Official
BASEBALL
GUIDE

1988 EDITION

Editor/Baseball Guide
DAVE SLOAN

Associate Editor/Baseball Guide
STEVE ZESCH

Contributing Editors/Baseball Guide
CRAIG CARTER
BARRY SIEGEL
LARRY WIGGE

President-Chief Executive Officer
RICHARD WATERS

Editor
TOM BARNIDGE

Director of Books and Periodicals
RON SMITH

Published by

The Sporting News

1212 North Lindbergh Boulevard
P.O. Box 56 — St. Louis, MO 63166

Copyright © 1988
The Sporting News Publishing Company

A Times Mirror
Company

ISBN 0-89204-264-8   ISSN 0078-3838

TABLE OF CONTENTS

For Index to Contents See Page 528

(Index to Minor League Cities on Page 523)

ON THE COVER: Chicago Cubs outfielder Andre Dawson captured the National League's Most Valuable Player award in 1987 after leading the league with 49 home runs, 137 runs batted in and 353 total bases.

—Photo by Rich Pilling

Offensive Outburst, Record Attendance Highlight 1987

By CLIFFORD KACHLINE

For a sport well into its second century, professional baseball continues to generate an amazing number of precedent-shattering headlines. The 1987 baseball year was no exception. Record attendance figures, the Minnesota Twins' surprising rise to their first world championship, an all-time high in home run production, a concerted move to bring more minorities into the sport at the executive and managerial levels, a decision by one of baseball's arbitrators upholding collusion charges against club owners and a massive turnover in top management personnel combined to write another interesting chapter in the game's rich history.

The attendance records were a direct result of four competitive divisional races combined with an offensive outburst that raised everybody's eyebrows and forced denials from several corners that the major leagues were playing with juiced-up baseballs. When all was said and done, the Twins were World Series champions, major league teams had produced more home runs than ever before and baseball was reporting its finest year ever at the turnstiles.

The minority issue surfaced as the indirect result of action taken by Commissioner Peter Ueberroth. Seeking to commemorate the 40th anniversary of Jackie Robinson's big-league debut, he decreed the season should be dedicated to the player chosen by Branch Rickey to break the color line. The concept led to the establishment of a program designed to elevate members of minority groups to the baseball hierarchy.

From the fans' viewpoint, the overriding focus of interest obviously involved what occurred on the field. With no team having repeated as world champion since 1978 and with parity being evidenced in other ways, the followers of almost every club found reasons for optimism.

All four divisions experienced torrid races. One wasn't decided until the final day of the season, and for the second time in three years, only one winner finished more than three games in front. In a touch of irony, three of the previous year's division winners wound up under the .500 level. The exception was the defending world-champion New York Mets.

The Minnesota Twins made the unlikely jump from also-rans to the top of the baseball world in 1987.

After having run away with the National League East a year earlier, the Mets failed to mount a serious challenge until late in the 1987 season. The absence of pitching star Dwight Gooden for the first two months due to drug rehabilitation, untimely injuries to other pitchers and internal strife contributed to the Mets' stumbling getaway.

At the same time, the St. Louis Cardinals shook off injuries to newly-acquired catcher Tony Pena and pitching ace John Tudor to grab an early lead. By July 23, Whitey Herzog's club boasted a 61-32 record and a 9½-game lead over the runner-up Montreal Expos, with the Mets another game back. But the Cardinals couldn't stand prosperity and struggled down the stretch, going 34-35 the remainder of the way. They still managed to hang on, however, and clinched the N.L. East title with an 8-2 victory over Montreal on October 1 at Busch Stadium. St. Louis' final edge was three games over New York, with the surprising Expos only four back.

The San Francisco Giants posted the biggest victory margin—six lengths over the Cincinnati Reds in the National League West—but not before experiencing a stiff battle. The Reds set the pace for most of the first 4½ months, and the Houston Astros posed a challenge in mid-August. However, a series of midsummer trades engineered by General Manager Al Rosen and a four-game sweep of the Reds at Candlestick Park in early August sparked a surge that led Roger Craig's club to the crown. The clincher came September 28, in a 5-4 victory at San Diego. Interestingly, only two years earlier the Giants had finished last and had lost a franchise-record 100 games.

Except for three days, the Minnesota Twins occupied first place in the American League West from July 6 on. Like the Giants, they clinched September 28, in a 5-3 triumph at Texas, though a letdown in the waning days slashed their final margin to two games over Kansas City and four over Oakland. At 85-77, rookie Manager Tom Kelly's squad produced the poorest record of the four division winners. The California Angels and Texas Rangers tied for the cellar, but finished only 10 lengths back. It was the smallest margin separating first and last place since division play began in 1969.

American League East fans witnessed the most spectacular race, with four teams figuring prominently at one time or another. In the beginning it was the Milwaukee Brewers, who opened the season with 13 consecutive victories, equaling the modern major league record set by the 1982 Atlanta Braves. The Brewers went on to win 20 of their first 23 games, but then encountered a 12-game losing streak that brought them back to earth.

The New York Yankees occupied the top rung much of the next 12 weeks, relinquishing it at times to the Toronto Blue Jays. Meanwhile, after a dismal 11-19 start, the Detroit Tigers zoomed into contention and finally reached first place August 19. With the Yankees slumping badly, it became a duel between Sparky Anderson's Tigers and Jimy Williams' Blue Jays down the stretch.

Entering a four-game showdown series in Toronto on September 24, the Blue Jays sported a 93-59 record to Detroit's 92-59. The Tigers lost the first three games, all by one run, but kept their flickering hopes alive by salvaging the Sunday contest, 3-2 in 13 innings. Still, Toronto led by 2½ games with six to play. When the Jays proceeded to drop three straight at home to Milwaukee while Detroit split four games at home with Baltimore, Toronto's edge was reduced to one game. The teams prepared for a season-ending series in Detroit. To the delight of Tiger fans, their club won all three contests, each again decided by a single run, with Larry Herndon's home run helping Frank Tanana beat Jimmy Key, 1-0, in the clincher. The sweep not only lifted the Tigers two games in front, but gave them the year's best record (98-64) and saddled the reeling Blue Jays with a seven-game losing streak.

Surprising results also were posted in both League Championship Series.

Although Minnesota's regular-season record would have resulted in a fifth-place finish in the A.L. East, 11 lengths back of Detroit, the Twins easily ousted the Tigers, four games to one, in the American League playoff. Kelly's crew won the first two games at home and then, after dropping the following game in Detroit, stunned the Tigers in the next two. Curiously, the Twins had compiled the worst road record ever (29-52) by a division leader.

In the National League playoff, the Cardinals found themselves without the services of their only acknowledged slugger, first baseman Jack Clark. He still was incapacitated by an ankle injury suffered in early September. Herzog's problem was compounded when the Giants took a 3-2 lead in games. When the series returned to St. Louis, Tudor (with late relief help) and Danny Cox pitched successive shutouts to lead the Cards to 1-0 and 6-0 victories, respectively, earning St. Louis its third N.L.

One of the highlights of the 1987 season was the 39-game hitting streak put together by Milwaukee's Paul Molitor.

pennant in six years.

The World Series was filled with drama. Under the rotation plan, it was the American League team's turn to host the opening games. As things turned out, this greatly benefitted the Twins, who boasted the year's best regular-season home record (56-25). Continuing their Metrodome mystique, they walloped the Cardinals, 10-1 and 8-4, in the first two games. When the Series switched to St. Louis, the momentum changed abruptly as the Cardinals rebounded for 3-1, 7-2 and 4-2 victories. But upon returning to Minnesota,

the Twins prevailed again, 11-5 and 4-2, with southpaw ace Frank Viola delivering the clincher. It marked the first time in World Series history that all games were won by the home team.

Four days after their decisive victory, the Twins flew to Washington as guests of President Ronald Reagan at a ceremony in the Rose Garden of the White House.

Subpar pitching and the umpire's shrinking strike zone were theories advanced as explanations for the record home run output. Over the first half of the 1987 campaign, the homer total was well ahead of the previous year's record clip, though the pace slowed slightly after the All-Star break.

Both leagues attained new home run highs. With American League hitters unloading 2,634 and the National League accounting for 1,824, the total of 4,458 amounted to nearly a 17 percent increase over the record of 3,813 set a year earlier. Six A.L. teams—Detroit, Toronto, Oakland, Texas, Kansas City and Cleveland—established new marks, as did three N.L. clubs—Chicago, San Francisco and New York. One of the more unusual homers was hit September 5 by California third baseman Jack Howell at Yankee Stadium. Facing reliever Tim Stoddard, Howell drove a pitch into the left-field stands, even though his bat broke in half about 12 inches from the knob.

Oakland first baseman Mark McGwire was the A.L.'s leading home run hitter with 49, smashing the rookie record of 38. Outfielder Andre Dawson also had 49 for the Chicago Cubs to pace the senior circuit. New York Yankee first baseman Don Mattingly accomplished two remarkable feats, equaling one record with home runs in eight consecutive games and establishing another by hitting six grand slams.

Several other notable hitting performances highlighted the season. Paul Molitor, Milwaukee's designated hitter, put together the seventh longest hitting streak in major league history. Starting July 16, he connected in 39 consecutive games before John Farrell, Cleveland rookie righthander, stopped him August 26. Benito Santiago, San Diego rookie catcher, set a rookie record by hitting safely in 34 successive games until Los Angeles' Orel Hershiser collared him October 3.

Boston's Wade Boggs captured his fourth American League batting championship in five years with a .363 average and enjoyed his fifth successive 200-hit season, while San Diego's Tony Gwynn batted .370 to lead the National League for

Philadelphia slugger Mike Schmidt became the 14th player in major league history to reach the 500-homer plateau when he hit a ninth-inning game-winner April 18.

the second time in four years and compiled his third 200-hit season in that stretch.

The home run barrage stirred speculation that the baseballs had been "juiced up." Denials by representatives of the manufacturer, Rawlings Sporting Goods Co., were met with skepticism, but scientific tests arranged separately by USA Today and the league offices confirmed that the 1987 baseballs were no livelier than those of recent years. The newspaper had Haller Testing Laboratories of Plainfield, N.J., perform tests early in July on 116 baseballs collected from all 26 teams. A few weeks later, at the request of the two leagues, the Science and Aeronautics Department of the University of Missouri at Rolla compared several dozen 1985 and 1987 balls manufactured by Rawlings.

The homer outburst also spawned several brawls and charges of cheating on the part of hitters as well as pitchers. Fourteen bench-clearing brawls erupted during the first half of the campaign. The biggest took place at Wrigley Field on July 7 after the Cubs' Dawson was struck on the face by a pitch from San Diego's Eric Show, causing wounds that required 24 stitches. Two days later, N.L. President A. Bartlett Giamatti issued an edict threatening "severe penalties, possibly including suspension," for any act clearly intended to maim or injure another player. The warning had a quick, positive effect.

Because certain pitchers long had been suspected of scuffing baseballs, Giamatti and his counterpart, A.L. President Bobby Brown, ordered umpires from both leagues to keep a close watch for illegal activity. And when the long-ball exploits of Mets infielder Howard Johnson, who hit 36 homers after totaling only 40 in five previous seasons, and other slightly-built players aroused suspicions of corked bats, Commissioner Ueberroth sent out an August 6 directive that permitted umpires to impound one bat per team per game upon request of the opposing manager. The confiscated bats were shipped to league headquarters to be X-rayed.

Three players, two of them pitchers, drew suspensions. Joe Niekro, veteran knuckleballer with Minnesota, was banned 10 days for doctoring baseballs; pitcher Kevin Gross of Philadelphia received the same sentence when umpires detected an illegal substance on his glove, and Billy Hatcher of Houston was suspended for 10 days for using a corked bat. No violations were found in the bats of other players that were examined.

The Niekro incident occurred in an August 3 game at Anaheim Stadium. A videotape carried on national network newscasts showed the Twins' hurler flipping away an emery board and a piece of sandpaper when ordered by the umpires to empty his pockets. Gross achieved notoriety exactly a week later when the umpires discovered a piece of sandpaper glued to the heel of his glove. Hatcher was caught September 1 when the barrel of the bat he used split, revealing it had been corked, as he grounded out. The Astros outfielder claimed the bat belonged to pitcher Dave Smith and that he (Hatcher) used it only because all of his bats were broken. The incident also cost Houston Manager Hal Lanier a fine under the directive on illegal bats.

While hitters generally fared well, pitchers struggled through a rough season. Boston's Roger Clemens and Oakland's Dave Stewart were the only hurlers to reach the coveted 20-victory level with 20-9 and 20-13 records, respectively. Clemens recorded his 20 wins despite a spring training holdout and 4-6 start. Rick Sutcliffe of the Chicago Cubs was the National League's top winner with 18 victories. Only four pitchers working the 162 innings required to qualify for earned-run honors finished under 3.00. The lone National League hurler to do so was veteran Nolan Ryan, who had a 2.76 ERA but a disappointing 8-16 record as a consequence of weak offensive support by his Houston mates. Jimmy Key of Toronto (2.76) edged Viola (2.90) and Clemens (2.97) for the American League's ERA title.

Other significant individual and team accomplishments included:

• Juan Nieves, 22-year-old Milwaukee southpaw, spiced the Brewers' season-opening winning streak with a 7-0 no-hitter at Baltimore on April 15. It was the year's lone no-hit performance.

• Mike Schmidt became the 14th player in major league history to reach the 500-homer plateau when he connected for a dramatic ninth-inning blow against Don Robinson with two on in an April 18 game at Pittsburgh. The homer lifted Philadelphia to an 8-6 victory. The Phillies' third baseman went on to hit 35 home runs and hike his career total to 530.

• Eric Davis, Cincinnati outfielder, hit his third grand slam of the month, equaling a major league record, to highlight a 6-2 victory at Pittsburgh on May 30. The blast also was his 19th homer, an N.L. record for home runs in April and May.

• Baltimore first baseman Eddie Murray hit home runs from both sides of the plate May 8 and 9 at Chicago to become the first player ever to accomplish the feat in successive games.

• Steve Bedrosian, Philadelphia relief ace, set a major league record by registering saves in 13 consecutive appearances from May 25 through June 30. Houston ended the streak by tagging him for three ninth-inning runs and a 7-6 loss July 2.

• Boston's Don Baylor marked his 38th birthday June 28 by getting hit by a Rick Rhoden pitch at Yankee Stadium. It was the 244th time Baylor had been struck by a pitched ball, breaking Ron Hunt's career record of 243.

• Baseball history was made July 11 in Baltimore when second baseman Bill Ripken, just up from Rochester, joined his brother, shortstop Cal Ripken Jr., in the Orioles' lineup, filled out by their father, Manager Cal Ripken Sr. It marked the first time that a big league manager had two sons playing for him.

• Kirby Puckett, Minnesota center fielder, tied a major league record with 10 hits in successive games at Milwaukee on August 29 and 30. After going 4 for 5, including two homers, in a 12-3 victory on Saturday night, he equaled an A.L. record the next afternoon with a four-RBI, 6-for-6 performance, and also robbed the Brewers' Robin Yount of a grand slam with a leaping, over-the-fence catch to feature a 10-6 victory.

• Led by catcher Ernie Whitt's three homers, the Toronto Blue Jays blasted a record 10 home runs while handing visiting Baltimore an 18-3 pasting September 14. Rance Mulliniks and George Bell each added two homers while Lloyd Moseby and rookies Bob Ducey and Fred McGriff contributed one. The Jays broke the old record of eight round-trippers in a game.

• Cal Ripken Jr.'s feat of playing 8,243 consecutive innings, believed to be the longest streak ever, ended in that same September 14 game at Toronto when he was replaced at shortstop by Ron Washington in the bottom of the eighth inning. However, Ripken played in all of the Orioles' remaining games to extend his consecutive-game streak to 927, sixth longest in major league annals.

• California catcher Bob Boone broke Al Lopez' 40-year-old record for most games caught in the majors when he worked his 1,919th game behind the plate September 16 at Kansas City. Boone had extended his record to 1,931 by season's end.

• Mets infielder Howard Johnson cracked his 36th homer, a grand slam, in an 8-1 victory at Chicago on September 21 to break the 53-year-old N.L. record for most home runs in a season by a switch-hitter. The old record was set by Rip Collins with the St. Louis Cardinals.

• Kansas City third baseman Kevin Seitzer became the 13th player in major league history—and the first since Tony Oliva of Minnesota in 1964—to collect 200 hits in his rookie season. No. 200 came in a September 28 game against Seattle.

Few rookies captured the spotlight or became the center of controversy as quickly as another Kansas City youngster, Vincent (Bo) Jackson. The former Auburn University football star and Heisman Trophy winner had signed a three-year, $1.066 million contract with the Royals the previous summer after spurning an offer from the National Football League's Tampa Bay Buccaneers, who had picked him No. 1 in the draft. With only half a season of pro baseball experience, the 24-year-old Jackson opened the '87 campaign as the Royals' left fielder and hit a solid .344 with 15 RBIs in his first 17 games. He subsequently cooled off, but had 18 homers and 45 RBIs—both team highs—at the All-Star break. He also carried a suspect .254 average and had struck out 115 times in 81 games.

On July 11, two days before the break, Jackson stunned his Kansas City teammates by announcing that he intended to pursue a pro football career as "a hobby" once the baseball season ended. That announcement was made after Jackson, unhappy with the way he was being used by Royals Manager Billy Gardner, conferred with co-Owner Avron Fogelman and agreed to a compromise that included eliminating the no-football clause from his Kansas City contract. Bo later signed a five-year contract with the Los Angeles Raiders, who had claimed him in the 1987 NFL draft.

At the time of Jackson's announcement, the Royals were 46-40 and only two games out of first place. When word of his decision reached the locker room, some of Jackson's Royal teammates expressed anger that the club would allow him to play both sports. Kansas City fans treated Jackson to a chorus of boos for most of the remaining home schedule. In August, fielding lapses and weak hitting led to his benching as the Royals fell back in the pennant chase. Over the last half of the season, Bo batted just .188 in 37 games to close the year with a .235 average that included 22 homers and 158 strikeouts in 118 games.

Capitalizing on the summer-long run of excitement, the major leagues attracted a record 52,011,506 fans for the regular sea-

Dick Howser, weak from his battle against a malignant brain tumor, resigned as Royals manager after two days of spring training.

son. This represented a 9½ percent increase over the previous year and marked the fifth time in six years that a new high was achieved. Both leagues exceeded their former record. The 14 American League teams played before 27,277,351 fans while the 12-team National League drew 24,734,155. The 26 teams averaged just over 2 million.

For the second straight year and second time ever, every team drew a million or better at home. More significantly, the National League-champion St. Louis Cardinals and the team they dethroned, the New York Mets, attracted 3,072,122 and 3,034,129, respectively. It marked the first time that any club other than the Los Angeles Dodgers had reached the 3-million level. The Dodgers have done it seven times. The Cardinal total was especially noteworthy considering that the St. Louis metropolitan area has a much smaller population base than Los Angeles or New York City.

In addition to the Cardinals and Mets, five other teams established all-time franchise attendance records. They were the Toronto Blue Jays, with 2,778,429; Kansas City Royals, 2,392,471; Minnesota Twins, 2,081,976; San Francisco Giants, 1,917,168, and the Texas Rangers, 1,763,053.

Four teams changed managers during the season and another after the campaign concluded. It was the smallest managerial turnover since 1971.

The year's first managerial shift occurred in spring training, but that wasn't precipitated by performance level. Forced to step aside the previous summer because of a brain tumor, Dick Howser attempted to resume his job as manager of the Kansas City Royals. After two days of workouts by Royals' pitchers and catchers, however, Howser announced February 23 that he was quitting. After waging a valiant battle against cancer, Howser, his weight down to 150 pounds, 17 fewer than before his two operations and radiation treatments, said he was too fatigued to carry on. New third base coach Billy Gardner took over as manager.

Howser underwent surgery a third time for the cancerous brain tumor March 20 at Huntington Memorial Hospital in Pasadena, Calif. He was able to attend several games at Royals Stadium early in the season, but when his condition took a turn for the worse, he entered St. Luke's Hospital in Kansas City on June 3. He died there exactly two weeks later at age 51. To honor his memory, the club formally retired Howser's No. 10 in ceremonies July 3, and the Royals' players wore a special patch bearing his number on their uniform sleeves the remainder of the season.

It wasn't until June 18 that the first managerial firing occurred. The victim was John Felske of Philadelphia. The 29-32 Phillies were turned over to third base coach Lee Elia.

Cleveland's Pat Corrales became the second casualty July 16. Coming off their best finish in 18 years, the Indians began the season with high expectations. Some prognosticators even picked them to lead the division. But by the All-Star break, the Indians were 31-56 and mired in last place in the A.L. East. Just hours before the schedule resumed, bullpen coach Howard (Doc) Edwards was elevated to the helm.

Gardner's tenure as Kansas City manager ended August 27 when he was dismissed after exhausting the patience of Royals' management. The position originally was offered to batting coach Hal McRae, who had been dropped from the team's active roster five weeks earlier, but he turned it down when club officials declined to give him a contract beyond the end of the season. John Wathan, who was working his first managerial assignment with the Royals' Omaha (American Association) farm team, became the next choice to succeed Gardner. The 62-64 Royals were still in contention at the time, 3½ games behind Minnesota in the A.L. West.

Gene Michael drove the final nail in his Chicago coffin when he disclosed in a radio interview September 7 that he had decided not to return as manager in '88. The following day he was relieved of his duties by General Manager Dallas Green, who then named Frank Lucchesi, former Philadelphia and Texas manager, on an interim basis to finish out the season. Luc-

chesi, who had been the club's "eye in the sky" coach, thus became the Cubs' sixth pilot in Green's six years with the club. The team was in fifth place with a 68-68 record when the change became effective.

Elia, Edwards and Wathan later received contract extensions, while the Cubs named Don Zimmer as their new manager November 20.

In a bizarre though not unexpected move, the New York Yankees shuffled managers again October 19, bringing Billy Martin back for a fifth term and transferring Lou Piniella to the front office as general manager. The announcement, coming on an off day during the World Series, captured the attention of the sports public everywhere. The date long will be remembered as Black Monday, not because of the Yankees' action, but because of the upheaval in the financial world. It was on that same date that the stock market experienced its biggest one-day drop in history, with the Dow Jones industrial index plummeting a record 508 points.

By bringing back Martin, whom he previously had fired four times, George Steinbrenner made his 14th managerial change in 14 years as owner of the Yankees. The 59-year-old Martin had spent the last two seasons as one of the team's television broadcasters and as a consultant to Steinbrenner. Piniella, who had one year left on his contract, had succeeded Martin after the 1985 season and was the only manager other than Billy in 1976-77 to lead the Yankees for two consecutive complete campaigns during Steinbrenner's regime. The Yanks finished fourth last season in the A.L. East with an 89-73 mark.

Two other clubs were left with lame-duck managers by announcements on the final weekend of the regular season. In a surprise development, the Mets informed the media October 3 that Dave Johnson would step aside after completing his three-year contract in 1988, though he would continue with the club as an assistant to the general manager. Dick Williams then shocked Seattle officials by disclosing that he planned to retire after the '88 season. "I've decided that 42 years (in professional baseball) is long enough," said the 58-year-old Mariners skipper, who has produced 1,546 victories, 13th on the all-time list, in his 20 seasons as a major league manager.

The Mets' decision was the culmination of a rift between Johnson and Frank Cashen, the club's executive vice-president and general manager. Johnson had ap-

Former Dodger official Al Campanis made some ill-advised comments on ABC-TV's Nightline show and stirred up a national hornet's nest.

proached Cashen late in August about a contract extension. But nothing came out of the meeting and Cashen made the surprise announcement that Johnson will not return after the '88 campaign. Johnson managed the Mets to the 1986 World Series championship and has produced more victories (388) in his first four major league seasons than any manager in history.

The commemoration of the 40th anniversary of Jackie Robinson's big-league debut began as a low-key event. Robinson's former uniform number (42) was emblazoned on second base in all 26 major league parks for the season opener. Many clubs staged special tributes and numerous private groups observed the occasion in various ways. In Montreal, a monument of Robinson was unveiled May 16 at the downtown site of the park where Jackie broke in with the then-Brooklyn Dodgers' International League farm team in 1946. The Baseball Writers' Association of America joined the celebration by voting to name its annual rookie of the year award after the former Dodger great.

Just hours after the Los Angeles Dodgers' April 6 season opener, the Robinson tribute took an unexpected turn that sent shockwaves through baseball and created a nationwide furor. It came about

when ABC-TV dedicated a segment of its "Nightline" show to Jackie's memory. Host Ted Koppel had arranged to have two men who were closely associated with the late Dodger great, former teammate Don Newcombe and author and former New York sportswriter Roger Kahn, as guests on the program.

Unfortunately, Newcombe, director of community relations for the Dodgers in Los Angeles, missed plane connections and was unable to reach New York in time. To replace him, Koppel contacted Al Campanis, the Dodgers' vice-president of player personnel. Campanis, who played shortstop alongside Robinson at Montreal in '46, was in Houston with Owner Peter O'Malley for the Dodgers' opener.

While the "Nightline" show was intended to be a memorial to Robinson, it wound up being something else. Early in the program Campanis recalled some of his 1946 experiences with Jackie in Montreal. "I was his enforcer," Campanis explained. "He took a lot of guff. He couldn't fight— Mr. (Branch) Rickey wouldn't let him— but I could." Later the discussion switched to the subject of blacks in baseball today, and some of Koppel's questions elicited comments from Campanis that were blatant racial slurs.

When Koppel asked why there were no

black managers or general managers in the major leagues, the 70-year-old Dodger executive commented: "I can't answer that question directly. The only thing I can say is you have to pay your dues to become a manager. Generally you have to go to the minor leagues. There's not very much pay involved, and some of the better-known black players have been able to get into other fields and make a pretty good living in that way."

Characterizing the reply as "a lot of baloney," Koppel then inquired: "Is there still that much prejudice in baseball today?" To which Campanis responded: "No, I don't believe it's prejudice. It's just that they (blacks) may not have some of the necessities to be, let's say, a field manager or perhaps a general manager." The comments shocked Koppel, who proceeded to ask whether he really believed that. "Well, I don't say that all of them, but they certainly are short," Campanis answered. "How many quarterbacks do you have? How many pitchers do you have that are black?"

The inflammatory comments quickly stirred an outcry of protest. Many who knew Campanis for all or most of his long career as a Dodger official said they couldn't believe the opinions he expressed were truly his. Some felt that, either because of his age or the glitter of national television, his thoughts became sidetracked.

O'Malley viewed a tape of the program the next morning, and when the media asked if Campanis' job was in jeopardy, the Dodger owner declared: "Absolutely not." Later that day both O'Malley and Campanis issued apologies for the controversial remarks. "I apologize to the American people, particularly to all black Americans, for my statements and my inability under the circumstances to express accurately my beliefs," Campanis said.

The apologies fell on deaf ears. The next day, two hours prior to the Dodgers' third game against Houston, O'Malley announced that he had asked Campanis for his resignation. "The comments Al made were so removed, so distant from what I believe the organization believes, that it was impossible for Al to continue the responsibilities he has had with us," the Dodger boss said. He immediately appointed Fred Claire to assume Campanis' duties. Claire already was the Dodgers' second in command in his position of executive vice-president.

Two nights after Campanis' appearance, Koppel had Commissioner Ueberroth, Reggie Jackson of the Oakland A's,

former Dodger catcher John Roseboro and Dr. Harry Edwards, associate professor of sociology at the University of California at Berkeley, as guests on "Nightline." Ueberroth pointed out that he had called for improved job opportunities for minorities at the December 1986 baseball meetings and reiterated that he believed strongly in the issue. "We would not have brought it up (at the winter meetings) and gone public with it and blatantly said baseball needs to improve if we didn't intend to do something about it," the commissioner said. "We would have ignored it." Roseboro termed as "hogwash" the "dues" reference by Campanis, saying: "We simply haven't been given a chance." He added that Campanis' remarks might create a breakthrough for blacks in baseball.

An unofficial survey by USA Today revealed that of the 879 top administrative positions in major league baseball, only 17 —or 1.9 percent—were held at that point by blacks and 13 by Hispanics and Asians. California teams employed 19 of the 30 minorities, with six of them on the Dodger staff. In a separate article, USA Today revealed that a study by Simmons Market Research Bureau showed black attendance at baseball games was only 6.8 percent, which was lower than for other major sports.

The uproar created by Campanis' gaffe brought the teams in all professional sports under close scrutiny for their minority hiring practices. Some black politicians called for boycotts and demonstrations against teams that declined to meet with them to discuss the employment of more minorities in front-office positions. Various civil rights organizations became similarly involved.

The Rev. Jesse Jackson, a leading civil rights activist and former presidential candidate, pressed the subject in meetings with Ueberroth and National Football League Commissioner Pete Rozelle in New York on May 5 and 6. After his session with Ueberroth, Jackson announced that if the major leagues failed to adopt a coherent affirmative action plan by July 4, former players would picket the parks "in a national day of justice in sports."

Jackson separately addressed the club owners of each league in Philadelphia on June 10 during the magnates' quarterly gathering. Afterward, the commissioner disclosed that he had asked the 26 clubs to complete affirmative action plans within 30 days, and Jackson subsequently called off the proposed July 4 boycott because, he said, he was encouraged by the program instituted by baseball.

To coordinate the program, Ueberroth disclosed June 13 that he had hired Dr. Edwards as a special consultant. An outspoken civil rights activist, the 44-year-old black professor already was serving as a consultant to the San Francisco 49ers of the National Football League and the Golden State Warriors of the National Basketball Association. His newest assignment was to locate and evaluate black and Hispanic former players who might be interested in a baseball job, thus creating a job bank. Ueberroth also arranged for Alexander and Associates, a Washington, D.C., consulting firm headed by Clifford Alexander, a former Secretary of the Army, to help implement and monitor baseball's affirmative action progress.

A group of current and former players held a two-hour meeting with Ueberroth and Edwards to discuss the plan the day before the All-Star Game in Oakland. Two of the attendees, Dave Winfield and Don Baylor, had compiled and sent to the commissioner a list of black and Hispanic former players they felt were qualified to become managers. "The door is open and players are stepping forward," Winfield said after the meeting. "They're working on strategies, methods, putting a system in place. They want to see that the transition is gradual, intelligent, permanent."

In an ironic twist, Edwards extended an invitation to Campanis to give lectures and seminars on baseball administration to prospective candidates among college students and former players. "To slam the door in his (Campanis') face, that is not only cruel, it is stupid," Edwards said. "I look forward to the day when Mr. Campanis can go back on 'Nightline' and say with just as much honesty, 'Not only have I met many black people who have all the necessities, but I have helped many of them get jobs in major league baseball.' That is the way that story should end."

Led by former players Frank Robinson, Willie Stargell and Ray Burris and former scout Ben Moore, a group of approximately 50 present and former black players formed an organization early in November called The Baseball Network. Its purpose was to assist in the affirmative action process. Moore was named acting executive director of the organization.

In the 40 years since Jackie Robinson broke the color line, only three blacks—Frank Robinson, Larry Doby and Maury Wills—have advanced to the managerial ranks in the majors. Hal McRae would have been the fourth had he agreed to accept Kansas City's late-season offer. The

lone black to serve as general manager was the late Bill Lucas of Atlanta. His brother-in-law, Henry Aaron, director of player development with the Braves, was the highest ranking black in the majors when the '87 season began. But that situation began changing later in the year.

Shortly after the Campanis incident, several clubs named blacks to their staffs. The Milwaukee Brewers hired Burris in the dual role of assistant to General Manager Harry Dalton and minor league instructor, while the Dodgers, who already were employing former players Newcombe, Roy Campanella, Tommy Davis and Lou Johnson in community relations or instructional jobs, added Roseboro as a minor league catching instructor. When the Milwaukee organization experienced a pitching shortage early in the season, the 36-year-old Burris resumed his pitching career, first while working with the club's Stockton (California) farm team and then briefly with Denver (American Association) before making the Brewer roster late in July.

In June, the Phillies brought back former outfielder Garry Maddox to serve as a broadcaster on their cable telecasts and also to work in marketing community relations and the spring and fall instructional camps. The Detroit Tigers appointed Michael Wilson, 25-year-old certified public accountant and former University of Michigan football player, as controller. Wilson was the highest-ranking black in the business side of a major league front office at the time.

Calvin Hill, a former NFL running back, became the first black to hold a high post with the Baltimore Orioles when owner Edward Bennett Williams named him to the club's board of directors July 21. Hill was employed with Fleet Financial Services in Washington, D.C., which provides comprehensive assistance to athletes and entertainers. He replaced Jack Dunn III, who had died, on the Oriole board. Former first baseman Chris Chambliss returned to the Yankees' payroll in June as an organizational hitting instructor and part-time scout. And in September the Cardinals hired former outfielder Ted Savage as assistant community relations director and minor league instructor.

The affirmative action process accelerated once the season closed. On October 28, the Dodgers announced the appointment of Tommy Hawkins, former basketball star and long-time Los Angeles sports announcer, to the newly-created position of vice-president of communications. It made him the highest-ranking black in the club's history. The 50-year-old Hawkins was to oversee the departments handling publicity, community services and marketing-promotions.

As part of a front-office overhaul, Orioles Owner Williams moved two blacks into key positions November 10, five weeks after firing Executive Vice-President and General Manager Hank Peters and Tom Giordano, the team's scouting and farm director. Frank Robinson, an Oriole coach the last two seasons, was named front-office advisor to Williams, while Peters' post was filled with the hiring of Roland Hemond as vice-president of baseball operations and the appointing of Calvin Hill as vice-president of administrative personnel. Hemond, former Chicago White Sox general manager, had been a special assistant on the commissioner's staff the past year and a half.

The Orioles' dismissal of Peters, the appointment of Piniella as Yankee general manager and the earlier ouster of Campanis by the Dodgers were part of the unusually heavy turnover of top-level executives. Being president or general manager of a team once was regarded as a guarantee of security, but the fact that 13 of the 26 clubs welcomed a top-level executive during the year further demonstrated the changing character of the sport.

Three changes were announced in January. Roy Eisenhardt relinquished the presidency of the Oakland A's for a role as executive vice-president when his father-in-law, Walter A. Haas Jr., took over as chief executive with the title of owner/managing general partner. Jerry Bell, former executive director of the Sports Facilities Commission that operates the Metrodome in Minneapolis, was appointed president of the Minnesota Twins on January 21. He replaced Howard Fox, who remained on the Twins' payroll as a consultant. Two days later, Peter Bavasi resigned as president of the Cleveland Indians to head up Telerate Sports, an information disseminating organization located in Scarsdale, N.Y. The Cleveland position remained vacant until November 2 when Peters was named president and chief operating officer of the Indians.

Ballard Smith, son-in-law of Owner Joan Kroc, stepped down as president of the San Diego Padres on May 26 to pursue other business ventures. Two weeks later, Chub Feeney, former National League president, came out of retirement to assume the Padres presidency. Murray Cook resigned as vice-president/general manager of the Montreal Expos on August 11 and was succeeded by another Expos vice-president, Bill Stoneman. Cook became general manager of the Cincinnati Reds two months later, following the October 12 firing of Bill Bergesch.

In other postseason changes, Dick Wagner resigned as president/general manager of the Houston Astros on October 14 and was replaced in early December by Bill Wood, the Astros' assistant general manager since July 1985; Malcolm (Mac) Prine quit as president of the Pittsburgh Pirates on October 23 in the wake of a power struggle with General Manager Syd Thrift and later was replaced by Carl F. Barger, with Douglas D. Danforth becoming chairman; Woody Woodward, who had given up his role as Yankee general manager a week earlier, joined the Phillies on October 28 as vice-president for player personnel, and Dallas Green resigned as president/general manager of the Cubs on October 29 with two years remaining on his contract. Two weeks later, in the ultimate irony, the Cubs appointed Jim Frey, whom Green had hired and fired as the club's manager, to succeed him with the title of executive vice-president for baseball operations. Frey had spent the summer as a Cubs' radio broadcaster.

In contrast to the front-office upheaval, ownership remained stable. The only shift among a team's primary shareholders involved the Boston Red Sox. It came in the spring when President Jean Yawkey bought out one of the team's two other general partners, Edward (Buddy) LeRoux, for an estimated $7 million. The transaction left Mrs. Yawkey and Haywood Sullivan, the Red Sox's chief operating officer, in full control and ended years of unrest and legal fights among the three partners.

Three franchises were up for sale early in the year, but later were taken off the block. At a joint media conference in San Diego on March 26, George Argyros and Mrs. Joan Kroc announced that Argyros planned to sell the Seattle Mariners and buy the Padres from Mrs. Kroc for a reported $60 million. The deal eventually fell through, at least partially because no one would meet Argyros' price, believed to be $45 million, for the Mariners. However, it also was speculated that owners of other N.L. teams were unlikely to approve of his acquisition of the Padres. As a consequence, both Argyros and Mrs. Kroc disclosed May 29 that they intended to retain ownership of their respective teams.

Argyros' attempted switch produced an

interesting—and costly—sidelight. On April 16, after the Padres defeated Los Angeles for only their second victory of the young season after eight losses, Argyros placed a phone call to the office of San Diego's rookie manager, Larry Bowa, to offer congratulations. By coincidence, General Manager Jack McKeon and N.L. President Giamatti both were in the office with Bowa when the call arrived. The incident prompted Ueberroth to slap Argyros with a $10,000 fine.

Texas Rangers Owner Eddie Chiles also was unable to find a buyer at his price and announced in mid May that he was removing the team from the market. Chiles was believed to be asking $80 million for his 53.65 percent of the Rangers and the lease-option he held on the 140 acres of land encompassing Arlington Stadium. Shortly after the season closed he exercised his option with the city to acquire full ownership of the complex.

Baseball's club owners were confronted with a serious new problem late in the year. The owners were ruled guilty of collusion by arbitrator Thomas T. Roberts in connection with the 1985 class of free agents. The decision, announced September 21, upheld the Players Association's claim that the owners conspired to constrict the movement of that group of players in violation of the Basic Agreement that stipulates "clubs shall not act in concert with other clubs."

Roberts' verdict was in response to a grievance filed by the Players Association on February 3, 1986, on behalf of the 62 players who became free agents at the close of the '85 season. The most prominent of those players were Kirk Gibson, Carlton Fisk, Donnie Moore, Phil and Joe Niekro and Tommy John.

In considering the case, Roberts conducted 32 hearings over an 11-month period. The process was interrupted temporarily in August 1986 when the Player Relations Committee, management's labor arm, fired Roberts because of his unfavorable ruling in another grievance. Another arbitrator subsequently reinstated him for the remainder of the case.

The hearings, which produced 5,682 pages of transcripts and 288 exhibits, were completed May 20 with Ueberroth as the final witness. Earlier witnesses included owners Steinbrenner, Williams and Milwaukee's Bud Selig as well as various other club officials and numerous lawyers and agents who represent individual players.

Under the Basic Agreement, the document binding the players and manage-

ment, a player qualifies for free agency if he has had six or more years of major league service and his contract has expired. In the first nine years of free agency, many eligible players changed teams amid an economic escalation that saw salaries skyrocket, with a few soaring beyond $2 million per year. But the spirited competition among clubs for free agents failed to materialize after the 1985 season.

In his 16-page opinion, Roberts noted that the bidding for free agents ceased coincident with meetings held by the owners and general managers shortly after the 1985 season. Nothing in the history of free agency, he wrote, explained "the sudden and abrupt termination of all efforts to secure the services of free agents from other clubs." Furthermore, he pointed out, no clubs pursued free agents during the winter of 1985-86 unless the player's '85 club exhibited no interest in keeping him. He concluded that that practice "in itself constitutes a strong indication of concerted action" on the part of the clubs.

Roberts also made the point that destruction of free agency could lead to the absence of long-term contracts. While the owners would favor this development, it could "only be accomplished within the constraints . . . of the Basic Agreement," the arbitrator wrote.

In his ruling, Roberts prescribed no penalties or remedies. Instead he said he would conduct further hearings to resolve that issue. He said he suggested to the chief labor representatives of the two parties, Barry Rona of the Player Relations Committee and Donald Fehr of the Players Association, "that they take a few days to re-read the award and consult their constituents, frame their thoughts and then get back to me and we will calendar any future hearings."

As the year drew to a close, both parties of the baseball dispute still were awaiting a final resolution of the collusion case as well as a ruling on a similar grievance involving the 1986 class of free agents. Another arbitrator, George Nicolau, was handling Conspiracy Case II. The grievance related not only to the way the clubs avoided that winter's group of free agents, but also to players who filed for salary arbitration.

Earlier in the year, Nicolau had delivered decisions in two other grievances filed by the Players Association. On February 7, he ruled that, contrary to an opinion rendered by the Player Relations Committee, clubs were prohibited from negotiating until May 1 with any of their free-agent players who remained unsigned after the January 8 deadline and refused salary arbitration. Shortly after the season began, Nicolau upheld the owners' move in reducing rosters to 24 players—rather than the usual 25—for the 1986 and '87 seasons.

The premier performers among '86 free agents involved in Conspiracy Case II were Jack Morris, Lance Parrish, Tim Raines, Andre Dawson, Bob Horner, Ron Guidry, Rich Gedman, Bob Boone, Doyle Alexander and Ray Knight. Of the 10, four signed with new teams—Parrish, Dawson, Horner and Knight, Horner deciding to play in Japan.

Morris, Detroit's long-time pitching ace, figured in an interesting free-agent scenario. Rejecting a two-year offer from the Tigers, he aggressively shopped his services—but with no success. The veteran righthander, a native of St. Paul, Minn., first tried to interest the Minnesota Twins. He made proposals based on a two-year package, a three-year package and a four-year package. He also offered to sign a one-year contract, with his salary to be determined by an arbitrator. When the Twins passed, Morris made a similar pitch to the Yankees, but Steinbrenner spurned the offer. After the Phillies also passed, Morris decided just hours before the deadline to accept salary arbitration and remain with the Tigers.

Knight, the 1986 World Series MVP, became the first of the group to change uniforms. He wanted $1 million for one season or a two-year, $1.6 million guaranteed contract to remain with the Mets. Miffed because they offered him one year at $800,000, Knight rejected the offer. Later, after the Mets declined to offer him arbitration, Knight was forced to accept Baltimore's lower offer, estimated at $475,000 plus a potential $150,000 in incentive bonuses.

Dawson also experienced an unusual free-agent scenario. Montreal offered him a two-year pact that Dawson turned down. Knee problems prompted the outfielder to set his sights on joining a team that played on natural grass. Finding no takers, he tried a novel approach: The Chicago Cubs were notified that Dawson was willing to sign a blank contract with General Manager Dallas Green to fill in the salary. After the March signing, Green inserted the figures: $500,000 in salary plus $150,000 if Dawson remained off the disabled list until the All-Star Game and another $50,000 for making the All-Star team. Dawson, of course, went on to have a spectacular season that earned him

MVP honors.

Parrish, Morris' Detroit batterymate, signed with Philadelphia on March 12 after nearly two months of on-again, off-again negotiations fraught with legal hangups. He wound up accepting less than the $1.2 million offered by his former team. Parrish, who earned $850,000 in 1986, reached agreement with Phils' President Bill Giles on February 19 on financial terms—a guaranteed $800,000 salary and another $200,000 if he had no significant problems with his chronic back ailment before the All-Star Game.

Horner pursued an entirely different course. The Atlanta Braves wanted him to take a sizeable cut in his last salary of $1.8 million, but he refused. When he failed to receive an acceptable offer from another major league club, he signed a one-year contract April 14 with the Yakult Swallows of Japan's Central League. It reportedly paid him more than $2 million in salary and bonuses.

Raines, Gedman, Guidry and Boone all agreed to terms with their old teams May 1—a month into the season. Each signed for approximately the same amount he rejected in January—Raines with Montreal at three years for $5 million; Gedman with Boston, two years for $1.8 million; Guidry with the Yankees, two years for $1,558,242, and Boone with California, one year at $747,153. Raines, the 1986 N.L. batting champion, broke in with a bang one day later, going 4 for 5 with a game-winning grand-slam in the 10th inning to help the Expos whip the Mets, 11-7.

Alexander was the last of the premier free agents to return to uniform, re-signing with Atlanta on May 5. Instead of the two-year, $1.87 million package reportedly offered by the Braves in January, he had to settle for $400,000 in salary and a possible $400,000 in incentives over two years.

Alexander finished the season pitching for the A.L. East Division-champion Detroit Tigers after an August trade.

The 1987 salary arbitration hearings provided a windfall for two players. Morris' gamble paid off when an arbitrator granted him the $1,850,000 contract that he sought from the Tigers, a half million more than Detroit had offered. That stood as the biggest arbitration award ever until Don Mattingly, New York Yankee first baseman, won a $1,975,000 salary four days later. Of the 26 players who went to salary arbitration, 10 were winners and 16 had to settle for the club's figure.

The 10 players who won their salary arbitration cases, with the team's offer in

Montreal's Tim Raines didn't begin his season until May, but quickly made up for lost time.

parentheses, were; Mattingly, $1,975,000 ($1,700,000); Morris, $1,850,000 ($1,350,000); Ron Darling, New York Mets, $1,050,000 ($800,000); Charlie Leibrandt, Kansas City, $850,000 ($725,000); Phil Bradley, Seattle, $750,000 ($550,000); Kevin Bass, Houston, $630,000 ($560,000); Greg Harris, Texas, $620,000 ($575,000); Dennis Walling, Houston, $595,000 ($450,000); Andy Hawkins, San Diego, $535,000 ($450,000), and Dick Schofield, California, $475,000 ($305,000).

The salaries of the 16 losers, with player's rejected figure in parentheses: Orel Hershiser, Los Angeles, $800,000 ($1,100,000); Brett Butler, Cleveland, $765,000 ($875,000); Bruce Hurst, Boston, $700,000 ($845,000); Kevin McReynolds, New York Mets, $625,000 ($825,000); Bill Doran, Houston, $625,000 ($825,000); Danny Cox, St. Louis, $600,000 ($875,000); Oil Can Boyd, Boston, $550,000 ($695,000); Jay Howell, Oakland, $530,000 ($630,000); Ted Power, Cincinnati, $500,000 ($610,000); Ken Schrom, Cleveland, $450,000 ($545,000); Kevin Gross, Philadelphia, $420,000 ($530,000); Gary Pettis, California, $400,000 ($550,000); Jim Acker, Atlanta, $350,000 ($450,000); Ken Phelps, Seattle, $300,000 ($515,000); Alejandro Pena, Los Angeles, $280,000 ($367,500), and Darryl Motley, Atlanta, $210,000 ($257,500).

A four-year contract signed just hours before the April 6 season openers assured major league umpires of a larger share of the sport's rising revenues. The agreement was hammered out in an all-night negotiating session, thus averting a threatened strike by the umpires. The pact provided for significant increases in salary, daily expense payments, postseason compensation, spring training pay, life insurance and retirement benefits.

During the first three years of the agreement, salaries will range from $40,000 for rookie umpires to $100,000 for those in their 20th year of major league service. This compared with the former scale that began at $30,000 for rookies and rose to a maximum of $80,000. In the final year of the contract, the range will be $41,000 to $105,000. The per diem figure for hotels, meals, cabs, etc., was hiked from $104 to $148 and spring training payments went from $100 to $150 per game and from $85 to $117 per day for expenses.

The postseason pool, in which all umpires share, was raised from $631,000 to $800,000, while life insurance was increased from $250,000 to $450,000 and pensions from $1,100 for each year of service to $2,000 with a ceiling of 20 years, making the maximum annual pension $40,000. In addition, umpires were assured of severance pay for the first time, with the one-time payments ranging from $30,000 for an umpire with 10 years of service to $100,000 for a 20-year veteran.

Seventy-six players filed for free agency after the 1987 season. Morris again headed a list that also included St. Louis slugger Jack Clark, Yankee relief ace Dave Righetti, Minnesota third baseman Gary Gaetti, California ace Mike Witt, Milwaukee's Paul Molitor and Houston reliever Dave Smith. Four other players—Rick Reuschel of San Francisco, Jeff Reardon of Minnesota, Alfredo Griffin of Oakland and Greg Harris of Texas—exercised their right to demand a trade and stood to become free agents unless they were swapped or their contracts were upgraded.

Here's the complete list of the 76 filing for free agency:

American League: Boston—Steve Crawford, Joe Sambito; California—Ruppert Jones, Gary Lucas, Greg Minton, Jerry Reuss, Mike Witt; Chicago—Dave LaPoint; Cleveland—Chris Bando, Brett Butler, Ed Vande Berg; Detroit—Mike Heath, Larry Herndon, Bill Madlock, Jack Morris, Frank Tanana; Kansas City —Thad Bosley, Gene Garber, Charlie Leibrandt, Jamie Quirk; Milwaukee—Len Barker, Mark Clear, Rick Manning, Paul Molitor; Minnesota—Juan Berenguer, George Frazier, Gary Gaetti, Tim Laudner; New York—Bill Gullickson, Tommy John, Dave Righetti; Oakland—Joaquin Andujar, Mike Davis, Moose Haas, Steve Henderson, Gary Lavelle, Dwayne Murphy; Seattle—Gary Matthews; Texas—Tom Paciorek; Toronto—Garth Iorg.

National League: Atlanta—Ken Griffey, Glenn Hubbard, Graig Nettles, David Palmer; Chicago—Bob Dernier, Ed Lynch, Dickie Noles, Manny Trillo; Cincinnati—Dave Collins; Houston—Larry Andersen, Jose Cruz, Danny Darwin, Dave Smith; Los Angeles—Phil Garner, Ken Landreaux; Montreal—Dave Engle, Vance Law, Charlie Lea, Dennis Martinez, Bob McClure, Reid Nichols, Bryn Smith; New York—Bill Almon, John Candelaria, Lee Mazzilli; Philadelphia—None; Pittsburgh—Terry Harper; St. Louis— Jack Clark; San Diego—Bruce Bochy, Steve Garvey; San Francisco—Chili Davis, Atlee Hammaker, Dave Henderson, Mike LaCoss, Eddie Milner, Joe Price, Joel Youngblood.

Several of the game's top stars who

Yankee relief ace Dave Righetti tested the free-agent waters before returning to Owner George Steinbrenner's fold.

could have opted for free agency were rewarded with lucrative contracts before the filing period. Atlanta gave Dale Murphy a three-year, $6 million guaranteed package, Philadelphia signed Mike Schmidt to a two-year, $4.5 million deal, with only the first year guaranteed, and Baltimore handed Cal Ripken Jr. a one-year, $1.7 million contract.

Indications that the owners might be abandoning their alleged freezeout of free agents surfaced December 1 when San Francisco signed Cleveland outfielder Brett Butler to a two-year guaranteed contract worth an estimated $700,000 a season plus a $400,000 signing bonus. Later that same day, San Francisco outfielder Chili Davis accepted a one-year pact calling for $815,000 in salary and a potential $150,000 in bonus from California. The Phillies signed Chicago Cubs center fielder Bob Dernier less than a week later.

Drug and alcohol problems continued to plague baseball, though the number of incidents dwindled. The situation involving Gooden created the biggest headlines, but two other former Cy Young Award choices also made the news because of chemical dependency. In addition, four other 1987 players entered rehabilitation centers during or after the season for drug or alcohol treatment, while a fifth player was suspended after an apparent relapse.

The disclosure about Gooden stunned the defending-champion Mets and their fans. Cashen called a team meeting in St. Petersburg on April 1 to inform the players that Gooden had tested positive for cocaine use several days earlier and would enter a program that could keep him off the mound for an indefinite period. Curiously, when the 22-year-old pitcher had signed a $1.5 million contract earlier in the spring, he had insisted on the inclusion of a voluntary drug-testing clause to "end all those allegations," as he put it, that he used drugs. "He had to want to get caught," said Manager Johnson.

The Mets arranged for Gooden to fly to New York on April 2, and that same day he entered the Smithers Alcoholism and Treatment Center in Manhattan. A television station in his hometown of Tampa, Fla., promptly killed a public service announcement that featured the pitcher advising youngsters to "Say no to drugs." After a 28-day treatment program, Gooden was released from the Smithers Center and rejoined the Mets. Ueberroth issued a statement wishing him well while warning that a relapse into drug abuse would trigger suspension for a minimum

Dwight Gooden didn't make his 1987 Mets' debut until June 5, but still finished with a 15-7 mark.

of one year.

After working out 12 days, Gooden returned to action with the Mets' Tidewater (International) farm team May 12. He pitched in four games for Tidewater before making his Mets' debut June 5. A near-capacity crowd of 51,402 turned out at Shea Stadium that night to welcome Gooden and gave him a pair of thundering standing ovations—when he took the mound and when he departed in the seventh inning of a 5-1 victory over Pittsburgh. Despite missing the first two months, Gooden went on to lead the Mets' staff with a 15-7 record.

The two other former Cy Young winners who were in the limelight because of drugs were Vida Blue and LaMarr Hoyt.

Blue, one of 21 players disciplined by Ueberroth early in 1986 for drug use, became a free agent after pitching for San Francisco in '86 and signed with Oakland on January 21 for a reported $300,000. One day before the A's batterymen were due to report for spring training, however, the 37-year-old southpaw announced he was retiring. It subsequently was disclosed that court documents showed Blue tested positive for cocaine three times during the 1986 season and in November had been ordered to spend 90 days in a drug aftercare program. Probation officers had administered the tests, which were required as part of Blue's 1983 conviction for cocaine possession. Officials of both the Giants and A's said they were not aware of the results.

Hoyt was released from federal prison in mid-February after serving 38 days following his December conviction for federal drug violations. Shortly after he got out of prison, Ueberreth announced the pitcher was being suspended for the entire 1987 season. Meanwhile, the San Diego Padres released Hoyt, who had three years left—at a total of $3.2 million—on his contract. The club also asked that the pact be dissolved, claiming he had breached the contract through repeated drug problems. The actions resulted in the players' union filing a grievance.

Arbitrator Nicolau heard the case and ruled June 16 that the Padres' release of the player was invalid. He also ordered the one-year suspension imposed by Ueberroth reduced to 60 days. "There is not a sliver of evidence that Hoyt used cocaine at any time during his major league career," the arbitrator wrote. "Nor is there any evidence that he sold, distributed or facilitated the distribution of drugs at any time." Nicolau went on to note that doctors found Hoyt, a 1983 Cy Young Award winner for the Chicago White Sox, was suffering from a sleep disorder called intractable insomnia and it was that condition that led the pitcher to go to Mexico for pills in violation of federal drug statutes.

One day after Nicolau's ruling, the Padres agreed to pay Hoyt the money due under the contract. But they also released him again. The Chicago White Sox signed the troubled righthander to a minor league contract July 1, but when the team physician discovered damage to Hoyt's right shoulder, he was ordered not to do any pitching and instead was put on a light workout program. Hoyt made headlines again in early December when he was arrested at his Columbia, S.C., apartment and charged with possession with intent to distribute cocaine. If convicted, Hoyt could face a minimum 10-year prison sentence.

San Francisco outfielder Eddie Milner voluntarily entered a one-month drug rehabilitation program in San Jose, California on April 17. After two drunk driving arrests in less than a month, California pitcher John Candelaria enrolled in an alcohol rehab center May 15 on orders from Ueberroth. Outfielder Otis Nixon, who began the season with Cleveland but was farmed to Buffalo (American Association) in May, was arrested for alleged cocaine possession in Buffalo on July 30 and subsequently underwent four weeks of treatment for substance abuse. Floyd Youmans, Montreal pitcher who was a high school teammate of Gooden in Tampa, entered a drug and alcohol rehabilitation program October 12.

Infielder Alan Wiggins of Baltimore, another of the 21 players disciplined by Ueberroth in '86, was placed under indefinite suspension without pay by the commissioner August 31 for "improper behavior" after allegedly testing positive for drugs. The Orioles released him a month later. Under terms of a settlement, the club agreed to pay Wiggins for the last 15 days of the season and the player agreed to forfeit one-third of his guaranteed $800,000 contract for 1988.

In an interview early in the season, Ueberroth told the New York Times that he felt drug usage by players had been "drastically reduced." At the same time, he disclosed he had levied "six-figure fines" against some teams for failure to report drug incidents among their players, but he declined to specify the amounts or to identify the teams.

On September 10, he reportedly tagged the Texas Rangers with a $250,000 fine—the largest the commissioner is authorized to levy—for calling up pitcher Steve Howe prematurely. Howe had been suspended by National Association President John Johnson for substance abuse for the fifth time following a disputed test while with San Jose (California) in 1986. Shortly after his reinstatement, the Rangers signed him July 12 to an Oklahoma City (American Association) contract. In the ensuing three weeks he passed more than 15 drug screenings. Impressed by his pitching, Rangers Owner Chiles and President Mike Stone flew to New York on August 5 to meet with Ueberroth to discuss Howe's situation. The commissioner reportedly asked that Howe be left at Oklahoma City until the close of the farm team's season in keeping with his policy

Toronto's George Bell posted some big 1987 numbers and captured the American League Most Valuable Player Award.

that a recovering drug offender spends enough time in the minor leagues to demonstrate that he can perform as well as stay drug-free. But the Rangers added the pitcher to their roster the next day anyway.

Problems created by excessive ball park drinking led to action in numerous cities. Beer and baseball, of course, long have been linked. Not only do breweries advertise heavily in the sport, but two teams are owned by breweries—the Cardinals by Anheuser-Busch and the Blue Jays by La-

batt's—and the Expos are owned by the family that runs the Seagrams liquor business. Nevertheless, in an attempt to reduce fan rowdiness induced by alcohol, a number of teams decided to ban beer vendors from the stands, forcing fans to go to the concession stands to buy beer, and some teams halted beer sales after the seventh inning. In addition, by midsummer 11 teams had designated certain seating areas in their parks as family sections where the sale of alcohol was prohibited.

Two more clubs also issued directives

banning alcoholic beverages from team flights, bus rides and the clubhouse, both home and road. Following the lead taken by the Padres in 1986, the Angels put such a rule in effect June 11 in the wake of Candelaria's two arrests. The White Sox followed suit a few weeks later. In each instance, officials emphasized the move was designed to protect the team in case of player accidents.

Toronto slugger George Bell topped the list of postseason award winners by walking away with the American League's Most Valuable Player Award and being named The Sporting News' Major League Player of the Year. Bell, who hit 47 home runs and drove in 134 runs, edged out Detroit shortstop Alan Trammell in MVP voting by the Baseball Writers' Association of Amercia. Andre Dawson captured N.L. honors after hitting 49 homers and driving in 137 runs for the Cubs. Results of the MVP voting in both leagues, with each first-place designation worth 14 points, second good for nine, third for eight, and on down, follow:

AMERICAN LEAGUE

Player—Club	1	2	3	4	5	6	7	8	9	10	Pts.
George Bell, Toronto	16	12	—	—	—	—	—	—	—	—	332
Alan Trammell, Detroit	12	15	1	—	—	—	—	—	—	—	311
Kirby Puckett, Minnesota	—	—	17	6	3	1	—	—	—	—	201
Dwight Evans, Boston	—	—	3	5	3	5	2	4	1	3	127
Paul Molitor, Milwaukee	—	1	3	2	3	4	9	1	—	1	125
Mark McGwire, Oakland	—	—	1	7	3	3	2	1	2	4	109
Don Mattingly, New York	—	—	1	2	2	4	5	3	3	3	92
Tony Fernandez, Toronto	—	—	1	2	5	2	1	3	2	—	79
Wade Boggs, Boston	—	—	1	3	1	1	1	5	1	3	64
Gary Gaetti, Minnesota	—	—	—	—	3	1	4	1	1	3	47
Jeff Reardon, Minnesota	—	—	—	—	1	3	1	1	4	1	37
Darrell Evans, Detroit	—	—	—	1	—	1	—	1	2	2	21
Doyle Alexander, Detroit	—	—	—	—	2	—	—	—	2	1	17
Tom Henke, Toronto	—	—	—	—	1	—	—	2	1	3	17
Wally Joyner, California	—	—	—	—	1	—	—	5	2	17
Kent Hrbek, Minnesota	—	—	—	—	—	1	—	2	—	—	11
Danny Tartabull, Kansas City	—	—	—	—	—	—	2	—	1	—	10
Robin Yount, Milwaukee	—	—	—	—	—	—	—	2	1	—	8
Roger Clemens, Boston	—	—	—	—	1	—	—	—	—	1	7
Jack Morris, Detroit	—	—	—	—	—	1	—	—	—	—	5
Kevin Seitzer, Kansas City	—	—	—	—	—	—	—	1	1	—	5
Ruben Sierra, Texas	—	—	—	—	—	—	—	1	1	—	5
Jose Canseco, Oakland	—	—	—	—	—	—	1	—	—	—	4
Matt Nokes, Detroit	—	—	—	—	—	—	—	—	—	1	1

NATIONAL LEAGUE

Player—Club	1	2	3	4	5	6	7	8	9	10	Pts.
Andre Dawson, Chicago	11	11	2	—	—	—	—	—	—	—	269
Ozzie Smith, St. Louis	9	1	2	1	3	1	2	—	1	2	193
Jack Clark, St. Louis	3	4	6	4	3	1	1	1	1	—	186
Tim Wallach, Montreal	1	4	7	5	1	1	2	1	1	—	165
Will Clark, San Francisco	—	1	4	4	2	4	3	4	1	1	128
Darryl Strawberry, New York	—	—	—	2	6	5	2	2	3	—	95
Tim Raines, Montreal	—	1	—	3	1	4	3	3	1	1	80
Tony Gwynn, San Diego	—	2	1	2	3	1	1	—	1	6	75
Eric Davis, Cincinnati	—	—	1	3	2	—	2	6	3	—	73
Howard Johnson, New York	—	—	1	—	1	1	4	1	1	2	42
Dale Murphy, Atlanta	—	—	—	—	1	2	4	3	3	34
Vince Coleman, St. Louis	—	—	—	—	1	—	1	2	1	2	20
Juan Samuel, Philadelphia	—	—	—	—	1	1	—	—	3	2	19
Mike Schmidt, Philadelphia	—	—	—	—	—	2	—	—	1	1	13
Pedro Guerrero, Los Angeles	—	—	—	—	—	2	—	—	1	—	12
Steve Bedrosian, Philadelphia	—	—	—	—	—	—	—	—	2	2	6
Milt Thompson, Philadelphia	—	—	—	—	—	—	1	—	—	—	4
Bill Doran, Houston	—	—	—	—	—	—	—	—	—	1	1
Terry Pendleton, St. Louis	—	—	—	—	—	—	—	—	—	1	1

Philadelphia relief ace Steve Bedrosian posted a 5-3 record and 40 saves for a team that won just 80 games and walked away with the National League Cy Young award.

Boston righthander Roger Clemens became the American League's first repeat Cy Young Award winner since Baltimore's Jim Palmer accomplished the feat in 1975 and '76. Clemens, who won just four of his first 10 decisions after a 30-day holdout that began in spring training, went on to record a 20-9 record and 2.97 earned-run average after his 24-4 1986 campaign. In the National League, Philadelphia reliever Steve Bedrosian was named the Cy Young winner. The big righthander recorded 40 saves and a 5-3 record for a team that won just 80 games. A breakdown of the Cy Young poll, with a first-place vote worth five points, second good for three and third for one:

National League

Pitcher	1	2	3	Pts.
Steve Bedrosian, Phil.	9	2	6	57
Rick Sutcliffe, Chicago	4	9	8	55
Rick Reuschel, Pitt-S.F.	8	4	2	54
Orel Hershiser, L.A.	2	0	4	14
Dwight Gooden, N.Y.	1	2	1	12
Nolan Ryan, Houston	0	4	0	12
Mike Scott, Houston	0	3	0	9
Bob Welch, L.A.	0	0	3	3

American League

Pitcher—Club	1	2	3	Pts.
Roger Clemens, Boston	21	6	1	124
Jimmy Key, Toronto	4	13	5	64
Dave Stewart, Oakland	2	4	10	32
Doyle Alexander, Detroit	1	0	3	8
Mark Langston, Seattle	0	2	1	7
Teddy Higuera, Milwaukee	0	1	2	5
Frank Viola, Minnesota	0	0	5	5
Jeff Reardon, Minnesota	0	1	1	4
Jack Morris, Detroit	0	1	0	3

Both winners in the BBWAA's Rookie of the Year polls were unanimous choices. Oakland's slugging first baseman Mark McGwire, who set a rookie record by hitting a league-leading 49 home runs, was the selection in the American League. San Diego catcher Benito Santiago, who carved out a rookie-record 34-game hitting streak, was the N.L. winner.

Sparky Anderson, who guided the Detroit Tigers to the A.L. East Division title, and Buck Rodgers, who directed the Montreal Expos to a surprising third-place finish in the N.L. East, were named the top managers by both the BBWAA and The Sporting News.

The Sporting News honored Al Rosen, general manager of the N.L. West Division-winning San Francisco Giants, as its Executive of the Year.

AMERICAN LEAGUE

Including

Team Reviews of 1987 Season

Team Day-by-Day Scores

1987 Standings, Home-Away Records

1987 Pitching Against Each Club

1987 Official A.L. Batting Averages

1987 Official A.L. Fielding Averages

1987 Official A.L. Pitching Averages

Big first baseman Kent Hrbek contributed 34 home runs and 90 RBIs to Minnesota's high-scoring offense.

Twins Fulfill Unlikely Dream

By PAT REUSSE

They planted spies in the center field stands to steal the opposing catcher's signs. They turned on air conditioners to blow their own fly balls over the outfield wall. They left the roof of the Metrodome painted off-white so that the unadapted eyes of the visitors would spin helplessly while tracking pop-ups.

At least that's what frustrated opponents alleged.

They were accused of being a nefarious bunch, these Minnesota Twins, but, truth be told, they hardly were vicious types.

They ranked tenth in the American League in batting (.261) and earned-run average (tie, 4.63). They were outscored, 806-786. They had the third-poorest road mark (29-52) in the league. And come October 17, the Twins had the poorest record and second-fewest wins of any A.L. team —to ever play in the World Series.

In one of the most dramatic turnarounds ever, Minnesota captured its first division title since 1970, blitzed the Detroit Tigers in five games in the A.L. Championship Series and, in its first World Series appearance since 1965, defeated the St. Louis Cardinals in seven games.

Only the year before, the Twins had been buried in sixth place in the A.L. West with a 71-91 record. The local optimism for 1987 was reflected in the sale of a paltry 4,000 season tickets.

But what the Twins did best was win when they had to, particularly in the Metrodome, where they were 6-0 in the postseason. The Twins' 56-25 home record was the best in the major leagues and pushed their overall mark to 85-77. And although they didn't run away from the pack—they were 36-37 and won only nine road games after the All-Star break—the Twins led the West for all but six days after June 9.

The Minnesota revival began February 3, two weeks before the start of spring training, when General Manager Andy MacPhail acquired ace reliever Jeff Reardon from the Montreal Expos. In 1986, the Twins had blown nearly 30 games after leading in the seventh inning or later.

"We felt the talent here was better than the record, but we weren't going to be a contender unless we found someone to finish games for us," MacPhail said. "I probably shouldn't have said it, but I told my wife that the happiest day of my life was the day we traded for Reardon."

Jeff Reardon was acquired from Montreal and literally saved the relief-starved Twins.

The Twins gave up starter Neal Heaton, catcher Jeff Reed and two pitching prospects, but Reardon was worth the price. After a shaky start, when his ERA was 10.80 in mid-May, Reardon was consistently remarkable. He finished 8-8 but saved 31 games, a performance that made him co-winner of The Sporting News' Fireman of the Year award.

"That guy," Manager Tom Kelly said, "made me a whole lot smarter."

Equally important, however, were Reardon's setup men, Juan Berenguer and Keith Atherton.

Berenguer, signed in January after being released by the San Francisco Giants, was invaluable during the first half, when most of the staff struggled. The hard-throwing righthander was 2-0 in five starts from May 15 to June 7 and finished 8-1 with a 3.94 ERA and four saves.

Atherton, acquired from Oakland the previous May, finished 7-5 with two saves in 59 games.

SCORES OF MINNESOTA TWINS' 1987 GAMES

APRIL

Date	W/L	Score	Winner	Loser
7—Oakland	W	5-4†	Frazier	Krueger
8—Oakland	W	4-1	Viola	Plunk
9—Oakland	W	5-4	Berenguer	Howell
10—At Seattle	W	8-1	Smithson	Morgan
11—At Seattle	L	5-6	Nunez	Reardon
12—At Seattle	W	8-5	Blyleven	Langston
13—At Oak.	L	3-6	Howell	Frazier
14—At Oak.	W	9-8	Atherton	Codiroli
15—At Oak.	W	5-2	Smithson	Stewart
17—At Calif.	L	1-2	Witt	Blyleven
18—At Calif.	L	0-1	Candelaria	Viola
19—At Calif.	W	6-5	Portugal	Sutton
20—Seattle	W	13-5	Smithson	Morgan
21—Seattle	W	6-1	Straker	Trujillo
22—Seattle	L	3-4	Langston	Frazier
23—California	L	3-7	Candelaria	Viola
24—California	L	1-8	Sutton	Portugal
25—California	W	8-7	Reardon	Finley
26—California	W	10-5	Frazier	Cook
28—At Toronto	L	1-5	Clancy	Viola
29—At Toronto	L	1-8	Johnson	Smithson
Won 12, Lost 9				

MAY

Date	W/L	Score	Winner	Loser
1—New York	W	7-4	Blyleven	Rhoden
2—New York	L	4-6	John	Viola
3—New York	W	4-3	Frazier	Stoddard
5—Baltimore	L	4-5	Bell	Smithson
6—Baltimore	L	0-6	McGregor	Blyleven
7—Baltimore	W	5-2	Viola	Flanagan
8—At N.Y.	L	7-11	Guante	Reardon
9—At N.Y.	W	2-0	Straker	Rasmussen
10—At N.Y.	L	1-6	Hudson	Smithson
11—At Balt.	W	10-4	Blyleven	McGregor
12—At Balt.	L	7-10	Dixon	Reardon
13—Toronto	L	0-7	Clancy	Portugal
14—Toronto	L	4-16	Stieb	Straker
15—Boston	W	3-1	Frazier	Hurst
16—Boston	L	1-6	Clemens	Blyleven
17—Boston	W	10-8†	Atherton	Schiraldi
19—At Cleve.	L	3-4	Schrom	Portugal
20—At Cleve.	W	8-2	Berenguer	Candiotti
21—At Cleve.	L	3-6	Swindell	Blyleven
22—Detroit	L	2-3	Morris	Viola
23—Detroit	W	7-5	Anderson	Terrell
24—Detroit	L	2-7	Robinson	Atherton
26—Milwaukee	W	4-2	Blyleven	Nieves
27—Milwaukee	W	7-2	Viola	Wegman
28—Milwaukee	W	13-1	Berenguer	Birkbeck
29—At Detroit	L	7-15	Terrell	Straker
31—At Detroit	W	9-5	Reardon	King
31—At Detroit	W	11-3	Frazier	Tanana
Won 14, Lost 14				

JUNE

Date	W/L	Score	Winner	Loser
1—At Boston	W	9-5	Viola	Clemens
2—At Boston	L	5-6	Schiraldi	Reardon
3—At Boston	L	6-7†	Schiraldi	Klink
5—Texas	L	9-15	Harris	Blyleven
6—Texas	W	3-2x	Atherton	Williams
7—Texas	W	7-4	Atherton	Russell
8—Kan. City	W	5-3	Niemann	Gubicza
9—Kan. City	W	5-2	Niekro	Jackson
10—Kan. City	W	4-3†	Reardon	Gleaton
12—At Chicago	W	5-2	Viola	Long
12—At Chicago	W	7-4	Berenguer	Nielsen
13—At Chicago	L	2-6	Dotson	Straker
14—At Chicago	W	6-3	Niekro	DeLeon
15—At Milw.	W	5-0	Blyleven	Wegman
16—At Milw.	W	7-3	Viola	Crim
17—At Milw.	L	5-8	Clear	Straker
19—Chicago	W	7-6	Reardon	Winn
20—Chicago	L	5-10	DeLeon	Blyleven
21—Chicago	W	8-6	Berenguer	Winn
23—Cleveland	W	9-4	Smithson	Candiotti
24—Cleveland	W	14-8	Straker	Swindell
25—Cleveland	W	4-3	Blyleven	Niekro
26—At Texas	L	0-1	Witt	Viola
27—At Texas	L	6-11	Correa	Frazier
27—At Texas	L	2-7	Hough	Atherton
28—At Texas	L	3-6	Guzman	Smithson
29—At Kan. C.	L	2-3*	Jackson	Straker
30—At Kan. C.	W	3-1	Blyleven	Leibrandt
Won 17, Lost 11				

JULY

Date	W/L	Score	Winner	Loser
1—At Kan. C.	L	3-4	Quisenberry	Atherton
2—At Kan. C.	L	3-10	Saberhagen	Niekro
3—Baltimore	W	6-5‡	Reardon	Niedenfuer
4—Baltimore	W	4-1	Straker	Bell
5—Baltimore	W	4-3	Blyleven	Niedenfuer
6—At N.Y.	W	2-0	Viola	Guidry
7—At N.Y.	L	7-12	Stoddard	Atherton
8—At N.Y.	L	4-13	Rhoden	Smithson
9—At Balt.	W	3-1	Straker	Bell
10—At Balt.	L	12-13	Williamson	Frazier
11—At Balt.	W	2-1	Viola	Griffin
12—At Balt.	L	0-5	Schmidt	Niekro
16—Toronto	L	2-5	Key	Blyleven
17—Toronto	W	3-2	Viola	Eichhorn
18—Toronto	L	5-7	Stieb	Niekro
19—Toronto	W	7-6	Schatzeder	Lavelle
20—New York	L	1-7	John	Straker
21—New York	W	2-1	Blyleven	Stoddard
22—New York	W	3-1	Viola	Rhoden
23—At Toronto	L	3-4	Stieb	Frazier
24—At Toronto	L	6-8	Eichhorn	Reardon
25—At Toronto	W	13-9	Schatzeder	Musselman
26—At Toronto	L	2-4	Key	Blyleven
27—At Seattle	W	4-3	Viola	Nunez
28—At Seattle	L	1-6	Morgan	Niekro
29—At Seattle	L	3-8	Guetterman	Smithson
31—At Oak.	W	5-3	Blyleven	Lamp
Won 13, Lost 14				

AUGUST

Date	W/L	Score	Winner	Loser
1—At Oak.	L	2-3	Stewart	Viola
2—At Oak.	L	5-6‡	Nelson	Reardon
3—At Calif.	W	11-3	Schatzeder	Witt
4—At Calif.	L	3-12	Sutton	Carlton
5—At Calif.	L	1-6	Candelaria	Blyleven
6—Oakland	W	9-4	Viola	Stewart
7—Oakland	W	9-4	Niekro	Lamp
8—Oakland	W	9-2	Carlton	Young
9—Oakland	W	7-5	Blyleven	Ontiveros
11—California	W	7-2	Viola	Candelaria
12—California	L	2-8	McCaskill	Straker
13—California	L	1-5	Witt	Carlton
14—Seattle	W	6-3	Blyleven	Morgan
15—Seattle	W	14-4	Smith	Guetterman
16—Seattle	W	5-1	Viola	Moore
17—Seattle	W	4-2	Straker	Langston
18—At Detroit	L	2-11	Morris	Carlton
19—At Detroit	L	1-7	Terrell	Blyleven
20—At Detroit	L	0-8	Alexander	Niekro
21—At Boston	L	3-11	Clemens	Viola
22—At Boston	L	5-6	Schiraldi	Straker
23—At Boston	L	4-6	Sellers	Carlton
24—Detroit	W	5-4	Reardon	King
25—Detroit	L	4-5	Alexander	Niekro
26—Detroit	L	8-10	Petry	Reardon
28—At Milw.	L	0-1	Bosio	Straker
29—At Milw.	W	12-3	Blyleven	Barker
30—At Milw.	W	10-6	Atherton	Crim
Won 13, Lost 15				

SEPTEMBER

Date	W/L	Score	Winner	Loser
1—Boston	L	0-9	Sellers	Niekro
2—Boston	W	5-4	Straker	Nipper
3—Boston	W	2-1†	Atherton	Gardner
4—Milwaukee	W	2-1§	Berenguer	Plesac
5—Milwaukee	W	2-1	Atherton	Crim
6—Milwaukee	L	0-6	Higuera	Carlton
7—Chicago	W	8-1	Bittiger	LaPoint
8—Chicago	L	3-4	Bannister	Blyleven
9—Chicago	W	2-1	Viola	Winn
11—At Cleve.	W	13-10†	Reardon	Gordon
12—At Cleve.	L	4-5	Jones	Berenguer
13—At Cleve.	W	7-3†	Reardon	Candiotti
14—At Chicago	L	2-8	LaPoint	Viola
15—At Chicago	L	2-6	McDowell	Niekro
16—At Chicago	L	10-13	DeLeon	Smithson
18—Cleveland	W	9-4	Blyleven	Akerfelds
19—Cleveland	W	3-1	Viola	Candiotti
20—Cleveland	W	3-2	Straker	Yett
22—Texas	W	6-4	Niekro	Harris
23—Texas	W	4-2	Berenguer	Guzman
24—Texas	W	4-0	Viola	Hough
25—At Kan. City	L	4-6	Farr	Schatzeder
26—At Kan. City	L	4-7	Davis	Reardon
27—At Kan. City	W	8-1	Blyleven	Leibrandt
28—At Texas	W	5-3	Berenguer	Guzman
29—At Texas	L	5-7	Hough	Atherton
30—At Texas	L	1-2	Witt	Straker
Won 16, Lost 11				

OCTOBER

Date	W/L	Score	Winner	Loser
2—At Kan. C.	L	3-6	Saberhagen	Viola
3—At Kan. C.	L	2-4	Leibrandt	Blyleven
4—At Kan. C.	L	1-10	Gubicza	Niekro
Won 0, Lost 3				

*5 innings. †10 innings. ‡11 innings. §12 innings. x13 innings.

Twins third baseman Gary Gaetti won a Gold Glove while hitting 31 homers and driving in 109 runs.

The three relievers were the life-support of a rotation that was shaky beyond Frank Viola and Bert Blyleven.

Viola, the majors' winningest lefthander over the last four seasons with 69 victories, topped the staff with a 17-10 record and ranked second in the league with a 2.90 ERA. From the end of May through mid-August, Viola was 12-2 with a 1.99 ERA. His 197 strikeouts were a career high.

Blyleven, 15-12 with a 4.01 ERA and 196 strikeouts, pitched his best down the stretch.

After their two front-liners, the Twins offered Les Straker (8-10), a 27-year-old rookie and veteran of 10 minor league seasons; two 42-year-olds, Joe Niekro (4-9), acquired in June from the New York Yankees, and Steve Carlton (1-5), acquired July 31 from Cleveland; Mike Smithson (4-7), and Mark Portugal (1-3), who was sent down June 8.

The Twins' core of stars was still the same—Gold Glove center fielder Kirby Puckett, right fielder Tom Brunansky, Gold Glove third baseman Gary Gaetti and first baseman Kent Hrbek—but the unsung heroes had their days, too.

Shortstop Greg Gagne batted a career-high .265. Second baseman Steve Lombardozzi (.238) drilled a three-run homer and a game-winning single as the Twins defeated the Texas Rangers, 5-3, September 28 to clinch the division. Catcher Tim Laudner batted only .191, but the Twins were 46-30 when he started during the regular season.

Dan Gladden (.249), acquired from San Francisco at the end of spring training, took over in left field, led the Twins with 25 stolen bases and was infectious as a scrappy leadoff hitter.

"He made us tougher," Brunansky said. "You watch him play and you want to give as much as you have, too."

Randy Bush, the fourth outfielder, drove in 46 runs in 293 at-bats. Roy Smalley (.275) was productive as the early season designated hitter, rookie Gene Larkin (.266) contributed in the middle and veteran Don Baylor, obtained August 31 from the Boston Red Sox, hit .286 for the Twins down the stretch.

The role players helped the stars, who continued to produce in a big way.

Puckett tied for the league lead with 207 hits, ranked fourth with a career-high .332 average and belted 28 homers with 99 runs batted in. Gaetti led the team with 109 RBIs and swatted 31 home runs. Hrbek tied for the league lead among first basemen with a .996 fielding average while hitting a career-high 34 homers with 90 RBIs. Brunansky matched personal bests with 32 homers and 85 RBIs.

The Twins' 98 errors were the fewest in the league.

"Defense is as big a reason for our success this season as anything," Reardon said. "That's what impressed me right away in spring training about this team—the defense and the power. I didn't realize how many guys the Twins had who could hit the ball out of the park until I came over here."

Which made Kelly's job a little easier in his first full season. "I just like to let them play," the low-key skipper said. "I wasn't always looking over their shoulders. If they made a mistake, I wanted to talk to them about it. But after it was over, it was over. I always tried to keep things on an even keel."

Danny Tartabull, acquired from Seattle in the off-season, emerged as the
Royals' power man, hitting 34 homers and driving in 101 runs.

Royals Endure '87 Nightmare

By BOB NIGHTENGALE

The 1987 season was perhaps the most traumatic in Kansas City Royals history.

The Royals' anguish began when they watched their beloved manager, Dick Howser, depart on the fourth day of spring training. Howser was too weak to manage after undergoing chemotherapy and two operations on a malignant brain tumor. He died June 17.

Third-base coach Billy Gardner was named as Howser's replacement. The Royals started fairly quickly under their new skipper and owned a five-game lead in the American League West on May 26. But they never played consistently good the rest of the way. On August 27, sitting 3½ games behind the Minnesota Twins with a 62-64 record, the Royals fired Gardner. They won their first two games under John Wathan, whose previous managerial experience consisted of five months with the Royals' Class AAA club in Omaha (American Association), and pulled within two games of the Twins on August 28. They never came closer.

"The whole traumatic thing about this year was that we could have won it; we could have won the whole thing," said second baseman Frank White, who won his eighth Gold Glove. "No one in our division played well this year."

The Royals' only consolation was that they finished the season with five straight victories and nine wins in their last 11 games. That flourish enabled them to finish second with an 83-79 record, two games behind the Twins.

"It was an embarrassing season in a lot of ways," pitcher Charlie Leibrandt said, "from the front office to the players. We just weren't able to put anything together all season. We're all frustrated."

It became evident early that this would be a trying season for the Royals.

Ed Hearn, who was acquired from the New York Mets in hopes of solving the Royals' catching woes, suffered a torn rotator cuff. He did not play after April 18.

George Brett went on the disabled list April 20 with a pulled muscle in his rib cage. He was reactivated May 13, but two days later he caught his spikes in the artificial turf at Royals Stadium and tore a knee ligament, resulting in another disabled stint. He missed 45 of the Royals' first 56 games and became so frustrated that he threatened to retire. Brett finished his agonizing season batting .290 with 22 home runs and 78 runs batted in.

The Royals' pitchers, although spared any injuries, were equally frustrated. The staff compiled the league's second-best earned-run average (3.86) and allowed fewer homers (128) than any team in the league, but several individuals struggled.

Lefthander Danny Jackson, who many thought would contend for the Cy Young Award, instead almost became the Royals' first 20-game loser when he finished with a 9-18 record and a 4.02 ERA. Righthander Mark Gubicza (13-18, 3.98) wasn't much better, though he did pace the staff with 166 strikeouts.

Bret Saberhagen enjoyed the best start of any pitcher in the majors by heading into the All-Star break with a 15-3 record and 2.47 ERA. Dreams of a second Cy Young Award in three years were dashed, however, when the righthander flopped after the All-Star break. He finished at 18-10 with a 3.36 ERA, 15 complete games and four shutouts. Leibrandt (16-11) was the team's most consistent starter, although a late-season slump kept the lefty from winning the A.L. title. He finished sixth with a 3.41 mark. Lefthander Bud Black, a part-time starter, was 8-6 with a 3.60 ERA.

Kansas City's relief corps compiled only 26 saves, a total surpassed by all but two A.L. teams. Most indicative of the bullpen's woes is the fact that Gene Garber, acquired August 31 from Atlanta, tied Dan Quisenberry for the team high in saves with eight in just one month's work.

Kansas City's top relievers were Garber and rookie John Davis (2.27 ERA). Lefthander Jerry Don Gleaton (4.26 ERA, five saves), the most frequently used reliever, and Steve Farr (4.15) were less steady.

In what he called the most frustrating season of his career, Quisenberry pitched a career-low 49 innings and had just one save opportunity after the All-Star break. Quisenberry's disenchantment led him to request a trade after the season.

He was one of several Royals who indicated they weren't sure they wanted to be around for another year.

Among the disgruntled was veteran left fielder/designated hitter Lonnie Smith, who was called up from Omaha in July but played in just six of the Royals' final 25 games. He hit .251.

Steve Balboni, who was moved from first base to DH to the bench, expressed his desire to be traded if not guaranteed a

SCORES OF KANSAS CITY ROYALS' 1987 GAMES

APRIL

Date	W/L	Score	Winner	Loser
6—Chicago	L	4-5	Dotson	Jackson
8—Chicago	W	9-3	Leibrandt	Bannister
9—Chicago	L	0-6	DeLeon	Gubicza
10—New York	W	13-1	Saberhagen	Rhoden
11—New York	L	2-15	Rasmussen	Jackson
12—New York	W	8-2	Leibrandt	Niekro
14—Detroit	W	10-1	Gubicza	Petry
15—Detroit	W	2-1	Saberhagen	Terrell
18—At N.Y.	L	6-7	Righetti	Farr
19—At N.Y.	L	0-5	Hudson	Leibrandt
19—At N.Y.	L	0-1	Clements	Gubicza
20—At Boston	W	10-2	Saberhagen	Hurst
21—At Boston	L	0-8	Clemens	Anderson
22—At Boston	L	0-1	Stanley	Jackson
24—At Detroit	W	7-3	Leibrandt	Petry
25—At Detroit	L	2-13	Morris	Gubicza
26—At Detroit	W	6-1	Saberhagen	Terrell
28—Baltimore	L	0-3	Boddicker	Jackson
29—Baltimore	W	5-4	Quisenberry	Schmidt

Won 9, Lost 10

MAY

Date	W/L	Score	Winner	Loser
1—Cleveland	L	0-2	Niekro	Gubicza
2—Cleveland	W	5-4	Saberhagen	Yett
3—Cleveland	W	2-1	Jackson	Schrom
5—Toronto	W	6-4	Leibrandt	Johnson
6—Toronto	W	6-3	Black	Key
8—At Cleve.	W	9-6	Gubicza	Schrom
9—At Cleve.	W	4-0	Saberhagen	Candiotti
10—At Cleve.	L	2-4	Swindell	Jackson
11—At Toronto	L	0-4	Key	Leibrandt
12—At Toronto	W	3-1	Black	Cerutti
13—At Balt.	W	8-7§	Farr	Williamson
14—At Balt.	L	3-4	Schmidt	Saberhagen
15—Milwaukee	W	4-3	Quisenberry	Clear
16—Milwaukee	W	13-0	Leibrandt	Wegman
17—Milwaukee	W	3-2	Farr	Birkbeck
18—Boston	W	4-2	Gubicza	Nipper
19—Boston	W	4-1	Saberhagen	Stanley
20—Boston	L	1-7	Hurst	Jackson
22—At Texas	W	8-1	Leibrandt	Loynd
23—At Texas	L	4-6	Hough	Black
24—At Texas	W	5-2	Gleaton	Guzman
25—At Chicago	W	6-1	Saberhagen	Davis
26—At Chicago	W	5-4	Jackson	Long
27—At Chicago	L	2-3	Dotson.	Leibrandt
29—Texas	L	5-16	Hough	Gubicza
30—Texas	W	12-7	Saberhagen	Guzman
31—Texas	L	2-3†	Mohorcic	Gleaton

Won 18, Lost 9

JUNE

Date	W/L	Score	Winner	Loser
1—At Milw.	L	2-3	Wegman	Leibrandt
2—At Milw.	L	3-14	Crim	Black
3—At Milw.	L	2-4	Barker	Gubicza
4—At Seattle	W	6-1	Saberhagen	Morgan
5—At Seattle	L	2-7	Guetterman	Jackson
6—At Seattle	W	5-2	Leibrandt	Bankhead
7—At Seattle	W	9-1	Black	Moore
8—At Minn.	L	3-5	Niemann	Gubicza
9—At Minn.	L	2-5	Niekro	Jackson
10—At Minn.	L	3-4†	Reardon	Gleaton
12—California	W	1-0	Saberhagen	Witt
13—California	L	0-4	Fraser	Gubicza
14—California	L	0-12	Sutton	Jackson
15—Oakland	L	6-7	Leiper	Farr
16—Oakland	L	1-11	Ontiveros	Anderson
17—Oakland	W	10-5	Saberhagen	Stewart
18—At Calif.	W	10-4	Gubicza	Fraser
19—At Calif.	W	2-0	Jackson	Sutton
20—At Calif.	W	8-4	Leibrandt	Lazorko
21—At Calif.	L	0-8	Reuss	Stoddard
22—At Oak.	L	1-4	Ontiveros	Saberhagen
23—At Oak.	W	4-0	Gubicza	Rijo
24—At Oak.	L	2-4	Young	Jackson
26—Seattle	L	1-5	Morgan	Leibrandt
27—Seattle	W	6-0	Saberhagen	Guetterman
28—Seattle	W	8-3	Gubicza	Moore
29—Minnesota	W	3-2*	Jackson	Straker
30—Minnesota	L	1-3	Blyleven	Leibrandt

Won 12, Lost 16

JULY

Date	W/L	Score	Winner	Loser
1—Minnesota	W	4-3	Quisenberry	Atherton
2—Minnesota	W	10-3	Saberhagen	Niekro
3—Toronto	W	6-4	Gubicza	Clancy
3—Toronto	W	5-4	Farr	Henke
4—Toronto	W	9-1	Black	Wells
5—Toronto	W	4-3†	Quisenberry	Eichhorn
6—At Cleve.	L	7-9	Stewart	Saberhagen
7—At Cleve.	L	4-6	Jones	Quisenberry
8—At Cleve.	L	8-9	Stewart	Gleaton
9—At Toronto	L	1-7	Nunez	Black
10—At Toronto	L	0-7	Stieb	Leibrandt
11—At Toronto	W	2-1	Saberhagen	Key
12—At Toronto	L	2-3	Clancy	Black
16—Baltimore	L	4-5	Boddicker	Leibrandt
17—Baltimore	L	1-3	Bell	Gubicza
18—Baltimore	L	7-11	Flanagan	Jackson
19—Baltimore	L	1-5	Schmidt	Black
20—Cleveland	L	5-9	Niekro	Saberhagen
21—Cleveland	W	3-2	Leibrandt	Bailes
22—Cleveland	W	5-1	Gubicza	Akerfelds
23—At Balt.	L	1-2	Bell	Jackson
24—At Balt.	L	1-3	Niedenfuer	Farr
25—At Balt.	L	3-4	Williamson	Saberhagen
26—At Balt.	W	4-0	Leibrandt	Dixon
28—At N.Y.	L	1-2	Rhoden	Gubicza
29—At N.Y.	L	0-4	Stoddard	Jackson
30—At N.Y.	L	3-6	John	Black
31—Boston	L	0-4	Clemens	Saberhagen

Won 10, Lost 18

AUGUST

Date	W/L	Score	Winner	Loser
1—Boston	W	4-0	Leibrandt	Sellers
2—Boston	W	13-5	Gubicza	Stanley
3—At Detroit	W	4-2†	Gleaton	Morris
4—At Detroit	W	8-4	Jackson	Petry
5—At Detroit	L	2-4	Terrell	Saberhagen
7—At Boston	L	3-4	Sellers	Leibrandt
8—At Boston	L	3-8	Hurst	Gubicza
9—At Boston	W	8-3	Davis	Crawford
10—New York	W	10-1	Jackson	Arnsberg
11—New York	W	8-5	Saberhagen	Guidry
12—New York	W	2-1	Leibrandt	Rhoden
13—Detroit	L	1-4	Morris	Gubicza
14—Detroit	W	7-5	Black	Terrell
15—Detroit	L	4-8	King	Jackson
16—Detroit	L	6-10	Robinson	Gleaton
17—At Texas	W	7-6	Davis	Russell
18—At Texas	L	1-3	Hough	Gubicza
19—At Texas	W	11-6	Stoddard	Witt
21—At Milw.	L	0-3	Barker	Jackson
22—At Milw.	W	8-7	Gleaton	Knudson
23—At Milw.	L	5-10	Aldrich	Stoddard
24—Texas	L	2-4	Witt	Gubicza
25—Texas	L	8-15	Howe	Stoddard
26—Texas	W	3-0	Jackson	Hough
27—Texas	W	3-2†	Davis	Mohorcic
28—At Chicago	W	9-3	Leibrandt	LaPoint
29—At Chicago	L	2-7	Bannister	Gubicza
30—At Chicago	W	11-7	Black	Dotson
31—At Chicago	L	3-5	DeLeon	Jackson

Won 16, Lost 13

SEPTEMBER

Date	W/L	Score	Winner	Loser
1—Milwaukee	L	0-2	Higuera	Saberhagen
2—Milwaukee	L	2-3	Wegman	Leibrandt
3—Milwaukee	L	2-8	Bosio	Gubicza
4—Chicago	W	6-2	Perez	Dotson
5—Chicago	W	4-2	Jackson	DeLeon
6—Chicago	L	4-5‡	Thigpen	Davis
7—At Calif.	W	5-2	Leibrandt	Witt
8—At Calif.	W	4-2	Gubicza	Fraser
10—At Oak.	L	2-3	Plunk	Davis
11—At Oak.	W	9-0	Saberhagen	Ontiveros
12—At Oak.	W	10-7	Leibrandt	Stewart
13—At Oak.	W	6-5	Gubicza	Honeycutt
14—California	W	8-5	Black	Lazorko
15—California	L	1-7	Fraser	Jackson
16—California	L	4-6	Minton	Saberhagen
17—California	W	7-6	Davis	Minton
18—Oakland	L	0-4	Ontiveros	Gubicza
19—Oakland	L	5-9	Davis	Perez
20—Oakland	L	6-7	Young	Jackson
21—At Seattle	L	1-5	Campbell	Saberhagen
22—At Seattle	W	4-3†	Gleaton	Reed
23—At Seattle	W	9-0	Gubicza	Langston
25—At Minn.	W	6-4	Farr	Schatzeder
26—At Minn.	W	7-4	Davis	Reardon
27—At Minn.	L	1-8	Blyleven	Leibrandt
28—Seattle	L	1-5	Guetterman	Gubicza
29—Seattle	W	6-3	Black	Langston
30—Seattle	W	7-3	Jackson	Morgan

Won 15, Lost 13

OCTOBER

Date	W/L	Score	Winner	Loser
2—Minnesota	W	6-3	Saberhagen	Viola
3—Minnesota	W	4-2	Leibrandt	Blyleven
4—Minnesota	W	10-1	Gubicza	Niekro

Won 3, Lost 0

*5 innings. †10 innings. ‡11 innings. §12 innings.

Kansas City rookie Kevin Seitzer impressed everybody with his .323 average and 207 hits.

starting role. He batted just .207 but had 24 homers and 60 RBIs in 386 at-bats.

One definite departure was Hal McRae, the Royals' longtime DH. He began the season as the club's hitting coach/DH, then was released as a player in July. Not wanting to return as hitting coach in 1988, McRae was released after the season.

Once again, the Royals were unable to find a bona fide starting shortstop or catcher. The Royals platooned Jamie Quirk (.236) and Larry Owen (.189) behind the plate and tried five different shortstops, all with little success. Buddy Biancalana and Angel Salazar opened the season at shortstop, but by September, Biancalana (.213) was wearing a Houston Astros uniform and Salazar (.205) was riding the bench with back problems. Bill Pecota (.276) and Ross Jones (.254) finished the season at short.

The Royals' offense again was weak. They batted .262 collectively, a 10-point improvement over 1986, but scored a league-low 715 runs and were shut out a league-high 17 times.

Yet, in a season of considerable unrest, newcomers Kevin Seitzer and Danny Tartabull gave reason for hope.

Seitzer, who inherited Brett's position at third base when Brett opted for first, tied for the A.L. lead with 207 hits, making him just the 13th player in major league

history to collect 200 hits as a rookie. He hit a team-high .323, smacked 15 homers, drove in 83 runs and scored 105 while shattering virtually every Royals rookie record. He finished second to Oakland's Mark McGwire in the A.L. Rookie of the Year voting.

Tartabull, who joined the Royals in an off-season trade with Seattle, certainly lived up to expectations. The right fielder hit .309 with 34 homers, 101 RBIs and a league-high 21 game-winning RBIs.

Another positive story was that of Jim Eisenreich, who had been out of baseball since 1984 with a nervous disorder. Attempting a comeback with the Royals, Eisenreich was assigned to Memphis (Southern), where he tore the league apart (.382). He was called up to Kansas City on June 16, and though his playing time was limited—he hit .238 in just 105 at-bats as a DH—at least he was back.

A couple of longtime veterans held their own. Center fielder Willie Wilson batted .279, hit a league-high 15 triples and stole 59 bases, one behind the league leader. White struggled with his average (.245) but continued to show good power, hitting 17 homers with 78 RBIs.

And then there was Bo Jackson.

Jackson, the 1985 Heisman Trophy winner, made the club the last week of spring training and quickly became the talk of baseball. The left fielder hit .500 the first seven games of the season (14 for 28) and was batting .324 at the end of April. His average fell to .254 by the All-Star break, but he still was leading the Royals with 18 homers and 45 RBIs (tied with Tartabull).

But on July 11, Jackson announced that he would play for the Los Angeles Raiders of the National Football League after the baseball season. That could have been the turning point for the Royals. Team unity went out the window as many players became enraged that the front office had allowed Jackson to play football.

The rookie's production dropped off even more and he spent much of the second half on the bench. Jackson, who finished with an alarming 158 strikeouts in 396 at-bats, left on a bitter note with his teammates still distressed.

"It was a major distraction; it just ruined our season," said Tartabull, Jackson's closest friend on the team.

Kansas City fans viewed Jackson's decision to play football as betrayal, and they let him know it by booing him loudly for several weeks. Nevertheless, the Royals set a club attendance record by drawing 2,392,471 fans to Royals Stadium.

The A's youthful 1-2 punch of Mark McGwire (left) and Jose Canseco combined for 80 home runs and 231 RBIs in 1987.

A's See a Star-Studded Future

By KIT STIER

Oakland Athletics Manager Tony LaRussa, a man not given to palm readers and crystal balls, can look to the stars and see a bright future.

Astrological prophecies? Never.

Oakland's assets are 100 percent tangible, as in budding *super*stars. They made the 1987 season a break-even proposition: good signs in bad times.

Mark McGwire, the 1987 American League Rookie of the Year, blasted 49 home runs, 11 more than any other first-year player in history. Slugging left fielder Jose Canseco, the 1986 A.L. Rookie of the Year, matured in 1987, cutting his strikeouts by 18 and his error total in half. And rookie Terry Steinbach, jumping from Class AA Huntsville, showed signs of becoming one of the majors' best catchers.

They were visions of beauty in an ugly finish, as the A's engine stalled during the stretch drive for the A.L. West title.

The club had played itself into contention, overcoming a 3-10 start to rise to second place by mid-June. The A's hovered in second or third (they even forged into first for three days) and entered September just 1½ games out of first. Four weeks later, the A's were eliminated after they lost six of seven games to Cleveland and Chicago, last-place teams in their respective divisions.

Oakland finished 81-81, good for a second straight third-place finish but the club's most victories since 1980.

"We did a lot of things right," LaRussa said. "I just think there are a lot of real positive things going on here. And I think the fans should get excited about it.

"I think we can get better with what we have. Firming up our defense would be a step in the right direction. I think we can do that by paying some attention to detail. Execution is the key."

The A's turned 122 double plays, last in the league, and only three A.L. teams committed more errors (142). Second basemen Tony Phillips and Tony Bernazard combined for 22 errors and shortstop Alfredo Griffin committed 24 before bowing out as a starter September 16 with a sprained left thumb.

LaRussa expects his team to bear down from Day 1 through Day 162 next year but can understand the struggle in 1987.

How many clubs receive a retirement notice the day before spring training begins from a pitcher expected to be a key starter? Oakland did, from lefthander Vida Blue.

Bad luck turned rotten with injuries to righthanded starters Joaquin Andujar and Moose Haas, who both opened the season on the disabled list. Andujar was disabled three other times, finished 3-5 and pitched only 60⅔ innings. Haas (2-2, 5.75 earned-run average) made only nine starts before undergoing elbow surgery in June.

With three-fifths of the projected starting staff unavailable for most of the season, LaRussa and pitching coach Dave Duncan scrambled. Thirteen different pitchers started games while one served as the rotation's anchor.

Righthander Dave Stewart (20-13, 3.68 ERA), cast off from the Philadelphia Phillies early in the 1986 season, was one of two 20-game winners in the majors and the first Athletic to reach the mark since Mike Norris won 22 in 1980. Stewart became only the second Oakland pitcher to fan 200 batters, striking out 205, second to Blue's 301 in 1971.

LaRussa could also lean on lefthander Curt Young. Though he missed three weeks at midseason with a strained left bicep, Young finished 13-7 with career highs in strikeouts (124) and complete games (six).

The rest of the staff, however, was part of LaRussa's juggling act. Reliever Steve Ontiveros, who also opened the season on the disabled list, became a regular member of the rotation in June and finished 10-8 in 22 starts and 13 relief appearances.

Hard-throwing righthander Jose Rijo (2-7, 5.90 ERA) was an inconsistent starter and sent to the minors twice. Eric Plunk (4-6), who was 1-2 in nine starts to open the season, also had two stints in Tacoma. Storm Davis, acquired August 30 from San Diego, was 1-1 in five starts, while Rick Honeycutt, picked up a day earlier from Los Angeles, won one of four starts. The victory ended a personal 13-game losing streak.

With the medley of starters combining for only 18 complete games, the A's relievers overcame a formidable challenge. The bullpen saved 40 games despite—what else?—a season-ending injury to stopper Jay Howell.

Howell (3-4, 5.89 ERA) saved 15 games through July 6 then broke down in the second half. He recorded only one more save, on August 21, before bone chips in his right

SCORES OF OAKLAND ATHLETICS' 1987 GAMES

APRIL

Date		Score	Winner	Loser
7—At Minn.	L	4-5*	Frazier	Krueger
8—At Minn.	L	1-4	Viola	Plunk
9—At Minn.	L	4-5	Berenguer	Howell
10—California	L	4-6	McCaskill	Stewart
11—California	L	3-6	Fraser	Krueger
12—California	W	7-1	Young	Witt
13—Minnesota	W	6-3	Howell	Frazier
14—Minnesota	L	8-9	Atherton	Codiroli
15—Minnesota	L	2-5	Smithson	Stewart
16—At Seattle	L	5-6	Trujillo	Rijo
17—At Seattle	L	2-4	Langston	Young
18—At Seattle	W	7-5	Howell	Moore
19—At Seattle	L	1-8	Bankhead	Codiroli
20—At Calif.	W	10-5	Stewart	Lucas
21—At Calif.	L	5-8	Cook	Eckersley
22—At Calif.	W	7-6	Young	Witt
24—Seattle	L	3-6	Moore	Krueger
25—Seattle	W	7-3	Stewart	Bankhead
26—Seattle	L	5-8	Trujillo	Rijo
27—Boston	W	5-2	Young	Stanley
28—Boston	W	7-1	Eckersley	Sellers
29—Milwaukee	L	7-8	Bosio	Nelson
30—Milwaukee	W	4-1	Stewart	Wegman

Won 9, Lost 14

MAY

Date		Score	Winner	Loser
1—Detroit	W	2-1§	Eckersley	Kelly
2—Detroit	W	3-2§	Leiper	Snell
3—Detroit	W	2-0	Plunk	King
5—At Boston	L	0-6	Hurst	Stewart
6—At Boston	L	2-6	Schiraldi	Eckersley
8—At Detroit	W	7-2	Young	Tanana
9—At Detroit	W	8-7	Nelson	Thurmond
10—At Detroit	L	6-7	Snell	Ontiveros
12—At Milw.	W	10-8	Stewart	Mirabella
13—At Milw.	W	8-2	Young	Higuera
15—Toronto	L	2-3	Johnson	Plunk
16—Toronto	W	10-3	Haas	Key
17—Toronto	W	3-0	Stewart	Cerutti
18—New York	L	1-2	John	Young
19—New York	W	4-2	Eckersley	Rasmussen
20—New York	W	7-5	Nelson	Hudson
22—Baltimore	L	6-10	Schmidt	Haas
23—Baltimore	L	4-5	Boddicker	Stewart
24—Baltimore	L	3-4	Ballard	Young
25—Baltimore	L	3-4	Bell	Eckersley
27—At Toronto	W	4-1	Haas	Johnson
28—At Toronto	W	4-3	Stewart	Clancy
29—At N.Y.	W	13-5	Young	Rasmussen
30—At N.Y.	W	4-3	Andujar	Niekro
31—At N.Y.	L	5-9	John	Eckersley

Won 15, Lost 10

JUNE

Date		Score	Winner	Loser
1—At Balt.	W	9-6	Nelson	Dixon
2—At Balt.	L	2-9	Boddicker	Stewart
3—At Balt.	W	7-3	Young	Ballard
5—Cleveland	L	3-4	Candiotti	Andujar
6—Cleveland	W	6-4	Eckersley	Swindell
7—Cleveland	L	2-12	Carlton	Stewart
8—Chicago	W	9-3	Ontiveros	Bannister
9—Chicago	W	8-3	Young	DeLeon
10—Chicago	W	5-2	Eckersley	Allen
12—At Texas	W	6-1	Stewart	Harris
13—At Texas	W	10-8	Ontiveros	Kilgus
14—At Texas	L	1-5	Hough	Plunk
15—At Kan. C.	W	7-6	Leiper	Farr
16—At Kan. C.	W	11-1	Ontiveros	Anderson
17—At Kan. C.	L	5-10	Saberhagen	Stewart
19—Texas	L	2-4	Hough	Haas
20—Texas	L	6-7	Witt	Young
21—Texas	W	7-3	Stewart	Guzman
21—Texas	L	3-13	Correa	Plunk
22—Kan. City	W	4-1	Ontiveros	Saberhagen
23—Kan. City	L	0-4	Gubicza	Rijo
24—Kan. City	W	4-2	Young	Jackson
26—At Cleve.	W	5-0	Stewart	Carlton
27—At Cleve.	W	13-3	Andujar	Schrom
28—At Cleve.	W	10-0	Ontiveros	Candiotti
29—At Chicago	L	2-5	Dotson	Young
30—At Chicago	L	3-12	Nielsen	Rijo

Won 16, Lost 11

JULY

Date		Score	Winner	Loser
1—At Chicago	L	3-5*	Winn	Howell
2—Boston	W	5-3	Andujar	Nipper
3—Boston	L	0-2	Sellers	Ontiveros
4—Boston	W	9-5	Rijo	Hurst
5—Boston	W	6-3	Stewart	Boyd
6—Detroit	W	5-3	Nelson	King
7—Detroit	L	4-6	Tanana	Andujar
8—Detroit	L	5-9	Robinson	Ontiveros
9—Milwaukee	L	3-8	Bosio	Rijo
10—Milwaukee	W	7-3	Stewart	Knudson
11—Milwaukee	W	6-5	Eckersley	Plesac
12—Milwaukee	L	3-4	Nieves	Howell
16—At Boston	W	11-6*	Cadaret	Stanley
17—At Boston	W	8-3	Stewart	Clemens
18—At Boston	L	3-5*	Hurst	Eckersley
19—At Boston	W	5-3†	Howell	Stanley
20—At Detroit	L	4-5	Henneman	Nelson
21—At Detroit	L	5-6*	King	Howell
22—At Detroit	W	10-1	Lamp	Tanana
23—At Milw.	L	5-12	Bosio	Andujar
24—At Milw.	L	2-10	Nieves	Ontiveros
25—At Milw.	W	13-4	Young	Knudson
26—At Milw.	L	4-7	Higuera	Lamp
27—California	W	6-1	Stewart	McCaskill
28—California	L	2-9	Witt	Andujar
29—California	L	4-5	Sutton	Ontiveros
31—Minnesota	L	3-5	Blyleven	Lamp

Won 12, Lost 15

AUGUST

Date		Score	Winner	Loser
1—Minnesota	W	3-2	Stewart	Viola
2—Minnesota	W	6-5†	Nelson	Reardon
3—Seattle	L	3-4	Morgan	Andujar
4—Seattle	W	9-3	Ontiveros	Guetterman
5—Seattle	W	3-1	Rijo	Bankhead
6—At Minn.	L	4-9	Viola	Stewart
7—At Minn.	L	4-9	Niekro	Lamp
8—At Minn.	L	2-9	Carlton	Young
9—At Minn.	L	5-7	Blyleven	Ontiveros
10—At Seattle	W	15-4	Stewart	Bankhead
11—At Seattle	L	2-8	Moore	Rijo
12—At Seattle	L	3-4	Langston	Nelson
14—At Calif.	W	7-6‡	Rodriguez	Buice
15—At Calif.	W	13-3	Stewart	Candelaria
16—At Calif.	W	9-6	Cadaret	Finley
17—At Calif.	L	4-6	Witt	Leiper
18—Toronto	L	1-2	Stieb	Eckersley
19—Toronto	W	7-3	Stewart	Cerutti
20—Toronto	L	6-7	Lavelle	Cadaret
21—New York	W	6-4	Ontiveros	Guidry
22—New York	W	6-0	Nelson	Trout
23—New York	L	0-4	Rhoden	Stewart
24—Baltimore	W	7-3	Cadaret	Boddicker
25—Baltimore	W	9-7	Young	Bell
27—At Toronto	L	4-9	Key	Cadaret
28—At Toronto	W	3-2	Stewart	Stieb
29—At Toronto	W	6-5*	Plunk	Eichhorn
30—At Toronto	L	3-13	Clancy	Rijo
31—At N.Y.	L	1-4	Guidry	Young

Won 15, Lost 14

SEPTEMBER

Date		Score	Winner	Loser
1—At N.Y.	W	8-3	Ontiveros	Hudson
2—At N.Y.	L	2-3*	Righetti	Honeycutt
4—At Balt.	L	2-5	Boddicker	Nelson
5—At Balt.	W	7-2	Young	Bell
6—At Balt.	L	6-7	Niedenfuer	Eckersley
7—Texas	W	2-1	Stewart	Williams
8—Texas	L	1-12	Hough	Nelson
9—Texas	W	11-7	Cadaret	Witt
10—Kan. City	W	3-2	Plunk	Davis
11—Kan. City	L	0-9	Saberhagen	Ontiveros
12—Kan. City	L	7-10	Leibrandt	Stewart
13—Kan. City	L	5-6	Gubicza	Honeycutt
14—At Texas	L	1-2†	Mohorcic	Ontiveros
15—At Texas	W	6-5	Plunk	Mohorcic
16—At Texas	L	1-4	Hough	Stewart
18—At Kan. C.	W	4-0	Ontiveros	Gubicza
19—At Kan. C.	W	9-5	Davis	Perez
20—At Kan. C.	W	7-6	Young	Jackson
21—At Cleve.	L	3-6	Jones	Stewart
22—At Cleve.	W	10-2	Honeycutt	Farrell
23—At Cleve.	L	6-8	Vande Berg	Plunk
24—Chicago	L	2-4	Bannister	Davis
25—Chicago	L	1-2*	Thigpen	Eckersley
26—Chicago	L	2-3	James	Plunk
27—Chicago	L	0-5	LaPoint	Honeycutt
29—Cleveland	W	5-4	Ontiveros	Jones
30—Cleveland	W	4-3	Stewart	Akerfelds

Won 12, Lost 15

OCTOBER

Date		Score	Winner	Loser
1—Cleveland	W	9-5	Cadaret	Candiotti
2—At Chicago	W	4-3†	Cadaret	James
3—At Chicago	L	1-17	LaPoint	Honeycutt
4—At Chicago	L	2-5	Bannister	Stewart

Won 2, Lost 2

*10 innings. †11 innings. ‡12 innings. §13 innings.

elbow forced him to the operating table.

Setup man Dennis Eckersley, who had started 359 of 376 career games before 1987, was a worthy replacement. Acquired from the Chicago Cubs four days before the season, the veteran righthander recorded his first save since 1976 on April 25 and finished the season with 16, a 6-8 record and 3.03 ERA.

Middle reliever Gene Nelson (6-5, 3.93 ERA, three saves) tied Eckersley for the team lead in appearances (54) and made six starts in August and early September. Rookie lefthander Greg Cadaret provided a second-half lift, going 6-2 in 29 games.

Pitchers weren't the only key players to be injured.

On April 22 in California, center fielder Dwayne Murphy tore up his right knee in a bone-jarring collision with right fielder Mike Davis. Murphy returned June 27 after surgery but appeared in only 82 games all season. He had a .233 average with eight home runs and 35 RBIs.

Davis' injury was the most upsetting. In the first game following the All-Star break, Davis kicked a door in Fenway Park after he failed to drive in a runner on third. The outburst earned him a damaged knee and his production plummeted. After batting .292 with 20 home runs and 53 RBIs through the break, Davis hit only two more home runs with 19 RBIs. His average dipped to .265.

Phillips' injury was almost as discouraging. He missed six weeks when his left wrist was broken July 11 by a McGwire line drive in batting practice. He hit only .188 after returning and finished the year at .240 with a career-high 10 home runs. Bernazard, acquired from Cleveland when Phillips went down, hit .266 for the A's with only three home runs.

Designated hitter/right fielder Reggie Jackson was limited to one start and 15 pinch-hitting appearances after August due to a hamstring injury. Jackson, who intimated that the '87 season would be the last in his outstanding career, hit 15 home runs with 43 RBIs. After 21 seasons, Jackson had 563 home runs (sixth on all-time list), 1,702 RBIs (13th), 2,597 strikeouts (first) and 2,584 hits.

Veteran third baseman Carney Lansford hit a team-leading .289 with 19 home runs and 76 RBIs. Griffin collected 20 RBIs in August and finished with 60 and a .263 average.

But it was youth that carried the A's in 1987.

McGwire's 49 homers also set an A's single-season record and his 118 RBIs tied the team mark. The big first baseman led the

Oakland righthander Dave Stewart surprised everybody by recording a 20-13 record.

league with a .618 slugging average. Canseco, the first Athletic to record consecutive 100-RBI seasons, had 31 homers, 113 RBIs and tied for second in the league with 17 game-winning RBIs. Steinbach shook off a .224 average for April to hit .284 with 16 home runs and 56 RBIs. Rookie Luis Polonia, called up to replace Murphy, had a team-high 17-game hitting streak, led the A's in stolen bases (29), tied for second in the league in triples (10) and batted .287, mostly as the leadoff hitter. And in September, flashy shortstop Walt Weiss arrived to hit .462.

"I think the club is headed in the right direction," LaRussa said, "but I don't think we are there yet. It's a learning experience."

Mariner lefthander Mark Langston won 19 times in '87 while leading the A.L. in strikeouts for the third time in the last four seasons.

Mariners Show Improvement

By JIM STREET

The 1987 Seattle Mariners could have given up before getting started. Memories of last place lingered from a season earlier as a for-sale sign was nailed into the coffin oddsmakers had reserved for a club that had been buried under the American League West four previous times.

By midseason, the sign was down and Seattle was, very much, alive. Owner George Argyros had struck out in his bid to buy the San Diego Padres and the Mariners were fighting for first place. They did, in fact, own first for one day, May 14, and avoided the basement all year.

Six months after being given up for dead, the Mariners had won more games than ever before (78) and finished in fourth place, matching the best finish in the franchise's 11-year history. They trailed the division champion Minnesota Twins by only seven games, escaping double figures for the first time.

It was a season of improvement, a new beginning, hope for the future. The Mariners set or tied 30 club records, had their first 19-game winner in Mark Langston and their first stolen-base champion in second baseman Harold Reynolds, who swiped a club-record 60 bases. They also had their second 19-game loser in Mike Moore.

Langston (19-13) was the cornerstone of the starting staff. The lefthander led the league in strikeouts for the third time in his four major league seasons by recording a franchise- and career-high 262. He ranked among the league leaders with 272 innings pitched, 14 complete games, three shutouts and was awarded his first Gold Glove.

"When you talk about lefthanded pitchers in the big leagues, Langston is one of the premier ones," General Manager Dick Balderson said. "He came of age this season, made some giant strides."

So, too, did Reynolds and shortstop Rey Quinones, who formed a promising keystone combination.

"I think that is probably our biggest strength, the play up the middle," Balderson said. "We're very fortunate to have two young guys at those positions. Not only can they play defense, but (they) became offensive players, as well. They'll be very key factors in the success we have in the future."

Besides winning the stolen-base title, Reynolds raised his batting average from

Designated hitter Ken Phelps hit 27 home runs in the Mariners' season of improvement.

.222 in 1986 to .275 last season and tied for fifth in the league with eight triples. Quinones, who hit .189 in 36 games with the Mariners in '86, hit .276 in 1987 with 12 home runs.

"Both of them gave us more offense than we expected," Manager Dick Williams said.

But the biggest surprises were pitchers Lee Guetterman and Bill Wilkinson, neither of whom figured in the team's plans at the beginning of the season.

Guetterman, a tall lefthander used as a spot starter and long reliever in 1986, wasn't even invited to spring training after an 0-4 season. He was promoted from the Class AAA Calgary farm club on May 21 and proceeded to compile an 11-4 record in 25 appearances, including 17 starts.

Wilkinson, a starter in the minor leagues, had been a question mark because of off-season elbow surgery. He emerged as a dependable stopper and finished with 10 saves. There was even talk of moving the rookie lefthander into the starting rotation. "But I'd prefer to have him available five times a week," Williams said. "Unless we make a trade for a stopper, he could be our Dave Righetti-type reliever."

SCORES OF SEATTLE MARINERS' 1987 GAMES

APRIL

Date	W/L	Score	Winner	Loser
7—At Calif.	L	1-7	Witt	Langston
8—At Calif.	L	1-7	Candelaria	Moore
9—At Calif.	W	7-2	Bankhead	Sutton
10—Minnesota	L	1-8	Smithson	Morgan
11—Minnesota	W	6-5	Nunez	Reardon
12—Minnesota	L	5-8	Blyleven	Langston
13—California	L	3-5*	Moore	Nunez
14—California	W	6-4	Bankhead	Sutton
15—California	L	0-4	McCaskill	Morgan
16—Oakland	W	6-5	Trujillo	Rijo
17—Oakland	W	4-2	Langston	Young
18—Oakland	L	5-7	Howell	Moore
19—Oakland	W	8-1	Bankhead	Codiroli
20—At Minn.	L	5-13	Smithson	Morgan
21—At Minn.	L	1-6	Straker	Trujillo
22—At Minn.	W	4-3	Langston	Frazier
24—At Oak.	W	6-3	Moore	Krueger
25—At Oak.	L	3-7	Stewart	Bankhead
26—At Oak.	W	8-5	Trujillo	Rijo
27—Detroit	W	5-2	Langston	King
28—Detroit	W	6-4	Morgan	Robinson
29—Boston	L	5-11	Nipper	Moore
30—Boston	W	11-2	Bankhead	Hurst

Won 12, Lost 11

MAY

Date	W/L	Score	Winner	Loser
1—Milwaukee	L	8-10	Mirabella	Wilkinson
2—Milwaukee	L	4-6	Clear	Langston
3—Milwaukee	W	7-3	Morgan	Higuera
5—At Detroit	W	7-5	Clarke	Robinson
6—At Detroit	L	5-7	Terrell	Bankhead
8—At Milw.	W	4-3‡	Clarke	Bosio
9—At Milw.	W	8-2	Morgan	Nieves
10—At Milw.	W	5-1	Moore	Wegman
11—At Boston	W	4-3	Bankhead	Clemens
12—At Boston	L	2-3	Sellers	Trujillo
13—At Boston	W	5-4	Langston	Sambito
15—New York	L	3-7	Hudson	Morgan
16—New York	W	10-8	Shields	Guante
17—New York	L	3-8	Niekro	Moore
18—Baltimore	L	0-6	Boddicker	Langston
19—Baltimore	L	4-15	Ballard	Trujillo
20—Baltimore	W	6-2	Morgan	Dixon
22—Toronto	L	5-7	Eichhorn	Bankhead
23—Toronto	L	2-6	Clancy	Moore
24—Toronto	W	5-2	Langston	Stieb
25—Toronto	L	5-6	Key	Morgan
27—At N.Y.	W	6-5	Guetterman	Guidry
28—At N.Y.	L	2-5	Rhoden	Moore
29—At Balt.	W	7-3	Langston	Ballard
30—At Balt.	W	12-0	Morgan	Bell
31—At Balt.	W	8-5	Guetterman	Habyan

Won 14, Lost 12

JUNE

Date	W/L	Score	Winner	Loser
1—At Toronto	W	2-0	Bankhead	Johnson
2—At Toronto	L	3-4	Musselman	Moore
3—At Toronto	L	2-7	Stieb	Langston
4—Kan. City	L	1-6	Saberhagen	Morgan
5—Kan. City	W	7-2	Guetterman	Jackson
6—Kan. City	L	2-5	Leibrandt	Bankhead
7—Kan. City	L	1-9	Black	Moore
8—Texas	W	6-0	Langston	Jeffcoat
9—Texas	L	0-3	Guzman	Morgan
10—Texas	L	5-9	Williams	Wilkinson
12—Cleveland	L	6-10	Huismann	Trujillo
13—Cleveland	L	1-6	Niekro	Langston
14—Cleveland	W	4-3*	Nunez	Yett
15—Chicago	W	8-2	Guetterman	Bannister
16—Chicago	W	8-6	Wilkinson	Winn
17—Chicago	W	2-0	Bankhead	Long
19—At Cleve.	W	7-4	Langston	Niekro
20—At Cleve.	L	2-9	Carlton	Morgan
21—At Cleve.	W	5-0	Guetterman	Schrom
22—At Chicago	W	3-0	Moore	Nielsen
23—At Chicago	L	3-13	Long	Bankhead
24—At Chicago	W	10-7	Langston	Dotson
26—At Kan. C.	W	5-1	Morgan	Leibrandt
27—At Kan. C.	L	0-6	Saberhagen	Guetterman
28—At Kan. C.	L	3-8	Gubicza	Moore
29—At Texas	L	3-4	Williams	Clarke
30—At Texas	W	5-2	Langston	Loynd

Won 13, Lost 14

JULY

Date	W/L	Score	Winner	Loser
1—At Texas	L	3-7	Hough	Morgan
2—Detroit	W	5-2	Guetterman	Tanana
3—Detroit	L	2-5	Robinson	Moore
4—Detroit	L	3-7	Morris	Campbell
5—Detroit	L	5-7	Petry	Langston
6—Milwaukee	W	3-2	Morgan	Wegman
7—Milwaukee	W	9-5	Guetterman	Nieves
8—Milwaukee	W	5-2†	Wilkinson	Plesac
9—Boston	W	11-5	Thomas	Gardner
10—Boston	L	4-7	Schiraldi	Langston
11—Boston	L	4-10	Clemens	Morgan
12—Boston	W	6-1	Guetterman	Nipper
16—At Detroit	L	2-3	Terrell	Moore
17—At Detroit	L	0-7	Tanana	Langston
18—At Detroit	L	6-10	Henneman	Reed
19—At Detroit	W	5-4	Nunez	Hernandez
20—At Milw.	L	11-13	Crim	Morgan
21—At Milw.	L	4-6	Higuera	Moore
22—At Milw.	W	2-1	Langston	Wegman
24—At Boston	L	4-5	Hurst	Guetterman
25—At Boston	L	5-11	Bolton	Clarke
26—At Boston	L	1-11	Clemens	Moore
27—Minnesota	L	3-4	Viola	Nunez
28—Minnesota	W	6-1	Morgan	Niekro
29—Minnesota	W	8-3	Guetterman	Smithson
31—At Calif.	L	2-8	Lazorko	Bankhead

Won 10, Lost 16

AUGUST

Date	W/L	Score	Winner	Loser
1—At Calif.	L	3-4	Fraser	Moore
2—At Calif.	W	5-4	Shields	Minton
3—At Oak.	W	4-3	Morgan	Andujar
4—At Oak.	L	3-9	Ontiveros	Guetterman
5—At Oak.	L	1-3	Rijo	Bankhead
6—California	W	15-4	Moore	Fraser
7—California	W	14-0	Langston	McCaskill
8—California	W	5-3	Morgan	Witt
9—California	L	5-7	Buice	Powell
10—Oakland	L	4-15	Stewart	Bankhead
11—Oakland	W	8-2	Moore	Rijo
12—Oakland	W	4-3	Langston	Nelson
14—At Minn.	L	3-6	Blyleven	Morgan
15—At Minn.	L	4-14	Smith	Guetterman
16—At Minn.	L	1-5	Viola	Moore
17—At Minn.	L	2-4	Straker	Langston
18—New York	L	3-4	Stoddard	Wilkinson
19—New York	L	0-8	Hudson	Morgan
20—New York	W	4-3‡	Reed	Arnsberg
21—Baltimore	W	3-2	Moore	Flanagan
22—Baltimore	W	14-6	Langston	Schmidt
23—Baltimore	L	5-6	Dixon	Powell
24—Toronto	L	3-7	Cerutti	Morgan
25—Toronto	L	3-6	Clancy	Moore
28—At N.Y.	W	10-4	Trujillo	Hudson
29—At N.Y.	W	7-1	Langston	Rhoden
29—At N.Y.	L	2-4	John	Campbell
30—At N.Y.	L	1-4	Gullickson	Moore
31—At Balt.	L	3-4	Griffin	Morgan

Won 12, Lost 17

SEPTEMBER

Date	W/L	Score	Winner	Loser
1—At Balt.	W	5-0	Bankhead	Habyan
2—At Balt.	W	8-6	Langston	Ballard
4—At Toronto	L	5-6*	Nunez	Powell
5—At Toronto	L	0-3	Flanagan	Campbell
6—At Toronto	L	2-3†	J. Nunez	E. Nunez
7—At Cleve.	W	6-4	Langston	Candiotti
8—At Cleve.	W	7-0	Morgan	Yett
9—At Cleve.	W	9-4	Moore	Easterly
11—Chicago	L	1-5	DeLeon	Campbell
12—Chicago	W	12-2	Bankhead	Long
13—Chicago	L	0-2	Bannister	Langston
14—Cleveland	L	2-4	Bailes	Morgan
15—Cleveland	L	2-4	Schrom	Moore
16—Cleveland	W	5-3	Wilkinson	Stewart
17—At Chicago	L	8-9*	Thigpen	Wilkinson
18—At Chicago	W	1-0	Langston	Bannister
19—At Chicago	L	8-10	Thigpen	Nunez
20—At Chicago	L	3-5	McDowell	Moore
21—Kan. City	W	5-1	Campbell	Saberhagen
22—Kan. City	L	3-4*	Gleaton	Reed
23—Kan. City	L	0-9	Gubicza	Langston
25—Texas	W	12-3	Morgan	Witt
26—Texas	W	2-1	Moore	Kilgus
27—Texas	W	5-3	Trujillo	Williams
28—At Kan. C.	W	5-1	Guetterman	Gubicza
29—At Kan. C.	L	3-6	Black	Langston
30—At Kan. C.	L	3-7	Jackson	Morgan

Won 13, Lost 14

OCTOBER

Date	W/L	Score	Winner	Loser
1—At Texas	W	8-6	Moore	Williams
2—At Texas	W	5-4	Powell	Mohorcic
3—At Texas	W	6-4	Guetterman	Guzman
4—At Texas	W	7-4	Langston	Hough

Won 4, Lost 0

*10 innings. †11 innings. ‡12 innings.

Seattle third baseman Jim Presley hit 24 home runs, but fell far short of offensive expectations.

Edwin Nunez, whom the Mariners were counting on as a righthanded stopper, had a good start (seven saves through May 11) but wasn't the same after being KO'd by the chicken pox in mid-May. He registered only five more saves the rest of the season and only one after August 3. Jerry Reed became the team's most effective righthanded closer and had six saves in his last 10 save situations. His 3.42 earned-run average ranked second on the team. Mike Trujillo was 4-4 but had a lofty 6.17 ERA.

The team's biggest disappointment was Moore. Considered at the outset to be a possible 20-game winner, the righthander came oh-so-close to being the franchise's first 20-game loser. He won his last two starts to avert that dubious distinction and finished with 12 complete games.

"I don't think he will have two years like this one," Williams said. "It was like a dark cloud hovered over him all season. When something went bad, he always seemed to be the one on the mound."

The opposition scored more unearned runs off Moore (24) than off any other Seattle starter.

"He was a major disappointment, no doubt about that. But he still shows you what you want to see. He pitched better

the second half of the season, but we need Mike Moore to be 19-9, not 9-19," Balderson said.

Righthanded starter Mike Morgan was 12-17, one win better than in '86.

The off-season trade of powerful Danny Tartabull and minor league pitcher Rick Luecken to the Kansas City Royals for outfielder Mike Kingery and pitchers Scott Bankhead and Steve Shields looked good at the start.

Bankhead won five of his first seven decisions but developed shoulder problems and finished 9-8. He entered the off-season under a surgeon's knife. Kingery performed well as the primary right fielder, batting .280 with nine homers and 52 runs batted in, but Shields spent most of the season in the minors.

Tartabull's 34 home runs and 101 RBIs with Kansas City changed the perspective of the trade, and the Mariners' brass entered the off-season trying to find a righthanded power hitter.

Although first baseman Alvin Davis and designated hitter Ken Phelps had career highs in home runs with 29 and 27, respectively, the Mariners finished last in the American League in homers (161) despite playing half their games in a stadium built for fence-busting.

Third baseman Jim Presley hit 24 home runs but struck out 157 times. Gary Matthews, acquired from the Chicago Cubs in July, hit only three homers as a part-time DH. But rookie Mickey Brantley overcame strained rib-cage muscles to clout 14 homers and hit .302 as he replaced John Moses (.246) in center field.

Catcher Scott Bradley, a .302 hitter after coming to Seattle from the Chicago White Sox in 1986, continued his impressive batting, finishing with a .278 average. His platoon partner, David Valle, hit 12 homers and knocked in 53 runs.

As a team, the Mariners had a club-record .272 batting average, but hitting coach Bobby Tolan was fired because of "lack of communication."

Left fielder Phil Bradley didn't lack in communication. He announced in August that he wanted to be traded. Despite his obvious disenchantment, Bradley made a bid at a fourth consecutive .300-season but fell short with a .297 mark.

Bradley finished among the league leaders with 179 hits, 38 doubles, 10 triples, 84 walks and 40 stolen bases. His 67 RBIs ranked fourth on the club behind Davis' 100, Presley's 88 and Phelps' 68.

"We made some strides this season," Balderson said, "but we still have some work to do."

White Sox officials were pleasantly surprised by Ivan Calderon's .293, 83-RBI 1987 performance.

June Swoon Ruins White Sox

By JOE GODDARD

The Chicago White Sox had to crawl before they could walk in 1987, but once they were on their feet, they ran.

Before the end of June—a month in which they went 7-21—the White Sox were at the bottom of the American League West. After June 28, however, they astounded their starved fans by posting a 52-39 mark the rest of the way, easily the best in the West during that span. The White Sox won 17 of their last 21 games to finish 77-85, eight games out of first.

"If it weren't for June, we'd have been in the crowd," veteran Carlton Fisk said of a division title race that included everyone but the White Sox.

Chicago's surprising fifth-place finish after 3½ months in the basement was a credit to Manager Jim Fregosi, who held the team together, especially when first-year General Manager Larry Himes (1) failed to make a major trade during the season; (2) came into the clubhouse to fine players who weren't wearing socks with their street shoes, and (3) imposed an alcohol ban on a team that wasn't known to have an alcohol problem.

Thus, Himes deserved credit, too. His policies inadvertently drew the players together. "If that's what it takes," he said.

Chicago's biggest problem in 1987 was hitting. The White Sox ranked near the bottom of the league with a .258 composite batting average and 748 runs, and their .319 on-base percentage was the league low.

Chicago's most productive hitters were first baseman Greg Walker and designated hitter Harold Baines. Walker didn't raise his average over .200 until May 26 but still finished with 27 home runs, a team-high 94 runs batted in and a .256 average. Baines missed the first month of the season after undergoing arthroscopic knee surgery and played only eight games in right field. But he made up for lost time by batting .293 with 20 homers and 93 RBIs.

Baines was replaced in right field by Ivan Calderon, who had been obtained from Seattle the year before and was the team's most pleasant surprise of 1987. He helped boost the club's strength from the right side of the plate by leading the team with a .293 average (tied with Baines), 28 homers, 38 doubles and 93 runs scored. He also drove in 83 runs.

The outfield emerged as a promising unit. Joining Calderon were rookie Ken Williams in center and Daryl Boston and Gary Redus in left. Williams, who was recalled from Hawaii (Pacific Coast) on May 18, batted .281 with 11 homers and 21 stolen bases, while Boston (.258, 10 homers) showed signs of reaching his potential after returning from a trip to Hawaii in August. Boston, however, had only 29 RBIs in 337 at-bats. Redus batted just .236 but had 12 homers and stole 52 bases after coming from Philadelphia in a late-March trade.

At age 39, Fisk drove catcher Ron Karkovice back to the minors by hitting 23 homers and driving in 71 runs. He also joined Yogi Berra and Johnny Bench as the only catchers with 300 homers and 1,000 RBIs in their major league careers.

In all, the White Sox hit 173 homers, 52 more than in 1986.

The best of Chicago's non-power hitters was Ozzie Guillen, who had 25 steals and hit .279, including a .311 average against righthanders. But the lefthanded-hitting shortstop was walked only 22 times, which was too seldom for a player who often batted in the leadoff spot.

An eye problem cut short second baseman Donnie Hill's first half of the season, and he was disabled again in the second half with a hamstring injury. Hill finished with a .239 average after losing his starting job to rookie Fred Manrique, who hit .258 in 298 at-bats and teamed with Guillen to form a double-play combination of the future. The White Sox tied Baltimore for the A.L. high by turning 174 double plays.

Steve Lyons did his best to play third base, batting .280 in 193 at-bats. But Lyons, Hill, Tim Hulett, Jerry Royster and others failed to produce runs from that position.

Chicago's pitching was fairly solid, particularly in the second half of the season, when the team made its surge. Though White Sox pitchers registered only 792 strikeouts, the A.L. low, they combined for a 4.30 earned-run average, which ranked fourth in the league.

Most notable were a remarkable turnaround by lefthander Floyd Bannister and the emergence of rookie Bobby Thigpen as a closer. Bannister had a 12-3 record and a 2.62 ERA after the All-Star Game, including a one-hit shutout against Seattle in which he faced the minimum 27 batters. He finished with a 16-11 mark, a 3.58 ERA

SCORES OF CHICAGO WHITE SOX' 1987 GAMES

APRIL

Date	W/L	Score	Winner	Loser
6—At Kan. C.	W	5-4	Dotson	Jackson
8—At Kan. C.	L	3-9	Leibrandt	Bannister
9—At Kan. C.	W	6-0	DeLeon	Gubicza
10—Detroit	L	4-11	Tanana	Allen
11—Detroit	L	1-7	Morris	Dotson
12—Detroit	L	1-7	Robinson	Davis
14—At Toronto	L	3-4x	Eichhorn	McKeon
15—At Toronto	W	5-0	DeLeon	Stieb
17—At Detroit	L	1-3	Tanana	Dotson
18—At Detroit	L	2-3	King	Thigpen
19—At Detroit	W	7-2	Bannister	Petry
20—Milwaukee	L	4-5	Crim	DeLeon
21—Milwaukee	W	7-1	Davis	Ciardi
24—Toronto	L	2-4†	Eichhorn	James
25—Toronto	W	5-4	James	Eichhorn
26—Toronto	L	2-5	Key	DeLeon
28—At Cleve.	L	0-1	Schrom	Davis
29—At Cleve.	L	5-6	Yett	James

Won 6, Lost 12

MAY

Date	W/L	Score	Winner	Loser
1—At Balt.	W	5-1	Bannister	McGregor
2—At Balt.	W	7-3	DeLeon	Flanagan
3—At Balt.	W	4-3	Thigpen	Boddicker
4—New York	L	1-6	Hudson	Dotson
5—New York	W	2-0	Long	Niekro
6—New York	L	1-4	Rhoden	Bannister
8—Baltimore	L	6-7	Dixon	Searage
9—Baltimore	L	6-15	Schmidt	McKeon
10—Baltimore	L	4-6	Bell	Dotson
11—At N.Y.	L	2-3	Rhoden	Bannister
12—At N.Y.	L	4-5x	Guante	Thigpen
13—Cleveland	L	5-7	Schrom	DeLeon
14—Cleveland	W	4-3	Thigpen	Yett
15—Texas	W	5-0	Dotson	Witt
16—Texas	L	2-7	Mohorcic	Winn
17—Texas	W	8-5	McKeon	Harris
19—At Milw.	W	5-1	DeLeon	Higuera
20—At Milw.	L	1-5	Nieves	Davis
22—At Boston	W	4-3	Winn	Clemens
23—At Boston	W	9-1	Bannister	Nipper
24—At Boston	W	4-1†	Searage	Stanley
25—Kan. City	L	1-6	Saberhagen	Davis
26—Kan. City	L	4-5	Jackson	Long
27—Kan. City	W	3-2	Dotson	Leibrandt
29—Boston	W	8-6	Winn	Stanley
30—Boston	W	3-2†	James	Gardner
31—Boston	L	9-10	Schiraldi	Searage

Won 14, Lost 13

JUNE

Date	W/L	Score	Winner	Loser
1—At Texas	L	9-11§	Mohorcic	Davis
2—At Texas	W	15-5	Long	Hough
3—At Texas	L	3-14	Guzman	Bannister
4—At Calif.	L	2-3	Lazorko	DeLeon
5—At Calif.	L	4-6	Candelaria	Allen
6—At Calif.	L	1-2†	Witt	James
7—At Calif.	W	4-0	Long	Fraser
8—At Oak.	L	3-9	Ontiveros	Bannister
9—At Oak.	L	3-8	Young	DeLeon
10—At Oak.	L	2-5	Eckersley	Allen
12—Minnesota	L	2-5	Viola	Long
12—Minnesota	L	4-7	Berenguer	Nielsen
13—Minnesota	W	6-2	Dotson	Straker
14—Minnesota	L	3-6	Niekro	DeLeon
15—At Seattle	L	2-8	Guetterman	Bannister
16—At Seattle	L	6-8	Wilkinson	Winn
17—At Seattle	L	0-2	Bankhead	Long
19—At Minn.	L	6-7	Reardon	Winn
20—At Minn.	W	10-5	DeLeon	Blyleven
21—At Minn.	L	6-8	Berenguer	Winn
22—Seattle	L	0-3	Moore	Nielsen
23—Seattle	W	13-3	Long	Bankhead
24—Seattle	L	7-10	Langston	Dotson
26—California	L	1-3	Reuss	DeLeon
27—California	L	1-3	Witt	Bannister
28—California	L	3-13	Fraser	Long
29—Oakland	W	5-2	Dotson	Young
30—Oakland	W	12-3	Nielsen	Rijo

Won 7, Lost 21

JULY

Date	W/L	Score	Winner	Loser
1—Oakland	W	5-3†	Winn	Howell
2—At Cleve.	L	1-2‡	Jones	James
3—At Cleve.	W	14-9	Winn	Stewart
4—At Cleve.	W	3-2	Dotson	Bailes
5—At Cleve.	W	17-0	Nielsen	Niekro
6—At Balt.	L	1-4	Griffin	DeLeon
7—At Balt.	W	9-3	Bannister	Habyan
8—At Balt.	L	5-6†	Boddicker	Winn
9—At N.Y.	W	6-3	Dotson	Tewksbury

JULY

Date	W/L	Score	Winner	Loser
10—At N.Y.	L	5-9	Rasmussen	Nielsen
11—At N.Y.	W	5-2y	Long	Clements
12—At N.Y.	L	2-6	John	Bannister
16—Cleveland	L	3-4	Bailes	Dotson
17—Cleveland	W	4-3†	James	Jones
18—Cleveland	W	6-3	Thigpen	Candiotti
19—Cleveland	W	9-7	Nielsen	Carlton
20—Baltimore	L	1-4*	Griffin	Allen
21—Baltimore	L	6-11	Williamson	Long
22—Baltimore	L	5-10	Habyan	DeLeon
24—New York	W	5-2	Bannister	Trout
25—New York	W	3-2	Searage	Clements
26—New York	L	2-5	Guidry	Dotson
27—At Detroit	L	1-4	Tanana	Nielsen
28—At Detroit	L	1-3	Robinson	Long
29—At Detroit	W	4-0	Bannister	Morris
30—At Milw.	L	1-6	Knudson	Allen
31—At Milw.	W	8-6	Dotson	Higuera

Won 14, Lost 13

AUGUST

Date	W/L	Score	Winner	Loser
1—At Milw.	W	3-2	LaPoint	Wegman
2—At Milw.	W	7-3	Long	Bosio
3—Toronto	L	5-14	Musselman	Bannister
4—Toronto	L	1-4	Cerutti	Allen
5—Toronto	L	2-3	Key	Dotson
7—Milwaukee	L	4-7†	Clear	Thigpen
8—Milwaukee	L	3-5	Burris	DeLeon
8—Milwaukee	W	8-6	Bannister	Bosio
9—Milwaukee	L	4-8	Nieves	Allen
10—Detroit	W	8-4	Dotson	Terrell
11—Detroit	L	6-9	Tanana	Nielsen
12—Detroit	L	7-8	Hernandez	Thigpen
13—At Toronto	W	10-3	Bannister	Niekro
14—At Toronto	L	2-3	Cerutti	DeLeon
15—At Toronto	W	1-0	Dotson	Clancy
16—At Toronto	L	4-6	Eichhorn	Searage
17—Boston	W	2-1	LaPoint	Sellers
18—Boston	L	8-14	Nipper	Bannister
19—Boston	W	8-3	DeLeon	Hurst
20—At Texas	L	1-5	Guzman	Dotson
21—At Texas	W	5-1	Long	Kilgus
22—At Texas	L	6-8	Hough	LaPoint
23—At Texas	W	8-1	Bannister	Russell
24—At Boston	W	6-3	DeLeon	Hurst
25—At Boston	L	3-7	Crawford	Dotson
26—At Boston	W	5-3	Long	Clemens
28—Kan. City	L	3-9	Leibrandt	LaPoint
29—Kan. City	W	7-2	Bannister	Gubicza
30—Kan. City	L	7-11	Black	Dotson
31—Kan. City	W	8-6	DeLeon	Jackson

Won 14, Lost 16

SEPTEMBER

Date	W/L	Score	Winner	Loser
1—Texas	L	4-6	Guzman	Long
2—Texas	W	5-0	LaPoint	Kilgus
3—Texas	W	5-2	Bannister	Witt
4—At Kan. C.	L	2-6	Perez	Dotson
5—At Kan. C.	L	2-4	Jackson	DeLeon
6—At Kan. C.	W	5-4‡	Thigpen	Davis
7—At Minn.	L	1-8	Bittiger	LaPoint
8—At Minn.	W	4-3	Bannister	Blyleven
9—At Minn.	L	1-2	Viola	Winn
11—At Seattle	W	5-1	DeLeon	Campbell
12—At Seattle	L	2-12	Bankhead	Long
13—At Seattle	W	2-0	Bannister	Langston
14—Minnesota	W	8-2	LaPoint	Viola
15—Minnesota	W	6-2	McDowell	Niekro
16—Minnesota	W	13-10	DeLeon	Smithson
17—Seattle	W	9-8†	Thigpen	Wilkinson
18—Seattle	L	0-1	Langston	Bannister
19—Seattle	W	10-8	Thigpen	Nunez
20—Seattle	W	5-3	McDowell	Moore
21—At Calif.	W	5-3	DeLeon	Finley
22—At Calif.	L	3-5	Witt	James
23—At Calif.	L	6-10	Minton	Thigpen
24—At Oak.	W	4-2	Bannister	Davis
25—At Oak.	W	2-1†	Thigpen	Eckersley
26—At Oak.	W	3-2	James	Plunk
27—At Oak.	W	5-0	LaPoint	Honeycutt
29—California	W	1-0	Bannister	Witt
30—California	W	5-2	Dotson	Reuss

Won 19, Lost 9

OCTOBER

Date	W/L	Score	Winner	Loser
1—California	W	6-3	McDowell	Fraser
2—Oakland	L	3-4‡	Cadaret	James
3—Oakland	W	17-1	LaPoint	Honeycutt
4—Oakland	W	5-2	Bannister	Stewart

Won 3, Lost 1

*5 innings. †10 innings. ‡11 innings. §12 innings. x13 innings. y15 innings.

Chicago first baseman Greg Walker slumped early but finished with 27 home runs and a team-leading 94 RBIs.

and 11 complete games. Thigpen returned from an aborted attempt to make him a starter at Hawaii to finish the season with a 7-5 record, a team-high 16 saves and a 2.73 ERA.

The other regular starters, righthanders Richard Dotson and Jose DeLeon, both had 11-12 records, while rookie righthander Bill Long made 23 starts and finished 8-8 with a 4.37 ERA. After the season, Dotson was traded with reliever Scott Nielsen to the New York Yankees for outfielder Dan Pasqua, catcher Mark Salas and reliever Steve Rosenberg.

Lefthander Dave LaPoint was acquired from the St. Louis Cardinals in July and posted a 6-3 mark with a 2.94 ERA, but another former Cardinal, Neil Allen, went 0-7 in 15 games before being released.

Righthander Jack McDowell, the club's No. 1 pick in the June 1987 free-agent draft, was 3-0 with a 1.93 ERA in four late-season starts.

Middle relief was a problem. Former closer Bob James had a shoulder injury and staggered home with a 4.67 ERA and 10 saves, all in the first half. Jim Winn, Nielsen and Ray Searage were a combined 9-14 with 10 saves.

Overall, though, the White Sox were excited about their second-half performance. And shortly after the season, Fregosi was rewarded with a new multiyear contract.

"I'm thrilled to death," Fregosi said. "I wanted to come back. Hopefully, before I leave here, there will be a championship year in the city of Chicago."

Youngster Ruben Sierra emerged in 1987 as the big gun in the Rangers' attack, hitting 30 homers and driving in a team-leading 109 runs.

'Bizarre' Rangers Tumble

By JIM REEVES

The calendar said 1987, but the tale of the Texas Rangers was classic pulp magazine, a strange but true story of sensational injuries and mysterious phenomena.

Consider the bizarre:

• Righthander Edwin Correa was lost for the second half of the season when doctors discovered he had been pitching with a stress fracture in his right shoulder.

"He was throwing the ball 90 miles an hour," Manager Bobby Valentine said. "That amazes me."

Despite the break, Correa was 3-5 in 15 starts.

• Greg Harris, the Rangers' bullpen stopper with 20 saves in 1986, had none in 1987 and was converted into a starter. In August and early September, he was sidelined 19 days with a swollen right elbow—from flicking sunflower seeds to a friend in the stands.

"I held them on my left hand and flicked them with the middle finger of my right hand," Harris said. "I was getting a few of them up past the first aisle."

He finished with a 5-10 record.

• Outfielder Oddibe McDowell slashed his right hand when he tried to cut a dinner roll at the Rangers' "welcome home" luncheon in April. In May, he sprained his left ankle while playing tennis. And July 1, McDowell injured his neck and right shoulder when he tried to make a diving catch.

The Rangers were the Charles Atlas ad revisited. The hitters were bullies who pounded 194 homers and scored 823 runs, both club records. The pitchers were rather sickly; altogether, seven were sidelined at various times. And in the field, Texas had sand kicked in its face as it set a modern major league record for passed balls (73) and ranked 13th in the American League in fielding.

It was a dramatic letdown from 1986, when a rookie-laden team surprised baseball with 87 victories and a second-place finish in the A.L. West.

"This year was a learning experience for us," Valentine said. "But some things you wish you didn't have to learn."

A 1-10 start set the tone. The Rangers never advanced past third place, seldom saw .500 and ultimately sank into a last-place tie with the California Angels. They finished 75-87, 10 games behind the division champion Minnesota Twins.

"We had our share of injuries," Valentine said, "and there were some strange ones. But that's part of the game. We just didn't have the depth to recover when we were hit with injuries, particularly to some of our pitchers."

Though their injuries were less-than-fantastic, Dale Mohorcic, Jeff Russell, Jose Guzman, Bobby Witt and Paul Kilgus all were ailing.

Mohorcic, who ranked among A.L. leaders with 74 appearances and a team-high 16 saves, missed two weeks in August due to gastro-intestinal bleeding. He finished 7-6 with a 2.99 earned-run average.

Russell opened the season on the disabled list following elbow surgery in March. He returned May 15, appeared in 52 games for the season and finished 5-4 with three saves.

Kilgus, 2-7 as a rookie starter and reliever, developed a stiff left shoulder and pitched in only one game after September 13.

Guzman, bothered by back spasms in May and June, finished 14-14 after a 2-5 start. He was second on the staff in wins and complete games (six).

And Witt, coming off an 11-9 season as a rookie, missed a month with shoulder problems. He won his final start to finish 8-10, but more importantly, pitched his first complete game after 55 career starts. Witt also led the majors with 140 walks in 143 innings.

Witt wasn't the only wild Ranger. The staff led the majors with 760 walks and 55 hit batsmen, both club records. But paced by Charlie Hough, Texas also topped the league with a club-high 1,103 strikeouts.

Hough, a 39-year-old knuckleballer, fanned a career-high 223 batters on his way to an 18-13 season. He led the majors in both starts (40) and innings ($285\frac{1}{3}$) and finished among the league leaders with a 3.79 ERA and 13 complete games.

Mitch Williams ranked second in the league with 85 appearances, breaking his club record of 80, set in 1986. The hard-throwing lefthander was 8-6 with six saves in his second season.

Reliever Steve Howe, out of the majors since 1985 due to drug problems, was 3-3 in his comeback season.

The Rangers' hitters had their share of injuries, too—slugger Pete Incaviglia missed most of September with an injured left ankle and catcher Mike Stanley caught both the chicken pox and pneumo-

SCORES OF TEXAS RANGERS' 1987 GAMES

APRIL

Date	W/L	Score	Winner	Loser
6—At Balt.	L	1-2	Aase	Harris
8—At Balt.	W	6-4	Mohorcic	Williamson
9—At Balt.	L	6-8	Dixon	Mason
10—Milwaukee	L	8-11	Nieves	Guzman
11—Milwaukee	L	6-8	Higuera	Hough
12—Milwaukee	L	5-7§	Clear	Anderson
14—At Boston	L	1-4	Nipper	Correa
15—At Boston	L	4-5	Hurst	Mohorcic
17—At Milw.	L	2-10	Higuera	Mason
18—At Milw.	L	3-4	Wegman	Witt
19—At Milw.	L	4-6	Clear	Harris
21—Baltimore	W	6-4	Hough	Flanagan
22—Baltimore	L	2-3†	Schmidt	Williams
23—Baltimore	W	9-4	Loynd	Bell
24—Boston	W	6-4†	Harris	Schiraldi
25—Boston	W	2-1	Guzman	Hurst
26—Boston	W	5-3x	Williams	Schiraldi
28—New York	W	3-1	Correa	Rasmussen
29—New York	W	8-7	Williams	Guante

Won 8, Lost 11

MAY

Date	W/L	Score	Winner	Loser
1—At Toronto	L	2-3†	Musselman	Williams
2—At Toronto	L	8-9	Eichhorn	Harris
3—At Toronto	L	1-3	Clancy	Correa
5—Cleveland	W	6-5†	Williams	Wills
6—Cleveland	W	7-2	Hough	Niekro
8—Toronto	L	4-7	Clancy	Guzman
9—Toronto	L	4-15	Stieb	Correa
10—Toronto	W	9-8	Witt	Eichhorn
11—At Cleve.	W	6-3*	Meridith	Niekro
12—At Cleve.	W	6-1	Hough	Carlton
13—At N.Y.	W	8-6	Guzman	John
14—At N.Y.	L	1-9	Rasmussen	Correa
15—At Chicago	L	0-5	Dotson	Witt
16—At Chicago	W	7-2	Mohorcic	Winn
17—At Chicago	L	5-8	McKeon	Harris
18—Detroit	L	3-6	Robinson	Guzman
19—Detroit	W	10-8	Mohorcic	King
20—Detroit	L	4-6	Petry	Witt
22—Kan. City	L	1-8	Leibrandt	Loynd
23—Kan. City	W	6-4	Hough	Black
24—Kan. City	L	2-5	Gleaton	Guzman
25—At Detroit	L	5-8	Tanana	Correa
26—At Detroit	L	7-8‡	Henneman	Mohorcic
27—At Detroit	L	3-4	Morris	Loynd
29—At Kan. C.	W	16-5	Hough	Gubicza
30—At Kan. C.	L	7-12	Saberhagen	Guzman
31—At Kan. C.	W	3-2†	Mohorcic	Gleaton

Won 11, Lost 16

JUNE

Date	W/L	Score	Winner	Loser
1—Chicago	W	11-9§	Mohorcic	Davis
2—Chicago	L	5-15	Long	Hough
3—Chicago	W	14-3	Guzman	Bannister
5—At Minn.	W	15-9	Harris	Blyleven
6—At Minn.	L	2-3x	Atherton	Williams
7—At Minn.	L	4-7	Atherton	Russell
8—At Seattle	L	0-6	Langston	Jeffcoat
9—At Seattle	W	3-0	Guzman	Morgan
10—At Seattle	W	9-5	Williams	Wilkinson
12—Oakland	L	1-6	Stewart	Harris
13—Oakland	L	8-10	Ontiveros	Kilgus
14—Oakland	W	5-1	Hough	Plunk
15—At Calif.	W	9-7	Russell	Finley
16—At Calif.	W	5-4	Guzman	Candelaria
17—At Calif.	L	1-6	Witt	Harris
19—At Oak.	W	4-2	Hough	Haas
20—At Oak.	W	7-6	Witt	Young
21—At Oak.	L	3-7	Stewart	Guzman
21—At Oak.	W	13-3	Correa	Plunk
22—California	L	3-7	Buice	Harris
23—California	L	6-8	Fraser	Hough
24—California	L	1-4	Sutton	Loynd
26—Minnesota	W	1-0	Witt	Viola
27—Minnesota	W	11-6	Correa	Frazier
27—Minnesota	W	7-2	Hough	Atherton
28—Minnesota	W	6-3	Guzman	Smithson
29—Seattle	W	4-3	Williams	Clarke
30—Seattle	L	2-5	Langston	Loynd

Won 16, Lost 12

JULY

Date	W/L	Score	Winner	Loser
1—Seattle	W	7-3	Hough	Morgan
3—At N.Y.	W	9-0	Witt	Tewksbury
3—At N.Y.	L	1-3	Rhoden	Guzman
4—At N.Y.	L	3-4	Rasmussen	Harris
5—At N.Y.	W	10-4	Russell	Bordi
6—At Toronto	L	4-6	Key	Hough
7—At Toronto	L	2-6	Clancy	Loynd
8—At Toronto	L	2-5	Musselman	Witt

JULY

Date	W/L	Score	Winner	Loser
9—Cleveland	L	4-10	Jones	Guzman
10—Cleveland	W	10-4	Harris	Niekro
11—Cleveland	W	6-2	Hough	Carlton
12—Cleveland	W	7-6	Guzman	Jones
16—New York	L	3-12	Guidry	Hough
17—New York	L	4-8	Rhoden	Witt
18—New York	W	7-2	Guzman	Hudson
19—New York	W	20-3	Harris	Trout
20—Toronto	L	3-5	Cerutti	Hough
21—Toronto	W	6-4	Mohorcic	Musselman
22—Toronto	W	5-3	Russell	Lavelle
23—At Cleve.	L	2-4	Candiotti	Guzman
24—At Cleve.	W	6-3	Russell	Carlton
25—At Cleve.	W	7-3	Hough	Niekro
26—At Cleve.	W	11-3	Kilgus	Bailes
27—Milwaukee	W	5-4	Williams	Plesac
28—Milwaukee	L	2-9	Bosio	Guzman
29—Milwaukee	L	8-9§	Plesac	Kilgus
31—Baltimore	L	4-8	Habyan	Hough

Won 14, Lost 13

AUGUST

Date	W/L	Score	Winner	Loser
1—Baltimore	L	1-7	Dixon	Kilgus
2—Baltimore	W	5-2	Witt	Boddicker
3—Boston	L	2-11	Hurst	Guzman
4—Boston	L	6-8	Schiraldi	Mohorcic
5—Boston	W	9-8	Guzman	Sambito
7—At Balt.	L	2-9	Dixon	Kilgus
8—At Balt.	W	11-5	Witt	Boddicker
9—At Balt.	L	4-5	Habyan	Hough
10—At Milw.	L	3-4§	Aldrich	Russell
11—At Milw.	W	7-1	Harris	Knudson
12—At Milw.	W	12-3	Kilgus	Burris
14—At Boston	L	3-9	Hurst	Howe
14—At Boston	W	9-4	Hough	Nipper
15—At Boston	L	6-7	Gardner	Howe
16—At Boston	L	2-12	Stanley	Harris
17—Kan. City	L	6-7	Davis	Russell
18—Kan. City	W	3-1	Hough	Gubicza
19—Kan. City	L	6-11	Stoddard	Witt
20—Chicago	W	5-1	Guzman	Dotson
21—Chicago	L	1-5	Long	Kilgus
22—Chicago	W	8-6	Hough	LaPoint
23—Chicago	L	1-8	Bannister	Russell
24—At Kan. C.	W	4-2	Witt	Gubicza
25—At Kan. C.	W	15-8	Howe	Stoddard
26—At Kan. C.	L	0-3	Jackson	Hough
27—At Kan. C.	L	2-3†	Davis	Mohorcic
28—At Detroit	W	5-3	Williams	Morris
29—At Detroit	L	1-4	Terrell	Witt
30—At Detroit	L	0-7	Alexander	Hough

Won 12, Lost 17

SEPTEMBER

Date	W/L	Score	Winner	Loser
1—At Chicago	W	6-4	Guzman	Long
2—At Chicago	L	0-5	LaPoint	Kilgus
3—At Chicago	L	2-5	Bannister	Witt
4—Detroit	L	2-11	Alexander	Hough
5—Detroit	W	8-7	Howe	Hernandez
6—Detroit	W	9-3	Guzman	Robinson
7—At Oak.	L	1-2	Stewart	Williams
8—At Oak.	W	12-1	Hough	Nelson
9—At Oak.	L	7-11	Cadaret	Witt
10—At Calif.	L	7-8†	Buice	Howe
11—At Calif.	W	7-2	Guzman	Candelaria
12—At Calif.	W	4-3	Hough	Witt
13—At Calif.	W	8-2	Russell	Reuss
14—Oakland	W	2-1‡	Mohorcic	Ontiveros
15—Oakland	L	5-6	Plunk	Mohorcic
16—Oakland	W	4-1	Hough	Stewart
18—California	W	5-1	Guzman	Reuss
19—California	W	4-3†	Williams	Buice
20—California	W	2-1†	Howe	Minton
22—At Minn.	L	4-6	Niekro	Harris
23—At Minn.	L	2-4	Berenguer	Guzman
24—At Minn.	L	0-4	Viola	Hough
25—At Seattle	L	3-12	Morgan	Witt
26—At Seattle	L	1-2	Moore	Kilgus
27—At Seattle	L	3-5	Trujillo	Williams
28—Minnesota	L	3-5	Berenguer	Guzman
29—Minnesota	W	7-5	Hough	Atherton
30—Minnesota	W	2-1	Witt	Straker

Won 14, Lost 14

OCTOBER

Date	W/L	Score	Winner	Loser
1—Seattle	L	6-8	Moore	Williams
2—Seattle	L	4-5	Powell	Mohorcic
3—Seattle	L	4-6	Guetterman	Guzman
4—Seattle	L	4-7	Langston	Hough

Won 0, Lost 4

*5 innings. †10 innings. ‡11 innings. §12 innings. x13 innings.

Designated hitter Larry Parrish slid into the Ranger record book in '87 by enjoying his second 100-RBI season.

nia—but their story was one of hard knocks and deep shots.

Designated hitter Larry Parrish set Ranger records with 32 home runs and a second 100-RBI season (100 in '87, 101 in '84). In May, he was the A.L. Player of the Month with seven homers, 35 RBIs and a .393 average.

Second-year outfielder Ruben Sierra, only 21, blossomed into the star Valentine had predicted, batting .263 with 30 homers and a team-leading 109 RBIs.

"He's as good a talent as I've ever seen, at any age," veteran outfielder Tom Paciorek said. "He can do so much. He's becoming better and better defensively.... He might, at one point, hit 40 homers and steal 30 bases." Sierra swiped 16 in 1987.

Incaviglia, another young lion, added 27 homers and 80 RBIs despite missing 23 games with the ankle injury. His average was up to .271 after a .250 rookie season, and his strikeouts declined to 168 from 185, which had set an A.L. record.

More power was supplied by first baseman Pete O'Brien (23 homers, 88 RBIs, 14 game-winning RBIs), McDowell (14 homers), rookie outfielder Bob Brower (14) and third baseman Steve Buechele (13).

Second baseman Jerry Browne was the Rangers' rookie star of 1987. The leadoff hitter, Browne topped the team with 27 stolen bases while batting .271. He teamed at the keystone with shortstop Scott Fletcher, who followed a .300 season in 1986 with a .287 mark in '87.

Geno Petralli (.302) was one of four catchers but the only Ranger to hit .300. He set a modern major league record with 35 passed balls (32 with Hough pitching). Don Slaught (.224), Darrell Porter (.238) and Stanley (.273) also worked behind the plate.

"Ruben's continued progress, the improvement shown by Jose, the play of Jerry Browne at second, those were some of the highlights for us," Valentine said. "From an individual standpoint, it was far from a lost cause."

From a team standpoint, however, it was a long drop from the heights of 1986.

California's Wally Joyner picked up right where he left off in his 1986 rookie campaign, hitting 34 homers and driving in 117 runs in '87.

Angels Hit Rock Bottom

By TOM SINGER

Coming off their third division title, the California Angels owed their 1987 season to franchise tradition—They fell hard. This time, all the way to last place.

In 1980 and 1983, the Angels trailed by 31 and 29 games, respectively, after winning the American League West title the previous seasons. Their demise of 1987 was of historic proportions.

California became only the second team —besides the 1914-15 Philadelphia Athletics—to tumble from first to last place in consecutive seasons, finishing 75-87 and in a sixth-place tie with the Texas Rangers.

"I'm sick about our standing," Manager Gene Mauch said. "To start the season with justifiably high hopes and not have them materialize was a very disappointing experience."

The Angels' experience was one of being so close, yet so far.

On August 5, they were in third place, half a game out. They struggled home at 19-35, a pace more indicative of their general character all season. As contenders go, California's title temperament had peaked at five games above .500 (11-6) on April 24.

The Angels embarked on their title defense with an altered cast, fielding an opening-day lineup that had three newcomers and four players who were 24 or younger. "We felt we could put young people out there because of our pitching staff," Mauch said. "It was our great stabilizer."

Before long, it was tottering precariously.

Three-fifths of the rotation broke down: Kirk McCaskill underwent elbow surgery April 27 and finished 4-6. John Candelaria, beset by personal problems, spent two months on the disabled list. He went 8-6 and was traded to the New York Mets in September. Urbano Lugo was demoted May 25 after an 0-2 start with a 9.32 earned-run average.

The challenge was too much for the other starters, Mike Witt and Don Sutton. Witt, 16-14, notched half of California's 20 complete games but allowed a club-record 128 runs in 36 starts. The Angels' lone representative at the All-Star Game, Witt won only one of his last nine starts. Sutton, 11-11, moved into 11th place on the all-time wins list (321) and recorded his 3,500th career strikeout. He also set an Angels record by allowing 38 home runs and was given his unconditional release after the season.

In 1986, the big four of Witt, Sutton, Candelaria and McCaskill combined for 60 wins. In 1987, their take was 39.

Aging Jerry Reuss went 4-5 after he was signed in June, but Chuck Finley, pegged as a starter in 1988, was winless in three starts after he was moved from the bullpen in September. He finished 2-7.

After saving 52 games over the previous two seasons, relief ace Donnie Moore was rendered invisible by a sore right side. He appeared in only 14 games, finishing 2-2 with five saves. A 29-year-old rookie, DeWayne Buice (6-7, 17 saves), and a released National League veteran, Greg Minton, (5-4, 10 saves) kept the bullpen afloat.

By design, the Angels' offense was expected to be only be an accessory. And despite brilliant individual efforts, it couldn't compensate for the ailing staff. California finished last in the league in batting (.252) and 11th in home runs (172).

First baseman Wally Joyner, improving on his stellar 1986 rookie season, led the club with 34 home runs and 117 runs batted in. Joyner, a .285 hitter in '87, became the first Angel to record 100 RBIs twice.

Brian Downing, a content designated hitter until the signing of Bill Buckner in late July forced him back to left field, set a personal high with 29 homers. His club-record 106 walks tied for the league lead, contributed to his .400 on-base average and helped him lead the team with 110 runs.

Outfielder Devon White, an early candidate for rookie honors, ranked third on the team in home runs (24) and second in both RBIs (87) and runs (103). He topped the team with 32 stolen bases and tied Joyner for the lead with 33 doubles.

Catcher Bob Boone, a free agent until he re-signed May 1, caught his 1,919th career game on September 16 to break Al Lopez's major league record. He also won his fifth Gold Glove.

Otherwise, inconsistency ruled. Center fielder Gary Pettis (.208, 17 RBIs, 124 strikeouts) and third baseman Doug DeCinces (.234) were inept, and Ruppert Jones (.245) and George Hendrick (.241) couldn't repeat their heroics off the bench. DeCinces was cut loose September 22, six days after Candelaria departed.

Mauch never could fully implement the

SCORES OF CALIFORNIA ANGELS' 1987 GAMES

APRIL

Date	W/L	Score	Winner	Loser
7—Seattle	W	7-1	Witt	Langston
8—Seattle	W	7-1	Candelaria	Moore
9—Seattle	L	2-7	Bankhead	Sutton
10—At Oak.	W	6-4	McCaskill	Stewart
11—At Oak.	W	6-3	Fraser	Krueger
12—At Oak.	L	1-7	Young	Witt
13—At Seattle	W	5-3*	Moore	Nunez
14—At Seattle	L	4-6	Bankhead	Sutton
15—At Seattle	W	4-0	McCaskill	Morgan
17—Minnesota	W	2-1	Witt	Blyleven
18—Minnesota	W	1-0	Candelaria	Viola
19—Minnesota	L	5-6	Portugal	Sutton
20—Oakland	L	5-10	Stewart	Lucas
21—Oakland	W	8-5	Cook	Eckersley
22—Oakland	L	6-7	Young	Witt
23—At Minn.	W	7-3	Candelaria	Viola
24—At Minn.	W	8-1	Sutton	Portugal
25—At Minn.	L	7-8	Reardon	Finley
26—At Minn.	L	5-10	Frazier	Cook
27—Milwaukee	L	7-10‡	Mirabella	Finley
28—Milwaukee	W	10-5	Buice	Crim
29—Detroit	L	1-2*	King	Moore
30—Detroit	L	4-12	Morris	Fraser
Won 12, Lost 11				

MAY

Date	W/L	Score	Winner	Loser
1—Boston	L	3-12	Clemens	Lugo
2—Boston	W	4-2	Witt	Stanley
3—Boston	W	11-4	Candelaria	Nipper
5—At Milw.	W	2-0	Sutton	Wegman
6—At Milw.	W	3-0	Witt	Birkbeck
8—At Boston	L	4-6	Sambito	Buice
9—At Boston	W	8-1	Fraser	Nipper
10—At Boston	L	0-7	Hurst	Sutton
11—At Detroit	W	5-1	Witt	Terrell
12—At Detroit	L	2-15	Petry	Lugo
13—At Detroit	L	7-10	Tanana	Candelaria
15—Baltimore	W	7-6*	Moore	O'Connor
16—Baltimore	L	2-4	McGregor	Witt
17—Baltimore	L	2-3	Schmidt	Buice
18—Toronto	L	0-12	Clancy	Cook
19—Toronto	W	2-1	Buice	Musselman
20—Toronto	W	5-4*	Lucas	Henke
22—New York	L	2-7	Rhoden	Witt
23—New York	L	0-3	Niekro	Fraser
24—New York	L	8-10*	Righetti	Moore
25—New York	L	3-6	John	Lazorko
27—At Balt.	L	6-8	Habyan	Lucas
28—At Balt.	L	7-8‡	Williamson	Buice
29—At Toronto	L	1-3	Stieb	Sutton
30—At Toronto	L	3-4*	Eichhorn	Lazorko
31—At Toronto	L	2-7	Cerutti	Candelaria
Won 9, Lost 17				

JUNE

Date	W/L	Score	Winner	Loser
1—At N.Y.	W	9-2	Witt	Hudson
2—At N.Y.	L	2-3	Righetti	Fraser
3—At N.Y.	L	3-9	Bordi	Sutton
4—Chicago	W	3-2	Lazorko	DeLeon
5—Chicago	W	6-4	Candelaria	Allen
6—Chicago	W	2-1*	Witt	James
7—Chicago	L	0-4	Long	Fraser
8—Cleveland	L	0-2	Niekro	Sutton
9—Cleveland	W	6-5	Lazorko	Yett
10—Cleveland	W	10-7	Minton	Bailes
12—At Kan. C.	L	0-1	Saberhagen	Witt
13—At Kan. C.	W	4-0	Fraser	Gubicza
14—At Kan. C.	W	12-0	Sutton	Jackson
15—Texas	L	7-9	Russell	Finley
16—Texas	L	4-5	Guzman	Candelaria
17—Texas	W	6-1	Witt	Harris
18—Kan. City	L	4-10	Gubicza	Fraser
19—Kan. City	L	0-2	Jackson	Sutton
20—Kan. City	L	4-8	Leibrandt	Lazorko
21—Kan. City	W	8-0	Reuss	Stoddard
22—At Texas	W	7-3	Buice	Harris
23—At Texas	W	8-6	Fraser	Hough
24—At Texas	W	4-1	Sutton	Loynd
26—At Chicago	W	3-1	Reuss	DeLeon
27—At Chicago	W	3-1	Witt	Bannister
28—At Chicago	W	13-3	Fraser	Long
29—At Cleve.	W	11-4	Sutton	Swindell
30—At Cleve.	L	1-2	Niekro	Lazorko
Won 17, Lost 11				

JULY

Date	W/L	Score	Winner	Loser
1—At Cleve.	W	10-5	Reuss	Carlton
2—Milwaukee	W	9-7§	Finley	Clear
3—Milwaukee	L	4-6	Higuera	Fraser
4—Milwaukee	L	1-2	Bosio	Sutton
5—Milwaukee	W	4-3‡	Finley	Clear
6—Boston	W	10-7‡	Minton	Gardner
7—Boston	W	9-4	Witt	Nipper
8—Boston	W	5-3	Fraser	Sellers
9—Detroit	W	5-2	Sutton	Morris
10—Detroit	L	4-9	King	Lazorko
11—Detroit	L	5-12	Henneman	Reuss
12—Detroit	W	5-4	Witt	Tanana
16—At Milw.	L	4-6	Higuera	McCaskill
17—At Milw.	L	2-12	Wegman	Witt
18—At Milw.	W	12-6	Buice	Plesac
19—At Milw.	W	8-5	Lazorko	Aldrich
20—At Boston	W	3-2	Minton	Sellers
21—At Boston	L	0-3	Clemens	McCaskill
22—At Boston	W	6-5	Witt	Boyd
24—At Detroit	L	3-6	Henneman	Finley
25—At Detroit	L	4-5*	Henneman	Minton
26—At Detroit	L	2-6	Terrell	Fraser
27—At Oak.	L	1-6	Stewart	McCaskill
28—At Oak.	W	9-2	Witt	Andujar
29—At Oak.	W	5-4	Sutton	Ontiveros
31—Seattle	W	8-2	Lazorko	Bankhead
Won 15, Lost 11				

AUGUST

Date	W/L	Score	Winner	Loser
1—Seattle	W	4-3	Fraser	Moore
2—Seattle	L	4-5	Shields	Minton
3—Minnesota	L	3-11	Schatzeder	Witt
4—Minnesota	W	12-3	Sutton	Carlton
5—Minnesota	W	6-1	Candelaria	Blyleven
6—At Seattle	L	4-15	Moore	Fraser
7—At Seattle	L	0-14	Langston	McCaskill
8—At Seattle	L	3-5	Morgan	Witt
9—At Seattle	W	7-5	Buice	Powell
11—At Minn.	L	2-7	Viola	Candelaria
12—At Minn.	W	8-2	McCaskill	Straker
13—At Minn.	W	5-1	Witt	Carlton
14—Oakland	L	6-7‡	Rodriguez	Buice
15—Oakland	L	3-13	Stewart	Candelaria
16—Oakland	L	6-9	Cadaret	Finley
17—Oakland	W	6-4	Witt	Leiper
18—Baltimore	L	1-4	Dixon	McCaskill
19—Baltimore	L	1-2	Boddicker	Sutton
20—Baltimore	L	2-4‡	Williamson	Buice
21—Toronto	W	3-1	Reuss	Niekro
22—Toronto	L	0-2	Nunez	Witt
23—Toronto	W	5-2	McCaskill	Stieb
24—New York	L	2-3†	Hudson	Lucas
25—New York	W	5-1	Candelaria	Rasmussen
27—At Balt.	L	5-9	Flanagan	Reuss
28—At Balt.	L	5-6	Williamson	Finley
29—At Balt.	W	6-5	Fraser	Williamson
30—At Balt.	W	6-2	Sutton	Bell
31—At Toronto	W	8-7†	Fraser	Henke
Won 13, Lost 16				

SEPTEMBER

Date	W/L	Score	Winner	Loser
1—At Toronto	L	3-4*	Musselman	Witt
2—At Toronto	L	6-7	Wells	Buice
4—At N.Y.	L	4-8	Gullickson	McCaskill
5—At N.Y.	L	6-7	Guidry	Sutton
6—At N.Y.	W	3-1	Candelaria	John
7—Kan. City	L	2-5	Leibrandt	Witt
8—Kan. City	L	2-4	Gubicza	Fraser
10—Texas	W	8-7*	Buice	Howe
11—Texas	L	2-7	Guzman	Candelaria
12—Texas	L	3-4	Hough	Witt
13—Texas	L	2-8	Russell	Reuss
14—At Kan. C.	L	5-8	Black	Lazorko
15—At Kan. C.	W	7-1	Fraser	Jackson
16—At Kan. C.	W	6-4	Minton	Saberhagen
17—At Kan. C.	L	6-7	Davis	Minton
18—At Texas	L	1-5	Guzman	Reuss
19—At Texas	L	3-4*	Williams	Buice
20—At Texas	L	1-2*	Howe	Minton
21—Chicago	L	3-5	DeLeon	Finley
22—Chicago	W	5-3	Witt	James
23—Chicago	W	10-6	Minton	Thigpen
25—At Cleve.	L	5-7	Jones	Lucas
26—At Cleve.	W	10-11*	Ritter	Lucas
27—At Cleve.	W	11-8	Sutton	Schrom
29—At Chicago	L	0-1	Bannister	Witt
30—At Chicago	L	2-5	Dotson	Reuss
Won 7, Lost 19				

OCTOBER

Date	W/L	Score	Winner	Loser
1—At Chicago	L	3-6	McDowell	Fraser
2—Cleveland	W	10-4	Sutton	Yett
3—Cleveland	W	12-5	Lazorko	Schrom
4—Cleveland	L	6-10	Farrell	Witt
Won 2, Lost 2				

*10 innings. †11 innings. ‡12 innings. §13 innings.

Angel righthander Mike Witt slumped in 1987 but still managed to record 16 victories.

full-throttle running game he envisioned with White, Pettis, shortstop Dick Schofield (.251) and rookie second baseman Mark McLemore. He hoped for 160 steals; he got 100. After White, McLemore had 25, Pettis, 24, and Schofield, 19.

By August, the Angels had decided to halt their youth movement. Veterans Tony Armas (.198) and Buckner (.306) were reeled in off the waiver list. An August 29 trade with the Pittsburgh Pirates for second baseman Johnny Ray (.346 with California) benched McLemore, who hit .236 while fielding brilliantly.

California lost 10 of its first 12 games in September and the season ended in shambles. The nosedive almost overshadowed a few encouraging indicators: Righthander Willie Fraser (10-10, 3.92 as a spot starter) was one of the league's better rookie pitchers. Jack Howell, who inherited third base from DeCinces, belted 23 homers. Journeyman Jack Lazorko was surpris-

ingly effective when given a chance to start, going at least seven innings in eight of 11 assignments. Reliever Gary Lucas rebounded from back problems and surrendered only 11 earned runs in his final 40 appearances.

But ultimately, the Angels' greatest feat was drawing 2,696,299 fans to view a last-place team.

As things unraveled, General Manager Mike Port became embroiled in a war of words with the players. Port said they "lack what it takes inside." When released, DeCinces responded: "There isn't a guy in the clubhouse who has any respect for Port."

In the end, Port hinted at additional movement. "On the basis of ability, this was not a last-place club," he said. "I have a positive feeling about the nucleus, but then I look at the standings. Obviously, this is not the time to sit tight and stand pat."

Shortstop Alan Trammell became the Tigers' cleanup hitter in 1987 and drove in a career-high 105 runs.

Tigers Roar to the Top

By TOM GAGE

In 1987, the Detroit Tigers' stumbling blocks became their stepping stones.

The Tigers admitted their shortcomings, then rectified them. When others saw vulnerability, Detroit saw the key to winning. In the end, a club originally labeled an also-ran was the surprise of the American League East. More important, the Tigers were division champions.

And fittingly, the Tigers capped their success story with an edge-of-the-seat ending. They went head to head with the front-running Toronto Blue Jays seven times in their last 11 games. Each game was decided by a run, the first three in the Jays' favor. The final four were all that mattered, however, and Detroit won them all, including the season finale, 1-0, to clinch the East title.

Along the way, Detroit needed a catcher, a cleanup hitter, a bullpen stopper, a righthanded hitter and a starting pitcher.

The Tigers' spring lineup was not unlike the one that won the World Series in 1984: Kirk Gibson, Chet Lemon and Larry Herndon roamed the outfield, Alan Trammell and Lou Whitaker were keystone partners and Darrell Evans returned his lusty bat as the first baseman/designated hitter.

But following a 9-20 preseason tuneup, the Tigers stumbled to a 9-16 start and were buried 11 games back on May 5. Skipper Sparky Anderson, the A.L. Manager of the Year, ventured onto a limb. "I don't know if we'll win it, but we'll be heard from before the season ends," he declared.

Two moves sent them on their way.

Trammell was moved to the cleanup spot to fill a gaping hole left by catcher Lance Parrish, who was lost to free agency. Previously an excellent No. 2 hitter, Trammell batted .343, ripped 28 homers, scored 109 runs and had 105 runs batted in, including 16 game-winners. He became the first Tiger since Al Kaline in 1955 to collect 200 hits and 100 RBIs in the same season. ". . .He's grown up, he's gotten strong and he knows how to drive the ball," Anderson said.

"I've never been one to declare myself a leader," Trammell said. "It's not done that way. It's done by example. I feel I've been around long enough to be an example."

And after sifting through the pretenders, the Tigers settled on a platoon of rookie Matt Nokes and Mike Heath to replace

Detroit's 40-year-old Darrell Evans slugged 34 home runs and drove in 99 runs.

Parrish behind the plate. Nokes hit .289, powered 32 homers, drove in 87 and was named to the A.L. All-Star squad. Heath's .281 average matched his career high.

"I never knew we'd get that kind of production behind the plate," Anderson said, "but I never knew we'd hit all season the way we did."

The Tigers led the major leagues with 225 home runs, a club record, and 896 runs. Their .272 average was third-best overall, tied with Seattle.

Just as pressing a need was the Tigers' want of a stopper. Willie Hernandez missed most of the first six weeks and encountered one frustration after another when he returned. By the end of the season, Hernandez (3-4, eight saves) was persona non grata at Tiger Stadium and booed every time he appeared. After the season, the lefthander said he would "prefer to go elsewhere."

"If it hadn't been for Mike Henneman," Anderson said, "I don't know where we would have ended up. Certainly not where we did."

Henneman, The Sporting News' A.L. Rookie Pitcher of the Year, was the bulwark of the bullpen. His second appearance, May 12 in a 15-2 rout of the California Angels, marked the start of the long road back. Twelve victories in the next 14

SCORES OF DETROIT TIGERS' 1987 GAMES

APRIL

			Winner	Loser
6—New York	L	1-2*	Righetti	Morris
8—New York	L	5-6	Hudson	Hernandez
9—New York	W	9-3	Terrell	Tewksbury
10—At Chicago	W	11-4	Tanana	Allen
11—At Chicago	W	7-1	Morris	Dotson
12—At Chicago	W	7-1	Robinson	Davis
14—At Kan. C.	L	1-10	Gubicza	Petry
15—At Kan. C.	L	1-2	Saberhagen	Terrell
17—Chicago	W	3-1	Tanana	Dotson
18—Chicago	W	3-2	King	Thigpen
19—Chicago	L	2-7	Bannister	Petry
20—At N.Y.	L	2-8	Rhoden	Morris
21—At N.Y.	L	1-3	Niekro	Terrell
22—At N.Y.	L	1-4	Shirley	Tanana
24—Kan. City	L	3-7	Leibrandt	Petry
25—Kan. City	W	13-2	Morris	Gubicza
26—Kan. City	L	1-6	Saberhagen	Terrell
27—At Seattle	L	2-5	Langston	King
28—At Seattle	L	4-6	Morgan	Robinson
29—At Calif.	W	2-1*	King	Moore
30—At Calif.	W	12-4	Morris	Fraser

Won 9, Lost 12

MAY

			Winner	Loser
1—At Oak.	L	1-2§	Eckersley	Kelly
2—At Oak.	L	2-3§	Leiper	Snell
3—At Oak.	L	0-2	Plunk	King
5—Seattle	L	5-7	Clarke	Robinson
6—Seattle	W	7-5	Terrell	Bankhead
8—Oakland	L	2-7	Young	Tanana
9—Oakland	L	7-8	Nelson	Thurmond
10—Oakland	W	7-6	Snell	Ontiveros
11—California	L	1-5	Witt	Terrell
12—California	W	15-2	Petry	Lugo
13—California	W	10-7	Tanana	Candelaria
15—Cleveland	W	4-3	Henneman	Huismann
16—Cleveland	W	5-3	Morris	Niekro
17—Cleveland	W	8-4	Terrell	Carlton
18—At Texas	W	6-3	Robinson	Guzman
19—At Texas	L	8-10	Mohorcic	King
20—At Texas	W	6-4	Petry	Witt
22—At Minn.	W	3-2	Morris	Viola
23—At Minn.	L	5-7	Anderson	Terrell
24—At Minn.	W	7-2	Robinson	Atherton
25—Texas	W	8-5	Tanana	Correa
26—Texas	W	8-7†	Henneman	Mohorcic
27—Texas	W	4-3	Morris	Loynd
29—Minnesota	W	15-7	Terrell	Straker
31—Minnesota	L	5-9	Reardon	King
31—Minnesota	L	3-11	Frazier	Tanana

Won 15, Lost 11

JUNE

			Winner	Loser
1—At Cleve.	L	6-9	Niekro	Petry
3—At Cleve.	W	15-3	Morris	Schrom
4—At Boston	L	5-8	Hurst	Terrell
5—At Boston	W	4-2	Robinson	Nipper
6—At Boston	W	5-3x	King	Gardner
7—At Boston	W	18-8	Henneman	Leister
9—Milwaukee	W	8-5	Morris	Higuera
10—Milwaukee	L	5-8*	Plesac	King
11—Milwaukee	L	5-8	Wegman	King
12—Boston	W	11-4	Tanana	Clemens
13—Boston	W	6-4	Petry	Crawford
14—Boston	W	2-1	Morris	Hurst
15—At Toronto	W	2-1	Terrell	Key
16—At Toronto	L	4-10	Lavelle	Robinson
17—At Toronto	W	3-2	Tanana	Clancy
19—At Balt.	W	5-3	Morris	Williamson
21—At Balt.	L	5-9y	Bell	Terrell
21—At Balt.	W	9-3	Petry	Dixon
22—Toronto	W	2-0	Tanana	Clancy
23—Toronto	L	7-8	Stieb	Robinson
24—Toronto	L	3-5	Cerutti	Morris
26—Baltimore	W	9-0	Terrell	Griffin
27—Baltimore	L	2-4	Niedenfuer	Tanana
28—Baltimore	W	8-7†	Hernandez	Corbett
29—At Milw.	W	11-1	Morris	Bosio
30—At Milw.	W	8-5	Petry	Clear

Won 17, Lost 9

JULY

			Winner	Loser
1—At Milw.	L	2-13	Wegman	Terrell
2—At Seattle	L	2-5	Guetterman	Tanana
3—At Seattle	W	5-2	Robinson	Moore
4—At Seattle	W	7-3	Morris	Campbell
5—At Seattle	W	7-5	Petry	Langston
6—At Oak.	L	3-5	Nelson	King
7—At Oak.	W	6-4	Tanana	Andujar
8—At Oak.	W	9-5	Robinson	Ontiveros
9—At Calif.	L	2-5	Sutton	Morris

JULY

			Winner	Loser
10—At Calif.	W	9-4	King	Lazorko
11—At Calif.	W	12-5	Henneman	Reuss
12—At Calif.	L	4-5	Witt	Tanana
16—Seattle	W	3-2	Terrell	Moore
17—Seattle	W	7-0	Tanana	Langston
18—Seattle	W	10-6	Henneman	Reed
19—Seattle	L	4-5	Nunez	Hernandez
20—Oakland	W	5-4	Henneman	Nelson
21—Oakland	W	6-5*	King	Howell
22—Oakland	L	1-10	Lamp	Tanana
24—California	W	6-3	Henneman	Finley
25—California	W	5-4*	Henneman	Minton
26—California	W	6-2	Terrell	Fraser
27—Chicago	W	4-1	Tanana	Nielsen
28—Chicago	W	3-1	Robinson	Long
29—Chicago	L	0-4	Bannister	Morris
31—At N.Y.	L	5-6	Righetti	Henneman

Won 17, Lost 9

AUGUST

			Winner	Loser
1—At N.Y.	W	10-5	Tanana	Rasmussen
2—At N.Y.	L	5-8	Rhoden	Robinson
3—Kan. City	L	2-4*	Gleaton	Morris
4—Kan. City	L	4-8	Jackson	Petry
5—Kan. City	W	4-2	Terrell	Saberhagen
6—New York	W	12-5	Tanana	Guidry
7—New York	W	8-0	Robinson	Rhoden
8—New York	L	0-7	John	King
9—New York	W	15-4	Petry	Rasmussen
10—At Chicago	L	4-8	Dotson	Terrell
11—At Chicago	W	9-6	Tanana	Nielsen
12—At Chicago	W	8-7	Hernandez	Thigpen
13—At Kan. C.	W	4-1	Morris	Gubicza
14—At Kan. C.	L	5-7	Black	Terrell
15—At Kan. C.	W	8-4	King	Jackson
16—At Kan. C.	W	10-6	Robinson	Gleaton
18—Minnesota	W	11-2	Morris	Carlton
19—Minnesota	W	7-1	Terrell	Blyleven
20—Minnesota	W	8-0	Alexander	Niekro
21—At Cleve.	L	4-12	Easterly	Petry
21—At Cleve.	L	3-8	Farrell	Tanana
22—At Cleve.	W	8-6	Henneman	Bailes
23—At Cleve.	W	4-3	Morris	Candiotti
24—At Minn.	L	4-5	Reardon	King
25—At Minn.	W	5-4	Alexander	Niekro
26—At Minn.	W	10-8	Petry	Reardon
28—Texas	L	3-5	Williams	Morris
29—Texas	W	4-1	Terrell	Witt
30—Texas	W	7-0	Alexander	Hough
31—Cleveland	L	2-7	Farrell	Tanana

Won 19, Lost 11

SEPTEMBER

			Winner	Loser
1—Cleveland	W	6-5‡	Hernandez	Gordon
2—Cleveland	W	2-1	Morris	Candiotti
3—Cleveland	W	3-1	Terrell	Yett
4—At Texas	W	11-2	Alexander	Hough
5—At Texas	L	7-8	Howe	Hernandez
6—At Texas	L	3-9	Guzman	Robinson
7—At Balt.	W	12-4	Morris	Ballard
9—At Balt.	W	7-4	Terrell	Dixon
9—At Balt.	W	6-0	Alexander	Boddicker
10—At Milw.	L	3-4	Nieves	Tanana
11—At Milw.	L	2-5	Higuera	Henneman
12—At Milw.	L	2-11	Wegman	Morris
13—At Milw.	W	5-1	Terrell	Bosio
14—Boston	W	3-0	Alexander	Clemens
15—Boston	W	9-8	Petry	Crawford
16—Boston	W	4-1	Morris	Sellers
18—Milwaukee	W	7-6	Terrell	Wegman
19—Milwaukee	W	5-2	Alexander	Bosio
20—Milwaukee	L	4-11	Nieves	Morris
21—At Boston	L	4-9	Nipper	Snell
22—At Boston	W	8-5	Terrell	Woodward
23—At Boston	W	4-0	Alexander	Hurst
24—At Toronto	L	3-4	Flanagan	Morris
25—At Toronto	L	2-3	Musselman	Hernandez
26—At Toronto	L	9-10	Nunez	Henneman
27—At Toronto	W	3-2§	Henneman	Nunez
28—Baltimore	L	0-3	Habyan	Morris
29—Baltimore	W	10-1	Tanana	Bell
30—Baltimore	L	3-7	Mesa	Petry

Won 17, Lost 12

OCTOBER

			Winner	Loser
1—Baltimore	W	9-5	Terrell	Boddicker
2—Toronto	W	4-3	Alexander	Clancy
3—Toronto	W	3-2‡	Henneman	Musselman
4—Toronto	W	1-0	Tanana	Key

Won 4, Lost 0

*10 innings. †11 innings. ‡12 innings. §13 innings. x14 innings. ySuspended game, began June 20.

Rookie Matt Nokes caught Detroit's attention in '87 with 32 homers and 87 RBIs.

games repaired the Tigers' confidence. Henneman would help keep it with an 11-3 record, seven saves and a 2.98 earned-run average.

The Tigers were vulnerable against left-handers until 14-year veteran Bill Madlock, released by the Los Angeles Dodgers, was signed June 4. Used mainly at DH, Madlock hit .279 with 14 homers and 50 RBIs.

"More than just getting Madlock's bat," pitcher Jack Morris said, "it proved to us that the front office was committed to winning. They were going to do what was needed to build a winner."

By mid-June, the Tigers had climbed to third place. By mid-July, they were only four games back. But by mid-August, the Tigers still needed another starter. Dan Petry, the No. 2 man behind Morris when the season opened, was inconsistent all year (9-7, 5.61 ERA). Rookie Jeff Robinson (9-6, 5.37 ERA) couldn't be asked to shoulder the burden of a pennant race. Detroit looked up a few sleeves and found an ace in Atlanta.

Doyle Alexander, obtained August 12 for John Smoltz, a top pitching prospect, pitched perfectly down the stretch. The veteran righthander finished 9-0 with three shutouts and a 1.53 ERA for the Tigers.

"He was the difference between first place and the cemetery," Anderson said.

After August 11, the Tigers occupied either first or second. They had the majors' best record after the All-Star break, 50-27, and the best in the end, too, at 98-64. They finished two games ahead of Toronto.

The season wasn't just one of additions; it had its ups, downs and vanishing acts.

After an excellent first year with Detroit, third baseman Darnell Coles plunged into a hitting (.181) and fielding slump (17 errors, 36 games) he never escaped. One night, the disgusted Coles threw a ball over the Tiger Stadium roof. He was traded August 7 to Pittsburgh for third baseman Jim Morrison (.205), but veteran Tom Brookens (.241, 13 homers, 59 RBIs) handled most of the third-base duty.

Whitaker's batting average declined for the fourth straight year, to .265, but he scored a team-leading 110 runs and rapped 38 doubles to rank among the league leaders.

Evans became the first 40-year-old to finish a season with at least 30 home runs. He tagged a team-leading 34, tying for third in the league, and contributed 99 RBIs.

"The man was an inspiration to us," said Gibson, who missed the first 24 games with a torn side muscle. Once back, he provided his usual solid offense—24 homers, 79 RBIs and a .277 average—as he switched from right to left field for 1987.

Right field was crowded. Herndon, a regular platoon there, hit a career-high .324. His ninth homer of '87 gave the Tigers a 1-0 victory over Toronto and the division title on the final day. Heath, Pat Sheridan (.259) and rookie Scott Lusader (.319 as Sheridan's late-season replacement) also played in right.

Lemon was on par with his 1984 season, hitting 20 homers, driving in 75 and batting .277.

The Tigers' rotation featured a "Big Three" of Morris (18-11, 3.38 ERA, 208 strikeouts), Walt Terrell (17-10 and winner of his last eight decisions) and Frank Tanana (15-10). Backing Henneman in the pen were Eric King (6-9, nine saves), Mark Thurmond (0-1, five saves) and, after September 1, Nate Snell (1-2), who was released after the season.

Although they fell in five games to the Minnesota Twins in the A. L. Championship Series, the Tigers focused on their deficiencies and turned a bad season into an excellent one.

"All the more satisfying," Trammell said.

Toronto lefthander Jimmy Key emerged as the ace of the Blue Jays' staff, recording 17 wins and a league-leading 2.76 ERA in 1987.

Late Swoon Kills Toronto

By NEIL MacCARL

Don't expect the Toronto Blue Jays to laugh at the ludicrous wisdom of Yogi Berra. They learned the hard way that "it ain't over until it's over."

There they were in first place on September 26 with 96 wins, a 3½-game lead and seven games to play. They were on a tear, having just won their seventh straight game after a six-game spurt two weeks earlier.

But one wonderful season for Manager Jimy Williams and the Blue Jays was ruined by one terrible week in which the Jays lost their final seven games, including a decisive three-game title showdown with the Detroit Tigers on the final weekend.

Toronto was dealt two crippling blows in the final two weeks. First, Gold Glove shortstop Tony Fernandez fractured his right elbow September 24 when he was upended by Detroit's Bill Madlock on a double play. Five games later, catcher Ernie Whitt suffered cracked ribs when he slid into the knee of Milwaukee Brewers second baseman Paul Molitor.

Fernandez and Whitt were missed, but the Blue Jays' plunge was the direct result of an offense that coughed, sputtered and then stalled completely. Toronto set club records in 1987 with 845 runs and 215 home runs but had only a .211 team batting average over the final seven games.

Left fielder George Bell, the A.L. Most Valuable Player and The Sporting News' A.L. Player of the Year, managed only three hits and two runs batted in in his final 26 at-bats. Gold Glove right fielder Jesse Barfield, whose 40 home runs led the majors in 1986, dropped to 28 homers in '87 and failed to hit one in his last 21 games. Center fielder Lloyd Moseby was the lone regular to hit consistently (11 for 23) over the final stretch.

Toronto fans, expecting a division title and a chance to avenge the playoff loss of 1985, turned out to Exhibition Stadium in record numbers all season. They set a club single-game attendance record of 47,828 for a July 1 game against the New York Yankees and a four-game series mark of 181,434 for the final home series against the Tigers in September. For the year, the Blue Jays drew 2,778,429, a record for an American League East team.

For much of the season the Blue Jays were incredible, as they were September 14, when they bombarded the Baltimore Orioles with a major league record 10 home runs. Whitt tied the Jays' single-game record with three, Bell and Rance Mulliniks hit two apiece, Moseby hit one, rookie Rob Ducey hit his first in the major leagues and Fred McGriff hit his 19th, a team record for a rookie.

But at other times, the Jays were totally frustrating. In June they had a team-record 11-game winning streak, then lost eight straight two weeks later, including four games in Kansas City, where they didn't win all season. And then came the fateful final week, when the Blue Jays staged one of the most memorable collapses ever and skidded from a division-leading 96-59 to 96-66 at season's end, two games behind the Tigers. Toronto had won 19 of its first 24 games in September.

Lefthander Jimmy Key, The Sporting News' A.L. Pitcher of the Year, led the league with a 2.76 earned-run average and was a model of consistency. He tied a team record with 17 victories, failed to go five innings only once in 36 starts and pitched eight complete games. But even he could not prevent the Blue Jays' self-destruction. He pitched a three-hitter in the season finale against Detroit, but Toronto lost, 1-0, on Larry Herndon's second-inning home run. A Jays' victory would have forced a one-game playoff for the A.L. East title.

The rest of the Blue Jays' starting rotation varied from streaky to inconsistent, although the staff led the league with a 3.74 ERA.

Righthander Jim Clancy became the second Toronto hurler to win 10 games by the All-Star break (Dave Stieb did it in 1983), but he won only five more in the second half.

The Jays lit up the scoreboard when Stieb (13-9) pitched, but the righthander didn't win a game after August 18.

Righthander Joe Johnson, who won seven starts in 1986 after being acquired from the Atlanta Braves, was a disappointing 3-5 in '87 and sent to the minors. Rookie lefthander David Wells (4-3) replaced him, was demoted to Syracuse after failing in two starts, then returned to pitch effectively in relief in September.

Lefthander John Cerutti was 11-4 while shuffling between the rotation and bullpen.

Rookie righthander Jose Nunez, left unprotected by Kansas City in December's major league draft, struck out 11 in his

SCORES OF TORONTO BLUE JAYS' 1987 GAMES

APRIL

			Winner	Loser
6—Cleveland	W	7-3	Key	Candiotti
8—Cleveland	W	5-1	Clancy	Swindell
9—Cleveland	L	3-14	Niekro	Johnson
10—At Boston	L	0-3	Hurst	Stieb
11—At Boston	W	11-1	Key	Clemens
12—At Boston	L	3-8	Stanley	Clancy
14—Chicago	W	4-3§	Eichhorn	McKeon
15—Chicago	L	0-5	DeLeon	Stieb
16—Boston	W	4-2	Key	Clemens
17—Boston	W	10-5	Cerutti	Stanley
18—Boston	L	4-6	Sellers	Clancy
19—Boston	L	1-4	Nipper	Johnson
20—At Cleve.	W	8-7*	Musselman	Jones
21—At Cleve.	L	0-5	Candiotti	Key
22—At Cleve.	W	6-3	Eichhorn	Carlton
24—At Chicago	W	4-2*	Eichhorn	James
25—At Chicago	L	4-5	James	Eichhorn
26—At Chicago	W	5-2	Key	DeLeon
28—Minnesota	W	5-1	Clancy	Viola
29—Minnesota	W	8-1	Johnson	Smithson

Won 12, Lost 8

MAY

			Winner	Loser
1—Texas	W	3-2*	Musselman	Williams
2—Texas	W	9-8	Eichhorn	Harris
3—Texas	W	3-1	Clancy	Correa
5—At Kan. C.	L	4-6	Leibrandt	Johnson
6—At Kan. C.	L	3-6	Black	Key
8—At Texas	W	7-4	Clancy	Guzman
9—At Texas	W	15-4	Stieb	Correa
10—At Texas	L	8-9	Witt	Eichhorn
11—Kan. City	W	4-0	Key	Leibrandt
12—Kan. City	L	1-3	Black	Cerutti
13—At Minn.	W	7-0	Clancy	Portugal
14—At Minn.	W	16-4	Stieb	Straker
15—At Oak.	W	3-2	Johnson	Plunk
16—At Oak.	L	3-10	Haas	Key
17—At Oak.	L	0-3	Stewart	Cerutti
18—At Calif.	W	12-0	Clancy	Cook
19—At Calif.	L	1-2	Buice	Musselman
20—At Calif.	L	4-5*	Lucas	Henke
22—At Seattle	W	7-5	Eichhorn	Bankhead
23—At Seattle	W	6-2	Clancy	Moore
24—At Seattle	L	2-5	Langston	Stieb
25—At Seattle	W	6-5	Key	Morgan
27—Oakland	L	1-4	Haas	Johnson
28—Oakland	L	3-4	Stewart	Clancy
29—California	W	3-1	Stieb	Sutton
30—California	W	4-3*	Eichhorn	Lazorko
31—California	W	7-2	Cerutti	Candelaria

Won 16, Lost 11

JUNE

			Winner	Loser
1—Seattle	L	0-2	Bankhead	Johnson
2—Seattle	W	4-3	Musselman	Moore
3—Seattle	W	7-2	Stieb	Langston
5—Baltimore	W	6-2	Key	Bell
6—Baltimore	W	8-5†	Musselman	Dixon
7—Baltimore	W	3-2	Eichhorn	Boddicker
8—At N.Y.	W	11-0	Stieb	Rhoden
9—At N.Y.	W	7-2	Cerutti	Guidry
10—At N.Y.	W	4-1	Key	John
11—At Balt.	W	8-6	Johnson	Habyan
12—At Balt.	W	8-5	Eichhorn	Boddicker
13—At Balt.	W	8-2	Cerutti	McGregor
14—At Balt.	L	5-8	Schmidt	Eichhorn
15—Detroit	L	1-2	Terrell	Key
16—Detroit	W	10-4	Lavelle	Robinson
17—Detroit	L	2-3	Tanana	Clancy
18—Milwaukee	L	3-6	Nieves	Stieb
19—Milwaukee	W	15-6	Musselman	Clear
20—Milwaukee	L	2-3	Wegman	Key
21—Milwaukee	W	7-6	Musselman	Crim
22—At Detroit	L	0-2	Tanana	Clancy
23—At Detroit	W	8-7	Stieb	Robinson
24—At Detroit	W	5-3	Cerutti	Morris
26—At Milw.	L	5-10	Plesac	Henke
27—At Milw.	W	8-1	Clancy	Nieves
28—At Milw.	L	5-11	Higuera	Stieb
29—New York	L	14-15	Righetti	Henke
30—New York	L	0-4	Guidry	Wells

Won 17, Lost 11

JULY

			Winner	Loser
1—New York	L	1-6‡	Clements	Musselman
3—At Kan. C.	L	4-6	Gubicza	Clancy
3—At Kan. C.	L	4-5	Farr	Henke
4—At Kan. C.	L	1-9	Black	Wells
5—At Kan. C.	L	3-4*	Quisenberry	Eichhorn
6—Texas	W	6-4	Key	Hough
7—Texas	W	6-2	Clancy	Loynd
8—Texas	W	5-2	Musselman	Witt
9—Kan. City	W	7-1	Nunez	Black
10—Kan. City	W	7-0	Stieb	Leibrandt
11—Kan. City	L	1-2	Saberhagen	Key
12—Kan. City	W	3-2	Clancy	Black
16—At Minn.	W	5-2	Key	Blyleven
17—At Minn.	L	2-3	Viola	Eichhorn
18—At Minn.	W	7-5	Stieb	Niekro
19—At Minn.	L	6-7	Schatzeder	Lavelle
20—At Texas	W	5-3	Cerutti	Hough
21—At Texas	L	4-6	Mohorcic	Musselman
22—At Texas	L	3-5	Russell	Lavelle
23—Minnesota	W	4-3	Stieb	Frazier
24—Minnesota	W	8-6	Eichhorn	Reardon
25—Minnesota	L	9-13	Schatzeder	Musselman
26—Minnesota	W	4-2	Key	Blyleven
27—Boston	W	10-8	Musselman	Schiraldi
28—Boston	W	5-4	Musselman	Sambito
29—Boston	L	5-6	Schiraldi	Lavelle
31—Cleveland	W	8-3	Key	Ritter

Won 15, Lost 12

AUGUST

			Winner	Loser
1—Cleveland	L	0-3	Bailes	Clancy
2—Cleveland	W	11-5	Stieb	Akerfelds
3—At Chicago	W	14-5	Musselman	Bannister
4—At Chicago	W	4-1	Cerutti	Allen
5—At Chicago	W	3-2	Key	Dotson
6—At Cleve.	L	5-14	Bailes	Clancy
7—At Cleve.	W	15-1	Stieb	Akerfelds
8—At Cleve.	L	1-3	Candiotti	Nunez
9—At Cleve.	W	5-1	Cerutti	Schrom
10—At Boston	L	1-9	Clemens	Clancy
11—At Boston	W	8-3	Key	Stanley
12—At Boston	W	10-4	Stieb	Sellers
13—Chicago	L	3-4	Bannister	Niekro
14—Chicago	W	3-2	Cerutti	DeLeon
15—Chicago	L	0-1	Dotson	Clancy
16—Chicago	W	6-4	Eichhorn	Searage
18—At Oak.	W	2-1	Stieb	Eckersley
19—At Oak.	L	3-7	Stewart	Cerutti
20—At Oak.	W	7-6	Lavelle	Cadaret
21—At Calif.	L	1-3	Reuss	Niekro
22—At Calif.	W	2-0	Nunez	Witt
23—At Calif.	L	2-5	McCaskill	Stieb
24—At Seattle	W	7-3	Cerutti	Morgan
25—At Seattle	W	6-3	Clancy	Moore
27—Oakland	W	9-4	Key	Cadaret
28—Oakland	L	2-3	Stewart	Stieb
29—Oakland	L	5-6*	Plunk	Eichhorn
30—Oakland	W	13-3	Clancy	Rijo
31—California	L	7-8†	Fraser	Henke

Won 17, Lost 12

SEPTEMBER

			Winner	Loser
1—California	W	4-3*	Musselman	Witt
2—California	W	7-6	Wells	Buice
4—Seattle	W	6-5*	Nunez	Powell
5—Seattle	W	3-0	Flanagan	Campbell
6—Seattle	W	3-2†	J. Nunez	E. Nunez
7—At Milw.	W	5-3	Ward	Plesac
8—At Milw.	L	4-6	Bosio	Stieb
9—At Milw.	L	4-6	Clear	Wells
11—New York	W	6-5*	Wells	Righetti
12—New York	W	13-1	Key	Rhoden
13—New York	L	5-8	Hudson	Cerutti
14—Baltimore	W	18-3	Clancy	Dixon
15—Baltimore	W	6-2	Flanagan	Mesa
16—Baltimore	W	7-0	Key	Boddicker
17—At N.Y.	L	5-6	Righetti	Henke
18—At N.Y.	W	6-3	Clancy	Allen
19—At N.Y.	L	2-4	Gullickson	Flanagan
20—At N.Y.	W	6-2	Wells	Leiter
21—At Balt.	W	2-1	Cerutti	Boddicker
22—At Balt.	W	8-4	Wells	Ballard
23—At Balt.	W	6-1	Clancy	Habyan
24—Detroit	W	4-3	Flanagan	Morris
25—Detroit	W	3-2	Musselman	Hernandez
26—Detroit	W	10-9	Nunez	Henneman
27—Detroit	L	2-3§	Henneman	Nunez
28—Milwaukee	L	4-6	Wegman	Flanagan
29—Milwaukee	L	3-5	Bosio	Key
30—Milwaukee	L	2-5	Nieves	Stieb

Won 19, Lost 9

OCTOBER

			Winner	Loser
2—At Detroit	L	3-4	Alexander	Clancy
3—At Detroit	L	2-3‡	Henneman	Musselman
4—At Detroit	L	0-1	Tanana	Key

Won 0, Lost 3

*10 innings. †11 innings. ‡12 innings. §13 innings.

first major league start—a 1-0 victory over the Royals—but worked mostly in relief. He finished 5-2.

With no one secure behind Clancy, Key and Stieb, the Jays' search for experience turned first to veteran knuckleballer Phil Niekro, who was released after just three starts and two losses to make room for longtime Baltimore lefthander Mike Flanagan. The Blue Jays surrendered two minor league pitchers to land Flanagan—and guaranteed his contract for next season—but he was a sound investment, winning three games in September while posting a 2.37 ERA.

The Blue Jays' bullpen, meanwhile, was solid from opening day: Righthander Tom Henke led the league with 34 saves, a Toronto record; righthander Mark Eichhorn topped the league with a team-record 89 appearances and was 10-6, and rookie lefthander Jeff Musselman was 12-5 in 67 relief spots.

But as tough as the relievers were, no one dominated the junior loop like Bell, who became the first Blue Jay selected to the All-Star team by the fans. Besides posting career highs with 47 home runs and a league-leading 134 RBIs, Bell was second in the league in runs (111) and slugging average (.605), sixth in hits (188) and tied for fifth in game-winning RBIs (16) while batting .308.

He was joined in the midsummer classic by Henke and Fernandez, who was headed toward his second 200-hit season when he was injured. The switch-hitting shortstop finished with 186 hits and a team-leading .322 average.

Moseby set career highs in home runs (26) and RBIs (96) and matched his best in stolen bases with a team-leading 39. And Barfield, the right-field third of perhaps the majors' most powerful outfield, added 84 RBIs.

More muscle was provided by Whitt (19 homers, 75 RBIs) and Toronto's designated hitters, who set a team record with 38 home runs. McGriff (20 homers, 18 as a DH) and Cecil Fielder (14, 11 as DH) shared regular DH duty.

Veteran Juan Beniquez, acquired from Kansas City at the All-Star break, provided righthanded punch off the bench by delivering 21 RBIs in only 81 at-bats with Toronto. Rick Leach (.282) took care of lefthanded-hitting detail.

There were, however, disappointments.

First baseman Willie Upshaw, who hit only nine home runs in 1986, had three in his first five games in '87 but only four after the All-Star break. He finished with 15, a .244 batting average and a career-

Toronto's Tony Fernandez provided his usual sparkling defense in 1987 and batted .322 before a September injury ended his season.

low 58 RBIs.

Toronto broke up the Rance Mulliniks/Garth Iorg platoon at third base and gave the job to Kelly Gruber (.235, 12 homers), but he failed to hit consistently and shared time with Mulliniks (.310, 11 homers) during the second half.

Second base was unsettled until mid-August. Iorg replaced rookie Mike Sharperson early, but with Fernandez slowed by a knee injury, the Jays suffered from a lack of speed. Rookie Nelson Liriano was called up from Syracuse in late August and provided hope for the future. Installed in the leadoff spot, he hit .241 but showed great speed and good range in the field.

Paul Molitor finished with an impressive .353 batting average and Milwaukee recorded a 76-42 record when he was in the lineup.

Brewers Streak to Third

By TOM FLAHERTY

For the Milwaukee Brewers, 1987 was the year of the streak.

They won 13 consecutive games to start the season, tying the major league record set by the Atlanta Braves in 1982. In the ninth game, Juan Nieves pitched the first no-hitter in franchise history.

On May 3, they lost their first of 12 straight games, a team record.

After the All-Star break, Paul Molitor returned to the lineup with a 39-game hitting streak, the seventh-longest in major league history.

Teddy Higuera pitched three straight shutouts on the way to pitching 32 straight scoreless innings, a team record. He had a negative streak, too, losing five straight and seven of eight decisions from May 3 to June 24. Higuera then won seven straight starts in August and September and finished 18-10.

If nothing else, rookie Manager Tom Trebelhorn's first season was anything but dull.

The Brewers, who had finished sixth or seventh for three straight seasons, finished in third place in the American League East with a 91-71 record, their first above .500 since 1983.

"We were picked to be seventh," Trebelhorn said. "Some people were kind to us and picked us sixth. I think a lot of people underestimated us.

"We finished where we deserved to be. We played third-place baseball. We finished third because of the way we played, not because someone else failed."

Despite their success, one question remained: How much higher would the Brewers have finished with a healthy Molitor available every day?

Molitor missed 44 games in the first half with hamstring and elbow injuries as the Brewers fell from 20-3 on May 2 to a 42-43 mark at the All-Star break.

He returned to the lineup and started his hitting streak the first game after the recess. The Brewers were 49-28 in the second half, second only to the Detroit Tigers in the major leagues.

How valuable was Molitor? When he was in the lineup, the Brewers were 76-42. Without him, they were 15-29.

Molitor finished with a .353 batting average, the highest in team history and second in the league to Boston's Wade Boggs (.363). Despite missing the 44 games, Molitor led the league with 114 runs scored and 41 doubles. He also led the team with 45 stolen bases.

Molitor's streak ended in Milwaukee on August 26, when he was hitless in four at-bats against Cleveland Indians rookie John Farrell. Molitor was the on-deck batter when pinch-hitter Rick Manning's 10th-inning single off Doug Jones gave the Brewers a 1-0 victory.

"Out of spring training, my goal year in and year out has been to stay as healthy as possible," said Molitor, who has played in 152 or more games only twice in his 10 major league seasons. "It started out in disappointing fashion. (But) starting out as I did in the second half and finishing up the way I did made it very satisfying."

The offense wasn't a one-man show. Milwaukee ranked second in the league with a .276 average and led the circuit with 176 stolen bases.

Center fielder Robin Yount enjoyed his best season since he was named the A.L. Most Valuable Player in 1982. Yount batted .312, hit 21 home runs and had 103 runs batted in.

"Overall, it's been a pretty good season," Yount said. "We learned a lot about ourselves and what we're capable of doing."

First baseman Greg Brock, acquired in the off-season from the Los Angeles Dodgers, had a career-high .299 average and 85 RBIs. Rookie catcher B.J. Surhoff batted .299 with 68 RBIs. Bill Schroeder, playing behind Surhoff, chipped in a .332 average, 14 homers and 42 RBIs in 75 games.

Some of the biggest hits came from a surprise source. Dale Sveum, who became the Brewers' shortstop because of injuries to Ernest Riles and rookie Kiki Diaz, batted only .252 but walloped 25 homers with 95 RBIs. He was steady—and sometimes brilliant—in the field.

At second base, Juan Castillo (.224) took over when Jim Gantner's injured hamstring kept him out for the second half. At third, Riles (.261) filled in for Molitor, who replaced Cecil Cooper (.248, six homers) as the DH in the second half.

Left fielder Rob Deer led the club with 28 homers and knocked in 80 runs. He batted only .238, however, and set an A.L. record with 186 strikeouts. Right fielder Glenn Braggs had a .269 average with 13 home runs and 77 RBIs in his first full major league season. Mike Felder (.266, 34 stolen bases) and Manning (.228) filled backup roles.

SCORES OF MILWAUKEE BREWERS' 1987 GAMES

APRIL

Date	W/L	Score	Winner	Loser
6—Boston	W	5-1	Higuera	Stanley
8—Boston	W	3-2	Crim	Gardner
9—Boston	W	12-11	Bosio	Crawford
10—At Texas	W	11-8	Nieves	Guzman
11—At Texas	W	8-6	Higuera	Hough
12—At Texas	W	7-5§	Clear	Anderson
13—At Balt.	W	6-3	Bosio	McGregor
14—At Balt.	W	7-4	Ciardi	Dixon
15—At Balt.	W	7-0	Nieves	Flanagan
17—Texas	W	10-2	Higuera	Mason
18—Texas	W	4-3	Wegman	Witt
19—Texas	W	6-4	Clear	Harris
20—At Chicago	W	5-4	Crim	DeLeon
21—At Chicago	L	1-7	Davis	Ciardi
24—Baltimore	W	6-4	Higuera	McGregor
25—Baltimore	W	8-2	Wegman	Dixon
26—Baltimore	W	5-3	Birkbeck	Flanagan
27—At Calif.	W	10-7§	Mirabella	Finley
28—At Calif.	L	5-10	Buice	Crim
29—At Oak.	W	8-7	Bosio	Nelson
30—At Oak.	L	1-4	Stewart	Wegman

Won 18, Lost 3

MAY

Date	W/L	Score	Winner	Loser
1—At Seattle	W	10-8	Mirabella	Wilkinson
2—At Seattle	W	6-4	Clear	Langston
3—At Seattle	L	3-7	Morgan	Higuera
5—California	L	0-2	Sutton	Wegman
6—California	L	0-3	Witt	Birkbeck
8—Seattle	L	3-4§	Clarke	Bosio
9—Seattle	L	2-8	Morgan	Nieves
10—Seattle	L	1-5	Moore	Wegman
12—Oakland	L	8-10	Stewart	Mirabella
13—Oakland	L	2-8	Young	Higuera
15—At Kan. C.	L	3-4	Quisenberry	Clear
16—At Kan. C.	L	0-13	Leibrandt	Wegman
17—At Kan. C.	L	2-3	Farr	Birkbeck
19—Chicago	L	1-5	DeLeon	Higuera
20—Chicago	W	5-1	Nieves	Davis
22—Cleveland	W	4-2	Wegman	Niekro
23—Cleveland	L	2-6	Carlton	Birkbeck
24—Cleveland	L	3-5	Schrom	Higuera
26—At Minn.	L	2-4	Blyleven	Nieves
27—At Minn.	L	2-7	Viola	Wegman
28—At Minn.	L	1-13	Berenguer	Birkbeck
29—At Cleve.	L	6-9	Bailes	Higuera
30—At Cleve.	W	6-5†	Clear	Huismann
31—At Cleve.	W	7-1	Nieves	Swindell

Won 6, Lost 18

JUNE

Date	W/L	Score	Winner	Loser
1—Kan. City	W	3-2	Wegman	Leibrandt
2—Kan. City	W	14-3	Crim	Black
3—Kan. City	W	4-2	Barker	Gubicza
4—New York	W	9-3	Higuera	Niekro
5—New York	L	1-13	John	Nieves
6—New York	W	7-6	Plesac	Righetti
7—New York	L	3-5	Bordi	Crim
9—At Detroit	L	5-8	Morris	Higuera
10—At Detroit	W	8-5†	Plesac	King
11—At Detroit	W	8-5	Wegman	King
12—At N.Y.	L	3-8	Rasmussen	Crim
13—At N.Y.	L	1-4	Rhoden	Nieves
14—At N.Y.	W	6-4	Plesac	Righetti
15—Minnesota	L	0-5	Blyleven	Wegman
16—Minnesota	L	3-7	Viola	Crim
17—Minnesota	W	8-5	Clear	Straker
18—At Toronto	W	6-3	Nieves	Stieb
19—At Toronto	L	6-15	Musselman	Clear
20—At Toronto	W	3-2	Wegman	Key
21—At Toronto	L	6-7	Musselman	Crim
22—At Boston	L	2-5*	Boyd	Johnson
23—At Boston	L	5-9	Crawford	Wegman
24—At Boston	L	7-8	Hurst	Higuera
26—Toronto	W	10-5	Plesac	Henke
27—Toronto	L	1-8	Clancy	Nieves
28—Toronto	W	11-5	Higuera	Stieb
29—Detroit	L	1-11	Morris	Bosio
30—Detroit	L	5-8	Petry	Clear

Won 13, Lost 15

JULY

Date	W/L	Score	Winner	Loser
1—Detroit	W	13-2	Wegman	Terrell
2—At Calif.	L	7-9x	Finley	Clear
3—At Calif.	W	6-4	Higuera	Fraser
4—At Calif.	W	2-1	Bosio	Sutton
5—At Calif.	L	3-4§	Finley	Clear
6—At Seattle	L	2-3	Morgan	Wegman
7—At Seattle	L	5-9	Guetterman	Nieves
8—At Seattle	L	2-5‡	Wilkinson	Plesac
9—At Oak.	W	8-3	Bosio	Rijo
10—At Oak.	L	3-7	Stewart	Knudson
11—At Oak.	L	5-6	Eckersley	Plesac
12—At Oak.	W	4-3	Nieves	Howell
16—California	W	6-4	Higuera	McCaskill
17—California	W	12-2	Wegman	Witt
18—California	L	6-12	Buice	Plesac
19—California	L	5-8	Lazorko	Aldrich
20—Seattle	W	13-11	Crim	Morgan
21—Seattle	W	6-4	Higuera	Moore
22—Seattle	L	1-2	Langston	Wegman
23—Oakland	W	12-5	Bosio	Andujar
24—Oakland	W	10-2	Nieves	Ontiveros
25—Oakland	L	4-13	Young	Knudson
26—Oakland	W	7-4	Higuera	Lamp
27—At Texas	L	4-5	Williams	Plesac
28—At Texas	W	9-2	Bosio	Guzman
29—At Texas	W	9-8§	Plesac	Kilgus
30—Chicago	W	6-1	Knudson	Allen
31—Chicago	L	6-8	Dotson	Higuera

Won 15, Lost 13

AUGUST

Date	W/L	Score	Winner	Loser
1—Chicago	L	2-3	LaPoint	Wegman
2—Chicago	L	3-7	Long	Bosio
4—Baltimore	W	9-8§	Knudson	Williamson
5—Baltimore	W	5-1	Higuera	Bell
6—Baltimore	W	11-8	Aldrich	Griffin
7—At Chicago	W	7-4†	Clear	Thigpen
8—At Chicago	W	5-3	Burris	DeLeon
8—At Chicago	L	6-8	Bannister	Bosio
9—At Chicago	W	8-4	Nieves	Allen
10—Texas	W	4-3§	Aldrich	Russell
11—Texas	L	1-7	Harris	Knudson
12—Texas	L	3-12	Kilgus	Burris
13—At Balt.	L	4-5	Boddicker	Bosio
14—At Balt.	W	6-2	Nieves	Bell
15—At Balt.	L	1-2	Flanagan	Higuera
16—At Balt.	W	6-2	Crim	Schmidt
17—At Cleve.	W	5-3	Knudson	Bailes
18—At Cleve.	L	8-9§	Farrell	Burris
19—At Cleve.	W	13-2	Nieves	Candiotti
20—At Cleve.	W	14-2	Higuera	Schrom
21—Kan. City	W	3-0	Barker	Jackson
22—Kan. City	L	7-8	Gleaton	Knudson
23—Kan. City	W	10-5	Aldrich	Stoddard
25—Cleveland	W	10-9	Nieves	Schrom
26—Cleveland	W	1-0†	Higuera	Jones
27—Cleveland	W	4-3	Knudson	Akerfelds
28—Minnesota	W	1-0	Bosio	Straker
29—Minnesota	L	3-12	Blyleven	Barker
30—Minnesota	L	6-10	Atherton	Crim

Won 18, Lost 11

SEPTEMBER

Date	W/L	Score	Winner	Loser
1—At Kan. C.	W	2-0	Higuera	Saberhagen
2—At Kan. C.	W	3-2	Wegman	Leibrandt
3—At Kan. C.	W	8-2	Bosio	Gubicza
4—At Minn.	L	1-2§	Berenguer	Plesac
5—At Minn.	L	1-2	Atherton	Crim
6—At Minn.	W	6-0	Higuera	Carlton
7—Toronto	L	3-5	Ward	Plesac
8—Toronto	W	6-4	Bosio	Stieb
9—Toronto	W	6-4	Clear	Wells
10—Detroit	W	4-3	Nieves	Tanana
11—Detroit	W	5-2	Higuera	Henneman
12—Detroit	W	11-2	Wegman	Morris
13—Detroit	L	1-5	Terrell	Bosio
14—At N.Y.	W	6-4	Stapleton	Gullickson
15—At N.Y.	L	3-4	Leiter	Nieves
16—At N.Y.	W	5-4	Higuera	Stoddard
18—At Detroit	L	6-7	Terrell	Wegman
19—At Detroit	L	2-5	Alexander	Bosio
20—At Detroit	W	11-4	Nieves	Morris
22—New York	W	7-2	Higuera	John
22—New York	L	8-10	Clements	Crim
23—New York	W	8-7†	Crim	Righetti
24—Boston	W	7-6	Clear	Sambito
25—Boston	L	2-9	Clemens	Nieves
26—Boston	W	3-2	Stapleton	Nipper
27—Boston	W	9-6	Burris	Stanley
28—At Toronto	W	6-4	Wegman	Flanagan
29—At Toronto	W	5-3	Bosio	Key
30—At Toronto	W	5-2	Nieves	Stieb

Won 20, Lost 9

OCTOBER

Date	W/L	Score	Winner	Loser
2—At Boston	L	2-3§	Gardner	Higuera
3—At Boston	W	8-4	Wegman	Leister
4—At Boston	L	0-4	Clemens	Bosio

Won 1, Lost 2

*7 innings. †10 innings. ‡11 innings. §12 innings. x13 innings.

Dale Sveum took over Milwaukee's shortstop job and impressed everybody with his defense and timely hitting.

"Pitching is one of the things we're looking for," General Manager Harry Dalton said, "and preferably a lefthanded-hitting outfielder. Somebody who can spell Braggs and Deer."

The Brewers got unexpected pitching help in '87.

Righthander Chuck Crim, invited to spring training only as an extra body due to injuries and contract hassles, surprised everyone by making the opening-day roster. That was just the beginning. He finished with a 6-8 record, a 3.67 earned-run average and 12 saves, all of them after the All-Star break.

Crim helped avert trouble when Dan Plesac (5-6, 23 saves) missed most of the last six weeks with a sore elbow. Elbow problems also plagued Mark Clear (8-5, six saves) at midseason, but he rebounded and surrendered only two earned runs in his final 15 appearances. Rookie Jay Aldrich (3-1) allowed only eight of 40 runners he inherited to score, the best success on the team. Overall, Milwaukee ranked second in the American League with 45 saves.

The Brewers' young starting staff continued to mature. Higuera failed to repeat as a 20-game winner but was among the league leaders with his 18 victories, 14 complete games, three shutouts and 240 strikeouts.

Nieves, who was 3-9 in the second half of his rookie season in 1986, won seven straight in the second half of '87 and finished 14-8. He set the tone for a successful year with the no-hitter in his second start, April 15 against Baltimore. Bill Wegman, in his second full season, ranked second on the staff with seven complete games and pitched better than his 12-11 record indicated.

Trebelhorn's biggest problem in the first half was finding a fourth and fifth starter. He never found a fifth man, but rookie Chris Bosio stepped into the fourth spot at midseason. After struggling as a setup man, Bosio posted an 8-6 record in the rotation and was 11-8 overall.

Mark Knudson (4-4), Mike Birkbeck (1-4) and Len Barker (2-1) all were tested as starters.

The Brewers aren't likely to be taken lightly in 1988, especially if Dalton completes his shopping. Trebelhorn will see that Milwaukee is prepared.

"The boys thought spring training was a lot of work last year," he said. "Wait until next year."

Yankee first baseman Don Mattingly went on a 1987 record binge, homering in eight consecutive games and blasting six grand slams.

Hopeful Yanks Fall Hard

By BILL MADDEN

The New York Yankees have never offered anything less than great theater. And when Billy Martin was rehired October 19 to become manager for the fifth time, a chorus of guffaws signaled that perhaps Owner George Steinbrenner had staged his greatest tragicomedy yet.

"Let's see if they're laughing at the end of next year," countered Lou Piniella, who wasn't exactly the merry manager in 1987 as the Yankees skidded to a fourth-place finish.

Piniella moved out of the Yankee hot seat, where 13 managers (including Martin four times, and Gene Michael and Bob Lemon, twice) have squirmed in the last 14 seasons, and into the general manager's chair, complete with a contract extension. The shakeup stole the spotlight from a 1987 season that produced some big numbers. Unfortunately for the Yankees, too many were negative.

New York set a club record by using 48 players. The turnover was most debilitating to the starting staff, where 15 different pitchers were used in the rotation. Among the starters, only Tommy John (13-6) and Rick Rhoden (16-10) were with the club all season.

All told, 12 Yankees went on the disabled list, most notably center fielder Rickey Henderson (.291, 17 home runs, 41 stolen bases) for 55 games in June, July and August, and second baseman Willie Randolph (.305, 67 runs batted in) for 26 games in July and August. As the injuries took their toll, the Yankees sank lower and lower. After leading the American League East for 65 days between May 14 and August 8, New York finished nine games behind the division champion Detroit Tigers at 89-73.

Don Mattingly provided a respite. Though sidelined himself for 18 games with a back injury in June, Mattingly tied Dale Long's major league record by hitting home runs in eight consecutive games, between July 8 and 18. And although he had never hit a grand slam in the majors, Mattingly set a single-season record by blasting six in 1987. The first baseman won his third straight Gold Glove and led the club with a .327 average and 115 RBIs. He was second on the team with 30 homers.

Reliever Dave Righetti also was his outstanding self, finishing 8-6 with 31 saves. He was named co-winner of The Sporting News' A.L. Fireman of the Year award.

A busy off-season gave the Yankees high hopes for 1987. Starters Rhoden and Charles Hudson were acquired from the Pittsburgh Pirates and Philadelphia Phillies, respectively, and hard-hitting outfielder Gary Ward was signed as a free agent. And indeed, the Yankees broke out of the gate with one of their best starts ever. They were 13-3 on April 23 with only the record-breaking start by the Milwaukee Brewers keeping them out of first place.

The Brewers, as expected, cooled, and Piniella's charges moved into first on May 14. On May 23, the Yankees' pennant hopes again were heightened when free-agent Ron Guidry rejoined the club. Guidry's layoff and lack of spring camp conditioning proved detrimental. Disabled by a sore elbow, he didn't pitch after September 5 and posted his third losing record (5-8) in the last four seasons.

Hudson, after a 6-0 start, was hit hard and demoted June 20 to Class AAA Columbus for two weeks. He finished 11-7 and led all starters with a 3.61 earned-run average and six complete games.

The Yankees didn't break down as a unit until after the All-Star break, when injuries mounted, trading acumen failed and the customary owner/manager dispute erupted.

At the break, New York was 55-34 with a comfortable three-game lead over the second-place Toronto Blue Jays. If the A.L. Most Valuable Player vote had been taken then, right fielder Dave Winfield (.295, 20 homers, 68 RBIs) and Ward (10 homers, 61 RBIs) would have been candidates. After the recess, Winfield hit just .250 with seven homers and 29 RBIs, missing the 100-RBI plateau for the first time as a Yankee (excluding the strike-shortened '81 season). He did, however, win his seventh career Gold Glove. Ward hit just .218 with 17 RBIs. Both were visible symbols of the team's collapse.

Once again, the Yankees felt Steinbrenner's presence as the team's fortunes began to fade. In the midst of a 2-8 road trip in early August, Piniella missed a phone call from Steinbrenner. Both became edgy. In a newspaper interview days later, the Yankee owner said: "Lou Piniella has no reason to be hurt. I do. I've made every player move he's asked for since Day One and this is what happens. If anyone should be hurt, it's me. I've done

SCORES OF NEW YORK YANKEES' 1987 GAMES

APRIL

Date	W/L	Score	Winner	Loser
6—At Detroit	W	2-1*	Righetti	Morris
8—At Detroit	W	6-5	Hudson	Hernandez
9—At Detroit	L	3-9	Terrell	Tewksbury
10—At Kan. C.	L	1-13	Saberhagen	Rhoden
11—At Kan. C.	W	15-2	Rasmussen	Jackson
12—At Kan. C.	L	2-8	Leibrandt	Niekro
13—Cleveland	W	11-3	Hudson	Swindell
14—Cleveland	W	10-6	Guante	Carlton
15—Cleveland	W	4-3	Rhoden	Waddell
18—Kan. City	W	7-6	Righetti	Farr
19—Kan. City	W	5-0	Hudson	Leibrandt
19—Kan. City	W	1-0	Clements	Gubicza
20—Detroit	W	8-2	Rhoden	Morris
21—Detroit	W	3-1	Niekro	Terrell
22—Detroit	W	4-1	Shirley	Tanana
23—At Cleve.	W	5-4	Rasmussen	Swindell
24—At Cleve.	L	5-6	Carlton	Righetti
25—At Cleve.	L	1-2	Bailes	Rhoden
26—At Cleve.	W	14-2	John	Candiotti
28—At Texas	L	1-3	Correa	Rasmussen
29—At Texas	L	7-8	Williams	Guante

Won 14, Lost 7

MAY

Date	W/L	Score	Winner	Loser
1—At Minn.	L	4-7	Blyleven	Rhoden
2—At Minn.	W	6-4	John	Viola
3—At Minn.	L	3-4	Frazier	Stoddard
4—At Chicago	W	6-1	Hudson	Dotson
5—At Chicago	L	0-2	Long	Niekro
6—At Chicago	W	4-1	Rhoden	Bannister
8—Minnesota	W	11-7	Guante	Reardon
9—Minnesota	L	0-2	Straker	Rasmussen
10—Minnesota	W	6-1	Hudson	Smithson
11—Chicago	W	3-2	Rhoden	Bannister
12—Chicago	W	5-4§	Guante	Thigpen
13—Texas	L	6-8	Guzman	John
14—Texas	W	9-1	Rasmussen	Correa
15—At Seattle	W	7-3	Hudson	Morgan
16—At Seattle	L	8-10	Shields	Guante
17—At Seattle	W	8-3	Niekro	Moore
18—At Oak.	W	2-1	John	Young
19—At Oak.	L	2-4	Eckersley	Rasmussen
20—At Oak.	L	5-7	Nelson	Hudson
22—At Calif.	W	7-2	Rhoden	Witt
23—At Calif.	W	3-0	Niekro	Fraser
24—At Calif.	W	10-8*	Righetti	Moore
25—At Calif.	W	6-3	John	Lazorko
27—Seattle	L	5-6	Guetterman	Guidry
28—Seattle	W	5-2	Rhoden	Moore
29—Oakland	L	5-13	Young	Rasmussen
30—Oakland	L	3-4	Andujar	Niekro
31—Oakland	W	9-5	John	Eckersley

Won 17, Lost 11

JUNE

Date	W/L	Score	Winner	Loser
1—California	L	2-9	Witt	Hudson
2—California	W	3-2	Righetti	Fraser
3—California	W	9-3	Bordi	Sutton
4—At Milw.	L	3-9	Higuera	Niekro
5—At Milw.	W	13-1	John	Nieves
6—At Milw.	L	6-7	Plesac	Righetti
7—At Milw.	W	5-3	Bordi	Crim
8—Toronto	L	0-11	Stieb	Rhoden
9—Toronto	L	2-7	Cerutti	Guidry
10—Toronto	L	1-4	Key	John
12—Milwaukee	W	8-3	Rasmussen	Crim
13—Milwaukee	W	4-1	Rhoden	Nieves
14—Milwaukee	L	4-6	Plesac	Righetti
15—Baltimore	W	9-2	John	Bell
16—Baltimore	W	6-5	Bordi	Williamson
17—Baltimore	W	4-3	Rasmussen	Boddicker
18—Baltimore	W	6-3	Rhoden	McGregor
19—At Boston	W	10-5§	Hudson	Sambito
20—At Boston	L	4-9	Nipper	John
21—At Boston	L	2-4	Clements	Tewksbury
22—At Balt.	W	7-3	Rasmussen	DeLeon
23—At Balt.	W	2-1	Rhoden	Corbett
24—At Balt.	L	0-4	Schmidt	Guidry
26—Boston	W	12-11*	Stoddard	Schiraldi
27—Boston	W	9-1	Tewksbury	Boyd
28—Boston	L	2-6	Nipper	Rhoden
29—At Toronto	W	15-14	Righetti	Henke
30—At Toronto	W	4-0	Guidry	Wells

Won 17, Lost 11

JULY

Date	W/L	Score	Winner	Loser
1—At Toronto	W	6-1‡	Clements	Musselman
3—Texas	L	0-9	Witt	Tewksbury
3—Texas	W	3-1	Rhoden	Guzman
4—Texas	W	4-3	Rasmussen	Harris
5—Texas	L	4-10	Russell	Bordi
6—Minnesota	L	0-2	Viola	Guidry
7—Minnesota	W	12-7	Stoddard	Atherton
8—Minnesota	W	13-4	Rhoden	Smithson
9—Chicago	L	3-6	Dotson	Tewksbury
10—Chicago	W	9-5	Rasmussen	Nielsen
11—Chicago	L	2-5x	Long	Clements
12—Chicago	W	6-2	John	Bannister
16—At Texas	W	12-3	Guidry	Hough
17—At Texas	W	8-4	Rhoden	Witt
18—At Texas	L	2-7	Guzman	Hudson
19—At Texas	L	3-20	Harris	Trout
20—At Minn.	W	7-1	John	Straker
21—At Minn.	L	1-2	Blyleven	Stoddard
22—At Minn.	L	1-3	Viola	Rhoden
24—At Chicago	L	2-5	Bannister	Trout
25—At Chicago	L	2-3	Searage	Clements
26—At Chicago	W	5-2	Guidry	Dotson
28—Kan. City	W	2-1	Rhoden	Gubicza
29—Kan. City	W	4-0	Stoddard	Jackson
30—Kan. City	W	6-3	John	Black
31—Detroit	W	6-5	Righetti	Henneman

Won 15, Lost 11

AUGUST

Date	W/L	Score	Winner	Loser
1—Detroit	L	5-10	Tanana	Rasmussen
2—Detroit	W	8-5	Rhoden	Robinson
3—At Cleve.	L	0-2	Candiotti	Trout
4—At Cleve.	L	3-15	Schrom	John
5—At Cleve.	W	5-2	Arnsberg	Niekro
6—At Detroit	L	5-12	Tanana	Guidry
7—At Detroit	L	0-8	Robinson	Rhoden
8—At Detroit	W	7-0	John	King
9—At Detroit	L	4-15	Petry	Rasmussen
10—At Kan. C.	L	1-10	Jackson	Arnsberg
11—At Kan. C.	L	5-8	Saberhagen	Guidry
12—At Kan. C.	L	1-2	Leibrandt	Rhoden
14—Cleveland	L	5-6	Candiotti	Arnsberg
15—Cleveland	W	11-2	Rasmussen	Schrom
16—Cleveland	L	0-1	Yett	Guidry
18—At Seattle	W	4-3	Stoddard	Wilkinson
19—At Seattle	W	8-0	Hudson	Morgan
20—At Seattle	L	3-4‡	Reed	Arnsberg
21—At Oak.	L	4-6	Ontiveros	Guidry
22—At Oak.	L	0-6	Nelson	Trout
23—At Oak.	W	4-0	Rhoden	Stewart
24—At Calif.	W	3-2†	Hudson	Lucas
25—At Calif.	L	1-5	Candelaria	Rasmussen
28—Seattle	L	4-10	Trujillo	Hudson
29—Seattle	L	1-7	Langston	Rhoden
29—Seattle	W	4-2	John	Campbell
30—Seattle	W	4-1	Gullickson	Moore
31—Oakland	W	4-1	Guidry	Young

Won 11, Lost 17

SEPTEMBER

Date	W/L	Score	Winner	Loser
1—Oakland	L	3-8	Ontiveros	Hudson
2—Oakland	W	3-2*	Righetti	Honeycutt
4—California	W	8-4	Gullickson	McCaskill
5—California	W	7-6	Guidry	Sutton
6—California	L	1-3	Candelaria	John
7—At Boston	W	9-5	Rhoden	Hurst
8—At Boston	L	6-8	Nipper	Gullickson
9—At Boston	L	3-5	Clemens	Hudson
11—At Toronto	L	5-6*	Wells	Righetti
12—At Toronto	L	1-13	Key	Rhoden
13—At Toronto	W	8-5	Hudson	Cerutti
14—Milwaukee	L	4-6	Stapleton	Gullickson
15—Milwaukee	W	4-3	Leiter	Nieves
16—Milwaukee	L	4-5	Higuera	Stoddard
17—Toronto	W	6-5	Righetti	Henke
18—Toronto	L	3-6	Clancy	Allen
19—Toronto	W	4-2	Gullickson	Flanagan
20—Toronto	L	2-6	Wells	Leiter
22—At Milw.	L	2-7	Higuera	John
22—At Milw.	W	10-8	Clements	Crim
23—At Milw.	L	7-8*	Crim	Righetti
25—At Balt.	W	8-4	Leiter	Mesa
26—At Balt.	W	2-0	Filson	Boddicker
27—At Balt.	L	5-9	O'Connor	Clements
28—Boston	W	9-7	Fulton	Sambito
29—Boston	W	6-0	Hudson	Hurst
30—Boston	L	0-7	Clemens	Leiter

Won 13, Lost 14

OCTOBER

Date	W/L	Score	Winner	Loser
1—Boston	L	5-7	Nipper	Righetti
2—Baltimore	W	3-1	John	Ballard
3—Baltimore	W	6-2	Gullickson	Habyan
4—Baltimore	L	2-4	Bell	Hudson

Won 2, Lost 2

*10 innings. †11 innings. ‡12 innings. §13 innings. x15 innings.

Injuries to second baseman Willie Randolph (left) and center fielder Rickey Henderson helped drop the Yankees out of contention.

everything for this guy. I gave him a chance to manage the New York Yankees without going to the minors first. In retrospect, maybe that was a mistake."

Days later, on August 9, Detroit bombed the dispirited Yankees, 15-4, and New York fell out of first for good.

But even before that, the Yankees had made two trades that went nowhere.

On June 10, they shipped two prospects, outfielder Keith Hughes and third baseman Shane Turner, to Philadelphia to reacquire Mike Easler, who had left in the Hudson deal. And on July 13, sometime-starter Bob Tewksbury (1-4) and two promising young pitchers, Rich Scheid and Dean Wilkins, were sent to the Chicago Cubs for lefthander Steve Trout.

Easler, who became a part-time designated hitter after Ron Kittle (.277, 12 homers) was sidelined in the second half with a neck injury, contributed just 21 RBIs in 167 at-bats. Trout was a monumental failure. Not only did he fail to win a game (0-4) but seldom could he find the plate. In 46⅓ innings, Trout yielded 37 walks and nine wild pitches.

And in yet another deal, the club traded lefthander Dennis Rasmussen (9-7), the Yankees' ace in 1986 with an 18-6 record, to the Cincinnati Reds for Bill Gullickson, who went 4-2 in eight starts.

Rookie Al Leiter was a bright spot during a dark ending, however, going 2-2 in four starts with 28 strikeouts in 22⅔ innings.

"He's something special," John said. "You just don't see kids coming along today who throw as hard as he does. He's maybe one in a thousand."

Relievers Tim Stoddard (4-3, 3.50 ERA, eight saves) and Pat Clements (3-3, seven saves) were two who fared better than most of the other 21 Yankee hurlers. Teamed with Righetti, they helped New York lead the league with 47 saves.

By the time Henderson rejoined the lineup in September, the Yankees already were five games off the pace. Shortstop Wayne Tolleson was out with an injured shoulder, but he hit only .221, anyway. Rhoden and Guidry went out with three weeks left. The catchers—Joel Skinner, Rick Cerone and Mark Salas—had combined for a .206 average. Outfielder Dan Pasqua hit 17 home runs but batted only .233.

The disappointments took some of the gleam off third baseman Mike Pagliarulo's team-leading 32 home runs (his .234 average didn't help, either) and the steady play of reserve outfielder Claudell Washington (.279) and backup shortstop/second baseman Bobby Meacham (.271).

There wasn't much to smile about at the end, save for the fifth coming of Martin, who, like Piniella, didn't take kindly to the snickering.

"I know Billy Martin and I know every time I've been here we've been a winner," he said. "And the last laugh is going to be mine."

Dwight Evans made the switch from the outfield to first base and enjoyed a remarkable 1987 season for the Boston Red Sox.

Roof Caves In on Red Sox

By JOE GIULIOTTI

The Boston Red Sox never had a chance to defend their American League championship. Their 1987 season was, arguably, over before it ever started.

A black cloud had appeared on the horizon the previous October, when the Red Sox were one strike away from winning the sixth game of the World Series and their first fall classic since 1918. They lost a two-run lead, the game and, eventually, the series to the New York Mets, who rebounded from a 3-0 deficit to win Game 7.

The problems continued in the off-season. Pitcher Tom Seaver, 42 years old and recovering from knee surgery, turned down a $600,000 contract. He wanted almost $1 million and retired when he couldn't get it. Catcher Rich Gedman wanted $1.1 million despite sub-par totals in every offensive category and a league-leading 14 passed balls in 1986. When the team offered $2.65 million for three years, he declared his free agency and didn't return until May 2. Once back, he didn't hit (.205) or field (eight passed balls) and wrapped up his season with thumb surgery in August.

The loss of Seaver and Gedman could have been overcome, but the frustration involving mound aces Roger Clemens and Dennis (Oil Can) Boyd was too much.

Clemens was seeking $1 million a year after his sensational 24-4 season in 1986, when he was named the A.L. Most Valuable Player, the Cy Young Award winner and The Sporting News' Player of the Year. The Red Sox offered $500,000 plus incentives, effectively insulting Clemens. On the day he was scheduled to open the 1987 exhibition season, Clemens walked out of training camp. He stayed away until April 4, didn't win his first game until April 21 and was only 6-6 through June.

With Clemens in spring exile, Boyd became the key to Manager John McNamara's rotation. Boyd, who had won 16 games in 1986, appeared to overcome early spring tightness in his shoulder and was named to replace Clemens as the opening-day starter. But on March 26, after pitching six innings in Vero Beach, Fla., against the Los Angeles Dodgers, his shoulder knotted up. Boyd didn't start a game until June 22, made only seven appearances all year (1-3, 5.89 earned-run average) and ended the season on the operating table.

McNamara's third choice to open the season was Bob Stanley, a reliever who had started only two games in the last six seasons. It was a grand experiment that, like the season, never got off the ground. Boston lost three straight at Milwaukee to open the year, setting the tone for a 78-84 fifth-place finish, 20 games behind the East division champion Detroit Tigers. The Red Sox climbed above .500 only once, on April 22, when they were 8-7.

The three losses to the Brewers also established a pattern that haunted the team and led to its worst road record in 22 years. The Red Sox were 28-54 away from Fenway Park, the second-worst road mark in the league.

Bruce Hurst was a case in point. Despite losing seven of his last eight starts, Hurst was 12-4 at home and a dismal 3-9 on the road. He did, however, pitch 15 complete games and contradict the adage about Fenway, where lefthanders aren't supposed to win.

Stanley won 75 percent of his games at home—three. The veteran righthander suffered through the worst season of his career, finishing 4-15 with a 5.01 ERA.

Al Nipper finished 11-12, one win better than in 1986, but owned the New York Yankees. Nipper pitched three of his six complete games against the Yanks and beat them four times.

Jeff Sellers, 7-8 in his third season split between Boston and the minors, had two shutouts and four complete games in 22 starts but a 5.28 ERA.

Despite his slow start, Clemens again was the success story of the Red Sox and the American League. He won the Cy Young Award for the second straight year, the first pitcher to do so since Jim Palmer in 1975 and 1976. When he shut out Milwaukee, 4-0, on the final day of the season, Clemens became one of only two 20-game winners in the majors and the first Boston hurler to win 20 in back-to-back seasons since Luis Tiant in 1973 and 1974. He led the league with seven shutouts and 18 complete games, ranked second in strikeouts (256) and innings (281⅔), and finished third in ERA (2.97).

McNamara built his bullpen around a pair of young arms—Calvin Schiraldi, a brilliant stopper in the final two months of 1986, and Wes Gardner, who had undergone shoulder surgery the previous July. Like most everything else in 1987, the plan fell flat. Gardner finished with 10 saves, a

SCORES OF BOSTON RED SOX' 1987 GAMES

APRIL

Date			Winner	Loser
6—At Milw.	L	1-5	Higuera	Stanley
8—At Milw.	L	2-3	Crim	Gardner
9—At Milw.	L	11-12	Bosio	Crawford
10—Toronto	W	3-0	Hurst	Stieb
11—Toronto	L	1-11	Key	Clemens
12—Toronto	W	8-3	Stanley	Clancy
14—Texas	W	4-1	Nipper	Correa
15—Texas	W	5-4	Hurst	Mohorcic
16—At Toronto	L	2-4	Key	Clemens
17—At Toronto	L	5-10	Cerutti	Stanley
18—At Toronto	W	6-4	Sellers	Clancy
19—At Toronto	W	4-1	Nipper	Johnson
20—Kan. City	L	2-10	Saberhagen	Hurst
21—Kan. City	W	8-0	Clemens	Anderson
22—Kan. City	W	1-0	Stanley	Jackson
24—At Texas	L	4-6†	Harris	Schiraldi
25—At Texas	L	1-2	Guzman	Hurst
26—At Texas	L	3-5x	Williams	Schiraldi
27—At Oak.	L	2-5	Young	Stanley
28—At Oak.	L	1-7	Eckersley	Sellers
29—At Seattle	W	11-5	Nipper	Moore
30—At Seattle	L	2-11	Bankhead	Hurst

Won 9, Lost 13

MAY

Date			Winner	Loser
1—At Calif.	W	12-3	Clemens	Lugo
2—At Calif.	L	2-4	Witt	Stanley
3—At Calif.	L	4-11	Candelaria	Nipper
5—Oakland	W	6-0	Hurst	Stewart
6—Oakland	W	6-2	Schiraldi	Eckersley
8—California	W	6-4	Sambito	Buice
9—California	L	1-8	Fraser	Nipper
10—California	W	7-0	Hurst	Sutton
11—Seattle	L	3-4	Bankhead	Clemens
12—Seattle	W	3-2	Sellers	Trujillo
13—Seattle	L	4-5	Langston	Sambito
15—At Minn.	L	1-3	Frazier	Hurst
16—At Minn.	W	6-1	Clemens	Blyleven
17—At Minn.	L	8-10†	Atherton	Schiraldi
18—At Kan. C.	L	2-4	Gubicza	Nipper
19—At Kan. C.	L	1-4	Saberhagen	Stanley
20—At Kan. C.	W	7-1	Hurst	Jackson
22—Chicago	L	3-4	Winn	Clemens
23—Chicago	L	1-9	Bannister	Nipper
24—Chicago	L	1-4†	Searage	Stanley
25—Cleveland	W	10-6	Crawford	Huismann
26—Cleveland	W	6-5	Nipper	Swindell
27—Cleveland	W	1-0	Clemens	Niekro
28—Cleveland	W	12-8	Crawford	Yett
29—At Chicago	L	6-8	Winn	Stanley
30—At Chicago	L	2-3†	James	Gardner
31—At Chicago	W	10-9	Schiraldi	Searage

Won 13, Lost 14

JUNE

Date			Winner	Loser
1—Minnesota	L	5-9	Viola	Clemens
2—Minnesota	W	6-5	Schiraldi	Reardon
3—Minnesota	W	7-6†	Schiraldi	Klink
4—Detroit	W	8-5	Hurst	Terrell
5—Detroit	L	2-4	Robinson	Nipper
6—Detroit	L	3-5y	King	Gardner
7—Detroit	W	8-18	Henneman	Leister
8—At Balt.	W	6-2	Stanley	Ballard
9—At Balt.	W	2-1	Hurst	Dixon
10—At Balt.	W	15-4	Nipper	Bell
12—At Detroit	L	4-11	Tanana	Clemens
13—At Detroit	L	4-6	Petry	Crawford
14—At Detroit	L	1-2	Morris	Hurst
16—At Cleve.	L	7-8	Huismann	Nipper
17—At Cleve.	W	4-0	Clemens	Candiotti
18—At Cleve.	L	5-7	Armstrong	Stanley
19—New York	L	5-10x	Hudson	Sambito
20—New York	W	9-4	Nipper	John
21—New York	W	4-2	Clemens	Tewksbury
22—Milwaukee	W	5-2*	Boyd	Johnson
23—Milwaukee	W	9-5	Crawford	Wegman
24—Milwaukee	W	8-7	Hurst	Higuera
26—At N.Y.	L	11-12†	Stoddard	Schiraldi
27—At N.Y.	L	1-9	Tewksbury	Boyd
28—At N.Y.	W	6-2	Nipper	Rhoden
29—Baltimore	W	14-3	Hurst	Schmidt
30—Baltimore	W	13-9	Crawford	Williamson

Won 15, Lost 12

JULY

Date			Winner	Loser
1—Baltimore	W	6-2	Clemens	Griffin
2—At Oak.	L	3-5	Andujar	Nipper
3—At Oak.	W	2-0	Sellers	Ontiveros
4—At Oak.	L	5-9	Rijo	Hurst
5—At Oak.	L	3-6	Stewart	Boyd
6—At Calif.	L	7-10§	Minton	Gardner

JULY

Date			Winner	Loser
7—At Calif.	L	4-9	Witt	Nipper
8—At Calif.	L	3-5	Fraser	Sellers
9—At Seattle	L	5-11	Thomas	Gardner
10—At Seattle	W	7-4	Schiraldi	Langston
11—At Seattle	W	10-4	Clemens	Morgan
12—At Seattle	L	1-6	Guetterman	Nipper
16—Oakland	L	3-6	Stewart	Clemens
17—Oakland	L	6-11†	Cadaret	Stanley
18—Oakland	W	5-3†	Hurst	Eckersley
19—Oakland	L	3-5‡	Howell	Stanley
20—California	L	2-3	Minton	Sellers
21—California	W	3-0	Clemens	McCaskill
22—California	L	5-6	Witt	Boyd
24—Seattle	W	5-4	Hurst	Guetterman
25—Seattle	W	11-5	Bolton	Clarke
26—Seattle	W	11-1	Clemens	Moore
27—At Toronto	L	8-10	Musselman	Schiraldi
28—At Toronto	L	4-5	Musselman	Sambito
29—At Toronto	W	6-5	Schiraldi	Lavelle
31—At Kan. C.	W	4-0	Clemens	Saberhagen

Won 11, Lost 15

AUGUST

Date			Winner	Loser
1—At Kan. C.	L	0-4	Leibrandt	Sellers
2—At Kan. C.	L	5-13	Gubicza	Stanley
3—At Texas	W	11-2	Hurst	Guzman
4—At Texas	W	8-6	Schiraldi	Mohorcic
5—At Texas	L	8-9	Guzman	Sambito
7—Kan. City	W	4-3	Sellers	Leibrandt
8—Kan. City	W	8-3	Hurst	Gubicza
9—Kan. City	L	3-8	Davis	Crawford
10—Toronto	W	9-1	Clemens	Clancy
11—Toronto	L	3-8	Key	Stanley
12—Toronto	L	4-10	Stieb	Sellers
14—Texas	W	9-3	Hurst	Howe
14—Texas	L	4-9	Hough	Nipper
15—Texas	W	7-6	Gardner	Howe
16—Texas	W	12-2	Stanley	Harris
17—At Chicago	L	1-2	LaPoint	Sellers
18—At Chicago	W	14-8	Nipper	Bannister
19—At Chicago	L	3-8	DeLeon	Hurst
21—Minnesota	W	11-3	Clemens	Viola
22—Minnesota	W	6-5	Schiraldi	Straker
23—Minnesota	W	6-4	Sellers	Carlton
24—Chicago	L	3-6	DeLeon	Hurst
25—Chicago	W	7-3	Crawford	Dotson
26—Chicago	L	3-5	Long	Clemens
29—At Cleve.	L	2-7	Candiotti	Stanley
29—At Cleve.	L	1-2	Yett	Hurst
30—At Cleve.	W	7-3	Clemens	Bailes

Won 14, Lost 13

SEPTEMBER

Date			Winner	Loser
1—At Minn.	W	9-0	Sellers	Niekro
2—At Minn.	W	4-5	Straker	Nipper
3—At Minn.	L	1-2†	Atherton	Gardner
4—Cleveland	W	5-2	Clemens	Bailes
5—Cleveland	L	2-15	Farrell	Stanley
6—Cleveland	L	1-3	Akerfelds	Sellers
7—New York	L	5-9	Rhoden	Hurst
8—New York	W	8-6	Nipper	Gullickson
9—New York	W	5-3	Clemens	Hudson
10—Baltimore	W	5-4	Sambito	Niedenfuer
11—Baltimore	W	9-3	Sellers	Habyan
12—Baltimore	W	4-3	Hurst	Niedenfuer
14—At Detroit	L	0-3	Alexander	Clemens
15—At Detroit	L	8-9	Petry	Crawford
16—At Detroit	L	1-4	Morris	Sellers
18—At Balt.	L	4-9	Habyan	Hurst
18—At Balt.	W	10-7	Woodward	Ballard
20—At Balt.	W	5-1	Clemens	Mesa
20—At Balt.	W	6-3	Gardner	DeLeon
21—Detroit	W	9-4	Nipper	Snell
22—Detroit	L	5-8	Terrell	Woodward
23—Detroit	L	0-4	Alexander	Hurst
24—At Milw.	W	6-7	Clear	Sambito
25—At Milw.	W	9-2	Clemens	Nieves
26—At Milw.	L	2-3	Stapleton	Nipper
27—At Milw.	L	6-9	Burris	Stanley
28—At N.Y.	L	7-9	Fulton	Sambito
29—At N.Y.	L	0-6	Hudson	Hurst
30—At N.Y.	W	7-3	Clemens	Leiter

Won 13, Lost 16

OCTOBER

Date			Winner	Loser
1—At N.Y.	W	7-5	Nipper	Righetti
2—Milwaukee	W	3-2§	Gardner	Higuera
3—Milwaukee	L	4-8	Wegman	Leister
4—Milwaukee	W	4-0	Clemens	Bosio

Won 3, Lost 1

*7 innings. †10 innings. ‡11 innings. §12 innings. x13 innings. y14 innings.

Rookie Mike Greenwell broke into Boston's starting lineup and batted .328 with 19 homers and 89 RBIs.

3-6 record, 5.42 ERA and surrendered 17 homers in 89⅔ innings. Schiraldi had six saves, an 8-5 record, a 4.41 ERA and gave up 15 homers in 83⅔ innings. Led by Hurst's 35 gopher balls, the Red Sox set a club record by allowing 190 homers. They ranked last in the league with 16 saves and 24th in the majors with a 4.77 ERA.

With the Red Sox out of the race by mid-June, they wisely shifted to a youth movement. Three aging heroes from 1986 were shipped out. First baseman Bill Buckner was released, designated hitter Don Baylor was traded to the Minnesota Twins and outfielder Dave Henderson was dealt to the San Francisco Giants.

Rookies Mike Greenwell, Ellis Burks,

Sam Horn, Todd Benzinger and John Marzano showed why hopes are high for the future.

Greenwell wielded a smoking stick, finishing with a .328 average, 19 home runs and 89 RBIs after earning a regular outfield berth in July.

Burks fit in as the regular center fielder, adding a dimension that has been missing for years—speed. He swiped 27 bases in 33 attempts, powered 20 homers, hit .272 and tallied 15 assists.

Horn, who hit 30 homers at Class AAA Pawtucket before his promotion, was used strictly as a designated hitter. He stroked 14 homers and hit .278 in only 158 at-bats.

The switch-hitting Benzinger also earned a promotion and came on strong in the final weeks. He hit seven of his eight homers from September 8-26 and finished at .278 with 43 RBIs, mainly as the right fielder.

Gedman's early season replacement, Marc Sullivan, hit a paltry .169 with two home runs and 10 RBIs. Marzano promoted July 30, hit .244 with 24 RBIs in 52 games.

Among the veterans, Dwight Evans made the switch from right field to first base and established career highs with 34 homers, 123 RBIs and a .305 average.

Marty Barrett topped the league's second basemen with a .988 fielding average and hit a solid .293. His keystone partner, shortstop Spike Owen, matched a personal high with a .259 average.

Outfielder Jim Rice, who finished third in the 1986 MVP balloting behind Clemens and the Yankees' Don Mattingly, suffered a series of injuries that contributed to his most disappointing season. A career .303 hitter who had averaged almost 30 homers and more than 100 runs batted in a year, Rice hit only .277 with 13 homers and 62 RBIs. He underwent arthroscopic surgery on both knees after the season.

And, as usual, there was Wade Boggs, who paced the league's top hitting (.278) team. The majors' supreme hitter captured his third straight batting crown—and fourth in five seasons—with a .363 mark. Boggs augmented his refined craft with a bit of rough-housing—he ripped 24 home runs (his previous high was eight) and knocked in 89 runs. The steady third baseman missed the final two weeks with an injured left knee and underwent surgery October 1.

Despite the positive signs, the negatives were strong enough to keep the Red Sox in fifth place from June 10 until the end of the season. Youth, however, offered hope for 1988.

Baltimore's Big Two of Cal Ripken (left) and Eddie Murray were not as consistent offensively in 1987 as they had been in past years.

Orioles' Slide Continues

By JIM HENNEMAN

After heading downhill the previous two seasons, the Baltimore Orioles only gained momentum in 1987.

The Orioles finished 67-95, their worst record since 1955, and in sixth place in the American League East, 31 games back. And although the breakdown was a team effort, General Manager Hank Peters and farm director Tom Giordano paid the price in the end—they were fired a day after the season closed.

It was a year that began with shakeups, too.

First-year Manager Cal Ripken Sr., searching for better fielding and speed, benched outfielder Lee Lacy and outfielder/designated hitter Larry Sheets when the season opened. The Orioles' fielding did improve (111 errors compared to 135 in 1986) but the gain was insignificant—Baltimore ranked next-to-last in the league in both hitting (tie, .258) and pitching (5.01 earned-run average).

The downfall was punctuated by a running feud between Ripken and infielder Alan Wiggins, who was later released and suspended indefinitely by the commissioner's office.

Except for the first week, when they sent out false signals by winning five of six games, the Orioles' predicament was painfully clear. They got a preview of coming distractions when the Milwaukee Brewers' Juan Nieves victimized them for a no-hitter on April 15. And although they still were in third place on May 28 with a 26-20 record, the Orioles won only five of their next 35 games to fall 19½ games behind on July 5.

Ripken maintained a cautious optimism after the first half of the season. "It's not like teams are dominating us," he said, "because they aren't. There have been very few games in which we haven't competed."

He couldn't say the same in the second half despite an 11-game winning streak after the All-Star break. The Orioles lost 42 of their final 64 games, including 17 of 18 in September. The Orioles were 18-60 against their division but had the league's third-best record (49-35) against the West. Baltimore also had the worst record in the league at home (31-51).

Asked if the other Eastern clubs were that much better, Ripken could only say: "Evidently they are. When you can only beat a team once or twice, there isn't

Oriole newcomer Terry Kennedy caught a club-record 135 games and contributed a career-high 18 home runs.

much you can say."

The Orioles' pitching was, again, a glaring weakness. The staff allowed 226 home runs, a major league record, and 1,555 hits and 880 runs, both club records. Baltimore tied a team mark for fewest complete games (17).

With such a calamity, the rookies got experience—in a hurry. Ripken started rookie pitchers in 63 games. Lefthander Eric Bell (10-13) tied for the team lead in wins and led all major league rookies with 29 starts. John Habyan was 2-7 as a starter but 4-0 with a 3.19 ERA in 14 relief appearances. Jeff Ballard won his first two decisions but lost his final eight. Jose Mesa, obtained when veteran Mike Flanagan (3-6) was traded to Toronto, was 1-3 in a September crash course.

Mike Boddicker again was the workhorse starter, but he slumped in the second half and posted a career-low 10 victories. Scott McGregor (2-7) was plagued by injuries and pitched only 38 innings after May 16. Three hurlers worked in both

SCORES OF BALTIMORE ORIOLES' 1987 GAMES

APRIL

Date	W/L	Score	Winner	Loser
6—Texas	W	2-1	Aase	Harris
8—Texas	L	4-6	Mohorcic	Williamson
9—Texas	W	8-6	Dixon	Mason
10—At Cleve.	W	12-11†	Williamson	Camacho
11—At Cleve.	W	7-3	Schmidt	Candiotti
12—At Cleve.	W	7-1	Bell	Schrom
13—Milwaukee	L	3-6	Bosio	McGregor
14—Milwaukee	L	4-7	Ciardi	Dixon
15—Milwaukee	L	0-7	Nieves	Flanagan
17—Cleveland	W	4-1	Boddicker	Candiotti
18—Cleveland	W	16-3	Bell	Schrom
19—Cleveland	L	0-3	Swindell	McGregor
19—Cleveland	L	7-8	Carlton	Williamson
21—At Texas	L	4-6	Hough	Flanagan
22—At Texas	W	3-2†	Schmidt	Williams
23—At Texas	L	4-9	Loynd	Bell
24—At Milw.	L	4-6	Higuera	McGregor
25—At Milw.	L	2-8	Wegman	Dixon
26—At Milw.	L	3-5	Birkbeck	Flanagan
28—At Kan. C.	W	3-0	Boddicker	Jackson
29—At Kan. C.	L	4-5	Quisenberry	Schmidt

Won 9, Lost 12

MAY

Date	W/L	Score	Winner	Loser
1—Chicago	L	1-5	Bannister	McGregor
2—Chicago	L	3-7	DeLeon	Flanagan
3—Chicago	L	3-4	Thigpen	Boddicker
5—At Minn.	W	5-4	Bell	Smithson
6—At Minn.	W	6-0	McGregor	Blyleven
7—At Minn.	L	2-5	Viola	Flanagan
8—At Chicago	W	7-6	Dixon	Searage
9—At Chicago	W	15-6	Schmidt	McKeon
10—At Chicago	W	6-4	Bell	Dotson
11—Minnesota	L	4-10	Blyleven	McGregor
12—Minnesota	W	10-7	Dixon	Reardon
13—Kan. City	L	7-8§	Farr	Williamson
14—Kan. City	W	4-3	Schmidt	Saberhagen
15—At Calif.	L	6-7†	Moore	O'Connor
16—At Calif.	W	4-2	McGregor	Witt
17—At Calif.	W	3-2	Schmidt	Buice
18—At Seattle	W	6-0	Boddicker	Langston
19—At Seattle	W	15-4	Ballard	Trujillo
20—At Seattle	L	2-6	Morgan	Dixon
22—At Oak.	W	10-6	Schmidt	Haas
23—At Oak.	W	5-4	Boddicker	Stewart
24—At Oak.	W	4-3	Ballard	Young
25—At Oak.	W	4-3	Bell	Eckersley
27—California	W	8-6	Habyan	Lucas
28—California	W	8-7§	Williamson	Buice
29—Seattle	L	3-7	Langston	Ballard
30—Seattle	L	0-12	Morgan	Bell
31—Seattle	L	5-8	Guetterman	Habyan

Won 17, Lost 11

JUNE

Date	W/L	Score	Winner	Loser
1—Oakland	L	6-9	Nelson	Dixon
2—Oakland	W	9-2	Boddicker	Stewart
3—Oakland	L	3-7	Young	Ballard
5—At Toronto	L	2-6	Key	Bell
6—At Toronto	L	5-8‡	Musselman	Dixon
7—At Toronto	L	2-3	Eichhorn	Boddicker
8—Boston	L	2-6	Stanley	Ballard
9—Boston	L	1-2	Hurst	Dixon
10—Boston	L	4-15	Nipper	Bell
11—Toronto	L	6-8	Johnson	Habyan
12—Toronto	L	5-8	Eichhorn	Boddicker
13—Toronto	L	2-8	Cerutti	McGregor
14—Toronto	W	8-5	Schmidt	Eichhorn
15—At N.Y.	L	2-9	John	Bell
16—At N.Y.	L	5-6	Bordi	Williamson
17—At N.Y.	L	3-4	Rasmussen	Boddicker
18—At N.Y.	L	3-6	Rhoden	McGregor
19—Detroit	L	3-5	Morris	Williamson
21—Detroit	W	9-5x	Bell	Terrell
21—Detroit	L	3-9	Petry	Dixon
22—New York	L	3-7	Rasmussen	DeLeon
23—New York	L	1-2	Rhoden	Corbett
24—New York	W	4-0	Schmidt	Guidry
26—At Detroit	L	0-9	Terrell	Griffin
27—At Detroit	W	4-2	Niedenfuer	Tanana
28—At Detroit	L	7-8‡	Hernandez	Corbett
29—At Boston	L	3-14	Hurst	Schmidt
30—At Boston	L	9-13	Crawford	Williamson

Won 5, Lost 23

JULY

Date	W/L	Score	Winner	Loser
1—At Boston	L	2-6	Clemens	Griffin
3—At Minn.	L	5-6‡	Reardon	Niedenfuer
4—At Minn.	L	1-4	Straker	Bell
5—At Minn.	L	3-4	Blyleven	Niedenfuer
6—Chicago	W	4-1	Griffin	DeLeon
7—Chicago	L	3-9	Bannister	Habyan
8—Chicago	W	6-5†	Boddicker	Winn
9—Minnesota	L	1-3	Straker	Bell
10—Minnesota	W	13-12	Williamson	Frazier
11—Minnesota	L	1-2	Viola	Griffin
12—Minnesota	W	5-0	Schmidt	Niekro
16—At Kan. C.	W	5-4	Boddicker	Leibrandt
17—At Kan. C.	W	3-1	Bell	Gubicza
18—At Kan. C.	W	11-7	Flanagan	Jackson
19—At Kan. C.	W	5-1	Schmidt	Black
20—At Chicago	W	4-1*	Griffin	Allen
21—At Chicago	W	11-6	Williamson	Long
22—At Chicago	W	10-5	Habyan	DeLeon
23—Kan. City	W	2-1	Bell	Jackson
24—Kan. City	W	3-1	Niedenfuer	Farr
25—Kan. City	W	4-3	Williamson	Saberhagen
26—Kan. City	L	0-4	Leibrandt	Dixon
28—At Cleve.	L	3-4†	Stewart	Niedenfuer
29—At Cleve.	W	7-4	Bell	Candiotti
30—At Cleve.	L	4-6†	Stewart	Williamson
31—At Texas	W	8-4	Habyan	Hough

Won 16, Lost 10

AUGUST

Date	W/L	Score	Winner	Loser
1—At Texas	W	7-1	Dixon	Kilgus
2—At Texas	L	2-5	Witt	Boddicker
4—At Milw.	L	8-9§	Knudson	Williamson
5—At Milw.	L	1-5	Higuera	Bell
6—At Milw.	L	8-11	Aldrich	Griffin
7—Texas	W	9-2	Dixon	Kilgus
8—Texas	L	5-11	Witt	Boddicker
9—Texas	W	5-4	Habyan	Hough
10—Cleveland	W	4-3	Williamson	Gordon
11—Cleveland	L	3-6	Bailes	Schmidt
12—Cleveland	L	6-8	Akerfelds	Griffin
13—Milwaukee	W	5-4	Boddicker	Bosio
14—Milwaukee	L	2-6	Nieves	Bell
15—Milwaukee	W	2-1	Flanagan	Higuera
16—Milwaukee	L	2-6	Crim	Schmidt
18—At Calif.	W	4-1	Dixon	McCaskill
19—At Calif.	W	2-1	Boddicker	Sutton
20—At Calif.	W	4-2§	Williamson	Buice
21—At Seattle	L	2-3	Moore	Flanagan
22—At Seattle	L	6-14	Langston	Schmidt
23—At Seattle	W	6-5	Dixon	Powell
24—At Oak.	L	3-7	Cadaret	Boddicker
25—At Oak.	L	7-9	Young	Bell
27—California	W	9-5	Flanagan	Reuss
28—California	W	6-5	Williamson	Finley
29—California	L	5-6	Fraser	Williamson
30—California	L	2-6	Sutton	Bell
31—Seattle	W	4-3	Griffin	Morgan

Won 13, Lost 15

SEPTEMBER

Date	W/L	Score	Winner	Loser
1—Seattle	L	0-5	Bankhead	Habyan
2—Seattle	L	6-8	Langston	Ballard
4—Oakland	W	5-2	Boddicker	Nelson
5—Oakland	L	2-7	Young	Bell
6—Oakland	W	7-6	Niedenfuer	Eckersley
7—Detroit	L	4-12	Morris	Ballard
9—Detroit	L	4-7	Terrell	Dixon
9—Detroit	L	0-6	Alexander	Boddicker
10—At Boston	L	4-5	Sambito	Niedenfuer
11—At Boston	L	3-9	Sellers	Habyan
12—At Boston	L	3-4	Hurst	Niedenfuer
14—At Toronto	L	3-18	Clancy	Dixon
15—At Toronto	L	2-6	Flanagan	Mesa
16—At Toronto	L	0-7	Key	Boddicker
18—Boston	W	9-4	Habyan	Hurst
18—Boston	L	7-10	Woodward	Ballard
20—Boston	L	1-5	Clemens	Mesa
20—Boston	L	3-6	Gardner	DeLeon
21—Toronto	L	1-2	Cerutti	Boddicker
22—Toronto	L	4-8	Wells	Ballard
23—Toronto	L	1-6	Clancy	Habyan
25—New York	L	4-8	Leiter	Mesa
26—New York	L	0-2	Filson	Boddicker
27—New York	W	9-5	O'Connor	Clements
28—At Detroit	W	3-0	Habyan	Morris
29—At Detroit	L	1-10	Tanana	Bell
30—At Detroit	W	7-3	Mesa	Petry

Won 6, Lost 21

OCTOBER

Date	W/L	Score	Winner	Loser
1—At Detroit	L	5-9	Terrell	Boddicker
2—At N.Y.	L	1-3	John	Ballard
3—At N.Y.	L	2-6	Gullickson	Habyan
4—At N.Y.	W	4-2	Bell	Hudson

Won 1, Lost 3

*5 innings. †10 innings. ‡11 innings. §12 innings. xSuspended game, began June 20.

starting and relief roles: Ken Dixon (7-10), Mike Griffin (3-5) and Dave Schmidt (10-5, 3.77 ERA), perhaps the best pitcher on the staff until he was sidelined the final six weeks with a bone spur in his elbow.

Relief ace Don Aase, who saved 34 games in 1986, pitched only eight innings all year due to an injured shoulder. Tom Niedenfuer, obtained May 23 from the Los Angeles Dodgers, took over the stopper's role and finished 3-5 with 13 saves, including 11 in 13 opportunities after the All-Star break. Rookie Mark Williamson (8-9, 4.03 ERA) ranked among the league leaders with 61 appearances and finished strong. He had a 6-4 record and 3.19 ERA after July 4.

Baltimore also uncovered a few bright spots on offense. Rookie Bill Ripken was promoted from Class AAA Rochester on July 11 to join his brother, the shortstop, and father, the manager. He was hardly a curiosity item, hitting .308 in 58 games. He made only three errors at second base before an ankle injury forced him out September 15.

Rookie Pete Stanicek, promoted in September, also left an impression with a .274 average and eight stolen bases in nine attempts. An infielder by trade, the switch-hitter was used primarily as a leadoff DH.

Sheets shunned his reserve status early and was named the team's most valuable player. He led the Orioles with a .316 average and 31 home runs and was second to Cal Ripken Jr. with 94 runs batted in.

Ripken notched 98 RBIs with 27 homers but hit a career-low .252. First baseman Eddie Murray also had a career-low .277 mark but slammed 30 homers and drove in 91.

Terry Kennedy set a club record by starting 135 games behind the plate and hit 18 homers, the second-highest total of his career. Outfielder/DH Jim Dwyer belted a career-high 15 homers while hitting .274.

There were, however, some disappointments. Outfielder/DH Mike Young struggled to a .240 finish that included 16 home runs but only 39 RBIs. Rookie outfielder Ken Gerhart suffered a fractured wrist August 12. He finished with 14 homers and a .243 average. Outfielder Fred Lynn (.253) missed 43 games due to injuries but hit 23 homers. Third baseman Ray Knight tailed off to a .256 average but tied a career high with 14 homers. Lacy hit only .244, his lowest average since 1973.

Despite the troubles on the field, the Orioles drew 1,835,692 fans in 78 home dates, the fifth-highest total in club history but a drop for the third straight year.

Second baseman Billy Ripken batted a surprising .308 after joining his brother and father in Baltimore on July 11.

Cleveland third baseman Brook Jacoby matured in 1987, hitting .300 with 32 home runs while dropping his strikeout total from 137 to 73.

Indians Fade Fast in the East

By SHELDON OCKER

In 1987, no team in the major leagues dashed the hopes of its fans more completely than the Cleveland Indians.

In the face of unprecedented preseason hype, the Tribe failed miserably. Several national publications had predicted that Cleveland would be the next mecca of the American League East. Instead, the Indians lost more than 100 games for the second time in three seasons. At 61-101, they finished 37 games behind the division champion Detroit Tigers.

The boosters who jumped on the bandwagon ignored the warnings of Cleveland's own front-office executives.

"We are hoping that sometime during the season, we will have an average pitching staff," Vice President Joe Klein said. It was a modest goal and one the Indians never came close to reaching. When the struggle was over, Cleveland's earned-run average was 5.28, the highest since the Washington Senators had a 5.33 ERA in 1956.

That three pitchers could tie for the team lead with only seven victories apiece was indicative of Cleveland's most glaring shortcoming.

The ace of the staff, knuckleball specialist Tom Candiotti, finished 7-18 with a 4.78 ERA. Plagued by poor support all season (3.7 runs per game), Candiotti was 2-9 at the All-Star break. He did rebound in the second half, when he won three straight starts in August and pitched two one-hitters: a 2-0 victory over the New York Yankees on August 3 and a 2-1 loss at Detroit on September 2.

For the second straight year, lefthander Scott Bailes had to serve as both a starter and bullpen stopper. Filling two roles, Bailes developed a sore shoulder that limited him to one appearance after September 4. He finished 7-8 and was second on the team with six saves.

Lefthander Greg Swindell (3-8, 5.10 ERA) was sabotaged by a balky elbow and spent most of the second half on the disabled list. After winning 14 games in 1986 and being selected to the A.L. All-Star squad, Ken Schrom's record sank to 6-13 with a 6.50 ERA. Rookie John Farrell offered hope for 1988 by posting a 5-1 record and 3.39 ERA after joining the club in August, but Rich Yett (3-9, 5.25 ERA overall) and Darrel Akerfelds (2-6, 6.75 ERA overall) were inconsistent in the rotation.

The Indians had hoped that aging Phil Niekro and Steve Carlton would be effective stop-gap pitchers until the farm system was ready to produce, but both were traded to contenders. Even after Niekro was dealt August 9 to the Toronto Blue Jays with a 7-11 record, no Indian was able to surpass his victory total.

Just as frustrating was the plight of the bullpen, which ranked 13th in the league with 25 saves. Anticipated stopper Ernie Camacho, who saved 20 games in 1986 and a club-record 23 in 1984, was sent to the minors May 30 after he managed only a 0-1 record, one save and a 9.22 ERA. Mark Huismann, acquired from the Seattle Mariners May 12, lost in three of his first four appearances with the Indians and finished 2-3.

Cleveland heaped the relief burden upon Ed Vande Berg and rookie Doug Jones. Vande Berg led the club with 55 appearances and recorded his first—and only—victory since June 1986 on September 23 against Oakland. Jones, who was sent to Class AAA Buffalo after a rocky start, was 6-4 with eight saves and a 2.68 ERA after being recalled June 28. He finished 6-5 with a 3.15 ERA.

A 31-56 record at the All-Star break—the worst in the American League—signaled the end for Manager Pat Corrales, who was fired July 16 and replaced by bullpen coach Doc Edwards, a four-time manager of the year in the minors.

Corrales had led the Indians to their best record since 1968 with an 84-78 finish in 1986. On the strength of that team's .284 batting average and 831 runs, both major league highs, Corrales and Klein believed the offense could carry the club in '87. But when the pitchers fell behind in the early innings, the offense also faltered.

Outfielder/first baseman Joe Carter, who led the majors in 1986 with 121 runs batted in, was one of three Indians with more than 30 home runs in '87, which tied an A.L. record. Despite 32 homers (a career high), 106 RBIs and 31 stolen bases, Carter did not consider his season a good one.

"I've had ample opportunity to drive in runs, but I have not taken advantage of these chances the way I should have," he said. "Besides, when you lose nobody remembers individual statistics."

Carter had only a .250 average with runners in scoring position, struck out 105 times and hit .264 overall, down from .302

SCORES OF CLEVELAND INDIANS' 1987 GAMES

APRIL			Winner	Loser
6—At Toronto	L	3-7	Key	Candiotti
8—At Toronto	L	1-5	Clancy	Swindell
9—At Toronto	W	14-3	Niekro	Johnson
10—Baltimore	L	11-12†	Williamson	Camacho
11—Baltimore	L	3-7	Schmidt	Candiotti
12—Baltimore	L	1-7	Bell	Schrom
13—At N.Y.	L	3-11	Hudson	Swindell
14—At N.Y.	L	6-10	Guante	Carlton
15—At N.Y.	L	3-4	Rhoden	Waddell
17—At Balt.	L	1-4	Boddicker	Candiotti
18—At Balt.	L	3-16	Bell	Schrom
19—At Balt.	W	3-0	Swindell	McGregor
19—At Balt.	W	8-7	Carlton	Williamson
20—Toronto	L	7-8†	Musselman	Jones
21—Toronto	W	5-0	Candiotti	Key
22—Toronto	L	3-6	Eichhorn	Carlton
23—New York	L	4-5	Rasmussen	Swindell
24—New York	W	6-5	Carlton	Righetti
25—New York	W	2-1	Bailes	Rhoden
26—New York	L	2-14	John	Candiotti
28—Chicago	W	1-0	Schrom	Davis
29—Chicago	W	6-5	Yett	James
Won 8, Lost 14				

MAY			Winner	Loser
1—At Kan. C.	W	2-0	Niekro	Gubicza
2—At Kan. C.	L	4-5	Saberhagen	Yett
3—At Kan. C.	L	1-2	Jackson	Schrom
5—At Texas	L	5-6†	Williams	Wills
6—At Texas	L	2-7	Hough	Niekro
8—Kan. City	L	6-9	Gubicza	Schrom
9—Kan. City	L	0-4	Saberhagen	Candiotti
10—Kan. City	W	4-2	Swindell	Jackson
11—Texas	L	3-6*	Meridith	Niekro
12—Texas	L	1-6	Hough	Carlton
13—At Chicago	W	7-5	Schrom	DeLeon
14—At Chicago	L	3-4	Thigpen	Yett
15—At Detroit	L	3-4	Henneman	Huismann
16—At Detroit	L	3-5	Morris	Niekro
17—At Detroit	L	4-8	Terrell	Carlton
19—Minnesota	W	4-3	Schrom	Portugal
20—Minnesota	L	2-8	Berenguer	Candiotti
21—Minnesota	W	6-3	Swindell	Blyleven
22—At Milw.	L	2-4	Wegman	Niekro
23—At Milw.	W	6-2	Carlton	Birkbeck
24—At Milw.	W	5-3	Schrom	Higuera
25—At Boston	L	6-10	Crawford	Huismann
26—At Boston	L	5-6	Nipper	Swindell
27—At Boston	L	0-1	Clemens	Niekro
28—At Boston	L	8-12	Crawford	Yett
29—Milwaukee	W	9-6	Bailes	Higuera
30—Milwaukee	L	5-6†	Clear	Huismann
31—Milwaukee	L	1-7	Nieves	Swindell
Won 8, Lost 20				

JUNE			Winner	Loser
1—Detroit	W	9-6	Niekro	Petry
3—Detroit	L	3-15	Morris	Schrom
5—At Oak.	W	4-3	Candiotti	Andujar
6—At Oak.	L	4-6	Eckersley	Swindell
7—At Oak.	W	12-2	Carlton	Stewart
8—At Calif.	W	2-0	Niekro	Sutton
9—At Calif.	L	5-6	Lazorko	Yett
10—At Calif.	L	7-10	Minton	Bailes
12—At Seattle	W	10-6	Huismann	Trujillo
13—At Seattle	W	6-1	Niekro	Langston
14—At Seattle	L	3-4†	Nunez	Yett
16—Boston	W	8-7	Huismann	Nipper
17—Boston	L	0-4	Clemens	Candiotti
18—Boston	W	7-5	Armstrong	Stanley
19—Seattle	L	4-7	Langston	Niekro
20—Seattle	W	9-2	Carlton	Morgan
21—Seattle	L	0-5	Guetterman	Schrom
23—At Minn.	L	4-9	Smithson	Candiotti
24—At Minn.	L	8-14	Straker	Swindell
25—At Minn.	L	3-4	Blyleven	Niekro
26—Oakland	L	0-5	Stewart	Carlton
27—Oakland	L	3-13	Andujar	Schrom
28—Oakland	L	0-10	Ontiveros	Candiotti
29—California	L	4-11	Sutton	Swindell
30—California	W	2-1	Niekro	Lazorko
Won 10, Lost 15				

JULY			Winner	Loser
1—California	L	5-10	Reuss	Carlton
2—Chicago	W	2-1‡	Jones	James
3—Chicago	L	9-14	Winn	Stewart
4—Chicago	L	2-3	Dotson	Bailes
5—Chicago	L	0-17	Nielsen	Niekro
6—Kan. City	W	9-7	Stewart	Saberhagen
7—Kan. City	W	6-4	Jones	Quisenberry

JULY			Winner	Loser
8—Kan. City	W	9-8	Stewart	Gleaton
9—At Texas	W	10-4	Jones	Guzman
10—At Texas	L	4-10	Harris	Niekro
11—At Texas	L	2-6	Hough	Carlton
12—At Texas	L	6-7	Guzman	Jones
16—At Chicago	W	4-3	Bailes	Dotson
17—At Chicago	L	3-4†	James	Jones
18—At Chicago	L	3-6	Thigpen	Candiotti
19—At Chicago	L	7-9	Nielsen	Carlton
20—At Kan. C.	W	9-5	Niekro	Saberhagen
21—At Kan. C.	L	2-3	Leibrandt	Bailes
22—At Kan. C.	L	1-5	Gubicza	Akerfelds
23—Texas	W	4-2	Candiotti	Guzman
24—Texas	L	3-6	Russell	Carlton
25—Texas	L	3-7	Hough	Niekro
26—Texas	L	3-11	Kilgus	Bailes
28—Baltimore	W	4-3†	Stewart	Niedenfuer
29—Baltimore	L	4-7	Bell	Candiotti
30—Baltimore	W	6-4†	Stewart	Williamson
31—At Toronto	L	3-8	Key	Ritter
Won 10, Lost 17				

AUGUST			Winner	Loser
1—At Toronto	W	3-0	Bailes	Clancy
2—At Toronto	L	5-11	Stieb	Akerfelds
3—New York	W	2-0	Candiotti	Trout
4—New York	W	15-3	Schrom	John
5—New York	L	2-5	Arnsberg	Niekro
6—Toronto	W	14-5	Bailes	Clancy
7—Toronto	L	1-15	Stieb	Akerfelds
8—Toronto	W	3-1	Candiotti	Nunez
9—Toronto	L	1-5	Cerutti	Schrom
10—At Balt.	L	3-4	Williamson	Gordon
11—At Balt.	W	6-3	Bailes	Schmidt
12—At Balt.	W	8-6	Akerfelds	Griffin
14—At N.Y.	W	6-5	Candiotti	Arnsberg
15—At N.Y.	L	2-11	Rasmussen	Schrom
16—At N.Y.	W	1-0	Yett	Guidry
17—Milwaukee	L	3-5	Knudson	Bailes
18—Milwaukee	W	9-8§	Farrell	Burris
19—Milwaukee	L	2-13	Nieves	Candiotti
20—Milwaukee	L	2-14	Higuera	Schrom
21—Detroit	W	12-4	Easterly	Petry
21—Detroit	W	8-3	Farrell	Tanana
22—Detroit	L	6-8	Henneman	Bailes
23—Detroit	L	3-4	Morris	Candiotti
25—At Milw.	L	9-10	Nieves	Schrom
26—At Milw.	L	0-1†	Higuera	Jones
27—At Milw.	L	3-4	Knudson	Akerfelds
29—Boston	W	7-2	Candiotti	Stanley
29—Boston	W	2-1	Yett	Hurst
30—Boston	L	3-7	Clemens	Bailes
31—At Detroit	W	7-2	Farrell	Tanana
Won 15, Lost 15				

SEPTEMBER			Winner	Loser
1—At Detroit	L	5-6§	Hernandez	Gordon
2—At Detroit	L	1-2	Morris	Candiotti
3—At Detroit	L	1-3	Terrell	Yett
4—At Boston	L	2-5	Clemens	Bailes
5—At Boston	W	15-2	Farrell	Stanley
6—At Boston	W	3-1	Akerfelds	Sellers
7—Seattle	L	4-6	Langston	Candiotti
8—Seattle	L	0-7	Morgan	Yett
9—Seattle	L	4-9	Moore	Easterly
11—Minnesota	L	10-13‡	Reardon	Gordon
12—Minnesota	W	5-4	Jones	Berenguer
13—Minnesota	L	3-7†	Reardon	Candiotti
14—At Seattle	W	11-8	Bailes	Morgan
15—At Seattle	W	4-2	Schrom	Moore
16—At Seattle	L	3-5	Wilkinson	Stewart
18—At Minn.	L	4-9	Blyleven	Akerfelds
19—At Minn.	L	1-3	Viola	Candiotti
20—At Minn.	L	2-3	Straker	Yett
21—Oakland	W	6-3	Jones	Stewart
22—Oakland	L	2-10	Honeycutt	Farrell
23—Oakland	W	8-6	Vande Berg	Plunk
25—California	W	7-5	Jones	Lucas
26—California	W	11-10†	Ritter	Lucas
27—California	L	8-11	Sutton	Schrom
29—At Oak.	L	4-5	Ontiveros	Jones
30—At Oak.	L	3-4	Stewart	Akerfelds
Won 9, Lost 17				

OCTOBER			Winner	Loser
1—At Oak.	L	5-9	Cadaret	Candiotti
2—At Calif.	L	4-10	Sutton	Yett
3—At Calif.	L	5-12	Lazorko	Schrom
4—At Calif.	W	10-6	Farrell	Witt
Won 1, Lost 3				

*5 innings. †10 innings. ‡11 innings. §12 innings.

Cory Snyder took over Cleveland's right-field job and hit a team-high 33 homers while striking out 166 times.

in 1986.

Carter wasn't the only Indian trying to duplicate an outstanding '86 season. Right fielder Cory Snyder hit a team-high 33 homers, up from 24 as a rookie, but set a club record with 166 strikeouts. His average plunged 36 points to .236.

The strikeout record Snyder wiped out had belonged to Brook Jacoby, who set the mark by whiffing 137 times in 1986. But in 1987, the third baseman's strikeout total fell to 73 as he posted career highs with 32 home runs and a .300 average.

"Brook has really matured this year," Edwards said. "He is much more selective at the plate. . . . I would like to see Carter and Snyder do the same thing and hit for a better average."

Shortstop Julio Franco led the team and ranked eighth in the league with a .319 average, but elbow problems diminished his effectiveness in the second half. And despite an 0-for-33 skid that dropped his average from .322 to .307, first baseman/designated hitter Pat Tabler had his best offensive season with 11 home runs, 86 RBIs and 13 game-winning RBIs.

Center fielder Brett Butler also thrived in 1987. The Indians' leadoff hitter ranked among the league leaders with eight triples, 91 walks, a .399 on-base average and 33 stolen bases. His .295 average was the second best of his career. Outfielder Mel

Hall had another solid season with 18 homers, 76 RBIs and a .280 average.

Behind the plate, injuries felled Chris Bando (.218) and Rick Dempsey (.177), but Andy Allanson (.266) closed the season impressively.

The most startling replacement was at second base, where rookie Tommy Hinzo replaced Tony Bernazard, who was traded to Oakland at the All-Star break. Hinzo, who started the season at Class A Kinston, closed with a .303 spurt to finish at .265.

The Indians' most baffling episode concerned the treatment of veteran DH Andre Thornton, who batted only 85 times all year. While Thornton sat, Carmen Castillo (.250, 11 home runs) helped fill the void.

Thoroughly disillusioned by season's end, Thornton resigned his captaincy. "There's no sense being captain, because they (front office) have destroyed my credibility with the players," he said.

The Indians set a club record with 187 home runs, but Edwards was more concerned with their league-high 153 errors.

"If we strengthen our pitching and our defense, we can be right in the hunt," Edwards said.

"Defense can help make your pitching. A good defense won't win that many games, but it will give your offense a chance to win."

American League Averages for 1987

CHAMPIONSHIP WINNERS IN PREVIOUS YEARS

1900—Chicago* ...... .607	1929—Philadelphia ...... .693	1958—New York ...... .597
1901—Chicago ...... .610	1930—Philadelphia ...... .662	1959—Chicago ...... .610
1902—Philadelphia ...... .610	1931—Philadelphia ...... .704	1960—New York ...... .630
1903—Boston ...... .659	1932—New York ...... .695	1961—New York ...... .673
1904—Boston ...... .617	1933—Washington ...... .651	1962—New York ...... .593
1905—Philadelphia ...... .622	1934—Detroit ...... .656	1963—New York ...... .646
1906—Chicago ...... .616	1935—Detroit ...... .616	1964—New York ...... .611
1907—Detroit ...... .613	1936—New York ...... .667	1965—Minnesota ...... .630
1908—Detroit ...... .588	1937—New York ...... .662	1966—Baltimore ...... .606
1909—Detroit ...... .645	1938—New York ...... .651	1967—Boston ...... .568
1910—Philadelphia ...... .680	1939—New York ...... .702	1968—Detroit ...... .636
1911—Philadelphia ...... .669	1940—Detroit ...... .584	1969—Baltimore (East) ...... .673
1912—Boston ...... .691	1941—New York ...... .656	1970—Baltimore (East) ...... .667
1913—Philadelphia ...... .627	1942—New York ...... .669	1971—Baltimore (East) ...... .639
1914—Philadelphia ...... .651	1943—New York ...... .636	1972—Oakland (West) ...... .600
1915—Boston ...... .669	1944—St. Louis ...... .578	1973—Oakland (West) ...... .580
1916—Boston ...... .591	1945—Detroit ...... .575	1974—Oakland (West) ...... .556
1917—Chicago ...... .649	1946—Boston ...... .675	1975—Boston (East) ...... .594
1918—Boston ...... .595	1947—New York ...... .630	1976—New York (East) ...... .610
1919—Chicago ...... .629	1948—Cleveland† ...... .626	1977—New York (East) ...... .617
1920—Cleveland ...... .636	1949—New York ...... .630	1978—New York (East) ...... .613
1921—New York ...... .641	1950—New York ...... .636	1979—Baltimore (East) ...... .642
1922—New York ...... .610	1951—New York ...... .636	1980—Kansas City (West) ...... .599
1923—New York ...... .645	1952—New York ...... .617	1981—New York (East) ...... .551
1924—Washington ...... .597	1953—New York ...... .656	1982—Milwaukee (East) ...... .586
1925—Washington ...... .636	1954—Cleveland ...... .721	1983—Baltimore (East) ...... .605
1926—New York ...... .591	1955—New York ...... .623	1984—Detroit (East) ...... .642
1927—New York ...... .714	1956—New York ...... .630	1985—Kansas City (West) ...... .562
1928—New York ...... .656	1957—New York ...... .636	1986—Boston (East) ...... .590

*Not recognized as major league in 1900. †Defeated Boston in one-game playoff for pennant.

STANDING OF CLUBS AT CLOSE OF SEASON

EAST DIVISION

Club	Det.	Tor.	Mil.	N.Y.	Bos.	Balt.	Clev.	Minn.	K.C.	Oak.	Sea.	Chi.	Tex.	Cal.	W.	L.	Pct.	G.B.
Detroit	..	7	6	5	11	9	9	8	5	5	7	9	8	9	98	64	.605	......
Toronto	6	..	4	7	7	12	8	9	4	5	10	8	9	7	96	66	.593	2
Milwaukee	7	9	..	7	7	11	9	3	8	6	4	6	9	5	91	71	.562	7
New York	8	6	6	..	6	10	7	6	7	5	7	7	5	9	89	73	.549	9
Boston	2	6	6	7	..	12	7	7	6	4	7	3	7	4	78	84	.481	20
Baltimore	4	1	2	3	1	..	7	5	9	7	4	8	7	9	67	95	.414	31
Cleveland	4	5	4	6	6	6	..	3	6	4	5	5	2	5	61	101	.377	37

WEST DIVISION

Club	Minn.	K.C.	Oak.	Sea.	Chi.	Tex.	Cal.	Det.	Tor.	Mil.	N.Y.	Bos.	Balt.	Clev.	W.	L.	Pct.	G.B.
Minnesota	..	5	10	9	7	6	5	4	3	9	6	5	7	9	85	77	.525	......
Kansas City	8	..	5	9	7	7	8	7	8	4	5	6	3	6	83	79	.512	2
Oakland	3	8	..	5	4	6	7	7	7	6	7	8	5	8	81	81	.500	4
Seattle	4	4	8	..	7	9	6	5	2	8	5	5	8	7	78	84	.481	7
Chicago	6	6	9	6	..	7	5	3	4	6	5	9	4	7	77	85	.475	8
Texas	7	6	7	4	6	..	8	4	3	3	7	5	5	10	75	87	.463	10
California	8	5	6	7	8	5	..	3	5	7	3	8	3	7	75	87	.463	10

Championship Series—Minnesota defeated Detroit, four games to one.

SHUTOUT GAMES

Club	Bos.	Chi.	Det.	Mil.	Sea.	Oak.	N.Y.	Cle.	Tor.	Bal.	K.C.	Cal.	Tex.	Min.	W.	L.	Pct.
Boston	..	0	0	1	0	2	1	2	1	0	3	2	0	1	13	4	.765
Chicago	0	..	1	0	1	1	1	1	2	0	1	2	2	0	12	4	.750
Detroit	2	0	..	0	1	0	1	0	2	2	0	0	1	1	10	4	.714
Milwaukee	0	0	0	..	0	0	0	1	0	1	2	0	0	2	6	5	.545
Seattle	0	3	0	0	..	0	0	2	1	2	0	1	1	0	10	9	.526
Oakland	0	0	1	0	0	..	1	2	1	0	1	0	0	0	6	6	.500
New York	1	0	1	0	1	1	..	0	1	1	3	1	0	0	10	11	.476
Cleveland	0	1	0	0	0	0	2	..	2	1	1	1	0	0	8	9	.471
Toronto	0	0	0	0	1	0	1	0	..	1	2	2	0	1	8	10	.444
Baltimore	0	0	1	0	1	0	1	0	0	..	1	0	0	2	6	9	.400
Kansas City	1	0	0	1	2	2	0	1	0	1	..	2	1	0	11	17	.393
California	0	0	0	2	1	0	0	0	0	0	3	..	0	1	7	11	.389
Texas	0	0	0	0	1	0	1	0	0	0	0	0	..	1	3	6	.333
Minnesota	0	0	0	1	0	0	2	0	0	0	0	0	1	..	4	9	.308

RECORD AT HOME
EAST DIVISION

Club	Det.	Tor.	N.Y.	Bos.	Mil.	Cle.	Balt.	Min.	K.C.	Tex.	Oak.	Sea.	Cal.	Chi.	W.	L.	Pct.
Detroit	....	4-2	4-3	6-0	3-3	6-1	4-3	4-2	2-4	5-1	3-3	4-2	5-1	4-2	54	27	.667
Toronto	4-3	....	2-4	4-3	2-5	4-2	6-0	5-1	4-2	6-0	2-4	5-1	5-1	3-3	52	29	.642
New York	5-1	2-5	....	4-3	3-3	4-2	6-1	4-2	6-0	3-3	3-3	3-3	4-2	4-2	51	30	.630
Boston	2-5	3-3	4-2	....	5-1	5-2	6-0	5-1	4-2	5-1	3-3	4-2	3-3	1-5	50	30	.625
Milwaukee	4-3	4-2	4-3	6-1	....	4-2	6-0	2-4	5-1	4-2	3-3	2-4	2-4	2-4	48	33	.593
Cleveland	3-3	3-4	4-3	4-2	2-5	....	2-4	3-3	4-2	1-5	2-4	1-5	3-3	3-3	35	46	.432
Baltimore	1-5	1-6	2-4	1-6	2-5	3-4	....	3-3	4-2	4-2	3-3	1-5	4-2	2-4	31	51	.378

WEST DIVISION

Club	Min.	K.C.	Tex.	Oak.	Sea.	Cal.	Chi.	Det.	Tor.	N.Y.	Bos.	Mil.	Cle.	Balt.	W.	L.	Pct.
Minnesota	....	4-2	5-1	7-0	6-1	3-4	4-2	2-4	2-4	4-2	4-2	5-1	6-0	4-2	56	25	.691
Kansas City	6-1	....	3-4	1-5	4-2	3-4	3-3	3-3	6-0	5-1	4-2	3-3	4-2	1-5	46	35	.568
Texas	6-1	2-4	....	3-3	2-5	3-3	4-3	3-3	3-3	4-2	4-2	1-5	5-1	3-3	43	38	.531
Oakland	3-3	3-4	3-4	....	3-3	2-4	3-4	4-2	3-3	4-2	5-1	3-3	4-2	2-4	42	39	.519
Seattle	3-3	2-5	4-2	5-2	....	4-3	4-2	3-3	1-5	2-4	3-3	4-2	2-4	3-3	40	41	.494
California	4-2	1-5	2-5	2-5	4-2	....	5-2	2-4	4-2	1-5	5-1	3-3	4-2	1-5	38	43	.469
Chicago	4-3	3-4	4-2	5-1	4-3	3-3	....	1-5	1-5	3-3	4-2	2-4	4-2	0-6	38	43	.469

RECORD ABROAD
EAST DIVISION

Club	Det.	Tor.	Mil.	N.Y.	Balt.	Bos.	Cle.	Chi.	Oak.	Sea.	Cal.	K.C.	Tex.	Min.	W.	L.	Pct.
Detroit	....	3-4	3-4	1-5	5-1	5-2	3-3	5-1	2-4	3-3	4-2	3-3	3-3	4-2	44	37	.543
Toronto	2-4	....	2-4	5-2	6-1	3-3	4-3	5-1	3-3	5-1	2-4	0-6	3-3	4-2	44	37	.543
Milwaukee	3-3	5-2	....	3-3	5-2	1-5	5-2	4-2	3-3	2-4	3-3	3-3	5-1	1-5	43	38	.531
New York	3-4	4-2	3-4	....	4-2	2-4	3-4	3-3	2-4	4-2	5-1	1-5	2-4	2-4	38	43	.469
Baltimore	3-4	0-6	0-6	1-6	....	0-6	4-2	6-0	4-2	3-3	5-1	5-1	3-3	2-4	36	44	.450
Boston	0-6	3-4	1-6	3-4	6-1	....	2-4	2-4	1-5	3-3	1-5	2-4	2-4	2-4	28	54	.341
Cleveland	1-6	2-4	2-4	2-4	4-3	2-5	....	2-4	2-4	4-2	2-4	2-4	1-5	0-6	26	55	.321

WEST DIVISION

Club	Chi.	Oak.	Sea.	Cal.	K.C.	Tex.	Min.	Det.	Tor.	Mil.	N.Y.	Balt.	Bos.	Cle.	W.	L.	Pct.
Chicago	....	4-3	2-4	2-5	3-3	3-4	2-4	2-4	3-3	4-2	2-4	4-2	5-1	3-3	39	42	.481
Oakland	1-5	....	2-5	5-2	5-1	3-3	0-7	3-3	4-2	3-3	3-3	3-3	4-2		39	42	.481
Seattle	3-4	3-3	....	2-4	2-4	5-2	1-6	2-4	1-5	4-2	3-3	5-1	2-4	5-1	38	43	.469
California	3-3	4-2	3-4	....	4-3	3-3	4-3	1-5	1-5	4-2	2-4	2-4	3-3	3-3	37	44	.457
Kansas City	4-3	4-3	5-2	5-1	....	4-2	2-4	4-2	2-4	1-5	0-6	2-4	2-4	2-4	37	44	.457
Texas	2-4	4-3	2-4	5-2	4-3	....	1-5	1-5	0-6	2-4	3-3	2-4	1-5	5-1	32	49	.395
Minnesota	3-4	3-3	3-3	3-2	1-6	1-6	....	2-4	1-5	4-2	2-4	3-3	1-5	3-3	29	52	.358

1987 A.L. Pitching Against Each Club

BALTIMORE—67-95

Pitcher	Bos. W-L	Cal. W-L	Chi. W-L	Clev. W-L	Det. W-L	K.C. W-L	Mil. W-L	Min. W-L	N.Y. W-L	Oak. W-L	Sea. W-L	Tex. W-L	Tor. W-L	Totals W-L
Aase	0-0	0-0	0-0	0-0	0-0	0-0	0-0	0-0	0-0	0-0	0-0	1-0	0-0	1-0
Ballard	0-2	0-0	0-0	0-0	0-1	0-0	0-0	0-0	0-1	1-1	1-2	0-0	0-1	2-8
Bell	0-1	0-1	1-0	3-0	1-1	2-0	0-2	1-2	1-1	1-2	0-1	0-1	0-1	10-13
Boddicker	0-0	1-0	1-1	1-0	0-2	2-0	1-0	0-0	0-2	3-1	1-0	0-2	0-4	10-12
Corbett	0-0	0-0	0-0	0-0	0-1	0-0	0-0	0-0	0-1	0-0	0-0	0-0	0-0	0-2
DeLeon	0-1	0-0	0-0	0-0	0-0	0-0	0-0	0-0	0-1	0-0	0-0	0-0	0-0	0-2
Dixon	0-1	1-0	1-0	0-0	0-2	0-1	0-2	1-0	0-0	0-1	1-1	3-0	0-2	7-10
Flanagan	0-0	1-0	0-1	0-0	0-0	1-0	1-2	0-1	0-0	0-1	0-1	0-0	0-0	3-6
Griffin	0-1	0-0	2-0	0-1	0-1	0-0	0-1	0-1	0-0	0-0	1-0	0-0	0-0	3-5
Habyan	1-1	1-0	1-1	0-0	1-0	0-0	0-0	0-0	0-1	0-0	0-2	2-0	0-2	6-7
McGregor	0-0	1-0	0-1	0-1	0-0	0-0	0-0	0-2	1-1	0-1	0-0	0-0	0-1	2-7
Mesa	0-1	0-0	0-0	0-0	1-0	0-0	0-0	0-0	0-1	0-0	0-0	0-0	0-1	1-3
Niedenfuer	0-2	0-0	0-0	0-1	1-0	1-0	0-0	0-2	0-0	1-0	0-0	0-0	0-0	3-5
O'Connor	0-0	0-1	0-0	0-0	0-0	0-0	0-0	0-0	1-0	0-0	0-0	0-0	0-0	1-1
Schmidt	0-1	1-0	1-0	1-1	0-0	2-1	0-1	1-0	1-0	1-0	0-1	1-0	1-0	10-5
Williamson	0-1	3-1	1-0	2-2	0-1	1-1	0-1	1-0	0-1	0-0	0-0	0-1	0-0	8-9
Totals	1-12	9-3	8-4	7-6	4-9	9-3	2-11	5-7	3-10	7-5	4-8	7-5	1-12	67-95

No Decisions—Arnold, Kinnunen.

BOSTON—78-84

Pitcher	Balt. W-L	Cal. W-L	Chi. W-L	Clev. W-L	Det. W-L	K.C. W-L	Mil. W-L	Min. W-L	N.Y. W-L	Oak. W-L	Sea. W-L	Tex. W-L	Tor. W-L	Totals W-L
Bolton	0-0	0-0	0-0	0-0	0-0	0-0	0-0	0-0	0-0	0-0	1-0	0-0	0-0	1-0
Boyd	0-0	0-1	0-0	0-0	0-0	0-0	1-0	0-0	0-1	0-1	0-0	0-0	0-0	1-3
Clemens	2-0	2-0	0-2	4-0	0-2	2-0	2-0	2-1	3-0	0-1	2-1	0-0	1-2	20-9
Crawford	1-0	0-0	1-0	2-0	0-2	0-1	1-1	0-0	0-0	0-0	0-0	0-0	0-0	5-4
Gardner	1-0	0-1	0-1	0-0	0-1	0-0	1-1	0-1	0-0	0-0	0-1	1-0	0-0	3-6
Hurst	3-1	1-0	0-2	0-1	1-2	2-1	1-0	0-1	0-2	2-1	1-1	3-1	1-0	15-13
Leister	0-0	0-0	0-0	0-0	0-1	0-0	0-1	0-0	0-0	0-0	0-0	0-0	0-0	0-2

Pitcher	Balt. W-L	Cal. W-L	Chi. W-L	Clev. W-L	Det. W-L	K.C. W-L	Mil. W-L	Min. W-L	N.Y. W-L	Oak. W-L	Sea. W-L	Tex. W-L	Tor. W-L	Totals W-L
Nipper..........	1-0	0-3	1-1	1-1	1-1	0-1	0-1	0-1	4-0	0-1	1-1	1-1	1-0	11-12
Sambito	1-0	1-0	0-0	0-0	0-0	0-0	0-1	0-0	0-2	0-0	0-1	0-1	0-1	2-6
Schiraldi.....	0-0	0-0	1-0	0-0	0-0	0-0	0-0	3-1	0-1	1-0	1-0	1-2	1-1	8-5
Sellers	1-0	0-2	0-1	0-1	0-1	1-1	0-0	2-0	0-0	1-1	1-0	0-0	1-1	7-8
Stanley........	1-0	0-1	0-2	0-3	0-0	1-2	0-2	0-0	0-0	0-3	0-0	1-0	1-2	4-15
Woodward .	1-0	0-0	0-0	0-0	0-1	0-0	0-0	0-0	0-0	0-0	0-0	0-0	0-0	1-1
Totals	12-1	4-8	3-9	7-6	2-11	6-6	6-7	7-5	7-6	4-8	7-5	7-5	6-7	78-84

No Decisions—None.

CALIFORNIA—75-87

Pitcher	Balt. W-L	Bos. W-L	Chi. W-L	Clev. W-L	Det. W-L	K.C. W-L	Mil. W-L	Min. W-L	N.Y. W-L	Oak. W-L	Sea. W-L	Tex. W-L	Tor. W-L	Totals W-L
Buice	0-3	0-1	0-0	0-0	0-0	0-0	2-0	0-0	0-0	0-1	1-0	2-1	1-1	6-7
Candelaria ..	0-0	1-0	1-0	0-0	0-1	0-0	0-0	3-1	2-0	0-1	1-0	0-2	0-1	8-6
Cook	0-0	0-0	0-0	0-0	0-0	0-0	0-0	0-1	0-0	1-0	0-0	0-0	0-1	1-2
Finley..........	0-1	0-0	0-1	0-0	0-1	0-0	2-1	0-1	0-0	0-1	0-0	0-1	0-0	2-7
Fraser	1-0	2-0	1-2	0-0	0-2	2-2	0-1	0-0	0-2	1-0	1-1	1-0	1-0	10-10
Lazorko.......	0-0	0-0	1-0	2-1	0-1	0-2	1-0	0-0	0-1	0-0	1-0	0-0	0-1	5-6
Lucas..........	0-1	0-0	0-0	0-2	0-0	0-0	0-0	0-0	0-1	0-1	0-0	0-0	1-0	1-5
Lugo	0-0	0-1	0-0	0-0	0-1	0-0	0-0	0-0	0-0	0-0	0-0	0-0	0-0	0-2
McCaskill....	0-1	0-1	0-0	0-0	0-0	0-0	0-1	1-0	0-1	1-1	1-1	0-0	1-0	4-6
Minton........	0-0	2-0	1-0	1-0	0-1	1-1	0-0	0-0	0-0	0-0	0-1	0-1	0-0	5-4
Moore..........	1-0	0-0	0-0	0-0	0-1	0-0	0-0	0-0	0-0	1-0	0-0	0-0	0-0	2-2
Reuss..........	0-1	0-0	1-1	1-0	0-1	1-0	0-0	0-0	0-0	0-0	0-0	0-2	1-0	4-5
Sutton........	1-1	0-1	0-0	3-1	1-0	1-1	1-1	2-1	0-2	1-0	0-2	1-0	0-1	11-11
Witt............	0-1	3-0	3-1	0-1	2-0	0-2	1-1	2-1	1-1	2-2	1-1	1-1	0-2	16-14
Totals	3-9	8-4	8-5	7-5	3-9	5-8	7-5	8-5	3-9	6-7	7-6	5-8	5-7	75-87

No Decisions—Garcia, Harvey.

CHICAGO—77-85

Pitcher	Balt. W-L	Bos. W-L	Cal. W-L	Clev. W-L	Det. W-L	K.C. W-L	Mil. W-L	Min. W-L	N.Y. W-L	Oak. W-L	Sea. W-L	Tex. W-L	Tor. W-L	Totals W-L
Allen	0-1	0-0	0-1	0-0	0-1	0-0	0-2	0-0	0-0	0-1	0-0	0-0	0-1	0-7
Bannister....	2-0	1-1	1-1	0-0	2-0	1-1	1-0	1-0	1-3	2-1	1-2	2-1	1-1	16-11
Davis..........	0-0	0-0	0-0	0-1	0-1	0-1	1-1	0-0	0-0	0-0	0-0	0-1	0-0	1-5
DeLeon........	1-2	2-0	1-2	0-1	0-0	2-1	1-2	2-1	0-0	0-1	1-0	0-0	1-2	11-12
Dotson........	0-1	0-1	1-0	1-1	1-2	2-2	1-0	1-0	1-2	1-0	0-1	1-1	1-1	11-12
James..........	0-0	1-0	0-2	1-2	0-0	0-0	0-0	0-0	0-0	1-1	0-0	0-0	1-1	4-6
LaPoint	0-0	1-0	0-0	0-0	0-0	0-1	1-0	1-1	0-0	2-0	0-0	1-1	0-0	6-3
Long	0-1	1-0	1-1	0-0	0-1	0-1	1-0	0-1	2-0	0-0	1-2	2-1	0-0	8-8
McDowell ...	0-0	0-0	1-0	0-0	0-0	0-0	0-0	1-0	0-0	0-0	1-0	0-0	0-0	3-0
McKeon......	0-1	0-0	0-0	0-0	0-0	0-0	0-0	0-0	0-0	0-0	1-0	0-1	0-1	1-2
Nielsen........	0-0	0-0	0-0	2-0	0-2	0-0	0-0	0-1	0-1	1-0	0-1	0-0	0-0	3-5
Searge	0-1	1-1	0-0	0-0	0-0	0-0	0-0	0-0	1-0	0-0	0-0	0-0	0-1	2-3
Thigpen......	1-0	0-0	0-1	2-0	0-2	1-0	0-1	0-0	0-1	1-0	2-0	0-0	0-0	7-5
Winn	0-1	2-0	0-0	1-0	0-0	0-0	0-0	0-3	0-0	1-0	0-1	0-1	0-0	4-6
Totals	4-8	9-3	5-8	7-5	3-9	6-7	6-6	6-7	5-7	9-4	6-7	7-6	4-8	77-85

No Decisions—Citarella, Clark, Pawlowski, Peterson.

CLEVELAND—61-101

Pitcher	Balt. W-L	Bos. W-L	Cal. W-L	Chi. W-L	Det. W-L	K.C. W-L	Mil. W-L	Min. W-L	N.Y. W-L	Oak. W-L	Sea. W-L	Tex. W-L	Tor. W-L	Totals W-L
Akerfelds ...	1-0	1-0	0-0	0-0	0-0	0-1	0-1	0-1	0-0	0-1	0-0	0-0	0-2	2-6
Armstrong..	0-0	1-0	0-0	0-0	0-0	0-0	0-0	0-0	0-0	0-0	0-0	0-0	0-0	1-0
Bailes..........	1-0	0-2	0-1	1-1	0-1	0-1	1-1	0-0	1-0	0-0	1-0	0-1	2-0	7-8
Camacho	0-1	0-0	0-0	0-0	0-0	0-0	0-0	0-0	0-0	0-0	0-0	0-0	0-0	0-1
Candiotti	0-3	1-1	0-0	0-1	0-2	0-1	0-1	0-4	2-1	1-2	0-1	1-0	2-1	7-18
Carlton	1-0	0-0	0-1	0-1	0-1	0-0	1-0	0-0	1-1	1-1	1-0	0-3	0-1	5-9
Easterly......	0-0	0-0	0-0	0-0	1-0	0-0	0-0	0-0	0-0	0-0	0-1	0-0	0-0	1-1
Farrell	0-0	1-0	1-0	0-0	2-0	0-0	0-0	0-0	0-0	0-1	0-0	0-0	0-0	5-1
Gordon	0-1	0-0	0-0	0-0	0-1	0-0	0-0	0-1	0-0	0-0	0-0	0-0	0-0	0-3
Huismann....	0-0	1-1	0-0	0-0	0-1	0-0	0-1	0-0	0-0	0-0	1-0	0-0	0-0	2-3
Jones	0-0	0-0	1-0	1-1	0-0	1-0	0-1	1-0	0-0	1-1	0-0	1-1	0-0	6-5
Niekro	0-0	0-1	2-0	0-1	1-1	2-0	0-1	0-1	0-1	0-0	1-1	0-4	1-0	7-11
Ritter.........	0-0	0-0	1-0	0-0	0-0	0-0	0-0	0-0	0-0	0-0	0-0	0-0	0-1	1-1
Schrom........	0-2	0-0	0-2	2-0	0-1	0-2	1-2	1-0	1-1	0-1	1-1	0-0	0-1	6-13
Stewart	2-0	0-0	0-0	0-1	0-0	2-0	0-0	0-0	0-0	0-0	0-1	0-0	0-0	4-2
Swindell......	1-0	0-1	0-1	0-0	0-0	1-0	0-1	1-1	0-2	0-1	0-0	0-0	0-1	3-8
Vande Berg	0-0	0-0	0-0	0-0	0-0	0-0	0-0	0-0	0-0	1-0	0-0	0-0	0-0	1-0
Waddell	0-0	0-0	0-0	0-0	0-0	0-0	0-0	0-0	0-1	0-0	0-0	0-0	0-0	0-1
Wills..........	0-0	0-0	0-0	0-0	0-0	0-0	0-0	0-0	0-0	0-0	0-0	0-1	0-0	0-1
Yett............	0-0	1-1	0-2	1-1	0-1	0-1	0-0	0-1	1-0	0-0	0-2	0-0	0-0	3-9
Totals	6-7	6-7	5-7	5-7	4-9	6-6	4-9	3-9	6-7	4-8	5-7	2-10	5-8	61-101

No Decisions—Kaiser.

DETROIT—98-64

Pitcher	Balt. W-L	Bos. W-L	Cal. W-L	Chi. W-L	Clev. W-L	K.C. W-L	Mil. W-L	Min. W-L	N.Y. W-L	Oak. W-L	Sea. W-L	Tex. W-L	Tor. W-L	Totals W-L
Alexander...	1-0	2-0	0-0	0-0	0-0	0-0	1-0	2-0	0-0	0-0	0-0	2-0	1-0	9-0
Henneman..	0-0	1-0	3-0	0-0	2-0	0-0	0-1	0-0	0-1	1-0	1-0	1-0	2-1	11-3
Hernandez..	1-0	0-0	0-0	1-0	1-0	0-0	0-0	0-0	0-1	0-0	0-1	0-1	0-1	3-4
Kelly	0-0	0-0	0-0	0-0	0-0	0-0	0-0	0-0	0-0	0-1	0-0	0-0	0-0	0-1
King	0-0	1-0	2-0	1-0	0-0	1-0	0-2	0-2	0-1	1-2	0-1	0-1	0-0	6-9
Morris.........	2-1	2-0	1-1	1-1	4-0	2-1	2-2	2-0	0-2	0-0	1-0	1-1	0-2	18-11
Petry..........	1-1	2-0	1-0	0-1	0-2	0-3	1-0	1-0	1-0	0-0	1-0	1-0	0-0	9-7
Robinson.....	0-0	1-0	0-0	2-0	0-0	1-0	0-0	1-0	1-1	1-0	1-2	1-1	0-2	9-6
Snell	0-0	0-1	0-0	0-0	0-0	0-0	0-0	0-0	0-0	1-1	0-0	0-0	0-0	1-2
Tanana.......	1-1	1-0	1-1	4-0	0-2	0-0	0-1	0-1	2-1	1-2	1-1	1-0	3-0	15-10
Terrell........	3-1	1-1	1-1	0-1	2-0	1-3	2-1	2-1	1-1	0-0	2-0	1-0	1-0	17-10
Thurmond...	0-0	0-0	0-0	0-0	0-0	0-0	0-0	0-0	0-0	0-1	0-0	0-0	0-0	0-1
Totals	9-4	11-2	9-3	9-3	9-4	5-7	6-7	8-4	5-8	5-7	7-5	8-4	7-6	98-64

No Decisions—Madden, Noles.

KANSAS CITY—83-79

Pitcher	Balt. W-L	Bos. W-L	Cal. W-L	Chi. W-L	Clev. W-L	Det. W-L	Mil. W-L	Min. W-L	N.Y. W-L	Oak. W-L	Sea. W-L	Tex. W-L	Tor. W-L	Totals W-L
Anderson....	0-0	0-1	0-0	0-0	0-0	0-0	0-0	0-0	0-0	0-1	0-0	0-0	0-0	0-2
Black	0-1	0-0	1-0	1-0	0-0	1-0	0-1	0-0	0-1	0-0	2-0	0-1	3-2	8-6
Davis..........	0-0	1-0	1-0	0-1	0-0	0-0	0-0	1-0	0-0	0-1	0-0	2-0	0-0	5-2
Farr	1-1	0-0	0-0	0-0	0-0	0-0	1-0	1-0	0-1	0-1	0-0	0-0	1-0	4-3
Gleaton......	0-0	0-0	0-0	0-0	0-1	1-1	1-0	0-1	0-0	0-0	1-0	1-1	0-0	4-4
Gubicza......	0-1	2-1	2-1	0-2	2-1	1-2	0-2	1-1	0-2	2-1	2-1	0-3	1-0	13-18
D. Jackson .	0-3	0-2	1-2	2-2	1-1	1-1	0-1	1-1	1-2	0-2	1-1	1-0	0-0	9-18
Leibrandt...	1-1	1-1	2-0	2-1	1-0	1-0	1-2	1-2	2-1	1-0	1-1	1-0	1-2	16-11
Perez..........	0-0	0-0	0-0	1-0	0-0	0-0	0-0	0-0	0-0	0-1	0-0	0-0	0-0	1-1
Quisenberry	1-0	0-0	0-0	0-0	0-1	0-0	1-0	1-0	0-0	0-0	0-0	1-0	1-0	4-1
Saberhagen	0-2	2-1	1-1	1-0	2-2	2-1	0-1	2-0	2-0	2-1	2-1	1-0	1-0	18-10
Stoddard....	0-0	0-0	0-1	0-0	0-0	0-0	0-1	0-0	0-0	0-0	0-0	1-1	0-0	1-3
Totals	3-9	6-6	8-5	7-6	6-6	7-5	4-8	8-5	5-7	5-8	9-4	7-6	8-4	83-79

No Decisions—Garber, Gumpert, Shirley.

MILWAUKEE—91-71

Pitcher	Balt. W-L	Bos. W-L	Cal. W-L	Chi. W-L	Clev. W-L	Det. W-L	K.C. W-L	Min. W-L	N.Y. W-L	Oak. W-L	Sea. W-L	Tex. W-L	Tor. W-L	Totals W-L
Aldrich........	1-0	0-0	0-1	0-0	0-0	0-0	1-0	0-0	0-0	0-0	0-0	1-0	0-0	3-1
Barker........	0-0	0-0	0-0	0-0	0-0	0-0	2-0	0-1	0-0	0-0	0-0	0-0	0-0	2-1
Birkbeck.....	1-0	0-0	0-1	0-0	0-1	0-0	0-1	0-1	0-0	0-0	0-0	0-0	0-0	1-4
Bosio	1-1	1-1	1-0	0-2	0-0	0-3	1-0	1-0	0-0	3-0	0-1	1-0	2-0	11-8
Burris	0-0	1-0	0-0	1-0	0-1	0-0	0-0	0-0	0-0	0-0	0-1	0-0	0-0	2-2
Ciardi.........	1-0	0-0	0-0	0-1	0-0	0-0	0-0	0-0	0-0	0-0	0-0	0-0	0-0	1-1
Clear..........	0-0	1-0	0-2	1-0	1-0	0-1	0-1	1-0	0-0	0-0	1-0	2-0	1-1	8-5
Crim...........	1-0	1-0	0-1	1-0	0-0	0-0	1-0	0-3	1-3	0-0	1-0	0-0	0-1	6-8
Higuera.......	2-1	1-2	2-0	0-2	2-2	1-1	1-0	1-0	3-0	1-1	1-1	2-0	1-0	18-10
Johnson......	0-0	0-1	0-0	0-0	0-0	0-0	0-0	0-0	0-0	0-0	0-0	0-0	0-0	0-1
Knudson	1-0	0-0	0-0	1-0	2-0	0-0	0-1	0-0	0-0	0-2	0-0	0-1	0-0	4-4
Mirabella	0-0	0-0	1-0	0-0	0-0	0-0	0-0	0-0	0-0	0-1	1-0	0-0	0-0	2-1
Nieves........	2-0	0-1	0-0	2-0	3-0	2-0	0-0	0-1	0-3	2-0	0-2	1-0	2-1	14-8
Plesac.........	0-0	0-0	0-1	0-0	0-0	1-0	0-0	0-1	2-0	0-1	0-1	1-1	1-1	5-6
Stapleton ...	0-0	1-0	0-0	0-0	0-0	0-0	0-0	0-0	1-0	0-0	0-0	0-0	0-0	2-0
Wegman.....	1-0	1-1	1-1	0-1	1-0	3-1	2-1	0-2	0-0	0-1	0-3	1-0	2-0	12-11
Totals	11-2	7-6	5-7	6-6	9-4	7-6	8-4	3-9	7-6	6-6	4-8	9-3	9-4	91-71

No Decisions—Madrid.

MINNESOTA—85-77

Pitcher	Balt. W-L	Bos. W-L	Cal. W-L	Chi. W-L	Clev. W-L	Det. W-L	K.C. W-L	Mil. W-L	N.Y. W-L	Oak. W-L	Sea. W-L	Tex. W-L	Tor. W-L	Totals W-L
Anderson....	0-0	0-0	0-0	0-0	0-0	1-0	0-0	0-0	0-0	0-0	0-0	0-0	0-0	1-0
Atherton	0-0	2-0	0-0	0-0	0-0	0-1	0-1	2-0	0-1	1-0	0-0	2-2	0-0	7-5
Berenguer ..	0-0	0-0	0-0	2-0	1-1	0-0	0-0	2-0	0-0	1-0	0-0	2-0	0-0	8-1
Bittiger......	0-0	0-0	0-0	1-0	0-0	0-0	0-0	0-0	0-0	0-0	0-0	0-0	0-0	1-0
Blyleven......	2-1	0-1	0-2	0-2	2-1	0-1	2-1	3-0	2-0	2-0	2-0	0-1	0-2	15-12
Carlton	0-0	0-1	0-2	0-0	0-0	0-1	0-0	0-1	0-0	1-0	0-0	0-0	0-0	1-5
Frazier	0-1	1-0	1-0	0-0	0-0	1-0	0-0	0-0	1-0	1-1	0-1	0-1	0-1	5-5
Klink	0-0	0-1	0-0	0-0	0-0	0-0	0-0	0-0	0-0	0-0	0-0	0-0	0-0	0-1
Niekro	0-1	0-1	0-0	1-1	0-0	0-2	1-2	0-0	0-0	1-0	0-1	1-0	0-1	4-9
Niemann	0-0	0-0	0-0	0-0	0-0	0-0	1-0	0-0	0-0	0-0	0-0	0-0	0-0	1-0
Portugal	0-0	0-0	1-1	0-0	0-1	0-0	0-0	0-0	0-0	0-0	0-0	0-0	0-1	1-3
Reardon	1-1	0-1	1-0	1-0	2-0	2-1	1-1	0-0	0-1	0-1	0-1	0-0	0-1	8-8
Schatzeder	0-0	0-0	1-0	0-0	0-0	0-0	0-1	0-0	0-0	0-0	0-0	0-0	2-0	3-1
Smith..........	0-0	0-0	0-0	0-0	0-0	0-0	0-0	0-0	0-0	0-0	1-0	0-0	0-0	1-0
Smithson ...	0-1	0-0	0-0	0-1	1-0	0-0	0-0	0-0	0-2	1-0	2-1	0-1	0-1	4-7
Straker	2-0	1-1	0-1	0-1	0-0	0-1	0-1	0-2	1-1	0-0	2-0	0-1	0-1	8-10
Viola	2-0	1-1	1-2	2-1	1-0	0-1	0-1	2-0	2-1	2-1	2-0	1-1	1-1	17-10
Totals	7-5	5-7	5-8	7-6	9-3	4-8	5-8	9-3	6-6	10-3	9-4	6-7	3-9	85-77

No Decisions—None.

NEW YORK—89-73

Pitcher	Balt. W-L	Bos. W-L	Cal. W-L	Chi. W-L	Clev. W-L	Det. W-L	K.C. W-L	Mil. W-L	Min. W-L	Oak. W-L	Sea. W-L	Tex. W-L	Tor. W-L	Totals W-L
Allen	0-0	0-0	0-0	0-0	0-0	0-0	0-0	0-0	0-0	0-0	0-0	0-0	0-1	0-1
Arnsberg	0-0	0-0	0-0	0-0	1-1	0-0	0-1	0-0	0-0	0-0	0-1	0-0	0-0	1-3
Bordi	1-0	0-0	1-0	0-0	0-0	0-0	0-0	1-0	0-0	0-0	0-0	0-1	0-0	3-1
Clements	0-1	0-0	0-0	0-2	0-0	0-0	1-0	1-0	0-0	0-0	0-0	0-0	1-0	3-3
Filson	1-0	0-0	0-0	0-0	0-0	0-0	0-0	0-0	0-0	0-0	0-0	0-0	0-0	1-0
Fulton	0-0	1-0	0-0	0-0	0-0	0-0	0-0	0-0	0-0	0-0	0-0	0-0	0-0	1-0
Guante	0-0	0-0	0-0	1-0	1-0	0-0	0-0	0-0	1-0	0-0	0-1	0-1	0-0	3-2
Guidry	0-1	0-0	1-0	1-0	0-1	0-1	0-1	0-0	0-1	1-1	0-1	1-0	1-1	5-8
Gullickson	1-0	0-1	1-0	0-0	0-0	0-0	0-0	0-1	0-0	0-0	1-0	0-0	1-0	4-2
Hudson	0-1	2-1	1-1	1-0	1-0	1-0	1-0	0-0	1-0	0-2	2-1	0-1	1-0	11-7
John	2-0	0-1	1-1	1-0	1-1	1-0	1-0	1-1	2-0	2-0	1-0	0-1	0-1	13-6
Leiter	1-0	0-1	0-0	0-0	0-0	0-0	0-0	1-0	0-0	0-0	0-0	0-1	0-0	2-2
Niekro	0-0	0-0	1-0	0-1	0-0	1-0	0-1	0-1	0-0	0-1	1-0	0-0	0-0	3-4
Rasmussen	2-0	0-0	0-1	1-0	2-0	0-2	1-0	1-0	0-1	0-2	0-0	2-1	0-0	9-7
Rhoden	2-0	1-1	1-0	2-0	1-1	2-1	1-2	1-0	1-2	1-0	1-1	2-0	0-2	16-10
Righetti	0-0	0-1	2-0	0-0	0-1	2-0	1-0	0-3	0-0	1-0	0-0	0-0	2-1	8-6
Shirley	0-0	0-0	0-0	0-0	0-0	1-0	0-0	0-0	0-0	0-0	0-0	0-0	0-0	1-0
Stoddard	0-0	1-0	0-0	0-0	0-0	0-0	1-0	0-1	1-2	0-0	1-0	0-0	0-0	4-3
Tewksbury	0-0	1-1	0-0	0-1	0-0	0-1	0-1	0-0	0-0	0-0	0-0	0-1	0-0	1-4
Trout	0-0	0-0	0-0	0-1	0-1	0-0	0-0	0-0	0-0	0-0	0-1	0-0	0-1	0-4
Totals	10-3	6-7	9-3	7-5	7-6	8-5	7-5	6-7	6-6	5-7	7-5	5-7	6-7	89-73

No Decisions—Cerone, Holland.

OAKLAND—81-81

Pitcher	Balt. W-L	Bos. W-L	Cal. W-L	Chi. W-L	Clev. W-L	Det. W-L	K.C. W-L	Mil. W-L	Min. W-L	N.Y. W-L	Sea. W-L	Tex. W-L	Tor. W-L	Totals W-L
Andujar	0-0	1-0	0-1	0-0	1-1	0-1	0-0	0-1	0-0	1-0	0-1	0-0	0-0	3-5
Cadaret	1-0	1-0	1-0	1-0	1-0	0-0	0-0	0-0	0-0	0-0	0-0	1-0	0-2	6-2
Codiroli	0-0	0-0	0-0	0-0	0-0	0-0	0-0	0-0	0-1	0-0	0-1	0-0	0-0	0-2
S. Davis	0-0	0-0	0-0	0-1	0-0	0-0	1-0	0-0	0-0	0-0	0-0	0-0	0-0	1-1
Eckersley	0-2	1-2	0-1	1-1	1-0	1-0	0-0	1-0	0-0	1-1	0-0	0-0	0-1	6-8
Haas	0-1	0-0	0-0	0-0	0-0	0-0	0-0	0-0	0-0	0-0	0-1	2-0	0-0	2-2
Honeycutt	0-0	0-0	0-0	0-2	1-0	0-0	0-1	0-0	0-0	0-1	0-0	0-0	0-0	1-4
Howell	0-0	1-0	0-0	0-1	0-0	0-1	0-0	0-1	1-1	0-0	1-0	0-0	0-0	3-4
Krueger	0-0	0-0	0-1	0-0	0-0	0-0	0-0	0-0	0-1	0-0	0-1	0-0	0-0	0-3
Lamp	0-0	0-0	0-0	0-0	0-0	1-0	0-0	0-1	0-2	0-0	0-0	0-0	0-0	1-3
Leiper	0-0	0-0	0-1	0-0	0-0	1-0	1-0	0-0	0-0	0-0	0-0	0-0	0-0	2-1
G. Nelson	1-1	0-0	0-0	0-0	0-0	2-1	0-0	0-1	1-0	2-0	0-1	0-1	0-0	6-5
Ontiveros	0-0	0-1	0-1	1-0	2-0	0-2	3-1	0-1	0-1	2-0	1-0	1-1	0-0	10-8
Plunk	0-0	0-0	0-0	0-1	0-1	1-0	1-0	0-0	0-1	0-0	0-0	1-2	1-1	4-6
Rijo	0-0	1-0	0-0	0-1	0-0	0-0	0-1	0-1	0-0	0-0	1-3	0-0	0-1	2-7
Rodriguez	0-0	0-0	1-0	0-0	0-0	0-0	0-0	0-0	0-0	0-0	0-0	0-0	0-0	1-0
Stewart	0-2	2-1	3-1	0-1	2-2	0-0	0-2	3-0	1-2	0-1	2-0	3-1	4-0	20-13
Young	3-1	1-0	2-0	1-1	0-0	1-0	2-0	2-0	0-1	1-2	0-1	0-1	0-0	13-7
Totals	5-7	8-4	7-6	4-9	8-4	7-5	8-5	6-6	3-10	7-5	5-8	6-7	7-5	81-81

No Decisions—Caudill, Lavelle, Otto, Von Ohlen.

SEATTLE—78-84

Pitcher	Balt. W-L	Bos. W-L	Cal. W-L	Chi. W-L	Clev. W-L	Det. W-L	K.C. W-L	Mil. W-L	Min. W-L	N.Y. W-L	Oak. W-L	Tex. W-L	Tor. W-L	Totals W-L
Bankhead	1-0	2-0	2-1	2-1	0-0	0-1	0-1	0-0	0-0	0-0	1-3	0-0	1-1	9-8
Campbell	0-0	0-0	0-0	0-1	0-0	0-1	1-0	0-0	0-0	0-1	0-0	0-0	0-1	1-4
Clarke	0-0	0-1	0-0	0-0	0-0	1-0	0-0	1-0	0-0	0-0	0-0	0-1	0-0	2-2
Guetterman	1-0	1-1	0-0	1-0	1-0	1-0	2-1	1-0	1-1	1-0	0-1	1-0	0-0	11-4
Langston	3-1	1-1	1-1	2-1	2-1	1-2	0-2	1-1	1-2	1-0	2-0	3-0	1-1	19-13
Moore	1-0	0-2	1-2	1-1	1-1	0-2	0-2	1-1	0-1	0-3	2-1	2-0	0-3	9-19
Morgan	2-1	0-1	1-1	0-0	1-2	1-0	1-2	3-1	1-3	0-2	1-0	1-2	0-2	12-17
Nunez	0-0	0-0	0-1	0-1	1-0	0-0	0-0	0-0	1-1	0-0	0-0	0-0	0-1	3-4
Powell	0-1	0-0	0-1	0-0	0-0	0-0	0-0	0-0	0-0	0-0	1-0	0-0	0-1	1-3
Reed	0-0	0-0	0-0	0-0	0-0	0-1	0-1	0-0	0-0	1-0	0-0	0-0	0-0	1-2
Shields	0-0	0-0	1-0	0-0	0-0	0-0	0-0	0-0	0-0	1-0	0-0	0-0	0-0	2-0
Thomas	0-0	1-0	0-0	0-0	0-0	0-0	0-0	0-0	0-0	0-0	0-0	0-0	0-0	1-0
Trujillo	0-1	0-1	0-0	0-0	0-1	0-0	0-0	0-0	0-1	1-0	2-0	1-0	0-0	4-4
Wilkinson	0-0	0-0	0-0	1-1	1-0	0-0	0-0	1-1	0-0	0-1	0-0	0-1	0-0	3-4
Totals	8-4	5-7	6-7	7-6	7-5	5-7	4-9	8-4	4-9	5-7	8-5	9-4	2-10	78-84

No Decisions—Brown, Huismann, Monteleone, Parker.

TEXAS—75-87

Pitcher	Balt. W-L	Bos. W-L	Cal. W-L	Chi. W-L	Clev. W-L	Det. W-L	K.C. W-L	Mil. W-L	Min. W-L	N.Y. W-L	Oak. W-L	Sea. W-L	Tor. W-L	Totals W-L
Anderson	0-0	0-0	0-0	0-0	0-0	0-0	0-0	0-1	0-0	0-0	0-0	0-0	0-0	0-1
Correa	0-0	0-1	0-0	0-0	0-0	0-1	0-0	0-0	1-0	1-1	1-0	0-0	0-2	3-5
Guzman	0-0	2-1	3-0	3-0	1-2	1-1	0-2	0-2	1-2	2-1	0-1	1-1	0-1	14-14
Harris	0-1	1-1	0-2	0-1	1-0	0-0	0-0	1-1	1-1	1-1	0-1	0-0	0-1	5-10
Hough	1-2	1-0	1-1	1-1	4-0	0-2	3-1	0-1	2-1	0-1	4-0	1-1	0-2	18-13

Knuckleballer Charlie Hough led Texas with 18 victories in 1987, including four each against Cleveland and Oakland.

Pitcher	Balt. W-L	Bos. W-L	Cal. W-L	Chi. W-L	Clev. W-L	Det. W-L	K.C. W-L	Mil. W-L	Min. W-L	N.Y. W-L	Oak. W-L	Sea. W-L	Tor. W-L	Totals W-L
Howe	0-0	0-2	1-1	0-0	0-0	1-0	1-0	0-0	0-0	0-0	0-0	0-0	0-0	3-3
Jeffcoat.....	0-0	0-0	0-0	0-0	0-0	0-0	0-0	0-0	0-0	0-0	0-0	0-1	0-0	0-1
Kilgus..........	0-2	0-0	0-0	0-2	1-0	0-0	0-0	1-1	0-0	0-0	0-1	0-1	0-0	2-7
Loynd	1-0	0-0	0-1	0-0	0-0	0-1	0-1	0-0	0-0	0-0	0-0	0-1	0-1	1-5
Mason.........	0-1	0-0	0-0	0-0	0-0	0-0	0-0	0-1	0-0	0-0	0-0	0-0	0-0	0-2
Meridith......	0-0	0-0	0-0	0-0	1-0	0-0	0-0	0-0	0-0	0-0	0-0	0-0	0-0	1-0
Mohorcic ...	1-0	0-2	0-0	2-0	0-0	1-1	1-1	0-0	0-0	0-0	1-1	0-1	1-0	7-6
Russell	0-0	0-0	2-0	0-1	1-0	0-0	0-1	0-1	0-1	1-0	0-0	0-0	1-0	5-4
Williams......	0-1	1-0	1-0	0-0	1-0	1-0	0-0	1-0	0-1	1-0	0-1	2-2	0-1	8-6
Witt	2-0	0-0	0-0	0-2	0-0	0-2	1-1	0-1	2-0	1-1	1-1	0-1	1-1	8-10
Totals	5-7	5-7	8-5	6-7	10-2	4-8	6-7	3-9	7-6	7-5	7-6	4-9	3-9	75-87

No Decisions—Creel, Henry, Malloy, Mielke.

TORONTO—96-66

Pitcher	Balt. W-L	Bos. W-L	Cal. W-L	Chi. W-L	Clev. W-L	Det. W-L	K.C. W-L	Mil. W-L	Min. W-L	N.Y. W-L	Oak. W-L	Sea. W-L	Tex. W-L	Totals W-L
Cerutti........	2-0	1-0	1-0	2-0	1-0	1-0	0-1	0-0	0-0	1-1	0-2	1-0	1-0	11-4
Clancy.........	2-0	0-3	1-0	0-1	1-2	0-3	1-1	1-0	2-0	1-0	1-1	2-0	3-0	15-11
Eichhorn.....	2-1	0-0	1-0	3-1	1-0	0-0	0-1	0-0	1-1	0-0	0-1	1-0	1-1	10-6
Flanagan	1-0	0-0	0-0	0-0	0-0	1-0	0-0	0-1	0-0	0-1	0-0	1-0	0-0	3-2
Henke	0-0	0-0	0-2	0-0	0-0	0-0	0-1	0-1	0-0	0-2	0-0	0-0	0-0	0-6
Johnson	1-0	0-1	0-0	0-0	0-1	0-0	0-1	0-0	1-0	0-0	1-1	0-1	0-0	3-5
Key	2-0	3-0	0-0	2-0	2-1	0-2	1-2	0-2	2-0	2-0	1-1	1-0	1-0	17-8
Lavelle	0-0	0-1	0-0	0-0	0-0	1-0	0-0	0-0	0-1	0-0	1-0	0-0	0-0	2-3
Musselman .	1-0	2-0	1-1	1-0	1-0	1-1	0-0	2-0	0-1	0-1	0-0	1-0	2-1	12-5
Niekro	0-0	0-0	0-1	0-1	0-0	0-0	0-0	0-0	0-0	0-0	0-0	0-0	0-0	0-2
Nunez	0-0	0-0	1-0	0-0	0-1	1-1	1-0	0-0	0-0	0-0	0-2	2-0	0-0	5-2
Stieb..........	0-0	1-1	1-1	0-1	2-0	1-0	1-0	0-4	3-0	1-0	1-1	1-1	1-0	13-9
Ward	0-0	0-0	0-0	0-0	0-0	0-0	0-0	1-0	0-0	0-0	0-0	0-0	0-0	1-0
Wells...........	1-0	0-0	1-0	0-0	0-0	0-0	0-1	0-1	0-0	2-1	0-0	0-0	0-0	4-3
Totals	12-1	7-6	7-5	8-4	8-5	6-7	4-8	4-9	9-3	7-6	5-7	10-2	9-3	96-66

No Decisions—Gordon.

OFFICIAL AMERICAN LEAGUE BATTING AVERAGES

Compiled by Elias Sports Bureau

CLUB BATTING

Club	AVG.	G	AB	R	H	TB	2B	3B	HR	RBI	GW RBI	SH	SF	HP	BB	IB	SO	SB	CS	GI DP	LOB	SHO	SLG	OBP
Boston	.278	162	5586	842	1554	2401	273	26	174	802	76	52	58	57	606	41	825	77	45	129	1197	4	.430	.352
Milwaukee	.276	162	5625	862	1552	2405	272	46	163	832	86	63	50	32	598	40	1040	176	74	104	1152	5	.428	.346
Seattle	.272	162	5508	760	1499	2360	282	48	161	717	73	38	50	43	500	19	863	174	73	132	1081	9	.428	.335
Detroit	.272	162	5649	896	1535	2548	274	32	225	840	88	39	56	46	653	44	913	106	50	108	1227	4	.451	.349
Toronto	.269	162	5635	845	1514	2512	277	38	215	790	90	30	35	38	555	45	970	126	50	136	1126	10	.446	.336
Texas	.266	162	5564	823	1478	2394	264	35	194	772	71	42	35	24	555	34	1081	120	71	116	1077	6	.430	.333
Cleveland	.263	162	5606	742	1476	2364	267	30	187	691	56	44	51	31	489	30	977	140	54	103	1133	9	.422	.324
Kansas City	.262	162	5499	715	1443	2266	239	40	168	677	81	34	42	30	523	32	1034	125	43	127	1144	17	.412	.328
New York	.262	162	5511	788	1445	2304	239	16	196	749	85	38	42	28	604	37	949	105	43	150	1119	11	.418	.336
Minnesota	.261	162	5511	786	1422	2338	258	35	196	733	81	47	38	36	523	45	898	113	65	128	1041	9	.430	.328
Oakland	.260	162	5441	806	1432	2358	263	33	199	761	77	50	39	36	523	39	1056	140	63	113	1095	6	.428	.333
Baltimore	.258	162	5576	729	1437	2329	219	20	211	701	64	31	48	22	593	29	939	69	45	139	1104	9	.418	.322
Chicago	.258	162	5538	748	1427	2301	283	36	173	706	76	54	32	33	524	35	971	138	52	117	1061	9	.415	.319
California	.252	162	5570	770	1406	2231	257	26	172	709	70	70	36	35	590	35	926	125	44	115	1145	11	.401	.326
Totals	.265	1134	77819	11112	20620	33111	3667	461	2634	10480	1074	632	629	493	7812	505	13442	1734	772	1717	15702	114	.425	.333

INDIVIDUAL BATTING

(Top Fifteen Qualifiers for Batting Championship—502 or More Plate Appearances)

(*Lefthanded Batter   †Switch-hitter)

Player, Club	AVG.	G	AB	R	H	TB	2B	3B	HR	RBI	GW RBI	SH	SF	HP	BB	IB	SO	SB	CS	GI DP	SLG	OBP
Boggs, Wade, Bos.*	.363	147	551	108	200	324	40	6	24	89	15	1	8	2	105	19	48	1	3	13	.588	.461
Molitor, Paul, Mil.	.353	118	465	114	164	263	41	5	16	75	3	5	1	2	69	2	67	45	10	4	.566	.438
Trammell, Alan, Det.	.343	151	597	109	205	329	34	3	28	105	16	2	6	3	60	8	47	21	2	11	.551	.402
Puckett, Kirby, Minn.	.332	157	624	96	207	333	32	5	28	99	12	0	6	6	32	7	91	12	7	16	.534	.367
Mattingly, Donald, N.Y.*	.327	141	569	93	186	318	38	2	30	115	8	1	8	1	51	13	38	1	4	16	.559	.378
Seitzer, Kevin, K.C.	.323	161	641	105	207	301	33	8	15	83	9	1	2	2	80	4	85	12	7	18	.470	.399
Fernandez, O. Antonio, Tor.†	.322	146	578	90	186	246	29	8	5	67	10	4	5	5	51	3	48	32	12	14	.426	.379
Franco, Julio, Clev.	.319	128	495	86	158	212	24	3	8	52	3	0	3	3	57	1	56	32	9	23	.428	.389
Sheets, Larry, Balt.*	.316	135	469	74	148	264	23	0	31	94	10	0	5	3	31	3	67	1	1	16	.563	.358
Yount, Robin, Mil.	.312	158	635	99	198	304	25	9	21	103	17	6	5	1	76	2	94	19	9	9	.479	.384
Tartabull, Danilo, K.C.	.309	158	582	95	180	315	27	3	34	101	21	0	5	1	79	10	136	9	4	14	.541	.390
Bell, George, Tor.	.308	156	610	111	188	369	34	4	47	134	16	3	9	7	39	9	75	5	1	17	.605	.352
Tabler, Patrick, Clev.	.307	151	553	66	170	243	34	3	11	86	13	3	5	6	51	6	84	5	2	6	.439	.369
Randolph, William, N.Y.	.305	120	449	96	137	186	24	2	7	67	7	5	5	2	82	1	25	11	6	15	.414	.411
Evans, Dwight, Bos.	.305	154	541	109	165	308	37	2	34	123	8	0	7	3	106	6	98	6	6	10	.569	.417

ALL PLAYERS LISTED ALPHABETICALLY
(*Lefthanded Batter †Switch-Hitter)

Player, Club	AVG.	G	AB	R	H	TB	2B	3B	HR	RBI	GW RBI	SH	SF	HP	BB	IB	SO	SB	CS	GI DP	SLG	OBP
Allanson, Andrew, Clev.	.266	50	154	17	41	56	6	1	3	16	1	4	5	0	9	0	30	1	1	2	.364	.298
Armas, Antonio, Cal.	.198	28	81	8	16	30	3	—	3	9	—	1	1	0	9	0	11	1	0	3	.370	.205
Baines, Harold, Chi.*	.293	132	505	59	148	242	26	4	20	93	10	0	2	1	46	2	82	0	0	12	.479	.352
Baker, Douglas, Det.†	.000	8	1	0	0	0	0	0	0	0	—	0	0	0	0	0	1	0	0	0	.000	.000
Balboni, Stephen, K.C.	.207	121	386	44	80	165	11	0	24	60	3	0	3	2	34	1	97	0	0	11	.427	.273
Bando, Christopher, Clev.†	.218	89	211	20	46	70	9	0	5	16	1	0	0	3	12	0	28	0	0	6	.332	.260
Barfield, Jesse, Tor.	.263	159	590	89	155	270	25	3	28	84	12	1	2	3	58	7	141	3	5	13	.458	.331
Barrett, Martin, Bos.	.293	137	559	72	164	196	23	0	3	43	6	6	5	1	51	0	38	15	3	11	.351	.351
Baylor, Donald, Bos.-Minn.	.245	128	388	67	95	152	9	0	16	63	6	0	6	28	45	0	59	5	1	13	.392	.360
Bean, William, Det.*	.258	26	66	6	17	19	2	0	0	4	0	0	0	0	5	0	11	0	0	1	.288	.310
Beane, William, Minn.	.267	12	15	—	4	6	2	0	0	—	—	0	0	0	0	0	6	0	1	0	.400	.267
Bell, George, Tor.	.308	156	610	111	188	369	32	4	47	134	16	0	9	7	39	9	75	5	1	17	.605	.352
Bell, Jay, Clev.	.216	38	125	14	27	44	9	1	2	13	1	3	0	2	8	0	31	2	0	0	.352	.269
Beniquez, Juan, K.C.-Tor.	.251	96	255	20	64	102	12	1	8	47	6	2	3	2	16	1	39	5	4	12	.400	.297
Benzinger, Todd, Bos.†	.278	73	223	36	62	99	11	—	8	43	4	3	3	1	22	3	41	2	1	5	.444	.344
Bergman, David, Det.*	.273	91	172	25	47	78	7	3	6	22	4	0	3	1	30	4	23	5	0	1	.453	.379
Bernazard, Antonio, Clev.-Oak.†	.250	140	507	73	127	199	26	2	14	49	2	7	3	2	55	2	79	11	8	10	.393	.323
Biancalana, Roland, K.C.†	.213	37	47	4	10	14	1	0	1	7	0	7	0	0	1	0	10	0	1	0	.298	.229
Boddicker, Michael, Balt.		34	0	0	0	0	0	0	0	0	—	1	0	0	—	—	0	0	0	0		
Boggs, Wade, Bos.*	.363	147	551	108	200	324	40	6	24	89	15	1	8	2	105	19	48	0	3	13	.588	.461
Bonilla, Juan, N.Y.	.255	23	55	6	14	20	3	0	1	3	0	3	0	0	5	0	6	1	2	2	.364	.317
Boone, Robert, Cal.	.242	128	389	42	94	121	18	0	7	33	1	14	3	8	35	0	36	1	2	10	.311	.304
Bosley, Thaddis, K.C.*	.279	80	140	13	39	50	6	1	1	16	3	0	3	0	9	0	26	2	6	2	.357	.318
Boston, Daryl, Chi.*	.258	103	337	51	87	142	21	2	10	29	2	4	3	0	25	2	68	12	6	5	.421	.307
Bradley, Philip, Sea.	.297	158	603	101	179	279	38	10	14	67	8	4	5	8	84	2	119	40	10	18	.463	.387
Bradley, Scott, Sea.*	.278	102	342	34	95	127	15	1	5	43	3	2	4	3	15	1	18	0	0	13	.371	.310
Braggs, Glenn, Mil.	.269	132	505	67	136	217	28	7	13	77	8	2	7	4	47	7	96	12	5	20	.430	.332
Brantley, Michael, Sea.	.302	92	351	52	106	175	23	2	14	54	4	0	3	0	24	0	44	13	4	2	.499	.344
Brett, George, K.C.*	.290	115	427	71	124	212	18	2	22	78	8	0	8	1	72	14	47	6	4	10	.496	.388
Brock, Gregory, Mil.*	.299	141	532	81	159	233	29	3	13	85	8	9	3	6	57	4	63	5	4	9	.438	.371
Brookens, Thomas, Det.	.241	143	444	59	107	167	15	3	13	59	4	9	3	2	33	3	63	7	4	8	.376	.295
Brower, Robert, Tex.	.261	127	303	63	79	137	10	3	14	46	5	7	2	0	36	3	66	15	9	2	.452	.338
Browne, Jerome, Tex.†	.271	132	454	63	123	154	16	6	6	38	1	1	1	0	61	0	50	27	17	6	.339	.358
Brunansky, Thomas, Minn.	.259	155	532	83	138	260	22	2	32	85	8	1	2	4	74	5	104	11	11	12	.489	.352
Buckner, William, Bos.-Cal.*	.286	132	469	39	134	171	18	2	5	74	8	4	6	0	22	2	26	2	3	13	.365	.314
Buechele, Steven, Tex.	.237	136	363	45	86	145	20	2	13	50	1	0	4	1	28	3	66	2	2	7	.399	.290
Buhner, Jay, N.Y.	.227	7	22	0	5	7	2	0	0	1	—	1	0	0	1	0	6	0	2	1	.318	.261
Burks, Ellis, Bos.	.272	133	558	94	152	246	30	2	20	59	6	4	1	2	41	0	98	27	6	7	.441	.324
Burleson, Richard, Balt.	.209	62	206	26	43	65	14	1	2	14	0	6	0	3	17	0	30	0	3	7	.316	.279
Bush, R. Randall, Minn.*	.253	122	293	46	74	121	10	2	11	46	6	5	5	3	43	5	49	10	3	6	.413	.349
Butera, Salvatore, Minn.	.171	51	111	7	19	27	5	0	1	12	—	2	2	1	7	0	16	0	0	7	.243	.217
Butler, Brett, Clev.*	.295	137	522	91	154	222	25	8	9	41	3	4	2	1	91	6	55	33	16	3	.425	.399
Calderon, Ivan, Chi.	.293	144	542	93	159	285	38	3	28	83	3	0	4	2	60	2	109	10	5	13	.526	.362
Canseco, Jose, Oak.	.257	159	630	81	162	296	35	3	31	113	17	1	9	9	50	6	157	15	3	16	.470	.310
Carter, Joseph, Clev.	.264	149	588	83	155	282	27	2	32	106	12	0	4	2	27	6	105	31	6	8	.480	.304
Castillo, Juan, Mil.†	.224	116	321	44	72	100	11	4	3	28	3	14	1	3	33	0	76	15	7	2	.312	.302
Castillo, M. Carmelo, Clev.	.250	89	220	27	55	105	17	0	11	31	0	1	4	0	16	0	52	1	1	0	.477	.296

Player, Club	AVG.	G	AB	R	H	TB	2B	3B	HR	RBI	GW RBI	SH	SF	HP	BB	IB	SO	SB	CS	GI DP	SLG	OBP
Cerone, Richard, N.Y.	.243	113	284	28	69	95	12	1	4	23	2	5	4	4	30	0	46	0	1	8	.335	.320
Cey, Ronald, Oak.	.221	45	104	12	23	41	6	0	2	11	2	1	1	1	22	1	32	0	0	4	.394	.359
Christensen, John, Sea.	.242	53	132	19	32	46	6	1	1	12	2	2	0	0	12	0	28	2	0	3	.348	.306
Clark, David, Clev.★	.207	29	87	11	18	32	5	0	2	12	0	2	0	0	12	0	24	1	0	4	.368	.225
Coles, Darnell, Det.	.181	53	149	14	27	46	5	1	4	15	1	0	1	2	15	1	23	1	1	1	.309	.263
Cooper, Cecil, Mil.★	.248	63	250	25	62	93	13	0	6	36	5	2	3	0	17	2	51	1	1	4	.372	.293
Cotto, Henry, N.Y.	.235	68	149	21	35	60	10	0	1	20	1	0	0	1	6	0	35	4	2	7	.403	.269
Davidson, J. Mark, Minn.	.267	102	150	32	40	49	4	1	1	14	0	4	0	0	13	1	26	9	0	4	.327	.321
Davis, Alvin, Sea.★	.295	157	580	86	171	299	37	2	29	100	8	0	8	2	72	6	84	0	7	17	.516	.370
Davis, Michael, Oak.★	.265	139	494	69	131	231	32	1	22	72	6	4	6	1	42	5	94	19	4	13	.468	.320
DeCinces, Douglas, Cal.	.234	133	453	65	106	177	23	0	16	63	5	2	3	2	70	6	87	3	0	10	.391	.337
Deer, Robert, Mil.	.238	134	474	71	113	216	15	2	28	80	8	0	1	5	86	6	186	12	0	4	.456	.360
Dempsey, J. Rikard, Clev.	.177	60	141	16	25	38	10	0	1	9	1	4	1	0	23	0	29	0	0	4	.270	.295
Destrade, Orestes, N.Y.†	.263	9	19	5	5	5	0	0	0	1	0	0	0	0	5	0	5	0	0	1	.263	.417
DeWillis, Jeffrey, Tor.	.120	13	25	5	3	7	1	0	0	2	0	0	0	0	2	0	12	0	0	0	.280	.185
Diaz, Mario, Sea.	.304	11	23	2	7	9	0	1	0	3	0	0	0	0	0	1	4	0	0	0	.391	.304
Dodson, Patrick, Bos.★	.167	26	42	4	7	16	3	0	2	6	0	2	2	0	8	0	13	0	0	0	.381	.288
Dorsett, Brian, Clev.	.273	5	11	4	3	6	0	0	1	3	0	0	0	0	0	0	3	0	0	0	.545	.333
Downing, Brian, Cal.	.272	155	567	110	154	276	29	3	29	77	11	0	3	17	106	6	85	5	5	10	.487	.400
Ducey, Robert, Tor.★	.188	34	48	12	9	13	1	0	1	6	1	1	1	0	3	0	10	2	5	0	.271	.298
Dwyer, James, Balt.★	.274	92	241	54	66	120	7	1	15	33	4	0	1	1	37	4	57	4	1	4	.498	.371
Easler, Michael, N.Y.★	.281	65	167	13	47	65	6	0	6	21	4	0	2	0	14	2	32	1	1	4	.389	.337
Eisenreich, James, K.C.★	.238	44	105	10	25	49	8	2	4	21	4	2	3	0	7	0	13	1	0	2	.467	.278
Eppard, James, Cal.★	.333	8	9	2	3	3	0	0	0	0	0	0	0	0	2	0	0	0	0	1	.333	.455
Espy, Cecil, Tex.†	.000	14	8	1	0	0	0	0	0	0	0	1	0	0	1	0	3	2	0	0	.000	.111
Evans, Darrell, Det.★	.257	150	499	90	128	250	20	0	34	99	7	2	6	2	100	8	84	6	5	2	.501	.379
Evans, Dwight, Bos.	.266	154	541	109	165	308	37	2	34	123	8	0	7	3	106	6	98	4	6	10	.569	.417
Felder, Michael, Mil.†	.305	108	289	48	77	102	5	7	2	31	5	9	2	0	28	0	23	34	8	3	.353	.329
Fernandez, O. Antonio, Tor.†	.322	146	578	90	186	246	29	8	5	67	10	4	4	5	51	3	48	32	12	14	.426	.379
Fielder, Cecil, Tor.	.269	82	175	30	47	98	7	1	14	32	3	0	1	1	20	2	48	0	1	6	.560	.345
Fimple, John, Cal.	.200	13	10	1	2	2	0	0	0	1	0	1	0	0	1	0	2	0	0	0	.200	.273
Fisk, Carlton, Chi.	.256	135	454	68	116	209	22	1	23	71	17	0	6	8	39	8	72	1	4	9	.460	.321
Fletcher, Scott, Tex.	.287	156	588	82	169	220	28	4	5	63	4	12	5	5	61	3	66	13	12	14	.374	.358
Franco, Julio, Clev.	.319	128	495	86	158	212	24	3	8	52	3	3	2	3	57	2	56	32	7	23	.428	.389
Frobel, Douglas, Clev.★	.100	29	40	5	4	10	0	0	2	5	1	0	1	0	5	1	13	0	0	1	.250	.196
Gaetti, Gary, Minn.	.257	154	584	95	150	283	36	2	31	109	14	1	3	3	37	7	92	10	9	25	.485	.303
Gagne, Gregory, Minn.	.265	137	437	68	116	188	28	7	10	40	6	10	2	4	25	0	84	6	6	3	.430	.310
Gallagher, David, Clev.	.111	15	36	2	4	7	1	0	0	1	0	1	0	0	2	0	5	2	0	1	.194	.158
Gallego, Michael, Oak.	.250	72	124	18	31	43	6	0	2	14	3	5	1	1	12	0	21	0	1	5	.347	.319
Gantner, James, Mil.★	.272	81	265	37	72	98	14	0	4	30	4	4	3	0	19	2	22	6	2	7	.370	.331
Gedman, Richard, Bos.★	.205	52	151	11	31	42	8	0	1	13	0	1	1	5	10	0	24	0	2	2	.278	.250
Gerhart, H. Kenneth, Balt.	.243	92	284	41	69	125	10	3	14	34	11	1	4	5	17	0	53	9	7	7	.440	.286
Gibson, Kirk, Det.★	.277	128	487	95	135	238	25	2	24	79	7	1	2	3	71	8	117	26	9	5	.489	.372
Gladden, C. Daniel, Minn.	.249	121	438	69	109	158	21	3	8	38	8	2	0	0	38	2	72	25	8	8	.361	.312
Gonzales, Rene, Balt.	.267	37	60	14	16	23	2	0	1	7	0	0	0	6	3	0	11	1	2	2	.383	.302
Greenwell, Michael, Bos.★	.328	125	412	71	135	235	31	6	19	89	8	2	3	4	35	2	40	5	7	7	.570	.386
Griffin, Alfredo, Oak.†	.263	144	494	69	130	172	23	5	3	60	6	10	2	0	28	2	41	26	13	9	.348	.306
Grubb, John, Det.★	.202	59	114	9	23	35	6	1	2	13	1	1	2	7	15	0	16	0	4	9	.307	.290
Gruber, Kelly, Tor.	.235	138	341	50	80	136	14	3	12	36	4	4	2	1	17	2	70	12	2	11	.399	.283
Guillen, Oswaldo, Chi.★	.279	149	560	64	156	198	22	7	2	51	4	13	8	1	22	2	52	25	8	10	.354	.303

Player, Club	AVG.	G	AB	R	H	TB	2B	3B	HR	RBI	GW RBI	SH	SF	HP	BB	1B	SO	SB	CS	GI DP	SLG	OBP
Gutierrez, Joaquin, Balt.	.000	3	1	0	0	0	0	0	0	0	0	0	0	0	0	0	0	0	0	0	.000	.000
Hairston, Jerry, Chi.†	.230	66	126	14	29	52	8	0	5	20	2	1	2	1	25	0	25	0	0	4	.413	.357
Hall, Melvin, Clev.*	.280	142	485	57	136	213	21	1	18	76	4	0	2	1	20	6	68	5	4	7	.439	.309
Harper, Brian, Oak.	.235	11	17	1	4	5	1	0	0	3	0	1	1	0	0	0	4	0	0	2	.294	.222
Harper, Terry, Det.	.203	31	64	4	13	25	3	0	3	10	0	1	0	0	9	0	8	1	0	1	.391	.301
Hart, Michael, Balt.*	.158	34	76	7	12	26	2	0	4	12	1	2	1	0	6	0	19	1	0	9	.342	.217
Hassey, Ronald, Chi.*	.214	49	145	15	31	49	9	0	3	3	0	0	0	0	17	0	11	0	0	1	.338	.303
Hearn, Edward, K.C.	.294	6	17	2	5	7	2	0	0	3	2	0	1	2	4	0	2	0	0	5	.412	.429
Heath, Michael, Det.	.281	93	270	34	76	116	16	0	8	33	1	0	2	0	21	2	42	1	1	3	.430	.339
Henderson, David, Bos.	.234	75	184	30	43	77	10	3	8	25	4	0	0	3	22	0	48	1	0	10	.418	.313
Henderson, Rickey, N.Y.	.291	95	358	78	104	178	17	3	17	37	1	0	1	2	80	1	52	41	8	0	.497	.423
Henderson, Stephen, Oak.	.289	46	114	14	33	49	7	0	3	9	7	4	2	2	12	0	19	0	0	7	.430	.357
Hendrick, George, Cal.	.241	65	162	14	39	64	10	0	5	25	0	0	0	2	14	1	18	0	0	8	.395	.301
Hengel, David, Sea.	.316	10	19	2	6	9	0	0	1	0	3	0	0	0	0	0	4	0	0	2	.474	.316
Henneman, Michael, Det.	.000	55		0	0	0	0	0	0	0	0	0	0	0	0	0	1	0	0	0	.000	.000
Herndon, Larry, Det.	.324	89	225	32	73	117	13	2	9	47	3	0	6	0	23	0	35	1	0	12	.520	.378
Hill, Donald, Chi.†	.239	111	410	57	98	151	14	6	9	46	8	6	4	1	30	0	35	0	0	11	.368	.290
Hinzo, Thomas, Clev.†	.265	67	257	31	68	92	17	3	3	21	1	0	1	2	14	1	47	4	4	6	.358	.296
Hoffman, Glenn, Bos.	.200	21	55	5	11	14	9	0	0	6	0	10	0	2	3	0	9	0	0	2	.255	.267
Horn, Samuel, Bos.*	.278	46	158	31	44	93	3	0	14	34	4	0	2	2	17	0	55	0	0	2	.589	.356
Howell, Jack, Cal.*	.245	138	449	64	110	207	7	5	23	64	6	1	5	2	57	0	118	4	1	5	.461	.331
Hrbek, Kent, Minn.*	.285	143	477	85	136	260	18	1	34	90	10	0	5	0	84	4	60	5	3	13	.545	.389
Hughes, Keith, N.Y.*	.000	4	4	0	0	0	0	0	0	0	0	0	0	0	0	0	2	0	0	0	.000	.000
Hulett, Timothy, Chi.	.217	68	240	20	52	83	10	0	7	28	3	5	2	0	10	1	41	0	2	6	.346	.246
Incaviglia, Peter, Tex.	.271	139	509	85	138	253	26	4	27	80	7	0	5	1	48	1	168	9	3	8	.497	.332
Infante, F. Alexis, Tor.		1		0														0				
Iorg, Garth, Tor.	.210	122	310	35	65	88	11	0	4	30	3	6	2	2	21	0	52	2	2	8	.284	.262
Jackson, Reginald, Oak.*	.220	115	336	42	74	135	14	1	15	43	3	0	1	4	33	0	97	2	2	3	.402	.297
Jackson, Vincent, K.C.	.235	116	396	46	93	180	17	2	22	53	3	0	2	5	30	0	158	10	4	4	.455	.296
Jacoby, Brook, Clev.	.300	155	540	73	162	292	26	4	32	69	3	0	2	3	75	3	73	2	3	19	.541	.387
Javier, Stanley, Oak.†	.185	81	151	22	28	39	3	1	2	9	0	6	0	0	19	0	33	3	2	2	.258	.276
Jones, Ross, K.C.	.254	39	114	10	29	37	4	2	0	10	1	0	3	1	5	0	15	1	0	5	.325	.285
Jones, Ruppert, Cal.*	.245	85	192	25	47	83	8	2	8	28	4	0	3	0	20	2	38	2	1	4	.432	.316
Joyner, Wallace, Cal.*	.285	149	564	100	161	298	33	1	34	117	7	1	0	5	72	12	64	8	2	14	.528	.366
Karkovice, Ronald, Chi.	.071	39	85	7	6	12	0	0	2	7	1	2	0	2	7	0	40	0	0	2	.141	.160
Kearney, Robert, Sea.	.170	24	47	5	8	14	4	1	0	1	0	5	1	0	7	0	9	0	0	0	.298	.188
Keedy, C. Patrick, Chi.	.171	17	41	6	7	14	1	0	2	7	1	3	2	0	1	0	14	0	0	0	.341	.209
Kelly, Roberto, N.Y.	.269	23	52	12	14	20	3	1	1	7	1	0	6	1	2	0	15	9	3	3	.385	.328
Kennedy, Terrence, Balt.*	.250	143	512	51	128	197	13	3	18	62	7	1	3	2	35	6	112	0	0	13	.385	.299
Kiefer, Steven, Mil.	.202	28	99	17	20	39	4	0	5	17	2	2	1	1	7	0	28	0	0	3	.394	.257
Kingery, Michael, Sea.*	.280	120	354	38	99	159	25	4	9	52	5	5	0	2	27	0	43	7	9	4	.449	.329
Kittle, Ronald, N.Y.	.277	59	159	21	44	85	5	0	12	28	3	3	0	6	10	1	36	0	1	4	.535	.318
Knight, C. Ray, Balt.	.256	150	563	46	144	210	24	1	14	65	7	0	1	0	39	3	90	0	0	16	.373	.310
Komminsk, Brad, Mil.	.067	7	15	0	1	1	0	0	0	0	0	1	3	0	1	0	7	0	0	0	.067	.125
Kunkel, Jeffrey, Tex.	.219	15	32	1	7	10	0	0	1	2	0	2	2	9	0	0	10	0	0	0	.313	.242
Lacy, Leondaus, Balt.	.244	87	258	35	63	103	13	3	7	28	3	5	2	2	32	3	49	3	1	5	.399	.326
Lansford, Carney, Oak.	.289	151	554	89	160	252	27	4	19	76	9	3	1	1	60	11	44	27	8	9	.455	.366
Larkin, Eugene, Minn.†	.266	85	233	23	62	89	11	2	4	28	5	2	3	3	25	3	31	1	4	4	.382	.340
Laudner, Timothy, Minn.	.191	113	288	30	55	112	7	1	16	43	5	5	2	2	23	0	80	1	0	4	.389	.252
Leach, Richard, Tor.*	.282	98	195	26	55	79	13	1	3	25	5	3	1	3	25	2	25	0	1	3	.405	.371

Player, Club	AVG.	G	AB	R	H	TB	2B	3B	HR	RBI	GW RBI	SH	SF	HP	BB	IB	SO	SB	CS	GI DP	SLG	OBP
Lee, Manuel, Tor.†	.256	56	121	14	31	42	2	3	1	11	1	1	1	0	6	0	13	2	0	1	.347	.289
LeMaster, Johnnie, Oak.	.083	20	24	3	2	2	0	0	0	1	0	0	0	0	1	0	4	0	0	0	.083	.120
Lemon, Chester, Det.	.277	146	470	75	130	226	30	3	20	75	6	0	5	8	70	7	82	13	9	17	.481	.376
Lindsey, William, Chi.	.188	9	16	2	3	3	0	0	0	0	0	2	1	0	0	0	3	0	0	0	.188	.176
Liriano, Nelson, Tor.†	.241	37	158	29	38	54	6	2	2	10	0	2	0	0	16	1	22	13	2	2	.342	.310
Lombardi, Phillip, N.Y.	.125	5	8	0	1	1	0	0	0	0	0	0	1	0	0	0	2	0	0	0	.125	.125
Lombardozzi, Stephen, Minn.	.238	136	432	51	103	152	19	3	8	38	4	9	0	4	33	0	66	5	1	10	.352	.298
Lowry, Dwight, Det.★	.200	13	25	0	5	7	2	1	0	4	0	0	0	0	0	0	6	0	0	0	.280	.200
Lusader, Scott, Det.★	.319	23	47	8	15	23	3	1	1	8	2	0	1	0	5	1	7	3	3	0	.489	.377
Lynn, Frederic, Balt.★	.253	111	396	49	100	193	24	1	23	60	5	4	2	4	39	6	72	3	7	8	.487	.320
Lyons, Stephen, Chi.★	.280	76	193	26	54	70	11	0	1	19	3	1	1	1	12	0	37	4	1	4	.363	.320
Macfarlane, Michael, K.C.	.211	8	19	4	4	5	1	0	0	3	0	0	0	0	2	0	2	0	0	1	.263	.286
Madison, C. Scott, K.C.†	.267	7	15	4	4	7	3	0	0	0	0	1	0	0	1	0	5	0	0	0	.467	.313
Madlock, Bill, Det.	.279	87	326	56	91	150	17	1	14	50	10	0	4	0	28	1	45	4	3	10	.460	.351
Manning, Richard, Mil.★	.228	97	114	21	26	35	7	1	0	13	2	8	1	0	12	0	18	4	3	3	.307	.299
Manrique, R. Fred, Chi.	.258	115	298	30	77	108	13	2	4	29	2	2	3	1	19	1	69	5	0	4	.362	.302
Martinez, Edgar, Sea.	.372	13	43	6	16	25	5	0	0	5	0	0	0	3	2	0	5	0	1	0	.581	.413
Marzano, John, Bos.	.244	52	168	20	41	67	11	0	5	24	1	2	2	1	7	0	41	0	0	2	.399	.283
Matthews, Gary, Sea.	.235	45	119	10	28	38	1	2	3	15	3	0	1	0	15	0	22	1	4	6	.319	.319
Mattingly, Donald, N.Y.★	.327	141	569	93	186	318	38	2	30	115	8	0	8	1	51	13	38	0	1	16	.559	.378
McCaskill, Kirk, Cal.		15																				
McDowell, Oddibe, Tex.★	.241	128	407	65	98	174	26	4	14	52	6	3	2	5	51	0	99	24	2	8	.428	.324
McGriff, Frederick, Tor.★	.247	107	295	58	73	149	16	0	20	43	5	0	0	5	60	4	104	3	1	3	.505	.376
McGwire, Mark, Oak.	.289	151	557	97	161	344	28	4	49	118	14	0	8	5	71	8	131	1	1	6	.618	.370
McLemore, Mark, Cal.†	.236	138	433	61	102	130	13	3	3	41	7	15	3	0	48	0	72	25	8	7	.300	.310
McRae, Harold, K.C.	.313	18	32	5	10	16	3	1	1	9	1	0	1	0	5	1	1	0	0	1	.500	.405
Meacham, Robert, N.Y.	.271	77	203	28	55	83	11	3	0	21	2	2	1	2	19	0	33	6	5	2	.409	.349
Meier, David, Tex.	.286	13	21	4	6	7	1	0	0	0	0	0	0	0	0	0	4	6	0	0	.333	.286
Mercado, Orlando, Det.	.136	10	22	2	3	3	0	0	0	1	1	5	1	1	2	0	0	0	0	0	.136	.208
Miller, Darrell, Cal.	.241	53	108	14	26	43	5	1	4	16	3	5	3	1	9	2	13	0	0	5	.398	.303
Molitor, Paul, Mil.	.353	118	465	114	164	263	41	5	16	75	7	4	1	2	69	2	67	45	10	4	.566	.438
Moore, Charles, Tor.	.215	51	107	15	23	38	10	1	1	7	1	7	0	1	13	0	12	0	0	2	.355	.306
Moore, Michael, Sea.	.000	33	11	0	0	0	0	0	0	0	0	1	0	0	0	0	0	0	0	0	.000	.000
Moronko, Jeffrey, N.Y.	.091	7	11	0	1	1	0	0	0	0	0	0	0	0	0	0	2	0	0	0	.091	.167
Morris, John, Det.	.000	36		0	0	0	0	0	0	0	0	0	0	0	0	0	0	0	0	0	.000	.000
Morrison, James, Det.	.205	34	117	15	24	39	3	0	4	16	0	0	0	0	2	0	26	2	2	1	.333	.221
Moseby, Lloyd, Tor.★	.282	155	592	106	167	280	27	4	26	96	8	3	2	2	70	4	124	39	15	11	.473	.358
Moses, John, Sea.†	.246	116	390	58	96	129	16	4	3	38	3	8	3	3	29	2	49	23	1	6	.331	.301
Mulliniks, S. Rance, Tor.★	.310	124	332	37	103	166	28	1	11	44	3	3	3	3	34	1	55	1	4	10	.500	.371
Murphy, Dwayne, Oak.★	.233	82	219	39	51	82	7	0	8	35	1	3	4	3	58	2	61	0	4	5	.374	.388
Murray, Eddie, Balt.†	.277	160	618	89	171	295	28	3	30	91	8	0	3	0	73	6	80	0	0	15	.477	.352
Myers, Gregory, Tor.★	.111	7	9	1	1	1	0	0	0	0	0	0	0	0	0	0	3	0	1	2	.111	.111
Narron, Jerry, Sea.★	.000	4	8	0	0	0	0	0	0	0	0	0	0	0	0	0	2	0	0	0	.000	.000
Nelson, Robert, Oak.	.167	7	24	1	4	5	1	0	0	0	0	0	0	0	0	0	12	0	0	0	.208	.167
Nelson, W. Eugene, Oak.		55																				
Newman, Albert, Minn.†	.221	110	307	44	68	93	15	5	0	29	4	7	1	3	34	0	27	15	11	5	.303	.298
Nichols, Carl, Balt.	.381	13	21	4	8	9	1	0	0	3	0	1	0	0	1	0	4	0	1	0	.429	.409
Nieto, Thomas, Minn.	.200	41	105	7	21	33	7	1	1	12	2	5	0	3	8	0	24	2	0	1	.314	.276
Nixon, Otis, Clev.†	.059	19	17	2	1	1	0	0	0	1	0	0	0	0	3	0	4	2	3	0	.059	.200
Nixon, R. Donell, Sea.	.250	46	132	17	33	46	4	0	3	12	2	4	0	2	13	0	28	21	7	3	.348	.327

Player, Club	AVG.	G	AB	R	H	TB	2B	3B	HR	RBI	GW RBI	SH	SF	HP	BB	IB	SO	SB	CS	GI DP	SLG	OBP
Noboa, Milciades, Clev.	.225	39	80	7	18	22	2	1	0	7	1	5	0	0	3	1	6	1	0	1	.275	.253
Nokes, Matthew, Det.*	.289	135	461	69	133	247	14	2	32	87	6	3	3	6	35	2	70	2	1	13	.536	.345
Nunez, Jose, Tor.	.000	38	4	0	0	0	0	0	0	0	0	0	0	0	0	0	0	0	1	0	.000	....
O'Brien, Charles, Mil.	.200	10	35	2	7	12	3	1	0	0	0	1	0	0	4	0	4	0	1	0	.343	.282
O'Brien, Peter, Tex.*	.286	159	569	84	163	260	26	1	23	88	14	0	10	0	59	6	61	0	4	9	.457	.348
O'Malley, Thomas, Tex.*	.274	45	117	10	32	43	8	0	1	12	1	0	2	0	15	1	9	0	0	7	.368	.351
Orta, Jorge, K.C.*	.180	21	50	3	9	19	4	0	2	4	2	0	0	0	3	1	8	0	0	0	.380	.226
Owen, Lawrence, K.C.	.189	76	164	17	31	52	6	0	5	14	4	7	4	1	16	0	51	0	0	5	.317	.260
Owen, Spike, Bos.†	.259	132	437	50	113	150	17	5	5	48	3	9	4	2	53	2	43	11	8	9	.343	.337
Paciorek, James, Mil.	.228	48	101	16	23	34	5	0	2	10	0	0	3	0	12	0	20	1	0	3	.337	.302
Paciorek, Thomas, Tex.	.283	27	60	6	17	29	5	0	2	12	0	7	1	1	1	0	19	0	0	3	.483	.302
Pagliarulo, Michael, N.Y.*	.234	150	522	76	122	250	26	3	32	87	12	2	3	2	53	9	111	1	3	9	.479	.305
Parrish, Larry, Tex.	.268	152	557	79	149	269	22	1	32	100	9	0	3	0	49	7	154	3	1	10	.483	.328
Parsons, Casey, Clev.*	.160	18	25	2	4	7	0	1	0	5	0	2	0	1	0	0	5	0	0	2	.280	.160
Pasqua, Daniel, N.Y.*	.233	113	318	42	74	134	7	1	17	42	7	0	2	0	40	3	99	0	2	7	.421	.319
Pecota, William, K.C.	.276	66	156	22	43	59	5	1	3	14	2	2	1	1	15	0	25	5	0	3	.378	.343
Petralli, Eugene, Tex.†	.302	101	202	28	61	97	11	2	7	31	3	1	0	2	27	2	29	0	2	4	.480	.388
Pettis, Gary, Cal.†	.208	133	394	49	82	102	13	2	1	17	0	6	1	1	52	5	124	24	5	8	.259	.302
Phelps, Kenneth, Sea.*	.259	120	332	68	86	182	13	0	27	68	6	0	4	0	80	10	75	1	1	7	.548	.410
Phillips, K. Anthony, Oak.†	.240	111	379	48	91	141	20	0	10	46	5	2	3	0	57	1	76	3	6	9	.372	.337
Pittaro, Christopher, Minn.†	.333	14	12	6	4	4	0	0	0	0	0	0	0	0	0	0	0	0	0	0	.333	.385
Polidor, Gustavo, Cal.	.263	63	137	12	36	45	9	0	0	15	3	8	0	0	2	0	15	1	7	3	.328	.277
Polonia, Luis, Oak.*	.287	125	435	78	125	173	16	10	4	49	6	2	1	1	32	0	64	29	7	4	.398	.335
Porter, Darrell, Tex.*	.238	85	130	19	31	55	3	0	7	21	4	1	2	2	30	1	43	0	0	2	.423	.387
Presley, James, Sea.	.247	152	575	78	142	249	23	6	24	88	6	0	6	2	38	4	157	2	7	15	.433	.296
Puckett, Kirby, Minn.	.332	157	624	96	207	333	32	5	28	99	12	0	3	6	32	12	91	12	7	16	.534	.367
Quinones, Rey, Sea.	.276	135	478	55	132	190	18	2	12	56	8	6	3	1	26	7	71	1	3	14	.397	.317
Quirk, James, K.C.*	.236	109	296	24	70	102	17	0	5	33	2	2	4	0	28	1	56	1	1	8	.345	.307
Ramos, Domingo, Sea.	.311	42	103	9	32	44	6	0	2	11	1	5	0	0	3	0	12	0	0	1	.427	.336
Randolph, William, N.Y.	.305	120	449	96	137	186	24	2	7	67	7	2	5	1	82	0	25	11	1	15	.414	.411
Ray, Johnny, Cal.†	.346	30	127	16	44	55	11	0	2	15	0	0	1	0	3	1	10	1	1	4	.433	.359
Rayford, Floyd, Balt.	.220	20	50	5	11	17	0	0	2	3	0	3	0	3	9	0	9	0	0	2	.340	.250
Redus, Gary, Chi.	.236	130	475	78	112	186	26	6	12	48	3	1	2	1	69	0	90	52	11	7	.392	.328
Reed, Jody, Bos.	.300	9	30	4	9	12	1	1	0	8	0	3	0	0	4	0	2	1	0	0	.400	.382
Renteria, Richard, Sea.	.100	12	10	2	1	2	1	0	0	0	0	0	0	0	1	0	2	0	1	1	.200	.182
Reynolds, Harold, Sea.†	.275	160	530	73	146	196	31	8	1	35	4	8	5	0	39	1	34	60	20	7	.370	.325
Rice, James, Bos.	.277	108	404	66	112	165	14	0	13	62	7	0	3	2	45	3	77	1	0	22	.408	.357
Riles, Ernest, Mil.*	.261	83	276	38	72	97	11	1	4	38	8	3	6	1	30	3	47	3	4	6	.351	.329
Ripken, Calvin, Balt.	.252	162	624	97	157	272	28	3	27	98	11	0	11	1	81	27	77	3	5	19	.436	.333
Ripken, William, Balt.	.308	58	234	27	72	87	9	0	2	20	3	7	1	1	21	0	23	4	1	3	.372	.363
Robidoux, William, Mil.*	.194	23	62	9	12	12	0	0	0	4	0	0	2	0	8	0	17	0	0	0	.194	.286
Romero, Edgardo, Bos.	.272	88	235	23	64	69	5	0	0	14	0	2	0	1	18	0	22	1	2	9	.294	.322
Romine, Kevin, Bos.	.292	9	24	5	7	9	2	0	0	2	0	0	0	0	0	0	6	2	0	0	.375	.346
Royster, Jeron, Chi.-N.Y.	.265	73	196	26	52	86	13	0	7	27	3	2	2	0	23	1	32	4	2	5	.439	.342
Ryal, Mark, Cal.*	.200	58	100	7	20	41	6	0	5	18	0	1	2	0	3	1	15	0	2	0	.410	.223
Sakata, Lenn, N.Y.	.267	19	45	5	12	20	2	0	2	4	0	8	0	0	2	0	4	0	0	2	.444	.313
Salas, Mark, Minn.-N.Y.*	.250	72	160	21	40	64	6	0	6	21	2	1	2	3	15	1	23	0	1	1	.400	.322
Salazar, Argenis, K.C.	.205	116	317	24	65	78	7	0	2	21	1	8	0	0	6	0	46	4	4	6	.246	.219
Sanchez, Alejandro, Oak.	.000	2	3	0	0	0	0	0	0	0	0	0	0	0	0	0	1	0	0	0	.000	.000
Sax, David, Bos.	.000	2	3	0	0	0	0	0	0	0	0	0	0	0	0	0	1	0	0	0	.000	.000

Player, Club	AVG.	G	AB	R	H	TB	2B	3B	HR	RBI	GW RBI	SH	SF	HP	BB	IB	SO	SB	CS	GI DP	SLG	OBP
Schofield, Richard, Cal.	.251	134	479	52	120	170	17	3	9	46	3	10	3	2	37	0	63	19	3	4	.355	.305
Schroeder, A. William, Mil.	.332	75	250	35	83	137	12	0	14	42	4	1	0	3	16	0	56	5	2	3	.548	.379
Seitzer, Kevin, K.C.	.323	161	641	105	207	301	33	8	15	83	9	1	1	2	80	0	85	12	7	18	.470	.399
Sharperson, Michael, Tor.	.208	32	96	4	20	26	4	1	0	9	0	1	1	1	7	0	15	2	1	2	.271	.269
Sheaffer, Danny, Bos.	.121	25	66	5	8	12	1	0	1	5	1	1	0	0	1	1	14	0	0	2	.182	.119
Sheets, Larry, Balt.*	.316	135	469	74	148	264	23	0	31	94	10	0	5	3	31	1	67	1	1	16	.563	.358
Shelby, John, Balt.†	.188	21	32	4	6	9	0	0	1	3	0	1	0	0	0	0	13	18	13	0	.281	.212
Sheridan, Patrick, Det.*	.259	141	421	57	109	152	19	3	6	49	5	2	5	1	44	4	90	16	11	7	.361	.327
Sierra, Ruben, Tex.†	.263	158	643	97	169	302	35	4	30	109	11	3	12	2	39	4	114	16	11	18	.470	.302
Simmons, Nelson, Balt.†	.265	16	49	3	13	19	1	0	1	4	1	1	0	0	3	0	8	0	0	3	.388	.296
Sinatro, Matt, Oak.	.000	6	3	0	0	0	0	0	0	0	0	0	0	0	0	0	1	0	0	1	.000	.000
Skinner, Joel, N.Y.	.137	64	139	9	19	32	4	2	3	14	2	4	2	1	8	0	46	0	0	9	.230	.187
Slaught, Donald, Tex.	.224	95	237	25	53	96	15	1	8	16	1	4	0	1	24	3	51	2	3	7	.405	.298
Smalley, Roy, Minn.†	.275	110	309	32	85	127	16	1	8	34	1	0	1	0	36	1	52	0	0	7	.411	.352
Smith, Brick, Sea.	.125	5	8	1	1	1	0	0	0	0	0	1	0	0	2	0	4	0	0	0	.125	.300
Smith, Lonnie, K.C.	.251	48	167	26	42	60	7	1	3	8	1	2	2	4	24	0	31	9	4	3	.359	.355
Snyder, J. Cory, Clev.	.236	157	577	74	136	263	24	2	33	82	12	0	6	1	31	4	166	9	1	2	.456	.273
Stanicek, Peter, Balt.†	.274	30	113	9	31	34	3	0	0	9	1	1	0	2	8	1	19	5	0	0	.301	.333
Stanicek, Stephen, Mil.	.286	4	7	2	2	2	0	0	0	0	0	0	0	0	0	0	2	8	0	0	.286	.286
Stanley, R. Michael, Tex.	.273	78	216	34	59	87	8	1	6	37	3	3	4	1	31	0	48	3	2	6	.403	.361
Stark, Matthew, Tor.	.083	5	12	0	1	1	0	0	0	0	0	0	0	0	0	0	0	0	0	0	.083	.083
Steinbach, Terry, Oak.	.284	122	391	66	111	181	16	3	16	56	5	6	3	9	32	2	66	1	0	10	.463	.349
Stieb, David, Tor.		34	0	0	0	0	0	0	0	0	0	6	0	0	0	0	0	0	0	0		
Sullivan, Marc, Bos.	.169	60	160	11	27	38	5	0	2	10	0	5	1	2	4	0	43	0	0	5	.237	.198
Surhoff, William J., Mil.*	.299	115	395	50	118	167	22	3	7	68	9	5	9	0	36	1	30	11	10	13	.423	.350
Sveum, Dale, Mil.†	.252	153	535	86	135	243	27	3	25	95	6	5	5	1	40	4	133	2	6	11	.454	.303
Tabler, Patrick, Clev.	.307	151	553	66	170	243	34	3	11	86	13	0	5	6	51	6	84	5	5	2	.439	.369
Tabor, Gregory, Tex.	.111	9	9	4	1	2	1	0	0	1	0	5	0	0	0	0	4	0	0	0	.222	.111
Tartabull, Danilo, K.C.	.309	158	582	95	180	315	27	3	34	101	21	2	5	1	79	2	136	9	1	14	.541	.390
Tettleton, Mickey, Oak.†	.194	82	211	19	41	68	3	0	8	26	0	2	2	0	30	0	65	1	0	3	.322	.292
Thornton, Andre, Clev.	.118	36	85	8	10	12	2	0	0	5	0	0	2	0	10	0	25	0	1	1	.141	.206
Thornton, Louis, Tor.*	.500	12	2	5	1	1	0	0	0	0	1	5	0	0	1	0	0	7	2	1	.500	.667
Thurman, Gary, K.C.	.296	27	81	12	24	26	2	1	0	5	4	0	0	0	8	0	20	5	3	1	.321	.360
Tolleson, J. Wayne, N.Y.†	.221	121	349	48	77	84	4	0	0	22	0	6	1	1	43	1	72	0	2	3	.241	.306
Tolman, Timothy, Det.	.083	9	12	3	1	2	1	0	0	1	0	2	0	0	7	0	2	0	0	1	.167	.429
Trammell, Alan, Det.	.343	151	597	109	205	329	34	3	28	105	16	3	6	3	60	8	47	21	11	11	.551	.402
Upshaw, Willie, Tor.*	.244	150	512	68	125	200	22	4	15	58	9	0	4	3	58	4	78	10	2	7	.391	.324
Valle, David, Sea.	.256	95	324	40	83	141	16	3	12	53	9	0	0	3	15	2	46	0	0	13	.435	.292
Van Gorder, David, Balt.	.238	12	21	4	5	8	0	0	1	4	0	2	0	0	3	0	6	2	0	1	.381	.333
Velarde, Randy, N.Y.	.182	8	22	1	4	4	0	1	0	1	0	1	0	0	0	0	6	0	1	1	.182	.182
Walewander, James, Det.†	.241	53	54	24	13	21	3	2	1	4	0	2	0	5	7	0	6	9	1	1	.389	.328
Walker, Gregory, Chi.*	.256	157	566	85	145	263	33	1	27	94	8	0	5	1	75	7	112	2	2	12	.465	.346
Ward, Gary, N.Y.	.248	146	529	65	131	203	22	0	16	78	11	1	4	0	33	2	101	10	9	20	.384	.291
Washington, Claudell, N.Y.*	.279	102	312	42	87	131	17	1	9	44	4	2	0	0	27	2	54	10	5	3	.420	.336
Washington, Ronald, Balt.	.203	26	79	7	16	24	3	0	1	6	1	0	0	0	2	0	15	1	0	2	.304	.213
Weaver, James, Sea.*	.000	7	4	2	0	0	0	0	0	0	0	4	0	0	1	0	3	3	1	0	.000	.333
Weiss, Walter, Oak.†	.462	16	26	3	12	16	4	0	0	1	0	4	4	1	2	0	11	1	2	0	.615	.500
Whitaker, Louis, Det.*	.265	149	604	110	160	258	38	6	16	59	8	14	2	2	71	2	108	13	5	5	.427	.341
White, Devon, Cal.†	.263	159	639	103	168	283	33	5	24	87	11	4	4	2	39	2	135	32	11	8	.443	.306
White, Frank, K.C.	.245	154	563	67	138	225	32	2	17	78	12	4	4	2	51	5	86	1	3	16	.400	.308

Player, Club	AVG	G	AB	R	H	TB	2B	3B	HR	RBI	GW RBI	SH	SF	HP	BB	IB	SO	SB	CS	GI DP	SLG	OBP
Whitt, L. Ernest, Tor.*	.269	135	446	57	120	203	24	1	19	75	8	3	3	1	44	4	50	1	1	17	.455	.334
Wiggins, Alan, Balt.†	.232	85	306	37	71	82	4	2	1	15	2	6	1	1	28	0	34	20	7	6	.268	.298
Wilkerson, Curtis, Tex.†	.268	85	138	28	37	54	5	3	0	14	1	0	0	2	6	0	16	6	3	2	.391	.308
Willard, Gerald, Oak.*	.167	7	6	0	1	1	0	0	0	1	0	0	0	0	2	0	1	0	0	0	.167	.375
Williams, Edward, Clev.	.172	22	64	9	11	18	4	0	1	4	1	0	1	1	9	0	19	0	0	2	.281	.280
Williams, Kenneth, Chi.	.281	116	391	48	110	165	18	0	11	50	4	3	0	9	10	0	83	21	10	5	.422	.314
Wilson, Michael, Cal.	.500	7	2	5	1	1	0	0	0	0	0	1	0	0	1	0	0	0	0	0	.500	.667
Wilson, Willie, K.C.†	.279	146	610	97	170	230	18	15	4	30	2	1	3	0	32	2	88	59	11	9	.377	.320
Winfield, David, N.Y.	.275	156	575	83	158	263	22	1	27	97	8	0	5	6	76	5	96	5	6	20	.457	.358
Witt, Robert, Tex.	.000	27	1	4	0	0	0	0	0	0	0	4	0	0	0	0	1	0	0	0	.000	.277
Wynegar, Harold, Cal.†	.207	31	92	4	19	21	2	0	0	5	0	1	0	0	9	0	13	0	0	2	.228	.277
Young, Curtis, Oak.	.000	31	1	0	0	0	0	0	0	0	0	0	0	0	0	0	0	0	0	0	.000	.000
Young, Michael, Balt.†	.240	110	363	46	87	147	10	1	16	39	4	0	1	2	46	2	91	10	7	7	.405	.328
Yount, Robin, Mil.	.312	158	635	99	198	304	25	9	21	103	17	6	5	1	76	10	94	19	9	9	.479	.384
Zuvella, Paul, N.Y.	.176	14	34	2	6	6	0	0	0	2	0	2	0	0	0	0	4	0	0	1	.176	.176

PLAYERS WITH TWO OR MORE CLUBS DURING 1987 SEASON

(Listed alphabetically, first club on top)

Player, Club	AVG	G	AB	R	H	TB	2B	3B	HR	RBI	GW RBI	SH	SF	HP	BB	IB	SO	SB	CS	GI DP	SLG	OBP
Baylor, Donald, Bos.	.239	108	339	64	81	137	8	0	16	57	6	0	6	24	40	3	47	5	2	10	.404	.355
Baylor, Donald, Minn.	.286	20	49	3	14	15	1	0	0	6	0	2	0	4	5	1	12	0	1	3	.306	.397
Beniquez, Juan, K.C.	.236	57	174	14	41	57	7	0	3	26	4	0	2	1	11	1	26	0	0	3	.328	.282
Beniquez, Juan, Tor.	.284	39	81	6	23	45	5	1	5	21	2	2	1	1	5	0	13	0	0	3	.556	.330
Bernazard, Antonio, Clev.	.239	79	293	39	70	117	12	1	11	30	2	4	1	0	25	2	49	7	4	4	.399	.300
Bernazard, Antonio, Oak.	.266	61	214	34	57	82	14	1	3	19	2	3	2	0	30	0	30	4	4	6	.383	.354
Buckner, William, Bos.	.273	75	286	23	78	92	6	1	2	42	6	0	5	0	13	1	19	1	3	10	.322	.299
Buckner, William, Cal.	.306	57	183	16	56	79	12	1	3	32	2	1	1	1	9	1	7	1	0	3	.432	.337
Royster, Jeron, Chi.	.240	55	154	25	37	69	11	0	7	23	3	3	2	1	19	0	28	2	2	2	.448	.324
Royster, Jeron, N.Y.	.357	18	42	1	15	17	2	0	0	4	2	2	0	0	4	1	4	2	1	0	.405	.413
Salas, Mark, Minn.	.378	22	45	8	17	28	2	0	3	9	0	0	1	0	5	1	6	0	1	0	.622	.431
Salas, Mark, N.Y.	.200	50	115	13	23	36	4	0	3	12	1	1	3	3	10	0	17	0	0	2	.313	.279

OFFICIAL AMERICAN LEAGUE DESIGNATED HITTING

CLUB DESIGNATED HITTING

Club	AVG	G	AB	R	H	TB	2B	3B	HR	RBI	GW RBI	SH	SF	HP	BB	IB	SO	SB	CS	GI DP	SLG	OBP
California	.278	162	630	106	175	300	35	3	28	89	9	3	3	12	95	5	74	3	5	13	.476	.381
Milwaukee	.273	162	662	96	181	277	36	3	16	98	9	2	6	1	70	5	132	24	11	11	.418	.341
New York	.271	162	627	93	170	297	31	3	30	85	9	0	2	3	66	4	124	19	6	16	.474	.342
Chicago	.271	162	642	83	174	288	35	5	23	105	10	1	4	4	64	3	103	1	9	13	.449	.340
Minnesota	.265	162	585	69	155	243	28	3	18	70	5	1	8	8	65	5	99	5	2	11	.415	.344
Texas	.262	162	606	90	159	280	26	1	31	100	11	1	2	4	72	7	177	4	3	13	.462	.342
Toronto	.258	162	592	101	153	305	32	3	38	97	13	1	4	8	83	6	160	3	3	11	.515	.353
Seattle	.258	162	573	93	148	272	18	0	34	109	15	2	5	8	103	5	122	2	5	13	.475	.374
Detroit	.254	162	635	109	161	282	25	3	32	112	11	9	10	9	78	3	108	6	5	19	.444	.339

Club	AVG.	G	AB	R	H	TB	2B	3B	HR	RBI	GW RBI	SH	SF	HP	BB	1B	SO	SB	CS	GI DP	SLG	OBP
Cleveland	.249	162	607	77	151	235	40	1	14	80	12	2	7	6	63	4	124	10	5	12	.387	.322
Boston	.248	162	600	114	149	270	19	0	34	105	10	7	6	27	75	4	113	5	4	22	.450	.355
Baltimore	.235	162	630	76	148	215	14	1	17	60	6	7	8	2	67	3	123	14	2	17	.341	.310
Kansas City	.215	162	599	78	129	246	14	6	25	91	11	2	8	4	61	8	113	7	5	11	.411	.289
Oakland	.203	162	617	81	125	219	30	2	22	74	8	4	8	5	65	2	163	5	5	15	.355	.281
Totals	.253	1134	8605	1266	2178	3729	393	36	362	1275	131	34	75	98	1027	62	1735	108	66	199	.433	.337

INDIVIDUAL DESIGNATED HITTING
(Listed Alphabetically)

Player, Club	AVG.	G	AB	R	H	TB	2B	3B	HR	RBI	GW RBI	SH	SF	HP	BB	1B	SO	SB	CS	GI DP	SLG	OBP
Baines, Chi.*	.290	117	466	56	135	223	23	4	19	89	10	0	2	0	42	1	75	1	0	10	.479	.348
Balboni, K.C.	.189	52	180	23	34	74	5	0	11	25	2	0	2	0	20	1	55	0	0	4	.411	.267
Baylor, Bos.-Minn.	.242	111	376	66	91	147	8	1	16	60	6	0	4	27	44	3	56	5	3	13	.391	.359
Bell, Tor.	.250	7	28	5	7	15	1	0	2	5	1	0	0	1	2	2	7	0	0	1	.536	.323
Beniquez, K.C.-Tor.*	.216	30	88	7	19	32	4	0	3	17	0	1	1	0	8	0	13	0	0	6	.364	.286
Bergman, Det.*	.143	7	7	0	1	1	0	0	0	1	1	0	0	0	2	0	1	0	0	0	.143	.222
Bernazard, Oak.†	.100	3	10	2	1	1	0	0	0	0	0	0	1	0	2	0	0	0	0	0	.100	.250
Biancalana, K.C.†		1	0	1	0	0	0	0	0	0	0	0	0	0	0	0	0	0	0	0		.600
Boggs, Bos.*	.500	1	4	0	2	6	0	0	0	0	0	0	0	0	1	2	0	0	0	0	1.500	.600
Bonilla, N.Y.	1.000	1	1	0	1	1	0	0	0	0	0	1	0	0	0	1	0	0	0	0	1.000	1.000
Boone, Cal.	.234	13	47	5	11	17	3	0	1	7	0	0	1	0	3	2	4	0	0	0	.362	.250
Bosley, K.C.*	.200	5	5	4	1	2	1	0	0	0	0	0	0	0	0	0	1	0	0	0	.400	.200
Boston, Chi.*	.231	6	13	0	3	3	0	0	0	3	1	0	1	0	0	0	7	0	0	0	.231	.286
S. Bradley, Sea.*	.267	8	30	3	8	11	3	0	0	6	0	0	0	0	1	0	8	0	0	3	.367	.303
Braggs, Mil.	.267	8	30	17	8	14	1	1	2	7	1	0	0	0	2	1	12	1	1	0	.467	.281
Brantley, Sea.	.287	21	80	2	23	48	8	1	5	14	4	0	1	0	3	2	1	0	0	1	.600	.370
Brett, K.C.*	.400	7	5	0	2	3	0	1	0	0	0	0	0	0	1	0	1	0	0	0	.600	.625
Browne, Tex.*	.000	1	1	2	0	0	0	0	0	0	0	0	0	0	3	0	1	1	1	0	.000	.000
Browne, Tex.†	.237	17	59	10	14	33	4	0	5	13	2	0	0	0	7	2	11	5	1	0	.559	.313
Brunansky, Minn.	.275	39	149	14	41	60	10	0	3	23	0	1	0	0	9	0	5	1	0	3	.403	.314
Buckner, Cal.*	.133	1	15	0	2	3	1	0	0	0	0	1	0	0	0	1	0	0	0	0	.200	.188
Burks, Bos.	.200	9	25	1	5	9	1	1	0	3	0	0	0	0	5	0	3	1	0	1	.360	.355
Burleson, Balt.	.167	3	6	0	1	1	0	0	0	0	0	0	0	1	3	1	0	0	0	0	.167	.444
Bush, Minn.*	.256	30	117	16	30	53	6	1	5	19	4	0	3	0	8	0	30	2	0	4	.453	.302
Calderon, Chi.	.176	5	17	0	3	4	1	0	0	4	0	0	0	0	0	1	3	1	0	0	.235	.176
Canseco, Oak.	.241	43	137	16	33	61	13	0	5	18	1	0	3	1	10	0	34	1	0	3	.445	.287
Carter, Clev.	.200	30	75	11	15	28	4	0	3	7	0	1	1	0	17	2	29	0	0	0	.373	.351
Castillo, Clev.	.400	8	15	3	6	10	1	0	1	2	0	0	0	0	3	0	4	1	0	3	.667	.500
Cey, Oak.	.275	12	40	7	11	21	4	0	2	5	0	0	0	0	2	1	10	0	0	3	.525	.310
Christensen, Sea.	.143	3	7	0	1	1	0	0	0	0	0	0	0	0	0	0	2	0	0	0	.143	.143
Clark, Clev.*	.249	62	249	25	62	93	13	1	6	36	5	0	3	0	17	2	50	1	0	4	.373	.294
Coles, Det.	.000	3	7	4	0	0	0	0	0	0	0	0	0	0	0	0	0	0	0	0	.000	.000
Cooper, Mil.*	.130	14	46	3	6	11	2	0	0	4	0	0	0	0	3	0	9	0	0	1	.239	.176
Davidson, Minn.	.000	1	1	0	0	0	0	0	0	0	0	0	0	0	0	0	0	0	0	0	.000	.000
M. Davis, Oak.*	.143	4	14	0	2	3	1	0	0	1	0	0	0	0	0	0	5	0	0	1	.214	.200
DeCinces, Cal.	.333	4	6	2	2	2	0	0	0	1	0	0	1	0	3	2	1	0	0	1	.333	.556
Deer, Mil.	.000	1	2	0	0	0	0	0	0	0	0	0	0	0	0	0	1	0	0	1	.000	.000
Destrade, N.Y.*	.143	4	14	2	2	2	0	0	0	0	0	0	0	0	3	0	5	2	0	0	.214	.200
Dodson, Bos.*	.333	2	6	0	2	3	1	0	0	1	0	0	0	0	0	2	0	0	0	1	.333	.333
Downing, Cal.	.273	118	444	85	121	221	22	3	24	63	9	2	2	12	84	4	63	2	4	10	.498	.400

Player, Club	AVG.	G	AB	R	H	TB	2B	3B	HR	RBI	GW RBI	SH	SF	HP	BB	IB	SO	SB	CS	GI DP	SLG	OBP
Ducey, Tor.★	.295	41	122	31	36	64	4	0	8	15	2	1	0	0	18	0	25	1	0	0	.525	.390
Dwyer, Balt.	.276	32	98	7	27	37	4	0	2	15	2	0	0	1	9	2	17	1	1	2	.378	.343
Easler, N.Y.★	.213	26	89	8	19	36	4	0	2	9	1	0	3	0	5	0	11	1	0	1	.404	.247
Eisenreich, K.C.★	.255	44	145	26	37	77	7	2	3	16	1	1	3	0	28	2	28	2	2	2	.531	.369
Evans, Det.★	.267	4	15	2	4	4	0	0	0	2	0	0	0	0	4	1	3	0	0	0	.267	.421
Evans, Bos.	.200	3	5	1	1	1	0	0	0	0	0	0	0	0	1	0	1	0	0	0	.200	.333
Felder, Mil.†	.283	55	127	24	36	77	6	1	11	25	2	0	1	1	14	0	31	0	0	4	.606	.357
Fielder, Tor.	.154	7	26	4	4	6	1	0	0	3	0	0	0	1	3	1	4	0	0	0	.231	.267
Fisk, Chi.	.231	8	26	4	6	7	1	0	0	3	0	0	0	1	6	0	3	0	0	1	.269	.382
Franco, Clev.	.083	5	12	2	1	4	0	0	1	3	0	0	1	1	4	0	3	0	0	0	.333	.313
Frobel, Clev.★	.429	2	7	3	3	6	0	0	1	1	0	0	0	1	1	0	1	0	0	0	.857	.500
Gaetti, Minn.		1	0	4	0	0	0	0	0	0	0	0	0	0	0	0	0	0	0	0		
Gagne, Minn.	.000	4	1	0	0	0	0	0	0	0	0	0	0	0	0	0	1	0	0	0	.000	.000
Gantner, Mil.★	.154	4	13	4	2	3	1	0	0	0	0	0	0	1	2	0	4	2	1	0	.231	.188
Gibson, Det.★	.263	15	57	8	15	22	4	0	1	7	0	0	0	0	7	0	5	1	0	2	.386	.354
Gladden, Minn.	.257	16	35	4	9	15	3	0	1	5	1	0	0	1	6	0	7	2	0	1	.429	.357
Greenwell, Bos.★	.286	13	42	8	12	20	5	0	2	4	0	0	1	0	11	0	7	0	0	2	.476	.444
Grubb, Det.★	.290	14	31	2	9	14	2	0	0	6	0	0	0	0	4	1	6	0	0	1	.452	.389
Gruber, Tor.	.200	7	15	1	3	4	1	0	0	3	0	0	0	0	0	0	7	2	0	0	.267	.188
Hairston, Chi.†	.156	15	32	3	5	11	0	0	2	4	0	0	0	1	3	0	4	1	1	2	.344	.229
Hall, Clev.★	.190	18	63	5	12	19	4	0	1	5	0	1	0	0	5	1	5	0	0	1	.302	.261
Harper, Oak.	1.000	1	1	0	1	1	0	0	0	1	0	0	0	0	0	0	0	0	0	0	1.000	1.000
Harper, Det.	.255	24	98	18	25	46	4	1	5	9	2	0	0	1	21	0	17	12	3	2	.469	.387
Hassey, Chi.★	.150	9	20	1	3	6	0	0	1	3	0	0	0	0	0	0	3	0	0	0	.300	.150
Heath, Det.	.000	5	4	0	0	0	0	0	0	0	0	0	0	0	0	0	0	0	0	0	.000	.000
Henderson, Bos.	.288	79	252	28	45	85	7	0	11	32	2	0	2	2	26	0	76	2	1	7	.475	.371
Henderson, N.Y.	.000	1	4	2	0	0	0	0	0	0	0	0	0	0	0	0	1	0	0	5	.000	.000
Henderson, Oak.	.283	23	59	10	17	28	2	0	3	13	3	0	0	0	9	0	7	2	0	0	.475	.371
Hendrick, Cal.	.000	1	1	0	0	0	0	0	0	0	0	0	0	0	0	0	0	0	0	0	.000	.000
Hengel, Sea.	.300	4	4	0	3	9	0	0	3	0	0	0	0	0	0	0	0	0	0	0	.605	.363
Herndon, Det.	.000	40	152	31	43	92	7	0	14	33	4	0	2	2	17	2	53	0	1	5	.000	.000
Hill, Chi.†	.179	1	1	0	0	0	0	0	0	0	0	0	0	0	1	0	0	0	0	0	.000	.500
Horn, Bos.★	.000	6	20	5	6	9	0	0	1	1	0	0	0	2	0	0	10	0	0	0	.000	.333
Hrbek, Minn.★	.273	151	9	0	0	0	0	0	0	0	0	0	0	0	0	0	1	0	0	5	.450	.500
Incaviglia, Tex.	.000	14	252	28	45	85	7	0	12	32	3	1	2	2	26	0	76	2	1	0	.337	.333
Iorg, Tor.	.667	1	4	0	3	6	0	0	0	3	0	0	0	0	0	0	1	0	0	2	.000	.000
Jackson, Oak.★		2	11	2	3	6	2	0	0	0	0	0	1	0	5	0	0	0	1	0	.545	.260
B. Jackson, K.C.	.000	4	3	0	0	2	0	0	0	0	0	0	0	0	2	0	0	2	0	0	.000	.500
Jacoby, Clev.	.278	49	0	0	0	0	0	0	0	0	0	0	3	0	0	0	0	0	0	0	.545	.000
Javier, Oak.†	.220	14	0	0	0	2	0	0	0	0	0	0	0	0	0	1	0	0	0	0	.667	.800
Jones, Cal.★	.667	1	3	0	0	4	0	0	0	0	0	0	0	0	0	0	1	0	0	0		
Karkovice, Chi.		3	0	2	0	0	0	0	0	0	0	0	0	0	0	0	1	0	0	0		
Keedy, Chi.		1	0	0	0	0	0	0	0	0	0	0	0	0	0	0	0	0	0	0		
Kelly, N.Y.	.000	2	3	2	0	0	0	0	0	0	0	0	0	0	0	0	0	0	0	0	.000	.000
Kingery, Sea.★	.278	4	0	0	0	83	5	0	0	27	3	2	3	0	7	0	35	0	2	4	.550	.304
Kittle, N.Y.	.220	49	50	21	42	13	2	0	12	8	1	0	0	0	5	0	7	0	0	3	.260	.291
Knight, Balt.	.220	14	3	2	11	0	0	0	0	0	0	0	0	0	1	0	3	1	0	0	.550	.250
Komminsk, Mil.	.000	1	1	0	0	0	0	0	0	0	0	0	0	0	0	0	0	0	0	0	.000	.000
Kunkel, Tex.	.000	1	3	0	0	0	0	0	0	0	0	0	0	0	0	0	1	0	0	0	.000	.000
Lacy, Balt.	.222	4	9	2	2	2	0	0	0	1	0	2	0	0	1	0	0	0	2	0	.222	.300
Lansford, Oak.	.286	4	14	4	4	4	0	0	0	0	0	0	0	0	1	0	0	0	0	0	.286	.333

Player, Club	AVG.	G	AB	R	H	TB	2B	3B	HR	RBI	GW RBI	SH	SF	HP	BB	IB	SO	SB	CS	GI DP	SLG	OBP
Larkin, Minn†	.264	40	140	14	37	54	9	1	2	12	2	0	2	1	17	2	17	1	4	2	.386	.344
Laudner, Minn.	.000	2	5	1	0	0	0	0	0	0	0	0	0	0	1	0	1	0	0	0	.000	.167
Leach, Tor.*	.278	30	72	9	20	32	4	1	2	11	4	0	1	2	10	1	11	0	0	1	.444	.376
Lee, Tor.†	...	1	0	0	0	0	0	0	0	0	0	0	0	0	0	0	0	0	0	0	...	...
LeMaster, Oak.	...	1	0	0	0	0	0	0	0	0	0	0	0	0	0	0	0	0	0	0	...	...
Lusader, Det.*	.000	8	30	1	3	7	1	0	1	2	0	0	0	0	0	0	7	0	0	2	.233	.100
Lynn, Balt.*	.100	6	30	1	3	7	1	0	0	0	0	0	0	0	0	0	0	0	0	0	.000	.000
Lyons, Chi.*	.000	64	1	0	0	0	0	0	0	0	0	0	0	0	0	0	0	0	0	0	.000	.000
Madlock, Det.	.263	2	247	37	65	106	11	0	10	38	7	0	1	8	19	1	36	2	3	9	.429	.335
Manning, Mil.*	.500	5	4	2	2	2	0	0	0	1	0	0	0	0	1	0	0	0	1	1	.500	.500
Manrique, Chi.	...	1	0	1	0	0	0	0	0	0	0	0	0	0	0	0	0	0	1	0	...	...
Martinez, Sea.	.000	39	1	0	0	0	0	0	0	0	0	2	0	0	0	0	0	0	0	0	.000	.000
Matthews, Sea.	.241	1	116	10	28	38	1	0	3	14	2	0	1	0	12	2	21	0	1	6	.328	.310
Mattingly, N.Y.*	.200	90	5	0	1	2	0	0	0	1	0	0	0	0	0	0	0	3	0	0	.400	.333
McGriff, Tor.*	.254	3	256	53	65	134	15	0	18	39	5	0	0	0	49	0	89	3	2	3	.523	.376
McLemore, Cal.†	.000	7	1	1	0	0	0	0	0	0	0	0	0	1	4	2	1	0	0	0	.000	.000
McRae, K.C.	.318	1	22	5	7	13	3	0	1	6	1	0	0	0	0	0	0	0	0	1	.591	.423
Meacham, N.Y.	...		0	0	0	0	0	0	0	0	0	0	0	0	0	0	0	0	0	0	...	...
Miller, Cal.	...		0	1	0	0	0	0	0	0	0	0	0	0	0	0	1	0	0	0	...	.440
Molitor, Mil.	.350	58	237	56	83	136	18	4	9	42	1	2	2	1	38	0	38	23	3	1	.574	.440
Morris, Det.	.125	8	24	0	3	6	0	0	1	4	0	0	0	0	2	0	4	0	0	0	.250	.192
Morrison, Det.	.000	2	1	2	0	0	0	0	0	0	0	0	0	0	0	0	0	0	0	0	.000	.000
Moseby, Tor.*	.000	2	3	0	0	0	0	0	0	0	0	0	0	0	0	0	0	0	0	0	.000	.000
Moses, Sea.†	.241	22	58	1	14	24	4	0	2	8	1	1	0	0	4	0	13	0	0	1	.414	.290
Mulliniks, Tor.†	.188	4	16	5	3	4	0	0	0	4	0	0	0	0	1	0	2	0	0	0	.250	.235
Murray, Balt.†	...	1	0	0	0	0	0	0	0	0	0	0	0	0	0	0	0	0	0	0	...	...
G. Nelson, Oak.	.429	5	7	2	3	4	0	0	0	1	0	0	0	0	3	1	1	0	2	0	.571	.500
Newman, Minn.†	1.000	1	1	0	1	1	0	0	0	0	0	0	0	0	0	0	0	0	1	0	1.000	1.000
Nieto, Minn.	...	2	0	2	0	0	0	0	0	0	0	0	0	0	0	0	0	0	0	0	...	...
Nixon, Clev.†	...	6	0	0	0	0	0	0	0	0	0	0	0	0	3	1	6	0	1	0	...	.278
Nixon, Sea.	.133	19	15	2	2	2	0	0	0	4	2	0	0	0	7	0	13	0	0	1	.133	.278
Noboa, Clev.	...	1	0	0	0	0	0	0	0	0	0	1	0	0	1	0	4	0	0	0	...	.408
Nokes, Det.*	.355	12	62	15	22	36	2	0	4	15	2	0	2	0	3	0	13	2	0	1	.581	.408
O'Brien, Tex.*	...	2	0	0	0	0	0	0	0	0	0	0	0	1	7	1	4	1	0	0	1.000	1.000
Orta, K.C.*	.171	3	41	3	7	16	0	0	2	3	1	0	0	0	3	0	1	0	0	0	.390	.227
Paciorek, Mil.	.143		7	0	1	1	0	0	0	3	0	0	0	0	0	0	3	2	1	10	.143	.143
Paciorek, Tex.	.000		4	0	0	0	0	0	0	0	0	0	0	0	0	0	0	0	0	2	.000	.200
Parrish, Clev.	.269	122	458	62	123	223	20	0	26	84	8	0	4	1	40	5	125	0	0	10	.487	.326
Parsons, Clev.*	.077	5	13	2	1	4	0	1	1	4	0	0	0	0	7	1	4	0	1	2	.308	.077
Pasqua, N.Y.*	.211	20	57	7	12	21	1	0	2	5	1	0	0	0	0	0	22	0	0	1	.368	.297
Pecota, K.C.	.000	1	1	0	0	0	0	0	0	0	0	0	0	0	1	0	0	1	0	0	.000	.297
Petralli, Tex.†	.000	2	1	1	0	0	0	0	0	0	0	0	0	0	0	0	0	0	0	0	.000	.000
Phelps, Sea.*	.262	114	325	67	85	178	13	0	26	66	6	0	4	8	78	5	72	1	7	7	.548	.412
Phillips, Oak.†	...	1	0	0	0	0	0	0	0	0	0	0	0	0	0	0	0	0	0	0	...	...
Pittaro, Minn.†	.265	18	34	11	9	11	2	0	0	2	0	0	0	0	4	0	5	2	1	1	.324	.342
Polonia, Oak.*	.239	35	88	15	21	35	2	0	4	12	3	0	1	2	24	2	30	0	0	0	.398	.409
Porter, Tex.*	1.000	1	1	1	1	4	0	0	1	3	0	0	0	0	0	0	0	0	0	0	4.000	1.000
Presley, Sea.	.344	8	32	6	11	19	2	1	2	7	3	1	0	1	1	0	4	0	1	1	.594	.364
Pucket, Minn.	1.000	2	2	0	2	2	0	0	0	0	0	0	0	0	2	0	0	0	0	0	1.000	1.000
Ramos, Sea.	1.000	1	2	2	2	2	0	0	0	0	0	0	0	0	1	0	0	1	0	0	1.000	1.000
Randolph, N.Y.	.800	1	5	3	4	5	1	0	0	0	0	0	0	0	2	0	0	0	0	1	1.000	.857

Player, Club	AVG.	G	AB	R	H	TB	2B	3B	HR	RBI	GW RBI	SH	SF	HP	BB	IB	SO	SB	CS	GI DP	SLG	OBP
Ray, Cal.†	.500	1	4	1	2	2	0	0	0	0	0	0	0	0	0	0	0	0	0	0	.500	.500
Rayford, Balt.	.000	1	1	0	0	0	0	0	0	0	0	0	0	0	0	0	0	0	0	0	.000	.000
Redus, Chi.	.500	4	6	1	3	3	0	0	0	0	0	0	0	0	0	0	2	0	0	0	.500	.500
Renteria, Sea	.000	4	4	1	0	0	0	0	0	0	0	0	0	0	1	0	0	1	0	0	.000	.200
Rice, Bos.	.158	12	38	6	6	12	0	0	2	6	1	0	1	0	6	1	5	0	0	5	.316	.283
Robidoux, Mil.*	.200	10	40	7	8	8	0	0	0	4	0	0	0	0	5	1	11	1	0	0	.200	.289
Romine, Bos.	.000	2	1	0	0	0	0	0	0	0	0	0	0	0	0	0	0	0	0	0	.000	.000
Royster, Chi.	.214	4	14	2	3	8	2	0	1	1	0	0	0	0	0	0	4	0	0	0	.571	.214
Ryal, Cal.*	.235	5	17	2	4	8	1	0	1	2	0	0	0	0	0	0	3	0	0	1	.471	.235
Salas, N.Y.*	.167	4	6	1	1	2	1	0	0	0	0	0	0	0	1	0	1	0	0	0	.333	.286
Sanchez, Oak	.000	1	1	0	0	0	0	0	0	0	0	0	0	0	0	0	0	0	0	0	.000	.000
Schofield, Cal.	.750	1	4	0	3	5	0	1	0	1	0	0	0	0	0	0	0	0	0	0	1.250	.750
Schroeder, Mil.	.100	2	10	0	1	2	1	0	0	1	0	0	0	0	0	0	3	0	0	0	.200	.100
Seitzer, K.C.	.250	1	4	0	1	1	0	0	0	0	0	0	0	0	0	0	0	0	0	0	.250	.250
Sheets, Balt.*	.364	7	22	5	8	11	0	0	1	5	0	0	0	0	1	0	2	1	0	1	.500	.391
Shelby, Balt.†	.000	1	1	0	0	0	0	0	0	0	0	0	0	0	0	0	0	0	0	0	.000	.000
Simmons, Balt.†	.000	5	3	1	0	0	0	0	0	0	0	0	0	0	0	0	0	0	0	0	.000	.000
Slaught, Tex.	.231	5	13	0	3	5	2	0	0	3	0	0	0	0	0	0	3	0	0	0	.385	.231
Smalley, Minn.†	.269	73	249	25	67	101	11	1	7	28	1	0	1	1	28	1	41	1	0	7	.406	.344
Smith, Sea.	1.000	1	1	0	1	1	0	0	0	0	0	0	0	0	0	0	0	0	0	0	1.000	1.000
Smith, K.C.	.167	15	48	8	8	10	2	0	0	2	0	0	0	0	7	0	11	4	1	0	.208	.273
Stanicek, Balt.†	.270	10	37	8	10	11	1	0	0	2	0	1	0	0	2	0	7	4	1	0	.297	.308
Stanicek, Mil.	.250	5	4	1	1	1	0	0	0	0	0	0	0	0	0	0	1	2	0	0	.250	.250
Stanley, Tex.	.308	5	13	0	4	5	1	0	0	1	0	0	0	0	2	0	4	0	0	0	.385	.400
Steinbach, Oak	.320	8	25	6	8	15	1	0	2	3	0	0	0	0	2	1	3	0	0	3	.600	.393
Stieb, Tor.		7	0	0																		
Surhoff, Mil.*	.192	7	26	2	5	6	1	0	0	4	0	0	1	0	0	0	1	0	0	0	.231	.185
Tabler, Clev.	.306	66	248	36	76	104	17	1	3	34	4	1	0	0	23	2	41	4	1	2	.419	.372
Tabor, Tex.	.000	6	23	1	0	0	0	0	0	0	0	0	0	0	0	0	0	0	0	0	.000	.000
Tartabull, K.C.†	.348	6	23	4	8	17	3	0	2	7	0	0	1	0	4	0	7	0	1	0	.739	.429
Tettleton, Oak.†	.270	21	37	1	10	17	1	0	2	7	0	0	0	0	9	0	11	0	0	0	.459	.413
Thornton, Clev.	.111	21	72	7	8	10	2	0	0	3	0	0	0	0	9	0	18	0	0	1	.139	.207
Thornton, Tor.*		6	0	2														1				
Tolman, Det.	.000	2	2	0	0	0	0	0	0	0	0	0	0	0	0	0	1	0	0	0	.000	.000
Valle, Sea.	.279	14	43	5	12	20	2	0	2	14	5	0	2	0	3	0	7	0	1	1	.465	.333
Walewander, Det.†	.333	8	9	7	3	3	0	0	0	0	0	4	0	0	0	0	0	4	0	0	.333	.333
Walker, Chi.*	.333	3	3	1	1	2	1	0	0	1	0	0	0	0	0	0	2	1	0	0	.667	.333
Ward, N.Y.	.287	36	136	23	39	75	10	1	8	23	0	0	0	1	5	0	21	3	1	4	.551	.326
Washington, N.Y.*	.297	13	37	5	11	17	3	0	1	6	0	0	0	0	1	0	5	1	0	0	.459	.326
Washington, Balt.	.000	2	2	0	0	0	0	0	0	0	0	0	0	0	0	0	1	0	0	0	.000	.000
Weiss, Oak.†	.000	2	6	0	0	0	0	0	0	0	0	4	0	0	0	0	1	0	0	0	.000	.000
White, K.C.	.250	1	4	0	1	1	0	0	0	0	0	0	0	0	0	0	1	0	0	0	.250	.250
Wiggins, Balt.†	.236	44	157	18	37	39	2	0	0	8	0	4	0	0	13	0	26	8	4	3	.248	.297
Wilkerson, Tex.†	.000	4	4	2	0	0	0	0	0	0	0	0	0	0	2	0	0	0	0	0	.000	.333
Willard, Oak.*	.250	3	4	1	1	1	0	0	0	1	0	0	0	0	0	0	1	0	0	0	.250	.250
Wilson, Cal.	1.000	2	1	1	1	1	0	0	0	0	0	0	0	0	0	1	0	0	0	0	1.000	1.000
Wilson, K.C.†	.222	2	9	4	2	4	2	0	0	4	0	0	0	0	2	0	4	3	0	0	.444	.364
Winfield, N.Y.	.214	8	28	2	6	7	1	0	0	4	0	0	1	0	4	1	0	1	0	2	.250	.313
Wynegar, Cal.†	.000	1	1	0	0	0	0	0	0	0	0	0	0	0	0	0	1	0	0	0	.000	.000
Young, Balt.†	.224	47	161	18	36	61	4	0	7	19	2	0	0	0	25	1	41	3	5	2	.379	.326
Yount, Mil.	.219	8	32	2	7	13	1	1	1	4	1	0	0	0	5	2	9	5	0	4	.406	.324

OFFICIAL AMERICAN LEAGUE FIELDING AVERAGES
CLUB FIELDING

Club	PCT	G	PO	A	E	TC	DP	TP	PB
Minnesota	.984	162	4282	1609	98	5989	147	0	21
New York	.983	162	4339	1685	102	6126	155	0	22
Baltimore	.982	162	4319	1747	111	6177	174	0	5
Toronto	.982	162	4362	1700	111	6173	148	0	13
Boston	.982	162	4308	1684	110	6102	158	0	30
Chicago	.981	162	4343	1782	116	6241	174	0	11
California	.981	162	4372	1640	117	6129	162	0	11
Detroit	.980	162	4368	1703	122	6193	147	0	13
Seattle	.980	162	4292	1756	122	6170	150	0	4
Kansas City	.979	162	4272	1853	131	6256	151	0	17
Oakland	.977	162	4337	1649	142	6128	122	0	18
Milwaukee	.976	162	4392	1606	145	6143	155	0	13
Texas	.976	162	4333	1685	151	6169	148	0	73
Cleveland	.975	162	4268	1626	153	6047	128	0	16
Totals	.979	1134	60587	23725	1731	84043	2119	0	267

INDIVIDUAL FIELDING

FIRST BASEMEN
(*Throws Lefthanded)

Leader, Club	PCT	G	PO	A	E	TC	DP
MATTINGLY, N.Y.*	.996	140	1239	91	5	1335	122

Player, Club	PCT	G	PO	A	E	TC	DP
Balboni, K.C.	.989	55	521	41	6	568	39
Beniquez, K.C.-Tor.	1.000	8	57	1	0	58	6
Benzinger, Bos.	1.000	2	9	1	0	10	0
Bergman, Det.*	.992	65	353	29	3	385	33
Boggs, Bos.	1.000	1	1	0	0	1	0
Brett, K.C.	.993	83	798	50	6	854	69
Brock, Mil.	.993	141	1065	109	8	1182	111
Buckner, Bos.-Cal.*	.992	79	640	60	6	706	54
Bush, Minn.*	.968	9	57	4	2	63	4
Carter, Clev.	.983	84	644	45	12	701	61
Cerone, N.Y.	1.000	2	4	0	0	4	0
Cey, Oak.	.982	7	55	1	1	57	3
Coles, Det.	1.000	9	50	3	0	53	1
Davis, Sea.	.994	157	1386	96	9	1491	133
DeCinces, Cal.	1.000	4	22	1	0	23	3
Deer, Mil.	.982	12	48	6	1	55	6
Destrade, N.Y.	1.000	3	20	1	0	21	2
Dodson, Bos.*	1.000	21	99	4	0	103	12
Evans, Det.	.997	105	810	100	3	913	86
Evans, Bos.	.982	79	619	41	12	672	72
Fielder, Tor.	1.000	16	98	6	0	104	12
Fisk, Chi.	.981	9	44	9	1	54	7
Hairston, Chi.	.984	7	55	5	1	61	7
Heath, Det.	1.000	4	20	1	0	21	3
Hendrick, Cal.	.984	9	56	4	1	61	7
Hrbek, Minn.	.996	137	1179	68	5	1252	112
Jacoby, Clev.	1.000	7	58	7	0	65	5
Javier, Oak.	.976	9	38	2	1	41	1
Joyner, Cal.*	.993	149	1276	92	10	1378	133
Keedy, Chi.	1.000	2	4	1	0	5	0
Knight, Balt.	.984	6	59	2	1	62	7
Kunkel, Tex.	.500	1	1	0	1	2	0
Lansford, Oak.	1.000	17	58	9	0	67	5
Larkin, Minn.	.989	26	165	10	2	177	12
Laudner, Minn.	1.000	7	30	1	0	31	3
Leach, Tor.*	1.000	5	6	0	0	6	0
Lowry, Det.	1.000	1	2	1	0	3	0
Madison, K.C.	1.000	4	20	2	0	22	4
Madlock, Det.	.989	22	167	11	2	180	14

Player, Club	PCT	G	PO	A	E	TC	DP
Mattingly, N.Y.*	.996	140	1239	91	5	1335	122
McGriff, Tor.*	.983	14	108	7	2	117	5
McGwire, Oak.	.992	145	1173	90	10	1273	91
Morrison, Det.	1.000	1	2	0	0	2	1
Moses, Sea.	.981	16	51	2	1	54	3
Murphy, Oak.	1.000	1	2	0	0	2	0
Murray, Balt.	.993	156	1371	145	10	1526	146
R. Nelson, Oak.*	.968	7	49	11	2	62	6
O'Brien, Tex.*	.992	158	1233	146	11	1390	118
Paciorek, Mil.	.980	21	93	6	2	101	8
Paciorek, Tex.	1.000	12	63	7	0	70	9
Pagliarulo, N.Y.	1.000	1	1	0	0	1	0
Parsons, Clev.	1.000	1	3	0	0	3	0
Pasqua, N.Y.*	1.000	12	82	8	0	90	2
Petralli, Tex.	1.000	5	10	0	0	10	0
Phelps, Sea.*	1.000	1	8	0	0	8	0
Porter, Tex.	1.000	5	11	1	0	12	2
Robidoux, Mil.	.983	10	53	4	1	58	9
Romero, Bos.	1.000	8	22	2	0	24	0
Ryal, Cal.*	.938	4	29	1	2	32	1
Schroeder, Mil.	1.000	4	10	1	0	11	4
Seitzer, K.C.	.990	25	183	23	2	208	19
Sheets, Balt.	.941	3	14	2	1	17	1
Smith, Sea.	.963	3	24	2	1	27	1
Stanley, Tex.	1.000	12	58	9	0	67	6
Steinbach, Oak.	1.000	1	1	0	0	1	0
Surhoff, Mil.	1.000	1	1	1	0	2	0
Tabler, Clev.	.984	82	650	75	12	737	49
Tettleton, Oak.	1.000	1	2	1	0	3	0
Upshaw, Tor.*	.993	146	1169	127	9	1305	114
Valle, Sea.	1.000	2	2	0	0	2	0
Walker, Chi.	.994	154	1402	80	9	1491	135
Ward, N.Y.	1.000	15	118	8	0	126	11
Willard, Oak.	1.000	1	1	0	0	1	1

FIRST BASEMEN WITH TWO OR MORE CLUBS

Player, Club	PCT	G	PO	A	E	TC	DP
Beniquez, K.C.	1.000	6	50	1	0	51	6
Beniquez, Tor.	1.000	2	7	0	0	7	0
Buckner, Bos.*	.991	74	605	58	6	669	53
Buckner, Cal.*	1.000	5	35	2	0	37	1

SECOND BASEMEN

Leader, Club	PCT	G	PO	A	E	TC	DP
BARRETT, BOS.	.988	137	320	438	9	767	108

Player, Club	PCT	G	PO	A	E	TC	DP
Baker, Det.		1	0	0	0	0	0
Barrett, Bos.	.988	137	320	438	9	767	108
Bell, Tor.	1.000	1	1	0	0	1	0
Bernazard, Clev.-Oak.	.971	137	243	335	17	595	61
Biancalana, K.C.	1.000	12	9	18	0	27	6

Player, Club	PCT	G	PO	A	E	TC	DP
Bonilla, N.Y.	.965	22	40	43	3	86	10
Brookens, Det.	.930	11	20	20	3	43	10
Browne, Tex.	.980	130	258	338	12	608	66
Buechele, Tex.	1.000	18	20	36	0	56	7
Burleson, Balt.	.977	55	112	145	6	263	39
Castillo, Mil.	.973	97	181	219	11	411	54
Felder, Mil.	1.000	1	2	3	0	5	0
Franco, Clev.	.979	9	18	28	1	47	3

SECOND BASEMEN—Continued

Player, Club	PCT	G	PO	A	E	TC	DP
Gagne, Minn.	....	1	0	0	0	0	0
Gallego, Oak.	.968	31	49	73	4	126	22
Gantner, Mil.	.984	57	95	153	4	252	36
Gonzales, Balt.	1.000	6	0	4	0	4	1
Griffin, Oak.	1.000	1	5	3	0	8	1
Gruber, Tor.	1.000	7	3	4	0	7	1
Gutierrez, Balt.	....	1	0	0	0	0	0
Heath, Det.	....	1	0	0	0	0	0
Hill, Chi.	.987	84	153	223	5	381	47
Hinzo, Clev.	.973	67	115	204	9	328	44
Hoffman, Bos.	1.000	2	0	2	0	2	0
Howell, Cal.	.909	13	4	6	1	11	2
Hulett, Chi.	.972	8	11	24	1	36	4
Iorg, Tor.	.982	91	139	195	6	340	33
Jones, K.C.	1.000	3	4	2	0	6	2
Keedy, Chi.	1.000	1	2	3	0	5	0
Kiefer, Mil.	1.000	4	1	8	0	9	1
Kunkel, Tex.	.955	10	17	25	2	44	8
Lee, Tor.	.966	27	51	61	4	116	16
LeMaster, Oak.	.955	5	8	13	1	22	1
Liriano, Tor.	.995	37	83	107	1	191	28
Lombardozzi, Minn.	.977	133	245	356	14	615	77
Lyons, Chi.	1.000	1	1	0	0	1	0
Manrique, Chi.	.984	92	147	234	6	387	58
McLemore, Cal.	.974	132	291	358	17	666	96
Meacham, N.Y.	.980	25	40	57	2	99	11
Molitor, Mil.	1.000	19	35	49	0	84	16
Morrison, Det.	1.000	3	9	5	0	14	2
Murphy, Oak.	1.000	1	0	1	0	1	0
Newman, Minn.	.988	47	54	111	2	167	20
Noboa, Clev.	.983	21	19	39	1	59	6
O'Malley, Tex.	....	1	0	0	0	0	0
Pecota, K.C.	1.000	15	20	27	0	47	6
Petralli, Tex.	1.000	4	1	1	0	2	0

Player, Club	PCT	G	PO	A	E	TC	DP
Phillips, Oak.	.974	87	160	260	11	431	40
Pittaro, Minn.	1.000	8	10	6	0	16	3
Polidor, Cal.	1.000	3	3	8	0	11	3
Ramos, Sea.	1.000	6	10	12	0	22	2
Randolph, N.Y.	.981	119	286	338	12	636	89
Ray, Cal.	.986	29	52	90	2	144	19
Reed, Bos.	1.000	2	3	10	0	13	2
Renteria, Sea.	.833	4	2	3	1	6	0
Reynolds, Sea.	.977	160	347	507	20	874	111
B. Ripken, Balt.	.990	58	133	162	3	298	53
Romero, Bos.	.973	29	65	81	4	150	19
Royster, Chi.-N.Y.	1.000	6	17	11	0	28	2
Sakata, N.Y.	1.000	6	5	7	0	12	3
Schofield, Cal.	1.000	2	1	3	0	4	0
Sharperson, Tor.	.971	32	64	69	4	137	16
Stanicek, Balt.	.975	19	36	42	2	80	15
Sveum, Mil.	.966	13	21	35	2	58	7
Tabor, Tex.	.938	4	4	11	1	16	2
Walewander, Det.	1.000	24	16	38	0	54	10
Washington, Balt.	1.000	3	3	2	0	5	0
Whitaker, Det.	.976	148	275	416	17	708	99
White, K.C.	.987	152	320	458	10	788	89
Wiggins, Balt.	.983	33	78	98	3	179	21
Wilkerson, Tex.	1.000	28	31	46	0	77	9
Zuvella, N.Y.	1.000	7	17	18	0	35	5

SECOND BASEMEN WITH TWO OR MORE CLUBS

Player, Club	PCT	G	PO	A	E	TC	DP
Bernazard, Clev.	.983	78	153	200	6	359	39
Bernazard, Oak.	.953	59	90	135	11	236	22
Royster, Chi.	1.000	5	12	5	0	17	1
Royster, N.Y.	1.000	1	5	6	0	11	1

THIRD BASEMEN

Leader, Club	PCT	G	PO	A	E	TC	DP
LANSFORD, OAK.	.980	142	98	249	7	354	15

Player, Club	PCT	G	PO	A	E	TC	DP
Baker, Det.	....	1	0	0	0	0	0
Bell, Tor.	....	1	0	0	0	0	0
Beniquez, K.C.	.800	6	0	4	1	5	0
Boggs, Bos.	.965	145	111	277	14	402	37
Bonilla, N.Y.	1.000	1	0	1	0	1	0
S. Bradley, Sea.	1.000	8	5	10	0	15	0
Brett, K.C.	.897	11	7	19	3	29	3
Brookens, Det.	.954	122	85	208	14	307	15
Buechele, Tex.	.964	123	68	175	9	252	13
Castillo, Mil.	.900	7	2	7	1	10	1
Cey, Oak.	1.000	3	1	3	0	4	1
Coles, Det.	.847	36	31	63	17	111	5
DeCinces, Cal.	.948	128	83	226	17	326	24
Evans, Det.	.929	7	5	8	1	14	0
Fielder, Tor.	....	2	0	0	0	0	0
Gaetti, Minn.	.973	150	134	261	11	406	28
Gallego, Oak.	1.000	24	5	24	0	29	1
Gantner, Mil.	.970	38	24	40	2	66	8
Gonzales, Balt.	.963	29	18	34	2	54	2
Grubb, Det.	....	1	0	0	0	0	0
Gruber, Tor.	.948	119	52	168	12	232	11
Gutierrez, Balt.	....	1	0	0	0	0	0
Heath, Det.	.750	4	1	2	1	4	0
Hill, Chi.	.885	32	14	55	9	78	8
Hoffman, Bos.	1.000	3	1	0	0	1	0
Howell, Cal.	.967	48	31	85	4	120	13
Hulett, Chi.	.953	61	44	118	8	170	15
Iorg, Tor.	.973	28	10	26	1	37	3
Jacoby, Clev.	.946	144	134	254	22	410	19
Keedy, Chi.	.943	11	9	24	2	35	2
Kiefer, Mil.	.966	26	15	42	2	59	3
Knight, Balt.	.956	130	110	282	18	410	28
Kunkel, Tex.	1.000	3	1	2	0	3	0
Lansford, Oak.	.980	142	98	249	7	354	15
LeMaster, Oak.	1.000	8	2	6	0	8	2
Lyons, Chi.	.971	51	35	99	4	138	11
Madlock, Det.	1.000	1	0	1	0	1	0
Martinez, Sea.	1.000	12	13	19	0	32	1
McGwire, Oak.	.813	8	2	11	3	16	0

Player, Club	PCT	G	PO	A	E	TC	DP
Miller, Cal.	1.000	1	1	0	0	1	0
Molitor, Mil.	.947	41	25	64	5	94	8
Moronko, N.Y.	1.000	3	1	7	0	8	0
Morrison, Det.	.962	16	10	41	2	53	1
Mulliniks, Tor.	.927	96	29	137	13	179	14
Newman, Minn.	1.000	12	4	11	0	15	0
Noboa, Clev.	.917	5	2	9	1	12	0
Nokes, Det.	....	2	0	0	0	0	0
O'Malley, Tex.	.962	40	21	56	3	80	3
Paciorek, Mil.	.829	15	13	16	6	35	4
Pagliarulo, N.Y.	.959	147	96	297	17	410	35
Parrish, Tex.	.918	28	19	26	4	49	6
Pecota, K.C.	.909	17	7	23	3	33	2
Petralli, Tex.	.882	17	8	7	2	17	2
Phillips, Oak.	.920	11	3	20	2	25	4
Polidor, Cal.	1.000	11	1	7	0	8	0
Presley, Sea.	.953	148	113	311	21	445	28
Ramos, Sea.	1.000	7	5	6	0	11	0
Rayford, Balt.	.800	1	2	2	1	5	1
Reed, Bos.	....	1	0	0	0	0	0
Riles, Mil.	.935	65	41	103	10	154	11
Romero, Bos.	.974	24	13	24	1	38	0
Royster, Chi.-N.Y.	.954	43	26	57	4	87	6
Sakata, N.Y.	.929	12	3	23	2	28	1
Seitzer, K.C.	.947	141	105	292	22	419	32
Smalley, Minn.	.850	14	7	10	3	20	0
Stanicek, Balt.	.714	2	1	4	2	7	0
Steinbach, Oak.	1.000	10	1	4	0	5	0
Surhoff, Mil.	1.000	10	2	6	0	8	2
Tolleson, N.Y.	1.000	3	0	5	0	5	2
Walewander, Det.	.947	17	7	11	1	19	0
Washington, Balt.	1.000	20	15	40	0	55	3
Wilkerson, Tex.	.923	18	7	5	1	13	1
Willard, Oak.	....	1	0	0	0	0	0
Williams, Oak.	.982	22	17	37	1	55	6
Zuvella, N.Y.	....	1	0	0	0	0	0

THIRD BASEMEN WITH TWO OR MORE CLUBS

Player, Club	PCT	G	PO	A	E	TC	DP
Royster, Chi.	.969	30	22	41	2	65	4
Royster, N.Y.	.909	13	4	16	2	22	2

SHORTSTOPS

Leader, Club	PCT	G	PO	A	E	TC	DP
SCHOFIELD, CAL.	.984	131	204	348	9	561	76

Player, Club	PCT	G	PO	A	E	TC	DP
Baker, Det.	1.000	6	2	8	0	10	1
Bell, Clev.	.947	38	67	93	9	169	22
Biancalana, K.C.	.886	22	12	27	5	44	4
Brookens, Det.	.955	16	14	28	2	44	8
Castillo, Mil.	1.000	13	7	25	0	32	4
Coles, Det.	1.000	1	0	1	0	1	0
DeCinces, Cal.	....	1	0	0	0	0	0
Diaz, Sea.	.972	10	10	25	1	36	6
Fernandez, Tor.	.979	146	270	396	14	680	88
Fletcher, Tex.	.966	155	249	413	23	685	98
Franco, Clev.	.963	111	157	285	17	459	53
Gagne, Minn.	.970	136	194	391	18	603	75
Gallego, Oak.	.920	17	21	25	4	50	6
Gonzales, Balt.	1.000	1	4	5	0	9	2
Griffin, Oak.	.963	137	245	386	24	655	72
Gruber, Tor.	.980	21	20	28	1	49	7
Guillen, Chi.	.975	149	266	475	19	760	105
Heath, Det.	1.000	2	0	1	0	1	0
Hoffman, Bos.	.984	16	14	49	1	64	9
Jones, K.C.	.974	36	42	109	4	155	13
Keedy, Chi.	1.000	1	2	4	0	6	3
Kunkel, Tex.	....	1	0	0	0	0	0
Lee, Tor.	.987	26	26	49	1	76	10
LeMaster, Oak.	1.000	7	4	5	0	9	2
Manrique, Chi.	.988	23	29	52	1	82	6
McLemore, Cal.	1.000	6	2	5	0	7	2
Meacham, N.Y.	.961	56	70	127	8	205	25
Moronko, N.Y.	1.000	2	0	2	0	2	1
Morrison, Det.	1.000	3	1	5	0	6	1
Mulliniks, Tor.	....	1	0	0	0	0	0
Newman, Minn.	.982	55	62	103	3	168	24
Noboa, Clev.	.962	8	7	18	1	26	2
Owen, Bos.	.975	130	176	336	13	525	69
Pecota, K.C.	.977	36	40	85	3	128	20
Phillips, Oak.	.971	9	14	19	1	34	3
Polidor, Cal.	.983	46	42	77	2	121	11
Presley, Sea.	1.000	4	0	4	0	4	1
Quinones, Sea.	.959	135	204	384	25	613	76
Quirk, K.C.	....	1	0	0	0	0	0
Ramos, Sea.	.953	25	32	70	5	107	17
Reed, Bos.	1.000	4	8	16	0	24	7
Renteria, Sea.	1.000	1	1	1	0	2	1
Riles, Mil.	.966	21	35	49	3	87	14
C. Ripken, Balt.	.973	162	240	480	20	740	103
Romero, Bos.	.985	24	22	44	1	67	9
Royster, N.Y.	1.000	1	1	6	0	7	1
Salazar, K.C.	.981	116	134	332	9	475	56
Schofield, Cal.	.984	131	204	348	9	561	76
Smalley, Minn.	1.000	4	2	1	0	3	0
Snyder, Clev.	.918	18	30	37	6	73	6
Sveum, Mil.	.965	142	221	361	21	603	82
Tolleson, N.Y.	.970	119	162	321	15	498	64
Trammell, Det.	.971	149	222	421	19	662	94
Velarde, N.Y.	.933	8	8	20	2	30	3
Walewander, Det.	1.000	3	3	9	0	12	2
Washington, Balt.	....	1	0	0	0	0	0
Weiss, Oak.	.974	11	8	30	1	39	4
Wilkerson, Tex.	.946	33	41	47	5	93	8
Zuvella, N.Y.	1.000	6	3	7	0	10	0

OUTFIELDERS

Leader, Club	PCT	G	PO	A	E	TC	DP
WILSON, K.C.	.997	143	342	3	1	346	1

Player, Club	PCT	G	PO	A	E	TC	DP
Armas, Cal.	1.000	27	36	0	0	36	0
Baines, Chi.*	1.000	8	13	0	0	13	0
Barfield, Tor.	.992	158	341	17	3	361	4
Bean, Det.*	1.000	24	54	1	0	55	0
Beane, Minn.	1.000	7	8	0	0	8	0
Bell, Tor.	.960	148	248	14	11	273	1
Beniquez, K.C.-Tor.	.976	29	40	0	1	41	0
Benzinger, Bos.	.987	61	146	6	2	154	2
Bergman, Det.*	1.000	7	4	0	0	4	0
Bosley, K.C.*	.966	28	28	0	1	29	0
Boston, Chi.*	.991	92	207	3	2	212	3
P. Bradley, Sea.	.983	158	273	13	5	291	1
S. Bradley, Sea.	....	2	0	0	0	0	0
Braggs, Mil.	.972	123	301	6	9	316	1
Brantley, Sea.	.982	82	163	3	3	169	1
Brower, Tex.	.964	106	183	2	7	192	0
Brunansky, Minn.	.990	138	273	10	3	286	1
Buechele, Tex.	1.000	2	1	0	0	1	0
Buhner, N.Y.	1.000	7	11	1	0	12	1
Burks, Bos.	.988	132	320	15	4	339	2
Bush, Minn.	.982	75	107	1	2	110	0
Butler, Clev.*	.990	136	393	4	4	401	2
Calderon, Chi.	.984	139	295	8	5	308	3
Canseco, Oak.	.975	130	263	12	7	282	3
Carter, Clev.	.965	62	138	1	5	144	0
Castillo, Clev.	1.000	23	29	3	0	32	0
Christensen, Sea.	1.000	43	60	3	0	63	1
Clark, Clev.	1.000	13	24	1	0	25	0
Coles, Det.	1.000	8	3	0	0	3	0
Cotto, N.Y.	.989	57	89	2	1	92	0
Davidson, Minn.	1.000	86	102	3	0	105	0
M. Davis, Oak.*	.942	124	210	3	13	226	1
Deer, Mil.	.974	123	256	10	7	273	1
Downing, Cal.	1.000	34	47	2	0	49	0
Ducey, Tor.	1.000	28	31	0	0	31	0
Dwyer, Balt.*	1.000	30	57	1	0	58	0
Easler, N.Y.	1.000	15	24	1	0	25	0
Eppard, Cal.*	1.000	1	1	0	0	1	0
Espy, Tex.	1.000	8	8	1	0	9	1
Evans, Bos.	.993	77	134	5	1	140	0
Felder, Mil.	.975	99	188	7	5	200	3
Fisk, Chi.	1.000	2	3	0	0	3	0
Frobel, Clev.	1.000	12	6	0	0	6	0
Gagne, Minn.	1.000	4	2	0	0	2	0
Gallagher, Clev.	.972	14	34	1	1	36	1
Gerhart, Balt.	.973	91	174	3	5	182	0
Gibson, Det.*	.974	121	253	6	7	266	0
Gladden, Minn.	.987	111	223	9	3	235	2
Greenwell, Bos.	.971	91	162	8	5	175	0
Grubb, Det.	1.000	31	42	1	0	43	0
Gruber, Tor.	1.000	2	1	0	0	1	0
Hairston, Chi.	1.000	13	27	0	0	27	0
Hall, Clev.*	.989	122	264	3	3	270	2
Harper, Oak.	....	1	0	0	0	0	0
Harper, Det.	.952	14	20	0	1	21	0
Hart, Balt.*	1.000	32	74	0	0	74	0
Heath, Det.	1.000	24	26	1	0	27	0
Henderson, Bos.	.958	64	114	0	5	119	0
Henderson, N.Y.*	.980	69	189	3	4	196	1
Henderson, Oak.	.943	31	33	0	2	35	0
Hendrick, Cal.	.967	45	58	1	2	61	0
Hengel, Sea.	.875	7	7	0	1	8	0
Herndon, Det.	.989	57	82	4	1	87	1
Howell, Cal.	.987	89	150	4	2	156	0
Incaviglia, Tex.	.945	132	216	8	13	237	0
Jackson, Oak.*	1.000	20	30	0	0	30	0
B. Jackson, K.C.	.955	113	180	9	9	198	1
Javier, Oak.	.983	71	111	3	2	116	3
Jones, Cal.*	.965	66	81	1	3	85	0
Keedy, Chi.	....	1	0	0	0	0	0
Kelly, N.Y.	.955	17	42	0	2	44	0
Kingery, Sea.*	.992	114	226	15	2	243	3
Kittle, N.Y.	1.000	2	4	1	0	5	0
Komminsk, Mil.	1.000	5	10	0	0	10	0
Kunkel, Tex.	....	3	0	0	0	0	0
Lacy, Balt.	.973	80	135	11	4	150	2
Leach, Tor.*	.981	43	51	1	1	53	0
Lemon, Det.	.992	145	350	4	3	357	1
Lusader, Det.*	.967	22	29	0	1	30	0
Lynn, Balt.*	.991	101	229	2	2	233	1
Lyons, Chi.	1.000	15	33	2	0	35	1
Manning, Mil.	.958	78	68	1	3	72	0
McDowell, Tex.*	.989	125	263	5	3	271	1
McGwire, Oak.	1.000	3	1	0	0	1	0
Meier, Tex.	.917	8	11	0	1	12	0

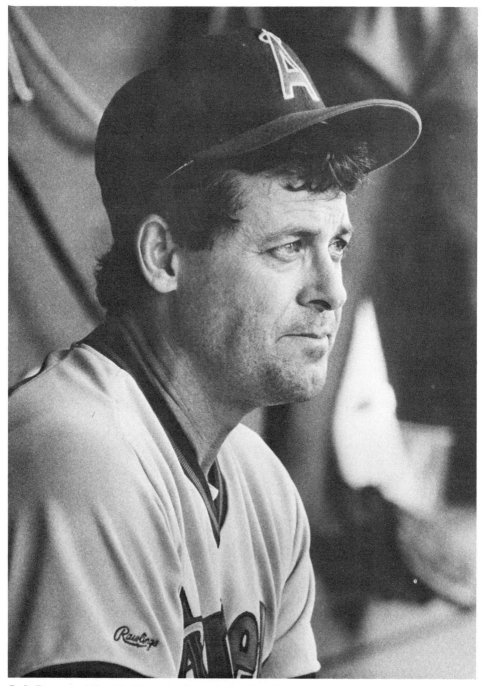

Bob Boone of the California Angels broke Al Lopez's 40-year-old record for most games as a catcher when he caught his 1,919th game on September 16 in Kansas City. Boone, a 16-year veteran who broke into the majors with the Philadelphia Phillies in 1972, finished the 1987 season with 1,935 games caught.

OUTFIELDERS—Continued

Player, Club	PCT	G	PO	A	E	TC	DP
Miller, Cal.	1.000	18	20	0	0	20	0
Moore, Tor.	.667	5	1	1	1	3	0
Moronko, N.Y.	....	2	0	0	0	0	0
Morrison, Det.	1.000	3	5	0	0	5	0
Moseby, Tor.	.980	153	294	7	6	307	1
Moses, Sea.	.987	100	220	5	3	228	0
Murphy, Oak.	.984	79	185	1	3	189	0
Newman, Minn.	....	2	0	0	0	0	0
Nixon, Clev.	1.000	17	21	0	0	21	0
Nixon, Sea.	1.000	32	76	1	0	77	0
Nokes, Det.	1.000	3	5	0	0	5	0
O'Brien, Tex.★	....	2	0	0	0	0	0
Paciorek, Mil.	1.000	5	7	0	0	7	0
Paciorek, Tex.	.950	12	19	0	1	20	0
Parrish, Tex.	....	1	0	0	0	0	0
Parsons, Clev.	1.000	2	1	0	0	1	0
Pasqua, N.Y.★	.985	74	132	2	2	136	0
Petralli, Tex.	.667	3	2	0	1	3	0
Pettis, Cal.	.980	131	344	2	7	353	2
Phillips, Oak.	1.000	2	2	0	0	2	0
Polonia, Oak.★	.979	104	235	2	5	242	1
Puckett, Minn.	.986	147	341	8	5	354	2
Redus, Chi.	.979	123	262	13	6	281	4
Rice, Bos.	.977	94	155	12	4	171	2
Romine, Bos.	1.000	7	10	1	0	11	1
Royster, Chi.-N.Y.	1.000	14	22	1	0	23	0
Ryal, Cal.★	.955	21	21	0	1	22	0
Salas, N.Y.	....	1	0	0	0	0	0
Sanchez, Oak.	1.000	1	1	0	0	1	0
Seitzer, K.C.	1.000	3	2	0	0	2	0
Sheets, Balt.	.975	124	229	5	6	240	2
Shelby, Balt.	1.000	19	25	0	0	25	0
Sheridan, Det.	.976	137	236	6	6	248	1
Sierra, Tex.	.963	157	272	17	11	300	6
Simmons, Balt.	1.000	13	24	2	0	26	1
Smith, K.C.	.915	32	52	2	5	59	0
Snyder, Clev.	.971	139	283	16	9	308	3
Stanley, Tex.	1.000	1	1	0	0	1	0
Tartabull, K.C.	.976	149	228	11	6	245	1
Thornton, Tor.	....	4	0	0	0	0	0
Thurman, K.C.	.971	27	61	5	2	68	1
Tolman, Det.	1.000	7	8	0	0	8	0
Valle, Sea.	....	1	0	0	0	0	0
Ward, N.Y.	.985	94	200	2	3	205	0
Washington, N.Y.★	.988	72	166	3	2	171	1
Washington, Balt.	1.000	2	1	0	0	1	0
Weaver, Sea.★	1.000	4	4	1	0	5	0
White, Cal.	.980	159	424	16	9	449	3
Wiggins, Balt.	.889	5	8	0	1	9	0
Williams, Chi.	.981	115	303	5	6	314	2
Wilson, Cal.	1.000	4	1	0	0	1	0
Wilson, K.C.	.997	143	342	3	1	346	1
Winfield, N.Y.	.989	145	253	6	3	262	1
Young, Minn.	.975	60	117	0	3	120	0
Yount, Mil.	.987	150	380	5	5	390	2

OUTFIELDERS WITH TWO OR MORE CLUBS

Player, Club	PCT	G	PO	A	E	TC	DP
Beniquez, K.C.	1.000	22	33	0	0	33	0
Beniquez, Tor.	.875	7	7	0	1	8	0
Royster, Chi.	1.000	13	22	1	0	23	0
Royster, N.Y.	....	1	0	0	0	0	0

CATCHERS

Leader, Club	PCT	G	PO	A	E	TC	DP	PB
CERONE, N.Y.	.998	111	538	38	1	577	6	13

Player, Club	PCT	G	PO	A	E	TC	DP	PB
Allanson, Clev.	.986	50	252	22	4	278	3	3
Bando, Clev.	.990	86	351	34	4	389	8	9
Boone, Cal.	.983	127	684	56	13	753	11	7
S. Bradley, Sea.	.983	82	433	29	8	470	4	2
Butera, Minn.	.983	51	213	21	4	238	3	9
Cerone, N.Y.	.998	111	538	38	1	577	6	13
Dempsey, Clev.	.984	59	293	18	5	316	3	3
DeWillis, Tor.	.964	13	49	5	2	56	1	0
Dorsett, Clev.	1.000	4	12	0	0	12	0	1
Fimple, Cal.	.913	13	18	3	2	23	0	0
Fisk, Chi.	.990	122	550	57	6	613	15	7
Gedman, Bos.	.976	51	306	14	8	328	1	8
Greenwell, Bos.	.750	1	3	0	1	4	0	0
Hassey, Chi.	1.000	24	114	12	0	126	4	2
Hearn, K.C.	1.000	5	25	0	0	25	0	1
Heath, Det.	.989	67	337	38	4	379	5	5
Karkovice, Chi.	.982	37	147	20	3	170	3	2
Kearney, Sea.	.981	24	94	10	2	106	0	0
Kennedy, Balt.	.993	142	750	58	6	814	11	4
Laudner, Minn.	.987	101	517	28	7	552	2	10
Lindsey, Clev.	1.000	9	28	4	0	32	1	0
Lombardi, N.Y.	1.000	3	7	1	0	8	0	0
Lowry, Det.	1.000	12	38	1	0	39	0	0
Macfarlane, K.C.	1.000	8	29	2	0	31	0	0
Madison, K.C.	.750	3	8	1	3	12	0	0
Marzano, Bos.	.986	52	337	24	5	366	7	9
Mercado, Det.	.980	10	40	8	1	49	1	1
Miller, Cal.	.984	33	110	15	2	127	1	3
Moore, Tor.	.984	44	236	10	4	250	0	4
Myers, Tor.	1.000	7	24	1	0	25	0	0
Narron, Sea.	1.000	3	9	0	0	9	0	0
Nichols, Balt.	1.000	13	39	3	0	42	1	0
Nieto, Minn.	.996	40	210	17	1	228	5	0
Nokes, Det.	.992	109	595	32	5	632	2	7
O'Brien, Mil.	1.000	10	78	11	0	89	0	1
Owen, K.C.	.983	76	370	38	7	415	4	5
Petralli, Tex.	.995	63	349	26	2	377	2	35
Porter, Tex.	1.000	7	10	1	0	11	0	0
Quirk, K.C.	.986	108	532	40	8	580	3	11
Rayford, Balt.	.980	17	92	8	2	102	3	1
Salas, Minn.-N.Y.	.996	55	258	16	1	275	0	10
Sax, Bos.	1.000	2	9	0	0	9	1	0
Schroeder, Mil.	.995	67	363	26	2	391	4	3
Sheaffer, Bos.	.977	25	121	5	3	129	1	2
Sinatro, Oak.	1.000	6	4	0	0	4	0	0
Skinner, N.Y.	.984	64	232	18	4	254	2	1
Slaught, Tex.	.985	85	429	39	7	475	5	20
Stanley, Tex.	.980	61	330	17	7	354	1	18
Stark, Tor.	1.000	5	25	1	0	26	0	1
Steinbach, Oak.	.986	107	640	40	10	690	6	14
Sullivan, Bos.	.994	60	303	29	2	334	6	11
Surhoff, Mil.	.984	98	645	49	11	705	10	9
Tettleton, Oak.	.987	80	433	28	6	467	1	4
Valle, Sea.	.989	75	420	34	5	459	2	2
Van Gorder, Balt.	.978	12	44	1	1	46	0	0
Whitt, Tor.	.994	131	803	55	5	863	10	8
Wynegar, Cal.	.994	28	162	12	1	175	3	1

CATCHERS WITH TWO OR MORE CLUBS

Player, Club	PCT	G	PO	A	E	TC	DP	PB
Salas, Minn.	.989	14	86	3	1	90	0	2
Salas, N.Y.	1.000	41	172	13	0	185	0	8

PITCHERS

Leader, Club	PCT	G	PO	A	E	TC	DP
MORRIS, DET.	1.000	34	31	18	0	49	1
TANANA, DET.★	1.000	34	14	35	0	49	2

Player, Club	PCT	G	PO	A	E	TC	DP
Aase, Balt.	1.000	7	0	1	0	1	0
Akerfelds, Clev.	.917	16	0	11	1	12	1
Aldrich, Mil.	.917	31	6	5	1	12	0
Alexander, Chi.	1.000	11	4	14	0	18	1
Allen, Chi.-N.Y.	.933	23	7	7	1	15	1
Anderson, Minn.★	1.000	4	1	0	0	1	0
Anderson, K.C.	1.000	6	1	3	0	4	0
Anderson, Tex.	1.000	8	2	3	0	5	1

PITCHERS—Continued

Player, Club	PCT	G	PO	A	E	TC	DP
Andujar, Oak.	.857	13	1	11	2	14	1
Armstrong, Clev.	.750	14	1	2	1	4	0
Arnold, Balt.	1.000	27	5	17	0	22	2
Arnsberg, N.Y.	1.000	6	1	5	0	6	0
Atherton, Minn.	.938	59	3	12	1	16	0
Bailes, Clev.*	.926	39	6	19	2	27	0
Ballard, Balt.*	1.000	14	5	10	0	15	1
Bankhead, Sea.	1.000	27	9	9	0	18	1
Bannister, Chi.*	.970	34	10	22	1	33	0
Barker, Mil.	1.000	11	3	6	0	9	0
Bell, Balt.*	1.000	33	8	16	0	24	2
Berenguer, Minn.	.923	47	5	7	1	13	0
Birkbeck, Mil.	.938	10	2	13	1	16	0
Bittiger, Minn.	1.000	3	0	2	0	2	0
Black, K.C.*	1.000	29	4	19	0	23	0
Blyleven, Minn.	.938	37	17	43	4	64	3
Boddicker, Balt.	.970	33	18	46	2	66	5
Bolton, Bos.*	1.000	29	3	9	0	12	1
Bordi, N.Y.	.750	16	2	1	1	4	0
Bosio, Mil.	.905	46	14	24	4	42	5
Boyd, Bos.	1.000	7	4	11	0	15	0
Brown, Sea.	...	1	0	0	0	0	0
Buice, Cal.	.947	57	3	15	1	19	2
Burris, Mil.	1.000	10	3	3	0	6	0
Cadaret, Oak.*	1.000	29	6	6	0	12	1
Camacho, Clev.	1.000	15	1	5	0	6	0
Campbell, Sea.	1.000	9	6	5	0	11	0
Candelaria, Cal.*	1.000	20	4	23	0	27	1
Candiotti, Clev.	.979	32	17	29	1	47	1
Carlton, Clev.-Minn.*	.963	32	3	23	1	27	2
Caudill, Oak.	...	6	0	0	0	0	0
Cerone, N.Y.	...	2	0	0	0	0	0
Cerutti, Tor.*	.952	44	5	15	1	21	1
Ciardi, Mil.	1.000	4	0	3	0	3	0
Citarella, Chi.	1.000	5	0	1	0	1	0
Clancy, Tor.	.968	37	25	36	2	63	4
Clark, Chi.*	1.000	11	0	1	0	1	0
Clarke, Sea.*	1.000	22	1	2	0	3	0
Clear, Mil.	.952	58	8	12	1	21	0
Clemens, Bos.	1.000	36	15	25	0	40	1
Clements, N.Y.*	1.000	55	5	15	0	20	2
Codiroli, Oak.	1.000	3	1	1	0	2	0
Cook, Cal.	1.000	16	4	8	0	12	1
Corbett, Balt.	1.000	11	2	5	0	7	2
Correa, Tex.	.824	15	5	9	3	17	1
Crawford, Bos.	1.000	29	8	10	0	18	2
Creel, Tex.	1.000	6	1	3	0	4	0
Crim, Mil.	.886	53	14	17	4	35	3
S. Davis, Oak.	1.000	5	1	0	0	1	0
Davis, Chi.	.857	13	5	1	1	7	1
Davis, K.C.	.923	27	5	7	1	13	1
DeLeon, Chi.	.889	33	10	14	3	27	0
DeLeon, Balt.	1.000	11	2	0	0	2	0
Dixon, Balt.	.960	34	17	7	1	25	1
Dotson, Chi.	.963	31	14	38	2	54	4
Easterly, Clev.*	1.000	16	3	4	0	7	0
Eckersley, Oak.	.944	54	4	13	1	18	0
Eichhorn, Tor.	.970	89	2	30	1	33	2
Farr, K.C.	.818	47	3	6	2	11	0
Farrell, Clev.	.882	10	8	7	2	17	1
Filson, N.Y.*	1.000	7	1	7	0	8	0
Finley, Cal.*	.944	35	6	11	1	18	1
Flanagan, Balt.-Tor.*	.962	23	8	17	1	26	2
Fraser, Cal.	.955	36	6	15	1	22	0
Frazier, Minn.	.909	54	2	8	1	11	0
Fulton, N.Y.	1.000	3	0	1	0	1	0
Garber, K.C.	1.000	13	2	3	0	5	0
Garcia, Cal.*	1.000	1	0	1	0	1	0
Gardner, Bos.	1.000	49	2	7	0	9	0
Gleaton, K.C.*	.933	48	2	12	1	15	1
Gordon, Tor.-Clev.	.875	26	3	11	2	16	1
Griffin, Balt.	.875	23	6	8	2	16	0
Guante, N.Y.	.750	23	1	2	1	4	0
Gubicza, K.C.	.973	35	32	40	2	74	7
Guetterman, Sea.*	1.000	25	7	22	0	29	3
Guidry, N.Y.*	1.000	22	4	14	0	18	1
Gullickson, N.Y.	1.000	8	2	5	0	7	0
Gumpert, K.C.	1.000	8	1	4	0	5	1
Guzman, Tex.	.960	37	14	34	2	50	3
Haas, Oak.	1.000	9	2	5	0	7	0
Habyan, Balt.	1.000	27	15	17	0	32	2
Harris, Tex.	.872	42	14	20	5	39	1
Harvey, Cal.	...	3	0	0	0	0	0
Henke, Tor.	1.000	72	9	12	0	21	1
Henneman, Det.	1.000	55	8	11	0	19	2
Henry, Tex.	1.000	5	2	1	0	3	0
Hernandez, Det.*	.857	45	2	4	1	7	1
Higuera, Mil.*	.941	35	9	23	2	34	3
Holland, N.Y.*	1.000	3	0	1	0	1	0
Honeycutt, Oak.*	1.000	7	1	3	0	4	0
Hough, Tex.	.987	40	30	46	1	77	3
Howe, Tex.*	1.000	24	4	4	0	8	0
Howell, Oak.	.875	36	3	4	1	8	0
Hudson, N.Y.	1.000	35	9	14	0	23	1
Huismann, Sea.-Clev.	.800	26	4	8	3	15	0
Hurst, Bos.*	.939	33	12	34	3	49	2
D. Jackson, K.C.*	.947	36	13	23	2	38	2
James, Chi.	.800	43	3	9	3	15	1
Jeffcoat, Tex.*	...	2	0	0	0	0	0
John, N.Y.*	.875	33	4	31	5	40	1
Johnson, Mil.*	1.000	10	0	5	0	5	1
Johnson, Tor.	1.000	14	7	8	0	15	0
Jones, Clev.	.808	49	8	13	5	26	3
Kaiser, Clev.*	1.000	2	1	0	0	1	0
Kelly, Det.	...	5	0	0	0	0	0
Key, Tor.*	.953	36	17	44	3	64	5
Kilgus, Tex.*	.800	25	7	9	4	20	2
King, Det.	.974	55	15	22	1	38	3
Kinnunen, Balt.*	1.000	18	0	2	0	2	0
Klink, Minn.*	1.000	12	0	2	0	2	1
Knudson, Mil.	.900	15	5	4	1	10	0
Krueger, Oak.*	...	9	0	0	0	0	0
Lamp, Oak.	1.000	36	1	9	0	10	0
Langston, Sea.*	.961	35	8	41	2	51	3
LaPoint, Chi.*	.962	14	2	23	1	26	0
Lavelle, Tor.-Oak.*	1.000	29	4	5	0	9	0
Lazorko, Cal.	1.000	26	8	25	0	33	1
Leibrandt, K.C.*	.946	35	15	55	4	74	4
Leiper, Oak.*	.944	45	5	12	1	18	1
Leister, Bos.	1.000	8	2	2	0	4	0
Leiter, N.Y.*	1.000	4	0	2	0	2	0
Long, Chi.	.929	29	14	25	3	42	2
Loynd, Tex.	.786	26	5	6	3	14	0
Lucas, Cal.*	.909	48	3	17	2	22	1
Lugo, Cal.	1.000	7	2	2	0	4	0
Madden, Det.*	...	2	0	0	0	0	0
Madrid, Mil.	...	3	0	0	0	0	0
Malloy, Tex.	1.000	2	0	1	0	1	0
Mason, Tex.*	.857	8	1	5	1	7	1
McCaskill, Cal.	.952	14	8	12	1	21	1
McDowell, Chi.	1.000	4	1	6	0	7	0
McGregor, Balt.*	.970	26	7	25	1	33	1
McKeon, Chi.*	1.000	13	4	0	0	4	0
Meridith, Tex.*	1.000	11	0	5	0	5	1
Mesa, Balt.	1.000	6	1	1	0	2	0
Mielke, Tex.	...	3	0	0	0	0	0
Minton, Cal.	1.000	41	5	19	0	24	1
Mirabella, Mil.*	.923	29	7	5	1	13	1
Mohorcic, Tex.	.941	74	9	23	2	34	3
Monteleone, Sea.	1.000	3	0	3	0	3	0
Moore, Cal.	1.000	14	0	2	0	2	0
Moore, Sea.	.966	33	22	34	2	58	4
Morgan, Sea.	.964	34	18	35	2	55	5
Morris, Det.	1.000	34	31	18	0	49	1
Musselman, Tor.*	1.000	68	9	15	0	24	2
G. Nelson, Oak.	.913	54	8	13	2	23	0
Niedenfuer, Balt.	.889	45	5	3	1	9	1
Niekro, N.Y.-Minn.	.931	27	11	16	2	29	1
Niekro, Clev.-Tor.	1.000	25	13	17	0	30	1
Nielsen, Chi.	.867	19	4	9	2	15	0
Niemann, Minn.*	1.000	6	0	1	0	1	0
Nieves, Mil.*	.853	34	6	23	5	34	2
Nipper, Bos.	.959	30	20	27	2	49	2
Noles, Bos.	1.000	4	0	1	0	1	0
Nunez, Sea.	1.000	48	2	5	0	7	0
Nunez, Tor.	1.000	37	5	7	0	12	1
O'Connor, Balt.*	.833	29	3	2	1	6	1
Ontiveros, Oak.	.977	35	14	29	1	44	0

OFFICIAL BASEBALL GUIDE

PITCHERS—Continued

Player, Club	PCT	G	PO	A	E	TC	DP
Otto, Oak.★	1.000	3	1	0	0	1	0
Parker, Sea.	1.000	3	0	1	0	1	0
Pawlowski, Chi.	....	2	0	0	0	0	0
Perez, K.C.	.000	3	0	0	1	1	0
Peterson, Chi.	1.000	1	1	0	0	1	0
Petry, Det.	.949	30	16	21	2	39	0
Plesac, Mil.★	.857	57	0	12	2	14	1
Plunk, Oak.	1.000	32	1	9	0	10	0
Portugal, Minn.	1.000	13	1	6	0	7	2
Powell, Sea.★	1.000	16	2	6	0	8	0
Quisenberry, K.C.	1.000	47	6	13	0	19	3
Rasmussen, N.Y.★	.966	26	6	22	1	29	0
Reardon, Minn.	1.000	63	2	6	0	8	1
Reed, Sea.	1.000	39	10	8	0	18	1
Reuss, Cal.★	.962	17	7	18	1	26	3
Rhoden, N.Y.	.974	30	14	24	1	39	2
Righetti, N.Y.★	.938	60	3	12	1	16	0
Rijo, Oak.	.952	21	10	10	1	21	0
Ritter, Clev.	.900	14	4	5	1	10	0
Robinson, Det.	.920	29	14	9	2	25	2
Rodriguez, Oak	1.000	15	2	6	0	8	1
Russell, Tex.	1.000	52	11	17	0	28	2
Saberhagen, K.C.	.965	33	21	34	2	57	5
Sambito, Bos.★	1.000	47	1	4	0	5	0
Schatzeder, Minn.★	1.000	30	2	5	0	7	0
Schiraldi, Bos.	.929	62	3	10	1	14	0
Schmidt, Balt.	.952	35	6	14	1	21	2
Schrom, Clev.	.960	32	11	13	1	25	1
Searage, Chi.★	1.000	58	1	9	0	10	0
Sellers, Bos.	.943	25	13	20	2	35	0
Shields, Sea.	1.000	20	1	5	0	6	0
Shirley, N.Y.-K.C.★	1.000	15	2	3	0	5	0
Smith, Minn.	1.000	7	0	2	0	2	0
Smithson, Minn.	1.000	21	6	11	0	17	1
Snell, Det.	1.000	22	6	1	0	7	0
Stanley, Bos.	.974	34	15	24	1	38	4
Stapleton, Mil.★	1.000	4	0	2	0	2	0
Stewart, Oak.	.974	37	18	20	1	39	0
Stewart, Clev.	1.000	25	1	3	0	4	2
Stieb, Tor.	.961	33	24	25	2	51	2
Stoddard, K.C.	1.000	17	4	10	0	14	1
Stoddard, N.Y.	.941	57	8	8	1	17	0
Straker, Minn.	.958	31	5	18	1	24	0
Sutton, Cal.	1.000	35	8	18	0	26	1
Swindell, Clev.★	.929	16	0	13	1	14	1
Tanana, Det.★	1.000	34	14	35	0	49	2
Terrell, Det.	.961	35	24	25	2	51	3
Tewksbury, N.Y.	1.000	8	3	5	0	8	1
Thigpen, Chi.	.917	51	8	14	2	24	1
Thomas, Sea.	1.000	8	0	1	0	1	0
Thurmond, Det.★	1.000	48	2	9	0	11	0
Trout, N.Y.★	1.000	14	5	6	0	11	0
Trujillo, Sea.	1.000	28	5	3	0	8	2
Vande Berg, Clev.★	.947	55	7	11	1	19	1
Viola, Minn.★	.930	36	6	34	3	43	1
Von Ohlen, Oak.★	....	4	0	0	0	0	0
Waddell, Clev.	....	6	0	0	0	0	0
Ward, Tor.	1.000	12	2	2	0	4	0
Wegman, Mil.	.966	34	29	27	2	58	2
Wells, Tor.★	1.000	18	2	4	0	6	1
Wilkinson, Sea.★	.875	56	1	6	1	8	0
Williams, Tex.★	.870	85	5	15	3	23	3
Williamson, Balt.	.949	61	20	17	2	39	1
Wills, Clev.	1.000	6	0	2	0	2	0
Winn, Chi.	.970	56	4	28	1	33	5
Witt, Cal.	.940	36	18	29	3	50	2
Witt, Tex.	1.000	26	8	17	0	25	1
Woodward, Bos.	1.000	9	2	1	0	3	0
Yett, Clev.	1.000	37	6	9	0	15	0
Young, Oak.★	.977	31	15	28	1	44	2

PITCHERS WITH TWO OR MORE CLUBS

Player, Club	PCT	G	PO	A	E	TC	DP
Allen, Chi.	.917	15	6	5	1	12	1
Allen, N.Y.	1.000	8	1	2	0	3	0
Carlton, Clev.★	.944	23	2	15	1	18	1
Carlton, Minn.★	1.000	9	1	8	0	9	1
Flanagan, Balt.★	.947	16	5	13	1	19	1
Flanagan, Tor.★	1.000	7	3	4	0	7	1
Gordon, Tor.	1.000	5	0	1	0	1	0
Gordon, Clev.	.867	21	3	10	2	15	1
Huismann, Sea.	.750	6	2	4	2	8	0
Huismann, Clev.	.857	20	2	4	1	7	0
Lavelle, Tor.★	1.000	23	4	5	0	9	0
Lavelle, Oak.★	....	6	0	0	0	0	0
Niekro P., N.Y.	.909	8	5	5	1	11	0
Niekro P., Minn.	.944	19	6	11	1	18	1
Niekro J., Clev.	1.000	22	12	17	0	29	1
Niekro J., Tor.	1.000	3	1	0	0	1	0
Shirley, N.Y.★	1.000	12	1	3	0	4	0
Shirley, K.C.★	1.000	3	1	0	0	1	0

OFFICIAL AMERICAN LEAGUE PITCHING AVERAGES

CLUB PITCHING

Club	W-L	ERA	G	CG	SHO	SV	IP	H	TBF	R	ER	HR	SH	SF	HB	BB	IB	SO	WP	BK
Toronto	96-66	3.74	162	18	8	43	1454.0	1323	6103	655	605	158	56	32	22	567	65	1064	56	14
Kansas City	83-79	3.86	162	44	11	26	1424.0	1424	6114	691	610	128	33	44	36	548	27	923	54	6
Detroit	98-64	4.02	162	33	10	31	1456.0	1430	6267	735	651	180	35	48	35	563	61	976	72	6
Chicago	77-85	4.30	162	29	8	37	1447.2	1436	6188	746	691	189	50	29	35	531	28	792	35	3
Oakland	81-81	4.32	162	18	6	40	1445.2	1442	6238	789	694	176	43	46	36	542	21	1042	52	10
New York	89-73	4.36	162	19	10	47	1446.1	1475	6225	758	700	179	51	48	32	542	31	900	61	9
California	75-87	4.38	162	20	7	36	1457.1	1481	6221	803	709	212	50	34	32	497	30	941	54	7
Seattle	78-84	4.49	162	20	10	33	1430.2	1503	6167	801	713	199	50	59	28	499	19	919	47	9
Milwaukee	91-71	4.62	162	39	6	45	1464.0	1548	6345	817	752	169	38	50	26	529	33	1039	45	8
Minnesota	85-77	4.63	162	28	4	39	1427.1	1465	6205	806	734	210	27	49	50	564	40	990	62	10
Texas	75-87	4.63	162	16	3	27	1444.1	1388	6390	849	743	199	42	45	55	760	34	1103	61	26
Boston	78-84	4.77	162	47	13	16	1436.0	1584	6265	825	761	190	60	46	31	517	38	1034	37	9
Baltimore	67-95	5.01	162	17	6	30	1439.2	1555	6278	880	801	226	41	39	27	547	50	870	52	8
Cleveland	61-101	5.28	162	24	8	25	1422.2	1566	6395	957	835	219	56	60	50	606	28	849	74	12
Totals	1134-1134	4.46	1134	372	114	475	20195.2	20620	87401	11112	9999	2634	632	629	493	7812	505	13442	762	137

PITCHERS' RECORDS

(Top Fifteen Qualifiers for Earned-Run Average Leadership—162 or More Innings)

Pitcher, Club	W	L	PCT	ERA	G	GS	CG	GF	SHO	SV	IP	H	TBF	R	ER	HR	SH	SF	HB	BB	IB	SO	WP	BK
Key, James, Tor.*	17	8	.680	2.76	36	36	8	0	1	0	261.0	210	1033	93	80	24	11	3	2	66	6	161	8	5
Viola, Frank, Minn.*	17	10	.630	2.90	36	36	7	0	1	0	251.2	230	1037	91	81	29	7	3	6	66	4	197	1	1
Clemens, W. Roger, Bos.	20	9	.690	2.97	36	36	18	0	7	0	281.2	248	1157	100	93	19	6	4	6	83	2	256	4	3
Saberhagen, Bret, K.C.	18	10	.643	3.36	33	33	15	0	4	0	257.0	246	1048	99	96	27	8	5	6	53	2	163	6	1
Morris, John, Det.	18	11	.621	3.38	34	34	13	0	0	0	266.0	227	1101	111	100	39	6	5	1	93	7	208	9	3
Leibrandt, Charles, K.C.*	16	11	.593	3.41	35	35	8	0	3	0	240.1	235	1015	103	91	23	5	5	1	74	5	151	12	1
Clancy, James, Tor.	15	11	.577	3.54	37	37	11	0	0	0	241.1	234	1008	100	95	24	9	4	1	80	5	180	5	0
Bannister, Floyd, Chi.*	16	11	.593	3.58	34	34	8	0	2	0	228.2	216	939	91	91	38	7	3	0	49	2	124	11	9
Stewart, David, Oak.*	20	13	.606	3.68	37	37	13	0	1	0	261.1	224	1103	107	107	24	5	5	6	105	0	205	12	9
Hough, Charles, Tex.	18	13	.581	3.79	40	40	13	0	0	0	285.1	242	1231	159	120	36	12	9	19	124	1	223	12	2
Langston, Mark, Sea.*	19	13	.594	3.84	35	35	14	0	3	0	272.0	236	1152	132	116	30	6	9	5	114	0	262	4	1
Higuera, Teodoro, Mil.*	18	10	.643	3.85	35	35	14	1	0	0	261.2	236	1084	120	112	24	6	7	3	87	2	240	9	0
Rhoden, Richard, N.Y.	16	10	.615	3.86	30	30	4	0	3	0	181.2	184	764	84	78	22	8	5	5	61	5	107	6	1
Tanana, Frank, Det.*	15	10	.600	3.91	34	34	5	0	1	1	218.2	216	924	106	95	27	11	11	5	56	5	146	12	
Fraser, William, Cal.	10	10	.500	3.92	36	23	2	6	0	1	176.2	160	744	85	77	26	5	4	6	63	3	106		

ALL PLAYERS LISTED ALPHABETICALLY

(*Lefthanded Pitcher)

Pitcher, Club	W	L	PCT	ERA	G	GS	CG	GF	SHO	SV	IP	H	TBF	R	ER	HR	SH	SF	HB	BB	IB	SO	WP	BK
Aase, Donald, Balt.	1	1	1.000	2.25	7	0	0	6	0	2	8.0	8	33	2	2	1	0	0	0	4	0	3	0	0
Akerfelds, Darrel, Clev.	2	6	.250	6.75	16	13	1	9	0	0	74.2	84	347	60	56	2	2	4	0	38	1	42	7	1
Aldrich, Jay, Mil.	3	1	.750	4.94	31	0	0	9	0	0	58.1	71	253	33	32	8	3	3	2	13	3	22	1	0
Alexander, Doyle, Det.	9	0	1.000	1.53	11	11	3	0	3	0	88.1	63	340	16	15	3	1	0	0	26	0	44	1	1
Allen, Neil, Chi.-N.Y.	0	8	.000	5.93	23	11	0	6	0	0	74.1	97	342	52	49	8	4	2	0	36	1	42	1	0
Anderson, Allan, Minn.*	1	0	1.000	10.95	4	2	0	0	0	0	12.1	20	61	15	15	3	0	0	2	10	2	3	0	0

Pitcher, Club	W	L	PCT	ERA	G	GS	CG	SHO	GF	SV	IP	H	TBF	R	ER	HR	SH	SF	HB	BB	IB	SO	WP	BK
Anderson, Richard, K.C.	0	2	.000	13.85	6	0	0	0	1	0	13.0	26	77	22	20	3	0	0	2	9	1	12	0	0
Anderson, Scott, Tex.	0	1	.000	9.53	8	2	0	0	2	0	11.1	17	59	12	12	0	1	0	1	8	2	6	2	0
Andujar, Joaquin, Oak.	3	5	.375	6.08	13	13	1	0	0	0	60.2	63	265	43	41	11	0	1	3	26	6	32	0	1
Armstrong, Michael, Clev.	1	0	1.000	8.68	14	0	0	0	2	0	18.2	27	91	18	18	4	1	0	0	10	0	9	2	0
Arnold, Tony, Balt.	0	3	.000	5.77	27	0	0	0	10	0	53.0	71	239	35	34	8	4	1	2	17	5	18	1	0
Arnsberg, Bradley, N.Y.	1	3	.250	5.59	6	2	0	0	2	0	19.1	22	91	12	12	5	4	2	0	13	3	14	1	0
Atherton, Keith, Minn.	4	4	.500	4.54	59	0	0	0	29	6	79.1	81	348	40	40	10	2	3	4	30	4	51	1	0
Bailes, Scott, Clev.*	7	8	.467	4.64	39	14	2	0	15	0	120.1	145	551	75	62	21	4	6	4	47	1	65	3	0
Ballard, Jeffrey, Balt.*	2	8	.200	6.59	14	14	0	0	1	0	69.2	100	327	60	51	15	3	1	3	35	0	27	0	0
Bankhead, M. Scott, Sea.	9	8	.529	5.42	27	25	2	2	0	0	149.1	168	642	96	90	35	3	6	0	37	1	95	2	1
Bannister, Floyd, Chi.*	16	11	.593	3.58	34	34	4	0	0	0	228.2	216	939	100	91	38	9	3	2	49	0	124	1	1
Barker, Leonard, Mil.	2	1	.667	5.36	11	11	0	0	1	0	43.2	54	198	27	26	6	1	0	0	17	7	22	1	1
Bell, Eric, Balt.*	10	13	.435	5.45	33	29	2	2	0	0	165.0	174	729	113	100	32	4	2	1	78	0	111	6	0
Berenguer, Juan, Minn.	8	1	.889	3.94	47	6	1	0	13	4	112.0	100	473	51	49	10	2	2	0	47	0	110	2	1
Birkbeck, Michael, Mil.	1	4	.200	6.20	10	10	0	0	0	0	45.0	63	210	33	31	8	0	0	1	19	0	25	0	0
Bittiger, Jeffrey, Minn.	0	1	.000	5.40	3	1	0	0	0	0	8.1	11	36	5	5	2	1	3	5	0	2	5	6	0
Black, Harry, K.C.*	8	6	.571	3.60	29	18	0	0	4	0	122.1	126	520	63	49	16	4	6	9	35	4	61	0	0
Blyleven, R. Aalbert, Minn.	15	12	.556	4.01	37	37	8	1	0	0	267.0	249	1122	132	119	46	7	4	9	101	2	196	6	0
Boddicker, Michael, Balt.	10	12	.455	4.18	33	33	8	2	0	0	226.0	212	950	114	105	29	3	3	7	78	0	152	13	0
Bolton, Thomas, Bos.*	0	1	.000	4.38	29	0	0	0	5	0	33.0	83	287	33	30	5	1	0	2	27	3	49	10	0
Bordi, Richard, N.Y.	3	1	.750	7.64	16	0	0	0	6	1	42.0	42	149	28	28	7	1	3	0	12	1	23	3	0
Bosio, Christopher, Mil.	11	8	.579	5.24	46	19	2	2	8	0	170.0	187	734	102	99	18	3	3	1	50	0	150	0	1
Boyd, Dennis, Bos.	1	3	.250	5.89	7	6	0	0	2	0	36.2	47	167	31	24	6	4	2	2	9	3	12	14	2
Brown, Michael G., Sea.	0	0	....	54.00	1	0	0	0	0	0	0.1	3	4	2	2	0	0	0	0	0	0	0	0	2
Buice, DeWayne, Cal.	6	7	.462	3.39	57	0	0	0	44	17	114.0	87	457	45	43	12	5	2	2	40	0	109	0	0
Burris, B. Ray, Mil.	6	6	.500	5.87	10	2	0	0	7	0	23.0	33	109	16	15	4	1	2	1	12	3	8	3	0
Cadaret, Gregory, Oak.*	6	2	.750	4.54	29	0	0	0	10	0	39.2	37	176	22	20	6	2	2	2	24	1	30	2	0
Camacho, Ernie, Clev.	1	1	.500	4.74	15	0	0	0	9	0	13.2	21	69	14	14	1	1	3	3	5	0	9	1	0
Campbell, Michael, Sea.	1	4	.200	4.71	9	9	1	1	0	0	49.1	41	215	29	26	9	0	2	1	25	1	35	0	0
Candelaria, John, Cal.*	8	6	.571	4.78	20	20	0	0	6	0	116.2	127	487	70	61	17	6	3	0	20	3	74	4	1
Candiotti, Thomas, Clev.	7	18	.280	5.74	32	32	7	2	5	0	201.2	193	888	132	107	28	8	5	4	93	2	111	13	0
Carlton, Steven, Clev.-Minn.*	6	14	.300	9.00	32	21	3	1	5	0	152.0	165	693	111	97	24	7	10	3	86	4	91	7	2
Caudill, William, Oak.	0	0	....	9.00	6	0	0	0	2	1	8.0	10	35	8	8	3	0	0	0	9	0	8	0	5
Cerone, Richard, N.Y.	0	0	....	0.00	2	0	0	0	0	0	2.0	3	7	0	0	0	0	0	0	1	0	1	0	0
Cerutti, John, Tor.*	11	4	.733	4.40	44	21	0	0	7	0	151.1	144	638	75	74	30	5	4	2	59	5	92	0	1
Ciardi, Mark, Mil.	1	1	.500	9.37	4	3	0	0	2	0	16.1	26	81	17	17	5	1	2	1	9	0	8	5	0
Citarella, Ralph, Chi.	0	0	....	7.36	3	0	0	0	0	0	11.0	13	49	9	9	4	0	2	0	4	5	9	5	0
Clancy, James, Tor.	15	11	.577	3.54	37	37	5	2	0	0	241.1	234	1008	103	95	24	5	5	2	80	0	180	3	0
Clark, Bryan, Chi.*	2	2	.500	2.41	11	0	0	0	18	2	18.2	19	77	14	14	1	3	0	5	8	1	8	0	0
Clarke, Stanley, Sea.*	0	0	....	5.48	22	1	0	0	0	0	23.0	31	107	39	39	7	2	1	9	10	3	13	12	0
Clear, Mark, Mil.	8	5	.615	4.48	58	0	0	0	20	6	78.1	70	360	44	39	9	6	0	3	55	4	81	3	3
Clemens, W. Roger, Bos.	20	9	.690	2.97	36	36	18	7	0	0	281.2	248	1157	100	93	19	6	4	9	83	4	256	9	3
Clements, Patrick, N.Y.*	3	3	.500	4.95	55	0	0	0	7	0	80.0	91	347	45	44	4	6	2	1	30	0	36	3	2
Codiroli, Christopher, Oak.	0	5	.000	8.74	3	3	0	0	0	0	11.1	12	54	11	11	1	6	0	5	8	2	4	4	0
Cook, Michael, Cal.	0	0	....	5.50	16	5	0	0	6	0	34.1	34	148	21	21	5	6	0	9	18	0	27	8	1
Corbett, Douglas, Balt.	0	3	.000	7.83	11	0	0	0	5	7	23.0	25	104	20	20	17	1	1	3	13	3	16	2	0
Correa, Edwin, Tex.	3	9	.250	7.89	15	15	2	0	0	0	70.0	83	339	63	59	13	1	2	1	52	2	61	3	0
Crawford, Steven, Bos.	5	4	.556	5.33	29	0	0	0	2	2	72.2	91	324	48	43	2	6	0	3	32	0	43	2	0
Creel, S. Keith, Tex.	0	0	....	4.66	6	0	0	0	0	0	9.2	12	46	5	5	15	1	0	0	5	5	5	9	0
Crim, Charles, Mil.	6	8	.429	3.67	53	0	0	0	18	12	130.0	133	549	60	53	3	6	3	1	39	0	56	2	2
Davis, George, Oak.	1	1	.500	3.26	5	5	0	0	0	0	30.1	28	128	13	11	3	0	1	0	11	0	28	2	0

Pitcher, Club	W	L	PCT	ERA	G	GS	CG	GF	SHO	SV	IP	H	TBF	R	ER	HR	SH	SF	HB	BB	IB	SO	WP	BK
Davis, Joel, Chi.	1	5	.167	5.73	13	9	1	1	0	0	55.0	56	243	35	35	7	1	1	0	29	1	25	4	0
Davis, John, K.C.	5	2	.714	2.27	27	0	0	12	0	1	43.2	29	181	13	11	1	0	4	2	26	4	24	1	1
DeLeon, Jose, Chi.	11	12	.478	4.02	33	31	2	0	0	0	206.0	177	889	106	92	24	6	6	10	97	4	153	2	1
DeLeon, Luis, Balt.	0	1	.000	4.79	33	0	0	3	0	1	20.2	19	89	15	11	4	0	4	2	8	4	13	6	0
Dixon, Kenneth, Balt.	7	10	.412	6.43	11	15	0	13	0	0	105.0	128	470	81	75	31	1	1	1	27	2	91	0	1
Dotson, Richard, Chi.	11	12	.478	4.17	34	31	7	0	2	0	211.1	201	900	109	98	24	4	3	0	86	1	114	5	0
Easterly, James, Clev.*	1	1	.500	4.55	31	0	0	1	0	0	31.2	26	137	17	16	4	2	3	1	13	4	22	5	0
Eckersley, Dennis, Oak.	6	8	.429	3.03	54	2	0	33	0	16	115.2	99	460	41	39	11	3	3	3	17	1	113	5	0
Eichhorn, Mark, Tor.	10	6	.625	3.17	89	0	0	27	0	4	127.2	110	540	47	45	14	7	4	6	52	3	96	3	0
Farr, Steven, K.C.	4	3	.571	4.15	47	9	1	19	0	1	91.0	97	408	47	42	9	0	3	2	44	13	88	3	1
Farrell, John, Clev.	5	1	.833	3.27	10	9	0	1	0	0	69.0	68	297	29	26	7	3	1	5	22	4	28	2	0
Filson, W. Peter, N.Y.*	1	0	1.000	4.67	7	2	1	3	0	0	22.0	26	99	10	8	2	2	0	1	9	1	10	1	1
Finley, Charles, Cal.*	2	7	.222	4.06	35	3	0	17	1	1	90.2	102	405	54	47	12	2	2	3	43	3	63	0	0
Flanagan, Michael, Balt.-Tor.*	6	8	.429	3.92	23	23	4	0	0	0	144.0	148	619	72	65	26	6	1	0	51	4	93	4	3
Fraser, William, Cal.	10	10	.500	4.98	36	23	5	6	1	3	176.2	160	744	85	77	9	5	10	6	63	3	106	3	0
Frazier, George, Minn.	5	5	.500	11.57	54	0	0	26	0	2	81.1	77	363	49	45	4	1	0	2	51	3	58	12	1
Fulton, William, N.Y.	1	0	1.000	2.51	13	0	0	1	0	0	4.2	13	24	6	6	1	0	0	1	1	0	2	6	0
Garber, H. Eugene, K.C.	0	0	....	16.20	49	1	1	12	0	8	14.1	3	55	5	4	0	0	0	0	3	3	3	0	0
Garcia, Miguel, Cal.*	0	0	....	5.42	48	0	0	0	0	0	1.2	3	11	4	3	0	0	0	3	42	0	0	1	0
Gardner, Wesley, Bos.	3	6	.333	4.26	49	1	0	29	0	10	89.2	98	401	55	54	17	4	2	0	28	7	70	4	0
Gleaton, Jerry, K.C.*	4	3	.500	4.09	48	0	0	22	0	5	50.2	38	210	28	24	4	3	3	4	15	3	44	4	1
Gordon, Donald, Tor.-Clev.	4	3	.500	4.36	26	0	0	9	0	1	50.2	57	228	36	23	5	1	3	3	33	3	23	4	0
Griffin, Michael, Balt.	3	5	.375	5.73	23	6	1	6	0	0	74.1	78	331	39	36	9	2	3	1	20	3	42	1	1
Guante, Cecilio, N.Y.	3	3	.600	3.98	23	0	0	9	0	0	44.0	42	195	30	28	8	0	3	6	120	0	46	3	1
Gubicza, Mark, K.C.	13	18	.419	3.98	35	35	10	0	2	0	241.2	231	1036	114	107	18	6	11	6	35	3	166	14	1
Guetterman, A. Lee, Sea.*	11	4	.733	3.81	25	17	2	3	1	0	113.1	117	483	60	48	13	2	5	1	38	2	42	3	0
Guidry, Ronald, N.Y.*	5	8	.385	3.67	22	17	1	4	0	0	117.2	111	493	50	48	14	4	2	4	11	1	96	3	2
Guillickson, William, N.Y.	4	2	.667	4.88	8	8	1	0	0	0	48.0	46	198	29	26	7	1	2	0	6	0	28	0	0
Gumpert, David, K.C.	0	0	....	6.05	8	0	0	3	0	0	19.1	27	88	16	13	3	0	1	3	82	1	13	1	0
Guzman, Jose, Tex.	14	14	.500	4.67	37	30	6	0	2	0	208.1	196	880	115	108	30	6	8	3	9	0	143	6	5
Haas, Bryan, Oak.	2	2	.500	5.75	9	9	0	0	0	0	40.2	57	181	29	26	7	2	1	0	40	0	13	0	1
Habyan, John, Balt.	6	7	.462	4.80	27	13	2	4	0	0	116.1	110	493	67	62	20	4	4	4	56	1	64	3	0
Harris, Greg, Tex.	5	10	.333	4.86	42	19	1	14	0	0	140.2	157	629	92	76	18	7	3	2	2	3	106	4	2
Harvey, Bryan, Cal.	0	0	....	0.00	3	0	0	2	0	0	5.0	6	22	0	0	0	0	0	0	25	0	3	3	0
Henke, Thomas, Tor.	0	6	.000	2.49	72	0	0	62	0	34	94.0	62	363	27	26	10	3	5	2	30	3	128	5	0
Henneman, Michael, Det.	11	3	.786	2.98	55	0	0	28	0	7	96.2	86	399	36	32	8	0	0	0	9	5	75	7	2
Henry, Dwayne, Tex.	0	0	....	9.00	5	0	0	1	0	0	10.0	12	50	10	10	2	3	2	3	20	0	7	1	0
Hernandez, Guillermo, Det.*	3	4	.429	3.67	45	0	0	31	0	8	49.0	53	217	27	20	8	0	3	0	87	7	30	4	0
Higuera, Teodoro, Mil.*	18	10	.643	3.85	35	35	14	0	3	0	261.2	236	1084	120	112	24	6	9	2	87	0	240	2	2
Holland, Alfred, N.Y.*	0	0	....	14.21	3	4	0	0	0	0	6.1	9	37	10	10	1	0	3	2	9	1	5	4	0
Honeycutt, Frederick, Oak.*	1	4	.200	5.32	40	24	0	1	0	0	23.2	25	106	17	14	36	5	14	19	124	5	10	0	1
Hough, Charles, Tex.	18	13	.581	3.79	40	40	13	0	3	0	285.1	238	1231	159	120	36	2	2	3	8	1	223	12	9
Howe, Steven, Tex.*	3	3	.500	4.31	24	0	0	15	0	2	31.1	33	131	15	15	2	3	6	1	21	1	19	2	1
Howell, Jay, Oak.	3	3	.500	5.89	36	0	0	27	0	16	44.1	48	200	30	29	6	4	8	3	57	1	35	4	0
Hudson, Charles, N.Y.	11	7	.611	3.61	36	16	0	7	0	0	154.2	137	641	63	62	19	5	7	2	12	0	100	5	0
Huismann, Mark, Sea.-Clev.	2	4	.400	5.04	26	0	0	11	0	2	50.0	48	212	32	28	7	8	4	1	76	5	38	3	0
Hurst, Bruce, Bos.*	15	13	.536	4.41	33	33	15	0	2	0	238.2	239	1001	124	117	35	7	0	7	109	1	190	3	0
Jackson, Danny, K.C.*	9	18	.333	4.02	36	34	11	0	3	0	224.0	219	981	115	100	11	11	2	7	17	6	152	5	0
James, Robert, Chi.	4	6	.400	4.67	43	0	0	32	0	10	54.0	54	238	32	28	10	4	0	4	4	0	34	3	0
Jeffcoat, J. Michael, Tex.*	0	0	1.000	12.86	2	2	0	0	0	0	7.0	11	35	10	10	0	0	1	0	47	0	1	0	0
John, Thomas, N.Y.*	13	6	.684	4.03	33	33	3	0	1	0	187.2	212	802	95	84	12	12	1	6	47	7	63	9	0

Pitcher, Club	W	L	PCT	ERA	G	GS	CG	GF	SHO	SV	IP	H	TBF	R	ER	HR	SH	SF	HB	BB	IB	SO	WP	BK
Johnson, John H., Mil.*	0	1	.000	9.57	10	2	0	0	0	0	26.1	42	134	30	28	10	1	1	0	18	1	18	1	0
Johnson, Joseph, Tor.	3	5	.375	5.13	14	14	0	0	0	0	66.2	77	289	44	38	8	5	1	2	18	0	27	3	0
Jones, Douglas, Clev.	6	5	.545	3.15	49	0	0	29	0	8	91.1	101	400	45	32	4	5	5	6	24	5	87	0	0
Kaiser, Jeffrey, Clev.*	0	0		16.20	2	0	0	0	0	0	3.1	4	18	6	6	1	0	0	0	3	0	2	0	0
Kelly, Bryan, Det.	0	1	.000	5.06	5	0	0	1	0	0	10.2	12	50	6	6	2	0	0	0	7	4	10	0	5
Key, James, Tor.*	17	8	.680	2.76	36	36	8	0	0	0	261.0	210	1033	93	80	24	11	3	2	66	6	161	8	0
Kilgus, Paul, Tex.*	2	7	.222	4.13	25	12	0	2	0	0	89.1	95	385	45	41	14	2	0	2	31	2	42	0	1
King, Eric, Det.	2	9	.400	4.89	55	4	0	26	0	9	116.0	111	513	67	63	15	3	3	4	60	10	89	5	0
Kinnunen, Michael, Balt.*	0	0		4.95	18	0	0	4	0	0	20.0	27	97	14	11	3	0	1	0	16	1	14	1	0
Klink, Joseph, Minn.*	0	1	.000	6.65	12	0	0	5	0	0	23.0	37	116	18	17	4	1	1	0	11	0	17	1	0
Knudson, Mark, Mil.	4	4	.500	5.37	15	8	1	3	0	0	62.0	88	288	46	37	7	3	5	0	14	3	26	0	2
Krueger, William, Oak.*	0	3	.000	9.53	9	5	0	1	0	0	5.2	9	33	7	6	0	0	0	1	8	3	7	1	0
Lamp, Dennis, Oak.	1	3	.250	5.08	36	0	0	10	0	0	56.2	76	262	38	32	5	3	3	1	22	0	36	0	1
Langston, Mark, Sea.*	19	13	.594	3.84	35	35	14	0	1	0	272.0	242	1152	132	116	30	12	6	5	114	4	262	4	0
LaPoint, David, Chi.-Oak.*	6	3	.667	2.94	14	12	2	0	1	0	82.2	69	341	29	27	7	1	0	1	31	5	43	9	3
Lavelle, Gary, Tor.-Oak.*	2	3	.400	5.91	29	0	0	11	0	1	32.0	40	157	24	21	2	2	2	0	22	2	23	3	0
Lazorko, Jack, Cal.	5	6	.455	4.59	26	11	0	5	0	0	117.2	108	487	68	60	20	3	3	2	44	6	55	1	0
Leibrandt, Charles, K.C.*	16	11	.593	3.41	35	35	8	0	3	0	240.1	235	1015	104	91	23	5	5	4	74	1	151	3	0
Leiper, David, Oak.*	2	1	.667	3.78	45	0	0	6	0	0	52.1	49	224	28	22	6	2	4	1	18	0	33	9	0
Leister, John, Bos.	0	2	.000	9.20	4	4	0	0	0	0	30.1	49	146	31	31	9	0	1	0	12	1	16	3	0
Leiter, Alois, N.Y.*	2	2	.500	6.35	4	4	0	0	0	0	22.2	24	104	16	16	2	1	0	0	15	0	28	4	1
Long, William, Chi.	8	8	.500	4.37	29	23	5	2	0	1	169.0	179	699	85	82	20	6	3	3	28	5	72	0	0
Loynd, Michael, Tex.	1	5	.167	6.10	26	8	0	6	0	0	69.1	82	328	53	47	14	1	2	1	38	0	48	4	0
Lucas, Gary, Cal.*	1	5	.167	3.63	48	0	0	21	0	3	74.1	66	320	41	30	7	7	2	2	35	5	44	3	1
Lugo, Urbano, Cal.	0	2	.000	9.32	7	5	0	0	0	0	28.0	42	143	34	29	8	1	2	0	18	0	24	3	0
Madden, Morris, Det.*	0	0		16.20	2	0	0	0	0	0	1.2	4	12	3	3	0	0	0	0	3	0	1	0	0
Madrid, Alexander, Mil.	0	0		15.19	3	0	0	0	0	0	5.1	11	28	9	9	1	0	0	0	1	0	8	0	0
Malloy, Robert, Tex.*	0	0	.000	6.55	2	0	0	1	0	0	11.0	13	51	11	8	6	0	1	4	3	2	3	0	0
Mason, Michael, Tex.*	0	2	.000	5.59	8	6	0	0	0	0	29.0	37	142	20	18	6	6	0	2	22	0	21	1	0
McCaskill, Kirk, Cal.	4	6	.400	5.67	14	13	0	0	0	0	74.2	84	334	52	47	14	3	5	2	34	2	56	1	0
McDowell, John, Chi.	3	0	1.000	1.93	4	4	1	0	0	0	28.0	16	103	6	6	1	0	1	0	6	0	15	0	0
McGregor, Scott, Balt.*	2	7	.222	6.64	26	15	8	0	1	0	85.1	112	393	69	63	15	3	5	1	35	5	39	0	3
McKeon, Joel, Chi.*	1	2	.333	9.43	13	0	0	4	0	0	21.0	27	102	22	22	8	6	1	2	15	1	14	3	4
Meridith, Ronald, Tex.*	1	0	1.000	6.10	6	0	0	3	0	0	20.2	25	96	18	14	7	1	2	1	12	0	17	1	0
Mesa, Jose, Balt.	1	3	.250	6.03	6	5	0	0	0	0	31.1	38	143	23	21	7	0	0	0	15	2	17	0	0
Mielke, Gary, Tex.	0	0		6.00	3	0	0	1	0	0	3.0	3	14	2	2	2	1	0	0	1	0	3	0	0
Minton, Gregory, Cal.	5	4	.556	3.08	41	0	0	27	0	10	76.0	71	313	28	26	4	5	2	0	29	4	35	2	0
Mirabella, Paul, Mil.*	2	2	.667	4.91	29	0	0	9	0	0	29.1	30	133	20	16	0	2	3	0	16	3	14	2	0
Mohorcic, Dale, Tex.	7	6	.538	2.99	74	0	0	54	0	16	99.1	88	390	34	33	11	7	2	2	19	6	48	3	4
Monteleone, Richard, Sea.	0	0		6.43	3	0	0	1	0	0	7.0	10	34	5	5	2	1	0	0	4	0	2	0	0
Moore, Donnie, Cal.	2	2	.500	2.70	14	0	0	12	0	5	26.2	28	122	12	8	8	1	0	0	13	3	17	4	0
Moore, Michael, Sea.	9	17	.321	4.71	33	33	12	0	2	0	231.0	268	1020	145	121	29	9	8	5	84	3	115	11	2
Morgan, Michael, Sea.	12	17	.414	4.65	34	31	8	0	2	0	207.0	245	898	117	107	25	8	5	3	53	3	85	24	1
Morris, John, Det.	18	11	.621	3.38	34	34	13	0	0	0	266.0	227	1101	111	100	39	6	5	3	93	7	208	5	3
Musselman, Jeffrey, Tor.*	12	5	.706	4.15	68	1	0	14	0	3	89.0	75	381	43	41	7	7	5	0	54	12	54	7	0
Nelson, W. Eugene, Oak.	6	5	.545	3.93	54	6	0	15	0	3	123.2	120	530	58	54	12	3	3	1	35	5	94	2	0
Niedenfuer, Thomas, Balt.	3	5	.375	4.99	45	0	0	39	0	13	52.1	55	233	32	29	11	0	5	3	22	4	37	13	0
Niekro, Joseph, N.Y.-Minn.	7	13	.350	5.33	27	26	1	0	0	0	147.0	155	655	101	87	15	2	2	0	64	1	84	10	3
Niekro, Phillip, Clev.-Tor.	7	13	.350	6.10	25	25	2	0	1	0	135.2	157	617	94	92	22	2	2	4	60	5	64	2	0
Nielsen, J. Scott, Chi.	3	5	.375	6.24	19	7	1	7	0	2	66.1	83	299	48	46	9	1	2	1	25	0	23	3	3
Niemann, Randy, Minn.*	1	0	1.000	8.44	6	0	0	3	1	0	5.1	3	28	5	5	0	2	0	2	7	0	1	1	0

Pitcher, Club	W	L	PCT	ERA	G	GS	CG	SHO	GF	SV	IP	H	TBF	R	ER	HR	SH	SF	HB	BB	IB	SO	WP	BK
Nieves, Juan, Mil.★	14	8	.636	4.88	34	33	3	1	0	0	195.2	199	867	112	106	24	3	7	2	100	5	163	4	0
Nipper, Albert, Bos.	11	12	.478	5.43	30	30	6	0	0	0	174.0	196	777	115	105	30	8	9	7	62	1	89	5	0
Noles, Dickie, Det.	0	0		4.50	4	0	0	0	3	0	2.0	3	9	1	1	1	0	0	0	1	0	0	0	0
Nunez, Edwin, Sea.	3	4	.429	3.80	48	0	0	0	40	12	47.1	45	198	20	20	7	3	4	1	18	8	34	2	1
Nunez, Jose, Tor.	5	2	.714	5.01	37	9	0	0	13	0	97.0	91	427	57	54	12	1	5	0	58	1	99	3	0
O'Connor, Jack, Balt.★	1	1	.500	4.30	29	3	0	0	7	2	46.0	46	202	23	22	5	6	3	4	23	3	33	3	1
Ontiveros, Steven, Oak.	10	8	.556	4.00	35	22	2	1	6	0	150.2	141	645	78	67	19	0	0	0	50	3	97	4	1
Otto, David, Oak.★	0	0		9.00	3	1	0	0	1	0	6.0	7	24	6	6	1	0	1	0	4	0	3	0	0
Parker, J. Clayton, Sea.	0	0		10.57	3	0	0	0	2	0	7.2	15	43	10	9	2	1	0	0	6	0	8	0	0
Pawlowski, John, Chi.	0	0		4.91	2	0	0	0	0	0	3.2	7	20	2	2	0	0	0	0	5	0	2	1	0
Perez, Melido, K.C.	1	1	.500	7.84	3	1	0	0	0	0	10.1	18	53	12	9	2	0	1	1	3	0	5	3	0
Peterson, Adam, Chi.	0	0		13.50	1	1	0	0	0	0	4.0	8	22	6	6	0	0	0	0	10	0	1	0	1
Petry, Daniel, Det.	9	7	.563	5.61	30	21	2	1	3	0	134.2	148	628	101	84	22	4	7	10	76	5	93	8	1
Plesac, Daniel, Mil.★	5	6	.455	2.61	57	0	0	0	47	23	79.1	63	325	30	23	8	3	2	3	23	3	89	8	2
Plunk, Eric, Oak.	4	6	.400	4.74	32	11	0	0	11	0	95.0	91	432	53	50	8	8	5	2	62	2	90	6	0
Portugal, Mark, Minn.	1	3	.250	7.77	16	7	0	0	3	0	44.0	58	204	40	38	13	3	1	0	24	0	28	5	0
Powell, Dennis, Sea.★	1	3	.250	3.15	13	3	0	0	7	0	34.1	32	147	13	12	3	2	2	1	15	3	17	2	0
Quisenberry, Daniel, K.C.	4	1	.800	2.76	47	0	0	0	39	8	49.0	58	215	15	15	1	5	1	7	10	4	17	0	0
Rasmussen, Dennis, N.Y.★	9	7	.563	4.75	26	25	2	0	0	0	146.0	145	627	78	77	31	1	5	1	55	3	89	0	0
Reardon, Jeffrey, Minn.	8	8	.500	4.48	63	0	0	0	58	31	80.1	70	337	41	40	14	5	3	4	28	4	83	8	0
Reed, Jerry, Sea.	1	2	.333	3.42	39	0	0	0	17	7	81.2	79	340	32	31	7	2	1	3	24	3	51	2	0
Reuss, Jerry, Cal.★	4	5	.444	5.25	37	16	0	1	1	0	82.1	112	368	60	48	16	1	7	2	17	5	37	3	1
Rhoden, Richard, N.Y.	16	10	.615	3.86	30	29	4	1	1	0	181.2	184	764	84	78	22	5	1	3	61	1	107	9	3
Righetti, David, N.Y.★	8	6	.571	3.51	60	0	0	0	54	31	95.0	95	419	45	37	9	6	7	3	44	4	77	1	0
Rijo, Jose, Oak.	9	7	.222	5.90	21	14	1	0	3	0	82.1	106	394	67	54	10	6	3	2	41	1	67	5	3
Ritter, Reggie, Clev.	0	1		6.08	14	0	0	0	7	0	26.2	33	130	21	18	5	0	1	0	16	1	11	1	0
Robinson, Jeffrey M., Det.	9	6	.600	5.37	29	21	2	0	2	0	127.1	132	569	86	76	16	3	0	7	54	3	98	4	3
Rodriguez, Ricardo, Oak.	1	0	1.000	2.96	15	0	0	0	11	0	24.1	32	112	8	8	1	2	2	1	15	1	9	0	0
Russell, Jeffrey, Tex.	5	4	.556	4.44	52	2	0	0	12	3	97.1	109	442	56	48	9	0	5	5	52	5	56	6	1
Saberhagen, Bret, K.C.	18	10	.643	3.36	33	33	15	4	0	0	257.0	246	1048	99	96	27	8	0	6	53	3	163	6	0
Sambito, Joseph, Bos.★	2	0	1.000	6.93	47	0	0	0	16	0	37.2	46	171	29	29	8	0	2	3	16	6	35	3	0
Schatzeder, Daniel, Minn.★	3	2	.600	6.39	30	1	0	0	5	1	43.2	64	208	37	31	15	2	0	0	18	2	30	8	2
Schiraldi, Calvin, Bos.	8	5	.571	4.41	62	14	0	0	52	6	83.2	75	361	45	41	13	8	2	1	40	1	93	5	2
Schmidt, David, Balt.	10	5	.909	3.77	35	29	4	2	7	1	124.0	128	515	56	52	13	0	3	0	26	3	30	4	2
Schrom, Kenneth, Clev.	6	13	.316	6.50	32	22	0	0	0	0	153.2	185	695	126	111	29	9	6	3	57	0	70	2	0
Searage, Raymond, Chi.★	2	3	.400	4.20	58	0	0	0	18	1	55.2	56	240	28	26	9	1	2	0	24	1	33	3	0
Sellers, Jeffrey, Bos.	7	8	.467	5.28	25	22	4	0	0	0	139.2	161	620	85	82	16	13	8	3	61	0	99	3	2
Shields, Stephen, Sea.	2	0	1.000	6.60	20	0	0	0	10	0	30.0	43	144	25	22	9	0	6	0	12	2	22	1	0
Shirley, Robert, N.Y.-K.C.★	1	0	1.000	6.31	15	1	0	0	7	0	41.1	46	189	32	29	5	6	1	2	22	3	13	0	0
Smith, LeRoy, Minn.	1	2	.333	4.96	7	1	0	0	0	0	16.1	20	78	10	9	1	2	5	0	6	3	8	4	0
Smithson, B. Mike, Minn.	4	15	.211	5.94	21	20	2	0	0	0	109.0	126	494	76	72	24	13	1	1	38	3	53	4	2
Snell, Nathaniel, Det.	4	2	.667	3.96	22	2	0	0	12	0	38.2	39	168	20	17	4	1	0	1	19	7	19	3	0
Stanley, Robert, Bos.	4	13	.235	5.01	34	20	0	0	5	0	152.2	198	676	96	85	16	7	4	3	42	3	67	7	0
Stapleton, David E., Mil.★	1	0	1.000	1.84	37	0	0	0	16	0	14.2	13	58	3	3	3	0	0	0	3	0	14	0	0
Stewart, David, Oak.	20	13	.606	3.68	37	37	8	1	0	0	261.1	224	1103	121	107	24	7	5	6	105	0	205	11	0
Stewart, Samuel, Clev.	4	2	.667	5.67	25	0	0	0	4	3	27.0	25	130	22	17	4	4	5	1	21	6	25	2	1
Stieb, David, Tor.	13	9	.591	4.09	33	31	3	1	0	0	185.0	164	789	92	84	16	5	5	7	87	1	115	4	0
Stoddard, Robert, K.C.	4	3	.571	4.28	17	0	0	0	6	0	40.0	51	190	26	19	3	1	1	3	22	7	23	4	0
Stoddard, Timothy, N.Y.	4	3	.571	3.50	57	0	0	0	23	8	92.2	83	386	38	36	13	6	6	0	30	9	78	3	5
Straker, Lester, Minn.	8	10	.444	4.37	31	26	1	0	0	0	154.1	150	656	79	75	13	6	5	2	59	6	76	3	5
Sutton, Donald, Cal.	11	11	.500	4.70	35	34	1	0	0	0	191.2	199	795	101	100	38	2	5	7	41	0	99	7	0

Pitcher, Club	W	L	PCT	ERA	G	GS	CG	GF	SHO	SV	IP	H	TBF	R	ER	HR	SH	SF	HB	BB	IB	SO	WP	BK
Swindell, F. Gregory, Clev.*	3	8	.273	5.10	16	15	4	0	0	0	102.1	112	441	62	58	18	4	3	4	37	1	97	0	1
Tanana, Frank, Det.*	15	10	.600	3.91	34	34	5	0	3	0	218.2	216	924	106	95	27	8	11	5	56	5	146	6	0
Terrell, C. Walter, Det.	17	10	.630	4.05	35	35	10	0	1	0	244.2	254	1057	123	110	30	3	10	3	94	7	143	8	0
Tewksbury, Robert, N.Y.	1	4	.200	6.75	8	6	0	1	0	0	33.1	47	149	26	25	5	2	0	0	7	0	12	0	0
Thigpen, Robert, Chi.	7	5	.583	2.73	51	0	0	37	0	16	89.0	86	369	30	27	10	6	3	1	24	5	52	0	1
Thomas, Roy, Sea.	1	1	1.000	5.23	8	0	0	2	0	0	20.2	23	92	12	12	2	0	0	0	11	0	14	2	0
Thurmond, Mark, Det.*	0	1	.000	4.23	48	0	0	23	0	0	61.2	83	280	32	29	5	1	4	3	24	4	21	4	0
Trout, Steven, N.Y.*	0	4	.000	6.60	14	9	0	2	0	5	46.1	51	224	36	34	4	1	0	1	37	0	27	9	1
Trujillo, Michael, Sea.	4	4	.500	6.17	28	7	0	6	0	0	65.2	70	284	45	45	12	0	2	0	26	0	36	6	0
Vande Berg, Edward, Clev.*	4	4	.500	5.10	55	0	0	18	0	1	72.1	96	321	42	41	9	7	5	2	21	2	40	5	1
Viola, Frank, Minn.*	17	10	.630	2.90	36	36	7	0	1	0	251.2	230	1037	91	81	29	0	3	0	66	0	197	1	0
Von Ohlen, David, Oak.*	0	0	–	7.50	4	0	0	3	0	0	6.0	10	27	5	5	1	1	1	0	1	0	3	0	0
Waddell,Thomas, Clev.	0	1	.000	14.29	6	0	0	2	0	0	5.2	7	32	10	9	0	0	0	1	7	0	6	1	0
Ward, R. Duane, Tor.	1	1	1.000	6.94	12	1	0	4	0	0	11.2	14	57	9	9	1	1	1	0	12	2	10	0	0
Wegman, William, Mil.	12	11	.522	4.24	34	33	7	0	0	0	225.0	229	934	113	106	31	4	6	6	53	2	102	4	2
Wells, David, Tor.*	4	3	.571	3.99	18	2	0	6	0	1	29.1	37	132	14	13	0	1	0	0	12	0	32	0	0
Wilkinson, William, Sea.*	3	4	.429	3.66	56	0	0	29	0	10	76.1	61	303	33	31	8	2	6	0	21	1	73	4	0
Williams, Mitchell, Tex.*	8	6	.571	3.23	85	1	0	32	0	6	108.2	63	469	47	39	9	4	3	0	94	7	129	4	2
Williamson, Mark, Balt.	8	9	.471	4.03	61	2	0	36	0	3	125.0	122	520	59	56	12	5	3	7	41	15	73	3	0
Wills, Frank, Clev.	0	1	.000	5.06	6	0	0	4	0	1	5.1	5	26	3	3	0	1	1	3	7	0	4	0	0
Winn, James, Chi.	1	6	.400	4.79	56	0	0	24	0	6	94.0	95	422	54	50	10	4	6	0	62	5	44	4	0
Witt, Michael, Cal.	16	14	.533	4.01	36	36	10	0	0	0	247.0	252	1065	128	110	34	6	6	6	84	1	192	6	0
Witt, Robert, Tex.	8	10	.444	4.91	26	25	1	0	0	0	143.0	114	673	82	78	10	5	5	4	140	0	160	7	2
Woodward, Robert, Bos.	1	1	.500	7.05	9	6	0	1	0	0	37.0	53	177	33	29	6	2	2	3	15	3	15	2	1
Yett, Richard, Clev.	3	9	.250	5.25	37	11	2	13	0	0	97.2	96	432	63	57	21	4	2	1	49	0	59	9	1
Young, Curtis, Oak.*	13	7	.650	4.08	31	31	6	0	0	0	203.0	194	828	102	92	38	6	4	3	44	3	124	2	1

PITCHERS WITH TWO OR MORE CLUBS IN 1987
(Listed alphabetically, first club on top)

Pitcher, Club	W	L	PCT	ERA	G	GS	CG	GF	SHO	SV	IP	H	TBF	R	ER	HR	SH	SF	HB	BB	IB	SO	WP	BK
Allen, Neil, Chi.	0	7	.000	7.07	15	10	3	2	0	0	49.2	74	236	40	39	6	3	2	2	26	0	26	1	0
Allen, Neil, N.Y.	0	0	.000	3.65	8	1	0	4	0	0	24.2	23	106	12	10	2	1	0	0	10	1	16	0	0
Carlton, Steven, Clev.*	5	9	.357	5.37	23	14	3	3	1	0	109.0	111	493	76	65	17	6	4	2	63	3	71	5	4
Carlton, Steven, Minn.*	1	5	.167	6.70	9	7	0	2	0	1	43.0	54	200	35	32	7	0	0	2	23	1	20	1	1
Flanagan, Michael, Balt.*	3	6	.333	4.94	16	16	4	0	0	0	94.2	102	410	57	52	9	6	1	0	36	1	50	1	0
Flanagan, Michael, Tor.*	3	2	.600	2.37	7	7	0	0	0	0	49.1	46	209	15	13	3	0	0	4	15	3	43	2	0
Gordon, Donald, Tor.	0	0	–	4.09	5	0	0	2	0	0	11.0	8	43	5	5	2	0	2	0	3	0	3	0	0
Gordon, Donald, Clev.	0	3	.000	4.08	21	0	0	7	0	1	39.2	49	185	31	18	3	1	1	4	12	3	20	0	0
Huismann, Mark, Sea.	2	3	.400	4.91	6	0	0	1	0	0	14.2	10	61	10	8	1	3	2	2	4	0	15	0	0
Huismann, Mark, Clev.	2	3	.400	5.09	20	0	0	10	0	2	35.1	38	151	22	20	6	1	1	0	8	0	23	3	1
Lavelle, Gary, Tor.*	2	3	.400	5.53	23	0	0	9	0	1	27.2	36	138	20	17	2	3	1	4	19	4	17	1	0
Lavelle, Gary, Oak.*	0	0	–	8.31	6	0	0	2	0	0	4.1	4	19	4	4	0	1	1	0	3	0	6	0	0
Niekro, Joseph, N.Y.	3	4	.429	3.55	8	8	1	0	0	0	50.2	40	211	25	20	4	1	4	4	19	0	30	0	0
Niekro, Joseph, Minn.	4	9	.308	6.26	19	18	2	0	0	0	96.1	115	444	76	67	11	2	5	6	45	0	54	13	0
Niekro, Phillip, Clev.	7	11	.389	5.89	22	22	2	0	0	0	123.2	142	561	83	81	18	4	0	4	53	0	57	9	2
Niekro, Phillip, Tor.	0	2	.000	8.25	3	3	0	0	0	0	12.0	15	56	11	11	4	0	0	0	7	0	7	1	1
Shirley, Robert, N.Y.*	1	0	1.000	4.50	12	1	0	6	0	0	34.0	36	152	20	17	4	0	6	0	16	0	12	0	0
Shirley, Robert, K.C.*	0	0	–	14.73	3	0	0	1	0	0	7.1	10	37	12	12	5	0	0	0	6	0	1	1	0

NATIONAL LEAGUE

Including

Team Reviews of 1987 Season

Team Day-by-Day Scores

1987 Standings, Home-Away Records

1987 Pitching Against Each Club

1987 Official N.L. Batting Averages

1987 Official N.L. Fielding Averages

1987 Official N.L. Pitching Averages

When third baseman Terry Pendleton hit his September 11 home run against the Mets, he set the course for the Cardinals' stretch drive.

Cardinals Regain '85 Form

By RICK HUMMEL

It was September 11 and midnight was approaching. Nearly 52,000 hostiles in New York were cheering the St. Louis Cardinals' darkest hour.

Only seven weeks earlier, the Cardinals had led the National League East by 9½ games. Now, they were within one strike of losing to the second-place Mets, who would climb to within half a game and, many believed, mark the beginning of the end of the Cardinals.

But between the dark and daylight came Terry Pendleton's hour and the Cardinals gained their most incredible victory in a fairly improbable season.

With a boisterous Shea Stadium crowd crowing last rites to the Redbirds, Willie McGee's two-strike, two-out single—only the Cardinals' second hit of the game—cut the Mets' lead to 4-2. Pendleton, the next batter, pounded sinkerballer Roger McDowell's first pitch into the dirt. He pounded the second, too, but sent it 420 feet away, beyond the center-field wall, to tie the score. The Cardinals won the game, 6-4, in the 10th, but more significantly, set the tone for the stretch.

"It was another chance for us to go for the jugular vein and we couldn't do it," Mets first baseman Keith Hernandez said after the game. "Give Pendleton some credit. . . . If they win it, that'll be the hit that did it."

Properly inspired, St. Louis finished 95-67 to win the East by three games over New York. The Cardinals also won their second pennant in three seasons—and lost their second World Series after leading three games to two in both 1985 and 1987.

It was evident to second baseman Tom Herr in spring training that things would be different from 1986, when St. Louis was the league's worst-hitting team and finished 28½ games behind New York.

"From Day One, you could sense the intensity and a better level of concentration," Herr said. "It was the best I'd seen in a few years. When we started the season, we knew we had as good a club as any in our division."

That specific club didn't last long. Catcher Tony Pena, acquired from Pittsburgh during spring training for Andy Van Slyke, Mike Dunne and Mike LaValliere, suffered a broken left thumb in the third game of the season. He missed six weeks. Nine days after Pena was hurt, ace lefthander John Tudor suffered a broken bone below his right knee when Mets catcher Barry Lyons leveled him in the dugout while chasing a pop foul. Tudor was out 3½ months. A week after the Tudor injury, Herr suffered a torn groin muscle that sidelined him almost three weeks. And rookie right fielder Jim Lindeman, who made Van Slyke expendable, twice went on the disabled list with back spasms that nagged him all season.

"I thought there was no way we could win," Manager Whitey Herzog said. "I didn't think any ball club could get by."

But here is where the Steve Lakes, Jose Oquendos, Curt Fords and Rod Bookers of the world came in.

Lake, who had only 329 major league at-bats in four seasons, hit .298 while Pena recovered. Oquendo, acquired from the Mets in an undistinguished 1985 trade, became the Cardinals' "Secret Weapon" as he started at seven positions, batted .286 for the season and was among the league's top pinch-hitters with a .385 average. Booker, a veteran of seven minor league seasons, was called up to replace Herr and hit .277 with St. Louis. Ford, who had hit only .248 in 1986, hit .336 for the first three months of the season in right field.

The starting rotation was dealt another blow when lefthander Greg Mathews lost his changeup and effectiveness. He was sent to Louisville for almost three weeks. Rookie lefthander Joe Magrane, called up after Tudor was felled, reeled off four quick victories to avert a potential disaster.

For the first 3½ months, the Cardinals' potent offense was their savior. The Cards averaged 5.6 runs per game while padding their record to 61-32, good for a 9½-game lead through July 23. They averaged 3.9 runs the rest of the way, sputtering home with a 34-35 record.

The Jack Clark factor was the most relative to the scoring trends.

Clark had a torrid first half with 26 home runs, 86 runs batted in and a .311 average. But in an injury-plagued second half, the big first baseman drove in only 20 more runs and hit nine homers. His season ended September 9 when he slid into first base and sprained his right ankle.

"Let's face it," Herzog said. "We're not nearly the same team with him out of the lineup. But for us to be a game-and-a-half up when he got hurt and to win was almost amazing."

Clark finished among the league leaders

SCORES OF ST. LOUIS CARDINALS' 1987 GAMES

APRIL

Date		W/L	Score	Winner	Loser
7—At Chicago		W	9-3	Tudor	Sutcliffe
9—At Chicago		W	4-2	Cox	Trout
10—At Pitts.		L	3-4	D. Robinson	LaPoint
11—At Pitts.		W	6-3	Forsch	Kipper
12—At Pitts.		L	4-7	Patterson	Tudor
13—At Pitts.		W	8-4	Cox	Drabek
14—Montreal		L	4-9	Tibbs	Mathews
16—Montreal		L	3-4	Heaton	Forsch
17—New York		W	4-3	Tudor	Ojeda
18—New York		W	12-8*	LaPoint	Orosco
19—New York		W	4-2	Mathews	Fernandez
21—Chicago		L	4-5	Noles	Dawley
22—Chicago		L	4-5	Sutcliffe	Dawley
23—Chicago		W	5-2	Cox	Maddux
24—At N.Y.		L	1-2	Fernandez	Mathews
25—At N.Y.		W	3-2	Magrane	Aguilera
26—At N.Y.		W	7-4	Forsch	Darling
28—San Diego		L	2-5	Whitson	Conroy
29—San Diego		W	10-6	Perry	McCullers
30—San Diego		W	5-4	Mathews	S. Davis
			Won 12, Lost 8		

MAY

Date		W/L	Score	Winner	Loser
1—Los Ang.		W	5-4*	Horton	Young
2—Los Ang.		L	6-7	Holton	Worrell
4—San Fran.		L	7-10	LaCoss	Dawley
5—San Fran.		L	6-10	Garrelts	Mathews
6—At S. Diego		W	3-0	Magrane	Whitson
7—At S. Diego		W	17-10	Forsch	Hawkins
8—At L.A.		W	5-1	Conroy	Pena
9—At L.A.		L	2-4	Valenzuela	Cox
10—At L.A.		L	6-7	Young	Perry
12—At S. Fran.		W	6-5	Magrane	Davis
13—At S. Fran.		W	7-6	Soff	J. Robinson
15—Cincinnati		W	5-4	Cox	Power
16—Cincinnati		W	6-5	Conroy	Soto
17—Cincinnati		W	10-2	Tunnell	Reuss
19—At Atlanta		L	5-6	Garber	Worrell
20—At Atlanta		W	5-4	Horton	Garber
21—At Atlanta		W	7-2	Forsch	Smith
22—At Hous.		W	7-5	Conroy	Ryan
23—At Hous.		W	4-3	Perry	Knepper
24—At Hous.		W	8-2	Magrane	Scott
25—Atlanta		L	5-14	Smith	Cox
26—Atlanta		L	4-5	Alexander	Dawley
28—Atlanta		W	11-5	Dawley	Mahler
29—Houston		W	8-2	Tunnell	Lopez
30—Houston		W	3-2	Cox	Knepper
31—Houston		L	7-8	Deshaies	Mathews
			Won 17, Lost 9		

JUNE

Date		W/L	Score	Winner	Loser
1—At Cinn.		W	8-6*	Worrell	Robinson
2—At Cinn.		L	2-3	Hoffman	Tunnell
3—At Cinn.		L	4-6	Pacillo	Conroy
4—At Chicago		W	3-1	Cox	Maddux
5—At Chicago		W	5-1	Mathews	Sanderson
6—At Chicago		L	5-6	Moyer	Forsch
7—At Chicago		W	13-9	Dawley	Mason
8—At Phila.		W	12-8	Horton	Carman
9—At Phila.		L	2-3	Ruffin	Cox
10—At Phila.		W	3-1	Mathews	Gross
12—Chicago		W	4-1	Forsch	Moyer
13—Chicago		W	9-2	Tunnell	Sutcliffe
14—Chicago		W	3-2	Cox	Sanderson
15—Pittsburgh		L	1-3	Dunne	Mathews
16—Pittsburgh		W	11-1	Dawley	Drabek
17—Pittsburgh		L	1-4	Reuschel	Forsch
18—Pittsburgh		W	8-6*	Dawley	Robinson
19—Montreal		L	7-8†	McClure	Dawley
20—Montreal		L	5-7	Parrett	Worrell
21—Montreal		W	7-3	Magrane	Sebra
23—Phila.		L	1-4	Rawley	Tunnell
24—Phila.		W	5-3	Worrell	Jackson
25—Phila.		W	3-0	Mathews	Ruffin
26—At Mon.		L	1-5	Sebra	Magrane
27—At Mon.		W	15-5	Forsch	Smith
28—At Mon.		W	7-6†	Dayley	Parrett
29—At N.Y.		W	8-7†	Worrell	Orosco
30—At N.Y.		L	2-3	Gooden	Mathews
			Won 17, Lost 11		

JULY

Date		W/L	Score	Winner	Loser
1—At N.Y.		L	6-9	Myers	Dawley
3—At Atlanta		W	9-1	Forsch	Puleo
4—At Atlanta		W	3-0	Cox	Smith
5—At Atlanta		W	4-1	Mathews	Alexander
7—Los Ang.		W	5-4	Worrell	Leary
7—Los Ang.		W	5-4*	Dayley	Howell
8—Los Ang.		W	6-3	Forsch	Valenzuela
8—Los Ang.		W	8-7*	Perry	Hershiser

JULY

Date		W/L	Score	Winner	Loser
9—San Fran.		W	7-6*	Horton	Garrelts
10—San Fran.		W	7-5‡	Tunnell	Lefferts
11—San Fran.		L	1-3	Downs	Magrane
12—San Fran.		W	3-2	Horton	Hammaker
16—At S. Diego		L	8-9*	McCullers	Worrell
17—At S. Diego		W	4-3	Mathews	Grant
18—At S. Diego		L	3-4*	Gossage	Dayley
19—At S. Diego		W	5-4*	Dayley	Gossage
21—At L.A.		W	6-1	Forsch	Valenzuela
22—At L.A.		W	3-1	Dayley	Welch
23—At L.A.		W	9-6	Dayley	Young
24—At S. Fran.		L	3-4	Hammaker	Horton
25—At S. Fran.		L	4-5	Garrelts	Dawley
26—At S. Fran.		L	3-6*	Garrelts	Worrell
26—At S. Fran.		L	2-5	LaCoss	Mathews
28—New York		L	4-6	Darling	Worrell
29—New York		L	4-6*	McDowell	Perry
30—New York		L	3-5	Gooden	Mathews
31—Pittsburgh		W	4-3	Dayley	Jones
			Won 16, Lost 11		

AUGUST

Date		W/L	Score	Winner	Loser
1—Pittsburgh		W	7-6*	Worrell	Jones
2—Pittsburgh		W	9-1	Magrane	Pena
3—At Mon.		W	5-2	Horton	Smith
4—At Mon.		L	5-10	McClure	Tunnell
5—At Mon.		L	1-2‡	St. Claire	Dayley
6—At Phila.		W	5-2	Tudor	Hume
7—At Phila.		L	5-15	Rawley	Magrane
8—At Phila.		W	9-5	Worrell	Carman
9—At Phila.		L	7-8§	Ritchie	Horton
10—At Pitts.		W	6-0	Forsch	Fisher
11—At Pitts.		W	6-5	Dayley	Reuschel
12—At Pitts.		L	0-11	Walk	Magrane
13—Phila.		L	2-4‡	Bedrosian	Dayley
14—Phila.		W	8-4	Mathews	Ruffin
15—Phila.		L	2-5	Gross	Forsch
16—Phila.		L	3-4	Rawley	Tudor
18—At Hous.		L	0-4	Ryan	Cox
19—At Hous.		L	1-2	Knepper	Magrane
20—At Hous.		L	4-5	Childress	Dayley
21—At Cinn.		W	2-1	Tudor	Hoffman
22—At Cinn.		W	9-7	Perry	Murphy
23—At Cinn.		W	12-6	Cox	Gullickson
24—Houston		L	2-5	Knepper	Magrane
25—Houston		W	7-1	Mathews	Darwin
26—Houston		W	5-4	Dayley	Agosto
28—Atlanta		W	4-3	Worrell	Garber
29—Atlanta		W	4-2	Magrane	Puleo
30—Atlanta		W	4-3	Dawley	Acker
31—Cincinnati		W	4-0	Tudor	Power
			Won 17, Lost 12		

SEPTEMBER

Date		W/L	Score	Winner	Loser
1—Cincinnati		L	4-7	Hoffman	Horton
2—Cincinnati		L	1-3	Williams	Cox
4—San Diego		W	4-2	Worrell	M. Davis
5—San Diego		L	1-4	Grant	Mathews
6—San Diego		W	6-4	Tudor	Show
7—At Mon.		L	2-9	Perez	Cox
8—At Mon.		L	1-4	Smith	Forsch
9—At Mon.		L	3-8	Martinez	Magrane
11—At N.Y.		W	6-4*	Dayley	Orosco
12—At N.Y.		W	8-1	Mathews	Gooden
13—At N.Y.		L	2-4	Cone	Cox
14—At Phila.		L	2-3†	Calhoun	Dayley
15—At Phila.		W	4-3	Horton	Gross
16—At Pitts.		W	8-5	Tudor	Drabek
17—At Pitts.		W	0-1	Dunne	Mathews
18—Chicago		L	1-8	Sutcliffe	Cox
19—Chicago		W	5-3	Magrane	Sanderson
20—Chicago		W	10-2	Forsch	Maddux
21—Phila.		W	3-1	Tudor	Carman
22—Phila.		W	3-2	Cox	Rawley
23—Pittsburgh		L	0-2	Fisher	Mathews
24—Pittsburgh		W	3-2	Horton	J. Robinson
25—At Chicago		L	1-2	Sanderson	Forsch
26—At Chicago		W	5-3	Tudor	Sutcliffe
27—At Chicago		L	3-7	Lancaster	Cox
29—Montreal		W	1-0	Magrane	Martinez
29—Montreal		W	3-0	Mathews	Smith
30—Montreal		L	1-6	Perez	Forsch
			Won 14, Lost 14		

OCTOBER

Date		W/L	Score	Winner	Loser
1—Montreal		W	8-2	Cox	Tibbs
2—New York		W	3-2	Tudor	Mitchell
3—New York		L	1-7	Aguilera	Tunnell
4—New York		L	6-11	Myers	Dawley
			Won 2, Lost 2		

*10 innings. †11 innings. ‡13 innings. §14 innings.

Cardinal first baseman Jack Clark set a torrid offensive pace until his season ended September 9.

in home runs, RBIs and game-winning RBIs (15), and topped the league in walks (a team-record 136), on-base percentage (.459) and slugging average (.597).

With Clark out, McGee was the man on the spot—the No. 5 spot—and he delivered, driving in a career-high 105 runs to rank fifth in the league. The fleet center fielder ranked third in triples (11), set a personal high with 11 home runs and batted .285, up from .256 in 1986.

Pendleton was equally productive, proving his contributions weren't limited to his "Hot Corner Houdini" act, which earned him a Gold Glove. Pendleton blasted 12 home runs and drove in 96 (both career highs), giving the Cardinals 307 RBIs from the meat of their order.

That they could do that was a credit to Vince Coleman and Ozzie Smith.

Coleman, prone in the past to extended hitting slumps, avoided them in 1987. Batting leadoff, he hit a career-high .289, was second in the league in runs (121), fourth in hits (180) and fifth in triples (10). He became the first player to steal more than 100 bases in each of his first three seasons, swiping 109 to lead the majors.

Smith had, arguably, the finest year of any Cardinal. The Gold Glove shortstop

led the team with a .303 average (his first .300 season), tied for second in the league with 40 doubles, was third in hits (182), sixth in walks (89) and seventh in stolen bases (43). But perhaps most impressive were Ozzie's 75 RBIs—without a home run —as the No. 2 hitter.

Herr, batting third, contributed 14 game-winning RBIs, including a dramatic 10th-inning grand slam to beat the Mets on April 18. He finished the season with 83 RBIs and a .263 average.

Feast turned to famine with the Cardinals' seventh and eighth hitters: Lindeman and Pena. Lindeman hit only .208 as a right fielder/first baseman. Pena, a .286 career hitter, slumped to .214.

Rookie John Morris (.261) teamed with Ford (.285) in right to give Herzog flexibility. Veteran Dan Driessen, called up from Louisville when Clark was injured, provided experience at first.

Though no starter won more than 11 games, revitalized pitching helped the Cardinals through the second half.

Tudor returned August 1 and won eight of nine decisions to finish 10-2. Mathews, clearly helped by his stint in the minors, was 11-11 and pitched into the seventh inning in 17 of his last 25 starts. Magrane (9-7) ranked among the league leaders with a 3.54 earned-run average and led the staff with four complete games. Righthander Danny Cox (11-9) lost five of six decisions in September but pitched complete games when the Cardinals clinched the division and the pennant. Veteran righthander Bob Forsch was 10-3 through early August and finished 11-7.

Lefthander Ricky Horton (8-3) was the link between the bullpen and rotation, making five of his six starts in July, when Cox suffered a broken bone in his right foot. Horton also finished second on the club with seven saves.

Righthander Todd Worrell (8-6, 2.66 ERA), the 1986 Rookie of the Year and league leader in saves (36), had another strong year with 33 saves, although he missed in 14 opportunities.

Ken Dayley, who underwent off-season elbow surgery, made his first appearance May 21 and provided the perfect lefthanded complement to Worrell. Dayley finished 9-5 with a 2.66 ERA and four saves in 53 games.

"Without him, we'd have been in fourth place," Herzog said. "It's that simple."

Yet for the third time in six seasons, the Cardinals were N.L. champions. And for the first time in club history, the Cardinals drew 3 million fans as they topped the majors in attendance (3,072,122).

Howard Johnson took over the Mets' third-base job and surprised every-body with his 36-homer, 99-RBI offensive explosion.

Injury Bug Cripples Mets

By JACK LANG

Pitching was a major part of the New York Mets' success story of 1986. And, as expected, it also told the story in 1987, when the defending World Series champions were overwhelming favorites to repeat.

Trouble is, the pitchers determined the Mets' destiny in absentia.

From the outset, injuries crippled the staff and, consequently, the Mets' chances of becoming the first back-to-back World Series champions since the 1977-78 New York Yankees. After rolling to a 108-54 record and 21½-game advantage over their closest pursuer in 1986, the Mets were forced to play catch-up in 1987. They finished 92-70, three games behind the National League East champion St. Louis Cardinals.

If it was any comfort, Manager Davey Johnson could begin preparing for difficult times even before the season began.

On March 30, relief ace Roger McDowell underwent hernia surgery that sidelined him until May 14. Without McDowell, who won 14 games and saved 22 in 1986, the Mets were 14-17. Stopper Jesse Orosco could not shoulder the burden alone and was 1-4 (but with seven saves) in those first five weeks.

The loss of McDowell was a blow, but the departure of Dwight Gooden was a jolt from which New York never fully recovered. On April 1, the Mets' ace righthander left the team to enter a drug rehabilitation center. He didn't return until June 5. And although Gooden finished strong—15-7 with a 3.21 earned-run average—the Mets struggled to stay near .500 in his absence.

Lefthander Bob Ojeda made only four starts before he developed a sore elbow. He started only one of the next 13 games, then lasted only an inning on May 9. Surgery followed and the man who had won 18 games in 1986 was wearing a cast for most of '87. He returned in September but was only 3-5 for the season.

Rick Aguilera, tabbed before the season as the No. 5 starter, moved into the forefront, then suffered damaged elbow ligaments in late May. He was sidelined until August 14 but still finished 11-3 with a 3.60 ERA.

Lefthander Sid Fernandez, 16-6 in 1986, missed two starts in May with a strained left knee. A sore shoulder in August, however, rendered him virtually useless for the month. Fernandez finished 12-8.

Rookie David Cone, obtained from the Kansas City Royals at the end of spring training, was pressed into service as a starter. He pitched effectively until May 27, when he fractured a finger while trying to bunt. He wasn't activated until August 13 and finished 5-6.

Ron Darling was the one starter to remain healthy—for most of the season. The man famous for good games and no decisions held true to form. The former Yale ace was 2-0 in his first four starts then made 14 more before he won his next game, on July 7. Then on September 11, he fell victim to the injury jinx.

In a crucial matchup with the first-place Cardinals at Shea Stadium, Darling suffered torn thumb ligaments when he dived for a bunt in the sixth inning. He lasted into the seventh but then departed after having surrendered only one hit. The Mets got to within a strike of cutting the St. Louis lead to half a game, but McDowell surrendered a game-tying two-run homer to Terry Pendleton. The Mets lost the game, 6-4, in 10 innings, and St. Louis came to life down the stretch.

Darling led the Mets with 167 strikeouts and finished 12-8.

As their pitchers fell, the Mets dipped into the farm system for help. Tom Edens, Bob Gibson, Jeff Innis, Terry Leach, John Mitchell and Don Schulze joined the team.

Leach proved to be one of the most valuable members of the staff, going 10-0 before suffering his first loss August 15. But even he was not immune from injury. Leach suffered torn cartilage in his right knee July 11 and was out three weeks. He finished 11-1 with a 3.22 ERA in 44 appearances, including 12 starts.

Mitchell started 19 games and finished 3-6.

The pitching loss ultimately led to the Mets' demise, but there were other discomforting developments.

Internal bickering coincided with the club's disappointing start. By mid-May the Mets were under .500, in fifth place and pitchers were questioning the defense. When Darryl Strawberry reported he had the flu during an important June 29-July 1 series against St. Louis, Lee Mazzilli and Wally Backman accused the right fielder of not giving his best. Name-calling and a team meeting followed. Johnson, who deplores meetings, called no fewer than five during the season.

Len Dykstra and Mookie Wilson, un-

SCORES OF NEW YORK METS' 1987 GAMES

APRIL

Date		Score	Winner	Loser
7—Pittsburgh	W	3-2	Ojeda	Patterson
9—Pittsburgh	W	4-2	Walter	Easley
10—Atlanta	W	6-3	Fernandez	Palmer
11—Atlanta	L	3-4	Garber	Cone
12—Atlanta	L	4-12	O'Neal	Ojeda
14—At Phila.	W	7-5	Darling	Bedrosian
15—At Phila.	W	4-1	Fernandez	Gross
16—At Phila.	W	9-3	Aguilera	Cowley
17—At St. L.	L	3-4	Tudor	Ojeda
18—At St. L.	L	8-12*	LaPoint	Orosco
19—At St. L.	L	2-4	Mathews	Fernandez
20—At Pitts.	L	6-9	Easley	Myers
21—At Pitts.	W	9-6	Ojeda	Kipper
22—At Pitts.	W	8-7	Darling	Patterson
24—St. Louis	W	2-1	Fernandez	Mathews
25—St. Louis	L	2-3	Magrane	Aguilera
26—St. Louis	L	4-7	Forsch	Darling
27—Houston	L	1-11	Deshaies	Cone
29—Houston	W	2-1	Fernandez	Scott
30—Montreal	W	11-3	Aguilera	Tibbs

Won 11, Lost 9

MAY

Date		Score	Winner	Loser
1—Montreal	W	7-6	Orosco	McClure
2—Montreal	L	7-11*	St. Claire	Orosco
3—Montreal	L	0-2	McClure	Ojeda
5—Cincinnati	L	0-2	Power	Fernandez
6—Cincinnati	W	3-2	Aguilera	Soto
8—At Atlanta	L	3-4*	Garber	Orosco
9—At Atlanta	L	4-5	Palmer	Ojeda
10—At Atlanta	L	7-8	Dedmon	Orosco
11—At Cinn.	L	2-12	Soto	Aguilera
12—At Cinn.	W	6-2	Cone	Reuss
13—At Hous.	L	1-2*	Meads	Walter
14—At Hous.	L	4-5	Meads	Walter
15—San Fran.	W	8-3	Fernandez	Krukow
16—San Fran.	L	4-5*	Garrelts	Innis
17—San Fran.	W	6-4	Cone	Hammaker
18—San Diego	L	5-7	Dravecky	Darling
19—San Diego	W	5-4	McDowell	Show
20—San Diego	W	10-3	Aguilera	Whitson
22—Los Ang.	W	6-4	Leach	Young
23—Los Ang.	L	2-4	Welch	Darling
24—Los Ang.	L	6-8	Hershiser	McDowell
25—At S. Fran.	W	8-7	Leach	Grant
26—At S. Fran.	W	3-2	Sisk	J. Robinson
27—At S. Fran.	W	4-3	McDowell	J. Robinson
29—At S. Diego	W	5-4	Leach	Lefferts
30—At S. Diego	W	3-0	Fernandez	Show
31—At S. Diego	L	0-1	Whitson	Mitchell

Won 13, Lost 14

JUNE

Date		Score	Winner	Loser
1—At L.A.	W	5-2	Leach	Valenzuela
2—At L.A.	L	3-6	Welch	Orosco
3—At L.A.	L	2-5	Hershiser	Darling
5—Pittsburgh	W	5-2	Gooden	Dunne
6—Pittsburgh	W	4-2	Fernandez	Drabek
7—Pittsburgh	W	5-4*	McDowell	D. Robinson
7—Pittsburgh	L	9-10	Taylor	McDowell
8—At Chicago	L	2-4	Smith	Sisk
9—At Chicago	L	5-6	Noles	Myers
10—At Chicago	W	13-2	Gooden	Sanderson
12—At Pitts.	W	10-2	Fernandez	Reuschel
13—At Pitts.	L	3-4	D. Robinson	Myers
14—At Pitts.	W	7-3	Sisk	Fisher
15—At Mon.	L	0-4	Martinez	Gooden
16—At Mon.	W	7-3	Leach	Sebra
17—At Mon.	L	1-9	Smith	Fernandez
18—At Mon.	W	10-7	Sisk	Heaton
19—Phila.	W	8-1	Mitchell	Carman
20—Phila.	W	3-2	Gooden	Tekulve
21—Phila.	W	8-3	Fernandez	Gross
23—Chicago	L	1-4	Sutcliffe	Darling
24—Chicago	W	2-1	McDowell	Smith
25—Chicago	W	8-2	Gooden	Trout
26—At Phila.	L	2-5	Gross	Fernandez
27—At Phila.	W	5-4	Leach	Rawley
28—At Phila.	L	4-5	Bair	McDowell
29—St. Louis	L	7-8†	Worrell	Orosco
30—St. Louis	W	3-2	Gooden	Mathews

Won 16, Lost 12

JULY

Date		Score	Winner	Loser
1—St. Louis	W	9-6	Myers	Dawley
2—At Cinn.	W	5-0	Leach	Robinson
3—At Cinn.	L	3-8	Hoffman	Darling
4—At Cinn.	L	3-7	Gullickson	Mitchell
5—At Cinn.	L	5-7	Browning	Gooden
7—At Atlanta	W	6-2	Leach	Mahler
7—At Atlanta	W	5-1	Darling	Dedmon

JULY

Date		Score	Winner	Loser
8—At Atlanta	L	3-5	Puleo	Fernandez
9—At Hous.	L	3-4	Smith	Myers
10—At Hous.	W	7-3	Gooden	Scott
11—At Hous.	W	9-6	Myers	Darwin
12—At Hous.	W	5-2	Darling	Knepper
16—Cincinnati	W	9-0	Gooden	Gullickson
17—Cincinnati	L	2-5	Williams	Darling
18—Cincinnati	L	3-7	Power	Fernandez
19—Cincinnati	W	6-5†	Orosco	Scherrer
20—Atlanta	W	9-2	Schulze	O'Neal
21—Atlanta	L	3-8	Alexander	Gooden
22—Atlanta	W	4-3	Darling	Smith
24—Houston	W	5-2	Fernandez	Ryan
24—Houston	W	7-4	Mitchell	Knepper
25—Houston	L	5-7	Deshaies	Schulze
26—Houston	L	2-5	Smith	Orosco
28—At St. L.	W	6-4	Darling	Worrell
29—At St. L.	W	6-4*	McDowell	Perry
30—At St. L.	W	5-3	Gooden	Mathews
31—At Mon.	L	3-13	Martinez	Mitchell

Won 16, Lost 11

AUGUST

Date		Score	Winner	Loser
1—At Mon.	W	12-4	Leach	Youmans
2—At Mon.	W	7-4	Darling	Sebra
3—Phila.	W	3-2†	McDowell	Tekulve
4—Phila.	W	5-3	Gooden	Ruffin
5—Phila.	W	13-3	Mitchell	Gross
6—Chicago	W	7-6	McDowell	Smith
7—Chicago	W	7-1	Darling	Sutcliffe
8—Chicago	L	3-5	Mason	Schulze
9—Chicago	L	3-6	Sanderson	Gooden
10—Montreal	L	1-2	Martinez	Mitchell
11—Montreal	W	6-2	Leach	Youmans
12—Montreal	W	4-2	Darling	Sebra
13—At Chicago	L	5-7	DiPino	McDowell
14—At Chicago	L	1-6	Sanderson	Mitchell
15—At Chicago	L	3-7	Moyer	Leach
16—At Chicago	W	23-10	Darling	Maddux
18—San Fran.	W	7-2	Gooden	Hammaker
19—San Fran.	L	6-10*	Garrelts	McDowell
20—San Fran.	W	7-4	Cone	Downs
21—San Diego	L	2-6	Jones	Darling
22—San Diego	L	3-8	M. Davis	Fernandez
23—San Diego	W	9-2	Gooden	Nolte
24—Los Ang.	W	1-0	Aguilera	Hillegas
25—Los Ang.	L	1-3	Valenzuela	Cone
26—Los Ang.	W	3-2	Darling	Welch
28—At S. Fran.	W	4-0	Gooden	LaCoss
29—At S. Fran.	L	1-9	Hammaker	Fernandez
30—At S. Fran.	W	5-3	Aguilera	Reuschel
31—At S. Diego	W	6-5*	Orosco	Comstock

Won 18, Lost 11

SEPTEMBER

Date		Score	Winner	Loser
1—At S. Diego	W	9-1	Cone	Jones
2—At S. Diego	W	4-3	Gooden	Whitson
4—At L.A.	W	5-1	Aguilera	Hillegas
5—At L.A.	W	4-3	Darling	Valenzuela
6—At L.A.	L	2-3§	Belcher	Myers
7—Phila.	L	3-5	Carman	Gooden
8—Phila.	W	5-2	Leach	Ruffin
9—Phila.	W	11-5	Aguilera	Rawley
11—St. Louis	L	4-6*	Dayley	Orosco
12—St. Louis	L	1-8	Mathews	Gooden
13—St. Louis	W	4-2	Cone	Cox
14—Chicago	W	6-5	Aguilera	Hall
15—Chicago	W	12-4	Fernandez	Maddux
16—At Mon.	W	10-0	Gooden	Lea
17—At Mon.	L	1-4	Perez	Cone
18—At Pitts.	L	9-10	Smiley	Myers
19—At Pitts.	W	5-4	Aguilera	Palacios
20—At Pitts.	L	8-9‡	Smiley	Ojeda
21—At Chicago	W	7-1	Gooden	Lancaster
22—At Chicago	L	2-6	Sutcliffe	Cone
23—Montreal	W	4-3	Candelaria	Smith
24—Montreal	L	4-5	Martinez	Aguilera
25—Pittsburgh	W	10-2	Fernandez	Bielecki
26—Pittsburgh	L	2-8	Drabek	Gooden
27—Pittsburgh	W	12-3	Ojeda	Dunne
28—At Phila.	W	1-0	Candelaria	Gross
29—At Phila.	L	0-3	Carman	Cone
30—At Phila.	L	3-4*	Calhoun	Orosco

Won 16, Lost 12

OCTOBER

Date		Score	Winner	Loser
2—At St. L.	L	2-3	Tudor	Mitchell
3—At St. L.	W	7-1	Aguilera	Tunnell
4—At St. L.	W	11-6	Myers	Dawley

Won 2, Lost 1

*10 innings. †11 innings. ‡14 innings. §16 innings.

Dwight Gooden managed to record 15 victories despite missing much of the first half of the season.

happy with their platoon roles in center field, both asked to be traded. They were not, although the Mets admitted they would try to accommodate Wilson, who hit .299 with nine home runs. Dykstra finished at .285 with 10 homers.

The Mets' lineup had become more powerful with the addition of left fielder Kevin McReynolds. The former San Diego Padre lived up to expectations with a .276 average, 29 homers and 95 runs batted in.

Howard Johnson, given a chance to play third base regularly, slugged a career-high 36 home runs, which established an N.L. single-season record for most homers by a switch-hitter. Johnson, who also tallied 99 RBIs, was accused by the Houston Astros and St. Louis Cardinals of using a corked bat, an allegation X-rays failed to confirm.

Strawberry overcame the internal bickering to have the type of season long expected of him. He recorded career highs with a .284 average, 39 home runs and 104 RBIs.

First baseman Keith Hernandez, elected as the team's first-ever captain, was his consistent self with a .290 average, 18 homers and 89 RBIs.

Tim Teufel had an outstanding season with a .308 average, 14 homers and 61 RBIs, but Backman, his second-base pla-

toon partner, dropped to .250 after hitting .320 in 1986. Shortstop Rafael Santana checked in at .255.

Catcher Gary Carter suffered through one of his most disappointing seasons, hitting only .235. He did, however, stroke 20 homers and knock in 83.

Among the reserves, rookie Dave Magadan hit .318 as a backup at third and first, while Mazzilli batted .306.

The Mets wound up leading the league with a .268 average and 823 runs. And their bullpen of McDowell (7-5, 25 saves), Orosco (3-9, 16 saves) Randy Myers (3-6, six saves) and Doug Sisk (3-1, three saves) combined to lead to the league with 51 saves (including Cone's one save).

But the Mets could lead the East for only 15 days in April. They overcame a 10½-length deficit on July 23 to fight to within 1½ games September 19, but the Cardinals, buoyed by taking two of three games in New York September 11-13, were not to be denied. The final blow for the Mets was watching from a private box in Busch Stadium on October 1 as the Cardinals clinched the division.

While the Mets were being eliminated, General Manager Frank Cashen announced that Johnson would manage the club in 1988 but then become his "special assistant" in 1989.

Smooth-fielding Montreal first baseman Andres Galarraga batted .305 and drove in 90 runs.

Expos Take a Giant Step

By IAN MacDONALD

If ever numbers lied in the final standings, they did so in 1987. The Montreal Expos, the No. 4 team in the National League East in 1986, rose to No. 3. "One" step at a time—a philosophy best suited for babies learning to walk.

But numbers are hardly the proper yardstick for measuring the Expos' achievement. The standings don't show the Expos intruding upon the division's darlings, the St. Louis Cardinals and New York Mets, in the midst of a pennant fight. And they don't report that these upstarts nearly bumped off both of them.

After finishing 29½ games behind the World Series champion Mets in 1986, Montreal went into battle in 1987 without its biggest guns. Gone were ace reliever Jeff Reardon and slugging outfielder Andre Dawson. Batting champion Tim Raines was unavailable until at least May 1 while he explored free agency.

Their absence showed. The Expos lost their first five games. By May 1, they had a lock on fifth place. It was then that Buck Rodgers, the N.L. Manager of the Year, pulled his troops together.

"...He did a remarkable job of keeping our spirits up," reliever Bob McClure said. "We had a tough start, but just after Raines came back (May 2) he called a team meeting. He told us to take a long look at ourselves in the mirror, to have some guts, because we had built-in crutches. If we lost, we were supposed to lose. He told us we could win. He made us realize we could play well and that losing was a horrible shame."

The introspective Expos found themselves and the winning touch. By June, they had control of third place. Over the next four months, they had a dogfight with the Mets for second. And with seven games to play, they arrived in St. Louis for a four-game series, trailing the first-place Cardinals by three games.

"I hope the pennant is on the line when we get in St. Louis," Rodgers had remarked just weeks earlier. "All we want is the chance to determine our fate."

They won the chance but lost the showdown. The Cardinals swept a doubleheader to open the series, dropping Montreal five games back with five to play. The Expos regrouped to win the next game but were eliminated the following day, when the Cardinals clinched the title with an 8-2 victory.

The final numbers showed Montreal four games behind the Cardinals with a 91-71 record, the second-best mark in franchise history.

"This was a season of turning points, but the biggest thing, by far, is that we didn't allow ourselves to be buried early," Rodgers said.

"When we started the season we were scuffling for pitchers and scuffling for outfielders. We lost our first five games and were still on the road. We could have been buried.

"...We managed to stay close for months with different players in key roles. Everybody did their share. Nobody on this club had to back up to the pay window."

The Expos marched forward behind the heroics of three All-Star Game selections —Raines, Tim Wallach and Hubie Brooks —and a probable selection in years ahead, Andres Galarraga.

Wallach, voted the team's player of the year, set a club record with 123 runs batted in, the most by an N.L. third baseman since Joe Torre knocked in 137 with St. Louis in 1971. A .298 hitter, Wallach led the league with 42 doubles, was second in RBIs and tied for the lead with 16 game-winning RBIs. His 177 hits and .514 slugging average also ranked among the leaders.

Raines hit .330, just four points less than his league-leading total of 1986, to finish third in the N.L. batting race. Despite missing nearly a month, the Expos' left fielder topped the league with 123 runs and ranked among the leaders with 175 hits, eight triples, 90 walks, 50 stolen bases, a .429 on-base average and .526 slugging average.

After fracturing his wrist in the third game of the season, shortstop Hubie Brooks missed six weeks. He didn't hit his first home run until June 2 but finished with 14 as he led the team down the stretch. His 29 RBIs in September set a club record for the month and helped push his season total to 72.

Galarraga, the smooth-fielding first baseman, hit .305 in just his second full season. His 90 RBIs and 40 doubles ranked second on the club.

From the start, however, pitching was the big issue. The Expos began the season with a rotation of Floyd Youmans, Jay Tibbs, Neal Heaton, Bob Sebra and Lary Sorensen. At the end, Dennis Martinez, Pascual Perez, Bryn Smith and Heaton

SCORES OF MONTREAL EXPOS' 1987 GAMES

APRIL

Date		Score	Winner	Loser
6—At Cinn.	L	5-11	Landrum	Youmans
8—At Cinn.	L	2-7	Gullickson	Tibbs
10—At Hous.	L	1-6	Darwin	Heaton
11—At Hous.	L	2-3	Lopez	Parrett
12—At Hous.	L	0-1	Knepper	Sebra
14—At St. L.	W	9-4	Tibbs	Mathews
16—At St. L.	W	4-3	Heaton	Forsch
17—At Chicago	L	0-7	Sutcliffe	Youmans
18—At Chicago	W	4-2	Sebra	Maddux
19—At Chicago	W	3-1	Sorensen	Moyer
20—Phila.	L	3-4	Schatzeder	Tibbs
22—Phila.	W	7-3	Heaton	Cowley
23—Phila.	W	6-5	St. Claire	Jackson
24—Chicago	L	4-6	Moyer	Sebra
25—Chicago	L	4-9	Sanderson	Tibbs
26—Chicago	L	1-7	Trout	Sorensen
27—At Phila.	W	6-4	Heaton	Gross
28—At Phila.	W	7-1	Youmans	Cowley
29—At Phila.	L	0-5	Rawley	Sebra
30—At N.Y.	L	3-11	Aguilera	Tibbs

Won 8, Lost 12

MAY

Date		Score	Winner	Loser
1—At N.Y.	L	6-7	Orosco	McClure
2—At N.Y.	W	11-7*	St. Claire	Orosco
3—At N.Y.	W	2-0	McClure	Ojeda
4—At Atlanta	L	7-10	Palmer	Sebra
5—At Atlanta	W	6-4	Tibbs	Mahler
6—At Atlanta	W	6-2	Smith	O'Neal
8—Houston	L	0-3	Scott	Heaton
9—Houston	W	3-1	Sebra	Deshaies
10—Houston	W	6-2	Tibbs	Darwin
11—Atlanta	W	7-6*	Sorensen	Acker
12—Atlanta	L	2-5	Smith	Heredia
13—Cincinnati	L	6-12	Browning	St. Claire
14—Cincinnati	L	9-10	Robinson	St. Claire
15—Los Ang.	W	6-3	Tibbs	Valenzuela
16—Los Ang.	W	10-3	Smith	Welch
17—Los Ang.	W	8-3	McClure	Hershiser
18—San Fran.	W	7-2	Heaton	Downs
19—San Fran.	L	2-6	LaCoss	Youmans
20—San Fran.	L	7-9	J. Robinson	St. Claire
22—At S. Diego	L	3-5	Hawkins	Brown
23—At S. Diego	W	6-0	Heaton	Dravecky
24—At S. Diego	W	2-1	Youmans	Show
25—At L.A.	W	3-1	Sorensen	Honeycutt
26—At L.A.	W	8-3	Sebra	Pena
27—At L.A.	L	4-6	Valenzuela	Smith
29—At S. Fran.	W	10-4	Heaton	LaCoss
30—At S. Fran.	W	6-4	Youmans	Krukow
31—At S. Fran.	L	0-8	Downs	Sebra

Won 17, Lost 11

JUNE

Date		Score	Winner	Loser
2—San Diego	W	6-2	Smith	Jones
3—San Diego	W	4-3	Heaton	Hawkins
4—San Diego	W	8-5	Youmans	S. Davis
5—At Phila.	L	6-7	Gross	McGaffigan
6—At Phila.	L	3-4	Rawley	Sebra
7—At Phila.	L	1-3	Jackson	Smith
8—Pittsburgh	W	7-1	Heaton	Fisher
9—Pittsburgh	L	1-8	Dunne	Sorensen
10—Pittsburgh	W	4-3†	McClure	D. Robinson
12—Phila.	W	13-6	Smith	Rawley
13—Phila.	W	7-5	Heaton	Jackson
14—Phila.	L	6-11	Carman	Sorensen
15—New York	W	4-0	Martinez	Gooden
16—New York	L	3-7	Leach	Sebra
17—New York	W	9-1	Smith	Fernandez
18—New York	L	7-10	Sisk	Heaton
19—At St. L.	W	8-7†	McClure	Dawley
20—At St. L.	W	7-5	Parrett	Worrell
21—At St. L.	L	3-7	Magrane	Sebra
23—At Pitts.	W	8-2	Heaton	Kipper
24—At Pitts.	L	6-9	Fisher	Fischer
25—At Pitts.	W	7-2	Martinez	Dunne
26—St. Louis	W	5-1	Sebra	Magrane
27—St. Louis	L	5-15	Forsch	Smith
28—St. Louis	L	6-7†	Dayley	Parrett
29—Chicago	L	5-9	Lancaster	Sorensen
30—Chicago	W	5-4	Martinez	Trout

Won 15, Lost 12

JULY

Date		Score	Winner	Loser
1—Chicago	L	0-1	Maddux	Sebra
3—San Diego	W	2-1	Youmans	Hawkins
4—San Diego	W	4-3	Burke	Gossage
5—San Diego	L	2-3	Gossage	Parrett
6—At Hous.	L	3-9	Darwin	Martinez
7—At Hous.	W	2-0	Sebra	Knepper
8—At Hous.	W	1-0	Youmans	Ryan
9—At Cinn.	L	2-7	Gullickson	Heaton
10—At Cinn.	W	5-1	Smith	Browning
11—At Cinn.	W	11-5	Martinez	Power
12—At Cinn.	W	4-2	Sebra	Hoffman
16—Atlanta	W	2-0	Youmans	Alexander
17—Atlanta	W	5-4	Burke	Acker
18—Atlanta	W	3-2	Parrett	Garber
19—Atlanta	W	2-1†	McGaffigan	Acker
20—Houston	W	4-1	Martinez	Deshaies
21—Houston	L	2-4	Darwin	Youmans
22—Houston	L	0-7	Scott	Sebra
23—Cincinnati	L	4-8	Power	Smith
24—Cincinnati	W	3-2	Heaton	Hoffman
25—Cincinnati	W	4-3‡	McGaffigan	Landrum
26—Cincinnati	W	6-0	Youmans	Gullickson
28—At Chicago	L	3-8	Sutcliffe	McGaffigan
29—At Chicago	W	11-3	Smith	Maddux
30—At Chicago	W	6-1	Heaton	Tewksbury
31—New York	W	13-3	Martinez	Mitchell

Won 18, Lost 8

AUGUST

Date		Score	Winner	Loser
1—New York	L	4-12	Leach	Youmans
2—New York	L	4-7	Darling	Sebra
3—St. Louis	L	2-5	Horton	Smith
4—St. Louis	W	10-5	McClure	Tunnell
5—St. Louis	W	2-1§	St. Claire	Dayley
6—At Pitts.	W	6-3	Parrett	Gott
7—At Pitts.	L	3-9	Walk	Sebra
8—At Pitts.	L	2-5	Drabek	Smith
9—At Pitts.	L	3-4	Dunne	Parrett
10—At N.Y.	W	2-1	Martinez	Mitchell
11—At N.Y.	L	2-6	Leach	Youmans
12—At N.Y.	L	2-4	Darling	Sebra
13—Pittsburgh	W	9-7	McGaffigan	Gideon
14—Pittsburgh	W	4-3	McClure	Smiley
15—Pittsburgh	W	6-3	Burke	Fisher
16—Pittsburgh	W	10-7	Parrett	Gideon
18—Los Ang.	W	2-1	Burke	Hershiser
19—Los Ang.	L	9-10	Pena	Parrett
20—Los Ang.	L	2-7	Valenzuela	Heaton
21—San Fran.	L	3-6	Dravecky	Martinez
22—San Fran.	W	5-4*	Burke	Lefferts
23—San Fran.	L	3-5	Downs	Sebra
25—At S. Diego	L	1-5	Grant	Heaton
26—At S. Diego	W	6-5‡	Burke	McCullers
27—At S. Diego	W	3-0	Smith	Jones
28—At L.A.	W	2-1‡	Burke	Leary
29—At L.A.	W	6-5*	McGaffigan	Crews
30—At L.A.	W	5-4	Parrett	Valenzuela
31—At S. Fran.	L	0-5	Dravecky	Martinez

Won 15, Lost 14

SEPTEMBER

Date		Score	Winner	Loser
1—At S. Fran.	L	4-14	Reuschel	Youmans
2—At S. Fran.	W	7-3	Perez	LaCoss
4—At Atlanta	L	4-7	Mahler	Heaton
5—At Atlanta	W	4-1	Martinez	Coffman
6—At Atlanta	W	5-2	Youmans	Z. Smith
7—St. Louis	W	9-2	Perez	Cox
8—St. Louis	W	4-1	Smith	Forsch
9—St. Louis	W	8-3	Martinez	Magrane
11—At Chicago	L	4-8	Lancaster	Youmans
12—At Chicago	W	7-1	Perez	Moyer
13—At Chicago	L	2-5	Sutcliffe	Smith
14—At Pitts.	W	6-4x	McGaffigan	Gideon
15—At Pitts.	L	1-5	Bielecki	Heaton
16—New York	L	0-10	Gooden	Lea
17—New York	W	4-1	Perez	Cone
18—Phila.	W	6-3	Smith	Ruffin
19—Phila.	W	12-4	Martinez	Rawley
20—Phila.	L	1-4	Gross	Heaton
21—Pitts.	L	2-5	Drabek	Sebra
22—Pitts.	W	4-3	Perez	Gott
23—At N.Y.	L	3-4	Candelaria	Smith
24—At N.Y.	W	5-4	Martinez	Aguilera
25—At Phila.	L	2-4	Carman	Heaton
26—At Phila.	W	7-4	Perez	Rawley
27—At Phila.	W	5-3	Parrett	Jackson
29—At St. L.	L	0-1	Magrane	Martinez
29—At St. L.	L	0-3	Mathews	Smith
30—At St. L.	W	6-1	Perez	Forsch

Won 16, Lost 12

OCTOBER

Date		Score	Winner	Loser
1—At St. L.	L	2-8	Cox	Tibbs
2—Chicago	W	7-1	Heaton	Maddux
3—Chicago	W	5-4	Parrett	Lancaster
4—Chicago	L	5-7	Moyer	Parrett

Won 2, Lost 2

*10 innings. †11 innings. ‡12 innings. §13 innings. x14 innings.

were the front-liners.

Youmans reported out of shape and never reached the potential he showed in 1986, when he won 13 games. He was disabled three times in 1987 and finished 9-8.

Smith began the season in the minors on injury rehabilitation after off-season elbow surgery. He finished 10-9 but was nagged by a sore shoulder the last month and a half.

Heaton, the principal in the deal that sent Reardon to the Minnesota Twins, was 10-4 through the All-Star break. He lost six straight down the stretch, however, and finished 13-10.

Martinez, re-signed May 6 by the organization as a free agent, was called up from Class AAA Indianapolis on June 8. He became the big winner for much of the season, finishing 11-4.

Perez provided the late-season spark with a brilliant 7-0 record in September. Also signed as a free agent, Perez was recalled in August after going 9-7 with a 3.79 earned-run average for Indianapolis. He was named the American Association's pitcher of the year.

Although the Expos' starters were inconsistent, they were saved by what truly was a bullpen by committee.

Tim Burke (7-0, 18 saves, 1.19 ERA), McClure (6-1, five saves, 3.44), Andy McGaffigan (5-2, 12 saves, 2.39), Jeff Parrett (7-6, six saves) and Randy St. Claire (3-3, seven saves) were outstanding.

"When we traded Reardon," Rodgers said, "people said we dumped a salary. We felt we had a good bullpen. The way those guys came through is probably my greatest satisfaction from the season."

Among the other players, Mitch Webster contributed in all departments. He showed power (15 homers, including two grand slams), speed (33 stolen bases), consistency (.281 average) and production (101 runs, 63 RBIs) as he switched from center to right field for 1987.

Versatile rookie Casey Candaele started at five positions, batted .272 and struck out only 28 times in 449 at-bats.

Second baseman Vance Law hit .273, his best average since 1982, with 12 homers and 56 RBIs. His platoon partner late in the season, Tom Foley, hit a career-high .293.

Platooning in center field with Candaele and Reid Nichols (.265), Herm Winningham hit only .239 but had career highs in doubles (20), RBIs (41) and stolen bases (29).

Wallace Johnson tied for the league lead with 17 pinch-hits, and utility man Dave

Neal Heaton gave Montreal 10 victories by the All-Star break but finished a disappointing 13-10.

Engle drove home 12 runs with 11 pinch-hits.

Catching wasn't a strong point. Mike Fitzgerald, hampered by a bad finger, hit .240 and had trouble throwing out runners. Jeff Reed, acquired in the Reardon/Heaton trade, was solid defensively but batted only .213.

But then, as Rodgers said, "There is no reason to dwell on low points because the high points completely overshadowed them."

Free-agent catcher Lance Parrish didn't live up to expectations and the Phillies never really contended in the National League East.

Phillies Swallow a Bitter Pill

By BILL BROWN

The 1987 season was a bitter pill to swallow for a hungry Philadelphia Phillies team.

When they signed free-agent catcher Lance Parrish and traded for fireballer Joe Cowley during spring training, the Phils were prepared to join the contenders in the National League East. Not in their worst dreams would they have imagined finishing 15 games removed from first place.

Even N.L. Cy Young Award winner Steve Bedrosian, who led the majors with a club-record 40 saves, and the slugging tandem of third baseman Mike Schmidt and second baseman Juan Samuel could lift Philadelphia no higher than fourth place all season. The Phillies finished 80-82 and tied for fourth with the Pittsburgh Pirates.

Philadelphia's new battery mates did, in fact, guide the team, but it was a trail that helped lead to the dismissal of Manager John Felske and a long season of mediocrity.

Though Parrish and Cowley weren't entirely to blame for the team's losing season, they helped set the pace early.

Parrish, a slow starter, had a .188 batting average and only three home runs in April. He hit one homer in May and finished the season with 17, his lowest total since 1981, 67 runs batted in and a .245 average. Over the previous five seasons, Parrish had averaged 28 homers and 92 RBIs with the Detroit Tigers.

Cowley, acquired from the Chicago White Sox for outfielder Gary Redus, served notice early that his reputation for wildness was well deserved.

In his first start, Cowley allowed the Chicago Cubs seven runs on the strength of three hits and four walks. He retired only two batters.

By May 8, Cowley was 0-4 and back in the minor leagues for the rest of the season. In five appearances—including four starts—with Philadelphia, Cowley surrendered 20 earned runs, 21 hits and 17 walks in 11⅔ innings. He wasn't much better at Maine (3-9, 7.86 earned-run average, 76 walks, 63 innings) and ended the season still seeking the form that enabled him to pitch a no-hitter for the White Sox in 1986.

The Phillies stumbled through April and by May 8 had a firm grip on last place with an 8-18 record. They were, however, 15-11 during May to briefly take pressure off the beleaguered Felske. But even with Schmidt and Samuel pounding the ball and the bullpen choking the opposition, Philadelphia couldn't maintain momentum. On June 18 in Chicago, with the Phils 9½ games out of first place at 29-32, Felske was fired. Since taking over before the 1985 season, he had posted a 190-194 record.

Schmidt provided some of the few early season highlights. On April 18 in Pittsburgh, he became the 14th player to hit 500 career home runs when he stroked a three-run, ninth-inning shot to beat the Pirates' Don Robinson. On June 14 in Montreal, Schmidt homered off Curt Brown for his 2,000th career hit. By season's end, he had hit 35 homers and moved into ninth place on the all-time home run list with 530. Schmidt led the Phils with 113 RBIs, hit .293, posted a .548 slugging average and was named to the N.L. All-Star team for the 11th time.

Samuel, who joined Schmidt on the N.L. squad, provided plenty of excitement along the way to his best season. The speedy second baseman led the league with 15 triples and ranked among the leaders in runs (113), hits (178), doubles (37), home runs (28), RBIs (100) and stolen bases (35). A .272 hitter in 1987, Samuel became the first player to record double figures in doubles, triples, home runs, and stolen bases in his first four seasons.

Bedrosian (5-3, 2.83 ERA) set a major league record by recording saves in 13 straight opportunities. He solidified a bullpen that had been a question mark in spring training but which set a club record with 48 saves. Forty-year-old Kent Tekulve also became the oldest pitcher to lead the league in appearances by pitching in 90 games. He finished 6-4 with a 3.09 ERA.

With those players leading the way, newly appointed Manager Lee Elia, Felske's dugout assistant, was hoping to duplicate the second half of 1986, when the Phils overcame a slow start to finish 86-75 and in second place behind the New York Mets.

"Lee is Philadelphia-born and -raised and he makes a lot of sense to me," club President Bill Giles said in announcing the managerial change. "Plus, he has the respect of the players and is a good communicator."

The Phillies lost their first four games under the former Cubs pilot but rallied to

SCORES OF PHILADELPHIA PHILLIES' 1987 GAMES

APRIL

Date		Score	Winner	Loser
7—At Atlanta	L	0-6	Mahler	Rawley
9—At Atlanta	L	7-8*	Garber	Schatzeder
10—Chicago	L	3-4	Lynch	Gross
11—Chicago	L	1-9	Sutcliffe	Cowley
12—Chicago	W	9-8*	Bedrosian	Smith
13—Chicago	L	2-5	Moyer	Carman
14—New York	L	5-7	Darling	Bedrosian
15—New York	L	1-4	Fernandez	Gross
16—New York	L	3-9	Aguilera	Cowley
17—At Pitts.	W	6-2*	Bedrosian	Jones
18—At Pitts.	W	8-6	Tekulve	D. Robinson
19—At Pitts.	L	2-5	Drabek	Ruffin
20—At Mon.	W	4-3	Schatzeder	Tibbs
22—At Mon.	L	3-7	Heaton	Cowley
23—At Mon.	L	5-6	St. Claire	Jackson
25—Pittsburgh	W	3-2	Carman	Drabek
26—Pittsburgh	W	6-4	Ruffin	Reuschel
27—Montreal	L	4-6	Heaton	Gross
28—Montreal	L	1-7	Youmans	Cowley
29—Montreal	W	5-0	Rawley	Sebra

Won 7, Lost 13

MAY

Date		Score	Winner	Loser
1—Cincinnati	L	5-8	Soto	Carman
2—Cincinnati	W	8-3	Ruffin	Browning
3—Cincinnati	L	6-9	Gullickson	Gross
5—Houston	L	1-5	Darwin	Rawley
6—Houston	L	2-3	Andersen	Tekulve
8—At Cinn.	L	3-4	Browning	Ruffin
9—At Cinn.	W	4-2	Gross	Gullickson
10—At Cinn.	W	4-3	Rawley	Power
11—At Hous.	W	7-6	Schatzeder	Andersen
12—At Hous.	L	2-5	Knepper	Jackson
13—Atlanta	L	5-10	Palmer	Ruffin
14—Atlanta	W	5-4	Gross	Mahler
15—San Diego	W	7-4	Rawley	Whitson
16—San Diego	W	9-0	Carman	Jones
17—San Diego	L	5-6	Hawkins	Jackson
18—Los Ang.	W	5-3	Ruffin	Honeycutt
21—Los Ang.	W	6-3	Rawley	Pena
22—San Fran.	L	1-2	Hammaker	Carman
23—San Fran.	W	9-8	Bedrosian	J. Robinson
24—San Fran.	L	3-6	LaCoss	Tekulve
25—At S. Diego	W	6-4	Schatzeder	Dravecky
26—At S. Diego	W	3-1	Rawley	Jones
27—At S. Diego	W	6-4	Carman	Hawkins
29—At L.A.	L	0-6	Welch	Ruffin
30—At L.A.	W	3-0	Gross	Hershiser
31—At L.A.	W	3-1	Rawley	Honeycutt

Won 15, Lost 11

JUNE

Date		Score	Winner	Loser
1—At S. Fran.	L	2-9	Hammaker	Carman
2—At S. Fran.	W	7-6	Ritchie	Davis
3—At S. Fran.	L	1-4	LaCoss	Ruffin
5—Montreal	W	7-6	Gross	McGaffigan
6—Montreal	W	4-3	Rawley	Sebra
7—Montreal	W	3-1	Jackson	Smith
8—St. Louis	L	8-12	Horton	Carman
9—St. Louis	W	3-2	Ruffin	Cox
10—St. Louis	L	1-3	Mathews	Gross
12—At Mon.	L	6-13	Smith	Rawley
13—At Mon.	L	5-7	Heaton	Jackson
14—At Mon.	W	11-6	Carman	Sorensen
15—At Chicago	W	3-2	Tekulve	Smith
16—At Chicago	L	2-7	Trout	Gross
17—At Chicago	L	3-5	Moyer	Rawley
18—At Chicago	L	7-9	Sutcliffe	Jackson
19—At N.Y.	L	1-8	Mitchell	Carman
20—At N.Y.	L	2-3	Gooden	Tekulve
21—At N.Y.	L	3-8	Fernandez	Gross
23—At St. L.	W	4-1	Rawley	Tunnell
24—At St. L.	L	3-5	Worrell	Jackson
25—At St. L.	L	0-3	Mathews	Ruffin
26—New York	W	5-2	Gross	Fernandez
27—New York	L	4-5	Leach	Rawley
28—New York	W	5-4	Bair	McDowell
29—Pittsburgh	W	6-5	Jackson	Jones
29—Pittsburgh	W	11-3	Bair	Dunne
30—Pittsburgh	W	6-4	Gross	Drabek

Won 13, Lost 15

JULY

Date		Score	Winner	Loser
1—Pittsburgh	W	11-4	Rawley	Taylor
2—Houston	L	6-7	Andersen	Bedrosian
3—Houston	W	2-1	Ruffin	Ryan
4—Houston	W	9-3	Hume	Deshaies
5—Houston	L	2-8	Scott	Gross
6—At Cinn.	W	9-6	Jackson	Power
7—At Cinn.	W	10-8*	Tekulve	Franco
8—At Cinn.	W	7-2	Ruffin	Hoffman

JULY

Date		Score	Winner	Loser
9—At Atlanta	L	6-11	Dedmon	Hume
10—At Atlanta	W	5-2	Rawley	Alexander
11—At Atlanta	L	4-5	Mahler	Carman
12—At Atlanta	L	3-9	O'Neal	Ruffin
16—At Hous.	L	1-2	Darwin	Jackson
17—At Hous.	W	2-1	Rawley	Scott
18—At Hous.	W	4-2	Carman	Knepper
19—At Hous.	W	4-1	Ruffin	Ryan
20—Cincinnati	L	6-10†	Franco	Jackson
21—Cincinnati	L	3-4	Gullickson	Gross
22—Cincinnati	W	5-3	Rawley	Browning
23—Atlanta	W	5-1	Carman	Puleo
24—Atlanta	W	11-5	Ruffin	Mahler
25—Atlanta	L	1-2	Palmer	Hume
26—Atlanta	W	7-3	Tekulve	Alexander
28—At Pitts.	W	5-2	Rawley	Reuschel
29—At Pitts.	W	4-3	Carman	Drabek
30—At Pitts.	W	1-0	Ruffin	Smiley
31—At Chicago	W	8-5	Tekulve	Sanderson

Won 18, Lost 9

AUGUST

Date		Score	Winner	Loser
1—At Chicago	L	3-5	Lancaster	Hume
2—At Chicago	L	2-3*	Smith	Calhoun
3—At N.Y.	L	2-3†	McDowell	Tekulve
4—At N.Y.	L	3-5	Gooden	Ruffin
5—Houston	L	3-13	Mitchell	Gross
6—St. Louis	L	2-5	Tudor	Hume
7—St. Louis	W	15-5	Rawley	Magrane
8—St. Louis	L	5-9	Worrell	Carman
9—St. Louis	W	8-7§	Ritchie	Horton
10—Chicago	W	4-2	Frohwirth	Moyer
11—Chicago	W	9-8‡	Gross	Tewksbury
12—Chicago	W	13-7	Calhoun	Lynch
13—At St. L.	W	4-2‡	Bedrosian	Dayley
14—At St. L.	L	4-8	Mathews	Ruffin
15—At St. L.	W	5-2	Gross	Forsch
16—At St. L.	W	4-3	Rawley	Tudor
18—San Diego	L	4-9†	Gossage	Ritchie
19—San Diego	W	6-5	Ruffin	Grant
20—San Diego	W	10-2	Toliver	Show
21—Los Ang.	W	2-1†	Tekulve	Young
21—Los Ang.	W	7-3	Rawley	Leary
22—Los Ang.	W	2-0	Maddux	Honeycutt
23—Los Ang.	L	1-5	Hershiser	Carman
24—San Fran.	L	1-6	Reuschel	Ruffin
25—San Fran.	L	2-3	Garrelts	Gross
26—San Fran.	L	0-2	D. Robinson	Rawley
28—At S. Diego	W	8-1	Carman	Whitson
29—At S. Diego	L	1-3	Nolte	Ruffin
30—At S. Diego	L	1-6	Grant	Gross
31—At L.A.	W	4-2	Rawley	Welch

Won 15, Lost 15

SEPTEMBER

Date		Score	Winner	Loser
1—At L.A.	W	7-5	Ritchie	Leary
2—At L.A.	W	6-2	Carman	Hershiser
4—At S. Fran.	L	2-3*	D. Robinson	Ritchie
5—At S. Fran.	L	3-6	Dravecky	Rawley
6—At S. Fran.	L	1-4	Reuschel	Toliver
7—At N.Y.	W	5-3	Carman	Gooden
8—At N.Y.	L	2-5	Leach	Ruffin
9—At N.Y.	L	5-11	Aguilera	Rawley
11—Pittsburgh	L	2-4	Drabek	Gross
12—Pittsburgh	L	4-12	Dunne	Carman
13—Pittsburgh	L	1-6	Fisher	Ruffin
14—St. Louis	L	3-2†	Calhoun	Dayley
15—St. Louis	L	3-4	Horton	Gross
16—Chicago	W	8-5	Maddux	Smith
17—Chicago	W	4-3	Carman	Moyer
18—At Mon.	L	3-6	Smith	Ruffin
19—At Mon.	L	4-12	Martinez	Rawley
20—At Mon.	W	4-1	Gross	Heaton
21—At St. L.	L	1-3	Tudor	Carman
22—At St. L.	L	2-3	Cox	Rawley
23—At Chicago	W	5-0	Ruffin	Moyer
24—At Chicago	W	3-2†	Bedrosian	Baller
25—Montreal	W	4-2	Carman	Heaton
26—Montreal	L	4-7	Perez	Rawley
27—Montreal	L	3-5	Parrett	Jackson
28—New York	L	0-1	Candelaria	Gross
29—New York	W	3-0	Carman	Cone
30—New York	W	4-3*	Calhoun	Orosco

Won 12, Lost 16

OCTOBER

Date		Score	Winner	Loser
2—At Pitts.	L	4-6	Walk	Jackson
3—At Pitts.	L	5-10	Palacios	Gross
4—At Pitts.	L	2-4	Dunne	Bedrosian

Won 0, Lost 3

*10 innings. †11 innings. ‡13 innings. §14 innings.

Phillies lefthander Shane Rawley produced 17 victories, but a late-season slump cost him a shot at the N.L. Cy Young Award.

go 18-9 in July. The team peaked on August 22, climbing nine games above .500 (66-57) and 6½ games out of first. A four-game losing skid followed, however, and Philadelphia never rejoined the pennant race.

Pitching was an ongoing problem.

Shane Rawley (17-11) finished second in the league in victories as the Phillies' most consistent starter. He appeared to be a strong candidate for the Cy Young, going 17-6 through August 31, but couldn't win in his last seven starts.

Don Carman, meanwhile, won six of his last eight decisions to finish 13-11. Carman, a former reliever who had come within three outs of pitching a perfect game at San Francisco in 1986, had another near-miss in 1987. On September 29 in Philadelphia, he allowed only a fourth-inning infield single to Mookie Wilson and the Mets.

Kevin Gross, who suffered a herniated disc prior to spring training, had a disappointing 9-16 season. Adding embarrassment to injury, Gross was ejected from an August 10 game against the Cubs and eventually suspended for 10 games for affixing sandpaper to his glove.

Lefthander Bruce Ruffin, who was 9-4 in 1986 after being promoted from the minors, was 11-14 in his first full major league season.

Two rookies in 1987, Wally Ritchie and Mike Jackson, helped in the bullpen. Ritchie was 3-2 with a 3.75 ERA in 49 games, while Jackson was 3-10 in 55 appearances, including seven starts. He had a 3.09 ERA in 48 relief spots. Jeff Calhoun (3-1) posted a team-low 1.48 ERA in 42 appearances.

With the starters inconsistent, the Phillies had to rely on offense but ranked tenth in the league with a .254 batting average. They also ranked first in strikeouts (1,109) with Samuel leading the way (162).

Milt Thompson was a bright spot in center field. He led the team—and finished among the N.L. leaders—with a .302 average, nine triples and 46 stolen bases. Chris James opened the season in the majors, was sent down to Maine on May 21, then hit .298 after being recalled June 2. He finished the season as the starting left fielder, hitting .293 with 17 home runs overall.

Right fielder Glenn Wilson and first baseman Von Hayes couldn't duplicate their 1986 seasons but still chipped in. Wilson led N.L. outfielders in assists (18) for the third straight year but had only 54 RBIs after 84 in 1986 and 102 in '85. Hayes' average dipped 28 points, to .277, but he hit a career-high 21 homers and notched 84 RBIs. He was second in the league with 121 walks and seventh in on-base percentage (.404).

Shortstop Steve Jeltz wasn't expected to hit and didn't, batting .232 for the season. He shared time with Luis Aguayo, who hit a career-high 12 home runs but batted only .206.

Greg Gross recorded 15 pinch-hits to push his career total to 123 and tie Jerry Morales for third place on the major league career list.

**Andy Van Slyke came to Pittsburgh via St. Louis and hit a solid .293 with
21 homers and 82 RBIs.**

Young Pirates Raise Eyebrows

By BOB HERTZEL

He won no style points for modesty, but General Manager Syd Thrift best summarized the season the Pittsburgh Pirates escaped the National League East basement in one vaunted statement:

"No one in baseball has done a better job than I have. It ain't easy to resurrect the dead."

For a while, Thrift himself appeared bound for a nether world.

Fans howled as the Pirates' former scouting supervisor made daring trades without blinking, jockeyed the lineup without hesitating—and turned a team that had finished last three straight seasons into one of the National League's best second-half teams of 1987.

The club that had lost 104 games in 1985 and finished 44 games back in 1986 charged to within a notch of .500 in 1987 (80-82) and into a fourth-place tie with the Philadelphia Phillies.

The Pirates had the fourth-best record in the league after the All-Star break (41-34) and third-best after August 31 (20-11). Such success usually is an omen of good things to come, which is why Thrift and Manager Jim Leyland were rewarded with contract extensions after the season.

The Pirates filled in the gaps with trades that could have cleaned out Three Rivers Stadium:

● Just weeks after the 1986 season, Pittsburgh dealt 15-game winner Rick Rhoden and relievers Cecilio Guante and Pat Clements to the New York Yankees for pitchers Brian Fisher, Doug Drabek and Logan Easley, none of whom had pitched a full season in the majors.

● On April 1, Thrift traded popular catcher Tony Pena, a .286 career hitter, to the St. Louis Cardinals for outfielder Andy Van Slyke, catcher Mike LaValliere and minor league pitcher Mike Dunne.

● On July 31, bullpen stopper Don Robinson was traded to the San Francisco Giants for minor league catcher Mackey Sasser. Days later, reliever Jim Gott was claimed on waivers from the Giants.

● On August 7, third baseman Jim Morrison, the Pirates' power source in 1986 (23 home runs, 88 runs batted in), was shipped to the Detroit Tigers for infielder/outfielder Darnell Coles.

● On August 21, All-Star pitcher Rick Reuschel was sent to San Francisco for reliever Jeff Robinson and minor league pitcher Scott Medvin.

● And finally, on August 29, Thrift traded second baseman Johnny Ray, a .288 career hitter in six seasons with the Pirates, to the California Angels for two minor league prospects.

What bordered on the outrageous turned out to be simply outstanding.

Dunne was named The Sporting News' top N.L. rookie pitcher after posting a 13-6 record and 3.03 earned-run average, the No. 2 mark in the league. Called up from Vancouver on June 1, he became the anchor of the starting rotation with Fisher (11-9) and Drabek (11-12). Jeff Robinson and Gott became bullpen stoppers, Van Slyke was sometimes unstoppable (.293 batting average, 21 home runs, 82 RBIs), LaValliere surprised everyone by hitting .300 and winning a Gold Glove and Coles flashed the power he had shown all through 1986.

Two other new arrivals, fleet outfielder John Cangelosi from the Chicago White Sox and shortstop Al Pedrique from the New York Mets, also helped fill holes.

That was the essence of the Pirates.

While most clubs would have been content just to consummate so many trades, the insatiable Thrift and Leyland went one step further and shuffled the lineup like card-sharps, using 105 variations in all.

Before season's end, Van Slyke was moved from right field to center, Barry Bonds from center to left, Bobby Bonilla from the outfield to third base and Fisher from the bullpen to the starting rotation, where he pitched six complete games. And with Ray gone, the Pirates brought up Jose Lind from Vancouver to play second base.

"I'm not saying he's the best second baseman in the league, but there is no second baseman with more range," Leyland said of Lind, who batted .322 in 35 games.

All of the shuffling brought out the best in everyone.

Bonilla appeared to benefit the most as he recorded 15 home runs, 77 RBIs and a .300 average, the tenth-best mark in the league. A switch-hitter, Bonilla also became the first Pirate in history to homer from each side of the plate in one game, July 3 against Los Angeles.

Pedrique was just one of nine players used at shortstop but, by far, the most productive. He won the job by batting .294 in his rookie season. Rafael Belliard, the reg-

SCORES OF PITTSBURGH PIRATES' 1987 GAMES

APRIL

Date		W/L	Score	Winner	Loser
7—At N.Y.		L	2-3	Ojeda	Patterson
9—At N.Y.		L	2-4	Walter	Easley
10—St. Louis		W	4-3	D. Robinson	LaPoint
11—St. Louis		L	3-6	Forsch	Kipper
12—St. Louis		W	7-4	Patterson	Tudor
13—St. Louis		L	4-8	Cox	Drabek
15—At Chicago		W	3-1*	D. Robinson	Noles
16—At Chicago		W	6-0	Kipper	Lynch
17—Phila.		L	2-6*	Bedrosian	Jones
18—Phila.		L	6-8	Tekulve	D. Robinson
19—Phila.		W	5-2	Drabek	Ruffin
20—New York		W	9-6	Easley	Myers
21—New York		L	6-9	Ojeda	Kipper
22—New York		L	7-8	Darling	Patterson
25—At Phila.		L	2-3	Carman	Drabek
26—At Phila.		L	4-6	Ruffin	Reuschel
28—Los Ang.		W	6-1	Kipper	Valenzuela
29—Los Ang.		L	2-10	Welch	Patterson
30—Los Ang.		W	5-4	Smiley	Hershiser

Won 8, Lost 11

MAY

Date		W/L	Score	Winner	Loser
1—San Fran.		W	4-2	Reuschel	Davis
2—San Fran.		W	1-0	Smiley	Downs
4—At S. Diego		L	5-9	S. Davis	Patterson
5—At S. Diego		W	10-8	Walk	Show
6—At L.A.		L	1-2	Hershiser	Reuschel
7—At L.A.		L	3-6	Honeycutt	Kipper
8—At S. Fran.		L	2-4	Downs	Fisher
9—At S. Fran.		L	4-9	Hammaker	Walk
10—At S. Fran.		W	4-1†	D. Robinson	Garrelts
12—San Diego		W	12-5	Reuschel	Hawkins
13—San Diego		W	9-5	Walk	Lefferts
14—San Diego		W	10-3	Fisher	Show
15—Atlanta		L	3-9	Assenmacher	Pena
16—Atlanta		L	8-10	Dedmon	Smiley
17—Atlanta		W	6-5	D. Robinson	Olwine
18—Houston		L	1-4	Scott	Kipper
19—Houston		W	5-2	Smiley	Meads
20—Houston		W	5-3	Taylor	Darwin
22—At Cinn.		W	4-1	Reuschel	Robinson
23—At Cinn.		W	3-2	Kipper	Pacillo
24—At Cinn.		W	7-2	Fisher	Browning
25—At Hous.		L	2-7	Deshaies	Taylor
26—At Hous.		L	3-10	Meads	Pena
27—At Hous.		L	2-7	Lopez	D. Robinson
29—Cincinnati		L	6-13	Hoffman	Kipper
30—Cincinnati		L	2-6	Gullickson	Taylor
31—Cincinnati		L	2-5	Power	Drabek

Won 13, Lost 14

JUNE

Date		W/L	Score	Winner	Loser
2—At Atlanta		W	4-1	Reuschel	Mahler
3—At Atlanta		W	4-1	Kipper	Palmer
4—At Atlanta		L	3-8	Smith	Fisher
5—At N.Y.		L	1-5	Gooden	Dunne
6—At N.Y.		L	2-4	Fernandez	Drabek
7—At N.Y.		L	4-5*	McDowell	D. Robinson
7—At N.Y.		W	10-9	Taylor	McDowell
8—At Mon.		L	1-7	Heaton	Fisher
9—At Mon.		W	8-1	Dunne	Sorensen
10—At Mon.		L	3-4†	McClure	D. Robinson
12—New York		L	2-10	Fernandez	Reuschel
13—New York		W	4-3	D. Robinson	Myers
14—New York		L	3-7	Sisk	Fisher
15—At St. L.		W	3-1	Dunne	Mathews
16—At St. L.		L	1-11	Dawley	Drabek
17—At St. L.		W	4-1	Reuschel	Forsch
18—At St. L.		L	6-8*	Dawley	D. Robinson
19—At Chicago		W	4-0	Fisher	Noles
20—At Chicago		W	8-2	Dunne	Maddux
21—At Chicago		L	3-6	Trout	Drabek
22—At Chicago		L	2-3	Moyer	Reuschel
23—Montreal		L	2-8	Heaton	Kipper
24—Montreal		W	9-6	Fisher	Fischer
25—Montreal		L	2-7	Martinez	Dunne
26—Chicago		W	5-2	Jones	Maddux
27—Chicago		W	7-0	Reuschel	Moyer
28—Chicago		W	6-2	Jones	Sutcliffe
29—At Phila.		L	5-6	Jackson	Jones
29—At Phila.		L	3-11	Bair	Dunne
30—At Phila.		L	4-6	Gross	Drabek

Won 13, Lost 17

JULY

Date		W/L	Score	Winner	Loser
1—At Phila.		L	4-11	Rawley	Taylor
3—Los Ang.		W	6-0	Reuschel	Valenzuela
4—Los Ang.		W	4-2	Kipper	Welch
5—Los Ang.		L	1-6	Hershiser	Fisher
6—San Fran.		L	5-7	Dravecky	Dunne
6—San Fran.		L	4-7	LaCoss	Drabek

JULY

Date		W/L	Score	Winner	Loser
7—San Fran.		W	6-4‡	Gideon	Price
8—San Fran.		L	4-8§	J. Robinson	Gideon
10—San Diego		W	6-5†	D. Robinson	Gossage
11—San Diego		L	1-3	Grant	Fisher
12—San Diego		W	4-2	Dunne	Show
16—At L.A.		L	0-7	Valenzuela	Kipper
17—At L.A.		L	2-3*	Young	D. Robinson
18—At L.A.		W	4-2	Drabek	Hershiser
19—At L.A.		W	7-2	Dunne	Honeycutt
20—At S. Fran.		W	7-6	Fisher	LaCoss
21—At S. Fran.		L	0-7	Dravecky	Kipper
22—At S. Fran.		W	4-0	Reuschel	Downs
23—At S. Diego		L	1-2	Show	Drabek
24—At S. Diego		W	3-2	Dunne	Jones
25—At S. Diego		W	9-3	Fisher	Hawkins
26—At S. Diego		L	4-7	Whitson	Kipper
28—Phila.		L	2-5	Rawley	Reuschel
29—Phila.		L	3-4	Carman	Drabek
30—Phila.		L	0-1	Ruffin	Smiley
31—At St. L.		L	3-4	Dayley	Jones

Won 11, Lost 15

AUGUST

Date		W/L	Score	Winner	Loser
1—At St. L.		L	6-7*	Worrell	Jones
2—At St. L.		L	1-9	Magrane	Pena
3—Chicago		W	6-4	Drabek	Maddux
4—Chicago		L	2-3†	Mason	Gideon
5—Chicago		W	10-0	Fisher	Moyer
6—Montreal		L	3-6	Parrett	Gott
7—Montreal		W	9-3	Walk	Sebra
8—Montreal		W	5-2	Drabek	Smith
9—Montreal		W	4-3	Dunne	Parrett
10—St. Louis		L	0-6	Forsch	Fisher
11—St. Louis		L	5-6	Dayley	Reuschel
12—St. Louis		W	11-0	Walk	Magrane
13—At Mon.		L	7-9	McGaffigan	Gideon
14—At Mon.		L	3-4	McClure	Smiley
15—At Mon.		L	3-6	Burke	Fisher
16—At Mon.		L	7-10	Parrett	Gideon
18—At Cinn.		W	7-4	Walk	Murphy
19—At Cinn.		L	10-9	Drabek	Browning
20—At Cinn.		L	3-5	Power	Dunne
21—At Atlanta		L	4-5	Smith	Smiley
22—At Atlanta		L	3-10	Glavine	Walk
23—At Atlanta		L	2-6	Palmer	Bielecki
24—Cincinnati		W	5-4	Drabek	Browning
25—Cincinnati		W	1-0	Dunne	Power
26—Cincinnati		W	6-5	J. Robinson	Franco
28—Houston		W	4-2	Walk	Scott
29—Houston		W	8-2	Bielecki	Ryan
30—Houston		W	7-0	Drabek	Knepper
31—Atlanta		W	7-3	Dunne	Dedmon

Won 15, Lost 14

SEPTEMBER

Date		W/L	Score	Winner	Loser
1—Atlanta		L	0-4	Z. Smith	Fisher
2—Atlanta		W	2-0	Walk	Glavine
4—At Hous.		L	0-2	Ryan	Bielecki
5—At Hous.		L	1-5	Knepper	Drabek
6—At Hous.		W	4-3	Dunne	Hernandez
7—At Chicago		W	3-2	Fisher	Moyer
8—At Chicago		W	4-1	Palacios	Sutcliffe
9—At Chicago		W	4-3	J. Robinson	Smith
11—At Phila.		W	4-2	Drabek	Gross
12—At Phila.		W	12-4	Dunne	Carman
13—At Phila.		W	6-1	Fisher	Ruffin
14—Montreal		L	4-6§	McGaffigan	Gideon
15—Montreal		W	5-1	Bielecki	Heaton
16—St. Louis		L	5-8	Tudor	Drabek
17—St. Louis		W	1-0	Dunne	Mathews
18—New York		W	10-9	Smiley	Myers
19—New York		L	4-5	Aguilera	Palacios
20—New York		W	9-8§	Smiley	Ojeda
21—At Mon.		W	5-2	Drabek	Sebra
22—At Mon.		L	3-4	Perez	Gott
23—At St. L.		W	2-0	Fisher	Mathews
24—At St. L.		L	2-3	Horton	J. Robinson
25—At N.Y.		L	2-10	Fernandez	Bielecki
26—At N.Y.		W	8-2	Drabek	Gooden
27—At N.Y.		L	3-12	Ojeda	Dunne
30—Chicago		W	5-3	Fisher	Sutcliffe
30—Chicago		L	8-10	Hall	Smiley

Won 16, Lost 11

OCTOBER

Date		W/L	Score	Winner	Loser
1—Chicago		W	12-3	Drabek	Sanderson
2—Phila.		W	6-4	Walk	Jackson
3—Phila.		W	10-5	Palacios	Gross
4—Phila.		W	4-2	Dunne	Bedrosian

Won 4, Lost 0

*10 innings. †11 innings. ‡12 innings. §14 innings.

ular at the end of '86, hit only .207.

Mike Diaz continued to hit with power, notching 16 home runs as a part-time outfielder and backup to first baseman Sid Bream (.275, 13 homers, 65 RBIs). Diaz was the Bucs' top pinch-hitter, collecting 11 of his 48 RBIs in that role.

Junior Ortiz was solid as LaValliere's backup, hitting .271 while appearing in a career-high 75 games.

Next to shortstop, left and right fields were busiest as seven players started at each position during the season.

Bonds, finishing in left, led the Pirates with 25 home runs while hitting .261 and driving in 59. He was among the league leaders in runs (99) and triples (nine), while Van Slyke finished near the top in doubles (36) and triples (11). R.J. Reynolds played mostly in right, hitting .260 with 51 RBIs, while Cangelosi saw duty at all three outfield positions and batted .275. Coles started 23 games in right and, during the Pirates' final home stand, hit .400 (8 for 20) with four home runs and 10 RBIs while at third base.

It took time, however, for all of the shuffling to pay dividends. Leyland had expected as much.

"We're hoping to get our pitching in place by July 1," he said early in the season.

But it wasn't until Gott and Robinson arrived in August that the staff came completely together. Gott became the stopper Pittsburgh had been seeking since Kent Tekulve faded away, recording 13 saves in 16 save opportunities with the Pirates. Robinson was 2-1 with four saves in 18 games. His 81 appearances overall ranked fourth in the league.

Don Robinson (6-6, 12 saves) had been the workhorse early but got help from rookies John Smiley (5-5, four saves, 63 appearances), Easley (1-1) and, after midseason, Brett Gideon (1-5). Two more rookies, opening-day starter Bob Patterson (1-4) and Dorn Taylor (2-3), worked in starting and relief roles, but both spent time at Vancouver. Bob Walk (8-2, 3.31 ERA) helped ease the youth crisis, pitching as a spot starter and in relief. Bob Kipper was 5-9 in 20 starts and four relief spots.

Struggling for identity, the Pirates hit their low point August 21-23 while losing a three-game series at Atlanta. The team truly was down, shocked by the trade of Reuschel (8-6, 2.75 ERA).

When Pittsburgh returned home, Thrift organized a clubhouse meeting in which Gott set a team goal: 25 victories in the final 38 games.

Mike Dunne, another St. Louis acquisition, produced 13 victories and was named The Sporting News' top rookie pitcher of 1987.

"I tried to talk him out of it," Thrift said. "I told him he had to be realistic with his goals. That was playing .667 ball and we were (17) under. But he said, 'We can do it.' "

They did even better and won 27 times. On the final day of the season, they moved into fourth place with the Phillies.

Rick Sutcliffe was a Chicago Cubs bright spot, producing a league-leading 18 victories and a career-high 174 strikeouts.

Enigmatic Cubs Finish Last

By DAVE VAN DYCK

Perhaps the fairest label to put on the Chicago Cubs came from team superscout Charlie Fox. "This team is an enigma," he said.

Fox glowed at the talent at each position then growled about the standings. "This is not a last-place team," he said.

And yet the cold, hard reality is that since the Cubs won the National League East title in 1984, they have finished in fourth, fifth and, now, sixth place.

Even with another managerial change and despite hitting the most home runs (209) in the league since the 1956 Cincinnati Reds, Chicago finished the 1987 season with a 76-85 record, 18½ games behind the division champion St. Louis Cardinals.

The Cubs had been in first "as late" as May 20, but by September 20 they were mired in last place. It was little consolation that they became the National League's first last-place team to draw 2 million fans.

President and General Manager Dallas Green protested loudly, accusing the players of playing for themselves, not for the team. A week before the season ended, he blasted the players, saying he was "slapped in the face and so were the Cub fans."

". . . We quit with a capital 'Q' " he said.

On October 29, Green quit himself. He resigned because of "basic philosophical differences with management," but reports indicated that he had been relieved of much of his power by Tribune Co. executives.

(One report said that Green had planned to become manager in 1988 and groom coach John Vukovich for the job in '89. He backed off, the report said, when he believed his authority would be usurped while stationed in the dugout.)

Some players and many of the fans, however, felt Green had given up at the All-Star break, when he dealt Steve Trout, the Cubs' top lefthanded starter, to the New York Yankees for righthander Bob Tewksbury and two minor league pitchers. Trout was 6-3 at the time, had pitched complete-game shutouts in his last two starts and had a 3.00 earned-run average. Tewksbury went 0-4 for Chicago with a 6.50 ERA after a 1-4 start with New York.

Even award-winning seasons from right fielder Andre Dawson and pitcher Rick Sutcliffe couldn't halt the slide or keep the interest of Manager Gene Mi-

Cubs rookie Rafael Palmeiro got his chance and hit 14 home runs in his short major league visit.

chael, who told a radio reporter September 7 that he did not want to return in 1988. The Cubs were in fifth place at 68-68.

Michael, in effect, had resigned—before he could be fired—and coach Frank Lucchesi, the team's eye in the sky, took over

SCORES OF CHICAGO CUBS' 1987 GAMES

APRIL

Date		Score	Winner	Loser
7—St. Louis	L	3-9	Tudor	Sutcliffe
9—St. Louis	L	2-4	Cox	Trout
10—At Phila.	W	4-3	Lynch	Gross
11—At Phila.	W	9-1	Sutcliffe	Cowley
12—At Phila.	L	8-9†	Bedrosian	Smith
13—At Phila.	W	5-2	Moyer	Carman
15—Pittsburgh	L	1-3†	D. Robinson	Noles
16—Pittsburgh	L	0-6	Kipper	Lynch
17—Montreal	W	7-0	Sutcliffe	Youmans
18—Montreal	L	2-4	Sebra	Maddux
19—Montreal	L	1-3	Sorensen	Moyer
21—At St. L.	W	5-4	Noles	Dawley
22—At St. L.	W	5-4	Sutcliffe	Dawley
23—At St. L.	L	2-5	Cox	Maddux
24—At Mon.	W	6-4	Moyer	Sebra
25—At Mon.	W	9-4	Sanderson	Tibbs
26—At Mon.	W	7-1	Trout	Sorensen
28—San Fran.	L	2-6	Krukow	Sutcliffe
29—San Fran.	W	8-4	Maddux	Mason
30—San Fran.	L	4-5	Garrelts	Smith

Won 10, Lost 10

MAY

Date		Score	Winner	Loser
1—San Diego	W	7-5	DiPino	McCullers
2—San Diego	W	7-3	Trout	Whitson
3—San Diego	W	4-2	Sutcliffe	Hawkins
4—Los Ang.	W	5-4	Noles	Howell
5—Los Ang.	L	1-3	Welch	Moyer
6—At S. Fran.	W	9-4	Sanderson	Davis
7—At S. Fran.	L	1-11	LaCoss	Lynch
8—At S. Diego	W	6-3	Sutcliffe	S. Davis
9—At S. Diego	W	5-2	Maddux	Show
10—At S. Diego	L	2-14	Whitson	Moyer
11—At L.A.	W	6-3	Sanderson	Hershiser
12—At L.A.	L	0-7	Honeycutt	Lynch
13—At L.A.	W	5-0	Sutcliffe	Pena
15—At Hous.	W	3-1	Maddux	Darwin
16—At Hous.	W	2-1	Moyer	Ryan
17—At Hous.	W	6-4	Mason	Knepper
19—Cincinnati	W	9-2	Sutcliffe	Browning
20—Cincinnati	L	2-6	Gullickson	Maddux
21—Cincinnati	W	8-7	Smith	Franco
22—Atlanta	L	5-9	Palmer	Sanderson
23—Atlanta	W	7-6y	Moyer	Acker
24—Atlanta	W	3-2§	Noles	Dedmon
25—At Cinn.	L	4-5	Gullickson	Maddux
26—At Cinn.	L	2-3	Franco	Smith
27—At Cinn.	W	4-1	Moyer	Reuss
29—At Atlanta	L	5-6§	Garber	Lynch
30—At Atlanta	W	11-6	Maddux	Smith
31—At Atlanta	L	1-2†	Garber	Lynch

Won 18, Lost 10

JUNE

Date		Score	Winner	Loser
1—Houston	L	5-6†	Andersen	DiPino
2—Houston	W	13-2	Mason	Ryan
3—Houston	W	22-7	Sutcliffe	Knepper
4—St. Louis	L	1-3	Cox	Maddux
5—St. Louis	L	1-5	Mathews	Sanderson
6—St. Louis	W	6-5	Moyer	Forsch
7—St. Louis	L	9-13	Dawley	Mason
8—New York	W	4-2	Smith	Sisk
9—New York	W	6-5	Noles	Myers
10—New York	L	2-13	Gooden	Sanderson
12—At St. L.	L	1-4	Forsch	Moyer
13—At St. L.	L	2-9	Tunnell	Sutcliffe
14—At St. L.	L	2-3	Cox	Sanderson
15—Phila.	L	2-3	Tekulve	Smith
16—Phila.	W	7-2	Trout	Gross
17—Phila.	W	5-3	Moyer	Rawley
18—Phila.	W	9-7	Sutcliffe	Jackson
19—Pittsburgh	L	0-4	Fisher	Noles
20—Pittsburgh	L	2-8	Dunne	Maddux
21—Pittsburgh	W	6-3	Trout	Drabek
22—Pittsburgh	W	3-2	Moyer	Reuschel
23—At N.Y.	W	4-1	Sutcliffe	Darling
24—At N.Y.	L	1-2	McDowell	Smith
25—At N.Y.	L	2-8	Gooden	Trout
26—At Pitts.	L	2-5	Jones	Maddux
27—At Pitts.	L	0-7	Reuschel	Moyer
28—At Pitts.	L	2-6	Jones	Sutcliffe
29—At Mon.	W	9-5	Lancaster	Sorensen
30—At Mon.	L	4-5	Martinez	Trout

Won 12, Lost 17

JULY

Date		Score	Winner	Loser
1—At Mon.	W	1-0	Maddux	Sebra
3—San Fran.	L	1-3	Downs	Moyer
4—San Fran.	W	5-3	Sutcliffe	Hammaker
5—San Fran.	L	5-7	Price	Lynch
6—San Diego	W	7-0	Trout	Grant
7—San Diego	W	7-5	Sanderson	Show
8—San Diego	W	12-8	Lancaster	McCullers
10—Los Ang.	W	12-5z	Sutcliffe	Honeycutt
11—Los Ang.	L	4-5†a	Young	Smith
11—Los Ang.	W	7-0	Trout	Leary
12—Los Ang.	L	0-12	Welch	Lancaster
16—At S. Fran.	W	4-1	Moyer	Dravecky
17—At S. Fran.	W	5-1	Sutcliffe	Downs
18—At S. Fran.	L	2-9	Hammaker	Maddux
19—At S. Fran.	L	3-4	Garrelts	Sanderson
20—At S. Diego	L	4-7	McCullers	Tewksbury
21—At S. Diego	L	3-4	M. Davis	Moyer
22—At S. Diego	W	6-3	Sutcliffe	Grant
24—At L.A.	W	6-4	Maddux	Leary
25—At L.A.	L	2-7	Howell	Tewksbury
26—At L.A.	L	6-7	Holton	DiPino
28—Montreal	W	8-3	Sutcliffe	McGaffigan
29—Montreal	L	3-11	Smith	Maddux
30—Montreal	L	1-6	Heaton	Tewksbury
31—Phila.	L	5-8	Tekulve	Sanderson

Won 12, Lost 13

AUGUST

Date		Score	Winner	Loser
1—Phila.	W	5-3	Lancaster	Hume
2—Phila.	W	3-2†	Smith	Calhoun
3—At Pitts.	L	4-6	Drabek	Maddux
4—At Pitts.	W	3-2‡	Mason	Gideon
5—At Pitts.	L	0-10	Fisher	Moyer
6—At N.Y.	L	6-7	McDowell	Smith
7—At N.Y.	L	1-7	Darling	Sutcliffe
8—At N.Y.	W	5-3	Mason	Schulze
9—At N.Y.	W	6-3	Sanderson	Gooden
10—At Phila.	L	2-4	Frohwirth	Moyer
11—At Phila.	L	8-9x	Gross	Tewksbury
12—At Phila.	L	7-13	Calhoun	Lynch
13—New York	W	7-5	DiPino	McDowell
14—New York	W	6-1	Sanderson	Mitchell
15—New York	W	7-3	Moyer	Leach
16—New York	L	10-23	Darling	Maddux
18—At Atlanta	L	5-9	Mahler	Lynch
19—At Atlanta	W	9-1	Sanderson	Puleo
20—At Atlanta	L	4-13	Acker	Moyer
21—Houston	W	7-5	DiPino	Deshaies
22—Houston	L	4-5‡	Andersen	DiPino
23—Houston	L	2-4	Heathcock	Sutcliffe
27—Atlanta	L	2-5	Smith	Moyer
27—Atlanta	W	8-6*	Lancaster	Mahler
28—At Cinn.	W	6-5†	Smith	Franco
29—At Cinn.	L	1-4	Browning	Sanderson
30—At Cinn.	W	3-1	Lynch	Rasmussen
31—At Hous.	W	4-3	Lancaster	Darwin

Won 14, Lost 14

SEPTEMBER

Date		Score	Winner	Loser
1—At Hous.	W	3-2	Moyer	Hernandez
2—At Hous.	L	1-10	Scott	Sutcliffe
4—Cincinnati	L	3-4	Williams	Smith
5—Cincinnati	L	5-10	Rasmussen	Lynch
6—Cincinnati	W	3-1	Lancaster	Power
7—Pittsburgh	L	2-3	Fisher	Moyer
8—Pittsburgh	L	1-4	Palacios	Sutcliffe
9—Pittsburgh	L	3-4	J. Robinson	Smith
11—Montreal	W	8-4	Lancaster	Youmans
12—Montreal	L	1-7	Perez	Moyer
13—Montreal	W	5-2	Sutcliffe	Smith
14—At N.Y.	L	5-6	Aguilera	Hall
15—At N.Y.	L	4-12	Fernandez	Maddux
16—At Phila.	L	5-8	Maddux	Smith
17—At Phila.	L	3-4	Carman	Moyer
18—At St. L.	W	8-1	Sutcliffe	Cox
19—At St. L.	L	3-5	Magrane	Sanderson
20—At St. L.	L	2-10	Forsch	Maddux
21—New York	L	1-7	Gooden	Lancaster
22—New York	W	6-2	Sutcliffe	Cone
23—Phila.	L	0-5	Ruffin	Moyer
24—Phila.	L	2-3‡	Bedrosian	Baller
25—St. Louis	W	2-1	Sanderson	Forsch
26—St. Louis	L	3-5	Tudor	Sutcliffe
27—St. Louis	W	7-3	Lancaster	Cox
30—At Pitts.	L	3-5	Fisher	Sutcliffe
30—At Pitts.	W	10-8	Hall	Smiley

Won 9, Lost 18

OCTOBER

Date		Score	Winner	Loser
1—At Pitts.	L	3-12	Drabek	Sanderson
2—At Mon.	L	1-7	Heaton	Maddux
3—At Mon.	L	4-5	Parrett	Lancaster
4—At Mon.	W	7-5	Moyer	Parrett

Won 1, Lost 3

*7 innings. †10 innings. ‡11 innings. §12 innings. x13 innings. y16 innings. zSuspended game, began July 9. aSuspended game, began July 10.

for the finish.

Lucchesi showed some spark—he was suspended for two games after a run-in with umpire Joe West—but the Cubs went 8-17 after the switch and didn't win two straight games after September 1.

That they still were battling the Pittsburgh Pirates to stay out of last place up until the final weekend was due to Dawson, who picked up the club all season and was named the N.L. Most Valuable Player. The former Montreal Expos star batted .287 and led the National League in home runs (49) and runs batted in (137), the best power totals since Cincinnati's George Foster had 52 homers and 149 RBIs in 1977. Dawson's 16 game-winning RBIs also tied for the league lead, and he received the seventh Gold Glove of his career.

While most free agents sat unsigned with the season due to open, Dawson, eager to leave Montreal for the friendly natural-grass confines in Chicago, presented a blank contract to the Cubs. Green filled in the salary amount at $500,000 for one year and Dawson proceeded to play like a million.

When Dawson strode to the plate for his last home at-bat of the season, more than 33,000 fans stood and roared in appreciation. Dawson bid them thanks and farewell by whaling a home run out of Wrigley Field and onto Waveland Avenue.

"It's been that way all year. . . . The adoration and love affair that's developed allows me to relax and just play the game," Dawson said.

Sutcliffe, who had offered to give up $100,000 of his salary to help sign Dawson, rebounded from two injury-plagued seasons to post a league-leading 18 victories, a career-high 174 strikeouts and a 3.68 ERA. He did, however, go from July 29 through September 12 without a victory and injured his right elbow in his last start of the season. Nevertheless, he was named The Sporting News' N.L. Pitcher of the Year.

But while the Cubs produced some good individual statistics—not only Dawson, but Keith Moreland (27), Leon Durham (27), Jerry Mumphrey (13), Manny Trillo (eight) and Bob Dernier (eight) had career highs in home runs—they were lacking in team totals, finishing last in stolen bases (109), walks allowed (628) and balks (29), and next-to-last in ERA (4.55) and shutouts (five).

The numbers reflected a particularly troublesome year for the pitching staff, which, besides Sutcliffe and Trout, managed only two complete games. They came from Jamie Moyer and Greg Maddux, two youngsters who were expected to turn around a staff that had the league's worst ERA (4.49) in 1986.

Moyer helped the club early, going 8-4 through mid-June, but finished with a 12-15 record and 5.10 ERA. Maddux had a rocky 6-14 rookie season, but another promising youngster emerged in Les Lancaster, who was 8-3 for the Cubs while dividing the season between Chicago and Iowa.

Veteran Scott Sanderson was 8-9 in 22 starts and 10 relief appearances, while Ed Lynch finished 2-9 in long relief, short relief and as a starter.

"I (felt) like the little Dutch boy with his finger in the dike," said Lynch, who appeared in 58 games.

Lee Smith (4-10) ranked second in the National League with a career-high 36 saves, but it was lefthander Frank DiPino who was consistently effective. The former Houston Astro was 3-3 with a 3.15 ERA in 69 appearances.

As shaky as the pitching was, the slide of the team corresponded with the losses of second baseman Ryne Sandberg and shortstop Shawon Dunston, who each missed more than a month in midseason due to injuries. Sandberg still managed to win his fifth Gold Glove and hit .294 with 16 home runs and 59 RBIs, but Dunston hit .246 with only five homers after clouting 17 in 1986.

Moreland, moved to third for 1987, was second on the club in RBIs with 88, finishing ahead of Durham, the first baseman, who had 63. Trillo backed up both players and hit .294.

The Cubs were able to look at two farm system graduates, center fielder Dave Martinez (.292, eight homers, eight triples) and left fielder/first baseman Rafael Palmeiro (.276, 14 homers), as they installed a revolving door in left and center. Mumphrey, who played at each position, led the team with a .333 average, followed by Dernier (.317), who played in center and pinch hit. Brian Dayett compiled a .277 average while batting fourth and playing left field.

Catcher Jody Davis again was near the 20-homer mark, hitting 19 while driving in 51 runs. The Cubs finally were able to rest him this season after acquiring Jim Sundberg (.201) from the Kansas City Royals.

As the Cubs packed up for the winter, none was overheard saying, "See you next year."

But one thing is for certain: A new braintrust can't take the Cubs any lower.

First baseman Will Clark (right) and right fielder Candy Maldonado helped power San Francisco to the 1987 N.L. West Division title.

Giants Stand Tall in the West

By NICK PETERS

Manager Roger Craig's power of positive thinking and General Manager Al Rosen's snappy summer deals to bolster the pitching staff made the San Francisco Giants the National League's comeback story of 1987.

Merely two seasons after suffering a franchise-record 100 losses, the Giants finished 90-72, overwhelmed the N.L. West down the stretch and captured their first division crown since 1971 with a deft blend of pitching, power and defense.

Just one more victory in the N.L. Championship Series would have given the Giants their first pennant since 1962, but the St. Louis Cardinals, down three games to two, rallied to win Game 6, 1-0, and Game 7, 6-0.

When Craig and Rosen had boldly predicted a division championship during spring training, skeptics shrugged it off as gushing optimism. Others suggested that the broiling Arizona sun was playing tricks with the mind.

But Craig and Rosen backed up their boast by performing astutely in the dugout and front office. Their work also paid off at the gate as a record 1,917,863 fans flocked to Candlestick Park to support a revitalized team.

The foundation was set in 1986, when the Giants improved to 83-79 and finished third. Rosen was the mover behind the jump of first baseman Will Clark and second baseman Robby Thompson from the minor leagues into the Giants' starting lineup. Craig impressed with his aggressive "Humm-Baby" approach, fielding a club that executed well and used the element of surprise to become a winner.

It was done differently in 1987. Craig again had to cope with injuries but was rewarded with brilliant play off the bench from infielder Chris Speier and outfielder/first baseman Mike Aldrete. And the Giants' attack rekindled memories of the big lumber wielded by Willie Mays, Willie McCovey and Orlando Cepeda.

The 1987 Giants didn't dazzle with finesse as much as they bludgeoned foes. Their 205 home runs established a franchise record, topping the old mark of 204, set in 1962. Clark led the way with 35 homers, the most by a San Francisco first baseman since McCovey hammered 39 in 1970.

Clark had a lot of company. Eight teammates hit 10 or more homers and 11 were belted by pinch-hitters, one shy of the major league mark. Center fielder Chili Davis and right fielder Candy Maldonado attained career highs with 24 and 20 home runs, respectively.

Defensively, shortstop Jose Uribe was the glue of a team that topped the majors with 183 double plays, a franchise record. That helped the pitching staff post a 3.68 earned-run average, also the best in the majors.

Yet it all didn't come together until July 4, the day Rosen swapped third baseman Chris Brown and pitchers Mark Davis, Mark Grant and Keith Comstock to the San Diego Padres for lefthanders Dave Dravecky and Craig Lefferts and third baseman Kevin Mitchell.

Dravecky was the key and he didn't disappoint, going 7-5 with three shutouts and a 3.20 ERA for his new club. Mitchell was the surprise. He fielded well at third and batted .306 for the Giants after a .245 start with the Padres. Overall, Mitchell blasted a career-high 22 homers and drove in 70 runs.

"We became a team July 4," observed veteran Mike Krukow, a 20-9 pitcher in 1986 who was far more valuable to the '87 title drive than his 1-6 first half would suggest. The club was struggling at 39-40 when the holiday blockbuster was announced.

A 16-7 start had given credence to the optimism of Craig and Rosen, but the Giants soon hit on hard times despite the impressive slugging of left fielder Jeffrey Leonard and Maldonado. Uribe went on the disabled list three times with a hamstring injury and Thompson's back trouble sidelined him from April 28 through May 13.

After the trade, the Giants were better equipped to sustain themselves. Improved pitching and Uribe's return compensated for Maldonado's absence June 28 to August 7 due to a broken finger and a dropoff by Leonard, whose four off-season surgeries (both knees, left shoulder, right wrist) began taking their toll, along with a hamstring problem.

Moreover, the Giants acquired reliever Don Robinson from the Pittsburgh Pirates on July 31, just as the club was losing five of six games at Cincinnati and Houston. The Giants slipped to third place, five lengths behind the first-place Reds and 1½ behind the Astros.

But suddenly, the pieces started fitting.

SCORES OF SAN FRANCISCO GIANTS' 1987 GAMES

APRIL			Winner	Loser
6—San Diego	W	4-3‡	J. Robinson	Dravecky
7—San Diego	W	4-3	LaCoss	Whitson
8—San Diego	W	2-1	Mason	Hawkins
9—At L.A.	W	8-1	Davis	Welch
10—At L.A.	W	5-4†	Garrelts	Leary
11—At L.A.	L	1-5	Hershiser	Krukow
12—At L.A.	L	5-7	Valenzuela	LaCoss
13—At S. Diego	W	13-6	Gott	Dravecky
14—At S. Diego	W	3-2	Grant	Wojna
15—At S. Diego	W	1-0	Downs	S. Davis
17—Atlanta	L	0-2	Smith	Krukow
18—Atlanta	W	2-1*	Garrelts	Garber
19—Atlanta	W	4-3	J. Robinson	Assenmacher
20—Los Ang.	W	4-3	Davis	Hershiser
21—Los Ang.	L	8-11*	Howell	Garrelts
22—Los Ang.	L	3-5	Valenzuela	Krukow
24—At Atlanta	W	7-5	Minton	Acker
25—At Atlanta	L	3-5	Garber	Garrelts
26—At Atlanta	W	6-4	Davis	Palmer
27—At Atlanta	W	7-3	Downs	Mahler
28—At Chicago	W	6-2	Krukow	Sutcliffe
29—At Chicago	L	4-8	Maddux	Mason
30—At Chicago	W	5-4	Garrelts	Smith
Won 16, Lost 7				

MAY			Winner	Loser
1—At Pitts.	L	2-4	Reuschel	Davis
2—At Pitts.	L	0-1	Smiley	Downs
4—At St. L.	W	10-7	LaCoss	Dawley
5—At St. L.	W	10-6	Garrelts	Mathews
6—Chicago	L	4-9	Sanderson	Davis
7—Chicago	W	11-1	LaCoss	Lynch
8—Pittsburgh	W	4-2	Downs	Fisher
9—Pittsburgh	W	9-4	Hammaker	Walk
10—Pittsburgh	L	1-4†	D. Robinson	Garrelts
12—St. Louis	L	5-6	Magrane	Davis
13—St. Louis	L	6-7	Soff	J. Robinson
15—At N.Y.	L	3-8	Fernandez	Krukow
16—At N.Y.	W	5-4*	Garrelts	Innis
17—At N.Y.	L	4-6	Cone	Hammaker
18—At Mon.	L	2-7	Heaton	Downs
19—At Mon.	W	6-2	LaCoss	Youmans
20—At Mon.	W	9-7	J. Robinson	St. Claire
22—At Phila.	W	2-1	Hammaker	Carman
23—At Phila.	L	8-9	Bedrosian	J. Robinson
24—At Phila.	W	6-3	LaCoss	Tekulve
25—New York	L	7-8	Leach	Grant
26—New York	L	2-3	Sisk	J. Robinson
27—New York	L	3-4	McDowell	J. Robinson
29—Montreal	L	4-10	Heaton	LaCoss
30—Montreal	L	4-6	Youmans	Krukow
31—Montreal	W	8-0	Downs	Sebra
Won 11, Lost 15				

JUNE			Winner	Loser
1—Phila.	W	9-2	Hammaker	Carman
2—Phila.	W	6-7	Ritchie	Davis
3—Phila.	W	4-1	LaCoss	Ruffin
5—At Hous.	L	1-6	Scott	Krukow
6—At Hous.	W	4-3‡	Comstock	Andersen
7—At Hous.	L	0-3	Ryan	Hammaker
8—At Cinn.	L	6-7	Franco	Garrelts
9—At Cinn.	W	10-2	Davis	Pacillo
10—At Cinn.	W	9-4	Comstock	Gullickson
11—San Diego	W	1-0	Downs	Show
12—San Diego	L	0-5	Whitson	LaCoss
13—San Diego	L	2-11	Hawkins	Hammaker
14—San Diego	L	1-4	Dravecky	Davis
16—At Atlanta	L	2-7	Alexander	Downs
17—At Atlanta	L	1-6	Mahler	J. Robinson
18—At S. Diego	L	1-3	S. Davis	Hammaker
19—At S. Diego	W	7-6	J. Robinson	McCullers
20—At S. Diego	L	4-10	Jones	J. Robinson
21—At S. Diego	W	11-2	Downs	Show
23—Cincinnati	L	1-4	Robinson	Hammaker
24—Cincinnati	L	4-5*	Franco	Garrelts
25—Cincinnati	W	7-6	Garrelts	Murphy
26—Houston	L	6-9	Knepper	LaCoss
27—Houston	L	5-6	Deshaies	Downs
28—Houston	W	8-4	Hammaker	Ryan
29—Atlanta	L	0-1	Smith	Grant
30—Atlanta	W	5-2	J. Robinson	Alexander
Won 11, Lost 16				

JULY			Winner	Loser
1—Atlanta	L	3-8	Mahler	LaCoss
3—At Chicago	W	3-1	Downs	Moyer
4—At Chicago	L	3-5	Sutcliffe	Hammaker
5—At Chicago	W	7-5	Price	Lynch
6—At Pitts.	W	7-5	Dravecky	Dunne
6—At Pitts.	W	7-4	LaCoss	Drabek

JULY			Winner	Loser
7—At Pitts.	L	4-6‡	Gideon	Price
8—At Pitts.	W	8-4x	J. Robinson	Gideon
9—At St. L.	L	6-7*	Horton	Garrelts
10—At St. L.	L	5-7§	Tunnell	Lefferts
11—At St. L.	W	3-1	Downs	Magrane
12—At St. L.	L	2-3	Horton	Hammaker
16—Chicago	L	1-4	Moyer	Dravecky
17—Chicago	L	1-5	Sutcliffe	Downs
18—Chicago	W	9-2	Hammaker	Maddux
19—Chicago	W	4-3	Garrelts	Sanderson
20—Pittsburgh	L	6-7	Fisher	LaCoss
21—Pittsburgh	W	7-0	Dravecky	Kipper
22—Pittsburgh	L	0-4	Reuschel	Downs
24—St. Louis	W	4-3	Hammaker	Horton
25—St. Louis	W	5-4	Garrelts	Dawley
26—St. Louis	W	6-3*	Garrelts	Worrell
26—St. Louis	W	5-2	LaCoss	Mathews
27—At L.A.	L	5-6‡	Leary	Garrelts
28—At L.A.	L	2-4	Hershiser	Hammaker
29—At L.A.	W	16-2	Krukow	Honeycutt
31—At Cinn.	L	2-9	Robinson	Dravecky
Won 14, Lost 13				

AUGUST			Winner	Loser
1—At Cinn.	W	7-3	LaCoss	Gullickson
2—At Cinn.	L	4-5†	Montgomery	J. Robinson
3—At Hous.	L	3-5§	Agosto	Price
4—At Hous.	L	4-5	Heathcock	Lefferts
5—At Hous.	L	5-6†	Andersen	J. Robinson
7—Cincinnati	W	3-1	LaCoss	Gullickson
8—Cincinnati	W	5-2	Hammaker	Browning
9—Cincinnati	W	3-2	Krukow	Power
9—Cincinnati	W	5-2	Downs	Hoffman
10—Houston	W	6-5	D. Robinson	Meads
11—Houston	L	3-7	Heathcock	LaCoss
12—Houston	W	8-1	Hammaker	Scott
13—Houston	W	7-6†	Lefferts	Childress
14—Los Ang.	L	3-4	Hillegas	Downs
15—Los Ang.	W	5-0	Dravecky	Valenzuela
16—Los Ang.	W	1-0*	LaCoss	Leary
18—At N.Y.	L	2-7	Gooden	Hammaker
19—At N.Y.	W	10-6*	Garrelts	McDowell
20—At N.Y.	L	4-7	Cone	Downs
21—At Mon.	W	6-3	Dravecky	Martinez
22—At Mon.	L	4-5*	Burke	Lefferts
23—At Mon.	W	5-3	Downs	Sebra
24—At Phila.	W	6-1	Reuschel	Ruffin
25—At Phila.	W	3-2	Garrelts	Gross
26—At Phila.	W	2-0	D. Robinson	Rawley
28—New York	L	0-4	Gooden	LaCoss
29—New York	W	9-1	Hammaker	Fernandez
30—New York	L	3-5	Aguilera	Reuschel
31—Montreal	W	5-0	Dravecky	Martinez
Won 18, Lost 11				

SEPTEMBER			Winner	Loser
1—Montreal	W	14-4	Reuschel	Youmans
2—Montreal	L	3-7	Perez	LaCoss
4—Phila.	W	3-2*	D. Robinson	Ritchie
5—Phila.	W	6-3	Dravecky	Rawley
6—Phila.	W	4-1	Reuschel	Toliver
7—At Hous.	L	2-4	Scott	LaCoss
8—At Hous.	W	6-4	D. Robinson	Andersen
9—At Hous.	L	2-4	Ryan	Hammaker
11—At Cinn.	L	3-4	Rasmussen	Dravecky
12—At Cinn.	W	7-1	Reuschel	Power
13—At Cinn.	W	6-1	LaCoss	Browning
14—San Diego	W	4-3	Lefferts	McCullers
15—San Diego	W	13-3	Hammaker	Nolte
16—Houston	W	7-1	Dravecky	Scott
17—Houston	W	4-0	Reuschel	Darwin
19—Cincinnati	W	5-1	LaCoss	Browning
20—Cincinnati	L	6-10	Murphy	D. Robinson
21—Los Ang.	L	2-4	Welch	Downs
22—Los Ang.	L	3-4	Valenzuela	Dravecky
23—Los Ang.	W	9-8	Lefferts	Hershiser
25—At Atlanta	W	9-2	Krukow	Glavine
26—At Atlanta	L	5-10	Puleo	Reuschel
27—At Atlanta	W	15-6	Price	Cary
28—At S. Diego	W	5-4	D. Robinson	McCullers
29—At S. Diego	W	5-3	Downs	Jones
30—At L.A.	W	3-0	Krukow	Belcher
Won 18, Lost 8				

OCTOBER			Winner	Loser
1—At L.A.	L	0-7	Welch	Reuschel
2—Atlanta	L	4-6	Coffman	Dravecky
3—Atlanta	W	6-3	Downs	Clary
4—Atlanta	W	5-4*	Bockus	Acker
Won 2, Lost 2				

*10 innings. †11 innings. ‡12 innings. §13 innings. x14 innings.

The Giants returned to Candlestick, swept the Reds in four games and completed a 9-2 home stand that created a first-place tie. Momentum gained strength when veteran righthander Rick Reuschel was obtained from Pittsburgh on August 21.

In only 49 days, Rosen had snatched a division championship from under the noses of the front offices in Cincinnati and Houston. The four new pitchers completely changed the complexion of the pitching staff, making it perhaps the major leagues' best.

"Al did his job, now I have to do mine," Craig said. "We're going to win this thing unless I mess it up."

Not to worry. From August 7 through the end of the season, the Giants went 37-17 and ran away from the pack, finishing six games ahead of the Reds. Dravecky, Reuschel, Robinson and Lefferts were a combined 20-12 with 11 saves for San Francisco, and Robinson finished with a career-high 19 saves overall. Fittingly, his homer clinched the division title at San Diego on September 28.

Reuschel, 13-9 for the year and winner of a Gold Glove, tied for the league lead in complete games (12) and shutouts (four) and was fourth in ERA (3.09). Dravecky was eighth in ERA (3.43) while Lefferts was sixth in total games (77).

Among the old guard, Atlee Hammaker bounced back from rotator cuff and knee surgeries in 1986 to go 10-10 with a 3.58 ERA. Scott Garrelts was 11-7 with a 3.22 ERA and 12 saves despite missing most of the final month with a finger fracture. Mike LaCoss went 13-10 in 39 appearances, including 26 starts. Kelly Downs pitched three shutouts and was 12-9 in 28 starts and 13 relief appearances. Krukow didn't lose the last four months and finished 5-6 after spending almost all of June on the disabled list.

Speier was voted the club's most inspirational player for providing a spark off the bench in Uribe's and Thompson's absences. The 37-year-old infielder hit 11 home runs, including two grand slams. Aldrete earned team most valuable player honors for batting .325 and filling in for Maldonado. The "Candy Man" still notched 85 runs batted in, giving him 170 in only 251 games over two years.

Leonard got healthy just in time to hammer a record four homers in the first four playoff games, bat .417 for the series and win the playoff MVP award. He had 19 home runs, 63 RBIs and a .280 batting average for the season. Uribe's glovework overshadowed a solid .291 average. Bob Brenly and Bob Melvin combined behind

The July 4 trade that brought Dave Dravecky to San Francisco was the key to the Giants' title drive.

the plate for 29 home runs and 82 RBIs. As a pinch-batter, Joel Youngblood had a .295 average with three homers and nine RBIs. Eddie Milner (.252) was solid as a defensive replacement in the outfield. This was a team in every sense of the word.

"We have no real superstars—just a bunch of guys who don't know how to quit and who keep rising to the occasion," said Clark, who batted .308 with a team-leading 91 RBIs. "It's someone different every day. We have a lot of heroes."

Beginning with Craig and Rosen, who believed all along and heartily enjoyed the last laugh.

The hot bat of Eric Davis literally carried Cincinnati's offense through the first half of the 1987 season.

Unarmed Reds Fall Hard

By HAL McCOY

Worse than leaving their hearts in San Francisco, the Cincinnati Reds left a division title there.

The Reds, who had led the National League West since May 29, arrived in San Francisco on August 7 for a four-game series with the Giants. Four losses later, the Reds stumbled out of town and into a rut that led to a 9-20 record for the month. When September arrived, Cincinnati was buried six games behind San Francisco.

Why so sickening a fall after a remarkable rise?

"The last seven games we played against San Francisco we scored 13 total runs and lost six (games)," Manager Pete Rose said after the Giants took two of three games September 11-13. A Cincinnati sweep would have pulled the Reds to within two games.

Having fended off the challengers, the Giants coasted to the West title while the Reds claimed second—for the third straight year—with an 84-78 record, six games behind the Giants.

For most of the season, Cincinnati had been expected to collapse because of an unsteady starting rotation.

• Veteran Mario Soto couldn't rebound from shoulder surgery the previous August and made only six early season starts.

• Jerry Reuss, signed in April and released in June, was 0-5 in seven starts.

• Tom Browning was demoted to the minors for a month and finished 10-13 with a 5.02 earned-run average.

• Bill Gullickson started fast, faltered and was traded August 26 to the New York Yankees for Dennis Rasmussen, who was 4-1 in seven starts for the Reds. Still, no one could surpass Gullickson's 10 victories.

• Ted Power lost his last six decisions, finished 10-13, and was traded with infielder Kurt Stillwell after the season to the Kansas City Royals for lefthander Danny Jackson and shortstop Angel Salazar.

• Ron Robinson, one of the Reds' top relievers, was pressed into starting duty and finished 7-5. Guy Hoffman was 9-10 while filling two roles. Both pitched with sore arms in the second half and underwent arthroscopic elbow surgery in October.

Clearly, Cincinnati wasn't armed for a pennant fight. But when Rose tapped the Reds' relief pipeline, he created an emergency situation—for the opposition.

The Reds' relievers compiled a 3.10 ERA, tops in the majors, and combined for 392 appearances, a major league record.

"Our bullpen has been our strong point in 1987," Rose said. "The job it's done sticks out. When we went to spring training, we knew we'd use the bullpen a lot.

"We happen to have the kind of arms that can pitch two or three days in a row. Obviously, I would have liked our starters to pitch more innings. But they didn't and you've got to pitch somebody. . . ."

Rob Murphy (8-5, 3.04 ERA, three saves) set a major league record for lefthanders by pitching in 87 games. "Amazingly, I feel as if it's April 1," Murphy said after the record-setting appearance that broke Wilbur Wood's mark of 86, set in 1968.

Righthander Frank Williams, summoned 85 times, topped the staff with a 2.30 ERA and was 4-0 in his first season with the Reds. Lefthander John Franco, named to the N.L. All-Star squad, was 8-5 in 68 games and fourth in the league in saves (32). Rookie Bill Landrum was 3-2 in 44 appearances.

"Appearances by relief pitchers might be a dubious record," Franco observed, "but the good thing is that we proved we're the best."

Cincinnati's offense was one of the best —second in the league in average (.266) and runs batted in (747), and tied for third in runs (783) and home runs (192)—yet it reversed roles with the pitching down the stretch.

"In the second half, our pitching was good enough that we allowed less runs per game (3.93 ERA compared to 4.51)," Rose said. "But we scored less per game (5.1 to 4.5) the second half. Our hitting went south."

Individual totals, however, were high.

Right fielder/first baseman Dave Parker, subjected to frequent knee drainings, hit only .253 but had 26 homers, 97 RBIs and tied for the league lead with 16 game-winning RBIs.

"And how can you complain about Eric Davis when he hit .293, drove in 100, stole 50 bases and played highlight film defense?" Rose asked. Davis' only weakness was injury—he missed 35 starts, including 18 in September. His torrid beginning, however, was one of the best ever. He was the N.L. Player of the Month in both April and May, when he combined for 19 homers and 52 RBIs. The Reds' center

SCORES OF CINCINNATI REDS' 1987 GAMES

APRIL			Winner	Loser
6—Montreal	W	11-5	Landrum	Youmans
8—Montreal	W	7-2	Gullickson	Tibbs
10—San Diego	W	6-3	Murphy	Dravecky
11—San Diego	W	5-1	Browning	Show
12—San Diego	L	2-5	Whitson	Hoffman
13—At Atlanta	W	7-2	Gullickson	Smith
14—At Atlanta	W	6-3	Power	Palmer
15—At Atlanta	L	3-4	Mahler	Browning
17—Houston	W	9-8	Murphy	Knepper
18—Houston	W	8-0	Gullickson	Ryan
19—Houston	L	3-7	Scott	Browning
19—Houston	W	6-2	Power	Darwin
20—At S. Diego	W	12-3	Hoffman	S. Davis
21—At S. Diego	L	2-3	McCullers	Murphy
22—At S. Diego	L	3-6	Whitson	Landrum
23—At S. Diego	W	3-2	Browning	Hawkins
24—At Hous.	W	4-3†	Murphy	Kerfeld
25—At Hous.	W	3-0*	Franco	Andersen
26—At Hous.	W	11-3	Soto	Knepper
28—Atlanta	L	3-7	O'Neal	Browning
29—Atlanta	L	2-5	Smith	Gullickson
30—Atlanta	W	9-8†	Landrum	Ziem
		Won 15, Lost 7		

MAY			Winner	Loser
1—At Phila.	W	8-5	Soto	Carman
2—At Phila.	L	3-8	Ruffin	Browning
3—At Phila.	W	9-6	Gullickson	Gross
5—At N.Y.	W	2-0	Power	Fernandez
6—At N.Y.	L	2-3	Aguilera	Soto
8—Phila.	W	4-3	Browning	Ruffin
9—Phila.	L	2-4	Gross	Gullickson
10—Phila.	L	3-4	Rawley	Power
11—New York	W	12-2	Soto	Aguilera
12—New York	L	2-6	Cone	Reuss
13—At Mon.	W	12-6	Browning	St. Claire
14—At Mon.	W	10-9	Robinson	St. Claire
15—At St. L.	L	4-5	Cox	Power
16—At St. L.	L	5-6	Conroy	Soto
17—At St. L.	L	2-10	Tunnell	Reuss
19—At Chicago	L	2-9	Sutcliffe	Browning
20—At Chicago	W	6-2	Gullickson	Maddux
21—At Chicago	L	7-8	Smith	Franco
22—Pittsburgh	L	1-4	Reuschel	Robinson
23—Pittsburgh	L	2-3	Kipper	Pacillo
24—Pittsburgh	L	2-7	Fisher	Browning
25—Chicago	W	5-4	Gullickson	Maddux
26—Chicago	W	3-2	Franco	Smith
27—Chicago	L	1-4	Moyer	Reuss
29—At Pitts.	W	13-6	Hoffman	Kipper
30—At Pitts.	W	6-2	Gullickson	Taylor
31—At Pitts.	W	5-2	Power	Drabek
		Won 13, Lost 14		

JUNE			Winner	Loser
1—St. Louis	L	6-8*	Worrell	Robinson
2—St. Louis	W	3-2	Hoffman	Tunnell
3—St. Louis	W	6-4	Pacillo	Conroy
5—Los Ang.	W	8-6	Hoffman	Howell
6—Los Ang.	W	5-2	Power	Valenzuela
7—Los Ang.	L	7-13	Welch	Reuss
8—San Fran.	W	7-6	Franco	Garrelts
9—San Fran.	L	2-10	Davis	Pacillo
10—San Fran.	W	4-9	Comstock	Gullickson
11—Atlanta	L	4-6	Puleo	Murphy
12—Atlanta	L	3-4	Mahler	Reuss
13—Atlanta	W	5-2	Hoffman	Palmer
14—Atlanta	W	4-3	Murphy	Garber
15—At Hous.	L	0-4	Scott	Gullickson
16—At Hous.	L	1-4	Deshaies	Power
17—At Hous.	W	9-1	Robinson	Ryan
18—At Atlanta	W	8-4	Hoffman	Palmer
19—At Atlanta	L	5-16	Smith	Pacillo
20—At Atlanta	L	6-8	Alexander	Gullickson
21—At Atlanta	W	6-5*	Landrum	Garber
23—At S. Fran.	W	4-1	Robinson	Hammaker
24—At S. Fran.	W	5-4*	Franco	Garrelts
25—At S. Fran.	L	6-7	Garrelts	Murphy
26—At L.A.	W	6-0	Power	Honeycutt
27—At L.A.	L	3-4*	Young	Franco
28—At L.A.	L	2-4	Valenzuela	Hoffman
30—Houston	W	5-4*	Franco	Andersen
		Won 14, Lost 13		

JULY			Winner	Loser
1—Houston	W	6-4	Scherrer	Darwin
2—New York	L	0-5	Leach	Robinson
3—New York	W	8-3	Hoffman	Darling
4—New York	W	7-3	Gullickson	Mitchell
5—New York	W	7-5	Browning	Gooden
6—Phila.	L	6-9	Jackson	Power

JULY			Winner	Loser
7—Phila.	L	8-10*	Tekulve	Franco
8—Phila.	L	2-7	Ruffin	Hoffman
9—Montreal	W	7-2	Gullickson	Heaton
10—Montreal	L	1-5	Smith	Browning
11—Montreal	L	5-11	Martinez	Power
12—Montreal	L	2-4	Sebra	Hoffman
16—At N.Y.	L	0-9	Gooden	Gullickson
17—At N.Y.	W	5-2	Williams	Darling
18—At N.Y.	W	7-3	Power	Fernandez
19—At N.Y.	L	5-6†	Orosco	Scherrer
20—At Phila.	W	10-6†	Franco	Jackson
21—At Phila.	W	4-3	Gullickson	Gross
22—At Phila.	L	3-5	Rawley	Browning
23—At Mon.	W	8-4	Power	Smith
24—At Mon.	L	2-3	Heaton	Hoffman
25—At Mon.	L	3-4‡	McGaffigan	Landrum
26—At Mon.	L	0-6	Youmans	Gullickson
28—San Diego	W	8-7	Franco	M. Davis
29—San Diego	W	15-5	Murphy	Show
30—San Diego	L	8-12	Jones	Hoffman
31—San Fran.	W	9-2	Robinson	Dravecky
		Won 13, Lost 14		

AUGUST			Winner	Loser
1—San Fran.	L	3-7	LaCoss	Gullickson
2—San Fran.	W	5-4†	Montgomery	J. Robinson
3—Los Ang.	L	2-7	Hershiser	Power
4—Los Ang.	W	10-4	Hoffman	Leary
5—Los Ang.	W	6-3	Robinson	Valenzuela
7—At S. Fran.	L	1-3	LaCoss	Gullickson
8—At S. Fran.	L	2-5	Hammaker	Browning
9—At S. Fran.	L	2-3	Krukow	Power
9—At S. Fran.	L	2-5	Downs	Hoffman
10—At L.A.	W	4-3	Williams	Valenzuela
11—At L.A.	L	2-7	Welch	Montgomery
12—At L.A.	L	0-1	Leary	Gullickson
13—At L.A.	W	5-2	Murphy	Hershiser
14—At S. Diego	W	2-0	Power	Show
14—At S. Diego	L	8-15	Booker	Hoffman
16—At S. Diego	W	2-0	Robinson	Whitson
18—Pittsburgh	L	4-7	Walk	Murphy
19—Pittsburgh	L	9-10	Drabek	Browning
20—Pittsburgh	W	5-3	Power	Dunne
21—St. Louis	L	1-2	Tudor	Hoffman
22—St. Louis	L	7-9	Perry	Murphy
23—St. Louis	L	6-12	Cox	Gullickson
24—At Pitts.	L	4-5	Drabek	Browning
25—At Pitts.	L	0-1	Dunne	Power
26—At Pitts.	L	5-6	J. Robinson	Franco
28—Chicago	L	5-6*	Smith	Franco
29—Chicago	W	4-1	Browning	Sanderson
30—Chicago	L	1-3	Lynch	Rasmussen
31—At St. L.	L	0-4	Tudor	Power
		Won 9, Lost 20		

SEPTEMBER			Winner	Loser
1—At St. L.	W	7-4	Hoffman	Horton
2—At St. L.	W	3-1	Williams	Cox
4—At Chicago	W	4-3	Williams	Smith
5—At Chicago	W	10-5	Rasmussen	Lynch
6—At Chicago	L	1-3	Lancaster	Power
7—Los Ang.	W	3-2§	Hume	Holton
8—Los Ang.	L	3-5	Hershiser	Robinson
9—Los Ang.	W	4-1	Browning	Belcher
11—San Fran.	W	4-3	Rasmussen	Dravecky
12—San Fran.	L	1-7	Reuschel	Power
13—San Fran.	L	1-6	LaCoss	Browning
14—At Atlanta	W	2-3	Glavine	Hoffman
15—At Atlanta	W	21-6	Robinson	Palmer
17—At L.A.	W	3-2*	Franco	Valenzuela
17—At L.A.	L	3-6	Welch	Power
19—At S. Fran.	L	1-5	LaCoss	Browning
20—At S. Fran.	W	10-6	Murphy	D. Robinson
22—San Diego	W	5-3	Rasmussen	Grant
23—San Diego	L	4-6§	M. Davis	Montgomery
24—San Diego	W	5-4	Pacillo	McCullers
25—Houston	W	4-1	Browning	Scott
26—Houston	L	3-5	Darwin	Robinson
27—Houston	W	4-2	Murphy	Knepper
28—Atlanta	W	6-5	Montgomery	Z. Smith
29—Atlanta	W	5-4	Perry	Acker
30—At S. Diego	W	3-1	Browning	Hawkins
		Won 17, Lost 9		

OCTOBER			Winner	Loser
1—At S. Diego	W	4-3	Pacillo	Nolte
2—At Hous.	W	12-7	Rasmussen	Childress
3—At Hous.	L	4-6	Heathcock	Power
4—At Hous.	W	2-1	Browning	Ryan
		Won 3, Lost 1		

*10 innings. †11 innings. ‡12 innings. §13 innings.

Reds left fielder Kal Daniels missed 54 games but still managed to hit 26 homers and bat .334.

fielder finished among the league leaders in seven offensive categories: home runs, RBIs, stolen bases, runs (120), walks (84), on-base average (.399) and slugging average (.593). He also won his first Gold Glove.

Kal Daniels hit .334, ripped 26 homers, drove in 64 runs and stole 26 bases in just his second season. The left fielder also

missed 54 games, some when he was platooned early but most due to a bad knee that required midseason surgery.

Nick Esasky tore up the American Association during a 20-day rehabilitation for a broken wrist, then returned to claim first base. He clubbed a career-high 22 homers, drove in 59 runs and hit .272 in only 100 games.

Veteran Dave Concepcion, in his 18th season with the Reds, batted a career-high .319 as he filled in around the infield.

Steady Buddy Bell put on a defensive clinic at third base. He committed only seven errors while hitting .284 with 17 homers and 70 RBIs.

Catcher Bo Diaz, a member of the N.L. All-Star squad, drove in 82 runs, clubbed 15 homers and batted .270.

Things weren't as rosy elsewhere.

Shortstop Barry Larkin suffered an early season knee injury and was slow recovering. He finished with a .244 average.

Second baseman Ron Oester suffered a season-ending knee injury July 5 and was released in October. Stillwell, once projected as the shortstop of the future, was unsteady there and at second. He became a forgotten man when rookie Jeff Treadway batted .333 after being called up in September.

Tracy Jones hit .290 and stole 31 bases but was unhappy with his platoon situation in the outfield.

In mid-August, after the Reds lost three straight one-run games in Pittsburgh, Owner Marge Schott responded with an announcement: "The only good thing about this is that if we don't win, it's not my fault. It's (General Manager Bill) Bergesch's and Pete's fault. They run the baseball."

Bergesch, criticized for not making trades for pitching help, paid a stiff price. He was fired October 12 and replaced by Murray Cook, who had resigned as the Montreal Expos' general manager on August 11.

"I don't know what happened," Bergesch said. "Little by little we deteriorated and we lost our spirit. We went through the motions. No heart."

The Reds remained as the only West division club without a title in the 1980s.

"We have the best combined record (in the N.L. West) for three years (259-232) ... but I guess you don't consider it a good year unless you win," Rose said. "We had identical records at home and away (42-39) and we beat Houston 13 of 18 after losing 14 of 18 last year. So we got rid of them but we couldn't beat San Francisco when we had to."

First baseman Glenn Davis contributed 27 homers and 93 RBIs to Houston's offense, but still was dropped from the cleanup spot.

Road Problems Doom Astros

By NEIL HOHLFELD

Though their pitching almost spoiled matters, the Houston Astros upheld the "no-repeat" axiom that has prevailed for the National League's divisional races of the 1980s.

After winning the N.L. West title in 1986 with a club-record 96 victories, the Astros slipped to third place in 1987 at 76-86, their worst record since 1978.

But even as they fell, the Astros were contenders.

On August 24, they were 65-60 and trailed the San Francisco Giants by half a game. With everything to gain, the Astros made their move—downward. They lost seven straight, closed the season with an 11-26 performance and finished 14 games behind the Giants.

Their collapse wasn't hard to figure.

"You don't have to go much further than our road record to see what happened," Manager Hal Lanier said. "You can look at that and our hitting and put your finger on it."

The Astros, a bad road club all season, were 5-17 on their last three trips. For the year, they were 29-52 outside the Astrodome.

"I guess 'nightmare' is the word to use for what . . . happened," Lanier said.

It didn't matter where they were when batting. The Astros ranked 11th in the league in average (.253) and runs scored (648), were tied for last in total bases (2,046) and finished last in hits (1,386). Houston's pitchers, meanwhile, were first in strikeouts (1,137), tied for first in shutouts (13) and tied for third in earned-run average (3.84).

No pitcher was hurt more by the lack of offense than Nolan Ryan. The 40-year-old righthander led the league with a 2.76 ERA and 270 strikeouts, but his record was a staggering 8-16.

Ryan extended his major league record for most seasons with 200 or more strikeouts (11) and, joining Rube Waddell and Jim Bunning, became only the third pitcher to win strikeout crowns in both leagues.

Righthander Mike Scott, who won the Cy Young Award in 1986, was second to Ryan in strikeouts (233) and also among the league leaders in victories (16), ERA (3.23), innings (247⅔), complete games (eight) and shutouts (three).

His season was, however, slightly uneven. Scott was 10-3 with a 2.20 ERA at home but 6-10 with a 4.26 ERA on the road. He was 9-4 through June but 7-9 thereafter.

"I know that everyone will judge me by 1986," Scott said. "But that was just an extraordinary year. . . . If you throw out 1986, this season looks pretty good compared to the rest of my career."

Scott was 33-25 in his three seasons with Houston before '86.

Lefthander Jim Deshaies also sparkled early, winning six straight decisions on his way to an 8-2 record through June. Recurring shoulder pain limited his effectiveness in the second half and he finished 11-6 in his second full major league season. A slight tear in his rotator cuff was repaired after the season.

Danny Darwin, acquired for the stretch drive in 1986, was better than his 9-10 record suggested. Houston scored a total of 24 runs in his 10 losses as the veteran righthander posted a 3.59 ERA.

In the bullpen, Houston was well equipped for the late innings. Righthander Dave Smith posted 24 saves without surrendering a home run. Larry Andersen was 9-5 with five saves in a team-leading 67 appearances. Juan Agosto was impressive (1-1, 2.63 ERA, 27 games) after a promotion from Class AAA Tucson.

There were, however, disappointments.

Starter Bob Knepper struggled with his mechanics for all but one stretch in August and finished 8-17 with a 5.27 ERA. The lefthander had posted 47 wins in his previous three seasons.

Middle relief was an ongoing problem. Charlie Kerfeld, who was 11-2 as a rookie in 1986, never hit his stride in '87. He was 0-2 with a 9.24 ERA in April and sent to the minors. His weight at the time, reportedly 265 pounds, didn't help matters. After he returned in July—about 20 pounds lighter—Kerfeld spent nearly two months on the disabled list with an injured elbow.

With Kerfeld out, the Astros relied on Rocky Childress (1-2, 2.98 ERA, 32 games), Jeff Heathcock (4-2, 3.16, 17 relief spots) and Dave Meads (5-3, 5.55, 45 games).

Still, the pitching was good enough for a club to contend seriously. The Astros' downfall was due to inadequate run production.

Strangely, no player had a marked dropoff from 1986. In fact, outfielder Billy Hatcher, catcher Alan Ashby and second baseman Bill Doran enjoyed their best

SCORES OF HOUSTON ASTROS' 1987 GAMES

APRIL			Winner	Loser
6—Los Ang.	W	4-3	Scott	Hershiser
7—Los Ang.	W	6-5	Andersen	Young
8—Los Ang.	W	7-3	Ryan	Young
10—Montreal	W	6-1	Darwin	Heaton
11—Montreal	W	3-2	Lopez	Parrett
12—Montreal	W	1-0	Knepper	Sebra
13—At L.A.	L	2-4	Holton	Ryan
14—At L.A.	L	2-3‡	Niedenfuer	Kerfeld
15—At L.A.	W	4-0	Scott	Pena
17—At Cinn.	L	8-9	Murphy	Knepper
18—At Cinn.	L	0-8	Gullickson	Ryan
19—At Cinn.	W	7-3	Scott	Browning
19—At Cinn.	L	2-6	Power	Darwin
21—Atlanta	W	7-6	Andersen	Garber
22—Atlanta	W	6-0	Deshaies	Palmer
23—Atlanta	W	5-3	Meads	Mahler
24—Cincinnati	L	3-4†	Murphy	Kerfeld
25—Cincinnati	L	0-3*	Franco	Andersen
26—Cincinnati	L	3-11	Soto	Knepper
27—At N.Y.	W	11-1	Deshaies	Cone
29—At N.Y.	L	1-2	Fernandez	Scott
Won 12, Lost 9				

MAY			Winner	Loser
1—At Atlanta	W	12-3	Ryan	Mahler
2—At Atlanta	L	4-12	O'Neal	Deshaies
3—At Atlanta	L	3-5	Smith	Scott
5—At Phila.	W	5-1	Darwin	Rawley
6—At Phila.	W	3-2	Andersen	Tekulve
8—At Mon.	W	3-0	Scott	Heaton
9—At Mon.	L	1-3	Sebra	Deshaies
10—At Mon.	L	2-6	Tibbs	Darwin
11—Phila.	L	6-7	Schatzeder	Andersen
12—Phila.	W	5-2	Knepper	Jackson
13—New York	W	2-1*	Meads	Walter
14—New York	W	5-4	Meads	Walter
15—Chicago	L	1-3	Maddux	Darwin
16—Chicago	L	1-2	Moyer	Ryan
17—Chicago	L	4-6	Mason	Knepper
18—At Pitts.	W	4-1	Scott	Kipper
19—At Pitts.	L	2-5	Smiley	Meads
20—At Pitts.	L	3-5	Taylor	Darwin
22—St. Louis	L	5-7	Conroy	Ryan
23—St. Louis	L	3-4	Perry	Knepper
24—St. Louis	L	2-8	Magrane	Scott
25—Pittsburgh	W	7-2	Deshaies	Taylor
26—Pittsburgh	W	10-3	Meads	Pena
27—Pittsburgh	W	7-2	Lopez	D. Robinson
29—At St. L.	L	2-8	Tunnell	Lopez
30—At St. L.	L	2-3	Cox	Knepper
31—At St. L.	W	8-7	Deshaies	Mathews
Won 12, Lost 15				

JUNE			Winner	Loser
1—At Chicago	W	6-5*	Andersen	DiPino
2—At Chicago	L	2-13	Mason	Ryan
3—At Chicago	L	7-22	Sutcliffe	Knepper
5—San Fran.	W	6-1	Scott	Krukow
6—San Fran.	L	3-4‡	Comstock	Andersen
7—San Fran.	W	3-0	Ryan	Hammaker
8—San Diego	L	4-5	Lefferts	Knepper
9—San Diego	W	1-0	Darwin	Dravecky
10—San Diego	W	10-1	Scott	S. Davis
11—At L.A.	W	1-0	Deshaies	Valenzuela
12—At L.A.	W	5-1	Ryan	Welch
13—At L.A.	L	1-7	Hershiser	Knepper
14—At L.A.	W	4-1	Darwin	Leary
15—Cincinnati	W	4-0	Scott	Gullickson
16—Cincinnati	W	4-1	Deshaies	Power
17—Cincinnati	L	1-9	Robinson	Ryan
18—Los Ang.	L	4-6†	Pena	Mathis
19—Los Ang.	W	3-2†	Meads	Hershiser
20—Los Ang.	W	3-2	Scott	Leary
21—Los Ang.	W	6-1	Deshaies	Honeycutt
23—At S. Diego	L	1-4	Whitson	Ryan
24—At S. Diego	W	12-7	Andersen	McCullers
25—At S. Diego	L	1-4	Dravecky	Scott
26—At S. Fran.	W	9-6	Knepper	LaCoss
27—At S. Fran.	W	6-5	Deshaies	Downs
28—At S. Fran.	L	4-8	Hammaker	Ryan
30—At Cinn.	L	4-5*	Franco	Andersen
Won 16, Lost 11				

JULY			Winner	Loser
1—At Cinn.	L	4-6	Scherrer	Darwin
2—At Phila.	W	7-6	Andersen	Bedrosian
3—At Phila.	L	1-2	Ruffin	Ryan
4—At Phila.	L	3-9	Hume	Deshaies
5—At Phila.	W	8-2	Scott	Gross
6—Montreal	W	9-3	Darwin	Martinez
7—Montreal	L	0-2	Sebra	Knepper

JULY			Winner	Loser
8—Montreal	L	0-1	Youmans	Ryan
9—New York	W	4-3	Smith	Myers
10—New York	L	3-7	Gooden	Scott
11—New York	L	6-9	Myers	Darwin
12—New York	L	2-5	Darling	Knepper
16—Phila.	W	2-1	Darwin	Jackson
17—Phila.	L	1-2	Rawley	Scott
18—Phila.	L	2-4	Carman	Knepper
19—Phila.	L	1-4	Ruffin	Ryan
20—At Mon.	L	1-4	Martinez	Deshaies
21—At Mon.	W	4-2	Darwin	Youmans
22—At Mon.	W	7-0	Scott	Sebra
24—At N.Y.	L	2-5	Fernandez	Ryan
24—At N.Y.	L	4-7	Mitchell	Knepper
25—At N.Y.	W	7-5	Deshaies	Schulze
26—At N.Y.	W	5-2	Smith	Orosco
28—At Atlanta	L	1-6	Smith	Scott
29—At Atlanta	L	3-5	Puleo	Ryan
30—At Atlanta	W	8-5	Knepper	Mahler
31—San Diego	L	2-6	Whitson	Darwin
Won 10, Lost 17				

AUGUST			Winner	Loser
1—San Diego	L	0-6	Nolte	Heathcock
2—San Diego	W	6-0	Scott	Grant
3—San Fran.	W	5-3§	Agosto	Price
4—San Fran.	W	5-4	Heathcock	Lefferts
5—San Fran.	W	6-5†	Andersen	J. Robinson
7—At S. Diego	L	1-7	M. Davis	Scott
8—At S. Diego	L	3-4*	Gossage	Meads
9—At S. Diego	L	3-4	Show	Knepper
10—At S. Fran.	L	5-6	D. Robinson	Meads
11—At S. Fran.	W	7-3	Heathcock	LaCoss
12—At S. Fran.	L	1-8	Hammaker	Scott
13—At S. Fran.	L	6-7†	Lefferts	Childress
14—Atlanta	W	8-4	Knepper	Puleo
15—Atlanta	W	8-0	Darwin	Mahler
16—Atlanta	W	6-2	Deshaies	Smith
17—Atlanta	W	11-2	Scott	Glavine
18—St. Louis	W	4-0	Ryan	Cox
19—St. Louis	W	2-1	Knepper	Magrane
20—St. Louis	W	5-4	Childress	Dayley
21—At Chicago	L	5-7	DiPino	Deshaies
22—At Chicago	W	5-4†	Andersen	DiPino
23—At Chicago	W	4-2	Heathcock	Sutcliffe
24—At St. L.	W	5-2	Knepper	Magrane
25—At St. L.	L	1-7	Mathews	Darwin
26—At St. L.	L	4-5	Dayley	Agosto
28—At Pitts.	L	2-4	Walk	Scott
29—At Pitts.	L	2-8	Bielecki	Ryan
30—At Pitts.	L	0-7	Drabek	Knepper
31—Chicago	L	3-4	Lancaster	Darwin
Won 15, Lost 14				

SEPTEMBER			Winner	Loser
1—Chicago	L	2-3	Moyer	Hernandez
2—Chicago	W	10-1	Scott	Sutcliffe
4—Pittsburgh	W	2-0	Ryan	Bielecki
5—Pittsburgh	W	5-1	Knepper	Drabek
6—Pittsburgh	L	3-4	Dunne	Hernandez
7—San Fran.	W	4-2	Scott	LaCoss
8—San Fran.	L	4-6	D. Robinson	Andersen
9—San Fran.	W	4-2	Ryan	Hammaker
10—At S. Diego	L	7-8	Gossage	Hernandez
11—At S. Diego	L	0-11	Show	Scott
13—At S. Diego	L	2-10	Jones	Deshaies
14—At L.A.	W	8-1	Ryan	Hillegas
15—At L.A.	L	2-3	Belcher	Knepper
16—At S. Fran.	L	1-7	Dravecky	Scott
17—At S. Fran.	L	0-4	Reuschel	Darwin
18—San Diego	L	1-2	McCullers	Smith
19—San Diego	L	1-2x	Leiper	Hernandez
20—San Diego	W	3-2	Scott	M. Davis
22—At Atlanta	L	2-6	Coffman	Knepper
23—At Atlanta	L	4-5	Acker	Smith
24—At Atlanta	L	7-8	Acker	Heathcock
25—At Cinn.	L	1-4	Browning	Scott
26—At Cinn.	W	5-3	Darwin	Robinson
27—At Cinn.	L	2-4	Murphy	Knepper
28—Los Ang.	W	11-5	Deshaies	Hershiser
29—Los Ang.	L	1-6	Hillegas	Ryan
30—Atlanta	L	1-3	Cary	Smith
Won 9, Lost 18				

OCTOBER			Winner	Loser
1—Atlanta	W	6-5	Andersen	Acker
2—Cincinnati	L	7-12	Rasmussen	Childress
3—Cincinnati	W	6-4	Heathcock	Power
4—Cincinnati	L	1-2	Browning	Ryan
Won 2, Lost 2				

*10 innings. †11 innings. ‡12 innings. §13 innings. x14 innings.

seasons.

Hatcher was headed toward his first .300 season when he was caught using a corked bat on September 1. After a 10-game suspension, Hatcher hit only .208 and his average dropped from .311 to .296. He finished third in the league in stolen bases (53) and had career highs in doubles (28), home runs (11) and runs batted in (63).

Ashby set personal highs in batting (.288), hits (111), home runs (14) and RBIs (63). Doran (.283) ranked among the league leaders in hits (177) and game-winning RBIs (13) and set a Houston record for second basemen with 16 home runs and 79 RBIs.

The emergence of rookie center fielder Gerald Young was one of the few bright spots of the second half. Young was promoted from Tucson in July and hit .321 with 26 stolen bases.

Right fielder Kevin Bass came within one homer of a second straight 20-20 season in home runs and stolen bases. He finished with 19 homers, 21 stolen bases, a .284 average and a career-high 85 RBIs.

First baseman Glenn Davis led the team with 27 homers and 93 RBIs, but Lanier wasn't satisfied with his clutch hitting. He dropped Davis from the cleanup spot for most of the second half.

Rookie third baseman Ken Caminiti broke in with a flourish in July, hitting safely in 10 of his first 12 games, but tailed off to a .246 average. He shared third with veteran Denny Walling (.283).

With no steady backups at shortstop, veteran Craig Reynolds started most games (108) and batted .254. His platoon partner in 1986, Dickie Thon, was placed on the disqualified list in July after he left the team due to vision problems. The shortstop's career had been unsettled since he was hit just above the left eye by a pitch in 1984.

"If I get better, maybe I'll try playing again," Thon said. "But if I don't, then I won't. . . . It's difficult to walk away from a game that I would do anything to play again."

Left fielder Jose Cruz, a fan favorite for 13 seasons, played his final season for the Astros. Cruz, 40, hit .241 with 11 homers but was informed that he would not be offered a 1988 contract. He left the team as the all-time leader in games (1,870), hits (1,937), triples (80), RBIs (942) and total bases (2,746).

And after the season, President and General Manager Dick Wagner resigned following several disputes with Lanier. Lanier, hired by Wagner after the 1985

Houston right fielder Kevin Bass put together a solid 19-homer 1987 season.

season, was openly critical of the club's lack of trading in '87.

"I owe Dick Wagner a great deal," Lanier said. "He gave me an opportunity to become a major league manager, but our not getting along was not good for the ball club. . . ."

Dodger righthander Orel Hershiser compiled a mediocre 16-16 record while finishing third in the N.L. with a 3.06 ERA.

Proud Dodgers Continue Slide

By GORDON VERRELL

All through the 1940s and 1950s, Dodgers fans sounded a memorable lament: "Wait until next year."

And now, long after the Brooklyn team traversed the continent following the 1957 season, the elegy is reborn.

Only thing is, the Dodgers are grieving washed-out seasons, not World Series setbacks.

For the second year in a row, the Los Angeles Dodgers finished 73-89, laboring through their first back-to-back losing seasons since 1967-68. They landed in fourth place in the National League West, 17 games behind the division champion San Francisco Giants.

Injuries, again, took a toll. Thirteen times the Dodgers used the disabled list, actually an improvement from 1986, when they had 16 disabling injuries.

And, again, the Dodger organization encountered a crushing setback before the team so much as got out of the box.

In 1986, it was Pedro Guerrero's left knee, shattered less than a week before the start of the season. In 1987, it was an entirely different blow.

On opening night, April 6 in Houston, Al Campanis, the Dodgers' vice president in charge of player personnel, appeared on ABC's "Nightline," ostensibly to talk about former minor league teammate Jackie Robinson. The line of questioning shifted quickly, Campanis got sidetracked, and he wound up insulting blacks and embarrassing himself, the Dodgers and all of baseball.

The next night, Dodgers President Peter O'Malley issued an earnest apology, as did Campanis, in hopes of quieting the fire storm that was brewing. It did no good. On April 8, Campanis was asked to resign.

In the midst of all this, the Dodgers lost their first five games, recovered only slightly to close to within 2½ games with a 19-15 record on May 12, then lost seven games in a row and never again reached .500.

While Guerrero was the source of the Dodgers' decline in 1986, the year after they won the division, he was a symbol of stability in 1987. Guerrero played in 152 games, finished the year with a 17-game hitting streak and led the club in virtually every offensive category: average (.338), runs (89), hits (184), total bases (294), home runs (27), runs batted in (89), game-winning RBIs (11) and walks (74).

Only second baseman Steve Sax played in more games (157) than the Dodger left fielder.

Guerrero also was a central figure in two of three flareups involving right fielder Mike Marshall, who missed 58 games because of various ailments but still batted .294 with 16 homers and 72 RBIs.

On June 11, after the Dodgers lost to Houston, 1-0, Guerrero had a shouting match with Marshall, who had not played. In Montreal on August 19, Manager Tom Lasorda used 20 players to outlast the Expos, 10-9, and Marshall wasn't one of them. That provoked another confrontation between Guerrero and Marshall. Then, before a game on September 2, Marshall and utility infielder Phil Garner exchanged blows.

It was an unsettling year all season for the Dodgers, beginning with the shocking ouster of Campanis, a company man for four decades. Fred Claire, the Dodgers' executive vice president, assumed Campanis' duties and immediately began reworking the roster.

Two days into the job, Claire pared veteran lefthander Jerry Reuss and signed free-agent Mickey Hatcher. In his first major league trade, on May 22, Claire shipped righthanded reliever Tom Niedenfuer to Baltimore for outfielder John Shelby and lefthander Brad Havens, both of whom were playing for the Orioles' Class AAA Rochester farm team.

The trade was generally panned at the time—the bullpen, after all, was a trouble spot—but Shelby became the Dodgers' everyday center fielder and hit .277 for the season. He had career highs in hits (132), doubles (26), home runs (21) and RBIs (69).

Hatcher and Shelby weren't the only retreads signed by Claire, who will continue in his personnel duties, the club announced after the season. Nor was Reuss the only veteran shown the door.

On May 29, Claire cut loose third baseman Bill Madlock. In subsequent deals he acquired free-agent Danny Heep, picked up Garner from the Houston Astros for a minor leaguer, signed free-agent Tito Landrum, landed shortstop Glenn Hoffman in a deal with the Boston Red Sox and, on August 29, shipped hard-luck lefthander Rick Honeycutt (who had lost a club-record 11 consecutive decisions) to the Oakland Athletics. In return, the Dodgers received minor league pitcher

SCORES OF LOS ANGELES DODGERS' 1987 GAMES

APRIL

Date	W/L	Score	Winner	Loser
6—At Hous.	L	3-4	Scott	Hershiser
7—At Hous.	L	5-6	Andersen	Young
8—At Hous.	L	3-7	Ryan	Young
9—San Fran.	L	1-8	Davis	Welch
10—San Fran.	L	4-5†	Garrelts	Leary
11—San Fran.	W	5-1	Hershiser	Krukow
12—San Fran.	W	7-5	Valenzuela	LaCoss
13—Houston	W	4-2	Holton	Ryan
14—Houston	W	3-2‡	Niedenfuer	Kerfeld
15—Houston	L	0-4	Scott	Pena
16—At S. Diego	L	2-3*	McCullers	Young
17—At S. Diego	W	5-3	Valenzuela	Whitson
18—At S. Diego	W	5-2	Howell	McCullers
19—At S. Diego	W	9-1	Welch	Wojna
20—At S. Fran.	L	3-4	Davis	Hershiser
21—At S. Fran.	W	11-8*	Howell	Garrelts
22—At S. Fran.	W	5-3	Valenzuela	Krukow
24—San Diego	W	5-0	Welch	Wojna
25—San Diego	W	4-2	Hershiser	S. Davis
26—San Diego	L	0-4	Show	Honeycutt
28—At Pitts.	L	1-6	Kipper	Valenzuela
29—At Pitts.	W	10-2	Welch	Patterson
30—At Pitts.	L	4-5	Smiley	Hershiser

Won 12, Lost 11

MAY

Date	W/L	Score	Winner	Loser
1—At St. L.	L	4-5*	Horton	Young
2—At St. L.	W	7-6	Holton	Worrell
4—At Chicago	L	4-5	Noles	Howell
5—At Chicago	W	3-1	Welch	Moyer
6—Pittsburgh	W	2-1	Hershiser	Reuschel
7—Pittsburgh	W	6-3	Honeycutt	Kipper
8—St. Louis	L	1-5	Conroy	Pena
9—St. Louis	W	4-2	Valenzuela	Cox
10—St. Louis	W	7-6	Young	Perry
11—Chicago	L	3-6	Sanderson	Hershiser
12—Chicago	W	7-0	Honeycutt	Lynch
13—Chicago	L	0-5	Sutcliffe	Pena
15—At Mon.	L	3-6	Tibbs	Valenzuela
16—At Mon.	L	3-10	Smith	Welch
17—At Mon.	L	3-8	McClure	Hershiser
18—At Phila.	L	3-5	Ruffin	Honeycutt
21—At Phila.	L	3-6	Rawley	Pena
22—At N.Y.	L	4-6	Leach	Young
23—At N.Y.	W	4-2	Welch	Darling
24—At N.Y.	W	8-6	Hershiser	McDowell
25—Montreal	L	1-3	Sorensen	Honeycutt
26—Montreal	L	3-8	Sebra	Pena
27—Montreal	W	6-4	Valenzuela	Smith
29—Phila.	W	6-0	Welch	Ruffin
30—Phila.	L	0-3	Gross	Hershiser
31—Phila.	L	1-3	Rawley	Honeycutt

Won 11, Lost 15

JUNE

Date	W/L	Score	Winner	Loser
1—New York	L	2-5	Leach	Valenzuela
2—New York	W	6-3	Welch	Orosco
3—New York	W	5-2	Hershiser	Darling
5—At Cinn.	L	6-8	Hoffman	Howell
6—At Cinn.	L	2-5	Power	Valenzuela
7—At Cinn.	W	13-7	Welch	Reuss
8—At Atlanta	W	6-3	Hershiser	Palmer
9—At Atlanta	W	5-3	Leary	Smith
10—At Atlanta	L	1-7	Alexander	Honeycutt
11—Houston	L	0-1	Deshaies	Valenzuela
12—Houston	L	1-5	Ryan	Welch
13—Houston	W	7-1	Hershiser	Knepper
14—Houston	L	1-4	Darwin	Leary
16—At S. Diego	L	2-3	McCullers	Pena
17—At S. Diego	L	7-8	Lefferts	Holton
18—At Hous.	W	6-4†	Pena	Mathis
19—At Hous.	L	2-3†	Meads	Hershiser
20—At Hous.	L	2-3	Scott	Leary
21—At Hous.	L	1-6	Deshaies	Honeycutt
23—Atlanta	W	3-2	Valenzuela	Puleo
24—Atlanta	W	5-4*	Young	Garber
25—Atlanta	W	2-1	Hershiser	Alexander
26—Cincinnati	L	0-6	Power	Honeycutt
27—Cincinnati	W	4-3*	Young	Franco
28—Cincinnati	W	4-2	Valenzuela	Hoffman
29—San Diego	L	0-3	Jones	Welch
30—San Diego	W	4-0	Hershiser	Dravecky

Won 13, Lost 14

JULY

Date	W/L	Score	Winner	Loser
1—San Diego	L	0-4	Show	Honeycutt
3—At Pitts.	L	0-6	Reuschel	Valenzuela
4—At Pitts.	L	2-4	Kipper	Welch
5—At Pitts.	W	6-1	Hershiser	Fisher
7—At St. L.	L	4-5	Worrell	Leary
7—At St. L.	L	4-5*	Dayley	Howell
8—At St. L.	L	3-6	Forsch	Valenzuela
8—At St. L.	L	7-8*	Perry	Hershiser
10—At Chicago	L	5-12y	Sutcliffe	Honeycutt
11—At Chicago	W	5-4*z	Young	Smith
11—At Chicago	L	0-7	Trout	Leary
12—At Chicago	W	12-0	Welch	Lancaster
16—Pittsburgh	W	7-0	Valenzuela	Kipper
17—Pittsburgh	W	3-2*	Young	Robinson
18—Pittsburgh	L	2-4	Drabek	Hershiser
19—Pittsburgh	L	2-7	Dunne	Honeycutt
21—St. Louis	L	1-6	Forsch	Valenzuela
22—St. Louis	L	1-3	Dayley	Welch
23—St. Louis	L	6-9	Dayley	Young
24—Chicago	L	4-6	Maddux	Leary
25—Chicago	W	7-2	Howell	Tewksbury
26—Chicago	W	7-6	Holton	DiPino
27—San Fran.	W	6-5‡	Leary	Garrelts
28—San Fran.	W	4-2	Hershiser	Hammaker
29—San Fran.	L	2-16	Krukow	Honeycutt
31—At Atlanta	W	9-5	Valenzuela	Alexander

Won 10, Lost 16

AUGUST

Date	W/L	Score	Winner	Loser
1—At Atlanta	W	5-2	Welch	Palmer
2—At Atlanta	L	5-10	Smith	Howell
3—At Cinn.	W	7-2	Hershiser	Power
4—At Cinn.	L	4-10	Hoffman	Leary
5—At Cinn.	L	3-6	Robinson	Valenzuela
7—Atlanta	L	3-4	Smith	Welch
8—Atlanta	L	7-9	Palmer	Hershiser
9—Atlanta	W	5-2	Hillegas	Puleo
10—Cincinnati	L	3-4	Williams	Valenzuela
11—Cincinnati	W	7-2	Welch	Montgomery
12—Cincinnati	W	1-0	Leary	Gullickson
13—Cincinnati	L	2-5	Murphy	Hershiser
14—At S. Fran.	W	4-3	Hillegas	Downs
15—At S. Fran.	L	0-5	Dravecky	Valenzuela
16—At S. Fran.	L	0-1*	LaCoss	Leary
18—At Mon.	L	1-2	Burke	Hershiser
19—At Mon.	W	10-9	Pena	Parrett
20—At Mon.	W	7-2	Valenzuela	Heaton
21—At Phila.	L	1-2†	Tekulve	Young
21—At Phila.	L	3-7	Rawley	Leary
22—At Phila.	L	0-2	Maddux	Honeycutt
23—At Phila.	W	5-1	Hershiser	Carman
24—At N.Y.	L	0-1	Aguilera	Hillegas
25—At N.Y.	W	3-1	Valenzuela	Cone
26—At N.Y.	L	2-3	Darling	Welch
28—Montreal	L	1-2‡	Burke	Leary
29—Montreal	L	5-6*	McGaffigan	Crews
30—Montreal	L	4-5	Parrett	Valenzuela
31—Phila.	L	2-4	Rawley	Welch

Won 10, Lost 19

SEPTEMBER

Date	W/L	Score	Winner	Loser
1—Phila.	L	5-7	Ritchie	Leary
2—Phila.	L	2-6	Carman	Hershiser
4—New York	L	1-5	Aguilera	Hillegas
5—New York	L	3-4	Darling	Valenzuela
6—New York	W	3-2x	Belcher	Myers
7—At Cinn.	L	2-3§	Hume	Holton
8—At Cinn.	W	5-3	Hershiser	Robinson
9—At Cinn.	L	1-4	Browning	Belcher
11—At Atlanta	W	5-2	Valenzuela	Coffman
12—At Atlanta	L	9-10*	Acker	Pena
13—At Atlanta	W	6-2	Hershiser	P. Smith
14—Houston	L	1-8	Ryan	Hillegas
15—Houston	W	3-2	Belcher	Knepper
17—Cincinnati	L	2-3*	Valenzuela	Franco
17—Cincinnati	W	6-3	Welch	Power
18—Atlanta	W	7-4	Hershiser	P. Smith
19—Atlanta	L	7-10	Boever	Young
20—Atlanta	W	5-3	Belcher	Puleo
21—At S. Fran.	W	4-2	Welch	Downs
22—At S. Fran.	W	4-3	Valenzuela	Dravecky
23—At S. Fran.	L	8-9	Lefferts	Hershiser
25—San Diego	W	5-3	Belcher	Whitson
26—San Diego	W	3-1	Welch	Nolte
27—San Diego	W	4-3	Crews	Gossage
28—At Hous.	L	5-11	Deshaies	Hershiser
29—At Hous.	W	6-1	Hillegas	Ryan
30—San Fran.	L	0-3	Krukow	Belcher

Won 14, Lost 13

OCTOBER

Date	W/L	Score	Winner	Loser
1—San Fran.	W	7-0	Welch	Reuschel
2—At S. Diego	W	10-3	Valenzuela	Grant
3—At S. Diego	L	0-1	Jones	Hershiser
4—At S. Diego	W	5-3	Hillegas	Whitson

Won 3, Lost 1

*10 innings. †11 innings. ‡12 innings. §13 innings. x16 innings. ySuspended game, began July 9. zSuspended game, began July 10.

Pedro Guerrero rebounded from his injury-plagued 1986 season and led the Dodgers in most offensive categories.

Tim Belcher, a promising righthander who was 4-2 for Los Angeles in five starts and one relief appearance.

But the many changes left Lasorda with new faces practically every night; in all, he had to devise 125 different lineups.

The veterans Claire brought in were used often. Hatcher and Garner shared third base with Dave Anderson in Madlock's absence. Anderson (.234) and Garner (.206) were weak at the plate, but Hatcher hit enough (.282) to earn additional time as Franklin Stubbs' backup at first base.

Out three weeks with a dislocated right shoulder, Stubbs had fewer home runs (16) and RBIs (52) than he did in '86 but improved his batting average—from .226 to .233. He and Guerrero switched positions at the end of the season.

Hoffman saw plenty of action at shortstop with often-injured Mariano Duncan on the disabled list twice. Hoffman hit only .220, five points better than Duncan

managed in 76 games.

The Dodgers' pinch-hitters and part-time outfielders, Heep, Landrum and Ken Landreaux, were equally pathetic, hitting a combined .199.

The Dodgers did get some production from their catchers. Mike Scioscia and Alex Trevino hit a combined .255 for the second straight year while driving in 54 runs. And Sax, a year after finishing second in the league in hitting, batted .280 and led the Dodgers with 37 stolen bases.

But when all was done, the Dodgers finished with the poorest batting average in the league (.252), scored the fewest runs (635), were shut out the most times (16) and committed the most errors (155). They also tied for the fewest saves (32) but received a late-season boost from Alejandro Pena, a reliever-turned-starter-turned-reliever who recorded nine of his 11 saves in September and October.

Orel Hershiser (16-16), Bob Welch (15-9) and Fernando Valenzuela (14-14) accounted for well over half of the Dodgers' wins. As a staff, the Dodgers' 3.72 earned-run average ranked second in the league. Their 29 complete games ranked first, fortunately, for the Dodgers' bullpen could have dropped Los Angeles to last in the West if given the opportunity.

Early season closer Matt Young lost the second and third games of the season and five by the end of May. He finished the year with 11 saves, a 5-8 record and a 4.47 ERA. Ken Howell didn't slam many doors, either, and wound up 3-4 with a 4.91 ERA.

Tim Leary, acquired from the Milwaukee Brewers for first baseman Greg Brock over the winter, was ineffective as both a middle reliever and starter. The righthander finished 3-11 with a 4.76 ERA. Havens compiled a 4.33 ERA in middle relief.

Three rookies, however, provided hope. Tim Crews, acquired in the Brock deal, was 1-1 with three saves and a 2.48 ERA in 20 appearances. Brian Holton, solid in both middle- and late-inning relief, was 3-2 with a 3.89 ERA in 53 appearances. Shawn Hillegas started 10 games and was 4-3 with a 3.57 ERA.

The Dodgers finished with a 40-41 record at Dodger Stadium, only the third time in their 30 years in Los Angeles they fell below .500 at home. And attendance dropped for the second straight year. That the Dodgers drew fewer than 3 million (2,800,409) for the first time since 1981 did not surprise O'Malley.

"Not at all," he said. "The fans are the smartest people of all. They know how they want to spend their money."

Newcomer Dion James hit a surprising .312 and added lightning to Atlanta's offense.

Bad News Braves Run in Place

By GERRY FRALEY

The San Francisco Giants reached the National League playoffs in 1987, two seasons after they lost 100 games.

"That gives you a reason to be optimistic," Atlanta Braves outfielder Dale Murphy said. "I feel good about the direction this club is going. I'm always optimistic, but San Francisco tells you that optimism can be realistic.

"It tells you things can change in a hurry."

Barring a miracle, it won't happen that quickly for the Braves. They finished 1987 in fifth place in the N.L. West with their fourth straight losing record, 69-92. And at the end, the Braves committed to the obvious: They are a team in need of an overhaul.

"We haven't given up on winning, especially in our division," General Manager Bobby Cox said. "But we are doing some things with an eye to the future."

The Braves were thinking of the future on August 13, when they traded 36-year-old starting pitcher Doyle Alexander to the Detroit Tigers for John Smoltz, a promising but untested 20-year-old right-hander.

The Braves were thinking of the future on August 30, when they traded 39-year-old reliever Gene Garber to the Kansas City Royals for catcher Terry Bell, a former first-round draft choice stuck at Class AA.

"We're trying to rebuild and stay competitive at the same time," Cox said. "We'll never give up the idea of winning in our division. But our plan is for the future. We've got a lot of kids. I've never seen so much excitement about the young pitchers we have."

But only one of their young starters, lefthander Tom Glavine, showed he was ready for the majors. Glavine, 21, was 2-4 with a 5.54 earned-run average in nine starts after his promotion from Class AAA Richmond in August. But he showed rapid improvement, lasting at least seven innings in four starts.

Second baseman Ron Gant, 22, possibly the best farm system product in several years, also showed promise in September. An All-Star selection with Greenville in the Class AA Southern League, Gant hit .265 in 83 at-bats for Atlanta. He and 21-year-old shortstop Jeff Blauser (.242) played well in the middle.

The immediate options dwindle thereaf-

Dale Murphy rose above the Braves' 1987 disaster by hitting 44 homers and driving in 105 runs.

ter. The Braves have other young pitchers, but all need time to develop. Kevin Coffman (2-3, five starts) and Pete Smith (1-2, six starts) both jumped from Greenville to Atlanta in September. Reliever Chuck Cary, recalled from Richmond in September, was 1-1 with a 3.78 ERA but allowed six of seven inherited runners to score.

The Braves do not have enough young players ready to attempt a transformation like San Francisco did in 1986 or the San Diego Padres did in '87.

The telling point for Atlanta is that despite finishing last in 1986, they began the 1987 season without a rookie. The Braves did not get a hit from a rookie until Blauser's infield single at San Diego on August 12. They did not get a win from a rookie until Glavine beat Pittsburgh on August 22.

After an 8-6 victory over Cincinnati on June 20, the Braves were 34-33 and tied for third place in the West, 2½ games out of first. They were 35-59 the rest of the season and almost overtaken by last-place San Diego. Atlanta's 28-46 record after the All-Star break was the worst in the majors.

SCORES OF ATLANTA BRAVES' 1987 GAMES

APRIL			Winner	Loser
7—Phila.	W	6-0	Mahler	Rawley
9—Phila.	W	8-7†	Garber	Schatzeder
10—At N.Y.	L	3-6	Fernandez	Palmer
11—At N.Y.	W	4-3	Garber	Cone
12—At N.Y.	W	12-4	O'Neal	Ojeda
13—Cincinnati	L	2-7	Gullickson	Smith
14—Cincinnati	L	3-6	Power	Palmer
15—Cincinnati	W	4-3	Mahler	Browning
17—At S. Fran.	W	2-0	Smith	Krukow
18—At S. Fran.	L	1-2†	Garrelts	Garber
19—At S. Fran.	L	3-4	J. Robinson	Assenmacher
21—At Hous.	L	6-7	Andersen	Garber
22—At Hous.	L	0-6	Deshaies	Palmer
23—At Hous.	L	3-5	Meads	Mahler
24—San Fran.	L	5-7	Minton	Acker
25—San Fran.	W	5-3	Garber	Garrelts
26—San Fran.	L	4-6	Davis	Palmer
27—San Fran.	L	3-7	Downs	Mahler
28—At Cinn.	W	7-3	O'Neal	Browning
29—At Cinn.	W	5-2	Smith	Gullickson
30—At Cinn.	L	8-9‡	Landrum	Ziem
Won 9, Lost 12				

MAY			Winner	Loser
1—Houston	L	3-12	Ryan	Mahler
2—Houston	W	12-4	O'Neal	Deshaies
3—Houston	W	5-3	Smith	Scott
4—Montreal	W	10-7	Palmer	Sebra
5—Montreal	L	4-6	Tibbs	Mahler
6—Montreal	L	2-6	Smith	O'Neal
8—New York	W	4-3†	Garber	Orosco
9—New York	W	5-4	Palmer	Ojeda
10—New York	W	8-7	Dedmon	Orosco
11—At Mon.	L	6-7†	Sorensen	Acker
12—At Mon.	W	5-2	Smith	Heredia
13—At Phila.	W	10-5	Palmer	Ruffin
14—At Phila.	L	4-5	Gross	Mahler
15—At Pitts.	W	9-3	Assenmacher	Pena
16—At Pitts.	W	10-8	Dedmon	Smiley
17—At Pitts.	L	5-6	D. Robinson	Olwine
19—St. Louis	W	6-5	Garber	Worrell
20—St. Louis	L	4-5	Horton	Garber
21—St. Louis	L	2-7	Forsch	Smith
22—At Chicago	W	9-5	Palmer	Sanderson
23—At Chicago	L	6-7x	Moyer	Acker
24—At Chicago	L	2-3§	Noles	Dedmon
25—At St. L.	W	14-5	Smith	Cox
26—At St. L.	W	5-4	Alexander	Dawley
28—At St. L.	L	5-11	Dawley	Mahler
29—Chicago	W	6-5§	Garber	Lynch
30—Chicago	L	6-11	Maddux	Smith
31—Chicago	W	2-1†	Garber	Lynch
Won 16, Lost 12				

JUNE			Winner	Loser
2—Pittsburgh	L	1-4	Reuschel	Mahler
3—Pittsburgh	L	1-4	Kipper	Palmer
4—Pittsburgh	W	8-3	Smith	Fisher
5—San Diego	L	3-10	Show	Alexander
6—San Diego	L	3-5	Whitson	McWilliams
7—San Diego	W	13-12	Garber	Booker
8—Los Ang.	L	3-6	Hershiser	Palmer
9—Los Ang.	L	3-5	Leary	Smith
10—Los Ang.	W	7-1	Alexander	Honeycutt
11—At Cinn.	W	6-4	Puleo	Murphy
12—At Cinn.	W	4-3	Mahler	Reuss
13—At Cinn.	L	2-5	Hoffman	Palmer
14—At Cinn.	L	3-4	Murphy	Garber
16—San Fran.	W	7-2	Alexander	Downs
17—San Fran.	W	6-1	Mahler	J. Robinson
18—Cincinnati	L	4-8	Hoffman	Palmer
19—Cincinnati	W	16-5	Smith	Pacillo
20—Cincinnati	W	8-6	Alexander	Gullickson
21—Cincinnati	L	5-6†	Landrum	Garber
23—At L.A.	L	2-3	Valenzuela	Puleo
24—At L.A.	L	4-5†	Young	Garber
25—At L.A.	L	1-2	Hershiser	Alexander
26—At S. Diego	L	1-5	Show	Mahler
27—At S. Diego	L	4-8	McCullers	Dedmon
28—At S. Diego	W	5-2	Puleo	Whitson
29—At S. Fran.	W	1-0	Smith	Grant
30—At S. Fran.	L	2-5	J. Robinson	Alexander
Won 11, Lost 16				

JULY			Winner	Loser
1—At S. Fran.	W	8-3	Mahler	LaCoss
3—St. Louis	L	1-9	Forsch	Puleo
4—St. Louis	L	0-3	Cox	Smith
5—St. Louis	L	1-4	Mathews	Alexander
7—New York	L	2-6	Leach	Mahler

JULY			Winner	Loser
7—New York	L	1-5	Darling	Dedmon
8—New York	W	5-3	Puleo	Fernandez
9—Phila.	W	11-6	Dedmon	Hume
10—Phila.	L	2-5	Rawley	Alexander
11—Phila.	W	5-4	Mahler	Carman
12—Phila.	W	9-3	O'Neal	Ruffin
16—At Mon.	L	0-2	Youmans	Alexander
17—At Mon.	L	4-5	Burke	Acker
18—At Mon.	L	2-3	Parrett	Garber
19—At Mon.	L	1-2‡	McGaffigan	Acker
20—At N.Y.	L	2-9	Schulze	O'Neal
21—At N.Y.	W	8-3	Alexander	Gooden
22—At N.Y.	L	3-4	Darling	Smith
23—At Phila.	L	1-5	Carman	Puleo
24—At Phila.	L	5-11	Ruffin	Mahler
25—At Phila.	W	2-1	Palmer	Hume
26—At Phila.	L	3-7	Tekulve	Alexander
28—Houston	W	6-1	Smith	Scott
29—Houston	W	5-3	Puleo	Ryan
30—Houston	L	5-8	Knepper	Mahler
31—Los Ang.	L	5-9	Valenzuela	Alexander
Won 9, Lost 17				

AUGUST			Winner	Loser
1—Los Ang.	L	2-5	Welch	Palmer
2—Los Ang.	W	10-5	Smith	Howell
4—San Diego	W	12-7	Puleo	Show
5—San Diego	L	3-7	Jones	Alexander
6—San Diego	L	4-7	McCullers	Garber
7—At L.A.	W	4-3	Smith	Welch
8—At L.A.	W	9-7	Palmer	Hershiser
9—At L.A.	L	2-5	Hillegas	Puleo
10—At S. Diego	L	0-2	Jones	Alexander
11—At S. Diego	L	6-7	M. Davis	Garber
12—At S. Diego	W	2-1	Smith	Nolte
13—At S. Diego	L	3-5	Grant	Palmer
14—At Hous.	L	4-8	Knepper	Puleo
15—At Hous.	L	0-8	Darwin	Mahler
16—At Hous.	L	2-6	Deshaies	Smith
17—At Hous.	L	2-11	Scott	Glavine
18—Chicago	W	9-5	Mahler	Lynch
19—Chicago	L	1-9	Sanderson	Puleo
20—Chicago	W	13-4	Acker	Moyer
21—Pittsburgh	W	5-4	Smith	Smiley
22—Pittsburgh	W	10-3	Glavine	Walk
23—Pittsburgh	W	6-2	Palmer	Bielecki
27—At Chicago	W	5-2	Smith	Moyer
27—At Chicago	L	6-8*	Lancaster	Mahler
28—At St. L.	L	3-4	Worrell	Garber
29—At St. L.	L	2-4	Magrane	Puleo
30—At St. L.	L	3-4	Dawley	Acker
31—At Pitts.	L	3-7	Dunne	Dedmon
Won 11, Lost 17				

SEPTEMBER			Winner	Loser
1—At Pitts.	W	4-0	Z. Smith	Fisher
2—At Pitts.	L	0-2	Walk	Glavine
4—Montreal	W	7-4	Mahler	Heaton
5—Montreal	L	1-4	Martinez	Coffman
6—Montreal	L	2-5	Youmans	Z. Smith
7—San Diego	L	4-11	Jones	Glavine
8—San Diego	W	4-2	P. Smith	Whitson
9—San Diego	W	3-2	Palmer	Nolte
11—Los Ang.	L	2-5	Valenzuela	Coffman
12—Los Ang.	W	10-9†	Acker	Pena
13—Los Ang.	L	2-6	Hershiser	P. Smith
14—Cincinnati	W	3-2	Glavine	Hoffman
15—Cincinnati	L	6-21	Robinson	Palmer
16—At S. Diego	L	0-3	Grant	Coffman
17—At S. Diego	L	1-7	Show	Z. Smith
18—At L.A.	L	4-7	Hershiser	P. Smith
19—At L.A.	W	10-7	Boever	Young
20—At L.A.	L	3-5	Belcher	Puleo
22—Houston	W	6-2	Coffman	Knepper
23—Houston	W	5-4	Acker	Smith
24—Houston	W	8-7	Acker	Heathcock
25—San Fran.	L	2-9	Krukow	Glavine
26—San Fran.	W	10-5	Puleo	Reuschel
27—San Fran.	L	6-15	Price	Cary
28—At Cinn.	L	5-6	Montgomery	Z. Smith
29—At Cinn.	L	4-5	Perry	Acker
30—At Hous.	W	3-1	Cary	Smith
Won 12, Lost 15				

OCTOBER			Winner	Loser
1—At Hous.	L	5-6	Andersen	Acker
2—At S. Fran.	W	6-4	Coffman	Dravecky
3—At S. Fran.	L	3-6	Downs	Clary
4—At S. Fran.	L	4-5†	Bockus	Acker
Won 1, Lost 3				

*7 innings. †10 innings. ‡11 innings. §12 innings. x16 innings.

"We knew when we came here this wouldn't be an easy job," said Manager Chuck Tanner, whose personal record is 99 games under .500 (273-372) in the last four seasons. "But we're getting it going in the right direction. There was a lot of improvement this year. There really was."

It was hard to find.

The Braves ranked last in the league with a 4.63 ERA, their second-highest figure since 1935. They were last in shutouts (four), saves (tie, 32) and strikeouts (837).

The saving grace was Zane Smith, who became the lefthanded starter the Braves have desired for a generation. Smith, who was winless in his last 12 starts in 1986, had a 7-1 streak after the All-Star break in 1987 and finished with 15 victories, the most by a Braves lefthander since the franchise moved to Atlanta in 1966. The Braves were 22-14 in games Smith started.

The Braves' other starters—12 altogether—combined for just 30 wins. David Palmer (8-11), Rick Mahler (8-13) and Charlie Puleo (6-8) were relied upon, as were Alexander (5-10) and Randy O'Neal (4-2 overall) before being traded.

The rotation's low victory total was partly due to the bullpen, which Tanner considered "our biggest disappointment." Garber (8-10) was the Braves' early season closer but blew eight of 17 save opportunities. Workhorse Jim Acker (4-9, 68 games) took over the role and finished with 14 saves. Jeff Dedmon (3-4, 53 games) and Paul Assenmacher (1-1, 52 games) worked mostly in middle relief.

Without Bob Horner, who took his power to Japan, the offense was expected to die. But for two months, it thrived. The Braves led the majors in scoring as late as May 30 and averaged 5.4 runs per game through 67 contests. Their success ended when the league stopped serving up fastballs.

Murphy rose above the disaster. With his strength preserved by a switch to right field, Murphy hit a career-high 44 homers and tied for fifth in the league with 105 runs batted in. The loss of Horner from the order was reflected in Murphy's career-high 115 walks, but the league could not avoid him.

Nor could it calm Dion James. Acquired from the Milwaukee Brewers for Brad Komminsk, James was the lightning in the Braves' attack. He hit .312 and rapped 37 doubles to rank among the league leaders in just his first N.L. season. And among N.L. outfielders who played in more than 100 games, James ranked first with a .996

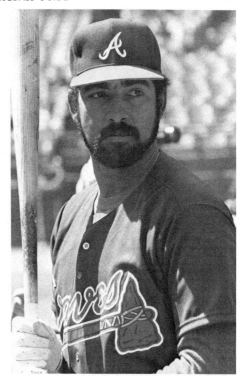

Braves catcher Ozzie Virgil muscled up and hit a career-high 27 home runs in 1987.

fielding average.

Speed, hardly the essence of the Braves over the years, couldn't be overlooked in 1987. First baseman Gerald Perry swiped a club-record 42 bases, clubbed 12 homers and ranked second on the team with 74 RBIs. Outfielder Albert Hall stole 33 bases in only 92 games and hit .284.

The Braves' customary power was supplied by Murphy, Perry, James (10 home runs), catcher Ozzie Virgil (27), left fielder Ken Griffey (14) and outfielder Gary Roenicke (nine). Overall, the Braves' 152 homers were their most since 1973.

In the field, the Braves tied for the league lead for fewest errors (116) and set a club record with a .982 fielding average. Ken Oberkfell (.280, 48 RBIs) set a franchise fielding record for third basemen (.979) playing in more than 100 games, and second baseman Glenn Hubbard (.264 batting) reduced his errors from 19 in 1986 to 11 last season. Shortstop Andres Thomas, the regular in '86, was disabled much of the season.

The Giants set a pace the Braves could hardly equal. But the example they set offers hope for the future.

The Padres lost 97 games despite the impressive efforts of Tony Gwynn, a .370 hitter and the 1987 N.L. batting champion.

Padres Survive Disaster

By MARK KREIDLER

When Larry Bowa was appointed manager of the San Diego Padres in October 1986, he knew the '87 season could be a long one. What he didn't perceive was that he would hardly know how to vent his frustration.

A season reserved for rebuilding nearly crumbled into total ruin. Bowa simmered, screamed and, once, nearly engaged in a fistic interlude.

A 12-42 start put the club in such a hole that by June, the team was playing strictly to salvage some pride and get an inside track on starting jobs in 1988. The Padres managed to play close to .500 (53-55) after June 4, but they lost 10 of their final 11 games to cinch last place in the National League West at 65-97 and finish off Bowa's gastro-intestinal structure. The manager, given a one-year contract extension, headed home vowing that nearly every position would be open in 1988.

The problems in 1987 were threefold: pitching, hitting and fielding.

San Diego's poor start wasn't deceiving —game after game slipped away due to sloppy fielding and offensive gaffes that ruined budding rallies. The Padres were 10th in the league in errors (tie, 147) and runs batted in (621).

The pitching staff simply collapsed. Eric Show, the second-winningest pitcher in club history, finished 8-16. Andy Hawkins, who had won 28 games over the last two seasons, went 3-10 and appeared in only five games after July 25 because of tendinitis in his right shoulder. Storm Davis, acquired from the Baltimore Orioles for catcher Terry Kennedy, was unhappy in San Diego. He posted a 2-7 record and 6.18 earned-run average before he was traded to Oakland on August 30. Righthander Ed Wojna stuck with the team long enough to go 0-3 in five games. He was sent to Class AAA Las Vegas in April.

The Padres started their season with veteran Steve Garvey at first base and rookie Joey Cora at second, but neither lasted through June. Garvey, lost for the year when he underwent shoulder surgery in May, gave way to a Carmelo Martinez-John Kruk platoon. The Padres said they would not offer Garvey a contract in 1988. Cora endured a brutal two months, with error compounding error, before Bowa sent the shaken rookie to Las Vegas the first week of June. Cora didn't return until rosters were expanded in September.

Bowa, who guided Las Vegas to the Pacific Coast League championship as a first-year manager in 1986, described the Padres' season as the most frustrating in his life—and it showed.

The low point emotionally came May 12, when Bowa and rookie outfielder Stan Jefferson had a heated shouting match. When fisticuffs appeared imminent, the normally soft-spoken Jefferson was dragged from the clubhouse by five teammates.

After the Padres lost three straight games in Montreal to fall 30 games below .500 on June 4, Bowa and General Manager Jack McKeon began a desperate overhaul. Tim Flannery replaced Cora, and catcher Benito Santiago, the N.L. Rookie of the Year, was rested. Kruk, the Padres' rookie of the year in '86, played first daily, and Martinez was moved to left field.

Though the season was to be a proving ground for the young players, Bowa needed to win some games.

The plan worked, even as the youngsters slowly rejoined the lineup. The Padres were 15-12 in June, 11-14 in July and 16-12 in August, a composite 42-38 mark that was the best in the N.L. West over that period. Kruk, given the job at first, launched an offensive tear that would yield him a .313 batting average, 20 home runs and 91 RBIs. Randy Ready also responded to regular duty at second and third base, hitting .309 with 12 homers and 54 RBIs in only 350 at-bats.

The Padres attempted another shakeup July 4, when they dealt versatile pitcher Dave Dravecky, reliever Craig Lefferts and third baseman Kevin Mitchell to the San Francisco Giants for third baseman Chris Brown and pitchers Mark Grant, Mark Davis and Keith Comstock.

The immediate results were not completely encouraging. While Dravecky, Lefferts and Mitchell were credited with helping the Giants to the division title, Brown missed several games with injuries and batted only .232 for San Diego. Comstock, who pitched in only five of the Padres' last 31 games, had an 0-1 record with a 5.50 ERA in San Diego.

Grant and Davis, however, rebounded from rough starts. Grant lost four of his first five decisions but captured five of his next six and finished 6-7 with a 4.66 ERA for San Diego. Davis allowed only nine earned runs in his final 25 games and was 5-3 with a 3.18 ERA as a reliever.

SCORES OF SAN DIEGO PADRES' 1987 GAMES

APRIL

Date		Score	Winner	Loser
6—At S. Fran.	L	3-4‡	J. Robinson	Dravecky
7—At S. Fran.	L	3-4	LaCoss	Whitson
8—At S. Fran.	L	1-2	Mason	Hawkins
10—At Cinn.	L	3-6	Murphy	Dravecky
11—At Cinn.	L	1-5	Browning	Show
12—At Cinn.	W	5-2	Whitson	Hoffman
13—San Fran.	L	6-13	Gott	Dravecky
14—San Fran.	L	2-3	Grant	Wojna
15—San Fran.	L	0-1	Downs	S. Davis
16—Los Ang.	W	3-2*	McCullers	Young
17—Los Ang.	L	3-5	Valenzuela	Whitson
18—Los Ang.	L	2-5	Howell	McCullers
19—Los Ang.	L	1-9	Welch	Wojna
20—Cincinnati	L	3-12	Hoffman	S. Davis
21—Cincinnati	W	3-2	McCullers	Murphy
22—Cincinnati	W	6-3	Whitson	Landrum
23—Cincinnati	L	2-3	Browning	Hawkins
24—At L.A.	L	0-5	Welch	Wojna
25—At L.A.	L	2-4	Hershiser	S. Davis
26—At L.A.	W	4-0	Show	Honeycutt
28—At St. L.	W	5-2	Whitson	Conroy
29—At St. L.	L	6-10	Perry	McCullers
30—At St. L.	L	4-5	Mathews	S. Davis
Won 6, Lost 17				

MAY

Date		Score	Winner	Loser
1—At Chicago	L	5-7	DiPino	McCullers
2—At Chicago	L	3-7	Trout	Whitson
3—At Chicago	L	2-4	Sutcliffe	Hawkins
4—Pittsburgh	W	9-5	S. Davis	Patterson
5—Pittsburgh	L	8-10	Walk	Show
6—St. Louis	L	0-3	Magrane	Whitson
7—St. Louis	L	10-17	Forsch	Hawkins
8—Chicago	L	3-6	Sutcliffe	S. Davis
9—Chicago	L	2-5	Maddux	Show
10—Chicago	W	14-2	Whitson	Moyer
12—At Pitts.	L	5-12	Reuschel	Hawkins
13—At Pitts.	L	5-9	Walk	Lefferts
14—At Pitts.	L	3-10	Fisher	Show
15—At Phila.	L	4-7	Rawley	Whitson
16—At Phila.	L	0-9	Carman	Jones
17—At Phila.	W	6-5	Hawkins	Jackson
18—At N.Y.	W	7-5	Dravecky	Darling
19—At N.Y.	L	4-5	McDowell	Show
20—At N.Y.	L	3-10	Aguilera	Whitson
22—Montreal	W	5-3	Hawkins	Brown
23—Montreal	L	0-6	Heaton	Dravecky
24—Montreal	L	1-2	Youmans	Show
25—Phila.	L	4-6	Schatzeder	Dravecky
26—Phila.	L	1-3	Rawley	Jones
27—Phila.	L	4-6	Carman	Hawkins
29—New York	L	4-5	Leach	Lefferts
30—New York	L	0-3	Fernandez	Show
31—New York	W	1-0	Whitson	Mitchell
Won 6, Lost 22				

JUNE

Date		Score	Winner	Loser
2—At Mon.	L	2-6	Smith	Jones
3—At Mon.	L	3-4	Heaton	Hawkins
4—At Mon.	L	5-8	Youmans	S. Davis
5—At Atlanta	W	10-3	Show	Alexander
6—At Atlanta	W	5-3	Whitson	McWilliams
7—At Atlanta	L	12-13	Garber	Booker
8—At Hous.	W	5-4	Lefferts	Knepper
9—At Hous.	L	0-1	Darwin	Dravecky
10—At Hous.	L	1-10	Scott	S. Davis
11—At S. Fran.	L	0-1	Downs	Show
12—At S. Fran.	W	5-0	Whitson	LaCoss
13—At S. Fran.	W	11-2	Hawkins	Hammaker
14—At S. Fran.	W	4-1	Dravecky	Davis
16—Los Ang.	W	3-2	McCullers	Pena
17—Los Ang.	W	8-7	Lefferts	Holton
18—San Fran.	W	3-1	S. Davis	Hammaker
19—San Fran.	L	6-7	J. Robinson	McCullers
20—San Fran.	W	10-4	Jones	J. Robinson
21—San Fran.	L	2-11	Downs	Show
23—Houston	W	4-1	Whitson	Ryan
24—Houston	L	7-12	Andersen	McCullers
25—Houston	W	4-1	Dravecky	Scott
26—Atlanta	W	5-1	Show	Mahler
27—Atlanta	W	8-4	McCullers	Dedmon
28—Atlanta	L	2-5	Puleo	Whitson
29—At L.A.	W	3-0	Jones	Welch
30—At L.A.	L	0-4	Hershiser	Dravecky
Won 15, Lost 12				

JULY

Date		Score	Winner	Loser
1—At L.A.	W	4-0	Show	Honeycutt
3—At Mon.	L	1-2	Youmans	Hawkins
4—At Mon.	L	3-4	Burke	Gossage
5—At Mon.	W	3-2	Gossage	Parrett
6—At Chicago	L	0-7	Trout	Grant
7—At Chicago	L	5-7	Sanderson	Show
8—At Chicago	L	8-12	Lancaster	McCullers
10—At Pitts.	L	5-6†	D. Robinson	Gossage
11—At Pitts.	W	3-1	Grant	Fisher
12—At Pitts.	L	2-4	Dunne	Show
16—St. Louis	W	9-8*	McCullers	Worrell
17—St. Louis	L	3-4	Mathews	Grant
18—St. Louis	W	4-3*	Gossage	Dayley
19—St. Louis	L	4-5*	Dayley	Gossage
20—Chicago	W	7-4	McCullers	Tewksbury
21—Chicago	W	4-3	M. Davis	Moyer
22—Chicago	L	3-6	Sutcliffe	Grant
23—Pittsburgh	W	2-1	Show	Drabek
24—Pittsburgh	L	2-3	Dunne	Jones
25—Pittsburgh	L	3-9	Fisher	Hawkins
26—Pittsburgh	W	7-4	Whitson	Kipper
28—At Cinn.	L	7-8	Franco	M. Davis
29—At Cinn.	L	5-15	Murphy	Show
30—At Cinn.	W	12-8	Jones	Hoffman
31—At Hous.	W	6-2	Whitson	Darwin
Won 11, Lost 14				

AUGUST

Date		Score	Winner	Loser
1—At Hous.	W	6-0	Nolte	Heathcock
2—At Hous.	L	0-6	Scott	Grant
4—At Atlanta	L	7-12	Puleo	Show
5—At Atlanta	W	7-3	Jones	Alexander
6—At Atlanta	W	7-4	McCullers	Garber
7—Houston	W	7-1	M. Davis	Scott
8—Houston	W	4-3*	Gossage	Meads
9—Houston	W	4-3	Show	Knepper
10—Atlanta	W	2-0	Jones	Alexander
11—Atlanta	W	7-6	M. Davis	Garber
12—Atlanta	L	1-2	Smith	Nolte
13—Atlanta	W	5-3	Grant	Palmer
14—Cincinnati	L	0-2	Power	Show
14—Cincinnati	W	15-8	Booker	Hoffman
16—Cincinnati	L	0-2	Robinson	Whitson
18—At Phila.	W	9-4†	Gossage	Ritchie
19—At Phila.	L	5-6	Ruffin	Grant
20—At Phila.	L	2-10	Toliver	Show
21—At N.Y.	W	6-2	Jones	Darling
22—At N.Y.	W	8-3	M. Davis	Fernandez
23—At N.Y.	L	2-9	Gooden	Nolte
25—Montreal	W	5-1	Grant	Heaton
26—Montreal	L	5-6‡	Burke	McCullers
27—Montreal	L	0-3	Smith	Jones
28—Phila.	L	1-8	Carman	Whitson
29—Phila.	W	3-1	Nolte	Ruffin
30—Phila.	W	6-1	Grant	Gross
31—New York	L	5-6*	Orosco	Comstock
Won 16, Lost 12				

SEPTEMBER

Date		Score	Winner	Loser
1—New York	L	1-9	Cone	Jones
2—New York	L	3-4	Gooden	Whitson
4—At St. L.	L	2-4	Worrell	M. Davis
5—At St. L.	L	4-1	Grant	Mathews
6—At St. L.	L	4-6	Tudor	Show
7—At Atlanta	W	11-4	Jones	Glavine
8—At Atlanta	L	2-4	P. Smith	Whitson
9—At Atlanta	L	2-3	Palmer	Nolte
10—Houston	W	8-7	Gossage	Hernandez
11—Houston	W	11-0	Show	Scott
13—Houston	W	10-2	Jones	Deshaies
14—At S. Fran.	L	3-4	Lefferts	McCullers
15—At S. Fran.	L	3-13	Hammaker	Nolte
16—Atlanta	W	3-0	Grant	Coffman
17—Atlanta	W	7-1	Show	Z. Smith
18—At Hous.	W	2-1	McCullers	Smith
19—At Hous.	W	2-1x	Leiper	Hernandez
20—At Hous.	L	2-3	Scott	M. Davis
22—At Cinn.	L	3-5	Rasmussen	Grant
23—At Cinn.	W	6-4§	M. Davis	Montgomery
24—At Cinn.	L	4-5	Pacillo	McCullers
25—At L.A.	L	3-5	Belcher	Whitson
26—At L.A.	L	1-3	Welch	Nolte
27—At L.A.	L	3-4	Crews	Gossage
28—San Fran.	L	4-5	D. Robinson	McCullers
29—San Fran.	L	3-5	Downs	Jones
30—Cincinnati	L	1-3	Browning	Hawkins
Won 10, Lost 17				

OCTOBER

Date		Score	Winner	Loser
1—Cincinnati	L	3-4	Pacillo	Nolte
2—Los Ang.	L	3-10	Valenzuela	Grant
3—Los Ang.	W	1-0	Jones	Hershiser
4—Los Ang.	L	3-5	Hillegas	Whitson
Won 1, Lost 3				

*10 innings. †11 innings. ‡12 innings. §13 innings. x14 innings.

Padres catcher Benito Santiago earned rookie honors with a season that included a .300 average and a rookie-record 34-game hitting streak.

The best of the Padres' bright spots were Santiago and right fielder Tony Gwynn.

Santiago earned N.L. rookie honors with a captivating season that he capped with a 34-game hitting streak, the longest ever by a rookie and tops in the league in 1987. The 22-year-old catcher finished with a .300 average, 18 home runs and 79 RBIs. He was impressive defensively, as well.

Gwynn, in his fourth full season, led the majors with a .370 batting average, the first time an N.L. player has hit the .370 mark since Stan Musial in 1948. He led the league with 218 hits and ranked second with 13 triples, 56 stolen bases and a .447 on-base average. Gwynn also captured his second straight Gold Glove.

Though Jefferson (.230, 29 RBIs) was a mild disappointment, rookies Shane Mack and Shawn Abner served notice they will challenge for starting outfield jobs. Martinez had a strong finish and posted a .273 average with 15 homers and 70 RBIs. Shortstop Garry Templeton, however, hit a career-low .222.

Bowa found candidates for the starting rotation in Grant, rookie Jimmy Jones and Eric Nolte. Jones, who began the season at Las Vegas, won seven of his last 10 decisions and finished 9-7. Nolte, promoted from Class AA Wichita in July, had a 3.21 ERA in 12 starts despite finishing 2-6. Ed Whitson topped all starters with 10 victories but didn't win a game after July. He served up a club-record 36 homers, and the entire staff surrendered a league-leading 175.

The bullpen fared well with Rich Gossage (5-4, 11 saves, 3.12 ERA), Greg Booker (1-1, 3.16 ERA) and Lance McCullers (8-10, 3.72 ERA), who finished among the league leaders with 78 appearances and 16 saves.

The sense of upheaval was reflected in the front office, where Owner Joan Kroc first announced a sale of the club to Seattle Mariners Owner George Argyros, then called it off. In June, her son-in-law, Ballard Smith, resigned as president of the team and Kroc brought in former National League president Chub Feeney to serve out the term. Like Bowa and McKeon, Feeney said he would return in 1988.

National League Averages for 1987

CHAMPIONSHIP WINNERS IN PREVIOUS YEARS

1876—Chicago ... .788	1913—New York ... .664	1950—Philadelphia ... .591
1877—Boston ... .646	1914—Boston ... .614	1951—New York† ... .624
1878—Boston ... .683	1915—Philadelphia ... .592	1952—Brooklyn ... .627
1879—Providence ... .705	1916—Brooklyn ... .610	1953—Brooklyn ... .682
1880—Chicago ... .798	1917—New York ... .636	1954—New York ... .630
1881—Chicago ... .667	1918—Chicago ... .651	1955—Brooklyn ... .641
1882—Chicago ... .655	1919—Cincinnati ... .686	1956—Brooklyn ... .604
1883—Boston ... .643	1920—Brooklyn ... .604	1957—Milwaukee ... .617
1884—Providence ... .750	1921—New York ... .614	1958—Milwaukee ... .597
1885—Chicago ... .777	1922—New York ... .604	1959—Los Angeles‡ ... .564
1886—Chicago ... .726	1923—New York ... .621	1960—Pittsburgh ... .617
1887—Detroit ... .637	1924—New York ... .608	1961—Cincinnati ... .604
1888—New York ... .641	1925—Pittsburgh ... .621	1962—San Francisco§ ... .624
1889—New York ... .659	1926—St. Louis ... .578	1963—Los Angeles ... .611
1890—Brooklyn ... .667	1927—Pittsburgh ... .610	1964—St. Louis ... .574
1891—Boston ... .630	1928—St. Louis ... .617	1965—Los Angeles ... .599
1892—Boston ... .680	1929—Chicago ... .645	1966—Los Angeles ... .586
1893—Boston ... .662	1930—St. Louis ... .597	1967—St. Louis ... .627
1894—Baltimore ... .695	1931—St. Louis ... .656	1968—St. Louis ... .599
1895—Baltimore ... .669	1932—Chicago ... .584	1969—New York (East) ... .617
1896—Baltimore ... .698	1933—New York ... .599	1970—Cincinnati (West) ... .630
1897—Boston ... .705	1934—St. Louis ... .621	1971—Pittsburgh (East) ... .599
1898—Boston ... .685	1935—Chicago ... .649	1972—Cincinnati (West) ... .617
1899—Brooklyn ... .677	1936—New York ... .597	1973—New York (East) ... .509
1900—Brooklyn ... .603	1937—New York ... .625	1974—Los Angeles (West) ... .630
1901—Pittsburgh ... .647	1938—Chicago ... .586	1975—Cincinnati (West) ... .667
1902—Pittsburgh ... .741	1939—Cincinnati ... .630	1976—Cincinnati (West) ... .630
1903—Pittsburgh ... .650	1940—Cincinnati ... .654	1977—Los Angeles (West) ... .605
1904—New York ... .693	1941—Brooklyn ... .649	1978—Los Angeles (West) ... .586
1905—New York ... .686	1942—St. Louis ... .688	1979—Pittsburgh (East) ... .605
1906—Chicago ... .763	1943—St. Louis ... .682	1980—Philadelphia (East) ... .562
1907—Chicago ... .704	1944—St. Louis ... .682	1981—Los Angeles (West) ... .573
1908—Chicago ... .643	1945—Chicago ... .636	1982—St. Louis (East) ... .568
1909—Pittsburgh ... .724	1946—St. Louis* ... .628	1983—Philadelphia (East) ... .556
1910—Chicago ... .675	1947—Brooklyn ... .610	1984—San Diego (West) ... .568
1911—New York ... .647	1948—Boston ... .595	1985—St. Louis (East) ... .623
1912—New York ... .682	1949—Brooklyn ... .630	1986—New York (East) ... .667

*Defeated Brooklyn, two games to none, in playoff for pennant. †Defeated Brooklyn, two games to one, in playoff for pennant. ‡Defeated Milwaukee, two games to none, in playoff for pennant. §Defeated Los Angeles, two games to one, in playoff for pennant.

STANDING OF CLUBS AT CLOSE OF SEASON

EAST DIVISION

Club	St.L.	N.Y.	Mon.	Phil.	Pitt.	Chi.	S.F.	Cin.	Hou.	L.A.	Atl.	S.D.	W.	L.	Pct.	G.B.
St. Louis	..	9	7	10	11	12	5	8	7	9	9	8	95	67	.586	......
New York	9	..	10	13	12	9	9	5	6	6	5	8	92	70	.568	3
Montreal	11	8	..	10	11	8	5	6	5	9	9	9	91	71	.562	4
Philadelphia	8	5	8	..	11	10	2	7	6	10	5	8	80	82	.494	15
Pittsburgh	7	6	7	7	..	14	6	8	6	6	5	8	80	82	.494	15
Chicago	6	9	10	8	4	..	5	6	8	6	5	9	76	85	.472	18½

WEST DIVISION

Club	S.F.	Cin.	Hou.	L.A.	Atl.	S.D.	St.L.	N.Y.	Mon.	Phil.	Pitt.	Chi.	W.	L.	Pct.	G.B.
San Francisco	..	11	8	8	10	13	7	3	7	10	6	7	90	72	.556	......
Cincinnati	7	..	13	10	10	12	4	7	6	5	4	6	84	78	.519	6
Houston	10	5	..	12	10	5	5	6	7	6	6	4	76	86	.469	14
Los Angeles	10	8	6	..	12	11	3	6	3	2	6	6	73	89	.451	17
Atlanta	8	8	8	6	..	6	3	7	3	7	7	6	69	92	.429	20½
San Diego	5	6	13	7	12	..	4	4	3	4	4	3	65	97	.401	25

Championship Series—St. Louis defeated San Francisco, four games to three.

SHUTOUT GAMES

Club	Pitt.	St.L.	Hou.	N.Y.	Phil.	S.F.	Cin.	Mon.	Chi.	S.D.	Atl.	L.A.	W.	L.	Pct.
Pittsburgh	..	3	1	0	0	2	1	0	4	0	1	1	13	6	.684
St. Louis	1	..	0	0	1	0	1	2	0	1	1	0	7	4	.636
Houston	1	1	..	0	0	1	1	3	0	2	2	2	13	8	.619
New York	0	0	0	..	1	1	2	1	0	1	0	1	7	5	.583
Philadelphia	1	0	0	1	..	0	0	1	1	1	0	2	7	5	.583
San Francisco	1	0	1	0	1	..	0	2	0	2	0	3	10	8	.556
Cincinnati	0	0	2	1	0	0	..	0	0	2	0	1	6	7	.462
Montreal	0	0	2	2	0	0	1	..	0	2	1	0	8	11	.421
Chicago	0	0	0	0	0	0	0	2	..	1	0	2	5	7	.417
San Diego	0	0	2	1	0	1	0	0	0	..	2	4	10	14	.417
Atlanta	1	0	0	0	1	2	0	0	0	0	..	0	4	7	.364
Los Angeles	1	0	0	0	1	1	1	0	2	2	0	..	8	16	.333

RECORD AT HOME

EAST DIVISION

Club	N.Y.	St.L.	Mon.	Pitt.	Phil.	Chi.	Hou.	S.F.	Atl.	Cin.	L.A.	S.D.	W.	L.	Pct.
New York	....	4-5	5-4	7-2	8-1	6-3	3-3	4-2	3-3	3-3	3-3	3-3	49	32	.605
St. Louis	4-5	....	4-5	6-3	5-4	6-3	4-2	3-3	4-2	4-2	5-1	4-2	49	32	.605
Montreal	4-5	6-3	....	7-2	6-3	3-6	3-3	2-4	5-1	3-3	4-2	5-1	48	33	.593
Pittsburgh	4-5	4-5	5-4	....	4-5	7-2	5-1	3-3	3-3	3-3	4-2	5-1	47	34	.580
Philadelphia	4-5	4-5	5-4	6-3	....	6-3	2-4	1-5	4-2	2-4	5-1	4-2	43	38	.531
Chicago	6-3	3-6	4-5	2-7	5-4	....	3-3	2-4	3-2	3-3	3-3	6-0	40	40	.500

WEST DIVISION

Club	Hou.	S.F.	Atl.	Cin.	L.A.	S.D.	N.Y.	St.L.	Mon.	Pitt.	Phil.	Chi.	W.	L.	Pct.
Houston	....	7-2	8-1	3-6	7-2	4-5	3-3	3-3	4-2	5-1	2-4	1-5	47	34	.580
San Francisco	6-3	....	5-4	6-3	4-5	6-3	1-5	4-2	3-3	3-3	5-1	3-3	46	35	.568
Atlanta	7-2	4-5	....	4-5	3-6	4-5	4-2	1-5	2-4	4-2	5-1	4-2	42	39	.519
Cincinnati	7-2	4-5	5-4	....	6-3	6-3	4-2	2-4	3-3	1-5	1-5	3-3	42	39	.519
Los Angeles	4-5	5-4	6-3	5-4	....	6-3	3-3	2-4	1-5	4-2	1-5	3-3	40	41	.494
San Diego	8-1	2-7	7-2	3-6	4-5	....	1-5	2-4	2-4	3-3	2-4	3-3	37	44	.457

RECORD ABROAD

EAST DIVISION

Club	St.L.	Mon.	N.Y.	Phil.	Chi.	Pitt.	S.F.	Cin.	L.A.	Hou.	S.D.	Atl.	W.	L.	Pct.
St. Louis	....	3-6	5-4	5-4	6-3	5-4	2-4	4-2	4-2	3-3	4-2	5-1	46	35	.568
Montreal	5-4	....	4-5	4-5	5-4	4-5	3-3	3-3	5-1	2-4	4-2	4-2	43	38	.531
New York	5-4	5-4	....	3-6	5-4	5-4	5-1	2-4	3-3	3-3	5-1	2-4	43	38	.531
Philadelphia	4-5	3-6	1-8	....	4-5	5-4	1-5	5-1	5-1	4-2	4-2	1-5	37	44	.457
Chicago	3-6	6-3	3-6	3-6	....	2-7	3-3	3-3	3-3	5-1	3-3	2-4	36	45	.444
Pittsburgh	3-6	2-7	2-7	3-6	7-2	....	3-3	5-1	2-4	1-5	3-3	2-4	33	48	.407

WEST DIVISION

Club	S.F.	Cin.	L.A.	Hou.	S.D.	Atl.	St.L.	Mon.	N.Y.	Phil.	Chi.	Pitt.	W.	L.	Pct.
San Francisco	....	5-4	4-5	2-7	7-2	5-4	3-3	4-2	2-4	5-1	4-2	3-3	44	37	.543
Cincinnati	3-6	....	4-5	6-3	6-3	5-4	2-4	3-3	3-3	4-2	3-3	3-3	42	39	.519
Los Angeles	5-4	3-6	....	2-7	5-4	6-3	1-5	2-4	3-3	1-5	3-3	2-4	33	48	.407
Houston	3-6	2-7	5-4	....	1-8	2-7	2-4	3-3	3-3	4-2	3-3	1-5	29	52	.358
San Diego	3-6	3-6	3-6	5-4	....	5-4	2-4	1-5	3-3	2-4	0-6	1-5	28	53	.346
Atlanta	4-5	4-5	3-6	1-8	2-7	....	2-4	1-5	3-3	2-4	2-3	3-3	27	53	.338

1987 N.L. Pitching Against Each Club

ATLANTA—69-92

Pitcher	Chi. W—L	Cin. W—L	Hou. W—L	L.A. W—L	Mtl. W—L	N.Y. W—L	Phil. W—L	Pitt. W—L	St.L. W—L	S.D. W—L	S.F. W—L	Totals W—L
Acker	1—1	0—1	2—1	1—0	0—3	0—0	0—0	0—0	0—1	0—0	0—2	4—9
Alexander	0—0	1—0	0—0	1—2	0—1	1—0	0—2	0—0	1—1	0—3	1—1	5—10
Assenmacher	0—0	0—0	0—0	0—0	0—0	0—0	0—0	1—0	0—0	0—0	0—1	1—1
Boever	0—0	0—0	0—0	1—0	0—0	0—0	0—0	0—0	0—0	0—0	0—0	1—0
Cary	0—0	0—0	1—0	0—0	0—0	0—0	0—0	0—0	0—0	0—0	0—1	1—1
Clary	0—0	0—0	0—0	0—0	0—0	0—0	0—0	0—0	0—0	0—0	0—1	0—1
Coffman	0—0	0—0	1—0	0—0	0—1	0—1	0—0	0—0	0—0	0—1	1—0	2—3
Dedmon	0—1	0—0	0—0	0—0	0—0	1—1	0—0	1—1	0—0	0—1	0—0	3—4
Garber	2—0	0—2	0—1	0—1	0—1	2—0	1—0	0—0	1—2	1—2	1—1	8—10
Glavine	0—0	1—0	0—1	0—0	1—1	0—1	0—0	0—1	0—0	0—0	0—0	2—4
Mahler	1—1	2—0	0—4	0—0	1—1	0—1	0—1	2—2	0—1	0—1	2—1	8—13
McWilliams	0—0	0—0	0—0	0—0	1—0	0—0	0—0	0—0	0—0	0—1	0—0	0—1
O'Neal	0—0	1—0	1—0	0—0	0—0	1—1	1—0	0—0	0—0	0—0	0—0	4—2
Olwine	0—0	0—0	0—0	0—0	0—0	0—0	0—0	0—1	0—0	0—0	0—0	0—1
Palmer	1—0	0—4	0—1	1—2	1—0	1—1	2—0	1—1	0—0	1—1	0—1	8—11
Puleo	0—1	1—0	1—1	0—3	0—0	1—0	0—1	0—0	0—2	2—0	1—0	6—8
P. Smith	0—0	0—0	0—0	0—2	0—0	0—0	0—0	0—0	1—0	0—0	0—0	1—2
Z. Smith	1—1	2—2	2—1	2—1	1—1	0—1	0—0	3—0	1—2	1—1	2—0	15—10
Ziem	0—0	0—1	0—0	0—0	0—0	0—0	0—0	0—0	0—0	0—0	0—0	0—1
Totals	6—5	8—10	8—10	6—12	3—9	7—5	7—5	7—5	3—9	6—12	8—10	69—92

No Decisions—Niekro.

CHICAGO—76-85

Pitcher	Atl. W—L	Cin. W—L	Hou. W—L	L.A. W—L	Mtl. W—L	N.Y. W—L	Phil. W—L	Pitt. W—L	St.L. W—L	S.D. W—L	S.F. W—L	Totals W—L
Baller	0—0	0—0	0—0	0—0	0—0	0—0	0—1	0—0	0—0	0—0	0—0	0—1
DiPino	0—0	0—0	1—2	0—1	0—0	1—0	0—0	0—0	0—0	1—0	0—0	3—3
Hall	0—0	0—0	0—0	0—0	0—0	0—1	0—0	1—0	0—0	0—0	0—0	1—1
Lancaster	1—0	1—0	1—0	0—1	2—1	0—1	1—0	0—0	1—0	1—0	0—0	8—3
Lynch	0—3	1—1	0—0	0—1	0—0	0—0	1—1	0—1	0—0	0—0	0—2	2—9
Maddux	1—0	0—2	1—0	1—0	1—3	0—2	0—0	0—3	0—3	1—0	1—1	6—14

OFFICIAL BASEBALL GUIDE

Pitcher	Atl. W—L	Cin. W—L	Hou. W—L	L.A. W—L	Mtl. W—L	N.Y. W—L	Phil. W—L	Pitt. W—L	St.L. W—L	S.D. W—L	S.F. W—L	Totals W—L
Mason	0—0	0—0	2—0	0—0	0—0	1—0	0—0	1—0	0—1	0—0	0—0	4—1
Moyer	1—2	1—0	2—0	0—1	2—2	1—0	2—3	1—3	1—1	0—2	1—1	12—15
Noles	1—0	0—0	0—0	1—0	0—0	1—0	0—0	0—2	1—0	0—0	0—0	4—2
Sanderson	1—1	0—1	0—0	1—0	1—0	2—1	0—1	0—1	1—3	1—0	1—1	8—9
Smith	0—0	2—2	0—0	0—1	0—0	1—2	1—3	0—1	0—0	0—0	0—0	4—10
Sutcliffe	0—0	1—0	1—2	2—0	3—0	2—1	2—0	0—3	2—3	3—0	2—1	18—10
Tewksbury	0—0	0—0	0—0	0—1	0—1	0—0	0—1	0—0	0—0	0—1	0—0	0—4
Trout	0—0	0—0	0—0	1—0	1—1	0—1	1—0	1—0	0—1	2—0	0—0	6—3
Totals	5—6	6—6	8—4	6—6	10—8	9—9	8—10	4—14	6—12	9—3	5—7	76—85

No Decisions—R. Davis.

CINCINNATI—84-78

Pitcher	Atl. W—L	Chi. W—L	Hou. W—L	L.A. W—L	Mtl. W—L	N.Y. W—L	Phil. W—L	Pitt. W—L	St.L. W—L	S.D. W—L	S.F. W—L	Totals W—L
Browning	0—2	1—1	2—1	1—0	1—1	1—0	1—2	0—3	0—0	3—0	0—3	10—13
Franco	0—0	1—2	2—0	1—1	0—0	0—0	1—1	0—1	0—0	1—0	2—0	8—5
Gullickson	1—2	2—0	1—1	0—1	2—1	1—1	2—1	1—0	0—1	0—0	0—3	10—11
Hoffman	2—1	0—0	0—0	2—1	0—2	1—0	0—1	1—0	2—1	1—3	0—1	9—10
Hume	0—0	0—0	0—0	1—0	0—0	0—0	0—0	0—0	0—0	0—0	0—0	1—0
Landrum	2—0	0—0	0—0	0—0	1—1	0—0	0—0	0—0	0—0	0—1	0—0	3—2
Montgomery	1—0	0—0	0—0	0—1	0—0	0—0	0—0	0—0	0—0	0—1	1—0	2—2
Murphy	1—1	0—0	3—0	1—0	0—0	0—0	0—0	0—1	0—1	2—1	1—1	8—5
Pacillo	0—1	0—0	0—0	0—0	0—0	0—0	0—1	1—0	2—0	0—1	0—0	3—3
Perry	1—0	0—0	0—0	0—0	0—0	0—0	0—0	0—0	0—0	0—0	0—0	1—0
Power	1—0	0—1	1—2	2—2	1—1	2—0	0—2	2—1	0—2	1—0	0—2	10—13
Rasmussen	0—0	1—1	1—0	0—0	0—0	0—0	0—0	0—0	0—0	1—0	1—0	4—1
Reuss	0—1	0—1	0—0	0—1	0—0	0—0	0—1	0—0	0—1	0—0	0—0	0—5
Robinson	1—0	0—0	1—1	1—1	1—0	0—1	0—0	0—1	0—1	1—0	2—0	7—5
Scherrer	0—0	0—0	1—0	0—0	0—0	0—1	0—0	0—0	0—0	0—0	0—0	1—1
Soto	0—0	0—0	1—0	0—0	0—0	1—1	1—0	0—0	0—1	0—0	0—0	3—2
Williams	0—0	1—0	0—0	1—0	0—0	1—0	0—0	0—0	1—0	0—0	0—0	4—0
Totals	10—8	6—6	13—5	10—8	6—6	7—5	5—7	4—8	4—8	12—6	7—11	84—78

No Decisions—O'Neill.

HOUSTON—76-86

Pitcher	Atl. W—L	Chi. W—L	Cin. W—L	L.A. W—L	Mtl. W—L	N.Y. W—L	Phil. W—L	Pitt. W—L	St.L. W—L	S.D. W—L	S.F. W—L	Totals W—L
Agosto	0—0	0—0	0—0	0—0	0—0	0—0	0—0	0—0	0—1	1—0	0—0	1—1
Andersen	2—0	2—0	0—2	1—0	0—0	0—0	2—1	0—0	0—0	1—0	1—2	9—5
Childress	0—0	0—0	0—1	0—0	0—0	0—0	0—0	0—0	1—0	0—0	0—1	1—2
Darwin	1—0	0—2	1—2	0—0	3—1	0—1	2—0	0—1	0—1	1—1	1—0	9—10
Deshaies	2—1	0—1	1—0	3—0	0—2	2—0	0—1	1—0	1—0	0—1	1—0	11—6
Heathcock	0—1	1—0	1—0	0—0	0—0	0—0	0—0	0—0	0—1	2—0	0—0	4—2
Hernandez	0—0	0—1	0—0	0—0	0—0	0—0	0—0	0—1	0—0	0—2	0—0	0—4
Kerfeld	0—0	0—0	0—1	0—1	0—0	0—0	0—0	0—0	0—0	0—0	0—0	0—2
Knepper	2—1	0—2	0—3	0—0	1—1	0—2	1—1	1—1	2—2	0—2	1—0	8—17
Lopez	0—0	0—0	0—0	0—0	1—0	0—0	0—0	1—0	0—0	0—0	0—0	2—1
Mathis	0—0	0—0	0—0	0—1	0—0	0—0	0—0	0—0	0—0	0—0	0—0	0—1
Meads	1—0	0—0	0—0	1—0	0—0	2—0	0—0	1—1	0—0	0—1	0—0	5—3
Ryan	1—1	0—0	0—2	3—2	0—1	0—1	0—2	1—1	1—1	0—1	2—1	8—16
Scott	1—2	1—0	2—1	3—0	2—0	0—2	1—1	1—1	0—1	3—3	2—2	16—13
Smith	0—2	0—0	0—0	0—0	0—0	2—0	0—0	0—0	0—0	0—1	0—0	2—3
Totals	10—8	4—8	5—13	12—6	7—5	6—6	6—6	5—7	5—13	10—8	6—6	76—86

No Decisions—Mallicoat, Solano.

LOS ANGELES—73-89

Pitcher	Atl. W—L	Chi. W—L	Cin. W—L	Hou. W—L	Mtl. W—L	N.Y. W—L	Phil. W—L	Pitt. W—L	St.L. W—L	S.D. W—L	S.F. W—L	Totals W—L
Belcher	1—0	0—0	0—1	1—0	0—0	1—0	0—0	0—0	0—0	1—0	0—1	4—2
Crews	0—0	0—0	0—0	0—0	0—1	0—0	0—0	0—0	0—0	1—0	0—0	1—1
Hershiser	4—1	0—1	2—1	1—3	0—2	2—0	1—2	2—2	0—1	2—1	2—2	16—16
Hillegas	1—0	0—0	0—0	1—1	0—0	0—2	1—0	0—0	0—0	1—0	1—0	4—3
Holton	0—0	1—0	0—1	1—0	0—0	0—0	0—0	0—0	1—0	0—1	0—0	3—2
Honeycutt	0—1	1—1	0—1	0—1	0—1	0—0	0—3	1—1	0—0	0—2	0—1	2—12
Howell	0—1	1—1	0—1	0—0	0—0	0—0	0—0	0—0	0—1	1—0	1—0	3—4
Leary	1—0	0—2	1—1	0—2	0—1	0—1	0—2	0—0	0—1	0—1	1—2	3—11
Niedenfuer	0—0	0—0	0—0	1—0	0—0	0—0	0—0	0—0	0—0	0—0	0—0	1—0
Pena	0—1	0—1	0—0	1—1	1—1	0—0	0—1	0—0	0—1	0—1	0—0	2—7
Valenzuela	3—0	0—0	1—4	0—1	2—2	1—2	0—0	1—2	1—2	2—0	3—1	14—14
Welch	1—1	2—0	3—0	0—1	0—1	2—1	1—1	1—1	0—1	3—1	2—1	15—9
Young	1—1	1—0	1—0	0—2	0—0	0—1	0—1	1—0	1—2	0—1	0—0	5—8
Totals	12—6	6—6	8—10	6—12	3—9	6—6	2—10	6—6	3—9	11—7	10—8	73—89

No Decisions—Davis, Havens, Krueger, Reuss, Savage.

MONTREAL—91-71

Pitcher	Atl. W—L	Chi. W—L	Cin. W—L	Hou. W—L	L.A. W—L	N.Y. W—L	Phil. W—L	Pitt. W—L	St.L. W—L	S.D. W—L	S.F. W—L	Totals W—L
Brown	0—0	0—0	0—0	0—0	0—0	0—0	0—0	0—0	0—0	0—1	0—0	0—1
Burke	1—0	0—0	0—0	0—0	2—0	0—0	0—0	1—0	0—0	2—0	1—0	7—0
Fischer	0—0	0—0	0—0	0—0	0—0	0—0	0—0	0—1	0—0	0—0	0—0	0—1
Heaton	0—1	2—0	1—1	0—2	0—1	0—1	3—2	2—1	1—0	2—1	2—0	13—10
Heredia	0—1	0—0	0—0	0—0	0—0	0—0	0—0	0—0	0—0	0—0	0—0	0—1
Lea	0—0	0—0	0—0	0—0	0—0	0—1	0—0	0—0	0—0	0—0	0—0	0—1
Martinez	1—0	1—0	1—0	1—1	0—0	4—0	1—0	1—0	1—1	0—0	0—2	11—4
McClure	0—0	0—0	0—0	0—0	1—0	1—1	0—0	2—0	2—0	0—0	0—0	6—1
McGaffigan	1—0	0—1	1—0	0—0	1—0	0—0	0—1	2—0	0—0	0—0	0—0	5—2
Parrett	1—0	1—1	0—0	0—1	1—1	0—0	1—0	2—1	1—1	0—1	0—0	7—6
Perez	0—0	1—0	0—0	0—0	0—0	1—0	1—0	1—0	2—0	0—0	1—0	7—0
Sebra	0—1	1—2	1—0	2—2	1—0	0—3	0—2	0—2	1—1	0—0	0—2	6—15
Smith	1—0	1—1	1—1	0—0	1—1	1—1	2—1	0—1	1—3	2—0	0—0	10—9
Sorensen	1—0	1—2	1—0	0—0	1—0	0—0	0—1	0—1	0—0	0—0	0—0	3—4
St. Claire	0—0	0—0	0—2	0—0	0—0	1—0	1—0	0—0	1—0	0—0	0—1	3—3
Tibbs	1—0	0—1	0—1	1—0	1—0	0—1	0—1	0—0	1—1	0—0	0—0	4—5
Youmans	2—0	0—2	1—1	1—1	0—0	0—2	1—0	0—0	0—0	3—0	1—2	9—8
Totals	9—3	8—10	6—6	5—7	9—3	8—10	10—8	11—7	11—7	9—3	5—7	91—71

No Decisions—Campbell, Hesketh, Law, Wallach.

NEW YORK—92-70

Pitcher	Atl. W—L	Chi. W—L	Cin. W—L	Hou. W—L	L.A. W—L	Mtl. W—L	Phil. W—L	Pitt. W—L	St.L. W—L	S.D. W—L	S.F. W—L	Totals W—L
Aguilera	0—0	1—0	1—1	0—0	2—0	1—1	2—0	1—0	1—1	1—0	1—0	11—3
Candelaria	0—0	0—0	0—0	0—0	0—0	1—0	1—0	0—0	0—0	0—0	0—0	2—0
Cone	0—1	0—1	1—0	0—1	0—1	0—1	0—1	0—0	1—0	1—0	2—0	5—6
Darling	2—0	2—1	0—2	1—0	2—2	2—0	1—0	1—1	0—2	0—0	1—0	12—8
Fernandez	1—1	1—0	0—2	2—0	0—0	0—1	2—1	3—0	1—1	1—1	1—1	12—8
Gooden	0—1	3—1	1—1	1—0	0—0	1—1	2—1	1—1	2—1	2—0	2—0	15—7
Innis	0—0	0—0	0—0	0—0	0—0	0—0	0—0	0—0	0—0	0—0	0—1	0—1
Leach	1—0	0—1	1—0	0—0	2—0	3—0	2—0	0—0	0—0	1—0	1—0	11—1
McDowell	0—0	2—1	0—0	0—0	0—1	0—0	1—1	1—1	1—0	1—0	1—1	7—5
Mitchell	0—0	0—1	0—1	1—0	0—0	0—2	2—0	0—0	0—1	0—1	0—0	3—6
Myers	0—0	0—1	0—0	1—1	0—1	0—0	0—0	0—3	2—0	0—0	0—0	3—6
Ojeda	0—2	0—0	0—0	0—0	0—0	0—1	0—0	3—1	0—1	0—0	0—0	3—5
Orosco	0—2	0—0	0—1	0—0	0—1	1—1	0—1	0—0	0—3	1—0	0—0	3—9
Schulze	1—0	0—1	0—0	0—1	0—0	0—0	0—0	0—0	0—0	0—0	0—0	1—2
Sisk	0—0	0—1	0—0	0—0	0—0	1—0	0—0	1—0	0—0	0—0	1—0	3—1
Walter	0—0	0—0	0—0	0—2	0—0	0—0	0—0	1—0	0—0	0—0	0—0	1—2
Totals	5—7	9—9	5—7	6—6	6—6	10—8	13—5	12—6	9—9	8—4	9—3	92—70

No Decisions—Edens, Gibson.

PHILADELPHIA—80-82

Pitcher	Atl. W—L	Chi. W—L	Cin. W—L	Hou. W—L	L.A. W—L	Mtl. W—L	N.Y. W—L	Pitt. W—L	St.L. W—L	S.D. W—L	S.F. W—L	Totals W—L
Bair	0—0	0—0	0—0	0—0	0—0	0—0	1—0	1—0	0—0	0—0	0—0	2—0
Bedrosian	0—0	2—0	0—0	0—1	0—0	0—0	0—1	1—1	1—0	0—0	1—0	5—3
Calhoun	0—0	1—1	0—0	0—0	0—0	0—0	1—0	0—0	1—0	0—0	0—0	3—1
Carman	1—1	1—1	0—1	1—0	1—1	2—0	2—1	2—1	0—3	3—0	0—2	13—11
Cowley	0—0	0—1	0—0	0—0	0—0	0—2	0—1	0—0	0—0	0—0	0—0	0—4
Frohwirth	0—0	1—0	0—0	0—0	0—0	0—0	0—0	0—0	0—0	0—0	0—0	1—0
K. Gross	1—0	1—2	1—2	0—1	1—0	2—1	1—4	1—2	1—2	0—1	0—1	9—16
Hume	0—2	0—1	0—0	1—0	0—0	0—0	0—0	0—0	0—1	0—0	0—0	1—4
M. Jackson	0—0	0—1	1—1	0—2	0—0	1—3	0—0	1—1	0—1	0—1	0—0	3—10
Maddux	0—0	1—0	0—0	0—0	1—0	0—0	0—0	0—0	0—0	0—0	0—0	2—0
Rawley	1—1	0—1	2—0	1—1	4—0	2—3	0—2	2—0	3—1	2—0	0—2	17—11
Ritchie	0—0	0—0	0—0	0—0	1—0	0—0	0—0	0—0	1—0	0—1	1—1	3—2
Ruffin	1—2	1—0	2—1	2—0	1—1	0—1	0—2	2—2	1—2	1—1	0—2	11—14
Schatzeder	0—1	0—0	0—0	1—0	0—0	1—0	0—0	0—0	0—0	1—0	0—0	3—1
Tekulve	1—0	2—0	1—0	0—1	1—0	0—0	0—2	1—0	0—0	0—0	0—1	6—4
Toliver	0—0	0—0	0—0	0—0	0—0	0—0	0—0	0—0	0—0	1—0	0—1	1—1
Totals	5—7	10—8	7—5	6—6	10—2	8—10	5—13	11—7	8—10	8—4	2—10	80—82

No Decisions—Newell, Wilson.

PITTSBURGH—80-82

Pitcher	Atl. W—L	Chi. W—L	Cin. W—L	Hou. W—L	L.A. W—L	Mtl. W—L	N.Y. W—L	Phil. W—L	St.L. W—L	S.D. W—L	S.F. W—L	Totals W—L
Bielecki	0—1	0—0	0—0	0—1	0—0	1—0	0—1	0—0	0—0	0—0	0—0	2—3
Drabek	0—0	2—1	2—1	1—1	1—0	2—0	1—1	2—3	0—3	0—1	0—1	11—12
Dunne	1—0	1—0	1—1	1—0	1—0	2—1	0—2	2—1	2—0	2—0	0—1	13—6
Easley	0—0	0—0	0—0	0—0	0—0	0—0	0—1	0—0	0—0	0—0	0—0	1—1
Fisher	0—2	4—0	1—0	0—0	0—1	1—2	0—1	1—0	1—1	2—1	1—1	11—9
Gideon	0—0	0—1	0—0	0—0	0—0	0—3	0—0	0—0	0—0	0—0	1—1	1—5
Gott	0—0	0—0	0—0	0—0	0—0	0—2	0—0	0—0	0—0	0—0	0—0	0—2
Jones	0—0	2—0	0—0	0—0	0—0	0—0	0—0	0—2	0—2	0—0	0—0	2—4
Kipper	1—0	1—0	1—1	0—1	2—2	0—1	0—1	0—0	0—1	0—1	0—1	5—9

Pitcher	Atl. W—L	Chi. W—L	Cin. W—L	Hou. W—L	L.A. W—L	Mtl. W—L	N.Y. W—L	Phil. W—L	St.L. W—L	S.D. W—L	S.F. W—L	Totals W—L
Palacios	0—0	1—0	0—0	0—0	0—0	0—0	0—1	1—0	0—0	0—0	0—0	2—1
Patterson	0—0	0—0	0—0	0—0	0—1	0—0	0—2	0—0	1—0	0—1	1—0	1—4
Pena	0—1	0—0	0—0	0—1	0—0	0—0	0—0	0—0	0—1	0—0	0—0	0—3
Reuschel	1—0	1—1	1—0	0—0	1—1	0—0	0—1	0—2	1—1	1—0	2—0	8—6
D. Robinson	1—0	1—0	0—0	0—1	0—1	0—1	1—1	0—1	1—1	1—0	1—0	6—6
J. Robinson	0—0	1—0	1—0	0—0	0—0	0—0	0—0	0—0	0—1	0—0	0—0	2—1
Smiley	0—2	0—1	0—0	1—0	1—0	0—1	2—0	0—1	0—0	0—0	1—0	5—5
Taylor	0—0	0—0	0—1	1—1	0—0	0—0	1—0	0—1	0—0	0—0	0—0	2—3
Walk	1—1	0—0	1—0	1—0	0—0	1—0	0—0	1—0	1—0	2—0	0—1	8—2
Totals	5—7	14—4	8—4	6—6	6—6	7—11	6—12	7—11	7—11	8—4	6—6	80—82

No Decisions—Drummond, Garcia, Johnson, Ross.

ST. LOUIS—95-67

Pitcher	Atl. W—L	Chi. W—L	Cin. W—L	Hou. W—L	L.A. W—L	Mtl. W—L	N.Y. W—L	Phil. W—L	Pitt. W—L	S.D. W—L	S.F. W—L	Totals W—L
Conroy	0—0	0—0	1—1	1—0	1—0	0—0	0—0	0—0	0—0	0—1	0—0	3—2
Cox	1—1	4—2	2—1	1—1	0—1	1—1	0—1	1—1	1—0	0—0	0—0	11—9
Dawley	2—1	1—2	0—0	0—0	0—0	0—1	0—2	0—0	2—0	0—0	0—2	5—8
Dayley	0—0	0—0	0—0	1—1	3—0	1—1	1—0	0—2	2—0	1—1	0—0	9—5
Forsch	2—0	2—2	0—0	0—0	2—0	1—3	1—0	0—1	2—1	1—0	0—0	11—7
Horton	1—0	0—0	0—1	0—0	1—0	1—0	0—0	2—1	1—0	0—0	2—1	8—3
LaPoint	0—0	0—0	0—0	0—0	0—0	0—0	1—0	0—0	0—1	0—0	0—0	1—1
Magrane	1—0	1—0	0—0	1—2	0—0	2—2	1—0	0—1	1—1	1—0	1—1	9—7
Mathews	1—0	1—0	0—0	1—1	0—0	1—1	2—3	3—0	0—3	2—1	0—2	11—11
Perry	0—0	0—0	1—0	1—0	1—1	0—0	0—1	0—0	0—0	1—0	0—0	4—2
Soff	0—0	0—0	0—0	0—0	0—0	0—0	0—0	0—0	0—0	0—0	1—0	1—0
Tudor	0—0	2—0	2—0	0—0	0—0	0—0	2—0	2—1	1—1	1—0	0—0	10—2
Tunnell	0—0	1—0	1—1	1—0	0—0	0—1	0—1	0—1	0—0	0—0	1—0	4—4
Worrell	1—1	0—0	1—0	0—0	1—1	0—1	1—1	2—0	1—0	1—1	0—1	8—6
Totals	9—3	12—6	8—4	7—5	9—3	7—11	9—9	10—8	11—7	8—4	5—7	95—67

No Decisions—O'Neal, Oquendo, Peters, Terry.

SAN DIEGO—65-97

Pitcher	Atl. W—L	Chi. W—L	Cin. W—L	Hou. W—L	L.A. W—L	Mtl. W—L	N.Y. W—L	Phil. W—L	Pitt. W—L	St.L. W—L	S.F. W—L	Totals W—L
Booker	0—1	0—0	1—0	0—0	0—0	0—0	0—0	0—0	0—0	0—0	0—0	1—1
Comstock	0—0	0—0	0—0	0—0	0—0	0—0	0—1	0—0	0—0	0—0	0—0	0—1
M. Davis	1—0	1—0	1—1	1—1	0—0	0—0	1—0	0—0	0—0	0—1	0—0	5—3
S. Davis	0—0	0—1	0—1	0—1	0—1	0—1	0—0	0—0	1—0	0—1	1—1	2—7
Dravecky	0—0	0—0	0—1	1—1	0—1	0—1	1—0	0—1	0—0	0—0	1—2	3—7
Gossage	0—0	0—0	0—0	2—0	0—1	1—1	0—0	1—0	0—1	1—1	0—0	5—4
Grant	2—0	0—2	0—1	0—1	0—1	1—0	0—0	1—1	1—0	1—1	0—0	6—7
Hawkins	0—0	0—1	0—2	0—0	0—0	1—2	0—0	1—1	0—2	0—1	1—1	3—10
Jones	3—0	0—0	1—0	1—0	2—0	0—2	1—1	0—2	0—1	0—0	1—1	9—7
Lefferts	0—0	0—0	0—0	1—0	1—0	0—0	0—1	0—0	0—1	0—0	0—0	2—2
Leiper	0—0	0—0	0—0	1—0	0—0	0—0	0—0	0—0	0—0	0—0	0—0	1—0
McCullers	2—0	1—2	1—1	1—1	2—1	0—1	0—0	0—0	0—0	1—1	0—3	8—10
Nolte	0—2	0—0	0—1	1—0	0—1	0—0	0—1	1—0	0—0	0—0	0—1	2—6
Show	3—1	0—0	0—3	2—0	2—0	0—1	0—2	0—1	1—3	0—1	0—2	8—16
Whitson	1—2	1—1	2—1	2—0	0—3	0—0	1—2	0—2	1—0	1—1	1—1	10—13
Wojna	0—0	0—0	0—0	0—0	0—2	0—0	0—0	0—0	0—0	0—0	0—1	0—3
Totals	12—6	3—9	6—12	13—5	7—11	3—9	4—8	4—8	4—8	4—8	5—13	65—97

No Decisions—Gorman, Hayward, Salazar.

SAN FRANCISCO—90-72

Pitcher	Atl. W—L	Chi. W—L	Cin. W—L	Hou. W—L	L.A. W—L	Mtl. W—L	N.Y. W—L	Phil. W—L	Pitt. W—L	St.L. W—L	S.D. W—L	Totals W—L
Bockus	1—0	0—0	0—0	0—0	0—0	0—0	0—0	0—0	0—0	0—0	0—0	1—0
Comstock	0—0	0—0	1—0	1—0	0—0	0—0	0—0	0—0	0—0	0—0	0—0	2—0
M. Davis	1—0	0—1	1—0	0—0	2—0	0—0	0—0	0—1	0—1	0—1	0—1	4—5
Downs	2—1	1—1	1—0	0—1	0—2	2—1	0—1	0—0	1—2	1—0	4—0	12—9
Dravecky	0—1	0—1	0—2	1—0	1—1	2—0	0—0	1—0	2—0	0—0	0—0	7—5
Garrelts	1—1	2—0	1—2	0—0	1—2	0—0	2—0	1—0	0—1	3—1	0—0	11—7
Gott	0—0	0—0	0—0	0—0	0—0	0—0	0—0	0—0	0—0	0—0	1—0	1—0
Grant	0—1	0—0	0—0	0—0	0—0	0—0	0—1	0—0	0—0	0—0	1—0	1—2
Hammaker	0—0	1—1	1—1	2—2	0—1	0—0	1—2	2—0	1—0	1—1	1—2	10—10
Krukow	1—1	1—0	1—0	0—1	2—2	0—1	0—1	0—0	0—0	0—0	0—0	5—6
LaCoss	0—1	1—0	4—0	0—3	1—1	1—2	0—1	2—0	1—1	2—0	1—1	13—10
Lefferts	0—0	0—0	0—0	1—1	1—0	0—1	0—0	0—0	0—1	1—0	0—0	3—3
Mason	0—0	0—1	0—0	0—0	0—0	0—0	0—0	0—0	0—0	0—0	1—0	1—1
Minton	1—0	0—0	0—0	0—0	0—0	0—0	0—0	0—0	0—0	0—0	0—0	1—0
Price	1—0	1—0	0—0	0—1	0—0	0—0	0—0	0—0	0—1	0—0	0—0	2—2
Reuschel	0—1	0—0	1—0	1—0	0—1	1—0	0—1	2—0	0—0	0—0	0—0	5—3
D. Robinson	0—0	0—0	0—1	2—0	0—0	0—0	0—0	2—0	0—0	0—0	1—0	5—1
J. Robinson	2—1	0—0	0—1	0—1	0—0	1—0	0—2	0—1	1—0	0—1	2—1	6—8
Totals	10—8	7—5	11—7	8—10	8—10	7—5	3—9	10—2	6—6	7—5	13—5	90—72

No Decisions—Burkett, Perlman.

OFFICIAL NATIONAL LEAGUE BATTING AVERAGES

Compiled by Elias Sports Bureau

CLUB BATTING

Club	AVG.	G	AB	R	H	TB	2B	3B	HR	RBI	GW RBI	SH	SF	HP	BB	IB	SO	SB	CS	GI DP	LOB	SHO	SLG	OBP
New York	.268	162	5601	823	1499	2430	287	34	192	771	85	70	39	31	592	74	1012	159	49	94	1189	5	.434	.339
Cincinnati	.266	162	5560	783	1478	2374	262	29	192	747	80	57	34	31	514	55	928	169	46	129	1068	7	.427	.330
Montreal	.265	162	5527	741	1467	2215	310	39	120	695	80	57	42	35	501	77	918	166	74	100	1091	11	.401	.328
Pittsburgh	.264	162	5536	723	1464	2229	282	45	131	684	75	71	51	29	535	67	914	140	58	121	1163	6	.403	.330
Chicago	.264	161	5583	720	1475	2412	244	33	209	683	75	59	52	21	504	45	1064	109	48	109	1154	7	.432	.326
St. Louis	.263	162	5500	798	1449	2081	252	49	94	746	90	84	51	18	644	61	933	248	72	126	1140	4	.378	.340
San Diego	.260	162	5456	668	1419	2063	209	48	113	621	61	81	36	27	577	75	992	198	91	122	1166	14	.378	.332
San Francisco	.260	162	5608	783	1458	2411	274	32	205	731	83	55	35	39	511	73	1094	126	97	99	1079	8	.430	.324
Atlanta	.258	161	5428	747	1401	2189	284	24	152	696	64	86	34	38	641	82	834	135	68	133	1173	7	.403	.339
Philadelphia	.254	162	5475	702	1390	2247	248	51	169	662	77	63	40	25	587	51	1109	111	49	133	1138	5	.410	.327
Houston	.253	162	5485	648	1386	2046	238	28	122	603	70	58	50	24	526	52	936	162	46	115	1158	8	.373	.318
Los Angeles	.252	162	5517	635	1389	2046	236	23	125	594	69	82	39	31	445	70	923	128	59	126	1094	16	.371	.309
Totals	.261	971	66276	8771	17275	26743	3126	435	1824	8233	909	823	481	349	6577	782	11657	1851	757	1407	13613	98	.404	.328

INDIVIDUAL BATTING

(Top Fifteen Qualifiers for Batting Championship—502 or More Plate Appearances)

(*Lefthanded Batter †Switch-hitter)

Player, Club	AVG.	G	AB	R	H	TB	2B	3B	HR	RBI	GW RBI	SH	SF	HP	BB	IB	SO	SB	CS	GI DP	SLG	OBP
Gwynn, Anthony, S.D.*	.370	157	589	119	218	301	36	13	7	54	5	2	4	3	82	26	35	56	12	13	.511	.447
Guerrero, Pedro, L.A.	.338	152	545	89	184	294	25	1	27	89	11	0	7	4	74	18	85	9	7	16	.539	.416
Raines, Timothy, Mtl.†	.330	139	530	123	175	279	34	8	18	68	8	3	4	4	90	26	52	50	5	9	.526	.429
Kruk, John, S.D.*	.313	138	447	72	140	218	14	2	20	91	5	3	5	0	73	15	93	18	10	8	.488	.406
James, Dion, Atl.*	.312	134	494	80	154	233	37	6	10	61	3	5	3	2	70	10	63	10	8	8	.472	.397
Clark, William, S.F.*	.308	150	529	89	163	307	29	5	35	91	11	3	2	5	49	13	98	5	8	2	.580	.371
Galarraga, Andres, Mtl.	.305	147	551	72	168	253	40	3	13	90	8	0	5	10	41	13	127	7	17	11	.459	.361
Smith, Osborne, St.L.†	.303	158	600	104	182	230	40	4	0	75	9	12	4	1	89	10	36	43	10	9	.383	.392
Thompson, Milton, Phil.*	.302	150	527	86	159	224	26	9	7	43	10	3	4	0	42	3	87	46	9	5	.425	.351
Bonilla, Roberto, Pitt.†	.300	141	466	58	140	224	33	3	15	77	10	0	8	2	39	4	64	3	5	8	.481	.351
Santiago, Benito, S.D.	.300	146	546	64	164	255	33	2	18	79	10	1	2	5	16	2	112	21	12	12	.467	.324
Wallach, Timothy, Mtl.	.298	153	593	89	177	305	42	4	26	123	16	0	7	7	37	5	98	9	6	9	.514	.343
Hatcher, William, Hou.	.296	141	564	96	167	234	28	3	11	63	4	7	5	9	42	1	70	53	9	11	.415	.352
Murphy, Dale, Atl.	.295	159	566	115	167	328	27	1	44	105	7	0	5	7	115	29	136	16	6	11	.580	.417
Sandberg, Ryne, Chi.	.294	132	523	81	154	231	25	2	16	59	10	1	2	2	59	4	79	21	2	11	.442	.367

ALL PLAYERS LISTED ALPHABETICALLY
(*Lefthanded Batter   †Switch-Hitter)

Player, Club	AVG.	G	AB	R	H	TB	2B	3B	HR	RBI	GW RBI	SH	SF	HP	BB	IB	SO	SB	CS	GI DP	SLG	OBP
Abner, Shawn, S.D.	.277	16	47	5	13	24	3	1	2	7	0	0	0	0	2	0	8	1	0	0	.511	.306
Acker, James, Atl.	.214	68	14	1	3	3	1	0	0	2	0	0	0	0	1	0	8	0	0	0	.214	.267
Afenir, M. Troy, Hou.	.300	10	20	1	6	7	1	0	0	1	0	0	0	0	0	0	12	0	0	0	.350	.300
Agosto, Juan, Hou.*	.000	27	1	0	0	0	0	0	0	0	0	3	0	0	0	0	1	0	0	0	.000	.000
Aguayo, Luis, Phil.	.206	94	209	25	43	90	9	1	12	21	4	6	2	5	15	1	56	6	0	5	.431	.273
Aguilera, Richard, N.Y.	.225	18	40	5	9	13	1	0	1	3	0	4	0	0	0	0	17	0	0	0	.325	.244
Aldrete, Michael, S.F.*	.325	126	357	50	116	165	18	0	9	51	8	6	2	5	43	5	50	6	0	6	.462	.396
Alexander, Doyle, Atl.	.029	16	35	1	1	1	0	0	0	1	0	4	0	1	0	0	13	0	0	0	.029	.056
Almon, William, Pitt.-N.Y.	.230	68	74	13	17	21	4	0	0	5	0	6	0	0	9	0	21	6	1	0	.284	.313
Andersen, Larry, Hou.	.167	67	6	1	1	1	0	0	0	1	1	0	0	0	1	0	4	0	0	1	.167	.286
Anderson, David, L.A.	.234	108	265	32	62	83	12	0	0	13	0	6	1	1	24	2	43	9	5	2	.313	.299
Ashby, Alan, Hou.†	.288	125	386	53	111	169	16	0	14	63	4	0	4	1	50	0	52	0	1	14	.438	.367
Assenmacher, Paul, Atl.*	.000	52	4	1	0	0	0	0	0	0	0	2	0	0	1	0	2	0	0	0	.000	.200
Backman, Walter, N.Y.†	.250	94	300	43	75	86	6	1	0	23	0	9	1	1	25	0	43	11	3	5	.287	.307
Bailey, J. Mark, Hou.†	.203	35	64	5	13	14	1	0	0	3	2	1	0	0	10	0	21	1	1	3	.219	.311
Bair, C. Douglas, Phil.	.000	11	1	0	0	0	0	0	0	0	0	0	0	0	0	0	0	0	0	0	.000	.000
Baller, Jay, Chi.	1.000	23	1	0	1	1	0	0	0	0	0	0	0	0	0	0	0	0	0	0	1.000	1.000
Barnes, William, St.L.	.250	4	4	1	1	4	0	0	1	3	0	0	0	0	0	0	0	0	0	0	1.000	.250
Bass, Kevin, Hou.†	.284	157	592	83	168	266	31	5	19	85	11	1	5	4	53	13	77	21	8	15	.449	.344
Bedrosian, Stephen, Phil.	.000	65	4	0	0	0	0	0	0	0	0	0	0	0	0	0	3	0	0	0	.000	.000
Belcher, Timothy, L.A.	.200	6	10	0	2	2	0	0	0	1	0	2	0	0	0	0	4	0	0	0	.200	.200
Bell, David, Cin.	.284	143	522	74	148	222	19	2	17	70	8	9	2	1	71	3	39	4	1	14	.425	.369
Bell, Terrence, Atl.	.000	1	1	0	0	0	0	0	0	0	0	0	0	0	0	0	0	0	0	0	.000	.000
Belliard, Rafael, Pitt.	.207	81	203	26	42	55	4	3	0	15	0	2	1	3	20	6	25	5	1	4	.271	.286
Benedict, Bruce, Atl.	.147	37	95	4	14	18	1	0	1	5	0	2	0	2	17	3	15	0	1	2	.189	.277
Berra, Dale, Hou.	.178	19	45	3	8	11	3	0	0	2	0	0	1	0	8	0	12	0	0	0	.244	.296
Berryhill, Damon, Chi.†	.179	12	28	2	5	6	1	0	0	1	0	0	0	0	3	0	5	0	0	1	.214	.258
Biancalana, Roland, Hou.†	.042	18	24	1	1	1	0	0	0	0	0	1	0	0	0	0	12	0	0	0	.042	.080
Bielecki, Michael, Pitt	.063	8	16	0	1	1	0	0	0	0	0	2	0	0	1	0	8	0	0	0	.063	.063
Blauser, Jeffrey, Atl	.242	51	165	11	40	58	6	3	2	15	1	2	0	3	18	1	34	2	3	4	.352	.328
Bochy, Bruce, S.D.	.160	38	75	8	12	21	3	0	2	11	1	0	0	1	11	1	21	0	0	3	.280	.264
Bockus, Randy, S.F.*	.000	12	0	0	0	0	0	0	0	0	0	0	0	0	0	0	0	0	0	0	.000	.000
Boever, Joseph, Atl.		14	0	0	0	0	0	0	0	0	0	0	0	0	0	0	0	0	0	0		
Bonds, Barry, Pitt.*	.261	150	551	99	144	271	34	9	25	59	6	0	3	3	54	3	88	32	10	4	.492	.329
Bonilla, Roberto, Pitt.†	.300	141	466	58	140	224	33	3	15	77	10	0	8	2	39	4	64	3	5	8	.481	.351
Booker, Gregory, S.D.	.000	44	6	0	0	0	0	0	0	0	0	0	0	0	0	0	2	0	0	0	.000	.000
Booker, Roderick, St.L.*	.277	44	47	9	13	16	1	1	0	8	0	7	0	0	7	0	7	2	0	0	.340	.370
Bream, Sidney, Pitt.*	.275	149	516	64	142	212	25	3	13	65	3	3	4	3	49	11	69	9	8	19	.411	.336
Brenly, Robert, S.F.	.267	123	375	55	100	175	19	1	18	51	8	3	6	6	47	3	85	10	7	5	.467	.348
Brooks, Hubert, Mtl.	.263	112	430	57	113	183	22	3	14	72	10	3	4	3	24	2	72	4	3	7	.426	.301
Brown, Curtis, Mtl.		5	0	0	0	0	0	0	0	0	0	0	0	0	0	0	0	0	0	0		
Brown, J. Christopher, S.F.-S.D.	.237	82	287	34	68	113	9	0	12	40	4	3	0	6	20	1	46	4	4	14	.394	.299
Browning, Thomas, Cin.*	.154	34	52	2	8	10	0	1	0	6	0	6	0	0	3	0	21	2	1	1	.192	.200
Brumley, A. Michael, Chi.†	.202	39	104	8	21	30	2	2	1	9	1	1	1	1	10	2	30	7	1	2	.288	.276
Bryant, Ralph, L.A.*	.246	46	69	7	17	27	2	1	2	10	0	2	0	1	10	2	24	4	1	0	.391	.346
Burke, Timothy, Mtl.	.000	55	10	0	0	0	0	0	0	0	0	1	0	0	0	0	6	0	0	0	.000	.000
Burkett, John, S.F.	.000	3	1	0	0	0	0	0	0	0	0	0	0	0	0	0	1	0	0	0	.000	.000

Player, Club	AVG.	G	AB	R	H	TB	2B	3B	HR	RBI	GW RBI	SH	SF	HP	BB	IB	SO	SB	CS	GI DP	SLG	OBP
Butera, Salvatore, Cin.	.182	5	11	1	2	5	0	0	0	2	0	0	0	0	1	0	6	0	0	0	.455	.250
Byers, Randell, S.D.*	.313	10	16	1	5	6	1	0	0	2	0	0	0	0	1	0	5	1	0	0	.375	.353
Calhoun, Jeffrey, Phil.*	.000	42	1	0	0	0	0	0	0	0	0	0	0	0	0	0	1	0	0	0	.000	.000
Caminiti, Kenneth, Hou.†	.246	63	203	10	50	68	7	0	3	23	2	2	1	0	12	1	44	0	0	6	.335	.287
Campbell, William, Mtl.	.000	7	1	0	0	0	0	0	0	0	0	0	0	0	1	0	1	0	0	0	.000	.500
Candaele, Casey, Mtl.†	.272	138	449	62	122	156	23	4	1	18	2	2	2	0	38	3	28	7	10	5	.347	.330
Candelaria, John, N.Y.	.200	3	5	0	1	1	0	0	0	0	0	1	0	0	0	0	0	0	0	0	.200	.200
Cangelosi, John, Pitt.†	.275	104	182	44	50	76	8	3	4	4	1	0	1	3	46	1	33	21	6	3	.418	.427
Carman, Donald, Phil.*	.082	35	61	2	5	5	0	0	0	1	0	1	0	0	1	0	23	0	1	2	.082	.111
Carreon, Mark, N.Y.	.250	9	12	0	3	3	0	0	0	0	0	0	0	0	1	0	1	1	1	0	.250	.308
Carter, Gary, N.Y.	.235	139	523	55	123	205	18	2	20	83	9	1	6	0	42	0	73	0	1	14	.392	.290
Cary, Charles, Atl.*	.000	13	1	0	0	0	0	0	0	0	0	0	0	0	0	0	0	0	0	0	.000	.000
Childress, Rodney, Hou.	.000	32	2	0	0	0	0	0	0	0	0	0	0	0	0	0	0	0	0	0	.000	.000
Clark, Jack, St.L.	.286	131	419	93	120	250	23	1	35	106	15	0	3	3	136	13	139	1	2	5	.597	.459
Clark, William, S.F.*	.308	150	529	89	163	307	29	5	35	91	11	3	2	5	49	11	98	5	17	2	.580	.371
Clary, Martin, Atl.	.000	7	7	0	0	0	0	0	0	0	0	1	0	0	0	0	0	0	0	0	.000	.000
Coffman, Kevin, Atl.	.100	5	10	0	1	1	0	0	0	0	0	2	0	0	1	0	5	0	0	0	.100	.182
Coleman, Vincent, St.L.†	.289	151	623	121	180	223	14	10	3	43	2	5	1	3	70	2	126	109	22	7	.358	.363
Coles, Darnell, Pitt.	.227	40	119	20	27	53	8	0	6	24	2	3	2	1	19	0	20	9	3	3	.445	.333
Collins, David, Cin.†	.294	57	85	19	25	30	5	0	0	5	0	2	0	2	11	0	12	9	1	1	.353	.388
Comstock, Keith, S.F.-S.D.*	.000	41	2	0	0	0	0	0	0	0	0	1	0	0	0	0	1	0	0	0	.000	.000
Concepcion, David, Cin.	.319	104	279	32	89	107	15	1	1	33	4	3	3	0	28	1	24	4	4	10	.384	.377
Concepcion, Onix, Pitt.	1.000	1	1	0	1	1	0	0	0	0	0	0	0	0	0	0	0	0	0	0	1.000	1.000
Cone, David, N.Y.*	.065	21	31	0	2	3	1	0	0	0	0	3	0	0	0	0	14	0	0	1	.097	.094
Conroy, Timothy, St.L.*	.000	10	15	0	0	0	0	0	0	0	0	1	0	0	0	0	8	0	0	0	.000	.000
Cora, Jose, S.D.†	.237	77	241	23	57	68	7	2	0	13	1	4	0	1	28	1	26	15	11	4	.282	.317
Cowley, Joseph, Phil.	.333	5	3	0	1	2	1	0	0	0	0	0	0	0	0	0	0	0	0	0	.667	.333
Cox, Danny, St.L.	.116	32	69	3	8	10	2	0	0	1	0	10	0	0	1	0	25	0	0	0	.145	.129
Crews, Timothy, L.A.	.000	20	2	0	0	0	0	0	0	0	0	1	0	0	0	0	2	0	0	0	.000	.000
Cruz, Jose, Hou.†	.241	126	365	47	88	146	17	4	11	38	5	0	3	0	36	3	65	4	5	4	.400	.307
Daniels, Kalvoski, Cin.*	.334	108	368	73	123	227	24	1	26	64	3	0	0	2	60	11	62	26	8	6	.617	.429
Darling, Ronald, N.Y.	.123	32	65	5	8	13	5	0	0	4	0	4	0	0	2	0	22	0	0	0	.200	.149
Darwin, Danny, Hou.	.182	35	66	2	12	16	2	1	0	4	1	0	0	0	2	0	40	1	0	0	.242	.206
Daugherty, John, Mtl.†	.100	11	10	1	1	2	1	0	0	1	0	0	0	0	0	0	3	0	0	0	.200	.100
Daulton, Darren, Phil.*	.194	53	129	10	25	40	6	0	3	13	2	1	0	2	16	1	37	0	0	0	.310	.281
Davis, Charles, S.F.†	.250	149	500	80	125	221	22	1	24	76	5	0	4	2	72	15	109	16	9	8	.442	.344
Davis, Eric, Cin.	.293	129	474	120	139	281	23	4	37	100	10	0	3	1	84	8	134	50	6	6	.593	.399
Davis, George, S.D.	.063	21	16	1	1	1	0	0	0	1	0	1	0	0	0	0	10	4	1	0	.063	.063
Davis, Glenn, Hou.	.251	151	578	70	145	265	35	2	27	93	11	0	5	5	47	10	84	0	2	16	.458	.310
Davis, Jody, Chi.	.248	125	428	57	106	179	12	0	19	51	5	1	2	2	52	2	91	1	0	14	.418	.331
Davis, Mark, S.F.-S.D.*	.233	64	30	3	7	10	1	0	0	1	0	2	0	0	0	0	6	0	0	0	.333	.233
Davis, Ronald, Chi.-L.A.	.000	25	3	0	0	0	0	0	0	0	0	1	0	0	0	0	0	0	0	0	.000	.000
Davis, Trench, Atl.*	.143	6	7	3	1	2	0	0	0	0	0	0	0	0	1	0	1	0	0	0	.286	.250
Davis, Wallace, Pitt.	.167	7	12	1	2	2	0	0	0	1	0	0	0	0	2	0	3	0	0	0	.167	.286
Dawley, William, St.L.	.000	60	2	0	0	0	0	0	0	0	0	1	0	0	0	0	2	0	0	0	.000	.000
Dawson, Andre, Chi.	.287	153	621	90	178	353	24	2	49	137	16	0	2	7	32	7	103	11	3	15	.568	.328
Dayett, Brian, Chi.	.277	97	177	20	49	80	14	1	5	25	3	0	1	0	20	0	37	0	0	3	.452	.348
Dayley, Kenneth, St.L.*	.222	53	9	1	2	4	2	0	0	0	0	1	0	0	0	0	0	0	0	0	.444	.222
DeCinces, Douglas, St.L.	.250	4	16	2	4	5	1	0	0	1	0	0	0	0	1	0	2	0	0	0	.313	.294
Dedmon, Jeffrey, Atl.*	.000	53	3	0	0	0	0	0	0	0	0	0	0	0	0	0	3	0	0	0	.000	.000

Player, Club	AVG.	G	AB	R	H	TB	2B	3B	HR	RBI	GW RBI	SH	SF	HP	BB	IB	SO	SB	CS	GI DP	SLG	OBP
DeJesus, Ivan, S.F.	.200	9	10	0	2	2	0	0	0	1	0	0	0	0	0	0	2	0	1	0	.200	.200
Dernier, Robert, Chi.	.317	93	199	38	63	99	4	4	8	21	5	4	0	1	19	0	19	16	7	4	.497	.379
Deshaies, James, Hou.*	.094	26	53	2	5	5	0	0	0	3	0	4	0	0	7	0	29	0	0	1	.094	.200
Devereaux, Michael, L.A.	.222	19	54	7	12	15	3	0	0	4	1	1	0	0	3	1	10	3	1	0	.278	.263
Diaz, Baudilio, Cin.	.270	140	496	49	134	209	28	1	15	82	4	0	6	5	19	3	73	1	0	16	.421	.300
Diaz, Michael, Pitt.	.241	103	241	28	58	118	8	2	16	48	6	0	7	3	31	0	42	0	0	6	.490	.326
DiPino, Frank, Chi.*	.500	69	2	0	1	1	0	0	0	0	0	1	0	0	0	0	0	0	0	0	.500	.500
Doran, William, Hou.†	.283	162	625	82	177	254	23	3	16	79	13	2	7	3	82	3	64	31	11	11	.406	.365
Dowell, Kenneth, Phil.	.128	15	39	4	5	5	0	0	0	1	0	1	0	0	2	0	5	0	0	1	.128	.171
Downs, Kelly, S.F.	.143	41	56	1	8	9	1	0	0	6	1	7	1	0	1	0	23	0	0	0	.161	.155
Drabek, Douglas, Pitt.	.119	30	59	2	7	8	1	0	0	4	0	7	0	0	2	0	24	0	1	1	.136	.159
Dravecky, David, S.D.-S.F.	.143	49	56	3	8	9	1	0	0	0	0	4	1	0	4	0	27	0	0	0	.161	.200
Driessen, Daniel, St.L.*	.233	24	60	5	14	19	2	0	1	11	1	4	0	0	7	0	8	1	0	2	.317	.309
Drummond, Timothy, Pitt	.000	6	1	0	0	0	0	0	0	0	0	0	0	0	0	0	1	0	0	0	.000	.000
Duncan, Mariano, L.A.†	.215	76	261	31	56	84	8	1	6	18	3	0	2	2	17	1	62	11	1	4	.322	.267
Dunne, Michael, Pitt.	.094	23	53	2	5	7	2	0	0	3	0	6	2	0	5	0	18	0	0	0	.132	.172
Dunston, Shawon, Chi.	.246	95	346	40	85	124	18	3	5	22	4	7	2	2	10	1	68	12	3	6	.358	.267
Durham, Leon, Chi.*	.273	131	439	70	120	225	22	1	27	63	5	0	2	0	51	9	92	8	3	6	.513	.348
Dykstra, Leonard, N.Y.*	.285	132	431	86	123	196	37	3	10	43	4	4	1	4	40	3	67	27	7	2	.455	.352
Easler, Michael, Phil.*	.282	33	110	7	31	38	5	1	0	10	0	0	0	0	6	3	20	0	1	6	.345	.316
Easley, K. Logan, Pitt.	.000	17	2	0	0	0	0	0	0	0	0	0	0	0	0	0	1	0	0	1	.000	.000
Edens, Thomas, N.Y.	.000	2	3	0	0	0	0	0	0	0	0	0	0	0	0	0	3	0	0	0	.000	.000
Elster, Kevin, N.Y.	.400	5	10	1	4	6	2	0	0	1	1	0	0	0	0	0	1	1	0	1	.600	.400
Engle, R. David, Mtl.	.226	59	84	7	19	26	4	0	1	14	5	0	1	0	6	0	11	0	1	5	.310	.278
Esasky, Nicholas, Cin.	.272	100	346	48	94	183	19	2	22	59	5	2	0	2	29	7	76	2	3	10	.529	.327
Fermin, Felix, Pitt.	.250	23	68	6	17	17	0	0	0	4	0	2	1	1	4	1	9	0	0	3	.250	.301
Fernandez, C. Sidney, N.Y.*	.163	29	43	2	7	10	1	1	0	2	1	10	0	2	0	0	19	0	0	2	.233	.178
Fischer, Jeffrey, Mtl.	.200	4	5	0	1	1	0	0	0	0	0	0	0	1	0	0	2	0	0	0	.200	.200
Fischlin, Michael, Atl.	----	1	0	0	0	0	0	0	0	0	0	0	0	1	0	0	0	0	0	0	----	----
Fisher, Brian, Pitt.	.190	37	58	6	11	18	1	0	2	9	1	5	0	0	5	0	28	0	1	0	.310	.277
Fitzgerald, Michael, Mtl.	.240	107	287	32	69	89	11	0	3	36	5	3	3	2	42	7	54	2	4	10	.310	.338
Flannery, Timothy, S.D.*	.228	106	276	23	63	70	5	1	0	20	5	4	3	0	42	4	30	3	4	6	.254	.332
Foley, Thomas, Mtl.*	.293	106	280	35	82	121	18	3	5	28	5	1	1	0	11	4	40	9	10	6	.432	.322
Ford, Curtis, St.L.*	.285	89	228	32	65	93	9	2	5	26	3	1	2	1	14	0	32	6	8	5	.408	.325
Forsch, Robert, St.L	.298	34	57	9	17	29	6	0	2	8	1	11	3	0	3	0	17	0	0	1	.509	.333
Franco, John, Cin.*	.000	68	2	0	0	0	0	0	0	0	0	1	0	0	0	0	1	0	0	0	.000	.000
Francona, Terry, Cin.*	.227	102	207	16	47	61	5	0	3	12	4	0	0	0	10	1	12	2	0	5	.295	.266
Frohwirth, Todd, Phil	.000	10	1	0	0	0	0	0	0	0	0	1	0	0	0	0	1	0	0	0	.000	.000
Gainey, Telmanch, Hou.*	.125	18	24	1	3	3	0	0	0	1	0	0	0	1	2	0	9	1	1	0	.125	.192
Galarraga, Andres, Mtl.	.305	147	551	72	168	253	40	3	13	90	9	1	4	0	41	13	127	7	10	11	.459	.361
Gant, Ronald, Atl.	.265	21	83	9	22	32	2	1	2	9	1	0	0	0	1	0	11	4	2	2	.386	.271
Garber, H. Eugene, Atl.	.000	49	4	0	0	0	0	0	0	0	0	0	1	0	1	0	2	0	0	0	.000	.200
Garcia, Leonardo, Cin.*	.200	31	30	8	6	9	3	0	0	2	2	0	0	0	4	0	8	3	1	3	.300	.286
Garcia, Miguel, Pitt.*	----	1	0	0	0	0	0	0	0	0	0	0	0	0	0	0	0	0	0	0	----	----
Garner, Philip, Hou.-L.A.	.206	113	238	29	49	73	9	0	5	23	4	5	4	0	28	8	44	6	6	5	.307	.285
Garrelts, Scott, S.F.	.200	65	10	1	2	3	1	0	0	2	0	0	0	0	0	0	5	0	0	0	.300	.200
Garvey, Steven, S.D.	.211	27	76	5	16	21	2	0	1	9	2	0	0	1	1	1	10	0	0	3	.276	.231
Gibson, Robert, N.Y.	----	1	0	0	0	0	0	0	0	0	0	0	0	0	0	0	0	0	0	0	----	----
Gideon, B. Brett, Pitt.	1.000	29	1	0	1	1	0	0	0	2	0	0	0	0	0	0	0	0	0	0	1.000	1.000
Glavine, Thomas, Atl.*	.125	9	16	0	2	2	0	0	0	1	0	0	0	0	1	0	4	0	0	0	.125	.176

Player, Club	AVG.	G	AB	R	H	TB	2B	3B	HR	RBI	GW RBI	SH	SF	HP	BB	IB	SO	SB	CS	GI DP	SLG	OBP
Gonzalez, Denio, Pitt.	.000	5	7	1	0	0	0	0	0	0	0	0	0	0	1	0	2	0	0	0	.000	.125
Gonzalez, Jose, L.A.	.188	19	16	2	3	5	2	0	0	1	0	0	1	0	1	0	2	5	0	1	.313	.222
Gooden, Dwight, N.Y.	.219	25	64	4	14	14	0	0	0	4	0	5	0	0	0	0	9	0	0	1	.219	.227
Gorman, Thomas, S.D.*	.....	6	0	0	0	0	0	0	0	0	0	0	0	0	0	0	0	0	0	0	.....	.....
Gossage, Richard, S.D.	.000	40	4	0	0	0	0	0	0	0	0	0	0	0	0	0	2	0	0	0	.000	.000
Gott, James, S.F.-Pitt.	.091	55	11	1	1	1	0	0	0	0	0	0	0	0	0	0	4	0	0	0	.091	.091
Grant, Mark, S.F.-S.D.	.091	34	44	2	4	4	0	0	0	2	0	6	0	0	3	0	16	0	1	0	.091	.149
Green, David, St.L.	.267	14	30	4	8	15	1	0	2	1	0	0	0	0	2	0	5	0	0	0	.500	.313
Gregg, W. Thomas, Pitt.*	.250	10	8	3	2	3	1	0	0	0	0	1	0	0	0	0	1	1	0	0	.375	.250
Griffey, G. Kenneth, Atl.*	.286	122	399	65	114	182	24	1	14	64	8	0	4	1	46	11	54	4	7	12	.456	.358
Gross, Gregory, Phil.*	.286	114	133	14	38	47	4	1	1	12	1	1	3	0	25	4	12	0	0	2	.353	.395
Gross, Kevin, Phil.	.190	34	63	4	12	16	1	0	1	4	1	8	0	0	2	0	25	0	0	2	.254	.215
Guerrero, Pedro, L.A.	.338	152	545	89	184	294	25	2	27	89	11	0	7	4	74	18	85	9	7	16	.539	.416
Gullickson, William, Cin.	.208	27	53	4	11	16	2	0	1	3	0	4	0	0	0	0	11	0	0	2	.302	.208
Gwynn, Anthony, S.D.*	.370	157	589	119	218	301	36	13	7	54	5	2	4	3	82	26	35	56	12	13	.511	.447
Gwynn, Christopher, L.A.*	.219	17	32	5	7	8	1	0	0	2	0	1	1	0	1	0	7	0	1	0	.250	.242
Hall, Albert, Atl.†	.284	92	292	54	83	120	20	4	3	24	2	4	1	2	38	3	36	33	10	5	.411	.369
Hall, Andrew, Chi.*	.000	21	4	0	0	0	0	0	0	0	0	0	0	0	0	0	3	0	0	0	.000	.000
Hamilton, Jeffrey, L.A.	.217	35	83	5	18	21	3	0	1	1	0	2	0	1	0	0	22	0	0	1	.253	.286
Hammaker, C. Atlee, S.F.†	.123	31	57	8	7	7	0	0	0	3	0	7	0	0	1	0	11	0	1	0	.123	.138
Harper, Terry, Pitt.	.288	36	66	8	19	25	3	0	1	7	0	0	0	0	7	1	19	2	3	6	.379	.356
Hatcher, Michael, L.A.	.282	101	287	27	81	123	19	1	7	42	3	3	3	1	20	4	21	2	3	6	.429	.328
Hatcher, William, Hou.	.296	141	564	96	167	234	28	3	11	63	6	7	5	9	42	1	70	53	9	11	.415	.352
Havens, Bradley, L.A.*	.000	31	2	1	0	0	0	0	0	0	0	0	0	0	0	0	1	0	0	0	.000	.000
Hawkins, M. Andrew, S.D.	.156	24	32	2	5	5	0	0	0	0	0	5	0	0	0	0	11	0	0	0	.156	.156
Hayes, Von, Phil.*	.277	158	556	84	154	263	36	5	21	84	6	0	4	3	121	12	77	16	7	12	.473	.404
Hayward, Raymond, S.D.*	.000	4	1	0	0	0	0	0	0	0	0	1	0	0	0	0	0	0	0	1	.000	.000
Heathcock, R. Jeffrey, Hou.	.000	19	10	0	0	0	0	0	0	0	0	6	0	0	0	0	4	0	0	0	.000	.000
Heaton, Neal, Mtl.*	.209	32	67	6	14	16	2	0	0	6	3	6	0	0	1	0	14	1	0	6	.239	.221
Heep, Daniel, L.A.*	.163	60	98	7	16	20	4	0	0	9	0	0	0	0	8	0	10	2	0	0	.204	.226
Henderson, David, S.F.	.238	15	21	2	5	7	2	0	0	1	0	0	0	0	8	0	5	0	0	1	.333	.448
Heredia, Ubaldo, Mtl.	.000	2	2	0	0	0	0	0	0	0	0	0	0	0	0	0	1	0	0	0	.000	.000
Hernandez, Keith, N.Y.*	.290	154	587	87	170	256	28	2	18	89	13	0	4	0	81	8	104	0	2	15	.436	.377
Hernandez, Manuel, Hou.	.000	6	5	0	0	0	0	0	0	0	0	0	0	0	0	0	3	0	0	0	.000	.000
Herr, Thomas, St.L.†	.263	141	510	73	134	169	29	0	2	83	14	3	12	0	68	3	62	19	4	12	.331	.346
Hershiser, Orel, L.A.	.211	40	90	10	19	24	5	0	0	7	1	10	0	0	2	0	17	1	0	1	.267	.228
Hesketh, Joseph, Mtl.*	.000	18	4	0	0	0	0	0	0	0	0	1	0	0	0	0	3	0	0	0	.000	.000
Hillegas, Shawn, L.A.	.125	12	14	0	0	0	0	0	0	0	0	5	0	0	0	0	10	0	1	4	.000	.125
Hoffman, Glenn, L.A.	.220	40	132	10	29	34	5	0	0	10	4	3	0	2	2	0	23	0	0	0	.258	.270
Hoffman, Guy, Cin.*	.111	36	45	2	5	6	1	0	0	5	2	0	0	0	7	1	15	0	1	4	.133	.111
Holton, Brian, L.A.	.200	53	5	0	1	1	0	0	0	1	0	3	0	0	0	0	1	0	1	0	.200	.200
Honeycutt, Frederick, L.A.*	.233	27	30	3	7	8	1	0	0	2	0	3	0	0	2	0	8	0	1	0	.267	.281
Horton, Ricky, St.L.*	.172	68	29	2	5	6	1	0	0	2	1	4	0	0	4	0	9	2	0	1	.207	.200
Householder, Paul, Hou.†	.083	14	12	1	1	2	0	0	0	1	0	4	0	6	0	0	2	0	1	0	.167	.200
Howell, Kenneth, L.A.	.250	40	4	1	1	1	0	0	0	0	0	4	0	1	7	0	1	0	0	0	.250	.250
Hubbard, Glenn, Atl.	.264	141	443	69	117	169	33	2	5	38	4	0	3	3	77	17	57	1	1	11	.381	.378
Hughes, Keith, Phil.*	.263	37	76	8	20	22	2	0	0	10	2	0	0	6	1	0	11	0	0	1	.289	.333
Hume, Thomas, Phil.-Cin.	.200	49	15	1	3	4	1	0	0	0	0	0	0	0	0	0	4	0	0	0	.267	.200
Hurdle, Clinton, N.Y.*	.333	3	3	0	1	1	0	0	0	0	0	0	0	0	0	0	1	0	0	0	.333	.333
Innis, Jeffrey, N.Y.	.000	17	3	0	0	0	0	0	0	0	0	0	0	0	0	0	1	0	0	0	.000	.000

Player, Club	AVG.	G	AB	R	H	TB	2B	3B	HR	RBI	GW RBI	SH	SF	HP	BB	IB	SO	SB	CS	GI DP	SLG	OBP
Jackson, Charles, Hou.	.211	35	71	3	15	21	3	0	0	6	0	3	0	0	7	0	19	1	1	0	.296	.282
Jackson, Darrin, Chi.	.800	7	5	2	4	5	1	0	0	1	0	0	0	0	0	0	0	0	0	0	1.000	.800
Jackson, Kenneth, Phil.	.250	8	16	1	4	6	2	0	0	0	1	0	0	1	1	1	4	0	0	0	.375	.333
Jackson, Michael, Phil.	.118	55	17	2	2	2	0	0	0	2	0	3	0	1	1	0	3	0	0	8	.118	.167
James, Dion, Atl.*	.312	134	494	80	154	233	37	6	10	61	3	5	3	2	70	2	63	10	8	4	.472	.397
James, D. Christopher, Phil.	.293	115	358	48	105	188	20	6	17	54	2	1	3	2	27	0	67	3	1	6	.525	.344
Jefferies, Gregg, N.Y.†	.500	6	6	0	3	4	1	0	0	2	0	0	0	0	0	0	0	0	0	0	.667	.500
Jefferson, Stanley, S.D.†	.230	116	422	59	97	143	8	7	8	29	4	3	3	2	39	2	92	34	11	6	.339	.296
Jelks, Gregory, Phil.	.091	10	11	2	1	2	1	0	0	0	0	0	0	0	0	0	4	1	0	0	.182	.286
Jeltz, L. Steven, Phil.†	.232	114	293	37	68	89	9	6	0	12	2	4	0	0	39	4	54	0	2	13	.304	.324
Jimenez, Alfonso, Pitt.	.000	5	6	0	0	0	0	0	0	0	0	0	0	0	0	0	2	0	0	0	.000	.143
Johnson, David, Pitt.		5	0	0	0	0	0	0	0	0	0	0	0	0	1	0	0	0	0	0		
Johnson, Howard, N.Y.†	.265	157	554	93	147	279	22	1	36	99	16	0	3	5	83	18	113	32	10	8	.504	.364
Johnson, K. Lance, St.L.*	.220	33	59	4	13	17	2	0	0	7	1	0	0	0	4	1	6	6	1	0	.288	.270
Johnson, Wallace, Mtl.†	.247	75	85	7	21	29	5	0	1	14	1	0	2	0	7	1	6	5	0	0	.341	.298
Jones, Barry, Pitt.	.000	32	3	0	0	0	0	0	0	0	0	0	0	0	1	0	1	0	0	0	.000	.250
Jones, James, S.D.	.163	32	49	7	8	11	0	0	1	3	1	8	0	0	2	0	18	0	0	0	.224	.196
Jones, Tracy, Cin.	.290	117	359	53	104	157	17	3	10	44	7	0	5	3	23	4	40	31	8	10	.437	.333
Kerfeld, Charles, Hou.	.000	21	3	0	0	0	0	0	0	0	0	0	0	0	0	0	1	0	0	0	.000	.000
Khalifa, Sam, Pitt.	.176	5	17	1	3	3	0	0	0	2	0	3	0	0	0	0	2	0	0	0	.176	.176
Kipper, Robert, Pitt.	.242	26	33	3	8	10	2	0	0	0	1	9	0	0	1	0	12	0	0	0	.303	.242
Knepper, Robert, Hou.*	.098	33	51	2	5	7	2	0	0	1	0	0	0	0	0	0	24	0	0	0	.137	.113
Krueger, William, L.A.*		2	0	0	0	0	0	0	0	0	0	0	0	0	1	0	0	0	0	0		
Kruk, John, S.D.*	.313	138	447	72	140	218	14	2	20	91	5	3	4	1	73	15	93	18	10	6	.488	.406
Krukow, Michael, S.F.	.167	30	54	1	9	11	2	0	0	7	1	5	0	0	2	0	27	0	0	0	.204	.196
Kutcher, Randy, S.F.	.188	14	16	7	3	6	0	0	1	1	0	0	0	0	1	0	5	1	1	1	.375	.235
LaCoss, Michael, S.F.	.060	39	50	2	3	3	0	0	0	3	1	4	2	0	2	0	16	0	0	1	.060	.113
Laga, Michael, St.L.*	.138	17	29	4	4	8	1	0	2	4	0	0	1	0	2	1	7	0	0	2	.276	.182
Lake, Steven, St.L.	.251	74	179	19	45	62	7	1	2	19	2	5	0	1	10	4	18	0	0	0	.346	.289
Lancaster, Lester, Chi.	.082	27	49	2	4	5	1	0	0	2	0	1	2	0	1	0	19	0	3	1	.102	.100
Landreaux, Kenneth, L.A.*	.203	115	182	17	37	59	4	2	6	23	4	3	1	0	16	2	28	5	3	2	.324	.269
Landrum, Terry, St.L.-L.A.	.222	81	117	13	26	33	4	0	1	10	2	1	2	1	10	2	30	3	2	1	.282	.289
Landrum, T. William, Cin.	.200	44	5	0	1	1	0	0	0	0	1	0	0	1	0	0	0	0	0	1	.200	.200
LaPoint, David, St.L.*	.000	6	4	0	0	0	0	0	0	0	0	1	2	0	0	0	3	0	0	0	.000	.000
Larkin, Barry, Cin.	.244	125	439	64	107	163	16	2	12	43	9	5	3	5	36	3	52	21	6	8	.371	.306
LaValliere, Michael, Pitt.*	.300	121	340	33	102	124	19	0	1	36	5	3	3	1	43	9	32	0	0	4	.365	.377
Law, Vance, Mtl.	.273	133	436	52	119	184	27	2	12	56	6	2	3	0	51	5	62	8	5	8	.422	.347
Lawless, Thomas, St.L.	.080	19	25	5	2	3	1	0	0	0	0	0	0	0	3	0	5	2	0	1	.120	.179
Lea, Charles, Mtl.		1	0	0	0	0	0	0	0	0	0	0	0	0	0	0	0	0	0	0		
Leach, Terry, N.Y.	.061	44	33	1	2	2	0	0	0	0	0	4	0	0	2	0	14	0	0	0	.061	.114
Leary, Timothy, L.A.	.304	39	23	1	7	8	1	0	0	5	0	3	0	0	0	0	5	0	0	0	.348	.304
Lefferts, Craig, S.D.-S.F.*	.286	77	7	0	2	3	1	0	0	1	0	0	0	0	0	0	4	0	0	0	.429	.286
Legg, Gregory, Phil.	.000	3	2	1	0	0	0	0	0	0	0	0	0	0	0	0	0	0	0	0	.000	.000
Leiper, David, S.D.*		12	0	0	0	0	0	0	0	0	0	0	0	0	0	0	0	0	0	0		
Leonard, Jeffrey, S.F.	.280	131	503	70	141	235	29	4	19	63	6	0	5	2	21	6	68	16	7	17	.467	.309
Lind, Jose, Pitt.	.322	35	143	21	46	62	8	4	0	11	0	6	0	0	8	0	12	2	1	5	.434	.358
Lindeman, James, St.L.	.208	75	207	20	43	80	13	0	8	28	4	2	4	3	11	2	56	3	1	4	.386	.253
Lopes, David, Hou.	.233	47	43	4	10	15	2	0	1	6	0	0	0	0	13	0	8	2	0	0	.349	.411
Lopez, Aurelio, Hou.	.000	26	1	0	0	0	0	0	0	0	0	1	0	0	0	0	1	0	0	0	.000	.000
Lynch, Edward, Chi.	.188	58	16	1	3	3	0	0	0	0	0	2	0	0	0	0	9	0	0	0	.188	.188

Player, Club	AVG	G	AB	R	H	TB	2B	3B	HR	RBI	GW RBI	SH	SF	HP	BB	IB	SO	SB	CS	GI DP	SLG	OBP
Lyons, Barry, N.Y.	.254	53	130	15	33	51	4	1	4	24	2	0	3	2	8	1	24	0	0	1	.392	.301
Mack, Shane, S.D.	.239	105	238	28	57	86	11	3	4	25	3	6	2	3	18	0	47	4	6	11	.361	.299
Maddux, Gregory, Chi.	.119	34	42	3	5	5	0	0	0	2	1	7	0	0	0	0	9	0	1	0	.119	.119
Maddux, Michael, Phil.	.000	7	3	0	0	0	0	0	0	0	0	1	0	0	0	0	2	0	0	0	.000	.000
Madlock, Bill, L.A.	.180	21	61	5	11	21	1	0	3	7	1	1	0	1	6	0	5	0	0	4	.344	.265
Magadan, David, N.Y.*	.318	85	192	21	61	85	13	1	3	24	4	0	1	0	22	2	22	0	0	5	.443	.386
Magrane, Joseph, St.L.	.135	28	52	5	7	12	2	0	1	3	0	6	0	0	4	0	22	0	0	1	.231	.196
Mahler, Richard, Atl.	.169	40	65	4	11	15	4	0	0	5	0	7	1	0	2	0	19	0	0	0	.231	.194
Maldonado, Candido, S.F.	.292	118	442	69	129	225	28	4	20	85	12	0	7	6	34	4	78	8	8	9	.509	.346
Mallicoat, Robin, Hou.*		4																				
Manwaring, Kirt, S.F.	.143	6	7	0	1	1	0	0	0	0	0	0	0	1	0	0	1	0	0	0	.143	.250
Marshall, Michael, L.A.	.294	104	402	45	118	185	19	0	16	72	8	1	4	4	18	2	79	0	0	13	.460	.327
Martinez, Carmelo, S.D.	.273	139	447	59	122	192	21	2	15	70	7	1	4	3	70	5	82	5	5	11	.430	.372
Martinez, David, Chi.*	.292	142	459	70	134	192	18	8	8	36	6	4	1	2	57	4	96	16	5	3	.418	.372
Martinez, J. Dennis, Mtl.	.065	22	46	5	3	3	0	0	0	0	0	3	0	0	3	0	17	0	0	0	.065	.122
Mason, Michael, Chi.*	.222	18	9	1	2	2	0	0	0	0	0	0	0	0	1	0	4	0	0	0	.222	.300
Mason, Roger, S.F.	.125	5	8	0	1	1	0	0	0	3	0	7	0	0	1	0	3	0	0	0	.125	.222
Mathews, Gregory, St.L.	.191	32	68	5	13	14	1	0	0	8	0	0	0	0	3	0	21	0	0	1	.206	.225
Mathis, Ronald, Hou.	.000	8	2	0	0	0	0	0	0	0	0	0	0	0	0	0	1	0	0	0	.000	.000
Matthews, Gary, Chi.	.262	44	42	3	11	14	3	0	0	8	3	0	0	0	4	0	11	0	0	3	.333	.326
Matuszek, Leonard, L.A.*	.067	16	15	0	1	1	0	0	0	0	0	1	0	0	1	0	4	0	0	0	.067	.125
Mazzilli, Lee, N.Y.†	.306	88	124	26	38	57	8	1	3	24	3	0	3	0	21	3	14	5	3	1	.460	.399
McClendon, Lloyd, Cin.	.208	45	72	8	15	26	5	0	2	13	0	2	1	0	4	0	15	1	0	0	.361	.247
McClure, Robert, Mtl.	.000	52	2	0	0	0	0	0	0	0	0	1	0	1	0	0	0	0	0	0	.000	.000
McCullers, Lance, S.D.	.071	78	14	1	1	1	0	0	0	1	0	0	0	0	1	0	5	0	0	0	.071	.133
McDowell, Roger, N.Y.	.231	56	13	1	3	4	1	0	0	0	0	0	0	0	1	0	5	0	0	0	.308	.286
McGaffigan, Andrew, Mtl.	.000	69	17	0	0	0	0	0	0	0	0	3	0	0	0	0	12	0	0	0	.000	.000
McGee, Willie, St.L.†	.285	153	620	76	177	269	37	11	11	105	8	1	5	2	24	5	90	16	9	24	.434	.312
McGriff, Terence, Cin.	.225	34	89	6	20	29	3	0	2	11	1	0	0	0	8	0	17	0	0	3	.326	.289
McReynolds, W. Kevin, N.Y.	.276	151	590	86	163	292	32	5	29	95	9	7	8	1	39	5	70	14	6	13	.495	.318
McWilliams, Larry, Atl.*	.200	9	5	0	1	1	0	0	0	0	0	1	0	0	0	0	2	0	0	0	.200	.200
Meads, David, Hou.*	.333	45	3	1	1	1	0	0	0	1	0	0	0	0	1	0	1	0	0	0	.333	.500
Melendez, Francisco, S.F.*	.313	12	16	2	5	8	1	1	0	0	0	3	0	0	0	0	3	0	0	0	.500	.313
Melvin, Robert, S.F.	.199	84	246	31	49	90	8	0	11	31	6	1	2	0	17	3	44	3	0	7	.366	.249
Mercado, Orlando, L.A.	.600	7	5	3	3	4	1	0	0	1	0	0	0	0	1	0	1	0	0	0	.800	.667
Miller, Keith, N.Y.	.373	25	51	14	19	25	2	2	0	0	0	3	0	1	2	0	6	8	3	2	.490	.407
Milligan, Randy, N.Y.	.000	3	1	0	0	0	0	0	0	0	0	0	0	0	0	0	1	0	0	0	.000	.000
Milner, Eddie, S.F.*	.252	101	214	38	54	80	14	0	4	19	4	5	0	0	24	3	33	10	9	10	.374	.328
Minton, Gregory, S.F.†	.000	15	2	0	0	0	0	0	0	0	0	0	0	0	0	0	1	0	0	0	.000	.000
Mitchell, John, N.Y.	.114	20	35	1	4	5	1	0	0	1	0	3	0	0	0	0	14	0	0	0	.143	.114
Mitchell, Kevin, S.D.-S.F.	.280	131	464	68	130	220	20	2	22	70	6	2	0	2	48	4	88	9	3	15	.474	.350
Montgomery, Jeffrey, Cin.	.000	14	2	0	0	0	0	0	0	0	0	1	0	0	0	0	1	0	0	0	.000	.000
Moreland, B. Keith, Chi.	.266	153	563	63	150	262	29	1	27	88	7	0	9	0	39	4	66	3	2	15	.465	.309
Morris, John, St.L.*	.261	101	157	22	41	64	6	4	3	23	2	0	0	1	11	3	22	5	0	2	.408	.314
Morrison, James, Pitt.	.264	96	348	41	92	143	22	1	9	46	6	1	5	1	27	3	57	8	5	9	.411	.315
Motley, Darryl, Atl.	.000	6	8	0	0	0	0	0	0	1	0	0	0	0	0	0	1	0	0	0	.000	.000
Moyer, Jamie, Chi.†	.230	39	61	3	14	15	1	0	0	3	1	7	0	0	6	0	17	0	0	0	.246	.294
Mumphrey, Jerry, Chi.†	.333	118	309	41	103	165	19	2	13	44	4	1	1	0	35	6	47	0	0	5	.534	.400
Murphy, Dale, Atl.	.295	159	566	115	167	328	27	1	44	105	7	0	5	7	115	29	136	16	6	11	.580	.417
Murphy, Robert, Cin.*	.200	87	5	0	1	1	0	0	0	0	0	1	0	0	0	0	2	0	0	0	.200	.200

Player, Club	AVG.	G	AB	R	H	TB	2B	3B	HR	RBI	GW RBI	SH	SF	HP	BB	1B	SO	SB	CS	GI DP	SLG	OBP
Myers, Randall, N.Y.*	.286	54	7	1	2	2	0	0	0	0	0	0	0	0	0	0	3	0	0	0	.286	.286
Nelson, Robert, S.D.*	.091	10	11	0	1	1	0	0	0	1	0	0	0	0	1	0	8	0	0	0	.091	.167
Nettles, Graig, Atl.*	.209	112	177	16	37	62	8	1	5	33	4	0	2	0	22	4	25	1	0	6	.350	.294
Newell, Thomas, Phil.	.000	2	2	0	0	0	0	0	0	0	0	0	0	0	0	0	0	0	0	0	.000	.000
Nichols, T. Reid, Mtl.	.265	77	147	22	39	63	8	2	4	20	3	2	2	1	14	4	13	2	1	4	.429	.329
Niedenfuer, Thomas, L.A.	......	15	0	0	0	0	0	0	0	0	0	0	0	0	0	0	0	0	0	0	......	......
Niekro, Phillip, Atl.	.000	1	1	0	0	0	0	0	0	0	0	0	0	0	0	0	0	0	0	0	.000	.000
Noce, Paul, Chi.	.228	70	180	17	41	63	9	2	3	14	1	4	0	2	6	1	49	5	3	2	.350	.261
Noles, Dickie, Chi.	.091	41	11	0	1	1	0	0	0	0	0	0	0	0	0	0	5	0	0	0	.091	.091
Nolte, Eric, S.D.*	.095	12	21	0	2	2	0	0	0	0	0	0	0	0	1	0	11	0	0	0	.095	.136
Norman, Nelson, Mtl.†	.000	1	4	0	0	0	0	0	0	0	0	0	0	0	0	0	1	0	0	0	.000	.000
Oberkfell, Kenneth, Atl.*	.280	135	508	59	142	184	29	2	3	48	3	0	3	2	48	5	29	3	3	13	.362	.342
Oester, Ronald, Cin.†	.253	69	237	28	60	87	9	6	2	23	4	5	0	0	22	4	51	3	3	8	.367	.317
Ojeda, Robert, N.Y.*	.071	10	14	3	1	1	0	0	0	0	0	2	0	0	2	0	4	0	0	0	.071	.188
Olwine, Edward, Atl.	......	27	0	0	0	0	0	0	0	0	0	0	0	0	0	0	0	0	0	0	......	......
O'Neal, Randall, Atl.-St.L.	.150	18	20	4	3	3	0	1	0	1	0	1	0	0	1	0	4	0	0	0	.150	.190
O'Neill, Paul, Cin.*	.256	84	160	24	41	78	14	1	7	28	2	0	0	0	18	1	29	2	2	3	.488	.331
Oquendo, Jose, St.L.†	.286	116	248	43	71	83	9	0	1	24	4	6	4	0	54	6	29	4	1	6	.335	.408
Orosco, Jesse, N.Y.	.000	58	8	0	0	0	0	0	0	0	0	1	0	0	0	0	7	0	0	0	.000	.000
Ortiz, Adalberto, Pitt.	.271	75	192	16	52	65	8	0	1	22	3	5	1	0	15	2	23	2	2	6	.339	.322
Pacillo, Patrick, Cin.	.091	13	11	1	1	2	1	0	0	0	0	1	0	0	1	0	6	0	0	0	.182	.167
Pagnozzi, Thomas, St.L.	.188	27	48	8	9	16	1	0	2	9	0	1	0	0	4	1	13	1	1	1	.333	.250
Palacios, Vicente, Pitt.	.111	6	9	1	1	1	0	0	0	0	0	0	0	0	0	0	4	0	0	0	.111	.111
Palmeiro, Rafael, Chi.*	.276	84	221	32	61	120	15	1	14	30	2	0	2	0	20	4	26	2	2	4	.543	.336
Palmer, David, Atl.	.125	28	48	4	6	10	1	0	1	5	2	8	0	0	1	0	15	0	0	1	.208	.143
Pankovits, James, Hou.	.230	50	61	7	14	19	2	0	1	8	0	0	0	0	6	0	13	2	2	2	.311	.299
Parent, Mark, S.D.	.080	12	25	0	2	2	0	0	0	2	0	0	0	0	0	0	9	0	0	0	.080	.080
Parker, David, Cin.*	.253	153	589	77	149	255	28	0	26	97	16	0	6	8	44	13	104	7	3	14	.433	.311
Parrett, Jeffrey, Mtl.	.000	45	5	0	0	0	0	0	0	0	0	4	0	0	0	0	3	0	0	0	.000	.000
Parrish, Lance, Phil.	.245	130	466	42	114	186	21	0	17	67	4	1	3	1	47	2	104	0	1	23	.399	.313
Patterson, Robert, Pitt.	.083	15	12	1	1	1	0	0	0	0	0	1	0	0	0	0	3	0	0	0	.083	.083
Pedrique, Alfredo, N.Y.-Pitt.	.294	93	252	24	74	89	10	0	1	27	5	6	1	3	19	4	29	4	4	7	.353	.349
Pena, Adalberto, Hou.	.152	21	46	5	7	7	0	0	0	0	0	1	0	1	2	0	7	0	0	3	.152	.204
Pena, Alejandro, L.A.	.077	37	13	0	1	1	0	0	0	0	0	1	0	0	0	0	5	0	0	0	.077	.077
Pena, Antonio, St.L.	.214	116	384	40	82	118	13	0	5	44	3	2	2	1	36	9	54	6	9	19	.307	.281
Pena, Hipolito, Pitt.*	.167	16	6	0	1	1	0	0	0	0	0	0	0	0	0	0	3	0	0	0	.167	.167
Pendleton, Terry, St.L.†	.286	159	583	82	167	240	29	4	12	96	4	9	9	2	70	6	74	19	12	18	.412	.360
Perez, Pascual, Mtl.	.042	12	24	3	1	1	0	0	0	0	0	3	0	0	0	0	8	0	0	0	.042	.042
Perlman, Jonathan, S.F.*	......	10	0	0	0	0	0	0	0	0	0	0	0	0	0	0	0	0	0	0	......	......
Perry, Gerald, Atl.*	.270	142	533	77	144	219	35	4	12	74	12	3	5	2	48	1	63	42	16	18	.411	.329
Perry, W. Patrick, St.L.-Cin.*	.143	57	7	0	1	1	0	0	0	0	0	0	0	0	0	0	1	0	0	0	.143	.143
Peters, Steven, St.L.*	.000	12	2	0	0	0	0	0	0	0	0	0	0	0	0	0	2	0	0	0	.000	.000
Powell, Alonzo, Mtl.	.195	14	41	3	8	11	3	0	0	4	0	0	0	0	5	0	17	5	5	0	.268	.283
Power, Ted, Cin.	.119	35	59	3	7	11	1	0	1	4	0	9	0	1	3	0	31	0	0	1	.186	.175
Prince, Joseph, S.F.	.167	20	6	1	1	1	0	0	0	1	0	0	0	0	0	0	3	0	0	0	.167	.167
Prince, Thomas, Pitt.	.222	4	9	1	2	6	1	0	1	2	0	1	1	0	1	0	2	0	0	1	.667	.222
Puhl, Terrance, Hou.*	.230	90	122	9	28	39	5	0	2	15	4	6	0	0	11	1	16	1	1	3	.320	.293
Puleo, Charles, Atl.	.179	36	28	3	5	8	0	0	1	1	0	0	0	0	1	0	13	0	0	1	.286	.207
Quinones, Luis, Chi.†	.218	49	101	12	22	28	6	0	0	8	1	1	0	0	10	0	16	0	5	0	.277	.288
Raines, Timothy, Mtl.†	.330	139	530	123	175	279	34	8	18	68	8	0	3	4	90	26	52	50	5	9	.526	.429

Player, Club	AVG.	G	AB	R	H	TB	2B	3B	HR	RBI	GW RBI	SH	SF	HP	BB	IB	SO	SB	CS	GI DP	SLG	OBP
Ramirez, Rafael, Atl.	.263	56	179	22	47	62	12	0	1	21	4	4	1	2	8	0	16	6	3	3	.346	.300
Ramsey, Michael, L.A.†	.232	48	125	18	29	37	4	2	0	12	0	2	1	0	10	0	32	2	4	3	.296	.287
Rasmussen, Dennis, Cin.*	.067	7	15	1	1	1	0	0	0	0	0	1	0	0	1	0	7	1	0	0	.067	.125
Rawley, Shane, Pitt.†	.152	37	79	5	12	15	1	1	0	4	0	12	1	0	1	0	31	1	0	1	.190	.160
Ray, Johnny, Pitt.†	.273	123	472	48	129	169	19	3	5	54	7	0	5	0	41	4	36	4	2	18	.358	.328
Ready, Randy, S.D.	.309	124	350	69	108	182	26	6	12	54	7	2	1	3	67	2	44	7	3	7	.520	.423
Reed, Jeffrey, Mtl.*	.213	75	207	15	44	58	11	0	1	21	5	4	4	1	12	1	20	0	0	8	.280	.254
Reid, Jessie, S.F.*	.125	6	8	0	1	4	0	0	1	1	1	0	0	0	1	0	5	0	0	1	.500	.222
Reuschel, Ricky, Pitt.-S.F.	.139	34	79	8	11	17	3	0	1	10	0	7	0	0	5	0	26	0	0	1	.215	.190
Reuss, Jerry, L.A.-Cin.*	.125	8	8	0	1	2	1	0	0	0	0	2	0	0	0	0	5	0	0	1	.250	.125
Reyes, Gilberto, L.A.	---	1	0	0	0	0	0	0	0	0	0	0	0	0	0	0	0	0	0	0	---	---
Reynolds, G. Craig, Hou.*	.254	135	374	35	95	130	17	3	4	28	6	4	8	0	30	8	44	1	1	4	.348	.303
Reynolds, Robert J., Pitt.†	.260	117	335	47	87	134	24	1	7	51	6	0	6	0	34	8	80	14	1	5	.400	.323
Reynolds, Ronn, Hou.	.167	38	102	5	17	24	4	0	1	7	1	1	1	0	3	0	29	0	0	3	.235	.189
Ritchie, Wallace, Phil.*	.250	49	4	0	1	1	0	0	0	0	0	0	0	0	0	0	1	0	0	0	.250	.250
Rivera, Luis, Mtl.	.156	18	32	2	5	7	2	0	0	1	1	0	0	0	1	0	8	0	0	0	.219	.182
Robinson, Don, Pitt.-S.F.	.222	69	18	1	4	8	1	0	1	2	2	0	0	0	1	0	4	0	0	0	.444	.263
Robinson, Jeffrey D., SF-Pitt.	.136	81	22	1	3	6	0	0	1	2	2	0	0	0	0	0	9	0	0	1	.273	.136
Robinson, Ronald, Cin.	.194	48	36	4	7	7	0	0	0	2	0	5	1	0	0	0	14	0	0	1	.194	.189
Roenicke, Gary, Atl.	.219	67	151	25	33	68	8	0	9	28	2	0	3	1	32	1	23	0	0	4	.450	.353
Roenicke, Ronald, Phil.†	.167	63	78	9	13	21	3	0	0	0	0	3	0	0	14	1	15	1	0	2	.269	.293
Romano, Thomas, Mtl.	.000	7	3	1	0	0	0	0	0	0	0	0	0	0	0	0	1	0	0	0	.000	.000
Ross, Mark, Pitt.	---	—	0	0	0	0	0	0	0	0	0	0	0	0	0	0	0	0	0	0	---	---
Rowdon, Wade, Chi.	.226	11	31	2	7	13	1	0	1	4	1	6	0	0	3	0	10	2	2	3	.419	.294
Ruffin, Bruce, Phil.	.055	35	73	3	4	5	1	0	0	3	0	7	2	0	2	0	39	0	0	1	.068	.080
Runge, Paul, Atl.	.213	27	47	9	10	20	1	0	3	8	1	1	5	0	5	0	10	5	0	1	.426	.288
Russell, John, Phil.	.145	24	62	5	9	19	1	0	3	7	0	7	0	0	3	0	17	1	1	4	.306	.185
Ryan, L. Nolan, Hou.	.062	34	65	2	4	7	0	0	1	4	0	7	0	0	1	0	22	0	0	2	.108	.076
Salazar, Luis, S.D.	.254	84	189	13	48	62	5	0	3	26	2	1	2	2	14	2	30	3	3	2	.328	.302
Samuel, Juan, Phil.	.272	160	655	113	178	329	37	15	28	100	11	0	6	5	60	5	162	35	15	12	.502	.335
Sandberg, Ryne, Chi.	.294	132	523	81	154	231	25	2	16	59	10	0	2	2	59	4	79	21	2	11	.442	.367
Sanderson, Scott, Chi.	.075	32	40	2	3	6	0	0	1	2	0	4	0	0	3	0	20	0	0	1	.150	.140
Santana, Rafael, N.Y.	.255	139	439	41	112	152	21	2	5	44	7	8	0	1	29	10	57	1	1	11	.346	.302
Santiago, Benito, S.D.	.300	146	546	64	164	255	33	2	18	79	10	4	6	5	16	2	112	21	12	12	.467	.324
Santovenia, Nelson, Mtl.	.000	2	2	0	0	0	0	0	0	0	0	0	0	0	0	0	0	0	0	0	.000	.000
Sasser, Mackey, S.F.-Pitt.*	.185	14	27	2	5	5	0	0	0	2	1	0	0	0	0	0	2	0	0	1	.185	.185
Savage, John, L.A.	---	3	0	0	0	0	0	0	0	0	0	0	0	0	0	0	0	0	0	0	---	---
Sax, Stephen, L.A.	.280	157	610	84	171	225	22	7	6	46	5	5	6	3	44	5	61	37	11	13	.369	.331
Schatzeder, Daniel, Phil.*	.167	26	12	1	2	2	0	0	0	0	0	0	0	0	1	0	6	0	0	1	.167	.231
Scherrer, William, Cin.*	.000	23	1	0	0	0	0	0	0	0	0	0	0	0	0	0	0	0	0	0	.000	.000
Schmidt, Michael, Phil.	.293	147	522	88	153	286	28	0	35	113	11	0	6	2	83	15	80	2	1	17	.548	.388
Schu, Richard, Phil.	.235	92	196	24	46	79	6	3	7	23	4	1	2	2	20	1	36	7	2	1	.403	.311
Schulze, Donald, N.Y.	.000	5	2	0	0	0	0	0	0	0	0	0	0	0	2	0	2	0	0	0	.000	.500
Scioscia, Michael, L.A.*	.265	142	461	44	122	168	26	1	6	38	9	4	2	1	55	9	23	7	4	13	.364	.343
Scott, Michael, Hou.	.125	36	80	4	10	10	0	0	0	3	0	8	0	0	3	0	32	0	0	0	.125	.157
Sebra, Robert, Mtl.	.157	36	51	2	8	9	1	0	0	1	1	4	0	0	2	0	16	0	0	0	.176	.189
Sharperson, Michael, L.A.	.273	10	33	7	9	11	2	0	0	1	0	0	0	0	4	1	5	0	0	0	.333	.351
Shelby, John, L.A.†	.277	120	476	61	132	221	26	0	21	69	9	0	9	1	31	0	97	16	6	9	.464	.317
Shines, Raymond, Mtl.†	.222	9	9	0	2	2	0	0	0	0	0	0	0	0	2	0	1	0	0	1	.222	.364
Shipley, Craig, L.A.	.257	26	35	3	9	10	1	0	0	2	0	0	0	0	0	0	6	0	0	2	.286	.257

Player, Club	AVG.	G	AB	R	H	TB	2B	3B	HR	RBI	GW RBI	SH	SF	HP	BB	IB	SO	SB	CS	GI DP	SLG	OBP
Show, Eric, S.D.	.071	34	70	5	5	6	1	0	0	2	0	7	1	0	0	0	28	0	0	3	.086	.070
Simmons, Ted, Atl.†	.277	73	177	20	49	69	8	0	4	30	5	0	2	0	21	5	23	1	1	4	.390	.350
Sisk, Douglas, N.Y.	.000	55	5	0	0	0	0	0	0	0	0	0	0	0	0	0	3	0	0	0	.000	.000
Smiley, John, Pitt.★	.143	63	7	1	1	2	1	0	0	1	0	0	0	0	1	0	1	0	0	0	.286	.143
Smith, Bryn, Mtl.	.136	26	44	2	6	9	3	0	1	4	0	7	2	0	1	0	10	0	0	0	.205	.149
Smith, David, Hou.	.500	50	2	0	1	1	0	0	0	0	0	0	0	0	0	0	1	0	0	0	.500	.667
Smith, Lee, Chi.	.000	63	2	0	0	0	0	0	0	0	0	0	0	0	0	0	1	0	0	0	.000	.000
Smith, Osborne, St.L.†	.303	158	600	104	182	230	40	4	0	75	9	12	4	0	89	3	36	43	9	9	.383	.392
Smith, Peter, Atl.	.091	6	11	0	1	1	0	0	0	0	0	1	0	1	3	0	1	0	0	0	.091	.091
Smith, Zane, Atl.★	.132	41	76	6	10	13	1	0	1	6	0	14	1	0	0	0	14	1	1	3	.171	.175
Soff, Raymond, St.L.	.000	12	1	0	0	0	0	0	0	0	0	0	0	1	0	0	1	0	0	0	.000	.000
Solano, Julio, Hou.	.000	11	2	0	0	0	0	0	0	0	0	0	0	0	0	0	2	0	0	0	.000	.000
Sorensen, Lary, Mtl.	.000	23	8	0	0	0	0	0	0	0	0	2	0	0	1	0	5	0	0	0	.000	.111
Soto, Mario, Cin.	.083	6	12	1	1	1	0	0	0	0	0	0	0	0	0	0	3	0	0	0	.083	.083
Speier, Chris, S.F.	.249	111	317	39	79	125	13	0	11	39	5	1	1	3	42	5	51	4	7	3	.394	.342
Spilman, W. Harry, S.F.★	.267	83	90	5	24	32	5	0	1	14	2	0	2	0	9	0	20	1	1	3	.356	.327
St. Claire, Randy, Mtl.	.333	44	6	0	2	2	0	0	0	0	0	2	1	0	0	0	1	0	0	0	.333	.333
Steels, James, S.D.★	.191	62	68	9	13	16	1	0	1	6	0	0	0	2	11	0	14	3	2	2	.235	.300
Stefero, John, Mtl.★	.196	18	56	4	11	14	0	0	1	3	1	0	2	3	3	1	17	0	0	5	.250	.237
Stillwell, Kurt, Cin.†	.258	131	395	54	102	148	20	7	4	33	3	3	2	7	32	2	50	4	6	2	.375	.316
Stone, Jeffery, Phil.★	.256	66	125	19	32	44	7	1	1	16	5	0	3	1	8	0	38	3	1	2	.352	.316
Strawberry, Darryl, N.Y.★	.284	154	532	108	151	310	32	5	39	104	7	1	7	0	97	13	122	36	12	4	.583	.398
Stubbs, Franklin, L.A.★	.233	129	386	48	90	160	16	3	16	52	5	1	2	1	31	9	85	8	1	7	.415	.290
Sundberg, James, Chi.	.201	61	139	9	28	42	2	0	2	15	0	0	1	0	19	3	40	0	0	3	.302	.306
Sutcliffe, Richard, Chi.★	.148	35	81	8	12	19	5	1	0	6	0	10	0	3	7	0	19	0	0	2	.235	.213
Taylor, Donald, Pitt.	.167	15	18	1	3	3	0	0	0	0	0	0	1	1	0	0	3	0	0	0	.167	.167
Tekulve, Kenton, Phil.	.000	90	1	1	0	0	0	0	0	0	0	1	0	0	1	0	0	0	0	0	.000	.500
Templeton, Garry, S.D.†	.222	148	510	42	113	151	13	5	5	48	5	5	3	1	42	11	92	14	3	15	.296	.281
Terry, Scott, St.L.	.000	11	2	0	0	0	0	0	0	0	0	0	0	0	0	0	0	0	0	0	.000	.000
Teufel, Timothy, N.Y.	.308	97	299	55	92	163	29	0	14	61	5	3	2	2	44	2	53	3	2	7	.545	.398
Tewksbury, Robert, Chi.	.000	7	5	0	0	0	0	0	0	0	0	4	0	0	0	0	4	0	0	0	.000	.000
Thomas, Andres, Atl.	.231	82	324	29	75	101	11	0	5	39	4	3	3	0	14	2	50	6	5	7	.312	.268
Thompson, Milton, Phil.★	.302	150	527	86	159	224	26	9	7	43	10	6	3	8	42	3	87	46	10	5	.425	.351
Thompson, Robert, S.F.	.262	132	420	62	110	176	26	5	10	44	2	0	0	0	40	3	91	16	11	8	.419	.338
Thon, Richard, Hou.	.212	32	66	6	14	18	1	0	1	3	1	2	0	0	16	0	13	3	0	1	.273	.366
Tibbs, Jay, Mtl.	.120	19	25	4	3	4	1	0	0	0	0	0	0	0	3	0	10	0	0	0	.160	.214
Toliver, Freddie, Phil.	.000	10	5	1	0	0	0	0	0	0	0	3	0	4	0	0	2	0	0	0	.000	.000
Treadway, H. Jeffrey, Cin.★	.333	23	84	9	28	38	4	0	2	4	0	1	1	0	2	2	6	1	0	1	.452	.356
Trevino, Alejandro, L.A.	.222	72	144	16	32	50	7	0	3	16	3	4	1	0	6	0	28	0	1	7	.347	.271
Trillo, J. Manuel, Chi.	.294	108	214	27	63	95	8	0	8	26	9	3	0	7	25	2	37	0	0	6	.444	.367
Trout, Steven, Chi.★	.154	11	26	1	4	4	0	0	0	0	0	3	0	0	0	0	9	0	0	1	.154	.154
Tudor, John, St.L.★	.200	17	35	1	7	7	0	0	0	5	0	5	0	0	2	0	6	0	0	0	.200	.243
Tunnell, B. Lee, St.L.	.235	33	17	1	4	4	0	0	0	5	1	8	1	1	0	0	5	0	0	0	.235	.235
Uribe, Jose, S.F.†	.291	95	309	44	90	131	16	5	5	30	3	0	3	0	24	9	35	12	2	4	.424	.343
Valenzuela, Fernando, L.A.★	.141	38	92	13	13	17	1	0	1	8	1	7	0	4	0	0	11	0	0	6	.185	.141
Van Slyke, Andrew, Pitt.★	.293	157	564	93	165	286	36	11	21	82	9	2	2	0	56	4	122	34	8	8	.507	.359
Venable, W. McKinley, Cin.★	.143	7	7	2	1	1	0	0	0	2	1	1	1	0	0	0	0	0	0	0	.143	.143
Virgil, Osvaldo, Atl.	.247	123	429	57	106	202	13	0	27	72	4	0	2	0	47	4	81	0	1	18	.471	.331
Walk, Robert, Pitt.	.231	39	26	6	6	6	0	0	0	5	1	1	0	0	0	0	6	0	0	1	.231	.231
Walker, Cleotha, Chi.†	.200	47	105	15	21	25	4	0	0	7	0	2	2	0	12	1	23	11	4	1	.238	.277

Player, Club	AVG.	G	AB	R	H	TB	2B	3B	HR	RBI	GW RBI	SH	SF	HP	BB	IB	SO	SB	CS	GI DP	SLG	OBP
Wallach, Timothy, Mtl.	.298	153	593	89	177	305	42	4	26	123	16	0	7	7	37	5	98	9	5	6	.514	.343
Waller, E. Tyrone, Hou.	.167	11	6	1	1	2	1	0	0	0	0	0	0	0	0	0	3	0	0	0	.333	.167
Walling, Dennis, Hou.*	.283	110	325	45	92	136	21	4	5	33	6	2	4	0	39	1	37	5	1	9	.418	.356
Walter, Gene, N.Y.*	.000	21	1	0	0	0	0	0	0	0	0	1	0	0	1	0	0	0	0	0	.000	.500
Washington, U.L., Pitt.†	.300	10	10	1	3	3	0	0	0	0	0	2	0	0	1	0	3	2	0	0	.300	.417
Wasinger, Mark, S.F.	.275	44	80	16	22	28	3	0	1	3	0	2	0	0	8	0	14	2	0	3	.350	.341
Webster, Mitchell, Mtl.†	.281	156	588	101	165	256	30	8	15	63	4	8	4	6	70	5	95	33	10	6	.435	.361
Welch, Robert, L.A.	.157	38	83	5	13	13	0	0	0	5	1	8	0	0	7	0	24	0	0	0	.157	.222
Wellman, Brad, L.A.	.250	3	4	1	1	1	0	0	0	1	0	0	0	0	0	0	1	0	0	0	.250	.250
Whitson, Eddie, S.D.	.123	36	65	1	8	9	1	0	0	4	1	10	0	0	1	0	17	0	0	2	.138	.136
Wilfong, Robert, S.F.*	.125	2	8	0	1	4	0	0	1	2	0	0	0	0	1	0	2	1	0	0	.500	.222
Williams, Frank, Cin.	.000	85	5	0	0	0	0	0	0	0	0	1	0	1	1	0	1	0	0	0	.000	.000
Williams, Matthew, S.F.	.188	84	245	28	46	83	9	2	8	21	1	3	1	0	16	4	68	4	3	1	.339	.240
Williams, Reginald, L.A.	.111	39	36	6	4	4	0	0	0	4	0	0	0	1	5	0	9	3	0	2	.111	.214
Wilson, Glenn, Phil.	.264	154	569	55	150	217	21	2	14	54	9	0	6	1	38	2	82	3	6	18	.381	.308
Wilson, William, N.Y.†	.299	124	385	58	115	175	19	7	9	34	2	2	2	0	35	8	85	21	6	0	.455	.359
Wine, Robert, Hou.	.103	14	29	1	3	4	1	0	0	0	0	1	0	0	1	0	10	0	0	0	.138	.133
Winningham, Herman, Mtl.*	.239	137	347	34	83	121	20	3	4	41	4	0	4	0	34	7	68	29	10	0	.349	.304
Wojna, Edward, S.D.	.000	5	5	0	0	0	0	0	0	0	0	0	0	0	0	0	1	0	0	0	.000	.000
Woodard, Michael, S.F.*	.211	10	19	4	4	5	1	0	0	1	0	0	0	0	0	0	6	1	1	0	.263	.211
Woodson, Tracy, L.A.	.228	53	136	14	31	44	8	0	1	11	2	0	1	0	9	2	37	1	0	2	.324	.284
Worrell, Todd, St.L.	.100	75	10	0	1	1	0	0	0	0	0	4	0	0	0	0	6	0	0	0	.100	.100
Wynne, Marvell, S.D.*	.250	98	188	17	47	65	8	2	2	24	2	1	1	1	20	0	27	11	6	3	.346	.321
Youmans, Floyd, Mtl.	.150	23	40	2	6	11	2	0	1	3	0	4	0	0	0	0	16	0	0	0	.275	.150
Young, Gerald, Hou.†	.321	71	274	44	88	104	9	2	1	15	1	0	2	0	26	0	57	26	9	1	.380	.380
Young, Matthew, L.A.*	.000	47	3	3	0	0	0	0	0	0	0	0	0	0	0	0	2	0	0	0	.000	.000
Youngblood, Joel, S.F.	.253	69	91	9	23	35	3	0	3	11	0	0	1	0	5	0	13	1	1	3	.385	.296
Ziem, Stephen, Atl.	....	2	....	....	....	....	....	....	....	....	....	....	....	....	....	....	....	....	....	....	....	....

PLAYERS WITH TWO OR MORE CLUBS DURING 1987 SEASON
(Listed alphabetically, first club on top)

Player, Club	AVG.	G	AB	R	H	TB	2B	3B	HR	RBI	GW RBI	SH	SF	HP	BB	IB	SO	SB	CS	GI DP	SLG	OBP
Almon, Pitt.	.200	19	20	5	4	5	1	0	0	1	0	0	0	0	1	0	5	0	0	0	.250	.238
Almon, N.Y.	.241	49	54	8	13	16	3	0	0	4	1	0	0	0	8	0	16	1	1	0	.296	.339
Brown, S.F.	.242	38	132	17	32	56	6	0	6	17	2	2	1	3	9	1	16	1	3	7	.424	.306
Brown, S.D.	.232	44	155	17	36	57	3	0	6	23	2	3	1	3	11	1	30	3	1	7	.368	.294
Comstock, S.F.	.000	15	1	0	0	0	0	0	0	0	0	0	0	0	0	0	1	0	0	0	.000	.000
Comstock, S.D.	.000	26	1	0	0	0	0	0	0	0	0	0	0	0	0	0	0	0	0	0	.000	.000
M. Davis, S.F.	.217	21	23	3	5	8	1	1	0	1	0	2	0	0	0	0	5	0	0	0	.348	.217
M. Davis, S.D.	.286	43	7	0	2	2	0	0	0	0	0	0	0	0	0	0	1	0	0	0	.286	.286
R. Davis, Chi.	....	21	0	0	0	0	0	0	0	0	0	0	0	0	0	0	0	0	0	0	....	....
R. Davis, L.A.	....	4	0	0	0	0	0	0	0	0	0	0	0	0	0	0	0	0	0	0	....	....
Dravecky, S.D.	.167	31	18	0	3	3	0	0	0	0	0	2	0	0	1	0	9	0	1	0	.167	.211
Dravecky, S.F.	.132	18	38	3	5	6	1	0	0	0	0	2	0	0	3	0	18	1	0	0	.158	.195
Garner, Hou	.223	43	112	15	25	39	5	0	3	15	3	1	3	0	8	1	20	1	0	2	.348	.268
Garner, L.A.	.190	70	126	14	24	34	4	0	2	8	1	4	1	0	20	7	24	5	1	3	.270	.299

Player, Club	AVG.	G	AB	R	H	TB	2B	3B	HR	RBI	GW RBI	SH	SF	HP	BB	IB	SO	SB	CS	GI DP	SLG	OBP
Gott, S.F.	.100	30	10	2	1	4	0	0	1	2	0	0	0	0	0	0	3	0	0	0	.400	.100
Gott, Pitt.	.000	25	1	0	0	0	0	0	0	0	0	0	0	0	0	0	1	0	0	0	.000	.000
Grant, S.F.	.083	16	12	1	1	1	0	0	0	0	0	3	0	0	1	0	4	0	0	0	.083	.154
Grant, S.D.	.094	18	32	0	3	3	0	0	0	1	0	3	0	0	2	0	12	0	0	1	.094	.147
Hume, Phil.	.200	38	15	1	3	4	1	0	0	0	0	0	0	0	0	0	4	1	0	1	.267	.200
Hume, Cin.	....	11	0	0	0	0	0	0	0	0	0	0	0	0	0	0	0	0	0	0	....	....
Landrum, St.L.	.200	30	50	5	10	11	1	0	0	6	0	0	0	0	7	2	14	1	1	1	.220	.298
Landrum, L.A.	.239	51	67	8	16	22	3	0	1	4	1	1	0	1	3	0	16	1	1	0	.328	.282
Lefferts, S.D.	.333	33	3	0	1	1	0	0	0	0	0	0	0	0	0	0	2	0	0	0	.333	.333
Lefferts, S.F.	.250	44	4	0	1	2	1	0	0	1	0	1	0	0	0	0	2	0	0	0	.500	.250
Mitchell, S.D.	.245	62	196	19	48	78	7	1	7	26	2	0	1	0	20	3	38	0	0	5	.398	.313
Mitchell, S.F.	.306	69	268	49	82	142	13	1	15	44	4	0	0	2	28	1	50	9	6	5	.530	.376
O'Neal, Atl	.105	17	19	4	2	2	0	0	0	1	0	1	0	0	1	0	4	0	0	0	.105	.150
O'Neal, St.L.	1.000	1	1	0	1	1	0	0	0	0	0	0	0	0	0	0	0	0	0	0	1.000	1.000
Pedrique, N.Y.	.000	5	6	1	0	0	0	0	0	0	0	1	0	0	1	0	2	0	0	0	.000	.143
Pedrique, Pitt.	.301	88	246	23	74	89	10	1	1	27	5	6	1	3	18	4	27	5	4	7	.362	.354
Perry, St.L	.143	45	7	0	1	1	0	0	0	0	0	0	0	0	0	0	1	1	0	0	.143	.143
Perry, Cin.	....	12	0	0	0	0	0	0	0	0	0	0	0	0	0	0	0	0	0	0	....	....
Reuschel, Pitt	.150	25	60	7	9	14	2	0	1	5	1	6	0	0	4	0	23	0	0	0	.233	.203
Reuschel, S.F.	.105	9	19	1	2	3	1	0	0	5	0	1	0	0	1	0	3	0	0	0	.158	.150
Reuss, L.A.	....	1	0	0	0	0	0	0	0	0	0	0	0	0	0	0	0	0	0	0	....	....
Reuss, Cin.	.125	7	8	0	1	2	1	0	0	0	0	2	0	0	0	0	5	1	0	0	.250	.125
D. Robinson, Pitt.	.143	44	7	0	1	1	0	0	0	1	0	0	0	0	1	0	2	0	0	0	.143	.250
D. Robinson, S.F.	.273	25	11	2	3	7	1	0	1	1	1	0	0	0	0	0	2	0	0	0	.636	.273
J. Robinson, S.F.	.111	63	18	0	2	2	0	0	0	1	0	0	0	0	0	0	7	0	0	0	.111	.111
J. Robinson, Pitt.	.250	18	4	1	1	4	0	0	1	1	1	1	0	0	0	0	2	0	0	0	1.000	.250
Sasser, S.F.	.000	2	4	0	0	0	0	0	0	0	0	0	0	0	0	0	0	0	0	0	.000	.000
Sasser, Pitt.	.217	12	23	2	5	5	0	0	0	2	0	0	0	0	0	0	2	0	0	1	.217	.217

OFFICIAL NATIONAL LEAGUE FIELDING AVERAGES

CLUB FIELDING

Club	PCT	G	PO	A	E	TC	DP	TP	PB
St. Louis	.982	162	4398	1870	116	6384	172	0	16
Atlanta	.982	161	4283	1921	116	6320	170	0	11
Houston	.981	162	4324	1617	116	6057	113	1	11
Pittsburgh	.980	162	4335	1834	123	6292	147	1	9
Philadelphia	.980	162	4345	1711	121	6177	137	0	17
San Francisco	.980	162	4413	1861	129	6403	183	0	15
Chicago	.979	161	4304	1787	130	6221	154	0	13
Cincinnati	.979	162	4357	1643	130	6130	137	0	13
New York	.978	162	4362	1797	137	6296	137	0	9
San Diego	.976	162	4300	1799	147	6246	135	0	22
Montreal	.976	162	4351	1679	147	6177	122	0	8
Los Angeles	.975	162	4365	1790	155	6310	144	0	8
Totals	.979	971	52137	21309	1567	75013	1751	2	152

INDIVIDUAL FIELDING

(*Throws lefthanded)

FIRST BASEMEN

Leader, Club	PCT	G	PO	A	E	TC	DP
STUBBS, L.A.*	.994	111	802	78	5	885	65

Player, Club	PCT	G	PO	A	E	TC	DP
Aldrete, S.F.*	.995	33	187	15	1	203	20
Almon, N.Y.	1.000	2	5	0	0	5	0
Bonilla, Pitt.	1.000	6	19	1	0	20	1
Bream, Pitt.*	.988	144	1236	127	17	1380	109
Brenly, S.F.	1.000	6	43	2	0	45	4
Candaele, Mtl.	1.000	1	1	0	0	1	0
Carter, N.Y.	1.000	4	10	0	0	10	1
Clark, St.L.	.989	126	1151	77	14	1242	116
Clark, S.F.*	.991	139	1253	103	13	1369	130
Coles, Pitt.	1.000	1	2	0	0	2	0
Concepcion, Cin.	1.000	26	118	10	0	128	3
Daugherty, Mtl.*	1.000	1	1	1	0	2	0
Daulton, Phil.	1.000	1	10	1	0	11	2
Davis, Hou.	.991	151	1283	112	12	1407	89
Diaz, Pitt.	.984	32	230	20	4	254	14
Driessen, St.L.	.993	21	141	10	1	152	13
Durham, Chi.*	.990	123	1049	57	11	1117	90
Engle, Mtl.	1.000	2	3	0	0	3	0
Esasky, Cin.	.994	93	772	40	5	817	72
Fitzgerald, Mtl.	1.000	1	1	0	0	1	0
Francona, Cin.*	.995	57	373	45	2	420	38
Galarraga, Mtl.	.993	146	1300	103	10	1413	96
Garvey, S.D.	1.000	20	138	11	0	149	10
Green, St.L.	1.000	3	4	0	0	4	1
Griffey, Atl.*	.962	3	24	1	1	26	2
G. Gross, Phil.*	1.000	11	20	1	0	21	1
Guerrero, L.A.	.981	40	319	38	7	364	30
Hatcher, L.A.	.992	37	234	24	2	260	29
Hayes, Phil.	.990	144	1164	78	12	1254	100
Heep, L.A.*	1.000	6	29	4	0	33	2
Hernandez, N.Y.*	.993	154	1298	149	10	1457	110
Hurdle, N.Y.	1.000	1	1	0	0	1	0
Jelks, Phil.	1.000	2	14	0	0	14	0

TRIPLE PLAY: Bream, Pitt.; Davis, Hou.

Player, Club	PCT	G	PO	A	E	TC	DP
Johnson, Mtl.	.972	9	68	2	2	72	4
Kruk, S.D.*	.996	101	870	75	4	949	74
Laga, St.L.*	.973	12	66	7	2	75	10
Landrum, St.L.	1.000	1	4	0	0	4	0
Law, Mtl.	.990	17	89	9	1	99	5
Lindeman, St.L.	.992	20	118	10	1	129	10
Madlock, L.A.	....	1	0	0	0	0	0
Magadan, N.Y.	.975	13	71	7	2	80	4
Martinez, S.D.	.990	65	475	36	5	516	41
Matuszek, L.A.	1.000	3	4	1	0	5	0
Mazzilli, N.Y.	1.000	13	58	2	0	60	1
McClendon, Cin.	.968	5	29	1	1	31	2
Melendez, S.F.*	1.000	5	19	0	0	19	0
Melvin, S.F.	1.000	1	7	1	0	8	1
Moreland, Chi.	....	1	0	0	0	0	0
Nelson, S.D.*	1.000	2	14	0	0	14	1
Nettles, Atl.	1.000	6	49	10	0	59	7
O'Neill, Cin.*	1.000	2	17	0	0	17	2
Oquendo, St.L.	1.000	3	17	0	0	17	2
Pagnozzi, St.L.	1.000	1	8	1	0	9	2
Palmeiro, Chi.*	.992	18	112	8	1	121	15
Parker, Cin.	.988	9	76	4	1	81	7
Pena, St.L.	1.000	4	7	0	0	7	0
Perry, Atl.	.990	136	1288	72	14	1374	118
Roenicke, Atl.	1.000	9	50	7	0	57	8
Salazar, S.D.	1.000	1	3	0	0	3	0
Schmidt, Phil.	.982	9	51	3	1	55	7
Schu, Phil.	.994	28	169	9	1	179	9
Shines, Mtl.	1.000	2	13	1	0	14	2
Simmons, Atl.	.984	28	216	23	4	243	24
Spilman, S.F.	.976	9	39	1	1	41	4
Stubbs, L.A.*	.994	111	802	78	5	885	65
Teufel, N.Y.	.667	1	1	1	1	3	1
Trillo, Chi.	.994	47	283	23	2	308	32
Van Slyke, Pitt.	1.000	1	10	0	0	10	3
Walling, Hou.	1.000	16	95	9	0	104	8
Woodson, L.A.	1.000	7	22	3	0	25	3

SECOND BASEMEN

Leader, Club	PCT	G	PO	A	E	TC	DP
DORAN, HOU.	.992	162	300	431	6	737	70

Player, Club	PCT	G	PO	A	E	TC	DP
Aguayo, Phil.	1.000	6	4	16	0	20	1
Almon, N.Y.	.917	10	4	7	1	12	1
Anderson, L.A.	1.000	5	1	5	0	6	0
Backman, N.Y.	.983	87	131	210	6	347	44
Belliard, Pitt.	1.000	7	9	15	0	24	2
Berra, Hou.	1.000	3	1	1	0	2	0
Biancalana, Hou.	1.000	3	1	2	0	3	1
Booker, St.L.	.960	18	24	24	2	50	3
Brumley, Chi.	....	1	0	0	0	0	0
Candaele, Mtl.	.985	68	76	125	3	204	18
Concepcion, Cin.	.992	59	125	133	2	260	36
Cora, S.D.	.975	66	118	192	8	318	31

Player, Club	PCT	G	PO	A	E	TC	DP
Doran, Hou.	.992	162	300	431	6	737	70
Duncan, L.A.	1.000	7	11	22	0	33	3
Fitzgerald, Mtl.	....	1	0	0	0	0	0
Flannery, S.D.	.986	84	139	207	5	351	40
Foley, Mtl.	.982	39	69	93	3	165	22
Gant, Atl.	.972	20	45	59	3	107	17
Garner, Hou.-L.A.	.920	14	6	17	2	25	2
Herr, St.L.	.989	137	306	350	7	663	103
Hubbard, Atl.	.986	139	284	478	11	773	114
Jimenez, Pitt.	1.000	2	2	0	0	2	0
Kutcher, S.F.	1.000	2	4	3	0	7	1
Law, Mtl.	.980	106	158	276	9	443	47
Lawless, St.L.	1.000	7	5	14	0	19	3
Legg, Phil.	1.000	1	3	1	0	4	1
Lind, Pitt.	.995	35	53	139	1	193	12

SECOND BASEMEN—Continued

Player, Club	PCT	G	PO	A	E	TC	DP
Miller, N.Y.	.967	16	21	38	2	61	6
Morrison, Pitt.	1.000	9	19	29	0	48	8
Noce, Chi.	.983	36	73	99	3	175	24
Oberkfell, Atl.	1.000	11	13	17	0	30	3
Oester, Cin.	.974	69	183	186	10	379	37
Oquendo, St.L.	1.000	32	50	65	0	115	20
Pankovits, Hou.	1.000	9	8	10	0	18	3
Pedrique, N.Y.-Pitt.	.800	3	1	3	1	5	0
Quinones, Chi.	1.000	4	3	7	0	10	1
Ray, Pitt.	.981	119	248	358	12	618	84
Ready, S.D.	.984	51	65	124	3	192	24
Runge, Atl.	1.000	2	2	4	0	6	1
Samuel, Phil.	.978	160	374	434	18	826	99
Sandberg, Chi.	.985	131	294	375	10	679	84
Sax, L.A.	.982	152	342	420	14	776	92
Sharperson, L.A.	.933	6	1	13	1	15	2
Speier, S.F.	.989	55	80	105	2	187	23
Stillwell, Cin.	.975	37	61	97	4	162	15
Teufel, N.Y.	.972	92	138	213	10	361	43
Thompson, S.F.	.972	126	246	341	17	604	99
Treadway, Cin.	.958	21	44	48	4	96	14
Trillo, Chi.	1.000	10	7	7	0	14	1
Wasinger, S.F.	1.000	10	12	18	0	30	4
Wellman, L.A.	1.000	1	0	1	0	1	0
Wilfong, S.F.	.833	2	2	3	1	6	2
Woodard, S.F.	1.000	8	13	15	0	28	4

TRIPLE PLAY: Doran, Hou., Ray, Pitt.

SECOND BASEMEN WITH TWO OR MORE CLUBS

Player, Club	PCT	G	PO	A	E	TC	DP
Garner, Hou.	1.000	2	0	1	0	1	0
Garner, L.A.	.917	12	6	16	2	24	2
Pedrique, N.Y.	1.000	1	1	2	0	3	0
Pedrique, Pitt.	.500	2	0	1	1	2	0

THIRD BASEMEN

Leader, Club	PCT	G	PO	A	E	TC	DP
BELL, CIN.	.979	142	93	241	7	341	17

Player, Club	PCT	G	PO	A	E	TC	DP
Aguayo, Phil.	1.000	2	1	2	0	3	0
Almon, Pitt.	....	1	0	0	0	0	0
Anderson, L.A.	.978	35	11	33	1	45	4
Barnes, St.L.	....	1	0	0	0	0	0
Bell, Cin.	.979	142	93	241	7	341	17
Bonilla, Pitt.	.932	89	53	138	14	205	12
Booker, St.L.	1.000	4	1	3	0	4	2
Brenly, S.F.	1.000	2	0	1	0	1	0
Brown, S.F.-S.D.	.923	80	60	132	16	208	17
Caminiti, Hou.	.949	61	50	98	8	156	11
Coles, Pitt.	.903	10	9	19	3	31	0
Concepcion, Cin.	1.000	13	5	20	0	25	2
DeCinces, St.L.	.833	3	3	7	2	12	0
Engle, Mtl.	1.000	1	0	1	0	1	0
Esasky, Cin.	.500	1	0	1	1	2	0
Flannery, S.D.	.913	8	2	19	2	23	2
Foley, Mtl.	1.000	9	1	4	0	5	0
Garner, Hou.-L.A.	.947	82	57	121	10	188	8
Hamilton, L.A.	.935	31	27	60	6	93	5
Hatcher, L.A.	.929	49	37	81	9	127	7
Jackson, Hou.	.957	16	6	38	2	46	4
Jelks, Phil.	.750	4	1	2	1	4	0
Johnson, N.Y.	.938	140	82	235	21	338	15
Kutcher, S.F.	1.000	2	2	1	0	3	0
Law, Mtl.	.971	22	11	22	1	34	2
Lawless, St.L.	1.000	3	0	1	0	1	0
Legg, Phil.	....	1	0	0	0	0	0
Madlock, L.A.	.912	16	8	23	3	34	2
Magadan, N.Y.	.981	50	17	85	2	104	5
McClendon, Cin.	1.000	1	1	0	0	1	0
Mitchell, S.D.-S.F.	.954	119	73	239	15	327	19
Moreland, Chi.	.934	150	99	300	28	427	27
Morrison, Pitt.	.975	82	46	151	5	202	11
Nettles, Atl.	.951	40	12	46	3	61	6
Nichols, Mtl.	.667	3	1	1	1	3	0
Noce, Chi.	1.000	2	1	0	0	1	0
Oberkfell, Atl.	.979	126	76	248	7	331	20
Oquendo, St.L.	.909	8	6	14	2	22	1
Pankovits, Hou.	1.000	4	0	2	0	2	0
Pedrique, Pitt.	1.000	3	0	1	0	1	0
Pena, Hou.	....	1	0	0	0	0	0
Pendleton, St.L.	.949	158	117	369	26	512	27
Quinones, Chi.	....	1	0	0	0	0	0
Ramirez, Atl.	.947	12	7	11	1	19	3
Ready, S.D.	.912	52	30	95	12	137	11
C. Reynolds, Hou.	1.000	2	0	2	0	2	0
Rowdon, Chi.	.818	9	3	15	4	22	0
Runge, Atl.	.923	10	9	15	2	26	3
Salazar, S.D.	.957	38	17	49	3	69	4
Sax, L.A.	....	1	0	0	0	0	0
Schmidt, Phil.	.971	138	87	315	12	414	28
Schu, Phil.	.905	45	24	62	9	95	2
Sharperson, L.A.	1.000	7	3	15	0	18	0
Shipley, L.A.	.857	6	3	3	1	7	0
Simmons, Atl.	1.000	2	2	2	0	4	0
Speier, S.F.	.991	44	22	84	1	107	10
Spilman, S.F.	.875	10	1	6	1	8	1
Stillwell, Cin.	.977	20	9	33	1	43	1
Trevino, L.A.	....	1	0	0	0	0	0
Trillo, Chi.	.926	35	7	18	2	27	2
Walker, Chi.	....	2	0	0	0	0	0
Wallach, Mtl.	.952	150	128	292	21	441	21
Walling, Hou.	.948	79	72	109	10	191	13
Washington, Pitt.	....	1	0	0	0	0	0
Wasinger, S.F.	.973	21	6	30	1	37	4
Wellman, L.A.	1.000	1	2	1	0	3	1
Williams, S.F.	.968	17	6	24	1	31	3
Woodson, L.A.	.958	45	36	55	4	95	4
Youngblood, S.F.	1.000	2	0	1	0	1	0

THIRD BASEMEN WITH TWO OR MORE CLUBS

Player, Club	PCT	G	PO	A	E	TC	DP
Brown, S.F.	.905	37	33	62	10	105	5
Brown, S.D.	.942	43	27	70	6	103	12
Garner, Hou.	.976	36	28	54	2	84	3
Garner, L.A.	.923	46	29	67	6	104	5
Mitchell, S.D.	.945	51	29	108	8	145	9
Mitchell, S.F.	.962	68	44	131	7	182	10

SHORTSTOPS

Leader, Club	PCT	G	PO	A	E	TC	DP
SMITH, ST.L.	.987	158	245	516	10	771	111

Player, Club	PCT	G	PO	A	E	TC	DP
Aguayo, Phil.	.971	78	81	154	7	242	29
Almon, Pitt.-N.Y.	.963	26	17	35	2	54	6
Anderson, L.A.	.977	65	91	169	6	266	29
Belliard, Pitt.	.979	71	104	176	6	286	29
Berra, Hou.	.963	18	13	39	2	54	4
Biancalana, Hou.	.889	16	8	16	3	27	2
Blauser, Atl.	.962	50	65	166	9	240	28
Booker, St.L.	1.000	1	0	1	0	1	0
Brooks, Mtl.	.953	109	131	271	20	422	53
Brown, S.F.	....	1	0	0	0	0	0
Brumley, Chi.	.965	34	43	93	5	141	24
Candaele, Mtl.	.962	25	28	48	3	79	10
Concepcion, Cin.	.727	2	2	6	3	11	2
Cora, S.D.	.867	5	5	8	2	15	1
DeJesus, S.F.	.840	14	7	14	4	25	2
Doran, Hou.	.500	3	0	1	1	2	0
Dowell, Phil.	1.000	15	17	36	0	53	7
Duncan, L.A.	.930	67	90	191	21	302	37
Dunston, Chi.	.969	94	160	271	14	445	54
Elster, N.Y.	.909	3	4	6	1	11	0
Fermin, Pitt.	.980	23	36	62	2	100	13

SHORTSTOPS—Continued

Player, Club	PCT	G	PO	A	E	TC	DP
Flannery, S.D.	1.000	2	1	0	0	1	0
Foley, Mtl.	.963	49	64	93	6	163	21
Garner, L.A.	.889	2	2	6	1	9	0
Gonzalez, Pitt.	1.000	1	2	1	0	3	0
Hamilton, L.A.	....	1	0	0	0	0	0
Hoffman, L.A.	.966	40	70	101	6	177	19
Jackson, Hou.	1.000	1	0	1	0	1	0
K. Jackson, Phil.	.955	8	6	15	1	22	1
Jeltz, Phil.	.971	114	191	271	14	476	55
Jimenez, Pitt.	1.000	2	1	8	0	9	1
Johnson, N.Y.	.955	38	36	70	5	111	12
Khalifa, Pitt.	.917	5	5	6	1	12	1
Kutcher, S.F.	1.000	1	0	1	0	1	0
Larkin, Cin.	.965	119	168	358	19	545	72
Legg, Phil.	....	1	0	0	0	0	0
McGee, St.L.	1.000	1	1	1	0	2	0
Mitchell, S.F.	1.000	1	0	1	0	1	0
Morrison, Pitt.	.931	17	7	20	2	29	5
Noce, Chi.	.981	35	43	58	2	103	15
Norman, Mtl.	.667	1	1	1	1	3	0
Oquendo, St.L.	.968	23	11	50	2	63	7
Pedrique, N.Y.-Pitt.	.969	80	117	192	10	319	43
Pena, Hou.	.982	19	19	35	1	55	3
Quinones, Chi.	.965	28	32	51	3	86	9
Ramirez, Atl.	.946	38	59	99	9	167	30
C. Reynolds, Hou.	.970	129	160	290	14	464	43
Rivera, Mtl.	.923	15	9	27	3	39	4
Runge, Atl.	1.000	9	4	8	0	12	1
Salazar, S.D.	.923	22	27	45	6	78	7
Santana, N.Y.	.973	138	213	396	17	626	82
Schmidt, Phil.	1.000	3	0	1	0	1	0
Shipley, L.A.	.949	18	12	25	2	39	2
Smith, St.L.	.987	158	245	516	10	771	111
Speier, S.F.	.982	22	16	40	1	57	8
Stillwell, Cin.	.914	51	74	117	18	209	22
Templeton, S.D.	.972	146	253	447	20	720	77
Thomas, Atl.	.953	81	128	276	20	424	56
Thon, Hou.	.925	31	21	53	6	80	7
Trillo, Chi.	1.000	6	4	5	0	9	0
Uribe, S.F.	.971	95	145	286	13	444	62
Washington, Pitt.	.833	1	1	4	1	6	0
Wasinger, S.F.	1.000	2	3	2	0	5	1
Wellman, L.A.	1.000	1	1	1	0	2	0
Williams, S.F.	.975	70	104	210	8	322	49

TRIPLE PLAY: Gonzalez, Pitt., C. Reynolds, Hou.

SHORTSTOPS WITH TWO OR MORE CLUBS

Player, Club	PCT	G	PO	A	E	TC	DP
Almon, Pitt.	.944	4	9	8	1	18	3
Almon, N.Y.	.972	22	8	27	1	36	3
Pedrique, N.Y.	1.000	4	2	7	0	9	0
Pedrique, Pitt.	.968	76	115	185	10	310	43

OUTFIELDERS

Leader, Club	PCT	G	PO	A	E	TC	DP
JAMES, ATL.*	.996	126	262	4	1	267	1

Player, Club	PCT	G	PO	A	E	TC	DP
Abner, S.D.	.926	14	23	2	2	27	1
Aldrete, S.F.*	.986	79	141	3	2	146	1
Almon, Pitt.-N.Y.	....	3	0	0	0	0	0
Bass, Hou.	.987	155	287	11	4	302	2
Bonds, Pitt.*	.986	145	330	15	5	350	3
Bonilla, Pitt.	.972	46	70	0	2	72	0
Bryant, L.A.	.917	19	22	0	2	24	0
Byers, S.D.*	1.000	5	6	1	0	7	0
Candaele, Mtl.	.985	67	132	3	2	137	0
Cangelosi, Pitt.*	.962	47	74	3	3	80	0
Carreon, N.Y.*	.800	5	4	0	1	5	0
Carter, N.Y.	1.000	1	2	0	0	2	0
Clark, St.L.	1.000	1	1	0	0	1	0
Coleman, St.L.	.970	150	274	16	9	299	3
Coles, Pitt.	1.000	26	28	1	0	29	0
Collins, Cin.*	1.000	21	36	0	0	36	0
Comstock, S.F.*	....	1	0	0	0	0	0
Cruz, Hou.*	.984	97	178	5	3	186	3
Daniels, Cin.	.968	94	178	5	6	189	0
C. Davis, S.F.	.975	135	265	6	7	278	2
Davis, Cin.	.990	128	380	10	4	394	4
Davis, Pitt.	1.000	1	3	0	0	3	0
Dawson, Chi.	.986	152	271	12	4	287	0
Dayett, Chi.	1.000	78	72	2	0	74	0
Dernier, Chi.	.989	71	86	2	1	89	1
Devereaux, L.A.	1.000	18	21	1	0	22	0
Diaz, Pitt.	.960	37	46	2	2	50	0
Duncan, L.A.	....	2	0	0	0	0	0
Dykstra, N.Y.*	.988	118	239	4	3	246	1
Easler, Phil.	.981	30	49	4	1	54	2
Engle, Mtl.	1.000	11	19	1	0	20	0
Esasky, Cin.	1.000	1	1	0	0	1	0
Ford, St.L.	.981	75	157	2	3	162	0
Francona, Cin.*	1.000	8	4	0	0	4	0
Gainey, Hou.*	1.000	6	10	0	0	10	0
Garcia, Cin.*	1.000	14	19	0	0	19	0
Gonzalez, L.A.	1.000	16	19	1	0	20	0
Green, St.L.	.882	10	14	1	2	17	0
Gregg, Pitt.*	1.000	4	1	0	0	1	0
Griffey, Atl.*	.995	107	181	7	1	189	1
G. Gross, Phil.*	1.000	50	33	1	0	34	0
Guerrero, L.A.	.971	109	163	6	5	174	0
Gwynn, S.D.*	.981	156	298	13	6	317	1
Gwynn, L.A.*	1.000	10	12	0	0	12	0
Hall, Atl.	.981	69	148	5	3	156	1
Harper, Pitt.	1.000	20	25	0	0	25	0
Hatcher, L.A.	1.000	7	6	0	0	6	0
Hatcher, Hou.	.986	140	276	16	4	296	6
Hayes, Phil.	.982	32	52	2	1	55	0
Heep, L.A.*	.962	22	23	2	1	26	1
Henderson, S.F.	1.000	9	10	1	0	11	0
Horton, St.L.*	....	1	0	0	0	0	0
Householder, Hou.	1.000	7	3	0	0	3	0
Hughes, Phil.*	.963	19	26	0	1	27	0
Jackson, Hou.	1.000	13	6	0	0	6	0
Jackson, Chi.	1.000	5	1	0	0	1	0
James, Atl.*	.996	126	262	4	1	267	1
James, Phil.	.990	108	198	5	2	205	1
Jefferson, S.D.	.987	107	232	3	3	238	1
Jelks, Phil.	1.000	1	4	0	0	4	0
Jeltz, Phil.	1.000	1	1	0	0	1	0
Johnson, N.Y.	....	2	0	0	0	0	0
Johnson, St.L.*	.931	25	27	0	2	29	0
Jones, Cin.	.990	95	189	2	2	193	0
Kruk, S.D.*	.978	29	41	3	1	45	0
Kutcher, S.F.	1.000	6	8	0	0	8	0
Landreaux, L.A.	.951	63	72	5	4	81	3
Landrum, St.L.-L.A.	.987	54	73	2	1	76	0
Lawless, St.L.	....	1	0	0	0	0	0
Leonard, S.F.	.966	127	193	7	7	207	2
Lindeman, St.L.	.976	49	78	4	2	84	3
Lopes, Hou.	.857	5	6	0	1	7	0
Mack, S.D.	.982	91	159	1	3	163	0
Maldonado, S.F.	.973	116	176	7	5	188	0
Marshall, L.A.	.987	102	147	4	2	153	0
Martinez, S.D.	.968	78	116	6	4	126	0
Martinez, Chi.*	.980	139	283	10	6	299	1
Matthews, Chi.	1.000	2	2	0	0	2	0
Mazzilli, N.Y.	1.000	25	24	1	0	25	0
McClendon, Cin.	1.000	1	1	0	0	1	0
McGee, St.L.	.981	152	353	9	7	369	1
McReynolds, N.Y.	.987	150	286	8	4	298	0
Milner, S.F.*	.993	84	135	0	1	136	0
Mitchell, S.D.-S.F.	1.000	6	3	0	0	3	0
Morris, St.L.*	.989	74	86	0	1	87	0
Motley, Atl.	1.000	2	2	0	0	2	0
Mumphrey, Chi.	.992	85	124	5	1	130	0
Murphy, Atl.	.977	159	325	14	8	347	1
Nichols, Mtl.	.990	59	97	4	1	102	0
O'Neill, Cin.*	.949	42	73	2	4	79	0
Oquendo, St.L.	1.000	46	65	4	0	69	1
Palmeiro, Chi.*	1.000	45	64	1	0	65	1
Pankovits, Hou.	1.000	6	11	3	0	14	0

OUTFIELDERS—Continued

Player, Club	PCT	G	PO	A	E	TC	DP
Parker, Cin.	.967	142	278	13	10	301	3
Pena, St.L.	1.000	2	2	0	0	2	0
Perry, Atl.	1.000	7	9	0	0	9	0
Powell, Mtl.	1.000	11	13	0	0	13	0
Puhl, Hou.	.980	40	48	0	1	49	0
Raines, Mtl.	.987	139	297	9	4	310	1
Ramsey, L.A.	.973	43	70	1	2	73	0
Ready, S.D.	1.000	16	29	1	0	30	0
Reid, S.F.★	1.000	3	3	0	0	3	0
Reynolds, Pitt.	.993	99	134	7	1	142	2
Roenicke, Atl.	.968	44	60	0	2	62	0
Roenicke, Phil.★	.964	26	26	1	1	28	0
Romano, Mtl.	....	3	0	0	0	0	0
Russell, Phil.	.955	10	20	1	1	22	0
Salazar, S.D.	1.000	10	9	0	0	9	0
Sax, L.A.	1.000	1	1	0	0	1	0
Shelby, L.A.	.972	117	269	9	8	286	3
Steels, S.D.★	.960	28	23	1	1	25	0
Stone, Phil.	1.000	25	32	3	0	35	1
Strawberry, N.Y.★	.972	151	272	6	8	286	3
Stubbs, L.A.★	1.000	18	28	1	0	29	0
Thompson, Phil.	.989	146	354	4	4	362	1
Trevino, L.A.	1.000	2	1	0	0	1	0
Van Slyke, Pitt.	.988	150	328	10	4	342	6
Venable, Cin.	1.000	4	3	0	0	3	0
Walker, Chi.	.974	33	37	0	1	38	0
Waller, Hou.	1.000	3	2	0	0	2	0
Walling, Hou.	1.000	7	8	1	0	9	0
Webster, Mtl.★	.982	153	266	8	5	279	0
Williams, L.A.	.913	30	21	0	2	23	0
Wilson, Phil.	.968	154	315	18	11	344	2
Wilson, N.Y.	.963	109	205	3	8	216	2
Winningham, Mtl.	.975	131	225	5	6	236	1
Worrell, St.L.	....	1	0	0	0	0	0
Wynne, S.D.★	.981	71	100	2	2	104	0
Young, Hou.	.980	67	143	5	3	151	1
Youngblood, S.F.	1.000	22	24	2	0	26	0

OUTFIELDERS WITH TWO OR MORE CLUBS

Player, Club	PCT	G	PO	A	E	TC	DP
Almon, Pitt.	....	2	0	0	0	0	0
Almon, N.Y.	....	1	0	0	0	0	0
Landrum, St.L.	1.000	23	41	1	0	42	0
Landrum, L.A.	.971	31	32	1	1	34	0
Mitchell, S.D.	1.000	3	3	0	0	3	0
Mitchell, S.F.	....	3	0	0	0	0	0

CATCHERS

Leader, Club	PCT	G	PO	A	E	TC	DP	PB
ASHBY, HOU.	.993	110	778	46	6	830	6	6

Player, Club	PCT	G	PO	A	E	TC	DP	PB
Afenir, Hou.	.974	10	35	2	1	38	1	3
Ashby, Hou.	.993	110	778	46	6	830	6	6
Bailey, Hou.	.985	27	126	7	2	135	0	0
Benedict, Atl.	.989	35	165	21	2	188	3	1
Berryhill, Chi.	.909	11	37	3	4	44	0	0
Bochy, S.D.	.962	23	95	7	4	106	0	0
Brenly, S.F.	.988	108	642	83	9	734	10	11
Butera, Cin.	.920	5	19	4	2	25	0	1
Carter, N.Y.	.991	135	874	70	9	953	13	5
Daulton, Phil.	.991	40	200	12	2	214	4	1
J. Davis, Chi.	.989	123	749	79	9	837	11	12
Diaz, Cin.	.992	137	747	70	7	824	6	9
Diaz, Pitt.	1.000	8	27	1	0	28	0	1
Engle, Mtl.	1.000	6	11	1	0	12	0	0
Fitzgerald, Mtl.	.981	104	602	27	12	641	2	4
Lake, St.L.	.996	59	253	21	1	275	2	1
LaValliere, Pitt.	.992	112	584	70	5	659	11	2
Lyons, N.Y.	.984	49	223	17	4	244	0	4
Manwaring, S.F.	.909	6	9	1	1	11	0	0
McClendon, Cin.	.981	12	49	4	1	54	1	2
McGriff, Cin.	.983	33	160	14	3	177	1	1
Melvin, S.F.	.998	78	407	43	1	451	7	4
Mercado, L.A.	1.000	7	13	0	0	13	0	0
Ortiz, Pitt.	.975	72	313	39	9	361	2	6
Pagnozzi, St.L.	1.000	25	53	4	0	57	0	1
Parent, S.D.	1.000	10	36	3	0	39	0	0
Parrish, Phil.	.989	127	724	66	9	799	1	15
Pena, St.L.	.988	112	615	51	8	674	8	14
Prince, Pitt.	1.000	4	14	3	0	17	0	0
Reed, Mtl.	.970	74	357	36	12	405	6	4
Reyes, L.A.	1.000	1	2	0	0	2	0	0
R. Reynolds, Hou.	.975	38	216	16	6	238	1	1
Russell, Phil.	1.000	7	28	0	0	28	0	1
Santiago, S.D.	.976	146	817	80	22	919	12	22
Santovenia, Mtl.	1.000	1	1	0	0	1	0	0
Sasser, S.F.-Pitt.	1.000	6	29	0	0	29	0	0
Scioscia, L.A.	.989	138	925	80	11	1016	11	6
Simmons, Atl.	.987	15	64	10	1	75	1	2
Spilman, S.F.	....	1	0	0	0	0	0	0
Stefero, Mtl.	.981	17	90	12	2	104	0	0
Sundberg, Chi.	.994	57	273	34	2	309	2	1
Trevino, L.A.	.987	45	205	22	3	230	3	2
Virgil, Atl.	.989	122	654	74	8	736	12	8
Wine, Hou.	.979	12	40	7	1	48	2	1

TRIPLE PLAY: Ortiz, Pitt.

CATCHERS WITH TWO OR MORE CLUBS

Player, Club	PCT	G	PO	A	E	TC	DP	PB
Sasser, S.F.	1.000	1	7	0	0	7	0	0
Sasser, Pitt.	1.000	5	22	0	0	22	0	0

PITCHERS

Leader, Club	PCT	G	PO	A	E	TC	DP
WELCH, L.A.	1.000	35	25	38	0	63	3

Player, Club	PCT	G	PO	A	E	TC	DP
Acker, Atl.	1.000	68	6	23	0	29	2
Agosto, Hou.★	.929	27	3	10	1	14	1
Aguilera, N.Y.	.947	18	7	29	2	38	1
Alexander, Atl.	1.000	16	6	10	0	16	1
Andersen, Hou.	.880	67	12	10	3	25	0
Assenmacher, Atl.★	1.000	52	2	3	0	5	0
Bair, Phil.	.667	11	1	1	1	3	0
Baller, Chi.	.750	23	0	3	1	4	0
Bedrosian, Phil.	1.000	65	3	7	0	10	0
Belcher, L.A.	1.000	6	1	5	0	6	0
Bielecki, Pitt.	.917	8	6	5	1	12	0
Bockus, S.F.	.750	12	0	3	1	4	0
Boever, Atl.	1.000	14	0	2	0	2	0
Booker, S.D.	.941	44	8	8	1	17	1
Brown, Mtl.	.667	5	0	2	1	3	0
Browning, Cin.★	.903	32	5	23	3	31	1
Burke, Mtl.	1.000	55	6	17	0	23	0
Burkett, S.F.	1.000	3	0	1	0	1	1
Calhoun, Phil.★	1.000	42	4	8	0	12	0
Campbell, Mtl.	1.000	7	0	2	0	2	0
Candelaria, N.Y.★	1.000	3	2	1	0	3	0
Carman, Phil.★	1.000	35	7	21	0	28	0
Cary, Atl.★	1.000	13	1	3	0	4	0
Childress, Hou.	1.000	32	2	6	0	8	0
Clary, Atl.	1.000	7	0	2	0	2	0
Coffman, Atl.	1.000	5	1	9	0	10	1
Comstock, S.F.-S.D.★	1.000	41	2	4	0	6	1
Cone, N.Y.	.957	21	12	10	1	23	0
Conroy, St.L.★	.875	10	3	4	1	8	1
Cowley, Phil.	.500	5	1	0	1	2	0
Cox, St.L.	.979	31	23	24	1	48	1
Crews, L.A.	1.000	20	2	5	0	7	0
Darling, N.Y.	.952	32	17	43	3	63	5
Darwin, Hou.	.941	33	10	22	2	34	0
S. Davis, S.D.	.941	21	7	9	1	17	0
M. Davis, S.F.-S.D.★	.923	63	4	20	2	26	3
Davis, Chi.-L.A.	1.000	25	1	3	0	4	2

PITCHERS—Continued

Player, Club	PCT	G	PO	A	E	TC	DP
Dawley, St.L.	1.000	60	10	17	0	27	2
Dayley, St.L.*	1.000	53	3	4	0	7	1
Dedmon, Atl.	1.000	53	10	17	0	27	1
Deshaies, Hou.*	.964	26	5	22	1	28	0
DiPino, Chi.*	.947	69	2	16	1	19	2
Downs, S.F.	.875	41	11	10	3	24	0
Drabek, Pitt.	.959	29	24	23	2	49	0
Dravecky, S.D.-S.F.*	.958	48	16	30	2	48	2
Drummond, Pitt.	1.000	6	0	2	0	2	0
Dunne, Pitt.	.980	23	18	32	1	51	3
Easley, Pitt.	1.000	17	2	8	0	10	1
Edens, N.Y.	.800	2	0	4	1	5	0
Fernandez, N.Y.*	.941	28	4	12	1	17	0
Fischer, Mtl.	1.000	4	1	2	0	3	0
Fisher, Pitt.	.971	37	13	20	1	34	1
Forsch, St.L.	1.000	33	9	25	0	34	2
Franco, Cin.*	1.000	68	4	7	0	11	0
Frohwirth, Phil.	1.000	10	1	1	0	2	1
Garber, Atl.	.958	49	4	19	1	24	2
Garcia, Pitt.*		1	0	0	0	0	0
Garrelts, S.F.	.938	64	5	10	1	16	1
Gibson, N.Y.	1.000	1	1	0	0	1	0
Gideon, Pitt.	1.000	29	1	5	0	6	0
Glavine, Atl.*	.933	9	1	13	1	15	0
Gooden, N.Y.	.925	25	15	22	3	40	3
Gorman, S.D.*		6	0	0	0	0	0
Gossage, S.D.	1.000	40	2	5	0	7	0
Gott, S.F.-Pitt.	.938	55	5	10	1	16	0
Grant, S.F.-S.D.	.886	33	10	21	4	35	0
K. Gross, Phil.	.923	34	13	23	3	39	1
Gullickson, Cin.	1.000	27	14	16	0	30	0
Hall, Chi.*	1.000	21	3	3	0	6	0
Hammaker, S.F.*	1.000	31	7	23	0	30	1
Havens, L.A.*	1.000	31	1	3	0	4	0
Hawkins, S.D.	1.000	24	8	18	0	26	3
Hayward, S.D.*	1.000	4	1	3	0	4	1
Heathcock, Hou.	.909	19	3	7	1	11	0
Heaton, Mtl.*	.917	32	5	28	3	36	1
Heredia, Mtl.	1.000	2	0	2	0	2	1
Hernandez, Hou.	.857	6	2	4	1	7	0
Hershiser, L.A.	.934	37	37	34	5	76	6
Hesketh, Mtl.*	.667	18	1	1	1	3	0
Hillegas, S.D.	.857	12	4	2	1	7	0
Hoffman, Cin.*	1.000	36	3	21	0	24	0
Holton, L.A.	1.000	53	8	14	0	22	2
Honeycutt, L.A.*	.913	27	4	17	2	23	0
Horton, St.L.	.956	67	12	31	2	45	2
Howell, L.A.	1.000	40	5	5	0	10	0
Hume, Phil.-Cin.	1.000	49	2	17	0	19	0
Innis, N.Y.	1.000	17	3	2	0	5	0
M. Jackson, Phil.	.944	55	5	12	1	18	0
Johnson, Pitt.	1.000	5	1	1	0	2	1
Jones, Pitt.	.909	32	3	7	1	11	1
Jones, S.D.	1.000	30	15	28	0	43	1
Kerfeld, Hou.	.889	21	5	3	1	9	0
Kipper, Pitt.*	1.000	24	3	16	0	19	1
Knepper, Hou.*	.958	33	7	39	2	48	2
Krueger, L.A.*		2	0	0	0	0	0
Krukow, S.F.	.975	30	9	30	1	40	5
LaCoss, S.F.	.967	39	15	43	2	60	4
Lancaster, Chi.	1.000	27	12	14	0	26	0
Landrum, Cin.	1.000	44	3	12	0	15	4
LaPoint, St.L.*	1.000	6	0	3	0	3	0
Law, Mtl.	1.000	3	0	1	0	1	0
Lea, Mtl.		1	0	0	0	0	0
Leach, N.Y.	.951	44	18	21	2	41	3
Leary, L.A.	1.000	39	9	18	0	27	2
Lefferts, S.D.-S.F.*	.889	77	5	11	2	18	1
Leiper, S.D.*	.667	12	0	2	1	3	0
Lopez, Hou.	.875	26	0	7	1	8	0
Lynch, Chi.	1.000	58	9	17	0	26	2
Maddux, Chi.	.943	30	16	50	4	70	7
Maddux, Chi.	.667	7	1	1	1	3	0
Magrane, St.L.	.923	27	10	26	3	39	3
Mahler, Atl.	.982	39	13	42	1	56	2
Mallicoat, Hou.*	1.000	4	1	1	0	2	0
Martinez, Mtl.	.971	22	10	23	1	34	3
Mason, Chi.*	1.000	17	1	5	0	6	1
Mason, S.F.	1.000	5	3	3	0	6	2
Mathews, St.L.*	.895	32	3	31	4	38	2
Mathis, Hou.	.800	8	2	2	1	5	0
McClure, Mtl.*	1.000	52	3	8	0	11	0
McCullers, S.D.	.929	78	9	17	2	28	1
McDowell, N.Y.	1.000	56	10	17	0	27	1
McGaffigan, Mtl.	.846	69	5	17	4	26	2
McWilliams, Atl.*	1.000	9	1	3	0	4	1
Meads, Hou.*	1.000	45	1	4	0	5	1
Minton, S.F.	1.000	15	2	4	0	6	1
Mitchell, N.Y.	.860	20	16	21	6	43	3
Montgomery, Cin.	1.000	14	1	3	0	4	0
Moyer, Chi.*	.929	35	15	37	4	56	3
Murphy, Cin.*	1.000	87	7	14	0	21	0
Myers, N.Y.*	.933	54	5	9	1	15	0
Newell, Phil.		2	0	0	0	0	0
Niedenfuer, L.A.	1.000	15	2	3	0	5	1
Niekro, Atl.		1	0	0	0	0	0
Noles, Chi.	1.000	41	6	14	0	20	0
Nolte, S.D.*	1.000	12	5	7	0	12	0
Ojeda, N.Y.*	1.000	10	5	6	0	11	2
Olwine, Atl.*	.750	27	0	3	1	4	0
O'Neal, Atl.-St.L.	1.000	17	4	17	0	21	1
O'Neill, Cin.*		1	0	0	0	0	0
Oquendo, St.L.		1	0	0	0	0	0
Orosco, N.Y.*	1.000	58	4	9	0	13	1
Pacillo, Cin.	1.000	12	2	5	0	7	0
Palacios, Pitt.	1.000	6	2	1	0	3	0
Palmer, Atl.	.971	28	9	25	1	35	2
Parrett, Mtl.	.857	45	3	9	2	14	1
Patterson, Pitt.*	1.000	15	0	7	0	7	0
Pena, L.A.	.833	37	4	1	1	6	0
Pena, Pitt.*	1.000	16	1	4	0	5	0
Perez, Mtl.	.885	10	6	17	3	26	0
Perlman, S.F.	.750	10	2	1	1	4	0
Perry, St.L.-Cin.*	.960	57	12	12	1	25	2
Peters, St.L.*	1.000	12	1	5	0	6	1
Power, Cin.	.929	34	9	17	2	28	0
Price, S.F.*	1.000	20	1	2	0	3	0
Puleo, Atl.	1.000	35	6	10	0	16	0
Rasmussen, Cin.*	.889	7	0	8	1	9	0
Rawley, Phil.*	.976	36	6	34	1	41	2
Reuschel, Pitt.-S.F.	.969	34	25	38	2	65	2
Reuss, L.A.-Cin.*	1.000	8	1	3	0	4	1
Ritchie, Phil.*	1.000	49	1	9	0	10	0
D. Robinson, Pitt.-S.F.	1.000	67	8	12	0	20	0
J. Robinson, S.F.-Pitt.	1.000	81	14	18	0	32	6
Robinson, Cin.	.821	48	5	18	5	28	1
Ross, Pitt.	1.000	1	0	1	0	1	0
Ruffin, Phil.*	.951	35	7	32	2	41	3
Ryan, Hou.	.967	34	11	18	1	30	1
Salazar, S.D.	1.000	2	0	1	0	1	0
Sanderson, Chi.	.923	32	10	14	2	26	3
Savage, L.A.		3	0	0	0	0	0
Schatzeder, Phil.*	.800	26	2	2	1	5	0
Scherrer, Cin.*	1.000	23	3	3	0	6	0
Schulze, N.Y.	1.000	5	6	6	0	12	0
Scott, Hou.	.961	36	17	32	2	51	2
Sebra, Mtl.	.941	36	11	21	2	34	0
Show, S.D.	.925	34	10	27	3	40	2
Sisk, N.Y.	1.000	55	5	19	0	24	0
Smiley, Pitt.*	1.000	63	7	9	0	16	2
Smith, Mtl.	.969	26	10	21	1	32	2
Smith, Hou.	1.000	50	4	4	0	8	0
Smith, Chi.	1.000	62	3	8	0	11	0
P. Smith, Atl.	.750	6	1	2	1	4	0
Z. Smith, Atl.*	1.000	36	15	43	0	58	4
Soff, St.L.	1.000	12	1	2	0	3	0
Solano, Hou.	1.000	11	1	3	0	4	0
Sorensen, Mtl.	.889	23	3	5	1	9	0
Soto, Cin.	1.000	6	2	6	0	8	0
St. Claire, Mtl.	1.000	44	1	9	0	10	2
Sutcliffe, Chi.	.943	34	12	54	4	70	4
Taylor, Pitt.	.800	14	3	5	2	10	3
Tekulve, Phil.	.969	90	11	20	1	32	0
Terry, St.L.	1.000	11	0	4	0	4	0
Tewksbury, Chi.	.500	7	0	1	1	2	0
Tibbs, Mtl.	1.000	19	7	8	0	15	1
Toliver, Phil.	1.000	10	1	6	0	7	0
Trout, Chi.*	1.000	11	2	15	0	17	1

PITCHERS—Continued

Player, Club	PCT	G	PO	A	E	TC	DP
Tudor, St.L.★	1.000	16	4	20	0	24	2
Tunnell, St.L.	1.000	32	6	12	0	18	1
Valenzuela, L.A.★	.944	34	15	53	4	72	2
Walk, Pitt.	.939	39	9	22	2	33	2
Wallach, Mtl.	......	1	0	0	0	0	0
Walter, N.Y.★	.800	21	2	2	1	5	1
Welch, L.A.	1.000	35	25	38	0	63	3
Whitson, S.D.	.971	36	14	19	1	34	0
Williams, Cin.	.931	85	8	19	2	29	5
Wilson, Phil.	1.000	1	0	1	0	1	0
Wojna, S.D.	1.000	5	3	5	0	8	0
Worrell, St.L.	1.000	75	0	17	0	17	0
Youmans, Mtl.	1.000	23	16	10	0	26	1
Young, L.A.★	.667	47	3	1	2	6	0
Ziem, Atl.	......	2	0	0	0	0	0

PITCHERS WITH TWO OR MORE CLUBS

Player, Club	PCT	G	PO	A	E	TC	DP
Comstock, S.F.★	1.000	15	2	3	0	5	1
Comstock, S.D.★	1.000	26	0	1	0	1	0
M. Davis, S.F.★	.909	20	0	10	1	11	1
M. Davis, S.D.★	.933	43	4	10	1	15	2
R. Davis, Chi.	1.000	21	1	1	0	2	1
R. Davis, L.A.	1.000	4	0	2	0	2	1
Dravecky, S.D.★	.941	30	5	11	1	17	1
Dravecky, S.F.★	.968	18	11	19	1	31	1

Player, Club	PCT	G	PO	A	E	TC	DP
Gott, S.F.	.909	30	2	8	1	11	0
Gott, Pitt.	1.000	25	3	2	0	5	0
Grant, S.F.	.909	16	3	7	1	11	0
Grant, S.D.	.875	17	7	14	3	24	0
Hume, Phil.	1.000	38	2	15	0	17	0
Hume, Cin.	1.000	11	0	2	0	2	0
Lefferts, S.D.★	.875	33	2	5	1	8	1
Lefferts, S.F.★	.900	44	3	6	1	10	0
O'Neal, Atl.	1.000	16	4	15	0	19	1
O'Neal, St.L.	1.000	1	0	2	0	2	0
Perry, St.L.★	.950	45	9	10	1	20	2
Perry, Cin.★	1.000	12	3	2	0	5	0
Reuschel, Pitt.	.960	25	17	31	2	50	2
Reuschel, S.F.	1.000	9	8	7	0	15	0
Reuss, L.A.★	....	1	0	0	0	0	0
Reuss, Cin.★	1.000	7	1	3	0	4	1
D. Robinson, Pitt.	1.000	42	4	9	0	13	0
D. Robinson, S.F.	1.000	25	4	3	0	7	0
J. Robinson, S.F.	1.000	63	11	14	0	25	4
J. Robinson, Pitt.	1.000	18	3	4	0	7	2

OFFICIAL NATIONAL LEAGUE PITCHING AVERAGES

CLUB PITCHING

Club	W-L	ERA	G	CG	SHO	SV	IP	H	TBF	R	ER	HR	SH	SF	HB	BB	IB	SO	WP	BK
San Francisco	90-72	3.68	162	19	10	38	1471.0	1407	6202	669	601	146	74	36	27	547	86	1038	59	25
Los Angeles	73-89	3.72	162	29	8	32	1455.0	1415	6238	675	601	130	65	27	28	565	62	1097	54	18
Houston	76-86	3.84	162	13	13	33	1441.1	1363	6114	678	615	141	76	33	26	525	61	1137	39	14
New York	92-70	3.84	162	16	7	51	1454.0	1407	6191	698	621	135	68	47	34	510	51	1032	42	13
St. Louis	95-67	3.91	162	10	7	48	1466.0	1484	6254	693	637	129	71	33	27	533	79	873	46	13
Montreal	91-71	3.92	162	16	8	50	1450.1	1428	6151	720	631	145	69	43	26	446	45	1012	47	22
Philadelphia	80-82	4.18	162	13	7	48	1448.1	1453	6265	749	673	167	68	51	35	587	86	877	35	14
Pittsburgh	80-82	4.20	162	25	13	39	1445.0	1377	6131	744	674	164	67	40	22	562	60	914	61	23
Cincinnati	84-78	4.24	162	7	6	44	1452.1	1486	6188	752	685	170	72	49	22	485	68	919	33	18
San Diego	65-97	4.27	162	14	5	33	1433.1	1402	6206	763	680	175	59	31	36	602	62	897	55	13
Chicago	76-85	4.55	161	11	4	48	1434.2	1524	6311	801	726	159	71	42	27	628	67	1024	58	21
Atlanta	69-92	4.63	161	16	10	32	1427.2	1529	6270	829	734	163	63	49	39	587	55	837	42	29
Totals	971-971	4.08	971	189	98	496	17379.0	17275	74521	8771	7878	1824	823	481	349	6577	782	11657	571	219

PITCHERS' RECORDS

(Top Fifteen Qualifiers for Earned-Run Average Leadership—162 or More Innings)

Pitcher, Club	W	L	PCT	ERA	G	GS	CG	GF	SHO	SV	IP	H	TBF	R	ER	HR	SH	SF	HB	BB	IB	SO	WP	BK
Ryan, L. Nolan, Hou.	8	16	.333	2.76	34	34	0	0	1	0	211.2	154	873	75	65	14	9	1	4	87	2	270	10	2
Dunne, Michael, Pitt.	13	6	.684	3.03	23	23	5	0	1	0	163.1	143	680	66	55	10	11	4	1	68	8	72	6	4
Hershiser, Orel, L.A.	16	16	.500	3.06	37	35	10	2	1	0	264.2	247	1093	105	90	17	8	2	1	74	5	190	11	6
Reuschel, Ricky, Pitt.-S.F.	13	9	.591	3.09	34	33	12	0	0	1	227.0	207	920	91	78	13	8	6	8	42	3	107	7	4
Gooden, Dwight, N.Y.	15	7	.682	3.21	25	25	7	0	3	0	179.2	162	730	68	64	11	5	5	2	53	6	148	7	0
Welch, Robert, L.A.	15	9	.625	3.22	35	35	7	0	4	0	251.2	204	1027	94	90	21	10	6	4	86	6	196	1	1
Scott, Michael, Hou.	16	13	.552	3.23	36	36	8	0	3	0	247.2	199	1010	94	89	21	8	3	4	79	6	233	4	2
Dravecky, David, S.D.-S.F.*	10	12	.455	3.43	48	28	8	8	3	0	191.1	186	801	82	73	18	7	4	5	64	6	138	10	1
Magrane, Joseph, St.L.*	9	7	.563	3.54	27	26	8	0	3	0	170.1	157	722	75	67	9	9	5	6	60	10	101	2	7
Hammaker, C. Atlee, S.F.*	10	10	.500	3.58	31	27	0	2	0	1	168.1	159	706	73	67	22	3	3	3	57	11	107	9	7
Darwin, Danny, Hou.	9	10	.474	3.59	33	30	3	1	1	0	195.2	184	833	87	78	17	8	3	5	69	11	134	8	1
Downs, Kelly, S.F.	12	9	.571	3.63	41	28	4	4	3	4	186.0	185	797	83	75	14	1	7	1	67	14	137	3	4
Sutcliffe, Richard, Chi.	18	10	.643	3.68	34	34	6	0	1	0	237.1	223	1012	106	97	24	9	8	4	106	12	174	12	4
LaCoss, Michael, S.F.	13	10	.565	3.68	39	34	2	2	4	2	171.0	184	728	78	70	16	9	3	8	63	5	79	9	1
Mathews, Gregory, St.L.*	11	11	.500	3.73	32	32	0	0	0	0	197.2	184	822	87	82	17	9	2	2	71	—	108	7	2

ALL PLAYERS LISTED ALPHABETICALLY

(*Lefthanded Pitcher)

Pitcher, Club	W	L	PCT	ERA	G	GS	CG	GF	SHO	SV	IP	H	TBF	R	ER	HR	SH	SF	HB	BB	IB	SO	WP	BK
Acker, James, Atl.	4	9	.308	4.16	68	0	0	41	0	14	114.2	109	491	57	53	11	3	3	4	51	8	68	1	0
Agosto, Juan, Hou.*	4	4	.500	2.63	27	0	0	13	0	2	27.1	26	118	12	8	1	3	0	0	10	1	6	9	0
Aguilera, Richard, N.Y.	11	3	.786	3.60	18	17	1	0	0	0	115.0	124	494	53	46	12	3	2	0	33	5	77	2	0
Alexander, Doyle, Atl.	5	10	.333	4.13	16	16	3	0	0	0	117.2	115	481	57	54	21	7	3	3	27	10	64	0	0
Andersen, Larry, Hou.	9	5	.643	3.45	67	0	0	31	0	5	101.2	95	440	46	39	7	8	4	2	41	4	94	2	0
Assenmacher, Paul, Atl.*	1	1	.500	5.10	52	0	0	10	0	2	54.2	58	251	41	31	8	2	1	1	24	5	39	0	0
Bair, C. Douglas, Phil.	1	0	1.000	5.93	11	0	0	2	0	0	13.2	17	61	9	9	4	0	0	0	5	2	10	0	0
Baller, Jay, Chi.	0	1	.000	6.75	23	0	0	9	0	0	29.1	38	139	22	22	4	2	0	0	20	2	27	5	2

Pitcher, Club	W	L	PCT	ERA	G	GS	CG	SHO	GF	SV	IP	H	TBF	R	ER	HR	SH	SF	HB	BB	IB	SO	WP	BK
Bedrosian, Stephen, Phil.	5	3	.625	2.83	65	0	0	0	56	40	89.0	79	366	31	28	11	2	1	1	28	5	74	3	1
Belcher, Timothy, L.A.	4	2	.667	2.38	6	6	2	0	0	0	34.0	30	135	11	9	1	2	1	0	7	0	23	3	1
Bielecki, Michael, Pitt.	2	3	.400	4.73	8	8	2	0	0	0	45.2	43	192	25	24	6	5	2	1	12	0	25	0	0
Bockus, Randy, S.F.	1	0	1.000	3.63	12	0	0	0	2	0	17.1	17	68	8	7	2	0	1	0	4	1	9	3	0
Boever, Joseph, Atl.	1	0	1.000	7.36	14	0	0	0	10	1	18.1	29	93	15	15	4	2	0	0	12	1	18	0	0
Booker, Gregory, S.D.	0	1	.500	3.16	44	0	0	0	16	0	68.1	62	288	29	24	5	1	1	3	30	7	17	1	1
Brown, Curtis, Mtl.	0	1	.000	7.71	5	0	0	0	1	0	7.0	10	35	6	6	3	0	0	0	4	0	6	1	0
Browning, Thomas, Cin.*	10	13	.435	5.02	32	31	2	0	0	0	183.0	201	791	107	102	27	7	7	5	61	6	117	2	2
Burke, Timothy, Mtl.	7	0	1.000	1.19	55	0	0	0	30	18	91.0	64	354	18	12	3	8	2	0	17	7	58	2	4
Burkett, John, S.F.	0	0	----	4.50	3	0	0	0	1	0	6.0	8	28	4	3	2	0	0	0	3	0	5	0	0
Calhoun, Jeffrey, Phil.*	3	0	.750	1.48	42	0	0	0	15	0	42.2	25	183	13	7	1	5	2	0	26	8	31	2	0
Campbell, William, Mtl.	0	0	----	5.84	7	0	0	0	1	0	10.0	18	55	12	9	2	1	1	1	4	4	5	0	0
Candelaria, John, N.Y.*	2	0	1.000	8.10	3	3	0	0	0	0	12.1	17	57	8	8	1	0	1	0	3	0	10	0	1
Carman, Donald, Phil.*	13	11	.542	4.22	35	35	3	2	0	0	211.0	194	886	110	99	34	11	5	5	69	7	125	3	1
Cary, Charles, Atl.*	1	2	.500	3.78	13	0	0	0	6	0	16.2	17	70	7	7	3	3	0	0	4	3	15	1	0
Childress, Rodney, Hou.	0	1	.333	2.98	32	1	0	0	12	1	48.1	46	201	17	16	4	1	3	1	18	6	26	0	0
Clary, Martin, Atl.	0	3	.000	6.14	7	5	0	0	2	0	14.2	20	68	13	10	2	3	0	0	4	0	7	0	1
Coffman, Kevin, Atl.	2	1	.400	4.62	5	5	0	0	0	0	25.1	31	126	14	13	2	1	1	1	22	0	14	1	1
Comstock, Keith, S.F.-S.D.*	2	1	.667	4.61	41	0	0	0	15	1	56.2	52	244	30	29	5	3	4	3	31	5	59	6	4
Cone, David, N.Y.	5	6	.455	3.71	21	13	0	0	3	1	99.1	87	420	46	41	11	4	3	0	44	3	68	2	0
Conroy, Timothy, St.L.*	3	2	.600	5.53	10	9	0	0	0	0	40.2	48	188	26	25	0	3	0	5	25	1	22	2	0
Cowley, Joseph, Phil.	0	4	.000	15.43	5	4	0	0	0	0	11.2	21	73	20	20	2	0	4	2	17	0	5	0	1
Cox, Danny, St.L.	11	9	.550	3.88	31	31	2	1	0	0	199.1	224	864	99	86	17	14	1	3	71	6	101	5	0
Crews, S. Timothy, L.A.	1	1	.500	2.48	31	0	0	0	7	0	29.0	30	124	11	8	2	1	1	3	8	3	20	0	0
Darling, Ronald, N.Y.	12	8	.600	4.29	32	32	2	0	0	0	207.2	183	891	111	99	24	5	3	3	96	3	167	6	3
Darwin, Danny, Hou.	9	10	.474	3.59	33	30	3	1	0	0	195.2	184	833	87	78	17	8	2	5	69	12	134	3	1
Davis, George, S.D.	2	7	.222	6.18	21	10	0	0	5	0	62.2	48	292	48	43	5	7	1	6	36	6	37	5	1
Davis, Mark, S.F.-S.D.*	9	8	.529	3.99	63	11	0	0	18	2	133.0	123	566	64	59	14	2	6	2	59	8	98	7	2
Davis, Ronald, Chi.-L.A.	2	8	----	5.94	25	0	0	0	8	2	36.1	50	169	27	24	8	1	2	6	18	8	32	6	2
Dawley, William, St.L.	5	8	.385	4.47	60	0	0	0	17	2	96.2	93	406	51	48	15	6	2	1	38	11	65	3	2
Dayley, Kenneth, St.L.*	9	5	.643	2.66	53	0	0	0	29	4	61.0	52	260	21	18	2	2	2	2	33	8	63	4	1
Dedmon, Jeffrey, Atl.	3	4	.429	3.91	53	3	0	0	14	4	89.2	82	384	46	39	8	9	5	1	42	1	40	5	0
Deshaies, James, Hou.*	11	6	.647	4.62	26	25	1	0	0	0	152.0	149	648	78	78	22	6	3	2	57	7	104	2	5
DiPino, Frank, Chi.*	3	3	.500	3.15	69	0	0	0	20	4	80.0	75	343	31	28	7	7	4	0	34	2	61	4	0
Downs, Kelly, S.F.	11	9	.571	3.63	41	28	4	3	4	0	186.0	185	797	83	75	14	3	1	1	67	11	137	12	4
Drabek, Douglas, Pitt.	11	12	.478	3.88	29	28	1	3	0	0	176.1	165	721	86	76	22	7	4	4	46	2	120	5	1
Dravecky, David, S.D.-S.F.*	10	12	.455	3.43	48	28	5	3	8	0	191.1	186	801	82	73	18	7	6	5	64	7	138	2	1
Drummond, Timothy, Pitt.	0	0	----	4.50	6	0	0	0	2	0	6.0	5	26	3	3	0	0	0	1	3	0	5	0	0
Dunne, Michael, Pitt.	13	6	.684	3.03	23	23	5	3	0	0	163.1	143	680	66	55	10	11	4	0	68	8	72	6	4
Easley, K. Logan, Pitt.	1	0	.500	5.47	17	0	0	0	7	1	26.1	23	118	17	16	5	3	0	1	17	4	21	2	1
Edens, Thomas, N.Y.	0	1	.000	6.75	2	2	0	0	0	0	8.0	15	42	7	6	2	1	0	0	4	0	4	2	0
Fernandez, C. Sidney, N.Y.*	12	8	.600	3.81	28	27	3	1	0	0	156.0	130	665	75	66	16	6	6	8	67	8	134	2	0
Fischer, Jeffrey, Mtl.	0	0	----	8.56	4	2	0	0	0	0	13.2	21	66	14	13	3	3	0	0	5	0	6	3	0
Fisher, Brian, Pitt.	11	9	.550	4.52	28	26	6	1	1	0	185.1	185	792	90	93	27	6	2	7	72	7	117	3	3
Forsch, Robert, St.L.	11	7	.611	4.32	37	30	2	0	2	0	179.0	189	755	90	86	15	5	5	0	45	4	89	1	1
Franco, John, Cin.*	8	5	.615	2.52	68	0	0	0	60	32	82.0	76	344	26	23	6	6	6	1	27	6	61	0	0
Frohwirth, Todd, Phil.	1	0	1.000	0.00	10	0	0	0	2	0	11.0	12	43	0	0	0	3	0	0	2	2	9	0	0
Garber, H. Eugene, Atl.	8	10	.444	4.41	49	0	0	0	43	10	69.1	87	320	39	34	7	8	3	1	28	10	48	4	1
Garcia, Miguel, Pitt.*	0	0	----	0.00	1	0	0	0	1	0	0.2	0	2	0	0	0	0	0	0	0	0	0	0	0
Garrelts, Scott, S.F.	11	7	.611	3.22	64	0	0	0	43	12	106.1	70	428	41	38	10	0	2	0	55	4	127	5	0
Gibson, Robert, N.Y.	0	0	----	0.00	1	0	0	0	0	0	1.0	0	4	0	0	0	0	0	0	1	0	2	0	0

Pitcher, Club	W	L	PCT	ERA	G	GS	CG	GF	SHO	SV	IP	H	TBF	R	ER	HR	SH	SF	HB	BB	IB	SO	WP	BK
Gideon, B. Brett, Pitt.	1	5	.167	4.66	29	0	0	17	0	0	36.2	34	153	22	19	6	2	0	1	10	3	31	2	0
Glavine, Thomas, Atl.*	2	4	.333	5.54	9	9	0	0	0	0	50.1	55	238	34	31	5	2	3	3	33	4	20	1	1
Gooden, Dwight, N.Y.	15	7	.682	3.21	25	25	7	0	3	0	179.2	162	730	68	64	11	5	5	2	53	2	148	5	1
Gorman, Thomas, S.D.*	0	0	....	4.09	6	0	0	2	0	0	11.0	11	47	5	5	1	0	0	0	8	2	8	0	0
Gossage, Richard, S.D.	5	4	.556	3.12	40	0	0	30	0	11	52.0	47	217	18	18	4	2	0	0	19	6	44	2	0
Gott, James, S.F.-Pitt.	1	2	.333	3.41	55	0	0	30	0	13	87.0	81	382	43	33	4	4	3	2	40	6	90	5	0
Grant, Mark, S.F.-S.D.	7	9	.438	4.24	33	25	2	2	0	0	163.1	170	720	88	77	22	2	1	1	73	7	90	8	3
Gross, Kevin, Phil.	9	16	.360	4.35	34	33	3	1	1	0	200.2	205	878	107	97	26	6	6	10	87	8	110	3	7
Gullickson, William, Cin.*	10	11	.476	4.85	27	27	3	0	0	0	165.0	172	698	99	89	33	8	6	2	39	7	89	1	1
Hall, Andrew, Chi.*	1	1	.500	6.89	21	0	0	7	0	0	32.2	40	147	31	25	4	6	2	0	14	9	20	4	0
Hammaker, C. Atlee, S.F.*	10	10	.500	3.58	31	27	2	0	1	0	168.1	159	706	73	67	22	1	3	0	57	10	107	1	7
Havens, Bradley, L.A.*	0	0	....	4.33	31	1	0	10	0	1	35.1	30	157	18	17	2	3	0	2	23	11	23	8	3
Hawkins, M. Andrew, S.D.	3	10	.231	5.05	24	20	0	2	0	0	117.2	131	516	71	66	16	5	3	3	49	2	51	2	3
Hayward, Raymond, S.D.*	0	2	....	16.50	4	2	0	0	0	0	6.0	12	31	11	11	3	1	0	0	3	0	2	2	0
Heathcock, R. Jeffrey, Hou.	4	2	.667	3.16	19	2	0	2	0	1	42.2	44	174	15	15	9	2	3	1	9	3	15	2	1
Heaton, Neal, Mtl.	13	10	.565	4.52	32	32	3	0	1	0	193.1	207	807	103	97	25	5	5	3	37	1	105	1	5
Heredia, Ubaldo, Mtl.	0	0	....	5.40	2	0	0	0	0	0	10.0	10	42	6	6	2	0	0	0	5	1	6	0	0
Hernandez, Manuel, Hou.	0	4	.000	5.40	6	3	0	2	0	0	21.2	25	95	15	13	2	0	0	0	9	2	12	2	2
Hershiser, Orel, L.A.	16	16	.500	3.06	37	35	10	0	8	0	264.2	247	1093	105	90	17	4	2	1	74	5	190	11	0
Hesketh, Joseph, Mtl.*	4	3	.571	3.14	18	10	0	3	0	0	28.2	23	128	12	10	2	8	0	2	15	3	31	4	1
Hillegas, Shawn, L.A.	4	3	.571	3.57	12	12	0	0	0	0	58.0	52	252	27	23	5	2	1	2	31	0	51	3	2
Hoffman, Guy, Cin.*	9	10	.474	4.37	36	22	3	1	1	1	158.2	160	669	83	77	20	8	5	2	49	5	87	0	0
Holton, Brian, L.A.	3	2	.600	3.89	53	1	0	26	0	1	83.1	87	360	39	36	11	2	5	1	32	11	58	3	0
Honeycutt, Frederick, L.A.*	2	12	.143	4.59	27	20	1	0	0	0	115.2	133	525	74	59	10	8	3	0	45	4	92	4	0
Horton, Ricky, St.L.*	8	3	.727	3.82	67	6	0	24	0	7	125.0	127	533	58	53	15	2	3	0	42	10	55	5	0
Howell, Kenneth, L.A.	3	4	.429	4.91	40	6	0	17	0	2	55.0	54	239	32	30	7	2	0	2	29	2	60	3	0
Hume, Thomas, Phil-Cin.	2	4	.333	5.36	49	0	0	5	0	0	84.0	89	379	54	50	10	6	4	5	43	5	33	3	0
Innis, Jeffrey, N.Y.	0	0	....	3.16	17	0	0	8	0	0	25.2	29	109	9	9	0	3	0	0	4	1	28	0	0
Jackson, Michael, Phil.	3	10	.231	4.20	55	7	0	8	0	1	109.1	88	468	55	51	16	3	0	6	56	6	93	1	8
Johnson, David, Pitt.	0	0	....	9.95	5	0	0	3	0	0	6.1	13	31	7	7	1	0	0	0	2	0	4	0	0
Jones, Barry, Pitt.	2	4	.333	5.61	32	0	0	10	0	0	43.1	55	203	34	27	6	3	2	2	23	6	28	3	0
Jones, James, S.D.	9	7	.563	4.14	30	22	2	4	1	0	145.2	154	639	85	67	14	5	5	0	54	12	51	3	0
Kerfeld, Charles, Hou.	0	0	....	6.67	21	0	0	11	0	0	29.2	34	137	22	22	3	4	1	0	21	5	17	3	2
Kipper, Robert, Pitt.*	5	9	.357	5.94	24	20	1	1	0	0	110.2	117	493	82	73	25	4	2	1	52	2	83	0	0
Knepper, Robert, Hou.*	8	17	.320	5.27	33	31	3	0	0	0	177.2	226	792	118	104	26	7	4	4	54	3	76	1	0
Krueger, William, L.A.*	0	0	....	0.00	2	0	0	0	0	0	2.1	3	13	2	0	0	0	0	0	1	0	2	0	0
Krukow, Michael, S.F.	5	6	.455	4.80	30	28	2	0	0	0	163.0	182	699	98	87	24	8	8	2	46	6	104	0	0
LaCoss, Michael, S.F.	13	10	.565	3.68	39	26	3	4	2	0	171.0	184	728	78	70	16	9	3	1	63	12	79	6	1
Lancaster, Lester, Chi.	8	3	.727	4.90	27	18	0	4	0	2	132.1	138	578	76	72	14	5	6	1	51	5	78	7	8
Landrum, T. William, Cin.	3	2	.600	4.71	44	0	0	14	0	0	65.0	92	276	35	34	3	7	2	4	34	6	42	4	1
LaPoint, David, St.L.*	1	1	.500	6.75	6	2	0	3	0	0	16.0	26	79	12	12	4	0	0	0	5	0	8	1	0
Law, Vance, Mtl.	0	1	.000	5.40	3	0	0	0	0	0	3.1	5	15	2	2	0	0	0	0	2	0	2	0	0
Lea, Charles, Mtl.	0	1	....	36.00	1	1	0	0	0	0	1.0	4	9	4	4	1	0	0	0	2	0	1	0	1
Leach, Terry, N.Y.	11	1	.917	3.22	44	12	1	7	1	0	131.1	132	542	54	47	14	8	1	2	29	5	61	3	1
Leary, Timothy, L.A.	3	11	.214	4.76	39	12	0	5	0	0	107.2	121	469	62	57	15	6	2	2	36	5	61	6	0
Lefferts, Craig, S.D.-S.F.*	5	5	.500	3.83	77	0	0	19	0	6	98.2	92	416	47	42	13	2	2	2	33	11	57	0	3
Leiper, David, S.D.*	1	0	1.000	4.50	12	0	0	2	0	0	16.0	16	67	8	8	1	5	0	0	5	6	10	1	1
Lopez, Aurelio, Hou.	2	1	.667	4.50	26	0	0	5	0	0	38.0	39	164	22	19	6	2	0	0	12	5	21	1	0
Lynch, Edward, Chi.	2	9	.182	5.38	58	8	0	19	0	4	110.1	181	498	74	66	17	7	2	2	48	7	80	4	0
Maddux, Gregory, Chi.	6	14	.300	5.61	30	27	1	2	0	0	155.2	181	701	111	97	17	6	4	4	74	13	101	4	7
Maddux, Michael, Phil.	2	0	1.000	2.65	7	2	0	0	0	0	17.0	17	72	5	5	0	7	0	0	5	0	15	1	0

Pitcher, Club	W	L	PCT	ERA	G	GS	CG	GF	SHO	SV	IP	H	TBF	R	ER	HR	SH	SF	HB	BB	IB	SO	WP	BK
Magrane, Joseph, St.L.*	9	7	.563	3.54	27	26	4	0	2	0	170.1	157	722	75	67	9	9	3	10	60	6	101	9	7
Mahler, Richard, Atl.	8	13	.381	4.98	39	28	3	1	1	0	197.0	212	849	118	109	24	9	3	2	85	8	95	5	2
Mallicoat, Robin, Hou.*	0	0		6.75	4	0	0	1	0	0	6.2	8	31	8	5	0	0	0	0	6	0		0	0
Martinez, J. Dennis, Mtl.	11	4	.733	3.30	22	22	2	0	1	0	144.2	133	599	59	53	9	4	3	6	40	2	84	4	2
Mason, Michael, Chi.*	4	1	.800	5.68	17	4	2	3	0	0	38.0	43	173	25	24	4	4	3	1	23	0	28	1	0
Mason, Roger, S.F.	1	1	.500	4.50	5	5	0	0	0	0	26.0	30	110	15	13	4	1	0	0	10	0	18	7	1
Mathews, Gregory, St.L.*	11	11	.500	3.73	32	32	2	0	1	0	197.2	184	822	87	82	17	9	2	0	71	5	108	0	2
Mathis, Ronald, Hou.	0	1	.000	5.25	8	0	0	3	0	0	12.0	20	55	8	7	2	1	0	0	11	0	8	5	0
McClure, Robert, Mtl.*	6	1	.857	3.44	52	0	0	16	0	5	52.1	47	222	30	20	8	5	2	1	20	3	33	5	1
McCullers, Lance, S.D.	8	10	.444	3.72	78	0	0	41	0	16	123.1	115	540	60	51	11	6	2	2	59	11	126	6	1
McDowell, Roger, N.Y.	7	5	.583	4.16	56	0	0	45	0	25	88.2	95	384	41	41	7	5	5	2	28	4	32	1	3
McGaffigan, Andrew, Mtl.	5	2	.714	2.39	69	0	0	30	0	12	120.1	105	500	38	32	5	5	5	3	42	7	100	1	0
McWilliams, Larry, Atl.*	0	3	.000	5.75	9	2	0	4	0	0	20.1	25	95	15	13	2	2	1	1	7	2	13	7	0
Meads, David, Hou.*	5	3	.625	5.55	45	0	0	21	0	0	48.2	60	209	31	30	8	2	0	1	16	3	32	11	0
Minton, Gregory, S.F.	3	0	1.000	3.47	15	0	0	2	0	1	23.1	30	105	30	9	2	1	5	2	10	3	9	3	1
Mitchell, John, N.Y.	3	6	.333	4.11	20	19	1	0	0	0	111.2	124	493	64	51	6	6	0	0	36	9	57	0	0
Montgomery, Jeffrey, Cin.	2	2	.500	6.52	14	0	0	6	0	0	19.1	25	89	15	14	2	0	0	5	9	1	13	1	1
Moyer, Jamie, Chi.*	12	15	.444	5.10	35	33	1	0	0	0	201.0	210	899	127	114	28	14	7	0	97	9	147	4	2
Murphy, Robert, Cin.*	8	5	.615	3.04	87	0	0	21	0	3	100.2	91	415	37	34	7	1	2	5	32	5	99	3	0
Myers, Randall, N.Y.*	3	6	.333	3.96	54	0	0	18	0	6	75.0	61	314	36	33	6	7	6	0	30	5	92	1	0
Newell, Thomas, Phil.	0	0		36.00	2	0	0	0	0	0	1.0	4	10	4	4	1	0	0	0	3	0	1	0	0
Niedenfuer, Thomas, L.A.	0	0		2.76	15	0	0	8	0	1	16.1	13	70	5	5	0	0	0	0	9	3	10	0	2
Niekro, Phillip, Atl.	1	0	1.000	15.00	1	1	0	0	0	0	3.0	6	20	5	5	1	0	1	0	6	1	0	0	1
Noles, Dickie, Chi.	4	2	.667	3.50	41	1	0	16	0	2	64.1	59	285	31	25	6	5	0	5	27	9	33	2	0
Nolte, Eric, S.D.*	2	6	.250	3.21	12	12	1	0	0	0	67.1	57	293	28	24	6	2	4	2	36	1	44	3	0
Ojeda, Robert, N.Y.*	3	5	.375	3.88	10	7	0	0	0	0	46.1	45	192	23	20	5	3	2	3	10	1	21	5	0
Olwine, Edward, Atl.*	0	1	.000	5.01	27	0	0	9	0	1	23.1	25	104	16	13	4	1	0	1	8	3	12	1	0
O'Neal, Randall, Atl.-St.L.	4	2	.667	5.32	17	11	0	2	0	0	66.0	81	300	39	39	12	2	5	7	26	3	37	0	2
O'Neill, Paul, Cin.*	0	0		13.50	1	0	0	0	0	0	2.0	2	11	3	3	0	0	0	0	4	0	2	0	0
Oquendo, Jose, St.L.	0	0		27.00	1	0	0	1	0	0	1.0	2	9	3	3	1	0	0	1	1	0	0	2	0
Orosco, Jesse, N.Y.*	3	9	.250	4.44	58	0	0	41	0	16	77.0	78	335	41	38	0	5	2	2	31	9	78	3	0
Pacillo, Patrick, Cin.	2	2	.500	6.13	12	7	0	2	0	0	39.2	41	176	30	27	5	2	1	1	19	1	23	3	2
Palacios, Vicente, Pitt.	2	1	.667	4.30	6	4	0	0	0	0	29.1	27	120	14	14	5	2	0	0	9	1	13	5	0
Palmer, David, Atl.	8	11	.421	4.90	28	28	4	0	0	0	152.1	169	687	94	83	17	9	7	3	64	4	111	6	1
Parrett, Jeffrey, Mtl.	7	6	.538	4.21	45	0	0	26	0	6	62.0	53	267	33	29	8	5	0	0	30	4	56	1	0
Patterson, Robert, Pitt.*	1	4	.200	6.70	15	7	0	17	0	0	43.0	49	201	34	34	8	6	9	3	22	5	27	0	2
Pena, Alejandro, L.A.	2	7	.222	3.50	37	0	0	2	0	11	87.1	82	377	41	34	5	5	8	1	37	4	76	1	0
Pena, Hipolito, Pitt.*	0	3	.000	4.56	16	1	0	2	0	1	25.2	16	115	14	13	9	2	8	5	26	5	16	2	1
Perez, Pascual, Mtl.	7	0	1.000	2.30	10	10	3	0	4	0	70.1	60	273	21	18	2	3	2	8	16	7	58	3	2
Perlman, Jonathan, S.F.	0	0		3.97	10	0	0	3	0	0	11.1	11	50	7	5	5	0	0	1	4	1	3	3	1
Perry, W. Patrick, St.L.-Cin.*	5	2	.714	3.56	57	0	0	16	0	2	81.0	60	324	34	32	7	3	7	1	25	4	39	1	0
Peters, Steven, St.L.*	2	0		1.80	12	0	0	4	0	1	15.0	17	64	3	3	1	1	0	0	6	0	11	1	0
Power, Ted, Cin.	10	13	.435	4.50	34	34	0	5	0	1	204.0	213	887	115	102	28	8	9	3	71	7	133	10	2
Price, Joseph, S.F.*	2	2	.500	2.57	34	0	0	0	0	0	35.0	19	137	10	10	5	0	3	0	13	1	42	0	0
Puleo, Charles, Atl.	6	8	.429	4.23	20	16	0	2	0	0	123.1	122	524	63	58	11	7	8	3	40	7	99	1	1
Rasmussen, Dennis, Cin.*	4	1	.800	3.97	35	7	0	0	0	0	45.1	39	187	22	20	5	3	8	0	12	0	39	0	2
Rawley, Shane, Phil.*	17	11	.607	4.39	36	36	12	0	3	0	229.2	250	1005	118	112	23	10	1	5	86	8	123	2	3
Reuschel, Ricky, Pitt-S.F.	13	9	.591	3.09	34	34	4	0	4	0	227.0	207	920	91	78	13	8	2	8	42	3	107	3	0
Reuss, Jerry, L.A-Cin.*	0	5	.000	7.61	8	3	0	3	0	0	36.2	54	171	32	31	8	3	3	1	12	1	12	1	1
Ritchie, Wallace, Phil.*	3	2	.600	3.75	49	0	0	13	0	3	62.1	60	273	27	26	7	5	2	1	29	11	45	2	3
Robinson, Don, Pitt.-S.F.	11	7	.611	3.42	67	0	0	54	0	19	108.0	105	460	42	41	13	7	3	0	40	6	79	7	1

Pitcher, Club	W	L	PCT	ERA	G	GS	CG	GF	SHO	SV	IP	H	TBF	R	ER	HR	SH	SF	HB	BB	IB	SO	WP	BK
Robinson, Jeffrey, S.F.-Pitt	8	9	.471	2.85	81		0	40	0	14	123.1	89	495	43	39	11	10	4	1	54	11	101	5	2
Robinson, Ronald, Cin	7	5	.583	3.68	48	18	0	14	1	4	154.0	148		71	63	14	8	7	1	43	8	99	0	0
Ross, Mark, Pitt	0	0		9.00	1		0	1	0	0	1.0		4			1	0	0	0	0	4	0	6	0
Ruffin, Bruce, Phil.★	11	14	.440	4.35	35	35	3	0	1	0	204.2	236	884	118	99	17	8	10	2	73	4	93	0	2
Ryan, L. Nolan, Hou	8	16	.333	2.76	34	34	0	0	1	0	211.2	154	873	75	65	14	9	1	4	87	2	270	10	0
Salazar, Luis, S.D.	0	0		4.50	2		0	2	0	2	2.0		9			0	0	0	0	1	0		2	0
Sanderson, Scott, Chi	8	9	.471	4.29	32	22	0	5	0	0	144.2	156	631	72	69	23	4	5	3	50	5	106	1	0
Savage, John, L.A.	0	0		2.70	3		0		0	0	3.1	4	14	1	1	0	0	0	0	0	0		0	0
Schatzeder, Daniel, Phil.★	3	1	.750	4.06	26		0	8	0	0	37.2	40	164	21	17	4	2	4	0	14	7	28	0	0
Scherrer, William, Cin.★	1	1	.500	4.36	23		0	10	0	0	33.0	43	151	17	16	3	1	3	1	16	4	24	2	0
Schulze, Donald, N.Y.	1	2	.333	6.23	5	4	0	1	0	0	21.2	24	91	15	15	4	3	2	4	6	0	5	0	2
Scott, Michael, Hou	16	13	.552	3.23	36	36	8	0	3	0	247.2	199	1010	94	89	21	8	3	3	79	6	233	10	2
Sebra, Robert, Mtl	2	5	.286	4.42	36	27	4	3	1	0	177.1	184	765	99	87	15	12	7	9	67	0	156	8	8
Show, Eric, S.D.	8	16	.333	3.84	34	34	5	0	3	0	206.1	188	887	99	88	26	9	5	3	85	7	117	6	5
Sisk, Douglas, N.Y.	3	1	.750	3.46	55		0	17	0	3	78.0	83	339	38	30	5	5	2	0	22	4	37	6	0
Smiley, John, Pitt.★	5	5	.500	5.76	63		0	19	0	4	75.0	83	336	49	48	5	0	3	2	50	8	58	5	1
Smith, Bryn, Mtl	10	9	.526	4.37	26	26	6	0	0	0	150.1	164	643	81	73	16	7	5	5	31	4	94	2	0
Smith, David, Hou	2	3	.400	1.65	50		0	44	0	24	60.0	39	240	13	11	4	3	2	0	21	8	73	5	2
Smith, Lee, Chi	4	10	.286	3.12	62		0	55	0	36	83.2	84	360	30	29	4	0	5	0	32	5	96	2	0
Smith, Peter, Atl	1	2	.333	4.83	6	6	0	0	0	0	31.2	39	143	21	17	3	4	1	5	14	6	11	4	2
Smith, Zane, Atl.★	15	10	.600	4.09	36	36	9	0	3	0	242.0	245	1035	130	110	19	12	0	5	91	6	130	4	0
Soff, Raymond, St.L.	1	0	1.000	6.46	12		0	4	0	1	15.1	18	68	17	11	3	1	2	1	5	1	9	3	1
Solano, Julio, Hou.	0	0		7.65	6		0	6	0	0	20.0	25	94	17	17	5	2	5	0	9	0	12	5	0
Sorensen, Lary, Mtl	3	4	.429	4.72	44	5	0	14	0	7	47.2	56	215	32	25	7	4	1	3	12	2	21	0	0
Soto, Mario, Cin	3	2	.600	5.12	14	6	0	0	0	0	31.2	34	138	18	18	7	1	3	0	12	1	11	0	0
St. Claire, Randy, Mtl.	3	3	.500	4.03	23		0	24	0	3	67.0	64	282	31	30	9	4	3	0	20	2	43	1	0
Sutcliffe, Richard, Chi	18	10	.643	3.68	34	34	6	0	1	0	237.1	223	1012	106	97	24	9	8	4	106	14	174	4	0
Taylor, Donald, Pitt	2	3	.400	5.74	14	8	0	0	0	0	53.1	48	226	35	34	10	1	2	1	28	1	37	9	0
Tekulve, Kenton, Phil	6	4	.600	3.09	90		0	38	0	0	105.0	96	432	38	36	8	5	8	1	29	13	60	3	0
Terry, Scott, St.L	0	0		3.38	7		0	2	0	3	13.1	13	59	5	5	0	1	0	0	8	2	9	2	0
Tewksbury, Robert, Chi	0	4	.000	6.50	19	3	0	3	0	0	18.0	32	93	15	13	1	3	3	0	13	3	10	0	2
Tibbs, Jay, Mtl	4	5	.444	4.99	10	12	0	2	0	0	83.0	95	366	55	46	10	2	0	1	34	3	54	1	1
Toliver, Freddie, Phil.★	1	1	.500	5.64	11	4	0	2	0	0	30.1	34	139	19	19	9	1	1	2	17	1	25	1	1
Trout, Steven, Chi★	6	3	.667	3.00	16	11	0	0	0	0	75.0	72	308	27	25	2	3	2	1	27	0	32	1	0
Tudor, John, St.L.★	10	2	.833	3.84	16	16	3	0	0	0	96.0	100	405	43	41	11	2	2	3	32	1	54	3	0
Tunnell, B. Lee, St.L	4	4	.500	4.84	32	9	0	3	0	0	74.1	90	335	45	40	5	1	2	1	34	7	49	1	5
Valenzuela, Fernando, L.A.★	14	14	.500	3.98	34	34	12	0	1	0	251.0	254	1116	120	111	25	18	4	4	124	4	190	2	1
Walk, Robert, Pitt.	8	2	.800	3.31	39	12	1	6	0	2	117.0	107	498	52	43	11	6	2	3	51	2	78	14	3
Wallach, Timothy, Mtl.★	0	0		0.00	1		0	1	0	0	1.0		3			0	0	0	0	0	0	0	7	0
Walter, Gene, N.Y.★	1	2	.333	3.20	25		0	6	0	2	19.2	18	89	10	7	1	10	1	1	13	3	11	0	0
Welch, Robert, L.A.	15	9	.625	3.22	35	35	6	0	4	0	251.2	204	1027	90	90	21	4	6	4	86	6	196	1	4
Whitson, Eddie, S.D.	10	13	.435	4.73	36	34	3	0	1	0	205.2	197	858	113	108	36	5	2	3	64	3	135	4	0
Williams, Frank, Cin.	4	0	1.000	2.30	85		0	19	0	0	105.2	101	446	37	27	5	0	6	2	39	9	60	4	1
Wilson, Glenn, Phil.	0	0		0.00	5		0	1	0	2	1.0		3			0	1	0	0	0	0	1	4	0
Wojna, Edward, S.D.	0	3	.000	5.89	23	3	0	0	0	0	18.1	25	84	12	12	2	3	2	0	6	0	13	0	0
Worrell, Todd, St.L.	8	6	.571	2.66	75		0	54	0	33	94.2	86	395	29	28	8	4	5	1	34	11	92	3	3
Youmans, Floyd, Mtl.	9	8	.529	4.64	25	23	3	0	3	0	116.1	112	505	63	60	13	6	2	0	47	2	94	3	1
Young, Matthew, L.A.★	5	8	.385	4.47	47		0	31	0	11	54.1	62	234	30	27	3	1	5	1	17	5	42	3	0
Ziem, Stephen, Atl	0	1	.000	7.71	2		0	1	0	0	2.1	4	12	3	2	3	0		0	1	0	0	0	0

PITCHERS WITH TWO OR MORE CLUBS IN 1987
Listed alphabetically, first club on top

Pitcher, Club	W	L	PCT	ERA	G	GS	CG	GF	SHO	SV	IP	H	TBF	R	ER	HR	SH	SF	HB	BB	IB	SO	WP	BK
Comstock, S.F.	2	0	1.000	3.05	15	0	0	3	0	0	20.2	19	87	8	7	1	1	1	0	10	2	21	3	1
Comstock, S.D.	0	1	.000	5.50	26	0	1	12	0	0	36.0	33	157	22	22	4	2	3	0	21	3	38	3	0
M. Davis, S.F.	4	5	.444	4.71	20	11	1	1	0	0	70.2	72	301	38	37	9	3	2	4	28	1	51	4	2
M. Davis, S.D.	5	3	.625	3.18	43	0	0	17	0	2	62.1	51	265	26	22	5	4	0	2	31	7	47	2	0
R. Davis, Chi.	0	0	.....	5.85	21	0	0	6	0	0	32.1	43	144	23	21	8	0	0	1	12	1	31	1	2
R. Davis, L.A.	0	0	.....	6.75	4	0	0	2	0	0	4.0	7	25	4	3	0	0	1	1	6	1	2	2	0
Dravecky, S.D.	3	7	.300	3.76	30	10	1	8	0	0	79.0	71	335	39	33	10	2	3	3	31	4	60	1	1
Dravecky, S.F.	7	5	.583	3.20	18	18	4	0	3	0	112.1	115	466	43	40	8	5	2	2	33	3	78	1	0
Gott, S.F.	1	0	1.000	4.50	30	3	0	8	0	0	56.0	53	253	32	28	4	1	1	0	32	5	63	3	1
Gott, Pitt.	0	2	.000	1.45	25	0	0	22	0	13	31.0	28	129	11	5	0	7	0	0	8	5	27	2	0
Grant, S.F.	1	2	.333	3.54	16	8	0	2	0	1	61.0	66	264	29	24	6	7	1	0	21	5	32	2	2
Grant, S.D.	6	7	.462	4.66	17	17	2	0	1	0	102.1	104	456	59	53	16	8	0	0	52	3	58	6	1
Hume, Phil.	1	4	.200	5.60	38	6	0	3	0	0	70.2	75	325	48	44	10	7	2	4	41	5	29	3	0
Hume, Cin.	1	0	1.000	4.05	11	0	0	2	0	0	13.1	14	54	6	6	1	1	1	1	2	1	4	0	0
Lefferts, S.D.	2	2	.500	4.38	33	0	0	8	0	2	51.1	56	225	29	25	9	2	0	2	15	5	39	5	2
Lefferts, S.F.	3	3	.500	3.23	44	0	0	14	0	4	47.1	36	191	18	17	4	4	2	1	18	6	18	1	1
O'Neal, Atl.	4	0	.667	5.61	16	10	1	2	0	0	61.0	79	279	41	38	12	1	2	0	24	3	33	9	0
O'Neal, St.L.	2	0	.....	1.80	1	1	0	0	0	0	5.0	2	21	1	1	1	1	0	2	2	0	4	0	1
Perry, St.L.	4	2	.667	4.39	45	0	0	13	0	1	65.2	54	269	34	32	7	2	2	1	21	3	33	3	0
Perry, Cin.	1	0	1.000	0.00	12	0	0	3	0	0	15.1	6	55	0	0	0	1	0	2	4	1	6	0	0
Reuschel, Pitt.	8	6	.571	2.75	25	25	9	0	3	0	177.0	163	715	63	54	12	4	7	6	35	1	80	5	0
Reuschel, S.F.	5	3	.625	4.32	9	8	3	0	1	0	50.0	44	205	28	24	4	4	1	2	7	2	27	2	0
Reuss, L.A.	0	0	.....	4.50	1	0	0	0	0	0	2.0	2	8	1	1	0	0	1	0	0	2	2	0	1
Reuss, Cin.	0	5	.000	7.79	7	7	0	0	0	0	34.2	52	163	31	30	2	2	1	1	12	2	10	1	1
D. Robinson, Pitt.	6	6	.500	3.86	42	0	0	37	0	12	65.1	66	276	29	28	6	6	1	0	22	3	53	6	1
D. Robinson, S.F.	5	1	.833	2.74	25	0	0	17	0	7	42.2	39	184	13	13	1	1	2	0	18	3	26	1	0
J. Robinson, S.F.	6	8	.429	2.79	63	0	0	33	0	10	96.2	69	395	34	30	10	9	4	1	48	10	82	3	2
J. Robinson, Pitt.	2	1	.667	3.04	18	0	0	7	0	4	26.2	20	100	9	9	1	0	0	1	19	2	19	4	0

American League Combined Shutouts

Following pitchers combined to pitch shutout games: Baltimore (1)—Habyan and Niedenfuer. California (4)—Candelaria and Moore; Sutton and Moore; Witt and Buice; Sutton and Minton. Chicago (4)—DeLeon and Thigpen; DeLeon and Searage; LaPoint and Thigpen; Bannister and Thigpen. Cleveland (2)—Niekro and Yett; Niekro and Bailes; Bailes and Stewart; Yett and Jones. Detroit (2)—Alexander and Henneman 2. Milwaukee (1)—Barker and Crim. Minnesota (1)—Straker, Berenguer and Reardon; Viola and Berenguer. New York (7)—John, Clements and Righetti; Niekro and Righetti; Guidry and Stoddard; Trout, Stoddard and Righetti; John and Hudson; Rhoden and Stoddard; Filson, Stoddard and Righetti. Oakland (4)—Plunk and Howell; Stewart and G. Nelson; G. Nelson, Lamp, Cadaret and Eckersley; Ontiveros, Plunk and Eckersley. Seattle (4)—Bankhead and Wilkinson 2; Bankhead and Nunez; Moore and Wilkinson. Texas (3)—Guzman, Kilgus and Mohorcic; Witt and Mohorcic; Witt, Russell and Kilgus. Toronto (5)—Clancy and Henke; Stieb and Eichhorn; Nunez and Henke; Flanagan and Henke; Key, Musselman and Henke.

National League Combined Shutouts

Following pitchers combined to pitch shutout games: Chicago (1)—Sutcliffe and Smith. Cincinnati (4)—Power and Franco 2; Power, Franco and Williams; Robinson and Franco. Houston (9)—Deshaies, Andersen and Smith 2; Knepper, Andersen and Smith; Ryan, Lopez and Smith; Darwin and Smith; Scott and Smith; Scott and Childress; Ryan and Smith; Ryan and Agosto. Los Angeles (1)—Leary, Crews and Young. Montreal (2)—Youmans, McClure and Burke; Smith, Hesketh, McClure and McGaffigan. New York (2)—Aguilera, Myers and McDowell; Candelaria, Aguilera and Myers. Philadelphia (2)—Ruffin and Bedrosian; Maddux, M. Jackson, Calhoun and Tekulve. Pittsburgh (3)—Walk, Easley, Smiley and D. Robinson; Walk and Gott; Dunne, J. Robinson and Gott. St. Louis (3)—Cox, Horton and Worrell; Tudor and Worrell; Mathews and Worrell. San Diego (4)—Whitson and Gossage; S. Davis and Jones; Nolte and Comstock; Jones and McCullers. San Francisco (2)—Dravecky and D. Robinson; Krukow and Price.

1987 CHAMPIONSHIP SERIES

Including

American League Review

American League Box Scores

American League Composite Box Score

National League Review

National League Box Scores

National League Composite Box Score

Minnesota third baseman Gary Gaetti clutches his American League Championship Series Most Valuable Player trophy and wipes a tear from his eye during a welcome-home celebration at the Metrodome.

Twins Rip Sleeping Tigers

By LARRY WIGGE

When Matt Nokes grounded back to the mound with two out in the ninth inning of Game 5 of the 1987 American League Championship Series, Minnesota reliever Jeff Reardon made the easy toss to first baseman Kent Hrbek and the Twins were A.L. champions. The Detroit Tigers were down and out after compiling the best regular-season record of any of the four division winners.

It was fitting that Reardon would be involved in the 9-5 victory that put Minnesota into the World Series for the first time since 1965.

"I watched these guys hit the ball and couldn't believe they didn't finish higher than sixth," Reardon said, recalling his first glimpse of the Twins in spring training after being acquired from the Montreal Expos. "At first, I must admit I wasn't so sure that being traded from Montreal to Minnesota was in my best interests. But. . . .

"After seeing these guys in spring training, I figured even if our pitching staff was mediocre, this team could contend."

Reardon, of course, was the puzzle piece that helped reshape the Twins' mediocre pitching staff. The hard-throwing right-hander posted 31 saves during the regular season. He also was credited with a victory in relief of Frank Viola in Game 1 of the Championship Series and had saves in Games 4 and 5.

Even Reardon, however, fell short in his assessment of the 1987 Twins. That the Twins could contend in the American League West, especially with the addition of Reardon, was generally accepted. But most baseball followers were quick to concede that anything beyond a division title was wishful thinking.

After all, the Tigers had won 98 games, the Twins 85. In fact, the Twins' 85-77 record would have placed them no better than fifth in the A.L. East.

"We were the champions in the A.L. West, but everybody said, 'So what?' " said Viola.

The odds clearly were stacked against the Twins, who tackled them one by one:

• The Tigers had righthander Doyle Alexander primed for the first game of the Championship Series. Alexander had compiled a sparkling 9-0 record with Detroit after being obtained from Atlanta in September. Even more impressive was the 11-0 mark recorded by the Tigers in

games that Alexander started.

• Detroit's Game 2 starter, Jack Morris, boasted a career record of 11-0 in games he had pitched in Minnesota. The St. Paul native also remembered the Twins' lack of interest when he was walking the free-agent trail in late 1986 and let them know that he would like to come home.

• Game 3 starter Walt Terrell boasted a 32-7 career mark, including 13-2 in 1987, in games that he pitched at Tiger Stadium.

But a funny thing happened on the way to the World Series. . . .

"There were a lot of things that were against us when you looked at this series on paper—the winning streaks by their starting pitchers and our lousy record on the road—but those things actually helped to drive us," said Twins third baseman Gary Gaetti, who batted .300 with two home runs and five RBIs en route to Most Valuable Player honors in the Championship Series.

Who would have thought that Gaetti would set a Championship Series record by connecting for homers in his first two at-bats against Alexander? Who would have thought that Twins catcher Tim Laudner, a .191 hitter in '87, would find a magic wand in Game 2 and provide the game-winning hit? Who would have thought that the Twins would win while Kent Hrbek and Kirby Puckett were struggling to a combined .182 (8 for 44) average? And who would have dreamed that Twins shortstop Greg Gagne would outhit (.278 to .200) his Detroit counterpart, Alan Trammell, and drive in more runs (3-2)?

Though the Twins had compiled the best home record (56-25) in the majors in '87, they had lost four of six meetings against the Tigers at the Metrodome. But, as Gaetti pointed out, paper lions don't always have the sharpest claws.

The Twins got all the big two-out hits. They were brilliant in the field. They won the battle of the bullpens and outpitched the best starting rotation in the A.L. They outhit the lineup that scored the most runs in baseball. And they beat the big guys in their own park—twice. When the Twins recorded victories in Games 4 and 5 at Tiger Stadium, it marked the first time since August 29 and 30 that the Twins had won consecutive games on the road.

"The turning point in the series was Game 4," said Gaetti. "They had just come

Jeff Reardon, who literally saved the day for the 1987 Twins, recorded a pair of saves in the team's Championship Series victory over Detroit.

back for a dramatic victory (7-6 with two runs in the eighth inning) in Game 3 and we stopped their momentum in their park."

Though the Twins had never won a

Championship Series contest before (they were swept three straight by Baltimore in 1969 and 1970), they jumped on the Tigers quickly. They knocked off Alexander, 8-5, in the first game and beat Morris, 6-3, in

Game 2. Then they hit the road, where they were a dreadful 29-52 (9-25 after the All-Star break). But these amazing Twins rallied from a 5-0 deficit in Game 3 to take the lead before falling, 7-6. Then they recorded 5-3 and 9-5 decisions on Tiger turf. Pretty good for a team that lost its last five and eight of nine road games down the stretch.

The Twins used the experience of 38-year-old veteran Don Baylor and took advantage of the Tigers' shaky relief pitching to rally from a 5-4 deficit in the bottom of the eighth inning and post their 8-5 Game 1 triumph.

Dan Gladden led off the decisive eighth with a single. After Greg Gagne popped up attempting to sacrifice, Puckett doubled to left-center field and Gladden beat the relay to the plate to score the tying run.

Rookie Mike Henneman replaced Alexander and added gasoline to the fire by walking Hrbek and Gaetti to load the bases. With the crowd of 53,269 in a frenzy, veteran lefthander Willie Hernandez replaced Henneman and Baylor was summoned to hit for lefthanded designated hitter Randy Bush.

Baylor, who had been obtained from Boston on August 31 for pennant insurance, paid a big dividend when he lined a 2-2 offering to left field to give the Twins a 6-5 lead. Tom Brunansky then added a pair of insurance runs with his second double of the game.

Alexander had taken a 5-4 lead into the Twins' half of the eighth after successive sacrifice flies by pinch-hitter Dave Bergman and Chet Lemon.

"Now the Tigers have to think about a split here," said Baylor, whose RBI single extended his Championship Series hitting streak to 11 games. "The pressure's on them."

The loss was the first Championship Series defeat for Detroit Manager Sparky Anderson in 10 games.

Things were supposed to get better for Anderson in Game 2 with Morris on the mound. But the Twins struck for three runs in the second inning and two more in the fourth as they rallied from a 2-0 deficit for a 6-3 victory and a commanding 2-0 lead in the series.

A two-run homer by Lemon had staked Morris to a 2-0 lead in the second inning, but the veteran righthander yielded doubles to Gaetti and Brunansky in the bottom half of the inning. With two out, Gagne, the No. 8 hitter in the Minnesota lineup, coaxed a walk from Morris. That brought up Laudner, a .191 hitter during the regular season with a propensity to

strike out (80 times in 288 at-bats). However, this time Laudner ripped Morris' first delivery into the left-field corner, scoring Brunansky and Gagne and giving the Twins a 3-2 lead.

With one out in the fifth, Bush singled and stole second and third. Morris' control got the best of him once again as he walked Brunansky and Gagne. This time, Laudner struck out. But Gladden responded with a two-run single to boost the Twins' lead to 5-2.

"The story of the first two games is that they've come up with the big hits and we haven't," said Trammell.

Trammell and Kirk Gibson, two of the main reasons for the Tigers' 1987 success, were a combined 2 for 16 in the first two games, explaining much of Detroit's predicament.

Former Tiger reliever Juan Berenguer earned the save in Game 2 by retiring five straight batters, including all three he faced in the ninth inning. His playful gestures of shooting down the Detroit batters, however, incensed many Tigers.

Surprisingly, the Twins came within five outs of taking a 3-0 lead when the series shifted to Detroit. But with Minnesota holding a 6-5 lead with Reardon on the mound in the eighth inning, Detroit's Pat Sheridan spoiled that plan by hitting a two-run homer to lift the Tigers to victory.

Larry Herndon had greeted Reardon with a single to open the eighth. After Tom Brookens popped up attempting to sacrifice, Sheridan, who had lost his right-field job to rookie Scott Lusader down the stretch when he was just 5 for 66, blasted Reardon's first delivery into the upper deck in right field.

"It was hard, one of the hardest things I've ever had to do," Sheridan said of his long stay on the bench. "I thought it would be a few days—not three to four weeks."

But Sheridan knew he would get another chance if the Tigers made the playoffs because Lusader had been called up too late to be eligible for postseason play.

Sheridan had triggered a five-run third-inning explosion with a double. After Lou Whitaker singled and Darrell Evans walked to load the bases, Gibson forced Evans at second as the first run crossed the plate. Gibson then stole second and, when Minnesota starter Les Straker committed a balk, Whitaker scored and Gibson went to third. Before the inning had ended, Trammell had singled home one run and Herndon had connected for a two-run pinch double.

Minnesota chipped away at that lead,

scoring twice in the fourth on a solo homer by Gagne and an RBI single by Bush. Brunansky smashed a two-run homer in the sixth and the Twins went ahead in the seventh on Gaetti's two-out, two-run single.

Though no team had ever come back from a five-run deficit to win a Championship Series contest, the Twins were headed in that direction before Sheridan's heroics capped a three-hour, 29-minute thriller, the longest nine-inning game in A.L. Championship Series history.

In Game 4, Puckett and Gagne ended slumps with home runs and a couple of blunders by Detroit veteran Darrell Evans helped the Twins register a 5-3 victory and take a 3-1 series lead.

Puckett, who had managed just one hit in 14 at-bats, hit a solo homer in the third inning. Gagne, who was 1 for 11, put the Twins ahead, 2-1, with a fourth-inning homer. The Twins added single runs in the fifth and sixth on Gaetti's sacrifice fly and Gene Larkin's RBI pinch double.

Detroit closed to 4-3 with one run in the sixth, but Evans' baserunning gaffe cost the Tigers at least one run. Leadoff singles by Lemon and Evans knocked out Viola and placed runners on first and third. Bergman's pinch single to the opposite field off Keith Atherton scored Lemon and Mike Heath's sacrifice advanced both runners.

At this point, Berenguer replaced Atherton and, on the first pitch to Whitaker, taken for a ball, Laudner's throw to Gaetti embarrassingly picked Evans off third base. But the horrifying night wasn't over for the 40-year-old slugger.

In the eighth, Evans, who had been switched from first base to third, failed to come up with Laudner's grounder. After reaching first base on Evans' error, Laudner went to second on a wild pitch and to third on a groundout. Lombardozzi plated him with a single past Evans' glove.

"I missed two balls I should have caught," Evans admitted later. "I hurt the team. But when I got home, I slept well. My wife made me laugh. My kids still love me. They all put bags over their heads, but what the heck."

The Twins, who trailed at one point in each of the first four games, jumped on Alexander for four runs in the second inning of Game 5 and went on to post a 9-5 victory.

Brunansky, who had seven hits in 17 at-bats in the series, including four doubles, a pair of home runs and nine RBIs, highlighted the Twins four-run second with a two-run double and then homered in the ninth. His nine RBIs were one short of Baylor's Championship Series record set in 1982 when Baylor was with California.

Gladden and Puckett added RBI singles in the second, Bush had a sacrifice fly in the seventh, the Twins scored a run in the eighth on a forceout and, after Brunansky's one-out homer in the ninth, Gladden and Gagne hit back-to-back RBI doubles.

Homers by Nokes, Lemon and Brunansky in Game 5 gave the teams 15 for the series, breaking the playoff record of 13 set by Los Angeles and Philadelphia in 1978 and equalled by California and Boston in 1986.

In eliminating the Tigers in five games, the Twins joined the 1973 New York Mets as the only division winner with fewer than 90 victories to advance to the World Series.

"They didn't give us a chance to regroup," said Henneman. "Every time we made a mistake, they cashed in."

In the process, Minnesota's Tom Kelly became only the sixth manager to win a Championship Series in his rookie season, following in the footsteps of Anderson with Cincinnati in 1970, Tommy Lasorda with Los Angeles in 1977, Jim Frey (Kansas City) and Dallas Green (Philadelphia) in 1980, and Harvey Kuenn with Milwaukee in 1982.

"For a while we could bang our chests and say we were the best team in baseball," Morris said. "But that was a week ago. Now, it's the Twins' turn."

GAME OF WEDNESDAY, OCTOBER 7
AT MINNESOTA (N)

Detroit	AB.	R.	H.	RBI.	PO.	A.
Whitaker, 2b	4	0	0	0	2	2
Madlock, dh	5	0	0	0	0	0
Gibson, lf	4	2	1	3	1	0
Trammell, ss	4	1	1	0	0	3
Herndon, rf	3	1	1	0	0	0
Bergman, ph	0	0	0	1	0	0
Sheridan, lf	0	0	0	0	0	0
Lemon, cf	3	0	2	1	3	0
Evans, 1b	4	0	2	0	10	0
Brookens, 3b	3	0	0	0	0	2
Grubb, ph	1	0	1	0	0	0
Heath, c	3	1	2	2	6	0
Nokes, ph	1	0	0	0	0	0
Alexander, p	0	0	0	0	0	1
Henneman, p	0	0	0	0	0	0
Hernandez, p	0	0	0	0	0	0
King, p	0	0	0	0	0	0
Totals	35	5	10	5	24	9

Minnesota	AB.	R.	H.	RBI.	PO.	A.
Gladden, lf	4	1	2	1	2	0
Gagne, ss	4	0	0	0	0	2
Puckett, cf	4	1	1	1	1	0
Hrbek, 1b	3	1	0	0	9	1
Gaetti, 3b	3	3	2	2	0	2
Bush, dh	3	1	1	0	0	0

	AB.	R.	H.	RBI.	PO.	A.
Baylor, ph	1	0	1	1	0	0
Brunansky, rf	4	1	2	3	3	0
Lombardozzi, 2b	3	0	1	0	2	0
Laudner, c	3	0	0	0	10	0
Viola, p	0	0	0	0	0	1
Reardon, p	0	0	0	0	0	0
Totals	32	8	10	8	27	6

Detroit .... 0 0 1   0 0 1   1 2 0—5
Minnesota .... 0 1 0   0 3 0   0 4 x—8

Detroit	IP.	H.	R.	ER.	BB.	SO.
Alexander (Loser)	7⅓	8	6	6	0	5
Henneman	0*	0	2	2	2	0
Hernandez	⅓	2	0	0	0	0
King	⅓	0	0	0	0	0

Minnesota	IP.	H.	R.	ER.	BB.	SO.
Viola	7*	9	5	5	1	6
Reardon (Winner)	2	1	0	0	1	3

*Pitched to two batters in eighth.

Game-winning RBI—Baylor.
Left on bases—Detroit 7, Minnesota 3. Two-base hits—Brunansky 2, Trammell, Puckett. Three-base hit—Bush. Home runs—Gaetti 2, Heath, Gibson. Sacrifice hit—Lombardozzi. Sacrifice flies—Bergman, Lemon. Umpires—Brinkman, Merrill, Coble, Clark, Reilly and McKean. Time—2:46. Attendance—53,269.

GAME OF THURSDAY, OCTOBER 8
AT MINNESOTA (N)

Detroit	AB.	R.	H.	RBI.	PO.	A.
Whitaker, 2b	3	1	2	1	2	4
Evans, 1b	4	0	2	0	6	0
Gibson, lf	4	0	0	0	0	0
Trammell, ss	4	0	0	0	2	1
Nokes, dh-c	4	1	1	0	1	0
Lemon, cf	4	1	1	2	2	0
Sheridan, rf	4	0	1	0	4	0
Brookens, 3b	2	0	0	0	1	3
Heath, c	2	0	0	0	6	0
Grubb, ph	1	0	0	0	0	0
Morris, p	0	0	0	0	0	0
Totals	32	3	7	3	24	8

Minnesota	AB.	R.	H.	RBI.	PO.	A.
Gladden, lf	4	0	1	2	1	0
Lombardozzi, 2b	4	0	0	0	3	3
Puckett, cf	4	0	0	0	2	0
Hrbek, 1b	4	1	1	1	8	0
Gaetti, 3b	4	1	1	0	1	1
Bush, dh	4	1	1	0	0	0
Brunansky, rf	2	2	1	1	1	0
Gagne, ss	1	1	0	0	1	3
Laudner, c	3	0	1	2	10	1
Blyleven, p	0	0	0	0	0	1
Berenguer, p	0	0	0	0	0	0
Totals	30	6	6	6	27	9

Detroit .... 0 2 0   0 0 0   0 1 0—3
Minnesota .... 0 3 0   2 1 0   0 0 x—6

Detroit	IP.	H.	R.	ER.	BB.	SO.
Morris (Loser)	8	6	6	6	3	7

Minnesota	IP.	H.	R.	ER.	BB.	SO.
Blyleven (Winner)	7⅓	7	3	3	1	6
Berenguer (Save)	1⅔	0	0	0	0	4

Game-winning RBI—Laudner.
Error—Trammell. Double plays—Detroit 1, Minnesota 1. Left on bases—Detroit 4, Minnesota 3. Two-base hits—Gaetti, Brunansky, Laudner. Home runs—Lemon, Hrbek, Whitaker. Stolen bases—Whitaker, Sheridan, Bush 2. Sacrifice hit—Brookens. Umpires—Merrill, Coble, Clark, Reilly, McKean and Brinkman. Time—2:54. Attendance—55,245.

GAME OF SATURDAY, OCTOBER 10,
AT DETROIT

Minnesota	AB.	R.	H.	RBI.	PO.	A.
Gladden, lf	3	1	1	0	2	0
Gagne, ss	5	2	1	1	3	1
Puckett, cf	5	0	0	0	1	0
Hrbek, 1b	3	1	0	0	5	2
Gaetti, 3b	5	0	2	2	2	0
Bush, dh	3	1	1	1	0	0
Brunansky, rf	3	1	1	2	2	0
Lombardozzi, 2b	3	0	0	0	1	1
Butera, c	3	0	2	0	6	0
Davidson, pr	0	0	0	0	0	0
Laudner, c	1	0	0	0	1	0
Straker, p	0	0	0	0	0	2
Schatzeder, p	0	0	0	0	1	0
Berenguer, p	0	0	0	0	0	0
Reardon, p	0	0	0	0	0	0
Totals	34	6	8	6	24	6

Detroit	AB.	R.	H.	RBI.	PO.	A.
Whitaker, 2b	4	1	1	0	1	3
Evans, 1b	1	0	0	0	11	1
Gibson, lf	5	1	1	1	1	0
Trammell, ss	4	1	1	1	2	0
Nokes, c	3	0	0	0	5	2
Lemon, cf	3	1	0	0	4	0
Bergman, dh	1	0	0	0	0	0
Herndon, dh	3	0	2	2	0	0
Morris, pr	0	1	0	0	0	0
Brookens, 3b	4	0	0	0	0	4
Sheridan, rf	4	2	2	2	3	0
Terrell, p	0	0	0	0	0	1
Henneman, p	0	0	0	0	0	1
Totals	32	7	7	6	27	12

Minnesota .... 0 0 0   2 0 2   2 0 0—6
Detroit .... 0 0 5   0 0 0   0 2 x—7

Detroit	IP.	H.	R.	ER.	BB.	SO.
Straker	2⅔	3	5	5	4	1
Schatzeder	3⅓†	2	0	0	0	5
Berenguer	1	0	0	0	1	1
Reardon (Loser)	1	2	2	2	1	0

Detroit	IP.	H.	R.	ER.	BB.	SO.
Terrell	6*	7	6	6	4	4
Henneman (Winner)	3	1	0	0	3	1

*Pitched to two batters in seventh.
†Pitched to one batter in seventh.

Game-winning RBI—Sheridan.
Error—Lombardozzi. Left on bases—Minnesota 8, Detroit 8. Two-base hits—Sheridan, Herndon. Home runs—Gagne, Brunansky, Sheridan. Stolen bases—Gibson 2. Hit by pitcher—By Schatzeder (Evans). Balk—Straker. Umpires—Coble, Clark, Reilly, McKean, Brinkman and Merrill. Time—3:29. Attendance—49,730.

GAME OF SUNDAY, OCTOBER 11,
AT DETROIT (N)

Minnesota	AB.	R.	H.	RBI.	PO.	A.
Gladden, lf	3	0	0	0	3	0
Newman, 2b	2	0	0	0	0	1
Larkin, ph	1	0	1	1	0	0
Lonbardozzi, pr-2b	1	0	1	1	2	1
Puckett, cf	5	2	2	1	1	0
Gaetti, 3b	4	0	0	1	3	4
Baylor, dh	4	0	1	0	0	0
Brunansky, rf	3	0	0	0	1	0
Hrbek, 1b	5	0	0	0	8	0
Gagne, ss	4	2	2	1	2	4
Laudner, c	2	1	0	0	7	1
Viola, p	0	0	0	0	0	0
Atherton, p	0	0	0	0	0	0
Berenguer, p	0	0	0	0	0	0
Reardon, p	0	0	0	0	0	0
Totals	34	5	7	5	27	11

Detroit	AB.	R.	H.	RBI.	PO.	A.
Whitaker, 2b	2	2	0	0	3	2
Morrison, dh	4	0	1	0	0	0
Nokes, ph	1	0	0	0	0	0
Gibson, lf	4	0	1	1	3	0
Trammell, ss	3	0	1	0	1	3
Herndon, rf	3	0	0	0	2	0
Lemon, cf	4	1	1	0	2	0
Evans, 1b-3b	4	0	1	0	7	1
Brookens, 3b	2	0	0	0	1	6
Bergman, ph-1b	2	0	1	1	6	0
Heath, c	2	0	0	0	2	0
Grubb, ph	1	0	1	0	0	0
Sheridan, pr	0	0	0	0	0	0
Tanana, p	0	0	0	0	0	1
Petry, p	0	0	0	0	0	1
Thurmond, p	0	0	0	0	0	0
Totals	32	3	7	2	27	14

Minnesota.............................. 0 0 1   1 1 1   0 1 0—5
Detroit................................... 1 0 0   0 1 1   0 0 0—3

Minnesota	IP.	H.	R.	ER.	BB.	SO.
Viola (Winner)	5*	5	3	2	4	3
Atherton	⅓	1	0	0	0	0
Berenguer	2⅔	0	0	0	2	1
Reardon (Save)	1	1	0	0	0	2

Detroit	IP.	H.	R.	ER.	BB.	SO.
Tanana (Loser)	5⅓	6	4	3	4	1
Petry	3⅓	1	1	0	0	1
Thurmond	⅓	0	0	0	0	0

*Pitched to two batters in sixth.

Game-winning RBI—Gagne.
Errors—Gagne, Herndon, Evans 2. Double play —Minnesota 1. Left on bases—Minnesota 11, Detroit 9. Two-base hits—Gagne, Larkin. Home runs —Puckett, Gagne. Sacrifice hits—Newman, Heath. Sacrifice fly—Gaetti. Hit by pitcher—By Tanana (Gladden 2, Baylor). Wild pitches—Tanana, Berenguer, Petry. Umpires—Clark, Reilly, McKean, Brinkman, Merrill and Coble. Time— 3:24. Attendance—51,939.

GAME OF MONDAY, OCTOBER 12, AT DETROIT

Minnesota	AB.	R.	H.	RBI.	PO.	A.
Gladden, lf	6	3	3	2	4	0
Gagne, ss	4	0	2	1	3	3
Puckett, cf	6	0	2	1	2	0
Hrbek, 1b	5	1	2	0	10	0
Gaetti, 3b	4	1	1	0	2	0

	AB.	R.	H.	RBI.	PO.	A.
Bush, dh	2	1	0	1	0	0
Brunansky, rf	5	1	3	3	3	0
Lombardozzi, 2b	4	2	2	0	0	4
Laudner, c	5	0	0	0	3	0
Blyleven, p	0	0	0	0	0	0
Schatzeder, p	0	0	0	0	0	1
Berenguer, p	0	0	0	0	0	0
Reardon, p	0	0	0	0	0	1
Totals	41	9	15	8	27	9

Detroit	AB.	R.	H.	RBI.	PO.	A.
Whitaker, 2b	4	0	0	0	3	3
Evans, 1b	4	0	0	0	9	2
Gibson, lf	4	1	3	1	3	0
Trammell, ss	5	1	1	1	1	2
Nokes, c	5	1	1	2	5	0
Lemon, cf	4	1	1	1	2	0
Grubb, dh	4	0	2	0	0	0
Sheridan, rf	2	0	0	0	0	1
Brookens, 3b	2	0	0	0	1	0
Bergman, ph	1	0	0	0	0	0
Morrison, 3b	1	1	1	0	1	2
Alexander, p	0	0	0	0	1	0
King, p	0	0	0	0	1	1
Henneman, p	0	0	0	0	0	1
Robinson, p	0	0	0	0	0	1
Totals	36	5	9	5	27	13

Minnesota.............................. 0 4 0   0 0 0   1 1 3—9
Detroit................................... 0 0 0   3 0 0   0 1 1—5

Minnesota	IP.	H.	R.	ER.	BB.	SO.
Blyleven (Winner)	6	5	3	3	2	3
Schatzeder	1	0	0	0	0	0
Berenguer	⅔	1	1	1	0	0
Reardon (Save)	1⅓	3	1	1	1	0

Detroit	IP.	H.	R.	ER.	BB.	SO.
Alexander (Loser)	1⅔	6	4	4	1	0
King	5	3	1	1	2	4
Henneman	2	5	4	4	1	2
Robinson	⅓	1	0	0	0	0

Game-winning RBI—Brunansky.
Errors—Gagne, Evans. Double play—Minnesota 1. Left on bases—Minnesota 12, Detroit 9. Two-base hits—Gagne 2, Brunansky, Gibson, Gladden 2. Home runs—Nokes, Lemon, Brunansky. Stolen bases—Bush, Puckett, Gibson. Sacrifice fly— Bush. Hit by pitcher—By Alexander (Gagne), by Blyleven (Sheridan 2), by King (Gaetti). Wild pitches—King, Reardon. Passed ball—Nokes. Umpires—Reilly, McKean, Brinkman, Merrill, Coble and Clark. Time—3:14. Attendance—47,448.

MINNESOTA TWINS' BATTING & FIELDING AVERAGES

Player—Position	G.	AB.	R.	H.	TB.	2B.	3B.	HR.	RBI.	B.A.	PO.	A.	E.	F.A.
Larkin, ph	1	1	0	1	2	1	0	0	1	1.000	0	0	0	.000
Butera, c	1	3	0	2	2	0	0	0	0	.667	6	0	0	1.000
Brunansky, rf	5	17	5	7	17	4	0	2	9	.412	10	0	0	1.000
Baylor, ph-dh	2	5	0	2	2	0	0	0	1	.400	0	0	0	.000
Gladden, lf	5	20	5	7	9	2	0	0	5	.350	12	0	0	1.000
Gaetti, 3b	5	20	5	6	13	1	0	2	5	.300	8	7	0	1.000
Gagne, ss	5	18	5	5	14	3	0	2	3	.278	9	13	2	.917
Lombardozzi, 2b-pr	5	15	2	4	4	7	0	0	1	.267	8	9	1	.944
Bush, dh	4	12	4	3	5	0	1	0	2	.250	0	0	0	.000
Puckett, cf	5	24	3	5	9	1	0	1	3	.208	7	0	0	1.000
Hrbek, 1b	5	20	4	3	6	0	0	1	1	.150	40	3	0	1.000
Laudner, c	5	14	1	1	2	1	0	0	0	.071	31	2	0	1.000
Berenguer, p	4	0	0	0	0	0	0	0	0	.000	0	0	0	.000
Reardon, p	4	0	0	0	0	0	0	0	0	.000	0	1	0	1.000
Blyleven, p	2	0	0	0	0	0	0	0	0	.000	0	1	0	1.000
Schatzeder, p	2	0	0	0	0	0	0	0	0	.000	1	1	0	1.000
Viola, p	2	0	0	0	0	0	0	0	0	.000	0	1	0	1.000
Atherton, p	1	0	0	0	0	0	0	0	0	.000	0	0	0	.000
Davidson, pr	1	0	0	0	0	0	0	0	0	.000	0	0	0	.000
Straker, p	1	0	0	0	0	0	0	0	0	.000	0	2	0	1.000
Newman, 2b	1	2	0	0	0	0	0	0	0	.000	0	1	0	.000
Totals	5	171	34	46	85	13	1	8	33	.269	132	41	3	.983

DETROIT TIGERS' BATTING & FIELDING AVERAGES

Player—Position	G.	AB.	R.	H.	TB.	2B.	3B.	HR.	RBI.	B.A.	PO.	A.	E.	F.A.
Grubb, ph-dh	4	7	0	4	4	0	0	0	0.	.571	0	0	0	.000
Morrison, dh-3b	2	5	1	2	2	0	0	0	0	.400	1	2	0	1.000
Herndon, rf-ph-dh	3	9	1	3	4	1	0	0	2	.333	2	0	1	.667
Sheridan, rf-pr	5	10	2	3	7	1	0	1	2	.300	7	1	0	1.000
Evans, 1b-3b	5	17	0	5	5	0	0	0	0	.294	43	4	3	.940
Gibson, lf	5	21	4	6	10	1	0	1	4	.286	10	1	0	1.000
Heath, c	3	7	1	2	5	0	0	1	2	.286	14	0	0	1.000
Lemon, cf	5	18	4	5	11	0	0	2	4	.278	13	0	0	1.000
Bergman, ph-dh-1b	4	4	0	1	1	0	0	0	2	.250	6	0	0	1.000
Trammell, ss	5	20	3	4	5	1	0	0	2	.200	6	9	1	.938
Whitaker, 2b	5	17	4	3	6	0	0	1	1	.176	11	14	0	1.000
Nokes, ph-dh-c	5	14	2	2	5	0	0	1	2	.143	11	2	0	1.000
Henneman, p	3	0	0	0	0	0	0	0	0	.000	0	2	0	1.000
Alexander, p	2	0	0	0	0	0	0	0	0	.000	1	1	0	1.000
King, p	2	0	0	0	0	0	0	0	0	.000	1	1	0	1.000
Morris, p-pr	2	0	1	0	0	0	0	0	0	.000	0	0	0	.000
Hernandez, p	1	0	0	0	0	0	0	0	0	.000	0	0	0	.000
Petry, p	1	0	0	0	0	0	0	0	0	.000	0	1	0	1.000
Robinson, p	1	0	0	0	0	0	0	0	0	.000	0	1	0	1.000
Tanana, p	1	0	0	0	0	0	0	0	0 ·	.000	0	1	0	1.000
Terrell, p	1	0	0	0	0	0	0	0	0	.000	0	1	0	1.000
Thurmond, p	1	0	0	0	0	0	0	0	0	.000	0	0	0	.000
Madlock, dh	1	5	0	0	0	0	0	0	0	.000	0	0	0	.000
Brookens, 3b	5	13	0	0	0	0	0	0	0	.000	3	15	0	1.000
Totals	5	167	23	40	65	4	0	7	21	.240	129	56	5	.974

MINNESOTA TWINS' PITCHING RECORDS

Pitcher	G.	GS.	CG.	IP.	H.	R.	ER.	BB.	SO.	HB.	WP.	W.	L.	Pct.	ERA.
Schatzeder	2	0	0	4⅓	2	0	0	0	5	1	0	0	0	.000	0.00
Atherton	1	0	0	⅓	1	0	0	0	0	0	0	0	0	.000	0.00
Berenguer	4	0	0	6	1	1	1	3	6	0	1	0	0	.000	1.50
Blyleven	2	2	0	13⅓	12	6	6	3	9	2	0	2	0	1.000	4.05
Reardon	4	0	0	5⅓	7	3	3	3	5	0	1	1	1	.500	5.06
Viola	2	2	0	12	14	8	7	5	9	0	0	1	0	1.000	5.25
Straker	1	1	0	2⅔	3	5	5	4	1	0	0	0	0	.000	16.88
Totals	16	5	0	44	40	23	22	18	35	3	2	4	1	.800	4.50

No shutouts. Saves—Berenguer, Reardon 2.

DETROIT TIGERS' PITCHING RECORDS

Pitcher	G.	GS.	CG.	IP.	H.	R.	ER.	BB.	SO.	HB.	WP.	W.	L.	Pct.	ERA.
Petry	1	0	0	3⅓	1	1	0	0	1	0	1	0	0	.000	0.00
Hernandez	1	0	0	⅓	2	0	0	0	0	0	0	0	0	.000	0.00
Robinson	1	0	0	⅓	1	0	0	0	0	0	0	0	0	.000	0.00
Thurmond	1	0	0	⅓	0	0	0	0	0	0	0	0	0	.000	0.00
King	2	0	0	5⅓	3	1	1	2	4	1	1	0	0	.000	1.69
Tanana	1	1	0	5⅓	6	4	3	4	1	3	1	0	1	.000	5.06
Morris	1	1	1	8	6	6	6	3	7	0	0	0	1	.000	6.75
Terrell	1	1	0	6	7	6	6	4	4	0	0	0	0	.000	9.00
Alexander	2	2	0	9	14	10	10	1	5	1	0	0	2	.000	10.00
Henneman	3	0	0	5	6	6	6	6	3	0	0	1	0	1.000	10.80
Totals	14	5	1	43	46	34	32	20	25	5	3	1	4	.200	6.70

No shutouts or saves.

COMPOSITE SCORE BY INNINGS

Minnesota	0	8	1	5	5	3	3	6	3 — 34
Detroit	1	2	6	3	1	2	1	6	1 — 23

Game-winning RBIs—Baylor, Laudner, Sheridan, Gagne, Brunansky.

Sacrifice hits—Lombardozzi, Brookens, Newman, Heath.

Sacrifice flies—Bergman, Lemon, Gaetti, Bush.

Stolen bases—Whitaker, Sheridan, Bush 3, Gibson 3, Puckett.

Caught stealing—Gladden.

Double plays—Gagne, Lombardozzi and Hrbek; Whitaker, Trammell and Evans; Gaetti, Lombardozzi and Hrbek; Lombardozzi, Gagne and Hrbek.

Left on bases—Minnesota 3, 3, 8, 11, 12—37; Detroit 7, 4, 8, 9, 9—37.

Hit by pitcher—By Schatzeder (Evans), by Tanana (Gladden 2, Baylor), by Alexander (Gagne), by Blyleven (Sheridan 2), by King (Gaetti).

Passed ball—Nokes.

Balk—Straker.

Time of games—First game, 2:46; second game, 2:54; third game, 3:29; fourth game, 3:24; fifth game, 3:14.

Attendance—First game, 53,269; second game, 55,245; third game, 49,730; fourth game, 51,939; fifth game, 47,448.

Umpires—Brinkman, Merrill, Coble, Clark, Reilly and McKean.

Official scorers—Bob Beebe, Minnesota official scorer; Rich Shook, United Press International (Detroit).

Cardinal utilityman Jose Oquendo had plenty to smile about after hitting a Game 7 homer against San Francisco in the N.L. Championship Series.

Cardinals Slip Past Giants

By LARRY WIGGE

"Do something during the game to make this night memorable." That was the challenge thrown out to Jose Oquendo by his wife, Zenaida, on October 14, 1987, the day their daughter Adianez turned 3.

"My wife asked me to do something special for my daughter," Oquendo said. "So when I hit the home run, I was thinking about Adianez."

The home run was indeed memorable.

Oquendo's unlikely three-run blast highlighted a four-run second inning and powered the St. Louis Cardinals to a 6-0 victory over the San Francisco Giants in Game 7 of the National League Championship Series. And it enabled the Cardinals to go to the World Series for the third time in six years.

"I stayed up late last night studying Rod Carew's (his boyhood hero) hitting video and came out early to take extra batting practice," Oquendo said. "But I'm lucky to hit a home run. I didn't think it was going out. I thought it was a good line drive until I heard the boom (from the fireworks that are ignited at Busch Stadium after each Cardinals' home run)."

Oquendo, the Cardinals' utility man supreme, came into the playoffs with just two career home runs in 903 at-bats before connecting against San Francisco lefthander Atlee Hammaker.

Ironically, Oquendo's other two big league homers also came against Giants' lefthanders—August 21, 1983, as a pinch-hitter against Gary Lavelle (when Oquendo was a member of the New York Mets) and July 25, 1987, against Craig Lefferts.

While Oquendo's surprising display of power highlighted the Cardinals' amazing comeback from a 3-2 series deficit, it was the St. Louis pitching that really saved the day.

The Giants had pulled within one victory of their first World Series appearance since 1962 by hitting nine home runs and scoring 23 runs in the first five games. But when the scene shifted to St. Louis for the final two games, the Cardinals recorded a Championship Series-record two straight shutouts.

John Tudor combined with Todd Worrell and Ken Dayley for a 1-0 decision in Game 6 and Danny Cox stymied the Giants on eight hits for a 6-0 final-game triumph.

In all, Cardinals' pitchers strung together 22 consecutive shutout innings, another Championship Series record. The Giants got only one runner as far as third base in the final two games.

"We came in here needing just one win and we didn't even score a run," said San Francisco Manager Roger Craig. "I wouldn't have believed it."

Cox, who also pitched the regular-season division-clinching victory, was scheduled to start Game 1, but was sidelined with a stiff neck. Lefthander Greg Mathews, however, proved a capable substitute, allowing only four hits over 7⅓ innings and singling home two runs to help the Cardinals record a 5-3 victory.

"Yesterday I played 18 holes of golf and I got away from my normal off-day high-carbohydrate diet and ate at Jack in the Box," said Mathews, who had an 0-2 record in three starts against the Giants in 1987 and gave up 14 runs and 21 hits in 16⅔ innings. "So much for being superstitious."

The Cardinals' sixth-inning uprising turned out to be the difference. With runners on second and third and one out, Terry Pendleton broke a 2-2 tie with a bloop single just inside the foul line in left field. Curt Ford singled to load the bases, but catcher Tony Pena fouled out. That brought Mathews to the plate.

Mathews, a .191 hitter in the regular season, looped Rick Reuschel's 1-2 delivery to center, scoring Willie McGee and Pendleton.

After Mathews walked Robby Thompson with one out in the eighth, Worrell came in and retired only one of the four batters he faced. However, Dayley came in to put out the fire, retiring Will Clark on a long fly to right-center with the bases loaded. He also induced Bob Melvin to hit into a game-ending double play in the ninth.

"I really don't know how we did it," said St. Louis Manager Whitey Herzog.

Herzog, of course, was referring to the absence of Cardinals' slugger Jack Clark (tendon tear in his ankle) and the emergency call that went out to Mathews after Cox couldn't answer the bell. The Cardinals were 20-16 without Clark in the lineup, but their run production fell from 5.31 per game to 3.61.

The Cardinals' meager attack was notable in Game 2 as Will Clark and Jeffrey Leonard flexed their home-run muscles and Dave Dravecky pitched a record-

John Tudor's Game 6 pitching stopped the Giants and kept the Cardinals alive in the N.L. Championship Series.

tying two-hitter in leading the Giants to a 5-0 victory. It was the first home loss in Championship Series competition in seven games for the Cardinals.

Clark slugged a two-run homer in the second inning and Leonard added a lead-off round-tripper in the fourth, his second homer in as many games. The Giants' victory sent the best-of-seven series to Candlestick Park tied at one victory apiece.

The only hits off Dravecky, acquired July 4 from San Diego, were singles by Jim Lindeman in the second and Tom Herr in the fourth. Previous Championship Series two-hit efforts had been turned in by Cincinnati's Ross Grimsley in 1972, Jon Matlack of the New York Mets in 1973 and Oakland's Vida Blue in 1974.

The Cardinals had only one baserunner after Herr's hit in the fourth as they were shut out at home for only the second time all season.

The Giants appeared to be in control of Game 3 after bolting to a 4-0 lead. Three second-inning runs and Leonard's record-tying third homer in as many games provided the cushion. The Giants almost broke the game open in the fifth, but St. Louis reliever Bob Forsch wriggled out of a bases-loaded jam.

The Giants would later have reason to look back and lament that failure to score. Lindeman, a .208 regular-season hitter who was replacing Jack Clark in the cleanup spot, got the Cardinals back in the game with a two-run, sixth-inning home run. And suddenly the momentum was on the Cardinals' side.

With their 17-inning scoreless streak a thing of the past, the Cardinals added a seventh-inning run on Dan Driessen's single and scored four more times in the eighth, two runs coming on Vince Coleman's single and another on Lindeman's sacrifice fly. Forsch held off the Giants and was credited with his first victory at Candlestick Park since August 1979.

But even with their dramatic comeback victory the Cardinals had reason for concern. Third baseman Pendleton sprained his ankle during an off-day workout and was relegated to limited duty.

Cox finally made his first start in Game 4, facing Mike Krukow, the first San Francisco starter in the series who was a member of the Giants' opening-day roster. Krukow won the battle of righthanders, 4-2.

While Krukow was scattering nine hits and benefitting from four double plays, Thompson, Leonard and Bob Brenly all hit homers as the Giants erased a 2-0 second-inning St. Louis lead.

Thompson broke an 0-for-11 slump with a two-out solo homer in the fourth, Leonard put the Giants in front for good with a two-out, two-run homer in the fifth and Brenly's homer put icing on the cake in the eighth. Leonard set a playoff record by slugging four homers in as many games, equaling the Championship Series mark of four homers in one series set by Pittsburgh's Bob Robertson in 1971 and tied by San Diego's Steve Garvey in 1978.

The Cardinals took a 3-2 lead into the bottom of the fourth inning in Game 5, but lost Mathews with a thigh injury and wound up losing, 6-3.

Bullpens were the key in this contest. Veteran San Francisco lefthander Joe Price replaced Reuschel in the fifth and retired 15 of the 17 batters he faced. Meanwhile, Forsch, the winning pitcher in Game 3, replaced Mathews to open the fourth and failed to get a batter out.

Chili Davis singled on Forsch's first delivery and went to third on Clark's hit-and-run single. After Brenly walked to load the bases, Jose Uribe, who was sent by the Cardinals to San Francisco in 1985 as part of the five-player deal involving Jack Clark, lined Forsch's first pitch to right for a two-run single. Pinch-hitter Mike Aldrete then delivered a sacrifice fly and Thompson capped the uprising with an triple.

Meanwhile, Price, who had been released by Cincinnati in the off-season and had been toiling in the minors for half a season before the Giants called him up, hurled one-hit ball over the final five innings while striking out six.

The Giants returned to St. Louis with high hopes that Dravecky could perform a replay of his Game 2 masterpiece. Left-handers had been poison to the Cardinals in the first five games of the series, combining for an earned-run average of 1.23 while holding the Redbirds to a woeful .171 batting average. But. . . .

The Cardinals, playing on the brink for most of September while fighting the Mets and Montreal Expos for first place in the N.L. East, rebounded, winning by the barest of margins, 1-0.

In a tense matchup that began with left-handers Dravecky and Tudor trading changeups and strikeouts, the Cardinals touched Dravecky for a tainted run when Pena led off the St. Louis second inning with a triple, a hit that Giants right fielder Candy Maldonado misplayed when he lost the ball in the lights.

One out later, Oquendo hit a short fly ball down the right-field line. Maldonado caught it, but his throw home was up the third-base line, Pena stepping around Melvin's tag. It was the first run off Dravecky, ending his playoff record scoreless streak at 16⅓ innings.

Tudor worked around six hits and two walks in 7⅓ innings. Worrell came in to finish off the eighth and struck out Will Clark leading off the ninth.

But when Craig sent Harry Spilman up to pinch hit, Herzog remembered a regular-season homer Spilman had hit off Worrell in San Francisco. In came the lefthanded Dayley, with Worrell moving to right field in case he was needed for one more batter. He wasn't.

Chris Speier, who was sent in to bat for Spilman, took a third strike and Uribe grounded out.

The Cardinals didn't leave anything to chance in the decisive seventh game, scoring four times in the second inning and riding Cox's pitching to a 6-0 victory.

San Francisco's Jeffrey Leonard hit four Championship Series home runs and infuriated the Cardinals with his 'one-flap-down' homer trot.

After Pena and Pendleton singled with one out in the second, McGee staked Cox to the only run he would need with a single past Giants shortstop Uribe. That's when Oquendo stepped to the plate with birthday wishes dancing in his head.

Moments later, Oquendo sent Hammaker's 3-2 pitch over the left-field wall. Herr added a two-run single in the sixth.

In the Giants' locker room, Leonard, who was outspoken and controversial throughout the series, was silent, even though he had been named the Most Valuable Player.

"It's bittersweet," said Leonard, who backed up his words with a .417 average and tied Championship Series records with four home runs, 10 hits and 22 total bases. "This is probably the only award that will be on my mantelpiece that will make me feel awful when I look at it."

Cox, who said he thought the Giants would walk Oquendo with first base open to get to him, said the sight of that homer was something else.

"When I saw him take that swing, I thought to myself, 'Jose what are you doing,' " said Cox. "But after it jumped off his bat, boy, was it a pretty sight."

It was an improbable finish to an improbable season for the Cardinals.

GAME OF TUESDAY, OCTOBER 6, AT ST. LOUIS (N)

San Francisco	AB.	R.	H.	RBI.	PO.	A.
Thompson, 2b	3	2	0	0	3	4
Mitchell, 3b	4	0	1	0	1	1
Leonard, lf	4	1	2	1	3	0
Maldonado, rf	4	0	1	2	3	0
C. Davis, cf	3	0	0	0	2	0
W. Clark, 1b	4	0	1	0	7	1
Brenly, c	4	0	0	0	3	1
Uribe, ss	4	0	2	0	1	2
Reuschel, p	1	0	0	0	0	2
Lefferts, p	0	0	0	0	0	1
Speier, ph	1	0	0	0	0	0
Garrelts, p	0	0	0	0	1	0
Melvin, ph	1	0	0	0	0	0
Totals	33	3	7	3	24	12

St. Louis	AB.	R.	H.	RBI.	PO.	A.
Coleman, lf	3	0	1	1	2	0
Smith, ss	3	1	1	0	0	4
Herr, 2b	4	0	0	0	4	2
Driessen, 1b	4	1	2	0	8	0
McGee, cf	4	1	2	1	2	0
Pendleton, 3b	4	1	1	1	0	2
Ford, rf	4	0	1	0	3	0
Pena, c	3	1	1	0	8	1
Mathews, p	1	0	1	2	0	0
Worrell, p	0	0	0	0	0	0
Dayley, p	0	0	0	0	0	0
Totals	30	5	10	5	27	9

San Francisco	1 0 0	1 0 0	0 1 0—3
St. Louis	0 0 1	1 0 3	0 0 x—5

San Francisco	IP	H.	R.	ER.	BB.	SO.
Reuschel (Loser)	6	9	5	5	2	1
Lefferts	1	1	0	0	1	0
Garrelts	1	0	0	0	0	2

St. Louis	IP.	H.	R.	ER.	BB.	SO.
Mathews (Winner)	7⅓	4	3	2	1	7
Worrell	⅓	2	0	0	1	0
Dayley (Save)	1⅓	1	0	0	0	1

Game-winning RBI—Pendleton.
Error—Driessen, Uribe. Double plays—San Francisco 1, St. Louis 1. Left on bases—San Francisco 6, St. Louis 6. Two-base hits—Maldonado, Driessen 2. Three-base hit—Smith. Home run—Leonard. Stolen base—W. Clark. Sacrifice hits—Mathews 2, Reuschel. Umpires—Kibler, Montague, Pallone, Gregg, Quick and Engel. Time—2:34. Attendance—55,331.

GAME OF WEDNESDAY, OCTOBER 7, AT ST. LOUIS

San Francisco	AB.	R.	H.	RBI.	PO.	A.
Thompson, 2b	5	0	0	0	3	3
Mitchell, 3b	5	0	0	0	0	4
Leonard, lf	4	2	3	1	4	0
Maldonado, rf	4	2	2	0	2	0
C. Davis, cf	3	0	1	0	0	0
Milner, pr-cf	0	0	0	0	3	0
W. Clark, 1b	3	1	2	2	7	0
Melvin, c	3	0	0	0	6	1
Uribe, ss	4	0	1	0	2	1
Dravecky, p	4	0	1	0	0	0
Totals	35	5	10	3	27	9

St. Louis	AB.	R.	H.	RBI.	PO.	A.
Coleman, lf	3	0	0	0	1	0
Smith, ss	3	0	0	0	0	2
Herr, 2b	4	0	1	0	3	1
Pendleton, 3b	3	0	0	0	1	1
McGee, cf	3	0	0	0	1	0
Lindeman, 1b	3	0	1	0	8	1
Oquendo, rf	2	0	0	0	3	0
Pena, c	2	0	0	0	10	0
Tudor, p	2	0	0	0	0	3
Pagnozzi, ph	1	0	0	0	0	0
Forsch, p	0	0	0	0	0	0
Totals	26	0	2	0	27	8

San Francisco	0 2 0	1 0 0	0 2 0—5
St. Louis	0 0 0	0 0 0	0 0 0—0

San Francisco	IP.	H.	R.	ER.	BB.	SO.
Dravecky (Winner)	9	2	0	0	4	6

St. Louis	IP.	H.	R.	ER.	BB.	SO.
Tudor (Loser)	8	10	5	3	2	6
Forsch	1	0	0	0	0	2

Game-winning RBI—W. Clark.
Error—Smith. Double plays—San Francisco 2. Left on bases—San Francisco 6, St. Louis 3. Two-base hit—Uribe. Home runs—W. Clark, Leonard. Sacrifice hit—Milner. Umpires—Montague, Pallone, Gregg, Quick, Engel and Kibler. Time—2:33. Attendance—55,331.

GAME OF FRIDAY, OCTOBER 9, AT SAN FRANCISCO (N)

St. Louis	AB.	R.	H.	RBI.	PO.	A.
Coleman, lf	4	1	1	2	1	0
Smith, ss	5	1	3	0	1	4
Herr, 2b	4	0	0	0	0	0
Lindeman, 1b	3	1	1	3	11	0
McGee, cf	4	0	1	0	3	0
Pena, c	4	0	1	0	9	1
Oquendo, rf-3b	4	1	1	0	1	0
Lawless, 3b	2	0	1	0	0	3
Ford, ph-rf	1	1	1	0	1	0
Magrane, p	1	0	0	0	0	1
J. Clark, ph	1	0	0	0	0	0
Forsch, p	0	0	0	0	0	1
Driessen, ph	1	0	1	1	0	0
Johnson, pr	0	1	0	0	0	0
Worrell, p	1	0	0	0	0	0
Totals	35	6	11	6	27	10

San Francisco	AB.	R.	H.	RBI.	PO.	A.
Thompson, 2b	2	0	0	0	3	3
Spilman, ph	1	1	1	1	0	0
Mitchell, 3b	5	0	1	0	0	2
Leonard, lf	3	1	1	1	2	0
Maldonado, rf	4	0	0	0	0	0
C. Davis, cf	3	1	1	0	3	1
Milner, cf	1	0	0	0	1	0
W. Clark, 1b	4	1	2	1	13	0
Brenly, c	4	1	1	1	5	0
Uribe, ss	4	0	0	0	0	5
Hammaker, p	3	0	0	0	0	0
D. Robinson, p	0	0	0	0	0	0
Lefferts, p	0	0	0	0	0	1
LaCoss, p	0	0	0	0	0	1
Aldrete, ph	1	0	0	0	0	0
Totals	35	5	7	4	27	13

St. Louis .... 0 0 0   0 0 2   4 0 0—6
San Francisco .... 0 3 1   0 0 0   0 0 1—5

St. Louis	IP.	H.	R.	ER.	BB.	SO.
Magrane	4	4	4	4	2	3
Forsch (Winner)	2	1	0	0	0	1
Worrell (Save)	3	2	1	1	0	4

San Francisco	IP.	H.	R.	ER.	BB.	SO.
Hammaker	6*	7	3	3	0	4
D. Robinson (Loser)	0†	3	3	3	0	0
Lefferts	1	1	0	0	0	0
LaCoss	2	0	0	0	2	1

*Pitched to one batter in seventh.
†Pitched to three batters in seventh.
Game-winning RBI—Coleman.
Errors—Mitchell, Herr. Double plays—San Francisco 2. Left on bases—St. Louis 6, San Francisco 6. Two-base hits—C. Davis, Brenly, W. Clark. Three-base hit—McGee. Home runs—Leonard, Lindeman, Spilman. Stolen bases—Thompson, Herr, Johnson. Sacrifice hit—Herr. Sacrifice fly—Lindeman. Hit by pitcher—By Forsch (Leonard). Wild pitch—Magrane. Umpires—Pallone, Gregg, Quick, Engel, Kibler and Montague. Time—3:27. Attendance—57,913.

GAME OF SATURDAY, OCTOBER 10, AT SAN FRANCISCO (N)

St. Louis	AB.	R.	H.	RBI.	PO.	A.
Coleman, lf	4	0	2	1	1	1
Smith, ss	4	0	0	0	0	4
Herr, 2b	4	0	1	0	1	1
Driessen, 1b	3	0	0	0	9	2
McGee, cf	4	0	1	0	1	0
Pendleton, 3b	4	0	1	0	0	1
Ford, rf	4	1	1	0	2	0
Pena, c	3	1	2	0	8	0
Cox, p	3	0	1	1	2	3
Totals	33	2	9	2	24	12

San Francisco	AB.	R.	H.	RBI.	PO.	A.
Milner, cf	4	0	0	0	3	0
Mitchell, 3b	4	1	2	0	0	1
Leonard, lf	2	1	1	2	0	0
W. Clark, 1b	4	0	2	0	12	3
Aldrete, rf	4	0	1	0	3	0
Brenly, c	4	1	2	1	3	0
Thompson, 2b	4	1	1	1	1	4
Uribe, ss	4	0	0	0	3	3
Krukow, p	2	0	0	0	2	2
Totals	32	4	9	4	27	13

St. Louis .... 0 2 0   0 0 0   0 0 0—2
San Francisco .... 0 0 0   1 2 0   0 1 x—4

St. Louis	IP.	H.	R.	ER.	BB.	SO.
Cox (Loser)	8	9	4	4	3	6

San Francisco	IP.	H.	R.	ER.	BB.	SO.
Krukow (Winner)	9	9	2	2	1	3

Game-winning RBI—Leonard.

Errors—Thompson, W. Clark. Double plays—San Francisco 4. Left on bases—St. Louis 5, San Francisco 7. Two-base hits—Mitchell, W. Clark. Home runs—Thompson, Leonard, Brenly. Umpires—Gregg, Quick, Engel, Kibler, Montague and Pallone. Time—2:23. Attendance—57,997.

GAME OF SUNDAY, OCTOBER 11, AT SAN FRANCISCO

St. Louis	AB.	R.	H.	RBI.	PO.	A.
Coleman, lf	4	1	2	0	1	0
Smith, ss	2	0	0	1	0	0
Herr, 2b	3	0	0	1	3	1
Driessen, 1b	3	0	0	0	5	0
Lindeman, ph-1b	1	0	0	0	1	0
McGee, cf	4	0	2	0	4	0
Pendleton, 3b	4	1	1	0	1	5
Morris, rf	2	0	0	0	1	0
Forsch, p	0	0	0	0	0	0
Horton, p	0	0	0	0	0	0
Lawless, ph-rf	2	0	0	0	1	0
Pena, c	2	1	1	0	6	2
Mathews, p	1	0	1	0	0	0
Ford, rf	0	0	0	0	0	0
Oquendo, ph-rf	2	0	0	0	1	0
Dayley, p	0	0	0	0	0	0
Totals	30	3	7	2	24	8

San Francisco	AB.	R.	H.	RBI.	PO.	A.
Thompson, 2b	2	1	1	1	1	4
Mitchell, 3b	4	1	2	1	1	1
Leonard, lf	4	0	0	0	1	0
Maldonado, rf	4	0	1	0	0	0
C. Davis, cf	3	1	1	0	3	0
Milner, cf	1	0	0	0	1	0
W. Clark, 1b	3	1	1	0	9	2
Brenly, c	1	1	0	0	7	1
Uribe, ss	4	1	1	2	4	2
Reuschel, p	1	0	0	0	0	1
Aldrete, ph	0	0	0	1	0	0
Price, p	1	0	0	0	0	0
Totals	28	6	7	6	27	11

St. Louis .... 1 0 1   1 0 0   0 0 0—3
San Francisco .... 1 0 1   4 0 0   0 0 x—6

St. Louis	IP.	H.	R.	ER.	BB.	SO.
Mathews	3	2	2	2	2	3
Forsch (Loser)	0*	3	4	4	1	0
Horton	3	2	0	0	0	2
Dayley	2	0	0	0	2	2

San Francisco	IP.	H.	R.	ER.	BB.	SO.
Reuschel	4	6	3	2	0	1
Price (Winner)	5	1	0	0	1	6

*Pitched to four batters in fourth.
Game-winning RBI—Uribe.
Error—Reuschel. Double plays—St. Louis 1, San Francisco 1. Left on bases—St. Louis 4, San Francisco 5. Two-base hit—Coleman. Three-base hits—Pendleton, Thompson. Home run—Mitchell. Stolen bases—Thompson, Mitchell, Uribe. Sacrifice hit—Smith. Sacrifice flies—Herr, Smith, Aldrete. Hit by pitcher—By Dayley (Thompson). Wild pitch—Reuschel. Umpires—Quick, Engel, Kibler, Montague, Pallone and Gregg. Time—2:48. Attendance—59,363.

GAME OF TUESDAY, OCTOBER 13, AT ST. LOUIS (N)

San Francisco	AB.	R.	H.	RBI.	PO.	A.
Thompson, 2b	3	0	0	0	0	1
Mitchell, 3b	4	0	1	0	0	1
Leonard, lf	3	0	1	0	3	0
Maldonado, rf	3	0	0	0	2	0
Aldrete, ph-rf	1	0	0	0	0	0
C. Davis, cf	4	0	0	0	1	0
W. Clark, 1b	3	0	0	0	9	0
Melvin, c	3	0	3	0	8	0

	AB.	R.	H.	RBI.	PO.	A.
Milner, pr	0	0	0	0	0	0
D. Robinson, p	0	0	0	0	0	0
Spilman, ph	0	0	0	0	0	0
Speier, ph	1	0	0	0	0	0
Uribe, ss	3	0	1	0	0	4
Dravecky, p	2	0	0	0	0	2
Brenly, ph-c	1	0	0	0	1	0
Totals	31	0	6	0	24	8

St. Louis	AB.	R.	H.	RBI.	PO.	A.
Coleman, lf	4	0	0	0	1	0
Smith, ss	4	0	0	0	3	0
Herr, 2b	3	0	2	0	1	2
Lindeman, 1b	3	0	0	0	6	0
Pendleton, 3b	3	0	0	0	1	2
Pena, c	3	1	1	0	9	1
McGee, cf	3	0	0	0	5	0
Oquendo, rf	2	0	0	1	1	0
Worrell, p-rf	0	0	0	0	0	0
Tudor, p	2	0	0	0	0	1
Morris, rf	1	0	0	0	0	0
Dayley, p	0	0	0	0	0	0
Totals	28	1	5	1	27	6

San Francisco .... 0 0 0   0 0 0   0 0 0—0
St. Louis .... 0 1 0   0 0 0   0 0 x—1

San Francisco	IP.	H.	R.	ER.	BB.	SO.
Dravecky (Loser)	6	5	1	1	0	8
D. Robinson	2	0	0	0	0	1

St. Louis	IP.	H.	R.	ER.	BB.	SO.
Tudor (Winner)	7⅓	6	0	0	3	6
Worrell	1	0	0	0	0	2
Dayley (Save)	⅔	0	0	0	0	1

Game-winning RBI—Oquendo.
Left on bases—San Francisco 8, St. Louis 4. Three-base hit—Pena. Sacrifice hit—Uribe. Sacrifice fly—Oquendo. Umpires—Engel, Kibler, Montague, Pallone, Gregg and Quick. Time—3:09. Attendance—55,331.

GAME OF WEDNESDAY, OCTOBER 14, AT ST. LOUIS (N)

San Francisco	AB.	R.	H.	RBI.	PO.	A.
Aldrete, rf	4	0	0	0	2	0
Mitchell, 3b	4	0	1	0	2	1
Leonard, lf	4	0	2	0	1	1
W. Clark, 1b	4	0	1	0	6	1
C. Davis, cf	4	0	0	0	2	0

	AB.	R.	H.	RBI.	PO.	A.
Brenly, c	3	0	1	0	9	0
Speier, 2b	3	0	0	0	1	3
Uribe, ss	3	0	2	0	1	3
Hammaker, p	0	0	0	0	0	1
Milner, ph	1	0	1	0	0	0
Price, p	0	0	0	0	0	0
Downs, p	0	0	0	0	0	0
Thompson, ph	1	0	0	0	0	0
Garrelts, p	0	0	0	0	0	0
Lefferts, p	0	0	0	0	0	0
LaCoss, p	0	0	0	0	0	1
Spilman, ph	1	0	0	0	0	0
D. Robinson, p	0	0	0	0	0	0
Totals	32	0	8	0	24	11

St. Louis	AB.	R.	H.	RBI.	PO.	A.
Coleman, lf	4	1	1	0	2	0
Smith, ss	4	0	1	0	6	5
Herr, 2b	5	0	2	2	0	4
Lindeman, 1b	3	0	0	0	7	1
Driessen, ph-1b	1	0	0	0	4	1
Pendleton, 3b	1	1	1	0	0	0
Lawless, ph-3b	2	0	1	0	0	1
Pena, c	4	1	2	0	5	0
McGee, cf	4	1	2	1	0	0
Oquendo, rf	2	2	1	3	1	0
Cox, p	3	0	1	0	2	2
Totals	33	6	12	6	27	14

San Francisco .... 0 0 0   0 0 0   0 0 0—0
St. Louis .... 0 4 0   0 0 2   0 0 x—6

San Francisco	IP.	H.	R.	ER.	BB.	SO.
Hammaker (Loser)	2	5	4	4	0	3
Price	⅔	2	0	0	0	1
Downs	1⅓	1	0	0	0	0
Garrelts	1⅔	2	2	2	4	2
Lefferts	0*	1	0	0	0	0
LaCoss	1⅓	1	0	0	1	1
D. Robinson	1	0	0	0	0	2

St. Louis	IP.	H.	R.	ER.	BB.	SO.
Cox (Winner)	9	8	0	0	0	5

*Pitched to one batter in sixth.

Game-winning RBI—McGee.
Error—C. Davis. Double plays—St. Louis 3. Left on bases—San Francisco 5, St. Louis 9. Two-base hit—McGee. Home run—Oquendo. Stolen bases—Coleman, Pena. Sacrifice hit—Cox. Wild pitch—Garrelts. Passed ball—Brenly. Umpires—Kibler, Montague, Pallone, Gregg, Quick and Engel. Time—2:59. Attendance—55,331.

ST. LOUIS CARDINALS' BATTING & FIELDING AVERAGES

Player—Position	G.	AB.	R.	H.	TB.	2B.	3B.	HR.	RBI.	B.A.	PO.	A.	E.	F.A.
Mathews, p	2	2	0	2	2	0	0	0	2	1.000	0	0	0	.000
Pena, c	7	21	5	8	10	0	1	0	0	.381	55	5	0	1.000
Ford, rf-ph	4	9	2	3	3	0	0	0	0	.333	6	0	0	1.000
Cox, p	2	6	0	2	2	0	0	0	1	.333	4	5	0	1.000
Lawless, 3b-ph-rf	3	6	0	2	2	0	0	0	0	.333	1	4	0	1.000
McGee, cf	7	26	2	8	11	1	1	0	2	.308	16	0	0	1.000
Lindeman, 1b-ph	5	13	1	4	7	0	0	1	3	.308	33	2	0	1.000
Coleman, lf	7	26	3	7	8	1	0	0	4	.269	9	1	0	1.000
Driessen, 1b-ph	5	12	2	3	5	2	0	0	1	.250	26	3	1	.967
Herr, 2b	7	27	0	6	6	0	0	0	3	.222	12	11	1	.958
Pendleton, 3b	6	19	3	4	6	0	1	0	1	.211	3	11	0	1.000
Smith, ss	7	25	2	5	7	0	1	0	1	.200	10	19	1	.967
Oquendo, rf-3b-ph	5	12	3	2	5	0	0	1	4	.167	7	0	0	1.000
Dayley, p	3	0	0	0	0	0	0	0	0	.000	0	0	0	.000
Forsch, p	3	0	0	0	0	0	0	0	0	.000	0	1	0	1.000
Horton, p	1	0	0	0	0	0	0	0	0	.000	0	0	0	.000
Johnson, pr	1	0	1	0	0	0	0	0	0	.000	0	0	0	.000
Clark, ph	1	1	0	0	0	0	0	0	0	.000	0	0	0	.000
Magrane, p	1	1	0	0	0	0	0	0	0	.000	0	1	0	1.000
Pagnozzi, ph	1	1	0	0	0	0	0	0	0	.000	0	0	0	.000
Worrell, p-rf	3	1	0	0	0	0	0	0	0	.000	0	0	0	.000
Morris, rf	2	3	0	0	0	0	0	0	0	.000	1	0	0	1.000
Tudor, p	2	4	0	0	0	0	0	0	0	.000	0	4	0	1.000
Totals	7	215	23	56	74	4	4	2	22	.260	183	67	3	.988

SAN FRANCISCO GIANTS' BATTING & FIELDING AVERAGES

Player—Position	G.	AB.	R.	H.	TB.	2B.	3B.	HR.	RBI.	B.A.	PO.	A.	E.	F.A.
Spilman, ph	3	2	1	1	4	0	0	1	1	.500	0	0	0	.000
Melvin, ph-c	3	7	0	3	3	0	0	0	0	.429	14	1	0	1.000
Leonard, lf	7	24	5	10	22	0	0	4	5	.417	14	1	0	1.000
Clark, 1b	7	25	3	9	14	2	0	1	3	.360	63	7	1	.986
Uribe, ss	7	26	1	7	8	1	0	0	2	.269	11	20	1	.969
Mitchell, 3b	7	30	2	8	12	1	0	1	2	.267	4	11	1	.938
Brenly, c-ph	6	17	3	4	8	1	0	1	2	.235	28	2	0	1.000
Maldonado, rf	5	19	2	4	5	1	0	0	2	.211	7	0	0	1.000
Dravecky, p	2	6	0	1	1	0	0	0	0	.167	0	2	0	1.000
Davis, cf	6	20	2	3	4	1	0	0	0	.150	11	1	1	.923
Milner, pr-cf-ph	6	7	0	1	1	0	0	0	0	.143	8	0	0	1.000
Thompson, 2b-ph	7	20	4	2	7	0	1	1	2	.100	11	19	1	.968
Aldrete, ph-rf	5	10	0	1	1	0	0	0	1	.100	5	0	0	1.000
Downs, p	1	0	0	0	0	0	0	0	0	.000	0	0	0	.000
Garrelts, p	2	0	0	0	0	0	0	0	0	.000	1	0	0	1.000
Lefferts, p	3	0	0	0	0	0	0	0	0	.000	0	2	0	1.000
Robinson, p	3	0	0	0	0	0	0	0	0	.000	0	0	0	.000
LaCoss, p	2	0	0	0	0	0	0	0	0	.000	0	2	0	1.000
Price, p	2	1	0	0	0	0	0	0	0	.000	0	0	0	.000
Krukow, p	1	2	0	0	0	0	0	0	0	.000	2	2	0	1.000
Reuschel, p	2	2	0	0	0	0	0	0	0	.000	0	3	1	.750
Hammaker, p	2	3	0	0	0	0	0	0	0	.000	0	1	0	1.000
Speier, ph-2b	3	5	0	0	0	0	0	0	0	.000	1	3	0	1.000
Totals	7	226	23	54	90	7	1	9	20	.239	180	77	6	.977

ST. LOUIS CARDINALS' PITCHING RECORDS

Pitcher	G.	GS.	CG.	IP.	H.	R.	ER.	BB.	SO.	HB.	WP.	W.	L.	Pct.	ERA.
Dayley	3	0	0	4	1	0	0	2	4	1	0	0	0	.000	0.00
Horton	1	0	0	3	2	0	0	0	2	0	0	0	0	.000	0.00
Tudor	2	2	0	23⅓	16	5	3	5	12	0	0	1	1	.500	1.76
Worrell	3	0	0	7⅔	4	1	1	1	6	0	0	0	0	.000	2.08
Cox	2	2	2	17	17	4	4	3	11	0	0	1	1	.500	2.12
Mathews	2	2	0	17⅔	6	5	4	3	10	0	0	1	0	1.000	3.48
Magrane	1	1	0	4	4	4	4	2	3	0	1	0	0	.000	9.00
Forsch	3	0	0	3	4	4	4	1	3	1	0	1	1	.500	12.00
Totals	7	7	2	61	54	23	20	17	51	2	1	4	3	.571	2.95

Shutouts—Tudor-Worrell-Dayley (combined); Cox. Saves—Dayley 2, Worrell.

SAN FRANCISCO GIANTS' PITCHING RECORDS

Pitcher	G.	GS.	CG.	IP.	H.	R.	ER.	BB.	SO.	HB.	WP.	W.	L.	Pct.	ERA.
Price	2	0	0	5⅔	3	0	0	1	7	0	0	1	0	1.000	0.00
LaCoss	2	0	0	3⅓	1	0	0	3	2	0	0	0	0	.000	0.00
Lefferts	3	0	0	2	3	0	0	1	0	0	0	0	0	.000	0.00
Downs	1	0	0	1⅓	1	0	0	0	0	0	0	0	0	.000	0.00
Dravecky	2	2	1	15	7	1	1	4	14	0	0	1	1	.500	0.60
Krukow	1	1	0	9	9	2	2	1	3	0	0	1	0	1.000	2.00
Reuschel	2	2	0	10	15	8	7	2	2	0	1	0	1	.000	6.30
Garrelts	2	0	0	2⅔	2	2	2	4	4	0	1	0	0	.000	6.75
Hammaker	2	2	0	8	12	7	7	0	7	0	0	0	1	.000	7.88
Robinson	3	0	0	3	3	3	3	0	3	0	0	0	1	.000	9.00
Totals	7	7	2	60	56	23	22	16	42	0	2	3	4	.429	3.30

Shutout—Dravecky. No saves.

COMPOSITE SCORE BY INNINGS

St. Louis	1	7	2	2	0	7	4	0	0 — 23
San Francisco	2	5	2	7	2	0	0	4	1 — 23

Game-winning RBIs—Pendleton, W. Clark, Coleman, Leonard, Uribe, Oquendo, McGee.

Sacrifice hits—Mathews 2, Reuschel, Milner, Herr, Smith, Uribe, Cox.

Sacrifice flies—Lindeman, Herr, Smith, Aldrete, Oquendo.

Stolen bases—W. Clark, Thompson 2, Herr, Johnson, Mitchell, Uribe, Coleman, Pena.

Caught stealing—Coleman 2, Pena, Uribe, W. Clark, McGee, Thompson 2.

Double plays—Lefferts, Thompson, Uribe & W. Clark; Smith, Herr & Driessen; Uribe & W. Clark; Mitchell, Thompson & W. Clark; Davis & W. Clark; Uribe, Thompson & W. Clark; Thompson & W. Clark; Uribe & W. Clark; W. Clark & Uribe; Thompson, Uribe & W. Clark 2; Pendleton, Herr & Driessen; Lindeman, Smith & Cox; Cox, Smith & Lindeman; Herr, Smith & Lindeman.

Left on bases—St. Louis 6, 3, 6, 5, 4, 4, 9—37; San Francisco 6, 6, 6, 7, 5, 8, 5—43.

Hit by pitcher—By Forsch (Leonard), by Dayley (Thompson).

Passed ball—Brenly.

Balks—None.

Time—First game, 2:34; second game, 2:33; third game, 3:27; fourth game, 2:23; fifth game, 2:48; sixth game, 3:09; seventh game, 2:59.

Attendance—First game, 55,331; second game, 55,331; third game, 57,913; fourth game, 57,997; fifth game, 59,363; sixth game, 55,331; seventh game, 55,331.

Umpires—Kibler, Montague, Pallone, Gregg, Quick & Engel.

Official scorers—Jack Herman, St. Louis official scorer; Dave Nightingale, The Sporting News; Nick Peters, Oakland Tribune.

1987 WORLD SERIES

Including

Review of 1987 Series

Official Play-by-Play, Each Game

Official Composite Box Score

World Series Tables—Attendance, Money, Results

Happy Twins pitcher Frank Viola holds up the Most Valuable Player trophy he was presented after Game 7 of the 1987 World Series.

Twins Enjoy Home Cooking

By LARRY WIGGE

John Viola and Donna Litt wanted to get married in June or July of 1987. But John also wanted his brother to be able to attend and so the couple scheduled the wedding for October instead, figuring that Frank Viola, pitcher for the Minnesota Twins, would be free. So much for careful planning.

Nobody bothered to consider the possibility that the Twins, lowly and hopeless for so many years, would be participating in the 1987 World Series. But there it was, Twins vs. Cardinals, and John Viola's best man was unable to make it to the church on time. The New York wedding went off without another hitch and Frank, a stylish lefthander, turned out to be a different kind of best man as he pitched the Twins to their first-ever World Series title. He recorded two victories over the Cardinals, including a solid six-hit effort over eight innings in the decisive seventh game, a 4-2 triumph.

"Who would have thought we'd go from 71-91 last year to the World Series this year?" asked Viola, shaking his head.

Pitching on three days rest for the second time in the Series, the 27-year-old Viola gave up two runs on four hits in the second inning, then permitted only two more baserunners in an eight-inning stint that included seven strikeouts and no walks before he gave way to ace reliever Jeff Reardon, who retired the side in the ninth.

It was Viola's 11th victory in 16 Metrodome starts since May 22, keeping him undefeated since that date. The victory also helped Viola redeem himself for his poor outing against the Cardinals in Game 4, when he was charged with five earned runs on six hits in 3⅓ innings in St. Louis after hurling eight strong innings and yielding only five hits in the Twins' 10-1 victory in the first game of the Series.

"I flew my mother and father, my brother and his new bride in for the game, but once it started I didn't think about anything but the game," Viola said shortly after learning that he had been named the Most Valuable Player of the Series.

It was the first title for this franchise since 1924, when the club was known as the Washington Senators.

While Viola was performing his magic, other Minnesota players were stepping to the forefront. Steve Lombardozzi and Greg Gagne, two light-hitting middle in-

Twins third baseman Gary Gaetti leaps on top of relief ace Jeff Reardon and catcher Tim Laudner after the final out of the '87 Series.

fielders, produced the game-winning hits in Games 6 and 7, respectively, rallying the the Twins from early-inning deficits both times. The Twins had limped back to the Metrodome after the Cardinals had burst their bubble in St. Louis with three straight victories and a 3-2 Series lead. The Redbirds were looking for the knock-out punch.

But that was not to be. Back in the Metrodome's cozy confines, the Twins came alive and completed their shocking rise to baseball's highest plateau. And they did it in a sometimes whacky Series that, for the first time in history, was decided by the home-field edge. All seven games were

Rabid Twins fans wave their Homer Hankies while celebrating Gary Gaetti's Game 2 home run against the Cardinals.

won by the home team.

Playing indoors clearly was the 1987 Twins' biggest edge. When the dust had cleared on the '87 regular season, the Twins had compiled a 56-25 home record and they went on to post a 6-0 mark in postseason play.

Incredibly, the Twins outscored the Cardinals, 33-12, at the Metrodome. They batted .336 (46-140) in the four home games with six homers. Their St. Louis numbers were significantly different. The Twins hit just .184 (18-98) with one homer at Busch Stadium. The Cardinals, on the other hand, batted .296 (29-98) in St. Louis, but hit just .231 (31-134) in Minnesota. The Redbirds outscored the Twins in St. Louis, 14-5.

The first World Series game played indoors came as something of a shock for the Cardinals. The Twins exploded for seven runs in the fourth inning and coasted to a

10-1 rout.

Ironically, the Twins had been held hitless through the first three innings by rookie lefthander Joe Magrane and trailed 1-0 before ending St. Louis' streak of 25 scoreless innings in postseason play. But Gary Gaetti, Don Baylor and Tom Brunansky singled to load the bases in the fourth and Kent Hrbek, a .150 hitter in the playoffs, singled to center to score two runs. Hrbek went to second base on McGee's throw to third. After Lombardozzi walked to reload the bases, Bob Forsch replaced Magrane on the mound.

Tim Laudner touched Forsch for an RBI single to increase Minnesota's lead to 3-1. Then Dan Gladden hit a 1-2 pitch into the left-field stands to become the 13th player in World Series history to hit a grand slam and the first since October 13, 1970, when Baltimore pitcher Dave McNally accomplished the feat against Cincinnati.

The seven runs represented the biggest output in one inning in 19 years—since Detroit scored 10 runs against St. Louis on October 9, 1968.

Lombardozzi belted a two-run homer down the left-field line off Forsch in the fifth and Gladden accounted for his fifth RBI of the game in the seventh when he lined a two-out double into the right-field corner. The outburst was more than enough to back Viola's five-hit pitching over eight innings and enabled the Twins to become the first team to win Game 1 at home since 1981.

Gladden's five RBIs were the most in a World Series game since Detroit's Kirk Gibson drove in five runs October 14, 1971, and left him one short of the Series record of six set by Bobby Richardson of the New York Yankees on October 8, 1960.

"It's hard to believe one swing of the bat could cause this much chaos," said Gladden, who had struggled through the second half of the regular season, batting just .195 after the All-Star break with only 12 RBIs.

While Gladden fell just short of the record book, Gaetti didn't. The third baseman singled and doubled in the fourth-inning, becoming the 17th player in Series history to get two hits in one inning and the first since October 11, 1971, when Baltimore's Merv Rettenmund turned the trick.

Bert Blyleven improved his career postseason pitching record to 5-0 one night later, hurling seven strong innings in an 8-4 victory as the Twins took a commanding 2-0 lead in the Series. For the second straight night, the Twins took command with a fourth-inning explosion.

Twins righthander
Juan Berenguer
kicks at the dirt
after letting the
Cardinals rally in
the seventh inning
of Game 3.

Gaetti opened the Game 2 scoring when he homered into the left-field stands with one out in the second, setting the stage for the big fourth.

With one out, Kirby Puckett and Hrbek singled. They both advanced on a wild pitch, before Gaetti walked to load the bases. Two runs scored when Randy Bush doubled into the right-field corner over the outstretched glove of leaping first baseman Dan Driessen.

After Tom Brunansky walked to reload the bases and Lombardozzi flied to left, Laudner pulled Danny Cox's first pitch through the left side of the infield for a two-run single. Bush scored the second run by eluding Pena's tag with a headfirst slide at home plate.

Gladden followed with an RBI single, chasing Cox in favor of Lee Tunnell. Then

Gagne greeted the reliever by looping a double down the right-field line to push the Twins advantage to 7-0.

The Twins struck early and often in the first two games, nicking St. Louis starters Magrane and Cox for 12 runs and 10 hits over 6⅔ innings. In seven games in the N.L. Championship Series, the Cardinals' starters had given up just 18 runs in 46⅔ innings.

"If I go to the track tomorrow, I'm betting on No. 4," Minnesota Manager Tom Kelly said in reference to the fourth-inning rallies that had netted the Twins 13 runs in the first two games.

Counting the A.L. Championship Series, the Twins became the first team to score five or more runs in seven straight post-season contests. And the 18-5 deficit was the widest margin of defeat in the first two games of the Series since 1937 when the Yankees outscored the New York Giants, 16-2.

"Two things mean nothing—last year and yesterday," said a bedraggled St. Louis Manager Whitey Herzog.

When the scene shifted to St. Louis for Game 3, the Cardinals rallied for three seventh-inning runs and a 3-1 victory, leaving Kelly and the Twins at the mercy of some heavy second-guessing.

The Twins were holding a 1-0 lead, courtesy of Brunansky's sixth-inning RBI single, when Kelly removed starter Les Straker before the start of the seventh inning. Straker, who had stymied St. Louis on four hits, was replaced by playoff hero Juan Berenguer. The Cardinals promptly routed the chunky righthander, who faced only five batters in one-third of an inning.

Jose Oquendo singled to center on Berenguer's first pitch. Pena, after failing on two bunt attempts, grounded a single to right that put runners on first and second and brought up another bunting situation. Herzog called on Terry Pendleton to pinch hit for John Tudor. Pendleton laid down a perfect bunt, advancing Oquendo to third and Pena to second and bringing up Vince Coleman.

Coleman, who had gone 1 for 11 in the Series, fell behind in the count, 0-2.

"I was determined not to get called out," said Coleman. "I just wanted to get the ball in play. I felt if I did, it would be a run and the game would be tied."

But Coleman didn't just tie the game, he went one better, lacing an inside fastball down the third-base line past a diving Gaetti to score two runs. He then stole his second base of the game and scored on a single by Ozzie Smith.

After the game Kelly bristled when questioned repeatedly about removing a pitcher who is throwing a shutout.

"I think I know my ball club better than you do," he snapped. "Juan pitched great for me in the Championship Series and he's done the job for me in that situation all year. He just didn't have it tonight.

"If you look at Les' history, after the sixth or seventh inning he gets shaky. They were getting runners on base in every inning and he was getting out of it. I wanted to get two innings out of Berenguer and one out of Reardon."

Meanwhile, Tudor was silencing the Twins' big bats. The lefthander was masterful for seven innings, allowing only four hits before turning things over to Todd Worrell, who hurled two scoreless innings in relief.

The Cardinals' offensive struggle could be traced back to the early-September ankle injury that sidelined slugging first baseman Jack Clark (35 homers, 106 RBIs in 131 games) and a rib-cage injury that limited third baseman Pendleton (12 homers, 96 RBIs) to a designated hitting role. As is often the case, however, their replacements produced some surprising performances.

Jim Lindeman, subbing for Clark, twice singled runs home and Tom Lawless, playing for Pendleton, clubbed a three-run homer to lead the Cardinals to a 7-2 Game 4 victory, knotting the Series at two games apiece.

After Gagne touched St. Louis starter Greg Mathews for his third homer in post-season play to give the Twins a 1-0 lead in the top of the third, the Cardinals came back in their half of the inning to tie the score on an RBI single by Lindeman. Then, the Cardinals gave the Twins a dose of their own medicine, scoring six times in the fourth.

Viola walked Pena to open the inning. Oquendo singled Pena to third and then Lawless, who had managed just two hits in 25 regular-season at-bats with no RBIs, belted an 0-1 delivery over the left-field wall to give the Cardinals a lead they never relinquished.

One out later, Coleman walked, chasing Viola in favor of Dan Schatzeder. After Ozzie Smith struck out, Coleman stole second and Herr then received an intentional walk. Lindeman made it 5-1 with an RBI single to left-center and advanced to second when Puckett bobbled the ball for an error. Willie McGee capped the uprising with a two-run double to left-center.

Mathews gave way to Forsch in the fourth inning after reinjuring a thigh muscle. Then Forsch gave way to Ken Dayley, who worked out of a bases-loaded jam with one out in the seventh inning and then finished the contest to record his first Series save.

The postgame spotlight definitely belonged to Lawless, who surprised even himself by flipping the bat in the air like it was just another day at the office after hitting his home run.

"I thought I hit the ball pretty well, but this is a big ball park and I didn't think it was going to go out," Lawless said. "There were runners on first and third at the time and I just stood there because I knew if it was going to be caught, it was going to be a sacrifice fly and I couldn't pass Jose (Oquendo). Then I saw the ball go over the wall and I said to myself, 'Holy cow, it went out.' My mind went blank for a moment because I couldn't believe it went

The unlikeliest of heroes, St. Louis backup third baseman Tom Lawless, celebrates with teammate Jose Oquendo after hitting a Game 4 home run to help the Cardinals square the 1987 World Series with the Twins.

Umpire Terry Tata gets help from Minnesota's Dan Gladden in calling Tom Brunansky safe at the plate in the fifth-inning of Game 6.

out. I flipped the bat, I guess, but I don't honestly remember doing it."

It was only the second career homer for Lawless, who didn't have a hit in '87 until August 12 at Pittsburgh. His first career homer came April 25, 1984, when he played for Cincinnati and, ironically, it came off Dayley, who was then pitching for Atlanta.

"He's never let me forget it either," said Dayley. "Now I'm off the hook."

Lawless became the first player to homer in the World Series without hitting a homer in the regular season since Oakland pitcher Ken Holtzman accomplished the feat in Game 4 of the 1974 Series.

The only thing positive about this contest for the Twins was the appearance of veteran righthander Joe Niekro, who pitched a scoreless fifth and sixth in relief. In the process, Niekro established a record for most years (19 years, 138 days) playing in the major leagues before appearing in his first World Series.

Getting production from the top of its batting order proved crucial once again to St. Louis in Game 5. In the first two games, the Cardinal speedsters, Coleman and Smith, managed only two hits in 16 at-bats and only one stolen base. In the next three games, which St. Louis won, the duo went 7 for 23 with six runs scored and seven steals. Coleman's base-stealing, in fact, was the key to the Cardinals' 4-2 Game 5 victory which gave the St. Louisans a 3-2 Series lead.

A routine ground ball by Coleman that took a funny hop at the edge of the sliding pit near first base and handcuffed Hrbek in the sixth inning led to three runs. Smith followed with a bunt that Blyleven tried to barehand, but dropped to give the Cardinals runners at first and second and none out.

After Herr flied out, Blyleven walked Driessen intentionally to load the bases. The Twins' veteran righthander looked to be out of trouble when he struck out McGee. But Curt Ford, another unlikely hero off the Cardinals bench, stroked a single to center to score two runs. Driessen scored the third run of the inning when Gagne booted Oquendo's grounder for an error.

The Cardinals made it 4-0 in the seventh as Coleman walked, went to second on a balk, stole third for his sixth stolen base of the Series and scored on a single by Smith.

The Twins had been held to only five runs in three games at Busch Stadium and trailed 5-2 after 4½ innings of Game 6, played, of course, at the Metrodome. Facing elimination, the Twins staged a four-run rally and went on to thump the Cardinals, 11-5.

Puckett led off the fifth with his third of four singles and Gaetti followed with an RBI double. Don Baylor, the veteran slugger acquired from Boston for the stretch run, then jolted the first pitch from St. Louis' John Tudor deep over the left-field wall to tie the score, 5-5. The go-ahead run scored when Brunansky singled, took second on a grounder to the mound and scored on Lombardozzi's two-out single, just beating a strong throw to the plate by McGee.

One inning later, the Twins scored four more runs. Gagne opened the sixth with a single. Puckett walked and the runners advanced to second and third on Pena's passed ball. After Gaetti popped out, Baylor was walked intentionally. One out later, Dayley replaced Forsch and was quickly jolted when Hrbek, 0 for 11 in the Series against lefthanders, belted a grand slam over the center-field fence.

It marked the first time that one team had connected for two grand slams in the same Series since 1956 when Yogi Berra and Bill Skowron did it for the Yankees against the Brooklyn Dodgers.

"I only wish," Hrbek would say later, "that I could have run around the bases twice, because that was something I will never feel again."

For the third straight year, the Series was going the limit.

Lindeman and Steve Lake stroked RBI singles to give the Cardinals a 2-0 lead in the second inning of Game 7. Lombardozzi provided an RBI single in the Twins' half of the second and they tied the score, 2-2, on a run-scoring double by Puckett in the fifth, setting the stage for the go-ahead run in the Minnesota sixth.

Brunansky and Hrbek were walked by Cox to start the rally. Laudner fouled to first and Bush was walked by Worrell to load the bases. After Worrell struck out Gladden, Gagne smashed a 3-2 pitch down the third-base line. Lawless made a diving stop, but his long throw to first base was late and Brunansky scored to give the Twins a 3-2 lead.

Gladden doubled home an insurance run in the eighth and Reardon came on in the ninth to preserve Viola's 4-2 victory.

"I can remember sitting in the stands watching the Twins lose," said Hrbek, a Minneapolis native. Hrbek, Viola, Gaetti, Brunansky, Bush, Laudner, Sal Butera and Roy Smalley were the remaining holdovers who labored through a 60-102 season in 1982.

"I was a fan," said Hrbek. "I watched the Vikings lose, the North Stars lose and I even watched Hubert Humphrey and Walter Mondale lose. It was tough."

Game 1

At Minnesota
October 17

St. Louis (N.L.)	AB.	R.	H.	RBI.	PO.	A.
Coleman, lf	4	0	0	0	0	0
Smith, ss	4	0	0	0	1	4
Herr, 2b	4	0	0	0	3	3
Lindeman, 1b	4	1	2	0	11	0
McGee, cf	3	0	2	0	2	1
Pena, c	3	0	0	1	2	0
Lake, c	0	0	0	0	0	0
Oquendo, rf	3	0	0	0	4	0
Pagnozzi, dh	3	0	1	0	0	0
Lawless, 3b	3	0	0	0	1	4
Magrane, p	0	0	0	0	0	0
Forsch, p	0	0	0	0	0	0
Horton, p	0	0	0	0	0	0
Totals	31	1	5	1	24	12

Minnesota (A.L.)	AB.	R.	H.	RBI.	PO.	A.
Gladden, lf	4	1	2	5	3	0
Gagne, ss	5	0	0	0	1	5
Puckett, cf	5	0	1	0	1	0
Gaetti, 3b	5	1	2	0	0	4
Baylor, dh	5	1	1	0	0	0
Brunansky, rf	3	1	1	0	1	0
Davidson, rf	0	0	0	0	0	0
Hrbek, 1b	2	2	1	2	12	0
Larkin, 1b	0	0	0	0	1	0
Lombardozzi, 2b	3	3	2	2	3	2
Laudner, c	3	1	1	1	5	0
Viola, p	0	0	0	0	0	4
Atherton, p	0	0	0	0	0	0
Totals	35	10	11	10	27	15

St. Louis	0 1 0	0 0 0	0 0 0— 1
Minnesota	0 0 0	7 2 0	1 0 x—10

St. Louis	IP.	H.	R.	ER.	BB.	SO.
Magrane (L)	3*	4	5	5	4	1
Forsch	3	4	4	2	0	0
Horton	2	3	1	1	0	1

Minnesota	IP.	H.	R.	ER.	BB.	SO.
Viola (W)	8	5	1	1	0	5
Atherton	1	0	0	0	0	0

*Pitched to five batters in fourth.

Bases on balls—Off Magrane 4 (Brunansky, Hrbek, Lombardozzi, Laudner), off Forsch 2 (Gladden, Hrbek).
Strikeouts—By Magrane 1 (Gagne), by Horton 1 (Laudner), by Viola 5 (Coleman, Smith, Oquendo, Lawless 2).
Game-winning RBI—Hrbek.
Error—Lawless. Double plays—Gaetti, Lombardozzi and Hrbek; Lawless, Herr and Lindeman. Left on bases—St. Louis 3, Minnesota 7. Two-base hits—Lindeman, Gaetti, Gladden. Home runs—Gladden, Lombardozzi. Stolen base—Gladden. Umpires—Phillips (A.L.) plate, Weyer (N.L.) first base, Kosc (A.L.) second base, McSherry (N.L.) third base, Kaiser (A.L.) left field, Tata (N.L.) right field. Time—2:39. Attendance—55,171.

FIRST INNING

Cardinals—Coleman bunted the first pitch down the third-base line and was thrown out, Viola to Hrbek, who scooped the ball out of the dirt for the out. Smith struck out. Herr bounced back to Viola. No runs, no hits, no errors, none left.

Twins—Gladden bounced to Smith. Gagne struck out. Puckett's high chop over the mound was fielded by Herr, who made an off-balanced and low throw which was caught on one hop at first base by Lindeman for the out. No runs, no hits, no errors, none left.

SECOND INNING

Cardinals—Puckett misjudged Lindeman's pop to short center field and it fell in front of him for a double. McGee flied to Puckett in right-center, Lindeman advancing to third just beating a strong throw by Puckett. Pena bounced to Gagne, who threw to Hrbek for the out at first base with Lindeman scoring on the play to give the Cardinals a 1-0 lead. Oquendo fouled to Gladden. One run, one hit, no errors, none left.

Twins—Gaetti flied to Oquendo. Baylor also flied to Oquendo. Brunansky walked. Hrbek walked on a 3-2 pitch. Lombardozzi popped to Lindeman. No runs, no hits, no errors, two left.

THIRD INNING

Cardinals—Pagnozzi grounded to Gaetti. Lawless struck out. Coleman also struck out. No runs, no hits, no errors, none left.

Twins—Laudner drew a leadoff walk. Gladden forced Laudner at second base, Lawless to Herr. Gagne fouled to Herr. On a 1-0 pitch to Puckett, Gladden stole second. Puckett bounced to Herr. No runs, no hits, no errors, one left.

FOURTH INNING

Cardinals—Smith hit a checked swing roller to Lombardozzi. Herr grounded to Gaetti, whose throw pulled Hrbek off the bag at first, but Hrbek was able to tag Herr for the out. Lindeman grounded a single to right. McGee was credited with an infield hit when Gagne backhanded his grounder deep in the hole and threw too late to second base in an attempt to force Lindeman. Pena bounced back to the mound, Viola to Hrbek for the out. No runs, two hits, no errors, two left.

Twins—Lawless made a diving stop of Gaetti's smash down the third-base line, but his throw to first base was late, giving the Twins their first hit of the game. Baylor smacked Magrane's first pitch up the middle for another hit, Gaetti stopping at second. Brunansky lined a single to center, loading the bases. Hrbek grounded an 0-1 pitch to center for a single, scoring Gaetti and Baylor with Brunansky going to third and Hrbek to second on McGee's throw to third base. The run tied the game, 1-1, and snapped the Cardinals postseason scoreless streak at 25 innings. Lombardozzi walked to load the bases once again. Forsch replaced Magrane on the mound for the Cardinals. Laudner grounded an 0-1 delivery to right field, scoring Brunansky to give the Twins a 3-1 lead. Gladden hit a 1-2 pitch into the stands in left-center field for a grand slam, the 13th grand slam in World Series history and the first since Baltimore's Dave McNally connected against Cincinnati in the third game of the 1970 Series, giving the Twins a 7-1 cushion. Gagne flied to Oquendo in right-center. Puckett grounded to Smith. Gaetti was credited with a double when Coleman lost his pop to short left in the white roof of the Metrodome. Baylor grounded out, Lawless to Lindeman, who scooped up a low throw. Seven runs, seven hits, no errors, one left.

FIFTH INNING

Cardinals—Oquendo grounded to Gagne, who momentarily fumbled the ball but recovered in time to throw to Hrbek at first base for the out. Pagnozzi bounced back to Viola. Lawless struck out. No runs, no hits, no errors, none left.

Twins—Brunansky bounced to Lawless. Hrbek walked. Lombardozzi blasted a 1-1 pitch into the left-field seats for a homer, scoring Hrbek and giving the Twins a 9-1 lead. Laudner flied to McGee. Gladden walked. Gagne flied to Oquendo. Two runs, one hit, no errors, one left.

SIXTH INNING

Cardinals—Coleman flied to Brunansky. Smith grounded to Gagne. Herr also bounced to Gagne. No runs, no hits, no errors, none left.

Twins—Puckett popped to Lindeman near the pitcher's mound. Gaetti was safe at first base on a throwing error by Lawless. Baylor bounced to Smith, who threw to Lindeman at first for the out, Gaetti advancing to second on the play. Brunansky flied to McGee. No runs, no hits, one error, one left.

SEVENTH INNING

Cardinals—Lindeman lined to Gagne. McGee lined a single to center. Pena grounded into a double play, Gaetti to Lombardozzi to Hrbek. No runs, one hit, no errors, none left.

Twins—Horton replaced Forsch on the mound for the Cardinals. Hrbek popped to Lawless. Lombardozzi singled past Horton up the middle. Laudner struck out. With Lombardozzi running on a 3-2 pitch, Gladden lined a double into the right-field corner, Lombardozzi scoring to give the Twins a 10-1 lead. Gagne grounded to Smith. One run, two hits, no errors, one left.

EIGHTH INNING

Cardinals—Oquendo struck out. Pagnozzi lined a single to center. Lawless popped to Lombardozzi, who collided with Gagne but made the catch in short-center field. Coleman forced Pagnozzi at second base, Gagne to Lombardozzi. No runs, one hit, no errors, one left.

Twins—Lake went in to catch for the Cardinals. Puckett lined a single to right. McGee dropped Gaetti's pop to short center, but recovered the ball in time to throw to Smith at second base to force Puckett. Baylor bounced into a double play, Lawless to Herr to Lindeman. No runs, one hit, no errors, none left.

NINTH INNING

Cardinals—Atherton replaced Viola on the mound, Larkin went in to play first base and Davidson went to right field for the Twins. Smith flied to Gladden. Herr also flied to Gladden. Lindeman grounded to Gaetti. No runs, no hits, no errors, none left.

Game 2

At Minnesota
October 18

St. Louis (N.L.)	AB.	R.	H.	RBI.	PO.	A.
Coleman, lf	4	1	1	0	1	0
Smith, ss	4	0	1	0	1	2
Herr, 2b	4	0	0	0	1	3
Driessen, 1b	4	1	1	1	10	0
McGee, cf	4	0	1	1	4	0
Pendleton, dh	4	1	1	0	0	0
Ford, rf	3	0	2	0	2	0
Oquendo, 3b	4	0	1	0	0	3
Pena, c	4	0	1	2	5	1
Cox, p	0	0	0	0	0	0
Tunnell, p	0	0	0	0	0	1

	AB.	R.	H.	PO.	A.	E.
Dayley, p	0	0	0	0	0	0
Worrell, p	0	0	0	0	0	0
Totals	35	4	9	4	24	10

Minnesota (A.L.)	AB.	R.	H.	RBI.	PO.	A.
Gladden, lf	5	0	1	1	3	0
Gagne, ss	4	0	1	1	0	3
Puckett, cf	4	1	1	0	0	1
Hrbek, 1b	3	1	1	0	11	0
Gaetti, 3b	3	2	2	1	1	1
Bush, dh	3	1	1	2	0	0
aLarkin	1	0	0	0	0	0
Brunansky, rf	3	1	0	0	3	0
Lombardozzi, 2b	3	0	0	0	1	4
bSmalley	1	0	1	0	0	0
cNewman, 2b	0	0	0	0	0	0
Laudner, c	3	2	2	3	8	0
Blyleven, p	0	0	0	0	0	0
Berenguer, p	0	0	0	0	0	0
Reardon, p	0	0	0	0	0	0
Totals	33	8	10	8	27	9

St. Louis .... 0 0 0 0 1 0 1 2 0—4
Minnesota .... 0 1 0 6 0 1 0 0 x—8

St. Louis	IP.	H.	R.	ER.	BB.	SO.
Cox (L)	3⅔	6	7	7	2	3
Tunnell	2⅓	3	1	1	1	1
Dayley	1⅓	0	0	0	0	1
Worrell	⅔	1	0	0	1	0

Minnesota	IP.	H.	R.	ER.	BB.	SO.
Blyleven (W)	7	6	2	2	1	8
Berenguer	1	3	2	2	0	0
Reardon	1	0	0	0	0	0

Bases on balls—Off Cox 2 (Gaetti, Brunansky),
off Tunnell 1 (Hrbek), off Worrell 1 (Laudner),
off Blyleven 1 (Ford).
Strikeouts—By Cox 3 (Bush, Brunansky,
Laudner), by Tunnell 1 (Lombardozzi), by Dayley 1 (Gaetti), by Blyleven 8 (Coleman 2, Smith,
Driessen, McGee 2, Oquendo, Pena).
Game-winning RBI—Gaetti.
aFlied out for Bush in eighth. bDoubled for
Lombardozzi in eighth. cRan for Smalley in
eighth. Errors—None. Left on bases—St. Louis 5,
Minnesota 5. Two-base hits—Bush, Gagne, Driessen, Smalley. Home runs—Gaetti, Laudner. Stolen
base—Coleman. Wild pitch—Cox. Umpires—
Weyer (N.L.) plate, Kosc (A.L.) first base,
McSherry (N.L.) second base, Kaiser (A.L.) third
base, Tata (N.L.) left field, Phillips (A.L.) right
field. Time—2:42. Attendance—55,257.

FIRST INNING

Cardinals—Coleman was called out on strikes.
Smith lined a single to center field. With Smith
running, Herr bounced to Gagne, who threw to
Hrbek for the out at first base. Driessen struck
out. No runs, one hit, no errors, one left.

Twins—Gladden lined to Herr on Cox' first
pitch of the game. Gagne flied to Ford. Smith
fielded Puckett's chopper over the mound on the
second-base side of the bag and made an off-balanced throw to Driessen at first base for the out.
No runs, no hits, no errors, none left.

SECOND INNING

Cardinals—McGee grounded to Lombardozzi.
Pendleton bounced to Gagne. Ford blooped a sin-
gle to left field. Oquendo was called out on strikes.
No runs, one hit, no errors, one left.

Twins—Hrbek bounced to Oquendo. Gaetti
ripped an 0-1 pitch into the left-field stands for a
home run. Bush was called out on strikes. Brunansky struck out swinging. One run, one hit, no
errors, none left.

THIRD INNING

Cardinals—Pena struck out. Coleman grounded to Lombardozzi. Smith bounced to Gagne. No
runs, no hits, no errors, none left.

Twins—Lombardozzi flied to McGee in short-
center field. Laudner struck out. Gladden flied to
Ford in right-center. No runs, no hits, no errors,
none left.

FOURTH INNING

Cardinals—Herr grounded out Hrbek unassisted. Hrbek also fielded Driessen's chopper and
made the play unassisted. McGee struck out. No
runs, no hits, no errors, none left.

Twins—Gagne bounced to Driessen unassisted.
Puckett lined a single to right-center field. Hrbek
blooped a single to right, Puckett stopping at second base. With a 2-0 count on Gaetti, Cox un-
corked a wild pitch, Puckett advancing to third
and Hrbek to second. Gaetti walked to load the
bases. Bush lined an 0-2 pitch into the right-field
corner for a double, scoring Puckett and Hrbek
with Gaetti stopping at third to give the Twins a
3-0 lead. Brunansky was walked intentionally to
reload the bases. Lombardozzi flied to Coleman in
medium left field, the runners holding their bases.
Laudner smashed Cox' first delivery into the hole
between short and third for a single, scoring Gaetti and Bush, who just beat Coleman's throw to the
plate with a headfirst fallaway slide, with Brunansky stopping at second on the play. Gladden
lined a 2-2 pitch into left field for a single, scoring
Brunansky with Laudner stopping at second.
Tunnell replaced Cox on the mound for the Cardinals. Gagne blooped a 1-0 delivery just inside the
right-field line for a double, scoring Laudner and
sending Gladden to third to give the Twins a 7-0
lead. Puckett bounced to Oquendo. Six runs, six
hits, no errors, two left.

FIFTH INNING

Cardinals—Pendleton's liner went to the right-
field wall, but he had to settle for a single when
Brunansky quickly returned the ball to the infield. Ford walked. Lombardozzi bobbled Oquendo's potential double-play grounder, but recovered in time to throw to Hrbek at first base for the
out, Pendleton stopping at third and Ford going to
second on the play. Pena bounced to Gaetti, who
threw to Hrbek at first for the out, Pendleton
scoring on the play and Ford going to third to cut
the Twins lead to 7-1. Coleman was called out on
strikes. One run, one hit, no errors, one left.

Twins—Hrbek walked on four pitches. Gaetti
grounded a single to left field, Hrbek stopping at
second. Bush forced Gaetti at second base, Herr to
Smith, Hrbek going to third on the play. With
Brunansky at the plate, Bush was picked off first
base, Pena to Driessen. Brunansky flied to McGee.
No runs, one hit, no errors, one left.

SIXTH INNING

Cardinals—Smith was called out on strikes.
Herr flied to Gladden. Driessen flied to Brunansky, who made the catch near the right-field
line. No runs, no hits, no errors, none left.

Twins—Lombardozzi struck out. Laudner
blasted 2-1 pitch over the center-field wall for a
home run, giving the Twins an 8-1 lead. Tunnell
made a good play on Gladden's shot back to the
mound and threw to Driessen at first base for the
out. Gagne bounced to Smith. One run, one hit, no
errors, none left.

SEVENTH INNING

Cardinals—McGee struck out. Pendleton flied
to Gladden on the warning track in left-center
field. Ford grounded a single up the middle.

Oquendo lined a single to center, Ford stopping at second. Pena blooped a single to center, scoring Ford to cut the Twins lead to 8-2, but Oquendo was thrown out trying to go to third, Puckett to Gaetti. One run, three hits, no errors, one left.

Twins—Dayley replaced Tunnell on the mound for the Cardinals. Puckett grounded to Herr, who came in for the short hop and made an off-balanced throw to Driessen at first base for the out. Hrbek also grounded to Herr. Gaetti struck out. No runs, no hits, no errors, none left.

EIGHTH INNING

Cardinals—Berenguer replaced Blyleven on the mound for the Twins. Coleman grounded a single to left. With Smith at the plate, Coleman stole second on the first pitch. Smith flied to Brunansky on the warning track in right field, Coleman advancing to third after the catch. Lombardozzi made a nice backhanded grab of Herr's soft liner behind second base. Driessen lined a double off the right-field wall, scoring Coleman to cut the Twins lead to 8-3. McGee blooped a single to left-center, scoring Driessen to make it 8-4. Pendleton grounded sharply to Lombardozzi, who knocked it down and threw to Hrbek at first base for the out. Two runs, three hits, no errors, one left.

Twins—Larkin, pinch-hitting for Bush, flied to McGee. Worrell replaced Dayley on the mound for the Cardinals. Brunansky grounded to Oquendo, who went to his left to field the one-hopper and threw to Driessen at first base for the out. Smalley batted for Lombardozzi and looped the first pitch to left-center field for a double, just beating Coleman's throw to Herr at second base. Newman ran for Smalley. Laudner walked. Gladden lined hard to McGee in right-center field. No runs, one hit, no errors, two left.

NINTH INNING

Cardinals—Reardon replaced Berenguer on the mound for the Twins and Newman stayed in the game at second base. Ford flied to Brunansky at the base of the wall in right field. Oquendo flied to Gladden. Pena grounded to Hrbek, who made the play unassisted at first base. No runs, no hits, no errors, none left.

Game 3

At St. Louis
October 20

Minnesota (A.L.)	AB.	R.	H.	RBI.	PO.	A.
Gladden, lf	4	0	1	0	1	0
Gagne, ss	3	1	1	0	1	3
Puckett, cf	3	0	1	0	4	0
Gaetti, 3b	4	0	0	0	0	2
Brunansky, rf	4	0	1	1	0	0
Hrbek, 1b	4	0	0	0	10	0
Laudner, c	3	0	2	0	5	1
cBush	1	0	0	0	0	0
Lombardozzi, 2b	3	0	0	0	3	5
Straker, p	2	0	0	0	0	0
aLarkin	1	0	0	0	0	0
Berenguer, p	0	0	0	0	0	0
Schatzeder, p	0	0	0	0	0	0
Totals	32	1	5	1	24	11

St. Louis (N.L.)	AB.	R.	H.	RBI.	PO.	A.
Coleman, lf	4	1	1	2	1	0
Smith, ss	4	0	2	1	0	3
Herr, 2b	4	0	1	0	3	1
Driessen, 1b	4	0	0	0	6	0
Worrell, p	0	0	0	0	0	0
McGee, cf	4	0	2	0	4	0
Ford, rf	4	0	1	0	2	0
Oquendo, 3b	3	1	1	0	1	1
Pena, c	2	1	1	0	9	0
Tudor, p	2	0	0	0	0	2

	AB.	R.	H.	PO.	A.	E.
aPendleton	0	0	0	0	0	0
Lindeman, 1b	0	0	0	0	1	0
Totals	31	3	9	3	27	7

Minnesota	0 0 0	0 0 1	0 0 0—1
St. Louis	0 0 0	0 0 0	3 0 x—3

Minnesota	IP.	H.	R.	ER.	BB.	SO.
Straker	6	4	0	0	2	4
Berenguer (L)	⅓	4	3	3	0	0
Schatzeder	1⅔	1	0	0	0	1

St. Louis	IP.	H.	R.	ER.	BB.	SO.
Tudor (W)	7	4	1	1	2	7
Worrell (S)	2	1	0	0	0	1

Bases on balls—Off Straker 2 (Oquendo, Pena), off Tudor 2 (Gagne, Puckett).

Strikeouts—By Straker 4 (Coleman, Ford, Tudor 2), by Schatzeder 1 (McGee), by Tudor 7 (Gaetti, Brunansky, Hrbek, Laudner, Lombardozzi, Straker 2), by Worrell 1 (Gladden).

Game-winning RBI—Coleman.

aGrounded out for Straker in seventh. bSacrificed for Tudor in seventh. cFlied out for Laudner in ninth. Errors—Pena, Gagne. Double play—Gagne, Lombardozzi and Hrbek. Two-base hits—McGee, Laudner, Coleman. Three-base hit—Puckett. Stolen bases—Coleman 2. Caught stealing—Ford. Sacrifice hit—Pendleton. Balk—Straker. Umpires—Kosc (A.L.) plate, McSherry (N.L.) first base, Kaiser (A.L.) second base, Tata (N.L.) third base, Phillips (A.L.) left field, Weyer (N.L.) right field. Time—2:45. Attendance—55,347.

FIRST INNING

Twins—Gladden flied to Ford. Gagne popped to Herr in short right field. Puckett grounded to Herr. No runs, no hits, no errors, none left.

Cardinals—Coleman was tagged out by Hrbek attempting to beat out a bunt down the first-base line on the first delivery by Straker. Smith grounded a single to left off Gagne's glove deep in the hole. Herr bounced into a double play, Gagne to Lombardozzi to Hrbek. No runs, one hit, no errors, none left.

SECOND INNING

Twins—Gaetti flied to McGee. Brunansky struck out. Tudor fielded Hrbek's tapper in front of the plate and threw to Driessen at first base for the out. No runs, no hits, no errors, none left.

Cardinals—Driessen's hard liner to left-center field was snared by Puckett, who made a long run and nice backhanded catch. McGee blooped a single to left. Ford lined hard to Puckett. With a 1-0 count on Oquendo, Straker was called for a balk, McGee advancing to second on the play. Oquendo walked. Pena bounced to Lombardozzi. No runs, one hit, no errors, two left.

THIRD INNING

Twins—Laudner lined a single to center. Pena was charged with an error when he missed Lombardozzi's foul pop near the Cardinals dugout. However, Tudor pitched around the error when he caught Lombardozzi looking at a third strike. Straker, batting for the first time in his major league career, tried to bunt with two strikes on him but missed. Gladden lined a single to left, Laudner stopping at second base. Gagne flied to McGee. No runs, two hits, no errors, two left.

Cardinals—Tudor struck out. Coleman reached first base on a throwing error by Gagne. Coleman stole second on Straker's first pitch to Smith. Smith then grounded out, Hrbek unassisted, with Coleman advancing to third. Herr grounded to Lombardozzi. No runs, no hits, one error, one left.

FOURTH INNING

Twins—Puckett hit a soft liner to Herr. Gaetti was called out on strikes. Brunansky flied to Coleman. No runs, no hits, no errors, none left.

Cardinals—Driessen flied to Gladden. McGee lined a double off the right-field wall. Ford was called out on strikes. Oquendo flied to Puckett. No runs, one hit, no errors, one left.

FIFTH INNING

Twins—Hrbek was called out on strikes. Laudner lined a double into the right-field corner. Lombardozzi bounced to Smith, who threw to Driessen at first base for the out, Laudner advancing to third on the play. Straker struck out. No runs, one hit, no errors, one left.

Cardinals—Pena walked. Tudor struck out, bunting foul for the third strike. Coleman was called out on strikes. Smith grounded to Lombardozzi. No runs, no hits, no errors, one left.

SIXTH INNING

Twins—Gladden bounced back to the mound, Tudor to Driessen at first base for the out. Gagne walked. Puckett also walked. Gaetti fouled to Pena at the top step of the Cardinals dugout, Gagne advancing to third after the catch. Brunansky had a broken bat single to right-center field on a 2-2 pitch, scoring Gagne to give the Twins a 1-0 lead and sending Puckett to third. Smith made a backhanded stop of Hrbek's grounder in the hole and his strong throw to Driessen at first base just nipped Hrbek. One run, one hit, no errors, two left.

Cardinals—Herr lined a single to center. With Herr running, Driessen bounced to Gagne, who threw to Hrbek at first base for the out. Gagne fielded McGee's bouncer near second base and threw to Hrbek at first base for the out, Herr holding at second. Ford flied to Puckett in left-center field. No runs, one hit, no errors, one left.

SEVENTH INNING

Twins—Laudner was called out on strikes. Lombardozzi flied to McGee. Larkin batted for Straker and grounded to Oquendo. No runs, no hits, no errors, none left.

Cardinals—Berenguer replaced Straker on the mound for the Twins. Oquendo lined Berenguer's first pitch to center for a single. After failing to bunt twice, Pena grounded an 0-2 pitch to right for a single, Oquendo stopping at second base. Pendleton, batting for Tudor, sacrificed Oquendo to third and Pena to second and was out on a close play at first base, Gaetti making a barehanded pickup and throw to Hrbek for the out. Coleman hit an 0-2 pitch past the third base bag and into the Twins bullpen for a double, scoring Oquendo and Pena to give the Cardinals a 2-1 lead. On the first pitch to Smith, Coleman stole third base. Smith then lined a 1-1 pitch to right for a single, scoring Coleman for a 3-1 Cardinals lead. Schatzeder replaced Berenguer on the mound for the Twins. Herr forced Smith at second, Gaetti to Lombardozzi, who dropped the ball and lost the opportunity to complete a double play. Driessen bounced to Lombardozzi. Three runs, four hits, no errors, one left.

EIGHTH INNING

Twins—Worrell replaced Tudor on the mound and Lindeman went in to play first base for the Cardinals. Gladden struck out. Herr struggled, but caught Gagne's popup to short right field near the line. Puckett lined a triple into the right-field corner. Gaetti lined hard right at Oquendo. No runs, one hit, no errors, one left.

Cardinals—McGee struck out. Ford bunted safely past Schatzeder for a single. Oquendo

popped to Lombardozzi in short right field. With Pena at the plate, Ford was caught stealing, Laudner to Gagne. No runs, one hit, no errors, none left.

NINTH INNING

Twins—Brunansky flied to McGee. Hrbek grounded to Smith. Bush, batting for Laudner, flied to Ford. No runs, no hits, no errors, none left.

Game 4

At St. Louis
October 21

Minnesota (A.L.)	AB.	R.	H.	RBI.	PO.	A.
Gladden, lf	5	0	1	0	4	0
Newman, 2b	3	0	1	0	1	1
dBaylor	1	0	1	0	0	0
Puckett, cf	4	0	1	1	1	0
Gaetti, 3b	3	0	1	0	1	1
Brunansky, rf	4	0	0	0	2	0
Hrbek, 1b	4	0	1	0	7	0
Laudner, c	3	0	0	0	8	0
Butera, c	0	0	0	0	0	0
Gagne, ss	4	1	1	1	0	3
Viola, p	1	0	0	0	0	0
Schatzeder, p	0	0	0	0	0	0
aLarkin	0	1	0	0	0	0
Niekro, p	0	0	0	0	0	1
bSmalley	1	0	0	0	0	0
Frazier, p	0	0	0	0	0	1
cDavidson	1	0	0	0	0	0
Totals	34	2	7	2	24	7

St. Louis (N.L.)	AB.	R.	H.	RBI.	PO.	A.
Coleman, lf	4	1	1	0	3	0
Smith, ss	4	1	0	0	1	4
Herr, 2b	3	1	2	0	6	3
Lindeman, 1b	4	1	2	2	6	1
McGee, cf	4	0	2	2	1	0
Pena, c	3	1	1	0	8	0
Oquendo, rf	4	1	1	0	1	0
Lawless, 3b	4	1	1	3	0	1
Mathews, p	1	0	0	0	0	1
Forsch, p	2	0	0	0	1	0
Dayley, p	1	0	0	0	0	0
Totals	34	7	10	7	27	10

Minnesota	001	010	000—2
St. Louis	001	600	00x—7

Minnesota	IP.	H.	R.	ER.	BB.	SO.
Viola (L)	3⅓	6	5	5	3	4
Schatzeder	⅔	2	2	2	1	1
Niekro	2	1	0	0	1	1
Frazier	2	1	0	0	0	2

St. Louis	IP.	H.	R.	ER.	BB.	SO.
Mathews	3⅔	2	1	1	2	3
Forsch (W)	2⅔	4	1	1	1	3
Dayley (S)	2⅔	0	0	0	0	2

Bases on balls—Off Viola 3 (Coleman, Smith, Pena), off Schatzeder 1 (Herr), off Niekro 1 (Herr), off Mathews 2 (Newman, Laudner), off Forsch 1 (Larkin).

Strikeouts—By Viola 4 (Coleman, Lindeman, McGee, Lawless), by Schatzeder 1 (Smith), by Niekro 1 (McGee), by Frazier 2 (Lawless, Dayley), by Mathews 3 (Gladden, Hrbek, Viola), by Forsch 3 (Gladden, Newman, Gagne), by Dayley 2 (Gaetti, Gagne).

Game-winning RBI—Lawless.

aWalked for Schatzeder in fifth. bReached safely on two-base error for Niekro in seventh. cFlied out for Frazier in ninth. dSingled for Newman in ninth. Errors—Puckett, Lindeman. Double play—Lindeman, Smith and Forsch. Left on bases—Minnesota 10, St. Louis 9. Two-base hits—McGee, Coleman. Home runs—Gagne, Lawless. Stolen bases—Gaetti, Brunansky, Coleman. Hit by pitcher—By Mathews (Gaetti), by Niekro (Lindeman), by Forsch (Puckett). Wild pitch—Mathews. Umpires—McSherry (N.L.) plate, Kaiser (A.L.) first base, Tata (N.L.) second base, Phillips (A.L.) third base, Weyer (N.L.) left field, Kosc (A.L.) right field. Time—3:11. Attendance—55,347.

FIRST INNING

Twins—Gladden struck out. Newman popped to Herr in short right-center field. Puckett lined hard to Coleman. No runs, no hits, no errors, none left.

Cardinals—Coleman struck out. Smith grounded to Newman. Herr bounced to Gagne. No runs, no hits no errors, none left.

SECOND INNING

Twins—Gaetti was hit by a pitch. Brunansky popped to Herr in short right field. With Hrbek at the plate, Gaetti stole second base and one pitch later he went to third on a wild pitch by Mathews. Hrbek then struck out. Laudner grounded to Lindeman, who made the play unassisted at first base. No runs, no hits, no errors, one left.

Cardinals—Lindeman struck out. McGee lined a single to center. Pena blooped a single to left-center, McGee stopping at second on the play. Gladden made a nice running catch of Oquendo's liner to left-center. Lawless was called out on strikes. No runs, two hits, no errors, two left.

THIRD INNING

Twins—Gagne blasted a 2-0 delivery into the left-field stands for a home run, giving the Twins a 1-0 lead. Viola struck out. Gladden flied to Coleman. Newman walked. Puckett forced Newman at second base, Smith to Herr. One run, one hit, no errors, one left.

Cardinals—Mathews grounded to Gagne. Coleman hit a sinking liner to right that Brunansky caught at his knees while tumbling to the ground. Smith walked. Herr looped a single to center on a hit-and-run play, Smith advancing to third. Lindeman lined a single to left, scoring Smith to enable the Cardinals to tie the score, 1-1, with Herr stopping at second base. McGee struck out. One run, two hits, no errors, two left.

FOURTH INNING

Twins—Gaetti lined a single to left. Mathews knocked down Brunansky's broken-bat smash back to the mound and threw to Herr at second base to force Gaetti. Hrbek flied to Oquendo. Brunansky stole second. With a 2-0 count on Laudner, Forsch replaced Mathews on the mound for the Cardinals. Forsch completed the walk to Laudner. Gagne struck out. No runs, one hit, no errors, two left.

Cardinals—Pena walked on four pitches. Oquendo lined a single to right-center field, sending Pena to third. Lawless belted an 0-1 pitch over the left-field wall for only his second career big league home run, giving the Cardinals a 4-1 lead. Forsch lined to Gladden. Coleman walked. Schatzeder replaced Viola on the mound for the Twins. Smith was called out on strikes. With Herr at the plate, Coleman stole second base. Herr was then walked intentionally. Lindeman looped an 0-1 pitch into left-center field for a single, scoring Coleman, sending Smith to third and Lindeman went to second when Puckett bobbled the ball for an error. McGee lined the first pitch to him to the left-center field wall for a double, scoring Herr and Lindeman to boost the Cardinals lead to 7-1. Pena flied to Puckett. Six runs, four hits, one error, one left.

FIFTH INNING

Twins—Larkin batted for Schatzeder and walked. Gladden lined a single to right-center, sending Larkin to third. Newman was called out on strikes. Lawless knocked down Puckett's smash down the third-base line with a diving stop, but Puckett had a single, Larkin scoring to cut the Cardinals lead to 7-2 with Gladden stopping at second. Smith made a diving stop of Gaetti's smash in the hole and threw to Herr at second to force Puckett, with Gladden advancing to third on the play. Coleman then made a diving shoestring grab of Brunansky's liner. One run, two hits, no errors, two left.

Cardinals—Niekro replaced Schatzeder on the mound for the Twins. Oquendo flied to Brunansky. Lawless lined to Newman. Forsch grounded to Gagne. No runs, no hits, no errors, none left.

SIXTH INNING

Twins—Hrbek grounded a single to right. Laudner bounced into a double play, Lindeman to Smith to Forsch covering first base. Gagne grounded to Lawless. No runs, one hit, no errors, none left.

Cardinals—Coleman lined a double into the right-field corner. Niekro reached high to stab Smith's bouncer back to the mound and threw to Hrbek at first base for the out, Coleman advancing to third on the play. Herr walked on four pitches. Lindeman was hit by a pitch, loading the bases. McGee struck out. Pena grounded out, Gaetti to Hrbek. No runs, one hit, no errors, three left.

SEVENTH INNING

Twins—Smalley, batting for Niekro, reached second base on a two-base error charged to Lindeman. Gladden struck out. Newman singled off Forsch's glove, Smalley advancing to third on the play. Puckett was hit by a pitch, loading the bases. Dayley replaced Forsch on the mound for the Cardinals. Gaetti struck out. Brunansky fouled to Lindeman. No runs, one hit, one error, three left.

Cardinals—Frazier replaced Niekro on the mound for the Twins. Oquendo bounced back to the mound, Frazier to Hrbek, who scooped up a throw in the dirt for the out. Lawless was called out on strikes. Dayley was also caught looking at a third strike. No runs, no hits, no errors, none left.

EIGHTH INNING

Twins—Hrbek bounced to Herr. Laudner also grounded to Herr. Gagne struck out. No runs, no hits, no errors, none left.

Cardinals—Butera went in to catch for the Twins. Coleman lined to Gaetti. Smith flied to Gladden in left-center field. Herr grounded a single to right. Lindeman flied to Gladden. No runs, one hit, no errors, one left.

NINTH INNING

Twins—Davidson, batting for Frazier, flied to McGee on the warning track in center field. Gladden grounded to Herr. Baylor batted for Newman and grounded a single to left. Puckett forced Baylor at second base, Smith to Herr. No runs, one hit, no errors, one left.

Game 5

At St. Louis
October 22

Minnesota (A.L.)	AB.	R.	H.	RBI.	PO.	A.
Gladden, lf	3	1	1	0	1	0
Gagne, ss	4	1	1	0	1	1
fBaylor	1	0	0	0	0	0
Puckett, cf	4	0	0	0	1	0

	AB.	R.	H.	PO.	A.	E.
Hrbek, 1b	4	0	1	0	9	0
Gaetti, 3b	4	0	1	2	2	2
Brunansky, rf	4	0	1	0	1	0
Laudner, c	2	0	0	0	8	1
cNewman	1	0	0	0	0	0
Lombardozzi, 2b	2	0	1	0	1	6
dSmalley	0	0	0	0	0	0
Blyleven, p	1	0	0	0	0	1
aLarkin	1	0	0	0	0	0
Atherton, p	0	0	0	0	0	0
Reardon, p	0	0	0	0	0	0
eBush	1	0	0	0	0	0
Totals	32	2	6	2	24	11

St. Louis (N.L.)	AB.	R.	H.	RBI.	PO.	A.
Coleman, lf	3	2	1	0	2	0
Smith, ss	4	1	2	1	1	2
Herr, 2b	4	0	0	0	6	2
Driessen, 1b	3	1	1	0	7	1
Dayley, p	0	0	0	0	0	0
Worrell, p	0	0	0	0	0	0
McGee, cf	4	0	0	0	3	0
Ford, rf	4	0	1	2	0	0
Oquendo, 3b	4	0	2	0	0	4
Pena, c	4	0	3	0	6	0
bJohnson	0	0	0	0	0	0
Lake, c	0	0	0	0	0	0
Cox, p	2	0	0	0	1	1
Lindeman, 1b	1	0	0	0	1	0
Totals	33	4	10	3	27	10

Minnesota	0 0 0 0 0 0 0 2 0—2
St. Louis	0 0 0 0 0 3 1 0 x—4

Minnesota	IP.	H.	R.	ER.	BB.	SO.
Blyleven (L)	6	7	3	2	1	4
Atherton	⅓	0	1	1	1	0
Reardon	1⅔	3	0	0	0	3

St. Louis	IP.	H.	R.	ER.	BB.	SO.
Cox (W)	7⅓	5	2	2	3	6
Dayley	⅓	0	0	0	0	0
Worrell (S)	1⅓	1	0	0	2	0

Bases on balls—Off Blyleven 1 (Driessen), off Atherton 1 (Coleman), off Cox 3 (Gladden, Laudner, Lombardozzi), off Worrell 2 (Smalley, Gladden).

Strikeouts—By Blyleven 4 (Coleman, McGee 2, Cox), by Reardon 3 (McGee, Oquendo, Lindeman), by Cox 6 (Gagne, Gaetti 2, Brunansky, Laudner, Blyleven).

Game-winning RBI—Ford.

aFlied out for Blyleven in seventh. bRan for Pena in eighth. cGrounded out for Laudner in ninth. dWalked for Lombardozzi in ninth. ePopped out for Reardon in ninth. fPopped out for Gagne in ninth. Error—Gagne. Double play—Laudner and Gaetti. Left on bases—Minnesota 9, St. Louis 8. Three-base hit—Gaetti. Stolen bases—Gladden, Coleman 2, Smith 2, Johnson. Caught stealing—Oquendo. Sacrifice hits—Cox, Blyleven. Balk—Atherton. Umpires—Kaiser (A.L.) plate, Tata (N.L.) first base, Phillips (A.L.) second base, Weyer (N.L.) third base, Kosc (A.L.) left field, McSherry (N.L.) right field. Time—3:21. Attendance—55,347.

FIRST INNING

Twins—Gladden grounded to Smith. Gagne bounced to Herr. Puckett popped to Herr in short right field. No runs, no hits, no errors, none left.

Cardinals—Coleman struck out. Smith bounced to Lombardozzi. Lombardozzi ranged far to his right to make a backhanded stop of Herr's grounder and threw to Hrbek at first base to nip Herr for the out. No runs, no hits, no errors, none left.

SECOND INNING

Twins—Hrbek grounded to Driessen unassisted. Gaetti struck out. Brunansky lined a single to left. Laudner walked. Lombardozzi popped to Smith in short left field. No runs, one hit, no errors, two left.

Cardinals—Driessen flied to Brunansky. McGee grounded to Lombardozzi. Ford popped to Gaetti. No runs, no hits, no errors, none left.

THIRD INNING

Twins—Blyleven struck out. Gladden walked. Gagne was called out on strikes. Gladden stole second base. Puckett hit a high chopper to Oquendo, who threw to Driessen at first base for the out. No runs, no hits, no errors, one left.

Cardinals—Oquendo looped a single down the left-field line. Pena grounded a hit-and-run single to right, sending Oquendo to third. Cox sacrificed Pena to second, Blyleven to Hrbek. Oquendo tried to score on Coleman's bouncer to Gagne, but was tagged out at the plate by Laudner, Pena holding second on the play. Smith grounded to Lombardozzi. No runs, two hits, no errors, two left.

FOURTH INNING

Twins—Hrbek grounded a single to right. Gaetti forced Hrbek at second base, Oquendo to Herr. Brunansky forced Gaetti at second, Oquendo to Herr, but Herr's throw to Driessen at first base was in the dirt trying to complete a double play. Laudner grounded to Smith, who threw to Driessen at first for the out. No runs, one hit, no errors, one left.

Cardinals—Gaetti knocked down Herr's liner and threw to Hrbek at first base for the out. Driessen grounded to Hrbek unassisted. McGee struck out. No runs, no hits, no errors, none left.

FIFTH INNING

Twins—Lombardozzi lined a single to center. Blyleven sacrificed Lombardozzi to second, Cox to Herr covering first base. Gladden fouled to Driessen. Gagne grounded to Driessen, who threw to Cox covering first for the out. No runs, one hit, no errors, one left.

Cardinals—Ford grounded to Lombardozzi. Oquendo lined a single to left-center field. Pena lined a hit-and-run single past a diving Lombardozzi, sending Oquendo to third. Cox struck out trying to lay down a squeeze bunt and Oquendo was doubled up off third, Laudner to Gaetti. No runs, two hits, no errors, one left.

SIXTH INNING

Twins—Puckett bounced to Oquendo. Hrbek flied to Coleman in short left field. Gaetti was called out on strikes. No runs, no hits, no errors, none left.

Cardinals—Coleman beat out a bad-hop grounder to Hrbek. Smith beat out a bunt when Blyleven had trouble making a barehanded pickup. After failing to bunt twice, Herr lined hard to Gladden near the left-field line. Coleman and Smith pulled off a double steal. After running the count to 3-0 on Driessen, Blyleven walked him intentionally to load the bases. McGee was called out on strikes. Ford lined a 2-1 pitch up the middle for a single, scoring Coleman and Smith to give the Cardinals a 2-0 lead with Driessen advancing to third base and Ford to second on Puckett's throw to third. Gaetti booted Oquendo's grounder for an error, Driessen scoring and Ford going to third on the play. Pena forced Oquendo at second base, Gaetti to Lombardozzi. Three runs, three hits, one error, two left.

SEVENTH INNING

Twins—Brunansky was called out on strikes. Laudner also struck out. Lombardozzi walked. Larkin, batting for Blyleven, flied to Coleman just short of the warning track in left-center field. No runs, no hits, no errors, one left.

Cardinals—Atherton came in to pitch for the Twins. Cox grounded to Lombardozzi. Coleman walked. Coleman went to second base on a balk and, after Reardon replaced Atherton on the mound for the Twins, he stole third. With the infield in for a play at the plate, Smith singled off the glove of a diving Lombardozzi, scoring Coleman to give the Cardinals a 4-0 lead. Smith stole second. Herr lined to Gagne. Gagne went to his right to field Driessen's grounder, but Driessen beat the throw to first base for a hit, Smith going to third. McGee struck out. One run, two hits, no errors, two left.

EIGHTH INNING

Twins—Gladden lined a single to right. Gagne beat out a bunt down the third-base line. Puckett flied to McGee. Dayley replaced Cox on the mound and Lindeman went in to play first base for the Cardinals. Hrbek flied to McGee in left-center field. Worrell replaced Dayley on the mound for the Cardinals. Gaetti tripled on a 2-2 pitch off the glove of McGee, who leaped high against the center-field wall, scoring Gladden and Gagne to cut the Cardinals lead to 4-2. Brunansky flied to McGee in left-center. Two runs, three hits, no errors, one left.

Cardinals—Ford flied to Puckett. Oquendo struck out. Pena bounced a single up the middle. Johnson came in to pinch-run for Pena and promptly stole second. Lindeman struck out. No runs, one hit, no errors, one left.

NINTH INNING

Twins—Newman batted for Laudner and grounded to Herr. Smalley, batting for Lombardozzi, walked. Bush batted for Reardon and popped to Herr in short right field. Gladden walked. Baylor, batting for Gagne, popped to Herr in short right field. No runs, no hits, no errors, two left.

Game 6

At Minnesota
October 24

St. Louis (N.L.)	AB.	R.	H.	RBI.	PO.	A.
Coleman, lf	5	0	0	0	1	0
Smith, ss	4	1	1	0	3	3
Herr, 2b	5	1	3	1	3	3
Driessen, 1b	2	1	1	0	4	0
bPagnozzi	1	0	0	0	0	0
Morris, rf	2	0	0	0	2	0
McGee, cf	4	1	2	1	4	0
Pendleton, dh	3	1	2	1	0	0
Ford, rf	1	0	0	0	1	0
aLindeman, rf-1b	3	0	0	0	4	0
Oquendo, 3b	3	0	1	0	2	2
Pena, c	3	0	1	0	2	0
Tudor, p	0	0	0	0	0	2
Horton, p	0	0	0	0	0	1
Forsch, p	0	0	0	0	0	0
Dayley, p	0	0	0	0	0	0
Tunnell, p	0	0	0	0	0	0
Totals	36	5	11	5	24	11

Minnesota (A.L.)	AB.	R.	H.	RBI.	PO.	A.
Gladden, lf	5	1	2	0	1	0
Gagne, ss	5	1	1	0	1	4
Puckett, cf	4	4	4	1	4	0
Gaetti, 3b	5	1	1	1	1	0
Baylor, dh	3	2	2	3	0	0
cBush	1	0	0	0	0	0

	AB.	R.	H.	PO.	A.	E.
Brunansky, rf	4	1	1	1	5	0
Hrbek, 1b	4	1	1	4	9	1
Laudner, c	5	0	0	0	5	0
Lombardozzi, 2b	4	0	3	1	1	5
Straker, p	0	0	0	0	1	0
Schatzeder, p	0	0	0	0	0	0
Berenguer, p	0	0	0	0	0	0
Reardon, p	0	0	0	0	0	0
Totals	40	11	15	11	27	10

St. Louis .... 1 1 0   2 1 0   0 0 0— 5
Minnesota .... 2 0 0   0 4 4   0 1 x—11

St. Louis	IP.	H.	R.	ER.	BB.	SO.
Tudor (L)	4†	11	6	6	1	1
Horton	1‡	2	1	1	0	0
Forsch	⅔	0	2	2	2	0
Dayley	⅓	1	1	1	0	0
Tunnell	2	1	1	0	1	0

Minnesota	IP.	H.	R.	ER.	BB.	SO.
Straker	3*	5	4	4	1	2
Schatzeder (W)	2	1	1	1	2	1
Berenguer	3	3	0	0	0	1
Reardon	1	2	0	0	0	0

*Pitched to three batters in fourth.
†Pitched to four batters in fifth.
‡Pitched to one batter in sixth.

Bases on balls—Off Tudor 1 (Brunansky), off Forsch 2 (Puckett, Baylor), off Tunnell 1 (Hrbek), off Straker 1 (Pendleton), off Schatzeder 2 (Pena, Smith).

Strikeouts—By Tudor 1 (Brunansky), by Straker 2 (Coleman, Herr), by Schatzeder 1 (Pendleton), by Berenguer 1 (Coleman).

Game-winning RBI—Lombardozzi.

aFouled out for Ford in fourth. bFlied out for Driessen in fifth. cReached first base on error for Baylor in eighth. Errors—McGee, Lindeman. Double play—Lombardozzi, Gagne and Hrbek. Left on bases—St. Louis 8, Minnesota 9. Two-base hits—Driessen, Lombardozzi, Gaetti. Three-base hit—Gladden. Home runs—Herr, Baylor, Hrbek. Stolen bases—Puckett, Pendleton 2. Sacrifice fly—Oquendo. Passed ball—Pena. Umpires—Tata (N.L.) plate, Phillips (A.L.) first base, Weyer (N.L.) second base, Kosc (A.L.) third base, McSherry (N.L.) left field, Kaiser (A.L.) right field. Time—3:22. Attendance—55,293.

FIRST INNING

Cardinals—Coleman struck out. Smith flied to Puckett. Herr blasted an 0-2 pitch from Straker into the upper deck down the right-field line for a home run, giving the Cardinals a 1-0 lead. Driessen grounded to Hrbek, who threw to Straker covering first base for the out. One run, one hit, no errors, none left.

Twins—Gladden's smash past the first-base bag went into the right-field corner for a triple. Herr fielded Gagne's one-hopper, looked Gladden back to third base and threw to Driessen at first for the out. Puckett grounded Tudor's first pitch into left field for a single, scoring Gladden to tie the score at 1-1. Gaetti bounced to Oquendo, who charged in and made an off-balanced throw to Driessen for the out, Puckett advancing to second on the play. Baylor lined a single to right, scoring Puckett to give the Twins a 2-1 lead. Brunansky was called out on strikes. Two runs, three hits, no errors, one left.

SECOND INNING

Cardinals—Lombardozzi fielded McGee's high chopper behind second base and threw to Hrbek at first base for the out. Pendleton walked on four pitches. Ford grounded to Lombardozzi, who bobbled the ball and lost his play on Pendleton at second base but recovered in time to get Ford at first. With Pendleton running on a 3-2 delivery, Oquendo lined a single to right to enable the Cardinals to tie the score, 2-2. Pena flied to Puckett. One run, one hit, no errors, one left.

Twins—McGee dropped Hrbek's long fly ball to the warning track in right-center field for a two-base error after a near collision with Ford. Hrbek was picked off, Tudor to Herr. Laudner bounced back to the m und, Tudor to Driessen for the out. Lombardozzi lined a single to right-center. Gladden lined a single to center, sending Lombardozzi to third. Gagne forced Gladden at second base, Smith to Herr. No runs, two hits, one error, two left.

THIRD INNING

Cardinals—Coleman bounced to Lombardozzi. Smith flied to Brunansky on the warning track in right field. Herr struck out. No runs, no hits, no errors, none left.

Twins—Puckett lined a single to center. Gaetti flied to Ford just in front of the warning track in right field. Baylor fouled to Pena. Puckett stole second. Brunansky walked on four pitches. Hrbek flied to Coleman. No runs, one hit, no errors, two left.

FOURTH INNING

Cardinals—Driessen lined a double off the right-field wall. McGee lined a single to center, Driessen stopping at third and McGee going to second when Puckett's throw to the plate missed the cutoff man. Pendleton got an infield hit when he grounded to Hrbek, but beat Straker in a race to the bag, Driessen scoring to give the Cardinals a 3-2 lead while McGee advanced to third on the play. Schatzeder replaced Straker on the mound for the Twins. Lindeman, batting for Ford, fouled to Gaetti. Oquendo hit a sacrifice fly to Brunansky near the right-field line, McGee scoring after the catch to boost the Cardinals lead to 4-2 with Pendleton advancing to second. Pendleton then stole third. Pena walked. Coleman flied to Puckett on the warning track in center field. Two runs, three hits, no errors, two left.

Twins—Lindeman stayed in the game and played right field for the Cardinals. Laudner flied to McGee. Lombardozzi's smash hit the third-base bag and went into short left field for a double. Gladden flied to McGee in left-center field, McGee and Coleman avoiding a near collision. Gagne grounded out, Smith to Driessen. No runs, one hit, no errors, one left.

FIFTH INNING

Cardinals—Smith walked. With Smith running, Herr bounced out, Gagne to Hrbek. Pagnozzi, batting for Driessen, flied to Brunansky, Smith advancing to third after the catch. McGee singled to right on Schatzeder's first delivery to him, scoring Smith to give the Cardinals a 5-2 lead. Pendleton struck out. One run, one hit, no errors, one left.

Twins—Morris went in to play right field and Lindeman moved to first base for the Cardinals. Puckett lined Tudor's first pitch to center for a single. Gaetti drilled a 1-1 delivery into the left-field corner for a double, scoring Puckett. Baylor belted the first pitch to him into the left-field stands for a home run to pull the Twins into a 5-5 tie. Brunansky lined a single to left. Horton replaced Tudor on the mound for the Cardinals. Hrbek flied to McGee. Laudner bounced back to the mound, Horton to Lindeman for the out at first base, Brunansky advancing to second on the play. Lombardozzi lined a single to center, scoring Brunansky, who just beat McGee's throw to the plate to give the Twins a 6-5 lead. Gladden lined to Smith. Four runs, five hits, no errors, one left.

SIXTH INNING

Cardinals—Berenguer replaced Schatzeder on the mound for the Twins. Lindeman grounded to Lombardozzi. Oquendo grounded to Gagne. Pena bounced to Gagne, who fielded the ball behind second base and threw to Hrbek for the out. No runs, no hits, no errors, none left.

Twins—Gagne's high chopper off the plate went for a hit when Smith fielded the ball behind the mound but his throw was too late to first base. Forsch replaced Horton on the mound for the Cardinals. Puckett walked on four pitches. Gagne went to third and Puckett to second on a passed ball by Pena. Gaetti popped to Smith in short center. Baylor was walked intentionally to load the bases. Brunansky popped to Smith in short center field. Dayley replaced Forsch on the mound for the Cardinals. Hrbek, 0-for-16 against lefthanded pitchers in the Series, smashed Dayley's first pitch over the center-field fence for a grand slam, boosting the Twins lead to 10-5. Laudner grounded to Herr. Four runs, two hits, no errors, none left.

SEVENTH INNING

Cardinals—Coleman struck out. Smith lined a single to right. Herr bounced a single to right, Smith stopping at second base. Morris bounced into a double play, Lombardozzi to Gagne to Hrbek. No runs, two hits, no errors, one left.

Twins—Tunnell replaced Dayley on the mound for the Cardinals. Lombardozzi flied to Morris. Gladden also flied to Morris. Gagne grounded to Herr, who made a nice play to his right. No runs, no hits, no errors, none left.

EIGHTH INNING

Cardinals—McGee grounded to Hrbek unassisted. Pendleton lined a single off the right-field wall, Brunansky making a quick recovery to prevent a double. Lindeman flied to Brunansky. Pendleton stole second base. Oquendo flied to Puckett in left-center field. No runs, one hit, no errors, one left.

Twins—Puckett got his fourth hit of the game when Herr knocked down his grounder up the middle but had no play. Gaetti flied to McGee. Bush, batting for Baylor, reached first base when Lindeman booted his bouncer for an error, Puckett going to third on the play. Oquendo made a diving stop behind third base and a strong throw to first to retire Brunansky, Puckett scoring to give the Twins an 11-5 lead and Bush going to second on the play. Hrbek was walked intentionally. Laudner forced Hrbek at second base, Smith to Herr. One run, one hit, one error, two left.

NINTH INNING

Cardinals—Reardon replaced Berenguer on the mound for the Twins. Pena lined a single to left-center field. Lombardozzi fielded Coleman's squibber behind second base and stepped on the bag to force Pena. Smith flied to Brunansky at the base of the wall in right field. Herr grounded a hit-and-run single to right, sending Coleman to third. Herr swiped second unmolested, but was not credited with a stolen base. Morris fouled to Laudner. No runs, two hits, no errors, two left.

Game 7

St. Louis (N.L.)	AB.	R.	H.	RBI.	PO.	A.
Coleman, lf	4	0	0	0	2	2
Smith, ss	4	0	0	0	0	1
Herr, 2b	4	0	1	0	1	2
Lindeman, 1b	3	1	1	0	5	1
cFord	1	0	0	0	0	0
McGee, cf	4	1	1	0	3	0
Pena, dh	3	0	2	1	0	0

	AB.	R.	H.	PO.	A.	E.
Oquendo, rf	3	0	0	0	2	0
Lawless, 3b	3	0	0	0	2	1
Lake, c	3	0	1	1	8	1
Magrane, p	0	0	0	0	1	1
Cox, p	0	0	0	0	0	0
Worrell, p	0	0	0	0	0	0
Totals	32	2	6	2	24	9

Minnesota (A.L.)	AB.	R.	H.	RBI.	PO.	A.
Gladden, lf	5	0	1	1	0	0
Gagne, ss	5	1	2	1	2	1
Puckett, cf	4	0	2	1	4	0
Gaetti, 3b	3	0	0	0	1	5
Baylor, dh	3	0	1	0	0	0
Brunansky, rf	3	2	1	0	2	0
Hrbek, 1b	3	0	0	0	10	1
Laudner, c	3	1	2	0	7	0
Lombardozzi, 2b	2	0	1	1	0	2
aSmalley	0	0	0	0	0	0
bNewman, 2b	1	0	0	0	0	1
Viola, p	0	0	0	0	1	1
Reardon, p	0	0	0	0	0	0
Totals	32	4	10	4	27	11

St. Louis .... 0 2 0   0 0 0   0 0 0—2
Minnesota .... 0 1 0   0 1 1   0 1 x—4

St. Louis	IP.	H.	R.	ER.	BB.	SO.
Magrane	4⅓	5	2	2	1	4
Cox (L)	⅔*	2	1	1	3	0
Worrell	3	3	1	1	1	2

Minnesota	IP.	H.	R.	ER.	BB.	SO.
Viola (W)	8	6	2	2	0	7
Reardon (S)	1	0	0	0	0	0

*Pitched to two batters in sixth.

Bases on balls—Off Magrane 1 (Laudner), off Cox 3 (Gaetti, Brunansky, Hrbek), off Worrell 1 (Smalley). Strikeouts—By Magrane 4 (Gagne 2, Baylor, Hrbek), by Worrell 2 (Gladden, Puckett), by Viola 7 (Coleman 2, Herr, Lindeman, McGee, Pena, Oquendo).

Game-winning RBI—Gagne. aWalked for Lombardozzi in sixth. bRan for Smalley in sixth. cPopped out for Lindeman in ninth. Error—Lindeman. Left on bases—St. Louis 3, Minnesota 10. Two-base hits—Puckett, Pena, Gladden. Stolen bases—Gaetti, Pena. Caught stealing—Herr. Hit by pitcher—By Magrane (Baylor). Umpires—Phillips (A.L.) plate, Weyer (N.L.) first base, Kosc (A.L.) second base, McSherry (N.L.) third base, Kaiser (A.L.) left field, Tata (N.L.) right field. Time—3:04. Attendance—55,376.

FIRST INNING

Cardinals—Coleman struck out. Smith flied to Puckett in right-center field. Herr bounced to Gaetti. No runs, no hits, no errors, none left.

Twins—Lindeman went to his right to field Gladden's grounder and threw to Magrane covering first base for the out. Gagne struck out. Puckett beat out a slow roller to Lawless at third. Gaetti flied to Oquendo, who raced into right-center field to make a shoetop catch. No runs, one hit, no errors, one left.

SECOND INNING

Cardinals—Lindeman looped a single to center field. McGee lined a single to left, Lindeman stopping at second base. Pena lined a 1-1 pitch to center, scoring Lindeman to give the Cardinals a 1-0 lead, McGee stopping at second on the play. Oquendo popped to Hrbek. Lawless flied to Puckett on the warning track in right-center, McGee advancing to third after the catch. Lake lined a

single to left on the first pitch, McGee scoring to boost the Cardinals lead to 2-0 and Pena stopping at second. Coleman popped to Gagne in short center. Two runs, four hits, no errors, two left.

Twins—Baylor was hit by a pitch. Brunansky grounded a single to left, Baylor stopping at second base. Hrbek struck out. Laudner grounded a single to left and Baylor, attempting to score, was thrown out at the plate on a controversial tag play, Coleman to Lake, with Brunansky stopping at second. Lombardozzi lined a 2-0 pitch to center for a single, Brunansky scoring to cut the lead to 2-1 and Laudner stopping at second. Gladden popped to Herr. One run, three hits, no errors, two left.

THIRD INNING

Cardinals—Smith bounced to Gaetti. Herr struck out. Lindeman also struck out. No runs, no hits, no errors, none left.

Twins—Gagne struck out. Puckett flied to McGee, who made a leaping catch against the wall in center field. Gaetti grounded to Lawless and was safe at first base when Lindeman dropped the throw for an error. Gaetti stole second base. Baylor struck out. No runs, no hits, one error, one left.

FOURTH INNING

Cardinals—McGee struck out. Pena also struck out, becoming Viola's fourth consecutive strikeout victim. Oquendo grounded to Gaetti. No runs, no hits, no errors, none left.

Twins—Brunansky flied to Coleman in short left field. Hrbek was thrown out attempting to bunt, Magrane to Lindeman. Laudner walked. Lombardozzi flied to McGee. No runs, no hits, no errors, one left.

FIFTH INNING

Cardinals—Lawless fouled to Hrbek. Lake grounded to Lombardozzi. Coleman struck out. No runs, no hits, no errors, none left.

Twins—Gladden grounded to Smith. Gagne was credited with a single when Lindeman fielded his high bouncer and threw to Magrane, who had trouble touching the first base bag, Gagne reaching safely. Cox replaced Magrane on the mound for the Cardinals. Puckett lined Cox's first pitch to the wall in right-center field for a double, plating Gagne to tie the score, 2-2. Gaetti walked. Puckett was thrown out at third base, Lake to Lawless, on a pitch that bounced in front of the plate, Gaetti advancing to second on the play. Baylor lined a single to left and Gaetti, attempting to score, was thrown out at the plate, Coleman to Lake, as he tried to bowl over the St. Louis catcher. One run, three hits, no errors, one left.

SIXTH INNING

Cardinals—Smith fouled to Gagne. Herr grounded a single up the middle. Herr was picked off first and caught in a rundown, Viola to Hrbek to Lombardozzi to second on the play. Lindeman flied to Brunansky. No runs, one hit, no errors, none left.

Twins—Brunansky walked. Hrbek also walked. Worrell replaced Cox on the mound for the Cardinals. Cox had words with plate umpire Phillips upon leaving and was ejected from the game. Laudner, after failing to bunt twice, fouled to Lindeman. Smalley, batting for Lombardozzi, walked on a 3-2 pitch to load the bases. Newman pinch-ran for Smalley. Gladden struck out. Lawless made a diving backhanded stop of Gagne's smash behind third base but his long throw to first base was too late and Brunansky scored to give the Twins a 3-2 lead. Puckett struck out. One run, one hit, no errors, three left.

SEVENTH INNING

Cardinals—Newman stayed in the game and played second base for the Twins. McGee grounded to Gagne. Pena lined a double off the right-field wall. Oquendo struck out. Pena stole third base. Lawless flied to Puckett. No runs, one hit, no errors, one left.

Twins—Gaetti flied to McGee in short center field. Baylor flied to Oquendo. Brunansky popped to Lawless. No runs, no hits, no errors, none left.

EIGHTH INNING

Cardinals—Lake bounced to Gaetti. Coleman flied to Brunansky near the right-field line. Smith grounded to Newman. No runs, no hits, no errors, none left.

Twins—Hrbek grounded to Herr. Laudner grounded a single to left. Newman fouled to Coleman. Gladden lined a 1-0 pitch to the wall in right-center field for a double, scoring Laudner, who slid in safely when the relay throw from Herr bounced over Lake's glove, to give the Twins a 4-2 lead. Gagne hit a hard one-hopper to Herr, who threw to Lindeman at first base for the out. One run, two hits, no errors, one left.

NINTH INNING

Cardinals—Reardon replaced Viola on the mound for the Twins. Herr flied to Puckett. Ford, batting for Lindeman, popped to Gaetti in short left field. McGee bounced to Gaetti. No runs, no hits, no errors, none left.

MINNESOTA TWINS' BATTING AND FIELDING AVERAGES

Player—Position	G.	AB.	R.	H.	TB.	2B.	3B.	HR.	RBI.	BB.	IBB.	SO.	B.A.	PO.	A.	E.	F.A.
Smalley, ph	4	2	0	1	2	1	0	0	0	2	0	0	.500	0	0	0	.000
Lombardozzi, 2b	6	17	3	7	11	1	0	1	4	2	0	2	.412	9	24	0	1.000
Baylor, dh-ph	5	13	3	5	8	0	0	1	3	1	1	1	.385	0	0	0	.000
Puckett, cf	7	28	5	10	13	1	1	0	3	2	0	1	.357	15	1	1	.941
Laudner, c	7	22	4	7	11	1	0	1	4	5	0	4	.318	46	2	0	1.000
Gladden, lf	7	31	3	9	16	2	1	1	7	3	0	4	.290	12	0	0	1.000
Gaetti, 3b	7	27	4	7	14	2	1	1	4	2	0	5	.259	6	15	0	1.000
Hrbek, 1b	7	24	4	5	8	0	0	1	6	5	1	3	.208	68	2	0	1.000
Gagne, ss	7	30	5	6	10	1	0	1	3	1	0	6	.200	6	20	2	.929
Brunansky, rf	7	25	5	5	5	0	0	0	2	4	1	4	.200	14	0	0	1.000
Newman, pr-2b-ph	4	5	0	1	1	0	0	0	0	1	0	1	.200	1	2	0	1.000
Bush, dh-ph	4	6	1	1	2	1	0	0	2	0	0	1	.167	0	0	0	.000
Larkin, 1b-ph	5	3	1	0	0	0	0	0	0	1	0	0	.000	1	0	0	1.000
Straker, p	2	2	0	0	0	0	0	0	0	0	0	2	.000	1	0	0	1.000
Blyleven, p	2	1	0	0	0	0	0	0	0	0	0	1	.000	0	1	0	1.000
Davidson, rf-ph	2	1	0	0	0	0	0	0	0	0	0	0	.000	0	0	0	.000
Viola, p	3	1	0	0	0	0	0	0	0	0	0	1	.000	1	5	0	1.000
Atherton, p	2	0	0	0	0	0	0	0	0	0	0	0	.000	0	0	0	.000
Berenguer, p	3	0	0	0	0	0	0	0	0	0	0	0	.000	0	0	0	.000
Butera, c	1	0	0	0	0	0	0	0	0	0	0	0	.000	0	0	0	.000
Frazier, p	1	0	0	0	0	0	0	0	0	0	0	0	.000	0	1	0	1.000
Niekro, p	1	0	0	0	0	0	0	0	0	0	0	0	.000	0	1	0	1.000
Reardon, p	4	0	0	0	0	0	0	0	0	0	0	0	.000	0	0	0	.000
Schatzeder, p	3	0	0	0	0	0	0	0	0	0	0	0	.000	0	0	0	.000
Totals	7	238	38	64	101	10	3	7	38	29	3	36	.269	180	74	3	.988

Baylor—Singled for Newman in ninth inning of fourth game; popped out for Gagne in ninth inning of fifth game.

Bush—Flied out for Laudner in ninth inning of third game; popped out for Reardon in ninth inning of fifth game; reached base on error for Baylor in eighth inning of sixth game.

Davidson—Flied out for Frazier in ninth inning of fourth game.

Larkin—Flied out for Bush in eighth inning of second game; grounded out for Straker in seventh inning of third game; walked for Schatzeder in fifth inning of fourth game; flied out for Blyleven in seventh inning of fifth game.

Newman—Ran for Smalley in eighth inning of second game; grounded out for Laudner in ninth inning of fifth game; ran for Smalley in sixth inning of seventh game.

Smalley—Doubled for Lombardozzi in eighth inning of second game; reached on two-base error for Niekro in seventh inning of fourth game; walked for Lombardozzi in ninth inning of fifth game; walked for Lombardozzi in sixth inning of seventh game.

ST. LOUIS CARDINALS' BATTING AND FIELDING AVERAGES

Player—Position	G.	AB.	R.	H.	TB.	2B.	3B.	HR.	RBI.	BB.	IBB.	SO.	B.A.	PO.	A.	E.	F.A.
Pendleton, dh-ph	3	7	2	3	3	0	0	0	1	1	0	1	.429	0	0	0	.000
Pena, c-dh	7	22	2	9	10	1	0	0	4	3	0	2	.409	32	1	1	.971
McGee, cf	7	27	2	10	12	2	0	0	4	0	0	9	.370	21	1	1	.957
Lindeman, 1b-ph-rf	6	15	3	5	6	1	0	0	2	0	0	3	.333	28	2	3	.909
Lake, c	3	3	0	1	1	0	0	0	1	0	0	0	.333	8	1	0	1.000
Ford, rf-ph	5	13	1	4	4	0	0	0	2	1	0	1	.308	5	0	0	1.000
Herr, 2b	7	28	2	7	10	0	0	1	1	2	1	2	.250	23	17	0	1.000
Oquendo, rf-3b	7	24	2	6	6	0	0	0	2	1	0	4	.250	8	10	0	1.000
Pagnozzi, dh-ph	2	4	0	1	1	0	0	0	0	0	0	0	.250	0	0	0	.000
Driessen, 1b	4	13	3	3	5	2	0	0	1	1	1	1	.231	27	1	0	1.000
Smith, ss	7	28	3	6	6	0	0	0	2	2	0	3	.214	7	19	0	1.000
Coleman, lf	7	28	5	4	6	2	0	0	2	2	0	10	.143	10	2	0	1.000
Lawless, 3b	3	10	1	1	4	0	0	1	3	0	0	4	.100	3	6	1	.900
Cox, p	3	2	0	0	0	0	0	0	0	0	0	1	.000	1	1	0	1.000
Forsch, p	3	2	0	0	0	0	0	0	0	0	0	0	.000	1	0	0	1.000
Morris, rf	1	2	0	0	0	0	0	0	0	0	0	0	.000	2	0	0	1.000
Tudor, p	2	2	0	0	0	0	0	0	0	0	0	2	.000	0	4	0	1.000
Dayley, p	4	1	0	0	0	0	0	0	0	0	0	1	.000	0	0	0	.000
Mathews, p	1	1	0	0	0	0	0	0	0	0	0	0	.000	0	1	0	1.000

Player—Position	G.	AB.	R.	H.	TB.	2B.	3B.	HR.	RBI.	BB.	IBB.	SO.	B.A.	PO.	A.	E.	F.A.
Horton, p..................	2	0	0	0	0	0	0	0	0	0	0	0	.000	0	1	0	1.000
Johnson, pr..................	1	0	0	0	0	0	0	0	0	0	0	0	.000	0	0	0	.000
Magrane, p..................	2	0	0	0	0	0	0	0	0	0	0	0	.000	1	1	0	1.000
Tunnell, p..................	2	0	0	0	0	0	0	0	0	0	0	0	.000	0	1	0	1.000
Worrell, p..................	4	0	0	0	0	0	0	0	0	0	0	0	.000	0	0	0	.000
Totals..................	7	232	26	60	74	8	0	2	25	13	2	44	.259	177	69	6	.976

Ford—Popped out for Lindeman in ninth inning of seventh game.
Johnson—Ran for Pena in eighth inning of fifth game.
Lindeman—Fouled out for Ford in fourth inning of sixth game.
Pagnozzi—Flied out for Driessen in fifth inning of sixth game.
Pendleton—Sacrificed for Tudor in seventh inning of third game.

MINNESOTA TWINS' PITCHING RECORDS

Pitcher	G.	GS.	CG.	IP.	H.	R.	ER.	HR.	BB.	IBB.	SO.	HB.	WP.	W.	L.	Pct.	ERA.
Reardon..................	4	0	0	4⅔	5	0	0	0	0	0	3	0	0	0	0	.000	0.00
Frazier..................	1	0	0	2	1	0	0	0	0	0	2	0	0	0	0	.000	0.00
Niekro..................	1	0	0	2	1	0	0	0	1	0	1	1	0	0	0	.000	0.00
Blyleven..................	2	2	0	13	13	5	4	0	2	1	12	0	0	1	1	.500	2.77
Viola..................	3	3	0	19⅓	17	8	8	1	3	0	16	0	0	2	1	.667	3.72
Straker..................	2	2	0	9	9	4	4	1	3	0	6	0	0	0	0	.000	4.00
Schatzeder..................	3	0	0	4⅓	4	3	3	0	3	1	3	0	0	1	0	1.000	6.23
Atherton	2	0	0	1⅓	0	1	1	0	1	0	0	0	0	0	0	.000	6.75
Berenguer..................	3	0	0	4⅓	10	5	5	0	0	1	1	0	0	0	1	.000	10.38
Totals..................	7	7	0	60	60	26	25	2	13	2	44	1	0	4	3	.571	3.75

No shutouts. Save—Reardon.

ST. LOUIS CARDINALS' PITCHING RECORDS

Pitcher	G.	GS.	CG.	IP.	H.	R.	ER.	HR.	BB.	IBB.	SO.	HB.	WP.	W.	L.	Pct.	ERA.
Worrell..................	4	0	0	7	6	1	1	0	4	0	3	0	0	0	0	.000	1.29
Dayley	4	0	0	4⅔	2	1	1	0	3	0	3	0	0	0	0	.000	1.93
Tunnell	2	0	0	4⅓	4	2	1	1	2	1	1	0	0	0	0	.000	2.08
Mathews..................	1	1	0	3⅔	2	1	1	1	2	0	3	1	1	0	0	.000	2.45
Tudor	2	2	0	11	15	7	7	1	3	0	8	0	0	1	1	.500	5.73
Horton	2	0	0	3	5	2	2	0	0	1	0	0	0	0	0	.000	6.00
Cox	3	2	0	11⅔	13	10	10	1	8	1	9	0	1	1	2	.333	7.71
Magrane..................	2	2	0	7⅓	9	7	7	0	5	0	5	1	0	0	1	.000	8.59
Forsch..................	3	0	0	6⅓	8	7	7	2	5	1	3	1	0	1	0	1.000	9.95
Totals..................	7	7	0	59	64	38	37	7	29	3	36	3	2	3	4	.429	5.64

No shutouts. Saves—Worrell 2, Dayley.

COMPOSITE SCORE BY INNINGS

Minnesota......................................	2	2	1	13	8	7	1	4	0 — 38
St. Louis	1	4	1	8	2	3	5	2	0 — 26

Game-winning RBI—Hrbek, Gaetti, Coleman, Lawless, Ford, Lombardozzi, Gagne.
Sacrifice hits—Pendleton, Cox, Blyleven.
Sacrifice fly—Oquendo.
Stolen bases—Coleman 6, Gladden 2, Gaetti 2, Smith 2, Pendleton 2, Brunansky, Johnson, Puckett, Pena.
Caught stealing—Ford, Oquendo, Herr.
Double plays—Gaetti, Lombardozzi and Hrbek; Lawless, Herr and Lindeman, Gagne, Lombardozzi and Hrbek; Lindeman, Smith and Forsch; Laudner and Gaetti; Lombardozzi, Gagne and Hrbek.
Passed ball—Pena.
Hit by pitcher—By Mathews (Gaetti), by Niekro (Lindeman), by Forsch (Puckett), by Magrane (Baylor).
Balks—Straker, Atherton.
Bases on balls—Off Schatzeder 3 (Herr, Smith, Pena), off Straker 3 (Oquendo, Pena, Pendleton), off Viola 3 (Coleman, Pena, Smith), off Blyleven 2 (Driessen, Ford), off Atherton 1 (Coleman), off Niekro 1 (Herr), off Cox 8 (Gaetti 2, Brunansky 2, Gladden, Hrbek, Laudner, Lombardozzi), off Forsch 5 (Baylor, Gladden, Hrbek, Larkin, Puckett), off Magrane 5 (Laudner 2, Brunansky, Hrbek, Lombardozzi), off Worrell 4 (Smalley 2, Gladden, Laudner), off Tudor 3 (Brunansky, Gagne, Puckett), off Mathews 2 (Laudner, Newman), off Tunnell 2 (Hrbek 2).
Strikeouts—By Viola 16 (Coleman 4, Lawless 3, Lindeman 2, McGee 2, Oquendo 2, Herr, Smith, Pena), by Blyleven 12 (McGee 4, Coleman 3, Cox, Driessen, Oquendo, Pena, Smith), by Straker 6 (Coleman 2, Tudor 2, Ford, Herr), by Reardon 3 (Lindeman, McGee, Oquendo), by Schatzeder 3 (McGee, Pendleton, Smith), by Frazier 2 (Dayley, Lawless), by Berenguer 1 (Coleman), by Niekro 1 (McGee), by Cox 9 (Brunansky 2, Gaetti 2, Laudner 2, Blyleven, Bush, Gagne), by Tudor 8 (Brunansky 2, Straker 2, Gaetti, Hrbek, Laudner, Lombardozzi), by Magrane 5 (Gagne 3, Baylor, Hrbek), by Dayley 3 (Gaetti 2, Gagne), by Forsch 3 (Gagne, Gladden, Newman), by Mathews 3 (Gladden, Hrbek, Viola), by Worrell 3 (Gladden 2, Puckett), by Horton 1 (Laudner), by Tunnell 1 (Lombardozzi).
Left on bases—St. Louis 43—3, 5, 7, 9, 8, 8, 3; Minnesota 56—7, 5, 6, 10, 9, 9, 10.
Time of games—First game, 2:39; second game, 2:42; third game, 2:45; fourth game, 3:11; fifth game, 3:21; sixth game, 3:22; seventh game, 3:04.
Attendance—First game, 55,171; second game, 55,257; third game, 55,347; fourth game, 55,347; fifth game, 55,347; sixth game, 55,293; seventh game, 55,376.
Umpires—Phillips (A.L.), Weyer (N.L.), Kosc (A.L.), McSherry (N.L.), Kaiser (A.L.), Tata (N.L.).
Official scorers—Jack Herman, St. Louis official scorer; Rick Hummel, St. Louis Post-Dispatch; Dave Nightingale, The Sporting News; Howard Sinker, Minneapolis Star and Tribune.

1987 ALL-STAR GAME

Including

Review of 1987 Game

Official Box Score

Official Play-by-Play

Results of Previous Games

One of the key plays of the 1987 All-Star Game occurred in the ninth inning when N.L. catcher Ozzie Virgil tagged out Yankee outfielder Dave Winfield in a bruising collision at home plate.

N.L. Wins Pitching Duel

By DAVE SLOAN

Let it be told that 1987 was a new beginning, an age in which a higher form of home-run hitter enjoyed long-ball everlasting and the pitcher paid his penance. A new breed of baseball was created for this new era and it was called "rabbit."

And then, at the 58th annual All-Star Game, major league baseball rested.

The so-called lively ball, inferior pitching and almighty hitting that dominated the early season headlines were all absent July 14 in Oakland. The game's only runs didn't come until two were out in the 13th inning, when Montreal Expos outfielder Tim Raines stroked a two-run triple off Oakland Athletics reliever Jay Howell to give the National League a 2-0 victory. The smash to left-center field, only the third extra-base hit of the game, capped a 3-for-3 night for Raines, the game's Most Valuable Player.

"You get to see the other league's pitchers only once a year, and they come in and throw hard for a couple of innings and then they leave," Chicago Cubs second baseman Ryne Sandberg said. "I think it's a pitchers' game most of the time."

It certainly was on this night. A total of 15 pitchers allowed only 14 hits. Until Raines' game-winning blow, only two players managed extra-base hits: Cubs outfielder Andre Dawson, who doubled in the first, and New York Yankees right fielder Dave Winfield, who doubled an inning later. Neither league advanced a runner to third base until the ninth inning, when both did.

"Without making any alibis, it was awfully hard seeing the ball," said Philadelphia Phillies third baseman Mike Schmidt, who had one single in two at-bats. "You couldn't pick up the spin or the rotation."

Because of television commitments, the game started at 5:40 p.m. local time, perfect for a large East Coast viewing audience but the absolute worst time for the hitters. The late-afternoon collage of sunlight and shadows at Oakland-Alameda County Coliseum played havoc with the game's best batsmen.

"It was extremely tough," said St. Louis Cardinals first baseman Jack Clark, who had knocked in 86 runs to lead the majors at the All-Star break. "You really had to concentrate just to make sure you didn't get hurt."

"Hell, even I couldn't see home plate," said Detroit Tigers righthander Jack Morris, who struck out two and walked one in two innings for the American League. "Catfish Hunter (the former Oakland star who was honorary captain of the A.L. team) told me that this was the time of day when he pitched his perfect game here (in 1968)."

Even with the difficult conditions for the hitters, it was ironic that no one homered. Eighteen players already had hit 20 or more home runs before the break and both leagues had combined for 2,513. Before the All-Star break in 1986, just eight players had 20 or more, with 2,059 homers overall. Clearly, the hitters were dominating the pitchers.

The closest thing to a home run came in the seventh inning. With a runner aboard and two out, Oakland rookie sensation Mark McGwire belted a shot deep into the right-field corner. But Atlanta Braves' Gold Glove outfielder Dale Murphy ran the drive down, making the catch near the wall. McGwire, the first member of the 1984 U.S. Olympic team to play in an All-Star Game, led the major leagues with 33 home runs at the break.

Before the 13th inning, the closest thing to a run came in the bottom of the ninth. With Winfield on second base and Boston's Dwight Evans on first with one out, the Seattle Mariners' Harold Reynolds grounded to first baseman Keith Hernandez. The Mets' Gold Glover fired the ball to second to force Evans, but Montreal shortstop Hubie Brooks' return throw to pitcher Steve Bedrosian, covering first, was a wild one.

Bedrosian, the Philadelphia Phillies' ace reliever who had set a record in 1987 with 13 saves in 13 consecutive appearances, made a game-saving fielding play. He dived to his right to snare Brooks' throw, scrambled to his feet and pegged a strike home as Winfield bore down on catcher Ozzie Virgil of the Atlanta Braves. Virgil caught the throw, braced himself, then made the tag as he survived a bone-jarring collision with the 6-foot-6, 220-pound Winfield, the only man to play the entire game.

"It was do-or-die," Bedrosian said of his diving stab at first. "If I don't catch the ball, the game is over.

"When I hit the ground, my first reaction was to see what the runner was doing. And then I had to make some kind of accurate throw. I was kind of surprised to

Montreal's Tim Raines is congratulated by third-base coach Hal Lanier after breaking open the 1987 All-Star Game with a 13th-inning double.

see (Winfield) go."

Bedrosian's big play sent the contest into extra innings, a good omen for the National League. In the seven previous extra-inning All-Star contests, the senior circuit had never lost.

It also set the stage for Raines, perhaps the best of the many free-agents who were ignored and left unsigned during the previous off-season. Raines eventually re-signed with Montreal on May 1 and, despite missing 21 games, made the N.L. All-Star squad for the seventh consecutive year. Raines, the 1986 N.L. batting champion with a .334 average, was second at the break with a .346 mark.

Raines entered the game in the sixth in-

ning and singled in his first two at-bats. In the ninth, he had been stranded at third base after stealing second on a pick-off play and continuing to third when McGwire threw the ball into left field. But Juan Samuel's fly to the rifle-armed Evans in short right field and Jeffrey Leonard's pop foul to Detroit Tigers catcher Matt Nokes ended the inning.

In the 13th, following singles by Virgil and Brooks, Raines tagged Howell for a triple to the wall in left-center field. The Nationals had the game's first runs, Raines had the MVP trophy sewn up and, even more important for him, his first All-Star Game hits. The outfielder had been 0-for-7 in his six previous games.

"Yeah, everybody had really been gettin' on me about it, including my wife and my (Montreal) teammates," Raines said. "But I did promise my wife I'd get at least one hit, so I guess that I came through all right."

The victory increased the Nationals' series lead to 37-20-1.

NATIONALS	AB.	R.	H.	RBI.	PO.	A.
Davis, (Reds) lf..............	3	0	0	0	1	0
Raines, (Expos) lf	3	0	3	2	1	0
Sandberg, (Cubs) 2b	2	0	0	0	0	2
Samuel, (Phillies) 2b ...	4	0	0	0	7	2
Dawson, (Cubs) cf-rf...	3	0	1	0	3	0
Reuschel, (Pirates) p...	0	0	0	0	0	0
Leonard, (Giants) rf....	2	0	0	0	0	0
Schmidt, (Phillies) 3b..	2	0	1	0	0	1
Wallach, (Expos) 3b	3	0	0	0	0	2
Clark, (Cardinals) 1b ..	3	0	0	0	7	1
Hernandez, (Mets) 1b..	2	0	1	0	4	2
Strawberry, (Mets) rf .	2	0	0	0	0	0
Diaz, (Reds) c..............	1	0	0	0	1	0
Virgil, (Braves) c	2	1	1	0	7	0
Carter, (Mets) c...........	1	0	0	0	1	0
Hershiser, (Dodgers) p	0	0	0	0	0	0
Murphy, (Braves) rf....	1	0	0	0	1	0
Franco, (Reds) p	0	0	0	0	0	0
Bedrosian, (Phillies) p.	0	0	0	0	0	2
eGuerrero (Dodgers) ...	1	0	0	0	0	0
L. Smith, (Cubs) p........	1	0	0	0	0	2
S. Fernandez, (Mets) p	0	0	0	0	0	0
O. Smith, (Cards) ss.....	2	0	0	0	3	2
Brooks, (Expos) ss	3	1	1	0	1	2
Scott, (Astros) p...........	0	0	0	0	0	0
aGwynn (Padres)	1	0	0	0	0	0
Sutcliffe, (Cubs) p	0	0	0	0	0	0
McGee, (Cardinals) cf .	4	0	0	0	2	0
Totals	46	2	8	2	39	18

AMERICANS	AB.	R.	H.	RBI.	PO.	A.
Henderson, (Yanks) cf	3	0	1	0	0	0
McGwire, (A's) 1b	3	0	0	0	7	0
Mattingly, (Yanks) 1b	1	0	0	0	10	0
Seitzer, (Royals) 3b......	2	0	0	0	0	0
Boggs, (Red Sox) 3b.....	3	0	0	0	0	3
Langston, (Mar.) p.......	0	0	0	0	0	0
Plesac, (Brewers) p......	0	0	0	0	0	0
dBaines (White Sox)	1	0	0	0	0	0
Righetti, (Yanks) p.......	0	0	0	0	0	0
Henke, (Blue Jays) p...	0	0	0	0	0	1
fParrish (Rangers)	1	0	1	0	0	0
Howell, (A's) p	0	0	0	0	0	0
gTabler (Indians)	1	0	0	0	0	0
Bell, (Blue Jays) lf	3	0	0	0	1	0
Nokes, (Tigers) c..........	2	0	0	0	8	0
Winfield, (Yanks) rf-lf	5	0	1	0	2	0
Ripken, (Orioles) ss......	2	0	1	0	0	5
T. F'rndez, (B. Jays) ss	2	0	0	0	1	3
Kennedy, (Orioles) c....	2	0	0	0	3	1
Evans, (Red Sox) rf	2	0	2	0	2	0
Randolph, (Yanks) 2b .	1	0	0	0	0	1
Reynolds, (Mar.) 2b	3	0	0	0	4	4
Saberhagen, (Roy.) p...	0	0	0	0	0	0
bTrammell (Tigers)	1	0	0	0	0	0
Morris, (Tigers) p.........	0	0	0	0	0	0
cPuckett, (Twins) cf....	4	0	0	0	1	0
Totals	42	0	6	0	39	18

Nationals.............. 0 0 0	0 0 0	0 0 0	0 0 0	2—2
Americans.............. 0 0 0	0 0 0	0 0 0	0 0 0	0—0

NATIONALS	IP.	H.	R.	ER.	BB.SO.	
Scott (Astros)	2	1	0	0	0	1
Sutcliffe (Cubs)	2	1	0	0	1	0
Hershiser (Dodgers) ..	2	1	0	0	1	0
Reuschel (Pirates)	1⅓	1	0	0	0	1

NATIONALS	IP.	H.	R.	ER.	BB.SO.	
Franco (Reds)	⅔	0	0	0	0	0
Bedrosian (Phillies) ...	1	0	0	0	2	0
L. Smith (Cubs)	3	2	0	0	0	4
S. Fernandez (Mets) ..	1	0	0	0	1	1

AMERICANS	IP.	H.	R.	ER.	BB.SO.	
Saberhagen (Royals) .	3	1	0	0	0	0
Morris (Tigers)	2	1	0	0	1	2
Langston (Mariners) .	2	0	0	0	0	3
Plesac (Brewers)	1	0	0	0	0	1
Righetti (Yankees)	⅓	1	0	0	0	0
Henke (Blue Jays)	2⅔	2	0	0	0	1
Howell (A's)	2	3	2	2	0	3

Winning pitcher—L. Smith. Losing pitcher—Howell.

Game-winning RBI—Raines.

aGrounded out for Scott in third. bReached first base on error for Saberhagen in third. cGrounded out for Morris in fifth. dPopped out for Plesac in eighth. eLined out for Bedrosian in tenth. fSingled for Henke in eleventh. gStruck out for Howell in thirteenth. Errors—Scott, O. Smith, McGwire. Double plays—Clark and O. Smith; Hernandez, Brooks, Bedrosian and Virgil. Left on bases—Nationals 6, Americans 11. Two-base hits—Dawson, Winfield. Three-base hit—Raines. Stolen base—Raines. Caught stealing—Schmidt. Sacrifice hits—Reynolds, T. Fernandez, Nokes. Bases on balls—Off Sutcliffe 1 (Mattingly), off Hershiser 1 (Mattingly), off Bedrosian 2 (Winfield, Evans), off S. Fernandez 1 (Seitzer), off Morris 1 (Carter). Strikeouts—By Scott 1 (Kennedy), by Reuschel 1 (Puckett), by L. Smith 4 (Puckett 2, McGwire, T. Fernandez), by S. Fernandez 1 (Tabler), by Morris 2 (Dawson, Clark), by Langston 3 (Davis, Wallach, Clark), by Plesac 1 (Brooks), by Henke 1 (Samuel), by Howell 3 (Wallach, Hernandez, L. Smith). Umpires—Denkinger (A.L.) plate, Stello (N.L.) first, Voltaggio (A.L.) second, West (N.L.) third, Cousins (A.L.) left field, Davidson (N.L.) right field. Official scorers—Gerry Fraley, Atlanta Constitution; Glenn Schwarz, San Francisco Examiner; Chuck Dybdal, Contra Costa Times. Players listed on roster but not used: N.L.—none; A.L.—Hurst, Witt. Time—3:39. Attendance—49,671.

FIRST INNING

Nationals—Davis grounded to Ripken. Sandberg hit a high chopper to Boggs, who threw to Mattingly at first base for the out. Dawson lined the first pitch down the left-field line for a double. Schmidt's checked-swing roller was fielded by Boggs, who threw to first for the out. No runs, one hit, no errors, one left.

Americans—Sandberg fielded Henderson's bouncer up the middle and threw to Clark at first base for the out. Mattingly reached first safely when his grounder went off Scott's glove and rolled behind the mound for an error. Boggs grounded into a force play, Sandberg to O. Smith, to retire Mattingly at second. Bell popped to O. Smith in short center field. No runs, no hits, one error, one left.

SECOND INNING

Nationals—Clark popped to Mattingly, who had to shield his eyes from the sun to make the catch. Strawberry grounded to Randolph. Carter bounced to Ripken. No runs, no hits, no errors, none left.

Americans—Winfield's smash went past Schmidt at third base and into the left-field corner for a double. Ripken lined Scott's 1-0 pitch to Clark, who made a leaping grab and fired to second, where O. Smith beat Winfield back to the bag for a double play. Kennedy struck out. No runs, one hit, no errors, none left.

THIRD INNING

Nationals—O. Smith lined to Bell. Gwynn, batting for Scott, grounded to Ripken. Davis bounced to Boggs. No runs, no hits, no errors, none left.

Americans—Sutcliffe came in to pitch for the Nationals. Randolph flied to Davis in left-center field. Trammell batted for Saberhagen and reached first base when his one-hopper glanced off O. Smith's glove for an error. Henderson flied to Dawson in right-center. Mattingly walked. Boggs flied to Dawson. No runs, no hits, one error, two left.

FOURTH INNING

Nationals—Morris came in to pitch and Reynolds took over at second base for the Americans. Sandberg grounded to Ripken, who made a backhanded stop and threw to Mattingly at first base for the out. Dawson tried to check his swing but couldn't, striking out. Schmidt looped a single to right. With Clark batting, Schmidt was thrown out at second base on a delayed steal attempt, Kennedy to Reynolds. No runs, one hit, no errors, none left.

Americans—Samuel came in to play second base for the Nationals. Bell's checked-swing roller hit the first-base bag and bounced up to Clark, who made the putout unassisted. Winfield's chopper over the mound was fielded by Samuel, who threw to first for the out. Ripken lined a single to left. Kennedy grounded into a forceout, O. Smith to Samuel, to retire Ripken at second base. No runs, one hit, no errors, one left.

FIFTH INNING

Nationals—Clark struck out. Strawberry grounded to Reynolds. Carter walked. O. Smith grounded into a forceout, Ripken to Reynolds, to retire Carter at second base. No runs, no hits, no errors, one left.

Americans—Hershiser came in to pitch, Diaz entered to catch and McGee took over in center field with Dawson moving to right for the Nationals. Reynolds grounded to O. Smith. Puckett, batting for Morris, bounced to Samuel. Henderson was credited with an infield hit when his chopper up the middle went off Samuel's glove. Mattingly walked on four pitches. Boggs hit a one-hopper to Schmidt, who threw to Samuel to force Mattingly at second base. No runs, one hit, no errors, two left.

SIXTH INNING

Nationals—Puckett remained in the game and played center field, Langston came in to pitch, Seitzer went in to play third base, McGwire took over at first base and T. Fernandez entered at shortstop for the Americans. McGee grounded to Reynolds. Davis was called out on strikes. Samuel hit a roller to Reynolds, who threw to McGwire at first base for the out. No runs, no hits, no errors, none left.

Americans—Wallach came in to play third base and Raines took over in left field for the Nationals. Bell grounded to Wallach. Winfield lined to Dawson, who made the catch just above his shoetops after misjudging the ball in the sun. T. Fernandez flied to McGee. No runs, no hits, no errors, none left.

SEVENTH INNING

Nationals—Nokes came in to catch, Evans took over in right field and Winfield moved to left for the Americans. Dawson grounded to T. Fernandez. Wallach struck out. Clark was called out on strikes. No runs, no hits, no errors, none left.

Americans—Reuschel came in to pitch, Hernandez took over at first base, Murphy went in to play right field and Brooks entered at shortstop for the Nationals. Evans lined Reuschel's first pitch to left field for a single. Reynolds sacrificed Evans to second base, Hernandez to Samuel covering first base for the out. Puckett struck out. McGwire sent an 0-1 pitch deep into the right-field corner, where Murphy made a fine running catch. No runs, one hit, no errors, one left.

EIGHTH INNING

Nationals—Plesac came in to pitch for the Americans. Diaz flied to Evans, who had to battle the sun to make the catch. Murphy fouled out to T. Fernandez, who made a nice running catch. Brooks struck out. No runs, no hits, no errors, none left.

Americans—Virgil came in to catch for the Nationals. Seitzer popped to Samuel. When Baines was announced as a pinch-hitter for Plesac, National League Manager Johnson made a double switch, bringing in Franco to pitch and Leonard to play left field. Baines popped to Samuel. Nokes flied to Raines in short left field. No hits, no errors, none left.

NINTH INNING

Nationals—Righetti came in to pitch for the Americans. McGee grounded to Reynolds. Raines lined a single to center for the National League's first hit since the fourth inning. With a 1-2 count on Samuel, Raines stole second on a pickoff play and continued to third when McGwire's throw to second went into left field for an error. Righetti was replaced on the mound by Henke. Samuel flied to Evans in short right field, Raines holding at third base as Evans made a perfect one-bounce throw to the plate. Leonard fouled to Nokes, who made the catch at the screen. No runs, one hit, one error, one left.

Americans—Bedrosian came in to pitch for the Nationals. Winfield walked. T. Fernandez sacrificed Winfield to second base, Bedrosian to Hernandez. Evans walked. Reynolds hit a 1-1 pitch to the right of Hernandez, who threw to Brooks at second base to force Evans, but the relay to first was too late to retire Reynolds. Bedrosian, who had to make a diving stab to keep Brooks' throw from getting away, jumped to his feet in time to throw home to retire Winfield, who crashed into Virgil, for a double play. No runs, no hits, no errors, one left.

TENTH INNING

Nationals—Wallach bounced back to the mound, Henke to McGwire for the out. Hernandez blooped a single to center field. Virgil flied to Winfield. Guerrero batted for Bedrosian and lined softly to Reynolds. No runs, one hit, no errors, one left.

Americans—L. Smith came in to pitch for the Nationals. Puckett struck out. McGwire also fanned. Seitzer flied to McGee, who made the catch on the warning track in dead center field. No runs, no hits, no errors, none left.

ELEVENTH INNING

Nationals—Brooks flied to Puckett in left-center field. McGee grounded to T. Fernandez. Raines lined a single to left. With Raines running on the pitch, Samuel was called out on strikes. No runs, one hit, no errors, one left.

Americans—Parrish, batting for Henke, lined a single to right-center field for the American League's first hit since the seventh inning. Nokes sacrificed Parrish to second base, L. Smith to Hernandez. Winfield bounced to Brooks, who threw to Hernandez at first for the out, Parrish advancing to third on the play. T. Fernandez was called out on strikes. No runs, one hit, no errors, one left.

TWELFTH INNING

Nationals—Howell came in to pitch for the Americans. Leonard grounded to T. Fernandez. Wallach struck out. Hernandez also fanned. No runs, no hits, no errors, none left.

Americans—Evans grounded a single up the middle. Reynolds, attempting to sacrifice, popped to Hernandez. Puckett struck out for the third straight time. McGwire bounced back to the mound, L. Smith to Hernandez for the out. No runs, one hit, no errors, one left.

THIRTEENTH INNING

Nationals—Virgil lined a single to left-center field on a 1-2 count. L. Smith, attempting to sacrifice, struck out. Brooks sent a 1-1 pitch through the hole between first and second for a single, Virgil stopping at second base. McGee lined to Winfield in medium left field, Virgil and Brooks holding. Raines laced a 2-0 pitch to the wall in left-center field for a triple, scoring Virgil and Brooks. Samuel lined to Reynolds, who made a leaping catch. Two runs, three hits, no errors, one left.

Americans—S. Fernandez, the last of the 28 players on the National League roster, came in to pitch. Seitzer walked. Tabler, batting for Howell, struck out. Nokes fouled to Virgil behind the plate. Winfield grounded to Wallach, who threw to Samuel to force Seitzer at second base for the game's final out. No runs, no hits, no errors, one left.

RESULTS OF PREVIOUS GAMES

1933—At Comiskey Park, Chicago, July 6. Americans 4, Nationals 2. Managers—Connie Mack, John McGraw. Winning pitcher—Lefty Gomez. Losing pitcher—Bill Hallahan. Attendance—47,595.

1934—At Polo Grounds, New York, July 10. Americans 9, Nationals 7. Managers—Joe Cronin, Bill Terry. Winning pitcher—Mel Harder. Losing pitcher—Van Mungo. Attendance—48,363.

1935—At Municipal Stadium, Cleveland, July 8. Americans 4, Nationals 1. Managers—Mickey Cochrane, Frankie Frisch. Winning pitcher—Lefty Gomez. Losing pitcher—Bill Walker. Attendance—69,831.

1936—At Braves Field, Boston, July 7. Nationals 4, Americans 3. Managers—Charlie Grimm, Joe McCarthy. Winning pitcher—Dizzy Dean. Losing pitcher—Lefty Gomez. Attendance—25,556.

1937—At Griffith Stadium, Washington, July 7. Americans 8, Nationals 3. Managers—Joe McCarthy, Bill Terry. Winning pitcher—Lefty Gomez. Losing pitcher—Dizzy Dean. Attendance—31,391.

1938—At Crosley Field, Cincinnati, July 6. Nationals 4, Americans 1. Managers—Bill Terry, Joe McCarthy. Winning pitcher—Johnny Vander Meer. Losing pitcher—Lefty Gomez. Attendance—27,067.

1939—At Yankee Stadium, New York, July 11. Americans 3, Nationals 1. Managers—Joe McCarthy, Gabby Hartnett. Winning pitcher—Tommy Bridges. Losing pitcher—Bill Lee. Attendance—62,892.

1940—At Sportsman's Park, St. Louis, July 9. Nationals 4, Americans 0. Managers—Bill McKechnie, Joe Cronin. Winning pitcher—Paul Derringer. Losing pitcher—Red Ruffing. Attendance—32,373.

1941—At Briggs Stadium, Detroit, July 8. Americans 7, Nationals 5. Managers—Del Baker, Bill McKechnie. Winning pitcher—Ed Smith. Losing pitcher—Claude Passeau. Attendance—54,674.

1942—At Polo Grounds, New York, July 6. Americans 3, Nationals 1. Managers—Joe Cronin,

Leo Durocher. Winning pitcher—Spud Chandler. Losing pitcher—Mort Cooper. Attendance—34,178.

1943—At Shibe Park, Philadelphia, July 13 (night). Americans 5, Nationals 3. Managers—Joe McCarthy, Billy Southworth. Winning pitcher—Dutch Leonard. Losing pitcher—Mort Cooper. Attendance—31,938.

1944—At Forbes Field, Pittsburgh, July 11 (night). Nationals 7, Americans 1. Managers—Billy Southworth, Joe McCarthy. Winning pitcher—Ken Raffensberger. Losing pitcher—Tex Hughson. Attendance—29,589.

1945—No game played.

1946—At Fenway Park, Boston, July 9. Americans 12, Nationals 0. Managers—Steve O'Neill, Charlie Grimm. Winning pitcher—Bob Feller. Losing pitcher—Claude Passeau. Attendance—34,906.

1947—At Wrigley Field, Chicago, July 8. Americans 2, Nationals 1. Managers—Joe Cronin, Eddie Dyer. Winning pitcher—Frank Shea. Losing pitcher—Johnny Sain. Attendance—41,123.

1948—At Sportsman's Park, St. Louis, July 13. Americans 5, Nationals 2. Managers—Bucky Harris, Leo Durocher. Winning pitcher—Vic Raschi. Losing pitcher—Johnny Schmitz. Attendance—34,009.

1949—At Ebbets Field, Brooklyn, July 12. Americans 11, Nationals 7. Managers—Lou Boudreau, Billy Southworth. Winning pitcher—Virgil Trucks. Losing pitcher—Don Newcombe. Attendance—32,577.

1950—At Comiskey Park, Chicago, July 11. Nationals 4, Americans 3 (14 innings). Managers—Burt Shotton, Casey Stengel. Winning pitcher—Ewell Blackwell. Losing pitcher—Ted Gray. Attendance—46,127.

1951—At Briggs Stadium, Detroit, July 10. Nationals 8, Americans 3. Managers—Eddie Sawyer, Casey Stengel. Winning pitcher—Sal Maglie. Losing pitcher—Ed Lopat. Attendance—52,075.

1952—At Shibe Park, Philadelphia, July 8. Nationals 3, Americans 2 (five innings—rain). Managers—Leo Durocher, Casey Stengel. Winning pitcher—Bob Rush. Losing pitcher—Bob Lemon. Attendance—32,785.

1953—At Crosley Field, Cincinnati, July 14. Nationals 5, Americans 1. Managers—Chuck Dressen, Casey Stengel. Winning pitcher—Warren Spahn. Losing pitcher—Allie Reynolds. Attendance—30,846.

1954—At Municipal Stadium, Cleveland, July 13. Americans 11, Nationals 9. Managers—Casey Stengel, Walter Alston. Winning pitcher—Dean Stone. Losing pitcher—Gene Conley. Attendance—68,751.

1955—At Milwaukee County Stadium, Milwaukee, July 12. Nationals 6, Americans 5 (12 innings). Managers—Leo Durocher, Al Lopez. Winning pitcher—Gene Conley. Losing pitcher—Frank Sullivan. Attendance—45,643.

1956—At Griffith Stadium, Washington, July 10. Nationals 7, Americans 3. Managers—Walter Alston, Casey Stengel. Winning pitcher—Bob Friend. Losing pitcher—Billy Pierce. Attendance—28,843.

1957—At Busch Stadium, St. Louis, July 9. Americans 6, Nationals 5. Managers—Casey Stengel, Walter Alston. Winning pitcher—Jim Bunning. Losing pitcher—Curt Simmons. Attendance—30,693.

1958—At Memorial Stadium, Baltimore, July 8. Americans 4, Nationals 3. Managers—Casey Stengel, Fred Haney. Winning pitcher—Early Wynn. Losing pitcher—Bob Friend. Attendance—48,829.

1959 (first game)—At Forbes Field, Pittsburgh, July 7. Nationals 5, Americans 4. Managers—Fred Haney, Casey Stengel. Winning pitcher—Johnny

Antonelli. Losing pitcher—Whitey Ford. Attendance—35,277.

1959 (second game)—At Memorial Coliseum, Los Angeles, August 3. Americans 5, Nationals 3. Managers—Casey Stengel, Fred Haney. Winning pitcher—Jerry Walker. Losing pitcher—Don Drysdale. Attendance—55,105.

1960 (first game)—At Municipal Stadium, Kansas City, July 11. Nationals 5, Americans 3. Managers—Walter Alston, Al Lopez. Winning pitcher—Bob Friend. Losing pitcher—Bill Monbouquette. Attendance—30,619.

1960 (second game)—At Yankee Stadium, New York, July 13. Nationals 6, Americans 0. Managers—Walter Alston, Al Lopez. Winning pitcher—Vernon Law. Losing pitcher—Whitey Ford. Attendance—38,362.

1961 (first game)—At Candlestick Park, San Francisco, July 11. Nationals 5, Americans 4 (10 innings). Managers—Danny Murtaugh, Paul Richards. Winning pitcher—Stu Miller. Losing pitcher—Hoyt Wilhelm. Attendance—44,115.

1961 (second game)—At Fenway Park, Boston, July 31. Americans 1, Nationals 1 (nine-inning tie, stopped by rain). Managers—Paul Richards, Danny Murtaugh. Attendance—31,851.

1962 (first game)—At District of Columbia Stadium, Washington, July 10. Nationals 3, Americans 1. Managers—Fred Hutchinson, Ralph Houk. Winning pitcher—Juan Marichal. Losing pitcher—Camilo Pascual. Attendance—45,480.

1962 (second game)—At Wrigley Field, Chicago, July 30. Americans 9, Nationals 4. Managers—Ralph Houk, Fred Hutchinson. Winning pitcher—Ray Herbert. Losing pitcher—Art Mahaffey. Attendance—38,359.

1963—At Municipal Stadium, Cleveland, July 9. Nationals 5, Americans 3. Managers—Alvin Dark, Ralph Houk. Winning pitcher—Larry Jackson. Losing pitcher—Jim Bunning. Attendance—44,160.

1964—At Shea Stadium, New York, July 7. Nationals 7, Americans 4. Managers—Walter Alston, Al Lopez. Winning pitcher—Juan Marichal. Losing pitcher—Dick Radatz. Attendance—50,850.

1965—At Metropolitan Stadium, Bloomington (Minnesota), July 13. Nationals 6, Americans 5. Managers—Gene Mauch, Al Lopez. Winning pitcher—Sandy Koufax. Losing pitcher—Sam McDowell. Attendance—46,706.

1966—At Busch Memorial Stadium, St Louis, July 12. Nationals 2, Americans 1 (10 innings). Managers—Walter Alston, Sam Mele. Winning pitcher—Gaylord Perry. Losing pitcher—Pete Richert. Attendance—49,936.

1967—At Anaheim Stadium, Anaheim (California), July 11. Nationals 2, Americans 1 (15 innings). Managers—Walter Alston, Hank Bauer. Winning pitcher—Don Drysdale. Losing pitcher—Jim Hunter. Attendance—46,309.

1968—At Astrodome, Houston, July 9 (night). Nationals 1, Americans 0. Managers—Red Schoendienst, Dick Williams. Winning pitcher—Don Drysdale. Losing pitcher—Luis Tiant. Attendance—48,321.

1969—At Robert F. Kennedy Memorial Stadium, Washington, July 23. Nationals 9, Americans 3. Managers—Red Schoendienst, Mayo Smith. Winning pitcher—Steve Carlton. Losing pitcher—Mel Stottlemyre. Attendance—45,259.

1970—At Riverfront Stadium, Cincinnati, July 14 (night). Nationals 5, Americans 4 (12 innings). Managers—Gil Hodges, Earl Weaver. Winning pitcher—Claude Osteen. Losing pitcher—Clyde Wright. Attendance—51,838.

1971—At Tiger Stadium, Detroit, July 13 (night). Americans 6, Nationals 4. Managers—

Earl Weaver, George (Sparky) Anderson. Winning pitcher—Vida Blue. Losing pitcher—Dock Ellis. Attendance—53,559.

1972—At Atlanta Stadium, Atlanta, July 25 (night). Nationals 4, Americans 3 (10 innings). Managers—Danny Murtaugh, Earl Weaver. Winning pitcher—Tug McGraw. Losing pitcher—Dave McNally. Attendance—53,107.

1973—At Royals Stadium, Kansas City, July 24 (night). Nationals 7, Americans 1. Managers—George (Sparky) Anderson, Dick Williams. Winning pitcher—Rick Wise. Losing pitcher—Bert Blyleven. Attendance—40,849.

1974—At Three Rivers Stadium, Pittsburgh, July 23 (night). Nationals 7, Americans 2. Managers—Yogi Berra, Dick Williams. Winning pitcher—Ken Brett. Losing pitcher—Luis Tiant. Attendance—50,706.

1975—At Milwaukee County Stadium, Milwaukee, July 15 (night). Nationals 6, Americans 3. Managers—Walter Alston, Alvin Dark. Winning pitcher—Jon Matlack. Losing pitcher—Jim Hunter. Attendance—51,480.

1976—At Veterans Stadium, Philadelphia, July 13 (night). Nationals 7, Americans 1. Managers—George (Sparky) Anderson, Darrell Johnson. Winning pitcher—Randy Jones. Losing pitcher—Mark Fidrych. Attendance—63,974.

1977—At Yankee Stadium, New York, July 19 (night). Nationals 7, Americans 5. Managers—Alfred (Billy) Martin, George (Sparky) Anderson. Winning pitcher—Don Sutton. Losing pitcher—Jim Palmer. Attendance—56,683.

1978—At San Diego Stadium, San Diego, July 11 (night). Nationals 7, Americans 3. Managers—Alfred (Billy) Martin, Thomas Lasorda. Winning pitcher—Bruce Sutter. Losing pitcher—Rich Gossage. Attendance—51,549.

1979—At Kingdome, Seattle, July 17. Nationals 7, Americans 6. Managers—Chuck Tanner, Bob Lemon. Winning pitcher—Bruce Sutter. Losing pitcher—Jim Kern. Attendance—58,905.

1980—At Dodger Stadium, Los Angeles, July 8. Nationals 4, Americans 2. Managers—Chuck Tanner, Earl Weaver. Winning pitcher—Jerry Reuss. Losing pitcher—Tommy John. Attendance—56,088.

1981—At Municipal Stadium, Cleveland, August 9 (night). Nationals 5, Americans 4. Managers—Dallas Green, Jim Frey. Winning pitcher—Vida Blue. Losing pitcher—Rollie Fingers. Attendance—72,086.

1982—At Olympic Stadium, Montreal, July 13 (night). Nationals 4, Americans 1. Managers—Thomas Lasorda, Alfred (Billy) Martin. Winning pitcher—Steve Rogers. Losing pitcher—Dennis Eckersley. Attendance—59,057.

1983—At Comiskey Park, Chicago, July 6 (night). Americans 13, Nationals 3. Managers—Harvey Kuenn, Dorrel (Whitey) Herzog. Winning pitcher—Dave Stieb. Losing pitcher—Mario Soto. Attendance—43,801.

1984—At Candlestick Park, San Francisco, July 10 (night). Nationals 3, Americans 1. Managers—Paul Owens, Joseph Altobelli. Winning pitcher—Charlie Lea. Losing pitcher—Dave Stieb. Attendance—57,756.

1985—At Metrodome, Minneapolis, July 16 (night). Nationals 6, Americans 1. Managers—Dick Williams, George (Sparky) Anderson. Winning pitcher—LaMarr Hoyt. Losing pitcher—Jack Morris. Attendance—54,960.

1986—At Astrodome, Houston, July 15 (night). Americans 3, Nationals 2. Managers—Dick Howser, Dorrel (Whitey) Herzog. Winning pitcher—Roger Clemens. Losing pitcher—Dwight Gooden. Attendance—45,774.

BATTING, PITCHING FEATURES

Including

No-Hit Pitching Performances

Low-Hit Pitching Performances

Top Strikeout Performances

Baseball's Top Firemen

Pitchers Winning 1-0 Games

Multi-Home Run Performances

Batters Hitting Grand Slams

Top One-Game Hitting Performances

Baseball's Top Pinch-Hitters

Top Performances in Debuts

Homers by Parks

Award Winners

Hall of Fame Electees

Hall of Famers List, Years Selected

Major League Draft

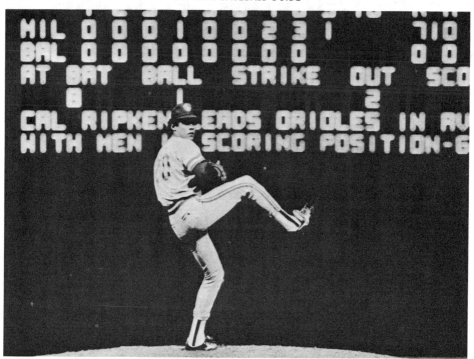

Juan Nieves of the Milwaukee Brewers pitches to Cal Ripken, Jr. (above) and then is mobbed by his teammates after retiring Eddie Murray for the final out in his 7-0 no-hitter at Baltimore last April 15.

Nieves' No-Hitter Spices Streak

By DAVE SLOAN

The Milwaukee Brewers captured the nation's attention by winning their first 13 games of the 1987 season, tying a major league record. One of the most memorable of those victories came April 15 in Baltimore, when lefthander Juan Nieves pitched a no-hitter for Milwaukee's ninth straight win.

Nieves' 7-0 gem was the first ever thrown by a Brewer pitcher in the club's 18-year history, the first thrown against the Orioles at Memorial Stadium and the only no-hitter in the major leagues in 1987. Nieves, who had struggled to an 11-12 record as a rookie in 1986 after being 10-3 at one point, threw 128 pitches against Baltimore in winning his second game of 1987.

"I was taking it hitter by hitter," said Nieves, whose previous best major league performance was a four-hitter against Seattle in '86. "The Oriole lineup is the toughest. Every time I walked a batter, I got intense, but always knew enough to pitch inside myself and control my emotions."

Nieves walked five and struck out seven in becoming the first pitcher to no-hit the Orioles since California's Nolan Ryan on June 1, 1975.

The 22-year-old Nieves was dominant at times, shaky at times, and was almost lifted by Brewers Manager Tom Trebelhorn in the sixth inning with Milwaukee leading, 1-0.

"At one point, I said to Harty (pitching coach Chuck Hartenstein), 'We've got the welcome home luncheon tomorrow. He's thrown a lot of pitches. What if I take him out with a no-hitter? Think we'll get welcomed back?' " asked Trebelhorn.

"I felt bad," said Nieves. "I couldn't throw a slider. My change-up was up. I didn't have a good fastball.

Although no Baltimore player reached second base, Nieves needed four fine defensive plays to accomplish the no-hitter. Rookie left fielder Jim Paciorek robbed Eddie Murray to start the second inning and third baseman Paul Molitor made key plays in the fourth and fifth innings to keep the Orioles hitless. But the biggest defensive play of the night came on the game's final out.

After Nieves retired Ken Gerhart and Rick Burleson on two pitches to start the bottom of the ninth inning, he walked the

Nieves' No-Hitter

Milwaukee	AB.	R.	H.	RBI.	E.
Molitor, 3b	4	0	1	1	0
Yount, cf	5	0	1	0	0
Braggs, rf	5	1	1	1	0
Cooper, dh	5	1	1	0	0
Sveum, ss	4	2	2	1	0
Brock, 1b	3	1	1	3	0
Paciorek, lf	3	1	1	0	0
Schroeder, c	4	1	2	0	0
Gantner, 2b	3	0	0	0	0
Totals	36	7	10	6	0

Baltimore	AB.	R.	H.	RBI.	E.
Gerhart, lf	3	0	0	0	1
Burleson, 2b	4	0	0	0	0
Ripken, ss	3	0	0	0	0
Murray, 1b	3	0	0	0	0
Lynn, cf	3	0	0	0	0
Knight, 3b	2	0	0	0	0
Lacy, dh	2	0	0	0	0
Shelby, rf	3	0	0	0	0
Rayford, c	3	0	0	0	0
Totals	26	0	0	0	1

Milwaukee .... 000 100 231—7
Baltimore .... 000 000 000—0

Milwaukee	IP.	H.	R.	ER.	BB.	SO.
NIEVES (W. 2-0)	9	0	0	0	5	7

Baltimore	IP.	H.	R.	ER.	BB.	SO.
Flanagan (L. 0-1)	6⅓	5	3	3	4	5
Schmidt	2⅔	5	4	4	1	1

Game-winning RBI—Sveum.

DP—Milwaukee 1, Baltimore 1. LOB—Milwaukee 7, Baltimore 4. 2B—Paciorek, Molitor, Sveum, Schroeder. HR—Sveum, Brock, Braggs. PB—Rayford. T—2:36. A—11,407.

next batter, Cal Ripken, on four. Murray then hit a drive to right-center field that looked to be a certain hit.

"When it came off the bat, it started to hang a little bit, and I thought (center fielder) Robin (Yount) wouldn't have any problem with it," Trebelhorn said. "Then it started to die, and I thought, 'Oh gee, there goes the kid's no-hitter.'

But Yount, a former shortstop, ran about 15 yards to his left, dove and caught the ball 18 inches off the turf with his body parallel to the ground. Nieves' no-hitter was preserved and his teammates mobbed him on the mound.

Nieves became the first Puerto Rican-born pitcher to throw a no-hitter and the youngest—at 22 years, three months and 10 days—since the Chicago Cubs' Burt Hooton beat Philadelphia, 4-0, April 16, 1972.

"I'm just happy that my team won," Nieves said. "All I care about is that we win. We have a great thing going right now."

White Sox Spoil Low-Hit Gems

By DAVE SLOAN

The Chicago White Sox may have compiled the second-lowest team batting average (.258) in the American League in 1987, but they certainly had a knack for making those hits count, especially when they were playing the role of spoilers.

On May 5 against the Yankees at Comiskey Park, the White Sox were held to just two hits by New York righthander Joe Niekro—singles in the third inning by Gary Redus and Ron Hassey. Those hits produced two runs, however, and the Sox held on to win, 2-0. Chicago righthander Bill Long also yielded just two hits—singles by Dan Pasqua in the second and seventh innings—to pick up his first major league victory.

On September 13 at Seattle, the White Sox pulled out another 2-0 victory despite being held to two hits by the Mariners' Mark Langston. This time both hits were homers—by Pat Keedy in the third inning and Donnie Hill in the seventh. And fellow lefthander Floyd Bannister of the Sox did Langston one better, giving up only a third-inning single to Harold Reynolds.

There were 58 low-hit performances (one- and two-hitters) in the major leagues in 1987, 35 in the American League and 23 in the National. The White Sox, Yankees and Houston Astros were involved in nine each, the most of any clubs. The White Sox won seven of their low-hit games and lost two, while the Yankees and Astros were both 5-4. Every major league team was involved in at least one low-hit game, with the Braves (0-3), Cubs (0-1) and Angels (0-1) failing to win any.

The Angels had a strange turnaround in low-hit games from the previous season. In 1986, the Angels played in a major league-leading 17 low-hit games en route to the American League Western Division title. Last season, the Angels lost their lone low-hit game, 12-0, to Toronto's Jim Clancy on May 18.

Seven pitchers—Houston's Mike Scott, Cleveland's Tom Candiotti, Milwaukee's Ted Higuera, Kansas City's Bret Saberhagen and Charlie Leibrandt, the White Sox's Bannister and Seattle's Langston—had two complete-game, low-hit performances in 1987.

The leader in the category, however, was veteran righthander Rick Reuschel, who was traded by Pittsburgh to San Francisco on August 21. Reuschel threw a

The Phillies' Mike Jackson nearly no-hit Montreal June 7 in his first major-league victory.

two-hitter for the Pirates against the Braves on June 2, a two-hitter against the Phillies on September 6 and a two-hitter against the Astros on September 17, the last two coming as a member of the Giants. Reuschel was the only pitcher to throw low-hit games for two different teams.

Philadelphia's Mike Jackson came closest to throwing a no-hitter and joining Milwaukee's Juan Nieves in that select company. On June 7, Jackson held the Montreal Expos hitless until Tim Raines led off the ninth inning with a double. Raines scored after a wild pitch and sacrifice fly to ruin Jackson's shutout bid. The rookie righthander needed final-out relief help from Steve Bedrosian to post a 3-1 victory, his first in the major leagues.

On five occasions, the club throwing the low-hit game lost. In addition to the White Sox's victories over the Yankees and Mariners, the Astros beat the Padres, 1-0, June

Houston's Mike Scott threw two complete-game, low-hit games before being named the N.L.'s starting pitcher for the All-Star Game in Oakland.

9 with third-inning singles by Alan Ashby and Dickie Thon. The Twins beat the White Sox, 2-1, September 9 on homers by Kirby Puckett and Tim Laudner.

The Detroit Tigers beat Candiotti and the Indians, 2-1, September 2, though managing just an eighth-inning single by Matt Nokes themselves. The Tigers' first run scored on a walk, an error, a sacrifice bunt and a groundout in the fifth inning. Another walk, a passed ball and Nokes' single produced the second run in the eighth.

Twelve of the 58 low-hit games were one-hitters.

A complete list of one- and two-hit games for the 1987 season follows:

NATIONAL LEAGUE
One-Hit Games

April 15—Scott, Houston vs. Los Angeles, 4-0—Duncan, single in third.

July 8—Youmans, Montreal vs. Houston, 1-0—Bass, single in eighth.

Sept. 29—Carman, Philadelphia vs. New York, 3-0—Wilson, single in fourth.

Oct. 1—Welch, Los Angeles vs. San Francisco, 7-0—Aldrete, single in sixth.

Two-Hit Games

April 25—Power (7⅓ innings), Franco (1⅔ innings) and Williams (one inning), Cincinnati vs. Houston, 3-0—Ashby, singles in fifth and eighth.

May 8—Scott, Houston vs. Montreal, 3-0—Candaele, triple in sixth; Stefero, single in eighth.

May 23—Heaton, Montreal vs. San Diego, 6-0—Gwynn, single in seventh; Salazar, single in eighth.

June 2—Reuschel, Pittsburgh vs. Atlanta, 4-1—Oberkfell, single in fourth; Thomas, single in fourth.

June 5—Mathews (7⅓ innings) and Worrell (1⅔ innings), St. Louis vs. Chicago, 5-1—Davis, double in first and single in fourth.

June 7—Jackson (8⅔ innings) and Bedrosian (⅓ inning), Philadelphia vs. Montreal, 3-1—Raines, double in ninth; Foley, single in ninth.

June 9—Dravecky (six innings) and McCullers (two innings), San Diego vs. Houston, 0-1—Ashby, single in third; Thon, single in third.

June 14—Darwin, Houston vs. Los Angeles, 4-1—Guerrero, homer in first; Marshall, single in first.

June 23—Whitson, San Diego vs. Houston, 4-1—C. Reynolds, double in fifth; Puhl, single in seventh.

June 29—Davis (one inning) and Jones (eight innings), San Diego vs. Los Angeles, 3-0—Hamilton, single in third; Marshall, single in fourth.

July 2—Leach, New York vs. Cincinnati, 5-0—Oester, single in third; Diaz, single in eighth.

Aug. 10—Jones, San Diego vs. Atlanta, 2-0—Oberkfell, single in fourth; Perry, single in fourth.

Aug. 25—Dunne, Pittsburgh vs. Cincinnati, 1-0—Parker, double in second; Bell, single in fourth.

Sept. 4—Ryan (seven innings) and Agosto (two innings), Houston vs. Pittsburgh, 2-0—Bonds, single in second; Bonilla, single in seventh.

Sept. 6—Reuschel, San Francisco vs. Philadelphia, 4-1—Samuel, single in fourth; Schmidt, double in fourth.

Sept. 9—Browning, Cincinnati vs. Los Angeles, 4-1—Devereaux, double in sixth; Sax, double in sixth.

Sept. 16—Grant, San Diego vs. Atlanta, 3-0—James, single in first; Perry, single in seventh.

Sept. 17—Reuschel, San Francisco vs. Houston, 4-0—Doran, single in first; Young, single in sixth.

Sept. 23—Fisher, Pittsburgh vs. St. Louis, 2-0—Pena, single in fifth; Johnson, single in eighth.

Kansas City's Bret Saberhagen pitched two-hitters against the Yankees and Indians last season.

AMERICAN LEAGUE
One-Hit Games

April 28—Boddicker, Baltimore vs. Kansas City, 3-0—Wilson, single in sixth.

May 16—Leibrandt, Kansas City vs. Milwaukee, 13-0—Schroeder, single in sixth.

June 9—Young, Oakland vs. Chicago, 8-3—Williams, homer in eighth.

June 26—Witt (eight innings) and Mohorcic (one inning), Texas vs. Minnesota, 1-0—Smalley, single in second.

Aug. 3—Candiotti, Cleveland vs New York, 2-0—Easler, single in eighth.

Sept. 1—Higuera, Milwaukee vs. Kansas City, 2-0—Jones, triple in.eighth.

Sept. 2—Candiotti (eight innings), Cleveland vs. Detroit, 1-2—Nokes, single in eighth.

Sept. 13—Bannister, Chicago vs. Seattle, 2-0—Reynolds, single in third.

Two-Hit Games

April 10—Saberhagen, Kansas City vs. New York, 13-1—Pasqua, double in eighth; Tolleson, single in ninth.

April 10—Hurst, Boston vs. Toronto, 3-0—Iorg, single in third; Fernandez, single in sixth.

April 21—Niekro (six innings) and Guante (three innings), New York vs. Detroit, 3-1—Whitaker, single in fourth; Grubb, single in seventh.

April 28—Correa (7⅔ innings) and Mohorcic (1⅓ innings), Texas vs. New York, 3-1—Randolph, single in eighth; Mattingly, double in eighth.

May 3—Clancy (8⅓ innings) and Henke (⅔ inning), Toronto vs. Texas, 3-1—O'Brien, single in fifth; Petralli, double in ninth.

May 5—Long, Chicago vs. New York, 2-0—Pasqua, singles in second and seventh.

May 5—Niekro (eight innings), New York vs. Chicago, 0-2—Redus, single in third; Hassey, single in third.

May 6—Rhoden, New York vs. Chicago, 4-1—Karkovice, single in third; Hassey, single in fourth.

May 9—Saberhagen, Kansas City vs. Cleveland, 4-0—Butler, single in seventh; Thornton, single in ninth.

May 18—Clancy, Toronto vs. California, 12-0—McLemore, single in sixth; White, single in seventh.

May 23—Bannister, Chicago vs. Boston, 9-1—Gedman, double in sixth; Burks, homer in ninth.

June 8—Langston, Seattle vs. Texas, 6-0—Sierra, single in fourth; Buechele, single in ninth.

June 19—Hough (7⅓ innings) and Mohorcic (1⅔ innings), Texas vs. Oakland, 4-2—Jackson, double in seventh; Polonia, single in eighth.

June 28—Ontiveros, Oakland vs. Cleveland, 10-0—Butler, single in first; Tabler, double in fourth.

July 12—Schmidt, Baltimore vs. Minnesota, 5-0—Gagne, single in sixth; Newman, single in seventh.

July 26—Leibrandt, Kansas City vs. Baltimore, 4-0—Gerhart, single in sixth; B. Ripken, single in ninth.

Aug. 8—John, New York vs. Detroit, 7-0—Herndon, single in fifth; Morrison, single in fifth.

Aug. 23—Rhoden (five innings) and Stoddard (four innings), New York vs. Oakland, 4-0—Lansford, single in fifth; Bernazard, single in sixth.

Aug. 27—Key (six innings), Eichhorn (⅔ inning), Musselman (1⅓ innings) and Henke (one inning), Toronto vs. Oakland, 9-4—Canseco, single in first; Lansford, homer in first.

Aug. 28—Bosio, Milwaukee vs. Minnesota, 1-0—Gagne, single in first; Hrbek, single in sixth.

Aug. 29—Yett, Cleveland vs. Boston, 2-1—Greenwell, singles in second and seventh.

Sept. 6—Higuera, Milwaukee vs. Minnesota, 6-0—Puckett, single in first; Davidson, single in third.

Sept. 9—Dotson (one inning), LaPoint (five innings) and Winn (two innings), Chicago vs. Minnesota, 1-2—Puckett, homer in fourth; Laudner, homer in ninth.

Sept. 13—Langston, Seattle vs. Chicago, 0-2—Keedy, homer in third; Hill, homer in seventh.

Sept. 23—Alexander, Detroit vs. Boston, 4-0—Burks, single in first; Barrett, single in first.

Sept. 27—LaPoint, Chicago vs. Oakland, 5-0—Steinbach, single in fifth; Gallego, double in eighth.

Oct. 4—Clemens, Boston vs. Milwaukee, 4-0—Felder, double in third; Sveum, double in eighth.

Ryan Again Leads in 10-K's

By DAVE SLOAN

By almost any standard, the 1987 season was a bizarre one for Houston Astros righthander Nolan Ryan. The 40-year-old fireballer led the National League with a 2.76 earned-run average and 270 strikeouts—the eighth time in his 21-year major league career that he has led his league in that category.

But Ryan won just eight of his 34 starts, a victory total surpassed by 46 other pitchers in the N.L. alone. Toronto's Jimmy Key compiled a 2.76 ERA in the American League and won 17 games.

But Ryan has always stood out as a master of the 10-strikeout game, and 1987 was no exception. Ryan struck out 10 or more batters in a game 12 times, more than any other pitcher, to extend his major league record in that category to 174 games. Baseball's all-time strikeout king, Ryan also extended his record for career strikeouts to 4,547 and had the 1987 season's single-game high with 16 strikeouts against the New York Mets on September 9.

Not surprisingly, the Astros again led all teams with 20 10-strikeout performances, up slightly from their major-league leading total of 18 in 1986. The Boston Red Sox were second with 12 such performances, with Roger Clemens leading the staff with nine. The only other pitcher with nine 10-strikeout games was Seattle's Mark Langston, the only Mariners pitcher to perform the feat. Langston led the American League with 262 strikeouts, a figure surpassed only by Ryan.

The Mets and Milwaukee Brewers, with 11 each, were the only other clubs in double figures.

Five teams—the Cubs, Dodgers, Red Sox, Royals and Yankees—had four pitchers throw at least one 10-strikeout game. The Atlanta Braves, St. Louis Cardinals and San Francisco Giants were shut out in the 10-strikeout department.

Following is a list of all pitchers who recorded at least 10 strikeouts in a game in 1987, with the number of times the feat was accomplished:

Houston's Nolan Ryan.

AMERICAN LEAGUE: Baltimore (1)—Bell. Boston (12)—Clemens 9, Hurst, Schiraldi, Sellers. California (3)—Witt 3. Chicago (3)—DeLeon 2, Bannister. Cleveland (4)—Swindell 3, Carlton. Detroit (7)—Morris 6, Robinson. Kansas City (5)—Gubicza 2, Jackson, Leibrandt, Saberhagen. Milwaukee (11)—Higuera 7, Bosio 2, Nieves 2. Minnesota (7)—Blyleven 3, Viola 3, Berenguer. New York (5)—Guidry 2, Gullickson, Hudson, Leiter. Oakland (5)—Stewart 3, Plunk, Young. Seattle (9)—Langston 9. Texas (7)—Witt 4, Hough 3. Toronto (3)—Clancy 2, Nunez.

NATIONAL LEAGUE: Atlanta—None. Chicago (4)—Maddux, Moyer, Sanderson, Sutcliffe. Cincinnati (1)—Power. Houston (20)—Ryan 12, Scott 7, Deshaies. Los Angeles (6)—Valenzuela 3, Hershiser, Honeycutt, Welch. Montreal (4)—Sebra 2, Perez, Youmans. New York (11)—Gooden 5, Darling 3, Fernandez 3. Philadelphia (1)—Rawley. Pittsburgh (1)—Fisher. St. Louis—None. San Diego (1)—Whitson. San Francisco—None.

1987 Games With 15 or More Strikeouts

Date	Pitcher—Club—Opp.	Place	IP.	H.	R.	ER.	BB.	SO.	Result
Sept. 9—Ryan, Astros vs. Giants		Houston	8	6	2	2	2	16	W 4-2
May 10—Swindell, Indians vs. Royals		Cleveland	9	11	2	2	2	15	W 4-2

Bedrosian Paces Firemen

By LARRY WIGGE

After his first six 1987 games, Philadelphia relief ace Steve Bedrosian had been rocked for 10 earned runs and 11 hits and had an unsightly earned-run average of 10.80. He had yielded four homers in just eight-plus innings. Hardly numbers to write home about.

But that's when Bedrosian went to work. He changed the mechanics of his delivery and developed a second fastball. He was Mr. Consistency the rest of the season.

From May 10 through June 30, Bedrosian recorded 19 saves and one victory in 20 appearances. That string included a major league record 13 saves in consecutive appearances. The previous record was 11 set by former Yankee ace Sparky Lyle in 1973.

Bedrosian played a major role in more than half of the Phillies' 80 victories, chalking up 40 saves and posting another five relief wins.

With one point being awarded for each save or relief win, Bedrosian edged St. Louis' Todd Worrell, 45-41, for The Sporting News' National League Fireman of the Year Award. The American League Fireman Award was shared by Jeff Reardon of the Twins and Dave Righetti of the Yankees, each hurler posting 31 saves and eight relief wins.

Worrell was second in the N.L. with 33 saves and eight wins, followed by Cincinnati's John Franco (32 saves, eight wins) and Chicago's Lee Smith (36 saves, four wins). The closest pursuer in the A.L. was Toronto's Tom Henke, who had 34 saves and no wins.

Reardon and Righetti are each two-time winners. Reardon earned the N.L. award when he was with Montreal in 1985 and finished second to Worrell in 1986, before being sent to Minnesota in a February 1987 trade. Righetti was the A.L. Fireman of the Year in '86, when he garnered a major league-record 46 saves.

It was the fifth time a member of the Twins had been named Fireman of the Year. Ron Perranoski accomplished the feat in 1969 and '70, Bill Campbell won it in 1976 and Mike Marshall shared the award with Texas' Jim Kern in 1979. Previous Yankees to win the Fireman Award are Luis Arroyo (1961), Lyle (1972) and Goose Gossage (1978).

Following is a complete list of major league players who recorded saves or relief wins in 1987:

The Yankees' Dave Righetti.

AMERICAN LEAGUE

Pitcher—Club	Saves	Relief Wins	Tot. Pts.
Reardon, Minnesota	31	8	39
Righetti, New York	31	8	39
Henke, Toronto	34	0	34
Plesac, Milwaukee	23	5	28
Buice, California	17	6	23
Mohorcic, Texas	16	7	23
Thigpen, Chicago	16	7	23
Eckersley, Oakland	16	6	22
Howell, Oakland	16	3	19
Henneman, Detroit	7	11	18
Crim, Milwaukee	12	5	17
Niedenfuer, Baltimore	13	3	16
King, Detroit	9	6	15
Minton, California	10	5	15
Musselman, Toronto	3	12	15
Nunez, Seattle	12	3	15
Clear, Milwaukee	6	8	14
Eichhorn, Toronto	4	10	14
James, Chicago	10	4	14
Jones, Cleveland	8	6	14
Schiraldi, Boston	6	8	14
Williams, Texas	6	8	14
Gardner, Boston	10	3	13
Wilkinson, Seattle	10	3	13
Quisenberry, Kansas City	8	4	12
Stoddard, New York	8	4	12
Hernandez, Detroit	8	3	11
Williamson, Baltimore	3	8	11
Berenguer, Minnesota	4	6	10
Clements, New York	7	3	10
Winn, Chicago	6	4	10
Atherton, Minnesota	2	7	9
Gleaton, Kansas City	5	4	9
Bailes, Cleveland	6	2	8
Garber, Kansas City	8	0	8
G. Nelson, Oakland	3	5	8
Reed, Seattle	7	1	8
Russell, Texas	3	5	8
Davis, Kansas City	2	5	7
Dixon, Baltimore	5	2	7
Frazier, Minnesota	2	5	7
Moore, California	5	2	7
Schmidt, Baltimore	1	6	7
Stewart, Cleveland	3	4	7
Cadaret, Oakland	0	6	6
Bosio, Milwaukee	2	3	5
Crawford, Boston	0	5	5
Farr, Kansas City	1	4	5
Habyan, Baltimore	1	4	5
Hudson, New York	0	5	5
Plunk, Oakland	2	3	5

Pitcher—Club	Saves	Relief Wins	Tot. Pts.	Pitcher—Club	Saves	Relief Wins	Tot. Pts.
Shields, Seattle	3	2	5	O'Connor, Baltimore	2	1	3
Thurmond, Detroit	5	0	5	Schatzeder, Minnesota	0	3	3
Wells, Toronto	1	4	5	Trujillo, Seattle	1	2	3
Fraser, California	1	3	4	Armstrong, Cleveland	1	1	2
Guante, New York	1	3	4	Black, Kansas City	1	1	2
Howe, Texas	1	3	4	Cerutti, Toronto	0	2	2
Huismann, Sea.-Cleveland	2	2	4	Clarke, Seattle	0	2	2
Lucas, California	3	1	4	Finley, California	0	2	2
Mirabella, Milwaukee	2	2	4	Knudson, Milwaukee	0	2	2
Searage, Chicago	2	2	4	Lazorko, California	0	2	2
Aase, Baltimore	2	1	3	Long, Chicago	1	1	2
Aldrich, Milwaukee	0	3	3	Loynd, Texas	1	1	2
Bordi, New York	0	3	3	Noles, Detroit	2	0	2
Carlton, Clev.-Minnesota	1	2	3	Ontiveros, Oakland	1	1	2
Guzman, Texas	0	3	3	Petry, Detroit	0	2	2
Lavelle, Tor.-Oakland	1	2	3	Sambito, Boston	0	2	2
Leiper, Oakland	1	2	3	Stapleton, Milwaukee	0	2	2
Nielsen, Chicago	2	1	3	Stoddard, Kansas City	1	1	2
Nunez, Toronto	0	3	3	Yett, Cleveland	1	1	2

One save—DeLeon, Baltimore; Camacho, Cleveland; Caudill, Oakland; Corbett, Baltimore; Griffin, Baltimore; Gordon, Toronto-Cleveland; Wills, Cleveland.

One relief win—Bolton, Boston; Burris, Milwaukee; Cook, California; Easterly, Cleveland; Farrell, Cleveland; Fulton, New York; Guetterman, Seattle; Harris, Texas; McKeon, Chicago; Meridith, Texas; Niemann, Minnesota; Powell, Seattle; Ritter, Cleveland; Robinson, Detroit; Rodriguez, Oakland; Snell, Detroit; Sutton, California; Thomas, Seattle; Vande Berg, Cleveland; Ward, Toronto.

NATIONAL LEAGUE

Pitcher—Club	Saves	Relief Wins	Tot. Pts.	Pitcher—Club	Saves	Relief Wins	Tot. Pts.
Bedrosian, Philadelphia	40	5	45	Landrum, Cincinnati	2	3	5
Worrell, St. Louis	33	8	41	Meads, Houston	0	5	5
Franco, Cincinnati	32	8	40	Robinson, Cincinnati	4	1	5
Smith, Chicago	36	4	40	Calhoun, Philadelphia	1	3	4
McDowell, New York	25	7	32	Crews, Los Angeles	3	1	4
D. Robinson, Pitts.-San Francisco	19	11	30	Gideon, Pittsburgh	3	1	4
Smith, Houston	24	2	26	Heathcock, Houston	1	3	4
Burke, Montreal	18	7	25	Leach, New York	0	4	4
McCullers, San Diego	16	8	24	Lynch, Chicago	4	0	4
Garrelts, San Francisco	12	11	23	Agosto, Houston	2	1	3
J. Robinson, S.F.-Pittsburgh	14	8	22	Assenmacher, Atlanta	2	1	3
Orosco, New York	16	3	19	Comstock, S.F.-San Diego	1	2	3
Acker, Atlanta	14	4	18	Hoffman, Cincinnati	0	3	3
Garber, Atlanta	10	8	18	Howell, Los Angeles	1	2	3
McGaffigan, Montreal	12	5	17	Jackson, Philadelphia	1	2	3
Gossage, San Diego	11	5	16	Jones, Pittsburgh	1	2	3
Young, Los Angeles	11	5	16	Lopez, Houston	1	2	3
Andersen, Houston	5	9	14	Price, San Francisco	1	2	3
Gott, S.F.-Pittsburgh	13	1	14	Sanderson, Chicago	2	1	3
Dayley, St. Louis	4	9	13	Schatzeder, Philadelphia	0	3	3
Horton, St. Louis	7	6	13	Bair, Philadelphia	0	2	2
Parrett, Montreal	6	7	13	Booker, San Diego	1	1	2
Pena, Los Angeles	11	2	13	Cary, Atlanta	1	1	2
Lefferts, S.D.-San Francisco	6	5	11	Cone, New York	1	1	2
McClure, Montreal	5	6	11	Downs, San Francisco	1	1	2
Murphy, Cincinnati	3	8	11	Easley, Pittsburgh	1	1	2
St. Claire, Montreal	7	3	10	Grant, S.F.-San Diego	1	1	2
Myers, New York	6	3	9	Jones, San Diego	0	2	2
Smiley, Pittsburgh	4	5	9	Leary, Los Angeles	1	1	2
Tekulve, Philadelphia	3	6	9	Leiper, San Diego	1	1	2
M. Davis, S.F.-San Diego	2	5	7	Mahler, Atlanta	0	2	2
Dawley, St. Louis	2	5	7	Mason, Chicago	0	2	2
Dedmon, Atlanta	4	3	7	Minton, San Francisco	1	1	2
DiPino, Chicago	4	3	7	Montgomery, Cincinnati	0	2	2
Perry, St.L.-Cincinnati	2	5	7	Niedenfuer, Los Angeles	1	1	2
Noles, Chicago	2	4	6	Puleo, Atlanta	0	2	2
Ritchie, Philadelphia	3	3	6	Sorensen, Montreal	1	1	2
Sisk, New York	3	3	6	Tunnell, St. Louis	0	2	2
Williams, Cincinnati	2	4	6	Walk, Pittsburgh	0	2	2
Holton, Los Angeles	2	3	5				

One save—Havens, Los Angeles; Hershiser, Los Angeles; Hesketh, Montreal; Olwine, Atlanta; H. Pena, Pittsburgh; Peters, St. Louis.

One relief win—Belcher, Los Angeles; Bockus, San Francisco; Boever, Atlanta; Childress, Houston; Frohwirth, Philadelphia; K. Gross, Philadelphia; Hall, Chicago; Hammaker, San Francisco; Hume, Philadelphia-Cincinnati; LaCoss, San Francisco; Lancaster, Chicago; LaPoint, St. Louis; Maddux, Philadelphia; Moyer, Chicago; Pacillo, Cincinnati; Scherrer, Cincinnati; Soff, St. Louis; Taylor, Pittsburgh; Walter, New York.

Best 1-0 Game Saved For Last

By DAVE SLOAN

Major league teams played 33 games in 1987 that ended in 1-0 scores, but they saved the best for last.

That was the Detroit Tigers' October 4 victory over the Toronto Blue Jays that decided the American League East Division championship. The Tigers, who held a one-game lead over the Blue Jays entering the season's final day, got the only run they needed on Larry Herndon's second-inning homer off Jimmy Key. Frank Tanana's six-hit pitching enabled Detroit to record its third straight triumph over the Jays and avoid a playoff.

Herndon's blast was one of four homers that decided 1-0 games. A day earlier, Stanley Jefferson's second-inning shot off Dodger righthander Orel Hershiser had made a winner of San Diego's Jimmy Jones. Jerry Mumphrey's July 1 ninth-inning homer off Bob Sebra gave Cubs righthander Greg Maddux a victory over the Expos and Candy Maldonado's seventh-inning homer off the Padres' Storm Davis provided the Giants' Kelly Downs with his victory margin April 15.

Downs, Pittsburgh rookie Mike Dunne and veteran lefthander John Candelaria were the only pitchers to win two 1-0 games. Sebra, California's Mike Witt and Minnesota's Frank Viola all lost two times. Floyd Bannister of the White Sox, Tim Leary of the Dodgers and John Smiley of the Pirates all split two 1-0 decisions. Smiley's victory came May 2 against the Giants' Downs, the only pitcher involved in three 1-0 decisions.

The Giants, Dodgers and Padres led all clubs by playing in five 1-0 games. The Giants won three and lost two, the Padres were 2-3 and the Dodgers' only victory came August 12 against Cincinnati when Leary drove in the game's lone run with a fifth-inning single off Bill Gullickson.

Candelaria won 1-0 games for two clubs. He pitched the California Angels over the Twins' Viola on April 18 and, after his September 15 trade to the Mets, pitched New York to a 1-0 victory over Philadelphia.

On August 26 at Milwaukee, Paul Molitor's 39-game hitting streak—the fifth-longest in major league history—ended in the Brewers' 1-0 triumph over the Cleveland Indians.

The Indians' Phil Niekro was stopped by Boston's Roger Clemens in a 1-0 effort May 27, keeping the veteran knuckleballer from tying the major league record for most wins by a brother combination. Before the season ended, however, the Niekros (Phil and Joe) had surpassed the Perrys (Gaylord and Jim), 538 victories to 529.

Nineteen of the 1-0 games were played in the National League, and the only clubs not involved in at least one were the Baltimore Orioles and Oakland A's.

The complete list of 1-0 games, including the winning and losing pitchers and the inning in which the run was scored, follows:

NATIONAL LEAGUE (19)

APRIL—

Date	Winner	Loser	Inning
12	—*Knepper, Hou.	*Sebra, Mon.	5
15	— Downs, S.F.	*Davis, S.D.	7

MAY—

Date	Winner	Loser	Inning
2	—*Smiley, Pitt.	Downs, S.F.	8
31	—*Whitson, S.D.	*Mitchell, N.Y.	5

JUNE—

Date	Winner	Loser	Inning
9	—*Darwin, Hou.	*Dravecky, S.D.	3
11	—*Deshaies, Hou.	Valenzuela, L.A.	3
11	— Downs, S.F.	*Show, S.D.	3
29	— Smith, Atl.	*Grant, S.F.	7

JULY—

Date	Winner	Loser	Inning
1	— Maddux, Chi.	Sebra, Mon.	9
8	— Youmans, Mon.	*Ryan, Hou.	1
30	—*Ruffin, Phil.	*Smiley, Pitt.	9

AUGUST—

Date	Winner	Loser	Inning
12	—*Leary, L.A.	*Gullickson, Cin.	5
16	— LaCoss, S.F.	*Leary, L.A.	10
24	—*Aguilera, N.Y.	*Hillegas, L.A.	4
25	— Dunne, Pitt.	*Power, Cin.	1

SEPTEMBER—

Date	Winner	Loser	Inning
17	—*Dunne, Pitt.	*Mathews, St. L.	1
28	—*Candelaria, N.Y.	*Gross, Phil.	2
29	— Magrane, St. L.	*Martinez, Mon.	6

OCTOBER—

Date	Winner	Loser	Inning
3	—*Jones, S.D.	Hershiser, L.A.	2

AMERICAN LEAGUE (14)

APRIL—

Date	Winner	Loser	Inning
18	—*Candelaria, Cal.	Viola, Minn.	7
19	—*Clements, N.Y.	*Gubicza, K.C.	8
22	— Stanley, Bos.	Jackson, K.C.	4
28	— Schrom, Cle.	Davis, Chi.	9

MAY—

Date	Winner	Loser	Inning
27	— Clemens, Bos.	Niekro, Cle.	5

JUNE—

Date	Winner	Loser	Inning
12	— Saberhagen, K.C.	Witt, Cal.	4
26	—*Witt, Tex.	Viola, Minn.	1

AUGUST—

Date	Winner	Loser	Inning
15	— Dotson, Chi.	*Clancy, Tor.	1
16	—*Yett, Cle.	*Guidry, N.Y.	8
26	— Higuera, Mil.	*Jones, Cle.	10
28	— Bosio, Mil.	*Straker, Minn.	6

SEPTEMBER—

Date	Winner	Loser	Inning
18	— Langston, Sea.	Bannister, Chi.	6
29	—*Bannister, Chi.	Witt, Cal.	5

OCTOBER—

Date	Winner	Loser	Inning
4	— Tanana, Det.	Key, Tor.	2

*Did not pitch complete game.

McGwire, Bell Led in Multi-HR

By DAVE SLOAN

Mark McGwire was not exactly a household name prior to the 1987 season. But everybody knows him now.

McGwire, a member of the 1984 U.S. Olympic team, blasted a league-leading 49 homers for the Oakland A's last season en route to the American League Rookie of the Year award. And the 6-foot-5, 215-pound first baseman was never better than on the weekend of June 27-28 in Cleveland, when he hit three home runs in a 13-3 A's victory and followed up that performance with two more homers in a 10-0 Oakland triumph. McGwire tied a major league record for most home runs in consecutive games.

McGwire was one of 135 players, 77 American Leaguers, to hit two or more homers in a game last season. Overall, there were 156 multi-homer performances in the A.L., 110 in the National League. The only player to do it for more than one team was infielder-outfielder Kevin Mitchell, who hit two homers for the Padres against the Dodgers on July 1 and, following a trade, two in his first game with the Giants on July 5 against the Cubs.

Two players had multi-homer performances in the same game 17 times in 1987, with the feat occurring 10 times in the American League. Teammates did it in the same game on 10 occasions, with one player from each club doing it in the same game seven times. Jose Canseco joined McGwire with a two-homer day of his own on June 28 against the Indians.

Cleveland was a leader when it came to three-homer games, both good and bad. Fifteen players hit three homers in a game last season, with three players—Cory Snyder, Joe Carter and Brook Jacoby—doing it for the Tribe. No other club in major league history had had more than two players accomplish the feat.

Unfortunately for the Indians, they also were victimized by three-homer games three times—by McGwire on June 27, by Seattle's Mickey Brantley on September 14 and by the Angels' Wally Joyner on October 3.

The Toronto Blue Jays led all major league clubs with 20 multi-homer performances, while the San Francisco Giants paced the N.L. with 16 such games.

American League Most Valuable Player George Bell of the Jays led all players with

Oakland's Mark McGwire belted five homers in consecutive games June 27-28 at Cleveland.

nine multi-homer performances, while N.L. MVP Andre Dawson of the Cubs was runner-up with eight. Dawson had consecutive multi-homer games on June 1-2 against the Astros. The only other player to accomplish that feat was outfielder Kirby Puckett of the Twins, who tagged the Milwaukee Brewers for back-to-back multi-homer games on August 29-30. Puckett's homers came during a streak of 10 straight hits.

The game with the most home runs came September 14 at Toronto, when the Blue Jays slugged a record 10 homers in an 18-3 victory over Baltimore. Catcher Ernie Whitt hit three, Bell and Rance Mulliniks hit two each and Rob Ducey,

Brook Jacoby's three-homer performance July 3 was the record third by an Indians player last season.

Fred McGriff and Lloyd Moseby one apiece in the Toronto rout.

Following is a list of players who had multi-homer games in '87 and the number of times:

AMERICAN LEAGUE: Baltimore (14) —Sheets 5, Murray 3, Gerhart 2, Lynn 2, Young 2. Boston (12)—Evans 4, Baylor 3, Horn 2, Boggs, Burks, Marzano. California (8)—Joyner 4, Downing, Howell, Ryal, White. Chicago (7)—Calderon 3, Fisk 2, Boston, Walker. Cleveland (12)— Carter 4, Jacoby 3, Snyder 3, Bernazard, Hall. Detroit (9)—Nokes 3, Lemon 2, Evans, Herndon, Madlock, Whitaker. Kansas City (8)—Jackson 3, Tartabull 2, Balboni, Brett, Seitzer. Milwaukee (7)— Deer 4, Sveum 2, Schroeder. Minnesota (7)—Puckett 2, Brunansky, Gagne, Laudner, Lombardozzi, Salas. New York (12)—Pagliarulo 4, Winfield 4, Mattingly 2, Henderson, Ward. Oakland (12)— McGwire 7, Canseco 4, Steinbach. Seattle (14)—Phelps 5, Presley 3, Davis 2, P. Bradley, S. Bradley, Brantley, Valle. Texas (14)—Sierra 3, Brower 2, Incaviglia 2, O'Brien 2, Buechele, McDowell, Parrish, Petralli, Slaught. Toronto (20)—Bell 9, Barfield 2, Moseby 2, Mulliniks 2, Whitt 2, Gruber, Iorg, McGriff.

NATIONAL LEAGUE: Atlanta (9)— Murphy 5, Virgil 3, Roenicke. Chicago (14)—Dawson 8, Durham 3, J. Davis, Dayett, Moreland. Cincinnati (9)—Daniels 2, Davis 2, Esasky 2, Parker 2, Diaz. Houston (7)—Bass 2, Doran 2, Cruz, Davis, C. Reynolds. Los Angeles (7)— Guerrero 2, Marshall 2, Shelby 2, Stubbs. Montreal (2)—Wallach, Webster. New York (13)—Strawberry 4, McReynolds 3, Carter 2, Dykstra, Hernandez, Johnson, Teufel. Philadelphia (11)—Samuel 3, Schmidt 3, Aguayo 2, Hayes 2, James. Pittsburgh (10)—Bonds 2, Bonilla 2, Morrison 2, Bream, Coles, Diaz, Van Slyke. St. Louis (8)—Clark 6, Ford, Lindeman. San Diego (4)—Kruk, Martinez, Mitchell, Santiago. San Francisco (16)—Clark 4, Davis 2, Leonard 2, Maldonado 2, Melvin 2, Aldrete, Mitchell, Speier, Williams.

A recap of the three-homer games:

Date	Player—Club—Opp.	Place	AB.	R.	H.	2B.	3B.	HR.	RBI.	Result
May 3	Davis, Reds vs. Phillies	A	5	4	4	0	0	3	6	W 9-6
May 4	Wallach, Expos vs. Braves	A	4	3	3	0	0	3	6	L 7-10
May 21	Snyder, Indians vs. Twins	H	4	3	3	0	0	3	3	W 6-3
May 28	Carter, Indians vs. Red Sox	A	5	3	4	0	0	3	5	L 8-12
June 14	Schmidt, Phillies vs. Expos	A	4	3	3	0	0	3	6	W 11-6
June 27	McGwire, A's vs. Indians	A	5	5	4	0	0	3	5	W 13-3
June 28	Madlock, Tigers vs. Orioles (11 innings)	H	5	3	3	0	0	3	4	W 8-7
July 3	Jacoby, Indians vs. White Sox	H	4	3	3	0	0	3	3	L 9-14
July 17	Sveum, Brewers vs. Angels	H	4	3	3	0	0	3	6	W 12-2
Aug. 1	Dawson, Cubs vs. Phillies	H	4	3	3	0	0	3	5	W 5-3
Sept. 10	Davis, Astros vs. Padres	A	4	3	3	0	0	3	5	L 7-8
Sept. 14	Brantley, Mariners vs. Indians	H	6	3	5	0	0	3	7	L 8-11
Sept. 14	Whitt, Blue Jays vs. Orioles	H	5	3	3	0	0	3	5	W 18-3
Sept. 30	Coles, Pirates vs. Cubs	H	4	3	4	0	0	3	6	L 8-10
Oct. 3	Joyner, Angels vs. Indians	H	3	3	3	0	0	3	3	W 12-5

Mattingly Hits Record 6 Slams

By DAVE SLOAN

Entering the 1987 season, everybody wondered what New York Yankees first baseman Don Mattingly could possibly do for an encore. He had led the American League in five offensive categories in '86 while hitting .352 with 31 home runs and 113 runs batted in. There wasn't much that the 25-year-old slugger had not already accomplished in his short major league career, but. . . .

On May 14, Mattingly hit his first career grand slam off Texas' Mike Mason in a 9-1 Yankee victory. There was no stopping him after that. Mattingly went on to hit five more slams, breaking the old mark of five set by Ernie Banks in 1955 and equaled by Jim Gentile in 1961. The record-breaker came September 29 off Boston's Bruce Hurst in a 6-0 New York win.

Mattingly's outburst helped the Yankees tie a major league record with 10 grand slams. Mike Pagliarulo (two) and Joel Skinner and Dave Winfield (one each) accounted for the other Yankee slams. The Boston Red Sox had eight players combine for nine slams and the New York Mets led the National League with seven slams hit by six different players.

All major league clubs except San Diego hit at least one grand slam in 1987, and all pitching staffs except Seattle's yielded at least one.

Outfielder Eric Davis of the Cincinnati Reds finished second to Mattingly with three slams, all coming in the month of May (to tie a major league record) and all hit in the state of Pennsylvania. Davis connected for slams on May 1 and 3 against the Phillies' Don Carman and Dan Schatzeder, respectively, and on May 30 against Pittsburgh rookie Dorn Taylor.

Including Mattingly, Davis and Pagliarulo, 13 players hit at least two slams last season, with Milwaukee's Rob Deer hitting his on consecutive days (August 19-20) against Cleveland. Fred Lynn accounted for the only two slams hit by Baltimore in 1987, ending a streak of five straight seasons in which the Orioles either led or tied for major league team honors.

There were 100 grand slams, 55 in the American League. Teammates hit slams in the same game on four occasions, increasing to 39 the number of times that has happened in major league history. In a wild 22-7 Chicago victory over Houston on

The Yankees' Don Mattingly was a terror to pitchers in 1987 when the bases were loaded.

June 3 at Wrigley Field, Brian Dayett and Keith Moreland of the Cubs and Billy Hatcher of the Astros all clubbed grand slams.

The slams by Dayett and Moreland were two of a record-tying nine yielded by Houston pitchers last season, the most in the majors. Julio Solano gave up three slams and Mike Scott and Aurelio Lopez yielded two each.

Minnesota reliever Jeff Reardon was the only other pitcher to give up three slams, but two hurlers were hit for slams while pitching for different clubs. Veterans Steve Carlton (Indians and Twins) and Rick Reuschel (Pirates and Giants) were victimized in two uniforms.

Perhaps the season's most dramatic grand slam came on May 2 at Shea Stadium, when Montreal's Tim Raines hit a 10th-inning blast (his fourth hit of the game) off the Mets' Jesse Orosco to give the Expos an 11-7 triumph in a nationally televised game. Raines, the 1986 N.L. batting champion who was ignored by other clubs after applying for free agency the previous winter, was playing his first game of 1987 with the Expos after re-signing with the team the day before.

Milwaukee's Rob Deer hit grand slams in consecutive games August 19-20 against Cleveland.

The complete list of grand slams, with the inning in which each was hit in parentheses, follows:

AMERICAN LEAGUE (55)

APRIL—

9	—Snyder, Cleveland vs. Johnson, Toronto	(1)
14	—Skinner, New York vs. Carlton, Cleveland	(5)
14	—Jackson, Kansas City vs. Snell, Detroit	(6)
15	—Evans, Boston vs. Mohorcic, Texas	(6)
20	—Phillips, Oakland vs. Lucas, California	(9)
30	—Nokes, Detroit vs. Cook, California	(7)

MAY—

3	—DeCinces, California vs. Gardner, Boston	(6)
8	—Pagliarulo, New York vs. Reardon, Minnesota	(9)
12	—Lynn, Baltimore vs. Reardon, Minnesota	(8)
14	—Mattingly, New York vs. Mason, Texas	(4)
20	—Brunansky, Minnesota vs. Candiotti, Cleveland.	(6)
25	—Burks, Boston vs. Huismann, Cleveland	(5)
29	—Brookens, Detroit vs. Klink, Minnesota	(5)

JUNE—

1	—McDowell, Texas vs. Davis, Chicago	(12)
2	—Walker, Chicago vs. Meridith, Texas	(2)
5	—O'Brien, Texas vs. Portugal, Minnesota	(6)
10	—Bernazard, Cleveland vs. Candelaria, California	(5)
10	—Burks, Boston vs. Bell, Baltimore	(4)
10	—Barrett, Boston vs. O'Connor, Baltimore	(7)
11	—Bell, Toronto, vs. Habyan, Baltimore	(5)
14	—Laudner, Minnesota vs. DeLeon, Chicago	(2)
14	—Schofield, California vs. Shirley, Kansas City	(9)
21	—Brower, Texas vs. Plunk, Oakland	(2)

23	—Upshaw, Toronto vs. Robinson, Detroit	(4)
26	—Rice, Boston vs. Bordi, New York	(2)
27	—Stanley, Texas vs. Reardon, Minnesota	(8)
29	—Mattingly, New York vs. Cerutti, Toronto	(2)
29	—Winfield, New York vs. Henke, Toronto	(8)
29	—Boggs, Boston vs. McGregor, Baltimore	(6)

JULY—

3	—*Stanley, Texas vs. Guante, New York	(6)
6	—Snyder, Cleveland vs. Farr, Kansas City	(8)
10	—Mattingly, New York vs. McKeon, Chicago	(2)
16	—Mattingly, New York vs. Hough, Texas	(2)

AUGUST—

2	—Kingery, Seattle vs. McCaskill, California	(1)
4	—Kiefer, Milwaukee vs. McGregor, Baltimore	(3)
6	—Parsons, Cleveland vs. Eichhorn, Toronto	(6)
10	—Horn, Boston vs. Nunez, Toronto	(8)
13	—Lynn, Baltimore vs. Bosio, Milwaukee	(4)
17	—White, California vs. Leiper, Oakland	(7)
19	—Deer, Milwaukee vs. Gordon, Cleveland	(4)
20	—Deer, Milwaukee vs. Vande Berg, Cleveland	(6)
22	—Quirk, Kansas City vs. Knudson, Milwaukee	(6)
23	—Baylor, Boston vs. Carlton, Minnesota	(5)
25	—White, Kansas City vs. Henry, Texas	(6)
27	—Bell, Toronto vs. Cadaret, Oakland	(5)
28	—Davis, Seattle vs. Hudson, New York	(6)
30	—Seitzer, Kansas City vs. Nielsen, Chicago	(8)

SEPTEMBER—

4	—Pagliarulo, New York vs. McCaskill, California	(1)
5	—Evans, Detroit vs. Russell, Texas	(4)
10	—Ryal, California vs. Mohorcic, Texas	(9)
15	—Benzinger, Boston vs. Tanana, Detroit	(1)
25	—Mattingly, New York vs. Mesa, Baltimore	(2)
26	—Nokes, Detroit vs. Cerutti, Toronto	(3)
29	—Mattingly, New York vs. Hurst, Boston	(3)

OCTOBER—

2	—Tartabull, Kansas City vs. Viola, Minnesota	(5)

NATIONAL LEAGUE (45)

APRIL—

13	—Thompson, San Fran. vs. Gorman, San Diego	(7)
17	—Stillwell, Cincinnati vs. Lopez, Houston	(5)
18	—Herr, St. Louis vs. Orosco, New York	(10)
22	—Dawson, Chicago vs. Worrell, St. Louis	(7)
26	—Parrish, Philadelphia vs. Reuschel, Pittsburgh.	(1)

MAY—

1	—Davis, Cincinnati vs. Carman, Philadelphia	(3)
2	—Raines, Montreal vs. Orosco, New York	(10)
2	—Nettles, Atlanta vs. Lopez, Houston	(6)
2	—James, Atlanta vs. Solano, Houston	(7)
3	—Davis, Cincinnati vs. Schatzeder, Philadelphia ..	(4)
5	—Speier, San Francisco vs. Soff, St. Louis	(6)
9	—Speier, San Francisco vs. Easley, Pittsburgh....	(5)
13	—Webster, Montreal vs. Browning, Cincinnati	(2)
17	—Pagnozzi, St. Louis vs. Hoffman, Cincinnati	(5)
24	—Clark, St. Louis vs. Scott, Houston	(2)
30	—Davis, Cincinnati vs. Taylor, Pittsburgh	(3)

JUNE—

1	—Dawson, Chicago vs. Solano, Houston	(8)
3	—Dayett, Chicago vs. Knepper, Houston	(1)
3	—Hatcher, Houston vs. Sutcliffe, Chicago	(4)
3	—Moreland, Chicago vs. Solano, Houston	(6)
10	—Ashby, Houston vs. S. Davis, San Diego	(4)
12	—Teufel, New York vs. Walk, Pittsburgh	(6)
17	—Fitzgerald, Montreal vs. Fernandez, New York .	(2)

JULY—

7	—Diaz, Cincinnati vs. Bair, Philadelphia	(2)
8	—Sundberg, Chicago vs. McCullers, San Diego	(8)
9	—Murphy, Atlanta vs. Bair, Philadelphia	(6)
31	—Webster, Montreal vs. Myers, New York	(5)

AUGUST—

1	—Johnson, New York vs. St. Claire, Montreal	(6)
3	—Marshall, Los Angeles vs. Power, Cincinnati	(3)
12	—Brenly, San Francisco vs. Scott, Houston	(7)
12	—Samuel, Philadelphia vs. Lynch, Chicago	(8)
15	—Law, Montreal vs. Fisher, Pittsburgh	(9)
16	—Davis, Chicago vs. Darling, New York	(4)
20	—Lyons, New York vs. Downs, San Francisco	(6)
29	—Van Slyke, Pittsburgh vs. Andersen, Houston.	(8)
30	—Carter, New York vs. Reuschel, San Francisco..	(1)

SEPTEMBER—

15	—McGriff, Cincinnati vs. Clary, Atlanta	(4)
16	—Dykstra, New York vs. Sebra, Montreal	(8)
19	—Hernandez, New York vs. Palacios, Pittsburgh .	(5)
20	—Coles, Pittsburgh vs. Fernandez, New York	(6)
20	—Esasky, Cincinnati vs. Perlman, San Francisco.	(9)
21	—Johnson, New York vs. Lynch, Chicago	(2)
26	—Brooks, Montreal vs. Rawley, Philadelphia	(7)
27	—Maldonado, San Francisco vs. Cary, Atlanta	(4)
28	—Puhl, Houston vs. Hershiser, Los Angeles	(5)

*First game of doubleheader.

Puckett, Seitzer Get 6 Hits

By DAVE SLOAN

Paul Molitor's 39-game hitting streak earned more headlines, but Kirby Puckett's two-day late-August assault on Milwaukee Brewer pitching was almost as impressive.

Puckett, the sparkplug center fielder for the World Series-champion Minnesota Twins, hit two homers and two singles in the Twins' 12-3 victory over Milwaukee on August 29 and followed that with six hits in six at-bats in a 10-6 win the following day. Puckett tied an American League record with his six-hit game and had hits in 10 consecutive at-bats over the two games.

Puckett led the major leagues with six multi-hit (four or more) performances last season. The only other major leaguer to have a six-hit game in 1987 was Kansas City rookie third baseman Kevin Seitzer, who led the Royals to a 13-5 victory over Boston on August 2 with two homers, a double and three singles in six plate appearances.

Another rookie third baseman, San Francisco's Mark Wasinger, belted three doubles and a homer in a 9-4 victory over Pittsburgh on May 9. The hits were Wasinger's first in the major leagues.

There were 290 multi-hit performances, 11 more than in 1986. A.L. hitters accounted for 154, National League hitters 136. A total of 184 players had at least one multi-hit performance, with veteran outfielder Mike Easler the only player to accomplish the feat in both leagues. As a member of the Philadelphia Phillies, Easler had four singles in an April 14 game against the Mets and, following his trade to the Yankees, hit four singles in a June 15 game against Baltimore.

All major league teams had at least one player with a multi-hit performance. The Cincinnati Reds led the senior circuit with 19 while the cross-state Cleveland Indians led the A.L. with 17. Eight different players contributed to the Reds' total; 10 players did it for the Indians.

For the second year in a row, San Diego outfielder Tony Gwynn led the N.L. with five multi-hit games. The major leagues' batting leader in 1987 (.370), Gwynn was also the only player with two five-hit performances, doing it on April 16 against the Dodgers and August 11 against the Braves.

Not counting Puckett and Seitzer, 14 players other than Gwynn had five-hit games. The club with the five-hit player won the game on all but two of those occasions. Ironically, one of those losses came the only time the five-hit player hit three home runs. On September 14 at Seattle, rookie Mickey Brantley drove in seven runs with three homers and two singles, but the Mariners still lost, 11-8, to Cleveland.

Another rookie, Mark McGwire of Oakland, had better luck against the Indians, hitting five homers in back-to-back multi-hit games June 27 and 28 in Cleveland. The A's won both games.

Four players hit for the cycle (single, double, triple, homer), all in the National League. Andre Dawson of the Cubs did it April 29 against San Francisco; the Giants' Candy Maldonado did it May 4 against the Cardinals; Tim Raines of the Expos did it August 16 against the Pirates, and Atlanta's Albert Hall did it September 23 against the Astros. Hall's performance was particularly noteworthy—he became the first Braves player to hit for the cycle since Billy Collins in 1910.

For the second consecutive year, 24 players compiled hitting streaks of 15 or more games. Detroit shortstop Alan Trammell was the only player to do it twice, with streaks of 21 and 18.

Molitor's 39-game streak from July 16 through August 25 was the season's longest and seventh longest in baseball history. The second-longest streak of 1987 was compiled by San Diego catcher Benito Santiago, whose 34-game streak from August 25 through October 2 set a rookie record. Ironically, Santiago's streak began on the day Molitor's ended.

Besides Molitor, Santiago and Trammell, the following players compiled hitting streaks of 15 or more games in 1987: 25 games—Wade Boggs, Red Sox; 19 games—Brett Butler, Indians; Terry Pendleton, Cardinals; Steve Sax, Dodgers; 18 games—Harold Baines, White Sox; Tony Fernandez, Blue Jays; 17 games—Buddy Bell, Reds; George Bell, Blue Jays; Brian Downing, Angels; Pedro Guerrero, Dodgers; Keith Hernandez, Mets; Luis Polonia, A's; 16 games—George Brett, Royals; Billy Hatcher, Astros; 15 games—Jerry Browne, Rangers; Scott Fletcher, Rangers; Don Mattingly, Yankees; Dale Murphy, Braves; Eddie Murray, Orioles; Pete O'Brien, Rangers; Ed Romero, Red Sox.

Minnesota's Kirby Puckett had six hits in one game and hits in 10 consecutive at-bats last year.

The complete list of players with four or more hits in one game follows:

AMERICAN LEAGUE: Baltimore (6) —Murray 3, Burleson, Knight, Sheets. Boston (13)—Barrett 4, Boggs 4, Rice 2, Horn, Owen, Reed. California (7)—Downing 2, Joyner 2, Howell, McLemore, White. Chicago (13)—Guillen 3, Baines 2, Calderon 2, Lyons 2, Hill, Redus, Walker, Williams. Cleveland (17)—Carter 3, Bernazard 2, Franco 2, Hall 2, Hinzo 2, Tabler 2, Allanson, Butler, Jacoby, Snyder. Detroit (13)—Trammell 3, Heath 2, Madlock 2, Bean, Bergman, Gibson, Lemon, Nokes, Whitaker. Kansas City (11)—Wilson 3, Jackson 2, Seitzer 2, Pecota, Smith, Tartabull, White. Milwaukee (16)—Brock 4, Molitor 3, Schroeder 2, Braggs, Castillo, Deer, Felder, Gantner, Surhoff, Yount. Minnesota (10)—Puckett 6, Gaetti, Gladden, Hrbek, Smalley. New York (8)— Mattingly 2, Randolph 2, Easler, Henderson, Washington, Winfield. Oakland (14) —McGwire 4, Polonia 3, Steinbach 2, Canseco, Davis, Griffin, Henderson, Weiss. Seattle (10)—Brantley 2, Moses 2, P. Bradley, Matthews, Phelps, Quinones, Ramos, Valle. Texas (6)—Brower, Browne, Fletcher, McDowell, Sierra, Stanley. Toronto (10)—Barfield 4, Fernandez 2, Bell, Gruber, Moseby, Whitt.

NATIONAL LEAGUE: Atlanta (9)— James 4, Hall, Murphy, Perry, Ramirez, Thomas. Chicago (16)—Dawson 3, Dunston 2, Moreland 2, J. Davis, Durham, Martinez, Mumphrey, Noce, Palmeiro, Sandberg, Sundberg, Trillo. Cincinnati (19)—Daniels 4, Concepcion 3, Diaz 3, Parker 3, Esasky 2, Jones 2, Davis, Oester. Houston (11)—Bass 4, Hatcher 2, Young 2, Davis, Puhl, Walling. Los Angeles (7)— Guerrero 2, Marshall 2, Sax, Scioscia, Shelby. Montreal (12)—Raines 3, Brooks 2, Galarraga 2, Wallach 2, Webster 2, Candaele. New York (11)—Carter 2, Magadan 2, McReynolds 2, Teufel 2, Dykstra, Johnson, Strawberry. Philadelphia (5)— Thompson 2, Easler, James, Hayes. Pittsburgh (14)—Morrison 3, Bonds 2, Belliard, Bream, Cangelosi, Coles, Diaz, LaValliere, Pedrique, Ray, Van Slyke. St. Louis (6)— Herr 2, Smith 2, Coleman, Pendleton. San Diego (10)—Gwynn 5, Jefferson 2, Flannery, Kruk, Salazar. San Francisco (16)— Davis 2, Leonard 2, Maldonado 2, Aldrete, Brenly, Melendez, Melvin, Milner, Mitchell, Spilman, Thompson, Uribe, Wasinger.

The records of all players with six and five hits in a game follows:

Date	Player—Club—Opp.	Place	AB.	R.	H.	2B.	3B.	HR.	RBI.	Result
Aug. 2	Seitzer, Royals vs. Red Sox	H	6	4	6	1	0	2	7	W 13-5
Aug. 30	Puckett, Twins vs. Brewers	A	6	4	6	2	0	2	4	W 10-6
April 12	Hayes, Phillies vs. Cubs (10 innings)	H	6	1	5	1	0	0	2	W 9-8
April 16	Gwynn, Padres vs. Dodgers (10 innings)	A	5	1	5	2	0	0	1	W 3-2
April 29	Dawson, Cubs vs. Giants	H	5	1	5	1	1	1	2	W 8-4
May 13	Wilson, Royals vs. Orioles (12 innings)	A	6	2	5	0	0	0	0	W 8-7
June 11	Felder, Brewers vs. Tigers	A	6	1	5	0	1	0	2	W 8-5
June 12	Brooks, Expos vs. Phillies	H	5	2	5	2	0	1	6	W 13-6
July 9	Guillen, White Sox vs. Yankees	A	5	1	5	1	0	0	1	W 6-3
July 11	Trammell, Tigers vs. Angels	A	6	2	5	1	0	0	3	W 12-5
July 24	Magadan, Mets vs. Astros	H	5	1	5	0	0	0	1	W 7-4
Aug. 5	Milner, Giants vs. Astros (11 innings)	A	6	2	5	3	0	0	1	L 5-6
Aug. 11	Thompson, Phillies vs. Cubs (13 innings)	H	7	1	5	1	1	0	3	W 9-8
Aug. 11	Gwynn, Padres vs. Braves	H	5	4	5	0	0	1	1	W 7-6
Aug. 16	Raines, Expos vs. Pirates	H	5	4	5	2	1	1	1	W 10-7
Sept. 5	Hinzo, Indians vs. Red Sox	A	6	1	5	1	0	0	1	W 15-2
Sept. 14	Brantley, Mariners vs. Indians	H	6	3	5	0	0	3	7	L 8-11
Sept. 15	Parker, Reds vs. Braves	A	5	4	5	1	0	2	8	W 21-6

Ward, Griffey Led in Pinch-Hits

Veteran Graig Nettles of the Atlanta Braves was baseball's most productive pinch-hitter in 1987, with three home runs and 23 RBIs in 72 at-bats.

By DAVE SLOAN

When the California Angels came to bat in the ninth inning of a September 10 game at Anaheim Stadium against the Texas Rangers, they trailed, 7-3, and appeared headed for their seventh defeat in eight games.

But the Angels gave their fans some hope when they loaded the bases without hitting the ball out of the infield against Ranger relievers Mitch Williams and Dale Mohorcic. The next batter, Mark Ryal, pinch-hitting for Gary Pettis, then drilled a 1-2 pitch from Mohorcic over the right-field wall for a grand slam to tie the game at 7-7. Devon White's solo homer in the 10th inning gave the Angels an 8-7 victory.

Ryal's home run was the club-record ninth by California pinch-hitters in 1987, tops in the American League. The Angels also led the A.L. in club pinch-hitting average (.327) and hits (48) while tying the Yankees with 35 runs batted in.

Team pinch-hitting was more balanced in the National League, with the Mets leading in average (.284), the Giants in homers (11), the Reds in hits (66) and the Braves in RBIs (49).

Nearly half of the Braves' runs batted in came from the bat of veteran Graig Nettles, who drove in a major-league leading 23 runs as a pinch-hitter. No other player had more than 13 RBIs in pinch roles.

Nettles and Ryal were two of six players to hit pinch grand slams in 1987, joining the Rangers' Mike Stanley, the Cubs' Jim Sundberg, the Indians' Casey Parsons and the Giants' Candy Maldonado.

Five players hit three home runs as a pinch-hitter, including Nettles, the Giants' Joel Youngblood, the Yankees' Dan Pasqua, the Rangers' Darrell Porter and George Hendrick of the Angels.

Among those players with at least 10 pinch-hit at-bats, Gary Ward of the Yankees (8 for 12, .667) and Ken Griffey of the Braves (11 for 18, .611) paced the A.L. and N.L., respectively.

Lee Mazzilli of the Mets and Wallace Johnson of the Expos led the N.L. with 17 pinch-hits each while the Royals' Thad Bosley led the A.L. with 12.

Following is a list of all pinch-hitters with at least 10 at-bats in 1987:

AMERICAN LEAGUE PINCH-HITTING
(Compiled by Elias Sports Bureau)

Club Pinch-Hitting

Club	AB.	H.	HR.	RBI.	Pct.	Club	AB.	H.	HR.	RBI.	Pct.
California	147	48	9	35	.327	Detroit	172	39	1	28	.227
Baltimore	86	27	5	23	.314	Seattle	89	20	3	27	.225
Minnesota	134	34	5	25	.254	Oakland	112	24	3	15	.214
Boston	80	20	2	16	.250	Chicago	89	18	3	15	.202
Kansas City	125	31	3	16	.248	New York	153	30	6	35	.196
Milwaukee	77	19	1	9	.247	Texas	154	30	6	24	.195
Toronto	167	39	3	28	.234	Cleveland	129	24	3	19	.186
						Totals	1714	403	50	315	.235

Individual Pinch-Hitting
(10 or More At-Bats)

Player-Club	AB.	H.	HR.	RBI.	Pct.
Ward, N.Y.	12	8	0	5	.667
Evans, Det.	10	6	0	4	.600
Buckner, Cal.	15	8	0	5	.533
Lemon, Det.	11	5	0	3	.455
Hendrick, Cal.	15	6	3	10	.400
Young, Balt.	10	4	0	3	.400
Herndon, Det.	21	8	0	5	.381
Manning, Mil.	16	6	0	3	.375
McRae, K.C.	11	4	0	3	.364
Baylor, Minn.	17	6	0	4	.353
S. Bradley, Sea.	12	4	0	4	.333
Eisenreich, K.C.	15	5	1	4	.333
Howell, Cal.	18	6	2	3	.333
Lacy, Balt.	12	4	0	3	.333
Mulliniks, Tor.	24	8	0	2	.333
Ryal, Cal.	31	10	2	8	.323
Surhoff, Mil.	10	3	0	1	.300
Wiggins, Balt.	10	3	0	1	.300
Greenwell, Bos.	17	5	1	6	.294
Larkin, Minn.	17	5	0	6	.294
Dwyer, Balt.	24	7	2	7	.292
Bosley, K.C.	42	12	0	3	.286
Parsons, Clev.	14	4	1	5	.286
Balboni, K.C.	15	4	2	5	.267
Easler, N.Y.	19	5	1	7	.263
Beniquez, Tor.	23	6	1	7	.261
Fisk, Chi.	12	3	0	2	.250
Hairston, Chi.	32	8	2	10	.250
Heath, Det.	12	3	0	1	.250
Leach, Tor.	28	7	0	3	.250
Jackson, Oak.	29	7	1	5	.241
Bush, Minn.	30	7	0	7	.233
Slaught, Tex.	22	5	0	0	.227
Jones, Cal.	27	6	2	6	.222
Fielder, Tor.	19	4	1	3	.211
Nokes, Det.	19	4	0	4	.211
Salas, N.Y.	19	4	2	5	.211
Boston, Chi.	10	2	0	0	.200
Iorg, Tor.	15	3	0	3	.200
Porter, Tex.	36	7	3	8	.194
Smalley, Minn.	31	6	1	2	.194
Petralli, Tex.	26	5	2	6	.192
Bergman, Det.	21	4	0	3	.190
Grubb, Det.	21	4	1	2	.190
Washington, N.Y.	21	4	1	4	.190
M. Davis, Oak.	11	2	0	0	.182
Castillo, Clev.	29	5	1	3	.172
Matthews, Sea.	12	2	0	4	.167
Phelps, Sea.	12	2	0	0	.167
Christensen, Sea.	13	2	0	2	.154
Pasqua, N.Y.	22	3	3	6	.136
Frobel, Clev.	15	2	1	2	.133
Thornton, Clev.	15	2	0	2	.133
Gruber, Tor.	16	2	0	1	.125
Sheridan, Det.	16	2	0	3	.125
Hall, Clev.	17	2	0	0	.118
Valle, Sea.	10	1	0	3	.100
Henderson, Oak.	11	1	0	0	.091
McDowell, Tex.	11	1	0	0	.091
Whitt, Tor.	12	1	0	3	.083
Kittle, N.Y.	13	1	0	0	.077
McGriff, Tor.	14	1	1	1	.071
Cotto, N.Y.	11	0	0	0	.000

Kansas City's Thad Bosley led the American League with 12 pinch-hits in 1987.

NATIONAL LEAGUE PINCH-HITTING
(Compiled by Elias Sports Bureau)

Club Pinch-Hitting

Club	AB.	H.	HR.	RBI.	Pct.	Club	AB.	H.	HR.	RBI.	Pct.
New York	215	61	7	31	.284	San Francisco	279	65	11	46	.233
St. Louis	182	48	1	33	.264	Philadelphia	258	60	4	21	.233
Cincinnati	260	66	5	38	.254	Pittsburgh	244	56	4	27	.230
Montreal	228	56	2	33	.246	Atlanta	209	47	6	49	.225
Chicago	262	64	8	47	.244	San Diego	229	48	1	34	.210
Houston	260	62	0	21	.238	Los Angeles	303	50	4	40	.165
						Totals	2929	683	53	420	.233

Individual Pinch-Hitting
(10 or More At-Bats)

Player-Club	AB.	H.	HR.	RBI.	Pct.	Player-Club	AB.	H.	HR.	RBI.	Pct.
Griffey, Atl.	18	11	0	8	.611	Ready, S.D.	25	6	0	4	.240
Leonard, S.F.	11	6	2	4	.545	Collins, Cin.	35	8	0	1	.229
Walling, Hou.	15	8	0	2	.533	Landrum, L.A.	35	8	1	4	.229
Kruk, S.D.	12	6	1	5	.500	Dernier, Chi.	31	7	1	6	.226
Teufel, N.Y.	18	8	1	3	.444	Booker, St.L.	18	4	0	3	.222
Hughes, Phil.	19	8	0	3	.421	Dayett, Chi.	32	7	0	4	.219
Ford, St.L.	18	7	0	1	.389	Diaz, Pitt.	32	7	2	11	.219
Oquendo, St.L.	26	10	1	6	.385	Pankovits, Hou.	32	7	0	3	.219
Scioscia, L.A.	11	4	0	5	.364	Spilman, S.F.	61	13	1	11	.213
LaValliere, Pitt.	14	5	0	0	.357	Trevino, L.A.	33	7	1	7	.212
Speier, S.F.	14	5	0	5	.357	Milner, S.F.	19	4	0	1	.211
Bonilla, Pitt.	17	6	0	5	.353	Foley, Mon.	24	5	0	0	.208
Mumphrey, Chi.	35	12	2	12	.343	Bryant, L.A.	29	6	1	5	.207
Concepcion, Cin.	24	8	0	2	.333	Cangelosi, Pitt.	50	10	1	1	.200
Morris, St.L.	30	10	0	8	.333	Landreaux, L.A.	50	10	1	7	.200
Thompson, Phil.	15	5	0	0	.333	Magadan, N.Y.	30	6	2	3	.200
Wilson, N.Y.	32	10	0	4	.313	Roenicke, Atl.	15	3	1	2	.200
Simmons, Atl.	29	9	2	8	.310	Wynne, S.D.	30	6	0	10	.200
Mazzilli, N.Y.	55	17	2	11	.309	Nichols, Mon.	16	3	0	2	.188
Trillo, Chi.	23	7	1	5	.304	Palmeiro, Chi.	27	5	2	4	.185
Puhl, Hou.	53	16	0	5	.302	Almon, N.Y.	22	4	0	0	.182
O'Neill, Cin.	37	11	2	13	.297	Nettles, Atl.	72	13	3	23	.181
Youngblood, S.F.	44	13	3	9	.295	Quinones, Chi.	23	4	0	1	.174
Lake, St.L.	14	4	0	0	.286	Cruz, Hou.	29	5	0	1	.172
Hall, Atl.	25	7	0	1	.280	Backman, N.Y.	12	2	0	0	.167
Johnson, Mon.	61	17	1	12	.279	Daniels, Cin.	12	2	0	1	.167
Dykstra, N.Y.	18	5	0	2	.278	Garner, L.A.	24	4	0	2	.167
Stillwell, Cin.	29	8	0	2	.276	Salazar, S.D.	18	3	0	1	.167
Clark, S.F.	11	3	0	2	.273	Lindeman, St.L.	13	2	0	2	.154
G. Gross, Phil.	55	15	0	7	.273	C. Davis, S.F.	20	3	1	1	.150
Martinez, Chi.	11	3	0	0	.273	Mack, S.D.	20	3	0	2	.150
Stubbs, L.A.	11	3	0	2	.273	Heep, L.A.	35	5	0	4	.143
Engle, Mon.	41	11	1	12	.268	Roenicke, Phil.	38	5	1	1	.132
Reynolds, Pitt.	23	6	0	3	.261	Aguayo, Phil.	18	2	1	1	.111
Steels, S.D.	31	8	0	3	.258	Melendez, S.F.	10	1	1	1	.100
Francona, Cin.	43	11	0	3	.256	James, Atl.	11	1	0	1	.091
Candaele, Mon.	12	3	0	0	.250	Wasinger, S.F.	11	1	0	0	.091
Daulton, Phil.	12	3	0	0	.250	Flannery, S.D.	23	2	0	1	.087
Lopes, Hou.	28	7	0	3	.250	Bochy, S.D.	12	1	0	1	.083
McClendon, Cin.	24	6	1	7	.250	Schu, Phil.	24	2	0	1	.083
C. Reynolds, Hou.	12	3	0	0	.250	Ashby, Hou.	16	1	0	0	.063
Winningham, Mon.	20	5	0	1	.250	Harper, Pitt.	16	1	0	0	.063
Matthews, Chi.	37	9	0	6	.243	Hatcher, L.A.	16	1	0	2	.063
Stone, Phil.	37	9	0	2	.243	Gainey, Hou.	11	0	0	0	.000
Aldrete, S.F.	25	6	1	3	.240	Matuszek, L.A.	13	0	0	0	.000
Jones, Cin.	25	6	1	3	.240						

PINCH-HOMERS FOR 1987

AMERICAN LEAGUE: Baltimore (5)—Dwyer 2, Lynn, Rayford, Sheets. Boston (2)—Greenwell, Henderson. California (9)—Hendrick 3, Howell 2, Jones 2, Ryal 2. Chicago (3)—Hairston 2, Baines. Cleveland (3)—Castillo, Frobel, Parsons. Detroit (1)—Grubb. Kansas City (3)—Balboni 2, Eisenreich. Milwaukee (1)—Kiefer. Minnesota (2)—Salas, Smalley. New York (6)—Pasqua 3, Easler, Salas, Washington. Oakland (3)—Steinbach 2, Jackson. Seattle (3)—Hengel, Kingery, Presley. Texas (6)—Porter 3, Petralli 2, Stanley. Toronto (3)—Beniquez, Fielder, McGriff.

NATIONAL LEAGUE: Atlanta (6)—Nettles 3, Simmons 2, Roenicke. Chicago (8)—Mumphrey 2, Palmeiro 2, Sundberg, Dernier, Trillo. Cincinnati (5)—O'Neill 2, Jones, Larkin, McClendon. Houston—None. Los Angeles (4)—Bryant, Landreaux, Landrum, Trevino. Montreal (2)—Engle, Johnson. New York (7)—Magadan 2, Mazzilli 2, Lyons, Strawberry, Teufel. Philadelphia (4)—Aguayo, James, Roenicke, Russell. Pittsburgh (4)—Diaz 2, Cangelosi, Van Slyke. St. Louis (1)—Oquendo. San Diego (1)—Kruk. San Francisco (11)—Youngblood 3, Leonard 2, Aldrete, Brenly, C. Davis, Maldonado, Melendez, Spilman.

Californians Dominate Debuts

By DAVE SLOAN

Fame can be fleeting, especially for a rookie in major league baseball.

When the Detroit Tigers called up outfielder Billy Bean from their Triple-A affiliate at Toledo (International) on April 25, Manager Sparky Anderson immediately placed the 22-year-old rookie in the starting lineup for that day's home game against the Kansas City Royals.

Bean's debut was nothing short of spectacular. Playing left field and batting leadoff, he had two doubles and two singles in six at-bats, drove in one run and scored twice in pacing the Tigers to a 13-2 victory. Bean doubled on the third pitch thrown by righthander Mark Gubicza, hit safely in his first three plate appearances and became the first major leaguer to get four hits in his debut game since Minnesota's Kirby Puckett on May 8, 1984.

But Bean's success story was short. Five weeks later, after compiling a .258 average in 66 at-bats over 26 games, he was sent back to the Toledo Mud Hens.

Bean was one of 155 players to make his major league debut in 1987, one of 78 in the American League. Pitchers accounted for 69 of the debuts, non-pitchers 86, and nine players made their debut in their club's season-opening game.

Like Bean, outfielder Chris Gwynn of the Los Angeles Dodgers was penciled in the starting lineup by Manager Tommy Lasorda when he was summoned from Class AAA Albuquerque (Pacific Coast) on August 14. Gwynn, the younger brother of San Diego's two-time National League batting champion Tony, singled three times in four at-bats and drove in two runs in a 4-3 win over San Francisco.

Boston's Sam Horn started slowly, striking out in the first inning and hitting into a double play in the third as the Red Sox's designated hitter against Seattle on July 25 at Fenway Park. But Horn homered in his next at-bat for the game-winning RBI in an 11-5 Boston victory. For good measure, Horn homered again and drove in three runs in the Red Sox's 11-1 win over the Mariners the following day.

Houston third baseman Ken Caminiti homered and tripled in three at-bats in the Astros' 2-1 victory over Philadelphia on July 16.

When 22-year-old second baseman Billy Ripken made his debut for the Baltimore Orioles on July 11, he became a part of baseball history. Playing alongside shortstop-brother Cal Ripken Jr., on a team managed by father Cal Sr., it marked the first time in major league history that two brothers played together on a club managed by their father.

It also was the first time brothers had combined to play the keystone positions since the O'Briens (second baseman Johnny and shortstop Eddie) did it for Pittsburgh in 1956.

Two New York pitchers had debut performances that they would prefer to forget.

Bill Fulton of the Yankees yielded consecutive homers to Toronto's Ernie Whitt, Jesse Barfield and Kelly Gruber in the eighth inning of a 13-1 Blue Jays victory on September 12. Fulton gave up five earned runs in 1⅔ innings but was not tagged with the defeat.

Jeff Innis of the Mets yielded a 10th-inning homer to San Francisco's Jeffrey Leonard and took a 5-4 loss May 16, just hours after being called up from the Mets' Triple-A affiliate at Tidewater (International).

Relief pitcher Mike Henneman, who debuted with the Tigers on May 11, won his first eight decisions in the major leagues and finished the season with an 11-3 record. He played an important part in Detroit's run to the American League Eastern Division title.

Lefthander Joe Magrane of the Cardinals had a memorable rookie season. Magrane beat the defending world champion New York Mets, 3-2, at Shea Stadium on April 25. Exactly six months later to the day, Magrane started Game 7 of the World Series against the Minnesota Twins.

The youngest player to make his debut was 20-year-old infielder Gregg Jefferies of the Mets, who pinch-hit against the Dodgers on September 6. The oldest player was pitcher Ubaldo Heredia of the Expos, who was 31 when he threw his first major league pitch May 12 against Cincinnati.

Thirty players making debuts in 1987 were native Californians, far and away the most from any state. Texas and Illinois were next with nine apiece. Twenty-one debuts were made by foreign-born players.

An alphabetical list of the players who made their debuts in '87 follows:

Player	Pos.	Club	Date and Place of Birth	Debut
Abner, Shawn Wesley	PH	San Diego	6-17-66—Hamilton, O.	9- 8
Afenir, Michael Troy	PH	Houston	9-21-63—Escondido, Calif.	9-14
Aldrich, Jay Robert	P	Milwaukee	4-14-61—Alexandria, La.	6- 5
Anderson, Scott Richard	P	Texas	8- 1-62—Corvallis, Ore.	4- 8
Ballard, Jeffrey Scott	P	Baltimore	8-13-63—Billings, Mont.	5- 9
Bean, William Daro	OF	Detroit	5-11-64—Santa Ana, Calif.	4-25
Belcher, Timothy Wayne	P	Los Angeles	10-19-61—Mount Gilead, O.	9- 6
Benzinger, Todd Eric	PH	Boston	2-11-63—Dayton, Ky.	6-21
Berryhill, Damon Scott	C	Chicago N.L.	12- 3-63—South Laguna, Calif.	9- 5
Blauser, Jeffrey Michael	PH	Atlanta	11- 8-65—Los Gatos, Calif.	7- 5
Bolton, Thomas Edward	P	Boston	5- 6-62—Nashville, Tenn.	5-17
Booker, Roderick Stewart	2B	St. Louis	9- 4-58—Los Angeles, Calif.	4-29
Brumley, Anthony Michael	SS	Chicago N.L.	4- 9-63—Oklahoma City, Okla.	6-16
Buhner, Jay Campbell	OF	New York A.L.	8-13-64—Louisville, Ky.	9-11
Buice, DeWayne Allison	P	California	8-20-57—Lynwood, Calif.	4-25
Burkett, John David	P	San Francisco	11-28-64—New Brighton, Pa.	9-15
Burks, Ellis Rena	OF	Boston	9-11-64—Vicksburg, Miss.	4-30
Byers, Randell Parker	PH	San Diego	10- 2-64—Bridgeton, N.J.	9- 7
Cadaret, Gregory James	P	Oakland	2-27-62—Detroit, Mich.	7- 5
Caminiti, Kenneth Gene	3B	Houston	4-21-63—Hanford, Calif.	7-16
Campbell, Michael Thomas	P	Seattle	2-17-64—Seattle, Wash.	7- 4
Carreon, Mark Steven	PH	New York N.L.	7-19-63—Chicago, Ill.	9- 8
Ciardi, Mark Thomas	P	Milwaukee	8-19-61—New Brunswick, N.J.	4- 9
Clary, Martin Keith	P	Atlanta	4- 3-62—Detroit, Mich.	9- 5
Coffman, Kevin Reese	P	Atlanta	1-19-65—Austin, Tex.	9- 5
Cora, Jose Manuel	2B	San Diego	5-14-65—Caguas, P.R.	4- 6
Crews, Stanley Timothy	P	Los Angeles	4- 3-61—Ocoee, Fla.	7-27
Crim, Charles Robert	P	Milwaukee	7-23-61—Van Nuys, Calif.	4- 8
Daugherty, John Michael	PH	Montreal	6- 3-60—Hialeah, Fla.	9- 1
Davis, John Kirk	P	Kansas City	1- 5-63—Chicago, Ill.	7-24
Destrade, Orestes	PH	New York A.L.	5- 8-62—Santiago, Cuba	9-11
Devereaux, Michael	OF	Los Angeles	4-10-63—Casper, Wyo.	9- 2
DeWillis, Jeffrey Allen	C	Toronto	4-13-65—Houston, Tex.	4-19
Diaz, Mario Rafael	SS	Seattle	1-10-62—Humacao, P.R.	9-12
Dorsett, Brian Richard	PH	Cleveland	4- 9-61—Terre Haute, Ind.	9- 8
Dowell, Kenneth Allen	SS	Philadelphia	1-19-61—Sacramento, Calif.	6-24
Drummond, Timothy Darnell	P	Pittsburgh	12-24-64—La Plata, Md.	9-12
Ducey, Robert Thomas	OF	Toronto	5-24-65—Toronto, Can.	5- 1
Dunne, Michael Dennis	P	Pittsburgh	10-27-62—South Bend, Ind.	6- 5
Easley, Kenneth Logan	P	Pittsburgh	11- 4-61—Salt Lake City, Utah	4- 9
Edens, Thomas Patrick	P	New York N.L.	6- 9-61—Ontario, Ore.	6- 2
Eppard, James Gerhard	PH	California	4-27-60—South Bend, Ind.	9- 8
Farrell, John Edward	P	Cleveland	8- 4-62—Monmouth Park, N.J.	8-18
Fermin, Felix Jose	SS	Pittsburgh	10- 9-63—Mao, Valverde, D.R.	7- 8
Fischer, Jeffrey Thomas	P	Montreal	8-17-63—West Palm Beach, Fla.	6-19
Frohwirth, Todd Gerald	P	Philadelphia	9-28-62—Milwaukee, Wis.	8-10
Fulton, William David	P	New York A.L.	10-22-63—Pittsburgh, Pa.	9-12
Gallagher, David Thomas	OF	Cleveland	9-20-60—Trenton, N.J.	4-12
Gant, Ronald Edwin	PH	Atlanta	3- 2-65—Victoria, Tex.	9- 6
Garcia, Leonardo Antonio	PH	Cincinnati	11- 6-62—Santiago, D.R.	4- 6
Garcia, Miguel Angel	P	California	4-19-66—Caracas, Venezuela	4-30
Gideon, Byron Brett	P	Pittsburgh	8- 8-63—Georgetown, Tex.	7- 5
Glavine, Thomas Michael	P	Atlanta	3-25-66—Concord, Mass.	8-17
Gregg, William Thomas	PH	Pittsburgh	7-29-63—Boone, N.C.	9-14
Gwynn, Christopher Karlton	OF	Los Angeles	10-13-64—Long Beach, Calif.	8-14
Harvey, Bryan Stanley	P	California	6- 2-63—Chattanooga, Tenn.	5-16
Henneman, Michael Alan	P	Detroit	12-11-61—St. Charles, Mo.	5-11
Heredia, Ubaldo Jose	P	Montreal	4- 5-56—Isla Margarita, Ven.	5-12
Hillegas, Shawn Patrick	P	Los Angeles	8-21-64—Dos Palos, Calif.	8- 9
Hinzo, Thomas Lee	2B	Cleveland	6-18-64—San Diego, Calif.	7-16
Horn, Samuel Lee	DH	Boston	11- 2-63—Dallas, Tex.	7-25
Hughes, Keith Wills	PH	New York A.L.	9-12-63—Bryn Mawr, Pa.	5-19
Infante, Fermin Alexis	PR	Toronto	12- 4-62—Barquisimeto, Ven.	9-27
Innis, Jeffrey David	P	New York N.L.	7- 5-62—Decatur, Ill.	5-16
Jackson, Charles Leo	3B	Houston	3-19-63—Seattle, Wash.	5-26
Jackson, Kenneth Bernard	SS	Philadelphia	8-21-63—Shreveport, La.	9-12
Jefferies, Gregory Scott	PH	New York N.L.	8- 1-67—Burlingame, Calif.	9- 6
Jelks, Gregory Dion	3B	Philadelphia	8-16-61—Cherokee, Ala.	8-20
Johnson, David Wayne	P	Pittsburgh	10-24-59—Middle River, Md.	5-29
Johnson, Kenneth Lance	PH	St. Louis	7- 7-63—Lincoln Heights, O.	7-10
Kelly, Roberto Conrado	OF	New York A.L.	10- 1-64—Panama City, Pan.	7-29
Kilgus, Paul Nelson	P	Texas	2- 2-62—Bowling Green, Ky.	6- 7
Klink, Joseph Charles	P	Minnesota	2- 3-62—Johnstown, Pa.	4- 9
Lancaster, Lester Wayne	P	Chicago N.L.	4-21-62—Dallas, Tex.	4- 7
Larkin, Eugene Thomas	DH	Minnesota	10-24-62—Flushing, N.Y.	5-22
Leister, John William	P	Boston	1- 3-61—San Antonio, Tex.	5-28
Leiter, Alois Terry	P	New York A.L.	10-23-65—Toms River, N.J.	9-15
Lind, Jose	2B	Pittsburgh	5- 1-64—Toabaja, P.R.	8-28
Lindsey, William Donald	C	Chicago A.L.	4-12-60—Staten Island, N.Y.	7-18

Player	Pos.	Club	Date and Place of Birth	Debut
Liriano, Nelson Arturo	2B	Toronto	6- 3-64—Puerto Plata, D.R.	8-25
Lusader, Scott Edward	DH	Detroit	9-30-64—Chicago, Ill.	9- 1
Macfarlane, Michael Andrew	C	Kansas City	4-12-64—Stockton, Calif.	7-23
Mack, Shane Lee	OF	San Diego	12- 7-63—Los Angeles, Calif.	5-25
Madden, Morris DeWayne	P	Detroit	8-31-60—Laurens, S.C.	6-11
Madrid, Alexander	P	Milwaukee	4-18-63—Springerville, Ariz.	7-20
Magrane, Joseph David	P	St. Louis	7- 2-64—Des Moines, Ia.	4-25
Mallicoat, Robin Dale	P	Houston	11-16-64—St. Helens, Ore.	9-11
Malloy, Robert William	P	Texas	11-24-64—Garland, Tex.	5-26
Manwaring, Kirt Dean	C	San Francisco	7-15-65—Elmira, N.Y.	9-15
Martinez, Edgar	3B	Seattle	1- 2-63—New York, N.Y.	9-12
Marzano, John Robert	C	Boston	2-14-63—Philadelphia, Pa.	7-31
McClendon, Lloyd Glenn	PH	Cincinnati	1-11-59—Gary, Ind.	4- 6
McDowell, Jack Burns	P	Chicago A.L.	1-16-66—Van Nuys, Calif.	9-15
McGriff, Terence Roy	C	Cincinnati	9-23-63—Fort Pierce, Fla.	7-11
Meads, David Donald	P	Houston	1- 7-64—Montclair, N.J.	4-13
Mesa, Jose Ramon	P	Baltimore	5-22-66—Azua, D.R.	9-10
Mielke, Gary Roger	P	Texas	1-28-63—St. James, Minn.	8-19
Miller, Keith Alan	2B	New York N.L.	6-12-63—Midland, Mich.	6-16
Milligan, Randall Andre	PH	New York N.L.	11-27-61—San Diego, Calif.	9-12
Monteleone, Richard	P	Seattle	3-22-63—Tampa, Fla.	4-15
Montgomery, Jeffrey Thomas	P	Cincinnati	1- 7-62—Wellston, O.	8- 1
Myers, Gregory Richard	C	Toronto	4-14-66—Riverside, Calif.	9-12
Newell, Thomas Dean	P	Philadelphia	5-17-63—Covina, Calif.	9- 9
Nixon, Robert Donell	OF	Seattle	12-31-61—Evergreen, N.C.	4- 7
Noce, Paul David	2B	Chicago N.L.	12-16-59—San Francisco, Calif.	6- 1
Nolte, Eric Carl	P	San Diego	4-28-64—Canoga Park, Calif.	8- 1
Nunez, Jose	P	Toronto	1-13-64—Jarabocoa, D.R.	4- 9
Otto, David Alan	P	Oakland	11-12-64—Chicago, Ill.	9- 8
Pacillo, Patrick Michael	P	Cincinnati	7-23-63—Rutherford, N.J.	5-23
Paciorek, James Joseph	1B	Milwaukee	6- 7-60—Detroit, Mich.	4- 9
Pagnozzi, Thomas Alan	C	St. Louis	7-30-62—Tucson, Ariz.	4-12
Palacios, Vicente	P	Pittsburgh	7-19-63—Veracruz, Mex.	9- 4
Parker, James Clayton	P	Seattle	12-19-62—Columbia, La.	9-14
Pawlowski, John	P	Chicago A.L.	9- 6-63—Johnson City, N.Y.	9-19
Pedrique, Alfredo Jose	SS	New York N.L.	8-11-60—Aragua, Venezuela	4-14
Perez, Melido Gross	P	Kansas City	2-15-66—San Cristobal, D.R.	9- 4
Peters, Steven Bradley	P	St. Louis	11-14-62—Oklahoma City, Okla.	8-11
Peterson, Adam Charles	P	Chicago A.L.	12-11-65—Long Beach, Calif.	9-19
Polonia, Luis Andrew	OF	Oakland	10-12-64—Santiago City, D.R.	4-24
Powell, Alonzo Sidney	OF	Montreal	12-12-64—San Francisco, Calif.	4- 6
Prince, Thomas Albert	C	Pittsburgh	8-13-64—Kankakee, Ill.	9-22
Ramsey, Michael James	OF	Los Angeles	7- 8-60—Harlem, Ga.	4- 6
Reed, Jody Eric	PR	Boston	7-26-62—Tampa, Fla.	9-12
Reid, Jessie Thomas	PH	San Francisco	6- 1-62—Honolulu, Haw.	9- 9
Ripken, William Oliver	2B	Baltimore	12-16-64—Havre de Grace, Md.	7-11
Ritchie, Wallace Reid	P	Philadelphia	7-12-65—Glendale, Calif.	5- 1
Robinson, Jeffrey Mark	P	Detroit	12-14-61—Ventura, Calif.	4-12
Romano, Thomas Michael	PH	Montreal	10-25-58—Syracuse, N.Y.	9- 1
Santovenia, Nelson Gil	C	Montreal	7-27-61—Pino del Rio, Cuba	9-16
Sasser, Mackey Daniel	PH	San Francisco	8- 3-62—Fort Gaines, Ga.	7-17
Savage, John Joseph	P	Los Angeles	4-22-64—Louisville, Ky.	9-14
Sharperson, Michael Tyrone	2B	Toronto	10- 4-60—Orangeburg, S.C.	4- 6
Sheaffer, Danny Todd	C	Boston	8- 2-61—Jacksonville, Fla.	4- 9
Smith, Brick Dudley	1B	Seattle	5- 2-59—Charlotte, N.C.	9-13
Smith, Peter John	P	Atlanta	2-27-66—Abington, Mass.	9- 8
Stanicek, Peter Louis	DH	Baltimore	4-16-63—Harvey, Ill.	9- 1
Stanicek, Stephen Blair	PH	Milwaukee	6- 9-61—Lake Forest, Ill.	9-16
Stapleton, David Earl	P	Milwaukee	10-16-61—Miami, Ariz.	9-14
Stark, Matthew Scott	C	Toronto	1-21-65—Whittier, Calif.	4- 8
Steels, James Earl	OF	San Diego	5-30-61—Jackson, Miss.	4- 6
Straker, Lester Paul	P	Minnesota	10-10-59—Ciudad Bolivar, Ven.	4-11
Surhoff, William James	C	Milwaukee	8- 4-64—Bronx, N.Y.	4- 8
Tabor, Greg Steven	DH	Texas	5-21-61—Castro Valley, Calif.	9-10
Taylor, Donald Clyde	P	Pittsburgh	8-11-58—Abington, Pa.	4-30
Thurman, Gary Montez	OF	Kansas City	11-12-64—Indianapolis, Ind.	8-30
Treadway, Hugh Jeffrey	2B	Cincinnati	1-22-63—Columbus, Ga.	9- 4
Velarde, Randy Lee	SS	New York A.L.	11-24-62—Midland, Tex.	8-20
Walewander, James	2B	Detroit	5- 2-61—Chicago, Ill.	5-31
Weiss, Walter William	PR	Oakland	11-28-63—Tuxedo, N.Y.	7-12
Wells, David Lee	P	Toronto	5-20-63—Torrance, Calif.	6-30
Williams, Matthew Derrick	SS	San Francisco	11-28-65—Bishop, Calif.	4-11
Williamson, Mark Alan	P	Baltimore	7-21-59—Lemon Grove, Calif.	4- 8
Woodson, Tracy Michael	1B-3B	Los Angeles	10- 5-62—Richmond, Va.	4- 7
Young, Gerald Anthony	OF	Houston	10-22-64—Tele, Honduras	7- 8
Ziem, Stephen Graeling	P	Atlanta	10-24-61—Milwaukee, Wis.	4-30

Homers by Parks for 1987

National League

	At Atl.	At Chi.	At Cin.	At Hou.	At L.A.	At Mont.	At N.Y.	At Phil.	At Pitt.	At St.L.	At S.D.	At S.F.	Totals 1987	1986
Atlanta	82	7	12	4	8	2	6	7	6	6	6	6	152	138
Chicago	7	114	6	6	8	14	9	17	8	4	10	6	209	155
Cincinnati	22	9	94	5	9	7	3	11	7	7	10	8	192	144
Houston	5	7	13	51	6	3	5	2	4	3	6	17	122	125
Los Angeles	8	8	9	5	52	5	5	2	3	8	14	6	125	130
Montreal	6	6	5	2	2	62	9	6	12	4	3	3	120	110
New York	3	17	6	7	5	10	93	10	20	6	10	5	192	148
Philadelphia	6	10	13	5	4	14	9	80	6	8	9	5	169	154
Pittsburgh	5	11	11	0	2	3	7	9	71	1	7	4	131	111
St. Louis	2	6	2	3	5	7	3	5	9	42	6	4	94	58
San Diego	11	3	7	3	3	3	4	3	4	4	60	8	113	136
San Francisco	13	6	13	6	4	6	3	6	5	9	16	118	205	114
1987 Totals	170	204	191	97	108	136	156	158	155	102	157	190	1824	......
1986 Totals	148	168	159	105	103	98	124	135	124	90	158	111	......	1523

AT ATLANTA (170): Atlanta (82)—Murphy 25, Virgil 15, Griffey 8, Roenicke 8, James 5, Thomas 4, Hall 3, Hubbard 3, Nettles 2, Oberkfell 2, Perry 2, Benedict, Blauser, Gant, Runge, Simmons. **Chicago** (7)—J. Davis 2, Dawson 2, Sandberg 2, Palmeiro. **Cincinnati** (22)—Bell 3, Daniels 3, Davis 3, Parker 3, Esasky 2, Larkin 2, Garcia, Jones, McClendon, McGriff, Oester, Stillwell. **Houston** (5)—Bass 2, Davis, Doran, Ryan. **Los Angeles** (8)—Guerrero 2, Marshall 2, Shelby 2, Bryant, Stubbs. **Montreal** (6)—Wallach 3, Galarraga, Law, Raines. **New York** (3)—Strawberry 2, Johnson. **Philadelphia** (6)—Schmidt 2, Hayes, James, Samuel, Thompson. **Pittsburgh** (5)—Diaz 2, Bonds, Coles, Van Slyke. **St. Louis** (2)—Clark, Morris. **San Diego** (11)—Kruk 4, Jefferson 2, Bochy, Brown, Gwynn, Salazar, Santiago. **San Francisco** (13)—C. Davis 3, Brown 2, Clark 2, Leonard 2, Maldonado 2, Brenly, Thompson.

AT CHICAGO (204): Atlanta (7)—Murphy 3, James 2, Perry, Puleo. **Chicago** (114)—Dawson 27, Moreland 19, Durham 16, Sandberg 8, J. Davis 7, Mumphrey 7, Trillo 6, Martinez 5, Palmeiro 5, Dernier 4, Dunston 3, Noce 3, Sundberg 2, Dayett 2, Sanderson. **Cincinnati** (9)—Diaz 2, Larkin 2, Davis, Esasky, Jones, O'Neill, Parker. **Houston** (7)—Bass 2, Doran 2, Hatcher 2, Cruz. **Los Angeles** (8)—Guerrero 2, Shelby 2, Hatcher, Landreaux, Madlock, Stubbs. **Montreal** (6)—Webster 2, Brooks, Foley, Law, Wallach. **New York** (17)—Johnson 4, Teufel 4, Hernandez 3, McReynolds 3, Carter, Dykstra, Strawberry, Wilson. **Philadelphia** (10)—James 3, Aguayo, Daulton, Parrish, Russell, Samuel, Schu, Thompson. **Pittsburgh** (11)—Bonds 3, Morrison 2, Reynolds 2, Bream, Diaz, Harper, J. Robinson, Van Slyke. **St. Louis** (6)—Pendleton 3, Clark, Driessen, McGee. **San Diego** (3)—Brown, Kruk, Templeton. **San Francisco** (6)—Mitchell 2, Brown, C. Davis, Leonard, Williams.

AT CINCINNATI (191): Atlanta (12)—Griffey 3, Perry 2, Virgil 2, Murphy, Palmer, Ramirez, Roenicke, Simmons. **Chicago** (6)—Dawson 2, J. Davis, Durham, Palmeiro, Sandberg. **Cincinnati** (94)—Davis 17, Parker 14, Daniels 13, Esasky 10, Bell 8, Diaz 8, Larkin 6, Jones 4, O'Neill 4, Stillwell 3, Francona 2, Treadway 2, Concepcion, McGriff, Power. **Houston** (13)—Ashby 2, Bass 2, Doran 2, Cruz, Davis, Garner, Hatcher, Pankovits, Puhl, Walling. **Los Angeles** (9)—Shelby 4, Marshall 3, Guerrero, Sax. **Montreal** (5)—Law 3, Wallach, Webster. **New York** (6)—Johnson 2, Teufel 2, Dykstra, Wilson. **Philadelphia** (13)—Parrish 3, Wilson 3, Aguayo 2, Schmidt 2, Hayes, Roenicke, Samuel. **Pittsburgh** (11)—Bonds 4, Bonilla 3, Cangelosi, Fisher, Reuschel, Van Slyke. **St. Louis** (7)—Lindeman, Pena. **San Diego** (7)—Kruk 2, Ready 2, Garvey, Jones, Mitchell. **San Francisco** (13)—Clark 4, C. Davis 2, Mitchell 2, Maldonado, Melvin, Speier, Williams, Youngblood.

AT HOUSTON (97): Atlanta (4)—Blauser, Griffey, Murphy, Runge. **Chicago** (6)—Dayett 2, Sandberg 2, Dunston, Trillo. **Cincinnati** (5)—Parker 2, Daniels, Jones, Oester. **Houston** (51)—Davis 12, Bass 10, Ashby 8, Doran 7, Cruz 6, Hatcher 3, Caminiti 2, Walling 2, Puhl. **Los Angeles** (5)—Stubbs 2, Anderson, Marshall, Shelby. **Montreal** (2)—Brooks, Law. **New York** (7)—Johnson 4, McReynolds 3. **Philadelphia** (5)—Samuel 3, Schmidt 2. **Pittsburgh**—None. **St. Louis** (3)—Clark 3. **San Diego** (3)—Salazar, Santiago, Templeton. **San Francisco** (6)—Mitchell 3, Clark 2, C. Davis.

AT LOS ANGELES (108): Atlanta (8)—Murphy 4, Perry 2, James, Thomas. **Chicago** (8)—Dawson 4, Dayett, Dunston, Martinez, Moreland. **Cincinnati** (9)—Davis 2, Esasky 2, Bell, Daniels, Diaz, Jones, Parker. **Houston** (6)—Bass, Davis, Doran, Garner, Hatcher, Walling. **Los Angeles** (52)—Guerrero 12, Shelby 8, Stubbs 6, Marshall 5, Hatcher 4, Landreaux 4, Duncan 3, Sax 2, Scioscia 2, Trevino 2, Landrum, Madlock, Valenzuela, Woodson. **Montreal** (2)—Wallach, Winningham. **New York** (5)—McReynolds 2, Aguilera, Hernandez, Strawberry. **Philadelphia** (4)—Parrish, Samuel, Schmidt, Schu. **Pittsburgh** (2)—Bream, Cangelosi. **St. Louis** (5)—Clark 3, McGee, Pendleton. **San Diego** (3)—Mitchell 2, Ready. **San Francisco** (4)—C. Davis 2, Brown, Clark.

AT MONTREAL (136): Atlanta (2)—Murphy, Virgil. **Chicago** (14)—Durham 4, Dawson 3, Moreland 2, Mumphrey 2, Palmeiro 2, Dernier. **Cincinnati** (7)—Davis 2, Parker 2, Diaz, Francona, Larkin. **Houston** (3)—Ashby, Doran, Garner. **Los Angeles** (5)—Guerrero, Landreaux, Madlock, Sax, Scioscia. **Montreal** (62)—Wallach 13, Brooks 9, Raines 9, Webster 9, Galarraga 7, Foley 3, Law 3, Nichols 3, Winningham 2, Candaele, Engle, Fitzgerald, Reed. **New York** (10)—Strawberry 4, Johnson 2, McReynolds 2, Carter, Dykstra. **Philadelphia** (14)—Schmidt 4, Hayes 2, Samuel 2, Aguayo, Daulton, K. Gross, James, Parrish, Wilson. **Pittsburgh** (3)—Bonds 2, Van Slyke. **St. Louis** (7)—Ford 2, Pena 2, Clark, Lindeman, McGee. **San Diego** (3)—Kruk 2, Gwynn. **San Francisco** (6)—Leonard 3, Melvin 2, Aldrete.

AT NEW YORK (156): Atlanta (6)—Murphy 3, James, Oberkfell, Virgil. **Chicago** (9)—Dawson 3, J. Davis 2, Brumley, Durham, Moreland, Sandberg. **Cincinnati** (3)—Bell, Diaz, Esasky. **Houston** (5)—Davis 3, Hatcher 2. **Los Angeles** (5)—Guerrero 3, Bryant, Shelby. **Montreal** (9)—Raines 3, Brooks, Fitzgerald, Foley, Galarraga, Johnson, Stefero. **New York** (93)—Strawberry 20, McReynolds 18, Johnson 13, Carter 9, Dykstra 7, Hernandez 6, Wilson 5, Lyons 4, Teufel 4, Mazzilli 3, Magadan 2, Santana 2.

Philadelphia (9)—Wilson 3, Parrish 2, James, Russell, Samuel, Schmidt. **Pittsburgh (7)**—Van Slyke 3, Bonds, Diaz, Prince, Reynolds. **St. Louis (3)**—Clark 2, Pendleton. **San Diego (4)**—Kruk 2, Martinez, Ready. **San Francisco (3)**—Brenly, Clark, Leonard.

AT PHILADELPHIA (158): Atlanta (7)—Virgil 3, Murphy 2, Hubbard, Perry. **Chicago (17)**—Dernier 3, Mumphrey 3, J. Davis 2, Dawson 2, Martinez 2, Dayett, Durham, Moreland, Rowdon, Sundberg. **Cincinnati (11)**—Davis 5, Bell 2, Daniels, Diaz, Gullickson, O'Neill. **Houston (2)**—Davis, Lopes. **Los Angeles (2)**—Guerrero, Hatcher. **Montreal (6)**—Brooks 2, Law, Wallach, Webster, Youmans. **New York (10)**—Strawberry 3, Carter 2, Johnson 2, Hernandez, Santana, Teufel. **Philadelphia (80)**—Samuel 15, Schmidt 15, Hayes 14, James 9, Aguayo 5, Parrish 5, Schu 5, Wilson 5, Thompson 3, Daulton, Easler, Russell, Stone. **Pittsburgh (9)**—Bonilla 3, Diaz 2, Bream, Ortiz, Reynolds, Van Slyke. **St. Louis (5)**—Clark 2, Herr, Morris, Pena. **San Diego (3)**—Santiago 2, Mitchell. **San Francisco (6)**—Speier 2, Brenly, Maldonado, Thompson, Uribe.

AT PITTSBURGH (155): Atlanta (6)—Virgil 3, Simmons 2, Perry. **Chicago (8)**—Palmeiro 4, Dawson 2, Durham, Sundberg. **Cincinnati (7)**—Davis 2, Daniels, Esasky, Jones, O'Neill, Parker. **Houston (4)**—Ashby, Cruz, Davis, Thon. **Los Angeles (3)**—Duncan, Guerrero, Stubbs. **Montreal (12)**—Raines 4, Galarraga 2, Webster 2, Fitzgerald, Law, Nichols, Wallach. **New York (20)**—Carter 3, Hernandez 3, Strawberry 3, Teufel 3, Johnson 2, McReynolds 2, Wilson 2, Magadan, Santana. **Philadelphia (6)**—Hayes 2, Schmidt 2, Parrish, Thompson. **Pittsburgh (71)**—Bonds 12, Van Slyke 11, Bream 10, Diaz 9, Bonilla 7, Morrison 6, Coles 5, Ray 5, Cangelosi 2, Reynolds 2, Fisher, LaValliere. **St. Louis (9)**—Lindeman 4, Clark 2, Laga, Lake, Pendleton. **San Diego (4)**—Jefferson, Kruk, Mack, Santiago. **San Francisco (5)**—Aldrete, Brenly, Clark, C. Davis, Leonard.

AT ST. LOUIS (102): Atlanta (6)—Griffey 2, Murphy 2, Perry, Virgil. **Chicago (4)**—Dawson 2, J. Davis, Moreland. **Cincinnati (7)**—Bell, Daniels, Davis, Diaz, Esasky, Jones, McClendon. **Houston (3)**—Bass, Davis, Hatcher. **Los Angeles (6)**—Guerrero 2, Duncan, Garner, Hatcher, Marshall, Scioscia, Trevino. **Montreal (4)**—Wallach 2, Galarraga, Law. **New York (6)**—Johnson 3, Carter, Hernandez, Strawberry. **Philadelphia (8)**—Schmidt 5, Parrish 2, Thompson. **Pittsburgh (1)**—Diaz. **St. Louis (42)**—Clark 17, McGee 6, Pendleton 5, Coleman 3, Lindeman 2, Pagnozzi 2, Ford, Green, Herr, Lake, Magrane, Morris, Pena. **San Diego (4)**—Brown, Ready, Santiago, Templeton. **San Francisco (9)**—C. Davis 3, Brenly 2, Speier 2, Maldonado, Mitchell.

AT SAN DIEGO (157): Atlanta (6)—Nettles 2, Perry 2, Murphy, Virgil. **Chicago (10)**—J. Davis 2, Dawson 2, Durham 2, Moreland, Mumphrey, Palmeiro, Sandberg. **Cincinnati (10)**—Esasky 3, Daniels 2, Parker 2, Bell, Butera, Davis. **Houston (6)**—Davis 3, Ashby, Jackson, R. Reynolds. **Los Angeles (14)**—Marshall 3, Shelby 3, Stubbs 3, Guerrero 2, Duncan, Sax, Scioscia. **Montreal (3)**—Wallach 2, Galarraga. **New York (10)**—Hernandez 3, Johnson 2, Strawberry 2, Backman, Carter, Santana. **Philadelphia (9)**—Aguayo 3, G. Gross, Hayes, James, Samuel, Schmidt, Wilson. **Pittsburgh (7)**—Bonds 3, Belliard, Bonilla, Reynolds, Van Slyke. **St. Louis (6)**—Clark 3, Barnes, Forsch, McGee. **San Diego (60)**—Santiago 11, Martinez 10, Kruk 8, Ready 7, Gwynn 5, Jefferson 5, Brown 3, Mack 2, Mitchell 2, Templeton 2, Wynne 2, Abner, Bochy, Salazar. **San Francisco (16)**—Brenly 2, Clark 2, C. Davis 2, Leonard 2, Melvin 2, Gott, Maldonado, Reid, D. Robinson, Thompson, Williams.

AT SAN FRANCISCO (190): Atlanta (6)—Gant, Hubbard, James, Murphy, Nettles, Runge. **Chicago (6)**—J. Davis 2, Durham, Moreland, Sandberg, Trillo. **Cincinnati (8)**—Daniels 3, Davis 3, Esasky, Larkin. **Houston (17)**—C. Reynolds 4, Davis 3, Cruz 2, Doran 2, Ashby, Bass, Caminiti, Hatcher, Walling, Young. **Los Angeles (6)**—Stubbs 2, Garner, Marshall, Sax, Scioscia. **Montreal (3)**—Raines, Wallach, Winningham. **New York (5)**—Carter 2, Strawberry 2, Johnson. **Philadelphia (5)**—Samuel 2, James, Parrish, Wilson. **Pittsburgh (4)**—Bonilla, Morrison, Pedrique, Van Slyke. **St. Louis (4)**—Forsch, McGee, Oquendo, Pendleton. **San Diego (6)**—Martinez 4, Abner, Mack, Mitchell, Santiago. **San Francisco (118)**—Clark 22, Maldonado 14, Brenly 10, C. Davis 9, Leonard 9, Aldrete 7, Mitchell 7, Thompson 7, Melvin 6, Speier 6, Williams 5, Milner 4, Uribe 4, Brown 2, Youngblood 2, Melendez, Spilman, Wasinger, Wilfong.

American League

	At Balt.	At Bos.	At Cal.	At Chi.	At Clev.	At Det.	At K.C.	At Mil.	At Min.	At N.Y.	At Oak.	At Sea.	At Tex.	At Tor.	Totals 1987	1986
Baltimore	110	2	11	17	14	7	5	5	4	5	8	10	11	2	211	169
Boston	8	86	12	4	9	3	7	6	8	4	3	11	7	6	174	144
California	11	4	88	9	6	3	4	6	9	8	4	8	5	7	172	167
Chicago	12	7	12	72	2	7	2	6	9	8	9	5	15	7	173	121
Cleveland	10	12	11	5	94	6	5	5	7	7	4	7	5	9	187	157
Detroit	14	10	10	7	7	125	2	8	7	8	4	5	9	9	225	198
Kansas City	4	5	10	11	9	10	73	5	7	3	5	12	11	3	168	137
Milwaukee	12	2	6	5	12	10	3	72	4	6	8	8	7	8	163	127
Minnesota	7	12	3	8	5	12	3	9	106	6	4	9	7	5	196	196
New York	6	8	8	4	11	8	2	6	8	98	8	13	7	9	196	188
Oakland	7	4	11	4	18	13	11	7	4	10	88	7	8	7	199	163
Seattle	10	1	6	4	5	7	1	4	5	5	2	103	6	2	161	158
Texas	11	2	10	2	12	8	9	6	9	6	11	6	93	9	194	184
Toronto	13	6	6	10	8	7	3	6	11	12	5	14	13	101	215	181
1987 Totals	235	161	204	162	212	226	130	151	198	186	163	218	204	184	2634	
1986 Totals	189	140	172	114	160	179	106	142	223	189	156	196	148	176		2290

AT BALTIMORE (235): Baltimore (110)—Sheets 21, C. Ripken 17, Murray 14, Kennedy 11, Lynn 11, Young 11, Knight 8, Gerhart 5, Dwyer 3, Burleson 2, Hart 2, Lacy 2, Gonzales, Rayford, Van Gorder. **Boston (8)**—Burks 2, Horn 2, Barrett, Benzinger, Dodson, Evans. **California (11)**—Joyner 3, Downing 2, Howell 2, Armas, DeCinces, Jones, Schofield. **Chicago (12)**—Walker 3, Calderon 2, Fisk 2, Baines, Boston, Hassey, Hulett, Redus. **Cleveland (10)**—Carter 4, Snyder 4, Butler, Hall. **Detroit (14)**—Nokes 3, Trammell 3, Evans 2, Gibson 2, Lemon 2, Madlock, Whitaker. **Kansas City (4)**—Salazar, Seitzer, Smith, White. **Milwaukee (12)**—Sveum 3, Brock 2, Molitor 2, Braggs, Deer, Gantner, Riles, Yount. **Minnesota**

(7)—Brunansky 2, Bush, Gaetti, Hrbek, Laudner, Nieto. **New York (6)**—Winfield 2, Henderson, Mattingly, Ward, Washington. **Oakland (7)**—McGwire 2, Canseco, M. Davis, Lansford, Phillips, Tettleton. **Seattle (10)**—Presley 3, Phelps 2, Valle 2, P. Bradley, Kingery, Quinones. **Texas (11)**—McDowell 2, Parrish 2, Sierra 2, Buechele, Incaviglia, O'Malley, Slaught, Stanley. **Toronto (13)**—Bell 3, Barfield 2, Fernandez 2, Gruber 2, Beniquez, Moseby, Upshaw, Whitt.

AT BOSTON (161): Baltimore (2)—Murray, Sheets. **Boston (86)**—Evans 14, Burks 11, Baylor 10, Boggs 10, Greenwell 8, Rice 7, Horn 6, Benzinger 5, Henderson 4, Marzano 4, Barrett 2, Owen 2, Dodson, Gedman, Sullivan. **California (4)**—Downing, Joyner, Miller, White. **Chicago (7)**—Fisk 4, Baines, Hassey, Walker. **Cleveland (12)**—Carter 7, Tabler 2, Bernazard, Castillo, Snyder. **Detroit (10)**—Brookens 2, Nokes 2, Trammell 2, Herndon, Lemon, Madlock, Sheridan. **Kansas City (5)**—White 2, Owen, Seitzer, Tartabull. **Milwaukee (2)**—Schroeder, Yount. **Minnesota (12)**—Brunansky 4, Gaetti 3, Hrbek 3, Gladden, Smalley. **New York (8)**—Pagliarulo 3, Cerone, Pasqua, Randolph, Ward, Washington. **Oakland (4)**—Canseco, Lansford, McGwire, Tettleton. **Seattle (1)**—Nixon. **Texas (2)**—Incaviglia, Petralli. **Toronto (6)**—Barfield 3, Gruber, Iorg, Upshaw.

AT CALIFORNIA (204): Baltimore (11)—Lynn 4, Dwyer 3, Kennedy 3, Murray. **Boston (12)**—Boggs 4, Evans 4, Baylor 2, Henderson, Rice. **California (88)**—Joyner 19, Howell 15, Downing 11, White 11, DeCinces 10, Schofield 4, Jones 3, McLemore 3, Miller 3, Ryal 3, Buckner 2, Armas, Boone, Hendrick, Pettis. **Chicago (12)**—Fisk 4, Walker 3, Calderon 2, Williams 2, Baines. **Cleveland (11)**—Snyder 3, Hall 2, Allanson, Bernazard, Carter, Clark, Jacoby, Tabler. **Detroit (10)**—Nokes 5, Bergman 2, Gibson 2, Lemon. **Kansas City (10)**—Tartabull 3, Brett 2, Balboni, Quirk, Seitzer, White, Wilson. **Milwaukee (6)**—Braggs 2, Deer, Felder, Riles, Yount. **Minnesota (3)**—Gaetti 2, Lombardozzi. **New York (8)**—Pasqua 3, Henderson, Mattingly, Pagliarulo, Skinner, Winfield. **Oakland (11)**—Canseco 2, McGwire 2, Steinbach 2, Jackson, Javier, Lansford, Murphy, Phillips. **Seattle (6)**—Presley 2, Valle 2, Davis, Kingery. **Texas (10)**—O'Brien 3, Incaviglia 2, Brower, Buechele, Paciorek, Parrish, Sierra. **Toronto (6)**—Moseby 2, Barfield, McGriff, Mulliniks, Whitt.

AT CHICAGO (162): Baltimore (17)—Murray 4, Gerhart 3, Dwyer 2, Lynn 2, Sheets 2, Kennedy, Knight, Lacy, C. Ripken. **Boston (4)**—Boggs, Buckner, Burks, Evans. **California (9)**—Howell 2, Joyner 2, White 2, Downing, Hendrick, Jones. **Chicago (72)**—Calderon 15, Baines 12, Walker 12, Boston 5, Fisk 5, Redus 4, Williams 4, Hulett 3, Royster 3, Guillen 2, Hairston 2, Manrique 2, Hassey, Hill, Karkovice. **Cleveland (5)**—Carter 3, Hall, Snyder. **Detroit (7)**—Nokes 2, Trammell 2, Evans, Lemon, Whitaker. **Kansas City (11)**—White 3, Balboni 2, Wilson 2, Orta, Quirk, Seitzer, Tartabull. **Milwaukee (5)**—Deer 2, Brock, Schroeder, Sveum. **Minnesota (8)**—Gagne 2, Brunansky, Bush, Gladden, Hrbek, Laudner, Smalley. **New York (5)**—Pagliarulo, Pasqua, Ward, Winfield. **Oakland (4)**—M. Davis, Jackson, McGwire, Murphy. **Seattle (4)**—Davis 2, Kingery, Presley. **Texas (2)**—Incaviglia, Sierra. **Toronto (10)**—Bell 3, Barfield 2, McGriff 2, DeWillis, Fielder, Gruber.

AT CLEVELAND (212): Baltimore (14)—C. Ripken 3, Knight 2, Murray 2, Dwyer, Gerhart, Lacy, Rayford, Shelby, Wiggins, Young. **Boston (9)**—Evans 3, Baylor 2, Burks 2, Greenwell, Rice. **California (6)**—Downing 2, DeCinces, Joyner, Schofield, White. **Chicago (2)**—Fisk, Williams. **Cleveland (94)**—Jacoby 21, Snyder 17, Carter 9, Castillo 8, Hall 8, Franco 5, Tabler 5, Butler 4, Bernazard 3, Hinzo 3, Allanson 2, Bando 2, Frobel 2, Bell, Clark, Dempsey, Dorsett, Parsons. **Detroit (7)**—Brookens, Gibson, Lemon, Madlock, Morrison, Trammell, Whitaker. **Kansas City (9)**—Beniquez 2, B. Jackson 2, Balboni, Bosley, Eisenreich, Pecota, Tartabull. **Milwaukee (12)**—Brock 3, Deer 3, Sveum 2, Cooper, Kiefer, Molitor, Yount. **Minnesota (5)**—Brunansky, Gladden, Hrbek, Laudner, Lombardozzi. **New York (11)**—Henderson 4, Winfield 4, Pagliarulo 2, Sakata. **Oakland (18)**—McGwire 5, Canseco 4, Jackson 2, Lansford 2, Steinbach 2, Murphy, Phillips, Polonia. **Seattle (5)**—Brantley, Phelps, Presley, Quinones, Ramos. **Texas (12)**—Brower 3, Incaviglia 3, Parrish 3, Buechele, O'Brien, Sierra. **Toronto (8)**—Barfield 2, Bell 2, Beniquez, McGriff, Moseby, Upshaw.

AT DETROIT (226): Baltimore (7)—Lynn 2, Kennedy, Knight, Lacy, C. Ripken, Young. **Boston (3)**—Benzinger, Burks, Greenwell. **California (3)**—Ryal 2, Boone. **Chicago (7)**—Hill 2, Boston, Fisk, Hairston, Hulett, Walker. **Cleveland (6)**—Hall 2, Bando, Bernazard, Butler, Tabler. **Detroit (125)**—Evans 19, Gibson 14, Nokes 14, Trammell 13, Lemon 10, Whitaker 10, Heath 8, Herndon 7, Madlock 7, Brookens 6, Bergman 4, Coles 3, Sheridan 3, Grubb 2, Harper 2, Lusader, Morrison, Walewander. **Kansas City (10)**—Balboni 3, White 2, Brett, B. Jackson, Orta, Smith, Tartabull. **Milwaukee (10)**—Braggs 2, Molitor 2, Sveum 2, Cooper, Schroeder, Surhoff, Yount. **Minnesota (12)**—Hrbek 2, Laudner 2, Salas 2, Brunansky, Bush, Gaetti, Larkin, Lombardozzi, Smalley. **New York (8)**—Ward 3, Cerone, Kelly, Mattingly, Pagliarulo, Pasqua. **Oakland (13)**—McGwire 7, M. Davis 2, Bernazard, Canseco, Jackson, Phillips. **Seattle (7)**—Phelps 2, Quinones 2, Davis, Kingery, Moses. **Texas (8)**—Sierra 4, O'Brien 3, Kunkel. **Toronto (7)**—Bell 2, Mulliniks 2, Lee, McGriff, Upshaw.

AT KANSAS CITY (130): Baltimore (5)—Lacy, Murray, B. Ripken, C. Ripken, Young. **Boston (7)**—Evans 2, Baylor, Boggs, Burks, Greenwell, Horn. **California (4)**—Boone, Downing, Hendrick, Schofield. **Chicago (2)**—Calderon, Fisk. **Cleveland (5)**—Hall 2, Bernazard, Franco, Snyder. **Detroit (2)**—Morrison, Trammell. **Kansas City (73)**—Tartabull 15, Brett 14, B. Jackson 14, Balboni 8, Seitzer 7, White 6, Eisenreich 3, Owen 2, Biancalana, McRae, Salazar, Smith. **Milwaukee (3)**—Braggs, Deer, Schroeder. **Minnesota (3)**—Brunansky, Laudner, Puckett. **New York (2)**—Meacham, Pasqua. **Oakland (11)**—M. Davis 3, Canseco 2, McGwire 2, Jackson, Lansford, Murphy, Phillips. **Seattle (1)**—Davis. **Texas (9)**—Sierra 3, O'Brien 2, Parrish 2, Buechele, Incaviglia. **Toronto (3)**—Fielder 2, McGriff.

AT MILWAUKEE (151): Baltimore (5)—Gerhart, Knight, Lynn, Murray, C. Ripken. **Boston (6)**—Horn 2, Benzinger, Boggs, Henderson, Sheaffer. **California (6)**—Downing 2, Howell 2, Hendrick, Joyner. **Chicago (6)**—Fisk 2, Calderon, Hulett, Lyons, Walker. **Cleveland (5)**—Butler, Carter, Castillo, Jacoby, Tabler. **Detroit (8)**—Brookens 2, Trammell 2, Evans, Gibson, Madlock, Nokes. **Kansas City (5)**—Quirk 2, Tartabull 2, Brett. **Milwaukee (72)**—Yount 12, Deer 11, Sveum 9, Molitor 7, Brock 5, Schroeder 5, Surhoff 5, Braggs 4, Cooper 4, Kiefer 4, Castillo 3, Felder, Paciorek, Riles. **Minnesota (9)**—Puckett 4, Hrbek 2, Bush, Gaetti, Larkin. **New York (6)**—Winfield 2, Cerone, Kittle, Pasqua, Randolph. **Oakland (7)**—M. Davis 2, Canseco, Gallego, Henderson, Jackson, Steinbach. **Seattle (4)**—Phelps 2, Davis, Presley. **Texas (6)**—Incaviglia 2, Brower, Parrish, Porter, Slaught. **Toronto (6)**—Bell 2, Barfield, McGriff, Moseby, Whitt.

AT MINNESOTA (198): Baltimore (4)—Murray 2, Dwyer, C. Ripken. **Boston (8)**—Boggs 3, Greenwell 2, Buckner, Evans, Henderson. **California (9)**—Joyner 3, Downing 2, Jones 2, DeCinces,

White. **Chicago** (9)—Redus 3, Baines 2, Boston 2, Hairston, Manrique. **Cleveland** (7)—Bernazard 3, Bando, Clark, Jacoby, Snyder. **Detroit** (7)—Lemon 2, Evans, Gibson, Morrison, Trammell, Whitaker. **Kansas City** (7)—Tartabull 3, Balboni, Brett, B. Jackson, Quirk. **Milwaukee** (4)—Braggs, Deer, Gantner, Schroeder. **Minnesota** (106)—Hrbek 20, Brunansky 19, Gaetti 18, Puckett 18, Gagne 7, Laudner 7, Smalley 5, Gladden 4, Bush 3, Lombardozzi 3, Butera, Salas. **New York** (8)—Kittle, Mattingly, Pagliarulo, Pasqua, Randolph, Salas, Washington, Winfield. **Oakland** (4)—M. Davis, Gallego, Griffin, Henderson. **Seattle** (5)—Phelps 2, Davis, Presley, Quinones. **Texas** (9)—McDowell 5, O'Brien 2, Buechele, Petralli. **Toronto** (11)—McGriff 2, Moseby 2, Mulliniks 2, Whitt 2, Bell, Fielder, Upshaw.

AT NEW YORK (186): Baltimore (5)—Gerhart, Lynn, C. Ripken, Sheets, Young. **Boston** (4)—Evans, Greenwell, Horn, Rice. **California** (8)—Howell 2, White 2, Armas, DeCinces, Joyner, Schofield. **Chicago** (8)—Fisk 2, Royster 2, Baines, Calderon, Hill, Redus. **Cleveland** (7)—Jacoby 3, Carter 2, Hall 2. **Detroit** (8)—Gibson 2, Brookens, Evans, Harper, Lemon, Sheridan, Whitaker. **Kansas City** (3)—Balboni, B. Jackson, Seitzer. **Milwaukee** (6)—Sveum 3, Gantner, Riles, Schroeder. **Minnesota** (6)—Brunansky 2, Davidson, Gladden, Hrbek, Laudner. **New York** (98)—Mattingly 17, Pagliarulo 17, Winfield 11, Henderson 10, Kittle 7, Ward 7, Pasqua 6, Cotto 5, Washington 5, Randolph 3, Easler 2, Meacham 2, Salas 2, Bonilla, Cerone, Sakata, Skinner. **Oakland** (10)—Canseco 2, M. Davis 2, McGwire 2, Steinbach 2, Cey, Murphy. **Seattle** (2)—P. Bradley, Brantley, Davis, Matthews, Phelps. **Texas** (6)—Parrish 2, Stanley 2, Buechele, Slaught. **Toronto** (12)—Bell 4, McGriff 2, Upshaw 2, Barfield, Beniquez, Liriano, Whitt.

AT OAKLAND (163): Baltimore (8)—Lynn 2, Sheets 2, Dwyer, Knight, Lacy, Murray. **Boston** (3)—Greenwell, Rice, Sullivan. **California** (4)—Downing 2, Polidor, White. **Chicago** (9)—Calderon 3, Fisk, Hill, Keedy, Redus, Walker, Williams. **Cleveland** (4)—Carter 2, Jacoby, Williams. **Detroit** (4)—Evans 2, Madlock, Nokes. **Kansas City** (5)—Balboni 3, Beniquez, Brett. **Milwaukee** (8)—Deer 2, Sveum 2, Braggs, Brock, Molitor, Yount. **Minnesota** (4)—Brunansky, Gaetti, Larkin, Puckett. **New York** (8)—Winfield 2, Easler, Mattingly, Meacham, Pagliarulo, Randolph, Ward. **Oakland** (88)—McGwire 21, Canseco 16, M. Davis 9, Lansford 9, Jackson 7, Steinbach 6, Phillips 5, Tettleton 5, Cey 3, Griffin 2, Murphy 2, Henderson, Javier, Polonia. **Seattle** (2)—Presley 2. **Texas** (11)—Parrish 4, Brower 2, Fletcher, Incaviglia, O'Brien, Petralli, Sierra. **Toronto** (5)—Bell 3, Barfield 2.

AT SEATTLE (218): Baltimore (10)—Dwyer 3, Sheets 2, Gerhart, Hart, Kennedy, Murray, B. Ripken. **Boston** (11)—Evans 4, Boggs 2, Greenwell 2, Baylor, Burks, Rice. **California** (8)—Downing 3, White 3, Joyner, Polidor, Schofield. **Chicago** (5)—Calderon, Hill, Keedy, Redus, Walker. **Cleveland** (7)—Jacoby 3, Bell, Butler, Carter, Franco. **Detroit** (5)—Evans 2, Herndon, Lemon, Madlock. **Kansas City** (12)—Balboni 3, B. Jackson 2, Brett 2, Brett, Owen, Pecota, Tartabull, White, Wilson. **Milwaukee** (8)—Deer 2, Schroeder 2, Braggs, Gantner, Paciorek, Sveum. **Minnesota** (9)—Puckett 3, Bush 2, Gaetti 2, Laudner, Lombardozzi. **New York** (13)—Pagliarulo 3, Kittle 2, Mattingly 2, Pasqua 2, Meacham, Skinner, Tolleson, Ward. **Oakland** (7)—Bernazard 2, M. Davis, Lansford, McGwire, Murphy, Tettleton. **Seattle** (103)—Davis 18, Phelps 15, P. Bradley 12, Brantley 11, Presley 11, Valle 8, Quinones 7, S. Bradley 5, Kingery 5, Christensen 2, Matthews 2, Moses 2, Nixon 2, Hengel, Ramos, Reynolds. **Texas** (6)—Buechele, Incaviglia, O'Brien, Parrish, Porter, Sierra. **Toronto** (14)—Bell 5, Gruber 3, Moseby 2, Whitt 2, Fernandez, McGriff.

AT TEXAS (204): Baltimore (11)—Gerhart 2, Murray 2, Sheets 2, Dwyer, Kennedy, Simmons, Washington, Young. **Boston** (7)—Evans 3, Boggs, Greenwell, Horn, Marzano. **California** (5)—Joyner 2, White 2, Buckner. **Chicago** (15)—Walker 4, Baines 2, Calderon 2, Royster 2, Williams 2, Boston, Hill, Karkovice. **Cleveland** (5)—Snyder 2, Carter, Castillo, Jacoby. **Detroit** (9)—Evans 3, Trammell 2, Brookens, Coles, Nokes, Sheridan. **Kansas City** (11)—Tartabull 5, Balboni 2, Brett, B. Jackson, Seitzer, White. **Milwaukee** (7)—Molitor 2, Yount 2, Brock, Deer, Sveum. **Minnesota** (7)—Bush 2, Hrbek 2, Gagne, Laudner, Lombardozzi. **New York** (7)—Mattingly 4, Easler, Pagliarulo, Washington. **Oakland** (8)—McGwire 3, Steinbach 3, Canseco, Jackson. **Seattle** (6)—Davis 3, Brantley, Phelps, Presley. **Texas** (93)—Parrish 16, Sierra 15, Incaviglia 11, O'Brien 9, Brower 7, Buechele 6, McDowell 5, Slaught 5, Fletcher 4, Petralli 4, Porter 4, Stanley 3, Paciorek 2, Browne, Wilkerson. **Toronto** (13)—Barfield 3, Bell 3, Iorg 2, Moseby 2, Fernandez, McGriff, Upshaw.

AT TORONTO (184): Baltimore (2)—Hart, C. Ripken. **Boston** (6)—Boggs, Burks, Greenwell, Henderson, Horn, Rice. **California** (7)—DeCinces 2, Downing 2, Hendrick, Jones, White. **Chicago** (7)—Hill 2, Hairston, Hulett, Manrique, Redus, Williams. **Cleveland** (9)—Snyder 3, Bando, Bernazard, Butler, Carter, Franco, Tabler. **Detroit** (9)—Nokes 3, Evans 2, Gibson, Madlock, Trammell, Whitaker. **Kansas City** (3)—Owen, Pecota, Tartabull. **Milwaukee** (8)—Deer 3, Molitor, Schroeder, Surhoff, Sveum, Yount. **Minnesota** (5)—Gaetti 2, Hrbek, Larkin, Puckett. **New York** (9)—Winfield 3, Mattingly 2, Henderson, Kittle, Pagliarulo, Ward. **Oakland** (7)—Bernazard 2, M. Davis 2, McGwire 2, Polonia. **Seattle** (2)—Phelps, Presley. **Texas** (9)—Incaviglia 3, McDowell 2, O'Brien, Porter, Sierra, Wilkerson. **Toronto** (101)—Bell 19, Moseby 15, Barfield 11, Whitt 11, Fielder 10, McGriff 7, Upshaw 7, Mulliniks 6, Gruber 5, Leach 3, Beniquez 2, Ducey, Fernandez, Iorg, Liriano, Moore.

THE SPORTING NEWS AWARDS
THE SPORTING NEWS MVP AWARDS

AMERICAN LEAGUE			NATIONAL LEAGUE		
Year Player Club	Points		Player Club	Points
1929—Al Simmons, Philadelphia, of	40		No selection	
1930—Joseph Cronin, Washington, ss	52		William Terry, New York, 1b	47
1931—H. Louis Gehrig, New York, 1b	40		Charles Klein, Philadelphia, of	40
1932—James Foxx, Philadelphia, 1b	46		Charles Klein, Philadelphia, of	46
1933—James Foxx, Philadelphia, 1b	49		Carl Hubbell, New York, p	64
1934—H. Louis Gehrig, New York, 1b	51		Jerome Dean, St. Louis, p	57
1935—Henry Greenberg, Detroit, 1b	64		J. Floyd Vaughan, Pittsburgh, ss	42
1936—H. Louis Gehrig, New York, 1b	55		Carl Hubbell, New York, p	61
1937—Charles Gehringer, Detroit, 2b	78		Joseph Medwick, St. Louis, of	70
1938—James Foxx, Boston, 1b	304		Ernest Lombardi, Cincinnati, c	229
1939—Joseph DiMaggio, New York, of	280		William Walters, Cincinnati, p	303
1940—Henry Greenberg, Detroit, of	292		Frank McCormick, Cincinnati, 1b	274
1941—Joseph DiMaggio, New York, of	291		Adolph Camilli, Brooklyn, 1b	300
1942—Joseph Gordon, New York, 2b	270		Morton Cooper, St. Louis, p	263
1943—Spurgeon Chandler, New York, p	246		Stanley Musial, St. Louis, of	267
1944—Robert Doerr, Boston, 2b			Martin Marion, St. Louis, ss	
1945—Edward J. Mayo, Detroit, 2b			Thomas Holmes, Boston, of	

THE SPORTING NEWS PLAYER, PITCHER OF YEAR

AMERICAN LEAGUE	NATIONAL LEAGUE
1948—Louis Boudreau, Cleveland, ss Robert Lemon, Cleveland, p	1948—Stanley Musial, St. Louis, of-1b John Sain, Boston, p
1949—Theodore Williams, Boston, of Ellis Kinder, Boston, p	1949—Enos Slaughter, St. Louis, of Howard Pollet, St. Louis, p
1950—Philip Rizzuto, New York, ss Robert Lemon, Cleveland, p	1950—Ralph Kiner, Pittsburgh, of C. James Konstanty, Philadelphia, p
1951—Ferris Fain, Philadelphia, 1b Robert Feller, Cleveland, p	1951—Stanley Musial, St. Louis, of Elwin Roe, Brooklyn, p
1952—Luscious Easter, Cleveland, 1b Robert Shantz, Philadelphia, p	1952—Henry Sauer, Chicago, of Robin Roberts, Philadelphia, p
1953—Albert Rosen, Cleveland, 3b Erv (Bob) Porterfield, Washington, p	1953—Roy Campanella, Brooklyn, c Warren Spahn, Milwaukee, p
1954—Roberto Avila, Cleveland, 2b Robert Lemon, Cleveland, p	1954—Willie Mays, New York, of John Antonelli, New York, p
1955—Albert Kaline, Detroit, of Edward Ford, New York, p	1955—Edwin Snider, Brooklyn, of Robin Roberts, Philadelphia, p
1956—Mickey Mantle, New York, of W. William Pierce, Chicago, p	1956—Henry Aaron, Milwaukee, of Donald Newcombe, Brooklyn, p
1957—Theodore Williams, Boston, of W. William Pierce, Chicago, p	1957—Stanley Musial, St. Louis, 1b Warren Spahn, Milwaukee, p
1958—Jack Jensen, Boston, of Robert Turley, New York, p	1958—Ernest Banks, Chicago, ss Warren Spahn, Milwaukee, p
1959—J. Nelson Fox, Chicago, 2b Early Wynn, Chicago, p	1959—Ernest Banks, Chicago, ss Samuel Jones, San Francisco, p
1960—Roger Maris, New York, of Charles Estrada, Baltimore, p	1960—Richard Groat, Pittsburgh, ss Vernon Law, Pittsburgh, p
1961—Roger Maris, New York, of Edward Ford, New York, p	1961—Frank Robinson, Cincinnati, of Warren Spahn, Milwaukee, p
1962—Mickey Mantle, New York, of Richard Donovan, Cleveland, p	1962—Maurice Wills, Los Angeles, ss Donald Drysdale, Los Angeles, p
1963—Albert Kaline, Detroit, of Edward Ford, New York, p	1963—Henry Aaron, Milwaukee, of Sanford Koufax, Los Angeles, p
1964—Brooks Robinson, Baltimore, 3b Dean Chance, Los Angeles, p	1964—Kenton Boyer, St. Louis, 3b Sanford Koufax, Los Angeles, p
1965—Pedro (Tony) Oliva, Minnesota, of James Grant, Minnesota, p	1965—Willie Mays, San Francisco, of Sanford Koufax, Los Angeles, p
1966—Frank Robinson, Baltimore, of James Kaat, Minnesota, p	1966—Roberto Clemente, Pittsburgh, of Sanford Koufax, Los Angeles, p
1967—Carl Yastrzemski, Boston, of Jim Lonborg, Boston, p	1967—Orlando Cepeda, St. Louis, 1b Mike McCormick, San Francisco, p
1968—Ken Harrelson, Boston, of Denny McLain, Detroit, p	1968—Pete Rose, Cincinnati, of Bob Gibson, St. Louis, p
1969—Harmon Killebrew, Minnesota, 1b-3b Denny McLain, Detroit, p	1969—Willie McCovey, San Francisco, 1b Tom Seaver, New York, p
1970—Harmon Killebrew, Minnesota, 3b Sam McDowell, Cleveland, p	1970—Johnny Bench, Cincinnati, c Bob Gibson, St. Louis, p
1971—Pedro (Tony) Oliva, Minnesota, of Vida Blue, Oakland, p	1971—Joe Torre, St. Louis, 3b Ferguson Jenkins, Chicago, p
1972—Richie Allen, Chicago, 1b Wilbur Wood, Chicago, p	1972—Billy Williams, Chicago, of Steve Carlton, Philadelphia, p
1973—Reggie Jackson, Oakland, of Jim Palmer, Baltimore, p	1973—Bobby Bonds, San Francisco, of Ron Bryant, San Francisco, p

PLAYER, PITCHER OF YEAR—Continued

AMERICAN LEAGUE

1974—Jeff Burroughs, Texas, of
      Jim Hunter, Oakland, p
1975—Fred Lynn, Boston, of
      Jim Palmer, Baltimore, p
1976—Thurman Munson, New York, c
      Jim Palmer, Baltimore, p
1977—Rod Carew, Minnesota, 1b
      Nolan Ryan, California, p
1978—Jim Rice, Boston, of
      Ron Guidry, New York, p
1979—Don Baylor, California, of
      Mike Flanagan, Baltimore, p
1980—George Brett, Kansas City, 3b
      Steve Stone, Baltimore, p
1981—Tony Armas, Oakland, of
      Jack Morris, Detroit, p
1982—Robin Yount, Milwaukee, ss
      Dave Stieb, Toronto, p
1983—Cal Ripken, Baltimore, ss
      LaMarr Hoyt, Chicago, p
1984—Don Mattingly, New York, 1b
      Willie Hernandez, Detroit, p
1985—Don Mattingly, New York, 1b
      Bret Saberhagen, Kansas City, p
1986—Don Mattingly, New York, 1b
      Roger Clemens, Boston, p
1987—George Bell, Toronto, of
      Jimmy Key, Toronto, p

NATIONAL LEAGUE

1974—Lou Brock, St. Louis, of
      Mike Marshall, Los Angeles, p
1975—Joe Morgan, Cincinnati, 2b
      Tom Seaver, New York, p
1976—George Foster, Cincinnati, of
      Randy Jones, San Diego, p
1977—George Foster, Cincinnati, of
      Steve Carlton, Philadelphia, p
1978—Dave Parker, Pittsburgh, of
      Vida Blue, San Francisco, p
1979—Keith Hernandez, St. Louis, 1b
      Joe Niekro, Houston, p
1980—Mike Schmidt, Philadelphia, 3b
      Steve Carlton, Philadelphia, p
1981—Andre Dawson, Montreal, of
      Fernando Valenzuela, Los Angeles, p
1982—Dale Murphy, Atlanta, of
      Steve Carlton, Philadelphia, p
1983—Dale Murphy, Atlanta, of
      John Denny, Philadelphia, p
1984—Ryne Sandberg, Chicago, 2b
      Rick Sutcliffe, Chicago, p
1985—Willie McGee, St. Louis, of
      Dwight Gooden, New York, p
1986—Mike Schmidt, Philadelphia, 3b
      Mike Scott, Houston, p
1987—Andre Dawson, Chicago, of
      Rick Sutcliffe, Chicago, p

FIREMAN (Relief Pitcher) OF THE YEAR

Year	Player	Club	Player	Club
1960—Mike Fornieles, Boston			Lindy McDaniel, St. Louis	
1961—Luis Arroyo, New York			Stu Miller, San Francisco	
1962—Dick Radatz, Boston			Roy Face, Pittsburgh	
1963—Stu Miller, Baltimore			Lindy McDaniel, Chicago	
1964—Dick Radatz, Boston			Al McBean, Pittsburgh	
1965—Eddie Fisher, Chicago			Ted Abernathy, Chicago	
1966—Jack Aker, Kansas City			Phil Regan, Los Angeles	
1967—Minnie Rojas, California			Ted Abernathy, Cincinnati	
1968—Wilbur Wood, Chicago			Phil Regan, L.A.-Chicago	
1969—Ron Perranoski, Minnesota			Wayne Granger, Cincinnati	
1970—Ron Perranoski, Minnesota			Wayne Granger, Cincinnati	
1971—Ken Sanders, Milwaukee			Dave Giusti, Pittsburgh	
1972—Sparky Lyle, New York			Clay Carroll, Cincinnati	
1973—John Hiller, Detroit			Mike Marshall, Montreal	
1974—Terry Forster, Chicago			Mike Marshall, Los Angeles	
1975—Rich Gossage, Chicago			Al Hrabosky, St. Louis	
1976—Bill Campbell, Minnesota			Rawly Eastwick, Cincinnati	
1977—Bill Campbell, Boston			Rollie Fingers, San Diego	
1978—Rich Gossage, New York			Rollie Fingers, San Diego	
1979—Mike Marshall, Minnesota			Bruce Sutter, Chicago	
Jim Kern, Texas				
1980—Dan Quisenberry, Kansas City			Rollie Fingers, San Diego	
			Tom Hume, Cincinnati	
1981—Rollie Fingers, Milwaukee			Bruce Sutter, St. Louis	
1982—Dan Quisenberry, Kansas City			Bruce Sutter, St. Louis	
1983—Dan Quisenberry, Kansas City			Al Holland, Philadelphia	
			Lee Smith, Chicago	
1984—Dan Quisenberry, Kansas City			Bruce Sutter, St. Louis	
1985—Dan Quisenberry, Kansas City			Jeff Reardon, Montreal	
1986—Dave Righetti, New York			Todd Worrell, St. Louis	
1987—Dave Righetti, New York			Steve Bedrosian, Philadelphia	
Jeff Reardon, Minnesota				

THE SPORTING NEWS ROOKIE AWARDS

1946—Combined selection—Delmer Ennis, Philadelphia, N. L., of
1947—Combined selection—Jack Robinson, Brooklyn, 1b
1948—Combined selection—Richie Ashburn, Philadelphia, N. L., of

AMERICAN LEAGUE

Year	Player	Club
1949—Roy Sievers, St. Louis, of		
1950—Combined selection—Edward Ford, New York, A. L., p		
1951—Orestes Minoso, Chicago, of		
1952—Clinton Courtney, St. Louis, c		
1953—Harvey Kuenn, Detroit, ss		

NATIONAL LEAGUE

Player	Club
Donald Newcombe, Brooklyn, p	
Willie Mays, New York, of	
Joseph Black, Brooklyn, p	
James Gilliam, Brooklyn, 2b	

THE SPORTING NEWS ROOKIE AWARDS—Continued

AMERICAN LEAGUE

Year	Player	Club
1954	Robert Grim, New York, p	
1955	Herbert Score, Cleveland, p	
1956	Luis Aparicio, Chicago, ss	
1957	Anthony Kubek, New York, inf-of	
	(No pitcher named)	
1958	Albert Pearson, Washington, of	
	Ryne Duren, New York, p	
1959	W. Robert Allison, Washington, of	
1960	Ronald Hansen, Baltimore, ss	
1961	Richard Howser, Kansas City, ss	
	Donald Schwall, Boston, p	
1962	Thomas Tresh, New York, of-ss	
1963	Peter Ward, Chicago, 3b	
	Gary Peters, Chicago, p	
1964	Pedro (Tony) Oliva, Minnesota, of	
	Wallace Bunker, Baltimore, p	
1965	Curtis Blefary, Baltimore, of	
	Marcelino Lopez, California, p	
1966	Tommie Agee, Chicago, of	
	James Nash, Kansas City, p	
1967	Rod Carew, Minnesota, 2b	
	Tom Phoebus, Baltimore, p	
1968	Del Unser, Washington, of	
	Stan Bahnsen, New York, p	
1969	Carlos May, Chicago, of	
	Mike Nagy, Boston, p	
1970	Roy Foster, Cleveland, of	
	Bert Blyleven, Minnesota, p	
1971	Chris Chambliss, Cleveland, 1b	
	Bill Parsons, Milwaukee, p	
1972	Carlton Fisk, Boston, c	
	Dick Tidrow, Cleveland, p	
1973	Al Bumbry, Baltimore, of	
	Steve Busby, Kansas City, p	
1974	Mike Hargrove, Texas, 1b	
	Frank Tanana, California, p	
1975	Fred Lynn, Boston, of	
	Dennis Eckersley, Cleveland, p	
1976	Butch Wynegar, Minnesota, c	
	Mark Fidrych, Detroit, p	
1977	Mitchell Page, Oakland, of	
	Dave Rozema, Detroit, p	
1978	Paul Molitor, Milwaukee, 2b	
	Rich Gale, Kansas City, p	
1979	Pat Putnam, Texas, 1b	
	Mark Clear, California, p	
1980	Joe Charboneau, Cleveland, of	
	Britt Burns, Chicago, p	
1981	Rich Gedman, Boston, c	
	Dave Righetti, New York, p	
1982	Cal Ripken, Baltimore, ss-3b	
	Ed Vande Berg, Seattle, p	
1983	Ron Kittle, Chicago, of	
	Mike Boddicker, Baltimore, p	
1984	Alvin Davis, Seattle, 1b	
	Mark Langston, Seattle, p	
1985	Ozzie Guillen, Chicago, ss	
	Teddy Higuera, Milwaukee, p	
1986	Jose Canseco, Oakland, of	
	Mark Eichhorn, Toronto, p	
1987	Mark McGwire, Oakland, 1b	
	Mike Henneman, Detroit, p	

NATIONAL LEAGUE

Player	Club
Wallace Moon, St. Louis, of	
William Virdon, St. Louis, of	
Frank Robinson, Cincinnati, of	
Edward Bouchee, Philadelphia, 1b	
Jack Sanford, Philadelphia, p	
Orlando Cepeda, San Francisco, 1b	
Carlton Willey, Milwaukee, p	
Willie McCovey, San Francisco, 1b	
Frank Howard, Los Angeles, of	
Billy Williams, Chicago, of	
Kenneth Hunt, Cincinnati, p	
Kenneth Hubbs, Chicago, 2b	
Pete Rose, Cincinnati, 2b	
Raymond Culp, Philadelphia, p	
Richard Allen, Philadelphia, 3b	
William McCool, Cincinnati, p	
Joseph Morgan, Houston, 2b	
Frank Linzy, San Francisco, p	
Tommy Helms, Cincinnati, 3b	
Donald Sutton, Los Angeles, p	
Lee May, Cincinnati, 1b	
Dick Hughes, St. Louis, p	
Johnny Bench, Cincinnati, c	
Jerry Koosman, New York, p	
Coco Laboy, Montreal, 3b	
Tom Griffin, Houston, p	
Bernie Carbo, Cincinnati, of	
Carl Morton, Montreal, p	
Earl Williams, Atlanta, c	
Reggie Cleveland, St. Louis, p	
Dave Rader, San Francisco, c	
Jon Matlack, New York, p	
Gary Matthews, San Francisco, of	
Steve Rogers, Montreal, p	
Greg Gross, Houston, of	
John D'Acquisto, San Francisco, p	
Gary Carter, Montreal, of-c	
John Montefusco, San Francisco, p	
Larry Herndon, San Francisco, of	
Butch Metzger, San Diego, p	
Andre Dawson, Montreal, of	
Bob Owchinko, San Diego, p	
Bob Horner, Atlanta, 3b	
Don Robinson, Pittsburgh, p	
Jeff Leonard, Houston, of	
Rick Sutcliffe, Los Angeles, p	
Lonnie Smith, Philadelphia, of	
Bill Gullickson, Montreal, p	
Tim Raines, Montreal, of	
Fernando Valenzuela, Los Angeles, p	
Johnny Ray, Pittsburgh, 2b	
Steve Bedrosian, Atlanta, p	
Darryl Strawberry, New York, of	
Craig McMurtry, Atlanta, p	
Juan Samuel, Philadelphia, 2b	
Dwight Gooden, New York, p	
Vince Coleman, St. Louis, of	
Tom Browning, Cincinnati, p	
Robby Thompson, San Francisco, 2b	
Todd Worrell, St. Louis, p	
Benito Santiago, San Diego, c	
Mike Dunne, Pittsburgh, p	

MAJOR LEAGUE EXECUTIVE

Year	Executive	Club	Year	Executive	Club
1936	Branch Rickey, St. Louis NL		1947	Branch Rickey, Brooklyn NL	
1937	Edward Barrow, New York AL		1948	Bill Veeck, Cleveland AL	
1938	Warren Giles, Cincinnati NL		1949	Robt. Carpenter, Phila'phia NL	
1939	Larry MacPhail, Brooklyn NL		1950	George Weiss, New York AL	
1940	W. O. Briggs, Sr., Detroit AL		1951	George Weiss, New York AL	
1941	Edward Barrow, New York AL		1952	George Weiss, New York AL	
1942	Branch Rickey, St. Louis NL		1953	Louis Perini, Milwaukee NL	
1943	Clark Griffith, Washington AL		1954	Horace Stoneham, N. York NL	
1944	Wm. O. DeWitt, St. Louis AL		1955	Walter O'Malley, Brooklyn NL	
1945	Philip K. Wrigley, Chicago NL		1956	Gabe Paul, Cincinnati NL	
1946	Thomas A. Yawkey, Boston AL		1957	Frank Lane, St. Louis NL	

MAJOR LEAGUE EXECUTIVE—Continued

Year	Executive	Club
1958	Joe L. Brown, Pittsburgh NL	
1959	E. J. (Buzzie) Bavasi, L.A. NL	
1960	George Weiss, New York AL	
1961	Dan Topping, New York AL	
1962	Fred Haney, Los Angeles AL	
1963	Vaughan (Bing) Devine, St.L.NL	
1964	Vaughan (Bing) Devine, St.L.NL	
1965	Calvin Griffith, Minnesota AL	
1966	Lee MacPhail, Commissioner's Office	
1967	Dick O'Connell, Boston AL	
1968	James Campbell, Detroit AL	
1969	John Murphy, New York NL	
1970	Harry Dalton, Baltimore AL	
1971	Cedric Tallis, Kansas City AL	
1972	Roland Hemond, Chicago AL	
1973	Bob Howsam, Cincinnati NL	
1974	Gabe Paul, New York AL	
1975	Dick O'Connell, Boston AL	
1976	Joe Burke, Kansas City AL	
1977	Bill Veeck, Chicago AL	
1978	Spec Richardson, San Fran. NL	
1979	Hank Peters, Baltimore AL	
1980	Tal Smith, Houston NL	
1981	John McHale, Montreal NL	
1982	Harry Dalton, Milwaukee AL	
1983	Hank Peters, Baltimore AL	
1984	Dallas Green, Chicago NL	
1985	John Schuerholz, Kansas City AL	
1986	Frank Cashen, New York NL	
1987	Al Rosen, San Francisco NL	

MAJOR LEAGUE MANAGER

Year	Manager	Club
1936	Joe McCarthy, New York AL	
1937	Bill McKechnie, Boston NL	
1938	Joe McCarthy, New York AL	
1939	Leo Durocher, Brooklyn NL	
1940	Bill McKechnie, Cincinnati NL	
1941	Billy Southworth, St. Louis NL	
1942	Billy Southworth, St. Louis NL	
1943	Joe McCarthy, New York AL	
1944	Luke Sewell, St. Louis AL	
1945	Ossie Bluege, Washington AL	
1946	Eddie Dyer, St. Louis NL	
1947	Bucky Harris, New York AL	
1948	Bill Meyer, Pittsburgh NL	
1949	Casey Stengel, New York AL	
1950	Red Rolfe, Detroit AL	
1951	Leo Durocher, New York NL	
1952	Eddie Stanky, St. Louis NL	
1953	Casey Stengel, New York AL	
1954	Leo Durocher, New York NL	
1955	Walter Alston, Brooklyn NL	
1956	Birdie Tebbetts, Cincinnati NL	
1957	Fred Hutchinson, St. Louis NL	
1958	Casey Stengel, New York AL	
1959	Walter Alston, Los Angeles NL	
1960	Danny Murtaugh, Pitts. NL	
1961	Ralph Houk, New York AL	
1962	Bill Rigney, Los Angeles AL	
1963	Walter Alston, Los Angeles NL	
1964	Johnny Keane, St. Louis NL	
1965	Sam Mele, Minnesota AL	
1966	Hank Bauer, Baltimore AL	
1967	Dick Williams, Boston AL	
1968	Mayo Smith, Detroit AL	
1969	Gil Hodges, New York NL	
1970	Danny Murtaugh, Pittsb'gh NL	
1971	Charlie Fox, San Francisco NL	
1972	Chuck Tanner, Chicago AL	
1973	Gene Mauch, Montreal NL	
1974	Bill Virdon, New York AL	
1975	Darrell Johnson, Boston AL	
1976	Danny Ozark, Philadelphia NL	
1977	Earl Weaver, Baltimore AL	
1978	George Bamberger, Milw'kee AL	
1979	Earl Weaver, Baltimore AL	
1980	Bill Virdon, Houston NL	
1981	Billy Martin, Oakland AL	
1982	Whitey Herzog, St. Louis NL	
1983	Tony LaRussa, Chicago AL	
1984	Jim Frey, Chicago NL	
1985	Bobby Cox, Toronto AL	
1986	John McNamara, Boston AL	
	Hal Lanier, Houston NL	
1987	Sparky Anderson, Detroit AL	
	Buck Rodgers, Montreal NL	

MAJOR LEAGUE PLAYER

Year	Player	Club
1936	Carl Hubbell, New York NL	
1937	Johnny Allen, Cleveland AL	
1938	Johnny Vander Meer, Cinn. NL	
1939	Joe DiMaggio, New York AL	
1940	Bob Feller, Cleveland AL	
1941	Ted Williams, Boston AL	
1942	Ted Williams, Boston AL	
1943	Spud Chandler, New York AL	
1944	Marty Marion, St. Louis NL	
1945	Hal Newhouser, Detroit AL	
1946	Stan Musial, St. Louis NL	
1947	Ted Williams, Boston AL	
1948	Lou Boudreau, Cleveland AL	
1949	Ted Williams, Boston AL	
1950	Phil Rizzuto, New York AL	
1951	Stan Musial, St. Louis NL	
1952	Robin Roberts, Philadelphia NL	
1953	Al Rosen, Cleveland AL	
1954	Willie Mays, New York NL	
1955	Duke Snider, Brooklyn NL	
1956	Mickey Mantle, New York AL	
1957	Ted Williams, Boston AL	
1958	Bob Turley, New York AL	
1959	Early Wynn, Chicago AL	
1960	Bill Mazeroski, Pittsburgh NL	
1961	Roger Maris, New York AL	
1962	Maury Wills, Los Angeles NL	
	Don Drysdale, Los Angeles NL	
1963	Sandy Koufax, Los Angeles NL	
1964	Ken Boyer, St. Louis NL	
1965	Sandy Koufax, Los Angeles NL	
1966	Frank Robinson, Baltimore AL	
1967	Carl Yastrzemski, Boston AL	
1968	Denny McLain, Detroit AL	
1969	Willie McCovey, San Fran. NL	
1970	Johnny Bench, Cin. NL	
1971	Joe Torre, St. Louis NL	
1972	Billy Williams, Chicago NL	
1973	Reggie Jackson, Oakland AL	
1974	Lou Brock, St. Louis NL	
1975	Joe Morgan, Cincinnati NL	
1976	Joe Morgan, Cincinnati NL	
1977	Rod Carew, Minnesota AL	
1978	Ron Guidry, New York AL	
1979	Willie Stargell, Pittsburgh NL	
1980	George Brett, Kansas City AL	
1981	Fernando Valenzuela, Los Angeles NL	
1982	Robin Yount, Milwaukee AL	
1983	Cal Ripken, Baltimore AL	
1984	Ryne Sandberg, Chicago NL	
1985	Don Mattingly, New York AL	
1986	Roger Clemens, Boston AL	
1987	George Bell, Toronto AL	

MINOR LEAGUE EXECUTIVE (HIGHER CLASSIFICATIONS)
(Restricted to Class AAA Starting in 1963)

Year	Executive	Club
1936	Earl Mann, Atlanta, Southern	
1937	Robt. LaMotte, Savannah, Sally	
1938	Louis McKenna, St. Paul, A.A.	
1939	Bruce Dudley, Louisville, A.A.	
1940	Roy Hamey, Kansas City, A.A.	
1941	Emil Sick, Seattle, PCL	
1942	Bill Veeck, Milwaukee, A.A.	
1943	Clar. Rowland, Los Angeles, PCL	
1944	William Mulligan, Seattle, PCL	
1945	Bruce Dudley, Louisville, A.A.	
1946	Earl Mann, Atlanta, Southern	
1947	Wm. Purnhage, Waterloo, I.I.I.	
1948	Ed. Glennon, Bir'ham, Southern	
1949	Ted Sullivan, Indianapolis, A.A.	
1950	Cl. (Brick) Laws, Oakland, PCL	
1951	Robert Howsam, Denver, West.	
1952	Jack Cooke, Toronto, Int.	
1953	Richard Burnett, Dallas, Texas	
1954	Edward Stumpf, Indpls., A.A.	
1955	Dewey Soriano, Seattle, PCL	
1956	Robert Howsam, Denver, A.A.	
1957	John Stiglmeier, Buffalo, Int.	
1958	Ed. Glennon, Bir'ham, Southern	
1959	Ed. Leishman, Salt Lake, PCL	
1960	Ray Winder, Little Rock, Sou.	
1961	Elten Schiller, Omaha, A.A.	
1962	Geo. Sisler, Jr., Rochester, Int.	
1963	Lewis Matlin, Hawaii, PCL	
1964	Ed. Leishman, San Diego, PCL	
1965	Harold Cooper, Columbus, Int.	
1966	John Quinn, Jr., Hawaii, PCL	
1967	Hillman Lyons, Richmond, Int.	
1968	Gabe Paul, Jr., Tulsa, PCL	
1969	Bill Gardner, Louisville, Int.	
1970	Dick King, Wichita, A.A.	
1971	Carl Steinfeldt, Jr., Roch'ter, Int.	
1972	Don Labbruzzo, Evansville, A.A.	
1973	Merle Miller, Tucson, PCL	
1974	John Carbray, Sacramento, PCL	
1975	Stan Naccarato, Tacoma, PCL	
1976	Art Teece, Salt Lake City, PCL	
1977	George Sisler, Jr., Col'bus, Int.	
1978	Willie Sanchez, Albu'que, PCL	
1979	George Sisler, Jr., Col'bus, Int.	
1980	Jim Burris, Denver, A.A.	
1981	Pat McKernan, Albuquerque, PCL	
1982	A. Ray Smith, Louisville, A.A.	
1983	A. Ray Smith, Louisville, A.A.	
1984	Mike Tamburro, Pawtucket, Int.	
1985	Patty Cox Hampton, Okla City, A.A.	
1986	Bob Goughan, Rochester, Int.	
1987	Stu Kehoe, Vancouver PCL	

MINOR LEAGUE EXECUTIVE (LOWER CLASSIFICATIONS)
(Separate Awards for Class AA and Class A Started in 1963)

Year	Executive	Club
1950	H. Cooper, Hutch'son, West. A.	
1951	O. W. (Bill) Hayes, T'ple, B.S.	
1952	Hillman Lyons, Danville, MOV	
1953	Carl Roth, Peoria, III	
1954	James Meaghan, Cedar R., III	
1955	John Petrakis, Dubuque, MOV	
1956	Marvin Milkes, Fresno, Calif.	
1957	Richard Wagner, L'coln, West.	
1958	Gerald Waring, Macon, Sally	
1959	Clay Dennis, Des Moines, III	
1960	Hubert Kittle, Yakima, Northw.	
1961	David Steele, Fresno, California	
1962	John Quinn, Jr., S. Jose, Calif.	
1963	Hugh Finnerty, Tulsa, Texas	
	Ben Jewell, M. Valley, Pioneer	
1964	Glynn West, Birmingham, Sou.	
	Jas. Bayens, Rock Hill, W. Car.	
1965	Dick Butler, Dallas-Ft.W., Tex.	
	Ken. Blackman, Quad C., Midw.	
1966	Tom Fleming, Evansville, South.	
	Cappy Harada, Lodi, California	
1967	Robt. Quinn, Reading, East.	
	Pat Williams, Spar'burg, W. C.	
1968	Phil Howser, Charlotte, South.	
	Merle Miller, Burlington, Midw.	
1969	Charlie Blaney, Albuq., Texas	
	Bill Gorman, Visalia, Calif.	
1970	Carl Sawatski, Arkansas, Texas	
	Bob Williams, Bakersfield, Calif.	
1971	Miles Wolff, Savannah, Dixie A.	
	Ed Holtz, Appleton, Midwest	
1972	John Begzos, S. Antonio, Texas	
	Bob Piccinini, Modesto, Calif.	
1973	Dick Kravitz, Jacksonville, Sou.	
	Fritz Colschen, Clinton, Midw.	
1974	Jim Paul, El Paso, Texas	
	Bing Russell, Portland, N'west	
1975	Jim Paul, El Paso, Texas	
	Cordy Jensen, Eugene, N'west	
1976	Woodrow Reid, Chat'ooga, Sou.	
	Don Buchheister, Ced. Rap., Mid.	
1977	Jim Paul, El Paso, Texas	
	Harry Pells, Quad Cities, Midw.	
1978	Larry Schmittou, Nashville, Sou.	
	Dave Hersh, Appleton, Midwest	
1979	Bill Rigney Jr., Midland, Tex.	
	Tom Romenesko, G'sboro, W.C.	
1980	Frances Crockett, C'lotte, Sou.	
	Tom Romenesko, G'sboro, W.C.	
1981	Allie Prescott, Memphis, Southern	
	Dan Overstreet, Hagerstown, Caro.	
1982	Art Clarkson, Birmingham, Sou.	
	Bob Carruesco, Stockton, Calif.	
1983	Edward Kenney, New Britain, East.	
	Terry Reynolds, Vero Beach, Fla. St.	
1984	Bruce Baldwin, Greenville, Sou.	
	Dave Tarrolly, Beloit, Midwest	
1985	Ben Bernard, Albany-Colonie, Eastern	
	Pete Vonachen, Peoria, Midwest	
1986	Bill Davidson, Midland, Texas	
	Rob Dlugozima, Durham, Carolina	
1987	Joe Preseren, Tulsa, Texas	
	Skip Weisman, Greensboro, So. Atl.	

MINOR LEAGUE MANAGER

Year	Manager	Club
1936	Al Sothoron, Milwaukee, A.A.	
1937	Jake Flowers, Salis'y, East. Sh.	
1938	Paul Richards, Atlanta, South.	
1939	Bill Meyer, Kansas City, A.A.	
1940	Larry Gilbert, Nashville, South.	
1941	Burt Shotton, Columbus, A.A.	
1942	Eddie Dyer, Columbus, A.A.	
1943	Nick Cullop, Columbus, A.A.	
1944	Al Thomas, Baltimore, Int.	
1945	Lefty O'Doul, San Fran., PCL	
1946	Clay Hopper, Montreal, Int.	
1947	Nick Cullop, Milwaukee, A.A.	
1948	Casey Stengel, Oakland, PCL	
1949	Fred Haney, Hollywood, PCL	
1950	Rollie Hemsley, Columbus, A.A.	
1951	Charlie Grimm, Milw., A.A.	
1952	Luke Appling, Memphis, South.	
1953	Bobby Bragan, Hollywood, PCL	

MINOR LEAGUE MANAGER—Continued

Year	Manager	Club
1954—Kerby Farrell, Indpls., A.A.		
1955—Bill Rigney, Minneapolis, A.A.		
1956—Kerby Farrell, Indpls., A.A.		
1957—Ben Geraghty, Wichita, A.A.		
1958—Cal Ermer, Birmingham, South.		
1959—Pete Reiser, Victoria, Texas		
1960—Mel McGaha, Toronto, Int.		
1961—Kerby Farrell, Buffalo, Int.		
1962—Ben Geraghty, Jackson'le, Int.		
1963—Rollie Hemsley, Indpls., Int.		
1964—Harry Walker, Jacks'vle., Int.		
1965—Grady Hatton, Okla. City, PCL		
1966—Bob Lemon, Seattle, PCL		
1967—Bob Skinner, San Diego, PCL		
1968—Jack Tighe, Toledo, Int.		
1969—Clyde McCullough, Tide., Int.		
1970—Tom Lasorda, Spokane, PCL		

Year	Manager	Club
1971—Del Rice, Salt Lake City, PCL		
1972—Hank Bauer, Tidewater, Int.		
1973—Joe Morgan, Charleston, Int.		
1974—Joe Altobelli, Rochester, Int.		
1975—Joe Frazier, Tidewater, Int.		
1976—Vern Rapp, Denver, A.A.		
1977—Tommy Thompson, Arkan., Tex.		
1978—Les Moss, Evansville, A.A.		
1979—Vern Benson, Syracuse, Int.		
1980—Hal Lanier, Springfield, A.A.		
1981—Del Crandall, Albuquerque, PCL		
1982—George Scherger, Indianapolis, A.A.		
1983—Bill Dancy, Reading, East.		
1984—Bob Rodgers, Indianapolis, A.A.		
1985—Jim Fregosi, Louisville, A.A.		
1986—Joe Sparks, Indianapolis, A.A.		
1987—Terry Collins, Albuquerque, PCL		

MINOR LEAGUE PLAYER

Year	Player	Club
1936—Jn. Vander Meer, Durham, Pied.		
1937—Charlie Keller, Newark, Int.		
1938—Fred Hutchinson, Seattle, PCL		
1939—Lou Novikoff, Tulsa-Los A'les.		
1940—Phil Rizzuto, Kansas City, A.A.		
1941—John Lindell, Newark, Int.		
1942—Dick Barrett, Seattle, PCL		
1943—Chet Covington, Scranton, East.		
1944—Rip Collins, Albany, Eastern		
1945—Gil Coan, Chattanooga, South.		
1946—Sibby Sisti, Indianapolis, A.A.		
1947—Hank Sauer, Syracuse, Int.		
1948—Gene Woodling, S. F., PCL		
1949—Orie Arntzen, Albany, Eastern		
1950—Frank Saucier, San Ant'o, Tex.		
1951—Gene Conley, Hartford, Eastern		
1952—Bill Skowron, Kans. City, A.A.		
1953—Gene Conley, Toledo, A.A.		
1954—Herb Score, Indianapolis, A.A.		
1955—John Murff, Dallas, Texas		
1956—Steve Bilko, Los Angeles, PCL		
1957—Norm Siebern, Denver, A.A.		
1958—Jim O'Toole, Nashville, South.		
1959—Frank Howard, Victoria-Spok.		
1960—Willie Davis, Spokane, PCL		
1961—Howie Koplitz, Bir'ham, South.		

Year	Player	Club
1962—Bob Bailey, Columbus, Int.		
1963—Don Buford, Indianapolis, Int.		
1964—Mel Stottlemyre, Richm'd., Int.		
1965—Joe Foy, Toronto, International		
1966—Mike Epstein, Rochester, Int.		
1967—Johnny Bench, Buffalo, Int.		
1968—Merv Rettenmund, Roch'ter, Int.		
1969—Danny Walton, Okla. City, A.A.		
1970—Don Baylor, Rochester, Int.		
1971—Bobby Grich, Rochester, Int.		
1972—Tom Paciorek, Albuq'que, PCL		
1973—Steve Ontiveros, Phoenix, PCL		
1974—Jim Rice, Pawtucket, Int.		
1975—Hector Cruz, Tulsa, A.A.		
1976—Pat Putnam, Asheville, W. Car.		
1977—Ken Landreaux, S.L.C., PCL-El Paso, Tex.		
1978—Champ Summers, Indi'polis, A.A.		
1979—Mark Bomback, Vancouver, PCL		
1980—Tim Raines, Denver, A.A.		
1981—Mike Marshall, Albuquerque, PCL		
1982—Ron Kittle, Edmonton, PCL		
1983—Kevin McReynolds, Las Vegas, PCL		
1984—Alan Knicely, Wichita, A.A.		
1985—Jose Canseco, Hunt., Sou.-Tac., PCL		
1986—Tim Pyznarski, Las Vegas, PCL		
1987—Randy Milligan, Tidewater, Int.		

Major League All-Star Teams

1925

Bottomley, St. Louis NL	1B
Hornsby, St. Louis NL	2B
Wright, Pittsburgh NL	SS
Traynor, Pittsburgh NL	3B
Cuyler, Pittsburgh NL	OF
Carey, Pittsburgh NL	OF
Goslin, Washington AL	OF
Cochrane, Philadelphia AL	C
Johnson, Washington AL	P
Rommel, Philadelphia AL	P
Vance, Brooklyn NL	P

1926

G. Burns, Cleve. AL
Hornsby, St. Louis NL
J. Sewell, Cleve. AL
Traynor, Pittsburgh NL
Goslin, Wash'ton AL
Mostil, Chicago AL
Ruth, New York AL
O'Farrell, St. Louis NL
Pennock, N. Y. AL
Uhle, Cleveland AL
Alexander, St. L. NL

1927

1B	Gehrig, N. Y. AL
2B	Hornsby, N. Y. NL
SS	Jackson, N. Y. AL
3B	Traynor, Pitts. NL
OF	Ruth, New York AL
OF	Simmons, Phila. AL
OF	P. Waner, Pitts. NL
C	Hartnett, Chicago NL
P	Root, Chicago NL
P	Lyons, Chicago AL

1928

Gehrig, New York AL	1B
Hornsby, Boston NL	2B
Jackson, New York NL	SS
Lindstrom, N. Y. NL	3B
Ruth, New York AL	OF
Manush, St. Louis AL	OF
P. Waner, Pittsburgh NL	OF
Cochrane, Philadelphia AL	C
Grove, Philadelphia AL	P
Hoyt, New York AL	P

1929

Foxx, Phila'phia AL
Hornsby, Chicago NL
Jackson, N. Y. NL
Traynor, Pittsb'gh NL
Simmons, Phila. AL
L. Wilson, Chi. NL
Ruth, New York AL
Cochrane, Phila. AL
Grove, Phila'phia AL
Grimes, Pittsburgh NL

1930

1B	Terry, New York NL
2B	Frisch, St. Louis NL
SS	Cronin, Wash'ton AL
3B	Lindstrom, N. Y. NL
OF	Simmons, Phila. AL
OF	L. Wilson, Chi. NL
OF	Ruth, New York AL
C	Cochrane, Phila AL
P	Grove, Phila'phia AL
P	W. Ferrell, Cleve. AL

1931

Gehrig, New York AL 1B
Frisch, St. Louis NL 2B
Cronin, Washington AL .... SS
Traynor, Pittsburgh NL 3B
Simmons, Philadelphia AL ...... OF
Averill, Cleveland AL .... OF
Ruth, New York AL .... OF
Cochrane, Philadelphia AL C
Grove, Philadelphia AL .... P
Earnshaw, Philadelphia AL .... P

1932

Foxx, Phila'phia AL
Lazzeri, N. Y. AL
Cronin, Wash'ton AL
Traynor, Pittsb'gh NL
O'Doul, Brooklyn NL
Averill, Cleveland AL
Klein, Philadelphia NL
Dickey, New York AL
Grove, Phila'phia AL
Warneke, Chicago NL

1933

1B—Foxx, Phila'phia AL
2B—Gehringer, Det. AL
SS—Cronin, Wash'ton AL
3B—Traynor, Pitts. NL
OF—Simmons, Chi. AL
OF—Berger, Boston NL
OF—Klein, Phila'phia NL
C—Dickey, N. Y. AL
P—Crowder, Wash. AL
P—Hubbell, N. Y. NL

1934

Gehrig, New York AL 1B
Gehringer, Detroit AL............... 2B
Cronin, Washington AL .... SS
Higgins, Philadelphia AL 3B
Simmons, Chicago AL............... OF
Averill, Cleveland AL .... OF
Ott, New York NL .... OF
Cochrane, Detroit AL............... C
Gomez, New York AL .... P
Rowe, Detroit AL....................... P
J. Dean, St. Louis NL .... P

1935

Greenberg, Det. AL
Gehringer, Det. AL
Vaughan, Pitts. NL
J. Martin, St. L. NL
Medwick, St. L. NL
Cramer, Phila. AL
Ott, New York NL
Cochrane, Detroit AL
Hubbell, N. Y. NL
J. Dean, St. Louis NL

1936

1B—Gehrig, New York AL
2B—Gehringer, Det. AL
SS—Appling, Chicago AL
3B—Higgins, Phila. AL
OF—Medwick, St. L. NL
OF—Averill, Cleve. AL
OF—Ott, New York NL
C—Dickey, N. Y. AL
P—Hubbell, N. Y. NL
P—J. Dean, St. Louis NL

1937

Gehrig, New York AL 1B
Gehringer, Detroit AL............... 2B
Bartell, New York NL .... SS
Rolfe, New York AL 3B
Medwick, St. Louis NL .... OF
J. DiMaggio, New York AL ..... OF
P. Waner, Pittsburgh NL .... OF
Hartnett, Chicago NL C
Hubbell, New York NL.............. P
Ruffing, New York AL .... P

1938

Foxx, Boston AL
Gehringer, Detroit AL
Cronin, Boston AL
Rolfe, New York AL
Medwick, St. Louis NL
J. DiMaggio, N. Y. AL
Ott, New York NL
Dickey, New York AL
Ruffing, New York AL
Gomez, New York AL
Vander Meer, Cin. NL

1939

1B—Foxx, Boston AL
2B—Gordon, N. Y. AL
SS—Cronin, Boston AL
3B—Rolfe, New York AL
OF—Medwick, St. L. NL
OF—J. DiMaggio, N. Y. AL
OF—Williams, Boston AL
C—Dickey, N. Y. AL
P—Ruffing, N. Y. AL
P—Feller, Cleveland AL
P—Walters, Cin. NL

1940

F. McCormick, Cin. NL 1B
Gordon, New York AL 2B
Appling, Chicago AL .... SS
Hack, Chicago NL 3B
Greenberg, Detroit AL .... OF
J. DiMaggio, New York AL ..... OF
Williams, Boston AL .... OF
Danning, New York NL C
Feller, Cleveland AL................. P
Walters, Cincinnati NL............. P
Derringer, Cincinnati NL......... P

1941

Camilli, Brooklyn NL
Gordon, N. Y. AL
Travis, Wash'ton, AL
Hack, Chicago NL
Williams, Boston AL
J. DiMaggio, N. Y. AL
Reiser, Brooklyn NL
Dickey, New York AL
Feller, Cleveland AL
Wyatt, Brooklyn NL
Lee, Chicago NL

1942

1B—Mize, New York NL
2B—Gordon, N. Y. AL
SS—Pesky, Boston AL
3B—Hack, Chicago NL
OF—Williams, Boston AL
OF—J. DiMaggio, N. Y. AL
OF—Slaughter, St. L. NL
C—Owen, Brooklyn NL
P—M. Cooper, St. L. NL
P—Bonham, N. Y. AL
P—Hughson, Boston AL

1943

York, Detroit AL....................... 1B
Herman, Brooklyn NL.............. 2B
Appling, Chicago AL .... SS
Johnson, New York AL............. 3B
Wakefield, Detroit AL............... OF
Musial, St. Louis NL.................. OF
Nicholson, Chicago NL .... OF
W. Cooper, St. Louis NL C
Chandler, New York AL........... P
M. Cooper, St. Louis NL........... P
Sewell, Pittsburgh NL .... P

1944

Sanders, St. Louis NL
Doerr, Boston AL
Marion, St. Louis NL
Elliott, Pittsburgh NL
Musial, St. Louis NL
Wakefield, Detroit AL
F. Walker, Brkn. NL
W. Cooper, St. L. NL
Newhouser, Det. AL
M. Cooper, St. L. NL
Trout, Detroit AL

1945

1B—Cavarretta, Chi. NL
2B—Stirnweiss, N. Y. AL
SS—Marion, St. Louis NL
3B—Kurowski, St. L. NL
OF—Holmes, Boston NL
OF—Pafko, Chicago NL
OF—Rosen, Brooklyn NL
C—Richards, Detroit AL
P—Newhouser, Det. AL
P—Ferriss, Boston AL
P—Borowy, Chicago NL

1946

Musial, St. Louis NL.................. 1B
Doerr, Boston AL 2B
Pesky, Boston AL....................... SS
Kell, Detroit AL......................... 3B
Williams, Boston AL .... OF
D. DiMaggio, Boston AL........... OF
Slaughter, St. Louis NL .... OF
Robinson, New York AL........... C
Newhouser, Detroit AL............. P
Feller, Cleveland AL.................. P
Ferriss, Boston AL..................... P

1947

Mize, New York NL
Gordon, Cleveland AL
Boudreau, Cleve. AL
Kell, Detroit AL
Williams, Boston AL
J. DiMaggio, N. Y. AL
Kiner, Pittsburgh NL
W. Cooper, N. Y. NL
Blackwell, Cin. NL
Feller, Cleveland AL
Branca, Brooklyn NL

1948

1B—Mize, New York NL
2B—Gordon, Cleve. AL
SS—Boudreau, Cleve. AL
3B—Elliott, Boston NL
OF—Williams, Boston AL
OF—J. DiMaggio, N. Y. AL
OF—Musial, St. Louis NL
C—Tebbetts, Boston AL
P—Sain, Boston NL
P—Lemon, Cleveland AL
P—Brecheen, St. L. NL

1949
Henrich, New York AL............. 1B
Robinson, Brooklyn NL............. 2B
Rizzuto, New York AL............. SS
Kell, Detroit AL 3B
Williams, Boston AL .... OF
Musial, St. Louis NL................. OF
Kiner, Pittsburgh NL................ OF
Campanella, Brooklyn NL....... C
Parnell, Boston AL .... P
Kinder, Boston AL .... P
Page, New York AL .... P

1950
Dropo, Boston AL 1B
Robinson, Brkn. NL
Rizzuto, New York AL
Kell, Detroit AL
Musial, St. Louis NL
Kiner, Pittsburgh NL
Doby, Cleveland AL
Berra, New York AL
Raschi, New York AL
Lemon, Cleveland AL
Konstanty, Phila. NL

1951
1B—Fain, Phila. AL
2B—Robinson, Brkn. NL
SS—Rizzuto, N. Y. AL
3B—Kell, Detroit AL
OF—Musial, St. Louis NL
OF—Williams, Boston AL
OF—Kiner, Pittsburgh NL
C—Campanella, Brkn. NL
P—Maglie, N. Y. NL
P—Roe, Brooklyn NL
P—Reynolds, N. Y. AL

1952
Fain, Philadelphia AL 1B
Robinson, Brooklyn NL............. 2B
Rizzuto, New York AL............. SS
Kell, Boston AL 3B
Musial, St. Louis NL................. OF
Sauer, Chicago NL..................... OF
Mantle, New York AL .... OF
Berra, New York AL................. C
Roberts, Philadelphia NL .... P
Shantz, Philadelphia AL........... P
Reynolds, New York AL........... P

1953
Vernon, Wash'ton AL
Schoendienst, St. L. NL
Reese, Brooklyn NL
Rosen, Cleveland AL
Musial, St. Louis NL
Snider, Brooklyn NL
Furillo, Brooklyn NL
Campanella, Brkn. NL
Roberts, Phila'phia NL
Spahn, Milwaukee NL
Porterfield, Wash. AL

1954
1B—Kluszewski, Cin. NL
2B—Avila, Cleveland AL
SS—Dark, New York NL
3B—Rosen, Cleveland AL
OF—Mays, New York NL
OF—Musial, St. Louis NL
OF—Snider, Brooklyn NL
C—Berra, New York AL
P—Lemon, Cleveland AL
P—Antonelli, N. Y. NL
P—Roberts, Phila. NL

1955
Kluszewski, Cincinnati NL 1B
Fox, Chicago AL 2B
Banks, Chicago NL.................... SS
Mathews, Milwaukee NL......... 3B
Snider, Brooklyn NL .... OF
Williams, Boston AL .... OF
Kaline, Detroit AL.................... OF
Campanella, Brooklyn NL....... C
Roberts, Philadelphia NL .... P
Newcombe, Brooklyn NL......... P
Ford, New York AL .... P

1956
Kluszewski, Cin. NL
Fox, Chicago AL
Kuenn, Detroit AL
Boyer, St. Louis NL
Mantle, New York AL
Aaron, Milwaukee NL
Williams, Boston AL
Berra, New York AL
Newcombe, Brkn. NL
Ford, New York AL
Pierce, Chicago AL

1957
1B—Musial, St. Louis NL
2B—Scho'st, N.Y.-Mil. NL
SS—McDougald, N. Y. AL
3B—Mathews, Milw. NL
OF—Mantle, N. Y. AL
OF—Williams, Boston AL
OF—Mays, New York NL
C—Berra, New York AL
P—Spahn, Milw. NL
P—Pierce, Chicago NL
P—Bunning, Detroit AL

1958
Musial, St. Louis NL................. 1B
Fox, Chicago AL 2B
Banks, Chicago NL.................... SS
Thomas, Pittsburgh NL 3B
Williams, Boston AL .... OF
Mays, San Francisco NL .... OF
Aaron, Milwaukee NL .... OF
Crandall, Milwaukee NL C
Turley, New York AL .... P
Spahn, Milwaukee NL .... P
Friend, Pittsburgh NL.............. P

1959
Cepeda, San Fran. NL
Fox, Chicago AL
Banks, Chicago NL
Mathews, Milw. NL
Minoso, Cleveland AL
Mays, San Fran. NL
Aaron, Milwaukee NL
Lollar, Chicago AL
Wynn, Chicago AL
S. Jones, S. Fran. NL
Antonelli, S. Fran. NL

1960
1B—Skowron, N. Y. AL
2B—Mazeroski, Pitts. NL
SS—Banks, Chicago NL
3B—Mathews, Milw. NL
OF—Minoso, Chicago AL
OF—Mays, San Fran. AL
OF—Maris, New York AL
C—Crandall, Milw. NL
P—Law, Pittsburgh NL
P—Spahn, Milw. NL
P—Broglio, St. Louis NL

1961—National
1B—Orlando Cepeda, S.F.
2B—Frank Bolling, Milw.
SS—Maury Wills, L.A.
3B—Ken Boyer, St. Louis
OF—Willie Mays, S.F.
OF—Frank Robinson, Cin.
OF—Roberto Clemente, Pitts.
C—Smoky Burgess, Pitts.
P—Joey Jay, Cincinnati
P—Warren Spahn, Milw.

1961—American
1B—Norm Cash, Detroit
2B—Bobby Richardson, N.Y.
SS—Tony Kubek, N.Y.
3B—Brooks Robinson, Balt.
OF—Mickey Mantle, N.Y.
OF—Roger Maris, N.Y.
OF—Rocky Colavito, Detroit
C—Elston Howard, N.Y.
P—Whitey Ford, N.Y.
P—Frank Lary, Detroit

1962—National
1B—Orlando Cepeda, S.F.
2B—Bill Mazeroski, Pitts.
SS—Maury Wills, L.A.
3B—Ken Boyer, St. Louis
OF—Tommy Davis, L.A.
OF—Willie Mays, S.F.
OF—Frank Robinson, Cin.
C—Del Crandall, Milw.
P—Don Drysdale, L.A.
P—Bob Purkey, Cin.

1962—American
1B—Norm Siebern, K.C.
2B—Bobby Richardson, N.Y.
SS—Tom Tresh, N.Y.
3B—Brooks Robinson, Balt.
OF—Leon Wagner, L.A.
OF—Mickey Mantle, N.Y.
OF—Al Kaline, Detroit
C—Earl Battey, Minnesota
P—Ralph Terry, N.Y.
P—Dick Donovan, Cleve.

1963—National
1B—Bill White, St. Louis
2B—Jim Gilliam, L.A.
SS—Dick Groat, St. Louis
3B—Ken Boyer, St. Louis
OF—Tommy Davis, L.A.
OF—Willie Mays, S.F.
OF—Hank Aaron, Milw.
C—John Edwards, Cin.
P—Sandy Koufax, L.A.
P—Juan Marichal, S.F.

1963—American
1B—Joe Pepitone, N.Y.
2B—Bobby Richardson, N.Y.
SS—Luis Aparicio, Balt.
3B—Frank Malzone, Boston
OF—Carl Yastrzemski, Boston
OF—Albie Pearson, L.A.
OF—Al Kaline, Detroit
C—Elston Howard, N.Y.
P—Whitey Ford, N.Y.
P—Gary Peters, Chicago

1964—American
1B—Dick Stuart, Boston
2B—Bobby Richardson, N.Y.
SS—Jim Fregosi, L.A.
3B—Brooks Robinson, Balt.
OF—Harmon Killebrew, Minn.
OF—Mickey Mantle, N.Y.
OF—Tony Oliva, Minn.
C—Elston Howard, N.Y.
P—Dean Chance, L.A.
P—Gary Peters, Chicago

1964—National
1B—Bill White, St. Louis
2B—Ron Hunt, New York
SS—Dick Groat, St. Louis
3B—Ken Boyer, St. Louis
OF—Billy Williams, Chicago
OF—Willie Mays, San Fran.
OF—Roberto Clemente, Pitts.
C—Joe Torre, Milwaukee
P—Sandy Koufax, L.A.
P—Jim Bunning, Phila.

1965—American
1B—Fred Whitfield, Cleveland
2B—Bobby Richardson, N.Y.
SS—Zoilo Versalles, Minnesota
3B—Brooks Robinson, Balt.
OF—Carl Yastrzemski, Boston
OF—Jimmie Hall, Minnesota
OF—Tony Oliva, Minnesota
C—Earl Battey, Minnesota
P—Jim Grant, Minnesota
P—Mel Stottlemyre, N.Y.

1965—National
1B—Willie McCovey, S.F.
2B—Pete Rose, Cincinnati
SS—Maury Wills, Los Angeles
3B—Deron Johnson, Cincinnati
OF—Willie Stargell, Pitts.
OF—Willie Mays, San Fran.
OF—Hank Aaron, Milwaukee
C—Joe Torre, Milwaukee
P—Sandy Koufax, L.A.
P—Juan Marichal, S.F.

1966—American
1B—Boog Powell, Baltimore
2B—Bobby Richardson, N.Y.
SS—Luis Aparicio, Baltimore
3B—Brooks Robinson, Balt.
OF—Frank Robinson, Balt.
OF—Al Kaline, Detroit
OF—Tony Oliva, Minnesota
C—Paul Casanova, Wash.
P—Jim Kaat, Minnesota
P—Earl Wilson, Detroit

1966—National
1B—Felipe Alou, Atlanta
2B—Pete Rose, Cincinnati
SS—Gene Alley, Pittsburgh
3B—Ron Santo, Chicago
OF—Willie Stargell, Pittsburgh
OF—Willie Mays, San Fran.
OF—Roberto Clemente, Pitts.
C—Joe Torre, Atlanta
P—Sandy Koufax, L.A.
P—Juan Marichal, S.F.

1967—American
1B—Harmon Killebrew, Minn.
2B—Rod Carew, Minnesota
SS—Jim Fregosi, California
3B—Brooks Robinson, Balt.
OF—Carl Yastrzemski, Boston
OF—Al Kaline, Detroit
OF—Frank Robinson, Balt.
C—Bill Freehan, Detroit
P—Jim Lonborg, Boston
P—Earl Wilson, Detroit

1967—National
1B—Orlando Cepeda, St. Louis
2B—Bill Mazeroski, Pittsburgh
SS—Gene Alley, Pittsburgh
3B—Ron Santo, Chicago
OF—Hank Aaron, Atlanta
OF—Jim Wynn, Houston
OF—Roberto Clemente, Pitts.
C—Tim McCarver, St. Louis
P—Mike McCormick, S.F.
P—Ferguson Jenkins, Chi.

1968—American
1B—Boog Powell, Baltimore
2B—Rod Carew, Minnesota
SS—Luis Aparicio, Chicago
3B—Brooks Robinson, Balt.
OF—Ken Harrelson, Boston
OF—Willie Horton, Detroit
OF—Frank Howard, Wash.
C—Bill Freehan, Detroit
P—Dave McNally, Balt.
P—Denny McLain, Detroit

1968—National
1B—Willie McCovey, S.F.
2B—Tommy Helms, Cincinnati
SS—Don Kessinger, Chicago
3B—Ron Santo, Chicago
OF—Billy Williams, Chicago
OF—Curt Flood, St. Louis
OF—Pete Rose, Cincinnati
C—Johnny Bench, Cincinnati
P—Bob Gibson, St. Louis
P—Juan Marichal, S.F.

1969—American
1B—Boog Powell, Baltimore
2B—Rod Carew, Minnesota
SS—Rico Petrocelli, Boston
3B—Harmon Killebrew, Minn.
OF—Frank Howard, Wash.
OF—Paul Blair, Baltimore
OF—Reggie Jackson, Oak.
C—Bill Freehan, Detroit
RHP—Denny McLain, Detroit
LHP—Mike Cuellar, Baltimore

1969—National
1B—Willie McCovey, S.F.
2B—Glenn Beckert, Chicago
SS—Don Kessinger, Chicago
3B—Ron Santo, Chicago
OF—Cleon Jones, New York
OF—Matty Alou, Pittsburgh
OF—Hank Aaron, Atlanta
C—Johnny Bench, Cincinnati
RHP—Tom Seaver, New York
LHP—Steve Carlton, St. Louis

1970—American
1B—Boog Powell, Baltimore
2B—Dave Johnson, Baltimore
SS—Luis Aparicio, Chicago
3B—Harmon Killebrew, Minn.
OF—Frank Howard, Wash.
OF—Reggie Smith, Boston
OF—Tony Oliva, Minnesota
C—Ray Fosse, Cleveland
RHP—Jim Perry, Minnesota
LHP—Sam McDowell, Cleve.

1970—National
1B—Willie McCovey, S.F.
2B—Glenn Beckert, Chicago
SS—Don Kessinger, Chicago
3B—Tony Perez, Cincinnati
OF—Billy Williams, Chicago
OF—Bobby Tolan, Cincinnati
OF—Hank Aaron, Atlanta
C—Johnny Bench, Cincinnati
RHP—Bob Gibson, St. Louis
LHP—Jim Merritt, Cincinnati

1971—American
1B—Norm Cash, Detroit
2B—Cookie Rojas, K.C.
SS—Leo Cardenas, Minnesota
3B—Brooks Robinson, Balt.
OF—Merv Rettenmund, Balt.
OF—Bobby Murcer, N.Y.
OF—Tony Oliva, Minnesota
C—Bill Freehan, Detroit
RHP—Jim Palmer, Baltimore
LHP—Vida Blue, Oakland

1971—National
1B—Lee May, Cincinnati
2B—Glenn Beckert, Chicago
SS—Bud Harrelson, New York
3B—Joe Torre, St. Louis
OF—Willie Stargell, Pittsburgh
OF—Willie Davis, Los Angeles
OF—Hank Aaron, Atlanta
C—Manny Sanguillen, Pitts.
RHP—Ferguson Jenkins, Chi.
LHP—Steve Carlton, St. Louis

1972—American
1B—Dick Allen, Chicago
2B—Rod Carew, Minnesota
SS—Luis Aparicio, Boston
3B—Brooks Robinson, Balt.
OF—Joe Rudi, Oakland
OF—Bobby Murcer, N.Y.
OF—Richie Scheinblum, K.C.
C—Carlton Fisk, Boston
RHP—Gaylord Perry, Cleveland
LHP—Wilbur Wood, Chicago

1972—National
1B—Willie Stargell, Pittsburgh
2B—Joe Morgan, Cincinnati
SS—Chris Speier, San Fran.
3B—Ron Santo, Chicago
OF—Billy Williams, Chicago
OF—Cesar Cedeno, Houston
OF—Roberto Clemente, Pitts.
C—Johnny Bench, Cincinnati
RHP—Ferguson Jenkins, Chi.
LHP—Steve Carlton, Phila.

1973—American
1B—John Mayberry, K.C.
2B—Rod Carew, Minnesota
SS—Bert Campaneris, Oak.
3B—Sal Bando, Oakland
OF—Reggie Jackson, Oak.
OF—Amos Otis, Kansas City
OF—Bobby Murcer, N.Y.
C—Thurman Munson, N.Y.
RHP—Jim Palmer, Baltimore
LHP—Ken Holtzman, Oakland

1973—National
1B—Tony Perez, Cincinnati
2B—Dave Johnson, Atlanta
SS—Bill Russell, Los Angeles
3B—Darrell Evans, Atlanta
OF—Bobby Bonds, San Fran.
OF—Cesar Cedeno, Houston
OF—Pete Rose, Cincinnati
C—Johnny Bench, Cincinnati
RHP—Tom Seaver, New York
LHP—Ron Bryant, San Fran.

1974—American
1B—Dick Allen, Chicago
2B—Rod Carew, Minnesota
SS—Bert Campaneris, Oak.
3B—Sal Bando, Oakland
OF—Joe Rudi, Oakland
OF—Paul Blair, Baltimore
OF—Jeff Burroughs, Texas
C—Thurman Munson, N.Y.
DH—Tommy Davis, Baltimore
RHP—Jim Hunter, Oakland
LHP—Mike Cuellar, Baltimore

1974—National
1B—Steve Garvey, Los Angeles
2B—Joe Morgan, Cincinnati
SS—Dave Concepcion, Cin.
3B—Mike Schmidt, Phila.
OF—Lou Brock, St. Louis
OF—Jim Wynn, Los Angeles
OF—Richie Zisk, Pittsburgh
C—Johnny Bench, Cincinnati
RHP—Andy Messersmith, L.A.
LHP—Don Gullett, Cincinnati

1975—American
1B—John Mayberry, K.C.
2B—Rod Carew, Minnesota
SS—Toby Harrah, Texas
3B—Graig Nettles, New York
OF—Jim Rice, Boston
OF—Fred Lynn, Boston
OF—Reggie Jackson, Oakland
C—Thurman Munson, N.Y.
DH—Willie Horton, Detroit
RHP—Jim Palmer, Baltimore
LHP—Jim Kaat, Chicago

1975—National
1B—Steve Garvey, Los Ang.
2B—Joe Morgan, Cincinnati
SS—Larry Bowa, Philadelphia
3B—Bill Madlock, Chicago
OF—Greg Luzinski, Phila.
OF—Al Oliver, Pittsburgh
OF—Dave Parker, Pittsburgh
C—Johnny Bench, Cincinnati
RHP—Tom Seaver, New York
LHP—Randy Jones, San Diego

1976—American
1B—Chris Chambliss, N.Y.
2B—Bobby Grich, Baltimore
3B—George Brett, K.C.
SS—Mark Belanger, Balt.
OF—Joe Rudi, Oakland
OF—Mickey Rivers, N.Y.
OF—Reggie Jackson, Balt.
C—Thurman Munson, N.Y.
DH—Hal McRae, Kansas City
RHP—Jim Palmer, Baltimore
LHP—Frank Tanana, Calif.

1976—National
1B—Willie Montanez, S.F.-Atl.
2B—Joe Morgan, Cincinnati
3B—Mike Schmidt, Phila.
SS—Dave Concepcion, Cin.
OF—George Foster, Cincinnati
OF—Cesar Cedeno, Houston
OF—Ken Griffey, Cincinnati
C—Bob Boone, Philadelphia
RHP—Don Sutton, Los Angeles
LHP—Randy Jones, San Diego

1977—American
1B—Rod Carew, Minn.
2B—Willie Randolph, N.Y.
3B—Graig Nettles, N.Y.
SS—Rick Burleson, Boston
OF—Jim Rice, Boston
OF—Larry Hisle, Minn.
OF—Bobby Bonds, Calif.
C—Carlton Fisk, Boston
DH—Hal McRae, K.C.
RHP—Nolan Ryan, Calif.
LHP—Frank Tanana, Calif.

1977—National
1B—Steve Garvey, L.A.
2B—Joe Morgan, Cincinnati
3B—Mike Schmidt, Phila.
SS—Garry Templeton, St. L.
OF—George Foster, Cin.
OF—Dave Parker, Pitts.
OF—Greg Luzinski, Phila.
C—Ted Simmons, St. Louis
RHP—Rick Reuschel, Chicago
LHP—Steve Carlton, Phila.

1978—American
1B—Rod Carew, Minnesota
2B—Frank White, K.C.
3B—Graig Nettles, N.Y.
SS—Robin Yount, Milw.
OF—Jim Rice, Boston
OF—Larry Hisle, Milw.
OF—Fred Lynn, Boston
C—Jim Sundberg, Texas
DH—Rusty Staub, Detroit
RHP—Jim Palmer, Balt.
LHP—Ron Guidry, N.Y.

1978—National
1B—Steve Garvey, L.A.
2B—Dave Lopes, Los Angeles
3B—Pete Rose, Cincinnati
SS—Larry Bowa, Phila.
OF—George Foster, Cin.
OF—Dave Parker, Pitts.
OF—Jack Clark, San Fran.
C—Ted Simmons, St. Louis
RHP—Gaylord Perry, S.D.
LHP—Vida Blue, San Fran.

1979—American
1B—Cecil Cooper, Milw.
2B—Bobby Grich, Calif.
3B—George Brett, K.C.
SS—Roy Smalley, Minn.
OF—Jim Rice, Boston
OF—Fred Lynn, Boston
OF—Ken Singleton, Balt.

C—Darrell Porter, K.C.
DH—Don Baylor, Calif.
RHP—Jim Kern, Texas
LHP—Mike Flanagan, Balt.

1979—National
1B—Keith Hernandez, St. L.
2B—Dave Lopes, Los Angeles
3B—Mike Schmidt, Phila.
SS—Garry Templeton, St. L.
OF—Dave Kingman, Chicago
OF—Omar Moreno, Pittsburgh
OF—Dave Winfield, San Diego

C—Ted Simmons, St. Louis
RHP—Joe Niekro, Houston
LHP—Steve Carlton, Phila.

1980—American
1B—Cecil Cooper, Milw.
2B—Willie Randolph, N.Y.
3B—George Brett, K.C.
SS—Robin Yount, Milw.
OF—Ben Oglivie, Milw.
OF—Al Bumbry, Baltimore
OF—Reggie Jackson, N.Y.
DH—Reggie Jackson, N.Y.
C—Rick Cerone, N.Y.
RHP—Steve Stone, Balt.
LHP—Tommy John, N.Y.

1980—National
1B—Keith Hernandez, St. L.
2B—Manny Trillo, Phila.
3B—Mike Schmidt, Phila.
SS—Garry Templeton, St. L.
OF—Dusty Baker, L.A.
OF—Cesar Cedeno, Houston
OF—George Hendrick, St. L.
C—Gary Carter, Montreal
RHP—Jim Bibby, Pittsburgh
LHP—Steve Carlton, Phila.

1981—American
1B—Cecil Cooper, Milw.
2B—Bobby Grich, Calif.
3B—Buddy Bell, Texas
SS—Rick Burleson, Calif.
OF—Rickey Henderson, Oak.
OF—Dwayne Murphy, Oak.
OF—Tony Armas, Oak.
C—Jim Sundberg, Texas
DH—Richie Zisk, Seattle
RHP—Jack Morris, Detroit
LHP—Ron Guidry, N.Y.

1981—National
1B—Pete Rose, Phila.
2B—Manny Trillo, Phila.
3B—Mike Schmidt, Phila.
SS—Dave Concepcion, Cin.
OF—George Foster, Cin.
OF—Andre Dawson, Mon.
OF—Pedro Guerrero, L.A.
C—Gary Carter, Montreal
RHP—Tom Seaver, Cincinnati
LHP—Fernando Valenzuela, L.A.

1982—American
1B—Cecil Cooper, Milw.
2B—Damaso Garcia, Tor.
3B—Doug DeCinces, Calif.
SS—Robin Yount, Milw.
OF—Dave Winfield, N.Y.
OF—Gorman Thomas, Milw.
OF—Dwight Evans, Boston
C—Lance Parrish, Detroit
DH—Hal McRae, K.C.
RHP—Dave Stieb, Toronto
LHP—Geoff Zahn, Calif.

1982—National
1B—Al Oliver, Montreal
2B—Manny Trillo, Phila.
3B—Mike Schmidt, Phila.
SS—Ozzie Smith, St. Louis
OF—Lonnie Smith, St. Louis
OF—Dale Murphy, Atlanta
OF—Pedro Guerrero, L.A.
C—Gary Carter, Montreal
RHP—Steve Rogers, Montreal
LHP—Steve Carlton, Phila.

1983—American
1B—Eddie Murray, Balt.
2B—Lou Whitaker, Detroit
3B—Wade Boggs, Boston
SS—Cal Ripken, Balt.
OF—Jim Rice, Boston
OF—Dave Winfield, N.Y.
OF—Lloyd Moseby, Toronto
C—Carlton Fisk, Chicago
DH—Greg Luzinski, Chicago
RHP—LaMarr Hoyt, Chicago
LHP—Ron Guidry, New York

1983—National
1B—George Hendrick, St. L.
2B—Glenn Hubbard, Atlanta
3B—Mike Schmidt, Phila.
SS—Dickie Thon, Houston
OF—Dale Murphy, Atlanta
OF—Andre Dawson, Montreal
OF—Tim Raines, Montreal
C—Tony Pena, Pittsburgh
RHP—John Denny, Phila.
LHP—Larry McWilliams, Pitts.

1984—American
1B—Don Mattingly, N.Y.
2B—Lou Whitaker, Detroit
3B—Buddy Bell, Texas
SS—Cal Ripken, Baltimore
OF—Tony Armas, Boston
OF—Dwight Evans, Boston
OF—Dave Winfield, N.Y.
C—Lance Parrish, Detroit
DH—Dave Kingman, Oak.
RHP—Mike Boddicker, Balt.
LHP—Willie Hernandez, Det.

1984—National
1B—Keith Hernandez, N.Y.
2B—Ryne Sandberg, Chicago
3B—Mike Schmidt, Phila.
SS—Ozzie Smith, St. Louis
OF—Dale Murphy, Atlanta
OF—Jose Cruz, Houston
OF—Tony Gwynn, S.D.
C—Gary Carter, Montreal
RHP—Rick Sutcliffe, Chicago
LHP—Mark Thurmond, S.D.

1985—American
1B—Don Mattingly, N.Y.
2B—Damaso Garcia, Tor.
3B—Wade Boggs, Boston
SS—Cal Ripken, Balt.
OF—Rickey Henderson, N.Y.
OF—Harold Baines, Chicago
OF—Phil Bradley, Seattle
C—Carlton Fisk, Chicago
DH—Don Baylor, New York
RHP—Bret Saberhagen, K.C.
LHP—Ron Guidry, New York

1985—National
1B—Keith Hernandez, N.Y.
2B—Tom Herr, St. Louis
3B—Tim Wallach, Mon.
SS—Ozzie Smith, St. L.
OF—Dave Parker, Cin.
OF—Willie McGee, St. Louis
OF—Dale Murphy, Atlanta
C—Gary Carter, N.Y.
RHP—Dwight Gooden, N.Y.
LHP—John Tudor, St. Louis

1986—American
1B—Don Mattingly, N.Y.
2B—Tony Bernazard, Cleve.
3B—Wade Boggs, Boston
SS—Tony Fernandez, Tor.
OF—Jim Rice, Boston
OF—George Bell, Toronto
OF—Kirby Puckett, Minn.
C—Rich Gedman, Boston
DH—Don Baylor, Boston
RHP—Roger Clemens, Boston
LHP—Teddy Higuera, Milw.

1986—National
1B—Keith Hernandez, N.Y.
2B—Steve Sax, L.A.
3B—Mike Schmidt, Phila.
SS—Ozzie Smith, St. Louis
OF—Tim Raines, Montreal
OF—Tony Gwynn, San Diego
OF—Dave Parker, Cincinnati
C—Gary Carter, New York
RHP—Mike Scott, Hou.
LHP—Fernando Valenzuela, L.A.

1987—American
1B—Don Mattingly, N.Y.
2B—Willie Randolph, N.Y.
3B—Wade Boggs, Boston
SS—Alan Trammell, Det.
OF—George Bell, Toronto
OF—Kirby Puckett, Minn.
OF—Dwight Evans, Bos.
C—Matt Nokes, Detroit
DH—Paul Molitor, Milw.
RHP—Roger Clemens, Bos.
LHP—Jimmy Key, Toronto

1987—National
1B—Jack Clark, St. Louis
2B—Juan Samuel, Philadelphia
3B—Tim Wallach, Montreal
SS—Ozzie Smith, St. Louis
OF—Andre Dawson, Chicago
OF—Tony Gwynn, San Diego
OF—Eric Davis, Cincinnati
C—Benito Santiago, S.D.
RHP—Rick Sutcliffe, Chicago
LHP—Zane Smith, Atlanta

Gold Glove Fielding Teams

1957 Majors
P—Shantz, N.Y. AL
C—Lollar, Chicago AL
1B—Hodges, Brooklyn
2B—Fox, Chicago AL
3B—Malzone, Boston
SS—McMillan, Cin.
OF—Minoso, Chicago AL
OF—Mays, N.Y. NL
OF—Kaline, Detroit

1958 American
P—Shantz, New York
C—Lollar, Chicago
1B—Power, Cleveland
2B—Bolling, Detroit
3B—Malzone, Boston
SS—Aparicio, Chicago
OF—Siebern, New York
OF—Piersall, Boston
OF—Kaline, Detroit

1958 National
P—Haddix, Cincinnati
C—Crandall, Milwaukee
1B—Hodges, Los Angeles
2B—Mazeroski, Pitt.
3B—Boyer, St. Louis
SS—McMillan, Cin.
OF—Robinson, Cin.
OF—Mays, San Fran.
OF—Aaron, Milwaukee

1959 American
P—Shantz, New York
C—Lollar, Chicago
1B—Power, Cleveland
2B—Fox, Chicago
3B—Malzone, Boston
SS—Aparicio, Chicago
OF—Minoso, Cleveland
OF—Kaline, Detroit
OF—Jensen, Boston

1959 National
P—Haddix, Pittsburgh
C—Crandall, Milwaukee
1B—Hodges, Los Angeles
2B—Neal, Los Angeles
3B—Boyer, St. Louis
SS—McMillan, Cincinnati
OF—Brandt, San Fran.
OF—Mays, San Francisco
OF—Aaron, Milwaukee

1960 American
P—Shantz, New York
C—Battey, Washington
1B—Power, Cleveland
2B—Fox, Chicago
3B—Robinson, Baltimore
SS—Aparicio, Chicago
OF—Minoso, Chicago
OF—Landis, Chicago
OF—Maris, New York

1960 National
P—Haddix, Pittsburgh
C—Crandall, Milwaukee
1B—White, St. Louis
2B—Mazeroski, Pittsburgh
3B—Boyer, St. Louis
SS—Banks, Chicago
OF—Moon, Los Angeles
OF—Mays, San Francisco
OF—Aaron, Milwaukee

1961 American
P—Lary, Detroit
C—Battey, Chicago
1B—Power, Cleveland
2B—Richardson, N.Y.
3B—Robinson, Baltimore
SS—Aparicio, Chicago
OF—Kaline, Detroit
OF—Piersall, Cleveland
OF—Landis, Chicago

1961 National
P—Shantz, Pittsburgh
C—Roseboro, Los Angeles
1B—White, St. Louis
2B—Mazeroski, Pittsburgh
3B—Boyer, St. Louis
SS—Wills, Los Angeles
OF—Mays, San Francisco
OF—Clemente, Pittsburgh
OF—Pinson, Cincinnati

1962 American
P—Kaat, Minnesota
C—Battey, Minnesota
1B—Power, Minnesota
2B—Richardson, N.Y.
3B—Robinson, Baltimore
SS—Aparicio, Chicago
OF—Landis, Chicago
OF—Mantle, New York
OF—Kaline, Detroit

1962 National
P—Shantz, St. Louis
C—Crandall, Milwaukee
1B—White, St. Louis
2B—Hubbs, Chicago
3B—Davenport, S.F.
SS—Wills, Los Angeles
OF—Mays, San Francisco
OF—Clemente, Pittsburgh
OF—Virdon, Pittsburgh

1963 American
P—Kaat, Minnesota
C—Howard, New York
1B—Power, Minnesota
2B—Richardson, N.Y.
3B—Robinson, Baltimore
SS—Versalles, Minnesota
OF—Kaline, Detroit
OF—Yastrzemski, Boston
OF—Landis, Chicago

1963 National
P—Shantz, St. Louis
C—Edwards, Cincinnati
1B—White, St. Louis
2B—Mazeroski, Pittsburgh
3B—Boyer, St. Louis
SS—Wine, Philadelphia
OF—Mays, San Francisco
OF—Clemente, Pittsburgh
OF—Flood, St. Louis

1964 American
P—Kaat, Minnesota
C—Howard, New York
1B—Power, Los Angeles
2B—Richardson, N.Y.
3B—Robinson, Baltimore
SS—Aparicio, Baltimore
OF—Kaline, Detroit
OF—Landis, Chicago
OF—Davalillo, Cleveland

1964 National
P—Shantz, Philadelphia
C—Edwards, Cincinnati
1B—White, St. Louis
2B—Mazeroski, Pittsburgh
3B—Santo, Chicago
SS—Amaro, Philadelphia
OF—Mays, San Francisco
OF—Clemente, Pittsburgh
OF—Flood, St. Louis

1965 American
P—Kaat, Minnesota
C—Freehan, Detroit
1B—Pepitone, New York
2B—Richardson, N.Y.
3B—Robinson, Baltimore
SS—Versalles, Minnesota
OF—Kaline, Detroit
OF—Tresh, New York
OF—Yastrzemski, Boston

1965 National
P—Gibson, St. Louis
C—Torre, Atlanta
1B—White, St. Louis
2B—Mazeroski, Pittsburgh
3B—Santo, Chicago
SS—Cardenas, Cincinnati
OF—Mays, San Francisco
OF—Clemente, Pittsburgh
OF—Flood, St. Louis

1966 American
P—Kaat, Minnesota
C—Freehan, Detroit
1B—Pepitone, New York
2B—Knoop, California
3B—B. Robinson, Balt.
SS—Aparicio, Baltimore
OF—Kaline, Detroit
OF—Agee, Chicago
OF—Oliva, Minnesota

1966 National
P—Gibson, St. Louis
C—Roseboro, Los Angeles
1B—White, Philadelphia
2B—Mazeroski, Pittsburgh
3B—Santo, Chicago
SS—Alley, Pittsburgh
OF—Mays, San Francisco
OF—Flood, St. Louis
OF—Clemente, Pittsburgh

1967 American
P—Kaat, Minnesota
C—Freehan, Detroit
1B—Scott, Boston
2B—Knoop, California
3B—B. Robinson, Balt.
SS—Fregosi, California
OF—Yastrzemski, Boston
OF—Blair, Baltimore
OF—Kaline, Detroit

1967 National
P—Gibson, St. Louis
C—Hundley, Chicago
1B—Parker, Los Angeles
2B—Mazeroski, Pittsburgh
3B—Santo, Chicago
SS—Alley, Pittsburgh
OF—Clemente, Pittsburgh
OF—Flood, St. Louis
OF—Mays, San Francisco

1968 American
P—Kaat, Minnesota
C—Freehan, Detroit
1B—Scott, Boston
2B—Knoop, California
3B—B. Robinson, Balt.
SS—Aparicio, Chicago
OF—Stanley, Detroit
OF—Yastrzemski, Boston
OF—Smith, Boston

1968 National
P—Gibson, St. Louis
C—Bench, Cincinnati
1B—Parker, Los Angeles
2B—Beckert, Chicago
3B—Santo, Chicago
SS—Maxvill, St. Louis
OF—Mays, San Francisco
OF—Clemente, Pittsburgh
OF—Flood, St. Louis

1969 American
P—Kaat, Minnesota
C—Freehan, Detroit
1B—Pepitone, New York
2B—Johnson, Baltimore
3B—B. Robinson, Balt.
SS—Belanger, Baltimore
OF—Blair, Baltimore
OF—Stanley, Detroit
OF—Yastrzemski, Boston

1969 National
P—Gibson, St. Louis
C—Bench, Cincinnati
1B—Parker, Los Angeles
2B—Millan, Atlanta
3B—Boyer, Atlanta
SS—Kessinger, Chicago
OF—Clemente, Pittsburgh
OF—Flood, St. Louis
OF—Rose, Cincinnati

1970 American
P—Kaat, Minnesota
C—Fosse, Cleveland
1B—Spencer, California
2B—Johnson, Baltimore
3B—B. Robinson, Balt.
SS—Aparicio, Chicago
OF—Stanley, Detroit
OF—Blair, Baltimore
OF—Berry, Chicago

1970 National
P—Gibson, St. Louis
C—Bench, Cincinnati
1B—Parker, Los Angeles
2B—Helms, Cincinnati
3B—Rader, Houston
SS—Kessinger, Chicago
OF—Clemente, Pittsburgh
OF—Agee, New York
OF—Rose, Cincinnati

1971 American
P—Kaat, Minnesota
C—Fosse, Cleveland
1B—Scott, Boston
2B—Johnson, Baltimore
3B—B. Robinson, Balt.
SS—Belanger, Baltimore
OF—Blair, Baltimore
OF—Otis, Kansas City
OF—Yastrzemski, Boston

1971 National
P—Gibson, St. Louis
C—Bench, Cincinnati
1B—Parker, Los Angeles
2B—Helms, Cincinnati
3B—Rader, Houston
SS—Harrelson, New York
OF—Clemente, Pittsburgh
OF—Bonds, San Francisco
OF—Davis, Los Angeles

1972 American
P—Kaat, Minnesota
C—Fisk, Boston
1B—Scott, Milwaukee
2B—Griffin, Boston
3B—Robinson, Baltimore
SS—Brinkman, Detroit
OF—Blair, Baltimore
OF—Murcer, New York
OF—Berry, California

1972 National
P—Gibson, St. Louis
C—Bench, Cincinnati
1B—Parker, Los Angeles
2B—Millan, Atlanta
3B—Rader, Houston
SS—Bowa, Philadelphia
OF—Clemente, Pittsburgh
OF—Cedeno, Houston
OF—Davis, Los Angeles

1973 American
P—Kaat, Chicago
C—Munson, New York
1B—Scott, Milwaukee
2B—Grich, Baltimore
3B—Robinson, Baltimore
SS—Belanger, Baltimore
OF—Blair, Baltimore
OF—Otis, Kansas City
OF—Stanley, Detroit

1973 National
P—Gibson, St. Louis
C—Bench, Cincinnati
1B—Jorgensen, Montreal
2B—Morgan, Cincinnati
3B—Rader, Houston
SS—Metzger, Houston
OF—Bonds, San Francisco
OF—Cedeno, Houston
OF—Davis, Los Angeles

1974 American
P—Kaat, Chicago
C—Munson, New York
1B—Scott, Milwaukee
2B—Grich, Baltimore
3B—Robinson, Baltimore
SS—Belanger, Baltimore
OF—Blair, Baltimore
OF—Otis, Kansas City
OF—Rudi, Oakland

1974 National
P—Messersmith, L.A.
C—Bench, Cincinnati
1B—Garvey, Los Angeles
2B—Morgan, Cincinnati
3B—Rader, Houston
SS—Concepcion, Cincinnati
OF—Cedeno, Houston
OF—Geronimo, Cincinnati
OF—Bonds, San Francisco

1975 American
P—Kaat, Chicago
C—Munson, New York
1B—Scott, Milwaukee
2B—Grich, Baltimore
3B—Robinson, Baltimore
SS—Belanger, Baltimore
OF—Blair, Baltimore
OF—Rudi, Oakland
OF—Lynn, Boston

1975 National
P—Messersmith, L.A.
C—Bench, Cincinnati
1B—Garvey, Los Angeles
2B—Morgan, Cincinnati
3B—Reitz, St. Louis
SS—Concepcion, Cincinnati
OF—Cedeno, Houston
OF—Geronimo, Cincinnati
OF—Maddox, Philadelphia

1976 American
P—Palmer, Baltimore
C—Sundberg, Texas
1B—Scott, Milwaukee
2B—Grich, Baltimore
3B—Rodriguez, Detroit
SS—Belanger, Baltimore
OF—Rudi, Oakland
OF—Evans, Boston
OF—Manning, Cleveland

1976 National
P—Kaat, Philadelphia
C—Bench, Cincinnati
1B—Garvey, Los Angeles
2B—Morgan, Cincinnati
3B—Schmidt, Philadelphia
SS—Concepcion, Cincinnati
OF—Cedeno, Houston
OF—Geronimo, Cincinnati
OF—Maddox, Philadelphia

1977 American
P—Palmer, Baltimore
C—Sundberg, Texas
1B—Spencer, Chicago
2B—White, Kansas City
3B—Nettles, New York
SS—Belanger, Baltimore
OF—Beniquez, Texas
OF—Yastrzemski, Boston
OF—Cowens, Kansas City

1977 National
P—Kaat, Philadelphia
C—Bench, Cincinnati
1B—Garvey, Los Angeles
2B—Morgan, Cincinnati
3B—Schmidt, Philadelphia
SS—Concepcion, Cincinnati
OF—Geronimo, Cincinnati
OF—Maddox, Philadelphia
OF—Parker, Pittsburgh

1978 American
P—Palmer, Baltimore
C—Sundberg, Texas
1B—Chambliss, New York
2B—White, Kansas City
3B—Nettles, New York
SS—Belanger, Baltimore
OF—Lynn, Boston
OF—Evans, Boston
OF—Miller, California

1978 National
P—Niekro, Atlanta
C—Boone, Philadelphia
1B—Hernandez, St. Louis
2B—Lopes, Los Angeles
3B—Schmidt, Philadelphia
SS—Bowa, Philadelphia
OF—Maddox, Philadelphia
OF—Parker, Pittsburgh
OF—Valentine, Montreal

1979 American
P—Palmer, Baltimore
C—Sundberg, Texas
1B—Cooper, Milwaukee
2B—White, Kansas City
3B—Bell, Texas
SS—Burleson, Boston
OF—Evans, Boston
OF—Lezcano, Milwaukee
OF—Lynn, Boston

1979 National
P—Niekro, Atlanta
C—Boone, Philadelphia
1B—Hernandez, St. Louis
2B—Trillo, Philadelphia
3B—Schmidt, Philadelphia
SS—Concepcion, Cincinnati
OF—Maddox, Philadelphia
OF—Parker, Pittsburgh
OF—Winfield, San Diego

1980 American
P—Norris, Oakland
C—Sundberg, Texas
1B—Cooper, Milwaukee
2B—White, Kansas City
3B—Bell, Texas
SS—Trammell, Detroit
OF—Lynn, Boston
OF—Murphy, Oakland
OF—Wilson, Kansas City

1980 National
P—Niekro, Atlanta
C—Carter, Montreal
1B—Hernandez, St. Louis
2B—Flynn, New York
3B—Schmidt, Philadelphia
SS—Smith, San Diego
OF—Dawson, Montreal
OF—Maddox, Philadelphia
OF—Winfield, San Diego

1981 American
P—Norris, Oakland
C—Sundberg, Texas
1B—Squires, Chicago
2B—White, Kansas City
3B—Bell, Texas
SS—Trammell, Detroit
OF—Murphy, Oakland
OF—Evans, Boston
OF—Henderson, Oakland

1981 National
P—Carlton, Philadelphia
C—Carter, Montreal
1B—Hernandez, St. Louis
2B—Trillo, Philadelphia
3B—Schmidt, Philadelphia
SS—Smith, San Diego
OF—Dawson, Montreal
OF—Maddox, Philadelphia
OF—Baker, Los Angeles

1982 American
P—Guidry, New York
C—Boone, California
1B—Murray, Baltimore
2B—White, Kansas City
3B—Bell, Texas
SS—Yount, Milwaukee
OF—Evans, Boston
OF—Winfield, New York
OF—Murphy, Oakland

1982 National
P—Niekro, Atlanta
C—Carter, Montreal
1B—Hernandez, St. Louis
2B—Trillo, Philadelphia
3B—Schmidt, Philadelphia
SS—O. Smith, St. Louis
OF—Dawson, Montreal
OF—Murphy, Atlanta
OF—Maddox, Philadelphia

1983 American
P—Guidry, New York
C—Parrish, Detroit
1B—Murray, Baltimore
2B—Whitaker, Detroit
3B—Bell, Texas
SS—Trammell, Detroit
OF—Evans, Boston
OF—Winfield, New York
OF—Murphy, Oakland

1983 National
P—Niekro, Atlanta
C—Pena, Pittsburgh
1B—Hernandez, St.L.-N.Y.
2B—Sandberg, Chicago
3B—Schmidt, Philadelphia
SS—O. Smith, St. Louis
OF—Dawson, Montreal
OF—Murphy, Atlanta
OF—McGee, St. Louis

1984 American
P—Guidry, New York
C—Parrish, Detroit
1B—Murray, Baltimore
2B—Whitaker, Detroit
3B—Bell, Texas
SS—Trammell, Detroit
OF—Evans, Boston
OF—Winfield, New York
OF—Murphy, Oakland

1984 National
P—Andujar, St. Louis
C—Pena, Pittsburgh
1B—Hernandez, New York
2B—Sandberg, Chicago
3B—Schmidt, Philadelphia
SS—O. Smith, St. Louis
OF—Murphy, Atlanta
OF—Dernier, Chicago
OF—Dawson, Montreal

1985 American
P—Guidry, New York
C—Parrish, Detroit
1B—Mattingly, New York
2B—Whitaker, Detroit
3B—Brett, Kansas City
SS—Griffin, Oakland
OF—Pettis, California
OF—Winfield, New York
OF—Evans, Boston (tie)
—Murphy, Oakland (tie)

1985 National
P—Reuschel, Pittsburgh
C—Pena, Pittsburgh
1B—Hernandez, New York
2B—Sandberg, Chicago
3B—Wallach, Montreal
SS—O. Smith, St. Louis
OF—McGee, St. Louis
OF—Murphy, Atlanta
OF—Dawson, Montreal

1986 American
P—Guidry, New York
C—Boone, California
1B—Mattingly, New York
2B—White, Kansas City
3B—Gaetti, Minnesota
SS—Fernandez, Toronto
OF—Pettis, California
OF—Barfield, Toronto
OF—Puckett, Minnesota

1986 National
P—Valenzuela, Los Angeles
C—Davis, Chicago
1B—Hernandez, New York
2B—Sandberg, Chicago
3B—Schmidt, Philadelphia
SS—Smith, St. Louis
OF—Gwynn, San Diego
OF—Murphy, Atlanta
OF—McGee, St. Louis

1987 American
P—Langston, Seattle
C—Boone, California
1B—Mattingly, New York
2B—White, Kansas City
3B—Gaetti, Minnesota
SS—Fernandez, Toronto
OF—Barfield, Toronto
OF—Puckett, Minnesota
OF—Winfield, New York

1987 National
P—Reuschel, Pitt.-S.F.
C—LaValliere, Pittsburgh
1B—Hernandez, New York
2B—Sandberg, Chicago
3B—Pendleton, St. Louis
SS—Smith, St. Louis
OF—Davis, Cincinnati
OF—Gwynn, San Diego
OF—Dawson, Chicago

Silver Slugger Teams

1980 American
1B—Cecil Cooper, Milw.
2B—Willie Randolph, N.Y.
3B—George Brett, K.C.
SS—Robin Yount, Milw.
OF—Ben Oglivie, Milw.
OF—Al Oliver, Texas
OF—Willie Wilson, K.C.
C—Lance Parrish, Detroit
DH—Reggie Jackson, N.Y.

1980 National
1B—Keith Hernandez, St.L.
2B—Manny Trillo, Phila.
3B—Mike Schmidt, Phila.
SS—Garry Templeton, St.L.
OF—Dusty Baker, Los Angeles
OF—Andre Dawson, Montreal
OF—George Hendrick, St.L.
C—Ted Simmons, St. Louis
P—Bob Forsch, St. Louis

1981 American
1B—Cecil Cooper, Milw.
2B—Bobby Grich, Calif.
3B—Carney Lansford, Bos.
SS—Rick Burleson, Calif.
OF—Rickey Henderson, Oak.
OF—Dwight Evans, Boston
OF—Dave Winfield, N.Y.
C—Carlton Fisk, Chicago
DH—Al Oliver, Texas

1981 National
1B—Pete Rose, Philadelphia
2B—Manny Trillo, Phila.
3B—Mike Schmidt, Phila.
SS—Dave Concepcion, Cin.
OF—Andre Dawson, Montreal
OF—George Foster, Cincinnati
OF—Dusty Baker, Los Angeles
C—Gary Carter, Montreal
P—Fernando Valenzuela, L.A.

1982 American
1B—Cecil Cooper, Milw.
2B—Damaso Garcia, Tor.
3B—Doug DeCinces, Calif.
SS—Robin Yount, Milw.
OF—Dave Winfield, N.Y.
OF—Willie Wilson, K.C.
OF—Reggie Jackson, Calif.
C—Lance Parrish, Detroit
DH—Hal McRae, K.C.

1982 National
1B—Al Oliver, Montreal
2B—Joe Morgan, S.F.
3B—Mike Schmidt, Phila.
SS—Dave Concepcion, Cin.
OF—Dale Murphy, Atlanta
OF—Pedro Guerrero, L.A.
OF—Leon Durham, Chicago
C—Gary Carter, Montreal
P—Don Robinson, Pittsburgh

1983 American
1B—Eddie Murray, Balt.
2B—Lou Whitaker, Detroit
3B—Wade Boggs, Boston
SS—Cal Ripken, Baltimore
OF—Jim Rice, Boston
OF—Dave Winfield, N.Y.
OF—Lloyd Moseby, Toronto
C—Lance Parrish, Detroit
DH—Don Baylor, New York

1983 National
1B—George Hendrick, St.L.
2B—Johnny Ray, Pittsburgh
3B—Mike Schmidt, Phila.
SS—Dickie Thon, Houston
OF—Andre Dawson, Montreal
OF—Dale Murphy, Atlanta
OF—Jose Cruz, Houston
C—Terry Kennedy, San Diego
P—Fernando Valenzuela, L.A.

1984 American
1B—Eddie Murray, Balt.
2B—Lou Whitaker, Detroit
3B—Buddy Bell, Texas
SS—Cal Ripken, Baltimore
OF—Tony Armas, Boston
OF—Jim Rice, Boston
OF—Dave Winfield, N.Y.
C—Lance Parrish, Detroit
DH—Andre Thornton, Cleve.

1984 National
1B—Keith Hernandez, N.Y.
2B—Ryne Sandberg, Chicago
3B—Mike Schmidt, Phila.
SS—Garry Templeton, S.D.
OF—Dale Murphy, Atlanta
OF—Jose Cruz, Houston
OF—Tony Gwynn, San Diego
C—Gary Carter, Montreal
P—Rick Rhoden, Pittsburgh

1985 American
1B—Don Mattingly, N.Y.
2B—Lou Whitaker, Detroit
3B—George Brett, K.C.
SS—Cal Ripken, Baltimore
OF—Rickey Henderson, N.Y.
OF—Dave Winfield, N.Y.
OF—George Bell, Toronto
C—Carlton Fisk, Chicago
DH—Don Baylor, New York

1985 National
1B—Jack Clark, St. Louis
2B—Ryne Sandberg, Chi.
3B—Tim Wallach, Montreal
SS—Hubie Brooks, Montreal
OF—Willie McGee, St. Louis
OF—Dale Murphy, Atlanta
OF—Dave Parker, Cincinnati
C—Gary Carter, New York
P—Rick Rhoden, Pittsburgh

1986 American
1B—Don Mattingly, N.Y.
2B—Frank White, K.C.
3B—Wade Boggs, Boston
SS—Cal Ripken, Baltimore
OF—George Bell, Toronto
OF—Kirby Puckett, Minn.
OF—Jesse Barfield, Toronto
C—Lance Parrish, Detroit
DH—Don Baylor, Boston

1986 National
1B—Glenn Davis, Houston
2B—Steve Sax, L.A.
3B—Mike Schmidt, Phila.
SS—Hubie Brooks, Montreal
OF—Tony Gwynn, San Diego
OF—Tim Raines, Montreal
OF—Dave Parker, Cincinnati
C—Gary Carter, New York
P—Rick Rhoden, Pittsburgh

1987 American
1B—Don Mattingly, N.Y.
2B—Lou Whitaker, Det.
3B—Wade Boggs, Boston
SS—Alan Trammell, Det.
OF—George Bell, Toronto
OF—Dwight Evans, Boston
OF—Kirby Puckett, Minn.
C—Matt Nokes, Detroit
DH—Paul Molitor, Milw.

1987 National
1B—Jack Clark, St. Louis
2B—Juan Samuel, Philadelphia
3B—Tim Wallach, Montreal
SS—Ozzie Smith, St. Louis
OF—Andre Dawson, Chicago
OF—Eric Davis, Cincinnati
OF—Tony Gwynn, San Diego
C—Benito Santiago, S.D.
P—Bob Forsch, St. Louis

Baseball Writers' Association Awards
Most Valuable Player Citations

CHALMERS AWARD

AMERICAN LEAGUE			NATIONAL LEAGUE		
Year Player Club		Points	Player Club		Points
1911—Tyrus Cobb, Detroit, of		64	Frank Schulte, Chicago, of		29
1912—Tristram Speaker, Boston, of		59	Lawrence Doyle, New York, 2b		48
1913—Walter Johnson, Washington, p		54	Jacob Daubert, Brooklyn, 1b		50
1914—Edward Collins, Philadelphia, 2b		63	John Evers, Boston, 2b		50

LEAGUE AWARDS

AMERICAN LEAGUE			NATIONAL LEAGUE		
Year Player Club		Points	Player Club		Points
1922—George Sisler, St. Louis, 1b		59	No selection		
1923—George Ruth, New York, of		64	No selection		
1924—Walter Johnson, Washington, p		55	Arthur Vance, Brooklyn, p		74
1925—Roger Peckinpaugh, Washington, ss		45	Rogers Hornsby, St. Louis, 2b		73
1926—George Burns, Cleveland, 1b		63	Robert O'Farrell, St. Louis, c		79
1927—H. Louis Gehrig, New York, 1b		56	Paul Waner, Pittsburgh, of		72
1928—Gordon Cochrane, Philadelphia, c		53	James Bottomley, St. Louis, 1b		76
1929—No selection			Rogers Hornsby, Chicago, 2b		60

BASEBALL WRITERS' ASSOCIATION MVP AWARDS

AMERICAN LEAGUE			NATIONAL LEAGUE		
Year Player Club		Points	Player Club		Points
1931—Robert Grove, Philadelphia, p		78	Frank Frisch, St. Louis, 2b		65
1932—James Foxx, Philadelphia, 1b		75	Charles Klein, Philadelphia, of		78
1933—James Foxx, Philadelphia, 1b		74	Carl Hubbell, New York, p		77
1934—Gordon Cochrane, Detroit, c		67	Jerome Dean, St. Louis, p		78
1935—Henry Greenberg, Detroit, 1b		*80	Charles Hartnett, Chicago, c		75
1936—H. Louis Gehrig, New York, 1b		73	Carl Hubbell, New York, p		60
1937—Charles Gehringer, Detroit, 2b		78	Joseph Medwick, St. Louis, of		70
1938—James Foxx, Boston, 1b		305	Ernest Lombardi, Cincinnati, c		229
1939—Joseph DiMaggio, New York, of		280	William Walters, Cincinnati, p		303
1940—Henry Greenberg, Detroit, of		292	Frank McCormick, Cincinnati, 1b		274
1941—Joseph DiMaggio, New York, of		291	Adolph Camilli, Brooklyn, 1b		300
1942—Joseph Gordon, New York, 2b		270	Morton Cooper, St. Louis, p		263
1943—Spurgeon Chandler, New York, p		246	Stanley Musial, St. Louis, of		267
1944—Harold Newhouser, Detroit, p		236	Martin Marion, St. Louis, ss		190
1945—Harold Newhouser, Detroit, p		236	Philip Cavarretta, Chicago, 1b		279
1946—Theodore Williams, Boston, of		224	Stanley Musial, St. Louis, 1b		319
1947—Joseph DiMaggio, New York, of		202	Robert Elliott, Boston, 3b		205
1948—Louis Boudreau, Cleveland, ss		324	Stanley Musial, St. Louis, of		303
1949—Theodore Williams, Boston, of		272	Jack Robinson, Brooklyn, 2b		264
1950—Philip Rizzuto, New York, ss		284	C. James Konstanty, Philadelphia, p		286
1951—Lawrence Berra, New York, c		184	Roy Campanella, Brooklyn, c		243
1952—Robert Shantz, Philadelphia, p		280	Henry Sauer, Chicago, of		226
1953—Albert Rosen, Cleveland, 3b		*336	Roy Campanella, Brooklyn, c		297
1954—Lawrence Berra, New York, c		230	Willie Mays, New York, of		283
1955—Lawrence Berra, New York, c		218	Roy Campanella, Brooklyn, c		226
1956—Mickey Mantle, New York, of		*336	Donald Newcombe, Brooklyn, p		223
1957—Mickey Mantle, New York, of		233	Henry Aaron, Milwaukee, of		239
1958—Jack Jensen, Boston, of		233	Ernest Banks, Chicago, ss		283
1959—J. Nelson Fox, Chicago, 2b		295	Ernest Banks, Chicago, ss		232½
1960—Roger Maris, New York, of		225	Richard Groat, Pittsburgh, ss		276
1961—Roger Maris, New York, of		202	Frank Robinson, Cincinnati, of		219
1962—Mickey Mantle, New York, of		234	Maurice Wills, Los Angeles, ss		209
1963—Elston Howard, New York, c		248	Sanford Koufax, Los Angeles, p		237
1964—Brooks Robinson, Baltimore, 3b		269	Kenton Boyer, St. Louis, 3b		243
1965—Zoilo Versalles, Minnesota, ss		275	Willie Mays, San Francisco, of		224
1966—Frank Robinson, Baltimore, of		*280	Roberto Clemente, Pittsburgh, of		218
1967—Carl Yastrzemski, Boston, of		275	Orlando Cepeda, St. Louis, 1b		*280
1968—Dennis McLain, Detroit, p		*280	Robert Gibson, St. Louis, p		242
1969—Harmon Killebrew, Minnesota, 1-3b		294	Willie McCovey, San Francisco, 1b		265
1970—John (Boog) Powell, Baltimore, 1b		234	Johnny Bench, Cincinnati, c		326
1971—Vida Blue, Oakland, p		268	Joseph Torre, St. Louis, 3b		318
1972—Richie Allen, Chicago, 1b		321	Johnny Bench, Cincinnati, c		263
1973—Reggie Jackson, Oakland, of		*336	Pete Rose, Cincinnati, of		274
1974—Jeff Burroughs, Texas, of		248	Steve Garvey, Los Angeles, 1b		270
1975—Fred Lynn, Boston, of		326	Joe Morgan, Cincinnati, 2b		321½
1976—Thurman Munson, New York, c		304	Joe Morgan, Cincinnati, 2b		311
1977—Rod Carew, Minnesota, 1b		273	George Foster, Cincinnati, of		291
1978—Jim Rice, Boston, of		352	Dave Parker, Pittsburgh, of		320
1979—Don Baylor, California, of		347	Willie Stargell, Pittsburgh, 1b		216
			Keith Hernandez, St. Louis, 1b		216

BASEBALL WRITERS' ASSOCIATION MVP AWARDS—Cont.

Year	AMERICAN LEAGUE Player, Club	Points	NATIONAL LEAGUE Player, Club	Points
1980	George Brett, Kansas City, 3b	335	Mike Schmidt, Philadelphia, 3b	*336
1981	Rollie Fingers, Milwaukee, p	319	Mike Schmidt, Philadelphia, 3b	321
1982	Robin Yount, Milwaukee, ss	385	Dale Murphy, Atlanta, of	283
1983	Cal Ripken, Baltimore, ss	322	Dale Murphy, Atlanta, of	318
1984	Willie Hernandez, Detroit, p	306	Ryne Sandberg, Chicago, 2b	326
1985	Don Mattingly, New York, 1b	367	Willie McGee, St. Louis, of	280
1986	Roger Clemens, Boston, p	339	Mike Schmidt, Philadelphia, 3b	287
1987	George Bell, Toronto, of	332	Andre Dawson, Chicago, of	269

*Unanimous selection.

BASEBALL WRITERS' ASSOCIATION ROOKIE AWARDS

1947—Combined selection—Jack Robinson, Brooklyn, 1b.
1948—Combined selection—Alvin Dark, Boston, N. L., ss.

Year	AMERICAN LEAGUE Player, Club	Votes	NATIONAL LEAGUE Player, Club	Votes
1949	Roy Sievers, St. Louis, of	10	Donald Newcombe, Brooklyn, p	21
1950	Walter Dropo, Boston, 1b	15	Samuel Jethroe, Boston, of	11
1951	Gilbert McDougald, New York, 3b	13	Willie Mays, New York, of	18
1952	Harry Byrd, Philadelphia, p	9	Joseph Black, Brooklyn, p	19
1953	Harvey Kuenn, Detroit, ss	23	James Gilliam, Brooklyn, 2b	11
1954	Robert Grim, New York, p	15	Wallace Moon, St. Louis, of	17
1955	Herbert Score, Cleveland, p	18	William Virdon, St. Louis, of	15
1956	Luis Aparicio, Chicago, ss	22	Frank Robinson, Cincinnati, of	*24
1957	Anthony Kubek, New York, inf-of	23	John Sanford, Philadelphia, p	16
1958	Albert Pearson, Washington, of	14	Orlando Cepeda, San Francisco, 1b	*†21
1959	W. Robert Allison, Washington, of	18	Willie McCovey, San Francisco, 1b	*24
1960	Ronald Hansen, Baltimore, ss	22	Frank Howard, Los Angeles, of	12
1961	Donald Schwall, Boston, p	7	Billy Williams, Chicago, of	10
1962	Thomas Tresh, New York, of-ss	13	Kenneth Hubbs, Chicago, 2b	19
1963	Gary Peters, Chicago, p	10	Peter Rose, Cincinnati, 2b	17
1964	Pedro (Tony) Oliva, Minnesota, of	19	Richard Allen, Philadelphia, 3b	18
1965	Curtis Blefary, Baltimore, of	12	James Lefebvre, Los Angeles, 2b	13
1966	Tommie Agee, Chicago, of	16	Tommy Helms, Cincinnati, 3b	12
1967	Rod Carew, Minnesota, 2b	19	Tom Seaver, New York, p	11
1968	Stan Bahnsen, New York, p	17	Johnny Bench, Cincinnati, c	10½
1969	Lou Piniella, Kansas City, of	9	Ted Sizemore, Los Angeles, 2b	14
1970	Thurman Munson, New York, c	23	Carl Morton, Montreal, p	11
1971	Chris Chambliss, Cleveland, 1b	11	Earl Williams, Atlanta, c	18
1972	Carlton Fisk, Boston, c	*24	Jon Matlack, New York, p	19
1973	Al Bumbry, Baltimore, of	13½	Gary Matthews, San Francisco, of	11
1974	Mike Hargrove, Texas, 1b	16½	Bake McBride, St. Louis, of	16
1975	Fred Lynn, Boston, of	23	John Montefusco, San Francisco, p	12
1976	Mark Fidrych, Detroit, p	22	Butch Metzger, San Diego, p	11
			Pat Zachry, Cincinnati, p	11
1977	Eddie Murray, Baltimore, dh-1b	12½	Andre Dawson, Montreal, of	10
1978	Lou Whitaker, Detroit, 2b	21	Bob Horner, Atlanta, 3b	12½
1979	John Castino, Minnesota, 3b	7	Rick Sutcliffe, Los Angeles, p	20
	Alfredo Griffin, Toronto, ss	7		
1980	Joe Charboneau, Cleveland, of	103	Steve Howe, Los Angeles, p	80
1981	Dave Righetti, New York, p	127	Fernando Valenzuela, Los Angeles, p	107
1982	Cal Ripken, Baltimore, ss-3b	132	Steve Sax, Los Angeles, 2b	63
1983	Ron Kittle, Chicago, of	104	Darryl Strawberry, New York, of	109
1984	Alvin Davis, Seattle, 1b	134	Dwight Gooden, New York, p	118
1985	Ozzie Guillen, Chicago, ss	101	Vince Coleman, St. Louis, of	*120
1986	Jose Canseco, Oakland, of	110	Todd Worrell, St. Louis, p	118
1987	Mark McGwire, Oakland, 1b	*140	Benito Santiago, San Diego, c	*120

*Unanimous selection. †Three writers did not vote.

Boston's Roger Clemens last season became the first pitcher to win back-to-back Cy Young Awards since Baltimore's Jim Palmer in 1975-76.

CY YOUNG MEMORIAL AWARD

Year	Pitcher Club	Votes
1956	Donald Newcombe, Brooklyn	10
1957	Warren Spahn, Milwaukee	15
1958	Robert Turley, New York, A.L.	5
1959	Early Wynn, Chicago, A.L.	13
1960	Vernon Law, Pittsburgh	8
1961	Edward Ford, New York, A.L.	9
1962	Don Drysdale, Los Angeles, N.L.	14
1963	Sanford Koufax, Los Angeles, N.L.	*20
1964	Dean Chance, Los Angeles, A.L.	17
1965	Sanford Koufax, Los Angeles, N.L.	*20
1966	Sanford Koufax, Los Angeles, N.L.	*20
1967	A. L.—Jim Lonborg, Boston	18
	N. L.—M. McCormick, San Francisco	18
1968	A. L.—Dennis McLain, Detroit	*20
	N. L.—Bob Gibson, St. Louis	*20
1969	A. L.—Dennis McLain, Detroit	10
	Mike Cuellar, Baltimore	10
	N. L.—Tom Seaver, New York	23
1970	A. L.—Jim Perry, Minnesota	†55
	N. L.—Bob Gibson, St. Louis	†118
1971	A. L.—Vida Blue, Oakland	†98
	N. L.—Fergy Jenkins, Chicago	†97
1972	A. L.—Gaylord Perry, Cleveland	†64
	N. L.—Steve Carlton, Philadelphia	.*†120
1973	A. L.—Jim Palmer, Baltimore	†88
	N. L.—Tom Seaver, New York	†71
1974	A. L.—Jim Hunter, Oakland	†90
	N. L.—Mike Marshall, Los Angeles	†96

Year	Pitcher Club	Votes
1975	A. L.—Jim Palmer, Baltimore	†98
	N. L.—Tom Seaver, New York	†98
1976	A. L.—Jim Palmer, Baltimore	†108
	N. L.—Randy Jones, San Diego	†96
1977	A. L.—Sparky Lyle, New York	†56½
	N. L.—Steve Carlton, Philadelphia	.*†104
1978	A. L.—Ron Guidry, New York	*†140
	N. L.—Gaylord Perry, San Diego	‡116
1979	A. L.—Mike Flanagan, Baltimore	†136
	N. L.—Bruce Sutter, Chicago	†72
1980	A. L.—Steve Stone, Baltimore	100
	N. L.—Steve Carlton, Philadelphia	118
1981	A. L.—Rollie Fingers, Milwaukee	126
	N. L.—Fernando Valenzuela, Los Ang.	70
1982	A. L.—Pete Vuckovich, Milwaukee	87
	N. L.—Steve Carlton, Philadelphia	112
1983	A. L.—LaMarr Hoyt, Chicago	116
	N. L.—John Denny, Philadelphia	103
1984	A. L.—Willie Hernandez, Detroit	88
	N. L.—Rick Sutcliffe, Chicago	*120
1985	A. L.—Bret Saberhagen, Kansas City.	127
	N. L.—Dwight Gooden, New York	*120
1986	A. L.—Roger Clemens, Boston	*140
	N. L.—Mike Scott, Houston	98
1987	A. L.—Roger Clemens, Boston	124
	N. L.—Steve Bedrosian, Philadelphia	57

*Unanimous selection. †Point system used.

Stargell Enters Hall on 1st Try

By LARRY WIGGE

The Pittsburgh Pirates were known as the Lumber Co. in the 1970s because of their fearsome hitting attack. And no one exemplified the spirit of the Pirates or wielded more fearsome lumber than one Willie Stargell.

So respected was Stargell by 1979 that fans and foes alike, knowing that he was nearing the twilight of his career, almost expected the big first baseman to carry the Pirates to victory in the World Series against the Baltimore Orioles. And he didn't disappoint. Playing a big part in the Pirates' comeback from a 3-1 deficit, the 38-year-old Stargell punctuated his big season with a 4-for-5 performance that included a two-run, sixth-inning homer in the decisive seventh game.

That victory came October 17, 1979, eight years to the day after Stargell had singled and scored the deciding run in the eighth inning as the Pirates defeated the Orioles, 2-1, in the seventh game of the '71 World Series.

Stargell, whose trademark was the tape-measure home run, spent his entire career with the Pirates, playing on six National League East Division titlists in addition to the World Series winners in 1971 and '79.

A winner. A leader. A force to be reckoned with. That was Willie Stargell, who finished his 21 major league seasons with a .282 lifetime average, 475 homers and 1,540 runs batted in. No other Pirate player ever hit as many as 400 homers.

That's why it came as no surprise that Stargell earned election to the Hall of Fame in 1987 on his first try, becoming only the 17th player to be inducted in the first year of eligibility.

"To be enshrined in the same room as Babe (Ruth), Hank (Aaron) and Ernie (Banks), what a feeling, what an honor," Stargell said of his election at Cooperstown. "All that hard work and sacrifice, I never thought it would feel like this. I never thought I would have a day like this. I'm overwhelmed."

Stargell was named on 352 of 427 ballots or 31 more than the required 75 percent of the ballots cast by 10-year members of the Baseball Writers Association of America. Jim Bunning, who posted a 224-184 career record, had no-hitters in each league and 40 shutouts in his 17 years with Detroit, Philadelphia, Pittsburgh and Los Angeles, finished second with 317 votes, four short

Willie Stargell is only the 17th player to be elected to the Hall of Fame in his first year of eligibility.

of election. Bunning had missed election in 1986 by 21 votes.

Only Pie Traynor in 1947 and Nellie Fox in 1985 missed getting into the Hall of Fame by slimmer margins than Bunning.

Unusual in this year's voting was that nine ballots were signed and returned showing no affirmation for any of the eligible candidates.

Following Stargell and Bunning were Tony Oliva with 202 votes, Orlando Cepeda (199) and Roger Maris (184).

Born in Earlsboro, Okla., Stargell broke into the majors in 1962, but didn't earn an everyday job with the Pirates until 1964. For the next 13 seasons, he hit 20 or more homers. Six times he hit 30 or more, and twice he led the National League—with 48 in 1971 and 44 in '73. Five times he topped the 100-RBI mark.

"In the eighth and ninth innings, when we were two down and needed a long ball, Willie had the ability to come up with it at just the right time," said Al Oliver, one of Stargell's longtime Pittsburgh teammates.

Willie was chosen as an outfielder on The Sporting News National League All-Star team in 1965, '66 and '71 and was the first baseman on that team in 1972.

Still his greatest tribute came in 1979. That's when the grizzled veteran was co-Most Valuable Player with St. Louis' Keith Hernandez after a 32-homer, 82-RBI season and was chosen MVP in the Championship Series and World Series, knocking in six runs with a .455 average against Cincinnati and hitting three homers, with seven RBIs and a .400 average against Baltimore in the World Series. He was named The Sporting News Major League Player of the Year in '79.

In that Series, Willie established records for most total bases in a seven-game series (25) and his four doubles and three homers are still a standard in World Series competition for long hits in a seven-game series.

Al Oliver once said: "If Willie told us to jump off the Fort Pitt Bridge, we'd ask him what kind of dive he wanted."

That's the kind of leadership Willie Stargell displayed.

The complete 1988 Hall of Fame voting totals follow: Stargell, 352; Bunning, 317; Oliva, 202; Cepeda, 199; Maris, 184; Harvey Kuenn, 168; Bill Mazeroski, 143; Luis Tiant, 132; Maury Wills, 127; Ken Boyer, 109; Mickey Lolich, 109; Ron Santo, 108; Minnie Minoso, 90; Elroy Face, 79; Vada Pinson, 67; Joe Torre, 60; Sparky Lyle, 56; Elston Howard, 53; Dick Allen, 52; Curt Flood, 48; Thurman Munson, 32; Don Larsen, 31; Wilbur Wood, 30; Bobby Bonds, 27; Manny Mota, 18; Mark Belanger, 16; Bill Lee, 3; Reggie Smith, 3; Lee May, 2; Al Hrabosky, 1.

Failing to receive votes: Stan Bahnsen, Ross Grimsley, Larry Hisle, Grant Jackson, Randy Jones, John Mayberry, Lynn McGlothen, Doc Medich, John Milner, Willie Montanez, Joe Rudi, Jim Spencer, Del Unser, Rick Wise.

Following is a complete list of those enshrined in the Hall of Fame prior to 1988 with the vote by which each enrollee was elected:

Following is a complete list of those enshrined in the Hall of Fame prior to 1984 with the vote by which each enrollee was elected:

1936—Tyrus Cobb (222), John (Honus) Wagner (215), George (Babe) Ruth (215), Christy Mathewson (205), Walter Johnson (189), named by Baseball Writers' Association of America. Total ballots cast, 226.

1937—Napoleon Lajoie (168), Tristram Speaker (165), Denton (Cy) Young (153), named by the BBWAA. Total ballots cast, 201. George Wright, Morgan G. Bulkeley, Byron Bancroft Johnson, John J. McGraw, Cornelius McGillicuddy (Connie Mack),

named by Centennial Commission.

1938—Grover C. Alexander (212), named by BBWAA. Total ballots, 262. Henry Chadwick, Alexander J. Cartwright, named by Centennial Commission.

1939—George Sisler (235), Edward Collins (213), William Keeler (207), Louis Gehrig, named by BBWAA (Gehrig by special election after retirement from game was announced). Total ballots cast, 274. Albert G. Spalding, Adrian C. Anson, Charles A. Comiskey, William (Buck) Ewing, Charles Radbourn, William A. (Candy) Cummings, named by committee of old-time players and writers.

1942—Rogers Hornsby (182), named by BBWAA. Total ballots cast, 233.

1944—Judge Kenesaw M. Landis, named by committee on old-timers.

1945—Hugh Duffy, Jimmy Collins, Hugh Jennings, Ed Delahanty, Fred Clarke, Mike Kelly, Wilbert Robinson, Jim O'Rourke, Dennis (Dan) Brouthers and Roger Bresnahan, named by committee on old-timers.

1946—Jesse Burkett, Frank Chance, Jack Chesbro, Johnny Evers, Clark Griffith, Tom McCarthy, Joe McGinnity, Eddie Plank, Joe Tinker, Rube Waddell and Ed Walsh, named by committee on old-timers.

1947—Carl Hubbell (140), Frank Frisch (136), Gordon (Mickey) Cochrane (128) and Robert (Lefty) Grove (123), named by BBWAA. Total ballots, 161.

1948—Herbert J. Pennock (94) and Harold (Pie) Traynor (93), named by BBWAA. Total ballots cast, 121.

1949—Charles Gehringer (159), named by BBWAA in runoff election. Total ballots cast, 187. Charles (Kid) Nichols and Mordecai (Three-Finger) Brown, named by committee on old timers.

1951—Mel Ott (197) and Jimmie Foxx (179), named by BBWAA. Total ballots cast, 226.

1952—Harry Heilmann (203) and Paul Waner (195), named by BBWAA. Total ballots cast, 234.

1953—Jerome (Dizzy) Dean (209) and Al Simmons (199), named by BBWAA. Total ballots cast, 264. Charles Albert (Chief) Bender, Roderick (Bobby) Wallace, William Klem, Tom Connolly, Edward G. Barrow and William Henry (Harry) Wright, named by the new Committee on Veterans.

1954—Walter (Rabbit) Maranville (209), William Dickey (202) and William Terry (195), named by BBWAA. Total ballots cast, 252.

1955—Joe DiMaggio (223), Ted Lyons (217), Arthur (Dazzy) Vance (205) and Charles (Gabby) Hartnett (195), named by BBWAA. Total ballots cast, 251. J. Franklin (Home Run) Baker and Ray Schalk, named by Committee on Veterans.

1956—Hank Greenberg (164) and Joe

Cronin (152), named by BBWAA. Total ballots cast, 193.

1957—Joseph V. McCarthy and Sam Crawford, named by Committee on Veterans.

1959—Zachariah (Zack) Wheat, named by Committee on Veterans.

1961—Max Carey and William Hamilton, named by Committee on Veterans.

1962—Bob Feller (150) and Jackie Robinson (124), named by BBWAA. Total ballots cast, 160. Bill McKechnie and Edd Roush, named by Committee on Veterans.

1963—Eppa Rixey, Edgar (Sam) Rice, Elmer Flick and John Clarkson, named by Committee on Veterans.

1964—Luke Appling (189), named by BBWAA in runoff election. Total ballots cast, 225. Urban (Red) Faber, Burleigh Grimes, Tim Keefe, Heinie Manush, Miller Huggins and John Montgomery Ward, named by Committee on Veterans.

1965—James (Pud) Galvin, named by Committee on Veterans.

1966—Ted Williams (282), named by BBWAA. Total ballots cast, 302. Casey Stengel, named by Committee on Veterans.

1967—Charles (Red) Ruffing (266), named by BBWAA in runoff election. Total ballots cast, 306. Branch Rickey and Lloyd Waner, named by Committee on Veterans.

1968—Joseph (Ducky) Medwick (240), named by BBWAA. Total ballots cast, 283. Leon (Goose) Goslin and Hazen (Kiki) Cuyler, named by Committee on Veterans.

1969—Stan (The Man) Musial (317) and Roy Campanella (270), named by BBWAA. Total ballots cast, 340. Stan Coveleski and Waite Hoyt, named by Committee on Veterans.

1970—Lou Boudreau (232), named by BBWAA. Total ballots cast, 300. Earle Combs, Jesse Haines and Ford Frick, named by Committee on Veterans.

1971—Chick Hafey, Rube Marquard, Joe Kelley, Dave Bancroft, Harry Hooper, Jake Beckley and George Weiss, named by Committee on Veterans. Satchel Paige, named by Special Committee on Negro Leagues.

1972—Sandy Koufax (344), Yogi Berra (339) and Early Wynn (301), named by BBWAA. Total ballots cast, 396. Lefty Gomez, Will Harridge and Ross Youngs, named by Committee on Veterans. Josh Gibson and Walter (Buck) Leonard, named by Special Committee on Negro Leagues.

1973—Warren Spahn (316), named by BBWAA. Total ballots cast, 380. Roberto Clemente (393), in special election by BBWAA in which 424 ballots were cast. Billy Evans, George Kelly and Mickey Welch, named by Committee on Veterans. Monte Irvin, named by Special Committee on Negro Leagues.

1974—Mickey Mantle (322) and Whitey Ford (284), named by BBWAA. Total ballots cast, 365. Jim Bottomley, Sam Thompson and Jocko Conlan, named by Committee on Veterans. James (Cool Papa) Bell, named by Special Committee on Negro Leagues.

1975—Ralph Kiner (273), named by BBWAA. Total ballots cast, 362. Earl Averill, Bucky Harris and Billy Herman, named by Committee on Veterans. William (Judy) Johnson, named by Special Committee on Negro Leagues.

1976—Robin Roberts (337) and Bob Lemon (305), named by BBWAA. Total ballots cast, 388. Roger Connor, Cal Hubbard and Fred Lindstrom, named by Committee on Veterans. Oscar Charleston, named by Special Committee on Negro Leagues.

1977—Ernie Banks (321), named by BBWAA. Total ballots cast, 383. Joe Sewell, Al Lopez and Amos Rusie, named by Committee on Veterans. Martin Dihigo and John Henry Lloyd, named by Special Committee on Negro Leagues.

1978—Eddie Mathews (301), named by BBWAA. Total ballots cast, 379. Larry MacPhail and Addie Joss, named by Committee on Veterans.

1979—Willie Mays (409), named by BBWAA. Total ballots cast, 432. Hack Wilson and Warren Giles, named by Committee on Veterans.

1980—Al Kaline (340) and Duke Snider (333), named by BBWAA. Total ballots cast, 385. Chuck Klein and Tom Yawkey, named by Committee on Veterans.

1981—Bob Gibson (337), named by BBWAA. Total ballots cast, 401. Johnny Mize and Rube Foster, named by Committee on Veterans.

1982—Henry Aaron (406) and Frank Robinson (370), named by BBWAA. Total ballots cast, 415. Albert B. (Happy) Chandler and Travis Jackson, named by Committee on Veterans.

1983—Brooks Robinson (344) and Juan Marichal (313), named by BBWAA. Total ballots cast, 374. George Kell and Walter Alston, named by Committee on Veterans.

1984—Luis Aparicio (341), Harmon Killebrew (335) and Don Drysdale (316), named by BBWAA. Total ballots cast, 403. Rick Ferrell and Pee Wee Reese, named by Committee on Veterans.

1985—Hoyt Wilhelm (331) and Lou Brock (315), named by BBWAA. Total ballots cast, 395. Enos Slaughter and Joseph (Arky) Vaughn, named by Committee on Veterans.

1986—Willie McCovey (346), named by BBWAA. Total ballots cast, 425. Bobby Doerr and Ernie Lombardi, named by Committee on Veterans.

1987—Billy Williams (354) and Jim (Catfish) Hunter (315), named by BBWAA. Total ballots cast, 413. Ray Dandridge, named by Committee on Veterans.

Pitchers a Premium in ML Draft

By DAVE SLOAN

For the second year in a row, pitchers were at a premium in the major league draft held at baseball's winter meetings.

In 1986, eight of the 10 players drafted were pitchers. In 1987, selecting teams opted for pitchers on six of their nine selections during the December 7 draft in Dallas. Righthander Joe Johnson was the only player chosen with major league experience. The 26-year-old Johnson was taken third overall by the Angels from the Blue Jays' Triple-A affiliate at Syracuse (International). Johnson finished the '87 season with a 3-5 record for Toronto and has a 20-18 record in three big-league campaigns.

Ironically, the player taken No. 1 in the draft was not a pitcher. Todd Pratt, a 20-year-old catcher in the Boston Red Sox's farm system, was drafted by Cleveland from the Sox's Triple-A Pawtucket (International) club. Pratt batted .258 with 12 home runs and 65 runs batted in with Winter Haven (Florida State) in 1987.

The Orioles, participating in the major league draft for the first time in 10 years, made pitcher Jose Bautista the No. 2 selection. Bautista, 23, was 10-5 with a 3.24 earned-run average at Jackson (Texas) in 1987, his seventh professional season. Bautista was drafted from the Mets' Triple-A Tidewater (International) club.

Each player selected in the draft costs $50,000, and if that player fails to make the season-opening roster, he must be returned to his old club for half the draft price.

No team drafted more than one player, though the Blue Jays and Pirates each lost two prospects.

Draft choices in order of selection:

Indians—Catcher Todd Pratt from Pawtucket (International) of the Red Sox' organization.

Orioles—Pitcher Jose Bautista from Tidewater (International) of the Mets' organization.

Angels—Pitcher Joe Johnson from Syracuse (International) of the Blue Jays' organization.

Astros—Pitcher Scott Medvin from Vancouver (Pacific Coast) of the Pirates' organization.

White Sox—Infielder Santiago Garcia from Syracuse (International) of the Blue Jays' organization.

Red Sox—Pitcher John Trautwein from Indianapolis (American Association) of the Expos' organization.

A's—Outfielder Doug Jennings from Edmonton (Pacific Coast) of the Angels' organization.

Expos—Pitcher Richard Sauveur from Vancouver (Pacific Coast) of the Pirates' organization.

Tigers—Pitcher John Wetteland from Albuquerque (Pacific Coast) of the Dodgers' organization.

Major League Attendance for 1987

NATIONAL LEAGUE	Home	Road
Atlanta	1,217,402	1,912,843
Chicago	2,035,130	2,088,113
Cincinnati	2,185,205	2,140,241
Houston	1,909,902	1,894,294
Los Angeles	2,797,409	2,120,115
Montreal	1,850,324	2,008,030
New York	3,034,129	2,323,808
Philadelphia	2,100,110	2,061,384
Pittsburgh	1,161,193	1,901,676
St. Louis	3,072,122	2,321,960
San Diego	1,454,061	1,805,278
San Francisco	1,917,168	2,156,413
Total	24,734,155	24,734,155

AMERICAN LEAGUE	Home	Road
Baltimore	1,835,692	1,880,669
Boston	2,231,551	1,999,414
California	2,696,299	1,877,630
Chicago	1,208,060	1,860,940
Cleveland	1,077,898	1,779,735
Detroit	2,061,830	2,018,317
Kansas City	2,392,471	2,047,056
Milwaukee	1,909,244	1,999,766
Minnesota	2,081,976	1,880,273
New York	2,427,672	2,451,506
Oakland	1,678,921	1,930,731
Seattle	1,134,255	1,795,683
Texas	1,763,053	1,796,351
Toronto	2,778,429	1,959,280
Total	27,277,351	27,277,351

MAJOR LEAGUE TRANSACTIONS

NECROLOGY

Rosen Swings Giant Deals

By DAVE SLOAN

The building of a championship baseball team requires many ingredients, but none more important than pitching. The 1987 season was proof positive. The Minnesota Twins, San Francisco Giants and Detroit Tigers all won division titles and all three teams can credit their success to the trades they made to acquire both bullpen and starting help.

On February 3, the Twins traded starting pitcher Neal Heaton, catcher Jeff Reed and two minor league pitchers to Montreal for relief pitcher Jeff Reardon and catcher Tom Nieto.

Although Heaton won 13 games for the surprising Expos, the Twins got exactly what they needed in Reardon, the righthander who filled a gaping hole in the Minnesota bullpen. In 1986, the entire Twins pitching staff combined for an American League-low 24 saves as Minnesota finished in sixth place in the A.L. West, 21 games behind the California Angels.

Reardon, who had saved 162 games in eight major league seasons prior to 1987, notched 31 and the Twins captured their first division title since 1970. He saved three more in postseason competition as the Twins went on to win their first-ever World Series.

The Giants' 1987 success was even more stunning. Just two seasons after losing 100 games and finishing last in the National League West, the Giants won their first division title in 16 years. Their turnabout could be traced to deals made by President/General Manager Al Rosen, who for his efforts was named The Sporting News' 1987 Major League Executive of the Year.

Rosen acquired five key players—four of them pitchers—in three trades over a 49-day span to enable the Giants to overtake Cincinnati and defending-champion Houston in the N.L. West.

On July 5, Rosen obtained pitchers Dave Dravecky and Craig Lefferts and infielder Kevin Mitchell from San Diego for infielder Chris Brown and pitchers Keith Comstock, Mark Davis and Mark Grant.

Dravecky, who was 3-7 with the Padres, compiled a 7-5 mark with the Giants and pitched a two-hit shutout against St. Louis in Game 2 of the N.L. Championship Series.

On July 31, Rosen acquired relief pitcher Don Robinson from Pittsburgh for minor league catcher Mackey Sasser and

Rick Reuschel won five of nine starts for the Giants after his trade from Pittsburgh on August 31.

$50,000. Robinson, who was 6-6 with the Pirates, posted a 5-1 record and seven saves with the Giants.

On August 31, Rosen made another trade with the Pirates and picked up starting pitcher Rick Reuschel for pitchers Jeff Robinson and Scott Medvin. Reuschel won five of nine starts for San Francisco down the stretch and finished the season as the Giants' most reliable starter.

The Tigers won their second A.L. East title in four seasons largely as the result of an August 12 trade with Atlanta.

The Tigers shipped a minor league pitcher to the Braves for veteran pitcher Doyle Alexander, who had re-signed with Atlanta as a free agent May 5 after receiving no offers from other clubs the previous off-season.

Alexander, a 36-year-old righthander who had compiled a 160-135 record in 16 major-league seasons prior to 1987, was a disaster with the Braves early in the year. He had a 5-10 record and 4.13 earned-run average in 16 starts before his trade to Detroit.

Alexander's relocation, however, did wonders for his career. He won his first nine decisions for the Tigers, finishing with a 9-0 record and 1.53 ERA in the American League.

A number of prominent players were released during the '87 season and, in some cases, were signed by other clubs.

On July 21, the Kansas City Royals bid farewell to designated hitter Hal McRae, who had been with the team for more than 14 years. McRae, who has a son playing in the Royals' minor-league system, was offered the Kansas City managerial job on an interim basis following the August 27 firing of Billy Gardner. McRae declined the offer, however, and the job instead went to John Wathan.

The Los Angeles Dodgers released four-time N.L. batting champion Bill Madlock on May 29. Madlock, a third baseman, batted just .180 in 21 games with Los Angeles. He received a reprieve, however, when Detroit signed him June 4. Madlock hit .279 with 14 homers and 50 runs batted in with the Tigers.

The Boston Red Sox gave first baseman Bill Buckner his unconditional release July 23. Buckner had three fine seasons with the Red Sox but probably will be remembered most for letting Mookie Wilson's ground ball go through his legs in the 10th inning of Boston's 6-5 loss to the Mets in Game 6 of the 1986 World Series. Buckner was signed by California five days after his Boston release and batted .306 in 57 games with the Angels.

Knuckleballer Phil Niekro, who at age 48 was the oldest player in the major leagues last season, apparently has reached the end of his career after 24 seasons and 318 wins. Niekro began the '87 season with Cleveland, was traded to Toronto on August 9 and released by the Blue Jays 22 days later. He was signed by his old club, the Atlanta Braves, September 23 and pitched his final game for the Braves against the Giants on September 27. He was released by Atlanta on November 10.

One of the season's saddest stories reached its culmination June 17 when the San Diego Padres cut much-troubled pitcher LaMarr Hoyt. Hoyt, the 1983 Cy Young Award winner and 1985 All-Star Game Most Valuable Player, was involved in three drug-related scrapes in 1986 and did not pitch during the 1987 season. Hoyt was signed to a minor-league contract by his former team, the Chicago White Sox, on July 1 but later was arrested in South Carolina and charged with possession with intent to distribute cocaine and marijuana.

A number of former stars received unconditional releases from their teams after the season ended. Among those were 321-game winner Don Sutton, released by the Angels on October 30; infielder Davey Lopes, a 16-year veteran released by the Astros on November 12; outfielder Lonnie Smith, cut loose by the Royals on December 15; and pitcher Steve Carlton, a four-time Cy Young Award recipient and winner of 329 major league games. The Minnesota Twins—the fifth team for which Carlton had pitched in two seasons—released the veteran pitcher December 21.

Five off-season deals made late in 1987 stand out:

• The Kansas City Royals shipped pitcher Danny Jackson and infielder Angel Salazar to the Cincinnati Reds on November 6 for shortstop Kurt Stillwell and pitcher Ted Power. The Royals believe Stillwell is the answer to their shortstop problem while the Reds hope Jackson—an 18-game loser last season—can fulfill his limitless potential with a change of scenery.

• The Reds further bolstered their pitching December 8 by acquiring young pitchers Jose Rijo and Tim Birtsas from the Oakland A's in exchange for 36-year-old outfielder Dave Parker. Rijo and Birtsas figure to help Cincinnati for years to come while Parker—a six-time All-Star—will make an already-formidable Oakland lineup even stronger.

• The Boston Red Sox acquired ace reliever Lee Smith from the Chicago Cubs for pitchers Al Nipper and Calvin Schiraldi on December 8. The Bosox hope Smith can do for them in 1988 what Reardon did for Minnesota in '87. Boston pitchers saved a major league-low 16 games last season.

• The Philadelphia Phillies traded outfielder Glenn Wilson, pitcher Mike Jackson and a minor league outfielder to the Seattle Mariners on December 9 for outfielder Phil Bradley and a minor league pitcher. Bradley figures to bat leadoff and give the Phils some much-needed speed. Wilson will add power to the Mariners' lineup while the promising Jackson is only 23 years old.

• In a blockbuster three-way deal finalized at the conclusion of the winter meetings December 11, the New York Mets shipped relief pitcher Jesse Orosco to the Oakland A's. The A's, in turn, traded Orosco, shortstop Alfredo Griffin and reliever Jay Howell to the Los Angeles Dodgers for pitchers Bob Welch, Matt Young and Jack Savage. The A's then traded Savage and two minor league pitchers to the Mets.

The Dodgers hope Orosco and Howell can fill the club's desperate need for relief pitching and that Griffin can take over at short. The A's are counting on Welch to become a mainstay in their starting rotation. The Mets received no immediate help but figure to benefit in years to come from their three young pitchers.

Following is a list of all player transactions for the 1987 calendar year:

January 5—Yankees traded pitcher Scott Nielsen and infielder Mike Soper to White Sox for pitcher Pete Filson and infielder Randy Velarde.

January 6—Blue Jays re-signed pitcher Jim Clancy, a free agent.

January 6—Astros re-signed third baseman Phil Garner, a free agent.

January 6—Angels' Edmonton affiliate signed pitcher Jack Lazorko, a free agent.

January 7—Orioles signed infielder Rick Burleson, a free agent formerly with the Angels.

January 7—Angels' Edmonton affiliate signed catcher Jack Fimple, a free agent.

January 8—Yankees re-signed pitcher Tommy John and second baseman Willie Randolph, both free agents.

January 8—Angels re-signed outfielder Brian Downing and third baseman Doug DeCinces, both free agents.

January 8—Reds traded outfielder Eddie Milner to Giants for pitchers Frank Williams, Timber Mead and Mike Villa.

January 8—Blue Jays re-signed catcher Ernie Whitt, a free agent.

January 8—Yankees' Columbus affiliate signed second baseman Juan Bonilla, a free agent.

January 9—Twins signed pitcher Juan Berenguer, a free agent.

January 12—Royals re-signed shortstop Buddy Biancalana, designated hitter Hal McRae and outfielder Jorge Orta, all free agents.

January 13—Padres' Las Vegas affiliate signed pitcher Tom Gorman, a free agent.

January 16—Twins signed pitcher Randy Niemann, a free agent, and assigned him to Portland.

January 19—Cardinals re-signed pitcher Ken Dayley and signed pitcher Dave LaPoint, both free agents.

January 19—Expos signed catcher Dave Engle, a free agent, and assigned him to Indianapolis.

January 20—Brewers traded outfielder Dion James to Braves for outfielder Brad Komminsk.

January 20—Pirates' Vancouver affiliate re-signed shortstop U.L. Washington, a free agent.

January 20—A's signed pitcher Vida Blue, a free agent formerly with the Giants.

January 21—White Sox signed infielder Jerry Royster, a free agent formerly with the Padres.

January 22—Orioles signed pitcher Dave Schmidt, a free agent.

January 22—A's Tacoma affiliate signed shortstop Luis Quinones, a free agent.

January 23—Braves signed outfielder Gary Roenicke, a free agent formerly with the Yankees.

January 24—Astros re-signed pitcher Ron Mathis, a free agent.

January 26—Cardinals' Louisville affiliate signed infielder Skeeter Barnes, a free agent.

January 27—Indians signed pitcher Ed Vande Berg, a free agent.

January 27—Braves traded outfielders Terry Harper and Freddy Tiburcio to Tigers for pitchers Randy O'Neal and Chuck Cary.

January 28—Yankees re-signed pitcher Bob Shirley, a free agent.

January 30—A's traded shortstop Luis Quinones

to Cubs for third baseman Ron Cey.

January 30—Orioles' Rochester affiliate signed pitcher Jack O'Connor, a free agent.

February 2—Blue Jays traded second baseman Damaso Garcia and pitcher Luis Leal to Braves for pitcher Craig McMurtry; Braves assigned Leal to Greenville.

February 2—Tigers' Toledo affiliate signed pitcher Nate Snell, a free agent.

February 3—Expos traded pitcher Jeff Reardon and catcher Tom Nieto to Twins for pitchers Neal Heaton, Al Cardwood and Yorkis Perez and catcher Jeff Reed.

February 4—Tigers' Toledo affiliate signed pitcher Bill Laskey and outfielders Mike Stenhouse and Jerry Davis, all free agents.

February 4—Mariners signed outfielder Steve Henderson, a free agent, and assigned him to Calgary.

February 4—Giants re-signed pitcher Atlee Hammaker, a free agent.

February 5—Indians signed pitcher Dennis Lamp, a free agent.

February 5—Giants signed pitcher Joe Price, a free agent formerly with the Reds.

February 6—Royals' Omaha affiliate signed pitcher Bob Stoddard, a free agent.

February 6—Indians signed catcher Rick Dempsey, a free agent formerly with the Orioles.

February 9—Mets signed catcher-infielder Clint Hurdle, a free agent, and assigned him to Tidewater.

February 9—Pirates' Vancouver affiliate signed shortstop Onix Concepcion, a free agent.

February 11—Dodgers' Albuquerque affiliate signed second baseman Jack Perconte, a free agent.

February 12—Orioles signed third baseman Ray Knight, a free agent formerly with the Mets.

February 13—Yankees signed catcher Rick Cerone, a free agent formerly with the Brewers.

February 13—White Sox signed pitcher Juan Agosto, a free agent, and assigned him to Hawaii.

February 13—Angels released pitcher Chris Green.

February 14—Brewers' Denver affiliate signed pitcher Paul Mirabella, a free agent.

February 16—Expos' Indianapolis affiliate signed pitcher Pascual Perez and re-signed pitcher Charlie Lea, both free agents.

February 17—Cubs traded pitcher Guy Hoffman to Reds for a player to be named; Cubs acquired infielder Wade Rowdon on February 23 and assigned him to Iowa.

February 19—Giants' Phoenix affiliate signed pitcher Ray Fontenot, a free agent.

February 19—Angels' Edmonton affiliate re-signed pitcher Vern Ruhle, a free agent.

February 20—Twins traded pitcher Mike Shade to Expos for infielder Al Newman; Expos assigned Shade to Indianapolis.

February 20—Mets' Tidewater affiliate signed outfielder Andre David, a free agent.

February 20—Cardinals' Louisville affiliate signed infielder Ivan DeJesus, a free agent.

February 23—Indians traded pitcher Curt Wardle to A's for pitcher Jeff Kaiser.

February 24—Twins signed outfielder Billy Sample, a free agent formerly with the Braves.

February 24—Tigers re-signed first baseman Darrell Evans, a free agent.

February 25—Royals re-signed first baseman

Steve Balboni, a free agent.

February 26—Dodgers' Albuquerque affiliate signed pitcher Jaime Cocanower, a free agent.

February 26—Rangers signed pitcher Frank Pastore, a free agent formerly with the Twins, and assigned him to Oklahoma City.

February 27—Expos re-signed pitcher Bryn Smith, a free agent.

February 27—Mets' Tidewater affiliate signed pitcher Chris Green, a free agent.

March 6—Expos' Indianapolis affiliate signed pitcher Bill Campbell, a free agent.

March 9—Cubs signed outfielder Andre Dawson, a free agent formerly with the Expos.

March 11—Expos released pitcher Bruce Berenyi.

March 11—White Sox signed pitcher Kevin Hickey, a free agent, and assigned him to Hawaii.

March 13—Phillies signed catcher Lance Parrish, a free agent formerly with the Tigers.

March 18—Giants released pitcher Ray Fontenot.

March 18—Indians released catcher Kevin Buckley.

March 19—Mariners released pitcher Steve Fireovid.

March 20—Mariners released catcher Donnie Scott.

March 20—A's released outfielder Rusty Tillman.

March 20—Reds traded pitcher Derek Botelho to Royals for infielder Eddie Tanner and outfielder Pete Carey; Reds assigned Tanner and Carey to Nashville.

March 20—Expos sold catcher Dann Bilardello to Pirates.

March 20—Expos released pitcher Len Barker.

March 20—Angels' Edmonton affiliate signed outfielder Tack Wilson, a free agent.

March 22—Giants' Phoenix affiliate purchased first baseman Francisco Melendez from Phillies.

March 22—A's released pitcher Carlos Diaz.

March 23—Indians released pitchers Kurt Kepshire and Dennis Lamp.

March 23—White Sox released second baseman Julio Cruz.

March 23—Cubs released catcher Mike Martin.

March 23—Tigers released outfielder Brian Harper.

March 23—Reds signed first baseman-outfielder Terry Francona, a free agent formerly with the Cubs.

March 24—Rangers traded catcher Orlando Mercado to Tigers for a player to be named; Rangers acquired outfielder Ruben Guzman on May 8 and assigned him to Tulsa.

March 25—Mariners released pitcher Bobby Castillo.

March 25—Astros signed pitcher Ray Fontenot, a free agent, and assigned him to Tucson.

March 26—Phillies traded outfielder Gary Redus to White Sox for pitcher Joe Cowley and cash.

March 26—Blue Jays released outfielder Ron Shepherd.

March 27—Giants reclaimed pitcher Charlie Corbell from Mets, who had selected him from Phoenix in the 1986 major league draft. Giants assigned Corbell to Phoenix.

March 27—Pirates traded pitcher Jim Winn to White Sox for a player to be named; Pirates ac-

quired outfielder John Cangelosi on March 30.

March 27—Twins released pitcher John Butcher.

March 27—Yankees released pitcher Rod Scurry.

March 27—Mets traded catcher Ed Hearn and pitchers Rick Anderson and Mauro Gozzo to Royals for pitcher David Cone and catcher Chris Jelic; Mets assigned Jelic to Lynchburg and Royals assigned Gozzo to Memphis.

March 27—Royals released outfielder Rudy Law.

March 29—Reds released outfielder Max Venable.

March 29—Orioles' Rochester affiliate signed catcher Donnie Scott, a free agent.

March 30—White Sox released outfielder Reid Nichols and pitcher Bob Gibson.

March 30—Red Sox released pitcher Tim Lollar.

March 30—Twins released infielder Ron Washington.

March 30—Cubs traded outfielder Thad Bosley and pitcher Dave Gumpert to Royals for catcher Jim Sundberg.

March 30—Braves released outfielder Darryl Motley.

March 30—Orioles released pitcher Rich Bordi.

March 30—Royals released infielder Greg Pryor.

March 31—Mariners' Calgary affiliate released outfielder Steve Henderson.

March 31—Twins released outfielder Mickey Hatcher.

March 31—Pirates released outfielder Mike Brown.

March 31—Mariners released pitcher Pete Ladd and infielder Dave Stapleton.

March 31—Giants traded outfielder Dan Gladden and pitcher David Blakley to Twins for pitchers Jose Dominguez and Ray Velasquez and a player to be named; Giants acquired pitcher Bryan Hickerson on June 15.

March 31—Expos released outfielder Dave Collins.

April 1—Cardinals traded outfielder Andy Van Slyke, catcher Mike LaValliere and pitcher Mike Dunne to Pirates for catcher Tony Pena; Pirates assigned Dunne to Vancouver.

April 1—Brewers released catcher Charlie O'Brien.

April 1—Braves signed third baseman Graig Nettles, a free agent formerly with the Padres.

April 1—Blue Jays released pitcher Bill Caudill.

April 2—Astros traded pitcher Jeff Calhoun to Phillies for catcher Ronn Reynolds; Phillies assigned Calhoun to Maine and Astros assigned Reynolds to Tucson.

April 2—Angels traded catcher Stan Cliburn to Braves for third baseman Joe Redfield.

April 2—Padres signed infielder Luis Salazar, a free agent, and assigned him to Las Vegas.

April 3—Brewers reclaimed outfielder Bob Simonson from Expos, who had selected him from Denver in the 1986 major league draft. Brewers assigned Simonson to Stockton.

April 3—Pirates reclaimed pitcher Vicente Palacios from Brewers, who had selected him from Vancouver in the 1986 major league draft. Pirates assigned Palacios to Vancouver.

April 3—Expos signed outfielder Reid Nichols, a free agent.

April 3—Cubs traded pitcher Dennis Eckersley

and infielder Dan Rohn to A's for outfielder Dave Wilder, infielder Brian Guinn and pitcher Mark Leonette; Cubs assigned all to Pittsfield.

April 4—Indians signed pitcher Steve Carlton, a free agent formerly with the White Sox.

April 4—Twins traded pitcher Dominic Iasparro to Mets, completing deal in which Mets traded shortstop Ron Gardenhire to Twins for a player to be named, November 12, 1986. Mets assigned Iasparro to Lynchburg.

April 4—Braves released pitcher Jeff Bittiger.

April 5—Braves' Greenville affiliate signed infielder Mike Fischlin, a free agent.

April 6—Blue Jays reclaimed pitcher Cliff Young from A's, who had selected him from Syracuse in the 1986 major league draft. Blue Jays assigned Young to Knoxville.

April 6—Cubs signed pitcher Dickie Noles, a free agent formerly with the Indians.

April 6—Pirates released pitcher Larry McWilliams.

April 6—Angels released second baseman Rob Wilfong and catcher Jerry Narron.

April 6—Orioles signed infielder Ron Washington, a free agent, and assigned him to Rochester.

April 6—Pirates' Vancouver affiliate sold pitcher Lee Tunnell to Cardinals' Louisville affiliate.

April 7—Mets' Tidewater affiliate signed pitcher Bob Gibson, a free agent.

April 7—Orioles' Rochester affiliate released catcher Donnie Scott.

April 7—Giants re-signed pitcher Jim Gott, a free agent.

April 9—Reds re-signed outfielder Max Venable, a free agent.

April 10—Dodgers released pitcher Jerry Reuss.

April 10—Dodgers signed outfielder Mickey Hatcher, a free agent.

April 10—Yankees' Columbus affiliate signed pitchers Al Holland and Rich Bordi, both free agents.

April 13—Dodgers signed pitcher Pete Ladd, a free agent, and assigned him to Albuquerque.

April 13—Orioles signed pitcher Chris Green, a free agent, and assigned him to Rochester.

April 14—Miami (Independent) signed pitcher Dennis Martinez, a free agent formerly with the Expos.

April 14—Yakult Swallows of Japanese Baseball League signed third baseman Bob Horner, a free agent formerly with the Braves.

April 15—Twins' Portland affiliate signed pitcher Jeff Bittiger, a free agent.

April 17—A's signed outfielder Steve Henderson, a free agent, and assigned him to Tacoma.

April 17—Mariners signed catcher Jerry Narron, a free agent, and assigned him to Calgary.

April 17—White Sox' Hawaii affiliate signed pitcher Ray Krawczyk, a free agent.

April 18—Reds' Nashville affiliate signed pitcher Jerry Reuss, a free agent.

April 19—Brewers sold outfielder Jim Adduci to Giants; Giants assigned him to Phoenix. Sale was cancelled on April 26 and Brewers assigned him to Denver.

April 21—Brewers sold pitcher Dave Schuler to Giants; Giants assigned Schuler to Phoenix.

April 24—Indians signed pitcher Mike Armstrong, a free agent, and assigned him to Buffalo.

April 25—Giants traded pitcher Colin Ward and infielder Steve Miller to Padres for pitcher Tim Meagher and infielder Mark Wasinger; Ward and Miller were assigned to Las Vegas, Meagher to Fresno and Wasinger to Phoenix.

April 26—Giants signed outfielder Rusty Tillman, a free agent, and assigned him to Phoenix.

April 27—A's signed pitcher Dennis Lamp, a free agent, and assigned him to Tacoma.

April 28—Brewers signed pitcher Len Barker, a free agent, and assigned him to Denver.

April 30—A's signed pitcher Bill Caudill, a free agent, and assigned him to Tacoma.

May 1—Expos released pitcher Bill Campbell.

May 1—Yankees re-signed pitcher Ron Guidry, a free agent.

May 1—Angels re-signed catcher Bob Boone, a free agent.

May 2—Expos re-signed outfielder Tim Raines, a free agent.

May 2—Red Sox re-signed catcher Rich Gedman, a free agent.

May 3—San Jose (Independent) signed outfielder-catcher Brian Harper, a free agent.

May 4—Expos released infielder Nelson Norman.

May 5—Tigers traded catcher Orlando Mercado to Dodgers' Albuquerque affiliate for pitcher Balvino Galvez; Tigers assigned Galvez to Glens Falls.

May 5—Giants' Phoenix affiliate signed second baseman Rob Wilfong, a free agent.

May 5—Braves re-signed pitcher Doyle Alexander, a free agent.

May 5—Indians' organization traded pitcher Jose Roman to Mets' organization for outfielder Mike Westbrook.

May 6—Brewers' El Paso affiliate signed catcher Donnie Scott, a free agent.

May 6—Miami (Independent) released pitcher Dennis Martinez.

May 6—Expos re-signed pitcher Dennis Martinez, a free agent, and assigned him to Indianapolis.

May 7—Dodgers reclaimed pitcher Jeff Edwards from Astros, who had selected him from Albuquerque in the 1986 major league draft; Dodgers assigned Edwards to Albuquerque.

May 10—Twins traded pitcher Bill Latham to Mets for outfielder Jayson Felice; Twins assigned Felice to Orlando and Mets assigned Latham to Tidewater.

May 11—Indians' Buffalo affiliate traded pitcher Don Schulze to Mets' Tidewater affiliate for outfielder Ricky Nelson.

May 12—A's purchased outfielder-catcher Brian Harper from San Jose (Independent) and assigned him to Tacoma.

May 12—Mariners traded pitcher Mark Huismann to Indians for outfielder Dave Gallagher; Mariners assigned Gallagher to Calgary.

May 13—Giants released infielder Rob Wilfong.

May 15—Rangers traded pitcher Mike Mason to Cubs for a player to be named; Rangers acquired pitcher Dave Pavlas on June 6 and assigned him to Tulsa.

May 16—Astros signed outfielder Paul Householder, a free agent formerly with the Brewers.

May 18—Braves' Greenville affiliate signed pitcher Larry McWilliams, a free agent.

May 18—Royals' Omaha affiliate signed outfielder Lonnie Smith, a free agent.

May 19—Reds released catcher Sal Butera.

May 19—Angels re-signed pitcher Doug Corbett, a free agent, and assigned him to Edmonton.

May 22—Dodgers traded pitcher Tom Niedenfuer to Orioles for outfielder John Shelby and pitcher Brad Havens.

May 22—Twins' Portland affiliate signed catcher Sal Butera, a free agent.

May 28—Giants released pitcher Greg Minton.

May 29—Mets traded infielder Al Pedrique and outfielder Scott Little to Pirates for infielder-outfielder Bill Almon; Pirates assigned Little to Salem.

May 29—Dodgers released third baseman Bill Madlock.

May 30—Orioles traded pitcher Ricky Jones to Twins for a player to be named; Twins assigned Jones to Portland. Orioles' Rochester affiliate acquired pitcher Ron Musselman on June 12.

June 1—White Sox signed outfielder Mike Brown, a free agent, and assigned him to Hawaii.

June 1—Angels signed pitcher Greg Minton, a free agent.

June 2—Astros traded outfielder Eric Bullock to Twins for pitcher Clay Christiansen; Twins assigned Bullock to Portland and Astros assigned Christiansen to Tucson.

June 4—Orioles released pitcher Tippy Martinez.

June 4—Tigers signed third baseman Bill Madlock, a free agent.

June 4—Indians signed pitcher Sammy Stewart, a free agent formerly with the Red Sox, and assigned him to Buffalo.

June 4—Padres traded pitcher Tom Gorman to Twins for pitcher Dave Blakley; Twins assigned Gorman to Portland and Padres assigned Blakley to Reno.

June 4—Brewers released outfielder Jim Adduci.

June 4—Mariners traded infielder Ross Jones to Royals for a player to be named; Royals assigned Jones to Omaha. Mariners acquired pitcher Ricky Rojas on October 19 and assigned him to Calgary.

June 5—Blue Jays signed outfielder Charlie Moore, a free agent formerly with the Brewers.

June 5—Yankees released pitcher Bob Shirley.

June 5—Giants purchased infielder Ivan DeJesus from Cardinals.

June 7—Yankees traded pitcher Joe Niekro and cash to Twins for catcher Mark Salas.

June 9—Cardinals' Louisville affiliate signed infielder Dan Driessen, a free agent.

June 10—Phillies traded outfielder Mike Easler to Yankees for outfielder Keith Hughes and infielder Shane Turner; Phillies assigned Hughes to Maine and Turner to Reading.

June 12—Dodgers signed first baseman Danny Heep, a free agent formerly with the Mets, and assigned him to San Antonio.

June 13—Royals signed pitcher Bob Shirley, a free agent.

June 14—Reds released pitcher Jerry Reuss.

June 15—Pirates released infielder Onix Concepcion.

June 15—Twins signed pitcher Terry Forster, a free agent formerly with the Angels, and assigned him to Portland.

June 17—Padres released pitcher LaMarr Hoyt.

June 17—Royals released outfielder Jorge Orta.

June 18—Tigers purchased pitcher Ron Meridith from Rangers and assigned him to Toledo.

June 19—Astros traded infielder Phil Garner to Dodgers for a player to be named; Astros acquired pitcher Jeff Edwards on June 26 and assigned him to Tucson.

June 19—Angels signed pitcher Jerry Reuss, a free agent.

June 19—Angels released pitcher Doug Corbett.

June 19—Reds' Nashville affiliate signed outfielder-first baseman Dave Collins, a free agent.

June 22—Astros released pitcher Aurelio Lopez.

June 22—Tigers traded pitcher Bryan Kelly to Mariners for pitcher Karl Best; Mariners assigned Kelly to Calgary and Tigers assigned Best to Toledo.

June 22—Brewers' Denver affiliate signed pitcher Roy Lee Jackson, a free agent formerly with the Twins.

June 22—Yankees' organization acquired pitcher Alan Mills, completing deal in which Yankees traded catcher Butch Wynegar to Angels for pitcher Ron Romanick and a player to be named, December 19, 1986.

June 23—Orioles signed pitcher Doug Corbett, a free agent.

June 23—Dodgers traded pitcher Tim Meeks to A's for pitcher Bill Krueger; Dodgers assigned Krueger to Albuquerque and A's assigned Meeks to Tacoma.

June 24—Phillies traded pitcher Dan Schatzeder and cash to Twins for pitcher Danny Clay and third baseman Tom Schwarz; Phillies assigned Clay to Maine and Schwarz to Reading.

June 25—Rangers traded second baseman Jose Mota to Dodgers for first baseman Larry See; Dodgers assigned Mota to San Antonio and Rangers assigned See to Oklahoma City.

June 26—Tigers traded outfielder Terry Harper to Pirates for pitcher Shawn Holman and first baseman Pete Rice; Tigers assigned Holman and Rice to Glens Falls.

June 29—A's traded pitcher Bill Mooneyham to Brewers for first baseman-third baseman Russ McGinnis; A's assigned McGinnis to Madison and Brewers assigned Mooneyham to El Paso.

June 29—Giants released infielder Mike Woodard.

June 30—Tigers sold pitcher John Pacella to Tokyo Whales of Japanese Baseball League.

June 30—Expos traded pitcher Curt Brown to Brewers for a player to be named; Brewers assigned Brown to Denver.

July 1—White Sox signed pitcher LaMarr Hoyt, a free agent, and assigned him to Daytona Beach.

July 1—Angels' Edmonton affiliate signed outfielder Tony Armas, a free agent formerly with the Red Sox.

July 2—A's traded pitcher Eric Broersma to Brewers for a player to be named; Brewers assigned Broersma to El Paso. A's acquired pitcher Curt Brown on August 5.

July 2—Astros signed infielder Mike Woodard, a free agent, and assigned him to Tucson.

July 4—Royals released pitcher Bob Shirley.

July 4—Cardinals released outfielder Tito Landrum.

July 5—Padres traded pitchers Dave Dravecky and Craig Lefferts and infielder Kevin Mitchell to Giants for third baseman Chris Brown and pitchers Keith Comstock, Mark Davis and Mark Grant.

July 10—Dodgers signed outfielder Tito Landrum, a free agent.

July 11—Orioles released infielder Rick Burleson.

July 11—Cubs traded outfielder Gary Matthews to Mariners for a player to be named; Cubs acquired pitcher Dave Hartnett on July 12 and assigned him to Peoria.

July 11—Giants signed first baseman Dave Kingman, a free agent formerly with the A's, and assigned him to Phoenix.

July 11—Rangers signed pitcher Steve Howe, a free agent, and assigned him to Oklahoma City.

July 11—Cardinals' Louisville affiliate signed outfielder David Green, a free agent.

July 11—Mariners released catcher Bob Kearney.

July 13—Cubs traded pitcher Steve Trout to Yankees for pitchers Bob Tewksbury, Rich Scheid and Dean Wilkins; Cubs assigned Scheid to Pittsfield and Wilkins to Winston-Salem.

July 13—Reds' Nashville affiliate signed outfielder Jim Wohlford, a free agent.

July 14—Royals traded outfielder Juan Beniquez to Blue Jays for pitcher Luis Aquino; Royals assigned Aquino to Omaha.

July 15—Indians traded second baseman Tony Bernazard to A's for pitcher Darrel Akerfelds and catcher Brian Dorsett; Indians assigned Dorsett to Buffalo.

July 15—A's released third baseman Ron Cey.

July 16—Brewers' Denver affiliate purchased infielder Skeeter Barnes from Cardinals.

July 20—Dodgers' Albuquerque affiliate signed second baseman Julio Cruz, a free agent.

July 21—Royals released designated hitter Hal McRae.

July 23—Red Sox released first baseman Bill Buckner.

July 23—Royals' Omaha affiliate purchased catcher Dann Bilardello from Pirates.

July 23—A's Tacoma affiliate signed catcher Bob Kearney, a free agent.

July 23—Phillies' Maine affiliate signed pitcher Doug Bair, a free agent.

July 25—Cardinals traded pitcher Joe Boever to Braves for pitcher Randy O'Neal; Cardinals assigned O'Neal to Louisville.

July 25—Braves released pitcher Larry McWilliams.

July 28—Angels signed first baseman Bill Buckner, a free agent.

July 29—A's released shortstop Johnnie LeMaster.

July 30—Royals traded shortstop Buddy Biancalana to Astros for pitcher Mel Stottlemyre Jr.; Royals assigned Stottlemyre to Memphis.

July 30—Cardinals traded pitcher Dave LaPoint to White Sox for pitcher Bryce Hulstrom; Cardinals assigned Hulstrom to Springfield.

July 31—Indians traded pitcher Steve Carlton to Twins for a player to be named; Indians acquired pitcher Jeff Perry on August 18 and assigned him to Williamsport.

July 31—Yankees signed pitcher Bob Shirley, a free agent, and assigned him to Columbus.

July 31—Pirates traded pitcher Don Robinson to Giants for catcher Mackey Sasser and $50,000; Pirates assigned Sasser to Vancouver.

August 3—Pirates claimed pitcher Jim Gott on waivers from Giants.

August 4—Cubs released pitcher Ron Davis.

August 5—Mariners released pitcher Roy Thomas.

August 6—Rangers' Oklahoma City affiliate signed pitcher Larry McWilliams, a free agent.

August 6—White Sox' Hawaii affiliate signed shortstop Johnnie LeMaster, a free agent.

August 7—Pirates traded third baseman Jim Morrison to Tigers for third baseman Darnell Coles and a player to be named; Pirates acquired pitcher Morris Madden on August 12 and assigned him to Vancouver.

August 8—Indians' Buffalo affiliate signed pitcher Roy Thomas, a free agent.

August 9—Indians traded pitcher Phil Niekro to Blue Jays for outfielder Darryl Landrum and a player to be named; Indians acquired pitcher Don Gordon on August 10.

August 10—Phillies released pitcher Tom Hume.

August 11—Orioles traded outfielder Nelson Simmons to Mariners for a player to be named; Mariners assigned Simmons to Calgary. Orioles acquired pitcher Mike Brown on August 26 and assigned him to Rochester.

August 12—Braves traded pitcher Doyle Alexander to Tigers for pitcher John Smoltz; Braves assigned Smoltz to Richmond.

August 13—Dodgers signed pitcher Ron Davis, a free agent, and assigned him to Albuquerque.

August 13—Rangers traded pitcher Greg Ferlenda to Orioles for catcher Kurt Beamesderfer; Orioles assigned Ferlenda to Rochester and Rangers assigned Beamesderfer to Tulsa.

August 18—Reds signed pitcher Tom Hume, a free agent.

August 21—Red Sox traded infielder Glenn Hoffman to Dodgers for a player to be named; Red Sox acquired pitcher Billy Bartels on December 8.

August 21—Pirates traded pitcher Rick Reuschel to Giants for pitchers Jeff Robinson and Scott Medvin; Pirates assigned Medvin to Vancouver.

August 21—Orioles released pitcher Doug Corbett.

August 25—Blue Jays released pitcher Gary Lavelle.

August 26—Reds traded pitcher Bill Gullickson to Yankees for pitcher Dennis Rasmussen.

August 26—White Sox traded infielders Jerry Royster and Mike Soper to Yankees for pitcher Ken Patterson and a player to be named; Yankees assigned Patterson to Hawaii. White Sox acquired pitcher Jeff Pries on September 19.

August 29—Pirates traded second baseman Johnny Ray to Angels for third baseman Billie Merrifield and a player to be named; Pirates acquired pitcher Miguel Garcia on September 3.

August 29—White Sox released pitcher Neil Allen.

August 29—Dodgers traded pitcher Rick Honeycutt to A's for a player to be named; Dodgers acquired pitcher Tim Belcher on September 3.

August 30—Padres traded pitcher Storm Davis to A's for two players to be named; Padres acquired pitcher Dave Leiper on August 31 and first baseman Rob Nelson on September 8.

August 31—Cardinals traded pitcher Pat Perry to Reds for a player to be named; Cardinals acquired pitcher Scott Terry on September 3.

August 31—A's signed pitcher Gary Lavelle, a free agent.

August 31—Blue Jays released pitcher Phil Niekro.

August 31—Braves traded pitcher Gene Garber to Royals for a player to be named; Braves acquired catcher Terry Bell on September 3.

August 31—Orioles traded pitcher Mike Flanagan to Blue Jays for pitcher Oswald Peraza and a player to be named; Orioles acquired pitcher Jose Mesa on September 4.

August 31—Red Sox traded designated hitter Don Baylor to Twins for a player to be named; Red Sox acquired pitcher Enrique Rios on December 18.

September 1—Red Sox traded outfielder Dave Henderson to Giants for a player to be named; Red Sox acquired outfielder Randy Kutcher on December 9.

September 4—Yankees signed pitcher Neil Allen, a free agent.

September 15—Angels traded pitcher John Candelaria to Mets for pitchers Shane Young and Jeff Richardson.

September 22—Blue Jays traded infielder Mike Sharperson to Dodgers for pitcher Juan Guzman.

September 22—Cubs traded pitcher Dickie Noles to Tigers for a player to be named; returned to Cubs on October 23.

September 23—Angels released third baseman Doug DeCinces.

September 29—Cardinals signed third baseman Doug DeCinces, a free agent.

September 29—Orioles released second baseman Alan Wiggins.

September 30—Mariners released outfielder Dave Gallagher.

September 30—Astros traded pitcher Julio Solano to Mariners for pitcher Doug Givler.

October 2—Cardinals released pitcher Ray Soff.

October 5—Padres traded pitcher Ed Wojna to White Sox for a player to be named.

October 5—Tigers traded outfielder Bruce Fields to Mariners for pitcher Stan Clarke.

October 5—Pirates released shortstop U.L. Washington.

October 6—Brewers' Denver affiliate purchased pitcher Tom Filer from Blue Jays.

October 7—Cardinals released third baseman Doug DeCinces.

October 8—Orioles released catcher Floyd Rayford, pitchers Tony Arnold, Mike Kinnunen and Luis DeLeon and outfielder Mike Hart.

October 12—A's released catchers Jerry Willard and Matt Sinatro and outfielder Brian Harper.

October 13—Astros released shortstop Dale Berra and catcher Ronn Reynolds.

October 15—Royals released shortstop Ross Jones and pitchers Theo Shaw and Bob Stoddard.

October 15—Phillies released outfielder Ron Roenicke.

October 16—Cubs traded outfielder Chico Walker to Angels for pitcher Todd Fischer.

October 16—Tigers released outfielder-designated hitter John Grubb, pitcher Nate Snell and catcher Dwight Lowry.

October 21—Reds released second baseman Ron Oester.

October 23—Rangers signed outfielder James Steels, a free agent.

October 23—Twins signed catcher Dwight Lowry, a free agent.

October 23—Blue Jays released catcher Charlie Moore.

October 26—Royals signed second baseman Brad Wellman, a free agent.

October 27—Reds released pitchers Tom Hume and Bill Scherrer.

October 28—Nippon Ham Fighters of Japanese Baseball League purchased outfielder Brian Dayett from Cubs.

October 29—Indians released catcher Rick Dempsey and pitchers Jamie Easterly and Sammy Stewart.

October 30—Angels released pitcher Don Sutton.

October 31—Rangers' organization signed catcher Dave Sax and outfielder Dallas Williams, both free agents.

November 2—Rangers traded catcher Don Slaught to Yankees for a player to be named; Rangers acquired pitcher Brad Arnsberg on November 10.

November 2—Yankees released pitcher Al Holland and infielders Lenn Sakata and Juan Bonilla.

November 6—Royals traded pitcher Danny Jackson and shortstop Angel Salazar to Reds for pitcher Ted Power and shortstop Kurt Stillwell.

November 6—Pirates traded outfielder Joe Orsulak to Orioles for shortstop Terry Crowley Jr. and third baseman Rico Rossy; Pirates assigned Crowley to Harrisburg.

November 9—Cardinals released first baseman Dan Driessen.

November 9—Indians released outfielder Miguel Roman.

November 9—Phillies released shortstop Ken Dowell.

November 11—Mets traded outfielder Terry Blocker to Braves for a player to be named; Mets acquired pitcher Kevin Dewayne Brown on December 8.

November 11—Brewers signed pitcher Odell Jones, a free agent, and re-signed pitchers Bill Mooneyham and Bryan Clutterbuck, both free agents.

November 11—Yankees signed pitcher Steve Shields, a free agent.

November 12—Astros released outfielder Davey Lopes.

November 12—Twins released pitcher Jeff Bittiger.

November 12—Pirates released pitcher Logan Easley.

November 12—Yankees traded outfielder Dan Pasqua, catcher Mark Salas and pitcher Steve Rosenberg to White Sox for pitchers Richard Dotson and Scott Nielsen.

November 12—Dodgers released pitcher Bill Krueger and catcher Orlando Mercado.

November 13—Braves re-signed outfielder Ken Griffey, a free agent.

November 18—Mariners released catcher Jerry Narron and outfielder Jim Weaver.

November 20—Pirates' Buffalo affiliate signed third baseman Skeeter Barnes, a free agent.

November 23—White Sox released pitcher Ray Krawczyk and infielder Pat Keedy.

November 24—Pirates' Buffalo affiliate signed outfielder Tom Romano, a free agent.

November 25—Giants re-signed pitcher Mike LaCoss, a free agent.

November 30—Indians released designated hitter Andre Thornton.

December 1—Giants signed outfielder Brett Butler, a free agent formerly with the Indians, and re-signed outfielder Joel Youngblood, a free agent.

December 1—Angels signed outfielder Chili Davis, a free agent formerly with the Giants.

December 1—Tigers re-signed catcher Mike Heath, a free agent.

December 3—Angels re-signed pitcher Greg Minton, a free agent.

December 3—Pirates' Buffalo affiliate signed

pitcher Logan Easley, a free agent.

December 5—Tigers traded pitcher Dan Petry to Angels for outfielder Gary Pettis.

December 5—Dodgers' Albuquerque affiliate signed pitchers Tony Arnold, Stan Kyles and Chuck Hensley, all free agents.

December 6—Braves' Greenville affiliate signed third baseman Graig Nettles, a free agent.

December 7—Expos' Indianapolis affiliate signed catcher Dave Engle, a free agent.

December 7—Twins signed pitchers Bryan Clark, a free agent formerly with the White Sox, and Don Schulze, a free agent formerly with the Mets; Twins assigned Clark to Portland.

December 7—Cubs re-signed second baseman Manny Trillo, a free agent.

December 7—Indians re-signed catcher Chris Bando, a free agent.

December 7—Royals re-signed pitcher Gene Garber, a free agent.

December 7—Expos re-signed pitcher Bob McClure, a free agent.

December 7—A's re-signed pitcher Gary Lavelle, a free agent.

December 7—Twins' Portland affiliate signed pitcher T.R. Bryden, a free agent.

December 8—Mets traded pitcher Doug Sisk to Orioles for pitcher Blaine Beatty and a player to be named; Mets acquired pitcher Greg Talamantez on December 11.

December 8—Phillies signed outfielder Bob Dernier, a free agent formerly with the Cubs.

December 8—Cubs traded pitcher Lee Smith to Red Sox for pitchers Al Nipper and Calvin Schiraldi.

December 8—Reds traded outfielder Dave Parker to A's for pitchers Jose Rijo and Tim Birtsas; Reds assigned Birtsas to Nashville.

December 8—Reds re-signed outfielder Dave Collins, a free agent.

December 8—Braves traded shortstop Rafael Ramirez and cash to Astros for third baseman Ed Whited and pitcher Mike Stoker, who were both assigned to Durham.

December 8—Rangers signed pitcher Craig McMurtry, a free agent, and assigned him to Oklahoma City.

December 9—Orioles traded pitcher Ken Dixon to Mariners for pitcher Mike Morgan.

December 9—A's signed catcher Ron Hassey, a free agent formerly with the White Sox.

December 9—Phillies traded outfielders Glenn Wilson and Dave Brundage and pitcher Mike Jackson to Mariners for outfielder Phil Bradley and pitcher Tim Fortugno; Phillies assigned Fortugno to Reading and Mariners assigned Brundage to Vermont.

December 9—A's Tacoma affiliate signed shortstop Ross Jones, a free agent.

December 10—White Sox traded pitcher Floyd Bannister and infielder Dave Cochrane to Royals for pitchers John Davis, Melido Perez, Chuck Mount and Greg Hibbard.

December 11—In a three-team deal, Mets traded pitcher Jesse Orosco to A's. A's then traded Orosco along with shortstop Alfredo Griffin and pitcher Jay Howell to Dodgers for pitchers Bob Welch, Matt Young and Jack Savage. A's then traded Savage along with pitchers Wally Whitehurst and Kevin Tapani to Mets.

December 11—Mets traded shortstop Rafael Santana and pitcher Victor Garcia to Yankees for outfielder Darren Reed, catcher Phil Lombardi and pitcher Steve Frey.

December 11—Mets signed outfielder Miguel Roman and shortstop Ken Dowell, both free agents.

December 14—Red Sox traded catcher Marc Sullivan to Astros for a player to be named.

December 14—Tigers re-signed outfielder Larry Herndon, a free agent.

December 14—Giants re-signed pitcher Joe Price, a free agent.

December 14—Cubs signed infielder Vance Law, a free agent formerly with the Expos.

December 14—Brewers re-signed pitcher Mark Clear, a free agent.

December 15—Royals released outfielder Lonnie Smith.

December 15—Dodgers signed outfielder Mike Davis, a free agent formerly with the A's.

December 16—Dodgers released infielder Glenn Hoffman.

December 16—Expos re-signed pitcher Bryn Smith, a free agent.

December 17—Mets re-signed outfielder Lee Mazzilli, a free agent.

December 18—Expos re-signed pitcher Dennis Martinez, a free agent.

December 18—Phillies signed pitcher David Palmer, a free agent formerly with the Braves.

December 21—Cardinals released pitchers Bob Forsch and Bill Dawley.

December 21—Orioles released infielder Ron Washington.

December 21—Angels released pitcher Stu Cliburn.

December 21—Twins released designated hitter Don Baylor, catcher Sal Butera and pitchers Steve Carlton, Mike Smithson and Dan Schatzeder.

December 21—Yankees re-signed pitcher Tommy John, a free agent.

December 21—Yankees released outfielders Mike Easler and Ron Kittle.

December 21—A's signed outfielder Dave Henderson, a free agent formerly with the Giants.

December 21—A's released infielders Tony Bernazard and Tony Phillips and pitcher Rick Rodriguez.

December 21—Royals released first baseman Steve Balboni.

December 21—Astros released shortstop Buddy Biancalana.

December 21—Cubs released pitcher Jay Baller.

December 21—White Sox released pitcher Bob James.

December 21—Mariners released outfielder John Moses and shortstop Domingo Ramos.

December 21—Giants released catcher Phil Ouellette.

December 21—Rangers released catcher Darrell Porter and pitcher Greg Harris.

December 22—Twins re-signed pitcher Juan Berenguer, a free agent.

December 22—Yankees traded pitcher Steve Trout and outfielder Henry Cotto to Mariners for pitchers Lee Guetterman, Clay Parker and Wade Taylor; Yankees assigned Taylor to Fort Lauderdale.

December 22—Angels re-signed pitcher Mike Witt, a free agent.

December 23—Yankees re-signed pitcher Dave Righetti, a free agent.

December 29—Tigers re-signed pitcher Jack Morris, a free agent.

Howser, Young Die in 1987

By DAVE SLOAN

Two men who shared the same first name and whose biggest contributions to baseball came off the playing field were among the most notable baseball personalities who died in 1987.

Dick Howser, whose greatest achievement came in the final two years of his life, and Dick Young, a noted sportswriter and columnist who covered baseball for half a century, both left imprints on the game that will last for many years.

Howser, a 29-year veteran of professional baseball whose finest moment came in 1985 when he managed the Kansas City Royals to their first-ever World Series title, died June 17 in a Kansas City hospital after a gallant fight against a malignant brain tumor. He was 51.

The malignancy was discovered two days after Howser had managed the American League to a 3-2 victory over the National League in the 1986 All-Star Game in Houston. Many of the players and coaches in the A.L. dugout that night later said the Royals' manager appeared muddled and confused, sometimes mistaking one player for another or forgetting names altogether. Howser checked himself into a hospital for tests because of persistent headaches and a stiff neck.

Tests revealed a tumor the size of a golf ball in the right frontal lobe of the brain, and Howser underwent surgery three times. The first surgery, performed July 22, 1986, resulted in the removal of most of the cancerous growth.

Howser then underwent a series of intensive radiation treatments in Kansas City before submitting to a radical procedure December 3 in Pasadena, Calif., in which millions of "killer cells" were introduced into the tumor cavity.

Howser, who had been replaced as the Royals' manager on an interim basis by third-base coach Mike Ferraro for the remainder of the '86 season, battled back to the point that he reported to the Royals' 1987 training camp in Florida last spring. But February 23, after just the third day of camp, Howser announced that he was too weak to continue as manager and resigned.

As a player, Howser was an All-America shortstop at Florida State University in 1957 and '58 before breaking into the major leagues with the Kansas City A's in 1961. He batted .281 that season and was named The Sporting News' A.L. Rookie Player of the Year.

Howser's first season was his best, however, and he retired as a player in 1968 after compiling a .248 career batting average in 789 games with the A's, Cleveland Indians and New York Yankees.

Following his retirement as an active player, Howser remained with the Yankees as a coach from 1968 through 1978, even managing the Yanks for one game in '78 following Billy Martin's resignation.

He returned to manage at Florida State in 1979 before being asked by Owner George Steinbrenner to manage the Yankees full-time in 1980. The Yanks won 103 games and the A.L. East Division crown, but Howser was forced to resign after New York was swept in three games by the Royals in the League Championship Series. Howser was only the fourth manager in major league history to win 100 games in his first season.

One year later, Howser accepted the Kansas City managing job after the dismissal of Jim Frey. He led the Royals to a half division title in the strike-torn '81 campaign and to A.L. West Division crowns in both 1984 and 1985. His '84 Royals were swept by Detroit in the LCS but his '85 edition battled back from three-games-to-one deficits in both the LCS against Toronto and the World Series against St. Louis.

Howser compiled a 507-425 managerial record in all or parts of eight major league seasons and the Royals retired his uniform No. 10 in ceremonies last July 3 in Kansas City.

Young was perhaps the most colorful, innovative, controversial and disliked sportswriter of the past 50 years. He was elected to the writers' wing of the Baseball Hall of Fame in 1978 and had been living in semiretirement in Boulder City, Nev., following intestinal surgery in late 1986. Young became ill while visiting New York in July 1987 and was hospitalized there after suffering complications from the previous surgery. He died August 31 at age 69.

His passions in addition to baseball were college basketball and professional boxing, and Young was not a writer to keep his opinions to himself, even if it brought him in conflict with others.

Young, whose father was a Russian Jew and whose mother was an American Jew of German descent, began his newspaper career in the depths of the Depression as a

Kansas City's Dick Howser peers from the dugout during the 1986 All-Star Game in Houston, his final game as manager. Two days later, a malignant brain tumor was found.

messenger boy for the New York Daily News. He rose through the ranks to become one of the most widely read sportswriters in the country. He had a syndicated column, "Young Ideas", and also was a regular columnist for The Sporting News from the late 1950s until 1985.

Young's first regular beat with the Daily News was the Brooklyn Dodgers, and the often-vengeful, belligerent style in which he covered the team got him in trouble on more than one occasion. Dodger Managers Burt Shotton and Leo Durocher barred Young temporarily from the clubhouse, but that didn't stop him from leading an editorial effort to keep the Dodgers in Brooklyn after Owner Walter O'Malley announced in 1957 his intention to move the team to Los Angeles.

When that effort failed, Young campaigned first for the formation of a third major league, and then for the placing of another National League team in the New York area. He got his wish when the expansion Mets played their first season there in 1962.

During his early years covering the Dodgers, Young set himself apart from his competition simply by outhustling other writers and coming up with information they didn't. He was one of the first morning-paper sportswriters to descend to the clubhouse for the purpose of gathering pregame information and quotes from players and club personnel, rather than just file the traditional on-deadline press box game story.

While covering the Dodgers, Young wrote a book about Roy Campanella and in 1956 won a Best Sports Stories award for a piece he did on pitcher Preacher Roe.

Young often waged personal vendettas in his column against prominent sports figures, including sportscaster Howard Cosell ("Howie the Shill", according to Young), heavyweight boxing champ Muhammad Ali, baseball union chief Marvin Miller, baseball's club owners (always referred to collectively as "the Lords of Baseball") and Jackie Robinson, whom Young had championed as the man to break baseball's color barrier, but who disliked the writer intensely for other than racial reasons.

According to one of Young's colleagues on the Dodgers beat at the time, the writer once confided, talking about Robinson, "I can never forget he's black." Robinson,

Travis Jackson (right) played for Manager John McGraw during most of his years with the New York Giants.

once he learned of Young's remarks, said, "I never want him to."

Young also railed against drug abuse in sports, other sportswriters he considered "establishment" and players he considered greedy for wanting bigger salaries. He came down particularly hard on Tom Seaver in 1977 when the Mets pitcher stated that he'd just as soon play elsewhere unless his contract was renegotiated.

That stance came back to haunt Young in 1982 when, after a 45-year association with the Daily News, he announced that he was leaving the paper to join the New York Post, a rival tabloid. Young defended his move by saying that the News, which had been put up for sale the previous year, could not guarantee his $100,000-plus annual salary. His critics said that he had two years left on his contract with the News, and that he should honor it.

The Daily News filed a $1.5-million breach-of-contract suit against Young, but it was later dismissed by a Manhattan judge.

Among those former players who died in 1987, the only one thus far to have made it to the Hall of Fame in Cooperstown, N.Y., was shortstop Travis Jackson, who died at Waldo, Ark., on July 17 at age 83.

Jackson, who was selected for the Hall by the Veterans Committee in 1982, batted .300 or better in six of his 15 major league seasons with the New York Giants from 1922-36. He finished his playing career in 1936 with a .291 average, 1,768 hits and 929 RBIs in 1,656 games.

Blessed with one of the best throwing arms ever for a major league shortstop, Jackson's best seasons were 1929, when he hit 29 home runs; 1930, when he batted a career-high .339, and 1934, when he drove in 101 runs. His offensive numbers would have been even more impressive had it not been for a series of injuries and sicknesses that dogged him throughout his career.

Jackson was a longtime minor league manager before retiring to Waldo in 1961.

Paul Derringer, the second-winningest pitcher in Cincinnati Reds history, died of cancer at Sarasota, Fla., on November 17. He was 81.

A righthander, Derringer won 161 games for the Reds between 1933-42, a Cincinnati victory total surpassed only by Hall of Famer Eppa Rixey (179).

Derringer began his major league career with the St. Louis Cardinals in 1931, posting an 18-8 record and leading the National League with a .632 winning percentage. He slumped to an 11-14 record

Paul Derringer (above) and Babe
Herman were two standout players
in the 1930s.

the following year and was traded in May 1933 to Cincinnati for shortstop Leo Durocher. Derringer lost 27 games that season with the last-place Reds despite posting a respectable 3.30 earned-run average.

He won 21 games in 1938, all complete-game efforts, and was 25-7 in 1939 as the Reds won the N.L. pennant. The following season, Derringer finished 20-12 and the Reds went on to a seven-game World Series victory over Detroit. Derringer won two games in the Series, including a 2-1 victory in Game 7.

Derringer won 223 games in 15 big league seasons but trivia buffs will remember him as the starting and winning Reds pitcher in the first night baseball game ever played May 24, 1935.

Another former Reds player who came up with a notable first in night baseball was outfielder Floyd (Babe) Herman, a colorful player who was often called "the other Babe" because his career paralleled that of Yankees slugger Babe Ruth.

Herman, whose finest moments in baseball came as a member of the Brooklyn Dodgers from 1926 to '31, slugged the first major league home run in a night game while playing for the Reds against his former team July 10, 1935.

Herman, who died at Glendale, Calif., on November 27, played six years for eight different minor league teams before joining the Dodgers as a rookie in 1926. He hit .319 his first year and .381 and .393, respectively, in 1929 and 1930 but didn't win a batting title either year. He was edged for the batting crown by Philadelphia's Frank O'Doul (.398) in '29 and the Giants' Bill Terry (.401) in '30.

Although he compiled a .324 batting mark in 13 major league seasons, his hitting ability was often overshadowed by his reputation as a clown prince. Known as a weak defensive outfielder, many stories were told about balls bouncing off his head and other zany happenings. The Dodgers were a poor club during much of the 1920s and early '30s, and Herman's colorful antics gave Brooklyn fans a bit of a respite from all the defeats.

Herman, who once homered as a pinch-hitter for Detroit playing Manager Ty Cobb in 1937, played six more seasons in the minor leagues in the early '40s before rejoining the Dodgers one final time as a pinch-hitter in 1945.

Among the other baseball personalities who died in 1987 were Jim Brewer, one of the game's most effective lefthanded relief pitchers during a 17-year career spent primarily with the Los Angeles Dodgers in the 1960s and '70s; Mike Burke, the man who as club president from 1966-73 tried unsuccessfully to restore the New York Yankees to their former prominence; Bobo Holloman, who as a member of the St. Louis Browns pitched a no-hitter in his first major league start on May 6, 1953, against the Philadelphia A's; Don McMahon, a relief specialist whose 874 pitching appearances between 1957 and 1974 rank fourth-best on the all-time list; Dale Mitchell, a player who struck out just 119 times in 3,984 big-league at-bats but is best remembered for striking out for the final out in Don Larsen's perfect game in the 1956 World Series; Phil Seghi, who had been associated with professional baseball for more than half a century in various front-office roles and was a consultant for the Cleveland Indians at the time of his death; George Selkirk, an eight-year minor league veteran who succeeded Babe Ruth as the Yankees' everyday right fielder in 1935; Luke Sewell, one of three brothers to play in the major leagues and manager of the St. Louis Browns' only American League championship club in 1944; and Dick Stello, a National League umpire who in 1987 completed his 19th season in the major leagues.

An alphabetical list of baseball deaths in 1987 follows:

Jerry K. Adair, 50, a slick-fielding utility infielder who played for four American League teams between 1958 and 1970, of liver cancer at Tulsa on May 31; was signed out of Oklahoma State University in 1958 by Baltimore and went on to play eight-plus seasons with the Orioles; set major league records for consecutive errorless games by a second baseman (89) and consecutive chances handled without an error (458) from July 22, 1964, through May 6, 1965, and led major league second basemen in putouts and assists in 1965 and in fielding percentage in 1964 and '65; was traded to the Chicago White Sox midway through the 1966 season and went to Boston in 1967, appearing in five World Series games for the Red Sox; was drafted by Kansas City in the A.L. expansion draft and spent two seasons with the Royals before getting his release; played briefly in the minor leagues and spent one season in Japan before returning to the United States and joining the Oakland A's as a coach in 1972; left the A's for a coaching position with the California Angels in 1975; compiled a .254 career batting average and a .981 career fielding mark in 1,165 major league games, 810 of which were spent at second base.

Lee Ballanfant, 91, who spent 22 years as a National League umpire before performing scouting duties for the Chicago Cubs, Houston Astros and Texas Rangers, at Dallas on July 15; spent six seasons with various Texas minor league clubs as a shortstop and second baseman in the 1920s; turned to umpiring in the Texas Association in 1926 after a broken leg had ended his playing career and moved on to the Texas League in 1929, where he spent seven years; made his major league debut in 1936 in a game at New York's Polo Grounds, marking the first time he had ever set foot in a major league park; the 5-foot-8, 130-pounder, one of the quickest umpires in the busi-

ness, worked six World Series and six All-Star Games before his career ended in 1957, primarily because of arthritis in his legs; turned to scouting before retiring in 1981.

Edward H. (Ed) Bastian, 58, who spent more than 20 years as a minor league club administrator in five baseball organizations before entering business for himself in 1973, at Knoxville on August 21; worked for the Baltimore Orioles, St. Louis Cardinals, New York Yankees, Atlanta Braves and New York Mets during a career that began in his native Rochester, N.Y., in 1950, when he was assistant to the concessions manager for the Red Wings.

Walter W. (Boom Boom) Beck, 82, a right-handed pitcher who compiled a 38-69 record with five major league teams in 12 seasons between 1924 and 1945, at Champaign, Ill., on May 7; made brief appearances with the St. Louis Browns between 1924 and 1928 after pitching a four-hit, 2-1 victory over the Chicago White Sox in his major league debut; spent 1929 through '32 in the minors before earning a spot in the 1933 Brooklyn Dodgers rotation; compiled a 12-20 mark that season and 2-6 the next; returned to the minors for four years before hooking on with the Philadelphia Phillies in 1939 and compiling a 7-14 mark; remained in the Phillies organization for five years before making later stops in Detroit, Cincinnati and Pittsburgh, where he compiled an 8-5 mark in 1945, his last major league season; played and managed in the minors until 1950 and later worked as a pitching coach for the Washington Senators, a scout for the Senators and a minor league pitching instructor for the Milwaukee Braves; retired after the 1971 season.

Henry (Hank) Behrman, 65, a free-spirited righthander who experienced rookie success with the Brooklyn Dodgers in 1946 but could not match that success later in his career, at New York on January 27; pitched for the Dodgers, Pittsburgh Pirates and New York Giants from 1946 to '49, compiling a 24-17 career record, mostly as a short reliever; was known for his disdain of curfews, which led to friction with Brooklyn managers Leo Durocher and Burt Shotton; enjoyed his best season in 1946, his rookie year, when he returned from military service to record an 11-5 record; was released by the Giants in 1949 and finished his career in the minors, pitching for Oakland, San Francisco, Oklahoma City and Charleston.

Joseph R. Bennett, 87, an infielder who appeared in one game with the 1923 Philadelphia Phillies and later formed a semi-pro team in New Jersey, at Morro Bay, Calif., on July 11; was a retired Army colonel who served in World War II and Korea before managing the officers' club at Fort Monmouth, N.J., after retirement from active duty.

Walter Martin (Huck) Betts, 90, a righthanded pitcher who compiled a 61-68 record for the Philadelphia Phillies and Boston Braves between 1920 and 1935, at Millsboro, Del., on June 13; pitched six seasons in Philadelphia, compiling an 18-27 mark; on the recommendation of old teammate Casey Stengel, was given a comeback by Boston in 1932 at age 35 and responded by giving the Braves 43 victories over the next four seasons; best campaigns were 1934 when he was 17-10 and 1932 when he was 13-11; retired in 1935 to his native Millsboro, where he operated a movie house and served on the Sussex County jury commission.

Henry John (Zeke) Bonura, 78, a colorful good-hit, no-field first baseman who in seven seasons prior to World War II compiled a .307 batting average with four major league teams, at New Orleans on March 9; drove in 100 or more runs four times and hit above .300 four times with his best season coming in 1936 when he batted .330 and set a Chicago White Sox record by driving in 138 runs; a former AAU javelin champion, Bonura spent five seasons in the minor leagues, primarily because of his fielding deficiencies, before the White Sox purchased his contract and gave him a chance; batted .302 with 27 home runs and 110 RBIs in his rookie campaign with a .545 slugging percentage; usually ranked among the fielding percentage leaders at first base, but only because he lacked range and speed; was traded to the Washington Senators in 1938 and drove in 114 runs; his career went downhill from there, with a stop in New York with the Giants, a return to Washington and a final stop with the Chicago Cubs; finished his career with 119 home runs and 704 RBIs in 917 games; spent the 1941 season in the minors with Minneapolis before joining the Army; after his discharge in 1945, returned to Minneapolis as a playing manager and later served in a similar capacity with four other minor league clubs before making three minor league stops as a manager; retired in 1957 to enter the real estate business in New Orleans; was known for his nonsensical on-field chatter, exaggerated gesturing and penchant for missing signs.

George V. (Pee Wee) Bourrette, 81, a former college football and basketball official who, following his retirement as a Kansas City-area high school teacher and coach, was a scout and coordinator of physical development for the Kansas City Royals, at Lee's Summit, Mo., on February 7.

Jim Brewer, 49, one of baseball's most effective lefthanded relief pitchers during a 17-year career spent primarily with the Los Angeles Dodgers, in an automobile crash near Carthage, Tex., on November 16; reached the major leagues with the Chicago Cubs in 1960 after spending four years in the minors and struggled to a 4-13 record while dividing time between the Cubs and their Salt Lake City farm club for four years; was involved in a brawl in which he was attacked by Cincinnati second baseman Billy Martin in 1960 and underwent two operations to repair bones around his eye socket; filed a $1 million damage suit against Martin which later was dropped; was traded to the Dodgers in late 1963 and came back in '64 to post his first winning record (4-3) in the majors; perfected a screwball that eventually made him the stopper in the Dodger bullpen and one of the most effective closers in the game; was 8-3 with a 2.49 ERA in 1968, the first of six straight years he would lead the staff in saves and appearances, although twice undergoing surgery to remove bone spurs in his left elbow; was relegated to a supporting role in 1974 with the arrival of workhorse Mike Marshall and pitched only 39 innings while serving two stints on the disabled list; was placed on waivers and claimed by the California Angels in 1975; spent most of his time on the disabled list and chose voluntary retirement at the end of the '76 season; returned to baseball the next spring as the Montreal Expos' pitching coach and later worked in the same capacity for Oral Roberts and Northwestern universities; rejoined the Dodgers in the spring of 1986 as pitching coach for their Great Falls (Pioneer) club; had just completed an Arizona Instructional League assignment for the Dodgers two weeks before the fatal crash; appeared in 584 major league games, 549 of them as a reliever, and amassed 132 saves to go with a 69-65 record and a 3.07 ERA; was the Dodgers' all-time leader in saves (125) and appeared in three World Series without a decision; pitched one scoreless inning in the 1973 All-Star Game.

Michael (Mike) Burke, 70, the man who tried unsuccessfully to restore the New York Yankees to baseball prominence from 1966 to 1973, at Dublin, Ireland, on February 5; enjoyed a colorful and multi-faceted career as a behind-the-lines espionage agent in Europe during World War II, a Hollywood script writer, an adviser to the High Commission for Germany, a circus manager and a network programming executive before being named vice-president of CBS Inc. and becoming involved with baseball; was named president of the Yankees in 1966 after CBS purchased the club; under Burke, the once-proud franchise struggled through a bleak period, managing to finish as high as second just one time; stayed on as part of the syndicate, headed by George Steinbrenner, that purchased the team in 1973; reached agreement with Steinbrenner shortly after the buyout that ended his active participation in the club's affairs; remained in New York to oversee the operation of Madison Square Garden Center, and as preident was in charge of the National Basketball Association's New York Knicks and the National Hockey League's New York Rangers; took a lot of heat when both franchises faltered and retired in 1981, moving to Ireland; worked as a gentleman farmer and wrote his autobiography entitled "Outrageous Good Fortune."

Joseph F. Burns, 98, who appeared in five major league games for the 1910 Cincinnati Reds and the 1913 Detroit Tigers, at Beverly, Mass., on July 12; was signed by the Reds in 1910 and appeared in one game that season, getting a single as a pinch-hitter in his only at-bat; played in the minors until Detroit purchased his contract in 1913; the lefthanded-hitting outfielder played four games for the Tigers, getting five hits in 13 at-bats; played in the minors until his career was interrupted in 1918 by World War I; played several more seasons in the minors after the War before retiring in 1927.

John Burrows Jr., 73, a lefthander who pitched professionally for 18 seasons, most of those in the minor leagues, in a fire that destroyed his Coal Run, O., home on April 27; the Louisiana native was signed originally by the Washington Senators in 1933, but didn't reach the major leagues until 10 years later with the Philadelphia A's; was 0-1 in his brief stint with the 1943 A's and was 0-2 after being acquired that season by the Chicago Cubs; appeared in three games without a decision for the 1944 Cubs before playing out his string in the minor leagues; continued his association with baseball after his 1950 retirement by touring South Africa with the financial backing of the African Baseball Board, giving clinics and staging games in 1952.

Edgar John Busch, 69, an infielder who compiled a .262 average in his 270-game, three-year major league career, in Illinois on January 17; began playing professionally in 1938 but didn't reach the major leagues until 1943; played three seasons with the Philadelphia A's, his best coming in 1944 when he hit .271 in 140 games.

Frank B. Callaway, 89, a utility infielder with Connie Mack's 1921 and '22 Philadelphia A's who founded a chain of sporting goods stores in Tennessee after an injury ended his baseball career, at Knoxville on August 21; signed his first professional contract with Knoxville in 1921 and appeared in 14 games at shortstop later that season for the A's, batting .240; batted .271 in 29 games the next season while playing second base, shortstop and third base before a knee injury forced him to give up baseball; became a founding partner later that year in the Athletic House sporting goods business in Knoxville; served as president of the chain for 45 years prior to his retirement in 1968.

Camilo G. Carreon, 50, a former catcher who played eight major league seasons with the Chicago White Sox, Cleveland Indians and Baltimore

Orioles from 1959 to 1966, at Tucson on September 2; a righthanded hitter, he posted a .264 career batting average in 354 games; batted .274 in 101 games for the 1963 White Sox in his best season; died without knowing his son Mark had been called up to the major leagues for the first time just two days earlier.

Edward Joseph (Cy) Cihocki, 80, a shortstop who played briefly with Connie Mack's Philadelphia Athletics in 1932 and '33 but enjoyed most of his success later in the minor leagues, at Newark, Del., on November 9; played in 34 games with the A's, all but one of them in 1933, batting .143; enjoyed his best minor league season with Los Angeles (Pacific Coast) in 1939, when he batted .280 and led PCL shortstops in fielding.

Ray J. Coles, 60, a retired Detroit Fire Department officer who once played minor league baseball and was a part-time scout for the New York Mets, Detroit Tigers, Chicago White Sox and California Angels, at Detroit on April 29; played in the New York Giants' farm system in the late 1940s.

Allen L. (Dusty) Cooke, 80, a promising outfielder whose career with the New York Yankees was sharply curtailed by an untimely shoulder injury in 1931, at Fuquay Varina, N.C., on November 21; joined the Yankees as a rookie in 1930 and hit .255 in 92 games after batting .358 at St. Paul in 1929; was given a starting outfield job in 1931, but dislocated his shoulder and tore ligaments when he tried to make a catch in April; sat out the rest of the '31 season after surgeons transplanted tendons from his leg to his shoulder and appeared in only three games in '32; never fully regained the strength in his throwing arm and was traded to Boston in 1933; enjoyed his best season in 1935 when he hit .306 in 100 games with the Red Sox; suffered a serious knee injury in 1936 and was shipped to Minneapolis in 1937; was later sold to Cincinnati and spent part of the 1938 season with the Reds before finishing his career in the minors in the early 1940s; batted .280 in 1,745 games in eight major league seasons; enlisted in the Navy in 1942 and became a pharmacist's mate, treating athletic and service-related injuries in a training command; that led to a job as trainer with the Philadelphia Phillies in 1946; managed the team for 10 days in 1948 when Ben Chapman was fired; remained with the Phillies until 1952, when he moved to Raleigh, N.C. to become a partner in an art supply business.

Warren P. (Pete) Cote, 85, who appeared in one game for the New York Giants in 1926 as a pinch-hitter and then was farmed out to Toledo, where he helped the Mud Hens win the Little World Series that season, at Middleton, Mass., on October 17; was an infielder who starred for the intercollegiate champion baseball team at Holy Cross College in 1926; also made minor league stops at Toronto and Buffalo of the International League.

Bob Crues, 67, who hit 69 home runs in 1948 while playing for the Amarillo Gold Sox in the Texas-New Mexico League, at Amarillo on December 26, 1986; began his professional career as a promising pitcher, but became an outfielder because of a shoulder injury; enjoyed his best season in '48 when he hit his 69 homers and drove in 254 runs in 140 games while batting .404 and collecting 479 total bases; shared the minor league home run record with Joe Hauser until Joe Bauman, a former teammate, hit 72 homers for Roswell, N.M., in 1954; played for various teams on the West Texas-New Mexico circuit until his retirement in 1953.

Lou Darvas, 73, one of America's top sports cartoonists for a quarter of a century whose work appeared regularly on the pages of The Sporting News in the 1950s and '60s, at Cleveland on February 10; began his career with the Toledo News-Bee in 1936 when he took over the cartoonist's board from the late Bud Fisher, creator of Mutt & Jeff; spent most of his career with the now-defunct Cleveland Press; was a quick worker once an idea was formed, often turning out quality work in 20 minutes; his cartoons could be funny or biting in their editorial comment, or pictorially attractive in their portraits of famous sports personalities; wrote a book in the early 1960s, detailing the art of cartoon drawing; was twice honored by the National Cartoonists Society as the country's top sports cartoonist, a plateau he shared with contemporary Willard Mullin of the New York World-Telegram and Sun.

C.V. (Carroll) Davis, 57, a former scout with the Houston Astros, a former director of minor league operations and scouting director for the Chicago White Sox, and a former director of player development for the Chicago Cubs, at Tifton, Ga., on March 3; was driving to the Astros' spring training camp in Kissimee, Fla., from his Chicago home when he apparently was stricken by a heart attack.

Paul Derringer, 81, the second-winningest pitcher in Cincinnati Reds history and the main man on a team that rose from the depths in the mid-1930s to win the 1939 National League championship and the 1940 World Series, of cancer at Sarasota, Fla., on November 17; was a righthander with a blazing fastball and over-the-top motion; was signed by the St. Louis Cardinals in 1927 and reached the major leagues four years later, carving an 18-8 rookie record while leading the N.L. in winning percentage; struggled to an 11-14 record and 4.05 earned-run average in 1932 and was traded in May 1933 to Cincinnati in the deal that brought shortstop Leo Durocher to the Cardinals; lost 27 games that season with the last-place Reds despite a respectable 3.30 ERA; won 21 games in 1938, all complete-game efforts, was 25-7 in 1939 as the Reds won the N.L. pennant, and finished 20-12 in 1940 as the Reds claimed a World Series title; won two games, including the seventh-game clincher, in the '40 fall classic; compiled a 223-212 record in a 15-year major league career that ended in 1945 after his third season with the Chicago Cubs; pitched 3,645 innings in 579 games and compiled a 3.46 ERA; won 161 games with the Reds in his nine-plus seasons, placing him second to Eppa Rixey's 179 wins; started for the Reds in the first night game ever played in major league baseball and carved out an impressive 1.13 ERA in four All-Star Game appearances; was a dapper dresser and a big tipper during his baseball-playing days, but fell on hard times when his post-baseball electric sign business failed; later relocated in Florida and fought weight and cancer problems, the latter eventually claiming his life.

Joseph Dickinson, 73, a former minor league pitcher who once made the Philadelphia A's roster, though he never pitched in the major leagues, at Cedarville, N.J., on April 4; the righthander broke in with Dayton in 1935 and pitched professionally until 1949, when he retired after spending the season with Hagerstown; his career was interrupted by Army service in World War II.

Jack Dunn III, 65, who had held a number of front-office positions with the Baltimore Orioles since 1954 and had owned the city's International League franchise before that, at Baltimore on June 11; was the Orioles' vice-president for stadium operations and a club director at the time of his death; previously had served the club as traveling secretary, assistant general manager, public relations director and play-by-play announcer over a 33-year period; was the grandson of Jack Dunn Sr., an infielder with the 1901 Orioles who later purchased the club, which then had International League ties; after Jack Dunn Sr.'s death in 1928, the club was taken over by his widow who in 1943 willed it to his grandson; the Princeton graduate took over operation of the club after World War II and served variously as manager, general manager, owner and president.

Willard C. Eckenroth, 66, a righthander who pitched briefly in the St. Louis Cardinals' and Washington Senators' organizations in the early 1940s before his career was ended by wounds suffered in World War II, at Mohnton, Pa., on May 23.

George S. Ferrell, 83, who spent 50 years in professional baseball as a player, manager and scout, and who was the brother of two men who had distinguished major league careers, at Greensboro, N.C., on October 6; was an outfielder-first baseman for 20 minor league seasons (1926-45) and never reached the major leagues, though he compiled an impressive .321 career average in 2,472 games; spent much of the latter half of his career as a playing manager and enjoyed success in the dual role, especially at Richmond; later managed exclusively and then turned to scouting with the St. Louis Cardinals (1952-57) and the Detroit Tigers (1958-75); was the brother of Hall of Famer Rick Ferrell and pitcher Wes Ferrell, who won 193 major league games and still holds the major league record for most career home runs by a pitcher (36).

Bill Boswell Flint, 65, a first baseman with Pulaski in the old Virginia League during the 1940s before and following World War II, at Roanoke, Va., on September 3.

Marshall B. Fox, 64, a minor league executive in the 1950s and '60s who was general manager at Tampa (Florida State) in 1965 when Johnny Bench played there as a rookie, at Naples, Fla., on July 10; also served as general manager of minor league operations at Lafayette (Mississippi-Ohio Valley) and Norfolk-Portsmouth (South Atlantic) before taking over at Tampa in 1957.

Larry French, 79, a lefthanded screwball artist who won 197 games with three National League clubs between 1929 and 1942, at San Diego on February 9; compiled a 197-171 record and a 3.44 earned-run average in 3,152 innings over 14 seasons with the Pittsburgh Pirates, Chicago Cubs and Brooklyn Dodgers; spent his first six seasons with the Pirates, but enjoyed his biggest success with the Cubs, compiling a 17-10 record for the 1935 N.L. champions and an 18-9 mark in 1936; slipped to 5-14 in 1941, but rebounded in 1942 for the Dodgers with a 15-4 record while leading the league with a .789 winning percentage and posting a 1.83 ERA; was 0-2 in seven World Series games with the 1935 and '38 Cubs and the '41 Dodgers; pitched the 40th shutout of his career, a one-hitter against the Phillies, in his final major league appearance; served in the Navy during World War II and announced his baseball retirement after the War; went back into the Navy during the Korean War and chose the service as his career.

Dr. Sidney Gaynor, 82, team physician for the New York Yankees from 1948 to 1976, at Columbus, Ind., on October 24.

Paul G. Gehrman, 74, a righthander who appeared in one game for the Cincinnati Reds in 1937, at Bend, Ore., on October 23; pitched in the minor leagues from 1938 to '48.

Edgar Hayes, 79, the former sports editor of the Detroit Times and the oldest member of the Detroit chapter of the Baseball Writers' Association of America, at Monroe, Mich., on June 22; worked for the Times until it was sold to the Detroit News in 1960; entered public relations and was named commissioner of horse racing for the

state of Michigan in 1961; later became a member of the Hazel Park Racing Association.

Floyd C. (Babe) Herman, 84, whose reputation as the clown prince of some pretty weak Brooklyn Dodgers teams in the 1920s and early '30s overshadowed his outstanding hitting ability, at Glendale, Calif., on November 27; compiled a .324 average in 13 major league seasons; was known as "the other Babe" because his career paralleled the career of Babe Ruth; played for eight clubs in six years in the minors before joining the Dodgers as a rookie in 1926 and hitting .319; batted .381 in 1929 and .393 in '30, but failed to win a batting title either year; was known as a weak defensive outfielder and many stories were told about fly balls bouncing off his head; was usually at the center of any zaniness involving the Dodgers; was idolized by Brooklyn fans because of his penchant for being involved in the unusual and his ability to hit the ball; Dodger fans howled in 1932 when he was traded to Cincinnati; batted .326 for the Reds but was traded to the Chicago Cubs in '33; went on to play for Pittsburgh, Cincinnati again and the Detroit Tigers between 1935 and '37; hit baseball's first home run during a night game with the Reds in 1935 and homered as a pinch-hitter for Detroit playing Manager Ty Cobb in 1937; spent the next six seasons in the minors with the Hollywood Stars before getting a final curtain call in 1945 with the Dodgers as a pinch-hitter; began a second career as a scout, first with Pittsburgh in 1946, then with the New York Yankees in 1953, the Phillies in 1955, the expansion New York Mets late in 1959, the Yankees again in 1962 and the San Francisco Giants in 1964; kept his hand in baseball as a consultant after his retirement.

Frank W. Hiller, 66, a righthanded pitcher who compiled a 30-32 record with the New York Yankees, Chicago Cubs, Cincinnati Reds and New York Giants between 1946 and '53, at West Chester, Pa., on January 8; was 5-6 as the forgotten man on the Yankee staff from 1946 to '49; compiled a 12-5 record after his 1950 trade to the Cubs, thanks to a forkball he had learned from former teammate Joe Bush; was 6-12 in 1951 for the Cubs, 5-8 in 1952 for the Reds and 2-1 in 1953 for the Giants; retired from the minor leagues in 1955 and went into the life insurance business in Philadelphia.

Oneal M. Hobbs, 92, a newspaper pressman who served as president of the old Western League from 1955 until it disbanded in 1958, at Pueblo, Colo., on October 7; was a former minor league player until he lost part of a hand in a printing press accident; was a longtime baseball booster in Pueblo and was involved in the operation of several Western League teams in the 1920s, '30s and '40s.

Alva Lee (Bobo) Holloman, 62, who on May 6, 1953, accomplished what no other major leaguer in the modern era ever has done when he threw a no-hitter in his first big-league start, at Athens, Ga., on May 1; pitched his no-hitter, a 6-0 decision over the Philadelphia A's, as a member of the St. Louis Browns on a damp and chilly spring night at old Sportsman's Park before 2,473 fans; had developed the reputation during his minor league days as a wild, but effective, flake; walked five and allowed another baserunner on his own error, but got a number of great fielding plays from his teammates; drove in half the Browns' runs himself with a pair of singles; went on to win two more games in nine decisions; after a horrible 1⅓-inning relief stint in a 13-4 loss to Washington on July 19, 1953, Browns Owner Bill Veeck sold Holloman's contract to Toronto (International); went from there to Columbus (American Association), St. Petersburg (Florida International) and

Augusta (South Atlantic) before returning home in a salary dispute; retired at the tender age of 27 to run a printing business in Athens.

Edwin T. (Ed) Honeywell, 72, a sportswriter who covered 2,065 consecutive home and away games involving professional baseball teams in Tacoma, Wash., at Tacoma on January 9; wrote for the Tacoma News Tribune for 46 years and was a correspondent for The Sporting News prior to his retirement in 1976; was voted the top writer in the country in 1961 by the minor league baseball writers' association, a group he served four times as president; was official scorer for Tacoma clubs in the old Western League for 11½ seasons and served in the same capacity for 17 years with Tacoma's Pacific Coast League teams.

Richard (Dick) Howser, 51, a 29-year veteran of professional baseball, both as a player and manager, who enjoyed his finest moments when he guided the 1985 Kansas City Royals to their first World Series title and then courageously battled a malignant brain tumor all the way to his deathbed, at Kansas City on June 17; the Miami, Fla., native was an All-America shortstop at Florida State in 1957 and '58 before turning professional and making his major league debut with the Kansas City A's in 1961; batted .281 that season and was named The Sporting News' A.L. Rookie Player of the Year; never could match that first season and went on to compile a .248 career average in 789 games with the A's, Cleveland Indians and New York Yankees; played in 85 games with the 1968 Yankees and then retired from active duty to become a Yankee coach; remained with the team through the 1978 season, in which he managed one game after Billy Martin's resignation; managed Florida State's baseball team in 1979 before being asked by Owner George Steinbrenner to manage the Yankees; led the 1980 Yanks to 103 victories and the A.L. East Division title, but watched his team get swept in the Championship Series by the Kansas City Royals and was pressured to resign; remained with the Yankees as a scout, but accepted a 1981 offer to manage the Royals; led the Royals to a half division title in the strike-torn 1981 season, and A.L. West titles in 1984 and '85; watched as his 1985 Royals came back from 3-1 deficits in both the A.L. Championship Series against Toronto and the World Series against St. Louis; began fighting his biggest battle, however, in 1986 when doctors discovered the brain tumor, diagnosed two days after Howser had guided the American Leaguers to a 3-2 victory in the All-Star Game; underwent surgery three times, a series of radiation treatments and a radical surgical treatment in which millions of "killer cells" were introduced into the tumor cavity; gallantly battled back to the point where he reported for 1987 spring training, but resigned on the third day of camp; his condition deteriorated quickly from that point; compiled a 507-425 managerial record in all or parts of eight seasons; until 1986, when Howser had to leave the 40-48 Royals after the All-Star Game, he had never managed a team that finished below second place.

Robert (Bobby) Hunter, 74, a businessman who served as president of the community-owned Toronto Maple Leafs during the minor league baseball franchise's final four seasons in Toronto (1964-67), at Toronto on August 25; a stockbroker, Hunter headed a group that bought the International League team from Jack Kent Cooke.

Travis C. Jackson, 83, who compiled a .291 career batting average in the 1920s and '30s as a star infielder with the New York Giants and was inducted into baseball's Hall of Fame in 1982 via the Veterans Committee selection process, at Waldo, Ark., on July 17; spent his first full major league season, 1923, as a backup for Giants shortstop Dave Bancroft and third baseman Heinie Groh; replaced the ailing Bancroft at shortstop the next season and batted .302, making it easy for Giants Manager John McGraw to trade Bancroft to the Boston Braves; went on to bat .300 or better in six of his 15 seasons in a Giants uniform; finished with career totals of 1,768 hits and 929 RBIs in 1,656 games; his best seasons were 1929, when he hit 21 home runs, 1930, when he batted a career-high .339, and 1934, when he drove in 101 runs; batted just .149 in four World Series with the Giants; his offensive numbers would have been more impressive if not for a series of injuries and sicknesses that dogged him throughout his career; was blessed with one of the best throwing arms ever for a major league shortstop; remained with the Giants organization after his 1936 retirement, managing at Jersey City (International) and coaching for the parent club under former teammates Mel Ott and Bill Terry; also managed in the minors for the Giants and Milwaukee Braves at Jackson, Tampa, Owensboro, Bluefield, Hartford, Appleton, Lawton, Midland, Eau Claire and Davenport before retiring and moving to Waldo in 1961; was the last member of the Giants 1928 infield to be inducted into the Hall of Fame.

Edward L. (Eddie) Jefferson, 64, who pitched in the Negro National League in the mid 1940s for the Philadelphia Stars and the Motor City Giants of Detroit, at Clinton, Md., on February 26.

Nicholas I. (Red) Jones, 82, who enjoyed a short but colorful and successful career as an American League umpire in the 1940s, at Miami, Fla., on March 19; began his professional career as a catcher, but turned to umpiring at age 24 when he realized his skills would never get him to the major leagues; struggled through the Depression years and finally landed his first full-time umpiring job in the Florida State League in 1935 at age 30; worked his way up through the minors and finally reached the major leagues in 1943; earned a reputation for fairness and consistency while maintaining his well-developed sense of humor; when his career ended in 1950 because of a stomach ulcer, Jones, an excellent storyteller, traveled the banquet circuit; eventually went to work in public relations for a Detroit brewery and later joined play-by-play announcer Bob Neal as a color man in the television broadcasting booth for Cleveland Indians games; had his own TV show in Detroit in the late 1960s while continuing to work for the brewery; worked with Al Ackerman as host of a pre-game show before the NBC telecasts of the 1968 World Series.

Danny Kaye, 74, a celebrated entertainer, singer, dancer, master of double talk and dialect and movie star who was a member of the limited partnership that helped the expansion Seattle Mariners get off the ground, on March 3; was a very talented star who also was a master chef, a licensed pilot and a conductor of remarkable ability, even though he could not even read music; starred in such motion pictures as "Up in Arms, The Kid From Brooklyn" and "The Secret Life of Walter Mitty," and was the goodwill ambassador for UNICEF, the charity for which he raised millions of dollars; formed a general partnership with Les Smith in 1976 that expanded to a limited partnership of Kaye and five businessmen and purchased the Mariners; when it became obvious four years later that rule by committee was not working out, Kaye and his partners sold out to George Argyros, who owns the team today; always a super fan, Kaye returned to that role and became a frequent visitor to Los Angeles Dodger games.

Robert G. (Bob) Kline, 77, a righthanded pitcher who compiled a 30-28 record with the Boston Red Sox, Philadelphia A's and Washington

Senators between 1930 and '34, at Westerville, O., on March 16; broke into professional baseball in 1929 and attracted attention because of his size (6-foot-4, 210 pounds) and a 23-9 record fashioned with Erie of the Central League; finished 5-5 in 1931, his rookie season with Boston, and followed that up with an 11-13 mark in 1932 and a 7-8 record in '33; was traded to Philadelphia and went 6-2 before finishing the 1934 season with Washington, where he won his only decision; played several more years in the minors, managed briefly in the minors and then scouted for the St. Louis Cardinals (1948-57) and the Kansas City Athletics (1958-59).

Thomas C. Lakos, 64, a rubber-armed pitcher who pitched for 11 years in the minor leagues, at Troy, Mich., on July 13; spent most of his career in the Dodgers' farm system and once was a pitching teammate of current Dodgers Manager Tommy Lasorda.

Horace (Hod) Lisenbee, 89, a righthander who beat the 1927 "Murderers' Row" New York Yankees five times in his rookie season with the Washington Senators, at Clarksville, Tenn., on November 14; compiled an 18-9 mark in that 1927 rookie season, but then never produced another winning record; served up No. 58 in Babe Ruth's record-setting string of 60 home runs in '27; pitched all or parts of eight seasons in the big leagues with Washington, the Boston Red Sox (1929-32), Philadelphia Athletics (1936) and Cincinnati Reds (1945), compiling a 37-58 record in 969 innings over 207 games; spent much of his 30-year baseball career in the minors, primarily with Memphis and Buffalo; after sitting out two seasons, he returned in 1944 at age 45 and pitched a no-hit game for Syracuse, a feat that earned him his final major league fling with the Reds.

Frederick Warrington Lucas, 84, a righthand-ed-hitting outfielder who appeared in 20 games with the 1935 Philadelphia Phillies, on March 11; began his professional career in 1923 and played for 12 years before reaching the major leagues; batted .265 in his short 1935 stay and was released in 1936.

Joseph Mancuso, 79, a scout for the Cleveland Indians between 1950 and 1967, at Lakeland, Fla., on March 20; the retired Ohio educator had worked as a spring training employee of the Detroit Tigers for the past 12 springs.

Ernest G. Maun, a righthander who compiled a 2-5 career mark in two major league seasons, on January 1; began his professional career in 1920 and reached the majors in 1924 with the New York Giants; after compiling a 1-1 mark in 22 games, he spent 1925 in the minors before getting another chance with the Philadelphia Phillies; was 1-4 in 1926 and never appeared in the major leagues again.

William (Fiddler Bill) McGee, a righthander who compiled a 46-41 record with the St. Louis Cardinals and New York Giants between 1935 and '42, at St. Louis on February 11; spent his first full major league season in St. Louis in 1936, where he compiled a 7-12 mark; enjoyed his best major league season in 1939 when he finished 12-5 and followed that up with a 16-10 effort in 1940; was traded to the Giants early in 1941 and slipped to a 2-9 mark; rebounded in 1942 with a 6-3 record and 2.93 ERA; chose to retire before the 1943 season; earned his nickname because he played the violin as a hobby.

Don McMahon, 57, a relief specialist who compiled a 90-68 record in 18 seasons with seven major league teams from 1957 to '74, at Los Angeles on July 22; collapsed while pitching batting practice for the Los Angeles Dodgers prior to a game at Dodger Stadium and died 1½ hours later; compiled a career 2.96 ERA in 874 appearances

(only two as a starter) for the Milwaukee Braves, Houston Colts, Cleveland Indians, Boston Red Sox, Chicago White Sox, Detroit Tigers and San Francisco Giants; his 874 appearances ranked fourth behind Hoyt Wilhelm, Lindy McDaniel and Cy Young in the major league record book; was a 20-game winner as a rookie for Owensboro (Kitty) in 1950, but was converted to the bullpen in 1954 in Atlanta (Southern Association); after reaching the majors in 1957 with the Braves, the sinkerballer led the National League with 15 saves in 1959; was traded to Houston three years later where he made his only two career starts (both losses) in 1963; was traded to Cleveland in 1964 and recorded 16 saves that summer for the Indians; pitched for three more teams before becoming a pitcher/pitching coach from 1970-74 with the Giants; remained on the Giants coaching staff one more season after retirement before performing similar duties for the Minnesota Twins (1976-77), San Francisco (1980-82) and Cleveland (1983-85); was a special assignments scout for the Dodgers at the time of his death.

Don Merry, 48, a longtime sportswriter for the Long Beach (Calif.) Press-Telegram, on October 6; covered the California Angels, Los Angeles Rams and Los Angeles Kings and was a columnist in his 16 years with the Press-Telegram; was a past member of the Los Angeles-Anaheim chapter of the Baseball Writers' Association of America.

Harry (Slugger) Mitauer, 81, a sportswriter who covered the St. Louis Cardinals and Browns baseball teams during a 50-year career with the now-defunct St. Louis Globe-Democrat, at St. Louis on June 10; the St. Louisan joined the Globe as a full-time employee in 1934 after working part-time as a statistician; served as secretary-treasurer of the St. Louis chapter of the Baseball Writers' Association of America for 25 years, including the two years following his 1984 retirement.

Dale Mitchell, 65, who compiled a .312 average in an 11-year major league career but was best remembered for making the final out in Don Larsen's perfect game during the 1956 World Series, at Tulsa on January 5; struck out only 119 times in 3,984 major league at-bats during a career spent mostly with the Cleveland Indians; spent seven years under contract to the Indians before turning professional at age 24; played for Oklahoma City in 1946 and won the Texas League batting championship with a .337 average; batted .423 in a late-season stint with the Indians at the end of the '46 season and was Cleveland's starting left fielder in 1947, batting .316 in his first full major league campaign; helped the Indians win the 1948 pennant with a .336 mark and led the A.L. in both hits (203) and triples (23) as a leadoff man in 1949; remained an outfield regular through 1953, when he was relegated to utility and pinch-hitting roles; made it to the World Series again in 1954 with the Indians and was acquired by the Dodgers in July of 1956, the year they faced the Yankees in the Series; was called on as a ninth-inning pinch-hitter for pitcher Sal Maglie in Game 5 and took a called third strike from Larsen, ending one of the most amazing pitching feats in baseball history; retired after the '56 season and went to work in the oil industry in Oklahoma and Texas.

Nicholas S. Mondero, 85, a righthander who pitched for various teams in the International, New York-Penn, Blue Ridge and Virginia leagues from 1924 to 1934 under the name of Nick Harrison, at Hazelton, Pa., on January 3; enjoyed his greatest success at Hagerstown, then a member of the Blue Ridge League, between 1924 and 1926 when he compiled a 44-23 record.

Julio Gonzalez Moreno, 65, a standout pitcher in Cuban baseball who pitched for the old Washington Senators from 1950 to '53, at Miami on January 2; held the Cuban amateur record for strikeouts in a game (21) before signing with the Havana Sugar Kings in 1947; pitched for the Sugar Kings until he was acquired by the Senators midway through the 1950 campaign; compiled an 18-22 mark in all or parts of four major league seasons; also played in the Mexican League and served as batting practice pitcher for the Detroit Tigers in 1968 and '69; was elected to the Cuban baseball hall of fame in 1983.

Tom Morgan, 56, a member of the original Los Angeles Angels expansion team in 1961 who compiled a 67-47 major league record as a pitcher for the New York Yankees, Kansas City A's, Detroit Tigers, Washington Senators and the Angels from 1951 to '63, at Anaheim on January 13; signed originally by the Yankees in 1949 and joined the Yankees in 1951, compiling a 9-3 record as a 21-year-old rookie and spot starter; enjoyed moderate success with the Yankees through 1956, with time out for military service in '53; was traded to the A's in 1957 and was sent a year later to Detroit; was acquired by Washington in 1960 and was purchased by the expansion Angels a year later; used strictly in relief, Morgan compiled an 8-2 record and 10 saves in '61 and went on to pitch two more seasons; became California's minor league pitching instructor in 1964 and later managed in the Angels' farm system in 1966 and '69; worked in the Yankee organization as a scout in 1971 and 1980 and as a coach in 1979; served twice as the Angels' pitching coach, 1972-74 and 1981-83; scouted for the Atlanta Braves in 1984 and '85 before coaching pitchers in the Braves' minor league system; compiled a career 3.61 earned-run average in 443 games and was 40-25 with 64 saves as a reliever; was 0-1 in three World Series with the Yankees.

Maurice (Mo) Mozzali, 65, chief scout for the St. Louis Cardinals and a player, coach and manager with the organization since 1947, at Lakeland, Fla., on March 2; the lefthanded-hitting outfielder-first baseman signed originally with the New York Giants in 1945 after three years of duty in the Navy's submarine service during World War II; was acquired by the Cardinals in a 1947 minor league trade; became a fixture in the American Association at Columbus and Omaha, where he was a popular and successful player; batted .290 in a decade in the American Association but never reached the majors because of the presence of such players as Stan Musial and Joe Cunningham; became a playing manager at Albany, Ga., in 1958 and joined the Cardinals' coaching staff the following year; managed again briefly before returning to scouting in 1961; was with the parent Cardinals as a coach in 1977 and '78; returned to full-time scouting in 1979 and boasted such top discoveries as Ted Simmons and Larry Jaster.

Francis J. (Bots) Nekola, 80, a retired scout for the Boston Red Sox whose most notable discoveries were Carl Yastrzemski and Rico Petrocelli, at Long Island, N.Y., on March 12; was a lefthanded pitcher who appeared in 11 major league games without a decision for the 1929 New York Yankees and 1933 Detroit Tigers; pitched in the minor leagues until 1938 and joined the Red Sox as a scout in '49; retired in 1976.

Fred Newman, 45, a righthanded pitcher who compiled a 33-39 record in six seasons with the Los Angeles/California Angels, in an auto accident at Framingham, Mass., on June 24; was signed originally by the Boston Red Sox in 1960 and was selected later that year by the Angels in the expansion draft; pitched two more seasons in the minors before joining the Angels at the end of

the 1962 season; had begun the '62 campaign with San Jose of the California League, where he won 15 of his first 16 decisions while carving out a 1.58 earned-run average; was 13-10 in 1964 and finished 14-16 in '65 with a 2.75 ERA; underwent shoulder surgery in 1966 and pitched in only three more major league games; retired in 1967 and became a firefighter in Brookline, Mass.

Lou Niss, 83, the first front-office employee hired by the New York Mets when the club was formed in 1960, at New York on April 30; began his career in 1923 as a sportswriter for the Brooklyn Times Union; when that paper merged 14 years later with the Brooklyn Eagle, he became assistant sports editor; became sports editor in 1941 and remained in that position until the paper went out of business in 1955; was long-time chairman of the Brooklyn chapter of the Baseball Writers' Association of America, was official scorer in the 1949 World Series and All-Star Game and originated the Brooklyn vs. the World sandlot game, which lasted for five years; took a job as publicity director at Yonkers Raceway in 1960 and then became publicity director with the New York team in the Continental League; served as publicity director and traveling secretary with the Mets in the team's formative years and later was just traveling secretary before retiring in 1980.

Wayne H. (Ossie) Osborne, 74, a righthander who pitched briefly with the Pittsburgh Pirates in 1935 and the Boston Braves in 1936, compiling a 1-1 record in seven major league games, at Portland, Ore., on March 13; lost the tip of his index finger on his pitching hand in a childhood accident and he had natural movement on his fastball because of the way he gripped the ball; spent the greater part of his pitching career in the Pacific Coast League, where he compiled a 134-145 mark with Portland, San Francisco and Hollywood.

Antonio (Tony) Pacheco, 59, who spent nearly 40 years in baseball as an infielder and manager in the minor leagues and coach and scout in the majors, primarily with the Cincinnati Reds and Houston Astros, at Miami; the native of Punta Brava, Cuba, was a shortstop and second baseman with Havana, Charleston, West Palm Beach, Cocoa, Monterrey and Savannah, among other clubs, before turning to managing in Havana (International) as a late-season replacement for Nap Reyes in 1958; also managed at Palatka, Cocoa, Newport News, Oklahoma City, San Antonio and Sarasota, in the winter leagues in Cuba, Venezuela and the Dominican Republic, and was the pilot of the Latin All-Stars who won the World Baseball Classic, a Triple-A postseason series, at Honolulu in 1972; was a player-coach, scout and manager in the Reds organization from 1955 to '60, and scouted Florida, the Caribbean and Cuba for the Reds and Astros; was a coach with the Astros from 1976 to '79 before returning to scouting; was elected to the Cuban baseball hall of fame in 1986.

Harold F. Parrott, 78, a former sportswriter and a longtime baseball official, at Nyak, N.Y., on July 30; was graduated from St. John's University at age 19 and joined the sports staff of the Brooklyn Eagle two years later, eventually serving as the paper's sports editor; was named traveling secretary of the Brooklyn Dodgers in 1943 and later became director of publicity and promotions; moved with the team to Los Angeles in 1958 and became director of ticket sales, a massive task in the Memorial Coliseum, the Dodgers' first West Coast home; left the Dodgers in 1969 for a front-office position with the expansion Seattle Pilots, a short-lived American League franchise; later filled front-office roles with the California Angels and San Diego Padres; an ardent tennis player, he was the first executive secretary of the

Northwest Tennis Association; after his retirement from baseball, he wrote an entertaining book about his years as a baseball executive entitled "Lords of Baseball."

Roy (Silent Roy) Partlow, 74, a lefthander who had a long career in the old Negro leagues and was briefly a teammate of Jackie Robinson and Don Newcombe with the Brooklyn Dodgers' Montreal farm team in 1946, at Cherry Hill, N.J., on April 19; pitched primarily for the Homestead Grays in a Negro league career that stretched from 1934 to 1950; the Georgian also played for the Cincinnati White Sox and Tigers, the Memphis Red Sox and the Philadelphia Stars, developing a reputation as a good hitter and effective pitcher; later pitched for Three Rivers in 1946 before returning to Homestead to complete his career.

John Petrakis, 73, president of the Dubuque (Ia.) Packers from 1955 to 1960 while the team was a member of the Class D Mississippi-Ohio Valley League and later the Midwest League, at Dubuque on August 1; was named The Sporting News' Executive of the Year following the 1955 campaign in which the Packers drew 95,000 fans en route to the league title.

Willie (Wee Willie) Powell, 85, a pitcher who played with four Negro league teams, primarily the Chicago American Giants, between 1926 and 1935, at Three Rivers, Mich.; had a 7-0 record in Negro league World Series play and was credited with a no-hitter during the 1927 regular season.

Tony George (Pug) Rensa, 86, a former catcher with the Detroit Tigers, Philadelphia Phillies, New York Yankees and Chicago White Sox at various times between 1930 and 1939, at Wilkes-Barre, Pa., on January 4; batted .261 in 200 major league games, but spent most of his 23-year baseball career in the minors with stops at Newark, Jersey City, Milwaukee and Columbus, among others; managed at Pittsfield and Union City between 1946 and '49.

Ed Rumill, 77, longtime baseball writer for The Christian Science Monitor, official scorer at Boston's major league parks for a quarter of a century and a regular contributor to a number of national sports publications, at Sun Lakes, Ariz., on September 18; joined the Monitor as a copy boy in 1927 and worked his way up through the ranks as a writer, editor and columnist; became the paper's chief baseball writer in 1930 and covered both the Red Sox and Braves, traveling with the clubs for many years; was official scorer at both Braves Field and Fenway Park in Boston and served as chief scorer during the 1961 World Series between the Cincinnati Reds and New York Yankees; served as national president for the Baseball Writers' Association of America in '61; was a former correspondent for The Sporting News and contributed to such publications as Baseball Digest, Baseball Magazine and Liberty; his column "Dugout," was syndicated at one time and appeared in more than 150 newspapers nationwide.

James W. (Jim) Russell, 69, an outfielder who compiled a .267 career average in all or parts of 10 major league seasons with the Pittsburgh Pirates, Boston Braves and Brooklyn Dodgers between 1942 and '51, aboard an airline flight from Tampa to Pittsburgh on November 24; the switch-hitting Russell reached the majors with Pittsburgh in 1942 and enjoyed his best season in '44, batting .312; never hit above .284 again; spent the 1948 and '49 seasons with Boston and 1950 and '51 with Brooklyn before spending his final two years in the minors at Portland; became a scout for the Brooklyn and Los Angeles Dodgers in 1954 and scouted for the Washington Senators in the early '60s; worked as a business machine salesman from 1965 to '85.

William C. (Broadway Bill) Schuster, 73, a colorful shortstop who played with Pittsburgh, the Boston Braves and Chicago Cubs between 1937 and 1945 but was best remembered for his ability and antics with the old Seattle Raniers and Los Angeles Angels of the Pacific Coast League, at El Monte, Calif., on June 28; his career as a player, coach and, briefly in 1951, a manager in the minors extended from 1935 through 1954 with periodic trips to the major leagues; appeared in three games for the Pirates in late 1937, two for the Braves in 1939 and 118 for the Cubs from 1943 to '45; compiled a major league average of .234; appeared in two World Series games for the Cubs against the Detroit Tigers in 1945, scoring the winning run in the 12th inning of the sixth game; was a fan favorite in Seattle and Los Angeles because of his hustle and unpredictable pranks; umpires usually tolerated his antics before throwing him out of the game; was an excellent baserunner and defensive infielder, adept at stealing home and at pulling the hidden-ball trick; retired at age 44 and settled in the Los Angeles area.

Phil Seghi, 68, who was associated with professional baseball for over half a century as a player and manager in the minors and a scout and front-office executive in the major leagues, at Thousand Oaks, Calif., on January 8; was a standout third baseman at Northwestern University and worked in the sports department of the Cedar Rapids (Ia.) Press Gazette after his graduation; decided to try his luck in professional baseball and began a minor league career that included stops at Cedar Rapids, Peoria, Winnipeg, Birmingham, Pensacola, Portsmouth and Wilkes-Barre before military service in the latter stages of World War II ended his career; accepted an offer form the Pittsburgh Pirates to manage their Hornell, N.Y., club, then moved to Keokuk in 1948 in the same capacity; piloted Cleveland minor league teams in Green Bay and Fargo from 1949 to '55 before joining the Cincinnati Reds as a scout in 1956; regarded as an astute judge of talent, he was tabbed by the Reds to become farm director in 1958 when Bill McKechnie Jr. resigned; was soon promoted to assistant general manager and spent 12 years in the Reds front office before leaving in 1968 to become director of minor league teams and scouting for Charley Finley's Oakland A's; remained there until December 1971, when he resigned to join the Indians as director of player personnel; was made vice-president and general manager of the Indians two years later and served in that capacity until 1985, when he was reassigned to lesser duties in a front-office shakeup; was still serving as a consultant at the time of his death.

George A. Selkirk, 79, the successor to Babe Ruth as the New York Yankees' right fielder in 1935 and the general manager of the Washington Senators in the 1960s, at Fort Lauderdale on January 19; spent more than 35 years in baseball as a player, minor league manager, farm system boss, front-office executive and scout; compiled a .290 average in 846 games over nine seasons with the Yankees after spending eight years in the minors; was called up by the Yankees late in 1934 after tearing up the International League at Newark with a .357 average; took over the right-field job in 1935 when the aging Ruth became a free agent and responded with a .312 average, 11 homers and 94 RBIs; was a big part of the Yankee teams that captured six American League pennants and five World Series titles between 1936 and '42; drove in more than 100 runs in 1936 and '39 and batted over .300 five times; wore Ruth's No. 3 until the number was retired by the Yankees; served in the Navy during World War II then ended his playing career at Newark in 1946; managed at Newark, Binghamton, Kansas City, Toledo and Wichita before becoming supervisor of player personnel for the Kansas City Athletics in 1957; moved to Baltimore as field coordinator for the Orioles in 1961; became general manager of the Senators in 1962 and later added the title of vice-president; remained with Washington through the 1969 season and then rejoined the Yankee organization as a scout in 1970.

Luke Sewell, 86, who managed the St. Louis Browns to their only American League championship in 1944, two years after ending his 20-year playing career, at Akron, O., on May 14; was one of three brothers who reached the major leagues; after attending the University of Alabama, Sewell, a catcher, reached the big leagues in 1921 with Cleveland, though he would not become a regular for six more years; spent 12 seasons with the Indians before going to the Washington Senators in 1933; went to the Chicago White Sox two years after ending his most productive offensive seasons; returned to Cleveland in 1939 as a player-coach and caught only 15 games; became the Indians' pitching coach in 1940 and was named player-manager of the Browns in June 1942; ended his playing days in 1942 when he went behind the plate in the late innings of six games; was responsible for most of the signings and trades that built the Browns into a contender and guided the 1944 Browns to the World Series against the Cardinals; the Browns captured the first game, but the Cardinals won the all-St. Louis Series in six games; was fired in 1946 after the Browns fell back to their second-division ways; was out of baseball until 1949, when he became manager of the Cincinnati Reds; remained in Cincinnati until he was fired in 1952; managed in the International League at Toronto in 1954 and '55 and at Seattle for part of the 1956 season; retired from baseball and returned to Akron; compiled a career .259 batting average in 1,630 games while hitting 20 home runs and driving in 696 runs.

John Thomas (Jack) Sheehan, 94, who spent more than half a century in Organized Baseball as a minor league player and manager and a major league scout and farm director, at West Palm Beach on May 29; was a switch-hitting infielder who enjoyed one brief fling in the major leagues with the Brooklyn Dodgers and played in the 1920 World Series, for which he was not eligible; while playing shortstop and managing at Winnipeg late in the 1920 season, his contract was purchased by the Dodgers, but he reported too late to be eligible for the World Series; became eligible, however, when Cleveland allowed Brooklyn to replace an injured player with Sheehan, after the Dodgers had given the Indians permission to replace Ray Chapman, the shortstop who had died after being hit by a Carl Mays pitch; played in the final three games of the Series, batting .182; played in five games for the Dodgers in 1921 before being sent to the minors for good; broke in with Champaign-Urbana in 1911 and played with 15 different clubs in 11 leagues before retiring in 1935; also managed clubs in Elmira, Columbus, Wheeling and Peoria before dropping out of baseball and returning to his native Chicago to run the city park district's baseball program; ran a summer baseball school opened by Cubs Owner P.K. Wrigley in 1939 and then served as director of the Cubs' farm system for 10 years; became the president of the Cubs' International League club in Springfield, Mass., in 1951 and became a scout for Cleveland in 1954; returned to Chicago as assistant farm director for the White Sox in 1956 and later scouted for the Washington Senators and Texas Rangers; retired for good in 1975.

John T. Skurski, 67, a scout for the Detroit Tigers, Philadelphia Phillies and St. Louis Cardinals from 1965 to '84, at Warren, Mich., on October 12.

George C. Smith, 49, an infielder with the Detroit Tigers and Boston Red Sox from 1963 to '66, at St. Petersburg, Fla., on June 15; played 89 games with the Tigers between 1963 and '65 and appeared in 128 games in 1966 with the Red Sox, compiling a career average of .205; spent a number of years between major league stints in the old Negro league and in the minors, retiring from baseball in 1969.

Harold (Bud) Smith, 84, a former sports promoter and a part-time scout for the Kansas City Royals, at Venice, Fla.; the Utica, N.Y., restaurateur promoted baseball barnstorming tours from as far north as Watertown, N.Y., to as far south as Biloxi, Miss.; scouted central New York state for the Royals.

Robert E. (Bob) Smith, 92, a righthander who pitched for 15 seasons in the major leagues, primarily for the Boston Braves when they were a second-division club, at Waycross, Ga., on July 19; pitched for the Braves, Chicago Cubs, Cincinnati Reds and the Braves again between 1923 and 1937, compiling a 106-139 record in 435 games, 229 as a starting pitcher; began his career as a light-hitting utility infielder, but made a successful switch to the mound; compiled his best record, 15-12, for the 1931 Cubs and followed that up with a 4-3 mark for the 1932 N.L. champions; was only with Cincinnati briefly in 1933 before being sold back to the Braves, for whom he pitched until his release in 1937; managed at Jacksonville in 1938 and then coached under Kiki Cuyler at two Southern League stops, Chattanooga (1939-42) and Atlanta (1943-48), before retiring from baseball.

Dick Stello, 53, a National League umpire since 1969, when he was crushed between two parked cars as he and an acquaintance stood beside a two-lane highway near Lakeland, Fla., on November 18; was victimized when a third car swerved off the highway and rear-ended one of the cars, pushing it into Stello; worked his first professional season in the Georgia-Florida League in 1963 and rose up through the ranks steadily; two years in the Texas League were followed by three in the International League and a fall 1968 trial in the N.L.; the N.L. purchased his contract and retained his service for the 1969 season; worked five N.L. Championship Series, two World Series and one All-Star Game in his 19 years of major league umpiring.

George Earl Toolson, 65, a minor league right-hander in the 1940s who was one of the early unsuccessful challengers to baseball's reserve clause, at Garden Grove, Calif., on November 22; pitched four seasons at Louisville around a stint in military service in World War II; was traded to the Yankee organization, which first assigned him to Newark, then to Binghamton; refused to report to Binghamton and was placed on the ineligible list; relocated in California and filed suit against the Yankees, both major leagues, the Pacific Coast League and two of its clubs, claiming that he had been effectively banned from baseball in violation of federal antitrust laws and asking for $375,000 in damages; the case was thrown out by a Los Angeles District Court judge in 1951, but the case reached the Supreme Court on appeal before a 1953 ruling was issued in baseball's favor.

Jack Wallaesa, 67, who appeared in 219 games for the Philadelphia Athletics and Chicago White Sox at shortstop and in the outfield between 1940 and 1948, at Easton, Pa., on December 27, 1986; compiled a .205 average in his brief major league tours and played in the minors until an injury ended his career in 1955; led the International League with 45 home runs while playing for Buffalo in 1951.

Lester E. (Les) Webber, 69, who overcame injuries and illnesses to put together a short but successful career as a relief pitcher for the Brooklyn Dodgers from 1942 to '46, at Santa Maria, Calif., on November 13; the righthander's early career was interrupted by chronic abdominal problems, an emergency appendectomy, torn arm ligaments and a rib injury; made it to the major leagues with the Dodgers in 1942 and went on to compile a 19-15 record over the next four seasons and even led the N.L. with 10 saves in 1943; was waived by Brooklyn in 1946 and was claimed by Cleveland, with whom he finished his major league career in 1948; finished his career with a 23-19 record in 154 games, almost all as a reliever.

Phil Weintraub, 79, a lefthanded-hitting outfielder-first baseman who once drove in 11 runs for the New York Giants in one 1944 game, at Palm Springs, Calif., on June 21; was billed by Giants Manager John McGraw as the big Jewish attraction he had been searching for, but never lived up to expectations, appearing in only 444 big-league games; compiled glittering minor league numbers, but was up and down in the majors and didn't really enjoy a productive season until the war year of 1944, when he hit .316 for the Giants; also played briefly with the Philadelphia Phillies and Cincinnati Reds in a career that ended after the 1945 season; drove in 11 runs, one short of the major league record, on April 30, 1944, with a home run, two doubles and a triple in the Giants' 26-8 mauling of the Brooklyn Dodgers; homered in his first major league at-bat and delivered the last hit in Philadelphia's Baker Bowl; played the accordion and was known as one of the flashiest dresser in baseball.

Arthur C. (Pinky) Whitney, 82, a star third baseman with the Philadelphia Phillies during a 12-year major league career from 1928 to '39, at Center, Tex., on September 1; the son of an immigrant Dutch father and a Swiss mother, Whitney was originally signed by Cleveland but was picked off the Indians' roster by the Phillies in the minor league draft of 1927; became the Phillies' third baseman and found his line-drive hitting style well-suited to the compact dimensions of the Baker Bowl; drove in 103 runs while compiling a .301 average in his 1928 rookie season; established himself as one of the top-fielding third basemen in the majors and hit a career-high .342 in 1930; was traded by the beleaguered Phillies to the Boston Braves in 1933 for three lesser players and his game suffered away from the Baker Bowl; after struggling through some mediocre seasons in Boston, he was traded back to Philadelphia and celebrated by earning a spot on the N.L. All-Star team; compiled a .341 average in 1937, his last big season; was shipped back to the minors in 1939 after battling kidney stones and played at Toledo and Tulsa before getting his release in 1941; returned to his native San Antonio where he operated a bowling alley, managed one of south Texas' top amateur baseball teams and did promotional work for the San Antonio Spurs of the National Basketball Association; later enjoyed a reputation, along with his second wife Harriet, as a lapidary and expert fashioner of jewelry.

Dan Wilson, 73, an infielder-outfielder who played with seven Negro league teams between 1937 and '47, in a fire at St. Louis; played the outfield, third base, second base and shortstop for such teams as the Pittsburgh Crawfords, St. Louis Stars, New York Black Yankees, New Orleans-St. Louis Stars, Harrisburg-St. Louis Stars, Homestead Grays and Philadelphia Stars.

Hugh Edward (Hughie) Wise, 81, who played, managed and scouted in professional baseball for more than 40 years and also designed and built a number of spring training baseball facilities, at Plantation, Fla., on July 21; was signed by the Brooklyn Dodgers off the Purdue campus in 1928 as a catcher and reached the majors for a two-game cup of coffee in 1930 with Detroit; played and managed in the minors until 1949; scouted for the Boston and Milwaukee Braves (1949-58), the New York Yankees (1959-61) and the Chicago White Sox (1962-72) and also was active as a scout in the Caribbean and in Venezuela; put his engineering degree from Purdue to use in the construction of four-diamond complexes for the Braves' organization at Myrtle Beach, S.C., and Waycross, Ga., and for the White Sox at Sarasota, Fla.; was the father of Dr. Hugh Wise and Dr. Kendall Wise, both of whom played professional baseball; Kendall, known as Casey, played in the major leagues from 1957 to 1960 with the Chicago Cubs, Milwaukee Braves and Detroit Tigers as a second baseman.

Dick Young, 69, a colorful, caustic and often-controversial sportswriter and columnist for the New York Daily News for 45 years before making a widely criticized move to the New York Post five years ago, at New York on August 31; began his newspaper career during the depression as a messenger boy for the Daily News and quickly rose through the ranks to become one of the most widely read sportswriters in the country; wrote a syndicated column, Young Ideas, and was a regular columnist for The Sporting News from the late 1950s until 1985; covered the Brooklyn Dodgers for the Daily News and his acid typewriter got him barred from the clubhouses of such managers as Burt Shotton and Leo Durocher; crusaded to keep the Dodgers in Brooklyn when Walter O'Malley announced in 1957 his intention to move the club to the West Coast and later campaigned for the formation of a third league and the placing of another team in New York; got his wish when the expansion Mets played their first season there in 1962; was considered at one time to be the guru of the new-breed sportswriters, always coming up with the controversial quote and making outrageous statements of his own; was one of the first morning-paper writers to descend to the clubhouse for pregame quotes and information rather than just file the traditional press-box game story; other areas of expertise included college basketball and professional boxing; was a powerful ally for those he backed, a hard-hitting opponent for the targets of his gibes; carried on feuds with such personalities as Howard Cosell, Muhammad Ali, Marvin Miller, Jackie Robinson and other sportswriters he considered "establishment"; was particularly vocal about the new breed of baseball stars in search of astronomical salaries; was particularly nasty in his 1977 chastisement of the Mets' Tom Seaver, who had announced that he wanted to renegotiate his contract or maybe play elsewhere; that story came back to haunt him in 1982, when Young announced that he was leaving the Daily News with two years remaining on his contract to work for the New York Post for $150,000 per year; drew the criticism of sportswriters throughout the country for what they believed was a hypocritical action; served two terms as chairman of the New York Chapter of the Baseball Writers' Association of America and remained active and vocal in its activities to his death; had been living in semiretirement in Boulder City, Nev., after undergoing intestinal surgery and became ill while visiting New York; was elected to the writers' wing of the Baseball Hall of Fame in 1978.

Edmund G. Zander, 49, a catcher-infielder who played seven seasons (1955 to '61) in the minors, at Yakima, Wash., on January 25; led the Northwest League in RBIs with 122 while playing for Yakima in 1960.

LEAGUE AND CLUB INFORMATION

Including

Major League Directory

American League Directory

American League Team Directories

National League Directory

National League Team Directories

Major League Players Association Directory

Minor League Presidents

Major League Farm Systems

MAJOR LEAGUE BASEBALL

OFFICE OF THE COMMISSIONER
Commissioner—Peter Ueberroth
Exec. V.P. & Chief Operating Officer—Ed Durso
BASEBALL OPERATIONS
Director—Bill Murray
Assistant Director—George Pfister
Manager, Player Records—Janice Micale
CORPORATE MARKETING
Director, Joel Rubenstein
DATA PROCESSING
Director—Dave Alworth
FINANCE, PERSONNEL & OFFICE MANAGEMENT
Chief Financial Officer—Don Marr
Controller—Frank Simio
Office Manager—Mary Ann Burns
LEGAL
Director, Legal Affairs—Tom Ostertag
Assistant Counsel—Stephanie Vardavas
Records Manager—Charlyne Sanders
LICENSING
Director, Licensing & V.P., MLBP—Rick White
Account Managers—Karyn Donohue, Carl Francis, Bonnie Powers
NEWS
Director—Richard Levin
Assistant Director—Jim Small
Manager, Club Relations—Susan Aglietti
Manager, Media Relations—Carole Coleman
Manager, Community Relations—Wally Weibel
SECURITY/FACILITY MANAGEMENT
Director—Kevin Hallinan
Regional Director, Central—Al Williams
BROADCASTING, MARKETING SUPPORT,
PUBLISHING, SPECIAL EVENTS
Senior Vice-President—Bryan Burns
Director, Broadcast Administration—Leslie Lawrence
Marketing Manager—Steve McKelvey
Publishing Manager—Cindy McManus
Special Events Manager—David Dziedzic

Headquarters—350 Park Avenue, New York, N.Y. 10022
Telephone—371-7800 (area code 212)
Teletype—910-380-9482

American League

Organized 1900

ROBERT W. BROWN, M.D.
President

JOHN E. FETZER, GENE AUTRY, CALVIN R. GRIFFITH
Vice-Presidents

RICHARD BUTLER, ROBERT O. FISHEL
Special Assistants to the President

DICK WAGNER
Special Assistant to Baseball

MARTIN J. SPRINGSTEAD
Chief Supervisor of Umpires

PHYLLIS MERHIGE
Director of Public Relations

TIM McCLEARY
Manager, Waivers & Player Records

TESS BASTA, CAROLYN COEN
Administrators

Headquarters—350 Park Avenue, New York, N. Y. 10022

Telephone—371-7600 (area code 212)

ASSISTANT SUPERVISORS OF UMPIRES—Henry Soar, Larry Napp, Jerry Neudecker.

UMPIRES—Lawrence Barnett, Nicholas Bremigan, Joseph Brinkman, Alan Clark, Drew Coble, Terrance Cooney, Derryl Cousins, Donald Denkinger, James Evans, Dale Ford, Richard Garcia, Ted Hendry, John Hirschbeck, Mark Johnson, Kenneth Kaiser, Greg Kosc, Tim McClelland, Larry McCoy, James McKean, Durwood Merrill, Dan Morrison, Stephen Palermo, David Phillips, Rick Reed, Michael Reilly, John (Rocky) Roe, Dale Scott, John Shulock, Tim Tschida, Vic Voltaggio, Tim Welke, Larry Young.

OFFICIAL STATISTICIANS—Elias Sports Bureau, Inc., 500 5th Ave., Suite 2114, New York, N.Y. 10036. Telephone—(212) 869-1530.

BALTIMORE ORIOLES

Chairman of the Board and President—Edward Bennett Williams

Vice-President of Baseball Operations—Roland A. Hemond
Vice-President/General Counsel—Lawrence Lucchino
Vice-President, Finance—Joseph P. Hamper, Jr.
Vice-President, Administrative Personnel—Calvin Hill
Vice-President, Business Affairs—Robert R. Aylward
Secretary/Treasurer—Robert J. Flanagan
Club Counsel—Lon Babby
Directors—Edward Bennett Williams, Joseph P. DiMaggio, George Will,
Jay Emmett, Robert J. Flanagan, Charles H. Hoffberger, Jerold C. Hoffberger,
Zanvyl Krieger, Lawrence Lucchino, Calvin Hill, Peter P. Weidenbruch, Jr.
Special Assistant to the President—Frank Robinson
Director of Player Personnel—R. Douglas Melvin
Scouting Director—Fred B. Uhlman
Executive Director, Sales and Tickets—Louis I. Michaelson
Public Relations Director—Robert W. Brown
Traveling Secretary—Philip E. Itzoe
Special Assignment and Projects/Baseball Operations—Kenneth E. Nigro
Corporate Marketing Director—Martin B. Conway
Director, Ticket Office—Roy A. Sommerhof
Media Information Director—Richard L. Vaughn
Director, Game Communications—Charles A. Steinberg, DDS
Director, Community Relations—Julia A. Wagner
Director, Washington Marketing—Julie Dryer
Director, Computer Services—James L. Kline
Group Sales Manager—Alan G. Locey
Promotions Manager—Jeffrey S. Urban
Stadium Operations, Manager—John J. McCall
Asst. Director, Sales and Tickets—J. Vince Dunbar
Manager, Orioles Designated Hitters—James B. Muno
Asst. Scouting Director/Player Development—Roy H. Krasik
Community Coordinator for Baseball Operations—Joseph V. Durham
Assistant Ticket Manager—Joseph B. Codd
Assistant Director, Ticket Office—Audrey Brown
Marketing Coordinator—Laurie D. Fleishman
Manager, Orioles Baseball Store—Bryan T. Hoffert
Washington Sales Representative—David B. Cope
Manager—Cal Ripken, Sr.
Club Physicians—Drs. Sheldon Goldgeier and Charles E. Silberstein
Executive Offices—Memorial Stadium, Baltimore, Md. 21218
Telephone—243-9800 (area code 301)

SCOUTS—Lefty Bagg, Carlos Bernhardt, Ray Crone, Ed Crosby, Will George, Jim Gilbert, Jesus Halabi, Len Johnston, Leo Labossiere, George Lauzerique, Bill Lawlor, Mike Ledna, Bill Miller, Carl Moesche, Kevin Murphy, Lamar North, Jim Pamlanye, Joe Robinson, Ed Sprague, John Stokoe, Bill Werle, Bennett Williams, Jerry Zimmerman.

PARK LOCATION—Memorial Stadium, 33rd Street, Ellerslie Avenue, 36th Street and Ednor Road.

Seating capacity—54,017.

FIELD DIMENSIONS—Home plate to left field at foul line, 309 feet; to center field, 405 feet; to right field at foul line, 309 feet.

BOSTON RED SOX

President—Jean R. Yawkey

Chief Executive Officer/Chief Operating Officer—Haywood C. Sullivan
Senior Vice-President, General Manager—James (Lou) Gorman
Vice-President & Chief Financial Officer—Robert C. Furbush
Executive Vice-President & Counsel—John F. Donovan Jr.
Vice President, Player Development—Edward F. Kenney
Director of Minor League Operations—Edward P. Kenney
Special Assistant to the General Manager—John M. Pesky
Executive Asst. & Dir. of Community Relations—Michael L. Silva
Director of Publications—Debra A. Matson
Controller—Stanley H. Tran
Director of Scouting—Edward M. Kasko
Vice President, Public Relations—Richard L. Bresciani
Vice-President, Transportation—John J. Rogers
Vice-President, Broadcasting & Advertising—James P. Healey
Vice-President, Property Management—Joseph F. McDermott
Director of Marketing—Lawrence C. Cancro
Director of Group Sales—Leslie Leary
Treasurer—John J. Reilly
Vice-President, Ticket Operations—Arthur J. Moscato
Director of Publicity—Josh S. Spofford
Manager—John F. McNamara
Club Physician—Dr. Arthur M. Pappas
Executive Offices—4 Yawkey Way, Boston, Mass. 02215
Telephone—267-9440 (area code 617)

SCOUTS—Rafael Batista, Milton Bolling, Ray Boone, Wayne Britton, Erwin Bryant, George Digby, Howard (Danny) Doyle, Bill Enos, Larry Flynn, Charles Koney, Jack Lee, Wilfrid (Lefty) Lefebvre, Don Lenhardt, Howard McCullough, Felix Maldonado, Frank Malzone, Sam Mele, Willie Paffen, Phillip Rossi, Edward Scott, Matt Sczesny, Joe Stephenson, Larry Thomas, Fay Thompson, Charlie Wagner.

PARK LOCATION—Fenway Park, Yawkey Way, Lansdowne Street and Ipswich Street.

Seating capacity—33,583.

FIELD DIMENSIONS—Home plate to left field at foul line, 315 feet; to center field, 420 feet; to right field at foul line, 302 feet; average right-field distance, 382 feet.

CALIFORNIA ANGELS

President and Chairman of the Board—Gene Autry

Sr. Vice-President and General Manager—Mike Port
Vice-President—Jackie Autry
Vice-President/Secretary-Treasurer—Michael Schreter
Sr. Vice-President, Marketing—John Hays
Sr. Vice-President, Finance and Administration—James Wilson
Vice-President, Public Relations—Tom Seeberg
Assistant to General Manager—Preston Gomez
Director Publicity—Tim Mead
Director Publications—John Sevano
Controller—Jim Kaczmarek
Director Scouting & Player Development—Bob Fontaine
Director Minor League Operations—Bill Bavasi
Adm. Asst., Player Personnel & Development—Frank Marcos
Director Ticket Department—Carl Gordon
Asst. Ticket Manager—Gen Linhoff
Manager, Data Operations—Bob Terzes
Manager, Data Processing—Ron Moore
Director Group Sales & Promotions—Lynn Kirchmann Biggs
Asst. Dir., Group Sales & Promotions—Bob Wagner
Assistant Director Marketing—Jean (Corky) Lippert
Traveling Secretary—Frank Sims
Manager Stadium Operations—Kevin Uhlich
Medical Director—Dr. Robert Kerlan
General Medicine—Dr. Jules Rasinski
Orthopedist—Dr. Lewis Yocum
Trainers—Rick Smith, Ned Bergert
Physical Therapist—Roger Williams
Manager—Gene Mauch
Executive Offices—Anaheim Stadium, 2000 State College Blvd.,
Anaheim, Calif. 92806
Telephone—937-6700 (area code 714) or 625-1123 (area code 213)

SCOUTS—Edmundo Borrome, George Bradley, Joe Carpenter, Pompeyo Dava-
lillo, Cliff Ditto, Jesse Flores, Oru Francuk, Bob Gardner, Lin Garrett, Red Gaskill,
Al Geddes, Steve Gruwell, Bruce Hines, Rick Ingalls, Nick Kamzic, Tim Kelly, Joe
Maddon, Jim McLaughlin, Bobby Myrick, Jon Neiderer, Eusebio Perez, Vic Power,
Phil Rizzo, Paul Robinson, Cookie Rojas, Rich Schlenker, Woody Smith, Mark Wie-
demaier.

PARK LOCATION—Anaheim Stadium, 2000 State College Blvd.

Seating capacity—64,573.

FIELD DIMENSIONS—Home plate to left field at foul line, 333 feet; to center
field, 404 feet; to right field at foul line, 333 feet.

CHICAGO WHITE SOX

Chairman, Board of Directors—Jerry M. Reinsdorf

President—Eddie M. Einhorn
Executive Vice-President—Howard C. Pizer
Vice-President/General Manager—Larry Himes
Senior Vice-President/Marketing & Sales—Mike McClure
Vice-President, Baseball Administration—Jack Gould
Vice-President, Finance—Timothy L. Buzard
Controller—Terry Savarise
General Counsel—Allan B. Muchin
Assistant V.P., Public Relations—Paul H. Jensen
Assistant V.P., Advertising & Promotions—Chuck Johnsen
Director of Scouting & Player Development—Al Goldis
Director of Ticket Administration—Millie Johnson
Director of Broadcast Sales—Edwin M. Doody
Director of Purchasing—Don Esposito
Special Assistant to the General Manager—Bart Johnson
Asst. Director of Scouting & Player Development—Steve Noworyta
Player Personnel Administrator—Dan Evans
Minor League Administrator—Mitch Lukevics
Administrative Asst., Baseball Operations—Jeff Chaney
Traveling Secretary—Glen Rosenbaum
Manager of Media Relations—Tim Clodjeaux
Manager of Community Relations—Paul Reis
Manager of Broadcast Operations—Laura Jane Hyde
Manager of Promotions & Special Events—Karen McDevitt
Accounting Manager—Sandra Grobarcik
Ticket Manager—Bob Devoy
Coordinator of Season Ticket Sales—Jeff Cieply
Coordinator of Group Ticket Sales—John Furrer
Trainer—Herman Schneider
Director of Physical Fitness—Al Vermeil
Team Physicians—Drs. James B. Boscardin,
Hugo Cuadros, David Orth
Manager—Jim Fregosi
Director of Park Operations—David M. Schaffer
Groundskeepers—Gene and Roger Bossard
Organist—Nancy Faust
Executive Offices—Comiskey Park, 324 W. 35th Street, Chicago, Ill. 60616
Telephone—924-1000 (area code 312)

SCOUTS—(Advance)—Bart Johnson, Larry Monroe. (Supervisors)—Larry Maxie, Danny Monzon, Lou Snipp. Juan Ramon Bernhardt, Mark Bernstein, Earl Brown Jr., Tom Calvano, Alex Cosmidis, Preston Douglas, Ed Ford, Rod Fridley, Mike Harris, Edward Ben Hays, Miguel Ibarra, Joe Ingalls, Reginald D. Lewis, Dario Lodigiani, Carlos Loreto, Jose Ortega, Ed Pebley, Garry Pellant, Victor Puig, Michael Rizzo, Bob Ray Sloan, Mark Snipp, Ron Vaughn, Craig Wallenbrock, Len Zabroski.

PARK LOCATION—Comiskey Park, 324 W. 35th Street, Chicago, Ill. 60616

Seating capacity—44,087.

FIELD DIMENSIONS—Home plate to left field at foul line, 347 feet; to center field, 409 feet; to right field at foul line, 347 feet.

CLEVELAND INDIANS

Board of Directors—Richard E. Jacobs, Chairman; David H. Jacobs, Vice-Chairman; Martin J. Cleary, Gary L. Bryenton

Chairman of the Board and Chief Executive Officer—Richard E. Jacobs
Vice-Chairman of the Board—David H. Jacobs
President and Chief Operating Officer—Hank Peters
Senior V.P., Baseball Administration & Player Relations—Dan O'Brien
Vice-President, Administration—Terry Barthelmas
Vice-President, Finance—Gregg Olson
Vice-President—Martin J. Cleary
Special Asst. to the President—Tom Giordano
Director, Publications/Advertising Sales—Valerie Arcuri
Director, Operations—Carl Hoerig
Director, Merchandising/Licensing—Mary Lisa Linsley
Director, Ticket Services—Connie Minadeo
Director, Public Relations—Rick Minch
Director, Player Development—Dan O'Dowd
Director, Scouting—Jeff Scott
Director, Team Travel—Mike Seghi
Director, Ticket Sales—Gary Sherwood
Director, Promotions/Sales—Jon Starrett
Controller—Diane Stuczynski
Administrator, Player Personnel—Phil Thomas
Manager, Indians Gift Shop—Terry Butler
Manager, Promotions/Sales—Nadine Glinski
Manager, Box Office—Tom Sullivan
Manager, Publications/Advertising Sales—Tim Needles
Manager, Season/Group Sales—Tony Seghy
Manager, Operations—Kerry Wimsatt
Account Executives, Ticket Sales—Chris Previte, Scott Sterneckert, Devore Whitt
Speakers Bureau—Bob Feller
Coordinator, Season/Group Sales—Lori Krzeminski
Coordinator, Computer Ticketing/Data Processing—Maria Miceli
Assistant to Director, Public Relations—Susie Gharrity
Manager—Doc Edwards
Medical Director—William T. Wilder, M.D.
Orthopedic Specialist—John Bergfeld, M.D.
Trainer—Jim Warfield
Assistant Trainer—Paul Spicuzza
Team Physicians—Drs. Tom Anderson, James R. Conforto, Godofredo Domingo, Mark Frankel, K.V. Gopal, Peter Greenwalt, Gus A. Kious
Executive Offices—Cleveland Stadium, Cleveland, Ohio 44114
Telephone—861-1200 (area code 216)

SCOUTS—Hector Acevedo, Rick Adair, John Burden, Dan Carnevale, Tom Chandler, Roy Clark, Tom Couston, Joe DeLuca, Connie Dettling, Trey Hillman, Luis Issac, Dave Koblentz, Joe Lewis, Bobby Malkmus, Jim Miller, Art Parrack, Mike Piatnik, Dave Roberts, Al Schoenberger, Dale Sutherland, Gary Sutherland, Birdie Tebbetts.

PARK LOCATION—Cleveland Stadium, Boudreau Blvd.

Seating capacity—74,208.

FIELD DIMENSIONS—Home plate to left field at foul line, 320 feet; to center field, 400 feet; to right field at foul line, 320 feet.

DETROIT TIGERS

Board of Directors
John E. Fetzer, Thomas S. Monaghan, James A. Campbell, Douglas J. Dawson

Chairman of the Board—John E. Fetzer
Vice-Chairman and Owner—Thomas S. Monaghan
President & Chief Executive Officer—James A. Campbell
Vice-President & General Manager—William R. Lajoie
Vice-President, Operations—William E. Haase
V.P., Player Procurement & Development—Joseph A. McDonald
V.P., Secretary/Treasurer—Alexander C. Callam
V.P., Marketing, Communications & P.R.—Jeffrey Odenwald
Director of Press & Public Relations—Dan Ewald
Controller—Michael Wilson
Director of Radio & TV—Neal Fenkell
Director of Stadium Operations—Ralph E. Snyder
Director of Ticket Sales—William H. Willis
Administrator of Player Development—Dave Miller
Executive Secretary/Baseball—Alice Sloane
Executive Secretary/Operations—Hazel McLane
Data Processing Manager—Richard Roy
Traveling Secretary—Bill Brown
Executive Consultant—Rick Ferrell
Special Assignment Scouts—Charles Day, Joseph Klein, Walter A. Evers,
Jerry Walker
Scouting Director—Jax Robertson
Western Scouting Supervisor—Dick Wiencek
Assistant Director of Public Relations—Greg Shea
Director of Marketing—Lew Matlin
Assistant Director of Public Relations/Community Relations—Vince Desmond
Group Sales Coordinator—Irwin Cohen
Assistant Director of Stadium Operations/Grounds Maintenance—Frank Feneck
Assistant Director of Stadium Operations/Grounds Maintenance—Ed Goward
Manager—Sparky Anderson
Club Physician—Clarence S. Livingood M.D.
Orthopedic Consultant—David Collon M.D.
Executive Offices—Tiger Stadium, Detroit, Mich. 48216
Telephone—962-4000 (area code 313)

SCOUTS—Mateo Alou, Rick Arnold, John Barkley, Ray Bellino, Jim Bierman, Wayne Blackburn, Charlie Gault, Richard Henning, Lee Irwin, Joe Lewis, Scott MacKenzie, Rick Magnante, Ramon Pena, Dee Phillips, Bill Schudlich, Steve Souchock, Richard Wilson, Marti Wolever.

PARK LOCATION—Tiger Stadium, Michigan Avenue, Cochrane Avenue, Kaline Drive and Trumbull Avenue.

Seating capacity—52,806.

FIELD DIMENSIONS—Home plate to left field at foul line, 340 feet; to center field, 440 feet; to right field at foul line, 325 feet.

KANSAS CITY ROYALS

Board of Directors
Joe Burke, William Deramus, III, Avron Fogelman, Charles Hughes,
Ewing Kauffman, Mrs. Ewing Kauffman, Earl Smith

Chairman of the Board (co-owner)—Ewing Kauffman
Vice Chairman of the Board (co-owner)—Avron Fogelman
President—Joe Burke
Executive Vice-President and General Manager—John Schuerholz
Executive Vice-President, Administration—Spencer (Herk) Robinson
Vice-President, Controller—Dale Rohr
Vice-President and Legal Counsel—Phil Koury
Vice-President, Public Relations—Dean Vogelaar
Vice-President, Marketing and Broadcasting—Dennis Cryder
Director of Scouting—Art Stewart
Director of Player Development—John Boles
Assistant to General Manager—Dean Taylor
Director of Event Personnel/Stadium Operations—Jay Hinrichs
Director of Ticket Operations—Glenn Loest
Director of Season Ticket Sales—Joe Grigoli
Director of Group Sales/Lancer Coordinator—Chris Muehlbach
Traveling Secretary—Dave Witty
Data Processing Manager—Loretta Kratzberg
Ticket Office Manager—Stacy Sherrow
Adm. Asst., Scouting & Player Development—Bob Hegman
Assistant Directors of Public Relations—Steve Fink, Ron Juanso
Assistant Directors of Marketing—Kevin Gray, Laura Collins
Accountants—Tom Pfannenstiel, Ken Willeke, Lisa Collins
Executive Secretary/Baseball—Peggy Mathews
Manager—John Wathan
Equipment Manager—Al Zych
Groundskeeper—George Toma
Stadium Engineer—Duane Robinson
Stadium Maintenance Coordinator—Dave Owen
Team Physician—Dr. Paul Meyer
Trainers—Mickey Cobb, Paul McGannon
Executive Offices—Royals Stadium, Harry S Truman Sports Complex
Mailing Address—P. O. Box 419969, Kansas City, Mo. 64141
Telephone—921-2200 (area code 816)

SCOUTS—Carl Blando, Gary Blaylock, Rick Cardenas, Bob Carter, Al Diez, Tom Ferrick, Rosey Gilhousen, Ken Gonzales, Guy Hansen, Dave Herrera, Gary Johnson, Al Kubski, Tony Levato, Chuck McMichael, Jim Moran, Brian Murphy, George Noga, Herb Raybourn, Jerry Stephens, Roy Tanner.

PARK LOCATION—Royals Stadium, Harry S Truman Sports Complex.

Seating capacity—40,625.

FIELD DIMENSIONS—Home plate to left field at foul line, 330 feet; to center field, 410 feet; to right field at foul line, 330 feet.

MILWAUKEE BREWERS

President, Chief Executive Officer—Allan H. (Bud) Selig

Executive Vice-President, General Manager—Harry Dalton
Vice-President, Marketing—Richard Hackett
Vice-President, Broadcast Operations—William Haig
Vice-President, Finance—Richard Hoffmann
Vice-President, Stadium Operations—Gabe Paul, Jr.
Asst. General Manager & Farm Director—Bruce Manno
Senior Advisor, Baseball Operations—Walter Shannon
Special Assistants to the General Manager—Dee Fondy, Sal Bando
Traveling Secretary—Jimmy Bank
Scouting Coordinator—Dick Foster
Major League Scouting—Harvey Kuenn
V.P., International Baseball Oper.—Ray Poitevint
Coord. of Player Development & Pitching—Bob Humphreys
Administrative Asst./Instructor—Ray Burris
Asst. Dir., Spring Training Operations—Freddie Frederico
Director of Publicity—Tom Skibosh
Assistant Director of Stadium Operations and Advertising—Jack Hutchinson
Director of Publications and Assistant Director of Publicity—Mario Ziino
Group Sales Director—Tim Trovato
Season Ticket Sales Director—Tom Osowski
Ticket Office Manager—John Barnes
Director of Ticket Office Computer Operations—Alice Boettcher
Manager—Tom Trebelhorn
Club Physician—Dr. Paul Jacobs
Trainers—John Adam, Al Price
Superintendent of Grounds and Maintenance—Harry Gill
Equipment Manager—Tony Migliaccio
P.A. Announcer—Bob Betts
Executive Offices—Milwaukee Brewers Baseball Club
Milwaukee County Stadium, Milwaukee, Wis. 53214
Telephone—933-4114 (area code 414)

SCOUTS—Supervisors: Julio Blanco-Herrera, Ken Bracey, Felix Delgado, Roland LeBlanc, Lee Sigman, Walter Youse. Regulars: Fred Beene, Tom Bourque, Derek Bryant, Nelson Burbrink, Ken Califano, Lou Cohenour, Warren Dewey, Jim Gabella, Dave Garcia, Gene Kerns, Phil Long, Steve McAllister, Jim McCray, Cal McLish, Ed Mathes, Gus Mureo, Johnny Neun, Frank Pena, Frank Piet, Reuben Rodriguez, Art Schuerman, Earl Silverthorn, Harry Smith, Mike Stafford, Sam Suplizio, Tommy Thompson, Edward Whitsett, George Zabala.

PARK LOCATION—Milwaukee County Stadium, S. 46th St. off Bluemound Rd.

Seating capacity—53,192.

FIELD DIMENSIONS—Home plate to left field at foul line, 315 feet; to center field, 402 feet; to right field at foul line, 315 feet.

MINNESOTA TWINS

Owner—Carl R. Pohlad

President—Jerry Bell
Chairman of Executive Committee—Howard Fox
Consultant—Calvin R. Griffith
Directors—Donald E. Benson, Paul R. Christen, James O. Pohlad, Robert C. Pohlad,
William M. Pohlad, Robert E. Woolley
Exec. Vice-President, Baseball Operations—Andy MacPhail
Vice-President, Player Personnel—Bob Gebhard
Vice-President, Baseball—Ralph Houk
Vice-President, Finance—Jim McHenry
Vice-President, Operations—Dave Moore
Director of Minor Leagues—Jim Rantz
Director of Scouting—Terry Ryan
Director of Media Relations—Tom Mee
Traveling Secretary—Laurel Prieb
Manager—Tom Kelly
Club Physicians—Dr. Leonard J. Michienzi, Dr. Harvey O'Phelan
Executive Offices—Hubert H. Humphrey Metrodome, 501 Chicago Ave. South,
Minneapolis, Minn. 55415
Telephone—375-1366 (area code 612)

SCOUTS—Floyd Baker, Vern Borning, Enrique Brito, Ellsworth Brown, Ramon
Conde, Larry Corrigan, Edward Dunn, Dan Durst, Marty Esposito, Jesse Flores, Jr.,
Jesse Flores, Sr., Angelo Giuliani, Bill Lohr, Mike Radcliff, Cobby Saatzer, Jeff Schu-
gel, Johnny Sierra, Dave Stabelfeldt, Herb Stein, Fred Waters.

PARK LOCATION—Hubert H. Humphrey Metrodome, 501 Chicago Ave. South.

Seating capacity—55,244.

FIELD DIMENSIONS—Home plate to left field at foul line, 343 feet; to center
field, 408 feet; to right field at foul line, 327 feet.

NEW YORK YANKEES

Principal Owner—George M. Steinbrenner

Partners—Harold M. Bowman, Daniel M. Crown, James S. Crown, Lester Crown, Michael Friedman, Marvin Goldklang, Barry Halper, Harvey Leighton, Daniel McCarthy, Harry Nederlander, James Nederlander, Robert Nederlander, William Rose Sr., Edward Rosenthal, Jack Satter, Joan Z. Steinbrenner, Charlotte Witkind, Richard Witkind

Exec. Vice-President, General Counsel—William F. Dowling
Associate General Counsel—John Ertmann
Vice-President, Marketing—Art Adler
Vice-President, Public Relations—John C. Fugazy
Vice-President, Community Relations—Richard Kraft
Vice-President, Publications—David S. Szen
Vice President—Ed Weaver
Controller—Bob Stoffel
Special Advisor—Clyde King
Vice President and General Manager—Lou Piniella
Vice-President, Baseball Administration—Bob Quinn
Director of Player Development—Bobby Hofman
Director of Scouting—Brian Sabean
Vice-President, Ticket Operations—Frank Swaine
Executive Director of Ticket Operations—Jeff Kline
Ticket Director—Jim Hodge
Director of Video Coordination—Jeff Sandler
Director of Computer Services—John Cook
Director of Group & Season Sales—Debbie Tymon
Assistant Player Development Director—Pete Jameson
Assistant Scouting Director—Kevin Elfering
Director of Media Relations—Harvey Greene
Assistant Media Relations Director—Lou D'Ermilio
Director of Customer Services—Joel S. White
Director of Scoreboard Operations—Betsy Leesman
Diamond Vision Director—John Franzone
Speakers Bureau—Bob Pelegrino
Editor/Yankees Magazine—Tom Bannon
Sales Manager—Kim Gasparini
Spring Training Coordinator—Marsh Samuel
Director, Alumni Association—Jim Ogle
Team Physician—Dr. John J. Bonamo
Manager—Billy Martin
Public Address Announcer—Bob Sheppard
Organist—Eddie Layton
Executive Offices—Yankee Stadium, Bronx, N.Y. 10451
Telephone—293-4300 (area code 212)

SCOUTS—Luis Arroyo, Mark Batchko, Hop Cassady, Al Cuccinello, Arturo Defreites, Joe DiCarlo, Tom Doyle, Fred Ferreira, Jack Gillis, Fernando Gonzalez, Dick Groch, Bill Haller, Bob Hartsfield, Clyde King, Bob Lemon, Don Lindeberg, Bill Livesey, Eddie Lopat, Gene Michael, Ramon Naranjo, Greg Orr, Roberto Rivera, Joe Robison, Stan Saleski, Rudy Santin, Charlie Silvera, Chris Smith, Jeff Taylor, Dick Tidrow, Paul Turco, Stan Williams, Jeff Zimmerman.

PARK LOCATION—Yankee Stadium, E. 161st St. and River Ave., Bronx, N.Y. 10451.

Seating capacity—57,545.

FIELD DIMENSIONS—Home plate to left field at foul line, 312 feet; to center field, 410 feet; to right field at foul line, 310 feet.

OAKLAND A's

Owner/Managing General Partner—Walter A. Haas, Jr.
Chief Operating Officer—Walter J. Haas
Executive Vice-President—Roy Eisenhardt
Vice-President, Baseball Operations—Sandy Alderson
Vice-President, Business Operations—Andy Dolich
Vice-President, Finance—Kathleen McCracken
Assistant to the Exec. V.P., Baseball Matters—Bill Rigney
Assistant to the V.P., Baseball Operations—Ron Schueler
Director of Player Development—Karl Kuehl
Director of Scouting—Dick Bogard
Director of Baseball Administration—Walt Jocketty
Director of Latin American Scouting—Juan Marichal
Director of Team Travel—Mickey Morabito
Director of Baseball Information—Jay Alves
Admin. Coordinator, Baseball Administration—Pamela Pitts
Admin. Assistant, Baseball Operations—Doreen Alves
Director of Broadcasting—David Rubinstein
Director of Media Relations—Kathy Jacobson
Director of Ticket Operations—Raymond B. Krise Jr.
Director of Community Affairs/Speakers Bureau—Dave Perron
Director of Stadium Operations & Security—Jorge Costa
Director of Publications—A.R. Worthington
Director of Broadcast Operations—Bill King
Director of Sales—Tom Cordova
Director of Special Projects—Steve Page
Director of Season Tickets—Barbara Reilly
Director of Group Sales—Bettina Flores
Executive Assistant—Sharon Jones
Promotions Director—Sharon Kelly
Manager—Tony LaRussa
Team Physician—Dr. Allan Pont
Team Orthopedist—Dr. Rick Bost
Trainers—Barry Weinberg, Larry Davis
Equipment Manager—Frank Ciensczyk
Visiting Clubhouse Manager—Steve Vucinich
Executive Offices—Oakland-Alameda County Coliseum,
P.O. Box 2220, Oakland, Calif. 94621
Telephone—638-4900 (area code 415)

SCOUTS—Mark Conkin, Grady Fuson, Bill Gayton, Butch Hughes, Mike Jones, Billy Merkel, Marty Miller, Ivan Murrell, Mel Nelson, Camilo Pascual, J.P. Ricciardi, Duane Schaffer, Mike Sgobba, Mike Squires, Ken Stauffer, Mike Sullivan.

PARK LOCATION—Oakland-Alameda County Coliseum, Nimitz Freeway and Hegenberger Road.

Seating capacity—50,219.

FIELD DIMENSIONS—Home plate to left field at foul line, 330 feet; to center field, 397 feet; to right field at foul line, 330 feet.

SEATTLE MARINERS

Chairman of the Board & Chief Executive Officer—George L. Argyros

President & Chief Operating Officer—Charles G. Armstrong
Vice President, Baseball Operations—Dick Balderson
Vice President, Finance & Administration—Brian Beggs
Vice President, Marketing and Sales—Bill Knudsen
Sr. Director of Communications—Randy Adamack
Director of Baseball Administration—Lee Pelekoudas
Director of Community Relations—Randy Stearnes
Director of Promotional Sales—Larry Sindall
Director of Public Relations—Bob Porter
Director of Scouting—Roger Jongewaard
Director of Stadium Operations—Jeff Klein
Director of Team Travel—Craig Detwiler
Director of Ticket Services—Doug Hopkins
Controller—Denise Podosek
Asst. to V.P., Baseball Operations & Special Assignments—Bob Harrison
Assistant Director of Public Relations—Ethan Kelly
Assistant Director of Marketing—Ross Skinner
Assistant Director of Ticket Services—John Ross Karnoski
Accounting Assistant—Shirley Shreve
Manager—Dick Williams
Trainer—Rick Griffin
Home Clubhouse & Equipment Manager—Henry Genzale
Club Physicians—Dr. Larry Pedegana, Dr. Mitchel Storey
Club Dentist—Dr. Richard Leshgold
Head Groundskeeper—Wilbur Loo
P.A. Announcers—Gary Spinnell, Bill Rice
Executive Offices—P.O. Box 4100
411 First Ave. S., Seattle, Washington 98104
Telephone—628-3555 (area code 206)

SCOUTS—Butch Baccala, Bill Barkley, Brian Granger, Joe Henderson, Doug Hopkins, Ken Houp, Pete Jones, Dave Karaff, Bill Kearns, Benny Looper, Ken Madeja, Jerry Marik, Tom Mooney, Joe Nigro, Fran Oneto, Myron Pine, Whitey Piurek, Mike Powers, Cananea Reyes, Rip Tutor, Steve Vrablik, Bob Wadsworth, Luke Wrenn.

PARK LOCATION—The Kingdome, 201 King Street, Seattle, Washington.

Seating capacity—58,850.

FIELD DIMENSIONS—Home plate to left field at foul line, 316 feet; to center field, 410 feet; to right field at foul line, 316 feet.

TEXAS RANGERS

Board of Directors—Eddie Chiles, Edward L. Gaylord, Fran Chiles, Michael H. Stone, Glenn Stinchcomb

Chairman of the Board, Chief Executive Officer—Eddie Chiles
President, Chief Operating Officer—Michael H. Stone
Vice President, General Manager—Thomas A. Grieve
Vice President, Finance and Secretary-Treasurer—Charles F. Wangner
General Counsel—John B. McAdams
Financial Consultant—Weldon Asten
Assistant G.M., Player Personnel and Scouting—Sandy Johnson
Assistant General Manager—Wayne Krivsky
Director, Player Development—Marty Scott
Director, Media Relations—John Blake
Director, Public Relations and Speakers Bureau—Bobby Bragan
Director, Sales, Broadcasting and Producer, Diamond Vision—Chuck Morgan
Director, Promotions and Director, Diamond Vision—Dave Fendrick
Director, Ticket Sales and Management—Mary Ann Bosher
Stadium Manager—Mat Stolley
Traveling Secretary—Dan Schimek
Controller—John McMichael
General Manager, Charlotte County Operations—Jay Miller
Assistant Director, Media Relations—Larry Kelly
Assistant Director, Ticket Sales & Management—John Schriever
Medical Director—Dr. Mike Mycoskie
Manager—Bobby Valentine
Field Superintendent—Jim Anglea
Assistant Field Superintendent—Brad Richards
Spring Training Director—John Welaj
Home Clubhouse and Equipment Manager—Joe Macko
Visiting Clubhouse Manager—Mike Wallace
Executive Offices—1250 Copeland Road, 11th Floor, Arlington, Tex. 76011
Arlington Stadium—1500 Copeland Road, Arlington, Tex. 76010
Mailing Address—P.O. Box 1111, Arlington, Tex. 76010
Telephone—273-5222 (area code 817)

SCOUTS—Manny Batista, Ray Blanco, Joe Branzell, Jose Cassino, Paddy Cottrell, Dick Coury, Henry Cruz, Amado Dinzey, Jim Dreyer, Bill Earnhart, Doug Gassaway, Mark Giegler, Tim Hallgren, Andy Hancock, Jack Hays, Bryan Lambe, Robert Lavallee, Omar Minaya, Omer Munoz, Elmo Plaskett, Luis Rosa, Bill Schmidt, Rick Schroeder, Mike Snyder, Len Strelitz, Randy Taylor, Rudy Terrasas, Danilo Troncoso, Jose Trujillo, Boris Villa, Bill Yates, John Young.

PARK LOCATION—Arlington Stadium, 1500 Copeland Road, Arlington, Tex.

Seating capacity—43,508.

FIELD DIMENSIONS—Home plate to left field at foul line, 330 feet; to center field, 400 feet; to right field at foul line, 330 feet.

TORONTO BLUE JAYS

Board of Directors—John Craig Eaton, L. G. Greenwood,
N. E. Hardy, R. Howard Webster, P. N. T. Widdrington
Chairman of the Board—R. Howard Webster
Vice-Chairman, Chief Executive Officer—N. E. Hardy
Executive Vice-President, Business—Paul Beeston
Executive Vice-President, Baseball—Pat Gillick
Vice-Presidents, Baseball—Bob Mattick, Al LaMacchia
Vice-President, Finance & Administration—Bob Nicholson
Director, Public Relations—Howard Starkman
Director, Ticket Operations—George Holm
Director, Operations—Ken Erskine
Director, Marketing—Paul Markle
Director, Canadian Scouting—Bob Prentice
Director, Florida Operations—Ken Carson
Administrator, Player Personnel—Gord Ash
Controller—Phil Martin
Manager, Group Sales—Maureen Haffey
Assistant Director, Public Relations—Gary Oswald
Assistant Director, Ticket Operations—Randy Low
Assistant Director, Operations—Len Frejlich
Manager, Promotions & Community Events—John Brioux
Manager, Stadium Promotions—Colleen Burns
Manager, Employee Compensation—Catherine Elwood
Manager, Information Systems—Kevin Worth
Manager, Team Travel—Mike Mitchell
Manager, Ticket Vault—Paul Goodyear
Manager, Ticket Revenue—Mike Maunder
Managers, Ticket Mail Services—Allan Koyanagi, Doug Barr
Manager, Event Personnel—Fred Wootton
Assistant Controller—Sue Sostarich
Systems Administrator—Mark Graham
Coordinator, Group Sales—Mark Edwards
Supervisor, Grounds—Brad Bujold
Supervisor, Security—Bob Sharpe
Supervisor, Office & Game Services—Dave Cox
Trainer—Tommy Craig
Manager—Jimy Williams
Team Physician—Dr. Ron Taylor
Executive Offices—Exhibition Stadium, Exhibition Place,
Toronto, Ontario M6K 3C3
Mailing Address—Box 7777, Adelaide St. P. O., Toronto, Ont. M5C 2K7
Telephone—595-0077 (area code 416)

SCOUTS—David Blume, Christopher Bourjos, Ellis Dungan, Robert Engle (Eastern Regional Scouting Director), Joe Ford, Epy Guerrero (Coordinator, Latin American Scouting & Player Development), Tom Hinkle, Jim Hughes, Moose Johnson (Special Assignment), Gordon Lakey (Special Assignment), Duane Larson, Ted Lekas, Ben McLure, Steve Minor, Wayne Morgan (Western Regional Scouting Director), Neil Summers, Don Welke, Tim Wilken, Dave Yoakum.

PARK LOCATION—Exhibition Stadium on the grounds of Exhibition Place. Entrances to Exhibition Place via Lakeshore Boulevard, Queen Elizabeth Way Highway and Dufferin and Bathurst Streets.

Seating capacity—43,737.

FIELD DIMENSIONS—Home plate to left field at foul line, 330 feet; to center field, 400 feet; to right field at foul line, 330 feet.

National League

Organized 1876

A. BARTLETT GIAMATTI
President and Treasurer

PHYLLIS B. COLLINS
Vice-President & Secretary

KATY FEENEY
Director of Media & Public Affairs

MARY LOU RISLEY
Executive Secretary & Office Manager

CATHY DAVIS
Administrative Assistant

NANCY CROFTS
Assistant Secretary

Headquarters—350 Park Avenue, New York, N. Y. 10022

Telephone—371-7300 (area code 212)

UMPIRES—Greg Bonin, Fred Brocklander, Gerald Crawford, Robert Davidson, Gerry Davis, Dana DeMuth, Robert Engel, Bruce Froemming, Eric Gregg, Tom Hallion, H. Douglas Harvey, John Kibler, Randall Marsh, John McSherry, Edward Montague, David Pallone, Frank Pulli, James Quick, Lawrence (Dutch) Rennert, Steve Rippley, Paul Runge, Terry Tata, Harry Wendelstedt, Joseph West, Lee Weyer, Charles Williams.

OFFICIAL STATISTICIANS—Elias Sports Bureau, Inc., 500 5th Ave., Suite 2114, New York, N.Y. 10036. Telephone—(212) 869-1530.

ATLANTA BRAVES

Chairman of the Board—William C. Bartholomay

President—Stan Kasten
Vice-President & General Manager—Robert J. Cox
Vice-President & Asst. General Manager—John W. Mullen
Vice-President and Business Manager—Charles S. Sanders
Vice-President, Player Development—Henry L. Aaron
Assistant Vice-President, Scouting—Paul L. Snyder, Jr.
Assistant Scouting Director—Rod Gilbreath
Director of Broadcasting—Wayne Long
Ticket Distribution Manager—Ed Newman
Director of Public Relations—Bob DiBiasio
Director of Promotions—Miles McRea
Assistant Public Relations Director—Jim Schultz
Publications Sales Manager—Peter Diffin
Director of Stadium Operations and Security—Ken Little
Director of Matrix Operations—Bob Larson
Assistant Controller—Martin Mathews
Traveling Secretary and Equipment Manager—Bill Acree
Director of Ticket Sales—Jack Tyson
Group Sales Manager—Donna Shepard
Manager—Chuck Tanner
Club Physician—Dr. David T. Watson
Executive Offices—P.O. Box 4064, Atlanta, Ga. 30302
Telephone—522-7630 (area code 404)

SCOUTS—Monty Aldrich, Mike Arbuckle, Cloyd Boyer, Forrest (Smoky) Burgess, Stu Cann, Joe Caputo, Kenny Lee Compton, Harold Cronin, Tony DeMacio, Dutch Dorman, Lou Fitzgerald, Darren Fleming, Ralph Garr, Pedro Gonzalez, Larry Grefer, John Groth, John Hageman, Gene Hassell, Herb Hippauf, Ray Holton, Jim Johnson, Dean Jongewaard, Charlie Kafoury, Robin Lynch, Burney R. (Dickey) Martin, Bob Mavis, Red Murff, Arthur Neal, Umberto Oropeza, Ernie Pedersen, Jack Pierce, Rance Pless, Rich Pohle, Jorge Posada, Harry Postove, Jim Procopio, Paul Ricciarini, Jose Salado, Bill Serena, Fred Shaffer, Charles Smith, Ted Sparks, Tony Stiel, Bob Turzilli, Wesley Westrum, William R. Wight, Don Williams, Bobby Wine, H.F. (Red) Wooten.

PARK LOCATION—Atlanta-Fulton County Stadium, on Capitol Avenue at the junction of Interstate Highways 20, 75 and 85.

Seating capacity—52,001.

FIELD DIMENSIONS—Home plate to left field at foul line, 330 feet; to center field, 402 feet; to right field at foul line, 330 feet.

CHICAGO CUBS

Board of Directors—Thomas G. Ayers, Stanton R. Cook
John W. Madigan, Andrew J. McKenna, Walter E. Massey
Chairman—John W. Madigan
Executive Vice-President, Baseball Operations—Jim Frey
Executive Vice-President, Business Operations—Don Grenesko
Vice-President, Business Operations—Mark McGuire
Vice-President, Minor Leagues & Scouting—Gordon Goldsberry
Vice-President—E.R. Saltwell
Special Player Consultants—Hugh Alexander, Charlie Fox, Billy Williams
General Counsel—Geoff Anderson
Corporate Secretary—Joyce Hutchinson
Director, Marketing—John McDonough
Director, Media Relations—Ned Colletti
Director, Minor League Operations—Bill Harford
Director, Planning & Control—Keith Bode
Director, Publications—Bob Ibach
Director, Stadium Operations—Tom Cooper
Director, Ticket Operations—Frank Maloney
Traveling Secretary—Peter Durso
Manager, EDP Systems—Joe Kirchen
Manager, Financial Accounting—Woodrow Broaders
Manager, Human Resources—Wendy Lewis
Assistant Director, Ticket Operations—Bill Galante
Assistant Director, Media Relations—Sharon Pannozzo
Assistant Director, Promotions and Community Services—Conrad Kowal
Assistant Director, Scouting—Scott Nelson
Assistant Director, Stadium Operations/Event Personnel—Paul Rathje
Assistant Director, Stadium Operations/Facilities—Lubie Veal
P.A. Announcer—Wayne Messmer
Team Photographer—Steve Green
Team Physician—Jacob Suker, M.D.
Trainer—John Fierro
Equipment Manager—Yosh Kawano
Manager—Don Zimmer
Executive Offices—Wrigley Field, 1060 West Addison Street, Chicago, Ill. 60613
Telephone—281-5050 (area code 312)

SCOUTS—(Major League)—Scott Reid. (National Supervisor)—Brandy Davis. (Regional Supervisors)—Harley Anderson, Tom Davis, Doug Mapson, Gary Nickels. (Latin American Supervisor)— Ruben Amaro. (Regular)—Billy Blitzer, Bill Capps, Billy Champion, Frank DeMoss, Ed DiRamio, Walt Dixon, Lou Garcia, Bobby Gardner, John Gracio, Gene Handley, John Hennessy, A.B. (Vedie) Himsl, Ron Hollingsworth, Toney Howell, Hank Izquierdo, John (Spider) Jorgensen, Doug Lauman, Noe Maduro, John (Buck) O'Neil, Luis Peraza, Andy Pienovi, Paul Provas, Joaquin Velilla, H.D. (Rube) Wilson, Earl Winn, Harold Younghans.

PARK LOCATION—Wrigley Field, Addison Street, N. Clark Street, Waveland Avenue and Sheffield Avenue.

Seating capacity—38,040.

FIELD DIMENSIONS—Home plate to left field at foul line, 355 feet; to center field, 400 feet; to right field at foul line, 353 feet.

CINCINNATI REDS

General Partner—Marge Schott

President and Chief Executive Officer—Marge Schott
Vice-President & General Manager—Murray Cook
Vice-President/Business & Marketing—Don Breen
Vice-President, Asst. General Manager—Sheldon Bender
Vice-President, Publicity—Jim Ferguson
Controller—Chris Krabbe
Director, Scouting—John Cox
Director, Minor Leagues—Branch Rickey
Director, Information & Publications—Jon Braude
Director, Stadium Operations—Tim O'Connell
Director, Promotions—Cal Levy
Director, Ticket Department—Bill Stewart
Director, Season Tickets—Pat McCaffrey
Director, Group Sales—Tony Harris
Director of Speakers Bureau—Gordy Coleman
Traveling Secretary—Brad Del Barba
Advance Scout—Jim Stewart
Assistant, Player Development and Scouting—Tom Kayser
Assistant Ticket Director—John O'Brien
Chief Administrative Assistant—Joyce Pfarr
Manager—Pete Rose
Executive Offices—100 Riverfront Stadium, Cincinnati, O. 45202
Telephone—421-4510 (area code 513)

SCOUTS—Larry Barton, Jr., Gene Bennett, Dave Calaway, Bill Clark, Martin Daily, Roger Ferguson, Edwin Howsam, Eddie Kolo, Chuck LaMar, Jeff McKay, Sam Mejias, Don Mitchell, Julian Mock, Chet Montgomery, Earl Rapp, Ed Roebuck, Tom Severtson, Robert Szymkowski, Mickey White, George Zuraw.

PARK LOCATION—Riverfront Stadium, downtown Cincinnati, bounded by Pete Rose Way to the Ohio River and from Walnut Street to Broadway.

Seating capacity—52,392.

FIELD DIMENSIONS—Home plate to left field at foul line, 330 feet; to center field, 404 feet; to right field at foul line, 330 feet.

HOUSTON ASTROS

Board of Directors—Dr. John J. McMullen, Chairman. Owners—Dr. John J. McMullen, Mrs. R.E. (Bob) Smith, Mrs. Thomas E. (Mimi) Dompier, James A. Elkins, Jr., Alfred C. Glassell, Jr., Bob Marco, Don Sanders, Jack T. Trotter, H.L. Brown and Jacqueline, Peter, Catherine and John McMullen, Jr.

General Manager—William J. Wood
President, Baseball Operations—Fred Stanley
Director of Minor League Operations—Fred Nelson
Director of Scouting—Dan O'Brien, Jr.
Director of Public Relations—Rob Matwick
Traveling Secretary—Barry Waters
Director of Marketing—Ted Haracz
Director of Broadcasting—Jamie Hildreth
Director of Special Events—Karen Williams
Director of Communications—Molly Glentzer
Special Assistant to the G.M.—Donald Davidson
Assistant Director of Public Relations—Chuck Pool
Assistant to the Dirs., Minor Leagues/Scouting—Lew Temple
Scoreboard Operations—Paul Darst
Broadcast Sales—Norm Miller
Ticket Manager—Charles Wall
Manager, Group & Season Ticket Sales—Veronica Stalica
Administrative Asst., Major League Operations—Chris Rice
Secretary, Public Relations—Meribeth Fuqua
Club Physicians—Dr. William Bryan, Dr. Michael Feltovich
Public Address Announcer—J. Fred Duckett
Manager—Hal Lanier
Executive Offices—The Astrodome, P.O. Box 288
Houston, Tex. 77001
Telephone—799-9500 (area code 713)
HOUSTON SPORTS ASSOCIATION, INC.
President and Chief Operating Officer—Robert G. Harter
Executive Vice-President—Neal Gunn
Executive Vice-President, Astrodome-Astrohall Stadium Corporation—Jimmie Fore
Vice-President, Operations—W. Gary Keller
Vice-President, Public Affairs—Jim Weidler
Treasurer—Gary Brooks
General Counsel—Frank Rynd
Controller—Adam C. Richards

SCOUTS—Clary Anderson, Stan Benjamin, Bob Blair, Jack Bloomfield, George Brophy, Gerry Craft, Walter Cress, Clark Crist, Shug DeFord, Doug Deutsch, Gary Elliott, Ben Galante, Carl Greene, Bill Hallauer, Red Hayworth, Dan Hutson, Bill Kelso, David Lakey, Julio Linares, Mike Maggart, Walter Matthews, Walter Millies, Hal Newhouser, Cotton Nix, Joe Nossek, Shawn Pender, Joe Pittman, Pico Prado, Ross Sapp, Lynwood Stallings, Reggie Waller, Paul Weaver, Tom Wheeler.

PARK LOCATION—The Astrodome, Kirby and Interstate Loop 610

Seating capacity—45,000.

FIELD DIMENSIONS—Home plate to left field at foul line, 330 feet; to center field, 400 feet; to right field at foul line, 330 feet.

LOS ANGELES DODGERS

Board of Directors—Peter O'Malley, President; Harry M. Bardt;
Roland Seidler, Vice-President and Treasurer;
Mrs. Roland (Terry) Seidler, Secretary

President—Peter O'Malley
Executive Vice-President, Player Personnel—Fred Claire
Vice-President, Communications—Tom Hawkins
Vice-President, Finance—Bob Graziano
Vice-President, Marketing—Merritt Willey
Vice-President, Treasurer—Roland Seidler
Assistant to the President—Ike Ikuhara
Assistant Secretary & General Counsel—Santiago Fernandez
Auditor—Michael Strange
Controller and Assistant Treasurer—Ken Hasemann
Director, Community Relations—Don Newcombe
Community Relations—Roy Campanella, Lou Johnson
Director, Dodgertown—Terry Reynolds
Director, Human Resources—Irene Tanji
Director, Data Processing—Mike Mularky
Director, Stadium Operations—Bob Smith
Director, Ticket Department—Walter Nash
Director, Stadium Club and Transportation—Bob Schenz
Director, Minor League Operations—Charlie Blaney
Director, Scouting—Ben Wade
Director, Media Services—Toby Zwikel
Director, Ticket Marketing and Promotions—Barry Stockhamer
Director, Community Services and Special Events—Bill Shumard
Traveling Secretary—Bill DeLury
Manager—Tom Lasorda
Club Physicians—Dr. Frank W. Jobe, Dr. Michael F. Mellman
Executive Offices—Dodger Stadium, 1000 Elysian Park Avenue,
Los Angeles, Calif. 90012
Telephone—224-1500 (area code 213)

SCOUTS—Eleodoro Arias, Ralph Avila, Eddie Bane, Boyd Bartley, Bob Bishop, Gib Bodet, Flores Bolivar, Mike Brito, Joe Campbell, Bob Darwin, Eddie Fajardo, Jim Garland, Manuel Gonzalez, Rafael Gonzalez, Michael Hankins, Dick Hanlon, Dennis Haren, Gail Henley, Elvio Jimenez, Hank Jones, John Keenan, Don LeJohn, Steve Lembo, Carl Loewenstine, Dale McReynolds, Bob Miske, Tommy Mixon, Luis Angel Montalvo, Ruben Morales, Victor Nazario, Regie Otero, Deni Pacini, Pablo Peguero, Bill Pleis, Dick Teed, Glen Van Proyen, Corito Varona, Miguel Angel Villaran. Special Assignment Scouts—Steve Boros, Mel Didier, Joe Ferguson, Phil Regan, Jerry Stephenson.

PARK LOCATION—Dodger Stadium, 1000 Elysian Park Avenue.

Seating capacity—56,000.

FIELD DIMENSIONS—Home plate to left field at foul line, 330 feet; to center field, 395 feet; to right field at foul line, 330 feet.

MONTREAL EXPOS

Board of Directors—Charles R. Bronfman, Lorne C. Webster, Claude R. Brochu, John J. McHale, Hugh Hallward, Sen. E. Leo Kolber, Arnold Ludwick

Honorary Directors—Louis R. Desmarais, Sydney Maislin

Chairman of the Board—Charles R. Bronfman
Deputy Chairman—John J. McHale
President & Chief Operating Officer—Claude R. Brochu
Honorary Treasurer—Arnold Ludwick
Vice-President, Baseball Operations & G.M.—Bill Stoneman
Assistant General Manager—David Dombrowski
Vice-President, Business Operations—Gerry Trudeau
Vice-President, Marketing—Claude Laberge
Controller—Raymond St. Pierre
Director, Player Development—Dan Duquette
Director of Scouting—Gary Hughes
Director, Team Travel—Dan Lunetta
Director of Stadium Operations—Monique Lacas
Director of Ticket Department—Claude Delorme
Director of Ticket Sales—Jean Drolet
Director of Promotions—Benoit Cartier
Director of Public Relations—Pierre Vidal
Assistant Director of Scouting—Frank Wren
Executive Asst., Minor League Clubs—Marilyn Elzer
Publicists—Monique Giroux, Richard Griffin
Coordinator, Spring Training—Kevin McHale
Manager—Buck Rodgers
Club Physician—Dr. Robert Brodrick
Club Orthopedist—Dr. Larry Coughlin
Mailing Address—P. O. Box 500, Station M, Montreal, Quebec,
Canada H1V 3P2
Telephone—253-3434 (area code 514)

SCOUTS—Jesus Alou, Kelvin Bowles, Pepito Centeno, Lloyd Christopher, Ed Creech, Pat Daugherty, Richard DeHart, Manny Estrada, Orrin Freeman, Joseph Frisina, Eddie Haas, Whitey Lockman, Eddie Lyons, Bill MacKenzie, Kevin Malone, Jethro McIntyre, Roy McMillan, Bob Oldis, Jose Perez, Cucho Rodriguez, Mark Servais, Angel Vazquez, Stan Zielinski, Greg Zunino.

PARK LOCATION—Olympic Stadium, 4545 Pierre de Coubertin St., Montreal, Quebec, Canada H1V 3N7.

Seating capacity—59,226.

FIELD DIMENSIONS—Home plate to left field at foul line, 325 feet; to center field, 404 feet; to right field at foul line, 325 feet.

NEW YORK METS

Chairman of the Board—Nelson Doubleday

Directors—Nelson Doubleday, Fred Wilpon, J. Frank Cashen,
Saul Katz, Marvin Tepper
Special Consultant to the Board of Directors—Richard Cummins
President & Chief Executive Officer—Fred Wilpon
Exec. Vice-President, G.M. & Chief Operating Officer—J. Frank Cashen
Vice-President, Operations—Bob Mandt
Vice-President, Baseball Administration—Alan E. Harazin
Vice-President, Baseball Operations—Joseph McIlvaine
Vice-President, Treasurer—Harold W. O'Shaughnessy
Vice-President, Marketing—Drew Sheinman
Director of Public Relations—Jay Horwitz
Director of Promotions—Michael Miller
Director of Broadcasting—Mike Ryan
Executive Asst. to General Manager—Jean Coen
Special Asst. to the G.M. & Team Travel Director—Arthur Richman
Ticket Manager—Bill Ianniciello
Controller—William Grundel
Director of Minor League Operations—Stephen Schryver
Director of Scouting—Roland Johnson
Stadium Manager—John McCarthy
Director of Amateur Baseball Relations—Tommy Holmes
Manager—Dave Johnson
Club Physician—Dr. James C. Parkes II
Team Trainer—Steve Garland
Executive Offices—William A. Shea Stadium, Roosevelt
Avenue and 126th Street, Flushing, N.Y. 11368
Telephone—507-6387 (area code 718)

SCOUTS—Paul Baretta, Phil Favia, Carmen Fusco, Dick Gernert, Rob Guzik, Marty Harvat, Reggie Jackson, Buddy Kerr, Joe Mason, Bob Minor, Harry Minor, Julian Morgan, Roy Partee, Carlos Pascual, Junior Roman, Marv Scott, Eddy Toledo, Terry Tripp, Bob Wellman, Jim Woodward, Jack Zduriencik.

PARK LOCATION—William A. Shea Stadium, Roosevelt Avenue and 126th Street, Flushing, N. Y. 11368.

Seating capacity—55,300.

FIELD DIMENSIONS—Home plate to left field at foul line, 338 feet; to center field, 410 feet; to right field at foul line, 338 feet.

PHILADELPHIA PHILLIES

President/General Partner—Bill Giles

Partners—John Drew Betz Associates, Tri-Play Associates,
Fitz Eugene Dixon Jr., Mrs. Rochelle Levy
Executive Vice-President—David Montgomery
Vice-President, Player Personnel—Woody Woodward
Vice-President, Finance—Jerry Clothier
Vice-President, Baseball Administration—Tony Siegle
Vice-President, Public Relations—Larry Shenk
Vice-President, Player Development and Scouting—Jim Baumer
Secretary and Counsel—William Y. Webb
Assistant to President—Paul Owens
Financial Consultant—Robert D. Hedberg
Director of Planning, Development & Super Boxes—Tom Hudson
Director of Promotions—Frank Sullivan
Traveling Secretary—Eddie Ferenz
Director of Sales and Ticket Operations—Richard Deats
Director of Scouting—Jack Pastore
Director of Community Relations—Chris Wheeler
Director of Marketing—Dennis Lehman
Director of Stadium Operations—Mike DiMuzio
Director of Operations—Pat Cassidy
Director of Management Information—Jeff Eisenberg
Controller—Mike Kent
Director of Publicity—Vince Nauss
Director of Group Sales—Bettyanne Joyce
Director of Season Ticket Sales—Dennis Mannion
Assistant Director of Promotions—Chris Legault
Assistant Director of Marketing—Jo-Anne Levy
Executive Secretary—Nancy Connor
Executive Secretary to Minor Leagues—Bill Gargano
Club Physician—Dr. Phillip Marone
Club Trainer—Jeff Cooper
Strength and Flexibility Instructor—Gus Hoefling
Manager—Lee Elia
Executive Offices—Philadelphia Veterans Stadium
Mailing Address—P.O. Box 7575, Philadelphia, Pa. 19101
Telephone—463-6000 (area code 215)

SCOUTS—(Special assignment)—Ray Shore and Jim Davenport. (Regular)—Bill
Adair, Oliver Bidwell, Edward Bockman, Wilfredo Calvino, Carlos Cervo, George
Farson, Tom Ferguson, Bill Harper, Ken Hultzapple, Jerry Jordan, Hank King, Jerry
Lafferty, Dick Lawlor, Anthony Lucadello, Fred Mazuca, Cotton Nye, Frank Perez,
Bob Poole, Bob Reasonover, Larry Reasonover, Joe Reilly, Jay Robertson, Tony
Roig, Randy Waddill, Don Williams.

PARK LOCATION—Philadelphia Veterans Stadium, Broad Street and Pattison
Avenue.

Seating capacity—62,382.

FIELD DIMENSIONS—Home plate to left field at foul line, 330 feet; to center
field, 408 feet; to right field at foul line, 330 feet.

PITTSBURGH PIRATES

Chairman & Chief Executive Officer—Douglas D. Danforth

President—Carl F. Barger
Senior V.P. & G.M./Baseball Operations—Syd Thrift
Senior Vice-President, Business Development—Bernard J. Mullin
Vice-President, Stadium Operations and Administration—Richard L. Andersen
Vice-President, Finance & Secretary—Ken Curcio
Vice-President, Public Relations—Rick Cerrone
Vice-President, Marketing—Steve Greenberg
Vice-President, Ticket Operations—Norman DeLuca
Vice-President—Harvey Walken
Director of Media Relations—Greg Johnson
Asst. Dir. of Media Relations/Publications Dir.—Jim Lachimia
Asst. Director of Public Relations—Sally O'Leary
Director of Scouting—Elmer Gray
Asst. Dir. of Minor Leagues & Scouting—James G. Bowden IV
Traveling Secretary—Charles Muse
Director of Broadcasting—Dean Jordan
Radio and TV Coordinator—Greg Brown
Community Relations Director—Patty Paytas
Manager—Jim Leyland
Club Physician—Dr. Richard Wechsler
Team Orthopedist—Dr. Jack Failla
Team Trainer—Kent Biggerstaff
Equipment Manager—John Hallahan
Executive Offices—Three Rivers Stadium, 600 Stadium Circle, Pittsburgh, Pa. 15212
Telephone—323-5000 (area code 412)

SCOUTS—(Supervisors)—Gene Baker, Jack Bowen, Bart Braun, Joe L. Brown, Bill Bryk, Joe Consoli, Pablo Cruz, Larry D'Amato, Steve Demeter, Angel Figueroa, Jerry Gardner, Pete Gebrian, Fred Goodman, Terry Logan, Bob Rossi, Don Scala, Lenny Yochim, Bob Zuk.

PARK LOCATION—Three Rivers Stadium, 600 Stadium Circle.

Seating capacity—58,727.

FIELD DIMENSIONS—Home plate to left field at foul line, 335 feet; to center field, 400 feet; to right field at foul line, 335 feet.

ST. LOUIS CARDINALS

Chairman of the Board, President and Chief Executive Officer—
August A. Busch, Jr.

Executive Vice-President, Chief Operating Officer—Fred L. Kuhlmann
Vice-Presidents—August A. Busch, III, Margaret S. Busch
Senior Vice-President—Stan Musial
Vice-President, Finance & Administration—Mark Gorris
Controller—John McMinn
Board of Directors—Adolphus A. Busch, IV, August A. Busch, Jr.,
August A. Busch, III, Frederic E. Giersch, Jr., Louis B. Hager, John Hayward,
Ben Kerner, Fred L. Kuhlmann, Stanley F. Musial, W.R. Persons,
Walter C. Reisinger, Louis B. Susman, John Valentine
Vice-President, General Manager—Dal Maxvill
Manager—Whitey Herzog
Admin. Asst. to Executive V.P. & Chief Operating Officer—Jacqueline Hunter
Admin. Asst. to Vice-President, General Manager—Judy Carpenter Barada
Admin. Asst. to Vice-President, Finance & Administration—Bernadine Hogan
Vice-President, Marketing—Marty Hendin
Manager, Special Events—Nancy McElroy
Director of Player Development—Lee Thomas
Director of Scouting—Fred McAlister
Assistant Director of Scouting—Marty Maier
Asst. to Player Development & Scouting—Scott Smulczenski
Director of Public Relations—Kip Ingle
Assistant Director of Public Relations—Brian Bartow
Director of Promotions—Dan Farrell
Director of Community Relations & Group Sales—Joe Cunningham
Director of Season Ticket Sales—Sue Ann McClaren
Manager of Group Sales—Bridget Wynn
Asst. to the Dir. of Community Relations/Minor League Instructor—Ted Savage
Director of Tickets and Stadium Operations—Mike Bertani
Assistant Director of Tickets—Josephine Arnold
Financial Analyst—Marian Rhodes
Supervisor of Office Services—Kevin Wade
Programming Analyst—Tim Busche
Traveling Secretary—C.J. Cherre
Club Physician—Dr. Stan London
Secretary and Treasurer—John L. Hayward
Assistant Secretary—Richard Schwartz
Executive Offices—Busch Stadium, 250 Stadium Plaza,
St. Louis, Mo. 63102
Telephone—421-4040 (area code 314)

SCOUTS—(Supervisors)—Jim Belz, Vern Benson, Steve Flores, Jim Johnson, Marty Keough, Tom McCormack, Joe Rigoli, Mike Roberts, Hal Smith, Charles (Tim) Thompson, Rube Walker (special assignment). (Part-time)—Jorge Aranzamendi, James Brown, Roberto Diaz, Cecil Espy, Manuel Guerra, Ray King, Juan Melo, Virgil Melvin, Ramon Ortiz, Bob Parks, Joe Popek, Kenneth Thomas.

PARK LOCATION—Busch Stadium, Broadway, Walnut Street, Stadium Plaza and Spruce Street.

Seating capacity—54,224.

FIELD DIMENSIONS—Home plate to left field at foul line, 330 feet; to center field, 414 feet; to right field at foul line, 330 feet.

SAN DIEGO PADRES

Board of Directors—Joan Kroc, Ballard F. Smith, Jr., Anthony J. Zulfer, Jr.

President—Chub Feeney
Exec. Vice-President, Chief Operating Officer—Dick Freeman
Senior Vice-President, Business Operations—Elten F. Schiller
Vice-President, Baseball Operations—Jack McKeon
Administrative Assistant—Rhoda Polley
Controller—Bob Wells
Major League Scout, Special Assignments—Dick Hager
Major League Scout, Special Assignments—Bill McKeon
Director, Minor Leagues and Scouting—Tom Romenesko
Director of Media Relations—Bill Beck
Assistant Director of Media Relations—Mike Swanson
Director of Broadcasting—Jim Winters
Director of Group Sales—Tom Mulcahy
Director of Marketing—Andy Strasberg
Director of Ticket Sales—Dave Gilmore
Traveling Secretary—John Mattei
Manager—Larry Bowa
Club Physician—Scripps Clinic
Executive Offices—P. O. Box 2000, San Diego, Calif. 92120
Telephone—283-7294 (area code 619)

SCOUTS—Santos Alomar, Dave Bartosch, Billy Castell, Ray Coley, Jose Cora, Manny Crespo, David Freeland, Denny Galehouse, Jose Garcia, Donald Hennelly, Ken Hennelly, Benny Jones, Pete Jones, Harvey Koepf, John Kosciak, Don LaBossiere, Manny Lantigue, Joe Lutz, Jim Marshall, Abe Martinez, Damon Oppenheimer, Tom Roberts, Ernie Sierra, Brad Sloan, Ed Stevens, Vince Valecce, Jose Valentin, Hector Valle, Bob Warner, Henry Weaver, Hank Zacharias.

PARK LOCATION—San Diego Jack Murphy Stadium, 9949 Friars Road.

Seating capacity—58,402.

FIELD DIMENSIONS—Home plate to left field at foul line, 330 feet; to center field, 405 feet; to right field at foul line, 330 feet.

SAN FRANCISCO GIANTS

Chairman—Robert A. Lurie

President & General Manager—Al Rosen
Executive Vice-President, Administration—Corey Busch
Vice-President, Baseball Operations—Bob Kennedy
Vice-President, Business Operations—Pat Gallagher
Assistant General Manager—Ralph Nelson Jr.
Director of Player Personnel and Scouting—Bob Fontaine
Director of Minor League Operations—Carlos Alfonso
Assistant Director of Minor Leagues/Scouting—Dave Nahabedian
Director of Travel—Dirk Smith
Special Assistants to the President and G.M.—Willie Mays, Willie McCovey
Administrative Assistant—Florence Myers
Director of Public Relations—Duffy Jennings
Director of Marketing—Mario Alioto
Director of Sales—Bob Gaillard
Director of Stadium Operations—Don Foreman
Director of Graphics and Photography—Dennis Desprois
Director of Retail Sales—Bob Tolifson
Ticket Manager—Arthur Schulze
Accounting Manager—Jeannie Adamo
Promotions Manager—Carlos Deza
Community Services Manager—Dave Craig
Retail Sales Manager—Dave Alioto
Group Sales Manager—Pennie Lundberg
Assistant Director of Public Relations—David Aust
Assistant Director of Stadium Operations—Gene Telucci
Assistant to the Executive Vice-President—Michael Shapiro, Esq.
Community Representative—Mike Sadek
Speakers Bureau—Joe Orengo
Director of Operations, GiantsVision—Karen Sisco
Director of Affiliate Relations, GiantsVision—Bob Hartzell
Marketing Manager, GiantsVision—Eva Bustos
Producer, GiantsVision—Jeff Kuiper
Manager—Roger Craig
Executive Offices—Candlestick Park, San Francisco, Calif. 94124
Telephone—468-3700 (area code 415)

SCOUTS—Harry Craft, Nino Escalera, Jim Fairey, Jack French, George M. Genovese, Milt Graff, Grady Hatton, Herman Hannah, Al Heist, Pete Jensen, Richard Klaus, Andy Korenek, Alan Marr, T. McCarthy, D. McMillan, Bob Miller, Frank Ontiveros, Jack Paepke, Bill Parese, Ken (Squeaky) Parker, Mike Reardon, Mike Russell, Hank Sauer, John Shafer, George Silvey, George Sobek, Bill Teed, Todd Thomas, Gene Thompson, Mike Toomey, Jack Uhey, John Van Ornum, Tom Zimmer.

PARK LOCATION—Candlestick Point, Bayshore Freeway.

Seating capacity—58,000.

FIELD DIMENSIONS—Home plate to left field at foul line, 335 feet; to center field, 400 feet; to right field at foul line, 330 feet.

𝕿𝖍𝖊 𝕾𝖕𝖔𝖗𝖙𝖎𝖓𝖌 𝕹𝖊𝖜𝖘 No. 1 MEN of 1987

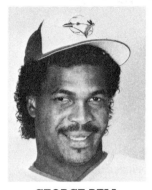

GEORGE BELL
● TORONTO BLUE JAYS ●
MAJOR LEAGUE
PLAYER OF THE YEAR

AL ROSEN
● SAN FRANCISCO GIANTS ●
MAJOR LEAGUE EXECUTIVE

BUCK RODGERS
● MONTREAL EXPOS ●
NATIONAL LEAGUE
MANAGER

SPARKY ANDERSON
● DETROIT TIGERS ●
AMERICAN LEAGUE
MANAGER

RANDY MILLIGAN
● TIDEWATER ●
MINOR LEAGUE PLAYER

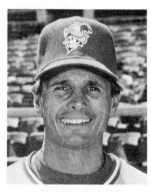

TERRY COLLINS
● ALBUQUERQUE ●
MINOR LEAGUE MANAGER

STU KEHOE
● VANCOUVER ●
MINOR LEAGUE EXECUTIVE
IN CLASS AAA

JOE PRESEREN
● TULSA ●
MINOR LEAGUE EXECUTIVE
IN CLASS AA

SKIP WEISMAN
● GREENSBORO ●
MINOR LEAGUE EXECUTIVE
IN CLASS A

Major League Players Association

805 Third Avenue
New York, N.Y. 10022
Telephone—(212) 826-0808

Executive Director & General Counsel—Donald Fehr
Special Assistant—Mark Belanger
Associate General Counsel—Eugene Orza
Assistant General Counsel—Lauren Rich
Counsel—Arthur Schack
Legal Assistant—Laura Sigal
Staff—Bonnie White, Virginia Carballo, Maureen Corless and Renee Ali

EXECUTIVE BOARD

Don Baylor—American League Representative
Paul Molitor—Alternate American League Representative
Bob Horner—National League Representative
Vance Law—Alternate National League Representative
Orel Hershiser—Pension Committee
Jimmy Key—Pension Committee Alternate
Rick Honeycutt—Pension Committee
Rick Horton—Pension Committee Alternate
Plus all remaining player representatives

NATIONAL LEAGUE PLAYER REPRESENTATIVES

Ken Oberkfell—Atlanta Braves
Scott Sanderson—Chicago Cubs
Ron Robinson—Cincinnati Reds
Bob Knepper—Houston Astros
Dave Anderson—Los Angeles Dodgers
Casey Candaele—Montreal Expos
Keith Hernandez—New York Mets
Shane Rawley—Philadelphia Phillies
Jim Gott—Pittsburgh Pirates
Danny Cox—St. Louis Cardinals
Keith Comstock—San Diego Padres
Bob Melvin—San Francisco Giants

AMERICAN LEAGUE PLAYER REPRESENTATIVES

Scott McGregor—Baltimore Orioles
Rich Gedman—Boston Red Sox
Mike Witt—California Angels
TBA—Chicago White Sox
Joe Carter—Cleveland Indians
Frank Tanana—Detroit Tigers
Kevin Seitzer—Kansas City Royals
Paul Molitor—Milwaukee Brewers
Bert Blyleven—Minnesota Twins
Dave Winfield—New York Yankees
TBA—Oakland A's
Dave Valle—Seattle Mariners
Geno Petralli—Texas Rangers
Willie Upshaw—Toronto Blue Jays

Minor League Presidents for '88

CLASS AAA

American Association—Ken Grandquist, 2nd & Riverside Drive, Des Moines, Ia. 50309

International League—Harold Cooper, P.O. Box 608, Grove City, Ohio 43123

Mexican League—Pedro Treto Cisneros, Angel Pola No. 16 Col. Periodista C.P. 11220, Mexico, D.F.

Pacific Coast League—Bill Cutler, 2101 E. Broadway Rd., Tempe, Ariz. 85282

CLASS AA

Eastern League—Charles Eshbach, P.O. Box 716, Plainville, Conn. 06062

Southern League—Jimmy Bragan, 235 Main St., Suite 103, Trussville, Ala. 35173

Texas League—Carl Sawatski, 10201 W. Markham St., Little Rock, Ark. 72205

CLASS A

California League—Joe Gagliardi, P.O. Box 26400, San Jose, Calif. 95159

Carolina League—John Hopkins, 4241 United Street, Greensboro, N.C. 27407

Florida State League—George MacDonald, Jr., P.O. Box 414, Lakeland, Fla. 33802

Midwest League—George Spelius, P.O. Box 936, Beloit, Wis. 53511

New York-Pennsylvania League—Leo A. Pinckney, 168 E. Genesee St., Auburn, N.Y. 13021

Northwest League—Jack Cain, P.O. Box 30025, Portland, Ore. 97230

South Atlantic League—John H. Moss, P.O. Box 49, Kings Mountain, N.C. 28086

ROOKIE CLASSIFICATION

Appalachian League—Bill Halstead, 157 Carson Lane, Bristol, Va. 24201

Gulf Coast League—Thomas J. Saffell, 11 Sunset Drive, Suite 501, Sarasota, Fla. 33577

Pioneer League—Ralph C. Nelles, P.O. Box 1144, Billings, Mont. 59103

Major League Farm Systems for '88

AMERICAN LEAGUE

BALTIMORE (5): AAA—Rochester. AA—Charlotte. A—Hagerstown, Newark. Rookie—Bluefield.

BOSTON (5): AAA—Pawtucket. AA—New Britain, Conn. A—Elmira, Lynchburg, Winter Haven.

CALIFORNIA (5): AAA—Edmonton. AA—Midland. A—Bend, Quad Cities, Palm Springs.

CHICAGO (6): AAA—Vancouver. AA—Birmingham. A—South Bend, Tampa, Utica. Rookie—Sarasota.

CLEVELAND (5): AAA—Colorado Springs. AA—Williamsport. A—Kinston, Waterloo. Rookie—Burlington, N.C.

DETROIT (5): AAA—Toledo. AA—Glens Falls. A—Lakeland, Fayetteville. Rookie—Bristol, Va.

KANSAS CITY (7): AAA—Omaha. AA—Memphis. A—Appleton, Baseball City, Fla., Eugene, Peninsula. Rookie—Boardwalk.

MILWAUKEE (5): AAA—Denver. AA—El Paso. A—Beloit, Stockton. Rookie—Helena.

MINNESOTA (5): AAA—Portland. AA—Orlando. A—Kenosha, Visalia. Rookie—Elizabethton.

NEW YORK (6): AAA—Columbus, O. AA—Albany-Colonie, N.Y. A—Fort Lauderdale, Oneonta, Prince William. Rookie—Sarasota.

OAKLAND (5): AAA—Tacoma. AA—Huntsville. A—Medford, Modesto, Madison.

SEATTLE (5): AAA—Calgary. AA—Vermont. A—Wausau, San Bernardino, Bellingham.

TEXAS (6): AAA—Oklahoma City. AA—Tulsa. A—Port Charlotte, Gastonia. Rookie—Butte, Sarasota.

TORONTO (6): AAA—Syracuse. AA—Knoxville. A—Myrtle Beach, Dunedin, St. Catharines, Ont. Rookie—Medicine Hat.

NATIONAL LEAGUE

ATLANTA (8): AAA—Richmond. AA—Greenville. A—Burlington, Ia., Durham, Sumter. Rookie—Bradenton, Idaho Falls, Pulaski.

CHICAGO (7): AAA—Iowa. AA—Pittsfield. A—Charleston, W. Va., Geneva, Peoria, Winston-Salem. Rookie—Wytheville.

CINCINNATI (6): AAA—Nashville. AA—Chattanooga. A—Cedar Rapids, Greensboro. Rookie—Billings, Sarasota.

HOUSTON (6): AAA—Tucson. AA—Columbus, Ga. A—Asheville, Auburn, Osceola, Fla. Rookie—Sarasota.

LOS ANGELES (6): AAA—Albuquerque. AA—San Antonio. A—Bakersfield, Vero Beach. Rookie—Great Falls, Sarasota.

MONTREAL (6): AAA—Indianapolis. AA—Jacksonville. A—Jamestown, Rockford, West Palm Beach. Rookie—Bradenton.

NEW YORK (6): AAA—Tidewater. AA—Jackson. A—Columbia, S.C., Little Falls, St. Lucie. Rookie—Kingsport.

PHILADELPHIA (5): AAA—Old Orchard Beach, Me. AA—Reading. A—Batavia, Clearwater, Spartanburg.

PITTSBURGH (6): AAA—Buffalo. AA—Harrisburg. A—Salem, Va., Augusta, Watertown. Rookie—Bradenton.

ST. LOUIS (7): AAA—Louisville. AA—Arkansas. A—Hamilton, Ont., St. Petersburg, Savannah, Springfield. Rookie—Johnson City.

SAN DIEGO (5): AAA—Las Vegas. AA—Wichita. A—Charleston, S.C., Riverside, Spokane.

SAN FRANCISCO (6): AAA—Phoenix. AA—Shreveport. A—Clinton, Everett, San Jose. Rookie—Pocatello.

OFFICIAL MINOR LEAGUE AVERAGES

Including

Official Averages of All Class AAA, Class AA, Class A and Rookie Leagues

American Association

CLASS AAA

Leading Batter
DALLAS WILLIAMS
Indianapolis

League President
JOE RYAN

Leading Pitcher
PASCUAL PEREZ
Indianapolis

CHAMPIONSHIP WINNERS IN PREVIOUS YEARS

1902—Indianapolis .683	1939—Kansas City .695	1961—Indianapolis .573
1903—St. Paul .657	Louisville (4th)‡ .490	Louisville (2nd)‡ .533
1904—St. Paul .646	1940—Kansas City .625	1962—Indianapolis .605
1905—Columbus .658	Louisville (4th)‡ .500	Louisville (4th)‡ .486
1906—Columbus .615	1941—Columbus† .621	1963-1968—Did not operate.
1907—Columbus .584	1942—Kansas City .549	1969—Omaha .607
1908—Indianapolis .601	Columbus (3rd)‡ .532	1970—Omaha° .529
1909—Louisville .554	1943—Milwaukee .596	Denver .504
1910—Minneapolis .637	Columbus (3rd)‡ .532	1971—Indianapolis .604
1911—Minneapolis .600	1944—Milwaukee .667	Denver° .521
1912—Minneapolis .636	Louisville (3rd)‡ .574	1972—Wichita .621
1913—Milwaukee .599	1945—Milwaukee .604	Evansville° .593
1914—Milwaukee .590	Louisville (3rd)‡ .545	1973—Iowa .610
1915—Minneapolis .597	1946—Louisville† .601	Tulsa° .504
1916—Louisville .605	1947—Kansas City .608	1974—Indianapolis .578
1917—Indianapolis .588	Milwaukee (3rd)‡ .513	Tulsa° .567
1918—Kansas City .589	1948—Indianapolis .649	1975—Evansville° .566
1919—St. Paul .610	St. Paul (3rd)‡ .558	Denver .596
1920—St. Paul .701	1949—St. Paul .608	1976—Denver° .632
1921—Louisville .583	Indianapolis (2nd)‡ .604	Omaha .574
1922—St. Paul .641	1950—Minneapolis .584	1977—Omaha .563
1923—Kansas City .675	Columbus (3rd)‡ .549	Denver° .522
1924—St. Paul .578	1951—Milwaukee† .623	1978—Indianapolis .578
1925—Louisville .635	1952—Milwaukee .656	Omaha° .489
1926—Louisville .629	Kansas City (2nd)‡ .578	1979—Evansville° .574
1927—Toledo .601	1953—Toledo .584	Oklahoma City .533
1928—Indianapolis .593	Kansas City (2nd)‡ .571	1980—Denver .676
1929—Kansas City .665	1954—Indianapolis .625	Springfield° .551
1930—Louisville .608	Louisville (2nd)‡ .556	1981—Denver .581
1931—St. Paul .623	1955—Minneapolis† .597	Denver° .559
1932—Minneapolis .595	1956—Indianapolis† .597	1982—Indianapolis° .551
1933—Columbus° .604	1957—Wichita .604	Omaha .518
Minneapolis .562	Denver (2nd)‡ .584	1983—Louisville .578
1934—Minneapolis .570	1958—Charleston .589	Denver‡ .545
Columbus° .556	Minneapolis (3rd)‡ .536	1984—Denver .513
1935—Minneapolis .591	1959—Louisville§ .599	Louisville‡ .510
1936—Milwaukee† .584	Omaha§ .516	1985—Oklahoma City .556
1937—Columbus† .584	Minneapolis (2nd)‡ .586	Louisville° .521
1938—St. Paul .596	1960—Denver .571	1986—Indianapolis° .563
Kansas City (2nd)‡ .556	Louisville (2nd)‡ .556	Denver .535

°Won playoff (East vs. West). †Won championship and four-team playoff. ‡Won four-team playoff. §Respective Eastern and Western division winners.

COMPOSITE STANDING OF CLUBS AT CLOSE OF SEASON, SEPTEMBER 3

Club	Den.	Lou.	Ind.	O.C.	Buf.	Iowa	Oma.	Nash.	W.	L.	T.	Pct.	G.B.
Denver (Brewers)	...	9	9	12	11	10	16	12	79	61	0	.564	...
Louisville (Cardinals)	11	...	11	12	9	12	12	11	78	62	0	.557	1
Indianapolis (Expos)	11	9	...	12	10	9	12	11	74	64	0	.536	4
Oklahoma City (Rangers)	8	8	8	...	11	12	11	11	69	71	0	.493	10
Buffalo (Indians)	9	11	10	9	...	10	10	7	66	74	0	.471	13
Iowa (Cubs)	10	8	9	8	10	...	7	12	64	74	0	.464	14
Omaha (Royals)	4	8	8	9	10	13	...	12	64	76	0	.457	15
Nashville (Reds)	8	9	9	9	13	8	8	...	64	76	0	.457	15

Iowa club represented Des Moines, Ia.

Major league affiliations in parentheses.

Playoffs—Denver defeated Oklahoma City, three games to two; Indianapolis defeated Louisville, three games to two; and Indianapolis defeated Denver, four games to one, to win league championship.

Regular-Season Attendance—Buffalo, 495,760; Denver, 314,549; Indianapolis, 250,250; Iowa, 257,857; Louisville, 516,329; Nashville, 378,715; Oklahoma City, 277,722; Omaha, 251,995. Total—2,743,177. Playoffs—46,337.

Managers—Buffalo, Orlando Gomez (through May 19), Steve Swisher (May 20 through end of season); Denver, Terry Bevington; Indianapolis, Joe Sparks; Iowa, Larry Cox; Louisville, Mike Jorgensen; Nashville, Jack Lind; Oklahoma City, Toby Harrah; Omaha, John Wathan (through August 26), Frank Funk (August 27 through end of season).

All-Star Team—1B-Jack Daugherty, Indianapolis; 2B-Billy Bates, Denver; SS-Luis Rivera, Indianapolis; 3B-Steve Kiefer, Denver; OF-Dave Clark, Buffalo; Dallas Williams, Indianapolis; Lance Johnson, Louisville; DH-Joey Meyer, Denver; C-Tom Pagnozzi, Louisville; Damon Berryhill, Iowa; RHP-Pascual Perez, Indianapolis; LHP-Paul Cherry, Louisville; Most Valuable Player-Lance Johnson, Louisville; Rookie of the Year-Lance Johnson, Louisville; Manager of the Year-Joe Sparks, Indianapolis.

(Compiled by Howe News Bureau, Boston, Mass.)

CLUB BATTING

Club	Pct.	G.	AB.	R.	OR.	H.	TB.	2B.	3B.	HR.	RBI.	GW.	SH.	SF.	HP.	BB.	Int. BB.	SO.	SB.	CS.	LOB.
Denver	.299	140	4834	928	829	1445	2405	272	56	192	871	76	26	47	25	585	24	813	172	68	972
Indianapolis	.290	138	4736	704	654	1372	2102	251	49	127	653	71	31	48	30	436	32	734	127	55	971
Louisville	.289	140	4799	812	705	1389	2179	302	43	134	742	71	29	46	34	558	50	787	122	56	1041
Buffalo	.287	140	4837	786	856	1389	2236	248	43	171	737	63	17	37	41	534	29	769	101	63	1020
Iowa	.285	138	4635	736	795	1321	2118	255	58	142	687	58	40	49	18	463	28	760	155	88	919
Oklahoma City	.285	140	4747	761	810	1351	2093	265	51	125	711	66	22	52	30	602	29	866	115	73	1032
Omaha	.265	140	4664	643	648	1234	1863	230	39	107	588	54	26	34	28	444	22	804	137	53	930
Nashville	.257	140	4667	598	671	1198	1702	211	34	75	535	59	42	42	32	460	36	666	129	44	978

INDIVIDUAL BATTING

(Leading Qualifiers for Batting Championship—378 or More Plate Appearances)

*Bats lefthanded. †Switch-hitter.

Player and Club	Pct.	G.	AB.	R.	H.	TB.	2B.	3B.	HR.	RBI.	GW.	SH.	SF.	HP.	BB.	Int. BB.	SO.	SB.	CS.
Williams, Dallas, Indianapolis*	.357	114	398	65	142	212	22	9	10	50	8	3	2	1	29	8	27	12	6
Stanicek, Stephen, Denver	.352	117	474	90	167	292	40	5	25	106	7	0	4	1	36	2	82	5	4
Clark, David, Buffalo*	.340	108	420	83	143	261	22	3	30	80	5	1	5	3	52	7	62	14	11
Rowdon, Wade, Iowa	.337	132	483	91	163	268	35	8	18	113	12	0	9	1	59	6	67	8	6
Johnson, Lance, Louisville*	.333	116	477	89	159	217	21	11	5	50	7	3	2	0	49	7	45	42	16
Kiefer, Steven, Denver	.330	90	361	90	119	241	21	4	31	95	9	0	4	2	37	3	63	11	2
Meier, David, Oklahoma City	.320	129	447	72	143	241	36	4	18	86	7	1	9	2	57	2	67	2	3
Bates, William, Denver†	.316	130	506	117	160	204	25	5	3	62	5	4	8	0	73	1	52	51	13
Treadway, Jeffrey, Nashville*	.315	123	409	66	129	188	28	5	7	59	6	2	6	3	52	3	41	2	1
Paredes, Johnny, Indianapolis	.312	130	493	80	154	209	19	6	8	47	2	10	2	3	44	0	57	30	11
Daugherty, John, Indianapolis*	.312	117	420	65	131	193	35	3	7	50	7	2	1	4	42	5	54	11	0
Rivera, Luis, Indianapolis	.312	108	433	73	135	191	26	3	8	53	4	3	3	2	32	2	73	24	11

Departmental Leaders: G—Tabor, 137; AB—Tabor, 528; R—Bates, 117; H—Stanicek, 167; TB—Stanicek, 292; 2B—Stanicek, 40; 3B—Quinones, 12; HR—Komminsk, 32; RBI—Rowdon, 113; GWRBI—Tanner, 13; SH—Venable, 11; SF—Ortiz, 10; HP—E. Williams, 15; BB—D. Walker, 87; IBB—Laga, 12; SO—Komminsk, 127; SB—Thurman, 58; CS—Varsho, 17.

(All Players—Listed Alphabetically)

Player and Club	Pct.	G.	AB.	R.	H.	TB.	2B.	3B.	HR.	RBI.	GW.	SH.	SF.	HP.	BB.	Int. BB.	SO.	SB.	CS.
Abrego, Johnny, Iowa	.000	20	10	0	0	0	0	0	0	0	0	1	0	0	0	0	5	0	0
Adduci, James, Denver*	.288	16	59	9	17	26	3	0	2	15	1	0	3	0	7	0	13	2	0
Agostinelli, Salvatore, Louisville	.000	1	1	0	0	0	0	0	0	0	0	0	0	0	0	0	1	0	0
Alfaro, Jesus, Denver	.272	46	180	27	49	83	10	3	6	21	2	1	1	1	15	2	29	1	2
Alicea, Luis, Louisville*	.305	29	105	18	32	52	10	2	2	20	3	1	1	1	9	1	9	4	2
Allanson, Andrew, Buffalo	.272	76	276	21	75	95	8	0	4	39	5	1	2	1	9	0	36	2	4
Allen, Roderick, Buffalo	.302	126	474	85	143	236	28	7	17	92	10	0	6	4	51	3	80	0	5
Angelero, Jose, Omaha	.000	7	0	0	0	0	0	0	0	0	0	0	1	0	0	0	0	0	0
Ayer, Jonathan, Louisville	.281	88	281	39	79	126	24	1	7	49	5	1	2	1	41	1	42	1	0
Baker, Derrell, Indianapolis	.000	2	3	1	0	0	0	0	0	0	0	0	0	0	0	0	0	0	0
Baller, Jay, Iowa	.000	44	2	0	0	0	0	0	0	0	0	0	0	0	0	0	1	0	0
Bargar, Gregory, Louisville	.125	37	16	1	2	2	0	0	0	0	0	0	0	0	0	0	10	0	0
Barker, Leonard, Denver	.000	13	1	0	0	0	0	0	0	0	0	0	1	0	0	0	0	0	0
Barnes, William, 62 Lou-48 Den	.304	110	431	79	131	222	33	5	16	76	10	2	6	2	41	1	38	17	5
Barrett, Timothy, Indianapolis*	.100	46	10	0	1	2	1	0	0	2	0	1	0	0	0	0	6	0	0
Bates, William, Denver†	.316	130	506	117	160	204	25	5	3	62	5	4	8	0	73	1	52	51	13
Bathe, William, Iowa	.331	46	130	17	43	61	7	1	3	22	4	0	1	1	17	2	18	0	2
Bell, Jay, Buffalo	.260	110	362	71	94	168	15	4	17	60	5	3	3	2	70	1	84	6	5
Bernstine, Nehames, Iowa†	.288	98	326	47	94	147	16	5	9	40	3	3	1	1	15	0	50	8	9
Berry, Mark, Nashvill	.230	75	217	20	50	59	6	0	1	22	2	2	2	1	45	1	35	1	1
Berryhill, Damon, Iowa†	.287	121	429	54	123	201	22	1	18	67	2	1	8	0	32	3	58	5	4
Beuerlein, John, Denver	.246	26	61	12	15	23	2	0	2	9	1	0	0	2	6	0	16	0	0
Biancalana, Roland, Omaha†	.100	3	10	1	1	1	0	0	0	2	1	0	0	0	3	0	3	1	0
Bilardello, Dann, Omaha	.183	22	71	6	13	26	5	1	2	7	1	2	0	0	4	0	15	0	1
Boever, Daniel, Nashville	.153	19	59	5	9	14	2	0	1	5	0	0	2	1	6	1	14	0	0
Booker, Roderick, Louisville*	.348	34	135	25	47	55	3	1	1	21	1	1	1	0	20	0	24	5	7
Brown, Curtis, 20 Ind-14 Den	.500	34	2	0	1	1	0	0	0	0	0	0	0	0	0	0	0	0	0
Browning, Thomas, Nashville*	.500	5	2	0	1	1	0	0	0	0	0	0	0	0	0	0	0	0	0
Brumley, Michael, Iowa†	.254	92	319	44	81	129	20	5	6	42	5	3	2	1	35	1	61	27	10
Brunenkant, Barry, Buffalo	.000	5	7	0	0	0	0	0	0	0	0	0	0	0	0	0	1	0	0

Player and Club	Pct.	G.	AB.	R.	H.	TB.	2B.	3B.	HR.	RBI.	GW.	SH.	SF.	HP.	BB.	Int. BB.	SO.	SB.	CS.
Buonantony, Richard, Louisville	.750	16	4	1	3	3	0	0	0	0	0	4	0	0	0	0	0	0	0
Calderon, Jose, Louisville*	.333	27	3	1	1	3	0	1	0	1	0	0	0	0	1	0	2	0	0
Capel, Michael, Iowa	.500	53	2	0	1	1	0	0	0	0	0	1	0	0	0	0	0	0	0
Capra, Nick, Oklahoma City	.303	97	353	69	107	134	18	3	1	39	3	6	3	0	62	3	53	21	13
Cartwright, Alan, Denver*	.236	71	216	30	51	85	8	1	8	43	2	1	1	2	18	2	41	4	2
Castillo, Juan, Denver†	.500	1	2	2	1	1	0	0	0	1	0	0	1	0	1	0	0	0	0
Charlton, Norman, Nashville*	.000	18	10	1	0	0	0	0	0	1	0	1	0	0	2	0	6	1	0
Cherry, Paul, Louisville*	.167	46	12	3	2	4	0	1	0	1	0	1	0	0	0	0	6	0	0
Citari, Joseph, Omaha	.281	113	381	55	107	197	24	0	22	58	6	1	4	5	49	1	91	0	2
Clark, David, Buffalo*	.340	108	420	83	143	261	22	3	30	80	5	1	5	3	52	7	62	14	11
Clemo, Scott, Indianapolis*	.273	4	11	2	3	6	1	1	0	2	0	0	0	0	2	0	3	0	0
Colbert, Richard, Louisville	.227	57	163	28	37	62	8	1	5	26	2	1	1	2	24	1	52	1	1
Cole, Rodger, Indianapolis	.000	3	2	0	0	0	0	0	0	0	0	0	0	0	0	0	2	0	0
Collins, David, Nashville†	.200	13	40	8	8	14	6	0	0	9	0	0	1	0	7	1	5	1	0
Corey, Mark, Indianapolis	.294	31	85	12	25	40	6	0	3	15	5	0	1	1	6	0	17	0	0
Costello, John, Louisville	.000	6	2	0	0	0	0	0	0	0	0	1	0	0	0	0	1	0	0
Crabbe, Bruce, Iowa	.251	95	251	38	63	92	11	0	6	23	0	7	0	1	28	1	36	1	0
Crone, William, Buffalo	.259	28	81	11	21	24	1	1	0	2	0	0	0	1	8	0	13	3	3
Cutshall, William, Nashville*	.000	26	9	1	0	0	0	0	0	0	0	0	0	0	3	0	6	0	0
Danek, William, Iowa	.200	9	10	1	2	2	0	0	0	0	0	0	0	0	0	0	4	0	0
Daugherty, John, Indianapolis†	.312	117	420	65	131	193	35	3	7	50	7	2	4	1	42	5	54	11	0
Davidsmeier, Daniel, Denver	.286	2	7	0	2	3	1	0	0	1	0	0	0	0	0	0	2	1	0
Davidson, Jackie, Iowa†	.286	20	7	0	2	3	1	0	0	1	0	0	0	0	0	0	2	0	0
DeJesus, Ivan, Louisville	.276	40	145	26	40	54	11	0	1	14	3	1	1	0	8	1	26	0	1
DeLosSantos, Luis, Omaha	.293	135	518	53	152	199	29	6	2	67	6	3	5	2	29	0	80	2	4
Diaz, Edgar, Denver	.272	48	162	24	44	58	10	2	0	15	0	1	1	0	18	0	14	5	4
Dibble, Robert, Nashville*	.333	45	3	0	1	2	1	0	0	0	0	0	0	0	0	0	0	0	0
Dorsett, Brian, Buffalo	.256	26	86	9	22	41	5	1	4	14	1	0	1	0	3	1	21	0	0
Dougherty, Mark, Louisville	.264	80	258	45	68	119	8	2	13	43	0	2	2	2	31	1	56	8	6
Driessen, Daniel, Louisville*	.244	58	176	30	43	75	9	1	7	35	1	0	4	0	31	7	24	2	0
Dunston, Shawon, Iowa	.421	5	19	1	8	9	1	0	0	2	0	0	0	0	0	0	3	1	1
Earley, William, Louisville	.000	52	2	0	0	0	0	0	0	0	0	0	0	0	0	0	0	0	0
Esasky, Nicholas, Nashville	.442	13	52	13	23	44	6	0	5	18	0	0	1	0	5	0	11	0	0
Espy, Cecil, Oklahoma City†	.302	118	443	76	134	167	18	6	1	37	2	4	3	1	31	2	66	46	14
Faulk, Kelly, Indianapolis	.000	32	5	0	0	0	0	0	0	0	0	0	0	0	0	0	3	0	0
Felder, Michael, Denver†	.363	27	113	26	41	57	6	2	2	20	4	1	1	1	14	1	6	17	1
Ficklin, Winston, Buffalo	.258	27	89	14	23	27	4	0	0	5	1	0	0	1	4	0	16	2	4
Finley, Brian, Nashville*	.222	10	27	2	6	9	1	1	0	1	0	0	0	1	9	0	4	1	2
Fischer, Jeffrey, Indianapolis	.250	24	16	1	4	6	2	0	0	3	0	0	0	0	0	0	4	0	0
Frobel, Douglas, Buffalo*	.301	58	209	34	63	122	12	1	15	42	0	0	1	2	20	0	36	3	1
Gallagher, David, Buffalo	.261	12	46	10	12	16	4	0	0	6	1	1	2	0	11	0	3	1	1
Garcia, Leonardo, Nashville*	.284	116	437	64	124	161	12	8	3	40	2	5	1	1	38	4	34	41	11
Gardner, Mark, Indianapolis	.000	9	2	0	0	0	0	0	0	0	0	0	0	0	0	0	0	0	0
Goldthorn, Burk, Oklahoma City*	.259	72	220	26	57	71	5	0	3	25	3	1	2	1	32	1	35	0	2
Gonzalez, Orlando, Nashville	.226	90	279	27	63	78	12	0	1	22	3	2	2	1	7	2	26	0	1
Grapenthin, Richard, Louisville	.400	55	5	1	2	2	0	0	0	1	0	0	0	0	1	0	1	0	0
Gray, Jeffrey, Nashville	.250	53	4	0	1	1	0	0	0	0	0	0	0	0	1	0	3	0	0
Green, David, Louisville	.356	50	180	38	64	99	21	1	4	27	4	0	0	3	15	0	29	3	1
Hall, Andrew, Iowa*	.500	35	2	1	1	1	0	0	0	0	0	0	0	0	0	0	1	0	0
Hamilton, Carlton, Iowa*	.000	29	13	3	0	0	0	0	0	0	0	1	0	0	1	0	4	0	0
Harris, Leonard, Nashville*	.248	120	403	45	100	124	12	3	2	31	3	2	2	5	27	4	43	30	12
Harrison, Ronald, Denver*	.167	4	6	1	1	1	0	0	0	0	0	0	0	0	0	0	0	0	0
Hayes, William, Iowa	.333	14	33	7	11	14	3	0	0	5	1	1	0	1	2	0	5	1	0
Henika, Ronald, Nashville*	.265	117	378	39	100	131	15	2	4	47	5	2	2	1	26	4	34	1	1
Heredia, Ubaldo, Indianapolis	.111	20	9	0	1	1	0	0	0	0	0	2	0	0	2	0	2	0	0
Hill, Orsino, Nashville*	.250	106	316	38	79	133	21	3	9	38	5	0	2	2	25	2	70	0	2
Holman, Brian, Indianapolis	.500	6	2	0	1	1	0	0	0	0	0	0	0	0	0	0	0	0	0
Jackson, Darrin, Iowa	.274	132	474	81	130	241	32	5	23	81	5	5	3	2	26	3	110	13	10
Jeffcoat, Michael, Oklahoma City*	.000	27	1	0	0	0	0	0	0	0	0	0	0	0	0	0	1	0	0
Johnson, Lance, Louisville*	.333	116	477	89	159	217	21	11	5	50	7	3	2	0	49	7	45	42	16
Johnson, Rowdin, Omaha	.254	134	503	58	128	162	14	7	2	53	3	6	2	0	39	3	54	23	12
Jones, Alfornia, Denver	.000	50	1	0	0	0	0	0	0	0	0	0	0	0	1	0	1	0	0
Jones, Ross, Omaha	.315	52	181	25	57	75	10	1	2	23	2	0	1	1	17	0	31	3	2
Jones, Timothy, Louisville*	.283	73	276	48	78	110	14	3	4	43	4	2	0	0	29	1	27	11	3
Jurak, Edward, Oklahoma City	.309	31	94	9	29	40	0	1	3	8	1	1	0	0	17	1	11	1	0
Kemp, Hubert, Nashville*	.238	30	21	3	5	7	2	0	0	7	1	1	0	0	2	0	3	0	0
Kemp, Steven, Oklahoma City*	.266	121	421	73	112	212	28	6	20	84	12	0	5	2	71	5	112	2	3
Kiefer, Steven, Denver	.330	90	361	90	119	241	21	4	31	95	9	0	4	2	37	3	63	11	2
Klipstein, David, Denver	.277	117	382	72	106	147	11	3	8	60	6	2	4	6	46	0	42	12	7
Knicely, Alan, Oklahoma City	.279	84	258	39	72	117	19	1	8	40	2	0	3	3	32	2	46	2	4
Komminsk, Brad, Denver	.298	135	494	110	147	282	31	4	32	95	11	0	5	4	66	2	127	18	9
Konderla, Michael, 37 Nash-11 Den	.000	48	7	0	0	0	0	0	0	0	0	0	0	0	0	0	3	0	0
Kopf, David, Iowa	.500	8	4	1	2	2	0	0	0	0	0	0	0	0	0	0	0	0	0
Kunkel, Jeffrey, Oklahoma City	.254	58	193	31	49	91	9	3	9	34	1	0	1	5	20	0	58	2	4
Laga, Michael, Louisville*	.304	116	418	80	127	253	35	2	29	91	7	0	5	4	48	12	93	1	1
Lancaster, Lester, Iowa	.200	15	5	0	1	1	0	0	0	0	0	0	0	0	0	0	2	0	0
Landrum, William, Nashville	.000	19	4	0	0	0	0	0	0	0	0	0	0	0	0	0	1	0	0
Landrum, Terry, Louisville	.188	5	16	2	3	4	1	0	0	1	0	0	0	1	1	0	4	1	0
LaPoint, David, Louisville*	1.000	14	1	0	1	1	0	0	0	0	0	0	0	0	0	0	0	0	0
Layton, Thomas, Iowa*	.000	21	2	0	0	0	0	0	0	0	0	2	0	0	0	0	2	0	0
Lea, Charles, Indianapolis	.000	5	2	0	0	0	0	0	0	0	0	0	0	0	0	0	1	0	0
Leonette, Mark, Iowa	.000	24	9	0	0	0	0	0	0	0	0	1	0	0	0	0	4	0	0
Lindeman, James, Louisville	.308	20	78	11	24	41	3	1	4	10	2	0	0	0	8	1	15	0	0
Lollar, Timothy, Louisville*	.083	13	12	1	1	2	1	0	0	0	0	0	0	0	1	0	3	0	0
Longenecker, Jere, Omaha	.167	5	12	1	2	2	0	0	0	0	0	0	0	0	0	0	2	0	0
Lopez, Robert, Nashville*	.000	7	5	0	0	0	0	0	0	0	0	0	0	0	0	0	1	0	0
Lovell, Donald, Buffalo*	.292	133	511	77	149	252	36	5	19	69	4	0	3	3	37	4	41	0	1
Lyons, William, Louisville	.315	66	216	40	68	96	10	3	4	23	1	1	0	5	29	1	39	6	3
Macfarlane, Michael, Omaha	.262	87	302	53	79	145	25	1	13	50	2	0	0	6	22	1	50	0	1
Madison, Scott, Omaha†	.271	125	454	68	123	224	31	2	22	83	11	1	5	2	60	7	50	3	2
Mahler, Michael, Louisville†	.000	14	3	0	0	0	0	0	0	0	0	0	0	0	0	0	2	0	0
Manfre, Michael, Nashville	.194	97	237	18	46	70	12	0	4	23	1	3	0	1	19	2	59	2	0

Player and Club	Pct.	G.	AB.	R.	H.	TB.	2B.	3B.	HR.	RBI.	GW.	SH.	SF.	HP.	BB.	Int. BB.	SO.	SB.	CS.
Martin, John, Louisville	.167	37	6	0	1	1	0	0	0	2	0	0	0	0	0	0	5	0	0
Martinez, Dennis, Indianapolis	.250	7	4	0	1	1	0	0	0	0	0	0	0	0	0	0	1	0	0
Martinez, Reynaldo, Omaha*	.215	35	121	14	26	44	10	1	2	14	1	0	0	0	11	0	43	0	0
Mason, Michael, Iowa*	.000	11	7	0	0	0	0	0	0	0	0	1	0	0	3	0	4	0	0
McClendon, Lloyd, Nashville	.286	26	84	11	24	39	6	0	3	14	0	0	2	2	17	0	15	1	1
McGrath, Charles, Louisville	.000	1	3	0	0	0	0	0	0	0	0	1	0	0	0	0	2	0	0
McGriff, Terence, Nashville	.272	67	228	36	62	109	11	3	10	33	3	0	5	0	25	5	47	0	0
Meier, David, Oklahoma City	.320	129	447	72	143	241	36	4	18	86	7	1	9	2	57	2	67	2	3
Meyer, Joe, Denver	.311	79	296	58	92	202	23	0	29	92	6	0	1	3	34	2	88	0	1
Montgomery, Jeff, Nashville	.133	24	15	1	2	2	0	0	0	0	0	2	0	0	0	0	5	0	0
Moore, William, Indianapolis	.249	102	321	55	80	146	24	3	12	60	9	0	6	5	63	3	68	2	3
Morris, John, Louisville*	.340	14	47	13	16	34	5	2	3	12	2	0	1	0	11	1	0	2	3
Murphy, John, Louisville	.243	76	239	43	58	83.	10	0	5	24	4	2	2	6	29	0	39	20	1
Nago, Garrett, Denver	.286	4	14	3	4	6	2	0	0	2	0	0	0	0	2	0	2	0	0
Nelson, James, Omaha	.222	6	18	3	4	5	1	0	0	2	0	0	0	0	7	0	4	0	0
Nelson, Ricky, Buffalo*	.234	49	167	18	39	58	9	2	2	17	2	1	1	0	8	2	23	5	1
Nixon, Otis, Buffalo†	.285	59	249	51	71	98	13	4	2	23	1	0	0	0	34	0	30	36	7
Noboa, Milciades, Buffalo	.315	43	149	26	47	57	6	2	0	14	0	1	1	0	18	0	16	2	2
Noce, Paul, Iowa	.269	47	167	30	45	77	5	3	7	25	2	2	2	0	19	1	39	13	5
Norman, Nelson, Indianapolis†	.292	76	219	30	64	89	11	1	4	30	3	1	6	0	23	3	14	1	0
O'Brien, Charles, Denver	.282	80	266	37	75	113	12	1	8	35	3	6	2	2	42	2	33	5	5
O'Malley, Thomas, Oklahoma City*	.311	109	431	83	134	201	27	2	12	70	11	0	3	4	69	6	62	4	6
O'Neal, Randall, Louisville	.286	7	7	1	2	2	0	0	0	0	0	0	0	0	1	0	1	0	1
O'Neill, Paul, Nashville*	.297	11	37	12	11	20	0	0	3	6	0	0	1	0	5	0	5	1	0
Ortiz, Javier, Oklahoma City	.276	119	381	58	105	187	23	7	15	69	7	1	10	4	58	2	99	5	2
Owen, Dave, 72 O.C.-21 Oma.†	.228	93	276	36	63	91	8	7	2	31	3	1	2	1	49	1	50	4	5
Pacillo, Patrick, Nashville	.100	16	10	0	1	1	0	0	0	1	0	0	0	1	1	0	3	0	0
Paciorek, James, Denver	.326	47	175	29	57	92	7	5	6	38	3	1	1	0	28	1	25	2	2
Pagnozzi, Thomas, Louisville	.313	84	320	53	100	166	20	2	14	71	10	0	6	3	30	0	50	0	0
Palmeiro, Rafael, Iowa*	.299	57	214	36	64	117	14	3	11	41	3	1	4	3	22	1	22	4	3
Paredes, Johnny, Indianapolis	.312	130	493	80	154	209	19	6	8	47	2	10	2	3	44	0	57	30	11
Parsons, Casey, Buffalo*	.288	82	278	40	80	135	15	2	12	51	4	0	3	3	36	4	38	2	5
Pecota, William, Omaha	.310	35	126	31	39	55	8	1	2	16	3	1	0	2	15	0	15	7	1
Pena, Antonio, Louisville	.375	2	8	0	3	3	0	0	0	0	0	0	0	0	0	0	2	0	0
Perez, Pascual, Indianapolis	.190	20	21	3	4	4	0	0	0	0	0	0	1	0	1	0	9	0	0
Peters, Steven, Louisville*	.000	11	1	0	0	0	0	0	0	0	0	0	0	0	0	0	1	0	0
Pevey, Marty, Louisville*	.237	16	38	5	9	14	2	0	1	5	0	0	1	0	0	0	10	0	0
Pico, Jeffrey, Iowa	.111	16	9	0	1	1	0	0	0	1	0	1	0	1	0	0	1	0	0
Potestio, Douglas, Iowa	.000	14	3	0	0	0	0	0	0	0	0	0	0	0	0	0	1	0	0
Powell, Alonzo, Indianapolis	.299	90	331	64	99	190	14	10	19	74	7	3	3	1	32	1	68	12	8
Pryor, Buddy, Nashville	.201	69	194	22	39	55	5	1	3	15	1	1	1	1	27	1	65	0	0
Pujols, Luis, Indianapolis	.310	9	29	4	9	12	3	0	0	2	0	0	0	0	1	0	1	0	0
Pyznarski, Timothy, Denver	.284	39	141	31	40	75	9	4	6	28	2	0	1	0	28	0	42	4	5
Quinones, Luis, Iowa†	.317	77	287	44	91	162	14	12	11	62	6	0	4	1	16	1	30	2	3
Ramos, Roberto, Omaha	.169	27	77	1	13	14	1	0	0	4	0	0	0	0	5	0	11	3	1
Reboulet, James, Louisville	.288	17	59	13	17	20	3	0	0	5	0	0	0	0	7	1	10	7	2
Reed, Jeffrey, Indianapolis*	.176	5	17	0	3	3	0	0	0	0	0	0	1	0	1	0	2	0	0
Renfroe, Cohen, Iowa	.000	8	0	0	0	0	0	0	0	0	0	1	0	0	0	0	0	0	0
Reuss, Jerry, Nashville*	.000	2	1	0	0	0	0	0	0	0	0	0	0	0	0	0	0	0	0
Reynolds, Jeffrey, Indianapolis	.245	116	420	61	103	187	19	1	21	76	10	1	5	5	29	1	95	4	2
Rivera, Luis, Indianapolis	.312	108	433	73	135	191	26	3	8	53	4	3	3	2	32	2	73	24	11
Robidoux, William, Denver*	.284	30	116	27	33	57	9	3	3	15	3	0	0	0	18	1	15	0	0
Robinson, Brian, Nashville	.313	4	16	1	5	5	0	0	0	0	0	0	0	0	2	0	4	0	0
Robinson, Michael, Louisville	.000	7	3	1	0	0	0	0	0	0	0	0	0	0	1	0	1	0	0
Rodriguez, Victor, Louisville	.294	116	422	44	124	170	33	2	3	54	3	0	8	3	15	2	42	0	0
Romano, Thomas, Indianapolis	.306	96	317	37	97	137	12	5	6	37	3	1	2	2	17	0	29	15	6
Rowdon, Wade, Iowa	.337	132	483	91	163	268	35	8	18	113	12	0	9	1	59	6	67	8	6
Sabo, Christopher, Nashville	.292	91	315	56	92	138	19	3	7	51	10	1	6	1	37	4	25	23	4
Scherrer, William, Nashville*	.000	33	1	0	0	0	0	0	0	0	0	0	0	0	0	0	0	0	0
Schulz, Jeffrey, Omaha*	.256	99	316	25	81	119	12	7	4	36	1	1	2	2	24	1	56	1	0
Scott, Donald, Denver†	.224	65	196	21	44	69	8	4	3	33	2	0	4	0	28	2	26	0	1
See, Laurence, Oklahoma City	.271	69	258	35	70	106	16	1	6	45	3	1	2	0	31	1	40	0	3
Shepherd, Ronald, Indianapolis	.291	102	358	45	104	167	22	1	13	53	3	0	3	2	21	1	64	13	4
Shines, Raymond, Indianapolis†	.279	92	305	52	85	129	18	4	6	51	4	0	7	4	52	6	45	1	2
Shirley, Steven, Omaha*	.000	44	1	0	0	0	0	0	0	0	0	0	0	0	0	0	1	0	0
Smajstrla, Craig, Buffalo	.282	111	432	63	122	170	19	4	7	51	7	6	2	1	40	1	41	14	7
Smith, Gregory, Oklahoma City*	.219	62	187	21	41	64	12	1	3	19	3	1	3	2	14	1	31	1	0
Smith, Lonnie, Omaha	.329	40	149	36	49	81	9	1	7	33	2	0	4	1	18	0	22	8	6
Smith, Michael, Indianapolis	.250	45	4	0	1	1	0	0	0	0	0	0	0	0	0	0	1	0	0
Smith, Keith, Denver†	.283	117	413	70	117	172	20	7	7	43	2	7	3	0	49	3	73	24	7
Snider, Van, Omaha*	.205	70	244	26	50	88	9	1	9	27	2	0	1	2	13	4	69	2	1
Soff, Raymond, Louisville	.000	23	4	0	0	0	0	0	0	0	0	0	0	0	0	0	1	0	0
Sorensen, Lary, Indianapolis	.250	21	4	0	1	1	0	0	0	0	0	0	0	0	0	0	1	0	0
Soto, Mario, Nashville	.000	2	2	0	0	0	0	0	0	0	0	0	0	0	0	0	0	0	0
Stanicek, Stephen, Denver	.352	117	474	90	167	292	40	5	25	106	7	0	4	1	36	2	82	5	4
Stanley, Michael, Oklahoma City	.335	46	182	43	61	114	8	3	13	54	2	2	3	29	1	36	2	0	
Stefero, John, Indianapolis*	.263	60	167	25	44	73	6	1	7	19	2	0	1	1	19	0	30	0	1
Stephens, Carl, Nashville	.133	9	30	1	4	4	0	0	0	2	1	0	1	0	5	1	9	0	1
Stephenson, Phillip, Iowa*	.305	105	298	53	91	149	24	2	10	56	5	2	7	1	62	2	56	4	6
Strode, Lester, Louisville*	.000	5	1	0	0	0	0	0	0	0	0	0	0	0	0	0	1	0	0
Surhoff, Richard, Iowa	.000	14	0	0	0	0	0	0	0	0	0	0	0	0	0	0	0	0	0
Syverson, Dain, Buffalo	.254	21	63	10	16	18	2	0	0	9	3	0	2	0	14	0	13	1	1
Tabor, Gregory, Oklahoma City	.303	137	528	78	160	231	35	6	8	66	7	4	3	2	31	1	82	22	14
Tanner, Edwin, Nashville†	.252	103	321	41	81	121	14	1	8	49	13	4	4	4	22	0	20	3	2
Taylor, Dwight, Omaha*	.213	86	211	35	45	55	5	1	1	14	2	4	1	0	17	1	35	23	11
Tejada, Wilfredo, Indianapolis	.247	91	299	28	74	95	10	1	3	29	4	0	3	2	18	2	49	2	2
Terry, Scott, Nashville	.227	27	22	3	5	9	1	0	1	2	0	2	0	0	0	0	7	0	0
Thurman, Gary, Omaha	.293	115	450	88	132	188	14	9	8	39	5	5	3	3	48	0	84	58	7
Tibbs, Jay, Indianapolis	.444	13	9	1	4	4	0	0	0	0	0	5	0	0	0	0	0	0	0
Tingley, Ronald, Buffalo	.269	57	167	27	45	78	8	5	5	30	3	0	1	4	25	1	42	1	2
Tomlin, David, Indianapolis*	.000	25	3	0	0	0	0	0	0	0	0	0	0	0	0	0	0	0	0
Treadway, Jeffrey, Nashville*	.315	123	409	66	129	188	28	5	7	59	6	2	6	3	52	3	41	2	1

Player and Club	Pct.	G.	AB.	R.	H.	TB.	2B.	3B.	HR.	RBI.	GW.	SH.	SF.	HP.	BB.	Int. BB.	SO.	SB.	CS.
Tudor, John, Louisville*	.000	2	3	0	0	0	0	0	0	0	0	0	0	0	0	0	2	0	0
Valdez, Julio, Iowa†	.276	63	192	24	53	69	10	0	2	14	1	0	0	11	2	28	3	2	
Valdez, Sergio, Indianapolis	.067	27	15	0	1	1	0	0	0	0	0	1	0	0	0	6	0	0	
Varsho, Gary, Iowa*	.302	132	504	87	152	220	23	9	9	48	6	3	4	3	41	2	65	37	17
Venable, William, Nashville*	.270	116	400	57	108	138	16	4	2	28	4	11	3	5	39	2	56	20	6
Walker, Bernard, Nashville*	.400	4	15	3	6	7	1	0	0	2	0	0	0	0	0	0	2	1	0
Walker, Cleotha, Iowa†	.244	90	315	64	77	120	13	3	8	31	3	0	3	0	65	3	52	28	9
Walker, Duane, Louisville*	.293	102	311	63	91	176	29	4	16	69	8	1	3	2	87	10	77	1	3
Washington, Randy, Buffalo	.290	100	283	46	82	139	12	0	15	48	5	3	2	1	39	0	56	3	1
Werner, Donald, Oklahoma City	.204	54	142	19	29	44	6	0	3	13	0	1	1	1	13	0	30	1	0
Williams, Dallas, Indianapolis*	.357	114	398	65	142	212	22	9	10	50	8	3	2	1	29	8	27	12	6
Williams, Edward, Buffalo	.291	131	488	90	142	241	29	2	22	85	6	0	2	15	55	5	117	6	2
Willis, Carl, Nashville*	.000	53	6	0	0	0	0	0	0	0	0	0	0	0	0	0	4	0	0
Wilson, Craig, Louisville	.214	21	70	10	15	20	2	0	1	8	0	2	1	0	3	0	5	0	2
Winters, Matthew, Omaha*	.280	50	182	30	51	86	8	0	9	34	2	0	4	1	17	2	36	1	0
Wohlford, James, Nashville	.210	33	81	5	17	22	2	0	1	11	0	1	0	0	11	0	9	0	0
Woods, Tony, Iowa	.206	40	102	11	21	29	3	1	1	13	0	2	2	0	8	0	27	0	1
Wotus, Ronald, Omaha	.256	91	262	27	67	79	12	0	0	16	3	2	2	0	34	2	40	2	2
Wright, Richard, Denver*	.000	15	3	0	0	0	0	0	0	0	0	0	0	0	0	0	0	0	0
Zwolensky, Mitchell, Iowa	.143	46	7	1	1	2	1	0	0	0	0	0	0	0	0	0	0	0	0

The following pitchers, listed alphabetically by club, with games in parentheses, had no plate appearances, primarily through use of designated hitters:

BUFFALO—Alba, Gibson (9); Armstrong, Michael (13); Camacho, Ernie (23); Easterly, James (2); Farrell, John (25); Huismann, Mark (13); Jones, Douglas (23); Kaiser, Jeffrey (22); Murphy, Kent (13); Murphy, Michael (37); Oelkers, Bryan (28); Pippin, Craig (19); Ritter, Reggie (16); Roberts, Scott (28); Roman, Jose (3); Schulze, Donald (5); Skalski, Joe (5); Stewart, Samuel (6); Thomas, Roy (10); Waddell, Thomas (28); Wills, Frank (36); Yett, Richard (7).

DENVER—Alba, Gibson (18); Aldrich, Jay (20); August, Donald (28); Birkbeck, Michael (1); Burris, Ray (1); Ciardi, Mark (20); Clay, David (6); Clutterbuck, Bryan (7); Gonzalez, Arturo (4); Jackson, Roy Lee (4); Johnson, John Henry (26); Kendrick, Peter (4); Knudson, Mark (14); Madrid, Alexander (27); Mirabella, Paul (25); Mooneyham, William (12); Scarpetta, Daniel (20); Schuler, David (3); Stapleton, David (44).

INDIANAPOLIS—Jones, Michael (15); Lewis, Richie (2); Parrett, Jeffrey (20); St. Claire, Randy (18).

IOWA—Davis, Ronald (1); Duquette, Bryan (25); Kraemer, Joseph (5); Maddux, Gregory (4); McKay, Alan (4); Noles, Dickie (3); Parmenter, Gary (2); Slowik, Thaddeus (5).

LOUISVILLE—Boever, Joseph (43); Conroy, Timothy (4); Dayley, Kenneth (1); Magrane, Joseph (3); Mathews, Gregory (3); Tunnell, Lee (6).

OKLAHOMA CITY—Anderson, Scott (49); Brown, Kevin (5); Cook, Glen (31); Creel, Keith (21); Henry, Dwayne (30); Howe, Steven (7); Kilgus, Paul (21); Killingsworth, Kirk (28); Knapp, Richard (2); Loynd, Michael (5); McWilliams, Larry (7); Meridith, Ronald (7); Mielke, Gary (28); Pastore, Frank (4); Rodgers, Timothy (33); Rucker, David (53); Russell, Jeffrey (4); Taylor, William (28); Witt, Robert (1); Zaske, Jeffrey (24).

OMAHA—Anderson, Richard (15); Aquino, Luis (14); Botelho, Derek (18); Davis, John (43); Farr, Steven (8); Gleaton, Jerry Don (6); Gumpert, David (35); Hargesheimer, Alan (9); Mullen, Thomas (31); Pippin, Craig (39); Rajsich, David (31); Sanchez, Israel (23); Stoddard, Robert (12); Swaggerty, William (27); Welchel, Donald (19).

GRAND SLAM HOME RUNS—Cartwright, D. Jackson, Kiefer, 2 each; Alicea, Bell, Clark, Dougherty, Felder, Goldthorn, Klipstein, Knicely, Laga, Macfarlane, Madison, Manfre, Meier, Meyer, Ortiz, Powell, Pryor, Reynolds, Rowdon, Shepherd, Snider, Stanicek, Tejada, Thurman, C. Walker, Winters, 1 each.

AWARDED FIRST BASE ON CATCHER'S INTERFERENCE—W. Barnes 3 (Berryhill, Tejada, Werner); Berryhill 2 (Stefero, Tejada); Daugherty (McGriff); Garcia (Colbert); R. Jones (Tejada); Snider (Tejada); Varsho (Berry).

CLUB FIELDING

Club	Pct.	G.	PO.	A.	E.	DP.	PB.	Club	Pct.	G.	PO.	A.	E.	DP.	PB.
Indianapolis	.975	138	3624	1434	130	141	14	Nashville	.972	140	3657	1432	145	131	21
Denver	.974	140	3640	1556	136	155	18	Omaha	.972	140	3612	1572	149	145	13
Oklahoma City	.974	140	3653	1556	138	147	13	Buffalo	.970	140	3650	1448	156	128	30
Louisville	.974	140	3639	1529	138	135	16	Iowa	.970	138	3531	1510	154	128	15

Triple Plays—Oklahoma City 2.

INDIVIDUAL FIELDING

*Throws lefthanded.

FIRST BASEMEN

Player and Club	Pct.	G.	PO.	A.	E.	DP.	Player and Club	Pct.	G.	PO.	A.	E.	DP.
Adduci, Denver*	1.000	1	6	2	0	1	Paciorek, Denver	.984	13	108	15	2	8
Ayer, Louisville	.994	19	160	9	1	13	Palmeiro, Iowa*	1.000	9	62	9	0	7
Barnes, 1 Lou-27 Denver	.989	28	250	23	3	37	Parsons, Buffalo	1.000	1	0	1	0	0
Bathe, Iowa	.975	6	37	2	1	3	Powell, Indianapolis	1.000	2	8	0	0	2
Berry, Nashville	.985	33	189	13	3	18	Pryor, Nashville	1.000	1	1	0	0	0
Berryhill, Iowa	1.000	1	4	1	0	0	Pyznarski, Denver	.988	17	156	15	2	14
Beuerlein, Denver	1.000	1	3	0	0	0	Robidoux, Denver	.980	22	184	14	4	16
Brunenkant, Buffalo	1.000	1	3	0	0	1	Rodriguez, Louisville	1.000	2	7	2	0	0
Citari, Omaha	.994	77	671	43	4	65	Rowdon, Iowa	.935	3	27	2	2	3
Crabbe, Iowa	1.000	6	39	6	0	6	Schulz, Omaha	.974	6	36	1	1	3
Daugherty, Indianapolis*	.993	92	749	76	6	83	Scott, Denver	1.000	1	2	0	0	0
DeLosSantos, Omaha	.977	42	356	20	9	35	See, Oklahoma City	.989	58	518	35	6	58
Driessen, Louisville	.989	22	164	9	2	17	Shines, Indianapolis	.995	43	330	33	2	37
Esasky, Nashville	1.000	12	102	7	0	11	G. Smith, Oklahoma City	.993	48	379	35	3	36
Frobel, Buffalo	.938	3	14	1	1	1	K. Smith, Denver	1.000	5	43	2	0	4
Henika, Nashville	.9889	103	825	62	10	79	Stanicek, Denver	.983	14	107	9	2	11
Knicely, Oklahoma City	.984	43	352	18	6	34	Stanley, Oklahoma City	1.000	4	38	4	0	3
Laga, Louisville*	.9890	102	922	67	11	98	Stephenson, Iowa*	.988	90	722	71	10	63
LOVELL, Buffalo*	.9893	133	1103	102	13	112	Syverson, Buffalo	1.000	4	21	2	0	2
Lyons, Louisville	1.000	6	11	1	0	2	Tanner, Nashville	.969	4	29	2	1	1
Madison, Omaha	.996	28	216	27	1	27	Tingley, Buffalo	1.000	5	47	3	0	3
Manfre, Nashville	.875	2	7	0	1	0	Valdez, Iowa	1.000	19	149	8	0	15
McClendon, Nashville	1.000	9	69	3	0	14	Woods, Iowa	.988	24	159	10	2	17
Meyer, Denver	.981	43	392	23	8	49	Wotus, Omaha	1.000	1	2	2	0	1
Moore, Indianapolis*	1.000	13	98	8	0	10							

Triple Plays—Knicely, See.

SECOND BASEMEN

Player and Club	Pct.	G.	PO.	A.	E.	DP.
Alfaro, Denver	1.000	4	9	9	0	4
Alicea, Louisville	.974	28	69	81	4	25
Bates, Denver	.974	126	254	393	17	93
Bell, Buffalo	1.000	1	3	3	0	1
Biancalana, Omaha	1.000	1	1	2	0	0
Booker, Louisville	.972	16	26	43	2	7
Brumley, Iowa	1.000	6	11	11	0	3
Crabbe, Iowa	.962	59	96	129	9	33
Crone, Buffalo	1.000	2	2	3	0	1
Davidsmeier, Denver	1.000	1	1	5	0	0
Dougherty, Louisville	.975	73	149	197	9	46
Felder, Denver	.000	1	0	0	1	0
Gonzalez, Nashville	1.000	20	43	46	0	12
Johnson, Omaha	.976	124	266	393	16	93
Kunkel, Oklahoma City	.980	10	13	37	1	3
Longenecker, Omaha	1.000	2	3	2	0	1
Lyons, Louisville	.984	12	21	42	1	5
Madison, Omaha	1.000	3	1	0	0	0
Noboa, Buffalo	.947	37	62	98	9	20
Noce, Iowa	.980	32	60	85	3	26
Norman, Indianapolis	.983	15	24	35	1	8
Owen, Oklahoma City	1.000	1	3	1	0	1
Paredes, Indianapolis	.978	128	234	387	14	89
Pecota, Omaha	1.000	2	3	4	0	0
Quinones, Iowa	.927	24	47	42	7	7
Reboulet, Louisville	1.000	1	3	1	0	1
Robinson, Nashville	1.000	2	3	7	0	1
Rodriguez, Louisville	1.000	7	17	17	0	6
Smajstrla, Buffalo	.970	108	195	295	15	74
Smith, Denver	1.000	12	22	32	0	7
Tabor, Oklahoma City	.972	132	275	387	19	94
Tanner, Nashville	.964	12	21	33	2	9
TREADWAY, Nashville	.980	116	236	362	12	72
Valdez, Iowa	.979	13	19	27	1	6
Walker, Iowa	.980	33	67	77	3	15
Wilson, Louisville	.961	10	17	32	2	4
Wotus, Omaha	.973	14	24	49	2	10

Triple Play—Tabor.

THIRD BASEMEN

Player and Club	Pct.	G.	PO.	A.	E.	DP.
Alfaro, Denver	.942	38	32	66	6	12
Barnes, 1 Lou-48 Denver	.912	49	26	99	12	11
Berry, Nashville	1.000	2	0	3	0	0
Booker, Louisville	.944	7	3	14	1	1
Clemo, Indianapolis	1.000	3	3	6	0	1
Crabbe, Iowa	1.000	10	7	13	0	2
Crone, Buffalo	1.000	1	0	1	0	0
Davidsmeier, Denver	.500	1	0	2	2	0
DeLosSantos, Omaha	.887	57	45	96	18	11
Dougherty, Louisville	1.000	1	1	0	0	0
Gonzalez, Nashville	.958	30	15	53	3	6
Harris, Nashville	.887	22	16	31	6	4
Jones, Omaha	1.000	1	0	2	0	0
Jurak, Oklahoma City	.927	17	13	25	3	3
Kiefer, Denver	.936	77	60	161	15	11
Kunkel, Oklahoma City	1.000	1	0	2	0	0
Lyons, Louisville	.938	12	12	33	3	2
Madison, Omaha	.924	47	26	108	11	13
Meier, Oklahoma City	1.000	10	8	22	0	2
Noce, Iowa	1.000	3	2	4	0	0
Norman, Indianapolis	.972	24	12	23	1	2
O'MALLEY, Oklahoma City	.972	104	112	198	9	22
Owen, 1 Okla City-1 Omaha	1.000	2	0	1	0	0
Paciorek, Denver	.857	10	3	15	3	1
Pagnozzi, Louisville	.800	2	0	4	1	0
Pecota, Omaha	.949	26	19	56	4	6
Pryor, Nashville	1.000	1	0	3	0	0
Reboulet, Louisville	.938	4	2	13	1	2
Reynolds, Indianapolis	.932	111	96	179	20	12
Robidoux, Denver	.000	1	0	0	1	0
Rodriguez, Louisville	.930	71	47	139	14	17
Rowdon, Iowa	.932	118	84	231	23	19
Sabo, Nashville	.938	75	43	137	12	19
See, Oklahoma City	.893	11	6	19	3	1
Shines, Indianapolis	.903	14	7	21	3	1
Smith, Denver	1.000	8	1	11	0	2
Stanicek, Denver	.833	11	5	20	5	0
Stefero, Indianapolis	.000	1	0	0	1	0
Syverson, Buffalo	.957	9	6	16	1	2
Tanner, Nashville	.969	30	17	45	2	2
Tingley, Buffalo	1.000	1	0	1	0	0
Valdez, Iowa	.976	15	9	31	1	1
Walker, Iowa	.750	2	0	6	2	0
Williams, Buffalo	.923	130	88	237	27	24
Wilson, Louisville	1.000	10	5	19	0	1
Woods, Iowa	.800	7	2	6	2	0
Wotus, Omaha	.944	25	14	54	4	6

Triple Play—Meier.

SHORTSTOPS

Player and Club	Pct.	G.	PO.	A.	E.	DP.
Alfaro, Denver	1.000	2	1	4	0	1
Angelero, Omaha	1.000	3	3	5	0	1
Bell, Buffalo	.945	109	198	322	30	67
Biancalana, Omaha	1.000	3	7	6	0	3
Booker, Louisville	.967	14	21	38	2	11
Brumley, Iowa	.938	85	131	229	24	44
Castillo, Denver	1.000	1	2	3	0	1
Crone, Buffalo	.971	24	35	67	3	13
DeJesus, Louisville	.966	38	57	111	6	21
Diaz, Denver	.960	48	95	144	10	30
Dunston, Iowa	.947	4	6	12	1	2
Espy, Oklahoma City	.956	51	80	157	11	37
Gonzalez, Nashville	.943	34	61	55	7	15
Harris, Nashville	.911	93	108	179	28	47
Johnson, Omaha	.918	12	15	30	4	7
R. Jones, Omaha	.959	50	74	136	9	18
T. Jones, Louisville	.962	73	112	221	13	40
Jurak, Oklahoma City	.981	13	16	37	1	6
Kunkel, Oklahoma City	.964	20	23	57	3	9
Lyons, Louisville	1.000	1	1	1	0	1
Noboa, Buffalo	.900	6	8	10	2	4
Noce, Iowa	.949	15	25	50	4	7
Norman, Indianapolis	.955	32	47	80	6	18
Owen, 67 Okla City-20 Omaha	.952	87	139	239	19	59
Pecota, Omaha	.895	10	16	18	4	2
Quinones, Iowa	.947	29	46	80	7	15
Rivera, Indianapolis	.964	107	190	291	18	84
Robinson, Nashville	1.000	2	2	5	0	2
Rodriguez, Louisville	.945	19	26	60	5	16
Rowdon, Iowa	.786	6	4	7	3	3
Smajstrla, Buffalo	1.000	1	3	3	0	0
SMITH, Denver	.966	94	147	309	16	74
Syverson, Buffalo	.964	6	7	20	1	3
Tabor, Oklahoma City	.938	4	5	10	1	3
Tanner, Nashville	.994	31	59	97	1	25
Valdez, Iowa	.966	18	23	34	2	6
Wotus, Omaha	.974	52	75	152	6	39

Triple Play—Espy.

OUTFIELDERS

Player and Club	Pct.	G.	PO.	A.	E.	DP.
Adduci, Denver°	1.000	11	19	2	0	0
Allen, Buffalo	1.000	4	1	0	0	0
Ayer, Louisville	.968	38	60	1	2	0
Barnes, 16 Lou-10 Denver	.957	26	39	5	2	2
Bernstine, Iowa	.971	80	101	1	3	0
Berry, Nashville	.875	6	7	0	1	0
Boever, Nashville	.905	16	18	1	2	0
Brumley, Iowa	1.000	1	5	0	0	0
Capra, Oklahoma City	.992	96	250	11	2	2
Cartwright, Denver°	.976	54	117	4	3	1
Clark, Buffalo	.971	107	181	22	6	4
Corey, Indianapolis	.933	10	13	1	1	0
Daughtry, Indianapolis°	.833	4	5	0	1	0
Espy, Oklahoma City	.960	62	115	4	5	0
Felder, Denver	1.000	27	75	3	0	0
Ficklin, Buffalo	.970	27	62	2	2	1
Finley, Nashville	1.000	9	18	0	0	0
Frobel, Buffalo	.990	49	101	3	1	0
Gallagher, Buffalo	1.000	12	34	1	0	0
Garcia, Nashville°	.982	113	262	13	5	2
Gonzalez, Nashville	1.000	1	4	0	0	0
Green, Louisville	.948	49	71	2	4	1
Harrison, Denver	1.000	4	5	0	0	0
Hill, Nashville	.974	96	140	7	4	0
Jackson, Iowa	.981	131	290	15	6	6
Johnson, Louisville°	.976	115	319	6	8	2
Jones, Omaha	1.000	2	2	0	0	0
Kemp, Oklahoma City°	.982	36	49	6	1	1

OUTFIELDERS—Continued

Player and Club	Pct.	G.	PO.	A.	E.	DP.	Player and Club	Pct.	G.	PO.	A.	E.	DP.
KLIPSTEIN, Denver	.994	112	314	3	2	0	Pyznarski, Denver	1.000	10	10	0	0	0
Komminsk, Denver	.983	133	269	16	5	2	Reboulet, Louisville	.905	12	17	2	2	0
Kunkel, Oklahoma City	.971	18	29	4	1	0	Reynolds, Indianapolis	1.000	3	2	0	0	0
Landrum, Louisville	1.000	5	7	1	0	0	Romano, Indianapolis	.984	86	175	5	3	1
Lindeman, Louisville	.938	14	14	1	1	1	Rowdon, Iowa	1.000	1	2	0	0	0
Lyons, Louisville	.959	34	71	0	3	0	Schulz, Omaha	.993	72	127	7	1	1
Madison, Omaha	1.000	21	24	0	0	0	Shepherd, Indianapolis	.979	95	177	7	4	1
Manfre, Nashville	.970	84	124	7	4	3	G. Smith, Oklahoma City	1.000	6	10	1	0	0
Martinez, Omaha*	.979	34	43	3	1	0	L. Smith, Omaha	.945	27	51	1	3	0
Meier, Oklahoma City	.966	112	163	9	6	1	Snider, Omaha	.974	65	105	7	3	1
Moore, Indianapolis*	.983	72	114	5	2	1	Stanicek, Denver	.975	64	114	1	3	0
Morris, Louisville*	1.000	14	20	2	0	1	Stephenson, Iowa*	1.000	7	13	0	0	0
Murphy, Louisville	.987	76	141	8	2	1	Tanner, Nashville	.950	13	19	0	1	0
Nelson, Buffalo	.979	38	85	7	2	2	Taylor, Omaha*	.987	75	141	7	2	1
Nixon, Buffalo	.983	58	170	3	3	0	Thurman, Omaha	.974	114	283	11	8	6
Noce, Iowa	1.000	1	1	0	0	0	Varsho, Iowa	.976	129	227	18	6	3
Norman, Indianapolis	1.000	1	1	0	0	0	Venable, Nashville	.977	112	212	5	5	2
O'Neill, Nashville*	1.000	10	19	1	0	0	B. Walker, Nashville	1.000	4	6	0	0	0
Ortiz, Oklahoma City	.974	117	209	16	6	3	C. Walker, Iowa	.966	46	79	7	3	0
Paciorek, Denver	1.000	19	27	0	0	0	D. Walker, Louisville*	.975	76	111	4	3	0
Palmeiro, Iowa*	.979	47	88	4	2	0	Washington, Buffalo	.988	94	158	3	2	1
Parsons, Buffalo	.993	70	145	3	1	0	Werner, Oklahoma City	.800	4	4	0	1	0
Pevey, Louisville	1.000	2	1	0	0	0	Williams, Indianapolis*	.964	98	178	9	7	1
Powell, Indianapolis	.970	82	155	6	5	3	Winters, Omaha	.970	47	90	7	3	1
Pryor, Nashville	1.000	1	1	0	0	0	Wohlford, Nashville	.967	14	26	3	1	0

Triple Play—Capra.

CATCHERS

Player and Club	Pct.	G.	PO.	A.	E.	DP.	PB.	Player and Club	Pct.	G.	PO.	A.	E.	DP.	PB.
Allanson, Buffalo	.974	76	428	30	12	2	12	Nelson, Omaha	.974	6	34	3	1	0	0
Bathe, Iowa	.980	24	139	8	3	1	0	O'Brien, Denver	.987	79	415	53	6	8	8
Berry, Nashville	.979	39	219	16	5	1	8	Pagnozzi, Louisville	.989	80	427	39	5	4	7
BERRYHILL, Iowa	.990	113	603	66	7	11	15	Pena, Louisville	1.000	2	7	1	0	0	0
Beuerlein, Denver	.969	14	60	2	2	0	3	Pevey, Louisville	1.000	6	34	2	0	1	0
Bilardello, Omaha	.991	20	96	13	1	3	0	Pryor, Nashville	.983	61	323	30	6	4	8
Brunenkant, Buffalo	1.000	2	2	0	0	0	0	Pujols, Indianapolis	1.000	8	52	6	0	0	0
Colbert, Louisville	.982	52	306	23	6	1	8	Ramos, Omaha	.993	26	114	24	1	1	3
Dorsett, Buffalo	.992	21	119	9	1	0	11	Reed, Indianapolis	1.000	5	27	2	0	0	0
Goldthorn, Oklahoma City	.977	68	375	45	10	7	6	Scott, Denver	.980	49	215	24	5	6	6
Hayes, Iowa	1.000	11	49	7	0	0	0	Stanley, Oklahoma City	.993	41	239	28	2	1	6
Knicely, Oklahoma City	1.000	4	12	1	0	0	0	Stefero, Indianapolis	.993	47	267	29	2	3	6
Macfarlane, Omaha	.987	76	408	37	6	3	9	Stephens, Louisville	.983	9	53	4	1	0	1
Madison, Oklahoma City	.984	21	108	14	2	4	1	Syverson, Buffalo	1.000	3	11	1	0	0	0
McClendon, Nashville	.750	1	3	0	1	0	1	Tejada, Indianapolis	.981	91	568	53	12	3	8
McGriff, Nashville	.992	54	343	36	3	2	4	Tingley, Buffalo	.980	51	259	33	6	4	7
Nago, Denver	1.000	4	22	3	0	0	1	Werner, Oklahoma City	.989	44	176	10	2	2	1

PITCHERS

Player and Club	Pct.	G.	PO.	A.	E.	DP.	Player and Club	Pct.	G.	PO.	A.	E.	DP.
Abrego, Iowa	.960	20	8	16	1	1	Easterly, Buffalo*	1.000	2	1	0	0	0
Alba, 9 Buf-18 Denver*	.889	27	1	7	1	0	Farr, Omaha	1.000	8	0	1	0	0
Aldrich, Denver	1.000	20	0	2	0	0	Farrell, Buffalo	.931	25	9	18	2	2
R. Anderson, Omaha	1.000	15	4	14	0	1	Faulk, Indianapolis	.955	32	7	14	1	3
S. Anderson, Oklahoma City	.933	49	5	9	1	0	Fischer, Indianapolis	.935	24	10	19	2	2
Aquino, Omaha	1.000	14	3	5	0	0	Gardner, Indianapolis	.857	9	3	3	1	0
Armstrong, Buffalo	1.000	13	2	1	0	0	Gleaton, Omaha*	1.000	6	0	3	0	0
AUGUST, Denver	1.000	28	18	29	0	4	A. Gonzalez, Denver	1.000	4	4	1	0	0
Baller, Iowa	1.000	44	4	4	0	1	Grapenthin, Louisville	.895	55	7	10	2	0
Bargar, Louisville	.971	36	8	25	1	1	Gray, Nashville	.941	53	13	3	1	0
Barker, Denver	1.000	13	6	8	0	1	Gumpert, Omaha	.857	35	3	9	2	2
Barrett, Indianapolis	.963	46	9	17	1	1	Hall, Iowa*	.929	35	2	11	1	0
Birkbeck, Denver	1.000	1	2	0	0	0	Hamilton, Iowa*	.864	27	6	13	3	0
Boever, Louisville	1.000	43	2	3	0	0	Hargesheimer, Omaha	1.000	9	1	0	0	0
Botelho, Oklahoma City	1.000	18	1	11	0	0	Henry, Oklahoma City	.889	30	3	5	1	1
C. Brown, 20 Ind-14 Denver	.833	34	7	8	3	0	Heredia, Indianapolis	.931	20	7	20	2	1
K. Brown, Oklahoma City	.714	5	2	3	2	0	Holman, Indianapolis	.875	6	4	3	1	0
Browning, Nashville*	.857	5	1	5	1	0	Howe, Oklahoma City*	1.000	7	2	6	0	1
Buonantony, Louisville	.923	16	1	11	1	0	Huismann, Buffalo	.857	13	3	3	1	0
Calderon, Louisville*	.882	27	2	13	2	0	Jackson, Denver	1.000	4	1	0	0	0
Camacho, Buffalo	.857	23	2	4	1	1	Jeffcoat, Oklahoma City*	.941	26	5	27	2	2
Capel, Iowa	.955	53	9	12	1	1	Johnson, Denver*	.857	26	1	5	1	1
Charlton, Nashville*	.955	18	6	15	1	0	A. Jones, Denver	1.000	50	4	9	0	1
Cherry, Louisville*	1.000	46	5	23	0	3	D. Jones, Buffalo	.846	23	3	8	2	1
Ciardi, Denver	.963	19	12	14	1	2	M. Jones, Indianapolis*	1.000	15	1	4	0	1
Clay, Denver	1.000	6	2	3	0	0	Kaiser, Denver*	.931	22	12	15	2	1
Clutterbuck, Denver	1.000	7	1	7	0	0	Kemp, Nashville	.933	27	11	17	2	1
Cole, Indianapolis	.000	3	0	0	1	0	Kendrick, Denver*	1.000	4	0	5	0	0
Conroy, Louisville*	1.000	4	0	3	0	0	Kilgus, Oklahoma City	.900	21	3	6	1	1
Cook, Oklahoma City	1.000	31	3	7	0	0	Killingsworth, Oklahoma City	.963	28	9	17	1	0
Creel, Oklahoma City	.909	21	11	29	4	3	Knapp, Oklahoma City	1.000	2	3	2	0	0
Cutshall, Nashville	1.000	26	6	11	0	0	Knudson, Denver	1.000	14	7	8	0	2
Danek, Iowa	1.000	9	4	4	0	0	Konderla, Denver	.867	48	3	10	2	0
Davidson, Iowa	.938	20	10	20	2	1	Kopf, Iowa	1.000	8	2	8	0	0
J. Davis, Omaha	.800	43	2	6	2	0	Lancaster, Iowa	1.000	15	1	10	0	1
R. Davis, Iowa	1.000	1	2	1	0	1	Landrum, Oklahoma City	.857	19	2	4	1	0
Dayley, Louisville*	1.000	1	0	1	0	0	LaPoint, Louisville*	1.000	14	3	15	0	2
Dibble, Nashville	.833	44	1	4	1	1	Layton, Iowa	1.000	21	5	11	0	0
Duquette, Iowa*	1.000	25	0	11	0	0	Lea, Indianapolis	1.000	5	5	4	0	2
Earley, Louisville*	1.000	52	5	8	0	1	Leonette, Iowa	.824	24	2	12	3	1

PITCHERS—Continued

Player and Club	Pct.	G.	PO.	A.	E.	DP.
Lollar, Louisville*	1.000	11	2	4	0	1
Lopez, Nashville	.875	7	2	5	1	0
Loynd, Oklahoma City	.667	5	0	2	1	2
Maddux, Iowa	1.000	4	5	1	0	1
Madrid, Denver	.947	27	7	11	1	0
Magrane, Louisville*	1.000	3	0	6	0	1
Mahler, Louisville*	1.000	13	2	8	0	0
Martin, Louisville	1.000	37	4	12	0	0
Martinez, Indianapolis	.824	7	3	11	3	1
Mason, Iowa*	.938	9	7	8	1	0
Mathews, Louisville*	1.000	3	0	4	0	1
McKay, Iowa*	1.000	4	0	1	0	1
McWilliams, Oklahoma City*	.667	7	1	1	1	0
Meridith, Oklahoma City*	1.000	7	1	2	0	0
Mielke, Oklahoma City	.929	28	3	10	1	1
Mirabella, Denver*	1.000	25	0	6	0	0
Montgomery, Nashville	.964	24	11	16	1	1
Mooneyham, Denver	.941	12	6	10	1	0
Mullen, Omaha	.919	31	14	20	3	2
K. Murphy, Buffalo*	1.000	13	3	10	0	0
M. Murphy, Buffalo	.971	37	17	17	1	2
Noles, Iowa	1.000	3	0	1	0	0
O'Neal, Louisville	.941	7	9	7	1	1
Oelkers, Buffalo*	.933	28	13	15	2	1
Pacillo, Nashville	.783	16	4	14	5	2
Parmenter, Iowa	.750	2	1	2	1	0
Parrett, Indianapolis	1.000	20	1	5	0	0
Pastore, Oklahoma City	1.000	4	1	7	0	0
Perez, Indianapolis	.933	19	13	15	2	1
Peters, Louisville*	1.000	11	1	0	0	0
Pico, Iowa	1.000	16	10	16	0	1
Pippin, 39 Omaha-19 Buffalo	.938	58	12	18	2	0
Potestio, Iowa	.857	14	3	9	2	1
Rajsich, Omaha*	.923	31	1	11	1	1
Renfroe, Iowa	1.000	8	2	4	0	1
Reuss, Nashville*	1.000	2	0	7	0	0
Ritter, Buffalo	.857	16	6	12	3	0
Roberts, Buffalo	.944	28	7	10	1	0

Player and Club	Pct.	G.	PO.	A.	E.	DP.
Rodgers, Oklahoma City	1.000	33	5	9	0	0
Rucker, Oklahoma City*	1.000	53	2	9	0	1
Russell, Oklahoma City	1.000	4	0	1	0	1
Sanchez, Omaha*	.892	23	9	24	4	1
Scarpetta, Denver*	.923	20	3	9	1	2
Scherrer, Nashville*	1.000	33	4	7	0	0
Schuler, Denver*	1.000	3	0	1	0	0
Schulze, Louisville*	1.000	5	3	5	0	0
Shirley, Omaha*	.929	44	4	9	1	0
Skalski, Buffalo	1.000	5	1	3	0	0
Slowik, Iowa	1.000	5	1	2	0	0
Smith, Indianapolis	.933	45	6	8	1	0
Soff, Louisville	.905	23	9	10	2	3
Sorensen, Indianapolis	1.000	21	3	9	0	0
Soto, Nashville	1.000	2	0	2	0	0
St. Claire, Indianapolis	1.000	18	2	1	0	0
Stapleton, Denver*	.892	44	11	22	4	2
Stewart, Buffalo	1.000	6	1	3	0	0
Stoddard, Omaha	.933	12	4	10	1	0
Strode, Louisville*	.800	5	0	4	1	1
Surhoff, Iowa	.500	14	1	1	2	0
Swaggerty, Omaha	.955	27	12	30	2	2
Tanner, Nashville	1.000	1	0	1	0	0
Taylor, Oklahoma City	.918	28	19	26	4	4
Terry, Nashville	.932	27	12	29	3	0
Thomas, Buffalo	1.000	10	0	2	0	0
Tibbs, Indianapolis	.909	12	3	7	1	0
Tomlin, Indianapolis*	.917	25	3	8	1	2
Tunnell, Louisville	1.000	6	4	10	0	1
Valdez, Indianapolis	.931	27	10	17	2	3
Waddell, Buffalo	.889	28	4	4	1	0
Welchel, Omaha	.905	19	7	12	2	1
Willis, Nashville	.929	53	1	12	1	2
Wills, Buffalo	.889	36	3	5	1	0
Wright, Denver*	1.000	14	1	5	0	0
Yett, Buffalo	1.000	7	5	5	0	0
Zaske, Oklahoma City	.895	23	4	13	2	0
Zwolensky, Iowa	1.000	44	11	23	0	1

Triple Play—Creel.

The following players do not have any recorded accepted chances at the positions indicated; therefore, are not listed in the fielding averages for those particular positions: Bates, ss; Beuerlein, p; Bilardello, 3b; Brunenkant, p; Burris, p; Clemo, 2b; Colbert, p; Costello, p; DeJesus, 3b; O. Gonzalez, p; Hayes, p; Henika, p; Klipstein, p; Kraemer, p; Lewis, p; Longenecker, 1b; R. Nelson, p; Noboa, 3b; Parsons, p; Pevey, p; M. Robinson, of; Roman, p; Scott, 3b, p; Tudor, p; C. Walker, ss; D. Williams, p; E. Williams, ss; Witt, p.

CLUB PITCHING

Club	ERA.	G.	CG	ShO.	Sv.	IP.	H.	R.	ER.	HR.	HB.	BB.	Int. BB.	SO.	WP.	Bk.
Nashville	4.27	140	19	7	36	1219.0	1270	671	579	115	25	536	35	868	69	17
Indianapolis	4.31	138	13	7	36	1208.0	1232	654	579	112	28	484	31	893	59	21
Omaha	4.31	140	14	4	32	1204.0	1301	648	577	104	24	461	34	728	66	13
Louisville	4.63	140	15	8	44	1213.0	1294	705	624	142	19	497	29	792	67	19
Oklahoma City	5.30	140	7	2	32	1217.2	1419	810	717	132	31	555	20	742	51	19
Iowa	5.37	138	11	6	28	1177.0	1347	795	702	150	56	549	51	755	71	23
Denver	5.54	140	19	1	32	1213.1	1462	829	747	142	21	442	23	653	38	10
Buffalo	5.58	140	9	1	31	1216.2	1374	856	754	176	34	558	27	768	61	20

PITCHERS' RECORDS

(Leading Qualifiers for Earned-Run Average Leadership — 112 or More Innings)

*Throws Lefthanded.

Pitcher—Club	W.	L.	Pct.	ERA.	G.	GS.	CG.	GF.	ShO.	Sv.	IP.	H.	R.	ER.	HR.	HB.	BB.	Int. BB.	SO.	WP.
Perez, Indianapolis	9	7	.563	3.79	19	18	8	0	2	0	133.0	128	65	56	12	1	34	4	125	4
Terry, Nashville	11	10	.524	3.96	27	27	10	0	0	0	181.2	199	94	80	13	3	48	1	91	2
Stapleton, Denver*	11	3	.786	4.05	44	9	4	16	1	5	129.0	141	64	58	7	1	28	4	74	2
Montgomery, Nashville	8	5	.615	4.14	24	21	1	0	0	0	139.0	132	76	64	17	3	51	3	121	3
Mullen, Omaha	8	8	.500	4.28	31	22	1	3	0	1	155.2	158	88	74	19	4	44	3	71	7
Pippin, Buffalo	4	7	.364	4.56	58	0	0	26	0	5	116.1	115	69	59	15	1	64	6	90	23
Sanchez, Omaha*	5	12	.294	4.62	23	21	3	0	0	0	124.2	162	74	64	6	5	46	3	74	8
Kemp, Louisville	6	10	.375	4.64	27	25	2	1	0	0	145.1	168	92	75	19	2	68	3	82	6
Cherry, Louisville*	11	5	.688	4.70	46	12	1	5	0	2	126.1	139	74	66	15	1	50	3	89	10
Jeffcoat, Oklahoma City*	11	8	.579	4.79	26	24	3	2	1	0	159.2	193	99	85	14	1	41	0	101	3

Departmental Leaders: G—Pippin, 58; W—Taylor, 12; L—Killingsworth, M. Murphy, 14; Pct.—Barrett, .909; GS—Killingsworth, Oelkers, Taylor, 28; CG—Terry, 10; GF—Baller, 40; ShO—Five pitchers with 2; Sv.—Boever, 21; IP—Terry, 181.2; H—August, 220; R—August, 124; ER—August, 111; HR—Farrell, 26; HB—Hamilton, 9; BB—Oelkers, 96; IBB—Capel, 11; SO—Valdez, 128; WP—Pippin, 23.

(All Pitchers—Listed Alphabetically)

Pitcher—Club	W.	L.	Pct.	ERA.	G.	GS.	CG.	GF.	ShO.	Sv.	IP.	H.	R.	ER.	HR.	HB.	BB.	Int. BB.	SO.	WP.
Abrego, Iowa	2	6	.250	8.74	20	14	1	2	0	0	68.0	91	72	66	15	5	41	0	38	4
Alba, 9 Buf-18 Denver*	6	5	.545	8.51	27	11	0	9	0	1	73.0	95	75	69	16	4	47	0	46	3
Aldrich, Denver	1	0	1.000	3.41	20	0	0	15	0	6	29.0	26	13	11	4	1	6	0	16	0
R. Anderson, Denver	6	5	.545	4.52	15	14	0	0	0	0	79.2	94	44	40	9	3	22	2	47	6
S. Anderson, Oklahoma City	5	3	.625	5.63	49	0	0	36	0	8	64.0	79	44	40	4	2	35	7	39	2
Aquino, Omaha	3	2	.600	2.31	14	4	1	5	1	1	50.2	42	15	13	2	1	16	1	29	0
Armstrong, Buffalo	2	4	.333	3.12	13	0	0	7	0	3	26.0	27	12	9	2	0	11	1	26	1
August, Denver	10	9	.526	5.57	28	27	8	1	0	0	179.1	220	124	111	16	5	55	3	91	4
Baller, Iowa	4	3	.571	3.64	44	0	0	40	0	15	59.1	50	24	24	7	3	24	4	62	3
Bargar, Louisville	10	7	.588	5.72	36	19	1	8	0	2	130.2	143	88	83	22	2	52	0	85	3
Barker, Denver	4	3	.571	4.69	13	8	0	3	0	0	48.0	48	27	25	2	0	29	2	36	2

Pitcher—Club	W.	L.	Pct.	ERA.	G.	GS.	CG.	GF.	ShO.	Sv.	IP.	H.	R.	ER.	HR.	HB.	BB.	Int. BB.	SO.	WP.
Barrett, Indianapolis	10	1	.909	3.57	46	1	0	19	0	2	93.1	90	38	37	9	0	38	3	61	5
Beuerlein, Denver	0	0	.000	15.75	3	0	0	3	0	0	4.0	8	7	7	3	0	3	0	0	0
Birkbeck, Denver	0	1	.000	9.64	1	1	0	0	0	0	4.2	9	11	5	0	0	3	0	1	0
Boever, Louisville	3	2	.600	3.36	43	0	0	36	0	21	59.0	52	22	22	7	1	27	2	79	1
Botelho, Omaha	3	9	.250	6.68	18	10	0	4	0	1	66.0	79	51	49	12	2	29	1	42	1
C. Brown, 20 Ind-14 Den	3	5	.375	7.36	34	1	0	19	0	6	51.1	73	46	42	7	0	10	0	23	2
K. Brown, Oklahoma City	0	5	.000	10.73	5	5	0	0	0	0	24.1	32	32	29	2	4	17	0	9	1
Browning, Nashville*	2	3	.400	6.07	5	5	1	0	1	0	29.2	37	22	20	5	0	12	0	28	1
Brunenkant, Buffalo	0	0	.000	9.00	1	0	0	1	0	0	2.0	3	2	2	0	2	2	0	0	0
Buonantony, Louisville	3	3	.500	4.50	16	13	1	1	1	0	72.0	88	46	36	5	2	32	2	41	9
Burris, Denver	0	0	.000	5.68	1	1	0	0	0	0	6.1	12	4	4	1	0	0	0	1	0
Calderon, Louisville*	4	6	.400	4.32	27	9	2	7	1	0	83.1	68	50	40	13	2	48	2	54	4
Camacho, Buffalo	1	3	.250	1.84	23	0	0	20	0	6	29.1	33	14	6	0	2	16	2	18	7
Capel, Iowa	7	10	.412	5.73	53	8	1	20	0	4	108.1	117	72	69	14	6	43	11	75	14
Charlton, Nashville*	2	8	.200	4.30	18	17	3	0	1	0	98.1	97	57	47	8	1	44	1	74	7
Cherry, Louisville*	11	5	.688	4.70	46	12	1	5	0	2	126.1	139	74	66	15	1	50	3	89	10
Ciardi, Denver	7	5	.583	5.61	19	19	2	0	0	0	112.1	134	82	70	18	1	31	1	42	4
Clay, Denver	1	0	1.000	7.94	6	0	0	1	0	0	11.1	18	10	10	1	2	5	0	7	1
Clutterbuck, Denver	3	2	.600	5.67	7	5	0	0	0	0	33.1	49	24	21	5	0	4	1	14	2
Colbert, Louisville	0	0	.000	27.00	1	0	0	1	0	0	0.1	2	1	1	0	0	0	0	0	1
Cole, Indianapolis	0	0	.000	1.80	3	0	0	0	0	0	5.0	1	1	1	1	0	2	0	2	1
Conroy, Louisville*	1	0	1.000	3.86	4	4	0	0	0	0	16.1	11	7	7	2	0	8	0	14	1
Cook, Oklahoma City	2	2	.500	4.53	31	0	0	8	0	4	57.2	54	33	29	7	1	23	0	36	3
Costello, Louisville	2	0	1.000	4.35	6	1	0	0	0	0	10.1	14	6	5	0	1	7	1	8	1
Creel, Oklahoma City	10	10	.500	4.92	21	21	4	0	0	0	146.1	176	91	80	21	6	41	0	99	3
Cutshall, Nashville	3	4	.429	5.13	26	16	1	6	0	0	93.0	73	59	53	7	5	85	0	56	10
Danek, Iowa	4	4	.500	4.09	9	9	4	0	1	0	50.2	50	26	23	5	2	23	0	27	2
Davidson, Iowa	3	10	.231	6.97	20	19	0	1	0	0	93.0	135	76	72	16	6	36	0	51	5
J. Davis, Omaha	4	3	.571	2.66	43	0	0	35	0	7	50.2	34	16	15	2	2	27	5	44	4
R. Davis, Iowa	0	0	.000	4.50	1	1	0	0	0	0	2.0	2	1	1	0	0	3	0	0	0
Dayley, Louisville*	0	0	.000	4.50	1	1	0	0	0	0	2.0	1	1	1	0	0	1	0	1	1
Dibble, Nashville	2	4	.333	4.72	44	0	0	19	0	4	61.0	72	34	32	5	1	27	4	51	5
Duquette, Iowa*	1	2	.333	6.08	25	0	0	4	0	0	26.2	30	20	18	3	1	24	6	17	1
Earley, Louisville*	2	3	.400	3.98	52	0	0	26	0	5	54.1	56	27	24	3	0	24	5	30	6
Easterly, Buffalo*	0	0	.000	0.00	2	0	0	2	0	1	2.2	0	0	0	0	0	0	0	3	0
Farr, Omaha	0	0	.000	1.42	8	0	0	8	0	4	12.2	6	3	2	0	0	6	1	15	0
Farrell, Buffalo	6	12	.333	5.83	25	24	2	1	0	0	156.0	155	109	101	26	8	64	2	91	9
Faulk, Indianapolis	3	3	.500	2.68	32	3	0	12	0	2	77.1	63	25	23	4	2	34	4	42	8
Fischer, Indianapolis	7	9	.438	5.44	24	24	0	0	0	0	145.2	179	93	88	20	2	55	2	76	7
Gardner, Indianapolis	3	3	.500	5.67	9	9	0	0	0	0	46.0	48	32	29	8	1	28	1	41	2
Gleaton, Omaha*	2	0	1.000	3.00	6	1	0	1	0	0	15.0	14	6	5	2	0	6	2	9	0
A. Gonzalez, Denver	2	0	1.000	3.65	4	4	0	0	0	0	24.2	27	10	10	1	0	5	0	11	2
O. Gonzalez, Nashville	0	0	.000	4.50	2	0	0	2	0	0	2.0	3	1	1	0	0	1	0	0	0
Grapenthin, Louisville	4	6	.400	3.64	55	0	0	19	0	8	99.0	107	50	40	9	0	32	6	49	0
Gray, Nashville	4	10	.286	4.86	53	0	0	29	0	14	83.1	97	52	45	9	0	26	9	70	6
Gumpert, Omaha	6	5	.545	3.89	35	5	0	15	0	6	74.0	79	40	32	9	1	36	5	47	2
Hall, Iowa*	6	3	.667	4.48	35	6	0	11	0	1	66.1	74	42	33	9	1	45	3	66	3
Hamilton, Iowa*	2	5	.286	5.99	26	17	0	2	0	0	94.2	103	74	63	10	9	85	2	63	5
Hargesheimer, Omaha	0	2	.000	3.50	9	2	0	5	0	2	18.0	20	9	7	1	0	9	0	10	0
Hayes, Iowa	0	0	.000	0.00	2	0	0	2	0	0	1.1	1	0	0	0	1	0	0	1	1
Henika, Nashville	0	0	.000	27.00	1	0	0	1	0	0	1.0	2	3	3	0	0	2	0	1	1
Henry, Oklahoma City	4	4	.500	4.96	30	8	0	15	0	3	69.0	66	39	38	11	0	50	3	55	3
Heredia, Indianapolis	7	8	.467	4.29	20	16	0	1	0	0	98.2	100	56	47	10	2	35	1	75	2
Holman, Indianapolis	0	4	.000	6.23	6	6	0	0	0	0	34.2	41	28	24	5	1	23	2	27	2
Howe, Oklahoma City*	2	2	.500	3.48	7	3	0	1	0	0	20.2	26	8	8	1	1	5	0	14	1
Huismann, Buffalo	1	1	.500	7.56	13	0	0	5	0	0	33.1	43	32	28	9	1	8	2	31	0
Jackson, Denver	0	0	.000	8.64	4	0	0	1	0	0	8.1	19	9	8	0	0	3	1	5	1
Jeffcoat, Oklahoma City*	11	8	.579	4.79	26	24	3	2	1	0	159.2	193	99	85	14	1	41	0	101	3
Johnson, Denver*	4	4	.500	3.72	26	0	0	11	0	3	46.0	44	23	19	0	0	20	1	33	1
A. Jones, Denver	3	6	.333	5.71	50	0	0	26	0	6	69.1	88	49	44	12	1	35	3	65	4
D. Jones, Buffalo	5	2	.714	2.04	23	0	0	20	0	7	61.2	49	18	14	3	0	12	2	61	4
M. Jones, Indianapolis*	3	1	.750	4.73	15	4	0	5	0	1	26.2	31	17	14	0	1	15	0	16	2
Kaiser, Buffalo*	5	3	.625	5.17	22	8	0	5	0	1	71.1	87	52	41	9	3	32	1	53	2
Kemp, Louisville	6	10	.375	4.64	27	25	2	1	0	0	145.1	168	92	75	19	2	68	3	82	6
Kendrick, Denver*	0	1	.000	8.59	4	3	0	0	0	0	14.2	20	15	14	3	1	10	0	7	0
Kilgus, Oklahoma City*	2	0	1.000	4.01	21	0	0	17	0	7	24.2	23	12	11	2	2	10	3	14	1
Killingsworth, Oklahoma City	6	14	.300	5.81	28	28	0	0	0	0	161.0	204	114	104	18	4	78	1	74	6
Klipstein, Denver	0	0	.000	4.50	2	0	0	2	0	0	2.0	3	1	1	0	0	1	0	1	0
Knapp, Oklahoma City	0	1	.000	6.59	2	2	0	0	0	0	13.2	17	10	10	6	0	4	0	3	1
Knudson, Denver	7	2	.778	5.86	14	14	1	0	0	0	78.1	89	53	51	11	2	30	0	37	4
Konderla, 37 Nash-11 Den	5	7	.417	4.16	48	3	0	16	0	2	101.2	103	56	47	5	0	60	4	87	7
Kopf, Iowa	2	2	.500	9.12	8	4	0	1	0	0	25.2	48	30	26	4	2	11	1	13	2
Kraemer, Iowa*	1	0	1.000	27.00	5	0	0	1	0	0	2.2	8	8	8	4	0	5	1	2	0
Lancaster, Iowa	5	3	.625	3.22	15	6	0	6	0	4	67.0	59	24	24	9	1	17	3	62	0
Landrum, Nashville	4	0	1.000	2.09	19	2	0	5	0	1	38.2	30	9	9	0	0	19	3	47	2
LaPoint, Louisville*	5	5	.500	4.03	14	13	4	0	0	0	91.2	93	45	41	8	0	27	0	70	4
Layton, Iowa	2	4	.333	4.85	21	2	0	3	0	0	42.2	56	30	23	1	2	13	0	20	5
Lea, Indianapolis	1	2	.333	4.44	5	5	0	0	0	0	24.1	23	13	12	2	0	15	2	19	0
Leonette, Iowa	1	4	.200	5.34	24	7	0	11	0	1	60.2	75	47	36	8	2	19	2	24	3
Lewis, Indianapolis	0	0	.000	9.82	2	0	0	2	0	0	3.2	6	4	4	2	0	0	0	3	0
Lollar, Louisville*	1	2	.333	9.40	11	6	0	2	0	0	29.2	36	34	31	6	1	27	0	10	4
Lopez, Nashville	0	0	.000	4.50	7	4	0	1	0	0	26.0	35	16	13	4	1	12	1	9	1
Loynd, Oklahoma City	0	0	.000	4.26	5	0	0	2	0	1	12.2	13	7	6	2	1	9	0	11	2
Maddux, Iowa	3	0	1.000	0.98	4	4	2	0	2	0	27.2	17	3	3	1	2	12	0	22	2
Madrid, Denver	5	7	.417	5.35	27	12	1	6	0	3	99.1	114	64	59	13	1	31	3	50	2
Magrane, Louisville*	1	0	1.000	1.93	3	3	1	0	1	0	23.1	16	7	5	1	0	3	0	17	0
Mahler, Louisville*	4	6	.400	6.57	13	10	0	0	0	0	61.2	73	47	45	11	1	33	1	37	3
Martin, Louisville	7	6	.538	4.68	37	13	0	6	0	0	107.2	117	59	56	14	2	44	5	63	8
Martinez, Indianapolis	3	2	.600	4.46	7	7	1	0	1	0	38.1	32	20	19	5	1	13	1	30	0
Mason, Iowa*	4	2	.667	3.50	9	9	2	0	0	0	54.0	53	28	21	1	2	27	2	41	6
Mathews, Louisville*	3	0	1.000	2.05	3	3	2	0	2	0	22.0	18	5	5	2	0	3	1	20	0
McGrath, Louisville	1	0	1.000	4.26	1	1	0	0	0	0	6.1	6	4	3	0	1	2	0	5	0

Pitcher—Club	W.	L.	Pct.	ERA	G.	GS.	CG.	GF.	ShO.	Sv.	IP.	H.	R.	ER.	HR.	HB.	BB.	Int. BB.	SO.	WP.
McKay, Iowa*	0	0	.000	22.09	4	0	0	1	0	0	3.2	7	9	9	0	0	4	1	1	1
McWilliams, Oklahoma City*	1	4	.200	11.28	7	6	0	0	0	0	22.1	44	29	28	1	1	20	0	13	2
Meridith, Oklahoma City*	1	0	1.000	0.00	7	0	0	5	0	0	12.1	10	2	0	0	0	5	1	5	0
Mielke, Oklahoma City	2	4	.333	4.10	28	0	0	15	0	3	37.1	36	20	17	0	1	16	2	34	0
Mirabella, Denver*	5	1	.833	2.31	25	0	0	18	0	6	39.0	39	11	10	5	1	10	1	28	0
Montgomery, Nashville	8	5	.615	4.14	24	21	1	0	0	0	139.0	132	76	64	17	3	51	3	121	3
Mooneyham, Denver	3	4	.429	4.78	12	12	2	0	0	0	69.2	76	42	37	7	1	38	1	36	1
Mullen, Omaha	8	8	.500	4.28	31	22	1	3	0	1	155.2	158	88	74	19	4	44	3	71	7
K. Murphy, Buffalo*	2	5	.286	6.84	13	9	0	0	0	0	51.1	63	42	39	16	0	22	0	32	0
M. Murphy, Buffalo	5	14	.263	6.29	37	19	0	11	0	2	136.0	167	108	95	18	3	69	4	46	4
Nelson, Buffalo	0	0	.000	0.00	1	0	0	1	0	0	0.1	2	1	0	0	0	1	0	0	0
Noles, Iowa	0	1	.000	10.80	3	0	0	2	0	0	5.0	8	6	6	2	1	3	1	3	1
O'Neal, Louisville*	3	1	.750	4.56	7	7	1	0	0	0	47.1	54	27	24	2	1	10	0	19	4
Oelkers, Buffalo*	11	8	.579	6.28	28	28	4	0	0	0	154.2	178	120	108	22	1	96	1	79	15
Pacillo, Nashville	8	4	.667	3.59	16	16	0	0	0	0	97.2	89	43	39	12	6	38	1	80	5
Parmenter, Iowa	1	0	1.000	0.00	2	1	0	0	0	0	10.0	3	0	0	0	0	6	0	7	0
Parrett, Indianapolis	2	1	.667	2.01	20	0	0	19	0	9	22.1	15	5	5	0	0	13	0	17	3
Parsons, Buffalo	0	0	.000	13.50	1	0	0	1	0	0	1.1	1	2	2	1	0	1	0	0	0
Pastore, Oklahoma City	1	3	.250	8.46	4	4	0	0	0	0	22.1	37	24	21	7	0	3	0	15	2
Perez, Indianapolis	9	7	.563	3.79	19	19	8	0	2	0	133.0	128	65	56	12	1	34	4	125	4
Peters, Louisville*	2	0	1.000	0.95	11	0	0	11	0	6	19.0	13	2	2	1	0	4	0	22	0
Pevey, Louisville	0	0	.000	0.00	1	0	0	1	0	0	0.2	1	0	0	0	0	0	0	0	0
Pico, Iowa	6	5	.545	4.80	16	16	1	0	0	0	93.2	118	57	50	9	2	27	3	45	2
Pippin, 39 Omaha-19 Buffalo	4	7	.364	4.56	58	0	0	26	0	5	116.1	115	69	59	15	1	64	6	90	23
Potestio, Iowa*	2	5	.286	7.94	14	10	0	1	0	0	56.2	81	56	50	16	2	19	2	20	2
Rajsich, Omaha*	1	5	.167	4.26	31	5	1	12	0	1	61.1	75	35	29	4	1	29	3	40	3
Renfroe, Iowa	0	1	.000	5.02	8	0	0	1	0	0	14.1	8	9	8	1	0	5	0	9	1
Reuss, Nashville*	0	2	.000	6.00	2	2	0	0	0	0	12.0	16	8	8	1	0	6	0	4	1
Ritter, Buffalo	6	4	.600	4.94	16	15	1	0	0	0	85.2	97	57	47	8	2	35	0	43	4
Roberts, Buffalo	5	3	.625	6.35	28	12	0	1	0	1	95.0	130	74	67	17	5	33	1	52	3
Rodgers, Oklahoma City	4	0	1.000	4.96	33	1	0	10	0	1	65.1	80	43	36	8	2	25	1	35	2
Roman, Buffalo	0	0	.000	17.47	3	0	0	0	0	0	5.2	11	11	11	2	0	4	0	10	1
Rucker, Oklahoma City*	3	2	.600	4.25	53	3	0	14	0	5	65.2	59	38	31	7	1	40	1	37	5
Russell, Oklahoma City	0	0	.000	1.42	4	0	0	2	0	0	6.1	5	1	1	0	0	1	0	5	0
Sanchez, Omaha*	5	12	.294	4.62	23	21	3	0	0	0	124.2	162	74	64	6	5	46	3	74	8
Scarpetta, Denver*	4	5	.444	7.20	20	12	1	0	0	0	75.0	99	63	60	11	0	24	1	31	1
Scherrer, Nashville*	4	1	.800	1.86	33	0	0	20	0	11	29.0	25	6	6	1	1	10	0	24	4
Schuler, Denver*	0	0	.000	6.75	3	0	0	1	0	0	4.0	9	5	3	1	0	1	1	1	0
Schulze, Buffalo	0	1	.000	9.67	5	5	0	0	0	0	22.1	33	25	24	2	2	12	0	13	1
Scott, Denver	0	0	.000	10.80	1	0	0	1	0	0	1.2	3	2	2	0	0	1	0	0	1
Shirley, Omaha*	4	2	.667	3.87	44	1	0	21	0	5	79.0	80	36	34	7	1	25	1	78	6
Skalski, Buffalo	0	3	.000	10.13	5	5	0	0	0	0	18.2	30	21	21	5	0	12	0	18	2
Slowik, Iowa	0	0	.000	9.00	5	0	0	2	0	0	8.0	9	9	8	2	0	6	0	6	2
Smith, Indianapolis	4	4	.500	4.69	45	2	0	26	0	6	86.1	85	51	45	2	6	43	4	90	6
Soff, Louisville	6	9	.400	5.64	23	13	1	2	0	0	83.0	109	63	52	11	4	34	1	35	5
Sorensen, Indianapolis	2	2	.500	4.29	21	3	0	3	0	0	50.1	54	29	24	8	1	11	0	30	2
Soto, Nashville	0	2	.000	11.91	2	2	0	0	0	0	11.1	17	16	15	3	0	8	0	8	1
St. Claire, Indianapolis	0	1	.000	2.18	18	0	0	14	0	7	20.2	12	5	5	1	0	12	1	15	0
Stapleton, Denver*	11	3	.786	4.05	44	9	4	16	1	5	129.0	141	64	58	7	1	28	4	74	2
Stewart, Buffalo	0	1	.000	9.26	6	0	0	3	0	2	11.2	18	13	12	2	0	6	0	8	1
Stoddard, Omaha	5	1	.833	3.84	12	11	1	0	1	0	63.1	62	28	27	3	0	27	2	36	2
Strode, Louisville*	0	0	.000	6.14	5	4	0	0	0	0	22.0	33	16	15	5	0	8	0	9	0
Surhoff, Iowa	1	0	1.000	2.76	14	0	0	3	0	0	29.1	29	16	9	4	1	15	3	17	1
Swaggerty, Omaha	10	12	.455	4.89	27	25	5	0	2	0	163.2	199	95	89	14	2	50	0	63	5
Tanner, Nashville	0	0	.000	4.50	1	0	0	1	0	0	2.0	2	1	1	1	0	1	0	1	0
Taylor, Oklahoma City	12	9	.571	5.61	28	28	0	0	0	0	168.1	198	122	105	10	2	91	0	100	8
Terry, Nashville	11	10	.524	3.96	27	27	10	0	0	0	181.2	199	94	80	13	3	48	1	91	2
Thomas, Buffalo	1	1	.500	4.29	10	0	0	2	0	1	21.0	19	12	10	3	1	12	1	17	0
Tibbs, Indianapolis	5	5	.500	2.99	12	12	2	0	1	0	81.1	64	31	27	6	1	22	0	55	0
Tomlin, Indianapolis*	3	2	.600	4.45	25	0	0	8	0	1	32.1	33	17	16	0	2	18	2	25	7
Tudor, Louisville*	1	0	1.000	7.88	2	2	0	0	0	0	8.0	11	8	7	2	0	1	0	3	0
Tunnell, Louisville	4	1	.800	3.41	6	6	1	0	1	0	37.0	33	16	14	3	0	19	0	32	2
Valdez, Indianapolis	10	7	.588	5.12	27	27	2	0	2	0	158.1	191	108	90	14	7	64	4	128	8
Waddell, Buffalo	5	3	.625	5.15	28	5	1	8	0	0	78.2	74	45	45	11	2	39	6	41	1
Welchel, Omaha	7	4	.636	4.82	19	19	2	0	0	0	112.0	126	62	60	5	1	44	1	70	2
Williams, Indianapolis*	0	0	.000	9.00	1	0	0	1	0	0	1.0	1	0	0	0	1	0	0	0	0
Willis, Nashville	6	4	.600	3.33	53	0	0	25	0	5	83.2	97	39	31	5	2	30	5	54	7
Wills, Buffalo	3	2	.600	3.34	36	0	0	30	0	6	56.2	53	28	21	5	0	22	2	45	1
Witt, Oklahoma City	1	0	1.000	9.00	1	1	0	0	0	0	5.0	5	5	5	1	0	3	0	2	0
Wright, Denver*	2	0	1.000	5.79	14	1	0	3	0	0	23.1	29	16	15	2	1	18	0	5	1
Yett, Buffalo	3	3	.500	3.05	7	7	1	0	0	0	44..1	38	17	15	7	1	18	0	33	2
Zaske, Oklahoma City	2	0	1.000	5.34	23	6	0	6	0	0	59.0	62	37	35	10	2	38	1	41	7
Zwolensky, Iowa	7	4	.636	4.43	44	5	0	13	0	3	105.2	115	56	52	9	6	35	6	64	5

BALKS—Danek, 5; Anderson, Montgomery, Zwolensky, 4 each; Alba, Calderon, Cherry, Davidson, Earley, Fischer, Hamilton, Heredia, Konderla, Kopf, Madrid, Mielke, Roberts, Wills, 3 each; K. Brown, Charlton, Cook, Creel, Cutshall, Grapenthin, Holman, Jeffcoat, Kaiser, Landrum, Layton, Loynd, Martinez, Perez, Pippin, Roman, Skalski, Taylor, Tunnell, Valdez, Waddell, 2 each; Abrego, Birkbeck, Botelho, C. Brown, Buonantony, Cole, J. Davis, Dibble, Farrell, Faulk, Gardner, Gray, Gumpert, Huismann, A. Jones, Kilgus, Killingsworth, Knudson, Lancaster, Lollar, Magrane, Martin, Mooneyham, K. Murphy, M. Murphy, Oelkers, Pacillo, Pastore, Pico, Russell, Sanchez, Shirley, Smith, Soff, St. Claire, Stoddard, Strode, Swaggerty, Tibbs, Willis, Yett, 1 each.

COMBINATION SHUTOUTS—Yett-Wills, Buffalo; Faulk-St. Claire, Indianapolis; Parmenter-Capel, Davidson-Capel-Baller, Abrego-Layton-Capel, Iowa; Bargar-Grapenthin, O'Neal-Earley, Louisville; Pacillo-Gray-Scherrer, Pacillo-Kemp-Gray-Scherrer, Montgomery-Scherrer, Cutshall-Gray, Terry-Willis, Nashville; Jeffcoat-Kilgus, Oklahoma City.

NO-HIT GAMES—None.

International League

CLASS AAA

Leading Batter
RANDY MILLIGAN
Tidewater

League President
HAROLD COOPER

Leading Pitcher
DeWAYNE VAUGHN
Tidewater

CHAMPIONSHIP WINNERS IN PREVIOUS YEARS

1884—Trenton	.520	
1885—Syracuse	.584	
1886—Utica	.646	
1887—Toronto	.644	
1888—Syracuse	.723	
1889—Detroit	.649	
1890 Detroit	.617	
1891—Buffalo (reg. season)	.727	
Buffalo (supplem'l)	.680	
1892—Providence	.615	
Binghamton°	.667	
1893—Erie	.606	
1894—Providence	.696	
1895—Springfield	.687	
1896—Providence	.602	
1897—Syracuse	.632	
1898—Montreal	.586	
1899—Rochester	.624	
1900—Providence	.616	
1901—Rochester	.642	
1902—Toronto	.669	
1903—Jersey City	.642	
1904—Buffalo	.657	
1905—Providence	.638	
1906—Buffalo	.607	
1907—Toronto	.619	
1908—Baltimore	.593	
1909—Rochester	.596	
1910—Rochester	.601	
1911—Rochester	.645	
1912—Toronto	.595	
1913—Newark	.625	
1914—Providence	.617	
1915—Buffalo	.632	
1916—Buffalo	.586	
1917—Toronto	.604	
1918—Toronto	.693	
1919—Baltimore	.671	
1920—Baltimore	.719	
1921—Baltimore	.717	
1922—Baltimore	.689	
1923—Baltimore	.677	
1924—Baltimore	.709	
1925—Baltimore	.633	
1926—Toronto	.657	
1927—Buffalo	.667	
1928—Rochester	.549	
1929—Rochester	.613	

1930—Rochester	.629	
1931—Rochester	.601	
1932—Newark	.649	
1933—Newark	.622	
Buffalo (4th)†	.494	
1934—Newark	.608	
Toronto (3rd)†	.559	
1935—Montreal	.597	
Syracuse (2nd)†	.565	
1936—Buffalo‡	.610	
1937—Newark‡	.717	
1938—Newark‡	.684	
1939—Jersey City	.582	
Rochester (2nd)†	.556	
1940—Rochester	.611	
Newark (2nd)†	.594	
1941—Newark	.649	
Montreal (2nd)†	.584	
1942—Newark	.601	
Syracuse (3rd)†	.513	
1943—Toronto	.625	
Syracuse (3rd)†	.536	
1944—Baltimore‡	.553	
1945—Montreal	.621	
Newark (2nd)†	.582	
1946—Montreal‡	.649	
1947—Jersey City	.610	
Syracuse (3rd)†	.575	
1948—Montreal‡	.614	
1949—Buffalo	.584	
Montreal (3rd)†	.545	
1950—Rochester	.609	
Baltimore (3rd)†	.556	
1951—Montreal‡	.617	
1952—Montreal	.629	
Rochester (3rd)†	.619	
1953—Rochester	.630	
Montreal (2nd)†	.586	
1954—Toronto	.630	
Syracuse (4th)§	.510	
1955—Montreal	.617	
Rochester (4th)†	.497	
1956—Toronto	.566	
Rochester (2nd)†	.553	
1957—Toronto	.575	
Buffalo (2nd)†	.571	
1958—Montreal‡	.588	
1959—Buffalo	.582	

Havana (3rd)†	.523	
1960—Toronto‡	.649	
1961—Columbus	.597	
Buffalo (3rd)†	.559	
1962—Jacksonville	.610	
Atlanta (3rd)†	.539	
1963 Syracuse x	.533	
Indianapolis‡	.562	
1964—Jacksonville	.589	
Rochester (4th)†	.532	
1965—Columbus	.582	
Toronto (3rd)†	.556	
1966—Rochester	.565	
Toronto (2nd-tied)†	.558	
1967—Richmond	.574	
Toledo (3rd)†	.525	
1968—Toledo	.565	
Jacksonville (4th)†	.514	
1969—Tidewater	.563	
Syracuse (3rd)†	.536	
1970—Syracuse‡	.600	
1971—Rochester‡	.614	
1972—Louisville	.563	
Tidewater (3rd)†	.545	
1973—Charleston	.586	
Pawtucket y†	.534	
1974—Memphis	.613	
Rochester x‡	.611	
1975—Tidewater‡	.610	
1976—Rochester	.638	
Syracuse (2nd)†	.590	
1977—Pawtucket	.571	
Charleston (2nd)‡	.557	
1978—Charleston	.607	
Richmond (4th)†	.511	
1979—Columbus‡	.612	
1980—Columbus‡	.593	
1981—Columbus‡	.633	
1982—Richmond	.590	
Tidewater (3rd)†	.540	
1983—Columbus	.593	
Tidewater (4th)†	.511	
1984—Columbus	.590	
Pawtucket (4th)†	.536	
1985—Syracuse	.564	
Tidewater (4th)†	.540	
1986—Richmond‡	.571	

°Won split-season playoff. †Won four-team playoff. ‡Won championship and four-team playoff. §Defeated Havana in game to decide fourth place, then won four-team playoff. xLeague was divided into Northern, Southern divisions. yLeague divided into American, National divisions. (NOTE—Known as Eastern League in 1884, New York State League in 1885, International League in 1886-87, International Association in 1888, International League in 1889-90, Eastern Association in 1891, and Eastern League from 1892 until 1912.)

STANDING OF CLUBS AT CLOSE OF SEASON, AUGUST 31

Club	Tide.	Col.	Roch.	Paw.	Tol.	Syr.	Me.	Rich.	W.	L.	T.	Pct.	G.B.
Tidewater (Mets)	....	13	7	10	11	11	15	14	81	59	0	.579	....
Columbus (Yankees)	7	....	11	9	11	14	11	14	77	63	0	.550	4
Rochester (Orioles)	13	9	....	10	12	9	9	12	74	65	0	.532	6½
Pawtucket (Red Sox)	10	11	10	....	5	13	12	12	73	67	0	.521	8
Toledo (Tigers)	9	9	8	15	....	8	12	9	70	70	0	.500	11
Syracuse (Blue Jays)	9	6	11	7	12	....	10	13	68	72	0	.486	13
Maine (Phillies)	5	9	11	8	8	10	....	9	60	80	0	.429	21
Richmond (Braves)	6	6	7	8	11	7	11	....	56	83	0	.403	24½

Maine club represented Old Orchard Beach, Me.

Tidewater club represented Norfolk and Portsmouth, Va.

Major league affiliations in parentheses.

Playoffs—Columbus defeated Rochester, three games to none; Tidewater defeated Pawtucket, three games to one; and Columbus defeated Tidewater, three games to none, to win Governor's Cup.

Regular-Season Attendance—Columbus, 570,599; Maine, 104,219; Pawtucket, 220,838; Richmond, 332,440; Rochester, 315,807; Syracuse, 211,315; Tidewater, 175,104; Toledo, 194,001. Total—2,124,323. Playoffs—25,795.

Managers—Columbus, Bucky Dent; Maine, Bill Dancy, Pawtucket, Ed Nottle; Richmond, Roy Majtyka; Rochester, John Hart; Syracuse, Doug Ault; Toledo, Leon Roberts.

All-Star Team—1B-Randy Milligan, Tidewater; 2B-Nelson Liriano, Syracuse; 3B-Jeff Moronko, Columbus; SS-Kevin Elster, Tidewater; C-Rey Palacios, Toledo; OF-Jay Buhner, Columbus; Mark Carreon, Tidewater; Roberto Kelly, Columbus; DH-Sam Horn, Pawtucket; Starting Pitcher-Brad Arnsberg, Columbus; Relief Pitcher-Don Gordon, Syracuse; Rookie of the Year-Randy Milligan, Tidewater; Most Valuable Player-Randy Milligan, Tidewater; Most Valuable Pitcher-Brad Arnsberg, Columbus; Manager of the Year-Ed Nottle, Pawtucket.

(Compiled by Howe News Bureau, Boston, Mass.)

CLUB BATTING

Club	Pct.	G.	AB.	R.	OR.	H.	TB.	2B.	3B.	HR.	RBI.	GW.	SH.	SF.	HP.	BB.	Int. BB.	SO.	SB.	CS.	LOB.
Tidewater	.282	140	4720	725	574	1331	2018	262	37	117	665	77	26	46	28	500	45	720	104	34	1013
Pawtucket	.271	140	4659	688	603	1261	1972	229	22	146	664	67	33	40	32	528	26	762	92	55	984
Columbus	.268	140	4701	699	611	1258	2056	221	59	153	653	73	35	42	39	477	29	892	139	52	972
Toledo	.267	140	4649	618	642	1240	1849	251	29	100	569	64	40	40	27	488	27	739	147	86	977
Rochester	.265	139	4614	630	601	1222	1901	234	20	135	583	69	47	42	36	466	41	736	76	54	947
Syracuse	.260	140	4745	635	684	1235	1853	208	64	94	571	65	29	39	27	404	25	847	184	88	921
Maine	.243	140	4414	537	662	1071	1638	189	30	106	489	56	39	39	30	502	26	760	108	71	921
Richmond	.240	139	4527	515	670	1086	1605	212	23	87	475	52	40	36	20	491	18	761	112	57	964

INDIVIDUAL BATTING

(Leading Qualifiers for Batting Championship—378 or More Plate Appearances)

*Bats lefthanded.   †Switch-hitter.

Player and Club	Pct.	G.	AB.	R.	H.	TB.	2B.	3B.	HR.	RBI.	GW.	SH.	SF.	HP.	BB.	Int. BB.	SO.	SB.	CS.
Milligan, Randy, Tidewater	.326	136	457	99	149	272	28	4	29	103	7	0	5	4	91	10	77	8	4
Tolman, Timothy, Toledo	.314	111	379	65	119	198	30	2	15	63	7	1	9	3	55	1	51	9	7
Carreon, Mark, Tidewater	.312	133	525	83	164	245	41	5	10	89	19	0	4	0	34	2	48	31	6
Blocker, Terry, Tidewater*	.312	124	525	89	164	213	21	5	6	37	5	4	2	0	26	0	71	33	11
Elster, Kevin, Tidewater	.310	134	549	83	170	241	33	7	8	74	7	3	3	1	35	4	62	7	3
Fields, Bruce, Toledo*	.305	123	446	75	136	185	32	4	3	51	7	1	1	1	41	4	48	24	8
David, Andre, Toledo*	.300	133	480	97	144	225	22	4	17	73	8	0	8	12	76	5	36	3	0
Sharperson, Michael, Syracuse	.299	88	338	67	101	147	21	5	5	26	1	2	1	1	40	0	41	14	10
Reed, Jody, Pawtucket	.296	136	510	77	151	198	22	2	7	51	2	8	5	2	69	0	23	9	7
Miller, Keith, Maine†	.292	122	383	61	112	184	16	4	16	54	4	2	2	4	55	3	72	20	5
Ducey, Robert, Syracuse*	.284	100	359	62	102	166	14	10	10	60	10	0	5	3	61	5	88	7	7

Departmental Leaders: G—Hill, 137; AB—Elster, 549; R—Milligan, 99; H—Elster, 170; TB—Milligan, 272; 2B—Carreon, 41; 3B—Campusano, Ducey, Liriano, 10; HR—Buhner, 31; RBI—Milligan, 103; GWRBI—Carreon, 19; SH—Palacios, 9; SF—Tolman, 9; HP—David, 12; BB—Milligan, 91; IBB—Dodson, Milligan, Traber, 10; SO—Hill, 152; SB—Kelly, 51; CS—Campusano, T. Davis, 15.

(All Players—Listed Alphabetically)

Player and Club	Pct.	G.	AB.	R.	H.	TB.	2B.	3B.	HR.	RBI.	GW.	SH.	SF.	HP.	BB.	Int. BB.	SO.	SB.	CS.
Aguilera, Richard, Tidewater	.000	3	1	0	0	0	0	0	0	0	0	0	0	0	1	0	1	0	0
Alvarez, Jesus, Columbus*	.203	19	64	9	13	14	1	0	0	2	1	0	0	0	7	0	10	0	0
Alvarez, Jose, Richmond	.111	22	9	0	1	2	1	0	0	0	0	0	0	0	0	0	1	0	0
Anderson, Brady, Pawtucket*	.380	23	79	18	30	40	4	0	2	8	2	0	0	0	16	3	8	2	1
Assenmacher, Paul, Richmond*	.000	4	2	0	0	0	0	0	0	0	0	0	0	0	0	0	2	0	0
Bair, Douglas, Maine	1.000	45	1	0	1	1	0	0	0	0	0	0	0	0	0	0	0	0	0
Baker, Douglas, Toledo†	.247	117	376	40	93	117	14	2	2	27	2	3	4	1	38	0	70	9	11
Barton, Shawn, Maine	.000	7	2	0	0	0	0	0	0	0	0	0	0	0	0	0	1	0	0
Bean, William, Toledo*	.275	104	357	51	98	144	18	2	8	43	3	3	3	7	38	3	52	14	11
Benzinger, Todd, Pawtucket†	.323	65	257	47	83	145	17	3	13	49	8	0	3	2	16	1	41	7	2
Blauser, Jeffrey, Richmond	.177	33	113	11	20	24	1	0	1	12	2	0	0	3	11	2	24	3	2
Blocker, Terry, Tidewater*	.312	124	525	89	164	213	21	5	6	37	5	4	2	0	26	0	71	33	11
Bonilla, Juan, Columbus	.240	7	25	1	6	6	0	0	0	1	1	1	0	0	1	0	6	0	0
Boudreaux, Eric, Maine	.000	7	6	1	0	0	0	0	0	0	0	2	0	0	2	0	3	0	0
Bowden, Mark, Maine*	.000	54	2	1	0	0	0	0	0	0	0	0	0	0	2	0	1	0	0
Brown, Michael, Richmond	.217	25	83	6	18	20	2	0	0	7	2	0	0	1	10	0	16	0	0
Buchanan, Robert, Tidewater*	.000	29	3	0	0	0	0	0	0	0	0	1	0	0	0	0	1	0	0
Buhner, Jay, Columbus	.279	134	502	83	140	258	23	1	31	85	12	2	2	2	55	6	124	4	2
Burks, Ellis, Pawtucket	.225	11	40	11	9	23	3	1	3	6	1	0	0	0	7	0	7	1	0
Campusano, Silvestre, Syracuse	.264	129	481	70	127	217	28	10	14	63	9	4	2	4	47	1	110	26	15
Cannizzaro, Chris, Pawtucket†	.235	95	328	37	77	112	18	1	5	29	1	3	1	2	46	3	41	4	1
Carlucci, Richard, Maine*	.000	19	2	0	0	0	0	0	0	0	0	0	0	0	0	0	1	0	0
Carreon, Mark, Tidewater	.312	133	525	83	164	245	41	5	10	89	19	0	4	0	34	2	48	31	6
Cary, Charles, Richmond*	.143	40	7	0	1	1	0	0	0	1	0	0	0	0	0	0	2	0	0
Castro, Jose, Syracuse	.277	61	184	26	51	80	14	0	5	21	6	0	1	5	21	0	14	0	1
Cathcart, Gary, Columbus*	.253	31	87	11	22	32	3	2	1	9	1	1	1	1	11	0	19	6	0
Chambers, Travis, Maine*	.000	64	3	0	0	0	0	0	0	0	0	2	0	0	0	0	2	0	0
Chavez, Pedro, Toledo	.285	54	165	23	47	71	9	0	5	15	2	8	2	1	10	0	29	6	4
Chiffer, Floyd, Richmond	.000	43	1	0	0	0	0	0	0	0	0	0	0	0	1	0	1	0	0
Childress, Willie, Richmond*	.246	48	179	29	44	67	8	3	3	20	2	2	2	0	10	0	24	0	1

Player and Club	Pct.	G.	AB.	R.	H.	TB.	2B.	3B.	HR.	RBI.	GW.	SH.	SF.	HP.	BB.	Int. BB.	SO.	SB.	CS.
Cijntje, Sherwin, Rochester*	.286	16	63	10	18	23	3	1	0	7	2	1	0	1	5	0	6	3	1
Cipolloni, Joseph, Maine	.212	87	222	13	47	71	13	1	3	16	1	1	2	3	27	1	33	0	1
Clary, Martin, Richmond	.105	26	19	1	2	3	1	0	0	1	0	3	0	0	1	0	8	0	0
Clay, Danny, Maine	.333	16	9	1	3	4	1	0	0	1	0	1	0	0	1	0	1	0	0
Cliburn, Stanley, Richmond	.148	19	54	6	8	9	1	0	0	1	0	1	0	1	11	0	12	0	0
Coles, Darnell, Toledo	.324	10	37	7	12	20	5	0	1	8	3	0	0	0	4	1	2	0	2
Corcoran, Timothy, Maine*	.242	66	211	20	51	67	8	1	2	18	2	3	2	1	19	3	14	1	2
Cotto, Henry, Columbus	.302	34	129	26	39	65	13	2	3	20	0	0	1	1	10	0	16	14	2
Cowley, Joseph, Maine	.000	13	5	0	0	0	0	0	0	0	0	0	0	0	0	0	2	0	0
Coyle, Rock, Syracuse	.219	14	32	3	7	7	0	0	0	1	0	0	0	1	0	0	4	1	1
Craig, Rodney, Rochester†	.179	13	39	2	7	8	1	0	0	5	1	0	3	0	4	1	8	2	1
Cuevas, Angelo, Tidewater*	.000	3	3	0	0	0	0	0	0	0	0	0	0	0	0	0	0	0	0
D'Alessandro, Salvatore, Richmond	.231	29	78	5	18	24	6	0	0	12	0	1	1	3	3	0	9	0	0
Dalena, Peter, Columbus*	.282	116	433	74	122	205	21	4	18	61	7	3	3	3	32	8	46	0	3
Dalton, Michael, Pawtucket	.667	40	3	2	2	2	0	0	0	2	0	0	0	1	0	0	0	0	0
Daulton, Darren, Maine*	.214	20	70	9	15	27	1	1	3	10	3	0	1	0	16	1	15	5	1
David, Andre, Tidewater*	.300	133	480	97	144	225	22	4	17	73	8	0	8	12	76	5	36	3	0
Davis, Gerald, Toledo	.203	51	118	9	24	28	4	0	0	12	2	0	1	0	15	1	18	1	2
Davis, Trench, Richmond*	.256	114	441	51	113	144	14	4	3	29	2	2	1	1	35	2	45	44	15
Day, Randall, Syracuse	.231	8	13	3	3	6	0	0	1	3	0	0	0	1	5	1	4	0	0
DeAngelis, Steven, Maine*	.156	16	45	2	7	8	1	0	0	3	1	1	1	1	4	0	13	0	2
Destrade, Orestes, Columbus†	.256	135	465	76	119	226	26	3	25	81	7	0	3	5	79	9	118	0	2
Dobie, Reginald, Richmond	.125	26	16	3	2	2	0	0	0	1	0	1	0	1	0	0	4	0	0
Dodson, Patrick, Pawtucket*	.275	111	367	59	101	172	15	1	18	72	9	0	5	0	67	10	83	4	1
Dowell, Kenneth, Maine	.283	102	307	34	87	107	11	0	3	31	4	8	1	1	40	0	77	7	9
Ducey, Rob, Syracuse*	.284	100	359	62	102	166	14	10	10	60	10	0	5	3	61	5	88	7	7
Earl, Scott, Toledo	.246	89	280	34	69	99	14	2	4	32	2	2	2	1	28	0	54	13	6
Edens, Thomas, Tidewater*	.000	25	7	0	0	0	0	0	0	1	0	3	0	0	1	0	2	0	0
Eichelberger, Juan, Richmond	.250	40	4	1	1	1	0	0	0	0	0	0	0	0	1	0	2	0	0
Elster, Kevin, Tidewater	.310	134	549	83	170	241	33	7	8	74	7	3	3	1	35	4	62	7	3
Escobar, Jose, Syracuse	.353	37	68	12	24	30	2	2	0	14	0	0	0	0	0	0	8	0	0
Espino, Juan, Columbus	.229	53	153	13	35	51	10	0	2	23	2	0	3	3	18	2	24	0	1
Estes, Frank, Syracuse*	.276	76	214	23	59	83	12	0	4	32	5	1	6	1	11	2	21	0	2
Falcone, David, Rochester*	.091	3	11	0	1	1	0	0	0	1	0	0	0	0	1	0	1	0	1
Felice, Jason, Tidewater	.150	8	20	2	3	7	1	0	1	3	1	0	0	0	1	0	6	0	1
Fields, Bruce, Toledo*	.305	123	446	75	136	185	32	4	3	51	7	1	1	1	41	4	48	24	8
Fischlin, Michael, Richmond	.203	103	306	32	62	73	9	1	0	20	4	6	2	1	47	2	50	5	2
Fortenberry, Jimmy, Maine*	.000	12	27	0	0	0	0	0	0	0	0	0	0	0	0	0	5	0	0
Freeman, Marvin, Maine	.167	10	6	0	1	1	0	0	0	0	0	0	0	0	0	0	5	0	0
Frohwirth, Todd, Maine	.000	27	2	0	0	0	0	0	0	0	0	0	0	0	0	0	2	0	0
Garcia, Damaso, Richmond	.000	1	1	0	0	0	0	0	0	0	0	0	0	0	0	0	1	0	0
Gelatt, David, Tidewater	.167	3	6	0	1	1	0	0	0	0	0	0	0	0	0	0	0	0	0
Geren, Robert, Columbus	.150	5	20	1	3	6	0	0	1	3	0	1	0	0	0	0	9	0	0
Gibbons, John, Tidewater	.266	103	323	43	86	147	25	0	12	61	2	1	4	5	49	6	97	0	0
Gibson, Kirk, Toledo*	.235	6	17	2	4	4	0	0	0	3	1	0	0	0	4	0	3	1	0
Gibson, Paul, Toledo	.000	28	1	0	0	0	0	0	0	0	0	0	0	0	0	0	0	0	0
Gibson, Robert, Tidewater	.048	25	21	0	1	1	0	0	0	0	0	0	0	0	1	0	9	0	1
Glavine, Thomas, Richmond*	.000	22	12	0	0	0	0	0	0	0	0	2	0	0	2	0	1	0	0
Glynn, Edward, Tidewater	.000	40	1	0	0	0	0	0	0	0	0	0	0	0	0	0	1	0	0
Gonzales, Rene, Rochester	.300	42	170	20	51	66	9	3	0	24	4	4	4	1	13	2	17	4	2
Gonzalez, Angel, Pawtucket	.400	10	35	4	14	18	4	0	0	6	0	1	0	0	3	0	4	0	1
Gooden, Dwight, Tidewater	.200	4	5	0	1	1	0	0	0	0	0	0	0	0	1	0	2	0	0
Green, Otis, Syracuse*	.256	131	473	62	121	169	21	6	5	60	5	3	5	5	45	4	96	15	10
Griffin, David, Richmond	.248	128	463	50	115	183	21	1	15	58	6	0	4	2	43	1	99	0	0
Guerrero, Inocencio, Richmond	.256	79	250	33	64	105	15	1	8	38	4	0	1	2	29	0	63	0	0
Gutierrez, Joaquin, Rochester	.255	92	333	32	85	106	9	3	2	25	3	4	3	3	19	3	42	7	5
Hart, Michael, Rochester*	.257	118	439	65	113	201	26	1	20	61	4	1	4	1	58	3	64	0	6
Hatcher, Johnny, Richmond	.229	61	179	9	41	56	10	1	1	19	1	1	1	0	4	0	26	5	4
Heath, Kelly, Richmond	.244	114	352	49	86	133	21	1	8	30	3	5	2	0	59	1	64	15	6
Hensley, Charles, Richmond*	.250	45	8	0	2	4	2	0	0	1	0	0	0	0	0	0	1	0	0
Hill, Glenallen, Syracuse	.235	137	536	65	126	211	25	6	16	77	10	1	5	1	25	1	152	22	9
Hoffman, Glenn, Pawtucket	.231	46	160	18	37	50	7	0	2	22	3	1	1	4	14	0	19	2	0
Holman, Dale, Richmond*	.242	67	165	17	40	57	9	1	2	21	1	1	3	2	21	4	25	3	1
Horn, Samuel, Pawtucket*	.321	94	333	57	107	216	19	0	30	84	8	0	2	5	33	3	88	0	0
Hudler, Rex, Rochester	.255	31	106	22	27	49	5	1	5	10	2	1	0	1	2	0	15	9	2
Hughes, Keith, 40 Col-50 Maine*	.294	90	316	48	93	167	15	4	17	57	3	0	2	3	37	2	58	4	2
Hurdle, Clinton, Tidewater*	.257	97	288	38	74	122	27	0	7	45	5	0	5	1	47	3	47	1	0
Infante, Alexis, Syracuse	.226	107	319	40	72	93	7	4	2	30	4	1	1	1	23	0	37	18	9
Innis, Jeffrey, Tidewater	.000	29	2	0	0	0	0	0	0	0	0	0	0	0	0	0	0	0	0
Jackson, Kenneth, Maine	.161	14	31	3	5	8	1	1	0	3	0	0	0	1	7	0	3	0	1
Jackson, Michael, Maine	.000	2	1	0	0	0	0	0	0	0	0	0	0	0	0	0	0	0	0
James, Christopher, Maine	.225	13	40	5	9	13	2	1	0	3	0	0	2	0	3	1	9	0	0
Jaster, Scott, Tidewater	.000	1	1	0	0	0	0	0	0	0	0	0	0	0	0	0	0	0	0
Jelks, Gregory, Maine	.266	123	433	67	115	209	17	4	23	79	13	2	6	2	52	1	82	14	9
Jeltz, Steven, Maine†	.333	24	72	6	24	31	7	0	0	3	0	1	0	1	13	0	8	1	0
Jones, Ronald, Maine*	.247	90	316	33	78	120	13	4	7	32	2	1	1	3	38	1	50	13	4
Kelly, Roberto, Columbus	.278	118	471	77	131	205	19	8	13	62	8	1	8	3	33	0	116	51	10
Kittle, Ronald, Columbus	.222	4	18	3	4	4	0	0	0	1	1	0	0	0	1	0	5	0	0
Latham, William, Tidewater*	.111	15	9	1	1	1	0	0	0	0	0	0	0	0	0	2	0	1	0	0
LeBoeuf, Alan, Maine*	.265	105	298	31	79	102	14	0	3	29	5	2	3	1	44	7	26	3	5
Lee, Manuel, Syracuse†	.203	74	251	25	51	71	9	5	3	26	4	3	2	0	10	0	50	2	2
Legg, Gregory, Maine	.241	95	348	48	84	120	16	4	4	30	2	1	3	1	27	1	47	8	2
Liriano, Nelson, Syracuse†	.250	130	531	72	133	202	19	10	10	55	4	5	6	2	44	3	76	36	10
Little, Bryan, Columbus†	.247	76	223	25	55	72	7	5	0	18	1	7	2	1	24	2	17	2	2
Lockwood, Richard, Tidewater†	.241	65	228	31	55	91	10	1	8	33	4	2	1	0	16	4	42	0	0
Lollar, Timothy, Toledo*	.200	10	5	0	1	1	0	0	0	0	0	0	0	0	0	0	2	0	0
Lomastro, Gerardo, Rochester	.264	21	72	9	19	29	2	1	2	12	1	0	2	3	5	0	12	1	0
Lombardi, Phillip, Columbus	.268	67	209	32	56	89	13	1	6	33	4	1	5	4	39	0	28	3	1
Lombarski, Thomas, Tidewater*	.214	73	173	21	37	47	6	2	0	19	4	0	1	0	22	2	31	1	1
Lowry, Dwight, Toledo*	.194	42	93	8	18	21	3	0	0	3	0	2	0	1	12	0	18	1	0
Loy, Darren, Maine	.138	56	109	7	15	16	1	0	0	6	0	3	2	1	10	5	21	1	1
Lusader, Scott, Toledo*	.269	136	505	78	136	232	29	8	17	80	3	2	4	1	50	2	93	19	5

Player and Club	Pct.	G.	AB.	R.	H.	TB.	2B.	3B.	HR.	RBI.	GW.	SH.	SF.	HP.	BB.	Int. BB.	SO.	SB.	CS.
Lyden, Mitchell, Columbus	.220	29	100	7	22	25	3	0	0	8	4	1	3	1	4	0	22	1	0
Maddux, Michael, Maine	.100	28	10	4	1	1	0	0	0	0	1	0	0	0	0	0	1	0	0
Marzano, John, Pawtucket	.282	70	255	46	72	124	22	0	10	35	5	2	1	5	21	0	50	2	3
McInnis, William, Pawtucket°	.205	21	78	7	16	21	5	0	0	5	0	1	0	0	4	0	15	2	2
McKnight, Jefferson, Tidewater†	.255	87	184	21	47	66	7	3	2	25	3	1	4	1	24	1	22	0	1
Meacham, Robert, Columbus	.273	40	154	28	42	62	5	3	3	23	1	4	2	2	26	0	24	10	7
Mesh, Michael, Pawtucket	.198	64	177	22	35	53	8	2	2	18	2	6	0	2	17	0	31	6	4
Miller-Jones, Gary, Pawtucket†	.245	127	420	60	103	156	15	4	10	60	9	6	5	4	44	2	61	8	8
Miller, Keith, Tidewater	.248	53	202	29	50	79	9	1	6	22	2	3	0	1	14	1	36	14	2
Miller, Keith, Maine†	.292	122	383	61	112	184	16	4	16	54	4	2	2	4	55	3	72	20	5
Milligan, Randy, Tidewater	.326	136	457	99	149	272	28	4	29	103	7	0	5	4	91	10	77	8	4
Mizerock, John, Richmond°	.278	90	277	21	77	103	20	0	2	30	6	2	3	0	28	2	38	3	0
Monell, Johnny, Tidewater†	.000	1	1	0	0	0	0	0	0	0	0	0	0	0	0	0	1	0	0
Moronko, Jeffrey, Columbus	.245	100	347	52	85	157	17	8	13	56	4	0	2	2	40	1	79	17	10
Motley, Darryl, Richmond	.254	113	422	54	107	172	24	1	13	58	8	0	3	3	32	1	65	6	5
Myers, Gregory, Syracuse°	.246	107	342	35	84	135	19	1	10	47	2	3	2	1	22	3	46	3	3
Nelson, Ricky, Tidewater°	.157	17	51	2	8	14	0	0	2	6	1	0	0	0	6	0	11	0	1
Newell, Thomas, Maine	.133	31	15	0	2	2	0	0	0	1	0	0	0	0	0	0	4	0	0
Newsom, Gary, Richmond	.171	10	35	2	6	9	0	0	1	3	1	2	0	0	1	0	4	1	1
Nichols, Carl, Rochester	.255	108	364	45	93	147	15	3	11	52	6	6	0	3	42	1	76	3	4
Nichols, Howard, Maine	.317	36	123	18	39	56	9	1	2	11	3	1	0	1	8	0	13	0	0
Olander, James, Maine	.214	43	145	17	31	41	7	0	1	8	0	1	0	0	13	1	30	2	2
Olson, Gregory, Tidewater	.283	47	120	15	34	50	8	1	2	15	3	2	2	0	14	1	13	0	0
Ortiz, Alejandro, Rochester	.167	2	6	0	1	2	1	0	0	1	1	0	0	1	0	0	1	0	0
Padget, Chris, Rochester°	.257	47	152	16	39	64	4	0	7	29	3	1	4	0	15	2	36	3	1
Palacios, Rey, Toledo	.258	133	449	50	116	181	22	2	13	60	10	9	3	2	34	2	86	6	7
Pardo, Alberto, Richmond†	.213	16	47	8	10	19	3	0	2	5	0	0	0	0	7	0	8	0	0
Pasqua, Daniel, Columbus	.341	23	85	16	29	53	6	0	6	15	2	1	0	1	5	0	21	2	0
Pedrique, Alfredo, Tidewater	.259	10	27	2	7	7	0	0	0	3	0	0	1	0	0	0	6	1	1
Rabb, John, Richmond	.226	121	403	57	91	172	15	3	20	50	4	1	4	2	50	2	87	11	11
Ransom, Jeffrey, Toledo†	.248	114	343	40	85	127	18	0	8	38	3	2	2	2	31	3	67	2	3
Rayford, Floyd, Rochester	.277	48	166	30	46	86	10	0	10	28	3	0	1	2	13	3	29	0	0
Reed, Darren, Columbus	.329	21	79	15	26	59	3	3	8	16	0	0	0	4	0		9	0	2
Reed, Jody, Pawtucket	.296	136	510	77	151	198	22	2	7	51	2	8	5	2	69	0	23	9	7
Rios, Carlos, Richmond	.274	52	190	21	52	68	10	3	0	17	0	4	5	0	10	1	16	2	1
Ripken, William, Rochester	.286	74	238	32	68	83	15	0	0	11	1	7	0	0	21	0	23	7	2
Rivera, German, Toledo	.260	112	408	53	106	170	24	2	12	70	12	0	6	3	29	4	45	9	2
Roenicke, Ronald, Maine†	.242	38	124	15	30	43	10	0	1	15	3	2	2	1	15	2	21	3	2
Roman, Ray, Maine	.225	38	89	10	20	31	5	0	2	12	1	1	0	0	1	0	28	0	1
Romine, Kevin, Pawtucket	.267	129	491	72	131	190	24	1	11	52	5	0	3	0	64	0	70	21	6
Roof, Eugene, Toledo†	.000	5	5	0	0	0	0	0	0	0	0	0	0	0	0	0	0	0	0
Runge, Paul, Richmond	.277	70	235	34	65	91	11	3	3	21	1	3	1	1	63	0	26	12	7
Russell, Anthony, Columbus	.333	15	51	11	17	24	2	1	1	4	1	2	0	1	6	0	12	6	2
Russell, John, Maine	.203	44	143	15	29	58	6	1	7	24	2	1	1	0	22	0	37	2	3
Sakata, Lenn, Columbus	.313	8	16	1	5	5	0	0	0	1	0	1	1	0	3	0	2	0	0
Salas, Mark, Columbus°	.233	12	43	5	10	17	1	0	2	4	0	0	0	0	5	0	8	0	0
Salcedo, Ronnie, Rochester°	.232	71	203	21	47	73	14	0	4	28	5	3	2	5	31	2	22	3	4
Sax, David, Pawtucket	.240	85	262	33	63	103	10	0	10	33	2	4	3	1	48	0	42	0	2
Schuler, David, Richmond	.000	13	2	0	0	0	0	0	0	0	0	0	0	0	0	0	1	0	0
Schulze, Donald, Tidewater	.000	15	8	0	0	0	0	0	0	0	0	0	0	0	0	0	1	0	0
Schwarz, Thomas, Maine	.118	6	17	2	2	5	0	0	0	3	0	0	1	0	1	0	4	0	0
Scott, Richard, Columbus	.199	51	166	14	33	45	6	0	2	15	1	3	0	1	9	0	33	0	2
Seibert, Gibson, Maine	.210	46	124	13	26	39	3	2	2	11	1	0	0	1	23	1	28	1	4
Sharperson, Michael, Syracuse	.299	88	338	67	101	147	21	5	5	26	1	2	1	1	40	0	41	14	10
Sheaffer, Danny, Pawtucket	.256	69	242	32	62	85	13	2	2	25	5	1	1	0	6	2	29	6	3
Shelby, John, Rochester†	.250	6	24	5	6	11	2	0	1	2	0	0	0	1	5	1	4	1	1
Sherlock, Glenn, Columbus°	.214	6	14	1	3	3	0	0	0	1	0	0	1	0	1	0	3	0	0
Simmons, Nelson, Rochester†	.271	64	207	25	56	77	10	1	3	21	2	0	3	0	21	1	28	0	0
Skinner, Joel, Columbus	.242	49	178	19	43	75	10	2	6	27	6	1	2	1	10	0	44	0	1
Smith, David, Rochester	.188	31	85	12	16	21	2	0	1	6	0	2	1	0	17	0	15	0	0
Smoltz, John, Richmond	.000	3	1	0	0	0	0	0	0	0	0	0	0	0	0	0	0	0	0
Speck, Clifford 20 Rich-8 Col.	.000	28	6	0	0	0	0	0	0	0	0	0	0	0	0	0	5	0	0
Springer, Steven, Columbus	.281	132	467	65	131	183	23	4	7	54	6	4	5	3	41	6	78	6	3
Stanicek, Peter, Rochester†	.297	38	145	29	43	62	13	0	2	16	2	1	2	2	24	1	21	8	4
Stenhouse, David, Syracuse	.221	64	140	6	31	38	7	0	0	9	2	6	0	0	19	0	29	1	0
Stenhouse, Michael, Toledo°	.280	117	343	39	96	146	15	1	11	42	6	5	2	3	63	5	46	7	2
Stone, Jeffrey, Maine°	.232	40	151	22	35	48	6	2	1	10	1	3	3	2	9	0	34	9	7
Strange, Douglas, Toledo†	.244	16	45	7	11	16	2	0	1	5	1	1	1	0	4	0	7	3	2
Strucher, Mark, Richmond	.230	27	87	9	20	29	3	0	2	7	1	0	0	1	4	0	13	1	1
Tarver, LaSchelle, Pawtucket°	.218	13	55	5	12	13	1	0	0	5	0	0	0	0	3	0	6	1	2
Thornton, Louis, Syracuse	.265	122	464	64	123	170	10	5	9	47	3	0	3	1	23	5	71	39	9
Tiburcio, Fredrick, Toledo°	.179	40	67	10	12	21	3	0	0	6	0	0	0	0	5	0	17	5	3
Toliver, Freddie, Maine	.143	25	14	2	2	2	0	0	0	2	1	2	1	0	0	0	6	0	0
Tolman, Timothy, Toledo	.314	111	379	65	119	198	30	2	15	63	7	1	9	3	55	1	51	9	7
Torve, Kelvin, Rochester°	.262	86	252	27	66	103	10	0	9	32	2	5	1	0	38	6	36	10	1
Traber, James, Rochester	.274	127	482	69	132	232	31	3	21	71	9	4	7	5	43	10	62	6	7
Tremblay, Gary, Pawtucket	.261	7	23	1	6	6	0	0	0	1	0	0	0	0	3	0	8	0	0
Tumpane, Robert, Richmond°	.175	33	57	5	10	19	3	0	2	9	3	0	0	0	7	0	11	0	0
Turner, Shane, Columbus°	.224	29	76	10	17	21	0	2	0	7	1	1	0	0	5	0	16	2	1
Ullger, Scott, Rochester	.277	96	307	52	85	140	19	0	12	38	5	2	0	2	39	1	84	1	3
Van Gorder, David, Rochester	.136	22	66	7	9	14	2	0	1	5	1	1	0	0	5	0	3	0	0
Vaughn, DeWayne, Tidewater	.167	50	6	0	1	1	0	0	0	1	0	1	0	0	1	0	1	0	0
Velarde, Randy, Columbus	.319	49	185	21	59	96	10	6	5	33	2	0	1	4	14	0	36	8	2
Wade, Scott, Pawtucket	.254	108	355	50	90	158	12	4	16	60	1	0	6	3	32	1	123	11	9
Walewander, James, Toledo†	.271	59	210	27	57	68	9	1	0	12	0	1	0	3	28	1	31	18	11
Walter, Gene, Tidewater°	.000	34	3	0	0	0	0	0	0	0	0	0	0	0	0	0	2	0	0
Ward, Kevin, Maine	.209	106	326	48	68	126	13	3	13	37	6	2	5		30	0	68	14	8
Washington, Ronald, Rochester	.320	70	272	50	87	151	17	1	15	43	4	0	3	3	10	0	62	8	7
Watts, Leonard, Maine°	.200	15	5	2	1	1	0	0	0	0	0	0	0	0	0	0	2	0	0
West, Matthew, Richmond†	.273	18	11	1	3	4	1	0	0	0	0	0	0	0	2	0	0	0	0
Wilborn, Thaddeus, Rochester†	.000	1	4	0	0	0	0	0	0	0	0	0	0	0	0	0	0	0	0
Williams, Dana, Pawtucket	.317	48	189	29	60	87	10	1	5	23	4	0	4	2	14	1	13	6	3
Worthington, Craig, Rochester	.258	109	383	46	99	136	14	1	7	50	8	3	2	2	32	3	62	0	2

Player and Club	Pct.	G.	AB.	R.	H.	TB.	2B.	3B.	HR.	RBI.	GW.	SH.	SF.	HP.	BB.	Int. BB.	SO.	SB.	CS.
Wyatt, David, Tidewater	.125	18	8	0	1	1	0	0	0	0	0	0	0	0	0	0	1	0	0
Yost, Edgar, Richmond	.304	9	23	3	7	11	1	0	1	1	0	1	0	0	0	0	6	1	0
Young, Michael, Rochester†	.320	7	25	4	8	16	0	1	2	5	0	0	0	0	3	0	7	0	0
Ziem, Stephen, Richmond	.400	23	5	0	2	2	0	0	0	2	1	2	0	0	0	0	2	0	0
Zuvella, Paul, Columbus	.301	69	269	47	81	110	15	4	2	25	4	3	2	3	22	1	21	13	2

The following pitchers, listed alphabetically by club, with games in parentheses, had no plate appearances, primarily through use of designated hitters:

COLUMBUS—Armstrong, Michael (3); Arnsberg, Bradley (19); Bordi, Richard (25); Carreno, Amalio (11); Clements, Patrick (4); Filson, Peter (22); Frey, Steven (23); Fulton, William (31); George, Stephen (2); Graham, Randle (41); Guidry, Ronald (1); Holland, Alfred (33); Hudson, Charles (5); Knox, Jeffrey (2); Layana, Timothy (13); Leiter, Alois (5); Pulido, Alfonso (34); Rasmussen, Dennis (1); Romanick, Ronald (18); Rosenberg, Steven (21); Shirley, Robert (5); Tewksbury, Robert (11); Thompson, Richard (2).

MAINE—Calhoun, Jeffrey (28); Riley, George (8); Ritchie, Wallace (13); Rozema, David (7); Smith, Daryl (4).

PAWTUCKET—Araujo, Anazario (43); Bolton, Thomas (5); Boyd, Dennis (3); Curry, Stephen (28); Davis, Charles (24); Ellsworth, Steven (27); Gardner, Wesley (5); Johnson, Mitchell (54); Leister, John (21); Rochford, Michael (22); Sellers, Jeffrey (5); Stewart, Hector (53); Woodward, Robert (21).

RICHMOND—Boever, Joseph (6); O'Neal, Randall (1); Olwine, Edward (22); Stringfellow, Thornton (8).

ROCHESTER—Alicea, Miguel (8); Arnold, Tony (6); Ballard, Jeffrey (23); Brown, Michael (1); Cooper, Donald (14); DeLeon, Luis (33); Dixon, Kenneth (5); Flanagan, Michael (3); Green, Christopher (9); Griffin, Michael (17); Habyan, John (7); Havens, Bradley (9); Householder, Brian (7); Huffman, Phillip (14); Kinnunen, Michael (48); Kucharski, Joseph (19); Long, Robert (10); McGregor, Scott (3); Musselman, Ronald (22); O'Connor, Jack (25); Oliveras, Francisco (6); Raczka, Michael (23); Rasmussen, Eric (49); Skinner, Michael (7); Strode, Lester (4); Telford, Anthony (1); Williamson, Mark (1).

SYRACUSE—Aquino, Luis (26); Davis, Steven (20); Filer, Thomas (8); Fireovid, Stephen (10); Gordon, Donald (41); Hudson, Anthony (40); Johnson, Joseph (13); Jones, Odell (31); Leal, Luis (4); McLaughlin, Colin (46); McMurtry, Craig (10); Segura, Jose (43); Stottlemyre, Todd (34); Ward, Duane (46); Wells, David (43).

TIDEWATER—Cone, David (3); Givens, Brian (1); McCarthy, Thomas (10); Mitchell, John (8); Myers, Randall (5); Roman, Jose (45).

TOLEDO—Barlow, Ricky (41); Best, Karl (28); Heinkel, Donald (29); Henneman, Michael (11); Hernandez, Guillermo (2); Jones, Jeffrey (18); Kelly, Bryan (6); Laskey, William (56); Madden, Morris (24); Meridith, Ronald (4); Mitchell, Charles (2); Murray, Jed (34); Pacella, John (26); Pena, Ramon (18); Searcy, Stephen (10); Snell, Nathaniel (12); Wright, Richard (20).

GRAND SLAM HOME RUNS—Gibbons, 2; Campusano, Cannizzaro, Dalena, David, Elster, Hatcher, Hoffman, Horn, Lusader, Meacham, Keith Miller (Maine), Miller-Jones, Milligan, Padgett, Pasqua, Romine, Tolman, Traber, Wade, 1 each.

AWARDED FIRST BASE ON CATCHER'S INTERFERENCE—Day 2 (Espino, Lyden); Gutierrez (Espino); Strucher (Lowry); Walter (Cipolloni).

CLUB FIELDING

Club	Pct.	G.	PO.	A.	E.	DP.	PB.	Club	Pct.	G.	PO.	A.	E.	DP.	PB.
Rochester	.979	139	3642	1473	109	135	10	Columbus	.974	140	3648	1529	139	136	9
Pawtucket	.977	140	3643	1479	122	133	16	Maine	.973	140	3541	1392	137	137	13
Tidewater	.977	140	3604	1523	122	119	4	Syracuse	.969	140	3679	1355	162	155	10
Richmond	.975	139	3597	1541	134	128	11	Toledo	.967	140	3643	1507	174	127	8

Triple Plays—Pawtucket, Rochester.

INDIVIDUAL FIELDING
FIRST BASEMEN

†Throws lefthanded.

Player and Club	Pct.	G.	PO.	A.	E.	DP.	Player and Club	Pct.	G.	PO.	A.	E.	DP.
Benzinger, Pawtucket	1.000	18	144	12	0	20	Lowry, Toledo	1.000	7	41	3	0	4
Corcoran, Maine*	.989	34	261	15	3	30	Loy, Maine	.971	8	63	5	2	4
Dalena, Columbus	.992	84	727	56	6	68	McKnight, Tidewater	1.000	12	18	4	0	2
Daulton, Maine	1.000	4	22	1	0	1	Miller-Jones, Pawtucket	1.000	5	31	3	0	1
David, Tidewater*	.993	15	141	7	1	12	Milligan, Tidewater	.990	101	858	88	10	66
Destrade, Columbus	.989	60	509	47	6	48	Palacios, Toledo	.983	20	113	6	2	7
Dodson, Pawtucket*	.986	109	926	84	14	86	Pedrique, Tidewater	1.000	2	3	1	0	0
Estes, Syracuse*	.979	29	222	15	5	29	Ransom, Toledo	.989	28	163	17	2	15
Falcone, Rochester	1.000	1	11	1	0	1	Rivera, Toledo	.974	4	32	6	1	4
Gonzales, Rochester	1.000	1	5	1	0	1	Roof, Toledo	1.000	1	3	0	0	0
Green, Rochester	.986	117	917	75	14	111	Sax, Pawtucket	.974	5	35	3	1	6
GRIFFIN, Richmond	.995	119	1012	99	6	94	Sheaffer, Pawtucket	1.000	6	48	8	0	2
Guerrero, Richmond	1.000	12	72	3	0	8	Stenhouse, Toledo	.992	80	667	64	6	55
Holman, Richmond	1.000	2	6	0	0	1	Strucher, Richmond	1.000	2	15	0	0	0
Horn, Pawtucket*	.938	4	28	2	2	3	Tiburcio, Toledo*	.500	1	1	0	1	0
Hughes, Maine*	1.000	2	3	0	0	0	Tolman, Toledo	.993	37	254	18	2	26
Hurdle, Tidewater	.995	24	199	9	1	16	Torve, Rochester	.996	77	632	48	3	62
Jelks, Maine	.994	62	432	35	3	38	Traber, Rochester*	.992	45	337	24	3	35
LeBoeuf, Maine	.992	49	353	19	3	40	Tumpane, Richmond*	.983	19	114	4	2	12
Lombarski, Tidewater	1.000	13	59	3	0	9	Ullger, Rochester	.992	29	222	17	2	20

Triple Plays—Sax, Torve.

SECOND BASEMEN

Player and Club	Pct.	G.	PO.	A.	E.	DP.	Player and Club	Pct.	G.	PO.	A.	E.	DP.
Blauser, Richmond	.955	13	24	40	3	8	MILLER-JONES, Pawtucket	.978	119	220	316	12	78
Bonilla, Columbus	1.000	5	10	13	0	5	K. Miller, Tidewater	.979	44	100	128	5	24
Cannizzaro, Pawtucket	.980	25	39	59	2	11	K. Miller, Maine	.965	72	123	183	11	41
Chavez, Toledo	.985	15	23	43	1	14	Newsom, Richmond	.925	6	11	26	3	1
Childress, Richmond	.980	9	13	35	1	3	Pedrique, Tidewater	1.000	4	9	8	0	2
Dowell, Maine	.972	6	18	17	1	7	Rabb, Richmond	.667	2	2	0	1	0
Earl, Toledo	.964	46	67	122	7	17	Rios, Richmond	.958	15	29	40	3	10
Escobar, Syracuse	1.000	3	4	5	0	2	Ripken, Rochester	.975	72	153	199	9	51
Gelatt, Tidewater	1.000	3	6	10	0	2	Runge, Rochester	.974	58	100	167	7	40
Gonzales, Rochester	.977	8	18	25	1	3	Sakata, Columbus	.975	8	13	26	1	6
Gutierrez, Rochester	1.000	4	6	6	0	3	Scott, Columbus	.993	26	51	85	1	23
Heath, Richmond	.981	40	96	115	4	38	Sharperson, Syracuse	.974	9	13	24	1	3
Hoffman, Pawtucket	1.000	3	1	3	0	0	Springer, Tidewater	.948	68	102	188	16	41
Hudler, Rochester	.955	5	8	13	1	7	Stanicek, Rochester	.958	36	71	90	7	31
Legg, Maine	.978	76	150	209	8	46	Tolman, Toledo	.947	35	71	91	9	22
Liriano, Syracuse	.969	130	246	346	19	96	Ullger, Rochester	.974	8	12	25	1	3
Little, Columbus	.982	59	106	118	4	27	Walewander, Toledo	.957	56	129	139	12	36
McKnight, Tidewater	.956	51	73	99	8	21	Washington, Rochester	.981	15	24	27	1	9
Meacham, Columbus	.993	31	59	80	1	16	Zuvella, Columbus	.982	24	52	57	2	14

Triple Plays—Miller-Jones, Stanicek.

THIRD BASEMEN

Player and Club	Pct.	G.	PO.	A.	E.	DP.	Player and Club	Pct.	G.	PO.	A.	E.	DP.
Alvarez, Columbus	.979	19	12	35	1	2	Mesh, Pawtucket	.926	33	27	61	7	8
Bonilla, Columbus	1.000	1	0	2	0	0	Miller, Maine	1.000	4	0	3	0	0
Cannizzaro, Pawtucket	.962	21	9	42	2	1	Moronko, Columbus	.957	78	57	165	10	16
Castro, Syracuse	.983	26	19	40	1	5	Newsom, Richmond	1.000	1	0	1	0	0
Chavez, Toledo	.891	25	16	41	7	2	Nichols, Maine	.934	35	24	47	5	5
Childress, Richmond	.954	39	26	98	6	6	Ortiz, Rochester	1.000	1	0	5	0	0
Coles, Toledo	1.000	8	4	7	0	0	Palacios, Toledo	.909	36	20	50	7	2
Dowell, Maine	1.000	4	0	5	0	0	Pedrique, Tidewater	1.000	3	1	5	0	0
Earl, Toledo	.925	15	9	28	3	2	Rabb, Richmond	.868	17	12	34	7	3
Escobar, Syracuse	.923	7	2	10	1	0	Ransom, Toledo	.934	24	20	37	4	1
Estes, Syracuse*	1.000	1	3	0	0	0	Rios, Richmond	.984	28	20	43	1	3
Gonzales, Rochester	.985	22	19	45	1	4	Rivera, Toledo	.928	38	12	78	7	2
Gonzalez, Pawtucket	.920	7	5	18	2	1	Runge, Richmond	1.000	13	9	23	0	0
Heath, Richmond	.900	35	14	67	9	8	Russell, Maine	1.000	3	1	4	0	0
Hoffman, Pawtucket	.961	45	34	88	5	9	Sax, Pawtucket	.886	45	39	62	13	4
Holman, Richmond	.800	2	1	3	1	1	Schwarz, Maine	1.000	6	1	12	0	0
Infante, Syracuse	.951	40	29	69	5	11	Scott, Columbus	1.000	14	7	18	0	2
James, Maine	1.000	6	3	4	0	0	Seibert, Maine	.955	29	28	36	3	6
Jelks, Maine	.915	50	39	80	11	5	Sharperson, Syracuse	.966	75	68	128	7	16
LeBoeuf, Maine	.870	8	5	15	3	2	Springer, Tidewater	.948	80	40	125	9	10
Legg, Maine	.852	12	6	17	4	1	Strange, Toledo	.933	16	14	28	3	2
Little, Columbus	1.000	20	9	34	0	2	Strucher, Richmond	.895	15	9	25	4	3
Lockwood, Tidewater	.989	42	19	73	1	10	Tolman, Toledo	.750	2	0	3	1	0
Lombardi, Columbus	.815	26	17	49	15	3	Ullger, Rochester	.900	6	4	5	1	2
Lombarski, Tidewater	.950	45	20	76	5	2	Washington, Rochester	.886	11	8	23	4	4
Loy, Maine	1.000	1	0	1	0	1	WORTHINGTON, Rochester	.935	101	79	211	20	16
McKnight, Tidewater	1.000	4	2	6	0	1							

Triple Plays—Hoffman.

SHORTSTOPS

Player and Club	Pct.	G.	PO.	A.	E.	DP.	Player and Club	Pct.	G.	PO.	A.	E.	DP.
Baker, Toledo	.957	115	190	342	24	81	Legg, Maine	.966	14	12	16	1	3
Blauser, Richmond	.942	21	32	66	6	13	McKnight, Tidewater	.933	3	7	7	1	3
Chavez, Toledo	.975	13	16	23	1	3	Meacham, Columbus	.957	11	23	44	3	11
Childress, Richmond	1.000	2	0	1	0	0	Mesh, Pawtucket	.976	9	16	25	1	9
Coles, Toledo	.667	1	1	1	1	0	Moronko, Columbus	.875	4	6	8	2	0
Dowell, Maine	.962	96	151	251	16	65	Newsom, Richmond	.929	3	5	8	1	2
Earl, Toledo	.947	20	18	53	4	7	Pedrique, Tidewater	1.000	1	1	3	0	1
Elster, Tidewater	.968	133	219	419	21	74	Reed, Pawtucket	.971	135	236	427	20	86
Escobar, Syracuse	.942	20	18	31	3	7	Rios, Richmond	.984	16	25	35	1	7
FISCHLIN, Richmond	.977	103	159	300	11	70	Ripken, Rochester	1.000	2	1	1	0	1
Gonzales, Rochester	.985	12	30	37	1	8	Scott, Columbus	.940	11	16	31	3	4
Gutierrez, Rochester	.969	87	135	269	13	57	Seibert, Maine	.967	10	10	19	1	5
Heath, Richmond	.875	8	5	9	2	1	Smith, Rochester	.967	31	31	85	4	20
Infante, Syracuse	.948	62	81	191	15	46	Springer, Tidewater	.972	5	11	24	1	4
Jackson, Maine	.935	12	13	30	3	9	Turner, Columbus	.917	24	35	53	8	14
Jelks, Maine	.900	3	3	6	1	1	Velarde, Columbus	.943	49	100	164	16	34
Jeltz, Maine	.954	24	45	79	6	18	Washington, Rochester	1.000	14	9	34	0	6
Lee, Syracuse	.928	74	120	177	23	47	Zuvella, Columbus	.957	45	79	121	9	25

Triple Play—Gonzales.

OUTFIELDERS

Player and Club	Pct.	G.	PO.	A.	E.	DP.	Player and Club	Pct.	G.	PO.	A.	E.	DP.
Anderson, Pawtucket*	1.000	23	48	1	0	0	Hughes, 35 Col-50 Maine*	.955	85	146	2	7	0
Bean, Toledo*	.970	104	228	1	7	0	Hurdle, Tidewater	.950	14	18	1	1	0
Benzinger, Pawtucket	.983	48	112	4	2	3	Infante, Syracuse	1.000	1	1	0	0	0
Blocker, Tidewater*	.977	123	286	8	7	6	James, Maine	1.000	7	19	0	0	0
Brown, Richmond	.946	25	34	1	2	0	Jelks, Maine	1.000	15	29	0	0	0
Buhner, Columbus	.980	133	275	20	6	6	Jones, Maine	.984	87	178	4	3	1
Burks, Pawtucket	1.000	11	25	0	0	0	Kelly, Columbus	.971	115	331	4	10	3
Campusano, Syracuse	.968	123	324	8	11	3	Lomastro, Rochester	.975	20	39	0	1	0
Cannizzaro, Pawtucket	.969	29	61	1	2	0	Lombardi, Columbus	1.000	14	20	1	0	0
Carreon, Tidewater*	.980	133	237	8	5	2	Lusader, Toledo*	.979	133	274	11	6	5
Castro, Syracuse	1.000	2	2	0	0	0	McInnis, Pawtucket*	1.000	21	48	1	0	0
Cathcart, Columbus*	1.000	28	58	2	0	0	McKnight, Tidewater	1.000	20	41	2	0	0
Cijntje, Rochester*	.944	16	34	0	2	0	Mesh, Pawtucket	.967	20	29	0	1	0
Coles, Toledo	1.000	2	2	0	0	0	K. Miller, Tidewater	1.000	6	12	1	0	0
Corcoran, Columbus*	.926	15	24	1	2	1	K. Miller, Maine	1.000	24	60	1	0	0
Cotto, Columbus	.974	32	73	3	2	0	Moronko, Columbus	.931	12	26	1	2	0
Coyle, Syracuse	.952	8	19	1	1	0	Motley, Richmond	.990	109	188	7	2	2
Craig, Rochester	1.000	8	13	0	0	0	Nelson, Tidewater	.938	17	30	0	2	0
Cuevas, Tidewater	1.000	3	2	0	0	0	Nichols, Rochester	.958	11	22	1	1	1
Dalena, Columbus	1.000	10	17	2	0	0	Olander, Maine	1.000	37	89	2	0	0
David, Tidewater*	.986	114	201	4	3	0	Padget, Rochester	.986	36	67	5	1	1
G. Davis, Toledo	.946	32	33	2	2	1	Palacios, Toledo	1.000	9	10	0	0	0
T. Davis, Richmond*.	.969	113	272	10	9	0	Pasqua, Columbus*	.982	20	55	0	1	0
DeAngelis, Maine*	1.000	10	13	0	0	0	Rabb, Richmond	.977	81	161	6	4	0
Ducey, Syracuse	.968	80	171	13	6	5	Ransom, Toledo	.833	5	5	0	1	0
Earl, Toledo	1.000	8	7	0	0	0	Reed, Columbus	.972	19	33	2	1	0
Felice, Tidewater	1.000	8	6	0	0	0	Roenicke, Maine*	.990	37	93	2	1	1
Fields, Toledo	.976	110	194	8	5	0	Romine, Pawtucket	.991	126	311	6	3	0
Fortenberry, Maine	1.000	10	10	0	0	0	A. Russell, Columbus	1.000	13	25	1	0	0
Green, Syracuse*	.929	13	22	4	2	0	J. Russell, Maine	.962	26	48	3	2	0
Guerrero, Richmond	1.000	3	6	0	0	0	Salcedo, Rochester	1.000	41	63	4	0	0
HART, Rochester*	.997	118	329	5	*1	0	Seibert, Maine	1.000	6	6	0	0	0
Hatcher, Richmond	.966	51	81	3	3	0	Sheaffer, Pawtucket	1.000	2	1	1	0	0
Heath, Richmond	1.000	29	36	7	0	3	Shelby, Rochester	1.000	6	14	0	0	0
Hill, Syracuse	.949	89	176	10	10	4	Simmons, Rochester	.972	63	103	3	3	0
Holman, Richmond	.960	34	46	2	2	0	Springer, Tidewater	1.000	5	5	0	0	0
Hudler, Rochester	.978	23	43	2	1	0	Stenhouse, Toledo	1.000	3	5	0	0	0

OUTFIELDERS—Continued

Player and Club	Pct.	G.	PO.	A.	E.	DP.	Player and Club	Pct.	G.	PO.	A.	E.	DP.
Stone, Maine	.978	38	89	1	2	1	Tumpane, Richmond*	1.000	3	2	0	0	0
Tarver, Pawtucket*	.967	12	29	0	1	0	Ullger, Rochester	.971	21	32	1	1	1
Thornton, Syracuse	.953	114	199	6	10	0	Wade, Pawtucket	.990	101	195	9	2	1
Tiburcio, Toledo*	.946	33	35	0	2	1	Ward, Maine	.958	86	151	7	7	0
Tolman, Toledo	.915	41	52	2	5	1	Washington, Rochester	.500	1	1	0	1	0
Traber, Rochester*	.969	81	154	3	5	1	Williams, Pawtucket	.984	45	115	5	2	2

CATCHERS

Player and Club	Pct.	G.	PO.	A.	E.	DP.	PB.	Player and Club	Pct.	G.	PO.	A.	E.	DP.	PB.
Cipolloni, Maine	.985	81	403	45	7	6	6	Olson, Tidewater	.987	39	219	12	3	1	0
Cliburn, Richmond	.977	18	115	15	3	0	4	Palacios, Toledo	.974	78	426	66	13	5	2
D'Alessandro, Richmond	.993	26	138	13	1	0	0	Pardo, Richmond	1.000	12	72	4	0	0	0
Daulton, Maine	1.000	16	116	11	0	2	1	Ransom, Toledo	.997	59	334	37	1	4	5
Espino, Columbus	.983	43	209	22	4	3	4	Rayford, Rochester	.986	23	131	11	2	1	1
Geren, Columbus	.958	5	20	3	1	1	1	Roman, Maine	.977	33	155	16	4	0	2
Gibbons, Tidewater	.987	99	506	31	7	3	3	Russell, Maine	1.000	14	58	7	0	0	2
Hurdle, Tidewater	.985	11	58	6	1	0	1	Salas, Columbus	1.000	9	46	5	0	3	1
Lombardi, Columbus	1.000	12	64	5	0	1	0	Sax, Pawtucket	.963	17	66	11	3	1	4
Lowry, Toledo	.962	21	66	10	3	1	1	Sheaffer, Pawtucket	.985	56	297	23	5	4	3
Loy, Maine	.991	26	98	9	1	2	2	Sherlock, Columbus	1.000	5	21	0	0	0	0
Lyden, Columbus	.970	24	120	11	4	1	2	Skinner, Columbus	.984	45	226	25	4	6	1
Marzano, Pawtucket	.978	66	326	36	8	5	7	Stenhouse, Syracuse	.988	64	303	20	4	4	2
Mizerock, Richmond	.977	87	504	54	13	7	7	Tremblay, Pawtucket	1.000	7	27	4	0	0	2
Myers, Syracuse	.984	106	637	50	11	6	8	Van Gorder, Rochester	.993	22	126	16	1	2	0
NICHOLS, Rochester	.988	99	595	64	8	9	9	Yost, Richmond	.897	7	31	4	4	0	0

PITCHERS

Player and Club	Pct.	G.	PO.	A.	E.	DP.	Player and Club	Pct.	G.	PO.	A.	E.	DP.
Aguilera, Tidewater	1.000	3	0	1	0	0	Habyan, Rochester	.900	7	3	6	1	0
Alicea, Rochester	1.000	8	0	2	0	0	Havens, Rochester*	1.000	9	2	5	0	0
Alvarez, Richmond	.950	22	12	26	2	1	Heinkel, Toledo	.976	29	16	25	1	3
Aquino, Syracuse	.923	26	5	7	1	0	Henneman, Toledo	1.000	11	2	6	0	0
Araujo, Pawtucket	.952	43	10	10	1	1	Hensley, Richmond*	.944	45	5	12	1	0
Arnold, Rochester	1.000	6	0	5	0	1	Holland, Columbus*	.923	33	2	10	1	5
Arnsberg, Columbus	.949	19	15	22	2	3	Householder, Rochester*	1.000	7	0	1	0	0
Assenmacher, Richmond*	1.000	4	1	3	0	0	A. Hudson, Syracuse	.864	40	5	14	3	2
Bair, Maine	.923	45	2	10	1	0	C. Hudson, Columbus	.500	5	0	1	1	0
Ballard, Rochester*	.958	23	4	19	1	0	Huffman, Rochester	.933	14	5	9	1	0
Barlow, Toledo	.778	41	9	12	6	1	Innis, Tidewater	.938	29	5	10	1	0
Barton, Maine*	.889	7	0	8	1	0	Jackson, Maine	1.000	2	0	3	0	0
Best, Toledo	1.000	28	2	6	0	0	J. Johnson, Syracuse	1.000	13	10	6	0	0
Boever, Richmond	1.000	6	2	0	0	0	M. Johnson, Pawtucket	1.000	24	3	6	0	0
Bolton, Pawtucket*	1.000	5	5	6	0	3	J. Jones, Toledo	.875	18	4	10	2	1
Bordi, Columbus	.875	25	5	2	1	0	O. Jones, Syracuse	.943	31	12	21	2	3
Boudreaux, Maine	1.000	7	0	12	0	1	Kelly, Maine	.800	6	2	2	1	0
Bowden, Maine*	.900	53	4	14	2	0	Kinnunen, Rochester*	1.000	48	4	19	0	1
Boyd, Pawtucket	1.000	3	2	5	0	0	Knox, Columbus	1.000	2	0	2	0	1
Brown, Rochester	1.000	1	1	1	0	0	Kucharski, Rochester	1.000	19	5	6	0	0
Buchanan, Tidewater*	1.000	29	4	16	0	1	Laskey, Toledo	.893	56	3	22	3	1
Calhoun, Maine*	1.000	28	3	8	0	0	Latham, Tidewater*	.933	15	4	10	1	1
Carlucci, Maine	1.000	19	2	5	0	0	Layana, Columbus	.926	13	8	17	2	1
Carreno, Columbus	1.000	11	0	2	0	0	Leal, Syracuse	1.000	4	0	3	0	0
Cary, Richmond*	.938	40	6	24	2	3	Leister, Pawtucket	.964	21	12	15	1	0
Chambers, Maine	.905	64	9	10	2	2	Leiter, Columbus*	1.000	5	2	6	0	3
Chiffer, Richmond	.875	43	1	6	1	0	Lollar, Toledo*	1.000	8	6	6	0	0
Clary, Richmond	.957	26	18	27	2	3	Long, Rochester	1.000	10	0	2	0	0
Clay, Maine	.917	15	6	16	2	2	Loy, Maine	1.000	4	0	1	0	0
Clements, Columbus*	1.000	4	3	4	0	1	Madden, Toledo*	1.000	24	3	12	0	0
Cone, Tidewater	1.000	3	2	1	0	0	Maddux, Maine	.923	18	9	15	2	0
Cooper, Rochester	1.000	14	2	7	0	1	McCarthy, Tidewater	1.000	10	2	3	0	0
Cowley, Maine	.944	13	2	15	1	3	McGregor, Rochester*	1.000	3	0	2	0	0
Curry, Pawtucket	.949	28	22	34	3	2	McKnight, Columbus*	1.000	1	0	1	0	0
Dalton, Pawtucket*	.964	39	10	17	1	4	McLaughlin, Syracuse	.833	46	2	3	1	0
C. Davis, Pawtucket	.900	24	5	4	1	0	McMurtry, Syracuse	1.000	9	3	8	0	1
S. Davis, Syracuse*	1.000	20	3	4	0	0	Meridith, Toledo*	1.000	4	1	3	0	0
DeLeon, Rochester	.857	33	0	6	1	0	C. Mitchell, Toledo	.750	2	1	2	1	1
Dixon, Rochester	1.000	5	1	2	0	1	J. Mitchell, Tidewater	.909	8	5	15	2	0
Dobie, Tidewater	.941	26	14	18	2	2	Murray, Toledo	.939	34	12	19	2	2
Edens, Tidewater	.864	25	11	8	3	0	Musselman, Rochester	.946	22	15	20	2	0
Eichelberger, Richmond	.941	40	14	18	2	1	Myers, Tidewater*	1.000	5	1	0	0	0
Ellsworth, Pawtucket	.958	27	8	15	1	0	Newell, Maine	.733	30	2	9	4	2
Filer, Syracuse	1.000	8	2	5	0	2	O'Connor, Rochester*	1.000	25	0	3	0	0
FILSON, Columbus*	1.000	22	3	40	0	1	O'Neal, Richmond	1.000	1	0	1	0	0
Fireovid, Syracuse	1.000	10	1	1	0	0	Oliveras, Rochester	1.000	6	0	4	0	0
Flanagan, Rochester*	1.000	3	0	3	0	0	Olwine, Richmond*	1.000	22	3	2	0	1
Freeman, Maine	.875	10	3	4	1	0	Pacella, Toledo	1.000	26	1	2	0	0
Frey, Columbus*	1.000	23	4	12	0	0	Pena, Toledo	.800	18	3	1	1	0
Frohwirth, Maine	1.000	27	1	8	0	0	Pulido, Columbus*	1.000	34	5	24	0	2
Fulton, Columbus	.875	31	12	23	5	1	Raczka, Rochester*	1.000	23	6	12	0	2
Gardner, Pawtucket	1.000	5	2	1	0	0	E. Rasmussen, Rochester	.941	49	3	13	1	0
P. Gibson, Toledo*	.912	27	10	21	3	1	Riley, Maine*	1.000	8	1	0	0	0
R. Gibson, Tidewater	.952	25	10	10	1	0	Ritchie, Maine*	1.000	13	0	4	0	0
Glavine, Richmond*	.950	22	14	24	2	0	Rochford, Pawtucket*	.905	22	7	12	2	2
Glynn, Tidewater*	1.000	40	2	5	0	0	Roman, Tidewater	.857	45	2	4	1	0
Gooden, Tidewater	1.000	4	2	2	0	0	Romanick, Columbus	1.000	18	6	17	0	1
Gordon, Syracuse	.929	41	2	11	1	1	Rosenberg, Columbus*	1.000	21	1	8	0	0
Graham, Columbus	1.000	41	2	7	0	0	Rozema, Maine	.800	7	0	4	1	2
Green, Rochester*	.750	9	2	1	1	0	Schulze, Tidewater	1.000	15	13	18	0	1
Griffin, Rochester	.952	17	6	14	1	0	Searcy, Toledo*	1.000	10	5	5	0	0
Guidry, Columbus*	1.000	1	0	1	0	0	Segura, Syracuse	.967	43	12	17	1	2

PITCHERS—Continued

Player and Club	Pct.	G.	PO.	A.	E.	DP.	Player and Club	Pct.	G.	PO.	A.	E.	DP.
Sellers, Pawtucket	1.000	5	4	7	0	0	Toliver, Maine	.923	22	5	19	2	4
Shirley, Columbus*	.750	5	0	3	1	0	Vaughn, Tidewater	.966	50	6	22	1	0
Skinner, Rochester	1.000	7	0	4	0	0	Walter, Tidewater*	.882	33	7	8	2	1
Smith, Maine	1.000	4	2	3	0	0	Ward, Syracuse	.938	46	6	9	1	0
Smoltz, Richmond	1.000	3	1	1	0	0	Watts, Maine*	1.000	14	3	4	0	0
Snell, Toledo	.941	12	8	8	1	1	Wells, Syracuse*	.944	43	7	10	1	1
Speck, 20 Rich-8 Col	1.000	28	8	9	0	1	West, Richmond	1.000	18	7	10	0	1
Stewart, Pawtucket*	1.000	53	4	11	0	3	Williamson, Rochester	1.000	1	2	0	0	0
Stottlemyre, Syracuse	.929	34	13	13	2	1	Woodward, Pawtucket	.955	21	21	21	2	3
Stringfellow, Richmond*	1.000	8	1	5	0	0	Wright, Toledo*	.727	20	0	8	3	0
Strode, Rochester*	1.000	4	0	1	0	0	Wyatt, Tidewater*	1.000	18	5	15	0	3
Tewksbury, Columbus	1.000	11	8	10	0	0	Ziem, Richmond	1.000	23	7	10	0	2
Thompson, Columbus	1.000	2	1	0	0	0							

The following players do not have any recorded accepted chances at the positions indicated; therefore, are not listed in the fielding averages for those particular positions: Armstrong, p; Dalena, p; Dalton, of; Estes, of; Garcia, 2b; George, p; P. Gibson, 1b; Givens, p; Gonzales, of; Gonzalez, 2b; D. Griffin, 3b; Gutierrez, 3b; Hatcher, 3b; Hernandez, p; Hudler, ss; Infante, 2b; Loy, of; Milligan, of; Monell, of; Ortiz, of; Ransom, p; D. Rasmussen, p; Rayford, of; R. Roman, of; Roof, p; Schuler, p; M. Stenhouse, 3b, p; Telford, p; Van Gorder, p.

CLUB PITCHING

Club	ERA.	G.	CG.	ShO.	Sv.	IP.	H.	R.	ER.	HR.	HB.	BB.	Int. BB.	SO.	WP.	Bk.
Tidewater	3.72	140	19	9	32	1201.1	1107	574	497	91	36	487	22	746	57	5
Columbus	3.90	140	23	9	36	1216.0	1297	611	527	98	17	380	28	664	32	13
Toledo	3.97	140	13	7	27	1214.1	1199	642	535	108	21	500	28	806	75	12
Pawtucket	4.01	140	31	6	30	1214.1	1243	603	541	135	16	425	31	686	49	10
Rochester	4.08	139	20	8	41	1214.0	1239	601	550	139	34	458	28	809	38	6
Richmond	4.36	139	19	7	26	1199.0	1245	670	581	107	41	493	21	819	71	7
Maine	4.41	140	18	7	27	1180.1	1152	662	578	126	37	587	52	789	58	16
Syracuse	4.43	140	4	11	41	1226.1	1222	684	603	134	37	526	27	898	67	10

PITCHERS' RECORDS
(Leading Qualifiers for Earned-Run Average Leadership — 112 or More Innings)

*Throws lefthanded.

Pitcher—Club	W.	L.	Pct.	ERA.	G.	GS.	CG.	GF.	ShO.	Sv.	IP.	H.	R.	ER.	HR.	HB.	BB.	Int. BB.	SO.	WP.
Vaughn, Tidewater	4	4	.500	2.66	50	2	0	20	0	7	122.0	103	40	36	4	1	39	3	72	3
Arnsberg, Columbus	12	5	.706	2.88	19	19	9	0	2	0	144.0	140	55	46	9	0	37	1	83	2
Ballard, Rochester*	13	4	.765	3.09	23	23	4	0	1	0	160.1	151	60	55	15	5	35	2	114	2
Glavine, Richmond*	6	12	.333	3.35	22	22	4	0	1	0	150.1	142	70	56	15	5	56	3	91	8
Eichelberger, Richmond	7	5	.583	3.38	40	9	2	18	1	5	127.2	105	53	48	6	5	38	3	86	6
P. Gibson, Toledo*	14	7	.667	3.47	27	27	7	0	2	0	179.0	173	83	69	14	3	57	6	118	6
Woodward, Pawtucket*	12	8	.600	3.51	21	21	5	0	0	0	136.0	134	65	53	12	1	62	2	82	6
Pulido, Columbus	9	5	.643	3.56	34	13	2	11	1	3	126.1	122	54	50	10	3	25	1	58	3
Edens, Tidewater	9	7	.563	3.59	25	22	0	1	0	1	138.0	140	69	55	10	7	55	0	61	2
Filson, Columbus*	12	4	.750	3.73	22	22	4	0	1	0	135.0	153	62	56	9	5	43	3	73	1

Departmental Leaders: G—Chambers, 64; W—P. Gibson, 14; L—Alvarez, Stottlemyre, 13; Pct.—Schulze, .917; GS—Stottlemyre, 34; CG—Arnsberg, 9; GF—Stewart, 38; ShO—Five pitchers with 2; Sv.—Kinnunen, 16; IP—Heinkel, 187.1; H—Heinkel, 208; R—Heinkel, Stottlemyre, 103; ER—Stottlemyre, 92; HR—Heinkel, O. Jones, 24; HB—Cowley, 16; BB—Stottlemyre, 87; IBB—Four pitchers with 7; SO—O. Jones, 147; WP—Barlow, 15.

(All-Pitchers—Listed Alphabetically)

Pitcher—Club	W.	L.	Pct.	ERA.	G.	GS.	CG.	GF.	ShO.	Sv.	IP.	H.	R.	ER.	HR.	HB.	BB.	Int. BB.	SO.	WP.
Aguilera, Tidewater	1	1	.500	0.69	3	3	0	0	0	0	13.0	8	2	1	0	0	1	0	10	0
Alicea, Rochester	0	1	.000	6.48	8	0	0	5	0	0	16.2	23	12	12	3	0	12	0	11	2
Alvarez, Richmond	9	13	.409	4.34	22	22	6	0	2	0	145.0	142	80	70	9	14	53	0	108	8
Aquino, Syracuse	6	7	.462	4.78	26	11	0	6	0	0	84.2	75	64	45	11	8	51	1	68	2
Araujo, Pawtucket	4	7	.364	3.44	43	5	3	21	1	4	96.2	99	40	37	12	1	16	5	43	4
Armstrong, Columbus	0	0	.000	0.00	3	0	0	1	0	1	1.1	0	2	0	0	0	3	0	0	0
Arnold, Rochester	2	1	.667	3.03	6	2	0	3	0	2	29.2	32	11	10	1	1	5	0	16	1
Arnsberg, Columbus	12	5	.706	2.88	19	19	9	0	2	0	144.0	140	55	46	9	0	37	1	83	2
Assenmacher, Richmond*	1	2	.333	3.65	4	4	0	0	0	0	24.2	30	11	10	4	0	8	1	21	0
Bair, Maine	6	3	.667	2.99	45	0	0	24	0	6	72.1	56	27	24	4	1	32	6	63	4
Ballard, Rochester*	13	4	.765	3.09	23	23	4	0	1	0	160.1	151	60	55	15	5	35	2	114	2
Barlow, Toledo	3	9	.250	6.01	41	11	0	10	0	2	97.1	95	82	65	8	1	76	3	56	15
Barton, Maine*	1	1	.500	4.39	7	4	0	3	0	1	26.2	25	14	13	2	0	15	1	19	3
Best, Toledo	3	5	.375	2.68	48	0	0	23	0	10	40.1	34	12	12	1	0	19	0	43	2
Boever, Richmond	1	0	1.000	1.00	6	0	0	4	0	1	9.0	8	1	1	0	1	4	1	8	0
Bolton, Pawtucket*	2	1	.667	5.40	5	4	0	1	0	0	21.2	25	14	13	0	0	12	1	8	1
Bordi, Columbus	2	2	.500	1.74	25	0	0	18	0	5	46.2	36	15	9	3	1	14	4	33	1
Boudreaux, Maine	2	5	.286	5.49	7	7	0	0	0	0	41.0	44	30	25	7	0	20	0	16	3
Bowden, Maine*	8	3	.727	3.63	53	6	0	9	0	4	96.2	103	46	39	9	0	35	7	57	9
Boyd, Pawtucket	1	1	.500	4.50	3	3	0	0	0	0	12.0	12	6	6	2	0	4	0	8	0
Brown, Rochester	0	0	.000	1.80	1	1	0	0	0	0	5.0	5	1	1	0	0	1	0	1	0
Buchanan, Tidewater*	4	4	.500	3.60	29	4	0	11	0	2	60.0	60	25	24	4	1	16	0	37	5
Calhoun, Maine*	1	1	.500	0.99	28	0	0	16	0	16	36.1	24	5	4	0	1	11	1	37	3
Carlucci, Maine	0	1	.000	6.87	19	0	0	12	0	0	36.2	38	30	28	6	3	16	1	16	1
Carreno, Columbus	1	1	.500	7.79	11	0	0	5	0	1	17.1	26	15	15	2	0	5	0	11	0
Cary, Richmond*	4	6	.400	4.68	40	9	1	16	0	3	105.2	104	64	55	12	0	43	0	128	8
Chambers, Maine	5	4	.556	4.31	64	1	0	23	0	5	94.0	91	52	45	10	5	65	6	51	4
Chiffer, Richmond	3	5	.375	4.66	43	0	0	17	0	4	56.0	65	34	29	6	4	19	2	34	1
Clary, Richmond	11	10	.524	3.74	26	26	5	0	0	0	178.0	180	86	74	13	4	75	2	91	10
Clay, Maine	4	6	.400	4.36	15	14	4	0	0	0	88.2	88	54	43	12	3	34	0	53	1
Clements, Columbus*	1	0	1.000	3.79	4	2	0	1	0	0	19.0	19	8	8	3	0	2	0	7	0
Cone, Tidewater	0	1	.000	5.73	3	3	0	0	0	0	11.0	10	8	7	1	1	6	0	7	0
Cooper, Rochester	2	2	.500	3.82	14	3	0	1	0	2	37.2	39	16	16	2	0	14	2	22	3
Cowley, Maine	3	9	.250	7.86	13	13	1	0	0	0	63.0	63	64	55	6	16	76	1	39	4
Curry, Pawtucket	11	12	.478	3.81	28	26	8	1	1	0	184.1	175	85	78	13	4	74	4	112	5
Dalena, Columbus	0	0	.000	0.00	1	0	0	0	0	0	1.0	0	0	0	0	0	0	1	1	0

Pitcher—Club	W.	L.	Pct.	ERA.	G.	GS.	CG.	GF.	ShO.	Sv.	IP.	H.	R.	ER.	HR.	HB.	BB.	Int. BB.	SO.	WP.
Dalton, Pawtucket*	1	2	.333	4.16	39	1	0	19	0	2	88.2	83	49	41	10	0	40	2	45	6
C. Davis, Pawtucket	5	2	.714	4.84	24	9	2	4	0	1	80.0	94	52	43	10	2	25	1	50	2
S. Davis, Syracuse*	1	5	.167	9.71	20	10	0	3	0	0	51.0	71	59	55	10	0	44	0	31	5
DeLeon, Rochester	3	3	.500	2.66	33	2	0	20	0	5	47.1	41	17	14	3	3	22	7	47	2
Dixon, Rochester	4	0	1.000	3.27	5	5	1	0	1	0	33.0	27	15	12	3	0	10	0	25	0
Dobie, Tidewater	12	10	.545	4.36	26	26	8	0	1	0	169.1	147	89	82	14	4	63	5	85	5
Edens, Tidewater	9	7	.563	3.59	25	22	0	1	0	1	138.0	140	69	55	10	7	55	0	61	2
Eichelberger, Richmond	7	5	.583	3.38	40	9	2	18	1	5	127.2	105	53	48	6	5	38	3	86	6
Ellsworth, Pawtucket	11	8	.579	4.29	27	26	5	1	1	0	165.2	182	85	79	19	3	46	1	89	5
Filer, Syracuse	1	0	1.000	1.46	8	4	0	2	0	0	24.2	23	6	4	1	0	6	2	9	0
Filson, Columbus*	12	4	.750	3.73	22	22	4	0	1	0	135.0	153	62	56	9	5	43	3	73	1
Fireovid, Syracuse	0	0	.000	6.50	10	0	0	2	0	0	18.0	31	15	13	3	0	6	1	4	1
Flanagan, Rochester*	0	0	.000	3.00	3	3	0	0	0	0	12.0	12	5	4	0	0	3	0	10	0
Freeman, Maine	0	7	.000	6.26	10	10	0	0	0	0	46.0	56	38	32	8	0	30	2	29	6
Frey, Columbus*	2	1	.667	3.04	23	0	0	11	0	6	47.1	45	19	16	2	0	10	0	35	4
Frohwirth, Maine	1	4	.200	2.51	27	0	0	18	0	3	32.1	30	12	9	3	0	15	7	21	0
Fulton, Columbus	7	8	.467	4.73	31	19	3	6	0	1	144.2	179	89	76	16	0	30	0	73	4
Gardner, Pawtucket	1	0	1.000	3.12	5	0	0	4	0	2	8.2	8	3	3	0	0	3	1	9	0
George, Columbus	1	1	.500	8.74	2	2	0	0	0	0	11.1	13	12	11	3	0	5	0	5	0
P. Gibson, Toledo*	14	7	.667	3.47	27	27	7	0	2	0	179.0	173	83	69	14	3	57	6	118	6
R. Gibson, Tidewater	11	7	.611	4.34	25	21	5	0	0	0	137.0	131	75	66	12	1	61	1	100	8
Givens, Tidewater	0	1	.000	24.55	1	1	0	0	0	0	3.2	9	10	10	0	0	6	0	3	2
Glavine, Richmond*	6	12	.333	3.35	22	22	4	0	1	0	150.1	142	70	56	15	5	56	3	91	8
Glynn, Richmond*	2	2	.500	2.72	40	0	0	18	0	1	43.0	34	16	13	4	0	26	1	30	2
Gooden, Tidewater	3	0	1.000	2.05	4	4	1	0	0	0	22.0	20	7	5	0	2	9	0	24	0
Gordon, Syracuse	4	6	.400	1.75	41	0	0	21	0	6	82.1	83	28	16	9	6	10	3	67	4
Graham, Columbus	3	2	.600	3.26	41	1	0	17	0	5	66.1	71	28	24	3	1	21	4	28	2
Green, Rochester*	0	2	.000	3.00	9	0	0	5	0	0	18.0	19	8	6	1	1	7	0	9	1
Griffin, Rochester	5	1	.833	3.28	17	10	1	4	0	1	74.0	74	33	27	8	1	21	1	53	0
Guidry, Columbus	1	0	1.000	0.00	1	1	0	0	0	0	5.0	3	2	0	0	0	2	0	3	0
Habyan, Rochester	3	2	.600	3.86	7	7	2	0	1	0	49.0	47	23	21	5	1	20	0	39	2
Havens, Rochester*	2	3	.400	6.03	9	6	0	1	0	0	31.1	36	22	21	3	1	17	0	16	1
Heinkel, Toledo	8	10	.444	3.99	29	27	3	1	2	1	187.1	208	103	83	24	2	49	2	132	5
Henneman, Toledo*	1	1	.500	1.47	11	0	0	9	0	4	18.1	5	3	3	0	0	3	0	19	1
Hensley, Richmond*	2	6	.250	4.98	45	4	0	23	0	4	86.2	94	49	48	10	3	48	4	73	3
Hernandez Toledo*	0	0	.000	3.00	2	0	0	0	0	0	3.0	4	1	1	0	0	1	0	2	0
Holland, Columbus*	4	6	.400	4.14	33	2	0	26	0	11	54.1	52	28	25	7	1	24	5	36	3
Householder, Rochester*	1	2	.333	4.91	7	2	0	2	0	1	18.1	15	10	10	1	1	13	0	15	2
A. Hudson, Syracuse	5	5	.500	4.59	40	3	2	16	1	1	96.0	113	62	49	10	2	31	4	47	2
C. Hudson, Columbus	0	2	.000	5.93	5	2	0	2	0	1	13.2	22	11	9	1	0	5	1	13	0
Huffman, Rochester	5	6	.455	4.78	14	14	4	0	0	0	86.2	86	55	46	15	7	38	1	54	2
Innis, Tidewater	6	1	.857	2.03	29	0	0	18	0	5	44.1	26	10	10	3	0	16	4	28	1
Jackson, Maine	1	0	1.000	0.82	2	2	0	0	0	0	11.0	9	2	1	0	0	5	1	13	2
J. Johnson, Syracuse	6	4	.600	4.26	13	13	0	0	0	0	76.0	88	41	36	7	3	18	1	24	1
M. Johnson, Pawtucket	2	4	.333	2.82	24	0	0	19	0	8	44.2	38	14	14	6	0	10	2	31	2
J. Jones, Toledo	4	3	.571	3.94	18	12	0	3	0	1	75.1	75	35	33	8	0	23	4	66	2
O. Jones, Syracuse	12	7	.632	4.03	31	27	0	0	0	0	167.2	142	80	75	24	3	81	0	147	6
Kelly, Toledo	2	1	.667	3.41	6	6	0	0	0	0	29.0	23	12	11	4	2	15	1	16	1
Kinnunen, Rochester*	6	4	.600	1.75	48	0	0	34	0	16	67.0	48	16	13	1	2	36	3	33	0
Knox, Columbus	0	1	.000	6.10	2	2	0	0	0	0	10.1	18	7	7	0	0	5	0	5	0
Kucharski, Rochester	4	6	.400	5.79	19	18	0	0	0	0	93.1	105	63	60	18	3	26	2	61	0
Laskey, Toledo	12	6	.667	3.86	56	0	0	27	0	3	100.1	90	51	43	12	4	31	4	73	2
Latham, Tidewater*	3	5	.375	5.79	15	13	0	0	0	0	65.1	95	47	42	7	2	14	0	31	2
Layana, Columbus	4	5	.444	4.76	13	13	0	0	0	0	70.0	77	37	37	6	1	37	2	36	3
Leal, Syracuse	2	1	.667	2.37	4	3	0	1	0	0	19.0	11	6	5	0	3	5	0	9	0
Leister, Pawtucket	11	5	.688	3.77	21	21	4	0	1	0	145.2	136	69	61	18	1	52	2	92	9
Leiter, Columbus*	1	4	.200	6.17	5	5	0	0	0	0	23.1	21	18	16	1	0	15	0	23	3
Lollar, Toledo*	2	2	.500	3.64	8	7	0	1	0	0	47.0	38	21	19	6	2	27	0	21	6
Long, Rochester	1	0	1.000	4.32	10	0	0	5	0	2	8.1	14	5	4	2	0	3	2	5	0
Loy, Maine	0	0	.000	0.00	4	0	0	4	0	0	6.0	6	0	0	0	1	0	0	0	0
Madden, Toledo*	4	2	.667	4.47	24	7	0	6	0	1	58.1	58	37	29	3	2	36	2	41	6
Maddux, Maine	6	6	.500	4.35	18	16	3	1	1	0	103.1	116	58	50	9	2	26	3	71	5
McCarthy, Tidewater	0	2	.000	4.26	10	0	0	2	0	0	19.0	22	17	9	2	0	16	2	7	1
McGregor, Rochester*	0	2	.000	3.06	3	3	0	0	0	0	17.2	17	6	6	2	0	5	0	15	0
McKnight, Tidewater	0	0	.000	0.00	1	0	0	1	0	0	2.0	0	0	0	0	0	0	0	0	0
McLaughlin, Rochester	4	5	.444	4.14	46	0	0	27	0	10	74.0	53	41	34	10	3	39	5	91	4
McMurtry, Syracuse	5	3	.625	3.52	9	8	1	0	1	0	53.2	46	23	21	6	0	15	0	31	2
Meridith, Toledo*	1	1	.500	6.23	4	3	0	0	0	0	17.1	28	13	12	2	0	3	0	7	1
C. Mitchell, Toledo	1	0	1.000	4.50	2	0	0	2	0	0	4.0	2	2	2	0	0	4	0	1	0
J. Mitchell, Tidewater	3	2	.600	3.33	8	8	1	0	1	0	48.2	44	24	18	2	3	20	0	16	4
Murray, Toledo	2	10	.167	5.43	34	15	1	11	0	1	107.2	122	79	65	15	2	41	3	62	7
Musselman, Rochester	6	6	.500	3.04	22	11	5	7	0	1	109.2	102	44	37	16	2	26	3	72	4
Myers, Tidewater*	0	0	.000	4.91	5	0	0	4	0	3	7.1	6	4	4	0	1	4	0	13	3
Newell, Maine	8	12	.400	4.35	30	28	3	0	2	0	163.1	168	87	79	15	1	79	6	127	6
O'Connor, Rochester*	3	0	1.000	2.67	25	0	0	8	0	3	33.2	28	11	10	2	0	9	1	19	1
O'Neal, Richmond	0	1	.000	3.60	1	1	0	0	0	0	5.0	4	3	2	1	0	1	0	5	0
Oliveras, Rochester	3	0	1.000	4.33	6	4	0	1	0	0	27.0	31	14	13	3	0	7	0	18	0
Olwine, Richmond*	3	0	1.000	1.91	22	0	0	16	0	8	33.0	34	8	7	1	1	7	1	19	4
Pacella, Toledo	2	3	.400	3.67	26	0	0	14	0	4	41.2	40	18	17	1	1	24	0	23	6
Pena, Toledo	0	1	.000	1.71	18	1	0	8	0	1	42.0	36	10	8	3	1	10	3	21	1
Pulido, Columbus*	9	5	.643	3.56	34	13	2	11	1	3	126.1	122	54	50	10	3	25	1	58	3
Raczka, Rochester*	4	8	.333	6.39	23	13	2	3	0	0	76.0	97	55	54	10	1	41	1	55	6
Ranson, Toledo	0	0	.000	0.00	2	0	0	2	0	0	2.1	0	0	0	0	0	0	0	1	1
D. Rasmussen, Columbus	1	0	1.000	1.29	1	1	0	0	0	0	7.0	5	1	1	0	0	0	0	4	0
E. Rasmussen, Rochester	6	8	.429	4.80	49	3	0	15	0	8	110.2	122	59	59	10	4	60	3	66	8
Riley, Maine*	0	1	.000	5.28	8	3	1	2	0	0	15.1	17	11	9	3	0	4	1	9	0
Ritchie, Maine*	3	1	.750	2.05	13	0	0	9	0	2	22.0	17	6	5	1	0	8	1	16	0
Rochford, Pawtucket*	8	8	.500	4.58	22	19	3	1	0	0	123.2	144	65	63	19	3	38	2	42	4
Roman, Tidewater	5	4	.556	3.07	45	0	0	34	0	9	55.2	46	21	19	3	2	39	5	65	4
Romanick, Columbus	5	8	.385	5.16	18	18	1	0	0	0	103.0	115	76	59	10	1	44	1	50	2
Roof, Toledo	0	0	.000	18.00	1	0	0	1	0	0	1.0	3	2	2	0	0	2	0	0	1
Rosenberg, Columbus*	4	1	.800	4.08	21	0	0	14	0	2	35.1	43	17	16	3	2	18	2	27	1

Pitcher—Club	W.	L.	Pct.	ERA.	G.	GS.	CG.	GF.	ShO.	Sv.	IP.	H.	R.	ER.	HR.	HB.	BB.	Int. BB.	SO.	WP.
Rozema, Maine	3	0	1.000	2.92	7	5	2	1	0	0	37.0	27	12	12	6	1	12	0	25	0
Schuler, Richmond*	0	2	.000	4.33	13	0	0	8	0	0	27.0	32	16	13	4	1	6	1	14	0
Schulze, Tidewater	11	1	.917	3.63	15	15	1	0	1	0	89.1	81	37	36	6	3	31	0	45	3
Searcy, Toledo*	3	4	.429	4.22	10	10	0	0	0	0	53.1	49	26	25	4	1	32	0	54	7
Segura, Syracuse	5	8	.385	6.56	43	12	0	12	0	4	107.0	136	90	78	13	1	59	2	54	14
Sellers, Pawtucket	3	2	.600	2.37	5	5	1	0	0	0	38.0	36	13	10	1	0	19	1	35	3
Shirley, Columbus*	0	5	.000	5.40	5	5	0	0	0	0	30.0	38	23	18	4	1	10	2	10	0
Skinner, Rochester	1	2	.333	6.39	7	6	1	0	1	0	31.0	38	22	22	5	1	20	0	21	0
Smith, Maine	1	3	.250	6.75	4	4	0	0	0	0	22.2	21	18	17	4	2	13	0	16	0
Smoltz, Richmond	0	1	.000	6.19	3	3	0	0	0	0	16.0	17	11	11	2	1	11	0	5	1
Snell, Toledo	6	1	.857	2.34	12	9	2	0	0	0	61.2	69	25	16	3	0	12	0	31	1
Speck, 20 Rich-8 Col	2	10	.167	5.40	28	15	2	8	0	0	105.0	113	73	63	13	2	50	4	85	11
Stenhouse, Toledo	0	0	.000	0.00	3	0	0	3	0	0	2.0	0	0	0	0	0	0	0	0	0
Stewart, Pawtucket*	1	7	.125	5.50	52	0	0	38	0	13	68.2	77	43	42	13	1	24	7	40	2
Stottlemyre, Syracuse	11	13	.458	4.44	34	34	1	0	0	0	186.2	189	103	92	14	6	87	3	143	10
Stringfellow, Richmond*	1	3	.250	5.79	8	6	0	1	0	0	32.2	44	25	21	3	0	14	0	14	4
Strode, Rochester*	0	1	.000	8.56	4	3	0	1	0	0	13.2	21	13	13	7	0	3	0	7	0
Telford, Rochester	0	0	.000	0.00	1	0	0	0	0	0	2.0	0	0	0	0	0	3	0	3	1
Tewksbury, Columbus	6	1	.857	2.53	11	11	3	0	0	0	74.2	68	23	21	5	1	11	0	32	0
Thompson, Columbus	0	0	.000	4.50	2	0	0	0	0	0	4.0	6	2	2	0	0	2	0	3	1
Toliver, Maine	6	9	.400	4.62	22	21	2	0	0	0	124.2	114	70	64	15	2	67	6	80	3
Van Gorder, Rochester	0	0	.000	18.00	1	0	0	1	0	0	1.0	3	2	2	2	0	0	0	1	0
Vaughn, Tidewater	4	4	.500	2.66	50	2	0	20	0	7	122.0	103	40	36	4	1	39	3	72	3
Walter, Tidewater*	1	4	.200	4.93	33	3	0	12	0	4	49.1	37	33	27	9	4	23	0	43	8
Ward, Syracuse	2	2	.500	3.89	46	3	0	29	0	14	76.1	59	35	33	7	2	42	1	67	7
Watts, Maine*	1	4	.200	5.23	14	6	0	0	0	0	41.1	39	26	24	5	0	24	2	31	1
Wells, Syracuse*	4	6	.400	3.87	43	12	0	17	0	6	109.1	102	49	47	9	0	32	4	106	9
West, Richmond	3	4	.429	5.78	18	12	0	4	0	0	67.0	79	50	43	3	0	47	1	22	4
Williamson, Rochester	0	1	.000	6.75	1	0	0	1	0	0	4.0	6	3	3	0	0	1	0	1	0
Woodward, Pawtucket	12	8	.600	3.51	21	21	5	0	0	0	136.0	134	65	53	12	1	62	2	82	6
Wright, Toledo*	2	4	.333	3.91	20	5	0	7	0	0	46.0	47	27	20	0	0	35	0	19	4
Wyatt, Tidewater*	6	3	.667	2.93	18	15	3	0	0	0	101.1	88	40	33	10	3	42	1	69	4
Ziem, Richmond	4	4	.500	6.02	23	8	0	9	0	1	55.1	77	43	37	6	0	24	0	30	5

BALKS—Curry, Heinkel, 5 each; Newell, Romanick, 4 each; Filson, 3; Barton, Ellsworth, Hensley, Pena, Roman, Rosenberg, Rozema, Searcy, Tewksbury, 2 each; Alvarez, Aquino, Arnold, Arnsberg, Assenmacher, Boudreaux, Bowden, Carlucci, Chambers, Chiffer, Cooper, Dalton, Edens, Eichelberger, Filer, Frohwirth, Fulton, P. Gibson, Gordon, Havens, A. Hudson, Huffman, Jackson, J. Johnson, J. Jones, O. Jones, Kucharski, Maddux, J. Mitchell, Musselman, Rochford, Schulze, Segura, Sellers, Smoltz, Snell, Stottlemyre, Toliver, Ward, Wells 1 each.

COMBINATION SHUTOUTS—Tewksbury-Holland, Leiter-Graham, Pulido-Frey, Fulton-Frey, Filson-Frey, Columbus; Maddux-Frohwirth-Bowden, Newell-Frohwirth, Rozema-Bowden-Bair, Clay-Bowden, Maine; Sellers-Stewart, Curry-Araujo, Pawtucket; Clary-Hensley-Chiffer, Ziem-Hensley-Chiffer, Eichelberger-Hensley, Richmond; Ballard-DeLeon, Griffin-Kinnunen, Raczka-Arnold, Musselman-Kinnunen, Rochester; Jones-Hudson-Gordon, Jones-Wells-McLaughlin, Wells-McLaughlin, Stottlemyre-Gordon, Jones-McLaughlin, Jones-Ward, Stottlemyre-Segura, McMurtry-Filer-Hudson, Leal-Hudson-Filer, Syracuse; Dobie-Glynn, Edens-Latham-Buchanan, Gooden-Roman, Schulze-Vaughn-Walter, Aguilera-Roman, Wyatt-Buchanan-Innis-Vaughn-Roman, Tidewater; Gibson-Henneman, Gibson-Laskey, Lollar-Snell-Best-Laskey, Toledo.

NO-HIT GAME—Curry, Pawtucket, defeated Richmond, 11-0, July 6.

Mexican League

CLASS AAA

CHAMPIONSHIP WINNERS IN PREVIOUS YEARS

1955—Mexico City Tigers° .... .539	1969—Reynosa .... .591	1978—Aguascalientes x .... .589
1956—Mexico City Reds .... .692	1970—Aguila§ .... .580	Union Laguna .... .523
1957—Yucatan .... .567	Mexico City Reds .... .607	1979—Saltillo .... .704
Mex. C. Reds (2nd)† .... .550	1971—Jalisco§ .... .558	Puebla x .... .628
1958—Nuevo Laredo .... .625	Saltillo .... .593	1980—No champion y
1959—Poza Rica .... .575	1972—Saltillo .... .636	1981—Mexico City Reds .... .615
Mex. C. Reds (3rd)† .... .507	Cordoba§ .... .541	Reynosa .... .492
1960—Mexico City Tigers .... .538	1973—Saltillo .... .656	1982—Ciudad Juarez x .... .570
1961—Veracruz .... .575	Mexico City Reds x .... .590	Mexico City Tigers .... .508
1962—Monterrey .... .592	1974—Jalisco .... .627	1983—Campeche z .... .614
1963—Puebla .... .606	Mexico City Reds x .... .551	Ciudad Juarez .... .535
1964—Mexico City Reds .... .586	1975—Tampico x .... .541	1984—Yucatan z .... .560
1965—Mexico City Tigers .... .590	Cordoba .... .649	Ciudad Juarez .... .509
1966—Mexico City Tigers‡ .... .614	1976—Mexico City Reds x .... .543	1985—Mexico City Reds z .... .606
Mexico City Reds .... .571	Union Laguna .... .547	Nuevo Laredo .... .5275
1967—Jalisco .... .607	1977—Mexico City Reds .... .623	1986—Puebla z .... .682
1968—Mexico City Reds .... .586	Nuevo Laredo x .... .507	Monclova .... .598

°Defeated Nuevo Laredo, two games to none, in playoff for pennant. †Won four-team playoff. ‡Won split-season playoff. §League divided into Northern, Southern divisions; won two-team playoff. xLeague divided into Northern, Southern zones; sub-divided into Eastern, Western divisions, won eight-team playoff. yA players strike on July 1 forced the cancellation of the regular season and playoff schedule. zLeague divided into Northern, Southern zones; four clubs from each zone qualified for postseason play. Won final series for league championship.

STANDING OF CLUBS AT CLOSE OF SEASON
NORTHERN ZONE

Club	Mon	Ags	N.L.	Mva	S.L.	U.L.	Sal	M.R.	Pue	M.T.	Leo	Cam	Tab	Yuc	W.	L.	T.	Pct.	G.B.
Monterrey	....	8	7	5	8	7	9	4	4	2	4	3	3	3	67	58	0	.536	....
Aguascalientes	6	....	8	10	8	7	8	3	2	3	4	1	3	2	65	60	1	.520	2
Nuevo Laredo	9	6	....	6	9	8	5	2	3	2	3	2	2	4	61	59	2	.508	3½
Monclova	9	4	8	....	4	11	8	1	3	4	2	4	2	3	63	61	2	.508	3½
San Luis	6	6	5	10	....	8	12	2	2	1	4	1	2	1	60	67	0	.472	8
Union Laguna	7	7	6	5	5	....	11	1	4	0	3	1	4	4	58	69	0	.457	10
Saltillo	5	6	5	6	4	3	....	2	0	3	1	1	4	1	41	81	2	.336	24½

SOUTHERN ZONE

Club	Mon	Ags	N.L.	Mva	S.L.	U.L.	Sal	M.R.	Pue	M.T.	Leo	Cam	Tab	Yuc	W.	L.	T.	Pct.	G.B.
Mexico City Reds............	2	3	4	5	4	5	4	....	7	10	6	6	8	11	75	49	1	.605	....
Puebla	2	3	2	3	4	2	6	7	....	10	6	8	9	9	71	52	1	.577	3½
Mexico City Tigers	4	3	4	2	5	6	3	6	3	....	6	5	9	12	68	58	1	.540	8
Leon	2	4	2	3	2	3	3	8	8	8	....	9	4	9	65	56	6	.537	8½
Campeche	1	4	3	0	5	5	5	4	6	8	4	....	5	8	58	57	3	.504	12½
Tabasco	3	3	3	3	4	2	2	6	5	5	9	8	....	7	60	62	3	.492	14
Yucatan	2	3	2	3	5	2	5	3	5	2	4	8	7	....	51	74	2	.408	24½

Playoffs—Nuevo Laredo defeated Monclova, four games to one, in Northern Zone finals. Mexico City Reds defeated Mexico City Tigers, four games to three, in Southern Zone finals. Mexico City Reds defeated Nuevo Laredo, four games to one, in final series to capture league championship.

Managers—Aguascalientes, Sergio Valenzuela; Campeche, Francisco Soto; Leon, Obed Placencia; Mexico City Reds, Benjamin Chavez; Mexico City Tigers, Roberto Mendez and Alfredo Uzcnaga; Monclova, Alfredo Rios and Carlos Paz; Monterrey, Manuel Magallon and Roberto Castellon; Nuevo Laredo, Jose Guerrero and Marcelo Juarez; Puebla, Rodolfo Sandoval and Roberto Mendez; Saltillo, Victor Fabela and Felipe Leal; San Luis, Gregorio Flores; Tabasco, Miguel Sotelo and Arturo Rubio; Union Laguna, Ramon Montoya; Yucatan, Carlos Paz and Francisco Baeza.

(Compiled by Ana Luisa Perea Talarico, League Statistician, Mexico, D.F.)

CLUB BATTING

Club	Pct.	G.	AB.	R.	OR.	H.	TB.	2B.	3B.	HR.	RBI.	GW.	SH.	SF.	HP.	BB.	Int. BB.	SO.	SB.	CS.	LOB.
Puebla	.321	124	4086	682	596	1310	1910	215	26	111	631	..	48	30	20	393	32	452	51	43	879
Leon	.317	127	4172	763	697	1323	1843	215	40	75	661	..	26	42	52	497	37	454	96	66	940
Aguascalientes	.311	126	4242	819	754	1320	2031	216	36	141	742	..	41	44	46	532	41	557	39	34	915
Mexico City Reds......	.309	125	4139	751	588	1278	1941	227	35	122	679	..	19	41	40	448	35	553	76	45	894
Union Laguna	.306	127	4284	706	748	1309	1908	196	20	121	645	..	39	37	35	432	45	612	83	53	915
San Luis	.301	127	4109	691	700	1238	1880	188	41	124	639	..	55	40	31	486	44	642	37	42	902
Monterrey.................	.297	125	3914	611	585	1164	1671	171	27	94	560	..	33	34	34	503	37	602	119	75	880
Saltillo	.296	124	4066	620	791	1204	1780	171	33	113	583	..	40	33	28	436	35	533	34	61	861
Monclova	.291	126	3978	662	747	1158	1743	181	21	121	593	..	37	32	36	510	46	573	40	44	884
Yucatan	.290	127	4030	638	657	1170	1677	171	24	96	582	..	48	39	34	450	39	499	92	54	841
Mexico City Tigers ...	.287	127	4041	653	673	1161	1636	158	31	85	588	..	89	31	40	561	38	517	54	55	922
Tabasco	.283	125	3909	498	559	1108	1428	166	20	38	440	..	50	40	30	400	40	416	103	63	862
Campeche	.280	118	3692	555	588	1035	1517	190	23	82	492	..	49	20	22	408	37	483	114	54	788
Nuevo Laredo	.280	122	3968	658	624	1110	1760	173	12	151	606	..	42	35	27	502	34	557	36	39	862

INDIVIDUAL BATTING
(Leading Qualifiers for Batting Championship—346 or More Plate Appearances)

°Bats lefthanded. †Switch-hitter.

Player and Club	Pct.	G.	AB.	R.	H.	TB.	2B.	3B.	HR.	RBI.	GW.	SH.	SF.	HP.	BB.	Int. BB.	SO.	SB.	CS.
Sanchez, Orlando, Puebla°	.415	123	439	95	182	293	34	1	25	115	..	0	2	2	48	8	37	6	3
Linares, Rufino, Mexico City Reds	.389	109	406	88	158	257	37	1	20	93	..	0	6	6	36	5	41	7	2
Cruz, Luis Alfonso, San Luis	.381	94	360	74	137	234	31	0	22	81	..	2	3	4	26	3	60	1	2
Vargas, Edilberto, Aguascalientes	.380	89	321	94	122	252	21	2	35	98	..	0	3	1	64	6	62	0	1
Payton, Eric, Union Laguna°	.379	124	477	105	181	299	32	4	26	114	..	1	10	1	62	8	60	23	5
Bellazetin, Jose, Mex City Tigers°	.371	120	455	91	169	216	28	5	3	56	..	6	3	5	71	10	25	14	7
Mora, Andres, Nuevo Laredo	.368	114	419	87	154	292	24	0	38	123	..	1	7	1	56	11	36	0	1
Olivares, Oswaldo 42 Yuc-80 Leon°	.365	122	449	97	164	217	20	12	3	52	..	2	1	2	75	4	25	21	14
Bronson, Eddie, Union Laguna	.365	109	400	81	146	237	28	3	19	75	..	2	3	4	42	8	48	10	4
Rodriguez, Juan, Leon	.362	121	439	101	159	188	15	7	0	61	..	7	8	8	72	0	15	14	6
Hernandez, Leo, Union Laguna	.359	103	390	92	140	271	21	1	36	123	..	0	3	3	42	8	33	10	5
Cole, Mike, Campeche°	.358	116	438	101	157	203	20	7	4	41	..	6	0	2	55	0	35	66	19
Bundy, Lorenzo, Mexico City Reds°	.357	100	356	94	127	226	18	6	23	81	..	0	3	3	61	13	45	14	1

Departmental Leaders: G—F. Guerrero, Pacho, 127; AB—Aguilar, 502; R—Aguilar, 108; H—O. Sanchez, 182; TB—N. Barrera, 309; 2B—Aguilar, 38; 3B—Villela, 13; HR—N. Barrera, 42; RBI—N. Barrera, 134; SH—A. Camacho, 24; SF—Castro, 11; HP—E. Miller, 13; BB—Greene, 106; IBB—N. Castaneda, 16; SO—Darkis, 101; SB—Cole, 66; CS—Ri. Herrera, 25.

(All Players—Listed Alphabetically)

Player and Club	Pct.	G.	AB.	R.	H.	TB.	2B.	3B.	HR.	RBI.	GW.	SH.	SF.	HP.	BB.	Int. BB.	SO.	SB.	CS.
Abrego, Jesus, Nuevo Laredo	.000	1	1	0	0	0	0	0	0	0	..	0	0	0	0	0	0	0	0
Acosta, Marco, Campeche	.299	44	77	7	23	41	2	2	4	11	..	1	0	0	9	2	27	0	0
Adams, Calvin, Tabasco	.326	26	86	12	28	42	6	1	2	13	..	0	2	1	11	2	10	1	2
Aguilar, Enrique, Aguascalientes	.325	123	502	108	163	287	38	1	28	116	..	1	6	5	35	4	37	5	5
Aguilera, Antonio, Yucatan	.281	74	171	37	48	73	12	2	3	27	..	3	1	2	26	3	30	7	2
Aikens, Willie, Puebla°	.354	77	268	59	95	167	17	2	17	67	..	0	4	0	50	4	38	0	0
Almodobar, Ricardo, Mex City Tigers.	.213	68	122	13	26	29	1	1	0	15	..	7	0	2	9	0	19	2	2
Alonso, Hermilo, Puebla	.336	53	110	15	37	47	5	1	1	19	..	3	0	0	8	0	10	1	3
Alvarez, Hector, Mexico City Tigers	.333	2	3	0	1	1	0	0	0	0	..	0	0	0	0	0	0	0	1
Alvarez, Juan Carlos, San Luis	.266	89	271	34	72	100	8	1	6	35	..	6	1	2	30	5	60	1	0
Alvarez, Ruben, Tabasco	.244	57	115	11	28	37	4	1	1	14	..	4	0	0	17	3	20	0	2
Andrade, Reynaldo, Monterrey°	.326	119	438	76	143	199	28	2	8	71	..	3	4	1	60	6	63	7	1
Angulo, Kenneth, Yucatan	.000	1	1	0	0	0	0	0	0	0	..	0	0	0	0	0	1	0	0
Arano, Ramon Jr., Saltillo	.500	9	2	2	1	1	0	0	0	1	..	0	0	0	0	0	0	0	0
Arce, Javier, 38 Yuc-38 San Luis	.239	76	218	21	52	72	6	1	4	30	..	1	3	5	29	0	42	0	1
Arzate, Martin, Aguascalientes	.281	65	217	43	61	82	7	4	2	23	..	4	1	1	36	2	37	5	1
Avila, Ruben, Union Laguna	.276	82	250	28	69	92	11	0	4	32	..	1	4	3	18	3	58	0	3
Ayala, Javier, 12 Leo-41 Puebla	.263	53	95	19	25	31	1	1	1	6	..	3	0	1	11	0	19	2	3
Baca, Manuel, Mexico City Reds	.306	109	356	49	109	159	27	1	7	49	..	1	1	5	25	2	48	4	7
Baez, Jesse, Mexico City Reds	.283	85	269	44	76	100	16	1	2	24	..	0	1	4	49	0	32	0	0
Barandica, Alberto, Union Laguna	.223	81	130	15	29	32	3	0	0	5	..	2	2	2	8	0	13	2	1
Barrera, Jesus Antonio, Nuevo Lar.	.269	66	227	14	61	75	6	1	2	21	..	2	0	1	13	1	24	1	1
Barrera, Nelson, Mexico City Reds	.349	118	438	97	153	309	26	2	42	134	..	0	5	2	43	8	70	6	4
Bazan, Pedro, Saltillo°	.273	58	176	27	48	70	5	1	5	25	..	0	0	1	28	8	24	0	0
Becerra, Juan, Mexico City Tigers	.375	8	16	2	6	6	0	0	0	3	..	0	0	0	2	0	3	0	0
Bellazetin, Jose Juan, MC Tigers°	.371	120	455	91	169	216	28	5	3	56	..	6	3	5	71	10	25	14	7
Beltran, Gerardo, Mex City Reds	.222	8	9	3	2	2	0	0	0	0	..	0	0	0	1	0	5	0	0
Bergie, Jordan, Nuevo Laredo°	.255	91	349	67	89	131	16	1	8	36	..	3	2	0	49	0	30	1	0
Bobadilla, Manuel, Monclova	.291	124	426	61	124	181	16	1	13	67	..	5	3	4	38	1	37	3	5
Bocardo, Manuel, Mexico City Reds	.260	26	50	10	13	23	1	0	3	9	..	0	2	0	5	0	13	0	0
Briones, Antonio, Tabasco	.272	105	389	56	106	118	10	1	0	22	..	7	1	7	42	1	23	38	21
Bronson, Eddie, Union Laguna	.365	109	400	81	146	237	28	3	19	75	..	2	3	4	42	8	48	10	4
Brown, Darrell, Leon	.366	48	194	28	71	85	14	0	0	29	..	1	1	0	10	3	11	3	3
Bryant, Derek, Monterrey	.337	89	297	59	100	186	17	3	21	68	..	1	1	0	58	5	49	8	6
Bundy, Lorenzo, Mexico City Reds°	.357	100	356	94	127	226	18	6	23	81	..	0	3	3	61	13	45	14	1
Burke, Norberto, 40 Tig-63 Yuc	.257	103	272	42	70	115	12	0	11	54	..	2	3	6	69	2	38	2	8
Bustamante, Miguel, Mex City Tigers.	.350	12	20	4	7	7	0	0	0	2	..	0	1	0	4	0	3	0	0
Cabrales, Sergio, Campeche	.000	2	3	0	0	0	0	0	0	0	..	0	0	0	0	0	0	0	0
Cabrera, J., 20 UL-9 Yuc-27 Agua	.226	56	137	24	31	39	5	0	1	15	..	0	1	1	19	0	23	0	0
Camacho, Adulfo, Mexico City Tigers	.280	122	368	65	103	135	14	3	4	56	..	24	3	7	48	0	58	8	8
Camacho, Marcos, Mexico City Tigers	.000	3	3	1	0	0	0	0	0	0	..	0	0	0	1	0	2	0	0
Camara, Jose, Campeche	.222	20	27	3	6	11	2	0	1	2	..	0	0	0	2	0	12	0	0
Campos, Rosendo, Tabasco	.185	49	65	5	12	12	0	0	0	3	..	1	0	0	3	0	16	2	0
Cano, Javier, Campeche	.273	77	161	26	44	48	4	0	0	8	..	4	0	0	22	0	31	1	2
Cantu, Gerardo, Saltillo	.000	5	4	0	0	0	0	0	0	0	..	0	0	0	4	0	0	0	0
Carrillo, Francisco, Mex City Tigers	.200	7	5	1	1	1	0	0	0	0	..	0	0	0	0	0	0	0	0
Castaneda, Antonio, Saltillo	.198	31	91	6	18	22	1	0	1	6	..	4	0	1	11	0	22	1	1
Castaneda, Maximiliano, U Laguna		3	0	1	0	0	0	0	0	0	..	0	0	0	0	0	0	0	0
Castanada, Nicolas, San Luis°	.370	55	165	47	61	115	9	0	15	46	..	0	0	0	57	16	39	0	1
Castelan, Miguel Angel, Puebla°	.301	102	349	39	105	143	15	7	3	46	..	2	3	1	26	3	62	18	9
Castilla, Vinicio, Saltillo	.185	13	27	0	5	7	2	0	0	1	..	0	0	1	0	0	5	0	0
Castillo, Esteban, Tabasco°	.304	115	404	47	123	162	18	0	7	52	..	3	2	0	46	11	21	5	2
Castillo, Raul, Tabasco	.193	74	187	14	36	50	11	0	1	23	..	7	3	3	13	0	46	1	0
Castro, Antonio, Mexico City Tigers°	.289	124	440	67	127	212	25	6	16	97	..	4	11	0	54	10	32	4	4
Cazarin, Manuel, Leon	.316	102	316	54	100	137	20	4	3	48	..	3	4	4	24	1	33	7	2
Chavez, Jose Angel, Mex City Reds	.250	9	24	3	6	6	0	0	0	2	..	1	2	0	0	0	3	0	0
Chavez, Jose Santos, Mex City Reds°	.231	51	130	16	30	45	9	0	2	20	..	0	5	1	18	1	22	0	2
Chavez, Juan de Dios, Saltillo	.250	15	32	3	8	14	3	0	1	6	..	1	1	0	4	0	7	0	0
Chavez, Ricardo, Campeche	.179	56	145	15	26	30	4	0	0	6	..	3	0	2	8	0	29	4	1
Clayton, Leonardo, San Luis†	.282	109	347	77	98	160	15	1	15	47	..	9	5	3	79	7	76	10	6
Cole, Mike, Campeche°	.358	116	438	101	157	203	20	7	4	41	..	6	0	2	55	0	35	66	19
Collins, James, Tabasco°	.329	122	428	67	141	203	22	5	10	67	..	2	3	5	35	10	69	5	6
Cosey, Donald Ray, Campeche	.283	103	382	56	108	179	23	3	14	79	..	0	3	0	32	8	34	2	3
Cotes, Eugenio, Yucatan°	.188	33	112	15	21	33	3	0	3	12	..	1	0	6	8	1	21	3	2
Craig, Rodney, 8 Nuevo Lar-29 Leo...	.353	37	119	19	42	65	7	2	4	21	..	0	2	2	12	0	14	13	4
Cruz, Fernando, Union Laguna	.303	108	360	38	109	142	19	1	4	45	..	5	6	2	45	1	21	1	1
Cruz, Javier, Mexico City Tigers	.158	20	38	4	6	6	0	0	0	4	..	0	0	0	5	0	11	0	0
Cruz, Luis Alfonso, San Luis	.381	94	360	74	137	234	31	0	22	81	..	2	3	4	26	3	60	1	2
Cruz, Todd, 38 Leo-6 Tig	.242	44	157	27	38	62	9	0	5	16	..	0	0	3	22	0	31	4	2

Player and Club	Pct.	G.	AB.	R.	H.	TB.	2B.	3B.	HR.	RBI.	GW.	SH.	SF.	HP.	BB.	Int. BB.	SO.	SB.	CS.
Darkis, Willie, 14 N. Lar-101 Tig......	.328	115	396	86	130	246	13	5	31	99	..	0	3	4	72	3	101	4	3
Daut, Manuel, Monclova	.279	66	201	30	56	93	13	0	8	31	..	5	0	0	20	1	37	1	2
Delgado, Tomas, Yucatan	.307	96	319	37	98	131	13	1	6	47	..	5	2	4	30	1	41	1	5
De Los Santos, Carlos, Monterrey.....	.254	29	59	13	15	15	0	0	0	2	..	1	0	1	13	0	7	0	2
Diaz, Luis Fernando, Nuevo Laredo	.314	64	194	38	61	98	15	2	6	29	..	1	1	1	31	1	18	1	1
Dominguez, David, San Luis	.304	126	438	85	133	226	18	6	21	91	..	2	4	2	59	5	75	5	0
Elizondo, Fernando, Puebla	.323	124	501	84	162	191	18	1	3	39	..	10	0	3	30	1	39	6	11
Escalante, Isidro, Aguascalientes	.216	41	111	15	24	33	3	3	0	13	..	1	1	1	11	0	10	3	1
Espinosa, Antonio, San Luis	.190	10	21	1	4	5	1	0	0	1	..	0	1	0	2	0	2	0	0
Esquer, Mercedes, Monterrey	.000	1	2	0	0	0	0	0	0	0	..	0	0	0	0	0	1	0	0
Esquer, Ramon, Leon	.250	5	4	2	1	1	0	0	0	1	..	0	0	0	1	0	1	0	0
Esquivias, Ruben, Union Laguna	.235	31	51	6	12	13	1	0	0	4	..	0	0	0	7	0	14	0	0
Estrada, Francisco, Campeche	.260	87	246	32	64	91	15	0	4	30	..	3	2	5	42	5	13	4	4
Estrada, Hector, Puebla	.304	33	69	9	21	30	2	2	1	7	..	0	0	0	6	0	19	0	0
Evans, John, Aguascalientes	.326	66	215	43	70	128	12	2	14	52	..	2	3	7	65	5	26	0	3
Fabela, Lorenzo, Yucatan	.250	13	16	2	4	6	2	0	0	2	..	1	0	0	0	0	2	0	0
Felix, Rodrigo, Campeche	.....	3	0	0	0	0	0	0	0	0	..	0	0	0	0	0	0	0	0
Fernandez, Daniel, M.C. Reds*	.331	118	432	102	143	199	25	8	5	46	..	6	3	8	69	4	53	34	20
Figueroa, Francisco, M.C. Reds	.000	7	7	0	0	0	0	0	0	0	..	0	0	0	0	0	2	0	0
Figueroa, Leobardo, Monclova	.100	5	10	0	1	1	0	0	0	0	..	0	0	0	0	0	3	0	1
Franco, Francisco, Puebla	.000	1	1	0	0	0	0	0	0	0	..	0	0	0	0	0	0	0	0
Fuson, Robin, Nuevo Laredo	.....	1	0	0	0	0	0	0	0	0	..	0	0	0	1	0	0	0	0
Garbey, Barbaro, Campeche	.195	24	82	15	16	27	5	0	2	11	..	0	1	0	6	2	11	1	0
Garcia, Jesus, Saltillo	.366	19	41	5	15	18	1	1	0	1	..	1	0	0	8	0	8	1	2
Garcia, Jose Luis, San Luis	.331	36	121	24	40	64	5	2	5	26	..	5	1	3	24	1	27	0	6
Garcia, Jose Luis, Tabasco*	.000	2	1	1	0	0	0	0	0	0	..	0	0	0	0	0	0	0	0
Garcia, Martin, Monterrey	.284	51	109	15	31	39	3	1	1	9	..	4	0	1	17	0	15	1	1
Garcia, N. Jesus, Nuevo Laredo	.231	25	39	12	9	12	0	0	1	3	..	0	0	1	4	0	10	0	0
Garibay, Roberto, Aguascalientes	.158	23	38	10	6	8	2	0	0	1	..	0	0	0	2	0	15	0	0
Garza, Adolfo, 23 Mva-81 Sal*	.280	104	357	46	100	153	20	0	11	70	..	2	2	2	38	3	43	0	2
Garza, Gerardo, Nuevo Laredo	.252	91	266	35	67	85	10	1	2	21	..	6	3	1	20	0	44	1	1
Garzon, Felix, Tabasco	.297	119	414	49	123	155	20	0	4	63	..	3	9	4	46	6	44	0	1
Gastelum, Carlos, Mexico City Reds	.286	23	70	10	20	22	2	0	0	7	..	0	1	0	3	0	9	0	1
Gomez, Alejandro, Tabasco	.271	121	406	43	110	124	8	3	0	45	..	5	7	3	27	0	45	16	7
Gomez, Graciano, 43 Leon-37 Saltillo	.271	80	266	34	72	93	8	5	1	32	..	2	2	2	17	0	27	1	4
Gonzalez, Efrain, San Luis	.271	66	192	22	52	77	8	1	5	18	..	3	0	0	9	1	23	1	0
Gonzalez, Jesus, Puebla	.296	124	483	79	143	200	29	2	8	71	..	7	6	3	41	0	39	0	2
Gonzalez, Juan, Aguascalientes	.219	38	114	12	25	33	5	0	1	18	..	0	0	3	3	0	30	0	0
Gonzalez, Leo, Union Laguna	.291	113	358	46	104	139	16	2	5	42	..	3	3	3	38	2	66	3	6
Gray, Gary, 36 Ags-31 Sal-44 Leo	.316	111	392	87	124	198	11	3	19	86	..	0	3	6	71	6	57	4	7
Green, David, Leon	.316	15	57	13	18	27	1	1	2	10	..	0	1	0	15	0	6	0	0
Greene, Altar, Monclova*	.325	114	348	81	113	206	14	2	25	83	..	0	3	3	106	12	80	7	3
Guerrero, Francisco, Union Laguna	.259	127	498	98	129	164	13	5	4	29	..	8	1	6	86	1	94	31	21
Guerrero, Jaime, Leon	.268	57	71	14	19	27	3	1	1	11	..	0	1	2	4	0	16	2	0
Guerrero, Leobardo, 29 Ags-80 Yuc.	.288	109	400	61	115	151	22	1	4	41	..	6	0	1	43	1	33	8	5
Guerrero, Victor Hugo, San Luis	.333	5	6	1	2	2	0	0	0	1	..	0	0	0	1	0	1	0	0
Gutierrez, Felipe, Mexico City Reds	.300	119	460	59	138	201	29	5	8	75	..	0	4	3	13	1	39	1	1
Gutierrez, Jose Luis, Yucatan	.000	2	0	0	0	0	0	0	0	0	..	0	0	0	2	0	0	0	0
Guzman, Andres, 64 Leo-15 Sal	.222	79	239	34	53	80	12	0	5	37	..	4	3	2	11	1	33	2	1
Guzman, Marco Antonio, Campeche	.255	117	389	54	99	139	17	1	7	54	..	1	5	5	62	7	51	3	3
Heras, Roberto, Monterrey	.238	95	302	25	72	107	12	1	7	39	..	0	3	2	8	0	42	1	0
Hernandez, Javier, Union Laguna*	.322	113	432	88	139	172	22	1	3	50	..	6	3	2	43	0	55	0	1
Hernandez, Jorge Luis, Puebla	.000	4	2	0	0	0	0	0	0	0	..	0	0	0	0	0	0	0	0
Hernandez, Juan, Monclova	.258	74	182	25	47	61	8	0	2	14	..	1	0	0	29	1	42	5	6
Hernandez, Leo, Union Laguna	.359	103	390	92	140	271	21	1	36	123	..	0	3	3	42	8	33	10	5
Hernandez, Miguel, M.C. Tigers	.251	114	327	44	82	95	11	1	0	28	..	7	1	7	52	0	37	3	5
Hernandez, Rodolfo, 87 Yuc-13 Mva.	.345	100	333	67	115	172	9	0	16	72	..	1	5	5	63	7	36	0	1
Herrera, Calixto, Mexico City Tigers ..	.167	18	18	2	3	4	1	0	0	1	..	1	0	0	0	0	4	0	0
Herrera, Raymundo, 8 Yuc-11 SL	.000	11	8	0	0	0	0	0	0	0	..	1	0	0	1	0	1	1	0
Herrera, Rene, Mexico City Reds	.245	72	163	26	40	46	4	1	0	10	..	5	1	1	15	0	26	5	2
Herrera, Ricardo, Monterrey	.314	109	414	70	130	151	15	3	0	31	..	0	2	2	53	2	32	34	25
Jimenez, Eduardo, Leon	.348	98	273	55	95	136	15	4	6	48	..	0	1	4	41	5	48	8	5
Jimenez, Leopoldo, Campeche	.357	13	14	1	5	6	1	0	0	3	..	0	0	0	3	0	2	1	0
Lavagnino, Jose Ernesto, San Luis	.341	28	85	11	29	41	2	2	2	12	..	0	0	0	8	0	17	0	0
Leal, Guadalupe, Union Laguna*	.280	100	279	31	78	122	8	0	12	53	..	2	1	1	28	4	47	2	1
Ledezma, Victor M., Agua	.000	1	1	0	0	0	0	0	0	0	..	0	0	0	0	0	1	0	1
Lezcano, Manuel, Yucatan	.233	16	60	9	14	28	2	3	2	7	..	1	0	1	5	3	6	0	0
Linares, Rufino, Mexico City Reds	.389	109	406	88	158	257	37	1	20	93	..	0	6	6	36	5	41	7	2
Lizarraga, Alejandro, Union Laguna	.298	98	302	35	90	112	10	0	4	33	..	3	1	4	16	2	20	2	7
Lopez, Alfonso, Mexico City Tigers	.322	97	342	45	110	132	14	1	2	41	..	10	3	2	21	1	22	2	4
Lopez, Antonio, Saltillo	.350	124	471	90	165	275	24	4	26	97	..	0	4	4	37	5	39	9	8
Lopez, Fernando, Mexico City Reds	.114	24	44	6	5	5	0	0	0	3	..	0	1	0	6	0	9	0	2
Lopez, Jaime, Leon*	.310	65	155	25	48	54	4	1	0	21	..	0	2	2	20	4	7	2	2
Lopez, Jesus Manuel, San Luis	.444	5	9	0	4	4	0	0	0	0	..	0	0	0	1	0	2	0	0
Lopez, Pablo, Saltillo	.253	71	182	26	46	66	5	0	5	15	..	1	1	1	16	1	20	0	3
Lopez, Salvador, Nuevo Laredo	.318	32	85	21	27	35	6	1	0	10	..	1	0	2	14	0	21	1	5
Lora, Luis, Yucatan*	.340	91	338	58	115	168	19	2	10	65	..	2	9	3	31	12	23	17	5
Loredo, Jorge Luis, Nuevo Laredo	.167	9	12	3	2	4	2	0	0	1	..	1	0	0	0	0	4	0	1
Luna, Jose Luis, 30 Sal-15 MC Reds.	.207	45	116	13	24	29	5	0	0	6	..	3	0	1	8	0	7	2	1
Machiria, Pablo, Mexico City Tigers	.295	107	319	52	94	136	10	4	8	50	..	10	1	4	27	2	43	6	5
Martinez, Francisco, Union Laguna	.273	106	308	36	86	108	12	2	2	25	..	7	0	2	14	0	32	1	1
Martinez, Grimaldo, Monclova	.243	39	37	6	9	10	1	0	0	4	..	0	0	0	4	0	8	1	1
Martinez, Raul, Monterrey	.275	92	258	28	71	92	8	2	3	42	..	4	7	1	26	1	31	0	3
Maza, Celerino, 10 Lag-2 SL	.238	12	21	1	5	5	0	0	0	1	..	0	0	0	0	0	7	0	0
McDonald, Tony, Aguascalientes	.347	123	498	105	173	225	27	5	5	66	..	4	5	7	48	4	36	11	8
Mendoza, Luis Alonso, Aguascalientes	.323	78	254	48	82	114	10	2	6	41	..	2	2	6	44	2	30	1	3
Mendoza, Mario, Aguascalientes*	.316	107	386	66	122	160	19	2	5	55	..	5	3	0	49	5	29	1	4
Mendoza, Porfirio, Campeche	.237	111	321	48	76	116	17	1	7	35	..	7	3	2	38	1	46	0	6
Mercado, Hector, Campeche	.250	9	8	1	2	3	1	0	0	0	..	0	0	0	0	0	2	0	0
Meza, Leonel, Monterrey	.184	40	76	5	14	14	0	0	0	5	..	1	0	0	5	0	16	1	0
Miller, Eddie, Monterrey	.293	100	338	69	99	172	15	5	16	70	..	0	4	13	60	9	70	32	6
Miller, Lemmie, Tabasco	.295	17	61	12	18	25	4	0	1	6	..	0	0	0	5	0	7	3	2

Player and Club	Pct.	G.	AB.	R.	H.	TB.	2B.	3B.	HR.	RBI.	GW.	SH.	SF.	HP.	BB.	Int. BB.	SO.	SB.	CS.
Milner, Ted, Leon	.368	22	57	16	21	24	1	1	0	10	..	0	0	4	15	1	11	5	2
Monroy, Victor Hugo, Monclova	.279	87	280	27	78	105	15	0	4	34	..	2	1	4	17	2	37	1	0
Mora, Andres, Nuevo Laredo	.368	114	419	87	154	292	24	0	38	123	..	1	7	1	56	11	36	0	1
Morales, Luis Arturo, Union Laguna	.000	5	3	0	0	0	0	0	0	1	..	1	1	1	0	0	1	0	0
Morales, Manuel, Mexico City Tigers	.268	113	358	58	96	118	14	1	2	42	..	14	2	5	49	0	18	4	5
Moreno, Roberto, Tabasco	.000	7	8	0	0	0	0	0	0	0	..	0	0	0	0	0	4	0	0
Morfin, Jorge, Aguascalientes°	.252	41	143	22	36	45	4	1	1	8	..	7	1	0	16	1	32	3	2
Morones, Martin, Monclova	.205	61	83	20	17	23	3	0	1	3	..	0	1	4	8	0	19	2	0
Navarrete, Juan, Saltillo°	.336	120	458	86	154	203	21	5	6	55	..	8	4	2	37	6	16	10	15
Navarro, Ruben, Mexico City Reds	.279	87	254	44	76	111	9	1	8	47	..	2	0	5	24	0	61	0	0
Nunez, Arturo, Nuevo Laredo	.053	11	19	1	1	1	0	0	0	0	..	1	0	0	3	0	6	0	1
Olivares, Oswaldo, 42 Yuc-80 Leo°	.365	122	449	97	164	217	20	12	3	52	..	2	1	2	75	4	25	21	14
Ortiz, Alejandro, Nuevo Laredo	.333	120	412	107	137	262	27	1	32	98	..	1	6	6	91	8	71	9	6
Ortiz, Alfredo, 3 Pue-3 MC Tigers°	.200	6	5	0	1	1	0	0	0	1	..	0	0	0	1	1	1	0	0
Pacho, Juan Jose, Yucatan	.291	127	416	67	121	161	11	4	7	40	..	13	5	2	35	1	30	8	6
Payton, Eric, Union Laguna°	.379	124	477	105	181	299	32	4	26	114	..	1	10	1	62	8	60	23	5
Peralta, Amado, Mexico City Tigers	.233	103	283	39	66	85	10	0	3	29	..	1	2	0	68	4	52	3	2
Perez, Jose Luis, Aguascalientes°	.303	108	370	74	112	172	17	5	11	61	..	5	2	3	55	6	76	1	1
Perez, Julian, Puebla	.403	26	77	11	31	44	5	1	2	15	..	0	0	2	16	1	6	1	1
Perez, Leonardo, Leon	.500	2	2	1	1	3	0	1	0	1	..	0	0	0	0	0	1	0	0
Perez Tovar, Raul, Campeche	.357	17	56	10	20	29	2	2	1	6	..	2	0	0	6	0	3	1	0
Picos, Tereso, Yucatan	.100	12	20	0	2	2	0	0	0	0	..	0	0	1	0	0	5	0	0
Pierce, Jack, 72 Leo-30 Tig°	.277	102	376	73	104	194	18	0	24	89	..	0	8	3	54	10	58	3	4
Ponce, Hector, Puebla	.275	110	345	42	95	119	14	2	2	30	..	12	1	0	14	0	34	10	2
Puente, Hugo, Yucatan	.000	7	10	1	0	0	0	0	0	0	..	0	0	0	1	0	5	0	0
Quintero, Guadalupe, 51 Sal-26 Leo	.310	77	226	28	70	87	11	0	2	25	..	2	2	3	19	2	21	2	4
Quintero, Victor, Puebla	.284	110	373	45	106	134	16	3	2	46	..	4	4	0	26	3	25	0	2
Quiroz, Jose Julian, Mexico City Tig°	.287	105	328	45	94	138	15	4	7	39	..	2	1	0	28	3	49	3	1
Ramirez, Enrique, Nuevo Laredo	.235	119	413	40	97	112	13	1	0	29	..	11	5	1	29	0	47	7	8
Ramirez, Gustavo, Tabasco	.250	11	20	1	5	5	0	0	0	3	..	0	0	1	1	0	5	0	1
Ramirez, Manuel, Tabasco	.231	76	216	20	50	67	9	1	2	23	..	3	3	2	17	1	11	1	0
Ramirez, Mario, Yucatan	.328	20	61	12	20	30	1	0	3	12	..	1	2	0	18	1	7	4	0
Rendon, Jose, Saltillo	.237	30	97	14	23	41	3	0	5	15	..	0	0	0	21	1	19	0	1
Reyes, Enrique, Nuevo Laredo	.222	48	126	8	28	35	4	0	1	10	..	3	2	2	19	1	19	0	1
Reyes, Gerardo, San Luis	.246	84	289	44	71	94	9	1	4	21	..	5	2	3	28	1	25	2	9
Reyes, Juan, Campeche	.287	107	370	48	106	183	24	1	17	71	..	2	5	0	28	6	64	3	1
Rios, Carlos, Campeche	.250	97	296	29	74	103	12	1	5	35	..	11	1	1	21	0	23	2	5
Rivera, Carlos, Saltillo	.287	48	164	29	47	87	9	2	9	27	..	0	3	2	16	2	42	0	1
Rivera, Eleazar, Monterrey	.097	19	31	1	3	3	0	0	0	1	..	0	1	0	1	0	13	0	0
Rivera, Jesus, Monterrey	.330	118	382	82	126	202	20	1	18	76	..	0	4	0	88	8	78	16	5
Rivera, Pablo, San Luis	.231	33	121	16	28	45	4	2	3	13	..	0	1	0	7	0	10	4	2
Rivero, Gener, Leon	.256	106	293	44	75	90	11	2	0	27	..	3	2	1	35	1	17	9	4
Robles, Humberto, Monterrey	.311	58	177	26	55	83	11	1	5	22	..	2	1	1	19	2	44	2	5
Robles, Sergio, Aguascalientes	.000	1	2	0	0	0	0	0	0	0	..	0	0	0	0	0	0	0	0
Rodriguez, Aurelio, Saltillo	.371	68	245	48	91	149	18	2	12	53	..	1	2	3	34	3	28	0	1
Rodriguez, Genaro, Monterrey	.308	78	234	30	72	106	13	3	5	43	..	4	2	2	23	1	33	6	4
Rodriguez, Guillermo, Puebla	.329	123	438	75	144	247	29	1	24	89	..	3	3	8	31	8	77	3	4
Rodriguez, Ignacio, Monclova	.000	2	1	0	0	0	0	0	0	0	..	0	0	0	0	0	0	0	0
Rodriguez, Jamie, Leon	.314	97	271	39	85	102	12	1	1	24	..	3	1	0	20	1	18	5	8
Rodriguez, Juan, Leon	.362	121	439	101	159	188	15	7	0	61	..	7	8	8	72	0	15	14	6
Romero, Marco Antonio, Puebla		2	0	0	0	0	0	0	0	0	..	0	0	0	0	0	0	0	0
Rosario, Alfonso, Monterrey	.300	122	437	92	131	232	31	2	22	99	..	3	8	7	54	6	63	3	6
Rosas, Clemente, Saltillo	.276	18	58	3	16	23	4	0	1	3	..	1	0	0	2	1	12	0	0
Rubio, Mauricio, San Luis	.176	27	17	9	3	3	0	0	0	2	..	0	0	0	2	0	4	0	0
Ruiz, Demetrio, Tabasco	.255	112	330	48	84	100	10	3	0	20	..	4	1	2	42	1	17	9	7
Ruiz, Porfirio, 20 Leon-45 Yuc	.320	65	169	17	54	69	12	0	1	23	..	2	3	1	17	0	20	1	2
Saenz, Ricardo, 14 Sal-56 Mva	.250	70	200	24	50	57	7	0	0	11	..	1	1	0	21	0	14	0	3
Saiz, Herminio, Monclova	.276	117	416	62	115	150	19	5	2	42	..	6	3	6	31	1	61	2	3
Samaniego, Manuel, Yucatan	.260	85	277	34	72	94	10	0	4	32	..	4	3	2	20	0	45	2	6
Sanchez, Andres, Mexico City Reds	.266	85	263	45	70	91	10	4	1	33	..	2	1	1	39	0	42	3	0
Sanchez, Armando, M.C. Reds°	.296	93	355	51	105	130	12	5	1	43	..	2	5	1	39	1	29	1	3
Sanchez, Gerardo, Nuevo Laredo	.271	121	472	71	128	178	18	1	10	44	..	4	6		37	0	50	5	6
Sanchez, Gustavo, Leon	.200	5	5	1	1	3	0	1	0	3	..	0	0	0	1	0	1	0	0
Sanchez, Orlando, Puebla°	.415	123	439	95	182	293	34	1	25	115	..	0	2	2	48	8	37	6	3
Serna, Joel, Monclova	.271	118	420	72	114	156	19	1	7	46	..	10	6	3	57	2	43	1	1
Serratos, Miguel, Campeche	.289	107	377	47	109	173	17	4	13	58	..	6	0	3	16	2	56	4	6
Sigler, Allan, Nuevo Laredo°	.279	87	258	53	72	131	14	3	13	44	..	3	2	2	66	7	70	3	3
Smith, Ken, Tabasco	.583	4	12	1	7	9	2	0	0	2	..	0	0	0	2	2	1	0	0
Smith, Robert, 85 Cam-27 Mon°	.339	112	398	82	135	190	25	3	8	56	..	4	1	4	69	5	53	28	9
Sommers, Jesus, Leon	.351	118	444	81	156	254	34	2	20	114	..	1	5	2	49	4	49	4	5
Soto, Carlos, Nuevo Laredo	.278	112	381	53	106	203	10	0	29	94	..	0	5	1	47	5	46	0	0
Stockstill, David, Puebla°	.323	123	434	92	141	234	26	2	21	70	..	1	6	1	84	4	37	1	3
Suarez, Miguel, Puebla°	.143	8	14	0	2	2	0	0	0	1	..	1	1	0	1	0	2	0	0
Tapia, Noe, Tabasco	.220	32	50	9	11	18	1	0	2	6	..	1	2	0	12	0	14	0	1
Tirado, Federico, Mexico City Tigers	.143	6	7	0	1	1	0	0	0	0	..	0	0	0	1	0	5	0	0
Tirado, Victor, Yucatan	.274	35	95	13	26	34	6	1	0	15	..	1	0	0	9	1	9	1	1
Torres, Eduardo, Saltillo	.196	46	138	26	27	47	8	0	4	17	..	1	1	2	43	2	32	0	6
Torres, Efrain, Nuevo Laredo	.217	86	221	33	48	61	4	0	3	19	..	4	0	2	13	0	50	2	4
Torres, Nemesio Jaime, Tabasco	.277	64	188	21	52	68	13	0	1	19	..	5	2	1	15	0	23	2	2
Torres, Raymundo, Yucatan	.290	123	431	93	125	229	18	1	28	95	..	3	4		74	8	84	16	3
Trower, Keith, Puebla	.321	6	28	5	9	14	3	1	0	1	..	0	0	0	1	0	1	3	1
Uzcanga, Ali, Saltillo	.291	93	316	48	92	120	7	6	3	30	..	3	1	4	36	0	50	1	3
Valdez, Baltazar, Monclova	.333	90	318	51	106	182	10	3	20	77	..	0	4	2	34	5	36	1	2
Valdez, Jesus, Monclova	.303	38	109	13	33	42	3	0	2	16	..	1	0	0	13	0	22	1	0
Valdez, Luis Alberto, Monterrey	.277	106	339	43	94	108	12	1	0	28	..	3	4	4	23	0	32	2	6
Valdez, Rodolfo, Campeche	.000	1	2	0	0	0	0	0	0	0	..	0	0	0	1	0	0	0	0
Valdivia, Arturo, Union Laguna	.333	6	6	0	2	2	0	0	0	1	..	0	0	0	0	0	1	0	0
Valencia, Carlos, Aguascalientes	.325	110	391	66	127	206	22	3	17	87	..	3	10	5	37	3	48	3	3
Valenzuela, Horacio, Union Laguna	.246	101	325	40	80	119	12	3	7	51	..	1	5	3	31	10	64	2	1
Valenzuela, Leonardo, Monclova°	.342	124	427	88	146	220	21	7	13	46	..	3	1	6	61	12	55	12	12
Valenzuela, Ricardo, San Luis	.328	115	430	66	141	199	28	3	8	82	..	6	5	3	20	3	45	1	1
Valle, Guadalupe, San Luis	.295	104	359	64	106	149	17	4	6	52	..	4	10	3	46	0	64	0	2

Player and Club	Pct.	G.	AB.	R.	H.	TB.	2B.	3B.	HR.	RBI.	GW.	SH.	SF.	HP.	BB.	Int. BB.	SO.	SB.	CS.
Valverde, Raul, Saltillo	.300	91	260	37	78	111	10	7	3	34	..	3	2	2	15	0	41	1	2
Vargas, Edilberto, Aguascalientes*	.380	89	321	94	122	252	21	2	35	98	..	0	3	1	64	6	62	0	1
Vargas, Ignacio, Yucatan	.231	27	65	6	15	26	4	2	1	4	..	0	0	1	2	0	26	0	1
Vargas, Trinidad, Yucatan	.180	25	50	3	9	11	2	0	0	3	..	0	0	0	1	0	17	1	0
Vega, Jesus, Aguascalientes	.000	1	1	0	0	0	0	0	0	0	..	0	0	0	0	0	1	0	0
Vega, Ramon, Aguascalientes	.268	62	220	17	59	71	8	2	0	18	..	6	3	1	9	1	26	0	0
Vergara, Salvador, San Luis	.286	8	7	1	2	2	0	0	0	1	..	0	0	0	0	0	0	0	0
Vila, Jesus, Union Laguna	.000	1	1	0	0	0	0	0	0	0	..	0	0	0	0	0	1	0	0
Villa, Victor, Puebla	.217	41	83	16	18	23	2	0	1	9	..	2	0	0	3	0	11	2	0
Villaescusa, Fernando, Yucatan*	.295	93	369	57	109	135	17	3	1	37	..	6	3	0	15	1	20	15	5
Villagomez, David, 76 Sal-44 Ags	.322	120	442	73	142	211	19	1	16	83	..	3	4	4	33	0	70	2	3
Villalobos, Enrique, Leon	.331	52	130	24	43	72	8	0	7	32	..	1	1	5	14	2	29	5	3
Villela, Carlos, San Luis	.283	122	453	76	128	186	14	13	6	58	..	7	3	1	52	2	62	9	5
Vizcarra, Roberto, Leon	.130	22	23	5	3	3	0	0	0	2	..	0	0	0	1	0	6	0	0
Vizcarra, Sergio, San Luis	.318	97	314	32	100	137	15	5	4	34	..	5	3	3	19	0	29	2	8
Wong, Julian, Saltillo	.240	82	217	27	52	73	8	2	3	21	..	6	2	0	24	1	31	6	5
Woods, Al, Tabasco	.331	48	142	26	47	72	10	0	5	24	..	0	1	0	27	0	13	1	0
Yepez, Jose Luis, Leon	.000	4	3	0	0	0	0	0	0	0	..	0	0	0	0	0	0	0	0
Zambrano, Rosario, Tabasco*	.328	117	387	55	127	161	18	5	2	35	..	5	4	1	39	3	46	18	9
Zuniga, Armando, Mexico City Tigers	.190	11	21	5	4	4	0	0	0	1	..	1	0	0	2	0	5	0	0

The following pitchers, listed alphabetically by club, with games in parentheses, had no plate appearances, primarily through use of designated hitters:

AGUASCALIENTES—Brusstar, Warren (20); Castaneda, Mario (1); Castillo, Feliciano (2); Delgadillo, Gustavo (30); Granillo, Carlos (29); Lopez, Hector (36); Martinez, Gabriel (23); Montano, Francisco (26); Munoz, Miguel (3); Padilla, Raymundo (10); Raygoza, Claudie (2); Rodriguez, Mario Alberto (37); Rojo, Gonzalo (31); Romero, Ramon (6); Solis, Miguel (17); Tafoya, Rodney (5); Valenzuela, Adan (7); Villanueva, Luis (41); Villegas, Mike (19).

CAMPECHE—Barraza, Ernesto (6); Dominguez, Herminio (26); Duran, Jesus (3); Flores, Jose Alberto (21); Hernandez, Angel (3); Huerta, Luis Enrique (30); Leal, Bernabe (2); Lizarraga, Cesar (2); Lunar, Luis (27); Mariscal, Tomas (2); Perez, Cipriano (15); Raygoza, Martin (3); Silva, Eduardo (20); Toledo, Mario (13); Velazquez, Ildefonso (27).

LEON—Beltran, Eleazar (26); Chavez, Guadalupe (41); Divison, Julio (2); Duarte, Florentino (22); Duckett, Bryant (3); Elvira, Narciso (33); Jaime Granillo, Ismael (49); Moreno, Abel (9); Osuna, Roberto (24); Sanchez, Martin (9); Sandoval, Guillermo (9); Soto, Fernando (24); Uribe, Juan Carlos (15); Valenzuela, Guillermo (2); Velazquez, Luis Alfonso (26); Yucupicio, Jesus Javier (40).

MEXICO CITY REDS—Armenta, Pedro (25); Barojas, Salome (53); Castaneda, Patricio (13); Elias Lomeli, Jorge (25); Felix, Antonio (22); Fowlkes, Alan (16); Kepshire, Kurt (4); Martin, John (6); Mendez, Luis Fernando (27); Sanchez, Felipe (10); Schuler, Dave (8); Solis, Ricardo (30); Sosa, Carlos (22).

MEXICO CITY TIGERS—Buitimea, Martin (31); Cruz, Jesus (5); Garcia, Juan (5); Herrera, Calixto (1); Menendez, Rolando (14); Moore, Robert (3); Moreno, Angel (30); Ordaz, Reynaldo (5); Palafox, Juan (6); Retes, Lorenzo (17); Rios, Jesus (28); Rivas, Martin (31); Rodriguez, Raul (6); Ruiz, Cecilio (5); Valdez, Armando (41); Valencia, Miguel Angel (25); Vidana, Alejandro (20); Zamudio, Aurelio (32).

MONCLOVA—Cano, Ezequiel (28); Garcia, Rogelio (28); Guzman, Ramon (30); Kaine, Martin (23); Luna, Jose Manuel (20); Menendez, Rolando (9); Mundo, Jesus (8); Norris, Mike (12); Pruneda, Armando (28); Ramirez, Roberto (9); Rivas, Lorenzo (4); Romero, Emigdio (2); Ruiz, Pablo (20); Sandate, Ricardo (4); Torres, Nelson (5); Valenzuela, Jaire (15); Vazquez, Florentino (32).

MONTERREY—Antunez, Martin (34); Gonzalez, Arturo (24); Gutierrez, Porfirio (18); Murillo, Felipe (1); Navarro, Adolfo (24); Osuna, Roberto (19); Pena, Jaime (20); Pulido, Antonio (37); Telechea, Gonzalo (2); Tellman, Tom (24); Uribe, Juan Carlos (10); Valenzuela, Ramon (1); Veliz, Francisco (17).

NUEVO LAREDO—Boyles, John (29); Carranza, Javier (30); Figueroa, Miguel (5); Lara, Hugo (5); Ledon, Juan Carlos (17); Leon, Maximino (14); Martinez, Antonio (36); Moreno, Jesus (24); Ochoa, Porfirio (36); Pollorena, Oscar (4); Romo, Manuel (34); Soto, Jose Luis (8); Tinoco, Ruben (4); Vizcarra, Faustino (18).

PUEBLA—Camarena, Martin (2); Castaneda, Aurelio (31); Cordova, Raul (4); Guzman, Gelacio (15); Jimenez, German (23); Jimenez, Isaac (10); Leal, Luis (19); Orozco, Jaime (25); Orozco, Octavio (2); Quijano, Enrique (5); Soto, Alvaro (37); Torrez, Martin (27); Urrea, Leonel (10).

SALTILLO—Aguilar, Miguel (28); Alvarez, Martin (32); Cartagena, Ruben (15); Castaneda, Mario (10); Espinosa, Roberto (3); Garcia, Jorge Luis (47); Leggatt, Richard (4); Mariscal, Tomas (5); Martin, John (1); Miranda, Julio Cesar (31); Moore, Gary (18); Mundo, Jesus (20); Munoz, Miguel (17); Munoz, Nelson (11); Padilla, Raymundo (19); Perez, Cipriano (10); Pollorena, Oscar (2); Rojo, Gonzalo (18); Rojo, Gustavo (14); Sanchez, Felipe (2); Shanks, William (2); Shimp, Tommy (6); Valenzuela, Adan (5); Valenzuela, Jaire (1); Villegas, Mike (3).

SAN LUIS—Armas, Isidro (31); Byron, Tim (6); Cardenas, Benito (20); Dimas, Rodolfo (34); Ek, Roberto (1); Findlay, Bill (20); Guzman, Benjamin (2); James, Duane (40); Katschke, Jim (25); Lizarraga, Hugo (1); Marquez, Isidro (1); Morales, Isidro (30); Ontiveros, Juan (48); Purata, Julio (29); Villegas, Ramon (12).

TABASCO—Castillejos, Jose (20); Colorado, Salvador (27); Cruz, Jesus (29); Divison, Julio (25); Erickson, Roger (5); Howe, Steve (10); Ibarra, Carlos (22); Leal, Barnabe (3); Matus, Nelson (5); Martinez, Victor (8); Moncada, Mario (20); Moya, Ramon (27); Rodriguez, Eulogio (13); Salas, Ernesto (28); Silva, Eduardo (16); Solis, Miguel (12); Vidana, Alejandro (2).

UNION LAGUNA—Diaz, Octavio (23); Escarrega, Ernesto (13); Franco, Francisco (8); Hernandez, Encarnacion (6); Kutsukos, Peter (11); Leal, Barnabe (5); Ledon, Juan Carlos (6); Matus, Nelson (10); Miranda, Francisco (26); Palafox, Juan (25); Renteria, Hilario (28); Rios, Sergio (4); Rivera, Juan Carlos (1); Saldana, Rodolfo (22); Salas, Ernesto (2); Serafin, Hector (38); Sombra, Francisco (33); Sosa, Carlos (2); Sosa, Victor (28); Tremblay, Wayne (4); Valenzuela, Jaire (1); Valverde, Alberto (2).

YUCATAN—Angulo, Kenneth (24); Arroyo, Freddie (25); Belman, Andres (20); Diaz, Cesar (19); Escarrega, Ernesto (4); Franco, Francisco (7); Gaxiola, Fernando (7); Guzman, Gelacio (12); Jimenez, Isaac (10); Montano, Nicolas (26); Orozco, Octavio (1); Pacheco, Alejandro (8); Quijano, Enrique (11); Retes, Lorenzo (18); Rodriguez, Pilar (13); Ruiz, Cecilio (10); Sauceda, Ramiro (37); Sosa, Elias (8); Urrea, Leonel (10); Villegas, Ramon (13).

GRAND SLAM HOME RUNS—Payton, 3; N. Barrera, L. Hernandez, Sommers, B. Valdez, 2 each; Aguilar, Aikens, Baca, Bobadilla, Darkis, Dominguez, A. Garza, Gray, R. Hernandez, An. Lopez, Lora, J.L. Perez, G. Quintero, Rendon, J. Reyes, C. Rios, Gu. Rodriguez, Rosario, Sigler, C. Soto, Valencia, E. Vargas, 1 each.

AWARDED FIRST BASE ON CATCHER'S INTERFERENCE—P. Mendoza (R. Vega); Navarrete (R. Castillo); Payton (G. Quintero); Gu. Rodriguez (F. Cruz); L. Valenzuela (O. Sanchez).

CLUB FIELDING

Club	Pct.	G.	PO.	A.	E.	DP.	PB.	Club	Pct.	G.	PO.	A.	E.	DP.	PB.
Mexico City Reds	.979	125	3084	1371	97	148	5	Aguascalientes	.972	126	3161	1517	136	165	9
Puebla	.978	124	3053	1373	98	142	14	Saltillo	.970	124	3081	1451	138	138	18
Leon	.978	127	3133	1423	101	139	13	Nuevo Laredo	.970	122	3049	1385	133	133	17
Campeche	.977	118	2850	1224	98	96	16	Union Laguna	.968	127	3172	1407	152	125	18
Tabasco	.976	125	3046	1457	109	113	6	Monclova	.966	126	3063	1265	152	131	17
Mexico City Tigers	.976	127	3195	1406	115	134	7	San Luis	.965	127	3125	1426	166	154	26
Monterrey	.974	125	3047	1292	118	113	29	Yucatan	.964	127	3071	1433	166	100	11

Triple Plays—Mexico City Reds 2, Campeche, Mexico City Tigers, Monterrey.

INDIVIDUAL FIELDING

*Throws lefthanded.

FIRST BASEMEN

Player and Club	Pct.	G.	PO.	A.	E.	DP.	Player and Club	Pct.	G.	PO.	A.	E.	DP.
H. Robles, Monterrey	1.000	34	261	20	0	21	J. Valdez, Monclova	.989	31	257	13	3	29
Ja. Lopez, Leon*	1.000	27	203	14	0	29	Lora, Yucatan*	.987	77	673	30	9	54
BUNDY, Mexico City Reds*	.997	99	874	64	3	111	Arce, San Luis	.987	13	72	4	1	7
Cosey, Campeche	.996	30	237	10	1	23	Ju. Perez, Puebla	.986	18	135	10	2	14
Garzon, Tabasco	.996	117	1056	86	5	91	Avila, Union Laguna	.986	44	330	18	5	12
Al. Lopez, Mexico City Tigers	.993	80	668	49	5	75	Peralta, Mexico City Tigers	.985	12	60	5	1	7
Gray, 32 Ags-24 Sal-41 Leo.....	.993	97	864	63	7	85	J. Reyes, Campeche	.985	45	368	20	6	36
Aikens, Puebla	.991	12	112	4	1	19	H. Valenzuela, Union Laguna	.984	95	775	35	13	67
Mora, Nuevo Laredo	.991	110	998	44	9	92	Quiroz, Mexico City Tigers*	.982	21	157	9	3	17
Gu. Rodriguez, Puebla	.991	96	855	37	8	92	Greene, Monclova	.981	40	291	18	6	32
Pierce, 55 Leo-30 Tig	.991	85	717	53	7	80	F. Gutierrez, Mexico City Reds .	.981	23	193	11	4	20
Villaescusa, Yucatan	.990	29	279	15	3	17	R. Hernandez, Yucatan	.980	19	188	12	4	14
M.A. Guzman, Campeche	.990	31	267	18	3	27	Ge. Rodriguez, Monterrey	.979	46	360	11	8	34
An. Lopez, Saltillo	.989	88	791	46	9	92	Clayton, San Luis	.977	108	921	74	23	121
B. Valdez, Monclova	.989	62	517	27	6	61	Heras, Monterrey	.977	51	411	17	10	39
E. Vargas, Aguascalientes	.989	89	845	56	10	98	E. Gonzalez, San Luis	.971	11	87	12	3	5

(Fewer Than Ten Games)

Player and Club	Pct.	G.	PO.	A.	E.	DP.	Player and Club	Pct.	G.	PO.	A.	E.	DP.
Lizarraga, Union Laguna	1.000	7	56	8	0	1	Alf. Ortiz, Puebla*	1.000	3	4	0	0	1
Sommers, Leon	1.000	9	54	4	0	6	Navarrete, Saltillo	1.000	1	3	1	0	1
T. Cruz, Leon	1.000	4	23	0	0	2	O. Sanchez, Puebla	1.000	2	4	0	0	1
C. Rios, Campeche	1.000	3	20	2	0	1	Payton, Union Laguna*	1.000	1	3	0	0	0
Diaz, Nuevo Laredo	1.000	3	19	1	0	3	L.A. Morales, Union Laguna	1.000	1	3	0	0	0
Meza, Monterrey	1.000	3	15	0	0	4	Loredo, Nuevo Laredo	1.000	1	2	0	0	0
Valle, San Luis	1.000	4	14	0	0	1	N.J. Garcia, Nuevo Laredo	1.000	1	2	0	0	0
Villagomez, Aguascalientes	1.000	2	10	0	0	1	Collins, Tabasco*	1.000	2	1	0	0	0
Vergara, San Luis	1.000	5	8	1	0	0	A. Garza, 1 Mva-8 Saltillo*	.989	9	87	5	1	7
Ja. Hernandez, Union Laguna	1.000	2	9	0	0	2	T. Vargas, Yucatan	.984	9	49	13	1	5
N. Barrera, Mexico City Reds	1.000	1	8	1	0	3	N. Torres, Tabasco	.977	7	80	4	2	10
Burke, Mexico City Tigers	1.000	4	7	2	0	3	Villalobos, Leon	.975	8	38	1	1	5
Bobadilla, Monclova	1.000	1	7	1	0	0	Baez, Mexico City Reds	.974	5	36	2	1	3
Bergie, Nuevo Laredo*	1.000	1	8	0	0	2	Soto, Nuevo Laredo	.973	7	70	2	2	13
Acosta, Campeche	1.000	3	6	1	0	0	Garbey, Campeche	.965	7	54	1	2	2
J. Cruz, Mexico City Tigers	1.000	2	6	0	0	0	Evans, Aguascalientes	.964	3	25	2	1	3
Esquivias, Union Laguna	1.000	1	5	0	0	0	C. Rivera, Saltillo	.939	5	42	4	3	5
Green, Leon	1.000	1	5	0	0	1	Man. Ramirez, Tabasco	.917	1	10	1	1	1
							Navarro, Mexico City Reds	.889	1	8	0	1	1

Triple Plays—Bundy 2, M.A. Guzman, Heras, Al. Lopez.

SECOND BASEMEN

Player and Club	Pct.	G.	PO.	A.	E.	DP.	Player and Club	Pct.	G.	PO.	A.	E.	DP.
Briones, Tabasco	.988	105	236	327	8	76	J. Barrera, Nuevo Laredo	.973	54	117	167	8	35
Ar. Sanchez, Mexico City Reds ..	.987	93	242	293	7	84	Ge. Sanchez, Nuevo Laredo	.973	79	185	240	12	59
J.F. Rodriguez, Leon	.987	120	296	453	10	101	Serna, Monclova	.971	113	266	294	17	72
M. Garcia, Monterrey	.986	36	76	69	2	17	C. Rios, Campeche	.970	69	161	190	11	31
S. Vizcarra, San Luis	.986	16	33	38	1	9	L. Guerrero, 27 Ags-55 Yuc	.969	82	181	230	13	48
N. Torres, Campeche	.986	14	26	43	1	8	Villaescusa, Yucatan	.968	63	122	182	10	37
R. Chavez, Campeche	.983	51	109	128	4	31	Barandica, Union Laguna	.967	71	101	130	8	31
Je. Gonzalez, Puebla	.983	124	271	364	11	106	F. Martinez, Union Laguna	.965	100	195	246	16	46
Re. Herrera, Mexico City Reds...	.983	18	27	30	1	7	Almodobar, Mexico City Tigers..	.959	28	50	44	4	9
L.A. Valdez, Monterrey	.982	101	244	295	10	66	Bustamante, Mexico City Tigers	.952	10	11	9	1	2
Ju. Gonzalez, Aguascalientes	.982	29	70	91	3	17	Wong, Saltillo	.945	20	38	48	5	10
A. Camacho, Mexico City Tigers	.980	112	261	320	12	79	Escalante, Aguascalientes	.944	10	23	28	3	10
Villela, San Luis	.980	119	316	357	16	102	G. Martinez, Monclova	.940	20	49	45	6	7
Navarrete, Saltillo	.979	113	295	357	14	93	T. Vargas, Yucatan	.938	10	19	26	3	4
An. Sanchez, Mexico City Reds..	.976	26	55	68	3	20	Campos, Tabasco	.925	14	18	19	3	4
McDonald, Aguascalientes	.974	65	156	186	9	38							

(Fewer Than Ten Games)

Player and Club	Pct.	G.	PO.	A.	E.	DP.	Player and Club	Pct.	G.	PO.	A.	E.	DP.
Garbey, Campeche	1.000	7	18	22	0	5	Gu. Sanchez, Leon	1.000	4	0	2	0	0
Rivero, Leon	1.000	5	6	10	0	0	Jo. L. Hernandez, Puebla	1.000	2	0	2	0	0
R. Vizcarra, Leon	1.000	4	7	7	0	2	De Los Santos, Monterrey	1.000	3	0	2	0	0
Sommers, Leon	1.000	3	2	10	0	1	Ju. Hernandez, Monclova	1.000	1	2	0	0	0
Ra. Herrera, Yucatan	1.000	5	6	4	0	3	Maza, San Luis	1.000	2	1	0	0	0
Rubio, San Luis	1.000	4	3	5	0	1	Esquivias, Union Laguna	1.000	1	1	0	0	1
Yepez, Leon	1.000	1	4	2	0	0	Fabela, Yucatan	.947	3	7	11	1	3
Peralta, Mexico City Tigers	1.000	1	3	3	0	2	Cabrera, Aguascalientes	.941	2	7	9	1	1
Burke, Mexico City Tigers	1.000	2	3	2	0	1	Alonso, Puebla	.923	7	3	9	1	1
Serratos, Campeche	1.000	2	1	4	0	0	Zuniga, Mexico City Tigers	.909	7	11	9	2	1
Ju. Chavez, Saltillo	1.000	1	2	1	0	1	Ri. Valenzuela, San Luis	.857	1	3	3	1	1

Triple Plays—A. Camacho, C. Rios, Ar. Sanchez.

THIRD BASEMEN

Player and Club	Pct.	G.	PO.	A.	E.	DP.	Player and Club	Pct.	G.	PO.	A.	E.	DP.
F. Gutierrez, Mexico City Reds ..	1.000	12	6	13	0	2	Sommers, Leon	.936	98	79	126	14	17
Castilla, Saltillo	.976	10	10	31	1	7	N. Gonzalez, Monterrey	.935	113	85	218	21	21
A. Camacho, MC Tigers	.974	19	10	27	1	1	L. Hernandez, Union Laguna	.935	102	86	202	20	20
N. BARRERA, MC Reds	.968	116	88	211	10	28	Ri. Valenzuela, San Luis	.934	115	98	243	24	31
Burke, 26 MC Tigers-63 Yuc	.953	89	57	164	11	10	T. Cruz, 12 Leon-6 MC Tigers...	.933	18	11	31	3	3
Serratos, Campeche	.950	104	80	208	15	16	N. Torres, Tabasco	.925	23	6	31	3	5
V. Quintero, Puebla	.947	98	70	162	13	12	C. Rivera, Saltillo	.923	27	19	53	6	2
E. Castillo, Tabasco	.945	105	96	233	19	21	Cabrera, 4 Yuc-19 U. Lag	.920	23	20	26	4	1
A. Rodriguez, Saltillo	.945	50	44	94	8	12	Campos, Tabasco	.917	10	5	6	1	0
Ale. Ortiz, Nu. Laredo	.942	120	107	234	21	24	Mar. Ramirez, Yucatan	.915	20	19	56	7	4
Alonso, Puebla	.941	39	30	50	5	7	Bobadilla, Monclova	.903	118	90	179	29	15
Meza, Monterrey	.941	20	8	24	2	0	Cazarin, Monclova	.892	34	22	36	7	3
Peralta, Mex City Tigers	.941	92	71	136	13	18	Arce, 34 Yuc-8 San Luis	.869	42	39	67	16	2
Wong, Saltillo	.941	33	20	59	5	2	Saiz, Monclova	.857	10	5	7	2	1
Aguilar, Aguascalientes	.938	123	110	254	24	30							

(Fewer Than Ten Games)

Player and Club	Pct.	G.	PO.	A.	E.	DP.	Player and Club	Pct.	G.	PO.	A.	E.	DP.
Garbey, Campeche	1.000	7	4	13	0	3	R. Vizcarra, Leon	1.000	3	3	0	0	0
C. Rios, Campeche	1.000	9	10	3	0	0	Ju. Perez, Puebla	1.000	1	1	1	0	0
Ju. Gonzalez, Aguascalientes	1.000	9	2	9	0	1	H. Robles, Monterrey	1.000	2	2	0	0	0
M. Camacho, MC Tigers	1.000	3	3	6	0	3	J. Barrera, Nuevo Laredo	1.000	2	1	1	0	0
R. Hernandez, Yucatan	1.000	3	2	6	0	0	Man. Ramirez, Tabasco	.938	5	6	9	1	0
J. Guerrero, Leon	1.000	4	2	4	0	0	V. Guerrero, San Luis	.917	3	2	9	1	1
Maza, Union Laguna	1.000	2	2	3	0	0	F. Martinez, U. Laguna	.900	4	3	6	1	1
Zuniga, MC Tigers	1.000	4	1	4	0	1	Picos, Yucatan	.826	7	5	14	4	0
An. Sanchez, MC Reds	1.000	3	1	3	0	1	An. Lopez, Saltillo	.765	7	4	9	4	2
Mercado, Campeche	1.000	3	3	1	0	1	P. Rivera, San Luis	.667	1	2	0	1	0
Fabela, Yucatan	1.000	6	1	3	0	0							

Triple Plays—M. Camacho, Serratos.

SHORTSTOPS

Player and Club	Pct.	G.	PO.	A.	E.	DP.	Player and Club	Pct.	G.	PO.	A.	E.	DP.
Ra. Herrera, 1 Yuc-9 San Luis	1.000	10	7	21	0	5	E. Ramirez, Nuevo Laredo	.962	120	253	381	25	78
De Los Santos, Monterrey	.985	24	25	39	1	8	Pacho, Yucatan	.960	127	261	429	29	77
ELIZONDO, Puebla	.979	123	219	445	14	102	Rivero, Leon	.956	102	126	285	19	66
Uzcanga, Saltillo	.978	90	172	314	11	69	Escalante, Aguascalientes	.954	20	44	60	5	12
T. Cruz, Leon	.973	14	24	46	2	13	S. Vizcarra, San Luis	.953	78	102	224	16	37
Re. Herrera, MC Reds	.970	40	74	90	5	25	J. Guerrero, Leon	.952	47	38	81	6	15
M. Mendoza, Aguascalientes	.969	107	229	389	20	96	Ri. Herrera, Monterrey	.951	108	160	329	25	79
P. Mendoza, Campeche	.968	111	221	329	18	53	Saiz, Monclova	.948	95	171	318	27	72
M. Morales, MC Tigers	.968	112	194	348	18	75	Almodobar, MC Tigers	.932	25	30	66	7	9
F. Gutierrez, MC Reds	.964	89	167	285	17	71	Valle, San Luis	.930	62	112	154	20	48
F. Guerrero, U. Laguna	.963	127	228	447	26	67	Ju. Hernandez, Monclova	.908	30	61	87	15	22
A. Gomez, Tabasco	.962	121	234	403	25	75	Wong, Saltillo	.837	20	37	50	7	14

(Fewer Than Ten Games)

Player and Club	Pct.	G.	PO.	A.	E.	DP.	Player and Club	Pct.	G.	PO.	A.	E.	DP.
V. Quintero, Puebla	1.000	6	8	11	0	2	A. Castaneda, Saltillo	.966	5	10	19	1	5
Campos, Tabasco	1.000	7	6	8	0	2	Ju. Chavez, Saltillo	.957	9	9	13	1	1
R. Vizcarra, Leon	1.000	4	7	3	0	1	Navarrete, Saltillo	.955	4	8	13	1	0
M. Garcia, Monterrey	1.000	3	6	4	0	2	McDonald, Aguascalientes	.953	8	19	22	2	9
Ju. Rodriguez, Leon	1.000	1	0	3	0	0	J.A. Chavez, MC Reds	.950	8	10	28	2	5
Je. Garcia, Saltillo	1.000	3	1	1	0	0	A. Camacho, MC Tigers	.941	4	4	12	1	3
Bobadilla, Monclova	1.000	1	0	2	0	0	C. Rios, Campeche	.931	9	14	13	2	4
Gu. Sanchez, Leon	1.000	1	1	1	0	1	Rubio, San Luis	.923	8	6	6	1	2
F. Figueroa, MC Reds	1.000	2	0	2	0	0	Moreno, Tabasco	.867	4	9	4	2	0
Barandica, Union Laguna	1.000	1	1	1	0	0	Loredo, Nuevo Laredo	.667	2	2	2	2	0
L. Jimenez, Campeche	1.000	3	1	1	0	0	Maza, Union Laguna	.500	2	1	0	1	0

Triple Plays—F. Gutierrez, Ri. Herrera.

OUTFIELDERS

Player and Club	Pct.	G.	PO.	A.	E.	DP.	Player and Club	Pct.	G.	PO.	A.	E.	DP.
G. Gomez, 39 Leon-37 Saltillo	1.000	76	141	6	0	0	Cosey, Campeche	.968	41	81	10	3	2
Perez Tovar, Campeche	1.000	17	34	2	0	1	I. Vargas, Yucatan	.968	20	35	5	1	0
Tapia, Tabasco	1.000	20	34	1	0	1	J. Rivera, Monterrey	.967	61	113	5	4	2
V. Tirado, Yucatan	1.000	16	33	1	0	0	Castelan, Puebla*	.967	98	199	5	7	0
H. Robles, Monterrey	1.000	16	23	2	0	0	Cole, Campeche*	.966	117	270	12	10	5
T. Cruz, Leon	1.000	10	21	2	0	0	Bellazetin, MC Tigers*	.965	95	131	7	5	2
Garibay, Aguascalientes	1.000	12	19	0	0	0	Craig, 8 N. Lar-29 Leon	.965	37	53	2	2	1
J.S. Chavez, MC Reds	1.000	12	15	1	0	0	Valencia, Aguascalientes	.963	108	195	15	8	1
F. Lopez, MC Reds	1.000	16	14	1	0	0	Quiroz, Mex. City Tigers*	.962	54	93	7	4	2
Je. Garcia, Saltillo	1.000	16	9	3	0	0	Aguilera, Yucatan	.961	60	91	8	4	1
STOCKSTILL, Puebla	.992	121	234	22	2	2	An. Lopez, Saltillo	.961	25	46	3	2	1
Ja. Rodriguez, Leon	.991	83	102	4	1	0	M. Guzman, Campeche	.959	47	66	4	3	1
Brown, Leon	.990	47	94	5	1	2	Ponce, Puebla	.959	106	175	11	8	1
Dominguez, San Luis	.986	116	200	12	3	4	Arzate, Aguascalientes	.958	60	104	9	5	1
Fernandez, MC Reds*	.986	118	268	10	4	2	E. Miller, Monterrey	.956	85	168	4	8	0
Andrade, Monterrey*	.986	88	130	7	2	2	G. Reyes, San Luis	.955	80	138	12	7	1
Ge. Sanchez, Nu. Laredo	.986	48	63	5	1	1	Ed. Torres, Saltillo	.955	44	101	6	5	0
Castro, Mex. City Tigers*	.985	118	190	10	3	0	Linares, Mexico City Reds	.953	86	133	10	7	0
Machiria, Mex. City Tigers	.984	94	173	7	3	1	D. Ruiz, Tabasco	.953	42	60	1	3	0
Ayala, 10 Leon-32 Puebla	.982	42	54	1	1	0	Bryant, Monterrey	.952	87	115	5	6	0
Greene, Monclova	.981	57	102	6	2	0	Jo. L. Garcia, San Luis	.952	33	56	3	3	0
Cazarin, Leon	.981	23	50	3	1	1	Morones, Monclova	.950	42	53	4	3	0
Baca, Mexico City Reds	.980	107	181	15	4	1	Ja. Hernandez, U. Laguna*	.950	14	18	1	1	0
Adams, Tabasco	.980	26	49	0	1	0	P. Rivera, San Luis	.949	30	56	0	3	0
Collins, Tabasco*	.980	121	233	7	5	1	E. Jimenez, Leon	.949	78	91	2	5	0
Villagomez, 76 Sal-30 Ags.	.979	106	168	18	4	1	Lavagnino, San Luis	.946	21	33	2	2	0
Morfin, Aguascalientes*	.979	37	89	4	2	0	Ef. Torres, N. Laredo	.944	69	96	6	6	0
Milner, Leon	.978	22	44	1	1	0	L. Guerrero, Yucatan	.944	28	49	2	3	0
Zambrano, Tabasco*	.978	117	214	10	5	1	Jo. L. Perez, Aguascalientes*	.941	87	128	16	9	1
Lizarraga, Union Laguna	.977	88	121	8	3	1	Darkis, 13 Lar-33 MC Tigers	.939	46	86	6	6	0
Cano, Campeche	.977	57	78	7	2	0	Ju. Hernandez, Monclova	.938	14	10	5	1	0
R. Smith, 84 Cam-27 Mon*	.977	111	204	5	5	1	Sigler, Nuevo Laredo	.937	86	143	5	10	1
Navarro, Mex. City Reds	.976	27	38	3	1	1	A. Castaneda, Saltillo	.936	25	35	9	3	3
R. Valverde, Saltillo	.976	84	153	10	4	0	Lora, Yucatan*	.933	18	26	2	2	0
L. Valenzuela, Monclova*	.976	119	266	14	7	1	Espinosa, San Luis	.933	10	13	1	1	1
Payton, Union Laguna*	.975	125	293	15	8	2	P. Lopez, Saltillo*	.932	50	51	4	4	0
Rosario, Monclova*	.974	114	206	15	6	2	Delgado, Yucatan	.931	76	126	9	10	1
Saenz, 12 Sal-42 Monclova	.973	54	102	8	3	1	R. Alvarez, Tabasco	.927	50	70	6	6	1
L.A. Cruz, San Luis	.973	93	199	15	6	11	Gu. Rodriguez, Puebla	.921	30	54	5	5	0
L. Miller, Tabasco	.972	17	34	1	1	0	Esquivias, Union Laguna	.917	10	10	1	1	1
Leal, Union Laguna*	.972	94	130	9	4	1	S. Lopez, Nuevo Laredo	.912	24	29	2	3	2
McDonald, Aguascalientes	.971	55	88	13	3	0	Lezcano, Yucatan	.909	15	26	4	3	0
R. Torres, Yucatan	.971	122	259	8	8	1	An. Sanchez, Mex City Reds*	.902	26	36	1	4	0
Bronson, Union Laguna	.970	86	156	8	5	1	Rendon, Saltillo	.892	28	30	3	4	0
Bergie, Nuevo Laredo*	.970	88	146	17	5	5	Woods, Tabasco	.875	11	14	0	2	0
Diaz, Nuevo Laredo	.969	50	91	3	3	1	Bazan, Yucatan	.857	13	14	4	3	0
Olivares, 42 Yuc-76 Leon*	.969	118	237	9	8	2	Ge. Rodriguez, Monterrey	.818	11	9	0	2	0

(Fewer Than Ten Games)

Player and Club	Pct.	G.	PO.	A.	E.	DP.	Player and Club	Pct.	G.	PO.	A.	E.	DP.
Re. Herrera, Mex. City Reds	1.000	6	10	0	0	0	E. Rivera, Monterrey	1.000	1	2	0	0	0
J. Cruz, Mex City Tigers	1.000	7	9	0	0	0	Suarez, Puebla°	1.000	4	2	0	0	0
C. Herrera, Mex. City Tigers	1.000	8	8	0	0	0	Vergara, San Luis	1.000	3	1	1	0	0
N. Je. Garcia, N. Laredo	1.000	6	5	0	0	0	Maza, San Luis	1.000	1	1	0	0	0
K. Smith, Tabasco	1.000	3	5	0	0	0	Cotes, Yucatan	1.000	2	1	0	0	0
H. Valenzuela, U. Laguna	1.000	3	4	0	0	0	G. Garza, Nuevo Laredo	1.000	1	1	0	0	0
Arce, San Luis	1.000	2	3	0	0	0	G. Ramirez, Tabasco	1.000	1	1	0	0	0
Trower, Puebla	1.000	3	3	0	0	0	S. Vizcarra, San Luis	.909	7	9	1	1	0
Almodobar, Mex. City Reds	1.000	3	3	0	0	0	M. Garcia, Monterrey	.833	8	5	0	1	1
H. Alvarez, Mex. City Tigers	1.000	1	3	0	0	0	L.A. Morales, U. Laguna	.800	2	4	0	1	0
Cabrera, Aguascalientes	1.000	1	2	1	0	0							

Triple Play—J. Rivera.

CATCHERS

Player and Club	Pct.	G.	PO.	A.	E.	DP.	PB.	Player and Club	Pct.	G.	PO.	A.	E.	DP.	PB.
Villalobos, Leon	1.000	19	71	11	0	0	4	G. Quintero, 37 Sal-26 Leo	.980	63	255	35	6	4	7
V. Tirado, Yucatan	1.000	18	47	10	0	0	3	E. Rivera, Monterrey	.979	18	41	5	1	4	1
E. Reyes, Nuevo Laredo	.995	44	183	27	1	8	3	O. Sanchez, Puebla	.978	98	449	36	11	5	11
F. ESTRADA, Campeche	.993	83	382	45	3	9	13	H. Estrada, Puebla	.977	23	75	10	2	0	2
R. Castillo, Tabasco	.990	73	258	53	3	6	5	J.C. Alvarez, San Luis	.977	87	366	58	10	11	20
G. Garza, Nuevo Laredo	.990	84	423	63	5	8	14	M.A. Guzman, Campeche	.977	41	146	23	4	3	3
Rosas, Saltillo	.989	18	82	10	1	0	2	Baez, Mexico City Reds	.977	81	342	35	9	4	5
R. Martinez, Monterrey	.989	90	476	59	6	9	23	Gastelum, Mexico City Reds	.975	23	102	15	3	1	0
Bocardo, Mexico City Reds	.988	24	70	9	1	0	0	D. Ruiz, Tabasco	.973	69	218	39	7	2	1
Villa, Puebla	.988	20	68	11	1	0	1	Cazarin, Leon	.973	38	157	24	5	3	3
A. Guzman, 51 Leo-12 Sal	.988	63	285	31	4	3	6	F. Cruz, Union Laguna	.972	103	471	54	15	2	14
Monroy, Monclova	.987	74	338	43	5	6	5	Luna, 30 Sal-14 MC Reds	.970	44	131	29	5	2	3
R. Vega, Aguascalientes	.987	60	250	45	4	2	5	Daut, Monclova	.966	58	244	38	10	3	12
M. Hernandez, MC Tigers	.987	114	584	79	9	16	1	Al. Lopez, Mexico City Tigers	.963	25	66	13	3	0	4
L.A. Mendoza, Agua	.986	71	305	48	5	4	4	Bazan, Saltillo	.963	48	199	35	9	3	6
P. Ruiz, 10 Leo-40 Yuc	.986	50	180	28	3	1	4	Avila, Union Laguna	.950	30	101	14	6	6	2
Heras, Monterrey	.981	42	230	24	5	3	5	Samaniego, Yucatan	.948	79	295	48	19	1	4
E. Gonzalez, San Luis	.981	52	174	29	4	6	6								

(Fewer Than Ten Games)

Player and Club	Pct.	G.	PO.	A.	E.	DP.	PB.	Player and Club	Pct.	G.	PO.	A.	E.	DP.	PB.
Acosta, Campeche	1.000	6	17	0	0	0	0	Cantu, Saltillo	1.000	1	5	0	0	0	0
Becerra, Mexico City Tigers	1.000	8	14	1	0	0	2	J. Vega, Aguascalientes	1.000	1	2	0	0	0	0
F. Tirado, Mexico City Tigers	1.000	5	12	0	0	0	0	Nunez, Nuevo Laredo	.971	7	30	3	1	0	0
S. Robles, Aguascalientes	1.000	1	7	0	0	0	0	Valdivia, Union Laguna	.938	4	14	1	1	0	1
Je. M. Lopez, San Luis	1.000	4	7	0	0	0	0								

PITCHERS

Player and Club	Pct.	G.	PO.	A.	E.	DP.	Player and Club	Pct.	G.	PO.	A.	E.	DP.
TELLMAN, Monterrey	1.000	24	11	42	0	1	Retes, 17 Tig-18 Yuc°	1.000	35	3	7	0	0
L. Leal, Puebla	1.000	19	9	33	0	7	Armenta, Mexico City Reds	1.000	25	2	7	0	1
Dominguez, Campeche	1.000	26	8	26	0	2	Sauceda, Yucatan	1.000	31	3	6	0	0
R. Villegas, 10 SL-13 Yuc	1.000	23	12	20	0	3	N. Montano, Yucatan	1.000	26	1	8	0	1
Moya, Tabasco	1.000	27	6	22	0	0	P. Castaneda, Mexico City Reds	1.000	13	4	5	0	1
Vazquez, Monclova	1.000	32	7	19	0	3	Camarena, Puebla	1.000	23	2	7	0	0
A. Valdez, Mexico City Tigers	1.000	41	5	21	0	1	Vidana, 2 Tab-20 Tig	1.000	22	6	3	0	0
Chavez, Leon	1.000	41	8	17	0	0	Osuna, 24 Leo-19 Mon	1.000	43	4	5	0	0
Beltran, Leon	1.000	26	10	15	0	1	Castillejos, Tabasco	1.000	20	1	7	0	2
Cano, Monclova°	1.000	28	7	17	0	1	F. Soto, Leon	1.000	24	4	4	0	0
I. Velazquez, Campeche	1.000	27	4	19	0	2	C. Perez, 10 Sal-15 Cam°	1.000	25	2	6	0	0
M. Alvarez, Saltillo	1.000	32	8	15	0	2	Menendez, 14 Tig-9 Mva	1.000	23	2	6	0	0
C. Ruiz, 10 Yuc-5 Tig°	1.000	15	1	21	0	1	Kutsukos, Union Laguna	1.000	11	1	6	0	2
Fowlkes, Mexico City Reds	1.000	16	5	17	0	1	Vizcarra, Nuevo Laredo	1.000	18	2	5	0	0
Delgadillo, Aguascalientes	1.000	30	8	14	0	0	E. Rodriguez, Tabasco	1.000	13	4	3	0	1
V. Sosa, Union Laguna	1.000	38	2	19	0	1	Moncada, Tabasco	1.000	20	1	6	0	0
Esquer, Monterrey°	1.000	23	3	18	0	0	F. Sanchez, 2 Sal-10 MC Reds	1.000	12	2	5	0	0
Buitimea, Mexico City Tigers	1.000	31	3	18	0	1	Quijano, 5 Pue-11 Yuc	1.000	16	2	5	0	0
Serafin, Union Laguna	1.000	38	2	18	0	0	Padilla, 19 Sal-10 Ags	1.000	29	2	5	0	1
Ontiveros, San Luis	1.000	48	8	12	0	0	A. Valenzuela, 7 Ags-5 Sal°	1.000	12	1	6	0	0
Valencia, Mexico City Tigers°	1.000	25	4	16	0	0	S. Rios, Union Laguna	1.000	24	3	3	0	0
M. Villegas, 19 Ags-3 Sal	1.000	22	7	13	0	1	Divison, 25 Tab-2 Leo	1.000	27	2	4	0	0
J. Rios, Mexico City Tigers	1.000	28	3	16	0	0	Cartagena, Saltillo	1.000	15	0	6	0	1
Lopez, Aguascalientes	1.000	22	3	15	0	0	Pena, Monterrey°	1.000	20	1	4	0	0
Gon. Rojo, 31 Ags-18 Sal	1.000	49	1	18	0	3	G. Guzman, 12 Yuc-15 Pue°	1.000	27	1	3	0	0
M. Munoz, 17 Sal-3 Ags	1.000	20	4	15	0	0	Luna, Monclova	1.000	20	0	4	0	0
Belman, Yucatan	1.000	20	1	17	0	0	Felix, Mexico City Reds	1.000	22	1	3	0	0
A. Soto, Puebla	1.000	37	1	16	0	0	P. Rodriguez, Yucatan	1.000	13	1	3	0	0
Granillo, Aguascalientes°	1.000	29	3	13	0	0	Toledo, Campeche	1.000	13	1	2	0	0
Durate, Leon	1.000	22	4	11	0	2	I. Rodriguez, Monclova	1.000	20	1	2	0	0
Uribe, 10 Mon-15 Leo	1.000	25	3	12	0	1	B. Leal, 3 Tab-5 Lag-2 Cam	1.000	10	0	2	0	0
Huerta, Campeche	1.000	30	2	12	0	0	R. Valenzuela, Monterrey	1.000	18	0	2	0	0
J. V'Inza, 1 Sal-1 Lag-15 Mva	1.000	17	1	13	0	2	Howe, Union Laguna	1.000	10	0	2	0	0
Jose L. Garcia, Tabasco°	1.000	41	6	7	0	0	Saldana, Union Laguna	1.000	12	0	2	0	0
Urrea, 10 Yuc-10 Puebla	1.000	20	5	8	0	1	Mar. Castaneda, 1 Ags-10 Sal	1.000	11	0	1	0	1
Romo, Nuevo Laredo	1.000	34	2	10	0	0	Colorado, Tabasco	.982	27	16	40	1	3
P. Gutierrez, Monterrey	1.000	18	3	9	0	0	Gonzalez, Monterrey	.974	24	10	28	1	1
Navarro, Monterrey	1.000	24	5	7	0	0	G. Jimenez, Puebla°	.973	23	8	35	1	4
G. Moore, Saltillo	1.000	18	2	10	0	0	Villanueva, Aguascalientes°°	.971	41	4	30	1	3
Flores, Campeche	1.000	21	4	7	0	0	Ibarra, Tabasco	.967	22	10	19	1	0
Antunez, Monterrey°	1.000	34	1	10	0	0	J. Cruz, 5 Tig-29 Tab°	.966	34	8	20	1	0
M. Rivas, Mexico City Tigers	1.000	31	1	10	0	0	R. Valdez, Campeche	.966	26	6	22	1	2
Cardenas, San Luis	1.000	20	4	7	0	2	Mundo, 8 Mva-20 Sal	.964	28	11	16	1	1
C. Sosa, 2 Lag-22 MC Reds	1.000	24	7	4	0	0	Carranza, Nuevo Laredo°	.963	30	6	20	1	3
R. Guzman, Monclova	1.000	30	3	7	0	1	Renteria, Union Laguna	.962	28	2	23	1	1
Franco, 8-Lag-7 Yuc-15 Pue	1.000	30	4	6	0	0	R. Solis, Mexico City Reds°	.961	30	8	41	2	5

PITCHERS—Continued

Player and Club	Pct.	G.	PO.	A.	E.	DP.	Player and Club	Pct.	G.	PO.	A.	E.	DP.
Dimas, San Luis	.960	34	9	15	1	1	J. Moreno, Nuevo Laredo	.917	24	5	39	4	5
Barojas, Mexico City Reds	.955	53	11	31	2	4	Silva, 20 Cam-16 Tab	.917	36	6	5	1	1
Jorge L. Garcia, Saltillo	.952	47	5	15	1	1	Norris, Monclova	.917	12	2	9	1	1
J. Miranda, Saltillo	.951	31	8	31	2	0	P. Ruiz, Monclova°	.917	20	2	9	1	1
Arroyo, Yucatan°	.951	25	14	44	3	5	G. Martinez, Aguascalientes	.917	23	1	10	1	0
Ochoa, Nuevo Laredo	.950	36	4	15	1	0	Mendez, Mexico City Reds	.914	27	6	26	3	1
M. Torres, Puebla	.947	27	1	17	1	1	Elias Lomeli, Mexico City Reds°	.913	25	2	19	2	3
Sombra, Union Laguna	.946	33	4	31	2	1	Zamudio, Mexico City Tigers	.912	32	3	28	3	1
Elvira, Leon°	.943	33	6	27	2	2	F. Miranda, Union Laguna	.909	26	3	7	1	3
Pruneda, Monclova	.943	28	10	23	2	1	Armas, San Luis	.900	31	6	12	2	2
Kaine, Monclova	.941	23	3	13	1	2	Matus, 5 Tab-10 Lag	.900	15	3	6	1	0
A. Castaneda, Puebla	.941	31	1	15	1	0	A. Martinez, Nuevo Laredo	.900	36	3	6	1	0
Leon, Nuevo Laredo	.941	14	5	11	1	3	C. Diaz, Yucatan	.900	19	2	9	1	1
Fuson, Nuevo Laredo	.940	22	6	41	3	4	Palafox, 6 Tig-25 Lag	.897	31	6	20	3	2
An. Moreno, MC Tigers°	.939	30	9	37	3	1	Vila, Union Laguna	.889	48	1	15	2	0
M. Raygoza, Campeche	.938	29	13	47	4	4	R. Garcia, Monclova	.889	28	2	6	1	1
Veliz, Monterrey°	.938	17	2	13	1	0	F. Montano, Aguascalientes	.886	26	7	24	4	5
Escarrega, 4 Yuc-13 Lag	.933	17	7	21	2	0	Boyles, Nuevo Laredo	.875	29	5	23	4	3
Pulido, Monterrey	.933	37	1	13	1	1	Angulo, Yucatan°	.875	24	3	18	3	1
M. Solis, 17 Ags-12 Tab	.931	29	5	22	2	3	Findlay, San Luis	.870	20	5	15	3	3
Purata, San Luis°	.931	29	8	19	2	2	Salas, 2 Lag-28 Tab	.867	30	5	8	2	1
Katschke, San Luis	.931	25	8	19	2	3	James, San Luis	.857	40	6	12	3	0
L.A. Velazquez, Leon	.929	26	11	28	3	2	Lunar, Campeche	.857	27	1	5	1	0
M.A. Rodriguez, Aguascalientes	.929	37	1	12	1	2	L. Perez, Leon	.842	34	5	11	3	3
Morales, San Luis	.926	30	8	17	2	1	I. Jimenez, 10 Pue-10 Yuc°	.833	20	2	18	4	2
Aguilar, Saltillo	.921	28	8	27	3	1	O. Diaz, Union Laguna	.800	23	2	2	1	0
J. Orozco, Puebla	.923	25	9	27	3	2	Brusstar, Aguascalientes	.750	20	0	3	1	0
Jaime Granillo, Leon	.923	49	2	10	1	0	Gus. Rojo, Saltillo	.667	14	0	2	1	0
Yucupicio, Leon	.923	40	7	5	1	0	Ledon, 17 Lar-6 Lag	.600	23	0	3	2	0

(Fewer Than Ten Games)

Player and Club	Pct.	G.	PO.	A.	E.	DP.	Player and Club	Pct.	G.	PO.	A.	E.	DP.
E. Sosa, Yucatan	1.000	8	3	5	0	0	V. Martinez, Tabasco	1.000	8	0	2	0	0
N. Torres, Monclova	1.000	5	1	5	0	0	Tinoco, Nuevo Laredo	1.000	6	0	2	0	1
Ramirez, Monclova	1.000	9	1	4	0	1	Mariscal, 2 Cam-5 Sal	1.000	7	1	0	0	0
G. Valenzuela, Leon	1.000	5	1	4	0	0	Pacheco, Yucatan	1.000	8	1	0	0	0
O. Orozco, 2 Pue-1 Yuc	1.000	3	0	4	0	0	Marquez, San Luis	1.000	1	1	0	0	0
Barraza, Campeche	1.000	6	0	5	0	0	Tremblay, Union Laguna	1.000	4	0	1	0	0
E. Hernandez, Union Laguna	1.000	6	0	5	0	0	B. Guzman, San Luis	1.000	2	0	1	0	0
Ju. Garcia, Mexico City Tigers	1.000	5	1	3	0	0	Duran, Campeche	1.000	3	0	1	0	0
Martin, 6 MC Reds-1 Sal	1.000	7	0	4	0	0	R. Rodriguez, MC Tigers	1.000	6	0	1	0	0
R. Moore, Mexico City Tigers	1.000	3	2	1	0	0	Kepshire, Mexico City Reds	1.000	4	0	1	0	0
Erickson, Tabasco	1.000	5	2	1	0	1	Schuler, Mexico City Reds	1.000	8	0	1	0	1
Lara, Nuevo Laredo	1.000	5	1	2	0	0	Ab. Moreno, Leon	1.000	9	0	1	0	0
Shimp, Saltillo	1.000	6	0	3	0	0	Shanks, Saltillo	1.000	2	0	1	0	0
Sandate, Monclova°	1.000	4	0	3	0	0	Figueroa, Nuevo Laredo	.750	5	1	2	1	1
Espinosa, Saltillo	1.000	3	0	2	0	0	Sandoval, Leon	.667	9	0	4	2	0
M. Sanchez, Leon	1.000	9	0	2	0	0	Ordaz, Mexico City Tigers	.500	5	0	1	1	0
Quiroz, MC Tigers°	1.000	8	0	2	0	0	R. Romero, Aguascalientes	.000	6	0	0	1	0

Triple Plays—Barojas, P. Castaneda.

CLUB PITCHING

Club	ERA.	G.	CG.	ShO.	Sv.	IP.	H.	R.	ER.	HR.	HB.	BB.	Int. BB.	SO.	WP.	Bk.
Tabasco	4.34	125	36	17	17	1015.1	1125	559	490	78	29	374	44	429	29	1
Monterrey	4.47	125	37	14	25	1015.2	1118	585	504	96	26	402	18	671	40	0
Nuevo Laredo	4.68	122	39	5	15	1016.1	1130	624	529	110	37	480	32	581	64	2
Yucatan	4.69	127	42	8	14	1023.2	1215	657	533	89	42	395	17	432	69	1
Mexico City Reds	4.75	125	39	10	20	1028.0	1166	588	542	100	37	452	15	485	46	1
Puebla	4.78	124	46	6	15	1017.2	1253	596	540	76	22	365	32	526	57	1
Mexico City Tigers	4.90	127	37	8	23	1065.0	1257	673	580	117	33	448	45	620	58	3
Campeche	4.93	118	38	6	16	950.0	1096	588	520	99	28	399	20	490	61	2
San Luis	5.03	127	24	3	19	1041.2	1175	700	582	124	24	587	47	511	53	2
Leon	5.40	127	31	3	26	1044.1	1223	697	627	99	36	532	75	568	63	3
Union Laguna	5.48	127	20	6	19	1057.1	1289	748	644	108	40	535	49	538	57	2
Aguascalientes	5.60	126	22	3	19	1053.2	1345	754	656	124	45	454	29	542	35	1
Monclova	5.72	126	28	9	22	1021.0	1231	747	649	132	39	571	44	530	61	2
Saltillo	6.22	124	26	3	19	1027.0	1265	791	710	122	37	564	73	527	66	2

PITCHERS' RECORDS
(Leading Qualifiers for Earned-Run Average Leadership — 102 or More Innings)

°Throws lefthanded.

Pitcher—Club	W.	L.	Pct.	ERA.	G.	GS.	CG.	GF.	ShO.	Sv.	IP.	H.	R.	ER.	HR.	HB.	BB.	Int. BB.	SO.	WP.
Fuson, Nuevo Laredo	14	8	.636	2.67	22	21	19	1	1	0	172.0	170	64	51	10	2	38	3	127	7
Tellman, Monterrey	15	4	.789	2.75	24	24	11	0	3	0	170.0	164	59	52	10	6	20	1	88	2
Dimas, San Luis	9	3	.750	2.88	34	0	1	34	0	3	115.2	102	39	37	12	1	32	5	68	5
L. Leal, Puebla	15	2	.882	2.97	19	19	7	0	0	0	136.1	151	48	45	5	0	41	3	77	4
Arroyo, Yucatan°	13	11	.542	3.05	25	25	17	0	0	0	189.0	190	81	64	11	4	35	3	76	5
Barojas, Mexico City Reds	13	4	.764	3.10	53	6	2	47	0	15	124.2	119	47	43	5	3	70	6	62	2
Colorado, Tabasco	15	9	.625	3.13	27	27	17	0	5	0	186.2	200	73	65	9	4	31	4	85	3
G. Jimenez, Puebla°	12	9	.571	3.31	23	23	13	0	3	0	168.1	178	72	62	6	1	42	3	108	3
J. Rios, Mexico City Tigers	16	9	.640	3.55	28	26	16	2	1	2	190.1	188	86	75	23	4	47	9	200	6
Gonzalez, Monterrey	12	6	.667	3.77	24	24	9	0	4	0	169.2	173	77	71	13	3	58	4	118	5
Villanueva, Aguascalientes°	7	7	.500	3.88	41	13	5	28	2	3	127.2	128	63	55	11	4	41	0	78	2
An. Moreno, MC Tigers°	14	7	.667	3.94	30	28	11	2	1	1	201.0	212	99	88	9	9	93	5	126	11
Ibarra, Tabasco	10	7	.588	3.99	22	21	5	1	3	0	119.2	117	53	53	14	4	57	3	47	1

Departmental Leaders: G—Barojas, 53; W—Mendez, Renteria, J. Rios, 16; L—Sombra, 16; Pct.—L. Leal, .882; GS—Purata, 29; CG—Fuson, 19; GF—Go. Rojo, 49; ShO—Colorado, 5; Sv.—Barojas, 15; IP—An. Moreno, 201.0; H—M. Raygoza, 237; R—R. Valdez, 126; ER—R. Valdez, 109; HR—Delgadillo, 27; HB—Sauceda, 12; BB—Carranza, 108; IBB—A. Soto, 14; SO—J. Rios, 200; WP—Angulo, Carranza, I. Jimenez, 17.

(All Pitchers—Listed Alphabetically)

Pitcher—Club	W.	L.	Pct.	ERA.	G.	GS.	CG.	GF.	ShO.	Sv.	IP.	H.	R.	ER.	HR.	HB.	BB.	Int. BB.	SO.	WP.
Aguilar, Saltillo	7	9	.438	5.74	28	26	2	2	0	0	138.0	184	96	88	17	6	60	5	57	8
Aguilera, Yucatan	0	1	.000	3.38	2	0	0	2	0	0	5.1	6	4	2	0	1	2	0	2	0
M. Alvarez, Saltillo	1	5	.167	6.73	32	3	0	22	0	0	104.1	121	82	78	13	4	74	10	65	9
R. Alvarez, Tabasco	0	0	.000	9.00	1	0	0	1	0	0	3.0	3	3	3	0	0	2	0	0	0
Angulo, Yucatan°	9	11	.450	4.49	24	23	10	1	0	0	148.1	173	97	74	10	1	66	1	79	17
Antunez, Monterrey°	10	6	.625	3.46	34	8	3	26	1	3	88.1	95	37	34	8	1	35	2	63	4
Armas, San Luis	5	8	.358	6.06	31	8	0	23	0	0	78.2	99	63	53	4	8	49	8	23	6
Armenta, Mexico City Reds	4	0	1.000	5.51	25	0	0	25	0	1	47.1	56	31	29	6	5	32	0	20	5
Arroyo, Yucatan°	13	11	.542	3.05	25	25	17	0	4	0	189.0	190	81	64	11	4	35	3	76	5
Barojas, Mexico City Reds	13	4	.764	3.10	53	6	2	47	0	15	124.2	119	47	43	5	3	70	6	62	2
Barraza, Campeche	0	2	.000	9.60	6	3	0	3	0	0	15.0	19	19	16	3	0	16	1	11	5
Belman, Yucatan	5	7	.417	5.63	20	13	1	7	0	1	76.2	96	57	48	5	5	43	1	20	8
Beltran, Leon	11	8	.579	5.87	26	26	6	0	1	0	153.1	206	107	100	14	6	43	7	64	4
Boyles, Nuevo Laredo	8	12	.400	4.58	29	25	5	4	3	2	149.1	152	87	76	16	1	87	4	98	6
Brusstar, Aguascalientes	2	1	.667	5.22	20	0	0	20	0	5	29.1	42	20	17	5	0	17	3	15	2
Buitimea, Mexico City Tigers	3	1	.750	4.98	31	3	0	28	0	2	77.2	92	51	43	9	5	35	7	32	3
Byron, San Luis	3	2	.600	6.16	6	6	1	0	0	0	38.0	36	27	26	3	1	20	0	19	1
Camara, Campeche	0	0	.000	18.00	1	0	0	1	0	0	1.0	3	2	2	0	0	1	0	0	2
Camarena, Puebla	3	1	.750	5.75	23	0	0	23	0	1	61.0	85	46	39	10	4	30	4	36	6
Cano, Monclova°	5	8	.385	6.24	28	16	2	12	1	0	115.1	140	88	80	11	11	69	6	52	4
Cardenas, San Luis	0	0	.000	4.77	20	1	0	19	0	0	45.1	50	28	24	2	1	25	3	16	4
Carranza, Nuevo Laredo°	9	8	.529	4.96	30	24	6	6	0	2	150.2	161	99	83	19	8	108	1	93	17
Cartagena, Saltillo	0	1	.000	5.88	15	0	0	15	0	0	26.0	30	19	17	4	1	9	1	14	0
A. Castaneda, Puebla	5	4	.556	6.08	31	10	2	21	0	1	111.0	146	83	75	9	3	54	1	48	10
Mar. Castaneda, 1 Ags-10 Sal°	0	0	.000	7.94	11	1	0	10	0	0	17.0	17	15	15	4	0	18	3	10	0
Max. Castaneda, Union Lag	0	0	.000	13.50	3	0	0	3	0	0	2.0	3	3	3	0	1	0	0	1	0
P. Castaneda, Mexico City Reds	1	2	.333	4.93	13	4	2	9	0	0	45.2	50	25	25	9	1	19	1	14	2
Castillejos, Tabasco	3	4	.429	6.91	20	4	0	16	0	2	41.2	71	33	32	4	1	11	5	10	1
Castillo, Aguascalientes	0	0	.000	0.00	2	0	0	2	0	0	2.2	4	0	0	0	0	4	0	0	0
Chavez, Leon	6	8	.429	5.65	41	12	4	29	1	2	106.2	127	72	67	11	3	48	8	40	5
Colorado, Tabasco	15	9	.625	3.13	27	27	17	0	5	0	186.2	200	73	65	9	4	31	4	85	3
Cordova, Puebla	0	0	.000	20.25	1	0	0	4	0	0	4.0	13	9	9	1	1	2	0	0	0
J. Cruz, 5 Tig-29 Tab°	7	10	.412	4.18	34	23	5	11	2	0	131.1	138	80	61	4	4	61	6	79	5
T. Cruz, Leon	0	0	.000	0.00	1	0	0	1	0	0	1.0	0	0	0	0	0	0	0	0	0
Delgadillo, Aguascalientes	13	7	.650	5.56	30	20	3	10	0	0	149.0	206	111	92	27	1	47	2	49	3
C. Diaz, Yucatan	3	6	.333	5.77	19	4	1	15	0	3	39.0	57	31	25	3	2	19	3	19	4
O. Diaz, Union Laguna	1	2	.333	6.45	23	0	0	23	0	0	22.1	23	17	16	2	1	23	2	14	1
Dimas, San Luis	9	3	.750	2.88	34	0	1	34	0	3	115.2	102	39	37	12	1	32	5	68	5
Divison, 25 Tab-2 Leo	4	5	.444	5.40	27	0	0	27	0	5	33.1	45	20	20	3	0	16	4	12	1
Dominguez, Campeche°	10	8	.556	4.61	26	25	8	1	0	0	158.0	168	89	81	17	1	65	3	106	5
Duarte, Leon	11	4	.733	5.50	22	17	2	5	0	0	93.1	118	67	57	14	4	35	2	29	6
Duckett, Leon	0	2	.000	7.94	3	0	0	3	0	0	5.2	5	5	5	0	0	9	2	4	0
Duran, Campeche	0	0	.000	36.00	3	0	0	3	0	0	1.0	2	4	4	0	0	6	0	0	0
Ek, San Luis	0	0	.000	0.00	1	0	0	1	0	0	0.2	1	0	0	0	0	2	0	0	0
Elias Lomeli, MC Reds°	5	8	.385	6.44	25	17	2	8	0	0	102.0	141	77	73	10	6	57	1	46	6
Elvira, Leon°	6	8	.429	5.27	33	19	4	14	0	4	109.1	104	75	64	13	3	62	4	80	8
Erickson, Tabasco	2	2	.500	3.46	5	1	0	4	0	0	13.0	14	6	5	1	0	3	0	8	0
Escarrega, 4 Yuc-13 Lag	4	5	.444	6.12	17	17	1	0	1	0	78.0	110	62	53	5	3	23	0	20	4
Espinosa, Saltillo	0	1	.000	10.32	3	3	0	0	0	0	11.1	18	14	13	2	0	11	0	9	1
Esquer, Monterrey°	8	10	.444	5.37	23	22	4	1	1	0	125.2	157	97	75	11	3	45	1	111	4
Felix, Mexico City Reds	1	1	.500	6.79	22	2	1	20	0	0	54.1	60	41	41	6	1	46	0	36	10
Figueroa, Nuevo Laredo	0	1	.000	11.68	5	1	0	4	0	1	12.1	20	17	16	1	2	5	0	5	4
Findlay, San Luis°	6	10	.375	5.45	20	20	4	0	2	0	104.0	123	82	63	9	1	66	3	45	4
Flores, Campeche	3	5	.375	3.86	21	5	1	16	1	0	63.0	73	32	27	2	3	30	3	35	7
Fowlkes, MC Reds	10	4	.714	3.88	16	14	8	2	2	0	102.0	103	48	44	9	4	15	1	39	2
Franco, 8 Lag-7 Yu-15 Pue	2	4	.333	6.42	30	7	1	23	0	1	81.1	106	61	58	7	5	31	1	19	3
Fuson, Nuevo Laredo	14	8	.636	2.67	22	21	19	1	1	0	172.0	170	64	51	10	2	38	3	127	7
Je. Garcia, Saltillo	0	0	.000	0.00	1	0	0	1	0	0	1.0	1	0	0	0	0	0	0	0	0
Jorge L. Garcia, Saltillo	4	10	.286	5.94	47	4	1	43	1	7	106.0	133	79	70	12	2	50	11	66	7
Jose L. Garcia, Tabasco°	1	0	1.000	4.95	41	1	0	40	0	4	43.2	55	32	24	4	4	19	5	19	2
Ju. Garcia, MC Tigers	0	2	.000	10.54	5	3	0	2	0	0	13.2	25	19	16	2	2	9	0	7	1
M. Garcia, Monterrey	0	0	.000	9.00	1	0	0	1	0	0	1.0	1	1	1	1	0	1	0	0	0
R. Garcia, Monclova	3	1	.750	6.14	28	0	0	28	0	1	55.2	71	46	38	9	0	22	6	17	3
Gaxiola, Yucatan	0	1	.000	7.27	7	1	0	6	0	0	8.2	13	11	7	1	1	5	0	2	1
Gonzalez, Monterrey	12	6	.667	3.77	24	24	9	0	4	0	169.2	173	77	71	13	3	58	4	118	5
Granillo, Aguascalientes°	12	3	.800	4.89	29	20	7	9	1	1	141.2	170	83	77	11	3	45	2	101	9
F. Gutierrez, MC Reds	0	0	.000	0.00	1	0	0	1	0	0	0.1	1	0	0	0	0	0	0	0	0
P. Gutierrez, Monterrey°	1	5	.167	6.79	18	11	1	7	0	0	61.0	93	58	46	7	2	29	3	38	5
B. Guzman, San Luis	1	0	1.000	2.25	2	0	0	2	0	0	4.0	3	1	1	0	0	6	0	2	0
G. Guzman, 12 Yuc-15 Pue°	4	0	1.000	4.83	27	0	0	27	0	0	41.0	52	27	22	3	0	20	3	10	1
R. Guzman, Monclova	2	3	.400	5.68	30	1	0	29	0	4	57.0	69	38	36	6	2	33	7	40	5
A. Hernandez, Campeche	1	0	1.000	1.29	5	0	0	5	0	3	7.0	4	1	1	0	0	1	0	1	0
E. Hernandez, Union Laguna	0	1	.000	2.75	6	3	0	3	0	0	19.2	17	9	6	0	0	9	0	12	0
Jo. L. Hernandez, Puebla	0	0	.000	0.00	1	0	0	1	0	0	0.2	1	0	0	0	0	0	0	0	0
Ju. Hernandez, Monclova	0	0	.000	3.86	1	0	0	1	0	0	4.2	5	2	2	0	0	4	0	2	0
Herrera, MC Tigers	0	0	.000	0.00	1	0	0	1	0	0	1.0	0	0	0	0	0	2	0	0	0
Howe, Tabasco	1	0	1.000	0.00	10	0	0	10	0	4	12.1	7	0	0	0	1	7	0	5	1
Huerta, Campeche	4	4	.500	3.74	30	1	0	4	0	0	65.0	72	32	27	5	2	24	1	39	5
Ibarra, Tabasco	10	7	.588	3.99	22	21	5	1	3	0	119.2	117	53	53	14	4	57	3	47	1
Jaime Granillo, Leon	8	4	.667	4.97	49	3	0	46	0	8	96.0	119	59	53	8	4	56	11	59	3
James, San Luis	3	6	.333	2.90	40	1	0	39	0	10	83.2	55	34	27	8	3	64	5	51	5
E. Jimenez, Leon	0	0	.000	0.00	1	0	0	1	0	0	1.0	1	0	0	0	0	0	0	0	0
G. Jimenez, Puebla°	12	9	.571	3.31	23	23	13	0	3	0	168.1	178	72	62	6	1	42	3	108	3
I. Jimenez, 10 Pu-10 Yuc°	5	10	.333	7.04	20	20	2	0	1	0	85.2	95	80	67	4	4	91	0	47	17
Kaine, Monclova	4	2	.667	3.95	23	0	0	23	0	11	43.1	38	23	19	2	0	21	5	19	1
Katschke, San Luis	5	13	.278	5.46	25	24	5	1	0	0	127.0	163	97	77	16	2	73	3	61	8
Kepshire, Mex City Reds	3	0	1.000	2.70	4	3	0	1	0	0	23.1	22	7	7	1	0	10	0	16	1
Kutsukos, Union Laguna	1	2	.333	9.00	11	0	0	11	0	2	15.0	24	18	15	0	3	12	4	7	1
Lara, Nuevo Laredo	1	3	.250	2.35	5	1	0	0	0	0	15.1	18	10	4	2	1	6	0	6	0
B. Leal, 5 Lag-3 Tab- 2 Cam	1	1	.500	9.25	10	4	0	6	0	0	24.1	38	33	25	5	1	21	1	14	3
L. Leal, Puebla	15	2	.882	2.97	19	19	7	0	0	0	136.1	151	48	45	5	0	41	3	77	4

Pitcher—Club	W.	L.	Pct.	ERA.	G.	GS.	CG.	GF.	ShO.	Sv.	IP.	H.	R.	ER.	HR.	HB.	BB.	Int. BB.	SO.	WP.
Ledon, 17 Lar-6 Lag	2	0	1.000	5.58	23	2	0	21	0	3	50.0	61	35	31	10	5	25	1	19	6
Leggatt, Saltillo	1	1	.500	6.00	4	0	0	4	0	0	9.0	8	6	6	1	2	4	1	4	3
Leon, Nuevo Laredo	6	3	.667	4.43	14	14	1	0	0	0	69.0	78	44	34	4	5	27	2	33	2
C. Lizarraga, Campeche	0	0	.000	6.23	2	0	0	2	0	0	4.1	6	3	3	0	0	3	0	1	0
H. Lizarraga, San Luis	0	0	.000	9.00	4	0	0	4	0	0	4.0	7	9	4	0	0	5	1	1	0
Lopez, Aguascalientes	5	3	.625	5.66	36	5	1	31	0	3	76.0	94	55	47	6	1	42	4	27	0
Luna, Monclova	1	0	1.000	10.38	20	0	0	20	0	0	39.0	78	49	45	6	1	21	1	15	1
Lunar, Campeche	4	1	.800	2.23	27	1	1	26	1	12	36.1	33	14	9	0	4	19	0	28	4
Mariscal, 2 Cam-5 Sal	0	1	.000	9.31	7	1	0	6	0	0	9.2	15	11	10	2	1	4	0	5	0
Marquez, San Luis	0	0	.000	4.15	1	1	0	0	0	0	4.1	5	3	2	1	0	5	0	3	1
Martin, 6 MCR-1 Sal	3	3	.500	6.81	7	7	1	0	0	0	37.0	46	30	28	5	2	18	1	11	0
A. Martinez, N. Laredo	3	5	.375	5.86	36	1	0	35	0	2	58.1	69	48	38	9	2	35	4	27	6
G. Martinez, Aguascalientes	3	4	.429	6.80	23	3	0	20	0	1	49.0	60	48	37	3	6	31	3	18	1
V. Martinez, Tabasco	0	0	.000	9.26	8	0	0	8	0	0	11.2	22	12	12	4	0	5	1	3	1
Matus, 5 Tab-10 Lag	0	5	.000	6.18	15	8	0	7	0	0	39.1	46	34	27	3	3	25	2	20	3
Mendez, Mex. City Reds	16	6	.727	4.02	27	26	11	1	2	0	174.2	166	83	78	17	5	51	2	106	2
Menendez, 14 Tig-9 Mva	2	7	.222	7.33	23	10	2	13	1	1	70.0	100	68	57	17	3	28	0	14	4
E. Miranda, Union Laguna	2	2	.500	6.71	26	0	0	26	0	1	57.2	61	48	43	6	0	46	1	50	3
J. Miranda, Saltillo	4	11	.267	5.20	31	18	6	13	0	0	135.0	151	94	78	14	4	77	7	70	9
Moncada, Tabasco	0	3	.000	6.50	20	3	1	17	0	0	45.2	57	38	33	2	1	29	1	33	2
F. Montano, Aguascalientes	6	12	.333	6.11	26	23	3	3	0	0	119.1	158	98	81	12	6	56	1	66	4
N. Montano, Yucatan	2	2	.500	4.59	26	3	0	23	0	1	68.2	84	47	35	11	2	24	0	31	3
G. Moore, Saltillo	1	3	.250	5.65	18	0	0	18	0	4	28.2	29	20	18	1	1	20	6	22	3
R. Moore, MC Tigers*	0	1	.000	6.94	3	3	0	0	0	0	11.2	18	11	9	1	0	9	1	4	1
Morales, San Luis*	11	9	.550	6.38	30	27	5	3	0	0	139.2	180	116	99	20	4	76	3	47	2
Ab. Moreno, Leon	0	0	.000	4.76	9	0	0	9	0	0	5.2	7	4	3	0	0	7	2	0	5
An. Moreno, MC Tigers*	14	7	.667	3.94	30	28	11	2	1	1	201.0	212	99	88	9	9	93	5	126	11
J. Moreno, Nuevo Laredo	10	6	.625	4.15	24	24	8	0	0	0	160.2	174	80	74	15	5	52	4	80	4
Moya, Tabasco	6	9	.400	4.55	27	23	4	4	1	0	148.1	158	92	75	15	2	62	4	56	3
Mundo, 8 Mva-20 Sal	7	11	.389	6.05	28	24	6	4	0	0	150.1	184	119	101	20	7	61	8	48	8
M. Munoz, 17 Sal-3 Ags	8	8	.500	5.19	20	20	5	0	0	0	109.1	133	75	63	10	3	50	5	54	7
N. Munoz, Saltillo	2	2	.500	9.19	11	0	0	11	0	2	15.2	22	16	16	1	0	12	2	13	0
Murillo, Monterrey	0	0	.000	9.00	1	0	0	1	0	0	1.0	1	1	1	1	0	0	0	0	0
Navarro, Monterrey	12	11	.522	5.22	24	24	7	0	1	0	131.0	130	84	76	12	3	77	2	87	6
Norris, Monclova	6	2	.750	3.96	12	12	3	0	0	0	61.1	67	30	27	4	4	25	0	55	1
Ochoa, Nuevo Laredo	5	6	.455	4.61	36	2	0	34	0	5	84.0	88	48	43	12	5	35	7	44	2
Ontiveros, San Luis	6	5	.545	5.77	48	0	0	48	0	6	96.2	118	70	62	17	1	47	10	44	6
Ordaz, Mex. City Tigers	0	0	.000	16.88	5	1	0	4	0	0	5.1	18	10	10	1	0	1	0	2	0
J. Orozco, Puebla	11	9	.550	4.19	25	21	12	4	0	1	154.2	186	81	72	11	2	20	1	97	3
O. Orozco, 2 Pue-1 Yuc	1	1	.500	8.22	3	3	0	0	0	0	15.1	20	14	14	3	0	7	0	5	0
Ortiz, Puebla*	0	0	.000	14.54	3	0	0	3	0	0	4.1	13	8	7	0	0	3	0	4	1
Osuna, 24 Leo-19 Mon	3	6	.333	4.00	43	0	0	43	0	2	92.1	79	50	41	4	4	62	6	73	5
Pacheco, Yucatan	1	0	1.000	0.69	8	0	0	8	0	0	13.0	11	1	1	0	0	6	0	7	0
Padilla, 19 Sal-10 Ags	3	2	.600	6.84	29	0	0	29	0	1	50.0	63	42	38	10	3	30	3	20	3
Palafox, 6 Tig-25 Lag	11	7	.611	4.20	31	22	6	9	0	2	148.0	178	80	69	12	7	46	3	57	5
Pena, Monterrey*	2	0	1.000	5.65	20	1	0	19	0	0	51.0	69	35	32	7	1	25	1	24	2
C. Perez, 10 Sal-15 Cam*	5	8	.385	5.40	25	12	3	13	0	1	80.0	94	52	48	11	5	37	1	35	6
L. Perez, Leon	3	4	.429	5.37	34	5	0	29	0	4	63.2	76	41	38	6	2	41	6	40	5
Pollorena, 2 Sal-4 Lar	0	0	.000	12.46	6	0	0	6	0	0	4.1	5	6	6	1	0	3	0	1	0
Pruneda, Monclova	14	11	.560	4.77	28	26	11	2	3	0	171.2	187	105	91	19	1	99	10	136	16
Pulido, Monterrey	2	3	.400	1.93	37	0	0	37	0	21	51.1	42	13	11	7	1	11	1	38	3
Purata, San Luis*	10	8	.556	4.16	29	29	6	0	1	0	147.0	160	91	68	19	1	87	4	106	10
Quijano, 5 Pue-11 Yuc	1	3	.250	7.02	16	2	0	14	0	1	42.1	63	37	33	7	1	25	1	12	6
Quiroz, Mex. City Tigers*	1	0	1.000	3.24	8	0	0	8	0	1	8.1	3	3	3	0	0	3	0	6	1
Ramirez, Monclova	0	0	.000	9.95	9	0	0	9	0	0	19.0	27	24	21	6	1	14	1	4	2
C. Raygoza, Aguascalientes	0	0	.000	7.71	2	0	0	2	0	0	2.1	3	2	2	0	0	4	0	1	0
M. Raygoza, Campeche	12	13	.480	4.57	29	28	14	1	1	0	195.0	237	110	99	22	5	68	5	82	8
Renteria, Union Laguna	16	7	.696	4.93	28	28	8	0	0	0	193.1	232	120	106	24	4	58	8	92	7
Retes, 17 Tig-18 Yuc*	4	7	.364	6.03	35	15	2	20	0	1	91.0	122	72	61	19	3	48	0	46	3
J. Rios, MC Tigers	16	9	.640	3.55	28	26	16	2	2	1	190.1	188	86	75	23	4	47	9	200	6
S. Rios, Union Laguna	0	2	.000	7.80	24	8	0	16	0	1	47.1	68	44	41	4	5	38	2	21	5
L. Rivas, Monclova	0	0	.000	13.50	4	0	0	4	0	0	7.1	18	14	11	0	0	3	0	2	0
M. Rivas, MC Tigers	5	6	.455	4.64	31	1	0	30	0	6	52.1	66	32	27	3	1	25	6	22	1
Rivera, Union Laguna*	0	0	.000	0.00	1	0	0	1	0	0	1.0	1	0	0	0	0	0	0	0	0
E. Rodriguez, Tabasco	0	1	.000	4.88	13	3	0	10	0	0	27.2	30	18	15	3	1	10	2	6	2
I. Rodriguez, Monclova	0	0	.000	7.32	20	4	0	16	0	0	39.1	53	38	32	3	2	36	1	27	8
M.A. Rodriguez, Aguascalientes	4	4	.500	4.95	37	9	0	28	0	2	103.2	135	68	57	12	11	50	3	38	5
P. Rodriguez, Yucatan	0	1	.000	4.24	13	0	0	13	0	1	17.0	22	12	8	3	1	7	0	7	2
R. Rodriguez, Monterrey	0	1	.000	14.85	6	1	0	5	0	0	6.2	16	11	11	2	0	4	0	3	1
Go. Rojo, 31 Ags-18 Sal	5	6	.455	4.46	49	0	0	49	0	8	72.2	79	38	36	8	4	41	6	41	3
Gu. Rojo, Saltillo	0	3	.000	10.80	14	3	0	11	0	0	30.0	39	38	36	10	1	35	4	20	1
E. Romero, Monclova	0	0	.000	4.50	2	0	0	2	0	0	8.0	11	7	4	0	0	3	1	2	0
R. Romero, Aguascalientes	0	1	.000	6.48	6	3	0	3	0	0	16.2	25	15	12	2	1	9	0	12	3
Romo, Nuevo Laredo*	2	4	.333	5.88	34	5	0	29	0	0	56.2	81	44	37	6	0	30	4	26	4
C. Ruiz, 10 Yuc-5 Tig*	5	5	.500	3.64	15	14	6	1	0	1	89.0	92	47	36	6	5	21	2	31	2
P. Ruiz, Monclova*	7	7	.500	5.16	20	20	3	0	1	0	90.2	99	58	52	14	2	80	0	56	7
Salas, 2 Lag-28 Tab	5	7	.417	6.08	30	6	1	24	0	1	71.0	85	53	48	5	3	27	3	25	2
Saldana, Union Laguna	0	0	.000	11.50	12	4	0	8	0	0	18.0	20	23	23	2	2	22	2	11	3
F. Sanchez, 2 Sal-10 MC Reds	1	0	1.000	5.54	12	0	0	12	0	0	26.0	43	19	16	1	1	12	1	9	1
M. Sanchez, Leon	1	0	1.000	4.50	9	0	0	9	0	0	16.0	16	10	8	0	1	7	1	11	0
Sandate, Monclova*	1	1	.500	2.37	4	2	1	2	0	0	19.0	16	5	5	2	0	4	0	7	0
Sandoval, Leon	0	0	.000	6.75	9	1	0	8	0	0	16.0	28	14	12	1	0	5	0	7	3
Sauceda, Yucatan	5	2	.714	5.66	31	0	0	31	0	3	47.2	68	30	30	6	12	13	3	26	4
Schuler, Mexico City Reds	0	2	.000	3.68	8	0	0	8	0	1	14.2	14	7	6	1	0	6	0	12	0
Serafin, Union Laguna	5	7	.417	4.56	38	12	1	26	0	4	116.1	144	76	59	15	0	57	5	70	6
Shanks, Saltillo	1	1	.500	5.91	2	1	0	1	0	0	10.2	14	7	7	1	0	4	0	3	1
Shimp, Saltillo	0	4	.000	8.89	6	6	0	0	0	0	26.1	47	29	26	2	1	15	3	19	1
Silva, 20 Cam-16 Tab	1	2	.333	4.57	36	0	0	36	0	2	69.0	87	37	35	6	3	21	2	28	5
M. Solis, 17 Ags-12 Tab	6	9	.400	4.14	29	18	4	11	1	1	111.0	117	61	51	10	5	34	9	37	1
R. Solis, Mexico City Reds*	12	8	.600	4.72	28	26	8	4	2	0	171.2	212	102	90	20	4	67	1	79	5
Sombra, Union Laguna*	3	16	.158	6.30	33	24	4	9	1	0	130.0	172	107	91	14	1	66	8	83	8
C. Sosa, 2 Lag-22 MC Reds	6	12	.333	5.88	24	21	4	3	0	0	111.2	145	82	73	14	5	55	2	38	10

Pitcher—Club	W.	L.	Pct.	ERA.	G.	GS.	CG.	GF.	ShO.	Sv.	IP.	H.	R.	ER.	HR.	HB.	BB.	Int. BB.	SO.	WP.
E. Sosa, Yucatan	1	2	.333	4.50	8	8	2	0	0	0	50.0	49	27	25	5	2	20	0	22	6
V. Sosa, Union Laguna	3	4	.429	4.81	28	1	0	27	0	0	76.2	91	47	41	7	5	38	5	26	2
A. Soto, Puebla	4	6	.400	5.53	37	1	0	36	0	11	57.0	79	36	35	7	2	29	14	30	4
F. Soto, Leon	5	4	.556	6.91	24	9	1	15	0	0	70.1	91	54	54	7	3	33	5	36	4
J.L. Soto, Nuevo Laredo	0	1	.000	11.74	8	0	0	8	0	0	7.2	15	11	10	1	1	7	0	5	0
Tafoya, Aguascalientes	0	2	.000	12.38	5	2	0	3	0	0	8.0	13	12	11	2	0	6	0	4	0
Telechea, Monterrey	0	0	.000	3.00	2	0	0	2	0	0	3.0	2	1	1	0	0	0	0	1	0
Tellman, Monterrey	15	4	.789	2.75	24	24	11	0	3	0	170.0	164	59	52	10	6	20	1	88	2
Tinoco, Nuevo Laredo	0	0	.000	4.22	6	0	0	6	0	0	10.2	8	7	5	1	0	3	0	8	1
Toledo, Campeche*	0	0	.000	9.92	13	0	0	13	0	0	16.1	27	20	18	1	1	10	0	6	1
M. Torres, Puebla*	10	10	.500	4.93	27	27	9	0	2	0	157.0	201	92	86	11	3	56	3	81	9
N. Torres, Monclova	0	1	.000	7.25	5	5	0	0	0	0	22.1	31	19	18	0	3	18	0	6	2
Tremblay, Union Laguna*	0	2	.000	9.42	4	4	0	0	0	0	14.1	19	15	15	2	2	14	1	6	2
Uribe, 10 Mon-15 Leo	3	4	.429	6.52	25	12	0	13	0	2	67.2	90	59	49	9	5	40	1	29	2
Urrea, 10 Yuc-10 Pue	4	7	.364	5.05	20	12	3	8	1	2	87.1	113	52	49	10	1	21	2	25	0
A. Valdez, Mexico City Tigers	7	9	.438	5.75	41	2	0	39	0	5	81.1	104	56	52	11	2	51	9	42	8
L.A. Valdez, Monterrey	1	0	1.000	8.53	7	0	0	7	0	0	6.1	6	6	6	1	0	8	2	4	0
R. Valdez, Campeche	9	12	.429	6.21	26	26	7	0	0	0	158.0	180	126	109	23	7	68	5	75	13
Valencia, Mexico City Tigers*	7	4	.636	4.70	25	17	4	8	3	0	107.1	111	69	56	14	3	57	1	53	4
A. Valenzuela, 5 Sal-7 Ags*	3	1	.750	4.29	12	9	0	3	0	0	48.1	56	24	23	3	3	24	1	19	3
G. Valenzuela, Leon	0	1	.000	6.48	5	2	0	3	0	0	16.2	16	15	12	3	0	10	3	7	0
J. V'lnza, 1 Sal-1 Lag-15 Mva	5	7	.417	7.22	17	17	3	0	0	0	81.0	116	72	65	20	0	28	2	23	1
R.L. Valenzuela, Monterrey	1	0	1.000	5.65	18	0	0	18	0	1	28.2	44	22	18	1	0	7	0	13	2
Valverde, Union Laguna	0	0	.000	0.00	1	0	0	1	0	0	1.0	2	1	0	0	0	0	0	0	0
Vazquez, Monclova	10	8	.556	5.38	32	11	2	21	1	6	103.2	114	75	62	14	5	63	3	52	5
I. Velazquez, Campeche	12	8	.600	4.69	27	26	7	1	1	0	170.2	188	96	89	18	4	56	0	80	7
L.A. Velazquez, Leon	9	8	.529	4.55	26	24	4	2	0	0	142.1	146	81	72	9	2	85	11	94	8
Veliz, Monterrey*	1	6	.143	5.40	17	8	2	9	0	0	70.0	77	46	42	11	2	48	0	50	5
Vidana, 2 Tab-20 Tig	2	1	.667	5.60	22	3	0	19	0	1	54.2	82	40	34	3	2	12	2	12	1
Vila, Union Laguna	11	6	.647	4.50	48	0	0	48	0	10	68.0	79	38	34	8	1	51	5	44	6
Villanueva, Aguascalientes*	7	7	.500	3.88	41	13	5	28	2	3	127.2	128	63	55	11	4	41	0	78	2
M. Villegas, 19 Ags-3 Sal	7	7	.500	7.16	22	15	3	7	0	0	104.1	144	90	83	12	3	44	5	75	4
R. Villegas, 12 SL-13 Yuc	3	11	.214	4.87	25	20	5	5	1	1	125.2	146	79	68	24	2	45	3	56	5
Vizcarra, Nuevo Laredo	1	2	.333	9.36	18	0	0	18	0	1	25.0	36	29	26	4	0	20	2	11	5
Yucupicio, Leon	1	2	.333	5.56	40	0	0	40	0	4	43.2	53	29	27	6	3	27	7	30	4
Zamudio, Mexico City Tigers	8	9	.471	4.16	32	19	4	13	0	3	129.2	147	75	60	9	2	52	3	60	11

BALKS—Armas, Beltran, Buitimea, Cano, Mar. Castaneda, Figueroa, Flores, Jorge L. Garcia, Jose L. Garcia, Morales, J. Moreno, F. Montano, J. Orozco, Palafox, Renteria, J. Rios, C. Sosa, E. Sosa, V. Sosa, F. Soto, Vazquez, I. Velazquez, Yucupicio, 1 each.

COMBINATION SHUTOUTS—Dominguez-Lunar, Huerta-Lunar, Campeche; Duarte-Yucupicio-Uribe, Leon; Elias Lomeli-Barojas, Kepshire-Barojas, Mendez-Barojas, C. Sosa-Barojas, Mexico City Reds; An. Moreno-Buitimea, Retes-A. Valdez, Mexico City Tigers; Norris-R. Guzman, Vazquez-Kaine, Monclova; Antunez-Pulido, Esquer-Pulido, Gonzalez-Antunez, Navarro-Pulido, Monterrey; Lara-Ochoa, Nuevo Laredo; Aguilar-G. Moore, A. Valenzuela-Shanks, Saltillo; Ibarra-Howe 2, Ibarra-Divison, M. Solis-Erickson, M. Solis-Howe, Tabasco; Escarrega-F. Miranda, Palafox-E. Hernandez, S. Rios-Palafox-Vila, Serafin-V. Sosa, Union Laguna; I. Jimenez-R. Villegas, E. Sosa-Sauceda, Yucatan.

NO-HIT GAMES—Pruneda, Monclova, defeated Mexico City Tigers, 1-0 (seven innings), May 17; I. Jimenez, Yucatan, defeated San Luis, 6-0, May 24.

Pacific Coast League

CLASS AAA

Leading Batter
JIM EPPARD
Edmonton

League President
BILL CUTLER

Leading Pitcher
VICENTE PALACIOS
Vancouver

CHAMPIONSHIP WINNERS IN PREVIOUS YEARS

Year	Team	Pct.
1903	Los Angeles	.630
1904	Tacoma	.589
	Tacoma§	.571
	Los Angeles§	.571
1905	Tacoma	.583
	Los Angeles°	.604
1906	Portland	.657
1907	Los Angeles	.608
1908	Los Angeles	.585
1909	San Francisco	.623
1910	Portland	.567
1911	Portland	.589
1912	Oakland	.591
1913	Portland	.559
1914	Portland	.574
1915	San Francisco	.570
1916	Los Angeles	.601
1917	San Francisco	.561
1918	Vernon	.569
	Los Angeles (2nd) x	.548
1919	Vernon	.613
1920	Vernon	.556
1921	Los Angeles	.574
1922	San Francisco	.638
1923	San Francisco	.617
1924	Seattle	.545
1925	San Francisco	.643
1926	Los Angeles	.599
1927	Oakland	.615
1928	San Francisco°	.630
	Sacramento§§	.626
	San Francisco§§	.626
1929	Mission	.643
	Hollywood°	.592
1930	Los Angeles	.576
	Hollywood°	.650
1931	Hollywood	.626
	San Francisco°	.608
1932	Portland	.587
1933	Los Angeles	.610
1934	Los Angeles z	.786
	Los Angeles z	.689

Year	Team	Pct.
1935	Los Angeles	.648
	San Francisco°	.608
1936	Portland‡	.549
1937	Sacramento	.573
	San Diego (3rd)†	.545
1938	Los Angeles	.590
	Sacramento (3rd)†	.537
1939	Seattle	.589
	Sacramento (4th)†	.500
1940	Seattle‡	.629
1941	Seattle‡	.598
1942	Sacramento	.590
	Seattle (3rd)†	.539
1943	Los Angeles	.710
	S. Francisco (2nd)†	.574
1944	Los Angeles	.586
	S. Francisco (3rd)†	.509
1945	Portland	.622
	S. Francisco (4th)†	.525
1946	San Francisco‡	.628
1947	Los Angeles††	.567
1948	Oakland‡	.606
1949	Hollywood‡	.583
1950	Oakland	.590
1951	Seattle‡	.593
1952	Hollywood	.606
1953	Hollywood	.589
1954	San Diego y	.604
1955	Seattle	.552
1956	Los Angeles	.637
1957	San Francisco	.601
1958	Phoenix	.578
1959	Salt Lake City	.552
1960	Spokane	.601
1961	Tacoma	.630
1962	San Diego	.604
1963	Spokane	.620
	Oklahoma City a	.632
1964	Arkansas	.609
	San Diego a	.576
1965	Oklahoma City a	.628
	Portland	.547

Year	Team	Pct.
1966	Seattle a	.561
	Tulsa	.578
1967	San Diego a	.574
	Spokane	.541
1968	Tulsa a	.642
	Spokane	.586
1969	Tacoma a	.589
	Eugene	.603
1970	Spokane a	.644
	Hawaii	.671
1971	Salt Lake City	.534
	Tacoma	.545
1972	Albuquerque	.622
	Eugene	.534
1973	Tucson	.583
	Spokane a	.563
1974	Spokane a	.549
	Albuqerque	.535
1975	Salt Lake City	.556
	Hawaii a	.611
1976	Salt Lake City	.625
	Hawaii a	.531
1977	Phoenix a	.579
	Hawaii	.541
1978	Tacoma b	.584
	Albuquerque b	.557
1979	Albuquerque	.581
	Salt Lake City c	.541
1980	Albuquerque°	.578
	Hawaii	.539
1981	Albuquerque°	.712
	Tacoma	.561
1982	Albuquerque°	.594
	Spokane	.545
1983	Albuquerque	.594
	Portland°	.528
1984	Hawaii	.621
	Edmonton°	.486
1985	Vancouver°	.552
	Phoenix	.563
1986	Vancouver	.616
	Las Vegas°	.563

°Won split-season playoff. †Won four-team playoff. ‡Won pennant and four-team playoff. §Tied for second-half title with Tacoma winning playoff. §§Tied for second-half title, with Sacramento winning playoff. ††Ended regular season in tie with San Francisco and won one-game playoff for pennant, then won four-club playoff. xWon playoff from first-place Vernon and awarded championship. yDefeated Hollywood in one-game playoff for pennant. zWon both halves, no playoff. aLeague was divided into Northern, Southern divisions in 1963, 1969-70-71, and Eastern, Western divisions in 1964 through 1968 and 1972 through 1977, won two-team playoff. bLeague divided into Eastern and Western divisions, Tacoma and Albuquerque declared co-champions following cancellation of four-team playoff due to continuing rain and wet grounds. cWon second-half title and defeated Hawaii in four-team playoff.

STANDING OF CLUBS AT CLOSE OF FIRST HALF, JUNE 20

NORTHERN DIVISION

Club	W.	L.	T.	Pct.	G.B.
Tacoma (A's)	39	32	0	.549	....
Calgary (Mariners)	38	32	0	.543	½
Vancouver (Pirates)	36	36	0	.500	3½
Edmonton (Angels)	35	36	0	.493	4
Portland (Twins)	20	49	0	.290	18

SOUTHERN DIVISION

Club	W.	L.	T.	Pct.	G.B.
Albuquerque (Dodgers)	43	27	1	.614	....
Phoenix (Giants)	39	33	0	.542	5
Tucson (Astros)	38	33	0	.535	5½
Hawaii (White Sox)	34	36	1	.486	9
Las Vegas (Padres)	32	40	0	.444	12

STANDING OF CLUBS AT CLOSE OF SECOND HALF, SEPTEMBER 1

NORTHERN DIVISION

Club	W.	L.	T.	Pct.	G.B.
Calgary (Mariners)	46	25	0	.648	....
Tacoma (A's)	39	33	0	.542	7½
Vancouver (Pirates)	36	36	0	.500	10½
Edmonton (Angels)	34	38	0	.472	12½
Portland (Twins)	25	47	0	.347	21½

SOUTHERN DIVISION

Club	W.	L.	T.	Pct.	G.B.
Las Vegas (Padres)	37	33	1	.529	....
Phoenix (Giants)	38	34	0	.528	½
Tucson (Astros)	37	34	0	.521	1
Albuquerque (Dodgers)	34	38	0	.472	4
Hawaii (White Sox)	31	39	1	.443	6

COMPOSITE STANDING OF CLUBS AT CLOSE OF SEASON, SEPTEMBER 1

NORTHERN DIVISION

Club	Cal.	Tac.	Van.	Edm.	Port.	Alb.	Phoe.	Tuc.	L.V.	Haw.	W.	L.	T.	Pct.	G.B.
Calgary (Mariners)	....	9	6	9	11	10	11	12	6	10	84	57	0	.596	....
Tacoma (A's)	7	....	10	11	10	7	6	11	6	10	78	65	0	.545	7
Vancouver (Pirates)	10	6	....	11	8	10	7	6	11	3	72	72	0	.500	13½
Edmonton (Angels)	6	5	5	....	12	5	11	6	8	11	69	74	0	.483	16
Portland (Twins)	5	6	8	4	....	4	5	4	6	3	45	96	0	.319	39

SOUTHERN DIVISION

Club	Cal.	Tac.	Van.	Edm.	Port.	Alb.	Phoe.	Tuc.	L.V.	Haw.	W.	L.	T.	Pct.	G.B.
Albuquerque (Dodgers)	6	9	6	11	10	....	9	7	10	9	77	65	1	.542	....
Phoenix (Giants)	5	10	9	5	11	7	....	9	13	8	77	67	0	.535	1
Tucson (Astros)	4	4	10	10	12	9	7	....	9	10	75	67	0	.528	2
Las Vegas (Padres)	10	10	5	8	10	6	3	6	....	11	69	73	1	.486	8
Hawaii (White Sox)	4	6	13	5	12	7	8	6	4	....	65	75	2	.464	11

Hawaii club represented Honolulu, Haw.

Major league affiliations in parentheses.

Playoffs—Albuquerque defeated Las Vegas, three games to none; Calgary defeated Tacoma, three games to two; Albuquerque defeated Calgary, three games to one, to win league championship.

Regular-Season Attendance—Albuquerque, 300,035; Calgary, 304,897; Edmonton, 229,381; Hawaii, 116,107; Las Vegas, 299,198; Phoenix, 183,798; Portland, 154,989; Tacoma, 293,366; Tucson, 157,744; Vancouver, 338,614. Total, 2,378,129. Playoffs, 52,076.

Managers—Albuquerque, Terry Collins; Calgary, Bill Plummer; Edmonton, John Kotchman; Hawaii, Bob Bailey; Las Vegas, Jack Krol; Phoenix, Wendell Kim; Portland, Charles Manuel; Tacoma, Keith Lieppman; Tucson, Bob Didier; Vancouver, Everett Bridges.

All-Star Team—1B—Jim Eppard, Edmonton; 2B—Jose Lind, Vancouver; 3B—Edgar Martinez, Calgary; SS—Brad Wellman, Albuquerque; OF—Jim Weaver, Calgary; Gerald Young, Tucson; Dave Hengel, Calgary; C—Mackey Sasser, Phoenix/Vancouver; DH—Francisco Melendez, Phoenix; RHP—Mike Campbell, Calgary; LHP—Ray Hayward, Las Vegas; Relief Pitcher—Todd Simmons, Las Vegas; Most Valuable Player—Mike Campbell, Calgary; Manager of the Year—Keith Lieppman, Tacoma.

(Compiled by William J. Weiss, League Statistician, San Mateo, Calif.)

CLUB BATTING

Club	Pct.	G.	AB.	R.	OR.	H.	TB.	2B.	3B.	HR.	RBI.	GW.	SH.	SF.	HP.	BB.	Int. BB.	SO.	SB.	CS.	LOB.
Calgary	.287	143	4813	837	655	1380	2095	277	39	120	758	71	52	40	28	657	46	649	133	73	1082
Edmonton	.281	143	4712	726	758	1326	1956	267	39	95	659	64	38	52	39	571	31	712	71	54	1059
Albuquerque	.281	143	4732	764	753	1328	1956	243	44	99	695	73	33	34	600	32	777	101	64	1066
Las Vegas	.271	143	4877	720	722	1323	1872	214	55	75	653	65	60	42	49	649	33	881	121	63	1198
Phoenix	.264	144	4830	766	757	1273	1806	224	51	69	694	67	48	52	42	690	50	844	121	53	1164
Tucson	.262	142	4643	733	703	1216	1808	234	71	72	645	65	55	41	37	665	42	828	227	95	1041
Tacoma	.261	143	4790	724	616	1248	1771	199	33	86	648	72	53	48	27	775	39	762	89	56	1174
Hawaii	.254	142	4565	633	716	1158	1733	211	32	100	569	53	22	100	39	550	28	747	115	56	988
Portland	.251	141	4555	549	779	1145	1603	189	37	65	503	42	25	30	31	506	19	688	106	46	973
Vancouver	.247	144	4752	580	573	1176	1609	195	38	54	524	67	37	43	36	533	38	738	143	86	989

INDIVIDUAL BATTING

(Leading Qualifiers for Batting Championship—389 or More Plate Appearances)

*Bats lefthanded.   †Switch-hitter.

Player and Club	Pct.	G.	AB.	R.	H.	TB.	2B.	3B.	HR.	RBI.	GW.	SH.	SF.	HP.	BB.	Int. BB.	SO.	SB.	CS.
Eppard, James, Edmonton*	.341	132	446	68	152	200	33	3	3	94	13	1	7	2	74	9	30	1	3
Martinez, Edgar, Calgary	.329	129	438	75	144	207	31	1	10	66	2	6	3	2	82	2	48	3	5
Melendez, Francisco, Phoenix*	.327	138	514	78	168	215	20	9	3	85	7	3	9	3	83	11	68	2	1
Sasser, Mackey, 87 Phoenix-28 Van*	.318	115	400	53	127	162	24	1	3	56	6	2	4	3	32	3	19	3	3
Wilson, Michael, Edmonton	.314	114	389	86	122	160	19	5	3	34	4	6	3	2	62	0	33	24	16
Garcia, Steven, Las Vegas*	.312	112	407	60	127	159	13	5	3	48	4	2	3	0	34	0	40	25	4
Coachman, Bobby, Edmonton	.309	115	440	82	136	180	26	3	4	43	4	2	5	44	0	33	9	5
Roberts, Leon, Las Vegas†	.306	98	359	66	110	151	18	10	1	38	4	6	1	3	37	3	39	27	14
Abner, Shawn, Las Vegas	.300	105	406	60	122	191	14	11	11	85	10	2	5	8	26	2	68	11	11
Bichette, Dante, Edmonton	.300	92	360	54	108	173	20	3	13	50	1	0	2	4	26	4	68	3	3

Departmental Leaders: G—Dunbar, 140; AB—Lind, 533; R—G. Jones, 102; H—Melendez, 168; TB—Merrifield, 231; 2B—Eppard, 33; 3B—Meadows, 14; HR—Hengel, 23; RBI—Hengel, 103; GWRBI—King, 14; SH—Green, 14; SF—Harper, 12; HP—Distefano, 15; BB—G. Jones, 123; IBB—Melendez, 11; SO—Nelson, 133; SB—Nixon, 46; CS—P. Wilson, 19.

(All Players—Listed Alphabetically)

Player and Club	Pct.	G.	AB.	R.	H.	TB.	2B.	3B.	HR.	RBI.	GW.	SH.	SF.	HP.	BB.	Int. BB.	SO.	SB.	CS.
Abner, Shawn, Las Vegas	.300	105	406	60	122	191	14	11	11	85	10	2	5	8	26	2	68	11	11
Adams, Patrick, Phoenix	.255	54	157	12	40	63	14	0	3	22	0	0	4	7	16	1	43	1	0
Adams, Ricky, Edmonton	.231	41	108	16	25	34	1	1	2	9	0	1	1	2	14	0	15	7	2
Agosto, Juan, Tucson*	.200	44	5	0	1	1	0	0	0	0	0	0	0	0	0	0	0	0	0
Allaire, Karl, Tucson*	.208	7	24	1	5	6	1	0	0	2	1	0	1	0	1	0	2	0	0

Player and Club	Pct.	G.	AB.	R.	H.	TB.	2B.	3B.	HR.	RBI.	GW.	SH.	SF.	HP.	BB.	Int. BB.	SO.	SB.	CS.
Amelung, Edward, Edmonton°	.259	124	386	52	100	144	23	3	5	58	3	3	6	2	25	5	47	3	6
Anderson, Kent, Edmonton	.232	57	181	27	42	65	4	5	3	20	2	5	1	3	19	0	26	2	1
Armas, Antonio, Edmonton	.250	29	108	11	27	42	4	1	3	16	2	0	0	1	6	1	25	0	2
Asadoor, Randall, Las Vegas	.248	96	270	39	67	97	13	4	3	28	2	1	1	8	47	1	58	1	4
Bailey, Mark, Tucson†	.138	11	29	1	4	4	0	0	0	2	0	1	0	0	4	1	10	0	0
Baker, Kerry, Vancouver†	.276	9	29	2	8	9	1	0	0	3	0	0	0	0	4	0	9	0	0
Beane, William, Portland	.285	123	463	63	132	200	28	8	8	71	5	0	5	4	36	2	77	18	5
Berra, Dale, Tucson	.270	116	389	60	105	163	19	6	9	59	6	3	5	3	61	6	70	11	9
Biancalana, Roland, Tucson†	.179	13	28	4	5	6	1	0	0	4	1	0	0	0	8	0	9	1	0
Bichette, Dante, Edmonton	.300	92	360	54	108	173	20	3	13	50	1	0	2	4	26	4	68	3	3
Bielecki, Michael, Vancouver	.233	26	30	3	7	7	0	0	0	1	0	2	0	0	2	0	12	0	0
Bilardello, Dann, Vancouver	.216	37	97	7	21	27	3	0	1	11	3	2	0	1	8	0	13	0	0
Bitker, Joseph, Las Vegas	.143	38	21	3	3	4	1	0	0	0	0	2	0	1	2	0	8	0	0
Blount, William, Las Vegas°	.500	20	12	0	6	6	0	0	0	3	0	0	0	0	0	0	3	0	0
Bockus, Randy, Phoenix°	.143	36	7	2	1	1	0	0	0	0	0	1	0	0	8	0	3	0	0
Boston, Daryl, Hawaii°	.299	21	77	14	23	41	3	0	5	13	2	0	0	1	10	1	10	10	0
Brantley, Jeffrey, Phoenix	.105	34	19	0	2	2	0	0	0	0	0	0	0	1	2	0	12	0	0
Brantley, Michael, Calgary	.240	13	50	13	12	20	0	1	2	6	1	0	0	1	7	1	4	3	2
Braun, Randall, Calgary°	.260	118	439	64	114	173	18	1	13	62	7	2	1	6	54	4	62	2	3
Brennan, William, Albuquerque	.200	28	20	1	4	5	1	0	0	1	0	0	0	0	0	0	8	0	0
Brouhard, Mark, Edmonton	.292	31	72	5	21	26	2	0	1	11	0	0	1	1	17	0	16	0	3
Brown, Michael, Hawaii	.291	67	230	46	67	105	13	2	7	32	3	1	2	4	32	3	30	1	2
Bryant, Ralph, Albuquerque°	.259	75	243	43	63	129	8	5	16	52	4	0	1	0	20	7	65	5	3
Buckley, Kevin, Las Vegas	.257	94	253	34	65	101	14	2	6	43	5	4	3	3	43	2	88	0	0
Bullock, Eric, 39 Tuc-67 Portland°	.267	106	330	42	88	119	13	6	2	34	3	1	2	2	42	7	27	14	7
Bundy, Lorenzo, Vancouver°	.455	4	11	3	5	8	1	1	0	1	0	0	0	0	2	0	0	0	0
Burrell, Kevin, Phoenix	.235	44	85	11	20	28	5	0	1	11	1	0	1	1	7	0	19	0	2
Burtt, Dennis, Albuquerque°	.125	31	24	2	3	4	1	0	0	1	0	3	0	0	1	0	5	0	0
Butera, Salvatore, Portland	.154	10	26	4	4	8	1	0	1	3	0	0	0	0	8	1	2	0	0
Byers, Randell, Las Vegas°	.274	121	463	58	127	203	22	9	12	76	12	4	4	2	31	5	64	14	5
Carpenter, Glenn, Tucson	.275	138	498	81	137	200	28	4	9	76	7	3	3	3	57	4	94	18	12
Carrasco, Norman, Edmonton	.202	30	84	12	17	27	5	1	1	8	1	2	0	0	4	0	7	1	0
Casey, Patrick, Portland	.215	48	144	20	31	46	6	0	3	13	1	0	1	0	32	0	25	0	1
Childress, Rodney, Tucson	.000	33	1	0	0	0	0	0	0	0	0	1	0	0	0	0	0	0	0
Christensen, John, Calgary	.326	13	46	11	15	22	4	0	1	12	2	1	0	1	8	0	8	1	0
Christiansen, Clay, 13 Port-19 Tuc	.000	32	11	0	0	0	0	0	0	0	0	2	0	0	1	0	7	0	0
Clark, Robert, Tacoma	.279	62	179	29	50	75	8	1	5	44	4	1	2	1	22	0	25	1	3
Clay, Danny, Portland	.000	17	0	1	0	0	0	0	0	0	0	0	0	0	0	0	0	0	0
Cliburn, Stanley, Edmonton	.227	23	66	15	15	29	5	0	3	13	1	0	1	2	9	0	11	0	0
Coachman, Bobby, Edmonton	.309	115	440	82	136	180	26	3	4	43	4	2	2	5	44	0	33	9	5
Cocanower, James, Albuquerque	.200	36	10	0	2	2	0	0	0	0	0	1	0	0	4	0	4	0	0
Cochrane, David, Hawaii†	.271	129	451	60	122	196	23	3	15	66	5	0	5	8	35	2	121	7	7
Cockrell, Alan, Phoenix	.257	129	432	82	111	177	23	5	11	72	5	5	4	3	69	4	131	7	3
Comstock, Keith, Phoenix°	.000	17	1	0	0	0	0	0	0	0	0	0	0	0	0	0	0	0	0
Cook, Dennis, Phoenix°	.231	12	13	1	3	3	0	0	0	0	0	1	0	0	1	0	4	0	0
Cora, Jose, Las Vegas†	.276	81	293	50	81	95	9	1	1	24	6	5	1	2	62	2	39	12	7
Corbell, Charles, Phoenix	.160	32	25	3	4	4	0	0	0	4	0	4	0	0	4	0	8	0	0
Corey, Mark, Portland	.259	48	139	22	36	63	5	2	6	24	2	0	0	0	29	0	35	0	0
Costello, Michael, Las Vegas	.167	12	6	1	1	1	0	0	0	0	0	2	0	0	0	0	3	0	0
Crews, Timothy, Albuquerque	.000	42	3	0	0	0	0	0	0	0	0	0	0	0	0	0	3	0	0
Crone, William, Tucson	.215	62	149	15	32	44	7	1	1	19	1	0	1	1	24	1	14	2	1
Cruz, Julio, Albuquerque†	.174	30	92	13	16	20	4	0	0	4	0	1	1	1	19	0	19	6	1
Davis, Wallace, Vancouver	.271	111	424	58	115	167	17	7	7	57	8	1	6	1	22	1	73	22	6
Debus, Jon, Albuquerque	.268	105	321	51	86	131	16	4	7	60	4	1	4	1	58	1	63	0	1
deJesus, Ivan, Phoenix	.259	17	54	8	14	20	4	1	0	2	0	1	0	0	12	0	9	1	1
Dempsey, Patrick, Portland	.240	89	296	24	71	117	20	1	8	42	2	1	0	0	7	0	48	0	0
Devereaux, Michael, Albuquerque	.273	3	11	2	3	7	1	0	1	1	1	0	0	0	0	0	2	1	0
Diaz, Mario, Calgary	.282	108	376	52	106	141	17	3	4	52	5	10	1	1	19	2	25	1	5
Distefano, Benito, Vancouver°	.278	130	431	67	120	193	20	4	15	77	9	0	4	15	77	7	53	7	6
Dorsett, Brian, Tacoma	.234	78	282	31	66	100	14	1	6	39	3	1	5	3	33	3	50	0	0
Drummond, Timothy, Vancouver	.200	46	5	0	1	1	0	0	0	0	0	0	0	0	0	0	3	0	0
Dugas, Shanie, Albuquerque°	.274	108	285	48	78	117	12	3	7	38	4	4	3	0	59	1	56	4	5
Dunbar, Thomas, Vancouver°	.267	140	501	76	134	179	32	2	3	77	10	3	4	1	91	5	73	16	9
Duncan, Mariano, Albuquerque†	.273	6	22	6	6	6	0	0	0	0	0	0	0	0	0	0	5	3	0
Dunne, Michael, Vancouver	.214	9	14	1	3	3	0	0	0	0	0	0	0	0	0	0	3	0	0
Easley, Logan, Vancouver	1.000	9	1	0	1	1	0	0	0	0	0	0	0	0	0	0	0	0	0
Edwards, Jeffrey, 6 Alb-20 Tuc°	.375	26	8	0	3	3	0	0	0	1	1	1	0	0	0	0	2	0	0
Engram, Graylyn, Hawaii	.000	5	2	0	0	0	0	0	0	0	0	0	0	0	1	0	2	0	0
Eppard, James, Edmonton°	.341	132	446	68	152	200	33	3	3	94	13	1	7	2	74	9	30	1	5
Escobar, Angel, Phoenix†	.265	130	434	68	115	150	13	8	2	50	5	6	1	2	73	5	59	11	7
Espinoza, Alvaro, Portland	.275	91	291	28	80	99	3	2	4	28	3	4	0	2	12	1	37	2	1
Fansler, Stanley, Vancouver	.300	25	20	1	6	7	1	0	0	1	0	3	0	0	3	0	4	0	0
Ferran, George, Phoenix	.167	40	6	0	1	1	0	0	0	0	0	0	0	0	0	0	2	0	0
Fimple, John, Edmonton	.292	71	226	30	66	87	15	0	2	24	0	1	5	3	33	0	46	1	0
Firova, Daniel, Calgary	.158	8	19	2	3	3	0	0	0	0	0	0	0	0	1	0	3	0	0
Fontenot, Ray, Tucson°	.333	17	3	1	1	1	0	0	0	0	0	0	0	0	1	0	1	0	0
Ford, Russell, Las Vegas	.000	43	7	0	0	0	0	0	0	1	0	0	0	0	0	0	5	0	0
Forrester, Thomas, Hawaii°	.190	58	179	16	34	62	10	0	6	26	2	0	0	0	12	2	30	1	0
Funk, Thomas, Tucson°	.222	39	9	1	2	3	1	0	0	0	0	0	0	0	0	0	2	0	0
Gainey, Telmanch, Tucson°	.290	123	421	83	122	201	28	6	13	72	8	0	5	0	82	6	92	8	8
Gallagher, David, Calgary	.306	75	268	45	82	122	27	2	3	46	6	8	3	0	37	1	36	12	4
Gallego, Michael, Tacoma	.268	10	41	6	11	15	0	2	0	6	0	0	0	0	7	0	7	1	2
Garcia, Steven, Las Vegas°	.312	112	407	60	127	159	13	5	3	48	4	2	5	0	34	0	40	25	4
Gardenhire, Ronald, Portland	.272	117	389	49	106	148	16	4	6	50	5	2	3	1	45	0	70	1	1
Giles, Brian, Hawaii	.220	132	449	60	99	144	21	3	6	47	3	5	4	5	64	1	71	19	3
Gillaspie, James, Las Vegas	.280	91	307	58	86	143	12	3	13	47	6	0	3	8	84	8	65	1	5
Gomez, Randall, Hawaii	.245	56	163	24	40	55	6	0	3	13	3	1	1	0	23	0	20	2	0
Gonzalez, Denio, Vancouver	.262	113	413	62	108	167	20	0	13	57	6	3	5	2	71	4	91	19	14
Gonzalez, Felipe, Vancouver	.250	8	16	1	4	4	0	0	0	1	1	0	0	0	0	0	1	0	0
Gonzalez, Jose, Albuquerque	.280	116	339	67	95	162	22	3	13	61	5	2	2	4	55	2	94	19	10
Gorman, Thomas, 1 LV-29 Port°	1.000	30	1	0	1	2	1	0	0	0	0	0	0	0	0	0	0	0	0
Graham, Everett, Phoenix°	.295	13	44	8	13	27	6	1	2	10	0	1	0	0	7	2	5	1	1

Player and Club	Pct.	G.	AB.	R.	H.	TB.	2B.	3B.	HR.	RBI.	GW.	SH.	SF.	HP.	BB.	Int. BB.	SO.	SB.	CS.
Grant, Mark, Phoenix	.000	3	6	1	0	0	0	0	0	0	0	1	0	0	0	0	2	0	0
Green, Gary, Las Vegas	.237	111	337	32	80	95	8	2	1	32	1	14	4	1	35	2	58	2	4
Guetterman, Lee, Calgary°	.000	16	0	0	0	0	0	0	0	0	0	1	0	0	0	0	0	0	0
Gwosdz, Douglas, Calgary	.228	66	167	26	38	61	11	3	2	28	4	4	3	3	22	1	30	3	2
Gwynn, Christopher, Albuquerque°	.279	110	362	54	101	134	12	3	5	41	8	1	0	1	36	5	38	5	7
Hagen, Kevin, 3 Port-33 Tuc	.063	36	16	0	1	1	0	0	0	1	0	4	0	0	2	0	7	0	0
Hamilton, Jeffrey, Albuquerque	.360	65	236	52	85	140	17	1	12	48	7	1	2	2	26	2	26	0	2
Hammaker, Atlee, Phoenix†	.333	3	3	0	1	1	0	0	0	0	0	0	0	0	2	0	0	0	0
Haro, Samuel, Vancouver	.227	69	238	26	54	69	15	0	0	22	3	3	2	3	22	4	35	14	5
Harper, Brian, Tacoma	.310	94	323	41	100	144	17	0	9	62	8	4	12	4	28	7	23	1	2
Harrison, Ronald, Vancouver°	.205	66	219	19	45	66	10	4	1	21	2	0	4	0	7	2	23	2	5
Hassey, Ronald, Hawaii°	.143	6	21	3	3	5	2	0	0	4	0	0	0	0	2	0	1	0	0
Havens, Bradley, Albuquerque°	.000	3	2	0	0	0	0	0	0	0	0	1	0	0	0	0	0	0	0
Hayward, Raymond, Las Vegas°	.167	35	30	3	5	5	0	0	0	3	0	2	1	0	0	0	4	0	0
Heath, David, Edmonton	.205	62	176	18	36	56	4	2	4	21	3	6	2	3	14	0	47	1	0
Heathcock, Jeffrey, Tucson	.059	22	17	1	1	2	1	0	0	0	0	1	0	0	0	0	7	0	0
Henderson, Stephen, Tacoma	.302	74	255	45	77	103	12	4	2	33	3	2	1	1	48	2	38	3	5
Hengel, David, Calgary	.295	117	448	80	132	230	25	2	23	103	12	0	6	7	45	5	73	5	2
Heredia, Hector, Albuquerque	.000	50	5	0	0	0	0	0	0	0	0	1	0	0	1	0	3	0	0
Hernandez, Manuel, Tucson	.000	9	8	0	0	0	0	0	0	0	0	2	0	0	2	0	7	0	0
Hill, Donald, Hawaii†	.391	7	23	10	9	17	2	0	2	6	0	0	0	0	2	0	1	2	0
Hillegas, Shawn, Albuquerque	.105	24	19	2	2	2	0	0	0	1	0	2	0	0	4	0	8	0	0
Hinshaw, George, Albuquerque	.338	103	296	53	100	152	18	2	10	63	8	0	2	4	32	5	49	10	3
Householder, Paul, Tucson†	.273	100	311	48	85	118	13	4	4	45	3	1	2	1	50	9	44	26	8
Howell, Kenneth, Albuquerque	.000	2	1	0	0	0	0	0	0	0	0	0	0	0	0	0	1	0	0
Howie, Mark, Tacoma	.236	44	148	22	35	39	1	0	1	13	1	0	1	1	22	1	23	0	2
Hulett, Timothy, Hawaii	.236	42	157	13	37	49	5	2	1	24	3	1	3	0	9	0	28	4	1
Jackson, Charles, Tucson	.289	80	291	51	84	111	10	4	3	43	2	4	4	1	36	1	42	13	9
James, Calvin, Tucson°	.286	11	35	7	10	12	0	1	0	4	1	0	0	0	3	0	2	2	0
Javier, Stanley, Tacoma†	.216	15	51	6	11	13	2	0	0	2	0	0	0	0	4	0	12	3	1
Jimenez, Alfonso, Vancouver	.237	49	131	16	31	38	3	2	0	6	1	1	2	0	15	4	14	7	2
Johns, Ronald, Vancouver	.175	18	57	4	10	11	1	0	0	8	1	2	1	1	3	0	9	0	0
Johnson, David, Vancouver	.065	23	31	0	2	2	0	0	0	1	0	1	0	0	1	0	6	0	0
Johnson, Roy, Tacoma°	.252	79	262	43	66	98	10	2	6	32	4	0	2	0	36	4	31	1	2
Jones, Barry, Vancouver	.000	20	2	0	0	0	0	0	0	0	0	0	0	0	0	0	1	0	0
Jones, Christopher, Phoenix°	.257	104	280	64	72	100	14	4	2	43	5	3	5	2	42	2	42	8	3
Jones, Gary, Tacoma°	.277	135	473	102	131	174	22	6	3	49	2	5	3	3	123	3	83	30	12
Jones, Ricky, Portland	.233	82	287	31	67	114	17	0	10	39	5	2	0	2	28	1	43	0	1
Jones, Ross, Calgary	.319	44	163	35	52	75	10	2	3	23	1	1	0	0	28	1	24	4	5
Karkovice, Ronald, Hawaii	.183	34	104	15	19	34	3	0	4	11	0	0	0	8	0	37	3	0	
Kearney, Robert, Tacoma	.177	22	62	6	11	14	0	0	1	8	1	1	0	0	6	0	8	1	0
Keedy, Patrick, Hawaii	.281	95	302	56	85	155	13	3	17	55	5	3	1	6	56	2	70	17	1
Kelley, Anthony, Tucson	.091	32	22	3	2	5	1	1	0	0	0	4	0	0	2	0	7	0	0
Kerfeld, Charles, Tucson	.000	32	6	0	0	0	0	0	0	0	0	0	0	0	0	0	2	0	0
Khalifa, Sam, Vancouver	.226	111	367	39	83	105	12	5	0	31	5	1	3	2	62	1	67	8	7
King, Kevin, Edmonton†	.285	119	404	59	115	208	27	3	20	85	14	0	6	3	55	3	123	8	5
Kingman, David, Phoenix	.203	20	59	11	12	21	3	0	2	11	1	0	1	1	12	0	11	0	0
Kipper, Robert, Vancouver	.000	6	1	0	0	0	0	0	0	0	0	0	0	0	0	0	1	0	0
Kramer, Randall, Vancouver	.500	11	2	0	1	1	0	0	0	0	0	0	0	0	0	0	0	0	0
Krauss, Timothy, Hawaii°	.237	100	287	35	68	85	11	0	2	12	0	1	0	3	50	2	28	2	3
Krawczyk, Raymond, Hawaii	.000	35	1	0	0	0	0	0	0	0	0	0	0	0	0	0	0	0	0
Krenchicki, Wayne, Hawaii	.234	126	465	48	109	149	19	0	7	56	8	4	2	0	47	2	61	3	2
Krueger, William, 10 Tac-16 Alb°	.133	26	15	2	2	3	1	0	0	1	0	1	0	0	1	0	4	0	0
Kutcher, Randy, Phoenix	.255	92	349	68	89	132	15	5	6	53	5	0	4	3	42	2	61	31	9
Kyles, Stanley, Tacoma	.000	44	1	0	0	0	0	0	0	0	0	0	0	0	0	0	0	0	0
Ladd, Peter, Albuquerque	.000	35	3	0	0	0	0	0	0	0	0	0	0	0	0	0	2	0	0
Lansford, Joseph, Las Vegas	.237	107	317	43	75	123	21	3	7	62	4	1	6	5	73	2	80	2	1
Larkin, Eugene, Portland†	.302	35	129	17	39	51	9	0	1	14	0	0	1	0	20	0	11	0	0
Leeper, David, Vancouver°	.277	72	191	17	53	78	14	1	3	29	2	1	1	1	6	1	19	1	2
LeMaster, Johnnie, 38 Tac-19 Haw ..	.269	57	167	20	45	53	3	1	1	14	3	5	3	0	14	1	30	4	1
Liddle, Steven, Portland	.000	3	10	0	0	0	0	0	0	0	0	0	0	0	0	0	1	0	0
Lind, Jose, Vancouver	.268	128	533	75	143	174	16	3	3	30	5	3	1	3	35	0	52	21	9
Lindsey, William, Hawaii	.195	15	41	6	8	17	0	0	3	8	1	0	0	1	5	0	5	0	0
Litton, Gregory, Phoenix	.217	60	203	24	44	59	8	2	1	22	2	2	3	2	18	1	40	0	1
Livingston, Dennis, Albuquerque	.000	56	3	0	0	0	0	0	0	0	0	0	0	0	0	0	2	0	0
Lopes, David, Tucson	.643	4	14	2	9	12	3	0	0	3	0	0	0	0	5	0	2	1	0
Lopez, Juan, Tucson	.214	21	28	3	6	8	2	0	0	3	0	1	0	0	4	0	7	1	0
Lyons, Stephen, Hawaii°	.285	47	167	26	48	65	11	0	2	16	5	1	1	1	22	1	27	7	5
Mack, Shane, Las Vegas	.336	39	152	38	51	79	11	1	5	26	3	0	1	1	19	0	32	13	0
Mallicoat, Robin, Tucson°	.333	3	3	1	1	1	0	0	0	0	0	1	0	0	1	0	0	0	0
Marte, Alexis, Portland°	.276	43	87	17	24	30	4	1	0	7	0	2	0	0	13	0	10	9	3
Martinez, Carlos, Hawaii	.247	83	304	32	75	101	15	1	3	36	1	1	3	0	14	1	50	3	2
Martinez, Edgar, Calgary	.329	129	438	75	144	207	31	1	10	66	2	6	3	2	82	2	48	3	5
Mason, Roger, Phoenix	.000	10	5	1	0	0	0	0	0	0	0	0	0	0	1	0	4	0	0
Mathis, Ronald, Tucson	.200	24	20	1	4	4	0	0	0	2	0	3	0	0	4	0	3	0	0
Mayberry, Gregory, Albuquerque°	.000	6	1	0	0	0	0	0	0	0	0	0	0	0	0	0	1	0	0
McDougal, Julius, Portland†	.190	64	216	17	41	52	5	3	0	20	1	0	2	2	22	0	40	9	3
McElroy, Glen, Hawaii	.259	14	27	7	7	8	1	0	0	1	0	1	0	0	6	0	1	1	0
McKnight, Jonathan, Phoenix	.000	12	2	0	0	0	0	0	0	0	0	0	0	0	0	0	0	0	0
Meadows, Michael, Tucson°	.258	129	426	70	110	189	21	14	10	76	7	0	7	5	70	3	87	26	8
Meads, David, Tucson°	.000	10	1	0	0	0	0	0	0	0	0	0	0	0	0	0	0	0	0
Medvin, Scott, 12 Phx-1 Van	.000	13	2	0	0	0	0	0	0	0	0	0	0	0	0	0	1	0	0
Meeks, Timothy, 21 Alb-13 Tac	.091	34	11	0	1	1	0	0	0	0	0	0	0	0	0	0	2	0	1
Melendez, Francisco, Phoenix°	.327	138	514	78	168	215	20	9	3	85	7	3	9	3	83	11	68	2	1
Mercado, Orlando, Albuquerque	.278	69	205	22	57	81	18	0	2	27	1	0	2	1	15	1	29	1	0
Merrifield, Billie, 127 Edm-3 Van	.283	130	481	79	136	231	30	4	19	76	5	0	5	0	51	3	85	2	2
Miller, Stephen, Phoenix	.091	9	11	1	1	1	0	0	0	0	0	1	0	0	3	1	2	0	0
Milner, Eddie, Phoenix°	.274	17	62	10	17	21	2	1	0	8	1	1	1	0	4	0	6	5	0
Miscik, Robert, Edmonton	.252	134	452	69	114	165	30	3	5	53	4	11	6	4	62	0	49	5	5
Montalvo, Rafael, Tucson	.000	59	5	0	0	0	0	0	0	0	0	1	0	0	0	0	4	0	0
Montgomery, Reginald, Edmonton	.253	72	245	23	62	85	11	0	4	28	7	0	3	2	23	4	38	1	0
Morhardt, Gregory, Portland°	.204	42	137	10	28	36	5	0	1	16	3	1	1	0	4	1	12	1	0

Player and Club	Pct.	G.	AB.	R.	H.	TB.	2B.	3B.	HR.	RBI.	GW.	SH.	SF.	HP.	BB.	Int. BB.	SO.	SB.	CS.
Morman, Russell, Hawaii	.269	89	294	52	79	129	19	2	9	53	8	0	3	1	60	3	56	5	3
Mulholland, Terence, Phoenix	.111	37	27	0	3	4	1	0	0	3	0	2	0	0	1	0	11	0	0
Murphy, Dwayne, Tacoma	.267	5	15	1	4	7	3	0	0	2	0	0	0	0	4	1	3	0	0
Narron, Jerry, Calgary°	.251	110	370	56	93	169	23	4	15	58	4	4	1	3	42	9	29	2	3
Nelson, Robert, Tacoma°	.215	120	413	68	89	174	19	3	20	74	11	0	6	3	97	4	133	5	2
Nieto, Thomas, Portland	.227	38	110	10	25	30	5	0	0	3	0	3	0	2	11	0	25	0	1
Nixon, Donell, Calgary	.323	82	328	72	106	141	18	1	5	52	4	3	2	0	51	5	51	46	16
Noble, Rayner, Tucson†	.000	2	0	0	0	0	0	0	0	0	0	1	0	0	0	0	0	0	0
Orsulak, Joseph, Vancouver°	.231	39	143	20	33	44	6	1	1	12	1	2	1	2	17	5	21	2	4
Ouellette, Philip, Phoenix†	.233	55	159	20	37	52	10	1	1	19	1	1	3	0	38	3	21	2	1
Palacios, Vicente, Vancouver†	.200	27	25	2	5	5	0	0	0	2	0	3	0	0	3	0	10	0	0
Pankovits, James, Tucson	.327	34	101	17	33	56	7	2	4	25	2	0	1	2	16	0	12	5	3
Parent, Mark, Las Vegas	.292	105	387	50	113	152	23	2	4	43	2	1	2	1	38	3	53	2	1
Parsons, Scott, Las Vegas	.264	37	129	16	34	47	7	0	2	19	1	1	1	4	18	1	26	0	0
Patterson, Robert, Vancouver	.000	14	4	2	0	0	0	0	0	0	0	1	0	0	1	0	3	0	0
Pederson, Stuart, Albuquerque°	.254	84	232	40	59	93	11	4	5	34	3	0	0	1	30	2	28	1	3
Pena, Adalberto, Tucson	.221	73	253	44	56	89	16	1	5	28	2	2	1	5	21	0	43	11	1
Pena, Hipolito, Vancouver°	.000	27	7	0	0	0	0	0	0	0	0	0	0	0	0	0	4	0	0
Perconte, John, Albuquerque°	.280	119	411	68	115	140	19	3	0	43	11	2	8	2	82	2	36	12	8
Perlman, Jonathan, Phoenix°	.000	52	6	0	0	0	0	0	0	1	0	0	0	0	1	0	3	0	0
Pettis, Gary, Edmonton†	.125	8	16	6	2	3	1	0	0	1	0	0	0	0	3	0	5	3	1
Phillips, Anthony, Tacoma†	.346	7	26	5	9	16	2	1	1	6	1	0	0	0	4	0	3	1	0
Pittaro, Christopher, Portland†	.286	127	447	77	128	153	13	6	0	43	5	3	10	3	67	2	49	16	4
Polonia, Luis, Tacoma†	.321	14	56	18	18	23	1	2	0	8	1	0	1	0	14	1	6	4	2
Portugal, Mark, Portland	.000	18	0	1	0	0	0	0	0	0	0	0	0	0	0	0	0	0	0
Poston, Mark, Las Vegas	.143	45	7	1	1	1	0	0	0	2	0	0	0	0	0	0	6	0	0
Pounders, Bradley, Las Vegas	.233	52	172	21	40	59	7	0	4	20	1	1	3	2	24	0	58	0	0
Powell, Dennis, Calgary°	.000	21	0	1	0	0	0	0	0	0	0	0	0	0	0	0	0	0	0
Price, Joseph, Phoenix	.167	17	6	2	1	1	0	0	0	1	0	0	0	0	1	0	4	0	0
Puikunas, Edmund, Phoenix	.000	24	1	1	0	0	0	0	0	0	0	0	0	0	1	0	1	0	0
Ramsey, Michael, Albuquerque†	.308	36	117	20	36	48	7	1	1	12	1	3	0	1	18	1	23	6	2
Randall, James, Edmonton†	.324	13	34	6	11	19	5	0	1	5	1	0	1	0	6	2	4	0	0
Ray, Larry, Vancouver°	.053	16	19	1	1	1	0	0	0	2	0	0	1	1	4	0	4	0	1
Reece, Thad, Tacoma°	.280	111	329	35	92	105	10	0	1	33	6	12	3	5	45	0	36	6	4
Reid, Jessie, Phoenix°	.270	128	433	83	117	197	22	5	16	84	9	1	3	5	84	8	80	19	8
Renteria, Richard, Calgary	.296	69	267	41	79	102	14	3	1	32	3	2	3	1	9	0	20	3	3
Reyes, Gilberto, Albuquerque	.272	89	265	42	72	109	18	2	5	46	1	1	2	6	30	0	57	0	1
Reynolds, Ronn, Tucson	.200	81	210	22	42	61	10	0	3	16	3	3	1	3	20	3	35	2	3
Roberts, Leon, Las Vegas†	.306	98	359	66	110	151	18	10	1	38	4	6	1	3	37	3	39	27	14
Roberts, Peter, Las Vegas°	.000	6	3	1	0	0	0	0	0	0	0	0	0	0	1	0	0	0	0
Rodriguez, Edwin, 60 LV-45 Port	.197	105	310	53	61	70	9	0	0	26	0	1	3	2	50	1	40	9	2
Rodriguez, Ricardo, Tacoma	1.000	22	1	0	1	1	0	0	0	0	0	0	0	0	0	0	0	0	0
Rodriguez, Ruben, Vancouver	.221	88	285	24	63	79	5	4	1	28	2	2	4	2	13	1	53	0	4
Rohn, Daniel, Tacoma°	.214	94	266	33	57	82	9	2	4	25	0	5	1	0	52	1	40	3	6
Rood, Nelson, Tucson	.282	92	163	37	46	53	5	1	0	12	1	6	0	2	33	0	13	18	4
Ross, Mark, Vancouver	.000	32	8	0	0	0	0	0	0	1	0	1	0	0	3	0	5	0	0
Rubel, Michael, Phoenix	.191	16	47	6	9	13	2	1	0	8	0	1	0	2	9	1	9	0	0
Ryal, Mark, Edmonton°	.429	16	49	10	21	28	3	2	0	12	0	0	0	0	5	0	7	0	0
Salazar, Luis, Las Vegas	.294	4	17	2	5	10	2	0	1	3	0	0	0	0	1	0	4	1	0
Salinas, Manuel, Hawaii°	.247	49	174	18	43	47	2	1	0	16	1	3	0	0	11	1	6	1	0
Sanchez, Alejandro, Tacoma	.310	53	203	43	63	99	9	6	5	32	3	0	0	4	29	3	30	9	4
Sasser, Mackey, 87 Phx-28 Van°	.318	115	400	53	127	162	24	1	3	56	6	2	4	3	32	3	19	3	3
Schaefer, Jeffrey, Albuquerque	.259	8	27	3	7	8	1	0	0	3	0	0	0	0	0	0	3	0	0
Schneider, Paul, Calgary	.000	51	0	1	0	0	0	0	0	0	0	0	0	0	0	0	0	0	0
Schuler, David, Phoenix	.333	15	3	0	1	1	0	0	0	0	0	0	0	0	0	0	1	0	0
Schweighoffer, Michael, Albuquerque	.143	17	7	0	1	1	0	0	0	0	0	0	0	0	2	0	1	0	0
Sconiers, Daryl, Hawaii°	.305	40	118	18	36	58	10	0	4	18	1	0	0	0	23	1	12	1	2
Scurry, Rodney, Phoenix°	.143	28	7	1	1	2	1	0	0	1	1	1	0	0	0	0	5	0	0
Searage, Raymond, Hawaii°	1.000	3	1	0	1	1	0	0	0	1	0	0	0	0	0	0	0	0	0
See, Laurence, Albuquerque	.304	66	257	45	78	118	18	2	6	44	5	0	3	0	26	2	32	1	2
Shields, Stephen, Calgary	.000	16	1	0	0	0	0	0	0	0	0	0	0	0	0	0	0	0	0
Shipley, Craig, Albuquerque†	.223	49	139	17	31	42	6	1	1	15	1	1	0	1	13	0	19	6	2
Simmons, Nelson, Calgary†	.309	18	68	14	21	35	5	0	3	13	3	0	1	0	10	0	10	1	2
Simmons, Todd, Las Vegas	.000	75	2	0	0	0	0	0	0	0	0	0	0	0	2	0	1	0	0
Sinatro, Matthew, Tacoma	.251	79	215	30	54	82	13	0	5	32	7	8	2	1	35	3	34	6	3
Siwy, James, Las Vegas	.000	36	5	0	0	0	0	0	0	0	0	0	0	0	0	0	1	0	0
Smith, Brick, Calgary	.261	84	314	47	82	130	15	0	11	48	3	3	4	1	53	1	41	1	0
Snyder, Brian, Las Vegas°	.333	39	3	0	1	2	1	0	0	0	0	0	0	0	0	0	2	0	0
Solano, Julio, Tucson	.000	43	3	0	0	0	0	0	0	0	0	2	0	0	0	0	2	0	0
Steels, James, Las Vegas	.321	15	53	12	17	22	3	1	0	5	0	0	0	1	8	0	7	3	1
Stockstill, David, Phoenix°	.170	18	47	3	8	17	1	1	2	9	2	0	0	0	6	1	4	0	0
Taylor, Donald, Vancouver	.000	9	7	0	0	0	0	0	0	0	0	0	0	0	0	0	2	0	0
Taylor, Michael, Hawaii	.223	98	242	36	54	80	14	3	2	21	1	4	1	5	29	1	45	13	10
Thomas, Todd, Phoenix°	.259	26	85	12	22	26	2	1	0	11	2	1	0	0	11	0	7	6	3
Thompson, Tommy, Hawaii°	.218	58	165	8	36	41	3	1	0	21	3	7	2	1	11	0	10	1	7
Thon, Richard, Tucson	.271	14	48	10	13	17	4	0	0	6	1	1	1	0	6	0	12	1	1
Tillman, Kerry, Phoenix	.316	94	304	50	96	142	12	2	10	52	7	2	5	2	32	2	54	8	2
Tolentino, Jose, Tacoma°	.228	59	202	16	46	63	8	0	3	26	2	2	0	0	21	0	29	0	0
Verducci, John, Phoenix	.173	30	75	7	13	14	1	0	0	4	0	2	0	3	12	1	20	0	1
Vosberg, Edward, Las Vegas°	.160	34	25	2	4	5	1	0	0	1	0	0	0	0	1	0	4	0	0
Walker, Anthony, 4 Tuc-44 Van	.226	48	146	17	33	42	4	1	1	9	1	0	1	0	10	1	22	4	5
Walker, Glen, Portland	.252	96	301	42	76	123	11	0	12	39	2	1	3	6	39	0	66	0	3
Waller, Tyrone, Tucson	.296	81	159	28	47	70	11	6	0	21	6	2	2	1	30	5	36	11	5
Ward, Colin, 3 Phx-12 LV°	.429	15	7	0	3	4	1	0	0	1	0	1	0	0	0	0	1	0	0
Washington, U.L., Vancouver	.238	73	261	28	62	82	10	2	2	21	3	1	2	0	40	1	46	19	7
Wasinger, Mark, 9 LV-41 Phx	.224	50	170	28	38	49	4	2	1	16	2	1	0	2	34	0	20	4	3
Watters, Michael, Calgary°	.278	112	418	74	116	165	25	6	4	43	4	4	3	0	58	3	53	14	12
Weaver, James, Calgary°	.280	124	472	95	132	222	25	7	17	91	8	3	7	1	95	9	104	31	8
Weiss, Walter, Tacoma†	.263	46	179	35	47	57	4	3	0	17	0	2	1	1	28	0	31	9	3
Wellman, Brad, Albuquerque	.306	88	317	50	97	124	11	5	2	38	4	3	2	5	36	0	38	9	7
Wiley, Craig, Las Vegas	.000	1	0	0	0	0	0	0	0	0	0	0	0	0	0	0	0	0	0
Wilfong, Robert, Phoenix°	.333	2	9	0	3	3	0	0	0	0	0	0	0	0	0	0	0	0	0

Player and Club	Pct.	G.	AB.	R.	H.	TB.	2B.	3B.	HR.	RBI.	GW.	SH.	SF.	HP.	BB.	Int. BB.	SO.	SB.	CS.
Willard, Gerald, Tacoma°	.298	67	215	42	64	97	15	0	6	38	5	3	3	0	56	3	33	0	1
Williams, Jaime, Portland	.221	38	113	7	25	32	7	0	0	9	1	1	2	2	9	0	18	0	0
Williams, Kenneth, Hawaii	.269	35	134	19	36	57	4	4	3	14	2	1	2	0	9	1	27	5	4
Williams, Matthew, Phoenix	.289	56	211	36	61	98	15	2	6	37	5	3	2	0	19	3	53	6	2
Williams, Reginald, Albuquerque	.307	58	166	24	51	68	8	3	1	17	4	3	2	2	16	1	28	11	5
Wilson, James, Portland	.268	45	157	16	42	58	7	0	3	24	1	0	1	1	18	0	34	2	0
Wilson, Michael, Edmonton	.314	114	389	86	122	160	19	5	3	34	4	6	3	2	82	0	33	24	16
Wilson, Phillip, Portland†	.227	130	458	50	104	132	14	7	0	26	4	3	1	3	58	4	52	35	17
Wine, Robert, Tucson	.240	76	262	35	63	125	21	7	9	62	6	1	4	4	30	1	88	5	4
Wishnevski, Michael, Calgary°	.329	60	161	33	53	77	9	3	3	23	2	0	2	1	36	2	27	1	1
Wojna, Edward, Las Vegas	.067	18	15	1	1	1	0	0	0	1	0	4	0	0	1	0	11	0	0
Woodard, Michael, 45 Phx-59 Tuc°	.250	104	381	56	95	115	10	5	0	36	5	5	2	3	47	1	30	23	8
Woodson, Tracy, Albuquerque	.290	67	259	37	75	107	13	2	5	44	1	0	4	2	17	0	22	1	1
Wrona, William, Las Vegas	.269	77	216	26	58	67	7	1	0	21	4	5	0	1	26	1	22	3	4
Yastrzemski, Michael, Hawaii†	.292	115	414	57	121	169	18	6	6	52	7	0	2	3	53	6	54	8	5
Young, Gerald, Tucson†	.291	86	340	59	99	130	15	5	2	31	3	2	2	3	47	0	32	43	12

The following pitchers, listed alphabetically by club, with games in parentheses, had no plate appearances, primarily through use of designated hitters:

ALBUQUERQUE—Davis, Ronald (7); Hartley, Michael (2); Heuer, Mark (1); Savage, John (13).

CALGARY—Best, Karl (27); Brown, Michael (22); Burroughs, Darren (2); Campbell, Michael (24); Clarke, Stanley (31); Ferreira, Anthony (32); Hanson, Erik (8); Kelly, Bryan (6); Monteleone, Richard (51); Parker, Clay (12); Reed, Jerry (1); Swift, William (6); Taylor, Terry (26); Thomas, Roy (14); Trujillo, Michael (5); Walker, James (5).

EDMONTON—Banning, Jack (6); Bryden, Thomas (41); Buice, DeWayne (5); Chadwick, Ray (27); Clark, Terry (33); Cliburn, Stewart (16); Cook, Michael (15); Corbett, Douglas (10); Corbett, Sherman (41); Fischer, Todd (31); Fossas, Anthony (40); Lazorko, Jack (10); Lugo, Urbano (15); McCaskill, Kirk (1); Morlock, Allen (28); Rios, Jesus (3); Ruhle, Vernon (25); Shipanoff, David (11); Smith, David (23).

HAWAII—Boling, John (9); Citarella, Ralph (29); Clark, Bryan (19); Conley, Virgil (6); Davis, Joel (17); Hardy, John (23); Hickey, Kevin (43); Long, William (2); McKeon, Joel (19); McLaughlin, Joey (31); Nielsen, Scott (10); Patterson, Kenneth (3); Rasmussen, James (28); Scott, Timothy (18); Tatsuno, Derek (22); Thigpen, Robert (9); White, David (31).

LAS VEGAS—Bauer, Eric (2); Jones, James (4); Mills, Michael (6).

PHOENIX—Hickey, Kevin (3).

PORTLAND—Anderson, Allan (21); Bianchi, Ben (8); Bittiger, Jeffrey (26); Clemons, Mark (7); Forster, Terry (13); Gasser, Steven (6); Gomez, Stephen (23); Higgs, Darrell (16); Huffman, Phillip (9); Klink, Joseph (12); Latham, William (6); Musselman, Ronald (14); Niemann, Randal (32); Perry, Jeffrey (10); Smith, Leroy (24); Smithson, Mike (6); Trudeau, Kevin (13).

TACOMA—Akersfelds, Darrel (19); Belcher, Timothy (29); Birtsas, Timothy (10); Broersma, Eric (9); Brown, Curtis (7); Burns, Todd (21); Cadaret, Gregory (7); Caudill, William (28); Codiroli, Christopher (19); Dozier, Thomas (32); Kibler, Russell (3); Lamp, Dennis (6); Law, Joseph (2); Leiper, David (5); Mooneyham, William (7); Ontiveros, Steven (1); Plunk, Eric (24); Rijo, Jose (10); Tanner, Bruce (4); Von Ohlen, David (52).

TUCSON—Mack, Tony (4); Miner, James (6).

VANCOUVER—Copp, William (3); Madden, Morris (6).

GRAND SLAM HOME RUNS—Wine 3; Hamilton, Hengel, Keedy, 2 each; Forrester, Gainey, R. Johnson, G. Jones, Meadows, Reid, 1 each.

AWARDED FIRST BASE ON CATCHER'S INTERFERENCE—Hengel 4 (Fimple 3, Sinatro); Berra 2 (Fimple 2); Amelung (Narron); Casey (Burrell); Heath (Rodriguez); Cruz (Gomez); Householder (Fimple); C. Jones (Narron); Wellman (Rodriguez).

CLUB FIELDING

Club	Pct.	G.	PO.	A.	E.	DP.	PB.	Club	Pct.	G.	PO.	A.	E.	DP.	PB.
Tacoma	.975	143	3817	1627	142	139	14	Calgary	.971	141	3720	1571	158	154	25
Edmonton	.974	143	3622	1490	137	116	21	Portland	.970	141	3583	1409	153	131	19
Las Vegas	.972	143	3755	1619	154	149	23	Phoenix	.967	144	3745	1605	181	140	27
Vancouver	.972	144	3836	1619	157	134	35	Albuquerque	.965	143	3618	1621	191	136	37
Hawaii	.971	142	3575	1501	151	152	11	Tucson	.965	142	3683	1543	192	139	23

INDIVIDUAL FIELDING

°Throws lefthanded.

FIRST BASEMEN

Player and Club	Pct.	G.	PO.	A.	E.	DP.	Player and Club	Pct.	G.	PO.	A.	E.	DP.
P. Adams, Phoenix	1.000	17	133	8	0	11	Meadows, Tucson°	.943	7	30	3	2	4
R. Adams, Edmonton	1.000	4	23	1	0	2	Melendez, Phoenix°	.988	127	1019	86	13	98
Asadoor, Las Vegas	1.000	2	11	1	0	1	Merrifield, Edmonton	.996	29	221	20	1	23
Bailey, Tucson	1.000	2	9	0	0	1	Morhardt, Portland°	.983	22	161	12	3	12
Braun, Edmonton°	.989	70	614	38	7	70	Morman, Hawaii	.995	41	355	28	2	35
Buckley, Las Vegas	.975	11	73	5	2	5	Narron, Calgary°	.993	107	970	70	7	84
Bundy, Vancouver	1.000	2	19	1	0	1	Nelson, Calgary°	.993	107	970	70	7	84
Carpenter, Tucson°	.991	138	1186	101	12	115	Nixon, Calgary	1.000	1	1	0	0	0
Casey, Portland	1.000	4	24	1	0	4	Pankovits, Tucson	1.000	5	32	4	0	4
Clark, Tacoma	1.000	2	13	2	0	0	Parent, Las Vegas	.970	3	30	2	1	1
Cochrane, Hawaii	.979	6	40	6	1	4	Parsons, Las Vegas	.977	20	198	12	5	16
Corey, Portland	.988	10	78	5	1	9	Pederson, Albuquerque°	1.000	1	6	1	0	0
Debus, Albuquerque	.967	45	344	33	13	32	Pittaro, Portland	1.000	8	59	3	0	8
DISTEFANO, Vancouver°	.995	109	992	61	5	85	Pounders, Las Vegas	.996	49	442	28	2	48
Dugas, Albuquerque	1.000	1	10	0	0	0	Randall, Edmonton	1.000	1	1	0	0	0
Eppard, Edmonton°	.990	115	936	85	10	77	Reyes, Albuquerque	.984	11	57	4	1	9
Espinoza, Portland	1.000	1	10	2	0	0	Rodriguez, Las Vegas	1.000	2	8	1	0	2
Forrester, Hawaii°	.992	54	449	32	4	47	Rubel, Phoenix	1.000	6	42	3	0	8
Gainey, Tucson	.750	1	3	0	1	1	Ryal, Edmonton°	1.000	3	35	0	0	6
Gardenhire, Portland	.997	46	329	33	1	29	Sasser, Vancouver	1.000	1	1	0	0	0
Javier, Tacoma	.833	2	5	0	1	1	Sconiers, Hawaii°	.984	34	237	13	4	28
Johns, Vancouver	.993	18	133	5	1	19	See, Albuquerque	.988	65	608	42	8	62
Jones, Calgary	1.000	3	28	2	0	2	Smith, Calgary	.999	67	610	58	1	71
Keedy, Hawaii	.990	25	189	18	2	18	Steels, Las Vegas°	.974	4	34	3	1	2
Kingman, Phoenix	1.000	4	27	1	0	7	Tolentino, Tacoma°	.977	32	279	15	7	27
Krenchicki, Tacoma	1.000	4	24	2	0	4	Waller, Tucson	1.000	1	1	0	0	0
Kutcher, Phoenix	1.000	1	12	0	0	0	Wellman, Albuquerque	1.000	2	1	0	0	0
Lansford, Las Vegas	.984	67	566	39	10	55	Willard, Tacoma°	.980	5	47	2	1	7
Larkin, Portland	.981	21	189	22	4	23	J. Wilson, Portland	.985	43	287	39	5	30
Leeper, Vancouver°	.995	20	186	16	1	12	Wine, Tucson	1.000	4	2	0	0	1
Lindsey, Hawaii	1.000	1	0	1	0	1	Woodson, Albuquerque	.986	36	258	30	4	24

SECOND BASEMEN

Player and Club	Pct.	G.	PO.	A.	E.	DP.	Player and Club	Pct.	G.	PO.	A.	E.	DP.
Adams, Edmonton	1.000	3	4	5	0	1	Lyons, Hawaii	.982	16	18	38	1	8
Asadoor, Las Vegas	1.000	1	1	2	0	0	Miller, Phoenix	1.000	1	2	1	0	0
Berra, Tucson	.957	14	25	42	3	13	Miscik, Edmonton	.965	16	30	52	3	7
Biancalana, Tucson	.900	5	10	8	2	2	Pankovits, Tucson	1.000	13	22	28	0	3
Carrasco, Edmonton	.974	18	32	43	2	6	Pena, Tucson	.857	2	4	2	1	0
Coachman, Edmonton	.981	115	228	342	11	61	Perconte, Albuquerque	.976	108	214	350	14	70
Cora, Las Vegas	.980	81	186	249	9	59	Phillips, Tacoma	1.000	4	7	6	0	1
Crone, Tucson	.985	61	106	150	4	31	PITTARO, Portland	.982	109	202	287	9	59
Cruz, Albuquerque	.967	20	39	49	3	11	Reece, Tacoma	.994	38	74	105	1	24
deJesus, Phoenix	1.000	7	11	18	0	3	Renteria, Calgary	.986	31	57	89	2	24
Dugas, Albuquerque	.929	11	16	23	3	4	L. Roberts, Las Vegas	.991	45	96	128	2	27
Engram, Hawaii	1.000	1	1	2	0	1	Rodriguez, LV-Port	.912	29	48	77	12	15
Gallego, Tacoma	.976	10	15	25	1	9	Rohn, Tacoma	.979	72	126	206	7	37
Garcia, Las Vegas	.953	19	49	53	5	13	Rood, Tucson	.946	23	37	51	5	13
Gardenhire, Portland	1.000	8	15	14	0	6	Salinas, Hawaii	.988	36	71	100	2	22
Giles, Hawaii	.978	40	73	104	4	28	Taylor, Hawaii	1.000	1	1	0	0	0
Hill, Hawaii	1.000	7	11	11	0	1	Thomas, Phoenix	.921	16	20	38	5	4
Hinshaw, Albuquerque	.833	3	5	5	2	1	Verducci, Phoenix	.968	28	51	70	4	18
Hulett, Hawaii	.875	3	9	5	2	2	Washington, Vancouver	.944	8	19	15	2	6
Jimenez, Vancouver	.927	10	20	31	4	8	Wasinger, LV-Phx	.926	12	29	21	4	5
G. Jones, Tacoma	.995	38	79	106	1	19	Watters, Calgary	.964	106	234	350	22	80
R. Jones, Calgary	.959	11	24	23	2	7	Wellman, Albuquerque	.989	16	33	53	1	10
Krauss, Hawaii	.975	67	107	164	7	38	Wilfong, Phoenix	1.000	1	3	2	0	1
Kutcher, Phoenix	1.000	10	11	22	0	2	Williams, Phoenix	.933	1	6	8	1	3
Lind, Vancouver	.973	128	311	432	21	84	Woodard, Phx-Tuc	.965	88	193	242	16	58
Litton, Phoenix	.974	55	139	161	8	35	Wrona, Las Vegas	1.000	3	3	4	0	0

THIRD BASEMEN

Player and Club	Pct.	G.	PO.	A.	E.	DP.	Player and Club	Pct.	G.	PO.	A.	E.	DP.
P. Adams, Phoenix	.906	16	8	40	5	4	C. Martinez, Hawaii	.913	29	24	49	7	4
R. Adams, Edmonton	1.000	2	1	2	0	0	E. Martinez, Calgary	.949	125	91	278	20	31
Asadoor, Las Vegas	.907	37	29	68	10	3	McDougal, Portland	.900	3	2	7	1	0
Berra, Tucson	.900	86	47	179	25	14	Merrifield, Edm-Van	.909	99	63	136	20	12
Biancalana, Tucson	.923	4	5	7	1	1	Miller, Phoenix	.800	3	0	4	1	11
Bichette, Edmonton	.947	5	4	14	1	0	Miscik, Edmonton	.941	43	26	69	6	3
Carrasco, Edmonton	.947	10	4	14	1	3	Pankovits, Tucson	.870	9	5	15	3	1
Cochrane, Albuquerque	.876	40	20	72	13	6	Parent, Las Vegas	1.000	1	1	2	0	0
Debus, Albuquerque	.862	14	4	21	4	0	Pena, Tucson	.926	10	6	19	2	0
deJesus, Phoenix	1.000	4	2	8	0	0	Phillips, Tacoma	1.000	3	1	4	0	0
Espinoza, Portland	.972	15	9	26	1	0	Reece, Tacoma	.927	21	7	31	3	1
Dugas, Albuquerque	.931	35	20	47	5	4	Renteria, Calgary	.964	10	7	20	1	6
Garcia, Las Vegas	.906	63	39	106	15	7	L. Roberts, Las Vegas	.872	12	13	21	5	2
Gardenhire, Portland	.971	45	36	63	3	6	Rodriguez, LV-Port	.932	28	18	64	6	5
Giles, Hawaii	1.000	1	1	0	0	0	Rohn, Tacoma	1.000	2	1	1	0	0
Gonzalez, Vancouver	.925	111	76	232	25	22	Rood, Tucson	1.000	8	0	3	0	0
Hamilton, Albuquerque	.929	64	43	102	11	14	Sasser, Phoenix	.857	5	3	9	2	0
Howie, Tacoma	1.000	3	2	6	0	0	Sinatro, Tacoma	1.000	1	1	4	0	0
Hulett, Hawaii	.927	42	38	76	9	7	Thomas, Phoenix	.895	8	6	11	2	2
Jackson, Tucson	.824	38	16	59	16	8	Waller, Tucson	.929	6	4	9	1	3
Jimenez, Vancouver	1.000	1	1	1	0	0	Washington, Vancouver	.938	31	17	58	5	5
Ri. Jones, Tacoma	.926	81	56	132	15	17	Wasinger, LV-Phx	.956	27	14	51	3	5
Ro. Jones, Calgary	.957	9	6	16	1	0	Wellman, Albuquerque	.889	7	0	8	1	2
Keedy, Hawaii	1.000	7	5	6	0	1	Willard, Tacoma	1.000	5	5	8	0	2
Krauss, Hawaii	.896	24	10	33	5	2	Williams, Phoenix	.935	53	45	128	12	15
KRENCHICKI, Tacoma	.954	123	66	222	14	17	Woodard, Phx-Tuc	.933	13	7	21	2	4
Kutcher, Phoenix	.952	33	29	71	5	6	Woodson, Albuquerque	.888	40	27	60	11	5
Lyons, Hawaii	.977	16	13	29	1	5	Wrona, Las Vegas	.958	32	14	54	3	4

SHORTSTOPS

Player and Club	Pct.	G.	PO.	A.	E.	DP.	Player and Club	Pct.	G.	PO.	A.	E.	DP.
Adams, Edmonton	.967	23	39	49	3	10	Lyons, Hawaii	1.000	1	2	1	0	0
Allaire, Tucson	1.000	7	11	27	0	9	Martinez, Hawaii	.897	16	23	38	7	9
Anderson, Edmonton	.967	57	112	154	9	36	McDougal, Portland	.961	60	129	170	12	36
Asadoor, Las Vegas	1.000	2	2	0	0	0	Miller, Phoenix	.857	3	2	4	1	3
Berra, Tucson	.937	19	32	42	5	7	Miscik, Edmonton	.967	69	100	191	10	35
Biancalana, Tucson	1.000	5	5	14	0	1	Pankovits, Tucson	1.000	1	3	2	0	0
Cruz, Albuquerque	.932	11	20	21	3	8	Pena, Tucson	.966	59	108	151	9	36
deJesus, Phoenix	.933	7	11	17	2	5	Perconte, Albuquerque	.750	1	0	3	1	0
Diaz, Calgary	.958	107	195	280	21	67	Pittaro, Portland	1.000	5	14	8	0	3
Dugas, Albuquerque	.918	25	25	64	8	14	Reece, Tacoma	.937	53	78	145	15	26
Duncan, Albuquerque	.920	6	8	15	2	6	Renteria, Calgary	.939	28	46	78	8	16
Escobar, Phoenix	.937	127	200	378	39	71	Rodriguez, Las Vegas	.949	17	19	37	3	5
Espinoza, Portland	.948	74	139	208	19	38	Rohn, Tacoma	.953	22	32	50	4	13
Gardenhire, Portland	.952	6	4	16	1	2	Rood, Tucson	.950	29	60	74	7	21
Giles, Hawaii	.931	99	170	288	34	67	Schaefer, Albuquerque	.939	8	14	17	2	5
GREEN, Las Vegas	.973	106	164	306	13	75	Shipley, Albuquerque	.950	43	70	101	9	25
Jackson, Tucson	.956	25	21	65	4	12	Thon, Tucson	.899	14	22	40	7	9
Jimenez, Vancouver	.977	8	10	32	1	6	Verducci, Phoenix	.889	1	4	4	1	0
Jones, Calgary	.962	15	19	32	2	9	Washington, Vancouver	.958	27	48	89	6	22
Keedy, Hawaii	.960	21	34	63	4	9	Wasinger, Phoenix	1.000	1	1	2	0	0
Khalifa, Vancouver	.937	111	193	325	35	49	Weiss, Tacoma	.952	45	76	140	11	32
Krauss, Hawaii	1.000	2	3	4	0	0	Wellman, Albuquerque	.946	62	89	192	16	34
Kutcher, Phoenix	.788	6	10	16	7	2	Williams, Phoenix	.667	1	2	0	1	0
LeMaster, Tac-Haw	.954	54	78	152	11	33	Wrona, Las Vegas	.941	49	61	98	10	22
Litton, Phoenix	1.000	5	7	12	0	2							

OUTFIELDERS

Player and Club	Pct.	G.	PO.	A.	E.	DP.
Abner, Las Vegas	.984	104	238	9	4	1
Adams, Edmonton	1.000	5	9	0	0	0
Amelung, Edmonton°	.979	105	221	7	5	0
Armas, Edmonton	1.000	27	60	1	0	0
Asadoor, Las Vegas	.939	46	72	5	5	2
Beane, Portland	.968	119	259	15	9	5
Bichette, Edmonton	.956	56	165	7	8	2
Boston, Hawaii°	1.000	21	43	3	0	0
Brantley, Calgary	.875	2	6	1	1	0
Braun, Calgary	1.000	4	4	0	0	0
Brouhard, Edmonton	.977	21	42	0	1	0
Brown, Hawaii	.988	60	156	7	2	1
Bryant, Albuquerque	.921	64	103	13	10	1
Bullock, Tuc-Port°	.987	77	145	5	2	0
BYERS, Las Vegas°	.995	117	189	14	1	4
Casey, Portland	.977	23	41	2	1	1
Christensen, Calgary	.923	13	24	0	2	0
Clark, Tacoma	1.000	15	25	2	0	1
Cochrane, Hawaii	.981	31	46	5	1	2
Cockrell, Phoenix	.977	125	204	9	5	1
Corey, Portland	.944	8	16	1	1	0
Davis, Vancouver	.984	108	232	8	4	2
Devereaux, Albuquerque	1.000	3	4	1	0	0
Distefano, Vancouver°	.982	22	50	6	1	2
Dugas, Albuquerque	1.000	2	1	0	0	0
Dunbar, Vancouver°	.991	122	223	8	2	1
Engram, Hawaii	1.000	2	1	0	0	0
Eppard, Edmonton°	.917	9	11	0	1	0
Gainey, Tucson	.944	99	182	5	11	1
Gallagher, Calgary	.974	73	143	5	4	1
Gillaspie, Las Vegas	.963	86	122	9	5	3
Gonzalez, Albuquerque	.963	106	225	10	9	2
Graham, Phoenix°	1.000	12	30	0	0	0
Gwynn, Albuquerque°	.993	100	141	5	1	0
Hagen, Tucson	1.000	1	1	0	0	0
Haro, Vancouver	.970	60	90	7	3	0
Harper, Tacoma	.984	76	113	8	2	2
Harrison, Vancouver	.991	62	105	4	1	1
Henderson, Tacoma	.984	65	122	4	2	1
Hengel, Calgary	.945	105	180	10	11	1
Hinshaw, Albuquerque	.972	88	134	7	4	0
Householder, Tucson	.965	74	133	4	5	2
Howie, Tacoma	.984	35	59	3	1	1
Jackson, Tucson	1.000	19	42	0	0	0
James, Tucson°	.950	8	18	1	1	0
Javier, Tacoma	.955	13	21	0	1	0
Johnson, Tacoma	.983	70	113	5	2	1
C. Jones, Phoenix°	.985	72	127	5	2	2
G. Jones, Tacoma	.981	100	203	4	6	1
R. Jones, Calgary	1.000	6	9	0	0	0
Keedy, Hawaii	.957	41	66	0	3	0
Kelley, Tucson	1.000	1	1	0	0	0
King, Edmonton°	.960	15	24	0	1	0
Kutcher, Phoenix	.970	44	91	7	3	1
Lansford, Las Vegas	.909	6	10	0	1	0
Larkin, Portland	1.000	4	2	0	0	0
Lyons, Hawaii	.977	27	40	3	1	1
Mack, Las Vegas	.990	39	97	3	1	0
Marte, Portland°	1.000	33	53	1	0	0
Martinez, Hawaii	.943	36	62	4	4	0
Meadows, Tucson°	.978	112	222	5	5	2
Melendez, Phoenix°	.947	7	17	1	1	0
Milner, Phoenix°	1.000	16	38	0	0	0
Miscik, Edmonton	.895	12	15	2	2	0
Montgomery, Edmonton	.969	62	118	5	4	0
Morhardt, Portland°	.902	19	37	0	4	0
Morman, Hawaii	.982	35	55	0	1	0
Murphy, Tacoma	1.000	5	6	0	0	0
Nelson, Tacoma°	1.000	1	1	0	0	0
Nixon, Calgary	.966	73	167	1	6	0
Orsulak, Vancouver°	.968	37	58	2	2	1
Pankovits, Tucson	1.000	4	5	0	0	0
Parsons, Las Vegas	1.000	10	12	0	0	0
Pederson, Albuquerque°	.957	59	89	1	4	0
Pettis, Edmonton	.889	6	7	1	1	0
Polonia, Tacoma°	.967	14	28	1	1	1
Ramsey, Albuquerque°	.966	35	55	1	2	0
Reece, Tacoma	1.000	3	1	0	0	0
Reid, Phoenix°	.986	122	274	9	4	2
L. Roberts, Las Vegas	.975	20	38	1	1	1
E. Rodriguez, LV-Port	.943	24	31	2	2	0
R. Rodriguez, Tacoma	1.000	1	2	0	0	0
Ryal, Edmonton°	1.000	6	9	0	0	0
Salazar, Las Vegas	1.000	4	5	0	0	0
Salinas, Hawaii	1.000	2	1	1	0	0
Sanchez, Tacoma	.949	53	105	6	6	3
Simmons, Calgary	.963	14	25	1	1	1
Sinatro, Tacoma	1.000	1	1	0	0	0
Solano, Tucson	1.000	1	0	0	0	0
Steels, Las Vegas°	1.000	10	12	1	0	0
Stockstill, Phoenix	.941	14	15	1	1	0
Taylor, Hawaii	.991	69	111	2	1	1
Thompson, Hawaii	.667	1	2	0	1	0
Tillman, Phoenix	.946	52	99	6	6	0
A. Walker, Tuc-Van	.961	48	72	2	3	0
G. Walker, Portland	.962	47	72	3	3	1
Waller, Tucson	.952	54	78	2	4	0
Wasinger, Phoenix	1.000	1	1	0	0	0
Watters, Calgary	1.000	4	11	0	0	0
Weaver, Calgary°	.982	119	218	6	4	1
Willard, Tacoma	.917	18	22	0	2	0
K. Williams, Hawaii	.974	33	75	1	2	0
R. Williams, Albuquerque	.984	44	58	2	1	0
M. Wilson, Edmonton	.986	112	275	13	4	2
P. Wilson, Portland	.972	129	328	19	10	2
Wishnevski, Calgary°	.949	26	37	0	2	0
Woodard, Phx-Tuc	1.000	5	7	0	0	0
Yastrzemski, Hawaii	.974	110	208	19	6	2
Young, Tucson	.972	85	232	7	7	2

CATCHERS

Player and Club	Pct.	G.	PO.	A.	E.	DP.	PB.
Bailey, Tucson	.967	5	23	6	1	2	0
Baker, Vancouver	1.000	8	39	6	0	2	1
Bilardello, Vancouver	.982	35	186	30	4	0	9
Buckley, Las Vegas	.991	61	292	26	3	4	11
Burrell, Phoenix	.952	35	126	13	7	4	4
Butera, Portland	1.000	10	46	7	0	0	2
Stan Cliburn, Edmonton	.990	22	89	11	1	0	2
Debus, Albuquerque	.993	26	125	14	1	0	9
Dempsey, Portland	.970	65	300	23	10	2	5
Dorsett, Tacoma	.990	56	341	51	4	9	7
Fimple, Edmonton	.978	71	383	60	10	4	11
Firova, Calgary	.976	8	37	4	1	0	2
Gomez, Hawaii	.989	50	253	17	3	1	3
Gonzalez, Phoenix	1.000	8	31	3	0	0	2
Gwosdz, Calgary	.978	63	288	29	7	2	14
Harper, Tacoma	.945	10	50	2	3	0	2
Heath, Edmonton	.972	59	246	30	8	3	8
Karkovice, Hawaii	.976	23	108	13	3	5	3
Kearney, Tacoma	.977	22	149	21	4	4	1
Liddle, Portland	1.000	3	12	4	0	1	2
Lindsey, Hawaii	.986	14	61	8	1	2	1
Lopez, Tucson	.983	21	52	5	1	1	2
McElroy, Hawaii	1.000	12	55	1	0	0	0
Mercado, Albuquerque	.984	67	327	47	6	2	8
Narron, Calgary	.981	99	525	41	11	7	9
Nieto, Portland	.977	37	193	15	5	1	5
Ouellette, Phoenix	.987	55	259	34	4	4	6
PARENT, Las Vegas	.988	98	525	54	7	8	12
Reyes, Albuquerque	.974	70	357	62	11	6	20
Reynolds, Tucson	.974	69	297	40	9	2	4
Rodriguez, Vancouver	.982	86	524	69	11	11	22
Sasser, Phx-Van	.976	100	584	63	16	10	18
Sinatro, Tacoma	.972	62	368	46	12	4	2
Thompson, Hawaii	.996	54	227	28	1	7	4
Wiley, Las Vegas	1.000	1	1	0	0	0	0
Willard, Tacoma	.979	10	43	4	1	2	2
Williams, Portland	.983	37	151	18	3	4	5
Wine, Tucson	.982	72	346	32	7	4	17

PITCHERS

Player and Club	Pct.	G.	PO.	A.	E.	DP.
Agosto, Tucson°	.952	44	8	12	1	1
Akerfelds, Tacoma	1.000	19	7	19	0	1
Anderson, Portland°	.933	19	7	21	2	0
Asadoor, Las Vegas	1.000	5	1	0	0	0
Banning, Edmonton	1.000	6	0	2	0	0
Bauer, Las Vegas°	.500	2	0	1	1	0
Belcher, Tacoma	.900	29	12	15	3	1
Berra, Tucson	1.000	1	0	1	0	0
Best, Calgary	1.000	27	1	3	0	0
Bielecki, Vancouver	.939	26	12	19	2	1
Birtsas, Tacoma°	.909	10	1	9	1	1
Bitker, Las Vegas	.818	36	7	20	4	0
Bittiger, Portland	.911	26	17	24	4	3
Blount, Las Vegas°	1.000	18	5	19	0	0

PITCHERS—Continued

Player and Club	Pct.	G.	PO.	A.	E.	DP.
Bockus, Phoenix	.931	36	10	17	2	2
Boling, Hawaii*	1.000	9	0	3	0	0
Brantley, Phoenix	1.000	29	10	23	0	1
Brennan, Albuquerque	.965	28	19	36	2	4
Broersma, Tacoma	1.000	9	0	1	0	1
C. Brown, Tacoma	1.000	7	0	3	0	0
M. Brown, Calgary	.971	22	7	26	1	0
Bryden, Edmonton	.929	41	2	11	1	0
Buckley, Las Vegas	1.000	2	0	1	0	1
Buice, Edmonton	1.000	5	0	1	0	0
Burns, Tacoma	1.000	21	1	4	0	0
Burtt, Albuquerque	.964	31	15	38	2	4
Cadaret, Tacoma*	1.000	7	0	3	0	0
Campbell, Calgary	.917	24	6	16	2	2
Caudill, Tacoma	1.000	28	1	5	0	1
Chadwick, Edmonton	.769	27	6	14	6	1
Childress, Tucson	1.000	33	2	8	0	0
Christiansen, Port-Tuc	1.000	32	9	14	0	2
Citarella, Hawaii	.917	29	3	8	1	0
B. Clark, Hawaii*	.970	19	7	25	1	2
T. Clark, Edmonton	.952	33	14	26	2	0
Clarke, Calgary*	.875	31	1	13	2	0
Clay, Portland	.929	16	7	6	1	3
Clemons, Portland	.909	7	2	8	1	2
Stew. Cliburn, Edmonton	1.000	16	3	2	0	0
Cocanower, Albuquerque	.846	35	6	27	6	4
Codiroli, Tacoma	.727	19	2	6	3	1
Comstock, Phoenix*	1.000	17	5	5	0	1
Conley, Hawaii*	.500	6	0	1	1	1
D. Cook, Phoenix*	1.000	12	2	15	0	1
M. Cook, Edmonton	1.000	15	8	6	0	0
Copp, Vancouver*	.500	3	0	1	1	0
Corbell, Phoenix	.938	30	12	18	2	4
D. Corbett, Edmonton	.857	10	4	2	1	0
S. Corbett, Edmonton*	1.000	41	3	7	0	3
Costello, Las Vegas	1.000	12	2	8	0	0
Crews, Albuquerque	.909	42	4	6	1	1
Davis, Hawaii	.957	17	10	12	1	2
Dozier, Tacoma	.864	32	10	9	3	1
Drummond, Vancouver	.875	46	2	5	1	0
Dunne, Vancouver	1.000	9	3	11	0	0
Easley, Vancouver	1.000	9	3	4	0	0
Edwards, Alb-Tuc*	1.000	26	3	6	0	0
Fansler, Vancouver	.967	25	9	20	1	1
Ferran, Phoenix	.955	40	9	12	1	0
Ferreira, Calgary*	.889	32	6	10	2	1
Fischer, Edmonton	1.000	31	5	9	0	0
Fontenot, Tucson*	1.000	17	3	7	0	0
Ford, Las Vegas	.950	43	2	17	1	1
Forster, Portland*	1.000	13	2	6	0	1
Fossas, Edmonton*	.971	40	7	27	1	0
Funk, Tucson*	.889	39	0	8	1	0
Gardenhire, Portland	1.000	2	0	1	0	0
Gasser, Portland	.500	6	0	1	1	0
Gomez, Portland	1.000	23	5	3	0	0
Gorman, LV-Port*	.933	30	7	7	1	2
Grant, Phoenix	.833	3	1	4	1	0
Guetterman, Calgary*	1.000	16	2	9	0	3
Hagen, Port-Tuc	.935	35	8	21	2	0
Hammaker, Phoenix*	1.000	3	3	1	0	0
Hanson, Calgary	1.000	8	2	6	0	0
Hardy, Hawaii	.909	22	1	9	1	2
Hartley, Albuquerque	1.000	2	2	0	0	0
Havens, Albuquerque*	1.000	3	1	1	0	0
Hayward, Las Vegas*	.947	23	10	26	2	4
Heathcock, Tucson	.976	22	16	25	1	2
Heredia, Albuquerque	.857	50	9	9	3	1
Hernandez, Tucson	.833	9	5	5	2	0
Heuer, Albuquerque	1.000	1	0	1	0	0
Hickey, Haw-Phx*	1.000	46	1	13	0	0
Higgs, Portland	1.000	16	0	3	0	0
Hillegas, Albuquerque	.974	24	10	28	1	2
Howell, Albuquerque	1.000	2	1	1	0	0
Huffman, Portland	1.000	9	0	1	0	0
Johnson, Vancouver	.894	23	10	32	5	2
B. Jones, Vancouver	1.000	20	1	3	0	0
J. Jones, Las Vegas	1.000	4	5	5	0	2
Kelley, Tucson	.979	31	14	33	1	4
Kelly, Calgary	1.000	6	1	5	0	0
Kerfeld, Tucson	.750	32	3	3	2	0
Kibler, Tacoma	1.000	3	3	1	0	0
Kipper, Vancouver*	1.000	6	2	2	0	0
Klink, Portland*	1.000	12	4	2	0	0
Kramer, Vancouver	.500	10	1	1	1	0
Krawczyk, Hawaii	.952	35	8	12	1	0
Krueger, Tac-Alb*	.964	24	5	22	1	3
Kyles, Tacoma	.972	38	10	25	1	3
Ladd, Albuquerque	1.000	35	1	2	0	0
Lamp, Tacoma	1.000	6	3	3	0	1
Latham, Portland*	1.000	6	4	4	0	0
Lazorko, Edmonton	.882	10	5	10	2	1
Law, Tacoma	.667	2	1	1	1	0
Leeper, Vancouver*	1.000	21	1	6	0	0
Leiper, Vancouver	1.000	5	0	2	0	0
Livingston, Albuquerque*	.917	56	6	16	2	0
Long, Hawaii	.750	2	2	1	1	1
Lugo, Edmonton	1.000	15	7	15	0	1
Madden, Vancouver*	.500	6	0	1	1	0
Mallicoat, Tucson*	1.000	2	1	1	0	0
Mason, Phoenix	1.000	10	6	6	0	0
Mathis, Tucson	.929	23	12	14	2	0
Mayberry, Albuquerque	1.000	6	0	4	0	0
McCaskill, Edmonton	1.000	1	1	2	0	0
McKeon, Hawaii*	1.000	19	2	12	0	0
McKnight, Phoenix	.889	12	3	5	1	1
McLaughlin, Hawaii	1.000	31	8	10	0	1
Meads, Tucson*	1.000	10	1	0	0	0
Medvin, Phx-Van	.667	13	1	1	1	0
Meeks, Alb-Tac	.952	33	6	34	2	2
Mills, Las Vegas	1.000	6	1	0	0	0
Miner, Tucson	1.000	6	1	2	0	0
Montalvo, Tucson	.909	59	8	22	3	3
Monteleone, Calgary	.938	51	0	15	1	2
Mooneyham, Tacoma	1.000	7	2	2	0	0
Morlock, Edmonton	.977	28	13	30	1	3
Mulholland, Phoenix*	.907	37	7	32	4	2
Musselman, Portland	.950	14	10	9	1	1
Nielsen, Hawaii	1.000	10	5	12	0	3
Niemann, Portland*	.962	32	5	20	1	3
Noble, Tucson*	1.000	2	1	0	0	0
Ontiveros, Tacoma	1.000	1	1	1	0	0
Palacios, Vancouver	.967	27	5	24	1	1
Parker, Calgary	.963	12	5	21	1	1
K. Patterson, Hawaii*	1.000	3	0	1	0	0
R. Patterson, Vancouver*	1.000	14	2	4	0	0
Pena, Vancouver*	1.000	27	2	9	0	0
Perlman, Phoenix	.966	52	10	18	1	0
Perry, Portland	1.000	10	5	5	0	1
Plunk, Tacoma	1.000	24	0	5	0	0
Portugal, Portland	.842	17	5	11	3	0
Poston, Las Vegas	1.000	45	5	15	0	2
Powell, Calgary*	.944	20	7	27	2	4
Price, Phoenix*	1.000	17	1	7	0	1
Puikunas, Phoenix*	.750	24	2	1	1	0
Rasmussen, Hawaii	1.000	28	5	10	0	2
Rijo, Tacoma	.917	9	2	9	1	1
Rios, Edmonton	1.000	3	0	4	0	0
P. Roberts, Las Vegas*	1.000	6	1	2	0	0
RODRIGUEZ, Tacoma*	1.000	21	10	24	0	3
Ross, Vancouver	.958	32	5	18	1	0
Ruhle, Edmonton	.938	25	8	7	1	1
Savage, Albuquerque	.667	13	1	1	1	0
Schneider, Calgary	.905	50	6	13	2	3
Schuler, Phoenix*	1.000	15	1	4	0	0
Schweighoffer, Albuquerque	.933	17	2	12	1	0
Scott, Hawaii	1.000	18	1	2	0	0
Scurry, Phoenix*	.833	28	2	8	2	0
Searage, Hawaii*	1.000	3	0	1	0	0
Shields, Portland	.778	16	4	3	2	0
Shipanoff, Edmonton	1.000	11	1	1	0	0
Simmons, Las Vegas	.950	75	8	11	1	1
Siwy, Las Vegas	1.000	36	6	11	0	0
D. Smith, Edmonton	1.000	12	4	1	0	1
L. Smith, Portland	.972	24	12	23	1	1
Smithson, Portland	.909	6	4	6	1	0
Snyder, Las Vegas*	.824	39	4	10	3	3
Solano, Tucson	.941	42	6	10	1	1
Swift, Calgary	1.000	5	5	4	0	4
Tanner, Tacoma	.833	4	2	3	1	0
Tatsuno, Hawaii*	.875	22	1	6	1	0
D. Taylor, Vancouver	.800	9	1	3	1	0
T. Taylor, Calgary	.868	25	14	19	5	1
Thigpen, Hawaii	1.000	9	10	7	0	3
Thomas, Calgary	1.000	14	3	5	0	1
Trudeau, Portland	1.000	13	4	4	0	0
Trujillo, Calgary	.889	5	1	7	1	1
VON OHLEN, Tacoma*	1.000	52	7	27	0	2
Vosberg, Las Vegas*	.872	34	8	33	6	2
Walker, Calgary	1.000	5	5	7	0	2
Ward, Phx-LV*	1.000	15	2	7	0	0
White, Hawaii	.979	31	17	29	1	3
Wojna, Las Vegas	.840	18	7	14	4	0

The following players do not have any recorded accepted chances at the positions indicated; therefore, are not listed in the fielding averages for those particular positions: Beane, 1b; Bianchi, p; Burroughs, p; Carpenter, of; Cochrane, p; Cora, ss; R. Davis, p; Dugas, p; Garcia, of; Harper, p; Hinshaw, 3b; Karkovice, of; Khalifa, of; Krauss, c; Lansford, 3b; Leeper, of; Mack, p; McKnight, of; Miller, p; Parent, of; Pederson, p; Reece, p; Reed, p; Reyes, p; Reynolds, 1b; Ru. Rodriguez, p; Rood, of; Rubel, 3b; See, 3b; Tolentino, p; Verducci, p; Waller, p; Wellman, c; Wrona, of.

CLUB PITCHING

Club	ERA	G	CG	ShO	Sv	IP	H	R	ER	HR	HB	BB	Int. BB	SO	WP	Bk.
Vancouver	3.30	144	33	16	34	1278.2	1143	573	469	68	43	617	24	895	70	15
Tacoma	3.78	143	14	7	29	1272.1	1171	616	535	68	37	692	29	919	92	17
Calgary	3.94	141	20	5	36	1240.0	1171	655	543	78	23	675	40	810	83	17
Tucson	4.22	142	11	7	28	1227.2	1307	703	575	59	24	524	33	689	82	13
Phoenix	4.55	144	14	2	39	1248.1	1360	757	631	84	35	588	26	761	76	30
Las Vegas	4.60	143	11	4	33	1251.2	1297	722	640	86	49	713	52	793	92	30
Albuquerque	4.65	143	23	8	31	1206.0	1258	753	623	80	32	656	19	788	136	13
Hawaii	4.86	142	20	11	32	1191.2	1298	716	643	104	33	525	41	651	58	12
Edmonton	5.00	143	24	8	22	1207.1	1271	758	671	117	47	616	60	676	60	11
Portland	5.06	141	27	3	15	1184.1	1297	779	666	91	39	590	33	644	72	18

PITCHERS' RECORDS
(Leading Qualifiers for Earned-Run Average Leadership — 115 or More Innings)

*Throws lefthanded.

Pitcher—Club	W	L	Pct.	ERA	G	GS	CG	GF	ShO	Sv	IP	H	R	ER	HR	HB	BB	Int. BB	SO	WP
Palacios, Vancouver	13	5	.722	2.58	27	26	7	0	5	0	185.0	140	63	53	10	5	85	1	148	5
Campbell, Calgary	15	2	.882	2.66	24	23	4	1	1	0	162.2	136	65	48	9	1	72	2	130	11
Hayward, Las Vegas*	8	5	.615	3.10	23	22	0	0	0	0	142.1	139	56	49	6	4	79	1	115	18
Christiansen, 13 Port-19 Tuc	8	9	.471	3.23	32	21	1	1	0	0	128.0	129	64	46	9	5	64	6	57	6
Hillegas, Albuquerque	13	5	.722	3.37	24	23	4	0	1	0	165.2	172	79	62	4	0	64	1	105	7
Bittiger, Portland	12	10	.545	3.40	26	24	9	2	2	0	180.0	171	84	68	13	2	57	2	94	9
Heathcock, Tucson	11	6	.647	3.47	22	22	6	0	2	0	142.2	145	67	55	8	1	28	1	71	3
Johnson, Vancouver	8	10	.444	3.51	23	22	9	1	2	0	153.2	133	74	60	9	10	68	0	76	8
B. Clark, Hawaii*	4	10	.286	3.53	19	18	3	0	1	0	122.1	113	58	48	7	3	56	3	64	9
Akerfelds, Tacoma	10	3	.769	3.54	19	19	3	0	0	0	129.2	117	52	51	9	4	57	1	84	9

Departmental Leaders: G—Simmons, 75; W—Campbell, 15; L—Monteleone, 13; Pct.—Campbell, .882; GS—Mulholland, 29; CG—Bittiger, Johnson, 9; GF—Simmons, 57; ShO—Palacios, 5; Sv.—Simmons, 22; IP—Palacios, 185.0; H—White, 214; R—Mulholland, 124; ER—Mulholland, White, 97; HR—Morlock, 22; HB—Brantley, Bryden, Fansler, 11; BB—Belcher, 133; IBB—Simmons, 16; SO—Palacios, 148; WP—Cocanower, 32.

(All Pitchers—Listed Alphabetically)

Pitcher—Club	W	L	Pct.	ERA	G	GS	CG	GF	ShO	Sv	IP	H	R	ER	HR	HB	BB	Int. BB	SO	WP
Agosto, Tucson*	4	2	.667	1.98	44	0	0	24	0	7	50.0	48	16	11	1	2	19	2	31	4
Akerfelds, Tacoma	10	3	.769	3.54	19	19	3	0	0	0	129.2	117	52	51	9	4	57	1	84	9
Anderson, Portland*	4	8	.333	5.60	19	15	3	3	0	0	98.0	127	77	61	9	1	49	4	45	5
Asadoor, Las Vegas	0	0	.000	0.00	3	0	0	2	0	0	5.1	4	0	0	0	1	1	0	4	1
Banning, Edmonton	0	0	.000	5.58	6	0	3	0	0	0	9.2	12	8	6	0	0	11	1	4	0
Bauer, Las Vegas*	0	1	.000	9.82	2	2	0	0	0	0	7.1	11	8	8	1	1	9	0	7	1
Belcher, Tacoma	9	11	.450	4.42	29	28	2	0	1	0	163.0	143	89	80	8	1	133	2	136	8
Berra, Tucson	0	0	.000	135.00	1	0	0	1	0	0	.1	4	5	5	0	0	2	0	0	1
Best, Calgary	2	6	.250	4.34	27	0	0	17	0	5	37.1	34	23	18	5	0	27	4	35	4
Bianchi, Portland	0	0	.000	9.28	8	0	0	6	0	1	10.2	9	13	11	2	2	16	0	9	0
Bielecki, Portland	12	10	.545	3.78	26	26	3	0	3	0	181.0	194	89	76	12	5	78	3	140	12
Birtsas, Tacoma*	7	2	.778	3.12	10	10	2	0	1	0	66.1	46	26	23	1	1	54	0	50	3
Bitker, Las Vegas	11	9	.550	4.83	36	27	3	2	0	1	160.1	184	97	86	14	7	79	1	80	9
Bittiger, Portland	12	10	.545	3.40	26	24	9	2	2	0	180.0	171	84	68	13	2	57	2	94	9
Blount, Las Vegas*	4	8	.333	5.93	18	15	2	1	1	0	82.0	110	61	54	10	3	37	1	44	4
Bockus, Phoenix	7	5	.583	4.49	36	13	2	19	0	7	108.1	133	60	54	7	2	41	4	64	4
Boling, Hawaii*	0	0	.000	3.97	9	0	0	2	0	0	11.1	8	5	5	2	1	7	2	6	3
Brantley, Phoenix	6	11	.353	4.65	29	28	2	0	0	0	170.1	187	110	88	13	11	82	3	111	5
Brennan, Albuquerque	10	9	.526	4.31	28	28	4	0	1	0	171.1	188	95	82	9	7	67	0	95	20
Broersma, Tacoma	0	1	.000	5.40	9	0	0	5	0	2	20.0	25	13	12	0	1	8	0	21	0
C. Brown, Tacoma	1	1	.500	3.00	7	0	0	6	0	0	12.0	15	4	4	1	0	0	0	5	0
M. Brown, Calgary	10	2	.833	4.25	22	19	3	1	0	0	125.0	117	68	59	9	2	62	3	63	3
Bryden, Edmonton	9	1	.900	6.35	41	1	0	26	0	2	72.1	75	52	51	7	11	47	7	53	6
Buckley, Las Vegas	0	0	.000	0.00	2	0	0	2	0	0	3.0	2	0	0	0	0	1	0	1	0
Buice, Edmonton	1	1	.500	1.08	5	0	0	4	0	2	8.1	4	5	1	0	0	7	1	7	0
Burns, Tacoma	2	2	.500	4.88	21	0	0	10	0	0	27.2	27	16	15	3	0	16	1	30	0
Burroughs, Calgary*	0	0	.000	13.50	2	0	0	0	0	0	2.0	5	3	3	0	0	1	0	2	1
Burtt, Albuquerque	9	8	.529	4.71	31	27	5	1	2	0	153.0	172	96	80	12	3	85	0	103	19
Cadaret, Tacoma*	1	2	.333	3.46	7	0	0	4	0	1	13.0	5	6	5	1	0	13	1	12	0
Campbell, Calgary	15	2	.882	2.66	24	23	4	1	1	0	162.2	136	65	48	9	1	72	2	130	11
Caudill, Tacoma	1	4	.200	2.57	28	0	0	21	0	7	35.0	32	17	10	0	0	16	1	35	1
Chadwick, Edmonton	7	10	.412	5.86	27	25	2	2	0	0	147.1	151	106	96	17	2	114	5	88	10
Childress, Tucson	3	3	.500	3.80	33	0	0	23	0	7	42.2	49	23	18	1	0	19	1	23	2
Christiansen, 13 Port-19 Tuc	8	9	.471	3.23	32	21	1	10	0	0	128.0	129	64	46	9	5	64	6	57	6
Citarella, Hawaii	3	8	.273	5.18	29	8	0	16	0	8	64.1	63	40	37	6	4	27	0	47	5
B. Clark, Hawaii*	4	10	.286	3.53	19	18	3	0	1	0	122.1	113	58	48	7	3	56	3	64	9
T. Clark, Edmonton	8	9	.471	3.84	33	20	5	6	1	4	154.2	140	79	66	13	7	56	8	88	4
Clarke, Calgary*	4	4	.500	2.92	31	2	1	10	0	2	64.2	46	23	21	4	3	34	8	42	2
Clay, Portland	1	5	.167	6.95	16	8	0	4	0	1	55.2	67	46	43	3	3	45	1	30	5
Clemons, Portland	0	2	.000	6.31	7	3	0	2	0	0	25.2	34	21	18	2	1	13	0	4	1
Cliburn, Edmonton	1	0	1.000	2.30	16	0	0	13	0	8	15.2	10	4	4	0	0	6	0	10	1
Cocanower, Albuquerque	7	8	.467	6.35	35	21	2	6	0	0	119.0	119	104	84	7	9	109	2	50	32
Cochrane, Hawaii	1	1	.500	7.15	8	1	0	6	0	0	11.1	15	9	9	0	0	11	0	6	1
Codiroli, Tacoma	2	7	.222	6.12	19	18	1	0	0	0	67.2	77	56	46	7	3	52	1	34	6
Comstock, Phoenix*	4	2	.667	2.77	17	1	0	7	0	2	39.0	24	12	12	0	0	23	0	35	1
Conley, Hawaii*	1	0	1.000	0.84	6	0	0	3	0	0	10.2	9	1	1	0	0	3	1	3	0
D. Cook, Phoenix*	2	5	.286	5.23	12	11	1	0	0	0	62.0	72	45	36	8	1	26	2	24	4
M. Cook, Phoenix	4	7	.364	6.48	15	15	4	0	2	0	83.1	81	64	60	8	1	54	1	54	12
Copp, Vancouver*	1	2	.333	5.73	3	3	0	0	0	0	11.0	18	10	7	0	1	4	0	6	0
Corbell, Phoenix	9	7	.563	4.80	30	28	3	0	1	0	172.1	212	109	92	10	5	48	2	81	4
D. Corbett, Edmonton	1	1	.500	1.69	10	0	0	3	0	0	21.1	22	5	4	2	0	11	3	9	0
S. Corbett, Edmonton*	6	6	.500	5.50	41	1	0	18	0	0	55.2	61	37	34	4	1	49	7	29	5
Costello, Las Vegas	3	5	.375	5.86	12	12	1	0	0	0	58.1	60	43	38	2	0	42	3	28	7
Crews, Albuquerque	7	2	.778	3.63	42	0	0	31	0	12	72.0	73	34	29	5	0	25	4	60	6
J. Davis, Hawaii	6	7	.462	3.71	17	16	4	1	1	0	111.2	90	54	46	8	1	45	0	52	4
R. Davis, Albuquerque	0	1	.000	4.82	7	0	0	2	0	0	9.1	6	6	5	1	2	7	0	8	0
Dozier, Tacoma	12	7	.632	3.95	32	19	0	7	0	0	152.2	153	80	67	10	1	90	0	117	17

Pitcher—Club	W.	L.	Pct.	ERA.	G.	GS.	CG.	GF.	ShO.	Sv.	IP.	H.	R.	ER.	HR.	HB.	BB.	Int. BB.	SO.	WP.
Drummond, Vancouver	2	6	.250	2.97	46	0	0	32	0	10	63.2	62	35	21	2	4	43	5	49	3
Dugas, Albuquerque	0	0	.000	0.00	2	0	0	2	0	0	2.0	1	0	0	0	0	0	0	1	0
Dunne, Vancouver	3	5	.375	1.76	9	9	3	0	1	0	61.1	61	21	12	2	2	23	1	41	1
Easley, Vancouver	2	2	.500	3.81	9	3	1	6	0	3	28.1	20	16	12	1	1	19	3	17	0
Edwards, 6 Alb-20 Tuc°	3	4	.429	4.85	26	10	1	5	0	0	68.2	59	45	37	3	2	50	2	43	9
Fansler, Vancouver	12	7	.632	3.80	25	25	4	0	1	0	161.0	138	76	68	5	11	107	0	77	17
Ferran, Phoenix	4	5	.444	4.19	40	1	0	9	0	1	73.0	81	40	34	3	3	37	3	51	2
Ferreira, Calgary°	2	5	.286	6.72	32	12	0	8	0	1	88.1	95	73	66	8	3	66	3	50	8
Fischer, Edmonton	5	6	.455	6.85	31	0	0	18	0	5	44.2	52	34	34	8	1	36	9	28	3
Fontenot, Tucson°	1	3	.250	6.75	17	8	0	2	0	1	52.0	67	50	39	4	2	22	0	24	6
Ford, Las Vegas	2	2	.500	6.46	43	1	0	12	0	0	85.0	100	69	61	8	4	63	6	41	7
Forster, Portland°	0	1	.000	7.27	13	0	0	5	0	0	17.1	25	16	14	0	1	18	1	3	1
Fossas, Edmonton°	6	8	.429	4.99	40	15	1	9	0	0	117.1	152	76	65	8	8	29	7	54	8
Funk, Tucson°	2	4	.333	4.99	39	3	0	9	0	1	61.1	79	49	34	5	0	27	3	35	7
Gardenhire, Portland	0	0	.000	9.00	2	0	0	2	0	0	4.0	8	5	4	1	0	1	0	0	0
Gasser, Portland	1	4	.200	8.27	6	6	0	0	0	0	20.2	21	25	19	1	0	37	1	18	12
Gomez, Portland	2	3	.400	5.91	23	0	0	17	0	4	32.0	37	22	21	2	0	19	5	11	4
Gorman, 1 LV-29 Port°	1	4	.200	3.02	30	1	0	22	0	5	44.2	37	19	15	3	2	25	8	22	7
Grant, Phoenix	2	1	.667	3.13	3	3	2	0	0	0	23.0	20	8	8	2	1	5	0	12	0
Guetterman, Calgary°	5	1	.833	2.86	16	2	1	5	0	1	44.0	41	14	14	1	1	17	1	29	3
Hagen, 3 Port-32 Tuc	8	6	.571	4.84	35	20	2	6	1	0	137.2	141	78	74	6	7	73	2	75	10
Hammaker, Phoenix°	1	2	.333	4.15	3	3	0	0	0	0	17.1	19	9	8	1	1	6	0	8	0
Hanson, Calgary	1	3	.250	3.61	8	7	0	0	0	0	47.1	38	23	19	4	2	21	0	43	2
Hardy, Hawaii	3	5	.375	3.40	22	0	0	15	0	3	39.2	35	16	15	3	2	18	4	31	2
Harper, Tacoma	0	0	.000	3.00	1	0	0	1	0	0	3.0	3	1	1	0	0	1	0	1	1
Hartley, Albuquerque	0	1	.000	6.75	2	0	0	0	0	0	2.2	5	3	2	0	0	3	1	3	0
Havens, Albuquerque°	0	1	.000	5.14	3	2	0	0	0	0	7.0	5	5	4	0	1	7	0	3	2
Hayward, Las Vegas°	8	5	.615	3.10	23	22	0	0	0	0	142.1	139	56	49	6	4	79	1	115	18
Heathcock, Tucson	11	6	.647	3.47	22	22	6	0	2	0	142.2	145	67	55	8	1	28	1	71	3
Heredia, Albuquerque	3	4	.429	4.22	50	3	0	18	0	4	98.0	90	56	46	8	0	61	1	75	5
Hernandez, Tucson	3	2	.600	3.00	9	9	0	0	0	0	54.0	42	21	18	2	0	15	2	42	0
Heuer, Albuquerque	1	0	1.000	0.00	1	0	0	0	0	0	2.0	2	0	0	0	0	1	0	2	1
Hickey, 43 Haw-3 Phx°	4	5	.444	5.01	46	4	0	18	0	8	82.2	88	52	46	8	1	36	4	48	3
Higgs, Portland	1	3	.250	4.40	16	0	0	10	0	3	28.2	24	14	14	0	1	18	2	21	0
Hillegas, Albuquerque	13	5	.722	3.37	24	24	4	0	1	0	165.2	172	79	62	4	0	64	1	105	7
Howell, Albuquerque	1	0	1.000	0.00	2	2	0	0	0	0	13.0	6	1	0	0	0	7	0	13	1
Huffman, Portland	1	2	.333	9.37	9	2	0	4	0	0	16.1	27	17	17	4	0	12	0	13	0
Johnson, Vancouver	8	10	.444	3.51	23	22	9	1	2	0	153.2	133	74	60	9	10	68	0	76	8
B. Jones, Vancouver	1	2	.333	3.20	20	0	0	20	0	11	25.1	21	9	9	2	0	14	1	27	0
J. Jones, Las Vegas	2	0	1.000	5.92	4	4	1	0	0	0	24.1	24	16	16	1	0	8	0	11	3
Kelley, Tucson	6	8	.429	5.20	31	27	2	0	2	0	159.1	189	99	92	8	2	63	2	62	4
Kelly, Calgary	2	1	.667	4.00	6	4	0	2	0	0	27.0	23	13	12	1	0	18	0	14	0
Kerfeld, Tucson	4	4	.500	4.74	32	3	0	12	0	4	62.2	61	36	33	3	1	27	2	59	8
Kibler, Tacoma	0	0	.000	11.81	3	0	0	1	0	0	5.1	7	7	7	1	0	3	0	1	0
Kipper, Vancouver°	0	2	.000	1.78	6	2	0	2	0	1	25.1	23	7	5	2	0	4	1	22	1
Klink, Portland°	0	0	.000	4.30	12	0	0	7	0	0	23.0	25	14	11	1	0	13	1	14	1
Kramer, Vancouver	0	0	.000	6.11	11	1	0	1	0	0	17.2	16	14	12	2	0	19	1	16	3
Krawczyk, Hawaii	11	6	.647	4.13	35	13	1	14	0	3	120.0	124	59	55	9	3	38	5	78	5
Krueger, 10 Tac-14 Alb°	9	7	.563	4.06	24	24	6	0	2	0	146.1	158	74	66	5	5	66	2	97	11
Kyles, Portland	7	4	.636	4.13	38	6	1	17	0	1	93.2	99	54	43	3	5	44	4	43	11
Ladd, Albuquerque	4	2	.667	6.42	35	0	0	16	0	4	47.2	61	40	34	4	3	21	2	43	6
Lamp, Tacoma	1	0	1.000	2.92	6	0	0	2	0	0	12.1	9	4	4	0	1	8	0	10	0
Latham, Portland°	0	5	.000	8.69	6	6	0	0	0	0	29.0	45	31	28	1	2	13	1	12	1
Law, Tacoma	0	1	.000	2.57	2	1	0	0	0	0	7.0	4	5	2	1	0	4	0	7	0
Lazorko, Edmonton	8	1	.889	3.50	10	10	4	0	1	0	69.1	63	32	27	3	2	32	1	35	1
Leeper, Vancouver°	3	4	.429	5.10	21	0	0	11	0	2	42.1	43	30	24	4	0	20	1	22	1
Leiper, Tacoma°	0	0	.000	0.00	5	0	0	5	0	1	9.0	3	0	0	0	1	0	6	0	
Livingston, Albuquerque°	4	7	.364	5.94	56	0	0	27	0	7	72.2	66	53	48	7	0	64	4	59	15
Long, Hawaii	2	0	1.000	4.15	2	2	0	0	0	0	13.0	15	7	6	0	0	4	0	6	0
Lugo, Edmonton	4	3	.571	3.67	15	14	4	0	2	0	90.2	89	46	37	8	2	46	2	47	0
Mack, Tucson	0	1	.000	4.26	4	0	0	1	0	0	6.1	10	3	3	2	0	3	0	8	0
Madden, Vancouver°	0	0	.000	8.59	6	0	0	3	0	0	7.1	8	8	7	0	1	10	1	4	3
Mallicoat, Tucson°	0	0	.000	3.72	2	2	0	0	0	0	9.2	9	5	4	0	0	7	0	8	2
Mason, Phoenix	5	1	.833	4.13	10	10	1	0	0	0	61.0	62	34	28	4	0	20	0	49	5
Mathis, Tucson	10	7	.588	3.60	23	21	1	1	1	0	132.2	133	67	53	7	3	42	3	85	11
Mayberry, Albuquerque	0	3	.000	8.41	6	5	0	0	0	0	20.1	18	19	19	1	1	17	0	14	2
McCaskill, Edmonton	1	0	1.000	3.00	1	1	0	0	0	0	6.0	3	2	2	0	0	4	0	4	0
McKeon, Hawaii°	6	4	.600	6.26	19	9	1	4	0	1	69.0	84	52	48	8	3	40	3	45	3
McKnight, Phoenix	2	2	.500	9.21	12	3	0	3	0	0	28.1	37	36	29	7	0	28	0	12	6
McLaughlin, Hawaii	3	3	.500	5.12	31	8	1	15	0	2	84.1	103	52	48	7	1	28	5	30	6
Meads, Tucson°	1	0	1.000	2.79	10	0	0	4	0	0	9.2	7	4	3	0	0	6	2	6	0
Medvin, 12 Phx-1 Van	0	1	.000	5.24	13	0	0	9	0	2	22.1	22	17	13	3	0	18	1	16	2
Meeks, 20 Alb-13 Tac	12	4	.750	4.03	33	20	4	3	0	2	149.2	150	78	67	11	3	46	1	86	10
Miller, Phoenix	0	0	.000	13.50	2	0	0	1	0	0	4.0	5	6	6	0	0	2	0	0	0
Mills, Las Vegas	0	1	.000	22.85	6	0	0	2	0	0	4.1	10	11	11	0	0	9	2	4	1
Miner, Phoenix	2	2	.500	6.92	6	1	0	0	0	0	13.0	15	10	10	0	0	13	1	7	1
Montalvo, Tucson	8	4	.667	3.52	59	2	0	27	0	4	94.2	113	56	37	0	2	41	4	43	8
Monteleone, Calgary	6	13	.316	5.51	51	0	0	33	0	15	65.1	59	45	40	5	2	63	8	38	4
Mooneyham, Tacoma	1	2	.333	4.67	7	0	0	1	0	0	17.1	13	10	9	0	3	15	3	8	3
Morlock, Tucson	6	11	.353	4.84	28	25	4	0	1	0	163.2	175	96	88	22	7	59	5	97	3
Mulholland, Phoenix°	7	12	.368	5.07	37	29	3	4	0	1	172.1	200	124	97	7	4	90	0	94	17
Musselman, Portland	3	10	.231	6.62	14	10	0	3	0	0	68.0	82	55	50	6	5	34	2	50	2
Nielsen, Hawaii	3	4	.429	3.97	10	10	3	0	0	0	68.0	74	36	30	5	3	30	3	21	2
Niemann, Portland°	4	7	.364	4.15	32	8	3	11	0	1	104.0	105	64	48	7	5	45	1	43	5
Noble, Tucson°	0	0	.000	11.37	2	1	0	0	0	0	6.1	12	8	8	0	1	4	0	4	0
Ontiveros, Tacoma	0	0	.000	3.00	1	1	0	0	0	0	3.0	1	1	1	0	0	2	0	1	1
Palacios, Vancouver	13	5	.722	2.58	27	26	7	0	5	0	185.0	140	63	53	10	5	85	1	148	5
Parker, Calgary	8	1	.889	2.93	12	12	4	0	0	0	86.0	78	35	28	4	0	28	1	44	4
K. Patterson, Hawaii°	0	6	.000	0.00	3	0	0	3	0	2	3.1	1	0	0	0	0	3	0	5	0
R. Patterson, Vancouver°	5	2	.714	2.12	14	12	5	1	1	0	89.0	62	21	21	5	0	30	0	92	2
Pederson, Albuquerque°	0	0	.000	18.00	1	0	0	0	0	0	1.0	1	2	2	0	0	0	0	0	0
Pena, Vancouver°	5	6	.455	3.72	27	7	0	15	0	4	77.1	69	37	32	4	0	37	0	62	10

Pitcher—Club	W.	L.	Pct.	ERA.	G.	GS.	CG.	GF.	ShO.	Sv.	IP.	H.	R.	ER.	HR.	HB.	BB.	Int. BB.	SO.	WP.
Perlman, Phoenix	12	6	.667	2.81	52	0	0	44	0	18	89.2	93	36	28	3	2	37	7	49	6
Perry, Portland	1	3	.250	6.18	10	7	1	0	1	0	43.2	49	31	30	5	3	30	1	16	3
Plunk, Tacoma	1	1	.500	1.56	24	0	0	19	0	9	34.2	21	8	6	1	0	17	2	56	6
Portugal, Portland	1	10	.091	6.00	17	16	2	1	0	0	102.0	108	75	68	9	1	50	0	69	5
Poston, Las Vegas	3	5	.375	4.73	45	2	0	18	0	1	93.1	108	55	49	9	2	35	5	35	7
Powell, Calgary°	4	8	.333	4.52	20	20	2	0	1	0	117.1	145	80	64	12	2	48	1	65	3
Price, Phoenix°	6	0	1.000	2.49	17	8	0	5	0	2	61.1	45	21	17	3	2	40	1	49	2
Puikunas, Phoenix°	5	1	.833	6.68	24	0	0	12	0	1	31.0	32	25	23	2	1	22	3	20	3
Rasmussen, Hawaii	6	5	.545	5.84	28	12	1	8	0	2	94.0	105	63	61	9	3	59	1	60	5
Reece, Tacoma	1	0	1.000	4.00	3	0	0	2	0	0	9.0	9	4	4	0	0	4	0	3	0
Reed, Calgary	0	0	.000	0.00	1	0	0	0	0	0	3.0	1	0	0	0	0	0	0	3	0
Reyes, Albuquerque	0	0	.000	0.00	1	0	0	1	0	0	0.1	0	0	0	0	0	1	0	1	0
Rijo, Tacoma	2	4	.333	3.95	9	8	0	0	0	0	54.2	44	27	24	5	1	28	0	67	8
Rios, Edmonton	0	2	.000	7.88	3	3	0	0	0	0	16.0	22	17	14	2	0	7	0	7	0
Roberts, Las Vegas°	1	0	1.000	4.55	6	5	0	0	0	0	29.2	34	16	15	2	1	15	1	21	3
Ri. Rodriguez, Tacoma	5	4	.556	3.31	21	9	2	4	1	0	92.1	90	39	34	5	5	36	4	52	1
Ru. Rodriguez, Vancouver	0	0	.000	18.00	1	0	0	1	0	0	1.0	1	2	2	0	0	3	0	0	0
Ross, Vancouver	5	6	.455	3.02	32	1	0	15	0	4	89.1	87	40	30	5	2	21	6	48	1
Ruhle, Edmonton	0	7	.000	6.26	25	9	0	9	0	0	77.2	100	63	54	8	5	28	1	37	5
Savage, Albuquerque	0	4	.000	4.20	13	0	0	9	0	1	15.0	20	15	7	2	2	11	3	13	1
Schneider, Calgary	4	3	.571	3.60	50	0	0	25	0	7	80.0	76	48	32	0	5	55	4	46	5
Schuler, Phoenix°	2	2	.500	3.57	15	1	0	6	0	1	35.1	36	19	14	6	0	12	0	14	0
Schweighoffer, Albuquerque	2	3	.400	5.33	17	4	0	4	0	1	50.2	62	39	30	9	2	29	1	22	7
Scott, Hawaii	0	0	.000	7.31	18	0	0	6	0	0	28.1	35	24	23	5	0	20	4	24	4
Scurry, Phoenix°	3	3	.500	3.77	28	3	0	11	0	4	59.2	53	27	25	4	1	41	0	57	9
Searage, Hawaii°	0	1	.000	3.68	3	1	0	1	0	1	7.1	6	5	3	1	0	3	0	5	0
Shields, Calgary	3	2	.600	2.25	16	0	0	14	0	4	24.0	16	7	6	2	0	11	1	15	1
Shipanoff, Edmonton	1	1	.500	6.31	11	2	0	5	0	0	25.2	35	21	18	5	0	7	0	16	1
Simmons, Las Vegas	7	7	.500	3.05	75	0	0	57	0	22	112.0	87	46	38	12	4	64	16	120	4
Siwy, Las Vegas	6	8	.429	5.78	36	2	0	17	0	8	71.2	68	47	46	2	6	48	6	53	5
D. Smith, Edmonton	1	0	1.000	3.21	12	2	0	3	0	1	28.0	24	11	10	2	0	13	2	9	1
L. Smith, Portland	9	12	.429	3.79	24	24	6	0	0	0	166.1	176	84	70	12	5	41	0	106	3
Smithson, Portland	2	3	.400	4.97	6	6	2	0	0	0	38.0	36	22	21	1	4	17	0	31	3
Snyder, Las Vegas°	5	4	.556	2.60	39	2	0	17	0	1	72.2	60	24	21	2	5	49	5	60	6
Solano, Tucson	5	5	.500	4.43	42	2	0	15	0	3	69.0	71	40	34	7	0	45	3	45	8
Swift, Calgary	0	0	.000	8.84	5	5	0	0	0	0	18.1	32	22	18	2	0	13	1	5	2
Tanner, Tacoma	3	0	1.000	3.05	4	3	0	1	0	0	20.2	22	10	7	2	0	7	0	4	3
Tatsuno, Hawaii°	1	3	.250	6.60	22	3	0	7	0	1	43.2	49	35	32	5	2	25	1	34	3
D. Taylor, Vancouver	0	3	.000	2.65	9	7	1	1	0	1	57.2	46	20	17	3	1	29	0	47	3
T. Taylor, Calgary	10	3	.769	3.65	25	23	3	0	1	0	138.0	131	69	56	6	0	90	0	107	16
Thigpen, Hawaii	2	3	.400	6.15	9	9	2	0	1	0	52.2	72	38	36	5	1	14	1	17	0
Thomas, Calgary	3	1	.750	3.45	14	4	0	4	0	0	47.0	36	22	18	1	2	34	3	39	12
Tolentino, Tacoma°	0	0	.000	0.00	1	0	0	1	0	0	0.2	0	0	0	0	0	0	0	0	0
Trudeau, Portland	0	1	.000	5.10	13	0	0	4	0	0	30.0	34	22	17	3	0	7	0	12	1
Trujillo, Calgary	3	1	.750	2.28	5	3	1	1	0	1	27.2	25	8	7	2	0	9	0	21	1
Verducci, Phoenix	0	0	.000	0.00	1	0	0	1	0	0	2.0	2	0	0	0	0	0	0	2	0
Von Ohlen, Tacoma°	5	4	.556	2.05	52	0	0	23	0	7	83.1	63	21	19	3	3	31	6	55	1
Vosberg, Las Vegas°	9	8	.529	3.92	34	24	3	1	0	0	167.2	154	88	73	11	5	97	3	98	6
Walker, Calgary	2	1	.667	3.60	5	5	1	0	1	0	35.0	37	14	14	3	0	6	0	19	1
Waller, Tucson	0	0	.000	0.00	2	0	0	2	0	0	2.1	2	1	0	0	0	0	0	2	0
Ward, 3 Phx-12 LV°	1	6	.143	10.13	15	10	0	0	0	0	42.2	64	51	48	2	1	41	0	34	10
White, Hawaii	9	10	.474	5.35	31	28	4	3	0	1	163.0	214	112	97	16	5	63	4	73	4
Wojna, Las Vegas	7	5	.583	4.03	18	16	1	1	1	0	96.0	97	50	43	4	5	42	2	47	4

BALKS—Vosberg, 11; Brantley, 7; Krueger, Palacios, 6 each; White, 5; T. Clark, D. Cook, Ferreira, Ford, T. Taylor, Ward, 4 each; Corbell, Johnson, Livingston, Meeks, Mulholland, Puikunas, L. Smith, 3 each; Bauer, Belcher, Bielecki, Blount, Broersma, Burns, Campbell, Citarella, Clay, Clemons, Cocanower, M. Cook, Fontenot, Fossas, Hayward, Hernandez, Kerfeld, Mathis, Portugal, Rasmussen, Rijo, Roberts, Scurry, 2 each; Agosto, Akerfelds, Anderson, Berra, Best, Bianchi, Bitker, Bittiger, Bockus, M. Brown, Bryden, Burtt, Christiansen, Clarke, Comstock, Dozier, Dunne, Fansler, Ferran, Gomez, Heathcock, Hickey, Higgs, Hillegas, Kelley, Kyles, Lamp, Latham, Lugo, Mallicoat, Mason, McKnight, Morlock, Musselman, Parker, R. Patterson, Pena, Perlman, Powell, Price, Ri. Rodriguez, Schneider, Scott, Simmons, Snyder, Swift, Thigpen, Trudeau, Von Ohlen, Wojna, 1 each.

COMBINATION SHUTOUTS—Brennan-Livingston-Crews, Brennan-Davis, Howell-Davis-Savage, Albuquerque; Kelly-Trujillo, Calgary; Morlock-Cliburn, Edmonton; Clark-Hickey-Krawczyk, Krawczyk-Conley-Citarella-Patterson, McKeon-Cochrane, Rasmussen-Hickey, Rasmussen-Scott-Hickey, Tatsuno-Krawczyk, White-Citarella, Hawaii; Hayward-Simmons, Vosberg-Simmons, Las Vegas; Brantley-Bockus, Phoenix; Belcher-Von Ohlen-Plunk, Birtsas-Leiper, Krueger-Lamp-Caudill, Tacoma; Hagen-Mack-Montalvo, Tucson; Copp-Pena, Pena-Drummond, Pena-Easley, Vancouver.

NO-HIT GAMES—Johnson, Vancouver, defeated Portland, 3-0, July 24; Krueger, Albuquerque, defeated Phoenix, 2-0 (seven innings, second game), August 14.

Eastern League

CLASS AA

Leading Batter
TOMMY GREGG
Harrisburg

League President
CHARLES ESHBACH

Leading Pitcher
ROB LOPEZ
Vermont

CHAMPIONSHIP WINNERS IN PREVIOUS YEARS

1923—Williamsport .... .661	1947—Utica† .... .652	1970—Waterbury a............................ .560
1924—Williamsport .... .654	1948—Scranton† .... .636	Reading a .... .553
1925—York§.................................... .583	1949—Albany.................................. .664	1971—Three Rivers .... .569
Williamsport§........................ .583	Binghamton (4th)‡............... .500	Elmira b................................. .561
1926—Scranton .... .627	1950—Wilkes-Barre‡ .... .652	1972—West Haven b........................ .600
1927—Harrisburg .... .630	1951—Wilkes-Barre...................... .612	Three Rivers .... .559
1928—Harrisburg .... .603	Scranton (2nd)† .... .562	1973—Reading b .... .551
1929—Binghamton .... .597	1952—Albany.................................. .603	Pittsfield................................. .551
1930—Wilkes-Barre.......................... .572	Binghamton (2nd)‡ .... .562	1974—Thetford Mines (2nd)c .... .536
1931—Harrisburg .... .597	1953—Reading................................ .682	Pittsfield (2nd)...................... .496
1932—Wilkes-Barre .... .561	Binghamton (2nd)‡ .... .636	1975—Reading................................ .613
1933—Binghamton .... .690	1954—Wilkes-Barre...................... .576	Bristol°................................. .587
1934—Binghamton .... .694	Albany (3rd)‡.................... .540	1976—Three Rivers .... .601
Williamsport°........................ .603	1955—Reading................................ .613	West Haven d........................ .576
1935—Scranton .... .657	Allentown (2nd)‡ .... .565	1977—West Haven e........................ .623
Binghamton°........................ .580	1956—Schenectady† .... .609	Three Rivers .... .551
1936—Scranton°.............................. .609	1957—Binghamton .... .607	1978—Reading................................ .642
Elmira................................. .629	Reading (3rd)‡................... .529	Bristol°................................. .580
1937—Elmira† .... .622	1958—Lancaster x............................ .568	1979—West Haven f........................ .597
1938—Binghamton .... .622	Binghamton (6th)‡............... .493	1980—Holyoke°.............................. .561
Elmira (3rd)‡....................... .522	1959—Springfield†............................ .607	Waterbury............................. .540
1939—Scranton† .... .571	1960—Williamsport y........................ .551	1981—Glens Falls .... .615
1940—Scranton .... .568	Springfield (3rd)y................ .496	Bristol°................................. .577
Binghamton (2nd)‡ .... .554	1961—Springfield............................ .612	1982—West Haven°........................ .614
1941—Wilkes-Barre .... .630	1962—Williamsport .... .593	Lynn..................................... .590
Elmira (3rd)‡....................... .514	Elmira (2nd)‡.................... .514	1983—Lynn..................................... .554
1942—Albany.................................. .600	1963—Charleston .... .593	New Britain‡.......................... .518
Scranton (2nd)‡ .... .593	1964—Elmira .... .586	1984—Waterbury............................. .543
1943—Scranton .... .630	1965—Pittsfield............................... .607	Vermont‡.............................. .536
Elmira (2nd)‡ .... .568	1966—Elmira .... .633	1985—Albany................................. .540
1944—Hartford .... .723	1967—Binghamton z .... .586	Vermont‡.............................. .514
Binghamton (4th)‡............... .474	Elmira................................. .532	1986—Reading................................ .566
1945—Utica..................................... .615	1968—Pittsfield............................... .604	Vermont‡.............................. .554
Albany (3rd)‡...................... .564	Reading (2nd)‡.................. .579	
1946—Scranton† .... .691	1969—York...................................... .640	

°Won split-season playoff. †Won championship and four-team playoff. ‡Won four-team playoff. §Tied for pennant, York winning playoff. xLeague was divided into Northern, Southern divisions and played a split season; Lancaster over-all season leader. yPlayoff finals canceled after one game because of rain with Williamsport and Springfield declared playoff co-champions. zLeague was divided into Eastern, Western divisions; Binghamton won playoff. aTied for pennant, Waterbury winning playoff. bLeague was divided into American, National divisions; won playoff. cLeague was divided into American and National divisions; won four-team playoff. dLeague was divided into Northern, Southern divisions, won playoff. eLeague was divided into New England and Canadian-American divisions; won playoff. fWon both halves of split season (no playoffs). (NOTE—Known as New York-Pennsylvania League prior to 1938.)

STANDING OF CLUBS AT CLOSE OF SEASON, SEPTEMBER 2

Club	Pitt.	Har.	Read.	Vmt.	Alb.	N.B.	Wpt.	G.F.	W.	L.	T.	Pct.	G.B.
Pittsfield (Cubs)	....	14	9	11	14	15	13	11	87	51	0	.630	......
Harrisburg (Pirates)	6	....	12	12	10	12	12	13	77	63	0	.550	11
Reading (Phillies)	11	8	....	11	10	12	11	13	76	63	0	.547	11½
Vermont (Reds)	9	8	9	....	10	10	12	15	73	67	0	.521	15
Albany (Yankees)	6	10	10	10	....	10	9	9	64	75	0	.460	23½
New Britain (Red Sox)	5	8	8	10	10	....	11	9	61	79	0	.436	27
Williamsport (Indians)	7	8	9	8	10	9	....	9	60	79	0	.432	27½
Glens Falls (Tigers)	7	7	6	5	11	11	11	....	58	79	0	.423	28½

Vermont club represented Burlington, Vt.

Major league affiliations in parentheses.

Playoffs—Harrisburg defeated Reading, three games to two; Vermont defeated Pittsfield, three games to one; Harrisburg defeated Vermont, three games to one, to win league championship.

Regular-Season Attendance—Albany, 285,016; Glens Falls, 79,303; Harrisburg, 212,141; New Britain, 83,338; Pittsfield, 51,551; Reading, 100,895; Vermont, 85,621; Williamsport, 77,140. Total—975,005. Playoffs—24,693. All-Star Game—3,548.

Managers—Albany, Tommy Jones; Glens Falls, Tom Burgess (through August 9), Tom Gamboa (August 10-15, 24-through end of season), Paul Felix (August 16-23); Harrisburg, Dave Trembley; New Britain, Dave Holt; Pittsfield, Jim Essian; Reading, George Culver; Vermont, Tom Runnels; Williamsport, Steve Swisher (through May 19), Orlando Gomez (May 20-through end of season).

All-Star Team—1B—Mark Grace, Pittsfield; 2B—Tom Barrett, Reading; 3B—Doug Strange, Glens Falls; SS—Ken Jackson, Reading; OF—Tommy Gregg, Harrisburg; Darren Reed, Albany; Dwight Smith, Pittsfield; C—Tom Prince, Harrisburg; DH—Mark Higgins, Williamsport; RHP—Rob Lopez, Vermont; LHP—Rich Sauveur, Harrisburg; Reliever—Todd Frohwirth, Reading; Most Valuable Player—Mark Grace, Pittsfield; Pitcher of the Year—Rob Lopez, Vermont; Manager of the Year—Dave Trembley, Harrisburg.

(Compiled by Howe News Bureau, Boston, Mass.)

CLUB BATTING

Club	Pct.	G.	AB.	R.	OR.	H.	TB.	2B.	3B.	HR.	RBI.	GW.	SH.	SF.	HP.	BB.	Int. BB.	SO.	SB.	CS.	LOB.
Harrisburg	.287	140	4704	721	664	1350	1898	213	49	79	653	66	46	50	41	469	43	621	185	88	1014
Reading	.286	139	4583	730	684	1309	1871	204	53	84	653	72	37	56	52	496	34	647	157	93	957
Pittsfield	.282	138	4619	740	599	1304	1966	235	62	101	663	78	57	44	50	527	41	719	239	92	1008
Glens Falls	.278	137	4581	692	718	1273	1869	225	16	113	636	54	52	52	29	473	52	717	80	64	939
New Britain	.272	140	4589	573	654	1248	1708	204	32	64	510	56	38	48	41	463	31	647	115	69	993
Albany	.266	140	4651	647	698	1238	1823	237	27	98	606	60	53	42	47	514	38	762	96	63	1017
Vermont	.259	140	4501	609	560	1168	1648	174	42	74	555	68	36	50	33	473	37	704	144	81	953
Williamsport	.259	139	4511	612	707	1169	1733	213	30	97	552	53	27	29	56	464	35	809	143	82	919

INDIVIDUAL BATTING

(Leading Qualifiers for Batting Championship—378 or More Plate Appearances)

*Bats lefthanded. †Switch-hitter.

Player and Club	Pct.	G.	AB.	R.	H.	TB.	2B.	3B.	HR.	RBI.	GW.	SH.	SF.	HP.	BB.	Int. BB.	SO.	SB.	CS.
Gregg, Thomas, Harrisburg*	.371	133	461	99	171	241	22	9	10	82	8	0	4	1	84	14	47	35	10
Smith, Dwight, Pittsfield*	.337	130	498	111	168	270	28	10	18	72	9	2	4	2	67	6	79	60	18
Turner, Shane, 20 Alb-74 Reading*	.334	94	356	69	119	164	19	7	4	55	8	2	2	4	33	1	38	5	7
Barrett, Thomas, Reading†	.334	136	485	107	162	203	20	9	1	55	8	12	5	6	95	5	45	30	17
Grace, Mark, Pittsfield*	.333	123	453	81	151	247	29	8	17	101	11	3	7	2	48	11	24	5	5
Morris, Harold, Albany*	.326	135	530	65	173	227	31	4	5	73	6	5	5	4	36	2	43	7	4
Medina, Luis, Williamsport	.320	96	341	61	109	184	15	6	16	68	9	0	8	5	48	6	75	10	2
Reed, Darren, Albany	.319	107	404	68	129	220	23	4	20	79	8	0	3	8	51	9	50	9	6
Reboulet, James, Harrisburg	.319	105	427	92	136	150	10	2	0	44	1	3	2	1	60	6	37	52	15
Jordan, Paul, Reading	.318	132	475	78	151	233	28	3	16	95	6	0	9	3	28	4	22	15	9
DeAngelis, Steven, Reading*	.315	116	422	70	133	216	23	3	18	84	14	0	4	12	58	13	53	5	7
Higgins, Mark, Williamsport	.312	108	394	76	123	203	21	1	19	79	7	0	1	5	54	9	57	4	2

Departmental Leaders: G—Barrett, 136; AB—Morris, 530; R—Dw. Smith, 111; H—Morris, 173; TB—Dw. Smith, 270; 2B—M. Roman, 35; 3B—Roomes, 12; HR—Brito, 24; RBI—Grace, 101; GWRBI—DeAngelis, 14; SH—Ruiz, 15; SF—Gutierrez, Jordan, 9; HP—House, 13; BB—Barrett, 95; IBB—Gregg, 14; SO—Roomes, 135; SB—Dw. Smith, 60; CS—Finley, House, Dw. Smith, 18.

(All Players—Listed Alphabetically)

Player and Club	Pct.	G.	AB.	R.	H.	TB.	2B.	3B.	HR.	RBI.	GW.	SH.	SF.	HP.	BB.	Int. BB.	SO.	SB.	CS.
Abner, Benjamin, Harrisburg	.213	26	61	3	13	16	3	0	0	5	1	0	0	2	2	0	6	0	2
Alvarez, Jesus, Albany*	.305	62	233	44	71	116	16	1	9	37	3	1	0	2	27	0	21	3	1
Amaral, Richard, Pittsfield	.254	104	315	45	80	98	8	5	0	28	1	6	1	3	43	2	50	28	6
Andersh, Kevin, Harrisburg	1.000	2	1	0	1	1	0	0	0	0	0	0	0	0	0	0	0	0	0
Anderson, Brady, New Britain*	.294	52	170	30	50	78	4	3	6	35	3	1	1	2	45	3	24	7	3
Armstrong, Jack, Vermont	.250	5	4	0	1	1	0	0	0	1	0	0	0	0	0	0	1	0	0
Baker, Kerry, Harrisburg†	.247	32	93	13	23	36	7	0	2	16	1	0	1	3	6	0	25	0	0
Barrett, Thomas, Reading†	.334	136	485	107	162	203	20	9	1	55	8	12	5	6	95	5	45	30	17
Barton, Shawn, Reading	.000	32	8	0	0	0	0	0	0	1	0	2	0	0	2	0	4	0	0
Beck, Dion, Reading*	.000	21	0	0	0	0	0	0	0	0	0	0	0	0	0	0	0	0	0
Beeler, Robert, Vermont	.182	6	11	0	2	2	0	0	0	1	0	0	0	0	0	0	3	0	0
Belen, Lance, Harrisburg	.290	122	420	69	122	193	18	4	15	93	11	2	8	9	48	3	75	4	1
Belliard, Rafael, Harrisburg	.338	37	145	24	49	58	5	2	0	9	1	2	0	0	6	0	16	7	5
Bennett, Keith, Williamsport	.195	46	128	23	25	29	2	1	0	7	0	0	2	3	36	0	26	13	6
Berry, Mark, Vermont	.321	32	112	22	36	50	4	2	2	18	3	0	2	1	30	1	8	7	2
Birriel, Jose, New Britain*	.292	117	390	50	114	165	21	0	10	57	6	3	6	3	70	4	57	1	3
Bishop, James, Williamsport	.190	20	58	3	11	13	2	0	0	1	0	0	0	0	9	0	17	0	1
Bochesa, Gregory, New Britain	.302	19	63	8	19	26	4	0	1	4	2	0	0	4	10	2	8	0	3
Boever, Daniel, Vermont	.301	101	355	57	107	165	14	1	14	61	12	0	7	0	40	5	50	7	1
Bonilla, Juan, Albany	.273	3	11	3	3	4	1	0	0	2	0	0	0	0	3	0	0	0	0
Boudreaux, Eric, Reading	.000	5	2	0	0	0	0	0	0	0	0	0	0	0	3	0	1	0	0
Bresnahan, David, Williamsport†	.150	52	147	12	22	27	3	1	0	5	1	0	0	2	25	5	36	2	0
Brink, Bradford, Reading	.111	12	9	0	1	1	0	0	0	0	0	0	0	0	0	0	4	0	0
Brito, Bernardo, Williamsport	.277	124	452	64	125	225	20	4	24	79	9	0	6	5	24	2	121	6	2
Brown, Anthony, Reading*	.293	72	242	36	71	105	13	3	5	51	6	0	6	3	14	1	39	7	6
Brown, Craig, Harrisburg	.268	127	411	54	110	164	23	5	7	40	1	6	3	1	30	6	47	11	10
Brown, Marty, Vermont	.264	134	470	69	124	196	17	5	15	74	8	1	7	4	59	3	93	23	14
Brown, Paul, New Britain*	1.000	7	1	0	1	1	0	0	0	0	0	0	0	0	0	0	0	0	0
Brundage, David, Reading*	.209	14	43	7	9	10	1	0	0	1	0	1	0	1	5	0	11	3	0
Bryant, John, Vermont	.256	87	254	45	65	90	15	2	2	14	1	0	1	5	40	3	34	8	5

Player and Club	Pct.	G.	AB.	R.	H.	TB.	2B.	3B.	HR.	RBI.	GW.	SH.	SF.	HP.	BB.	Int. BB.	SO.	SB.	CS.
Carroll, Carson, Albany	.250	17	44	10	11	18	4	0	1	9	2	0	2	0	17	0	11	1	2
Cathcart, Gary, Albany°	.237	77	245	33	58	79	15	0	2	31	1	2	0	0	32	2	41	8	4
Chavez, Pedro, Glens Falls	.339	63	236	55	80	115	12	1	7	38	3	3	6	2	20	0	27	4	3
Clements, Wesley, Glens Falls	.277	61	220	35	61	117	15	1	13	52	5	0	4	0	38	3	54	2	1
Close, Casey, Albany	.279	127	459	57	128	174	19	3	7	62	7	4	5	5	24	4	72	10	9
Concepcion, Onix, Harrisburg	.357	6	14	2	5	5	0	0	0	1	0	0	0	2	3	0	1	1	0
Cook, Jeffrey, Harrisburg†	.228	53	193	26	44	50	6	0	0	4	0	3	0	0	9	0	26	11	5
Cooper, David, Glens Falls	.000	33	1	0	0	0	0	0	0	0	0	0	0	0	0	0	1	0	0
Copp, William, Harrisburg	.000	5	0	0	0	0	0	0	0	0	0	0	0	0	2	0	0	0	0
Crouch, Zachary, New Britain°	.000	24	2	1	0	0	0	0	0	0	0	0	0	0	0	0	2	0	0
Damian, Leonard, Pittsfield	.167	26	24	2	4	5	1	0	0	1	0	0	0	0	1	0	3	0	0
Danek, William, Pittsfield	.000	6	10	0	0	0	0	0	0	0	0	1	0	0	0	0	3	0	0
Daniel, Clayton, Harrisburg†	.000	15	4	0	0	0	0	0	0	0	0	0	0	0	1	0	2	0	0
Dascenzo, Douglas, Pittsfield†	.306	134	496	84	152	205	32	6	3	56	12	7	5	1	73	5	38	36	7
Davidson, Jackie, Pittsfield†	.250	11	4	1	1	4	0	1	0	2	0	5	0	0	0	0	0	0	0
DeAngelis, Steven, Reading°	.315	116	422	70	133	216	23	3	18	84	14	0	4	12	58	13	53	5	7
DeFrancesco, Anthony, New Britain	.244	82	238	16	58	85	12	0	5	39	3	1	2	3	32	0	34	0	4
Deitz, Timothy, Vermont°	.500	20	2	0	1	1	0	0	0	1	0	0	0	0	0	0	1	0	0
Dimascio, Daniel, Glens Falls	.233	78	220	28	49	77	13	0	5	38	4	2	4	0	19	0	55	2	2
Dotzler, Michael, Harrisburg°	.250	18	48	5	12	18	1	1	1	8	1	0	1	0	3	0	9	1	0
Duffy, John, Glens Falls†	.000	51	1	0	0	0	0	0	0	0	0	0	0	0	0	0	1	0	0
Dunlap, Joseph, Vermont	.253	116	380	58	96	130	12	5	4	40	4	6	4	1	41	5	55	9	3
Edge, Gregory, Reading†	.250	18	52	8	13	14	1	0	0	5	0	0	0	0	8	0	2	2	2
Estrada, Eduardo, New Britain	.232	92	293	19	68	87	11	1	2	31	5	2	1	0	18	1	41	3	2
Felix, Paul, Glens Falls†	.250	79	292	39	73	121	12	0	12	47	2	2	4	3	16	5	65	0	2
Fermin, Felix, Harrisburg	.268	100	399	62	107	126	9	5	0	35	6	7	3	2	27	1	22	22	13
Ficklin, Winston, Williamsport	.310	98	361	67	112	155	20	4	5	37	1	0	0	3	42	1	47	47	16
Finley, Brian, Vermont°	.263	110	372	66	98	133	13	8	2	39	2	1	4	4	70	2	43	17	18
Flores, Jose, New Britain†	.198	31	96	6	19	20	1	0	0	6	1	1	0	2	8	1	23	0	2
Fortenberry, Jimmy, 43 Rea-43 Alb°	.253	86	289	32	73	114	10	2	9	46	6	1	4	2	15	2	48	2	6
Freeman, Marvin, Reading	.000	10	6	0	0	0	0	0	0	0	0	1	0	0	1	0	4	0	0
Frohwirth, Todd, Reading	.000	36	4	0	0	0	0	0	0	0	0	0	0	0	0	0	2	0	0
Galvez, Balvino, Glens Falls	.667	22	3	1	2	2	0	0	0	0	0	0	0	0	0	0	0	0	0
Gentile, Gene, Harrisburg°	.227	96	299	45	68	131	18	0	15	52	5	0	4	0	47	6	68	3	3
Geren, Robert, Albany	.221	78	213	33	47	91	7	2	11	31	5	4	5	2	21	2	42	1	1
Gergen, Robert, Williamsport	.305	85	295	46	90	144	26	2	8	49	4	1	4	3	30	1	41	3	4
Germann, Mark, Vermont	.221	71	199	19	44	52	3	1	1	11	1	1	2	1	25	1	14	3	0
Gideon, Brett, Harrisburg	.000	26	1	0	0	0	0	0	0	0	0	0	0	0	0	0	0	0	0
Gill, Turner, Williamsport	.189	130	438	41	83	117	14	1	6	32	5	6	1	10	19	0	108	11	8
Gonzalez, Angel, New Britain	.300	113	406	57	122	167	18	0	9	45	8	3	5	1	46	1	43	24	9
Gonzalez, Fredi, Albany	.125	26	48	6	6	8	2	0	0	6	2	1	0	0	11	0	13	0	0
Gordon, Kevin, Harrisburg	.500	25	2	0	1	1	0	0	0	1	0	0	0	0	0	0	0	0	0
Grace, Mark, Pittsfield°	.333	123	453	81	151	247	29	8	17	101	11	3	7	2	48	11	24	5	5
Granger, Lee, Glens Falls†	.286	11	28	7	8	12	4	0	0	1	0	0	0	0	1	0	1	2	0
Gregg, Thomas, Harrisburg°	.371	133	461	99	171	241	22	9	10	82	8	0	4	1	84	14	47	35	10
Guinn, Brian, Pittsfield°	.281	124	384	67	108	151	15	8	4	49	8	3	5	1	65	4	47	16	12
Gutierrez, Dimas, Harrisburg	.303	128	479	71	145	209	29	7	7	65	7	2	9	5	24	3	37	19	11
Guzman, Ruben, Glens Falls	.290	12	31	5	9	17	0	1	2	10	0	0	1	1	1	0	8	1	3
Haggerty, Roger, New Britain	.286	2	7	1	2	3	1	0	0	1	0	0	0	0	0	0	2	0	0
Hardgrave, Eric, Glens Falls	.348	9	23	1	8	10	2	0	0	4	0	0	1	0	3	0	5	0	0
Hauradou, Yanko, Albany	.233	49	120	9	28	35	4	0	1	11	2	6	2	2	6	0	22	1	1
Henderson, Ramon, Harrisburg	.261	75	226	28	59	81	20	1	0	27	4	0	3	0	19	1	34	6	4
Hermann, Jeffrey, Glens Falls°	.300	95	327	62	98	148	19	2	9	55	2	1	4	2	53	1	51	10	4
Hicks, Joseph, Albany	.282	27	78	10	22	29	4	0	1	5	0	0	0	0	23	0	27	1	0
Hicks, Robert, Reading	.077	48	13	1	1	1	0	0	0	1	1	3	0	0	1	0	3	0	0
Higgins, Mark, Williamsport	.312	108	394	76	123	203	21	1	19	79	7	0	1	5	54	9	57	4	2
Higgins, Theodore, Albany°	.244	61	193	23	47	58	11	0	0	25	1	0	2	2	25	1	43	2	0
Hinzo, Thomas, Williamsport†	.242	26	99	16	24	28	2	1	0	9	0	1	0	0	13	0	18	11	3
Hirsch, Jeffrey, Pittsfield†	1.000	34	2	1	2	2	0	0	0	0	0	0	0	0	0	0	0	0	0
Hoiles, Chris, Glens Falls	.276	108	380	47	105	156	12	0	13	53	5	4	3	3	35	4	37	1	5
Holman, Shawn, 27 Har-18 G.F.	.000	45	2	0	0	0	0	0	0	0	0	1	0	0	0	0	1	0	0
Hopkins, Richard, Pittsfield°	.225	75	169	19	38	67	9	1	6	28	3	4	2	3	16	1	27	2	1
House, Bryan, Pittsfield†	.269	133	491	66	132	190	29	4	7	59	6	6	6	13	45	2	83	33	18
Howard, James, Albany	.151	68	159	16	24	31	7	0	0	8	0	6	1	1	13	1	36	1	3
Iavarone, Gregory, Pittsfield	.000	3	1	0	0	0	0	0	0	0	0	0	0	0	0	0	1	0	0
Irvine, Daryl, New Britain	.000	37	2	0	0	0	0	0	0	0	0	0	0	0	0	0	2	0	0
Jackson, Kenneth, Reading	.289	112	377	54	109	154	12	6	7	44	4	1	4	4	46	4	68	13	5
Jefferson, James, Vermont	.000	41	3	0	0	0	0	0	0	0	0	0	0	0	0	0	3	0	0
Johns, Ronald, Harrisburg	.302	40	149	29	45	82	8	1	9	44	5	0	3	3	11	0	15	0	1
Jones, Brian, Harrisburg	.137	27	73	4	10	16	4	1	0	5	1	0	1	0	9	1	14	1	1
Jones, Christopher, Vermont	.230	113	383	50	88	137	11	4	10	39	5	2	3	4	23	4	99	13	10
Jordan, Paul, Reading	.318	132	475	78	151	233	28	3	16	95	6	0	9	3	28	4	22	15	9
Kaye, Jeffrey, Reading	.304	10	23	2	7	12	2	0	1	4	1	1	0	1	0	0	7	0	1
Kiecker, Dana, New Britain	.000	39	2	1	0	0	0	0	0	0	0	1	0	0	1	0	0	0	0
King, Jeffrey, Harrisburg	.240	26	100	12	24	37	7	0	2	25	2	0	4	0	4	0	27	0	1
Kopf, David, Pittsfield	.100	21	10	0	1	1	0	0	0	1	1	2	0	0	2	0	4	0	0
Kramer, Randall, Harrisburg†	.000	26	4	1	0	0	0	0	0	0	0	0	0	0	1	0	1	0	0
Langdon, Ted, Vermont	.000	21	6	0	0	0	0	0	0	0	0	0	0	0	0	0	3	0	0
Leiper, Timothy, Glens Falls†	.318	46	176	31	56	80	12	0	4	26	2	1	4	0	12	2	12	4	1
Leiva, Jose, Reading	.253	105	368	84	93	123	8	11	0	22	3	6	0	6	53	0	49	50	16
Leonette, Mark, Pittsfield	.000	25	1	1	0	0	0	0	0	0	0	0	0	0	0	0	1	0	0
Lewis, John, Pittsfield°	.400	3	5	2	2	2	0	0	0	0	0	0	0	0	0	0	0	1	0
Lind, Orlando, Harrisburg	.250	14	4	0	1	1	0	0	0	0	0	1	0	0	0	0	2	0	0
Little, Bryan, Albany†	.254	17	59	11	15	17	2	0	0	7	0	0	0	0	13	0	2	3	1
Lombardi, Phillip, Albany°	.250	20	60	9	15	27	3	0	3	8	2	0	0	0	11	0	10	1	1
Lombardozzi, Christopher, Albany°°	.210	28	105	8	22	30	5	0	1	11	1	0	0	0	5	0	18	0	1
Long, Bruce, Reading	1.000	4	2	1	2	2	0	0	0	0	0	0	0	0	0	0	0	0	0
Longenecker, Jere, Albany	.227	70	216	28	49	73	9	0	5	26	2	3	3	3	30	5	45	7	2
Lopez, Robert, Vermont°	.174	20	23	4	4	5	1	0	0	2	0	1	0	0	3	0	7	0	0
Lotzar, Gregory, Harrisburg°	.304	57	181	27	55	68	6	2	1	8	1	3	0	0	17	1	16	14	3
Lundblade, Frederick, Reading	.300	127	460	72	138	207	23	2	14	74	6	0	5	3	33	0	71	7	1
Lyden, Mitchell, Albany	.253	71	233	25	59	99	12	2	8	36	2	1	1	2	11	0	47	0	0

Player and Club	Pct.	G.	AB.	R.	H.	TB.	2B.	3B.	HR.	RBI.	GW.	SH.	SF.	HP.	BB.	Int. BB.	SO.	SB.	CS.
Machado, Julio, Reading	.350	22	20	1	7	7	0	0	0	0	0	1	0	0	1	0	6	0	1
Magee, Warren, Reading†	.375	13	8	1	3	6	1	1	0	0	0	0	0	0	2	0	1	0	0
Marigny, Ronald, Glens Falls	.143	18	49	8	7	9	0	1	0	3	1	3	0	0	14	0	11	0	0
Masters, David, Pittsfield	.105	25	19	2	2	5	0	0	1	3	0	3	0	0	1	0	3	0	0
McInnis, William, New Britain°	.226	100	327	42	74	89	11	2	0	15	3	4	1	3	27	5	29	7	7
McLarnan, John, Reading	.250	46	8	2	2	2	0	0	0	1	0	0	0	0	0	0	2	0	0
Medina, Luis, Williamsport	.320	96	341	61	109	184	15	6	16	68	9	0	8	5	48	6	75	10	2
Mejia, Oscar, Williamsport	.294	110	371	50	109	142	18	0	5	57	7	4	3	3	36	4	20	3	2
Melendez, Jose, Harrisburg	.000	6	1	0	0	0	0	0	0	0	1	0	0	0	1	0	0	0	0
Melton, Lawrence, Harrisburg	.111	12	9	0	1	1	0	0	0	0	0	1	0	0	0	0	5	0	0
Mesh, Michael, New Britain	.247	22	77	8	19	24	3	1	0	4	0	1	1	2	4	0	10	1	3
Miley, David, Vermont°	.182	15	33	2	6	6	0	0	0	1	0	0	0	0	3	0	1	0	0
Miller, Michael A., Reading°	.250	15	12	1	3	3	0	0	0	2	0	0	0	0	0	0	2	0	0
Miller, Michael R., Pittsfield	.211	11	19	2	4	5	1	0	0	2	0	1	0	0	1	0	5	0	0
Mills, Craig, Glens Falls	.196	15	51	5	10	13	3	0	0	7	1	0	0	0	4	0	10	2	0
Minutelli, Gino, Vermont	.400	6	5	0	2	2	0	0	0	1	0	0	0	0	1	0	2	0	0
Mirabito, Timothy, Vermont	.182	23	11	2	2	2	0	0	0	0	0	2	0	0	0	0	7	0	0
Mitchell, Charles, Glens Falls	.000	39	3	0	0	0	0	0	0	0	0	0	0	0	0	0	0	0	0
Monda, Gregory, Vermont°	.303	127	466	55	141	204	30	3	9	79	13	0	4	3	28	6	47	1	1
Moore, Bradley, Reading	.000	9	3	0	0	0	0	0	0	0	0	1	0	0	0	0	0	0	0
Morgan, Christopher, Glens Falls°	.272	131	459	65	125	185	28	1	10	71	8	2	4	5	52	4	58	4	5
Moritz, Christopher, New Britain	.292	91	322	64	94	117	13	5	0	30	4	5	2	3	28	4	59	18	8
Morris, Harold, Albany°	.326	135	530	65	173	227	31	4	5	73	6	5	5	4	36	2	43	7	4
Moses, Steven, Williamsport°	.285	89	298	48	85	103	12	3	0	17	0	2	2	5	38	1	22	17	10
Neal, Scott, Harrisburg†	.286	39	7	0	2	2	0	0	0	0	0	0	0	0	0	0	4	0	0
Neidlinger, James, Harrisburg†	.185	27	27	2	5	6	1	0	0	0	0	6	0	0	1	0	10	0	0
Nichols, Howard, Reading	.333	48	183	37	61	87	11	0	5	38	2	0	4	5	15	0	21	4	2
Noles, Dickie, Pittsfield	.000	1	1	0	0	0	0	0	0	0	0	0	0	0	0	0	0	0	0
Nunley, Angelo, Vermont	.272	87	302	32	82	99	7	5	0	29	0	2	4	0	21	0	39	14	4
Oliver, Joseph, Vermont	.305	66	236	31	72	119	13	2	10	60	10	1	7	3	17	2	30	0	3
Oliverio, Stephen, Vermont	.063	27	16	1	1	2	1	0	0	2	0	6	0	0	0	0	7	0	0
Pavlas, David, Pittsfield	.143	7	7	0	1	1	0	0	0	0	0	2	0	0	0	0	3	0	0
Phillips, James, Pittsfield	.273	45	11	0	3	3	0	0	0	0	0	0	0	0	0	0	4	0	1
Phillips, Stephen, Glens Falls°	.254	22	71	8	18	20	2	0	0	4	0	1	0	0	7	0	14	2	2
Pico, Jeffrey, Pittsfield	.250	13	12	0	3	3	0	0	0	1	0	0	0	0	1	0	2	0	0
Pike, Mark, Williamsport	.163	26	86	7	14	17	3	0	0	5	1	0	0	1	6	0	22	4	1
Polk, Riley, Williamsport	.212	33	104	9	22	28	3	0	1	7	0	0	0	3	13	0	19	5	4
Prince, Thomas, Harrisburg	.307	113	365	41	112	157	23	2	6	54	8	4	2	8	51	2	46	6	3
Quintana, Carlos, New Britain	.311	56	206	31	64	87	11	3	2	31	5	0	4	1	24	3	33	3	3
Reboulet, James, Harrisburg	.319	105	427	92	136	150	10	2	0	44	1	3	2	1	60	6	37	52	15
Reed, Darren, Albany	.319	107	404	68	129	220	23	4	20	79	8	0	3	8	51	9	50	9	6
Renfroe, Cohen, Pittsfield	.000	40	3	0	0	0	0	0	0	0	0	0	1	0	0	0	2	0	0
Rice, Cepedia, Glens Falls	.299	57	187	29	56	94	5	0	11	39	6	0	2	3	32	1	73	1	3
Rice, Timothy, Pittsfield	.000	55	3	0	0	0	0	0	0	0	0	0	0	0	0	0	0	0	0
Richardson, Jeffrey, Vermont	.209	35	134	24	28	32	4	0	0	8	0	2	0	1	5	0	25	5	0
Riley, Darren, Vermont°	.258	118	372	42	96	122	14	3	2	36	4	3	4	3	48	4	62	32	17
Ritter, Christopher, Harrisburg	.000	29	5	0	0	0	0	0	0	0	0	0	0	0	1	0	1	0	0
Roberts, John, New Britain	.277	79	278	20	77	84	7	0	0	20	0	8	3	1	20	0	15	18	7
Robles, Gabaliel, Pittsfield	.000	2	2	0	0	0	0	0	0	0	0	0	0	0	0	0	1	0	0
Roesler, Michael, Vermont	.000	22	1	0	0	0	0	0	0	0	0	0	0	0	0	0	1	0	0
Roman, Miguel, Williamsport	.261	124	459	47	120	193	35	4	10	63	4	4	4	5	19	3	98	5	11
Roman, Ray, Reading	.140	17	43	6	6	16	0	2	2	6	2	0	1	1	5	0	12	0	0
Roomes, Rolando, Pittsfield	.308	129	503	100	155	261	19	12	21	95	8	1	4	9	42	1	135	32	6
Rowland, Donald, Glens Falls	.275	83	295	41	81	109	8	4	4	25	1	9	4	1	19	0	44	3	4
Ruiz, Benny, Glens Falls	.294	110	412	67	121	146	14	1	3	48	5	15	3	0	42	5	55	2	3
Russell, Anthony, Albany	.244	93	312	58	76	116	11	4	7	26	1	8	1	5	66	9	55	25	12
Russell, Robert, Harrisburg°	.074	34	27	0	2	2	0	0	0	0	0	5	0	0	2	0	14	0	0
Sambo, Ramon, Vermont†	.226	11	31	3	7	8	1	0	0	1	0	0	0	0	1	0	2	1	2
Sauveur, Richard, Harrisburg°	.286	31	35	5	10	13	3	0	0	5	0	1	0	0	2	0	6	0	0
Scanlan, Robert, Reading	.158	27	19	1	3	3	0	0	0	0	0	0	3	0	1	0	10	0	0
Scheid, Richard, 9 Alb-11 Pitts.°	.000	20	2	0	0	0	0	0	0	0	0	0	0	0	0	0	2	0	0
Schwartz, Thomas, Reading	.292	17	48	5	14	26	3	0	3	11	0	0	0	0	9	0	4	0	1
Scott, Richard, Albany	.231	18	65	10	15	20	3	1	0	7	1	0	1	2	7	0	16	0	0
Scott, Tary, New Britain	.249	105	338	35	84	144	21	0	13	49	4	0	4	5	20	3	65	0	0
Seibert, Gibson, Reading	.254	50	130	14	33	40	2	1	1	15	1	1	3	1	25	0	22	1	4
Service, Scott, Reading	.000	5	2	0	0	0	0	0	0	0	0	0	0	0	0	0	0	0	0
Sferrazza, Matthew, Glens Falls	.259	124	436	55	113	139	20	0	2	25	5	7	3	1	47	1	41	23	10
Shaw, Scott, Albany	.288	58	219	27	63	86	13	2	2	23	2	2	3	3	16	2	34	1	3
Shelton, Michael, Albany°	.167	41	12	2	2	2	0	0	0	0	0	0	0	0	1	0	6	0	0
Sherlock, Glenn, Albany°	.250	4	12	0	3	4	1	0	0	2	0	1	1	0	1	0	2	0	0
Simpson, Gregory, Vermont°	.000	37	4	0	0	0	0	0	0	0	0	0	0	0	0	0	0	0	0
Smith, Daryl, 2 Wpt-20 Reading	.267	12	15	3	4	4	0	0	0	1	0	1	0	0	0	0	6	0	0
Smith, Dwight, Pittsfield°	.337	130	498	111	168	270	28	10	18	72	9	2	4	2	67	6	79	60	18
Smith, Michael, Vermont	.174	32	23	5	4	7	0	0	1	2	0	3	0	1	0	0	7	2	0
Soares, Todd, Reading	.180	49	139	14	25	39	4	2	2	14	2	1	2	1	15	2	33	5	4
Spagnola, Glenn, Vermont°	.241	28	29	6	7	10	3	0	0	5	0	1	0	0	4	0	15	1	0
Strange, Douglas, Glens Falls	.302	115	431	63	130	202	31	1	13	70	4	0	5	3	31	3	53	5	11
Swain, Robert, Williamsport	.162	35	111	8	18	25	4	0	1	3	0	1	0	0	8	1	23	1	3
Syverson, Dain, Williamsport	.218	67	220	22	48	70	12	2	2	23	2	3	0	2	35	2	29	4	1
Tenacen, Francisco, Vermont	.286	13	42	4	12	16	2	1	0	2	0	0	0	1	1	0	9	1	1
Thoma, Raymond, Pittsfield	.277	96	260	30	72	94	9	2	3	33	2	3	2	8	15	3	44	7	5
Thoutsis, Paul, New Britain°	.000	1	4	0	0	0	0	0	0	0	0	0	0	0	0	0	1	0	0
Tiburcio, Fredrick, Glens Falls°	.272	56	213	29	58	91	12	3	5	16	0	1	0	1	19	3	29	5	5
Toale, John, New Britain	.212	15	52	4	11	15	1	0	1	3	0	0	0	4	1	0	8	0	0
Todd, Kyle, Harrisburg	.284	82	215	32	61	94	9	6	4	24	2	2	0	2	11	1	30	2	4
Torres, Ricardo, Albany	.000	35	1	0	0	0	0	0	0	0	0	0	0	0	0	0	1	0	0
Tremblay, Gary, New Britain	.207	81	242	20	50	69	8	1	3	26	3	2	3	0	14	0	67	0	1
Tresh, Michael, Albany	.167	6	15	1	2	2	0	0	0	1	0	0	3	0	0	0	6	0	0
Turner, Shane, 20 Alb-74 Reading°	.334	94	356	69	119	164	19	7	4	55	8	2	4	3	33	1	38	5	7
Vargas, Hector, Albany†	.223	44	130	18	29	35	3	0	1	10	2	5	0	0	15	0	30	3	2
Vasquez, Luis, New Britain	.333	10	3	1	1	2	1	0	0	0	0	0	0	0	0	0	1	0	0
Velarde, Randy, Albany	.316	71	263	40	83	128	20	2	7	32	3	2	1	3	25	0	47	8	6

Player and Club	Pct.	G.	AB.	R.	H.	TB.	2B.	3B.	HR.	RBI.	GW.	SH.	SF.	HP.	BB.	Int. BB.	SO.	SB.	CS.
Villanueva, Hector, Pittsfield	.274	109	391	59	107	180	31	0	14	70	8	2	3	1	43	1	38	3	4
Walker, Anthony, Harrisburg	.315	64	222	30	70	88	7	4	1	40	5	0	5	2	20	0	29	10	3
Walker, Michael, Harrisburg	.000	4	1	0	0	0	0	0	0	0	0	0	0	0	0	0	0	0	0
Ward, Kevin, Reading	.250	16	56	9	14	21	5	1	0	6	1	0	1	1	6	0	12	5	2
Wellman, Phillip, Harrisburg†	.000	1	0	0	0	0	0	0	0	0	0	0	0	0	0	1	0	0	0
Wilder, David, Pittsfield	.223	98	274	40	61	89	13	3	3	31	5	1	2	6	51	2	74	11	8
Williams, Dana, New Britain	.335	78	310	48	104	137	18	3	3	38	3	0	7	6	9	0	16	10	3
Williams, Roger, Pittsfield	.290	31	31	5	9	16	1	0	2	6	2	1	0	0	4	0	14	0	0
Williams, Steven, Reading°	.206	83	247	20	51	71	9	1	3	32	4	0	3	1	23	2	33	1	2
Wilson, John, Glens Falls°	.139	27	36	10	5	6	1	0	0	2	0	1	0	1	8	0	12	7	0
Wilson, Doyle, Williamsport	.195	53	149	11	29	30	1	0	0	11	3	5	0	2	9	0	30	1	2
Wrona, Richard, Pittsfield	.220	70	218	22	48	67	10	3	1	25	2	2	3	1	7	3	32	5	1
Zambrano, Eduardo, New Britain	.246	33	118	16	29	48	11	1	2	11	1	1	1	2	10	1	21	1	2
Zambrano, Roberto, New Britain	.289	131	460	67	133	192	21	10	6	56	4	1	7	3	56	1	70	7	6
Zeratsky, Rodney, Vermont	.189	73	222	12	42	57	9	0	2	28	5	4	1	1	13	1	34	0	0
Zupka, William, New Britain	.000	55	1	0	0	0	0	0	0	0	0	0	0	0	0	0	1	0	0

The following pitchers, listed alphabetically by club, with games in parentheses, had no plate appearances, primarily through use of designated hitters:

ALBANY—Balabon, Richard (1); Blum, Brent (13); Bystrom, Martin (11); Carreno, Amalio (9); Davidson, Robert (14); Dersin, Eric (3); Frey, Steven (14); George, Stephen (16); Guercio, Maurice (24); Harrison, Matthew (27); Johnson, John (14); Kamieniecki, Scott (10); Knox, Jeffrey (23); Layana, Timothy (8); Leiter, Alois (15); Patterson, Kenneth (24); Pries, Jeffrey (7); Rosenberg, Steven (32); Schmidt, Eric (40); Thompson, Richard (5); Wilkins, Dean (2).

GLENS FALLS—Agar, Jeffrey (17); Cooper, William (26); Garces, Robinson (4); Jones, Jeffrey (10); Lee, Mark (7); McHugh, Charles (13); Moore, Robert (4); Pena, Ramon (43); Poissant, Rodney (30); Raubolt, Arthur (5); Ritz, Kevin (25); Smoltz, John (21).

HARRISBURG—Morrow, Benjamin (14); Rooker, David (9); Stading, Gregory (3); Taylor, Donald (3); Wilmet, Paul (5).

NEW BRITAIN—Bast, Steven (28); Clarkin, Michael (44); Dalton, Michael (4); Gakeler, Daniel (30); Manzanillo, Josias (2); Plympton, Jeffrey (23); Skripko, Scott (7).

PITTSFIELD—Bell, Gregory (5); Harkey, Michael (1); McKay, Alan (53).

READING—Bowden, Mark (10); Riley, George (9).

VERMONT—Brusky, Brad (46).

WILLIAMSPORT—Beasley, Christopher (11); Bellaman, Michael (27); Dube, Greg (8); Encarnacion, Luis (43); Hilton, Stan (12); Karpuk, Gregory (25); Kuykendall, Kevin (7); LaFever, Greg (27); Link, Robert (56); Morgan, Eugene (9); Murphy, Kent (9); Nichols, Rodney (16); Perry, Jeff (3); Poehl, Michael (5); Sabo, Scott (15); Scott, Charles (4); Skalski, Joe (18); Wilson, Roger (46).

GRAND SLAM HOME RUNS—Monda, 2; Anderson, Baker, Belen, Clements, Close, Felix, Grace, M. Higgins, House, Johns, Morris, Nichols, Oliver, Reed, C. Rice, T. Scott, Strange, Vargas, Villanueva, 1 each.

AWARDED FIRST BASE ON CATCHER'S INTERFERENCE—Monda 6 (Lundblade 2, Bresnahan, Dimascio, Hoiles, Prince); M. Brown (Syverson); Jackson (Dotzler); Morgan (Syverson); Roberts (Dotzler); Seibert (Prince); Dw. Smith (Hoiles).

CLUB FIELDING

Club	Pct.	G.	PO.	A.	E.	DP.	PB.	Club	Pct.	G.	PO.	A.	E.	DP.	PB.
Pittsfield	.972	138	3585	1532	148	110	12	Glens Falls	.967	137	3537	1449	171	120	10
Vermont	.971	140	3542	1475	148	119	15	Albany	.966	139	3618	1488	182	121	18
Reading	.971	139	3579	1563	153	132	19	Williamsport	.964	139	3525	1494	188	138	20
Harrisburg	.971	140	3602	1504	152	142	18	New Britain	.963	140	3584	1557	196	117	11

Triple Play—Pittsfield.

INDIVIDUAL FIELDING

°Throws lefthanded.

FIRST BASEMEN

Player and Club	Pct.	G.	PO.	A.	E.	DP.	Player and Club	Pct.	G.	PO.	A.	E.	DP.
Amaral, Pittsfield	1.000	9	69	13	0	9	Leiper, Glens Falls	.993	20	120	18	1	8
Baker, Harrisburg	1.000	3	21	3	0	2	Longenecker, Albany	.989	9	87	4	1	6
Belen, Harrisburg	.988	89	707	64	9	78	McInnis, New Britain°	1.000	1	11	0	0	2
Birriel, New Britain°	.991	79	599	57	6	55	Medina, Williamsport°	.984	13	120	5	2	7
Boever, Vermont	.993	17	137	8	1	11	Mesh, New Britain	1.000	1	1	0	0	1
Bresnahan, Williamsport	.976	11	77	5	2	6	Monda, Vermont°	.990	117	1043	74	11	93
Brito, Williamsport	.667	1	2	0	1	0	Morris, Albany°	.986	130	1085	79	17	100
Brown, Vermont	1.000	7	55	3	0	3	Nichols, Reading	1.000	2	4	0	0	0
Cathcart, Albany°	1.000	1	1	0	0	0	Oliver, Vermont	1.000	3	16	2	0	1
Estrada, New Britain	1.000	1	8	0	0	2	Rice, Glens Falls	.968	44	372	23	13	31
Felix, Glens Falls	.979	34	294	26	7	34	Roman, Williamsport	.963	5	22	4	1	1
Geren, Albany	.889	2	7	1	1	0	Sauveur, Harrisburg°	1.000	1	2	0	0	0
Gergen, Williamsport	.996	30	219	13	1	20	R. Scott, Albany	.941	1	15	1	1	0
Gonzalez, Albany	1.000	2	4	1	0	1	T. Scott, New Britain	.987	71	581	39	8	46
GRACE, Pittsfield°	.995	122	1054	96	6	84	Soares, Reading	1.000	2	14	0	0	1
Hardgrave, Glens Falls	1.000	4	39	4	0	5	Swain, Williamsport	1.000	1	4	0	0	0
Hermann, Glens Falls	.992	42	328	24	3	27	Syverson, Williamsport	1.000	1	9	0	0	0
Hicks, Albany	.923	4	20	4	2	3	Tremblay, New Britain	1.000	5	26	2	0	0
Higgins, Williamsport	.976	87	709	80	19	82	Villanueva, Pittsfield	1.000	14	79	10	0	4
Hoiles, Glens Falls	.955	6	19	2	1	3	Wilder, Pittsfield	.900	1	9	0	1	3
Johns, Harrisburg	.991	39	303	19	3	31	Williams, Reading	.993	18	125	13	1	8
Jordan, Reading	.994	127	1193	54	8	110	Wilson, Williamsport	1.000	1	1	0	0	0
King, Harrisburg	.992	14	107	10	1	10	Wrona, Pittsfield	1.000	3	6	0	0	0

Triple Play—Grace.

SECOND BASEMEN

Player and Club	Pct.	G.	PO.	A.	E.	DP.	Player and Club	Pct.	G.	PO.	A.	E.	DP.
Amaral, Pittsfield	.960	90	173	261	18	59	Gonzalez, New Britain	.963	102	236	316	21	61
BARRETT, Reading	.991	123	248	423	6	93	Hauradou, Albany	.972	37	70	67	4	20
Bennett, Williamsport	.977	39	70	103	4	19	Henderson, Reading	.979	20	37	56	2	15
Bonilla, Albany	1.000	3	11	8	0	2	Hinzo, Williamsport	.978	26	58	78	3	19
Carroll, Albany	.989	17	44	45	1	11	Hopkins, Pittsfield	.985	34	51	78	2	15
Dunlap, Vermont	.982	25	51	60	2	12	House, Pittsfield	.951	34	60	77	7	10
Estrada, New Britain	.966	26	52	60	4	10	Howard, Albany	.972	30	39	66	3	8
Fermin, Harrisburg	1.000	2	5	5	0	1	Jones, Harrisburg	.968	25	43	49	3	15
Flores, New Britain	.978	17	43	45	2	12	Little, Albany	.963	5	13	13	1	8

SECOND BASEMEN—Continued

Player and Club	Pct.	G.	PO.	A.	E.	DP.	Player and Club	Pct.	G.	PO.	A.	E.	DP.
Lombardozzi, Albany	.978	28	61	72	3	13	Ruiz, Glens Falls	.974	36	75	76	4	15
Longenecker, Albany	.966	8	10	18	1	3	Russell, Albany	.000	1	0	0	1	0
Marigny, Glens Falls	.911	18	45	37	8	11	Sambo, Vermont	.951	9	15	24	2	4
Mejia, Williamsport	.975	47	94	142	6	34	Scott, Albany	.985	11	34	31	1	10
Nunley, Vermont	.970	86	184	241	13	49	Strange, Glens Falls	1.000	6	11	14	0	3
Phillips, Glens Falls	1.000	3	7	7	0	3	Swain, Williamsport	.979	9	16	30	1	6
Polk, Williamsport	.986	31	74	70	2	20	Syverson, Williamsport	.750	1	1	2	1	0
Reboulet, Harrisburg	.968	96	229	249	16	54	Todd, Harrisburg	.990	29	44	56	1	14
Richardson, Vermont	.980	31	71	75	3	16	Turner, 19 Alb-2 Rea	.982	21	58	53	2	13
Rowland, Glens Falls	.973	80	185	207	11	57							

Triple Play—Amaral.

THIRD BASEMEN

Player and Club	Pct.	G.	PO.	A.	E.	DP.	Player and Club	Pct.	G.	PO.	A.	E.	DP.
Alvarez, Albany	.913	56	39	108	14	6	Longenecker, Albany	.941	15	8	24	2	2
Bennett, Williamsport	.909	3	2	8	1	0	Mejia, Williamsport	.929	56	33	98	10	9
Berry, Vermont	.929	10	15	24	3	2	Mills, Glens Falls	.870	14	12	28	6	3
Bishop, Williamsport	.913	19	15	27	4	2	Nichols, Reading	.890	47	21	76	12	4
BROWN, Vermont	.957	125	77	234	14	19	Phillips, Glens Falls	1.000	4	3	7	0	1
DeFrancesco, New Britain	.800	7	5	15	5	0	Richardson, Vermont	.750	3	2	1	1	0
Estrada, New Britain	.897	50	30	83	13	8	Ruiz, Glens Falls	.949	13	7	30	2	3
Gergen, Williamsport	.887	49	30	64	12	10	Schwarz, Reading	.850	7	3	14	3	1
Germann, Vermont	.846	4	3	8	2	0	Scott, Albany	1.000	2	0	3	0	0
Gonzalez, New Britain	1.000	4	0	2	0	0	Shaw, Albany	.915	53	44	106	14	11
Gutierrez, Harrisburg	.915	122	107	225	31	26	Strange, Glens Falls	.936	101	87	193	19	15
Hauradou, Albany	.600	3	0	3	2	0	Swain, Williamsport	.933	24	7	35	3	2
Henderson, Reading	.897	28	16	45	7	4	Syverson, Williamsport	.900	5	3	6	1	1
Hoiles, Glens Falls	.944	2	6	11	1	1	Thoma, Pittsfield	.951	62	37	99	7	8
Hopkins, Pittsfield	.885	11	8	15	3	1	Toale, New Britain	.833	15	7	23	6	2
House, Pittsfield	.897	89	53	138	22	10	Todd, Harrisburg	.879	21	12	39	7	4
Howard, Albany	.880	19	15	29	6	1	Turner, Reading	.956	66	44	109	7	6
Leiper, Glens Falls	.923	6	1	11	1	1	Williams, Reading	1.000	2	1	2	0	0
Little, Albany	.913	7	4	17	2	1	Zambrano, New Britain	.903	78	50	146	21	9

SHORTSTOPS

Player and Club	Pct.	G.	PO.	A.	E.	DP.	Player and Club	Pct.	G.	PO.	A.	E.	DP.
Barrett, Reading	.946	10	14	21	2	8	Longenecker, Albany	.947	25	32	57	5	7
Belliard, Harrisburg	.961	37	59	115	7	26	Mejia, Williamsport	.889	12	15	25	5	3
Bennett, Williamsport	.833	1	1	4	1	1	Mesh, New Britain	.926	19	27	60	7	14
Chavez, Glens Falls	.968	62	105	164	9	26	Moritz, New Britain	.956	81	141	250	18	39
Concepcion, Harrisburg	1.000	6	9	16	0	5	Phillips, Glens Falls	.963	10	17	35	2	8
Dunlap, Vermont	.953	88	128	240	18	45	Polk, Williamsport	.800	1	2	2	1	0
Edge, Reading	.943	17	22	61	5	13	Ruiz, Glens Falls	.960	65	112	203	13	44
Estrada, New Britain	1.000	4	6	10	0	4	Scott, Albany	.889	2	2	6	1	0
FERMIN, Harrisburg	.968	99	172	283	15	59	Strange, Glens Falls	.900	2	3	6	1	2
Flores, New Britain	.927	14	18	33	4	8	Syverson, Williamsport	.889	1	6	2	1	1
Germann, Vermont	.961	58	84	165	10	37	Thoma, Pittsfield	.956	27	42	89	6	21
Gill, Williamsport	.948	130	201	369	31	80	Todd, Harrisburg	.900	8	8	19	3	5
Gonzalez, New Britain	.852	7	8	15	4	3	Tresh, Albany	.938	5	4	11	1	0
Guinn, Pittsfield	.962	118	191	339	21	65	Turner, Reading	1.000	2	4	10	0	1
Hauradou, Albany	.800	3	6	2	2	0	Vargas, Albany	.874	42	48	111	23	22
Hopkins, Pittsfield	1.000	5	4	6	0	2	Velarde, Albany	.957	71	127	254	17	51
Howard, Albany	.864	9	4	15	3	1	Zambrano, New Britain	.919	21	31	60	8	13
Jackson, Reading	.952	112	154	376	27	72							

OUTFIELDERS

Player and Club	Pct.	G.	PO.	A.	E.	DP.	Player and Club	Pct.	G.	PO.	A.	E.	DP.
Abner, Harrisburg	1.000	12	15	1	0	0	House, Pittsfield	1.000	11	15	0	0	0
Anderson, New Britain*	.985	41	127	2	2	1	Jones, Vermont	.965	99	207	12	8	2
Barrett, Reading	.750	3	3	0	1	0	Leiper, Glens Falls	1.000	22	43	1	0	0
Bennett, Williamsport	1.000	3	2	1	0	0	Leiva, Reading	.971	102	224	8	7	1
Berry, Vermont	1.000	3	7	0	0	0	Lewis, Pittsfield	1.000	3	5	0	0	0
Birriel, New Britain*	.923	14	22	2	2	0	Longenecker, Albany	1.000	10	15	0	0	0
Boever, Vermont	.986	66	137	5	2	1	Lotzar, New Britain*	1.000	15	31	1	0	0
Brito, Williamsport	.904	36	46	1	5	0	Lundblade, Reading	1.000	16	17	3	0	0
A. Brown, Reading	.934	64	119	9	9	4	McInnis, New Britain*	.974	91	214	9	6	3
C. Brown, Harrisburg	.956	122	224	13	11	2	Medina, Williamsport*	.986	69	140	5	2	1
Brundage, Reading*	1.000	13	15	1	0	0	Mesh, New Britain	1.000	2	4	1	0	0
Bryant, Vermont	.943	50	94	5	6	1	Morgan, Glens Falls	.974	127	242	16	7	3
Cathcart, Albany*	.980	69	142	5	3	0	Moritz, New Britain*	1.000	2	1	0	0	0
Close, Albany	.981	106	192	12	4	1	Morris, Albany*	1.000	4	1	0	0	0
Cook, Harrisburg	1.000	49	103	2	0	0	Moses, Williamsport*	.984	84	176	6	3	2
DASCENZO, Pittsfield*	.987	126	299	5	4	1	Phillips, Glens Falls	1.000	2	3	0	0	0
DeAngelis, Reading*	.940	110	201	4	13	2	Pike, Williamsport	.978	26	85	3	2	2
DeFrancesco, New Britain.	1.000	5	6	0	0	0	Quintana, New Britain	.981	53	100	4	2	2
Dimascio, Glens Falls	.813	13	12	1	3	0	Reboulet, Harrisburg	1.000	13	21	3	0	0
Estrada, New Britain	.000	2	0	0	1	0	Reed, Albany	.978	104	174	6	4	1
Ficklin, Williamsport	.984	97	247	7	4	3	Riley, Vermont	.967	104	195	12	7	1
Finley, Vermont*	.979	104	230	8	5	2	Roberts, New Britain	.974	79	143	5	4	1
Fortenberry, 33 Rea-26 Alb	.964	59	127	5	5	1	Roman, Williamsport	.941	120	212	12	14	5
Gentile, Harrisburg*	.919	63	95	7	9	2	Roomes, Pittsfield	.979	124	268	13	6	1
Granger, Glens Falls	1.000	9	24	0	0	0	Russell, Albany	.988	90	243	8	3	3
Gregg, Harrisburg*	.973	120	242	12	7	1	Schwarz, Reading	.667	3	2	0	1	0
Guzman, New Britain	1.000	12	13	0	0	0	Seibert, Reading	.978	46	80	7	2	1
Haggerty, New Britain	1.000	2	1	0	0	0	Sferrazza, Glens Falls	.974	122	275	19	8	0
Hauradou, Albany	1.000	2	1	0	0	0	Smith, Pittsfield	.941	110	214	8	14	0
Henderson, Reading	1.000	4	6	0	0	0	Soares, Reading	.973	38	71	2	2	1
Hermann, Glens Falls	.947	56	107	0	6	0	Strange, Glens Falls	1.000	5	9	1	0	0
Higgins, Albany*	.946	29	68	2	4	0	Syverson, Williamsport	1.000	1	8	1	0	0

OUTFIELDERS—Continued

Player and Club	Pct.	G.	PO.	A.	E.	DP.	Player and Club	Pct.	G.	PO.	A.	E.	DP.
Tenacen, Vermont	.889	9	8	0	1	0	Ward, Reading	.938	14	30	0	2	0
Thoutsis, New Britain	1.000	1	2	0	0	0	Wilder, Pittsfield	1.000	66	112	10	0	2
Tiburcio, Glens Falls°	.973	55	142	4	4	1	Williams, New Britain	.969	71	148	7	5	1
Todd, Harrisburg	1.000	1	3	0	0	0	Wilson, Glens Falls	.969	25	29	2	1	0
Tremblay, New Britain	1.000	1	3	0	0	0	E. Zambrano, New Britain	.956	32	62	3	3	0
Velarde, Albany	1.000	1	1	0	0	0	R. Zambrano, New Britain	.948	31	51	4	3	0
Walker, Harrisburg	.994	63	152	7	1	1							

Triple Play—Dw. Smith.

CATCHERS

Player and Club	Pct.	G.	PO.	A.	E.	DP.	PB.	Player and Club	Pct.	G.	PO.	A.	E.	DP.	PB.
Baker, Harrisburg	.975	27	138	15	4	3	5	Lundblade, Reading	.986	75	379	33	6	3	5
Beeler, Vermont	.947	6	18	0	1	0	1	Lyden, Albany	.986	61	317	24	5	4	10
Berry, Vermont	.988	17	72	11	1	2	4	Mejia, Williamsport	1.000	4	8	0	0	0	1
Bochesa, New Britain	.974	19	103	10	3	1	5	Miley, Vermont	1.000	13	63	8	0	0	0
Bresnahan, Williamsport	.972	36	181	26	6	4	3	Miller, Pittsfield	1.000	11	34	3	0	0	0
Clements, Glens Falls	1.000	1	3	1	0	1	0	Oliver, Vermont	.964	49	231	33	10	2	4
DeFrancesco, New Britain	.976	66	284	44	8	2	3	Prince, Harrisburg	.985	108	622	88	11	9	11
Dimascio, Glens Falls	.979	62	285	48	7	3	5	Roman, Reading	.986	13	63	8	1	2	0
Dotzler, Harrisburg	.967	16	82	6	3	0	2	Sherlock, Albany	.967	4	24	5	1	0	1
Felix, Glens Falls	.944	5	32	2	2	1	1	Syverson, Williamsport	.968	60	281	50	11	5	3
GEREN, Albany	.994	71	312	44	2	2	2	Tremblay, New Britain	.982	69	325	49	7	4	3
Gonzalez, Albany	.963	23	66	11	3	3	4	Villanueva, Pittsfield	.991	80	410	48	4	1	8
Henderson, Reading	.970	17	85	12	3	0	3	Williams, Reading	.983	42	209	22	4	1	10
Hoiles, Glens Falls	.981	77	381	75	9	6	4	Wilson, Pittsfield	.979	52	248	34	6	6	13
Iavarone, Pittsfield	1.000	2	2	0	0	0	0	Wrona, Pittsfield	.974	68	293	49	9	4	4
Kaye, Reading	.979	7	40	6	1	1	1	Zeratsky, Vermont	.990	71	326	51	4	5	6
Lombardi, Albany	.973	10	29	7	1	2	1								

PITCHERS

Player and Club	Pct.	G.	PO.	A.	E.	DP.	Player and Club	Pct.	G.	PO.	A.	E.	DP.
Agar, Glens Falls	1.000	17	0	3	0	0	Kramer, Harrisburg	.947	26	5	13	1	0
Andersh, Harrisburg°	1.000	2	0	2	0	0	Kuykendall, Williamsport	1.000	7	2	2	0	1
Armstrong, Vermont	.917	5	3	8	1	0	LaFever, Williamsport	.976	27	11	29	1	3
Balabon, Albany	.000	1	0	0	2	0	Langdon, Vermont	.909	21	3	7	1	0
Barton, Reading°	.926	32	3	22	2	0	Layana, Albany	1.000	8	8	12	0	0
Bast, New Britain°	.951	28	7	32	2	0	Lee, Glens Falls°	.600	7	1	2	2	1
Beasley, Williamsport	.933	11	10	18	2	0	Leiter, Albany°	1.000	15	1	10	0	1
Beck, Reading°	1.000	21	1	3	0	0	Leonette, Pittsfield	1.000	25	1	4	0	0
Bellaman, Williamsport	.980	27	14	35	1	2	Lind, Harrisburg	.900	14	3	6	1	1
Birriel, New Britain°	.800	11	0	8	2	0	Link, Williamsport	.889	56	9	7	2	1
Blum, Albany°	1.000	13	4	6	0	0	Long, Reading	1.000	4	3	4	0	0
Boudreaux, Reading	1.000	5	2	4	0	0	Lopez, Vermont	.914	20	8	24	3	1
Bowden, Reading°	.833	10	3	2	1	0	Machado, Reading	.875	21	7	7	2	0
Brink, Reading	.867	12	6	7	2	1	Magee, Reading	.727	13	2	6	3	0
Brown, New Britain°	1.000	7	6	4	0	0	Manzanillo, New Britain	1.000	2	0	1	0	0
Brusky, Vermont	.952	46	6	14	1	3	Masters, Pittsfield	.824	25	9	19	6	1
Bystrom, Albany	1.000	11	6	4	0	0	McHugh, Glens Falls	1.000	13	7	9	0	1
Carreno, Albany	1.000	9	1	1	0	0	McKay, Pittsfield°	.810	53	5	12	4	1
Clarkin, New Britain	.905	44	9	10	2	0	McLarnan, Reading	1.000	46	3	14	0	0
Close, Albany	1.000	2	0	1	0	0	Melendez, Harrisburg	1.000	6	1	3	0	1
D. Cooper, Glens Falls	.833	33	0	5	1	0	Melton, Harrisburg	1.000	12	2	6	0	0
W. Cooper, Glens Falls	.923	26	8	16	2	1	Miller, Reading°	.944	15	5	12	1	0
Copp, Glens Falls°	1.000	5	1	11	0	2	Minutelli, Vermont	1.000	6	1	1	0	0
Crouch, New Britain	1.000	24	2	16	0	0	Mirabito, Vermont	1.000	23	4	11	0	1
Dalton, New Britain°	1.000	4	2	0	0	0	Mitchell, Glens Falls	.905	39	7	12	2	1
Damian, Pittsfield	.943	26	11	22	2	2	B. Moore, Reading	1.000	9	0	1	0	0
Danek, Pittsfield	1.000	6	3	6	0	0	Morgan, Williamsport	1.000	6	2	1	0	0
Daniel, Harrisburg°	1.000	15	0	4	0	0	Morrow, Harrisburg	1.000	14	1	1	0	0
J. Davidson, Pittsfield	.923	11	6	6	1	1	Murphy, Williamsport°	1.000	9	4	2	0	0
R. Davidson, Albany	.867	14	5	8	2	0	Neal, Harrisburg°	1.000	39	6	15	0	0
Deitz, Vermont	1.000	20	2	4	0	1	Neidlinger, Harrisburg	.953	26	21	20	2	0
Dube, Williamsport	1.000	8	1	4	0	1	Nichols, Williamsport	1.000	16	6	4	0	1
Duffy, Glens Falls°	.933	49	5	9	1	1	Oliverio, Vermont	.966	27	12	16	1	2
Dunlap, Vermont	1.000	2	0	1	0	0	Patterson, Albany°	.765	24	2	11	4	0
Encarnacion, Williamsport	1.000	43	5	6	0	1	Pavlas, Pittsfield	.941	7	2	14	1	0
Freeman, Reading	1.000	9	1	5	0	1	Pena, Glens Falls	.818	43	4	14	4	1
Frey, Albany°	1.000	14	0	6	0	0	Perry, Williamsport	1.000	3	2	1	0	0
Frohwirth, Reading	1.000	36	3	16	0	1	PHILLIPS, Pittsfield	1.000	45	8	19	0	3
Gakeler, New Britain	.911	30	14	27	4	1	Pico, Pittsfield	1.000	12	7	13	0	0
Galvez, Glens Falls	.920	22	6	17	2	0	Plympton, New Britain	.733	23	2	9	4	0
Garces, Glens Falls°	1.000	4	1	3	0	0	Poehl, Williamsport	.933	5	5	9	1	0
George, Albany°	1.000	16	2	10	0	0	Poissant, Glens Falls	.938	30	6	9	1	0
Gideon, Harrisburg	1.000	26	1	12	0	0	Pries, Albany	1.000	7	2	3	0	0
Gordon, Harrisburg	1.000	25	1	3	0	0	Raubolt, Glens Falls	.833	5	2	3	1	0
Guercio, Albany	.667	24	4	4	4	1	Renfroe, Pittsfield	.900	40	4	5	1	0
Harrison, Albany°	.911	27	10	31	4	2	Rice, Pittsfield°	1.000	55	9	4	0	0
Hicks, Reading	1.000	48	3	5	0	1	Riley, Reading°	1.000	9	1	1	0	1
Hilton, Williamsport	.786	12	2	9	3	0	Ritter, Harrisburg	.923	29	11	13	2	1
Hirsch, Pittsfield	1.000	34	4	7	0	0	Ritz, Glens Falls	.943	25	12	38	3	3
Holman, 27 Har-18 GF	.864	45	11	8	3	0	Robles, Pittsfield	1.000	2	1	2	0	0
Irvine, New Britain	.932	37	8	33	3	5	Roesler, Vermont	1.000	22	3	2	0	0
Jefferson, Vermont	.727	41	3	5	3	0	Rooker, Harrisburg	.875	9	2	5	1	2
Johnson, Albany	1.000	14	1	1	0	0	Rosenberg, Albany°	1.000	32	4	6	0	1
Jones, Glen Falls	1.000	10	5	2	0	0	Ruiz, Glens Falls	1.000	1	0	1	0	0
Kamieniecki, Albany	1.000	10	4	6	0	0	Russell, Harrisburg°	.941	34	2	14	1	1
Karpuk, Williamsport	1.000	25	7	13	0	3	Sabo, Williamsport°	1.000	15	3	3	0	0
Kiecker, New Britain	.933	39	15	27	3	3	Sauveur, Harrisburg	.986	30	13	56	1	4
Knox, Albany	.966	23	11	17	1	0	Scanlan, Reading	.978	27	9	36	1	2
Kopf, Pittsfield	1.000	21	12	11	0	2	Scheid, 9 Alb-11 Ptf°	.889	20	6	10	2	0

PITCHERS—Continued

Player and Club	Pct.	G.	PO.	A.	E.	DP.	Player and Club	Pct.	G.	PO.	A.	E.	DP.
Schmidt, Albany	1.000	40	2	7	0	1	Thoma, Pittsfield	1.000	1	1	0	0	0
Scott, Williamsport	1.000	4	1	2	0	0	Thompson, Albany	1.000	5	0	1	0	0
Service, Reading	1.000	5	2	2	0	1	Torres, Albany	.857	34	2	10	2	0
Shelton, Reading	.892	41	13	20	4	0	Vasquez, New Britain	1.000	10	2	8	0	1
Simpson, Vermont°	.923	37	2	10	1	0	Walker, Harrisburg	1.000	4	2	3	0	0
Skalski, Williamsport	.750	18	5	10	5	0	Wilkins, Albany	1.000	2	2	0	0	0
D. Smith, 2 Wpt-19 Rea	.818	21	7	11	4	0	Williams, Harrisburg	.976	28	14	26	1	1
M. Smith, Vermont	.828	27	14	34	10	2	Wilmet, Harrisburg	1.000	5	1	1	0	1
Smoltz, Glens Falls	.844	21	17	10	5	1	Wilson, Williamsport°	.865	45	10	22	5	3
Spagnola, Vermont	.958	28	12	34	2	3	Zupka, New Britain	.921	55	10	25	3	1
Taylor, Harrisburg	1.000	3	1	2	0	0							

The following players do not have any recorded accepted chances at the positions indicated: therefore, are not listed in the fielding averages for those particular positions: Bell, p; Bresnahan, 3b; Bryant, c; Dersin, p; Encarnacion, 1b; Geren, 3b; Germann, 2b; Hardgrave, of; Harkey, p; T. Higgins, p; Hopkins, c; Iavarone, 2b; Mejia, 1b, of, p; R. Moore, p; Noles, p; Patterson, of; Polk, 3b; Stading, p; Swain, of; Thoma, 2b; Torres, of; Villanueva, 3b; Wilder, 3b.

CLUB PITCHING

Club	ERA.	G.	CG.	ShO.	Sv.	IP.	H.	R.	ER.	HR.	HB.	BB.	Int. BB.	SO.	WP.	Bk.
Vermont	3.54	140	34	16	30	1180.2	1180	560	465	70	31	480	32	669	62	12
Pittsfield	3.87	138	18	6	35	1195.0	1238	599	514	77	50	441	58	704	56	14
New Britain	4.17	140	27	10	21	1194.2	1219	654	554	69	35	514	40	669	74	31
Harrisburg	4.24	140	29	8	31	1200.2	1268	664	566	92	46	529	31	790	60	17
Reading	4.40	139	12	4	44	1193.0	1255	684	583	96	45	473	37	747	60	23
Albany	4.43	139	15	8	33	1206.0	1271	698	593	81	38	488	35	716	67	14
Williamsport	4.52	139	23	3	27	1175.0	1297	707	590	108	59	447	23	675	76	22
Glens Falls	5.07	137	10	1	27	1179.0	1331	758	664	117	45	507	35	656	61	25

PITCHERS' RECORDS
(Leading Qualifiers for Earned-Run Average Leadership — 112 or More Innings)

°Throws lefthanded.

Pitcher — Club	W.	L.	Pct.	ERA.	G.	GS.	CG.	GF.	ShO.	Sv.	IP.	H.	R.	ER.	HR.	HB.	BB.	Int. BB.	SO.	WP.
Lopez, Vermont	13	4	.765	2.40	20	20	10	0	4	0	154.0	153	50	41	5	2	26	3	82	0
Knox, Albany	11	5	.688	2.64	22	22	1	0	1	0	143.0	129	51	42	5	5	36	1	47	5
Sauveur, Harrisburg°	13	6	.684	2.86	30	27	7	0	1	0	195.0	174	71	62	9	9	96	3	160	9
Oliverio, Vermont	14	7	.667	2.89	27	27	6	0	2	0	186.2	173	73	60	12	2	58	2	78	10
Damian, Pittsfield	13	9	.591	3.21	26	26	5	0	0	0	168.0	179	80	60	10	8	36	2	97	8
M. Smith, Vermont	8	12	.400	3.36	27	27	6	0	2	0	171.1	152	78	64	5	3	117	3	104	15
Masters, Pittsfield	13	3	.800	3.73	25	24	2	0	1	0	157.0	158	77	65	9	14	67	2	105	8
Kiecker, New Britain	7	10	.412	3.82	39	17	2	18	0	6	153.0	164	76	65	6	10	66	5	66	9
Shelton, Reading	10	8	.556	3.85	41	15	0	9	0	1	135.2	164	77	58	7	5	40	3	68	5
Spagnola, Vermont	11	8	.579	3.87	28	27	9	0	2	0	183.2	186	96	79	17	5	49	3	88	6

Departmental Leaders: G—Link, 56; W—Scanlan, 15; L—Bellaman, 14; Pct.—Masters, Russell, .800; GS—Seven pitchers with 27; CG—Lopez, 10; GF—Zupka, 39; ShO—Lopez, 4; Sv.—Frohwirth, 19; IP—Sauveur, 195.0; H—Harrison, 203; R—Harrison, 115; ER—LaFever, 94; HR—Russell, 21; HB—Masters, 14; BB—M. Smith, 117; IBB—Clarkin, Hirsch, Renfroe, 8; SO—Sauveur, 160; WP—Irvine, 16.

(All Pitchers—Listed Alphabetically)

Pitcher — Club	W.	L.	Pct.	ERA.	G.	GS.	CG.	GF.	ShO.	Sv.	IP.	H.	R.	ER.	HR.	HB.	BB.	Int. BB.	SO.	WP.
Agar, Glens Falls	3	4	.429	8.16	17	0	0	5	0	1	32.0	42	36	29	9	2	18	0	21	0
Andersh, Harrisburg°	0	1	.000	12.27	2	1	0	0	0	0	3.2	10	6	5	0	0	2	0	2	1
Armstrong, Vermont	1	2	.333	3.03	5	5	2	0	1	0	35.2	24	12	12	0	1	23	4	39	3
Balabon, Albany	0	1	.000	4.15	1	1	0	0	0	0	4.1	4	3	2	0	0	3	0	2	1
Barton, Reading°	6	5	.545	4.92	32	12	3	9	0	3	82.1	108	50	45	8	1	31	2	53	5
Bast, New Britain°	9	13	.409	4.46	28	26	6	1	1	1	175.2	183	96	87	13	4	63	7	93	6
Beasley, Williamsport	2	6	.250	6.65	11	11	1	0	0	0	66.1	93	63	49	8	3	30	1	37	5
Beck, Reading°	3	0	1.000	4.56	21	0	0	12	0	0	23.2	22	14	12	1	0	11	1	17	0
Bell, Pittsfield°	0	0	.000	12.60	5	0	0	0	0	0	5.0	8	8	7	1	1	8	1	5	2
Bellaman, Williamsport	6	14	.300	4.36	27	26	5	0	0	0	165.0	199	102	80	12	11	69	1	84	10
Birriel, New Britain°	5	2	.714	1.90	11	5	5	5	2	1	52.0	45	11	11	0	0	20	2	19	1
Blum, Albany°	1	0	1.000	4.91	12	0	0	5	0	2	25.2	31	17	14	0	1	6	1	14	0
Boudreaux, Reading	2	2	.500	3.72	5	5	1	0	0	0	29.0	23	13	12	1	1	13	2	13	0
Bowden, Reading°	1	1	.500	5.73	10	3	0	1	0	0	22.0	25	15	14	5	1	16	1	20	4
Brink, Reading	3	2	.600	5.00	12	11	1	0	0	0	72.0	76	42	40	7	5	23	2	50	3
Brown, New Britain°	0	1	.000	5.96	7	5	0	0	0	0	22.2	21	15	15	2	0	18	0	10	6
Brusky, Vermont	4	3	.571	4.04	46	0	0	22	0	2	62.1	70	32	28	5	2	34	3	37	4
Bystrom, Albany	3	3	.500	5.89	11	6	1	2	1	1	44.1	50	30	29	3	2	22	3	31	2
Carreno, Albany	0	3	.000	7.88	9	3	0	4	0	1	24.0	32	23	21	6	0	15	1	18	1
Clarkin, New Britain	7	7	.500	4.78	44	9	0	27	0	6	111.0	99	65	59	6	5	66	8	73	10
Close, Albany	0	0	.000	2.25	2	0	0	2	0	0	4.0	2	1	1	0	0	1	0	4	1
D. Cooper, Glens Falls	4	6	.400	5.01	33	0	0	24	0	8	46.2	49	29	26	8	3	23	6	29	0
W. Cooper, Glens Falls	7	7	.500	4.69	26	25	3	0	1	0	142.0	163	89	74	17	1	41	5	74	4
Copp, Harrisburg°	2	2	.500	4.40	5	5	0	0	0	0	30.2	33	17	15	2	0	17	1	11	1
Crouch, New Britain°	6	9	.400	3.90	24	19	5	1	1	0	131.2	129	63	57	9	1	61	3	90	4
Dalton, New Britain	0	0	.000	0.00	4	0	0	4	0	1	5.0	1	0	0	0	0	2	0	8	0
Damian, Pittsfield	13	9	.591	3.21	26	26	5	0	0	0	168.0	179	80	60	10	8	36	2	97	8
Danek, Pittsfield	2	1	.667	2.30	6	6	1	0	0	0	43.0	33	12	11	6	1	12	0	25	2
Daniel, Harrisburg°	4	2	.667	6.20	15	4	1	3	0	0	40.2	61	29	28	3	1	13	1	23	3
J. Davidson, Pittsfield	1	3	.250	4.15	11	4	0	1	0	0	52.0	56	27	24	3	4	17	2	26	1
R. Davidson, Albany	1	2	.333	2.41	14	6	0	4	0	0	59.2	63	24	16	1	1	16	4	46	2
Deitz, Vermont	2	5	.286	5.57	20	0	0	13	0	1	32.1	38	30	20	1	5	18	1	26	4
Dersin, Albany	0	0	.000	4.70	3	0	0	0	0	0	7.2	6	5	4	1	0	5	0	5	1
Dube, Williamsport	0	2	.000	8.35	8	3	0	1	0	0	18.1	27	19	17	2	2	12	1	10	5
Duffy, Glens Falls°	2	6	.250	4.83	49	1	0	19	0	2	91.1	112	56	49	9	2	32	3	61	3
Dunlap, Vermont	0	0	.000	0.00	2	0	0	2	0	0	3.0	1	0	0	0	0	0	0	1	0
Encarnacion, Williamsport	4	5	.444	3.90	43	1	0	35	0	12	55.1	61	24	24	5	6	22	5	34	1
Freeman, Reading	3	3	.500	5.07	9	9	0	0	0	0	49.2	45	30	28	7	0	32	1	19	1
Frey, Albany°	0	2	.000	1.93	14	0	0	10	0	1	28.0	20	6	6	0	0	7	1	19	1

Pitcher—Club	W.	L.	Pct.	ERA.	G.	GS.	CG.	GF.	ShO.	Sv.	IP.	H.	R.	ER.	HR.	HB.	BB.	Int. BB.	SO.	WP.
Frohwirth, Reading	2	4	.333	1.86	36	0	0	31	0	19	58.0	36	14	12	3	2	13	0	44	1
Gakeler, New Britain	8	13	.381	4.63	30	25	5	3	1	0	173.0	188	112	89	14	7	63	5	90	7
Galvez, Glens Falls	5	9	.357	4.63	22	21	3	1	0	0	116.2	148	69	60	7	3	54	3	53	5
Garces, Glens Falls°	3	1	.750	3.86	4	4	0	0	0	0	23.1	17	11	10	1	1	12	0	15	4
George, Albany°	1	7	.125	8.10	16	10	0	2	0	0	56.2	73	51	51	11	0	23	0	29	3
Gideon, Harrisburg	4	3	.571	1.98	26	0	0	24	0	12	36.1	27	10	8	2	1	10	2	39	1
Gordon, Harrisburg	3	4	.429	2.78	25	0	0	15	0	9	35.2	27	13	11	1	4	15	2	20	2
Guercio, Albany	1	1	.500	5.50	24	1	0	9	0	3	54.0	68	43	33	7	2	26	4	32	7
Harkey, Pittsfield	0	0	.000	0.00	1	0	0	0	0	0	2.0	1	0	0	0	0	0	0	2	0
Harrison, Albany°	8	11	.421	4.20	27	27	6	0	1	0	178.0	203	115	83	9	5	49	1	83	6
Hicks, Reading	6	8	.429	3.16	48	1	0	17	0	6	99.2	107	54	35	5	3	34	5	54	7
Higgins, Albany°	0	0	.000	9.00	1	0	0	1	0	0	1.0	1	1	1	0	0	1	0	0	0
Hilton, Williamsport	4	2	.667	3.29	12	5	0	2	0	0	52.0	54	24	19	6	3	17	2	28	4
Hirsch, Pittsfield	7	1	.875	4.11	34	0	0	23	0	8	46.0	51	22	21	1	1	25	8	39	7
Holman, 27 Har-18 G.F.	5	6	.455	4.66	45	5	0	16	0	3	104.1	116	65	54	10	8	60	4	49	6
Irvine, New Britain	4	13	.235	5.31	37	16	3	8	0	0	127.0	156	101	75	7	2	59	4	70	16
Jefferson, Vermont	3	9	.250	3.04	41	0	0	33	0	13	50.1	47	22	17	3	3	19	7	39	2
Johnson, Albany	5	5	.500	5.18	14	10	1	0	1	0	57.1	64	37	33	4	0	30	2	23	4
Jones, Glens Falls	1	2	.333	6.58	10	6	0	0	0	0	39.2	45	34	29	9	1	14	1	29	0
Kamienecki, Albany	1	3	.250	5.35	10	7	0	1	0	0	37.0	41	25	22	0	1	33	3	19	3
Karpuk, Williamsport	2	4	.333	4.40	25	3	0	7	0	0	73.2	76	37	36	2	3	32	1	31	2
Kiecker, New Britain	7	10	.412	3.82	39	17	2	18	0	6	153.0	164	76	65	6	10	66	5	66	9
Knox, Albany	11	5	.688	2.64	23	22	1	0	1	0	143.0	129	51	42	5	5	36	1	47	5
Kopf, Pittsfield	5	5	.500	4.21	21	15	3	3	0	0	94.0	89	49	44	6	5	26	2	43	2
Kramer, Harrisburg	4	5	.444	6.34	26	4	1	14	1	1	49.2	62	43	35	2	0	29	4	43	8
Kuykendall, Williamsport	0	1	.000	7.71	7	2	0	1	0	0	21.0	28	21	18	4	0	11	1	8	4
LaFever, Williamsport	8	13	.381	5.43	27	27	6	0	1	0	155.2	179	103	94	19	8	55	1	83	7
Langdon, Vermont	4	6	.400	4.35	21	12	0	2	0	0	80.2	83	48	39	5	3	49	0	45	8
Layana, Albany	2	4	.333	5.05	8	7	1	0	0	0	46.1	51	28	26	4	2	18	0	19	1
Lee, Glens Falls°	0	0	.000	8.64	7	0	0	4	0	0	8.1	13	9	8	1	0	1	0	3	1
Leiter, Albany°	3	3	.500	3.35	15	14	2	0	0	0	78.0	64	34	29	4	2	37	0	71	3
Leonette, Pittsfield	4	0	1.000	0.74	25	0	0	8	0	2	36.2	29	5	3	1	0	6	2	19	1
Lind, Harrisburg	1	8	.111	4.74	14	9	0	1	0	0	57.0	64	40	30	2	1	24	1	37	4
Link, Williamsport	6	5	.545	3.51	56	1	0	37	0	11	105.0	105	51	41	7	3	28	4	59	5
Long, Reading	0	2	.000	12.46	4	3	0	0	0	0	13.0	17	19	18	2	1	20	0	6	0
Lopez, Vermont	13	4	.765	2.40	20	20	10	0	4	0	154.0	153	50	41	5	2	26	3	82	0
Machado, Reading	4	5	.444	4.74	21	17	2	2	0	0	108.1	112	70	57	9	4	40	2	89	6
Magee, Reading	4	4	.500	4.91	13	10	1	2	1	0	55.0	50	36	30	1	4	36	2	43	11
Manzanillo, New Britain	2	0	1.000	4.50	2	2	0	0	0	0	10.0	8	5	5	1	0	8	0	12	0
Masters, Pittsfield	12	3	.800	3.73	25	24	2	0	1	0	157.0	158	77	65	9	14	67	2	105	8
McHugh, Glens Falls	4	7	.364	7.55	13	13	1	0	0	0	64.1	88	57	54	4	3	22	0	27	4
McKay, Pittsfield°	2	4	.333	3.36	53	0	0	15	0	4	67.0	53	29	25	5	1	35	7	60	4
McLarnan, Reading	7	5	.583	3.52	46	0	0	29	0	10	92.0	75	43	36	9	1	21	7	51	1
Mejia, Williamsport	0	0	.000	0.00	1	0	0	0	0	0	0.1	0	0	0	0	0	0	0	0	0
Melendez, Harrisburg	1	3	.250	10.80	6	6	0	0	0	0	18.1	28	24	22	4	0	11	0	13	0
Melton, Harrisburg	7	3	.700	3.89	12	12	4	0	0	0	76.1	74	41	33	6	5	30	1	60	2
Miller, Reading°	4	3	.571	5.69	15	11	0	2	0	0	61.2	85	42	39	7	0	22	0	26	1
Minutelli, Vermont	4	1	.800	3.18	6	6	0	0	0	0	39.2	34	15	14	3	2	16	0	39	2
Mirabito, Vermont	4	7	.364	4.93	23	16	1	3	0	1	98.2	125	62	54	10	2	34	2	41	6
Mitchell, Glens Falls	5	1	.833	2.40	39	0	0	28	0	7	78.2	63	23	21	4	4	26	6	55	4
Moore, Reading	0	1	.000	0.98	9	0	0	8	0	4	18.1	12	2	2	0	2	4	2	13	0
Moore, Glens Falls	0	2	.000	7.71	4	2	0	1	0	0	9.1	12	9	8	2	0	7	0	2	1
Morgan, Williamsport	1	0	1.000	7.71	6	0	0	4	0	2	7.0	12	8	6	2	0	2	0	4	0
Morrow, Harrisburg	0	0	.000	4.70	14	0	0	7	0	1	15.1	21	9	8	1	0	12	1	14	3
Murphy, Williamsport°	4	3	.571	6.49	9	9	2	0	1	0	43.0	58	35	31	6	1	17	0	27	5
Neal, Harrisburg°	5	6	.455	6.55	39	3	0	12	0	4	67.1	75	54	49	13	5	37	3	47	3
Neidlinger, Harrisburg	11	8	.579	3.96	26	26	7	0	0	0	170.2	183	92	75	9	5	61	4	96	6
Nichols, Williamsport	4	3	.571	3.69	16	16	1	0	0	0	100.0	107	53	41	9	9	33	0	60	5
Noles, Pittsfield	0	1	.000	6.00	1	1	0	0	0	0	3.0	4	2	2	1	1	1	0	5	1
Oliverio, Vermont	14	7	.667	2.89	27	27	6	0	2	0	186.2	173	73	60	12	4	58	2	78	10
Patterson, Albany°	3	6	.333	3.96	24	8	1	14	0	5	63.2	59	31	28	2	2	31	1	47	4
Pavlas, Pittsfield	6	1	.857	3.80	7	7	0	0	0	0	45.0	49	25	19	6	3	17	2	27	1
Pena, Glens Falls	5	6	.455	2.79	43	0	0	35	0	7	67.2	76	24	21	3	1	16	5	36	1
Perry, Williamsport	1	0	1.000	1.57	3	3	0	0	0	0	23.0	18	8	4	1	0	10	1	17	2
Phillips, Reading°	9	3	.750	3.48	45	7	0	14	0	2	95.2	111	49	37	6	4	29	5	51	0
Pico, Pittsfield	4	4	.500	3.87	12	12	1	0	0	0	79.0	74	38	34	1	1	23	5	52	2
Plympton, New Britain	4	1	.800	3.82	23	6	1	7	0	1	63.2	61	35	27	2	2	34	2	60	4
Poehl, Williamsport	2	2	.500	4.01	5	5	2	0	0	0	33.2	32	17	15	0	1	9	0	14	0
Poissant, Glens Falls	4	5	.444	6.17	30	10	1	4	0	1	105.0	129	82	72	15	7	43	1	49	9
Pries, Albany	1	1	.500	5.85	7	0	0	2	0	0	20.0	26	13	13	2	2	13	0	5	4
Raubolt, Glens Falls	2	2	.500	2.33	5	4	1	0	0	0	27.0	20	10	7	1	2	17	0	15	2
Renfroe, Pittsfield	4	5	.444	4.08	40	0	0	37	0	16	46.1	56	22	21	2	0	15	8	27	3
Rice, Pittsfield°	3	2	.600	4.43	55	0	0	15	0	3	44.2	48	23	22	5	0	22	5	19	2
Riley, Glens Falls	0	0	.000	4.66	9	0	0	3	0	0	9.2	14	8	5	2	0	3	1	4	0
Ritter, Harrisburg	8	4	.667	4.06	29	18	5	3	3	0	135.1	158	71	61	7	6	54	4	73	4
Ritz, Glens Falls	8	8	.500	4.89	25	25	1	0	0	0	152.2	171	95	83	5	4	71	1	78	11
Robles, Pittsfield	0	1	.000	6.10	2	2	0	0	0	0	10.1	16	8	7	0	4	4	1	5	2
Roesler, Vermont	4	2	.667	3.29	22	0	0	20	0	11	27.1	28	10	10	1	0	10	3	19	0
Rooker, Harrisburg	0	0	.000	3.26	9	0	0	3	0	0	19.1	20	11	7	0	1	17	0	7	3
Rosenberg, Albany°	4	4	.500	2.25	32	0	0	31	0	15	40.0	33	11	10	1	0	12	1	24	0
Ruiz, Glens Falls	0	0	.000	9.00	1	0	0	1	0	0	2.0	3	3	2	0	0	4	0	1	1
Russell, Harrisburg°	8	2	.800	3.94	34	20	4	10	0	1	155.1	149	75	68	21	4	49	1	96	5
Sabo, Williamsport°	1	0	1.000	5.21	15	0	0	6	0	0	19.0	18	13	11	2	1	12	2	16	2
Sauveur, Williamsport°	13	6	.684	2.86	30	27	7	0	1	0	195.0	174	71	62	9	9	96	3	160	9
Scanlan, Reading	15	5	.750	5.10	27	26	3	0	1	0	164.0	187	98	93	12	11	55	3	91	4
Scheid, 9 Alb-11 Pitts°	4	3	.571	6.16	20	15	1	2	1	0	76.0	88	60	52	3	6	52	1	46	7
Schmidt, Albany	9	8	.529	5.31	40	6	1	18	0	4	98.1	115	64	58	10	2	42	3	64	4
Scott, Williamsport	0	3	.000	4.00	4	4	0	0	0	0	27.0	29	16	12	4	0	6	0	14	0
Service, Reading	0	3	.000	7.78	5	4	0	0	0	0	19.2	22	19	17	5	0	16	1	12	1
Shelton, Reading	10	8	.556	3.85	41	15	0	9	0	1	135.2	164	77	58	7	5	40	3	68	5
Simpson, Vermont°	1	1	.500	4.42	37	0	0	11	0	1	55.0	66	32	27	3	1	27	1	31	2
Skalski, Williamsport	8	7	.533	4.20	18	18	5	0	0	0	113.2	105	62	53	15	5	35	0	76	5

Pitcher—Club	W.	L.	Pct.	ERA.	G.	GS.	CG.	GF.	ShO.	Sv.	IP.	H.	R.	ER.	HR.	HB.	BB.	Int. BB.	SO.	WP.
D. Smith, 2 Wpt-19 Rea	7	3	.700	3.92	21	14	1	2	0	1	87.1	86	46	38	6	4	46	2	58	6
M. Smith, Vermont	8	12	.400	3.36	27	27	6	0	2	0	171.1	152	78	64	5	3	117	3	104	15
Smoltz, Glens Falls	4	10	.286	5.68	21	21	0	0	0	0	130.0	131	89	82	17	7	81	2	86	6
Spagnola, Vermont	11	8	.579	3.87	28	27	9	0	2	0	183.2	186	96	79	17	5	49	3	88	6
Stading, Harrisburg	0	0	.000	6.75	3	0	0	2	0	0	1.1	1	1	1	0	0	3	0	0	0
Taylor, Harrisburg	1	0	1.000	0.00	3	1	0	2	0	1	8.0	6	0	0	0	0	1	0	10	1
Thoma, Pittsfield	0	0	.000	36.00	1	0	0	1	0	0	1.0	5	4	4	0	0	1	0	0	2
Thompson, Albany	0	0	.000	9.58	5	0	0	2	0	0	10.1	14	12	11	2	1	7	0	2	0
Torres, Albany	8	3	.727	3.34	34	0	0	16	0	0	64.2	60	29	24	2	1	22	4	71	9
Vasquez, New Britain	3	2	.600	2.80	10	9	0	0	0	0	61.0	63	23	19	4	1	19	0	26	0
Walker, Harrisburg	0	2	.000	9.00	4	4	0	0	0	0	15.0	20	17	15	2	0	9	0	9	4
Wilkins, Albany	0	0	.000	6.75	2	2	0	0	0	0	12.0	18	11	9	3	1	1	0	8	0
Williams, Pittsfield	13	8	.619	4.46	28	27	5	0	0	0	171.1	176	92	85	14	3	78	6	84	6
Wilmet, Harrisburg	1	1	.500	9.39	5	0	0	4	0	0	7.2	8	8	8	2	0	4	1	3	0
Wilson, Williamsport*	6	8	.429	3.48	45	3	1	23	0	2	88.0	85	43	34	3	3	44	3	68	12
Zupka, New Britain	5	8	.385	3.72	55	1	0	39	0	5	109.0	101	52	45	5	3	35	4	53	11

BALKS—Skalski, 10; Irvine, 9; Smoltz, 8; Bast, Machado, Sauveur, 7 each; Birriel, W. Cooper, Gakeler, Hirsch, Magee, Masters, Mitchell, Oliverio, Plympton, Ritz, Scheid, 3 each; Bellaman, Boudreaux, Brink, D. Cooper, Crouch, Encarnacion, Hicks, Karpuk, Leiter, Lind, Lopez, McKay, Neal, Pena, Rosenberg, M. Smith, Vasquez, 2 each; Agar, Armstrong, Barton, Brusky, Bystrom, Damian, Danek, Dube, Freeman, Galvez, Garces, George, Gordon, Guercio, Harrison, Kamieniecki, Kiecker, Kopf, LaFever, Layana, Link, McHugh, McLarnan, Melendez, Miller, Minutelli, Mirabito, Neidlinger, Nichols, Noles, Pavlas, Perry, Phillips, Poehl, Ritter, Scanlan, Schmidt, Shelton, D. Smith, Spagnola, Stading, Walker, Zupka, 1 each.

COMBINATION SHUTOUTS—Knox-Thompson, Johnson-Schmidt, Scheid-Rosenberg, Albany; Lind-Neal, Melendez-Ritter-Gideon-Russell, Taylor-Gordon, Harrisburg; Crouch-Clarkin, Kiecker-Irvine-Zupka, Clarkin-Zupka, Kiecker-Clarkin, Bast-Zupka, New Britain; Pico-Rice-Renfroe, Pico-McKay-Renfroe, Danek-Hirsch, Kopf-Hirsch, Damian-McKay-Phillips, Pittsfield; Magee-Moore, Reading; Smith-Jefferson, Mirabito-Simpson-Jefferson, Spagnola-Jefferson, Langdon-Jefferson, Oliverio-Roesler, Vermont; Encarnacion-Morgan, Williamsport.

NO-HIT GAMES—None.

Southern League

CLASS AA

Leading Batter
DAVE MYERS
Chattanooga

League President
JIMMY BRAGAN

Leading Pitcher
BRIAN HOLMAN
Jacksonville

CHAMPIONSHIP WINNERS IN PREVIOUS YEARS

1904—Macon .... .598	1938—Savannah .... .574	1965—Columbus .... .572
1905—Macon .... .625	Macon (2nd)† .... .570	1966—Mobile .... .629
1906—Savannah .... .637	1939—Columbus .... .601	1967—Birmingham .... .604
1907—Charleston .... .620	Augusta (2nd)† .... .597	1968—Asheville .... .614
1908—Jacksonville .... .694	1940—Savannah .... .627	1969—Charlotte .... .579
1909—Chattanooga° .... .738	Columbus (2nd)† .... .583	1970—Columbus .... .569
Augusta .... .702	1941—Macon .... .643	1971—Did not operate as league—clubs
1910—Columbus .... .588	Columbia (2nd)† .... .636	were members of Dixie Association.
1911—Columbus° .... .681	1942—Charleston .... .620	1972—Asheville .... .583
Columbia .... .710	Macon (2nd)† .... .585	Montgomery§ .... .561
1912—Jacksonville° .... .679	1943-45—Did not operate.	1973—Montgomery§ .... .580
Columbus .... .632	1946—Columbus .... .568	Jacksonville .... .559
1913—Savannah .... .754	Augusta (4th)† .... .547	1974—Jacksonville .... .565
Savannah .... .593	1947—Columbus .... .575	Knoxville§ .... .533
1914—Savannah° .... .667	Savannah (2nd)† .... .563	1975—Orlando .... .587
Albany .... .650	1948—Charleston .... .572	Montgomery§ .... .545
1915—Macon .... .588	Greenville (3rd)† .... .549	1976—Montgomery x .... .591
Columbus° .... .686	1949—Macon‡ .... .623	Orlando .... .540
1916—Augusta° .... .617	1950—Macon‡ .... .588	1977—Montgomery x .... .628
Columbia .... .631	1951—Montgomery .... .607	Jacksonville .... .522
1917—Charleston .... .741	1952—Columbia .... .649	1978—Knoxville x .... .611
Columbia° .... .667	Montgomery (3rd)† .... .558	Savannah .... .500
1918—Did not operate.	1953—Jacksonville .... .679	1979—Columbus .... .587
1919—Columbia .... .585	Savannah (2nd)† .... .571	Nashville x .... .576
1920—Columbia .... .633	1954—Jacksonville .... .593	1980—Memphis .... .576
1921—Columbia .... .642	Savannah (2nd)† .... .571	Charlotte x .... .500
1922—Charleston .... .625	1955—Columbia .... .636	1981—Nashville .... .566
1923—Charlotte° .... .653	Augusta (3rd)† .... .543	Orlando x .... .556
Macon .... .580	1956—Jacksonville‡ .... .621	1982—Jacksonville .... .576
1924—Augusta .... .612	1957—Augusta .... .636	Nashville x .... .535
1925—Spartanburg .... .620	Charlotte (2nd)† .... .562	1983—Birmingham x .... .628
1926—Greenville .... .662	1958—Augusta .... .550	Jacksonville .... .531
1927—Greenville .... .622	Macon (3rd)† .... .500	1984—Charlotte x .... .510
1928—Asheville .... .664	1959—Knoxville .... .557	Knoxville .... .483
1929—Asheville .... .605	Gastonia (4th)† .... .504	1985—Charlotte .... .545
Knoxville° .... .634	1960—Columbia .... .597	Huntsville x .... .542
1930—Greenville° .... .620	Savannah (3rd)† .... .561	1986—Huntsville .... .553
Macon .... .643	1961—Asheville .... .635	Columbus x .... .500
1931-35—Did not operate.	1962—Savannah .... .662	
1936—Jacksonville .... .652	Macon (3rd)† .... .576	
Columbus° .... .650	1963—Augusta° .... .661	
1937—Columbus .... .572	Lynchburg .... .662	
Savannah (3rd)† .... .565	1964—Lynchburg .... .579	

°Won split-season playoff. †Won four-club playoff. ‡Won championship and four-club playoff. §League was divided into Eastern and Western divisions; won playoff. xLeague was divided into Eastern and Western divisions and played split season; won playoff.

STANDING OF CLUBS AT CLOSE OF FIRST HALF, JUNE 17

EASTERN DIVISION						WESTERN DIVISION					
Club	W.	L.	T.	Pct.	G.B.	Club	W.	L.	T.	Pct.	G.B.
Charlotte (Orioles)	43	29	0	.597	....	Birmingham (White Sox)	41	31	0	.569	....
Jacksonville (Expos)	42	30	0	.583	1	Memphis (Royals)	38	33	0	.535	2½
Columbus (Astros)	40	32	0	.556	3	Huntsville (A's)	34	38	0	.472	7
Greenville (Braves)	29	42	0	.408	13½	Chattanooga (Mariners)	34	38	0	.472	7
Orlando (Twins)	27	45	0	.375	16	Knoxville (Blue Jays)	31	41	0	.431	10

STANDING OF CLUBS AT CLOSE OF SECOND HALF, SEPTEMBER 1

EASTERN DIVISION						WESTERN DIVISION					
Club	W.	L.	T.	Pct.	G.B.	Club	W.	L.	T.	Pct.	G.B.
Jacksonville (Expos)	43	29	0	.597	....	Huntsville (A's)	40	32	0	.556	....
Charlotte (Orioles)	42	31	0	.575	1½	Knoxville (Blue Jays)	37	35	0	.514	3
Greenville (Braves)	41	32	0	.562	2½	Chattanooga (Mariners)	34	37	0	.479	5½
Orlando (Twins)	34	37	0	.479	8½	Memphis (Royals)	34	38	0	.472	6
Columbus (Astros)	27	44	0	.380	15½	Birmingham (White Sox)	27	44	0	.380	12½

COMPOSITE STANDING OF CLUBS AT CLOSE OF SEASON, SEPTEMBER 1

Club	Jax.	Char.	Hunt.	Mem.	Grn.	Chat.	Birm.	Knox.	Col.	Orl.	W.	L.	T.	Pct.	G.B.
Jacksonville (Expos)	....	8	9	12	11	11	10	6	7	11	85	59	0	.590	....
Charlotte (Orioles)	9	....	7	10	10	9	11	11	9	9	85	60	0	.586	½
Huntsville (A's)	7	9	....	8	10	7	8	8	8	9	74	70	0	.514	11
Memphis (Royals)	4	6	8	....	7	9	9	8	11	10	72	71	0	.503	12½
Greenville (Braves)	5	6	6	9	....	7	8	11	8	10	70	74	0	.486	15
Chattanooga (Mariners)	5	7	9	7	9	....	7	8	6	10	68	75	0	.476	16½
Birmingham (White Sox)	6	5	8	6	8	9	....	10	8	8	68	75	0	.476	16½
Knoxville (Blue Jays)	10	5	8	8	5	8	6	....	8	10	68	76	0	.472	17
Columbus (Astros)	9	7	8	5	8	9	8	8	....	5	67	76	0	.469	17½
Orlando (Twins)	4	7	7	6	6	6	8	6	11	....	61	82	0	.427	23½

Major league affiliations in parentheses.

Playoffs—Birmingham defeated Huntsville, three games to none; Charlotte defeated Jacksonville, three games to two; Birmingham defeated Charlotte, three games to one, to win league championship.

Regular-Season Attendance—Birmingham, 147,279; Charlotte, 129,246; Chattanooga, 110,893; Columbus, 128,845; Greenville, 206,468; Huntsville, 256,090; Jacksonville, 190,456; Knoxville, 124,231; Memphis, 215,749; Orlando, 69,656. Total—1,578,913. Playoffs—18,942. All-Star Game—2,919.

Managers—Birmingham, Rico Petrocelli; Chattanooga, Sal Rende; Charlotte, Greg Biagini; Columbus, Tom Wiedenbauer; Greenville, Jim Beauchamp; Huntsville, Brad Fischer; Jacksonville, Tommy Thompson; Knoxville, Glenn Ezell; Memphis, Bob Schaefer; Orlando, George Mitterwald.

All-Star Team—1B—Dave Falcone, Charlotte; 2B—Ronnie Gant, Greenville; 3B—Ken Caminiti, Columbus; SS—Walt Weiss, Huntsville; OF—Geronimo Berroa, Knoxville; Larry Walker, Jacksonville; Rondal Rollin, Birmingham; Matt Winters, Memphis; Mike Berger, Jacksonville; C—Nelson Santovenia, Jacksonville; DH—Tom Dodd, Charlotte; RHP—Brian Holman, Jacksonville; LHP—Rob Mallicoat, Columbus; Relief Pitcher—Kevin Price, Jacksonville; Most Valuable Player—Tom Dodd, Charlotte; Manager of the Year—Tommy Thompson, Jacksonville.

(Compiled by Howe News Bureau, Boston, Mass.)

CLUB BATTING

Club	Pct.	G.	AB.	R.	OR.	H.	TB.	2B.	3B.	HR.	RBI.	GW.	SH.	SF.	HP.	BB.	Int. BB.	SO.	SB.	CS.	LOB.
Charlotte	.272	145	4830	750	655	1314	2009	222	43	129	667	77	32	39	37	581	23	834	178	89	1036
Knoxville	.268	144	4874	731	702	1307	2038	241	52	162	672	62	26	47	40	480	14	975	136	59	977
Chattanooga	.267	143	4776	626	623	1274	1803	236	37	73	567	66	47	59	30	432	22	636	107	70	970
Memphis	.263	143	4782	752	729	1259	2063	245	53	151	688	63	19	39	22	609	15	1036	106	60	996
Columbus	.262	143	4781	675	691	1252	1869	235	29	108	604	60	35	37	35	444	18	844	94	51	960
Birmingham	.260	143	4744	662	736	1232	1901	219	24	134	609	59	30	37	21	515	26	844	90	66	992
Jacksonville	.255	144	4796	670	585	1223	1881	210	35	126	615	79	43	32	53	513	23	779	100	60	1011
Huntsville	.251	144	4682	616	635	1177	1673	225	26	73	533	66	53	40	47	640	21	1017	165	69	1123
Orlando	.249	143	4692	600	722	1166	1755	196	30	111	538	50	38	29	38	478	15	698	97	50	968
Greenville	.245	144	4783	611	615	1172	1715	214	28	91	556	66	47	34	31	537	24	896	86	50	1040

INDIVIDUAL BATTING

(Leading Qualifiers for Batting Championship—389 or More Plate Appearances)

*Bats lefthanded.   †Switch-hitter.

Player and Club	Pct.	G.	AB.	R.	H.	TB.	2B.	3B.	HR.	RBI.	GW.	SH.	SF.	HP.	BB.	Int. BB.	SO.	SB.	CS.
Myers, David, Chattanooga	.328	130	488	72	160	224	33	2	9	69	8	5	5	1	30	0	33	1	5
Caminiti, Kenneth, Columbus†	.325	95	375	66	122	196	25	2	15	69	7	0	7	0	25	4	58	11	5
Stanicek, Peter, Charlotte†	.315	88	337	78	106	156	18	4	8	50	8	2	3	8	46	0	46	30	10
Cimo, Matthew, Charlotte	.308	108	406	73	125	212	21	6	18	64	7	2	3	2	31	1	85	13	7
Cijntje, Sherwin, Charlotte*	.304	111	405	59	123	166	19	6	4	44	7	3	0	1	50	2	44	31	14
Wetherby, Jeffrey, Greenville*	.303	140	488	67	148	223	31	4	12	78	8	2	2	2	63	5	87	7	4
Xavier, Joseph, Huntsville*	.301	137	492	74	148	211	37	7	4	53	9	12	5	5	77	3	72	23	15
Reyna, Luis, Knoxville*	.297	132	501	61	149	228	21	8	14	67	8	2	3	3	20	2	75	21	10
Berger, Michael, Jacksonville	.293	143	508	94	149	249	20	7	22	93	10	1	7	8	71	4	106	13	6
Falcone, David, Charlotte*	.293	132	478	74	140	213	25	3	14	92	11	1	3	1	67	7	76	15	3
Shaddy, Christopher, Knoxville	.291	125	475	87	138	236	35	3	19	77	8	8	9	4	59	1	110	10	6

Departmental Leaders: G—Berger, 143; AB—Pruitt, 542; R—Tatis, 101; H—Myers, 160; TB—Berroa, 297; 2B—Xavier, 37; 3B—Eisenreich, Fox, 10; HR—Rollin, 39; RBI—Dodd, 127; GWRBI—Dodd, L. Walker, 19; SH—Xavier, 12; SF—Dodd, 12; HP—Howard, 12; BB—Tubbs, 86; IBB—O'Dell, 9; SO—Rollin, 218; SB—Tatis, 55; CS—Tubbs, 19.

(All Players—Listed Alphabetically)

Player and Club	Pct.	G.	AB.	R.	H.	TB.	2B.	3B.	HR.	RBI.	GW.	SH.	SF.	HP.	BB.	Int. BB.	SO.	SB.	CS.
Afenir, Troy, Columbus	.202	31	99	15	20	34	8	0	2	11	0	2	0	0	6	0	20	0	0
Akins, Sidney, Columbus	.250	16	4	1	1	1	0	0	0	0	0	0	0	0	0	0	2	0	0
Alcala, Julio, Memphis	.200	26	105	14	21	26	1	2	0	5	0	1	0	0	4	0	11	2	2
Alcazar, Jorge, Birmingham	.200	43	125	9	25	33	2	0	2	14	1	2	1	2	10	1	29	2	1
Allaire, Karl, Columbus*	.249	110	341	51	85	102	13	2	0	26	2	4	2	1	50	2	79	7	6
Allen, Robert, Columbus	.188	31	85	4	16	22	3	0	1	7	0	0	0	0	7	0	15	0	0
Alva, John, Greenville	.246	19	65	8	16	21	2	0	1	7	1	2	0	1	1	0	14	0	0

Player and Club	Pct.	G.	AB.	R.	H.	TB.	2B.	3B.	HR.	RBI.	GW.	SH.	SF.	HP.	BB.	Int. BB.	SO.	SB.	CS.
Anderson, Roy, Huntsville	.237	72	198	29	47	77	10	1	6	31	4	6	1	2	33	0	53	0	0
Arias, Antonio, Huntsville	.261	15	46	8	12	18	0	0	2	6	0	0	0	1	2	0	9	0	2
Arndt, Larry, Huntsville	.244	124	422	48	103	132	18	1	3	31	2	6	2	1	60	2	111	17	5
Arnold, Timothy, Jacksonville	.194	38	108	6	21	29	2	0	2	8	1	1	1	2	12	0	15	0	2
Arnsberg, Timothy, Columbus	.000	13	1	0	0	0	0	0	0	0	0	0	0	0	0	0	0	0	0
Balelo, Onesimo, Chattanooga	.193	47	140	17	27	37	4	0	2	15	3	7	3	0	15	0	26	0	3
Bartley, Gregory, Chattanooga	.000	48	1	0	0	0	0	0	0	0	0	0	0	0	0	0	1	0	0
Beamesderfer, Kurt, Charlotte	.255	42	137	11	35	49	8	0	2	16	2	2	2	1	13	1	20	1	2
Beauchamp, Kash, Knoxville	.298	59	188	28	56	85	10	2	5	24	0	1	2	3	24	0	39	3	5
Bell, Terence, Memphis	.239	86	272	30	65	84	8	1	3	23	2	2	2	1	33	1	70	5	3
Beltre, Esteban, Jacksonville	.212	142	491	55	104	139	15	4	4	34	4	10	0	3	40	0	98	9	8
Bennett, James, Memphis°	.260	91	319	58	83	166	22	2	19	46	0	0	1	2	21	0	80	2	3
Berger, Michael, Jacksonville	.293	143	508	94	149	249	20	7	22	93	10	1	7	8	71	4	106	13	6
Berroa, Geronimo, Knoxville	.287	134	523	87	150	297	33	3	36	108	13	0	7	5	46	1	104	2	1
Bertolani, Jerry, Birmingham	.298	24	94	13	28	37	3	3	0	6	1	0	1	1	7	0	15	6	3
Bierley, Brad, Orlando°	.235	139	507	71	119	213	20	4	22	78	10	2	9	4	57	2	68	6	5
Blackwell, Larry, Orlando	.227	62	220	37	50	80	12	3	4	21	2	3	1	1	29	0	47	9	10
Blankenship, Kevin, Greenville	.000	40	4	0	0	0	0	0	0	0	0	0	0	0	0	0	3	0	0
Blankenship, Lance, Huntsville	.254	107	390	64	99	138	21	3	4	39	4	3	5	6	67	0	60	34	7
Blauser, Jeffrey, Greenville	.249	72	265	35	66	97	13	3	4	32	1	6	3	3	34	0	49	5	3
Borders, Patrick, Knoxville	.292	94	349	44	102	151	14	1	11	51	5	0	3	2	20	1	56	2	5
Borg, Gary, Orlando°	.225	52	169	20	38	62	7	4	3	18	0	2	0	0	24	2	25	1	0
Bowen, Kenneth, Memphis†	.196	48	143	20	28	40	4	1	2	14	1	1	2	2	16	0	30	4	0
Briley, Gregory, Chattanooga°	.275	137	539	81	148	200	21	5	7	61	3	2	8	2	41	0	58	34	14
Brilinski, Tyler, Huntsville°	.265	136	480	60	127	212	35	1	16	68	10	0	3	4	55	6	108	7	2
Brock, Norman, Columbus°	.287	113	362	54	104	139	15	7	2	33	2	6	4	0	34	0	68	22	5
Brumfield, Jacob, Memphis	.333	9	39	7	13	23	3	2	1	6	1	1	0	0	3	0	8	2	1
Bruzik, Robert, Chattanooga	.288	76	229	27	66	103	14	4	5	34	7	4	4	0	21	0	37	10	3
Caceres, Edgar, Jacksonville†	.129	18	62	7	8	10	0	1	0	3	0	0	0	0	3	0	7	2	0
Camelo, Peter, Jacksonville°	.222	98	324	36	72	125	16	2	11	39	1	2	3	2	29	3	55	6	5
Caminiti, Kenneth, Columbus†	.325	95	375	66	122	196	25	2	15	69	7	0	7	0	25	4	58	11	5
Caraballo, Wilmer, Birmingham	.265	52	166	24	44	68	12	0	4	35	4	0	4	1	7	0	28	0	0
Carroll, Carson, Memphis	.249	52	173	22	43	56	8	1	1	19	0	4	2	1	19	0	36	5	0
Cash, Earl, Columbus	.000	32	3	0	0	0	0	0	0	0	0	0	0	0	0	0	0	0	0
Chambers, Albert, Columbus°	.282	92	280	34	79	122	23	1	6	42	5	0	4	1	33	0	55	1	4
Childress, Willie, Greenville°	.215	90	335	43	72	106	16	0	6	36	1	5	4	1	34	3	55	10	5
Christensen, John, Chattanooga	.385	12	39	8	15	20	5	0	0	6	1	0	0	1	7	0	5	0	1
Cijntje, Sherwin, Charlotte°	.304	111	405	59	123	166	19	6	4	44	7	3	0	1	50	2	44	31	14
Cimo, Matthew, Charlotte	.308	108	406	73	125	212	21	6	18	64	7	2	3	2	31	1	85	13	7
Clemons, Mark, 6 Orl-13 Jax	.333	19	3	0	1	1	0	0	0	0	0	0	0	0	0	0	2	0	0
Coffman, Kevin, Greenville	.130	30	23	0	3	3	0	0	0	4	0	0	0	0	1	0	10	0	0
Colombino, Carlo, Columbus	.272	39	151	19	41	53	10	1	0	17	1	0	0	2	7	0	13	1	1
Cook, Mitchell, Columbus°	.500	6	4	0	2	2	0	0	0	0	0	1	0	0	0	0	1	0	0
Corsi, James, Huntsville	.000	28	1	0	0	0	0	0	0	0	0	0	0	0	0	0	0	0	0
Coyle, Rock, Knoxville	.326	67	236	45	77	125	18	3	8	39	5	1	1	3	36	1	20	8	3
Crew, Kenneth, 31 Mem-11 Col	.000	42	1	0	0	0	0	0	0	0	0	0	0	0	0	0	0	0	0
D'Alessandro, Salvatore, Greenville	.318	6	22	0	7	8	1	0	0	2	0	0	0	0	1	0	5	0	0
Datz, Jeffrey, Columbus	.248	121	408	55	101	146	21	0	8	42	4	3	2	5	30	0	69	1	4
David, Brian, Chattanooga	.278	120	410	63	114	157	28	3	3	45	6	4	7	4	65	3	37	10	8
Denson, Andrew, Greenville	.219	128	447	54	98	165	23	1	14	55	7	1	2	11	33	1	95	1	2
Dewey, Todd, Greenville†	.238	99	320	34	76	108	13	2	5	35	4	4	3	0	39	3	59	2	3
DeWillis, Jeffrey, Knoxville	.131	39	122	11	16	31	6	0	3	11	1	1	0	0	11	0	23	0	0
Diaz, Jose, Knoxville	.178	29	90	14	16	32	5	1	3	10	1	0	0	1	6	0	29	0	0
Dietrick, Patrick, Huntsville	.204	115	328	50	67	86	9	2	2	22	3	3	1	5	39	0	91	16	6
Dodd, Thomas, Charlotte	.289	136	494	99	143	288	24	5	37	127	19	0	12	3	77	7	77	9	4
Dopson, John, Jacksonville°	.083	21	12	0	1	1	0	0	0	0	0	1	0	0	0	0	6	0	0
Drew, Cameron, Columbus°	.280	133	490	66	137	216	26	1	17	70	8	0	5	3	25	4	81	8	1
Duffy, Darrin, Huntsville	.179	38	117	5	21	26	5	0	0	5	0	4	0	0	7	0	24	3	2
Dunster, Donald, Columbus	.500	11	2	0	1	1	0	0	0	2	0	1	0	0	0	0	1	0	0
Eave, Gary, Greenville	.000	25	3	0	0	0	0	0	0	0	0	0	0	0	0	0	0	0	0
Eccles, John, Orlando	.175	17	57	5	10	19	3	0	2	11	0	2	1	2	0	0	11	0	0
Eccleston, Thomas, Chattanooga°	.289	39	128	18	37	54	3	1	4	16	2	0	1	0	8	0	15	1	1
Eisenreich, James, Memphis°	.382	70	275	60	105	194	36	10	11	57	5	0	2	0	47	3	44	13	4
Elliott, John, Columbus	.273	3	11	0	3	3	0	0	0	0	0	0	0	0	0	0	1	0	1
Escobar, Jose, Knoxville	.141	26	92	4	13	16	3	0	0	4	1	1	0	1	4	0	11	2	1
Falcone, David, Charlotte°	.293	132	478	74	140	213	25	3	14	92	11	1	3	1	67	7	76	15	3
Farmar, Damon, Charlotte†	.280	37	132	25	37	63	9	4	3	9	3	3	0	0	10	1	31	9	2
Farmer, Bryan, Charlotte°	.000	39	0	0	0	0	0	0	0	0	0	1	0	0	0	0	0	0	0
Felice, Jason, Orlando	.284	103	377	56	107	178	23	0	16	61	8	0	1	5	43	3	54	1	3
Firova, Daniel, Chattanooga	.200	52	165	19	33	43	7	0	1	21	5	3	0	2	4	0	19	0	1
Fishel, John, Columbus	.276	130	457	78	126	231	29	2	24	88	7	0	2	8	55	3	78	7	4
Forrester, Thomas, Birmingham°	.289	59	204	27	59	97	8	0	10	27	3	0	0	1	21	0	45	0	4
Fowlkes, Alan, Jacksonville	.000	5	1	0	0	0	0	0	0	0	0	0	0	0	0	0	1	0	0
Fox, Eric, Chattanooga†	.266	134	523	76	139	211	28	10	8	54	5	4	5	2	40	5	93	22	10
Fuentes, Michael, Memphis	.276	128	457	70	126	212	20	3	20	69	10	1	3	3	64	4	103	4	2
Fulton, Gregory, Chattanooga†	.232	137	482	51	112	157	20	2	7	62	9	3	8	3	46	5	76	2	2
Funderburk, Mark, Orlando	.250	118	412	56	103	205	12	3	28	68	9	0	0	5	28	2	82	2	1
Funk, Thomas, Columbus°	.000	16	2	0	0	0	0	0	0	0	0	0	0	0	0	0	1	0	0
Gant, Ronald, Greenville	.247	140	527	78	130	205	27	3	14	82	12	3	7	2	59	0	92	24	4
Garcia, Santiago, Knoxville	.297	63	239	28	71	102	12	5	3	22	1	2	2	10	22	2	22	7	3
Gardner, Mark, Jacksonville	.333	17	12	1	4	4	0	0	0	2	1	1	0	0	0	0	2	0	0
Gatewood, Henry, Orlando	.244	51	123	10	30	33	3	0	0	7	0	3	0	0	16	0	20	0	0
Gibbons, John, Chattanooga	.265	120	423	63	112	160	16	4	8	45	6	1	3	2	56	4	49	7	8
Gonring, Douglas, Columbus°	.200	32	85	2	17	18	1	0	0	5	0	1	1	1	7	0	16	0	0
Graybill, David, Jacksonville	.000	11	4	0	0	0	0	0	0	0	0	0	0	0	0	0	1	0	0
Greene, Thomas, Greenville	.111	23	9	1	1	2	1	0	0	0	0	0	0	0	0	0	5	0	0
Guerrero, Inocencio, Greenville	.287	53	171	25	49	67	9	0	3	31	5	0	1	0	37	1	35	0	0
Hall, Matthew, Chattanooga°	.230	72	252	26	58	94	11	2	7	34	1	6	2	3	25	1	47	18	6
Hansen, Roger, Chattanooga	.281	98	335	33	94	123	12	1	5	34	4	0	2	4	30	2	45	0	3
Hatcher, Johnny, Greenville	.323	28	99	13	32	44	6	0	2	9	2	0	0	1	5	0	9	2	3
Hearron, Jeffrey, Knoxville	.220	37	118	19	26	40	9	1	1	15	1	1	2	5	16	0	30	0	1
Heise, Larry, Greenville°	.000	33	0	0	0	0	0	0	0	0	0	0	0	2	1	0	0	0	0

Player and Club	Pct.	G.	AB.	R.	H.	TB.	2B.	3B.	HR.	RBI.	GW.	SH.	SF.	HP.	BB.	Int. BB.	SO.	SB.	CS.
Hemond, Scott, Huntsville	.182	33	110	10	20	28	3	1	1	8	1	1	0	4	0	30	5	1
Hesketh, Joseph, Jacksonville°	.000	6	1	0	0	0	0	0	0	0	0	0	0	0	0	0	1	0	0
Holman, Brian, Jacksonville	.067	22	15	1	1	1	0	0	0	0	0	3	0	0	2	0	7	0	0
Holtz, Gerald, Charlotte	.280	89	343	70	96	132	19	4	3	30	5	3	1	1	65	0	37	21	11
Houston, Melvin, Jacksonville	.250	95	392	55	98	114	9	2	1	26	1	6	0	3	46	1	41	20	11
Howard, Steven, Huntsville	.255	133	439	79	112	176	17	4	13	66	9	5	6	12	76	2	142	9	8
Howie, Mark, Huntsville	.257	92	342	42	88	114	17	0	3	45	5	1	7	3	44	1	48	18	10
Ilsley, Blaise, Columbus°	.333	26	12	1	4	5	1	0	0	2	0	1	0	0	2	0	2	0	0
Ingle, Randy, Greenville	.207	47	121	10	25	28	3	0	0	9	3	2	1	0	5	0	30	0	1
Jarrell, Joseph, Charlotte	.219	91	324	41	71	128	14	2	13	55	3	1	5	6	24	0	105	7	3
Johnson, Randall, Jacksonville	.167	25	12	1	2	2	0	0	0	0	0	0	0	1	2	0	4	0	0
Johnson, Richard, Columbus	.254	139	508	62	129	199	23	1	15	71	9	0	4	8	44	1	112	0	4
Jones, Calvin, Chattanooga	.000	26	1	0	0	0	0	0	0	0	0	0	0	0	0	0	1	0	0
Jones, James, Huntsville	.269	72	227	27	61	70	9	0	0	23	3	3	1	2	48	2	39	2	2
Jones, Michael, Knoxville	.292	7	24	3	7	8	1	0	0	1	0	0	0	0	0	0	5	1	0
Jones, Ricky, Charlotte	.275	39	142	25	39	83	6	1	12	25	3	1	1	2	21	1	19	1	2
Jose, Felix, Huntsville†	.226	91	296	29	67	95	11	1	5	42	5	1	3	2	28	1	61	3	3
Justice, David, Greenville°	.227	93	348	38	79	117	12	4	6	40	6	1	3	0	53	6	48	3	2
Khoury, Scott, Charlotte°	.167	12	24	3	4	9	2	0	1	3	0	0	0	1	5	0	8	0	0
Kilner, John, Greenville°	.000	26	8	0	0	0	0	0	0	0	0	0	0	0	0	0	2	0	0
Kinnard, Kenneth, 37 Grv-54 Knx	.271	91	325	49	88	127	16	4	5	41	3	4	2	1	20	0	107	15	0
Kramer, Joseph, Huntsville	.184	42	103	8	19	34	2	3	3	9	0	1	1	0	18	0	34	3	3
Latmore, Robert, Charlotte	.273	4	11	5	3	3	0	0	1	1	0	0	0	0	2	0	4	1	0
Lawrence, Andy, Jacksonville	.290	131	479	60	139	202	25	1	12	76	8	1	2	2	34	3	68	7	5
Lemke, Mark, Greenville†	.231	6	26	0	6	6	0	0	0	4	0	1	0	0	0	0	4	0	0
Liddle, Steven, Orlando	.271	94	321	39	87	133	17	1	9	27	2	1	0	2	24	0	36	0	0
Linares, Rufino, Jacksonville	.250	1	4	0	1	1	0	0	0	0	0	0	0	0	0	0	0	0	0
Lindsey, William, Birmingham	.282	63	206	35	58	92	10	0	8	32	2	4	2	2	30	1	16	0	2
Livin, Jeffrey, Columbus	.000	38	5	0	0	0	0	0	0	0	0	0	0	0	1	0	4	0	0
Loggins, Michael, Memphis†	.282	110	440	73	124	189	27	7	8	49	2	2	1	2	50	1	75	17	11
Long, Bruce, Columbus	.000	9	2	0	0	0	0	0	0	0	0	0	0	0	0	0	2	0	0
Longenecker, Jere, Memphis	.269	28	67	12	18	24	3	0	1	11	1	0	0	0	11	0	6	2	1
Mack, Tony, Columbus	.000	37	2	0	0	0	0	0	0	0	0	1	0	0	0	0	2	0	0
Magrann, Thomas, Charlotte	.211	57	180	23	38	55	6	1	3	19	3	2	0	0	35	1	45	3	2
Malave, Omar, Knoxville	.200	2	5	1	1	1	0	0	0	1	0	0	0	0	1	0	0	0	0
Mallicoat, Robbin, Columbus	.000	25	7	0	0	0	0	0	0	0	0	1	0	0	0	0	3	0	0
Mann, Scott, Jacksonville°	.278	107	370	51	103	161	24	2	10	40	6	3	3	6	30	2	37	4	4
Marte, Alexis, Orlando°	.262	50	195	30	51	67	2	4	2	19	3	5	1	0	17	2	20	28	4
Martinez, Carlos, Birmingham	.233	9	30	2	7	8	1	0	0	0	0	0	0	1	0	0	6	2	2
Martinez, Reynaldo, Memphis°	.261	78	283	34	74	117	10	3	9	43	8	0	2	1	33	0	94	5	3
Mathews, Edward, Greenville	.000	37	2	0	0	0	0	0	0	0	0	0	0	0	0	0	1	0	0
McDougal, Julius, Orlando†	.216	62	218	24	47	55	6	1	0	9	2	1	1	3	20	0	38	17	5
McGuire, William, Chattanooga	.228	79	259	21	59	78	10	0	3	29	2	5	7	4	23	0	32	2	1
McPhail, Marlin, Birmingham°	.290	125	420	60	122	188	18	3	14	52	4	1	3	3	45	0	53	2	1
Merullo, Matthew, Birmingham°	.275	48	167	13	46	59	7	0	2	17	2	0	0	0	6	0	20	1	0
Mikulik, Joseph, Columbus	.242	133	488	88	118	189	17	9	12	57	6	4	2	5	36	0	93	11	5
Miller, Michael, Memphis	.217	91	258	42	56	80	12	3	2	31	3	5	4	0	30	0	61	9	4
Moreno, Armando, Jacksonville	.223	117	417	70	93	146	23	3	8	46	6	6	2	7	80	0	58	5	7
Morhardt, Gregory, Orlando°	.225	80	285	28	64	90	15	1	3	25	0	2	3	1	19	1	41	0	0
Morris, Angel, Memphis	.190	23	58	4	11	15	1	0	1	3	0	0	0	0	4	0	17	1	0
Myers, David, Chattanooga	.328	130	488	72	160	224	33	2	9	69	8	5	5	1	30	0	33	1	5
Nelson, James, Memphis	.289	68	228	47	66	106	12	2	8	36	6	0	2	1	56	0	46	3	1
Nichols, Ty, Charlotte†	.188	60	207	18	39	60	5	2	4	16	0	1	1	1	20	0	59	3	3
Nipper, Michael, Greenville	.203	38	123	18	25	42	8	0	3	11	0	0	1	1	16	1	29	0	0
O'Dell, James, Birmingham°	.254	131	449	67	114	191	20	0	19	78	6	0	5	2	53	9	56	2	1
Opie, James, Jacksonville	.219	37	128	13	28	38	8	1	0	11	1	1	2	1	8	0	31	1	0
Palmer, Douglas, Orlando	.281	126	480	67	135	170	18	4	3	45	1	4	2	5	58	1	47	12	7
Parker, Robert, Columbus°	.215	85	261	36	56	59	3	0	0	16	1	2	3	0	36	2	29	16	4
Peraza, Oswald, Knoxville	.000	28	3	0	0	0	0	0	0	0	0	0	0	0	0	0	2	0	0
Perez, Yorkis, Jacksonville°	.000	12	3	0	0	0	0	0	0	0	0	0	0	0	0	0	0	0	0
Peterson, Adam, Birmingham	.000	26	0	0	0	0	0	0	0	0	0	0	0	0	1	0	0	0	0
Pino, Rolando, Birmingham	.184	95	288	36	53	82	10	2	5	22	0	3	0	2	49	0	51	5	4
Price, Kevin, Jacksonville	.500	57	2	1	1	1	0	0	0	0	0	1	0	0	0	0	1	0	0
Pruitt, Darrell, Birmingham	.260	138	542	88	141	200	25	5	8	55	5	9	3	2	45	0	85	26	17
Ralston, Robert, Orlando	.258	79	267	28	69	76	7	0	0	18	2	4	1	2	28	0	27	10	7
Rather, Dody, Columbus	.111	26	9	2	1	4	0	0	1	2	0	0	0	0	3	0	5	0	0
Reboulet, Jeffery, Orlando	.256	129	422	52	108	128	15	1	1	35	5	5	0	1	58	0	56	9	5
Reyna, Luis, Knoxville°	.297	132	501	61	149	228	21	8	14	67	8	2	3	3	20	2	75	21	10
Richardson, Timothy, Charlotte	.143	2	7	0	1	2	1	0	0	1	0	0	0	0	0	0	2	0	0
Rios, Carlos, Greenville	.291	41	158	20	46	55	7	1	0	10	2	5	2	2	18	0	13	0	1
Rivera, Jose, Memphis	.239	120	431	49	103	199	20	2	24	73	3	0	1	3	40	1	130	9	6
Roberts, Norman, Charlotte	.050	8	20	3	1	4	0	0	1	1	0	1	0	0	0	0	6	2	0
Robertson, Andre, Chattanooga	.269	90	323	40	87	128	23	3	4	35	2	3	3	2	9	0	51	0	3
Roby, Ellis, Greenville†	.000	4	1	0	0	0	0	0	0	0	0	0	0	0	0	0	1	0	1
Rodiles, Jose, Columbus	.000	10	0	0	0	0	0	0	0	0	0	0	0	0	1	0	0	0	0
Rollin, Rondal, Birmingham	.244	140	513	90	125	270	28	0	39	106	10	1	6	3	65	6	218	4	5
Rossy, Elam, Charlotte	.287	127	471	69	135	175	22	3	4	50	2	3	1	3	43	0	38	20	9
Salcedo, Ronnie, Charlotte°	.333	8	27	3	9	13	4	0	0	2	0	0	0	0	2	0	2	1	1
Salinas, Manuel, Birmingham°	.279	76	305	40	85	137	22	3	8	32	3	2	3	1	22	3	10	0	6
Santarelli, Calvin, Columbus	.000	43	2	1	0	0	0	0	0	0	0	0	0	0	3	0	1	0	0
Santiago, Norman, Jacksonville	.243	61	140	12	34	43	6	0	1	17	3	4	1	2	13	1	16	0	1
Santovenia, Nelson, Jacksonville	.279	117	394	56	110	184	17	0	19	63	8	1	3	5	36	1	58	3	4
Schwarz, Thomas, Orlando	.227	68	233	25	53	83	14	2	4	36	0	3	3	1	25	0	24	0	3
Scott, Michael, Greenville	.400	18	5	1	2	2	0	0	0	0	0	0	0	0	1	0	3	0	0
Shaddy, Christopher, Knoxville	.291	125	475	87	138	236	35	3	19	77	8	8	9	4	59	1	110	10	6
Shade, Michael, Columbus	.200	38	5	0	1	1	0	0	0	0	0	0	0	0	0	0	4	0	0
Shaw, Theodore, Memphis	.000	46	1	0	0	0	0	0	0	0	0	0	0	0	0	0	1	0	0
Skeete, Rafael, Charlotte°	.281	11	32	5	9	10	1	0	0	2	1	0	0	0	2	0	10	2	1
Sliwinski, Kevin, Knoxville	.256	133	480	72	123	219	19	4	23	90	5	0	6	4	73	4	88	3	4
Smith, Alexander, Greenville	.138	9	29	1	4	4	0	0	0	0	0	0	0	0	0	0	2	0	0
Smith, Dana, Charlotte	.259	74	243	27	63	72	4	1	1	30	2	4	2	2	36	1	58	1	5
Smith, David, Charlotte	.249	64	205	21	51	62	8	0	1	17	0	1	4	1	20	1	28	3	5

Player and Club	Pct.	G.	AB	R	H	TB	2B	3B	HR	RBI	GW	SH	SF	HP	BB	Int. BB	SO	SB	CS
Smith, Peter, Greenville	.091	29	11	0	1	1	0	0	0	3	1	1	0	0	2	0	4	0	0
Snider, Van, Memphis°	.328	45	174	25	57	108	10	7	9	40	8	0	0	1	10	0	34	2	5
Sparks, Gregory, Huntsville°	.279	57	172	18	48	71	9	1	4	28	4	0	2	1	14	0	35	1	0
Springer, Gary, Memphis†	.237	92	342	60	81	114	13	1	6	33	1	2	4	0	47	2	61	0	2
Stanicek, Peter, Charlotte†	.315	88	337	78	106	156	18	4	8	50	8	2	3	8	46	0	46	30	10
Stark, Matthew, Knoxville	.299	25	87	10	26	39	3	2	2	18	1	0	1	1	13	0	9	0	0
Stottlemyre, Melvin, 19 Col-1 Mem...	.000	20	2	0	0	0	0	0	0	0	0	1	0	0	0	0	1	0	0
Stringfellow, Thornton, Greenville° ...	.333	20	9	2	3	3	0	0	0	0	0	1	0	0	0	0	1	0	0
Strucher, Mark, Greenville	.227	51	172	19	39	71	13	2	5	18	3	0	3	2	12	2	37	1	0
Sudo, Robert, Jacksonville	.000	11	2	0	0	0	0	0	0	0	0	0	0	0	0	0	1	0	0
Tackett, Jeffrey, Charlotte†	.224	61	205	18	46	54	6	1	0	13	2	1	1	2	12	0	34	5	5
Tatis, Bernardo, Knoxville†	.279	137	526	101	147	221	22	8	12	49	5	3	7	2	80	2	93	55	11
Thomas, James, Columbus†	.276	84	326	41	90	128	17	3	5	43	8	6	1	1	39	2	34	9	7
Thomas, Troy, Birmingham°	.287	128	460	69	132	176	24	1	6	59	9	1	5	1	69	5	78	21	7
Tolentino, Jose, Huntsville°	.237	49	173	20	41	65	6	0	6	25	4	1	1	1	21	2	28	1	0
Tonucci, Norman, Knoxville°	.224	135	482	58	108	195	15	6	20	55	5	2	3	3	39	0	176	3	4
Torve, Kenton, Birmingham°	.304	17	46	5	14	20	6	0	0	7	2	0	0	0	6	0	8	0	0
Traen, Thomas, 4 Jax-6 Orl†	.000	10	1	0	0	0	0	0	0	0	0	0	0	0	0	0	1	0	0
Trautwein, John, Jacksonville	.000	56	2	0	0	0	0	0	0	1	0	0	0	1	0	0	2	0	0
Tubbs, Gregory, Greenville	.269	141	540	97	145	187	19	7	3	40	3	7	1	2	86	2	86	24	19
Tumpane, Robert, Greenville	.219	57	192	26	42	73	2	1	9	24	5	0	0	0	19	0	45	1	2
Van Blaricom, Mark, Memphis	.249	115	374	64	93	137	18	4	6	42	5	0	6	4	61	0	59	16	7
Venturini, Peter, Birmingham	.254	96	378	37	96	125	12	4	3	30	5	4	2	0	33	0	48	9	9
Veras, Camilo, Huntsville°	.111	2	9	1	1	1	0	0	0	0	0	0	0	0	0	0	4	0	0
Vetsch, David, Orlando°	.243	87	309	40	75	133	18	2	12	50	5	0	5	4	22	2	82	2	0
Walker, Larry, Jacksonville°	.287	128	474	91	136	253	25	7	26	83	19	0	3	9	67	5	120	24	3
Wayne, Gary, Jacksonville°	1.000	56	2	1	2	2	0	0	0	1	0	0	0	0	1	0	0	0	1
Weinberger, Gary, Jacksonville°	.280	27	100	9	28	37	5	2	0	14	1	1	0	0	6	0	6	2	0
Weiss, Walter, Huntsville†	.285	91	337	43	96	119	16	2	1	32	3	6	2	2	47	2	67	23	3
Wetherby, Jeffrey, Greenville°	.303	140	488	67	148	223	31	4	12	78	8	2	2	2	63	5	87	7	4
Winters, James, Birmingham	.236	104	351	47	83	118	11	3	6	37	2	3	2	0	45	1	78	10	4
Winters, Matthew, Memphis°	.268	93	343	61	92	173	17	2	20	88	7	0	7	1	60	3	71	5	5
Wishnevski, Michael, Chattanooga°	.333	12	39	10	13	14	1	0	0	7	2	0	1	0	12	2	11	0	1
Wright, George, Jacksonville†	.262	87	328	50	86	137	15	3	10	58	9	0	4	2	33	3	32	4	3
Xavier, Joseph, Huntsville°	.301	137	492	74	148	211	37	7	4	53	9	12	5	5	77	3	72	23	15
Yanes, Edward, Orlando	.206	29	97	12	20	30	4	0	2	10	1	1	1	2	10	0	20	0	0
Yelding, Eric, Knoxville	.200	39	150	23	30	38	6	1	0	7	0	1	1	1	12	0	25	10	5
Yost, Edgar, Greenville	.165	40	115	6	19	23	1	0	1	8	1	3	1	0	8	0	24	0	0

The following pitchers, listed alphabetically by club, with games in parentheses, had no plate appearances, primarily through use of designated hitters.

BIRMINGHAM—Acker, Larry (12); Bettendorf, Jeffrey (43); Blasucci, Anthony (12); Boling, John (40); Conley, Virgil (17); Gaynor, Richard (51); Hall, Gardner (10); Hardy, John (9); Hickey, James (7); McDowell, Jack (4); Mecerod, George (9); Menendez, Antonio (27); Pall, Donn (30); Pawlowski, John (35); Rasmussen, James (7); Renz, Kevin (11); Scott, Timothy (11).

CHARLOTTE—Alicea, Miguel (37); Beatty, Blaine (15); Carriger, Ricky (5); Daniel, Jimmy (36); Dillard, Gordon (36); Green, Christopher (12); Hoover, John (22); Householder, Brian (15); Kaufman, Curt (9); Kucharski, Joseph (9); Long, Robert (43); Milacki, Robert (29); Oliveras, Francisco (23); Raczka, Michael (12); Rice, Richard (23); Stanhope, Chester (33); Talamantez, Gregory (4); Walton, Robert (4); Welsh, Christopher (4).

CHATTANOOGA—Beasley, Christopher (14); Burroughs, Darren (24); Christ, Michael (12); Givler, Douglas (42); Gunnarsson, Robert (11); Hanson, Erik (21); Mendek, William (39); Parker, Clayton (20); Potestio, Douglas (5); Schooler, Michael (28); Spratke, Kenneth (27); Walker, James (39); Wooden, Mark (14).

COLUMBUS—Baker, Mark (4); Clark, Robert (13); Edwards, Jeffrey (6); Grovom, Carl (2); Hall, Martin (3); Metoyer, Tony (4); Van Houten, James (1); Vargas, Jose (3).

GREENVILLE—Alvarez, Jose (9); DelRosario, Maximo (19); Gilliam, Keith (5); McWilliams, Larry (7); Palmer, David (1).

HUNTSVILLE—Birtsas, Timothy (17); Burns, Todd (34); Cadaret, Gregory (24); Carroll, James (3); Criswell, Brian (32); Cundari, Philip (5); Hilton, Stan (14); Kent, John (1); Kibler, Russell (41); Lambert, Reese (29); McDonald, Kirk (5); Mooneyham, William (12); Otto, David (9); Scherer, Douglas (38); Shaver, Jeffrey (24); Walton, Bruce (18); Wardle, Curtis (6); Whitehurst, Walter (29).

JACKSONVILLE—Cunningham, William (3); Devlin, Robert (13); Payne, Michael (10); Thompson, Richard (7); Youmans, Floyd (1).

KNOXVILLE—Bencomo, Omar (38); Brinson, Hugh (8); Burgos, Enrique (17); Chestnut, Troy (41); Davis, Steven (13); Englund, Timothy (20); Filer, Thomas (6); Gilliam, Keith (3); Leal, Luis (1); Linton, Douglas (1); McMurtry, Craig (12); Mesa, Jose (35); Mumaw, Stephen (6); Provence, Todd (58); Walsh, David (24); Yearout, Michael (34); Young, Clifford (42).

MEMPHIS—Acker, Larry (24); Blovin, Gary (7); Crouch, Matthew (16); DeJesus, Jose (25); George, Phillip (20); Gozzo, Mauro (19); Hibbard, Gregory (16); Lambert, Timothy (13); Luecken, Richard (28); Morgan, Eugene (24); Mount, Charles (15); Ownbey, Richard (4); Perez, Melido (20); Shiflett, Mark (47); Sparling, Donald (7); Stranski, Scott (12); Thompson, Richard (8).

ORLANDO—Bianchi, Ben (4); Bronkey, Jeffery (24); Bumgarner, Jeffrey (26); Gasser, Steven (20); Gomez, Steven (24); Higgs, Darrell (38); Morgan, Eugene (19); Nivens, Toby (14); Perry, Jeff (7); Pierorazio, Wesley (51); Smith, Daniel (20); Smith, Robert (22); Sontag, Alan (15); Trudeau, Kevin (19); Walker, Kurt (25); Young, John (11).

GRAND SLAM HOME RUNS—Berger, Felice, Fulton, Rivera, Rollin, Walker, M. Winters, 2 each; Alcazar, Alva, Berroa, Blauser, Brumfield, Caraballo, Childress, DeWillis, Eccleston, Fox, Gant, Howard, Ri. Johnson, Lawrence, Mann, R. Martinez, Mikulik, Santovenia, Schwarz, Sliwinski, Springer, Wetherby, Wright, 1 each.

AWARDED FIRST BASE ON CATCHER'S INTERFERENCE—Firova 3 (Merullo, Morris, Nipper); Arndt 2 (Borders, Tackett); Mikulik 2 (Magrann, Tackett); David Smith 2 (Hemond 2); Allen (Merullo); Bell (Tackett); Cimo (J. Jones); Dietrick (DeWillis); Eccleston (Merullo); Hall (Gatewood); Sliwinski (Liddle); Sparks (Eccles); Stanicek (Nelson); Tatis (Nelson); Venturini (Anderson); Wetherby (Borders).

CLUB FIELDING

Club	Pct.	G.	PO.	A.	E.	DP.	PB.	Club	Pct.	G.	PO.	A.	E.	DP.	PB.
Jacksonville	.974	144	3787	1432	139	118	15	Huntsville	.968	144	3731	1591	174	108	11
Greenville	.974	144	3780	1512	142	149	24	Orlando	.966	143	3676	1398	178	163	13
Charlotte	.973	145	3786	1433	147	128	16	Memphis	.966	143	3728	1509	185	155	12
Chattanooga	.972	143	3749	1480	149	132	21	Knoxville	.964	144	3749	1586	200	124	27
Columbus	.970	143	3668	1468	157	120	22	Birmingham	.963	143	3687	1358	195	118	29

Triple Plays—Greenville 2, Chattanooga.

INDIVIDUAL FIELDING

°Throws lefthanded.

FIRST BASEMEN

Player and Club	Pct.	G.	PO.	A.	E.	DP.	Player and Club	Pct.	G.	PO.	A.	E.	DP.
Afenir, Columbus	1.000	1	2	0	0	0	Arias, Huntsville	1.000	5	34	2	0	3

FIRST BASEMEN—Continued

Player and Club	Pct.	G.	PO.	A.	E.	DP.	Player and Club	Pct.	G.	PO.	A.	E.	DP.
Arndt, Huntsville	.964	8	51	2	2	2	Johnson, Columbus	.991	139	1189	81	11	105
Berger, Jacksonville	.994	21	153	9	1	15	Lawrence, Jacksonville	.990	126	1024	78	11	92
Borg, Orlando☆	.984	50	386	36	7	49	Longenecker, Memphis	1.000	20	111	7	0	12
BRILINSKI, Huntsville☆	.992	100	854	104	8	66	McDougal, Orlando	1.000	1	7	1	0	0
Caraballo, Birmingham	1.000	2	12	2	0	1	McPhail, Birmingham	1.000	14	67	2	0	5
Carroll, Memphis	.985	26	179	15	3	26	Miller, Memphis	1.000	10	74	3	0	13
Chambers, Columbus☆	1.000	1	10	0	0	1	Morhardt, Orlando☆	.982	72	574	43	11	72
Childress, Greenville	.944	2	15	2	1	4	Nelson, Memphis	.966	17	131	10	5	8
Datz, Columbus	1.000	3	12	0	0	1	O'Dell, Birmingham☆	.984	101	774	39	13	64
Denson, Greenville	.991	115	998	50	10	105	Reyna, Knoxville☆	.974	50	401	45	12	38
Dewey, Greenville	.967	4	27	2	1	3	Richardson, Charlotte	1.000	2	15	1	0	0
DeWillis, Knoxville	1.000	2	6	1	0	1	Santovenia, Jacksonville	1.000	1	5	0	0	0
Dodd, Charlotte	.993	14	136	7	1	15	Schwarz, Orlando	1.000	2	10	0	0	2
Falcone, Charlotte	.980	131	1111	78	24	107	Shaddy, Knoxville	1.000	2	16	1	0	3
Felice, Orlando	1.000	2	15	2	0	1	Sliwinski, Knoxville	.986	93	848	73	13	72
Forrester, Birmingham☆	.993	36	278	25	2	34	Smith, Charlotte	1.000	1	9	0	0	1
Fuentes, Memphis	.987	48	367	21	5	42	Sparks, Huntsville☆	.983	6	53	5	1	2
Fulton, Chattanooga	.990	129	1069	73	12	97	Springer, Memphis	1.000	3	22	4	0	4
Funderburk, Orlando	.981	26	196	13	4	21	Tatis, Knoxville	1.000	1	5	0	0	0
Gonring, Columbus	1.000	5	23	3	0	3	Tolentino, Huntsville☆	.986	37	387	30	6	26
Guerrero, Greenville	1.000	5	37	3	0	2	Torve, Birmingham	1.000	5	21	0	0	2
Hansen, Chattanooga	.986	28	195	14	3	23	Tumpane, Greenville☆	1.000	19	178	19	0	20
Hatcher, Greenville	1.000	1	3	0	0	0	Van Blaricon, Memphis	.976	4	39	1	1	4
Ingle, Greenville	1.000	2	8	0	0	1	Winters, Memphis	.977	37	313	24	8	33

Triple Plays—Denson 2, Hansen.

SECOND BASEMEN

Player and Club	Pct.	G.	PO.	A.	E.	DP.	Player and Club	Pct.	G.	PO.	A.	E.	DP.
Alcala, Memphis	.942	26	52	78	8	15	McPhail, Birmingham	.947	26	48	59	6	12
Allen, Columbus	1.000	8	12	18	0	4	Miller, Memphis	.971	23	44	57	3	12
Arndt, Huntsville	1.000	2	3	9	0	3	Moreno, Jacksonville	.985	27	58	70	2	16
Blankenship, Huntsville	.990	21	34	63	1	11	Palmer, Orlando	.971	77	141	193	10	55
Bowen, Memphis	.979	41	68	121	4	41	Parker, Columbus	.962	52	96	130	9	26
Briley, Chattanooga	.951	122	221	346	29	72	Pino, Birmingham	.970	45	75	116	6	26
Caceres, Jacksonville	.978	18	39	51	2	14	Ralston, Orlando	.950	33	69	101	9	28
Carroll, Memphis	1.000	6	11	18	0	4	Reboulet, Orlando	.956	35	71	103	8	33
David, Chattanooga	.990	25	33	67	1	20	Rossy, Charlotte	1.000	17	29	40	0	7
Diaz, Knoxville	1.000	2	2	4	0	0	Salinas, Birmingham	.979	76	177	198	8	33
Elliott, Columbus	1.000	3	3	7	0	0	Santiago, Jacksonville	.966	8	11	17	1	2
GANT, Greenville	.973	140	328	434	21	108	Shaddy, Knoxville	.972	52	104	141	7	35
Garcia, Knoxville	.937	62	139	187	22	36	Smith, Charlotte	.983	39	69	102	3	21
Houston, Jacksonville	.978	95	197	257	10	61	Springer, Memphis	.980	53	88	159	5	32
Howie, Huntsville	.957	67	100	165	12	26	Stanicek, Charlotte	.977	87	191	241	10	58
Ingle, Greenville	.977	9	15	27	1	5	Tatis, Knoxville	.974	34	64	87	4	20
Jones, Charlotte	1.000	4	6	13	0	3	Thomas, Columbus	.965	84	169	219	14	56
Latmore, Charlotte	1.000	2	2	9	0	1	Van Blaricom, Memphis	1.000	1	4	2	0	1
Longenecker, Memphis	.750	1	1	2	1	0	Venturini, Birmingham	1.000	1	1	3	0	0
Malave, Knoxville	1.000	1	5	3	0	3	Xavier, Huntsville	.984	64	122	185	5	28

Triple Play—Gant.

THIRD BASEMEN

Player and Club	Pct.	G.	PO.	A.	E.	DP.	Player and Club	Pct.	G.	PO.	A.	E.	DP.
Allen, Columbus	.800	1	0	4	1	0	Miller, Memphis	.917	15	7	26	3	3
Arias, Huntsville	.923	6	0	12	1	1	Moreno, Jacksonville	.957	91	79	187	12	22
Arndt, Huntsville	.915	112	80	221	28	16	MYERS, Chattanooga	.952	114	78	237	16	21
Berger, Jacksonville	1.000	3	3	2	0	0	Nichols, Charlotte	.982	20	7	26	4	3
Blankenship, Huntsville	.922	18	14	33	4	1	Nipper, Greenville	.789	8	7	8	4	0
Caminiti, Columbus	.925	93	55	205	21	16	Opie, Jacksonville	.953	37	39	84	6	6
Caraballo, Birmingham	.960	41	23	73	4	4	Palmer, Orlando	.904	39	22	63	9	6
Carroll, Memphis	1.000	14	12	26	0	1	Parker, Columbus	1.000	1	0	4	0	1
Childress, Greenville	.936	81	38	152	13	14	Pino, Birmingham	.867	9	3	10	2	1
Colombino, Columbus	.903	37	34	68	11	5	Pruitt, Birmingham	.889	7	3	5	1	1
David, Chattanooga	.904	23	11	36	5	4	Ralston, Orlando	.871	24	14	40	8	3
Dewey, Greenville	.808	10	2	19	5	1	Reboulet, Orlando	.875	4	2	5	1	1
Diaz, Knoxville	.895	7	3	14	2	1	Rivera, Memphis	.897	111	69	209	32	27
Eccles, Orlando	.750	1	1	2	1	1	Robertson, Chattanooga	.971	14	12	22	1	2
Fishel, Columbus	.906	14	9	20	3	3	Rossy, Charlotte	.942	104	92	214	19	22
Hemond, Huntsville	1.000	2	1	5	0	2	Santiago, Jacksonville	.978	18	12	32	1	4
Howie, Huntsville	.933	4	6	8	1	0	Schwarz, Orlando	.868	62	52	99	23	13
Ingle, Greenville	.955	12	3	18	1	0	Shaddy, Knoxville	1.000	5	5	8	0	1
Jarrell, Charlotte	1.000	2	1	4	0	0	A. Smith, Greenville	.778	4	1	6	2	1
Jones, Charlotte	.949	14	17	20	2	0	D. Smith, Charlotte	1.000	9	3	19	0	3
Lemke, Greenville	.941	6	4	12	1	3	Springer, Memphis	.895	6	5	12	2	2
Longenecker, Memphis	.800	3	1	3	1	1	Strucher, Greenville	.926	29	20	55	6	7
Martinez, Birmingham	.917	9	5	17	2	2	Tolentino, Huntsville☆	.000	1	0	0	1	0
McDougal, Orlando	.938	14	13	17	2	0	Tonucci, Knoxville	.921	135	98	289	33	26
McPhail, Birmingham	.871	89	64	159	33	17	Xavier, Huntsville	.960	10	4	20	1	3

SHORTSTOPS

Player and Club	Pct.	G.	PO.	A.	E.	DP.	Player and Club	Pct.	G.	PO.	A.	E.	DP.
ALLAIRE, Columbus	.956	107	139	312	21	54	David, Chattanooga	.952	27	37	81	6	14
Allen, Columbus	.918	19	28	50	7	9	Diaz, Knoxville,	.987	19	20	54	1	8
Alva, Greenville	.978	19	30	61	2	13	Duffy, Huntsville	.950	38	54	99	8	16
Balelo, Chattanooga	.963	46	61	121	7	24	Escobar, Knoxville	.958	25	38	77	5	16
Beltre, Jacksonville	.941	142	198	358	35	60	Ingle, Greenville	.903	14	13	43	6	5
Bertolani, Birmingham	.933	24	34	63	7	11	Jarrell, Charlotte	.813	5	10	16	6	4
Blauser, Greenville	.976	72	101	225	8	49	Jones, Charlotte	.938	17	20	55	5	10
Bowen, Memphis	.939	7	7	24	2	3	Latmore, Charlotte	1.000	2	4	4	0	1
Carroll, Memphis	.976	10	16	24	1	5	Longenecker, Memphis	.846	3	3	8	2	0

SHORTSTOPS—Continued

Player and Club	Pct.	G.	PO.	A.	E.	DP.	Player and Club	Pct.	G.	PO.	A.	E.	DP.
McDougal, Orlando	.931	46	79	123	15	32	Schwarz, Orlando	1.000	3	2	3	0	2
Miller, Memphis	1.000	2	4	6	0	2	Shaddy, Knoxville	.936	66	98	195	20	37
Nichols, Charlotte	.964	39	54	105	6	27	Dana Smith, Charlotte	.973	26	41	69	3	13
Parker, Columbus	.970	24	41	56	3	14	David Smith, Charlotte	.980	63	78	165	5	26
Pino, Birmingham	.938	36	68	83	10	24	Springer, Memphis	.955	24	39	67	5	16
Ralston, Orlando	.839	9	12	14	5	3	Van Blaricom, Memphis	.940	102	174	296	30	79
Reboulet, Orlando	.960	90	147	262	17	71	Venturini, Birmingham	.928	86	132	239	29	43
Rios, Greenville	.972	41	61	114	5	28	Weiss, Huntsville	.960	90	152	259	17	40
Robertson, Chattanooga	.959	76	111	215	14	44	Xavier, Huntsville	.966	24	27	57	3	11
Santiago, Jacksonville	1.000	9	7	12	0	3	Yelding, Knoxville	.918	38	64	92	14	22

Triple Plays—Alva, Rios, Robertson.

OUTFIELDERS

Player and Club	Pct.	G.	PO.	A.	E.	DP.	Player and Club	Pct.	G.	PO.	A.	E.	DP.
Anderson, Huntsville	1.000	3	1	0	0	0	Khoury, Charlotte*	1.000	1	1	0	0	0
Beamesderfer, Charlotte	1.000	6	8	0	0	0	Kinnard, 34 Grv-49 Knx	.972	83	173	3	5	1
Beauchamp, Knoxville	.989	39	88	3	1	0	Kramer, Huntsville	.968	33	61	0	2	0
Bennett, Memphis*	.983	65	113	3	2	1	Lawrence, Jacksonville	1.000	1	1	0	0	0
Berger, Jacksonville	.975	101	186	8	5	0	Loggins, Memphis*	.976	110	284	5	7	1
Berroa, Knoxville	.942	132	236	6	15	1	Longenecker, Memphis	1.000	1	1	0	0	0
Bierley, Orlando	.978	138	259	8	6	1	Mann, Jacksonville	.970	72	129	1	4	1
Blackwell, Orlando	.969	61	152	2	5	1	Marte, Orlando*	.984	49	121	3	2	0
Blankenship, Huntsville	.979	71	137	3	3	1	Martinez, Memphis*	.984	78	173	11	3	2
Brock, Columbus*	.958	81	133	4	6	0	McPhail, Birmingham	1.000	2	2	0	0	0
Brumfield, Memphis	.946	9	35	0	2	0	Mikulik, Columbus	.983	126	230	4	4	1
Bruzik, Chattanooga	.976	71	118	5	3	1	Miller, Memphis	.966	36	54	3	2	1
Camelo, Jacksonville*	.960	93	167	3	7	0	Morhardt, Orlando*	1.000	9	10	0	0	0
Caraballo, Birmingham	1.000	2	2	0	0	0	Myers, Chattanooga	1.000	5	8	1	0	1
Chambers, Columbus*	.917	12	21	1	2	0	O'Dell, Birmingham*	.938	13	14	1	1	0
Childress, Greenville	1.000	9	17	0	0	0	Pruitt, Birmingham	.975	133	390	7	10	2
Christensen, Chattanooga	1.000	6	10	1	0	1	Reyna, Knoxville*	.976	79	158	3	4	0
Cijntje, Charlotte*	.975	106	229	1	6	0	Roberts, Charlotte	.800	6	4	0	1	0
Cimo, Charlotte	.985	106	190	8	3	0	Rollin, Birmingham	.961	73	140	7	6	2
Coyle, Knoxville	.986	33	64	4	1	0	Rossy, Charlotte	1.000	9	8	1	0	0
Dietrick, Huntsville	.973	113	243	6	7	2	Salcedo, Charlotte	1.000	5	9	1	0	0
Dodd, Charlotte	1.000	6	12	0	0	0	Skeete, Charlotte*	.947	8	15	3	1	0
Drew, Columbus	.984	131	298	8	5	0	Sliwinski, Knoxville	1.000	2	2	0	0	0
Eccleston, Chattanooga*	.950	35	57	0	3	0	Smith, Greenville	1.000	1	1	0	0	0
Farmar, Charlotte	.961	35	69	4	3	0	Snider, Memphis	.962	45	95	6	4	2
Felice, Orlando	.969	75	121	5	4	1	Sparks, Huntsville	.961	38	47	2	2	0
Fishel, Columbus	.985	100	182	13	3	4	Springer, Memphis	.900	8	9	0	1	0
Fox, Chattanooga	.980	134	378	11	8	5	Tatis, Knoxville	.967	104	251	9	9	3
Fuentes, Memphis	.971	52	67	0	2	0	Thomas, Birmingham	.980	119	237	11	5	2
Fulton, Chattanooga	.967	19	25	4	1	1	Tubbs, Knoxville	.984	140	364	9	6	3
GIBBONS, Chattanooga*	.987	109	216	7	3	1	Veras, Huntsville*	1.000	2	4	0	0	0
Hall, Chattanooga*	.952	72	116	4	6	1	Vetsch, Chattanooga	.972	78	161	15	5	4
Hatcher, Greenville	.978	26	42	3	1	1	Walker, Jacksonville	.968	121	263	9	9	1
Holtz, Charlotte*	.963	85	181	2	7	0	Weinberger, Jacksonville*	.963	26	51	1	2	1
Howard, Huntsville	.930	119	197	1	15	0	Wetherby, Greenville*	.977	139	240	10	6	2
Howie, Huntsville	1.000	20	29	1	0	0	J. Winters, Birmingham	.966	98	191	10	7	1
Jarrell, Charlotte	.955	81	177	15	9	5	M. Winters, Memphis	.992	67	125	4	1	3
Jones, Knoxville	.941	6	16	0	1	0	Wishnevski, Chattanooga*	.895	8	17	0	2	0
Jose, Huntsville	.945	71	131	7	8	1	Wright, Jacksonville	.988	41	75	5	1	0
Justice, Greenville*	.962	91	199	4	8	0	Yanes, Orlando	.958	28	67	2	3	0

Triple Play—Gibbons.

CATCHERS

Player and Club	Pct.	G.	PO.	A.	E.	DP.	PB.	Player and Club	Pct.	G.	PO.	A.	E.	DP.	PB.
Afenir, Columbus	.981	20	140	16	3	2	2	Hearron, Knoxville	.981	35	187	24	4	1	6
Alcazar, Birmingham	.948	40	223	15	13	1	12	Hemond, Huntsville	.969	29	160	27	6	2	5
Anderson, Huntsville	.989	60	323	40	4	5	4	Jones, Huntsville	.988	65	301	40	4	3	2
Arnold, Jacksonville	.984	38	225	22	4	2	2	Liddle, Orlando	.987	93	606	77	9	12	11
Beamesderfer, Charlotte	.995	32	164	17	1	2	3	Lindsey, Birmingham	.986	62	376	50	6	7	5
Bell, Memphis	.986	85	445	35	7	3	8	Magrann, Charlotte	.985	57	371	34	6	3	7
Borders, Knoxville	.976	77	432	49	12	3	16	McGuire, Chattanooga	.989	79	477	43	6	4	12
D'Alessandro, Greenville	1.000	6	55	11	0	0	2	Merullo, Birmingham	.974	47	278	24	8	3	12
DATZ, Columbus	.993	107	675	74	5	7	16	Morris, Memphis	.991	20	101	5	1	0	0
Dewey, Greenville	.991	82	505	44	5	6	9	Nelson, Memphis	.976	52	300	24	8	3	4
DeWillis, Knoxville	.973	34	171	12	5	1	5	Nipper, Greenville	.972	24	126	13	4	1	8
Eccles, Orlando	.989	15	75	16	1	0	1	Santovenia, Jacksonville	.987	115	785	71	11	5	13
Firova, Chattanooga	.994	52	303	33	2	3	9	Stark, Knoxville	1.000	3	18	3	0	0	0
Fishel, Columbus	1.000	1	1	0	0	0	1	Strucher, Greenville	1.000	4	19	2	0	1	0
Gatewood, Orlando	.996	48	215	23	1	4	1	Tackett, Charlotte	.976	61	379	27	10	2	6
Gonring, Columbus	.971	24	97	5	3	0	3	Yost, Greenville	.981	35	197	15	4	2	5
Hansen, Chattanooga	1.000	25	119	10	0	2	0								

PITCHERS

Player and Club	Pct.	G.	PO.	A.	E.	DP.	Player and Club	Pct.	G.	PO.	A.	E.	DP.
Acker, 12 Bir-24 Mem*	.947	36	5	13	1	3	Birtsas, Huntsville*	.947	17	6	12	1	0
Akins, Greenville	1.000	16	3	4	0	2	Blankenship, Greenville	.926	40	4	21	2	0
Alicea, Greenville	1.000	37	4	7	0	1	Blasucci, Birmingham*	1.000	12	1	0	0	0
Alvarez, Greenville	1.000	9	0	2	0	0	Blouin, Memphis	.667	3	1	1	1	0
Arnsberg, Columbus	.714	13	2	3	2	0	Boling, Birmingham*	1.000	40	1	4	0	0
Bartley, Chattanooga	.882	48	1	14	2	0	Brinson, Knoxville	1.000	8	3	3	0	0
Beasley, Chattanooga	.769	14	3	7	3	0	Bronkey, Orlando	1.000	24	3	7	0	1
Beatty, Charlotte*	.917	15	4	7	1	0	Bumgarner, Orlando	.889	26	6	18	3	1
Bencomo, Knoxville	.923	38	16	20	3	0	Burgos, Knoxville*	1.000	17	0	9	0	0
Bettendorf, Birmingham	.840	43	2	19	4	3	Burns, Huntsville	1.000	34	6	10	0	1
Bianchi, Orlando*	.800	4	1	3	1	0	Burroughs, Chattanooga*	.909	24	4	6	1	1

PITCHERS—Continued

Player and Club	Pct.	G.	PO.	A.	E.	DP.
Cadaret, Huntsville*	.750	24	0	6	2	0
Carroll, Huntsville	1.000	3	0	2	0	0
Cash, Columbus	1.000	32	4	12	0	0
Chestnut, Knoxville	.950	41	8	11	1	0
Christ, Chattanooga	.938	12	5	10	1	0
Clark, Columbus*	1.000	13	2	4	0	0
Clemons, 6 Orl-12 Jax	1.000	18	6	11	0	3
Coffman, Greenville	.900	30	11	25	4	0
Cooley, Birmingham*	.789	17	6	9	4	1
Cook, Columbus	.800	6	0	4	1	0
Corsi, Huntsville	.917	28	5	6	1	0
Crew, 31 Mem-11 Clm	.920	42	5	18	2	1
Criswell, Huntsville*	1.000	32	12	13	0	0
Crouch, Memphis	.935	16	10	19	2	1
Cundari, Huntsville	1.000	5	6	3	0	1
Cunningham, Jacksonville*	1.000	3	1	5	0	0
Daniel, Charlotte	1.000	36	7	13	0	1
Davis, Knoxville*	1.000	13	1	5	0	0
DeJesus, Memphis	.909	25	12	18	3	2
DelRosario, Greenville	1.000	19	1	4	0	1
Devlin, Jacksonville	.667	13	2	2	2	0
Dillard, Charlotte*	.857	36	2	4	1	0
Dopson, Jacksonville	.958	21	11	12	1	0
Dunster, Columbus	.833	11	4	6	2	1
Eave, Greenville	1.000	25	1	6	0	1
Edwards, Columbus*	1.000	6	0	4	0	0
Englund, Knoxville	.900	20	0	9	1	1
Farmer, Greenville*	.900	39	3	6	1	2
Filer, Knoxville*	1.000	6	3	4	0	0
Forrester, Birmingham*	1.000	3	0	1	0	0
Fowlkes, Jacksonville	.750	5	1	2	1	0
Gardner, Jacksonville	.952	17	6	14	1	0
Gasser, Orlando	.846	20	4	7	2	2
Gaynor, Birmingham	.938	51	6	9	1	0
George, Memphis*	1.000	20	0	2	0	0
Givler, Chattanooga	.875	42	2	5	1	0
Gomez, Orlando	1.000	24	7	2	0	1
Gozzo, Memphis	1.000	19	11	12	0	1
Graybill, Jacksonville	1.000	11	3	6	0	0
Green, Charlotte*	.750	12	0	3	1	0
Greene, Greenville	.950	23	7	12	1	1
Grovon, Columbus*	1.000	2	0	1	0	0
Gunnarsson, Chattanooga*	.833	11	0	5	1	0
G. Hall, Birmingham*	1.000	10	2	12	0	1
M. Hall, Columbus	1.000	3	1	0	0	0
Hanson, Chattanooga	.960	21	10	14	1	1
Hardy, Birmingham	1.000	9	1	3	0	0
Heise, Greenville*	.800	33	1	3	1	2
Hesketh, Jacksonville*	.889	6	2	6	1	0
Hibbard, Memphis*	.975	16	8	31	1	2
Hickey, Birmingham	1.000	7	0	4	0	0
Higgs, Orlando	1.000	38	2	5	0	1
Hilton, Huntsville	.909	14	6	14	2	1
Holman, Jacksonville	1.000	22	11	11	0	0
Hoover, Charlotte	.880	22	9	13	3	0
Householder, Charlotte*	1.000	15	3	9	0	0
Ilsley, Columbus*	.945	26	14	38	3	2
Johnson, Jacksonville*	.826	25	4	15	4	1
Jones, Chattanooga	.929	26	6	7	1	0
Kaufman, Charlotte	1.000	9	0	1	0	0
Kibler, Huntsville	.905	41	10	9	2	0
Kilner, Greenville*	.889	26	6	10	2	1
Kucharski, Charlotte	1.000	9	2	3	0	0
R. Lambert, Huntsville*	1.000	29	1	7	0	0
T. Lambert, Memphis	.846	13	3	8	2	1
Livin, Columbus	.842	38	6	10	3	0
B. Long, Columbus	.700	9	4	3	3	0
R. Long, Charlotte	.846	43	6	5	2	1
Luecken, Memphis	.963	28	9	17	1	1
Mack, Columbus	1.000	37	2	6	0	1
Mallicoat, Columbus	.963	24	4	22	1	2
Mathews, Greenville	.917	37	7	15	2	2
McDonald, Huntsville	1.000	5	2	2	0	0
McDowell, Birmingham	1.000	4	0	1	0	0
McMurtry, Knoxville	.800	12	4	8	3	2
McWilliams, Greenville*	1.000	7	3	6	0	1
Mecerod, Birmingham	.875	9	0	7	1	0
Mendek, Chattanooga*	.870	39	5	15	3	2
Menendez, Birmingham	.813	27	1	12	3	3
Mesa, Knoxville	.946	35	11	24	2	1
Metoyer, Columbus	.400	4	0	2	3	0
MILACKI, Charlotte	1.000	29	13	23	0	2
Miller, Memphis	1.000	1	1	0	0	0
Mooneyham, Huntsville	.900	12	2	7	1	0
Morgan, 24 Mem-9 Orl	.962	33	7	18	1	1
Mount, Memphis	1.000	15	1	2	0	0
Mumaw, Knoxville*	1.000	6	4	3	0	0
Nivens, Orlando	.920	13	11	12	2	3
Oliveras, Charlotte	.952	23	5	15	1	4
Otto, Huntsville*	.875	9	5	9	2	1
Ownbey, Memphis	.000	4	0	0	1	0
Pall, Birmingham	.974	30	12	25	1	4
C. Parker, Chattanooga	.960	16	7	17	1	2
Pawlowski, Birmingham	1.000	35	3	2	0	0
Payne, Jacksonville	1.000	10	14	8	0	0
Peraza, Knoxville	.947	28	16	20	2	1
M. Perez, Memphis	.929	20	9	17	2	0
Y. Perez, Jacksonville*	.857	12	1	5	1	2
Perry, Orlando	1.000	7	2	3	0	0
Peterson, Birmingham	.963	26	10	16	1	2
Pierorazio, Orlando*	1.000	51	5	16	0	1
Potestio, Chattanooga	1.000	5	1	3	0	0
Price, Jacksonville	.933	57	2	12	1	1
Provence, Knoxville	.978	58	12	32	1	4
Raczka, Charlotte*	.889	12	3	5	1	1
Rasmussen, Birmingham	1.000	7	0	2	0	0
Rather, Columbus	.917	26	6	16	2	1
Renz, Birmingham	1.000	11	2	5	0	0
Rice, Charlotte	.833	23	3	7	2	1
Rodiles, Columbus	.800	10	3	1	1	0
Santarelli, Columbus	1.000	43	5	13	0	1
Scherer, Huntsville	.957	37	9	13	1	0
Schooler, Chattanooga	.960	28	10	14	1	0
M. Scott, Columbus	1.000	15	1	3	0	0
T. Scott, Birmingham	1.000	11	1	1	0	0
Shade, Jacksonville	1.000	38	6	5	0	1
Shaver, Huntsville	.933	23	19	23	3	2
Shaw, Memphis	.667	45	4	6	5	0
Shiflett, Memphis*	.880	47	3	19	3	1
D. Smith, Orlando*	1.000	20	4	3	0	1
P. Smith, Greenville	.889	29	9	15	3	1
R. Smith, Orlando	.931	22	8	19	2	0
Sontag, Orlando	.929	15	5	8	1	0
Sparks, Huntsville*	1.000	1	1	0	0	0
Spratke, Chattanooga	.886	27	17	14	4	0
Stanhope, Charlotte	1.000	33	11	14	0	1
Stottlemyre, 19 Clm-1 Mem	.846	20	9	13	4	1
Stranski, Memphis	1.000	12	0	2	0	0
Stringfellow, Greenville*	.957	20	4	18	1	0
Sudo, Jacksonville	1.000	11	1	15	0	0
Talamantez, Charlotte	1.000	4	1	1	0	0
Thomas, Birmingham	1.000	3	0	1	0	0
Thompson, 7 Jax-8 Mem	.667	15	0	2	1	0
Traen, 4 Jax-6 Orl*	1.000	10	1	8	0	0
Trautwein, Jacksonville	.947	56	6	12	1	0
Trudeau, Orlando	1.000	19	8	3	0	1
Van Houten, Columbus	1.000	1	1	2	0	0
Vargas, Columbus	1.000	3	1	3	0	0
J. Walker, Chattanooga	.960	39	6	18	1	0
K. Walker, Orlando	.833	25	2	3	1	0
Walsh, Knoxville*	1.000	24	5	15	0	0
B. Walton, Huntsville	.941	18	11	5	1	1
R. Walton, Charlotte	1.000	4	1	1	0	0
Wardle, Jacksonville	.600	6	4	2	4	0
Wayne, Jacksonville*	.952	56	5	15	1	1
Welsh, Charlotte*	1.000	4	0	1	0	0
Whitehurst, Huntsville	.935	28	16	42	4	1
Yearout, Huntsville	1.000	34	10	10	0	0
C. Young, Knoxville*	.973	42	9	27	1	1
J. Young, Orlando*	1.000	11	3	4	0	1

The following players do not have any recorded accepted chances at the positions indicated; therefore, are not listed in the fielding averages for those particular positions: Allen, p/ Baker, p; Balelo, p; Borders, 3b; Camelo, p; Carriger, p; Dodd, 3b; Funk, p; Gibbons, p; Gilliam, p; Houston, of; Kent, p; Kinnard, 1b; Leal, p; Lindsey, p; Linton, p; McDougal, of; Miller, c; Morhardt, p; Myers, p; O'Dell, p; Palmer, p; R. Parker, of, p; Ralston, of; Salinas, p; Santiago, of; Shaw, of; Sparling, p; Springer, p; Wooden, p; Youmans, p.

CLUB PITCHING

Club	ERA.	G.	CG.	ShO.	Sv.	IP.	H.	R.	ER.	HR.	HB.	BB.	Int. BB.	SO.	WP.	Bk.
Chattanooga	3.59	143	12	10	33	1249.2	1235	623	499	105	30	418	12	882	56	17
Jacksonville	3.68	144	10	12	46	1262.1	1118	585	516	116	38	568	14	976	45	7
Huntsville	3.79	144	12	7	36	1243.2	1257	635	524	91	18	450	23	762	64	10
Greenville	3.84	144	14	10	38	1260.0	1135	615	537	91	42	461	36	887	81	15
Charlotte	4.04	145	17	11	33	1262.0	1265	655	567	123	36	461	3	884	73	10
Knoxville	4.17	144	10	8	28	1249.2	1249	702	579	118	33	525	25	789	66	13
Columbus	4.25	144	16	4	27	1222.2	1267	691	577	128	34	537	25	898	51	8
Memphis	4.45	143	18	5	34	1242.2	1296	729	615	125	28	522	28	800	69	19
Birmingham	4.50	143	15	6	23	1229.0	1240	736	614	121	60	562	25	822	67	11
Orlando	4.52	143	12	8	36	1225.1	1314	722	616	140	35	545	10	859	67	11

PITCHERS' RECORDS
(Leading Qualifiers for Earned-Run Average Leadership — 115 or More Innings)

*Throws lefthanded.

Pitcher—Club	W.	L.	Pct.	ERA.	G.	GS.	CG.	GF.	ShO.	Sv.	IP.	H.	R.	ER.	HR.	HB.	BB.	Int. BB.	SO.	WP.
Holman, Jacksonville	14	5	.737	2.50	22	22	6	0	1	0	151.1	114	52	42	8	7	56	0	115	8
Hanson, Chattanooga	8	10	.444	2.60	21	21	1	0	0	0	131.1	102	56	38	10	3	43	0	131	11
Mallicoat, Columbus*	10	7	.588	2.89	24	24	3	0	0	0	152.1	132	68	49	13	5	78	2	141	8
Peraza, Knoxville	10	7	.588	3.12	28	19	3	6	0	1	132.2	122	63	46	16	2	33	1	105	6
Greene, Greenville	11	8	.579	3.29	23	23	4	0	2	0	142.1	103	60	52	13	4	66	1	101	7
P. Smith, Greenville	9	9	.500	3.35	29	25	5	2	1	1	177.1	162	76	66	10	3	67	0	119	11
Shaver, Huntsville	7	9	.438	3.39	23	23	2	0	0	0	140.2	147	69	53	14	0	51	1	85	3
M. Perez, Memphis	8	5	.615	3.43	20	20	5	0	2	0	133.2	125	60	51	13	0	20	1	126	4
Johnson, Jacksonville*	11	8	.579	3.73	25	24	0	1	0	0	140.0	100	63	58	10	9	128	0	163	12
Spratke, Chattanooga	8	10	.444	3.78	27	27	1	0	0	0	166.2	159	93	70	21	3	63	0	69	6

Departmental Leaders: G—Provence, 58; W—Trautwein, 15; L—Mesa, Provence, 13; Pct.—Bettendorf, .900; GS—Mesa, 35; CG—Holman, 6; GF—Price, 45; ShO—Bumgarner, Whitehurst, 3; Sv.—Price, 19; IP—Mesa, 193.1; H—Mesa, 206; R—Mesa, 131; ER—Mesa, 112; HR—Stanhope, 24; HB—Bettendorf, 12; BB—Coffman, 130; IBB—Five pitchers with 6; SO—Johnson, 163; WP—Coffman, 21.

(All Pitchers—Listed Alphabetically)

Pitcher—Club	W.	L.	Pct.	ERA.	G.	GS.	CG.	GF.	ShO.	Sv.	IP.	H.	R.	ER.	HR.	HB.	BB.	Int. BB.	SO.	WP.
Acker, 12 Bir-24 Mem*	8	10	.444	5.09	36	13	1	13	0	3	132.2	159	91	75	15	5	48	2	63	7
Akins, Greenville	3	1	.750	0.87	16	0	0	10	0	4	41.1	30	4	4	1	0	9	2	31	0
Alicea, Charlotte	2	2	.500	2.50	37	1	0	18	0	3	72.0	48	21	20	6	0	17	0	63	2
Alvarez, Greenville	1	0	1.000	0.84	9	0	0	8	0	5	21.1	14	2	2	0	0	8	2	20	0
Arnsberg, Columbus	2	1	.667	4.53	13	5	1	3	0	0	45.2	46	27	23	7	0	21	1	19	3
Baker, Columbus	0	1	.000	5.63	4	0	0	3	0	1	8.0	10	5	5	0	0	5	2	5	0
Bartley, Chattanooga	4	5	.444	3.71	48	0	0	32	0	13	63.0	66	34	26	7	2	26	4	37	4
Beasley, Chattanooga	2	4	.333	3.67	14	8	0	4	0	0	56.1	73	33	23	4	1	22	0	26	2
Beatty, Charlotte*	6	5	.545	3.07	15	15	3	0	1	0	105.2	110	38	36	2	1	20	2	57	4
Bencomo, Knoxville	8	11	.421	4.14	38	23	1	13	0	3	167.1	186	94	77	15	4	40	3	96	2
Bettendorf, Birmingham	9	1	.900	4.55	43	0	0	14	0	2	89.0	88	54	45	3	12	42	6	41	6
Bianchi, Orlando	1	1	.500	4.95	4	3	0	0	0	0	20.0	25	13	11	1	0	9	0	11	0
Birtsas, Huntsville*	5	10	.333	3.61	17	17	3	0	0	0	114.2	109	54	46	8	1	53	0	75	3
Blankenship, Greenville	4	7	.364	4.13	40	6	0	9	0	1	102.1	96	51	47	5	5	53	2	78	6
Blasucci, Birmingham*	1	0	1.000	2.70	12	0	0	4	0	0	13.1	7	4	4	1	0	7	0	16	1
Blouin, Memphis	2	1	.667	4.00	3	3	1	0	0	0	18.0	21	8	8	0	0	1	0	14	1
Boling, Birmingham*	6	1	.857	2.96	40	0	0	20	0	5	51.2	27	20	17	1	1	35	1	35	0
Brinson, Knoxville	0	1	.000	5.40	8	5	0	2	0	1	26.2	23	17	16	1	0	18	0	19	2
Bronkey, Orlando	1	6	.143	6.29	24	4	1	16	0	7	48.2	70	40	34	5	4	28	1	23	0
Bumgarner, Orlando	13	10	.565	4.38	26	26	4	0	3	0	168.1	174	96	82	14	5	94	0	87	16
Burgos, Knoxville*	2	3	.400	4.37	17	5	0	6	0	1	45.1	33	27	22	4	1	55	0	45	3
Burns, Huntsville	3	4	.429	2.97	34	0	0	27	0	7	63.2	49	24	21	4	1	17	4	54	3
Burroughs, Chattanooga*	4	1	.800	2.29	24	6	1	10	1	1	74.2	50	20	19	4	0	19	0	69	5
Cadaret, Huntsville*	5	2	.714	2.90	24	0	0	21	0	9	40.1	31	16	13	1	0	20	3	48	6
Camelo, Jacksonville*	0	0	.000	9.00	1	0	0	1	0	0	1.0	2	1	1	0	0	0	0	1	0
Carriger, Charlotte	0	0	.000	1.29	5	0	0	2	0	0	7.0	3	1	1	0	0	4	0	12	0
Carroll, Huntsville	0	0	.000	2.25	3	0	0	1	0	0	4.0	2	1	1	0	2	3	0	5	1
Cash, Columbus	3	5	.375	5.55	32	1	0	15	0	3	60.0	74	39	37	7	5	27	3	44	1
Chestnut, Knoxville	7	6	.538	3.77	41	4	0	19	0	4	76.1	74	39	32	10	2	26	6	26	1
Christ, Chattanooga	4	4	.500	3.56	12	11	1	1	0	0	65.2	66	33	26	1	3	28	0	30	4
Clark, Columbus*	1	1	.500	4.22	13	2	0	5	0	1	21.1	22	11	10	0	0	7	0	14	0
Clemons, 6 Orl-12 Jax	4	5	.545	4.19	18	17	0	1	0	1	103.0	112	59	48	9	4	20	1	46	1
Coffman, Greenville	11	11	.500	4.41	30	30	1	0	0	0	181.2	162	102	89	9	6	130	3	153	21
Conley, Birmingham*	3	9	.250	5.11	17	17	2	0	1	0	100.1	117	69	57	11	5	33	3	56	1
Cook, Columbus	4	1	.800	3.56	6	6	0	0	0	0	30.1	33	13	12	2	0	12	0	19	1
Corsi, Huntsville	8	1	.889	2.81	28	0	0	18	0	4	48.0	30	17	15	1	0	15	1	33	5
Crew, 31 Mem-11 Col	4	6	.400	3.88	42	6	1	19	1	4	102.0	118	54	44	10	2	42	6	85	6
Criswell, Huntsville*	7	5	.583	2.91	32	9	0	8	0	3	111.1	106	42	36	8	1	38	1	69	3
Crouch, Memphis	7	3	.700	4.00	16	14	1	1	0	0	90.0	103	49	40	6	2	26	0	47	9
Cundari, Huntsville	2	2	.500	7.66	5	5	0	0	0	0	24.2	36	23	21	3	1	15	0	10	0
Cunningham, Jacksonville*	0	1	.000	6.08	3	3	0	0	0	0	13.1	17	9	9	2	0	6	0	7	0
Daniel, Charlotte	4	7	.364	4.91	36	3	0	15	0	2	80.2	84	51	44	11	2	37	0	57	5
Davis, Knoxville*	6	2	.750	3.02	13	11	0	2	0	0	65.2	54	26	22	6	1	38	1	37	4
DeJesus, Memphis	4	11	.267	4.49	25	24	2	0	0	0	130.1	106	78	65	8	4	99	0	79	11
DelRosario, Greenville	0	3	.000	3.42	19	0	0	11	0	1	26.1	33	19	10	1	4	17	5	15	1
Devlin, Jacksonville	0	0	.000	7.96	13	0	0	5	0	1	26.0	27	24	23	3	4	23	1	24	1
Dillard, Charlotte*	5	2	.714	3.31	36	0	0	22	0	4	49.0	44	18	18	3	2	19	0	53	9
Dopson, Jacksonville	7	5	.583	3.80	21	21	1	0	1	0	118.1	123	58	50	8	1	30	1	75	0
Dunster, Columbus	4	5	.444	4.76	11	11	2	0	0	0	64.1	73	44	34	7	0	17	0	42	3
Eave, Greenville	2	5	.286	2.82	25	1	0	19	0	7	54.1	39	19	17	9	1	23	4	52	1
Edwards, Columbus*	0	0	.000	4.30	6	2	0	3	0	0	14.2	17	7	7	1	1	10	1	23	2
Englund, Knoxville	0	2	.000	7.98	20	0	0	11	0	2	38.1	55	37	34	5	5	13	0	19	4
Farmer, Greenville*	1	3	.250	3.43	39	0	0	20	0	1	60.1	57	23	23	4	1	19	3	32	4
Filer, Knoxville	2	0	1.000	0.87	6	3	1	3	1	1	20.2	13	2	2	0	0	4	0	14	1
Forrester, Birmingham*	0	0	.000	2.25	3	0	0	3	0	0	4.0	1	1	1	0	0	4	0	2	0
Fowlkes, Jacksonville	2	0	1.000	1.72	5	1	0	1	0	0	15.2	6	4	3	0	2	8	0	10	0
Funk, Columbus*	2	0	1.000	2.25	16	0	0	13	0	2	28.0	23	8	7	3	1	6	0	23	0
Gardner, Jacksonville	4	6	.400	4.19	17	17	1	0	0	0	101.0	101	50	47	13	0	42	0	78	4
Gasser, Orlando	9	8	.529	4.39	20	20	3	0	1	0	127.0	117	68	62	18	2	68	0	126	5
Gaynor, Birmingham	5	7	.417	3.40	51	7	0	32	0	5	98.0	89	46	37	7	4	61	3	71	12
George, Memphis*	4	2	.667	4.62	20	5	0	9	0	2	50.2	56	30	26	7	0	11	2	19	2
Gibbons, Chattanooga*	0	0	.000	0.00	2	0	0	2	0	0	2.1	1	0	0	0	0	1	0	0	0
Gilliam, 3 Knx-5 Grv*	1	0	1.000	4.66	8	0	0	1	0	0	9.2	3	5	5	0	1	17	0	5	4
Givler, Chattanooga	3	5	.375	4.25	42	1	0	19	0	1	91.0	102	50	43	8	3	46	2	79	6
Gomez, Orlando	0	1	.000	2.13	24	0	0	16	0	4	38.0	28	13	9	4	2	14	1	22	0
Gozzo, Memphis	6	5	.545	4.53	19	14	1	2	0	0	91.1	95	58	46	13	4	36	2	56	3
Graybill, Jacksonville	5	4	.556	4.21	11	11	1	0	1	0	66.1	66	34	31	10	2	22	0	29	0
Green, Charlotte*	1	3	.250	2.84	12	0	0	6	0	1	25.1	23	18	8	4	1	13	0	22	3
Greene, Greenville	11	8	.579	3.29	23	23	4	0	2	0	142.1	103	60	52	13	4	66	1	101	7
Grovom, Columbus*	0	2	.000	12.15	2	2	0	0	0	0	6.2	7	9	9	1	0	9	0	9	0
Gunnarsson, Chattanooga*	0	1	.000	5.40	11	0	0	3	0	0	18.1	19	14	11	3	0	9	0	9	0
G. Hall, Birmingham*	3	5	.375	3.72	10	10	1	0	0	0	58.0	54	28	24	4	2	20	1	30	3

Pitcher—Club	W.	L.	Pct.	ERA.	G.	GS.	CG.	GF.	ShO.	Sv.	IP.	H.	R.	ER.	HR.	HB.	BB.	Int. BB.	SO.	WP.
M. Hall, Columbus	0	1	.000	3.48	3	1	0	0	0	0	10.1	13	7	4	1	0	4	0	7	1
Hanson, Chattanooga	8	10	.444	2.60	21	21	1	0	0	0	131.1	102	56	38	10	3	43	0	131	11
Hardy, Birmingham	0	0	.000	1.64	9	0	0	7	0	3	11.0	5	2	2	1	1	1	0	12	0
Heise, Greenville*	2	2	.500	4.88	33	1	0	14	0	5	51.2	52	33	28	7	0	26	3	40	6
Hesketh, Jacksonville*	1	0	1.000	2.29	6	3	0	1	0	1	19.2	18	6	5	1	0	4	1	22	1
Hibbard, Memphis*	7	6	.538	3.23	16	16	3	0	1	0	106.0	102	48	38	7	2	21	1	56	1
Hickey, Birmingham	0	2	.000	6.29	7	1	1	2	0	0	24.1	28	20	17	8	1	7	0	14	0
Higgs, Orlando	5	3	.625	1.97	38	0	0	27	0	8	64.0	62	23	14	2	0	27	2	64	5
Hilton, Huntsville	2	4	.333	5.68	14	14	0	0	0	0	65.0	85	52	41	6	0	24	1	28	4
Holman, Jacksonville	14	5	.737	2.50	22	22	6	0	1	0	151.1	114	52	42	8	7	56	0	115	8
Hoover, Charlotte	9	8	.529	4.56	22	22	4	0	1	0	140.0	151	78	71	11	4	51	0	100	12
Householder, Charlotte*	8	1	.889	3.27	15	14	1	1	1	0	82.2	81	34	30	4	5	46	0	63	8
Ilsley, Columbus*	10	11	.476	3.86	26	26	3	0	0	0	167.2	162	84	72	13	4	63	1	130	6
Johnson, Jacksonville*	11	8	.579	3.73	25	24	0	1	0	0	140.0	100	63	58	10	9	128	0	163	12
Jones, Chattanooga	2	9	.182	4.98	26	10	0	12	0	2	81.1	90	58	45	5	2	38	0	77	4
Kaufman, Charlotte	0	0	.000	1.86	9	0	0	5	0	0	19.1	12	5	4	2	0	5	0	9	1
Kent, Huntsville	0	0	.000	0.00	1	0	0	0	0	0	1.0	0	0	0	0	0	1	0	0	0
Kibler, Huntsville*	5	1	.833	3.09	41	5	1	12	1	2	96.0	103	41	33	11	2	33	3	36	6
Kilner, Greenville*	7	8	.467	4.58	26	24	0	1	0	0	127.2	136	74	65	12	0	72	2	63	6
Kucharski, Charlotte	6	3	.667	3.83	9	9	1	0	1	0	56.1	54	28	24	8	1	13	0	43	1
R. Lambert, Huntsville*	3	2	.600	3.24	29	0	0	21	0	6	33.1	37	15	12	3	0	10	2	27	3
T. Lambert, Memphis	4	4	.500	5.61	13	10	2	1	0	0	61.0	72	45	38	8	2	34	1	21	7
Leal, Knoxville	1	0	1.000	0.00	1	1	0	0	0	0	6.0	5	0	0	0	0	2	0	7	0
Lindsey, Birmingham	0	0	.000	18.00	1	0	0	1	0	0	1.0	4	2	2	0	0	0	0	0	0
Linton, Knoxville	0	0	.000	9.00	1	1	0	0	0	0	3.0	5	3	3	0	1	1	0	1	0
Livin, Columbus	5	9	.357	5.06	38	7	0	17	0	2	101.1	102	66	57	19	3	51	3	63	4
B. Long, Columbus	0	4	.000	5.57	9	7	1	2	0	0	32.1	41	30	20	4	0	18	1	11	5
R. Long, Charlotte	6	3	.667	2.14	43	0	0	39	0	16	54.2	28	17	13	4	4	28	1	55	2
Luecken, Memphis	9	9	.500	4.75	28	24	2	0	0	0	146.0	163	86	77	12	3	53	3	88	5
Mack, Columbus	2	5	.286	2.83	37	0	0	27	0	10	57.1	60	26	18	6	0	23	2	46	1
Mallicoat, Columbus*	10	7	.588	2.89	24	24	3	0	0	0	152.1	132	68	49	13	5	78	2	141	8
Mathews, Greenville	3	7	.300	3.58	37	1	0	28	0	11	65.1	63	28	26	3	1	30	6	45	3
McDonald, Huntsville	0	1	.000	2.73	5	5	0	0	0	0	26.1	23	9	8	2	0	9	0	9	2
McDowell, Birmingham	1	2	.333	7.84	4	4	1	0	1	0	20.2	19	20	18	5	1	8	0	17	3
McMurtry, Knoxville	4	2	.667	2.77	12	11	1	0	0	0	78.0	64	28	24	3	0	20	0	56	2
McWilliams, Greenville*	1	2	.333	5.45	7	7	0	0	0	0	33.0	33	24	20	3	5	26	1	27	4
Mecerod, Birmingham	0	3	.000	7.18	9	6	0	1	0	0	31.1	39	29	25	7	3	23	1	19	4
Mendek, Chattanooga*	7	3	.700	4.03	39	6	0	14	0	4	76.0	79	35	34	6	1	35	0	56	3
Menendez, Birmingham	10	10	.500	4.83	27	27	4	0	1	0	173.1	193	111	93	19	7	76	1	102	12
Mesa, Knoxville	10	13	.435	5.21	35	35	4	0	2	0	193.1	206	131	112	19	3	104	0	115	13
Metoyer, Columbus	0	1	.000	6.60	4	1	0	0	0	0	15.0	26	14	11	3	0	8	0	9	0
Milacki, Charlotte	11	9	.550	4.56	29	24	2	2	0	1	148.0	168	86	75	10	3	66	0	101	10
Miller, Memphis	0	0	.000	0.00	1	0	0	0	0	0	0.1	0	0	0	0	0	0	0	0	0
Mooneyham, Huntsville	2	6	.250	4.75	12	11	0	0	0	0	60.2	68	36	32	2	1	25	0	39	2
Morgan, 24 Mem-9 Orl	4	4	.500	6.15	33	2	0	13	0	3	79.0	93	58	54	6	1	45	2	57	8
Morhardt, Orlando	0	1	.000	2.57	3	0	0	2	0	0	7.0	2	2	2	1	1	4	0	3	0
Mount, Memphis	0	0	.000	5.85	15	0	0	9	0	5	20.0	22	13	13	3	0	8	1	19	2
Mumaw, Knoxville*	0	0	.000	6.59	6	0	0	2	0	0	13.2	13	11	10	2	0	7	1	7	1
Myers, Chattanooga	0	0	.000	3.00	2	0	0	2	0	0	3.0	2	1	1	1	0	0	0	3	0
Nivens, Orlando	2	7	.222	4.14	13	13	2	0	0	0	82.2	101	47	38	9	2	39	1	46	6
O'Dell, Birmingham*	0	1	.000	17.61	6	0	0	3	0	0	7.2	10	15	15	2	0	12	0	4	1
Oliveras, Charlotte	4	3	.667	3.60	23	10	3	6	1	2	100.0	99	43	40	9	5	21	0	67	5
Otto, Huntsville*	4	1	.800	2.34	9	8	1	0	0	0	50.0	36	14	13	1	0	11	0	25	4
Ownbey, Memphis	0	0	.000	6.75	4	1	0	2	0	1	4.0	6	3	3	0	0	3	0	1	0
Pall, Birmingham	8	11	.421	4.27	30	23	3	3	0	0	158.0	173	100	75	18	8	63	4	139	9
Palmer, Greenville	1	0	1.000	0.00	1	1	0	0	0	0	5.0	3	0	0	0	0	3	0	6	0
C. Parker, Chattanooga	7	5	.583	2.73	16	16	5	0	1	0	112.0	103	47	34	7	1	14	1	60	2
R. Parker, Columbus	0	0	.000	2.70	4	0	0	4	0	0	3.1	5	2	1	1	0	4	0	1	0
Pawlowski, Birmingham	5	6	.455	4.70	35	8	0	27	0	3	69.0	69	44	36	7	2	38	1	57	1
Payne, Jacksonville	2	2	.500	4.95	10	7	0	0	0	0	36.1	37	22	20	4	0	16	0	22	0
Peraza, Knoxville	10	7	.588	3.12	28	19	3	6	0	1	132.2	122	63	46	16	2	33	1	105	6
M. Perez, Memphis	8	5	.615	3.43	20	20	5	0	2	0	133.2	125	60	51	13	0	20	1	126	4
Y. Perez, Jacksonville*	2	7	.222	4.05	12	10	1	1	1	1	60.0	61	34	27	4	1	30	0	60	4
Perry, Orlando	4	3	.571	4.31	7	6	0	1	0	0	39.2	42	21	19	3	1	14	0	34	5
Peterson, Birmingham	12	9	.571	3.90	26	26	2	0	1	0	170.2	165	79	74	12	7	73	1	124	6
Pierorazio, Birmingham	1	6	.143	4.70	51	1	0	29	0	7	90.0	77	52	47	12	3	48	0	76	2
Potestio, Chattanooga	1	1	.500	5.32	5	4	0	0	0	0	22.0	26	13	13	5	0	8	0	14	1
Price, Jacksonville	9	4	.692	2.40	57	0	0	45	0	19	97.2	71	29	26	12	2	24	4	63	2
Provence, Knoxville	6	13	.316	4.05	58	0	0	42	0	9	97.2	105	59	44	6	3	44	5	39	2
Raczka, Charlotte*	2	3	.400	8.84	12	5	0	5	0	0	36.2	48	41	36	8	2	21	0	31	0
Rasmussen, Birmingham	0	1	.000	3.06	7	1	0	2	0	2	17.2	15	6	6	2	1	3	0	15	1
Rather, Columbus	4	12	.250	5.46	26	22	2	0	1	0	128.2	142	90	78	16	3	65	0	80	7
Renz, Birmingham	1	0	1.000	3.55	11	0	0	4	0	3	25.1	21	12	10	1	0	11	1	8	1
Rice, Charlotte	2	1	.667	5.40	23	8	0	5	0	4	71.2	71	46	43	11	2	33	0	57	7
Rodiles, Charlotte	2	0	1.000	5.51	10	2	0	1	0	0	32.2	38	30	20	5	0	26	0	24	1
Salinas, Birmingham	0	0	.000	0.00	1	0	0	1	0	0	1.0	0	0	0	0	0	1	0	0	0
Santarelli, Columbus	8	4	.667	3.58	43	2	0	27	0	5	75.1	80	31	30	5	4	25	5	78	5
Scherer, Huntsville	8	5	.615	4.74	37	11	0	16	0	3	95.0	110	64	50	3	3	42	2	58	5
Schooler, Chattanooga	13	8	.619	3.96	28	28	3	0	2	0	175.0	183	87	77	14	6	48	1	144	4
M. Scott, Greenville	3	5	.375	6.98	15	11	1	3	1	0	59.1	59	51	46	4	8	50	1	41	5
T. Scott, Birmingham	1	2	.333	4.79	11	1	0	2	0	0	20.2	20	15	11	2	1	14	1	20	1
Shade, Jacksonville	2	3	.400	3.28	38	2	0	17	0	3	82.1	62	33	30	8	2	46	2	58	0
Shaver, Huntsville	7	9	.438	3.39	23	23	2	0	0	0	140.2	147	69	53	14	0	51	1	85	3
Shaw, Memphis	3	3	.500	5.57	45	1	0	26	0	4	74.1	73	52	46	10	3	52	2	64	5
Shiflett, Memphis*	4	4	.500	3.94	47	0	0	30	0	13	64.0	59	36	28	10	2	35	6	36	2
D. Smith, Orlando*	1	0	1.000	5.23	20	0	0	7	0	2	41.1	49	31	24	7	3	26	1	21	5
P. Smith, Orlando	9	9	.500	3.35	29	25	5	2	1	1	177.1	162	76	66	10	3	67	0	119	11
R. Smith, Orlando	8	9	.471	5.02	22	22	0	0	0	0	122.0	141	78	68	23	2	48	0	54	4
Sontag, Orlando	2	7	.222	6.53	15	11	1	1	0	0	73.0	89	59	53	13	2	25	2	35	2
Sparks, Huntsville*	0	0	.000	4.50	1	0	0	1	0	0	2.0	1	1	1	0	1	2	0	0	0
Sparling, Memphis	0	2	.000	9.00	3	3	0	0	0	0	10.0	16	12	10	5	0	8	0	4	0
Spratke, Chattanooga	8	10	.444	3.78	27	27	1	0	0	0	166.2	159	93	70	21	3	63	0	69	6

Pitcher—Club	W.	L.	Pct.	ERA.	G.	GS.	CG.	GF.	ShO.	Sv.	IP.	H.	R.	ER.	HR.	HB.	BB.	Int. BB.	SO.	WP.
Springer, Memphis	0	0	.000	0.00	1	0	0	1	0	0	1.0	0	0	0	0	0	1	0	1	0
Stanhope, Charlotte	12	7	.632	4.17	33	23	3	2	0	0	164.0	190	99	76	24	2	37	0	69	0
Stottlemyre, 19 Col-1 Mem	7	6	.538	4.31	20	20	4	0	1	0	127.1	125	68	61	12	8	41	2	85	2
Stranski, Memphis	1	1	.500	5.83	12	0	0	6	0	2	29.1	32	22	19	4	1	17	0	26	3
Stringfellow, Greenville*	10	3	.769	3.46	20	14	3	4	1	2	104.0	90	46	40	10	3	32	1	60	2
Sudo, Jacksonville	1	5	.167	7.14	11	9	0	1	0	0	51.2	70	43	41	8	1	29	0	33	2
Talamantez, Charlotte	2	2	.500	9.45	4	4	0	0	0	0	13.1	19	14	14	2	0	12	0	3	2
Thomas, Birmingham	0	0	.000	3.60	3	0	0	2	0	0	5.0	3	2	2	0	0	1	0	2	0
Thompson, 7 Jax-8 Mem	1	0	1.000	5.23	15	0	0	6	0	1	31.0	35	20	18	5	4	11	1	27	3
Traen, 4 Jax-6 Orl*	1	3	.250	4.56	10	6	0	2	0	1	51.1	42	29	26	8	3	22	2	38	5
Trautwein, Jacksonville	15	4	.789	2.87	56	1	0	25	0	8	106.2	92	43	34	8	2	42	3	85	4
Trudeau, Orlando	5	6	.455	5.57	19	13	0	5	0	1	84.0	111	64	52	12	1	31	0	83	4
Van Houten, Columbus	0	0	.000	0.00	1	0	0	0	0	0	2.0	1	0	0	0	0	0	0	0	0
Vargas, Columbus	2	0	1.000	3.00	3	3	0	0	0	0	21.0	20	7	7	1	0	10	1	9	0
J. Walker, Chattanooga	5	8	.385	3.51	39	5	0	21	0	7	92.1	100	40	36	9	4	18	3	64	4
K. Walker, Orlando	4	4	.500	2.98	25	0	0	25	0	7	48.1	46	20	16	2	1	5	0	39	1
Walsh, Knoxville*	2	4	.333	5.45	24	8	0	7	0	0	67.2	72	52	41	8	4	46	1	42	8
B. Walton, Huntsville	2	2	.500	3.10	18	2	0	6	0	2	58.0	61	24	20	4	1	13	1	40	4
R. Walton, Charlotte	2	0	1.000	3.79	4	4	0	0	0	0	19.0	18	9	8	3	1	10	0	6	1
Wardle, Huntsville*	0	5	.000	9.47	6	6	0	0	0	0	25.2	31	29	27	8	2	26	1	15	1
Wayne, Jacksonville*	5	1	.833	2.35	56	0	0	28	0	10	80.1	56	23	21	4	0	35	0	78	2
Welsh, Charlotte*	1	1	.500	3.24	4	3	0	0	0	0	16.2	14	8	6	1	1	8	0	16	1
Whitehurst, Huntsville	11	10	.524	3.98	28	28	5	0	3	0	183.1	192	104	81	12	2	42	3	106	9
Wooden, Chattanooga	0	1	.000	3.86	14	0	0	11	0	5	18.2	14	9	8	0	1	4	1	14	0
Yearout, Knoxville*	2	3	.400	3.13	34	6	0	13	0	5	95.0	71	42	33	8	4	24	2	79	5
Youmans, Jacksonville	1	0	1.000	3.00	1	1	0	0	0	0	6.0	4	2	2	1	0	3	0	6	0
C. Young, Knoxville*	8	9	.471	4.45	42	12	0	10	0	1	119.1	148	76	59	15	3	43	5	81	12
J. Young, Orlando*	2	6	.250	3.54	11	11	1	0	0	0	68.2	65	30	27	3	1	34	1	63	7

BALKS—Shiflett, 10; Schooler, 7; Bartley, Bencomo, Bumgarner, Criswell, Gozzo, Mesa, R. Smith, J. Young, 3 each; Blankenship, DeJesus, Farmer, Greene, Hilton, Holman, Hoover, Householder, Ilsley, Johnson, Kilner, Menendez, Pall, Perry, M. Scott, P. Smith, Sparling, Spratke, Stanhope, Stottlemyre, B. Walton, C. Young, 2 each; Acker, Birtsas, Blouin, Boling, Burgos, Cadaret, Cash, Coffman, Conley, Cunningham, Eave, Grovom, Gunnarsson, G. Hall, Hanson, R. Lambert, T. Lambert, Linton, R. Long, McDowell, Mendek, Metoyer, Oliveras, Pawlowski, Peraza, Price, Provence, Raczka, Rasmussen, Rather, Rice, Stringfellow, J. Walker, Walsh, Wayne, Wooden, 1 each.

COMBINATION SHUTOUTS—Peterson-Gaynor, Hall-Blasucci, Birmingham; Kucharski-Oliveras, Hoover-Long, Householder-Long, Welsh-Oliveras, Beatty-Long, Stanhope-Carriger-Dillard-Long, Charlotte; Parker-Givler, Christ-Jones, Hanson-Mendek-Walker, Beasley-Burroughs-Bartley, Burroughs-Jones, Walker-Wooden, Chattanooga; Cook-Cash, Stottlemyre-Mack, Columbus; Kilner-Mathews 2, Smith-Farmer-Blankenship, Kilner-Blankenship, Smith-Akins, Greenville; Criswell-Cadaret, Scherer-Criswell, Criswell-Lambert-Burns, Huntsville; Graybill-Price, Johnson-Devlin, Johnson-Price, Graybill-Shade, Dopson-Thompson, Clemons-Trautwein, Dopson-Wayne, Johnson-Shade-Wayne, Jacksonville; Bencomo-Yearout-Gilliam-Provence, McMurtry-Provence, Davis-Yearout-Bencomo, Leal-Brinson, Mesa-Yearout, Knoxville; DeJesus-Morgan, Memphis; Gasser-Higgs, Young-Gomez, Perry-Walker, Young-Walker, Orlando.

NO-HIT GAME—Milacki, Charlotte, lost no-hitter in 12th inning vs. Chattanooga, May 28.

Texas League

CLASS AA

Leading Batter
LAVELL FREEMAN
El Paso

League President
CARL SAWATSKI

Leading Pitcher
CHARLES McGRATH
Arkansas

CHAMPIONSHIP WINNERS IN PREVIOUS YEARS

1888—Dallas .... .671	1926—Dallas .... .574	1960—Rio Grande Valley .... .590
1889—Houston .... .551	1927—Wichita Falls .... .654	Tulsa (3rd)..................... .528
1890—Galveston............................. .705	1928—Houston° .... .679	1961—Amarillo .... .643
1892—Houston .... .741	Wichita Falls .... .731	San Antonio (3rd)§............. .532
Houston .... .613	1929—Dallas° .... .588	1962—El Paso .... .571
1895—Dallas .... .754	Wichita Falls .... .620	Tulsa (2nd)§..................... .550
Fort Worth° .... .750	1930—Wichita Falls .... .697	1963—San Antonio .... .564
1896—Fort Worth .... .757	Fort Worth° .... .632	Tulsa (3rd)§..................... .529
Houston° .... .679	1931—Houston a .... .625	1964—San Antonio‡..................... .607
Galveston............................. .548	Houston .... .734	1965—Tulsa......................... .574
1897—San Antonio† .... .657	1932—Beaumont° .... .640	Albuquerque b..................... .550
Galveston† .... .717	Dallas......................... .727	1966—Arkansas......................... .579
1898—League disbanded.	1933—Houston .... .623	1967—Albuquerque .... .557
1899—Galveston............................. .632	San Antonio (4th)§............. .523	1968—Arkansas......................... .586
Galveston............................. .762	1934—Galveston‡............................. .579	El Paso b......................... .562
1900-01—Did not operate.	1935—Oklahoma City‡..................... .590	1969—Amarillo .... .593
1902—Corsicana .... .866	1936—Dallas......................... .604	Memphis b......................... .504
Corsicana .... .682	Tulsa (3rd)§..................... .519	1970—Albuquerque a..................... .615
1903—Paris-Waco............................. .615	1937—Oklahoma City .... .635	Memphis......................... .507
Dallas° .... .648	Fort Worth (3rd)§............. .535	1971—Did not operate as league—clubs
1904—Corsicana° .... .615	1938—Beaumont .... .635	were members of Dixie Associa-
Fort Worth .... .800	1939—Houston .... .606	tion.
1905—Fort Worth .... .545	Fort Worth (4th)§............. .540	1972—Alexandria .... .600
1906—Fort Worth .... .677	1940—Houston‡......................... .652	El Paso b......................... .557
Cleburne x .... .609	1941—Houston .... .673	1973—San Antonio .... .590
1907—Austin .... .629	Dallas (4th)§......................... .519	Memphis b......................... .558
1908—San Antonio .... .664	1942—Beaumont .... .605	1974—Victoria b......................... .581
1909—Houston .... .601	Shreveport (2nd)§............. .576	El Paso .... .555
1910—Dallas† .... .586	1943-44-45—Did not operate.	1975—Lafayette c......................... .558
Houston† .... .586	1946—Fort Worth .... .656	Midland c......................... .604
1911—Austin .... .575	Dallas (2nd)§......................... .591	1976—Amarillo b......................... .600
1912—Houston .... .626	1947—Houston‡......................... .623	Shreveport......................... .515
1913—Houston .... .620	1948—Fort Worth‡......................... .601	1977—El Paso......................... .600
1914—Houston† .... .671	1949—Fort Worth .... .649	Arkansas d......................... .485
Waco† .... .671	Tulsa (2nd)§..................... .584	1978—El Paso d......................... .593
1915—Waco .... .592	1950—Beaumont .... .595	Jackson......................... .567
1916—Waco .... .587	San Antonio (4th)§............. .513	1979—Arkansas d......................... .571
1917—Dallas......................... .600	1951—Houston‡......................... .619	Midland......................... .563
1918—Dallas......................... .584	1952—Dallas......................... .571	1980—Arkansas d......................... .596
1919—Shreveport° .... .677	Shreveport (3rd)§............. .522	San Antonio......................... .544
Fort Worth .... .651	1953—Dallas‡......................... .571	1981—San Antonio......................... .571
1920—Fort Worth .... .703	1954—Shreveport .... .559	Jackson d......................... .507
Fort Worth .... .750	Houston (2nd)§ .... .553	1982—El Paso......................... .559
1921—Fort Worth .... .691	1955—Dallas......................... .581	Tulsa d......................... .515
Fort Worth .... .662	Shreveport (3rd)§............. .540	1983—Jackson......................... .507
1922—Fort Worth .... .694	1956—Houston‡......................... .623	Beaumont d......................... .500
Fort Worth .... .711	1957—Dallas......................... .662	1984—Beaumont......................... .654
1923—Fort Worth .... .632	Houston (2nd)§ .... .630	Jackson d......................... .610
1924—Fort Worth .... .689	1958—Fort Worth .... .582	1985—El Paso......................... .632
Fort Worth .... .763	Cor. Christi (3rd)§............. .507	Jackson d......................... .537
1925—Fort Worth .... .711	1959—Victoria .... .589	1986—El Paso d......................... .630
Fort Worth y .... .653	Austin (2nd)§ .... .548	Jackson......................... .533

°Won split-season playoff. †No playoff for title. ‡Finished first and won four-club playoff. §Won four-club playoff. xTitle to Cleburne by default. yTied with Dallas in second half and won playoff for championship. zFort Worth disbanded. aTied with Beaumont at end of first half and won title in best-of-five series played as part of second half schedule. bLeague divided into Eastern, Western divisions. cLeague divided into Eastern, Western divisions; won two-team playoff. cLeague divided into Eastern, Western divisions; declared co-champions when playoffs were not completed. dLeague divided into Eastern and Western divisions and played split-season; won playoffs. NOTE—Championship awarded to winner of four-team playoff, 1933-51; first-place team and playoff winner co-champions, 1952-64.

STANDING OF CLUBS AT CLOSE OF FIRST HALF, JUNE 16

EASTERN DIVISION

Club	W.	L.	T.	Pct.	G.B.
Shreveport (Giants)	40	26	0	.606	......
Arkansas (Cardinals)	36	29	0	.554	3½
Tulsa (Rangers)	27	39	0	.409	13
Jackson (Mets)	27	40	0	.403	13½

WESTERN DIVISION

Club	W.	L.	T.	Pct.	G.B.
Wichita (Padres)	39	27	0	.591	......
Midland (Angels)	35	31	0	.530	4
El Paso (Brewers)	34	33	0	.507	5½
San Antonio (Dodgers)	26	39	0	.400	12½

STANDING OF CLUBS AT CLOSE OF SECOND HALF, AUGUST 29

EASTERN DIVISION

Club	W.	L.	T.	Pct.	G.B.
Jackson (Mets)	43	26	0	.623	......
Shreveport (Giants)	38	31	0	.551	5
Arkansas (Cardinals)	36	34	0	.514	7½
Tulsa (Rangers)	25	45	0	.357	18½

WESTERN DIVISION

Club	W.	L.	T.	Pct.	G.B.
El Paso (Brewers)	41	26	0	.612	......
Midland (Angels)	40	30	0	.571	2½
Wichita (Padres)	30	38	0	.441	11½
San Antonio (Dodgers)	24	47	0	.338	19

COMPOSITE STANDING OF CLUBS AT CLOSE OF SEASON, AUGUST 29

Club	Shrv.	El.P.	Mid.	Ark.	Wich.	Jax.	Tul.	S.A.	W.	L.	T.	Pct.	G.B.
Shreveport (Giants)	....	6	5	16	4	19	23	5	78	57	0	.578	......
El Paso (Brewers)	4	....	17	5	17	6	7	19	75	59	0	.560	2½
Midland (Angels)	5	15	....	5	16	4	6	24	75	61	0	.551	3½
Arkansas (Cardinals)	16	4	5	....	5	19	17	6	72	63	0	.533	6
Wichita (Padres)	5	14	16	5	....	3	6	20	69	65	0	.515	8½
Jackson (Mets)	13	4	6	13	7	....	20	7	70	66	0	.515	8½
Tulsa (Rangers)	9	3	4	15	4	12	....	5	52	84	0	.382	26½
San Antonio (Dodgers)	5	13	8	4	12	3	5	....	50	86	0	.368	28½

Arkansas club represented Little Rock, Ark.

Major league affiliations in parentheses.

Playoffs—Jackson defeated Shreveport, two games to one; Wichita defeated El Paso, two games to one; Wichita defeated Jackson, four games to two, to win league championship.

Regular-Season Attendance—Arkansas, 256,365; El Paso, 180,633; Jackson, 131,248; Midland, 137,910; San Antonio, 122,277; Shreveport, 233,524; Tulsa, 170,932; Wichita, 150,952. Total—1,383,841. Playoffs—21,534. All-Star Game—2,476.

Managers—Arkansas, Jim Riggleman; El Paso, Duffy Dyer; Jackson, Tucker Ashford; Midland, Max Oliveras; San Antonio, Gary LaRocque; Shreveport, Jack Mull; Tulsa, Bill Stearns, Steve Smith.

All-Star Team—1B—Brad Pounders, Wichita; 2B—Luis Alicea, Arkansas; 3B—Joe Redfield, Midland; SS—Gregg Jefferies, Jackson; OF—Joaquin Contreras, Jackson; Lavell Freeman, El Paso; Mike Devereaux, San Antonio; C—Sandy Alomar, Wichita and Joe Szekely, San Antonio; DH—Doug Jennings, Midland; P—John Burkett, Shreveport; Dennis Cook, Shreveport; Dave West, Jackson; Steve Peters, Arkansas; Charles McGrath, Arkansas; Most Valuable Player—Gregg Jefferies, Jackson; Pitcher of the Year—Dennis Cook, Shreveport; Manager of the Year—Duffy Dyer, El Paso.

(Compiled by Howe News Bureau, Boston, Mass.)

CLUB BATTING

Club	Pct.	G.	AB.	R.	OR.	H.	TB.	2B.	3B.	HR.	RBI.	GW.	SH.	SF.	HP.	BB.	Int. BB.	SO.	SB.	CS.	LOB.
El Paso	.300	134	4839	893	813	1453	2338	272	23	189	813	68	12	33	30	581	34	968	83	42	1070
Midland	.294	136	4744	823	782	1395	2179	225	32	165	742	73	52	45	45	570	32	923	101	73	1028
Wichita	.293	134	4677	734	681	1371	2071	255	26	131	662	63	39	43	32	422	47	813	130	70	970
San Antonio	.273	136	4700	607	735	1283	1847	213	48	85	542	48	60	43	35	420	30	777	101	66	982
Jackson	.269	136	4514	605	608	1214	1772	238	34	84	553	66	45	44	50	466	47	924	140	74	983
Arkansas	.268	135	4409	598	566	1182	1750	247	36	83	546	65	55	39	40	439	49	798	181	86	911
Tulsa	.266	136	4577	544	727	1217	1702	202	26	77	490	48	33	35	40	519	28	819	109	61	1081
Shreveport	.263	135	4509	570	462	1185	1776	229	31	100	519	74	48	28	43	376	49	797	95	64	929

INDIVIDUAL BATTING

(Leading Qualifiers for Batting Championship—367 or More Plate Appearances)

°Bats lefthanded.   †Switch-hitter.

Player and Club	Pct.	G.	AB.	R.	H.	TB.	2B.	3B.	HR.	RBI.	GW.	SH.	SF.	HP.	BB.	Int. BB.	SO.	SB.	CS.
Freeman, Lavell, El Paso°	.395	129	526	117	208	330	42	4	24	96	8	0	3	3	70	7	95	13	3
Jefferies, Gregg, Jackson†	.367	134	510	81	187	305	48	5	20	101	10	0	6	5	49	18	43	26	10
Jurak, Edward, Tulsa	.346	98	338	67	117	172	19	3	10	47	4	0	1	1	70	2	44	19	6
Jennings, Douglas, Midland°	.338	126	464	106	157	282	33	4	30	104	13	2	4	13	94	11	136	7	3
Howard, Thomas, Wichita†	.332	113	401	72	133	210	27	4	14	60	5	8	1	1	36	9	72	26	8
Brown, Todd, El Paso	.330	105	418	77	138	204	23	2	13	82	6	0	2	4	47	2	72	4	7
Redfield, Joseph, Midland	.321	128	498	108	160	295	31	7	30	108	10	4	4	6	67	2	83	17	4
Alomar, Roberto, Wichita†	.319	130	536	88	171	256	41	4	12	68	5	1	7	2	49	5	74	43	15
Brassil, Thomas, Wichita	.318	106	390	59	124	188	23	1	13	54	2	0	3	2	12	1	38	3	3
Michel, Domingo, San Antonio	.314	102	363	64	114	174	20	5	10	49	5	0	5	4	25	1	47	0	0

Departmental Leaders: G—Devereaux, 135; AB—Devereaux, 562; R—Freeman, 117; H—Freeman, 208; TB—Freeman, 330; 2B—Jefferies, 48; 3B—Lawton, 10; HR—Holmes, Jennings, Redfield, 30; RBI—Fitzgerald, Redfield, 108; GWRBI—Fitzgerald, 15; SH—Allen, 9; SF—Devereaux, 11; HP—Jennings, 13; BB—Jennings, 94; IBB—Jefferies, 18; SO—Carter, 141; SB—Cole, 68; CS—Cole, 29.

(All Players—Listed Alphabetically)

Player and Club	Pct.	G.	AB.	R.	H.	TB.	2B.	3B.	HR.	RBI.	GW.	SH.	SF.	HP.	BB.	Int. BB.	SO.	SB.	CS.
Adams, Patrick, Shreveport	.266	50	169	20	45	72	9	0	6	20	5	0	0	7	23	3	49	0	2
Adams, Ricky, Midland	.268	34	127	18	34	43	3	0	2	16	2	0	2	1	10	0	21	11	2
Agostinelli, Salvatore, Arkansas	.242	84	186	25	45	61	9	2	1	20	4	3	1	4	24	1	17	9	3
Alexander, Gary, Tulsa	.281	23	96	9	27	45	3	0	5	14	2	1	0	2	5	0	16	0	0
Alexander, Tommy, Wichita	.000	53	5	0	0	0	0	0	0	0	0	0	0	0	0	0	4	0	0
Alfaro, Jesus, El Paso	.312	91	381	72	119	209	25	1	21	85	6	2	3	0	38	4	55	2	1
Alicea, Luis, Arkansas†	.270	101	337	57	91	123	14	3	4	47	12	5	5	2	49	2	28	13	8
Allen, Robert, Midland	.279	63	219	33	61	76	11	2	0	19	1	9	1	0	31	1	39	4	4
Alomar, Roberto, Wichita†	.319	130	536	88	171	256	41	4	12	68	5	1	7	2	49	5	74	43	15
Alomar, Santos, Wichita	.307	103	375	50	115	160	19	1	8	65	6	3	7	5	21	1	37	1	5
Armstrong, Kevin, Wichita	.000	15	10	0	0	0	0	0	0	0	0	2	0	0	0	0	3	0	0
Arnold, Scott, Arkansas	.091	29	33	3	3	4	1	0	0	1	0	3	0	0	0	0	9	0	0
Bauer, Eric, Wichita	.333	15	12	3	4	5	1	0	0	0	0	0	0	0	3	0	2	0	0
Bautista, Jose, Jackson	.314	29	35	4	11	12	1	0	0	5	2	5	1	0	1	0	12	0	0

Player and Club	Pct.	G.	AB.	R.	H.	TB.	2B.	3B.	HR.	RBI.	GW.	SH.	SF.	HP.	BB.	Int. BB.	SO.	SB.	CS.
Bayer, Christopher, Jackson†	.000	5	4	0	0	0	0	0	0	0	0	0	0	0	0	0	1	0	0
Beamesderfer, Kurt, Tulsa	.245	59	188	25	46	55	9	0	0	14	1	1	1	1	36	0	18	2	2
Bergendahl, Wray, Jackson	.000	12	3	0	0	0	0	0	0	0	1	0	0	0	0	0	1	0	0
Bootay, Kevin, Tulsa†	.229	29	105	12	24	30	4	1	0	6	0	1	0	0	9	0	12	5	9
Brady, Brian, Midland°	.288	100	281	46	81	127	17	1	9	50	8	1	5	4	44	4	47	4	7
Brantley, Jeffrey, Shreveport	.000	2	4	0	0	0	0	0	0	0	0	0	0	0	0	0	1	0	0
Brassil, Thomas, Wichita	.318	106	390	59	124	188	23	1	13	54	2	0	3	2	12	1	38	3	3
Breedlove, Larry, Arkansas	.222	7	9	1	2	3	1	0	0	0	0	0	0	0	2	0	0	0	0
Brouhard, Mark, Midland	.318	24	88	17	28	48	3	1	5	17	2	0	1	2	7	2	22	0	0
Brown, Jeffrey D., San Antonio°	.236	92	322	40	76	128	14	4	10	50	2	2	1	3	41	5	65	1	2
Brown, Jeffrey L., San Antonio	.337	56	193	19	65	93	11	1	5	35	1	3	4	1	6	1	29	2	3
Brown, Kevin, Wichita°	.063	33	16	0	1	1	0	0	0	0	0	0	0	0	0	0	5	0	0
Brown, Todd, El Paso	.330	105	418	77	138	204	23	2	13	82	6	0	2	4	47	2	72	4	7
Burkett, John, Shreveport	.051	27	39	0	2	2	0	0	0	1	0	0	0	0	0	0	20	0	0
Burns, Thomas, Jackson	.000	10	6	0	0	0	0	0	0	0	0	1	3	0	0	0	6	0	0
Bustabad, Juan, San Antonio°	.256	110	352	45	90	116	11	6	1	30	3	8	2	1	34	1	41	1	4
Canale, George, El Paso°	.257	65	253	38	65	100	10	2	7	36	2	0	0	2	20	1	69	3	2
Carmichael, Alan, Arkansas	.241	51	133	16	32	48	7	0	3	15	2	2	1	2	18	1	37	1	1
Carrasco, Norman, Midland	.294	60	245	36	72	98	11	0	5	39	5	2	4	1	6	0	26	5	7
Carter, Dennis, Arkansas	.249	115	386	46	96	166	21	8	11	54	5	1	3	7	30	3	141	3	4
Casey, Timothy, El Paso°	.268	77	246	53	66	135	13	1	18	60	5	0	1	2	39	6	87	2	2
Cecena, Jose, Tulsa	.000	43	1	0	0	0	0	0	0	0	0	0	0	0	0	0	0	0	0
Clark, Jerald, Wichita	.311	132	531	86	165	271	36	8	18	95	12	0	6	7	40	6	82	6	5
Clay, David, 16 EIP-9 San	.000	25	3	0	0	0	0	0	0	0	0	0	0	0	0	0	1	0	0
Clements, Wesley, Tulsa	.235	48	170	24	40	77	5	1	10	28	5	0	2	1	34	1	45	0	0
Cole, Alexander, Arkansas°	.256	125	477	68	122	148	12	4	2	27	2	5	1	0	44	5	55	68	29
Contreras, Joaquin, Jackson†	.307	132	482	65	148	215	34	3	9	78	10	1	7	9	46	4	104	17	13
Cook, Dennis, Shreveport	.200	19	25	3	5	8	0	0	1	1	0	3	0	0	3	0	5	0	0
Cortez, David, Wichita	.247	64	186	25	46	65	2	1	5	20	4	1	0	2	19	1	57	1	0
Costello, John, Arkansas°	.250	44	4	0	1	1	0	0	0	0	0	0	0	0	1	0	0	0	0
Costello, Michael, Wichita	.000	11	2	0	0	0	0	0	0	0	0	2	0	0	0	0	0	0	0
Cucjen, Romulo, Shreveport	.268	109	314	36	84	127	17	4	6	33	4	4	1	1	28	2	56	0	4
Cuevas, Angelo, Jackson°	.256	20	39	5	10	19	1	1	2	5	1	0	0	0	5	1	14	0	0
Dabney, Ty, Shreveport°	.307	119	436	55	134	213	35	7	10	67	8	0	5	2	28	6	60	5	4
Davidsmeier, Daniel, 3 EIP-62 Shr	.227	65	207	28	47	65	5	2	3	16	2	3	1	3	20	3	34	0	1
Davis, Douglas, Midland	.230	63	187	28	43	71	5	1	7	26	4	5	5	2	24	0	44	2	4
Davis, George, Wichita	.000	1	1	0	0	0	0	0	0	0	0	0	0	0	0	0	0	0	0
Davis, Gerald, Wichita	.290	14	31	5	9	14	2	0	1	7	1	0	1	0	10	1	6	0	0
Debus, Jon, San Antonio	.188	5	16	0	3	5	2	0	0	0	0	0	0	1	0	0	3	0	0
DeButch, Michael, Wichita	.291	114	446	76	130	147	15	1	0	32	5	7	2	4	49	1	66	25	16
DeLuca, Kurt, Jackson	.253	56	154	19	39	54	15	0	0	17	3	1	2	2	16	1	27	7	2
Devereaux, Michael, San Antonio	.301	135	562	90	169	293	28	9	26	91	11	1	11	2	48	8	65	33	18
Devine, Kevin, San Antonio	.000	6	2	0	0	0	0	0	0	0	0	0	0	0	1	0	1	0	0
DeWolf, Robert, El Paso°	.278	97	360	59	100	138	10	2	8	35	2	4	3	1	39	0	76	16	2
Dixon, Andrew, Shreveport	.272	71	287	42	78	96	12	3	0	28	4	1	1	2	12	0	35	37	13
Doran, Mark, Midland	.276	110	377	50	104	156	16	6	8	49	3	3	1	3	38	1	101	6	12
Duggan, Thomas, Tulsa	.274	91	288	30	79	102	14	0	3	32	4	4	2	2	30	4	63	1	0
Eichhorn, David, San Antonio	.143	40	14	1	2	2	0	0	0	0	0	1	0	0	0	0	3	0	0
Farmar, Damon, Midland†	.245	82	290	46	71	106	5	3	8	42	3	3	3	1	37	1	75	12	6
Farwell, Frederick, San Antonio°	.000	38	3	1	0	0	0	0	0	0	0	1	0	0	0	0	2	0	0
Fassero, Jeffrey, Arkansas°	.077	28	26	1	2	2	0	0	0	1	0	2	0	0	2	0	13	0	0
Fitzgerald, Michael, Arkansas	.286	126	447	72	128	253	36	4	27	108	15	0	7	4	35	6	94	3	3
Francois, Manuel, San Antonio†	.242	12	33	3	8	9	1	0	0	3	0	0	0	2	0	0	7	0	1
Freeland, Dean, Shreveport	.080	26	25	1	2	2	0	0	0	2	0	1	0	0	0	0	8	0	0
Freeman, David, Midland°	.395	129	526	117	208	330	42	4	24	96	8	0	3	3	70	7	95	13	3
Fregosi, James, Arkansas	.267	115	303	35	81	103	15	2	1	19	0	2	3	3	52	6	49	7	3
Gardner, Jeffrey, Jackson°	.273	119	399	55	109	125	10	3	0	30	2	5	2	3	58	1	55	1	5
Geivett, William, Midland	.262	44	149	31	39	51	5	2	1	6	1	5	0	0	30	0	34	10	3
Gideon, Ronnie, Jackson°	.105	7	19	1	2	3	1	0	0	0	0	0	0	0	5	1	9	0	1
Gillaspie, Mark, Wichita†	.324	41	148	27	48	79	8	1	7	22	1	1	0	0	26	3	24	0	2
Gobbo, Michael, El Paso	.286	54	175	25	50	79	11	0	6	26	2	0	4	0	24	0	39	0	0
Goldthorn, Burk, Tulsa°	.292	51	161	16	47	72	9	2	4	28	0	1	1	0	31	2	37	0	2
Gonzalez, Otto, Tulsa	.277	59	188	24	52	78	9	1	5	27	8	1	3	0	35	3	44	2	1
Graham, Everett, Shreveport°	.263	71	228	33	60	98	9	1	9	31	4	1	3	0	41	10	40	14	7
Grimes, John, Shreveport	.209	45	129	17	27	59	8	0	8	25	2	0	1	1	9	2	31	0	0
Guzman, Ruben, Tulsa	.270	73	256	34	69	83	7	2	1	12	0	2	2	3	17	1	59	22	7
Hamilton, Robert, San Antonio	.154	13	13	1	2	5	0	0	1	3	1	2	0	0	0	0	5	0	0
Hardgrave, Eric, El Paso	.243	51	173	19	42	62	8	0	4	18	2	0	2	2	13	0	35	0	1
Harman, David, Tulsa	.500	46	2	0	1	1	0	0	0	0	0	1	0	0	0	0	0	0	0
Harris, Gregory, Wichita	.154	28	26	0	4	4	0	0	0	1	0	2	1	0	0	0	7	0	0
Hartley, Michael, San Antonio	.000	25	3	0	0	0	0	0	0	0	0	0	0	0	0	0	0	0	0
Hartshorn, Kyle, Jackson°	.148	27	27	1	4	6	0	1	0	1	0	2	0	2	1	0	15	0	0
Harvey, Kenneth, San Antonio	.235	83	217	37	51	66	3	3	2	19	1	7	3	2	34	1	41	10	3
Hayden, Alan, Jackson°	.286	62	238	34	68	81	9	2	0	16	2	1	0	0	17	1	18	21	7
Hayes, Charles, Shreveport	.304	128	487	66	148	229	33	3	14	75	13	1	7	3	26	6	76	5	9
Heep, Daniel, San Antonio°	.340	11	47	6	16	23	1	0	2	9	0	0	0	1	4	0	7	0	0
Hernandez, Leonardo, El Paso	.250	14	44	7	11	18	2	1	1	5	3	0	1	0	1	0	6	0	0
Hernandez, Robert, Jackson°	.200	3	5	0	1	1	0	0	0	0	0	0	0	0	0	0	2	0	0
Hickerson, Bryan, Shreveport°	.000	4	4	0	0	0	0	0	0	0	0	0	0	0	0	0	2	0	0
Hill, Bradley, Tulsa°	.260	85	269	33	70	103	14	2	5	35	5	1	5	1	22	0	40	1	1
Hill, Kenneth, Arkansas°	.125	18	8	1	1	1	0	0	0	0	0	1	0	0	0	0	4	0	0
Hocutt, Michael, Jackson°	.244	111	357	46	87	158	15	1	18	57	7	1	3	3	38	3	106	1	2
Hogan, Michael, Shreveport	.286	34	7	0	2	2	0	0	0	1	0	0	0	0	0	0	0	0	0
Holmes, Stanley, Midland	.309	131	517	96	160	277	25	1	30	106	10	1	4	2	58	6	70	3	6
Hotchkiss, John, Midland	.295	113	417	57	123	170	26	0	7	56	5	4	7	2	40	1	69	0	3
Howard, Thomas, Wichita†	.332	113	401	72	133	210	27	4	14	60	5	8	1	1	36	9	72	26	8
Hubbard, Jeffrey, Tulsa	.172	21	58	4	10	14	0	2	0	1	2	0	3	0	9	0	21	2	2
Huff, Michael, San Antonio	.311	31	135	23	42	58	5	1	3	18	1	2	0	3	9	0	21	2	2
Infante, Kennedy, Arkansas	.290	108	348	35	101	140	21	0	6	44	3	4	4	8	9	3	67	2	3
Jefferies, Gregg, Jackson†	.367	134	510	81	187	305	48	5	20	101	10	0	6	5	49	18	43	26	10
Jelic, Christopher, Jackson	.246	50	183	22	45	74	10	2	5	24	3	1	3	3	27	1	40	1	3
Jennings, Douglas, Midland°	.338	126	464	106	157	282	33	1	30	104	13	2	4	13	94	11	136	7	3

Player and Club	Pct.	G.	AB.	R.	H.	TB.	2B.	3B.	HR.	RBI.	GW.	SH.	SF.	HP.	BB.	Int. BB.	SO.	SB.	CS.
Jirschele, Michael, Tulsa	.226	76	265	31	60	85	7	0	6	21	1	1	1	4	39	2	65	2	4
Johnson, Erik, Shreveport	.095	9	21	1	2	3	1	0	0	3	0	0	0	0	5	0	5	0	1
Jones, Geary, Jackson	.200	2	5	1	1	1	0	0	0	0	0	0	0	0	0	0	2	0	1
Jones, Robert, Tulsa°	.303	65	178	20	54	89	8	0	9	26	3	0	1	4	29	0	38	3	1
Jones, Timothy, Arkansas°	.330	61	176	23	58	79	12	0	3	26	1	3	3	2	29	4	16	16	10
Jurak, Edward, Tulsa	.346	98	338	67	117	172	19	3	10	47	4	0	1	1	70	2	44	19	6
Kinzer, Matthew, Arkansas	.000	17	17	0	0	0	0	0	0	0	0	2	0	0	0	0	5	0	0
Kirby, Wayne, San Antonio°	.238	24	80	7	19	27	1	2	1	9	1	3	0	0	4	0	7	6	4
Klein, Lawrence, Tulsa	.257	107	342	44	88	120	15	1	5	30	2	8	3	4	30	2	59	9	7
Kmak, Joseph, Shreveport	.195	15	41	5	8	10	0	1	0	3	0	0	1	3	0	4	0	0	0
Knabenshue, Christopher, Wichita°	.309	128	473	91	146	228	31	3	15	65	3	0	1	66	11	99	20	14	
Lawton, Marcus, Jackson†	.300	133	530	99	159	214	20	10	5	36	3	7	4	4	44	1	82	44	22
Lenderman, David, Jackson°	.000	17	1	0	0	0	0	0	0	0	0	0	0	0	0	0	0	0	0
Leopold, James, Arkansas	.000	18	1	0	0	0	0	0	0	0	0	0	1	0	0	0	0	0	0
Lewallyn, Dennis, San Antonio	.000	4	1	0	0	0	0	0	0	0	0	0	0	0	0	0	1	0	0
Liddell, David, Jackson	.120	10	25	2	3	3	0	0	0	0	0	0	0	0	3	0	8	0	0
Little, Scott, Jackson	.152	18	33	5	5	9	1	0	1	4	1	0	1	1	7	1	10	0	1
Litton, Gregory, Shreveport	.260	72	254	34	66	102	6	3	8	33	5	2	2	2	22	2	51	2	4
Lockwood, Richard, Jackson†	.219	60	215	22	47	75	14	1	4	25	3	0	3	1	32	4	31	2	0
Lundgren, Kurt, Jackson	.100	23	10	0	1	1	0	0	0	0	0	0	0	0	1	0	5	0	0
Lung, Rodney, Tulsa	.122	17	49	3	6	13	4	0	1	5	1	3	0	0	2	0	18	0	0
Lynch, Joseph, Wichita	.000	62	3	0	0	0	0	0	0	1	0	0	1	0	0	0	1	0	0
Malave, Benito, Arkansas	.000	28	1	0	0	0	0	0	0	0	0	0	0	0	0	0	1	0	0
Manwaring, Kirt, Shreveport	.267	98	307	27	82	105	13	2	2	22	5	2	0	8	19	2	33	1	2
Marquez, Edwin, Midland	.286	86	294	45	84	99	7	1	2	27	1	9	3	3	26	0	36	5	3
Mattox, Frank, El Paso†	.284	121	486	92	138	184	19	3	7	53	4	1	3	4	59	0	86	29	9
May, Scott, San Antonio	.167	33	12	2	2	3	1	0	0	2	4	0	0	1	0	8	0	0	
McCament, Randall, Shreveport	.000	52	4	0	0	0	0	0	0	0	2	0	0	0	0	0	2	0	0
McCarthy, Thomas, Jackson	.000	37	4	0	0	0	0	0	0	0	0	0	0	0	0	0	4	0	0
McConnell, Walter, San Antonio°	.234	39	141	19	33	54	7	1	4	13	1	0	1	2	14	1	31	0	1
McCue, Deron, Shreveport	.269	96	297	48	80	125	16	4	7	32	2	2	2	3	37	2	41	13	3
McDonald, Thomas, Shreveport	.259	33	116	19	30	50	9	1	3	12	4	3	0	2	15	2	19	2	4
McGrath, Charles, Arkansas	.233	32	30	4	7	11	1	0	1	2	1	4	0	0	0	0	11	0	0
McKnight, Jefferson, Jackson°	.203	16	59	5	12	21	3	0	2	8	0	0	1	4	0	12	1	1	
Medvin, Scott, Shreveport	.000	37	5	0	0	0	0	0	0	0	0	2	0	1	1	0	1	0	0
Melrose, Jeffrey, Tulsa°	.252	127	472	43	119	153	17	4	3	34	3	5	4	5	14	1	76	12	1
Mena, Andres, San Antonio	.136	34	22	1	3	7	1	0	1	1	0	1	0	0	0	0	8	0	0
Meyers, Paul, Shreveport†	.252	115	373	44	94	121	18	0	3	29	5	6	2	0	21	2	57	4	4
Michel, Domingo, San Antonio	.314	102	363	64	114	174	20	5	10	49	5	0	5	5	48	3	74	14	6
Millay, Garrick, Tulsa	.243	28	115	12	28	41	8	1	1	7	0	0	0	2	4	1	23	1	0
Miller, Stephen, Wichita°	.246	25	69	14	17	21	1	0	1	4	1	1	0	0	8	0	21	0	0
Mitchell, Joseph, El Paso	.291	81	326	55	95	194	27	0	24	76	8	1	1	1	23	2	73	1	2
Montgomery, Reginald, Midland	.344	44	180	33	62	96	10	0	8	33	4	0	0	1	13	2	27	2	1
Morris, David, Shreveport	.000	16	1	0	0	0	0	0	0	0	0	0	0	0	0	0	1	0	0
Mota, Jose, 21 Tul-54 San†	.249	75	261	34	65	77	6	3	0	15	1	5	1	2	34	1	46	5	6
Murray, David, Tulsa	.174	38	109	7	19	24	5	0	0	6	0	1	1	1	15	0	7	5	1
Nago, Garrett, El Paso†	.263	111	396	76	104	175	29	3	12	60	3	1	2	3	86	6	69	0	1
Nalls, Gary, Midland	.200	9	15	1	3	4	1	0	0	0	0	0	0	0	2	0	4	0	0
Nolte, Eric, Wichita°	.357	10	14	2	5	5	0	0	0	2	0	4	0	0	1	0	7	0	0
Norman, Scott, Arkansas	.000	5	2	0	0	0	0	0	0	0	0	0	0	0	0	0	1	0	0
Ohnoutka, Brian, Shreveport	.200	29	35	3	7	12	2	0	1	4	1	6	0	0	4	0	4	0	0
Olker, Joseph, Shreveport	.000	5	3	0	0	0	0	0	0	0	0	0	0	0	0	0	2	0	0
Opie, James, El Paso	.306	28	98	21	30	55	4	0	7	16	1	0	0	1	8	1	27	2	1
Orton, John, Midland	.154	5	13	1	2	3	1	0	0	0	0	0	0	1	2	0	3	0	0
Oyster, Jeffrey, Arkansas	.125	32	16	0	2	2	0	0	0	2	1	1	0	0	0	0	7	0	0
Pardo, Alberto, Jackson†	.328	25	61	2	20	29	6	0	1	13	0	0	2	0	5	1	15	0	0
Parsons, Scott, Wichita	.242	48	153	14	37	52	9	0	2	13	1	0	1	1	11	1	28	0	1
Pederson, Stuart, San Antonio°	.235	30	102	8	24	36	6	0	2	14	2	0	2	1	10	0	14	1	1
Pequignot, Jonathan, San Antonio°	.250	60	168	18	42	60	9	0	3	22	1	3	1	0	28	2	40	3	1
Perdomo, Felix, Jackson	.255	28	94	13	24	31	4	0	1	11	2	0	1	0	6	0	19	1	0
Perezchica, Antonio, Shreveport	.319	89	332	44	106	165	24	1	11	47	4	3	3	4	19	4	74	3	3
Peters, Steven, Arkansas°	.067	49	15	2	1	2	1	0	0	0	0	1	0	0	3	0	7	0	0
Pevey, Marty, Arkansas°	.279	80	197	28	55	77	11	1	3	16	1	1	1	1	10	2	33	6	1
Phillips, Stephen, Jackson°	.218	87	225	28	49	70	11	2	2	26	3	3	2	1	28	4	67	3	3
Pohle, Walter, El Paso	.251	104	327	48	82	124	18	0	8	51	3	2	3	6	30	0	49	3	2
Pounders, Bradley, Wichita	.314	79	309	63	97	194	16	0	27	89	10	0	4	3	33	5	79	0	0
Pruitt, Edwin, Jackson°	.000	43	0	0	0	0	0	0	0	0	0	1	0	1	0	0	0	0	0
Puikunas, Edmund, Shreveport	.000	32	6	0	0	0	0	0	0	0	0	1	0	0	0	0	3	0	0
Rainey, Scott, Wichita	.165	58	182	14	30	44	6	1	2	14	1	0	2	1	12	0	45	2	1
Ramsey, Michael, San Antonio†	.265	52	211	29	56	77	9	3	2	11	2	0	1	0	26	1	42	9	6
Reboulet, James, Arkansas	.286	21	77	11	22	28	6	0	0	10	3	2	0	0	15	0	7	14	3
Redfield, Joseph, Midland	.321	128	498	108	160	295	31	7	30	108	10	4	4	6	67	2	83	17	4
Reece, Jeffrey, Wichita°	.000	42	2	0	0	0	0	0	0	0	0	0	0	1	0	1	0	0	
Remlinger, Michael, Shreveport°	.000	6	8	0	0	0	0	0	0	0	0	0	0	0	0	0	4	0	0
Riggs, James, Wichita°	.320	10	25	4	8	15	1	0	2	4	1	0	0	0	0	0	4	0	0
Riles, Earnest, El Paso°	.340	41	153	45	52	80	10	6	6	24	0	0	2	0	28	1	24	1	1
Robinson, Michael, Arkansas	.278	122	410	62	114	184	27	8	9	54	2	6	3	5	22	3	88	19	5
Rodriguez, Angel, El Paso	.309	20	55	7	17	23	3	0	1	2	0	1	0	0	4	0	4	0	0
Rojas, Homar, San Antonio†	.237	28	97	6	23	33	5	1	1	7	0	0	1	0	2	0	11	0	0
Rowen, Robert, San Antonio°	.143	28	7	2	1	2	1	0	0	0	3	0	0	0	1	0	0	0	
Rubel, Michael, Shreveport	.213	39	141	15	30	54	6	0	6	17	6	0	1	2	17	1	37	0	1
Samuels, Roger, Shreveport°	.333	21	3	0	1	1	0	0	0	1	0	0	0	0	1	0	1	0	0
Sanchez, Zoilo, Jackson	.238	106	315	35	75	110	14	3	5	43	5	1	5	7	23	1	78	5	2
Santiago, Michael, Jackson°	.000	46	4	0	0	0	0	0	0	0	0	0	0	0	0	0	2	0	0
Savage, John, San Antonio	.000	49	3	0	0	0	0	0	0	0	0	1	0	0	0	0	1	0	0
Schaefer, Jeffrey, San Antonio	.304	101	368	39	112	134	18	2	0	37	1	7	4	3	13	0	49	2	4
Schweighoffer, Michael, San Antonio.	.167	19	12	1	2	3	1	0	0	0	1	1	0	0	3	0	6	0	0
Scott, Donald, El Paso†	.450	5	20	4	9	9	0	0	0	1	0	0	0	5	0	2	0	0	
Seoane, Mitchell, Midland	.250	8	28	4	7	7	0	0	0	1	0	0	0	0	0	0	2	0	0
Shipley, Craig, San Antonio	.236	33	127	14	30	47	5	3	2	9	1	0	1	1	5	0	17	2	1
Sierra, Ulises, Wichita	.091	19	22	0	2	3	1	0	0	1	0	1	0	0	0	0	6	0	0
Silver, Roy, Arkansas°	.322	110	320	51	103	153	26	3	6	47	6	1	4	0	37	9	38	6	6

Player and Club	Pct.	G.	AB.	R.	H.	TB.	2B.	3B.	HR.	RBI.	GW.	SH.	SF.	HP.	BB.	Int. BB.	SO.	SB.	CS.
Sonberg, Erik, San Antonio	.083	15	12	1	1	1	0	0	0	1	0	0	0	0	1	0	5	0	0
St. Laurent, James, Tulsa°	.287	132	533	53	153	200	29	3	4	70	7	1	5	1	39	7	76	7	9
Stephens, Carl, Arkansas	.251	100	307	35	77	121	20	0	8	42	4	2	2	3	37	4	68	6	2
Stewart, Jeffrey, Wichita	1.000	16	1	0	1	1	0	0	0	0	0	0	0	0	0	0	0	0	0
Szekely, Joseph, San Antonio°	.297	113	417	54	124	162	22	2	4	49	8	0	1	.5	33	3	65	4	2
Tate, Stuart, Shreveport	.200	34	5	1	1	1	0	0	0	0	0	0	0	0	1	0	3	0	0
Tellez, Alonso, San Antonio	.282	119	426	52	120	166	27	2	5	49	5	2	5	2	27	3	56	8	3
Thomas, Todd, Shreveport°	.245	57	155	25	38	45	4	0	1	10	0	2	0	0	18	1	20	9	1
Thomas, James, Midland†	.256	40	172	29	44	54	3	2	1	11	0	3	0	1	16	0	26	10	6
Threadgill, George, Tulsa	.288	93	323	42	93	128	14	3	5	36	2	2	2	8	36	0	59	16	8
Torres, Philip, San Antonio	.000	44	5	0	0	0	0	0	0	0	0	1	0	0	0	0	3	0	0
Valera, Alcadio, Jackson†	.154	5	13	1	2	2	0	0	0	0	0	0	0	0	1	0	3	0	0
VanBurkleo, Tyler, Midland°	.328	48	183	38	60	116	12	4	12	33	1	0	1	3	23	1	58	3	2
Van Stone, Paul, Shreveport†	.233	20	43	4	10	15	2	0	1	10	1	0	0	1	6	1	12	0	1
Walker, Cameron, 8 EIP-30 Wich	.000	38	1	0	0	0	0	0	0	0	0	0	0	0	0	0	1	0	0
Walters, Darryel, El Paso	.311	106	392	77	122	212	18	3	22	83	11	0	2	1	47	3	100	7	9
Wasem, James, Wichita	.179	10	28	4	5	6	1	0	0	5	0	0	2	0	5	0	4	0	0
Wasilewski, Thomas, Shreveport	.125	14	8	0	1	1	0	0	0	0	0	3	0	0	1	0	3	0	0
Weissman, Craig, Arkansas	.000	29	33	1	0	0	0	0	0	0	0	3	0	0	3	0	18	0	0
Welborn, Todd, Jackson	.000	12	2	0	0	0	0	0	0	0	0	0	0	0	0	0	0	0	0
West, David, Jackson°	.200	25	35	3	7	13	0	0	2	4	0	5	0	0	2	0	17	0	0
Weston, Michael, Jackson	.000	58	3	1	0	0	0	0	0	0	0	2	0	0	0	0	1	0	0
Wilmet, Paul, Arkansas	.000	17	1	0	0	0	0	0	0	0	0	0	0	0	1	0	0	0	0
Wilson, Craig, Arkansas	.290	66	238	37	69	87	13	1	1	26	5	3	2	1	30	1	19	9	6
Wilson, John, Jackson°	.245	44	98	15	24	27	3	0	0	10	2	0	0	2	7	1	41	8	0
Winters, Daniel, Jackson	.233	55	146	22	34	54	11	0	3	17	2	0	1	4	20	2	29	1	1
Wohler, Barry, San Antonio°	.143	28	21	1	3	3	0	0	0	0	0	3	0	0	4	0	12	0	0
Wrona, William, Wichita	.303	32	109	17	33	43	7	0	1	13	2	2	2	2	11	0	7	3	0
Young, John, Arkansas°	.250	12	4	0	1	1	0	0	0	0	0	0	0	0	0	0	3	0	0
Young, Shane, Jackson°	.190	33	42	2	8	11	0	0	1	6	2	3	0	0	1	0	10	0	0
Young, Michael, Wichita	.222	13	9	0	2	2	0	0	0	1	0	2	0	0	0	0	4	0	0
Yurtin, Jeffrey, Wichita°	.236	54	161	20	38	57	8	1	3	26	3	1	3	1	9	2	28	0	0

The following pitchers, listed alphabetically by club, with games in parentheses, had no plate appearances, primarily through use of designated hitters:

ARKANSAS—Calderon, Jose (6); Herzog, Hans (21).

EL PASO—Ambrose, Mark (17); Bass, Barry (53); Brisco, Jamie (52); Broersma, Eric (14); Castillo, Luis (14); Diaz, Derek (12); Duquette, Bryan (7); Gonzalez, Arturo (1); Hunter, James (16); Kendrick, Peter (10); Ludy, John (15); Miglio, John (56); Murphy, Daniel (22); Peterek, Jeffrey (9); Puig, Edward (1); Sadler, Alan (10); Scarpetta, Daniel (10); Stapleton, David (4); Wheeler, Bradley (34).

JACKSON—Roman, Jose (2).

MIDLAND—Cedeno, Vinicio (54); Collins, Christopher (23); Dacus, Barry (42); Garcia, Miguel (50); Harvey, Bryan (43); Lovelace, Vance (53); Mack, Tony (10); Martinez, David (12); McGuire, Stephen (10); Reed, Martin (26); Romanovsky, Michael (26); Smith, David (10); Venturino, Philip (27).

SAN ANTONIO—Heuer, Mark (4); Scott, Timothy (2); Tejeda, Felix (6).

SHREVEPORT—Hammaker, Atlee (1).

TULSA—Brown, Kevin (8); Couchee, Michael (2); Ferlenda, Gregory (9); Knapp, Richard (24); Malloy, Robert (16); Mielke, Gary (28); Money, Kyle (10); Odekirk, Richard (26); Pavlas, David (13); Raether, Eric (32); Rodgers, Timothy (3); Rogers, Kenneth (28); Valdez, Efrain (11); West, Thomas (26); Whitaker, Darrell (39); Witt, Robert (1); Zaske, Jeffrey (2).

WICHITA—Harris, Gregory S. (2); Luebber, Stephen (12).

GRAND SLAM HOME RUNS—Canale, Goldthorn, Yurtin, 2 each; Alicea, Jeffrey D. Brown, Carrasco, Casey, Fitzgerald, Hocutt, Hotchkiss, Jirschele, Jurak, Mattox, Michel, Perezchica, Pounders, Redfield, Tellez, Walters, 1 each.

AWARDED FIRST BASE ON CATCHER'S INTERFERENCE—Contreras 5 (Agostinelli, Gobbo, Kmak, Scott, Stephens); T. Brown 2 (S. Alomar 2); Pohle 2 (Jeffrey L. Brown, Marquez); Burkett (Carmichael); Graham (Carmichael).

CLUB FIELDING

Club	Pct.	G.	PO.	A.	E.	DP.	PB.	Club	Pct.	G.	PO.	A.	E.	DP.	PB.
El Paso	.974	134	3555	1480	132	132	17	Midland	.969	136	3616	1470	164	125	21
San Antonio	.973	136	3623	1494	142	125	18	Wichita	.968	134	3522	1381	162	118	14
Shreveport	.973	135	3537	1504	142	126	15	Arkansas	.966	135	3487	1420	173	118	7
Tulsa	.972	136	3528	1533	145	120	23	Jackson	.965	136	3546	1595	185	139	21

INDIVIDUAL FIELDING

°Throws lefthanded.

FIRST BASEMEN

Player and Club	Pct.	G.	PO.	A.	E.	DP.	Player and Club	Pct.	G.	PO.	A.	E.	DP.
Adams, Shreveport	.993	47	390	32	3	37	Hocutt, Jackson	.991	101	891	56	9	88
Alfaro, El Paso	.992	30	222	27	2	26	Holmes, Midland	.987	107	934	48	13	88
Brady, Midland°	.953	10	38	3	2	4	Hubbard, Tulsa	1.000	2	4	0	0	1
Brassil, Wichita	.980	43	323	21	7	27	Jones, Tulsa°	1.000	1	2	0	0	0
J.D. Brown, San Antonio	.990	81	748	52	8	69	Lockwood, Jackson	.990	30	274	27	3	29
J.L. Brown, San Antonio	.921	6	33	2	3	4	McKnight, Jackson	1.000	2	6	0	0	0
Canale, El Paso	.996	65	639	35	3	53	MELROSE, Tulsa°	.995	124	1153	72	6	94
Carmichael, Jackson	.000	1	0	0	1	0	Pardo, Jackson	.977	6	37	5	1	1
Carrasco, Midland	1.000	1	1	0	0	0	Parsons, Wichita	.954	13	94	9	5	7
Clements, Tulsa	.948	9	85	7	5	7	Pederson, San Antonio°	.969	10	60	3	2	4
Cortez, Wichita	1.000	1	6	0	0	0	Pequignot, San Antonio	1.000	2	7	4	0	0
Cucjen, Shreveport	.995	30	185	15	1	20	Perdomo, Jackson	1.000	1	6	0	0	0
Dabney, Shreveport	.990	31	255	28	3	28	Pevey, Arkansas	.985	37	180	21	3	19
Davis, Midland	.909	1	8	2	1	1	Pounders, Wichita	.989	78	693	39	8	62
Debus, San Antonio	1.000	2	14	0	0	3	Redfield, Midland	1.000	8	58	9	0	6
DeLuca, Jackson	.952	10	32	8	2	2	Rodriguez, El Paso	1.000	1	0	1	0	0
Duggan, Tulsa	.985	9	64	2	1	6	Rubel, Shreveport	.990	39	393	19	4	24
Fitzgerald, Arkansas	.973	111	839	76	25	81	Silver, Arkansas	.971	17	63	5	2	4
Fregosi, Arkansas	1.000	3	9	0	0	2	Szekely, San Antonio	1.000	3	29	2	0	0
Gideon, Jackson°	1.000	2	12	1	0	2	Tellez, San Antonio	.990	45	365	28	4	28
Gillaspie, Wichita	.944	3	16	1	1	2	VanBurkleo, Midland°	.980	23	133	11	3	12
Hardgrave, El Paso	.990	48	381	22	4	40	Van Stone, Shreveport	.923	2	11	1	1	1
Hernandez, El Paso	1.000	1	1	0	0	1	Yurtin, Wichita	1.000	4	25	3	0	1

SECOND BASEMEN

Player and Club	Pct.	G.	PO.	A.	E.	DP.
Adams, Midland	.965	13	23	32	2	6
Alfaro, El Paso	.971	12	33	35	2	12
ALICEA, Arkansas	.975	95	184	251	11	56
Allen, Midland	.933	5	14	14	2	2
Alomar, Wichita	.955	12	21	21	2	6
Bustabad, San Antonio	.972	40	70	103	5	20
Carrasco, Midland	.979	29	67	76	3	13
Cortez, Wichita	1.000	5	7	7	0	0
Davidsmeier, Shreveport	.990	42	64	135	2	26
DeButch, Wichita	.969	107	221	274	16	59
Francois, San Antonio	1.000	4	6	11	0	1
Gardner, Jackson	.989	86	195	246	5	65
Geivett, Midland	1.000	1	8	1	0	2
Harvey, San Antonio	.966	57	113	145	9	31
Hotchkiss, Midland	.986	45	96	116	3	23
Jirschele, Tulsa	1.000	7	12	19	0	5
Johnson, Shreveport	1.000	5	11	6	0	2
Jones, Arkansas	1.000	1	3	2	0	1
Jurak, Tulsa	.935	13	14	29	3	3
Klein, Tulsa	.971	70	153	214	11	45
Lawton, Jackson	.750	2	1	2	1	0
Litton, Shreveport	.996	52	85	155	1	24
Mattox, El Paso	.966	119	235	337	20	70
McCue, Shreveport	1.000	3	4	4	0	1
McKnight, Jackson	1.000	1	1	2	0	0
Miller, Wichita	.947	2	5	13	1	3
Mota, 20 Tul-49 SA	.976	69	138	190	8	38
Murray, Tulsa	.973	36	72	108	5	19
Perdomo, Jackson	.993	27	59	77	1	18
Perezchica, Shreveport	.967	29	50	69	4	20
Phillips, Jackson	.969	39	82	106	6	18
Pohle, El Paso	.892	8	12	21	4	7
Reboulet, Arkansas	.952	9	22	37	3	7
Redfield, Midland	1.000	7	13	14	0	4
Seoane, Midland	.936	8	23	21	3	5
J. Thomas, Midland	.951	39	103	91	10	28
T. Thomas, Shreveport	.909	16	15	35	5	4
Van Stone, Shreveport	1.000	12	9	24	0	6
Wasem, Wichita	1.000	1	2	0	0	0
Wilson, Arkansas	.965	34	89	103	7	23
Wrona, Wichita	.987	12	37	41	1	10

THIRD BASEMEN

Player and Club	Pct.	G.	PO.	A.	E.	DP.
Alfaro, El Paso	.974	47	26	86	3	11
Allen, Midland	.857	6	3	9	2	0
Brassil, Wichita	.892	24	16	42	7	3
Breedlove, Arkansas	1.000	3	0	3	0	1
Brown, San Antonio	.878	24	8	28	5	3
Bustabad, San Antonio	.920	17	3	20	2	0
Carrasco, Midland	.920	29	23	57	7	10
Clements, Tulsa	.800	5	2	10	3	0
Cortez, Wichita	.935	45	19	81	7	7
Cucjen, Shreveport	.879	26	19	39	8	8
Davidsmeier, 3 ElP-1 Shr	1.000	4	1	4	0	0
Davis, Midland	1.000	1	0	1	0	0
Debus, San Antonio	.500	2	0	2	2	0
Duggan, Tulsa	.953	41	31	70	5	4
Fregosi, Arkansas	.953	25	13	28	2	1
Geivett, Midland	.898	23	15	29	5	5
Harvey, San Antonio	1.000	2	1	6	0	0
HAYES, Shreveport	.934	119	100	212	22	20
Hernandez, El Paso	.000	1	0	0	1	0
Hocutt, Jackson	1.000	2	0	2	0	0
Holmes, Midland	.974	21	11	27	1	4
Hotchkiss, Midland	1.000	5	4	7	0	1
Hubbard, Tulsa	1.000	11	12	20	0	5
Infante, Arkansas	.900	92	67	132	22	8
Jefferies, Jackson	.963	30	19	60	3	8
Jirschele, Tulsa	.984	40	32	91	2	7
Johnson, Shreveport	1.000	1	0	1	0	0
Klein, Tulsa	.868	27	9	37	7	2
Lockwood, Jackson	.895	12	14	20	4	5
Marquez, Midland	.833	1	3	2	1	0
McConnell, San Antonio	.884	38	11	65	10	4
McKnight, Jackson	.962	8	3	22	1	2
Millay, Tulsa	.948	26	16	57	4	2
Miller, Wichita	.952	15	6	34	2	1
Mitchell, El Paso	.943	72	38	161	12	12
Pequignot, San Antonio	.873	34	21	41	9	3
Phillips, Jackson	.875	9	3	18	3	0
Pohle, El Paso	.957	19	12	32	2	3
Reboulet, Arkansas	1.000	3	0	1	0	0
Redfield, Midland	.884	66	61	114	23	7
Riggs, Wichita	.923	7	3	9	1	0
Sanchez, Jackson	.891	93	65	181	30	26
Shipley, San Antonio	.962	33	19	56	3	7
Silver, Arkansas	.938	15	12	18	2	2
Tellez, San Antonio	.750	6	2	1	1	0
Wasem, Wichita	.909	7	2	18	2	2
Wilson, Arkansas	.985	27	16	49	1	3
Wrona, Wichita	.932	16	11	30	3	5
Yurtin, Wichita	.975	35	19	60	2	8

SHORTSTOPS

Player and Club	Pct.	G.	PO.	A.	E.	DP.
Adams, Midland	.971	21	35	64	3	12
Alfaro, El Paso	.917	7	1	10	1	1
Allen, Midland	.965	52	69	149	8	29
Alomar, Wichita	.930	113	167	288	34	60
Brassil, Wichita	.965	19	22	61	3	7
Bustabad, San Antonio	.972	41	54	120	5	20
Cucjen, Shreveport	.930	35	35	72	8	16
Davidsmeier, Shreveport	.958	17	22	46	3	8
DeButch, Wichita	.500	1	0	1	1	0
Duggan, Tulsa	.992	25	35	82	1	14
Francois, San Antonio	1.000	1	1	4	0	2
Fregosi, Arkansas	.957	89	145	230	17	50
Gardner, Jackson	.907	37	49	97	15	15
Geivett, Midland	.915	8	13	30	4	7
Hotchkiss, Midland	.950	67	92	210	16	34
Jefferies, Jackson	.937	103	148	328	32	67
Jirschele, Tulsa	.975	33	41	75	3	14
Jones, Arkansas	.962	59	77	149	9	26
Jurak, Tulsa	.957	78	139	218	16	45
Klein, Tulsa	1.000	9	11	16	0	3
Litton, Shreveport	.974	20	32	44	2	8
McKnight, Jackson	1.000	1	0	1	0	0
Miller, Wichita	.800	3	4	8	3	0
Opie, El Paso	.979	22	34	59	2	9
Perdomo, Jackson	1.000	1	0	1	0	0
Perezchica, Shreveport	.959	61	94	189	12	42
Phillips, Jackson	1.000	2	3	4	0	0
Pohle, El Paso	.953	76	129	235	18	47
Riles, El Paso	.952	39	70	127	10	27
SCHAEFER, San Antonio	.950	101	165	330	26	73
Thomas, Shreveport	.918	18	26	41	6	4
Valera, Arkansas	1.000	4	6	13	0	3
Wilson, Arkansas	1.000	6	5	12	0	2
Wrona, Wichita	.923	3	2	10	1	2

OUTFIELDERS

Player and Club	Pct.	G.	PO.	A.	E.	DP.
Adams, Midland	1.000	1	1	0	0	0
Agostinelli, Arkansas	.917	18	11	0	1	0
Alexander, Tulsa	.949	23	34	3	2	0
Bootay, Tulsa	.943	29	64	2	4	1
Brady, Midland°	.965	60	103	8	4	0
Brouhard, Midland	1.000	10	13	0	0	0
J. Brown, San Antonio	1.000	2	5	0	0	0
T. Brown, El Paso	.960	96	229	8	10	1
Carter, Arkansas	.932	111	169	9	13	2
Casey, El Paso°	1.000	13	20	0	0	0
Clark, Wichita	.989	129	262	10	3	1
Clements, Tulsa	.889	4	8	0	1	0
Cole, Arkansas°	.968	121	289	14	10	5
Contreras, Jackson°	.973	131	244	7	7	3
Cortez, Wichita	.917	5	10	1	1	0
Cuevas, Jackson	1.000	11	27	2	0	0
Dabney, Shreveport	.956	69	102	6	5	1
D. Davis, Midland	1.000	2	1	0	0	0
G. Davis, Wichita	1.000	6	9	1	0	0
Deluca, Jackson	.920	34	22	1	2	0
DEVEREAUX, San Antonio	.991	133	339	7	3	1
DeWolf, El Paso°	.973	90	178	3	5	0
Dixon, Shreveport	.978	71	86	5	2	0
Doran, Midland	.972	107	205	6	6	1
Duggan, Tulsa	1.000	7	10	1	0	0
Farmar, Midland	.964	81	177	9	7	1
Freeman, El Paso°	.965	121	212	9	8	0
Geivett, Midland	1.000	9	6	0	0	0
Gillaspie, Wichita	.861	21	29	2	5	0
Graham, Shreveport°	.979	65	92	1	2	0
Guzman, Tulsa	.955	72	143	4	7	0
Hayden, Jackson°	.972	57	100	4	3	1
Heep, San Antonio°	1.000	6	9	1	0	0
Hill, Tulsa	.966	66	106	7	4	3
Hocutt, Jackson	1.000	2	3	0	0	0
Hotchkiss, Midland	1.000	3	6	1	0	0

OUTFIELDERS—Continued

Player and Club	Pct.	G.	PO.	A.	E.	DP.	Player and Club	Pct.	G.	PO.	A.	E.	DP.
Howard, Wichita	.975	104	226	6	6	1	Parsons, Wichita	1.000	15	18	0	0	0
Hubbard, Tulsa	.846	6	11	0	2	0	Pederson, San Antonio°	1.000	18	28	0	0	0
Huff, San Antonio	.964	31	52	2	2	0	Pequignot, San Antonio	1.000	12	21	0	0	0
Jelic, Jackson	.923	7	11	1	1	0	Pevey, Arkansas	1.000	7	5	0	0	0
Jennings, Midland°	.962	87	145	6	6	1	Phillips, Jackson	.957	38	20	2	1	0
Jones, Tulsa°	1.000	10	15	0	0	0	Rainey, Wichita	1.000	2	1	0	0	0
Kirby, San Antonio	.941	20	47	1	3	0	Ramsey, San Antonio°	.948	52	85	7	5	0
Knabenshue, Wichita	.977	126	277	14	7	3	Reboulet, Arkansas	1.000	8	15	1	0	0
Lawton, Jackson	.956	130	264	16	13	1	Robinson, Arkansas	.980	115	187	9	4	1
Little, Jackson	.955	13	20	1	1	0	Schweighoffer, San Antonio	1.000	1	1	0	0	0
Lockwood, Jackson	1.000	2	3	1	0	0	Silver, Arkansas	.971	59	98	2	3	0
Marquez, Midland	1.000	1	6	0	0	0	St. Laurent, Tulsa	.951	130	194	18	11	5
McCue, Shreveport	.949	82	108	4	6	1	Tellez, San Antonio	1.000	51	84	5	0	1
McDonald, Shreveport	.930	30	45	8	4	1	Thomas, Shreveport	.895	15	14	3	2	0
McKnight, Jackson	1.000	9	12	2	0	0	Threadgill, Tulsa	.979	87	141	2	3	0
Meyers, Shreveport°	.973	112	246	6	7	0	VanBurkleo, Midland°	.986	31	69	4	1	1
Michel, San Antonio	.936	91	140	6	10	1	Walters, El Paso	.989	92	166	7	2	0
Millay, Tulsa	1.000	2	2	1	0	0	C. Wilson, Arkansas	1.000	4	7	0	0	0
Montgomery, Midland	1.000	44	90	6	0	0	J. Wilson, Jackson	.927	20	38	0	3	0
Nalls, Midland	.929	9	13	0	1	0	Wohler, San Antonio°	1.000	1	1	0	0	0
Opie, El Paso	1.000	7	6	1	0	0	Yurtin, Wichita	.875	4	7	0	1	0

CATCHERS

Player and Club	Pct.	G.	PO.	A.	E.	DP.	PB.	Player and Club	Pct.	G.	PO.	A.	E.	DP.	PB.
Agostinelli, Arkansas	.978	43	244	28	6	2	2	Liddell, Jackson	.931	8	51	3	4	0	1
Alomar, Wichita	.978	90	606	50	15	6	5	Lung, Tulsa	.967	16	80	9	3	0	2
Beamesderfer, Tulsa	.984	57	335	43	6	4	7	Manwaring, Shreveport	.994	93	603	81	4	8	8
Brown, San Antonio	.991	29	195	21	2	2	4	Marquez, Midland	.980	84	521	73	12	4	12
Carmichael, Jackson	.970	37	233	24	8	7	7	NAGO, El Paso	.995	86	543	57	3	7	10
Carrasco, Midland	1.000	2	1	0	0	0	1	Orton, Midland	.969	5	26	5	1	0	3
Clements, Tulsa	.958	9	44	2	2	0	5	Pardo, Jackson	1.000	6	21	2	0	0	0
Davis, Midland	.989	54	326	47	4	5	5	Pevey, Arkansas	.972	22	98	6	3	0	0
DeLuca, Jackson	1.000	12	42	5	0	1	2	Rainey, Wichita	.991	48	308	39	3	7	9
Gobbo, El Paso	.978	35	198	27	5	2	7	Rodriguez, El Paso	.989	15	80	6	1	0	0
Goldthorn, Tulsa	.980	42	257	30	6	2	5	Rojas, San Antonio	.983	24	151	20	3	1	4
Gonzalez, Tulsa	.991	22	97	15	1	1	4	Scott, El Paso	.970	3	27	5	1	1	0
Grimes, Shreveport	.990	41	273	28	3	3	6	Silver, Arkansas	1.000	3	5	0	0	0	1
Jelic, Jackson	.976	44	256	34	7	4	5	Stephens, San Antonio	.992	89	553	75	5	4	4
Jones, Jackson	1.000	2	3	1	0	0	0	Szekely, San Antonio	.992	93	562	52	5	7	10
Kmak, Shreveport	.980	14	87	11	2	0	1	Winters Jackson	.986	38	195	16	3	2	6

PITCHERS

Player and Club	Pct.	G.	PO.	A.	E.	DP.	Player and Club	Pct.	G.	PO.	A.	E.	DP.
Alexander, Wichita	.933	53	4	10	1	0	Hill, Arkansas	.875	18	5	9	2	0
Ambrose, El Paso	.958	17	6	17	1	1	Hogan, Shreveport	.800	34	3	13	4	1
Armstrong, Wichita	.923	15	1	11	1	0	Holmes, Midland	1.000	3	1	0	0	0
Arnold, Arkansas	.879	29	15	14	4	1	Hunter, El Paso	1.000	16	7	19	0	3
Bass, El Paso	.852	53	5	18	4	2	Kendrick, El Paso°	1.000	10	3	10	0	0
Bauer, Wichita°	.944	14	1	16	1	1	Kinzer, Arkansas	.905	17	9	10	2	1
Bayer, Jackson	.875	5	1	6	1	0	Knapp, Tulsa	.978	24	6	38	1	0
Bergendahl, Jackson	.500	12	0	3	3	0	Lenderman, Jackson	1.000	17	3	8	0	2
Brantley, Shreveport	1.000	2	1	1	0	0	Leopold, Arkansas	1.000	18	1	2	0	1
Brisco, El Paso	.938	52	3	12	1	1	Lewallyn, San Antonio	1.000	4	0	3	0	0
Broersma, El Paso	1.000	14	0	1	0	1	Lovelace, Midland°	.957	53	3	19	1	0
J.K. Brown, Tulsa	.769	8	2	8	3	1	Ludy, El Paso	1.000	15	2	4	0	0
K.A. Brown, Wichita°	.947	33	5	13	1	2	Luebber, Wichita	1.000	12	1	4	0	0
Burkett, Shreveport	.980	27	19	29	1	1	Lundgren, Jackson	1.000	23	0	10	0	0
Burns, Jackson	1.000	10	1	4	0	0	Lynch, Wichita	.938	62	8	22	2	3
Castillo, El Paso	.958	14	5	18	1	0	Mack, Midland	1.000	10	1	4	0	1
Cecena, Tulsa	.923	43	1	11	1	1	Malave, Arkansas	.800	28	5	3	2	0
Cedeno, Midland	.882	53	8	7	2	0	Malloy, Tulsa	1.000	16	1	8	0	0
Clay, 16 EP-9 SA	1.000	25	2	10	0	1	Martinez, Midland	1.000	12	3	8	0	0
Collins, Midland	1.000	23	7	15	0	0	May, San Antonio	.900	30	7	11	2	0
Cook, Shreveport°	.941	16	3	13	1	0	McCament, Shreveport	1.000	52	7	28	0	5
J. Costello, Arkansas	.929	44	4	9	1	0	McCarthy, Jackson	.938	37	5	10	1	0
M. Costello, Wichita	1.000	11	4	9	0	0	McGrath, Arkansas	.969	32	14	17	1	0
Dacus, Midland	.895	42	6	11	2	1	McGuire, Midland	1.000	10	3	2	0	0
Davis, Midland	.000	1	0	0	1	0	Medvin, Shreveport	.864	37	6	13	3	0
Devine, San Antonio	1.000	6	3	1	0	0	Mena, San Antonio	.944	34	8	26	2	0
Diaz, El Paso	1.000	12	1	1	0	0	Mielke, Tulsa	.900	28	0	9	1	1
Duquette, El Paso°	1.000	7	1	0	0	0	Miglio, El Paso°	1.000	56	1	9	0	0
Eichhorn, San Antonio	1.000	40	10	26	0	1	Money, Tulsa	1.000	10	0	6	0	0
Farwell, San Antonio°	1.000	38	1	12	0	0	Morris, Shreveport	1.000	16	3	5	0	0
Fassero, Arkansas°	.911	28	9	32	4	3	Murphy, El Paso	.786	22	6	5	3	0
Ferlenda, Tulsa	.833	9	3	2	1	0	Nago, El Paso	1.000	1	0	2	0	0
Freeland, Shreveport	.950	26	10	28	2	2	Nolte, Wichita°	1.000	10	4	11	0	1
Garcia, Midland°	1.000	50	2	18	0	1	Norman, Arkansas	1.000	5	0	3	0	0
Gonzalez, El Paso	1.000	1	2	0	0	0	Odekirk, Tulsa°	.976	26	9	32	1	2
Hamilton, San Antonio	1.000	12	5	12	0	0	Ohnoutka, Shreveport	.906	27	10	19	3	1
Hammaker, Shreveport°	1.000	1	1	0	0	0	Olker, Shreveport°	1.000	5	0	5	0	0
Harman, Tulsa	1.000	46	8	17	0	2	Oyster, Arkansas	.783	32	4	14	5	1
G.W. Harris, Wichita	.962	27	7	18	1	3	Pavlas, Tulsa	.929	13	4	9	1	1
Hartley, San Antonio	1.000	25	3	9	0	2	Pequignot, San Antonio	1.000	3	1	0	0	0
Hartshorn, Jackson	.974	26	18	20	1	0	Peterek, El Paso	1.000	9	7	4	0	2
Harvey, Midland	1.000	43	1	5	0	0	Peters, Arkansas°	.938	47	3	12	1	0
Hernandez, Jackson°	1.000	3	0	3	0	0	Pruitt, Arkansas°	1.000	43	5	9	0	0
Herzog, Arkansas°	.833	21	0	5	1	0	Puig, El Paso°	1.000	1	0	2	0	1
Heuer, San Antonio	1.000	4	0	1	0	0	Puikunas, Shreveport°	.846	32	1	10	2	0
Hickerson, Shreveport°	.667	4	1	1	1	0	Raether, Tulsa	.875	32	0	7	1	0
							Reece, Wichita°	.938	42	1	14	1	1

PITCHERS—Continued

Player and Club	Pct.	G.	PO.	A.	E.	DP.	Player and Club	Pct.	G.	PO.	A.	E.	DP.
Reed, Midland°	.933	26	5	37	3	9	Torres, San Antonio	1.000	44	5	13	0	1
Remlinger, Shreveport°	1.000	6	0	1	0	0	Valdez, Tulsa°	.909	11	1	9	1	1
Rodgers, Tulsa	1.000	3	0	1	0	0	Venturino, Midland	.939	27	13	18	2	2
Rogers, Tulsa°	.818	28	6	21	6	2	Walker, 8 EP-30 Wich	1.000	38	3	19	0	1
Romanovsky, Midland°	1.000	26	3	23	0	0	Wasilewski, Shreveport	.929	14	9	4	1	0
Rowen, San Antonio°	.786	27	5	6	3	0	Weissman, Arkansas	.970	29	12	20	1	4
Sadler, El Paso	.824	10	5	9	3	1	Welborn, Jackson	1.000	12	3	3	0	0
Samuels, Shreveport°	.667	21	1	3	2	0	D. West, Jackson°	.939	25	7	39	3	3
Santiago, Jackson°	.968	46	6	24	1	1	T. West, Tulsa	.976	26	13	28	1	1
Savage, San Antonio	.941	49	4	12	1	0	Weston, Jackson	.952	58	6	14	1	0
Scarpetta, El Paso°	1.000	10	0	6	0	1	Wheeler, El Paso°	1.000	34	6	21	0	2
SCHWEIGHOFFER, SA	1.000	17	6	36	0	4	Whitaker, Tulsa	1.000	39	3	10	0	2
Sierra, Wichita	.958	19	6	17	1	2	Wilmet, Arkansas	1.000	17	0	5	0	0
Smith, Midland	1.000	10	3	1	0	0	Witt, Tulsa	1.000	1	0	2	0	0
Sonberg, San Antonio°	.933	15	6	8	1	2	Wohler, San Antonio°	.976	27	14	26	1	2
Stapleton, El Paso°	1.000	4	0	1	0	0	J. Young, Jackson°	1.000	12	1	4	0	0
Stewart, Wichita	1.000	16	0	5	0	0	M. Young, Wichita°	.871	13	4	23	4	1
Tate, Shreveport	1.000	34	5	11	0	1	S. Young, Jackson°	.968	27	7	23	1	2

The following players do not have any recorded accepted chances at the positions indicated; therefore, are not listed in the fielding averages for those particular positions: Breedlove, of; Calderon, p; Contreras, 1b; Couchee, p; Cucjen, of; DeWolf, p; G.S. Harris, p; Hotchkiss, p; Melrose, p; Perdomo, of, p; Peters, of; Phillips, p; Pohle, 1b; Roman, p; T. Scott, p; Tejeda, p; Zaske, p.

CLUB PITCHING

Club	ERA.	G.	CG.	ShO.	Sv.	IP.	H.	R.	ER.	HR.	HB.	BB.	Int. BB.	SO.	WP.	Bk.
Shreveport	2.85	135	11	15	43	1179.0	1062	462	374	53	58	470	32	946	62	18
Arkansas	3.61	135	17	9	39	1162.1	1145	566	466	88	32	454	48	877	55	10
Jackson	3.83	136	12	6	38	1182.0	1250	608	503	81	46	432	41	771	61	15
Wichita	4.58	134	20	6	30	1174.0	1251	681	597	156	25	518	33	890	70	24
San Antonio	4.75	136	14	7	23	1207.2	1366	735	638	136	33	484	46	871	76	10
Midland	4.88	136	12	9	42	1205.1	1448	782	654	138	37	507	37	861	86	9
Tulsa	4.90	136	11	4	34	1176.0	1300	727	640	118	46	457	45	782	95	11
El Paso	5.45	134	11	3	35	1185.0	1478	813	717	144	38	471	34	821	75	13

PITCHERS' RECORDS
(Leading Qualifiers for Earned-Run Average Leadership — 109 or More Innings)

°Throws lefthanded.

Pitcher—Club	W.	L.	Pct.	ERA.	G.	GS.	CG.	GF.	ShO.	Sv.	IP.	H.	R.	ER.	HR.	HB.	BB.	Int. BB.	SO.	WP.
McGrath, Arkansas	12	6	.667	2.69	32	18	4	3	0	1	143.2	117	53	43	9	2	35	2	97	3
D. West, Jackson°	10	7	.588	2.81	25	25	4	0	2	0	166.2	152	67	52	5	4	81	1	186	5
Ohnoutka, Shreveport	9	11	.450	2.99	27	27	3	0	1	0	162.1	147	67	54	6	9	74	2	128	16
Bautista, Jackson	10	5	.667	3.24	28	25	2	2	1	0	169.1	174	76	61	9	4	43	3	95	6
Freeland, Shreveport	12	9	.571	3.27	26	26	1	0	0	0	151.1	153	67	55	8	12	76	3	109	8
Burkett, Shreveport	14	8	.636	3.34	27	27	6	0	1	0	177.2	181	75	66	11	7	53	2	126	3
Wheeler, El Paso°	8	2	.800	3.55	34	12	2	7	1	2	111.2	110	46	44	6	3	35	5	75	6
Weissman, Arkansas	11	7	.611	3.77	29	27	4	0	0	0	171.2	189	83	72	20	2	42	3	95	1
S. Young, Jackson°	9	10	.474	3.85	27	27	4	0	1	0	175.1	176	91	75	15	5	54	2	111	5
Alexander, Wichita	6	5	.545	3.94	53	1	1	19	0	3	112.0	95	54	49	20	2	40	4	106	9

Departmental Leaders: G—Lynch, 62; W—Burkett, Reed, 14; L—Mena, 14; Pct.—Bauer, .900; GS—Arnold, 29; CG—G.W. Harris, 7; GF—Miglio, 49; ShO—Arnold, G.W. Harris, Venturino, D. West, 2; Sv.—Peters, 23; IP—Burkett, 177.2; H—Reed, 227; R—Romanovsky, 125; ER—Reed, 102; HR—G.W. Harris, 32; HB—Hartshorn, 15; BB—D. West, 81; IBB—Savage, 12; SO—D. West, 186; WP—Arnold, 17.

(All Pitchers—Listed Alphabetically)

Pitcher—Club	W.	L.	Pct.	ERA.	G.	GS.	CG.	GF.	ShO.	Sv.	IP.	H.	R.	ER.	HR.	HB.	BB.	Int. BB.	SO.	WP.
Alexander, Wichita	6	5	.545	3.94	53	1	1	19	0	3	112.0	95	54	49	20	2	40	4	106	9
Ambrose, El Paso	4	8	.333	8.20	17	17	1	0	0	0	90.0	148	100	82	16	4	45	0	64	9
Armstrong, Wichita	2	5	.286	6.78	15	15	0	0	0	0	73.0	103	63	55	11	0	42	2	36	4
Arnold, Arkansas	12	9	.571	4.05	29	29	4	0	2	0	169.0	151	84	76	15	14	74	6	120	17
Bass, El Paso	7	4	.636	3.82	53	0	0	24	0	9	94.1	114	44	40	4	1	32	5	59	6
Bauer, Wichita°	9	1	.900	4.16	14	14	3	0	1	0	97.1	97	46	45	13	4	36	1	64	9
Bautista, Jackson	10	5	.667	3.24	28	25	2	2	1	0	169.1	174	76	61	9	4	43	3	95	6
Bayer, Jackson	0	3	.000	8.27	5	5	0	0	0	0	20.2	26	21	19	4	3	15	0	6	1
Bergendahl, Jackson	0	3	.000	9.00	12	1	0	5	0	0	25.0	36	27	25	7	1	7	1	23	6
Brantley, Shreveport	0	1	.000	3.09	2	2	0	0	0	0	11.2	12	7	4	1	1	4	0	7	1
Brisco, El Paso	8	5	.615	3.41	52	0	0	16	0	3	97.2	114	48	37	7	5	39	1	67	6
Broersma, El Paso	1	0	1.000	2.39	13	0	0	5	0	1	26.1	21	7	7	1	3	10	1	19	0
J.K. Brown, Tulsa	1	4	.200	7.29	8	8	0	0	0	0	42.0	53	36	34	3	1	18	1	26	1
K.A. Brown, Wichita°	6	7	.462	5.50	33	17	2	4	0	1	122.2	130	81	75	18	1	68	0	76	5
Burkett, Shreveport	14	8	.636	3.34	27	27	6	0	1	0	177.2	181	75	66	11	7	53	2	126	3
Burns, Jackson	2	1	.667	5.66	10	7	0	2	0	1	35.0	42	26	22	4	5	14	0	16	5
Calderon, Arkansas°	1	0	1.000	3.00	6	0	0	1	0	0	9.0	9	4	3	1	0	7	1	11	1
Castillo, El Paso	4	6	.400	6.00	14	14	0	0	0	0	81.0	107	61	54	16	3	20	0	47	1
Cecena, Tulsa	3	3	.500	4.28	43	0	0	19	0	2	61.0	54	37	29	7	3	37	4	61	7
Cedeno, Midland	5	7	.417	4.43	53	0	0	32	0	10	81.1	85	54	40	11	6	51	8	64	11
Clay, 16 EIP-9 San	0	2	.000	6.51	25	2	0	7	0	1	56.2	82	44	41	6	4	19	2	22	1
Collins, Midland	7	6	.538	5.98	23	23	1	0	1	0	131.0	164	97	87	20	5	51	2	99	6
Cook, Shreveport	9	2	.818	2.13	16	16	1	0	1	0	105.2	94	32	25	1	1	20	1	98	4
J. Costello, Arkansas°	5	2	.714	2.31	44	0	0	25	0	7	74.0	64	27	19	5	3	22	5	67	2
M. Costello, Wichita	2	2	.500	6.34	11	10	0	0	0	0	59.2	68	46	42	18	1	23	0	44	1
Couchee, Wichita	0	0	.000	0.00	2	0	0	2	0	0	3.0	2	0	0	0	1	0	1	5	0
Dacus, Midland	4	4	.500	4.03	42	9	0	6	0	1	120.2	139	65	54	9	3	34	3	79	6
Davis, Wichita	0	1	.000	4.00	1	1	0	0	0	0	4.0	4	3	0	0	0	0	0	2	0
Devine, San Antonio	2	3	.400	5.08	6	4	1	2	0	0	28.1	29	18	16	5	0	5	1	19	0
DeWolf, El Paso°	0	0	.000	9.82	3	0	0	3	0	0	3.2	8	4	4	0	2	1	0	2	0
Diaz, El Paso	0	2	.000	6.75	12	0	0	4	0	0	20.0	28	15	15	2	0	12	2	11	5
Duquette, El Paso°	1	0	1.000	8.59	7	0	0	4	0	0	7.1	10	8	7	1	0	4	0	2	0
Eichhorn, San Antonio	3	8	.273	4.61	40	16	2	11	1	1	127.0	157	81	65	11	5	34	1	65	6

Pitcher—Club	W.	L.	Pct.	ERA.	G.	GS.	CG.	GF.	ShO.	Sv.	IP.	H.	R.	ER.	HR.	HB.	BB.	Int. BB.	SO.	WP.
Farwell, San Antonio*	2	0	1.000	4.31	38	1	1	7	0	1	54.1	72	29	26	3	0	19	5	37	4
Fassero, Arkansas*	10	7	.588	4.10	28	27	2	0	1	0	151.1	168	90	69	16	1	67	7	118	7
Ferlenda, Tulsa	2	4	.333	5.75	9	8	1	0	0	0	36.0	46	24	23	6	2	21	0	24	5
Freeland, Shreveport	12	9	.571	3.27	26	26	1	0	0	0	151.1	153	67	55	8	12	76	3	109	8
Garcia, Midland*	10	6	.625	2.59	50	0	0	25	0	5	87.0	86	35	25	3	0	34	7	67	9
Gonzalez, El Paso	1	0	1.000	3.38	1	1	0	0	0	0	5.1	5	2	2	1	0	0	0	3	1
Hamilton, San Antonio	4	6	.400	4.78	12	12	0	0	0	0	69.2	73	41	37	11	0	28	2	63	3
Hammaker, Shreveport*	0	1	.000	1.29	1	1	0	0	0	0	7.0	6	2	1	0	0	0	0	3	0
Harman, Tulsa	4	4	.500	3.67	46	3	0	18	0	3	95.2	97	43	39	6	3	30	11	40	2
G.S. Harris, Wichita	0	0	.000	4.50	2	0	0	0	0	0	2.0	2	1	1	0	0	4	0	0	0
G.W. Harris, Wichita	12	11	.522	4.28	27	27	7	0	2	0	174.1	205	103	83	32	3	49	3	170	7
Hartley, San Antonio	3	4	.429	1.32	25	0	0	19	0	3	41.0	21	8	6	2	2	18	5	37	6
Hartshorn, Jackson	11	11	.500	4.14	26	26	2	0	0	0	163.0	196	94	75	12	15	49	1	71	4
Harvey, Midland	2	2	.500	2.04	43	0	0	36	0	20	53.0	40	14	12	1	0	28	5	78	10
Hernandez, Jackson*	0	2	.000	7.56	3	3	0	0	0	0	16.2	22	14	14	3	0	3	0	8	0
Herzog, Arkansas*	1	1	.500	5.40	21	1	0	3	0	0	13.1	24	10	8	0	0	3	0	10	0
Heuer, San Antonio	0	0	.000	10.80	4	0	0	2	0	1	6.2	12	8	8	3	0	1	0	1	1
Hickerson, Shreveport*	1	2	.333	3.94	4	3	0	0	0	0	16.0	20	7	7	0	0	4	0	23	1
Hill, Arkansas*	3	5	.375	5.20	18	8	0	5	0	2	53.2	60	33	31	1	0	30	3	48	8
Hogan, Shreveport	4	2	.667	1.55	34	4	0	12	0	4	81.1	64	22	14	2	4	21	1	64	3
Holmes, Midland*	0	0	.000	0.00	3	0	0	3	0	0	6.1	6	0	0	0	0	2	0	3	0
Hotchkiss, Midland	0	1	.000	6.75	1	0	0	1	0	0	1.1	3	1	1	0	0	1	0	0	0
Hunter, El Paso	5	5	.500	4.61	16	15	1	1	0	0	95.2	117	60	49	14	2	33	1	62	4
Kendrick, El Paso*	7	2	.778	4.33	10	10	1	0	0	0	68.2	74	34	33	10	3	22	2	57	1
Kinzer, Arkansas	5	6	.455	4.73	17	16	1	0	1	0	91.1	82	57	48	10	1	34	1	74	5
Knapp, Tulsa	8	12	.400	4.33	24	24	4	0	1	0	153.2	163	89	74	14	6	43	5	98	4
Lenderman, Jackson	1	6	.143	9.66	17	6	0	7	0	2	36.1	55	44	39	3	3	29	6	24	6
Leopold, Arkansas	2	3	.400	2.51	18	0	0	15	0	3	32.1	32	13	9	1	1	12	3	24	0
Lewallyn, San Antonio	0	1	.000	1.23	4	0	0	4	0	0	7.1	8	1	1	0	0	5	3	7	0
Lovelace, Midland*	3	3	.500	3.23	53	1	0	14	0	4	83.2	73	40	30	8	3	60	1	91	13
Ludy, El Paso	3	1	.750	9.29	15	6	0	4	0	0	41.2	83	47	43	7	1	6	0	26	5
Luebber, Wichita	1	1	.500	3.97	12	0	0	6	0	0	22.2	21	11	10	1	1	8	2	13	0
Lundgren, Jackson	4	5	.444	3.96	23	9	0	5	0	1	77.1	83	40	34	6	1	29	4	47	4
Lynch, Wichita	6	7	.462	3.50	62	0	0	41	0	12	97.2	111	46	38	5	2	45	11	62	7
Mack, Midland	1	1	.500	5.12	10	0	0	5	0	2	19.1	20	12	11	3	1	12	0	16	1
Malave, Arkansas	1	4	.200	4.15	28	0	0	10	0	0	30.1	26	15	14	2	0	28	3	27	1
Malloy, Tulsa	2	10	.167	4.89	16	16	1	0	0	0	92.0	97	55	50	10	2	39	2	73	12
Martinez, Midland	3	6	.333	5.60	12	12	1	0	0	0	72.1	71	49	45	11	2	44	2	46	7
May, San Antonio	8	8	.500	5.98	30	16	2	4	1	0	111.1	136	83	74	19	1	52	1	108	11
McCament, Shreveport	4	3	.571	2.38	52	0	0	44	0	14	79.1	78	28	21	5	5	18	4	39	5
McCarthy, Jackson	1	4	.200	2.65	37	1	0	33	0	21	54.1	57	18	16	3	0	21	3	30	4
McGrath, Arkansas	12	6	.667	2.69	32	18	4	3	0	1	143.2	117	53	43	9	2	35	2	97	3
McGuire, Midland	6	4	.600	6.40	10	10	0	0	0	0	52.0	81	41	37	5	0	15	1	39	3
Medvin, Shreveport	7	1	.875	1.72	37	0	0	15	0	4	78.2	59	19	15	2	8	41	3	71	3
Melrose, Tulsa*	0	0	.000	0.00	1	0	0	1	0	0	1.2	0	0	0	0	0	2	0	0	0
Mena, San Antonio	7	14	.333	4.99	34	24	3	0	1	0	164.0	177	98	91	14	9	68	1	100	10
Mielke, Tulsa	3	3	.500	2.98	28	0	0	25	0	15	45.1	34	18	15	5	1	10	3	46	1
Miglio, El Paso*	7	2	.778	3.63	56	0	0	49	0	18	72.0	65	33	29	6	3	27	9	74	5
Money, El Paso	0	1	.000	8.75	10	0	0	2	0	1	23.2	26	24	23	2	4	22	1	13	2
Morris, Shreveport	1	1	.500	4.36	16	0	0	3	0	0	33.0	30	16	16	2	3	18	5	16	2
Murphy, El Paso	10	7	.588	5.12	22	22	5	0	1	0	135.1	152	88	77	18	1	69	3	107	8
Nago, El Paso	0	0	.000	0.00	1	0	0	0	0	0	1.0	2	0	0	0	0	0	0	0	0
Nolte, Wichita*	4	2	.667	2.88	10	10	2	0	1	0	75.0	62	28	24	4	2	19	0	67	3
Norman, Arkansas	0	1	.000	2.61	5	1	0	2	0	0	10.1	14	8	3	0	2	8	0	5	2
Odekirk, Tulsa*	9	13	.409	5.84	26	26	1	0	0	0	148.0	192	109	96	15	8	58	0	69	14
Ohnoutka, Shreveport	9	11	.450	2.99	27	27	3	0	1	0	162.1	147	67	54	6	9	74	2	128	16
Olker, Shreveport*	0	2	.000	5.24	5	5	0	0	0	0	22.1	28	15	13	2	1	9	0	17	0
Oyster, Arkansas	5	4	.556	3.33	32	8	2	3	0	0	97.1	111	47	36	2	2	38	4	67	1
Pavlas, Tulsa	1	6	.143	7.69	13	12	0	1	0	0	59.2	79	51	51	9	3	27	2	46	7
Pequignot, San Antonio	0	1	.000	12.00	3	0	0	3	0	0	6.0	11	8	8	3	0	3	0	4	0
Perdomo, Jackson	0	0	.000	4.50	1	0	0	1	0	1	2.0	2	1	1	0	0	2	0	1	0
Peterek, El Paso*	2	3	.400	8.52	9	9	0	0	0	0	49.2	80	53	47	6	0	16	0	38	5
Peters, Arkansas*	4	4	.500	1.57	47	0	0	37	0	23	74.1	51	16	13	1	1	24	5	78	1
Phillips, Jackson	0	0	.000	0.00	1	0	0	1	0	0	0.1	0	0	0	0	0	0	0	1	0
Pruitt, Jackson*	6	2	.750	3.83	43	0	0	21	0	1	51.2	51	24	22	2	3	15	9	31	1
Puig, El Paso*	0	1	.000	7.11	1	1	0	0	0	0	6.1	12	5	5	0	0	3	0	5	0
Puikunas, Shreveport*	3	3	.500	1.50	32	0	0	27	0	14	42.0	19	8	7	2	2	16	5	36	2
Raether, Tulsa	3	3	.500	4.76	31	0	0	26	0	3	34.0	34	19	18	6	3	12	3	38	2
Reece, Wichita*	5	5	.500	4.42	42	5	0	26	0	9	75.1	73	44	37	6	1	55	7	62	5
Reed, Midland*	14	8	.636	5.71	26	26	0	0	0	0	160.2	227	115	102	14	5	52	1	82	5
Remlinger, Shreveport*	4	2	.667	2.36	6	6	0	0	0	0	34.1	14	11	9	2	3	22	0	51	2
Rodgers, Midland	0	0	.000	4.00	3	0	0	2	0	0	9.0	15	4	4	0	0	2	0	7	0
Rogers, Tulsa*	1	5	.167	5.35	28	0	0	8	0	2	69.0	80	51	41	5	2	35	3	59	14
Roman, Jackson	0	0	.000	3.86	2	0	0	1	0	1	4.2	3	2	2	1	0	1	0	7	0
Romanovsky, Midland*	8	7	.533	6.29	26	26	2	0	0	0	141.2	211	125	77	23	5	62	1	97	9
Rowen, San Antonio*	2	8	.200	6.91	27	9	0	5	0	1	69.0	77	60	53	9	1	52	2	57	7
Sadler, El Paso	1	5	.167	8.37	10	9	0	0	0	0	43.0	57	52	40	9	2	35	1	17	4
Samuels, Shreveport*	3	1	.750	1.62	21	1	0	11	0	4	33.1	24	10	6	2	0	10	1	35	2
Santiago, Jackson*	4	2	.667	1.86	46	0	0	15	0	3	82.1	73	23	17	3	1	63	4	48	7
Savage, San Antonio	5	6	.455	2.60	49	0	0	37	0	10	69.1	64	22	20	2	3	31	12	67	2
Scarpetta, El Paso*	4	4	.500	5.89	10	9	1	0	1	0	55.0	60	36	36	6	1	20	3	48	5
Schweighoffer, San Antonio	4	4	.500	4.58	17	15	2	0	1	0	108.0	135	70	55	10	2	26	3	50	7
Scott, San Antonio	0	1	.000	16.88	2	2	0	0	0	0	5.1	14	10	10	2	1	2	0	6	1
Sierra, Wichita	8	5	.615	3.95	19	18	4	0	1	0	114.0	120	57	50	14	1	42	1	89	3
Smith, Midland	1	0	1.000	3.90	10	3	0	2	0	0	30.0	27	17	13	4	2	12	1	19	0
Sonberg, San Antonio*	2	7	.222	5.54	15	13	1	1	0	0	74.2	101	59	46	10	3	30	0	53	3
Stapleton, El Paso*	0	0	.000	1.74	4	0	0	3	0	2	10.1	9	2	2	0	0	0	0	10	0
Stewart, Shreveport	1	2	.333	4.50	16	1	0	8	0	2	24.0	24	13	12	1	1	18	1	16	2
Tate, Shreveport	5	5	.500	3.80	34	8	0	12	0	3	83.0	75	41	35	2	1	57	4	75	7
Tejeda, San Antonio*	0	0	.000	3.18	6	0	0	0	0	0	5.2	8	4	2	0	0	4	1	3	1
Tellez, San Antonio	0	0	.000	4.50	2	0	0	2	0	0	2.0	1	1	1	0	1	0	0	1	0
Torres, San Antonio	2	4	.333	3.21	44	0	0	20	0	5	75.2	66	30	27	14	1	32	5	73	5

Pitcher—Club	W.	L.	Pct.	ERA.	G.	GS.	CG.	GF.	ShO.	Sv.	IP.	H.	R.	ER.	HR.	HB.	BB.	Int. BB.	SO.	WP.
Valdez, Tulsa*	1	4	.200	7.11	11	8	1	1	1	0	49.1	62	44	39	9	2	24	3	38	3
Venturino, Midland	11	6	.647	5.51	27	26	3	0	2	0	165.0	215	117	101	26	5	49	5	81	6
Walker, 8 EIP-30 Wich	5	6	.455	5.82	38	10	0	10	0	3	94.1	115	69	61	18	5	52	1	58	7
Wasilewski, Shreveport	2	3	.400	3.90	14	9	0	0	0	0	60.0	58	35	26	5	1	27	1	48	3
Weissman, Arkansas	11	7	.611	3.77	29	27	4	0	0	0	171.2	189	83	72	20	2	42	3	95	1
Welborn, Jackson	4	1	.800	0.47	12	0	0	10	0	4	19.1	6	1	1	0	0	8	0	16	1
D. West, Jackson*	10	7	.588	2.81	25	25	4	0	2	0	166.2	152	67	52	5	4	81	1	186	5
T. West, Tulsa	9	10	.474	4.68	26	22	3	3	0	0	144.1	174	85	75	13	4	44	1	57	5
Weston, Jackson	8	4	.667	3.40	58	1	0	21	0	3	82.0	96	39	31	4	1	18	5	50	6
Wheeler, El Paso*	8	2	.800	3.55	34	12	2	7	1	2	111.2	110	46	44	6	3	35	5	75	6
Whitaker, Tulsa	3	1	.750	2.33	39	0	0	17	0	1	92.2	77	27	24	6	2	21	6	68	14
Wilmet, Arkansas	0	2	.000	4.70	17	0	0	10	0	3	23.0	23	15	12	2	2	18	2	18	2
Witt, Tulsa	0	1	.000	5.40	1	1	0	0	0	0	5.0	5	9	3	1	0	6	0	2	0
Wohler, San Antonio*	6	10	.375	4.57	27	23	2	1	1	0	155.2	172	89	79	15	3	65	3	107	9
J. Young, Arkansas*	0	2	.000	5.09	12	0	0	4	0	0	17.2	24	11	10	3	1	12	3	18	4
M. Young, Wichita*	4	6	.400	7.06	13	13	1	0	0	0	65.0	73	55	51	5	3	46	0	45	11
S. Young, Jackson*	9	10	.474	3.85	27	27	4	0	1	0	175.1	176	91	75	15	5	54	2	111	5
Zaske, Tulsa	2	0	1.000	1.64	2	2	0	0	0	0	11.0	10	2	2	1	0	5	0	12	2

BALKS—G.W. Harris, 6; Bauer, 5; Cook, Odekirk, Weissman, M. Young, 4 each; Bautista, Castillo, Eichhorn, Kendrick, Reed, Rowan, Wasilewski, D. West, T. West, S. Young, 3 each; Arnold, K.A. Brown, Freeland, Hogan, Kinzer, Knapp, Lenderman, Lovelace, Lundgren, Lynch, Murphy, Sadler, Wohler, 2 each; Alexander, Armstrong, Burkett, Cedeno, Clay, M. Costello, Diaz, Fassero, Ferlenda, Ludy, Martinez, May, McCarthy, Morris, Ohnoutka, Olker, Peters, Puikunas, Romanovsky, Samuels, Sierra, Tate, Tejeda, Venturino, Walker, Weston, Whitaker, 1 each.

COMBINATION SHUTOUTS—McGrath-Peters, Arnold-Peters, Weissman-Peters, Arnold-Costello, Weissman-Norman, Arkansas; Young-McCarthy, Hartshorn-Welborn, Jackson; Martinez-Mack, Romanovsky-Venturino-Lovelace, Venturino-Cedeno, Romanovsky-Cedeno, Smith-Lovelace-Garcia, Collins-Cedeno-Lovelace, Midland; Mena-Scott, Eichhorn-Hartley, San Antonio; Ohnoutka-Medvin 3, Freeland-Puikunas 2, Freeland-Cook, Cook-McCament-Puikunas, Cook-Puikunas, Cook-Hogan, Burkett-Puikunas, Remlinger-Tate, Tate-Samuels, Shreveport; Ferlenda-Mielke-Cecena, Pavlas-Whitaker-Raether, Tulsa; Nolte-Alexander, Wichita.

NO-HIT GAMES—Kinzer, Arkansas, defeated Tulsa, 10-0 (second game), June 6; G.W. Harris, Wichita, defeated Midland, 7-0, August 26.

California League

CLASS A

CHAMPIONSHIP WINNERS IN PREVIOUS YEARS

1914—Fresno	.571	1960—Reno	.614	1974—Fresno§	.607
1915—Modesto	.857	Reno	.657	San Jose	.579
1916-40—Did not operate.		1961—Reno	.743	1975—Reno	.614
1941—Fresno	.643	Reno	.643	Reno	.614
S. Barbara (2nd)*	.597	1962—San Jose§	.686	1976—Salinas	.650
1942—Santa Barbara†	.642	Reno	.587	Reno§	.547
1943-44-45—Did not operate.		1963—Modesto	.589	1977—Salinas	.564
1946—Stockton‡	.600	Stockton§	.687	Lodi§	.579
1947—Stockton‡	.679	1964—Fresno	.638	1978—Visalia§	.698
1948—Fresno	.607	Fresno	.600	Lodi	.607
S. Barbara (3rd)*	.529	1965—San Jose	.586	1979—San Jose§	.636
1949—Bakersfield	.612	Stockton§	.614	Reno	.525
San Jose (4th)*	.543	1966—Modesto	.577	1980—Stockton§	.638
1950—Ventura	.607	Modesto	.671	Visalia	.507
Modesto (2nd)*	.586	1967—San Jose§	.676	1981—Visalia	.621
1951—Santa Barbara‡	.599	Modesto	.586	Lodi§	.521
1952—Fresno‡	.629	1968—San Jose	.629	1982—Modesto§	.671
1953—San Jose‡	.664	Fresno§	.623	Visalia	.586
1954—Modesto‡	.623	1969—Stockton§	.600	1983—Visalia	.621
1955—Stockton	.733	Visalia	.614	Redwood§	.529
Fresno§	.718	1970—Bakersfield	.667	1984—Modesto§	.597
1956—Fresno‡	.650	Bakersfield	.671	Bakersfield	.486
1957—Visalia x	.622	1971—Visalia§	.583	1985—Fresno§	.575
Salinas (4th)*	.504	Fresno	.500	Stockton	.566
1958—Fresno*	.639	1972—Modesto§	.547	1986—Palm Springs	.613
Bakersfield	.672	Bakersfield	.629	Stockton§	.585
1959—Bakersfield	.592	1973—Lodi§	.657		
Modesto§	.643	Bakersfield	.571		

*Won four-club playoff. †League disbanded June 28. ‡Won championship and four-club playoff. §Won split-season playoff. xWon both halves of split-season.

STANDING OF CLUBS AT CLOSE OF FIRST HALF, JUNE 21

NORTHERN DIVISION

Club	W.	L.	T.	Pct.	G.B.
Stockton (Brewers)	49	22	0	.690	....
Modesto (A's)	39	32	0	.549	10
Salinas (Mariners)	31	40	0	.437	18
Reno (Padres)	30	41	0	.423	19
San Jose (Independent)	22	49	0	.310	27

SOUTHERN DIVISION

Club	W.	L.	T.	Pct.	G.B.
Fresno* (Giants)	42	30	0	.583	....
Bakersfield (Dodgers)	41	31	0	.569	1
San Bernardino (Independent)	35	36	0	.493	6½
Palm Springs (Angels)	34	37	0	.479	7½
Visalia (Twins)	33	38	0	.465	8½

STANDING OF CLUBS AT CLOSE OF SECOND HALF, AUGUST 30

NORTHERN DIVISION

Club	W.	L.	T.	Pct.	G.B.
Reno (Padres)	46	25	0	.648	....
Stockton (Brewers)	45	26	0	.634	1
Modesto (A's)	40	31	0	.563	6
Salinas (Mariners)	33	38	0	.465	13
San Jose (Independent)	11	60	0	.155	35

SOUTHERN DIVISION

Club	W.	L.	T.	Pct.	G.B.
Fresno (Giants)	38	33	0	.535	....
Bakersfield (Dodgers)	37	34	0	.521	1
Palm Springs (Angels)	35	36	0	.493	3
San Bernardino (Independent)	35	36	0	.493	3
Visalia (Twins)	35	36	0	.493	3

COMPOSITE STANDING OF CLUBS AT CLOSE OF SEASON, AUGUST 30

NORTHERN DIVISION

Club	Sto.	Mod.	Reno	Sal.	S.J.	Fr.	Bak.	S.B.	P.S.	Vis.	W.	L.	T.	Pct.	G.B.
Stockton (Brewers)	....	11	10	13	18	10	6	9	10	7	94	48	0	.662	....
Modesto (A's)	9	....	12	9	16	6	7	8	5	7	79	63	0	.556	15
Reno (Padres)	10	10	....	15	15	5	9	3	3	6	76	66	0	.535	18
Salinas (Mariners)	7	7	7	....	15	4	2	5	10	7	64	78	0	.451	30
San Jose (Independent)	2	4	5	5	....	2	2	2	5	6	33	109	0	.232	61

SOUTHERN DIVISION

Club	Sto.	Mod.	Reno	Sal.	S.J.	Fr.	Bak.	S.B.	P.S.	Vis.	W.	L.	T.	Pct.	G.B.
Fresno (Giants)	2	6	11	8	10	....	10	10	10	13	80	63	0	.559	....
Bakersfield (Dodgers)	6	7	3	10	10	11	....	10	10	11	78	65	0	.545	2
San Bernardino (Independent)	3	6	5	9	10	8	10	....	11	8	70	72	0	.493	9½
Palm Springs (Angels)	4	7	5	4	7	10	10	13	....	9	69	73	0	.486	10½
Visalia (Twins)	5	5	8	5	8	7	9	12	9	....	68	74	0	.479	11½

*Fresno defeated Bakersfield in one-game playoff for first-half, Southern Division title.

Major league affiliations in parentheses.

Playoffs—Reno defeated Stockton, two games to none; Fresno defeated Reno, four games to three, to win league championship.

Regular-Season Attendance—Bakersfield, 109,120; Fresno, 107,908; Modesto, 78,357; Palm Springs, 52,313; Reno, 109,002; Salinas, 42,552; San Bernardino, 158,896; San Jose, 69,120; Stockton, 61,794; Visalia, 60,818. Total, 849,880.

Managers—Bakersfield, Kevin Kennedy; Fresno, Bob Harrison; Modesto, Tommie Reynolds; Palm Springs, Bill Lachemann, Jr.; Reno, Dale Kelly; Salinas, Greg Mahlberg; San Bernardino, Rich Dauer; San Jose, Mike Verdi; Stockton, Dave Machemer; Visalia, Dan Schmitz.

All-Star Team—1B—Lee Stevens, Palm Springs; 2B—Kenny Grant, Palm Springs; 3B—Tony Pellegrino, Reno; SS—Gary Sheffield, Stockton; OF—Darryl Hamilton, Stockton; Jerome Nelson, Modesto; Daniel Grunhard, Palm Springs; C—Luis Lopez, Bakersfield; DH—Chris Calvert, Visalia; P—Taketo Kamei, San Jose; Mike Pitz, Bakersfield; Tim Burcham, Palm Springs; Mike Mills, Reno; Most Valuable Player—Luis Lopez, Bakersfield; Pitcher of the Year—Taketo Kamei, San Jose; Manager of the Year—Dave Machemer, Stockton.

(Compiled by William J. Weiss, League Statistician, San Mateo, Calif.)

CLUB BATTING

Club	Pct.	G.	AB.	R.	OR.	H.	TB.	2B.	3B.	HR.	RBI.	GW.	SH.	SF.	HP.	BB.	Int. BB.	SO.	SB.	CS.	LOB.
Reno	.268	142	4764	808	774	1279	1829	202	54	80	708	65	39	48	45	684	22	945	176	95	1097
Stockton	.259	142	4643	762	537	1202	1680	197	31	73	658	80	55	51	76	721	40	822	183	88	1099
Bakersfield	.258	143	4722	723	663	1219	1704	204	25	77	596	65	74	30	59	572	26	756	193	100	1037
Fresno	.258	143	4692	692	603	1211	1712	202	46	69	589	68	39	48	59	545	24	1055	146	100	1029
Palm Springs	.254	142	4673	703	750	1189	1685	204	41	70	623	60	46	40	34	695	21	1020	162	92	1040
San Bernardino	.253	142	4698	679	721	1190	1775	210	30	105	583	61	26	35	35	639	29	1098	152	84	1051
Visalia	.249	142	4576	680	619	1138	1637	201	26	82	598	61	56	55	66	713	13	957	129	90	1111
Salinas	.244	142	4620	562	620	1128	1480	165	41	35	473	52	48	37	42	565	12	972	163	147	1030
Modesto	.244	142	4589	684	613	1120	1554	200	36	54	580	65	38	47	70	738	27	1019	181	115	1126
San Jose	.207	142	4337	423	816	898	1206	136	26	40	347	26	56	35	33	525	17	1092	134	67	901

INDIVIDUAL BATTING
(Leading Qualifiers for Batting Championship—383 or More Plate Appearances)

°Bats lefthanded.   †Switch-hitter.

Player and Club	Pct.	G.	AB.	R.	H.	TB.	2B.	3B.	HR.	RBI.	GW.	SH.	SF.	HP.	BB.	Int. BB.	SO.	SB.	CS.
Lester, James, Reno	.331	97	369	69	122	171	22	6	5	82	6	1	3	11	48	1	66	8	5
Lopez, Luis, Bakersfield	.329	142	550	89	181	276	43	2	16	96	16	5	6	9	38	3	49	6	6
Hamilton, Darryl, Stockton°	.328	125	494	102	162	215	17	6	8	61	4	5	7	6	74	9	59	43	12
Sconiers, Daryl, San Jose°	.313	98	336	46	105	155	19	2	9	49	3	0	3	1	52	3	64	15	7
Grunhard, Daniel, Palm Springs°	.306	121	432	69	132	185	16	8	7	68	2	3	3	0	52	1	58	28	10
Davis, Harry, Fresno†	.296	116	415	76	123	184	39	2	6	58	8	4	7	6	47	6	87	21	13
Monico, Mario, Stockton°	.293	138	467	84	137	183	23	4	5	67	11	2	8	2	97	3	54	13	5
Calvert, Christopher, Visalia	.290	119	410	65	119	171	23	4	7	68	11	0	4	14	60	1	78	17	7
Stevenson, William, Reno°	.290	111	376	74	109	200	22	3	21	88	7	0	3	3	70	6	92	0	4
Odle, Page, 17 SB-118 Reno	.286	135	503	93	144	222	24	6	14	86	11	5	4	2	71	1	88	25	16

Departmental Leaders: G—Lopez, 142; AB—Lopez, 550; R—J. Carter, 109; H—Lopez, 181; TB—Lopez, 276; 2B—Lopez, 43; 3B—J. Carter, 11; HR—Stevenson, 21; RBI—Sheffield, 103; GWRBI—Lopez, 16; SH—Brocki, 12; SF—G. Connor, 9; HP—Gould, 21; BB—Grant, 107; IBB—Hamilton, 9; SO—Eccles, 127; SB—McCray, 65; CS—J. Carter, 25.

(All Players—Listed Alphabetically)

Player and Club	Pct.	G.	AB.	R.	H.	TB.	2B.	3B.	HR.	RBI.	GW.	SH.	SF.	HP.	BB.	Int. BB.	SO.	SB.	CS.
Abshier, Lanny, Palm Springs°	.071	6	14	1	1	1	0	0	0	1	0	1	0	0	3	0	8	0	0
Akimoto, Kohsaku, San Jose	.112	103	268	16	30	37	2	1	1	9	0	8	0	1	36	1	86	1	1
Alfonzo, Edgar, Palm Springs	.304	36	92	13	28	35	4	0	1	15	2	3	1	0	13	0	21	1	1
Alfredson, Thomas, Palm Springs	.299	52	184	32	55	96	4	5	9	45	2	0	2	2	32	2	61	9	7
Anderson, Michael, Palm Springs	.251	61	191	27	48	56	8	0	0	15	2	1	2	0	18	0	52	10	4
Anderson, Timothy, Bakersfield†	.210	29	62	7	13	16	3	0	0	5	0	2	1	1	8	0	7	6	1
Aragon, Joey, Visalia	.267	129	423	61	113	162	17	4	8	65	8	5	7	1	63	1	54	15	12
Azar, Todd, Salinas	.355	17	62	7	22	28	2	2	0	10	0	0	1	0	4	0	4	2	0
Baham, Leon, San Bernardino†	.279	132	484	78	135	188	23	3	8	72	8	2	6	1	61	3	78	13	9
Barry, John, Fresno	.271	110	395	35	107	117	10	0	0	33	4	3	3	4	41	2	72	7	6
Barton, Shawn, San Jose	.233	68	245	16	57	66	7	1	0	27	4	4	3	2	28	0	30	11	2
Battaglia, Jeffrey, San Bernardino	.259	56	174	29	45	84	13	1	8	19	2	0	3	2	18	0	63	8	4
Bell, Juan, Bakersfield†	.245	134	473	54	116	149	15	3	4	58	1	7	5	3	43	3	91	21	7
Bell, Robert, Palm Springs	.153	31	85	9	13	18	5	0	0	5	0	2	0	0	11	0	21	0	0
Benjamin, Michael, Fresno	.241	64	212	25	51	83	6	4	6	24	6	2	0	2	24	1	71	6	2
Bernardo, Robert, Salinas	.172	73	232	27	40	66	11	0	5	28	4	1	2	12	25	0	89	3	6
Bilello, John, San Jose	.250	9	4	0	1	1	0	0	0	0	0	0	0	0	0	0	3	0	1
Bishop, James, San Bernardino	.247	23	73	8	18	23	2	0	1	5	1	0	0	0	10	1	22	0	0
Blackwell, Larry, Visalia	.257	25	70	14	18	29	3	1	2	14	2	0	1	0	13	0	15	2	0
Blair, Paul, Fresno	.258	92	298	49	77	89	8	2	0	25	3	4	2	2	30	0	56	8	6
Blankenship, Lance, Modesto	.274	22	84	14	23	36	9	2	0	17	1	1	0	1	12	1	29	12	3
Bond, David, Reno°	.000	5	3	0	0	0	0	0	0	0	0	0	0	0	0	0	3	0	0
Bonilla, George, Fresno°	.273	36	11	1	3	4	1	0	0	1	0	0	0	0	0	0	5	0	0
Boone, Robert, Palm Springs	.111	3	9	0	1	2	1	0	0	0	0	0	0	0	0	0	1	0	0
Bordick, Michael, Modesto	.268	133	497	73	133	159	17	0	3	75	6	4	8	5	87	3	92	8	8
Borg, Gary, Visalia°	.287	81	282	45	81	127	20	4	6	41	7	1	3	1	54	3	48	7	2
Brandts, Michael, Salinas	.237	113	393	48	93	129	13	4	5	40	3	3	6	1	44	0	111	4	6
Britt, Patrick, Modesto	.237	92	308	33	73	90	11	0	2	39	6	0	4	1	34	1	67	2	2
Brocki, Michael, San Bernardino	.233	123	386	59	90	120	18	3	2	33	5	12	3	3	70	1	86	25	16
Brooks, Billy, Bakersfield	.000	49	1	0	0	0	0	0	0	0	0	0	0	0	1	0	1	0	0
Brown, Jeffrey B., Bakersfield°	.154	28	91	8	14	28	3	1	3	14	3	1	0	0	18	1	20	2	0
Brown, Jeffrey L., Bakersfield	.226	23	93	14	21	40	5	1	4	21	1	1	1	3	4	0	15	1	1
Brown, Renard, Stockton†	.220	60	182	40	40	47	1	3	0	13	1	2	0	3	45	0	38	23	5
Bruzik, Robert, Salinas†	.337	22	86	10	29	30	1	0	0	4	0	1	1	2	6	1	12	12	2
Burgos, Francisco, San Jose†	.227	69	229	20	52	68	9	2	1	14	2	3	0	1	10	2	30	4	1
Burke, Michael, Bakersfield°	.270	42	148	16	40	61	8	2	3	25	5	1	1	1	10	0	24	1	6
Cabrera, Victor, San Bernardino	.216	64	167	16	36	46	8	1	0	12	0	3	2	0	21	0	35	2	2
Calvert, Christopher, Visalia	.290	119	410	65	119	171	23	4	7	68	11	0	4	14	60	1	78	17	7
Canale, George, Stockton°	.280	66	246	42	69	110	18	1	7	48	4	2	2	1	38	3	59	5	4
Carter, Jeffrey, Fresno	.275	135	510	109	140	194	14	11	6	50	4	4	7	5	94	4	75	49	25
Carter, Ronnie, San Bernardino	.213	70	164	19	35	52	5	0	4	18	1	0	0	0	30	1	54	5	5
Castaneda, Nick, Stockton°	.000	1	1	0	0	0	0	0	0	0	0	0	0	0	0	0	0	0	0
Chandler, Brian, San Jose°	.162	22	68	3	11	12	1	0	0	2	0	1	1	1	5	1	25	0	2
Chapman, Christopher, Bakersfield°..	.267	65	206	37	55	112	15	0	14	42	7	2	1	3	38	6	53	0	4
Childers, Jeffrey, 7 SB-21 Reno	.000	28	3	0	0	0	0	0	0	0	0	1	0	0	0	0	1	0	0
Christman, Kevin, San Jose	.300	3	10	0	3	3	0	0	0	1	0	0	0	0	0	0	3	0	0
Clark, Anthony, San Jose	.111	18	45	1	5	7	0	1	0	1	0	0	0	2	5	0	14	0	0
Clark, Isaiah, Stockton	.230	112	383	47	88	127	21	3	4	43	2	8	4	10	27	0	49	3	8
Clark, Rodney, San Bernardino°	.211	6	19	2	4	5	1	0	0	3	0	1	0	0	3	0	5	0	0
Clem, John, Salinas†	.235	110	366	37	86	117	18	2	3	59	8	2	4	3	69	2	100	7	8
Colbert, Craig, Fresno°	.245	115	388	41	95	133	12	4	6	51	6	3	5	4	22	2	89	5	5
Combs, Marcus, San Bernardino°	.074	24	27	3	2	2	0	0	0	1	1	0	0	0	1	0	9	0	0
Conner, Gregory, Fresno	.242	129	480	51	116	182	26	5	10	70	7	0	9	9	24	0	122	11	7
Conner, Jeffrey, San Jose°	.000	32	1	0	0	0	0	0	0	0	0	0	0	0	0	0	0	0	0
Cooper, Craig, Reno	.269	129	438	69	118	185	26	4	11	82	12	0	5	2	65	0	104	0	0
Cox, Douglas, Bakersfield°	.091	25	11	2	1	2	1	0	0	1	0	0	0	0	2	0	2	0	0

Player and Club	Pct.	G.	AB.	R.	H.	TB.	2B.	3B.	HR.	RBI.	GW.	SH.	SF.	HP.	BB.	Int. BB.	SO.	SB.	CS.
Cron, Christopher, Palm Springs	.272	26	92	6	25	34	3	0	2	9	0	1	2	2	9	0	27	2	2
Cruz, Todd, San Bernardino	.205	91	298	38	61	112	11	2	12	35	2	1	2	4	34	2	80	7	2
Darby, Michael, Salinas	.000	25	0	1	0	0	0	0	0	0	0	0	0	0	0	0	0	0	0
Davis, Harry, Fresno†	.296	116	415	76	123	184	39	2	6	58	8	4	7	6	47	6	87	21	13
Davis, Kenneth, Visalia	.219	117	370	60	81	97	14	1	0	25	2	8	2	1	52	0	44	11	11
Dewolf, Robert, Stockton°	.600	3	15	6	9	14	2	0	1	4	0	0	0	0	2	0	1	1	0
Diaz, William, Salinas	.260	60	200	26	52	68	11	1	1	21	2	2	4	1	25	1	49	9	10
Dominguez, Jose, Fresno	.250	46	4	0	1	2	1	0	0	1	0	1	0	0	1	0	2	0	0
Duncan, Michael, Modesto°	.168	32	107	21	18	38	7	2	3	11	1	0	0	0	34	2	25	4	2
Eccles, John, Visalia	.227	107	383	48	87	161	17	0	19	64	8	3	5	5	36	0	127	1	2
Eccleston, Thomas, Salinas°	.214	62	220	23	47	64	6	4	1	19	3	2	2	1	21	1	34	6	6
Edwards, Jeffrey, San Bernardino	.140	19	50	4	7	7	0	0	0	1	0	0	1	0	2	0	18	0	0
Edwards, Jovon, Salinas°	.285	65	200	33	57	77	4	5	2	22	4	3	2	3	29	1	27	10	14
Erickson, Roger, San Jose	.500	30	2	0	1	1	0	0	0	0	0	0	0	0	0	0	1	0	0
Escalera, Ruben, Stockton°	.227	112	335	51	76	99	11	6	0	38	7	4	6	8	57	2	58	5	7
Espinoza, Andres, Palm Springs°	.260	77	242	21	63	85	16	0	2	26	6	3	2	0	21	0	68	1	1
Fazzini, Frank, Bakersfield	.234	41	137	21	32	58	6	1	6	21	2	0	0	1	24	2	49	2	2
Ferraro, Carl, Reno°	.167	39	6	0	1	1	0	0	0	0	0	0	0	0	0	0	3	0	0
Finley, David, Modesto	.202	32	89	14	18	25	5	1	0	5	0	0	1	0	13	1	25	1	0
Firova, Daniel, Salinas	.333	23	75	5	25	31	3	0	1	10	1	1	0	0	7	0	12	1	4
Fitzpatrick, Danny, Stockton	.000	37	1	0	0	0	0	0	0	0	0	0	0	0	0	0	0	0	0
Foley, Keith, Salinas	.249	79	265	25	66	89	11	0	4	29	2	7	1	2	20	1	34	2	5
Gastelum, Macario, Bakersfield	.000	2	1	0	0	0	0	0	0	0	0	0	0	0	0	0	1	0	0
Gavin, David, Modesto	.197	72	198	31	39	57	7	1	3	21	3	2	1	3	28	0	63	4	3
Gibree, Robert, Salinas	.196	46	148	18	29	45	10	0	2	15	3	0	1	2	18	0	37	3	4
Gilbert, Shawn, Visalia	.224	82	272	39	61	81	5	0	5	27	2	4	4	7	34	0	59	6	4
Goldstein, Ira, Visalia°	.174	55	109	11	19	26	1	0	2	15	0	3	2	1	30	1	37	1	3
Gonzalez, Eduardo, San Jose	.149	73	215	19	32	56	6	0	6	20	3	2	1	2	15	2	63	3	1
Gonzalez, Felipe, San Jose	.229	41	140	11	32	43	6	1	1	11	3	3	0	1	3	0	27	2	1
Gorski, Gary, Modesto	.250	44	128	21	32	42	7	0	1	12	2	2	0	5	32	2	34	5	1
Gould, Robert, Modesto	.280	99	336	58	94	134	20	4	4	45	8	1	4	21	65	2	71	25	17
Grant, Kenneth, Palm Springs	.280	137	515	103	144	216	30	6	10	59	10	8	4	5	107	4	85	20	14
Gray, Jeffrey, Reno	.245	106	355	59	87	113	14	6	0	42	3	1	1	3	41	0	77	20	6
Grunhard, Daniel, Palm Springs°	.306	121	432	69	132	185	16	8	7	68	2	3	3	0	52	1	58	28	10
Guerrero, Epifanio, Stockton	.301	52	183	22	55	72	11	0	2	25	3	1	0	1	19	2	31	6	3
Guzman, Juan, Bakersfield	.091	22	11	2	1	1	0	0	0	0	0	0	0	0	1	0	4	0	0
Hamilton, Darryl, Stockton°	.328	125	494	102	162	215	17	6	8	61	4	5	7	6	74	9	59	43	12
Hansen, David, Bakersfield°	.262	132	432	68	113	146	22	1	3	38	3	6	1	4	65	1	61	4	2
Hardgrave, Eric, Stockton	.056	5	18	1	1	1	0	0	0	1	0	0	0	0	1	0	8	0	0
Harper, Brian, San Jose	.310	8	29	5	9	18	0	0	3	8	0	0	1	0	2	0	1	1	0
Hartley, Michael, Bakersfield	.167	33	6	0	1	1	0	0	0	0	0	0	0	0	0	0	3	0	0
Hartsock, Brian, San Bernardino°	.270	115	352	54	95	133	18	1	6	47	4	2	4	1	55	2	82	3	1
Haruta, George, San Jose	.234	19	47	3	11	14	0	0	1	2	0	0	1	0	8	0	7	0	1
Harvey, Randall, San Bernardino°	.277	110	249	38	69	126	11	2	14	48	5	0	2	2	37	5	68	1	1
Henley, Daniel, Bakersfield	.229	83	258	36	59	75	11	1	1	28	2	5	1	2	40	0	51	4	0
Heredia, Gilbert, Fresno	.286	11	7	1	2	2	0	0	0	2	0	0	0	0	1	0	1	0	0
Hernandez, Carlos, Bakersfield	.228	48	162	22	37	54	6	1	3	22	3	1	2	3	14	0	23	8	4
Holcomb, Ted, Bakersfield°	.206	42	102	14	21	25	2	1	0	10	1	6	1	0	19	0	9	1	4
Holmes, Carl, San Bernardino	.157	19	51	7	8	14	3	0	1	4	0	0	0	2	0	0	22	0	0
Howitt, Dann, Modesto°	.208	109	336	44	70	109	11	2	8	42	3	3	3	4	59	1	110	7	9
Huth, Kenneth, San Bernardino†	.268	23	82	16	22	31	4	1	1	11	1	0	0	0	12	0	21	5	2
Iannini, Steven, Modesto	.194	36	98	20	19	27	2	0	2	7	0	1	4	1	20	0	26	7	9
Jacas, David, Visalia†	.224	46	107	18	24	29	5	0	0	6	1	2	1	5	4	0	26	5	2
Jones, Gary, Fresno†	.267	94	300	28	80	102	10	0	4	46	6	2	2	2	36	5	66	4	4
Jones, Robert, Stockton	.295	39	149	29	44	69	6	2	5	27	5	1	2	8	16	0	30	13	1
Kamei, Taketo, San Jose°	.500	34	2	0	1	1	0	0	0	0	0	0	0	0	0	0	0	0	0
Kating, James, Bakersfield	.263	128	456	84	120	185	20	3	13	63	8	6	4	10	82	6	53	15	17
Kemp, Joseph, Salinas°	.191	14	47	3	9	16	2	1	1	9	0	0	0	1	3	0	14	1	2
Kirby, Wayne, Bakersfield°	.269	105	416	77	112	132	14	3	0	34	2	5	2	3	49	1	41	56	21
Kleven, Mark, Reno†	.154	6	13	3	2	2	0	0	0	1	0	1	0	0	4	0	5	1	0
Kmak, Joseph, Fresno	.221	48	154	18	34	42	8	0	0	12	1	3	0	3	15	0	32	1	2
Kolovitz, Michael, Salinas	.000	30	1	0	0	0	0	0	0	0	0	0	0	0	0	0	1	0	0
Krause, Thomas, Salinas°	.246	99	349	34	86	104	14	2	0	23	3	4	1	0	39	0	41	13	14
Kroll, Todd, Bakersfield	.000	43	3	1	0	0	0	0	0	0	0	0	0	0	0	0	2	0	0
Kubala, Brian, San Jose	.154	20	26	0	4	4	0	0	0	0	0	0	0	1	3	0	8	0	0
Kyander, Michael, San Bernardino°	.225	64	160	20	36	53	8	0	3	16	3	1	2	0	28	1	31	1	2
Lange, Clark, Visalia	.148	40	88	16	13	15	2	0	0	5	1	1	2	2	27	2	31	1	1
Lanoux, Carol, Visalia°	.268	129	433	63	116	150	16	0	6	63	7	6	4	3	71	1	72	4	7
Larson, Daniel, Salinas	.235	99	345	38	81	105	12	3	2	43	1	4	3	6	54	1	60	13	15
Law, Rudy, San Bernardino°	.312	29	93	19	29	40	4	2	1	11	2	2	0	1	18	1	11	4	3
Lee, Harvey, San Jose	.240	106	325	40	78	109	9	8	2	26	2	1	2	1	56	1	65	24	8
Lester, James, Reno	.331	97	369	69	122	171	22	6	5	82	6	1	3	11	48	1	66	8	5
LeVasseur, Thomas, Reno	.275	106	389	68	107	120	7	3	0	48	7	3	4	1	55	1	53	19	16
Lincoln, Lance, Stockton	.200	42	110	16	22	23	1	0	0	10	1	3	1	7	27	1	26	3	0
Locklear, Keith, San Jose°	.178	21	73	6	13	21	5	0	1	8	0	0	1	0	4	0	20	0	2
Lopez, Luis, Bakersfield	.329	142	550	89	181	276	43	2	16	96	16	5	6	9	38	3	49	6	6
Loubier, Stephen, Reno	.000	13	3	0	0	0	0	0	0	0	0	1	0	0	2	0	2	0	0
MacArthur, Matthew, SB	.188	9	16	3	3	4	1	0	0	2	0	1	0	2	4	0	5	3	0
Malone, Rubio, San Bernardino†	.500	54	2	1	1	1	0	0	0	0	0	0	0	0	0	0	1	0	0
Mancini, Joseph, San Jose°	.276	27	87	13	24	30	3	0	1	8	1	1	1	0	12	1	23	5	1
Mangham, Eric, Bakersfield	.264	67	208	40	55	79	11	2	3	27	4	1	1	9	23	0	38	8	4
Manto, Jeffrey, Palm Springs	.256	112	375	61	96	146	21	4	7	63	8	5	7	8	102	1	85	8	2
Marx, William, Reno	.000	11	3	1	0	0	0	0	0	0	0	0	0	0	0	0	2	0	0
Masters, Frank, Salinas	.235	52	162	22	38	58	9	1	3	23	3	2	0	0	38	2	44	2	0
Matta, Robert, San Jose°	.074	10	27	2	2	3	1	0	0	1	0	1	0	0	3	0	10	0	0
McAnany, James, Palm Springs°	.143	10	35	6	5	6	1	0	0	2	0	1	0	0	5	0	7	1	0
McCatty, Steven, San Jose°	.071	35	28	2	2	2	0	0	0	1	0	0	0	0	4	0	13	0	0
McCoy, Timothy, Fresno	.000	38	1	0	0	0	0	0	0	0	0	0	0	0	0	0	1	0	0
McCray, Rodney, Reno	.211	117	413	69	87	108	11	5	0	26	0	9	3	10	69	3	96	65	16
McGinnis, Russell, Modesto	.255	47	165	24	42	75	9	0	8	31	4	3	3	2	23	1	33	1	1
McGrew, Charles, Stockton°	.253	100	297	51	75	120	13	1	10	55	6	3	2	2	48	5	61	0	3
McNealy, Robert, San Jose°	.231	31	108	21	25	30	3	1	0	5	1	1	0	0	14	1	14	14	2

Player and Club	Pct.	G.	AB.	R.	H.	TB.	2B.	3B.	HR.	RBI.	GW.	SH.	SF.	HP.	BB.	Int. BB.	SO.	SB.	CS.
Meagher, Thomas, 3 Reno-24 Fresno	.286	27	7	0	2	2	0	0	0	1	0	0	0	0	0	0	1	0	0
Meier, Kevin, Fresno	.250	13	4	0	1	1	0	0	0	0	0	0	0	0	1	0	1	0	0
Messier, Thomas, Fresno	.176	24	17	3	3	4	1	0	0	1	0	0	0	0	2	0	4	0	0
Meyer, Daniel, San Jose°	.250	3	12	0	3	4	1	0	0	1	0	0	0	0	0	0	0	0	0
Meyers, Glenn, Visalia	.232	54	190	22	44	64	12	1	2	22	2	1	1	4	14	0	31	1	1
Miller, Lemmie, San Jose	.067	6	15	0	1	1	0	0	0	0	0	1	0	3	0	4	2	0	
Miller, Todd, Fresno†	.167	61	144	19	24	27	3	0	0	9	0	0	2	2	18	0	53	3	4
Mills, Michael, Reno	.000	54	1	0	0	0	0	0	0	0	0	0	0	0	0	0	1	0	0
Milner, Theodore, 3 SB-55 PS°	.278	58	187	33	52	61	2	2	1	21	3	2	1	3	27	0	38	19	6
Minch, John, Modesto	.280	78	257	35	72	90	18	0	0	33	8	1	2	10	40	0	41	7	4
Monceratt, Pablo, Salinas°	.220	112	377	49	83	115	14	3	4	34	4	3	0	2	56	2	113	8	5
Monico, Mario, Stockton°	.293	138	467	84	137	183	23	4	5	67	11	2	8	2	97	3	54	13	5
Mons, Jeffrey, Bakersfield	.231	10	26	3	6	6	0	0	0	2	0	0	0	0	2	0	7	0	0
Montano, Martin, Stockton°	.000	46	5	1	0	0	0	0	0	0	0	0	0	0	1	0	2	0	0
Moore, Charles, San Jose	.207	34	111	12	23	36	7	0	2	13	1	1	1	0	19	1	24	1	1
Mora, Juan, Bakersfield	.200	16	45	2	9	13	1	0	1	8	1	1	0	1	0	0	12	0	1
Moralez, Paul, 24 Bak-53 SB	.238	77	210	24	50	62	3	0	3	27	5	0	1	3	13	0	23	0	2
Morgan, Kenneth, Visalia°	.235	89	268	33	63	80	10	2	1	26	3	1	2	3	32	0	69	10	8
Mori, Hiroyuki, San Jose°	.208	109	317	26	66	92	15	1	3	38	2	6	5	0	42	1	82	4	4
Morris, David, Fresno	.000	27	1	0	0	0	0	0	0	0	0	0	0	0	0	0	0	0	0
Morrison, Brian, San Bernardino	.256	118	395	44	101	168	18	2	15	66	8	0	4	3	50	2	120	8	3
Mota, Miguel, Bakersfield†	.247	98	271	40	67	71	2	1	0	21	0	8	0	2	17	1	46	33	6
Mueller, Peter, Visalia°	.247	25	89	15	22	44	4	0	6	18	0	0	1	4	20	1	23	1	0
Munoz, Michael, Bakersfield°	.167	53	6	0	1	1	0	0	0	0	0	0	2	0	0	0	5	0	1
Murray, Stephen, Salinas	.251	105	426	60	107	118	9	1	0	42	4	3	4	2	50	1	52	17	14
Nabekawa, Tsutomu, San Jose	.000	33	4	0	0	0	0	0	0	0	0	0	0	0	0	0	2	0	0
Nakamura, Hideo, San Jose	.137	76	183	7	25	27	2	0	0	10	0	2	1	4	20	0	59	2	2
Nalls, Gary, Palm Springs	.258	42	120	15	31	39	4	2	0	10	1	1	0	0	8	0	35	6	1
Nash, David, Fresno	.214	62	159	22	34	48	3	1	3	17	2	1	2	2	38	0	46	3	4
Nelson, Jeffrey, Salinas	.500	17	2	1	1	1	0	0	0	0	0	0	0	0	0	0	1	0	0
Nelson, Jerome, Modesto†	.263	125	437	92	115	150	15	10	0	40	2	7	5	2	99	3	69	51	20
Nelson, Richard, Fresno	.261	98	333	74	87	158	21	4	14	57	5	2	3	12	57	0	103	6	1
Newson, Warren, Reno°	.309	51	165	44	51	80	7	2	6	28	0	2	1	0	39	0	34	2	6
Nieporte, James, Reno	.270	93	318	45	86	114	13	3	3	41	6	2	7	2	27	1	66	5	1
Nolte, Eric, Reno°	.200	11	5	0	1	1	0	0	0	0	0	1	0	0	0	0	2	0	0
Nunez, Dario, Palm Springs	.236	136	517	67	122	153	16	6	1	50	3	7	1	4	47	0	88	13	14
Odle, Page, 17 SB-118 Reno	.286	135	503	93	144	222	24	6	14	86	11	5	4	2	71	1	88	25	16
Olker, Joseph, Fresno	.385	17	13	2	5	5	0	0	0	1	0	3	0	0	1	0	3	0	0
Osaka, Teruki, San Jose	.000	34	1	0	0	0	0	0	0	0	0	0	0	0	0	0	1	0	0
Pappas, Erik, Palm Springs	.243	119	395	50	96	131	20	3	3	64	8	3	7	0	66	0	77	16	6
Patterson, Michael, San Bernardino...	.223	89	238	31	53	65	10	1	0	17	3	2	1	3	30	0	46	0	2
Peguero, Jeremia, Modesto	.227	136	453	59	103	129	11	6	1	45	4	5	4	5	49	0	88	31	22
Pellegrino, Anthony, Reno.	.279	128	462	77	129	171	23	5	3	74	5	1	7	2	67	0	72	7	5
Pena, Jose, Fresno	.278	80	266	43	74	99	11	1	4	35	5	1	4	4	12	0	43	6	5
Penigar, Charles, Palm Springs†	.231	51	173	36	40	49	7	1	0	13	2	5	1	2	27	1	31	21	10
Perry, Steven, San Jose†	.194	11	31	1	6	6	0	0	0	0	0	1	0	0	5	0	14	0	0
Pettis, Stacey, San Jose	.104	15	48	4	5	6	1	0	0	4	0	0	2	0	7	0	24	1	1
Pilkington, Eric, Fresno°	.250	35	4	1	1	2	1	0	0	0	0	0	0	0	1	0	1	0	0
Pinelli, Willie, Bakersfield	.266	49	109	10	29	31	2	0	0	7	2	4	2	3	16	1	20	4	3
Pitz, Michael, Bakersfield	.000	30	6	1	0	0	0	0	0	0	0	0	0	0	3	0	5	0	0
Plesac, Joseph, Reno	.250	29	4	1	1	1	0	0	0	0	0	0	0	0	1	0	1	0	0
Polli, Gregory, San Jose°	.230	26	87	10	20	29	6	0	1	9	0	0	1	1	9	0	13	2	1
Pottinger, Mark, Stockton†	.182	50	165	24	30	33	3	0	0	14	3	4	0	1	27	1	28	13	6
Pust, John, Visalia	.175	32	80	7	14	20	3	0	1	8	1	1	1	1	9	0	22	0	1
Quinzer, Paul, Reno	.100	36	10	0	1	2	1	0	0	2	0	2	0	0	0	0	4	0	0
Reichle, Darrin, Reno†	1.000	4	1	1	1	4	0	0	1	1	0	0	0	0	0	0	0	0	0
Reitz, Kenneth, San Jose	.209	59	158	9	33	41	5	0	1	9	0	1	3	1	13	1	44	0	1
Richardson, Allen, Visalia°	.245	42	94	11	23	26	3	0	0	9	1	1	1	1	23	0	21	2	3
Rinaldi, Jude, San Jose	.216	25	74	8	16	22	0	0	2	10	2	0	1	0	7	0	14	1	1
Rivera, Pablo, Reno	.184	14	49	4	9	14	3	1	0	7	0	0	0	0	5	1	11	0	0
Roberts, Peter, Reno°	.000	17	4	1	0	0	0	0	0	0	0	0	0	0	1	0	2	0	0
Robinson, Marteese, Modesto	.222	48	171	18	38	52	5	3	1	22	3	1	2	1	16	0	39	7	3
Rodgers, Darrell, Fresno	.143	26	7	2	1	1	0	0	0	0	0	1	0	0	0	0	2	0	0
Rodriguez, Angel, Stockton	.264	49	178	23	47	76	12	1	5	40	6	1	3	1	13	0	39	2	0
Rojas, Homar, Bakersfield	.000	3	3	0	0	0	0	0	0	0	0	0	0	0	0	0	1	0	0
Rolland, David, San Jose	.214	100	299	41	64	88	16	1	2	23	2	5	3	9	47	0	85	16	7
Russ, Kevin, Reno°	.197	40	127	10	25	39	3	1	3	12	1	4	0	0	13	0	56	3	1
Samuels, Roger, Fresno°	.000	27	1	1	0	0	0	0	0	0	1	0	0	0	1	0	1	0	0
Savarino, William, Modesto°	.279	122	448	66	125	180	25	3	8	78	9	2	6	4	56	4	74	5	5
Sconiers, Daryl, Bakersfield	.313	98	336	46	105	155	19	2	9	49	3	0	3	1	52	3	64	15	7
Scott, Timothy, Bakersfield	.000	7	3	0	0	0	0	0	0	0	0	1	0	0	0	0	2	0	0
Seay, Mark, San Jose°	.089	30	56	2	5	5	0	0	0	2	0	0	2	0	11	0	31	3	1
Senne, Timothy, Visalia†	.265	76	211	29	56	81	10	0	5	31	2	7	5	0	35	1	54	2	6
Sheehy, Mark, Bakersfield	.667	2	3	1	2	2	0	0	0	0	0	0	0	0	0	0	1	0	0
Sheffield, Gary, Stockton	.277	129	469	84	130	210	23	3	17	103	14	6	6	8	81	8	48	25	15
Sheridan, Michael, San Bernardino°...	.000	3	3	0	0	0	0	0	0	0	0	0	0	0	0	0	1	0	0
Shinholster, Vincent, SB†	.280	55	125	25	35	50	5	2	2	25	1	0	0	8	15	1	23	1	1
Siler, Michael, Bakersfield	.000	28	8	1	0	0	0	0	0	0	0	2	0	0	1	0	2	0	0
Simonson, Robert, Stockton	.229	77	249	31	57	76	10	0	3	23	6	1	1	6	30	1	70	10	4
Sims, Timothy, San Jose	.169	24	77	7	13	13	0	0	0	3	0	0	1	0	17	0	24	3	1
Skurla, John, Fresno°	.276	129	456	77	126	201	25	10	10	91	11	2	3	2	66	4	99	15	13
Slominski, Richard, Salinas	.256	12	43	2	11	13	2	0	0	3	0	0	0	0	0	0	8	0	0
Smith, Bryan, Bakersfield	.000	8	1	0	0	0	0	0	0	0	0	0	0	0	0	0	1	0	0
Smith, Todd, San Jose†	.135	50	133	13	18	27	3	3	0	8	0	1	1	3	15	0	61	3	4
Sorrento, Paul, Palm Springs°	.224	114	370	66	83	125	14	2	8	45	2	0	3	3	78	7	95	1	2
Spagnuolo, Joseph, Bakersfield	.333	11	36	4	12	18	3	0	1	6	1	1	1	0	7	0	5	2	1
Springer, Gary, San Jose†	.231	21	78	18	18	24	3	0	1	7	0	1	0	1	15	2	13	2	1
Stearns, Donald, San Bernardino†	.184	48	152	18	28	48	4	2	4	12	1	0	0	2	14	2	53	15	4
Steen, Scott, San Bernardino	.083	9	24	4	2	2	0	0	0	1	0	0	0	0	5	0	10	0	0
Stein, John, Bakersfield°	.250	30	8	2	2	3	1	0	0	0	0	0	0	0	3	0	1	0	0
Stevens, Lee, Palm Springs°	.244	140	532	82	130	220	29	2	19	97	8	0	4	4	61	5	117	1	9
Stevens, John, San Bernardino	.333	3	6	1	2	2	0	0	0	1	0	0	0	0	0	0	2	0	0
Stevenson, William, Reno°	.290	111	376	74	109	200	22	3	21	88	7	0	3	3	70	6	92	0	4

Player and Club	Pct.	G.	AB.	R.	H.	TB.	2B.	3B.	HR.	RBI.	GW.	SH.	SF.	HP.	BB.	Int. BB.	SO.	SB.	CS.
Stratton, Drew, Modesto†	.211	89	304	35	64	92	11	1	5	32	2	3	1	4	32	4	83	2	6
Stull, Walter, San Bernardino	.000	29	2	1	0	0	0	0	0	0	0	0	0	0	0	0	2	0	0
Swan, Russell, Fresno°	.000	12	3	0	0	0	0	0	0	0	0	0	0	0	0	0	3	0	0
Tettleton, Mickey, Modesto†	.364	3	11	4	4	11	1	0	2	2	0	0	0	1	4	0	4	0	0
Torricelli, Timothy, Stockton	.224	94	250	35	56	75	10	0	3	39	2	2	4	2	47	1	46	10	6
Towers, Kevin, Reno	.000	47	2	0	0	0	0	0	0	0	0	1	0	0	0	0	0	0	0
Triplett, Antonio, San Bernardino	.317	85	312	40	99	123	12	3	2	37	3	0	2	2	30	2	63	24	10
Uribe, Jorge, Salinas	.258	118	376	54	97	129	10	5	4	24	5	6	1	2	38	0	117	27	14
Van Stone, Paul, Fresno†	.231	17	39	6	9	9	0	0	0	0	0	0	0	8	0	7	0	1
Vizquel, Omar, Salinas	.263	114	407	61	107	135	12	8	0	38	5	6	4	0	57	1	56	25	19
Ward, James, Bakersfield	.298	54	131	30	39	45	1	1	1	23	1	5	0	2	29	0	23	10	2
Wasem, James, Reno	.242	99	335	51	81	105	11	5	1	31	1	2	3	5	58	1	46	22	15
Washington, Glenn, Palm Springs	.180	24	50	6	9	9	0	0	0	3	0	0	0	4	0	21	5	2
Westbrooks, Elanis, Fresno	.259	24	58	8	15	21	2	2	0	3	0	1	0	5	0	10	1	2
White, Michael, Bakersfield°	.273	50	172	28	47	59	7	1	1	20	1	0	0	13	1	22	7	6
Whitfield, Terry, San Bernardino°	.305	21	59	8	18	26	2	0	2	6	1	0	0	1	9	1	6	2	2
Wiley, Craig, Reno†	.268	78	261	38	70	106	9	3	7	42	4	1	3	3	34	4	20	2	2
Williams, Fred, Stockton	.233	136	446	73	104	130	15	1	3	48	5	10	5	10	72	5	114	8	9
Williams, Jaime, Visalia	.280	10	25	4	7	13	3	0	1	3	0	0	0	0	6	1	1
Winters, Daniel, San Jose	.364	3	11	2	4	4	0	0	0	0	0	0	0	1	0	2	0	0
Wood, Brian, Reno°	.000	29	11	0	0	0	0	0	0	0	0	0	1	0	0	0	9	0	0
Yamano, Kazuaki, San Jose°	.245	110	327	43	80	100	6	4	2	17	0	10	3	1	34	0	89	15	11
Yanes, Edward, Visalia	.280	98	314	49	88	139	16	4	9	58	2	5	7	7	55	1	68	5	2
Young, Delwyn, San Bernardino†	.286	89	322	61	92	164	21	3	15	45	4	0	2	1	49	4	60	20	10
Yurtin, Jeffrey, Reno°	.358	61	201	43	72	107	13	2	6	28	4	0	4	1	27	3	35	2	1
Zellner, Joey, Visalia	.249	108	358	70	89	122	17	5	2	30	1	7	2	6	75	1	72	37	17
Zottman, Roger, Palm Springs	.254	23	67	4	17	20	3	0	0	12	1	0	0	7	0	24	0	1

The following pitchers, listed alphabetically by club, with games in parentheses, had no plate appearances, primarily through use of designated hitters:

BAKERSFIELD—Collins, Sherman (3); Farwell, Frederick (6); Noch, Douglas (3); Ray, Jay (21); Roche, Roderick (19); Rowen, Robert (1); Tejeda, Felix (1).

FRESNO—Hogan, Michael (1); Tate, Chuck (11).

MODESTO—Berg, Richard (21); Caraballo, Felix (12); Corsi, James (19); Fingers, Robert (27); Hayes, Christopher (11); Holcomb, Scott (28); Kent, John (49); Law, Joseph (18); Shotkoski, David (8); Tapani, Kevin (24); Veres, David (26); Walton, Bruce (16); Wernig, Patrick (22); Whitney, Jeffrey (22); Williamson, Kevin (34).

PALM SPRINGS—Burcham, Timothy (26); Carballo, Leandro (19); Charland, Colin (27); DiMichele, Frank (38); Eggertsen, Todd (17); Fetters, Michael (19); Heath, Allan (23); Marino, Mark (32); McCaskill, Kirk (2); Moore, Donnie (3); Shull, Michael (28); Spearnock, Michael (30); Vanderwel, William (25); Ward, Daniel (23); Ward, Colby (54).

RENO—Blakely, David (2); Davis, George (1); Estrada, Jay (12); Filippi, James (7); Harrison, Brian (1); Kelly, Patrick (2); Lewis, James (13).

SALINAS—Brinkman, Gregory (23); Burba, David (9); Fortugno, Timothy (46); Gunnarsson, Robert (35); Hull, Jeffrey (45); McClain, Michael (11); McCorkle, David (24); Moore, Richard (33); Snell, David (47); Thomas, Roy (4); Zavaras, Clinton (26).

SAN BERNARDINO—Chamberlain, Craig (11); Filippi, James (23); Greenlee, Robert (10); Hayes, Todd (56); Marrett, Scott (21); McCormack, Ronald (10); Rincon, John (8); Smith, Lawrence (50); Walker, Steven (22); Witt, Stephen (26).

SAN JOSE—Blobaum, Jeffrey (23); Brusstar, Warren (3); Bryan, Frank (16); Collishaw, David (1); de la Torre, Ernesto (7); Feola, Lawrence (10); Gonzalez, Julian (4); Haraguchi, Tetsuya (20); Kane, Douglas (14); Maye, Stephen (7); Moore, Robert (4); Sosa, Elias (3); Vaccaro, Salvatore (3); Watkins, Troy (9); Wheeler, Bradley (10).

STOCKTON—Ambrose, Mark (5); Burris, Ray (2); Castillo, Luis (8); Derksen, Robert (3); Fleming, Keith (51); Frew, Michael (21); Hunter, James (8); Kanwisher, Gary (4); Ludy, John (20); Moore, Sam (16); Moraw, Carl (17); Morris, James (4); Perez, Leonardo (2); Peterek, Jeffrey (17); Peters, Daniel (1); Puig, Edward (27); Sadler, Alan (4); Uribe, Juan (2); Vila, Jesus (6); Watkins, Timothy (25); Wheeler, Bradley (2).

VISALIA—Blakely, David (17); Bronkey, Jeffrey (27); Carrasco, Ernest (13); Casian, Lawrence (18); Cota, Timothy (8); Galloway, Troy (12); Guthrie, Mark (5); Heinle, Dana (25); Lee, Robert (20); O'Connor, Timothy (57); Perry, Jeffrey (14); Pittman, Park (31); Redding, Michael (26); Scanlon, Steven (19); Strube, Robert (33); Walker, Kurt (31); Williams, Jimmy (13).

GRAND SLAM HOME RUNS—Alfredson, McGrew, Mori, Rodriguez, Sheffield, Stevenson, 2 each; J. Bell, Chapman, Clem, Espinoza, Hamilton, Harvey, Hensley, Lanoux, Odle, Savarino, Sconiers, 1 each.

AWARDED FIRST BASE ON CATCHER'S INTERFERENCE—Zellner 2 (Jones, Mora); T. Anderson (Slominski); Burgos (Eccles); Gorski (Pappas); Lopez (Gibree); Mota (Gibree); Pellegrino (Pena); Robinson (Akimoto); Shinholster (Calvert); Simonson (Wiley); Slominski (Jones); Stevenson (Foley).

CLUB FIELDING

Club	Pct.	G.	PO.	A.	E.	DP.	PB.	Club	Pct.	G.	PO.	A.	E.	DP.	PB.
Stockton	.969	142	3752	1497	169	125	34	San Bernardino	.959	142	3703	1473	219	113	43
Modesto	.967	142	3699	1345	174	96	34	Reno	.959	142	3687	1578	223	136	32
Visalia	.962	142	3672	1531	208	120	35	Salinas	.957	142	3697	1477	231	113	45
Palm Springs	.961	142	3732	1550	213	116	47	Bakersfield	.955	143	3719	1574	248	110	34
Fresno	.961	143	3686	1559	212	120	37	San Jose	.949	142	3562	1377	264	111	52

Triple Plays—Fresno, Modesto.

INDIVIDUAL FIELDING
FIRST BASEMEN

°Throws lefthanded.

Player and Club	Pct.	G.	PO.	A.	E.	DP.	Player and Club	Pct.	G.	PO.	A.	E.	DP.
Barry, Fresno	.994	19	142	11	1	9	Cruz, San Bernardino	.968	3	25	5	1	3
Blair, Fresno	1.000	22	165	18	0	12	Duncan, Modesto°	.985	31	243	23	4	18
Borg, Visalia°	.994	72	613	58	4	57	Edwards, San Bernardino	.972	5	35	0	1	3
Brandts, Salinas	.977	42	316	27	8	25	Escalera, Stockton°	.990	38	274	15	3	25
J.D. Brown, Bakersfield	.984	27	237	13	4	13	Espinoza, Palm Springs°	.985	29	236	21	4	19
J.L. Brown, Bakersfield	.846	1	10	1	2	0	E. Gonzalez, San Jose	.941	4	15	1	1	2
Burke, Bakersfield°	.984	25	240	13	4	16	F. Gonzalez, San Jose	.917	4	9	2	1	2
Calvert, Visalia	.981	25	239	17	5	16	Gorski, Modesto	.975	6	34	5	1	2
Canale, Stockton	.994	66	615	33	4	47	Hardgrave, Stockton	1.000	5	43	2	0	3
Chandler, San Jose	.993	18	132	10	1	9	Hartsock, San Bernardino	.977	18	117	8	3	14
Chapman, Bakersfield	.978	36	294	19	7	22	Haruta, San Jose	.971	9	63	5	2	3
Clark, San Bernardino°	1.000	6	58	4	0	7	Harvey, San Bernardino°	.959	22	150	13	7	11
Clem, Salinas	.979	4	40	6	1	2	Henley, Bakersfield	1.000	7	62	5	0	5
Cooper, Reno	.984	113	832	65	15	99	Howitt, Modesto	.984	17	119	10	2	8

FIRST BASEMEN—Continued

Player and Club	Pct.	G.	PO.	A.	E.	DP.	Player and Club	Pct.	G.	PO.	A.	E.	DP.
Jones, Fresno	1.000	2	21	0	0	1	Patterson, San Bernardino	1.000	5	6	1	0	0
Kyander, San Bernardino*	.979	59	396	23	9	28	Pottinger, Stockton	1.000	1	10	0	0	0
Lange, Visalia	.984	21	110	14	2	13	Reitz, San Jose	.957	10	38	6	2	4
Lester, Reno	1.000	2	5	2	0	0	Rinaldi, San Jose	.964	8	71	10	3	8
Lincoln, Stockton	.986	19	136	8	2	8	Robinson, Modesto	.997	48	387	10	1	29
Lopez, Bakersfield	.983	44	368	28	7	26	Rodriguez, Stockton	1.000	4	19	0	0	2
MacArthur, San Bernardino	1.000	3	8	0	0	1	Rolland, San Jose	.946	6	32	3	2	2
Manto, Palm Springs	1.000	3	10	1	0	0	Sconiers, San Jose*	.987	84	633	53	9	55
Masters, Modesto	.984	31	226	21	4	16	Sheridan, San Bernardino	1.000	1	5	1	0	0
McCatty, San Jose	1.000	1	2	0	0	0	Skurla, Fresno*	.983	67	580	59	11	50
McGinnis, Modesto	.969	8	60	2	2	5	Steen, San Bernardino	.982	7	53	2	1	2
McGrew, Stockton	.994	18	151	7	1	21	STEVENS, Palm Springs*	.986	115	1028	66	16	80
Minch, Modesto	.953	15	97	4	5	3	Stevenson, Reno	.982	44	347	25	7	23
Monceratt, Salinas*	.980	102	873	58	19	67	Triplett, San Bernardino	.989	26	163	9	2	12
Moralez, Bak-SB	.979	43	306	20	7	19	Van Stone, Frenso	1.000	5	45	2	0	4
Mori, San Jose*	.989	15	90	4	1	15	Ward, Bakersfield	1.000	1	1	0	0	0
Mueller, Visalia*	.908	23	184	15	4	12	Williams, Stockton	1.000	1	2	0	0	0
Nakamura, San Jose	1.000	1	11	0	0	0	Yanes, Visalia	.969	8	58	4	2	3
Nelson, Fresno	.981	34	276	29	6	34							

Triple Play—Skurla.

SECOND BASEMEN

Player and Club	Pct.	G.	PO.	A.	E.	DP.	Player and Club	Pct.	G.	PO.	A.	E.	DP.
Akimomo, San Jose	.944	13	12	22	2	5	Murray, Salinas	.963	89	156	266	16	39
Alfonzo, Palm Springs	1.000	6	13	16	0	4	Nakamura, San Jose	.893	22	29	46	9	8
Anderson, Bakersfield	.926	25	41	47	7	10	Peguero, Modesto	.963	127	242	354	23	67
Aragon, Visalia	.970	87	173	247	13	46	Pellegrino, Reno	1.000	6	14	13	0	2
Baham, San Bernardino	.984	30	58	63	2	7	Perry, San Jose	.857	4	6	6	2	0
Barry, Fresno	1.000	1	1	0	0	0	Pinelli, Bakersfield	.958	44	59	101	7	15
Blair, Fresno	.911	9	19	22	4	5	Pottinger, Stockton	1.000	1	2	2	0	1
BROCKI, San Bernardino	.972	120	227	300	15	58	Pust, Visalia	.963	8	16	10	1	3
Burgos, San Jose	.930	16	32	21	4	7	Reitz, San Jose	.955	13	20	22	2	2
Carter, Fresno	.966	134	262	362	22	75	Richardson, Visalia	.973	22	27	45	2	10
Finley, Modesto	1.000	1	0	2	0	0	Rolland, San Jose	.968	58	104	140	8	28
F. Gonzalez, San Jose	.909	2	7	3	1	2	Savarino, Modesto	.977	23	29	57	2	4
Grant, Palm Springs	.947	137	286	363	36	78	Senne, Visalia	.944	39	65	86	9	20
Guerrero, Stockton	.969	39	62	93	5	17	Smith, San Jose	1.000	1	2	2	0	0
Haruta, San Jose	1.000	2	4	1	0	0	Spagnuolo, Bakersfield	.946	10	22	31	3	3
Henley, Bakersfield	.959	25	41	52	4	8	Springer, San Jose	.968	21	44	66	4	17
Holcomb, Bakersfield	.984	36	47	74	2	15	Stearns, San Bernardino	.923	14	12	24	3	3
Kleven, Reno	.750	1	1	2	1	0	Torricelli, Stockton	.850	6	6	11	3	1
Krause, Salinas	1.000	4	3	3	0	2	Van Stone, Fresno	1.000	1	1	0	0	0
Kubala, San Jose	.800	3	3	1	1	0	Vizquel, Salinas	1.000	4	9	10	0	1
Larson, Salinas	.955	52	91	140	11	32	Ward, Bakersfield	.958	38	60	124	8	20
Lee, San Jose	.875	4	3	4	1	1	Wasem, Reno	.969	59	127	216	11	45
Lester, Reno	.960	84	150	237	16	42	Wiley, Reno	1.000	1	1	0	0	0
Lincoln, Stockton	1.000	1	3	2	0	2	Williams, Stockton	.966	105	201	275	17	53
Matta, San Jose	.921	8	21	14	3	4	Young, San Bernardino	.500	3	1	0	1	0
McCatty, San Jose	1.000	1	1	3	0	0	Zellner, Visalia	.909	3	4	6	1	2

Triple Plays—Carter, Peguero.

THIRD BASEMEN

Player and Club	Pct.	G.	PO.	A.	E.	DP.	Player and Club	Pct.	G.	PO.	A.	E.	DP.
Abshier, Palm Springs	.750	1	0	3	1	0	Lester, Reno	.667	2	1	1	1	0
Alfonzo, Palm Springs	.769	4	2	8	3	0	Lincoln, Stockton	.944	7	4	13	1	1
Aragon, Visalia	1.000	4	1	1	0	0	Mancini, San Jose	.889	26	23	41	8	5
Baham, San Bernardino	.964	34	25	56	3	7	MacArthur, San Bernardino	.625	3	1	4	3	0
Barry, Fresno	1.000	2	1	6	0	1	Manto, Palm Springs	.899	111	83	245	37	16
Bell, Palm Springs	.750	6	5	4	3	0	Masters, Modesto	1.000	3	2	2	0	0
Bishop, San Bernardino	.915	20	25	29	5	3	McCatty, San Jose	.500	3	1	1	2	0
Blair, Fresno	.921	32	16	66	7	2	McGinnis, Modesto	.944	11	6	11	1	1
Blankenship, Modesto	.816	14	8	23	7	0	Minch, Modesto	.790	31	16	33	13	3
Brandts, Salinas	.896	61	55	100	18	8	Moore, San Jose	1.000	3	2	2	0	1
Brocki, San Bernardino	.750	3	2	1	1	1	Moralez, Bak-SB	.871	17	9	18	4	0
Burgos, San Jose	.862	19	10	15	4	2	Murray, Salinas	1.000	1	1	0	0	0
Carter, San Bernardino	.921	13	11	24	3	4	Nakamura, San Jose	.867	44	25	53	12	0
Clark, Stockton	.886	106	81	144	29	14	Pellegrino, Reno	.883	106	89	145	31	12
Colbert, Fresno	.901	113	86	225	34	22	Perry, San Jose	1.000	1	1	1	0	0
Cron, Palm Springs	.910	26	21	60	8	4	Pottinger, Stockton	.886	14	16	15	4	4
Cruz, San Bernardino	.833	16	15	30	9	3	Pust, Visalia	.000	1	0	0	1	0
Diaz, Salinas	.851	52	45	86	23	6	Reitz, San Jose	.850	19	8	26	6	2
Finley, Modesto	.915	30	28	47	7	2	Rolland, San Jose	.852	14	7	16	4	1
E. Gonzalez, San Jose	.788	36	26	37	17	2	Savarino, Modesto	.878	41	34	52	12	1
F. Gonzalez, San Jose	.750	1	1	2	1	0	Senne, Visalia	.938	21	15	30	3	4
Gorski, Modesto	.894	30	19	40	7	2	Shinholster, San Bernardino	.894	33	24	52	9	6
Guerrero, Stockton	1.000	2	2	1	0	0	Smith, San Jose	1.000	1	0	1	0	0
Hansen, Bakersfield	.859	114	77	198	45	13	Stearns, San Bernardino	.750	3	2	7	3	1
Harper, San Jose	.615	5	3	5	5	0	Torricelli, Stockton	.875	20	7	28	5	6
Haruta, San Jose	1.000	2	1	0	0	0	Triplett, San Bernardino	.923	22	9	39	4	1
Henley, Bakersfield	.911	30	24	48	7	3	Van Stone, Fresno	.600	3	1	5	4	0
Jones, Fresno	.667	1	1	1	1	1	Ward, Bakersfield	.500	2	0	2	2	0
Krause, Salinas	.915	33	19	56	7	1	Wasem, Reno	1.000	5	3	5	0	0
Kubala, San Jose	.875	4	3	4	1	0	Williams, Stockton	.944	7	7	10	1	0
Lange, Visalia	.882	20	13	17	4	1	Young, San Bernardino	.909	6	3	7	1	0
LANOUX, Visalia	.929	119	85	228	24	22	Yurtin, Reno	.918	37	31	59	8	7
Larson, Salinas	.500	2	0	3	3	0							

Triple Plays—Colbert, Finley.

SHORTSTOPS

Player and Club	Pct.	G.	PO.	A.	E.	DP.
Abshier, Palm Springs	.941	4	4	12	1	2
Alfonzo, Palm Springs	.950	4	8	11	1	1
Anderson, Bakersfield	.769	3	4	6	3	1
Aragon, Visalia	.938	37	59	93	10	13
Baham, San Bernardino	.937	78	134	194	22	37
Barry, Fresno	.918	78	108	194	27	43
Barton, San Jose	.968	67	136	198	11	44
Bell, Bakersfield	.926	134	235	431	53	71
Benjamin, Fresno	.930	63	89	188	21	41
Bilello, San Jose	1.000	1	1	2	0	0
Blair, Fresno	.839	12	10	16	5	2
Blankenship, Modesto	.929	3	6	7	1	2
BORDICK, Modesto	.968	131	216	305	17	53
Burgos, San Jose	.886	30	43	58	13	8
Clark, Stockton	.929	5	4	9	1	0
Cruz, San Bernardino	.933	71	99	181	20	30
Diaz, Salinas	.957	5	4	18	1	1
Erickson, San Jose	1.000	1	1	1	0	1
Gilbert, Visalia	.918	82	122	214	30	37
Gorski, Modesto	.667	1	2	2	2	0
Guerrero, Stockton	.933	7	12	16	2	1
Krause, Salinas	.917	29	35	76	10	18
Kubala, San Jose	.818	3	5	4	2	3
Larson, San Bernardino	1.000	4	4	6	0	2
Lester, Reno	.833	2	6	4	2	1
LeVasseur, Reno	.915	103	195	290	45	58
Lincoln, Stockton	.927	9	10	28	3	2
MacArthur, San Bernardino	1.000	1	0	1	0	0
Mancini, San Jose	1.000	1	2	1	0	1
Matta, San Jose	.917	2	3	8	1	1
Nakamura, San Jose	.857	4	2	4	1	1
Nunez, Palm Springs	.945	136	237	387	36	57
Peguero, Modesto	.931	10	11	16	2	3
Pellegrino, Reno	.929	18	33	46	6	14
Perry, San Jose	.708	6	8	9	7	1
Pottinger, Stockton	1.000	1	0	2	0	1
Pust, Visalia	.972	23	26	44	2	10
Rolland, San Jose	.931	15	19	35	4	7
Savarino, Modesto	1.000	1	0	1	0	0
Senne, Visalia	.923	11	9	15	2	3
Sheffield, Stockton	.937	129	235	345	39	77
Shinholster, San Bernardino	1.000	2	2	0	0	0
Sims, San Jose	.890	24	42	55	12	10
Spagnuolo, Bakersfield	.667	1	0	2	1	0
Van Stone, Fresno	.667	2	1	1	1	0
Vizquel, Salinas	.948	109	72	285	25	54
Ward, Bakersfield	.971	9	9	24	1	5
Wasem, Salinas	.968	28	44	78	4	13
Williams, Stockton	.909	2	4	6	1	0
Young, San Bernardino	.600	1	1	2	2	0

Triple Play—Bordick.

OUTFIELDERS

Player and Club	Pct.	G.	PO.	A.	E.	DP.
Abshier, Palm Springs	1.000	1	1	0	0	0
Alfredson, Palm Springs	1.000	49	77	10	0	1
Anderson, Palm Springs	.987	49	74	4	1	0
Azar, Salinas	1.000	17	23	0	0	0
Barton, San Jose	1.000	1	3	0	0	0
Battaglia, San Bernardino	.963	51	76	3	3	3
Bernardo, Salinas	.963	68	98	5	4	1
Blackwell, Visalia	.964	16	25	2	1	1
Blankenship, Modesto	1.000	6	12	0	0	0
Borg, Visalia*	.667	3	4	0	2	0
J. L. Brown, Bakersfield	1.000	5	3	0	0	0
R. Brown, Stockton	.990	54	100	2	1	1
Bruzik, Salinas	.971	21	32	2	1	1
Burgos, San Jose	1.000	1	1	0	0	0
Carter, San Bernardino	.966	30	28	0	1	0
Clark, San Jose	1.000	13	27	0	0	0
Clem, Salinas	.969	84	114	9	4	2
Combs, San Bernardino	1.000	12	8	0	0	0
Conner, Fresno	.966	113	141	2	5	0
H. Davis, Fresno	.972	107	235	8	7	2
K. Davis, Visalia*	.975	112	188	9	5	2
Dewolf, Stockton*	1.000	3	7	0	0	0
Duncan, Modesto	1.000	1	1	0	0	0
Eccleston, Salinas*	.946	55	83	4	5	1
Edwards, Salinas*	.991	60	108	4	1	0
Escalera, Stockton*	.974	71	105	6	3	3
Fazzini, Bakersfield	.974	29	37	1	1	0
Foley, Salinas	1.000	2	3	0	0	0
Gavin, Modesto	.944	49	67	1	4	0
E. Gonzalez, San Jose	.909	9	10	0	1	0
F. Gonzalez, San Jose	.800	2	4	0	1	0
Gorski, Modesto	1.000	5	9	2	0	0
Gould, Modesto	.975	87	153	4	4	1
Gray, Reno	.984	98	171	8	3	1
Grunhard, Palm Springs*	.944	106	186	16	12	2
HAMILTON, Stockton	.996	122	221	8	1	2
Hansen, Bakersfield	1.000	1	2	0	0	0
Harper, San Jose	1.000	3	4	0	0	0
Hartsock, San Bernardino	.979	71	88	6	2	2
Henley, Bakersfield	.938	9	15	0	1	0
Holmes, San Bernardino	.727	11	7	1	3	0
Howitt, Modesto	.975	88	144	13	4	6
Huth, San Bernardino	.957	22	40	4	2	2
Iannini, Modesto*	1.000	24	40	0	0	0
Jacas, Visalia	.955	41	61	3	3	0
Jones, Stockton	.985	38	65	1	1	0
Kamei, San Jose*	1.000	2	1	0	0	0
Kating, Bakersfield	.973	125	177	6	5	0
Kemp, Salinas*	.895	12	17	0	2	0
Kirby, Bakersfield	.950	104	213	13	12	2
Larson, San Bernardino	1.000	2	2	1	0	0
Law, San Bernardino*	1.000	25	43	0	0	0
Lee, San Jose	.914	87	157	13	16	1
Lincoln, Stockton	1.000	6	2	1	0	0
Locklear, San Jose	.969	19	28	3	1	0
Malone, San Bernardino*	.667	2	2	0	1	0
Mangham, Bakersfield	.927	56	73	3	6	1
McCray, Reno	.974	114	251	13	7	2
McNealy, San Jose	.962	31	69	6	3	0
Meyer, San Jose	1.000	1	1	0	0	0
Meyers, Visalia	.947	46	53	1	3	0
L. Miller, San Jose	1.000	3	2	1	0	0
T. Miller, Fresno	.935	48	85	2	6	1
Milner, SB-PS*	.981	51	99	3	2	2
Monceratt, Salinas*	.500	7	3	0	3	0
Monico, Stockton	.994	102	143	10	1	1
Montano, Stockton*	1.000	3	1	0	0	0
Moore, San Jose	.955	10	19	2	1	0
Moralez, San Bernardino	1.000	5	4	0	0	0
Morgan, Visalia*	.948	74	122	6	7	1
Mori, San Jose*	.956	63	125	6	6	0
Morrison, San Bernardino	.961	90	134	15	6	1
Mota, Bakersfield	.948	85	124	7	8	0
Nalls, Palm Springs	.980	31	45	3	1	0
Nash, Fresno	.934	45	54	3	4	0
J. Nelson, Modesto	.983	117	233	5	4	0
R. Nelson, Fresno	.972	60	97	6	3	1
Newson, Reno*	.890	48	60	5	8	1
Nieporte, Reno	1.000	3	9	1	0	1
Odle, San Bernardino-Reno	.951	129	184	12	10	3
Penigar, Palm Springs	.973	49	100	7	3	3
Perry, San Jose	1.000	1	2	0	0	0
Pettis, San Jose	.980	15	48	1	1	0
Polli, San Jose	1.000	23	40	3	0	1
Pottinger, Stockton	.984	34	60	2	1	0
Rinaldi, San Jose	1.000	1	1	0	0	0
Rivera, Reno	.957	14	20	2	1	1
Rolland, San Jose	.955	18	18	3	1	0
Russ, Reno*	.895	40	51	0	6	0
Seay, San Jose*	.900	26	44	1	5	1
Senne, Visalia	1.000	2	1	0	0	0
Sheehy, Bakersfield	1.000	2	2	0	0	0
Skurla, Fresno*	.981	59	99	4	2	1
Smith, San Jose	.910	47	88	3	9	0
Sorrento, San Bernardino	.971	91	123	10	4	0
Stearns, San Bernardino	.971	26	32	2	1	0
Stevens, Palm Springs*	.714	6	3	2	2	0
Stratton, Modesto	.976	77	114	6	3	2
Torricelli, Stockton	1.000	4	7	1	0	0
Triplett, San Bernardino	.963	117	220	11	9	3
Uribe, Salinas	.958	14	23	0	1	0
Washington, Palm Springs	.938	43	75	1	5	0
Westbrooks, Fresno	1.000	19	26	4	0	0
White, Bakersfield	.917	45	66	0	6	0
Whitfield, San Bernardino	.920	17	22	1	2	0
Williams, Stockton	1.000	18	23	1	0	0
Yamano, San Jose*	.975	104	222	11	6	2
Yanes, Visalia	.961	89	141	5	6	1
Young, San Bernardino	.969	71	120	6	4	0
Yurtin, Reno	.952	14	18	2	1	0
Zellner, Visalia	.954	100	156	11	8	1

CATCHERS

Player and Club	Pct.	G.	PO.	A.	E.	DP.	PB.
Akimoto, San Jose	.972	88	463	59	15	2	31
Battaglia, San Bernardino	.949	6	34	3	2	0	1
Bell, Palm Springs	1.000	9	59	12	0	0	1
Boone, Palm Springs	.955	3	17	4	1	0	0
Britt, Modesto	.981	56	375	31	8	2	1
J. L. Brown, Bakersfield	1.000	14	99	10	0	0	4

CATCHERS—Continued

Player and Club	Pct.	G.	PO.	A.	E.	DP.	PB.
Cabrera, San Bernardino	.974	61	363	47	11	4	12
Calvert, Visalia	.971	12	85	14	3	1	5
Carter, San Bernardino	1.000	4	3	2	0	0	0
Chandler, San Jose	1.000	1	1	0	0	0	1
Christman, San Jose	1.000	3	7	1	0	0	2
Eccles, Visalia	.985	99	685	93	12	7	17
Edwards, San Bernardino	.990	15	91	10	1	1	1
Firova, Salinas	1.000	23	170	21	0	2	7
Foley, Salinas	.974	71	481	52	14	6	19
Gibree, Salinas	.976	44	342	20	9	4	15
Goldstein, Visalia	.970	43	196	33	7	5	13
E. Gonzalez, San Jose	1.000	1	1	0	0	0	0
F. Gonzalez, San Jose	.985	32	164	27	3	1	6
Harper, San Jose	1.000	2	14	7	0	1	1
Hernandez, Bakersfield	.963	30	181	26	8	5	4
Jones, Fresno	.986	65	446	57	7	2	17
Kmak, Fresno	.989	45	323	35	4	1	14
LOPEZ, Bakersfield	.989	89	560	57	7	6	25
Masters, Modesto	.975	16	101	16	3	1	2
McAnany, Palm Springs	.933	3	24	4	2	0	0
McCatty, San Jose	.933	2	12	2	1	0	0
McGinnis, Modesto	.988	11	71	8	1	0	1
McGrew, Stockton	.991	63	392	52	4	5	15
Minch, Modesto	.985	19	127	8	2	2	2
Mons, Bakersfield	.977	7	40	2	1	0	1
Moore, San Jose	.978	20	116	17	3	0	4
Mora, Bakersfield	.990	14	90	11	1	0	0
Nieporte, Reno	.985	75	462	64	8	10	23
Pappas, Palm Springs	.988	116	775	82	10	4	37
Patterson, San Bernardino	.983	86	540	82	11	8	29
Pena, Fresno	.974	42	254	46	8	2	6
Reitz, San Jose	.975	8	36	3	1	0	6
Rinaldi, San Jose	1.000	3	12	0	0	0	1
Rodriguez, Stockton	.991	40	293	30	3	0	9
Savarino, Modesto	.991	56	374	54	4	5	18
Sheridan, San Bernardino	1.000	2	4	0	0	0	0
Slominski, Salinas	.973	12	93	16	3	2	4
Stevenson, Reno	1.000	4	27	7	0	1	0
Tettleton, Modesto	1.000	1	5	0	0	0	0
Torricelli, Stockton	.982	63	366	69	8	6	10
Wiley, Reno	.983	70	498	83	10	5	9
Williams, Visalia	.986	10	62	8	1	0	0
Winters, San Jose	1.000	3	22	2	0	0	0
Zellner, Visalia	1.000	1	1	0	0	0	0
Zottneck, Palm Springs	.993	22	115	22	1	1	9

PITCHERS

Player and Club	Pct.	G.	PO.	A.	E.	DP.
Akimoto, San Jose	1.000	1	0	1	0	0
Ambrose, Stockton	.875	5	1	6	1	0
Barton, San Jose	1.000	1	0	1	0	0
Bell, Palm Springs	1.000	2	0	1	0	0
Berg, Modesto	.933	21	3	11	1	2
Bilello, San Jose	.857	7	1	5	1	0
Blakley, Visalia-Reno	.800	19	0	4	1	0
Blobaum, San Jose	1.000	23	1	12	0	0
Bond, Reno*	1.000	5	0	5	0	0
Bonilla, Fresno*	1.000	36	9	23	0	4
Brinkman, Salinas	.865	23	10	22	5	0
Bronkey, Visalia	1.000	27	2	7	0	1
Brooks, Bakersfield	.902	47	14	23	4	2
Brusstar, San Jose	1.000	3	0	1	0	1
Bryan, San Jose	1.000	16	0	4	0	0
Burcham, Palm Springs	.956	26	9	34	2	2
Burba, Salinas	.950	9	4	15	1	0
Burris, Stockton	1.000	2	0	1	0	0
Caraballo, Modesto	1.000	12	0	3	0	0
Carballo, Palm Springs	.900	19	1	8	1	0
Carrasco, Visalia	.786	13	3	8	3	0
Casian, Visalia*	.974	18	6	31	1	1
Castillo, Stockton	.733	8	2	9	4	0
Chamberlain, San Bernardino	1.000	11	10	18	0	0
Charland, Palm Springs*	.900	27	5	13	2	0
Childers, SB-Reno	1.000	28	6	20	0	3
Collins, Bakersfield	1.000	3	3	0	0	0
Conner, San Jose*	.929	32	12	27	3	3
Corsi, Modesto	1.000	19	1	5	0	0
Cota, Visalia	1.000	8	1	3	0	0
Cox, Bakersfield*	.958	25	5	18	1	1
Darby, Salinas	.733	23	5	6	4	0
de la Torre, San Jose	1.000	7	0	3	0	0
DiMichele, Palm Springs*	.917	38	5	6	1	0
Dominguez, Fresno	.852	46	4	19	4	2
Eggertsen, Palm Springs	.852	17	7	16	4	0
Erickson, San Jose	.935	29	8	21	2	2
Estrada, Reno	.750	12	1	2	1	0
Farwell, Bakersfield*	1.000	6	1	1	0	0
Feola, San Jose*	.571	10	0	4	3	0
Ferraro, Reno*	.895	39	3	14	2	1
Fetters, Palm Springs	.885	19	8	15	3	1
Filippi, SB-Reno	.947	30	13	23	2	1
Fingers, Modesto	.714	27	3	2	2	0
Fitzpatrick, Stockton	1.000	37	1	20	0	0
Fleming, Stockton	1.000	51	11	20	0	0
Fortugno, Salinas*	.917	46	7	4	1	0
Frew, Stockton	.957	21	4	18	1	1
Galloway, Visalia*	.722	12	1	12	5	0
Gastelum, Bakersfield	.000	2	0	0	1	0
J. Gonzalez, San Jose	1.000	4	3	3	0	0
Greenlee, San Bernardino*	.750	10	1	2	1	0
Gunnarsson, Salinas*	.846	35	5	6	2	0
Guthrie, Visalia*	1.000	4	0	2	0	0
Guzman, Bakersfield	.905	22	5	14	2	2
Haraguchi, San Jose	.900	20	3	6	1	0
Hartley, Bakersfield	.917	33	3	8	1	1
Harvey, San Bernardino*	.875	27	8	20	4	1
C. Hayes, Modesto	1.000	11	7	6	0	0
T. Hayes, San Bernardino	.762	55	2	14	5	2
Heath, Palm Springs*	1.000	22	2	8	0	0
Heinle, Visalia	.917	25	2	20	2	2
Heredia, Visalia	1.000	11	2	11	0	0
Holcomb, Modesto*	.926	28	5	20	2	1
Howitt, Modesto	1.000	2	1	0	0	0
Hull, Salinas	.917	45	2	9	1	1
Hunter, Stockton	1.000	8	0	16	0	0
Kamei, San Jose*	.955	28	7	35	2	5
Kane, San Jose	.889	14	2	6	1	0
Kanwisher, Stockton	1.000	4	0	1	0	0
Kent, Modesto	.920	49	6	17	2	0
Kolovitz, Salinas	.926	30	7	18	2	0
Kroll, Bakersfield	.955	43	7	14	1	1
Kubala, San Jose	.800	11	0	4	1	0
Law, Modesto	.905	18	2	17	2	0
H. Lee, San Jose	1.000	1	1	0	0	0
R. Lee, Visalia	.667	20	3	1	2	0
Lewis, Reno	.818	13	3	6	2	0
Loubier, Reno	1.000	13	2	9	0	0
Ludy, Reno	1.000	20	8	16	0	1
Malone, San Bernardino*	.862	52	3	22	4	1
Marino, Palm Springs	.857	32	1	11	2	0
Marrett, San Bernardino	.867	21	4	9	2	0
Marx, Reno	1.000	9	3	4	0	0
Maye, San Jose	1.000	6	0	2	0	0
McCaskill, Palm Springs	1.000	2	1	1	0	0
McCatty, San Jose	.923	24	9	15	2	2
McClain, Salinas	.941	11	0	16	1	1
McCorkle, Salinas	.957	24	18	27	2	1
McCormack, San Bernardino	.857	10	2	4	1	1
McCoy, Fresno*	.875	28	8	20	4	0
Meagher, Reno-Fresno	.963	27	16	10	1	0
Meier, Fresno	1.000	13	6	5	0	1
Messier, Fresno*	.897	24	9	26	4	1
Mills, Reno	.950	54	4	15	1	1
Montano, Stockton	.958	43	3	20	1	2
D. Moore, Palm Springs	1.000	3	1	0	0	0
Ri. Moore, San Jose	1.000	33	6	18	0	3
Ro. Moore, San Jose	.750	4	1	2	1	0
S. Moore, Stockton	.846	16	4	7	2	0
Moraw, Stockton	.850	17	5	12	3	2
D. Morris, Fresno	1.000	27	2	4	0	0
J. Morris, Stockton*	.750	4	1	2	1	0
Munoz, Bakersfield*	.946	52	9	26	2	1
Nabekawa, San Jose	.944	32	3	14	1	2
Nelson, Salinas	.769	17	5	15	6	1
Noch, Bakersfield	1.000	3	0	2	0	0
Nolte, Reno*	.929	11	2	11	1	0
O'Connor, Visalia*	1.000	57	5	16	0	0
Olker, San Jose	.920	17	4	19	3	2
Osaka, San Jose	1.000	34	3	6	0	0
Perez, Stockton	1.000	2	0	1	0	0
Perry, Visalia	.917	14	1	10	1	0
Peterek, Stockton	.926	17	4	21	2	4
Peters, Stockton	1.000	1	0	1	0	0
Pilkington, Fresno*	1.000	35	8	12	0	2
Pittman, Stockton	.800	31	14	22	9	1
Pitz, Bakersfield	.943	30	18	32	3	2
Plesac, Reno	.897	29	14	21	4	2
Puig, Stockton*	.948	27	9	46	3	4
Quinzer, Reno	.864	36	7	12	3	0
Redding, Visalia	.912	26	14	17	3	0
Reichle, Reno	1.000	4	0	2	0	0
Reitz, San Jose	1.000	6	0	1	0	0
Rincon, San Bernardino	1.000	8	2	4	0	0
Roberts, Reno*	.882	17	2	13	2	1
Roche, Bakersfield	1.000	17	2	1	0	0
Rodgers, Fresno	.941	26	14	18	2	1
Sadler, Stockton	.667	4	0	2	1	0
Samuels, Fresno	.500	27	2	2	4	0

PITCHERS—Continued

Player and Club	Pct.	G.	PO.	A.	E.	DP.	Player and Club	Pct.	G.	PO.	A.	E.	DP.
Scanlon, Visalia	.917	19	4	7	1	1	Vanderwel, Palm Springs	.750	25	7	17	8	1
Scott, Bakersfield	1.000	7	3	8	0	0	Veres, Modesto	.848	26	14	25	7	2
Shinholster, San Bernardino	.951	14	6	10	1	0	Vila, Stockton	1.000	6	4	6	0	1
Shotkoski, Modesto	.750	8	0	3	1	0	K. Walker, Visalia	1.000	31	4	5	0	0
Shull, Palm Springs	.938	28	2	13	1	1	S. Walker, San Bernardino	.964	22	11	16	1	0
Siler, Bakersfield	.977	28	15	28	1	2	Walton, Modesto	.923	16	10	14	2	0
B. Smith, Bakersfield	.800	8	0	4	1	0	D. Ward, Bakersfield	1.000	23	7	5	0	0
L. Smith, San Bernardino	.957	50	19	26	2	2	R. C. Ward, Palm Springs	.941	54	3	13	1	0
Snell, Salinas	.867	47	8	18	4	1	Wasem, Reno	1.000	3	1	1	0	0
Sosa, San Jose	1.000	3	1	0	0	0	Ti. Watkins, Stockton	1.000	25	1	14	0	2
Spearnock, Palm Springs°	.923	30	2	10	1	0	Tr. Watkins, San Jose	.500	9	0	1	1	0
Stein, Bakersfield	.912	30	10	21	3	3	Wernig, Modesto°	.714	22	0	5	2	0
Strube, Visalia°	.931	33	8	19	2	3	Wheeler, SJ-Sto°	1.000	12	0	9	0	1
Stull, San Bernardino	.889	27	4	12	2	0	WHITNEY, Modesto	1.000	22	14	21	0	1
Swan, Fresno°	.947	12	8	10	1	2	Williams, Visalia°	.917	13	3	19	2	0
Tapani, Modesto	.957	24	9	35	2	1	Williamson, Modesto	.905	34	9	10	2	3
Tate, Fresno	1.000	11	3	2	0	0	Witt, San Bernardino	1.000	26	0	7	0	0
Towers, Reno	.960	47	8	16	1	0	Wood, Reno	.880	29	15	29	6	3
Vaccaro, San Jose°	1.000	3	0	1	0	0	Zavaras, Salinas	.821	26	6	17	5	0

Triple Play—Wernig.

The following players do not have any recorded accepted chances at the positions indicated; therefore, are not listed in the fielding averages for those particular positions: Akimoto, 3b, of; Barton, 3b; Bilello, 3b; Blankenship, 2b; Bruzik, p; Collishaw, p; Combs, 3b; Cooper, 3b; Cruz, p; Davis, p; Derksen, p; Finley, p; Gavin, p; Goldstein, of, p; Harrison, p; T. Hayes, of; Henley, ss, p; Hogan, p; Holcomb, 1b; Kelly, p; Kyander, p; Lanoux, p; Lee, ss; Mancini, of; McGrew, p; Mori, p; Nakamura, of; S. Perry, p; Pinelli, of; Ray, p; Reitz, p; Rinaldi, 2b, 3b; Rowen, p; Sconiers, p; Senne, p; Simonson, of; T. Smith, p; Steen, 3b; Stratton, 3b; Tejeda, p; Thomas, p; Torricelli, ss; Triplett, ss; Uribe, p; Yamano, p; Yurtin, p.

CLUB PITCHING

Club	ERA.	G.	CG.	ShO.	Sv.	IP.	H.	R.	ER.	HR.	HB.	BB.	Int. BB.	SO.	WP.	Bk.
Stockton	2.98	142	24	12	38	1250.2	1029	537	414	47	45	629	13	1010	100	5
Salinas	3.47	142	16	11	41	1232.1	1044	620	475	54	55	621	30	1037	114	5
Fresno	3.55	143	21	9	44	1228.2	1135	603	484	83	35	556	17	1008	99	5
Visalia	3.63	142	16	9	25	1224.0	1138	619	493	66	60	670	30	1025	121	8
Modesto	3.79	142	21	8	41	1233.0	1060	613	519	87	55	599	25	1019	124	1
Bakersfield	3.88	143	25	7	33	1239.2	1248	663	534	73	40	514	34	938	108	13
San Bernardino	4.04	142	25	8	30	1234.1	1126	721	555	104	66	722	17	999	140	18
Palm Springs	4.25	142	16	8	31	1244.0	1212	750	587	45	64	721	13	963	147	7
Reno	4.43	142	14	6	42	1229.0	1250	774	605	71	53	728	16	945	131	12
San Jose	4.65	142	49	6	6	1187.1	1332	816	613	55	46	637	37	792	134	8

PITCHERS' RECORDS
(Leading Qualifiers for Earned-Run Average Leadership — 114 or More Innings)

°Throws lefthanded.

Pitcher—Club	W.	L.	Pct.	ERA.	G.	GS.	CG.	GF.	ShO.	Sv.	IP.	H.	R.	ER.	HR.	HB.	BB.	Int. BB.	SO.	WP.
Snell, Salinas	5	4	.556	1.96	47	5	1	20	0	3	119.1	105	45	26	3	11	48	4	74	13
Peterek, Stockton	11	3	.786	2.02	17	17	5	0	1	0	129.1	101	43	29	3	1	52	1	105	7
Kamei, San Jose°	10	14	.417	2.42	28	26	16	0	3	0	201.0	184	89	54	7	2	90	4	187	12
McCorkle, Salinas	10	7	.588	2.59	24	23	6	0	3	0	152.2	140	66	44	6	5	41	5	91	0
Bonilla, Fresno°	12	8	.600	2.83	36	12	1	18	1	4	120.2	117	50	38	9	2	41	2	102	8
Law, Modesto	10	1	.909	2.88	18	18	5	0	2	0	118.2	87	45	38	11	4	40	1	123	1
McCatty, San Jose	8	13	.381	2.95	24	23	13	0	2	0	174.0	153	79	57	3	4	78	0	133	16
L. Smith, San Bernardino°	10	8	.556	2.96	50	5	0	19	0	4	152.0	129	65	50	8	3	71	2	113	12
Filippi, 23 S.B.-7 Reno	13	9	.591	3.11	30	24	4	2	1	0	165.1	122	81	57	17	5	104	4	114	8
Burcham, Fresno	17	6	.739	3.11	26	25	5	0	2	0	185.1	184	79	64	5	5	86	1	128	20
Pitz, Bakersfield	17	6	.739	3.11	30	29	8	0	1	0	205.1	198	92	71	11	8	52	2	141	15

Departmental Leaders: G—O'Connor, 57; W—Burcham, Pitz, 17; L—Kamei, 14; Pct.—Law, .909; GS—Pittman, Pitz, 29; CG—Kamei, 16; GF—Mills, 50; ShO—Kamei, McCorkle, Puig, 3; Sv.—Mills, 26; IP—Pitz, 205.1; H—Pitz, 198; R—Wood, 107; ER—Charland, 88; HR—Filippi, 17; HB—Snell, Wood, 11; BB—Pittman, 138; IBB—O'Connor, 11; SO—Pittman, 198; WP—Plesac, Veres, 29.

(All Pitchers—Listed Alphabetically)

Pitcher—Club	W.	L.	Pct.	ERA.	G.	GS.	CG.	GF.	ShO.	Sv.	IP.	H.	R.	ER.	HR.	HB.	BB.	Int. BB.	SO.	WP.
Akimoto, San Jose	0	0	.000	27.00	1	0	0	0	0	0	0.1	1	1	1	0	0	2	0	0	1
Ambrose, Stockton	3	1	.750	3.99	5	5	0	0	0	0	29.1	27	14	13	1	0	17	1	29	3
Barton, San Jose	0	0	.000	.000	1	0	0	1	0	0	2.0	2	0	0	0	0	1	0	0	0
Bell, Palm Springs	0	0	.000	4.50	2	0	0	2	0	0	4.0	5	2	2	0	0	3	0	2	0
Berg, Modesto	3	3	.500	4.24	21	2	0	11	0	1	51.0	45	29	24	2	4	37	2	38	12
Biello, San Jose	1	4	.200	3.34	7	4	2	2	0	0	35.0	32	15	13	2	1	10	1	22	4
Blakley, 17 Vis.-2 Reno	1	0	1.000	8.69	19	1	0	8	0	0	29.0	38	33	28	9	9	27	0	20	2
Blobaum, San Jose	2	6	.250	6.16	23	5	2	5	0	0	49.2	67	38	34	1	3	23	2	30	8
Bond, Reno°	1	2	.333	10.38	5	5	0	0	0	0	21.2	34	28	25	0	1	17	0	19	3
Bonilla, Fresno°	12	8	.600	2.83	36	12	1	18	1	4	120.2	117	50	38	9	2	41	2	102	8
Brinkman, Salinas	9	9	.500	3.35	23	22	0	0	0	0	131.2	126	73	49	8	7	50	1	88	11
Bronkey, Visalia	2	5	.286	3.82	27	0	0	20	0	5	35.1	26	21	15	2	6	32	6	31	5
Brooks, Bakersfield	7	8	.467	4.16	47	6	0	16	0	4	97.1	99	55	45	7	7	47	7	67	7
Brusstar, San Jose	0	1	.000	20.77	3	2	0	0	0	0	4.1	14	12	10	0	1	3	0	1	2
Bruzik, San Jose	0	0	.000	.000	1	0	0	1	0	0	1.0	1	0	0	0	0	0	0	0	0
Bryan, San Jose	1	4	.200	5.74	16	2	0	6	0	0	31.1	45	22	20	2	2	24	3	17	7
Burba, Salinas	1	6	.143	4.61	9	9	0	0	0	0	54.2	53	31	28	3	2	29	0	46	3
Burcham, Palm Springs	17	6	.739	3.11	26	25	5	0	2	0	185.1	184	79	64	5	5	86	1	128	20
Burris, Stockton	2	0	1.000	0.00	2	2	0	0	0	0	12.1	3	0	0	0	0	5	0	9	0
Caraballo, Modesto	2	0	1.000	0.96	12	0	0	5	0	1	28.0	19	4	3	1	0	7	1	22	2
Carballo, Palm Springs	2	1	.667	6.02	19	0	0	9	0	0	40.1	34	29	27	3	8	14	0	15	2
Carrasco, Visalia	4	4	.500	4.59	13	11	0	0	0	0	64.2	62	38	33	5	5	23	0	40	4
Casian, Visalia°	10	3	.769	2.51	18	15	3	1	2	0	97.0	89	35	27	3	7	49	0	96	7
Castillo, Stockton	5	1	.833	3.48	8	8	2	0	1	0	51.2	53	23	20	5	2	16	0	46	3
Chamberlain, San Bernardino	6	4	.600	2.43	11	11	5	0	2	0	85.1	63	33	23	3	4	39	0	65	9
Charland, Palm Springs°	6	12	.333	5.38	27	27	6	0	1	0	147.1	159	100	88	10	6	87	0	150	13

Pitcher—Club	W.	L.	Pct.	ERA.	G.	GS.	CG.	GF.	ShO.	Sv.	IP.	H.	R.	ER.	HR.	HB.	BB.	Int. BB.	SO.	WP.
Childers, 7 S.B.-21 Reno	13	2	.867	3.27	28	16	6	6	1	1	137.2	131	61	50	4	5	67	1	94	9
Collins, Bakersfield	2	1	.667	3.06	3	3	0	0	0	0	17.2	9	7	6	2	3	8	0	19	1
Collishaw, San Jose	0	1	.000	4.50	1	0	0	1	0	0	2.0	1	1	1	1	0	0	0	1	0
Conner, San Jose*	2	11	.154	4.32	32	11	7	12	0	2	108.1	135	74	52	4	3	40	7	68	13
Corsi, Modesto	3	1	.750	3.60	19	0	0	10	0	6	30.0	23	16	12	1	1	10	1	45	4
Cota, Visalia	0	3	.000	1.56	8	0	0	2	0	1	17.1	12	10	3	2	0	5	0	10	3
Cox, Bakersfield*	10	8	.556	4.53	25	22	3	0	1	0	137.0	145	83	69	11	0	56	3	102	11
Cruz, San Bernardino	0	0	.000	0.00	3	0	0	3	0	0	4.0	3	0	0	0	2	0	5	0
Darby, Salinas	5	6	.455	4.53	23	5	0	8	0	1	55.2	50	37	28	2	3	32	5	52	10
Davis, Reno	0	0	.000	3.60	1	1	0	0	0	0	5.0	2	2	2	0	0	6	0	5	0
de la Torre, San Jose	0	1	.000	3.60	7	0	0	3	0	0	10.0	9	4	4	1	0	6	1	2	2
Derksen, Stockton	1	0	1.000	1.59	3	1	0	2	0	0	11.1	9	6	2	0	3	5	0	9	1
DiMichele, Palm Springs*	6	9	.400	4.79	38	13	1	11	0	1	97.2	105	74	52	3	6	65	0	73	10
Dominguez, Fresno	4	6	.400	2.62	46	0	0	32	0	16	89.1	70	43	26	3	2	49	4	75	15
Eggertsen, Palm Springs*	4	6	.400	4.27	17	17	1	0	0	0	90.2	101	59	43	3	7	45	0	50	13
Erickson, San Jose	4	11	.267	3.18	29	18	4	10	1	2	141.2	149	78	50	4	1	50	3	93	11
Estrada, Reno	2	0	1.000	2.78	12	0	0	5	0	1	35.2	37	17	11	2	1	16	1	18	7
Farwell, Bakersfield*	1	0	1.000	0.00	6	0	0	1	0	0	8.0	5	0	0	0	1	5	0	13	1
Feola, San Jose*	1	3	.250	6.35	10	4	0	1	0	1	28.1	33	25	20	1	4	15	0	17	5
Ferraro, Reno*	5	5	.500	6.49	39	3	0	13	0	0	97.0	116	81	70	9	4	59	2	75	5
Fetters, Palm Springs	9	7	.563	3.57	19	19	2	0	0	0	116.0	106	62	46	2	6	73	0	105	22
Filippi, 23 S.B.-7 Reno	13	9	.591	3.10	30	24	4	2	1	0	165.1	122	81	57	17	5	104	4	114	8
Fingers, Modesto	2	0	1.000	2.96	27	0	0	11	0	3	54.2	47	21	18	6	3	16	0	37	7
Finley, Modesto	0	0	.000	4.50	1	0	0	1	0	0	4.0	6	2	2	0	0	0	0	1	0
Fitzpatrick, Stockton	6	2	.750	2.53	37	0	0	18	0	2	85.1	67	34	24	2	3	55	3	67	11
Fleming, Stockton	6	7	.462	2.04	51	1	0	38	0	16	92.2	57	27	21	0	4	37	0	89	4
Fortugno, Salinas*	8	2	.800	2.80	46	4	1	17	1	6	93.1	43	36	29	1	3	84	1	141	19
Frew, Stockton	7	6	.538	3.77	21	18	1	1	1	0	107.1	99	56	45	4	2	54	2	98	9
Galloway, Visalia*	4	7	.364	4.63	12	12	2	0	0	0	72.0	87	40	37	4	0	24	0	41	7
Gastelum, Bakersfield	1	0	1.000	9.00	2	0	0	0	0	0	3.0	1	3	3	0	0	8	0	4	0
Gavin, Modesto	0	0	.000	18.00	2	0	0	1	0	0	1.0	1	2	2	0	0	5	0	0	1
Goldstein, Visalia	0	0	.000		1	0	0	0	0	0	0.0	2	2	2	1	0	0	0	0	0
Gonzalez, San Jose	0	3	.000	5.96	4	4	1	0	0	0	22.2	28	23	15	0	4	24	2	12	6
Greenlee, San Bernardino*	0	2	.000	14.92	10	2	0	5	0	0	12.2	14	27	21	2	5	32	0	8	12
Gunnarsson, Salinas*	4	3	.571	2.29	35	1	1	17	1	8	63.0	46	18	16	4	0	17	1	57	2
Guthrie, Visalia*	2	1	.667	4.50	4	1	0	1	0	0	12.0	10	7	6	0	0	5	1	9	2
Guzman, Bakersfield	5	6	.455	4.75	22	21	0	0	0	0	110.0	106	71	58	4	1	84	0	113	19
Haraguchi, San Jose	0	12	.000	8.95	20	13	4	0	0	0	63.1	90	79	63	3	4	51	3	32	9
Harrison, Reno*	0	0	.000	7.36	1	1	0	0	0	0	3.2	6	5	3	0	0	5	0	2	0
Hartley, Bakersfield	5	4	.556	2.57	33	0	0	27	0	14	56.0	44	19	16	4	4	24	5	72	7
Harvey, San Bernardino*	11	12	.478	3.79	27	27	8	0	0	0	180.2	171	99	76	12	3	65	0	149	9
C. Hayes, Modesto	5	4	.556	3.50	11	6	1	3	0	0	54.0	47	29	21	5	3	28	0	55	2
T. Hayes, San Bernardino	9	1	.900	2.84	55	0	0	37	0	11	79.1	59	32	25	7	6	35	4	86	6
Heath, Palm Springs*	0	2	.000	6.18	22	1	0	10	0	0	43.2	53	39	30	1	1	41	1	37	8
Heinle, Visalia	1	1	.500	3.45	25	1	1	8	0	1	60.0	54	27	23	1	1	27	1	23	2
Henley, Bakersfield	0	0	.000	0.00	1	0	0	1	0	0	1.0	1	0	0	0	1	0	0	0	0
Heredia, Fresno	5	3	.625	2.90	11	11	5	0	2	0	80.2	62	28	26	8	0	23	1	60	2
Hogan, Fresno	0	0	.000	0.00	1	0	0	1	0	0	4.0	2	0	0	0	0	1	0	1	0
Holcomb, Modesto*	12	6	.667	3.38	28	27	1	0	0	0	151.2	138	64	57	13	7	86	1	111	11
Howitt, Modesto	0	0	.000	1.80	2	0	0	2	0	0	5.0	7	1	1	0	0	3	0	3	1
Hull, Salinas	4	6	.400	2.17	45	4	0	34	0	16	74.2	45	25	18	4	5	30	3	91	5
Hunter, Stockton	6	1	.857	2.45	8	8	0	0	0	0	51.1	39	16	14	1	5	20	0	44	2
Kamei, San Jose*	10	14	.417	2.42	28	26	16	0	3	0	201.0	184	89	54	7	2	90	4	187	12
Kane, San Jose	0	1	.000	2.32	14	0	0	7	0	0	31.0	27	18	8	2	0	21	1	26	2
Kanwisher, Stockton	1	0	1.000	8.53	4	2	0	1	0	1	12.2	17	12	12	2	0	14	0	13	0
Kelly, Reno	0	0	.000	0.00	1	0	0	1	0	0	0.1	0	0	0	0	0	0	0	1	0
Kent, Modesto	1	6	.143	2.27	49	0	0	47	0	24	79.1	48	33	20	3	7	35	3	60	10
Kolovitz, Salinas	5	7	.417	4.23	30	21	3	4	0	0	144.2	142	80	68	6	3	64	3	106	6
Kroll, Bakersfield	2	3	.400	4.58	43	0	0	13	0	1	76.2	98	55	39	6	1	23	5	46	6
Kubala, San Jose	1	7	.125	7.43	11	10	1	1	0	0	53.1	65	47	44	8	3	23	0	23	1
Kyander, San Bernardino*	0	0	.000	9.00	1	0	0	1	0	0	1.0	1	1	1	0	0	0	0	1	0
Lanoux, Visalia	0	0	.000	0.00	1	0	0	1	0	0	1.0	1	0	0	0	0	0	0	2	0
Law, Modesto	10	1	.909	2.88	18	18	5	0	2	0	118.2	87	45	38	11	4	40	1	123	1
H. Lee, San Jose	0	0	.000	0.00	1	0	0	0	0	0	2.0	1	2	0	0	1	0	1	0
R. Lee, San Jose	2	3	.400	5.17	20	5	0	5	0	0	55.2	60	38	32	3	1	39	0	58	5
Lewis, Reno	2	2	.500	6.14	13	2	1	3	1	0	29.1	34	26	20	3	1	21	0	28	2
Loubier, Reno	2	2	.500	4.15	13	4	0	4	0	1	34.2	34	22	16	0	1	19	2	27	7
Ludy, Stockton	7	3	.700	1.60	20	10	2	8	0	3	90.0	72	26	16	3	3	15	0	52	5
Malone, San Bernardino*	4	4	.500	2.08	52	4	0	36	0	14	108.1	83	36	25	5	4	69	4	130	5
Marino, Palm Springs	1	2	.333	6.75	32	0	0	10	0	0	66.2	76	63	50	3	6	47	0	53	5
Marrett, San Bernardino	2	5	.286	5.62	21	11	1	4	0	0	81.2	88	57	51	9	2	44	1	39	2
Marx, Reno	1	2	.333	5.71	9	9	0	0	0	0	41.0	49	33	26	6	1	23	0	30	5
Maye, San Jose	0	0	.000	3.21	6	0	0	1	0	0	14.0	15	6	5	1	0	4	0	10	2
McCaskill, Palm Springs	2	0	1.000	0.00	2	2	0	0	0	0	10.0	4	1	0	0	0	3	0	7	0
McCatty, San Jose	8	13	.381	2.95	24	23	13	0	2	0	174.0	153	79	57	3	4	78	0	133	16
McClain, Salinas	1	3	.250	2.91	11	6	1	3	0	0	52.2	47	25	17	4	1	29	3	12	0
McCorkle, Salinas	10	7	.588	2.59	24	23	6	0	3	0	152.2	140	66	44	6	5	41	5	91	0
McCormack, San Bernardino	2	1	.667	6.59	10	6	0	1	0	1	28.2	37	30	21	4	2	22	1	22	11
McCoy, Fresno*	14	9	.609	3.97	28	28	6	0	2	0	181.1	176	91	80	14	5	88	1	165	13
McGrew, Stockton	0	0	.000	0.00	1	0	0	1	0	0	1.0	2	1	0	0	0	0	0	1	0
Meagher, 3 Reno-24 Fresno	6	5	.545	3.30	27	19	5	3	0	0	133.2	122	60	49	4	10	41	0	99	10
Meier, Fresno	3	2	.600	3.65	13	3	0	2	0	1	49.1	45	22	20	4	0	18	0	26	4
Messier, Fresno*	10	7	.588	4.25	24	23	2	0	1	0	131.1	128	72	62	11	3	77	0	97	16
Mills, Reno	4	6	.400	2.39	54	0	0	50	0	26	83.0	64	38	22	1	1	44	2	57	8
Montano, Stockton*	6	3	.667	3.21	43	3	0	23	0	7	89.2	87	40	32	2	2	47	1	54	8
D. Moore, Palm Springs	0	0	.000	0.00	3	0	0	1	0	1	5.0	5	0	0	0	0	4	0	4	0
Ri. Moore, Salinas	2	6	.250	4.65	33	0	0	21	0	6	62.0	59	36	32	5	3	22	4	51	6
Ro. Moore, San Jose	2	2	.500	5.68	4	4	0	0	0	0	25.1	25	17	16	4	2	16	1	17	5
S. Moore, Stockton	4	5	.444	4.58	16	14	1	1	0	0	78.2	58	48	40	6	2	78	0	71	8
Moraw, Stockton	7	5	.583	3.58	17	17	2	0	2	0	103.0	76	54	41	2	3	69	0	80	19
Mori, San Jose*	0	0	.000	18.00	1	0	0	1	0	0	1.0	2	2	2	0	0	0	0	0	0
D. Morris, Fresno	3	1	.750	3.50	27	0	0	25	0	11	36.0	32	15	14	3	0	10	2	31	1

Pitcher—Club	W.	L.	Pct.	ERA.	G.	GS.	CG.	GF.	ShO.	Sv.	IP.	H.	R.	ER.	HR.	HB.	BB.	Int. BB.	SO.	WP.
J. Morris, Stockton*	1	0	1.000	0.75	4	0	0	0	0	0	12.0	6	5	1	0	0	12	0	9	0
Munoz, Bakersfield*	8	7	.533	3.74	52	12	2	23	0	8	118.0	125	68	49	5	0	43	3	80	6
Nabekawa, San Jose	1	5	.167	5.62	32	5	1	6	0	0	65.2	83	54	41	3	5	43	3	36	5
Nelson, Salinas	3	7	.300	5.74	17	16	1	0	0	0	80.0	80	61	51	2	4	71	0	43	17
Noch, Bakersfield	1	0	1.000	2.63	3	2	1	1	0	0	13.2	9	5	4	1	0	6	0	9	0
Nolte, Reno*	3	4	.429	4.36	11	11	1	0	0	0	64.0	76	38	31	4	1	24	0	47	2
O'Connor, Visalia*	3	6	.333	2.24	57	0	0	38	0	9	88.1	77	27	22	3	1	41	11	61	8
Olker, Fresno*	7	6	.538	3.11	17	17	2	0	0	0	107.0	98	45	37	4	1	36	1	97	4
Osaka, San Jose	0	7	.000	8.61	34	8	0	17	0	0	61.2	90	80	59	3	5	62	3	35	15
Perez, Stockton	0	0	.000	8.31	2	0	0	1	0	1	4.1	2	4	4	0	0	6	0	5	0
J. Perry, Visalia	5	6	.455	4.66	14	9	0	1	0	0	63.2	75	38	33	2	6	32	2	51	12
S. Perry, San Jose	0	0	.000	......	1	0	0	0	0	0	0.0	2	3	3	0	0	1	0	0	0
Peterek, Stockton	11	3	.786	2.02	17	17	5	0	1	0	129.1	101	43	29	3	1	52	1	105	7
Peters, Stockton	0	0	.000	9.00	1	0	0	0	0	0	3.0	4	3	3	1	0	1	0	1	0
Pilkington, Fresno*	3	4	.429	3.77	35	2	0	14	0	0	74.0	75	37	31	6	3	52	1	49	8
Pittman, Visalia	4	12	.250	3.28	31	29	1	0	0	0	161.2	109	81	59	4	2	138	1	198	24
Pitz, Bakersfield	17	6	.739	3.11	30	29	8	0	1	0	205.1	198	92	71	11	8	52	2	141	15
Plesac, Reno	7	4	.636	5.48	29	21	2	1	1	0	118.1	122	91	72	7	5	101	1	70	29
Puig, Stockton*	11	8	.579	3.29	27	23	7	0	3	0	167.0	161	78	61	10	9	64	3	123	11
Quinzer, Reno	9	10	.474	3.58	36	17	1	14	0	4	145.2	151	79	58	10	4	54	0	118	8
Ray, Bakersfield	3	5	.375	4.00	21	0	0	14	0	4	27.0	29	13	12	3	1	8	4	29	4
Redding, Visalia	8	9	.471	4.49	26	25	3	0	1	0	142.1	157	81	71	12	8	66	1	83	15
Reichle, Reno	0	3	.000	13.86	4	3	0	0	0	0	12.1	24	19	19	2	0	16	0	6	4
Reitz, San Jose	0	0	.000	5.91	6	0	0	5	0	0	10.2	13	8	7	0	0	1	0	2	2
Rincon, San Bernardino	3	3	.500	5.79	8	3	2	0	0	0	28.0	33	19	18	4	1	11	0	18	4
Roberts, Reno*	4	8	.333	3.09	17	12	2	1	1	0	84.1	92	41	29	4	5	51	0	68	8
Roche, Bakersfield	0	0	.000	8.34	17	0	0	13	0	0	22.2	32	22	21	6	1	21	0	17	7
Rodgers, Fresno	7	7	.500	3.79	26	16	0	3	0	1	97.1	90	61	41	8	6	58	2	76	10
Rowen, Bakersfield*	0	0	.000	18.00	1	0	0	0	0	0	1.0	2	2	2	0	0	1	0	1	1
Sadler, Stockton	0	0	.000	6.60	4	4	0	0	0	0	15.0	21	13	11	2	0	12	0	8	2
Samuels, Fresno*	1	2	.333	0.84	27	0	0	18	0	9	42.2	29	11	4	1	1	18	3	64	2
Scanlon, Visalia	1	1	.500	3.63	19	1	0	9	0	0	39.2	51	22	16	3	0	18	2	22	2
Sconiers, San Jose*	0	0	.000	13.50	1	0	0	1	0	0	0.2	1	1	1	0	0	1	0	0	0
Scott, Bakersfield	2	3	.400	4.45	7	5	1	1	0	0	32.1	33	19	16	2	1	10	1	29	2
Senne, Visalia	0	1	.000	6.75	1	0	0	1	0	0	1.1	2	2	1	0	0	3	0	0	1
Shinholster, San Bernardino	4	5	.444	4.54	14	12	2	1	0	0	73.1	72	56	37	10	7	34	1	47	6
Shotkoski, Modesto	1	4	.200	15.00	8	3	0	2	0	1	18.0	29	30	30	3	4	22	0	20	4
Shull, Palm Springs	4	5	.444	2.06	28	0	0	23	0	7	65.2	41	22	15	3	4	38	4	63	6
Siler, Bakersfield	11	7	.611	3.49	28	26	9	0	2	0	173.0	181	79	67	12	3	44	4	100	5
B. Smith, Bakersfield*	0	2	.000	4.95	8	4	0	2	0	0	20.0	14	14	11	1	1	23	0	17	2
L. Smith, San Bernardino*	10	8	.556	2.96	50	5	0	19	0	4	152.0	129	65	50	8	3	71	2	113	12
T. Smith, San Jose	0	0	.000	......	1	0	0	0	0	0	0.0	0	2	2	0	0	2	0	0	0
Snell, Salinas	5	4	.556	1.96	47	5	1	20	0	3	119.1	105	45	26	3	11	48	4	74	13
Sosa, San Jose	0	1	.000	9.95	3	1	0	0	0	0	6.1	12	8	7	1	2	9	1	2	0
Spearnock, Palm Springs*	5	1	.833	4.67	30	2	0	12	0	3	69.1	69	41	36	6	1	37	0	40	9
Stein, Bakersfield	3	5	.375	3.43	30	13	1	4	0	2	118.0	117	56	45	3	7	51	0	77	14
Strube, Visalia*	9	6	.600	3.90	33	19	5	4	0	0	147.2	135	72	64	7	5	71	1	119	11
Stull, San Bernardino	5	5	.500	5.03	27	14	0	1	0	0	91.1	91	62	51	8	8	76	0	87	17
Swan, Fresno*	6	3	.667	3.80	12	12	0	0	0	0	64.0	54	40	27	5	1	29	0	59	4
Tapani, Modesto	10	7	.588	3.76.	24	24	6	0	1	0	148.1	122	74	62	14	5	60	2	121	21
Tate, Fresno	0	0	.000	11.35	11	0	0	6	0	1	23.0	38	29	29	3	3	17	0	14	2
Tejeda, Bakersfield*	0	0	.000	0.00	1	0	0	1	0	0	2.0	0	0	0	0	0	0	0	2	0
Thomas, Salinas	0	0	.000	0.00	4	0	0	1	0	1	7.1	5	0	0	0	0	3	0	5	0
Towers, Reno	5	8	.385	4.68	47	6	0	26	0	9	109.2	95	72	57	4	8	80	4	116	19
Uribe, Stockton	0	0	.000	10.13	2	1	0	1	0	0	2.2	4	4	3	0	0	7	0	2	2
Vaccaro, San Jose*	0	1	.000	22.09	3	1	0	2	0	0	3.2	10	9	9	1	0	5	0	3	1
Vanderwel, Palm Springs	3	8	.273	4.76	25	25	0	0	0	0	121.0	100	85	64	3	5	105	0	103	16
Veres, Modesto	8	9	.471	4.79	26	26	2	0	0	0	148.1	124	90	79	9	6	108	3	124	29
Vila, Stockton	2	2	.500	2.58	6	6	3	0	0	0	38.1	30	15	11	2	3	16	0	25	0
K. Walker, Visalia	5	2	.714	0.83	31	0	0	27	0	9	54.1	30	12	5	1	2	13	2	80	1
S. Walker, San Bernardino	5	10	.333	4.53	22	20	3	0	2	0	113.1	107	75	57	5	7	85	1	72	28
Walton, Modesto	8	6	.571	2.88	16	16	3	0	1	0	106.1	97	44	34	6	4	27	0	84	2
D. Ward, Palm Springs	3	7	.300	4.27	23	11	1	8	0	1	92.2	96	57	44	2	3	31	0	48	7
R. C. Ward, Palm Springs	7	7	.500	2.64	54	0	0	44	0	18	88.2	74	37	26	1	6	42	7	85	16
Wasem, Reno	0	0	.000	11.25	3	0	0	3	0	0	4.0	7	7	5	0	0	3	0	1	1
Ti. Watkins, Stockton	7	1	.875	1.73	25	2	2	20	1	7	57.1	30	14	11	1	3	26	2	63	5
Tr. Watkins, San Jose	0	0	.000	6.00	9	0	0	2	0	0	12.0	14	10	8	2	0	15	1	5	2
Wernig, Modesto*	1	4	.200	4.99	22	3	0	9	0	1	39.2	40	24	22	3	3	33	4	29	5
Wheeler, 10 SJ-2 Sto*	3	0	1.000	1.21	12	0	0	9	0	1	22.1	23	4	3	0	0	7	1	19	0
Whitney, Modesto	4	5	.444	3.72	22	6	3	10	1	3	87.0	86	38	36	3	1	29	3	54	5
Williams, Visalia*	7	4	.636	2.22	13	13	2	0	0	0	85.0	66	38	21	5	5	62	2	81	10
Williamson, Modesto	9	7	.563	4.83	34	11	0	9	0	1	108.0	94	67	58	7	3	53	4	92	7
Witt, San Bernardino	1	4	.200	7.18	26	8	0	4	0	0	52.2	63	48	42	12	10	47	0	53	10
Wood, Reno	12	7	.632	4.51	29	26	1	1	0	0	167.2	156	107	84	12	11	100	2	145	15
Yamano, San Jose*	0	1	.000	5.00	4	1	0	0	0	0	9.0	10	6	5	0	0	9	0	5	2
Yurtin, Reno	0	0	.000	9.00	1	0	0	1	0	0	1.0	2	1	1	0	0	1	0	0	0
Zavaras, Salinas	7	12	.368	4.45	26	26	2	0	2	0	139.2	102	87	69	6	8	101	0	180	22

BALKS—Filippi, Wood, 4 each; Childers, Erickson, Fortugno, Pitz, Stull, 3 each; Brooks, Eggertsen, Fitzpatrick, Heredia, Kroll, Malone, McCoy, Pittman, Siler, L. Smith, Vanderwel, S. Walker, 2 each; Bilello, Bond, Carrasco, Castillo, Fetters, Galloway, Gunnarsson, Guzman, Harvey, T. Hayes, Kamei, Kent, Ludy, Marino, McCatty, McClain, McCormack, Munoz, Nabekawa, Nolte, Osaka, J. Perry, Puig, Quinzer, Ray, Redding, Reichle, Rincon, Roberts, Rodgers, Scanlon, Sconiers, Shinholster, Spearnock, Stein, Strube, 1 each.

COMBINATION SHUTOUTS—Collins-Munoz, Pitz-Stein, Siler-Hartley, Bakersfield; Messier-Dominguez 2, Bonilla-Dominguez, Fresno; Holcomb-Fingers, Tapani-Berg-Fingers, Veres-Corsi, Modesto; Burcham-C. Ward, Fetters-C. Ward-Shull, McCaskill-Moore-D. Ward, Vanderwel-Carballo, D. Ward-DiMichele-C. Ward, Palm Springs; Filippi-Mills, Quinzer-Mills, Reno; Brinkman-Gunnarsson, Darby-Gunnarsson, Nelson-Darby-Hull, Zavaras-Fortugno-Gunnarsson, Salinas; Chamberlain-Hayes, Harvey-Malone, San Bernardino; Ambrose-Perez, Hunter-Montano, Ludy-Morris-Fleming, Stockton; Casian-Heinle, Pittman-O'Connor, Pittman-Scanlon, Redding-O'Connor-Bronkey, Strube-Heinle-Bronkey, Strube-Walker, Williams-Bronkey, Visalia.

NO-HIT GAMES—Pittman-O'Connor, Visalia, defeated Palm Springs, 1-0, June 1; Collins-Munoz, Bakersfield, defeated San Jose, 4-0 (seven innings), August 12; Fortugno, Salinas, defeated Modesto, 6-0 (seven innings), August 12; Law, Modesto, defeated Stockton, 1-0, August 14.

Carolina League

CLASS A

CHAMPIONSHIP WINNERS IN PREVIOUS YEARS

1945—Danville .681	1961—Wilson .594	1973—Lynchburg .588
1946—Greensboro .599	1962—Durham .636	Winston-Salem‡ .557
Raleigh (2nd)† .563	Wilson .600	1974—Salem .671
1947—Burlington .613	Kinston (2nd)† .593	Salem .582
Raleigh (3rd)† .574	1963—Kinston§ .538	1975—Rocky Mount .667
1948—Raleigh .592	Greensboro§ .590	Rocky Mount .614
Martinsville (2nd)† .570	Wilson (2nd)† .535	1976—Winston-Salem .618
1949—Danville .601	1964—Kinston§ .572	Winston-Salem .551
Burlington (4th)† .500	Winston-Salem§† .590	1977—Lynchburg .591
1950—Winston-Salem° .693	1965—Peninsula§ .597	Peninsula‡ .556
1951—Durham .600	Durham§ .580	1978—Peninsula .696
Wins-Salem (2nd)† .583	Tidewater† .528	Lynchburg‡ .614
1952—Raleigh .581	1966—Kinston§ .547	1979—Winston-Salem a .607
Reidsville (4th)† .536	Winston-Salem§ .586	1980—Peninsula‡ .714
1953—Raleigh .593	Rocky Mount† .533	Durham .600
Danville (2nd)† .572	1967—Durham x (West.) .536	1981—Peninsula .522
1954—Fayetteville° .628	Raleigh (East.) .542	Hagerstown‡ .507
1955—HP-Thomasville .580	1968—Salem (West.) .607	1982—Alexandria‡ .597
Danville (2nd)† .533	Ral-Dur (East.) .597	Durham .588
1956—HP-Thomasville .591	HP-Thom. y (W.) .493	1983—Lynchburg‡ .691
Fayetteville (4th)† .523	1969—Rocky M (East.) .569	Winston-Salem .529
1957—Durham .632	Salem (West.) .542	1984—Lynchburg‡ .645
HP-Thomasville .622	Ral-Dur z (East.) .560	Durham .486
1958—Durham .576	1970—Winston-Salem‡ .586	1985—Lynchburg .679
Burlington (4th)† .511	Burlington .597	Winston-Salem‡ .417
1959—Raleigh .600	1971—Peninsula‡ .647	1986—Hagerstown .655
Wilson (2nd)† .550	Kinston .623	Winston-Salem‡ .594
1960—Greensboro‡ .636	1972—Salem‡ .657	
Burlington .586	Burlington .632	

°Won championship and four-club playoff. †Won four-club playoff. ‡Won split-season playoff. §League was divided into Eastern, Western divisions. xWon eight-club, two-division playoff. yWon eight-club, two-division playoff against Raleigh-Durham. zWon eight-club, two-division playoff against Burlington. aWon both halves of split-season (no playoffs).

STANDING OF CLUBS AT CLOSE OF FIRST HALF, JUNE 17

NORTHERN DIVISION

Club	W.	L.	T.	Pct.	G.B.
Hagerstown (Orioles)	40	30	0	.571	......
Salem (Pirates)	33	36	0	.478	6½
Prince William (Yankees)	33	37	0	.471	7
Lynchburg (Mets)	32	37	0	.464	7½

SOUTHERN DIVISION

Club	W.	L.	T.	Pct.	G.B.
Winston-Salem (Cubs)	41	29	0	.586	......
Peninsula (White Sox)	34	36	0	.486	7
Kinston (Indians)	33	37	0	.471	8
Durham (Braves)	33	37	0	.471	8

STANDING OF CLUBS AT CLOSE OF SECOND HALF, AUGUST 30

NORTHERN DIVISION

Club	W.	L.	T.	Pct.	G.B.
Salem (Pirates)	47	23	0	.671	......
Prince William (Yankees)	33	37	0	.471	14
Hagerstown (Orioles)	32	38	0	.457	15
Lynchburg (Mets)	31	39	0	.443	16

SOUTHERN DIVISION

Club	W.	L.	T.	Pct.	G.B.
Kinston (Indians)	42	28	0	.600	......
Peninsula (White Sox)	32	38	0	.457	10
Durham (Braves)	32	38	0	.457	10
Winston-Salem (Cubs)	31	39	0	.443	11

COMPOSITE STANDING OF CLUBS AT CLOSE OF SEASON, AUGUST 30

Club	Sal.	Kin.	W.S.	Hag.	P.W.	Pen.	Dur.	Lyn.	W.	L.	T.	Pct.	G.B.
Salem (Pirates)	....	13	8	13	13	10	12	11	80	59	0	.576	......
Kinston (Indians)	7	....	12	12	11	13	8	12	75	65	0	.536	5½
Winston-Salem (Cubs)	12	8	....	8	9	14	9	12	72	68	0	.514	8½
Hagerstown (Orioles)	7	8	12	....	9	8	13	15	72	68	0	.514	8½
Prince William (Yankees)	7	9	11	11	....	9	10	9	72	68	0	.471	14½
Peninsula (White Sox)	10	7	6	12	11	....	11	9	66	74	0	.471	14½
Durham (Braves)	8	12	11	7	10	9	....	8	65	75	0	.464	15½
Lynchburg (Mets)	8	8	8	5	11	11	12	....	63	76	0	.453	17

Major League affiliations in parentheses.

Playoffs—Kinston defeated Winston-Salem, two games to none; Salem defeated Hagerstown, two games to none; Salem defeated Kinston, three games to one, to win league championship.

Regular-Season Attendance—Durham, 217,012; Hagerstown, 135,059; Kinston, 68,199; Lynchburg, 88,370; Peninsula, 88,620; Prince William, 105,749; Salem, 111,661; Winston-Salem, 133,263. Total—947,933. Playoffs—10,106. All-Star Game—2631.

Managers—Durham, Brian Snitker; Hagerstown, Glenn Gulliver; Kinston, Mike Hargrove; Lynchburg, John Tamargo; Peninsula, Gil Granger; Prince William, Wally Moon; Salem, Steve Demeter; Winston-Salem, Jay Loviglio.

All-Star Team—1B—Rob Sepanek, Prince William; 2B—Mark Lemke, Durham; 3B—Lou Gomez, Hagerstown; SS—Jim Bullinger, Winston-Salem; OF—Tony Chance, Salem; Alex Smith, Durham; Mark Davis, Peninsula; C—Joe Girardi, Winston-Salem; DH—Casey Webster, Kinston; LHP—Blaine Beatty, Hagerstown; RHP—Dave Miller, Durham; Most Valuable Player—Casey Webster, Kinston; Pitcher of the Year—Blaine Beatty, Hagerstown; Manager of the Year—Mike Hargrove, Kinston.

(Compiled by Howe News Bureau, Boston, Mass.)

CLUB BATTING

Club	Pct.	G.	AB.	R.	OR.	H.	TB.	2B.	3B.	HR.	RBI.	GW.	SH.	SF.	HP.	BB.	Int. BB.	SO.	SB.	CS.	LOB.
Salem	.278	139	4783	771	640	1328	2042	197	35	149	688	67	44	56	42	500	19	902	220	77	994
Hagerstown	.272	140	4762	720	692	1296	1872	217	46	89	656	65	30	50	52	571	25	734	171	75	1048
Prince William	.266	140	4733	734	765	1257	1903	225	26	123	657	60	29	47	38	579	23	865	96	52	1041
Winston-Salem	.264	140	4661	647	736	1229	1730	183	45	76	574	60	58	35	35	507	26	706	188	65	1019
Peninsula	.263	140	4672	683	732	1229	1790	193	40	96	606	60	37	48	54	574	13	873	161	102	1025
Lynchburg	.262	139	4520	670	742	1185	1745	202	44	90	603	55	43	46	46	606	29	898	157	96	1019
Durham	.260	140	4699	647	640	1223	1762	217	26	90	583	60	40	45	44	501	19	768	138	71	1007
Kinston	.256	140	4574	737	662	1172	1748	195	39	101	660	66	23	59	66	737	12	995	180	70	1071

INDIVIDUAL BATTING

(Leading Qualifiers for Batting Championship—378 or More Plate Appearances)

°Bats lefthanded.   †Switch-hitter.

Player and Club	Pct.	G.	AB.	R.	H.	TB.	2B.	3B.	HR.	RBI.	GW.	SH.	SF.	HP.	BB.	Int. BB.	SO.	SB.	CS.
Gomez, Leonardo, Hagerstown	.326	131	466	94	152	251	38	2	19	110	10	1	10	2	95	3	85	6	2
Smith, Alexander, Durham	.323	115	461	82	149	208	27	1	10	68	9	0	6	6	34	3	54	10	7
Chance, Anthony, Salem	.318	133	525	99	167	271	23	6	23	96	15	1	5	10	50	1	104	26	13
Webster, Casey, Kinston	.318	138	485	86	154	251	25	6	20	111	9	0	15	15	78	0	98	5	1
Harper, Milton, Kinston°	.312	135	465	100	145	246	31	5	20	97	13	2	10	3	117	6	69	6	1
Richardson, Timothy, Hagerstown	.309	128	479	86	148	186	14	9	2	61	7	4	4	4	59	1	18	34	13
Sepanek, Robert, Prince William°	.306	139	517	92	158	266	25	4	25	106	11	1	6	2	85	6	99	6	6
Meulens, Hensley, Prince William	.300	116	430	76	129	240	23	2	28	103	8	0	6	9	53	3	124	14	3
Moser, Steven, Salem	.297	135	532	87	158	206	21	3	7	72	4	9	6	7	57	0	49	31	10
Morris, Richard, Durham	.294	100	340	63	100	144	14	0	10	57	2	0	6	7	67	0	69	8	5
Davis, Mark, Peninsula	.294	134	507	91	149	233	24	6	16	72	6	2	5	6	63	2	115	37	11
Wagner, Daniel, Peninsula	.293	138	518	83	152	217	21	4	12	93	10	1	12	6	44	0	83	15	11

Departmental Leaders: G—Sepanek, 139; AB—Rigos, 536; R—Harper, 100; H—Chance, 167; TB—Chance, 271; 2B—Gomez, 38; 3B—T. Richardson, 9; HR—Meulens, 28; RBI—Webster, 111; GWRBI—Chance, 15; SH—Moser, 9; SF—Webster, 15; HP—Webster, 15; BB—Harper, 117; IBB—Gideon, 9; SO—K. Richardson, 130; SB—C. Landrum, 79; CS—Waggoner, 23.

(All Players—Listed Alphabetically)

Player and Club	Pct.	G.	AB.	R.	H.	TB.	2B.	3B.	HR.	RBI.	GW.	SH.	SF.	HP.	BB.	Int. BB.	SO.	SB.	CS.
Akins, Sidney, Durham	.000	30	5	0	0	0	0	0	0	0	0	0	0	0	0	0	1	0	0
Albertson, John, Durham	.000	1	1	0	0	0	0	0	0	0	0	0	0	0	0	0	1	0	0
Alva, John, Durham	.255	111	388	46	99	122	14	3	1	49	1	5	4	0	27	2	36	17	5
Archibald, Jaime, Lynchburg°	.231	49	130	15	30	40	4	0	2	16	0	3	3	1	21	0	21	2	1
Arendas, Daniel, Prince William°	.265	64	204	24	54	71	6	1	3	20	3	1	2	1	12	1	17	2	1
Audain, Miguel, Peninsula	.154	36	91	4	14	14	0	0	0	2	0	0	1	0	10	0	22	2	2
Aviles, Brian, Durham	.111	16	9	0	1	1	0	0	0	1	1	0	0	0	2	0	3	0	0
Bafia, Robert, Winston-Salem	.249	129	473	61	118	209	32	7	15	69	5	0	3	2	47	0	108	11	5
Barringer, Reginald, Salem	.313	75	163	24	51	53	2	0	0	18	3	0	2	3	24	1	13	7	7
Bauer, Peter, Lynchburg	.500	6	2	0	1	1	0	0	0	1	0	4	0	0	0	0	0	0	0
Bautista, Bienvenido, Hagerstown†	.208	76	255	31	53	65	8	2	0	16	1	4	1	0	31	0	54	23	7
Bayer, Christopher, Lynchburg†	.056	27	18	1	1	2	1	0	0	0	0	1	0	1	2	0	10	0	1
Belle, Albert, Kinston	.324	10	37	5	12	23	2	0	3	9	1	0	0	0	8	0	16	0	1
Bellino, Frank, Hagerstown°	.269	114	387	60	104	171	15	5	14	70	9	0	3	2	41	7	33	2	1
Bennett, Keith, Kinston	.221	65	226	32	50	66	6	2	2	15	3	5	3	2	44	0	49	22	10
Billmeyer, Michael, Hagerstown†	.191	13	47	2	9	9	0	0	0	1	0	0	0	0	3	0	7	1	1
Bohlke, Scott, Durham	.194	43	134	7	26	29	3	0	0	13	0	1	2	0	13	0	19	0	3
Bonilla, Juan, Prince William	.308	44	130	26	40	54	11	0	1	19	1	0	3	1	31	0	16	0	0
Braxton, Glen, Peninsula°	.172	35	87	4	15	22	5	1	0	6	1	1	1	0	12	0	33	3	0
Bresnahan, David, Kinston†	.179	9	28	3	5	5	0	0	0	2	0	0	1	0	6	0	7	0	1
Brooks, Desmond, Peninsula°	.233	79	163	21	38	54	7	3	1	20	2	2	2	3	34	2	27	2	8
Brown, Kevin, Durham°	.133	13	15	1	2	2	0	0	0	1	0	1	0	0	1	0	3	0	0
Brown, Kurt, Peninsula	.253	104	344	29	87	120	15	0	6	40	5	3	1	3	24	0	72	0	2
Brunswick, Mark, Lynchburg	.167	16	36	4	6	7	1	0	0	2	0	1	0	0	8	0	8	1	0
Bruske, James, Kinston	.232	123	439	62	102	145	16	3	7	61	8	1	4	12	65	3	118	17	5
Bullinger, James, Winston-Salem	.256	129	437	58	112	157	12	3	9	48	7	5	3	3	50	5	79	3	5
Burke, Kevin, Hagerstown°	.270	14	37	3	10	16	0	0	2	3	1	0	0	0	5	1	6	2	1
Buss, Scott, Kinston	.226	10	31	4	7	9	2	0	0	0	0	0	0	0	5	0	5	1	0
Calvert, Arthur, Prince William	.273	119	411	72	112	187	32	2	13	53	4	2	0	3	18	0	85	9	2
Carpenter, Douglas, Hagerstown	.288	15	66	10	19	25	3	0	1	4	1	0	0	0	7	0	14	3	2
Carrillo, Matias, Salem°	.271	90	284	42	77	118	11	3	8	37	4	0	4	2	19	1	41	15	4
Carter, Frederick, Prince William	.258	36	89	9	23	35	6	0	2	9	4	1	1	2	11	0	20	0	0
Cento, Anthony, Peninsula	.160	17	50	5	8	8	0	0	0	1	0	3	0	1	4	0	15	0	0
Cepeda, Octavio, Salem°	.000	8	2	0	0	0	0	0	0	0	0	0	0	0	0	0	1	0	0
Chance, Anthony, Salem	.318	133	525	99	167	271	23	6	23	96	15	1	5	10	50	1	104	26	13
Ciszkowski, Jeffrey, Lynchburg	.375	22	8	2	3	4	1	0	0	0	0	0	0	0	2	0	2	0	0
Coleman, Dewayne, Winston-Salem	.667	17	3	2	2	3	1	0	0	0	0	0	0	0	0	0	1	0	0
Cook, Jeffrey, Salem	.339	69	298	48	101	121	9	4	1	26	0	4	3	1	26	1	30	39	7
Copp, William, Salem	.059	19	17	1	1	1	0	0	0	1	0	2	0	0	4	0	7	0	0
Criswell, Timothy, Durham	.245	89	278	34	68	88	12	1	2	27	4	7	3	3	20	0	34	2	4
Crowley, Terrence, Hagerstown†	.302	78	291	31	88	101	5	4	0	30	2	4	1	1	21	0	42	8	9
Cruz, Luis, Winston-Salem	.210	82	248	35	52	62	7	0	1	23	6	5	3	0	25	0	38	14	2
Cuevas, Angelo, Lynchburg°	.349	54	195	38	68	87	10	0	3	42	5	1	3	1	31	1	28	5	3
Cuevas, Johnny, Durham	.057	24	70	1	4	6	2	0	0	4	0	1	1	0	7	1	24	1	0
Curtis, Michael, Winston-Salem°	.174	32	23	0	4	4	0	0	0	3	0	5	0	0	5	0	5	0	0
Danek, William, Winston-Salem	.071	13	14	0	1	1	0	0	0	1	0	2	0	0	2	0	4	0	0
Davis, Kevin, Salem	.259	137	486	64	126	207	36	3	13	65	4	4	9	4	30	1	95	12	5
Davis, Mark, Peninsula	.294	134	507	91	149	233	24	6	16	72	6	2	5	6	63	2	115	37	11
DelRosario, Maximo, Durham	.000	41	2	0	0	0	0	0	0	0	0	0	0	0	0	0	2	0	0
Deluca, Kurt, Lynchburg	.340	58	206	32	70	101	12	2	5	22	1	3	2	1	30	1	24	6	9
Dotzler, Michael, Salem°	.260	72	231	34	60	106	16	0	10	36	3	0	1	0	23	5	66	5	5
Dulin, Timothy, Hagerstown	.283	124	446	67	126	168	23	2	5	52	5	3	8	4	49	0	50	10	10
Eave, Gary, Durham	.000	16	8	0	0	0	0	0	0	0	0	0	0	0	0	0	3	0	0
Englett, Todd, Salem	.000	2	1	0	0	0	0	0	0	0	0	0	0	0	0	0	1	0	0
Erickson, Donald, Lynchburg°	.333	12	6	2	2	5	0	0	1	3	1	0	0	0	1	0	6	1	0
Finley, Steven, Hagerstown°	.338	15	65	9	22	32	3	2	1	5	0	0	0	0	1	0	6	7	2

Player and Club	Pct.	G.	AB.	R.	H.	TB.	2B.	3B.	HR.	RBI.	GW.	SH.	SF.	HP.	BB.	Int. BB.	SO.	SB.	CS.
Franchi, Kevin, Salem°	.000	17	2	0	0	0	0	0	0	0	0	0	0	0	0	0	2	0	0
Fredymond, Juan, Durham	.115	28	52	3	6	6	0	0	0	1	0	1	0	0	6	1	17	1	1
Garcia, Cornelio, Peninsula°	.284	77	271	41	77	126	17	7	6	47	9	2	2	2	34	2	63	12	5
Gelatt, David, Lynchburg	.220	105	328	68	72	106	15	2	5	18	0	3	0	1	68	3	76	20	8
Gellinger, Michael, Peninsula†	.270	74	233	26	63	81	10	1	2	19	1	6	1	4	23	1	25	10	7
Gideon, Ronnie, Lynchburg°	.254	113	398	63	101	200	16	4	25	92	10	0	5	3	65	9	108	3	5
Ging, Adam, Lynchburg†	.194	29	103	7	20	26	1	1	1	10	1	0	0	2	4	1	15	1	0
Girardi, Joseph, Winston-Salem	.280	99	364	51	102	151	9	8	8	46	7	2	1	2	33	2	64	9	2
Givens, Brian, Lynchburg	.063	21	16	0	1	1	0	0	0	0	2	0	0	0	0	0	10	0	0
Gomez, Leonardo, Hagerstown	.326	131	466	94	152	251	38	2	19	110	10	1	10	2	95	3	85	6	2
Gonzalez, Eduardo, Prince William	.091	5	11	0	1	1	0	0	0	0	0	0	0	0	0	0	4	0	1
Gonzalez, Fredi, Prince William	.065	16	31	1	2	2	0	0	0	1	0	1	0	2	0	11	0	1
Gooden, Dwight, Lynchburg	.000	1	1	0	0	0	0	0	0	0	0	0	0	0	0	0	0	0	0
Gordon, Kevin, Salem	.000	9	1	0	0	0	0	0	0	0	0	0	0	0	0	0	0	0	0
Grebeck, Craig, Peninsula	.280	104	378	63	106	179	22	3	15	67	5	2	4	1	37	0	62	3	6
Green, John, Winston-Salem	.000	16	2	0	0	0	0	0	0	0	0	0	0	0	0	0	0	0	0
Greene, Jeffry, Peninsula°	.265	114	359	54	95	137	9	6	7	49	2	3	6	4	62	3	55	4	6
Greene, Jeffrey, Durham	.000	55	6	0	0	0	0	0	0	0	0	0	0	1	0	3	0	0
Grimes, Lee, Winston-Salem	.260	92	277	41	72	101	12	1	5	35	2	2	3	4	29	1	34	13	0
Gross, Kip, Lynchburg	.250	16	8	0	2	3	1	0	0	1	0	0	0	0	0	0	1	0	0
Gwinn, Anthony, Prince William	.244	75	209	33	51	72	9	0	4	25	2	1	2	0	27	0	36	4	3
Hannon, Phillip, Winston-Salem†	.357	8	14	2	5	5	0	0	0	3	0	1	0	2	0	0	2	1	0
Harper, Milton, Kinston°	.312	135	465	100	145	246	31	5	20	97	13	2	10	3	117	6	69	6	1
Hatfield, Robert, Salem	.000	27	1	1	0	0	0	0	0	0	1	0	1	0	3	0	1	0	0
Hauradou, Yanko, Prince William	.224	58	147	22	33	50	8	0	3	19	1	1	2	1	14	0	24	4	2
Hayden, Alan, Lynchburg°	.315	65	248	52	78	94	6	5	0	29	2	2	3	1	37	2	25	43	11
Hernandez, Martin, Salem	.000	19	9	0	0	0	0	0	0	0	0	2	0	0	0	0	3	0	0
Hicks, Joseph, Prince William	.250	73	180	20	45	84	9	0	10	30	2	0	2	2	35	1	59	1	1
Higgins, Theodore, Prince William	.255	31	94	13	24	39	5	2	2	20	1	1	0	0	10	0	14	1	2
Hillman, Thomas, Kinston	.172	62	174	23	30	35	3	1	0	6	0	3	1	2	26	0	39	2	1
Hinzo, Thomas, Kinston†	.278	65	266	64	74	87	11	1	0	25	2	0	0	3	32	0	44	49	10
Hirsch, Jeffrey, Winston-Salem†	1.000	27	1	0	1	1	0	0	0	0	0	0	0	0	0	0	0	0	0
Hood, Dennis, Durham	.269	120	438	73	118	184	19	4	13	62	7	3	2	4	51	0	115	32	12
Howard, Christian, Prince William	.240	86	258	35	62	90	11	1	5	27	0	4	1	4	10	0	43	2	2
Iasparro, Donnie, Lynchburg	.000	7	1	0	0	0	0	0	0	0	0	0	0	0	0	0	0	0	0
Iavarone, Gregory, Winston-Salem	.133	9	15	2	2	4	2	0	0	0	0	0	0	0	2	0	3	0	0
Isa, Kelsey, Peninsula†	.196	72	240	33	47	66	7	3	2	19	2	2	2	1	28	1	31	3	7
James, Troy, Lynchburg	.143	54	7	0	1	2	1	0	0	0	0	0	0	0	0	0	4	0	0
Jaster, Scott, Lynchburg	.262	120	428	49	112	161	20	7	5	53	4	3	2	4	39	2	81	22	15
Jelic, Christopher, Lynchburg	.330	71	224	47	74	116	8	5	8	48	2	0	3	0	49	1	30	4	4
Jimenez, Cesar, Durham	.200	30	10	0	2	2	0	0	0	0	0	0	0	0	0	0	3	0	0
Johnson, Dodd, Durham	.282	135	479	62	135	193	24	5	8	65	12	0	3	5	69	0	89	10	2
Jones, David, Durham	.000	27	3	0	0	0	0	0	0	0	0	0	0	0	0	0	1	0	0
Jones, Geary, Lynchburg	.200	34	85	8	17	23	6	0	0	6	1	0	1	0	15	1	26	1	2
Jones, Labarry, Durham°	.283	117	424	72	120	196	23	4	15	52	6	2	1	4	49	0	55	23	10
Jordan, Scott, Kinston	.282	123	447	97	126	196	21	8	11	73	9	3	4	10	78	0	113	37	10
Jundy, Lorin, Lynchburg	.000	6	6	0	0	0	0	0	0	0	0	0	0	0	0	0	4	0	0
Kallevig, Gregory, Winston-Salem	.333	27	3	0	1	1	0	0	0	1	0	0	0	0	0	0	2	0	0
Kazmierczak, William, W-S†	.211	19	19	0	4	4	0	0	0	2	0	2	0	0	3	0	6	0	0
Kent, Lewis, Kinston	.229	81	218	23	50	82	8	0	8	35	1	1	4	6	32	1	67	0	1
Khoury, Scott, Hagerstown°	.268	95	313	57	84	151	21	5	12	62	5	0	2	9	67	4	46	4	1
King, Jeffrey, Salem	.277	90	310	68	86	175	9	1	26	71	2	0	2	1	61	2	88	6	2
Kirk, Timothy, Salem°	.000	37	1	0	0	0	0	0	0	0	0	0	0	0	0	0	1	0	0
Koopmann, Robert, Salem°	.167	12	12	1	2	2	0	0	0	0	0	2	0	0	0	0	1	0	0
Kraemer, Joseph, Winston-Salem°	.000	41	2	0	0	0	0	0	0	0	0	1	0	0	0	0	1	0	0
Kraus, Ralph, Prince William°	.287	126	450	68	129	181	31	3	5	59	4	5	5	1	37	4	61	6	3
Kuld, Peter, Kinston	.183	35	115	12	21	39	4	1	4	15	2	0	0	0	11	0	42	0	3
Lambert, Robert, Prince William	.277	86	328	56	91	120	9	4	4	30	2	1	5	2	50	0	73	16	4
Landrum, Cedric, Winston-Salem°	.282	126	458	82	129	168	13	7	4	49	5	1	4	6	78	3	50	79	18
Landrum, Darryl, Winston-Salem	.179	10	28	3	5	5	0	0	0	0	0	0	0	0	4	0	11	3	1
Lemke, Mark, Durham†	.292	127	489	75	143	237	28	3	20	68	9	4	7	5	54	3	45	10	7
Lewis, John, Winston-Salem°	.288	98	323	59	93	122	11	6	2	36	3	0	1	0	51	1	41	19	6
Liddell, David, Lynchburg	.255	31	102	18	26	44	6	0	4	17	1	1	1	4	7	1	30	1	1
Lilliquist, Derek, Durham°	.222	3	9	2	2	2	0	0	0	0	0	0	0	0	0	0	1	0	0
Lind, Orlando, Salem	.133	11	15	2	2	2	0	0	0	0	0	0	0	0	0	0	3	0	0
Little, Scott, 19 Lyn-82 Sal	.292	101	339	65	99	157	12	5	12	55	12	2	8	1	51	1	61	19	7
Lomastro, Gerardo, Hagerstown	.262	82	282	46	74	126	21	2	9	49	5	0	6	10	21	3	42	1	1
Lombardozzi, Christopher, PW°	.257	102	338	57	87	137	14	3	10	45	5	0	3	2	70	3	48	11	6
Maas, Jason, Prince William	.197	45	117	19	23	29	6	0	0	12	3	0	1	1	19	2	20	4	1
Magallanes, Everardo, Kinston°	.244	58	205	20	50	66	4	3	2	23	3	2	0	1	16	0	18	2	0
Mallinak, Melvin, Hagerstown†	.206	76	233	23	48	61	8	1	1	21	2	4	3	1	19	0	53	4	1
Maloney, Richard, Durham	.247	20	73	7	18	24	4	1	0	6	2	0	0	0	12	1	10	0	1
Martin, Norberto, Peninsula†	.259	41	162	21	42	53	6	1	1	18	0	0	4	1	18	0	19	11	6
Martinez, Ricardo, Prince William	.278	7	18	3	5	5	0	0	0	0	0	1	0	0	0	0	3	0	1
Matas, James, Winston-Salem	.091	29	11	2	1	1	0	0	0	0	0	3	0	0	0	0	7	0	0
Mathews, Edward, Durham	.000	10	5	0	0	0	0	0	0	0	0	0	0	0	0	0	0	0	0
Maysonet, Gregory, Salem	.000	1	1	0	0	0	0	0	0	0	0	0	0	0	0	0	0	0	0
McElroy, Glen, Peninsula	.250	37	100	12	25	28	1	1	0	10	0	1	1	2	13	0	13	0	0
McMorris, Mark, Winston-Salem°	.264	119	444	52	117	168	23	2	8	59	11	0	3	5	34	6	37	1	2
Melendez, Jose, Salem	.000	20	12	0	0	0	0	0	0	0	0	1	0	0	0	0	7	0	0
Melton, Lawrence, Salem	.182	12	11	2	2	2	0	0	0	2	0	1	0	0	0	0	5	0	0
Mercedes, Guillermo, Salem	.000	19	4	0	0	0	0	0	0	0	0	0	0	0	0	0	1	0	0
Mercker, Kent, Durham°	.000	7	1	0	0	0	0	0	0	0	0	0	0	0	0	0	0	0	0
Meulens, Hensley, Prince William	.300	116	430	76	129	240	23	2	28	103	8	0	6	9	53	3	124	14	3
Miller, David, Durham	.345	30	29	5	10	11	1	0	0	5	0	2	0	0	3	0	3	0	0
Miller, Michael, Salem°	.000	2	2	0	0	0	0	0	0	0	0	0	0	0	0	0	1	0	0
Monell, Johnny, Lynchburg†	.328	29	122	20	40	68	13	3	3	17	5	1	1	0	7	1	10	3	1
Morales, William, Prince William	.304	26	46	5	14	17	3	0	0	7	2	0	0	2	0	0	8	0	0
Morris, Richard, Durham	.294	100	340	63	100	144	14	0	10	57	2	0	6	7	67	0	69	8	5
Morrow, Benjamin, Salem	.000	24	4	0	0	0	0	0	0	0	0	0	0	0	0	0	4	0	0
Moser, Steven, Salem	.297	135	532	87	158	206	21	3	7	72	4	9	6	7	57	0	49	31	10
Muratti, Rafael, Salem	.156	32	96	11	15	27	3	0	3	13	1	3	2	0	8	0	22	0	1

Player and Club	Pct.	G.	AB.	R.	H	TB.	2B.	3B.	HR.	RBI.	GW.	SH.	SF.	HP.	BB.	Int. BB.	SO.	SB.	CS.
Newsom, Gary, Durham	.221	93	303	39	67	81	12	1	0	16	0	2	3	4	37	0	25	18	9
Nipper, Michael, Durham	.261	7	23	3	6	12	0	0	2	5	0	0	0	3	1	7	0	0
Oertli, Charles, Winston-Salem	.283	62	205	29	58	73	9	0	2	31	3	2	2	0	18	1	32	2	0
Patterson, Gregg, Winston-Salem°	.111	15	9	0	1	1	0	0	0	1	0	1	0	0	1	0	2	0	0
Paulino, Ernesto, Hagerstown	.246	85	285	30	70	97	12	0	5	34	3	1	5	1	23	1	51	2	2
Perdomo, Felix, Lynchburg	.287	89	286	40	82	124	19	1	7	39	3	1	1	4	29	0	56	7	4
Perez, Hector, Lynchburg°	.278	102	353	57	98	155	19	4	10	54	3	2	3	4	34	3	63	13	7
Pfaff, Robert, Durham	.248	93	355	39	88	136	25	1	7	60	5	1	3	4	15	1	88	0	1
Pittman, Douglas, Salem	.235	73	234	41	55	92	8	1	9	35	6	0	3	1	22	1	51	2	1
Posey, John, Hagerstown	.261	103	349	46	91	140	23	1	8	50	5	0	4	7	43	2	47	3	1
Ramos, John, Prince William	.217	76	235	26	51	65	6	1	2	27	1	3	3	2	28	3	30	8	5
Rauth, Christopher, Lynchburg	.222	28	27	3	6	7	1	0	0	0	0	2	0	0	3	0	2	0	0
Reichard, Clyde, Salem	.667	22	3	1	2	2	0	0	0	0	0	0	0	0	0	0	1	0	0
Reichel, Thomas, Peninsula	.220	17	59	6	13	13	0	0	0	6	1	1	0	1	8	0	5	3	1
Repoz, Craig, Lynchburg	.232	115	358	49	83	121	9	1	9	47	5	1	6	5	65	0	100	13	7
Rice, Cepedia, Salem	.276	52	170	38	47	86	7	1	10	27	1	0	1	2	35	0	71	4	4
Richards, Russell, Durham°	.333	23	18	3	6	13	1	0	2	2	1	3	0	0	1	0	3	0	0
Richardson, Jeffrey, Lynchburg	.048	29	21	3	1	1	0	0	0	0	0	3	0	1	1	0	11	0	0
Richardson, Kerry, Kinston	.240	117	430	55	103	189	24	1	20	87	6	1	4	3	36	0	130	3	4
Richardson, Timothy, Hagerstown	.309	128	479	86	148	186	14	9	2	61	7	4	4	4	59	1	18	34	13
Rigos, John, Salem	.287	129	536	80	154	234	18	7	16	69	8	2	6	5	53	4	67	31	9
Roberts, Norman, Hagerstown	.284	76	250	36	71	111	12	5	6	38	2	6	2	3	31	0	59	17	8
Robles, Gabaliel, Winston-Salem	.125	20	8	0	1	1	0	0	0	1	0	1	0	0	0	0	3	0	0
Roby, Ellis, Durham†	.163	44	86	4	14	17	1	1	0	3	0	3	1	0	10	0	15	1	0
Roca, Gilberto, Salem	.300	54	170	19	51	77	12	1	4	35	4	1	1	3	7	0	22	1	1
Rodriguez, Richard, Lynchburg°	.000	69	1	0	0	0	0	0	0	0	0	0	0	0	1	0	1	0	0
Rohrmeier, Daniel, Peninsula	.329	68	243	43	80	112	13	2	5	34	4	2	3	2	29	0	37	2	3
Roth, Kris, Winston-Salem	.278	27	18	2	5	9	2	1	0	1	0	2	0	0	1	0	8	0	0
Ruskin, Scott, Salem†	.301	23	83	16	25	39	3	1	3	11	1	0	2	0	11	0	20	10	0
Salisbury, James, Durham	.000	12	9	0	0	0	0	0	0	0	0	1	0	0	1	0	3	0	0
Sampen, William, Salem	.053	26	19	1	1	1	0	0	0	1	0	2	0	0	0	0	4	0	0
Scott, Michael, Durham	.000	7	4	1	0	0	0	0	0	0	0	2	0	0	1	0	2	0	0
Scruggs, Ronald, Peninsula°	.226	81	252	44	57	99	13	1	9	34	4	0	1	4	46	2	69	2	6
Sepanek, Robert, Prince William°	.306	139	517	92	158	266	25	4	25	106	11	1	6	2	85	6	99	6	6
Siebert, Richard, Durham	.000	12	4	0	0	0	0	0	0	0	0	0	0	0	0	0	0	0	0
Singley, Joseph, Peninsula	.150	8	20	3	3	7	1	0	1	2	0	0	0	1	0	0	10	0	0
Skeete, Rafael, Hagerstown°	.277	98	364	69	101	123	7	3	3	38	3	3	0	6	35	2	71	39	12
Slocumb, Heath, Winston-Salem	.000	9	2	0	0	0	0	0	0	0	0	1	0	0	0	0	0	0	0
Slowik, Thaddeus, Winston-Salem	.200	49	5	1	1	1	0	0	0	0	0	0	0	0	0	0	0	0	0
Small, Jeffrey, Winston-Salem	.279	119	462	49	129	185	21	4	9	65	6	7	7	2	14	2	61	13	10
Smith, Alexander, Durham	.323	115	461	82	149	208	27	1	10	68	9	0	6	34	3	54	10	7
Smith, Todd, Salem†	.233	41	133	19	31	44	2	1	3	12	1	1	0	2	14	0	35	9	1
Stading, Gregory, Salem	.000	44	3	0	0	0	0	0	0	0	0	1	0	0	0	0	0	0	0
Stevanus, Michael, Salem†	.224	39	98	9	22	25	3	0	0	6	0	2	0	0	8	1	24	4	3
Stevens, Michael, Salem	.227	7	22	2	5	8	0	0	1	4	0	0	0	0	1	0	10	0	0
Stewart, John, Durham°	.000	35	3	0	0	0	0	0	0	0	0	0	0	0	0	0	1	0	0
Strickland, Robert, Winston-Salem°	.273	10	22	3	6	13	1	0	2	5	0	0	0	4	0	9	0	0
Strijek, Randy, Hagerstown	.181	34	94	14	17	25	2	3	0	4	1	0	1	2	13	0	33	3	1
Sutryk, Thomas, Peninsula	.264	90	276	37	73	91	12	0	2	32	3	4	2	9	23	0	38	1	4
Swain, Robert, Kinston	.288	63	208	45	60	76	11	1	1	25	3	2	4	45	1	37	4	5
Toler, Gregory, Prince William	.259	9	27	1	7	7	0	0	0	5	0	0	0	0	0	0	1	0	0
Tresh, Michael, Prince William†	.247	97	344	61	85	116	10	3	5	33	6	6	4	4	54	0	51	7	6
Tullier, Michael, Winston-Salem°	.290	105	317	45	92	132	14	1	8	48	1	2	4	0	59	4	41	6	4
Turgeon, David, Prince William	.288	18	66	6	19	23	1	0	1	5	0	0	1	6	0	13	0	1
Twardoski, Michael, Kinston°	.288	85	267	45	77	106	16	2	3	38	4	0	5	2	73	0	50	3	3
Valera, Alcadio, Lynchburg†	.252	78	202	27	51	66	10	1	1	20	3	3	2	5	14	0	45	0	4
Vargas, Hector, Prince William†	.226	34	53	8	12	12	0	0	0	2	0	1	0	0	5	0	5	1	1
Villanueva, Juan, Lynchburg	.229	100	336	32	77	97	14	3	0	33	3	2	7	5	28	1	62	4	2
Voigt, John, Hagerstown	.111	2	9	0	1	1	0	0	0	1	0	0	0	1	0	4	0	0
Wachs, Thomas, Lynchburg°	.000	17	4	0	0	0	0	0	0	0	0	1	0	0	0	0	4	0	0
Waggoner, Aubrey, Peninsula°	.265	115	426	82	113	172	15	4	12	51	4	4	2	5	87	2	88	52	23
Wagner, Daniel, Peninsula	.293	138	518	83	152	217	21	4	12	93	10	1	12	6	44	0	83	15	11
Walker, Michael, Salem	.250	21	16	1	4	6	2	0	0	4	2	1	0	1	0	2	0	0
Wallace, Timothy, Winston-Salem	.233	78	253	32	59	85	9	4	3	25	2	4	0	5	28	0	28	4	2
Walsh, Edward, Peninsula°	.179	22	56	2	10	12	2	0	0	4	1	0	0	2	8	0	18	1	2
Webster, Casey, Kinston	.318	138	485	86	154	251	25	6	20	111	9	0	15	15	78	0	98	5	1
Weiss, Jeffrey, Durham°	.238	60	160	25	38	47	7	1	0	17	1	0	3	1	19	2	32	5	4
Westbrook, Michael, 15 Lyn-82 Kin°	.200	97	270	45	54	68	4	5	0	12	0	1	2	2	32	0	36	29	9
Wilkins, Dean, Winston-Salem	.200	13	10	2	2	4	0	1	0	2	0	1	0	0	0	0	4	0	0
Williams, Walter, Durham°	.200	6	5	0	1	1	0	0	0	0	0	1	0	0	0	0	2	0	0
Wilmet, Paul, Salem	.000	22	2	0	0	0	0	0	0	0	0	0	0	0	0	0	1	0	0
Wilson, Doyle, Kinston	.225	59	191	18	43	51	8	0	0	22	2	2	3	1	29	1	35	1	3
Woods, Eric, Winston-Salem°	.270	76	211	35	57	60	3	0	0	16	2	6	1	4	26	1	29	13	8
Workman, Michael, Kinston	.169	22	71	2	12	12	0	0	0	7	0	1	1	3	0	13	1	2
Young, Ernest, Hagerstown†	.182	17	44	6	8	13	2	0	1	3	0	0	0	6	1	13	2	0
Zarranz, Fernando, Winston-Salem	.333	15	6	2	2	4	2	0	0	1	0	2	0	0	1	0	3	0	0

The following pitchers, listed alphabetically by club, with games in parentheses, had no plate appearances, primarily through use of designated hitters:

DURHAM—O'Quinn, Steven (1).

HAGERSTOWN—Berry, Dale (6); Beatty, Blaine (13); Borgatti, Michael (27); Bowden, Stephen (34); Burdick, Stacey (1); Carriger, Ricky (43); Cinnella, Douglas (19); Dillard, Gordon (14); Dubois, Brian (27); Ferlenda, Gregory (2); Harnisch, Peter (4); Heath, Allan (14); Hixon, Alan (1); Martinez, Felix (6); Michno, Thomas (14); Palermo, Peter (36); Rowe, Thomas (9); Sanchez, Geraldo (24); Skinner, Michael (2); Talamantez, Gregory (6); Telford, Anthony (2); Thorpe, Paul (13); Walton, Robert (13); Wilson, Wayne (15).

KINSTON—Dillmore, Phillip (25); Farr, Michael (47); Fedor, Francis (14); Ghelfi, Andrew (26); Ghelfi, Anthony (19); Gilles, Mark (30); Grossman, James (9); Kuykendall, Kevin (12); Nichols, Rodney (9); Poehl, Michael (22); Scott, Charles (19); Shamblin, William (39); Soos, Charles (47); Walker, Michael C. (3); Wickander, Kevin (25).

LYNCHBURG—Stiles, William (36); Welborn, Todd (37).

PENINSULA—Brennan, James (13); Carey, William (10); Conley, Virgil (9); Girdner, Troy (5); Hall, Todd (23); Hulstrom, Bryce (34); Kennedy, Bo (15); Kutzler, Jerry (10); Lahrman, Thomas (36); Ollom, Michael (26); Radinsky, Scott (12); Renz, Kevin (47); Reynolds, David (27); Scheer, Ronald (31); Tauken, Daniel (32); Villanueva, Gilbert (11).

PRINCE WILLIAM—Adkins, Steven (21); Balabon, Richard (11); Blum, Brent (28); Brill, Todd (4); Bystrom, Martin (7); Carreno, Amalio (26); Carroll, Christopher (25); Clayton, Royal (9); Clossen, William (9); Dacosta, William (4); Davidson, Robert (21); Figueroa, Fernando (19); Foster, Randy (3); George, Stephen (10); Giron, Ysidro (44); Imes, Rodney (10); Kamienicki, Scott (19); Layana, Timothy (7); Manon, Ramon (23); Mills, Alan (37); Tirado, Aristarco (32); Torres, Ricardo (17); Voeltz, William (7).

SALEM—Adams, Steven (3); Daniel, Clayton (3).

WINSTON-SALEM—Cloninger, Todd (2); Gardner, Jimmie (2).

GRAND SLAM HOME RUNS—Meulens, 3; King, 2; Bafia, Bellino, Cruz, K. Davis, M. Davis, Dulin, Harper, Higgins, Johnson, Morris, Perdomo, Repoz, Roberts, Sepanek, Wallace, 1 each.

AWARDED FIRST BASE ON CATCHER'S INTERFERENCE—Carrillo 3 (Bellino, Ku. Brown, Kent); Posey 3 (Kent, Liddell, Ramos); Rohrmeier 3 (Girardi, Posey, Ramos); Girardi 2 (Liddell, Pittman); King 2 (Pfaff, Ramos); Ku. Brown (Posey); Gelatt (Posey); Hood (Paulino); Jaster (Ku. Brown); Khoury (Pfaff); Repoz (Wilson); Roth (Pittman); Weiss (Ku. Brown).

CLUB FIELDING

Club	Pct.	G.	PO.	A.	E.	DP.	PB.	Club	Pct.	G.	PO.	A.	E.	DP.	PB.
Durham	.972	140	3668	1592	153	122	23	Hagerstown	.962	140	3707	1501	208	124	28
Kinston	.968	140	3671	1600	176	156	31	Lynchburg	.961	139	3549	1547	205	144	20
Winston-Salem	.963	140	3649	1565	202	137	20	Peninsula	.958	140	3660	1538	229	131	21
Salem	.962	139	3703	1494	205	125	16	Prince William	.957	140	3627	1455	229	120	20

Triple Play—Kinston.

INDIVIDUAL FIELDING

*Throws lefthanded.

FIRST BASEMEN

Player and Club	Pct.	G.	PO.	A.	E.	DP.	Player and Club	Pct.	G.	PO.	A.	E.	DP.
Archibald, Lynchburg*	.982	23	202	18	4	9	Perdomo, Lynchburg	1.000	14	81	7	0	13
Bafia, Winston-Salem	.970	18	145	16	5	21	Perez, Lynchburg*	1.000	5	39	4	0	3
Billmeyer, Hagerstown	.925	4	35	2	3	4	Pittman, Salem	.991	14	102	7	1	8
Brooks, Lynchburg	1.000	1	8	2	0	2	Rice, Salem	.975	38	330	27	9	32
Burke, Hagerstown*	.968	4	26	4	1	0	Richardson, Hagerstown	.990	117	1013	83	11	80
Criswell, Durham	.979	5	35	11	1	4	Rigos, Salem	.500	1	0	1	1	0
DeLuca, Lynchburg	1.000	1	4	1	0	0	Roca, Salem	1.000	3	19	0	0	3
Dotzler, Salem	1.000	1	5	0	0	1	Ruskin, Salem*	.994	23	151	16	1	14
Garcia, Peninsula	.988	27	225	22	3	18	Sepanek, Prince William*	.988	139	1167	84	15	102
Gideon, Lynchburg	.985	103	926	53	15	105	Smith, Durham	1.000	3	20	4	0	1
Greene, Peninsula*	.991	110	977	69	9	86	Stevens, Salem	1.000	1	4	1	0	1
Harper, Kinston*	.991	133	1230	111	12	137	Strickland, Winston-Salem*	.923	2	12	0	1	1
Hicks, Prince William	1.000	4	20	2	0	2	Sutryk, Peninsula	1.000	1	1	0	0	0
JOHNSON, Durham	.993	135	1230	94	9	102	Tullier, Winston-Salem*	.992	15	109	9	1	7
Kent, Kinston	.976	6	36	4	1	2	Twardoski, Kinston*	.981	6	51	1	1	6
Khoury, Hagerstown*	.973	7	67	5	2	9	Voigt, Hagerstown	.818	2	9	0	2	1
King, Salem	.993	65	554	55	4	51	Wagner, Peninsula	.935	6	41	2	3	1
Kraus, Prince William*	1.000	2	13	1	0	2	Walsh, Peninsula	.981	6	47	4	1	3
McMorris, Winston-Salem*	.991	112	976	57	9	91	Young, Hagerstown*	.964	12	97	9	4	12

Triple Play—Twardoski.

SECOND BASEMEN

Player and Club	Pct.	G.	PO.	A.	E.	DP.	Player and Club	Pct.	G.	PO.	A.	E.	DP.
Barringer, Salem	.973	11	16	20	1	3	Lombardozzi, Prince William	.934	53	75	108	13	21
Bennett, Kinston	.974	63	167	207	10	52	Mallinak, Hagerstown	.978	20	39	51	2	15
Bonilla, Prince William	.984	38	83	98	3	29	Martin, Peninsula	.931	39	94	108	15	18
Cruz, Winston-Salem	.925	7	19	18	3	9	Martinez, Prince William	.857	2	1	5	1	1
Dulin, Hagerstown	.969	124	268	330	19	79	Moser, Salem	.948	133	277	347	34	78
Fredymond, Durham	.857	4	7	5	2	3	Newsom, Durham	1.000	7	9	16	0	2
Gelatt, Lynchburg	.960	86	164	240	17	54	Perdomo, Lynchburg	.953	39	70	91	8	23
Gellinger, Peninsula	.972	39	83	93	5	24	Roby, Durham	.966	8	11	17	1	3
Ging, Lynchburg	1.000	5	5	10	0	2	Small, Winston-Salem	.970	111	252	335	18	69
Hauradou, Prince William	.988	24	32	50	1	10	Stevanus, Salem	1.000	1	3	6	0	2
Hillman, Kinston	.920	9	8	15	2	3	Sutryk, Peninsula	1.000	5	15	9	0	4
Hinzo, Kinston	.960	65	129	186	13	46	Swain, Kinston	1.000	8	15	11	0	2
Isa, Peninsula	.951	66	152	179	17	35	Valera, Lynchburg	.964	10	15	12	1	3
Lambert, Prince William	.956	48	102	94	9	19	Villanueva, Lynchburg	.963	20	48	56	4	16
LEMKE, Durham	.982	126	248	355	11	83	Wallace, Winston-Salem	.964	27	60	75	5	17

Triple Play—Hillman.

THIRD BASEMEN

Player and Club	Pct.	G.	PO.	A.	E.	DP.	Player and Club	Pct.	G.	PO.	A.	E.	DP.
Bafia, Winston-Salem	.900	92	58	193	28	16	Meulens, Prince William	.896	116	96	224	37	15
Barringer, Salem	.877	53	21	72	13	6	Morris, Durham	.914	91	60	185	23	11
Brooks, Lynchburg	1.000	3	0	4	0	0	Newsom, Durham	.966	51	30	85	4	9
Cruz, Winston-Salem	.825	15	8	25	7	3	Perdomo, Lynchburg	.863	29	15	54	11	3
DeLuca, Lynchburg	1.000	4	2	1	0	0	Posey, Hagerstown	1.000	2	2	1	0	0
Dotzler, Salem	.667	1	0	2	1	0	Reichel, Peninsula	.889	17	12	36	6	4
Gelatt, Lynchburg	1.000	2	0	3	0	0	Repoz, Lynchburg	.908	109	72	215	29	21
Gellinger, Peninsula	.909	29	21	49	7	2	K. Richardson, Kinston	.900	3	3	6	1	0
Ging, Lynchburg	.938	6	5	10	1	0	T. Richardson, Hagerstown	.875	5	1	6	1	1
Gomez, Hagerstown	.903	123	75	232	33	27	Rigos, Salem	.889	6	5	3	1	1
Hauradou, Prince William	.714	4	0	5	2	0	Rohrmeier, Peninsula	.891	68	47	124	21	13
Hillman, Kinston	1.000	3	1	4	0	1	Stevanus, Salem	.894	31	14	45	7	3
Isa, Peninsula	.500	1	0	1	1	1	Sutryk, Peninsula	.845	39	25	57	15	6
King, Salem	.885	20	18	51	9	4	Swain, Kinston	1.000	2	0	1	0	0
Little, Salem	.902	58	45	84	14	12	Turgeon, Prince William	.932	18	9	46	4	4
Lombardozzi, Prince William	.917	7	3	8	1	0	Wallace, Winston-Salem	.943	39	29	71	6	9
Mallinak, Hagerstown	.912	15	5	26	3	1	WEBSTER, Kinston	.934	137	105	303	29	30

Triple Play—K. Richardson.

SHORTSTOPS

Player and Club	Pct.	G.	PO.	A.	E.	DP.	Player and Club	Pct.	G.	PO.	A.	E.	DP.
ALVA, Durham	.961	111	185	377	23	69	Magallanes, Kinston	.936	57	79	169	17	36
Audain, Peninsula	.903	30	50	81	14	17	Mallinak, Hagerstown	.918	41	48	98	13	18
Barringer, Salem	1.000	5	4	9	0	2	Maloney, Durham	.961	20	36	63	4	13
Bennett, Kinston	.923	2	6	6	1	1	Martinez, Prince William	1.000	5	8	10	0	2
Bullinger, Winston-Salem	.955	129	210	383	28	92	Newsom, Durham	.907	12	13	26	4	6
Crowley, Hagerstown	.928	77	97	213	24	39	Repoz, Lynchburg	.750	1	4	2	2	2
Cruz, Winston-Salem	.936	14	12	32	3	8	Small, Winston-Salem	.000	1	0	0	1	0
Davis, Salem	.932	137	223	392	45	78	Stevanus, Salem	1.000	7	4	7	0	1
Gelatt, Lynchburg	.937	10	27	32	4	14	Strijek, Hagerstown	.929	33	48	97	11	14
Ging, Lynchburg	.957	9	8	37	2	4	Sutryk, Peninsula	.902	28	38	81	13	9
Gomez, Hagerstown	1.000	3	0	1	0	0	Swain, Kinston	.921	43	59	116	15	28
Grebeck, Peninsula	.963	91	137	278	16	51	Tresh, Prince William	.924	94	127	276	33	58
Hauradou, Prince William	.879	15	24	27	7	5	Valera, Lynchburg	.949	61	89	170	14	43
Hillman, Kinston	.973	51	72	147	6	30	Vargas, Prince William	.849	28	29	44	13	7
Lambert, Prince William	.792	8	5	14	5	3	Villanueva, Lynchburg	.935	74	89	215	21	35
Lombardozzi, Prince William	.939	15	13	33	3	5							

OUTFIELDERS

Player and Club	Pct.	G.	PO.	A.	E.	DP.	Player and Club	Pct.	G.	PO.	A.	E.	DP.
Arendas, Prince William*	.978	65	133	1	3	0	C. Landrum, Winston-Salem	.940	119	286	11	19	4
Bautista, Hagerstown	.958	70	133	4	6	3	D. Landrum, Kinston	1.000	7	14	0	0	0
Belle, Kinston	1.000	6	5	0	0	0	Lewis, Winston-Salem	.977	77	125	1	3	0
Bellino, Hagerstown	.923	43	68	4	6	1	Little, 17 Lyn-14 Sal	.984	31	60	2	1	0
Bohlke, Durham	.949	33	56	0	3	0	Lomastro, Winston-Salem	.962	62	95	6	4	0
Braxton, Peninsula*	.946	18	34	1	2	0	Maas, Prince William	.944	16	16	1	1	0
Brooks, Lynchburg	.977	37	41	2	1	1	Mallinak, Hagerstown	1.000	3	5	0	0	0
Bruske, Kinston	.951	122	188	7	10	2	Monell, Lynchburg	1.000	28	41	1	0	1
Buss, Kinston	.929	7	12	1	1	0	Muratti, Salem	.974	23	35	2	1	0
Calvert, Prince William	.962	118	224	3	9	1	Newsom, Durham	1.000	3	3	0	0	0
Carpenter, Hagerstown	.971	15	33	1	1	1	Paulino, Hagerstown	1.000	1	1	0	0	0
Carrillo, Salem*	.951	33	55	3	3	2	Perdomo, Lynchburg	1.000	2	1	0	0	0
Carter, Prince William	1.000	13	22	0	0	0	Perez, Lynchburg*	.984	73	122	3	2	1
Chance, Salem	.961	132	206	14	9	1	K. Richardson, Kinston	.979	95	134	5	3	0
Cook, Salem	.975	68	149	6	4	1	T. Richardson, Hagerstown	.875	4	7	0	1	0
Cruz, Winston-Salem	.968	37	59	2	2	0	RIGOS, Salem	.980	126	283	6	6	2
Cuevas, Lynchburg	.963	50	70	7	3	1	Roberts, Hagerstown	.935	72	125	4	9	1
Davis, Peninsula	.970	128	214	9	7	1	Roby, Durham	.913	11	20	1	2	0
DeLuca, Lynchburg	.975	51	116	1	3	1	Ruskin, Lynchburg	1.000	1	1	0	0	0
Finley, Hagerstown*	1.000	15	32	3	0	2	Scruggs, Peninsula*	.965	72	129	9	5	4
Fredymond, Durham	.862	15	24	1	4	0	Sepanek, Prince William*	1.000	5	2	0	0	0
Gellinger, Peninsula	1.000	5	10	0	0	0	Skeete, Hagerstown*	.956	94	234	6	11	0
Gonzalez, Prince William	1.000	1	1	0	0	0	A. Smith, Durham	.959	110	154	10	7	0
Grimes, Winston-Salem	.931	73	87	7	7	2	T. Smith, Winston-Salem	.957	33	61	5	3	0
Hannon, Winston-Salem	1.000	5	3	1	0	0	Stevens, Salem	1.000	1	2	0	0	0
Hauradou, Prince William	1.000	12	15	2	0	0	Strickland, Winston-Salem*	1.000	5	11	0	0	0
Hayden, Lynchburg*	.956	60	85	1	4	0	Sutryk, Peninsula	1.000	6	10	0	0	0
Higgins, Prince William	1.000	28	64	1	0	1	Tullier, Winston-Salem*	.974	81	143	8	4	1
Hood, Durham	.970	118	275	15	9	3	Waggoner, Peninsula	.970	112	283	10	9	3
Howard, Prince William*	.954	79	135	11	7	2	Wagner, Peninsula	.975	92	191	8	5	0
Jaster, Lynchburg	.931	117	260	9	20	1	Wallace, Winston-Salem	1.000	2	1	0	0	0
Jones, Durham	.978	110	210	16	5	0	Walsh, Peninsula	.750	1	3	0	1	0
Jordan, Kinston	.957	121	260	6	12	3	Weiss, Durham*	.939	36	44	2	3	0
Khoury, Hagerstown*	.973	76	140	6	4	3	Westbrook, 10 Lyn-62 Kin	.966	72	137	5	5	0
Kraus, Prince William*	.955	120	179	11	9	3	Woods, Winston-Salem*	.953	56	121	2	6	0
Lambert, Prince William	.990	39	94	1	1	0	Workman, Kinston	.909	19	30	0	3	0

CATCHERS

Player and Club	Pct.	G.	PO.	A.	E.	DP.	PB.	Player and Club	Pct.	G.	PO.	A.	E.	DP.	PB.
Bellino, Hagerstown	.667	3	3	1	2	0	1	Kent, Kinston	.975	51	236	32	7	3	9
Billmeyer, Lynchburg	1.000	3	14	3	0	0	0	Kuld, Kinston	.982	35	197	19	4	1	2
Bresnahan, Kinston	1.000	8	41	9	0	1	3	Liddell, Lynchburg	.964	30	174	15	7	2	8
Brooks, Lynchburg	.989	17	79	7	1	0	1	McElroy, Peninsula	.986	37	188	22	3	4	1
Brown, Peninsula	.964	100	479	59	20	3	15	Miller, Winston-Salem	1.000	1	2	0	0	0	0
Brunswick, Lynchburg	1.000	16	67	5	0	0	0	Morales, Prince William	.946	20	95	10	6	2	6
Cento, Peninsula	.979	17	81	11	2	0	5	Nipper, Durham	1.000	7	45	5	0	0	4
Criswell, Durham	.981	41	290	19	6	2	5	Oertli, Winston-Salem	.984	45	266	36	5	3	2
Cuevas, Durham	.987	24	135	12	2	0	2	Paulino, Hagerstown	.980	64	401	44	9	4	14
DeLuca, Lynchburg	1.000	1	1	0	0	0	0	Pfaff, Durham	.973	76	433	63	14	5	12
Dotzler, Salem	.982	63	429	66	9	3	9	Pittman, Salem	.985	41	294	29	5	4	4
Girardi, Winston-Salem	.973	95	569	74	18	4	17	Posey, Hagerstown	.979	76	492	58	12	5	13
Gonzalez, Prince William	1.000	14	56	1	0	0	0	Ramos, Prince William	.942	53	283	24	19	3	6
GWINN, Prince William	.988	74	378	49	5	3	8	Roca, Salem	.984	42	292	25	5	3	3
Iavarone, Winston-Salem	1.000	6	23	4	0	0	1	Toler, Prince William	.981	9	48	5	1	0	0
Jelic, Lynchburg	.978	61	346	45	9	3	8	Wilson, Kinston	.981	59	367	53	8	2	17
Jones, Lynchburg	.980	31	171	25	4	2	3								

PITCHERS

Player and Club	Pct.	G.	PO.	A.	E.	DP.	Player and Club	Pct.	G.	PO.	A.	E.	DP.
Adams, Salem	1.000	3	0	1	0	0	Brennan, Peninsula	1.000	13	1	5	0	0
Adkins, Prince William*	.958	21	4	19	1	1	Brill, Prince William*	1.000	4	2	1	0	1
Akins, Durham	1.000	30	6	8	0	1	Brown, Durham*	.941	13	2	14	1	0
Aviles, Durham	.947	16	6	12	1	0	Bystrom, Prince William	1.000	7	3	4	0	0
Balabon, Prince William	1.000	11	3	6	0	1	Carey, Peninsula	1.000	10	1	3	0	1
Barry, Prince William*	.750	6	1	2	1	0	Carreno, Prince William	.833	26	3	7	2	1
Bauer, Lynchburg	.938	61	5	10	1	1	Carriger, Hagerstown	.941	43	8	8	1	2
Bayer, Lynchburg	.944	26	8	26	2	3	Carroll, Prince William	.875	25	0	7	1	0
Beatty, Hagerstown*	.947	13	7	11	1	2	Cepeda, Salem	1.000	8	0	4	0	0
Blum, Prince William*	.957	28	6	16	1	1	Cinnella, Hagerstown	1.000	19	7	11	0	0
Borgatti, Hagerstown	.909	27	10	10	2	0	Ciszkowski, Lynchburg	.813	22	3	10	3	0
Bowden, Hagerstown	.917	34	11	11	2	0	Clayton, Prince William	1.000	9	4	8	0	0

PITCHERS—Continued

Player and Club	Pct.	G.	PO.	A.	E.	DP.
Cloninger, Winston-Salem*	1.000	2	0	1	0	0
Clossen, Prince William	.714	9	1	4	2	0
Coleman, Winston-Salem	1.000	17	1	3	0	0
Conley, Peninsula*	1.000	9	0	5	0	0
Copp, Salem*	.976	19	8	33	1	3
Curtis, Winston-Salem*	.895	30	4	30	4	2
Dacosta, Prince William	1.000	4	0	2	0	0
Danek, Winston-Salem	.840	13	6	15	4	0
Daniel, Salem*	.000	3	0	0	1	0
Davidson, Prince William	.969	21	11	20	1	0
DelRosario, Durham	.969	41	6	25	1	2
Dillard, Hagerstown*	1.000	14	0	2	0	1
Dillmore, Kinston*	.714	25	2	3	2	1
Dubois, Hagerstown*	.984	27	5	55	1	0
Eave, Durham	.909	16	11	9	2	1
Erickson, Lynchburg*	.857	12	4	2	1	1
Farr, Kinston	1.000	47	3	5	0	0
Fedor, Kinston	.833	14	3	2	1	0
Figueroa, Prince William*	.857	19	1	5	1	0
Foster, Prince William*	1.000	3	1	0	0	0
Franchi, Salem*	.875	17	1	6	1	1
Gardner, Winston-Salem	1.000	2	2	1	0	1
George, Prince William*	.846	10	4	7	2	1
And. Ghelfi, Kinston	.981	26	21	31	1	3
Ant. Ghelfi, Kinston	.962	18	11	14	1	3
Gilles, Kinston	.929	30	13	26	3	2
Girdner, Peninsula	1.000	5	1	0	0	1
Giron, Prince William	1.000	44	2	10	0	1
Givens, Lynchburg*	.920	21	3	20	2	1
Gordon, Salem	1.000	9	0	3	0	0
Green, Winston-Salem	.778	16	1	6	2	0
Greene, Durham	.944	55	6	11	1	0
Gross, Lynchburg	.957	16	5	17	1	0
Hall, Peninsula*	.914	23	9	23	3	2
Harnisch, Hagerstown	.800	4	1	3	1	0
Hatfield, Salem	.824	27	6	8	3	1
Heath, Hagerstown*	1.000	14	0	2	0	0
Hernandez, Salem	.900	19	4	5	1	0
Hirsch, Winston-Salem	.889	27	3	5	1	0
Howard, Prince William*	1.000	4	0	4	0	1
Hulstrom, Peninsula*	1.000	34	0	11	0	1
Iasparro, Lynchburg	1.000	7	1	2	0	0
Imes, Prince William	1.000	10	2	15	0	2
James, Lynchburg	.909	54	2	8	1	1
Jimenez, Durham	.941	30	8	8	1	1
D. Jones, Durham	.833	27	4	11	3	1
Jundy, Lynchburg	1.000	6	2	6	0	0
Kallevig, Winston-Salem	.889	27	4	12	2	1
Kamieniecki, Prince William	.938	19	10	20	2	3
Kazmierczak, Winston-Salem	1.000	19	9	23	0	0
Kennedy, Peninsula	.929	15	3	10	1	0
Khoury, Hagerstown*	1.000	4	1	2	0	0
Kirk, Salem	.917	37	1	10	1	0
Koopmann, Salem*	.897	12	3	23	3	0
Kraemer, Winston-Salem*	.889	41	1	7	1	0
Kutzler, Peninsula	.923	10	5	7	1	0
Kuykendall, Kinston	.800	12	1	3	1	1
Lahrman, Peninsula	1.000	36	9	25	0	1
Layana, Prince William	1.000	7	0	6	0	0
Lilliquist, Durham*	1.000	3	1	0	0	0
Lind, Salem	.957	11	10	12	1	3
Manon, Prince William	.750	23	2	10	4	0
Martinez, Hagerstown*	1.000	6	0	2	0	0
Matas, Winston-Salem	1.000	29	1	18	0	3
Mathews, Peninsula	1.000	10	2	13	0	0
Melendez, Salem	.909	20	9	11	2	1
Melton, Salem	1.000	12	5	10	0	4
Mercedes, Salem	1.000	19	2	12	0	0
Mercker, Durham*	1.000	3	0	3	0	0
Michno, Hagerstown	1.000	14	3	1	0	0
Miller, Durham	.982	30	16	38	1	3
Mills, Prince William	.909	35	11	19	3	0
Morrow, Salem	.500	24	0	2	2	0
Nichols, Kinston*	1.000	9	8	5	0	0
Ollom, Peninsula	.911	26	7	34	4	0
Palermo, Hagerstown	.923	36	6	18	2	0
Patterson, Winston-Salem*	1.000	15	0	13	0	1
POEHL, Kinston	1.000	22	12	25	0	3
Radinsky, Peninsula*	.923	12	2	10	1	1
Rauth, Lynchburg	.913	28	3	18	2	0
Reichard, Salem	1.000	22	4	3	0	0
Renz, Peninsula	.923	47	4	8	1	1
Reynolds, Peninsula	.921	27	9	26	3	6
Richards, Hagerstown	.947	22	10	26	2	1
Richardson, Lynchburg	.933	29	5	23	2	3
Robles, Winston-Salem	1.000	20	2	4	0	0
Rodriguez, Lynchburg*	.944	69	4	13	1	0
Roth, Winston-Salem	.976	27	12	28	1	5
Rowe, Hagerstown	.818	9	3	6	2	0
Salisbury, Durham	1.000	12	3	4	0	0
Sampen, Salem	.963	26	6	20	1	1
Sanchez, Hagerstown	1.000	24	13	16	0	0
Scheer, Peninsula	.797	31	15	32	12	2
C. Scott, Kinston	.966	19	12	16	1	2
M. Scott, Durham	.900	7	3	6	1	0
Shamblin, Kinston	.882	39	4	11	2	1
Siebert, Durham	.857	12	7	5	2	0
Skinner, Hagerstown	1.000	2	1	2	0	0
Slocumb, Winston-Salem	.714	9	2	8	4	2
Slowik, Winston-Salem	.920	49	6	17	2	2
Soos, Kinston	.957	47	8	14	1	0
Stading, Salem	.923	44	5	7	1	0
Stewart, Durham*	1.000	35	1	10	0	1
Stiles, Lynchburg	1.000	36	1	5	0	0
Talamantez, Hagerstown	1.000	6	2	6	0	0
Tauken, Peninsula	.850	32	5	12	3	2
Telford, Hagerstown	1.000	2	2	2	0	0
Thorpe, Hagerstown	1.000	33	5	17	0	1
Tirado, Prince William	.923	32	3	9	1	1
Torres, Prince William	1.000	17	2	7	0	0
Villanueva, Peninsula*	1.000	11	2	5	0	2
Wachs, Winston-Salem	1.000	17	3	23	0	0
M.A. Walker, Salem	1.000	21	10	17	0	1
M.C. Walker, Kinston	.667	3	1	1	1	0
Walton, Hagerstown	1.000	13	2	10	0	1
Welborn, Lynchburg	.800	37	3	5	2	0
Wickander, Kinston*	.963	25	6	20	1	0
Wilkins, Winston-Salem	.889	13	2	6	1	0
Williams, Durham*	1.000	6	3	7	0	0
Wilmet, Salem	1.000	22	1	5	0	0
Wilson, Hagerstown	.923	15	6	6	1	1
Zarranz, Winston-Salem	.938	15	7	8	1	1

The following players do not have any recorded accepted chances at the positions indicated; therefore, are not listed in the fielding averages for those particular positions: Audain, of; Barringer, of; Burdick, p; Ferlenda, p; Gelatt, p; Gellinger, ss; Ging, of; F. Gonzalez, 1b; Gooden, p; Grebeck, 3b; Grossman, p; Hixon, p; Howard, 1b; G. Jones, p; Lemke, 3b; Maysonet, p; Meulens, of; M. Miller, 3b; Morales, 3b; O'Quinn, p; Posey, of; A. Smith, 3b; Strijek, 3b; Tresh, 2b, of; Tullier, of; Twardoski, of; Voeltz, p.

CLUB PITCHING

Club	ERA.	G.	CG.	ShO.	Sv.	IP.	H.	R.	ER.	HR.	HB.	BB.	Int. BB.	SO.	WP.	Bk.
Salem	3.80	139	19	10	40	1234.1	1198	640	521	134	44	504	14	991	60	14
Durham	4.05	140	16	5	31	1222.2	1209	640	550	117	38	505	16	850	63	14
Kinston	4.05	140	26	9	29	1223.2	1214	662	551	86	51	536	16	832	102	8
Hagerstown	4.19	140	21	10	29	1235.2	1247	692	575	95	26	594	13	886	83	4
Winston-Salem	4.42	140	15	8	42	1216.1	1272	736	598	113	67	596	28	817	92	19
Peninsula	4.43	140	17	5	33	1220.0	1234	732	600	92	63	607	18	710	70	19
Lynchburg	4.64	139	12	3	27	1183.0	1281	742	610	81	43	594	41	811	99	13
Prince William	4.66	140	14	4	23	1209.0	1264	765	626	96	45	639	20	844	102	17

PITCHERS' RECORDS
(Leading Qualifiers for Earned-Run Average Leadership—112 or More Innings)

*Throws lefthanded.

Pitcher—Club	W.	L.	Pct.	ERA.	G.	GS.	CG.	GF.	ShO.	Sv.	IP.	H.	R.	ER.	HR.	HB.	BB.	Int. BB.	SO.	WP.
C. Scott, Kinston	9	6	.600	2.69	19	19	5	0	1	0	133.2	117	54	40	10	1	40	0	95	4
James, Lynchburg	7	3	.700	3.16	14	1	0	13	0	1	119.2	116	49	42	5	1	41	10	81	3
Wickander, Kinston*	9	6	.600	3.42	25	25	2	0	0	0	147.1	128	69	56	7	7	75	2	118	14
Miller, Durham	15	9	.625	3.59	30	27	8	2	0	0	205.1	188	92	82	19	3	53	1	155	8
M.A. Walker, Salem	12	5	.706	3.71	21	21	4	0	1	0	135.2	140	67	56	14	0	57	1	91	8
Lahrman, Peninsula	5	10	.333	3.74	36	17	2	10	0	3	158.2	170	75	66	13	5	42	1	64	5
Copp, Salem*	11	5	.688	3.82	29	19	8	0	3	0	129.2	126	64	55	13	4	32	0	98	2
Sampen, Salem	9	8	.529	3.84	26	26	2	0	1	0	152.1	126	77	65	16	7	72	1	137	3
Dubois, Hagerstown*	8	9	.471	3.89	27	25	3	0	0	0	155.0	162	81	67	13	5	73	2	96	5
Kazmierczak, Winston-Salem	9	5	.643	3.94	19	19	3	0	1	0	118.2	120	68	52	12	6	51	0	92	6

Departmental Leaders: G—Rodriguez, 69; W—Miller, 15; L—Ollom, Scheer, 13; Pct.—Beatty, .917; GS—Richardson, 28; CG—Copp, And. Ghelfi, Miller, 8; GF—Renz, 42; ShO—Copp, 3; Sv.—Renz, 20; IP—Miller, 205.1; H—And. Ghelfi, 192; R—Ollom, 117; ER—Roth, 90; HR—Ollom, 20; HB—Roth, 16; BB—Scheer, 118; IBB—Bauer, 12; SO—Miller, 155; WP—Givens, 19.

(All Pitchers—Listed Alphabetically)

Pitcher—Club	W.	L.	Pct.	ERA.	G.	GS.	CG.	GF.	ShO.	Sv.	IP.	H.	R.	ER.	HR.	HB.	BB.	Int. BB.	SO.	WP.
Adams, Salem	0	0	.000	7.71	3	0	0	2	0	0	7.0	14	7	6	1	0	2	0	3	0
Adkins, Prince William*	9	8	.529	4.82	21	20	0	0	0	0	115.2	120	72	62	11	3	70	1	84	12
Akins, Durham	3	5	.375	3.61	30	2	0	16	0	2	67.1	75	32	27	9	1	14	2	63	3
Aviles, Durham	3	8	.273	4.22	16	15	0	0	0	0	81.0	78	43	38	10	2	26	1	48	4
Balabon, Prince William	1	6	.143	7.17	11	11	0	0	0	0	47.2	58	48	38	7	2	40	1	40	7
Barry, Hagerstown*	0	2	.000	3.95	6	2	0	1	0	0	13.2	10	8	6	1	0	10	0	14	0
Bauer, Lynchburg	6	7	.462	4.22	61	0	0	28	0	5	91.2	103	51	43	10	1	48	12	73	4
Bayer, Lynchburg	4	10	.286	5.76	26	16	0	4	0	1	109.1	121	83	70	6	6	56	2	56	10
Beatty, Hagerstown*	11	1	.917	2.52	13	13	4	0	1	0	100.0	81	32	28	7	1	11	0	65	5
Blum, Prince William*	4	5	.444	4.17	28	11	2	9	0	4	99.1	109	52	46	7	4	25	0	50	5
Borgatti, Hagerstown	5	5	.500	4.68	27	19	2	4	0	2	138.1	152	93	72	15	3	58	0	90	2
Bowden, Hagerstown	4	7	.364	5.07	34	7	2	12	0	0	99.1	103	65	56	8	2	67	1	79	14
Brennan, Peninsula	1	0	1.000	3.07	13	0	0	8	0	0	29.1	21	11	10	4	0	16	0	15	1
Brill, Prince William*	0	0	.000	3.72	4	0	0	3	0	0	9.2	13	4	4	1	0	2	0	5	0
Brown, Durham*	4	4	.500	5.20	13	12	1	1	0	0	72.2	78	46	42	6	0	42	0	48	5
Burdick, Hagerstown	0	1	.000	9.00	1	1	0	0	0	0	5.0	6	6	5	0	1	2	0	5	0
Bystrom, Prince William	2	3	.400	3.48	7	7	0	0	0	0	31.0	41	16	12	2	3	9	0	13	0
Carey, Peninsula	0	2	.000	6.75	10	0	0	7	0	1	16.0	23	12	12	2	0	12	0	6	2
Carreno, Prince William	5	2	.714	3.03	26	4	2	14	0	2	62.1	53	30	21	2	1	30	2	49	14
Carriger, Hagerstown	9	8	.529	2.39	43	0	0	36	0	10	67.2	51	23	18	2	1	24	3	67	3
Carroll, Prince William	2	2	.500	3.92	25	0	0	15	0	3	39.0	33	19	17	4	8	23	2	29	2
Cepeda, Salem	1	4	.200	3.68	8	2	0	5	0	0	22.0	16	10	9	2	1	8	0	23	3
Cinnella, Hagerstown	3	5	.375	6.23	19	9	0	2	0	0	60.2	67	53	42	6	1	41	0	39	4
Ciszkowski, Lynchburg	2	7	.222	7.20	22	12	0	1	0	0	75.0	88	70	60	8	3	65	1	63	4
Clayton, Prince William	2	1	.667	4.58	9	4	0	4	0	0	37.1	49	25	19	4	0	17	0	20	1
Cloninger, Winston-Salem*	1	0	1.000	6.23	2	0	0	0	0	0	4.1	7	6	3	0	1	4	0	3	1
Clossen, Prince William	1	4	.200	4.84	9	9	0	0	0	0	44.2	38	27	24	5	1	24	0	31	2
Coleman, Winston-Salem	1	1	.500	5.83	17	0	0	5	0	3	29.1	42	19	19	1	1	14	1	19	5
Conley, Peninsula*	2	2	.500	0.96	9	0	0	6	0	1	18.2	15	3	2	0	0	2	0	13	1
Copp, Salem*	11	5	.688	3.82	19	19	8	0	3	0	129.2	126	64	55	13	4	32	0	98	2
Curtis, Winston-Salem*	6	9	.400	4.23	30	22	2	3	0	0	159.2	175	86	75	12	6	74	3	101	11
Dacosta, Prince William	1	1	.500	6.50	4	2	0	0	0	0	18.0	20	14	13	1	1	15	0	7	1
Danek, Winston-Salem	10	3	.769	2.71	13	13	2	0	2	0	89.2	83	29	27	5	2	28	0	53	7
Daniel, Salem*	0	1	.000	11.25	3	0	0	1	0	0	4.0	8	7	5	0	1	3	0	2	0
Davidson, Prince William	3	10	.231	3.98	21	16	5	2	1	0	124.1	140	65	55	6	3	33	1	70	8
DelRosario, Durham	2	5	.286	1.40	41	0	0	37	0	16	64.1	42	15	10	0	2	17	1	25	2
Dillard, Hagerstown*	2	1	.667	2.05	14	0	0	9	0	3	22.0	12	5	5	2	1	11	0	26	2
Dillmore, Kinston*	2	2	.500	8.49	25	2	0	10	0	2	23.1	28	23	22	3	1	33	1	18	7
Dubois, Hagerstown*	8	9	.471	3.89	27	25	3	0	0	0	155.0	162	81	67	13	5	73	2	96	5
Eave, Durham	5	4	.556	4.84	16	14	2	1	0	0	87.1	90	51	47	13	5	35	1	82	3
Erickson, Lynchburg	4	2	.667	8.63	12	6	0	2	0	0	32.1	37	32	31	4	4	36	0	32	4
Farr, Kinston	4	6	.400	3.95	47	0	0	40	0	17	57.0	48	29	25	8	1	39	4	63	11
Fedor, Kinston	0	1	.000	6.75	14	0	0	6	0	0	18.2	23	18	14	0	3	19	1	20	8
Ferlenda, Hagerstown	2	0	1.000	3.38	2	0	0	0	0	0	5.1	3	2	2	1	0	9	0	6	0
Figueroa, Prince William	1	1	.500	6.03	19	3	0	8	0	1	31.1	35	23	21	6	1	22	1	19	0
Foster, Prince William*	0	0	.000	6.75	3	0	0	1	0	0	1.1	2	2	1	0	1	1	0	1	0
Franchi, Salem*	0	1	.000	6.14	17	0	0	6	0	2	22.0	30	22	15	3	1	13	0	16	1
Gardner, Winston-Salem	1	0	1.000	3.68	2	0	0	0	0	0	7.1	5	7	3	0	0	11	0	7	3
Gelatt, Lynchburg	0	0	.000	0.00	1	0	0	0	0	0	1.0	2	0	0	0	0	1	0	0	0
George, Prince William*	3	3	.500	5.86	10	8	1	1	0	0	50.2	60	41	33	4	0	23	1	28	1
And. Ghelfi, Kinston	12	6	.667	4.29	26	26	8	0	1	0	182.2	192	97	87	16	9	42	0	81	5
Ant. Ghelfi, Kinston	3	7	.300	5.19	18	12	2	2	1	0	86.2	83	57	50	6	4	58	0	69	9
Gilles, Kinston	9	9	.500	4.49	30	22	4	3	1	1	154.1	185	101	77	12	9	63	2	81	12
Girdner, Peninsula	0	1	.000	2.57	5	0	0	5	0	2	7.0	4	2	2	0	0	4	0	4	2
Giron, Prince William	4	3	.571	4.21	44	0	0	21	0	1	66.1	65	37	31	7	0	34	2	58	7
Givens, Lynchburg	6	8	.429	4.65	21	20	3	0	0	0	112.1	112	79	58	8	4	69	0	96	19
Gooden, Lynchburg	0	0	.000	0.00	1	1	0	0	0	0	4.0	2	0	0	0	0	2	0	3	0
Gordon, Salem	1	0	1.000	4.58	9	0	0	3	0	0	17.2	23	11	9	1	3	12	0	14	2
Green, Winston-Salem	0	2	.000	6.43	16	0	0	9	0	2	21.0	30	17	15	3	2	7	1	7	1
Greene, Durham	9	7	.563	3.81	55	2	0	29	0	6	104.0	112	57	44	7	2	45	7	76	4
Gross, Lynchburg	7	4	.636	2.72	16	15	2	0	0	0	89.1	92	37	27	1	6	22	1	39	1
Grossman, Kinston	0	1	.000	2.08	9	0	0	5	0	0	17.1	14	7	4	2	3	6	0	6	0
Hall, Peninsula*	8	6	.571	4.26	23	21	4	2	2	0	133.0	137	73	63	7	7	60	2	94	3
Harnisch, Hagerstown	1	2	.333	2.25	4	4	0	0	0	0	20.0	17	7	5	0	0	14	0	18	3
Hatfield, Salem	2	3	.400	4.69	27	3	1	13	0	2	55.2	54	36	29	3	3	33	3	47	8
Heath, Hagerstown*	0	2	.000	4.41	14	0	0	4	0	0	16.1	16	9	8	1	0	13	0	20	1
Hernandez, Salem	4	8	.333	5.03	19	14	0	1	0	1	77.0	89	51	43	14	3	29	1	71	3
Hirsch, Winston-Salem	3	1	.750	1.50	27	0	0	25	0	16	36.0	27	11	6	0	4	11	2	38	4
Hixon, Hagerstown	0	1	.000	20.25	1	0	0	0	0	0	1.1	2	3	3	2	0	3	0	1	1
Howard, Prince William*	0	0	.000	10.29	4	0	0	0	0	0	7.0	9	8	8	0	1	8	0	1	0
Hulstrom, Peninsula*	9	2	.818	2.88	34	2	0	12	0	2	68.2	64	33	22	1	2	32	2	71	6
Iasparro, Lynchburg	0	0	.000	6.17	7	2	0	0	0	0	11.2	16	13	8	1	1	11	0	8	0
Imes, Prince William	2	3	.400	3.95	10	10	0	0	0	0	68.1	68	35	30	4	1	20	1	49	3
James, Lynchburg	7	3	.700	3.16	54	1	0	13	0	1	119.2	116	49	42	5	1	41	10	81	3
Jimenez, Durham	3	4	.429	3.82	30	2	0	14	0	6	68.1	57	36	29	8	0	28	1	53	4
D. Jones, Durham	1	2	.333	4.78	27	0	0	11	0	0	49.0	53	33	26	8	1	25	0	31	7
G. Jones, Lynchburg	0	0	.000	0.00	1	0	0	0	0	0	0.2	0	0	0	0	0	0	0	1	0
Jundy, Lynchburg	0	4	.000	10.38	6	4	0	0	0	0	21.2	28	25	25	4	0	14	0	15	3
Kallevig, Winston-Salem	4	3	.571	5.17	27	2	0	12	0	2	62.2	62	42	36	4	5	24	3	22	6
Kamieniecki, Prince William	9	5	.643	4.17	19	19	1	0	0	0	112.1	91	61	52	7	5	78	3	84	9
Kazmierczak, Winston-Salem	9	5	.643	3.94	19	19	3	0	1	0	118.2	120	68	52	12	6	51	0	92	6
Kennedy, Peninsula	1	1	.500	6.62	15	5	0	3	0	1	50.1	57	41	37	6	1	44	1	43	6
Khoury, Hagerstown*	0	0	.000	4.76	4	0	0	4	0	0	5.2	7	3	3	0	0	3	0	2	0
Kirk, Salem*	2	1	.667	3.42	37	1	0	10	0	4	55.1	58	33	21	10	0	24	1	40	5
Koopmann, Salem*	4	4	.500	4.68	12	12	0	0	0	0	75.0	93	47	39	7	1	19	0	33	6
Kraemer, Winston-Salem*	3	2	.600	2.73	41	0	0	27	0	13	52.2	49	20	16	4	2	41	2	43	3

Pitcher—Club	W.	L.	Pct.	ERA.	G.	GS.	CG.	GF.	ShO.	Sv.	IP.	H.	R.	ER.	HR.	HB.	BB.	Int. BB.	SO.	WP.
Kutzler, Peninsula	5	2	.714	4.10	10	9	2	1	1	0	63.2	53	34	29	1	3	24	1	30	2
Kuykendall, Kinston	1	2	.333	5.55	12	0	0	3	0	1	24.1	26	17	15	2	2	22	0	24	5
Lahrman, Peninsula	5	10	.333	3.74	36	17	2	10	0	3	158.2	170	75	66	13	5	42	1	64	5
Layana, Prince William	2	1	.667	6.35	7	3	0	2	0	0	22.2	29	22	16	3	1	11	0	17	5
Lilliquist, Durham*	2	1	.667	2.88	3	3	2	0	0	0	25.0	13	9	8	1	1	6	0	29	0
Lind, Salem	6	3	.667	2.22	11	11	1	0	0	0	81.0	72	31	20	10	0	27	0	54	3
Manon, Prince William	2	3	.400	7.32	23	3	0	4	0	1	39.1	45	36	32	1	0	41	0	28	7
Martinez, Hagerstown*	1	0	1.000	3.86	6	0	0	1	0	1	7.0	6	4	3	1	0	5	0	8	1
Matas, Winston-Salem	8	6	.571	4.15	29	18	2	5	2	0	119.1	112	67	55	9	8	65	1	85	14
Mathews, Durham	4	1	.800	1.94	10	6	0	2	0	1	51.0	42	11	11	4	1	10	0	29	0
Maysonet, Salem	0	0	.000	0.00	1	0	0	0	0	0	1.2	1	0	0	0	0	3	0	2	0
Melendez, Salem	9	6	.600	4.56	20	20	1	0	1	0	116.1	96	62	59	17	8	56	0	86	4
Melton, Salem	6	1	.857	3.38	12	9	0	0	0	0	58.2	57	25	22	3	3	24	2	43	1
Mercedes, Salem	2	0	1.000	3.96	19	0	0	6	0	3	36.1	42	25	16	7	2	10	1	28	2
Mercker, Durham*	0	1	.000	5.40	3	3	0	0	0	0	11.2	11	8	7	1	0	6	0	14	1
Michno, Hagerstown	1	0	1.000	8.14	14	0	0	8	0	1	24.1	33	24	22	2	0	22	0	23	7
Miller, Durham	15	9	.625	3.59	30	27	8	2	0	0	205.1	188	92	82	19	3	53	1	155	8
Mills, Prince William	2	11	.154	6.09	35	8	0	11	0	1	85.2	102	75	58	7	4	64	3	53	9
Morrow, Salem	4	5	.444	3.74	24	0	0	18	0	6	43.1	55	22	18	5	0	14	0	41	0
Nichols, Kinston	4	2	.667	4.02	9	8	1	1	1	0	56.0	53	27	25	3	1	14	0	61	4
O'Quinn, Durham	0	1	.000	32.40	1	1	0	0	0	0	1.2	4	6	6	0	0	4	0	0	0
Ollom, Peninsula	10	13	.435	4.82	26	26	3	0	0	0	166.1	188	117	89	20	15	61	0	75	11
Palermo, Hagerstown	7	1	.875	3.26	36	8	1	12	0	3	105.0	95	49	38	3	1	52	4	81	10
Patterson, Winston-Salem*	5	3	.625	3.89	15	9	0	0	0	0	69.1	73	35	30	5	2	24	1	60	3
Poehl, Kinston	9	10	.474	4.14	22	21	3	0	1	0	139.0	142	75	64	10	7	47	0	100	9
Radinsky, Peninsula*	1	7	.125	5.77	12	8	0	2	0	0	39.0	43	30	25	2	3	32	0	37	3
Rauth, Lynchburg	6	10	.375	4.67	28	27	3	0	0	0	160.0	182	101	83	12	7	56	0	109	12
Reichard, Salem	4	0	1.000	0.96	22	0	0	11	0	4	37.1	19	6	4	0	0	17	0	34	1
Renz, Peninsula	6	3	.667	3.69	47	0	0	42	0	20	70.2	76	34	29	5	4	24	4	52	2
Reynolds, Peninsula	10	7	.588	3.98	27	25	4	1	1	1	163.0	151	81	72	13	4	71	1	66	4
Richards, Durham	6	10	.375	4.54	22	20	1	1	0	0	125.0	138	73	63	14	9	50	1	62	3
Richardson, Lynchburg	6	12	.333	4.91	29	28	3	0	0	0	154.0	180	103	84	11	7	68	2	79	16
Robles, Winston-Salem	1	5	.167	8.25	20	8	0	4	0	0	60.0	83	66	55	17	2	36	0	37	5
Rodriguez, Lynchburg*	3	1	.750	2.78	69	0	0	30	0	5	68.0	69	23	21	3	0	26	6	59	8
Roth, Winston-Salem	10	10	.500	5.02	27	26	2	0	1	0	161.1	178	115	90	17	16	82	3	107	14
Rowe, Hagerstown	0	1	.000	1.46	9	0	0	6	0	3	24.2	21	8	4	1	1	6	0	21	1
Salisbury, Durham	2	2	.500	4.17	12	9	1	0	0	0	45.1	48	22	21	6	0	18	0	20	2
Sampen, Salem	9	8	.529	3.84	26	26	2	0	1	0	152.1	126	77	65	16	7	72	1	137	3
Sanchez, Hagerstown	2	9	.182	6.28	24	15	4	2	0	0	106.0	133	85	74	18	4	50	2	53	3
Scheer, Peninsula	6	13	.316	5.55	31	23	2	2	0	0	136.1	130	108	84	7	14	118	2	69	15
C. Scott, Kinston	9	6	.600	2.69	19	19	5	0	1	0	133.2	117	54	40	10	1	40	0	95	4
M. Scott, Durham	1	1	.500	4.91	7	7	0	0	0	0	33.0	28	23	18	0	5	29	0	12	5
Shamblin, Kinston	4	3	.571	4.05	39	2	1	16	0	0	80.0	79	41	36	6	3	33	3	43	6
Siebert, Durham	4	4	.500	4.07	11	10	1	0	1	0	55.1	61	30	25	3	2	39	0	49	1
Skinner, Hagerstown	0	0	.000	0.00	2	2	0	0	0	0	8.0	2	1	0	0	0	5	0	10	1
Slocumb, Winston	1	2	.333	6.26	9	4	0	1	0	0	27.1	26	25	19	1	0	26	0	27	0
Slowik, Winston-Salem	3	6	.333	4.41	49	0	0	27	0	5	69.1	63	40	34	5	8	51	11	45	4
Soos, Kinston	6	4	.600	3.27	47	0	0	28	0	7	82.2	79	40	30	1	0	31	3	34	6
Stading, Salem	1	4	.200	3.58	44	1	0	23	0	4	70.1	62	35	28	7	6	41	4	87	4
Stewart, Durham*	0	2	.000	6.69	35	2	0	10	0	0	40.1	60	33	30	5	3	28	1	31	7
Stiles, Lynchburg	3	3	.500	5.00	36	0	0	16	0	0	36.0	41	28	20	2	2	31	3	30	2
Talamantez, Hagerstown	0	4	.000	6.10	6	6	0	0	0	0	20.2	23	20	14	2	1	22	0	13	4
Tauken, Peninsula	2	4	.333	5.04	32	3	0	16	0	2	75.0	76	57	42	9	4	43	2	46	4
Telford, Hagerstown	1	0	1.000	1.59	2	2	0	0	0	0	11.1	9	2	2	0	1	5	0	10	0
Thorpe, Hagerstown	3	1	.750	2.57	33	0	0	17	0	6	56.0	59	18	16	0	1	21	1	35	5
Tirado, Prince William	8	1	.889	3.09	32	0	0	22	0	5	46.2	37	25	16	3	2	24	1	54	3
Torres, Prince William	3	1	.750	2.90	17	1	0	10	0	4	40.1	34	15	13	2	1	19	1	49	6
Tullier, Winston-Salem*	0	0	.000	2.25	4	0	0	4	0	0	4.0	6	1	1	0	0	3	0	3	0
Villanueva, Peninsula*	1	1	.500	6.66	11	1	0	6	0	0	24.1	26	21	18	2	1	22	2	25	3
Voeltz, Prince William*	0	0	.000	10.13	7	1	0	2	0	1	8.0	13	13	9	2	2	6	0	5	0
Wachs, Lynchburg*	4	4	.500	4.31	17	7	1	2	1	0	56.1	58	30	27	5	0	21	0	31	4
M.A. Walker, Salem	12	5	.706	3.71	21	21	4	0	1	0	135.2	140	67	56	14	0	57	1	91	8
M.C. Walker, Kinston	3	0	1.000	2.61	3	3	0	0	0	0	20.2	17	7	6	0	0	14	0	19	2
Walton, Hagerstown	8	2	.800	3.61	13	12	3	0	1	0	84.2	81	36	34	5	1	34	0	68	2
Welborn, Lynchburg	5	1	.833	2.48	37	0	0	31	0	15	40.0	34	18	11	1	1	25	4	36	9
Wickander, Kinston*	9	6	.600	3.42	25	25	2	0	1	0	147.1	128	69	56	7	7	75	2	118	14
Wilkins, Winston-Salem	4	4	.500	4.11	13	6	3	1	0	1	50.1	49	31	23	3	1	24	0	29	1
Williams, Durham*	1	4	.200	4.11	6	5	0	0	0	0	35.0	31	20	16	3	1	30	0	23	4
Wilmet, Salem	2	0	1.000	0.50	22	0	0	21	0	14	36.0	17	2	2	1	8	4	0	41	4
Wilson, Hagerstown	4	6	.400	5.56	15	15	2	0	0	0	77.2	96	55	48	5	1	33	0	36	10
Zarranz, Winston-Salem	2	6	.250	4.74	15	11	2	0	0	0	74.0	82	51	39	15	1	22	0	39	4

BALKS—Bauer, Koopmann, Matas, Stewart, 4 each; Balabon, Curtis, Hatfield, Ollom, Patterson, 3 each; Bayer, Brown, Clayton, Danek, Davidson, Givens, Greene, Kamieniecki, Layana, Manon, Miller, Poehl, Richardson, Roth, Sampen, Scheer, Shamblin, 2 each; Adkins, Akins, Blum, Cepeda, Cinnella, Copp, Farr, Figueroa, Franchi, And. Ghelfi, Gilles, Green, Gross, Hall, Harnisch, Hirsch, D. Jones Kraemer, Kuykendall, Melton, Radinsky, Rauth, Reynolds, Richards, Sanchez, Siebert, Slocumb, Stading, Stiles, Talamantez, Tauken, Torres, Villanueva, Zarranz, 1 each.

COMBINATION SHUTOUTS—Salisbury-Akins, Mathews-Jimenez, Aviles-Miller, Richards-DelRosario, Durham; Beatty-Bowden, Dubois-Martinez, Beatty-Carriger, Bowden-Palermo, Palermo-Carriger, Wilson-Carriger, Walton-Thorpe, Harnisch-Palermo, Hagerstown; Wickander-Farr, Wickander-Soos, Kinston; Gross-Givens-Rodriguez, Gross-Welborn, Lynchburg; Scheer-Renz, Peninsula; Clossen-Manon, Adkins-Torres, Bystrom-Giron-Blum-Layana, Prince William; Cepeda-Stading, Melendez-Franchi-Hatfield, Melendez-Wilmet, Hernandez-Wilmet, Salem; Matas-Slowik-Hirsch, Gardner-Slowik, Winston-Salem.

NO-HIT GAMES—None.

Florida State League

CLASS A

CHAMPIONSHIP WINNERS IN PREVIOUS YEARS

1919—Sanford°	.605	1951—DeLand§	.643	1970—Miami b	.662
Orlando°	.703	1952—DeLand x	.704	St. Petersburg	.600
1920—Tampa	.654	Palatka (3rd)‡	.569	1971—Miami b	.667
Tampa	.722	1953—Daytona Beach†	.657	Daytona Beach	.586
1921—Orlando	.635	DeLand	.703	1972—Miami c	.562
1922—St. Petersburg	.503	1954—Jacksonville Beach	.629	Daytona Beach	.606
St. Petersburg	.618	Lakeland†	.594	1973—St. Petersburg d	.575
1923—Orlando	.667	1955—Orlando	.671	West Palm Beach	.580
Orlando	.678	Orlando	.643	1974—West Palm Beach d	.598
1924—Lakeland	.695	1956—Cocoa	.614	Fort Lauderdale	.626
Lakeland	.683	Cocoa	.671	1975—St. Petersburg d	.652
1925—St. Petersburg	.667	1957—Palatka	.629	Miami	.581
Tampa†	.696	Tampa†	.681	1976—Tampa	.559
1926—Sanford	.647	1958—St. Petersburg	.732	Lakeland d	.536
Sanford	.623	St. Petersburg	.681	1977—Lakeland d	.616
1927—Orlando†	.600	1959—Tampa	.591	West Palm Beach	.583
Miami	.661	St. Petersburg†	.612	1978—Lakeland	.565
1928-35—Did not operate.		1960—Lakeland	.731	Miami§	.539
1936—Gainesville	.542	Palatka†	.614	1979—Fort Lauderdale	.643
St. Augustine (4th)†	.492	1961—Tampa†	.710	Winter Haven e	.577
1937—Gainesville§	.616	Sarasota	.696	1980—Daytona Beach	.628
1938—Leesburg	.626	1962—Sarasota	.689	Fort Lauderdale d	.606
Gainesville (2nd)‡	.615	Fort Lauderdale†	.623	1981—Fort Myers	.554
1939—Sanford§	.787	1963—Sarasota	.645	Daytona Beach f	.504
1940—Daytona Beach	.619	Sarasota	.667	1982—Fort Lauderdale f	.621
Orlando (4th)‡	.507	1964—Fort Lauderdale†	.629	Tampa	.546
1941—St. Augustine	.659	St. Petersburg	.594	1983—Daytona Beach	.634
Leesburg (4th)‡	.488	1965—Fort Lauderdale	.627	Vero Beach f	.515
1942-45—Did not operate.		Fort Lauderdale	.634	1984—Tampa	.532
1946—Orlando§	.681	1966—Leesburg†	.781	Fort Lauderdale f	.521
1947—St. Augustine	.625	St. Petersburg	.700	1985—Fort Myers g	.590
Gainesville (2nd)‡	.584	1967—St. Petersburg y	.691	Fort Lauderdale	.550
1948—Orlando	.643	Orlando	.638	1986—St. Petersburg g	.647
Daytona Beach (2nd)‡	.616	1968—Miami	.613	West Palm Beach	.593
1949—Gainesville	.635	Orlando z	.579		
St. Augustine (3rd)‡	.556	1969—Miami a	.606		
1950—Orlando	.629	Orlando	.606		
DeLand (3rd)‡	.590				

°Split-season playoff abandoned after each team won three games. †Won split-season playoff. ‡Won four-club playoff. §Won championship and four-club playoff. xWon both halves of split season. yLeague divided into Eastern and Western divisions with split season. St. Petersburg and Orlando won both halves of split season; St. Petersburg won playoff. zLeague divided into Eastern and Western divisions. Miami won regular-season pennant on basis of highest won-lost percentage. Orlando won four-club playoff involving first two teams in each division. aLeague divided into Southern and Central divisions. Miami won playoff between division leaders. (NOTE—Pennant awarded to playoff winner in 1936.) bLeague divided into Eastern and Western divisions. Miami won regular-season pennant on basis of highest won-loss percentage, and also won four-club playoff involving first two teams in each division. cLeague divided into Eastern and Western divisions. Won four-club playoff involving first two teams in each division. dLeague divided into Eastern and Western divisions. Won four-club playoff involving first two teams in each division. eLeague divided into Northern and Southern divisions. Same two clubs won both halves; won playoffs. fWon split-season playoff. gLeague divided into Western, Central and Southern divisions. Won four-club playoff.

STANDING OF CLUBS AT CLOSE OF SEASON, AUGUST 27

WESTERN DIVISION

Club	W.	L.	T.	Pct.	G.B.
St. Petersburg (Cardinals)	85	57	0	.599	....
Dunedin (Blue Jays)	76	64	0	.543	8
Clearwater (Phillies)	66	70	0	.485	16
Charlotte (Rangers)	69	74	0	.483	16½
Tampa (Reds)	64	76	0	.457	20
Fort Myers (Royals)	54	87	0	.383	30½

SOUTHERN DIVISION

Club	W.	L.	T.	Pct.	G.B.
Fort Lauderdale (Yankees)	85	53	0	.616	....
West Palm Beach (Expos)	75	63	0	.543	10
Vero Beach (Dodgers)	62	76	0	.449	23
Miami (Independent)	44	89	0	.331	38½

CENTRAL DIVISION

Club	W.	L.	T.	Pct.	G.B.
Osceola (Astros)	80	59	0	.576	....
Lakeland (Tigers)	74	61	0	.548	4
Daytona Beach (White Sox)	69	70	0	.496	11
Winter Haven (Red Sox)	67	71	0	.486	12½

COMPOSITE STANDING OF CLUBS AT CLOSE OF SEASON, AUGUST 27

Club	Ft.L.	St.P.	Osc.	Lak.	WPB	Dun.	Day.	W.H.	Clw.	Char.	Tam.	V.B.	Ft.M.	Mia.	W.	L.	T.	Pct.	G.B.
Fort Lauderdale (Yankees)	....	6	3	4	10	4	5	4	5	5	4	11	7	17	85	53	0	.616	....
St. Petersburg (Cardinals)	2	....	3	4	7	8	4	7	7	9	6	15	6	85	57	0	.599	2
Osceola (Astros)	5	4	....	9	5	2	12	11	5	3	6	6	5	7	80	59	0	.576	5½
Lakeland (Tigers)	4	3	11	....	3	4	9	9	2	5	7	4	5	8	74	61	0	.548	9½
West Palm Beach (Expos)	10	1	3	5	....	4	4	2	3	6	6	11	5	15	75	63	0	.543	10
Dunedin (Blue Jays)	3	8	6	4	4	....	4	4	6	11	7	4	10	5	76	64	0	.543	10
Daytona Beach (White Sox)	3	4	8	11	4	4	....	12	5	4	3	1	5	5	69	70	0	.496	16½
Winter Haven (Red Sox)	4	1	9	11	6	3	8	....	4	3	4	5	5	4	67.	71	0	.486	18
Clearwater (Phillies)	3	9	3	4	3	10	3	4	....	7	7	3	9	1	66	70	0	.485	18
Charlotte (Rangers)	3	9	5	3	2	5	3	5	9	....	9	4	7	5	69	74	0	.483	18½
Tampa (Reds)	3	7	2	1	2	9	5	3	9	7	....	3	9	4	64	76	0	.457	22
Vero Beach (Dodgers)	9	2	2	4	9	2	7	3	5	4	5	....	2	8	62	76	0	.449	23
Fort Myers (Royals)	1	1	3	1	3	6	3	3	7	9	7	6	....	4	54	87	0	.383	32½
Miami (Independent)	3	2	1	0	5	3	3	4	3	3	2	12	3	....	44	89	0	.331	38½

Major league affiliations in parentheses.

Playoffs—Fort Lauderdale defeated Lakeland, two games to none; Osceola defeated St. Petersburg, two games to none; Fort Lauderdale defeated Osceola, three games to one, to win league championship.

Regular-Season Attendance—Charlotte, 100,238; Clearwater, 55,370; Daytona Beach, 54,132; Dunedin, 20,905; Fort Lauderdale, 50,074; Fort Myers, 27,369; Lakeland, 61,255; Miami, 35,934; Osceola, 38,068; St. Petersburg, 121,732; Tampa, 62,394; Vero Beach, 82,676; West Palm Beach, 110,633; Winter Haven, 30,711. Total—851,491. Playoffs—4,017. All-Star Game 2,609.

Managers—Charlotte, Jim Skaalen; Clearwater, Rollie Dearmas; Daytona Beach, Marc Hill; Dunedin, Bob Bailor; Fort Lauderdale, Buck Showalter; Fort Myers, Jerry Terrell; Lakeland, John Wockenfuss; Miami, Dan Norman; Osceola, Ken Bolek; St. Petersburg, Dave Bialas; Tampa, Marc Bombard; Vero Beach, John Shoemaker; West Palm Beach, Felipe Alou; Winter Haven, Doug Camilli.

All-Star Team—1B-Terry Jones, Fort Myers; 2B-Andy Stankiewicz, Fort Lauderdale; 3B-John Toale, Winter Haven; SS-Jerry Bertolani, Daytona Beach; OF-Bernie Anderson, Lakeland; Mauricio Nunez, St. Petersburg; Jeff Baldwin, Osceola; DH-Kevin Maas, Fort Lauderdale; RHP-Jose Cano, Winter Haven; Ramon Martinez, Vero Beach; LHP-Rob Livchak, Osceola; Wayne Edwards, Daytona Beach; Relief Pitchers-Brian Meyer, Osceola; Dana Ridenour, Fort Lauderdale; Manager of the Year-Dave Bialas, St. Petersburg.

(Compiled by Howe News Bureau, Boston, Mass.)

CLUB BATTING

Club	Pct.	G.	AB.	R.	OR.	H.	TB.	2B.	3B.	HR.	RBI.	GW.	SH.	SF.	HP.	BB.	Int. BB.	SO.	SB.	CS.	LOB.
Fort Lauderdale	.275	138	4646	671	555	1277	1714	220	29	53	595	77	39	45	38	529	20	825	142	53	1083
Osceola	.269	139	4624	662	488	1246	1636	194	35	42	573	65	78	58	37	647	36	685	142	64	1166
St. Petersburg	.267	142	4618	659	562	1231	1614	206	30	39	588	77	41	49	31	518	25	699	129	64	1049
Vero Beach	.264	138	4639	623	658	1227	1655	183	28	63	547	53	33	52	49	481	26	689	112	66	1010
Daytona Beach	.263	139	4536	659	618	1194	1693	207	47	66	576	55	28	56	31	505	18	682	141	99	930
Lakeland	.261	135	4380	667	599	1143	1521	194	29	42	566	64	42	56	24	682	27	604	178	72	1059
Fort Myers	.257	141	4488	538	680	1153	1504	169	37	36	466	45	21	29	34	420	17	777	203	105	901
West Palm Beach	.256	138	4566	607	567	1169	1600	173	18	74	537	64	47	41	34	489	25	660	129	56	1017
Dunedin	.253	140	4596	584	556	1164	1600	186	32	62	521	67	12	39	36	474	17	885	196	87	941
Charlotte	.252	143	4726	549	574	1193	1602	186	44	45	485	59	33	33	32	411	24	789	112	54	1002
Tampa	.250	140	4427	510	623	1106	1420	182	24	28	436	58	49	37	36	538	22	694	159	56	1043
Winter Haven	.249	138	4526	642	660	1129	1618	191	20	86	574	59	28	43	49	619	22	869	92	42	1076
Clearwater	.244	136	4395	522	579	1074	1451	188	33	41	458	58	29	38	34	430	25	766	98	54	924
Miami	.244	133	4224	445	619	1030	1375	184	25	37	389	39	43	30	28	405	21	709	163	77	876

INDIVIDUAL BATTING

(Leading Qualifiers for Batting Championship—389 or More Plate Appearances)

*Bats lefthanded.   †Switch-hitter.

Player and Club	Pct.	G.	AB.	R.	H.	TB.	2B.	3B.	HR.	RBI.	GW.	SH.	SF.	HP.	BB.	Int. BB.	SO.	SB.	CS.
Culberson, Charles, Fort Myers	.320	116	388	57	124	146	16	3	0	46	4	1	5	3	27	0	65	47	9
James, Calvin, Osceola*	.319	109	408	72	130	169	17	5	4	45	4	7	3	2	58	2	59	22	8
Anderson, Bernard, Lakeland*	.318	118	384	65	122	162	23	4	3	69	8	0	5	4	114	6	35	17	6
Eveline, William, Daytona Beach*	.316	119	411	69	130	184	29	8	3	63	10	1	5	1	35	2	30	14	11
Jackson, Lavern, Winter Haven	.310	107	361	57	112	145	23	2	2	53	8	4	2	2	55	3	54	16	12
Leyritz, James, Fort Lauderdale†	.307	102	374	48	115	155	22	0	6	51	5	7	4	6	38	1	54	2	1
Stankiewicz, Andrew, Ft. Lauderdale	.307	119	456	80	140	178	18	7	2	47	4	7	1	4	62	1	84	26	13
Jones, Terence, Fort Myers*	.307	135	489	58	150	219	30	3	11	83	8	0	5	6	38	3	56	7	10
Mendez, Jesus, St. Petersburg*	.305	137	522	63	159	192	19	4	2	78	15	3	7	1	46	3	24	5	4
Baldwin, Jeffrey, Osceola*	.304	127	437	70	133	166	20	5	1	56	8	3	8	1	83	9	49	5	7
Bertolani, Jerry, Daytona Beach	.304	114	408	87	124	176	28	6	4	59	6	2	6	5	61	1	60	23	14
Richardson, Jeffrey, Tampa	.299	100	374	44	112	125	9	2	0	37	7	1	7	3	30	5	35	10	4
Brundage, David, Clearwater*	.299	101	338	49	101	134	14	5	3	36	5	2	3	3	50	0	37	16	7
Austin, Dominic, Lakeland	.297	115	451	92	134	163	10	5	3	41	6	5	3	1	64	2	38	45	11

Departmental Leaders: G—Senne, 140; AB—Harrison, 537; R—Austin, 92; H—Mendez, 159; TB—T. Jones, 219; 2B—Do. Martinez, 32; 3B—J. Brumfield, 10; HR—Sipe, 17; RBI—Sipe, 84; GWRBI—Mendez, 15; SH—Rohde, 10; SF—Batesole, Mills, 9; HP—Batesole, 13; BB—B. Anderson, 114; IBB—Snyder, 11; SO—Batiste, 136; SB—Batiste, 70; CS—Batiste, 25.

(All Players—Listed Alphabetically)

Player and Club	Pct.	G.	AB.	R.	H.	TB.	2B.	3B.	HR.	RBI.	GW.	SH.	SF.	HP.	BB.	Int. BB.	SO.	SB.	CS.
Adderley, Kenneth, Miami	.222	96	288	17	64	73	4	1	1	21	4	1	0	2	15	1	64	13	9
Afenir, Troy, Osceola	.276	79	294	60	81	145	20	1	14	68	6	0	8	2	33	1	75	1	0
Alyea, Brant, Miami	.280	116	414	43	116	162	29	1	5	63	4	1	3	3	20	1	66	3	2
Amante, Thomas, St. Petersburg	.292	30	106	16	31	45	7	2	1	12	2	0	2	2	18	0	22	0	2
Anderson, Bernard, Lakeland*	.318	118	384	65	122	162	23	4	3	69	8	0	5	4	114	6	35	17	6
Anderson, Timothy, Vero Beach	.400	3	10	0	4	4	0	0	0	0	0	0	0	0	1	0	3	0	1
Arendas, Daniel, Fort Lauderdale*	.254	36	126	17	32	37	5	0	0	14	1	2	2	2	15	0	17	3	1
Arnsberg, Timothy, Osceola	.200	22	5	3	1	2	1	0	0	1	0	0	0	1	1	0	0	0	0
Austin, Dominic, Lakeland	.297	115	451	92	134	163	10	5	3	41	6	5	3	1	64	2	38	45	11
Azocar, Oscar, Fort Lauderdale*	.359	53	192	25	69	104	11	3	6	39	9	0	0	3	0	18	5	5	
Baker, Derrell, West Palm Beach	.265	126	449	67	119	139	5	0	5	56	8	3	5	3	77	2	31	6	4
Baldwin, Jeffrey, Osceola*	.304	127	437	70	133	166	20	5	1	56	8	3	8	1	83	9	49	5	7
Balthazar, Doyle, Lakeland	.213	15	47	5	10	13	3	0	0	6	0	1	0	0	1	0	7	1	0
Bartels, Willliam, Vero Beach	.143	56	7	1	1	1	0	0	0	1	0	0	0	0	1	0	1	0	0
Bastinck, Derek, Lakeland	.200	29	85	11	17	24	4	0	1	8	1	0	1	0	19	0	11	0	0
Batesole, Michael, Vero Beach	.285	115	414	56	118	175	24	0	11	77	8	1	9	13	30	2	61	3	3
Batiste, Kevin, Dunedin	.267	130	514	65	137	164	12	3	3	28	2	2	2	7	58	2	136	70	25
Beck, Dion, Clearwater*	.000	27	0	0	0	0	0	0	0	0	0	0	0	0	1	0	0	0	0
Becker, Gregory, St. Petersburg*	.000	5	0	0	0	0	0	0	0	0	0	0	0	0	3	0	0	0	
Becker, Timothy, Fort Lauderdale†	.231	130	450	54	104	121	6	4	1	44	3	6	4	4	35	2	38	28	12
Beeler, Robert, Tampa	.264	79	231	24	61	81	18	1	0	24	5	2	1	2	14	1	32	4	1
Befort, Curtis, Clearwater	.000	11	0	0	0	0	0	0	0	0	0	0	0	0	0	0	0	0	0
Behnsch, Bobby, Clearwater*	.245	91	322	37	79	98	11	1	2	29	4	0	3	0	44	3	66	1	1
Benitez, Manuel, Vero Beach	.285	123	431	51	123	183	24	3	10	71	8	1	4	7	35	1	64	1	2
Benzo, Luis, Tampa†	.111	5	9	0	1	1	0	0	0	0	0	0	0	0	0	0	4	0	0
Berman, Gary, Clearwater	.249	133	454	61	113	169	25	2	9	65	10	3	7	5	63	4	76	4	2
Bernardo, Rick, Charlotte*	.277	138	483	68	134	175	19	8	2	56	7	2	3	6	41	2	84	4	4
Berry, Sean, Fort Myers	.254	66	205	26	52	69	7	2	2	30	6	1	1	3	43	2	65	4	4
Bertolani, Jerry, Daytona Beach	.304	114	408	87	124	176	28	6	4	59	6	2	6	5	61	1	60	23	14
Berube, Luc, Fort Lauderdale*	.172	8	29	2	5	6	1	0	0	3	1	0	0	0	0	0	6	0	0
Bierscheid, Eugene, Clearwater	.000	17	1	0	0	0	0	0	0	0	0	0	1	0	0	0	0	0	0
Billmeyer, Michael, 27 Clt-67 Mia†....	.266	94	305	31	81	112	15	2	4	25	1	0	0	1	34	4	50	2	1

Player and Club	Pct.	G.	AB.	R.	H.	TB.	2B.	3B.	HR.	RBI.	GW.	SH.	SF.	HP.	BB.	Int. BB.	SO.	SB.	CS.
Bishop, Timothy, Fort Lauderdale	.125	9	24	3	3	3	0	0	0	1	0	1	1	0	0	0	6	1	0
Blackshear, Steven, Clearwater†	.500	10	4	1	2	3	1	0	0	0	0	0	0	0	2	0	1	0	0
Blasucci, Anthony, Daytona Beach*	.000	34	1	0	0	0	0	0	0	0	0	0	0	0	0	0	1	0	0
Blowers, Michael, West Palm Beach	.253	136	491	68	124	208	30	3	16	71	13	0	3	0	48	0	118	4	4
Bochesa, Gregory, Winter Haven	.199	55	171	19	34	42	0	1	2	19	2	0	2	4	22	0	26	0	1
Borders, Patrick, Dunedin	.364	3	11	0	4	4	0	0	0	1	0	0	0	0	0	0	3	0	0
Boudreaux, Eric, Clearwater	.000	8	2	0	0	0	0	0	0	0	0	1	0	0	1	0	2	0	0
Bradshaw, Kevin, Lakeland	.226	115	337	52	76	87	11	0	0	30	2	8	6	0	41	0	28	5	5
Brink, Bradford, Clearwater	.000	17	11	0	0	0	0	0	0	0	0	0	0	0	0	0	4	0	0
Brow, Dennis, Fort Lauderdale	.281	67	196	24	55	74	9	2	2	29	0	2	3	0	25	0	40	1	2
Brown, Don, Tampa	.263	58	171	17	45	61	7	3	1	20	3	2	2	0	28	0	37	7	4
Brown, Michael, Osceola	.207	65	135	20	28	35	4	0	1	10	0	1	3	2	17	1	18	12	2
Brown, Jeffrey, Vero Beach	.198	25	81	14	16	28	6	0	2	9	1	0	1	0	5	0	14	1	1
Brumfield, Harvey, Clearwater*	.233	115	451	52	105	155	20	6	6	56	4	2	5	1	26	3	81	28	11
Brumfield, Jacob, Fort Myers	.245	114	379	56	93	145	14	10	4	34	3	1	0	0	45	2	78	43	14
Brundage, David, Clearwater*	.299	101	338	49	101	134	14	5	3	36	5	2	3	3	50	0	37	16	7
Buheller, Timothy, Winter Haven*	.207	60	188	35	39	42	3	0	0	12	3	2	1	0	35	0	35	9	3
Burke, Donald, West Palm Beach*	.243	108	292	33	71	78	7	0	0	23	3	3	2	0	47	6	38	3	7
Burke, Michael, Vero Beach*	.272	62	217	24	59	80	5	2	4	29	1	0	3	2	15	2	32	2	2
Butts, Randall, St. Petersburg*	.237	72	177	19	42	54	6	0	2	28	3	0	0	0	26	2	38	1	0
Caceres, Edgar, West Palm Beach†	.269	105	390	55	105	127	14	1	2	37	2	7	1	5	27	0	30	30	5
Caffrey, Robert, West Palm Beach	.221	42	154	15	34	55	9	0	4	15	3	0	1	0	12	0	39	1	1
Camilli, Kevin, Winter Haven*	.238	24	63	6	15	16	1	0	0	6	0	0	0	0	7	1	10	0	0
Campbell, Kevin, Vero Beach	.040	28	25	1	1	1	0	0	0	0	0	0	1	0	3	0	15	0	0
Campbell, Michael, Tampa	.333	6	3	0	1	2	1	0	0	1	0	0	0	0	1	0	1	0	0
Cano, Joselito, Osceola	.211	24	19	2	4	4	0	0	0	0	0	0	0	0	0	0	6	0	0
Caraballo, Ramon, Clearwater	.000	24	1	0	0	0	0	0	0	0	0	0	0	0	0	0	0	0	0
Cardoward, Alfredo, W. Palm Beach	.278	29	18	3	5	10	2	0	1	4	0	1	0	0	1	0	1	0	0
Carey, Peter, Tampa*	.218	103	271	40	59	84	14	1	3	22	3	4	2	2	74	2	49	14	4
Carpenter, Douglas, Miami	.290	97	331	39	96	128	21	4	1	38	6	1	5	1	54	2	57	40	14
Cartaya, Joel, Charlotte†	.246	104	370	34	91	102	9	1	0	24	3	2	2	1	34	0	27	7	3
Carter, Frederick, Fort Lauderdale	.270	25	74	11	20	27	2	1	1	8	1	0	0	0	10	0	14	1	0
Cento, Anthony, Daytona Beach	.400	9	15	0	6	7	1	0	0	1	0	0	0	0	0	0	2	0	0
Clark, Anthony, Charlotte	.239	24	71	5	17	24	2	1	1	5	1	0	1	2	1	0	19	2	1
Clark, Garry, Clearwater	.200	12	10	0	2	2	0	0	0	0	0	2	0	0	0	0	3	0	0
Clements, David, Tampa	.244	99	361	44	88	119	20	1	3	57	7	3	6	1	25	1	47	5	3
Collins, Allen, West Palm Beach	.375	34	8	0	3	3	0	0	0	1	0	0	0	0	0	0	3	0	0
Colombino, Carlo, Osceola	.267	92	330	48	88	107	12	2	1	50	5	5	7	10	33	0	24	5	4
Colston, Frank, Miami	.230	43	152	8	35	39	4	0	0	5	2	0	0	1	18	1	21	0	2
Converse, Michael, Tampa	.167	36	6	0	1	2	1	0	0	0	0	0	0	0	0	0	2	0	0
Coolbaugh, Scott, Charlotte	.275	66	233	27	64	91	21	0	2	20	3	1	2	0	24	1	56	0	1
Cooper, Gary, Osceola	.279	123	427	66	119	156	17	4	4	74	11	4	5	5	66	2	69	14	5
Corcino, Luis, Fort Myers	.261	76	203	21	53	60	7	0	0	16	2	2	2	2	13	0	35	3	4
Cota, Christopher, Daytona Beach	.210	108	314	32	66	79	7	3	0	20	2	2	0	0	30	2	48	7	10
Coveney, Patrick, Daytona Beach*	.159	29	82	10	13	21	2	0	2	7	0	0	0	1	4	0	16	2	0
Credeur, Todd, Osceola*	.200	16	5	0	1	1	0	0	0	0	0	0	0	0	1	0	2	0	0
Crofton, Kevin, Fort Lauderdale	.220	14	50	5	11	18	1	0	2	10	2	0	1	0	1	0	9	0	0
Cronkright, Daniel, Daytona Beach*	.244	122	409	55	100	164	17	4	13	69	3	2	8	1	68	6	80	6	5
Culberson, Charles, Fort Myers	.320	116	388	57	124	146	16	3	0	46	4	1	5	3	27	0	65	47	9
Cunningham, Joseph, St. Petersburg	.264	91	276	40	73	96	13	2	2	27	1	3	3	4	52	3	47	1	1
Cunningham, William, WPB*	.000	14	1	0	0	0	0	0	0	0	0	0	0	0	0	0	1	0	0
Cusack, David, Lakeland	.218	80	243	24	53	98	15	0	10	43	5	0	2	0	56	2	52	3	2
Daily, Richard, Lakeland†	.208	16	48	12	10	20	4	0	2	9	3	0	1	0	12	0	18	2	2
Daniels, Gregory, Miami*	.300	10	20	2	6	8	0	1	0	0	0	0	0	0	1	0	2	0	0
Dantzler, Shawn, Clearwater	.270	121	423	41	114	157	30	2	3	49	6	1	2	7	29	4	62	1	2
Daulton, Darren, Clearwater*	.227	9	22	1	5	11	3	0	1	5	0	0	1	0	4	0	3	0	0
David, Gregory, Dunedin*	.218	106	335	56	73	121	15	0	11	55	11	0	7	4	70	5	82	1	1
Davis, Geffrey, West Palm Beach	.224	91	281	32	63	93	9	0	7	39	8	1	4	3	28	0	25	1	2
Davis, Gerald, Lakeland	.254	19	63	15	16	20	1	0	1	9	0	0	2	1	21	0	9	0	0
Davis, Steven, Tampa*	.257	113	335	42	86	139	16	2	11	47	3	3	2	5	28	3	75	8	3
Dean, Kevin, West Palm Beach	.288	127	475	80	137	190	15	4	10	47	8	2	3	11	65	1	91	24	12
DeCordova, David, St. Petersburg*	.000	37	2	0	0	0	0	0	0	0	0	0	0	1	0	0	1	0	0
Deitz, Timothy, Tampa	.000	23	1	0	0	0	0	0	0	0	0	0	0	0	0	0	1	0	0
DeLaCruz, Hector, Dunedin	.259	130	425	57	110	140	20	2	2	42	6	1	2	3	56	0	75	32	15
DeLeon, Julio, Charlotte†	.171	16	41	2	7	10	1	1	0	3	0	1	0	0	1	0	10	0	0
Delgado, Juan, Osceola	.257	78	191	27	49	64	11	2	0	19	3	1	2	2	28	0	28	3	2
Dempsay, Adam, Lakeland	.218	46	133	11	29	36	7	0	0	14	1	1	3	0	11	0	23	3	1
Devine, Kevin, Vero Beach*	.000	30	3	1	0	0	0	0	0	0	0	0	0	0	3	0	2	0	0
Devlin, Robert, West Palm Beach	.000	36	1	0	0	0	0	0	0	0	0	0	1	0	0	0	0	0	0
Diaz, Carlos, Dunedin	.230	73	230	24	53	59	6	0	0	27	6	1	1	1	22	0	41	3	2
Dickerson, Bobby, Fort Lauderdale	.196	23	56	6	11	16	5	0	0	3	0	1	3	0	4	0	14	0	0
Dixon, Edward, West Palm Beach	.000	43	4	0	0	0	0	0	0	0	0	0	0	1	0	0	1	0	0
Duggan, Thomas, Charlotte	.229	26	83	12	19	25	4	1	0	10	1	0	0	1	12	0	18	2	1
Dunster, Donald, Osceola	.167	12	12	2	2	2	0	0	0	0	0	0	3	0	3	0	6	0	0
Edge, Gregory, Clearwater	.246	103	394	45	97	110	9	2	0	36	5	3	2	0	45	1	30	34	14
Elliot, Terrill, St. Petersburg	.246	64	203	28	50	62	7	1	1	19	2	2	1	1	14	0	31	0	1
Elliott, John, Osceola	.245	86	196	22	48	57	6	0	1	23	3	6	1	1	50	3	20	5	5
Engram, Graylyn, Daytona Beach	.289	72	249	38	72	97	11	4	2	26	4	0	0	2	27	0	31	15	6
Esteban, Philipe, Vero Beach	.286	6	7	0	2	2	0	0	0	0	0	0	0	0	0	0	1	0	0
Eveline, William, Daytona Beach*	.316	119	411	69	130	184	29	8	3	63	10	1	5	1	35	2	30	14	11
Falzone, James, Miami	.091	10	22	1	2	2	0	0	0	0	0	1	0	1	3	0	2	0	0
Fazzini, Frank, Vero Beach	.250	11	16	5	4	9	2	0	1	1	0	0	0	1	2	0	4	0	0
Ferradas, Miguel, Vero Beach	.000	1	2	0	0	0	0	0	0	0	0	0	0	0	1	0	1	0	0
Fletcher, Darrin, Vero Beach	.266	43	124	13	33	40	7	0	0	15	0	0	4	1	22	3	12	0	2
Fontes, Bradley, Charlotte	.243	12	37	2	9	9	0	0	0	5	0	0	1	0	4	0	14	0	0
Forney, Jeffrey, Tampa	.267	127	415	65	111	153	17	8	3	31	5	3	4	11	69	0	65	23	6
Forrest, Christopher, St. Petersburg	.143	24	7	1	1	1	0	0	0	0	0	1	0	0	1	0	0	0	0
Fox, Blane, Lakeland*	.251	117	383	59	96	127	18	2	3	45	5	0	4	2	60	4	46	28	11
Fox, Michael, St. Petersburg	.272	125	448	53	122	171	28	3	5	71	7	4	6	1	38	4	52	6	2
Francois, Manuel, Vero Beach†	.280	109	404	68	113	143	9	6	3	49	6	3	5	4	32	0	68	17	14
Freiling, Howard, Vero Beach*	.260	57	208	21	54	73	11	1	2	20	5	3	1	2	11	0	33	0	2
Frye, Paul, West Palm Beach	.224	36	116	14	26	42	4	0	4	14	0	1	2	0	14	0	21	0	1

Player and Club	Pct.	G.	AB.	R.	H.	TB.	2B.	3B.	HR.	RBI.	GW.	SH.	SF.	HP.	BB.	Int. BB.	SO.	SB.	CS.
Galvez, Balvino, Vero Beach	.000	6	3	0	0	0	0	0	0	0	0	1	0	0	0	0	1	0	0
Garcia, Cornelio, Daytona Beach°	.231	15	39	0	9	12	1	1	0	3	1	0	0	0	7	0	7	1	3
Garcia, Rene, Vero Beach°	.000	6	1	0	0	0	0	0	0	0	0	0	0	0	0	0	0	0	0
Garner, Michael, Vero Beach†	.250	94	264	38	66	77	6	1	1	18	1	1	0	5	26	0	39	25	7
Garrison, Webster, Dunedin	.283	128	477	70	135	157	14	4	0	44	5	0	5	0	57	0	53	27	9
Gaylor, Robert, West Palm Beach	.231	44	104	14	24	29	2	0	1	16	1	0	1	0	12	1	11	3	0
Gegen, Frederick, Vero Beach°	.281	128	452	63	127	173	22	3	6	55	4	2	6	4	63	5	87	10	2
Geist, Peter, Vero Beach	.222	98	316	36	70	98	10	0	6	36	2	3	4	1	30	5	47	3	4
Gellinger, Michael, Daytona Beach°	.375	12	32	5	12	12	0	0	0	3	0	1	1	0	3	0	1	0	2
Glasker, Stephen, Charlotte°	.263	132	487	53	128	164	11	8	3	41	4	8	2	4	29	5	99	23	9
Goff, Michael, Winter Haven	.212	31	99	14	21	31	4	0	2	6	1	0	0	2	17	0	19	0	0
Goff, Timothy, Fort Myers	.227	77	238	22	54	62	3	1	1	17	2	1	0	2	29	0	43	3	5
Gonzalez, Julian, Daytona Beach	.000	27	1	0	0	0	0	0	0	0	0	0	0	0	0	0	0	0	0
Green, Robert, Fort Lauderdale	.274	118	409	67	112	169	31	4	6	67	10	1	8	1	60	1	94	7	4
Green, Terry, Osceola	.288	99	351	37	101	132	18	2	3	42	8	6	5	1	14	1	44	13	8
Haggerty, Roger, Winter Haven	.241	84	245	29	59	99	8	1	10	41	3	2	2	3	22	1	51	0	0
Hammond, Christopher, Tampa°	.100	25	20	3	2	4	2	0	0	1	0	1	0	0	2	0	6	0	0
Hardgrave, Eric, Lakeland	.303	25	76	10	23	31	2	0	2	14	0	0	3	0	1	0	14	3	0
Harris, Tyrone, West Palm Beach	.200	26	20	0	4	5	1	0	0	2	0	1	0	0	2	0	10	0	0
Harris, Vincent, Daytona Beach†	.200	26	55	21	11	13	2	0	0	3	0	1	0	0	12	0	18	9	2
Harrison, Brett, St. Petersburg	.263	139	537	87	141	188	31	2	4	57	9	3	6	2	69	0	96	18	4
Hartman, Jeffrey, Vero Beach	.286	29	56	5	16	18	2	0	0	5	0	1	0	1	3	0	5	0	0
Hawley, William, Tampa	.000	5	2	0	0	0	0	0	0	0	0	0	0	0	0	0	0	0	0
Hernandez, Cesar, West Palm Beach .	.236	32	106	14	25	36	3	1	2	6	1	0	1	1	4	0	29	6	1
Hershman, William, St. Petersburg° ..	.167	28	6	1	1	1	0	0	0	0	0	0	0	0	1	1	5	0	0
Hershiser, Gordon, Vero Beach	.222	18	9	0	2	2	0	0	0	1	0	0	0	0	0	0	4	0	0
Herzog, Hans, St. Petersburg	.000	30	2	0	0	0	0	0	0	0	0	0	0	0	0	0	0	0	0
Heuer, Mark, Vero Beach	.000	8	1	0	0	0	0	0	0	0	0	0	0	0	1	0	1	0	0
Hickey, James, Daytona Beach	.000	15	0	0	0	0	0	0	0	0	0	0	0	0	1	0	0	0	0
Hilgenberg, Scott, Tampa°	.282	94	330	27	93	107	11	0	1	34	7	2	1	3	37	6	38	4	3
Hill, Kenneth, St. Petersburg	.000	18	1	0	0	0	0	0	0	0	0	0	0	0	0	0	0	0	0
Holmes, Darren, Vero Beach	.231	19	13	1	3	4	1	0	0	2	0	3	0	0	1	0	5	0	0
Hornacek, Jay, 34 VRB-39 Miami	.234	73	214	22	50	80	17	2	3	25	1	2	2	1	21	3	55	3	1
Horton, David, St. Petersburg	.235	73	166	23	39	46	3	2	0	17	0	2	3	0	21	0	29	4	3
Housie, Wayne, Lakeland†	.258	125	458	58	118	147	12	7	1	45	6	6	6	3	39	2	74	26	11
Houston, Melvin, West Palm Beach	.245	45	159	23	39	51	9	0	1	17	2	5	3	0	15	0	14	8	2
Howard, David, Fort Myers†	.194	89	289	26	56	76	9	4	1	19	3	7	0	0	30	0	68	11	10
Howey, Todd, Clearwater	.227	115	370	34	84	120	21	3	3	37	7	0	3	2	28	3	93	3	6
Huseby, Kenneth, Tampa	.000	9	0	0	0	0	0	0	0	0	0	1	0	0	1	0	3	0	0
Huson, Jeffrey, West Palm Beach°	.286	131	455	54	130	156	15	4	1	53	5	6	8	1	50	4	30	33	9
Ickes, Michael, Winter Haven	.196	56	143	16	28	36	6	1	0	13	0	3	2	1	14	0	36	0	2
Inagaki, Shuji, Miami	.260	74	192	19	50	66	8	4	0	17	2	5	1	1	24	0	42	9	3
Jackson, Lavern, Winter Haven	.310	107	361	57	112	145	23	2	2	53	8	0	4	2	55	3	54	16	12
Jackson, Mark, Tampa	.222	56	207	24	46	52	4	1	0	10	3	2	0	2	28	0	31	8	7
James, Calvin, Osceola°	.319	109	408	72	130	169	17	5	4	45	4	7	3	2	58	2	59	22	8
Jarner, Kenneth, Clearwater	.269	11	26	5	7	7	0	0	0	1	0	0	0	0	3	0	3	0	0
Jeter, Shawn, Dunedin°	.271	127	468	59	127	186	22	5	9	56	9	2	4	6	54	3	107	8	8
Johnson, Thomas, Fort Myers°	.275	97	324	45	89	128	15	3	6	45	6	1	2	0	34	0	53	4	4
Jones, Michael, Dunedin	.315	80	267	30	84	118	13	3	5	51	4	1	0	0	13	0	42	7	4
Jones, Terence, Fort Myers°	.307	135	489	58	150	219	30	3	11	83	8	0	5	6	38	3	56	7	10
Jose, Manuel, Winter Haven†	.252	54	214	42	54	74	5	3	3	17	1	1	4	0	34	0	53	42	11
Joslyn, John, Fort Myers°	.279	45	154	22	43	57	9	1	1	20	0	2	1	2	24	1	32	7	4
Kaiser, Bart, Clearwater°	.236	66	165	17	39	62	11	3	2	21	0	1	2	1	11	0	53	1	3
Kaye, Jeffrey, Clearwater	.255	60	153	27	39	64	9	2	4	16	1	1	1	2	23	1	51	0	0
Kelly, Jimy, Dunedin	.218	71	238	22	52	58	2	2	0	16	0	3	2	0	15	1	27	0	4
Kesselmark, Joseph, Vero Beach°	.274	125	424	56	116	166	26	3	6	48	7	2	4	2	45	6	46	8	5
Kindred, Curtis, Tampa	.000	17	12	0	0	0	0	0	0	0	0	1	0	0	1	0	5	0	0
Koslofski, Kevin, Fort Myers°	.242	109	330	46	80	98	12	3	0	25	1	3	2	7	46	3	64	25	9
Kramer, Mark, Charlotte°	.266	130	473	53	126	158	18	4	2	57	8	5	3	3	31	2	56	7	8
Kravec, Kenneth, Fort Myers°	.000	3	1	0	0	0	0	0	0	0	0	0	0	0	0	0	1	0	0
Kreuter, Chad, Clearwater	.217	85	281	36	61	108	18	1	9	40	7	2	1	1	31	2	32	1	1
Kristan, Kevin, West Palm Beach	.000	39	2	0	0	0	0	0	0	0	0	0	0	0	0	0	1	0	0
Laboy, Jose, Fort Lauderdale	.246	60	175	18	43	55	3	0	3	17	2	0	1	2	18	0	37	0	2
Lambert, Kenneth, Vero Beach	.254	77	244	30	62	75	4	0	3	26	3	1	3	0	27	0	12	3	3
Landrum, Darryl, Dunedin	.207	98	348	42	72	128	20	3	10	38	2	1	2	8	28	0	98	16	5
Langley, Wesley, Vero Beach	.000	5	1	0	0	0	0	0	0	0	0	0	0	0	0	0	1	0	0
Lara, Crucito, St. Petersburg	.231	134	445	53	103	123	18	1	0	39	4	4	2	5	36	5	83	9	8
Laseke, Eric, Winter Haven	.266	116	443	62	118	156	15	4	5	40	6	5	1	6	54	1	52	7	4
Latmore, Robert, Miami	.207	109	353	26	73	103	17	2	3	31	4	8	3	3	21	0	75	2	9
Lau, Charles, Miami	.125	12	32	2	4	5	1	0	0	0	0	0	0	0	2	0	13	0	0
Lea, Charles, West Palm Beach	.200	19	5	0	1	1	0	0	0	0	0	0	0	0	0	0	0	0	0
Leary, Robert, West Palm Beach	.198	64	192	20	38	52	11	0	1	18	0	2	0	5	15	1	39	1	1
Leyritz, James, Fort Lauderdale†	.307	102	374	48	115	155	22	0	6	51	5	7	4	6	38	1	54	2	1
Livchak, Robert, St. Petersburg°	.382	29	34	4	13	18	2	0	1	4	1	0	0	0	4	0	9	0	0
Long, Bruce, Osceola	.143	11	7	1	1	1	0	0	0	2	0	1	0	0	2	0	3	0	0
Lopez, Juan, Osceola	.250	21	56	5	14	14	0	0	0	0	0	1	0	1	0	0	7	0	0
Lovullo, Anthony, Lakeland†	.267	18	60	11	16	22	3	0	1	16	3	0	3	0	10	0	8	0	0
Luciani, Randall, Lakeland	.185	16	54	8	10	15	2	0	1	3	0	0	0	0	8	0	18	0	0
Lung, Rodney, Clearwater	.189	17	37	3	7	7	0	0	0	5	1	1	1	0	5	0	14	0	0
Maas, Jason, Fort Lauderdale°	.283	64	226	42	64	86	19	0	1	23	2	2	2	0	36	2	29	17	4
Maas, Kevin, Fort Lauderdale°	.278	116	439	77	122	191	28	4	11	73	12	0	8	2	53	4	108	14	4
Machado, Julio, Clearwater	.250	7	4	1	1	1	0	0	0	0	0	0	0	0	0	0	2	0	0
Magallanes, William, Daytona Beach ..	.267	69	221	30	59	104	4	4	11	44	3	1	5	5	24	0	64	5	7
Magee, Warren, Clearwater†	.333	28	6	2	2	2	0	0	0	0	0	0	0	0	0	0	1	0	0
Magrann, Thomas, Miami	.182	35	99	16	18	27	3	0	2	7	0	1	0	1	15	0	11	2	2
Malave, Benito, St. Petersburg	.000	24	3	0	0	0	0	0	0	0	0	0	0	0	0	0	3	0	0
Malave, Omar, Dunedin	.228	38	101	7	23	30	2	1	1	10	1	0	2	0	4	0	14	0	0
Malone, Charles, Clearwater	.143	34	21	3	3	3	0	0	0	0	0	0	0	0	1	0	5	0	0
Manering, Mark, Fort Lauderdale°...	.300	82	297	44	89	108	14	1	1	31	6	1	1	1	32	3	32	1	0
Marigny, Ronald, Lakeland	.246	70	187	16	46	54	8	0	0	20	2	5	2	0	25	0	20	3	4
Marino, John, West Palm Beach†	.000	28	2	0	0	0	0	0	0	0	0	0	0	0	0	0	0	0	0
Markley, Scott, Osceola°	.242	85	302	42	73	95	10	3	2	22	4	8	1	4	40	1	35	21	3

Player and Club	Pct.	G.	AB.	R.	H.	TB.	2B.	3B.	HR.	RBI.	GW.	SH.	SF.	HP.	BB.	Int. BB.	SO.	SB.	CS.
Martinez, Domingo, Dunedin	.257	118	435	53	112	172	32	2	8	65	12	0	2	3	41	2	88	8	3
Martinez, Luis, Tampa	.225	12	40	5	9	12	3	0	0	3	1	0	1	0	5	0	2	0	0
Martinez, Ramon, Vero Beach	.100	25	20	1	2	2	0	0	0	0	0	2	0	0	0	0	5	0	0
Martinez, Ricardo, Ft. Lauderdale	.143	3	7	1	1	1	0	0	0	0	0	0	0	0	0	0	3	0	1
Mauch, Thomas, St. Petersburg°	.143	33	7	0	1	1	0	0	0	0	0	1	0	0	0	0	2	0	0
McCall, Roy, Clearwater	.197	66	208	23	41	58	4	2	3	17	3	2	0	2	23	0	49	0	0
McElroy, Glen, Daytona Beach	.000	6	5	0	0	0	0	0	0	0	0	0	0	0	0	0	1	0	0
McKelvey, Mitch, West Palm Beach	.000	4	1	0	0	0	0	0	0	0	0	0	0	0	0	0	1	0	0
McRae, Brian, Fort Myers†	.252	131	481	62	121	140	14	1	1	31	3	0	0	6	22	1	70	33	18
Mead, Timber, Tampa	.231	29	13	1	3	3	0	0	0	0	0	0	0	0	2	0	6	0	0
Melendez, Luis, Lakeland	.125	7	16	2	2	2	0	0	0	1	0	1	0	0	4	0	5	0	0
Mendez, Jesus, St. Petersburg°	.305	137	522	63	159	192	19	4	2	78	15	3	7	1	46	3	24	5	4
Merullo, Matthew, Daytona Beach°	.260	70	250	26	65	100	11	6	4	47	6	0	6	0	20	1	18	1	1
Metoyer, Tony, Osceola	.400	23	10	1	4	7	0	0	1	1	0	1	0	0	0	0	0	0	1
Meulens, Hensley, Fort Lauderdale	.172	17	58	2	10	13	3	0	0	2	0	0	0	0	7	0	25	0	0
Meyer, Brian, Osceola	1.000	52	1	2	1	2	1	0	0	3	0	1	0	0	1	0	0	0	0
Milholland, Eric, Daytona Beach	.241	104	320	44	77	90	8	1	1	25	3	4	2	1	36	1	42	5	8
Millay, Garrick, Charlotte	.266	113	395	52	105	172	25	3	12	53	2	2	1	6	45	3	58	2	4
Miller, Kenny, Clearwater	.242	36	99	8	24	27	3	0	0	6	1	0	1	1	5	0	11	0	1
Miller, Michael, Clearwater°	.286	9	7	1	2	2	0	0	0	1	0	0	0	0	0	0	1	0	0
Mills, Craig, Lakeland	.267	113	397	70	106	156	28	2	6	58	7	0	9	7	55	2	73	13	4
Milstien, David, Winter Haven	.221	100	303	35	67	72	5	0	0	33	3	7	4	1	12	1	31	0	1
Mims, Larry, Miami†	.234	107	354	52	83	90	5	1	0	14	3	7	0	2	40	0	32	37	11
Minutelli, Gino, Tampa°	.091	20	11	1	1	1	0	0	0	1	1	1	0	0	2	0	2	0	0
Monzon, Jose, Lakeland	.000	4	5	0	0	0	0	0	0	0	0	2	0	0	0	0	4	0	0
Moore, Bradley, Clearwater	.000	5	3	0	0	0	0	0	0	0	0	0	0	0	0	0	0	0	0
Morris, Angel, Fort Myers	.233	43	133	15	31	36	2	0	1	10	1	0	2	0	11	0	20	3	2
Mulligan, William, Fort Myers°	.000	40	1	0	0	0	0	0	0	0	0	0	0	0	0	0	1	0	0
Munoz, Omer, West Palm Beach	.000	5	7	0	0	0	0	0	0	0	0	0	0	0	1	0	1	0	1
Munoz, Pedro, Dunedin	.235	92	341	55	80	125	11	5	8	44	5	1	4	2	34	0	74	13	4
Murdock, Kevin, Daytona Beach	.268	20	41	4	11	13	2	0	0	9	1	1	0	0	11	0	11	2	0
Murphy, John, St. Petersburg	.313	9	16	4	5	7	2	0	0	3	0	0	0	2	4	0	5	0	0
Murray, David, Charlotte	.235	25	68	11	16	17	1	0	0	3	0	0	0	0	10	0	10	2	0
Mustari, Frank, Vero Beach	.143	6	7	0	1	2	1	0	0	0	0	0	0	0	0	0	3	0	0
Nicholson, Keith, Lakeland	.000	25	0	0	0	0	0	0	0	0	0	0	0	0	0	0	1	0	0
Nieto, Andres, Daytona Beach	.277	76	188	27	52	56	2	1	0	13	0	4	1	2	10	0	13	3	2
Norman, Daniel, Miami	.261	23	69	8	18	24	3	0	1	7	0	0	1	0	6	1	7	1	0
North, Jay, St. Petersburg	.120	27	25	2	3	4	1	0	0	2	0	2	0	0	2	0	10	0	0
Novak, Thomas, Tampa	.000	29	4	1	0	0	0	0	0	0	0	0	0	0	0	0	2	0	0
Nowak, Matthew, Miami	.310	30	84	13	26	40	5	0	3	12	1	2	0	1	20	0	24	3	1
Nunez, Mauricio, St. Petersburg	.258	132	493	66	127	179	18	5	8	75	13	3	6	4	47	2	68	44	16
Ojeda, Luis, Miami	.221	82	271	28	60	72	9	0	1	34	5	1	5	3	25	2	15	4	1
Orsag, James, Winter Haven°	.257	94	265	47	68	99	13	3	4	34	3	0	2	3	44	0	70	7	1
Osteen, David, St. Petersburg	.300	19	20	4	6	7	1	0	0	1	0	3	0	0	1	0	8	0	0
Padilla, Livio, Winter Haven	.213	37	94	9	20	29	3	0	2	10	1	1	1	4	15	0	27	0	0
Pardini, William, Miami°	.224	53	156	15	35	44	9	0	0	15	0	0	2	3	14	0	15	3	1
Parker, Olen, Clearwater†	.270	63	185	28	50	53	1	1	0	13	1	2	1	0	20	2	30	3	2
Parker, Richard, Clearwater	.252	101	330	56	83	111	13	3	3	34	6	2	3	3	31	3	36	6	4
Pearn, Joseph, Charlotte	.221	55	140	6	31	33	2	0	0	15	1	1	0	0	17	0	29	0	0
Pearson, Kevin, Tampa	.255	125	420	38	107	134	16	1	3	52	9	5	5	5	43	2	62	10	2
Peel, Jack, Daytona Beach	.303	38	142	27	43	74	16	0	5	33	5	3	3	3	14	0	21	4	1
Perez, Yorkis, West Palm Beach°	.091	15	11	1	1	1	0	0	0	1	0	2	0	0	0	0	3	0	0
Pinol, Juan, Tampa	.222	55	185	15	41	48	5	1	0	14	0	1	2	0	19	0	36	1	3
Pottinger, Mark, Lakeland†	.299	31	67	13	20	24	2	1	0	11	2	0	1	1	12	0	14	4	1
Potts, David, Osceola	.167	36	6	1	1	1	0	0	0	0	0	0	0	0	0	0	2	0	0
Pratt, Todd, Winter Haven	.258	118	407	57	105	163	22	0	12	65	8	0	6	1	70	4	94	0	1
Prioleau, Thelanious, Lakeland†	.241	9	29	4	7	8	1	0	0	4	1	0	0	0	7	0	4	2	0
Randle, Randy, Osceola	.220	116	372	54	82	118	18	6	2	39	1	8	3	0	48	2	68	16	6
Reese, Kyle, Fort Myers	.144	43	125	10	18	22	4	0	0	10	0	1	2	0	5	1	41	0	0
Reichel, Thomas, Daytona Beach	.284	79	225	42	64	77	10	0	1	15	3	1	3	2	31	1	30	9	2
Reimer, Kevin, Clearwater°	.244	74	271	36	66	111	13	7	6	34	4	0	2	2	29	2	48	2	1
Rice, Thomas, Fort Myers	.400	3	10	3	4	4	0	0	0	0	0	0	0	0	4	0	2	0	0
Richardi, Richard, Miami†	.270	111	382	56	103	133	19	4	1	30	1	8	3	2	44	1	47	22	12
Richardson, Jeffrey, Tampa	.299	100	374	44	112	125	9	2	0	37	7	1	7	3	30	5	35	10	4
Richie, Robert, Lakeland°	.294	60	204	31	60	77	8	3	1	32	3	1	1	2	22	1	27	4	2
Rivers, Kenneth, Dunedin	.333	14	36	3	12	16	1	0	1	5	0	0	0	2	0		4	0	2
Robertson, Michael, St. Petersburg	.280	119	425	79	119	146	16	1	3	43	5	4	4	4	68	2	57	13	9
Rodriguez, Raul, Dunedin	.182	4	11	1	2	3	1	0	0	0	0	0	0	0	0	0	2	0	0
Rohde, David, Osceola	.286	103	377	57	108	140	15	1	5	42	5	10	4	4	50	1	58	12	6
Rojas, Ricardo, Fort Myers	.500	21	2	0	1	1	0	0	0	1	0	0	0	0	0	0	0	0	0
Rosario, Melvin, Fort Lauderdale	.169	46	124	9	21	27	6	0	0	18	3	3	1	1	10	0	44	0	0
Rousey, Stephen, West Palm Beach°	.000	5	1	0	0	0	0	0	0	0	0	0	0	0	0	0	0	0	0
Rowland, Donald, Lakeland	.276	26	87	17	24	30	3	0	1	17	2	3	1	1	14	0	11	3	4
Ruiz, Samuel, Miami°	.214	16	56	9	12	13	1	0	0	3	0	1	0	1	5	0	9	2	2
Ryan, Kevin, Vero Beach	.000	1	1	0	0	0	0	0	0	0	0	0	0	0	0	0	0	0	0
Sambo, Ramon, Tampa†	.268	88	302	66	81	93	10	1	0	17	1	5	0	0	65	0	43	60	12
Samson, Frederick, Charlotte	.285	83	270	27	77	94	12	1	1	40	7	3	4	2	25	1	53	3	2
Sanchez, Juan, Clearwater	.199	58	161	15	32	43	6	1	1	12	2	1	2	5	6	0	30	1	0
Sapienza, Michael, Tampa	.255	72	208	15	53	54	1	0	0	20	3	4	1	0	13	1	30	1	1
Sassone, Michael, St. Petersburg	.217	27	23	2	5	5	0	0	0	1	0	4	0	0	1	0	9	0	0
Scanlin, Michael, Charlotte°	.243	84	268	36	65	96	13	3	4	30	4	1	4	0	23	0	66	13	3
Schulte, Joseph, Osceola	.250	42	4	0	1	2	1	0	0	0	0	0	0	0	0	0	0	0	0
Schulte, Mark, Fort Myers°	.265	137	491	48	130	172	21	3	5	61	5	1	6	3	30	2	45	10	7
Schunk, Jerry, Dunedin	.246	98	358	40	88	119	15	2	4	39	4	0	2	2	17	0	38	11	4
Schwarz, Thomas, Clearwater	.289	26	83	9	24	32	5	0	1	11	1	1	0	1	10	0	9	0	0
Scott, Jerry, Tampa	.000	6	7	0	0	0	0	0	0	0	0	0	0	0	0	0	0	0	0
Scruggs, Anthony, Charlotte	.326	23	86	14	28	41	4	0	3	11	1	1	0	2	4	0	17	4	2
Sedar, Edward, Daytona Beach	.264	55	174	23	46	61	8	2	1	31	0	0	2	1	19	1	36	6	6
Senne, Michael, St. Petersburg	.261	140	505	79	132	196	28	3	10	82	13	2	8	4	55	3	90	16	6
Service, Scott, Clearwater	.000	21	15	1	0	0	0	0	0	0	0	0	3	0	0	0	4	0	0
Sharts, Stephen, Clearwater	.111	41	9	0	1	1	0	0	0	1	0	0	1	0	1	0	6	0	0
Shaw, Scott, Fort Lauderdale	.294	82	320	42	94	126	18	1	4	56	8	0	1	0	38	1	48	2	0

Player and Club	Pct.	G.	AB.	R.	H.	TB.	2B.	3B.	HR.	RBI.	GW.	SH.	SF.	HP.	BB.	Int. BB.	SO.	SB.	CS.
Simon, Richard, Osceola	.000	5	1	0	0	0	0	0	0	0	0	0	0	0	0	0	1	0	0
Simonds, Daniel, Miami	.229	11	35	3	8	11	0	0	1	3	0	1	0	0	2	0	4	1	0
Sims, Kinney, Vero Beach*	.267	14	15	3	4	7	1	1	0	1	0	1	0	0	1	0	6	0	0
Singley, Joseph, Daytona Beach	.111	9	18	1	2	2	0	0	0	0	0	0	0	0	1	0	5	0	1
Sipe, Patrick, West Palm Beach*	.274	129	478	70	131	212	24	3	17	84	7	0	4	2	23	10	62	1	1
Smith, Bryan, Vero Beach	.000	10	1	0	0	0	0	0	0	0	0	0	0	0	0	0	0	0	0
Smith, Bryn, West Palm Beach	.000	4	0	0	0	0	0	0	0	0	0	1	0	0	1	0	0	0	0
Smith, Dana, Miami	.192	24	73	7	14	19	2	0	1	2	0	1	0	2	11	0	12	1	0
Snyder, Doug, Osceola*	.282	109	309	43	87	115	14	4	2	42	4	2	6	1	84	11	60	11	3
Sonberg, Erik, Vero Beach	.000	7	2	0	0	0	0	0	0	0	0	0	0	0	0	0	2	0	0
Spagnuolo, Joseph, Vero Beach	.269	93	279	45	75	103	6	2	6	38	5	2	3	3	28	1	42	18	5
Stankiewicz, Andrew, Ft. Lauderdale	.307	119	456	80	140	178	18	7	2	47	4	7	1	4	62	1	84	26	13
Stoll, Richard, West Palm Beach	.000	13	0	0	0	0	0	0	0	0	0	1	0	0	0	0	0	0	0
Strichek, James, St. Petersburg	.000	17	2	0	0	0	0	0	0	0	0	0	0	0	0	0	1	0	0
Sudo, Robert, West Palm Beach	.143	17	7	0	1	1	0	0	0	0	0	0	2	0	1	0	2	0	0
Sugiura, Mamoru, Miami	.200	66	180	10	36	54	8	2	2	10	0	1	0	0	12	1	69	2	1
Sullivan, Carl, Daytona Beach	.228	108	337	41	77	109	18	4	2	28	2	2	3	4	18	0	70	21	10
Sullivan, Daniel, Winter Haven†	.242	106	339	50	82	111	14	0	5	46	6	1	2	4	65	1	52	4	1
Swob, Timothy, Tampa*	.071	26	14	0	1	2	1	0	0	1	0	1	0	0	1	0	8	0	0
Tabaka, Jeffrey, West Palm Beach	.111	28	9	0	1	1	0	0	0	1	0	0	0	0	0	0	5	0	0
Tapia, Jose, Vero Beach	.000	45	3	0	0	0	0	0	0	0	0	0	0	0	1	0	3	0	0
Thomas, Thomas, Vero Beach*	.296	114	416	72	123	144	9	6	0	31	2	2	5	1	82	1	25	20	13
Thomson, Robert, Lakeland	.228	71	206	21	47	62	12	0	1	22	3	6	1	0	25	1	30	2	0
Thoutsis, Paul, Winter Haven*	.247	105	336	47	83	122	14	2	7	41	5	2	2	7	35	3	50	2	1
Threadgill, George, Charlotte	.333	19	60	7	20	24	2	1	0	2	0	0	1	1	7	0	16	5	2
Tinkle, David, Fort Myers*	.220	81	245	21	54	69	6	3	1	18	1	0	1	0	19	2	38	3	5
Toale, John, Winter Haven*	.300	98	317	49	95	163	23	0	15	58	4	0	2	0	44	7	54	0	1
Torres, Philip, Vero Beach	.000	6	0	0	0	0	0	0	0	0	0	1	0	0	0	0	0	0	0
Torve, Kenton, Daytona Beach*	.247	52	150	13	37	52	7	1	2	16	1	1	3	0	18	2	34	1	3
Touma, Timothy, West Palm Beach	.258	59	124	14	32	34	2	0	0	9	1	6	1	1	13	0	15	0	2
Traen, Thomas, West Palm Beach†	.000	12	3	0	0	0	0	0	0	0	0	2	0	0	0	0	2	0	0
Trafton, Todd, Daytona Beach	.263	127	449	64	118	190	23	2	15	61	5	2	8	3	54	1	44	7	5
Vanderwal, John, West Palm Beach*	.286	50	189	29	54	75	11	2	2	22	2	1	3	0	30	0	25	8	3
Vargas, Jose A., Charlotte†	.215	127	493	60	106	121	9	3	0	29	5	3	5	1	22	2	48	35	12
Vargas, Jose E., Osceola	.190	23	21	1	4	4	0	0	0	3	1	4	1	0	0	0	5	0	0
Villa, Michael, Tampa*	.000	22	2	0	0	0	0	0	0	0	0	0	0	0	0	0	0	0	0
Walden, Travis, Clearwater*	.333	41	15	1	5	6	1	0	0	5	1	0	0	0	2	0	0	0	0
Walters, Daniel, Osceola	.249	99	338	23	84	95	8	0	1	30	2	5	5	0	33	2	42	2	4
Ward, Turner, Fort Lauderdale†	.294	130	493	83	145	185	15	2	7	55	8	7	3	6	64	4	83	25	3
Weidie, Stuart, Winter Haven*	.220	101	313	35	69	107	16	2	6	48	3	1	5	6	47	0	108	4	2
Wells, Terry, Osceola*	.100	28	10	3	1	2	1	0	0	0	0	1	0	0	2	0	2	0	0
Wetteland, John, Vero Beach	.077	27	26	1	2	2	0	0	0	1	0	1	0	0	0	0	5	0	0
Whitaker, Brian, Tampa	.156	15	32	4	5	6	1	0	0	2	0	0	0	5	0	5	6	3	0
White, Gary, Clearwater*	.162	12	37	0	6	6	0	0	0	3	0	1	0	2	0	6	0	0	0
White, Michael, Vero Beach*	.222	14	45	6	10	11	1	0	0	3	0	0	0	3	0	6	0	0	0
Wieligman, Richard, Lakeland*	.281	103	360	60	101	143	17	5	5	49	4	3	3	1	60	7	35	14	8
Wilborn, Thaddeus, Miami†	.224	19	49	3	11	12	1	0	0	5	1	0	1	0	6	2	5	2	1
Williams, Bernabe, Fort Lauderdale *	.155	25	71	11	11	14	3	0	0	4	0	2	0	3	18	1	22	9	1
Williams, Robert, West Palm Beach	.091	21	11	1	1	1	0	0	0	1	0	0	0	0	2	0	7	0	0
Williamson, Bret, Tampa	.218	103	289	23	63	89	16	2	2	28	0	4	1	0	29	1	56	0	3
Willis, Kenneth, Tampa	.200	25	20	1	4	5	1	0	0	1	0	1	1	0	1	0	4	0	0
Wilson, Craig, St. Petersburg	.358	38	162	35	58	72	6	4	0	28	2	0	0	0	14	0	5	12	8
Wisdom, Allen, Clearwater†	.000	8	1	0	0	0	0	0	0	0	0	0	0	0	0	0	0	0	0
Wood, Stephen, Vero Beach	.000	23	2	0	0	0	0	0	0	0	0	0	0	0	0	0	2	0	0
Woods, Tony, Miami	.249	73	261	31	65	110	11	2	10	35	4	1	5	0	17	3	53	12	4
Young, Raymond, Dunedin	.000	35	1	0	0	0	0	0	0	0	0	0	0	0	0	0	1	0	0
Zambrano, Eduardo, Winter Haven	.267	69	225	33	60	111	16	1	11	32	2	3	3	5	27	0	47	1	1
Zayas, Carlos, Clearwater	.203	21	64	4	13	14	1	0	0	5	1	0	1	1	4	0	8	0	1
Zeratsky, Rodney, Tampa	.248	38	129	10	32	43	8	0	1	13	0	1	1	2	15	0	7	1	0

The following pitchers, listed alphabetically by club, with games in parentheses, had no plate appearances, primarily through use of designated hitters:

CHARLOTTE—Barfield, John (25); Brown, Kevin (6); Cerny, Martin (34); Clawson, Kenneth (36); Harden, Ty (11); Lankard, Steven (66); Manuel, Barry (13); Mays, Jeffrey (9); Meadows, Jimmy (9); Morales, Edwin (16); Morse, Scott (13); Petkovsek, Mark (11); Raether, Eric (27); Rockman, Marvin (10); Rogers, Kenneth (5); Russell, Jeffrey (2); Schofield, John (37); Shiflett, Christian (1); Thomas, Mitchell (28); True, Steven (3); Valdez, Efrain (17); Wilson, Stephen (20).

CLEARWATER—McDevitt, Stephen (3); McElroy, Charles (2); Pruett, David (1).

DAYTONA BEACH—Abreu, Francisco (6); Allen, Neil (4); Brennan, James (14); Cauley, Chris (10); Cortes, Argenis (32); DeLaCruz, Carlos (7); Drees, Thomas (27); Edwards, Wayne (29); Girdner, Troy (20); Groom, Wedsel (11); Henry, Mark (30); Little, Douglas (29); Potestio, Frank (29); Reed, Kenneth (24); Roth, Rex (7).

DUNEDIN—Balsley, Darren (43); Blair, William (50); Brinson, Hugh (25); Castillo, Antonio (39); Cummings, Steven (32); Englund, Timothy (9); Filer, Thomas (6); Johnson, Dane (18); Jones, Christopher (27); Lavelle, Gary (9); Mumaw, Stephen (30); Newcomb, Joe (4); Saitta, Patrick (16); Sanders, Earl (29); Watts, Robert (5).

FORT LAUDERDALE—Adkins, Steven (5); Carroll, Christopher (19); Christopher, Michael (24); Eiland, David (8); Evers, Troy (24); Figueroa, Fernando (9); Gay, Scott (24); Guercio, Maurice (9); Guidry, Ronald (2); Hellman, Jeffrey (24); Marris, Mark (1); Patterson, Kenneth (9); Pries, Jeffrey (11); Ridenour, Dana (43); Rodriguez, Gabriel (14); Rose, Mark (17); Rub, Gerry (38); Scheid, Richard (9); Stoddard, Timothy (2); Voeltz, William (8); Wilkins, Dean (15).

FORT MYERS—Adams, Kenneth (14); Alexander, Jonathan (12); Blouin, Gary (17); Boroski, Stanley (8); Butcher, Michael (5); Champagne, Brannon (17); Crouch, Matthew (10); DeLeon, Jesus (3); Ellis, Rufus (29); Goodenough, Randy (15); Gordon, Thomas (3); Hibbard, Gregory (3); Jones, George (40); McIntyre, Richard (17); Meyers, Brian (4); Mount, Charles (16); Naworski, Andrew (17); Netemeyer, Daniel (9); Odom, Timothy (17); Perez, Melido (8); Pumphrey, Shawn (10); Studeman, Dennis (7); Trapp, Michael (9); Vasquez, Aguedo (8); Williams, Timothy (2).

LAKELAND—Carter, Richard (21); Cooper, David (23); Garces, Robinson (30); Gohmann, Kenneth (31); Hansen, Michael (22); Lacko, Richard (24); Lee, Mark (30); McHugh, Charles (3); Nosek, Randall (10); O'Neill, Daniel (5); Phillips, Charles (13); Raubolt, Arthur (28); Schultz, Scott (21); Schwabe, Michael (5); Slavik, Joseph (7); Vesling, Donald (1); Wenson, Paul (47); Williams, Kenneth (9).

MIAMI—Browning, Michael (17); Burdick, Stacey (4); Constant, Andres (6); Diez, Scott (28); Evans, Scott (2); Harrington, John (23); King, Kenneth (21); Martinez, Dennis (3); Matsubara, Yasushi (10); Matsuo, Hideharu (32); Peguero, Soto (21); Rohan, Edward (22); Rowe, Thomas (5); Sheary, Kevin (10); Talamantez, Gregory (3); Thorpe, Paul (8); Vazquez, Jesse (21); Walton, Robert (9); Watanabe, Mashahito (4); Wilson, Chaunan (3).

OSCEOLA—DeLeon, Pedro (5); Estes, Joel (47); Fascher, Stanley (4); Murphy, Gary (4).

ST. PETERSBURG—Zaltsman, Stanley (1).

TAMPA—Roesler, Michael (28); Vierra, Joseph (9); Williams, Dwayne (4).

VERO BEACH—Sepulveda, Jorge (10); Shea, Kevin (25).

WINTER HAVEN—Abril, Ernest (9); Brown, Paul (11); Coffey, Michael (40); Dedos, Felix (54); Gabriele, Daniel (26); Gomez, Dana (20); Haley, Bart (2); Hetzel, Eric (26); Livernois, Derek (20); Lockhart, Bruce (20); Shikles, Larry (27); Slifko, Paul (28).

GRAND SLAM HOME RUNS—Afenir, Brow, Magallanes, 2 each; David, S. Davis, Johnson, T. Jones, Leyritz, D. Martinez, Mendez, Nowak, Pratt, Sipe, D. Sullivan, Toale, Ward, Weide, Zambrano, 1 each.

AWARDED FIRST BASE ON CATCHER'S INTERFERENCE—Azocar 3 (Lau, McCall, Pratt); Baker 2 (Magrann, Reese); Dickerson 2 (Kreuter, Lambert); Gegen 2 (Merullo, Nowak); Kramer 2 (Hornacek, Nowak); Ward 2 (Morris, Nowak); Behnsch (Magrann); Berry (M. Fox); Billmeyer (Nowak); D. Burke (Pratt); Dempsay (Walters); Gaylor (Bartels); Kreuter (Magrann); Millay (Merullo); Mills (Lambert).

CLUB FIELDING

Club	Pct.	G.	PO.	A.	E.	DP.	PB.	Club	Pct.	G.	PO.	A.	E.	DP.	PB.
St. Petersburg	.971	142	3587	1541	154	133	21	Dunedin	.964	140	3639	1432	191	137	30
West Palm Beach	.971	138	3576	1490	153	138	17	Fort Myers	.960	141	3507	1363	205	117	24
Osceola	.970	139	3647	1444	158	101	17	Vero Beach	.959	138	3604	1477	216	119	38
Fort Lauderdale	.967	138	3602	1511	172	132	34	Miami	.959	133	3345	1440	205	124	24
Clearwater	.967	136	3469	1388	167	117	18	Charlotte	.959	143	3684	1566	225	126	23
Lakeland	.966	135	3486	1471	177	112	19	Winter Haven	.958	138	3546	1395	214	125	37
Daytona Beach	.964	139	3572	1564	190	134	29	Tampa	.956	140	3504	1497	232	119	29

Triple Plays—Clearwater, Lakeland, Vero Beach.

INDIVIDUAL FIELDING

*Throws lefthanded.

FIRST BASEMEN

Player and Club	Pct.	G.	PO.	A.	E.	DP.	Player and Club	Pct.	G.	PO.	A.	E.	DP.
Afenir, Osceola	.995	20	173	12	1	10	T. JONES, Fort Myers*	.992	103	831	52	7	81
Azocar, Fort Lauderdale*	1.000	1	1	0	0	0	Joslyn, Fort Myers*	.996	28	240	18	1	21
Bastinck, Lakeland	1.000	1	1	0	0	0	Kaiser, Clearwater	.982	16	106	6	2	11
Batesole, Vero Beach	1.000	2	9	1	0	0	Lau, Miami	1.000	6	55	5	0	1
Behnsch, Clearwater	.993	89	782	55	6	67	Lung, Charlotte	1.000	1	5	0	0	0
Berman, Clearwater	.986	31	266	15	4	24	Maas, Fort Lauderdale*	.986	76	667	51	10	67
Bernardo, Charlotte*	.986	138	1198	103	19	105	Malave, Dunedin	.979	14	83	9	2	4
Billmeyer, Miami	.990	25	185	12	2	23	Manering, Fort Lauderdale*	.996	55	535	34	2	44
Blowers, West Palm Beach	1.000	1	1	0	0	0	D. Martinez, Dunedin	.986	118	1014	78	16	101
Borders, Dunedin	1.000	2	21	1	0	1	L. Martinez, Tampa	1.000	4	32	6	0	0
Bradshaw, Lakeland	1.000	3	19	1	0	2	McCall, Clearwater	1.000	4	45	1	0	3
Brown, Vero Beach	.953	10	73	8	4	4	Mendez, St. Petersburg*	.991	125	1138	81	11	104
Burke, Vero Beach*	.992	59	469	37	4	38	Merullo, Daytona Beach	.964	3	27	0	1	4
Butts, St. Petersburg*	.984	17	115	6	2	9	Milholland, Daytona Beach	.857	3	6	0	1	1
Caffrey, West Palm Beach	.978	31	258	11	6	24	Mills, Lakeland	.965	13	101	9	4	8
Carey, Tampa*	.889	1	7	1	1	1	Morris, Fort Lauderdale	1.000	1	3	0	0	0
Carter, Fort Lauderdale	1.000	9	59	9	0	3	Murdock, Daytona Beach	1.000	1	3	0	0	0
Clements, Tampa	.984	12	111	9	2	8	Norman, Miami	.982	11	99	8	2	10
Colston, Miami	.917	4	32	1	3	6	Ojeda, Miami	.992	27	247	14	2	18
Cooper, Osceola	.988	37	305	16	4	26	Orsag, Winter Haven	.976	38	254	26	7	32
Cunningham, St. Petersburg	1.000	1	3	1	0	0	Pearn, Charlotte	1.000	2	3	0	0	0
Cusack, Lakeland	.982	22	159	9	3	13	Pratt, Winter Haven	.980	28	236	15	5	27
Daily, Lakeland	.986	16	126	13	2	10	Prioleau, Lakeland	1.000	1	5	0	0	0
Daulton, Clearwater	.818	2	7	2	2	0	Robertson, St. Petersburg	.900	3	18	0	2	2
David, Osceola	1.000	1	1	0	0	0	Scawlin, Charlotte*	.987	9	69	6	1	5
DeLaCruz, Dunedin	.985	9	58	7	1	8	Schulte, Fort Myers	.975	9	71	6	2	8
Diaz, Dunedin	1.000	2	16	1	0	0	Sedar, Daytona Beach	.979	8	42	4	1	3
Duggan, Charlotte	1.000	4	18	1	0	2	Shaw, Fort Lauderdale	1.000	1	9	1	0	1
Fazzini, Vero Beach	1.000	1	1	0	0	0	Sipe, West Palm Beach*	.991	114	955	73	9	94
Fox, St. Petersburg	1.000	2	18	1	0	4	Smith, Miami	1.000	1	10	1	0	1
Freiling, Vero Beach*	.994	52	467	33	3	42	Snyder, Osceola	.990	96	823	40	9	57
Garcia, Daytona Beach*	.982	14	106	5	2	11	Sullivan, Winter Haven	.982	82	601	40	12	52
Gegen, Vero Beach	.971	23	187	11	6	17	Toale, Winter Haven	.938	2	10	5	1	1
Hardgrave, Lakeland	1.000	7	34	1	0	2	Torve, Daytona Beach	1.000	6	30	2	0	1
Hilgenberg, Tampa*	.993	93	790	52	6	62	Trafton, Daytona Beach	.989	118	1033	73	12	100
Hornacek, 4 VB-1 Mia	.969	5	29	2	1	4	Weidie, Winter Haven	1.000	1	7	0	0	0
Inagaki, Miami	.987	67	505	33	7	48	Wieligman, Osceola*	.990	87	758	50	8	64
Johnson, Fort Myers*	1.000	3	9	0	0	0	Williamson, Tampa	.986	40	320	20	5	24
M. Jones, Dunedin	.950	2	16	3	1	2	Woods, Miami	1.000	12	76	8	0	2

Triple Plays—Berman, Freiling, Wieligman.

SECOND BASEMEN

Player and Club	Pct.	G.	PO.	A.	E.	DP.	Player and Club	Pct.	G.	PO.	A.	E.	DP.
Anderson, Vero Beach	1.000	2	2	6	0	2	Huson, West Palm Beach	1.000	1	0	1	0	0
Austin, Lakeland	.975	109	223	319	14	57	Ickes, Winter Haven	.902	11	32	23	6	9
Baker, West Palm Beach	1.000	4	6	12	0	1	Jarner, Clearwater	.818	2	3	6	2	2
Bochesa, Winter Haven	1.000	1	1	0	0	0	LASEKE, Winter Haven	.979	113	237	316	12	79
Brown, Osceola	.969	11	14	17	1	3	Malave, Dunedin	.933	6	8	6	1	0
Caceres, West Palm Beach	.989	94	168	267	5	54	Marigny, Lakeland	.982	25	48	60	2	11
Clements, Tampa	1.000	4	12	11	0	3	Martinez, Fort Lauderdale	1.000	2	2	2	0	1
Coolbaugh, Charlotte	1.000	1	2	5	0	0	McRae, Fort Myers	.972	130	284	346	18	75
Corcino, Fort Myers	.967	15	35	23	2	4	Millay, Charlotte	1.000	1	2	4	0	1
Dickerson, Fort Lauderdale	.976	8	13	27	1	1	Mims, Miami	.952	50	83	136	11	21
Elliott, Osceola	.952	66	122	153	14	27	Munoz, West Palm Beach	.833	1	2	3	1	0
Esteban, Vero Beach	1.000	5	2	9	0	0	Murray, Charlotte	.977	7	19	23	1	5
Eveline, Daytona Beach	.947	36	75	87	9	16	Nieto, Daytona Beach	.953	48	99	106	10	25
Francois, Vero Beach	.956	103	225	269	23	62	Pardini, Miami	.933	48	87	164	18	29
Garrison, Dunedin	.964	116	222	311	20	71	O. Parker, Clearwater	.961	58	111	160	11	38
Gaylor, West Palm Beach	.970	8	16	16	1	5	R. Parker, Clearwater	.959	39	79	109	8	14
Gellinger, Daytona Beach	.952	7	20	20	2	3	Pinol, Tampa	.977	8	16	27	1	5
Goff, Winter Haven	.925	18	35	39	6	5	Pottinger, Lakeland	1.000	2	0	4	0	0
Harrison, St. Petersburg	.973	131	274	367	18	88	Reichel, Daytona Beach	.985	31	50	78	2	14
Hartman, Vero Beach	.967	25	32	56	3	9	Richardi, Miami	.935	26	49	81	9	19
Horton, St. Petersburg	.917	7	7	15	2	2	Richardson, Tampa	.965	72	153	176	12	36
Houston, West Palm Beach	.959	38	61	101	7	13	Rohde, Osceola	.965	84	135	249	14	45

SECOND BASEMEN—Continued

Player and Club	Pct.	G.	PO.	A.	E.	DP.	Player and Club	Pct.	G.	PO.	A.	E.	DP.
Rowland, Lakeland	1.000	6	13	6	0	1	Spagnuolo, Vero Beach	1.000	22	39	56	0	9
Ruiz, Miami	.875	5	8	13	3	3	Stankiewicz, Fort Lauderdale	.973	118	233	347	16	83
Sambo, Tampa	.963	58	94	141	9	25	Tinkle, Fort Myers	1.000	2	2	2	0	0
Samson, Charlotte	.948	16	36	37	4	9	Torve, Daytona Beach	.967	42	67	108	6	28
Sanchez, Clearwater	.976	42	92	110	5	18	Touma, West Palm Beach	.941	17	13	19	2	6
Schunk, Dunedin	.968	22	55	65	4	13	Vargas, Charlotte	.952	126	270	327	30	72
Shaw, Fort Lauderdale	.966	13	27	29	2	7	Whitaker, Tampa	.952	8	8	12	1	2
Smith, Miami	.982	10	19	35	1	11	Wilson, St. Petersburg	1.000	9	14	31	0	4

Triple Plays—Austin, Francois.

THIRD BASEMEN

Player and Club	Pct.	G.	PO.	A.	E.	DP.	Player and Club	Pct.	G.	PO.	A.	E.	DP.
Batesole, Vero Beach	.905	100	84	163	26	14	Malave, Dunedin	.833	8	4	11	3	2
Benzo, Tampa	.667	1	0	2	1	0	Marigny, Lakeland	.971	14	9	25	1	4
Berman, Clearwater	.906	96	55	186	25	17	Meulens, Fort Lauderdale	.887	17	18	37	7	4
Berry, Fort Myers	.859	59	39	101	23	14	Milholland, Daytona Beach	1.000	2	1	0	0	0
BLOWERS, West Palm Beach	.9444	128	72	234	18	27	Millay, Charlotte	.893	55	33	109	17	10
Bradshaw, Lakeland	1.000	1	1	0	0	0	Mills, Lakeland	.9438	96	71	181	15	11
Brown, Osceola	.864	36	26	63	14	3	Mustari, Vero Beach	1.000	2	0	2	0	0
Brumfield, Fort Myers	.855	25	17	42	10	3	Nieto, Daytona Beach	1.000	6	3	3	0	1
Caceres, West Palm Beach	.750	1	2	1	1	0	Nowak, Miami	1.000	9	4	23	0	1
Cartaya, Charlotte	1.000	1	3	4	0	0	Ojeda, Miami	.907	37	30	48	8	2
Clements, Tampa	.912	76	61	146	20	12	R. Parker, Clearwater	.925	20	11	38	4	1
Colombino, Osceola	.939	88	59	173	15	19	Pearson, Tampa	.906	37	33	83	12	9
Coolbaugh, Charlotte	.921	64	40	146	16	9	Prioleau, Lakeland	1.000	1	1	0	0	0
Cooper, Osceola	.932	25	21	34	4	2	Reichel, Daytona Beach	.870	25	9	38	7	6
Corcino, Fort Myers	.864	23	10	28	6	1	Richardi, Miami	.926	21	13	37	4	4
Cronkright, Daytona Beach	.925	121	80	253	27	17	Richardson, Tampa	.961	22	15	34	2	3
Culberson, Fort Myers	1.000	1	1	0	0	0	Rowland, Lakeland	.929	14	5	21	2	1
Cunningham, St. Petersburg	.957	83	66	134	9	12	Samson, Charlotte	.957	24	13	53	3	6
DeLaCruz, Dunedin	.903	118	93	205	32	19	Sanchez, Clearwater	.783	6	4	14	5	2
Dickerson, Fort Lauderdale	.929	5	4	9	1	0	Sapienza, Tampa	.758	14	10	15	8	2
Duggan, Charlotte	.857	7	6	12	3	0	Schulte, Fort Myers	1.000	1	1	0	0	0
Elliott, Osceola	.500	2	0	1	1	0	Schunk, Dunedin	.879	9	12	17	4	3
Engram, Daytona Beach	.714	3	2	3	2	2	Schwarz, Clearwater	.896	17	14	29	5	2
Garrison, Dunedin	.824	7	9	5	3	0	Shaw, Fort Lauderdale	.954	63	40	126	8	11
Gaylor, West Palm Beach	1.000	3	1	2	0	0	Smith, Miami	1.000	6	3	11	0	0
Gegen, Vero Beach	.830	38	25	68	19	4	Spagnuolo, Vero Beach	.952	9	2	18	1	0
Gellinger, Daytona Beach	1.000	2	2	4	0	2	Sullivan, Winter Haven	1.000	5	6	8	0	2
Green, Osceola	1.000	2	2	1	0	0	Thomson, Lakeland	.000	2	0	0	1	0
Haggerty, Winter Haven	.907	78	48	128	18	15	Thoutsis, Winter Haven	1.000	1	1	1	0	1
Horton, St. Petersburg	.914	35	16	58	7	4	Tinkle, Fort Myers	.856	43	28	67	16	7
Jarner, Clearwater	.875	4	2	5	1	1	Toale, Winter Haven	.888	73	57	102	20	8
Kreuter, Charlotte	1.000	1	0	3	0	0	Touma, West Palm Beach	.941	13	8	24	2	3
Laboy, Fort Lauderdale	.855	43	21	73	16	6	Ward, Fort Lauderdale	1.000	1	2	1	0	1
Latmore, Miami	.938	9	4	11	1	1	Wilson, St. Petersburg	.931	31	21	60	6	1
Lovullo, Lakeland	.953	18	11	30	2	1	Woods, Miami	.887	59	52	121	22	14
Maas, Fort Lauderdale	.806	19	6	19	6	0							

SHORTSTOPS

Player and Club	Pct.	G.	PO.	A.	E.	DP.	Player and Club	Pct.	G.	PO.	A.	E.	DP.
Adderley, Miami	1.000	1	2	1	0	0	Laseke, Winter Haven	1.000	3	7	12	0	0
Anderson, Vero Beach	1.000	1	0	2	0	0	Latmore, Miami	.939	102	168	275	29	64
Becker, Fort Lauderdale	.956	130	233	396	29	80	Malave, Dunedin	.909	5	9	11	2	4
Bertolani, St. Petersburg	.935	113	190	358	38	64	Marigny, Lakeland	.915	29	39	69	10	14
Blowers, West Palm Beach	1.000	2	2	5	0	2	Milstien, Winter Haven	.898	100	142	281	48	49
Bradshaw, Lakeland	.939	111	169	358	34	51	Mims, Miami	.904	18	39	46	9	9
Caceres, West Palm Beach	1.000	1	0	1	0	0	Munoz, West Palm Beach	1.000	2	1	5	0	0
Cartaya, Charlotte	.919	98	152	282	38	55	Murray, Charlotte	.904	13	17	30	5	6
Clements, Tampa	1.000	2	1	6	0	1	Nieto, Daytona Beach	.825	19	19	33	11	6
Corcino, Fort Myers	.930	32	47	86	10	21	Ojeda, Miami	1.000	2	1	3	0	1
Cunningham, St. Petersburg	1.000	1	1	1	0	0	Pardini, Miami	1.000	2	2	4	0	0
Dickerson, Fort Lauderdale	.895	11	7	10	2	1	Parker, Clearwater	.894	32	40	87	15	15
Duggan, Charlotte	1.000	1	1	4	0	0	Pearson, Tampa	.917	88	121	288	37	43
EDGE, Clearwater	.960	102	183	320	21	59	Pinol, Tampa	.901	46	78	113	21	16
Elliott, Osceola	.952	15	15	25	2	2	Pottinger, Lakeland	1.000	1	4	4	0	0
Garrison, Dunedin	.917	4	1	10	1	0	Prioleau, Lakeland	.833	8	15	15	6	3
Gaylor, West Palm Beach	.895	10	16	18	4	6	Randle, Osceola	.939	115	158	317	31	53
Geist, Vero Beach	.926	98	117	283	32	54	Reichel, Daytona Beach	.972	24	24	80	3	14
Goff, Winter Haven	.935	11	19	24	3	5	Richardi, Miami	.909	12	17	23	4	5
Harrison, St. Petersburg	.913	13	14	28	4	3	Richardson, Tampa	.909	9	12	18	3	6
Houston, West Palm Beach	.943	9	10	23	2	4	Rohde, Osceola	.935	29	30	56	6	6
Howard, Fort Myers	.934	89	123	273	28	48	Rowland, Lakeland	.962	5	7	18	1	2
Huson, West Palm Beach	.944	124	232	346	34	70	Samson, Charlotte	.927	40	56	97	12	11
Ickes, Winter Haven	.909	43	59	91	15	24	Schunk, Dunedin	.952	68	102	193	15	36
Jarner, Clearwater	.952	4	7	13	1	1	Smith, Miami	.939	7	11	20	2	3
Kelly, Dunedin	.942	70	123	203	20	51	Spagnuolo, Vero Beach	.929	49	71	126	15	21
Laboy, Fort Lauderdale	.824	7	6	8	3	0	Tinkle, Fort Myers	.881	·32	32	57	12	12
Lara, St. Petersburg	.935	134	218	427	45	97	Touma, West Palm Beach	1.000	1	0	2	0	0

Triple Plays—Bradshaw, Geist.

OUTFIELDERS

Player and Club	Pct.	G.	PO.	A.	E.	DP.	Player and Club	Pct.	G.	PO.	A.	E.	DP.
Adderley, Miami	.970	80	185	7	6	2	Baldwin, Osceola*	.976	114	201	6	5	1
Alyea, Miami	.984	94	178	11	3	1	Bastinck, Lakeland	1.000	1	1	0	0	0
Amante, St. Petersburg	.909	26	58	2	6	0	Batiste, Dunedin	.986	129	347	16	5	5
Anderson, Lakeland*	.976	111	229	10	6	0	Benitez, Vero Beach	.953	88	157	7	8	1
Arendas, Fort Lauderdale*	.985	32	63	2	1	0	Berman, Clearwater	1.000	1	2	0	0	0
Azocar, Fort Lauderdale*	.975	51	111	4	3	2	Bishop, Fort Lauderdale	1.000	8	14	0	0	0
Baker, West Palm Beach	.988	105	167	4	2	1	Bochesa, Winter Haven	1.000	4	10	0	0	0

OUTFIELDERS—Continued

Player and Club	Pct.	G.	PO.	A.	E.	DP.
Brow, Fort Lauderdale	.976	51	78	2	2	0
D. Brown, Tampa	.893	55	86	6	11	1
M. Brown, Osceola	.750	4	3	0	1	0
H. Brumfield, Clearwater°	.983	101	284	9	5	0
J. Brumfield, Fort Myers	.962	83	218	11	9	1
Brundage, Clearwater°	.974	88	178	13	5	0
Buheller, Winter Haven°	.993	54	133	7	1	0
Burke, West Palm Beach°	.981	97	149	4	3	0
Carey, Tampa°	.959	66	111	7	5	1
Carpenter, Miami	.981	93	199	9	4	2
Carter, Fort Lauderdale	.818	7	8	1	2	0
Clark, Charlotte	.941	19	31	1	2	0
Cooper, Osceola	.990	66	95	1	1	0
Cota, Daytona	.963	107	193	16	8	3
Coveney, Daytona Beach°	.923	25	36	0	3	0
Culberson, Fort Myers	.968	93	211	4	7	0
Daniels, Miami°	1.000	7	8	1	0	0
Dantzler, Clearwater	.995	100	176	6	1	1
G. Davis, Lakeland	1.000	6	8	0	0	0
S. Davis, Tampa	.974	98	219	4	6	2
Dean, West Palm Beach	.978	127	252	13	6	6
DeLeon, Charlotte	1.000	12	11	0	0	0
Delgado, Osceola	.971	28	32	1	1	0
Dempsay, Lakeland	1.000	1	2	0	0	0
Duggan, Charlotte	.944	18	17	0	1	0
Engram, Daytona Beach	.978	66	126	6	3	3
Eveline, Daytona Beach	1.000	12	12	1	0	0
Fazzini, Vero Beach	1.000	4	0	1	0	0
Forney, Tampa	.957	117	194	4	9	0
B. Fox, Lakeland°	.959	92	154	10	7	3
M. Fox, St. Petersburg	.750	1	2	1	1	0
Frye, West Palm Beach	1.000	27	42	1	0	0
Garner, Vero Beach	.962	75	126	1	5	1
Garrison, Dunedin	1.000	1	1	0	0	0
Gegen, Vero Beach	1.000	35	48	5	0	0
Glasker, Charlotte°	.977	129	284	10	7	3
R. Green, Fort Lauderdale	.974	110	213	9	6	3
T. Green, Osceola	1.000	53	91	3	0	0
Harris, Daytona Beach	.978	20	42	3	1	0
Hernandez, West Palm Beach	.955	31	60	4	3	1
Horton, St. Petersburg	.933	9	13	1	1	0
Housie, Lakeland	.978	122	248	13	6	3
Houston, West Palm Beach	1.000	4	3	0	0	0
Howey, Clearwater	.979	102	180	8	4	3
Huson, West Palm Beach	1.000	1	2	0	0	0
Inagaki, Miami	1.000	4	7	0	0	0
L. Jackson, Winter Haven	.970	96	216	9	7	5
M. Jackson, Tampa	.946	56	120	2	7	0
James, Osceola°	.980	107	244	7	5	0
Jeter, Dunedin	.954	126	241	9	12	4
Johnson, Fort Myers°	.947	75	139	5	8	0
Jones, Dunedin	.984	71	119	3	2	0
Jose, Winter Haven	.949	53	146	4	8	0
Joslyn, Fort Myers°	1.000	1	1	0	0	0
Kaiser, Clearwater	.974	19	38	0	1	0
Kesselmark, Vero Beach°	.981	115	203	7	4	1
Koslofski, Fort Myers	.970	100	185	10	6	2
Kramer, Charlotte°	.954	124	180	7	9	1
Kreuter, Charlotte	1.000	2	3	0	0	0
Landrum, Dunedin	.962	96	166	11	7	1
Luciani, Lakeland	1.000	8	7	0	0	0
Maas, Fort Lauderdale	.935	23	41	2	3	1
Magallanes, Daytona Beach	.984	60	115	7	2	2
Malave, Dunedin	.900	5	8	1	1	0
Markley, Osceola	.990	81	191	3	2	1
Mendez, St. Petersburg°	1.000	16	27	0	0	0
Merullo, Daytona Beach	.800	2	3	1	1	0
Millay, Charlotte	.958	28	42	4	2	0
Miller, Clearwater	.941	11	16	0	1	0
Mills, Lakeland	1.000	3	1	0	0	0
Mims, Osceola	.969	41	88	7	3	3
Munoz, Dunedin	1.000	2	4	1	0	1
Nunez, St. Petersburg	.991	129	324	7	3	2
Orsag, Winter Haven	.920	13	23	0	2	0
Peel, Daytona Beach	1.000	35	66	1	0	1
Pottinger, Lakeland	1.000	15	26	0	0	0
Reimer, Charlotte	.939	20	31	0	2	0
Richardi, Miami	.979	53	90	5	2	1
Richie, Lakeland	.964	57	99	7	4	1
Robertson, St. Petersburg	.970	113	214	12	7	2
Ruiz, Miami	1.000	2	5	1	0	0
Sambo, Tampa	.971	15	34	0	1	0
Scanlin, Charlotte°	.954	71	101	2	5	0
Schulte, Fort Myers	.956	90	185	9	9	2
Scruggs, Charlotte	.894	22	41	1	5	0
Sedar, Daytona Beach	.985	37	58	6	1	2
SENNE, St. Petersburg	.9964	139	260	15	1	3
Sims, Vero Beach°	1.000	6	4	0	0	0
Snyder, Osceola	1.000	3	7	1	0	1
Spagnuolo, Vero Beach	1.000	6	5	0	0	0
Sugiura, Miami	.970	59	93	5	3	1
Sullivan, Daytona Beach	.975	106	227	4	6	1
Thomas, Vero Beach	.9960	111	243	9	1	3
Thoutsis, Winter Haven	1.000	63	126	7	0	0
Threadgill, Charlotte	.875	14	13	1	2	0
Vanderwal, West Palm Beach°.	.972	50	103	1	3	1
Ward, Fort Lauderdale	.977	129	330	10	8	2
Weidie, Winter Haven	.979	86	174	9	4	2
White, Vero Beach	1.000	8	11	0	0	0
Wieligman, Lakeland°	1.000	20	31	0	0	0
Williams, Fort Lauderdale	1.000	22	49	1	0	0
Williamson, Tampa	.979	40	46	1	1	0
Zambrano, Winter Haven	.978	67	167	7	4	2

CATCHERS

Player and Club	Pct.	G.	PO.	A.	E.	DP.	PB.
Afenir, Osceola	.980	37	180	18	4	1	10
Balthazar, Lakeland	.973	15	65	8	2	1	1
Bastinck, Lakeland	.973	27	201	14	6	2	4
Beeler, Tampa	.962	60	269	36	12	4	12
Billmeyer, Miami	.991	55	292	41	3	2	10
Bochesa, Winter Haven	.982	31	140	28	3	4	8
J. Brown, Vero Beach	1.000	13	56	3	0	1	5
M. Brown, Osceola	1.000	3	2	0	0	1	0
Caffrey, West Palm Beach	1.000	3	15	1	0	0	0
Cento, Daytona Beach	.964	9	26	1	1	1	2
Colston, Miami	.951	7	36	3	2	1	1
Crofton, Fort Lauderdale	.987	13	64	12	1	0	2
Daulton, Clearwater	.958	5	20	3	1	0	0
David, Dunedin	.982	61	341	35	7	6	20
Davis, West Palm Beach	.974	87	528	72	16	10	12
Dempsay, Lakeland	.975	43	202	33	6	5	5
Diaz, Dunedin	.985	71	416	42	7	6	6
Elliot, St. Petersburg	.980	52	247	47	6	6	4
Falzone, Miami	.953	9	39	2	2	1	0
Ferradas, Vero Beach	1.000	1	1	0	0	0	0
Fletcher, Vero Beach	.988	41	212	35	3	4	9
Fontes, Charlotte	.977	12	81	4	2	0	1
Fox, St. Petersburg	.986	90	428	75	7	5	16
Goff, Fort Myers	.995	70	339	52	2	3	11
Hornacek, Mia 27-VB 32	.972	59	284	26	9	2	16
Kaye, Clearwater	.984	31	166	14	3	1	2
Kreuter, Charlotte	.982	64	377	51	8	4	6
Lambert, Vero Beach	.973	74	447	50	14	6	12
Lau, Miami	.909	6	17	3	2	1	1
Leary, West Palm Beach	.993	82	371	41	3	5	5
Leyritz, Fort Lauderdale	.976	91	458	76	13	7	25
Lopez, Osceola	.991	21	96	14	1	1	1
Lung, Charlotte	.971	13	62	5	2	2	3
Magrann, Miami	.952	33	139	39	9	1	2
Martinez, Tampa	.967	6	28	1	1	0	0
McCall, Clearwater	.986	60	322	30	5	4	7
McElroy, Daytona Beach	1.000	6	16	2	0	0	1
Melendez, Lakeland	.975	7	37	2	1	0	1
Merullo, Daytona Beach	.982	39	197	27	4	1	3
Milholland, Daytona Beach	.989	98	469	61	6	6	20
Miller, Clearwater	1.000	20	71	5	0	0	2
Mills, Lakeland	.900	1	9	0	1	0	1
Monzon, Lakeland	.889	4	7	1	1	0	0
Morris, Fort Myers	.970	34	172	20	6	2	5
Murdock, Daytona Beach	.955	11	18	3	1	0	3
Murphy, St. Petersburg	1.000	9	29	4	0	0	1
Nowak, Miami	.886	16	57	13	9	1	7
Padilla, Winter Haven	.968	53	155	29	6	1	13
Pearn, Charlotte	.984	43	230	19	4	1	8
Pratt, West Palm Beach	.980	84	436	49	10	5	16
Reese, Fort Myers	.968	42	203	9	7	0	8
Rice, Fort Myers	1.000	3	16	1	0	0	0
Rivers, Dunedin	.985	13	57	7	1	1	3
Rodriguez, Dunedin	.818	4	8	1	2	0	1
Rohde, Osceola	1.000	1	2	3	0	1	0
Rosario, Fort Lauderdale	.975	45	205	33	6	1	7
Sapienza, Tampa	.975	52	238	37	7	3	9
Scott, Tampa	.833	3	5	0	1	0	0
Simonds, Miami	.969	11	52	10	2	0	3
Singley, Daytona Beach	.750	4	3	0	1	1	1
Thomson, Lakeland	.987	60	272	26	4	2	7
Touma, West Palm Beach	1.000	1	2	0	0	0	0
Trafton, Daytona Beach	1.000	2	3	1	0	0	0
WALTERS, Osceola	.992	93	540	62	5	6	5
White, Clearwater	.952	12	55	5	3	1	3
Zayas, Clearwater	.949	19	81	12	5	2	4
Zeratsky, Tampa	.987	35	208	23	3	2	8

Triple Play—Kaye.

PITCHERS

Player and Club	Pct.	G.	PO.	A.	E.	DP.
Abril, Winter Haven	.800	9	2	2	1	0
Adams, Fort Myers	1.000	4	0	3	0	0
Adkins, Fort Lauderdale°	1.000	5	0	5	0	1
Alexander, Fort Myers°	.857	12	0	6	1	0
Allen, Daytona Beach	1.000	4	2	5	0	1
Arnsberg, Osceola	.900	21	1	8	1	0
Balsley, Dunedin	.828	43	8	16	5	0
Barfield, Charlotte°	.936	25	17	27	3	0
Bartels, Vero Beach	.967	56	5	24	1	0
Beck, Clearwater°	1.000	27	3	4	0	0
Becker, St. Petersburg°	1.000	43	3	14	0	1
Befort, Clearwater	1.000	11	2	2	0	1
Bierscheid, Clearwater	.750	17	2	1	1	0
Blackshear, Clearwater	1.000	10	1	3	0	0
Blair, Dunedin	.938	50	5	10	1	1
Blasucci, Daytona Beach°	1.000	33	0	9	0	1
Blouin, Fort Myers	.952	17	9	11	1	1
Boroski, Fort Myers	1.000	8	3	11	0	1
Boudreaux, Clearwater	1.000	8	3	5	0	1
Brennan, Daytona Beach	.800	14	0	8	2	0
Brink, Clearwater	.962	17	10	15	1	2
Brinson, Dunedin	1.000	25	8	14	0	2
K. Brown, Charlotte	.867	6	5	8	2	0
M. Brown, Osceola	1.000	1	0	1	0	0
P. Brown, Winter Haven°	1.000	11	2	3	0	1
Browning, Miami	.929	37	6	7	1	0
Butcher, Fort Myers	1.000	5	3	0	0	0
K. Campbell, Vero Beach	.966	28	16	40	2	0
M. Campbell, Tampa	1.000	6	3	7	0	0
Cano, Osceola	.949	24	13	24	2	0
Caraballo, Clearwater	1.000	24	5	9	0	0
Cardwood, West Palm Beach	.944	28	4	13	1	2
Carroll, Fort Lauderdale	.700	19	3	4	3	0
Carter, Lakeland	.897	21	7	19	3	4
Castillo, Dunedin°	1.000	39	2	7	0	0
Cauley, Daytona Beach	1.000	10	2	5	0	1
Cerny, Charlotte°	.900	34	9	18	3	1
Champagne, Fort Myers	.800	17	1	3	1	1
Christopher, Fort Lauderdale	.963	24	17	35	2	5
Clark, Clearwater	.867	12	3	10	2	2
Clawson, Charlotte	.875	36	4	10	2	2
Coffey, Winter Haven	1.000	40	4	12	0	1
Collins, West Palm Beach	.900	34	7	11	2	0
Constant, Miami	1.000	6	2	2	0	0
Converse, Tampa	.722	36	5	8	5	0
Cooper, Lakeland	1.000	23	1	3	0	2
Cortes, Daytona Beach	.938	32	3	12	1	0
Credeur, Osceola°	.750	16	3	6	3	0
Crouch, Fort Myers	1.000	10	3	13	0	1
Cummings, Dunedin	.894	32	14	28	5	1
Cunningham, WPB°	.750	14	1	2	1	0
DeCordova, St. Petersburg°	1.000	37	7	16	0	1
Dedos, Winter Haven	.875	54	7	14	3	1
Deitz, Tampa	.909	23	1	9	1	1
DeLaCruz, Daytona Beach	.800	7	1	0	0	0
DeLeon, Osceola	1.000	5	0	2	0	0
Devine, Vero Beach	.880	29	7	15	3	3
Devlin, West Palm Beach	.938	36	4	11	1	2
Diez, Miami°	.900	28	5	13	2	0
Dixon, West Palm Beach	.882	43	4	11	2	1
Drees, Daytona Beach°	.977	27	15	27	1	0
Dunster, Osceola	.960	17	10	14	1	1
Edwards, Daytona Beach°	.935	29	12	31	3	3
Eiland, Fort Lauderdale	1.000	8	1	16	0	0
Ellis, Fort Myers	.870	29	10	10	3	2
Englund, Dunedin	1.000	9	4	4	0	0
Estes, Osceola°	.913	47	4	17	2	0
Evans, Miami	.500	2	1	0	1	0
Evers, Fort Lauderdale	.931	24	10	17	2	1
Figueroa, Fort Lauderdale°	.000	3	0	0	1	0
Filer, Dunedin	1.000	8	2	0	0	0
Forrest, St. Petersburg	.875	22	6	15	3	1
Gabriele, Winter Haven	1.000	26	13	15	0	0
Galvez, Vero Beach	.667	6	7	3	5	0
Garces, Lakeland°	.857	30	3	9	2	1
Garcia, Vero Beach	.500	6	0	1	1	0
Gay, Fort Lauderdale	.960	24	5	19	1	0
Girdner, Daytona Beach	.833	20	2	3	1	0
Gohmann, Lakeland	.889	31	5	11	2	1
Gomez, Winter Haven	1.000	20	4	7	0	0
Gonzalez, Daytona Beach	1.000	26	2	4	0	0
Goodenough, Fort Myers°	1.000	15	3	1	0	1
Gordon, Fort Myers	1.000	3	0	1	0	0
Groom, Daytona Beach°	.714	11	2	3	2	0
Guercio, Fort Lauderdale	1.000	9	4	0	0	0
Hammond, Tampa°	.896	25	11	32	5	0
Hansen, Lakeland	.931	22	7	20	2	1
Harden, Charlotte	.846	11	5	6	2	0
Harrington, Miami	.900	22	7	11	2	1
Harris, West Palm Beach	.868	26	11	22	5	1
Hawley, Tampa	1.000	5	0	1	0	0
Hellman, Fort Lauderdale	.909	24	4	6	1	0
Henry, Daytona Beach°	1.000	30	3	7	0	1
Hershman, St. Petersburg	.864	28	6	13	3	1
Hershiser, Vero Beach	.947	18	8	10	1	1
Herzog, St. Petersburg°	1.000	30	1	11	0	2
Hetzel, Winter Haven	.912	26	9	22	3	1
Heuer, Vero Beach	1.000	8	0	2	0	0
Hibbard, Fort Myers°	1.000	3	2	5	0	0
Hickey, Daytona Beach	1.000	15	5	0	0	0
Hill, St. Petersburg	1.000	18	2	4	0	0
Holmes, Vero Beach	.842	19	9	7	3	1
Huseby, Tampa	1.000	43	6	9	0	0
D. Johnson, Dunedin	.923	18	6	6	1	0
T. Johnson, Fort Myers°	1.000	1	1	0	0	0
C. Jones, Dunedin	.944	27	11	23	2	1
G. Jones, Fort Myers	1.000	40	6	11	0	1
Kindred, Tampa	.905	17	3	16	2	3
King, Miami	.923	21	8	28	3	0
Kravec, Fort Myers°	1.000	2	0	1	0	1
Kristan, West Palm Beach	.923	39	4	8	1	1
Lacko, Lakeland	.962	24	10	15	1	1
Langley, Vero Beach	.800	5	1	3	1	0
Lankard, Charlotte	1.000	66	3	21	0	1
Lavelle, Dunedin°	.667	9	0	2	1	0
Lea, West Palm Beach	.833	19	2	8	2	0
Lee, Lakeland°	1.000	30	4	7	0	0
Little, Daytona Beach	.929	28	14	25	3	3
Livchak, St. Petersburg°	.893	25	5	20	3	1
Livernois, Winter Haven	.792	20	5	14	5	1
Lockhart, Winter Haven°	1.000	20	0	3	0	1
Long, Osceola	1.000	11	7	11	0	2
Machado, Clearwater	1.000	7	1	2	0	1
Magee, Clearwater	.857	28	1	5	1	0
B. Malave, St. Petersburg	1.000	24	3	4	0	0
Malone, Charlotte	.905	34	7	12	2	2
Manuel, Charlotte	1.000	13	1	4	0	0
Marino, West Palm Beach°	.923	28	1	11	1	0
D. Martinez, Miami	1.000	3	0	5	0	0
R. Martinez, Vero Beach	.926	25	16	34	4	0
Matsubara, Miami°	.875	10	2	5	1	1
Matsuo, Miami	1.000	32	3	9	0	2
Mauch, St. Petersburg	.950	33	4	15	1	0
Mays, Charlotte	.917	9	4	7	1	1
McDevitt, Clearwater	1.000	3	2	0	0	0
McElroy, Clearwater°	1.000	2	1	1	0	0
McIntyre, Fort Myers	1.000	17	1	8	0	1
McKelvey, West Palm Beach	.500	4	0	1	1	0
Mead, Tampa	.921	29	10	25	3	2
Meadows, Charlotte	1.000	9	6	2	0	0
Metoyer, Osceola	.920	23	9	14	2	0
Meyer, Osceola	.955	52	9	12	1	1
Meyers, Fort Myers	1.000	4	2	2	0	0
Miller, Clearwater°	.889	9	4	4	1	0
Minutelli, Tampa°	.862	17	4	21	4	3
Moore, Clearwater	.857	53	4	8	2	1
Morales, Charlotte	.667	16	0	2	1	0
Morse, Charlotte	.875	13	1	6	1	0
Mount, Fort Myers	1.000	16	1	2	0	0
Mulligan, Fort Myers°	.923	39	4	8	1	1
Mumaw, Dunedin°	1.000	30	3	12	0	1
Murphy, Osceola	1.000	4	0	3	0	0
Naworski, Fort Myers	1.000	17	1	4	0	0
Newcomb, Daytona Beach	1.000	4	0	2	0	0
Nicholson, Lakeland	.852	25	8	15	4	2
North, St. Petersburg	.919	27	11	23	3	1
Nosek, Lakeland	.571	10	1	3	3	0
Novak, Tampa	1.000	29	6	6	0	1
O'Neill, Lakeland°	1.000	5	0	1	0	0
Odom, Fort Myers	.765	17	2	11	4	0
Osteen, St. Petersburg	.958	19	7	16	1	0
Patterson, Fort Lauderdale°	.722	9	3	10	5	0
Peguero, Miami	.889	21	6	18	3	0
M. Perez, Fort Myers	.938	8	6	9	1	0
Y. Perez, West Palm Beach°	.947	15	3	15	1	1
Petkovsek, Charlotte	1.000	11	2	10	0	0
Phillips, Lakeland	.923	13	2	10	1	1
Potestio, Daytona Beach	.947	29	10	26	2	1
Potts, Osceola	1.000	36	3	8	0	2
Pries, Fort Lauderdale	.923	11	3	9	1	1
Pruett, Clearwater	1.000	6	1	0	0	0
Pumphrey, Fort Myers	.750	10	0	3	1	0
Raether, Charlotte	.833	27	1	4	1	0
Raubolt, Lakeland	.714	28	3	7	4	0
Reed, Daytona Beach	.625	24	1	4	3	0
Ridenour, Fort Lauderdale	1.000	43	6	8	0	0
Rockman, Charlotte	1.000	10	2	2	0	0
Rodriguez, Fort Lauderdale	.875	14	3	4	1	0
Roesler, Tampa	1.000	28	0	3	0	0
Rogers, Charlotte°	1.000	5	4	3	0	0
Rohan, Miami	.976	22	15	25	1	2
Rojas, Fort Myers	.929	21	5	8	1	1
Rose, Fort Lauderdale	.826	17	6	13	4	4
Rousey, West Palm Beach	1.000	5	0	1	0	0

PITCHERS—Continued

Player and Club	Pct.	G.	PO.	A.	E.	DP.
Rowe, Miami	.667	5	0	2	1	0
Rub, Fort Lauderdale*	.941	38	6	10	1	2
Russell, Charlotte	1.000	2	1	1	0	0
Ryan, Vero Beach	.875	11	2	5	1	0
Saitta, Dunedin	.929	16	5	8	1	1
Sanders, Dunedin	.914	29	11	21	3	4
Sassone, St. Petersburg	.909	27	6	14	2	2
Scheid, Fort Lauderdale*	1.000	9	4	7	0	1
Schofield, Charlotte	.905	37	6	13	2	0
Schulte, Osceola	.917	42	5	6	1	0
Schultz, Lakeland	.875	21	4	10	2	0
Schwabe, Lakeland	1.000	5	2	4	0	0
Sepulveda, Vero Beach	1.000	9	0	1	0	0
Service, Clearwater	.905	21	5	14	2	4
SHARTS, Clearwater*	1.000	41	10	21	0	2
Shea, Vero Beach*	.800	25	1	3	1	1
Sheary, Miami	1.000	10	4	4	0	1
Shiflett, Charlotte	1.000	1	0	1	0	0
Shikles, Winter Haven	.944	27	15	19	2	2
Simon, Osceola	.667	5	0	2	1	0
Slavik, Lakeland*	1.000	7	1	1	0	0
Slifko, Winter Haven	.938	28	7	23	2	1
Bryan Smith, Vero Beach*	.833	10	0	5	1	0
Sonberg, Vero Beach*	1.000	7	3	7	0	0
Stoddard, Fort Lauderdale	1.000	2	0	1	0	0
Stoll, West Palm Beach	1.000	13	2	4	0	0
Strichek, St. Petersburg	1.000	17	1	2	0	0
Studeman, Fort Myers	1.000	7	0	1	0	0
Sudo, West Palm Beach	.971	17	7	27	1	5
Swob, Tampa*	.980	26	9	40	1	1
Tabaka, West Palm Beach*	.958	28	3	20	1	3
Talamantez, Miami	1.000	3	0	4	0	0
Tapia, Vero Beach	.875	45	5	9	2	1
Thomas, Charlotte	.975	28	10	29	1	2
Torres, Vero Beach	1.000	6	1	0	0	0
Traen, West Palm Beach*	.857	12	0	6	1	0
Trapp, Fort Myers*	.750	9	1	5	2	0
True, Charlotte*	.500	3	1	0	1	0
Valdez, Charlotte*	.933	17	4	10	1	1
Vargas, Osceola	.946	23	9	26	2	0
Vazquez, Miami*	1.000	21	3	4	0	1
Vesling, Lakeland*	1.000	1	1	0	0	0
Vierra, Tampa*	1.000	9	0	1	0	0
Villa, Tampa	1.000	22	3	5	0	0
Walden, Clearwater*	.714	41	4	6	4	0
Walton, Miami	1.000	9	8	10	0	1
Watanabe, Miami*	1.000	4	2	2	0	0
Watts, Dunedin	1.000	5	0	2	0	0
Wells, Osceola*	.955	26	7	14	1	0
Wenson, Lakeland	.889	47	7	9	2	1
Wetteland, Vero Beach	.814	27	16	19	8	3
Wilkins, Fort Lauderdale	.929	15	10	16	2	2
D. Williams, Tampa	1.000	4	1	1	0	0
K. Williams, Lakeland*	.857	9	2	10	2	0
R. Williams, West Palm Beach	.826	21	5	14	4	1
T. Williams, Fort Myers*	1.000	2	1	1	0	0
Willis, Tampa	.875	25	10	32	6	3
C. Wilson, Miami	1.000	8	0	5	0	0
S. Wilson, Charlotte*	.800	20	4	12	4	0
Wisdom, Clearwater*	1.000	8	4	5	0	0
Wood, Vero Beach	.778	23	5	9	4	0
Young, Dunedin	.870	34	5	15	3	2

The following players do not have any recorded accepted chances at the positions indicated; therefore, are not listed in the fielding averages for those particular positions: Abreu, p; Beeler, of; Blasucci, of; Burdick, p; Caffrey, of; Corcino, p; J. Cunningham, of; Cusack, p; Je. DeLeon, p; Elliott, p; Fascher, p; Guidry, p; Haley, of; Hornacek, 3b; Laboy, of; Latmore, of; Little, of; O. Malave, p; Marris, p; Ri. Martinez, ss; McHugh, p; Mills, ss; Morris, p; Murray, 3b; Mustari, ss; Netemeyer, p; Nieto, of; Pardini, of; O. Parker, 3b; Pratt, of; Reese, p; Reichel, of; Rivers, p; Roth, p; Bryn Smith, p; D. Smith, c; Thomson, p; Thorpe, p; Toale, ss; Vasquez, p; Voeltz, p; Wieligman, p; Zaltsman, p.

CLUB PITCHING

Club	ERA.	G.	CG.	ShO.	Sv.	IP.	H.	R.	ER.	HR.	HB.	BB.	Int. BB.	SO.	WP.	Bk.
Osceola	3.02	139	27	14	34	1215.2	1052	488	408	42	35	465	18	796	57	7
Charlotte	3.39	143	9	9	39	1228.0	1135	574	462	48	40	581	31	871	69	14
Fort Lauderdale	3.38	138	36	12	32	1200.2	1152	555	451	56	29	501	15	718	80	15
Dunedin	3.41	140	8	15	32	1213.0	1137	556	460	53	32	526	9	774	87	12
West Palm Beach	3.49	138	22	8	33	1192.0	1131	567	462	62	25	546	32	886	65	8
St. Petersburg	3.56	142	26	16	35	1195.2	1186	562	473	47	20	404	22	679	58	6
Clearwater	3.74	136	10	9	34	1156.1	1152	579	481	47	29	454	14	670	46	13
Vero Beach	3.84	138	26	8	16	1201.1	1197	658	512	63	42	605	32	842	88	14
Daytona Beach	3.83	139	40	13	19	1190.2	1230	618	507	43	48	500	29	685	72	9
Lakeland	3.88	135	23	10	33	1162.0	1127	599	501	45	50	566	28	745	63	9
Tampa	3.89	140	28	11	26	1168.0	1183	623	505	59	35	513	34	736	60	12
Miami	4.01	133	29	5	15	1115.0	1121	619	497	41	34	501	24	567	97	15
Winter Haven	4.03	138	33	5	28	1182.0	1285	660	529	54	33	532	16	677	70	5
Fort Myers	4.29	141	25	10	20	1169.0	1248	680	557	54	41	454	21	687	61	15

PITCHERS' RECORDS
(Leading Qualifiers for Earned-Run Average Leadership — 115 or More Innings)

*Throws lefthanded.

Pitcher—Club	W.	L.	Pct.	ERA.	G.	GS.	CG.	GF.	ShO.	Sv.	IP.	H.	R.	ER.	HR.	HB.	BB.	Int. BB.	SO.	WP.
Cano, Osceola	15	3	.833	1.94	24	23	6	0	0	0	167.1	137	50	36	5	3	47	4	99	2
R. Martinez, Vero Beach	16	5	.762	2.17	25	25	6	0	1	0	170.1	128	45	41	3	4	78	1	148	5
Vargas, Osceola	11	8	.579	2.33	23	23	7	0	5	0	158.2	124	46	41	5	3	42	2	108	7
Lacko, Lakeland	9	7	.563	2.41	24	24	8	0	4	0	153.0	125	52	41	3	2	71	4	133	9
Christopher, Fort Lauderdale	13	8	.619	2.44	24	24	9	0	4	0	169.1	183	63	46	5	0	28	1	81	4
Service, Clearwater	13	4	.765	2.48	21	21	5	0	2	0	137.2	127	46	38	4	4	32	0	73	1
Dunster, Osceola	7	4	.636	2.50	17	17	7	0	3	0	126.0	108	40	35	4	2	23	1	75	3
Sassone, St. Petersburg	11	7	.611	2.59	27	26	6	0	3	0	166.2	125	59	48	5	2	56	3	116	11
C. Jones, Dunedin	11	6	.647	2.63	27	25	3	1	0	0	157.1	119	48	46	7	2	57	0	95	6
Little, Daytona Beach	8	10	.444	2.64	28	21	8	5	1	1	163.1	151	61	48	6	9	46	2	108	7

Departmental Leaders: G—Lankard, 66; W—Cummings, 18; L—K. Campbell, Drees, Peguero, 14; Pct.—Cano, Cardwood, .833; GS—Cummings, 29; CG—Edwards, 15; GF—Dedos, 50; ShO—Vargas, 5; Sv.—Meyer, 25; IP—Edwards, 199.2; H—Edwards, 211; R—Peguero, 108; ER—Peguero, 94; HR—Four pitchers with 11; HB—Carter, 12; BB—Gabriele, 105; IBB—Bartels, 13; SO—Gabriele, 150; WP—Edwards, Wetteland, 17.

(All Pitchers—Listed Alphabetically)

Pitcher—Club	W.	L.	Pct.	ERA.	G.	GS.	CG.	GF.	ShO.	Sv.	IP.	H.	R.	ER.	HR.	HB.	BB.	Int. BB.	SO.	WP.
Abreu, Daytona Beach	0	1	.000	13.50	4	2	0	0	0	0	4.2	4	7	7	0	1	11	0	4	1
Abril, Winter Haven	1	3	.250	5.22	9	5	0	4	0	0	29.1	34	24	17	0	1	21	0	14	3
Adams, Fort Myers	1	3	.250	4.22	4	4	1	0	0	0	21.1	15	11	10	0	1	8	0	5	2
Adkins, Fort Lauderdale*	1	1	.500	4.64	5	3	0	1	0	0	21.1	26	11	11	2	0	8	0	7	3
Alexander, Fort Myers*	3	4	.429	4.16	12	12	1	0	1	0	67.0	63	33	31	4	1	29	0	37	6
Allen, Daytona Beach	0	1	.000	2.00	4	4	0	0	0	0	18.0	17	6	4	1	0	7	0	17	1
Arnsberg, Osceola	4	2	.667	3.77	21	3	1	12	0	2	57.1	59	27	24	0	3	26	2	34	3
Balsley, Dunedin	3	5	.375	3.29	43	0	0	31	0	9	79.1	67	35	29	1	2	30	3	49	2
Barfield, Charlotte*	10	7	.588	3.69	25	25	3	0	2	0	153.2	145	75	63	3	3	55	0	79	6
Bartels, Vero Beach	6	7	.462	2.84	56	0	0	36	0	4	88.2	81	43	28	0	8	59	13	73	15
Beck, Clearwater*	1	1	.500	2.72	27	1	0	16	0	8	43.0	39	14	13	3	2	17	0	35	1
Becker, St. Petersburg*	8	3	.727	3.10	43	0	0	22	0	6	90.0	89	37	31	4	2	23	2	49	3

Pitcher—Club	W.	L.	Pct.	ERA.	G.	GS.	CG.	GF.	ShO.	Sv.	IP.	H.	R.	ER.	HR.	HB.	BB.	Int. BB.	SO.	WP.
Befort, Clearwater	1	1	.500	5.63	11	0	0	4	0	0	24.0	27	21	15	2	2	11	1	12	2
Bierscheid, Clearwater	2	1	.667	2.72	17	1	0	4	0	0	36.1	35	13	11	0	0	12	0	15	0
Blackshear, Clearwater	2	2	.500	3.57	10	8	0	2	0	0	40.1	39	16	16	3	1	15	0	15	1
Blair, Dunedin	2	9	.182	4.43	50	0	0	45	0	13	85.1	99	51	42	5	1	29	0	72	9
Blasucci, Daytona Beach°	4	2	.667	2.31	33	2	0	17	0	9	58.1	38	20	15	4	1	26	3	64	4
Blouin, Fort Myers	9	6	.600	2.44	17	17	3	0	0	0	92.1	86	40	25	2	6	28	0	55	5
Boroski, Fort Myers	4	3	.571	3.69	8	8	2	0	1	0	46.1	48	22	19	1	1	10	0	23	1
Boudreaux, Clearwater	0	6	.000	7.59	8	6	0	1	0	0	32.0	44	31	27	1	1	11	0	15	3
Brennan, Daytona Beach	1	1	.500	4.76	14	6	1	3	1	0	51.0	63	30	27	2	1	30	1	16	2
Brink, Clearwater	4	7	.364	3.82	17	17	2	0	1	0	94.1	99	50	40	5	2	39	0	64	1
Brinson, Dunedin	11	5	.688	3.11	25	18	0	1	0	0	107.0	99	47	37	3	2	58	0	64	8
K. Brown, Charlotte	0	2	.000	2.72	6	6	1	0	0	0	36.1	33	14	11	1	0	17	0	21	1
M. Brown, Osceola	0	1	.000	18.00	1	0	0	0	0	0	1.0	1	2	2	0	0	4	0	0	0
P. Brown, Winter Haven°	4	2	.667	3.67	11	7	1	3	1	0	54.0	58	28	22	5	1	36	1	40	7
Browning, Miami	5	8	.385	2.04	37	0	0	36	0	12	57.1	55	23	13	0	2	15	3	40	5
Burdick, Miami	1	2	.333	4.73	4	2	0	0	0	0	13.1	17	15	7	1	0	17	0	9	0
Butcher, Fort Myers	2	2	.500	5.46	5	5	1	0	0	0	31.1	33	20	19	3	1	8	0	17	0
K. Campbell, Vero Beach	7	14	.333	3.91	28	28	5	0	1	0	184.0	200	100	80	11	9	64	4	112	11
M. Campbell, Tampa	0	3	.000	6.04	6	6	0	0	0	0	28.1	32	21	19	2	3	17	0	9	1
Cano, Osceola	15	3	.833	1.94	24	23	6	0	0	0	167.1	137	50	36	5	3	47	4	99	2
Caraballo, Clearwater	2	0	1.000	5.29	24	0	0	7	0	0	49.1	62	36	29	1	2	21	1	16	0
Cardwood, West Palm Beach	10	2	.833	3.35	28	16	1	4	1	0	113.0	82	47	42	8	2	81	3	83	8
Carroll, Fort Lauderdale	3	2	.600	3.60	19	0	0	12	0	3	40.0	39	18	16	1	3	23	4	28	2
Carter, Lakeland	7	3	.700	4.81	21	20	1	0	1	0	101.0	92	62	54	5	12	72	0	60	5
Castillo, Dunedin°	6	2	.750	3.36	39	0	0	18	0	6	69.2	62	30	26	2	5	19	1	62	4
Cauley, Daytona Beach	0	0	.000	0.00	10	0	0	3	0	0	15.1	15	3	0	0	0	5	2	6	3
Cerny, Charlotte°	5	4	.556	2.06	34	8	3	13	2	2	83.0	58	23	19	3	2	44	2	70	4
Champagne, Fort Myers	0	4	.000	5.32	17	6	0	4	0	1	47.1	56	33	28	3	0	25	1	27	5
Christopher, Fort Lauderdale	13	8	.619	2.44	24	24	9	0	4	0	169.1	183	63	46	5	0	28	1	81	4
Clark, Clearwater	3	5	.375	4.15	12	12	0	0	0	0	65.0	78	36	30	2	0	13	1	30	4
Clawson, Charlotte	6	3	.667	3.75	36	2	0	9	0	4	72.0	66	38	30	1	6	57	6	47	9
Coffey, Winter Haven	3	9	.250	3.81	40	6	2	16	0	4	106.1	110	60	45	2	9	51	2	47	8
Collins, West Palm Beach	8	6	.571	3.15	34	9	0	12	0	2	91.1	82	38	32	6	4	47	4	67	5
Constant, Miami	1	1	.500	2.25	6	2	1	2	0	0	20.0	20	9	5	0	1	4	0	9	2
Converse, Tampa	4	7	.364	3.96	36	11	2	13	0	0	97.2	103	53	43	4	5	49	3	54	5
Cooper, Lakeland	3	3	.500	1.93	23	0	0	19	0	10	37.1	26	13	8	2	1	15	3	22	2
Corcino, Fort Myers	0	0	.000	13.50	2	0	0	1	0	0	2.0	3	3	3	0	0	3	0	1	0
Cortes, Daytona Beach	1	5	.167	5.97	32	8	1	8	1	2	72.1	89	60	48	1	2	44	0	42	3
Credeur, Osceola°	3	3	.500	3.77	16	11	0	2	0	0	62.0	54	30	26	3	2	32	0	42	5
Crouch, Fort Myers	5	1	.833	1.85	10	10	2	0	0	0	73.0	65	23	15	0	4	14	0	47	2
Cummings, Daytona Beach	18	8	.692	2.94	32	29	2	1	2	0	186.2	189	80	61	8	2	60	0	111	12
Cunningham, West Palm Beach°	2	1	.667	5.49	14	1	0	4	0	0	19.2	19	14	12	2	0	14	0	23	1
Cusack, Lakeland	0	0	.000	0.00	1	0	0	1	0	0	1.2	2	0	0	0	0	1	0	1	0
DeCordova, St. Petersburg	5	9	.357	4.58	37	11	1	15	0	3	92.1	103	55	47	2	2	30	2	72	3
Dedos, Winter Haven	5	7	.417	2.32	54	0	0	50	0	23	89.1	98	34	23	2	3	38	7	49	8
Deitz, Tampa	2	5	.286	4.45	23	0	0	19	0	9	30.1	24	15	15	0	5	21	6	15	3
DeLaCruz, Daytona Beach	0	0	.000	8.22	7	0	0	4	0	0	7.2	11	7	7	0	1	8	0	7	1
J. DeLeon, Fort Myers	0	2	.000	5.52	3	3	1	0	0	0	14.2	10	9	9	0	1	8	0	11	1
P. DeLeon, Osceola	0	0	.000	5.54	5	0	0	4	0	0	13.0	16	8	8	1	1	6	0	9	2
Devine, Vero Beach	2	5	.286	5.27	29	8	1	11	0	0	80.1	105	61	47	5	3	28	1	40	3
Devlin, West Palm Beach	8	1	.889	0.85	36	0	0	29	0	15	53.0	35	11	5	1	1	16	3	34	0
Diez, Miami°	1	10	.091	4.13	28	13	5	8	0	0	104.2	107	55	48	4	3	49	3	48	11
Dixon, West Palm Beach	10	5	.667	2.27	43	0	0	18	0	4	87.1	82	35	22	5	0	28	7	72	2
Drees, Daytona Beach°	10	14	.417	3.74	27	26	8	1	3	0	168.2	195	87	70	10	6	58	4	76	9
Dunster, Osceola	7	4	.636	2.50	17	17	7	0	3	0	126.0	108	40	35	4	2	23	1	75	3
Edwards, Daytona Beach°	16	8	.667	3.61	29	28	15	0	2	0	199.2	211	91	80	4	9	68	3	121	17
Eiland, Fort Lauderdale	5	3	.625	1.88	8	8	4	0	1	0	62.1	57	17	13	0	0	8	0	28	1
Elliott, Osceola	0	0	.000	18.00	1	0	0	1	0	0	1.0	1	2	2	0	0	4	0	0	1
Ellis, Fort Myers	5	9	.357	4.62	29	14	1	4	1	0	103.1	125	69	53	6	1	51	1	52	13
Englund, Dunedin	5	2	.714	3.60	9	9	2	0	1	0	55.0	59	23	22	6	1	6	0	22	1
Estes, Osceola°	6	5	.545	2.51	47	2	0	13	0	1	68.0	53	27	19	1	2	30	4	57	6
Evans, Miami	0	1	.000	3.00	2	2	0	0	0	0	9.0	8	3	3	0	0	4	0	8	0
Evers, Fort Lauderdale	13	5	.722	3.11	24	22	7	0	2	0	147.2	126	61	51	6	3	52	0	60	4
Fascher, Osceola	1	0	1.000	9.00	4	3	0	1	0	0	7.0	10	8	7	0	0	3	0	10	0
Figueroa, Fort Lauderdale°	0	0	.000	12.27	3	0	0	2	0	0	7.1	11	12	10	4	0	9	0	4	1
Filer, Dunedin	0	0	.000	0.78	6	5	0	0	0	0	23.0	20	5	2	1	1	0	0	13	0
Forrest, St. Petersburg	4	4	.500	4.88	22	10	1	6	0	0	72.0	82	49	39	3	4	39	4	35	6
Gabriele, Winter Haven	13	8	.619	3.42	26	26	6	0	1	0	179.0	164	80	68	10	2	105	0	150	10
Galvez, Vero Beach	2	3	.400	3.23	6	6	2	0	0	0	39.0	39	20	14	3	1	13	0	21	4
Garces, Lakeland°	4	2	.667	3.70	30	0	0	8	0	3	58.1	47	30	24	3	5	36	1	53	11
Garcia, Vero Beach°	1	0	1.000	8.00	6	0	0	2	0	0	9.0	16	9	8	2	0	7	0	5	0
Gay, Fort Lauderdale	7	7	.500	4.65	24	17	4	3	0	2	120.0	122	70	62	11	4	78	2	71	11
Girdner, Daytona Beach	1	0	1.000	3.52	20	0	0	8	0	0	38.1	34	15	15	0	3	9	0	28	0
Gohmann, Lakeland	4	6	.400	3.89	31	2	1	10	1	2	76.1	65	41	33	0	4	26	0	54	3
Gomez, Winter Haven	1	0	1.000	5.12	20	0	0	17	0	0	38.2	53	26	22	7	1	14	0	10	2
Gonzalez, Daytona Beach	3	1	.750	3.81	26	0	0	15	0	4	26.0	14	13	11	1	2	19	1	20	1
Goodenough, Fort Myers°	1	1	.500	3.08	15	0	0	8	0	3	26.1	22	11	9	1	0	15	2	17	0
Gordon, Fort Myers	1	0	1.000	2.63	3	3	0	0	0	0	13.2	5	4	4	0	2	17	0	11	0
Groom, Daytona Beach°	7	2	.778	3.59	11	10	2	0	0	0	67.2	60	30	27	4	2	33	1	29	2
Guercio, Fort Lauderdale	2	2	.500	4.88	9	3	1	3	0	0	27.2	33	17	15	3	1	17	1	15	3
Guidry, Fort Lauderdale°	0	0	.000	0.00	2	0	0	0	0	0	6.0	4	0	0	0	0	1	0	7	0
Haley, Winter Haven°	0	0	.000	15.00	2	0	0	0	0	0	3.0	6	5	5	0	0	4	0	4	0
Hammond, Tampa°	11	11	.500	3.55	25	24	6	1	0	0	170.0	174	81	67	10	3	60	1	126	6
Hansen, Lakeland	8	6	.571	4.84	22	19	3	1	1	0	113.1	126	68	61	4	2	63	4	67	3
Harden, Charlotte	0	4	.000	4.67	11	6	0	1	0	0	44.1	52	39	23	1	2	27	2	28	0
Harrington, Miami	2	8	.200	4.91	22	12	2	6	0	0	95.1	100	67	52	5	2	72	2	35	11
Harris, West Palm Beach	9	7	.563	4.37	26	26	7	0	1	0	179.0	178	101	87	7	2	77	1	121	11
Hawley, Tampa	0	2	.000	5.73	5	2	0	2	0	0	11.0	12	7	7	3	1	4	0	8	1
Hellman, Fort Lauderdale	1	1	.500	2.40	24	1	0	11	0	6	56.1	58	25	15	5	4	25	1	26	4
Henry, Daytona Beach°	1	3	.250	4.47	30	1	0	9	0	1	40.0	36	21	19	2	2	26	0	24	3
Hershman, St. Petersburg	4	6	.400	5.11	28	16	1	4	0	0	104.0	106	64	59	6	1	54	0	49	5
Hershiser, Vero Beach	1	6	.143	3.23	18	11	2	1	1	1	78.0	71	42	28	6	2	34	1	61	5
Herzog, St. Petersburg°	6	2	.750	4.19	30	0	0	19	0	7	43.0	55	24	20	2	0	12	3	19	2

Pitcher—Club	W.	L.	Pct.	ERA.	G.	GS.	CG.	GF.	ShO.	Sv.	IP.	H.	R.	ER.	HR.	HB.	BB.	Int. BB.	SO.	WP.
Hetzel, Winter Haven	10	12	.455	3.55	26	26	11	0	0	0	192.2	186	94	76	6	1	87	1	136	12
Heuer, Vero Beach	1	2	.333	6.10	8	2	0	2	0	0	20.2	25	18	14	1	0	13	0	8	1
Hibbard, Fort Myers°	2	1	.667	1.88	3	3	3	0	1	0	24.0	20	5	5	0	1	3	0	20	0
Hickey, Daytona Beach	3	1	.750	1.93	15	2	0	4	0	0	32.2	25	12	7	1	1	10	1	18	2
Hill, St. Petersburg	1	3	.250	4.17	18	4	0	10	0	2	41.0	38	19	19	2	1	17	1	33	1
Holmes, Vero Beach	6	4	.600	4.52	19	19	1	0	1	0	99.2	111	60	50	4	1	53	0	46	5
Huseby, Tampa	1	1	.500	3.08	43	0	0	16	0	0	61.1	57	30	21	3	0	33	4	33	3
D. Johnson, Dunedin	2	5	.286	5.80	18	13	0	0	0	0	59.0	68	44	38	1	3	49	0	25	6
T. Johnson, Fort Myers°	0	0	.000	0.00	1	0	0	0	0	0	0.2	0	0	0	0	0	2	0	0	0
C. Jones, Dunedin	11	6	.647	2.63	27	25	3	1	0	0	157.1	119	48	46	7	2	57	0	95	6
G. Jones, Fort Myers	1	8	.111	6.46	40	0	0	23	0	1	69.2	97	60	50	2	4	20	3	30	0
Kindred, Tampa	7	7	.500	3.43	17	16	5	0	1	0	105.0	101	49	40	4	0	50	1	63	6
King, Miami	4	12	.250	3.07	21	20	7	1	0	0	132.0	140	62	45	9	1	38	4	57	4
Kravec, Fort Myers°	0	0	.000	4.50	2	0	0	2	0	0	4.0	6	2	2	0	0	1	0	3	0
Kristan, West Palm Beach	1	2	.333	3.83	39	0	0	14	0	2	47.0	57	30	20	5	3	18	2	31	5
Lacko, Lakeland	9	7	.563	2.41	24	24	8	0	4	0	153.0	125	52	41	3	2	71	4	133	9
Langley, Vero Beach°	1	1	.500	12.00	5	2	0	0	0	0	12.0	16	18	16	2	1	25	0	7	4
Lankard, Charlotte	9	7	.563	2.44	66	0	0	48	0	17	88.2	77	28	24	1	3	31	6	77	1
Latmore, Miami	0	0	.000	3.86	2	0	0	2	0	0	2.1	0	1	1	0	0	2	0	1	1
Lavelle, Dunedin°	0	1	.000	8.25	9	8	0	0	0	0	12.0	18	12	11	2	0	2	0	8	1
Lea, West Palm Beach	2	6	.250	3.68	19	17	0	0	0	0	71.0	70	33	29	6	1	27	1	54	5
Lee, Lakeland°	3	2	.600	2.55	30	0	0	15	0	4	53.0	48	17	15	1	1	18	3	42	1
Little, Daytona Beach	8	10	.444	2.64	28	21	8	5	1	1	163.1	151	61	48	6	9	46	2	108	7
Livchak, St. Petersburg°	14	5	.737	2.99	25	23	7	0	3	0	159.1	154	64	53	3	3	56	0	71	5
Livernois, Winter Haven	7	7	.500	4.92	20	15	2	2	0	0	113.1	133	80	62	5	3	48	2	64	5
Lockhart, Winter Haven°	3	0	1.000	6.87	20	1	0	11	0	0	38.0	50	32	29	4	0	17	0	11	0
Long, Osceola	4	5	.444	3.50	11	11	2	0	0	0	69.1	72	31	27	3	1	22	0	35	2
Machado, Clearwater	2	0	1.000	2.60	7	5	0	1	0	0	34.2	31	11	10	2	2	19	2	32	0
Magee, Clearwater	6	5	.545	3.38	28	4	0	13	0	1	66.2	39	32	25	1	2	38	0	60	7
B. Malave, St. Petersburg	1	1	.500	2.03	24	0	0	24	0	15	40.0	37	13	9	1	0	12	1	30	1
O. Malave, Dunedin	0	0	.000	0.00	1	0	0	0	0	0	2.0	1	0	0	0	0	1	0	1	0
Malone, Clearwater	6	8	.429	3.90	34	15	0	10	0	2	120.0	105	55	52	7	4	63	2	100	5
Manuel, Charlotte	1	2	.333	6.60	13	5	0	3	0	0	30.0	33	24	22	2	3	18	0	19	4
Marino, West Palm Beach°	0	0	.000	3.58	28	0	0	8	0	0	32.2	32	14	13	0	1	26	0	34	5
Marris, Fort Lauderdale	0	0	.000	3.00	1	0	0	1	0	0	3.0	3	1	1	0	0	1	0	1	0
D. Martinez, Miami	1	1	.500	6.16	3	3	0	0	0	0	19.0	21	14	13	0	3	3	0	11	2
R. Martinez, Vero Beach	16	5	.762	2.17	25	25	6	0	1	0	170.1	128	45	41	3	4	78	1	148	5
Matsubara, Miami°	2	2	.500	3.53	10	2	1	6	0	0	35.2	26	15	14	0	0	21	0	22	8
Matsuo, Miami	4	4	.500	2.81	32	2	0	20	0	0	80.0	66	35	25	1	6	44	3	37	10
Mauch, St. Petersburg	7	2	.778	4.44	33	6	0	8	0	1	77.0	77	45	38	3	4	21	2	52	11
Mays, Charlotte	2	3	.400	4.58	9	7	0	1	0	0	37.1	36	20	19	3	1	20	2	23	2
McDevitt, Clearwater	0	1	.000	10.97	3	3	0	0	0	0	10.2	14	14	13	1	1	11	0	6	1
McElroy, Clearwater°	1	0	1.000	0.00	2	0	0	0	0	0	7.1	1	1	0	0	0	4	0	7	0
McHugh, Lakeland	1	0	1.000	7.50	3	1	0	0	0	0	6.0	9	5	5	2	0	2	0	5	1
McIntyre, Fort Myers	1	4	.200	3.64	17	3	0	4	0	1	47.0	61	24	19	3	3	18	3	19	1
McKelvey, West Palm Beach	0	1	.000	4.00	4	2	0	1	0	0	9.0	9	5	4	1	0	8	2	14	1
Mead, Tampa	5	7	.417	5.00	29	15	1	9	1	1	102.2	105	72	57	8	3	44	1	83	5
Meadows, Charlotte	0	3	.000	6.23	9	4	0	1	0	0	26.0	34	19	18	2	0	8	1	16	0
Metoyer, Osceola	7	3	.700	2.72	23	17	2	1	1	0	112.1	99	46	34	8	4	38	1	67	3
Meyer, Osceola	8	9	.471	1.99	52	0	0	47	0	25	77.0	58	26	17	1	2	23	1	58	5
Meyers, Fort Myers	2	0	1.000	4.50	4	0	0	2	0	0	10.0	9	6	5	0	0	6	1	5	2
Miller, Clearwater°	4	3	.571	3.14	9	8	1	0	1	0	51.2	52	27	18	0	1	19	0	20	1
Minutelli, Tampa°	7	6	.538	3.80	17	15	5	1	1	0	104.1	98	51	44	4	5	48	4	70	13
Moore, Clearwater	4	7	.364	2.00	53	0	0	42	0	16	67.1	63	23	15	0	0	21	5	42	2
Morales, Charlotte	3	2	.600	3.34	16	0	0	4	0	0	29.2	30	16	11	0	0	17	2	32	2
Morris, Fort Myers	0	0	.000	6.75	1	0	0	0	0	0	1.1	2	1	1	1	0	0	0	0	0
Morse, Charlotte	4	4	.500	2.93	12	12	0	0	0	0	61.1	53	25	20	3	2	28	1	44	3
Mount, Fort Myers	1	1	.500	0.00	16	0	0	14	0	4	19.0	13	3	0	0	2	11	1	11	1
Mulligan, Fort Myers°	2	5	.286	5.66	39	4	0	17	0	5	82.2	102	56	52	8	1	18	2	60	4
Mumaw, Dunedin°	6	5	.545	2.13	30	1	0	10	0	3	76.0	68	23	18	3	2	23	3	73	8
Murphy, Osceola	0	0	.000	1.29	4	0	0	1	0	0	7.0	2	1	1	0	0	5	0	4	0
Naworski, Fort Myers	0	4	.000	3.80	17	0	0	13	0	3	23.2	17	12	10	2	2	17	4	16	0
Netemeyer, Fort Myers°	0	1	.000	5.21	9	1	0	5	0	0	19.0	17	13	11	0	1	15	0	10	2
Newcomb, Dunedin	0	0	.000	5.23	4	1	0	2	0	0	10.1	14	10	6	0	0	10	0	3	1
Nicholson, Lakeland	9	6	.600	4.07	25	24	3	1	1	1	135.0	143	73	61	5	8	56	2	75	3
North, St. Petersburg	13	9	.591	2.67	27	27	4	0	3	0	165.0	164	64	49	9	1	53	2	74	6
Nosek, Lakeland	2	4	.333	7.38	10	10	0	0	0	0	39.0	63	40	32	4	1	30	0	16	6
Novak, Tampa	0	1	.000	4.53	29	1	0	6	0	0	53.2	70	34	27	1	1	25	1	33	1
O'Neill, Lakeland°	0	0	.000	3.24	5	0	0	0	0	0	8.1	8	4	3	1	0	5	1	6	0
Odom, Fort Myers	4	8	.333	6.47	17	16	1	0	0	0	80.2	109	71	58	1	5	36	1	38	5
Osteen, St. Petersburg	10	3	.769	3.20	19	17	6	2	2	0	112.2	123	47	40	5	0	15	2	61	2
Patterson, Fort Lauderdale°	1	3	.250	6.33	9	9	0	0	0	0	42.2	46	34	30	0	2	31	0	36	5
Peguero, Miami	4	14	.222	6.38	21	21	4	0	0	0	132.2	172	108	94	7	3	42	3	59	10
M. Perez, Fort Myers	4	3	.571	2.38	8	8	5	0	1	0	64.1	51	20	17	3	0	7	0	51	3
Y. Perez, West Palm Beach°	6	2	.750	2.34	15	15	3	0	0	0	100.0	78	36	26	4	0	46	0	111	8
Petkovsek, Charlotte	3	4	.429	4.02	11	10	0	1	0	0	56.0	67	36	25	2	0	17	0	23	5
Phillips, Lakeland	3	4	.429	6.10	13	9	2	0	0	0	48.2	58	39	33	4	2	20	2	14	1
Potestio, Daytona Beach	11	13	.458	4.17	29	26	5	1	1	0	170.2	189	104	79	6	3	70	6	80	11
Potts, Osceola	2	2	.500	3.36	36	0	0	14	0	5	64.1	61	26	24	1	1	27	1	39	2
Pries, Fort Lauderdale	6	2	.750	4.57	11	10	2	1	1	0	65.0	67	39	33	6	5	24	1	25	2
Pruett, Clearwater	0	1	.000	12.00	6	1	0	2	0	0	12.0	16	17	16	3	1	11	0	10	2
Pumphrey, Fort Myers	0	2	.000	8.10	10	0	0	8	0	2	10.0	10	10	9	1	0	5	1	9	0
Raether, Charlotte	2	1	.667	1.11	27	0	0	25	0	15	40.2	30	8	5	0	1	16	1	35	3
Raubolt, Lakeland	5	6	.455	4.15	28	9	3	5	0	0	89.0	88	53	41	1	6	51	3	63	7
Reed, Daytona Beach	3	8	.273	6.36	24	5	0	16	0	2	52.1	71	43	37	1	4	19	5	25	4
Reese, Fort Myers	0	0	.000	0.00	1	0	0	0	0	0	0.1	0	0	0	0	0	0	0	1	1
Ridenour, Fort Lauderdale	5	4	.556	1.77	43	0	0	39	0	21	66.0	38	14	13	3	3	34	1	90	10
Rivers, Dunedin	0	0	.000	45.00	1	0	0	1	0	0	0.0	4	5	5	1	0	2	0	0	0
Rockman, Charlotte	0	1	.000	4.11	10	0	0	6	0	1	15.1	15	7	7	2	2	12	0	12	0
Rodriguez, Fort Lauderdale	3	3	.500	4.14	14	1	0	8	0	0	37.0	30	19	17	1	2	19	1	20	3
Roesler, Tampa	7	2	.778	2.23	28	0	0	24	0	11	36.1	30	14	9	0	0	15	4	29	2
Rogers, Charlotte°	0	3	.000	4.76	5	3	0	1	0	0	17.0	17	13	9	1	1	8	0	14	2
Rohan, Miami	5	12	.294	4.37	22	20	3	1	0	1	129.2	132	75	63	6	5	54	2	49	5

Pitcher—Club	W.	L.	Pct.	ERA.	G.	GS.	CG.	GF.	ShO.	Sv.	IP.	H.	R.	ER.	HR.	HB.	BB.	Int. BB.	SO.	WP.
Rojas, Fort Myers	6	10	.375	3.91	21	21	4	0	0	0	117.1	124	71	51	11	2	44	0	86	4
Rose, Fort Lauderdale	7	6	.538	3.49	17	16	3	0	0	0	95.1	102	51	37	4	1	38	0	43	6
Roth, Daytona Beach	0	0	.000	13.50	7	0	0	3	0	0	4.0	7	8	6	0	1	11	0	0	1
Rousey, West Palm Beach	0	0	.000	3.52	5	0	0	3	0	1	7.2	11	4	3	0	0	4	0	3	1
Rowe, Miami	1	1	.500	2.76	5	1	0	3	0	0	16.1	12	6	5	1	1	2	0	13	1
Rub, Fort Lauderdale*	2	1	.667	3.67	38	0	0	15	0	5	61.1	52	29	25	2	1	33	2	47	9
Russell, Charlotte	0	0	.000	2.45	2	2	0	0	0	0	11.0	8	3	3	1	0	5	0	3	0
Ryan, Vero Beach	1	1	.500	4.05	11	0	0	7	0	1	13.1	12	8	6	0	0	12	0	7	0
Saitta, Dunedin	2	2	.500	3.18	16	0	0	4	0	0	39.2	41	18	14	2	2	19	1	21	3
Sanders, Dunedin	7	11	.389	4.50	29	26	1	0	1	0	146.0	138	87	73	8	7	86	0	83	15
Sassone, St. Petersburg	11	7	.611	2.59	27	26	6	0	3	0	166.2	125	59	48	5	2	56	3	116	11
Scheid, Fort Lauderdale*	7	0	1.000	2.95	9	8	1	1	0	0	55.0	43	25	18	1	0	29	0	49	3
Schofield, Charlotte	6	4	.600	3.50	37	3	0	16	0	0	82.1	88	41	32	4	1	37	1	52	9
Schulte, Osceola	5	1	.833	3.03	42	1	0	15	0	1	71.1	53	29	24	1	7	39	2	57	4
Schultz, Lakeland	4	1	.800	4.42	21	3	0	8	0	0	57.0	66	31	28	4	2	19	2	21	3
Schwabe, Lakeland	2	1	.667	3.00	5	2	2	1	0	1	18.0	12	6	6	1	0	8	0	9	0
Sepulveda, Vero Beach	0	3	.000	6.94	9	0	0	3	0	0	11.2	13	9	9	3	2	6	0	12	0
Service, Clearwater	13	4	.765	2.48	21	21	5	0	2	0	137.2	127	46	38	8	4	32	0	73	1
Sharts, Clearwater*	9	6	.600	3.34	41	12	1	10	0	2	118.2	119	47	44	2	1	25	1	50	5
Shea, Vero Beach*	0	1	.000	5.33	25	0	0	14	0	2	25.1	27	16	15	3	1	13	0	24	2
Sheary, Miami	5	3	.625	3.90	10	9	4	1	0	0	67.0	68	34	29	4	2	20	1	39	2
Shiflett, Charlotte	0	0	.000	.000	1	0	0	0	0	0	0.2	0	2	0	0	0	1	0	0	0
Shikles, Winter Haven	12	11	.522	3.63	27	27	9	0	2	0	188.2	204	99	76	5	6	51	3	85	11
Simon, Osceola	1	3	.250	4.76	5	5	0	0	0	0	22.2	26	14	12	2	0	12	0	9	0
Slavik, Lakeland*	0	2	.000	6.17	7	0	0	4	0	0	11.2	17	8	8	0	0	10	1	10	0
Slifko, Winter Haven	8	12	.400	5.05	28	25	2	2	0	1	149.2	189	98	84	8	6	60	0	67	4
Bryan Smith, Miami	0	3	.000	5.96	10	1	0	3	0	0	22.2	30	25	15	0	0	23	1	17	4
Bryn Smith, W. Palm Beach	0	2	.000	4.08	4	4	0	0	0	0	17.2	19	10	8	2	3	1	0	16	1
Sonberg, Vero Beach*	1	5	.167	4.40	7	7	2	0	0	0	43.0	48	32	21	2	3	21	1	28	1
Stoddard, Fort Lauderdale	0	0	.000	0.00	2	0	0	0	0	0	2.0	1	0	0	0	0	0	0	1	0
Stoll, West Palm Beach	0	2	.000	6.12	13	1	0	9	0	1	25.0	26	19	17	3	2	11	1	17	0
Strichek, St. Petersburg	1	3	.250	5.40	17	2	0	6	0	1	31.2	30	20	19	2	0	15	0	16	1
Studeman, Fort Myers	0	0	.000	1.23	7	0	0	2	0	0	14.2	11	3	2	1	0	7	0	11	0
Sudo, West Palm Beach	4	7	.364	4.04	17	12	4	1	1	0	91.1	104	46	41	4	1	23	1	42	2
Swob, Tampa*	8	10	.444	3.16	26	25	5	1	1	0	170.2	163	76	60	5	3	67	3	98	8
Tabaka, West Palm Beach*	8	6	.571	4.17	28	15	0	8	0	5	95.0	90	46	44	3	3	58	3	71	6
Talamantez, Miami	0	0	.000	3.38	3	3	0	0	0	0	10.2	9	5	4	1	0	16	0	6	4
Tapia, Vero Beach	5	6	.455	5.47	45	2	0	25	0	4	77.1	85	53	47	7	5	43	7	60	8
Thomas, Charlotte	6	9	.400	3.24	28	25	1	0	0	0	161.1	138	62	58	7	8	92	3	147	9
Thomson, Lakeland	0	0	.000	13.50	1	0	0	1	0	0	0.2	3	1	1	0	0	1	0	1	0
Thorpe, Vero Beach	0	1	.000	0.96	8	0	0	7	0	2	9.1	4	2	1	0	0	3	0	11	1
Tinkle, Fort Myers	0	0	.000	36.00	1	0	0	0	0	0	1.0	3	4	4	0	0	2	0	0	0
Torres, Vero Beach	0	1	.000	4.91	6	0	0	5	0	4	7.1	9	4	4	0	0	2	0	7	0
Traen, West Palm Beach*	0	1	.000	3.49	12	0	0	5	0	3	28.1	21	13	11	0	1	15	0	19	2
Trapp, Fort Myers*	0	2	.000	7.20	9	1	0	5	0	0	20.0	30	17	16	0	1	13	1	3	0
True, Charlotte*	0	0	.000	15.75	3	0	0	2	0	0	4.0	7	8	7	0	1	2	0	4	1
Valdez, Charlotte*	3	6	.333	3.71	17	8	0	2	0	0	70.1	67	32	29	6	1	28	2	45	3
Vargas, Osceola	11	8	.579	2.33	23	23	7	0	5	0	158.2	124	46	41	5	3	42	2	108	7
Vasquez, Fort Myers	0	1	.000	6.32	8	0	0	2	0	0	15.2	24	12	11	1	1	8	0	7	0
Vazquez, Miami*	1	3	.250	5.90	21	0	0	11	0	0	39.2	43	29	26	1	3	24	2	25	10
Vesling, Lakeland*	0	0	.000	1.13	1	1	0	0	0	0	8.0	5	1	1	1	0	0	0	1	0
Vierra, Tampa*	1	1	.500	10.13	4	0	0	6	0	1	8.0	14	11	9	3	1	3	0	7	0
Villa, Tampa	3	1	.750	5.40	22	0	0	14	0	4	33.1	44	21	20	2	1	17	4	14	1
Voeltz, Fort Lauderdale*	1	0	1.000	5.59	8	0	0	4	0	0	9.2	16	8	6	0	1	4	0	3	2
Walden, Clearwater*	6	9	.400	3.95	41	15	1	14	0	5	114.0	126	68	50	4	2	53	1	56	7
Walton, Miami	4	3	.571	2.07	9	9	2	0	1	0	69.2	53	20	16	0	0	24	1	53	4
Watanabe, Miami*	1	0	1.000	3.57	4	4	0	0	0	0	22.2	27	15	9	0	1	10	0	12	3
Watts, Dunedin	0	0	.000	3.24	5	0	0	2	0	0	8.1	9	4	3	0	0	4	0	3	1
Wells, Osceola*	7	9	.438	4.76	26	23	2	1	0	0	130.1	118	74	69	7	4	82	0	93	13
Wenson, Lakeland	9	7	.563	2.81	47	0	0	36	0	12	83.1	70	31	26	3	3	33	2	61	2
Wetteland, Vero Beach	12	7	.632	3.13	27	27	7	0	2	0	175.2	150	81	61	11	2	92	0	144	17
Wieligman, Lakeland*	0	0	.000	7.71	1	0	0	1	0	0	2.1	2	2	2	0	0	1	0	1	1
Wilkins, Fort Lauderdale	8	5	.615	2.73	15	14	5	1	2	0	105.2	95	41	32	2	1	39	1	76	7
D. Williams, Tampa	1	1	.500	3.86	4	0	0	4	0	0	4.2	2	3	2	0	1	2	0	4	0
K. Williams, Lakeland*	2	0	1.000	2.66	9	0	0	7	0	1	61.0	52	22	18	1	1	29	0	30	5
R. Williams, W Palm Beach	7	12	.368	3.41	21	20	7	0	1	0	124.0	136	65	47	5	1	46	4	74	2
T. Williams, Fort Myers*	0	2	.000	15.19	2	2	0	0	0	0	5.1	11	12	9	0	0	5	0	4	3
Willis, Tampa	7	11	.389	3.94	25	25	4	0	1	0	150.2	154	85	66	10	3	58	2	90	5
C. Wilson, Miami	2	3	.400	4.44	8	8	0	0	0	0	48.2	41	26	24	1	1	37	0	23	3
S. Wilson, Charlotte*	9	5	.643	2.44	20	17	1	1	1	0	107.0	81	41	29	5	3	44	0	80	5
Wisdom, Clearwater*	0	3	.000	5.46	8	5	0	0	0	0	31.1	36	21	19	2	1	19	0	12	3
Wood, Vero Beach	0	2	.000	1.66	23	0	0	3	0	0	43.1	31	14	8	0	0	19	3	22	3
Young, Dunedin	3	2	.600	2.64	34	5	0	15	0	0	95.1	62	34	28	3	2	72	1	69	10
Zaltzman, St. Petersburg	0	0	.000	18.00	1	0	0	0	0	0	1.0	3	2	2	0	0	1	0	2	1

BALKS—Odom, 5; K. Campbell, Rose, Wilkins, 4 each; Barfield, Clawson, Hammond, Harris, Hetzel, G. Jones, Kindred, Lacko, Bryan Smith, Wisdom, Young, 3 each; Blasucci, Brinson, Devine, Ellis, Englund, Gay, Harrington, Hershman, Machado, R. Martinez, Metoyer, Peguero, Rohan, Sanders, Sassone, Valdez, Vazquez, Watanabe, Willis, S. Wilson, 2 each; Adkins, Bartels, Beck, Becker, Befort, Blouin, Boroski, Boudreaux, Brennan, P. Brown, Browning, Cano, Caraballo, Carter, Cerny, Coffey, Collins, Converse, Cortes, Crouch, Cummings, DeCordova, Deitz, Diez, Drees, Eiland, Estes, Evers, Garces, Girdner, Gohmann, Goodenough, Hershiser, Holmes, C. Jones, King, Kristan, Lankard, Little, Malone, Matsuo, Mead, Minutelli, Mulligan, Newcomb, Nicholson, Nosek, Patterson, Y. Perez, Petkovsek, Potestio, Potts, Reed, Rodriguez, Schofield, Service, Sharts, Simon, Stoll, Vargas, Walden, K. Williams, R. Williams, 1 each.

COMBINATION SHUTOUTS—Cerny-Wilson-Raether, Morse-Clawson-Lankard-Raether, Wilson-Raether, Thomas-Clawson-Lankard, Charlotte; Sharts-Moore-Walden, Service-Sharts-Moore, Clark-Moore-McGee, Service-Moore, Blackshear-Sharts-Beck, Clearwater; Potestio-Blasucci, Drees-Blasucci, Little-Henry-Gonzalez, Groom-Cauley-Henry-Gonzalez, Daytona Beach; Lavelle-Sanders-Blair, Jones-Blair, Cummings-Newcomb, Jones-Castillo, Dunedin; Guidry-Scheid, Christopher-Ridenour, Fort Lauderdale; Perez-Naworski, Rojas-Mulligan, Blouin-Champagne, Rojas-Mount, Blouin-Mount, Fort Myers; Schultz-Wenson, Williams-Schwabe, Lakeland; Rohan-Browning 2, King-Browning, Matsubara-Browning, Miami; Vargas-Potts, Metoyer-Meyer, Wells-Potts, Credeur-Arnsberg, Wells-Murphy-Schulte, Osceola; Forrest-Herzog, North-Malave, Hershman-Malave, North-DeCordova, Sassone-Becker, St. Petersburg; Swob-Roesler, Willis-Mead, Minutelli-Huseby-Roesler, Hammond-Roesler, Swob-Hammond, Willis-Deitz, Tampa; Martinez-Bartels 2, Vero Beach; Cardwood-Traen, Perez-Devlin, Collins-Devlin, Lea-Dixon-Devlin, West Palm Beach; Hetzel-Coffey, Winter Haven.

NO-HIT GAMES—None.

Midwest League

CLASS A

CHAMPIONSHIP WINNERS IN PREVIOUS YEARS

1947—Belleville................................ .667	1962—Dubuque z............................. .667	1975—Waterloo a........................... .727
Belleville................................ .672	Waterloo .... .625	Quad Cities .... .624
1948—West Frankfort°.................. .708	1963—Clinton .... .710	1976—Waterloo a........................... .600
1949—Centralia............................... .627	Clinton .... .629	Cedar Rapids........................ .595
Paducah (4th)†.................... .454	1964—Clinton .... .667	1977—Waterloo .... .580
1950—Centralia‡............................ .675	Fox Cities z .... .667	Burlington a........................... .511
1951—Paris§.................................... .700	1965—Burlington............................. .667	1978—Appleton a........................... .708
Danville (4th)†.................... .432	Burlington............................. .677	Burlington .... .500
1952—Danville x.............................. .685	1966—Fox Cities z .... .689	1979—Waterloo .... .600
Decatur (3rd)†.................... .584	Cedar Rapids........................ .762	Quad Cities a........................ .579
1953—Decatur°............................... .576	1967—Wisconsin Rapids .... .685	1980—Waterloo a........................... .610
1954—Decatur .... .587	Appleton z............................ .587	Quad Cities .... .532
Danville (2nd)‡.................. .528	1968—Decatur .... .656	1981—Wausau a............................. .636
1955—Dubuque°.............................. .587	Quad Cities z .... .648	Quad Cities .... .570
1956—Paris y.................................. .656	1969—Appleton.............................. .648	1982—Madison .... .626
Dubuque .... .603	Appleton.............................. .690	Appleton b........................... .579
1957—Decatur y.............................. .683	1970—Quincy z............................... .691	1983—Appleton c........................... .635
Clinton .... .623	Quad Cities .... .581	Springfield .... .576
1958—Michigan City .... .623	1971—Appleton.............................. .642	1984—Appleton c........................... .640
Waterloo z .... .613	Quad Cities a........................ .548	Springfield .... .504
1959—Waterloo .... .613	1972—Appleton.............................. .598	1985—Kenosha b............................ .568
Waterloo .... .613	Danville a .... .584	Peoria .... .536
1960—Waterloo .... .629	1973—Wisconsin Rapids a .... .562	1986—Springfield .... .621
Waterloo .... .677	Danville .... .537	Waterloo b........................... .557
1961—Waterloo .... .613	1974—Appleton.............................. .593	
Quincy z............................. .594	Danville a............................ .517	

°Won championship and four-club playoff. †Won four-club playoff. ‡Playoff finals canceled because of bad weather. §Won both halves of split-season. xWon first half of split-season and tied Paris for second-half title. yWon first-half title and four-team playoff. zWon split-season playoff. aLeague divided into Northern and Southern divisions and played split-season. Playoff winner. bLeague divided into Northern, Central and Southern divisions. Playoff winner. cLeague divided into Northern, Central and Southern divisions; regular-season and playoff winner. (NOTE—Known as Illinois State League in 1947-48 and Mississippi-Ohio Valley League from 1949 through 1955.)

STANDING OF CLUBS AT CLOSE OF SEASON, AUGUST 31

NORTHERN DIVISION

Club	W.	L.	T.	Pct.	G.B.
Kenosha (Twins)	82	58	0	.586	....
Appleton (Royals)	71	69	0	.507	11
Madison (A's)	63	77	0	.450	19
Wausau (Mariners)	57	83	0	.407	25

SOUTHERN DIVISION

Club	W.	L.	T.	Pct.	G.B.
Springfield (Cardinals)...........................	94	46	0	.671	....
Peoria (Cubs)	71	69	0	.507	23
Burlington (Expos)	62	75	0	.453	30½
Quad City (Angels)	47	91	0	.341	46

CENTRAL DIVISION

Club	W.	L.	T.	Pct.	G.B.
Beloit (Brewers)...................................	76	64	0	.543	....
Clinton (Giants)	72	67	0	.518	3½
Waterloo (Indians)	72	68	0	.514	4
Cedar Rapids (Reds).............................	70	70	0	.500	6

COMPOSITE STANDING OF CLUBS AT CLOSE OF SEASON, AUGUST 31

Club	Spr.	Ken.	Bel.	Cln.	Wat.	Peo.	App.	C.R.	Bur.	Mad.	Wau.	Q.C.	W.	L.	T.	Pct.	G.B.
Springfield (Cardinals)..............	....	5	5	5	8	13	7	7	12	7	9	16	94	46	0	.671	....
Kenosha (Twins)	5	....	6	4	5	3	10	6	8	11	17	7	82	58	0	.586	12
Beloit (Brewers).......................	5	4	....	10	10	7	2	12	6	6	7	7	76	64	0	.543	18
Clinton (Giants)	5	6	10	....	7	5	5	13	5	4	5	7	72	67	0	.518	21½
Waterloo (Indians)	2	5	10	13	....	3	6	9	4	6	5	9	72	68	0	.514	22
Peoria (Cubs)	7	7	3	5	7	....	4	6	13	5	7	7	71	69	0	.507	23
Appleton (Royals)	3	10	8	5	4	6	....	2	7	11	10	5	71	69	0	.507	23
Cedar Rapids (Reds)................	3	4	8	7	11	4	8	....	4	7	7	7	70	70	0	.500	24
Burlington (Expos)	8	2	4	4	6	7	3	6	....	4	5	13	62	75	0	.453	30½
Madison (A's)	3	9	4	6	4	5	9	3	6	....	10	4	63	77	0	.450	31
Wausau (Mariners)	1	3	3	5	5	3	10	3	5	10	....	9	57	83	0	.407	37
Quad City (Angels)	4	3	3	3	1	13	5	3	5	6	1	....	47	91	0	.341	46

Quad City's home games played in Davenport, Ia.

Major league affiliations in parentheses.

Playoffs—Kenosha defeated Beloit, two games to one; Springfield defeated Clinton, two games to one; Kenosha defeated Springfield, three games to one, to win league championship.

Regular-Season Attendance—Appleton, 81,208; Beloit, 87,419; Burlington, 71,098; Cedar Rapids, 144,279; Clinton, 112,826; Kenosha, 58,197; Madison, 84,381; Peoria, 195,832; Quad City, 60,999; Springfield, 154,148; Waterloo, 68,081; Wausau, 61,342. Total—1,179,810. Playoffs—11,447. All-Star Game—1,156.

Managers—Appleton, Ken Berry; Beloit, Gomer Hodge; Burlington, J.R. Miner; Cedar Rapids, Paul Kirsch; Clinton, Bill Evers; Kenosha, Don Leppert; Madison, Jim Nettles; Peoria, Jim Tracy; Quad City, Eddie Rodriguez; Springfield, Gaylen Pitts; Waterloo, Glenn Adams; Wausau, Bobby Cuellar.

All-Star Team—1B—Mark Leonard, Clinton; 2B—Francisco Laureano, Appleton; 3B—Keith Lockhart, Cedar Rapids; SS—Bienvenido Figueroa, Springfield; OF—Greg Vaughn, Beloit; Gregg Ritchie, Clinton; Jerome Walton, Peoria; C—Todd Zeile, Springfield; DH—Victor Garcia, Peoria; LHP—Trevor Wilson, Clinton; RHP—Robert Faron, Springfield; LH Reliever—Robert Glisson, Springfield; RH Reliever—Mike Perez, Springfield; Most Valuable Players—Greg Vaughn, Beloit and Todd Zeile, Springfield; Manager of the Year—Don Leppert, Kenosha.

(Compiled by Howe News Bureau, Boston, Mass.)

CLUB BATTING

Club	Pct.	G.	AB.	R.	OR.	H.	TB.	2B.	3B.	HR.	RBI.	GW.	SH.	SF.	HP.	BB.	Int. BB.	SO.	SB.	CS.	LOB.
Clinton	.265	139	4540	657	621	1204	1703	217	42	66	575	69	55	36	39	527	27	830	142	82	947
Kenosha	.265	140	4689	733	614	1242	1830	205	37	103	639	74	25	41	51	550	28	768	100	58	1072
Springfield	.263	140	4642	745	492	1220	1745	215	26	86	654	85	67	55	42	651	32	765	98	57	1091
Beloit	.262	140	4580	757	754	1199	1859	227	32	123	645	64	52	39	44	626	19	959	169	69	1007
Peoria	.261	140	4660	632	631	1216	1699	207	42	64	560	65	41	39	40	517	28	1025	157	85	1005
Madison	.261	140	4544	726	742	1185	1685	216	46	44	639	55	25	47	35	724	18	963	141	89	1093
Appleton	.260	140	4524	701	765	1176	1726	229	36	83	603	63	39	52	38	534	12	966	150	80	932
Waterloo	.249	140	4550	668	626	1132	1761	217	23	122	591	65	28	44	31	543	17	983	112	55	950
Burlington	.246	137	4548	601	585	1117	1759	256	31	108	537	56	53	32	52	455	27	944	103	61	932
Wausau	.243	140	4485	623	806	1091	1662	217	24	102	539	47	26	35	42	558	22	1030	226	100	933
Quad City	.237	138	4611	537	778	1094	1525	179	33	62	452	37	23	32	69	502	20	1119	84	66	1054
Cedar Rapids	.237	140	4583	585	551	1086	1637	198	22	103	514	63	38	30	57	462	27	968	172	77	912

INDIVIDUAL BATTING
(Leading Qualifiers for Batting Championship—378 or More Plate Appearances)

*Bats lefthanded.   †Switch-hitter.

Player and Club	Pct.	G.	AB.	R.	H.	TB.	2B.	3B.	HR.	RBI.	GW.	SH.	SF.	HP.	BB.	Int. BB.	SO.	SB.	CS.
Hale, Walter, Kenosha*	.345	87	339	65	117	164	12	7	7	65	13	0	7	4	33	4	26	3	3
Ritchie, Gregory, Clinton*	.337	124	416	102	140	193	19	11	4	49	10	5	3	3	90	8	80	41	21
Walton, Jerome, Peoria	.335	128	472	102	158	222	24	11	6	38	4	5	1	11	91	2	91	49	25
Laureano, Francisco, Appleton	.323	139	498	86	161	236	25	1	16	87	7	0	11	1	70	0	81	19	9
Leonard, Mark, Clinton*	.320	128	413	57	132	212	31	2	15	80	9	0	3	5	71	3	61	5	8
Lockhart, Keith, Cedar Rapids*	.313	140	511	101	160	276	37	5	23	84	11	1	6	13	86	7	70	20	8
Dull, Michael, Burlington*	.311	135	498	88	155	261	38	7	18	85	8	1	6	6	63	6	69	7	5
Baine, Thomas, Springfield	.306	139	496	95	152	198	29	4	3	62	3	7	6	4	91	2	32	21	8
Vaughn, Gregory, Beloit	.305	139	492	120	150	292	31	6	33	105	8	3	6	5	102	2	115	36	9
McIntosh, Timothy, Beloit	.302	130	461	83	139	235	30	3	20	85	14	1	3	7	49	2	96	7	4

Departmental Leaders: G—Lockhart, 140; AB—Randle, 565; R—Vaughn, 120; H—Randle, 166; TB—Vaughn, 292; 2B—Ronson, 44; 3B—Veras, 12; HR—Vaughn, 33; RBI—Zeile, 106; GWRBI—McIntosh, 14; SH—Figueroa, 12; SF—Laureano, 11; HP—Cron, 17; BB—Teixeira, 104; IBB—Balfanz, Ritchie, 8; SO—Williamson, 133; SB—Te. Williams, 74; CS—Walton, 25.

(All Players—Listed Alphabetically)

Player and Club	Pct.	G.	AB.	R.	H.	TB.	2B.	3B.	HR.	RBI.	GW.	SH.	SF.	HP.	BB.	Int. BB.	SO.	SB.	CS.
Abner, Benjamin, Springfield	.210	34	81	14	17	27	4	0	2	11	0	2	0	2	14	0	13	1	1
Adriance, Daniel, Beloit*	.667	34	3	1	2	2	0	0	0	0	0	0	0	0	1	0	1	0	0
Alberro, Hector, Beloit†	.189	75	222	25	42	47	5	0	0	21	2	8	2	5	21	0	33	4	6
Alfonzo, Edgar, Quad City	.253	51	198	25	50	77	9	3	4	25	1	3	3	2	12	0	35	3	7
Alou, Jose, Burlington	.251	102	319	40	80	124	18	1	8	45	7	7	3	3	32	0	83	14	7
Alvis, David, Waterloo*	.252	119	353	42	89	139	18	1	10	40	2	1	1	0	27	2	53	1	1
Amante, Thomas, Appleton	.279	62	229	38	64	84	9	1	3	33	6	0	6	2	32	1	28	2	0
Angelero, Jose, Appleton	.202	35	109	10	22	25	1	1	0	10	0	2	1	0	6	0	27	1	2
Ashley, Shon, Beloit	.246	121	419	62	103	173	20	7	12	62	7	6	4	5	40	2	121	16	4
Baca, Mark, Quad City	.291	60	213	32	62	77	11	2	0	16	2	4	1	6	29	0	24	11	4
Bailey, Patrick, Appleton*	.328	101	320	44	105	148	21	2	6	47	4	1	3	2	38	3	78	5	6
Baine, Thomas, Springfield	.306	139	496	95	152	198	29	4	3	62	3	7	6	4	91	2	32	21	8
Baldwin, Lloyd, Waterloo	.309	38	149	18	46	61	6	0	3	19	1	1	2	1	10	0	17	1	2
Balfanz, John, Springfield*	.243	82	243	42	59	88	8	0	7	28	4	1	1	5	58	8	59	0	1
Bandy, Kenneth, Quad City	.234	71	214	20	50	68	7	1	3	18	4	1	0	2	19	0	75	1	6
Barker, Timothy, Beloit	.272	138	511	93	139	177	20	3	4	36	3	10	3	1	76	0	78	39	14
Barns, Jeffrey, Quad City†	.258	64	221	29	57	71	7	2	1	18	0	3	0	1	22	2	26	8	2
Barragan, Gerald, Madison	.271	83	295	36	80	95	9	3	0	36	3	4	3	1	17	1	31	5	4
Beattie, Burt, Kenosha	.143	7	7	0	1	1	0	0	0	0	0	1	0	0	0	0	0	0	0
Bell, Leonard, Peoria	.255	54	184	20	47	66	14	1	1	25	1	1	1	2	15	2	63	2	0
Benavides, Alfredo, Cedar Rapids	.133	5	15	2	2	3	1	0	0	0	0	0	0	0	0	0	7	0	1
Bennett, Jose, Wausau	.223	55	193	24	43	63	8	0	4	22	0	0	1	0	13	0	63	1	1
Berringer, John, Peoria	.000	41	1	0	0	0	0	0	0	0	0	0	0	0	0	0	0	0	0
Birch, Brock, Clinton*	1.000	25	1	0	1	1	0	0	0	0	0	0	0	0	0	0	0	0	0
Bivens, William, Springfield	.154	31	13	1	2	2	0	0	0	0	0	2	0	1	0	0	6	0	0
Bolar, Wendell, Wausau	.242	103	327	56	79	124	18	6	5	25	6	2	2	10	32	1	93	24	8
Boskie, Shawn, Peoria	.053	26	19	1	1	3	0	1	0	2	0	1	0	0	2	0	7	0	0
Bottenfield, Kent, Burlington†	.214	27	14	0	3	3	0	0	0	0	0	0	0	1	0	0	8	0	0
Bowie, James, Wausau*	.266	127	448	56	119	175	26	0	10	66	7	3	5	3	56	3	67	8	3
Breedlove, Larry, Springfield	.218	77	248	38	54	67	8	1	1	18	6	2	0	0	46	2	44	2	5
Brown, Don, Cedar Rapids	.215	56	181	35	39	59	7	2	3	12	5	2	0	2	33	0	59	13	6
Brown, Kenosha	.188	43	117	17	22	37	4	1	3	16	1	1	2	2	19	0	24	6	2
Brown, Keith, Cedar Rapids	.200	17	15	1	3	3	0	0	0	0	0	1	0	0	2	0	5	0	0
Brown, Renard, Beloit	.105	6	19	3	2	3	1	0	0	1	0	1	0	0	5	0	5	1	2
Brown, Terence, Beloit	.208	97	288	42	60	84	10	1	4	34	6	2	2	5	48	0	90	5	9
Bruno, Joseph, Cedar Rapids	.000	36	1	0	0	0	0	0	0	0	0	0	0	0	0	0	1	0	0
Buffolino, Rocco, Clinton	.000	9	1	0	0	0	0	0	0	0	0	0	0	0	0	0	0	0	0
Caffrey, Robert, Burlington	.251	89	338	51	85	157	20	2	16	57	4	0	4	1	23	2	81	0	1
Cain, Calvin, Cedar Rapids*	.235	116	375	38	88	134	21	2	7	47	3	2	2	3	24	2	60	1	4
Calvert, Christopher, Kenosha	.500	1	4	1	2	2	0	0	0	0	0	0	0	0	0	0	0	0	0
Canan, Richard, Peoria	.197	45	157	20	31	43	9	0	1	24	3	0	1	1	14	1	42	2	1
Canseco, Osvaldo, Madison	.265	92	309	64	82	135	12	4	11	54	4	0	1	1	67	3	104	6	7
Capello, Peter, Appleton	.241	67	199	30	48	69	7	4	2	21	0	1	4	4	30	0	38	3	4
Carlson, William, Clinton	.220	20	50	5	11	13	2	0	0	8	0	0	1	1	4	0	8	0	0
Carr, Terence, Quad City	.204	100	357	52	73	99	12	1	4	28	3	3	2	7	62	1	99	14	8
Carrasco, Claudio, Waterloo†	.263	130	463	79	122	187	20	9	9	59	5	3	3	4	72	2	97	8	7
Cerny, Scott, Quad City	.261	84	303	48	79	100	7	7	0	20	3	3	1	5	66	1	40	7	4
Chireno, Manuel, Beloit	.097	23	62	7	6	7	1	0	0	3	0	1	1	2	2	0	17	1	0
Clemo, Scott, Burlington*	.258	104	314	50	81	137	20	3	10	33	6	2	3	1	39	2	57	9	5
Connelly, Daron, Clinton	.000	47	8	0	0	0	0	0	0	0	0	0	0	0	0	0	2	0	0
Conroy, Timothy, Springfield*	.000	1	1	0	0	0	0	0	0	0	0	0	0	0	0	0	1	0	0
Cron, Christopher, Quad City	.276	111	398	53	110	165	20	1	11	62	5	0	1	17	44	2	88	1	3
Cupples, Michael, Madison	.211	97	294	45	62	91	17	0	4	33	3	5	3	1	51	1	60	2	2
DeLima, Rafael, Kenosha*	.273	131	494	75	135	204	9	9	9	67	4	1	2	1	86	5	77	12	9

Player and Club	Pct.	G.	AB.	R.	H.	TB.	2B.	3B.	HR.	RBI.	GW.	SH.	SF.	HP.	BB.	Int. BB.	SO.	SB.	CS.
DeYoung, Robin, Burlington†	.000	46	4	0	0	0	0	0	0	0	0	0	0	0	0	0	0	0	0
Disher, Daniel, Wausau	.258	96	298	48	77	132	10	3	13	43	2	4	4	1	19	1	87	12	6
Dixon, Andrew, Clinton°	.333	58	243	34	81	103	12	5	0	23	2	0	0	0	17	0	35	34	13
Duffy, Darrin, Madison	.278	43	176	32	49	78	7	2	6	28	0	3	0	1	24	0	42	7	3
Duke, Douglas, Burlington	.237	123	439	51	104	197	25	1	22	75	7	3	4	6	27	4	101	2	2
Dull, Michael, Burlington°	.311	135	498	88	155	261	38	7	18	85	8	1	6	6	63	6	69	7	5
Dyson, Theodore, Quad City°	.266	65	218	32	58	112	13	1	13	37	4	0	1	3	29	2	78	1	1
Ealy, Thomas, Clinton†	.266	60	169	26	45	61	6	2	2	21	1	0	1	2	27	1	37	4	3
Eisenreich, Charles, Appleton°	.240	104	300	54	72	103	16	3	3	32	3	4	4	0	71	1	71	18	9
Engel, Steven, Springfield	.000	4	1	0	0	0	0	0	0	0	0	0	0	0	0	0	0	0	0
Escalera, Carlos, Appleton	.220	86	300	29	66	92	9	1	5	45	8	1	4	1	15	0	66	3	1
Espinal, Arismendy, Cedar Rapids	.500	27	2	2	1	1	0	0	0	0	0	0	0	0	1	0	0	0	0
Espinal, Sergio, Peoria	.249	76	209	24	52	65	5	1	2	20	2	0	2	3	22	1	56	5	3
Fairchild, Glenn, Waterloo†	.226	114	385	68	87	126	19	4	4	33	5	6	1	3	44	1	109	34	10
Farley, Brian, Springfield	.111	11	9	0	1	2	1	0	0	0	0	2	0	0	0	0	1	0	0
Faron, Robert, Springfield	.120	27	25	3	3	3	0	0	0	0	0	3	0	0	2	0	11	0	0
Figueroa, Bienvenido, Springfield	.278	134	489	52	136	161	13	3	2	83	10	12	7	4	34	2	46	7	7
Finigan, Kevin, Burlington	.127	23	55	4	7	7	0	0	0	3	0	0	0	0	2	0	23	2	2
Finley, David, Madison	.286	17	56	3	16	23	2	1	1	17	1	0	2	0	1	0	12	1	0
Flowers, Kim, Clinton	.248	66	218	36	54	87	7	1	8	32	3	1	0	2	23	1	66	2	2
Ford, Ondra, Appleton°	.265	93	309	53	82	123	31	2	2	45	2	2	5	1	29	1	75	19	6
Forgione, Christopher, Kenosha°	.244	112	393	59	96	137	11	3	8	42	4	1	2	4	32	3	45	6	7
Gallardo, Luis, Quad City	.286	22	77	6	22	27	3	1	0	7	1	1	0	0	4	0	17	2	1
Gamba, Thomas, Waterloo	.263	81	179	25	47	63	6	2	2	19	2	2	0	1	21	0	28	2	6
Garcia, Victor, Peoria	.263	123	479	53	126	206	24	4	16	104	8	0	5	3	25	1	112	2	1
Gay, Jeffrey, Quad City°	.212	63	217	12	46	55	6	0	1	20	1	0	2	0	10	3	51	0	0
Gaylor, Robert, Burlington	.250	31	112	11	28	32	4	0	0	6	2	3	2	0	11	0	9	6	3
Gilbert, Patrick, Madison	.275	99	345	66	95	140	25	4	4	58	5	2	7	7	65	1	60	5	6
Giles, Troy, Quad City	.172	38	128	15	22	30	3	1	1	9	0	0	1	0	14	1	57	2	0
Gilkey, Bernard, Springfield	.228	46	162	30	37	42	5	0	0	9	1	2	2	2	39	1	28	18	5
Glisson, Robert, Springfield°	.143	40	7	0	1	1	0	0	0	1	0	1	0	0	0	0	3	0	0
Goff, Jerry, Wausau°	.232	109	336	51	78	138	17	2	13	47	3	1	2	8	65	3	87	4	7
Goins, Scott, Clinton	.200	7	15	3	3	4	1	0	0	2	0	1	0	0	3	0	3	0	0
Gomez, Patrick, Peoria°	.100	20	10	0	1	2	1	0	0	0	0	0	0	0	0	0	3	0	0
Gonzalez, Carlos, Appleton	.194	86	248	25	48	67	10	0	3	18	2	8	1	0	23	1	72	3	7
Gonzalez, Felipe, Clinton	.205	29	73	7	15	22	1	0	2	6	2	1	1	1	2	0	8	1	2
Graham, Jeffrey, Springfield	.100	5	10	0	1	1	0	0	0	0	0	0	0	0	0	0	3	0	0
Graves, Christopher, Quad City	.166	74	247	31	41	55	4	2	2	13	1	1	1	1	35	2	102	15	12
Green, John, Peoria	.333	26	3	0	1	1	0	0	0	0	0	0	0	0	0	0	2	0	0
Grilione, David, Quad City†	.208	96	336	29	70	97	16	1	3	28	4	0	2	5	19	2	123	4	2
Gunn, Clay, Wausau	.233	71	223	21	52	81	9	1	6	23	2	0	0	2	17	2	43	3	2
Gust, Christopher, Madison†	.256	61	168	33	43	49	4	1	0	17	2	1	0	6	41	2	22	12	5
Hale, Walter, Kenosha°	.345	87	339	65	117	164	12	7	7	65	13	0	7	4	33	4	26	3	3
Hamilton, Scott, Springfield	.115	29	26	1	3	3	0	0	0	2	1	0	0	0	1	0	8	0	0
Hanker, Frederick, Madison	.290	26	93	11	27	39	9	0	1	14	1	0	0	0	8	0	18	0	1
Hardy, Mark, Burlington	.194	35	103	17	20	38	4	1	4	9	2	1	0	2	16	0	57	5	1
Harkey, Michael, Peoria	.214	12	14	0	3	3	0	0	0	0	0	1	0	0	0	0	5	0	0
Harrison, Phillip, Peoria°	.083	34	12	0	1	1	0	0	0	1	0	2	1	0	1	0	4	0	0
Harrison, Ronald, Beloit°	.299	41	144	24	43	64	10	4	1	28	0	0	4	1	6	0	9	8	2
Hartnett, David, 22 Wau-18 Peo°	.000	40	2	0	0	0	0	0	0	0	0	0	0	0	0	0	1	0	0
Headley, Kent, Appleton†	.230	65	213	30	49	56	3	2	0	18	2	7	1	2	28	1	43	8	1
Hemond, Scott, Madison	.289	90	343	60	99	152	21	4	8	52	5	0	2	1	40	1	79	27	12
Henry, Douglas, Beloit	.000	31	0	0	0	0	0	0	0	0	0	1	0	0	0	0	0	0	0
Hickerson, Bryan, Clinton°	.100	17	10	1	1	3	0	1	0	0	0	0	0	0	2	0	5	0	0
Higson, Charles, Clinton°	.000	28	2	0	0	0	0	0	0	0	0	0	0	0	0	0	1	0	0
Hilgenberg, Scott, Cedar Rapids°	.191	38	131	7	25	32	4	0	1	17	2	0	0	0	16	4	28	0	0
Hill, Stephen, Springfield°	.500	7	2	0	1	1	0	0	0	0	0	0	0	0	0	0	1	0	0
Hill, Steven, Peoria	.264	130	492	56	130	171	21	4	4	54	6	6	3	2	43	0	60	20	12
Hilton, Howard, Springfield	.000	62	5	0	0	0	0	0	0	0	0	1	0	0	1	0	4	0	0
Hisey, Steven, Wausau°	.267	41	131	20	35	68	9	0	8	28	2	0	0	0	17	0	25	1	2
Howes, John, Burlington°	.125	28	16	0	2	2	0	0	0	1	0	0	0	0	1	0	11	0	1
Iavarone, Gregory, Peoria	.204	24	49	1	10	11	1	0	0	2	0	1	0	1	4	0	12	0	0
Isaacson, Christopher, Waterloo	.281	41	114	19	32	72	5	1	11	28	3	0	1	1	12	1	30	0	2
Ishmael, Michael, Burlington	.106	20	47	4	5	5	0	0	0	0	0	0	0	0	1	4	0	9	2	0
Jacas, David, Kenosha†	.278	38	126	20	35	46	3	1	2	16	0	1	0	0	11	0	27	4	0
Jackson, Gregory, Quad City	.209	24	67	5	14	20	1	1	1	4	0	0	1	0	13	0	26	1	0
Jackson, Lloyd, Clinton°	.262	41	107	13	28	43	6	3	1	5	0	1	0	2	6	0	34	2	2
Jackson, Kenneth, Appleton	.268	134	512	86	137	249	43	6	19	67	8	1	3	11	48	3	90	15	13
Jacobson, Nels, Burlington	.000	30	7	0	0	0	0	0	0	0	0	3	0	0	0	0	1	0	0
Jaha, John, Beloit	.269	122	376	68	101	144	22	0	7	47	3	2	3	4	102	2	86	10	5
Jefferson, Reginald, Cedar Rapids°.	.222	15	54	9	12	26	5	0	3	11	2	0	0	3	1	0	12	1	1
Johnigan, Stephen, Waterloo	.186	22	70	4	13	14	1	0	0	9	3	0	2	0	7	1	6	2	1
Johns, Ronald, Springfield	.282	54	209	37	59	90	17	1	4	32	5	1	4	2	17	0	25	1	1
Johnson, Charles, Springfield	.188	18	69	8	13	15	2	0	0	7	1	2	1	0	6	0	11	9	1
Johnson, Deron, Wausau°	.224	102	321	30	72	104	17	0	5	45	3	1	3	0	45	4	60	4	4
Johnson, Scott, Waterloo°	.268	121	351	63	94	185	23	1	22	70	9	3	8	3	44	3	77	1	2
Johnson, Thomas, Appleton°	.000	2	4	1	0	0	0	0	0	0	0	0	0	0	0	0	3	1	0
Jones, James, Clinton†	.242	18	33	4	8	8	0	0	0	2	0	1	0	0	7	0	7	2	0
Jones, Kenneth, Madison	.243	48	189	25	46	62	6	2	2	21	2	3	7	1	16	1	36	12	6
Jones, Michael, Burlington°	.154	8	13	0	2	2	0	0	0	0	0	1	0	0	0	0	3	0	0
Jones, Robert, Beloit	.263	85	323	35	85	135	17	3	9	52	3	6	3	0	14	2	73	8	3
Jorgensen, Terry, Kenosha	.315	67	254	37	80	118	17	0	7	33	4	0	1	2	18	0	43	1	0
Kallevig, Gregory, Peoria	.333	10	3	0	1	2	1	0	0	0	0	0	0	0	0	0	2	0	0
Kazmierczak, William, Peoria†	.000	6	3	0	0	0	0	0	0	0	0	0	0	0	0	0	3	0	0
Kelly, Leonard, Burlington	.000	21	0	0	0	0	0	0	0	0	0	0	0	0	0	0	0	0	0
Kent, Bernard, Beloit°	.283	64	212	31	60	106	14	1	10	46	5	0	1	0	22	5	39	7	1
Kindred, Curtis, Cedar Rapids	.000	10	1	0	0	0	0	0	0	0	0	0	0	0	0	0	1	0	0
Kindred, Vincent, Springfield	.251	111	435	68	109	176	25	3	12	60	7	3	5	5	35	1	92	19	8
Knapp, Michael, Quad City	.257	91	327	34	84	107	14	3	1	31	2	0	7	4	27	0	48	1	6
Kosco, Andrew, Wausau°	.206	108	349	42	72	128	22	2	10	54	4	0	3	6	27	0	97	3	2
Kryzanowski, Rusty, Kenosha	.067	9	30	4	2	5	0	0	1	2	0	0	0	0	3	0	13	0	0
Kunkel, Kevin, Madison	.000	26	1	0	0	0	0	0	0	0	0	0	0	0	0	0	0	0	0

Player and Club	Pct.	G.	AB	R.	H.	TB.	2B.	3B.	HR.	RBI.	GW.	SH.	SF.	HP.	BB.	Int. BB.	SO.	SB.	CS.
Labozzetta, Albert, Cedar Rapids°	.250	8	4	2	1	1	0	0	0	0	0	0	0	0	1	0	0	0	0
Ladnier, Deric, Appleton†	.269	116	442	73	119	183	20	7	10	68	7	1	6	3	32	1	96	15	1
Lampkin, Thomas, Waterloo°	.266	118	398	49	106	150	19	2	7	55	5	1	6	2	34	2	41	5	0
Langdon, Ted, Cedar Rapids	.000	3	1	0	0	0	0	0	0	0	0	0	0	0	0	0	1	0	0
Lapenta, Gerald, Peoria°	.280	119	343	59	96	148	21	2	9	52	8	1	2	4	81	7	67	3	3
Larios, John, Appleton	.152	12	33	6	5	8	0	0	1	4	2	0	0	2	2	0	9	0	2
Laureano, Francisco, Appleton	.323	139	498	86	161	236	25	1	16	87	7	0	11	1	70	0	81	19	9
Lazor, Joseph, Cedar Rapids°	.231	26	13	0	3	3	0	0	0	1	0	0	0	0	0	0	5	0	0
Leius, Scott, Kenosha	.239	126	414	65	99	147	16	4	8	51	5	5	4	3	50	0	88	6	4
Lemons, Timothy, Springfield	.273	28	88	11	24	43	5	1	4	16	3	0	0	0	9	1	16	1	1
Lennon, Patrick, Wausau	.251	98	319	54	80	128	21	3	7	34	4	1	2	1	46	1	82	25	8
Leonard, Mark, Clinton°	.320	128	413	57	132	212	31	2	15	80	9	0	3	5	71	3	61	5	8
Lexa, Michael, Kenosha	.175	51	103	8	18	23	5	0	0	7	1	1	1	0	6	1	23	3	0
Liebert, Allen, Waterloo°	.330	35	97	17	32	70	8	0	10	26	2	0	2	0	9	0	22	1	0
Lincoln, Lance, Beloit	.098	21	61	3	6	8	2	0	0	5	0	2	1	0	12	0	16	0	1
Lockhart, Keith, Cedar Rapids°	.313	140	511	101	160	276	37	5	23	84	11	1	6	13	86	7	70	20	8
Lonigro, Gregory, Cedar Rapids	.244	121	426	51	104	132	20	1	2	36	4	7	1	3	20	2	51	10	8
Lono, Joel, Cedar Rapids°	.143	27	14	0	2	2	0	0	0	1	0	1	0	0	0	0	4	0	0
Mack, Quinn, Burlington°	.268	59	164	15	44	62	10	1	2	15	3	0	0	2	11	1	22	0	3
Mackie, Scott, Waterloo	.213	65	169	23	36	57	12	0	3	15	2	1	2	3	20	0	70	6	5
Maddox, Leland, Madison	.000	5	15	1	0	0	0	0	0	0	0	0	0	0	1	0	7	0	0
Mangham, Mark, Springfield	.100	22	10	1	1	1	0	0	0	0	0	0	0	0	0	0	5	0	0
Mann, Kelly, Peoria	.254	95	287	24	73	103	16	1	4	45	2	3	4	4	23	0	66	1	1
Marino, John, Burlington°	.333	5	3	1	1	1	0	0	0	0	0	0	0	0	1	0	1	0	0
Martinez, Luis, Madison†	.254	97	291	32	74	98	12	3	2	36	3	0	1	0	48	0	59	5	11
Marzan, Jose, Kenosha	.255	32	102	16	26	35	4	1	1	15	3	2	1	0	18	1	15	1	1
Masters, Frank, Madison	.216	42	148	17	32	45	7	0	2	14	0	0	1	1	15	1	49	0	1
Mattia, Tony, Quad City°	.178	56	191	20	34	59	4	0	7	32	1	0	3	3	28	1	49	0	2
May, Derrick, Peoria°	.298	128	439	60	131	193	19	8	9	52	11	0	5	1	42	4	106	5	7
McAnany, James, Quad City°	.250	32	112	9	28	36	3	1	1	11	1	0	1	4	7	0	34	1	1
McClellan, Clinton	.250	28	24	1	6	6	0	0	0	4	0	1	0	0	2	0	8	0	0
McCollom, James, Quad City	.273	88	322	35	88	133	21	0	8	36	1	0	1	5	31	3	57	3	1
McDonald, Michael, Wausau°	.255	100	302	45	77	122	19	1	8	43	3	1	3	2	62	2	71	8	7
McGinnis, Russell, Beloit	.307	51	189	34	58	107	10	0	13	35	5	1	0	2	19	2	36	1	2
McHugh, Scott, Burlington	.281	21	64	11	18	25	4	0	1	8	1	0	1	3	9	0	11	0	0
McIntosh, Timothy, Beloit	.302	130	461	83	139	235	30	3	20	85	14	1	3	7	49	2	96	7	4
McNamara, James, Clinton°	.247	110	385	43	95	134	22	1	5	53	3	2	7	0	19	1	52	4	2
Mejias, Simeon, Peoria†	.129	22	31	1	4	4	0	0	0	0	0	1	0	0	2	0	7	1	0
Melvin, Scott, Springfield	.292	115	411	77	120	176	19	5	9	69	11	7	9	7	56	5	76	1	4
Mendenhall, Shannon, Madison	.134	24	67	7	9	11	2	0	0	8	1	2	1	0	11	0	34	1	1
Meyer, Steven, Springfield°	.286	8	7	1	2	2	0	0	0	0	0	0	0	0	2	0	1	0	0
Meyers, Glenn, Kenosha	.272	32	81	18	22	34	4	1	2	14	6	1	1	0	8	0	19	0	0
Michalak, Anthony, Clinton	.280	44	164	23	46	52	6	0	0	14	3	4	1	1	16	1	15	6	1
Mijares, William, Clinton	.202	113	357	36	72	90	8	5	0	28	5	10	0	0	20	1	60	8	5
Miller, Michael, Peoria	.179	30	84	8	15	23	2	0	2	8	1	2	2	0	3	0	19	0	1
Montoyo, Carlos, Beloit	.266	55	188	46	50	78	9	2	5	19	1	1	1	4	52	0	22	8	0
Moore, Sam, Clinton	.500	11	2	0	1	1	0	0	0	0	0	0	0	0	0	0	0	0	0
Morrow, David, Burlington	.218	94	294	27	64	88	22	1	0	21	0	1	0	2	29	1	73	3	2
Moscrey, Michael, Cedar Rapids	.063	19	16	1	1	1	0	0	0	2	2	0	0	0	0	0	5	0	0
Mullino, Ray, Peoria	.000	17	1	0	0	0	0	0	0	0	0	0	0	0	0	0	0	0	0
Mullins, Ronald, Cedar Rapids	.000	34	1	0	0	0	0	0	0	0	0	0	0	0	0	0	1	0	0
Munoz, Omer, Burlington	.241	52	195	22	47	59	8	2	0	16	1	6	0	3	7	0	13	5	3
Murphy, John, Springfield	.147	30	68	8	10	17	4	0	1	7	0	1	1	2	8	0	21	0	0
Murphy, Miguel, Kenosha	.200	13	5	4	1	1	0	0	0	0	0	0	0	0	1	0	1	0	0
Murray, Scott, Clinton	.268	19	56	6	15	17	2	0	0	3	0	0	1	1	6	0	12	1	1
Naveda, Edgar, Kenosha	.278	136	511	65	142	220	34	1	14	77	8	4	7	3	37	4	74	5	8
Norman, Scott, Springfield	.333	23	6	1	2	5	0	0	1	1	0	1	0	0	0	0	2	0	0
Ojea, Alexander, Springfield†	.252	131	432	82	109	153	24	1	6	52	5	9	5	4	72	1	89	12	10
Ojeda, Raymond, Beloit	.000	42	3	0	0	0	0	0	0	0	0	0	0	0	0	0	1	0	0
Oller, Jeffrey, Burlington°	.244	110	406	53	99	174	24	3	15	54	7	5	2	6	54	3	105	2	6
Olson, James, Burlington	.200	14	10	1	2	3	1	0	0	0	0	1	0	1	0	0	4	0	0
Ortman, Douglas, Madison	.208	38	96	23	20	39	10	0	3	22	3	2	3	1	35	0	27	0	0
Parker, Stephen, Peoria°	.222	29	18	4	4	4	0	0	0	0	0	1	0	0	1	0	4	0	0
Parks, Derek, Kenosha	.247	129	466	70	115	210	19	2	24	94	7	0	6	10	77	5	111	1	1
Patterson, David, Clinton	.253	121	434	64	110	163	20	3	9	71	11	4	6	4	55	2	56	7	5
Paulino, Luis, Peoria°	.205	49	117	22	24	29	2	0	1	13	2	0	1	2	24	1	26	1	2
Pena, James, Clinton°	.174	26	23	1	4	5	1	0	0	1	0	1	0	0	1	0	3	0	0
Perez, Michael, Springfield	.250	58	4	0	1	1	0	0	0	1	0	0	0	0	0	0	1	0	0
Perry, Parnell, Peoria	.252	110	361	47	91	109	12	3	0	26	4	1	2	0	22	1	81	20	7
Pickett, Antoine, Appleton†	.262	25	61	13	16	25	2	2	1	6	2	0	0	4	5	0	11	2	1
Pike, Mark, Waterloo	.234	88	248	31	58	74	6	2	2	21	2	3	3	3	24	0	43	9	6
Pinol, Juan, Cedar Rapids	.188	12	32	3	6	8	0	1	0	1	0	0	0	0	3	0	11	0	2
Polk, Riley, Waterloo	.276	64	203	21	56	68	9	0	1	20	1	0	2	1	25	0	34	6	4
Pulliam, Harvey, Appleton	.276	110	395	54	109	158	20	1	9	55	7	1	3	3	26	0	79	21	7
Puzey, James, Springfield°	.213	17	47	10	10	18	1	2	1	6	0	0	1	0	13	1	4	1	0
Randle, Michael, Kenosha°	.294	139	565	110	166	198	22	5	0	53	5	6	2	13	53	4	51	45	18
Rannow, John, Clinton	.234	50	107	17	25	33	3	1	1	8	2	1	2	2	16	0	41	0	0
Raziano, Scott, Springfield	.274	102	317	52	87	119	17	0	5	50	10	8	4	2	43	0	44	2	2
Redick, Kevin, Clinton	.206	78	223	36	48	70	7	0	5	14	0	9	0	5	26	1	77	8	2
Reiser, James, Madison	.279	95	308	51	86	99	9	2	0	37	4	0	4	2	64	0	54	9	6
Remlinger, Michael, Clinton°	.000	6	2	0	0	0	0	0	0	0	0	0	0	0	0	0	1	0	0
Reyes, Giovanny, Quad City	.225	101	365	41	82	106	14	5	0	29	3	4	2	3	26	0	62	9	5
Richardson, James, Waterloo†	.247	133	470	79	116	150	20	1	4	49	12	4	4	3	91	1	91	27	6
Richmond, Robert, Clinton	.500	12	2	1	1	1	0	0	0	0	0	0	0	0	0	0	1	0	0
Ricker, Drew, Clinton°	.000	33	1	0	0	0	0	0	0	0	0	0	0	0	0	0	1	0	0
Ritchie, Gregory, Clinton°	.337	124	416	102	140	193	19	11	4	49	10	5	3	3	90	8	80	41	21
Roberts, Brent, Waterloo	.184	17	49	5	9	12	3	0	0	3	0	0	1	0	7	0	20	0	0
Robertson, Douglas, Clinton	.176	28	17	1	3	3	0	0	0	1	0	2	0	0	0	0	4	0	0
Robinson, Brian, Cedar Rapids	.211	131	470	67	99	152	16	2	11	45	2	8	1	1	70	1	85	28	9
Robles, Gabaliel, Peoria	.500	11	2	0	1	1	0	0	0	0	0	0	0	0	1	0	0	1	0
Rogers, Sebastian, Cedar Rapids†	.000	22	12	1	0	0	0	0	0	0	0	1	0	0	0	0	1	0	0
Rojas, Melquiades, Burlington	.148	25	27	1	4	4	0	0	0	4	0	1	0	0	1	0	8	0	0

Player and Club	Pct.	G.	AB.	R.	H.	TB.	2B.	3B.	HR.	RBI.	GW.	SH.	SF.	HP.	BB.	Int. BB.	SO.	SB.	CS.
Ronson, Tod, Clinton*	.291	133	488	82	142	224	44	4	10	92	12	2	7	2	67	7	80	11	8
Rooker, David, Beloit	.000	21	1	0	0	0	0	0	0	0	0	0	0	0	0	0	0	0	0
Rosario, David, Peoria*	.000	24	3	0	0	0	0	0	0	0	0	0	0	0	0	0	1	0	0
Rousey, Stephen, Burlington*	.000	29	6	0	0	0	0	0	0	0	0	2	0	0	1	0	2	0	0
Rush, Edward, Cedar Rapids	.275	24	80	9	22	26	4	0	0	10	1	1	0	2	8	0	18	2	1
Sala, David, Springfield*	.000	3	1	0	0	0	0	0	0	0	0	0	0	0	0	0	1	0	0
Santos, Donaciano, Waterloo	.193	25	57	7	11	19	8	0	0	7	1	0	1	1	3	0	19	0	0
Schueler, Russ, Burlington	.204	106	339	42	69	88	6	5	1	29	2	4	2	5	30	4	63	18	5
Schwarz, Jeffrey, Peoria	.200	20	10	2	2	2	0	0	0	1	0	2	0	0	0	0	2	0	0
Scudder, Scott, Cedar Rapids	.200	26	20	1	4	5	1	0	0	2	1	0	0	0	3	0	9	0	0
Seifert, Keith, Waterloo	.255	88	243	34	62	97	14	0	7	39	6	2	5	0	27	1	55	2	0
Sharpnack, Robert, Madison	.500	23	2	0	1	1	0	0	0	0	0	0	0	0	0	0	1	0	0
Shelton, Harry, Peoria*	.237	113	337	47	80	102	11	1	3	31	6	2	3	0	30	1	65	18	12
Shumake, Brooks, Cedar Rapids	.241	130	448	54	108	168	19	1	13	58	9	1	3	5	47	0	101	31	6
Silva, Ryan, Clinton	.143	5	14	1	2	5	0	0	1	1	0	0	0	0	1	0	2	0	0
Silverio, Francisco, Cedar Rapids	.231	99	308	32	71	100	13	2	4	30	3	2	2	1	20	3	104	12	5
Skodny, Joseph, Appleton*	.000	32	1	0	0	0	0	0	0	0	0	0	0	0	0	0	1	0	0
Slocumb, Heath, Peoria	.200	17	15	1	3	3	0	0	0	0	0	2	0	0	0	0	5	0	0
Smith, Gregory, Peoria†	.270	124	444	69	120	171	23	5	6	56	6	7	5	4	62	5	96	26	9
Smith, Robert, Beloit	.264	48	182	23	48	66	10	1	2	25	1	2	1	0	17	1	42	6	2
Snyder, Kendall, Kenosha†	.206	34	102	15	21	27	3	0	1	9	1	1	0	2	10	0	22	0	2
Sobczyk, Robert, Beloit	.111	8	9	0	1	1	0	0	0	0	1	0	0	0	0	0	3	0	0
Sparks, Gregory, Madison*	.297	58	222	25	66	92	15	1	3	41	6	1	4	0	26	3	38	3	1
Spiers, William, Beloit*	.298	64	258	43	77	98	10	1	3	26	4	2	0	3	15	0	38	11	5
Spitale, Benjamin, Burlington*	.250	57	168	18	42	58	9	2	1	21	2	3	0	4	18	3	27	5	3
St. Claire, Steven, Burlington	.242	63	165	27	40	69	15	1	4	15	2	0	0	4	15	0	53	5	2
Stancel, Mark, Madison	.000	9	0	0	0	0	0	0	0	0	0	0	0	0	1	0	0	0	0
Stewart, John, Cedar Rapids	.208	58	154	15	32	53	4	1	5	12	1	1	1	5	18	2	39	4	1
Stone, Brian, Beloit	.000	29	3	0	0	0	0	0	0	0	0	0	0	0	0	0	1	0	0
Takach, David, Springfield*	.000	39	4	0	0	0	0	0	0	0	0	0	0	0	0	0	4	0	0
Tartabull, Jose, Wausau	.278	91	295	49	82	105	9	1	4	32	2	3	3	1	61	2	39	23	13
Taylor, David, Beloit	.175	53	154	14	27	32	5	0	0	14	2	3	4	0	24	1	37	1	0
Taylor, Kenneth, Peoria	.182	8	11	1	2	2	0	0	0	1	0	1	0	1	3	2	3	0	0
Teixeira, Vincent, Madison	.251	122	438	85	110	152	18	3	6	54	4	2	4	5	104	1	103	15	8
Tenacen, Francisco, Cedar Rapids	.245	101	380	58	93	157	12	2	16	54	8	0	3	9	16	1	74	14	5
Tinkey, Robert, Kenosha	.245	127	436	67	107	170	20	2	13	61	10	0	2	7	71	1	89	4	3
Toal, John, Clinton	.245	126	420	51	103	132	19	2	2	53	5	6	2	8	41	1	61	5	5
Trout, Steven, Peoria*	.000	1	4	0	0	0	0	0	0	0	1	0	0	0	0	0	0	0	0
Van Stone, Paul, Clinton†	.321	8	28	5	9	11	0	1	0	2	0	0	0	5	0	3	1	2	
Vaughn, Gregory, Beloit	.305	139	492	120	150	292	31	6	33	105	8	3	6	5	102	2	115	36	9
Velasquez, Raymond, Clinton	.000	45	4	0	0	0	0	0	0	0	0	0	0	0	0	0	4	0	0
Veras, Camilo, Madison*	.294	129	470	79	138	215	20	12	11	76	6	0	2	5	61	2	90	26	9
Villa, Michael, Clinton*	.250	18	4	0	1	1	0	0	0	0	0	0	0	0	0	0	1	0	0
Viltz, Corey, Burlington	.146	13	41	8	6	8	2	0	0	1	0	1	0	0	6	0	8	2	1
Vincent, Michael, Cedar Rapids	.224	72	232	21	52	78	12	1	4	19	2	0	2	6	18	2	61	6	7
Vontz, Douglas, Burlington	.500	41	2	0	1	1	0	0	0	0	0	0	2	0	1	0	0	0	0
Wakamatsu, Donald, Cedar Rapids	.216	103	365	33	79	115	13	1	7	41	3	2	3	3	30	1	71	3	3
Walker, Bernard, Cedar Rapids*	.300	52	160	25	48	63	4	1	3	18	3	2	3	0	31	2	43	25	9
Walling, Kendall, Quad City	.240	29	100	9	24	31	4	0	1	8	0	0	2	1	5	0	28	0	1
Walton, Jerome, Peoria	.335	128	472	102	158	222	24	11	6	38	4	5	1	11	91	2	91	49	25
Watkins, Darren, Appleton	.111	12	18	3	2	2	0	0	0	1	0	0	0	1	0	2	10	1	0
Watkins, Keith, Madison	.243	50	173	27	42	60	10	4	0	17	1	0	2	2	19	1	31	4	5
Watson, DeJon, Appleton*	.240	91	254	48	61	92	10	3	5	50	5	2	3	2	66	1	53	5	6
Webster, Leonard, Kenosha	.250	52	140	17	35	51	7	0	3	17	2	0	3	0	17	0	20	2	0
Wedvick, Jeffrey, Burlington	.200	5	15	1	3	4	1	0	0	2	0	0	0	0	1	0	1	0	1
Weinberger, Gary, Burlington*	.283	79	304	44	86	124	21	1	5	33	2	2	4	2	29	0	27	7	6
Welborn, Anthony, Burlington	.200	20	15	2	3	6	0	0	1	3	0	2	0	0	0	0	9	1	1
Williams, Edward, Peoria*	.219	14	32	5	7	8	1	0	0	2	0	0	0	0	6	0	17	1	1
Williams, Ted, Wausau†	.257	120	460	63	118	145	16	1	3	31	5	6	2	4	35	2	84	74	21
Williams, Troy, Wausau	.203	19	59	7	12	15	1	1	0	4	0	1	0	2	8	0	30	6	3
Williamson, Raymond, Waterloo	.217	121	396	72	86	173	15	0	24	65	3	0	1	5	56	3	133	7	2
Willis, Scott, Cedar Rapids	.000	43	1	0	0	0	0	0	0	0	0	0	0	0	0	0	0	1	0
Wilson, David, Madison	.178	18	45	4	8	9	1	0	0	2	1	0	0	0	9	0	6	1	1
Wilson, Thomas, Cedar Rapids	.194	53	160	17	31	39	5	0	1	13	1	4	3	1	12	0	37	2	1
Wilson, Trevor, Clinton*	.125	26	16	1	2	5	0	0	1	2	1	2	1	0	0	0	8	0	0
Wolkoys, Robert, Appleton	.240	106	308	56	74	90	11	1	1	29	4	8	3	1	42	0	63	11	5
Wolten, Brad, Waterloo*	.192	60	156	12	30	44	5	0	3	14	1	1	0	0	10	0	38	0	1
Woods, Anthony, Wausau	.224	120	424	57	95	134	6	3	6	42	4	3	6	1	55	1	102	30	13
Woods, Eric, Peoria*	.000	6	4	3	0	0	0	0	0	0	0	0	0	0	0	0	1	0	
Young, Delwyn, Burlington†	.314	19	51	12	16	20	4	0	0	2	0	1	0	0	19	1	5	9	2
Zarranz, Fernando, Peoria	.125	14	8	2	1	1	0	0	0	0	0	2	1	0	1	0	1	0	0
Zeile, Todd, Springfield	.292	130	487	94	142	249	24	4	25	106	12	0	3	1	70	7	85	1	3

The following pitchers, listed alphabetically by club, with games in parentheses, had no plate appearances, primarily through use of designated hitters:

APPLETON—Butcher, Michael (20); Cassidy, William (4); Cruse, Jeffrey (20); Gilles, Thomas (1); Gilmore, William (27); Harlan, Daniel (11); Hibbard, Gregory (9); LeBlanc, Richard (16); Lee, Benjamin (40); Maldonado, Carlos (2); McKinzie, Philip (43); Meyers, Brian (3); Moeller, Dennis (18); Mount, Charles (28); Naworski, Andrew (22); Nocas, Luke (25); Peters, Gary (11); Poldberg, Brian (2); Pumphrey, Shawn (1); Rodriguez, Jose (9); Tresemer, Michael (23); Willis, James (32).

BELOIT—Birkbeck, Michael (1); Cangemi, Jamie (12); Carley, David (8); Diaz, Derek (37); Drahman, Brian (46); Elvira, Narcisso (4); Franchi, Kevin (8); Kanwisher, Gary (22); Kendrick, Peter (3); Kostichka, Steven (17); Monson, Steven (11); Shiver, Todd (21); Veres, Randolf (21); Watkins, Timothy (18).

BURLINGTON—Larsen, Daniel (4); McCormack, Ronald (13); Vaccaro, Salvatore (4).

CEDAR RAPIDS—Dale, Philip (46).

KENOSHA—Abbott, Paul (26); Bangston, Patrick (7); Buzzard, Lawrence (25); Cota, Timothy (7); Davins, James (48); DeJaynes, Paul (3); Dyer, Michael (27); Franchi, Kevin (12); Gonzalez, German (47); Heinle, Dana (13); Hernandez, Robert (3); Kline, Douglas (9); Rios, Enrique (30); Romero, Elvis (3); Satzinger, Jeffrey (5); Stowell, Steven (5); Swanson, Chad (3); Thomas, Carl (10); Wulf, Brian (3).

MADISON—Baez, Pedro (10); Beavers, Mark (27); Bradley, Bert (14); Carroll, James (47); Cundari, Philip (10); Deabenderfer, Blaine (17); Glover, Jeffrey (26); Kopyta, Jeffrey (48); Lambert, Reese (23); MacLeod, Kevin (10); Otto, David (1); Salcedo, Luis (36); Stocker, Robert (14); Weber, Weston (9).

PEORIA—Otten, Brian (58).

QUAD CITY—Bisceglia, James (36); Fix, Gregory (37); Green, Daryl (27); Hernandez, Roberto (7); Kannenberg, Scott (28); Kesler, Michael (42); Long, James (23); McKinnis, Timothy (14); Merejo, Luis (49); Morehouse, Richard (20); Pardo, Lawrence (38); Pineda, Rafael (5); Rivera, Elvin (6); Tapia, Jose (27); Vann, Brandy (27).

SPRINGFIELD—Agar, Jeffrey (9); Dayley, Kenneth (2); Hulstrom, Bryce (1); Tunnell, Lee (1).

WATERLOO—Bird, Steven (40); Chambers, Carl (16); Compres, Fidel (21); Egloff, Bruce (7); Gardner, Myron (7); Githens, John (41); Gonzales, Todd (25); Keliipuleole, Carl (29); Kurczewski, Tommy (4); Kuykendall, Kevin (23); Kuzniar, Paul (51); Madden, Scott (18); Mercado, Manuel (16); Ogden, Todd (13); Rountree, Michael (1); Seanez, Rudy (10); Shaw, Jeffrey (28); Walker, Michael (23).

WAUSAU—Blueberg, James (8); Eldredge, Edward (12); Frink, Keith (15); Gardiner, Michael (13); Gold, Mark (25); Intorcia, Trent (43); Little, Thomas (4); McLain, Timothy (7); Rice, Patrick (28); Ryan, Jody (27); Schreiber, Martin (6); Thorpe, Michael (36); Townsend, Howard (46); Webb, Charlie (10); Webster, Rudy (16); Wooden, Mark (34).

GRAND SLAM HOME RUNS—Garcia, V. Kindred, 2 each; Abner, Alou, Ashley, Bowie, Cupples, DeLima, Disher, Hale, Hemond, Hilgenberg, Steven Hill, Hisey, S. Johnson, R. Jones, Lemons, Masters, Mattia, McCollom, Melvin, Oller, Parks, Tenacen, Tinkey, Toal, Vaughn, Vincent, 1 each.

AWARDED FIRST BASE ON CATCHER'S INTERFERENCE—V. Kindred 4 (C. Gonzalez, Knapp, Mann, Morrow); Leonard 4 (Goff 2, Hemond, Johnigan); Amante 3 (Iavarone, Isaacson, Knapp); Bolar 3 (C. Gonzalez 2, Wakamatsu); Silverio 2 (Miller, Zeile); Bowie (C. Gonzalez); Figueroa (Goff); Headley (Gay); Iavarone (Zeile); Lexa (Miller); Masters (Knapp); McDonald (Gay); J. Murphy (Morrow); Parks (Knapp); Redick (Parks); Tenacen (Lampkin); Wedvick (Knapp).

CLUB FIELDING

Club	Pct.	G.	PO.	A.	E.	DP.	PB.	Club	Pct.	G.	PO.	A.	E.	DP.	PB.
Springfield	.973	140	3701	1540	148	116	21	Burlington	.959	137	3597	1506	219	113	22
Cedar Rapids	.969	140	3678	1522	168	130	7	Madison	.954	140	3543	1502	242	142	21
Kenosha	.965	140	3578	1327	177	127	20	Peoria	.954	140	3657	1518	251	106	25
Waterloo	.964	140	3565	1508	188	100	20	Quad City	.954	138	3581	1504	247	122	28
Beloit	.962	140	3602	1446	197	105	24	Wausau	.953	140	3557	1482	249	127	39
Clinton	.962	139	3614	1334	197	126	21	Appleton	.951	140	3561	1428	259	124	43

INDIVIDUAL FIELDING

*Throws lefthanded.

FIRST BASEMEN

Player and Club	Pct.	G.	PO.	A.	E.	DP.	Player and Club	Pct.	G.	PO.	A.	E.	DP.
Alvis, Waterloo*	.992	109	797	64	7	57	Ladnier, Appleton	.984	8	58	5	1	5
Amante, Springfield	.971	7	55	12	2	5	Lapenta, Peoria	.988	72	608	53	8	51
Bailey, Appleton	.984	47	325	35	6	29	Lemons, Springfield	.974	19	139	9	4	14
Baldwin, Waterloo	1.000	8	66	11	0	3	Leonard, Clinton	.986	84	610	47	9	66
Balfanz, Springfield	.987	71	632	46	9	54	Marzan, Kenosha	.984	32	232	14	4	27
Bell, Peoria	.986	12	61	10	1	6	Masters, Madison	1.000	6	47	2	0	8
BOWIE, Wausau*	.993	109	917	72	7	81	Mattia, Quad City	.923	2	12	0	1	3
Breedlove, Springfield	1.000	2	25	2	0	1	McCollom, Quad City	.980	59	509	25	11	49
Brown, Beloit	1.000	1	6	0	0	0	McGinnis, Beloit	.985	47	361	32	6	27
Caffrey, Burlington	.981	73	646	37	13	48	Melvin, Springfield	.970	11	87	11	3	7
Carlson, Clinton	1.000	8	41	5	0	4	Meyer, Springfield*	1.000	1	1	0	0	1
Duke, Burlington	.967	3	26	3	1	2	Morrow, Burlington	.988	37	302	29	4	31
Dyson, Quad City	.979	42	406	20	9	33	Oller, Burlington	1.000	2	4	0	0	1
Escalera, Appleton	.969	13	115	9	4	10	Ortman, Madison	.978	37	328	24	8	28
Finley, Madison	1.000	2	17	1	0	2	Patterson, Clinton	.990	14	83	15	1	6
Flowers, Clinton	.992	18	119	8	1	14	Paulino, Peoria	.984	38	280	21	5	17
Garcia, Peoria	.985	33	307	17	5	21	Polk, Waterloo	1.000	3	24	1	0	3
Goff, Wausau	1.000	1	5	0	0	1	Puzey, Springfield	1.000	2	8	1	0	1
Gonzalez, Clinton	1.000	2	12	0	0	1	Rannow, Clinton	.965	18	101	8	4	11
Grilione, Quad City	1.000	2	2	1	0	0	Santos, Waterloo	1.000	3	16	3	0	1
Gunn, Wausau	.972	6	32	3	1	0	Seifert, Waterloo	.981	45	304	14	6	25
Hanker, Madison	.981	26	193	16	4	15	Shumake, Cedar Rapids	.996	60	532	29	2	58
Hilgenberg, Cedar Rapids*	.991	38	327	14	3	25	Silva, Clinton	1.000	1	3	0	0	0
Hisey, Wausau	.964	3	22	5	1	0	Snyder, Kenosha	.977	30	199	14	5	17
G. Jackson, Quad City	.974	17	143	8	4	8	Sparks, Madison*	.979	51	393	21	9	36
K. Jackson, Appleton	1.000	1	1	0	0	0	Spitale, Burlington*	.961	32	232	16	10	15
Jaha, Beloit	.991	58	432	30	4	40	Tinkey, Kenosha	.990	86	655	40	7	64
Jefferson, Cedar Rapids*	.992	14	120	11	1	11	Van Stone, Clinton	.971	5	31	2	1	4
Johns, Springfield	.991	36	308	26	3	26	Veras, Madison*	.980	29	228	23	5	29
Johnson, Wausau	.981	27	201	10	4	27	Vincent, Cedar Rapids	1.000	37	302	23	0	23
J. Jones, Clinton	.962	3	25	0	1	2	Wakamatsu, Cedar Rapids	1.000	2	12	3	0	1
R. Jones, Beloit	.900	3	17	1	2	1	Walling, Quad City	.985	21	188	9	3	14
Kent, Beloit*	.979	48	345	29	8	25	Watson, Appleton*	.987	87	709	28	10	75
Kosco, Wausau	1.000	1	6	0	0	0							

SECOND BASEMEN

Player and Club	Pct.	G.	PO.	A.	E.	DP.	Player and Club	Pct.	G.	PO.	A.	E.	DP.
Alberro, Beloit	.930	8	18	22	3	7	Lockhart, Cedar Rapids	1.000	10	16	22	0	3
Alfonzo, Quad City	.967	39	85	119	7	28	Lonigro, Cedar Rapids	.964	114	219	294	19	72
Baldwin, Waterloo	.962	5	9	16	1	4	Maddox, Madison	1.000	4	6	11	0	2
Barker, Beloit	.955	66	100	157	12	20	Martinez, Madison	.935	74	146	197	24	43
Barragan, Madison	.950	9	19	19	2	8	Mejias, Peoria	1.000	4	7	5	0	0
Bolar, Wausau	.939	26	52	55	7	15	Melvin, Springfield	.957	23	37	52	4	14
Brown, Kenosha	.917	41	73	82	14	18	Mendenhall, Madison	1.000	1	2	5	0	2
Carrasco, Waterloo	.965	125	223	328	20	57	Michalak, Clinton	.905	3	12	7	2	2
Cerny, Quad City	.959	82	175	246	18	43	Montoyo, Beloit	.975	52	88	145	6	27
Chireno, Beloit	.949	15	35	40	4	6	OJEA, Springfield	.977	121	271	356	15	71
Clemo, Burlington	.948	94	174	246	23	51	Patterson, Clinton	.969	68	127	157	9	37
Eisenreich, Appleton	1.000	2	2	4	0	1	Pinol, Cedar Rapids	.909	2	4	6	1	1
Espinal, Peoria	.930	10	15	25	3	7	Polk, Waterloo	.981	11	22	30	1	6
Flowers, Clinton	.965	16	21	34	2	7	Reiser, Madison	.949	56	112	147	14	37
Gaylor, Burlington	1.000	12	29	23	0	6	Reyes, Quad City	.940	17	30	49	5	7
Goins, Clinton	.905	7	5	14	2	1	Rush, Cedar Rapids	.939	15	30	47	5	9
Gust, Madison	.958	7	13	10	1	2	Schueler, Burlington	.937	29	57	61	8	14
Hale, Kenosha	.975	86	164	233	10	59	Smith, Peoria	.952	5	4	16	1	3
Hill, Peoria	.959	125	232	347	25	56	Toal, Clinton	.958	51	106	120	10	30
Ishmael, Burlington	.938	7	5	10	1	3	Van Stone, Clinton	.857	1	4	2	1	1
Johnson, Wausau	1.000	1	0	1	0	0	Watkins, Madison	1.000	1	2	0	0	0
Jones, Clinton	1.000	1	1	0	0	1	Wilson, Madison	1.000	1	0	2	0	0
Laureano, Appleton	.941	135	228	376	38	81	Wolkoys, Appleton	.944	9	15	19	2	4
Lexa, Kenosha	.985	23	32	32	1	3	Woods, Wausau	.968	117	221	316	18	78
Lincoln, Beloit	.882	8	7	23	4	2	Young, Burlington	.938	11	24	21	3	2

THIRD BASEMEN

Player and Club	Pct.	G.	PO.	A.	E.	DP.
Baldwin, Waterloo	.900	5	2	7	1	1
Barker, Beloit	.929	75	37	133	13	10
Barns, Quad City	.958	27	26	65	4	4
Barragan, Madison	.818	9	5	13	4	3
Bell, Peoria	.890	42	31	74	13	6
Bolar, Wausau	.925	30	27	47	6	4
Breedlove, Springfield	.914	56	34	105	13	5
Canan, Peoria	.824	31	18	52	15	3
Cerny, Quad City	.833	1	2	3	1	0
Chireno, Beloit	.750	2	1	5	2	1
Clemo, Burlington	.750	1	1	2	1	0
Cron, Quad City	.893	106	84	218	36	27
Dull, Burlington	.667	4	4	4	4	2
Eisenreich, Appleton	.872	78	45	126	25	9
Escalera, Appleton	.822	19	10	27	8	1
Espinal, Peoria	.833	37	22	48	14	1
Finley, Madison	1.000	8	9	14	0	3
Flowers, Clinton	.833	4	2	3	1	0
Gallardo, Quad City	1.000	1	0	1	0	0
Garcia, Peoria	.918	35	30	60	8	4
Gaylor, Burlington	1.000	7	5	7	0	0
Goff, Wausau	.958	12	6	17	1	1
Ishmael, Burlington	1.000	2	1	2	0	0
Jaha, Beloit	.910	68	59	82	14	11
Johns, Springfield	.941	6	5	11	1	2
Johnson, Wausau	.805	24	21	45	16	10
Jones, Clinton	1.000	2	0	5	0	1
Knapp, Quad City	1.000	1	1	1	0	0
Kryzanowski, Kenosha	1.000	1	0	2	0	0
Ladnier, Appleton	.913	15	10	32	4	5
Lennon, Wausau	.863	85	67	179	39	18
Lexa, Kenosha	.920	13	8	15	2	1
Lincoln, Beloit	.818	5	4	5	2	0
Lockhart, Cedar Rapids	.924	127	69	270	28	33
McHugh, Burlington	.900	20	12	33	5	3
Mejias, Peoria	.692	5	6	3	4	1
Melvin, Springfield	.934	46	34	94	9	10
Michalak, Clinton	.917	28	18	48	6	5
Naveda, Kenosha	.918	124	84	217	27	18
Oller, Burlington	.895	108	86	220	36	20
Patterson, Clinton	.934	40	27	58	6	10
Polk, Waterloo	1.000	7	8	19	0	1
Raziano, Springfield	.946	40	18	88	6	9
Reiser, Madison	.950	14	4	34	2	6
Reyes, Quad City	.818	3	6	3	2	2
RICHARDSON, Waterloo	.948	131	107	275	21	19
Schueler, Burlington	1.000	2	0	3	0	0
Silva, Clinton	.333	1	0	1	2	0
Stewart, Cedar Rapids	.920	15	5	18	2	1
Taylor, Beloit	.750	2	1	2	1	1
Teixeira, Madison	.890	112	90	193	35	24
Tinkey, Kenosha	.813	9	5	8	3	1
Toal, Clinton	.838	69	42	103	28	11
Van Stone, Clinton	1.000	1	1	2	0	0
Walling, Quad City	1.000	3	1	2	0	0
Wolkoys, Appleton	.890	44	28	61	11	7
Zeile, Springfield	1.000	2	1	2	0	0

SHORTSTOPS

Player and Club	Pct.	G.	PO.	A.	E.	DP.
Alberro, Beloit	.891	66	99	172	33	26
Alfonzo, Quad City	.968	12	24	37	2	9
Angelero, Appleton	.894	35	41	94	16	17
Baldwin, Waterloo	.937	13	20	39	4	8
Barns, Quad City	.896	37	54	93	17	21
Barragan, Madison	.938	65	106	195	20	41
Benavides, Cedar Rapids	.778	4	7	7	4	2
Bolar, Wausau	.910	44	63	109	17	19
Canan, Peoria	.849	15	30	32	11	10
Capello, Appleton	.939	61	80	152	15	34
Chireno, Beloit	1.000	5	5	6	0	0
Cron, Quad City	1.000	4	4	7	0	1
Duffy, Madison	.923	41	60	133	16	29
Espinal, Peoria	.896	10	14	29	5	2
Fairchild, Waterloo	.920	98	173	242	36	40
FIGUEROA, Springfield	.951	133	178	368	28	70
Finley, Madison	1.000	2	2	3	0	2
Flowers, Clinton	.911	20	18	33	5	7
Gallardo, Quad City	.870	16	18	29	7	2
Gaylor, Burlington	.922	12	10	37	4	7
Ishmael, Burlington	1.000	7	18	20	0	2
Jaha, Beloit	1.000	1	2	1	0	0
Jones, Clinton	.800	7	2	2	1	0
Leius, Kenosha	.943	126	183	331	31	74
Lennon, Wausau	.944	5	6	11	1	1
Lexa, Kenosha	.800	7	4	8	3	3
Lincoln, Beloit	.844	10	10	17	5	1
Lonigro, Cedar Rapids	1.000	1	1	4	0	2
McDonald, Wausau	.899	99	142	269	46	51
McHugh, Burlington	1.000	1	2	1	0	0
Mejias, Peoria	.000	1	0	0	2	0
Mendenhall, Madison	.918	20	32	46	7	12
Michalak, Clinton	.938	16	22	39	4	10
Mijares, Clinton	.940	113	189	252	28	64
Montoyo, Beloit	1.000	3	3	10	0	1
Munoz, Burlington	.944	52	78	174	15	36
Naveda, Kenosha	.930	13	14	39	4	12
Ojea, Burlington	.976	11	13	27	1	5
Pinol, Cedar Rapids	1.000	4	5	11	0	2
Polk, Waterloo	.909	36	48	92	14	16
Reiser, Madison	.875	16	18	38	8	7
Reyes, Quad City	.941	76	114	219	21	38
Robinson, Cedar Rapids	.945	130	188	384	33	72
Rush, Cedar Rapids	.950	6	6	13	1	2
Schueler, Burlington	.921	73	103	201	26	32
Smith, Peoria	.915	117	189	331	48	59
Spiers, Peoria	.931	64	111	160	20	42
Van Stone, Clinton	1.000	1	2	3	0	1
Wolkoys, Appleton	.886	51	85	125	27	34
Young, Burlington	.500	1	2	1	3	0

OUTFIELDERS

Player and Club	Pct.	G.	PO.	A.	E.	DP.
Abner, Springfield	1.000	31	45	2	0	0
Alou, Burlington	.981	92	197	5	4	2
Amante, Springfield	.968	48	85	7	3	0
Ashley, Beloit	.945	71	133	5	8	1
Baca, Quad City	.959	58	135	4	6	2
Baine, Springfield	.978	130	208	13	5	1
Baldwin, Waterloo	1.000	11	22	2	0	0
Bandy, Quad City	.928	48	85	5	7	3
Barker, Beloit	1.000	3	3	0	0	0
Bennett, Wausau	.915	32	51	3	5	0
Bowie, Wausau*	1.000	2	2	0	0	0
D. Brown, Cedar Rapids	.942	54	95	3	6	0
J. Brown, Kenosha	.500	1	1	0	1	0
R. Brown, Beloit	1.000	4	9	0	0	0
T. Brown, Beloit	.985	63	131	4	2	0
Cain, Cedar Rapids*	.967	105	139	8	5	0
Canseco, Madison	.913	78	131	6	13	2
Carlson, Clinton	1.000	1	4	1	0	0
Carr, Quad City	.954	98	160	7	8	3
DeLima, Kenosha*	.965	131	272	6	10	2
Disher, Wausau	.954	93	154	12	8	2
Dixon, Clinton*	.992	58	112	5	1	1
Dull, Burlington	.961	133	184	14	8	1
Ealy, Clinton	.971	40	63	4	2	0
Eisenreich, Appleton	.929	18	25	1	2	0
Fairchild, Waterloo	.917	10	20	2	2	0
Figueroa, Springfield	1.000	1	2	0	0	0
Finigan, Burlington	.962	14	23	2	1	1
Flowers, Clinton	1.000	11	21	1	0	0
Ford, Appleton*	.911	83	131	12	14	2
Forgione, Kenosha*	.963	79	154	4	6	4
Gamba, Waterloo	.987	66	71	3	1	0
Gaylor, Burlington	1.000	1	0	2	0	0
Gilbert, Madison	.953	91	173	10	9	3
Giles, Quad City	.896	34	58	2	7	0
Gilkey, Springfield	.955	46	79	5	4	1
Graham, Springfield	1.000	5	7	0	0	0
Graves, Quad City	.957	73	191	10	9	3
Grilione, Quad City	.936	87	142	5	10	2
Gust, Madison	.966	56	108	5	4	0
Hardy, Burlington	.911	29	38	3	4	0
Harrison, Beloit	.975	37	73	5	2	1
Headley, Appleton	.951	63	132	5	7	1
Hemond, Madison	.714	7	5	0	2	0
Hisey, Wausau	1.000	28	38	0	0	0
Jacas, Kenosha	.948	29	53	2	3	0
K. Jackson, Appleton	.975	129	270	8	7	1
L. Jackson, Clinton*	.833	23	40	0	8	0
C. Johnson, Springfield	.974	18	36	1	1	1
D. Johnson, Wausau	.925	20	35	2	3	0
S. Johnson, Waterloo	.953	59	58	3	3	1
K. Jones, Madison	.953	47	96	5	5	3
R. Jones, Beloit	.955	75	120	8	6	0
Jorgensen, Kenosha	.921	31	54	4	5	0
Kindred, Springfield	.971	111	197	6	6	0
Kosco, Wausau	.950	72	104	11	6	2
Larios, Appleton	.917	12	11	0	1	0
Mack, Burlington*	.971	44	65	2	2	0
Mackie, Waterloo	.956	62	82	4	4	0
May, Peoria	.960	115	181	13	8	1

OUTFIELDERS—Continued

Player and Club	Pct.	G.	PO.	A.	E.	DP.
McCollom, Quad City	1.000	24	50	4	0	0
Melvin, Springfield	1.000	3	4	0	0	0
Meyers, Kenosha	.933	21	14	0	1	0
J. Murphy, Springfield	.000	2	0	0	1	0
M. Murphy, Kenosha	.800	4	4	0	1	0
Paulino, Peoria	1.000	2	2	0	0	0
Perry, Peoria	.971	99	158	10	5	2
Pickett, Appleton	.976	21	39	1	1	0
Pike, Waterloo	.976	85	156	8	4	1
Polk, Waterloo	1.000	1	1	0	0	0
Pulliam, Appleton	.971	108	195	8	6	0
Randle, Kenosha*	.986	138	269	20	4	3
Raziano, Springfield	.982	42	52	3	1	0
Redick, Clinton	.955	67	98	9	5	2
Reyes, Quad City	.933	6	13	1	1	0
Ritchie, Clinton*	.945	113	168	5	10	0
Roberts, Waterloo	.947	12	18	0	1	0
Ronson, Clinton	.950	126	196	12	11	3
Santos, Waterloo	1.000	11	8	1	0	0
Seifert, Waterloo	.958	25	22	1	1	0
Shelton, Peoria	.951	94	126	9	7	1
Shumake, Cedar Rapids	.966	33	55	2	2	0
Silva, Clinton	1.000	1	1	0	0	0
Silverio, Cedar Rapids	.981	94	198	5	4	1
Smith, Beloit	.945	48	77	9	5	2
Sparks, Madison*	1.000	7	13	1	0	0
St. Claire, Burlington	.964	49	49	5	2	1
Stewart, Cedar Rapids	.952	20	20	0	1	0
Tartabull, Wausau	.949	84	140	9	8	0
Teixeira, Madison	.875	6	7	0	1	0
Tenacen, Cedar Rapids	.951	99	169	4	9	0
Vaughn, Beloit	.963	135	247	11	10	2
VERAS, Madison*	.987	101	206	16	3	2
Viltz, Burlington*	.950	12	17	2	1	1
Vincent, Cedar Rapids	.967	19	28	1	1	0
Walker, Cedar Rapids	.944	37	48	3	3	0
Walton, Peoria	.974	125	255	9	7	3
D. Watkins, Appleton	.800	9	4	0	1	0
K. Watkins, Madison	.955	42	82	3	4	0
Watson, Appleton*	1.000	4	5	0	0	0
Weinberger, Burlington*	.961	66	121	1	5	0
E. Williams, Peoria*	1.000	9	16	0	0	0
Te. Williams, Wausau	.954	112	238	13	12	2
Tr. Williams, Wausau	.929	9	12	1	1	0
Williamson, Waterloo	.953	99	173	9	9	1
Wilson, Madison	.895	14	16	1	2	0
Wolkoys, Appleton	1.000	4	8	0	0	0
Wolten, Waterloo*	.940	51	73	6	5	2
Woods, Peoria*	1.000	5	8	0	0	0
Young, Burlington	1.000	2	1	0	0	0

CATCHERS

Player and Club	Pct.	G.	PO.	A.	E.	DP.	PB.
Bailey, Appleton	.980	46	228	22	5	1	11
Beattie, Kenosha	1.000	7	26	1	0	0	1
Caffrey, Burlington	.978	9	41	4	1	0	3
Cupples, Madison	.978	51	278	29	7	2	1
Duke, Burlington	.9912	90	605	69	6	8	8
Escalera, Appleton	.982	36	202	20	4	1	13
Garcia, Peoria	.986	22	126	14	2	2	2
Gay, Quad City	.975	47	270	42	8	2	17
Goff, Wausau	.977	93	578	73	15	5	32
C. Gonzalez, Appleton	.957	84	478	52	24	2	19
F. Gonzalez, Clinton	.971	20	141	25	5	2	0
Gunn, Wausau	.973	55	327	35	10	6	7
Hemond, Madison	.970	70	403	53	14	6	18
Iavarone, Peoria	.958	22	107	6	5	0	0
Isaacson, Waterloo	.975	23	100	16	3	0	5
Johnigan, Waterloo	.976	22	147	14	4	0	1
Knapp, Quad City	.971	67	382	53	13	4	7
Lampkin, Waterloo	.981	108	689	100	15	4	14
Liebert, Waterloo	1.000	1	2	0	0	0	0
Mann, Peoria	.986	86	582	63	9	7	16
Masters, Madison	.970	23	119	12	4	3	2
McAnany, Quad City	.984	30	158	26	3	1	4
McGinnis, Beloit	.960	2	23	1	1	0	2
McINTOSH, Beloit	.9914	92	624	71	6	3	12
McNamara, Clinton	.9911	108	908	90	9	13	18
Miller, Peoria	.968	28	173	11	6	2	7
Morrow, Burlington	.980	43	308	28	7	5	9
Murphy, Springfield	.992	21	108	10	1	1	9
Murray, Clinton	.985	17	126	6	2	1	2
Parks, Kenosha	.984	107	800	85	14	8	16
Puzey, Springfield	1.000	9	64	8	0	1	3
Rannow, Clinton	.960	8	47	1	2	0	1
Sobczyk, Beloit	1.000	6	17	1	0	0	0
D. Taylor, Beloit	.992	50	317	42	3	3	10
K. Taylor, Peoria	.889	2	7	1	1	0	0
Wakamatsu, Cedar Rapids	.985	97	678	66	11	5	3
Webster, Kenosha	.981	39	228	29	5	1	3
Wedvick, Burlington	.976	5	36	5	1	1	2
Wilson, Cedar Rapids	.992	49	341	33	3	1	4
Zeile, Springfield	.985	115	866	77	14	2	9

PITCHERS

Player and Club	Pct.	G.	PO.	A.	E.	DP.
Abbott, Kenosha	.909	26	9	21	3	4
Adriance, Beloit*	.826	34	5	14	4	1
Agar, Springfield	1.000	9	0	2	0	0
Baez, Madison	1.000	10	1	4	0	2
Bangston, Kenosha	1.000	7	2	6	0	1
Beavers, Madison*	.955	27	8	34	2	2
Berringer, Peoria	.941	41	4	12	1	1
Birch, Clinton*	1.000	25	1	10	0	1
Bird, Waterloo	1.000	40	3	5	0	0
Bisceglia, Quad City	1.000	36	1	8	0	1
Bivens, Springfield	.951	30	16	23	2	1
Blueberg, Wausau	.917	8	5	6	1	0
Boskie, Peoria	.867	26	12	27	6	2
Bottenfield, Burlington	.955	27	14	28	2	1
Bowie, Wausau*	1.000	1	2	0	0	0
Bradley, Madison	1.000	14	0	0	0	0
Brown, Cedar Rapids	.902	17	12	34	5	2
Bruno, Cedar Rapids	.846	36	3	8	2	0
Buffolino, Clinton	1.000	9	1	3	0	0
Butcher, Appleton	1.000	20	9	18	0	2
Buzzard, Kenosha	1.000	25	5	12	0	0
Cangemi, Beloit	.800	12	2	6	2	0
Carley, Beloit	1.000	8	1	2	0	0
Carroll, Madison	1.000	47	2	15	0	2
Cassidy, Appleton	.667	4	1	1	1	0
Chambers, Waterloo*	.778	16	2	5	2	0
Compres, Waterloo	.882	21	5	10	2	0
Connelly, Clinton	.955	47	3	18	1	1
Conroy, Springfield*	1.000	1	0	1	0	0
Cota, Kenosha	.929	7	4	9	1	0
Cruse, Appleton	.900	20	6	3	1	0
Cundari, Madison	.944	10	3	14	1	2
Dale, Cedar Rapids	1.000	46	5	16	0	0
Davins, Kenosha	.941	48	2	14	1	2
Deabenderfer, Madison	.917	17	1	10	1	0
DeJaynes, Kenosha	.000	3	0	0	1	0
DeYoung, Burlington	1.000	46	4	15	0	1
Diaz, Beloit	1.000	37	3	4	0	0
Drahman, Beloit	.962	46	7	18	1	2
Dyer, Kenosha	.871	27	7	20	4	2
Egloff, Waterloo	1.000	7	3	6	0	1
Eldredge, Wausau	.786	12	4	7	3	0
Elvira, Beloit*	1.000	4	1	4	0	0
Engel, Springfield*	1.000	4	5	5	0	0
Espinal, Cedar Rapids	1.000	27	1	10	0	1
Farley, Springfield	.923	11	5	7	1	1
FARON, Springfield	1.000	27	15	40	0	5
Fix, Quad City*	.900	37	1	8	1	0
Franchi, 8 Blt-12 Ken*	1.000	20	2	1	0	0
Frink, Wausau*	1.000	15	0	2	0	0
Gardiner, Wausau	.882	13	5	10	2	0
Gardner, Waterloo	1.000	7	3	2	0	0
Gilmore, Appleton	.933	27	2	12	1	1
Githens, Waterloo	.955	41	7	14	1	0
Glisson, Springfield*	.902	40	9	28	4	1
Glover, Madison	.972	26	11	24	1	2
Gold, Wausau	.818	25	3	6	2	1
Gomez, Peoria*	.862	20	4	21	4	0
Gonzales, Waterloo*	.971	25	7	26	1	1
Gonzalez, Kenosha	1.000	47	4	8	0	2
D. Green, Quad City	.850	27	9	25	6	1
J. Green, Peoria	1.000	26	0	5	0	0
Hamilton, Springfield	.976	26	17	23	1	3
Harkey, Peoria	.917	12	4	18	2	0
Harlan, Appleton	1.000	11	1	10	0	1
Harrison, Peoria*	.964	34	6	47	2	2
Hartnett, 22 Wau-18 Peo*	.931	40	6	21	2	0
Heine, Kenosha	.952	13	6	14	1	0
Henry, Beloit	.923	31	11	25	3	2
Robert Hernandez, Kenosha*	1.000	3	0	1	0	0
Roberto Hernandez, Quad City	.600	7	1	2	2	0
Hibbard, Appleton*	1.000	9	2	16	0	1
Hickerson, Clinton*	.857	17	0	12	2	0
Higson, Clinton	1.000	28	2	1	0	0
Hill, Springfield*	.900	7	1	8	1	1
Hilton, Springfield	.950	62	8	11	1	1
Howes, Burlington*	.946	28	6	29	2	1
Intorcia, Wausau*	1.000	43	7	22	0	2

PITCHERS—Continued

Player and Club	Pct.	G.	PO.	A.	E.	DP.
Jacobson, Burlington	1.000	30	9	19	0	1
Jones, Burlington*	1.000	8	2	13	0	1
Kallevig, Peoria	.800	10	3	5	2	0
Kannenberg, Quad City	.946	28	12	23	2	1
Kanwisher, Beloit	1.000	22	11	17	0	2
Kazmierczak, Peoria	1.000	6	0	9	0	1
Keliipuleole, Waterloo	.920	29	12	11	2	0
Kelly, Burlington	.833	21	4	6	2	1
Kendrick, Beloit*	1.000	3	1	3	0	0
Kesler, Quad City*	1.000	42	2	5	0	1
Kindred, Cedar Rapids	1.000	10	0	3	0	0
Kline, Kenosha	1.000	9	1	2	0	0
Kopyta, Peoria	1.000	48	11	16	0	1
Kostichka, Beloit	1.000	17	0	7	0	1
Kunkel, Madison	.917	22	2	9	1	1
Kurczewski, Waterloo	1.000	4	2	5	0	0
Kuykendall, Waterloo	.833	23	1	9	2	0
Kuzniar, Waterloo	.917	51	9	13	2	0
Labozzetta, Cedar Rapids*	.867	8	0	13	2	2
Lambert, Madison*	1.000	23	1	12	0	0
Langdon, Cedar Rapids	.833	3	2	3	1	1
Larsen, Burlington	1.000	4	0	2	0	0
Lazor, Cedar Rapids*	.917	26	6	27	3	3
LeBlanc, Appleton	.778	16	8	6	4	1
Lee, Appleton*	.895	40	6	11	2	0
Little, Wausau	1.000	4	1	1	0	0
Long, Quad City	1.000	23	1	7	0	1
Lono, Cedar Rapids*	.974	27	5	32	1	3
MacLeod, Madison*	1.000	10	3	12	0	3
Madden, Waterloo*	1.000	18	1	5	0	0
Mangham, Springfield	1.000	22	11	15	0	0
Marino, Burlington*	1.000	5	1	2	0	0
McClellan, Clinton	.892	28	14	19	4	3
McCormack, Burlington	.857	13	1	5	1	0
McKinnis, Quad City	1.000	14	0	3	0	1
McKinzie, Appleton*	.943	43	8	25	2	4
McLain, Wausau	1.000	7	2	5	0	0
Mercado, Waterloo*	.824	16	0	14	3	1
Merejo, Quad City*	1.000	49	4	25	0	3
Moeller, Appleton*	.857	18	3	9	2	0
Monson, Beloit	.900	11	2	7	1	0
Moore, Clinton	.700	11	2	5	3	0
Morehouse, Quad City	.923	20	3	21	2	1
Moscrey, Cedar Rapids	.913	19	5	16	2	0
Mount, Appleton	.917	28	2	9	1	2
Mullino, Peoria	1.000	17	0	8	0	0
Mullins, Cedar Rapids	.813	34	7	6	3	0
Naworski, Appleton	.938	22	5	10	1	0
Nocas, Appleton	.880	25	4	18	3	1
Norman, Springfield	.889	23	2	6	1	0
Ogden, Waterloo	.913	13	9	12	2	1
Ojeda, Beloit*	.895	14	2	15	2	1
Olson, Burlington	.826	14	3	16	4	1
Otten, Peoria	.889	58	0	16	2	1
Otto, Madison*	1.000	1	1	0	0	0
Pardo, Quad City	.636	38	4	3	4	0
Parker, Peoria*	.976	27	8	33	1	3
Pena, Clinton*	.913	26	7	35	4	3
Perez, Springfield	.833	58	4	6	2	1
Peters, Appleton	1.000	11	7	17	0	0
Pineda, Quad City	.667	5	1	1	1	0
Remlinger, Clinton*	1.000	6	1	2	0	0
Rice, Wausau	.949	28	17	20	2	0
Richmond, Clinton	1.000	12	0	2	0	0
Ricker, Clinton*	.857	33	1	5	1	0
Rios, Kenosha	.909	30	5	15	2	0
Rivera, Quad City	.833	6	1	4	1	0
Robertson, Clinton	.973	28	10	26	1	1
Robles, Peoria	1.000	11	0	1	0	0
Rodriguez, Appleton	1.000	9	2	8	0	0
Rogers, Cedar Rapids*	.969	21	3	28	1	1
Rojas, Burlington	.900	25	16	29	5	4
Romero, Kenosha*	1.000	3	0	1	0	0
Rooker, Beloit	1.000	20	7	20	0	0
Rosario, Peoria*	.800	23	0	4	1	0
Rousey, Burlington	1.000	28	9	13	0	1
Ryan, Wausau	.943	27	9	24	2	3
Sala, Springfield*	1.000	3	1	1	0	0
Salcedo, Madison	.900	36	4	14	2	0
Satzinger, Kenosha	.857	47	2	10	2	2
Schreiber, Wausau*	1.000	6	0	4	0	0
Schwarz, Peoria	.727	20	4	12	6	1
Scudder, Cedar Rapids	.935	26	8	35	3	1
Seanez, Waterloo	.833	10	3	2	1	1
Sharpnack, Madison	.909	23	7	13	2	0
Shaw, Waterloo	.943	28	19	31	3	1
Shiver, Beloit	1.000	21	2	4	0	0
Skodny, Appleton*	1.000	32	2	7	0	2
Slocumb, Peoria	.840	16	5	16	4	1
Stancel, Madison	.875	9	7	7	2	1
Stocker, Madison	.963	14	8	18	1	0
Stone, Madison	.974	29	13	24	1	1
Stowell, Kenosha*	.667	5	1	1	1	0
Swanson, Kenosha	1.000	13	2	3	0	0
Takach, Springfield*	.967	39	8	21	1	1
Tapia, Quad City	.854	27	7	28	6	2
Thomas, Kenosha*	1.000	36	10	23	0	1
Thorpe, Wausau	.909	46	5	15	2	3
Townsend, Appleton	1.000	21	12	32	0	0
Tresemer, Appleton	.882	23	5	10	2	0
Trout, Peoria*	1.000	1	1	3	0	1
Tunnell, Springfield	1.000	1	0	1	0	1
Vann, Quad City	.943	27	6	27	2	2
Velasquez, Clinton	1.000	45	7	13	0	3
Veres, Beloit	1.000	21	12	32	0	0
Villa, Clinton	1.000	18	4	11	0	2
Vontz, Burlington	.926	41	10	15	2	1
Walker, Waterloo	.915	23	15	28	4	1
Watkins, Beloit	.952	18	5	15	1	0
Webb, Wausau*	1.000	10	11	11	0	2
Weber, Madison	.875	9	2	12	2	1
Webster, Wausau	.889	16	3	5	1	0
Welborn, Burlington	.943	20	12	21	2	0
J. Willis, Appleton*	1.000	32	8	16	0	2
S. Willis, Cedar Rapids	.944	43	7	10	1	1
Wilson, Clinton*	.964	26	12	42	2	2
Wooden, Wausau	1.000	34	4	10	0	1
Zarranz, Peoria	.913	13	7	14	2	0

The following players do not have any recorded accepted chances at the positions indicated; therefore, are not listed in the fielding averages for those particular positions: Bandy, p; Birkbeck, p; Bivens, of; Capello, 3b; Carlson, 3b; Dayley, p; Disher, p; Eisenreich, ss; Figueroa, p; Gilles, p; Hulstrom, p; G. Jackson, p; K. Jackson, 3b; Jaha, p; Johnigan, p; Johns, of; T. Johnson, of; Kunkel, of; Lexa, of; Lincoln, p; Maldonado, p; McGinnis, 3b; B. Meyers, p; Morrow, 3b; Poldberg, p; Pumphrey, p; Raziano, ss; Stewart, 2b; Vaccaro, p; Walling, of; Wulf, p; Young, 1b.

CLUB PITCHING

Club	ERA.	G.	CG.	ShO.	Sv.	IP.	H.	R.	ER.	HR.	HB.	BB.	Int. BB.	SO.	WP.	Bk.
Springfield	3.10	140	18	9	49	1233.2	1130	492	425	98	32	333	19	1009	46	7
Burlington	3.31	137	31	9	19	1199.0	1062	585	441	72	35	552	20	980	95	8
Cedar Rapids	3.38	140	13	13	32	1226.0	1027	551	460	101	30	529	10	995	76	11
Peoria	3.59	140	18	8	37	1219.0	1159	631	486	67	63	550	32	950	86	26
Clinton	3.61	139	21	12	27	1204.2	1098	621	483	83	36	634	21	1188	70	20
Kenosha	3.86	140	15	6	43	1192.2	1059	614	511	74	35	675	18	1026	68	27
Waterloo	3.95	140	21	8	21	1188.1	1132	626	521	104	61	524	5	906	90	19
Madison	4.41	140	15	4	29	1181.0	1252	742	579	108	58	506	11	763	66	13
Beloit	4.50	140	16	4	38	1200.2	1273	754	600	73	43	573	29	961	89	13
Appleton	4.55	140	11	7	40	1187.0	1212	765	600	91	54	634	61	873	112	8
Quad City	4.70	138	18	4	24	1193.2	1211	778	623	73	34	676	34	792	111	11
Wausau	4.79	140	16	5	32	1185.2	1347	806	631	142	59	463	17	877	95	20

PITCHERS' RECORDS

(Leading Qualifiers for Earned-Run Average Leadership — 112 or More Innings)

*Throws lefthanded.

Pitcher—Club	W.	L.	Pct.	ERA.	G.	GS.	CG.	GF.	ShO.	Sv.	IP.	H.	R.	ER.	HR.	HB.	BB.	Int. BB.	SO.	WP.
Brown, Cedar Rapids	13	4	.765	1.59	17	17	3	0	1	0	124.1	91	28	22	5	3	27	0	86	3
Wilson, Clinton*	10	6	.625	2.01	26	26	3	0	2	0	161.1	130	60	36	3	6	77	0	146	9
Faron, Springfield	19	2	.905	2.14	27	27	7	0	2	0	201.2	179	57	48	13	5	30	2	146	5
Butcher, Appleton	10	4	.714	2.67	20	19	3	0	1	0	121.1	101	50	36	4	5	56	5	89	9
Welborn, Burlington	10	5	.667	2.72	20	19	7	1	0	1	129.0	103	57	39	5	7	59	1	105	10

Pitcher—Club	W.	L.	Pct.	ERA.	G.	GS.	CG.	GF.	ShO.	Sv.	IP.	H.	R.	ER.	HR.	HB.	BB.	Int. BB.	SO.	WP.
Howes, Burlington*	7	9	.438	2.75	28	17	6	4	3	0	134.0	114	52	41	9	6	64	1	103	7
Jacobson, Burlington	7	2	.778	2.81	30	16	3	6	0	1	121.2	95	45	38	5	2	70	0	135	11
Hamilton, Springfield	12	6	.667	2.85	26	25	4	1	1	0	164.1	151	62	52	13	1	34	0	132	3
Dyer, Kenosha	16	5	.762	3.07	27	27	2	0	0	0	167.0	124	72	57	9	8	84	1	163	7
Parker, Peoria*	7	8	.467	3.08	27	20	2	0	1	0	125.2	125	63	43	11	3	41	1	74	4

Departmental Leaders: G—Hilton, 62; W—Faron, 19; L—Kannenberg, 17; Pct.—Hickerson, 1.000; GS—Shaw, 28; CG—Walker, 8; GF—Perez, 51; ShO—Shaw, 4; Sv.—Perez, 41; IP—Faron, 201.2; H—Kannenberg, 230; R—Kannenberg, 132; ER—Kannenberg, 106; HR—Ryan, 31; HB—Boskie, 17; BB—Pardo, 110; IBB—McKinzie, 10; SO—McClellan, 209; WP—Pardo, 31.

(All Pitchers—Listed Alphabetically)

Pitcher—Club	W.	L.	Pct.	ERA.	G.	GS.	CG.	GF.	ShO.	Sv.	IP.	H.	R.	ER.	HR.	HB.	BB.	Int. BB.	SO.	WP.
Abbott, Kenosha	13	6	.684	3.65	26	25	1	0	0	0	145.1	102	76	59	11	3	103	0	138	11
Adriance, Beloit*	2	2	.500	4.63	34	0	0	12	0	2	79.2	100	58	41	4	2	41	5	76	6
Agar, Springfield	0	2	.000	9.35	9	0	0	3	0	0	17.1	30	20	18	3	1	8	0	20	3
Baez, Madison	2	1	.667	1.97	10	2	0	4	0	0	32.0	27	7	7	2	1	12	0	18	0
Bandy, Quad City	0	0	.000	13.50	2	0	0	2	0	0	1.1	3	2	2	0	0	3	0	0	0
Bangston, Kenosha	2	1	.667	3.66	7	6	1	0	0	0	32.0	27	15	13	0	2	17	0	21	2
Beavers, Madison*	9	12	.429	3.66	27	26	4	1	0	1	172.0	192	89	70	13	9	58	1	120	6
Berringer, Peoria	7	0	1.000	4.50	41	0	0	15	0	5	66.0	72	36	33	6	1	24	2	54	3
Birch, Clinton*	0	0	.000	3.88	25	3	0	14	0	1	51.0	54	30	22	5	1	32	2	26	3
Bird, Waterloo	5	1	.833	2.84	40	0	0	22	0	3	66.2	53	25	21	3	0	32	1	58	4
Birkbeck, Beloit	0	0	.000	2.08	1	1	0	0	0	0	4.1	4	4	1	0	0	1	0	7	0
Bisceglia, Quad City	2	3	.400	7.46	36	0	0	21	0	6	44.2	60	39	37	3	1	17	2	53	8
Bivens, Springfield	13	5	.722	3.81	30	24	2	2	1	0	170.0	164	80	72	18	1	50	1	165	3
Blueberg, Wausau	2	5	.286	6.43	8	8	0	0	0	0	42.0	53	40	30	6	3	19	0	31	5
Boskie, Peoria	9	11	.450	4.35	26	25	1	0	0	0	149.0	149	91	72	12	17	56	2	100	7
Bottenfield, Burlington	9	13	.409	4.53	27	27	6	0	3	0	161.0	175	98	81	12	2	42	0	103	9
Bowie, Wausau*	0	0	.000	0.00	1	0	0	1	0	0	2.0	2	0	0	0	0	3	0	2	0
Bradley, Madison	0	2	.000	1.52	14	0	0	10	0	1	29.2	26	10	5	1	0	7	1	27	4
Brown, Cedar Rapids	13	4	.765	1.59	17	17	3	0	1	0	124.1	91	28	22	5	3	27	0	86	3
Bruno, Cedar Rapids	3	3	.500	1.90	36	1	1	14	1	3	75.2	52	23	16	3	3	37	3	83	3
Buffolino, Clinton	0	3	.000	6.23	9	0	0	6	0	0	13.0	17	12	9	2	0	6	3	6	2
Butcher, Appleton	10	4	.714	2.67	20	19	3	0	1	0	121.1	101	50	36	4	5	56	5	89	9
Buzzard, Kenosha	6	4	.600	4.30	25	15	3	7	0	0	111.0	124	62	53	12	3	48	2	73	5
Cangemi, Beloit	3	3	.500	5.80	12	10	1	2	0	0	54.1	59	42	35	5	2	43	0	55	3
Carley, Beloit	0	1	.000	9.42	8	4	0	1	0	0	14.1	13	16	15	2	3	11	0	12	1
Carroll, Madison	8	5	.615	2.71	47	0	0	43	0	13	79.2	68	28	24	1	4	39	4	69	9
Cassidy, Appleton	0	2	.000	10.97	4	4	0	0	0	0	10.2	17	18	13	3	0	6	2	8	1
Chambers, Waterloo*	0	2	.000	6.75	16	3	0	5	0	0	30.2	35	29	23	2	1	32	0	18	1
Compres, Waterloo	3	2	.600	3.71	21	6	0	3	0	0	63.0	60	29	26	5	1	23	0	56	8
Connelly, Clinton	6	4	.600	2.76	47	3	0	17	0	3	88.0	81	35	27	5	3	32	5	71	2
Conroy, Springfield*	0	0	.000	18.00	1	1	0	0	0	0	2.0	6	4	4	1	0	1	0	1	1
Cota, Kenosha	3	3	.500	4.47	7	7	1	0	0	0	44.1	44	27	22	3	1	15	0	27	0
Cruse, Appleton	6	2	.750	3.81	20	1	0	6	0	1	49.2	46	25	21	4	2	23	2	39	5
Cundari, Madison	2	4	.333	3.86	10	10	0	0	0	0	49.0	53	29	21	4	1	15	0	25	1
Dale, Cedar Rapids	4	4	.500	2.95	46	0	0	39	0	12	73.1	67	30	24	9	2	20	1	57	4
Davins, Kenosha	6	4	.600	2.96	48	0	0	39	0	6	85.0	75	36	28	0	0	52	2	80	9
Dayley, Springfield*	0	0	.000	0.00	2	2	0	0	0	0	3.2	1	0	0	0	0	1	0	3	0
Deabenderfer, Madison	3	3	.500	9.48	17	9	0	0	0	0	50.1	61	67	53	10	6	48	0	19	6
DeJaynes, Kenosha	1	1	.500	6.14	3	3	0	0	0	0	14.2	18	11	10	1	2	11	1	4	0
DeYoung, Burlington	3	8	.273	3.98	46	1	0	35	0	9	86.0	65	43	38	7	6	47	2	115	3
Diaz, Beloit	3	2	.600	8.68	37	0	0	21	0	4	46.2	80	50	45	4	3	20	1	38	6
Disher, Wausau	0	0	.000	15.00	2	0	0	2	0	0	3.0	5	5	5	1	0	3	0	4	0
Drahman, Beloit	6	5	.545	2.16	46	0	0	41	0	18	79.0	63	28	19	2	3	22	3	60	5
Dyer, Kenosha	16	5	.762	3.07	27	27	2	0	0	0	167.0	124	72	57	9	8	84	1	163	7
Egloff, Waterloo	1	2	.333	5.16	7	7	0	0	0	0	22.2	30	14	13	1	4	10	0	14	1
Eldredge, Wausau	2	6	.250	7.38	12	12	1	0	0	0	57.1	73	55	47	11	10	46	1	29	8
Elvira, Beloit*	3	0	1.000	1.33	4	4	1	0	1	0	27.0	15	5	4	1	0	12	0	29	3
Engel, Springfield*	1	0	1.000	4.82	4	3	0	0	0	0	18.2	18	10	10	5	0	6	0	15	2
Espinal, Cedar Rapids	3	3	.500	2.65	27	2	0	7	0	1	51.0	44	20	15	4	0	25	1	27	6
Farley, Springfield	2	2	.500	4.10	11	9	0	0	0	0	48.1	46	27	22	5	2	14	0	37	5
Faron, Springfield	19	2	.905	2.14	27	27	7	0	2	0	201.2	179	57	48	13	5	30	2	146	5
Figueroa, Springfield	0	0	.000	0.00	1	0	0	1	0	0	0.2	0	0	0	0	0	0	0	0	0
Fix, Quad City*	3	3	.500	4.06	37	0	0	16	0	2	62.0	49	32	28	0	2	50	5	49	5
Franchi, 8 Bel-12 Ken*	1	1	.500	4.50	20	0	0	9	0	2	28.0	34	17	14	1	1	15	2	28	2
Frink, Wausau*	1	2	.333	5.23	15	2	0	4	0	1	32.2	28	25	19	4	1	21	1	30	0
Gardiner, Wausau	3	5	.375	5.22	13	13	2	0	1	0	81.0	91	54	47	9	3	33	2	80	3
Gardner, Waterloo	0	2	.000	7.58	7	3	0	1	0	0	19.0	24	17	16	1	0	14	0	9	6
Gilles, Appleton	0	0	.000	0.00	1	0	0	0	0	0	3.0	2	0	0	0	0	2	0	1	0
Gilmore, Appleton	1	2	.333	6.49	27	0	0	12	0	0	51.1	69	50	37	6	7	40	9	27	8
Githens, Waterloo	8	7	.533	4.49	41	10	0	6	0	1	120.1	109	71	60	19	11	34	1	85	5
Glisson, Springfield*	11	3	.786	3.31	40	16	3	15	0	1	138.2	147	55	51	7	7	31	1	78	2
Glover, Madison	7	13	.350	4.74	26	26	7	0	0	0	163.1	177	118	86	13	8	72	0	83	8
Gold, Wausau	1	0	1.000	4.96	25	0	0	8	0	5	52.2	69	39	29	5	5	33	0	41	8
Gomez, Peoria*	3	6	.333	4.31	20	17	1	3	0	0	94.0	88	55	45	4	1	71	2	95	13
Gonzales, Waterloo*	10	10	.500	3.46	25	24	5	0	1	0	151.0	147	69	58	11	7	64	0	83	7
Gonzalez, Kenosha	8	5	.615	2.51	47	0	0	40	0	19	82.1	70	26	23	6	0	22	2	92	0
D. Green, Quad City	6	14	.300	4.20	27	27	2	0	0	0	152.0	152	96	71	13	4	86	2	95	6
J. Green, Peoria	2	4	.333	3.05	26	0	0	15	0	3	38.1	26	18	13	1	4	18	5	30	0
Hamilton, Springfield	12	6	.667	2.85	26	25	4	1	1	0	164.1	151	62	52	13	1	34	0	132	3
Harkey, Peoria	2	3	.400	3.55	12	12	3	0	0	0	76.0	81	45	30	3	6	23	2	48	2
Harlan, Appleton	3	5	.375	3.49	11	9	1	0	0	0	56.2	62	30	22	5	1	19	2	28	4
Harrison, Peoria*	7	10	.412	3.66	34	16	2	4	0	2	132.2	110	63	54	9	2	82	4	118	11
Hartnett, 22 Wau-18 Peo*	7	4	.636	4.02	40	12	0	9	0	1	121.0	135	65	54	12	6	31	2	85	7
Heinle, Kenosha	3	5	.375	4.35	13	7	2	1	1	0	60.0	71	42	29	6	5	28	0	41	8
Henry, Beloit	8	9	.471	4.88	31	15	1	5	0	2	132.1	145	83	72	6	5	51	5	106	7
R'brt Hernandez, Kenosha*	0	0	.000	4.26	3	0	0	2	0	0	6.1	2	3	3	0	0	6	0	11	1
R'brto Hernandez, Quad City	2	3	.400	6.86	7	6	0	1	0	0	21.0	24	21	16	2	2	12	0	21	5
Hibbard, Appleton*	7	2	.778	1.11	9	9	2	0	1	0	64.2	53	17	8	3	2	18	3	61	2
Hickerson, Clinton*	11	0	1.000	1.24	17	10	2	3	1	1	94.0	60	17	13	1	1	37	0	103	5
Higson, Clinton	1	2	.333	4.96	28	0	0	13	0	4	49.0	41	33	27	7	2	21	2	54	4

Pitcher—Club	W.	L.	Pct.	ERA.	G.	GS.	CG.	GF.	ShO.	Sv.	IP.	H.	R.	ER.	HR.	HB.	BB.	Int. BB.	SO.	WP.
Hill, Springfield°	1	3	.250	6.66	7	7	0	0	0	0	24.1	38	20	18	3	0	10	0	21	0
Hilton, Springfield	8	6	.571	2.10	62	0	0	26	0	7	107.1	77	33	25	11	2	17	5	107	4
Howes, Burlington°	7	9	.438	2.75	28	17	6	4	3	0	134.0	114	52	41	9	6	64	1	103	7
Hulstrom, Springfield°	0	0	.000	0.00	1	0	0	1	0	0	1.0	2	0	0	0	0	0	0	2	0
Intorcia, Wausau°	4	5	.444	3.86	43	4	1	17	1	0	100.1	101	59	43	8	5	31	2	63	2
Jackson, Quad City	0	0	.000	13.50	1	0	0	0	0	0	1.1	2	2	2	1	0	0	0	2	0
Jacobson, Burlington	7	2	.778	2.81	30	16	3	6	0	1	121.2	95	45	38	5	2	70	0	135	11
Jaha, Beloit	0	0	.000	4.50	1	0	0	0	0	0	2.0	0	1	1	0	1	4	0	2	0
Johnigan, Waterloo	0	0	.000	9.00	1	0	0	1	0	0	1.0	2	1	1	0	1	0	0	0	0
Jones, Burlington°	3	4	.429	1.52	8	8	2	0	1	0	59.1	53	20	10	0	1	19	0	31	4
Kallevig, Peoria	3	1	.750	3.28	10	4	1	3	0	1	35.2	35	14	13	0	4	5	1	17	1
Kannenberg, Quad City	7	17	.292	5.45	28	26	6	0	0	0	175.0	230	132	106	14	5	47	5	89	7
Kanwisher, Beloit	12	4	.750	4.32	22	22	4	0	1	0	131.1	144	72	63	12	4	55	1	80	11
Kazmierczak, Peoria	0	0	.000	5.40	6	1	0	0	0	0	18.1	17	12	11	1	1	8	0	17	2
Keliipuleole, Waterloo	3	3	.500	2.43	29	0	0	18	0	6	59.1	38	21	16	3	0	22	0	50	5
Kelly, Burlington	1	1	.500	3.68	21	2	0	10	0	1	44.0	34	27	18	2	0	42	1	37	4
Kendrick, Beloit°	1	1	.500	2.57	3	3	0	0	0	0	14.0	16	5	4	1	0	1	0	7	1
Kesler, Quad City°	2	2	.500	5.37	42	0	0	8	0	1	63.2	74	46	38	3	2	60	4	31	11
Kindred, Cedar Rapids	1	1	.500	4.50	10	0	0	3	0	1	20.0	15	11	10	0	0	10	0	22	0
Kline, Kenosha	5	2	.714	4.28	9	9	1	0	1	0	54.2	48	27	26	5	1	25	1	62	7
Kopyta, Madison	2	4	.333	5.48	48	5	0	25	0	4	93.2	102	65	57	14	7	35	1	65	4
Kostichka, Beloit	1	0	1.000	4.22	17	0	0	4	0	1	21.1	24	11	10	1	0	13	0	11	8
Kunkel, Madison	3	2	.600	4.47	22	3	0	7	0	2	56.1	55	37	28	1	3	27	0	32	5
Kurczewski, Waterloo	4	1	.800	3.27	4	4	0	0	0	0	22.0	23	9	8	1	0	11	0	14	2
Kuykendall, Waterloo	4	1	.800	2.20	23	0	0	22	0	4	28.2	18	8	7	2	1	14	0	29	3
Kunzniar, Waterloo	6	6	.500	2.38	51	0	0	31	0	7	90.2	69	31	24	8	5	32	2	109	12
Labozzetta, Cedar Rapids°	2	4	.333	4.45	8	4	0	0	0	0	28.1	20	23	14	3	0	25	0	20	3
Lambert, Madison°	3	3	.500	3.06	23	0	0	22	0	6	35.1	36	16	12	2	1	10	1	33	2
Langdon, Cedar Rapids	1	1	.500	4.50	3	3	0	0	0	0	18.0	11	10	9	2	1	8	0	18	0
Larsen, Burlington	0	1	.000	9.00	4	0	0	2	0	0	6.0	8	7	6	0	2	3	0	5	3
Lazor, Cedar Rapids°	9	8	.529	3.57	26	26	1	0	0	0	163.2	132	68	65	15	1	52	1	155	7
LeBlanc, Appleton	3	8	.273	5.42	16	16	2	0	0	0	88.0	88	70	53	7	4	52	7	53	13
Lee, Appleton°	4	4	.500	5.45	40	1	0	24	0	5	71.0	82	55	43	7	1	47	5	67	6
Lincoln, Beloit	0	0	.000	0.00	1	0	0	1	0	0	1.0	1	1	0	0	0	3	0	0	1
Little, Wausau	0	0	.000	1.50	4	0	0	3	0	0	6.0	5	2	1	0	1	5	0	9	1
Long, Quad City	2	3	.400	1.85	23	0	0	17	0	7	43.2	30	14	9	1	2	22	5	39	2
Lono, Cedar Rapids°	12	11	.522	3.33	27	27	7	0	2	0	184.0	180	74	68	18	0	41	1	112	4
MacLeod, Madison°	1	3	.250	4.89	10	8	0	2	0	0	42.1	41	24	23	5	1	39	0	32	5
Madden, Waterloo°	4	0	1.000	4.11	18	1	0	8	0	0	30.2	32	17	14	5	0	6	0	23	1
Maldonado, Appleton	0	0	.000	11.57	2	0	0	1	0	0	2.1	4	3	3	0	0	3	0	4	1
Mangham, Springfield	7	7	.500	4.13	22	19	1	0	1	0	109.0	97	60	50	8	7	76	4	70	12
Marino, Burlington°	1	1	.500	2.78	5	5	2	0	0	0	32.1	26	12	10	3	0	4	1	33	0
McClellan, Clinton	12	10	.545	3.25	28	27	5	0	2	0	177.1	141	86	64	18	6	100	2	209	10
McCormack, Burlington	0	2	.000	2.64	13	0	0	6	0	1	30.2	33	17	9	1	0	16	1	28	6
McKinnis, Quad City	0	1	.000	3.79	14	0	0	7	0	0	19.0	16	9	8	1	0	10	0	19	2
McKinzie, Appleton°	2	5	.286	3.80	43	2	0	17	0	3	97.0	102	49	41	8	5	42	10	77	8
McLain, Wausau	3	2	.600	4.31	7	5	1	1	0	1	39.2	42	21	19	2	2	15	0	28	2
Mercado, Waterloo°	1	4	.200	7.64	16	9	0	2	0	0	50.2	51	49	43	7	8	49	0	35	6
Merejo, Quad City°	4	2	.667	4.13	49	0	0	31	0	7	76.1	67	48	35	3	2	33	3	48	3
Meyers, Appleton	0	0	.000	6.00	3	0	0	0	0	0	6.0	8	6	4	1	0	2	0	2	1
Moeller, Appleton	2	5	.286	7.20	18	13	0	0	0	0	55.0	72	63	44	5	1	45	3	49	6
Monson, Beloit	0	3	.000	6.32	11	7	0	2	0	0	37.0	47	34	26	3	0	19	0	23	6
Moore, Clinton	5	2	.714	3.63	11	6	3	1	0	0	44.2	38	22	18	3	3	32	0	46	3
Morehouse, Quad City	3	9	.250	4.45	20	19	1	1	1	0	95.0	104	56	47	3	1	64	2	52	8
Moscrey, Cedar Rapids°	8	4	.667	4.31	19	15	0	1	0	0	94.0	100	56	45	8	6	45	0	65	6
Mount, Appleton	0	1	.000	3.52	28	0	0	19	0	12	30.2	20	13	12	1	3	22	1	25	5
Mullino, Peoria	1	3	.250	4.84	17	0	0	7	0	0	35.1	42	27	19	2	2	21	1	36	5
Mullins, Cedar Rapids	3	1	.750	3.15	34	0	0	20	0	2	68.2	45	32	24	3	1	56	1	67	8
Naworski, Appleton°	0	2	.000	3.89	22	2	0	13	0	2	37.0	28	27	16	1	8	26	0	21	9
Nocas, Appleton	10	6	.625	4.58	25	24	1	0	0	0	118.0	115	74	60	9	7	62	4	87	10
Norman, Springfield	4	1	.800	2.37	23	2	0	12	0	0	49.1	42	15	13	1	2	12	2	26	1
Ogden, Waterloo	4	6	.400	4.66	13	12	2	0	0	0	67.2	81	44	35	3	3	33	0	39	5
Ojeda, Beloit°	3	5	.375	5.07	41	3	0	17	0	4	81.2	83	61	46	8	4	55	4	59	7
Olson, Burlington	3	6	.333	4.68	14	14	1	0	0	0	77.0	80	55	40	11	0	43	1	77	7
Otten, Peoria	6	6	.500	2.18	58	0	0	47	0	20	70.1	62	24	17	2	3	22	6	50	1
Otto, Madison°	0	0	.000	0.00	1	1	0	0	0	0	3.0	2	0	0	0	0	0	0	2	0
Pardo, Quad City	1	7	.125	9.04	38	5	0	12	0	0	71.2	75	85	72	6	5	110	2	63	31
Parker, Peoria°	7	8	.467	3.08	27	20	2	0	1	0	125.2	125	63	43	11	3	41	1	74	4
Pena, Clinton°	10	11	.476	3.97	26	26	6	0	2	0	161.0	158	90	71	15	3	80	0	142	6
Perez, Springfield	6	2	.750	0.85	58	0	0	51	0	41	84.1	47	12	8	2	2	21	3	119	2
Peters, Appleton	3	3	.500	4.81	11	9	1	1	1	0	48.2	50	34	26	5	1	28	1	38	4
Pineda, Quad City	0	1	.000	7.56	5	1	0	0	0	0	8.1	13	9	7	1	0	4	0	6	1
Poldberg, Appleton	0	0	.000	18.00	2	0	0	1	0	0	1.0	2	2	2	0	0	1	0	1	1
Pumphrey, Appleton°	0	1	.000	67.50	1	1	0	0	0	0	0.2	4	5	5	0	0	3	0	1	1
Remlinger, Clinton°	2	1	.667	3.30	6	5	0	0	0	0	30.0	21	12	11	2	1	14	0	43	3
Rice, Wausau	12	11	.522	3.84	28	27	4	0	1	0	166.1	192	100	71	13	7	43	2	127	15
Richmond, Clinton	0	2	.000	7.11	12	1	0	6	0	0	19.0	21	16	15	4	2	13	0	18	3
Ricker, Clinton°	1	2	.333	7.44	33	1	0	17	0	2	42.1	53	42	35	3	2	39	0	43	1
Rios, Kenosha	9	9	.500	4.26	30	27	3	2	1	1	162.2	147	85	77	7	2	100	2	120	4
Rivera, Quad City	1	1	.500	2.81	6	0	0	3	0	0	16.0	6	5	5	2	1	6	0	12	1
Robertson, Clinton	8	12	.400	5.10	28	27	2	0	0	0	164.0	185	115	93	10	2	95	3	173	9
Robles, Peoria	0	1	.000	4.21	11	1	0	6	0	0	25.2	32	16	12	1	0	11	0	13	1
Rodriguez, Appleton	3	2	.600	4.25	9	4	0	2	0	0	36.0	35	18	17	1	0	19	1	24	3
Rogers, Cedar Rapids°	3	7	.300	4.19	21	19	1	2	0	0	109.2	84	59	51	12	9	79	0	108	13
Rojas, Burlington	8	9	.471	3.80	25	25	4	0	1	0	158.2	146	84	67	10	3	67	1	100	8
Romero, Kenosha	0	0	.000	7.36	3	0	0	2	0	0	3.2	3	5	3	1	0	7	0	3	1
Rooker, Beloit	5	6	.455	4.65	20	16	0	1	0	0	81.1	84	57	42	6	4	49	1	69	10
Rosario, Peoria°	0	2	.000	3.55	23	0	0	16	0	5	25.1	23	14	10	1	4	24	0	13	4
Rousey, Burlington	1	5	.167	2.97	28	3	0	14	0	1	72.2	60	33	24	4	5	37	5	46	15
Ryan, Wausau	9	15	.375	4.92	27	27	6	0	0	0	173.2	196	119	95	31	6	54	1	114	9
Sala, Springfield°	1	0	1.000	0.90	3	3	0	0	0	0	10.0	5	1	1	0	0	3	0	10	0
Salcedo, Madison	5	4	.556	6.16	36	0	0	10	0	2	80.1	94	66	55	14	4	33	0	61	3

Pitcher—Club	W.	L.	Pct.	ERA.	G.	GS.	CG.	GF.	ShO.	Sv.	IP.	H.	R.	ER.	HR.	HB.	BB.	Int. BB.	SO.	WP.
Satzinger, Kenosha	5	6	.455	3.87	47	1	0	18	0	8	107.0	80	51	46	3	4	86	5	128	7
Schreiber, Wausau°	0	0	.000	5.40	6	0	0	5	0	1	10.0	10	8	6	2	0	6	0	4	0
Schwarz, Peoria	5	7	.417	4.58	20	13	2	1	2	0	92.1	79	59	47	7	8	59	1	91	9
Scudder, Cedar Rapids	7	12	.368	4.10	26	26	0	0	0	0	153.2	129	86	70	16	7	76	0	128	15
Seanez, Waterloo	0	4	.000	6.75	10	10	0	0	0	0	34.2	35	29	26	6	1	23	0	23	2
Sharpnack, Madison	7	10	.412	4.97	23	19	2	1	1	0	121.1	145	88	67	14	9	37	1	66	3
Shaw, Waterloo	11	11	.500	3.52	28	28	6	0	4	0	184.1	192	89	72	15	6	56	0	117	8
Shiver, Beloit	3	4	.429	3.62	21	0	0	8	0	4	37.1	33	16	15	1	2	19	5	39	1
Skodny, Appleton°	4	1	.800	2.30	32	0	0	27	0	15	43.0	28	12	11	4	1	16	3	29	3
Slocumb, Peoria	10	4	.714	2.60	16	16	3	0	1	0	103.2	97	44	30	2	3	42	3	81	15
Stancel, Madison	3	3	.500	4.25	9	9	0	0	0	0	48.2	43	30	23	5	3	26	2	33	3
Stocker, Madison	4	7	.364	4.19	14	14	2	0	0	0	77.1	86	47	36	5	0	21	0	40	5
Stone, Beloit	11	7	.611	4.97	29	25	1	2	0	0	146.2	162	97	81	8	5	55	0	109	4
Stowell, Kenosha°	0	2	.000	6.91	5	3	0	1	0	0	14.1	14	16	11	3	2	18	0	8	2
Swanson, Kenosha	4	3	.571	3.93	13	8	0	1	0	0	55.0	52	25	24	4	2	27	0	29	2
Takach, Springfield°	9	6	.600	3.59	39	1	1	10	0	0	80.1	76	35	32	8	2	18	1	54	3
Tapia, Quad City	7	10	.412	3.39	27	27	5	0	1	0	175.1	167	91	66	14	3	56	3	103	11
Thomas, Kenosha°	0	2	.000	6.66	10	2	1	3	0	0	25.2	30	24	19	1	1	25	1	17	3
Thorpe, Wausau	3	12	.200	4.93	36	14	0	13	0	5	111.1	134	74	61	13	5	32	2	83	13
Townsend, Wausau°	4	5	.444	3.86	46	0	0	30	0	2	74.2	85	46	32	8	2	21	1	50	6
Tresemer, Appleton	8	8	.500	5.25	23	20	1	0	0	0	121.2	124	75	71	8	2	52	3	90	8
Trout, Peoria°	1	0	1.000	0.00	1	1	0	0	0	0	8.0	6	0	0	0	1	0	0	6	1
Tunnell, Springfield	0	1	.000	3.38	1	1	0	0	0	0	2.2	4	1	1	0	0	0	0	3	0
Vaccaro, Burlington°	0	0	.000	1.93	4	0	0	2	0	0	4.2	2	2	1	0	0	3	0	2	1
Vann, Quad City	7	15	.318	3.98	27	27	4	0	0	0	167.1	140	90	74	6	4	96	1	110	10
Velasquez, Clinton	3	5	.375	3.26	45	2	0	32	0	13	60.2	49	23	22	3	2	39	2	73	7
Veres, Beloit	10	6	.625	3.12	21	21	6	0	0	0	127.0	132	63	44	5	4	52	2	98	8
Villa, Clinton	3	7	.300	3.65	18	2	0	9	0	3	49.1	49	28	20	2	2	17	2	35	3
Vontz, Burlington	8	9	.471	2.09	41	0	0	26	0	5	82.0	68	33	19	3	1	36	6	60	7
Walker, Waterloo	11	7	.611	3.59	23	23	8	0	1	0	145.1	133	74	58	11	13	68	1	144	14
Watkins, Beloit	5	5	.500	3.64	18	9	2	5	0	3	71.2	55	40	29	4	0	38	1	71	4
Webb, Wausau°	2	2	.500	3.92	10	5	1	3	0	0	39.0	37	20	17	2	0	24	3	34	7
Weber, Madison	4	1	.800	3.47	9	8	0	0	0	0	46.2	44	21	18	4	1	27	0	38	2
Webster, Wausau	0	9	.000	7.36	16	12	0	2	0	0	58.2	72	64	48	11	3	49	1	24	11
Welborn, Burlington	10	5	.667	2.72	20	19	7	1	0	1	129.0	103	57	39	5	7	59	1	105	10
J. Willis, Appleton°	5	6	.455	6.72	32	5	0	6	0	2	73.2	100	69	55	9	4	50	0	52	5
S. Willis, Cedar Rapids	1	7	.125	3.94	43	0	0	41	0	13	61.2	57	31	27	3	2	28	2	47	4
Wilson, Clinton°	10	6	.625	2.01	26	26	3	0	2	0	161.1	130	60	36	3	6	77	0	146	9
Wooden, Wausau	5	1	.833	3.33	34	0	0	31	0	17	51.1	55	24	19	7	1	6	1	54	1
Wulf, Kenosha°	0	0	.000	9.00	3	0	0	1	0	0	4.0	7	4	4	1	0	0	0	5	2
Zarranz, Peoria	7	2	.778	2.63	13	13	3	0	1	0	85.2	77	36	25	2	2	26	0	74	8

BALKS—Ryan, 8; Boskie, Rios, Robertson, Shaw, Zarranz, 5 each; Gonzalez, Harrison, Hartnett, Lazor, 4 each; Buzzard, Cota, Gardner, Glover, Gold, Gomez, Harkey, Satzinger, Scudder, Tapia, 3 each; Abbott, Birch, Bottenfield, Butcher, Chambers, Compres, Davins, Dyer, Eldredge, Farley, Glisson, Heinle, Higson, Kannenberg, Kanwisher, Kelly, Kopyta, McClellan, McCormack, Pena, Rosario, Salcedo, Seanez, Sharpnack, Stone, Vann, Veres, Wilson, 2 each; Baez, Blueberg, Cangemi, Carroll, Connelly, Dale, Deabenderfer, DeYoung, Drahman, Egloff, Espinal, Faron, Fix, Gardiner, Gonzales, J. Green, Harlan, Hilton, Keliipuleole, Kesler, Kindred, Kostichka, Kurczewski, Kuykendall, LeBlanc, Lee, Long, Mangham, Monson, Moore, Mullino, Nocas, Ojeda, Pineda, Remlinger, Rice, Ricker, Rodriguez, Rogers, Rooker, Schwarz, Swanson, Thorpe, Tresemer, Villa, Watkins, Weber, Welborn, 1 each.

COMBINATION SHUTOUTS—Nocas-Willis-Gilmore-Mount-Skodny, Tresemer-Willis-Mount, Hibbard-Mount, Butcher-Lee, Appleton; Stone-Drahman, Elvira-Shiver, Beloit; Olson-DeYoung-Vontz, Burlington; Lazor-Bruno 2, Scudder-Mullins-Willis, Labozzetta-Bruno-Espinal, Brown-Kindred, Brown-Willis, Lazor-Willis, Scudder-Dale, Cedar Rapids; McClellan-Hickerson, Wilson-Hickerson, Hickerson-Ricker, Remlinger-Birch-Connelly, Robertson-Velasquez, Clinton; Buzzard-Satzinger, Abbott-Satzinger-Gonzalez-Thomas, Abbott-Gonzalez, Kenosha; Beavers-Carroll, Deabenderfer-Lambert, MacLeod-Carroll, Madison; Boskie-Otten, Trout-Mullino, Parker-Green-Berringer-Otten, Peoria; Green-Long, Kannenberg-Hernandez, Quad City; Hamilton-Takach-Hilton, Sala-Norman, Hamilton-Perez, Glisson-Bivens, Springfield; Githens-Madden, Ogden-Bird-Kuzniar, Waterloo; Ryan-Hartnett, Webb-Thorpe, Wausau.

NO-HIT GAME—Schwarz, Peoria, defeated Kenosha, 4-0, July 10.

NY-Pennsylvania League

CLASS A

CHAMPIONSHIP WINNERS IN PREVIOUS YEARS

1939—Olean° .... .631	1958—Wellsville .... .556	1976—Elmira .... .727
1940—Olean° .... .625	Geneva (2nd)† .... .548	Elmira .... .703
1941—Jamestown .... .618	1959—Wellsville† .... .635	1977—Oneonta y .... .671
Bradford (2nd)† .... .549	1960—Erie .... .643	Batavia .... .600
1942—Jamestown° .... .672	Wellsville (2nd)† .... .535	1978—Oneonta .... .729
1943—Lockport .... .591	1961—Geneva .... .616	Geneva z .... .718
Wellsville (3rd)† .... .532	Olean (4th)† .... .512	1979—Geneva .... .725
1944—Lockport .... .608	1962—Jamestown .... .580	Oneonta z .... .618
Jamestown (2nd)† .... .565	Auburn (3rd)† .... .521	1980—Oneonta y .... .662
1945—Batavia° .... .677	1963—Auburn .... .585	Geneva .... .649
1946—Jamestown‡ .... .672	Batavia (3rd)† .... .485	1981—Oneonta y .... .658
Batavia‡ .... .672	1964—Auburn§ .... .622	Jamestown .... .649
1947—Jamestown° .... .690	1965—Binghamton .... .677	1982—Oneonta .... .566
1948—Lockport° .... .603	Binghamton .... .607	Niagara Falls y .... .553
1949—Bradford° .... .635	1966—Auburn x .... .620	1983—Utica y .... .649
1950—Hornell .... .653	Binghamton .... .646	Newark .... .649
Olean (2nd)† .... .568	1967—Auburn .... .667	1984—Newark .... .622
1951—Olean .... .622	1968—Auburn .... .645	Little Falls y .... .587
Hornell (3rd)† .... .568	Oneonta (2nd)° .... .558	1985—Oneonta° .... .705
1952—Hamilton .... .659	1969—Oneonta .... .662	Auburn .... .603
Jamestown (2nd)† .... .643	1970—Auburn .... .623	1986—Oneonta .... .766
1953—Jamestown° .... .704	1971—Oneonta .... .662	St. Catharines z .... .632
1954—Corning° .... .621	1972—Niagara Falls .... .686	
1955—Hamilton° .... .656	1973—Auburn .... .667	
1956—Wellsville° .... .617	1974—Oneonta .... .768	
1957—Wellsville .... .632	1975—Newark .... .688	
Erie (2nd)† .... .598	Newark .... .714	

°Won championship and four-club playoff. †Won four-club playoff. ‡Jamestown and Batavia declared co-champions; Batavia defeated Jamestown in final of four-club playoff. §Won championship and two-club playoff. xWon split-season playoff. yLeague divided into Eastern and Western Divisions; won playoff. zLeague divided into Wrigley and Yawkey Divisions; won playoff. (NOTE—Known as Pennsylvania-Ontario-New York League from 1939 through 1956.)

STANDING OF CLUBS AT CLOSE OF SEASON, SEPTEMBER 3

EASTERN DIVISION

Club	W.	L.	T.	Pct.	G.B.
Watertown (Pirates)	44	32	0	.579	......
Oneonta (Yankees)	41	34	0	.547	2½
Auburn (Astros)	39	36	0	.520	4½
Little Falls (Mets)	38	36	0	.514	5
Utica (Phillies)	31	43	0	.419	12
Elmira (Red Sox)	26	50	0	.342	18

WESTERN DIVISION

Club	W.	L.	T.	Pct.	G.B.
Geneva (Cubs)	48	28	0	.632	......
Jamestown (Expos)	44	33	0	.571	4½
Newark (Orioles)	42	32	0	.568	5
St. Catharines (Blue Jays)	41	36	0	.532	7½
Erie (Cardinals)	36	39	0	.480	11½
Batavia (Independent)	23	54	0	.299	25½

COMPOSITE STANDING OF CLUBS AT CLOSE OF SEASON, SEPTEMBER 3

Club	Gen.	Wat.	Jam.	New.	Ont.	St.C.	Aub.	L.F.	Eri.	Uti.	Elm.	Bat.	W.	L.	T.	Pct.	G.B.
Geneva (Cubs)	....	2	6	6	3	8	2	3	5	3	3	7	48	28	0	.632	......
Watertown (Pirates)	1	....	3	2	5	2	6	7	2	6	6	4	44	32	0	.579	4
Jamestown (Expos)	5	1	....	5	3	6	3	1	7	3	4	6	44	33	0	.571	4½
Newark (Orioles)	5	2	6	....	0	5	2	2	5	2	3	10	42	32	0	.568	5
Oneonta (Yankees)	1	6	1	4	....	0	6	3	4	4	9	3	41	34	0	.547	6½
St. Catharines (Blue Jays)	3	2	3	6	4	....	2	2	6	3	3	7	41	36	0	.532	7½
Auburn (Astros)	2	5	1	1	5	2	....	4	2	8	7	2	39	36	0	.520	8½
Little Falls (Mets)	1	4	3	2	7	2	4	....	0	5	7	3	38	36	0	.514	9
Erie (Cardinals)	6	3	2	4	3	0	5	2	....	4	3	2	5	36	39	0	.480	11½
Utica (Phillies)	1	5	1	1	4	1	3	5	1	....	5	4	31	43	0	.419	16
Elmira (Red Sox)	1	3	0	1	2	1	4	1	6	....		3	26	50	0	.342	22
Batavia (Independent)	2	0	5	1	1	4	2	1	6	0	1	....	23	54	0	.299	25½

Major league affiliations in parentheses.

Playoffs—Geneva defeated Watertown, two games to none, to win league championship.

Regular-Season Attendance—Auburn, 29,740; Batavia, 25,339; Elmira, 49,848; Erie, 59,698; Geneva, 19,918; Jamestown, 46,324; Little Falls, 32,536; Newark, 21,489; Oneonta, 48,903; St. Catharines, 48,015; Utica, 51,435; Watertown, 33,004. Total—466,249.

Managers—Auburn, Gary Tuck; Batavia, Art Mazmanian; Elmira, Bill Limoncelli; Erie, Joe Rigoli; Geneva, Tom Spencer; Jamestown, Gene Glynn; Little Falls, Rich Miller; Newark, Mike Hart; Oneonta, Gary Allenson; St. Catharines, Joe Lonnett; Utica, Tony Taylor; Watertown, Jeff Cox.

All-Star Team—1B—(tie) Jaime Barragan, Utica and Ernie Young, Newark; 2B—Williams Suero, St. Catharines; 3B—Jack Voigt, Newark; SS—Marty Rivero, Geneva; OF—Dan Nyssen, Auburn; Steve Finley, Newark; Steve Patrick, Utica; Jeff Ahr, Newark; C—Rich Wilkins, Geneva and Bob Natal, Jamestown; RHP—Doug Royalty, Auburn; Alex Sanchez, St. Catharines; LHP—Chris Pollack, Jamestown; Jerry Daniels, Erie; DH—Luc Berube, Oneonta; Manager of the Year—Tom Spencer, Geneva.

(Compiled by Howe News Bureau, Boston, Mass.)

CLUB BATTING

Club	Pct.	G.	AB.	R.	OR.	H.	TB.	2B.	3B.	HR.	RBI.	GW.	SH.	SF.	HP.	BB.	Int. BB.	SO.	SB.	CS.	LOB.
Newark	.269	74	2444	431	311	658	981	106	17	61	383	36	4	29	17	340	5	521	102	40	536
Oneonta	.266	75	2584	416	373	688	910	102	21	26	369	39	20	25	31	328	10	475	81	29	598
Jamestown	.253	77	2448	358	317	620	907	101	24	46	300	33	24	28	31	251	16	541	112	37	478
Auburn	.253	75	2551	342	342	645	877	96	17	34	291	34	44	18	42	285	18	525	81	37	610
Elmira	.251	76	2545	325	470	639	902	103	11	46	281	22	24	21	24	240	6	507	42	23	537

Club	Pct.	G.	AB.	R.	OR.	H.	TB.	2B.	3B.	HR.	RBI.	GW.	SH.	SF.	HP.	BB.	Int. BB.	SO.	SB.	CS.	LOB.
Watertown	.251	76	2538	409	349	637	924	123	22	40	329	35	26	30	23	319	12	613	158	64	525
St. Catharines	.247	77	2534	316	316	625	897	83	18	51	281	37	21	23	26	236	10	588	79	42	514
Little Falls	.245	74	2544	408	370	623	866	81	9	48	353	35	17	24	33	313	16	538	83	27	558
Utica	.241	74	2511	315	393	606	861	109	22	34	263	22	22	16	15	240	14	531	64	44	517
Geneva	.234	76	2466	353	274	578	779	104	14	23	302	42	38	17	37	316	30	527	89	35	566
Erie	.229	75	2410	298	348	553	734	96	8	23	249	30	26	20	22	303	14	541	92	37	544
Batavia	.219	77	2543	290	398	558	823	80	10	55	251	17	13	13	24	242	7	686	76	38	499

INDIVIDUAL BATTING
(Leading Qualifiers for Batting Championship—211 or More Plate Appearances)

*Bats lefthanded.   †Switch-hitter.

Player and Club	Pct.	G.	AB.	R.	H.	TB.	2B.	3B.	HR.	RBI.	GW.	SH.	SF.	HP.	BB.	Int. BB.	SO.	SB.	CS.
Voigt, John, Newark	.320	63	219	41	70	115	10	1	11	52	5	1	1	0	33	0	45	1	3
Barragan, Jaime, Utica*	.318	67	245	36	78	118	23	1	5	47	4	0	3	0	30	2	33	1	5
Suero, Williams, St. Catharines	.316	77	297	43	94	126	12	4	4	24	4	2	1	1	35	1	35	23	11
Nyssen, Daniel, Auburn	.315	74	305	39	96	138	18	3	6	55	5	2	0	3	15	1	36	3	4
Carter, Steven, Watertown*	.310	66	242	50	75	95	18	1	0	30	2	0	3	4	33	2	37	24	8
Jose, Elio, 51 Batavia-21 Geneva	.310	72	239	36	74	116	14	5	6	28	0	0	2	6	15	0	53	5	4
Weeks, Thomas, Oneonta*	.307	68	238	33	73	108	13	2	6	57	6	0	6	3	41	3	32	2	2
Zupcic, Robert, Elmira	.303	66	238	39	72	109	12	2	7	37	1	3	2	2	17	0	35	5	4
Berube, Luc, Oneonta*	.302	72	255	53	77	118	14	3	7	52	7	0	2	5	47	0	41	5	0
Renteria, Edinson, Auburn	.302	71	275	37	83	102	16	0	1	29	3	5	4	5	33	0	30	10	7
Sullivan, Glenn, Geneva*	.301	71	256	39	77	114	20	1	5	44	5	1	4	5	30	2	23	3	0
Ahr, Jeffery, Newark	.300	56	203	35	61	77	6	2	2	28	5	0	3	1	30	0	30	6	6

Departmental Leaders: G—B. Rodriguez, Suero, 77; AB—Nyssen, 305; R—Buford, 68; H—Nyssen, 96; TB—B. Rodriguez, 141; 2B—Barragan, 23; 3B—Kirkpatrick, 7; HR—Faulkner, 16; RBI—B. Rodriguez, 65; GWRBI—B. Rodriguez, 10; SH—Ru. Harris, 8; SF—B. Rodriguez, 7; HP—Owens, Shepherd, 9; BB—Ru. Harris, 63; IBB—Wilkins, 8; SO—Laboy, 86; SB—Buford, 35; CS—Christian, 16.

(All Players—Listed Alphabetically)

Player and Club	Pct.	G.	AB.	R.	H.	TB.	2B.	3B.	HR.	RBI.	GW.	SH.	SF.	HP.	BB.	Int. BB.	SO.	SB.	CS.
Acosta, Jose, Watertown*	.000	20	6	1	0	0	0	0	0	0	0	0	0	0	0	0	1	0	0
Ahr, Jeffery, Newark	.300	56	203	35	61	77	6	2	2	28	5	0	3	1	30	0	30	6	6
Aleshire, Troy, Auburn	.244	30	86	9	21	30	6	0	1	11	2	1	1	0	10	2	29	1	0
Allen, David, Utica	.000	5	2	0	0	0	0	0	0	0	0	0	0	0	0	0	1	0	0
Allen, Harold, Auburn*	.000	14	15	0	0	0	0	0	0	0	1	0	0	0	0	0	10	0	0
Alou, Moises, Watertown	.214	39	117	20	25	47	6	2	4	18	3	0	2	4	16	0	36	6	3
Andrade, Herberto, Geneva	.254	25	63	4	16	22	3	0	1	5	0	1	0	1	5	0	20	3	0
Arrington, Warren, Geneva	.214	23	84	13	18	39	5	0	0	12	2	0	1	2	11	1	20	7	2
Ashby, Andrew, Utica	.063	13	16	1	1	1	0	0	0	0	0	0	0	0	0	0	9	0	0
Aspray, Michael, Geneva	.000	23	3	0	0	0	0	0	0	0	0	3	0	0	0	0	0	0	0
Atha, Jeffrey, Jamestown*	.235	16	51	2	12	14	2	0	0	4	0	1	0	0	6	1	6	1	2
Ayers, Scott, Jamestown	.167	11	6	0	1	1	0	0	0	0	0	0	0	0	1	0	3	0	0
Barczi, Scott, Watertown	.308	40	117	25	36	54	9	3	1	10	3	0	3	4	22	0	22	15	5
Barnwell, Robert, Watertown	.000	15	2	0	0	0	0	0	0	0	0	0	0	0	0	0	1	0	0
Barragan, Jaime, Utica*	.318	67	245	36	78	118	23	1	5	47	4	0	3	0	30	2	33	1	5
Bastinck, Derek, Little Falls	.255	27	51	7	13	20	4	0	1	11	0	0	1	2	10	1	14	0	0
Batiste, Kimothy, Utica	.173	46	150	15	26	42	8	1	2	10	0	0	0	0	7	3	65	4	0
Bell, Derek, St. Catharines	.264	74	273	46	72	119	11	3	10	42	8	2	3	6	18	1	60	12	4
Bennett, Keith, Erie*	.000	11	1	0	0	0	0	0	0	0	0	0	0	0	0	0	1	0	0
Bergeron, Gilles, Jamestown	.200	13	5	0	1	1	0	0	0	0	0	0	0	0	0	0	2	0	0
Beriatua, Steven, St. Catharines	.201	55	149	8	30	34	4	0	0	11	1	5	0	3	18	2	38	0	0
Berube, Luc, Oneonta*	.302	72	255	53	77	118	14	3	7	52	7	0	2	5	47	0	41	5	0
Bishop, Timothy, Oneonta	.205	60	190	33	39	52	4	0	3	23	3	4	2	2	15	0	33	14	3
Bogar, Timothy, Little Falls	.234	58	205	31	48	57	9	0	0	23	3	0	2	3	18	0	39	2	2
Bond, Robert, Batavia	.000	34	35	5	0	0	0	0	0	0	0	0	0	0	3	0	22	0	0
Boswell, Michael, Geneva	.188	19	48	9	9	15	6	0	0	4	1	0	0	0	11	0	13	2	0
Bourne, Kendrick, Elmira†	.252	51	147	22	37	54	3	1	4	15	0	0	1	1	24	1	46	4	3
Boyd, Daryl, Watertown	.000	2	1	0	0	0	0	0	0	0	0	0	0	0	1	0	0	0	0
Brian, Braden, Jamestown*	.280	44	93	9	26	33	4	0	1	7	0	0	0	1	13	2	12	1	1
Brito, Mario, Jamestown	.263	15	19	1	5	5	0	0	0	1	0	0	0	0	0	0	5	0	0
Broadfoot, Scott, Erie	.240	16	25	4	6	8	2	0	0	4	0	3	0	0	3	0	6	1	0
Bromley, Norm, Watertown	.211	19	57	6	12	20	2	0	2	8	2	2	1	1	3	1	9	0	1
Brooks, Damon, Auburn	.242	53	153	22	37	45	5	0	1	8	0	3	0	2	16	0	39	13	2
Bross, Terrence, Little Falls	.333	10	3	0	1	2	1	0	0	1	0	0	0	0	0	0	2	0	0
Buford, Don, Newark†	.298	71	289	68	86	136	19	2	9	45	4	0	5	3	40	2	43	35	9
Burdick, Kevin, Watertown	.280	71	293	44	82	116	20	1	4	43	4	3	3	1	23	0	24	20	4
Bustamante, Rafael, Utica	.258	53	151	11	39	45	1	1	1	13	1	1	2	1	8	1	21	1	0
Caballero, Eduardo, Geneva	.167	14	12	0	2	2	0	0	0	2	0	0	0	0	1	0	1	0	0
Cakora, Matthew, Geneva*	.000	11	1	0	0	0	0	0	0	0	0	0	0	0	0	0	1	0	0
Carter, Edward, Erie*	.255	69	204	36	52	64	9	0	1	23	2	2	2	2	33	2	29	8	3
Carter, Jeffrey, Jamestown	.000	31	2	0	0	0	0	0	0	0	0	0	0	0	0	0	1	0	0
Carter, Steven, Watertown*	.310	66	242	50	75	95	18	1	0	30	2	0	3	4	33	2	37	24	8
Carver, Billy, Auburn	.185	46	151	15	28	39	3	1	2	16	3	0	1	4	14	2	28	1	1
Castillo, Frank, Geneva	.000	14	1	0	0	0	0	0	0	0	0	0	0	0	0	0	1	0	0
Castner, Rodger, Watertown	.000	15	4	0	0	0	0	0	0	0	0	0	0	0	0	0	4	0	0
Castro, Liliano, Batavia	.253	72	229	19	58	61	1	1	0	14	0	4	1	1	6	1	22	4	4
Cavalier, Kevin, Jamestown	.000	27	2	0	0	0	0	0	0	0	0	0	0	0	0	0	2	0	0
Chamberlain, Wesley, Watertown	.260	66	258	50	67	103	13	4	5	35	8	0	3	1	25	2	48	22	7
Chesney, Michael, St. Catharines	.412	12	17	6	7	15	0	1	2	7	2	0	0	1	4	0	7	0	1
Christian, Ricardo, Erie†	.234	72	252	37	59	70	7	2	0	15	5	2	1	6	21	1	60	30	16
Cianfrocco, Angelo, Jamestown	.247	70	251	28	62	84	8	4	2	27	3	4	4	1	9	2	59	2	0
Cobb, Mark, Utica	.206	55	180	20	37	52	6	3	1	14	3	5	0	0	12	1	46	5	4
Colavito, Steven, Batavia†	.152	17	46	1	7	7	0	0	0	2	0	0	0	0	1	0	7	0	0
Coulter, Darrell, Utica	.000	7	1	0	0	0	0	0	0	0	0	0	0	0	1	0	1	0	0
Cruz, Milton, Batavia	.143	21	42	3	6	7	1	0	0	4	0	1	0	0	6	0	16	1	0
Cunningham, Jim, Erie	.111	3	9	0	1	2	1	0	0	1	0	0	0	0	0	0	2	0	0
Daniels, Jerry, Erie*	.000	36	6	0	0	0	0	0	0	0	0	0	0	0	0	0	2	1	0
Degifico, Vincent, Elmira*	.254	46	130	11	33	46	4	0	3	17	1	1	1	1	9	0	21	1	2
Dell'Amico, Steven, Utica*	.286	11	7	1	2	4	0	0	0	0	1	0	0	1	1	0	2	0	0

Player and Club	Pct.	G.	AB.	R.	H.	TB.	2B.	3B.	HR.	RBI.	GW.	SH.	SF.	HP.	BB.	Int. BB.	SO.	SB.	CS.
DelRosario, Bautista, St. Catharines..	.135	28	52	7	7	8	1	0	0	3	1	0	1	0	4	0	16	0	0
Denkenberger, Ralph, Batavia°	.253	66	221	30	56	73	7	2	2	20	1	0	0	0	14	0	40	13	3
DeShields, Delino, Jamestown°	.219	34	96	16	21	29	1	2	1	5	0	2	1	1	24	1	28	14	4
Diaz, Alexis, Little Falls†	.340	12	47	7	16	22	4	1	0	8	0	0	0	0	2	0	3	2	2
Dickerson, Bobby, Oneonta	.278	8	18	4	5	9	1	0	1	4	0	0	0	0	2	0	1	1	0
Dickson, Kenneth, Auburn	.283	29	99	10	28	44	5	1	3	22	4	1	1	0	6	0	11	1	1
Didder, Rayborne, Oneonta	.185	14	27	6	5	7	2	0	0	2	0	0	0	0	6	1	9	2	0
Dillard, Michael, Elmira†	.294	18	34	4	10	10	0	0	0	2	0	0	0	1	4	0	3	1	3
Disabato, Patrick, Little Falls°	.250	15	4	1	1	1	0	0	0	0	0	1	0	0	0	0	0	0	0
Dorante, Luis, Elmira	.191	31	68	10	13	15	2	0	0	5	0	0	1	0	14	0	20	2	0
Doss, Larry, Jamestown	.200	35	55	8	11	11	0	0	0	2	0	0	0	0	3	0	16	2	0
Duncan, Calvin, Watertown	.000	24	5	0	0	0	0	0	0	0	0	0	0	0	1	0	3	0	0
Eberle, Michael, Newark	.325	24	77	9	25	36	8	0	1	17	1	0	3	0	5	0	14	0	0
Echevarria, Robert, Elmira	.141	36	92	5	13	17	1	0	1	4	1	1	0	2	11	0	30	2	3
Ehrhard, Rodney, Oneonta	.250	33	104	13	26	42	6	2	2	19	0	0	1	0	18	1	36	3	1
Elmore, Michael, Newark	.202	40	114	15	23	30	1	0	2	6	1	1	0	1	13	0	34	2	2
Erickson, Steven, Oneonta	.174	37	109	15	19	19	0	0	0	11	1	1	3	1	23	0	20	3	3
Esquer, David, Newark	.271	35	85	17	23	24	1	0	0	3	0	1	0	0	9	0	15	5	2
Etzweiler, Daniel, St. Catharines°	.071	4	14	1	1	1	0	0	0	0	0	0	0	0	3	0	5	0	0
Fagnano, Philip, Utica	.000	12	10	0	0	0	0	0	0	0	0	0	0	0	0	0	4	0	0
Farmer, Howard, Jamestown	.286	15	14	4	4	6	2	0	0	4	0	3	0	0	1	0	5	0	0
Faulkner, Craig, Batavia	.273	75	275	38	75	136	13	0	16	51	5	0	3	26	3	58	2	0
Fernandez, Reynaldo, Oneonta°	.067	9	15	0	1	1	0	0	0	0	0	0	0	1	0	0	6	0	0
Finley, Steven, Newark°	.293	54	222	40	65	91	13	2	3	33	3	1	2	2	22	0	24	26	5
Foster, Lindsay, St. Catharines	.264	74	288	40	76	97	7	4	2	23	2	5	2	0	16	1	51	10	5
Fox, Jay, Batavia	.000	18	2	0	0	0	0	0	0	0	0	0	0	0	0	0	2	0	0
Freeman, Peter, Watertown	.222	10	18	2	4	5	1	0	0	0	0	0	0	1	1	0	5	0	0
Galloway, Isaac, Utica	.183	33	82	8	15	16	1	0	0	4	0	0	0	1	6	0	20	1	1
Garrison, James, Watertown	.217	61	175	30	38	44	6	0	0	18	2	6	3	0	37	3	47	14	7
Geronimo, Angel, Batavia	.194	58	191	18	37	42	2	0	1	15	0	3	0	0	20	0	27	4	5
Gilmore, Matthew, St. Catharines	.333	2	3	1	1	1	0	0	0	0	0	0	0	0	0	0	1	0	0
Gomez, Henrique, Geneva	.200	11	10	1	2	2	0	0	0	0	0	1	0	0	1	0	6	0	0
Gonzalez, Javier, Little Falls	.262	40	145	18	38	61	6	1	5	25	2	1	2	0	14	1	36	2	1
Gordon, John, Batavia°	.210	43	143	14	30	45	6	3	3	18	0	0	1	0	25	1	43	3	5
Greene, Keith, Utica†	.217	7	23	5	5	6	1	0	0	1	0	1	0	0	1	0	3	2	1
Grier, Antron, Erie	.182	52	110	19	20	23	3	0	0	7	2	0	2	0	4	0	41	7	1
Griffin, Terry, Little Falls	.167	14	6	1	1	1	0	0	0	0	0	0	0	0	0	0	4	0	0
Griffith, Jeffrey, Little Falls	.180	41	133	10	24	34	4	0	2	10	1	0	0	2	11	1	58	3	3
Guzman, Jose, Oneonta	.000	1	0	0	0	0	0	0	0	0	0	0	0	0	1	0	0	0	0
Gwinn, Anthony, Oneonta	.183	25	93	10	17	23	6	0	0	11	0	1	1	0	10	0	29	0	1
Hailey, Freddie, Oneonta	.252	64	222	36	56	66	3	2	1	24	4	4	0	4	27	1	36	6	3
Halama, Scott, Erie	.000	11	2	0	0	0	0	0	0	0	0	1	0	0	0	0	1	0	0
Hannon, Phillip, Geneva†	.216	72	232	28	50	58	6	1	0	24	7	8	2	2	29	1	61	8	10
Hansen, Terrel, Jamestown	.239	29	67	8	16	22	3	0	1	14	1	0	2	0	10	1	20	1	2
Harms, Thomas, Newark	.259	58	201	36	52	74	13	0	3	32	3	0	5	1	34	2	35	9	4
Harris, Robert, Watertown	.272	49	180	34	49	69	6	4	2	23	1	3	2	1	25	0	48	30	7
Harris, Russell, Auburn†	.216	64	218	44	47	65	7	1	3	21	3	8	2	4	63	1	46	15	7
Hartline, Daniel, Newark	.239	27	67	12	16	22	4	1	0	11	3	0	0	0	11	0	23	3	1
Hartman, Edward, Watertown	.296	39	135	23	40	68	6	2	6	34	1	1	3	1	24	2	22	3	1
Harvick, Brad, Erie°	.143	15	7	1	1	1	0	0	0	0	0	0	0	0	0	0	3	0	0
Hawkins, Chris, Auburn°	.000	3	1	0	0	0	0	0	0	0	0	0	0	0	0	0	1	0	0
Height, Ronald, Little Falls	.254	63	228	43	58	71	8	1	1	20	1	1	0	8	37	0	39	12	1
Hellmann, David, 23 Bat-41 Gen	.218	64	188	28	41	48	4	0	1	16	3	4	2	1	28	1	49	0	2
Hennis, Randall, Auburn	.100	13	10	0	1	1	0	0	0	0	0	0	0	0	0	0	4	0	0
Hernandez, Jeremy, Erie	.150	16	20	0	3	4	1	0	0	1	0	1	0	0	0	0	5	0	0
Herrera, Hector, Auburn	.224	47	125	13	28	31	3	0	0	11	0	5	0	3	10	1	43	3	2
Hildreth, George, Batavia	.143	4	7	3	1	1	0	0	0	1	0	0	1	0	7	1	2	0	0
Hill, Lewellyn, Oneonta†	.282	14	39	9	11	15	0	2	0	0	0	0	0	0	3	0	16	0	0
Hillman, Eric, Little Falls°	.200	13	15	0	3	4	1	0	0	2	1	0	0	1	0	5	0	0
Hinkle, Michael, Erie	.000	16	9	1	0	0	0	0	0	0	0	0	0	0	0	0	3	0	0
Houser, Chris, Erie	.000	13	6	0	0	0	0	0	0	0	0	0	1	0	0	0	6	0	0
Hundley, Todd, Little Falls†	.146	34	103	12	15	22	4	0	1	10	1	0	0	3	12	2	27	0	0
Hunter, Robert, Oneonta	.200	10	5	4	1	1	0	0	0	0	0	0	0	0	2	0	2	2	0
Hurta, Robert, Utica°	.000	21	3	0	0	0	0	0	0	0	0	0	0	0	1	0	2	0	0
Ishmael, Michael, Jamestown	.167	46	120	13	20	20	0	0	0	7	2	4	2	1	9	0	16	2	4
Jeffers, Steven, Erie†	.234	70	209	19	49	55	6	0	0	12	0	4	1	3	22	0	19	8	3
Jimenez, Alejandro, Little Falls°	.243	68	239	41	58	98	10	0	10	60	4	0	5	3	28	2	37	4	0
Johnson, Gregory, Auburn	.000	24	4	0	0	0	0	0	0	0	0	1	0	0	2	0	4	0	0
Joiner, David, Little Falls	.193	36	109	9	21	27	3	0	1	10	1	3	0	2	7	1	18	2	0
Jongewaard, Steven, Erie	.333	21	6	2	2	2	0	0	0	2	0	1	0	1	0	1	1	0
Jose, Elio, 51 Batavia-21 Geneva	.310	72	239	36	74	116	14	5	6	28	0	0	2	6	15	0	53	5	4
Jundy, Lorin, Little Falls	.000	10	6	0	0	0	0	0	0	0	0	0	0	0	0	0	2	0	0
Kelley, Dean, Oneonta°	.246	62	224	46	55	77	9	2	3	27	2	1	1	3	32	2	31	9	0
Kelly, Michael, Elmira	.302	51	172	18	52	65	8	1	1	21	2	2	0	0	8	0	17	1	0
Kerrigan, Robert, Jamestown	.000	21	1	0	0	0	0	0	0	0	0	0	0	0	0	0	1	0	0
Kingston, Roger, Batavia°	.211	60	190	22	40	51	6	1	1	18	0	0	1	3	12	0	57	9	1
Kirkpatrick, Stephen, Utica°	.289	72	287	45	83	126	14	7	5	28	1	2	0	2	28	3	26	22	11
Koller, Mark, Watertown	.222	23	9	1	2	2	0	0	0	2	0	0	0	1	0	2	0	0
Laboy, Carlos, Auburn	.249	73	285	48	71	112	6	4	9	39	6	2	0	5	21	4	86	8	1
Lampe, Edward, Batavia†	.167	57	162	24	27	44	5	0	4	13	1	1	1	2	39	0	69	13	7
LaRosa, John, Utica°	.333	15	9	1	3	3	0	0	0	0	0	0	0	0	0	0	3	0	0
LaRose, Steven, Little Falls†	.000	26	5	0	0	0	0	0	0	0	0	0	0	0	1	0	1	0	0
Lehman, Michael, Newark	.237	40	139	18	33	40	4	0	1	13	0	0	1	1	18	1	32	4	2
Lemle, Robert, Little Falls	.293	26	92	16	27	35	3	1	1	7	2	0	0	0	15	2	20	11	1
Lewis, Daniel, Auburn°	.278	70	230	39	64	88	11	2	3	32	4	1	4	6	40	2	48	9	5
Lindsey, Douglas, Utica	.243	52	169	23	41	51	7	0	1	25	3	0	3	1	22	2	34	1	3
Lopez, Marc, Utica	.000	5	1	0	0	0	0	0	0	0	0	0	0	0	0	0	0	0	0
Macavage, Joseph, Watertown	.250	8	4	1	1	1	0	0	0	1	0	0	0	0	0	0	1	0	0
Marchok, Christopher, Jamestown°	.000	18	1	0	0	0	0	0	0	0	0	0	0	0	0	0	0	0	0
Marrs, Terry, Elmira	.148	29	54	4	8	11	1	1	0	2	0	1	1	0	7	0	23	0	1
Martin, Russell, Jamestown	.000	7	1	0	0	0	0	0	0	0	0	0	0	0	0	0	0	0	0
Martinez, Ricardo, Oneonta	.000	2	2	0	0	0	0	0	0	0	0	0	0	0	0	0	0	0	0

Player and Club	Pct.	G.	AB.	R.	H.	TB.	2B.	3B.	HR.	RBI.	GW.	SH.	SF.	HP.	BB.	Int. BB.	SO.	SB.	CS.
Martinez, Romulo, Batavia	.187	72	251	29	47	76	9	1	6	23	4	0	2	6	24	1	73	13	3
Massarelli, John, Auburn	.161	23	56	7	9	14	1	2	0	3	0	1	0	7	0	10	3	0
Massicotte, Jeffrey, Geneva	.000	35	1	0	0	0	0	0	0	1	0	0	0	0	1	0	1	0	0
Matilla, Pedro, Elmira°	.152	25	66	4	10	14	4	0	0	4	0	0	0	0	4	0	14	0	0
McAnarney, James, Little Falls	.188	18	16	2	3	3	0	0	0	1	0	0	0	1	0	0	5	0	0
McCarthy, Gregory, Utica°	.000	20	1	0	0	0	0	0	0	0	0	0	0	0	0	0	1	0	0
McClure, LaRue, Auburn	.000	21	1	0	0	0	0	0	0	0	0	0	0	0	0	0	0	0	0
McDaniel, Terrence, Little Falls†	.241	70	237	51	57	80	4	2	5	31	3	3	1	1	52	0	82	20	10
McDonald, Shelby, Utica	.000	29	2	0	0	0	0	0	0	0	0	0	0	0	0	0	1	0	0
McHugh, Scott, Jamestown	.254	40	114	18	29	49	9	1	3	15	2	1	1	1	18	0	15	1	0
McMahon, Sean, St. Catharines	.150	11	20	3	3	3	0	0	0	1	0	1	0	0	7	0	7	1	0
Mealy, Anthony, Batavia	.243	21	70	9	17	31	5	0	3	10	3	0	0	0	3	0	24	4	0
Meamber, Timothy, Erie	1.000	20	1	0	1	1	0	0	0	0	0	0	0	1	0	0	0	0	1
Mejias, Simeon, Geneva†	.279	60	179	34	50	54	2	1	0	19	1	7	0	2	25	1	25	12	6
Melton, Sam, Elmira	.224	55	170	22	38	41	3	0	0	9	0	3	0	5	17	0	36	2	0
Melvin, William, Geneva	.313	15	16	1	5	6	1	0	0	1	0	0	0	0	0	0	4	0	0
Merced, Orlando, Watertown†	.417	4	12	4	5	7	0	1	0	3	0	0	0	1	1	0	1	1	0
Merejo, Domingo, Watertown°	.136	35	88	5	12	15	1	1	0	4	0	0	1	0	4	0	23	0	2
Michael, Steven, Elmira	.250	17	4	0	1	1	0	0	0	0	0	0	0	0	0	0	1	0	0
Miller, Michael, Little Falls	.231	13	13	2	3	5	0	1	0	2	0	0	0	0	3	0	2	0	0
Mitchell, Jorge, Jamestown	.176	35	85	9	15	26	2	0	3	10	2	0	1	1	7	0	27	0	0
Mitchell, Mark, Oneonta	.344	45	154	20	53	57	4	0	0	11	2	1	0	4	12	2	20	2	5
Monegro, Miguel, Elmira	.214	51	145	17	31	36	3	1	0	9	1	1	0	2	11	2	22	3	2
Monteiro, David, Utica°	.087	30	46	3	4	4	0	0	0	3	0	0	1	0	3	0	26	1	0
Moore, Derek, Geneva†	.032	27	31	4	1	1	0	0	0	1	0	0	0	1	6	0	19	1	1
Moore, Patrick, Erie	.160	17	25	2	4	4	0	0	0	1	0	0	0	0	8	0	7	0	0
Moran, Frank, Erie	.269	70	216	30	58	79	10	1	3	34	1	2	2	1	33	0	45	4	1
Mota, Andres, Auburn	.263	70	255	26	67	90	9	1	4	14	2	5	1	5	16	0	42	6	5
Mullino, Ray, Geneva	.250	26	4	1	1	1	0	0	0	1	0	0	0	0	2	0	3	0	0
Murphy, Peter, Watertown°	.286	27	35	2	10	11	1	0	0	5	0	0	0	4	4	0	7	1	0
Natal, Robert, Jamestown	.322	57	180	26	58	95	8	4	7	32	4	0	3	3	12	1	25	6	4
Naughton, Daniel, Little Falls	.251	61	215	37	54	77	6	1	5	33	6	0	4	2	24	0	43	6	0
Nelson, Darren, Erie	.287	71	251	27	72	106	17	1	5	44	7	3	3	3	11	1	46	5	3
Newman, Todd, Auburn	.091	19	11	1	1	1	0	0	0	2	1	0	1	0	0	0	4	0	0
Newton, Stephen, Little Falls	.250	25	4	0	1	1	0	0	0	0	0	0	0	0	0	0	2	0	0
North, Mark, Geneva°	.200	15	15	1	3	3	0	0	0	2	0	2	0	0	0	0	3	0	0
Nowak, Matthew, Newark	.228	46	136	26	31	45	3	1	3	25	4	0	3	3	40	0	35	3	1
Nunez, Bernardino, St. Catharines	.204	66	225	23	46	79	10	1	7	22	3	0	3	1	15	3	77	2	1
Nyssen, Daniel, Auburn	.315	73	305	39	96	138	18	3	6	55	5	2	0	3	15	1	36	3	4
Olah, Robert, Little Falls	.241	37	83	11	20	37	2	0	5	16	2	0	1	0	14	1	15	0	0
Olmstead, Reed, Erie°	.230	62	161	12	37	45	5	0	1	18	0	0	1	2	25	2	39	3	2
Ortiz, Joseph, Auburn	.236	24	72	4	17	23	3	0	1	9	0	0	1	1	7	0	19	0	1
Osuna, Alfonso, Auburn	.000	8	1	0	0	0	0	0	0	0	0	0	0	0	0	0	1	0	0
Owens, Stephen, Geneva	.253	67	217	31	55	81	11	3	3	29	4	1	2	9	25	2	43	12	2
Pacholec, Joseph, Watertown	.000	15	15	0	0	0	0	0	0	0	0	3	0	0	1	0	4	0	0
Paredes, Jesus, Jamestown†	.150	8	20	4	3	3	0	0	0	1	0	0	0	0	5	0	7	2	2
Payton, David, Erie	.265	73	260	33	69	104	12	1	7	25	1	1	1	1	36	2	39	8	2
Peek, Timothy, Utica	.200	4	5	1	1	1	0	0	0	1	0	0	0	0	1	0	3	1	0
Pena, Luis, Newark	.254	41	130	16	33	61	5	1	7	26	3	0	1	2	6	0	36	0	0
Perez, Gorky, Auburn°	.258	52	151	22	39	45	2	2	0	15	1	1	1	2	22	5	15	8	1
Perez, Manlio, Utica	.168	38	95	12	16	19	3	0	0	5	2	3	1	0	9	0	24	2	3
Peyton, Michael, Watertown	.227	10	22	4	5	5	0	0	0	1	1	0	0	0	4	0	6	3	0
Pina, John, Elmira	.276	60	196	44	54	109	15	2	12	45	8	6	1	1	28	0	64	6	1
Plantier, Phillip, Elmira°	.175	28	80	7	14	22	2	0	2	9	1	1	1	0	9	0	9	0	0
Polanco, Radhames, Little Falls°	.277	73	285	44	79	115	10	1	8	49	5	2	4	1	28	3	58	0	2
Pollack, Christopher, Jamestown°	.100	14	10	1	1	1	0	0	0	0	0	0	0	0	2	0	4	0	0
Polverini, Stephen, Auburn	.333	21	3	0	1	1	0	0	0	0	0	0	0	0	0	0	1	0	0
Powers, Scott, Elmira	.235	58	213	35	50	66	11	1	1	16	2	2	4	1	24	1	43	6	2
Radcliffe, Ernest, Erie	.184	42	87	9	16	25	4	1	1	9	2	0	0	0	17	0	23	1	0
Raisanen, Keith, Watertown	.217	41	92	16	20	29	3	0	2	10	1	0	1	0	13	0	33	7	3
Rambo, Matthew, Utica°	.133	13	15	1	2	2	0	0	0	1	0	1	0	0	0	0	8	0	0
Ramon, Julio, Oneonta	.267	9	15	3	4	6	2	0	0	0	0	1	0	0	2	0	3	0	0
Ramsey, Fernando, Geneva	.161	39	56	9	9	10	1	0	0	3	1	2	0	0	5	1	10	2	0
Reaves, Scott, Utica	.185	19	54	4	10	18	1	2	1	7	1	0	1	1	7	0	8	0	2
Redman, Timothy, Erie	.221	55	136	18	30	41	3	1	2	18	0	1	1	1	24	0	34	4	2
Reeder, Michael, 50 Gen-25 Bat°	.184	75	234	28	43	66	7	2	4	23	4	1	1	3	30	4	76	1	1
Renteria, Edinson, Auburn	.302	71	275	37	83	102	16	0	1	29	3	5	4	5	33	0	30	10	7
Ricker, Troy, Jamestown	.258	75	260	32	67	88	12	3	1	25	3	2	0	3	12	2	53	24	3
Rivero, Martin, Geneva	.257	74	284	39	73	99	17	0	3	48	7	4	6	0	17	2	47	2	3
Rivers, Kenneth, St. Catharines	.263	49	171	21	45	69	6	0	6	27	2	2	1	1	10	0	25	2	0
Robinson, Brett, Geneva†	.067	18	15	0	1	1	0	0	0	1	0	1	0	0	6	0	5	0	0
Robinson, Kevin, Erie†	.202	59	124	15	25	31	4	1	0	15	5	2	2	2	19	4	25	5	0
Roche, Faustino, Little Falls°	.316	59	158	33	50	54	1	0	1	19	0	3	2	0	23	1	21	6	5
Rodriguez, Boi, Jamestown°	.281	77	274	51	77	141	9	5	15	65	10	0	7	3	37	5	58	14	8
Rodriguez, Gabriel, Geneva°	.000	24	5	0	0	0	0	0	0	0	0	0	0	0	0	0	1	0	0
Roman, Daniel, Oneonta	.291	58	206	36	60	74	8	3	0	32	6	2	2	2	17	0	35	7	1
Romero, Charles, St. Catharines	.242	53	198	14	48	54	2	2	0	13	1	2	1	3	6	0	51	14	10
Romo, Robert, Auburn	.167	17	6	2	1	1	0	0	0	0	0	1	0	0	1	0	3	0	0
Rosario, Jossy, Geneva	.083	4	12	0	1	1	0	0	0	0	0	0	0	0	1	0	2	0	0
Rosario, Julio, Elmira†	.309	45	162	18	50	55	5	0	0	14	1	1	0	1	7	0	20	4	0
Rose, Carl, Elmira	.233	39	120	14	28	55	4	1	7	14	1	0	1	1	11	0	46	0	0
Royalty, Douglas, Auburn	.125	16	16	4	2	2	0	0	0	2	0	4	0	1	3	0	6	0	0
Ruckman, Scott, Utica	.268	57	209	32	56	90	14	1	6	30	0	1	3	12	2	45	1	3	
Runge, Scott, Watertown	.000	10	5	0	0	0	0	0	0	0	0	0	0	0	0	0	3	0	0
Russo, Anthony, Erie	.000	36	1	0	0	0	0	0	0	0	0	0	0	0	0	0	1	0	0
Santos, Donaciano, Batavia	.080	7	25	0	2	2	0	0	0	0	0	1	0	0	0	0	9	0	0
Scannell, Lawrence, Elmira	.182	26	66	7	12	18	3	0	1	4	0	1	0	2	5	0	13	3	0
Schmitt, Gary, Batavia	.182	11	22	1	4	7	0	0	1	1	0	1	0	0	5	0	12	1	4
Scott, Jeffrey, Utica	.211	11	19	0	4	4	0	0	0	1	0	1	0	0	3	0	6	0	0
Sellick, John, Erie	.178	30	90	8	16	27	5	0	2	8	2	1	1	0	13	0	37	0	0
Shea, Edward, Watertown	.259	41	135	18	35	47	6	0	2	20	3	3	1	1	11	1	31	1	3
Shephard, Kelvin, Jamestown	.215	68	205	38	44	54	6	2	0	15	3	3	0	9	19	1	60	18	4

Player and Club	Pct.	G.	AB.	R.	H.	TB.	2B.	3B.	HR.	RBI.	GW.	SH.	SF.	HP.	BB.	Int. BB.	SO.	SB.	CS.
Shepherd, Keith, Watertown	.167	17	12	0	2	2	0	0	0	0	0	0	0	0	2	0	7	0	0
Shifflett, Barry, St. Catharines*	.276	59	192	36	53	85	8	0	8	31	5	0	4	1	43	0	39	3	1
Shiflett, Matthew, Jamestown	.200	14	15	2	3	6	0	0	1	1	0	1	0	0	0	0	5	0	0
Shoulders, Robert, Newark	.179	35	112	14	20	32	1	1	3	14	1	0	1	0	8	0	21	1	1
Simon, Richard, Auburn	.182	16	22	0	4	5	1	0	0	1	0	2	0	0	0	0	14	0	0
Sims, Joe, Jamestown	.241	58	162	14	39	54	9	0	2	22	1	1	3	3	19	0	41	1	0
Smith, Corey, Utica†	.000	9	8	0	0	0	0	0	0	0	0	0	0	0	2	0	6	0	0
Smith, Gregg, Erie	.137	45	102	16	14	21	4	0	1	4	1	1	0	0	21	1	36	3	3
Smith, Jeffrey, Little Falls	.000	13	1	0	0	0	0	0	0	0	0	0	0	0	0	0	1	0	0
Smith, Willie, Watertown	.500	5	2	0	1	1	0	0	0	0	0	0	0	0	0	0	1	0	0
Stepniak, Steven, Batavia	.181	38	105	8	19	29	4	0	2	10	1	0	1	1	7	0	46	2	0
Strijek, Randy, Newark	.251	66	203	30	51	66	6	3	1	23	2	0	2	1	29	0	64	4	3
Suero, Williams, St. Catharines	.316	77	297	43	94	126	12	4	4	24	4	2	1	1	35	1	35	23	11
Sullivan, Glenn, Geneva*	.301	71	256	39	77	114	20	1	5	44	5	1	4	5	30	2	23	3	0
Taylor, Kenneth, 4 Gen-17 Bat	.104	21	48	1	5	6	1	0	0	1	0	0	0	0	2	0	16	0	0
Tesmer, James, Little Falls	.179	46	106	6	19	22	0	0	1	7	2	0	1	1	5	1	14	1	0
Thomas, Mark, Watertown	.231	33	108	22	25	50	5	1	6	16	1	0	1	0	11	0	49	1	2
Thomas, Royal, Utica	.214	19	14	0	3	3	0	0	0	2	0	2	0	0	0	0	1	0	0
Thomas, Orlando, Erie	.200	43	90	9	18	21	3	0	0	8	2	1	2	1	11	1	30	3	0
Thornton, Albert, Elmira	.220	62	205	19	45	77	5	0	9	31	2	0	5	1	15	0	54	0	1
Tingle, Darrell, Oneonta	.209	66	239	33	50	62	10	1	0	22	0	3	2	2	29	0	64	7	2
Torborg, Douglas, Watertown	.133	16	15	1	2	3	1	0	0	0	0	3	0	0	0	0	5	0	0
Townley, Jason, St. Catharines	.175	60	177	21	31	55	4	1	6	17	2	0	3	2	27	0	47	1	1
Trautwein, David, Little Falls	.000	25	1	0	0	0	0	0	0	0	0	0	0	0	0	0	1	0	0
Trlicek, Richard, Utica	.000	10	5	0	0	0	0	0	0	0	0	0	0	0	0	0	1	0	0
Turgeon, David, Oneonta	.281	48	178	19	50	61	6	1	1	23	2	1	2	1	13	0	23	2	1
Valverde, Miguel, Batavia	.226	9	31	5	7	8	1	0	0	2	0	0	1	0	3	0	9	2	1
Vanderwal, John, Jamestown*	.478	18	69	24	33	60	12	3	3	15	0	0	1	0	3	0	14	3	2
Vargas, Hector, Oneonta†	.279	15	43	4	12	18	4	1	0	7	0	0	2	1	2	0	6	1	2
Vatcher, James, Utica	.269	67	249	44	67	95	15	2	3	21	3	2	1	2	28	0	31	10	5
Vaughn, Timothy, Watertown	.182	8	11	1	2	3	1	0	0	1	0	0	0	0	2	0	5	0	0
Ventress, Leroy, Utica	.208	44	120	15	25	33	3	1	1	11	0	1	1	1	14	0	39	3	1
Viltz, Corey, Jamestown†	.298	43	131	28	39	58	7	0	4	16	2	1	1	1	32	0	41	16	1
Vizcaino, Reyes, Watertown	.306	51	180	33	55	85	14	2	4	33	1	0	1	0	25	0	53	7	3
Voigt, John, Newark	.320	63	219	41	70	115	10	1	11	52	5	1	1	0	33	0	45	1	3
Wade, Darrin, St. Catharines*	.250	74	268	28	67	99	12	1	6	41	2	0	4	3	21	1	71	0	2
Walker, Lonnie, Little Falls	.235	56	153	35	36	50	5	0	3	19	1	0	1	7	18	1	41	15	3
Wallen, Walter, Little Falls	.000	5	4	0	0	0	0	0	0	0	0	0	0	0	0	0	2	0	0
Ward, Joseph, Batavia	.000	20	2	0	0	0	0	0	0	0	0	0	0	0	0	0	0	0	0
Ware, Derek, St. Catharines	.278	27	90	8	25	27	2	0	0	9	2	1	0	1	3	0	28	8	3
Warfel, Brian, Elmira	.311	45	132	19	41	62	8	2	3	19	0	1	3	0	18	2	19	1	1
Webb, Benjamin, Watertown	.333	23	3	1	1	1	0	0	0	0	0	1	0	0	1	0	1	0	0
Wedvick, Jeffrey, Jamestown	.246	44	134	21	33	46	7	0	2	12	0	1	2	3	7	0	14	4	0
Weeks, Thomas, Oneonta*	.307	69	238	33	73	108	13	2	6	57	6	0	6	3	41	3	32	2	2
White, Gary, Utica*	.267	38	105	9	28	39	5	0	2	11	2	2	0	0	12	0	33	1	2
Wilkins, Richard, Geneva*	.251	75	243	35	61	97	8	2	8	43	7	0	0	1	58	0	40	7	2
Willes, David, Utica	.304	42	161	25	49	78	7	2	6	27	2	2	2	0	27	0	13	5	3
Williams, Bernabe, Oneonta	.344	25	93	13	32	36	4	0	0	15	1	1	1	1	10	0	14	9	3
Williams, Edward, Geneva*	.230	71	269	46	62	83	12	3	1	21	0	4	0	8	29	4	55	24	6
Williams, Gerald, Oneonta	.365	29	115	26	42	58	6	2	2	29	5	0	0	1	16	0	18	6	2
Williams, Jody, Watertown	.149	24	47	5	7	7	0	0	0	4	1	1	2	0	16	0	19	0	5
Williams, Joseph, Utica	.179	24	56	3	10	10	0	0	0	0	1	0	0	1	4	0	9	5	3
Williams, Vaughn, Geneva	.216	26	74	12	16	18	2	0	0	7	1	0	0	1	9	3	25	5	1
Wilson, Craig, Elmira	.322	50	171	20	55	74	13	0	2	18	2	0	1	4	8	0	17	1	0
Wilson, Terrence, St. Catharines	.195	33	87	7	17	23	4	1	0	7	2	1	0	3	5	1	27	1	3
Young, Anthony, Little Falls	.100	14	10	1	1	1	0	0	0	0	0	1	0	0	0	0	4	0	0
Young, Ernest, Newark†	.279	70	247	54	69	132	12	3	15	55	1	0	0	2	42	0	70	3	1
Young, Mark, St. Catharines	.154	3	13	3	2	2	0	0	0	3	0	0	0	0	1	0	3	2	0
Zerb, Troy, Utica	.091	4	11	0	1	3	0	1	0	1	0	0	0	0	1	0	7	0	0
Zupcic, Robert, Elmira	.303	66	238	39	72	109	12	2	7	37	1	3	2	2	17	0	35	5	4

The following pitchers, listed alphabetically by club, with games in parentheses, had no plate appearances, primarily through use of designated hitters:

AUBURN—Hartgraves, Dean (23).

BATAVIA—Blundin, Barry (16); Casano, Andrew (14); Girouard, Michael (19); Halle, Andrew (17); Johnson, Lee (14); Ramos, Jose (19); Santana, Ernesto (9).

ELMIRA—Banasiak, Edward (15); Diaz, Johnny (17); Estrada, Peter (14); Harris, Reginald (9); McCollum, Gregory (22); Mosley, Anthony (17); Pemberton, Jose (10); Richardson, Ronnie (17); Romero, Antonio (19); Sepela, Thomas (15); Tejada, Joaquin (17); Whiting, Michael (1).

ERIE—Marte, Roberto (21).

GENEVA—Main, Kevin (12); Rosario, David (2).

JAMESTOWN—Leon, Danilo (3); Ramirez, Juan (1).

NEWARK—Bryan, Frank (17); Culkar, Steven (7); Evans, Scott (20); Gast, Joseph (2); Lopez, Craig (11); Ludwig, Frederick (1); Michno, Thomas (25); Pinder, Christopher (9); Sanchez, Geraldo (2); Sander, Michael (15); Sonneberger, Steven (13); Telford, Anthony (6); Williams, Robert (14); Wilson, Chaunan (13); Winzenread, Richard (20).

ONEONTA—Byrnes, John (20); Chapin, Darrin (25); Clayton, Royal (2); Dacosta, William (6); Eiland, David (5); Faccio, Luis (14); Foster, Randy (16); Gargin, Sean (13); Gedaminski, Todd (6); Gogolewski, Douglas (15); Imes, Rodney (4); Makemson, Jay (10); Marris, Mark (20); Martel, Edward (2); Morrison, Anthony (15); Popplewell, Thomas (16); Voeltz, William (17).

ST. CATHARINES—Beris, Robert (11); Butler, Alan (19); Hernandez, Xavier (13); Lariviere, Christopher (2); MacDonald, Robert (1); Richey, Rodney (6); Rogers, James (13); Sanchez, Alex (11); Silverstein, Allan (22); Towey, Steven (16); Trahey, James (6); Wapnick, Steven (20); Watts, Robert (28); Wishnevski, Robert (16); Woide, Steven (24).

UTICA—Carter, Andrew (12); Chadwick, Robert (25); Viggiano, Matthew (2).

WATERTOWN—Befort, Lyle (3).

GRAND SLAM HOME RUNS—Jimenez, Laboy, Thornton, Voigt, 2 each; Buford, Bustamante, Chesney, Gonzalez, Ro. Martinez, Nyssen, Pena, Pina, Shoulders, Vizcaino, E. Williams, 1 each.

AWARDED FIRST BASE ON CATCHER'S INTERFERENCE—Lewis 4 (Barczi, Faulkner, Gonzalez, Redman); Buford 2 (O. Thomas, Wilkins); Powers 2 (Gonzalez, Hundley); Colavito (Rivers); Height (Barczi); Jimenez (C. Wilson); Merced (C. Wilson); Monegro (Brian); Nyssen (Matilla); White (Hundley); E. Williams (Rivers); Jos. Williams (C. Wilson).

CLUB FIELDING

Club	Pct.	G.	PO.	A.	E.	DP.	PB.	Club	Pct.	G.	PO.	A.	E.	DP.	PB.
Newark	.966	74	1888	800	96	70	12	St. Catharines	.953	77	2014	713	134	49	23
Geneva	.963	76	1987	745	105	57	15	Watertown	.952	76	2029	776	141	68	21
Erie	.961	75	1944	862	115	69	13	Batavia	.951	77	1999	856	147	49	14
Auburn	.958	75	1990	845	123	56	25	Elmira	.946	76	1963	791	156	72	21
Utica	.954	74	1956	817	134	69	28	Oneonta	.946	75	1984	797	158	67	34
Little Falls	.954	74	1960	908	139	62	16	Jamestown	.945	77	1959	806	161	54	11

Triple Play—Auburn.

INDIVIDUAL FIELDING

°Throws lefthanded.

FIRST BASEMEN

Player and Club	Pct.	G.	PO.	A.	E.	DP.	Player and Club	Pct.	G.	PO.	A.	E.	DP.
Aleshire, Auburn	.933	4	14	0	1	1	Olah, Little Falls	.977	24	162	9	4	13
Barragan, Utica°	.988	62	529	29	7	47	Olmstead, Erie°	.982	52	402	33	8	32
Brian, Jamestown	1.000	3	20	0	0	1	Ortiz, Auburn	.989	11	81	6	1	3
Bustamante, Utica	.974	11	73	2	2	9	Pena, Newark°	.982	7	53	1	1	1
Cianfrocco, Jamestown	1.000	2	6	0	0	1	Radcliffe, Erie	.980	22	139	10	3	17
Daniels, Erie°	1.000	2	1	0	0	0	Reaves, Utica	1.000	1	1	0	0	0
Degifico, Elmira	.978	33	209	12	5	21	REEDER, 39 Gen.-25 Bat.°	.993	64	535	27	4	51
Denkenberger, Batavia°	.983	10	57	1	1	1	Rivero, Geneva	1.000	1	2	0	0	0
Dickson, Auburn	1.000	14	138	6	0	10	Roman, Oneonta	1.000	8	52	1	0	3
Erickson, Oneonta	.714	1	5	0	2	0	Rose, Batavia	.970	28	235	23	8	12
Faulkner, Batavia	1.000	1	2	1	0	1	Ruckman, Utica	1.000	1	2	0	0	0
Freeman, Watertown	.950	4	18	1	1	1	Sellick, Erie	.985	16	122	6	2	9
Griffith, Watertown	1.000	2	12	0	0	2	Shifflett, St. Catharines	1.000	6	36	1	0	1
Gwinn, Oneonta	.875	1	7	0	1	1	Sims, Jamestown	.972	52	354	34	11	28
Hansen, Jamestown	1.000	1	2	1	0	0	Smith, Utica	1.000	3	9	1	0	0
Hartman, Watertown	.986	32	262	22	4	19	Sullivan, Geneva°	.984	38	295	21	5	25
Herrera, Auburn	.500	2	1	0	1	1	Thornton, Elmira	.986	57	465	19	7	40
Jimenez, Little Falls°	.971	63	562	45	18	40	Townley, St. Catharines	1.000	2	6	0	0	1
Jose, 22 Batavia-1 Geneva°	.980	23	189	10	4	7	Vizcaino, Watertown	.987	44	352	36	5	37
Lewis, Auburn°	.984	54	492	13	8	33	Voigt, Newark	1.000	3	26	1	0	1
Massarelli, Auburn	1.000	1	2	0	0	0	Wade, St. Catharines°	.984	72	582	27	10	44
McHugh, Jamestown	.978	23	171	10	4	12	Wedvick, Jamestown	1.000	12	86	8	0	6
Mitchell, Oneonta	1.000	4	18	2	0	2	Weeks, Oneonta	.986	67	588	35	9	51
Mota, Auburn	1.000	1	2	0	0	1	White, Utica	1.000	4	24	1	0	3
Nelson, Erie	.963	6	25	1	1	5	Wilkins, Geneva	.952	3	20	0	1	0
Nyssen, Auburn	1.000	1	3	0	0	0	Young, Newark°	.992	67	584	38	5	60

Triple Play—Dickson.

SECOND BASEMEN

Player and Club	Pct.	G.	PO.	A.	E.	DP.	Player and Club	Pct.	G.	PO.	A.	E.	DP.
Atha, Jamestown	.943	16	31	52	5	10	McHugh, Jamestown	1.000	1	0	1	0	0
Bogar, Little Falls	.909	3	4	6	1	2	McMahon, St. Catharines	1.000	1	1	2	0	0
Boswell, Geneva	.976	11	20	20	1	3	Mejias, Geneva	.950	49	90	118	11	20
Buford, Newark	.965	70	140	194	12	48	Merced, Watertown	.900	4	11	7	2	1
Bustamante, Utica	.972	15	29	40	2	8	Mitchell, Jamestown	.500	1	0	1	1	0
Cianfrocco, Jamestown	.954	35	71	95	8	15	Monegro, Elmira	.936	39	74	88	11	27
Dickerson, Oneonta	1.000	1	1	3	0	0	Moran, Erie	.960	19	36	36	3	8
Didder, Oneonta	.929	6	8	5	1	1	Mota, Auburn	1.000	1	0	1	0	0
Echevarria, Elmira	.969	30	58	67	4	12	Paredes, Jamestown	.933	8	10	18	2	0
Garrison, Watertown	.950	61	115	153	14	28	Perez, Utica	.971	26	47	52	3	8
Geronimo, Batavia	.951	36	57	59	6	7	Powers, Elmira	.960	22	39	57	4	14
Gordon, Batavia	.980	36	80	121	4	22	Renteria, Auburn	.956	71	136	192	15	33
Height, Little Falls	.959	59	132	175	13	38	Rosario, Elmira	.818	2	6	3	2	1
Hellmann, 11 Bat.-25 Gen.	.953	36	73	70	7	17	Strijek, Newark	.870	4	8	12	3	1
Herrera, Auburn	.842	7	6	10	3	4	Suero, St. Catharines	.956	77	149	197	16	28
Hildreth, Batavia	.913	3	16	5	2	1	Tingle, Oneonta	.915	20	40	46	8	10
Ishmael, Jamestown	.971	28	43	56	3	10	Vaughn, Watertown	1.000	4	1	0	0	0
JEFFERS, Erie	.985	69	118	217	5	45	Willes, Utica	.977	40	100	111	5	30
Joiner, Little Falls	.949	15	26	48	4	3	Williams, Watertown	.952	19	29	51	4	9
Kelley, Oneonta	.947	59	110	158	15	30	Zerb, Utica	1.000	4	2	4	0	0

Triple Play—Renteria.

THIRD BASEMEN

Player and Club	Pct.	G.	PO.	A.	E.	DP.	Player and Club	Pct.	G.	PO.	A.	E.	DP.
Andrade, Geneva	.500	1	1	0	1	0	Melton, Elmira	.897	54	54	102	18	7
Batiste, Utica	.914	15	13	19	3	3	Monegro, Elmira	.808	7	6	15	5	0
Bowell, Geneva	.813	6	6	7	3	1	Moran, Erie	.714	4	1	4	2	1
Bromley, Watertown	.875	18	16	26	6	0	Mota, Auburn	.915	49	20	110	12	7
Bustamante, Utica	.800	3	5	7	3	0	Nowak, Newark	.833	9	4	16	4	1
Castro, Batavia	1.000	1	1	0	0	0	Ortiz, Auburn	.643	5	2	7	5	1
Cunningham, Erie	1.000	3	2	3	0	1	Owens, Geneva	.896	58	43	95	16	6
DelRosario, St. Catharines	.800	4	1	7	2	1	Payton, Erie	.884	70	43	133	23	9
Dickson, Auburn	.891	13	9	32	5	3	Perez, Utica	1.000	2	0	2	0	0
Didder, Oneonta	1.000	8	3	8	0	1	Plantier, Elmira	.793	21	12	34	12	4
Esquer, Newark	.933	8	4	10	1	1	Polanco, Little Falls	.902	73	34	160	21	12
Etzweiler, St. Catharines	.846	4	7	4	2	0	Reaves, Utica	.923	9	7	17	2	1
Foster, St. Catharines	.894	69	58	103	19	7	Rodriguez, Jamestown	.842	77	52	119	32	15
Geronimo, Batavia	1.000	2	1	4	0	0	Roman, Oneonta	.880	34	13	53	9	6
Gilmore, St. Catharines	.500	1	1	0	1	0	Rosario, Elmira	1.000	2	2	0	0	0
Griffith, Watertown	.850	39	25	43	12	6	Ruckman, Utica	.910	53	25	117	14	11
Hellmann, 3 Bat.-14 Gen.	.940	17	12	35	3	4	Santos, Batavia	1.000	2	1	0	0	1
Herrera, Auburn	.896	17	12	31	5	3	Taylor, Batavia	.500	4	1	0	1	1
Joiner, Little Falls	1.000	6	0	5	0	0	Thomas, Watertown	.882	29	15	45	8	5
Jose, Geneva	1.000	2	0	1	0	0	Turgeon, Oneonta	.907	43	16	81	10	7
Martinez, Batavia	.874	71	53	127	26	7	VOIGT, Newark	.941	60	37	140	11	16
McHugh, Jamestown	.750	6	0	6	2	0							

SHORTSTOPS

Player and Club	Pct.	G.	PO.	A.	E.	DP.	Player and Club	Pct.	G.	PO.	A.	E.	DP.
Batiste, Utica	.904	31	51	71	13	10	Mejias, Geneva	.500	1	1	0	1	0
Beriatua, St. Catharines	.900	54	60	120	20	18	Mitchell, Jamestown	.667	1	2	0	1	0
Bogar, Little Falls	.920	53	75	188	23	30	MORAN, Erie	.953	56	58	106	8	22
Burdick, Watertown	.920	71	106	204	27	42	Owens, Geneva	.800	3	3	5	2	3
Bustamante, Utica	.978	12	11	33	1	9	Perez, Utica	.867	6	5	8	2	0
Castro, Batavia	.945	71	112	196	18	24	Powers, Elmira	.866	38	56	86	22	22
Cianfrocco, Jamestown	.904	35	48	84	14	13	Renteria, Auburn	1.000	1	0	1	0	0
DelRosario, St. Catharines	.903	23	29	27	6	6	Rivero, Geneva	.924	70	99	194	24	37
DeShields, Jamestown	.796	27	25	57	21	8	Rodriguez, Jamestown	1.000	1	0	2	0	0
Diaz, Little Falls	.897	10	13	22	4	1	Roman, Oneonta	.813	13	17	22	9	3
Dickerson, Oneonta	.885	6	7	16	3	2	Rosario, Geneva	1.000	4	1	10	0	0
Dillard, Elmira	.917	13	11	22	3	4	Rosario, Elmira	.915	37	44	106	14	19
Echevarria, Elmira	1.000	3	5	2	0	1	Smith, Erie	.904	41	56	113	18	23
Esquer, Newark	.933	24	20	36	4	6	Strijek, Newark	.945	62	85	190	16	34
Foster, St. Catharines	.862	5	13	12	4	4	Taylor, Batavia	1.000	1	0	1	0	0
Gordon, Batavia	1.000	4	3	7	0	1	Tingle, Oneonta	.887	51	75	137	27	28
Harris, Auburn	.938	64	88	212	20	23	Turgeon, Oneonta	.500	1	0	1	1	0
Hellmann, 9 Bat.-1 Gen	.943	10	14	19	2	1	Vargas, Oneonta	.873	14	20	42	9	10
Herrera, Auburn	.885	12	14	32	6	3	Vatcher, Utica	1.000	1	0	1	0	0
Ishmael, Jamestown	.905	18	18	39	6	7	Vaughn, Watertown	.933	4	5	9	1	2
Joiner, Little Falls	.913	14	21	42	6	5	Ventress, Utica	.862	42	54	90	23	24
Martinez, Batavia	.750	3	1	2	1	0	Williams, Watertown	.769	5	1	9	3	0
McMahon, St. Catharines	.800	9	6	10	4	5							

Triple Play—Harris.

OUTFIELDERS

Player and Club	Pct.	G.	PO.	A.	E.	DP.	Player and Club	Pct.	G.	PO.	A.	E.	DP.
Ahr, Newark	.952	55	56	3	3	0	Merejo, Watertown*	.917	14	21	1	2	1
Alou, Watertown	.957	27	43	1	2	0	J. Mitchell, Jamestown	.968	28	26	4	1	1
Arrington, Geneva	1.000	22	34	2	0	0	M. Mitchell, Oneonta	.931	39	53	1	4	0
Bell, St. Catharines	.985	72	126	6	2	1	Monteiro, Utica*	.900	18	8	1	1	0
Bishop, Oneonta	.955	56	81	3	4	1	Moore, Geneva	.895	21	17	0	2	0
Bond, Batavia	1.000	25	14	1	0	1	Mota, Auburn	1.000	11	11	0	0	0
Bourne, Elmira	.968	36	58	3	2	0	Naughton, Little Falls	.968	57	57	3	2	1
Brian, Jamestown	1.000	1	1	0	0	0	NELSON, Erie	.990	58	91	8	1	1
Brooks, Auburn	.981	41	48	3	1	0	Nunez, St. Catharines	.938	59	101	4	7	0
E. Carter, Erie*	.945	62	82	4	5	2	Nyssen, Auburn	.979	71	139	3	3	0
S. Carter, Watertown	.944	61	132	4	8	1	Ortiz, Auburn	1.000	3	1	0	0	0
Chamberlain, Watertown	.949	64	121	9	7	3	Perez, Auburn*	.949	46	70	4	4	2
Christian, Erie	.954	66	118	7	6	2	Peyton, Watertown	1.000	5	2	0	0	0
Cobb, Utica	.975	55	72	7	2	1	Pina, Elmira	.968	52	84	8	3	0
Colavito, Batavia	.929	12	11	2	1	0	Raisanen, Watertown	.968	22	30	0	1	0
Denkenberger, Batavia*	.894	55	69	7	9	0	Ramsey, Geneva	.842	27	15	1	3	0
Doss, Jamestown	.960	22	19	5	1	1	Ricker, Jamestown	.961	74	118	5	5	0
Ehrhard, Oneonta	.974	15	35	2	1	1	Robinson, Erie*	.957	32	41	4	2	1
Elmore, Newark	.938	29	43	2	3	1	Roche, Little Falls*	.917	30	31	2	3	0
Fernandez, Oneonta*	1.000	3	2	0	0	0	Romero, St. Catharines	.937	53	71	3	5	1
Finley, Newark*	.970	54	122	7	4	2	Santos, Batavia	1.000	6	5	1	0	0
Galloway, Utica	.742	31	21	2	8	1	Scannell, Elmira	.971	19	32	2	1	1
Geronimo, Batavia	.000	2	0	0	2	0	Schmitt, Batavia	.900	11	8	1	1	0
Gordon, Batavia	1.000	1	1	0	0	0	Sellick, Erie	1.000	5	7	0	0	0
Greene, Utica	1.000	7	5	2	0	0	Shephard, Jamestown	.935	64	96	5	7	3
Grier, Erie	.978	35	42	3	1	0	Shoulders, Newark	.933	22	27	1	2	1
Hailey, Oneonta	.964	63	126	7	5	1	Stepniak, Batavia	.895	18	16	1	2	0
Hannon, Geneva	.985	70	126	4	2	1	Sullivan, Geneva*	.964	31	25	2	1	0
Hansen, Jamestown	.870	14	19	1	3	0	Tesmer, Little Falls	.963	31	48	4	2	0
Harms, Newark	.967	51	87	1	3	0	Valverde, Batavia	.947	9	16	2	1	0
Harris, Watertown	.954	46	58	4	3	0	Vanderwal, Jamestown*	1.000	18	20	0	0	0
Hartline, Newark	.913	18	21	0	2	0	Vatcher, Utica	.977	63	116	11	3	3
Hill, Oneonta	.950	14	19	0	1	0	Viltz, Jamestown*	.947	41	53	1	3	0
Hunter, Oneonta	1.000	4	7	0	0	0	Walker, Little Falls	.975	46	75	2	2	0
Jose, 8 Batavia-8 Geneva	.810	16	16	1	4	0	Ware, St. Catharines	.931	25	26	1	2	0
Kelly, Elmira	.961	48	68	6	3	1	Warfel, Elmira	1.000	20	41	1	0	0
Kingston, Batavia*	.943	54	80	2	5	0	Wedvick, Batavia	1.000	2	1	0	0	0
Kirkpatrick, Utica	.978	72	166	9	4	3	B. Williams, Oneonta	.952	24	40	0	2	0
Laboy, Auburn*	.921	70	85	8	8	0	E. Williams, Geneva*	.956	69	126	4	6	0
Lampe, Batavia	.939	54	87	6	6	1	G. Williams, Oneonta	.959	29	68	3	3	1
Lemle, Little Falls	1.000	24	47	1	0	1	J. Williams, Utica	1.000	15	19	1	0	0
Lewis, Auburn*	1.000	1	2	0	0	0	V. Williams, Geneva	.969	22	30	1	1	0
Marrs, Elmira	.968	28	29	1	1	0	Wilson, St. Catharines	.891	32	39	2	5	0
McDaniel, Little Falls	.928	67	101	15	9	3	Young, St. Catharines	.800	3	3	1	1	0
Mealy, Batavia	.951	21	37	2	2	0	Zupcic, Elmira	.971	60	131	1	4	0

CATCHERS

Player and Club	Pct.	G.	PO.	A.	E.	DP.	PB.	Player and Club	Pct.	G.	PO.	A.	E.	DP.	PB.
Aleshire, Auburn	.976	18	144	17	4	2	1	Gwinn, Oneonta	.973	24	188	27	6	4	11
Andrade, Geneva	.986	20	129	13	2	1	6	Hundley, Little Falls	.967	31	181	25	7	4	7
Barczi, Watertown	.970	40	273	15	9	1	12	Lehman, Newark	.975	40	275	32	8	2	8
Bastinck, Little Falls	1.000	13	68	10	0	1	0	Lindsey, Utica	.979	52	337	41	8	4	13
Brian, Jamestown	1.000	13	79	7	0	2	2	Massarelli, Auburn	.985	18	112	20	2	1	8
Bustamante, Utica	1.000	3	9	0	0	0	1	Matilla, Elmira	.959	21	99	17	5	2	9
Carver, Auburn	.981	44	334	29	7	1	16	Moore, Erie	.923	2	11	1	1	0	0
Chesney, St. Catharines	1.000	2	16	2	0	0	1	Natal, Jamestown	.984	46	321	52	6	4	9
Cruz, Batavia	.991	18	96	11	1	1	3	Nowak, Newark	.985	16	115	15	2	4	2
Dorante, Elmira	.956	28	114	16	6	1	4	Ramon, Oneonta	1.000	9	21	6	0	0	0
Eberle, Newark	.994	24	142	13	1	2	2	Redman, Erie	.975	53	284	34	8	3	8
Ehrhard, Oneonta	.974	16	104	10	3	3	10	Rivers, St. Catharines	.979	45	378	41	9	1	9
Erickson, Oneonta	.976	36	219	29	6	2	14	Scott, Utica	1.000	9	33	3	0	1	1
Faulkner, Batavia	.983	62	393	57	8	3	11	Shea, Watertown	.977	41	317	29	8	4	9
Freeman, Watertown	1.000	3	19	1	0	0	0	Smith, Utica	1.000	3	4	0	0	0	0
Gonzalez, Little Falls	.984	39	273	41	5	6	9	Taylor, 1 Gen-9 Bat	.952	10	53	7	3	0	0

CATCHERS—Continued

Player and Club	Pct.	G.	PO.	A.	E.	DP.	PB.
Thomas, Erie	.976	40	217	26	6	1	5
Thornton, Elmira	1.000	1	3	0	0	0	1
Townley, St. Catharines	.974	34	275	26	8	2	13
Wedvick, Jamestown	.972	31	217	30	7	2	1
White, Utica	.977	25	159	14	4	1	13
WILKINS, Geneva	.989	64	483	51	6	6	9
Wilson, Elmira	962	44	228	23	10	0	7

Triple Play—Carver.

PITCHERS

Player and Club	Pct.	G.	PO.	A.	E.	DP.
D. Allen, Utica	.333	5	0	1	2	0
H. Allen, Auburn*	.773	14	3	14	5	0
Ashby, Utica	.929	13	3	10	1	1
Aspray, Geneva	1.000	23	7	7	0	0
Ayers, Jamestown	1.000	11	4	6	0	1
Banasiak, Elmira	.833	15	4	11	3	0
Barnwell, Watertown	1.000	15	2	4	0	0
Befort, Watertown	1.000	3	0	3	0	0
Bennett, Erie	1.000	11	1	2	0	0
Bergeron, Jamestown	.800	13	1	3	1	0
Bevis, St. Catharines	1.000	11	2	4	0	1
Blundin, Batavia	.920	16	5	18	2	4
Bond, Batavia	.000	2	0	0	1	0
Boyd, Watertown	.000	2	0	0	1	0
Brito, Jamestown	.808	15	8	13	5	0
Broadfoot, Erie	.969	16	8	23	1	1
Bross, Little Falls	1.000	10	1	6	0	1
Bryan, Newark	1.000	17	5	8	0	1
Butler, St. Catharines*	.818	19	2	7	2	1
Byrnes, Oneonta*	.800	20	1	3	1	0
Caballero, Geneva	1.000	14	5	12	0	1
Cakora, Geneva*	1.000	11	1	1	0	0
A. Carter, Utica*	.600	12	1	2	2	0
J. Carter, Jamestown	1.000	31	5	10	0	0
Casano, Batavia	.762	14	2	14	5	2
Castillo, Geneva	1.000	1	1	1	0	0
Castner, Watertown	1.000	15	1	2	0	0
Cavalier, Jamestown	1.000	27	1	9	0	1
Chadwick, Utica*	1.000	25	2	7	0	0
Chapin, Oneonta	.889	25	3	5	1	0
Coulter, Utica	1.000	7	0	3	0	0
Culkar, Newark	.667	7	1	1	1	0
Dacosta, Oneonta	.833	6	2	3	1	1
Daniels, Erie*	.875	36	1	6	1	0
Dell'amico, Utica	.813	11	3	10	3	0
Diaz, Elmira*	1.000	17	0	3	0	0
Disabato, Little Falls*	.933	15	2	12	1	0
Duncan, Watertown	.923	24	3	9	1	2
Eiland, Oneonta	1.000	5	1	5	0	0
Estrada, Elmira	.929	14	4	9	1	0
Evans, Newark	.714	20	0	5	2	0
Faccio, Oneonta	1.000	14	1	6	0	0
Fagnano, Utica	1.000	12	0	10	0	0
Farmer, Jamestown	.853	15	9	20	5	1
Foster, Jamestown	1.000	16	7	13	0	1
Fox, Batavia	1.000	18	4	5	0	0
Gargin, Oneonta	1.000	13	3	5	0	0
Gast, Newark*	.000	2	0	0	2	0
Gedaminski, Oneonta*	1.000	6	0	2	0	0
Girouard, Batavia	.963	19	5	21	1	0
Gogolewski, Oneonta	.765	15	6	7	4	0
Gomez, Geneva	.875	10	3	4	1	2
Griffin, Little Falls	.944	14	4	13	1	2
Griffith, Watertown	.500	1	0	1	1	0
Halama, Erie	1.000	11	2	6	0	0
Halle, Batavia*	.941	17	1	15	1	0
Harris, Elmira	.727	9	1	7	3	0
Hartgraves, Auburn*	.800	23	0	4	1	0
Harvick, Erie*	.842	15	4	12	3	1
Hennis, Auburn	1.000	13	2	14	0	0
J. Hernandez, Erie	.931	16	7	20	2	1
X. Hernandez, St. Catharines	.923	13	3	9	1	2
Hillman, Little Falls*	.818	13	3	6	2	0
Hinkle, Erie	.958	12	11	12	1	1
Houser, Erie	1.000	13	5	8	0	0
Hurta, Utica*	.733	21	1	10	4	1
Imes, Oneonta	.857	4	2	4	1	3
G. Johnson, Auburn	.889	24	2	6	1	0
L. Johnson, Batavia	.923	13	9	27	3	1
Jongewaard, Erie	.875	20	1	6	1	0
Jundy, Little Falls	.813	10	3	10	3	0
Kerrigan, Jamestown	.923	21	7	5	1	2
Koller, Watertown	.818	23	3	6	2	3
Lariviere, St. Catharines	1.000	2	0	1	0	0
LaRosa, Utica*	.941	15	4	12	1	1
LaRose, Little Falls	.929	26	7	6	1	0
C. Lopez, Newark	1.000	11	3	8	0	0
M. Lopez, Utica	.500	5	0	2	2	0
Ludwig, Newark	1.000	1	0	2	0	1
Macavage, Watertown	.889	8	3	5	1	0
MacDonald, St. Catharines*	1.000	1	1	0	0	0
Main, Geneva	.750	12	1	2	1	1
Makemson, Oneonta	.833	10	1	4	1	0
Marchok, Jamestown*	.800	18	2	6	2	0
Marris, Oneonta	.667	20	4	2	3	1
Marte, Erie	1.000	21	2	4	0	1
Martin, Jamestown	.333	7	0	1	2	0
Massicotte, Geneva	1.000	35	2	8	0	0
McAmarney, Little Falls	.926	17	9	16	2	1
McCarthy, Utica*	.857	20	1	5	1	0
McClure, Auburn	1.000	21	2	1	0	0
McCollum, Elmira	.941	22	4	12	1	1
McDonald, Utica	.889	29	2	14	2	0
Meamber, Erie	.800	20	5	7	3	0
Melvin, Geneva	.875	15	4	10	2	1
Michael, Elmira	.931	16	6	21	2	3
Michno, Newark	1.000	25	5	9	0	0
Miller, Little Falls	1.000	13	2	14	0	1
Morrison, Oneonta*	.846	15	4	18	4	0
Mosley, Elmira*	1.000	17	2	4	0	1
Mullino, Geneva	.895	26	2	15	2	0
Murphy, Watertown	.958	14	8	15	1	1
Newman, Auburn*	.938	17	3	12	1	0
Newton, Little Falls	1.000	25	3	3	0	0
North, Geneva*	1.000	15	4	19	0	1
Osuna, Auburn*	1.000	8	0	3	0	0
Pacholec, Watertown	1.000	15	2	12	0	0
Peek, Utica	1.000	4	1	3	0	0
Pemberton, Elmira	1.000	10	1	0	0	0
Pinder, Newark*	1.000	9	0	2	0	0
POLLACK, Jamestown*	1.000	14	7	19	0	1
Polverini, Auburn	.750	21	0	6	2	0
Popplewell, Oneonta	.947	16	5	13	1	1
Rambo, Utica*	.867	13	1	12	2	0
Ramirez, Jamestown	.800	1	1	3	1	0
Ramos, Batavia*	.833	19	3	12	3	0
Richardson, Elmira	.933	17	5	9	1	2
Richey, St. Catharines	1.000	6	3	1	0	1
Robinson, Geneva	.966	18	9	19	1	1
Rodriguez, Geneva*	.867	24	2	11	2	0
Rogers, St. Catharines	.846	13	3	8	2	0
Romero, Elmira	.900	19	0	9	1	0
Romo, Auburn	.857	17	1	5	1	0
Rose, Batavia	.875	9	2	12	2	0
Royalty, Auburn	.972	16	4	31	1	3
Runge, Watertown	.900	10	2	7	1	0
Russo, Erie	1.000	36	1	7	0	0
A. Sanchez, St. Catharines	.850	17	6	11	3	1
G. Sanchez, Newark	1.000	2	2	1	0	0
Sander, Newark	1.000	15	5	17	0	1
Santana, Batavia	.333	9	0	2	4	1
Sepela, Elmira	.941	15	6	10	1	1
Shepherd, Watertown	.895	17	6	11	2	1
Shiflett, Jamestown	.958	14	5	18	1	0
Silverstein, St. Catharines	1.000	22	1	13	0	0
Simon, Auburn	1.000	16	7	12	0	2
J. Smith, Little Falls	.857	13	2	4	1	0
W. Smith, Watertown	.667	5	1	1	1	0
Sonneberger, Newark	.933	13	5	9	1	1
Tejada, Elmira	.875	17	2	5	1	0
Telford, Newark	1.000	6	2	2	0	0
Thomas, Jamestown	.889	19	1	15	2	2
Torborg, Watertown*	.950	16	6	13	1	1
Towey, St. Catharines	.857	16	0	6	1	0
Trahey, St. Catharines	1.000	6	0	2	0	0
Trautwein, Little Falls	.800	25	5	3	2	0
Trlicek, Utica	.714	10	0	5	2	0
Vizcaino, Watertown	.000	2	0	0	1	0
Voeltz, Oneonta*	.833	17	1	9	2	0
Wallen, Little Falls	.800	21	5	3	2	0
Wapnick, St. Catharines	1.000	20	3	7	0	0
Ward, Batavia	.917	20	3	8	1	0
Watts, St. Catharines	.895	28	1	16	2	3
Webb, Watertown	.875	23	1	6	1	0
Williams, Newark	.875	14	6	8	2	0
Wilson, Elmira	.933	13	5	9	1	0
Winzenread, Newark	.778	20	0	7	2	1
Wishnevski, St. Catharines	1.000	16	5	19	0	2
Woide, St. Catharines*	1.000	24	0	13	0	1
Young, Little Falls	1.000	14	4	9	0	0

The following players do not have any recorded accepted chances at the positions indicated; therefore, are not listed in the fielding averages for those particular positions: Bastinck, of; Beriatua, 2b; Boswell, ss, of; Bromley, p; Brooks, p; Bross, of; Burdick, 2b; Bustamante, of; Clayton, p; Denkenberger, p; Echevarria, 3b; Geronimo, ss; Gordon, 3b; Guzman, of; Hawkins, p; Jongewaard, 2b; Leon, p; Martel, p; Ri. Martinez, 2b; P. Moore, 3b; Payton, of; Radcliffe, p; Raisanen, ss; Rivero, 2b; D. Rosario, p; Rose, of; Viggiano, p; Wallen, of; Warfel, p; Whiting, p.

CLUB PITCHING

Club	ERA.	G.	CG.	ShO.	Sv.	IP.	H.	R.	ER.	HR.	HB.	BB.	Int. BB.	SO.	WP.	Bk.
Jamestown	3.13	77	13	6	20	653.0	601	317	227	36	22	246	3	602	31	7
Geneva	3.21	76	8	7	27	662.1	553	274	236	43	21	244	12	603	20	5
St. Catharines	3.32	77	1	11	24	671.1	534	316	248	39	35	307	15	670	38	4
Auburn	3.47	75	9	5	16	663.1	592	342	256	33	18	311	20	599	60	6
Newark	3.60	74	16	4	9	629.1	584	311	252	40	25	214	9	521	34	4
Watertown	3.62	76	3	6	23	676.1	617	349	272	29	31	317	13	582	49	6
Erie	3.67	75	4	3	19	648.0	654	348	264	62	20	235	16	511	40	8
Oneonta	3.70	75	2	10	23	661.1	635	373	272	28	25	335	19	531	60	3
Little Falls	3.94	74	4	4	17	653.1	660	370	286	47	24	243	14	519	55	4
Utica	3.93	74	6	2	12	652.0	651	393	285	34	32	322	19	520	46	9
Batavia	4.25	77	3	6	6	666.1	663	398	315	56	26	311	14	515	45	12
Elmira	4.84	76	11	2	7	654.1	686	470	352	40	46	328	4	420	54	4

PITCHERS' RECORDS
(Leading Qualifiers for Earned-Run Average Leadership — 62 or More Innings)

*Throws lefthanded.

Pitcher — Club	W.	L.	Pct.	ERA.	G.	GS.	CG.	GF.	ShO.	Sv.	IP.	H.	R.	ER.	HR.	HB.	BB.	Int. BB.	SO.	WP.
Wishnevski, St. Catharines	7	2	.778	1.53	16	15	1	0	0	0	88.0	58	18	15	2	6	39	1	71	6
Thomas, Utica	6	0	1.000	1.89	19	6	0	7	0	2	76.0	67	23	16	1	0	18	3	62	3
Pollack, Jamestown*	6	4	.600	2.07	14	14	2	0	1	0	87.0	80	37	20	2	1	31	0	108	1
Foster, Oneonta*	6	2	.750	2.26	16	9	1	3	0	1	75.2	68	35	19	0	3	28	3	74	7
C. Lopez, Newark	5	4	.556	2.33	11	3	0	1	0	0	65.2	52	21	17	4	3	24	1	54	2
Hinkle, Erie	5	4	.556	2.34	12	10	2	1	2	1	69.1	64	23	18	4	0	16	4	53	1
Robinson, Geneva	5	4	.556	2.40	18	14	3	3	1	1	97.2	71	32	26	3	3	29	2	76	0
Simon, Auburn	8	2	.800	2.59	16	16	1	0	1	0	107.2	104	41	31	4	1	43	1	80	5
A. Sanchez, St. Catharines	8	3	.727	2.64	17	17	0	0	0	0	95.1	72	33	28	3	5	38	0	116	6
Royalty, Auburn	10	4	.714	2.65	16	15	4	0	0	0	112.0	91	42	33	7	2	16	0	82	5

Departmental Leaders: G—Daniels, Russo, 36; W—Royalty, 10; L—Hennis, Michael, Ward, 9; Pct.—Daniels, .818; GS—A. Sanchez, 17; CG—Girouard, 6; GF—Massicotte, 28; ShO—Caballero, Hinkle, Murphy, 2; Sv.—Massicotte, 15; IP—Royalty, 112.0; H—Girouard, 107; R—Gogolewski, 73; ER—Gogolewski, 54; HR—Blundin, Casano, 11; HB—Michael, 9; BB—Morrison, 57; IBB—Chapin, Watts, 5; SO—A. Sanchez, 116; WP—Gogolewski, 15.

(All Pitchers—Listed Alphabetically)

Pitcher — Club	W.	L.	Pct.	ERA.	G.	GS.	CG.	GF.	ShO.	Sv.	IP.	H.	R.	ER.	HR.	HB.	BB.	Int. BB.	SO.	WP.
Acosta, Watertown*	2	3	.400	1.32	20	3	0	10	0	6	47.2	34	13	7	0	2	22	3	48	1
D. Allen, Utica	0	0	.000	0.93	5	0	0	1	0	0	9.2	8	4	1	0	0	7	0	10	2
H. Allen, Auburn*	2	8	.200	4.72	14	14	0	0	0	0	68.2	71	47	36	4	2	38	0	68	10
Ashby, Utica	3	7	.300	4.05	13	13	0	0	0	0	60.0	56	38	27	3	1	36	3	51	7
Aspray, Geneva	6	0	1.000	2.45	23	2	0	6	0	2	51.1	48	16	14	3	2	14	2	56	2
Ayers, Jamestown	2	4	.333	3.03	11	5	0	1	0	0	38.2	37	21	13	3	0	22	0	27	3
Banasiak, Elmira	0	6	.000	4.97	15	10	0	3	0	1	50.2	48	42	28	2	3	35	0	41	9
Barnwell, Watertown	0	1	.000	4.32	15	0	0	13	0	1	25.0	22	13	12	2	2	10	0	17	1
Befort, Watertown	0	0	.000	6.23	3	0	0	1	0	0	4.1	3	4	3	0	1	2	1	3	0
Bennett, Erie	0	1	.000	7.02	11	0	0	2	0	0	16.2	23	21	13	3	2	11	0	13	4
Bergeron, Jamestown	3	3	.500	3.66	13	8	0	4	0	1	51.2	48	30	21	3	1	26	0	47	1
Bevis, St. Catharines	2	3	.400	6.20	11	0	0	6	0	0	20.1	26	15	14	2	0	4	2	20	0
Blundin, Batavia	3	8	.273	4.48	16	14	4	2	0	0	94.1	100	61	47	11	5	34	1	59	4
Bond, Batavia	0	0	.000	31.50	2	0	0	0	0	0	2.0	5	7	7	0	0	4	0	2	0
Boyd, Watertown	0	0	.000	2.61	2	2	0	0	0	0	10.1	13	6	3	1	0	5	0	6	4
Brito, Jamestown	6	5	.545	3.02	15	15	3	0	0	0	95.1	83	50	32	6	2	40	0	89	3
Broadfoot, Erie	5	5	.500	2.74	16	16	1	0	0	0	101.2	96	40	31	10	2	17	1	67	2
Bromley, Watertown	0	0	.000	36.00	1	0	0	0	0	0	1.0	2	4	4	1	0	2	0	0	1
Brooks, Auburn	0	0	.000	4.91	2	0	0	2	0	0	3.2	3	2	2	0	1	4	0	1	1
Bross, Little Falls	2	0	1.000	3.86	10	3	0	1	0	0	28.0	22	23	12	3	0	20	0	21	1
Bryan, Newark	0	2	.000	5.61	17	3	0	3	0	0	51.1	65	37	32	4	5	17	2	26	2
Butler, St. Catharines*	2	2	.500	3.90	19	8	0	3	0	1	57.2	45	34	25	1	1	38	0	55	4
Byrnes, Oneonta*	1	0	1.000	5.59	20	0	0	7	0	1	29.0	38	26	18	0	1	11	0	23	3
Caballero, Geneva	8	4	.667	2.86	14	14	2	0	2	0	94.1	71	33	30	6	2	27	2	80	1
Cakora, Geneva*	2	3	.400	3.57	11	1	0	3	0	1	22.2	25	10	9	1	0	2	0	19	1
A. Carter, Utica*	0	1	.000	5.65	12	1	0	1	0	0	28.2	27	25	18	1	4	19	0	19	2
J. Carter, Jamestown	2	3	.400	2.34	31	0	0	20	0	5	42.1	39	15	11	1	0	17	0	42	5
Casano, Batavia	5	6	.455	4.14	14	11	5	2	1	0	87.0	82	41	40	11	3	48	3	71	7
Castillo, Geneva	1	0	1.000	0.00	1	1	0	0	0	0	6.0	3	1	0	0	0	1	0	6	0
Castner, Jamestown	2	1	.667	7.36	15	1	0	5	0	2	25.2	31	25	21	2	3	17	0	14	2
Cavalier, Jamestown	4	2	.667	3.38	27	0	0	17	0	9	48.0	37	20	18	5	0	17	2	48	0
Chadwick, Utica*	5	1	.833	4.26	25	0	0	16	0	3	38.0	33	24	18	2	1	22	1	32	3
Chapin, Oneonta	1	1	.500	0.68	25	0	0	21	0	12	40.0	31	8	3	1	0	17	5	26	6
Clayton, Oneonta	0	1	.000	2.25	2	0	0	1	0	0	4.0	4	1	1	0	0	2	0	3	0
Coulter, Utica	1	1	.500	3.21	7	0	0	5	0	1	14.0	15	8	5	0	2	9	1	11	1
Culkar, Newark	1	0	1.000	4.15	7	0	0	6	0	1	8.2	9	4	4	0	0	1	0	6	0
Dacosta, Oneonta	1	3	.250	5.60	6	6	0	0	0	0	27.1	37	22	17	3	2	16	1	12	1
Daniels, Erie*	9	2	.818	3.65	36	0	0	17	0	6	49.1	47	21	20	3	2	16	2	58	5
Dell'Amico, Utica	0	2	.000	7.55	11	5	0	3	0	0	31.0	42	35	26	1	8	16	0	17	2
Denkenberger, Batavia*	0	0	.000	13.50	1	0	0	1	0	0	2.0	5	3	3	0	0	0	0	0	0
Diaz, Elmira	3	2	.600	2.49	17	0	0	12	0	6	25.1	23	13	7	2	1	15	0	14	2
Disabato, Little Falls*	1	1	.500	4.60	15	5	0	3	0	0	43.0	52	29	22	3	0	15	0	30	3
Duncan, Watertown*	4	2	.667	2.36	24	0	0	16	0	4	49.2	45	20	13	1	3	22	3	57	4
Eiland, Oneonta	4	0	1.000	1.84	5	5	0	0	0	0	29.1	20	6	6	1	0	3	0	16	2
Estrada, Elmira	3	5	.375	5.26	14	10	1	0	0	0	63.1	63	42	37	4	5	24	0	31	4
Evans, Newark	1	2	.333	1.85	20	0	0	18	0	4	24.1	15	8	5	0	1	10	0	23	0
Faccio, Oneonta	1	1	.500	2.93	14	1	0	8	0	1	40.0	39	19	13	2	2	14	3	41	2
Fagnano, Utica	1	6	.143	5.00	12	11	0	0	0	0	54.0	67	43	30	3	0	16	1	37	3
Farmer, Jamestown	9	6	.600	3.27	15	15	3	0	1	0	96.1	93	42	35	4	3	30	0	63	4
Foster, Oneonta*	6	2	.750	2.26	16	9	1	3	0	1	75.2	68	35	19	0	3	28	3	74	7
Fox, Batavia	2	4	.333	4.30	18	2	0	14	0	1	46.0	38	29	22	4	1	29	2	58	6
Gargin, Oneonta	1	0	1.000	3.71	13	0	0	6	0	1	26.2	36	14	11	1	0	14	3	25	1
Gast, Newark*	0	1	.000	8.44	2	1	0	0	0	0	5.1	8	7	5	0	0	4	0	1	1
Gedaminski, Oneonta*	0	2	.000	5.59	6	1	0	4	0	0	9.2	13	8	6	2	0	11	1	5	1

Pitcher—Club	W.	L.	Pct.	ERA.	G.	GS.	CG.	GF.	ShO.	Sv.	IP.	H.	R.	ER.	HR.	HB.	BB.	Int. BB.	SO.	WP.
Girouard, Batavia	5	6	.455	2.69	19	10	6	7	1	1	100.1	107	40	30	6	3	33	1	69	5
Gogolewski, Oneonta	3	7	.300	6.63	15	14	0	0	0	0	73.1	81	73	54	6	3	51	0	62	15
Gomez, Geneva	3	3	.500	3.34	10	10	0	0	0	0	59.1	58	27	22	2	1	19	0	48	0
Griffin, Little Falls	3	3	.500	4.61	14	8	0	0	0	0	56.2	68	41	29	6	4	14	2	27	3
Griffith, Watertown	0	1	.000	7.71	1	0	0	1	0	0	2.1	5	4	2	0	0	0	1	1	1
Halama, Erie	1	1	.500	5.24	11	2	0	2	0	0	22.1	34	19	13	3	2	11	1	18	1
Halle, Batavia*	0	7	.000	4.91	17	9	2	3	0	0	66.0	75	53	36	6	2	33	2	63	4
Harris, Elmira	2	3	.400	5.01	9	8	1	0	1	0	46.2	50	29	26	3	6	22	0	25	3
Hartgraves, Auburn*	0	5	.000	3.98	23	0	0	12	0	2	31.2	31	24	14	1	1	27	4	42	1
Harvick, Erie*	5	6	.455	4.83	15	14	0	0	0	0	63.1	81	47	34	8	4	20	0	36	3
Hawkins, Auburn*	0	1	.000	9.00	3	2	0	1	0	0	8.0	13	11	8	1	0	8	0	4	1
Hennis, Auburn	3	9	.250	4.58	13	12	3	0	0	0	72.2	67	41	37	2	2	33	3	40	6
J. Hernandez, Erie	5	4	.556	2.81	16	16	1	0	0	0	99.1	87	36	31	7	2	41	3	62	7
X. Hernandez, St. Catharines	3	3	.500	5.07	13	11	0	0	0	0	55.0	57	39	31	4	4	16	0	49	2
Hillman, Little Falls*	6	4	.600	4.22	13	13	2	0	1	0	79.0	84	44	37	4	3	30	2	80	8
Hinkle, Erie	5	4	.556	2.34	12	10	2	1	2	1	69.1	64	23	18	4	0	16	4	53	1
Houser, Erie	3	3	.500	3.78	13	11	0	0	0	0	64.1	64	32	27	7	0	33	0	53	1
Hurta, Utica*	0	4	.000	5.70	21	1	0	7	0	0	36.1	44	32	23	3	1	20	0	40	3
Imes, Oneonta	4	0	1.000	0.33	4	4	1	0	1	0	27.2	16	1	1	0	0	5	0	10	0
G. Johnson, Auburn	6	2	.750	3.88	24	0	0	12	0	2	51.0	49	27	22	3	1	24	2	55	6
L. Johnson, Batavia	1	7	.125	4.67	13	12	1	0	0	0	69.1	58	47	36	3	4	41	0	38	6
Jongewaard, Erie	2	2	.500	3.38	20	2	0	8	0	1	45.1	36	23	17	2	0	23	1	47	2
Jundy, Little Falls	3	4	.429	3.98	10	9	1	0	0	0	54.1	59	28	24	3	1	14	0	45	1
Kerrigan, Jamestown	1	0	1.000	2.45	21	0	0	12	0	3	40.1	40	16	11	1	3	7	0	34	3
Koller, Watertown	3	2	.600	3.57	23	3	0	5	0	1	58.0	55	26	23	6	0	23	2	33	0
Lariviere, St. Catharines	0	0	.000	9.00	2	0	0	1	0	0	5.0	6	5	5	1	1	3	0	5	0
LaRosa, Utica*	3	5	.375	4.46	15	12	1	1	0	1	74.2	75	42	37	8	2	29	2	54	3
LaRose, Little Falls	3	4	.429	2.98	26	2	0	22	0	8	51.1	38	21	17	4	5	19	2	51	3
Leon, Jamestown	0	0	.000	16.20	3	0	0	1	0	0	1.2	4	3	3	0	2	1	0	3	0
C. Lopez, Newark	5	4	.556	2.33	11	11	3	0	1	0	65.2	52	21	17	4	3	24	1	54	2
M. Lopez, Utica	0	1	.000	9.82	5	0	0	1	0	0	7.1	7	8	8	1	2	11	0	5	2
Ludwig, Newark	0	0	.000	0.00	1	0	0	1	0	0	3.0	2	0	0	0	0	1	0	1	1
Macavage, Watertown	1	3	.250	2.59	8	3	0	2	0	0	24.1	18	10	7	1	2	13	0	20	3
MacDonald, St. Catharines*	0	0	.000	4.50	1	1	0	0	0	0	4.0	8	4	2	0	0	4	0	4	0
Main, Geneva	1	1	.500	6.84	12	3	0	5	0	1	25.0	34	22	19	2	2	15	2	24	2
Makemson, Oneonta	2	1	.667	3.49	10	3	0	2	0	2	28.1	24	15	11	1	4	18	0	15	5
Marchok, Jamestown*	2	3	.400	2.42	18	5	1	5	1	2	48.1	43	26	13	1	2	17	1	47	6
Marris, Oneonta	2	1	.667	3.79	20	0	0	10	0	4	38.0	25	20	16	1	2	29	0	40	3
Marte, Erie	0	1	.000	4.91	21	1	0	11	0	1	33.0	30	23	18	5	3	15	0	29	4
Martel, Oneonta*	1	0	1.000	3.00	2	0	0	1	0	0	3.0	2	1	1	0	0	3	0	2	1
Martin, Jamestown	0	0	.000	8.71	7	0	0	4	0	0	10.1	17	12	10	2	4	4	0	6	2
Massicotte, Geneva	4	0	1.000	2.23	35	0	0	28	0	15	44.1	29	14	11	4	2	31	2	58	4
McAnarney, Little Falls	5	4	.556	3.96	17	11	1	2	1	1	75.0	80	37	33	3	1	39	1	41	13
McCarthy, Utica*	4	1	.800	0.91	20	0	0	13	0	3	29.2	14	9	3	0	2	23	2	40	1
McClure, Auburn	1	0	1.000	0.90	21	0	0	17	0	12	30.0	16	4	3	1	1	14	1	42	0
McCollum, Elmira	2	3	.400	4.71	22	5	0	13	0	5	57.1	55	35	30	3	6	30	3	45	2
McDonald, Utica	1	4	.200	3.42	29	0	0	12	0	2	52.2	53	27	20	6	4	18	2	54	3
Meamber, Erie	0	5	.000	5.40	20	3	0	5	0	1	45.0	56	34	27	6	2	6	1	40	6
Melvin, Geneva	8	5	.615	3.48	15	15	2	0	0	0	85.1	58	39	33	4	4	50	0	81	6
Michael, Elmira	3	9	.250	4.10	16	16	5	0	0	0	105.1	106	65	48	5	9	32	0	96	7
Michno, Newark	3	1	.750	3.08	25	0	0	13	0	3	38.0	32	22	13	3	0	25	1	36	4
Miller, Little Falls	2	5	.286	4.01	13	13	0	0	0	0	76.1	87	40	34	5	3	12	0	44	8
Morrison, Oneonta*	4	6	.400	3.57	15	15	0	0	0	0	85.2	60	45	34	2	4	57	0	79	4
Mosley, Elmira*	3	2	.600	3.44	17	1	0	9	0	0	49.2	41	20	19	4	3	32	1	38	5
Mullino, Geneva	3	1	.750	1.78	26	1	0	17	0	6	50.2	40	11	10	1	1	13	2	49	0
Murphy, Watertown	9	3	.750	3.54	14	12	3	1	2	0	89.0	76	42	35	6	2	27	1	57	3
Newman, Auburn*	3	3	.500	2.67	17	13	0	1	0	0	77.2	47	35	23	4	3	45	2	70	12
Newton, Little Falls	3	0	1.000	2.20	25	0	0	17	0	7	41.0	18	12	10	4	1	15	2	46	5
North, Geneva*	5	4	.556	4.20	15	13	0	1	0	0	79.1	70	39	37	9	2	23	0	62	2
Osuna, Auburn*	1	0	1.000	5.74	8	0	0	3	0	0	15.2	16	16	10	1	0	14	2	20	0
Pacholec, Watertown	7	4	.636	3.76	15	15	0	0	0	0	79.0	82	46	33	3	1	45	0	80	9
Peek, Utica	1	1	.500	1.40	4	4	0	0	0	0	25.2	20	4	4	0	0	7	0	13	2
Pemberton, Elmira	0	0	.000	9.22	10	0	0	8	0	0	13.2	12	16	14	1	3	21	0	12	3
Pinder, Newark*	0	0	.000	3.38	9	1	0	4	0	0	13.1	17	5	5	0	1	7	0	17	1
Pollack, Jamestown*	6	4	.600	2.07	14	14	2	0	1	0	87.0	80	37	20	2	1	31	0	108	1
Polverini, Auburn	3	1	.750	3.80	21	0	0	13	0	0	45.0	47	25	19	2	2	20	1	44	1
Popplewell, Oneonta	4	6	.400	5.10	16	9	0	5	0	1	65.1	79	53	37	3	2	38	2	54	4
Radcliffe, Erie	0	0	.000	0.00	1	0	0	0	0	0	1.0	6	5	0	2	0	0	0	1	0
Rambo, Utica*	4	4	.500	3.74	13	13	4	0	0	0	74.2	79	41	31	3	3	36	2	52	3
Ramirez, Jamestown	0	0	.000	4.50	1	1	0	0	0	0	4.0	5	4	2	0	0	4	0	2	1
Ramos, Batavia*	4	0	1.000	2.95	19	2	2	7	1	2	58.0	49	23	19	2	1	25	0	50	6
Richardson, Elmira	5	8	.385	3.66	17	15	4	1	0	0	98.1	94	54	40	5	5	33	0	61	5
Richey, St. Catharines	0	1	.000	4.76	6	0	0	4	0	0	11.1	10	7	6	1	0	10	3	8	0
Robinson, Geneva	5	4	.556	2.40	18	14	3	3	1	1	97.2	71	32	26	3	3	29	2	76	0
Rodriguez, Geneva*	2	3	.400	4.68	24	2	1	4	0	1	42.1	43	27	22	7	2	18	0	40	1
Rogers, St. Catharines	2	4	.333	3.36	13	12	0	0	0	0	56.1	46	33	21	4	4	24	0	60	5
Romero, Elmira	2	2	.500	6.96	19	0	0	11	0	1	32.1	40	29	25	1	2	26	0	14	4
Romo, Auburn	2	1	.667	4.08	17	3	1	5	1	0	39.2	37	27	18	3	2	25	4	51	12
Rosario, Geneva*	0	0	.000	6.75	2	0	0	1	0	0	4.0	3	3	3	1	1	2	0	4	1
Rose, Batavia	2	3	.400	4.14	9	7	0	2	0	0	45.2	44	29	21	4	1	22	2	32	2
Royalty, Auburn	10	4	.714	2.65	16	15	4	0	0	0	112.0	91	42	33	7	2	16	0	82	5
Runge, Watertown	2	2	.500	5.00	10	8	0	1	0	0	45.0	46	30	25	2	2	19	0	35	7
Russo, Erie	1	5	.167	3.62	36	0	0	24	0	9	37.1	30	24	15	2	1	26	3	34	4
A. Sanchez, St. Catharines	8	3	.727	2.64	17	17	0	0	0	0	95.1	72	33	28	3	5	38	0	116	6
G. Sanchez, Newark	0	1	.000	8.22	5	2	0	0	0	0	7.2	10	7	7	0	0	5	0	4	0
Sander, Newark	9	4	.692	3.40	15	14	5	1	1	0	95.1	82	42	36	9	6	20	0	76	3
Santana, Batavia	0	4	.000	8.10	9	4	0	3	0	0	26.2	33	30	24	3	3	22	0	37	2
Sepela, Elmira	3	8	.273	7.09	15	11	0	1	0	0	59.2	91	70	47	5	1	23	0	24	6
Shepherd, Watertown	5	2	.714	4.20	17	13	1	0	1	0	70.2	66	40	33	0	5	42	0	57	4
Shiflett, Jamestown	9	3	.750	3.84	14	14	4	0	1	0	89.0	75	41	38	8	4	30	0	86	2
Silverstein, St. Catharines	3	3	.500	1.94	22	2	0	11	0	4	60.1	37	21	13	6	0	23	2	81	3
Simon, Auburn	8	2	.800	2.59	16	16	1	0	1	0	107.2	104	41	31	4	1	43	1	80	5

Pitcher—Club	W.	L.	Pct.	ERA.	G.	GS.	CG.	GF.	ShO.	Sv.	IP.	H.	R.	ER.	HR.	HB.	BB.	Int. BB.	SO.	WP.
J. Smith, Little Falls	1	1	.500	8.04	13	1	0	3	0	0	15.2	17	15	14	2	2	6	0	11	0
W. Smith, Watertown	2	0	1.000	4.43	5	4	0	1	0	1	20.1	15	13	10	1	3	10	0	24	1
Sonneberger, Newark	6	5	.545	4.67	13	13	3	0	0	0	86.2	90	50	45	7	2	21	0	66	7
Tejada, Elmira	0	2	.000	5.64	17	0	0	5	0	0	44.2	57	52	28	4	2	32	0	14	4
Telford, Newark	1	0	1.000	1.02	6	2	0	3	0	0	17.2	16	2	2	0	0	3	0	27	0
Thomas, Utica	6	0	1.000	1.89	19	6	0	7	0	2	76.0	67	23	16	1	0	18	3	62	3
Torborg, Watertown*	5	3	.625	3.14	16	12	0	1	0	1	83.0	72	35	29	2	2	38	0	86	3
Towey, St. Catharines	4	2	.667	5.63	16	4	0	1	0	0	38.1	26	26	24	3	7	53	0	42	5
Trahey, St. Catharines	0	1	.000	23.82	6	1	0	2	0	0	5.2	11	16	15	2	1	14	0	5	0
Trautwein, Little Falls	3	2	.600	3.60	25	0	0	9	0	0	40.0	46	23	16	1	1	16	1	37	3
Trlicek, Utica	2	5	.286	4.10	10	8	1	0	1	0	37.1	43	28	17	2	1	31	2	22	5
Viggiano, Utica	0	0	.000	3.86	2	0	0	1	0	0	2.1	1	2	1	0	1	4	0	1	1
Vizcaino, Watertown	0	0	.000	6.75	2	0	0	1	0	0	1.1	0	2	1	0	0	4	1	2	0
Voeltz, Oneonta*	6	3	.667	3.70	17	8	0	5	0	0	58.1	62	26	24	4	2	18	1	44	5
Wallen, Little Falls	3	4	.429	3.43	21	0	0	13	0	1	39.1	31	20	15	3	2	18	3	38	3
Wapnick, St. Catharines	3	4	.429	3.02	20	6	0	4	0	1	65.2	53	28	22	5	2	21	0	63	3
Ward, Batavia	1	9	.100	3.91	20	6	3	12	0	2	69.0	67	35	30	6	3	20	3	56	3
Warfel, Elmira	0	0	.000	5.40	2	0	0	1	0	0	5.0	6	3	3	0	0	1	0	5	0
Watts, St. Catharines	4	5	.444	2.39	28	0	0	25	0	8	52.2	41	18	14	2	4	10	5	37	2
Webb, Watertown	2	5	.286	2.50	23	0	0	15	0	7	39.2	32	16	11	1	3	16	2	42	5
Whiting, Elmira	0	0	.000	0.00	1	0	0	1	0	0	2.1	0	0	0	0	0	2	0	0	0
Williams, Newark	6	5	.545	3.60	14	14	3	0	0	0	95.0	83	50	38	5	3	32	2	75	8
Wilson, Newark	8	4	.667	3.09	13	13	2	0	1	0	81.2	61	35	28	6	3	25	2	69	2
Winzenread, Newark	2	3	.400	3.79	20	1	0	9	0	1	35.2	42	21	15	2	1	19	1	40	3
Wishnevski, St. Catharines	7	2	.778	1.53	16	15	1	0	0	0	88.0	58	18	15	2	6	39	1	71	6
Woide, St. Catharines*	3	3	.500	2.10	24	0	0	19	0	9	55.2	38	19	13	3	0	14	2	54	2
Young, Little Falls	3	4	.429	4.53	14	9	0	0	0	0	53.2	58	37	27	6	1	25	1	48	4

BALKS—Marte, Ward, 3 each; Cavalier, Estrada, Farmer, Halle, Houser, L. Johnson, McCarthy, Morrison, Mullino, Osuna, Pacholec, Silverstein, Sonneberger, 2 each; Acosta, H. Allen, Ayers, Bross, Butler, Caballero, A. Carter, Chadwick, Daniels, Dell'Amico, Disabato, Fox, Gargin, Girouard, Gomez, Griffith, Hennis, J. Hernandez, Hillman, Hinkle, LaRose, C. Lopez, Marchok, McDonald, Michael, Mosley, Newman, Rambo, Ramos, Robinson, Rose, Royalty, Sander, Santana, Shepherd, Shiflett, Thomas, Torborg, Trlicek, Wapnick, 1 each.

COMBINATION SHUTOUTS—Royalty-McClure, Allen-Romo, Newman-McClure, Auburn; Harris-Banasiak, Elmira; Hernandez-Hinkle, Erie; Caballero-Rodriguez-Massicotte, Melvin-Mullino, Robinson-Aspray, Aspray-Massicotte-Mullino, Geneva; Pollack-Carter, Bergeron-Kerrigan, Jamestown; Hillman-LaRose, Young-Newton, Little Falls; Sander-Evans, Newark; Foster-Marris-Byrnes-Chapin, Imes-Chapin, Dacosta-Popplewell, Eiland-Byrnes, Gogolewski-Foster-Chapin, Voeltz-Marris-Chapin, Foster-Marris, Popplewell-Marris, Voeltz-Chapin, Oneonta; Sanchez-Watts 2, Wishnevski-Silverstein 2, Wapnick-Silverstein, Wishnevski-Butler, Sanchez-Wapnick-Watts, Butler-Wapnick, Sanchez-Woide, Rogers-Woide, Wishnevski-Woide, St. Catharines; Thomas-LaRosa-Hurta, Utica; Boyd-Murphy-Webb, Pacholec-Castner-Koller, Torborg-Webb, Watertown.

NO-HIT GAMES—None.

Northwest League

CLASS A

CHAMPIONSHIP WINNERS IN PREVIOUS YEARS

1901—Portland	.675	
1902—Butte	.608	
1903—Butte	.578	
1904—Boise	.625	
1905—Vancouver	.586	
Everett°	.667	
1906—Tacoma	.600	
1907—Aberdeen	.625	
1908—Vancouver	.578	
1909—Seattle	.653	
1910—Spokane	.596	
1911—Vancouver	.628	
1912—Seattle	.600	
1913—Vancouver	.600	
1914—Vancouver	.632	
1915—Seattle	.564	
1916—Spokane	.622	
1917—Great Falls	.592	
1918—Seattle	.588	
1919—Seattle	.590	
1920—Victoria	.600	
1921—Yakima	.710	
Yakima	.660	
1922—Calgary†	.600	
1923-36—Did not operate.		
1937—Wenatchee	.603	
Tacoma°	.627	
1938—Yakima	.583	
Bellingham (2nd)†	.511	
1939—Wenatchee	.601	
Tacoma (2nd)†	.533	
1940—Spokane	.587	
Tacoma (4th)†	.500	
1941—Spokane	.669	
1942—Vancouver	.594	
1943-45—Did not operate.		

1946—Wenatchee	.622	
1947—Vancouver	.566	
1948—Spokane	.614	
1949—Yakima	.660	
Vancouver (2nd)†	.615	
1950—Yakima	.613	
1951—Spokane	.655	
1952—Victoria	.631	
1953—Salem	.635	
Spokane°	.590	
1954—Vancouver°	.636	
Lewiston	.629	
1955—Salem	.646	
Eugene°	.639	
1956—Yakima	.691	
Yakima	.619	
1957—Eugene°	.576	
Wenatchee°	.647	
1958—Lewiston	.621	
Yakima°	.594	
1959—Salem	.623	
Yakima°	.563	
1960—Yakima	.638	
Yakima	.562	
1961—Lewiston°	.621	
Yakima	.600	
1962—Wenatchee°	.574	
Tri-City	.580	
1963—Lewiston	.594	
Yakima°	.613	
1964—Eugene	.636	
Yakima°	.611	
1965—Lewiston	.667	
Tri-City°	.681	
1966—Tri-City	.679	
1967—Medford	.607	

1968—Tri-City	.600	
1969—Rogue Valley	.633	
1970—Lewiston a	.538	
Coos Bay-No. Bend	.563	
1971—Tri-City a	.625	
Bend	.538	
1972—Lewiston a	.675	
Walla Walla	.513	
1973—Walla Walla b	.638	
Portland	.563	
1974—Bellingham	.619	
Eugene c	.571	
1975—Portland	.545	
Eugene d	.684	
1976—Portland	.556	
Walla Walla d	.639	
1977—Bellingham e	.618	
Portland	.667	
1978—Grays Harbor f	.671	
Eugene	.514	
1979—Central Oregon d	.606	
Walla Walla	.571	
1980—Bellingham g	.643	
Eugene g	.529	
1981—Medford d	.600	
Bellingham	.557	
1982—Medford d	.757	
Salem d	.486	
1983—Medford h	.735	
Bellingham	.588	
1984—Tri-Cities h	.622	
Medford	.608	
1985—Everett h	.541	
Eugene	.541	
1986—Bellingham h	.608	
Eugene	.608	

°Won split-season playoff. †Won four-club playoff. §League disbanded June 18. aLeague divided into Northern and Southern divisions, declared champion under league rules. bLeague divided into Eastern and Western divisions, declared champion under league rules. cLeague divided into Eastern and Western divisions; won two-team playoff. dLeague divided into Northern and Southern divisions; won two-team playoff. eLeague divided into Affiliate and Independent divisions; won two-team playoff. fDeclared league champion after winning one-game playoff. Balance of playoff canceled due to rain and wet grounds. gDeclared co-champion after winning one game. Balance of playoff canceled due to rain and wet grounds. hLeague divided into Washington and Oregon divisions; won two-team playoff. (NOTE—Known as Pacific Northwest League 1901-02, Pacific National League 1903-04, Northwestern League 1905-18, Pacific Coast International League 1919-22 and Western International League 1937-54.)

STANDING OF CLUBS AT CLOSE OF SEASON, SEPTEMBER 1

EASTERN DIVISION

Club	Spo.	Bend	Med.	Boi.	Ev.	Eug.	Sal.	Bell.	W.	L.	T.	Pct.	G.B.
Spokane (Padres)	....	11	11	11	6	6	3	6	54	22	0	.711	....
Bend (Co-op)	4	....	8	10	1	3	4	3	33	42	0	.440	20½
Medford (A's)	5	9	....	6	1	1	5	4	31	45	0	.408	23
Boise (Independent)	5	6	9	....	2	2	0	2	26	50	0	.342	28

WESTERN DIVISION

Club	Spo.	Bend	Med.	Boi.	Ev.	Eug.	Sal.	Bell.	W.	L.	T.	Pct.	G.B.
Everett (Giants)	1	6	6	6	....	9	11	10	49	26	0	.653	....
Eugene (Royals)	2	3	5	5	6	....	13	11	45	30	0	.600	4
Salem (Angels)	4	3	3	6	4	4	....	10	34	41	0	.453	15
Bellingham (Mariners)	1	4	3	6	6	5	5	....	30	46	0	.395	19½

Major league affiliations in parentheses.

Playoff—Spokane defeated Everett, two games to one, to win league championship.

Regular-Season Attendance—Bellingham, 22,183; Bend, 36,131; Boise, 71,344; Eugene, 132,819; Everett, 58,823; Medford, 72,729; Salem, 34,181; Spokane, 113,865. Total, 542,075. Playoffs, 7,560.

Managers—Bellingham, Rick Sweet; Bend, Melvin Roberts; Boise, Derrel Thomas (June 16 through July 25) and Mal Fichman (July 26 through end of season); Eugene, Rick Mathews; Everett, Joe Strain; Medford, Dave Hudgens; Salem, Chris Smith; Spokane, Rob Picciolo.

All-Star Team—1B—Steve Hendricks, Spokane; 2B—Paul Faries, Spokane; 3B—Mark Owens, Everett; SS—Jose Valentin, Spokane; OF—Ken Griffey, Bellingham; Bob Moore, Eugene; Jeff Mace, Boise; C—Andy Skeels, Spokane; DH—Jorge Pedre, Eugene; RHP—Mike Erb, Salem; LHP—Jim Campbell, Eugene; Most Valuable Player—Steve Hendricks, Spokane; Manager of the Year—Rob Picciolo, Spokane.

(Compiled by William J. Weiss, League Statistician, San Mateo, Calif.)

CLUB BATTING

Club	Pct.	G.	AB.	R.	OR.	H.	TB.	2B.	3B.	HR.	RBI.	GW.	SH.	SF.	HP.	BB.	Int. BB.	SO.	SB.	CS.	LOB.
Spokane	.281	76	2651	473	317	744	1022	130	29	30	405	43	33	34	45	370	17	516	103	37	669
Boise	.263	76	2571	420	542	677	914	111	12	34	361	25	44	33	21	377	11	490	54	27	623
Eugene	.258	75	2602	439	342	672	931	113	16	38	369	38	19	22	47	353	7	570	101	32	599
Everett	.258	75	2617	430	311	675	961	107	10	53	371	44	11	16	38	348	8	528	68	17	619
Bend	.255	75	2591	372	432	661	914	115	12	38	318	26	23	22	38	267	15	563	93	32	581
Salem	.246	75	2509	372	383	618	858	119	17	29	309	26	27	27	43	326	16	562	134	46	564
Medford	.244	76	2550	376	499	621	848	109	17	28	308	27	19	27	28	372	4	658	76	35	616
Bellingham	.232	76	2578	392	448	599	879	86	13	56	337	27	15	22	23	377	10	626	101	42	594

INDIVIDUAL BATTING
(Leading Qualifiers for Batting Championship—205 or More Plate Appearances)

°Bats lefthanded.   †Switch-hitter.

Player and Club	Pct.	G.	AB.	R.	H.	TB.	2B.	3B.	HR.	RBI.	GW.	SH.	SF.	HP.	BB.	Int. BB.	SO.	SB.	CS.
Moore, Robert, Eugene	.374	57	235	40	88	112	13	4	1	25	2	2	1	1	14	2	22	23	1
Owens, Mark, Everett°	.357	65	227	55	81	145	14	1	16	54	9	0	2	3	52	4	54	0	1
Hendricks, Steven, Spokane	.356	75	303	52	108	170	25	5	9	75	6	0	3	2	36	0	38	4	4
Mace, Jeffrey, Boise	.340	75	285	57	97	143	11	1	11	56	4	2	6	0	47	3	43	5	1
Maasberg, Gary, Bend	.328	71	262	44	86	136	15	1	11	45	5	2	2	4	35	4	44	6	4
Griffey, Kenneth, Bellingham	.313	54	182	43	57	110	9	1	14	40	4	1	1	0	44	3	42	13	6
Hollins, David, Spokane†	.309	75	278	52	86	114	14	4	2	44	6	3	4	2	53	7	36	20	5
Faries, Paul, Spokane	.307	74	280	67	86	101	9	3	0	27	0	4	5	5	36	0	25	30	9
Cole, Stewart, Eugene	.305	63	243	42	74	102	17	1	3	51	5	3	4	1	34	1	45	3	1
Aldrete, Richard, Everett°	.300	59	220	36	66	82	13	0	1	29	4	1	1	0	29	1	29	0	1

Departmental Leaders: G—Maloney, 76; AB—Hendricks, 303; R—Faries, 67; H—Hendricks, 108; TB—Hendricks, 170; 2B—Hendricks, 25; 3B—Hillemann, 6, HR—Owens, 16; RBI—Hendricks, 75; GWRBI—Skeels, 11; SH—R. Farmer, 9; SF—Brosius, 7; HP—Hillemann, 16; BB—Skeels, 58; IBB—Hollins, 7; SO—R. Farmer, 85; SB—Faries, 30; CS—Amaro, 11.

(All Players—Listed Alphabetically)

Player and Club	Pct.	G.	AB.	R.	H.	TB.	2B.	3B.	HR.	RBI.	GW.	SH.	SF.	HP.	BB.	Int. BB.	SO.	SB.	CS.
Able, Wayne, Boise	.224	19	58	5	13	14	1	0	0	6	1	2	1	1	10	0	24	2	1
Abraham, Glenn, Everett†	.175	13	40	3	7	9	0	1	0	2	0	1	0	1	2	0	10	4	3
Abshier, Lanny, Salem°	.214	11	14	6	3	4	1	0	0	2	0	1	0	2	0	0	5	3	2
Alborano, Peter, Eugene°	.294	30	85	17	25	31	1	1	1	21	1	1	2	2	22	2	17	1	1
Aldrete, Richard, Everett°	.300	59	220	36	66	82	13	0	1	29	4	1	1	0	29	1	29	0	1
Amaro, Ruben, Salem†	.282	71	241	51	68	90	7	3	3	31	3	3	6	7	49	5	28	27	11
Angus, Robert, Boise°	.239	56	159	26	38	61	8	0	5	28	0	1	1	3	30	0	30	3	3
Aylward, James, Bend	.261	73	272	44	71	94	11	0	4	30	6	2	5	6	33	1	24	2	1
Azar, Todd, Bellingham	.265	44	166	23	44	55	2	3	1	23	3	0	3	1	20	2	15	2	1
Baca, Mark, Salem	.250	2	4	0	1	2	1	0	0	0	0	0	0	0	0	0	0	0	0
Bell, Robert, Boise	.231	41	104	13	24	31	2	1	1	10	1	0	1	1	10	0	25	6	1
Benoit, Dickens, Everett	.280	57	186	41	52	94	5	2	11	42	2	0	1	8	23	1	55	10	2
Berrios, Juan, Eugene	.200	13	40	8	8	10	2	0	0	5	0	0	0	8	0	18	0	1
Bock, Douglas, Eugene	.190	34	105	11	20	22	2	0	0	13	0	1	2	0	17	0	34	3	1
Bond, David, Spokane°	.000	10	2	0	0	0	0	0	0	0	0	0	0	0	0	0	2	0	0
Bowman, Tad, Boise	.256	18	39	3	10	13	1	1	0	9	0	1	0	0	1	0	8	1	0
Brito, Jorge, Medford	.182	40	110	7	20	24	1	0	1	15	2	1	2	1	12	0	54	0	0
Brooks, Monte, Spokane	.257	52	210	25	54	61	7	0	0	28	2	4	2	2	18	0	32	5	3
Brosius, Scott, Medford	.286	65	255	34	73	102	18	1	3	49	6	1	7	0	26	0	36	5	2
Buckels, Gary, Salem	.000	1	0	0	0	0	0	0	0	0	0	1	0	0	0	0	0	0	0
Burr, James, Boise°	.271	46	166	33	45	51	3	0	1	25	2	4	1	2	24	1	21	2	0
Burrus, Daryl, Bellingham°	.138	31	87	6	12	14	2	0	0	9	0	1	0	2	16	0	33	0	1
Carlisle, Dennis, Boise	.000	6	2	0	0	0	0	0	0	0	0	0	0	0	1	0	1	0	0
Carr, Charles, Bellingham	.242	44	165	31	40	46	1	1	1	11	0	3	0	1	12	0	38	20	1
Cash, Todd, Boise	.257	69	261	41	67	94	14	2	3	31	2	3	0	2	28	1	39	5	6
Cayson, Tony, Bellingham	.178	51	169	17	30	38	5	0	1	13	1	0	2	1	17	0	65	7	2
Ciprian, Francis, Medford	.133	26	75	6	10	13	3	0	0	6	2	1	0	0	16	0	22	0	1
Clements, Anthony, Eugene	.240	58	192	32	46	58	7	1	1	23	2	1	2	1	25	0	49	4	3
Cole, John, Boise	.247	25	73	4	18	20	2	0	0	10	0	3	2	1	13	0	10	1	3
Cole, Stewart, Eugene	.305	63	243	42	74	102	17	1	3	51	5	3	4	1	34	1	45	3	1
Coomer, Ronald, Medford	.345	45	168	23	58	75	10	2	1	26	3	0	1	0	19	0	22	1	1
Cooper, James, Everett†	.217	59	203	32	44	51	5	1	0	13	1	3	1	4	16	0	64	26	6
Daughtry, Dorian, Bellingham	.222	41	126	12	28	33	2	0	1	16	2	2	0	1	10	0	37	6	3
de Jesus, Carlos, Bend	.290	35	107	9	31	36	5	0	0	15	2	1	1	0	8	0	28	0	1
de la Rosa, Cesar, Bend	.233	68	232	22	54	71	9	1	2	29	2	4	1	1	6	0	65	4	1
Dewey, Mark, Everett	.200	19	5	0	1	1	0	0	0	0	0	0	0	0	0	0	3	0	0
Eldridge, Trevor, Medford†	.156	15	32	5	5	5	0	0	0	1	0	1	0	0	10	0	15	0	0
Enos, Eric, Bend	.249	65	217	30	54	83	14	0	5	35	2	0	3	27	6	39	0	1
Espinal, Josue, Medford	.196	43	158	30	31	38	3	2	0	13	1	6	1	4	15	0	35	8	5
Espinosa, Santiago, Salem	.038	17	26	4	1	1	0	0	0	0	0	0	0	0	6	0	10	1	0
Estrada, Jay, Spokane	.000	10	1	0	0	0	0	0	0	0	0	0	0	0	0	0	0	0	0
Fajardo, Victor, Spokane	.100	8	10	2	1	1	0	0	0	0	0	0	0	0	2	0	3	0	1
Faries, Paul, Spokane	.307	74	280	67	86	101	9	3	0	27	0	4	5	5	36	0	25	30	9
Farmer, Kevin, Spokane	.298	18	47	6	14	18	2	1	0	6	0	0	0	6	0	7	0	0
Farmer, Reginald, Spokane°	.253	69	241	49	61	78	4	5	1	24	3	9	4	0	36	2	85	12	6
Fellows, William, Boise	.300	5	10	3	3	3	0	0	0	2	0	1	0	1	0	0	4	0	1
Finley, David, Medford	.333	3	9	1	3	3	0	0	0	0	0	0	0	0	1	0	0	0	0
Flora, Kevin, Salem	.273	35	88	17	24	31	5	1	0	12	4	3	0	0	21	0	14	8	4
Foley, Martin, Bend	.265	73	291	29	77	103	10	2	4	31	2	1	2	7	8	0	62	9	4
Gainous, Russell, Eugene°	.288	56	208	39	60	72	8	2	0	22	3	1	0	7	34	0	32	18	5
Gallardo, Luis, Salem	.203	45	138	19	28	38	8	1	0	9	0	4	0	2	14	0	35	0	3
Gambee, Bradley, Everett	.333	7	3	0	1	1	0	0	0	0	0	0	0	0	0	0	1	0	0
Garner, Kevin, Spokane°	.274	36	106	19	29	53	7	1	5	25	3	0	3	1	16	1	28	0	0
Gay, Jeffery, Salem°	.500	2	4	0	2	2	0	0	0	1	0	0	0	0	0	0	1	0	0
Giles, Troy, Salem	.241	53	174	28	42	54	7	1	1	12	2	1	0	2	12	1	52	13	5
Gilmore, Terrance, Spokane	.500	14	4	1	2	3	1	0	0	1	0	0	0	2	0	2	0	0
Goins, Scott, Everett	.261	46	176	35	46	58	9	0	1	17	4	0	0	1	26	0	36	5	1
Gonzalez, Ruben, Bellingham	.304	40	125	24	38	69	10	0	7	29	2	0	4	0	17	0	12	2	0
Gorski, Gary, Medford	.150	15	20	1	3	3	0	0	0	0	0	0	0	1	4	0	4	0	0
Greene, Keith, Bend†	.269	54	234	36	63	76	9	2	0	25	3	3	3	5	8	1	41	27	8
Griffey, Kenneth, Bellingham°	.313	54	182	43	57	110	9	1	14	40	4	1	1	0	44	3	42	13	6
Grubb, Cary, Salem	.252	52	131	15	33	45	3	0	3	16	1	0	2	2	15	1	26	3	0
Gunderson, Eric, Everett	.000	15	3	0	0	0	0	0	0	0	0	1	0	0	0	0	2	0	0
Gust, Christopher, Medford°	.200	3	5	1	1	1	0	0	0	0	0	0	0	0	6	0	2	0	0
Ham, Michael, Everett	.248	39	129	13	32	39	4	0	1	21	2	0	1	0	12	0	24	0	1
Haney, Todd, Bellingham	.254	66	252	57	64	94	11	2	5	27	2	1	2	2	44	0	33	18	10
Hanker, Frederick, Medford	.277	41	148	20	41	57	10	0	2	21	1	0	3	1	20	0	20	2	3
Hawkins, Todd, Everett	.273	51	183	28	50	79	11	0	6	33	4	0	3	2	20	0	23	0	0
Hendricks, Steven, Spokane	.356	75	303	52	108	170	25	5	9	75	6	0	3	2	36	0	38	4	4
Heredia, Gilbert, Everett	.000	3	1	0	0	0	0	0	0	0	0	0	0	0	1	0	1	0	0
Hess, Mark, Boise	.000	1	2	0	0	0	0	0	0	0	0	0	0	0	0	0	1	0	0

Player and Club	Pct.	G.	AB.	R.	H.	TB.	2B.	3B.	HR.	RBI.	GW.	SH.	SF.	HP.	BB.	Int. BB.	SO.	SB.	CS.
Hillemann, Charles, Spokane	.285	65	242	54	69	93	9	6	1	30	4	4	2	16	21	0	59	17	0
Hisey, Steven, Bellingham	.271	22	70	12	19	33	5	0	3	17	2	0	1	0	19	0	10	1	1
Hoffinger, Glenn, Medford	.192	40	130	22	25	46	5	2	4	17	1	1	0	0	18	0	39	2	1
Hoffman, John, Bellingham	.124	37	89	10	11	11	0	0	0	4	0	0	0	0	17	1	14	0	1
Hollins, David, Spokane†	.309	75	278	52	86	114	14	4	2	44	6	3	4	2	53	7	36	20	5
Holmes, Carl, Spokane	.242	21	66	6	16	23	4	0	1	10	2	1	0	2	6	0	24	1	1
Holsman, Richard, Spokane°	1.000	34	1	0	1	1	0	0	0	0	0	0	0	0	0	0	0	0	0
Hooper, Jeffrey, Bellingham	.286	63	231	31	66	119	10	2	13	53	6	0	4	0	26	1	59	2	0
Houston, Ervin, Eugene	.186	32	86	14	16	17	1	0	0	7	1	1	0	2	14	0	17	5	2
Hupke, Douglas, Eugene†	.246	34	65	10	16	20	4	0	0	3	1	1	0	1	9	0	29	7	2
Jackson, Greg, Salem	.235	44	115	20	27	41	8	0	2	14	2	0	1	2	15	0	40	0	2
Jimenez, Geovanni, Medford	.159	24	69	15	11	24	2	1	3	8	2	0	0	2	15	2	35	2	0
Johnson, Ranfred, Bellingham	.000	13	2	0	0	0	0	0	0	0	0	0	0	0	0	0	1	0	0
Kemp, Joseph, Bellingham°	.300	23	80	11	24	40	4	3	2	14	0	1	1	2	12	2	19	4	2
Kleven, Mark, Spokane†	.125	14	16	1	2	3	1	0	0	0	0	0	0	0	3	0	7	0	1
Kocman, Chris, Everett	.284	41	148	26	42	70	7	0	7	27	3	0	0	3	20	1	27	2	0
Koehnke, Brandon, Boise	.239	28	67	16	16	17	1	0	0	8	2	2	0	1	18	0	11	0	1
Lee, Wiley, Salem°	.286	57	206	32	59	81	8	1	4	25	2	1	1	3	19	3	32	21	2
Leslie, Reginald, Spokane	.000	16	1	0	0	0	0	0	0	0	0	0	0	0	0	0	1	0	0
Lewis, Anthony, Spokane	.000	15	1	0	0	0	0	0	0	0	0	1	0	0	0	0	0	0	0
Lind, Randall, Everett	.227	46	128	24	29	49	5	0	5	24	4	0	0	2	21	0	45	5	1
List, Paul, Salem	.000	13	18	2	0	0	0	0	0	0	0	0	0	4	0	0	7	0	0
Lutticken, Robert, Spokane	.256	31	82	10	21	24	3	0	0	11	0	2	1	3	9	0	18	0	0
Maasberg, Gary, Bend	.328	71	262	44	86	136	15	1	11	45	5	2	2	4	35	4	44	6	4
Mace, Jeffrey, Boise	.340	75	285	57	97	143	11	1	11	56	4	2	6	0	47	3	43	5	1
Made, Carlo, Medford	.242	45	149	24	36	50	4	2	2	13	0	1	1	0	14	0	43	7	5
Malone, Jackson, Boise	.279	69	222	46	62	74	9	0	1	23	2	6	1	1	57	1	47	9	4
Maloney, Mark, Boise	.287	76	293	54	84	136	24	2	8	61	5	1	3	4	33	3	64	4	1
Martinez, Nicio, Bend†	.215	27	65	7	14	18	4	0	0	5	0	1	1	0	6	0	26	0	1
Martinez, Ramon, Salem	.189	44	106	8	20	21	1	0	0	13	0	1	1	0	10	0	23	1	0
Maxwell, Fernando, Boise	.000	32	0	0	0	0	0	0	0	0	0	0	0	0	1	0	0	0	0
McDonald, Steven, Boise	.232	66	207	30	48	58	8	1	0	21	2	4	5	2	18	1	32	0	2
Michalak, Anthony, Everett	.269	16	67	9	18	18	0	0	0	4	1	1	0	0	6	0	1	1	0
Molina, Mario, Salem°	.225	61	173	12	39	52	8	1	1	30	1	0	3	0	10	1	31	2	4
Montero, Jorge, Salem	.163	44	104	11	17	25	5	0	1	11	2	0	2	1	15	0	38	2	1
Moore, Robert, Eugene	.374	57	235	40	88	112	13	4	1	25	2	2	1	1	14	2	22	23	1
Morrison, Jeff, Bellingham	.185	38	119	7	22	29	4	0	1	15	0	0	1	1	11	0	30	2	0
Musolino, Michael, Salem°	.299	51	144	13	43	57	11	0	1	8	0	3	0	1	13	0	30	5	1
Myers, Michael, Spokane°	.333	20	3	0	1	2	1	0	0	0	0	0	1	0	0	0	1	0	0
Nina, Julio, Medford†	.207	33	111	9	23	35	4	1	2	9	1	0	1	1	16	0	36	4	1
Orton, John, Salem	.261	51	176	31	46	80	8	1	8	36	4	1	2	7	32	1	61	6	2
Owens, Mark, Everett°	.357	65	227	55	81	145	14	1	16	54	9	0	2	3	52	4	54	0	1
Papajohn, Michael, Boise	.200	25	50	10	10	13	1	1	0	1	0	3	0	1	13	0	13	1	1
Parry, Robert, Medford	.265	66	249	43	66	94	15	2	3	36	3	3	4	1	32	1	44	6	4
Patrick, Otis, Bellingham	.180	40	122	22	22	24	2	0	0	7	1	0	0	3	20	0	42	6	2
Paul, Corey, Bellingham°	.137	33	95	9	13	14	1	0	0	7	2	0	0	1	18	1	51	1	2
Pedre, Jorge, Eugene	.270	64	233	28	63	117	15	0	13	66	6	0	1	12	16	2	48	2	1
Perno, Donn, Everett°	.210	27	67	5	14	18	4	0	0	19	3	0	0	0	15	0	15	1	0
Peters, Reed, Salem	.265	71	234	47	62	92	17	2	3	25	1	5	0	2	55	0	25	22	6
Phillips, Lamont, Eugene	.246	50	138	27	34	65	5	1	8	29	1	1	2	4	43	0	28	3	2
Phillips, Lonnie, Everett	.317	27	41	9	13	24	3	1	2	8	0	0	0	0	13	0	7	0	0
Piazza, Anthony, Everett	.204	19	54	6	11	15	4	0	0	8	2	0	0	0	2	0	12	0	0
Pickett, Antoine, Eugene†	.190	34	100	27	19	24	3	1	0	8	0	1	0	2	19	0	23	7	2
Pierce, Benjamin, Eugene†	.000	14	1	0	0	0	0	0	0	0	0	0	0	0	0	0	0	0	0
Poche, Harold, Medford	.209	26	86	10	18	22	4	0	0	10	1	0	1	0	18	0	40	4	1
Ramirez, Fausto, Bellingham†	.157	49	172	12	27	31	4	0	0	12	1	2	0	2	13	0	37	6	6
Rasmus, Anthony, Salem	.300	49	120	20	36	49	5	4	0	19	0	3	1	3	7	0	27	10	2
Reichardt, Kevin, Bellingham	.284	64	222	56	63	99	13	1	7	30	1	0	1	5	51	0	63	11	4
Reichle, Darrin, Spokane†	.000	11	4	0	0	0	0	0	0	0	0	0	0	0	0	0	0	0	0
Reyna, Dionisio, Medford†	.282	48	142	22	40	68	10	0	6	24	1	0	0	4	29	1	33	3	2
Robinson, Darryl, Eugene	.246	55	199	30	49	65	7	0	3	27	5	2	2	2	17	0	37	1	0
Robinson, Marteese, Medford	.292	6	24	4	7	8	1	0	0	3	1	0	0	0	3	0	5	2	0
Robinson, William, Salem	.122	25	49	8	6	6	0	0	0	2	0	1	0	5	3	0	18	2	0
Rodriguez, Edgar, Salem°	.250	67	244	28	61	87	16	2	2	43	4	1	6	6	24	4	59	8	3
Rohn, Andrew, Everett	.233	43	146	25	34	40	6	0	0	14	0	1	2	5	25	0	15	4	1
Ryser, Michael, Medford°	.255	31	98	9	25	28	3	0	0	6	0	0	0	4	14	0	32	0	0
Sanchez, Osvaldo, Spokane°	.223	44	130	12	29	47	7	1	3	24	2	0	4	4	16	0	33	3	1
Sherman, James, Boise	.186	13	43	7	8	16	5	0	1	4	0	0	0	1	6	0	17	0	0
Shibata, Keith, Eugene°	1.000	22	1	0	1	1	0	0	0	0	0	0	0	0	0	0	0	0	0
Sholl, Derek, Eugene	.165	36	115	12	19	20	1	0	0	4	0	0	2	2	9	0	32	1	0
Shultis, Christopher, Boise°	.293	67	229	30	67	92	12	2	3	38	2	2	4	2	32	1	44	4	2
Shumpert, Terrance, Eugene	.290	48	186	38	54	84	16	1	4	22	3	0	2	3	27	0	41	16	4
Silva, Ryan, Everett	.200	20	65	8	13	18	0	1	1	7	1	0	1	2	6	0	17	0	0
Sims, Kinney, Bend°	.239	50	176	38	42	54	7	1	1	16	0	2	3	3	28	0	46	26	5
Sisco, Michael, Bellingham	.183	35	104	9	19	20	1	0	0	10	0	3	2	1	10	0	25	0	0
Skeels, Andrew, Spokane°	.289	72	270	48	78	118	23	1	5	64	11	0	5	5	58	5	46	1	1
Smith, Dwayne, Bend°	.233	38	120	16	28	36	3	1	1	5	0	2	0	1	5	2	31	5	0
Smith, Joel, Medford	.230	40	139	26	32	36	4	0	0	10	0	0	1	7	10	0	38	10	2
Smith, Roger, Boise°	.258	48	178	28	46	51	5	0	0	16	1	4	3	1	20	0	23	9	0
Soltero, Saul, Spokane	.000	28	2	0	0	0	0	0	0	0	0	0	0	0	0	0	1	0	0
Southland, Kip, Everett	.223	63	260	42	58	73	11	2	0	25	2	2	1	2	21	0	51	1	0
Stoerck, Scott, Bellingham	.000	26	0	0	0	0	0	0	0	0	0	0	0	1	0	0	0	0	0
Stone, David, Bend	.162	29	74	14	12	26	3	1	3	11	1	0	1	2	13	0	33	1	0
Thagard, Neil, Boise†	.113	29	71	7	8	10	2	0	0	5	0	4	3	0	8	0	21	0	0
Tinsley, Lee, Medford†	.174	45	132	22	23	30	3	2	0	13	0	1	4	2	35	0	57	9	3
Torchia, Todd, Spokane	.232	40	99	17	23	31	5	0	1	10	1	1	1	2	15	0	30	2	0
Trevino, Antonio, Bend	.229	73	275	43	63	97	15	2	5	38	1	3	2	4	39	1	62	11	3
Valentin, Jose, Spokane†	.250	70	244	52	61	79	8	2	2	24	3	0	3	1	35	2	38	8	5
Verstandig, Mark, 42 B'd-3 Spo.°	.296	45	125	19	37	45	8	0	0	19	1	1	0	2	35	0	19	0	1
Walker, Matthew, Everett	.217	42	120	22	26	32	1	1	1	7	1	0	1	2	15	0	32	0	0
Watkins, Darren, Eugene	.184	40	136	25	25	29	2	1	0	11	1	1	0	4	16	0	48	5	2
Watkins, Keith, Medford	.333	3	9	1	3	3	0	0	0	1	0	0	0	0	3	0	0	0	0

Player and Club	Pct.	G.	AB.	R.	H.	TB.	2B.	3B.	HR.	RBI.	GW.	SH.	SF.	HP.	BB.	Int. BB.	SO.	SB.	CS.
Willes, David, Bend	.233	23	90	14	21	27	1	1	1	12	1	1	1	0	13	0	8	2	2
Williams, Quinn, Boise	.232	20	56	7	13	17	2	1	0	6	1	1	2	0	6	0	12	2	0
Williams, Rodney, Medford	.176	26	74	7	13	14	1	0	0	7	1	1	0	1	16	0	27	2	1
Willson, Robert, Everett*	.255	48	145	11	37	45	5	0	1	17	1	1	2	3	23	1	13	1	0
Wilson, David, Medford	.342	40	158	34	54	69	8	2	1	20	1	2	1	3	20	0	19	9	3
Wright, Donald, Eugene	.235	63	234	39	55	82	9	3	4	32	7	3	2	3	29	0	50	2	4
Zerb, Troy, Bend	.169	18	59	7	10	14	1	0	1	4	0	0	0	0	5	0	35	0	0

The following pitchers, listed alphabetically by club, with games in parentheses, had no plate appearances, primarily through use of designated hitters:

BELLINGHAM—Baldwin, Brian (11); Bieksha, Stephen (21); Bryant, Erick (16); Burba, David (5); Cameron, Gary (5); Eldredge, Edward (3); Frink, Keith (7); Gardiner, Michael (2); Goff, Michael (13); Helton, Keith (28); Mangual, Victor (4); McGuire, Michael (14); Peters, Thomas (6); Taylor, Wade (12); Togneri, Paul (20); Webb, Charlie (4); Wilkinson, Brian (13).

BEND—Bryan, Frank (1); Cannon, Dana (3); Coulter, Darrell (11); Forbes, Willie (9); Frost, Robert (25); Goldsmith, Gary (24); Hansen, Todd (16); Limbach, Chris (41); Lopez, Marc (4); Roche, Roderick (12); Romero, Elvis (15); Smith, Bradley (3); Viggiano, Matthew (12); Vike, James (26); Vizcaino, Hector (12).

BOISE—Armstrong, Eldridge (6); Arnold, Gail (5); Cota, Stephen (17); Fontenot, Gregory (2); Haar, Matthew (33); Hatfield, Clinton (5); Larson, Dirk (6); Magnuson, Geoffrey (8); Mills, Steven (26); Resnikoff, Robert (17); Savage, John (8); Schmerer, Dana (17); Tate, Michael (26); Townsend, Benjamin (33).

EUGENE—Adams, Joseph (16); Appier, Kevin (15); Campbell, James (32); Gordon, Thomas (15); Hudson, James (16); Mallea, Luis (22); McCormack, Brian (17); Nelson, Douglas (22); Pickens, Kevin (21); Smith, Archie (16); Studeman, Dennis (21).

EVERETT—Bluhm, William (13); Comstock, Brad (16); Geiger, Gary (18); Hostetler, Thomas (14); MacKenzie, Shaun (16); Massey, James (2); Remlinger, Michael (2); Terrill, James (30); Wilson, John (9).

MEDFORD—Baez, Pedro (11); Beck, Rodney (17); Berg, Richard (1); Cabrera, Nasusel (22); Caraballo, Felix (8); Chenevey, James (9); Chiamparino, Scott (13); Claudio, Sindulfo (5); Dockery, Michael (17); Gilbert, Robbie (13); Hartley, Todd (15); Hill, Roy (20); Hosinski, Steven (8); Jones, Carl (11); MacLeod, Kevin (1); Schock, William (7); Shotkoski, David (4); Veilleux, Brian (8); Wernig, Patrick (1).

SALEM—Bobel, Jamea (13); Davis, Freddie (14); Dunn, Stephen (12); Erb, Michael (12); Goettsch, Jeffrey (18); Magnuson, Geoffrey (3); Mutz, Frank (15); Pineda, Rafael (4); Randolph, Scott (14); Reinholtz, Eric (26); Townsend, James (15); Wassenaar, Robert (31).

SPOKANE—Aquino, Pedro (18); de la Cruz, Francisco (7); Forbes, Willie (7); Vizcaino, Hector (1).

GRAND SLAM HOME RUNS—Benoit, Pedre, 2 each; Alborano, Cayson, Foley, Haney, Hawkins, Kocman, Maloney, Orton, Phillips (Eug.), D. Robinson, Shultis, Trevino, 1 each.

AWARDED FIRST BASE ON CATCHER'S INTERFERENCE—Parry 2 (Orton, Rodriguez); Angus (Brito); Rodriguez (Brito).

CLUB FIELDING

Club	Pct.	G.	PO.	A.	E.	DP.	PB.	Club	Pct.	G.	PO.	A.	E.	DP.	PB.
Spokane	.962	76	2039	807	113	65	19	Bend	.953	75	1977	870	141	68	27
Everett	.960	75	2009	807	117	73	11	Boise	.945	76	1968	811	161	54	17
Bellingham	.954	76	2005	762	133	67	29	Salem	.939	75	1989	743	177	60	31
Eugene	.953	75	2031	730	135	54	26	Medford	.933	76	1987	786	198	44	34

*Throws lefthanded.

INDIVIDUAL FIELDING

FIRST BASEMEN

Player and Club	Pct.	G.	PO.	A.	E.	DP.	Player and Club	Pct.	G.	PO.	A.	E.	DP.
Alborano, Eugene*	1.000	2	6	0	0	2	Lutticken, Spokane	1.000	4	7	2	0	0
Aldrete, Everett*	.917	4	21	1	2	2	Maasberg, Bend	1.000	3	31	1	0	1
Amaro, Salem	.978	22	170	8	4	15	Mace, Boise	.980	13	94	6	2	6
AYLWARD, Bend	.995	72	673	51	4	65	McDonald, Boise*	.950	14	91	5	5	5
Azar, Bellingham	.978	26	215	12	5	17	Morrison, Bellingham	.985	16	128	3	2	15
Brito, Medford	1.000	1	2	1	0	0	Musolino, Salem	.963	18	96	7	4	5
Brosius, Medford	.942	6	46	3	3	5	Pedre, Eugene	1.000	1	9	0	0	1
Burr, Boise*	.978	44	384	13	9	31	La. Phillips, Eugene	1.000	16	117	6	0	6
Coomer, Medford	1.000	2	21	2	0	3	Lo. Phillips, Everett	1.000	4	27	1	0	3
Gonzalez, Bellingham	.991	25	222	9	2	17	Rasmus, Salem	1.000	1	1	0	0	0
Grubb, Salem	.950	17	105	9	6	11	Reyna, Medford*	.955	17	143	6	7	10
Hanker, Medford	.965	12	102	7	4	6	Robinson, Medford	.972	6	68	1	2	1
Hendricks, Spokane	.989	74	608	42	7	51	Ryser, Medford	.909	2	9	1	1	0
Hisey, Bellingham	.983	5	57	2	1	6	Sherman, Boise	.982	12	105	4	2	10
Hoffinger, Medford	.986	34	252	28	4	12	Sisco, Bellingham	.857	2	6	0	1	1
Hooper, Bellingham	1.000	6	44	2	0	4	Torchia, Spokane	.923	4	23	1	2	1
Jackson, Salem	.983	43	277	8	5	22	Willson, Everett*	.980	48	406	25	9	33
Jimenez, Medford	.967	4	28	1	1	0	Wright, Eugene	.968	62	499	40	18	39
Kocman, Everett	.988	30	237	16	3	27							

SECOND BASEMEN

Player and Club	Pct.	G.	PO.	A.	E.	DP.	Player and Club	Pct.	G.	PO.	A.	E.	DP.
Amaro, Salem	1.000	2	5	7	0	2	Kleven, Spokane	1.000	1	4	4	0	1
Brooks, Spokane	1.000	3	6	6	0	0	Koehnke, Boise	.972	7	16	19	1	4
Brosius, Medford	.879	14	23	28	7	3	Lee, Salem	.968	53	127	143	9	33
Carr, Bellingham	.926	8	10	15	2	1	Made, Medford	1.000	2	2	2	0	1
Cash, Boise	.942	66	119	155	17	31	Malone, Boise	.925	7	16	21	3	5
Clements, Eugene	.667	1	1	1	1	1	Patrick, Bellingham	.986	14	29	41	1	8
Cole, Eugene	.949	34	58	90	8	15	Perno, Everett	.944	21	27	40	4	10
Eldridge, Medford	1.000	1	1	2	0	1	Rasmus, Salem	.916	30	41	57	9	11
Espinal, Medford	.890	37	56	89	18	12	Rohn, Everett	.990	20	36	61	1	15
Fajardo, Medford	1.000	2	1	1	0	0	Shumpert, Eugene	.945	45	81	107	11	23
FARIES, Spokane	.971	74	169	197	11	38	Trevino, Bend	.938	8	16	29	3	9
Foley, Bend	.957	29	66	90	7	22	Willes, Bend	.968	23	58	62	4	12
Goins, Everett	.967	41	86	121	7	26	Williams, Medford	.808	6	9	12	5	1
Gust, Medford	.667	1	1	1	1	0	Wilson, Medford	.913	20	40	55	9	7
Haney, Bellingham	.952	61	148	170	16	46	Zerb, Bend	.899	17	23	57	9	11
Jimenez, Medford	1.000	3	1	4	0	0							

THIRD BASEMEN

Player and Club	Pct.	G.	PO.	A.	E.	DP.	Player and Club	Pct.	G.	PO.	A.	E.	DP.
Amaro, Salem	.776	24	14	31	13	3	Burrus, Bellingham	.714	3	2	3	2	0
Brooks, Spokane	1.000	2	0	2	0	0	Carr, Bellingham	.846	3	2	9	2	0
Brosius, Medford	.823	26	20	59	17	3	Cole, Eugene	.800	12	5	11	4	2

THIRD BASEMEN—Continued

Player and Club	Pct.	G.	PO.	A.	E.	DP.
Coomer, Medford	.908	38	33	76	11	4
Foley, Bend	.879	37	25	62	12	2
Gallardo, Salem	.886	42	25	76	13	7
Grubb, Salem	.766	19	11	25	11	1
HOLLINS, Spokane	.938	75	59	167	15	12
Jimenez, Medford	1.000	3	1	4	0	0
Kleven, Spokane	1.000	2	1	3	0	0
Kocman, Everett	1.000	12	7	16	0	2
Maasberg, Bend	.910	40	31	70	10	8
Made, Medford	.875	7	2	5	1	0
Malone, Boise	.888	57	49	102	19	11
Martinez, Salem	1.000	1	0	3	0	0
Michalak, Everett	.667	4	0	2	1	0
Morrison, Bellingham	.941	7	2	14	1	1
Owens, Everett	.873	53	33	105	20	6
Phillips, Eugene	.829	15	8	21	6	3
Rasmus, Salem	.916	30	41	57	9	11
Reichardt, Bellingham	.903	53	38	101	15	13
Robinson, Eugene	.873	55	38	79	17	5
Rohn, Everett	.931	13	8	19	2	2
Shultis, Boise	.918	25	23	66	8	5
Sisco, Bellingham	.969	14	9	22	1	1
Williams, Boise	.667	3	1	3	2	0

SHORTSTOPS

Player and Club	Pct.	G.	PO.	A.	E.	DP.
Abshier, Salem	.833	9	2	3	1	0
Amaro, Salem	1.000	5	5	6	0	1
Brooks, Spokane	.923	7	8	16	2	2
Brosius, Medford	.893	20	34	58	11	9
Carr, Bellingham	.846	15	23	32	10	7
Clements, Eugene	.876	56	63	135	28	22
J. Cole, Boise	.872	21	34	61	14	9
S. Cole, Eugene	.955	21	24	60	4	10
DE LA ROSA, Bend	.931	68	109	202	23	45
Eldridge, Medford	.738	13	13	18	11	1
Finley, Medford	.909	3	0	10	1	1
Flora, Salem	.841	32	35	81	22	14
Gallardo, Salem	.750	3	1	2	1	1
Hess, Boise	1.000	1	0	1	0	0
Kleven, Spokane	.778	3	3	4	2	0
Kocman, Everett	.882	2	4	11	2	2
Koehnke, Boise	.921	16	19	39	5	6
Lee, Salem	.900	3	2	7	1	0
Made, Medford	.821	31	34	62	21	13
Malone, Boise	.667	2	1	3	2	0
N. Martinez, Bend	.853	17	19	45	11	8
R. Martinez, Salem	.855	43	27	91	20	18
Michalak, Everett	.905	13	21	36	6	12
Ramirez, Bellingham	.940	48	57	131	12	20
Rasmus, Salem	.000	2	0	0	1	0
Rohn, Everett	1.000	1	3	2	0	1
Shultis, Boise	.918	42	74	139	19	23
Sisco, Bellingham	.894	19	23	36	7	7
Southland, Everett	.930	63	95	183	21	41
Valentin, Spokane	.914	69	101	175	26	35
Williams, Medford	.854	19	25	45	12	3

OUTFIELDERS

Player and Club	Pct.	G.	PO.	A.	E.	DP.
Able, Boise	.941	17	31	1	2	0
Abraham, Everett	1.000	12	18	0	0	0
Alborano, Eugene*	.857	5	6	0	1	0
Aldrete, Everett*	.987	44	71	4	1	0
Amaro, Salem	1.000	24	49	1	0	0
Azar, Bellingham	.963	16	24	2	1	0
Baca, Salem	1.000	2	3	0	0	0
Bell, Boise	.925	37	59	3	5	0
Benoit, Everett	.932	54	67	2	5	0
Brooks, Spokane	.969	43	57	6	2	1
Carr, Bellingham	1.000	13	15	2	0	1
Cayson, Bellingham	.946	48	83	4	5	0
Cooper, Everett	.943	58	111	5	7	2
Daughtry, Bellingham	.957	35	61	6	3	1
Espinosa, Salem	1.000	9	10	0	0	0
K. Farmer, Spokane	1.000	2	2	0	0	0
R. Farmer, Spokane*	.937	69	97	7	7	0
Gainous, Eugene	.950	55	94	2	5	0
Giles, Eugene	.908	51	66	3	7	1
Greene, Bend	.951	53	93	4	5	0
GRIFFEY, BELLINGHAM*	.992	52	117	4	1	1
Gust, Medford	1.000	2	4	0	0	0
Hanker, Medford	1.000	8	11	0	0	0
Hillemann, Spokane	.984	64	117	3	2	0
Hisey, Bellingham	.947	11	18	0	1	0
Hoffinger, Medford	.875	7	7	0	1	0
Holmes, Spokane	.971	21	31	3	1	1
Houston, Eugene	.929	21	23	3	2	1
Hupke, Eugene	.962	21	25	0	1	0
Kemp, Bellingham*	1.000	22	38	3	0	1
Koehnke, Boise	1.000	1	1	0	0	0
Lind, Everett	.983	41	50	7	1	1
List, Salem	1.000	9	5	1	0	0
Maasberg, Bend	.955	15	20	1	1	0
Mace, Boise	.958	56	123	15	6	1
Maloney, Boise	.941	26	45	3	3	0
Martinez, Bend	.857	5	6	0	1	0
McDonald, Boise*	.944	48	60	7	4	0
Molina, Salem*	.925	54	61	1	5	0
Montero, Salem	.935	41	68	4	5	2
Moore, Eugene	.964	54	75	6	3	1
Nina, Medford*	.922	31	54	5	5	0
Orton, Salem	1.000	1	1	0	0	0
Papajohn, Boise	.941	20	26	6	2	0
Parry, Medford	.962	64	117	8	5	2
Patrick, Bellingham	.821	25	32	0	7	0
Paul, Bellingham*	.909	24	38	2	4	0
Peters, Salem	.952	69	114	6	6	0
Pickett, Eugene	.946	27	33	2	2	0
Poche, Medford	.950	21	36	2	2	0
Reyna, Medford*	1.000	22	33	4	0	1
Robinson, Salem	1.000	17	18	0	0	0
Rodriguez, Salem	.857	6	6	0	1	0
Sanchez, Spokane*	.978	33	43	2	1	1
Sholl, Eugene	1.000	28	46	1	0	0
Silva, Everett	1.000	10	13	1	0	0
Sims, Bend*	.921	45	55	3	5	0
D. Smith, Bend	.930	33	63	3	5	0
J. Smith, Medford	.929	39	76	3	6	1
R. Smith, Boise	.953	47	75	6	4	0
Stone, Bend	.933	20	28	0	2	0
Tinsley, Medford	.952	45	77	2	4	0
Torchia, Spokane	.923	26	23	1	2	0
Trevino, Bend	.939	66	96	11	7	3
Walker, Everett	.931	37	53	1	4	0
D. Watkins, Eugene	.976	40	73	7	2	2
K. Watkins, Medford	1.000	3	3	0	0	0
Williams, Medford	1.000	6	8	0	0	0
Wilson, Medford	1.000	1	1	0	0	0

CATCHERS

Player and Club	Pct.	G.	PO.	A.	E.	DP.	PB.
Angus, Boise	.976	51	279	11	7	1	8
Berrios, Eugene	1.000	13	109	8	0	1	8
Bock, Eugene	.982	33	299	33	6	0	9
Bowman, Boise	.985	17	59	5	1	0	2
Brito, Medford	.981	38	222	30	5	0	12
Burrus, Bellingham	.983	11	54	4	1	0	12
Ciprian, Medford	.989	26	163	11	2	0	12
de Jesus, Bend	.957	26	186	14	9	0	12
Enos, Bend	.995	35	189	27	1	2	6
K. Farmer, Spokane	.985	7	59	6	1	0	1
Fellows, Boise	1.000	5	26	1	0	0	0
Gay, Salem	1.000	2	5	0	0	0	0
Ham, Everett	.980	25	165	28	4	1	2
HAWKINS, Everett	.994	44	309	23	2	4	8
Hoffman, Bellingham	.967	34	189	17	7	1	7
Hooper, Bellingham	.969	34	228	19	8	2	5
Jackson, Salem	1.000	2	2	1	0	0	0
Lutticken, Spokane	.962	26	158	18	7	2	2
Morrison, Bellingham	1.000	8	56	1	0	0	5
Musolino, Salem	.971	5	32	2	1	0	2
Orton, Salem	.979	34	270	15	6	3	9
Owens, Everett	.960	8	42	6	2	1	0
Pedre, Eugene	.982	33	291	28	6	1	9
Piazza, Everett	1.000	15	57	3	0	0	1
Rodriguez, Salem	.979	40	299	28	7	0	20
Ryser, Medford	.989	24	154	18	2	3	10
Skeels, Spokane	.982	53	412	35	8	3	16
Thagard, Boise	.979	27	129	13	3	0	7
Verstandig, Bend	.983	22	147	25	3	0	9

PITCHERS

Player and Club	Pct.	G.	PO.	A.	E.	DP.
Adams, Eugene	.909	16	4	6	1	0
Appier, Eugene	.947	15	10	8	1	0
Aquino, Spokane*	.857	18	4	8	2	1
Armstrong, Boise	.667	6	1	1	1	0
Baez, Medford	1.000	11	2	7	0	0
Baldwin, Bellingham	.810	11	5	12	4	0
Beck, Medford	.938	17	12	18	2	1
Berg, Medford	1.000	1	1	0	0	0
Bieksha, Bellingham	.818	21	1	8	2	1
Bluhm, Everett	1.000	13	1	2	0	0
Bobel, Salem	.875	13	1	6	1	0
Bond, Spokane*	.857	10	4	8	2	0
Bryan, Bend	1.000	1	3	0	0	0
Bryant, Bellingham	.917	16	4	7	1	0
Buckels, Salem	.857	31	1	11	2	0
Burba, Bellingham	1.000	5	2	4	0	0
Cabrera, Medford	.938	22	10	20	2	1
Cameron, Bellingham*	1.000	5	0	1	0	0
Campbell, Eugene*	1.000	32	5	9	0	0
Caraballo, Medford	1.000	8	1	6	0	0
Carlisle, Boise	1.000	4	0	3	0	0
Chenevey, Medford*	1.000	9	0	2	0	0
Chiamparino, Medford	.833	13	6	4	2	1
Claudio, Medford*	1.000	5	0	2	0	1
Cole, Boise	1.000	2	1	1	0	0
Comstock, Everett	.857	16	3	3	1	0
Coomer, Medford	1.000	1	1	0	0	0
Cota, Bend	.882	17	5	10	2	0
Coulter, Bend	.875	11	3	4	1	0
Davis, Salem	.800	14	1	3	1	0
de la Cruz, Spokane	1.000	7	3	1	0	0
Dewey, Everett	.875	19	3	11	2	2
Dockery, Medford*	.667	17	1	5	3	0
Dunn, Salem*	1.000	12	5	11	0	0
Eldredge, Bellingham	.000	3	0	0	2	0
Erb, Salem	.895	12	6	11	2	0
Estrada, Spokane	1.000	10	2	2	0	0
Fontenot, Boise*	.000	2	0	0	1	0
Forbes, Bend-Spokane*	.957	16	5	17	1	0
Frink, Bellingham*	.750	7	1	2	1	0
Frost, Bend	1.000	25	3	16	0	0
Gambee, Everett	.818	7	2	7	2	1
Garner, Spokane	.900	6	4	5	1	1
Geiger, Everett	.944	18	6	11	1	3
Gilbert, Medford	.947	13	5	13	1	0
GILMORE, Spokane	1.000	14	8	19	0	2
Goettsch, Salem	.938	18	5	10	1	1
Goff, Bellingham	1.000	13	4	5	0	0
Goldsmith, Bend	.750	24	3	6	3	0
Gordon, Eugene	.947	15	8	10	1	1
Gorski, Medford	.667	10	0	2	1	0
Gunderson, Everett*	.882	15	5	10	2	0
Haar, Boise*	1.000	33	2	4	0	0
Hanker, Bellingham	1.000	1	1	0	0	0
Hansen, Bend*	.960	16	4	20	1	0
Hartley, Medford	.900	15	5	13	2	1
Hatfield, Boise	.333	5	1	0	2	0
Helton, Bellingham*	1.000	28	1	6	0	1
Heredia, Everett	.667	3	1	1	1	0
Hill, Medford	.750	20	3	3	2	0
Holsman, Spokane*	.857	34	1	11	2	0
Hosinski, Medford	1.000	8	3	1	0	0
Hostetler, Everett	.846	14	2	9	2	2
Hudson, Everett	.923	16	7	5	1	0
Johnson, Bellingham	1.000	13	4	6	0	0
Jones, Medford	.667	11	2	0	1	0
Larson, Boise*	.750	6	0	3	1	0
Leslie, Spokane	.727	16	3	5	3	0
Lewis, Spokane	.875	15	8	13	3	2
Limbach, Bend*	.950	41	3	16	1	0
Lopez, Bend	.600	4	0	3	2	0
MacKenzie, Everett	1.000	16	2	2	0	0
Magnuson, Boise-Salem*	.600	11	1	2	2	0
Mallea, Eugene	.800	22	1	3	1	0
Mangual, Bellingham	1.000	4	0	3	0	0
Maxwell, Boise	1.000	32	1	9	0	1
McCormack, Eugene	.889	17	2	6	1	0
McGuire, Bellingham	.938	14	6	9	1	1
Mills, Boise	1.000	26	3	13	0	1
Mutz, Salem	.840	15	7	14	4	0
Myers, Spokane	.933	20	4	10	1	1
Nelson, Eugene	1.000	22	2	3	0	0
Peters, Bellingham	.000	6	0	0	1	0
Phillips, Everett	.923	15	8	16	2	0
Pickens, Spokane	.909	21	2	8	1	1
Pierce, Eugene*	1.000	13	0	5	0	0
Pineda, Salem	1.000	4	1	0	0	0
Randolph, Salem	.850	14	2	15	3	0
Reichle, Spokane	.875	11	1	6	1	2
Reinholtz, Salem*	.846	26	3	8	2	0
Resnikoff, Boise*	1.000	17	2	19	0	0
Roche, Bend	1.000	12	4	3	0	0
Romero, Bend	.821	15	7	16	5	0
Ryser, Medford	1.000	1	1	0	0	0
Savage, Boise	.875	8	2	5	1	0
Schmerer, Boise*	.929	17	0	13	1	0
Schock, Medford	.857	7	1	5	1	2
Shibata, Eugene*	.800	21	0	8	2	0
Shotkoski, Medford	1.000	4	0	1	0	0
A. Smith, Eugene*	.958	16	7	16	1	3
B. Smith, Bend	1.000	3	1	0	0	0
Soltero, Spokane	.889	28	5	11	2	0
Stoerck, Bellingham	.875	26	1	6	1	0
Studeman, Eugene	1.000	21	0	3	0	0
Tate, Boise	.750	26	1	8	3	0
Taylor, Bellingham	1.000	12	5	7	0	0
Terrill, Everett*	1.000	30	6	10	0	1
Togneri, Bellingham*	1.000	20	0	8	0	0
B. Townsend, Boise	.889	33	3	13	2	1
J. Townsend, Salem*	1.000	15	1	15	0	1
Veilleux, Medford*	1.000	8	0	2	0	0
Viggiano, Bend	.857	12	4	8	2	1
Vike, Bend	.786	26	4	7	3	0
Vizcaino, Bend-Spokane	1.000	13	0	3	0	0
Wassenaar, Salem	1.000	31	3	7	0	0
Wernig, Medford*	1.000	1	0	1	0	0
Wilkinson, Bellingham	.882	13	3	12	2	1
Wilson, Everett*	1.000	9	3	6	0	2

The following players do not have any recorded accepted chances at the positions indicated; therefore, are not listed in the fielding averages for those particular positions: Abshier, 3b; Arnold, p; Brito, p; Brosius, p; Burrus, of; Cannon, p; Carlisle, 3b; Clements, of; K. Farmer, p; Gardiner, p; Grubb, ss; Haney, p; Koehnke, p; List, p; Lutticken, of; MacLeod, p; Made, p; Massey, p; La. Phillips, p; Remlinger, p; Sherman, 3b; Skeels, 1b; Verstandig, of; Webb, p.

CLUB PITCHING

Club	ERA	G.	CG.	ShO.	Sv.	IP.	H.	R.	ER.	HR.	HB.	BB.	Int. BB.	SO.	WP.	Bk.
Spokane	3.376655	76	11	6	23	679.2	598	317	255	30	23	359	15	616	57	9
Eugene	3.376661	75	0	6	19	677.0	553	342	254	25	38	338	11	696	49	15
Everett	3.45	75	11	8	15	669.2	615	311	257	40	26	297	4	549	45	7
Salem	3.77	75	10	5	12	663.0	614	383	278	43	35	310	5	592	55	5
Bend	4.53	75	6	5	13	659.0	671	432	332	40	25	412	14	525	86	8
Medford	4.80	76	5	1	15	662.1	737	499	353	24	32	339	10	545	77	11
Bellingham	4.96	76	0	2	16	668.1	675	448	368	40	53	382	3	512	96	10
Boise	5.64	76	8	2	11	656.0	804	542	411	64	51	353	26	478	58	13

PITCHERS' RECORDS
(Leading Qualifiers for Earned-Run Average Leadership — 61 or More Innings)

*Throws lefthanded.

Pitcher—Club	W.	L.	Pct.	ERA	G.	GS.	CG.	GF.	ShO.	Sv.	IP.	H.	R.	ER.	HR.	HB.	BB.	Int. BB.	SO.	WP.
Campbell, Eugene*	6	0	1.000	0.73	32	0	0	21	0	10	62.0	32	5	5	1	1	12	3	75	3
Holsman, Spokane*	6	4	.600	1.89	34	0	0	25	0	8	62.0	42	21	13	3	3	41	2	91	5
Erb, Salem	6	3	.667	2.44	12	12	4	0	1	0	85.0	65	33	23	3	2	20	0	98	0
Gunderson, Everett*	8	4	.667	2.46	15	15	5	0	3	0	98.2	80	34	27	4	3	34	1	99	4
Chiamparino, Medford	5	4	.556	2.53	13	11	3	1	1	0	67.2	64	29	19	2	3	20	0	65	6
Gilmore, Spokane	7	0	1.000	2.59	14	14	3	0	0	0	100.2	95	37	29	6	3	24	1	81	3
Gordon, Eugene	9	0	1.000	2.86	13	13	0	1	0	1	72.1	48	33	23	2	3	47	0	91	2
Myers, Spokane	7	1	.875	3.00	20	8	3	2	3	2	84.0	69	36	28	1	2	32	3	69	3
A. Smith, Eugene*	5	5	.500	3.02	16	14	0	0	0	0	80.1	75	47	27	2	5	29	0	76	3
Appier, Eugene	5	2	.714	3.04	15	15	0	0	0	0	77.0	81	43	26	2	2	29	0	72	7

Departmental Leaders: G—Limbach, 41; W—Gordon, Hostetler, 9; L—Romero, Tate, 9; Pct.—Gilmore, Gordon, 1.000; GS—11 pitchers with 15; CG—Gunderson, 5; GF—Limbach, 33; ShO—Gunderson, Myers, 3; Sv.—Helton, 13; IP—Gilmore, 100.2; H—Cota, 115; R—Hartley, 78; ER—Beck, 53; HR—Maxwell, 11; HB—Taylor, 13; BB—McGuire, 66; IBB—B. Townsend, 7; SO—Gunderson, 99; WP—McGuire, Resnikoff, 15.

(All Pitchers—Listed Alphabetically)

Pitcher—Club	W.	L.	Pct.	ERA.	G.	GS.	CG.	GF.	ShO.	Sv.	IP.	H.	R.	ER.	HR.	HB.	BB.	Int. BB.	SO.	WP.
Adams, Eugene	1	3	.250	4.70	16	4	0	4	0	0	38.1	22	21	20	3	3	34	1	29	4
Appier, Eugene	5	2	.714	3.04	15	15	0	0	0	0	77.0	81	43	26	2	2	29	0	72	7
Aquino, Spokane°	4	1	.800	3.83	18	5	1	4	0	0	51.2	57	31	22	1	0	36	1	42	5
Armstrong, Boise	0	0	.000	1.64	6	0	0	2	0	1	11.0	9	12	2	0	2	11	1	8	1
Arnold, Boise	0	1	.000	11.57	5	1	0	2	0	1	7.0	9	10	9	1	2	8	0	6	1
Baez, Medford	0	1	.000	3.32	11	0	0	7	0	2	21.2	27	14	8	0	0	10	1	17	0
Baldwin, Bellingham	2	4	.333	5.60	11	10	0	0	0	0	53.0	66	37	33	2	2	16	0	19	9
Beck, Medford	5	8	.385	5.18	17	12	2	1	0	0	92.0	106	74	53	5	4	26	0	69	12
Berg, Medford	0	0	.000	0.00	1	0	0	1	0	1	2.0	0	0	0	0	0	0	0	4	0
Bieksha, Bellingham	1	3	.250	4.23	21	3	0	5	0	1	61.2	62	33	29	6	1	36	1	41	8
Bluhm, Everett	1	1	.500	2.79	13	2	0	11	0	1	29.0	28	15	9	1	1	19	1	19	5
Bobel, Salem	2	4	.333	6.08	13	5	0	2	0	1	40.0	47	35	27	6	4	14	0	28	5
Bond, Spokane°	3	3	.500	4.33	10	10	0	0	0	0	54.0	53	29	26	1	1	36	0	46	9
Brito, Medford	0	0	.000	0.00	1	0	0	1	0	0	0.1	0	0	0	0	0	0	0	0	0
Brosius, Medford	0	0	.000	0.00	1	0	0	1	0	0	2.0	1	0	0	0	1	0	0	1	0
Bryan, Bend	1	0	1.000	1.00	1	1	1	0	0	0	9.0	6	1	1	0	0	2	0	1	0
Bryant, Bellingham	2	1	.667	4.74	16	1	0	6	0	0	43.2	54	30	23	3	1	22	1	32	4
Buckels, Salem	4	6	.400	4.18	31	0	0	16	0	0	56.0	53	34	26	1	0	38	3	63	8
Burba, Bellingham	3	1	.750	1.93	5	5	0	0	0	0	23.1	20	10	5	0	0	3	0	24	4
Cabrera, Medford	4	4	.500	4.42	22	3	0	7	0	1	77.1	89	52	38	1	1	28	0	53	9
Cameron, Bellingham°	0	2	.000	9.24	5	1	0	2	0	1	12.2	16	13	13	0	1	15	0	11	2
Campbell, Eugene°	6	0	1.000	0.73	32	0	0	21	0	10	62.0	32	5	5	1	1	12	3	75	3
Cannon, Bend	0	0	.000	9.00	3	0	0	1	0	0	3.0	7	4	3	0	1	3	0	4	0
Caraballo, Medford	1	2	.333	3.19	8	1	0	3	0	1	36.2	34	16	13	2	3	11	0	26	1
Carlisle, Boise	0	2	.000	5.89	4	4	0	0	0	0	18.1	22	12	12	0	1	6	0	5	0
Chenevey, Medford°	0	2	.000	5.03	9	5	0	0	0	0	19.2	16	13	11	0	0	19	1	27	9
Chiamparino, Medford	5	4	.556	2.53	13	11	3	1	1	0	67.2	64	29	19	2	3	20	0	65	6
Claudio, Medford°	0	0	.000	7.45	5	1	0	1	0	0	9.2	15	10	8	0	0	13	0	8	0
Cole, Boise	0	0	.000	0.00	2	0	0	1	0	0	1.1	1	0	0	0	1	1	0	1	0
Comstock, Everett	3	1	.750	3.89	16	2	1	7	1	2	41.2	42	19	18	6	2	21	0	26	5
Coomer, Medford	0	0	.000	45.00	1	0	0	1	0	0	1.0	4	5	5	1	0	1	0	0	0
Cota, Boise	4	7	.364	4.52	17	15	3	0	0	0	93.2	115	67	47	9	4	39	3	81	5
Coulter, Bend	4	3	.571	3.31	11	8	0	0	0	0	49.0	55	28	18	1	1	36	0	37	7
Davis, Salem	1	2	.333	7.18	14	0	0	4	0	0	26.1	28	27	21	1	2	35	1	15	3
de la Cruz, Spokane	1	0	1.000	5.40	7	0	0	6	0	0	6.2	3	4	4	0	0	9	0	4	1
Dewey, Everett	7	3	.700	3.30	19	10	1	5	0	1	84.2	88	39	31	2	2	26	1	67	1
Dockery, Medford°	1	3	.250	6.59	17	2	0	9	0	3	28.2	33	27	21	0	2	32	2	26	6
Dunn, Salem°	3	4	.429	3.38	12	9	2	1	1	0	69.1	73	34	26	7	3	19	0	52	0
Eldredge, Bellingham	0	0	.000	1.80	3	2	0	0	0	0	10.0	5	3	2	0	1	7	0	11	1
Erb, Salem	6	3	.667	2.44	12	12	4	0	1	0	85.0	65	33	23	3	2	20	0	98	0
Estrada, Spokane	2	1	.667	4.18	10	0	0	4	0	0	23.2	22	12	11	0	2	15	2	14	1
Farmer, Spokane	0	0	.000	15.43	1	0	0	0	0	0	2.1	2	4	4	0	0	2	0	1	1
Fontenot, Boise°	0	0	.000	19.64	2	1	0	0	0	0	3.2	9	8	8	1	0	4	0	2	0
Forbes, 9 Bend-6 Spok°	7	5	.583	3.34	15	15	2	0	1	0	97.0	93	44	36	6	2	38	1	74	9
Frink, Bellingham°	1	0	1.000	1.19	7	0	0	1	0	0	22.2	24	6	3	0	0	9	0	10	0
Frost, Bend	3	3	.500	5.32	25	2	0	7	0	2	64.1	62	41	38	9	1	35	2	42	12
Gambee, Everett	2	3	.400	7.27	7	7	0	0	0	0	34.2	37	31	28	3	2	34	0	22	3
Gardiner, Bellingham	2	0	1.000	0.00	2	1	0	0	0	0	10.0	6	0	0	0	1	1	0	11	0
Garner, Spokane	3	1	.750	2.02	6	6	1	0	0	0	35.2	18	8	8	1	1	16	0	42	2
Geiger, Everett	6	4	.600	4.54	18	11	0	1	0	0	83.1	87	47	42	5	2	41	0	61	6
Gilbert, Medford	1	7	.125	5.49	13	11	0	0	0	0	60.2	68	60	37	3	5	36	2	39	7
Gilmore, Eugene	7	0	1.000	2.59	14	14	3	0	0	0	100.2	95	37	29	6	3	24	1	81	3
Goettsch, Salem	2	1	.667	2.90	18	2	1	6	0	1	49.2	33	21	16	3	2	28	0	57	6
Goff, Bellingham	5	6	.455	7.31	13	13	0	0	0	0	60.1	80	58	49	8	5	23	0	56	10
Goldsmith, Bend	1	2	.333	6.53	24	1	0	7	0	1	40.0	43	32	29	5	2	27	1	38	5
Gordon, Eugene	9	0	1.000	2.86	15	13	0	1	0	1	72.1	48	33	23	2	3	47	0	91	2
Gorski, Medford	1	1	.500	6.14	10	0	0	8	0	1	14.2	21	13	10	1	0	4	0	14	0
Gunderson, Everett°	8	4	.667	2.46	15	15	5	0	3	0	98.2	80	34	27	4	3	34	1	99	4
Haar, Boise°	3	0	1.000	6.35	33	1	0	11	0	0	45.1	69	40	32	7	0	20	1	30	1
Haney, Bellingham	0	0	.000	0.00	1	0	0	1	0	0	1.0	0	0	0	0	0	0	0	0	0
Hanker, Medford	0	0	.000	0.00	1	0	0	1	0	0	1.2	3	0	0	0	0	0	0	0	0
Hansen, Bend°	4	6	.400	3.68	16	15	4	0	1	0	85.2	76	51	35	4	4	47	1	87	11
Hartley, Medford	3	8	.273	5.62	15	15	0	0	0	0	75.1	84	78	47	5	3	51	0	53	8
Hatfield, Boise	0	1	.000	30.86	5	1	0	0	0	0	4.2	15	19	16	1	2	8	0	2	1
Helton, Bellingham°	3	0	1.000	1.31	28	1	0	25	0	13	55.0	36	14	8	1	4	26	0	70	5
Heredia, Everett	2	0	1.000	3.60	3	3	1	0	0	0	20.0	24	8	8	2	0	1	0	11	0
Hill, Medford	2	1	.667	3.06	20	0	0	17	0	5	32.1	25	16	11	0	1	25	2	36	6
Holsman, Spokane°	6	4	.600	1.89	34	0	0	25	0	8	62.0	42	21	13	3	4	41	2	91	5
Hosinski, Medford°	0	2	.000	7.90	8	5	0	1	0	0	27.1	33	31	24	2	2	23	0	18	4
Hostetler, Everett	9	2	.818	3.08	14	13	2	0	0	0	90.2	77	37	31	10	2	34	0	89	4
Hudson, Eugene	3	4	.429	4.54	16	15	0	1	0	0	83.1	78	51	42	3	8	30	1	61	4
Johnson, Bellingham	1	3	.250	3.56	13	0	0	4	0	0	30.1	27	19	12	1	1	14	0	20	3
Jones, Medford	2	0	1.000	6.14	11	0	0	5	0	1	29.1	37	23	20	1	3	16	0	30	3
Koehnke, Boise	0	0	.000	0.00	1	0	0	1	0	0	1.0	1	0	0	0	0	0	0	1	0
Larson, Boise°	0	4	.000	7.78	6	5	0	1	0	0	19.2	29	25	17	2	2	14	0	19	5
Leslie, Spokane	3	2	.600	5.50	16	3	0	4	0	1	36.0	38	26	22	2	2	25	1	43	7
Lewis, Spokane	5	3	.625	5.14	15	12	2	1	1	0	75.1	73	50	43	9	3	51	1	42	4
Limbach, Bend°	6	4	.600	3.70	41	1	0	33	0	8	82.2	86	46	34	6	2	28	2	69	5
List, Salem	0	0	.000	....	1	0	0	0	0	0	0.0	1	0	0	0	0	1	0	0	1
Lopez, Bend	0	2	.000	5.02	4	4	0	0	0	0	14.1	11	11	8	0	2	16	0	15	1
MacKenzie, Everett	3	1	.750	5.10	16	1	0	6	0	0	30.0	34	21	17	1	5	26	0	15	1
MacLeod, Medford°	1	0	1.000	3.38	6	0	0	1	0	0	2.2	2	1	1	0	0	3	0	7	0
Made, Medford	0	0	.000	....	1	0	0	0	0	0	0.0	0	0	0	0	0	2	0	0	0
Magnuson, 8 Boi-3 Sal	0	4	.000	12.60	11	0	0	2	0	0	10.0	13	20	14	0	1	21	1	9	2
Mallea, Eugene	3	4	.429	1.60	22	3	0	12	0	1	45.0	31	11	8	2	3	27	3	48	3
Mangual, Bellingham	0	0	.000	3.18	4	0	0	2	0	0	5.2	3	2	2	0	0	3	0	3	3
Massey, Everett	1	0	1.000	1.80	2	0	0	1	0	0	5.0	4	1	1	1	0	6	0	6	0

Pitcher—Club	W.	L.	Pct.	ERA.	G.	GS.	CG.	GF.	ShO.	Sv.	IP.	H.	R.	ER.	HR.	HB.	BB.	Int. BB.	SO.	WP.
Maxwell, Boise	1	2	.333	6.75	32	1	0	14	0	3	64.0	92	56	48	11	7	17	3	64	0
McCormack, Eugene	1	3	.250	3.53	17	0	0	5	0	0	35.2	21	14	14	3	3	23	0	35	4
McGuire, Bellingham	3	8	.273	7.39	14	13	0	0	0	0	56.0	50	57	46	4	5	66	0	50	15
Mills, Boise	4	4	.500	4.41	26	3	0	10	0	0	67.1	63	43	33	6	5	44	4	49	10
Mutz, Salem	4	6	.400	3.33	15	15	1	0	0	0	83.2	83	51	31	7	5	35	0	67	8
Myers, Spokane	7	1	.875	3.00	20	9	3	2	3	2	84.0	69	36	28	1	2	32	3	69	3
Nelson, Eugene	4	5	.444	5.25	22	5	0	9	0	3	48.0	60	35	28	3	2	19	3	44	3
Peters, Bellingham	0	0	.000	14.46	6	0	0	2	0	0	9.1	5	17	15	2	4	21	0	9	10
La. Phillips, Eugene	0	0	.000	7.71	2	0	0	1	0	0	2.1	1	2	2	0	0	5	0	0	0
Lo. Phillips, Everett	5	5	.500	3.72	15	10	1	2	0	0	77.1	64	40	32	3	7	36	1	60	9
Pickens, Eugene	3	0	1.000	4.76	21	1	0	6	0	0	34.0	21	20	18	2	1	30	0	48	7
Pierce, Eugene°	1	0	1.000	8.10	13	0	0	2	0	1	16.2	23	21	15	0	2	18	0	17	3
Pineda, Salem	0	0	.000	20.25	4	2	0	0	0	0	4.0	9	10	9	1	0	7	0	4	1
Randolph, Salem	3	6	.333	5.21	14	14	1	0	1	0	57.0	57	43	33	3	2	34	0	28	6
Reichle, Spokane	4	1	.800	2.96	11	10	0	0	0	0	54.2	45	24	18	2	2	40	0	47	10
Reinholtz, Salem°	1	3	.250	3.16	26	1	0	9	0	2	51.1	43	28	18	4	1	14	0	33	1
Remlinger, Everett°	0	0	.000	3.60	2	1	0	0	0	0	5.0	1	2	2	0	0	5	0	11	1
Resnikoff, Boise°	5	6	.455	4.55	17	15	3	1	1	1	93.0	104	62	47	7	6	46	1	46	15
Roche, Bend	1	3	.250	4.83	12	3	0	3	0	0	31.2	40	22	17	1	0	9	1	27	0
Romero, Bend	5	9	.357	3.71	15	15	0	0	0	0	87.1	90	52	36	2	3	50	2	68	11
Ryser, Medford	0	0	.000	9.00	1	0	0	1	0	0	3.0	6	3	3	0	0	1	0	2	1
Savage, Boise	1	4	.200	5.05	8	8	0	0	0	0	35.2	49	37	20	3	2	16	1	17	3
Schmerer, Boise°	3	6	.333	4.54	17	14	2	2	1	0	73.1	79	50	37	7	2	36	0	55	6
Schock, Medford	1	1	.500	5.14	7	7	0	0	0	0	21.0	29	18	12	0	2	6	0	15	0
Shibata, Eugene°	3	4	.429	2.55	21	5	0	4	0	0	53.0	38	22	15	1	2	19	1	61	6
Shotkoski, Medford	2	0	1.000	1.93	4	3	0	1	0	0	18.2	19	7	4	0	2	6	0	16	4
A. Smith, Eugene°	5	5	.500	3.02	16	14	0	0	0	0	80.1	75	47	27	2	5	29	0	76	3
B. Smith, Bend	2	1	.667	4.70	3	3	0	0	0	0	15.1	9	8	8	1	0	8	0	9	1
Soltero, Spokane	5	3	.625	2.17	28	0	0	21	0	12	49.2	33	14	12	1	2	19	4	64	5
Stoerck, Bellingham	0	3	.000	3.88	26	1	0	19	0	0	46.1	44	30	20	3	5	30	1	36	6
Studeman, Eugene	1	0	1.000	3.41	21	0	0	9	0	3	29.0	22	17	11	1	3	16	0	39	0
Tate, Boise	1	9	.100	3.76	26	7	0	12	0	5	67.0	76	38	28	4	6	37	4	70	5
Taylor, Bellingham	3	5	.375	4.47	12	10	0	2	0	1	58.1	58	31	29	4	13	22	0	53	4
Terrill, Everett°	2	1	.667	1.02	30	0	0	24	0	11	53.0	35	9	6	2	0	12	0	55	4
Togneri, Bellingham°	2	2	.500	6.70	20	1	0	6	0	0	44.1	49	38	33	3	4	24	0	26	5
B. Townsend, Boise	4	0	1.000	9.76	33	0	0	9	0	0	43.1	54	51	47	5	8	33	7	14	4
J. Townsend, Salem°	5	2	.714	3.05	15	15	1	0	1	0	82.2	70	43	28	5	11	39	0	81	4
Veilleux, Medford°	1	1	.500	4.85	8	0	0	3	0	0	13.0	18	7	7	1	0	6	2	16	0
Viggiano, Bend	1	3	.250	4.89	12	11	0	0	0	0	49.2	51	38	27	2	4	44	1	33	12
Vike, Bend	2	2	.500	6.36	26	0	0	12	0	2	52.1	55	49	37	4	3	53	3	41	11
Vizcaino, 12 Bend-1 Spo	0	1	.000	8.57	13	3	0	5	0	0	21.0	35	26	20	2	2	29	0	10	2
Wassenaar, Salem	3	4	.429	2.14	31	0	0	26	0	8	54.2	48	18	13	2	3	18	1	65	11
Webb, Bellingham°	0	0	.000	0.00	4	1	0	1	0	0	6.0	6	0	0	0	3	0	4	0	
Wernig, Medford°	1	0	1.000	2.25	1	0	0	0	0	0	4.0	4	1	1	0	0	0	3	1	
Wilkinson, Bellingham	2	8	.200	7.06	13	13	0	0	0	0	58.2	64	50	46	3	6	40	0	26	7
Wilson, Everett°	0	1	.000	2.70	9	0	0	7	0	0	16.2	14	8	5	0	0	7	0	5	1

BALKS—Goff, Gordon, Schmerer, Shibata, 4 each; Gunderson, Hudson, 3 each; Adams, Aquino, Baez, Bobel, Bond, Cabrera, Chenevey, Dewey, Frost, Hansen, Hartley, Hill, Larson, Mills, J. Townsend, 2 each; Appier, Armstrong, Baldwin, Beck, Bryant, Cameron, Carlisle, Cota, Estrada, Gambee, Helton, Holsman, Johnson, Leslie, Lewis, Limbach, Lopez, MacKenzie, Mutz, Myers, Nelson, Resnikoff, Roche, Tate, Taylor, Vike, 1 each.

COMBINATION SHUTOUTS—Baldwin-Bieksha-Helton, Goff-Johnson-Stoerck, Bellingham; Lopez-Frost-Limbach, Romero-Limbach, Viggiano-Limbach, Bend; Appier-Pickens-McCormack-Shibata, Gordon-Campbell, Hudson-Campbell-Nelson, Shibata-Pickens-Studeman, Smith-Campbell-Nelson, Smith-Studeman, Eugene; Gambee-Terrill, Hostetler-Wilson, Hostetler-Terrill, Phillips-Comstock-Dewey, Everett; Bobel-Wassenaar, Salem; Bond-Holsman-Soltero, Garner-Soltero, Spokane.

NO-HIT GAMES—None.

South Atlantic League

CLASS A

CHAMPIONSHIP WINNERS IN PREVIOUS YEARS

1948—Lincolnton° .... .627	1966—Spartanburg .... .682	1977—Greenwood .... .557
1949—Newton-Conover .... .667	Spartanburg .... .767	Gastonia‡ .... .590
Ruth'ford Co. (2nd)† .... .627	1967—Spartanburg .... .730	1978—Greenwood .... .614
1950—Newton-Conover .... .627	Spartanburg .... .567	Greenwood .... .565
Lenoir (2nd)† .... .626	1968—Spartanburg .... .597	1979—Greenwood‡ .... .565
1951—Morganton .... .645	Greenwood‡ .... .597	Spartanburg .... .525
Shelby (2nd)† .... .604	1969—Greenwood‡ .... .587	1980—Greensboro .... .590
1952—Lincolnton .... .649	Shelby .... .565	Charleston .... .561
Shelby (2nd)† .... .645	1970—Greenville .... .576	1981—Greensboro‡ .... .695
1953-59—League inactive.	Greenville .... .619	Greenwood .... .549
1960—Lexington .... .707	1971—Greenwood .... .631	1982—Greensboro‡ .... .681
Salisbury (2nd)† .... .650	Greenwood .... .759	Florence .... .546
1961—Salisbury .... .627	1972—Spartanburg‡ .... .788	1983—Columbia .... .620
Shelby (4th)† .... .481	Greenville .... .652	Gastonia‡ .... .587
1962—Statesville .... .563	1973—Spartanburg‡ .... .646	1984—Charleston .... .549
Statesville .... .700	Gastonia .... .619	Asheville‡ .... .510
1963—Greenville† .... .576	1974—Gastonia .... .606	1985—Florence‡ .... .599
Salisbury .... .631	Gastonia .... .672	Greensboro .... .540
1964—Rock Hill .... .672	1975—Spartanburg .... .543	1986—Columbia‡ .... .682
Salisbury‡ .... .631	Spartanburg .... .614	Asheville .... .643
1965—Salisbury .... .641	1976—Asheville .... .544	
Rock Hill‡ .... .603	Greenwood‡ .... .600	

°Won championship and four-club playoff. †Won four-club playoff. ‡Won split-season playoff. (NOTE—Known as Western Carolina League from 1948 through 1962 and known as Western Carolinas League through 1979.)

STANDING OF CLUBS AT CLOSE OF FIRST HALF, JUNE 17

NORTHERN DIVISION

Club	W.	L.	T.	Pct.	G.B.
Asheville (Astros)	37	32	0	.536	....
Charleston (W.Va.) (Co-op)	37	33	0	.529	½
Greensboro (Red Sox)	33	37	0	.471	4½
Fayetteville (Tigers)	33	37	0	.471	4½
Spartanburg (Phillies)	30	40	0	.429	7½
Gastonia (Rangers)	30	40	0	.429	7½

SOUTHERN DIVISION

Club	W.	L.	T.	Pct.	G.B.
Myrtle Beach (Blue Jays)	42	28	0	.600	....
Sumter (Braves)	37	31	0	.544	4
Savannah (Cardinals)	37	32	0	.536	4½
Macon (Pirates)	35	34	0	.507	6½
Columbia (Mets)	35	35	0	.500	7
Charleston (S.C.) (Padres)	31	38	0	.449	10½

STANDING OF CLUBS AT CLOSE OF SECOND HALF, AUGUST 30

NORTHERN DIVISION

Club	W.	L.	T.	Pct.	G.B.
Asheville (Astros)	54	16	0	.771	....
Spartanburg (Phillies)	36	34	0	.514	18
Fayetteville (Tigers)	32	37	0	.464	21½
Charleston (W.Va.) (Co-op)	29	40	0	.420	24½
Gastonia (Rangers)	28	42	0	.400	26
Greensboro (Red Sox)	22	48	0	.314	32

SOUTHERN DIVISION

Club	W.	L.	T.	Pct.	G.B.
Myrtle Beach (Blue Jays)	41	28	0	.594	....
Macon (Pirates)	38	30	1	.559	2½
Sumter (Braves)	38	31	0	.551	3
Charleston (S.C.) (Padres)	37	33	0	.529	4½
Savannah (Cardinals)	32	37	1	.464	9
Columbia (Mets)	29	40	0	.420	12

COMPOSITE STANDING OF CLUBS AT CLOSE OF SEASON, AUGUST 30

Club	Ash.	M.B.	Sum.	Mac.	Sav.	Ch.S	CChWV	Spar.	Fay.	Col.	Gas.	Gbr.	W.	L.	T.	Pct.	G.B.
Asheville (Astros)	....	4	6	9	6	4	12	12	10	7	11	10	91	48	0	.655	....
Myrtle Beach (Blue Jays)	6	....	6	8	12	11	6	5	5	9	7	8	83	56	0	.597	8
Sumter (Braves)	3	9	....	8	11	9	6	7	6	6	5	5	75	62	0	.547	15
Macon (Pirates)	1	8	8	....	8	8	4	4	7	12	7	6	73	64	1	.533	17
Savannah (Cardinals)	4	4	5	6	....	8	6	3	9	8	8	8	69	69	1	.500	21½
Charleston (S.C.) (Padres)	6	5	6	8	8	....	5	3	6	7	8	6	68	71	0	.489	23
Charleston (W.Va.) (Co-op)	4	4	4	5	2	5	....	8	8	5	10	11	66	73	0	.475	25
Spartanburg (Phillies)	4	5	3	6	4	7	8	....	8	6	7	8	66	74	0	.471	25½
Fayetteville (Tigers)	6	5	4	3	7	4	8	8	....	7	7	6	65	74	0	.468	26
Columbia (Mets)	3	7	10	4	7	9	5	4	2	....	5	8	64	75	0	.460	27
Gastonia (Rangers)	5	3	5	3	2	2	6	9	9	5	....	9	58	82	0	.414	33½
Greensboro (Red Sox)	6	2	5	4	2	4	5	8	10	2	7	....	55	85	0	.393	36½

Major league affiliations in parentheses.

Playoffs—Myrtle Beach defeated Asheville, three games to two, to win league championship.

Regular-Season Attendance—Asheville, 104,060; Charleston (S.C.), 87,185; Charleston (W.Va.), 97,563; Columbia, 92,855; Fayetteville, 95,008; Gastonia, 71,110; Greensboro, 166,208; Macon, 41,728; Myrtle Beach, 74,179; Savannah, 33,363; Spartanburg, 36,286; Sumter, 26,081. Total—925,626. Playoffs—8,894. All-Star Game—2,961.

Managers—Asheville, Keith Bodie; Charleston (S.C.), Tony Torchia; Charleston (W.Va.), Hal Dyer; Columbia, Butch Hobson; Fayetteville, John Lipon; Gastonia, Chino Cadahia; Greensboro, Dick Berardino; Macon, Dennis Rogers; Myrtle Beach, Barry Foote; Savannah, Mark DeJohn; Spartanburg, Ramon Aviles; Sumter, Buddy Bailey.

All-Star Team—1B—Mike Simms, Asheville; 2B—Carlos Baerga, Charleston (S.C.) and Geronimo Pena, Savannah; 3B—Ed Whited, Asheville; SS—Lou Frazier, Asheville; OF—Junior Felix, Myrtle Beach; Mark Whiten, Myrtle Beach; Vince Holyfield, Spartanburg; C—Phil Clark, Fayetteville; DH—John Love, Macon; RHP—Doug Linton, Myrtle Beach; LHP—Charles McElroy, Spartanburg; Most Valuable Player—Ed Whited, Asheville; Manager of the Year—Keith Bodie, Asheville.

(Compiled by Howe News Bureau, Boston, Mass.)

CLUB BATTING

Club	Pct.	G.	AB.	R.	OR.	H.	TB.	2B.	3B.	HR.	RBI.	GW.	SH.	SF.	HP.	BB.	Int. BB.	SO.	SB.	CS.	LOB.
Asheville	.269	139	4471	809	587	1204	1858	228	24	126	697	73	26	56	42	607	29	909	335	121	895
Charleston (S.C.)	.260	139	4510	610	641	1174	1565	166	24	59	523	52	49	30	49	516	25	898	173	95	976
Macon	.259	138	4555	674	640	1182	1611	168	33	65	554	57	61	39	45	452	25	940	151	60	960
Spartanburg	.259	140	4646	652	675	1202	1732	196	29	92	578	60	42	36	63	482	27	839	173	100	992
Fayetteville	.257	139	4656	644	706	1197	1643	160	41	68	547	53	60	31	54	436	24	904	218	85	976
Myrtle Beach	.255	139	4556	660	542	1164	1756	195	32	111	558	67	18	40	66	425	28	1056	295	95	913
Columbia	.248	139	4577	615	593	1136	1628	189	27	83	524	57	41	34	42	536	24	924	122	49	1025
Greensboro	.246	140	4650	554	635	1142	1550	177	21	63	475	49	61	35	39	456	18	785	73	25	1028
Gastonia	.243	140	4672	591	726	1136	1588	179	18	79	489	50	19	36	46	441	10	949	123	62	933
Sumter	.243	137	4500	616	561	1093	1525	173	26	69	529	63	37	31	38	493	29	883	216	63	975
Charleston (W.Va.)	.238	139	4378	552	648	1044	1497	201	24	68	493	62	23	36	44	505	17	990	207	116	900
Savannah	.235	139	4436	583	606	1043	1445	161	17	69	488	58	44	34	51	563	28	925	187	60	1002

INDIVIDUAL BATTING

(Leading Qualifiers for Batting Championship—378 or More Plate Appearances)

°Bats lefthanded.   †Switch-hitter.

Player and Club	Pct.	G.	AB.	R.	H.	TB.	2B.	3B.	HR.	RBI.	GW.	SH.	SF.	HP.	BB.	Int. BB.	SO.	SB.	CS.
Whited, Edward, Asheville	.323	128	440	97	142	263	37	0	28	126	18	0	7	8	59	7	58	12	3
Love, John, Macon	.313	138	515	76	161	238	29	3	14	91	9	1	5	9	44	4	63	7	3
Perez, Julio, Macon	.308	115	393	67	121	153	12	7	2	49	7	4	3	6	27	0	31	29	11
Yelding, Eric, Myrtle Beach	.305	88	357	53	109	128	12	2	1	31	5	1	4	4	18	0	30	73	13
Baerga, Carlos, Charleston (S.C.)†	.305	134	515	83	157	219	23	9	7	50	5	6	2	12	38	7	107	26	21
Hithe, Victor, Asheville	.302	126	388	78	117	179	23	3	11	53	6	0	2	4	55	1	75	31	17
Clark, Phillip, Fayetteville	.295	135	542	83	160	228	26	9	8	79	11	1	8	6	25	0	43	25	9
Cuyler, Milton, Fayetteville†	.292	94	366	65	107	129	8	4	2	34	3	17	2	7	34	4	78	27	13
Holyfield, Vince, Spartanburg	.292	132	507	91	148	223	19	1	18	58	6	3	3	12	55	1	90	56	19
Mantrana, Manuel, 62 Fay-30 Clb	.292	92	343	59	100	131	16	0	5	34	3	4	5	4	36	2	47	35	10
Felix, Junior, Myrtle Beach†	.290	124	466	70	135	204	15	9	12	51	9	2	2	10	43	8	124	64	28
Taylor, William, Charleston (S.C.)	.288	120	416	70	120	130	5	1	1	40	7	3	1	2	41	2	90	56	15
Beyeler, Arnold, Fayetteville	.285	117	431	78	123	152	10	5	3	39	4	16	4	7	64	0	51	20	8
Peguero, Julio, Macon†	.285	132	520	88	148	183	11	6	4	53	7	1	4	1	56	3	76	23	9

Departmental Leaders: G—Whiten, 139; AB—P. Clark, 542; R—Hunter, 105; H—Love, 161; TB—Simms, 264; 2B—Whited, 37; 3B—Baerga, P. Clark, Felix, 9; HR—Simms, 39; RBI—Whited, 126; GWRBI—Whited, 18; SH—Cuyler, 17; SF—Knapp, 10; HP—Whiten, 16; BB—Basso, 83; IBB—Grotewald, Whiten, 10; SO—Simms, 167; SB—Pena, 80; CS—Felix, 28.

(All Players—Listed Alphabetically)

Player and Club	Pct.	G.	AB.	R.	H.	TB.	2B.	3B.	HR.	RBI.	GW.	SH.	SF.	HP.	BB.	Int. BB.	SO.	SB.	CS.
Abreu, Franklin, Savannah	.263	129	415	45	109	125	13	0	1	44	4	2	6	3	49	1	88	11	5
Adams, Steven, Asheville	.000	17	6	0	0	0	0	0	0	0	0	0	0	0	0	0	3	0	0
Adkins, Todd, Fayetteville†	.265	18	49	10	13	14	1	0	0	9	2	1	0	3	1	7	0	1
Aleshire, Troy, Asheville	.098	19	41	2	4	6	2	0	0	5	0	0	1	1	4	0	9	1	2
Alexander, Gary, Gastonia	.293	50	184	27	54	81	15	0	4	14	0	1	0	0	26	0	36	3	0
Allen, Larry, Charleston (W. Va.)°	.269	106	338	35	91	119	19	0	3	35	2	0	1	1	46	2	45	21	14
Alou, Moises, Macon	.125	4	8	1	1	1	0	0	0	0	0	0	0	0	2	0	4	0	0
Alvarez, Michael, Savannah†	.279	77	240	36	67	78	3	4	0	23	3	3	0	3	27	2	24	29	8
Andersh, Kevin, Macon	1.000	6	1	0	1	1	0	0	0	0	0	0	1	0	0	0	0	0	0
Anderson, Michael, Columbia	.053	25	19	0	1	1	0	0	0	0	0	4	0	0	2	0	4	0	0
Archibald, Jaime, Columbia°	.260	62	177	17	46	64	10	1	2	28	3	0	1	4	20	1	51	3	0
Ashby, Andrew, Spartanburg	.000	13	8	0	0	0	0	0	0	1	1	1	0	0	1	0	4	0	0
Audain, Miguel, Charleston (W. Va.)	.129	14	31	1	4	6	2	0	0	0	1	0	2	3	0	3	2	0
August, Samuel, Asheville	.263	19	19	3	5	5	0	0	0	4	0	0	0	2	0	5	0	0
Austin, James, Charleston (S.C.)	.269	35	26	9	7	10	3	0	0	2	0	1	0	0	5	0	0	0	0
Baerga, Carlos, Charleston (S.C.)†	.305	134	515	83	157	219	23	9	7	50	5	6	2	12	38	7	107	26	21
Bailey, Brandon, Columbia	.256	124	403	63	103	192	15	1	24	70	7	0	5	3	68	2	108	2	3
Baker, Michael, Greensboro	.232	83	228	25	53	59	6	0	0	13	1	9	3	2	34	0	42	4	2
Balthazar, Doyle, Charleston (W. Va.)	.218	36	87	10	19	20	1	0	0	2	2	2	0	0	11	0	20	5	0
Banister, Jeffery, Macon	.254	101	307	35	78	116	20	0	6	37	5	3	3	2	27	0	70	1	0
Barretto, Saul, Gastonia	.223	36	130	16	29	37	4	2	0	7	0	0	0	6	0	6	2	1
Basso, Michael, Charleston (S.C.)	.252	133	428	59	108	158	23	0	9	53	6	4	4	6	83	3	71	10	5
Bates, Steven, Spartanburg°	.299	80	304	46	91	116	15	5	0	32	4	2	2	1	28	1	19	7	12
Behny, Mark, Savannah	.000	23	10	0	0	0	0	0	0	0	0	1	0	0	4	0	5	0	0
Belinda, Stanley, Macon	.000	50	7	0	0	0	0	0	0	0	0	1	0	0	0	0	4	0	0
Bell, Michael, Sumter°	.244	133	443	54	108	146	17	3	5	51	9	0	1	3	54	3	95	11	9
Bell, Robert, Fayetteville	.095	15	42	0	4	4	0	0	0	1	0	0	0	4	1	10	0	0
Bernhardt, Cesar, Charles. (W. Va.)	.252	122	444	56	112	165	28	5	5	53	7	0	2	7	25	1	59	15	9
Beyeler, Arnold, Fayetteville	.285	117	431	78	123	152	10	5	3	39	4	16	4	7	64	0	51	20	8
Bierscheid, Eugene, Spartanburg	1.000	27	1	1	1	1	0	0	0	0	0	0	0	0	0	0	0	0	0
Biggio, Craig, Asheville	.375	64	216	59	81	129	17	2	9	49	9	1	2	2	39	0	33	31	10
Blakely, David, Charleston (S.C.)	.000	18	1	0	0	0	0	0	0	0	0	0	0	0	0	0	0	0	0
Bond, Daven, Asheville	.375	37	8	2	3	4	1	0	0	2	0	0	0	1	0	3	0	0
Bones, Ricardo, Charleston (S.C.)	.103	26	29	1	3	3	0	0	0	2	0	0	0	4	0	7	0	1
Bowen, Ryan, Asheville	.214	27	28	2	6	9	0	0	1	2	0	0	1	0	3	0	9	0	0
Boyd, Daryl, Macon	.000	20	1	0	0	0	0	0	0	0	0	1	0	0	1	0	0	0	0
Brantley, Clifford, Spartanburg	.111	20	18	0	2	2	0	0	0	1	0	4	0	0	0	0	2	0	0
Braxton, Glen, Charleston (W. Va.)°..	.191	26	68	6	13	19	4	1	0	9	1	0	1	2	10	0	23	3	7
Britt, Robert, Spartanburg°	.238	63	189	19	45	63	5	2	3	29	4	1	5	0	15	0	36	4	4
Brocail, Douglas, Charleston (S.C.)°..	.333	20	21	7	7	8	1	0	0	0	0	3	0	0	3	0	5	0	0
Brooks, Brian, Charleston (S.C.)°	.271	124	414	45	112	166	23	5	7	55	6	0	4	4	37	3	75	21	10
Brown, Kevin, Sumter°	.105	9	19	1	2	2	0	0	0	3	0	0	0	0	5	0	0	0
Brown, Richard, Columbia	.000	51	6	0	0	0	0	0	0	0	0	1	0	0	1	0	1	0	0
Brunelle, Rodney, Charleston (W. Va.)....	.249	119	385	47	96	150	18	3	10	53	7	0	2	5	41	1	108	14	7
Buheller, Timothy, Greensboro°	.233	40	129	21	30	35	5	0	0	4	1	6	2	0	28	0	21	9	1
Butts, David, Sumter°	.261	100	295	45	77	112	14	3	5	34	3	0	0	1	26	4	27	5	2
Cabrera, Basilio, Fayetteville	.251	122	442	55	111	140	10	2	5	48	4	2	1	3	26	1	85	38	8
Cabrera, Francisco, Myrtle Beach	.276	129	449	61	124	195	27	1	14	72	10	0	6	3	40	6	82	4	2
Callas, Peter, Charleston (W. Va.)°...	.255	93	271	32	69	104	14	0	7	45	6	0	4	0	69	5	82	2	6
Castro, Liliano, Fayetteville	.248	40	105	7	26	26	0	0	0	7	0	3	0	1	5	0	13	1	2

Player and Club	Pct.	G.	AB.	R.	H.	TB.	2B.	3B.	HR.	RBI.	GW.	SH.	SF.	HP.	BB.	Int. BB.	SO.	SB.	CS.
Cepeda, Octavio, Macon	.231	20	13	2	3	4	1	0	0	0	0	1	0	0	0	0	6	0	0
Chavez, Rafael, Charleston (S.C.)	.182	53	11	0	2	2	0	0	0	1	0	1	0	0	0	0	9	0	0
Christopher, Fredrick, Spartanburg	.136	30	22	2	3	3	0	0	0	1	0	1	0	0	0	0	3	0	1
Clark, Garry, Spartanburg	.500	6	2	0	1	1	0	0	0	0	0	0	0	0	0	0	0	0	0
Clark, Mark, Sumter	.167	10	12	1	2	2	0	0	0	1	0	1	0	0	1	0	2	0	0
Clark, Phillip, Fayetteville	.295	135	542	83	160	228	26	9	8	79	11	1	8	6	25	0	43	25	9
Cloninger, Gregory, Sumter°	.294	11	34	2	10	13	1	1	0	4	0	0	1	3	0		8	0	0
Cohen, Tommy, Macon	.136	29	22	2	3	4	1	0	0	1	0	3	0	0	1	0	8	0	0
Cohoon, Donald, Charles. (W. Va.)†	.277	48	137	11	38	46	6	1	0	10	1	1	1	0	9	0	24	4	4
Colescott, Robert, Columbia	.196	60	148	12	29	47	3	3	3	17	0	1	2	2	10	0	46	2	5
Colpitt, Michael, Spartanburg	.208	16	24	1	5	6	1	0	0	2	0	0	0	0	5	0	4	1	2
Cooper, Scott, Greensboro°	.251	119	370	52	93	163	21	2	15	63	6	0	6	2	58	7	69	1	0
Crosby, Todd, Spartanburg†	.230	103	300	50	69	80	6	1	1	25	3	4	0	2	52	4	29	21	9
Cruz, Rafael, Gastonia†	.219	38	114	19	25	31	6	0	0	15	2	0	2	0	17	2	25	16	3
Cuevas, Johnny, Charleston (W. Va.)	.194	47	139	9	27	35	3	1	1	15	1	0	1	0	8	0	29	0	1
Cuyler, Milton, Fayetteville†	.292	94	366	65	107	129	8	4	2	34	3	17	2	7	34	4	78	27	13
Czajkowski, James, Sumter	.000	50	3	0	0	0	0	0	0	0	0	0	0	0	0	0	1	0	0
D'Alessandro, Salvatore, Ch. WV	.224	25	85	8	19	30	5	0	2	10	0	0	1	2	7	0	9	0	2
Davis, Mark, Sumter	.288	22	52	8	15	21	6	0	0	8	1	0	1	4	2	0	10	0	0
Davis, Mark, Savannah°	.095	24	21	2	2	2	0	0	0	4	1	2	1	0	1	0	3	0	0
Davis, Wayne, Myrtle Beach	.237	137	518	78	123	213	25	1	21	76	7	0	7	8	28	1	166	46	13
Deak, Brian, Sumter	.202	92	252	50	51	102	6	0	15	49	9	0	5	2	68	2	89	7	1
DeCillis, Dean, Fayetteville	.238	49	160	24	38	46	6	1	0	10	1	2	2	1	17	1	31	5	5
Deiley, Louis, Asheville	.299	33	67	5	20	30	4	0	2	12	0	1	2	3	7	0	10	2	1
DeLaCruz, Francisco, Charles. (S.C.)	.000	6	1	0	0	0	0	0	0	1	0	0	0	0	1	0	0	0	0
DeLaRosa, Cesar, Spartanburg†	.149	17	47	1	7	7	0	0	0	4	0	3	1	0	3	0	11	2	1
DeLeon, Pedro, Asheville	.071	21	14	1	1	1	0	0	0	1	0	0	0	0	0	0	6	0	0
DeLoach, Bobby, Savannah	.250	28	64	4	16	17	1	0	0	5	2	1	0	0	2	0	13	1	2
Denkenberger, Ralph, Macon°	.200	4	5	0	1	1	0	0	0	0	0	0	0	0	0	0	3	0	0
Diaz, Jose, Myrtle Beach	.230	21	61	8	14	23	3	0	2	6	1	2	0	0	6	0	19	1	0
Donnels, Chris, Columbia°	.257	41	136	20	35	48	7	0	2	17	1	0	1	1	24	1	27	3	1
Doster, Zachery, Fayetteville	.201	110	333	34	67	86	7	3	2	22	3	0	1	3	54	2	104	13	9
Dumas, Donald, 17 Sav-8 Fay	.000	25	1	0	0	0	0	0	0	0	0	0	0	0	0	0	0	0	0
Durant, Richard, Columbia	.333	3	27	5	9	14	3	1	0	3	0	3	1	0	2	0	12	4	1
Dziadkowiec, Andrew, Myrtle Beach°	.282	17	39	6	11	12	1	0	0	1	0	1	0	0	8	1	9	0	0
Edwards, Jeffrey, Asheville	.276	14	29	4	8	11	0	0	1	2	0	0	2	0	0	0	4	1	1
Ellis, Douglas, Macon	.000	31	5	0	0	0	0	0	0	0	0	0	1	0	1	0	3	0	0
Englett, Todd, Macon	.000	1	2	0	0	0	0	0	0	0	0	0	0	0	0	0	0	0	0
Escobar, Santiago, Myrtle Beach	.267	120	445	62	119	154	16	2	5	47	5	2	3	8	25	0	44	20	8
Felix, Junior, Myrtle Beach†	.290	124	466	70	135	204	15	9	12	51	9	2	2	10	43	8	124	64	28
Fernandez, Joey, Savannah°	.271	63	177	33	48	82	11	1	7	25	4	3	1	0	39	2	28	1	3
Flores, Jose, Greensboro†	.262	51	149	19	39	44	3	1	0	5	2	4	1	1	9	0	34	3	1
Foley, Martin, Spartanburg	.056	8	18	0	1	1	0	0	0	0	0	0	0	0	0	0	5	0	0
Forrest, Joel, Macon°	.077	35	13	1	1	1	0	0	0	1	0	2	0	0	1	0	9	0	0
Foster, Lindsay, Myrtle Beach†	.186	21	59	9	11	14	3	0	0	7	0	0	0	0	4	0	13	1	1
Foster, Paul, Fayetteville	.271	137	535	73	145	235	22	7	18	93	11	0	3	1	41	6	96	13	5
Frazier, Arthur, Asheville†	.258	108	399	83	103	119	9	2	1	33	4	4	3	2	68	1	89	75	24
Friesen, Robert, Fayetteville°	.000	6	1	0	0	0	0	0	0	0	0	0	0	0	0	0	1	0	0
Frost, Jerald, Sumter	.250	70	176	19	44	45	1	0	0	15	3	7	0	3	13	2	28	11	1
Gaeckle, Christopher, Greensboro	.224	18	116	16	26	44	8	2	2	18	1	0	1	5	19	0	20	0	1
Garcia, Carlos, Macon	.255	110	373	44	95	124	14	3	3	38	2	2	2	6	23	2	80	20	10
Garcia, Victor, Columbia°	.083	34	12	1	1	1	0	0	0	0	0	0	0	0	1	0	4	0	0
Garner, Darrin, Gastonia	.233	103	343	53	80	86	6	0	0	28	0	5	3	9	59	1	66	39	8
Garrison, James, Macon	.194	15	31	7	6	6	0	0	0	2	0	2	1	0	3	0	4	2	0
Gervais, Patrice, Macon	.211	23	38	5	8	10	2	0	0	2	0	0	0	0	4	0	8	0	0
Ging, Adam, Columbia†	.266	106	387	49	103	144	18	1	7	46	3	4	0	2	59	6	58	6	1
Gonring, Douglas, Asheville°	.234	36	94	15	22	35	7	0	2	10	0	3	0	11	2	7	0	0	
Gonzalez, Clifford, Columbia°	.246	125	399	56	98	147	20	4	7	36	2	6	0	4	37	2	54	24	7
Gonzalez, Juan, Gastonia	.265	127	509	69	135	202	21	2	14	74	7	1	4	5	30	2	92	9	4
Gonzalez, Marcos, Fayetteville	.333	5	3	1	1	1	0	0	0	0	0	0	0	0	0	0	2	0	1
Graham, Jeffrey, Savannah	.233	111	400	52	93	135	17	2	7	51	5	2	2	12	48	1	104	4	4
Grater, Marc, Savannah	.000	50	4	0	0	0	0	0	0	0	0	0	0	0	0	0	1	0	0
Greene, Keith, Spartanburg†	.143	18	28	1	4	6	0	1	0	1	0	0	0	0	0	0	5	0	1
Grimsley, Jason, Spartanburg	.273	23	11	2	3	3	0	0	0	0	0	0	0	0	1	0	4	0	0
Gross, Bob, Gastonia	.266	59	169	19	45	61	10	0	2	14	1	2	3	2	18	1	18	0	1
Grotewald, Jeff, Spartanburg°	.252	113	381	56	96	167	22	2	15	70	6	0	3	4	47	10	114	4	6
Gsellman, Bob, Charleston (W. Va.)	.167	31	84	15	14	27	4	0	3	12	2	1	0	0	13	0	46	1	0
Gurtcheff, Jefferey, Macon	.192	10	26	2	5	8	3	0	0	2	0	0	0	0	3	0	11	0	0
Hall, Andrew, Macon	.185	12	27	6	5	8	0	0	1	2	0	1	0	1	5	0	12	0	0
Hall, Martin, Asheville	.125	23	8	0	1	1	0	0	0	0	0	0	1	0	1	0	3	0	0
Hall, Victor, Charleston (S.C.)	.242	109	297	37	72	88	5	1	3	42	1	0	3	7	46	0	47	5	7
Hansel, Damon, Macon	.231	70	169	25	39	55	9	2	1	16	1	3	1	0	23	1	73	7	2
Hansen, Raymond, Greensboro°	.205	103	307	34	63	84	10	1	3	28	3	0	1	2	36	1	65	1	1
Hansen, Todd, Macon°	.000	1	1	0	0	0	0	0	0	0	0	0	0	0	0	0	0	0	0
Harris, Gregory, Charleston (S.C.)	.111	21	9	2	1	2	1	0	0	0	0	3	0	0	0	0	4	1	0
Harrison, Brian, Charleston (S.C.)°	.077	38	13	1	1	1	0	0	0	0	0	0	0	0	0	0	5	0	0
Harrison, Keith, Charleston (S.C.)°	.203	102	212	39	43	45	2	0	0	17	0	4	1	3	38	0	75	17	11
Hartman, Edward, Macon	.190	20	42	6	8	10	1	0	0	2	0	0	0	0	7	0	13	2	0
Haselman, William, Gastonia	.306	61	235	35	72	111	13	1	8	33	3	0	1	1	19	0	46	1	2
Heakins, Craig, Macon	.190	11	21	5	4	4	0	0	0	2	0	0	2	0	11	2	9	2	1
Henion, Scott, Columbia	.000	54	6	1	0	0	0	0	0	0	0	0	0	0	2	0	2	0	0
Henry, Michael, Savannah	.095	27	21	1	2	2	0	0	0	1	0	3	1	0	1	0	8	0	0
Hernandez, Robert, Columbia°	.244	35	45	5	11	12	1	0	0	5	2	6	0	1	2	0	9	0	0
Hewes, Patrick, Savannah	.259	118	417	51	108	145	13	0	8	53	4	0	5	4	74	5	59	0	0
Hightower, Barry, Columbia	.000	16	1	1	0	0	0	0	0	0	0	0	1	0	0	0	1	0	0
Hill, Anthony, Greensboro	.227	106	331	36	75	91	8	1	2	26	4	3	2	2	24	0	88	13	3
Hill, Stephen, Savannah°	.000	6	8	1	0	0	0	0	0	0	0	0	0	0	0	0	5	0	0
Hithe, Victor, Greensboro	.302	126	388	78	117	179	23	3	11	53	6	0	2	4	55	1	75	31	17
Holyfield, Vince, Spartanburg	.292	132	507	91	148	223	19	1	18	58	6	3	3	12	55	1	90	56	19
Horta, Neder, Asheville	.209	65	172	15	36	41	3	1	0	16	0	1	2	2	26	2	36	12	5
Horton, David, Savannah	.286	2	7	0	2	2	0	0	0	0	0	0	0	0	0	0	2	0	0
Hubbard, Trent, Asheville†	.236	101	284	39	67	80	8	1	1	35	2	0	7	0	28	1	42	28	13

Player and Club	Pct.	G.	AB.	R.	H.	TB.	2B.	3B.	HR.	RBI.	GW.	SH.	SF.	HP.	BB.	Int. BB.	SO.	SB.	CS.
Hufford, Scott, Spartanburg	.244	49	168	18	41	64	8	3	3	20	3	2	0	1	19	0	32	1	6
Hunter, Bertram, Asheville	.262	130	473	105	124	194	26	7	10	71	8	0	5	5	51	0	103	56	16
Hursey, Darrin, Fayetteville*	.000	25	1	0	0	0	0	0	0	0	0	0	0	0	0	0	1	0	0
Iglesias, Luis, Greensboro	.274	134	457	73	125	201	20	1	18	82	10	2	7	8	62	1	69	10	9
Jacas, Andre, Columbia†	.344	29	90	18	31	41	5	1	1	13	1	0	2	4	14	0	13	12	3
Jackson, Ronald, Gastonia	.210	89	291	35	61	81	9	1	3	24	4	1	5	3	39	0	63	2	5
Jarner, Kenneth, Spartanburg	.291	96	296	35	86	98	6	3	0	20	1	3	1	5	18	4	27	19	8
Jimenez, Alejandro, Columbia*	.314	44	118	25	37	54	9	1	2	16	3	0	0	1	6	0	26	0	0
Johnson, Charles, Spartanburg	.233	114	395	37	92	118	13	2	3	39	3	4	4	5	22	0	77	23	5
Johnson, Cisco, Myrtle Beach	.000	3	1	0	0	0	0	0	0	0	0	0	0	0	0	0	0	0	0
Johnson, Jay, Sumter	.179	84	207	24	37	55	6	3	2	30	5	5	2	4	11	1	28	7	2
Jones-Pointer, Carl, Sumter	.225	110	351	60	79	116	19	0	6	39	5	1	1	3	47	4	90	35	6
Kane, Thomas, Greensboro	.000	29	1	0	0	0	0	0	0	0	0	0	0	0	0	0	1	0	0
Kennelley, Steve, Columbia	.179	9	28	3	5	6	1	0	0	2	0	0	0	0	2	0	12	0	0
King, Michael, Charleston (S.C.)*	.251	114	335	34	84	108	12	0	4	40	4	2	2	1	37	5	55	2	5
Kiser, Garland, Spartanburg*	.000	21	4	0	0	0	0	0	0	0	0	0	0	0	0	0	2	0	0
Knapp, John, Charleston (W. Va.)	.227	133	471	65	107	151	17	3	7	56	8	1	10	2	74	1	103	42	14
Knorr, Randy, Myrtle Beach	.264	46	129	17	34	56	4	0	6	21	3	0	2	0	6	0	46	0	0
Koopmann, Robert, Macon†	.333	15	12	2	4	4	0	0	0	2	0	1	0	0	2	0	5	0	0
LaMarche, Michel, Spartanburg†	.143	44	7	0	1	1	0	0	0	0	0	0	0	0	0	0	5	0	0
Lau, David, Columbia	.234	49	107	14	25	40	4	1	3	12	2	1	0	0	16	1	19	0	2
Lavender, Robert, Gastonia	.207	49	150	22	31	53	4	0	6	17	2	1	3	1	23	0	27	2	3
Lawrence, Scott, Savannah	.108	29	37	4	4	5	1	0	0	3	1	5	0	0	8	0	16	0	0
LeMasters, James, Sumter	.133	28	15	0	2	2	0	0	0	0	0	0	0	0	2	0	8	0	0
Lemle, Robert, Columbia	.218	37	87	6	19	22	1	1	0	3	2	0	1	2	3	0	22	5	3
Lewis, Craig, Macon	.000	6	2	0	0	0	0	0	0	0	0	0	2	0	0	0	1	0	0
Liddell, David, Columbia	.208	23	53	6	11	14	3	0	0	3	1	0	0	0	7	0	18	0	0
Liebert, Allen, Fayetteville*	.216	29	97	9	21	32	2	0	3	14	1	0	0	0	23	2	20	1	1
Liriano, Felix, Fayetteville	.000	23	1	0	0	0	0	0	0	0	0	0	0	0	0	0	1	0	0
Llanes, Pedro, Savannah	.250	12	12	0	3	3	0	0	0	1	0	1	0	0	1	0	7	0	0
Lockley, Blane, Macon*	.198	45	116	22	23	48	5	1	6	19	3	0	0	3	18	1	43	0	1
Longmire, Anthony, Macon†	.263	127	445	63	117	155	15	4	5	62	7	3	6	5	41	6	73	18	7
Longuil, Richard, Sumter	.143	28	28	5	4	10	0	0	2	3	0	0	0	4	0	9	0	0
Looper, Edward, Savannah	.228	69	237	31	54	73	5	1	4	26	2	1	1	2	24	0	32	5	1
Lopez, Juan, Asheville	.234	13	47	4	11	13	2	0	0	7	2	1	0	0	0	0	8	0	1
Love, John, Macon	.313	138	515	76	161	238	29	3	14	91	9	1	5	9	44	4	63	7	3
Lovullo, Anthony, Fayetteville†	.257	55	191	34	49	86	13	0	8	32	3	2	1	2	37	4	30	6	0
Luciani, Randall, Fayetteville	.253	81	253	27	64	104	16	0	8	30	1	1	0	7	20	0	96	2	3
Lundahl, Richard, Columbus	.240	104	292	28	70	91	10	1	3	25	3	0	1	0	22	2	76	2	0
Macavage, Joseph, Macon	.000	5	4	0	0	0	0	0	0	0	0	0	0	0	0	0	2	0	0
Maldonado, Peter, Spartanburg	.600	53	5	2	3	4	1	0	0	0	0	2	0	1	0	0	0	0	0
Maloney, Richard, Sumter	.270	110	397	63	107	122	7	4	0	26	0	1	5	3	64	0	47	25	6
Mantrana, Manuel, 62 Fay.-30 Col.	.292	92	343	59	100	131	16	0	5	34	3	4	5	4	36	2	47	35	10
Marak, Paul, Sumter	.000	50	13	0	0	0	0	0	0	0	0	0	0	1	0	0	1	0	0
Marchese, Joseph, Greensboro	.219	84	269	27	59	77	12	0	2	25	0	4	3	0	6	0	30	2	2
Marina, Juan, Columbia	.321	28	28	3	9	9	0	0	0	3	0	1	0	0	0	0	7	0	0
Martel, Jay Savannah	.000	42	11	1	0	0	0	0	0	0	0	0	0	2	0	0	6	0	0
Martin, Albert, Sumter*	.253	117	375	59	95	159	18	5	12	64	8	1	4	2	44	5	69	27	8
Martin, Darryl, Fayetteville	.226	118	425	50	96	129	17	5	2	52	4	3	2	5	21	0	64	25	8
Martin, Norberto, Ch'rln (W.Va.)†	.312	68	250	44	78	109	14	1	5	35	8	4	3	4	17	1	40	14	4
Martinez, Gilberto, Greensboro	.278	109	370	43	103	146	13	3	8	46	4	3	2	6	32	2	48	4	2
Martinez, Julian, Savannah	.227	123	427	67	97	142	17	2	8	31	5	1	1	1	48	2	110	20	8
Massarelli, John, Asheville	.353	6	17	6	6	6	0	0	0	1	0	0	0	0	2	0	1	3	0
Maysey, Matthew, Charleston (S.C.)	.074	41	27	0	2	2	0	0	0	1	0	1	0	0	1	0	10	0	0
McCall, Roy, Spartanburg	.232	33	112	15	26	40	6	1	2	12	1	0	1	1	10	1	26	2	1
McCutcheon, James, Gastonia	.190	45	142	10	27	32	5	0	0	7	1	1	0	0	18	0	55	2	0
McDevitt, Terrance, Ch'rln (S.C)*	.222	91	185	21	41	42	1	0	0	15	2	4	0	1	32	0	41	6	1
McElroy, Charles, Spartanburg*	.333	29	27	5	9	11	2	0	0	1	0	0	0	0	1	0	6	0	0
McGee, Timothy, Greensboro	.259	90	270	25	70	79	7	1	0	20	4	2	2	2	29	0	28	3	2
McKinley, Timothy, Macon	.257	61	167	26	43	47	4	0	0	25	4	2	1	1	27	1	38	3	2
McMahon, Sean, Myrtle Beach	1.000	3	1	2	1	1	0	0	0	0	0	0	0	0	0	0	0	0	0
McMillan, Timothy, Ch'rln (W. Va.)	.268	111	366	54	98	154	17	3	11	45	2	0	4	5	21	3	106	23	13
McMurtrie, Daniel, Columbia	.000	38	12	2	0	0	0	0	0	0	0	0	0	0	2	0	2	0	0
Mealy, Anthony, Macon	.171	31	70	9	12	15	3	0	0	4	0	1	1	0	2	0	18	2	0
Mehl, Steven, Charleston (W. Va.)†	.168	130	357	45	60	77	9	1	2	19	4	5	1	5	38	1	77	32	15
Meizoso, Agustin, 20 Gas.-24 Col.*	.000	44	1	0	0	0	0	0	0	0	0	1	0	0	0	0	1	0	0
Melendez, Luis, Fayetteville	.225	46	111	19	25	37	4	1	2	13	0	1	0	1	19	0	47	2	0
Mendoza, Jesus, Sumter	.154	7	13	0	2	3	1	0	0	1	0	0	0	0	2	0	6	0	0
Merced, Orlando, Macon*	.000	4	4	1	0	0	0	0	0	0	0	0	0	0	1	0	3	0	0
Mercedes, Guillermo, Macon	.000	18	1	0	0	0	0	0	0	0	0	0	0	0	0	0	0	0	0
Meyer, Steven, Savannah*	.223	104	354	36	79	119	16	0	8	61	9	1	5	4	32	4	52	2	1
Miller, Kenny, Spartanburg	.214	21	56	6	12	12	0	0	0	4	1	0	1	0	4	0	15	2	1
Minton, Jesse, Sumter*	.145	34	76	4	11	12	1	0	0	3	0	0	0	3	0	14	0	1
Molero, Juan, Greensboro	.227	90	273	28	62	84	11	1	3	28	2	9	0	1	27	0	56	1	0
Monell, Johnny, Columbia†	.282	100	358	61	101	144	21	5	4	41	2	1	5	5	33	2	40	20	8
Monzon, Jose, Fayetteville	.053	11	19	1	1	1	0	0	0	0	0	0	0	0	2	0	5	0	0
Muratti, Rafael, Macon	.249	79	273	38	68	95	7	1	6	37	3	2	4	2	30	1	65	9	6
Murphy, Brian, Sumter	1.000	8	1	0	1	1	0	0	0	0	0	0	0	0	0	0	0	0	0
Murphy, Peter, Macon*	.250	10	4	1	1	1	0	0	0	1	0	0	0	0	0	0	1	0	0
Murrell, Rodney, Columbia*	.281	126	406	63	114	167	18	4	9	60	12	0	5	3	60	2	78	10	0
Natera, Luis, Columbia	.216	125	403	40	87	111	13	1	3	33	3	4	3	1	21	1	79	4	4
Naughton, Daniel, Columbia	.250	27	36	5	9	12	3	0	0	2	0	0	0	0	8	0	9	0	0
Navilliat, James, Charleston (S.C.)*	.125	41	16	0	2	2	0	0	0	0	0	0	1	0	2	0	4	0	0
Nelson, Ronald, Spartanburg	.248	130	416	55	103	165	27	1	11	61	6	0	3	10	43	2	109	4	3
Nemeth, Carey, Savannah	.139	16	36	6	5	11	0	2	5	0	0	0	0	9	0	17	1	1
Newson, Warren, Charleston (S.C.)*	.346	58	191	50	66	103	12	2	7	32	0	2	1	0	52	1	35	13	7
Nezelek, Andrew, Sumter*	.214	12	14	2	3	5	0	0	0	1	0	1	0	1	0	3	0	0
Nichols, Scott, Columbia	.236	94	275	42	65	98	13	1	6	39	7	3	3	6	58	1	67	8	0
Normand, Guy, Asheville	.111	31	18	4	2	6	1	0	1	2	1	4	0	0	7	0	13	0	0
Nowlin, James, Sumter†	.200	42	10	0	2	2	0	0	0	0	0	2	0	0	1	0	5	0	0
O'Quinn, Steven, 3 CWV.-22 Sum.	.200	25	5	1	1	1	0	0	0	0	0	0	0	0	0	0	2	0	0
Oglesbee, Nathan, Asheville*	.244	95	234	42	57	108	10	1	13	42	3	0	2	3	43	1	56	1	2

Player and Club	Pct.	G.	AB.	R.	H.	TB.	2B.	3B.	HR	RBI.	GW.	SH.	SF.	HP.	BB.	Int. BB.	SO.	SB.	CS.
Olivares, Omar, Charleston (S.C.)	.200	37	30	6	6	10	1	0	1	5	1	0	0	3	0	0	7	0	0
Olmstead, Reed, Savannah°	.150	18	60	5	9	11	2	0	0	4	0	1	1	0	7	0	17	0	0
Olson, James, Asheville	.143	27	7	0	1	1	0	0	0	2	1	2	0	0	0	0	4	0	0
Palmer, Dean, Gastonia	.215	128	484	51	104	147	16	0	9	54	4	0	1	6	36	1	126	4	4
Paris, Juan, Greensboro	.259	125	498	60	129	169	17	7	3	41	5	3	3	1	39	0	70	13	4
Parker, Theodore, Savannah†	.091	14	33	5	3	3	0	0	0	2	0	0	0	2	7	3	5	1	1
Peek, Timothy, Spartanburg	.200	10	10	0	2	2	0	0	0	0	0	0	0	0	0	0	4	0	0
Peel, Jack, Charleston (W. Va.)	.288	67	208	31	60	85	12	2	3	33	6	3	3	3	32	0	27	8	8
Peguero, Julio, Macon†	.285	132	520	88	148	183	11	6	4	53	7	1	4	1	56	3	76	23	9
Pena, Geronimo, Savannah	.269	134	505	95	136	197	28	3	9	51	7	1	3	8	73	6	98	80	21
Pennington, Kenneth, Sumter	.247	103	372	50	92	129	13	0	8	48	4	2	1	8	31	2	55	12	5
Perez, Gorky, Asheville°	.263	46	133	22	35	51	8	1	2	12	1	0	2	2	14	2	26	4	2
Perez, Julio, Macon	.308	115	393	67	121	153	12	7	2	49	7	4	3	6	27	0	31	29	11
Perez, Vladimir, Spartanburg	.143	46	7	0	1	2	1	0	0	0	0	1	0	0	1	0	4	0	0
Picota, Lenin, Savannah	.167	28	36	1	6	7	1	0	0	0	0	4	0	0	0	0	10	0	0
Pifer, Gary, 21 CWV.-9 Fay.	.000	30	1	1	0	0	0	0	0	0	0	0	0	0	0	0	0	0	0
Pilkinton, Lemuel, Greensboro	.240	84	262	33	63	84	7	1	4	25	2	5	1	1	31	0	63	3	0
Plumb, David, Sumter	.318	86	292	47	93	136	26	1	5	43	5	0	2	0	30	4	46	3	2
Polka, Fredric, Columbia°	.207	106	299	49	62	93	10	0	7	41	6	2	4	4	66	4	74	2	1
Polley, Dale, Sumter	.125	7	8	1	1	1	0	0	0	0	0	2	0	0	2	0	3	0	0
Ponder, Kevin, Columbia°	.000	33	3	0	0	0	0	0	0	0	0	0	0	0	0	0	1	0	0
Postier, Paul, Gastonia	.231	118	398	36	92	105	13	0	0	37	4	3	2	2	37	1	57	2	4
Price, Phillip, Spartanburg	.222	35	9	3	2	3	1	0	0	0	0	1	0	0	1	0	2	0	0
Quinlan, Thomas, Myrtle Beach	.223	132	435	42	97	138	20	3	5	51	1	3	6	6	34	0	130	0	2
Reaves, Scott, Spartanburg	.286	47	182	21	52	81	10	2	5	26	1	0	1	3	17	1	28	0	2
Redington, Thomas, Sumter	.321	18	56	9	18	20	2	0	0	5	1	0	0	0	13	0	14	1	2
Reed, Richard, Macon	.429	46	7	2	3	4	1	0	0	1	0	1	0	0	0	0	1	0	0
Rhodes, Karl, Asheville°	.252	129	413	62	104	137	16	4	3	50	4	3	8	0	77	6	82	43	14
Richards, Russell, Sumter°	.286	10	7	1	2	3	1	0	0	2	0	1	0	0	0	0	2	0	0
Rivers, Kenneth, Myrtle Beach	.250	2	8	1	2	3	1	0	0	0	0	0	0	1	0	0	2	0	0
Roberts, John, Greensboro	.349	63	232	47	81	114	19	1	4	26	4	5	1	3	22	0	13	13	1
Robertson, Roderick, Spartanburg†	.210	92	300	39	63	82	10	3	1	20	3	5	1	6	12	2	65	14	4
Rodgers, Paul, Myrtle Beach†	.260	120	377	70	98	157	20	3	11	45	4	3	3	2	77	1	93	28	10
Rodriguez, Raul, Myrtle Beach	.167	8	12	1	2	2	0	0	0	0	0	0	0	0	2	0	2	1	0
Rogers, Danilo, Sumter	.181	73	155	16	28	41	8	1	1	17	1	2	0	1	13	0	37	4	3
Romero, Charles, Myrtle Beach	1.000	1	1	0	1	1	0	0	0	0	0	0	0	0	0	0	0	0	0
Romero, Ediberto, Spartanburg	.000	9	4	0	0	0	0	0	0	0	0	0	0	0	0	0	4	0	0
Rosario, Victor, Greensboro	.219	109	370	43	81	120	9	0	10	48	4	3	1	7	24	3	60	2	5
Rose, Carl, Macon	.000	8	3	0	0	0	0	0	0	0	0	0	0	0	0	0	1	0	0
Roseboro, Jaime, Columbia	.247	113	340	41	84	109	8	1	5	40	4	2	3	4	39	0	54	13	5
Ross, Sean, Sumter°	.245	118	462	51	113	141	12	2	4	43	5	4	3	2	21	2	82	43	7
Ruckman, Scott, Spartanburg	.056	11	18	1	1	1	0	0	0	2	0	0	0	0	0	0	4	0	0
Ruskin, Scott, Macon†	.297	81	239	37	71	111	9	2	9	42	4	1	1	0	25	0	64	7	0
Russ, Kevin, Charleston (S.C.)	.234	47	124	19	29	46	4	2	3	22	2	1	3	0	13	1	41	2	2
Sabino, Miguel, Sumter°	.251	112	319	39	80	99	9	2	2	31	4	5	6	0	30	0	81	25	8
Sanchez, Pedro, Asheville	.269	124	412	63	111	152	31	2	2	57	5	1	6	1	30	1	49	28	10
Sanchez, Rey, Gastonia	.219	50	160	19	35	43	1	2	1	10	1	3	0	2	22	0	17	6	3
Santana, Ernesto, Macon	.000	15	7	0	0	0	0	0	0	0	0	0	0	0	0	0	2	0	0
Sawyer, Randall, Gastonia	.267	5	15	3	4	4	0	0	0	1	0	0	0	1	0	0	3	0	0
Scanlin, Michael, Gastonia°	.222	45	167	19	37	60	2	0	7	22	4	0	2	1	28	2	47	4	7
Scarsone, Steven, Ch'ln (W. Va.)	.216	95	259	35	56	72	11	1	1	17	3	3	0	3	31	0	64	8	5
Schlopy, Clifford, Macon°	.000	15	0	0	0	0	0	0	0	0	0	0	0	0	0	0	0	0	0
Schnurbusch, Chris, Fayetteville	.217	19	60	4	13	13	0	0	0	3	0	1	0	4	2	0	11	0	0
Scruggs, Ronald, Ch'rln (W. Va.)°	.179	29	84	11	15	23	1	2	1	2	0	1	0	1	8	0	32	8	2
Scultz, Todd, Gastonia†	.243	28	70	8	17	18	1	0	0	6	0	1	0	0	9	0	16	2	1
Sellick, John, Savannah	.176	25	74	8	13	30	2	0	5	10	1	0	0	1	9	0	30	0	0
Sheehan, John, Asheville	.000	43	3	0	0	0	0	0	0	0	0	0	0	0	1	0	2	0	0
Siegel, Robert, Macon	.000	5	0	0	0	0	0	0	0	0	0	0	1	0	0	0	0	0	0
Simms, Michael, Asheville	.273	133	469	93	128	264	19	0	39	100	9	0	3	9	73	5	167	7	0
Sims, Mark, Spartanburg†	.263	28	19	3	5	5	0	0	0	2	0	2	0	0	4	0	6	0	0
Singletary, Nathan, Savannah†	.167	7	18	2	3	4	1	0	0	0	0	1	0	0	0	0	4	0	0
Sloan, Terry, Sumter°	.000	16	0	0	0	0	0	0	0	0	0	1	0	0	0	0	0	0	0
Sojo, Luis, Myrtle Beach	.211	72	223	23	47	66	5	4	2	15	2	4	1	0	17	0	18	5	1
Solano, Ramon, Fayetteville	.241	74	237	28	57	78	7	4	2	24	1	6	3	9	0	0	69	14	7
Sommers, Scott, Greensboro°	.230	81	269	28	62	82	8	0	4	33	4	5	3	0	20	5	33	1	0
Sosa, Samuel, Gastonia	.279	129	519	73	145	213	27	4	11	59	14	0	3	5	21	0	123	22	8
Stark, Jeffrey, Spartanburg	.283	130	453	77	128	186	25	3	9	68	8	0	4	4	58	0	77	19	9
Stevanus, Michael, Macon†	.282	24	85	11	24	25	1	0	0	6	1	1	0	0	8	0	28	1	1
Stoker, Michael, Asheville	.207	25	29	2	6	7	1	0	0	2	0	3	0	0	1	0	7	0	0
Strickland, Robert, Ch'rln (W.Va.)°†	.233	87	258	30	60	91	13	0	6	34	2	0	2	2	34	2	72	5	5
Strong, Steven, Fayetteville	.238	8	21	2	5	8	0	0	1	6	1	0	2	0	2	0	1	1	0
Talbott, Shawn, Asheville	.286	36	7	1	2	4	2	0	0	0	0	0	0	0	0	0	1	0	0
Tatum, James, Charleston (S.C.)	.280	128	468	52	131	184	22	2	9	72	7	4	9	8	46	2	65	8	5
Taylor, Andrew, Savannah	.143	45	7	1	1	4	0	0	1	2	0	3	0	0	0	0	3	0	0
Taylor, William, Charleston (S.C.)	.288	120	416	70	120	130	5	1	1	40	7	3	1	2	41	2	90	56	15
Toy, Tracy, 13 Mac.-16 CWV.	.200	29	5	0	1	1	0	0	0	0	0	0	0	0	0	0	3	0	0
Trapasso, Michael, Savannah°	.167	23	6	2	1	1	0	0	0	0	0	0	0	0	2	0	3	0	0
Turner, Matthew, Sumter	.100	39	10	0	1	1	0	0	0	0	0	0	0	0	0	0	6	0	0
Valdez, Jose, Fayetteville†	.000	4	5	0	0	0	0	0	0	1	0	0	0	0	0	0	1	0	0
Valdez, Rafael, Charleston (S.C.)	.264	127	435	42	115	150	16	2	5	44	7	3	0	2	22	1	69	4	5
Valera, Julio, Columbia	.219	22	32	2	7	8	1	0	0	4	0	3	0	2	0	7	0	0	0
Van Horn, Todd, Gastonia	.212	59	189	26	40	53	5	4	0	17	2	0	1	2	23	0	35	6	5
Vaughn, Timothy, Macon	.205	60	185	21	38	58	6	1	4	18	1	6	1	2	14	1	41	1	1
Velazquez, Guillermo, Ch'rln (S.C.)°	.220	102	295	32	65	86	12	0	3	30	4	1	0	0	16	0	65	2	0
Velez, Jose, Gastonia	.256	110	403	51	103	170	21	2	14	50	1	0	0	7	9	0	91	1	3
Wagner, Gerald, Sumter	.000	26	0	0	0	0	0	0	0	0	0	0	0	0	0	0	0	0	0
Walker, Clifton, Spartanburg	.000	7	1	0	0	0	0	0	0	0	0	0	0	0	0	0	1	0	0
Ward, Gregory, Savannah†	.182	54	121	15	22	28	4	1	0	8	0	0	1	0	18	1	35	1	0
Wasilewski, Kevin, Asheville	.500	31	2	0	1	2	1	0	0	1	0	0	0	0	0	0	1	0	0
Whited, Edward, Asheville°	.323	128	440	97	142	263	37	0	28	126	18	0	7	8	59	7	58	12	3
Whiten, Mark, Myrtle Beach	.253	139	494	90	125	202	22	5	15	64	11	0	1	16	76	10	149	49	14
Williams, Paul, Greensboro	.257	63	206	17	53	75	13	0	3	26	2	0	3	4	18	0	44	0	0

Player and Club	Pct.	G.	AB.	R.	H.	TB.	2B.	3B.	HR.	RBI.	GW.	SH.	SF.	HP.	BB.	Int. BB.	SO.	SB.	CS.
Williams, Walter, Sumter*	.429	25	28	4	12	23	5	0	2	9	0	1	0	0	4	0	10	0	0
Wilson, Allen, Charleston (W. Va.)	.143	19	56	4	8	14	3	0	1	8	0	1	0	0	8	0	21	0	0
Yacopino, Edward, Macon†	.247	117	344	67	85	114	13	2	4	38	2	5	4	7	43	3	52	17	6
Yan, Julian, Myrtle Beach	.231	132	481	67	111	187	21	2	17	71	9	0	5	8	41	1	129	3	3
Yelding, Eric, Myrtle Beach	.305	88	357	53	109	128	12	2	1	31	5	1	4	4	18	0	30	73	13
York, Michael, Macon	.111	28	36	2	4	6	2	0	0	2	1	5	0	0	1	0	9	0	0
Young, Michael, Charleston (S.C.)	.000	12	11	0	0	0	0	0	0	1	0	3	0	0	1	0	6	0	0
Zaltsman, Stanley, Savannah*	.429	43	7	0	3	3	0	0	0	0	1	0	0	0	0	0	1	0	0
Zayas, Carlos, Spartanburg	.281	68	235	29	66	95	11	0	6	36	2	4	3	5	21	0	27	7	2

The following pitchers, listed alphabetically by club, with games in parentheses, had no plate appearances, primarily through use of designated hitters:

ASHEVILLE—McClure, LaRue (18); Osuna, Alfonso (14).

CHARLESTON (W.Va.)—Abrell, Thomas (31); Abreu, Francisco (7); Garcia, Rene (21); Gardner, Jimmie (21); Grovom, Carl (26); Hendrix, James (41); LaPoint, Anthony (40); Main, Kevin (9); Melvin, William (17); Robinson, Randall (36); Sandoval, Jesus (4); Sossamon, Timothy (31); Villanueva, Gilbert (16); Weems, Danny (28).

COLUMBIA—Myres, Douglas (4); Welborn, Todd (8).

FAYETTEVILLE—Aldred, Scott (21); Belcher, Glenn (31); Berrios, Hector (47); Duquette, Charles (7); Nosek, Randall (16); O'Neill, Daniel (39); Parascand, Steven (32); Phillips, Charles (11); Ramos, Jose (10); Rightnowar, Ronald (39); Rivera, Carlos (6); Schwabe, Michael (11); Slavik, Joseph (14); Williams, Kenneth (17).

GASTONIA—Alvarez, Wilson (8); Bryant, Phillip (31); Burgos, John (21); Castillo, Felipe (26); Jones, Marshall (32); Lamle, Adam (15); Malloy, Robert (9); Mathews, Terry (34); Mays, Jeffrey (18); Meadows, Jimmy (14); Morales, Edwin (17); Patterson, Glenn (8); Pavlik, Roger (15); Rivera, Lino (51); Rosenthal, Wayne (56); Soto, Edwardo (6); Steiner, Brian (6); Taylor, David (13); Whitaker, Darrell (13).

GREENSBORO—Abbott, John (22); Carista, Michael (27); Hale, Daniel (6); Haley, Bart (30); McGowan, Donald (28); Morrison, James (5); Revak, Raymond (25); Ryan, Kenneth (28); Sanderski, John (35); Schilling, Curtis (29); Wacha, Charles (8); Walters, David (28).

MACON—Hatfield, Robert (4).

MYRTLE BEACH—Burgos, Enrique (23); Depastino, Richard (25); Diaz, Victor (34); Guenther, Robert (5); Hall, Darren (41); Hentgen, Patrick (32); Horsman, Vincent (30); Humphries, Bobbie (20); Jones, Dennis (21); Linton, Douglas (20); MacDonald, Robert (10); Mejia, Cesar (33); Saitta, Patrick (1); Sanchez, Alex (1); Shea, John (26); Tracy, James (28); Watts, Robert (10).

SAVANNAH—Hohn, Eric (3).

GRAND SLAM HOME RUNS—Whited, 4; Bailey, Deak, Newson, 2 each; Basso, Brooks, Callas, Cuevas, D'Allesandro, Graham, Haselman, Holyfield, Love, Murrell, Nichols, Oglesbee, Rosario, Roseboro, Ross, Stark, Strickland, Whiten, Yacopino, Zayas, 1 each.

AWARDED FIRST BASE ON CATCHER'S INTERFERENCE—M. Bell 7 (Polka 2, P. Clark, Colescott, Gonring, Inglesias, P. Williams); Roberts 4 (Heakins 2, F. Cabrera, Zayas); Love 3 (P. Clark, Cuevas, Lau); DeCillis 2 (F. Cabrera 2); Luciani 2 (Balthazar, Liddell); Allen (Deiley); Austin (Deak); Baerga (Nichols); Bailey (F. Cabrera); Baker (Liddell); Bierscheid (McKinley); Brunelle (Jackson); Callas (Basso); P. Clark (McCall); Gsellman (Zayas); K. Harrison (Deak); Murrell (Gurtcheff); Pena (Zayas); Plumb (P. Williams); Scultz (Grotewald).

CLUB FIELDING

Club	Pct.	G.	PO.	A.	E.	DP.	PB.	Club	Pct.	G.	PO.	A.	E.	DP.	PB.
Sumter	.961	137	3537	1465	203	102	18	Myrtle Beach	.955	139	3575	1309	229	105	25
Savannah	.960	139	3545	1546	212	122	14	Gastonia	.954	140	3644	1462	247	99	38
Spartanburg	.960	140	3615	1632	220	147	35	Charleston (S.C.)	.954	139	3555	1493	246	112	25
Asheville	.959	139	3567	1445	216	112	27	Charleston (W. Va.)	.953	139	3528	1548	252	128	14
Greensboro	.959	140	3619	1361	214	101	23	Macon	.951	138	3522	1360	251	100	20
Columbia	.959	139	3588	1466	218	109	23	Fayetteville	.940	139	3612	1522	328	117	31

INDIVIDUAL FIELDING

*Throws lefthanded.

FIRST BASEMEN

Player and Club	Pct.	G.	PO.	A.	E.	DP.	Player and Club	Pct.	G.	PO.	A.	E.	DP.
Allen, Charleston (W. Va.)	.985	76	635	36	10	46	A. Martin, Sumter*	1.000	3	19	2	0	1
Archibald, Columbia*	.991	15	96	11	1	5	D. Martin, Fayetteville	.971	19	160	7	5	10
Bailey, Columbia	.983	101	807	62	15	69	McCall, Spartanburg	.929	2	24	2	2	3
Banister, Macon	1.000	18	125	7	0	7	Mendoza, Sumter	.971	6	30	3	1	3
Basso, Charleston (S.C.)	.975	24	176	20	5	15	Meyer, Savannah*	.986	98	899	58	14	80
Bell, Sumter*	.985	122	1007	70	16	70	Minton, Sumter	.965	19	130	9	5	18
Brooks, Charleston (S.C.)*	1.000	1	2	0	0	1	NELSON, Spartanburg	.9929	113	918	67	7	105
Brunelle, Charleston (W. Va.)*	.978	12	85	4	2	8	Nemeth, Savannah	1.000	4	29	2	0	4
Callas, Charleston (W. Va.)*	.983	33	277	17	5	35	Nichols, Savannah	.989	22	171	13	2	16
Cohoon, Charleston (W. Va.)	.857	2	12	0	2	0	Oglesbee, Asheville*	.992	16	120	4	1	12
Colescott, Columbia	1.000	1	1	0	0	0	Olmstead, Savannah*	.963	17	145	10	6	10
Cooper, Greensboro	.980	11	86	12	2	7	Pennington, Sumter	1.000	1	2	0	0	0
Davis, Sumter	1.000	5	19	1	0	0	Pilkinton, Greensboro	.989	68	506	18	6	44
Denkenberger, Macon*	1.000	2	7	1	0	1	Postier, Gastonia	1.000	24	216	19	0	18
Foster, Fayetteville	.9921	121	1060	77	9	95	Quinlan, Myrtle Beach	1.000	2	11	0	0	1
Gross, Gastonia	.994	22	148	5	1	6	Ruskin, Macon*	.976	22	152	10	4	11
Grotewald, Spartanburg	.988	32	228	9	3	20	Scanlin, Gastonia*	1.000	3	17	1	0	1
Hall, Charleston (S.C.)	.994	43	301	12	2	22	Sellick, Savannah	.979	6	44	2	1	4
Hansel, Macon	.977	55	369	20	9	25	Simms, Asheville	.984	124	1089	45	19	88
Hartman, Macon	.978	16	81	10	2	6	Sommers, Greensboro	.997	77	546	27	2	40
Iglesias, Spartanburg	.990	14	95	9	1	4	Strickland, Charleston (W. Va.)	.976	30	229	13	6	25
Jimenez, Columbia*	.980	25	187	10	4	15	Velazquez, Charleston (S.C.)	.984	88	695	58	12	52
King, Charleston (S.C.)	.990	14	99	4	1	13	Velez, Gastonia	.981	101	794	68	17	56
Knorr, Myrtle Beach	.984	7	56	5	1	3	Ward, Savannah	1.000	1	2	0	0	0
Lau, Columbia	.974	9	33	4	1	1	Whited, Savannah	1.000	6	32	1	0	2
Lockley, Macon	.974	32	282	14	8	29	Yacopino, Macon*	.968	8	60	1	2	4
Love, Macon	.987	10	72	6	1	5	Yan, Myrtle Beach	.985	131	1047	87	17	90
Lundahl, Columbia	.974	12	71	3	2	4	Zayas, Spartanburg	1.000	1	5	3	0	0
Marchese, Greensboro	1.000	1	1	1	0	0							

SECOND BASEMEN

Player and Club	Pct.	G.	PO.	A.	E.	DP.	Player and Club	Pct.	G.	PO.	A.	E.	DP.
Abreu, Savannah	1.000	1	1	0	0	0	Bernhardt, Charleston (W. Va.)	.958	109	225	255	21	63
Adkins, Fayetteville	.936	14	17	27	3	6	Beyeler, Fayetteville	.938	63	110	190	20	42
Audain, Charleston (W. Va.)	1.000	1	2	2	0	0	Butts, Sumter	.956	61	91	126	10	29
Baerga, Charleston (S.C.)	.948	115	229	302	29	67	Castro, Fayetteville	1.000	1	0	2	0	0
Baker, Greensboro	.981	81	170	198	7	40	Cloninger, Sumter	1.000	3	2	2	0	0

SECOND BASEMEN—Continued

Player and Club	Pct.	G.	PO.	A.	E.	DP.
Cohoon, Charleston (W. Va.)	1.000	3	2	1	0	0
Crosby, Spartanburg	.952	83	177	178	18	52
Cruz, Gastonia	.975	21	35	42	2	9
DeCillis, Fayetteville	.857	3	5	7	2	0
Diaz, Myrtle Beach	1.000	6	18	12	0	3
Escobar, Myrtle Beach	.955	119	227	265	23	56
Flores, Greensboro	.964	12	25	29	2	6
Frost, Sumter	1.000	1	2	1	0	1
Garner, Gastonia	.963	99	188	256	17	45
Garrison, Macon	.966	7	11	17	1	3
Gervais, Macon	1.000	5	5	4	0	1
Ging, Columbia	.970	89	197	223	13	41
Horta, Asheville	.955	29	60	66	6	13
Hubbard, Asheville	.947	51	92	105	11	15
Jarner, Spartanburg	1.000	2	1	4	0	0
Johnson, Sumter	.966	75	122	163	10	30
Kennelley, Columbia	.917	8	15	18	3	4
Knorr, Myrtle Beach	1.000	1	1	0	0	0
Lovullo, Fayetteville	.970	7	9	23	1	4
Maloney, Sumter	.993	34	62	85	1	16
Mantrana, 50 Fay-30 Columbia	.934	80	188	193	27	43
Marchese, Greensboro	.951	62	114	121	12	25
Martin, Charleston (W. Va.)	1.000	1	2	0	0	0
Martinez, Savannah	1.000	9	16	17	0	3
McDevitt, Charleston (S.C.)	.947	36	39	86	7	13
Mehl, Charleston (W. Va.)	.947	5	6	12	1	2
Murrell, Columbia	.955	24	38	46	4	8
Nichols, Savannah	1.000	1	0	2	0	0
Peguero, Macon	.892	11	20	13	4	2
Pena, Savannah	.958	134	324	342	29	80
PEREZ, Macon	.964	104	188	263	17	49
Postier, Gastonia	.929	8	12	14	2	4
Robertson, Spartanburg	.956	70	160	190	16	59
Sanchez, Asheville	.954	81	142	192	16	47
Scarsone, Charleston (W. Va.)	.955	32	67	83	7	23
Schnurbusch, Fayetteville	.950	5	7	12	1	0
Scultz, Gastonia	.957	27	38	52	4	9
Sojo, Myrtle Beach	.961	18	45	29	3	11
Solano, Fayetteville	.909	5	11	9	2	1
Stevanus, Macon	.947	12	26	28	3	2
Tatum, Charleston (S.C.)	1.000	1	0	1	0	0
Valdez, Fayetteville	.833	3	7	3	2	0
Vaughn, Macon	.952	23	42	38	4	6
Whited, Asheville	1.000	1	0	1	0	0

THIRD BASEMEN

Player and Club	Pct.	G.	PO.	A.	E.	DP.
Audain, Charleston (W. Va.)	.852	8	6	17	4	1
Beyeler, Fayetteville	.898	59	39	119	18	10
Butts, Sumter	.897	20	5	30	4	2
Castro, Fayetteville	.857	4	3	3	1	0
Clark, Fayetteville	.739	9	4	13	6	2
Cohoon, Charleston (W. Va.)	.842	23	11	53	12	7
Colescott, Columbia	.940	21	18	29	3	4
Colpitt, Spartanburg	.875	2	3	4	1	0
Cooper, Greensboro	.917	91	68	141	19	12
Davis, Sumter	.870	8	4	16	3	1
DeCillis, Fayetteville	1.000	1	0	1	0	1
Diaz, Myrtle Beach	1.000	1	0	2	0	0
Donnels, Columbia	.922	39	32	86	10	10
Foster, Myrtle Beach	.880	10	6	16	3	1
Garner, Gastonia	1.000	2	0	2	0	1
Garrison, Macon	.750	2	1	2	1	0
Gervais, Macon	1.000	1	1	3	0	0
Gonring, Asheville	.500	1	0	1	1	0
Hall, Charleston (S.C.)	.788	13	8	18	7	3
Horta, Asheville	.875	4	3	4	1	0
Horton, Savannah	1.000	2	1	6	0	1
Hubbard, Asheville	.500	1	0	1	1	0
Iglesias, Spartanburg	.932	70	48	173	16	22
Jarner, Spartanburg	.852	21	8	38	8	5
Knapp, Charleston (W. Va.)	.934	100	84	199	20	18
Looper, Savannah	.904	61	32	128	17	6
Love, Macon	.906	120	93	236	34	23
Lovullo, Fayetteville	.871	49	32	110	21	9
Lundahl, Columbia	1.000	11	9	13	0	0
Maloney, Sumter	1.000	5	2	6	0	1
Mantrana, Fayetteville	.438	4	2	5	9	0
Martin, Fayetteville	.737	6	5	9	5	1
Martinez, Savannah	.907	75	59	176	24	17
McDevitt, Charleston (S.C.)	.920	13	7	16	2	2
Molero, Greensboro	.872	67	40	110	22	16
Murrell, Columbia	.931	86	54	162	16	15
Nemeth, Savannah	.923	5	3	9	1	1
Nichols, Savannah	.923	7	4	8	1	2
Palmer, Gastonia	.819	107	58	209	59	12
Pennington, Sumter	.879	100	86	196	39	26
Perez, Macon	1.000	3	1	1	0	0
Postier, Gastonia	.899	36	23	57	9	2
Quinlan, Myrtle Beach	.891	130	96	232	40	29
Reaves, Spartanburg	.913	46	26	100	12	10
Redington, Sumter	.932	17	12	29	3	1
Ruckman, Spartanburg	.636	6	0	7	4	0
Sanchez, Asheville	.922	23	13	46	5	2
Scarsone, Charleston (W. Va.)	1.000	8	4	7	0	1
Schnurbusch, Fayetteville	.711	14	7	25	13	5
Sellick, Savannah	.500	3	1	1	2	0
Simms, Asheville	1.000	1	0	2	0	0
Sojo, Myrtle Beach	.778	4	3	4	2	0
Stevanus, Macon	1.000	1	1	1	0	0
Strickland, Charleston (W. Va.)	.900	11	5	22	3	3
Tatum, Charleston (S.C.)	.935	127	87	257	24	19
Vaughn, Macon	.863	17	13	31	7	5
WHITED, Asheville	.944	121	75	248	19	23
Zayas, Spartanburg	.900	3	2	7	1	0

SHORTSTOPS

Player and Club	Pct.	G.	PO.	A.	E.	DP.
ABREU, Savannah	.915	129	178	424	56	69
Adkins, Fayetteville	.944	3	7	10	1	3
Audain, Charleston (W. Va.)	.909	5	10	10	2	1
Baerga, Charleston (S.C.)	.900	19	24	39	7	9
Baker, Greensboro	1.000	1	1	1	0	0
Butts, Sumter	.941	11	14	34	3	3
Castro, Fayetteville	.926	35	39	111	12	14
Cloninger, Sumter	.938	7	3	27	2	1
Cohoon, Charleston (W. Va.)	.970	16	15	49	2	9
Crosby, Spartanburg	.963	7	7	19	1	4
Cruz, Gastonia	.927	10	13	25	3	0
DeCillis, Fayetteville	.906	44	69	105	18	20
DeLaRosa, Spartanburg	.909	17	13	47	6	8
Diaz, Myrtle Beach	.919	14	18	39	5	10
Escobar, Myrtle Beach	.833	2	1	4	1	0
Flores, Greensboro	.883	29	20	63	11	7
Foley, Spartanburg	.963	8	12	14	1	3
Frazier, Asheville	.907	107	172	297	48	52
Frost, Sumter	.896	59	73	126	23	20
Garcia, Macon	.910	110	161	262	42	48
Garrison, Macon	.917	3	1	10	1	0
Ging, Columbia	.939	23	37	71	7	11
Horta, Asheville	.920	28	31	50	7	8
Iglesias, Spartanburg	.937	54	62	162	15	26
Jarner, Spartanburg	.921	50	70	162	20	33
Knapp, Charleston (W. Va.)	.936	33	45	101	10	15
Maloney, Sumter	.962	77	90	217	12	36
Marchese, Greensboro	.913	17	24	39	6	7
D. Martin, Fayetteville	1.000	1	2	0	0	0
N. Martin, Charleston (W. Va.)	.902	48	80	151	25	32
Martinez, Savannah	.870	17	15	45	9	10
McDevitt, Charleston (S.C.)	.829	12	7	22	6	7
Murrell, Columbia	1.000	5	3	0	0	1
Natera, Columbia	.907	125	144	356	51	57
Pena, Savannah	1.000	1	1	1	0	0
Postier, Gastonia	.977	31	53	72	3	19
Robertson, Spartanburg	.922	22	13	58	6	11
Rosario, Greensboro	.912	109	155	303	44	44
P. Sanchez, Asheville	.879	16	14	37	7	5
R. Sanchez, Gastonia	.933	47	88	162	18	25
Scarsone, Charleston (W. Va.)	.908	51	56	122	18	23
Sojo, Myrtle Beach	.939	42	49	90	9	18
Solano, Fayetteville	.873	67	116	180	43	33
Stevanus, Macon	.921	13	17	18	3	3
Tatum, Charleston (S.C.)	1.000	2	0	1	0	0
Valdez, Charleston (S.C.)	.902	122	145	343	53	49
VanHorn, Gastonia	.926	54	75	151	18	24
Vaughn, Macon	.945	22	35	51	5	9
Yelding, Myrtle Beach	.887	88	126	226	45	27

CATCHERS

Player and Club	Pct.	G.	PO.	A.	E.	DP.	PB.
Aleshire, Asheville	.991	17	105	6	1	1	3
Balthazar, Charles. (W. Va.)	.962	33	178	26	8	0	2
Banister, Macon	.968	64	415	46	15	7	4
Barretto, Gastonia	.974	29	206	18	6	2	5
Basso, Charleston (S.C.)	.976	105	628	78	17	6	17
Biggio, Asheville	.995	59	377	46	2	3	9
Brunelle, Charleston (W. Va.)	1.000	1	0	2	0	0	1
Cabrera, Myrtle Beach	.978	123	849	89	21	5	20

CATCHERS—Continued

Player and Club	Pct.	G.	PO.	A.	E.	DP.	PB.
Clark, Fayetteville	.961	80	452	67	21	4	23
Colescott, Columbia	.959	24	123	16	6	0	3
Cuevas, Charleston (W. Va.)	.980	47	257	35	6	4	3
D'Alessandro, Char. (WVa)	.988	25	139	29	2	2	1
Deak, Sumter	.983	77	576	55	11	3	7
Deiley, Asheville	.958	26	133	25	7	0	5
Dziadkowiec, Myrtle Beach	.985	12	62	5	1	0	0
Edwards, Asheville	1.000	14	54	13	0	0	3
Englett, Macon	1.000	1	7	0	0	0	0
Gaeckle, Greensboro	.990	25	171	19	2	0	5
Gonring, Asheville	.954	32	176	12	9	0	7
Gross, Gastonia	.969	25	143	11	5	0	10
Grotewald, Spartanburg	.956	50	319	52	17	4	16
Gsellman, Charles. (W. Va.)	.979	30	165	20	4	2	0
Gurtcheff, Macon	.939	6	43	3	3	0	1
A. Hall, Macon	.945	9	46	6	3	2	3
G. Hall, Charleston (S.C.)	.947	5	18	0	1	0	0
Haselman, Gastonia	.933	4	26	2	2	0	1
Heakins, Macon	.913	11	64	9	7	0	2
HEWES, Savannah	.992	114	644	97	6	4	9
Hubbard, Asheville	1.000	2	3	1	0	0	0
Jackson, Gastonia	.988	88	677	75	9	3	22
King, Charleston (S.C.)	.978	49	277	29	7	1	8
Knorr, Myrtle Beach	1.000	10	38	2	0	0	1
Lau, Columbia	.977	27	152	18	4	1	2
Liddell, Columbia	.930	19	90	16	8	2	3
Liebert, Fayetteville	.973	17	94	14	3	0	1
Lopez, Asheville	1.000	13	84	17	0	1	0
Massarelli, Asheville	1.000	6	33	2	0	0	0
McCall, Spartanburg	.979	29	165	23	4	2	8
McGee, Greensboro	.987	86	565	103	9	4	10
McKinley, Macon	.972	58	387	36	12	4	6
Melendez, Fayetteville	.970	43	231	26	8	3	3
Miller, Spartanburg	.944	4	17	0	1	0	1
Monzon, Fayetteville	.979	11	44	3	1	1	3
Nelson, Spartanburg	.981	14	93	10	2	1	1
Nichols, Savannah	.972	29	152	23	5	2	5
Pilkinton, Greensboro	.962	15	50	0	2	1	1
Plumb, Sumter	.981	66	402	58	9	1	11
Polka, Columbia	.982	93	569	45	11	3	15
Rivers, Myrtle Beach	1.000	2	18	1	0	0	1
Rodriguez, Myrtle Beach	1.000	7	33	4	0	1	3
Strickland, Charles. (W. Va.)	1.000	2	5	1	0	1	4
Strong, Fayetteville	.942	8	46	3	3	1	1
Williams, Greensboro	.962	35	202	23	9	1	7
Wilson, Charleston (W. Va.)	.982	18	92	18	2	1	3
Zayas, Spartanburg	.973	55	335	58	11	6	9

OUTFIELDERS

Player and Club	Pct.	G.	PO.	A.	E.	DP.
Alexander, Gastonia	.928	48	73	4	6	0
Allen, Charleston (W. Va.)°	.875	6	6	1	1	0
Alou, Macon	1.000	4	6	0	0	0
Alvarez, Savannah°	1.000	53	78	4	0	0
Archibald, Columbia°	.950	27	34	4	2	0
Balthazar, Charleston (W. Va.)	1.000	2	1	0	0	0
Basso, Charleston (S.C.)	1.000	3	7	0	0	0
Bates, Spartanburg	.964	74	102	4	4	1
Bell, Fayetteville	1.000	11	23	0	0	0
Biggio, Asheville	1.000	2	1	0	0	0
Braxton, Charleston (W. Va.)°	.971	23	32	2	1	1
Britt, Spartanburg°	.969	52	89	4	3	2
Brooks, Charleston (S.C.)°	.960	119	205	11	9	3
Brunelle, Charleston (W. Va.)	.925	100	142	6	12	0
Buheller, Greensboro°	.990	39	91	5	1	1
Cabrera, Fayetteville	.912	118	184	13	19	2
Clark, Fayetteville	.963	14	24	2	1	0
Cohoon, Charleston (W. Va.)	.750	3	3	0	1	0
Colpitt, Spartanburg	1.000	1	1	1	0	0
Cuyler, Fayetteville	.973	90	237	13	7	2
Davis, Myrtle Beach	.936	133	209	11	15	3
DeLoach, Savannah	1.000	4	2	0	0	0
Doster, Savannah	.959	90	154	10	7	4
Felix, Myrtle Beach	.956	85	188	8	9	1
Fernandez, Savannah	1.000	56	74	2	0	1
P. Foster, Fayetteville	.933	13	25	3	2	0
Gervais, Macon	.500	1	1	0	1	0
C. Gonzalez, Columbia	.956	113	208	7	10	4
J. Gonzalez, Gastonia	.953	126	234	10	12	1
M. Gonzalez, Fayetteville	1.000	2	4	0	0	0
Graham, Savannah	.948	108	156	7	9	0
Greene, Spartanburg	.933	11	14	0	1	0
Gross, Gastonia	1.000	1	2	0	0	0
Hall, Charleston (S.C.)	.950	41	51	6	3	1
Hansen, Greensboro°	.931	29	51	3	4	1
Harrison, Charleston (S.C.)°	.908	79	111	8	12	0
Hill, Greensboro	.938	91	101	4	7	0
Hithe, Asheville	.949	118	195	9	11	3
HOLYFIELD, Spartanburg	.985	128	245	10	4	2
Hubbard, Asheville	.938	28	29	1	2	0
Hufford, Spartanburg	.922	47	56	3	5	0
Hunter, Asheville	.959	128	266	15	12	0
Jacas, Columbia	.938	27	43	2	3	1
Jarner, Spartanburg	.933	11	14	0	1	0
Jimenez, Columbia°	.500	1	1	0	1	0
Ch. Johnson, Savannah	.978	112	255	7	6	1
Ci. Johnson, Myrtle Beach	1.000	1	1	0	0	0
Jones-Pointer, Sumter	.982	103	158	8	3	2
Lavender, Gastonia	.949	44	72	3	4	0
Lemle, Columbia	.979	33	44	3	1	1
Longmire, Macon	.956	108	167	5	8	1
Looper, Savannah	.800	7	8	0	2	0
Luciani, Fayetteville	.972	18	33	2	1	1
Lundahl, Columbia	.960	61	88	9	4	2
Mantrana, Fayetteville	1.000	2	4	0	0	0
Marchese, Greensboro	1.000	4	8	0	0	0
A. Martin, Sumter°	.932	103	118	5	9	0
D. Martin, Fayetteville	.958	78	155	4	7	0
N. Martin, Charleston (W. Va.)	1.000	2	2	1	0	0
G. Martinez, Greensboro	.942	103	177	3	11	0
J. Martinez, Savannah	.982	30	51	5	1	3
McCutcheon, Gastonia	.942	35	63	2	4	0
McDevitt, Charleston (S.C.)	1.000	1	2	1	0	0
McGee, Greensboro	1.000	2	5	0	0	0
McMillan, Charleston (W. Va.)°	.926	102	154	8	13	0
Mealy, Macon	.885	21	23	0	3	0
Mehl, Charleston (W. Va.)	.961	126	230	15	10	1
Merced, Macon	1.000	2	1	1	0	0
Miller, Spartanburg	.700	11	7	0	3	0
Monell, Columbia	.950	93	129	4	7	0
Muratti, Macon	.979	72	128	10	3	3
Murrell, Columbia	.818	11	8	1	2	0
Naughton, Columbia	.957	22	21	1	1	0
Newson, Charleston (S.C.)°	.977	58	81	4	2	1
Nichols, Savannah	.984	40	58	2	1	0
Oglesbee, Asheville°	1.000	12	13	0	0	0
Paris, Greensboro	.945	123	282	8	17	3
Parker, Savannah	.967	11	27	2	1	1
Peel, Charleston (W. Va.)	.942	55	107	6	7	2
Peguero, Asheville	.948	122	231	6	13	0
Perez, Asheville°	.942	38	46	3	3	0
Postier, Gastonia	1.000	18	34	2	0	0
Rhodes, Asheville°	.952	128	163	14	9	3
Roberts, Greensboro	.992	62	113	6	1	0
Rodgers, Myrtle Beach	.982	63	110	1	2	0
Rogers, Sumter	.944	50	47	4	3	1
Romero, Myrtle Beach	1.000	1	2	0	0	0
Roseboro, Columbia	.970	105	184	8	6	1
Ross, Sumter°	.971	111	226	9	7	1
Ruskin, Macon°	.941	26	31	1	2	0
Russ, Charleston (S.C.)	.941	45	63	1	4	0
Sabino, Savannah°	.970	92	151	8	5	2
Sawyer, Gastonia	1.000	5	4	1	0	0
Scanlin, Gastonia°	.974	40	72	2	2	1
Scruggs, Charleston (W. Va.)°	.959	28	44	3	2	0
Scultz, Gastonia	1.000	2	3	0	0	0
Sellick, Savannah	1.000	3	1	1	0	1
Singletary, Savannah	1.000	6	10	0	0	0
Sojo, Myrtle Beach	1.000	1	3	0	0	0
Sosa, Gastonia	.920	113	183	12	17	4
Stark, Spartanburg	.973	111	204	14	6	2
Strickland, Charleston (W. Va.)	.981	36	50	2	1	1
Taylor, Charleston (S.C.)	.951	115	204	10	11	3
Ward, Savannah	.973	24	33	3	1	0
Whiten, Myrtle Beach	.963	135	292	18	12	4
Yacopino, Macon°	.962	92	166	10	7	3

PITCHERS

Player and Club	Pct.	G.	PO.	A.	E.	DP.
Abbott, Greensboro°	.875	22	1	6	1	0
Abrell, Charleston (W. Va.)	.850	31	5	12	3	1
Abreu, Charleston (W. Va.)	1.000	7	0	1	0	0
Adams, Macon	1.000	17	1	10	0	1
Aldred, Fayetteville°	.962	21	4	21	1	1
Alvarez, Gastonia°	1.000	8	1	6	0	0
Andersh, Macon°	.833	6	0	5	1	1
Anderson, Columbia	.800	25	8	20	7	0
Ashby, Spartanburg	.867	13	5	8	2	1
AUGUST, Asheville	1.000	18	4	25	0	2
Austin, Charleston (S.C.)	.963	31	14	12	1	1
Behny, Savannah	1.000	23	3	9	0	0
Belcher, Fayetteville	.875	31	6	15	3	0
Belinda, Macon	.875	50	3	11	2	3

PITCHERS—Continued

Player and Club	Pct.	G.	PO.	A.	E.	DP.
Berrios, Fayetteville*	.867	45	2	24	4	0
Bierscheid, Spartanburg	.944	27	2	15	1	0
Blakley, Charleston (S.C.)	1.000	18	2	2	0	0
Bond, Asheville	.963	37	6	20	1	1
Bones, Charleston (S.C.)	.947	26	12	24	2	1
Bowen, Asheville	.870	26	3	17	3	0
Boyd, Macon	1.000	20	2	5	0	0
Brantley, Spartanburg	1.000	20	8	17	0	4
Brocail, Charleston (S.C.)	.958	19	9	14	1	2
K. Brown, Sumter*	1.000	9	2	15	0	0
R. Brown, Columbia	1.000	51	7	9	0	1
Bryant, Gastonia	.800	31	11	21	8	1
E. Burgos, Myrtle Beach*	.857	23	3	3	1	0
J. Burgos, Gastonia*	1.000	21	1	9	0	0
Carista, Greensboro	.962	27	6	19	1	0
Castillo, Gastonia	.964	26	6	21	1	4
Cepeda, Macon	.875	20	3	4	1	0
Chavez, Charleston (S.C.)	.857	53	4	14	3	0
Christopher, Spartanburg*	.920	28	3	20	2	0
G. Clark, Spartanburg	1.000	6	2	6	0	1
M. Clark, Sumter	.833	10	3	7	2	1
Cohen, Macon	1.000	29	3	9	0	0
Cooper, Greensboro	.667	2	2	0	1	0
Czajkowski, Sumter	1.000	50	8	8	0	1
Davis, Savannah*	1.000	20	3	12	0	0
DeLaCruz, Charleston (S.C.)	1.000	6	0	1	0	0
DeLeon, Asheville	.900	19	3	15	2	0
Depastino, Myrtle Beach	.778	25	2	5	2	0
J. Diaz, Myrtle Beach	1.000	1	1	0	0	0
V. Diaz, Myrtle Beach*	.909	34	0	10	1	1
Dumas, 17 Sav-8 Fay	1.000	25	1	4	0	0
Duquette, Fayetteville	1.000	7	0	1	0	0
Durant, Columbia	.912	23	13	18	3	1
Ellis, Macon	.680	31	4	13	8	3
Forrest, Macon*	.917	35	2	20	2	0
Friesen, Fayetteville	1.000	5	0	4	0	0
R. Garcia, Charleston (W. Va.)*	1.000	21	5	4	0	0
V. Garcia, Columbia	.938	34	6	9	1	1
Gardner, Charleston (W. Va.)	.808	21	4	17	5	0
Grater, Savannah	1.000	50	4	15	0	1
Grimsley, Spartanburg	.846	23	15	7	4	2
Grovom, Charleston (W. Va.)*	.956	26	6	59	3	1
Guenther, Myrtle Beach	1.000	5	1	2	0	0
Hale, Greensboro	1.000	6	1	4	0	0
Haley, Greensboro*	.684	30	5	8	6	0
D. Hall, Myrtle Beach	1.000	41	5	6	0	0
M. Hall, Asheville	.875	23	2	12	2	0
Hansen, Macon*	.833	10	2	3	1	0
Harris, Charleston (S.C.)	.929	20	3	10	1	0
Harrison, Charleston (S.C.)*	.846	37	0	11	2	0
Hatfield, Macon	1.000	4	0	4	0	0
Hendrix, Charleston (W. Va.)	.895	41	5	12	2	0
Henion, Columbia	1.000	54	5	17	0	1
Henry, Savannah	.967	27	12	17	1	3
Hentgen, Myrtle Beach	.897	32	13	13	3	0
Hernandez, Columbia*	.973	24	10	26	1	1
Hightower, Columbia*	1.000	16	0	2	0	0
Hill, Savannah*	1.000	6	2	7	0	0
Horsman, Myrtle Beach*	.923	30	7	17	2	2
Humphries, Myrtle Beach	1.000	20	3	8	0	0
Hursey, Fayetteville	.905	25	11	27	4	1
D. Jones, Myrtle Beach*	1.000	21	0	9	0	0
M. Jones, Gastonia	.913	32	17	25	4	0
Kane, Greensboro	.941	29	6	10	1	1
Kiser, Spartanburg*	1.000	21	1	7	0	0
Koopmann, Macon*	.957	15	4	18	1	0
LaMarche, Spartanburg	.889	44	6	18	3	0
Lamle, Gastonia*	.929	15	3	10	1	0
LaPoint, Charleston (W. Va.)	.833	40	2	3	1	0
Lawrence, Savannah	.886	29	15	24	5	2
LeMasters, Sumter	.905	28	8	11	2	0
Lewis, Macon	1.000	6	1	2	0	1
Linton, Myrtle Beach	.880	20	8	14	3	1
Liriano, Fayetteville	.909	23	13	7	2	0
Llanes, Savannah	.923	12	5	7	1	0
Longuil, Sumter	.829	27	10	19	6	0
Macavage, Macon	1.000	5	1	4	0	0
MacDonald, Myrtle Beach*	1.000	10	2	6	0	0
Main, Charleston (W. Va.)	.917	9	5	6	1	3
Maldonado, Spartanburg	.955	53	6	15	1	2
Malloy, Gastonia	.778	9	3	4	2	0
Marak, Sumter	.931	50	13	14	2	0
Marina, Columbia	.976	27	15	25	1	1
Martel, Savannah	.909	42	7	13	2	0
Mathews, Gastonia	.941	34	2	14	1	0
Mays, Gastonia	.882	18	7	8	2	1
Maysey, Charleston (S.C.)	.969	41	13	18	1	0

Player and Club	Pct.	G.	PO.	A.	E.	DP.
McClure, Asheville	.857	18	1	5	1	1
McElroy, Spartanburg*	.920	24	8	15	2	1
McGowan, Greensboro	.846	28	2	9	2	1
McMurtrie, Columbia	1.000	38	8	7	0	2
Meadows, Gastonia	.963	14	14	12	1	0
Meizoso, 20 Gas-24 Clb*	1.000	44	1	10	0	0
Mejia, Myrtle Beach	.909	33	7	23	3	1
Melvin, Charleston (W. Va.)	1.000	17	1	4	0	0
Mercedes, Macon	1.000	18	0	9	0	0
Morales, Gastonia	.909	17	3	7	1	0
Morrison, Greensboro	1.000	5	0	3	0	0
B. Murphy, Sumter	1.000	7	0	2	0	0
P. Murphy, Macon	1.000	10	3	4	0	0
Myres, Columbia	1.000	4	0	1	0	0
Navilliat, Charleston (S.C.)*	.970	40	10	22	1	1
Nezelek, Spartanburg	.935	12	13	16	2	2
Normand, Asheville*	.933	31	6	22	2	2
Nosek, Fayetteville	.500	16	3	2	5	0
Nowlin, Sumter	.920	41	5	18	2	0
O'Neill, Fayetteville*	.909	39	2	18	2	2
O'Quinn, 3 CWV-22 Sum	.867	25	4	9	2	0
Olivares, Charleston (S.C.)	.830	31	18	21	8	1
Olson, Asheville	1.000	27	5	12	0	2
Osuna, Asheville*	1.000	14	0	4	0	0
Parascand, Fayetteville*	.905	32	3	16	2	0
Patterson, Gastonia	1.000	8	1	0	0	0
Pavlik, Gastonia	.917	15	7	15	2	0
Peek, Spartanburg	.933	10	6	8	1	2
Perez, Spartanburg	.938	46	4	11	1	0
Phillips, Fayetteville	.955	11	5	16	1	1
Picota, Savannah	.854	28	14	27	7	3
Pifer, 19 CWV-8 Fay	.941	27	10	22	2	1
Polley, Sumter*	.857	7	2	10	2	1
Ponder, Columbia	1.000	33	4	6	0	1
Price, Spartanburg	1.000	35	7	13	0	1
Ramos, Fayetteville*	.000	10	0	0	1	0
Reed, Macon	.800	46	2	10	3	2
Revak, Greensboro*	.875	25	4	3	1	1
Richards, Sumter	1.000	10	2	11	0	1
Rightnowar, Fayetteville	.958	39	9	14	1	1
C. Rivera, Fayetteville	1.000	6	0	1	0	0
L. Rivera, Gastonia	.920	51	9	14	2	2
Robinson, Charleston (W. Va.)	.889	36	2	14	2	0
Romero, Spartanburg	.889	9	3	5	1	0
Rose, Macon	1.000	8	0	1	0	0
Rosenthal, Gastonia	.909	56	5	5	1	0
Ryan, Greensboro	.962	28	8	17	1	1
Saitta, Myrtle Beach	1.000	1	0	1	0	0
Sanderski, Greensboro	.750	35	3	6	3	0
Sandoval, Charleston (W. Va.)	1.000	4	0	1	0	0
Santana, Macon	.667	15	1	5	3	0
Schilling, Greensboro	.964	29	5	22	1	1
Schlopy, Macon*	1.000	15	0	8	0	1
Schwabe, Fayetteville	1.000	11	2	4	0	1
Shea, Myrtle Beach*	.941	26	5	27	2	3
Sheehan, Asheville	.933	43	3	11	1	0
Siegel, Macon	.714	5	1	4	2	0
Sims, Spartanburg*	.949	28	4	33	2	0
Slavik, Fayetteville*	.667	14	1	7	4	0
Sloan, Sumter	.923	16	3	9	1	0
Sossamon, Charleston (W. Va.)	.889	26	7	25	4	2
Soto, Gastonia	.833	6	2	3	1	1
Stoker, Greensboro	.886	25	10	21	4	3
Talbott, Asheville	1.000	36	2	8	0	1
A. Taylor, Savannah	.833	45	4	6	2	1
D. Taylor, Gastonia	1.000	13	1	4	0	0
Toy, 13 Mac-16 CWV	.969	29	4	17	1	3
Tracy, Myrtle Beach	.875	28	5	9	2	1
Trapasso, Savannah*	1.000	23	0	5	0	0
Turner, Sumter	.938	39	5	10	1	0
Valera, Columbia	.815	22	7	15	5	1
Villanueva, Charleston (W. Va.)*	.875	16	6	8	2	1
Wacha, Greensboro	1.000	8	1	5	0	0
Wagner, Sumter*	1.000	26	0	8	0	0
Walker, Spartanburg	1.000	7	2	2	0	0
Walters, Greensboro	1.000	28	3	12	0	2
Wasilewski, Asheville	.833	31	1	9	2	1
Watts, Myrtle Beach	.857	10	0	6	1	1
Weems, Charleston (W. Va.)	.841	28	7	30	7	3
Welborn, Columbia	1.000	8	0	2	0	0
Whitaker, Gastonia	1.000	13	0	1	0	0
K. Williams, Fayetteville*	.909	17	8	12	2	1
W. Williams, Sumter*	.882	24	6	9	2	1
York, Macon	.931	28	6	21	2	1
Young, Charleston (S.C.)*	.808	12	4	17	5	0
Zaltsman, Savannah*	1.000	43	1	5	0	1

The following players do not have any recorded accepted chances at the positions indicated; therefore, are not listed in the fielding averages for those particular positions: Baerga, of; Brooks, p; Cruz, 3b; Doster, 3b; L. Foster, of; Ging, 3b; G. Hall, p; Hernandez, of; Hohn, p; Hubbard, p; King, 3b, of; Luciani, p; Lundahl, 2b; McMahon, 2b; J. Perez, ss; Postier, p; A. Sanchez, p; Solano, 3b; Sommers, 2b; Steiner, p; R. Valdez, of; Van Horn, 1b; Velazquez, p.

CLUB PITCHING

Club	ERA.	G.	CG.	ShO.	Sv.	IP.	H.	R.	ER.	HR.	HB.	BB.	Int. BB.	SO.	WP.	Bk.
Myrtle Beach	3.13	139	6	13	39	1191.2	1065	542	414	89	43	417	23	990	80	11
Sumter	3.37	137	17	11	32	1179.0	1067	561	442	83	47	444	11	971	82	14
Columbia	3.50	139	13	10	31	1196.0	1142	593	465	88	39	491	41	907	89	13
Asheville	3.64	139	23	12	39	1189.0	1099	587	481	94	37	552	20	946	93	14
Charleston (W. Va.)	3.65	139	23	14	27	1176.0	1144	648	477	49	82	541	13	807	133	14
Savannah	3.67	139	21	10	28	1181.2	1121	606	482	83	66	479	32	771	87	18
Macon	3.70	138	9	6	38	1174.0	1160	640	482	81	56	471	12	939	89	18
Fayetteville	3.75	139	10	7	33	1204.0	1164	706	501	56	42	563	10	844	95	15
Greensboro	3.78	140	19	11	32	1206.1	1212	635	507	87	31	489	32	949	77	15
Charleston (S.C.)	3.86	139	20	4	25	1185.0	1146	641	508	72	41	424	27	901	79	12
Spartanburg	4.12	140	19	6	26	1205.0	1194	675	552	82	49	529	43	940	100	14
Gastonia	4.32	140	6	5	40	1214.2	1203	726	583	88	46	510	20	1037	115	10

PITCHERS' RECORDS

(Leading Qualifiers for Earned-Run Average Leadership — 112 or More Innings)

*Throws lefthanded.

Pitcher—Club	W.	L.	Pct.	ERA.	G.	GS.	CG.	GF.	ShO.	Sv.	IP.	H.	R.	ER.	HR.	HB.	BB.	Int. BB.	SO.	WP.
Linton, Myrtle Beach	14	2	.875	1.55	20	19	2	1	0	1	122.0	94	34	21	9	2	25	0	155	8
August, Asheville	12	1	.923	1.72	18	18	5	0	3	0	115.0	82	35	22	4	4	39	0	110	4
Hentgen, Myrtle Beach	11	5	.688	2.35	32	31	2	0	2	0	188.0	145	62	49	5	8	60	0	131	14
Grovom, Charleston (W. Va.)*	12	6	.667	2.44	26	24	6	1	4	0	170.0	143	63	46	7	4	70	1	147	19
Marina, Columbia	6	7	.462	2.59	27	20	0	4	0	2	128.2	116	50	37	4	5	59	4	80	6
Mejia, Myrtle Beach	7	4	.636	2.73	33	10	1	15	0	5	125.1	108	42	38	8	7	27	4	90	6
Valera, Columbia	8	7	.533	2.80	22	22	2	0	2	0	125.1	114	53	39	7	4	31	0	97	6
Longuil, Sumter	9	9	.500	2.89	27	23	6	3	0	2	152.2	148	66	49	8	7	45	0	100	11
Carista, Greensboro	13	6	.684	2.89	27	26	4	0	1	0	180.2	155	66	58	15	1	49	3	148	4
Stoker, Asheville	13	5	.722	2.91	25	25	6	0	2	0	164.0	129	60	53	9	2	86	0	124	11
Hernandez, Columbia*	11	10	.524	3.01	24	24	8	0	1	0	170.1	141	76	57	10	3	57	3	113	10

Departmental Leaders: G—Rosenthal, 56; W—York, 17; L—Schilling, 15; Pct.—August, .923; GS—Hentgen, 31; CG—Hernandez, Lawrence, Sossamon, 8; GF—Grovom, 4; Sv.—Rosenthal, 30; IP—Hentgen, 188.0; H—Bones 183; R—Bryant, 108; ER—Olivares, 87; HR—Horsman, 20; HB—Sossamon, 22; BB—York, 88; IBB—Maldonado, 10; SO—Schilling, 189; WP—Bryant, 22.

(All Pitchers—Listed Alphabetically)

Pitcher—Club	W.	L.	Pct.	ERA.	G.	GS.	CG.	GF.	ShO.	Sv.	IP.	H.	R.	ER.	HR.	HB.	BB.	Int. BB.	SO.	WP.
Abbott, Greensboro*	3	4	.429	3.39	22	6	0	6	0	0	82.1	87	44	31	4	2	39	1	68	7
Abrell, Charleston (W. Va.)	2	2	.500	5.43	31	8	0	7	0	3	64.2	73	53	39	4	4	34	0	33	9
Abreu, Charleston (W. Va.)*	0	0	.000	4.76	7	0	0	5	0	0	11.1	16	7	6	0	1	9	0	6	3
Adams, Macon	6	2	.750	1.66	17	3	0	3	0	1	43.1	40	12	8	1	1	8	1	23	2
Aldred, Fayetteville*	4	9	.308	3.57	21	20	0	0	0	0	110.0	101	56	44	5	3	69	0	91	8
Alvarez, Gastonia*	1	5	.167	6.47	8	6	0	1	0	0	32.0	39	24	23	5	4	23	0	19	0
Andersh, Macon*	3	3	.500	3.31	6	6	0	0	0	0	32.2	34	15	12	3	2	7	0	20	2
Anderson, Columbia	8	10	.444	3.59	25	24	3	0	0	0	145.1	139	86	58	17	4	66	2	102	10
Ashby, Spartanburg	4	6	.400	5.60	13	13	1	0	0	0	64.1	73	45	40	8	2	38	2	52	9
August, Asheville	12	1	.923	1.72	18	18	5	0	3	0	115.0	82	35	22	4	4	39	0	110	4
Austin, Charleston (S.C.)	7	10	.412	4.20	31	21	2	3	1	0	152.0	138	89	71	10	1	56	2	123	20
Behny, Savannah	3	6	.333	5.50	23	10	1	3	0	0	72.0	85	51	44	6	3	50	1	28	10
Belcher, Fayetteville	5	2	.714	4.41	31	5	0	11	0	3	85.2	92	57	42	3	0	38	0	55	1
Belinda, Macon	6	4	.600	2.09	50	0	0	45	0	16	82.0	59	26	19	4	4	27	1	75	4
Berrios, Charleston (S.C.)*	7	7	.500	2.79	45	0	0	25	0	7	87.0	70	46	27	5	4	35	3	93	10
Bierscheid, Spartanburg	1	2	.333	3.69	27	0	0	15	0	4	46.1	55	28	19	2	4	19	1	16	4
Blakley, Charleston (S.C.)	0	4	.000	5.79	18	0	0	12	0	2	18.2	18	12	12	2	4	9	0	7	3
Bond, Asheville	3	5	.375	4.95	37	9	0	19	0	6	87.1	96	61	48	8	2	38	1	66	10
Bones, Charleston (S.C.)	12	5	.706	3.65	26	26	4	0	1	0	170.1	183	81	69	9	6	45	4	130	5
Bowen, Asheville	12	5	.706	4.04	26	26	6	0	2	0	160.1	143	86	72	12	5	78	1	126	8
Boyd, Macon	1	2	.333	4.71	20	1	0	6	0	1	36.1	34	21	19	1	3	19	3	20	2
Brantley, Spartanburg	3	10	.231	4.81	20	20	3	0	0	0	110.1	114	69	59	2	9	58	2	86	10
Brocail, Charleston (S.C.)	2	6	.250	4.09	19	18	0	0	0	0	92.1	94	51	42	6	1	28	0	68	4
Brooks, Charleston (S.C.)	0	0	.000	2.08	3	0	0	2	0	0	4.1	3	1	1	0	0	4	0	3	0
K. Brown, Sumter*	7	1	.875	1.93	9	9	0	0	0	0	56.0	53	14	12	2	1	19	0	45	5
R. Brown, Columbia	6	7	.462	3.21	51	0	0	27	0	8	87.0	80	41	31	7	2	46	8	90	7
Bryant, Gastonia	9	11	.450	5.31	31	23	0	0	0	0	142.1	159	108	84	18	9	54	1	132	22
E. Burgos, Myrtle Beach*	5	2	.714	2.11	23	0	0	13	0	7	38.1	22	15	9	2	0	24	1	46	8
J. Burgos, Gastonia*	0	2	.000	5.24	21	3	0	6	0	0	55.0	61	34	32	4	2	14	2	42	4
Carista, Greensboro	13	6	.684	2.89	27	26	4	0	1	0	180.2	155	66	58	15	1	49	3	148	4
Castillo, Gastonia	7	8	.467	4.36	26	22	0	1	0	0	119.2	118	70	58	2	5	66	1	86	8
Cepeda, Macon	6	6	.500	4.26	20	18	1	1	1	0	80.1	75	53	38	4	2	44	0	63	11
Chavez, Charleston (S.C.)	8	5	.615	2.99	53	0	0	32	0	11	87.1	86	36	29	2	3	21	6	59	3
Christopher, Spartanburg*	9	11	.450	3.74	28	24	3	2	2	1	142.0	131	71	59	10	5	57	5	140	14
G. Clark, Spartanburg	0	0	.000	3.45	6	0	0	3	0	0	15.2	15	7	6	0	0	3	0	11	1
M. Clark, Sumter	4	4	.500	4.56	10	10	0	0	0	0	51.1	49	29	26	5	1	21	0	46	5
Cohen, Macon	5	8	.385	3.82	29	19	2	1	0	0	117.2	124	78	50	10	6	48	0	96	9
Cooper, Greensboro	0	0	.000	0.00	2	0	0	2	0	0	2.0	2	1	0	0	0	2	0	3	1
Czajkowski, Sumter	4	6	.400	2.23	50	0	0	40	0	20	68.2	63	26	17	2	2	17	3	59	4
Davis, Savannah*	6	5	.545	4.47	20	19	3	0	2	0	104.2	114	69	52	8	5	44	0	32	7
DeLaCruz, Charleston (S.C.)	0	1	.000	8.31	6	1	0	4	0	0	8.2	9	8	8	1	1	10	0	7	0
DeLeon, Asheville	7	5	.583	4.42	19	14	3	1	2	1	99.2	93	54	49	10	6	41	2	91	9
Depastino, Myrtle Beach	4	0	1.000	4.92	25	1	0	10	0	1	53.0	48	34	29	5	7	28	0	37	5
J. Diaz, Myrtle Beach	0	0	.000	16.62	1	0	0	1	0	0	4.1	8	8	8	3	0	3	0	1	1
V. Diaz, Myrtle Beach*	1	5	.167	3.53	34	0	0	26	0	9	43.1	39	24	17	1	0	27	3	41	2
Dumas, 17 Sav.-8 Fay.	1	3	.250	5.90	25	0	0	6	0	1	39.2	45	30	26	6	5	13	2	26	3
Duquette, Fayetteville	0	0	.000	0.66	7	0	0	5	0	1	13.2	9	2	1	0	1	3	0	13	2
Durant, Columbia	6	10	.375	4.05	23	20	0	0	0	0	126.2	129	67	57	11	3	41	3	78	7
Ellis, Macon	5	2	.714	2.91	31	5	0	12	0	3	77.1	76	35	25	4	2	31	0	62	5
Forrest, Macon*	4	6	.400	5.01	35	16	1	6	0	0	106.0	142	83	59	12	6	31	1	63	8
Friesen, Fayetteville	1	3	.250	7.29	5	4	0	0	0	0	21.0	25	18	17	3	0	18	0	13	0
R. Garcia, Charleston (W. Va.)	2	1	.667	3.00	21	0	0	14	0	4	24.0	19	11	8	0	1	10	1	17	4
V. Garcia, Columbia	3	8	.273	4.46	34	13	0	4	0	0	101.0	102	56	50	14	1	46	0	84	8
Gardner, Charleston (W. Va.)	2	9	.182	5.17	21	14	0	4	0	0	78.1	91	60	45	3	7	49	0	51	19
Grater, Savannah	6	10	.375	3.04	50	0	0	28	0	6	74.0	54	35	25	4	6	48	9	59	11

Pitcher—Club	W.	L.	Pct.	ERA.	G.	GS.	CG.	GF.	ShO.	Sv.	IP.	H.	R.	ER.	HR.	HB.	BB.	Int. BB.	SO.	WP.
Grimsley, Spartanburg	7	4	.636	3.16	23	9	3	7	0	0	88.1	59	48	31	4	6	54	2	98	12
Grovom, Charleston (W. Va.)	12	6	.667	2.44	26	24	6	1	4	0	170.0	143	63	46	7	4	70	1	147	19
Guenther, Myrtle Beach	0	0	.000	5.87	5	0	0	1	0	0	7.2	14	7	5	1	2	7	1	5	1
Hale, Greensboro	3	0	1.000	0.00	6	0	0	6	0	1	15.0	8	0	0	0	0	9	0	12	0
Haley, Greensboro*	3	11	.214	4.28	30	15	2	10	0	2	122.0	119	71	58	6	10	54	1	63	12
D. Hall, Myrtle Beach	5	5	.500	3.51	41	0	0	28	0	6	66.2	57	31	26	7	0	28	5	68	1
G. Hall, Charleston (S.C.)	0	0	.000	0.00	1	0	0	1	0	0	2.0	2	0	0	0	0	1	0	2	0
M. Hall, Asheville	5	5	.500	4.24	23	8	1	4	0	0	76.1	80	44	36	4	2	29	1	66	7
Hansen, Macon*	1	1	.500	6.23	10	0	0	3	0	1	13.0	15	13	9	1	0	12	1	13	3
Harris, Charleston (S.C.)	9	3	.750	2.77	20	15	2	1	0	0	94.1	75	34	29	3	2	24	2	74	3
Harrison, Charleston (S.C.)*	4	0	1.000	2.72	37	3	0	11	0	4	72.2	64	31	22	4	4	30	2	87	5
Hatfield, Macon	0	0	.000	1.93	4	1	0	0	0	0	9.1	8	4	2	0	2	5	0	6	0
Hendrix, Charleston (W. Va.)	4	4	.500	3.53	40	3	0	9	0	0	89.1	100	45	35	2	7	41	4	53	5
Henion, Columbia	3	9	.250	3.34	54	1	0	44	0	12	70.0	63	37	26	5	6	34	7	55	11
Henry, Savannah	8	5	.615	3.57	27	21	3	2	0	0	141.0	123	69	56	7	16	46	0	80	6
Hentgen, Myrtle Beach	11	5	.688	2.35	32	31	2	0	2	0	188.0	145	62	49	5	8	60	0	131	14
Hernandez, Columbia*	11	10	.524	3.01	24	24	8	0	1	0	170.1	141	76	57	10	3	57	3	113	10
Hightower, Columbia*	0	1	.000	6.26	16	1	0	5	0	1	27.1	32	25	19	1	3	25	0	22	7
Hill, Savannah*	2	3	.400	6.08	6	6	0	0	0	0	26.2	36	21	18	3	3	9	0	22	2
Hohn, Savannah*	0	0	.000	8.10	3	0	0	0	0	0	3.1	6	5	3	0	0	1	0	2	1
Horsman, Myrtle Beach*	7	7	.500	3.32	30	28	0	1	0	0	149.0	144	74	55	20	2	37	2	109	5
Hubbard, Asheville	0	0	.000	0.00	1	0	0	1	0	0	1.0	1	0	0	0	0	1	0	0	0
Humphries, Myrtle Beach	4	9	.308	5.95	20	10	0	7	0	3	65.0	78	53	43	5	5	27	0	58	10
Hursey, Fayetteville*	11	8	.579	3.11	25	23	1	0	0	0	139.0	132	65	48	5	2	57	0	77	9
D. Jones, Myrtle Beach*	6	5	.545	2.75	21	15	0	2	0	0	68.2	51	37	21	3	0	50	0	78	8
M. Jones, Gastonia	8	10	.444	4.65	32	18	2	4	0	0	147.0	152	91	76	11	2	52	2	105	8
Kane, Greensboro	4	6	.400	3.30	29	0	0	26	0	7	60.0	55	35	22	4	2	25	1	47	3
Kiser, Spartanburg*	0	5	.000	6.49	21	5	0	6	0	1	43.0	49	37	31	2	4	24	2	27	6
Koopmann, Macon*	3	4	.429	3.42	15	13	2	0	0	0	81.2	95	34	31	5	4	13	0	43	2
LaMarche, Spartanburg	4	7	.364	4.31	44	1	0	24	0	4	77.1	88	45	37	4	6	25	6	47	4
Lamle, Gastonia*	2	3	.400	4.31	15	5	0	3	0	0	48.0	62	32	23	7	0	10	0	29	1
LaPoint, Charleston (W. Va.)	5	5	.500	5.21	40	0	0	30	0	7	46.2	48	37	27	3	7	44	3	35	7
Lawrence, Savannah	13	8	.619	3.16	29	28	8	0	3	0	182.1	167	87	64	15	11	42	1	123	7
LeMasters, Sumter	5	9	.357	3.62	28	17	2	2	1	0	109.1	91	60	44	8	2	50	0	105	3
Lewis, Macon*	0	2	.000	6.65	6	5	0	0	0	0	21.2	28	18	16	1	2	14	0	17	2
Linton, Myrtle Beach	14	2	.875	1.55	20	19	2	1	0	1	122.0	94	34	21	9	2	25	0	155	8
Liriano, Fayetteville	2	5	.286	5.61	23	11	0	7	0	0	67.1	79	56	42	4	2	47	0	27	12
Llanes, Savannah	1	7	.125	4.62	12	12	1	0	1	0	74.0	73	44	38	11	1	30	2	43	7
Longuil, Sumter	9	9	.500	2.89	27	23	6	3	0	2	152.2	148	66	49	8	7	45	0	100	11
Luciani, Fayetteville	0	0	.000	54.00	2	0	0	1	0	0	0.2	4	4	4	0	1	4	0	0	1
Macavage, Macon	0	1	.000	3.21	5	1	0	1	0	0	14.0	14	7	5	2	1	5	0	11	1
MacDonald, Myrtle Beach*	2	1	.667	5.66	10	0	0	4	0	0	20.2	24	18	13	1	0	7	1	12	2
Main, Charleston (W. Va.)	1	3	.250	5.87	9	3	0	3	0	1	23.0	25	21	15	1	2	15	0	11	2
Maldonado, Spartanburg	8	7	.533	3.30	53	0	0	38	0	8	87.1	84	38	32	3	4	26	10	61	7
Malloy, Gastonia	5	0	1.000	2.53	9	9	1	0	0	0	57.0	51	21	16	5	0	13	0	66	5
Marak, Sumter	12	5	.706	3.13	50	6	0	14	0	2	118.0	101	50	41	6	6	44	1	98	9
Marina, Columbia	6	7	.462	2.59	27	20	0	4	0	2	128.2	116	50	37	4	5	59	4	80	6
Martel, Savannah	7	4	.636	3.19	42	10	1	12	1	2	104.1	97	53	37	6	3	53	7	104	7
Mathews, Gastonia	3	3	.500	5.59	34	1	0	13	0	0	48.1	53	35	30	5	2	32	4	46	7
Mays, Gastonia	4	5	.444	4.55	18	9	0	5	0	0	57.1	60	39	29	4	0	22	0	41	5
Maysey, Charleston (S.C.)	14	11	.560	3.17	41	18	5	21	0	7	150.1	112	71	53	13	5	59	4	143	13
McClure, Asheville	4	2	.667	2.45	18	0	0	11	0	3	25.2	21	15	7	1	1	18	2	32	3
McElroy, Spartanburg*	14	4	.778	3.11	24	21	5	0	2	0	130.1	117	51	45	6	0	48	2	115	7
McGowan, Greensboro	2	3	.400	2.11	28	0	0	20	0	6	64.0	41	25	15	2	3	29	0	64	4
McMurtrie, Columbia	8	2	.800	4.35	38	7	0	9	0	0	89.0	107	49	43	3	5	30	7	52	6
Meadows, Gastonia	4	7	.636	2.95	14	14	2	0	1	0	79.1	58	37	26	4	5	18	0	53	2
Meizoso, 20 Gas-24 Clb*	5	0	1.000	2.26	44	1	0	18	0	3	67.2	46	20	17	0	0	45	3	84	13
Mejia, Myrtle Beach	7	4	.636	2.73	33	10	1	15	0	5	125.1	108	42	38	8	7	27	4	90	6
Melvin, Charleston (W.Va.)	2	3	.400	3.42	17	3	1	8	0	1	47.1	41	23	18	2	2	34	1	32	2
Mercedes, Macon*	1	1	.500	2.25	18	0	0	13	0	4	32.0	22	13	8	1	0	5	0	29	3
Morales, Gastonia	1	4	.200	4.44	17	4	1	6	0	0	48.2	46	29	24	5	2	17	0	43	2
Morrison, Greensboro	1	2	.333	4.10	5	5	1	0	0	0	26.1	23	16	12	5	2	20	1	20	0
B. Murphy, Sumter	0	1	.000	2.35	7	0	0	4	0	1	7.2	3	3	2	0	1	6	0	9	3
P. Murphy, Macon	0	0	.000	7.27	10	2	0	6	0	2	26.0	32	21	21	5	1	10	0	17	3
Myers, Columbia	0	0	.000	3.68	4	0	0	2	0	0	7.1	9	4	3	1	0	5	1	14	2
Navilliat, Charleston (S.C.)*	5	6	.455	5.15	40	2	0	23	0	1	92.2	105	66	53	8	3	42	2	49	9
Nezelek, Sumter	6	3	.667	1.80	12	12	5	0	0	0	85.0	56	24	17	5	6	12	1	67	4
Normand, Asheville*	16	5	.762	3.48	31	25	2	1	0	0	157.2	154	73	61	18	6	71	2	103	14
Nosek, Fayetteville	4	11	.267	4.64	16	16	0	0	0	0	77.2	69	63	40	1	7	63	0	57	12
Nowlin, Sumter	6	5	.545	4.54	41	9	1	10	1	4	113.0	112	64	57	13	8	39	1	89	5
O'Neill, Fayetteville*	4	2	.667	2.49	39	0	0	28	0	10	72.1	60	29	20	4	0	20	2	75	3
O'Quinn, 3 CWV-22 Sum	3	5	.375	2.77	25	9	2	6	1	1	74.2	67	30	23	6	1	20	2	49	4
Olivares, Charleston (S.C.)	4	14	.222	4.60	31	24	5	3	0	0	170.1	182	107	87	9	7	57	4	86	3
Olson, Asheville	5	5	.500	3.99	27	12	0	7	0	1	90.1	92	53	40	7	3	61	2	73	13
Osuna, Asheville*	0	0	1.000	2.75	14	0	0	7	0	2	19.2	20	6	6	1	0	6	0	20	0
Parascand, Fayetteville*	0	4	.000	3.97	32	4	0	12	0	3	81.2	74	53	36	2	2	54	1	45	13
Patterson, Gastonia	0	0	.000	5.40	8	2	0	0	0	0	16.2	14	14	10	0	0	15	0	15	4
Pavlik, Gastonia	2	7	.222	4.95	15	14	0	0	0	0	67.1	66	46	37	3	5	42	0	55	6
Peek, Spartanburg	2	3	.400	3.21	10	9	1	0	0	0	56.0	50	24	20	6	1	16	0	39	2
Perez, Spartanburg	3	2	.600	4.36	46	1	0	17	0	5	74.1	81	46	36	9	1	42	4	50	2
Phillips, Fayetteville	5	2	.714	1.49	11	11	3	0	2	0	78.2	49	18	13	4	4	31	1	60	3
Picota, Savannah	10	9	.526	3.02	28	28	3	0	0	0	184.2	177	78	62	10	6	58	3	105	7
Pifer, 19 CWV-8 Fay	11	8	.579	4.09	27	23	2	2	0	0	158.1	172	97	72	7	10	44	2	85	11
Polley, Sumter*	3	1	.750	2.88	7	6	1	1	1	0	40.2	37	16	13	2	0	9	0	32	1
Ponder, Columbia	3	4	.429	4.22	33	6	0	11	0	2	74.2	79	38	35	8	3	27	4	61	4
Postier, Gastonia	0	0	.000	0.00	2	0	0	2	0	0	2.1	1	3	0	0	0	4	0	1	0
Price, Spartanburg	2	2	.500	4.60	35	2	1	8	0	3	72.1	83	40	37	8	1	25	3	43	2
Ramos, Fayetteville*	0	1	.000	4.05	10	0	0	9	0	0	13.1	16	8	6	0	0	8	0	10	1
Reed, Macon	8	4	.667	2.50	46	0	0	20	0	7	93.2	80	38	26	6	9	29	3	92	4
Revak, Greensboro*	3	7	.300	5.28	25	11	0	11	0	1	76.2	107	54	45	10	1	20	1	45	3
Richards, Sumter	3	3	.500	3.19	10	8	1	0	1	0	48.0	45	28	17	5	0	17	1	39	3
Rightnowar, Fayetteville	7	7	.500	4.96	39	10	2	19	0	6	101.2	115	70	56	7	4	37	1	65	4

Pitcher—Club	W.	L.	Pct.	ERA.	G.	GS.	CG.	GF.	ShO.	Sv.	IP.	H.	R.	ER.	HR.	HB.	BB.	Int. BB.	SO.	WP.
C. Rivera, Fayetteville	0	0	.000	4.50	6	0	0	0	0	0	12.0	14	12	6	1	2	8	0	2	2
L. Rivera, Gastonia	1	5	.167	2.69	51	2	0	22	0	5	103.2	92	41	31	4	0	38	3	93	11
Robinson, Charleston (W.Va.)	4	7	.364	3.06	36	7	3	19	1	5	79.1	74	39	27	4	4	14	0	53	7
Romero, Spartanburg	2	3	.400	3.24	9	9	0	0	0	0	41.2	41	27	15	1	1	22	2	31	5
Rose, Macon	0	1	.000	4.15	8	0	0	5	0	1	13.0	21	9	6	1	0	5	0	6	4
Rosenthal, Gastonia	1	5	.167	1.70	56	0	0	55	0	30	68.2	44	19	13	6	0	25	5	101	10
Ryan, Greensboro	3	12	.200	5.49	28	19	2	8	0	0	121.1	139	88	74	10	3	63	8	75	10
Saitta, Myrtle Beach	0	1	.000	6.00	1	0	0	0	0	0	3.0	2	2	2	1	0	1	0	0	0
Sanchez, Myrtle Beach	0	0	.000	3.00	1	0	0	1	0	1	3.0	2	1	1	1	0	0	0	4	0
Sanderski, Greensboro	2	3	.400	3.36	35	0	0	25	0	4	77.2	87	38	29	6	2	33	5	67	5
Sandoval, Charleston (W. Va.)	0	0	.000	1.93	4	0	0	3	0	1	4.2	4	1	1	0	0	2	0	2	1
Santana, Macon	0	3	.000	6.06	15	5	0	4	0	0	32.2	30	31	22	4	3	31	0	28	3
Schilling, Greensboro	8	15	.348	3.82	29	28	7	1	3	0	184.0	179	96	78	10	2	65	8	189	10
Schlopy, Macon*	3	3	.500	3.55	15	3	0	6	0	2	33.0	39	16	13	1	1	11	1	32	2
Schwabe, Fayetteville	1	1	.500	2.45	11	0	0	7	0	3	22.0	18	10	6	2	0	2	1	23	1
Shea, Myrtle Beach*	11	5	.688	3.47	26	23	1	1	1	0	140.0	147	67	54	13	5	42	1	92	2
Sheehan, Asheville	5	4	.556	3.41	43	2	0	33	0	14	71.1	61	32	27	5	2	36	6	59	7
Siegel, Macon	2	1	.667	4.43	5	5	0	0	0	0	20.1	16	11	10	2	4	11	0	20	4
Sims, Spartanburg*	7	8	.467	5.07	28	25	2	0	1	0	142.0	138	89	80	16	4	64	2	113	13
Slavik, Fayetteville*	4	3	.571	3.23	14	10	0	1	0	0	53.0	50	25	19	5	1	20	0	40	1
Sloan, Sumter	0	2	.000	5.19	16	3	0	5	0	0	34.2	30	22	20	3	3	18	0	26	2
Sossamon, Charleston (W.Va.)	13	10	.565	3.80	26	25	8	0	2	0	151.2	147	87	64	10	22	76	1	114	17
Soto, Gastonia	1	3	.250	11.88	6	4	0	1	0	0	16.2	26	23	22	0	2	18	1	11	6
Steiner, Gastonia*	0	1	.000	17.65	6	1	0	0	0	0	8.2	17	18	17	1	1	8	0	8	0
Stoker, Asheville	13	5	.722	2.91	25	25	6	0	2	0	164.0	129	60	53	9	2	86	0	124	11
Talbott, Asheville	3	2	.600	3.06	36	0	0	23	0	11	64.2	57	26	22	6	1	19	2	41	2
A. Taylor, Savannah	5	3	.625	3.44	45	1	0	36	0	13	70.2	62	30	27	4	4	26	2	44	3
D. Taylor, Gastonia	1	3	.250	4.46	13	3	0	2	0	2	38.1	48	26	19	3	2	12	0	30	4
Toy, 13 Mac-16 Char. (W.Va.)	4	8	.333	4.65	29	11	0	6	0	1	93.0	103	61	48	2	4	30	0	60	8
Tracy, Myrtle Beach	3	5	.375	2.17	28	2	0	18	0	5	74.2	69	26	18	3	4	17	3	53	5
Trapasso, Savannah*	1	1	.500	4.09	23	1	0	4	0	0	44.0	38	23	20	2	4	38	0	27	12
Turner, Sumter	2	3	.400	4.71	39	9	0	17	0	0	93.2	91	61	49	8	5	48	2	102	8
Valera, Columbia	8	7	.533	2.80	22	22	2	0	2	0	125.1	114	53	39	7	4	31	0	97	6
Velazquez, Charleston (S.C.)	0	0	.000	5.40	5	0	0	5	0	0	5.0	4	3	3	1	0	3	0	4	0
Villanueva, Charleston (W.Va.)*	5	5	.375	3.35	16	6	0	4	0	1	43.0	32	21	16	0	3	39	0	56	14
Wacha, Greensboro	2	2	.500	7.06	8	5	0	3	0	0	29.1	33	24	23	1	1	20	1	28	6
Wagner, Sumter*	4	2	.667	3.16	26	0	0	13	0	1	31.1	25	14	11	0	1	18	0	24	2
Walker, Spartanburg	0	0	.000	5.27	7	1	0	1	0	0	13.2	16	10	8	1	1	8	0	11	2
Walters, Greensboro	8	14	.364	3.38	28	25	3	3	1	1	165.0	177	77	62	14	2	61	2	120	12
Wasilewiat, Asheville	4	4	.500	6.11	31	0	0	9	0	1	56.0	70	42	38	9	3	29	1	35	5
Watts, Myrtle Beach	3	0	1.000	2.84	10	0	0	4	0	1	19.0	13	7	6	1	1	7	2	10	2
Weems, Charleston (W.Va.)	5	8	.385	3.39	28	25	2	1	2	1	164.2	159	91	62	7	9	58	0	100	12
Welborn, Columbia	0	0	.000	0.00	8	0	0	8	0	4	8.0	4	0	0	0	1	10	0	10	0
Whitaker, Gastonia	2	3	.400	2.13	13	0	0	7	0	2	25.1	17	7	6	1	5	5	0	26	2
K. Williams, Fayetteville*	6	6	.500	3.53	17	17	4	0	0	0	102.0	113	63	40	2	1	33	0	67	9
W. Williams, Sumter*	8	4	.667	3.91	24	18	0	5	0	1	112.2	105	58	49	11	4	64	1	88	13
York, Macon	17	6	.739	3.04	28	28	3	0	3	0	165.2	129	71	56	11	2	88	1	169	9
Young, Charleston (S.C.)*	3	6	.333	4.08	12	11	2	1	0	0	64.0	71	51	29	4	4	35	1	59	11
Zaltsman, Savannah*	7	6	.538	1.91	43	3	1	31	0	6	75.1	57	20	16	2	2	23	5	86	7

BALKS—Carista, Turner, 6 each; Cohen, Henry, Pifer, 5 each; Anderson, Durant, Normand, 4 each; Berrios, Brantley, Castillo, Gardner, Hentgen, Hursey, Koopmann, LaMarche, Lawrence, Maysey, Osuna, L. Rivera, Ryan, Shea, York, 3 each; Behny, Bones, Bowen, R. Brown, DeLeon, Haley, Harris, Horsman, LeMasters, Main, Maldonado, Martel, Nezelek, Nosek, Schilling, A. Taylor, D. Taylor, 2 each; Abrell, Aldred, Ashby, August, Austin, Blakley, Bond, Cepeda, Davis, Dumas, Ellis, Forrest, Grater, Grovom, Hansen, Harrison, Hendrix, Henion, Lamle, LaPoint, Linton, Liriano, Longuil, Marina, Mathews, McElroy, Morrison, B. Murphy, Nowlin, Olivares, Peek, Picota, Polley, Ponder, Rightnowar, Romero, Rose, Sanderski, Santana, Schlopy, Schwabe, Sims, Slavik, Sossamon, Stoker, Tracy, Walker, Watts, K. Williams, Young, 1 each.

COMBINATION SHUTOUTS—Bowen-Hall-McClure, August-Olson-Sheehan, Stoker-Bond, Asheville; Matsey-Chevez, Harris-Austin-Blakley-Navilliat, Charleston (S.C.); Gardner-Pifer, Grovom-Pifer, Pifer-Melvin, Robinson-Villanueva, Charleston (W.Va.); Hernandez-Welborn, Garcia-Welborn, Durant-Welborn, Marina-McMurtrie, Hernandez-Brown, Valera-Henion-Ponder, Valera-Ponder, Columbia; Hursey-Berrios 2, Slavik-Parascand, Phillips-O'Neill, Nosek-Duquette, Fayetteville; Bryant-Mathews-Rosenthal, Meadows-Steiner-Rosenthal, Jones-Rosenthal, Castillo-Rivera, Gastonia; Ryan-Walters, Carista-Kane, Walters-Sanderski, Walters-McGowan, Haley-Sanderski-Kane, Carista-Revak-Kane, Greensboro; Andersh-Ellis, Adams-Ellis-Belinda, York-Belinda, Macon; Hentgen-Horsman-Hall, Linton-Hall, Horsman-Humphries, Linton-Diaz, Horsman-Tracy-Diaz, Jones-Depastino-Tracy, Linton-Humphries, Linton-Burgos, Hentgen-Hall, Jones-Burgos, Myrtle Beach; Behny-Zaltsman-Grater, Picota-Dumas, Henry-Zaltsman, Savannah; McElroy-Grimsley, Spartanburg; Longuil-Czajkowski, LeMasters-Marak, Brown-Czajkowski, Marak-Czajkowski, O'Quinn-Nowlin, Longuil-Turner, Marak-Polley, Sumter.

NO-HIT GAME—Weems, Charleston (W.Va.), defeated Greensboro, 3-0 (first game), June 3.

Appalachian League

SUMMER CLASS A CLASSIFICATION

CHAMPIONSHIP WINNERS IN PREVIOUS YEARS

1921—Greenville .608	1948—Pulaski‡ .680	1970—Bluefield .638
Johnson City° .627	1949—Bluefield‡ .721	1971—Bluefield a .609
1922—Bristol .557	1950—Bluefield .600	Kingsport .559
1923—Knoxville .635	Bluefield z .745	1972—Bristol a .588
1924—Knoxville° .642	1951—Kingsport‡ .659	Covington .586
Bristol .607	1952—Johnson City .595	1973—Kingsport .757
1925—Greenville .667	Welch (3rd)† .509	1974—Bristol a .754
1926-36—Did not operate.	1953—Welch° .705	Bluefield .536
1937—Elizabethton .559	Johnson City .672	1975—Marion .515
Pennington Gap° .580	1954—Bluefield‡ .619	Johnson City a .603
1938—Elizabethton .664	1955—Salem°° .689	1976—Johnson City a .714
Greenville (3rd)† .571	1956—Did not operate.	Bluefield .600
1939—Elizabethton‡ .597	1957—Bluefield .701	1977—Kingsport .623
1940—Johnson City§ .726	1958—Johnson City .662	1978—Elizabethton .594
Elizabethton .750	1959—Morristown .603	1979—Paintsville .800
1941—Johnson City .614	1960—Wytheville .614	1980—Paintsville .657
Elizabethton° .661	1961—Middlesboro .591	1981—Paintsville .657
1942—Bristol .667	1962—Bluefield .671	1982—Bluefield a .681
Bristol x .660	1963—Bluefield .652	Johnson City .478
1943—Bristol .755	1964—Johnson City .662	1983—Paintsville .653
Bristol y .617	1965—Salem .614	1984—Elizabethton b .580
1944—Kingsport‡ .575	1966—Marion .623	Pulaski .536
1945—Kingsport‡ .670	1967—Bluefield .627	1985—Bristol c .638
1946—New River‡ .675	1968—Marion .583	1986—Johnson City .667
1947—Pulaski .648	1969—Pulaski a .576	Pulaski b .621
New River (3rd)† .516	Johnson City .544	

°Won split-season playoff. †Won four-team playoff. ‡Won championship and four-team playoff. §Johnson City, first-half winner, won playoff involving six clubs. xWon both halves and defeated second-place Elizabethton in playoff. yWon both halves, but Erwin won four-team playoff. zWon both halves, but Bristol won two-club playoff. °°Salem and Johnson City declared playoff co-champions when weather forced cancellation of final series. aLeague was divided into Northern, Southern divisions; declared league champion, based on highest won-lost percentage. bLeague was divided into Northern, Southern divisions; won playoff for league championship. cBristol declared league champion based on regular-season record.

STANDING OF CLUBS AT CLOSE OF SEASON, AUGUST 29

NORTHERN DIVISION

Club	W.	L.	T.	Pct.	G.B.
Burlington (Indians)	51	19	0	.729	....
Pulaski (Braves)	39	31	0	.557	12
Bluefield (Orioles)	37	32	0	.536	13½
Wytheville (Cubs)	32	38	0	.457	19

SOUTHERN DIVISION

Club	W.	L.	T.	Pct.	G.B.
Johnson City (Cardinals)	42	27	0	.609	....
Elizabethton (Twins)	29	40	0	.420	13
Kingsport (Mets)	28	42	0	.400	14½
Bristol (Tigers)	20	49	0	.290	22

COMPOSITE STANDING OF CLUBS AT CLOSE OF SEASON, AUGUST 29

Club	Bur.	J.C.	Pul.	Blu.	Wyt.	Eliz.	Kng.	Bri.	W.	L.	T.	Pct.	G.B.
Burlington (Indians)	....	5	11	9	10	5	5	6	51	19	0	.729	....
Johnson City (Cardinals)	3	....	4	4	5	6	10	10	42	27	0	.609	8½
Pulaski (Braves)	3	4	....	9	6	4	6	7	39	31	0	.557	12
Bluefield (Orioles)	3	4	3	....	9	7	5	6	37	32	0	.536	13½
Wytheville (Cubs)	2	3	6	5	....	6	6	4	32	38	0	.457	19
Elizabethton (Twins)	3	6	4	0	2	....	6	8	29	40	0	.420	21½
Kingsport (Mets)	3	4	2	3	2	6	....	8	28	42	0	.400	23
Bristol (Tigers)	2	1	1	2	4	6	4	....	20	49	0	.290	30½

Major league affiliations in parentheses.

Playoffs—Burlington defeated Johnson City, two games to none, to win league championship.

Regular-Season Attendance—Bluefield, 35,867; Bristol, 15,337; Burlington, 76,653; Elizabethton, 13,101; Johnson City, 22,271; Kingsport, 28,453; Pulaski, 14,468; Wytheville, 18,122. Total—224,272. Playoffs—2,129.

Managers—Bluefield, Jim Pamlayne; Bristol, Rick Magnante; Burlington, Tom Chandler; Elizabethton, Ray Smith; Johnson City, Dan Radison; Kingsport, Bobby Floyd; Pulaski, Grady Little; Wytheville, Brad Mills.

All-Star Team—1B—Troy Neel, Burlington; 2B—Rich Casarotti, Pulaski; 3B—Brian Champion, Pulaski; SS—Ray Narleski, Burlington; OF—Bo Allred, Burlington; Tracy Pancoski, Bluefield; Ray Lankford, Johnson City; C—Dan Simond, Bluefield; DH—Terry Brown, Bluefield; RHP—Frank Castillo, Wytheville; LHP—Rocky Elli, Kingsport; Player of the Year—Frank Castillo, Wytheville; Manager of the Year—Tom Chandler, Burlington.

(Compiled by Howe News Bureau, Boston, Mass.)

CLUB BATTING

Club	Pct.	G.	AB.	R.	OR.	H.	TB.	2B.	3B.	HR.	RBI.	GW.	SH.	SF.	HP.	BB.	Int. BB.	SO.	SB.	CS.	LOB.
Pulaski	.268	70	2374	388	326	637	972	116	9	67	328	32	12	14	33	250	10	539	92	34	506
Burlington	.264	70	2356	437	270	622	976	132	18	62	377	44	12	28	30	385	14	542	69	34	566
Wytheville	.264	70	2394	363	387	631	859	102	21	28	303	28	13	14	18	289	5	539	74	28	548
Bluefield	.258	69	2299	355	336	592	909	113	18	56	305	29	7	18	26	261	6	569	63	39	482
Johnson City	.256	69	2277	341	274	584	838	104	18	38	288	33	14	18	20	322	11	426	108	48	544
Elizabethton	.236	69	2305	317	384	544	713	84	8	23	254	25	11	16	36	305	9	508	71	29	540
Kingsport	.220	70	2222	311	391	489	668	76	11	27	256	19	18	21	28	316	2	596	103	40	500
Bristol	.217	69	2240	258	402	486	655	65	13	26	208	15	8	17	25	264	0	548	102	42	469

INDIVIDUAL BATTING

(Leading Qualifiers for Batting Championship—189 or More Plate Appearances)

*Bats lefthanded. †Switch-hitter.

Player and Club	Pct.	G.	AB.	R.	H.	TB.	2B.	3B.	HR.	RBI.	GW.	SH.	SF.	HP.	BB.	Int. BB.	SO.	SB.	CS.
Allred, Dale, Burlington*	.341	54	167	39	57	103	14	1	10	38	5	2	4	1	35	3	33	4	0
Narleski, William, Burlington	.324	60	225	55	73	96	13	2	2	33	5	2	2	0	43	0	31	5	1
Walbeck, Matthew, Wytheville	.314	51	169	24	53	71	9	3	1	28	1	0	3	0	22	0	39	0	1
Paulino, Luis, Wytheville*	.314	55	185	42	58	97	11	2	8	40	5	0	3	0	26	1	25	4	1
Lankford, Raymond, Johnson City*	.308	66	253	45	78	112	17	4	3	32	5	0	1	5	19	0	43	14	11
Casarotti, Richard, Pulaski†	.304	66	260	39	79	109	14	2	4	24	1	2	0	0	22	1	50	12	3
Hayden, Paris, Bluefield	.303	62	241	44	73	113	14	1	8	38	1	0	4	3	16	1	53	9	4
Maclin, Lonnie, Johnson City*	.301	62	229	45	69	86	6	1	3	22	4	0	1	1	24	0	32	22	5
Rosario, Jossy, Wytheville	.301	66	279	52	84	117	13	7	2	27	5	0	0	1	17	0	31	5	5
Baldwin, Anthony, Pulaski	.301	54	183	36	55	87	11	0	7	20	3	1	0	1	29	1	53	23	8
Arias, Alejandro, Wytheville	.296	61	233	41	69	76	7	0	0	24	2	0	1	1	27	0	29	16	6
Pancoski, Tracey, Bluefield	.294	64	218	45	64	121	13	4	12	49	6	1	1	9	30	1	44	5	4
Cloninger, Gregory, Pulaski*	.292	54	216	39	63	96	10	1	7	42	5	1	1	8	20	0	24	5	3

Departmental Leaders: G—Todd, 70; AB—J. Rosario, 279; R—Narleski, 55; H—J. Rosario, 84; TB—Fulton, 128; 2B—Wahlig, 19; 3B—J. Rosario, 7; HR—T. Brown, 14; RBI—Fulton, Neel, 59; GWRBI—T. Brown, Todd, 7; SH—Toney, 5; SF—Martin, 6; HP—Pancoski, 9; BB—Carmona, 50; IBB—Brewer, 5; SO—Shipman, 75; SB—Ale. Diaz, 34; CS—Lankford, 11.

(All Players—Listed Alphabetically)

Player and Club	Pct.	G.	AB.	R.	H.	TB.	2B.	3B.	HR.	RBI.	GW.	SH.	SF.	HP.	BB.	Int. BB.	SO.	SB.	CS.
Albertson, John, Pulaski	.191	34	68	10	13	17	1	0	1	11	2	0	2	2	13	0	33	1	0
Allison, James, Burlington*	.244	52	131	28	32	48	9	2	1	16	0	1	1	3	32	2	18	8	2
Allred, Dale, Burlington*	.341	54	167	39	57	103	14	1	10	38	5	2	4	1	35	3	33	4	0
Alvarez, Eduardo, Elizabethton	.125	20	48	9	6	7	1	0	0	3	0	0	0	0	7	0	14	0	1
Arias, Alejandro, Wytheville	.296	61	233	41	69	76	7	0	0	24	2	0	1	1	27	0	29	16	6
Arias, Pedro, Burlington	.167	23	60	7	10	18	2	0	2	5	1	1	0	1	5	0	28	2	2
Arrington, Warren, Wytheville	.276	50	181	46	50	71	8	2	3	18	0	0	1	3	44	1	45	6	4
Baldwin, Anthony, Pulaski	.301	54	183	36	55	87	11	0	7	20	3	1	0	1	29	1	53	23	8
Baldwin, Lloyd, Burlington	.302	28	96	19	29	37	3	1	1	12	1	0	0	0	10	0	14	2	3
Barranco, Vincent, Burlington*	.284	34	67	22	19	21	2	0	0	6	1	0	1	1	17	1	16	6	2
Barrs, Stanley, Johnson City	.278	32	79	10	22	33	5	0	2	12	0	0	1	2	13	0	14	0	0
Bautista, Ramon, Burlington	.203	27	79	12	16	27	7	2	0	7	1	1	2	0	15	1	23	1	1
Baxter, James, Burlington	.276	37	98	19	27	45	7	1	3	16	2	1	1	4	28	0	28	1	2
Belbru, Juan, Johnson City	.150	23	40	5	6	10	1	0	1	3	0	0	0	1	5	0	15	1	0
Berg, Richard, Pulaski	.292	41	106	15	31	41	4	0	2	14	1	0	1	3	15	0	19	1	1
Bettendorf, David, Bluefield*	.249	61	213	35	53	81	13	0	5	30	3	1	4	0	25	1	42	3	1
Biggers, Alan, Johnson City	.264	45	125	12	33	40	4	0	1	9	1	1	0	1	5	0	26	6	4
Biggs, Douglas, Bristol*	.149	49	94	11	14	18	2	1	0	4	0	1	0	3	25	0	33	7	0
Brewer, Rodney, Johnson City*	.252	67	238	33	60	105	11	2	10	42	5	0	2	3	36	5	40	2	2
Brown, Jarvis, Elizabethton	.244	67	258	52	63	77	9	1	1	15	0	3	0	5	48	1	50	30	2
Brown, Terry, Bluefield*	.286	65	231	44	66	127	7	6	14	43	7	0	3	1	27	0	74	7	3
Browning, Steven, Bluefield	.219	24	64	9	14	20	3	0	1	7	1	0	0	0	6	1	12	1	0
Cakora, Matthew, Wytheville*	.000	15	0	0	0	0	0	0	0	0	0	0	0	0	1	0	0	0	0
Calzado, Lorenzo, Johnson City	.296	12	27	3	8	13	2	0	1	4	0	0	0	0	1	0	11	1	0
Cameron, Stanton, Kingsport	.132	26	53	6	7	11	1	0	1	5	0	1	1	0	10	0	24	1	1
Campos, Frank, Wytheville	.000	18	2	0	0	0	0	0	0	0	1	0	0	0	0	0	0	0	0
Canino, Carlos, Wytheville	.111	6	9	1	1	1	0	0	0	1	0	0	0	0	0	0	5	0	0
Capellan, Carlos, Elizabethton	.261	64	253	34	66	85	13	3	0	31	4	4	3	1	15	2	13	5	5
Carmona, Gregorio, Johnson City†	.175	47	120	35	21	27	4	1	0	9	0	1	1	0	50	1	42	14	10
Carpenter, Danny, Wytheville	.295	46	149	29	44	60	6	2	2	18	1	1	3	2	24	0	53	13	1
Casarotti, Richard, Pulaski†	.304	66	260	39	79	109	14	2	4	24	1	2	0	0	22	1	50	12	3
Castillo, Alberto, Kingsport	.111	7	9	1	1	1	0	0	0	0	0	1	0	0	5	0	3	1	0
Castillo, Axel, Burlington	.240	51	175	19	42	65	6	1	5	26	3	0	1	3	14	1	48	2	1
Castillo, Frank, Wytheville	.000	12	17	0	0	0	0	0	0	0	0	1	0	0	1	0	6	0	0
Champion, Brian, Pulaski	.284	67	261	38	74	115	14	0	9	43	5	0	2	3	23	1	62	3	2
Cloninger, Gregory, Pulaski*	.292	54	216	39	63	96	10	1	7	42	5	1	1	8	20	0	24	5	3
Corbin, Archie, Kingsport	.500	6	2	0	1	1	0	0	0	0	0	0	0	0	0	0	1	0	0
Courtney, Shawn, Elizabethton	.225	24	80	7	18	18	0	0	0	5	0	0	0	0	10	1	10	1	0
Crowson, David, Kingsport*	.000	17	2	0	0	0	0	0	0	0	0	0	0	0	0	0	0	0	0
Cummings, Brian, Pulaski	.400	14	10	2	4	4	0	0	0	3	1	0	0	0	6	0	2	1	0
Dariah, Bruce, Burlington†	.158	7	19	2	3	3	0	0	0	1	0	0	0	0	2	0	5	1	0
Davis, Braz, Wytheville	.045	12	22	1	1	1	0	0	0	1	0	1	0	0	1	0	12	0	0
Diaz, Alberto, Kingsport	.208	22	53	8	11	14	1	1	0	3	0	0	0	0	2	0	8	0	0
Diaz, Alexis, Kingsport†	.264	54	212	29	56	67	9	1	0	13	1	4	1	1	16	0	31	34	9
Donnels, Chris, Kingsport*	.302	26	86	18	26	39	4	0	3	16	3	0	2	1	17	1	17	4	1
Dunham, Chris, Burlington	.210	35	62	14	13	27	2	0	4	10	2	0	2	5	33	1	12	0	3
Echoles, James, Kingsport	.059	11	17	3	1	1	0	0	0	0	0	0	0	0	3	0	11	1	0
Eddings, Jay, Wytheville	.125	21	8	1	1	1	0	0	0	1	0	0	0	0	0	0	4	0	0
Eggleston, Darren, Wytheville	.233	50	163	16	38	52	7	2	1	23	2	1	1	1	9	0	48	6	1
Elli, Rocky, Kingsport*	.000	14	14	0	0	0	0	0	0	0	0	0	0	0	0	0	5	0	0
Ericson, Mark, Elizabethton	.284	48	162	20	46	61	9	0	2	27	4	0	1	7	11	1	31	0	1
Espino, Francisco, Wytheville	.000	8	2	0	0	0	0	0	0	0	0	0	0	0	0	0	1	0	0
Ferretti, Sam, Burlington	.268	48	123	34	33	47	5	0	3	17	1	1	3	2	20	0	17	9	3
Fine, Thomas, Kingsport	.000	14	10	0	0	0	0	0	0	0	0	1	0	0	0	0	7	0	0
Fleming, Henrique, Wytheville*	.258	64	217	33	56	66	5	1	1	24	3	4	1	1	34	1	35	14	5
Flynn, Erroll, Pulaski*	.238	49	130	18	31	44	7	0	2	14	2	1	1	4	17	2	32	12	4
Fowler, Michael, Pulaski	.274	59	175	37	48	83	13	2	6	30	2	0	1	1	22	0	40	6	2
Franco, Matthew, Wytheville*	.248	62	202	25	50	65	10	1	1	21	2	0	0	0	26	1	41	4	1
Fryman, Travis, Bristol	.234	67	248	25	58	73	9	0	2	20	3	0	2	1	22	0	40	5	2
Fulton, Charles, Johnson City*	.290	67	245	36	71	128	16	1	13	59	5	0	5	2	36	3	42	4	2
Gabriel, Lico, Bluefield†	.186	53	167	19	31	39	8	0	0	14	3	0	2	3	16	1	54	6	7
Galarza, Edgar, Wytheville	.070	21	43	1	3	3	0	0	0	1	0	0	0	1	4	0	26	1	0
Galindo, Luis, Bristol	.282	29	103	8	29	31	2	0	0	10	0	0	0	1	19	0	14	0	2
Gardner, John, Wytheville	.000	12	6	0	0	0	0	0	0	0	0	0	0	0	1	0	2	0	0
Gentleman, Jean, Johnson City	.228	61	193	18	44	54	10	0	0	13	3	0	1	1	25	0	33	5	2
George, Jeffrey, Kingsport	.167	18	6	0	1	1	0	0	0	1	0	1	0	0	0	0	4	0	0
Gibbs, James, Johnson City	.364	12	11	1	4	6	2	0	0	2	1	0	0	0	2	0	2	0	0
Gomez, Fabio, Burlington	.184	22	76	6	14	22	2	0	2	9	0	0	1	1	2	0	23	2	2
Gonzalez, Marcos, Bristol	.048	12	21	1	1	1	0	0	0	0	0	0	0	3	0	0	14	0	0

Player and Club	Pct.	G.	AB.	R.	H.	TB.	2B.	3B.	HR.	RBI.	GW.	SH.	SF.	HP.	BB.	Int. BB.	SO.	SB.	CS.
Gourlay, Craig, Pulaski	.500	13	2	1	1	2	1	0	0	0	0	0	0	0	1	0	0	0	0
Halloran, Michael, Elizabethton	.255	40	141	14	36	40	4	0	0	15	1	1	0	2	15	0	24	0	1
Handel, Mark, Elizabethton*	.167	32	96	16	16	26	2	1	2	12	1	0	0	5	21	0	41	2	1
Harley, Christian, Bristol	.154	43	104	9	16	25	3	0	2	9	2	1	0	0	15	0	48	7	2
Harper, Gregory, Pulaski	.221	45	122	14	27	39	3	0	3	19	0	2	0	0	10	2	49	2	0
Harriger, Dennis, Kingsport	.000	12	2	0	0	0	0	0	0	1	0	0	0	0	1	0	1	0	0
Hartsfield, Randall, Pulaski	.667	6	3	0	2	2	0	0	0	1	0	0	0	0	0	0	0	0	0
Hathaway, Shawn, Johnson City	.600	26	5	1	3	3	0	0	0	2	0	2	0	0	0	0	0	0	0
Hayden, Paris, Bluefield	.303	62	241	44	73	113	14	1	8	38	1	0	4	3	16	1	53	9	4
Hempen, Hal, Johnson City	.000	13	3	0	0	0	0	0	0	0	0	0	0	0	0	0	1	0	0
Henderson, William, Bristol	.179	55	196	14	35	46	5	0	2	17	1	0	3	5	14	0	34	2	3
Hernandez, Rodolfo, Kingsport	.264	66	216	33	57	75	10	1	2	27	1	4	2	1	31	0	41	8	3
Hildebrandt, Vernon, Elizabethton	.237	35	118	18	28	35	7	0	0	7	0	1	0	1	27	0	25	2	0
Hildreth, George, Johnson City	.000	1	1	0	0	0	0	0	0	0	0	0	0	0	0	0	1	0	0
Hines, Timothy, Kingsport*	.141	29	71	4	10	10	0	0	0	2	0	0	0	2	9	0	14	2	0
Hitt, Daniel, Johnson City*	.000	22	1	0	0	0	0	0	0	0	0	0	0	0	0	0	0	0	0
Holland, Timothy, Bluefield	.274	53	157	20	43	65	8	1	4	19	1	1	0	1	15	0	47	4	0
Horsley, Clinton, Johnson City	.333	25	3	1	1	3	0	1	0	1	0	0	0	0	1	0	2	0	0
Howell, Patrick, Kingsport	.217	34	92	14	20	25	2	0	1	5	1	0	0	2	10	0	28	8	2
Huffman, Kris, Johnson City†	.233	64	206	26	48	59	5	3	0	20	3	2	2	0	48	1	29	21	5
Hunter, Brian, Pulaski	.231	65	251	38	58	96	10	2	8	30	2	0	1	5	18	0	47	3	2
Jackson, Gregory, Wytheville	.111	10	27	2	3	7	1	0	1	4	1	0	0	0	0	0	8	0	0
Johnston, Ryan, Johnson City	.247	62	223	26	55	74	9	2	2	30	5	0	3	3	23	1	30	10	5
Johnstone, John, Kingsport	.000	17	2	0	0	0	0	0	0	0	0	0	0	0	0	0	1	0	0
Jones, Charles, Elizabethton*	.239	61	218	30	52	66	8	0	2	23	4	0	2	3	36	3	53	3	1
Kler, William, Bluefield	.079	25	63	11	5	8	0	0	1	2	0	0	0	0	14	1	38	4	0
Knight, Larry, Pulaski†	1.000	18	1	0	1	1	0	0	0	0	0	1	0	0	0	0	0	0	0
Krogman, Monte, Kingsport	.250	11	4	0	1	1	0	0	0	0	0	0	0	0	1	0	3	0	0
Lankford, Raymond, Johnson City*	.308	66	253	45	78	112	17	4	3	32	5	0	1	5	19	0	43	14	11
Lara, Francisco, Bristol	.214	42	112	14	24	29	3	1	0	12	1	0	1	1	8	0	33	3	0
Liriano, Julio, Burlington	.324	44	148	26	48	73	16	0	3	22	3	0	0	0	7	0	29	1	1
Long, Lee, Pulaski*	.241	39	79	17	19	33	3	1	3	10	1	0	0	6	1	0	21	2	2
Maclin, Lonnie, Johnson City*	.301	62	229	45	69	86	6	1	3	22	4	0	1	1	24	0	32	22	5
Martin, Christopher, Elizabethton	.253	65	237	31	60	78	4	1	4	35	3	0	6	2	32	2	46	9	4
Martinez, Francis, Johnson City	.400	10	5	0	2	2	0	0	0	0	0	0	0	0	0	0	1	0	0
Martz, Franklyn, Bluefield	.224	23	58	6	13	15	2	0	0	5	0	1	1	0	8	0	17	0	1
Mateo, Hoascar, Bristol	.129	14	31	2	4	5	1	0	0	3	0	0	0	0	2	0	6	0	0
Mathiot, Michael, Elizabethton	.188	26	80	9	15	20	2	0	1	8	1	0	0	2	6	0	22	1	0
Maxey, Kevin, Johnson City	.242	38	95	20	23	33	5	1	1	11	1	0	0	0	14	0	22	6	2
May, Lee, Kingsport	.229	60	214	35	49	70	7	4	2	27	1	1	3	5	11	0	54	12	3
McBride, Ivan, Burlington	.218	41	101	11	22	31	4	1	1	12	3	2	0	2	9	1	13	3	4
Minton, Jesse, Pulaski*	.264	52	174	25	46	68	10	0	4	16	0	0	1	4	13	2	34	9	3
Mitchell, James, Burlington	.256	13	43	4	11	12	1	0	0	3	0	0	0	0	3	0	7	1	1
Monzon, Jose, Bristol	.250	7	12	3	3	4	1	0	0	1	0	0	0	0	0	0	1	0	0
Mota, Carlos, Bristol	.214	15	42	6	9	11	2	0	0	2	1	0	0	1	8	0	11	4	0
Murphy, Brian, Pulaski	.500	11	4	1	2	6	1	0	1	2	0	0	0	0	0	0	1	0	0
Murphy, James, Bristol*	.219	53	178	20	39	68	3	1	8	24	1	0	1	1	13	0	55	5	4
Murphy, Paul, Bluefield	.243	42	140	21	34	64	6	0	8	21	1	0	1	2	13	0	26	1	1
Myres, Douglas, Kingsport	.500	23	2	0	1	1	0	0	0	0	0	0	0	0	0	0	1	0	0
Narleski, William, Burlington	.324	60	225	55	73	96	13	2	2	33	5	2	2	0	43	0	31	5	1
Neel, Troy, Burlington*	.281	59	192	36	54	101	17	0	10	59	5	0	5	3	25	4	59	0	0
Nunez, Nelson, Wytheville	.000	18	0	0	0	0	0	0	0	0	0	0	0	0	1	0	0	0	0
Pancoski, Tracey, Bluefield	.294	64	218	45	64	121	13	4	12	49	6	0	1	9	30	1	44	5	4
Paulino, Luis, Wytheville*	.314	55	185	42	58	97	11	2	8	40	5	0	3	0	26	1	25	4	1
Pegues, Steven, Bristol	.284	59	236	36	67	89	6	5	2	23	1	0	2	0	16	0	43	22	7
Perry, Eric, Wytheville*	.288	66	243	36	70	108	15	1	7	41	5	0	0	2	33	1	51	3	1
Pierson, Larry, Johnson City	.238	13	21	6	5	5	0	0	0	1	0	3	0	0	3	0	7	0	0
Piskor, Stephen, Kingsport	.217	51	157	19	34	50	5	1	3	24	0	0	1	3	24	0	26	3	3
Polley, Dale, Pulaski	.000	13	1	0	0	0	0	0	0	0	0	0	0	0	0	0	1	0	0
Power, John, Burlington*	.226	16	53	5	12	17	2	0	1	10	0	0	1	1	6	0	12	1	0
Pride, Curtis, Kingsport*	.240	31	104	22	25	32	4	0	1	9	0	2	0	1	16	0	34	14	5
Pulliam, Timothy, Johnson City	.125	21	24	3	3	3	0	0	0	2	0	0	0	1	4	0	5	0	0
Ramirez, Nicolas, Bluefield	.230	50	200	25	46	55	5	2	0	16	1	1	0	3	22	0	51	12	8
Reeser, Seth, Pulaski*	.333	21	3	2	1	1	0	0	0	0	0	0	0	0	1	0	1	0	0
Reis, Paulo, Pulaski	.194	12	36	8	7	8	1	0	0	2	0	0	0	1	3	0	9	4	0
Richie, Robert, Bristol*	.250	3	12	2	3	3	0	0	0	5	0	0	0	0	1	0	2	1	0
Roberts, Brent, Burlington	.301	37	123	19	37	66	8	3	5	29	3	0	2	0	12	0	26	1	1
Rodriguez, Francisco, Kingsport	1.000	16	1	0	1	1	0	0	0	0	0	0	0	0	0	0	0	0	0
Rogers, Robert, Bristol	.203	38	79	12	16	24	5	0	1	9	1	0	0	2	12	0	22	0	3
Rosa, Julio, Bristol	.135	41	104	9	14	21	2	1	1	10	0	1	2	0	10	0	25	2	0
Rosario, Francisco, Johnson City	.229	38	105	11	24	33	5	2	0	8	1	1	1	0	11	0	18	2	0
Rosario, Jossy, Wytheville	.301	66	279	52	84	117	13	7	2	27	5	0	0	1	17	0	31	5	5
Rountree, Michael, Burlington*	.217	41	115	29	25	51	2	0	8	24	5	0	1	0	32	0	42	14	2
Sanchez, Samuel, Kingsport	.250	36	100	13	25	29	4	0	0	14	2	0	2	1	11	1	24	2	3
Schnurbusch, Chris, Bristol	.217	51	166	21	36	50	6	1	2	13	2	0	1	5	22	0	37	10	7
Schourek, Peter, Kingsport*	.000	12	9	0	0	0	0	0	0	0	0	1	0	0	0	0	2	0	0
Sebree, Kenneth, Johnson City	.167	8	6	1	1	4	0	0	1	1	0	0	0	0	0	0	2	0	0
Segui, Daniel, Kingsport	.170	38	112	14	19	26	1	0	2	11	0	1	1	3	11	0	30	1	4
Sherrill, Timothy, Johnson City*	.250	25	4	1	1	1	0	0	0	0	0	1	0	0	2	0	1	0	0
Shipman, Robert, Bristol†	.210	61	186	17	39	62	8	0	5	27	2	0	2	1	31	0	75	4	3
Simonds, Daniel, Bluefield	.270	54	178	25	48	57	6	0	1	23	1	0	4	4	22	0	33	3	3
Smith, Chad, Pulaski†	.200	12	10	3	2	2	0	0	0	0	0	1	0	0	1	0	4	0	0
Smith, Kenneth, Johnson City	.000	13	7	1	0	0	0	0	0	1	0	1	0	0	1	0	4	0	0
Smith, Marvin, Elizabethton	.224	47	165	24	37	58	8	2	3	27	2	0	2	2	27	0	49	11	6
Sommer, David, Wytheville	.000	16	1	0	0	0	0	0	0	0	0	0	0	0	1	0	1	0	0
Sommerkamp, Frank, Bristol	.244	38	82	13	20	31	3	4	0	11	1	1	0	0	13	0	25	0	0
Soto, Jose, Bluefield	.307	36	114	14	35	51	9	2	1	15	2	1	0	0	23	0	22	2	0
Spoolstra, Scott, Kingsport*	.240	57	175	26	42	57	4	1	3	28	1	0	2	0	38	0	44	1	1
Stanton, Michael, Pulaski*	.091	15	11	0	1	2	1	0	0	0	0	0	1	0	1	0	4	0	0
Stockham, Douglas, Pulaski*	.333	15	3	1	1	3	0	1	0	1	0	0	0	0	0	0	0	0	0
Strong, Steven, Bristol	.240	55	179	20	43	51	8	0	0	15	1	0	2	1	28	0	31	4	5
Stroud, Derek, Wytheville*	.250	19	4	0	1	1	0	0	0	1	0	1	0	0	0	0	2	0	0

Player and Club	Pct.	G.	AB.	R.	H.	TB.	2B.	3B.	HR.	RBI.	GW.	SH.	SF.	HP.	BB.	Int. BB.	SO.	SB.	CS.
Tatarian, Dean, Elizabethton	.243	40	136	16	33	42	9	0	0	11	2	1	1	4	19	0	34	2	3
Taylor, Kenneth, Wytheville	.115	9	26	0	3	4	1	0	0	3	0	0	1	2	3	0	9	1	0
Taylor, Scott, Wytheville	.234	32	111	8	26	33	7	0	0	17	0	2	0	2	6	0	26	1	1
Tilmon, Patton, Pulaski	.000	15	5	1	0	0	0	0	0	0	0	0	2	0	3	0	1	0	0
Todd, Theron, Pulaski°	.273	70	253	42	69	111	12	0	10	45	7	2	4	1	24	0	51	8	4
Tomberlin, Andy, Pulaski°	.286	14	7	1	2	2	0	0	0	1	0	0	0	0	0	0	0	0	0
Toney, Anthony, Bristol†	.236	68	258	46	61	79	6	3	2	14	1	5	1	6	35	0	57	30	7
Tucker, Horace, Wytheville	.133	19	45	2	6	9	0	0	1	5	1	0	0	2	5	0	22	0	0
Turtletaub, Gregory, Kingsport°	.276	59	181	28	50	72	14	1	2	29	2	0	2	2	35	0	34	6	1
Valdez, Frank, Elizabethton	.229	61	227	28	52	75	8	0	5	28	0	0	1	2	18	0	62	4	3
Vasquez, Julian, Kingsport	.333	25	3	1	1	1	0	0	0	0	0	0	0	0	0	0	1	0	0
Wacker, Wade, Elizabethton	.135	12	37	4	5	5	0	0	0	3	1	1	0	0	5	0	7	1	1
Wahlig, John, Bluefield†	.261	61	241	36	63	89	19	2	1	23	2	2	2	0	24	0	49	6	7
Walbeck, Matthew, Wytheville	.314	51	169	24	53	71	9	3	1	28	1	0	3	0	22	0	39	0	1
Wallman, Scott, Bluefield	.308	7	13	1	4	4	0	0	0	0	0	0	0	0	0	0	6	0	0
Watts, Walter, Elizabethton	.224	15	49	5	11	20	0	0	3	4	2	0	0	0	4	0	27	0	0
Weese, Dean, Johnson City	.222	13	9	1	2	4	2	0	0	5	0	1	0	0	0	0	4	0	0
Whitson, Anthony, Wytheville	.667	19	6	1	4	5	1	0	0	1	0	1	0	0	0	0	2	0	0
Wiese, Marc, Kingsport	.114	34	88	9	10	13	3	0	0	3	1	1	0	3	20	0	43	0	1
Williams, Edward, Wytheville	.227	16	44	2	10	11	1	0	0	4	0	0	0	0	4	0	16	0	1
Woods, Jason, Kingsport	.183	36	109	14	20	40	5	0	5	22	2	0	1	3	23	0	54	1	1
Young, Derrick, Kingsport	.172	45	116	14	20	30	2	1	2	16	4	0	3	0	22	0	48	4	2

The following pitchers, listed alphabetically by club, with games in parentheses, had no plate appearances, primarily through use of designated hitters:

BLUEFIELD—Amarena, Salvatore (11); Burdick, Stacey (10); Bushing, Christopher (20); Cavers, Michael (12); Culkar, Steven (4); Harnisch, Peter (9); Miller, David (12); Mondile, Steven (10); Myers, Chris (10); Olson, Daniel (17); Pilkinton, Marcus (19); Pinder, Christopher (8); Ricci, Charles (13); Rodriguez, Danilo (8); Steneman, Joseph (10); Williams, Steven (6).

BRISTOL—Canarte, Alvaro (9); Coker, Larry (23); Cook, Ronald (18); Dawson, David (5); Duquette, Charles (11); Everson, Charles (12); Hayes, James (11); Lott, Henry (8); McCarthy, Martin (7); Nozling, Paul (10); Pena, Franklin (11); Richards, David (20); Rivera, Carlos (12); Rudolph, Blaine (10); Schwabe, Michael (4); Steward, Charles (6); Vesling, Donald (12); Wilkins, Michael (11).

BURLINGTON—Baez, Angel (16); Bearse, Kevin (22); Garza, Guillermo (14); Harwell, David (19); Kramer, Thomas (12); Kurczewski, Tommy (9); Mercado, Manuel (4); Ogden, Todd (1); Olin, Steven (26); Oliveras, David (11); Ortiz, Angel (14); Roscoe, Gregory (13); Scaglione, Anthony (7); Stitz, John (1).

ELIZABETHTON—Anthony, Michael (6); Bangston, Patrick (13); Banks, Willie (13); Craskey, Robert (11); Delkus, Peter (21); Hernandez, Robert (2); Kline, Douglas (5); Kryzanowski, Rusty (18); Marten, Thomas (13); Meyer, Basil (14); Perez, Alexis (7); Richardson, David (9); Romero, Elvis (8); Schneider, Steven (6); Stowell, Steven (7); Villanueva, Eric (3); White, Frederick (11); Wulf, Brian (6).

KINGSPORT— Willoughby, Mark (17).

PULASKI—Reilley, John (7); Scarborough, Richard (4).

WYTHEVILLE—Quiles, Victor (18).

GRAND SLAM HOME RUNS—Bettendorf, 3; Brewer, Champion, Cloninger, Fulton, Liriano, Long, P. Murphy, Pegues, Perry, Schnurbusch, Roberts, Rountree, Woods, 1 each.

AWARDED FIRST BASE ON CATCHER'S INTERFERENCE—Davis (Piskor); Strong (Ericson); Wiese (Fulton).

CLUB FIELDING

Club	Pct.	G.	PO.	A.	E.	DP.	PB.	Club	Pct.	G.	PO.	A	E.	DP.	PB.
Johnson City	.959	69	1793	763	110	51	23	Wytheville	.950	70	1812	697	131	59	19
Pulaski	.958	70	1800	707	109	59	36	Kingsport	.949	70	1778	729	136	49	30
Burlington	.957	70	1849	689	114	48	25	Bristol	.946	69	1784	731	144	58	27
Bluefield	.951	69	1774	648	126	58	23	Elizabethton	.938	69	1803	729	166	62	13

Triple Play—Johnson City.

INDIVIDUAL FIELDING

°Throws lefthanded.

FIRST BASEMEN

Player and Club	Pct.	G.	PO.	A.	E.	DP.	Player and Club	Pct.	G.	PO.	A.	E.	DP.
Bettendorf, Bluefield	.968	57	425	34	15	39	Minton, Pulaski	1.000	9	63	3	0	8
Biggs, Bristol°	1.000	3	4	0	0	0	J. Murphy, Bristol	.977	51	440	25	11	34
BREWER, Johnson City°	.990	63	554	45	6	37	P. Murphy, Bluefield	1.000	1	1	0	0	1
Calzado, Johnson City	.919	4	32	2	3	1	Neel, Bristol	.981	56	424	33	9	28
Dunham, Bristol	.979	30	175	14	4	15	Paulino, Wytheville	.970	23	149	15	5	19
Fowler, Pulaski	1.000	1	6	0	0	1	Perry, Wytheville	.963	46	347	21	14	28
Franco, Wytheville	1.000	10	60	5	0	3	Rosario, Johnson City	1.000	6	50	4	0	3
Fulton, Johnson City	.833	1	5	0	1	0	Soto, Elizabethton	.982	15	104	5	2	10
Hunter, Pulaski°	.980	62	497	29	11	43	Spoolstra, Kingsport°	.988	44	370	26	5	21
Jones, Elizabethton	.972	31	249	25	8	23	Turtletaub, Kingsport°	1.000	2	3	0	0	1
Lara, Bristol	.975	28	177	21	5	14	Woods, Kingsport	.964	30	226	14	9	19
Martin, Elizabethton	.994	38	313	35	2	34							

Triple Play—Brewer.

SECOND BASEMAN

Player and Club	Pct.	G.	PO.	A.	E.	DP.	Player and Club	Pct.	G.	PO.	A.	E.	DP.
Arias, Bristol	.882	10	9	21	4	5	Galindo, Bristol	1.000	9	15	15	0	6
Baldwin, Bristol	.955	7	10	11	1	2	GENTLEMAN, Johnson City	.9641	52	89	153	9	25
Barrs, Johnson City	.972	10	11	24	1	2	Gomez, Bristol	.877	18	30	41	10	12
Berg, Pulaski	.913	10	17	25	4	4	Harley, Bristol	1.000	1	2	4	0	1
Capellan, Elizabethton	.956	45	108	151	12	33	Hernandez, Kingsport	.918	31	61	74	12	14
Carmona, Johnson City	.861	15	13	18	5	4	Hildebrandt, Elizabethton	.940	25	52	57	7	8
Casarotti, Pulaski	.9638	60	133	160	11	35	Martz, Bluefield	.958	7	10	13	1	4
Cloninger, Pulaski	1.000	1	0	2	0	0	Ramirez, Bluefield	1.000	4	6	9	0	0
Dariah, Bristol	1.000	7	5	15	0	3	Rosa, Bristol	.958	33	47	90	6	13
Diaz, Kingsport	.895	19	34	34	8	5	Rosario, Wytheville	.949	66	113	182	16	34
Eggleston, Wytheville	.938	6	12	18	2	3	Schnurbusch, Bristol	.938	34	59	91	10	19
Ferretti, Bristol	.943	48	78	87	10	13	Segui, Kingsport	.903	31	57	82	15	14
Franco, Wytheville	.500	1	0	1	1	0	Wahlig, Bluefield	.927	61	119	148	21	36

Triple Play—Gentleman.

THIRD BASEMEN

Player and Club	Pct.	G.	PO.	A.	E.	DP.	Player and Club	Pct.	G.	PO.	A.	E.	DP.
A. Arias, Wytheville	.879	30	18	40	8	1	Harley, Bristol	.882	38	23	52	10	3
P. Arias, Burlington	.750	5	4	2	2	0	Hernandez, Kingsport	.928	19	16	48	5	4
Baldwin, Burlington	.839	21	16	36	10	6	Hildebrandt, Elizabethton	.769	8	3	17	6	4
Barrs, Johnson City	.789	13	4	11	4	0	Holland, Bluefield	.873	26	15	40	8	1
Berg, Pulaski	.913	10	4	17	2	4	Huffman, Johnson City	.842	7	4	12	3	5
Biggers, Johnson City	.875	37	21	56	11	1	Jones, Elizabethton	.821	10	7	16	5	3
Carmona, Johnson City	.887	24	8	39	6	2	Lara, Elizabethton	.833	4	1	9	2	1
Castillo, Burlington	.865	36	14	50	10	1	Martz, Bluefield	.727	15	4	12	6	0
CHAMPION, Pulaski	.871	64	39	110	22	12	Murphy, Bluefield	.955	38	25	59	4	8
Cloninger, Pulaski	1.000	1	0	2	0	0	Narleski, Burlington	1.000	2	2	2	0	0
Courtney, Elizabethton	.792	21	16	26	11	1	Rogers, Burlington	.917	22	9	24	3	2
Donnels, Kingsport	.909	24	16	44	6	2	Schnurbusch, Bristol	.850	23	15	36	9	2
Franco, Wytheville	.848	48	35	82	21	10	Segui, Kingsport	.667	2	0	2	1	0
Galindo, Bristol	.925	16	14	23	3	3	Valdez, Elizabethton	.917	33	29	59	8	7
Gentleman, Johnson City	.750	4	0	3	1	0	Wiese, Kingsport	.853	30	20	44	11	5

SHORTSTOPS

Player and Club	Pct.	G.	PO.	A.	E.	DP.	Player and Club	Pct.	G.	PO.	A.	E.	DP.
A. Arias, Wytheville	.952	35	59	101	8	20	Gentleman, Johnson City	.917	5	1	10	1	2
P. Arias, Bristol	1.000	2	1	3	0	0	Hernandez, Kingsport	.931	16	20	47	5	7
Bautista, Burlington	.911	26	31	51	8	8	Holland, Bluefield	.899	27	31	58	10	10
Berg, Pulaski	.833	4	6	9	3	2	Huffman, Johnson City	.918	57	66	190	23	29
Biggers, Johnson City	.857	2	1	5	1	0	Narleski, Burlington	.942	46	58	122	11	21
Calzado, Johnson City	.800	1	1	3	1	1	Ramirez, Bluefield	.901	46	65	108	19	28
Carmona, Johnson City	.951	8	9	30	2	5	Reis, Pulaski	.956	12	19	24	2	5
Casarotti, Pulaski	.833	4	3	7	2	0	Rogers, Burlington	.947	4	9	9	1	2
CLONINGER, Pulaski	.938	53	57	155	14	27	Rosa, Pulaski	1.000	7	7	13	0	4
Alb. Diaz, Kingsport	1.000	1	1	2	0	0	Segui, Kingsport	.889	6	3	5	1	2
Ale. Diaz, Kingsport	.915	54	67	126	18	15	Tatarian, Elizabethton	.902	39	75	110	20	21
Eggleston, Wytheville	.913	39	55	81	13	13	Valdez, Elizabethton	.914	22	35	50	8	6
Fryman, Bristol	.927	66	103	187	23	41	Wacker, Elizabethton	.900	9	6	21	3	6
Galarza, Wytheville	.800	1	3	1	1	1							

Triple Play—Huffman.

OUTFIELDERS

Player and Club	Pct.	G.	PO.	A.	E.	DP.	Player and Club	Pct.	G.	PO.	A.	E.	DP.
Allison, Burlington*	.974	50	71	3	2	0	Kler, Bluefield	.964	23	24	3	1	0
Allred, Burlington*	.940	47	61	2	4	0	Lankford, Johnson City*	.968	66	143	7	5	1
Alvarez, Elizabethton	.923	18	9	3	1	0	Lara, Bristol	1.000	1	1	0	0	0
P. Arias, Burlington	1.000	6	4	0	0	0	Liriano, Burlington	.930	37	37	3	3	1
Arrington, Wytheville	.951	50	112	5	6	1	Maclin, Johnson City*	.922	62	70	1	6	1
Baldwin, Pulaski	.964	38	50	4	2	1	Martin, Elizabethton	.917	24	39	5	4	0
Barranco, Burlington*	.979	26	46	1	1	1	Mathiot, Elizabethton	.926	17	24	1	2	0
Belbru, Johnson City	.933	15	14	0	1	0	Maxey, Johnson City	.902	29	43	3	5	1
Berg, Pulaski	1.000	8	6	1	0	0	May, Kingsport	.936	57	124	7	9	3
Biggs, Bristol*	.933	29	27	1	2	0	McBride, Burlington	.933	37	41	1	3	0
Brewer, Johnson City*	1.000	3	3	0	0	0	Minton, Pulaski	.944	23	32	2	2	1
J. Brown, Elizabethton	.875	67	106	6	16	1	Pancoski, Bluefield*	.978	60	83	4	2	1
T. Brown, Bluefield	.909	11	9	1	1	0	Paulino, Wytheville	.868	26	41	5	7	0
Calzado, Johnson City	.000	3	0	0	1	0	Pegues, Bristol	.922	57	114	4	10	1
Cameron, Kingsport	.893	21	23	2	3	0	Power, Burlington*	1.000	8	8	0	0	0
Capellan, Elizabethton	1.000	16	25	3	0	0	Pride, Kingsport	.894	28	39	3	5	0
Carpenter, Wytheville	.926	40	56	7	5	2	Richie, Bristol	1.000	3	2	0	0	0
Echoles, Kingsport	1.000	2	1	0	0	0	Roberts, Burlington	.875	20	12	2	2	1
Eggleston, Wytheville	1.000	1	2	0	0	0	Rogers, Burlington	.667	5	2	0	1	0
Fleming, Wytheville	.938	62	115	5	8	0	Rountree, Burlington*	1.000	31	41	1	0	0
Flynn, Pulaski*	.956	45	63	2	3	0	Sanchez, Kingsport	.958	20	21	2	1	0
Fowler, Pulaski	.959	54	64	6	3	0	Shipman, Bristol	.952	56	76	4	4	1
Gabriel, Bluefield	.933	45	48	8	4	1	Smith, Elizabethton	.900	47	98	1	11	0
Galarza, Wytheville	1.000	12	8	1	0	1	Soto, Bluefield	.967	15	28	1	1	0
Gonzalez, Bristol	.933	11	13	1	1	0	Todd, Pulaski*	.940	68	119	6	8	0
Handel, Elizabethton	.950	24	35	3	2	0	Toney, Bristol	.918	67	121	2	11	2
Hayden, Bluefield	.956	62	103	5	5	0	Tucker, Wytheville	.913	15	21	0	2	0
Howell, Kingsport	.975	22	35	4	1	1	Turtletaub, Kingsport*	.971	52	96	4	3	0
Hunter, Pulaski*	1.000	1	1	0	0	0	Valdez, Elizabethton	.750	4	6	0	2	0
Jackson, Wytheville	1.000	6	4	0	0	0	Williams, Wytheville	.786	13	11	0	3	0
JOHNSTON, Johnson City	.980	56	92	5	2	0	Young, Kingsport	.965	33	55	0	2	0

CATCHERS

Player and Club	Pct.	G.	PO.	A.	E.	DP.	PB.	Player and Club	Pct.	G.	PO.	A.	E.	DP.	PB.
Albertson, Pulaski	.994	22	161	10	1	0	5	Mathiot, Elizabethton	.977	6	41	1	1	0	2
Baxter, Burlington	.982	37	243	33	5	1	10	Monzon, Bristol	.957	7	19	3	1	0	0
Berg, Pulaski	.978	6	42	3	1	0	3	Mota, Burlington	.976	15	111	9	3	0	10
Browning, Bluefield	.978	17	128	8	3	2	6	Piskor, Kingsport	.994	50	280	38	2	6	19
Castillo, Kingsport	1.000	6	21	4	0	0	4	Pulliam, Johnson City	1.000	8	18	0	0	0	2
Ericson, Elizabethton	.978	37	279	35	7	5	6	Rosario, Johnson City	.986	23	132	13	2	1	4
Fulton, Johnson City	.987	47	356	28	5	3	17	Simonds, Bluefield	.976	54	491	44	13	5	16
Halloran, Elizabethton	.960	28	201	17	9	0	5	Sommerkamp, Burlington	.996	38	252	21	1	4	5
Harper, Pulaski	.986	45	299	42	5	5	20	Strong, Bluefield	.969	25	137	20	5	1	8
Henderson, Bristol	.986	37	261	24	4	2	15	K. Taylor, Wytheville	1.000	9	73	9	0	0	6
Hines, Kingsport	.994	23	147	15	1	1	7	S. Taylor, Wytheville	.985	25	180	18	3	1	5
Huffman, Johnson City	1.000	1	2	0	0	0	0	WALBECK, Wytheville	.997	38	293	22	1	3	8
Long, Pulaski	.951	18	87	11	5	3	8	Wallman, Bluefield	.923	5	22	2	2	0	1
Mateo, Bristol	.954	12	55	7	3	0	4								

PITCHERS

Player and Club	Pct.	G.	PO.	A.	E.	DP.	Player and Club	Pct.	G.	PO.	A.	E.	DP.
Amarena, Bluefield	.875	11	2	12	2	1	Miller, Bluefield	.944	12	4	13	1	1
Baez, Burlington	1.000	16	2	1	0	0	Mondile, Bluefield	.833	10	4	1	1	0
Bangston, Elizabethton	.833	13	2	3	1	0	Murphy, Pulaski	1.000	11	3	1	0	0
Banks, Elizabethton	.591	13	4	9	9	0	Myers, Bluefield°	1.000	10	2	8	0	0
Bearse, Burlington°	.900	22	2	7	1	0	Myres, Kingsport	.947	23	7	11	1	1
Burdick, Bluefield	.800	10	5	3	2	1	Mozling, Bristol°	.800	10	0	4	1	0
Bushing, Bluefield	1.000	20	4	1	0	0	Nunez, Wytheville	1.000	18	2	4	0	0
Cakora, Wytheville°	1.000	15	2	3	0	1	Ogden, Burlington	1.000	1	1	0	0	0
Campos, Wytheville	1.000	18	7	9	0	0	Olin, Burlington	1.000	26	3	18	0	2
Canarte, Bristol	.500	9	2	1	3	0	Oliveras, Burlington	.857	11	2	4	1	1
F. Castillo, Wytheville	1.000	12	7	13	0	2	Olson, Bluefield	1.000	17	3	5	0	0
Cavers, Bluefield°	1.000	12	0	3	0	0	Ortiz, Burlington°	.929	14	1	12	1	0
Champion, Pulaski	1.000	1	0	1	0	0	Pena, Bristol	1.000	11	2	7	0	0
Coker, Bristol°	.840	23	5	16	4	1	Perez, Elizabethton	1.000	7	3	0	0	0
Cook, Bristol	.833	18	0	5	1	0	PIERSON, Johnson City	1.000	13	9	17	0	0
Corbin, Kingsport	1.000	6	4	5	0	0	Pilkinton, Bluefield	.900	19	0	9	1	0
Craskey, Elizabethton	.917	11	8	14	2	0	Pinder, Bluefield°	1.000	8	1	3	0	0
Crowson, Kingsport	1.000	17	1	6	0	1	Polley, Pulaski°	1.000	13	3	1	0	0
Culkar, Bluefield	1.000	4	0	1	0	0	Quiles, Wytheville	.667	18	3	1	2	0
Cummings, Pulaski	.900	14	9	9	2	1	Reeser, Pulaski	1.000	21	1	9	0	1
Davis, Wytheville	1.000	12	5	7	0	1	Reilley, Pulaski	1.000	7	1	2	0	1
Dawson, Bristol	1.000	5	2	1	0	0	Ricci, Bluefield	1.000	13	3	6	0	0
Delkus, Elizabethton	1.000	21	2	7	0	0	Richards, Bristol°	.833	20	3	2	1	0
Duquette, Bristol	.750	11	1	2	1	0	Richardson, Elizabethton°	1.000	9	2	2	0	0
Eddings, Wytheville	1.000	21	6	11	0	0	Rivera, Bristol	1.000	12	2	2	0	0
Elli, Kingsport°	.875	14	3	18	3	0	D. Rodriguez, Bluefield	1.000	8	2	2	0	0
Espino, Wytheville	1.000	8	3	3	0	0	F. Rodriguez, Kingsport	1.000	16	0	1	0	0
Everson, Bristol	.909	12	4	6	1	1	Romero, Elizabethton°	1.000	8	0	4	0	0
Fine, Kingsport	.813	14	5	8	3	0	Roscoe, Burlington	1.000	13	7	12	0	2
Gardner, Wytheville	.700	12	3	4	3	0	Rudolph, Bristol	1.000	10	3	5	0	0
Garza, Burlington	1.000	14	6	15	0	3	Scaglione, Burlington	1.000	7	3	6	0	0
George, Kingsport	1.000	18	0	7	0	2	Schneider, Elizabethton	1.000	5	3	3	0	0
Gibbs, Johnson City	.960	12	7	17	1	1	Schourek, Kingsport°	1.000	12	4	13	0	1
Gourlay, Pulaski	1.000	13	0	6	0	2	Schwabe, Bristol	1.000	4	1	1	0	0
Harnisch, Bluefield	.929	9	2	11	1	0	Sebree, Johnson City	.944	8	7	10	1	1
Harriger, Bluefield	.893	12	7	18	3	0	Sherrill, Johnson City°	1.000	25	3	4	0	0
Hartsfield, Pulaski	1.000	5	1	1	0	0	C. Smith, Pulaski°	.833	12	2	8	2	0
Harwell, Burlington	.875	19	10	4	2	0	K. Smith, Johnson City	1.000	13	6	14	0	1
Hathaway, Johnson City	.947	26	7	11	1	0	Sommer, Wytheville	.857	16	1	11	2	0
Hayes, Bristol	.636	11	1	6	4	0	Stanton, Pulaski°	1.000	15	3	11	0	0
Hempen, Johnson City	1.000	13	2	5	0	0	Steneman, Bluefield	1.000	10	1	8	0	0
Hernandez, Elizabethton°	1.000	2	0	1	0	0	Steward, Bristol	.909	6	3	7	1	1
Hitt, Johnson City°	.875	22	0	7	1	0	Stockham, Pulaski°	1.000	15	4	7	0	0
Horsley, Johnson City	1.000	25	2	5	0	1	Stowell, Elizabethton	1.000	7	1	7	0	0
Johnstone, Kingsport	1.000	17	5	5	0	0	Stroud, Wytheville°	1.000	19	4	8	0	0
Kline, Elizabethton	.625	5	1	4	3	0	Tilmon, Pulaski	.833	15	4	6	2	1
Knight, Pulaski°	.857	18	0	6	1	0	Tomberlin, Pulaski°	.909	12	1	9	1	1
Kramer, Burlington	.933	12	5	9	1	0	Vasquez, Kingsport	.667	25	1	1	1	1
Krogman, Kingsport	.889	12	1	6	1	1	Vesling, Bristol°	.920	12	7	16	2	0
Kryzanowski, Elizabethton	1.000	18	3	10	0	1	Weese, Johnson City	.909	13	6	4	1	0
Kurczewski, Burlington	1.000	9	3	4	0	0	White, Elizabethton	.818	11	4	5	2	1
Lott, Bristol	.800	8	0	4	1	0	Whitson, Wytheville	1.000	19	2	4	0	0
Marten, Elizabethton	.885	13	12	11	3	1	Wilkins, Bristol	.840	11	10	11	4	1
Martinez, Johnson City	1.000	10	2	7	0	0	Willoughby, Kingsport°	.857	17	3	3	1	0
McCarthy, Bristol	1.000	7	5	3	0	0	Wulf, Elizabethton°	1.000	6	0	2	0	0
Meyer, Elizabethton	.875	14	2	5	1	0							

The following players do not have any recorded accepted chances at the positions indicated; therefore, are not listed in the fielding averages for those particular positions: Anthony, p; A. Arias, of; Biggs, 3b, p; A. Castillo, p; Dunham, of; Eggleston, 3b; Flynn, p; Fulton, of; Hildebrandt, ss; Mercado, p; Minton, c; Mitchell, 3b, of; J. Murphy, 2b, of; Pulliam, ss, of, p; Rogers, 2b; Rosa, 3b, of, p; Scarborough, p; Stitz, p; S. Taylor, 3b; Villanueva, p; Watts, 1b; S. Williams, p.

CLUB PITCHING

Club	ERA.	G.	CG.	ShO.	Sv.	IP.	H.	R.	ER.	HR.	HB.	BB.	Int. BB.	SO.	WP.	Bk.
Burlington	2.85	70	4	11	22	616.1	496	270	195	25	26	271	6	606	30	8
Johnson City	3.39	69	11	10	16	597.2	583	274	225	45	11	162	15	494	24	3
Pulaski	4.02	70	7	7	13	600.0	526	326	268	28	32	344	16	588	44	6
Bluefield	4.09	69	4	2	13	591.1	585	336	269	39	21	320	7	619	42	4
Wytheville	4.17	70	6	2	12	604.0	584	387	280	62	47	317	2	535	55	6
Elizabethton	4.36	70	8	5	14	601.0	595	384	291	31	16	338	6	517	69	4
Kingsport	4.65	70	8	6	12	592.2	592	391	306	54	35	354	1	435	58	8
Bristol	4.78	69	1	3	9	594.2	624	402	316	43	28	286	4	473	53	8

PITCHERS' RECORDS
(Leading Qualifiers for Earned-Run Average Leadership — 56 or More Innings)

°Throws lefthanded.

Pitcher—Club	W.	L.	Pct.	ERA.	G.	GS.	CG.	GF.	ShO.	Sv.	IP.	H.	R.	ER.	HR.	HB.	BB.	Int. BB.	SO.	WP.
Tilmon, Pulaski	8	1	.889	1.56	15	10	1	3	1	0	80.2	55	20	14	1	3	22	1	101	5
Stockham, Pulaski°	6	0	1.000	1.68	15	7	2	5	2	0	64.1	46	13	12	0	4	14	1	80	3
Pierson, Johnson City	8	4	.667	1.68	13	13	5	0	5	0	85.2	67	21	16	4	1	10	0	72	5
Harwell, Burlington	4	1	.800	1.69	19	4	0	7	0	2	58.2	37	16	11	3	6	24	0	91	5
Bearse, Burlington°	7	1	.875	1.71	22	3	0	18	0	8	63.0	45	13	12	1	1	15	1	81	2
F. Castillo, Wytheville	10	1	.909	2.29	12	12	5	0	0	0	90.1	86	31	23	4	5	21	0	83	2
Olin, Burlington	4	4	.500	2.35	26	0	0	25	0	7	57.1	42	21	15	0	1	17	5	75	4
Elli, Kingsport°	9	3	.750	2.66	14	14	3	0	1	0	94.2	77	43	28	3	8	50	0	54	9
Burdick, Bluefield	7	2	.778	2.69	10	10	2	0	0	0	67.0	50	25	20	3	3	50	0	83	5
Roscoe, Burlington	7	2	.778	2.89	13	11	0	2	0	1	71.2	64	33	23	6	4	24	0	59	5
Kramer, Burlington	7	3	.700	3.01	12	11	2	1	1	1	71.2	57	31	24	2	1	26	0	71	0

Departmental Leaders: G—Hathaway, Olin, 26; W—F. Castillo, 10; L—Eddings, 10; Pct.—F. Castillo, .909; GS—Cummings, Elli, Ortiz, 14; CG—F. Castillo, Pierson, 5; GF—Olin, 25; ShO—Pierson, 5; Sv.—Bearse, Delkus, Sherrill, 8; IP—Elli, 94.2; H—Cummings, 96; R—Banks, 71; ER—Banks, 51; HR—Ricci, 11; HB—Elli, Gourlay, Sommer, 8; BB—Banks, 62; IBB—Hathaway, 6; SO—Tilmon, 101; WP—Banks, 28.

(All Pitchers—Listed Alphabetically)

Pitcher—Club	W.	L.	Pct.	ERA.	G.	GS.	CG.	GF.	ShO.	Sv.	IP.	H.	R.	ER.	HR.	HB.	BB.	Int. BB.	SO.	WP.
Amarena, Bluefield	5	3	.625	4.44	11	9	0	1	0	0	52.2	60	28	26	4	4	18	0	49	2
Anthony, Elizabethton*	0	0	.000	5.40	4	0	0	5	0	0	6.2	4	7	4	0	1	6	0	6	1
Baez, Burlington	3	1	.750	3.20	16	2	0	7	0	2	39.1	37	20	14	1	2	16	0	24	1
Bangston, Elizabethton	3	2	.600	1.85	13	1	1	9	1	3	34.0	24	13	7	1	2	12	2	34	1
Banks, Elizabethton	1	8	.111	6.99	13	13	0	0	0	0	65.2	73	71	51	3	3	62	0	71	28
Bearse, Burlington*	7	1	.875	1.71	22	3	0	18	0	8	63.0	45	13	12	1	1	15	1	81	2
Biggs, Bristol*	0	0	.000	4.50	1	0	0	1	0	0	2.0	3	3	1	1	0	1	0	1	1
Burdick, Bluefield	7	2	.778	2.69	10	10	2	0	0	0	67.0	50	25	20	3	3	50	0	83	5
Bushing, Bluefield	2	0	1.000	3.65	20	0	0	11	0	6	37.0	27	20	15	2	1	18	0	51	1
Cakora, Wytheville*	1	0	1.000	1.71	15	0	0	11	0	4	26.1	18	6	5	3	1	13	0	27	2
Campos, Wytheville	0	3	.000	4.76	18	2	0	11	0	4	39.2	29	23	21	4	4	24	0	34	4
Canarte, Bristol	0	0	.000	14.25	9	0	0	3	0	0	12.0	29	24	19	2	2	6	1	7	3
A. Castillo, Kingsport	0	0	.000	0.00	1	0	0	0	0	0	1.0	1	0	0	0	0	1	0	0	0
F. Castillo, Wytheville	10	1	.909	2.29	12	12	5	0	0	0	90.1	86	31	23	4	5	21	0	83	2
Cavers, Bluefield*	2	0	1.000	1.08	12	0	0	6	0	0	16.2	11	3	2	0	1	12	0	24	1
Champion, Pulaski	0	0	.000	0.00	1	0	0	0	0	0	1.2	1	0	0	0	0	2	0	1	0
Coker, Bristol*	3	3	.500	4.33	23	0	0	10	0	1	43.2	41	25	21	2	1	19	0	35	1
Cook, Bristol*	2	3	.400	2.39	18	2	0	8	0	1	49.0	44	19	13	1	3	16	0	52	4
Corbin, Kingsport	2	3	.400	6.31	6	6	0	0	0	0	25.2	24	21	18	3	2	26	0	17	6
Craskey, Elizabethton	4	3	.571	4.00	11	11	2	0	0	0	72.0	64	36	32	5	0	32	1	51	8
Crowson, Kingsport	0	5	.000	8.67	17	6	0	4	0	1	36.1	47	41	35	5	0	24	1	43	6
Culkar, Bluefield	0	0	.000	0.00	4	0	0	2	0	1	5.1	5	0	0	0	0	2	0	6	0
Cummings, Pulaski	6	3	.667	3.16	14	14	1	0	0	0	85.1	96	46	30	2	2	36	2	60	0
Davis, Wytheville	7	2	.778	3.19	12	12	0	0	0	0	73.1	67	36	26	6	2	38	0	52	4
Dawson, Bristol	0	1	.000	6.61	5	3	0	1	0	0	16.1	25	13	12	3	0	4	0	13	3
Delkus, Elizabethton	3	2	.600	1.19	21	0	0	20	0	8	37.2	29	6	5	1	1	7	1	44	0
Duquette, Bristol	1	3	.250	1.23	11	0	0	10	0	2	22.0	17	5	3	2	1	10	0	20	1
Eddings, Wytheville	2	10	.167	4.62	21	5	0	10	0	2	50.2	63	43	26	7	1	10	1	40	5
Elli, Kingsport*	9	3	.750	2.66	14	14	3	0	1	0	94.2	77	43	28	3	8	50	0	54	9
Espino, Wytheville	2	3	.400	5.25	8	7	1	0	0	0	36.0	42	29	21	3	1	14	0	26	9
Everson, Bristol	0	2	.000	1.61	12	0	0	10	0	5	22.1	13	5	4	0	2	8	3	22	1
Fine, Kingsport	1	7	.125	5.50	14	13	2	0	1	0	72.0	73	56	44	10	5	39	0	51	9
Flynn, Pulaski*	0	0	.000	0.00	1	0	0	1	0	0	1.0	1	0	0	0	0	0	0	1	0
Gardner, Wytheville	3	1	.750	3.42	12	8	0	2	0	1	47.1	27	23	18	7	7	34	0	51	5
Garza, Burlington	5	1	.833	3.64	14	4	0	3	0	1	54.1	39	23	22	2	3	26	0	39	3
George, Kingsport	2	3	.400	4.91	18	5	0	7	0	5	58.2	69	36	32	4	2	31	0	44	6
Gibbs, Johnson City	7	3	.700	3.24	12	12	1	0	0	0	75.0	69	31	27	9	1	17	1	53	3
Gourlay, Pulaski	1	2	.333	18.32	13	2	0	1	0	0	18.2	15	45	38	1	8	54	1	22	14
Harnisch, Bluefield	3	1	.750	2.56	9	9	0	0	0	0	52.2	38	19	15	0	1	26	1	64	4
Harriger, Kingsport	2	5	.286	4.33	12	7	0	2	0	0	43.2	43	31	21	3	4	22	0	24	1
Hartsville, Pulaski	0	0	.000	2.70	5	1	0	4	0	0	10.0	7	4	3	0	0	7	1	7	0
Harwell, Burlington	4	1	.800	1.69	19	4	0	7	0	2	58.2	37	16	11	3	6	24	0	91	5
Hathaway, Johnson City	4	1	.800	2.06	26	0	0	21	0	6	48.0	46	14	11	3	1	13	6	45	1
Hayes, Johnson City	0	7	.000	8.35	11	11	0	0	0	0	36.2	40	41	34	1	6	48	0	27	13
Hempen, Johnson City	2	3	.400	2.85	13	6	1	0	0	0	47.1	32	17	15	4	0	10	0	47	2
Hernandez, Elizabethton*	0	0	.000	0.00	2	0	0	0	0	0	3.2	3	0	0	0	1	0	0	5	0
Hitt, Johnson City*	1	2	.333	4.80	22	0	0	7	0	1	45.0	59	32	24	6	1	13	1	39	2
Horsley, Johnson City	3	0	1.000	3.38	25	0	0	8	0	1	45.1	41	18	17	2	1	15	1	39	3
Johnstone, Kingsport	1	1	.500	7.45	17	1	0	4	0	0	29.0	42	28	24	3	0	20	0	21	4
Kline, Elizabethton	1	1	.500	3.94	5	5	0	0	0	0	29.2	18	17	13	2	0	24	0	40	2
Knight, Pulaski*	1	0	1.000	4.80	18	0	0	8	0	1	30.0	31	19	16	1	3	28	1	25	2
Kramer, Burlington	7	3	.700	3.01	12	11	2	1	1	1	71.2	57	31	24	2	1	26	0	71	0
Krogman, Kingsport	2	2	.500	4.19	11	6	1	1	1	0	38.2	38	23	18	4	3	26	0	26	4
Kryzanowski, Elizabethton	3	1	.750	1.62	18	3	1	12	1	2	50.0	37	19	9	2	1	23	0	49	2
Kurczewski, Burlington	5	0	1.000	1.96	9	9	1	0	1	0	46.0	34	19	10	1	1	26	0	25	3
Lott, Bristol	0	1	.000	5.74	8	0	0	3	0	0	15.2	15	11	10	1	1	10	0	7	1
Marten, Elizabethton	6	4	.600	3.57	13	11	3	1	2	0	80.2	86	42	32	4	0	26	1	48	2
Martinez, Johnson City	2	2	.500	6.27	10	5	0	2	0	0	33.0	41	27	23	3	2	16	3	20	3
McCarthy, Bristol	0	2	.000	3.58	7	5	0	1	0	0	32.2	38	16	13	3	1	12	0	16	3
Mercado, Burlington*	1	0	1.000	4.63	4	2	0	1	0	0	11.2	14	10	6	0	0	10	0	9	0
Meyer, Elizabethton	1	2	.333	5.04	14	0	0	4	0	0	30.1	35	20	17	1	0	13	0	25	2
Miller, Bluefield	0	9	.000	5.49	12	12	1	0	0	0	60.2	72	48	37	7	2	29	1	63	3
Mondile, Bluefield	1	1	.500	4.43	10	0	0	4	0	0	22.1	20	12	11	2	2	21	1	15	1
Murphy, Pulaski	2	3	.400	6.91	11	4	0	6	0	3	27.1	25	22	21	2	3	24	1	25	3
Myers, Bluefield*	3	2	.600	2.32	10	10	0	0	0	0	50.1	36	18	13	1	0	28	0	60	1
Myres, Kingsport	2	4	.333	3.58	23	0	0	19	0	3	32.2	33	19	13	5	1	16	0	30	1
Nozling, Bristol*	0	3	.000	7.71	10	3	0	1	0	0	23.1	29	24	20	3	2	26	0	14	1
Nunez, Wytheville	0	3	.000	4.35	18	2	0	8	0	0	41.1	38	28	20	5	5	23	0	34	1
Ogden, Burlington	0	0	.000	0.00	1	0	0	0	0	0	2.0	0	1	0	0	1	2	0	2	0
Olin, Burlington	4	4	.500	2.35	26	0	0	25	0	7	57.1	42	21	15	0	1	17	5	75	4
Oliveras, Burlington	2	2	.500	4.80	11	6	0	1	0	0	30.0	31	25	16	2	3	29	0	24	1
Olson, Bristol	4	1	.800	6.37	17	0	0	10	0	1	41.0	46	35	29	4	3	28	0	55	9
Ortiz, Burlington*	5	3	.625	3.33	14	14	1	0	0	0	83.2	68	45	31	6	3	46	0	85	4
Pena, Bristol	3	5	.375	4.78	11	8	0	2	0	0	37.2	39	28	20	5	0	19	0	27	2
Perez, Elizabethton	0	0	.000	2.30	7	0	0	5	0	0	15.2	17	9	4	0	2	8	1	12	5
Pierson, Johnson City	8	4	.667	1.68	13	13	5	0	5	0	85.2	67	21	16	4	1	10	0	72	5
Pilkinton, Bluefield	1	3	.250	3.26	19	0	0	13	0	4	38.2	44	23	14	2	1	16	2	39	2
Pinder, Bluefield*	2	2	.500	4.82	8	1	0	7	0	1	18.2	20	12	10	2	0	9	1	22	3
Polley, Pulaski*	0	2	.000	1.75	13	1	0	8	0	5	25.2	18	7	5	1	0	9	0	37	1
Pulliam, Johnson City	0	0	.000	9.00	1	0	0	1	0	0	1.0	1	3	1	0	0	2	0	0	0
Quiles, Wytheville	0	0	.000	4.76	18	0	0	8	0	0	34.0	34	30	18	3	6	41	0	30	6
Reeser, Pulaski	2	2	.500	4.75	21	0	0	13	0	2	47.1	42	28	25	1	1	26	2	39	2
Reilley, Pulaski	2	2	.500	3.29	7	0	0	6	0	1	13.2	14	6	5	1	1	7	3	17	2
Ricci, Bluefield	5	5	.500	6.50	13	12	1	0	0	0	62.1	74	52	45	11	2	38	1	40	3
Richards, Bristol*	0	2	.000	4.40	20	2	0	9	0	0	45.0	49	26	22	2	1	20	0	56	1
Richardson, Elizabethton*	2	3	.400	4.46	9	6	0	0	0	0	34.1	36	20	17	3	2	23	0	23	1
Rivera, Bristol	0	0	.000	9.95	12	0	0	5	0	0	19.0	25	27	21	2	1	16	0	16	5

Pitcher—Club	W.	L.	Pct.	ERA	G	GS.	CG.	GF.	ShO.	Sv.	IP.	H.	R.	ER.	HR.	HB.	BB.	Int. BB.	SO.	WP.
D. Rodriguez, Bluefield	0	1	.000	9.16	8	2	0	3	0	0	18.2	29	23	19	1	1	10	0	10	2
F. Rodriguez, Kingsport	1	1	.500	6.85	16	0	0	4	0	0	22.1	19	22	17	2	2	21	0	17	3
Romero, Elizabethton*	0	1	.000	4.15	8	0	0	3	0	0	13.0	19	9	6	0	0	5	0	10	0
Rosa, Bristol	0	0	.000	9.00	1	0	0	1	0	0	1.0	2	1	1	0	0	0	0	1	0
Roscoe, Burlington	7	2	.778	2.89	13	11	0	2	0	1	71.2	64	33	23	6	4	24	0	59	5
Rudolph, Bristol	0	5	.000	5.40	10	6	0	0	0	0	35.0	37	28	21	2	1	26	0	24	4
Scaglione, Burlington	1	1	.500	3.24	7	4	0	1	0	0	25.0	22	10	9	1	0	11	0	21	2
Scarborough, Pulaski	0	0	.000	1.59	4	0	0	3	0	1	5.2	7	3	1	0	1	2	2	2	2
Schneider, Elizabethton	1	1	.500	13.50	5	0	0	1	0	0	8.0	10	12	12	2	0	13	0	5	3
Schourek, Kingsport*	4	5	.444	3.68	12	12	2	0	0	0	78.1	70	37	32	7	2	34	0	57	2
Schwabe, Bristol	2	1	.667	4.26	4	1	0	2	0	0	12.2	8	8	6	1	1	3	0	7	1
Sebree, Johnson City	5	2	.714	2.14	8	8	1	0	1	0	42.0	39	13	10	2	1	12	0	44	1
Sherrill, Johnson City*	3	4	.429	3.00	25	0	0	18	0	8	42.0	25	18	14	1	2	18	2	62	0
C. Smith, Pulaski*	3	6	.333	6.82	12	12	0	0	0	0	60.2	69	53	46	7	2	42	1	38	3
K. Smith, Johnson City	5	2	.714	3.60	13	13	3	0	1	0	80.0	88	38	32	6	1	18	1	38	0
Sommer, Wytheville	3	6	.333	4.86	16	9	0	5	0	1	63.0	62	44	34	6	8	45	1	68	6
Stanton, Pulaski*	4	8	.333	3.24	15	13	3	1	2	0	83.1	64	37	30	7	3	42	0	82	2
Steneman, Bluefield	1	1	.500	2.35	10	2	0	6	0	0	30.2	33	11	8	0	0	11	0	25	5
Steward, Bristol	1	2	.333	2.86	6	5	0	1	0	0	28.1	22	11	9	1	0	14	0	19	2
Stitz, Burlington	0	0	.000	9.00	1	0	0	0	0	0	2.0	6	3	2	0	1	0	0	0	0
Stockham, Pulaski*	6	0	1.000	1.68	15	7	2	5	2	0	64.1	46	13	12	0	4	14	1	80	3
Stowell, Elizabethton*	3	2	.600	4.22	7	7	1	0	0	0	49.0	44	26	23	1	2	33	0	40	6
Stroud, Wytheville*	3	4	.429	3.78	19	6	0	4	0	0	52.1	45	31	22	7	4	31	0	56	6
Tilmon, Pulaski	8	1	.889	1.56	15	10	1	3	1	0	80.2	55	20	14	1	3	22	1	101	5
Tomberlin, Pulaski*	4	2	.667	4.43	12	6	0	4	0	0	44.2	35	23	22	3	2	29	0	51	5
Vasquez, Kingsport	2	3	.400	3.29	25	0	0	10	0	3	41.0	36	20	15	5	6	22	0	36	6
Vesling, Bristol*	6	2	.750	3.14	12	12	1	0	0	0	80.1	83	36	28	5	2	11	0	52	4
Villanueva, Elizabethton*	0	1	.000	18.69	3	1	0	0	0	0	4.1	9	11	9	1	0	8	0	3	1
Weese, Johnson City	2	4	.333	5.91	13	10	0	1	0	0	53.1	75	42	35	5	0	18	0	35	4
White, Elizabethton	0	9	.000	7.53	11	11	0	0	0	0	55.0	76	62	46	5	2	35	0	45	6
Whitson, Wytheville	1	5	.167	8.34	19	7	0	5	0	0	49.2	73	63	46	7	3	23	0	34	5
Wilkins, Bristol	2	7	.222	5.70	11	11	0	0	0	0	60.0	65	51	38	6	3	15	0	47	2
Williams, Bluefield*	1	1	.500	2.70	6	2	0	2	0	0	16.2	20	7	5	0	0	4	0	13	0
Willoughby, Kingsport	0	0	.000	4.34	17	0	0	10	0	0	18.2	20	14	9	0	0	22	0	15	1
Wulf, Elizabethton*	1	0	1.000	3.18	6	0	0	1	0	1	11.1	11	4	4	0	0	7	0	6	1

BALKS—Banks, Roscoe, C. Smith, Vesling, 3 each; Baez, Crowson, Fine, Gibbs, Nunez, Rivera, 2 each; Bushing, F. Castillo, Cummings, Davis, Elli, Gardner, Harnisch, Hayes, Johnstone, Knight, Kurczewski, Lott, Miller, Oliveras, Ortiz, Pierson, Pinder, Rudolph, Scarborough, Schourek, Stowell, Vasquez, Whitson, 1 each.

COMBINATION SHUTOUTS—Williams-Cavers-Bushing, Myers-Pilkinton, Bluefield; Pena-Cook-Lott, Wilkins-Richards-Duquette, Cook-Everson, Bristol; Kurczewski-Bearse 2, Kurczewski-Bearse-Harwell, Kramer-Baez, Bearse-Oliveras-Harwell, Harwell-Baez, Oliveras-Garza-Olin, Ortiz-Harwell, Scaglione-Baez, Burlington; Richardson-Delkus, Elizabethton; Smith-Sherrill, Sebree-Hempen-Martinez, Gibbs-Sherrill, Johnson City; Elli-Vasquez, Elli-Krogman-Myers, Elli-Myers, Kingsport; Stockham-Reilley, Stockham-Reeser, Pulaski; Stroud-Gardner, Castillo-Cakora-Sommer, Wytheville.

NO-HIT GAMES—None.

Gulf Coast League

SUMMER CLASS A CLASSIFICATION

CHAMPIONSHIP WINNERS IN PREVIOUS YEARS

1964—Sarasota Braves .610	1973—Texas .732	1983—Texas .645
1965—Bradenton Astros .632	1974—Chicago N.L. .702	Los Angeles b .617
1966—New York A.L. .667	1975—Texas .774	1984—White Sox .651
1967—Kansas City .614	1976—Texas .704	Rangers b .571
1968—Oakland .650	1977—Chicago-A.L. .731	1985—Yankees c .705
1969—Montreal .585	1978—Texas .600	Rangers .532
1970—Chicago A.L. .600	1979—Houston .635	1986—Reds .548
1971—Kansas City .755	1980—Kansas City-Blue .635	Dodgers b .541
1972—Chicago N.L. a .651	1981—Kansas City-Gold .688	
Kansas City a .651	1982—New York-A.L. .667	

(Note—Known as Sarasota Rookie League in 1964 and Florida Rookie League in 1965.) aDeclared co-champions; no playoff. bLeague divided into Northern and Southern divisions; won one-game playoff for league championship. cYankees declared champion based on winning percentage when one-game playoff against Rangers was rained out.

STANDING OF CLUBS AT CLOSE OF SEASON, AUGUST 30

NORTHERN DIVISION   SOUTHERN DIVISION

Club	W.	L.	T.	Pct.	G.B.	Club	W.	L.	T.	Pct.	G.B.
Dodgers	43	20	0	.683	....	Royals	40	23	0	.635	....
Pirates	33	30	0	.524	10	White Sox	39	24	0	.619	1
Yankees	31	32	0	.492	12	Astros	32	30	0	.516	7½
Expos	21	42	0	.333	22	Reds	32	31	0	.508	8
Braves	20	43	0	.317	23	Rangers	23	39	0	.371	16½

COMPOSITE STANDING OF CLUBS AT CLOSE OF SEASON, AUGUST 30

Club	Dod.	Roy.	W.S.	Pir.	Ast.	Rds.	Yan.	Rng.	Exp.	Brv.	W.	L.	T.	Pct.	G.B.
Dodgers	....	5	4	3	7	3	4	7	5	5	43	20	0	.683	....
Royals	2	....	5	6	3	4	5	6	5	4	40	23	0	.635	3
White Sox	3	2	....	3	4	7	4	5	4	7	39	24	0	.619	4
Pirates	4	1	4	....	1	6	6	4	4	3	33	30	0	.524	10
Astros	0	4	3	6	....	2	4	4	5	4	32	30	0	.516	10½
Reds	4	3	0	1	5	....	4	4	6	5	32	31	0	.508	11
Yankees	3	2	3	1	3	3	....	6	5	5	31	32	0	.492	12
Rangers	0	1	2	3	2	3	1	....	5	6	23	39	0	.371	19½
Expos	2	2	3	3	2	1	2	2	....	4	21	42	0	.333	22
Braves	2	3	0	4	3	2	2	1	3	....	20	43	0	.317	23

Games played at Bradenton and Sarasota, Fla.

Club names are major league affiliations.

Playoffs—Dodgers defeated Royals, one game to none, to win league championship.

Regular-Season Attendance—No total official league attendance figures reported.

Managers—Astros, Julio Linares; Braves, Pedro Gonzalez; Dodgers, Jose Alvarez; Expos, Jethro McIntyre; Pirates, Woody Huyke; Rangers, Stan Hough; Reds, Sam Mejias; Royals, Luis Silverio; White Sox, Steve Dillard; Yankees, Fred Ferreira.

All-Star Team—1B—Ben Shelton, Pirates; 2B—Jose Munoz, Dodgers; 3B—Bob Knecht, Royals; SS—Jose Vizcaino, Dodgers; OF—Eric Anthony, Astros; Mark Merchant, Pirates; Lynn Robinson, Braves; C—Ruben Pujols, Royals; Starting Pitcher—Danny Newman, Astros; Relief Pitcher—Scott Jeffery, Reds; Manager of the Year—Luis Silverio, Royals.

(Compiled by Howe News Bureau, Boston, Mass.)

CLUB BATTING

Club	Pct.	G.	AB.	R.	OR.	H.	TB.	2B.	3B.	HR.	RBI.	GW.	SH.	SF.	HP.	BB.	Int. BB.	SO.	SB.	CS.	LOB.
Royals	.264	63	2104	349	263	555	757	80	34	18	293	32	16	25	15	254	15	351	104	36	445
Pirates	.252	63	2019	265	268	509	664	74	12	19	210	27	23	12	23	226	11	403	134	54	445
Rangers	.250	62	2071	270	336	517	674	66	17	19	226	18	10	19	16	221	12	401	81	43	436
White Sox	.246	63	2066	312	236	508	669	76	20	15	259	31	8	23	28	232	22	407	141	42	424
Dodgers	.246	63	2087	269	213	513	614	68	15	1	201	28	33	17	30	203	21	364	71	39	445
Astros	.244	62	1964	307	266	480	644	64	17	22	240	23	26	18	41	276	14	458	66	52	447
Yankees	.236	63	1960	250	250	462	558	54	9	8	216	28	19	26	26	257	11	404	77	45	452
Expos	.233	63	2065	253	323	481	657	85	17	19	208	18	16	19	36	191	8	436	105	35	425
Reds	.231	63	2076	284	307	480	620	66	19	12	227	22	28	15	21	234	12	407	99	41	437
Braves	.228	63	2132	223	320	487	639	79	11	17	192	18	33	19	19	209	11	430	63	31	471

INDIVIDUAL BATTING

(Leading Qualifiers for Batting Championship—170 or More Plate Appearances)

°Bats lefthanded.   †Switch-hitter.

Player and Club	Pct.	G.	AB.	R.	H.	TB.	2B.	3B.	HR.	RBI.	GW.	SH.	SF.	HP.	BB.	Int. BB.	SO.	SB.	CS.
Rodriguez, Henry, Dodgers°	.331	49	148	23	49	62	7	3	0	15	4	1	2	3	16	7	15	3	1
Munoz, Jose, Dodgers†	.321	54	187	31	60	67	7	0	0	22	7	2	1	3	26	3	22	6	5
Faulk, James, Expos°	.321	52	156	28	50	74	7	1	5	29	1	1	3	1	10	1	22	11	3
Knecht, Robert, Royals°	.308	61	208	55	64	102	12	10	2	44	4	0	2	1	43	6	23	31	6
Sable, Luke, Rangers	.303	56	228	29	69	75	6	0	0	23	1	1	2	2	9	0	14	25	5
Morales, William, Yankees	.294	51	180	25	53	66	11	1	0	24	2	0	4	0	12	2	21	18	7
Cedeno, Ramon, Astros	.292	60	216	39	63	82	9	2	2	27	3	0	5	1	24	0	26	5	8
Henry, Carlos, Astros°	.281	54	185	29	52	58	4	1	0	17	3	1	1	2	28	4	44	6	7
Taddeo, Stephen, Yankees°	.281	62	235	31	66	77	7	2	0	23	5	1	3	0	20	1	33	9	4
Brewer, Omar, Rangers†	.278	50	151	26	42	61	9	2	2	21	1	0	2	4	25	7	48	2	3

Player and Club	Pct.	G.	AB.	R.	H.	TB.	2B.	3B.	HR.	RBI.	GW.	SH.	SF.	HP.	BB.	Int. BB.	SO.	SB.	CS.
Robinson, Lynn, Braves†	.278	61	198	37	55	77	10	3	2	21	2	1	2	2	32	2	40	27	4
Williams, Flavio, Pirates	.278	42	144	18	40	45	3	1	0	16	4	3	4	0	19	0	17	14	5
Marabell, Scott, Dodgers	.277	55	184	23	51	69	14	2	0	32	5	1	4	4	11	0	34	5	3
Acta, Manuel, Astros	.268	59	235	37	63	78	5	2	2	13	0	3	0	2	13	0	37	5	10

Departmental Leaders: G—Penn, Taddeo, 62; AB—Acta, Taddeo, 235; R—Knecht, 55; H—Sable, 69; TB—Anthony, 110; 2B—Marabell, 14; 3B—Knecht, 10; HR—Anthony, 10; RBI—Anthony, 46; GWRBI—Munoz, Veras, 7; SH—Valdez, 7; SF—Bruckner, Cedeno, Torres, 5; HP—Penn, 15; BB—Knecht, 43; IBB—Brewer, H. Rodriguez, 7; SO—Vance, 59; SB—Merchant, 33; CS—Merchant, 13.

(All Players—Listed Alphabetically)

Player and Club	Pct.	G.	AB.	R.	H.	TB.	2B.	3B.	HR.	RBI.	GW.	SH.	SF.	HP.	BB.	Int. BB.	SO.	SB.	CS.
Acta, Manuel, Astros	.268	59	235	37	63	78	5	2	2	13	0	3	0	2	13	0	37	5	10
Adames, Herman, White Sox	.248	35	105	13	26	28	2	0	0	6	0	1	1	2	11	1	12	6	4
Alvarez, Clemente, White Sox	.182	25	55	8	10	14	1	0	1	4	0	0	0	0	7	0	8	1	1
Alvey, Andrew, Reds	.234	19	64	12	15	22	3	2	0	2	0	1	0	1	11	0	23	2	2
Amick, Adam, Astros	.000	6	4	1	0	0	0	0	0	0	0	1	0	0	0	0	2	0	0
Anderson, Timothy, Dodgers†	.230	44	122	16	28	31	1	1	0	8	0	4	0	1	15	0	20	5	5
Angelero, Jose, Royals	.290	25	93	17	27	36	2	2	1	10	1	2	1	0	12	1	14	4	2
Anthony, Eric, Astros°	.264	60	216	38	57	110	11	6	10	46	4	0	1	2	26	3	58	2	2
Apolinario, Oswaldo, Braves	.045	14	22	3	1	1	0	0	0	0	0	0	0	0	1	0	5	0	1
Arakawa, Tetsuo, Dodgers	.000	4	3	0	0	0	0	0	0	0	0	0	0	0	0	0	3	0	0
Atha, Jeffrey, Expos°	.226	29	62	9	14	18	4	0	0	4	0	1	0	2	6	1	7	2	0
Bailey, Gregory, Expos	.193	24	57	8	11	12	1	0	0	8	0	0	2	1	10	0	9	0	0
Bailey, James, Braves	.188	46	133	10	25	41	9	2	1	17	2	1	3	1	13	0	35	0	1
Barretto, Saul, Rangers	.255	43	137	18	35	49	6	1	2	17	2	0	1	1	8	0	17	0	3
Baum, Jeffrey, Astros°	.226	45	137	25	31	40	4	1	1	16	2	2	3	0	26	0	18	3	4
Bautista, Jose, Braves	.194	11	36	4	7	12	0	1	1	2	1	0	0	0	3	0	13	0	2
Beam, Keith, Reds	.400	3	5	1	2	3	1	0	0	0	0	0	0	0	1	0	1	0	0
Beams, Michael, Astros	.180	46	122	22	22	30	5	0	1	21	1	3	3	1	15	3	23	5	2
Belcher, Kevin, Rangers	.209	58	215	32	45	63	8	2	2	10	1	0	0	2	32	0	38	10	7
Bell, Rolando, Dodgers	.253	55	170	18	43	50	5	1	0	16	2	1	1	1	8	2	19	4	4
Beltran, Angel, Pirates	.207	19	58	7	12	13	1	0	0	5	1	0	0	0	5	1	9	1	1
Beniquez, Juan, Royals°	.263	7	19	6	5	9	2	1	0	0	0	0	0	2	0	4	1	1
Bennett, Brian, Astros	.200	25	75	4	15	17	2	0	0	9	1	0	1	1	10	0	23	1	1
Benzo, Luis, Reds†	.224	19	58	3	13	16	3	0	0	8	0	0	0	4	0	6	2	3
Bergquist, Patrick, Royals°	.263	57	194	33	51	65	6	1	2	34	2	1	3	1	33	2	31	24	7
Blackwell, Joe, Yankees	.222	14	18	0	4	4	0	0	0	0	1	0	0	0	4	0	5	0	0
Bluthart, Jay, Pirates°	.271	36	118	17	32	46	6	1	2	17	0	2	6	11	2	12	2	0
Bouman, Randall, Expos	.000	2	1	0	0	0	0	0	0	0	0	1	0	0	0	0	1	0	0
Brewer, Omar, Rangers†	.278	50	151	26	42	61	9	2	2	21	1	0	2	4	25	7	48	2	3
Brock, Reginald, Reds	.247	28	77	11	19	24	3	1	0	7	0	1	0	2	0	14	5	1
Bromby, Scott, Expos	.167	18	6	0	1	1	0	0	0	0	0	0	0	0	0	0	0	0	0
Bromley, Norman, Pirates	.213	14	47	4	10	15	2	0	1	6	0	1	0	1	2	0	5	0	2
Brown, Kenneth, Yankees	.180	34	61	10	11	13	0	1	0	14	3	0	2	1	6	0	22	3	2
Bruckner, Glen, Rangers	.251	47	183	23	46	65	7	3	2	20	1	1	5	1	12	0	38	4	2
Brune, James, Reds	.667	2	3	1	2	3	1	0	0	0	0	0	0	0	0	0	1	0	0
Byrnes, Timothy, Royals	.276	45	116	18	32	35	1	1	0	9	2	0	4	1	25	0	15	6	2
Caceras, Angel, Rangers	.190	25	63	6	12	12	0	0	0	2	0	1	1	0	16	1	15	2	3
Cantres, Angel, Yankees	.037	20	27	2	1	2	1	0	0	0	0	0	0	2	3	0	11	0	0
Carrion, Junior, Braves†	.253	36	87	7	22	22	0	0	0	4	1	4	0	1	4	0	10	1	2
Castillo, Braulio, Dodgers	.200	49	140	21	28	39	4	2	1	19	2	1	1	4	16	1	41	7	2
Cedeno, Ramon, Astros	.292	60	216	39	63	82	9	2	2	27	3	0	5	1	24	0	26	5	8
Cepero, Ismael, Dodgers°	.290	23	31	4	9	9	0	0	0	2	0	0	0	2	0	4	0	1
Cerny, Christopher, Dodgers°	.059	14	17	1	1	1	0	0	0	0	0	0	1	0	0	2	0	5	0	0
Chmielewski, Shon, Braves	.500	11	2	0	1	1	0	0	0	0	1	0	0	0	1	0	0	0
Clark, David, Expos°	.143	12	7	2	1	3	0	1	0	1	1	1	0	0	0	0	2	0	0
Cohen, Daniel, Braves°	.233	20	73	5	17	18	1	0	0	8	0	0	2	1	0	3	0	17	2	0
Colon, Cristobal, Rangers†	.257	46	136	12	35	38	3	0	0	9	0	2	1	0	3	0	12	5	1
Colon, David, Braves	.256	55	215	22	55	70	10	1	1	24	2	3	3	0	12	0	29	1	5
Colontino, Paul, White Sox	.172	16	29	8	5	7	2	0	0	1	0	1	1	0	4	0	10	0	0
Colsom, Bruce, Reds	.000	14	9	0	0	0	0	0	0	0	0	2	0	0	4	0	4	0	0
Conde, Hector, Royals†	.293	42	133	23	39	53	5	3	1	21	2	2	1	0	15	1	19	5	0
Costello, Fred, Astros	.091	13	11	0	1	1	0	0	0	1	0	5	0	5	0	7	0	0
Crockom, Kenneth, Astros	.209	45	139	25	29	37	8	0	0	12	0	1	2	4	37	0	31	12	6
Cruz, Bernardo, White Sox	.289	26	83	6	24	28	2	1	0	8	2	1	0	1	0	0	15	4	1
Cudjo, Lavelle, Reds	.143	37	105	14	15	18	1	1	0	8	1	0	0	0	8	0	31	7	3
Cunningham, David, Astros	.385	12	26	8	10	10	0	0	0	5	0	0	1	2	5	0	6	2	1
Currin, Wesley, Astros	.000	12	3	0	0	0	0	0	0	0	0	0	0	0	0	0	3	0	0
Davis, Brian, White Sox	.219	42	128	14	28	39	4	2	1	16	1	1	2	3	7	0	36	10	3
Davis, Mark, Braves	.277	37	141	16	39	68	8	0	7	22	0	0	1	1	8	1	23	2	0
Davis, Michael, Royals	.228	31	79	7	18	22	4	0	0	7	1	1	0	1	8	1	12	0	2
DeLeon, Julio, Rangers†	.245	44	151	18	37	51	7	2	1	13	2	1	0	0	11	0	33	4	3
DeLosSantos, Pedro, Astros	.234	46	137	17	32	40	2	3	0	13	1	3	0	3	14	1	33	7	3
DeShields, Delino, Expos°	.216	31	111	17	24	36	5	2	1	4	0	0	2	21	0	30	16	5
Diaz, Jose, White Sox	.087	14	23	1	2	2	0	0	0	0	0	0	0	0	2	0	11	2	3
Diaz, Junior, Reds	.000	7	1	0	0	0	0	0	0	0	0	0	0	0	0	0	0	0	0
Didder, Rayborne, Yankees	.205	17	39	6	8	13	1	2	0	6	1	0	0	0	4	0	8	1	1
Dilone, Rene, Pirates†	.308	6	13	2	4	4	0	0	0	0	0	0	0	0	1	0	2	1	0
Dooley, Marvin, Pirates	.000	6	2	0	0	0	0	0	0	0	0	0	0	0	0	0	1	0	0
Doss, Gregory, Braves	.125	12	24	2	3	5	2	0	0	1	0	0	0	0	5	0	4	0	0
Doss, Raymond, Pirates	.429	11	14	0	6	7	1	0	0	3	0	0	0	0	1	0	4	0	0
Downs, Ronald, Pirates	.000	21	3	0	0	0	0	0	0	0	0	0	0	0	0	0	2	0	0
Doyle, Shaun, White Sox°	.272	31	103	17	28	36	6	1	0	15	3	0	2	0	12	0	7	2	2
Duprey, Jose, Dodgers°	.000	3	1	0	0	0	0	0	0	0	0	0	0	0	0	0	0	0	0
Duran, Jose, Dodgers	.281	33	57	2	16	17	1	0	0	5	2	1	0	4	1	1	10	1	1
Dyer, Linton, Royals	.000	6	9	2	0	0	0	0	0	0	0	0	0	1	2	0	3	0	0
Elliott, David, Yankees°	.180	29	61	6	11	16	2	0	1	4	0	0	1	0	9	1	11	0	0
Englett, Todd, Pirates	.063	7	16	1	1	1	0	0	0	2	0	1	0	3	0	10	23	1	1
Esteban, Philipe, Dodgers°	.160	51	81	12	13	16	3	0	0	6	1	0	3	1	5	0	26	1	0
Eusebio, Raul, Astros	.208	42	125	26	26	34	1	2	1	15	3	0	0	7	18	0	19	8	2
Faulk, James, Expos°	.321	52	156	28	50	74	7	1	5	29	1	1	3	1	10	1	22	11	3
Feliz, Felix, Pirates	.284	28	67	7	19	23	4	0	0	4	0	5	0	0	7	0	8	2	1

Player and Club	Pct.	G.	AB.	R.	H.	TB.	2B.	3B.	HR.	RBI.	GW.	SH.	SF.	HP.	BB.	Int. BB.	SO.	SB.	CS.
Fernandez, Joseph, Dodgers†	.077	9	13	2	1	1	0	0	0	1	0	0	0	0	0	0	4	0	0
Fernandez, Reynaldo, Yankees°	.271	16	48	7	13	14	1	0	0	3	1	0	0	1	10	1	15	1	2
Ferradas, Miguel, Dodgers	.250	2	4	0	1	1	0	0	0	1	0	0	0	0	0	0	1	0	0
Finigan, Kevin, Expos	.333	14	3	1	1	2	1	0	0	0	0	0	0	0	2	0	0	0	0
Fletcher, Robert, Dodgers°	.400	18	5	0	2	2	0	0	0	2	0	0	0	0	0	0	0	0	0
Floyd, Daniel, Dodgers	.188	9	16	3	3	4	1	0	0	1	1	1	1	0	0	0	8	0	0
Fuller, Paul, White Sox°	.146	31	96	6	14	21	3	2	0	7	0	0	0	0	6	0	15	1	2
Garcia, Santos, Yankees	.317	25	41	6	13	16	0	0	1	8	0	0	1	1	5	0	14	2	0
Gardner, William, Royals	.316	37	98	19	31	37	3	0	1	15	2	0	1	0	13	0	25	2	2
Garman, James, Rangers	.000	1	1	0	0	0	0	0	0	0	0	0	0	0	0	0	1	0	0
Gastleum, Macario, Dodgers	.000	8	1	0	0	0	0	0	0	1	0	0	0	0	0	0	1	0	0
Gayo, Rene, Reds	.167	12	30	1	5	5	0	0	0	2	0	0	0	0	9	0	6	0	0
Gervais, Patrice, Pirates	.300	8	30	6	9	9	0	0	0	1	0	0	0	0	3	0	6	4	0
Giannelli, Thomas, Expos	.063	10	16	0	1	1	0	0	0	1	0	0	0	0	0	0	4	4	0
Gonzalez, Raul, Pirates	.133	18	45	4	6	8	2	0	0	1	0	0	0	0	0	0	8	0	0
Goshay, Henry, Dodgers	.246	54	191	27	47	53	4	1	0	11	1	2	1	3	19	1	34	16	3
Guzman, Jose, Yankees	.233	18	43	5	10	11	1	0	0	4	0	0	1	0	4	0	15	1	1
Hall, Andrew, Pirates	.455	3	11	2	5	6	1	0	0	0	0	0	0	0	1	0	1	0	0
Hall, Lamar, Braves	.206	38	97	11	20	21	1	0	0	4	0	4	0	1	5	1	17	3	1
Hamilton, David, Reds	.232	30	69	18	16	24	2	3	0	4	0	0	0	4	19	1	8	5	1
Hamilton, Michael, Rangers	.130	9	23	3	3	3	0	0	0	2	0	0	0	0	0	0	9	0	1
Hardwick, Darryl, Royals	.328	25	64	9	21	26	3	1	0	9	0	1	1	1	3	0	9	2	1
Harris, Franklyn, White Sox	.254	35	114	15	29	48	4	3	3	22	0	1	1	5	6	2	18	0	0
Harris, Keith, White Sox	.093	16	43	6	4	4	0	0	0	2	0	0	1	1	6	0	16	3	0
Harris, Vincent, White Sox†	.319	18	47	18	15	16	1	0	0	9	0	0	1	1	10	0	7	15	4
Haugh, Brendon, Royals	.212	44	118	17	25	39	3	4	1	17	2	0	1	1	10	1	17	2	2
Haywood, James, Pirates	.235	8	17	0	4	4	0	0	0	2	0	0	0	0	0	1	7	2	2
Henderson, David, Astros	.218	30	78	11	17	20	1	1	0	9	0	1	0	0	1	0	7	1	0
Henderson, Frank, Royals	.214	45	131	13	28	38	4	3	0	15	0	1	2	1	5	0	30	0	3
Henry, Carlos, Astros°	.281	54	185	29	52	58	4	1	0	17	3	1	1	2	28	4	44	6	7
Hernandez, Jose, Rangers	.173	24	52	5	9	12	1	1	0	2	0	1	0	1	9	0	25	2	1
Herrera, Jose, Yankees	.222	20	36	8	8	12	2	1	0	3	1	2	0	2	2	0	12	2	1
Higginbotham, Frankie, Astros	.000	5	2	0	0	0	0	0	0	0	0	0	0	0	0	0	1	0	0
Hill, Lewellyn, Yankees†	.169	31	89	11	15	20	0	1	1	8	1	0	0	3	4	0	31	6	1
Holmes, Timothy, Pirates	.000	8	3	1	0	0	0	0	0	0	0	0	0	0	1	0	1	0	0
Hook, Michael, Astros	.000	6	1	0	0	0	0	0	0	0	0	0	0	0	0	0	1	0	0
Hosey, Dwayne, White Sox	.279	41	129	26	36	43	2	1	1	10	2	0	2	3	18	1	22	19	4
Hunter, Robert, Yankees	.333	17	36	6	12	16	4	0	0	3	0	0	0	0	12	0	7	7	1
Isaac, Richard, Rangers	.286	27	105	13	30	36	4	1	0	10	0	0	1	0	9	0	13	6	3
Jackson, Troy, Pirates°	.149	16	47	4	7	8	1	0	0	3	0	0	0	0	4	0	17	2	1
Javier, Vicente, Reds	.299	24	67	12	20	24	4	0	0	7	0	5	0	1	8	0	14	3	2
Jeffery, Scott, Reds	.400	26	5	1	2	2	0	0	0	0	0	0	0	1	0	0	1	0	0
Jewett, Trent, Braves	.231	27	78	9	18	20	2	0	0	8	0	0	0	0	11	0	8	2	1
Jimenez, Ramon, Yankees°	.207	55	145	19	30	35	0	1	1	15	3	1	3	1	30	2	42	1	0
Jones, Eugene, Reds	.262	48	168	26	44	61	13	2	0	24	4	0	2	1	22	0	25	9	3
Joyner, Mack, Expos°	.000	4	2	0	0	0	0	0	0	0	0	0	0	0	0	0	1	0	0
Keays, Shayne, Expos	.000	16	1	0	0	0	0	0	0	0	0	1	0	0	0	0	0	0	0
Keelan, Douglas, Braves	.267	27	60	8	16	17	1	0	0	4	1	1	0	1	8	1	9	1	1
Kingwood, Tyrone, Expos	.265	46	151	17	40	58	7	4	1	26	5	0	1	1	7	0	31	8	4
Knecht, Robert, Royals°	.308	61	208	55	64	102	12	10	2	44	4	0	2	1	43	6	23	31	6
Koethke, Timothy, Pirates°	.222	15	27	3	6	7	1	0	0	2	1	0	0	0	6	0	7	0	0
Kovarick, Paul, Reds	.135	34	104	10	14	22	2	0	2	11	3	0	2	1	20	1	37	4	1
Kreuder, Daniel, Dodgers	.167	15	6	1	1	1	0	0	0	0	0	0	0	0	0	0	1	0	0
Lapaix, Rigoberto, Reds	.178	12	45	2	8	9	1	0	0	4	0	0	0	0	3	0	6	0	1
Lee, Christopher, Astros	.143	15	7	0	1	1	0	0	0	2	1	0	0	0	0	0	2	0	0
Lehnerz, Daniel, Reds	.250	16	4	0	1	1	0	0	0	0	0	0	1	0	0	0	0	0	0
Lemuth, Stephen, Expos°	.170	34	47	3	8	12	1	0	1	4	0	0	0	2	2	0	21	0	0
Lewis, Craig, Pirates	.167	8	6	1	1	1	0	0	0	0	0	0	0	1	4	0	0	0	0
Liendo, Temis, Yankees	.000	2	2	0	0	0	0	0	0	0	0	0	0	0	0	0	1	0	0
Lilliquist, Derek, Braves°	.500	2	2	0	1	1	0	0	0	0	0	0	0	0	0	0	0	0	0
Lilly, Michael, Dodgers	.000	16	1	0	0	0	0	0	0	0	0	0	0	0	0	0	1	0	0
Lipscomb, Brian, Pirates†	.212	15	33	8	7	7	0	0	0	1	1	0	0	1	6	0	12	2	0
Locke, Roger, Astros	.222	13	9	1	2	2	0	0	0	0	1	0	0	0	0	0	5	0	0
Logan, James, Yankees	.190	16	21	4	4	5	1	0	0	5	0	0	0	0	6	0	4	1	0
Losa, William, Rangers	.162	35	117	15	19	32	0	2	3	18	1	1	1	1	16	0	43	1	0
Luckham, Kenneth, Dodgers	.000	6	2	1	0	0	0	0	0	0	0	0	0	0	0	0	2	0	0
Lukachyk, Robert, White Sox°	.222	17	54	6	12	15	1	1	0	7	0	0	0	9	2		13	5	1
Maksodian, Michael, White Sox°	.349	34	109	23	38	58	11	3	1	28	6	0	2	1	19	4	13	7	2
Maldonado, Johnny, Braves	.000	17	3	0	0	0	0	0	0	0	0	2	0	0	0	0	3	0	0
Maldonado, Ricardo, Expos	.267	8	15	1	4	6	2	0	0	0	0	0	0	0	4	0	3	0	0
Marabell, Scott, Dodgers	.277	55	184	23	51	69	14	2	0	32	5	1	4	4	11	0	34	5	3
Marrero, Miguel, Braves°	.500	9	4	0	2	2	0	0	0	0	0	0	0	0	0	0	0	0	0
Marrero, Rogelio, Astros°	.111	17	9	2	1	1	0	0	0	0	0	0	0	0	3	0	7	0	0
Marsh, Quinn, Yankees	.500	1	2	0	1	1	0	0	0	0	0	0	0	0	0	0	1	0	0
Martinez, Luis, Reds	.294	45	153	24	45	64	8	1	3	24	3	0	1	1	10	4	11	5	0
Martinez, Ramon, Pirates	.000	18	5	0	0	0	0	0	0	0	0	0	0	0	0	0	3	0	0
Mason, Robert, Expos	.212	40	85	6	18	21	3	0	0	6	1	1	1	1	4	2	11	0	1
Mathews, Jeremy, Reds	.208	48	173	23	36	57	5	2	4	22	4	3	1	0	10	2	56	6	4
Matos, Ramon, Royals	.246	48	122	23	30	38	0	4	0	10	2	2	1	2	11	0	31	12	5
Maville, Randy, Expos	.244	37	82	7	20	24	4	0	0	5	1	0	2	0	10	0	16	0	0
Maysonet, Gregory, Pirates	.000	10	0	0	0	0	0	0	0	0	0	1	0	0	0	0	0	0	0
Mayz, Kelly, Pirates†	.242	24	62	8	15	16	1	0	0	5	2	3	0	0	5	0	13	0	1
Mealy, Anthony, Pirates	.337	28	104	15	35	47	7	1	1	17	3	1	1	2	7	0	19	15	4
Mee, James, Reds	.216	22	51	6	11	12	1	0	0	5	0	0	2	2	12	0	14	1	0
Meister, Ralph, Braves	.000	13	12	0	0	0	0	0	0	0	0	0	0	0	6	0	6	0	0
Mendoza, Jesus, Braves°	.218	36	119	11	26	32	4	1	0	14	2	4	2	4	15	0	26	0	2
Merchant, Mark, Pirates†	.265	50	185	32	49	65	5	1	3	17	1	0	4	1	30	4	29	33	13
Merejo, Jose, White Sox	.186	20	59	8	11	11	0	0	0	5	2	1	0	0	6	0	8	4	1
Mershon, Brian, Reds†	.235	34	102	15	24	24	0	0	0	11	1	3	1	2	10	2	13	11	3
Miguel, Tamares, Dodgers	.000	14	11	0	0	0	0	0	0	1	0	1	0	0	1	0	4	0	0
Milian, Carlos, Dodgers	.000	8	1	0	0	0	0	0	0	0	0	0	0	0	0	0	1	0	0
Miller, Paul, Pirates	.000	12	19	2	0	0	0	0	0	0	0	0	0	0	3	0	10	0	0

Player and Club	Pct.	G.	AB.	R.	H.	TB.	2B.	3B.	HR.	RBI.	GW.	SH.	SF.	HP.	BB.	Int. BB.	SO.	SB.	CS.
Minchey, Nathan, Expos	.000	12	8	0	0	0	0	0	0	0	0	0	0	0	0	0	5	0	0
Mitchell, Glenn, Braves	.000	14	2	0	0	0	0	0	0	0	0	1	0	0	0	0	0	1	0
Mitchell, Keith, Braves	.240	57	208	24	50	70	12	1	2	21	1	0	2	2	29	0	50	7	2
Mittan, James, Braves	.257	17	35	2	9	10	1	0	0	4	0	1	1	0	1	0	15	1	0
Mobley, Charlie, Braves*	.231	51	130	15	30	39	4	1	1	5	1	2	0	1	13	2	20	5	3
Mohr, Michael, Reds	.262	32	103	17	27	29	2	0	0	8	1	1	0	0	18	0	11	18	2
Moore, Franklin, Pirates*	.000	8	1	0	0	0	0	0	0	0	0	0	0	0	0	0	1	0	0
Mora, Juan, Dodgers	.287	27	87	8	25	33	4	2	0	6	0	0	1	0	2	0	11	1	0
Morabito, John, White Sox	.282	14	39	6	11	12	1	0	0	3	0	0	0	2	6	0	3	1	0
Morales, William, Yankees	.294	51	180	25	53	66	11	1	0	24	2	0	4	0	12	2	21	18	7
Mota, Yony, Expos	.000	13	1	0	0	0	0	0	0	0	0	0	0	0	0	0	1	0	0
Munoz, Jose, Dodgers†	.321	54	187	31	60	67	7	0	0	22	7	2	1	3	26	3	22	6	5
Murdock, Kevin, White Sox	.111	8	18	2	2	3	1	0	0	0	0	0	0	0	2	0	3	0	0
Murphy, Gary, Astros	.000	4	1	0	0	0	0	0	0	0	0	0	0	0	0	0	0	0	0
Newman, Daniel, Astros*	.000	12	9	0	0	0	0	0	0	0	0	0	0	0	2	0	5	0	0
Niethammer, Darren, Rangers	.247	52	178	23	44	53	6	0	1	29	1	0	2	1	14	1	14	10	4
Nordstrom, Carl, Reds	.429	15	7	1	3	4	1	0	0	2	0	1	0	0	1	0	1	0	0
Ocasio, Javier, White Sox	.343	29	105	24	36	43	5	1	0	18	2	0	0	3	13	0	11	7	2
Oliva, Roberto, Braves	.000	6	13	1	0	0	0	0	0	0	0	0	0	0	0	0	4	0	0
Ortiz, Joseph, Astros	.289	36	121	18	35	55	8	0	4	25	2	0	2	6	18	0	20	3	1
Ortiz, Julio, Dodgers	.000	25	2	0	0	0	0	0	0	0	0	1	0	0	0	0	1	0	0
Overeem, Steven, Expos	.000	10	6	0	0	0	0	0	0	0	0	0	0	0	0	0	1	0	0
Palos, Jose, Pirates	.189	12	37	5	7	8	1	0	0	3	0	1	0	1	2	0	8	1	0
Panizzi, David, Astros	.400	7	25	5	10	13	0	0	1	5	0	0	0	0	3	0	8	4	0
Paredes, Jesus, Expos†	.250	50	184	32	46	53	5	1	0	7	0	3	0	3	23	0	37	21	5
Parker, Jarrod, Braves	.125	12	8	0	1	1	0	0	0	0	0	1	0	0	0	0	5	0	0
Paulino, Elvys, Expos	.200	53	150	12	30	34	4	0	0	12	1	3	2	2	9	2	15	1	1
Payton, Raymond, White Sox	.182	13	33	4	6	10	1	0	1	5	1	0	0	0	3	0	7	1	0
Penn, Trevor, Expos*	.262	62	210	33	55	81	9	1	5	26	2	0	4	15	28	1	37	10	6
Perez, Beban, Yankees	.250	52	140	18	35	37	2	0	0	13	1	1	0	2	21	2	24	6	6
Perez, Eduardo, Braves	.202	31	89	8	18	22	1	0	1	5	1	1	1	1	8	0	14	0	0
Perez, Francisco, Astros	.071	12	14	1	1	1	0	0	0	0	0	3	0	0	4	0	10	0	0
Perez, Ozzie, Reds†	.176	30	85	8	15	15	0	0	0	7	1	2	0	1	17	1	12	5	1
Perez, Richard, Royals	.293	44	150	11	44	52	5	0	1	20	2	2	3	0	7	1	20	5	1
Perozo, Daniel, Reds	.254	50	189	35	48	68	7	5	1	29	2	0	0	4	15	1	39	6	3
Piechowski, Timothy, Expos*	.308	50	120	18	37	53	7	3	1	12	1	0	2	1	9	0	9	12	2
Pledger, Kinnis, White Sox*	.252	37	127	18	32	47	6	3	1	13	1	0	1	0	13	3	46	20	0
Polledo, Santiago, Expos	.263	22	38	4	10	11	1	0	0	6	0	0	0	2	2	0	8	1	0
Polo, Andres, Braves	.179	19	28	2	5	5	0	0	0	0	0	0	0	0	3	0	8	1	1
Pride, Troy, Dodgers	.158	22	19	3	3	3	0	0	0	1	0	0	0	0	1	0	4	1	1
Pujols, Ruben, Royals	.304	41	115	23	35	63	6	2	6	17	0	1	1	2	11	0	23	3	0
Ramirez, Juan, Astros	.000	12	9	0	0	0	0	0	0	0	0	1	0	0	0	0	5	0	0
Ramos, Paul, Yankees	.213	47	108	13	23	27	1	0	1	8	0	0	0	5	18	0	18	1	5
Reagans, Javan, Expos	.253	43	83	8	21	25	2	1	0	9	0	1	0	0	9	0	17	7	0
Redmond, Andre, Pirates	.234	20	47	8	11	12	1	0	0	2	0	1	0	2	4	0	11	6	1
Reilley, John, Braves	.000	14	1	0	0	0	0	0	0	0	0	1	0	0	0	0	0	0	0
Reis, Paulo, Braves	.223	40	139	16	31	39	6	1	0	12	1	2	1	2	12	2	34	5	2
Reyes, Rolando, Yankees	.133	20	45	1	6	6	0	0	0	2	0	1	0	1	0	0	12	0	1
Rice, Thomas, Royals	.259	22	54	12	14	16	2	0	0	8	0	1	0	0	4	1	11	0	0
Risley, William, Reds	.111	11	9	0	1	1	0	0	0	0	0	2	0	0	0	0	4	0	0
Rivera, Angel, Expos	.000	15	9	0	0	0	0	0	0	0	0	0	0	0	0	0	4	0	0
Rivera, Bienvenido, Braves	.143	16	7	0	1	1	0	0	0	0	0	1	0	0	0	0	6	0	0
Rivera, Hector, Expos	.000	14	14	0	0	0	0	0	0	0	0	0	0	0	0	0	4	0	0
Robinson, Barrington, Royals	.238	54	193	25	46	66	12	1	2	34	6	0	2	2	21	0	26	3	0
Robinson, Lynn, Braves†	.278	61	198	37	55	77	10	3	2	21	2	1	2	2	32	2	40	27	4
Robitaille, Martin, Expos*	.196	59	153	14	30	41	6	1	1	19	1	0	3	0	19	1	35	5	2
Rodriguez, Carlos, Yankees†	.157	50	115	15	18	18	0	0	0	11	1	6	1	1	23	0	8	2	1
Rodriguez, Henry, Dodgers*	.331	49	148	23	49	62	7	3	0	15	4	1	2	3	16	7	15	3	1
Rodriguez, Jorge, Rangers	.284	20	67	7	19	21	0	1	0	9	2	2	0	0	6	0	9	1	1
Rodriguez, Rosario, Reds*	.375	17	8	2	3	3	0	0	0	0	0	0	1	0	2	0	0	0	0
Rogers, Michael, Rangers	.214	49	145	16	31	39	4	2	0	17	3	0	3	1	38	0	45	0	2
Runge, Scott, Pirates	.333	4	3	0	1	2	1	0	0	0	0	0	0	0	0	0	1	0	0
Ruscitto, Andrew, Astros*	.180	45	122	13	22	29	4	0	1	10	1	0	2	6	20	1	47	4	4
Russell, Kal, Pirates*	.186	15	43	2	8	8	0	0	0	4	0	1	1	0	3	0	2	1	0
Ryan, Kevin, Dodgers	.000	19	3	0	0	0	0	0	0	0	0	1	0	0	1	0	0	0	0
Ryans, Dennis, Yankees	.218	25	55	3	12	13	1	0	0	6	1	1	0	0	3	0	11	1	0
Sable, Luke, Rangers	.303	56	228	29	69	75	6	0	0	23	1	1	2	2	9	0	14	25	5
Santiago, Delvy, Expos	.000	12	11	0	0	0	0	0	0	0	0	0	0	0	0	0	2	0	0
Santos, Luis, Dodgers	.238	57	147	15	35	43	4	2	0	14	1	2	0	3	15	0	20	12	3
Scarborough, Richard, Braves	.182	9	11	0	2	2	0	0	0	1	0	2	0	0	0	0	4	0	0
Schlopy, Clifford, Pirates*	.000	3	2	0	0	0	0	0	0	0	0	0	0	0	0	0	1	0	1
Schmitt, Gary, Pirates	.273	4	11	0	3	4	1	0	0	1	0	0	0	0	0	0	3	0	0
Scott, Jerry, Reds	.000	3	7	1	0	0	0	0	0	0	0	0	0	0	1	0	0	0	0
Scruggs, Anthony, Rangers	.345	30	119	24	41	64	5	0	6	24	3	0	0	2	12	3	22	12	5
Seymour, Winston, Pirates*	.264	19	53	3	14	22	2	0	2	7	1	0	0	1	6	1	10	2	1
Shelton, Ben, Pirates	.286	38	119	22	34	60	8	3	4	16	2	0	1	2	12	1	48	7	2
Shepherd, Michael, Reds	.233	41	129	10	30	36	3	0	1	12	1	2	2	2	10	0	25	4	2
Shinall, Zakary, Dodgers	.000	8	1	0	0	0	0	0	0	0	0	0	0	0	0	0	1	0	0
Siegel, Robert, Pirates†	.000	3	2	0	0	0	0	0	0	0	0	1	0	0	0	0	0	0	0
Simmonds, Leroy, Dodgers†	.172	22	29	5	5	7	2	0	0	1	0	0	0	1	2	0	8	0	1
Singley, Joseph, White Sox	.219	28	96	10	21	31	4	0	2	11	5	0	0	0	10	2	32	2	1
Slaughter, Garland, Pirates	.000	14	1	0	0	0	0	0	0	0	0	0	0	0	0	0	0	0	0
Smith, Edward, White Sox	.237	32	114	10	27	36	3	0	2	18	1	0	0	2	6	0	28	3	3
Smith, Willie, Pirates	.333	10	3	0	1	2	1	0	0	0	0	0	0	0	0	0	1	0	0
Solarte, Jose, Expos	.333	19	3	0	1	1	0	0	0	0	0	0	0	0	0	0	1	0	0
Solarte, Nollys, Pirates	.333	1	3	0	1	1	0	0	0	0	0	0	0	0	0	0	1	0	1
Soto, Mario, Reds	.000	2	2	0	0	0	0	0	0	0	0	0	0	0	0	0	1	0	0
Spriggs, George, Pirates	.281	37	128	15	36	43	8	0	1	12	0	1	0	3	11	0	30	16	4
Stewart, Andrew, Pirates*	.195	16	41	4	8	8	0	0	0	3	0	0	0	0	1	0	9	0	0
Storms, Steven, Reds	.333	20	3	1	1	2	1	0	0	0	0	0	0	0	0	0	0	0	0
Stout, Michael, Reds	.111	10	9	2	1	1	0	0	0	0	0	0	0	0	3	0	4	0	0
Stuart, Robert, Braves*	.239	50	142	14	34	45	8	0	1	15	3	0	0	2	15	2	15	8	2

Player and Club	Pct.	G.	AB.	R.	H.	TB.	2B.	3B.	HR.	RBI.	GW.	SH.	SF.	HP.	BB.	Int. BB.	SO.	SB.	CS.
Taddeo, Stephen, Yankees°	.281	62	235	31	66	77	7	2	0	23	5	1	3	0	20	1	33	9	4
Tafoya, Dennis, Astros	.000	19	4	1	0	0	0	0	0	0	1	0	1	0	1	0	2	0	0
Takacs, Jeff, Expos	.223	42	94	5	21	33	4	1	2	13	2	0	0	0	5	0	24	1	0
Tejada, Eugenio, White Sox	.152	11	33	4	5	6	1	0	0	3	1	0	2	0	0	0	7	0	2
Thomas, Dwight, White Sox	.191	24	68	10	13	20	4	0	1	10	0	0	1	2	8	0	31	1	0
Thomas, Mark, Pirates	.288	17	66	8	19	27	4	2	0	12	3	0	0	0	5	1	13	2	1
Thompson, Anthony, Pirates	.294	11	17	3	5	6	1	0	0	1	0	0	0	0	2	0	7	2	0
Torrez, Miguel, Yankees	.265	61	219	36	58	69	11	0	0	23	1	2	5	5	42	0	30	14	10
Trammell, Marcus, White Sox°	.233	37	103	23	24	28	2	1	0	11	0	1	1	1	16	3	8	17	4
Trochim, Scott, Reds	.224	45	152	18	34	45	4	2	1	22	1	1	3	0	15	0	15	3	4
Tunall, Steven, Pirates	.200	12	10	1	2	2	0	0	0	1	0	1	0	0	0	0	2	0	0
Turek, Joseph, Reds	.250	3	8	1	2	2	0	0	0	1	0	1	0	0	0	0	0	0	0
Urman, Michael, Braves	.191	18	47	3	9	9	0	0	0	3	0	2	0	1	11	0	19	0	1
Valdez, Amilcar, Dodgers	.238	60	181	23	43	48	5	0	0	16	0	7	3	2	19	4	20	1	3
Valverde, Miguel, Pirates†	.290	20	69	10	20	26	4	1	0	4	1	0	2	6	0	13	9	4
Vance, Ricky, Expos	.200	50	155	18	31	48	11	0	2	15	2	2	1	1	10	0	59	8	4
Vanzytveld, Jeffrey, Dodgers°	.333	9	6	0	2	2	0	0	0	0	0	0	0	0	0	0	1	0	0
Vasquez, Ernesto, Astros	.667	14	3	0	2	3	1	0	0	2	0	1	0	0	0	0	1	0	0
Vazquez, Marcos, Braves	.143	12	14	2	2	2	0	0	0	0	0	2	0	0	0	0	3	0	0
Ventura, Pablo, Royals	.197	30	71	11	14	20	6	0	0	7	4	0	1	3	0	20	1	0
Veras, Yovanny, Yankees	.260	55	196	18	51	68	8	0	3	33	7	0	4	2	18	2	50	1	2
Vierra, Joseph, Reds°	.333	14	3	0	1	1	0	0	0	0	0	1	0	0	0	0	0	0	0
Virgo, Ryan, Dodgers	.250	10	4	0	1	1	0	0	0	0	1	0	1	0	0	0	0	0	0
Vizcaino, Jose, Dodgers†	.253	49	150	26	38	45	5	1	0	12	2	2	1	0	22	1	24	8	5
Wadsworth, Randal, Dodgers	.150	13	20	2	3	4	1	0	0	1	0	1	0	0	2	0	1	0	0
Walker, Roosevelt, Expos	.250	28	24	10	6	9	1	1	0	1	0	0	0	0	9	2	2	2
Wall, Michael, Pirates	.312	27	77	10	24	32	3	1	1	12	2	1	1	0	6	1	11	1	2
Walsh, Edward, White Sox°	.397	18	58	4	23	26	3	0	0	14	3	0	2	0	5	1	10	0	0
Warren, Randy, White Sox	.274	38	95	22	26	37	6	1	1	13	1	3	3	1	27	1	10	10	2
Washington, David, Astros	.279	27	68	9	19	23	3	0	0	6	1	1	0	1	7	1	17	2	2
Wegman, Bruce, Expos	.000	13	2	0	0	0	0	0	0	0	0	0	0	0	0	0	1	0	0
Whitaker, Brian, Reds	.351	11	37	7	13	13	0	0	0	1	0	0	0	0	2	0	8	2	1
Williams, Flavio, Pirates	.278	42	144	18	40	45	3	1	0	16	4	3	4	0	19	0	17	14	5
Wilson, Randall, Yankees	.000	15	0	0	0	0	0	0	0	0	0	1	0	0	0	0	0	0	0
Wolfer, James, Reds°	.267	14	30	1	8	8	0	0	0	5	0	1	2	0	4	0	11	0	4
Wong, Nibaldo, Dodgers	.103	15	29	1	3	3	0	0	0	2	0	0	0	1	2	0	9	0	0
Wright, Brian, Braves°	.192	15	26	0	5	6	1	0	0	3	0	0	0	3	0	8	0	0
Yamasaki, Takeshi, Dodgers	.000	10	10	1	0	0	0	0	0	0	0	0	0	0	3	0	4	0	0
Yochum, Kenneth, Braves	.000	18	1	0	0	0	0	0	0	0	0	0	0	0	1	0	0	0	1
Young, John, Pirates	.240	38	121	23	29	49	6	1	4	18	1	1	1	1	24	0	23	6	4
Zeinert, Bradley, Dodgers	.286	22	7	0	2	2	0	0	0	4	0	1	0	0	0	0	1	0	0

The following pitchers, listed alphabetically by club, with games in parentheses, had no plate appearances, primarily through use of designated hitters:

ASTROS—Small, Christopher (3).

BRAVES—Barcelo, Jorge (10); Gillund, Robert (9); Nevada, Yonny (7); Rosario, Manuel (1).

DODGERS—Langley, Wesley (1); Riensche, Kenneth (6).

EXPOS—Hesketh, Joseph (2).

PIRATES—Befort, Lyle (6); Macavage, Joseph (2).

RANGERS—Alvarez, Wilson (10); Bohanon, Brian (5); Boron, Randy (25); Ebarb, Wayne (7); Hurst, Jonathan (12); Jaime, Jose (15); Javier, Carlos (12); Kopczynski, Todd (28); Lamle, Adam (3); Lopez, Jose (13); Lynch, David (13); Manuel, Barry (1); Mmahat, Kevin (12); Moss, Jan (12); Nen, Robb (2); Petkovsek, Mark (3); Rockman, Marvin (14); Rosario, Amado (4); Saavedra, Francisco (12); Steiner, Brian (4); Wilkinson, Spencer (8).

REDS—Keen, Rick (19).

ROYALS—Acevedo, Eugenio (1); Anderson, Mark (22); Clark, Dera (21); Daly, Shaun (13); DeLeon, Jesus (12); Drohan, William (12); Hill, Terry (16); Hoeme, Steven (15); Karklins, Gregory (15); Maldonado, Carlos (20); Meyers, Brian (13); Murray, Timothy (8); Netemeyer, Daniel (3); Pumphrey, Shawn (4); Shaw, Kevin (7); Vasquez, Aguedo (3); Wagner, Hector (13); Wellington, Robert (9).

WHITE SOX—Abreu, Francisco (6); Burroughs, Kenneth (7); Carey, William (9); Cauley, Chris (10); DeLaCruz, Carlos (10); DeVincenzo, Richard (5); Fella, Bradley (3); Garcia, Ramon (9); Groom, Wedsel (4); Hall, Gardner (3); Hasler, Curtis (12); Kennedy, Bo (9); Knackert, Brent (12); Kutzler, Jerry (4); Martinez, Gabriel (9); McDowell, Jack (2); Parks, Paul (1); Pena, Jose (11); Radinsky, Scott (11); Sabatino, John (16); Sandoval, Jesus (5); Schrenk, Steven (8).

YANKEES—Brill, Todd (12); Brito, Isaias (17); Candelaria, Jorge (14); Clayton, Royal (3); Cleto, Jose (5); Faccio, Luis (3); Figueroa, Fernando (14); Garcia, Robert (7); Gargin, Sean (2); Gedaminski, Todd (8); Gonzalez, Jose (10); Persia, Lauriano (10); Rodriguez, Gabriel (2); Ryan, Todd (3); Seaman, Christopher (9); Stanford, Donald (17).

GRAND SLAM HOME RUNS—Barretto, D. Colon, B. Davis, Maksodian, Payton, Penn, Shelton, 1 each.

AWARDED FIRST BASE ON CATCHER'S INTERFERENCE—Adames (Jo. Ortiz); Jimenez (Mason); Knecht (F. Harris).

CLUB FIELDING

Club	Pct.	G.	PO.	A.	E.	DP.	PB.	Club	Pct.	G.	PO.	A.	E.	DP.	PB.
Dodgers	.966	63	1689	723	85	64	16	Astros	.948	62	1578	678	125	32	10
White Sox	.957	63	1643	717	105	47	21	Royals	.946	63	1639	664	132	52	12
Braves	.956	63	1692	744	111	61	14	Rangers	.945	62	1600	689	133	43	12
Pirates	.953	63	1600	685	113	39	18	Expos	.944	63	1618	696	136	43	7
Yankees	.950	63	1587	694	120	44	14	Reds	.943	63	1656	759	145	49	14

Triple Plays—Reds 2, White Sox.

INDIVIDUAL FIELDING

°Throws lefthanded.

FIRST BASEMEN

Player and Club	Pct.	G.	PO.	A.	E.	DP.	Player and Club	Pct.	G.	PO.	A.	E.	DP.
Bailey, Braves	1.000	1	1	0	0	0	Fuller, White Sox	.980	6	46	3	1	4
Bluthart, Pirates	1.000	1	1	0	0	0	Gardner, Royals	.972	32	239	8	7	19
Caceras, Rangers	.980	19	137	13	3	12	Gayo, Reds	1.000	1	2	0	0	1
Cantres, Yankees	.981	14	51	2	1	2	Giannelli, Expos	1.000	7	25	1	0	0
Cohen, Braves	.989	17	161	13	2	18	Henry, Astros°	.974	16	141	6	4	4
Davis, Braves	.984	8	61	2	1	2	Jackson, Pirates°	.979	12	90	2	2	6
Elliott, Yankees°	1.000	15	119	2	0	12	JIMENEZ, Yankees°	.989	46	350	23	4	24
Eusebio, Astros	1.000	1	10	1	0	1	Jones, Reds	.984	40	330	29	6	26
Fernandez, Yankees°	.933	3	27	1	2	3	Keelan, Braves	1.000	4	9	0	0	2

FIRST BASEMEN—Continued

Player and Club	Pct.	G.	PO.	A.	E.	DP.	Player and Club	Pct.	G.	PO.	A.	E.	DP.
Koethke, Pirates*	.981	7	50	3	1	2	Robitaille, Expos	1.000	2	5	0	0	0
Kovarick, Reds	.990	29	277	21	3	16	Rodriguez, Dodgers*	.982	42	306	21	6	32
Lemuth, Expos*	1.000	1	1	0	0	0	Rogers, Rangers	.987	45	358	18	5	19
Losa, Rangers	1.000	1	6	1	0	0	Ruscitto, Astros	.992	40	344	27	3	15
Maksodian, White Sox	.987	26	220	15	3	16	Seymour, Pirates*	.972	16	125	12	4	7
Mendoza, Braves*	.984	35	333	25	6	29	Shelton, Pirates*	.990	35	290	15	3	18
Mittan, Braves	.957	7	41	3	2	4	Thomas, White Sox	.984	23	175	14	3	11
Niethammer, Rangers	.971	4	31	3	1	3	Valdez, Dodgers	.996	41	220	13	1	18
Ortiz, Astros	.980	10	95	2	2	6	Vizcaino, Dodgers	1.000	1	8	1	0	0
Penn, Expos*	.976	60	533	28	14	35	Walsh, White Sox	.993	16	139	7	1	11
Perez, Royals	.987	43	352	18	5	24	Yamasaki, Dodgers	1.000	5	12	0	0	4

Triple Plays—Kovarick, Thomas.

SECOND BASEMEN

Player and Club	Pct.	G.	PO.	A.	E.	DP.	Player and Club	Pct.	G.	PO.	A.	E.	DP.
Acta, Astros	.947	45	86	92	10	11	Logan, Yankees	1.000	3	0	4	0	1
Adames, White Sox	.947	26	35	73	6	8	Mayz, Pirates	.962	21	26	49	3	5
Alvey, Reds	.905	19	34	52	9	6	Merejo, White Sox	.944	5	7	10	1	2
Anderson, Dodgers	.961	17	34	39	3	10	Mitchell, Braves	.750	1	2	1	1	1
Apolinario, Braves	1.000	9	17	18	0	5	Munoz, Dodgers	.975	34	63	56	3	10
Atha, Expos	.967	21	23	36	2	5	PAREDES, Expos	.966	46	100	96	7	16
Baum, Royals	.958	33	59	79	6	15	Paulino, Expos	.900	13	18	18	4	2
Beams, Astros	.833	2	0	5	1	0	O. Perez, Reds	.842	5	4	12	3	1
Benzo, Reds	.958	5	8	15	1	1	R. Perez, Royals	1.000	1	4	2	0	1
Blackwell, Yankees	1.000	3	1	6	0	0	Reis, Braves	.961	30	70	77	6	14
Brock, Reds	.778	2	2	5	2	1	Robitaille, Expos	1.000	1	1	0	0	0
Bruckner, Rangers	.952	28	68	70	7	14	Rodriguez, Yankees	1.000	2	1	1	0	0
Conde, Royals	.928	34	60	68	10	10	Russell, Pirates	.932	14	30	25	4	6
Cunningham, Astros	1.000	2	4	5	0	0	Sable, Rangers	.975	17	35	42	2	9
Didder, Yankees	1.000	1	2	3	0	0	Stuart, Braves	.956	35	57	94	7	20
Esteban, Dodgers	.956	43	40	68	5	21	Torrez, Yankees	.956	60	135	149	13	29
Feliz, Pirates	.957	26	49	62	5	11	Trammell, White Sox	.957	31	58	77	6	13
Hamilton, Reds	.949	25	60	71	7	17	Warren, White Sox	.903	9	9	19	3	5
Isaac, Rangers	.906	17	41	36	8	2	Washington, Astros	.943	20	30	53	5	10
Javier, Reds	1.000	2	4	3	0	0	Whitaker, Reds	.923	9	15	21	3	6
Knecht, Royals	.875	2	6	8	2	3	Williams, Pirates	.901	16	30	34	7	3

THIRD BASEMEN

Player and Club	Pct.	G.	PO.	A.	E.	DP.	Player and Club	Pct.	G.	PO.	A.	E.	DP.
Acta, Astros	.792	14	12	30	11	3	Jones, Reds	.786	5	3	8	3	0
Adames, White Sox	.750	3	2	4	2	1	Knecht, Royals	.859	33	28	51	13	3
Anderson, Dodgers	1.000	1	1	0	0	0	Logan, Yankees	1.000	4	4	11	0	1
Apolinario, Braves	1.000	1	0	1	0	1	Losa, Rangers	1.000	1	0	2	0	0
Atha, Expos	.667	6	5	5	5	0	Mathews, Reds	.922	23	23	37	13	2
G. Bailey, Expos	.870	24	19	41	9	7	Mayz, Pirates	1.000	2	1	1	0	1
J. Bailey, Braves	.932	37	27	69	7	4	Niethammer, Rangers	.818	6	1	8	2	0
Beams, Astros	.874	31	21	55	11	5	Ortiz, Astros	.778	11	8	13	6	1
BELL, Dodgers	.946	48	28	77	6	6	Paulino, Expos	.943	11	8	25	2	1
Benzo, Reds	1.000	1	2	2	0	0	Perez, Royals	.500	3	0	2	2	0
Brewer, Rangers	.803	22	14	47	15	3	Reagans, Expos	.500	2	1	0	1	0
Bromley, Pirates	.813	12	10	16	6	2	Reyes, Yankees	.000	2	0	0	1	0
Byrnes, Royals	1.000	7	0	5	0	0	Robinson, Royals	.920	32	32	72	9	7
Cunningham, Astros	.750	4	2	10	4	0	Robitaille, Expos	.854	39	17	71	15	4
Davis, Braves	.877	30	22	49	10	4	Sable, Rangers	.921	35	28	77	9	3
DeLosSantos, Astros	.846	7	1	10	2	1	Smith, White Sox	.897	31	31	73	12	9
DeShields, Expos	1.000	1	1	2	0	0	Stuart, Braves	.875	5	1	6	1	1
Diaz, White Sox	1.000	13	6	14	0	0	Thomas, Pirates	.826	11	3	16	4	1
Didder, Yankees	.900	6	5	13	2	2	Torrez, Yankees	1.000	1	0	1	0	0
Doyle, White Sox	.957	23	18	48	3	3	Trammell, White Sox	1.000	1	0	1	0	0
Dyer, Royals	1.000	1	1	1	0	0	Trochim, Reds	.915	37	37	82	11	5
Esteban, Dodgers	1.000	1	1	1	0	1	Valdez, Dodgers	.946	31	36	52	5	3
Feliz, Pirates	1.000	1	1	1	0	0	Veras, Yankees	.884	54	48	97	19	4
Fuller, White Sox	1.000	1	1	0	0	0	Wall, Pirates	.968	21	12	48	2	2
Gervais, Pirates	.846	6	3	8	2	0	Yamasaki, Dodgers	1.000	1	1	0	0	1
Hamilton, Reds	.800	2	2	2	1	0	Young, Pirates	.860	15	13	24	6	1
Henderson, Astros	1.000	1	0	2	0	0							

Triple Play—Trochim.

SHORTSTOPS

Player and Club	Pct.	G.	PO.	A.	E.	DP.	Player and Club	Pct.	G.	PO.	A.	E.	DP.
Adames, White Sox	.909	4	4	6	1	2	Herrera, Yankees	.852	19	16	36	9	7
Anderson, Dodgers	1.000	1	1	3	0	0	Javier, Reds	.916	21	36	62	9	10
Angelero, Royals	.898	25	33	81	13	11	Knecht, Royals	.967	7	7	22	1	2
Arakawa, Dodgers	1.000	3	3	3	0	3	Mathews, Reds	.892	20	19	55	9	11
Bailey, Braves	1.000	3	4	4	0	1	Mayz, Pirates	.938	4	3	12	1	1
Baum, Royals	.000	1	0	0	1	0	Merejo, White Sox	.947	15	22	50	4	5
Beams, Astros	1.000	1	1	0	0	0	Munoz, Dodgers	.896	20	32	54	10	15
Blackwell, Yankees	.833	6	3	2	1	2	Ocasio, White Sox	.922	24	27	68	8	13
Brown, Yankees	.938	6	6	9	1	2	Paredes, Expos	.962	9	7	18	1	0
Byrnes, Royals	.942	37	50	96	9	19	Paulino, Expos	.910	29	40	82	12	6
Carrion, Braves	.873	33	50	74	18	12	Perez, Reds	.882	25	39	58	13	14
Colon, Braves	.877	45	40	102	20	13	Reis, Braves	.930	8	12	28	3	6
Cruz, White Sox	.895	25	34	60	11	9	C. RODRIGUEZ, Yankees	.950	50	78	167	13	19
Cunningham, Astros	1.000	3	3	12	0	2	H. Rodriguez, Dodgers*	1.000	1	3	2	0	0
DeLosSantos, Astros	.909	37	41	109	15	7	Ryans, Yankees	.714	3	4	6	4	1
DeShields, Expos	.860	30	47	88	22	12	Sable, Rangers	.765	3	2	11	4	0
Dilone, Pirates	.737	4	4	10	5	0	Simmonds, Dodgers	.900	5	6	12	2	3
Feliz, Pirates	.000	1	0	0	1	0	Spriggs, Pirates	.878	33	53	84	19	11
Hall, Braves	.943	36	52	97	9	18	Trochim, Reds	.917	4	3	8	1	0
Henderson, Astros	.888	26	25	62	11	8	Vizcaino, Dodgers	.929	47	65	106	13	23
Hernandez, Rangers	.932	24	30	38	5	7	Williams, Pirates	.865	27	31	65	15	10

Triple Plays—Cruz, Perez.

OUTFIELDERS

Player and Club	Pct.	G.	PO.	A.	E.	DP.
Anthony, Astros*	.957	54	100	11	5	1
Barretto, Rangers	1.000	2	1	0	0	0
Bautista, Braves	.933	10	13	1	1	0
Beams, Astros	1.000	5	1	1	0	0
Belcher, Rangers	.931	58	89	6	7	1
Bell, Dodgers	.970	11	29	3	1	0
Beniquez, Royals	1.000	4	6	0	0	0
Bergquist, Royals	.921	52	78	4	7	2
Bluthart, Pirates	.950	30	37	1	2	1
Brewer, Rangers	1.000	10	9	1	0	0
Brock, Reds	.974	18	34	4	1	1
Brown, Yankees	1.000	26	35	2	0	0
Bruckner, Rangers	.923	15	11	1	1	1
Cantres, Yankees	1.000	3	2	0	0	0
Castillo, Dodgers	.955	34	40	2	2	0
Cedeno, Astros	.966	59	104	9	4	0
Cepero, Dodgers*	1.000	7	9	0	0	0
Cohen, Braves	1.000	1	2	0	0	0
Colon, Braves	.973	55	99	8	3	3
Colontino, White Sox	.786	11	9	2	3	1
Conde, Royals	1.000	4	3	0	0	0
Crockom, Astros	.964	38	50	3	2	0
Cudjo, Reds	.925	30	31	6	3	0
Davis, White Sox	.941	36	61	3	4	0
DeLeon, Rangers	.979	43	88	4	2	1
Doyle, White Sox	1.000	4	2	0	0	0
Faulk, Expos*	.922	43	64	7	6	3
Garcia, Yankees	.000	1	0	0	1	0
Goshay, Dodgers	.975	55	68	9	2	2
Guzman, Yankees	1.000	12	16	2	0	1
Hardwick, Royals	.909	21	26	4	3	2
K. Harris, White Sox	1.000	16	26	2	0	1
V. Harris, White Sox	.889	14	16	0	2	0
Haugh, Royals	.963	37	75	4	3	1
Haywood, Pirates*	1.000	6	11	1	0	0
Henderson, Royals	.965	42	81	1	3	1
Henry, Astros*	1.000	34	66	2	0	0
Hill, Yankees	.932	29	54	1	4	0
Hosey, White Sox	1.000	32	65	3	0	0
Hunter, Yankees	.840	14	18	3	4	0
Isaac, Rangers	1.000	4	3	0	0	0
Kingwood, Expos	.957	44	83	6	4	0
Lapaix, Reds	.867	11	13	0	2	0
Lemuth, Expos*	1.000	8	3	0	0	0
Lipscomb, Pirates*	1.000	6	10	0	0	0
Losa, Rangers	1.000	3	5	0	0	0
Lukachyk, White Sox	1.000	10	17	0	0	0
Maksodian, White Sox	1.000	4	4	1	0	0
Marabell, Dodgers	.979	53	81	11	2	5
Matos, Royals	.909	42	57	3	6	0
Mealy, Pirates	.969	28	30	1	1	0
Merchant, Pirates	.971	46	98	4	3	2
Mershon, Reds	.962	26	47	3	2	1
Mitchell, Braves	.974	56	109	5	3	0
Mittan, Braves	.667	3	1	1	1	0
Mobley, Braves*	.973	42	66	7	2	2
Mohr, Reds	.980	32	48	1	1	0
Morabito, White Sox	1.000	4	6	0	0	0
Niethammer, Rangers	.929	13	12	1	1	1
Oliva, Braves	1.000	6	10	0	0	0
Palos, Pirates	.929	10	10	3	1	0
Panizzi, Astros	.833	6	5	0	1	0
Payton, White Sox	1.000	12	15	1	0	0
Penn, Expos*	1.000	2	4	0	0	0
Perez, Yankees*	.921	46	78	4	7	0
PEROZO, Reds	.981	49	96	5	2	2
Piechowski, Expos*	1.000	39	45	6	0	3
Pledger, White Sox	.976	37	39	2	1	0
Polo, Braves	.909	8	10	0	1	0
Pride, Dodgers	1.000	13	7	1	0	0
Ramos, Yankees	.980	33	47	3	1	0
Reagans, Expos	.857	18	17	1	3	0
Redmond, Pirates	1.000	15	24	0	0	0
Robinson, Braves	.982	40	48	7	1	2
Rodriguez, Rangers	1.000	18	16	1	0	0
Ryans, Yankees	1.000	4	5	0	0	0
Santos, Dodgers	.970	55	95	3	3	1
Schmitt, Pirates	1.000	4	1	0	0	0
Scruggs, Rangers	.957	27	39	6	2	2
Shepherd, Reds*	.959	39	45	2	2	0
Stewart, Pirates*	.818	12	9	0	2	0
Taddeo, Yankees*	.944	61	80	4	5	1
Takacs, Expos*	.957	36	44	1	2	0
Tejada, White Sox	.913	10	19	2	2	0
Thomas, Pirates	1.000	1	2	0	0	0
Thompson, Pirates	.750	3	3	0	1	0
Valverde, Pirates	.946	18	34	1	2	0
Vance, Expos	.957	48	61	6	3	1
Ventura, Royals	.914	30	31	1	3	0
Walker, Expos	1.000	7	9	1	0	0
Warren, White Sox	.976	26	39	1	1	1
Young, Pirates	1.000	19	35	2	0	0

Triple Play—Brock.

CATCHERS

Player and Club	Pct.	G.	PO.	A.	E.	DP.	PB.
Alvarez, White Sox	.983	25	103	16	2	1	5
Barretto, Rangers	.972	29	213	33	7	2	0
Beltran, Pirates	.984	18	104	20	2	1	6
Bennett, Astros	.987	22	131	17	2	2	2
Brune, Reds	.857	2	5	1	1	0	1
Davis, Royals	.995	31	163	18	1	2	4
Doss, Braves	1.000	12	56	7	0	0	4
Doyle, White Sox	.960	3	23	1	1	0	4
Duran, Dodgers	.986	33	125	19	2	2	5
Englett, Pirates	1.000	6	42	7	0	0	1
Eusebio, Astros	.982	30	194	23	4	2	4
Fernandez, Dodgers	1.000	7	29	4	0	0	1
Ferradas, Dodgers	1.000	2	7	0	0	0	0
Floyd, Dodgers	.936	8	39	5	3	2	3
Fuller, White Sox	1.000	9	48	4	0	0	3
Garcia, Yankees	.969	19	61	2	2	0	3
Gayo, Reds	.928	12	50	14	5	3	1
Gonzalez, Pirates	1.000	18	118	12	0	0	4
Hall, Pirates	1.000	3	24	8	0	0	1
Hamilton, Pirates	.952	8	53	7	3	1	1
Harris, White Sox	.979	29	201	29	5	3	4
Jewett, Pirates	.988	27	140	23	2	4	6
Keelan, Braves	.964	11	48	5	2	0	1
Losa, Rangers	.946	20	149	25	10	1	7
Maldonado, Expos	1.000	6	24	2	0	0	0
Martinez, Reds	.976	32	187	19	5	1	6
MASON, Expos	.995	39	174	33	1	3	0
Maville, Expos	.974	33	154	31	5	4	4
Mee, Reds	.973	20	97	13	3	0	1
Mora, Dodgers	.970	27	162	30	6	2	3
Morales, Pirates	.971	51	279	60	10	1	11
Murdock, White Sox	.886	8	30	1	4	0	0
Niethammer, Rangers	.991	11	91	14	1	1	4
Ortiz, Astros	.975	12	69	9	2	0	4
Perez, Braves	.980	31	161	31	4	2	3
Polledo, Expos	.972	16	57	12	2	0	3
Pujols, Royals	.975	30	143	13	4	0	6
Reyes, Yankees	.976	9	37	3	1	0	0
Rice, Royals	.950	22	80	16	5	1	2
Ryans, Yankees	1.000	1	1	0	0	0	0
Scott, Reds	1.000	3	15	2	0	0	0
Singley, White Sox	.966	9	51	5	2	0	5
Urman, Braves	.974	18	89	24	3	2	4
Wadsworth, Dodgers	1.000	10	34	6	0	0	1
Wolfer, Braves	.982	11	52	4	1	0	5
Wong, Dodgers	.988	14	70	11	1	0	3
Wright, Braves	.893	8	24	1	3	0	2

Triple Play—Wolfer.

PITCHERS

Player and Club	Pct.	G.	PO.	A.	E.	DP.
Abreu, White Sox	1.000	6	0	5	0	0
Alvarez, Rangers*	.889	10	0	8	1	0
Amick, Astros	1.000	6	1	0	0	0
M. Anderson, Royals	1.000	22	2	4	0	0
Barcelo, Braves	1.000	10	1	1	0	0
Befort, Pirates	1.000	6	0	2	0	0
Bohanon, Rangers*	.750	5	0	3	1	0
Boron, Rangers	1.000	25	5	6	0	1
Brill, Yankees*	.857	12	1	5	1	0
Brito, Yankees	1.000	17	1	3	0	0
Bromby, Expos	.833	18	3	7	2	0
Candelaria, Yankees	.692	14	4	5	4	0
Carey, White Sox	1.000	9	0	6	0	0
Cauley, White Sox	1.000	10	2	1	0	0
Cerny, Dodgers*	1.000	14	5	16	0	0
Chmielewski, Expos	.800	11	0	4	1	0
Da. Clark, Expos*	1.000	12	2	5	0	0
De. Clark, Royals	1.000	21	1	13	0	1
Clayton, Yankees	1.000	3	1	4	0	0
Cleto, Yankees	1.000	5	0	2	0	0
Colson, Reds	.828	14	5	19	5	0
Costello, Astros	.824	13	7	7	3	0
Currin, Braves*	.857	12	0	6	1	0
Daly, Royals*	.000	13	0	0	1	0
DeLaCruz, White Sox	.783	10	8	10	5	1
DeLeon, Royals	.867	12	4	9	2	1

PITCHERS—Continued

Player and Club	Pct.	G.	PO.	A.	E.	DP.
DeVincenzo, White Sox°	.833	5	0	5	1	0
Diaz, Reds	1.000	7	1	2	0	0
Dooley, Pirates	1.000	6	0	3	0	1
Doss, Pirates	.957	11	5	17	1	0
Downs, Pirates	.929	21	6	7	1	0
Drohan, Royals	.857	12	2	4	1	0
Duprey, Dodgers°	1.000	3	2	1	0	0
Ebarb, Rangers	.500	7	0	1	1	0
Faccio, Yankees	.800	3	2	2	1	0
Figueroa, Yankees°	1.000	14	3	7	0	0
Finigan, Expos	1.000	14	0	2	0	0
Fletcher, Dodgers°	.917	18	2	9	1	0
Ra. Garcia, White Sox	1.000	6	0	3	0	0
Ro. Garcia, Yankees	1.000	7	2	5	0	0
Gargin, Yankees	1.000	2	0	2	0	0
Gastleum, Dodgers	1.000	8	1	2	0	0
Gedaminski, Yankees°	.769	8	1	9	3	1
Gillund, Braves	1.000	9	1	1	0	0
Gonzalez, Yankees	.917	10	2	9	1	1
Groom, White Sox°	1.000	4	0	2	0	0
Hall, White Sox°	1.000	3	1	0	0	0
Hasler, White Sox	.952	12	7	13	1	0
Higginbotham, Astros	.833	5	1	4	1	0
Hill, Royals	.750	16	2	4	2	0
Hoeme, Royals	.429	15	0	3	4	0
Holmes, Pirates	.938	8	5	10	1	2
Hook, Astros°	.250	6	0	1	3	0
Hurst, Rangers	.867	12	2	11	2	1
Jaime, Rangers°	.875	15	2	5	1	1
Javier, Rangers	1.000	12	1	3	0	0
Jeffery, Reds	1.000	26	4	5	0	0
Joyner, Expos	1.000	4	0	3	0	0
Karklins, Royals	.955	15	6	15	1	2
Keays, Expos°	.714	16	2	3	2	0
Keen, Reds	.909	19	2	8	1	2
Kennedy, Royals	.857	9	2	10	2	0
Knackert, White Sox	.909	12	5	5	1	1
Kopczynski, Rangers	.933	28	5	23	2	2
Kreuder, Dodgers	1.000	15	3	9	0	1
Kutzler, White Sox	1.000	4	2	5	0	0
Lamle, Rangers°	1.000	3	1	7	0	1
Langley, Dodgers°	1.000	1	0	4	0	0
Lee, Astros	1.000	15	2	14	0	0
Lehnerz, Reds	1.000	16	3	6	0	0
Lewis, Pirates	1.000	8	4	4	0	0
Lilliquist, Braves°	1.000	2	1	2	0	0
Lilly, Dodgers	1.000	16	3	5	0	0
Locke, Astros	.833	13	4	16	4	1
Lopez, Rangers	.857	13	2	4	1	1
Luckham, Dodgers	1.000	6	2	4	0	0
Lynch, Rangers°	.962	13	6	19	1	0
Macavage, Pirates	1.000	2	1	0	0	0
C. Maldonado, Royals	.833	20	1	4	1	0
J. Maldonado, Braves	1.000	17	6	3	0	0
Manuel, Rangers	1.000	1	0	1	0	0
M. Marrero, Braves°	.900	9	5	4	1	0
R. Marrero, Astros°	1.000	16	0	8	0	0
Marsh, Reds	1.000	1	1	5	0	1
G. Martinez, White Sox	.750	9	1	2	1	0
R. Martinez, Pirates	.929	18	3	10	1	0
Maysonet, Pirates	1.000	10	2	2	0	0
McDowell, White Sox	1.000	2	0	1	0	0
Meister, Braves	1.000	13	5	9	0	0
Meyers, Royals	.889	13	3	5	1	0
Miguel, Dodgers	.941	14	3	13	1	0
Millen, Dodgers	1.000	8	1	1	0	0
Miller, Pirates	.960	12	4	20	1	0
Minchey, Expos	.833	12	1	9	2	0
Mitchell, Braves	.600	14	0	3	2	0
Mmahat, Rangers°	.833	12	4	11	3	0
Moore, Pirates°	1.000	8	0	4	0	0
Moss, Rangers	.500	12	0	1	1	0
Mota, Expos	1.000	13	2	1	0	0
Murphy, Astros	1.000	4	2	0	0	0
Murray, Rangers	1.000	8	1	1	0	0
Nevada, Braves	1.000	7	0	1	0	0
Newman, Astros°	.897	12	8	27	4	1
Nordstrom, Reds	.857	15	4	20	4	1
Ortiz, Dodgers	1.000	25	2	8	0	0
Overeem, Expos	.667	10	0	6	3	0
Parker, Braves	.400	10	1	1	3	0
Pena, White Sox°	.833	11	1	4	1	1
Perez, Astros	.867	12	0	13	2	0
Perozo, Reds	1.000	1	0	1	0	0
Persia, Yankees	.875	10	1	6	1	0
Petkovski, Rangers	1.000	3	0	2	0	0
Pumphrey, Royals	.500	4	0	1	1	0
Radinsky, White Sox°	1.000	11	4	18	0	1
Ramirez, Expos	.842	12	5	11	3	0
Reilley, Braves	.833	14	2	8	2	2
Rice, Royals	1.000	1	0	1	0	0
Riensche, Dodgers	1.000	6	1	2	0	0
Risley, Reds	.750	11	3	12	5	2
A. Rivera, Expos	.900	15	4	5	1	3
B. Rivera, Braves	.857	16	3	3	1	0
H. RIVERA, Expos	1.000	14	8	17	0	1
Rockman, Rangers	.800	14	0	8	2	0
R. Rodriguez, Reds°	.925	17	8	29	3	0
A. Rosario, Rangers	.750	4	0	3	1	0
Runge, Pirates	1.000	4	2	3	0	1
K. Ryan, Dodgers	1.000	19	1	4	0	0
T. Ryan, Yankees	.500	3	0	1	1	0
Saavedra, Rangers°	.750	12	1	2	1	0
Sabatino, White Sox	.857	16	1	5	1	0
Sandoval, White Sox	1.000	5	1	0	0	0
Santiago, Pirates	1.000	12	3	6	0	0
Scarborough, Braves	.963	9	3	23	1	1
Schlopy, Pirates°	1.000	3	0	4	0	0
Schrenk, White Sox	1.000	8	0	7	0	0
Seaman, Yankees°	.800	9	3	5	2	1
Shaw, Royals	.750	7	1	8	3	2
Shinall, Dodgers	.875	8	1	6	1	0
Siegel, Pirates	1.000	3	1	4	0	0
Slaughter, Pirates	.846	14	4	7	2	0
Small, Astros	.667	3	2	0	1	1
Smith, Pirates	1.000	10	0	2	0	0
Solarte, Expos	.750	19	0	3	1	0
Soto, Reds	1.000	2	1	2	0	0
Stanford, Rangers	.923	17	3	9	1	1
Steiner, Rangers°	1.000	4	1	2	0	0
Storms, Reds	.600	20	0	3	2	0
Stout, Reds	.920	10	4	19	2	0
Tafoya, Astros	.895	19	5	12	2	0
Tunall, Pirates	1.000	12	3	10	0	0
Turek, Reds	1.000	3	0	5	0	0
Vanzytveld, Dodgers	.867	9	4	9	2	1
A. Vasquez, Royals	1.000	3	0	2	0	0
E. Vasquez, Astros	1.000	14	2	7	0	0
Vazquez, Braves	.913	12	5	16	2	1
Vierra, Reds°	.857	14	0	6	1	0
Virgo, Dodgers	.800	1	0	4	1	1
Wagner, Royals	1.000	13	0	5	0	0
Wegman, Expos	.800	13	1	7	2	0
Wellington, Royals	.833	9	2	8	2	2
Wilkinson, Rangers	1.000	8	0	2	0	0
Wilson, Yankees	1.000	15	0	3	0	1
Yochum, Braves	1.000	18	3	1	0	1
Zeinert, Dodgers°	.850	22	3	14	3	0

Triple Play—Stout.

The following players do not have any recorded accepted chances at the positions indicated; therefore, are not listed in the fielding averages for those particular positions: Acevedo, p; T. Anderson, p; G. Bailey, 2b; Beam, of; Beams, p; Beltran, of; Beniquez, c; Benzo, ss; Bouman, p; Burroughs, p; Ju. DeLeon, ss; Jo. Diaz, 2b; Esteban, ss p; Fella, p; M. Hamilton, of; F. Harris of; F. Henderson, 2b; Hesketh, p; Marabell, 3b; L. Martinez, of; Mendoza, of; Morabito, 3b; Nen, p; Netemeyer, p; Parks, p; Pride, 1b; G. Rodriguez, p; Rogers, of; M Rosario, p; Ryans, 2b; Shepherd, p; N. Solarte, of; Tejada, ss; Trochim, of; Wong, p.

CLUB PITCHING

Club	ERA	G.	CG	ShO	Sv.	IP	H.	R.	ER.	HR.	HB.	BB.	Int. BB.	SO.	WP.	Bk.
White Sox	2.61	63	4	5	16	547.2	463	236	159	8	29	211	0	443	40	12
Dodgers	2.72	63	1	9	18	563.0	445	213	170	10	30	281	20	470	44	7
Yankees	2.98	63	15	6	10	529.0	492	250	175	10	19	188	1	374	29	8
Royals	3.16	63	1	4	17	546.1	517	263	192	10	27	207	2	369	40	5
Astros	3.29	62	9	4	15	526.0	483	266	192	22	15	171	6	368	54	8
Pirates	3.34	63	3	6	19	533.1	494	268	198	15	27	183	3	409	43	9
Expos	3.42	63	5	3	8	539.1	553	323	205	16	17	239	13	397	59	9
Reds	3.52	63	5	4	20	552.0	508	307	216	14	29	276	31	380	47	7
Braves	3.88	63	6	1	8	564.0	555	320	243	20	21	269	31	352	42	8
Rangers	4.29	62	2	3	8	533.1	482	336	254	25	41	278	9	499	52	25

PITCHERS' RECORDS
(Leading Qualifiers for Earned-Run Average Leadership — 50 or More Innings)

*Throws lefthanded.

Pitcher—Club	W.	L.	Pct.	ERA.	G.	GS.	CG.	GF.	ShO.	Sv.	IP.	H.	R.	ER.	HR.	HB.	BB.	Int. BB.	SO.	WP.
Lee, Astros	5	2	.714	1.15	15	6	1	6	0	4	55.0	37	12	7	1	2	16	1	59	1
Newman, Astros*	7	2	.778	1.41	12	11	3	1	1	0	76.2	55	21	12	5	1	12	0	59	6
Cerny, Dodgers*	6	3	.667	1.56	14	14	0	0	0	0	81.0	38	20	14	0	1	46	1	72	4
DeLaCruz, White Sox	5	3	.625	1.73	10	9	1	0	0	0	62.1	45	19	12	1	0	27	0	42	5
Gedaminski, Yankees*	3	3	.500	1.78	8	8	2	0	0	0	50.2	32	18	10	0	3	24	0	49	1
Miguel, Dodgers	4	3	.571	1.83	14	14	0	0	0	0	68.2	58	16	14	0	0	43	2	42	8
Hurst, Rangers	4	3	.571	1.88	12	12	0	0	0	0	57.1	34	19	12	0	2	32	1	59	0
Risley, Reds	1	4	.200	1.89	11	11	0	0	0	0	52.1	38	24	11	0	3	26	3	50	6
Colson, Reds	7	2	.778	2.12	14	8	3	1	2	0	68.0	59	24	16	1	1	26	3	43	6
Ramirez, Expos	1	7	.125	2.17	12	12	0	0	0	0	66.1	62	31	16	1	1	24	0	35	9

Departmental Leaders: G—Kopczynski, 28; W—Colson, Karklins, Newman, Nordstrom, 7; L—H. Rivera, 8; Pct.—A. Rivera, .857; GS—Cerny, Miguel, H. Rivera, 14; CG—Figueroa, 5; GF—Kopczynski, 24; ShO—Figueroa, 3; Sv.—Jeffery, 9; IP—H. Rivera, 86.2; H—Perez, 82; R—Keen, 47; ER—Perez, 35; HR—Alvarez, Locke, 6; HB—Boron, 8; BB—Keen, 50; IBB—Storms, 7; SO—Cerny, 72; WP—Boron, 15.

(All Pitchers—Listed Alphabetically)

Pitcher—Club	W.	L.	Pct.	ERA.	G.	GS.	CG.	GF.	ShO.	Sv.	IP.	H.	R.	ER.	HR.	HB.	BB.	Int. BB.	SO.	WP.
Abreu, White Sox	1	0	1.000	5.06	6	0	0	1	0	0	10.2	11	6	6	0	1	8	0	6	1
Acevedo, Royals	0	0	.000	0.00	1	0	0	1	0	0	1.0	1	0	0	0	0	1	0	2	0
Alvarez, Rangers*	2	5	.286	5.24	10	10	0	0	0	0	44.2	41	29	26	6	3	21	0	46	3
Amick, Astros	2	0	1.000	6.75	6	1	0	2	0	0	17.1	18	14	13	2	2	3	0	7	3
M. Anderson, Royals	3	0	1.000	2.57	22	0	0	17	0	6	28.0	27	14	8	0	0	5	1	21	3
T. Anderson, Dodgers	0	0	.000	0.00	1	0	0	1	0	0	1.0	0	0	0	0	0	1	0	1	0
Barcelo, Braves	0	1	.000	6.60	10	0	0	7	0	1	15.0	18	16	11	2	0	10	2	13	0
Beams, Astros	0	0	.000	9.00	1	0	0	1	0	0	1.0	1	1	1	0	0	1	0	1	0
Befort, Pirates	0	1	.000	0.00	6	0	0	4	0	0	10.0	10	2	0	0	0	6	0	6	1
Bohanon, Rangers*	0	2	.000	4.71	5	4	0	0	0	0	21.0	15	13	11	1	0	5	0	21	2
Boron, Rangers	3	3	.500	5.14	25	0	0	17	0	1	35.0	24	25	20	0	8	38	0	24	15
Bouman, Expos	0	1	.000	2.45	2	2	0	0	0	0	3.2	4	7	1	0	0	5	0	3	1
Brill, Yankees*	1	5	.167	3.66	12	7	0	2	0	1	39.1	54	27	16	1	1	14	0	23	1
Brito, Yankees	1	1	.500	3.10	17	1	0	10	0	2	29.0	29	18	10	1	2	11	0	22	1
Bromby, Expos	3	6	.333	3.63	18	4	0	10	0	3	57.0	67	31	23	1	1	12	3	48	1
Burroughs, White Sox	1	0	1.000	4.00	7	0	0	4	0	0	9.0	4	9	4	0	0	15	0	11	4
Candelaria, Yankees	2	4	.333	1.61	14	5	2	7	0	3	44.2	33	15	8	1	2	15	0	35	5
Carey, White Sox	3	0	1.000	1.61	9	1	0	2	0	0	22.1	16	5	4	0	0	7	0	26	5
Cauley, White Sox	1	1	.500	1.83	10	0	0	9	0	5	19.2	16	5	4	0	2	6	0	19	2
Cerny, Dodgers*	6	3	.667	1.56	14	14	0	0	0	0	81.0	38	20	14	0	1	46	1	72	4
Chmielewski, Braves	1	1	.500	6.27	11	0	0	5	0	0	18.2	22	17	13	2	0	16	0	12	5
Da. Clark, Expos*	1	2	.333	3.02	12	5	0	2	0	1	41.2	37	21	14	0	0	17	0	30	3
De. Clark, Royals	3	4	.429	2.24	21	0	0	8	0	4	56.1	42	20	14	1	1	17	5	51	3
Clayton, Dodgers	0	2	.000	3.48	3	1	0	2	0	0	10.1	12	5	4	0	0	2	1	5	0
Cleto, Yankees	0	0	.000	16.20	5	0	0	1	0	0	3.1	8	7	6	0	1	6	0	1	0
Colson, Reds	7	2	.778	2.12	14	8	3	1	2	0	68.0	59	24	16	1	1	26	3	43	6
Costello, Astros	5	7	.417	3.22	13	12	0	1	0	0	72.2	74	40	26	1	1	28	1	45	9
Currin, Braves*	3	1	.750	1.04	12	1	0	8	0	3	26.0	25	5	3	0	1	3	2	30	1
Daly, Royals*	1	0	1.000	3.86	13	0	0	6	0	0	9.1	6	5	4	0	1	6	1	8	1
DeLaCruz, White Sox	5	3	.625	1.73	10	9	1	0	0	0	62.1	45	19	12	1	0	27	0	42	5
DeLeon, Royals	4	1	.800	3.84	12	12	1	0	1	0	58.2	50	28	25	0	1	33	2	30	2
DeVincenzo, White Sox*	1	0	1.000	1.80	5	1	0	2	0	0	10.0	6	2	2	0	0	2	0	10	0
Diaz, Reds	1	0	1.000	2.70	7	0	0	3	0	0	13.1	13	6	4	0	0	7	0	9	1
Dooley, Pirates	0	2	.000	4.76	6	2	0	3	0	0	11.1	13	9	6	0	2	13	0	5	2
Doss, Pirates	4	4	.500	3.10	11	11	1	0	0	0	58.0	56	30	20	0	3	33	0	35	7
Downs, Pirates	2	4	.333	2.98	21	0	0	15	0	5	42.1	37	24	14	1	1	11	1	29	0
Drohan, Royals	5	3	.625	6.11	12	11	0	0	0	0	45.2	58	36	31	4	2	14	0	28	7
Duprey, Dodgers*	0	1	.000	5.63	9	0	0	2	0	0	8.0	9	9	5	0	3	2	0	3	3
Ebarb, Rangers	0	1	.000	14.04	7	0	0	1	0	0	8.1	14	15	13	1	3	5	0	6	0
Esteban, Dodgers	0	0	.000	9.00	1	0	0	1	0	0	2.0	3	3	2	0	1	2	0	1	0
Faccio, Yankees	1	0	1.000	3.29	3	2	0	1	0	0	13.2	13	5	5	0	1	4	0	13	2
Fella, White Sox*	0	1	.000	0.00	3	0	0	2	0	0	3.0	3	4	0	0	0	3	0	4	0
Figueroa, Yankees*	4	4	.500	2.77	14	6	5	4	3	1	61.2	44	22	19	1	2	11	0	51	3
Finigan, Expos	0	1	.000	1.26	14	0	0	10	0	2	28.2	25	10	4	2	1	8	1	26	2
Fletcher, Dodgers*	1	3	.250	4.11	18	5	0	3	0	2	46.0	43	24	21	1	4	27	3	48	1
Ra. Garcia, White Sox	1	0	1.000	1.50	6	0	0	2	0	0	12.0	8	3	2	0	2	5	0	6	1
Ro. Garcia, Yankees*	1	0	1.000	6.14	7	1	0	4	0	0	14.2	18	11	10	0	2	12	0	5	1
Gargin, Yankees	1	0	1.000	0.00	2	0	0	1	0	0	9.0	4	1	0	0	0	4	0	5	0
Gastleum, Dodgers	1	1	.500	3.86	9	2	0	4	0	0	16.1	11	9	7	0	0	14	1	16	7
Gedaminski, Yankees*	3	3	.500	1.78	8	8	2	0	0	0	50.2	32	18	10	0	3	24	0	49	1
Gillund, Braves	0	1	.000	2.84	9	0	0	3	0	0	19.0	21	6	6	0	0	5	2	9	0
Gonzalez, Yankees	4	2	.667	2.34	10	7	3	1	0	0	50.0	47	20	13	1	1	9	0	33	1
Groom, White Sox*	1	0	1.000	0.75	4	1	0	1	0	0	12.0	12	1	1	0	1	2	0	8	0
Hall, White Sox*	1	1	.500	4.09	3	1	0	1	0	0	11.0	12	7	5	0	0	2	0	11	0
Hasler, White Sox	4	3	.571	2.55	12	10	1	1	0	0	60.0	66	29	17	1	5	6	0	40	0
Hesketh, Expos*	0	0	.000	8.31	2	1	0	0	0	0	4.1	7	4	4	0	0	8	0	8	1
Higginbotham, Astros	0	2	.000	4.15	5	3	0	0	0	0	13.0	17	16	6	0	2	8	0	8	0
Hill, Royals	1	1	.500	1.93	16	0	0	10	0	1	23.1	21	8	5	0	1	6	2	14	2
Hoeme, Royals	2	0	1.000	5.70	15	0	0	2	0	0	23.2	33	23	15	1	3	11	1	16	3
Holmes, Pirates	4	1	.800	2.86	8	8	1	0	0	0	34.2	38	14	11	3	1	6	0	23	0
Hook, Astros*	1	1	.500	5.12	6	4	1	0	0	0	19.1	23	16	11	0	1	11	0	16	4
Hurst, Rangers	4	3	.571	1.88	12	12	0	0	0	0	57.1	34	19	12	0	2	32	1	59	0
Jaime, Rangers*	0	0	.000	5.96	15	0	0	1	0	0	25.2	26	27	17	2	3	16	0	21	2
Javier, Rangers*	0	1	.000	9.00	12	0	0	2	0	0	13.0	16	15	13	1	0	12	1	6	1
Jeffery, Reds	4	2	.667	2.93	26	0	0	16	0	9	40.0	45	17	13	1	2	13	4	32	1
Joyner, Royals*	0	0	.000	2.45	4	3	0	0	0	0	11.0	8	6	3	0	1	6	0	9	1
Karklins, Royals	7	2	.778	2.78	15	8	0	1	0	0	58.1	62	22	18	0	2	18	3	35	2
Keays, Expos*	0	2	.000	3.81	16	0	0	5	0	0	28.1	34	17	12	0	0	17	0	20	4
Keen, Expos	0	2	.000	8.53	19	0	0	8	0	1	31.2	34	47	30	1	5	50	6	14	4
Kennedy, White Sox	4	2	.667	2.72	9	8	0	1	0	0	53.0	45	23	16	1	1	19	0	50	3
Knackert, White Sox	6	2	.750	2.85	12	11	1	0	1	0	72.2	55	28	23	2	4	15	0	60	4
Kopczynski, Rangers	3	2	.600	1.27	28	1	0	24	0	3	49.2	44	13	7	1	2	5	1	43	2

Pitcher—Club	W.	L.	Pct.	ERA.	G.	GS.	CG.	GF.	ShO.	Sv.	IP.	H.	R.	ER.	HR.	HB.	BB.	Int. BB.	SO.	WP.
Kreuder, Dodgers	3	1	.750	1.82	15	2	0	2	0	0	39.2	39	12	8	0	2	12	0	29	4
Kutzler, White Sox	1	1	.500	4.95	4	3	0	0	0	0	20.0	14	13	11	1	2	7	0	16	1
Lamle, Rangers°	0	2	.000	2.57	3	3	0	0	0	0	14.0	18	11	4	1	1	0	0	12	0
Langley, Dodgers°	1	0	1.000	0.00	1	1	0	0	0	0	5.0	1	0	0	0	0	4	0	4	0
Lee, Astros	5	2	.714	1.15	15	6	1	6	0	4	55.0	37	12	7	1	2	16	1	59	1
Lehnerz, Reds	0	6	.000	5.74	16	8	0	4	0	0	53.1	57	40	34	2	7	31	1	40	9
Lewis, Pirates	3	0	1.000	2.05	8	4	0	4	0	1	30.2	21	9	7	1	1	10	0	29	1
Lilliquist, Braves°	0	0	.000	0.00	2	2	0	0	0	0	13.0	3	0	0	0	0	2	0	16	0
Lilly, Dodgers	4	2	.667	6.51	16	0	0	7	0	2	27.2	32	23	20	1	0	10	1	23	0
Locke, Astros	3	3	.500	4.73	13	13	0	0	0	0	59.0	56	34	31	6	1	27	0	46	11
Lopez, Rangers	1	1	.500	9.67	13	2	0	0	1	0	27.0	33	34	29	1	4	21	2	18	4
Luckham, Dodgers	2	0	1.000	1.32	6	6	1	0	1	0	27.1	21	4	4	0	2	8	2	21	1
Lynch, Rangers°	4	3	.571	2.29	13	9	1	0	1	0	55.0	38	18	14	1	3	29	0	55	5
Macavage, Pirates	0	0	.000	0.00	2	0	0	2	0	2	2.1	0	0	0	0	1	0	0	4	0
C. Maldonado, Royals	5	1	.833	2.48	20	0	0	8	0	4	58.0	32	18	16	2	2	19	2	56	2
J. Maldonado, Braves	0	6	.000	4.34	17	6	0	3	0	1	47.2	48	28	23	0	3	28	3	21	2
Manuel, Rangers	0	0	.000	18.00	1	0	0	0	0	0	1.0	3	2	2	0	0	1	0	1	2
M. Marrero, Braves°	2	4	.333	4.93	9	7	1	1	0	0	42.0	35	27	23	3	1	21	1	24	8
R. Marrero, Astros°	4	1	.800	1.48	16	0	0	10	0	3	42.2	21	12	7	2	1	16	0	36	5
Marsh, Reds	1	0	1.000	0.00	1	1	0	0	0	0	6.0	3	0	0	0	0	1	0	1	0
G. Martinez, White Sox	1	0	1.000	3.46	9	0	0	4	0	0	13.0	18	11	5	0	1	9	0	12	3
R. Martinez, Pirates	1	1	.500	1.93	18	0	0	9	0	4	42.0	36	12	9	1	1	11	0	23	2
Maysonet, Pirates	2	1	.667	6.50	10	0	0	4	0	0	18.0	16	13	13	1	0	5	0	27	4
McDowell, White Sox	0	1	.000	2.57	2	1	0	1	0	0	7.0	4	3	2	0	1	1	0	12	0
Meister, Braves	3	6	.333	3.69	13	13	2	0	0	0	68.1	68	39	28	2	2	22	3	53	3
Meyers, Royals	2	3	.400	1.45	13	1	0	1	0	0	37.1	35	13	6	2	3	12	3	22	1
Miguel, Dodgers	4	3	.571	1.83	14	14	0	0	0	0	68.2	58	16	14	0	4	43	2	42	8
Milian, Dodgers	0	1	.000	5.40	8	0	0	1	0	0	13.1	13	9	8	1	1	10	0	5	0
Miller, Pirates	3	6	.333	3.20	12	12	1	0	1	0	70.1	55	34	25	3	2	26	0	62	3
Minchey, Expos	3	4	.429	4.94	12	11	2	0	0	0	54.2	62	45	30	1	2	28	0	61	6
Mitchell, Braves	0	1	.000	6.61	14	3	0	4	0	1	32.2	39	26	24	5	2	26	0	18	3
Mmahat, Rangers°	3	3	.500	3.21	12	9	1	1	0	0	53.1	37	22	19	1	2	30	1	60	6
Moore, Pirates°	2	0	1.000	3.86	8	0	0	4	0	1	18.2	16	8	8	0	1	7	0	11	5
Moss, Rangers	2	2	.500	9.00	12	2	0	3	0	0	21.0	27	34	21	1	2	23	1	29	4
Mota, Expos	1	2	.333	4.34	13	1	0	5	0	0	18.2	18	10	9	0	1	10	1	14	1
Murphy, Astros	0	0	.000	6.30	4	0	0	4	0	1	10.0	10	7	7	0	0	4	1	7	2
Murray, Royals	0	1	.000	2.84	8	2	0	4	0	0	12.2	10	4	4	0	1	6	0	6	0
Nen, Rangers	0	0	.000	7.71	2	0	0	0	0	0	2.1	4	2	2	0	0	3	1	4	0
Netemeyer, Royals°	0	0	.000	0.96	3	0	0	6	0	0	9.1	7	4	1	0	1	11	0	13	3
Nevada, Braves	1	1	.500	4.26	7	0	0	6	0	0	12.2	10	7	6	0	0	11	3	8	2
Newman, Astros°	7	2	.778	1.41	12	11	3	1	1	0	76.2	55	21	12	5	1	12	0	59	6
Nordstrom, Reds	7	3	.700	3.89	15	11	1	2	0	0	76.1	69	42	33	5	0	39	0	55	9
Ortiz, Dodgers	5	1	.833	2.14	25	1	0	15	0	6	42.0	34	15	10	1	2	18	5	43	2
Overeem, Expos	0	4	.000	6.39	10	7	0	1	0	0	38.0	59	42	27	3	1	16	1	26	9
Parker, Braves	0	4	.000	6.55	10	5	0	3	0	0	34.1	32	33	25	3	1	29	1	14	7
Parks, White Sox	0	0	.000	0.00	1	0	0	1	0	0	1.0	0	1	0	0	0	1	0	1	0
Pena, White Sox°	2	1	.667	2.21	11	0	0	8	0	3	20.1	17	8	5	0	0	7	0	22	1
Perez, Astros	2	6	.250	3.92	12	12	4	0	0	0	80.1	82	41	35	3	1	28	0	51	9
Perozo, Reds	0	0	.000	0.00	1	0	0	1	0	0	1.2	1	0	0	0	0	0	0	0	0
Persia, Yankees	2	3	.400	3.55	10	7	0	1	0	0	38.0	42	24	15	0	2	14	0	14	1
Petkovsek, Rangers	0	0	.000	3.18	3	1	0	0	0	0	5.2	4	2	2	0	2	2	0	7	0
Pumphrey, Royals	0	0	.000	9.00	4	0	0	1	0	0	5.0	9	6	5	0	0	5	1	3	1
Radinsky, White Sox°	3	3	.500	2.31	11	10	0	0	0	0	58.1	43	23	15	1	4	39	0	41	5
Ramirez, Expos	1	7	.125	2.17	12	12	0	0	0	0	66.1	62	31	16	1	1	24	0	35	9
Reilley, Braves	1	2	.333	3.62	14	0	0	6	0	2	27.1	28	15	11	0	0	12	5	22	1
Rice, Royals	0	1	.000	21.00	1	0	0	1	0	0	3.0	7	9	7	0	1	4	1	1	0
Riensche, Dodgers	0	0	.000	3.60	6	1	0	1	0	0	5.0	3	3	2	1	1	9	0	4	1
Risley, Reds	1	4	.200	1.89	11	11	0	0	0	0	52.1	38	24	11	0	3	26	3	50	6
A. Rivera, Expos	6	1	.857	3.07	15	0	0	8	0	5	41.0	32	18	14	5	3	34	3	30	8
B. Rivera, Braves	1	5	.167	3.26	16	5	0	2	0	0	49.2	55	26	18	0	2	19	1	29	2
H. Rivera, Braves	5	8	.385	2.70	14	14	3	0	1	0	86.2	67	38	26	2	2	44	2	62	10
Rockman, Rangers	0	1	.000	1.93	14	0	0	7	0	4	37.1	32	12	8	0	3	8	0	36	2
G. Rodriguez, Yankees	1	0	1.000	2.08	2	1	0	0	0	0	8.2	7	5	2	0	1	1	0	9	0
R. Rodriguez, Reds°	1	5	.167	3.08	17	10	0	4	0	1	64.1	64	32	22	2	2	21	5	33	1
A. Rosario, Rangers	0	1	.000	10.80	4	0	0	1	0	0	3.1	9	9	4	3	0	1	0	1	0
M. Rosario, Braves	0	0	.000	54.00	1	0	0	1	0	0	1.0	3	6	6	0	1	3	0	1	1
Runge, Pirates	1	1	.500	5.02	4	2	0	1	0	1	14.1	16	9	8	2	0	4	0	9	1
K. Ryan, Royals	3	0	1.000	1.44	19	0	0	12	0	3	31.1	17	10	5	1	1	12	0	41	3
T. Ryan, Yankees	0	1	.000	0.00	3	0	0	1	0	0	6.2	5	2	0	0	0	5	0	8	1
Saavedra, Rangers°	1	2	.333	2.75	12	6	0	0	0	0	36.0	37	13	11	1	1	7	0	30	1
Sabatino, White Sox	2	3	.400	4.36	16	1	0	13	0	4	33.0	33	20	16	1	2	12	0	23	2
Sandoval, White Sox	0	0	.000	6.00	5	0	0	3	0	1	9.0	12	6	6	0	1	6	0	4	1
Santiago, Pirates	2	3	.400	4.09	12	9	0	1	0	0	55.0	55	30	25	4	6	15	1	37	2
Scarborough, Braves	4	3	.571	1.68	9	8	2	0	0	0	48.1	46	19	9	1	3	16	2	25	2
Schlopy, Pirates	1	0	1.000	0.00	3	0	0	1	0	0	14.2	5	1	0	0	0	4	0	16	1
Schrenk, White Sox	1	2	.333	0.95	8	6	1	0	0	1	28.1	23	10	3	0	2	12	0	19	2
Seaman, Yankees°	4	0	1.000	2.56	9	8	2	0	0	0	52.2	48	18	15	0	0	16	0	36	1
Shaw, Royals	3	2	.600	1.44	7	6	0	0	0	0	31.1	28	11	5	0	1	7	0	15	1
Shepherd, Reds°	0	0	.000	0.00	1	0	0	1	0	0	1.0	1	0	0	0	0	0	0	2	0
Shinall, Dodgers	1	2	.333	5.04	8	6	0	1	0	0	30.1	27	17	17	0	0	15	1	29	4
Siegel, Pirates	1	1	.500	5.06	3	1	0	1	0	0	10.2	12	7	6	1	3	2	0	9	3
Slaughter, Pirates	0	2	.000	4.94	14	0	0	7	0	1	23.2	30	25	13	0	2	11	0	18	6
Small, Astros	0	0	.000	12.27	3	0	0	1	0	0	3.2	11	6	5	0	2	1	0	1	0
Smith, Pirates	2	1	.667	1.40	10	1	0	5	0	4	19.1	12	4	3	0	1	11	1	27	2
Solarte, Expos	1	1	.500	2.25	19	0	0	14	0	2	32.0	30	14	8	1	3	8	2	11	2
Soto, Reds	0	1	.000	2.38	2	0	0	0	0	0	11.1	11	8	3	0	0	2	0	5	0
Stanford, Yankees	5	4	.556	3.76	17	7	1	7	0	0	64.2	65	33	27	2	0	26	0	47	5
Steiner, Rangers°	0	3	.000	9.00	4	3	0	0	0	0	12.0	16	13	12	4	0	7	0	13	3
Storms, Reds	2	0	1.000	6.57	20	0	0	9	0	1	37.0	43	34	27	1	2	33	7	20	9
Stout, Reds	4	4	.500	2.73	10	9	1	0	1	0	52.2	44	23	16	0	6	12	1	28	1
Tafoya, Astros	2	1	.667	2.61	19	0	0	16	0	5	41.1	35	22	12	0	2	14	0	39	3
Tunall, Pirates	5	2	.714	4.71	12	9	0	0	0	0	57.1	66	37	30	1	2	14	0	39	3

Pitcher—Club	W.	L.	Pct.	ERA.	G.	GS.	CG.	GF.	ShO.	Sv.	IP.	H.	R.	ER.	HR.	HB.	BB.	Int. BB.	SO.	WP.
Turek, Reds	3	0	1.000	2.05	3	3	0	0	0	0	22.0	15	6	5	1	0	10	1	19	0
Vanzytveld, Dodgers	4	1	.800	2.84	9	9	0	0	0	0	50.2	42	19	16	3	6	21	1	41	4
A. Vasquez, Royals	1	0	1.000	0.00	3	0	0	2	0	1	2.0	1	0	0	0	1	2	0	0	0
E. Vasquez, Astros	1	3	.250	5.03	14	0	0	11	0	0	34.0	43	24	19	1	2	7	1	16	1
Vazquez, Braves	3	5	.375	3.71	12	12	1	0	0	0	70.1	68	35	29	1	4	35	2	46	5
Vierra, Reds*	1	2	.333	0.86	14	0	0	11	0	8	21.0	11	4	2	0	0	5	0	29	0
Virgo, Dodgers	4	1	.800	4.64	10	2	0	1	0	0	21.1	18	12	11	1	5	7	2	13	0
Wagner, Royals	1	3	.250	3.06	13	12	0	0	0	0	53.0	63	26	18	0	2	12	0	28	0
Wegman, Expos	0	3	.000	4.61	13	3	0	3	0	0	27.1	41	29	14	0	1	10	0	14	1
Wellington, Royals	2	1	.667	2.97	9	8	0	0	0	0	30.1	25	16	10	0	4	18	0	20	9
Wilkinson, Rangers	0	2	.000	5.91	8	0	0	4	0	0	10.2	10	8	7	0	2	12	1	7	1
Wilson, Yankees	1	3	.250	4.22	15	2	0	6	0	0	32.0	31	19	15	3	1	14	0	17	6
Wong, Dodgers	0	0	.000	0.00	1	0	0	0	0	0	3.0	2	0	0	0	0	1	0	2	0
Yochum, Braves	1	2	.333	1.89	18	1	0	8	0	0	38.0	34	15	8	1	1	11	4	11	0
Zeinert, Dodgers*	4	0	1.000	1.25	22	0	0	13	0	5	43.1	34	8	6	0	1	18	1	32	2

BALKS—Boron, 6; Javier, 5; Lopez, Lynch, 4 each; Amick, Gonzalez, Luckham, Maysonet, R. Rodriguez, 3 each; Candelaria, DeLaCruz, Dooley, Joyner, Knackert, Mmahat, Newman, Pena, Ramirez, Reilley, Risley, B. Rivera, Santiago, 2 each; M. Anderson, Bromby, Cerny, Da. Clark, Cleto, DeVincenzo, Diaz, Fella, Fletcher, Gedaminski, Hasler, Jaime, Lewis, Lilly, Locke, C. Maldonado, J. Maldonado, R. Marrero, Meister, Meyers, Moore, Moss, Nordstrom, Parker, Persia, Radinsky, Rice, A. Rivera, H. Rivera, Rockman, Sandoval, Schrenk, Solarte, Steiner, Vanzytveld, E. Vasquez, Vazquez, Wellington, 1 each.

COMBINATION SHUTOUTS—Higginbotham-Marrero-Tafoya, Lee-Murphy, Locke-Tafoya, Astros; Currin-Gillund, Braves; Cerny-Ryan, Cerny-Ortiz, Cerny-Zeinert-Ryan, Gastleum-Zeinert, Luckham-Ortiz, Miguel-Zeinert, Miguel-Zeinert-Ortiz, Cerny-Lilly, Dodgers; Clark-Bromby, Joyner-Rivera, Expos; Doss-Schlopy-Lewis, Schlopy-Smith, Smith-Martinez, Holmes-Runge, Pirates; Hurst-Petkovsek-Rockman, Hurst-Rockman, Rangers; Stoudt-Jeffery, Reds; Netemeyer-Clark, Wagner-Maldonado, Shaw-Murray, Royals; Radinsky-Groom-Carey, Knackert-Groom, Kennedy-Pena, White Sox; Gedaminski-Wilson, Brill-Candelaria, Seaman-Stanford, Yankees.

NO-HIT GAME—Miller, Pirates, defeated Reds, 2-0 (first game), July 27.

Pioneer League

SUMMER CLASS A CLASSIFICATION

CHAMPIONSHIP WINNERS IN PREVIOUS YEARS

1939—Twin Falls* .581	1955—Boise .588	1973—Billings .629
1940—Salt Lake City .608	Magic Valley (4th)* .489	1974—Idaho Falls .569
Ogden (4th)* .492	1956—Boise .561	1975—Great Falls .577
1941—Boise .623	1957—Salt Lake City .650	1976—Great Falls .577
Ogden (2nd)* .598	Billings† .582	1977—Lethbridge .629
1942—Pocatello† .690	1958—Great Falls .582	1978—Billings x .735
Boise .683	Boise† .615	1979—Helena .623
1943-44-45—Did not operate.	1959—Boise .633	Lethbridge y .559
1946—Twin Falls‡ .585	Billings (2nd)* .523	1980—Lethbridge y .743
Salt Lake City† .585	1960—Boise† .686	Billings .629
1947—Salt Lake City .618	Idaho Falls .650	1981—Calgary .657
Twin Falls† .600	1961—Boise .638	Butte y .557
1948—Pocatello .611	Great Falls* .571	1982—Medicine Hat y .629
Twin Falls (2nd)* .595	1962—Boise§ .565	Idaho Falls .600
1949—Twin Falls .624	Billings† .706	1983—Billings y .614
Pocatello (3rd)* .595	1963—Idaho Falls .702	Calgary .600
1950—Pocatello .635	Magic Valley† .643	1984—Billings .691
Billings (3rd)* .571	1964—Treasure Valley .615	Helena y .647
1951—Salt Lake City .618	1965—Treasure Valley .530	1985—Great Falls .771
Great Falls (3rd)* .559	1966—Ogden .591	Salt Lake City y .657
1952—Pocatello .595	1967—Ogden .621	1986—Salt Lake City z .643
Idaho Falls (2nd)* .573	1968—Ogden .609	Great Falls .571
1953—Ogden .679	1969—Ogden .620	
Salt Lake C. (4th)* .527	1970—Idaho Falls .629	
1954—Salt Lake City .595	1971—Great Falls .643	
Great Falls (4th)* .530	1972—Billings .694	

*Won four-club playoff. †Won split-season playoff. ‡Ended first half in tie with Salt Lake City and won one-game playoff. §Ended first half in tie with Billings and Great Falls and won playoff. xBillings (first place) defeated Idaho Falls (second place) in First Place-Second Place playoff. yLeague divided into Northern and Southern divisions; won two-club playoff. zWon two-club playoff.

STANDING OF CLUBS AT CLOSE OF SEASON, AUGUST 30

NORTHERN DIVISION

Club	Hel.	Bil.	GF.	MH.	SLC.	IF.	Poc.	But.	W.	L.	T.	Pct.	G.B.
Helena (Brewers)	....	5	7	9	5	4	7	9	46	24	0	.657	....
Billings (Reds)	3		7	10	6	4	8	6	44	25	0	.638	1½
Great Falls (Dodgers)	7	6	....	9	0	4	2	7	35	34	0	.507	10½
Medicine Hat (Blue Jays)	5	4	5	....	0	2	6	4	26	43	0	.377	19½

SOUTHERN DIVISION

Club	Hel.	Bil.	GF.	MH.	SLC.	IF.	Poc.	But.	W.	L.	T.	Pct.	G.B.
Salt Lake City (Independent)	2	4	7	7	....	12	10	7	49	21	0	.700	....
Idaho Falls (Braves)	3	3	3	5	2	....	10	10	36	34	0	.514	13
Pocatello (Giants)	0	2	5	1	4	4	....	7	23	47	0	.329	26
Butte (Co-op)	4	1	0	2	4	4	4	....	19	50	0	.275	29½

Major league affiliations in parentheses.

Playoff—Salt Lake City defeated Helena, three games to one, to win league championship.

Attendance—Billings, 104,732; Butte, 19,669; Great Falls, 64,226; Helena, 27,020; Idaho Falls, 52,164; Medicine Hat, 25,948; Pocatello, 18,790; Salt Lake City, 170,134. Total, 482,683. Playoffs, 6,595.

Managers—Billings, Dave Keller; Butte, Ernest Rodriguez; Great Falls, Tim Johnson; Helena, Dave Huppert; Idaho Falls, Rod Gilbreath; Medicine Hat, Eduardo Dennis; Pocatello, Rafael Landestoy; Salt Lake City, Jim Gilligan.

All-Star Team—1B—Greg Vella, Medicine Hat; 2B—Bryan Foster, Helena; 3B—Alan Lewis, Great Falls; SS—Andres Santana, Pocatello; OF—Bernie Walker, Billings; Michael Malinak, Salt Lake City; Jon Mitchell, Idaho Falls; C—Frank Colston, Salt Lake City; DH—Mathis Huff, Salt Lake City; P—Sherman Collins, Great Falls; Tim Peters, Salt Lake City; Jaime Navarro, Helena; Manager of the Year—Tim Johnson, Great Falls.

(Compiled by William J. Weiss, League Statistician, San Mateo, Calif.)

CLUB BATTING

Club	Pct.	G.	AB.	R.	OR.	H.	TB.	2B.	3B.	HR.	RBI.	GW.	SH.	SF.	HP.	BB.	Int. BB.	SO.	SB.	CS.	LOB.
Salt Lake City	.320	70	2450	543	395	784	1110	133	26	47	470	33	33	29	41	390	16	447	185	42	594
Helena	.303	70	2453	451	334	744	1072	113	19	59	380	39	22	20	259	10	458	86	36	525
Idaho Falls	.282	70	2336	408	420	659	913	117	28	27	348	29	27	31	23	295	12	420	137	42	524
Pocatello	.264	70	2351	362	475	622	858	102	25	28	300	22	24	13	18	266	5	488	118	42	503
Butte	.262	69	2304	336	458	604	809	106	15	23	263	13	25	16	24	236	9	456	76	33	475
Great Falls	.261	69	2273	325	317	594	820	109	21	25	270	29	28	17	18	220	16	466	80	36	490
Billings	.259	69	2262	416	307	585	894	113	23	50	344	33	20	21	30	311	12	644	125	47	476
Medicine Hat	.252	69	2319	328	463	585	870	99	15	52	281	19	13	16	18	211	6	573	62	54	430

INDIVIDUAL BATTING

(Leading Qualifiers for Batting Championship—189 or More Plate Appearances)

*Bats lefthanded.   †Switch-hitter.

Player and Club	Pct.	G.	AB.	R.	H.	TB.	2B.	3B.	HR.	RBI.	GW.	SH.	SF.	HP.	BB.	Int. BB.	SO.	SB.	CS.
Huff, Mathis, Salt Lake City	.417	48	163	37	68	102	13	0	7	37	6	0	2	1	23	1	23	3	1
Colston, Frank, Salt Lake City*	.397	52	189	36	75	95	15	1	1	46	2	2	1	2	26	2	37	3	1
Nilsson, David, Helena*	.394	55	188	36	74	90	13	0	1	21	3	1	2	0	22	2	14	0	1
Casillas, Adam, Salt Lake City*	.385	60	208	45	80	100	15	1	1	44	6	1	6	1	40	3	12	3	0
Cassels, Christopher, Helena	.382	60	225	41	84	110	12	1	4	37	10	1	2	3	17	2	21	0	2
Mitchell, John, Idaho Falls*	.368	67	250	53	92	143	20	2	9	53	6	0	4	0	31	4	35	9	5

Player and Club	Pct.	G.	AB.	R.	H.	TB.	2B.	3B.	HR.	RBI.	GW.	SH.	SF.	HP.	BB.	Int. BB.	SO.	SB.	CS.
Sanchez, Rey, Butte	.365	49	189	36	69	91	10	6	0	25	3	3	2	2	21	1	11	22	6
Leake, Jon, Salt Lake City	.351	49	188	47	66	80	14	0	0	35	5	3	0	3	34	1	29	6	3
Dodig, Jeffrey, Idaho Falls*	.346	67	209	53	72	113	17	9	2	48	4	1	3	4	47	2	32	14	2
Argo, William, Great Falls†	.341	52	167	39	57	74	11	3	0	22	4	2	1	0	22	1	18	15	4

Departmental Leaders: G—Malinak, 69; AB—Malinak, 265; R—Blackmon, 61; H—Mitchell, 92; TB—Malinak, 148; 2B—Carlson, Mitchell, 20; 3B—Dodig, 9; HR—Malinak, 12; RBI—Carlson, 67; GWRBI—Cassels, 10; SH—Reynolds, 8; SF—Casillas, Glass, A. Lewis, 6; HP—Blackmon, 14; BB—Ferguson, 52; IBB—Taubensee, 5; SO—DeMerit, 74; SB—Santana, 45; CS—Santana, 10.

(All Players—Listed Alphabetically)

Player and Club	Pct.	G.	AB.	R.	H.	TB.	2B.	3B.	HR.	RBI.	GW.	SH.	SF.	HP.	BB.	Int. BB.	SO.	SB.	CS.
Abbatiello, Patrick, Idaho Falls	.303	56	165	25	50	68	10	1	2	30	1	1	4	0	17	0	47	7	3
Abraham, Glenn, Pocatello†	.246	26	69	13	17	24	4	0	1	5	1	2	0	1	7	0	23	3	3
Aguilar, Mark, 5 But-9 Hel	.233	14	43	8	10	11	1	0	0	4	0	0	0	0	5	0	11	2	0
Alberro, Hector, Helena†	.243	19	74	12	18	18	0	0	0	3	0	1	0	1	7	1	17	9	3
Allison, Jeffrey, Idaho Falls*	.224	59	134	22	30	42	6	0	2	14	1	2	0	0	15	1	30	9	1
Argo, William, Great Falls†	.341	52	167	39	57	74	11	3	0	22	4	2	1	0	22	1	18	15	4
Arias, Francisco, Pocatello	.667	18	3	0	2	2	0	0	0	0	0	0	0	0	0	0	0	0	0
Armstrong, Jack, Billings	.000	5	1	0	0	0	0	0	0	0	0	0	0	0	0	0	0	0	0
Barron, Anthony, Great Falls	.298	53	171	33	51	77	13	2	3	30	2	1	3	5	13	2	49	5	3
Baucom, Steven, Medicine Hat*	.242	58	231	32	56	76	11	0	3	21	1	2	0	4	15	0	19	3	9
Bennett, Thomas, Butte†	.129	33	62	11	8	9	1	0	0	1	0	0	0	0	4	0	27	4	0
Berriatua, Steven, Medicine Hat	.268	11	41	7	11	12	1	0	0	3	1	0	0	0	5	0	7	1	0
Beuder, Jon, Salt Lake City†	.339	49	174	49	59	89	5	5	5	29	2	2	0	3	23	0	27	14	4
Blackmon, Anthony, Salt Lake City†..	.259	65	212	61	55	83	8	4	4	35	1	2	2	14	44	2	42	10	8
Bland, Sam, Great Falls	.167	7	12	3	2	2	0	0	0	2	0	0	0	1	2	0	2	0	0
Blohm, Peter, Idaho Falls	.000	14	8	0	0	0	0	0	0	0	0	0	0	0	0	0	4	0	0
Bolick, Frank, Helena†	.250	52	156	41	39	79	8	1	10	28	2	1	0	3	41	1	44	4	0
Bournigal, Rafael, Great Falls	.146	30	82	5	12	16	4	0	0	4	0	1	0	1	3	0	7	0	1
Boze, Anthony, Helena	.310	24	71	15	22	38	7	0	3	12	1	2	0	0	12	0	15	0	2
Breitenbucher, Karl, Pocatello	.000	15	12	0	0	0	0	0	0	0	0	1	0	0	0	0	6	0	0
Brown, Winston, Medicine Hat*	.185	36	108	5	20	26	6	0	0	8	1	2	0	0	11	0	37	3	5
Brune, James, Billings	.236	25	72	10	17	22	5	0	0	4	1	1	0	1	4	0	27	0	0
Bryant, Christopher, Idaho Falls	.293	66	246	48	72	99	12	6	1	31	3	0	1	1	24	1	31	38	4
Buffolino, Rocco, Pocatello	.333	19	3	0	1	1	0	0	0	0	0	0	0	0	1	0	0	0	0
Carlson, William, Pocatello	.324	68	259	45	84	142	20	4	10	67	5	1	5	1	18	1	30	2	4
Carrasco, Carlos, Great Falls	.250	14	8	2	2	2	0	0	0	2	0	0	0	0	0	0	2	0	0
Casillas, Adam, Salt Lake City*	.385	60	208	45	80	100	15	1	1	44	6	1	6	1	40	3	12	3	0
Cassels, Christopher, Helena	.382	60	225	41	84	110	12	1	4	37	10	1	2	3	17	2	21	0	2
Chavez, Samuel, Billings*	.154	14	13	2	2	5	0	0	1	2	0	2	0	0	0	0	5	0	0
Citronnelli, Eddie, Salt Lake City	.303	67	238	50	72	119	15	1	10	57	3	0	3	2	32	1	70	9	5
Cole, Lucius, Butte	.242	42	120	27	29	37	6	1	0	12	1	0	1	3	17	0	24	8	1
Cole, Robert, Idaho Falls	.309	48	181	33	56	67	7	2	0	16	2	0	1	4	13	0	25	19	4
Collins, Sherman, Great Falls	.429	11	7	1	3	3	0	0	0	0	0	0	0	0	0	0	1	0	0
Colon, Antonio, Butte	.234	34	94	9	22	28	6	0	0	14	0	1	0	2	7	0	29	1	1
Colston, Frank, Salt Lake City*	.397	52	189	36	75	95	15	1	1	46	2	2	1	2	26	2	37	3	1
Connelly, David, Pocatello*	.333	2	3	0	1	1	0	0	0	0	0	0	0	0	0	0	0	0	0
Connolly, Stephen, Pocatello	.375	13	16	1	6	7	1	0	0	3	0	0	0	1	0	0	2	0	0
Cox, Darren, Idaho Falls	.000	14	5	0	0	0	0	0	0	0	0	0	0	0	1	0	2	0	0
Currie, Brian, Great Falls*	.000	17	2	0	0	0	0	0	0	0	0	0	0	0	0	0	0	0	0
de la Rosa, Domingo, Pocatello	.000	11	1	0	0	0	0	0	0	0	0	0	0	0	0	0	1	0	0
de la Rosa, Juan, Medicine Hat	.290	57	200	29	58	74	9	2	1	24	4	1	3	0	2	0	38	14	5
DeMerit, Thomas, Great Falls	.194	61	217	28	42	69	5	5	4	28	1	0	1	5	16	0	74	15	2
Dodd, William, Billings	.000	23	2	0	0	0	0	0	0	0	0	0	0	1	0	0	1	0	0
Dodig, Jeffrey, Idaho Falls*	.346	67	209	53	72	113	17	9	2	48	4	1	3	4	47	2	32	14	2
Dostal, Bruce, Great Falls*	.284	62	201	27	56	67	6	1	1	27	1	6	2	1	23	1	38	14	9
Duke, Richard, Idaho Falls	.100	22	40	6	4	4	0	0	0	0	0	0	0	0	8	0	10	0	2
Duncan, Alan, Idaho Falls*	.231	24	39	4	9	12	1	1	0	12	1	1	1	3	2	0	7	2	1
Dziadkowiec, Andrew, Medicine Hat*.	.271	65	228	30	62	84	13	3	1	25	1	3	1	3	16	0	36	4	2
Eastman, Douglas, Billings	.300	66	243	50	73	106	10	4	5	45	7	0	4	0	25	1	41	21	8
Economy, Scott, Billings	.250	17	8	1	2	4	2	0	0	3	0	0	0	0	0	0	4	0	0
Emmert, Brian, Great Falls*	.230	60	178	27	41	54	10	0	1	18	2	0	1	2	20	2	43	0	0
Etzweiler, Daniel, Medicine Hat*	.255	65	212	34	54	108	15	3	11	36	2	0	2	3	31	2	69	1	6
Falzone, James, Helena	.231	6	13	1	3	6	0	0	1	2	0	0	0	0	1	0	1	0	0
Fellows, William, Salt Lake City	.227	9	22	3	5	5	0	0	0	1	0	0	0	0	1	0	8	0	0
Ferguson, James, Salt Lake City	.327	65	214	59	70	88	7	1	3	40	1	1	5	5	52	0	32	6	5
Ferradas, Miguel, Great Falls	.083	19	48	3	4	4	0	0	0	0	0	2	0	1	6	0	14	0	1
Fillard, William, Medicine Hat	.244	40	119	14	29	50	4	1	5	18	4	0	1	1	20	0	41	6	5
Floyd, Christopher, Medicine Hat	.259	20	54	5	14	21	1	0	2	6	0	1	0	0	5	0	15	0	2
Floyd, Daniel, Great Falls*	.167	7	6	0	1	1	0	0	0	0	0	0	0	0	0	0	4	0	0
Flynn, William, Butte*	.143	20	35	4	5	5	0	0	0	1	0	0	0	0	7	0	10	0	1
Foster, Bryan, Helena	.302	56	212	42	64	86	6	2	4	32	3	2	3	0	9	0	36	9	3
Freiling, Howard, Great Falls*	.500	2	4	0	2	4	2	0	0	2	0	0	0	0	0	0	1	0	0
Ganter, Bryan, Billings	.228	39	92	20	21	31	5	1	1	9	1	1	1	5	17	0	20	6	2
Garcia, Librado, Helena	.247	26	73	8	18	32	1	2	3	7	0	1	2	1	4	0	28	2	4
Gastelum, Macario, Great Falls	.000	10	3	0	0	0	0	0	0	0	0	0	0	0	0	0	2	0	0
Gettler, Christopher, Great Falls	.200	10	5	1	1	1	0	0	0	2	0	0	0	0	0	0	0	0	0
Gilbert, Gregory, Idaho Falls	.250	64	188	32	47	57	7	0	1	21	2	5	3	2	22	1	36	8	3
Gilmore, Matthew, Medicine Hat	.248	46	153	20	38	43	2	0	1	18	0	0	2	0	13	1	42	4	3
Glass, Steven, Idaho Falls	.268	58	183	29	49	63	9	1	1	33	2	0	6	3	19	2	22	8	7
Gonzalez, Lawrence, Great Falls	.000	16	2	0	0	0	0	0	0	0	0	0	0	0	0	0	0	0	0
Green, Stephen, Great Falls	.253	53	178	21	46	58	6	0	2	14	3	1	1	0	19	2	40	9	5
Greenwood, Michael, Pocatello	.238	43	130	22	31	45	6	1	2	10	0	2	0	0	16	1	24	3	2
Griffin, Barry, Butte*	.227	34	22	2	5	8	0	0	1	3	0	0	0	0	2	0	11	0	0
Guerrero, Juan, Pocatello	.210	34	81	13	17	27	5	1	1	7	0	0	1	0	17	0	28	1	1
Guerrero, Miguel, Helena†	.221	52	181	22	40	45	3	1	0	14	2	4	0	0	16	0	43	8	6
Gunter, Reid, Pocatello	.000	21	2	0	0	0	0	0	0	0	0	0	0	0	0	0	1	0	0
Hawkins, Walter, Idaho Falls*	.154	8	13	2	2	2	0	0	0	1	0	0	0	0	3	0	2	1	0
Henry, Floyd, Billings*	.200	9	5	0	1	1	0	0	0	2	0	2	0	0	2	0	1	0	0
Hernandez, Arned, Helena	.250	7	8	2	2	2	0	0	0	1	0	0	0	0	2	0	0	0	0
Hester, Steven, Billings	.000	5	2	1	0	0	0	0	0	0	0	0	0	0	2	0	1	0	0
Hoff, Darren, 38 But-8 SLC	.300	46	140	19	42	58	8	1	2	20	2	0	0	1	22	2	29	2	3

Player and Club	Pct.	G.	AB.	R.	H.	TB.	2B.	3B.	HR.	RBI.	GW.	SH.	SF.	HP.	BB.	Int. BB.	SO.	SB.	CS.
Holland, Troy, Helena*	.260	32	50	11	13	22	1	1	2	8	0	0	0	1	5	0	18	5	0
Huff, Mathis, Salt Lake City	.417	48	163	37	68	102	13	0	7	37	6	0	2	1	23	1	23	3	1
James, Keith, Pocatello	.303	64	211	49	64	96	13	5	3	36	3	1	1	2	37	2	56	18	4
Jefferson, Reginald, Billings†	.364	8	22	10	8	12	1	0	1	9	1	0	0	1	4	1	2	1	0
Jenkins, Mack, Billings†	.000	13	13	0	0	0	0	0	0	0	0	0	2	0	0	0	8	0	0
Johnson, Cisco, Medicine Hat	.223	34	121	19	27	44	5	3	2	18	0	1	1	0	16	0	29	6	5
Johnson, Dante, Billings	.277	55	166	27	46	73	13	1	4	33	3	0	4	3	20	0	51	14	7
Johnson, Dominick, Pocatello	.000	18	3	0	0	0	0	0	0	0	0	0	0	0	0	0	3	0	0
Johnson, Eric, Great Falls	.179	34	78	8	14	23	3	0	2	8	0	0	1	0	17	1	19	0	0
Johnson, Erik, Pocatello	.264	43	129	19	34	53	7	0	4	12	0	3	0	0	13	0	21	6	2
Jones, James, Pocatello†	.245	29	49	15	12	14	2	0	0	5	0	3	1	2	15	0	8	5	2
Kaiser, Keith, Billings	.125	13	8	2	1	1	0	0	0	1	0	1	0	0	0	0	4	0	0
Knorr, Randy, Medicine Hat	.292	26	106	21	31	68	7	0	10	24	1	0	3	1	5	3	26	0	0
Koh, Joseph, Idaho Falls	.224	35	66	18	15	20	1	2	0	4	0	2	0	0	16	0	5	6	2
Lace, Jeffrey, Butte	.163	15	43	3	7	8	1	0	0	1	0	0	0	1	2	0	19	0	1
Lane, Brian, Billings	.200	56	175	19	35	52	6	1	3	16	0	3	1	1	18	0	73	2	0
Langley, Wesley, Great Falls	.200	12	5	0	1	1	0	0	0	0	0	0	0	0	0	0	2	0	0
Lavrusky, Charles, Idaho Falls	.000	21	4	0	0	0	0	0	0	0	0	0	0	0	0	0	2	0	0
Laya, Jesus, Pocatello	.290	28	69	7	20	22	2	0	0	10	0	2	1	0	3	0	14	1	1
Leake, Jon, Salt Lake City	.351	49	188	47	66	80	14	0	0	35	5	3	0	3	34	1	29	6	3
Lemons, Lenual, Butte	.274	27	95	20	26	36	2	1	2	15	2	1	1	1	16	0	16	8	3
Letterio, Shane, Billings	.284	64	229	42	65	83	11	2	1	25	3	0	3	2	25	0	48	14	7
Lewis, Alan, Great Falls*	.335	65	224	34	75	112	9	2	8	37	4	0	6	0	27	4	20	1	1
Lewis, Brett, Pocatello	.000	23	1	0	0	0	0	0	0	0	0	0	0	0	1	0	0	0	0
Lienhard, Steven, Pocatello	.154	14	13	2	2	2	0	0	0	3	0	2	0	0	3	0	4	1	0
Linarez, Jose, Pocatello	.227	27	75	4	17	21	4	0	0	13	2	1	0	0	9	0	16	1	1
Lomeli, Michael, Idaho Falls	.250	23	4	1	1	1	0	0	0	0	0	1	0	0	0	0	2	0	0
Maldonado, Phillip, Idaho Falls	.265	48	113	16	30	35	5	0	0	15	3	2	2	2	15	0	12	4	0
Malinak, Michael, Salt Lake City	.321	69	265	57	85	148	17	5	12	57	4	1	3	7	30	1	63	1	4
Malseed, James, Pocatello	.263	65	224	26	60	90	12	6	2	27	2	1	3	4	24	0	52	10	4
Marrero, Oreste, Helena*	.325	51	154	30	50	83	8	2	7	34	0	1	0	1	18	3	31	2	1
Marrero, Vilato, Helena	.288	61	233	35	67	105	14	3	6	47	3	0	0	2	12	1	34	1	1
Marsh, Quinn, Billings	.000	19	2	0	0	0	0	0	0	0	0	0	1	0	0	0	2	0	0
Martin, Mark, Idaho Falls	.226	32	93	13	21	29	2	0	2	14	1	3	1	2	12	0	21	3	3
Martinez, Luis, Great Falls	.264	64	261	31	69	90	13	4	0	15	5	6	1	1	13	1	24	15	3
McCarthy, Stephen, Billings	.286	13	7	3	2	3	1	0	0	2	0	1	0	1	1	0	4	0	0
McClintock, Ronald, Pocatello*	.232	40	112	10	26	33	2	1	1	17	1	1	0	1	10	1	24	3	0
McCutchen, James, Butte	.273	66	253	37	69	101	15	1	5	35	0	2	4	1	23	2	58	9	5
McNees, Kevin, Idaho Falls*	.328	60	198	28	65	89	9	3	3	33	2	1	2	0	18	1	34	6	4
Meier, Kevin, Pocatello	.500	6	4	1	2	2	0	0	0	1	0	0	0	1	1	0	0	0	0
Melisauskas, Todd, Great Falls	.188	23	48	7	9	11	2	0	0	2	0	2	0	0	3	0	12	0	0
Mendez, Eddy, Medicine Hat	.243	20	70	10	17	22	2	0	1	6	0	0	0	0	5	0	20	4	2
Messer, Douglas, Pocatello*	.500	16	2	0	1	1	0	0	0	1	0	0	0	0	0	0	0	0	0
Mitchell, John, Idaho Falls*	.368	67	250	53	92	143	20	2	9	53	6	0	4	0	31	4	35	9	3
Mons, Jeffrey, Great Falls	.283	33	113	18	32	46	9	1	1	25	3	1	0	0	16	2	24	0	1
Montoyo, Carlos, Helena	.289	13	45	12	13	18	1	2	0	2	0	0	1	0	12	0	3	2	1
Moore, Dwayne, Helena	.319	53	188	36	60	91	14	1	5	45	6	1	3	1	10	0	38	1	3
Morphew, Barry, Medicine Hat	.132	15	38	3	5	5	0	0	0	1	0	0	0	0	6	0	14	0	0
Murray, Scott, Pocatello	.500	2	10	2	5	10	0	1	1	1	0	0	0	0	0	0	1	0	0
Mustari, Frank, Great Falls	.305	62	226	32	69	99	15	3	3	30	2	0	0	1	17	0	59	6	5
Myers, James, Pocatello	.000	12	2	0	0	0	0	0	0	0	0	1	0	0	0	0	1	0	0
Nilsson, David, Helena*	.394	55	188	36	74	90	13	0	1	21	3	1	2	0	22	2	14	0	1
Noch, Douglas, Great Falls	.400	14	10	2	4	5	1	0	0	1	1	2	0	0	2	0	2	0	0
Noonan, Todd, Salt Lake City	.000	4	3	0	0	0	0	0	0	0	0	0	0	0	2	0	1	0	0
O'Hare, Sean, Billings*	.203	54	172	30	35	66	10	0	7	37	2	0	2	1	36	0	55	2	0
Okubo, Katsuya, Butte	.254	60	201	26	51	68	11	3	0	20	1	6	0	4	21	0	45	5	1
O'Leary, Troy, Helena†	.400	3	5	0	2	2	0	0	0	1	0	0	0	0	0	0	0	0	0
Ortiz, Joseph, Helena	.241	39	112	22	27	34	4	0	1	12	0	2	0	3	5	0	29	14	2
Peters, Daniel, Butte	.000	12	1	0	0	0	0	0	0	0	0	0	0	0	0	0	1	0	0
Peyton, Michael, Butte	.242	11	33	5	8	10	2	0	0	2	0	0	0	0	3	1	7	1	0
Piscetta, Robert, Great Falls	.000	10	2	1	0	0	0	0	0	0	0	1	0	0	0	0	1	0	0
Raley, Timothy, Helena*	.337	59	199	37	67	95	10	3	4	38	7	4	3	1	36	0	23	16	2
Ramirez, Frank, Idaho Falls	.222	15	9	0	2	2	0	0	0	0	0	1	0	0	0	0	4	0	0
Reynolds, Neil, Salt Lake City*	.277	68	256	44	71	101	14	2	4	43	0	8	1	2	44	4	49	4	3
Riccio, Robert, Billings	.194	50	124	20	24	34	2	1	2	13	1	2	3	2	20	1	41	5	2
Roberts, Steven, Medicine Hat	.172	31	87	6	15	19	1	0	1	6	0	1	0	1	3	0	31	0	0
Robinson, Brad, Billings	.268	52	168	32	45	84	9	3	8	35	4	2	0	1	23	1	58	7	0
Rodnunsky, Pierre, Butte	.235	58	166	22	39	43	4	0	0	9	0	4	0	3	23	0	32	12	9
Rush, Edward, Billings	.305	25	82	18	25	29	2	1	0	6	2	1	0	1	12	0	14	4	2
Russell, Daniel, Helena	.311	31	103	9	32	44	3	0	3	14	0	1	2	0	2	0	26	2	2
Sanchez, Rey, Butte	.365	49	189	36	69	91	10	6	0	25	3	3	2	2	21	1	11	22	6
Santana, Andres, Pocatello	.262	67	256	51	67	75	2	3	0	9	1	1	0	1	36	0	37	45	10
Sawyer, Randall, Butte	.317	42	161	18	51	72	9	0	4	24	1	0	0	0	10	0	8	1	1
Scott, Steven, Salt Lake City	.257	59	144	23	37	47	6	2	0	24	1	7	5	0	20	0	20	8	3
Sellner, Scott, Billings	.313	45	150	39	47	72	9	2	4	22	2	0	0	9	21	0	39	6	5
Seuberth, William, Butte†	.000	21	1	0	0	0	0	0	0	0	0	0	0	0	0	0	0	0	0
Shiverick, William, Billings	.000	20	2	0	0	0	0	0	0	0	0	0	0	0	0	0	2	0	0
Sloan, Gary, Billings†	.200	28	55	6	11	16	2	0	1	6	1	0	1	0	14	1	18	4	1
Smith, Edward, Medicine Hat	.133	12	15	2	2	2	0	0	0	0	0	1	0	0	1	0	12	0	0
Smith, Robert, Helena	.355	22	76	21	27	43	7	0	3	14	1	0	4	1	17	0	13	7	3
Sobczyk, Robert, Helena	.167	3	6	0	1	1	0	0	0	0	0	0	0	0	0	0	2	0	0
Speakes, Joseph, Pocatello	.220	20	59	7	13	15	2	0	0	2	0	2	0	0	3	0	23	0	0
Spear, Michael, Butte	.249	53	185	27	46	68	11	1	3	19	1	1	4	2	5	0	24	1	0
Spiers, William, Helena*	.409	6	22	4	9	10	1	0	0	3	0	0	0	0	3	0	1	0	0
Springer, Dennis, Great Falls	.000	23	2	1	0	0	0	0	0	0	0	0	0	0	0	0	1	0	0
Suttle, Matthew, Butte	.184	48	125	16	23	26	0	0	1	12	0	3	2	3	11	0	26	2	2
Takeda, Yasushi, Butte	.277	58	191	27	53	71	10	1	2	21	0	3	2	0	17	0	42	0	0
Taubensee, Edward, Pocatello*	.265	55	162	24	43	65	7	0	5	28	1	0	2	1	25	5	47	2	2
Thomas, Keith, Billings†	.254	45	142	22	36	58	6	2	4	24	3	1	0	0	7	1	45	11	4
Thompson, Ryan, Medicine Hat	.245	40	110	13	27	35	3	1	1	9	0	0	0	0	6	0	34	1	2
Tomasino, Vittorio, Billings	.188	14	32	2	6	9	0	0	1	6	0	0	0	0	3	0	13	0	1
Valdez, Ramon, Butte*	.272	52	184	30	50	71	10	1	3	27	2	1	0	1	25	3	37	1	0

Player and Club	Pct.	G.	AB.	R.	H.	TB.	2B.	3B.	HR.	RBI.	GW.	SH.	SF.	HP.	BB.	Int. BB.	SO.	SB.	CS.
Vella, Gregory, Medicine Hat*	.266	67	230	43	61	105	11	0	11	43	4	2	3	4	34	0	49	4	2
Vuz, John, Pocatello	.237	38	118	6	28	31	1	1	0	14	3	0	0	1	4	0	17	0	1
Wadsworth, Randal, Great Falls	.143	3	7	1	1	1	0	0	0	0	0	0	0	0	0	0	1	0	0
Walker, Bernard, Billings*	.354	33	113	36	40	68	12	5	2	17	1	0	1	0	35	1	22	26	6
Walker, William, Helena	.182	14	33	7	6	12	0	0	2	4	1	0	0	2	7	0	9	0	0
Wandler, Michael, Pocatello	.278	63	234	42	65	83	13	1	1	31	3	0	1	1	23	0	29	10	5
Wanish, John, Great Falls	.000	15	6	0	0	0	0	0	0	1	0	1	0	0	2	0	2	0	1
Ward, David, Salt Lake City	.238	58	160	28	38	47	3	3	0	21	2	6	1	1	19	1	32	10	4
Ward, Randall, Idaho Falls*	.167	15	6	1	1	1	0	0	0	0	0	0	0	0	0	0	5	0	0
Ware, Derek, Medicine Hat†	.253	27	91	11	23	24	1	0	0	8	0	0	0	0	7	0	27	7	3
Waznik, Allen, Idaho Falls*	.083	15	12	0	1	1	0	0	0	0	0	2	0	0	2	0	3	0	0
Westbrooks, Elanis, Pocatello	.282	19	78	12	22	25	1	1	0	10	1	0	0	0	8	0	11	7	2
Williams, Matthew, Pocatello	.202	30	89	10	19	22	3	0	0	9	0	0	0	2	11	0	34	1	0
Williams, Michael, Idaho Falls	.176	20	34	5	6	14	2	0	2	4	0	0	0	0	5	0	22	1	0
Williams, Theodore, Idaho Falls	.245	56	155	23	38	61	9	1	4	21	1	0	3	2	27	0	40	3	3
Wilson, Michael, Idaho Falls	.250	14	8	1	2	4	2	0	0	2	0	2	0	0	1	0	4	0	0
Wright, William, Idaho Falls	.000	26	2	0	0	0	0	0	0	0	0	0	0	0	0	0	1	0	0
Young, Mark, Medicine Hat	.333	29	105	24	35	52	7	2	2	7	0	0	1	0	10	0	27	4	3
Ziegler, Gregory, Idaho Falls	.000	11	5	0	0	0	0	0	0	0	0	1	0	0	2	0	4	0	0

The following pitchers, listed alphabetically by club, with games in parentheses, had no plate appearances, primarily through use of designated hitters:

BILLINGS—Hill, Milton (21); Turek, Joseph (9).

BUTTE—Anderson, Edwin (9); Burgos, John (10); Dolan, John (2); Elliott, Craig (4); Glover, Terence (9); Johnson, Carl (17); Kitano, Katsunori (13); Miranda, Angel (12); Tozuka, Tomoyuki (19); Wojda, Joseph (9).

GREAT FALLS—Johnson, Carl (4); Kreuder, Daniel (1); Luckham, Kenneth (3); Martin, David (18); Shinall, Zakary (1); Whatley, Leland (20).

HELENA—Carter, Larry (9); Chapman, Mark (27); Correa, Ramser (3); Johnson, Christopher (12); Kostichka, Steven (19); Kucera, Bradley (6); Miranda, Angel (13); Monson, Steven (14); Navarro, Jaime (13); Nelson, Scott (13); Shiver, Todd (5); Sparks, Steven (10); Tanner, Dean (2); Whitlock, Michael (16); Woodhouse, David (21).

IDAHO FALLS—Ferrebee, Anthony (9); Gillund, Robert (8).

MEDICINE HAT—Bevis, Robert (11); Castro, Pablo (1); Colon, Geovanny (12); Conliffe, Anthony (17); Cromwell, Nathaniel (15); Cuff, Robert (18); Foley, Timothy (5); Granato, Mark (18); Lariviere, Christopher (15); MacDonald, Robert (13); Maitia, Robert (24); Newcomb, Joe (11); Richey, Rodney (12); Timlin, Michael (13); Wilson, Terry (15).

POCATELLO—Figueroa, Jesus (15).

SALT LAKE CITY—Alleyne, Isaac (18); Collins, Timothy (2); Creekmore, Niles (23); Dolan, John (7); Groennert, John (14); Hetrick, Kent (21); Hiyama, Yasuhiro (10); Humphrey, Michael (15); Ikeue, Koichi (13); Peters, Timothy (38); Poss, David (6); Savage, John (4); Stange, Kurt (14); Wenrick, William (6).

GRAND SLAM HOME RUNS—Beuder, DeMerit, Martin, O'Hare, Thomas, B. Walker, 1 each.

AWARDED FIRST BASE ON CATCHER'S INTERFERENCE—Colston 2 (Duke, Ferradas); Casillas (Knorr).

CLUB FIELDING

Club	Pct.	G.	PO.	A.	E.	DP.	PB.	Club	Pct.	G.	PO.	A.	E.	DP.	PB.
Billings	.959	69	1779	707	106	51	25	Great Falls	.951	69	1738	638	122	55	21
Helena	.954	70	1832	688	121	46	19	Pocatello	.946	70	1771	791	146	63	24
Salt Lake City	.954	70	1847	748	126	49	19	Butte	.943	69	1756	706	149	43	10
Idaho Falls	.952	70	1782	759	129	68	24	Medicine Hat	.942	69	1797	752	158	65	14

Triple Play—Salt Lake City.

INDIVIDUAL FIELDING

*Throws lefthanded.

FIRST BASEMEN

Player and Club	Pct.	G.	PO.	A.	E.	DP.	Player and Club	Pct.	G.	PO.	A.	E.	DP.
Argo, Great Falls	1.000	1	11	1	0	1	McClintock, Pocatello*	.983	22	160	13	3	14
Barron, Great Falls	1.000	2	14	1	0	1	MITCHELL, Idaho Falls*	.991	52	430	24	4	45
Bland, Great Falls	1.000	3	9	1	0	0	O'Hare, Billings	.985	54	416	35	7	35
Carlson, Pocatello	.981	51	479	32	10	47	Reynolds, Salt Lake City	.984	63	573	28	10	32
Colon, Butte	.970	4	30	2	1	1	Roberts, Medicine Hat	.980	9	48	1	1	5
Eastman, Billings	.979	13	84	8	2	9	Robinson, Billings	.939	10	41	5	3	2
Emmert, Great Falls*	.972	55	389	33	12	32	Russell, Helena	.989	22	166	11	2	12
Flynn, Butte	.938	2	13	2	1	3	Sawyer, Butte	.982	7	53	1	1	2
Huff, Salt Lake City	.952	10	76	3	4	8	Suttle, Butte	.955	8	60	4	3	1
Jefferson, Billings*	1.000	3	21	1	0	1	Valdez, Butte*	.975	52	413	17	11	30
E. Johnson, Great Falls	.992	19	111	8	1	12	Vella, Medicine Hat*	.987	66	588	27	8	53
Leake, Salt Lake City	1.000	2	15	0	0	2	Walker, Helena	.944	12	63	4	4	6
O. Marrero, Helena*	.973	47	342	23	10	22	Williams, Idaho Falls	.986	26	191	13	3	14
V. Marrero, Helena	.800	1	4	0	1	0							

Triple Play—Reynolds.

SECOND BASEMEN

Player and Club	Pct.	G.	PO.	A.	E.	DP.	Player and Club	Pct.	G.	PO.	A.	E.	DP.
Abbatiello, Idaho Falls	1.000	4	2	8	0	3	Koh, Idaho Falls	.978	15	23	21	1	7
Aguilar, Butte-Helena	.945	11	27	25	3	7	Lace, Butte	.978	12	24	21	1	0
Alberro, Helena	.957	17	40	48	4	9	Leake, Salt Lake City	1.000	1	0	1	0	0
BAUCOM, Medicine Hat	.966	58	122	158	10	40	Lemons, Butte	.943	27	45	70	7	10
Blackmon, Salt Lake City	.921	59	126	119	21	23	Lewis, Great Falls	.917	2	6	5	1	1
Bournigal, Great Falls	.952	20	43	37	4	10	Linarez, Pocatello	.968	14	26	35	2	8
Bryant, Idaho Falls	.932	59	118	143	19	30	Montoyo, Helena	.964	13	29	25	2	9
Cole, Butte	.333	1	0	1	2	0	Morphew, Medicine Hat	.857	3	6	6	2	0
de la Rosa, Medicine Hat	.818	3	5	4	2	1	Mustari, Great Falls	.948	50	71	112	10	18
Etzweiler, Medicine Hat	.900	2	4	5	1	1	Ortiz, Helena	1.000	2	3	2	0	1
Ferguson, Salt Lake City	.913	8	12	9	2	2	Riccio, Billings	.974	34	60	54	3	13
Foster, Helena	.953	35	62	79	7	13	Rodnunsky, Butte	.962	28	48	52	4	10
Gilbert, Idaho Falls	.951	9	17	22	2	8	Rush, Billings	.943	9	14	19	2	3
J. Guerrero, Pocatello	.968	32	59	62	4	9	Scott, Salt Lake City	.915	20	18	36	5	7
M. Guerrero, Helena	.857	4	3	3	1	1	Sellner, Billings	.969	42	70	86	5	18
Hoff, Butte-Salt Lake City	1.000	4	6	10	0	0	Sloan, Billings	.667	3	2	2	2	0
E. Johnson, Pocatello	.977	27	61	65	3	10	Wandler, Pocatello	1.000	1	1	2	0	0
Jones, Pocatello	.957	12	25	20	2	6	Young, Medicine Hat	.917	6	8	14	2	2

THIRD BASEMEN

Player and Club	Pct.	G.	PO.	A.	E.	DP.
Abbatiello, Idaho Falls	.843	22	13	30	8	2
Barron, Great Falls	.750	3	4	2	2	0
Bland, Great Falls	.500	1	0	1	1	0
Bolick, Helena	.947	13	5	13	1	0
de la Rosa, Medicine Hat	1.000	2	1	7	0	1
Etzweiler, Medicine Hat	.882	50	43	99	19	12
Ferguson, Salt Lake City	1.000	6	4	11	0	0
Fillard, Medicine Hat	.600	2	3	0	2	0
Floyd, Medicine Hat	.867	11	5	8	2	0
GILBERT, Idaho Falls	.924	49	33	88	10	10
Gilmore, Medicine Hat	.750	1	1	2	1	0
Glass, Idaho Falls	.818	3	4	5	2	0
Hoff, Butte-Salt Lake City	.885	16	7	16	3	0
E. Johnson, Pocatello	.880	9	11	11	3	3
Jones, Idaho Falls	1.000	5	1	6	0	0
Koh, Idaho Falls	1.000	2	0	2	0	0
Lane, Billings	.922	54	35	107	12	3
Leake, Salt Lake City	.884	47	26	88	15	4
Lewis, Great Falls	.891	56	45	111	19	12
Linarez, Pocatello	.905	6	3	16	2	1
Maldonado, Idaho Falls	.667	3	1	1	1	0
Malinak, Salt Lake City	.688	4	2	9	5	0
V. Marrero, Pocatello	.915	55	39	101	13	8
Morphew, Medicine Hat	.857	3	6	6	2	0
Mustari, Great Falls	.879	11	7	22	4	1
Okubo, Butte	.838	58	47	82	25	3
Reynolds, Salt Lake City	.636	5	2	5	4	0
Riccio, Billings	.889	16	12	20	4	1
Rodnunsky, Butte	1.000	2	2	1	0	0
Rush, Billings	.923	4	4	8	1	1
Russell, Helena	.793	9	6	17	6	1
Scott, Salt Lake City	.926	14	3	22	2	1
Sloan, Billings	.909	11	2	18	2	0
Wandler, Pocatello	.918	57	39	128	15	12
Matt. Williams, Pocatello	1.000	1	1	0	0	0
T. Williams, Idaho Falls	.816	10	11	20	7	4

Triple Play—Leake.

SHORTSTOPS

Player and Club	Pct.	G.	PO.	A.	E.	DP.
Abbatiello, Idaho Falls	.865	25	26	70	15	11
Aguilar, Butte-Helena	.800	3	5	7	3	2
Alberro, Helena	.889	2	0	8	1	0
Bennett, Butte	.765	7	5	8	4	0
Berriatua, Medicine Hat	.930	11	14	26	3	6
Bournigal, Great Falls	1.000	10	6	10	0	2
Etzweiler, Medicine Hat	.892	16	22	44	8	6
FERGUSON, Salt Lake City	.969	54	75	171	8	26
Foster, Helena	.924	21	17	44	5	4
Gilbert, Idaho Falls	1.000	2	1	0	0	1
Gilmore, Medicine Hat	.845	45	74	122	36	26
Glass, Idaho Falls	.920	53	83	125	18	25
Guerrero, Helena	.936	47	72	118	13	17
Hoff, Butte	.906	6	12	17	3	3
E. Johnson, Pocatello	1.000	2	1	1	0	0
Jones, Pocatello	.889	7	3	5	1	0
Lace, Billings	1.000	3	1	1	0	0
Letterio, Billings	.922	61	80	146	19	27
V. Marrero, Helena	.800	2	3	1	1	0
Martinez, Great Falls	.918	63	103	143	22	32
Riccio, Billings	1.000	1	3	3	0	3
Rush, Billings	.945	14	20	32	3	7
Sanchez, Butte	.953	49	84	162	12	25
Santana, Pocatello	.878	66	94	202	41	34
Scott, Salt Lake City	.885	26	30	55	11	8
Spiers, Helena	.700	6	8	6	6	3
Wandler, Pocatello	1.000	3	4	6	0	2

Triple Play—Ferguson.

OUTFIELDERS

Player and Club	Pct.	G.	PO.	A.	E.	DP.
Abbatiello, Idaho Falls	1.000	4	3	0	0	0
Abraham, Pocatello	1.000	16	24	0	0	0
Allison, Idaho Falls°	.980	40	47	3	1	0
Argo, Great Falls	.943	45	64	2	4	0
Barron, Great Falls	.976	30	39	2	1	0
Bennett, Butte	.920	19	21	2	2	0
Beuder, Salt Lake City	.961	49	68	5	3	0
Blackmon, Salt Lake City	.800	6	4	0	1	0
Boze, Helena	.938	11	15	0	1	0
Brown, Medicine Hat	.957	34	45	0	2	0
Carlson, Pocatello	.880	10	20	2	3	0
Casillas, Salt Lake City°	.966	34	54	3	2	0
Cassels, Helena	.989	59	86	2	1	0
Citronnelli, Salt Lake City	.985	26	34	0	4	0
L. Cole, Butte	.838	29	29	2	6	1
R. Cole, Butte	.937	44	73	1	5	0
de la Rosa, Medicine Hat	.956	52	103	6	5	1
DeMerit, Great Falls	.952	40	39	1	2	1
Dodig, Idaho Falls	.982	61	107	3	2	0
Dostal, Great Falls	.965	52	78	4	3	1
Duncan, Idaho Falls	.875	9	7	0	1	0
Eastman, Billings	.992	55	115	3	1	0
Fillard, Medicine Hat	.949	34	35	2	2	0
Ganter, Billings	.957	36	42	2	2	0
Garcia, Helena	.935	25	42	1	3	0
Gilbert, Idaho Falls	1.000	2	2	0	0	0
Green, Great Falls	.960	51	90	7	4	2
Greenwood, Pocatello	.966	41	80	4	3	1
Hawkins, Idaho Falls°	1.000	4	5	0	0	0
Hernandez, Helena	.333	3	1	0	2	0
Hoff, Butte	.926	13	25	0	2	0
Holland, Helena°	.920	25	21	2	2	1
Huff, Salt Lake City	.667	2	2	0	1	0
James, Pocatello	.933	53	75	8	6	1
C. Johnson, Medicine Hat	.957	30	44	0	2	0
Da. Johnson, Billings	.893	48	62	5	8	0
Koh, Idaho Falls	1.000	2	1	0	0	0
Malinak, Salt Lake City.	.978	65	85	3	2	0
Malseed, Pocatello	.947	64	104	4	6	0
McCutchen, Butte	.920	63	145	4	13	0
McNees, Idaho Falls	.977	56	79	6	2	0
Mendez, Medicine Hat	1.000	9	13	4	0	0
Mitchell, Idaho Falls	.800	15	11	1	3	0
Moore, Helena	.891	39	54	3	7	0
Peyton, Butte	.917	11	10	1	1	0
RALEY, Helena	1.000	57	81	5	0	1
Reynolds, Salt Lake City	1.000	1	1	0	0	0
Roberts, Medicine Hat	1.000	9	10	0	0	0
Robinson, Billings	.918	37	41	4	4	1
Rodnunsky, Butte	1.000	11	17	1	0	0
Sawyer, Butte	.880	22	21	1	3	0
E. Smith, Medicine Hat	.800	9	4	0	1	0
R. Smith, Helena	.929	21	36	3	3	0
Speakes, Pocatello	.810	19	15	2	4	1
Spear, Butte	.958	40	64	5	3	0
Suttle, Butte	.968	30	53	7	2	0
Thomas, Billings	.833	30	24	1	5	0
Thompson, Medicine Hat	.935	29	56	2	4	1
Walker, Billings	.980	33	46	3	1	0
Ward, Salt Lake City	.968	55	87	5	3	0
Ware, Medicine Hat	1.000	12	17	1	0	0
Westbrooks, Pocatello	.953	19	37	4	2	1
Michael Williams, Pocatello	.818	7	9	0	2	0
Young, Medicine Hat	.979	21	31	8	1	1

CATCHERS

Player and Club	Pct.	G.	PO.	A.	E.	DP.	PB.
Brune, Billings	.955	25	154	17	8	0	6
Citronnelli, Salt Lake City	.981	24	142	17	3	1	7
Colon, Butte	.959	23	147	16	7	0	2
Colston, Salt Lake City	.968	49	312	47	12	0	12
Duke, Idaho Falls	.975	21	71	7	2	1	8
Dziadkowiec, Medicine Hat	.969	55	177	60	14	2	9
Falzone, Helena	.913	6	18	3	2	0	1
Fellows, Salt Lake City	1.000	9	62	5	0	1	8
Ferradas, Great Falls	.954	17	128	16	7	0	6
C. Floyd, Medicine Hat	1.000	7	28	8	0	0	2
D. Floyd, Great Falls	.917	6	11	0	1	0	2
Glass, Idaho Falls	1.000	1	0	1	0	0	0
Knorr, Medicine Hat	.949	12	70	5	4	0	3
Laya, Pocatello	.969	17	83	12	3	0	0
MALDONADO, Idaho Falls	.986	42	182	30	3	2	5
Martin, Idaho Falls	.985	21	117	11	2	1	2
Melisauskas, Great Falls	.974	22	134	18	4	4	7
Mons, Great Falls	.981	33	276	26	6	2	5
Murray, Pocatello	1.000	2	13	0	0	0	0
Myers, Pocatello	1.000	2	2	0	0	0	0
Nilsson, Helena	.981	44	329	28	7	0	7
Noonan, Salt Lake City	1.000	1	1	0	0	0	0
Ortiz, Helena	.985	31	214	48	4	0	8
Sobczyk, Helena	1.000	3	10	0	0	0	0
Suttle, Butte	1.000	7	46	6	0	1	1
Takeda, Butte	.982	47	276	48	6	2	7
Taubensee, Billings	.984	53	344	29	6	2	19
Tomasino, Billings	1.000	8	18	3	0	0	0
Vuz, Pocatello	.957	30	157	23	8	2	9
Wadsworth, Great Falls	1.000	3	19	6	0	0	1
Matt. Williams, Pocatello	.981	29	124	28	3	1	5
T. Williams, Idaho Falls	.981	15	89	14	2	0	8

PITCHERS

Player and Club	Pct.	G.	PO.	A.	E.	DP.
Alleyne, Salt Lake City*	.875	18	2	5	1	0
Arias, Pocatello	.800	18	4	4	2	0
Anderson, Butte	1.000	9	0	8	0	0
Armstrong, Billings	1.000	5	3	4	0	0
Bevis, Medicine Hat	1.000	11	1	3	0	0
Blohm, Idaho Falls	.889	14	5	11	2	0
Breitenbucher, Pocatello	.920	15	10	13	2	2
Buffolino, Pocatello	.900	19	3	6	1	1
Burgos, Butte*	.800	10	2	14	4	2
Carrasco, Great Falls	.769	13	4	6	3	0
Carter, Helena	1.000	9	2	2	0	0
Casillas, Salt Lake City*	1.000	3	0	1	0	0
Chapman, Helena	1.000	27	1	1	0	0
Chavez, Billings*	.941	14	7	25	2	3
Collins, Great Falls	.800	11	5	3	2	0
Colon, Medicine Hat	.667	12	0	4	2	0
Conliffe, Medicine Hat	1.000	17	2	1	0	0
Connolly, Pocatello	.895	13	2	15	2	0
Correa, Helena	.500	3	1	0	1	0
Cox, Idaho Falls*	.889	14	7	9	2	1
Creekmore, Salt Lake City	.955	23	5	16	1	2
Cromwell, Medicine Hat*	1.000	15	0	15	0	0
Cuff, Medicine Hat	.882	18	1	14	2	0
Currie, Great Falls*	.667	17	1	1	1	0
de la Rosa, Pocatello	.923	11	5	7	1	1
Dodd, Billings	1.000	23	9	6	0	0
Dolan, Butte-Salt Lake City*	1.000	9	2	4	0	1
Economy, Billings	1.000	17	8	7	0	0
Elliott, Butte	1.000	4	2	2	0	0
Ferrebee, Idaho Falls*	.800	9	0	4	1	0
Figueroa, Pocatello	.556	15	3	2	4	0
Foley, Medicine Hat	1.000	5	0	1	0	1
Gastelum, Great Falls	1.000	10	3	0	0	0
Gettler, Great Falls	1.000	10	4	0	0	0
Gillund, Idaho Falls	.667	8	2	0	1	1
Glover, Butte	1.000	9	2	1	0	0
Gonzalez, Great Falls	.875	16	3	4	1	0
Granato, Medicine Hat	.875	18	2	5	1	0
Griffin, Butte*	.917	14	2	9	1	0
Groennert, Salt Lake City	1.000	14	2	6	0	1
Gunter, Pocatello	1.000	21	6	8	0	0
Henry, Billings*	1.000	9	4	3	0	0
Hernandez, Helena	1.000	4	1	0	0	0
Hester, Billings	1.000	5	1	5	0	0
Hetrick, Salt Lake City	.889	21	3	13	2	1
Hill, Billings	1.000	21	4	5	0	1
Hiyama, Salt Lake City	1.000	10	3	2	0	1
Humphrey, Salt Lake City	.938	15	4	11	1	1
Ikeue, Salt Lake City	1.000	13	3	9	0	0
Jenkins, Billings	.960	13	10	14	1	2
Ca. Johnson, Butte-Great Falls	.556	17	1	4	4	0
Ch. Johnson, Helena	1.000	12	4	6	0	0
D. Johnson, Pocatello	.900	18	4	5	1	0
Kaiser, Billings	.909	13	11	9	2	0
Kitano, Butte*	.920	13	5	18	2	0
Kostichka, Helena	1.000	19	5	2	0	0
Kucera, Helena	1.000	6	1	4	0	0
Langley, Great Falls*	.950	12	2	17	1	1
Lariviere, Medicine Hat	.929	15	8	18	2	5
Lavrusky, Idaho Falls*	.929	21	5	8	1	0
Lewis, Pocatello	.889	23	4	4	1	0
Lienhard, Pocatello	.947	14	7	11	1	1
Lomeli, Idaho Falls	1.000	23	1	12	0	0
MacDonald, Medicine Hat	1.000	13	0	3	0	0
Maitia, Medicine Hat	.800	24	2	10	3	0
Marsh, Billings	1.000	19	2	5	0	0
Martin, Great Falls	1.000	18	0	2	0	0
McCarthy, Billings*	1.000	13	5	11	0	0
Meier, Pocatello	.714	6	0	5	2	0
Messer, Pocatello	.958	16	10	13	1	1
Miranda, Butte-Helena	1.000	25	1	3	0	1
Monson, Helena	.913	14	9	12	2	0
Myers, Pocatello	.875	10	1	6	1	0
Navarro, Helena	1.000	13	3	6	0	1
Nelson, Helena*	.818	13	0	9	2	2
NEWCOMB, Medicine Hat	1.000	11	4	30	0	2
Noch, Great Falls	.913	14	6	15	2	0
D. Peters, Butte	.893	12	6	19	3	0
T. Peters, Salt Lake City	.929	38	1	12	1	1
Piscetta, Great Falls	.750	10	1	2	1	0
Poss, Salt Lake City	1.000	6	0	3	0	0
Ramirez, Idaho Falls	1.000	15	4	19	0	0
Richey, Medicine Hat	.833	12	2	3	1	2
Savage, Salt Lake City	1.000	4	2	5	0	0
Seuberth, Butte	.857	21	4	14	3	1
Shiver, Medicine Hat	1.000	5	0	2	0	0
Shiverick, Billings	.857	20	1	5	1	0
Sparks, Helena	1.000	10	2	6	0	0
Springer, Great Falls	1.000	23	6	12	0	1
Stange, Salt Lake City	.950	14	7	12	1	1
Timlin, Medicine Hat	.875	13	3	11	2	2
Tozuka, Butte	1.000	19	2	11	0	0
Turek, Billings	1.000	9	2	0	0	0
Vuz, Pocatello	1.000	3	0	1	0	0
Wanish, Great Falls	.750	15	5	4	3	0
Ward, Idaho Falls*	1.000	15	1	8	0	1
Waznik, Idaho Falls*	.833	15	3	7	2	1
Wenrick, Salt Lake City*	1.000	6	0	3	0	0
Whatley, Great Falls	1.000	20	4	3	0	1
Whitlock, Helena*	1.000	16	4	17	0	1
M. Wilson, Idaho Falls	.846	14	4	18	4	1
T. Wilson, Medicine Hat	.818	15	2	7	2	0
Wojda, Butte	.750	9	1	5	2	2
Woodhouse, Helena	.833	21	7	3	2	0
Wright, Idaho Falls	.778	26	2	5	2	1
Ziegler, Idaho Falls	.929	11	4	9	1	1

The following players do not have any recorded accepted chances at the positions indicated; therefore, are not listed in the fielding averages for those particular positions: Barron, ss, c; Baucom, ss; Blackmon, ss; Bland, of; Castro, p; T. Collins, p; Fillard, 1b; J. Guerrero, 3b; Eric Johnson, of; Kreuder, p; Laya, 1b; Letterio, 1b; A. Lewis, ss; Linarez, ss; Luckham, p; Maldonado, ss; McCutchen, p; Noonan, of; O'Leary, of; Ortiz, 1b, of; Peyton, ss; Rodnunsky, p; Shinall, p; Tanner, p; Walker, p.

CLUB PITCHING

Club	ERA.	G.	CG.	ShO.	Sv.	IP.	H.	R.	ER.	HR.	HB.	BB.	Int. BB.	SO.	WP.	Bk.
Great Falls	3.48	69	12	5	10	579.1	538	317	224	34	20	288	11	559	46	7
Billings	3.61	69	4	2	16	593.0	579	307	238	32	16	232	4	532	60	10
Helena	3.98	70	6	4	22	610.2	582	334	270	41	21	279	13	579	44	5
Salt Lake City	4.65	70	7	4	15	615.2	672	395	318	37	29	216	12	505	51	10
Idaho Falls	4.98	70	3	0	26	594.0	683	420	329	28	24	309	19	470	58	16
Medicine Hat	5.24	69	4	1	13	599.0	709	463	349	38	25	285	8	471	69	18
Butte	5.44	69	15	1	6	585.1	666	458	353	49	30	295	2	453	56	12
Pocatello	5.70	70	6	2	8	590.1	748	475	374	52	27	284	18	384	58	13

PITCHERS' RECORDS
(Leading Qualifiers for Earned-Run Average Leadership—56 or More Innings)

*Throws lefthanded.

Pitcher—Club	W.	L.	Pct.	ERA.	G.	GS.	CG.	GF.	ShO.	Sv.	IP.	H.	R.	ER.	HR.	HB.	BB.	Int. BB.	SO.	WP.
Chavez, Billings*	6	4	.600	1.988	14	14	2	0	0	0	86.0	74	23	19	4	2	31	0	52	5
S. Collins, Great Falls	6	2	.750	1.989	11	10	3	0	0	0	63.1	39	27	14	3	1	31	0	77	6
Noch, Great Falls	5	3	.625	2.30	14	11	3	1	2	0	78.1	74	24	20	2	3	19	0	85	2
Langley, Great Falls*	4	4	.500	2.77	12	10	2	0	1	0	65.0	55	26	20	3	3	42	0	61	4
Springer, Great Falls	4	3	.571	2.88	23	5	1	13	0	6	65.2	70	38	21	3	2	16	2	54	4
Monson, Helena	10	1	.909	2.91	14	14	0	0	0	0	96.0	80	38	31	1	4	31	0	94	7
Whitlock, Helena*	6	3	.667	3.00	16	7	1	4	1	2	63.0	53	30	21	4	2	29	2	44	0
Kaiser, Billings	6	5	.545	3.08	13	13	2	0	0	0	76.0	67	37	26	3	3	39	0	71	9
Humphrey, Salt Lake City	5	2	.714	3.29	15	11	1	2	0	0	79.1	74	40	29	5	2	31	2	75	7
Carrasco, Great Falls	4	4	.500	3.36	13	13	11	1	0	0	69.2	69	38	26	4	3	34	1	63	9

Departmental Leaders: G—T. Peters, 38; W—Monson, 10; L—Kitano, 9; Pct.—Monson, .909; GS—Lariviere, 15; CG—D. Peters, 5; GF—T. Peters, 33; ShO—Ikeue, Noch, 2; Sv.—Chapman, Wright, 13; IP—Monson, 96.0; H—Lienhard, 109; R—Kitano, 70; ER—Kitano, 62; HR—Connolly, de la Rosa, Tozuka, 9; HB—M. Wilson, 9; BB—Tozuka, Waznik, M. Wilson, 45; IBB—Wright, 6; SO—Waznik, 102; WP—Waznik, 14.

(All Pitchers—Listed Alphabetically)

Pitcher—Club	W.	L.	Pct.	ERA	G.	GS.	CG.	GF.	ShO.	Sv.	IP.	H.	R.	ER.	HR.	HB.	BB.	Int. BB.	SO.	WP.
Alleyne, Salt Lake City°	1	2	.333	8.67	18	2	0	1	0	0	27.0	44	36	26	1	5	16	2	22	2
Anderson, Butte	1	3	.250	11.18	9	8	1	0	0	0	33.0	32	42	41	4	7	41	0	23	4
Arias, Pocatello	0	4	.000	6.68	18	0	0	4	0	0	32.1	45	30	24	2	3	17	0	10	1
Armstrong, Billings	2	1	.667	2.66	5	4	0	0	0	0	20.1	16	7	6	0	0	12	0	29	1
Bevis, Medicine Hat	1	1	.500	3.20	11	1	0	8	0	2	25.1	32	15	9	1	0	6	1	22	2
Blackmon, Salt Lake City	0	0	.000	......	1	0	0	0	0	0	0.0	1	0	0	0	0	1	0	0	0
Blohm, Idaho Falls	4	3	.571	5.49	14	10	0	3	0	0	62.1	75	48	38	3	2	32	1	33	1
Breitenbucher, Pocatello	5	8	.385	5.96	15	13	1	1	0	0	77.0	98	67	51	7	0	40	3	35	11
Buffolino, Pocatello	2	3	.400	1.97	19	0	0	17	0	5	32.0	27	10	7	2	1	12	5	28	0
Burgos, Butte°	4	6	.400	5.60	10	10	2	0	0	0	62.2	77	48	39	4	1	20	0	38	5
Carrasco, Great Falls	4	4	.500	3.36	13	12	1	1	0	0	69.2	69	38	26	4	3	34	1	63	9
Carter, Helena	1	2	.333	5.54	9	4	0	0	0	0	26.0	37	22	16	2	0	9	0	15	0
Casillas, Salt Lake City°	0	0	.000	9.00	3	0	0	1	0	0	3.0	5	3	3	0	0	2	0	0	0
Castro, Medicine Hat°	0	0	.000	36.00	1	0	0	0	0	0	1.0	4	4	4	1	0	0	0	1	1
Chapman, Helena	3	1	.750	1.31	27	0	0	22	0	13	34.1	28	5	5	2	1	9	2	51	5
Chavez, Billings°	6	4	.600	1.988	14	14	2	0	0	0	86.0	74	23	19	4	2	31	0	52	5
S. Collins, Great Falls	6	2	.750	1.989	11	10	3	0	0	0	63.1	39	27	14	3	1	31	0	77	6
T. Collins, Salt Lake City	0	0	.000	162.00	2	0	0	0	0	0	0.1	1	6	6	0	0	5	0	0	0
Colon, Medicine Hat	0	3	.000	8.04	12	4	0	3	0	0	31.1	44	33	28	2	4	13	1	27	1
Conliffe, Medicine Hat	0	1	.000	7.03	17	0	0	7	0	1	24.1	39	26	19	1	2	13	0	19	5
Connolly, Pocatello°	3	7	.300	4.25	13	13	1	0	1	0	72.0	89	52	34	9	2	18	1	46	5
Correa, Helena	0	1	.000	16.50	3	2	0	0	0	0	6.0	10	12	11	1	0	8	0	0	1
Cox, Idaho Falls°	3	3	.500	5.51	14	8	0	4	0	2	49.0	51	34	30	2	0	27	0	43	5
Creekmore, Salt Lake City	2	2	.500	4.42	23	3	0	6	0	1	59.0	72	36	29	2	5	21	0	42	5
Cromwell, Medicine Hat°	4	6	.400	4.31	15	11	1	2	0	0	54.1	54	36	26	1	1	37	0	47	10
Cuff, Medicine Hat	0	1	.000	6.79	18	3	0	6	0	1	50.1	85	57	38	5	2	18	1	22	4
Currie, Great Falls°	1	3	.250	4.91	17	1	0	3	0	0	22.0	26	16	12	1	1	8	1	19	1
de la Rosa, Pocatello	1	3	.250	6.25	11	6	0	4	0	0	36.0	41	30	25	9	1	20	0	20	1
Dodd, Billings	5	1	.833	3.96	23	0	0	8	0	1	52.1	52	29	23	1	1	18	0	59	3
Dolan, 2 But-7 SLC°	2	0	1.000	5.48	9	1	0	4	0	0	21.1	32	16	13	1	3	3	0	16	4
Economy, Billings	4	0	1.000	3.43	17	1	0	4	0	2	39.1	33	17	15	1	3	20	0	25	2
Elliott, Butte	0	1	.000	9.82	4	1	0	1	0	0	7.1	11	11	8	1	0	8	1	7	2
Ferrebee, Idaho Falls°	0	2	.000	10.42	9	3	0	3	0	0	19.0	29	26	22	2	1	17	0	12	8
Figueroa, Pocatello	0	0	.000	9.33	15	0	0	8	0	0	18.1	20	25	19	0	5	26	0	11	3
Foley, Medicine Hat	0	0	.000	8.68	5	0	0	1	0	0	9.1	14	10	9	0	1	2	0	6	1
Gastelum, Great Falls	0	1	.000	2.28	10	3	0	5	0	3	23.2	15	9	6	0	0	21	0	36	2
Gettler, Great Falls	3	1	.750	3.74	10	4	1	2	0	0	33.2	25	15	14	2	0	14	0	33	2
Gillund, Idaho Falls	1	0	1.000	6.60	8	0	0	5	0	0	15.0	19	13	11	1	1	6	0	9	1
Glover, Butte	0	1	.000	6.75	9	1	0	5	0	2	16.0	27	18	12	2	0	12	0	10	4
Gonzalez, Great Falls	1	2	.333	5.76	16	2	0	5	0	0	29.2	31	23	19	3	2	21	3	25	2
Granato, Medicine Hat	4	3	.571	6.80	18	6	0	5	0	0	46.1	62	45	35	6	3	26	1	39	3
Griffin, Butte°	3	4	.429	3.59	14	8	1	3	0	0	62.2	57	35	25	6	1	31	0	49	7
Groennert, Salt Lake City	3	4	.571	3.56	14	5	0	6	0	2	60.2	64	30	24	2	4	16	1	55	8
Gunter, Pocatello	2	5	.286	7.20	21	2	0	9	0	0	45.0	58	43	36	3	3	25	2	33	5
Henry, Billings°	4	0	1.000	4.63	9	5	0	2	0	1	35.0	37	21	18	3	1	12	1	38	4
Hernandez, Helena	0	0	.000	13.50	4	0	0	0	0	0	4.2	5	7	7	0	0	10	0	5	3
Hester, Billings	2	1	.667	5.76	5	5	0	0	0	0	25.0	33	20	16	4	0	12	0	21	3
Hetrick, Salt Lake City°	9	2	.818	4.84	21	9	2	7	0	1	70.2	85	45	38	8	1	26	2	63	7
Hiyama, Salt Lake City	3	1	.750	5.57	10	7	0	2	0	0	32.1	36	22	20	3	0	10	0	17	3
Humphrey, Salt Lake City	5	2	.714	3.29	15	11	1	2	0	0	79.1	74	40	29	5	2	31	2	75	7
Ikeue, Salt Lake City	6	3	.667	4.70	13	12	2	0	0	0	82.1	80	49	43	5	1	28	0	67	4
Jenkins, Billings	5	3	.625	3.51	13	12	0	0	0	0	77.0	84	38	30	6	2	24	0	67	2
Ca. Johnson, 17 But-4 GF	1	2	.333	5.02	21	1	0	15	0	1	37.2	36	27	21	1	4	11	0	48	3
Ch. Johnson, Helena	5	0	1.000	4.03	12	11	0	0	0	0	60.1	55	32	27	8	3	21	0	54	5
D. Johnson, Pocatello	1	2	.333	7.20	18	2	0	5	0	2	35.0	42	35	28	2	4	26	1	30	5
Kaiser, Billings	6	5	.545	3.08	13	13	2	0	0	0	76.0	67	37	26	3	3	39	0	71	9
Kitano, Butte°	1	9	.100	6.86	13	13	3	0	0	0	81.1	102	70	62	5	1	28	0	55	7
Kostichka, Helena	3	0	1.000	5.46	19	0	0	12	0	2	28.0	31	21	17	2	1	18	3	27	3
Kreuder, Great Falls	0	1	.000	19.29	1	1	0	0	0	0	2.1	7	8	5	1	0	2	0	1	1
Kucera, Helena°	1	1	.500	4.00	6	0	0	3	0	0	9.0	7	4	4	0	0	10	0	9	1
Langley, Great Falls°	4	4	.500	2.77	12	10	2	1	0	1	65.0	55	26	20	3	3	42	0	61	4
Lariviere, Medicine Hat	4	7	.364	3.86	15	15	0	0	0	0	81.2	89	46	35	2	0	29	0	47	6
Lavruskey, Idaho Falls°	4	1	.800	3.67	21	0	0	6	0	3	54.0	52	33	22	3	0	31	1	51	7
Lewis, Pocatello	1	0	1.000	5.32	23	2	0	6	0	1	47.1	62	40	28	5	2	24	4	34	6
Lienhard, Pocatello	3	6	.333	5.96	14	12	2	1	1	0	74.0	109	56	49	6	1	14	0	52	9
Lomeli, Idaho Falls	3	0	1.000	3.02	23	0	0	13	0	5	44.2	51	24	15	2	0	20	2	39	3
Luckham, Great Falls	0	0	.000	2.45	3	0	0	1	0	0	3.2	6	2	1	0	0	4	0	3	0
MacDonald, Medicine Hat°	3	1	.750	2.92	13	0	0	9	0	2	24.2	22	13	8	0	1	12	1	26	5
Maitia, Medicine Hat	1	3	.250	6.35	24	2	0	10	0	3	45.1	49	41	32	5	4	34	1	45	5
Marsh, Billings	2	2	.500	4.31	19	0	0	10	0	1	31.1	27	22	15	1	2	9	1	30	8
Martin, Great Falls	2	0	1.000	5.40	18	0	0	5	0	0	21.2	25	14	13	2	2	15	0	17	4
McCarthy, Billings°	4	4	.500	4.81	13	13	0	0	0	0	63.2	75	47	34	4	1	27	0	43	6
McCutchen, Butte	0	0	.000	0.00	1	0	0	1	0	0	1.0	0	0	0	0	0	3	0	1	0
Meier, Pocatello	3	0	1.000	3.22	6	5	1	1	0	0	36.1	39	16	13	0	0	11	0	24	3
Messer, Pocatello°	3	6	.333	5.97	16	13	1	1	0	0	60.1	84	47	40	4	3	33	1	44	4
Miranda, 12 But-13 Hel°	1	2	.333	3.12	25	0	0	13	0	3	43.1	27	22	15	5	1	26	2	60	1
Monson, Helena	10	1	.909	2.91	14	14	0	0	0	0	96.0	80	38	31	1	4	31	0	94	7
Myers, Pocatello	0	2	.000	8.69	10	2	0	4	0	0	19.2	29	21	19	1	1	16	1	12	5
Navarro, Helena	4	3	.571	3.57	13	13	3	0	0	0	85.2	87	37	34	5	1	18	1	95	5
Nelson, Helena°	4	3	.571	5.05	13	10	0	2	0	0	57.0	64	38	32	4	1	34	1	47	5
Newcomb, Medicine Hat	3	3	.500	4.86	11	11	1	0	0	0	66.2	67	46	36	8	2	33	0	43	3
Noch, Great Falls	5	3	.625	2.30	14	11	3	1	2	0	78.1	74	24	20	2	3	19	0	85	2
D. Peters, Butte	3	6	.333	4.34	12	11	5	1	1	0	83.0	94	60	40	7	0	35	0	63	6
T. Peters, Salt Lake City	9	3	.750	2.10	38	0	0	33	0	11	55.2	39	21	13	1	1	20	4	57	2
Piscetta, Great Falls	2	2	.333	6.20	10	3	0	1	0	0	20.1	24	16	14	2	0	12	0	18	2
Poss, Salt Lake City	0	1	.000	7.90	6	2	0	2	0	0	13.2	25	16	12	1	2	5	1	11	1
Ramirez, Idaho Falls	7	1	.875	3.44	15	0	0	2	0	1	65.1	75	32	25	1	3	26	3	41	6
Richey, Medicine Hat	1	2	.333	2.08	12	0	0	10	0	4	21.2	16	9	5	0	0	9	2	26	4
Rodnunsky, Butte	0	0	.000	0.00	4	0	0	4	0	0	4.0	0	0	0	0	0	6	0	0	0
Savage, Salt Lake City	2	0	1.000	6.61	4	3	0	0	0	0	16.1	20	15	12	2	2	5	0	10	1
Seuberth, Butte	2	7	.222	3.48	21	4	3	15	0	1	72.1	77	40	28	3	5	32	1	68	4

Pitcher—Club	W.	L.	Pct.	ERA.	G.	GS.	CG.	GF.	ShO.	Sv.	IP.	H.	R.	ER.	HR.	HB.	BB.	Int. BB.	SO.	WP.
Shinall, Great Falls	0	0	.000	47.25	1	0	0	0	0	0	1.1	4	8	7	1	1	5	0	0	0
Shiver, Helena	1	2	.333	2.53	5	0	0	4	0	0	10.2	6	5	3	1	0	7	1	9	0
Shiverick, Billings	1	1	.500	4.62	20	1	0	16	0	3	39.0	38	25	20	4	1	14	0	47	10
Sparks, Helena	6	3	.667	4.68	10	9	2	0	0	0	57.2	68	44	30	8	4	20	1	47	5
Springer, Great Falls	4	3	.571	2.88	23	5	1	13	0	6	65.2	70	38	21	3	2	16	2	54	4
Stange, Salt Lake City	3	2	.600	5.33	14	13	2	1	0	0	79.1	92	55	47	6	5	20	0	51	5
Tanner, Helena	0	0	.000	3.00	2	0	0	0	0	0	3.0	3	1	1	0	0	2	0	2	0
Timlin, Medicine Hat	4	8	.333	5.14	13	12	2	0	0	0	75.1	79	50	43	4	5	26	0	66	9
Tozuka, Butte	2	8	.200	5.11	19	9	0	6	0	2	75.2	96	63	43	9	6	45	0	49	10
Turek, Billings	0	2	.000	5.87	9	1	0	6	0	1	15.1	18	11	10	0	0	10	0	10	2
Vuz, Pocatello	0	0	.000	5.40	3	0	0	3	0	0	5.0	5	3	3	0	1	2	0	5	0
Walker, Helena	0	0	.000	0.00	1	0	0	1	0	0	0.1	0	0	0	0	0	1	0	1	0
Wanish, Great Falls	2	7	.222	3.94	15	7	1	0	1	0	48.0	37	35	21	5	1	32	0	41	6
Ward, Idaho Falls*	3	2	.600	5.48	15	5	1	6	0	2	46.0	48	31	28	5	0	19	2	30	2
Waznik, Idaho Falls	4	4	.500	3.52	15	12	1	0	0	0	84.1	81	44	33	1	3	45	1	102	14
Wenrick, Salt Lake City*	3	0	1.000	3.92	6	2	0	1	0	0	20.2	14	12	9	1	1	9	0	22	2
Whatley, Great Falls	2	1	.667	4.68	20	0	0	15	0	0	25.0	28	18	13	2	1	12	4	21	1
Whitlock, Helena*	6	3	.667	3.00	16	7	1	4	1	2	63.0	53	30	21	4	2	29	2	44	0
M. Wilson, Idaho Falls	4	6	.400	6.24	14	13	0	0	0	0	70.2	90	63	49	4	9	45	2	52	5
T. Wilson, Medicine Hat	1	4	.200	5.23	15	4	0	4	0	0	41.1	53	32	24	2	0	27	0	35	10
Wojda, Butte	1	2	.333	6.33	9	3	0	1	0	0	27.0	33	24	19	2	1	16	0	17	3
Woodhouse, Helena	2	3	.400	4.75	21	0	0	8	0	2	47.1	36	29	25	2	4	36	0	47	4
Wright, Idaho Falls	3	6	.333	3.48	26	0	0	25	0	13	33.2	34	21	13	0	1	14	6	32	1
Ziegler, Idaho Falls	0	6	.000	7.74	11	11	1	0	0	0	50.0	78	51	43	4	4	27	1	26	5

BALKS—Tozuka, 6; Timlin, 5; Cuff, 4; Cox, Economy, Gunter, Meier, Stange, T. Wilson, Ziegler, 3 each; Alleyne, Blohm, Carrasco, Creekmore, de la Rosa, Dodd, Ch. Johnson, Kaiser, Maitia, Newcomb, Ward, M. Wilson, 2 each; Arias, Carter, Chavez, Conliffe, Elliott, Ferrebee, Figueroa, Gonzalez, Griffin, Henry, Hetrick, Hiyama, Kitano, Langley, Lariviere, Lewis, Lienhard, Lomeli, McCarthy, Miranda, Monson, Navarro, Noch, Piscetta, Poss, Ramirez, Seuberth, Shinall, Vuz, Waznik, Wojda, 1 each.

COMBINATION SHUTOUTS—Kaiser-Dodd 2, Billings; Gettler-Currie-Martin, Piscetta-Whatley, Great Falls; Johnson-Woodhouse-Whitlock, Navarro-Correa-Chapman, Nelson-Hernandez-Kostichka, Helena; Granato-Bevis, Medicine Hat; Humphrey-Alleyne-Creekmore, Ikeue-Peters, Salt Lake City.

NO-HIT GAMES—None.

Index to Minor League Clubs, Cities

1988 A.L. EAST DIVISION SLATE...

1988	AT MILWAUKEE	AT DETROIT	AT CLEVELAND	AT TORONTO	AT BALTIMORE	AT NEW YORK	AT BOSTON
EAST							
MILWAUKEE...		May 24*, 25*, 26* Sept. 1*, 2*, 3*, 4	May 27*, 28*, 29 Aug. 16*, 17*, 18*	May 30*, 31* June 1* Aug. 19*, 20, 21	April 4, 6*, 7* Aug. 5*, 6*, 7	April 8*, 9*, 10 July 25*, 26*, 27*, 28*	April 11, 12, 13, 14 July 29*, 30, 31
DETROIT.........	May 16*, 17*, 18 Aug. 26*, 27*, 28		June 9*, 10*, 11, 12 Sept. 26*, 27*, 28*	June 24*, 25, 26 Sept. 12*, 13*, 14*	June 6*, 7*, 8* Sept. 22*, 23*, 24*, 25	June 27*, 28*, 29* Sept. 8*, 9*, 10, 11	April 4, 6, 7 Aug. 12*, 13, 14
CLEVELAND ...	May 12*, 13*, 14, 15 Aug. 22*, 23*, 24	June 3*, 4*, 5 Sept. 19*, 20*, 21*		June 13*, 14*, 15 Sept. 15*, 16*, 17, 18	April 15*, 16*, 17 Aug. 2*, 3*, 4*	June 23*, 24*, 25*, 26 Sept. 5, 6*, 7*	June 27*, 28*, 29* Sept. 9*, 10, 11
TORONTO	May 20*, 21*, 22, 23* Aug. 29*, 30*, 31	June 16*, 17*, 18, 19 Sept. 5*, 6*, 7*	June 6*, 7*, 8* Sept. 23*, 24*, 25		June 27*, 28*, 29* Sept. 9*, 10*, 11	April 22*, 23*, 24 Aug. 9*, 10*, 11*	June 2*, 3*, 4, 5 Sept. 26*, 27*, 28*
BALTIMORE....	April 19*, 20*, 21 Aug. 12*, 13*, 14, 15*	June 13*, 14*, 15* Sept. 16*, 17*, 18	April 8*, 9, 10, 11* July 26*, 27*, 28*	June 20*, 21*, 22*, 23* Sept. 30* Oct. 1, 2		June 10*, 11, 12 Sept. 19*, 20*, 21*	June 24*, 25, 26 Sept. 12*, 13*, 14*
NEW YORK	April 15, 16, 17 Aug. 2*, 3*, 4*	June 20*, 21*, 22* Sept. 30* Oct. 1, 2	June 17*, 18, 19 Sept. 12*, 13*, 14*	April 11, 12*, 13*, 14 July 29*, 30, 31	June 3*, 4*, 5 Sept. 26*, 27*, 28*, 29*		June 13*, 14*, 15* Sept. 15*, 16*, 17, 18
BOSTON.........	April 22*, 23, 24 Aug. 9*, 10*, 11	April 19*, 20*, 21 Aug. 4*, 5, 6, 7	June 20*, 21*, 22* Sept. 29*, 30* Oct. 1, 2	June 10*, 11, 12 Sept. 19*, 20*, 21*	June 16*, 17*, 18, 19 Sept. 5*, 6*, 7*	June 6*, 7*, 8* Sept. 23*, 24*, 25	
SEATTLE........	June 13*, 14*, 15 Sept. 9*, 10*, 11	April 29*, 30* May 1 July 4, 5*, 6*	April 26*, 27*, 28* July 1*, 2*, 3	May 10*, 11*, 12* July 8*, 9, 10	May 20*, 21*, 22 Aug. 22*, 23*, 24*	May 16*, 17*, 18* Aug. 19*, 20*, 21	May 13*, 14, 15* Aug. 16*, 17*, 18*
OAKLAND	June 20*, 21*, 22 Sept. 23*, 24, 25	May 2*, 3 July 7*, 8*, 9, 10	April 29*, 30 May 1 July 4, 5*, 6	April 26*, 27*, 28* July 1, 2, 3	May 13*, 14*, 15 Aug. 16*, 17*, 18*	May 20*, 21*, 22 Aug. 22*, 23*, 24*	May 16*, 17*, 18* Aug. 19*, 20, 21
CALIFORNIA...	June 2*, 3*, 4*, 5 Sept. 27*, 28*	April 26*, 27*, 28* July 1*, 2, 3	May 2*, 3* July 7*, 8*, 9, 10	April 29*, 30* May 1 July 4*, 5*, 6*	May 17*, 18*, 19* Aug. 19*, 20*, 21	May 13*, 14, 15 Aug. 16*, 17*, 18*	May 20*, 21, 22 Aug. 22*, 23*, 24*
TEXAS	May 4*, 5 July 21*, 22*, 23*, 24	April 12, 14 July 29 (Tn), 30*, 31	April 19*, 20* Aug. 11*, 12*, 13, 14	May 17*, 18* Sept. 1*, 2*, 3, 4	May 2*, 3* July 7*, 8*, 9*, 10	April 29*, 30* May 1 July 18*, 19*, 20*	April 15, 16, 17*, 18 Aug. 2*, 3*
KANSAS CITY	April 29*, 30 May 1 July 18*, 19*, 20	April 15*, 16, 17 July 26*, 27*, 28*	May 30, 31* June 1* Aug. 19*, 20, 21	April 19*, 20* Aug. 5*, 6, 7, 8*	April 12*, 13*, 14* July 29*, 30*, 31	April 26*, 27*, 28* July 8*, 9*, 10	May 2*, 3* July 14*, 15*, 16, 17
MINNESOTA...	May 2*, 3* July 1*, 2, 3, 4*	May 13*, 14, 15 Aug. 15*, 16*, 17	April 12*, 13*, 14* July 29*, 30, 31	April 15*, 16, 17 Aug. 1, 2*, 3*	May 4*, 5* Aug. 1, 2*, 3*	April 5, 6, 7* Aug. 5*, 6*, 7	April 29*, 30 May 1 July 18*, 19*, 20*
CHICAGO........	June 16*, 17*, 18*, 19 Sept. 5, 7*	May 31* June 1* Aug. 18*, 19*, 20*, 21	May 17*, 18*, 19* Sept. 2*, 3, 4	May 27*, 28, 29 Aug. 22*, 23*, 24	May 6*, 7*, 8, 9* July 19*, 20*	May 10*, 11* July 14*, 15*, 16, 17	May 4*, 5* July 21*, 22*, 23, 24
1988	81 HOME DATES 51 NIGHTS	80 HOME DATES 54 NIGHTS	81 HOME DATES 56 NIGHTS	81 HOME DATES 49 NIGHTS	81 HOME DATES 66 NIGHTS	81 HOME DATES 61 NIGHTS	81 HOME DATES 46 NIGHTS

*NIGHT GAME
NIGHT GAME: Any game starting after 5:00 p.m.
HEAVY BLACK FIGURES DENOTE SUNDAY

AND COMPLETE WEST SCHEDULES

1988	WEST						
	AT SEATTLE	AT OAKLAND	AT CALIFORNIA	AT TEXAS	AT KANSAS CITY	AT MINNESOTA	AT CHICAGO
MILWAUKEE...	June 6*, 7*, 8* Sept. 16*, 17*, 18	June 27*, 28*, 29 Sept. 30* Oct. 1, 2	June 24*, 25*, 26 Sept. 19*, 20*, 21*	April 26*, 27* July 14*, 15*, 16*, 17	May 6*, 7*, 8 July 5*, 6*, 7*	May 9*, 10*, 11* July 8*, 9*, 10	June 10*, 11*, 12 Sept. 12*, 13*, 14*
DETROIT.........	May 6*, 7*, 8 July 18*, 19*, 20	May 9*, 10*, 11 July 22*, 23, 24	May 4*, 5* July 14*, 15*, 16, 17	April 22*, 23*, 24 Aug. 8*, 9*, 10*	April 8*, 9, 10 Aug. 1*, 2*, 3*	May 27*, 28*, 29 Aug. 22*, 23*, 24*	May 20*, 21, 22 Aug. 29*, 30*, 31*
CLEVELAND ...	May 4*, 5* July 14*, 15*, 16*, 17	May 6*, 7, 8 July 18*, 19*, 20	May 9*, 10*, 11* July 22*, 23*, 24	April 4*, 6*, 7* Aug. 5*, 6*, 7*	May 20*, 21*, 22 Aug. 29*, 30*, 31*	April 22*, 23*, 24 Aug. 8*, 9*, 10*	May 23*, 24*, 25* Aug. 26*, 27*, 28
TORONTO	May 2*, 3* July 21*, 22*, 23*, 24	May 4*, 5 July 14*, 15*, 16, 17	May 6*, 7*, 8 July 18*, 19*, 20*	May 24*, 25*, 26* Aug. 26*, 27*, 28*	April 4*, 6*, 7* Aug. 12*, 13*, 14	April 8*, 9, 10 July 25*, 26*, 27	May 13*, 14*, 15, 16* Aug. 16*, 17*
BALTIMORE....	May 30, 31* June 1 Sept. 2*, 3*, 4	May 23*, 24*, 25 Aug. 26*, 27, 28	May 27*, 28*, 29 Aug. 29*, 30*, 31*	May 10*, 11*, 12* July 1*, 2*, 3*	April 22*, 23, 24 Aug. 9*, 10*, 11*	April 26*, 27*, 28 July 22*, 23*, 24	April 29*, 30* May 1 July 4*, 5*, 6
NEW YORK	May 27*, 28*, 29 Aug. 29*, 30*, 31*	May 30*, 31 June 1 Sept. 2*, 3, 4	May 23*, 24*, 25* Aug. 26*, 27, 28	May 6*, 7*, 8 July 4*, 5*, 6*	May 4*, 5* July 21*, 22*, 23*, 24	April 18*, 19*, 20* Aug. 12, 13, 14	May 2*, 3* June 30* July 1*, 2, 3
BOSTON	May 23*, 24*, 25* Aug. 26*, 27*, 28	May 27*, 28, 29 Aug. 29*, 30*, 31	May 30, 31* Sept. 1*, 2*, 3*, 4	April 8*, 9*, 10 July 25*, 26*, 27*	May 9*, 10* July 1*, 2*, 3, 4*	May 6*, 7, 8 July 5*, 6*, 7*	April 26*, 27*, 28* July 8*, 9*, 10
SEATTLE........		April 4*, 5*, 6 Aug. 4*, 5*, 6, 7	April 21*, 22*, 23*, 24 Aug. 8*, 9*, 10*	June 20*, 21*, 22* Sept. 23*, 24*, 25	June 2*, 3*, 4*, 5 Sept. 26*, 27*, 28*	June 17*, 18*, 19 Sept. 5, 6*, 7*	April 8*, 9*, 10 July 25*, 26*, 27
OAKLAND	April 12*, 13*, 14* July 29*, 30*, 31		April 8*, 9*, 10 July 25*, 26*, 27	June 9*, 10*, 11*, 12* Sept. 5*, 6*, 7*	June 6*, 7*, 8* Sept. 8*, 9*, 10*, 11	June 3*, 4*, 5 Sept. 27*, 28*, 29	April 21*, 22*, 23*, 24 Aug. 1*, 2*, 3*
CALIFORNIA ...	April 15*, 16*, 17 Aug. 1*, 2*, 3	April 18*, 19*, 20 Aug. 11*, 12*, 13, 14		June 6*, 7*, 8* Sept. 8*, 9*, 10*, 11	June 17*, 18*, 19 Sept. 5*, 6*, 7*	June 20*, 21*, 22 Sept. 30* Oct. 1*, 2	April 4, 6*, 7 July 28*, 29*, 30, 31
TEXAS	June 27, 28*, 29* Sept. 29*, 30* Oct. 1*, 2	June 17*, 18, 19 Sept. 13*, 14*, 15	June 14*, 15*, 16 Sept. 16*, 17, 18		May 27*, 28*, 29 Aug. 15*, 16*, 17*	May 30, 31* June 1* Aug. 18*, 19*, 20*, 21	June 2*, 3*, 4*, 5 Sept. 26*, 27*, 28*
KANSAS CITY	June 24*, 25*, 26 Sept. 19*, 20*, 21	June 14*, 15*, 16 Sept. 16*, 17, 18	June 10*, 11, 12, 13* Sept. 13*, 14*, 15*	May 13*, 14*, 15, 16* Aug. 22*, 23*, 24*		May 17*, 18*, 19 Sept. 1*, 2, 3, 4	June 20*, 21*, 22* Sept. 23*, 24*, 25
MINNESOTA ...	June 9*, 10*, 11*, 12 Sept. 12*, 13*, 14*	June 24*, 25, 26-26 Sept. 19*, 20*, 21	June 27, 28*, 29* Sept. 22*, 23*, 24*, 25	May 20*, 21*, 22 Aug. 29*, 30*, 31*	May 23*, 24*, 25* Aug. 26*, 27*, 28		June 6*, 7*, 8* Sept. 9*, 10*, 11
CHICAGO........	April 18*, 19*, 20 Aug. 11*, 12*, 13*, 14	April 15*, 16*, 17 Aug. 8*, 9*, 10	April 12*, 13*, 14 Aug. 5*, 6*, 7	June 24*, 25*, 26* Sept. 19*, 20*, 21*	June 27*, 28*, 29* Sept. 29*, 30* Oct. 1*, 2	June 13*, 14*, 15* Sept. 15*, 16*, 17, 18	
1988	81 HOME DATES 61 NIGHTS	80 HOME DATES 41 NIGHTS	81 HOME DATES 60 NIGHTS	81 HOME DATES 73 NIGHTS	81 HOME DATES 65 NIGHTS	81 HOME DATES 56 NIGHTS	81 HOME DATES 62 NIGHTS

JULY 12—ALL-STAR GAME AT CINCINNATI
AUGUST 1—HALL OF FAME GAME AT COOPERSTOWN, N.Y. (Chicago Cubs vs. Cleveland Indians)

1988 N.L. EAST DIVISION SLATE...

1988	EAST					
	AT CHICAGO	**AT MONTREAL**	**AT NEW YORK**	**AT PHILADELPHIA**	**AT PITTSBURGH**	**AT ST. LOUIS**
CHICAGO........		April 8*, 9*, **10** July 26*, 27* Sept. 26*, 27*, 28*, 29*	June 2*, 3*, 4, **5** August 2*, 3*, 4 Sept. 14*, 15	June 20*, 21*, 22 July 28*, 29*, 30*, **31** Sept. 12*, 13*	April 22*, 23, **24** June 7*, 8*, 9* Sept. 23*, 24*, **25**	April 11*, 12*, 13 June 10*, 11*, **12** Sept. 9*, 10, **11**
MONTREAL	April 19, 20, 21 June 17, 18, **19** Sept. 19, 20, 21		April 12, 14 August 12*, 13, **14-14** Sept. 16*, 17, **18**	April 22*, 23*, **24** June 13*, 14*, 15* Sept. 23*, 24*, **25**	June 2*, 3*, 4*, **5** August 2*, 3*, 4* Sept. 7*, 8*	June 27*, 28*, 29* August 5*, 6, **7**, 8* Sept. 5*, 6*
NEW YORK	June 23, 24, 25, **26** August 9, 10, 11 Sept. 7, 8	April 4, 6*, 7* June 10*, 11*, **12** Sept. 9*, 10*, **11**		April 8*, 9, **10** July 25*, 26*, 27* Sept. 26*, 27*, 28*	June 27*, 28*, 29* August 5*, 6*, **7**, 8* Sept. 5, 6*	April 22*, 23*, **24** June 6*, **7**, 8* Sept. 23*, 24, **25**
PHILADELPHIA	June 27, 28, 29 August 5, 6, **7**, 8 Sept. 5, 6	April 15*, 16*, **17** June 6*, 7*, 8* Sept. 30* Oct. 1*, **2**	April 18*, 19*, 20* June 17*, 18*, **19** Sept. 20*, 21*, 22*		April 11*, 13*, 14* June 10*, 11*, **12** Sept. 9*, 10*, **11**	June 23*, 24*, 25*, **26** August 2*, 3*, 4 Sept. 7*, 8*
PITTSBURGH..	April 15, 16, **17** June 13, 14, 15 Sept. 30 Oct. 1, **2**	June 23*, 24*, 25*, **26** August 9*, 10*, 11* Sept. 14*, 15*	June 20*, 21*, 22 July 29*, 30*, **31** August 1* Sept. 12*, 13	April 5*, 6*, 7* August 12*, 13*, **14** Sept. 16*, 17*, **18**		April 8*, 9*, **10** July 25*, 26*, 27* Sept. 19*, 20*, 21*
ST. LOUIS	May 17, 18, 19 August 12, 13, **14** Sept. 16, 17, **18**	June 20*, 21*, 22* July 28*, 29*, 30*, **31** Sept. 12*, 13*	April 15*, 16, **17** June 13*, 14*, 15* Sept. 30* Oct. 1, **2**	June 2*, 3*, 4*, **5** August 9*, 10*, 11 Sept. 14*, 15	April 19*, 20*, 21* June 17*, 18*, **19** Sept. 26*, 27*, 28*	
ATLANTA.......	May 23, 24, 25 August 19, 20, **21**	May 4*, 5* June 30* July 1*, 2*, **3**	May 2*, 3* July 21*, 22*, 23, **24**	April 29*, 30 May 1 July 18*, 19*, 20*	May 20*, 21*, **22** August 15*, 16*, 17*	May 13*, 14*, **15** August 22*, 23*, 24*
CINCINNATI ...	May 30, 31 June 1 Sept. 2, 3, **4**	April 26*, 27* July 14*, 15*, 16*, **17**	May 6*, 7, **8** July 4*, 5*, 6*	May 9*, 10*, 11* July 1, 2, **3**	May 13*, 14*, **15** August 22*, 23*, 24*	May 23*, 24*, 25 August 19*, 20, **21**
HOUSTON.......	May 27, 28, **29** August 22, 23, 24	May 6*, 7*, **8** July 18*, 19*, 20*	May 4*, 5* June 30* July 1*, 2*, **3**	May 2*, 3* July 14*, 15*, 16*, **17**	May 23*, 24*, 25* August 19*, 20*, **21**	May 20*, 21*, **22** August 16*, 17*, 18*
LOS ANGELES	May 9, 10 July 14, 15, 16, **17**	May 27*, 28*, **29** August 29*, 30*, 31*	May 30, 31* June 1* Sept. 2*, 3, **4**	May 24*, 25*, 26* August 26*, 27*, **28**	May 11*, 12* July 21*, 22*, 23*, **24**	May 6*, 7*, **8** July 18*, 19*, 20
SAN DIEGO.....	May 11, 12 July 21, 22, 23, **24**	May 24*, 25*, 26* August 26*, 27*, **28**	May 27*, 28*, **29** August 29*, 30*, 31	May 30*, 31* June 1* Sept. 2*, 3*, **4**	May 6*, 7, **8** July 18*, 19*, 20*	May 9*, 10* July 14*, 15*, 16*, **17**
SAN FRAN.	May 6, 7, **8** July 18, 19, 20	May 30*, 31* June 1* Sept. 2*, 3*, **4**	May 24*, 25*, 26* August 26*, 27*, **28**	May 27*, 28, **29** August 29*, 30*, 31*	May 9*, 10* July 14*, 15*, 16*, **17**	May 11, 12 July 21*, 22*, 23, **24**
1988	81 HOME DATES 0 NIGHTS	81 HOME DATES 67 NIGHTS	80 HOME DATES 52 NIGHTS	81 HOME DATES 61 NIGHTS	81 HOME DATES 65 NIGHTS	81 HOME DATES 58 NIGHTS

*NIGHT GAME
NIGHT GAME: Any game starting after 5:00 p.m.
HEAVY BLACK FIGURES DENOTE SUNDAY

AND COMPLETE WEST SCHEDULES

1988 — WEST

	AT ATLANTA	AT CINCINNATI	AT HOUSTON	AT LOS ANGELES	AT SAN DIEGO	AT SAN FRANCISCO
CHICAGO........	April 5*, 6* Aug. 25*, 26*, 27, **28**	May 20*, 21*, **22** August 16*, 17*, 18*	May 13*, 14, **15** August 29*, 30*, 31	April 26*, 27*, 28* July 1*, 2*, **3**	May 2*, 3*, 4* July 8*, 9*, **10**	April 29*, 30 May **1** July 4, 5*, 6
MONTREAL	May 9*, 10*, 11* July 8*, 9*, **10**	May 2*, 3* July 21*, 22*, 23, **24**	April 29*, 30* May **1** July 4*, 5*, 6*	May 17*, 18*, 19* August 19*, 20*, 21	May 13*, 14*, **15** August 16*, 17*, 18	May 20*, 21, **22** August 22*, 23*, 24
NEW YORK	April 26*, 27* July 14*, 15*, 16*, **17**	April 29*, 30* May **1** July 18*, 19*, 20*	May 9*, 10*, 11* July 8*, 9, **10**	May 20*, 21*, **22** August 22*, 23*, 24*	May 16*, 17*, 18*, 19 August 19*, **21**	May 13*, 14, **15** August 16*, 17*, 18
PHILADELPHIA	May 6*, 7*, **8** July 4*, 5*, 6*	May 4*, 5* July 7*, 8*, 9*, **10**	April 26*, 27* July 21*, 22*, 23*, **24**	May 13*, 14*, **15** August 16*, 17*, 18	May 20*, 21*, **22** August 22*, 23*, 24*	May 16*, 17*, 18 August 19*, 20, **21**
PITTSBURGH..	May 30, 31* June 1* Sept. 2*, 3*, **4**	May 27*, 28*, **29** August 29*, 30*, 31*	May 16*, 17*, 18* August 26*, 27*, **28**	May 2*, 3*, 4* July 8*, 9*, **10**	April 29*, 30* May **1** July 4*, 5*, 7	April 26*, 27*, 28 July 1*, 2, **3**
ST. LOUIS	May 27*, 28, **29** August 29*, 30*, 31*	April 4, 6*, 7 August 26*, 27*, **28**	May 30*, 31* June 1* Sept. 2*, 3*, **4**	April 29*, 30* May **1** July 4*, 5*, 6*	April 26*, 27*, 28 July 1*, 2*, **3**	May 2*, 3*, 4 July 8*, 9, **10**
ATLANTA.......		May 16*, 17*, 18* August 12*, 13*, **14** Sept. 30* Oct. 1, **2**	April 19*, 20*, 21* June 10*, 11*, **12**, 13* Sept. 21*, 22*	April 15*, 16, **17** June 20*, 21*, 22* Sept. 12*, 13*, 14*	June 3*, 4*, **5** August 1*, 2*, 3* Sept. 9*, 10*, **11**	June 7*, 8*, 9 July 29*, 30, **31-31** Sept. 7*, 8*
CINCINNATI ...	April 22*, 23, **24** July 26*, 27*, 28* Sept. 23*, 24*, **25**		April 14*, 15*, 16, **17** June 20*, 21*, 22* Sept. 5*, 6*	June 3*, 4, **5** August 1*, 2*, 3* Sept. 9*, 10*, **11**	June 6*, 7*, 8*, 9 July 29*, 30*, **31** Sept. 7*, 8*	April 11*, 12*, 13 June 10*, 11, **12** Sept. 26*, 27*, 28*
HOUSTON.......	April 11*, 12*, 13* June 17*, 18*, **19** Sept. 27*, 28*, 29*	April 8*, 9, **10** June 14*, 15*, 16* Sept. 13*, 14*, 15*		June 6*, 7*, 8*, 9 July 29*, 30*, **31** Sept. 7*, 8*	April 22*, 23*, **24** July 26*, 27*, 28 Sept. 23*, 24*, **25**	June 3*, 4, **5** August 1*, 2*, 3 Sept. 9*, 10, **11**
LOS ANGELES	April 7*, 8*, 9*, **10** June 14*, 15*, 16* Sept. 5*, 6*	June 24*, 25*, **26** August 9*, 10*, 11* Sept. 16*, 17*, **18**	June 27*, 28*, 29 August 5*, 6*, **7**, 8* Sept. 19*, 20*		April 12*, 13*, 14 June 10*, 11*, **12** Sept. 26*, 27*, 28*	April 22*, 23, **24** July 25*, 26*, 27* Sept. 23*, 24, **25**
SAN DIEGO.....	June 24*, 25*, **26** August 9*, 10*, 11* Sept. 16*, 17*, **18**	June 27*, 28*, 29*, 30 August 5*, 6*, **7** Sept. 19*, 20	April 5*, 6 Aug. 12*, 13*, **14**, 15* Sept. 30* Oct. 1*, **2**	April 18*, 19*, 20*, 21* June 17*, 18, **19** Sept. 21*, 22*		April 7*, 8*, 9, **10** June 20*, 21*, 22 Sept. 5, 6*
SAN FRAN......	June 27*, 28*, 29* August 5*, 6*, **7**, 8* Sept. 19*, 20*	April 18*, 19*, 20*, 21 June 17*, 18, **19** Sept. 21*, 22	June 24*, 25*, **26** August 9*, 10*, 11* Sept. 16*, 17*, 18	April 4, 5* Aug. 12*, 13*, **14**, 15* Sept. 30* Oct. 1, **2**	April 15*, 16*, **17** June 13*, 14*, 15 Sept. 12*, 13*, 14*	
1988	81 HOME DATES 64 NIGHTS	81 HOME DATES 58 NIGHTS	81 HOME DATES 61 NIGHTS	81 HOME DATES 61 NIGHTS	81 HOME DATES 60 NIGHTS	80 HOME DATES 42 NIGHTS

JULY 12—ALL-STAR GAME AT CINCINNATI
AUGUST 1—HALL OF FAME GAME AT COOPERSTOWN, N.Y. (Chicago Cubs vs. Cleveland Indians)

Index to Contents

AMERICAN LEAGUE

NATIONAL LEAGUE

1987 Game Scores

1987 Game Scores

NATIONAL ASSOCIATION (MINOR LEAGUE) AVERAGES